INDEX OF MAJORS AND GRADUATE DEGREES

1993

Fifteenth Edition

College Entrance Examination Board
New York

A message about the College Board

The College Board is a nonprofit membership association composed of colleges, schools, systems, and education associations and agencies serving secondary and higher education. The Board helps students who are making the transition from high school to college through programs and services that include guidance, admissions, placement, credit by examination, and financial aid.

The College Handbook is an official publication of the College Board. Institutions that are College Board members are identified by the oak leaf symbol ⬥ following their names. As College Board members, these institutions—through the participation of their representatives in national and regional meetings, councils, advisory committees, and task forces—voice concerns about significant educational issues and help shape Board-sponsored programs and services used by more than 2.5 million students every year. Virtually every high school and college in the nation is affected by these services.

The more than 3,200 postsecondary institutions described in the *Handbook*—both College Board members and nonmembers—voluntarily provide the information presented here to assist students in making informed college choices. These institutions are committed to increasing students' awareness of their options, thus expanding their educational opportunities. *The College Handbook* has become the leading authoritative source of information on colleges and universities in the United States and is a trusted resource for students in the midst of the school-to-college transition.

The College Board is a nonprofit membership organization that provides tests and other educational services for students, schools, and colleges. The membership is composed of more than 2,800 colleges, schools, school systems, and education associations. Representatives of the members serve on the Board of Trustees and advisory councils and committees that consider the Board's programs and participate in the determination of its policies and activities.

Copies of this book are available from your local bookseller or may be ordered from College Board Publications, Box 886, New York, New York 10101-0886. The price is $16.

Editorial inquiries concerning this book should be directed to Guidance Publishing, The College Board, 45 Columbus Avenue, New York, New York 10023-6992.

Contents

This edition of **Index of Majors and Graduate Degrees** *is dedicated to the memory of Jean Marzone, who died in January 1992. In her eight-year career at the College Board, Ms. Marzone was involved in every aspect of the work of the delivery of data-based guidance information to students and educators. For the past four years, she directed the Annual Survey of Colleges. She was dedicated to the work of the College Board and to providing accurate and useful data to students and researchers. Her keen intelligence, good humor, and kindness will be greatly missed by her colleagues in the educational community at large.*

Introduction

Two of the most important factors to students deciding where to apply to college are programs of study and college location. The *Index of Majors and Graduate Degrees* is designed to help students find out which colleges offer the particular fields of study that interest them and are in the location they prefer. In addition, the *Index* includes lists of colleges that offer special academic programs.

There are nearly 600 majors listed in the *Index*. Each is listed alphabetically, and the colleges and graduate schools that offer a major in that field are listed state by state. Some institutions listed here do not offer majors in the traditional sense, but do provide in-depth specialization that approximates the course work usually required for a degree.

The new title of this book is intended to reflect its contents more accurately. *The Index of Majors and Graduate Degrees, 1993* is based on all-new curriculum and academic program information supplied by approximately 2,900 institutions in the College Board's Annual Survey of Colleges, 1992–93. Every effort has been made to ensure that the listings of colleges under each major are as complete and accurate as possible. However, students are urged to contact institutions directly to confirm the information.

Colleges eligible for listing

To be included in the *Index of Majors and Graduate Degrees*, an institution must meet the criteria set by the U.S. Department of Education Division of Eligibility and Agency Evaluation. The *Index* includes colleges accredited by a nationally recognized accrediting agency or approved by a state department of education or a state university; colleges that have attained preaccredited status with a nationally recognized accrediting agency; and public and nonprofit colleges whose credits have been accepted as if coming from an accredited institution by at least three accredited institutions.

Institutions offering graduate-level curriculums only, as well as undergraduate, are included. Institutions in foreign countries are included here on the basis of their membership in the College Board.

Tips on using this book

It is important to attend a college that has the major or majors of interest to you. A major (also called field of study, or program of study) is an academic field of specialization, so-called because students take the majority of courses in this field during their college studies. At most colleges students are expected to take a broad range of courses before declaring (committing to) a major.

All users, even those with a clear idea of their intended major, may find it useful to first browse through the three-page list of "Major fields of study by discipline." Students who know the broad discipline in which they are interested but who seek information about what specific majors are offered within that area should also consult this list.

Students may find several majors of interest—even related majors—under different disciplines. For example, the chart below shows the various majors involving textiles (left column) and the broad academic areas, or disciplines, those majors fall into (right):

Major	*Discipline*
Fibers/textiles/weaving	Crafts and design
Textiles and clothing	Home economics
Textile technology	Industrial production
Clothing and textiles management	Vocational home economics
Textile engineering	Engineering

Users can speed their search for all majors of interest by going to the index at the back of the book which lists all majors in alphabetical order: in a glance one can see all majors that begin with a certain key word.

Major fields of study

The list of majors used in the *Index* is based on the Classification of Instructional Programs (CIP) used by the National Center for Educational Statistics. Colleges were provided with the list of fields and asked to use it to report their majors, even though their own titles for some majors might not match the CIP exactly. Colleges could and did add names of other majors they felt did not conform closely enough to any title listed; these additional fields are *not* included in the *Index*, but can be found in *The College Handbook*.

The levels at which colleges offer specific majors are designated by the following letters found after the colleges' names:

C	Certificate or diploma
A	Associate degree
B	Bachelor's degree
M	Master's degree
D	Doctoral degree
F	First professional degree
W	Work beyond doctorate or first professional degree

Undergraduate

Certificate and diploma. These are nondegree offerings below the associate degree and are most often found under technical and vocational fields of study. They generally lead to employment in an occupational field.

Associate. Two types of associate majors are offered: (1) technologies and vocational specialities that are generally completed in two years of college study and are usually sufficient for entrance into an occupational field, and (2) college- or university-parallel programs, that are like the first two years of a four-year college curriculum. Students obtaining a degree in a nonvocational area often transfer to four-year colleges where they complete the requirements for a bachelor's degree in a specific major.

Bachelor's. Sometimes called baccalaureate degrees, these degree programs generally require four or five years of study. The bachelor of arts (BA) and bachelor of science (BS) are the most common baccalaureates, and both include general education courses, a major, and electives. The bachelor of science is more likely to be awarded in the sciences and for professional or technical fields of study. Bachelor of arts degrees are awarded more often in the humanities and arts. However, there are no absolute differences between the degrees, and policies concerning their award vary from college to college.

Graduate

Graduate programs vary in length and may lead to a master's degree, a doctorate, or a first professional degree.

Master's. Master of arts (MA) and master of science (MS) programs lead to the customary first graduate degrees in the liberal arts and sciences and usually take one to two academic years of study to complete. There are many other master's degrees offered, such as the MBA (master of business administration), MLS (master of library science), MSW (master of social work). *See also* "Work beyond the doctorate or first professional degree" below.

Doctorate. The doctoral degree may be the doctor of philosophy (PhD), awarded in many of the humanities, arts, and sciences, or another doctoral degree such as the doctor of education (EdD), or doctor of public health (DPH). Doctoral programs usually consist of course work and independent research culminating in a dissertation or other formal presentation of the results of independent study.

First professional. The first professional programs listed in the *Index* are those recognized by the U.S. Department of Education and defined as requiring at least two academic years of previous college work for entrance and a total of at least six years of college work for completion. The degrees awarded upon completion of these programs are:

D.C.	Chiropractic
D.D.S. or D.M.D.	Dentistry
J.D.	Law
M.D.	Medicine
O.D.	Optometry
D.O.	Osteopathic medicine
Pharm.D.	Pharmacy
D.P.M.	Podiatry or podiatric medicine
D.V.M.	Veterinary medicine
B.Div., M.Div., Rabbinical, or Talmudical	Theological professions

Work beyond the doctorate or first professional degree: Work beyond the doctorate or first professional degree is advanced graduate study usually consisting of research or other independent pursuits.

In some fields, the master's degree is the next highest degree awarded *after* completion of the first professional degree. The degrees M or D listed in this book in the fields of Dental specialities, Medical specialties, and Podiatry or podiatric medicine are awarded after the first professional degree has been earned.

Special academic programs

There are 18 special academic programs listed in this section: ▪ accelerated study ▪ combined bachelor's/graduate degree ▪ cooperative education ▪ double major ▪ external degree ▪ honors program ▪ independent study ▪ internship ▪ liberal arts and career combination ▪ semester at sea ▪ student-designed major ▪ study abroad ▪ teacher preparation ▪ telecourses ▪ United Nations semester ▪ visiting/exchange student program ▪ Washington semester ▪ weekend college.

The programs are described in the glossary at the beginning of the *Index*. For each program, there is a state-by-state listing of colleges that offer that option. Institutions that offer these programs through cross-registration are generally *not* listed. However, colleges that offer combined bachelor's/graduate degree programs and liberal arts and career combinations through joint programs with other institutions are included here.

Colleges included in this book

In this list colleges are listed by state by their characterization of themselves as any of the following:

▪ two-year	▪ four-year
▪ two-year upper-division	▪ five-year
▪ three-year	▪ graduate

Generally, two-year colleges offer associate degrees only. In a few cases—usually at branch campuses of university systems—a junior or community college awards a bachelor's degree as well. Two-year upper-division institutions and colleges offering three or more years of study usually grant bachelor's degrees. Many of these colleges also offer degrees at the graduate and associate levels.

An address to which students can write for additional information is included for each college.

Glossary of special programs

Accelerated program. A college program of study completed in less time than is usually required, most often by attending in summer or by carrying extra courses during the regular academic term. Completion of a bachelor's degree program in three years is an example of acceleration.

Combined bachelor's/graduate degree. A program to which students are accepted for study at both the undergraduate and graduate levels. The program usually can be completed in less time than two individual programs.

Cooperative education. A college program in which a student alternates between semesters (or other periods) of full-time study and full-time employment in related work. Students are paid for their work at the prevailing rate. Typically, five years are required to complete a bachelor's degree program under the cooperative plan, but graduates have the advantage of having completed about a year's practical experience in addition to their studies.

Double major. Any program of study in which a student completes the requirements of two majors concurrently.

External degree. A program of college study in which students earn credits toward a degree through independent study, college courses, proficiency examinations, and personal experience. External degree programs require minimal or no classroom attendance.

Honors program. Any special program for very able students offering the opportunity for educational enrichment, independent study, acceleration, or some combination of these.

Independent study. Any arrangement that allows students to complete some of their college program by studying independently instead of attending scheduled classes and completing group assignments. Typically, students plan programs of study in consultation with a faculty adviser or committee to whom they may report periodically and submit a final report for evaluation.

Internship. Any short-term, supervised work experience, usually related to a student's major field, for which the student earns academic credit. The work can be full or part time, on or off campus, paid or unpaid. Student teaching and apprenticeships are examples of internships.

Liberal arts and career combination. A program in which a student typically completes three years of study in a liberal arts field followed by two years of professional/technical study (for example, engineering, allied health, or forestry) at the end of which the student is awarded bachelor of arts and bachelor of science degrees. The combination is sometimes referred to as a 3 + 2 program.

Semester at sea. A program for credit, usually for students with majors in oceanography or marine-related fields, in which students live for part of a semester on a ship, frequently a research vessel. Academic courses are generally taken in conjunction with the sea experience or at separate times during the semester.

Student-designed major. A program that allows a student to construct a major field of study not formally offered by the college. Often nontraditional and interdisciplinary in nature, the major is developed by the student with the approval of a designated college officer or committee.

Study abroad. Any arrangement by which a student completes part of the college program—typically the junior year but frequently only a semester or a summer—studying in another country. A college may operate a campus abroad or it may have a cooperative agreement with some other American college or an institution of the other country.

Teacher preparation. A college program designed to prepare students to meet the requirements for certification as teachers in elementary and secondary schools.

Telecourses. Televised courses that are broadcast via public or cable stations and which may be viewed in the home (or on campus equipment) for credit.

United Nations semester. A program in which students generally take courses at a college in the New York City metropolitan area while participating in an internship program at the United Nations.

Visiting/exchange student program. Any arrangement between a student and a college that permits study for a semester or more at another college without extending the amount of time required for a degree.

Washington semester. A program in which students participate in an internship program with a government agency or department in the Washington, D.C., metropolitan area. Students earn field service credit for their work and frequently take courses at area colleges.

Weekend college. A program that allows students to take a complete course of study and attend classes only on weekends. These programs are generally restricted to a few areas of study at a college and require more than the traditional number of years to complete.

Major fields of study by discipline

Agribusiness and agricultural production

Agribusiness
Agricultural business and
    management
Agricultural economics
Agricultural mechanics
Agricultural production
Agricultural products and
    processing
Equestrian science
Horticulture
International agriculture

Agricultural sciences

Agricultural sciences
Agronomy
Animal sciences
Dairy
Food sciences
Horticultural science
Ornamental horticulture
Plant protection (pest
    management)
Soil sciences

Allied health services

Allied health
Community health work
Dental laboratory technology
Geriatric aide
Medical assistant
Medical illustrating
Medical records technology
Mental health/human services
Ophthalmic services
Physician's assistant
Practical nursing
Rehabilitation counseling/services
Veterinarian's assistant

Architecture

Architecture

Area studies

African studies
American studies
Asian studies
Canadian studies
Caribbean studies
East Asian studies
Eastern European studies
European studies
Latin American studies
Middle Eastern studies
Pacific area studies
Russian and Slavic studies
Scandinavian studies
South Asian studies
Southeast Asian studies
Western European studies

Biology

Biochemistry
Biology
Biophysics
Biotechnology
Cell biology
Microbiology
Molecular biology

Botany

Bacteriology
Botany
Mycology
Plant genetics
Plant pharmacology
Plant physiology

Business and management

Accounting
Aviation management
Business administration and
    management
Business economics
Business and management
Business statistics
Contract management and
    procurement/purchasing
Engineering management
Finance
Food management
Hotel/motel and restaurant
    management
Human resources development
Institutional management
Insurance and risk management
International business
    management
Investments and securities
Labor/industrial relations
Management information systems
Management science
Marketing management
Marketing research
Music business management
Operations research (quantitative
    methods)
Organizational behavior
Personnel management
Real estate
Small business management and
    ownership
Sports management
Taxation
Trade and industrial supervision
    and management
Transportation management

Business and office

Business computer, console, and
    peripheral equipment opera-
    tion

Business data entry equipment operation

Business data processing and
    related programs
Business data programming
Business and office
Business systems analysis
Court reporting
Legal secretary
Medical secretary
Office supervision and manage-
    ment
Secretarial and related programs
Word processing

Chemistry

Analytical chemistry
Chemistry
Inorganic chemistry
Organic chemistry
Pharmaceutical chemistry
Physical chemistry

Civil technologies

Civil technology
Drafting and design technology
Survey and mapping technology
Urban planning technology

Communications

Advertising
Communications
Communications research
Journalism (mass communication)
Public relations
Radio/television (includes news
    broadcast)
Telecommunications

Communication technologies

Educational media technology
Interpreter for the deaf
Motion picture technology
Photographic technology
Radio/television technology

Computer and information sciences

Computer graphics
Computer and information
    sciences
Computer mathematics
Computer programming
Data processing
Information sciences and systems
Microcomputer software
Robotics
Systems analysis

Construction trades

Carpentry
Construction
Electrical installation
Masonry, tile setting
Plumbing/pipefitting/steamfitting

Crafts and design

Ceramics
Crafts
Enameling
Fiber/textiles/weaving
Glass
Graphic arts technology
Graphic design
Illustration design
Industrial design
Metal/jewelry
Printmaking
Theater design

Diagnostic and treatment services

Electrodiagnostic technologies
Emergency medical technologies
    (including ambulance and
    paramedic)
Medical radiation dosimetry
Nuclear medical technology
Radiograph medical technology
Respiratory therapy technology
Surgical technology
Ultrasound therapy

Education administration

Administration of special
    education

Adult and continuing education administration
Community college education administration
Education administration
Educational supervision
Higher education administration

Education, general

Adult and continuing education research
Curriculum and instruction
Education
Educational statistics and research
Educational testing/evaluation/ measurement
Higher education research
International and comparative education
School psychology
Social foundations
Student counseling and personnel services

Engineering

Aerospace, aeronautical, and astronautical engineering
Agricultural engineering
Architectural engineering
Bioengineering and biomedical engineering
Ceramic engineering
Chemical engineering
Civil engineering
Computer engineering
Electrical, electronics, and communications engineering
Engineering
Engineering mechanics
Engineering physics
Engineering science
Environmental health engineering
Geological engineering
Geophysical engineering
Industrial engineering
Materials engineering
Mechanical engineering
Metallurgical engineering
Mining and mineral engineering
Naval architecture and marine engineering
Nuclear engineering
Ocean engineering
Paper engineering
Petroleum engineering
Preengineering
Surveying and mapping sciences
Systems engineering
Textile engineering

Engineering technologies

Architectural technologies
Computer technology
Electrical technology
Electronic technology
Engineering and engineering related technologies
Laser electro-optic technology
Mining and petroleum technologies
Occupational safety and health technology
Quality control technology

Environmental control technologies

Air conditioning/heating/ refrigeration technology
Air pollution control technology
Energy conservation and use technology
Sanitation technology
Solar heating and cooling technology
Water and wastewater technology

Environmental design

City/community/regional planning
Environmental design
Historic preservation
Interior design
Landscape architecture
Urban design

Ethnic studies

Afro-American (black) studies
American Indian studies
Hispanic American studies
Islamic studies
Jewish studies
Mexican American studies

Fine arts

Art conservation
Art history
Arts management
Drawing
Fine arts
Painting
Sculpture
Studio art

Geological sciences

Geochemistry
Geology
Geophysics and seismology
Paleontology

Health science

Basic clinical health sciences
Chiropractic (includes all work except D.C. or D.C.M. degree)
Clinical laboratory science
Dental specialties (includes work beyond first professional degree only)
Emergency/disaster science
Gerontology
Health care administration
Health sciences
Medical records administration
Medical specialties (includes work beyond first professional degree only)
Nurse anesthetist
Nursing
Optometry (includes all work except O.D. degree)
Pharmacy (includes all work except Pharm. D. degree)
Population and family planning
Predentistry
Premedicine
Prepharmacy
Preveterinary
Public health laboratory science (includes epidemiology)
Speech pathology/audiology
Sports medicine

Home economics

Business home economics
Family and community services
Family/consumer resource management
Fashion design
Food science and nutrition
Geriatric services
Home economics
Human environment and housing
Individual and family development
International/comparative home economics
Marriage and family counseling
Textiles and clothing

Industrial production

Chemical manufacturing technology
Industrial technology
Manufacturing technology
Optical technology
Plastic technology
Textile technology
Welding technology

Languages

African languages (non-Semitic)
Arabic

Chinese
Foreign languages (multiple emphasis)
French
German
Greek (classical)
Greek (modern)
Hebrew
Indic languages (including Hindi and Sanskrit)
Iranian languages
Italian
Japanese
Korean
Latin
Native American languages
Portuguese
Russian
Scandinavian languages
Slavic languages (other than Russian)
Spanish
Yiddish

Law

Law (includes all work except J.D. degree)
Legal assistant/paralegal
Prelaw

Letters/literature

American literature
Classics
Comparative literature
Creative writing
English
English literature
Folklore and mythology
Language interpretation and translation
Linguistics (includes phonetics, semantics, and philology)
Medieval studies
Rhetoric
Speech, debate, and forensics
Technical and business writing

Library and archival sciences

Archival science

Library assistant

Library science
Museum studies

Life sciences, specialized areas

Anatomy
Biomedical science
Biometrics and biostatistics
Ecology
Embryology
Environmental science

Histology
Marine biology
Neurosciences
Nutritional sciences
Parasitology
Radiobiology
Toxicology

Marketing and distribution

Apparel and accessories
  marketing
Fashion merchandising
Hospitality and recreation
  marketing
Insurance marketing
Marketing and distribution
Personal services
Retailing
Tourism
Transportation and travel
  marketing

Mathematics

Actuarial sciences
Applied mathematics
Mathematics
Pure mathematics
Statistics

Mechanical and electromechanical technologies

Aeronautical technology
Automotive technology
Biomedical equipment technology
Computer servicing technology
Electromechanical technology
Instrumentation technology
Mechanical design technology

Mechanics and repairers

Air conditioning/heating/
  refrigeration mechanics
Aircraft mechanics
Automotive mechanics
Diesel engine mechanics
Electrical and electronics
  equipment repair
Industrial equipment
  maintenance and repair
Power plant operation and
  maintenance (stationary
  energy sources)

Medical laboratory technologies

Cytotechnology
Medical laboratory science

Military sciences

Aerospace science (Air Force)
Coast Guard science
Merchant Marine

Military science (Army)
Naval science (Navy, Marines)

Multi/interdisciplinary studies

Biological and physical
  sciences
Clinical pastoral care
Engineering and other disciplines
Humanities
Humanities and
  social sciences
International studies
Liberal/general studies
Peace studies
Women's studies

Music

Music
Music history and appreciation
Music performance
Music theory and composition

Parks and recreation

Parks and recreation
  management
Recreation and community
  services technologies
Water resources

Philosophy

Philosophy

Physical sciences

Astronomy
Astrophysics
Atmospheric sciences and
  meteorology
Earth sciences
Metallurgy
Oceanography
Physical sciences
Planetary science

Physics

Atomic/molecular physics
Electron physics
Elementary particle physics
Fluids and plasmas
Nuclear physics
Optics
Physics
Solid state physics

Precision production

Commercial art
Drafting
Graphic and printing
  production
Machine tool operation/
  machine shop
Precision metal work
Woodworking

Protective services

Criminal justice studies
Criminal justice technology
Fire control and safety technology
  (includes firefighting)
Fire protection
Forensic studies
Law enforcement and corrections
Law enforcement and corrections
  technologies
Protective services

Psychology

Clinical psychology
Cognitive psychology
Community psychology
Comparative psychology
Counseling psychology
Developmental psychology
Experimental psychology
Industrial and organizational
  psychology
Personality psychology
Psychology
Physiological psychology
Psycholinguistics
Psychometrics
Quantitative psychology
Social psychology

Public affairs

Community services
Funeral services/mortuary
  science
International public service
Medical social work
Public administration
Public affairs
Public policy studies
Public utilities
Social work

Rehabilitation services

Art therapy
Dance therapy
Music therapy
Occupational therapy
Occupational therapy assistant
Physical therapy
Physical therapy assistant
Recreation therapy
Respiratory therapy

Religion

Religion

Renewable natural resources

Conservation and regulation
Fishing and fisheries
Forest products processing
  technology
Forestry and related sciences

Forestry production and
  processing
Renewable natural resources
Wildlife management

Science technologies
Biological laboratory technology
Nuclear technologies
Oceanographic technologies
Science technologies

Social sciences

Anthropology
Archaeology
Behavioral sciences
Criminology
Demography
Economics
Geography
History
International development
International relations
Political science and government
Rural sociology
Social sciences
Sociology
Urban studies

Special education

Bilingual/bicultural education
Education of the culturally
  disadvantaged
Education of the deaf and hearing
  impaired
Education of the emotionally
  handicapped
Education of exceptional children,
  not otherwise classified
Education of the gifted and
  talented
Education of the mentally
  handicapped
Education of the physically
  handicapped
Education of the visually
  handicapped
Remedial education
Special education
Specific learning disabilities
Speech correction
Teaching English as a second
  language/foreign language

Teacher education, general

Early childhood education
Elementary education
Junior high education
Secondary education
Teacher's aide

Teacher education, specific subjects

Agricultural education
Art education

Business education
Driver and safety education
English education
Foreign languages education
Health education
Home economics education
Industrial arts education
Marketing and distributive
    education
Mathematics education
Music education
Nursing education
Nutritional education
Physical education
Reading education
Science education
Social science education
Social studies education
Speech/communication/theater
    education
Technical education
Trade and industrial education

Theology

Bible studies
Biblical languages
Missionary studies
Religious education
Religious music
Theological studies

Transportation

Airline piloting and navigation
Air traffic control
Aviation computer technology
Flight attendant
Marine maintenance
Vehicle and equipment operation

Visual and performing arts

Cinematography/film
Dance
Dramatic arts
Film animation
Film arts
Jazz
Musical theater
Photography
Video
Visual and performing arts

Vocational home economics

Child development, care, and
    guidance
Clothing and textiles manage-
    ment, production, and services
Dietetic aid/assistant
Food production, management,
    and services
Home furnishings and equipment
    management, production, and
    services
Institutional/home management,
    and supporting programs

Zoology

Entomology
Genetics, human and animal
Pathology, human and animal
Pharmacology, human and
    animal
Physiology, human and animal
Zoology

First professional degrees

Chiropractic (D.C. degree)
Dentistry (D.D.S. or D.M.D.
    degrees)
Law (J.D. degree)
Medicine (M.D. degree)
Optometry (O.D. degree)
Osteopathic medicine (D.O.
    degree)
Pharmacy (Pharm. D. degree)
Podiatry (D.P.M. degree,
    includes chiropody)
Theological professions (B. Div.,
    M. Div., Rabbinical, or
    Talmudical)
Veterinary medicine (D.V.M.
    degree)

Accounting

Alabama

Alabama Agricultural and
Mechanical University B
Alabama State University B
Athens State College B
Auburn University
Auburn B,M
Montgomery B
Bessemer State Technical College A
Birmingham-Southern College B
Bishop State Community College A
Central Alabama Community
College: Childersburg Campus C
Chattahoochee Valley Community
College A
Douglas MacArthur State Technical
College A
Draughons Junior College A
Faulkner University B
Huntingdon College B
Jacksonville State University B
Jefferson State Community
College A
John C. Calhoun State Community
College C,A
Lawson State Community
College A
Livingston University A,B
Lurleen B. Wallace State Junior
College C
Mobile College B
Northeast Alabama State Junior
College A
Oakwood College A,B
Samford University B
Selma University A
Shoals Community College C
Spring Hill College B
Troy State University
Montgomery B
Troy B
Tuskegee University B
University of Alabama
Birmingham B,M
Huntsville C,B
Tuscaloosa B,M,D
University of Montevallo B
University of North Alabama B
University of South Alabama B,M
Walker State Technical College A
Wallace State Community College
at Hanceville A

Alaska

Alaska Pacific University A,B
University of Alaska
Anchorage A,B
Fairbanks A,B

Arizona

Arizona State University B,M
Cochise College A
DeVry Institute of Technology:
Phoenix B
Glendale Community College A
Grand Canyon University B
Lamson Junior College C,A
Mesa Community College A
Mohave Community College C,A
Northern Arizona University B
Northland Pioneer College C
Paradise Valley Community College
C,A
Pima Community College C,A
Rio Salado Community College A
Scottsdale Community College C,A
University of Arizona B,M

Western International University
B,M
Yavapai College C,A

Arkansas

Arkansas College B
Arkansas State University B
Arkansas Tech University B
Capital City Junior College A
Central Baptist College A
Garland County Community
College A
Harding University B,M
Henderson State University B
Hendrix College B
John Brown University B
Ouachita Baptist University B
Shorter College A
Southern Arkansas Community
College A
Southern Arkansas University B
University of Arkansas
Fayetteville B,M
Little Rock B
Monticello B
Pine Bluff B
University of Central Arkansas B
University of the Ozarks B
Westark Community College A

California

Allan Hancock College C,A
Armstrong College A,B,M
Azusa Pacific University B
Bakersfield College A
Barstow College C,A
Biola University B
California Lutheran University B
California State Polytechnic
University: Pomona B
California State University
Bakersfield B
Chico M
Dominguez Hills B
Fresno B,M
Fullerton B,M
Hayward B,M
Long Beach B
Los Angeles B,M
Northridge M
Sacramento B,M
San Marcos B
Stanislaus B
Central California Commercial
College A
Cerritos Community College A
Chabot College A
Chaffey Community College A
Chapman University B
Christ College Irvine B
Citrus College C
City College of San Francisco C,A
Claremont McKenna College B
Coastline Community College A
College of the Desert A
College of Marin: Kentfield A
College of Notre Dame C,B
College of the Sequoias C
Compton Community College A
Cosumnes River College C,A
Crafton Hills College C,A
De Anza College C,A
DeVry Institute of Technology: City
of Industry B
Diablo Valley College A
East Los Angeles College A
El Camino College A
Evergreen Valley College C
Feather River College A
Foothill College A
Fresno City College C,A
Fresno Pacific College A,B

Gavilan Community College A
Glendale Community College C,A
Golden Gate University C,B,M
Golden West College C,A
Grossmont Community College C,A
Heald Business College
San Jose C,A
Walnut Creek C,A
Heald College
Sacramento A
Santa Rosa C,A
Humphreys College A,B
Irvine Valley College C,A
John F. Kennedy University B
Kelsey-Jenney College C,A
Kings River Community College A
La Sierra University B
Lake Tahoe Community College
C,A
Laney College C,A
Lassen College A
Lincoln University B
Long Beach City College C,A
Los Angeles City College A
Los Angeles Harbor College C,A
Los Angeles Mission College A
Los Angeles Pierce College A
Los Angeles Trade and Technical
College A
Los Angeles Valley College C
Los Medanos College C,A
Loyola Marymount University B
Marymount College A
Mendocino College C,A
Merced College A
MiraCosta College C,A
Mission College C,A
Modesto Junior College A
Monterey Peninsula College C,A
Moorpark College A
Mount St. Mary's College A,B
Mount San Antonio College C,A
Napa Valley College A
National University B,M
Ohlone College C,A
Orange Coast College C,A
Oxnard College C,A
Pacific Union College B
Palomar College C,A
Pasadena City College C,A
Pepperdine University B
Phillips Junior College
Fresno Campus C,A
San Fernando Valley
Campus C
Point Loma Nazarene College B
Rio Hondo College A
Saddleback College C,A
St. Mary's College of California B
San Diego City College C,A
San Diego Mesa College C,A
San Diego Miramar College A
San Diego State University B
San Francisco State University B,M
San Joaquin Delta College A
San Jose City College A
San Jose State University B,M
Santa Barbara City College C
Santa Clara University B
Santa Monica College A
Santa Rosa Junior College C,A
Sierra College A
Skyline College A
Solano Community College A
Southern California College B
Southwestern College A
Taft College C,A
United States International
University B
University of La Verne B
University of the Pacific B
University of Redlands B

University of San Diego B
University of San Francisco B,M
University of Southern California
B,M
Ventura College C,A
West Coast University C,A,B,M
West Hills Community College A
West Valley College A
Woodbury University B,M
Yuba College C,A

Colorado

Adams State College B
Aims Community College A
Arapahoe Community College C,A
Blair Junior College A
Colorado Christian University B
Colorado Mountain College
Alpine Campus A
Timberline Campus A
Colorado State University B,M
Community College of Denver C,A
Denver Technical College A
Fort Lewis College B
Front Range Community College
C,A
Mesa State College A,B
Metropolitan State College of
Denver B
Morgan Community College A
National College A
Northeastern Junior College A
Otero Junior College C
Parks Junior College A
Pikes Peak Community College C,A
Pueblo Community College A
Red Rocks Community College C,A
Regis College of Regis University B
Trinidad State Junior College A
University of Colorado
Boulder B
Colorado Springs B
Denver B,M
University of Denver B,M
University of Northern Colorado B
University of Southern Colorado B
Western State College of
Colorado B

Connecticut

Albertus Magnus College B
Asnuntuck Community College C,A
Briarwood College A
Central Connecticut State
University B
Fairfield University B
Housatonic Community College A
Manchester Community College
C,A
Mattatuck Community College C,A
Middlesex Community College A
Mitchell College A
Northwestern Connecticut
Community College A
Norwalk Community College A
Quinebaug Valley Community
College A
Quinnipiac College B
Sacred Heart University A,B
St. Joseph College B
South Central Community
College A
Southern Connecticut State
University B
Teikyo-Post University A,B
Tunxis Community College C,A
University of Bridgeport B
University of Connecticut B
University of Hartford B,M
University of New Haven B,M
Western Connecticut State
University B,M

Delaware

Delaware State College B
Delaware Technical and
    Community College
        Southern Campus A
        Stanton/Wilmington
            Campus A
        Terry Campus A
Goldey-Beacom College A,B
University of Delaware B,M
Wesley College B
Wilmington College B

District of Columbia

American University B,M
Catholic University of America B,M
Gallaudet University B
George Washington University
    B,M,D
Georgetown University B
Howard University B
Southeastern University A,B,M
University of the District of
    Columbia A,B

Florida

Barry University B,M
Bethune-Cookman College B
Broward Community College A
Daytona Beach Community College
    C,A
Edison Community College C,A
Flagler College B
Florida Agricultural and Mechanical
    University B
Florida Atlantic University B,M
Florida Community College at
    Jacksonville A
Florida Institute of Technology B
Florida International University
    B,M
Florida Memorial College B
Florida Southern College B,M
Florida State University B,M,D
Fort Lauderdale College A,B
Gulf Coast Community College C,A
Hillsborough Community College C
Indian River Community College A
Jacksonville University B
Jones College A,B
Keiser College of Technology A
Lynn University B
Miami-Dade Community College
    C,A
Nova University B,M
Okaloosa-Walton Community
    College A
Orlando College A,B
Palm Beach Community College A
Pensacola Junior College A
Phillips Junior College:
    Melbourne A
St. Petersburg Junior College A
St. Thomas University B,M
Santa Fe Community College C,A
South College: Palm Beach Campus
    C,A
South Florida Community College
    C,A
Stetson University C,B,M
Tampa College A,B
University of Central Florida B,M
University of Florida B,M,D
University of Miami B,M
University of North Florida B,M
University of South Florida B,M
University of Tampa B
University of West Florida B,M
Valencia Community College A
Webber College A,B

Georgia

Abraham Baldwin Agricultural
    College A
Albany State College B
Athens Area Technical Institute
    C,A
Atlanta Metropolitan College A
Augusta College B
Augusta Technical Institute C,A
Bainbridge College A
Berry College B
Brenau Women's College B
Brewton-Parker College B
Brunswick College A
Chattahoochee Technical Institute
    C,A
Clark Atlanta University B
Clayton State College A,B
Columbus College B
Dalton College A
Darton College A
DeKalb College A
DeKalb Technical Institute C,A
DeVry Institute of Technology:
    Atlanta B
East Georgia College A
Emory University B,M
Floyd College A
Fort Valley State College B
Gainesville College A
Georgia College B
Georgia Southern University B
Georgia Southwestern College A,B
Georgia State University B,M,D
Gordon College A
Kennesaw State College B,M
LaGrange College B
Macon College C,A
Meadows College of Business A
Mercer University
    Atlanta B,M
    Macon B,M
Middle Georgia College A
Morehouse College B
Morris Brown College B
North Georgia College B
Oglethorpe University B
Piedmont College B
Reinhardt College A
Savannah State College B
Savannah Technical Institute C,A
Shorter College B
South College C,A
South Georgia College A
Truett-McConnell College A
University of Georgia B,M
Valdosta State College B
Waycross College C
West Georgia College B,M

Hawaii

Brigham Young University-Hawaii
    C,A,B
Cannon's International Business
    College of Honolulu A
Chaminade University of
    Honolulu B
Hawaii Pacific University A,B,M
University of Hawaii
    Kapiolani Community College
        C,A
    Kauai Community College C,A
    Leeward Community College
        C,A
    Manoa B,M

Idaho

Albertson College B
Boise State University B
College of Southern Idaho A
Idaho State University B
ITT Technical Institute: Boise C

Lewis Clark State College A
Northwest Nazarene College B
Ricks College A
University of Idaho B

Illinois

Augustana College B
Aurora University B
Barat College B
Black Hawk College C,A
Blackburn College B
Bradley University B
Carl Sandburg College C,A
Chicago State University B
City Colleges of Chicago
    Chicago City-Wide College
        C,A
    Malcolm X College A
    Olive-Harvey College C,A
    Richard J. Daley College A
    Wright College C,A
College of DuPage C,A
College of Lake County C,A
College of St. Francis B
Concordia University B
De Paul University B,M
DeVry Institute of Technology
    Chicago B
    Lombard B
Eastern Illinois University B
Elgin Community College C,A
Elmhurst College B
Eureka College B
Gem City College C,A
Greenville College B
Highland Community College C,A
Illinois Benedictine College B
Illinois Central College C,A
Illinois College B
Illinois Eastern Community
    Colleges: Olney Central
    College A
Illinois Institute of Technology B
Illinois State University B,M
Illinois Valley Community College
    C,A
Illinois Wesleyan University B
John A. Logan College A
Joliet Junior College A
Judson College B
Kishwaukee College C,A
Lake Land College A
Lewis and Clark Community
    College A
Lewis University B
Lincoln Land Community
    College A
Loyola University of Chicago B
MacCormac Junior College A
MacMurray College B
McKendree College B
Midstate College C,A
Millikin University B
Monmouth College B
Morton College C,A
National-Louis University C,B
North Central College B
North Park College and Theological
    Seminary B
Northeastern Illinois University B
Northern Illinois University B,M
Northwestern University M,D
Oakton Community College C,A
Olivet Nazarene University B
Parkland College C,A
Phillips College of Chicago A
Quincy College B
Rend Lake College A
Richland Community College A
Robert Morris College: Chicago A
Rock Valley College A
Rockford College B

Roosevelt University B,M
Rosary College B,M
St. Augustine College C,A
St. Xavier University C,B
Sangamon State University B,M
Shawnee Community College A
Southern Illinois University
    Carbondale B,M,D
    Edwardsville B
Spoon River College A
State Community College A
Trinity Christian College B
Trinity College B
Triton College C,A
University of Chicago M,D
University of Illinois
    Chicago B,M,D
    Urbana-Champaign B,M,D
Waubonsee Community College
    C,A
Western Illinois University B,M
William Rainey Harper College C,A

Indiana

Ancilla College C,A
Anderson University B
Ball State University B
Bethel College B
Butler University B
Calumet College of St. Joseph
    C,A,B
Franklin College B
Goshen College B
Grace College B
Huntington College A,B
Indiana Institute of Technology A,B
Indiana State University B
Indiana University
    Bloomington B,M,D
    East A,B
    Kokomo B
    Northwest B
    South Bend B
    Southeast B
Indiana University—Purdue
    University
    Fort Wayne A,B
    Indianapolis B
Indiana Vocational Technical
    College
    Central Indiana A
    Columbus C,A
    Eastcentral C,A
    Kokomo C,A
    Lafayette C,A
    Northcentral C,A
    Northeast C,A
    Northwest C,A
    Southcentral C,A
    Southeast C,A
    Southwest C,A
    Wabash Valley C,A
    Whitewater C,A
Indiana Wesleyan University A,B
International Business College A
ITT Technical Institute:
    Indianapolis A
Manchester College A,B,M
Marian College A,B
Martin University B
Oakland City College A,B
Purdue University
    Calumet B
    North Central Campus A,B
    West Lafayette B,M,D
St. Francis College A,B
St. Joseph's College B
St. Mary-of-the-Woods College B
Taylor University B
Tri-State University A,B
University of Evansville B
University of Indianapolis B,M

University of Notre Dame *B*
University of Southern Indiana *C,B*
Valparaiso University *B*
Vincennes University *A*

Iowa

American Institute of Business *C,A*
American Institute of Commerce *C,A*
Briar Cliff College *B*
Buena Vista College *B*
Central College *B*
Clarke College *B*
Clinton Community College *A*
Coe College *B*
Des Moines Area Community College *A*
Dordt College *B*
Drake University *B*
Graceland College *B*
Grand View College *B*
Hawkeye Institute of Technology *C,A*
Iowa Central Community College *A*
Iowa Lakes Community College *A*
Iowa State University *B*
Iowa Wesleyan College *B*
Iowa Western Community College *A*
Kirkwood Community College *A*
Loras College *B*
Luther College *B*
Morningside College *B*
Mount Mercy College *B*
Mount St. Clare College *B*
Muscatine Community College *A*
North Iowa Area Community College *C,A*
Northeast Iowa Community College *A*
Northwest Iowa Technical College *A*
Northwestern College *B*
St. Ambrose University *B,M*
Scott Community College *A*
Simpson College *B*
Southeastern Community College: North Campus *A*
Southwestern Community College *A*
Teikyo Marycrest University *B*
Teikyo Westmar University *B*
University of Dubuque *A,B*
University of Iowa *B,M,D*
University of Northern Iowa *B*
Upper Iowa University *B*
Waldorf College *A*
Wartburg College *B*
William Penn College *B*

Kansas

Baker University *B*
Barton County Community College *A*
Benedictine College *A,B*
Bethany College *B*
Bethel College *B*
Brown Mackie College *A*
Butler County Community College *C*
Central College *A*
Cloud County Community College *A*
Coffeyville Community College *A*
Colby Community College *A*
Cowley County Community College *A*
Dodge City Community College *A*
Emporia State University *B*
Fort Hays State University *B*
Fort Scott Community College *A*
Friends University *A,B*

Haskell Indian Junior College *A*
Highland Community College *A*
Hutchinson Community College *A*
Johnson County Community College *A*
Kansas City Kansas Community College *A*
Kansas Newman College *B*
Kansas State University *B,M*
Kansas Wesleyan University *B*
Labette Community College *A*
McPherson College *B*
MidAmerica Nazarene College *B*
Neosho County Community College *A*
Ottawa University *B*
Pittsburg State University *B,M*
Pratt Community College *C,A*
St. Mary College *B*
Seward County Community College *C,A*
Sterling College *B*
Tabor College *B*
University of Kansas *B*
Washburn University of Topeka *B*
Wichita State University *B,M*

Kentucky

Alice Lloyd College *B*
Bellarmine College *B*
Brescia College *B*
Campbellsville College *B*
Cumberland College *B*
Eastern Kentucky University *B*
Franklin College *A*
Georgetown College *B*
Jefferson Community College *A*
Kentucky Wesleyan College *B*
Lexington Community College *A*
Lindsey Wilson College *B*
Madisonville Community College *A*
Morehead State University *B*
Murray State University *B*
Northern Kentucky University *B*
Paducah Community College *A*
Prestonburg Community College *A*
Sue Bennett College *A*
Sullivan College *A,B*
Thomas More College *A,B*
Union College *A,B*
University of Kentucky *B,M*
University of Louisville *B*
Watterson College *A*
Western Kentucky University *B*

Louisiana

Centenary College of Louisiana *B*
Dillard University *B*
Grambling State University *A,B*
Louisiana College *B*
Louisiana State University
    Agricultural and Mechanical College *B,M,D*
    Shreveport *B*
Louisiana Tech University *B,M*
Loyola University *B*
McNeese State University *B*
Nicholls State University *B*
Northeast Louisiana University *B*
Northwestern State University *A,B*
Southeastern Louisiana University *B*
Southern University
    New Orleans *B*
    Shreveport *A*
Southern University and Agricultural and Mechanical College *B,M*
University of New Orleans *B,M*
University of Southwestern Louisiana *B*
Xavier University of Louisiana *B*

Maine

Andover College *A*
Beal College *A*
Casco Bay College *A*
Husson College *A,B*
St. Joseph's College *B*
Thomas College *C,B,M*
University of Maine
    Augusta *A,B*
    Machias *A,B*
    Orono *B*
    Presque Isle *B*
University of Southern Maine *B*
Westbrook College *B*

Maryland

Anne Arundel Community College *A*
Catonsville Community College *C,A*
Cecil Community College *C,A*
Charles County Community College *C,A*
Chesapeake College *C,A*
Columbia Union College *A,B*
Dundalk Community College *C,A*
Essex Community College *C,A*
Frederick Community College *A*
Frostburg State University *B*
Garrett Community College *A*
Hagerstown Business College *C,A*
Hagerstown Junior College *A*
Harford Community College *C,A*
Howard Community College *A*
Loyola College in Maryland *B*
Montgomery College
    Germantown Campus *A*
    Rockville Campus *A*
    Takoma Park Campus *A*
Morgan State University *B*
Mount St. Mary's College *B*
New Community College of Baltimore *A*
Prince George's Community College *C,A*
Salisbury State University *B*
Sojourner-Douglass College *B*
Towson State University *B*
University of Baltimore *B*
University of Maryland
    College Park *B*
    Eastern Shore *B*
Villa Julie College *A,B*
Wor-Wic Tech Community College *A*

Massachusetts

American International College *B*
Anna Maria College for Men and Women *B*
Aquinas College at Milton *A*
Aquinas College at Newton *C,A*
Assumption College *B,M*
Atlantic Union College *A,B*
Babson College *B,M*
Bay Path College *A*
Bay State College *A*
Becker College
    Leicester Campus *A*
    Worcester Campus *A*
Bentley College *B,M*
Boston College *B*
Boston University *A,B*
Bridgewater State College *C,B*
Bristol Community College *A*
Bunker Hill Community College *A*
Cape Cod Community College *A*
College of the Holy Cross *B*
Elms College *B*
Emmanuel College *B*
Endicott College *A*
Fisher College *A*
Fitchburg State College *B*

Gordon College *B*
Greenfield Community College *A*
Harvard University *M,D*
Holyoke Community College *A*
Lasell College *A*
Marian Court Junior College *A*
Massachusetts Bay Community College *C,A*
Massachusetts Institute of Technology *M,D*
Massasoit Community College *A*
Merrimack College *A,B*
Middlesex Community College *A*
Mount Ida College *A*
Mount Wachusett Community College *A*
New England Banking Institute *C,A*
Newbury College *A*
Nichols College *B*
North Adams State College *B*
North Shore Community College *A*
Northeastern University *C,A,B,M*
Northern Essex Community College *A*
Pine Manor College *B*
Quincy College *C,A*
Quinsigamond Community College *C,A*
Roxbury Community College *A*
Salem State College *B*
Simmons College *B*
Springfield Technical Community College *A*
Stonehill College *B*
Suffolk University *B*
University of Massachusetts
    Amherst *B,M*
    Dartmouth *B*
    Lowell *A,B*
Western New England College *B,M*

Michigan

Adrian College *A,B*
Alpena Community College *A*
Andrews University *A,B*
Aquinas College *B*
Baker College
    Auburn Hills *C,A*
    Cadillac *C,A*
    Flint *C,A,B*
    Mount Clemens *C,A*
    Muskegon *C,A,B*
    Owosso *C,A,B*
    Port Huron *A*
Calvin College *B*
Central Michigan University *B*
Charles Stewart Mott Community College *A*
Cleary College *A,B*
Davenport College of Business *A,B*
Delta College *A*
Detroit College of Business *A,B*
Eastern Michigan University *B,M*
Ferris State University *B,M*
Glen Oaks Community College *C*
GMI Engineering & Management Institute *B*
Grand Rapids Baptist College and Seminary *B*
Grand Rapids Community College *A*
Grand Valley State University *B,M*
Great Lakes Junior College of Business *C,A*
Henry Ford Community College *A*
Hillsdale College *B*
Hope College *B*
Jackson Community College *A*
Jordan College *A*
Kalamazoo Valley Community College *A*
Kellogg Community College *C,A*

Kirtland Community College *A*
Lake Superior State University *A,B*
Lansing Community College *A*
Lawrence Technological
University *B*
Lewis College of Business *A*
Macomb Community College *C,A*
Madonna University *B*
Marygrove College *A,B*
Michigan Christian College *C,A*
Michigan State University *B,M,D*
Mid Michigan Community
College *A*
Montcalm Community College *A*
Muskegon Community College *A*
Northern Michigan University *B*
Northwestern Michigan College *A*
Northwood Institute *A,B*
Oakland Community College *C,A*
Oakland University *B*
Olivet College *B*
Saginaw Valley State University
B,M
St. Clair County Community
College *A*
Schoolcraft College *C,A*
Siena Heights College *A,B*
Southwestern Michigan College *A*
Spring Arbor College *B*
Suomi College *A*
University of Detroit Mercy *B*
University of Michigan
Ann Arbor *D*
Dearborn *B*
Flint *B*
Walsh College of Accountancy and
Business Administration *B,M*
Wayne State University *B,M*
West Shore Community College *A*
Western Michigan University *B,M*

Minnesota

Alexandria Technical College *A*
Anoka-Ramsey Community
College *A*
Augsburg College *B*
Austin Community College *A*
Bemidji State University *B*
Bethel College *B*
College of St. Benedict *B*
College of St. Catherine: St.
Catherine Campus *B*
College of St. Scholastica *B*
Concordia College: Moorhead *B*
Concordia College: St. Paul *B*
Gustavus Adolphus College *B*
Inver Hills Community College *A*
Itasca Community College:
Arrowhead Region *A*
Lakewood Community College *A*
Mankato State University *B,M*
Metropolitan State University *B*
Minneapolis Community College *A*
Moorhead State University *B*
Normandale Community College *A*
Northland Community College *A*
Northwestern College *A,B*
Rainy River Community College
C,A
St. Cloud State University *B,M*
St. John's University *B*
St. Mary's College of Minnesota *B*
St. Paul Technical College *C,A*
Southwest State University *A,B*
University of Minnesota
Crookston *A*
Duluth *B*
Twin Cities *B*
University of St. Thomas *B*
Vermilion Community College *C,A*
Willmar Community College *A*
Willmar Technical College *C,A*

Winona State University *B*

Mississippi

Alcorn State University *B*
Belhaven College *B*
Copiah-Lincoln Community
College *A*
Delta State University *B*
Jackson State University *B,M*
Jones County Junior College *A*
Mary Holmes College *A*
Millsaps College *B*
Mississippi College *B*
Mississippi Gulf Coast Community
College
Jackson County Campus *A*
Jefferson Davis Campus *A*
Mississippi State University *B,M*
Mississippi University for Women *B*
Northeast Mississippi Community
College *A*
Phillips Junior College
Jackson *A*
Mississippi Gulf Coast *A*
Rust College *B*
Tougaloo College *B*
University of Mississippi *B,M,D*
University of Southern Mississippi
B,M

Missouri

Avila College *B,M*
Central Methodist College *B*
Central Missouri State University
B,M
College of the Ozarks *B*
Columbia College *B*
Culver-Stockton College *B*
DeVry Institute of Technology:
Kansas City *B*
Drury College *B*
East Central College *C,A*
Evangel College *A,B*
Fontbonne College *B*
Hannibal-LaGrange College *B*
Jefferson College *A*
Lincoln University *B*
Lindenwood College *M*
Longview Community College *A*
Maple Woods Community College
C,A
Maryville University *B*
Missouri Baptist College *B*
Missouri Southern State College
A,B
Missouri Valley College *B*
Missouri Western State College *A,B*
Moberly Area Community College
C,A
National College *C*
North Central Missouri College *C,A*
Northeast Missouri State University
B,M
Northwest Missouri State
University *B*
Park College *B*
Penn Valley Community College
C,A
Phillips Junior College *A*
Rockhurst College *B*
St. Charles Community College *A*
St. Louis Community College
Florissant Valley *C*
Forest Park *C,A*
Meramec *C,A*
St. Louis University *B,M,D*
Southeast Missouri State
University *B*
Southwest Baptist University *B*
Southwest Missouri State University
B,M
State Fair Community College *A*

Three Rivers Community College *A*
University of Missouri
Columbia *B,M,D*
Kansas City *B,M*
St. Louis *M*
Webster University *B*
Westminster College *B*
William Jewell College *B*
William Woods College *B*

Montana

Carroll College *B*
College of Great Falls *A,B*
Eastern Montana College *B*
Flathead Valley Community
College *A*
Miles Community College *A*
Montana College of Mineral
Science and Technology *B*
Montana State University *B*
Rocky Mountain College *B*
University of Montana *B,M*

Nebraska

Bellevue College *B*
Central Community College *C,A*
Chadron State College *B*
College of St. Mary *A,B*
Concordia College *B*
Creighton University *B*
Dana College *B*
Doane College *B*
Hastings College *B*
Lincoln School of Commerce *C,A*
McCook Community College *A*
Metropolitan Community College *A*
Midland Lutheran College *A,B*
Northeast Community College *A*
Peru State College *B*
Southeast Community College:
Beatrice Campus *A*
Union College *B*
University of Nebraska
Lincoln *B,M*
Omaha *B,M*
Wayne State College *B*
Western Nebraska Community
College
Scottsbluff Campus *A*
Sidney Campus *A*

Nevada

Community College of Southern
Nevada *A*
Northern Nevada Community
College *C*
Truckee Meadows Community
College *A*
University of Nevada
Las Vegas *B,M*
Reno *B*
Western Nevada Community
College *A*

New Hampshire

Castle College *C,A*
Daniel Webster College *A*
Franklin Pierce College *A,B*
Hesser College *A*
McIntosh College *A*
New England College *B*
New Hampshire College *A,B,M*
New Hampshire Technical College
Berlin *A*
Laconia *C,A*
Nashua *A*
Stratham *C,A*
Plymouth State College of the
University System of New
Hampshire *B*
Rivier College *A,B*

New Jersey

Atlantic Community College *A*
Bergen Community College *A*
Berkeley College of Business *C,A*
Bloomfield College *C,B*
Brookdale Community College *A*
Burlington County College *C,A*
Caldwell College *C*
Camden County College *A*
Centenary College *B*
College of St. Elizabeth *C,B*
County College of Morris *A*
Cumberland County College *A*
Essex County College *C,A*
Fairleigh Dickinson University *B,M*
Georgian Court College *B*
Glassboro State College *B*
Gloucester County College *C,A*
Jersey City State College *B*
Kean College of New Jersey *B*
Mercer County Community
College *A*
Monmouth College *B*
Ocean County College *C,A*
Passaic County Community
College *A*
Ramapo College of New Jersey *B*
Rider College *B*
Rutgers—The State University of
New Jersey
Camden College of Arts and
Sciences *B*
Douglass College *B*
Livingston College *B*
Newark College of Arts and
Sciences *B*
Rutgers College *B*
University College Camden *B*
University College New
Brunswick *B*
University College Newark *B*
St. Peter's College *B*
Seton Hall University *B,M*
Stockton State College *B*
Thomas Edison State College *C,A,B*
Trenton State College *B*
Union County College *A*
Upsala College *B*
William Paterson College of New
Jersey *B*

New Mexico

Albuquerque Technical-Vocational
Institute *A*
Clovis Community College *A*
College of Santa Fe *A,B*
College of the Southwest *B*
Dona Ana Branch Community
College of New Mexico State
University *A*
Eastern New Mexico University
Portales *B,M*
Roswell Campus *C*
National College *A,B*
New Mexico Junior College *A*
New Mexico State University
Carlsbad *C*
Las Cruces *B,M*
Northern New Mexico Community
College *C,A*
Parks College *C,A*
San Juan College *A*
University of New Mexico *B,M*
Western New Mexico University *B*

New York

Adelphi University *B,M*
Adirondack Community College *A*
Alfred University *B*
Berkeley College *A*
Berkeley School: New York City
C,A

Bramson ORT Technical Institute
C,A
Broome Community College A
Bryant & Stratton Business Institute
Albany C,A
Buffalo C,A
Rochester A
Syracuse A
Canisius College B,M
Cazenovia College A
Central City Business Institute A
City University of New York
Baruch College B,M,D
Borough of Manhattan
Community College A
Brooklyn College B,M
College of Staten Island B
Hostos Community College A
Hunter College B
Kingsborough Community
College A
La Guardia Community
College A
Lehman College B,M
Medgar Evers College B
New York City Technical
College A
Queens College B
Queensborough Community
College A
York College B
Clarkson University B,M
Clinton Community College A
College of St. Rose B
Columbia-Greene Community
College C,A
Community College of the Finger
Lakes A
Cornell University M,D
Corning Community College C,A
Daemen College B
Dominican College of Blauvelt B
Dowling College B
Dutchess Community College A
D'Youville College B
Elmira College B
Five Towns College A
Fordham University B,M
Fulton-Montgomery Community
College A
Genesee Community College C,A
Hartwick College B
Herkimer County Community
College A
Hilbert College A
Hofstra University B,M
Houghton College B
Hudson Valley Community College
C,A
Iona College B,M
Ithaca College B
Jamestown Business College C,A
Jamestown Community College A
Jefferson Community College C,A
King's College B
Le Moyne College B
Long Island University
Brooklyn Campus B,M
C. W. Post Campus B,M
Southampton Campus B
Manhattan College B
Maria College A
Marist College B
Marymount Manhattan College B
Mercy College C,B
Mohawk Valley Community College
. C,A
Molloy College B
Monroe College A
Monroe Community College A
Mount St. Mary College B
Nassau Community College A

Nazareth College of Rochester B
New York Institute of Technology
A,B
New York University B,M,D
Niagara County Community
College A
Niagara University B
Onondaga Community College A
Orange County Community
College A
Pace University
College of White Plains A,B,M
New York A,B,M
Pleasantville/Briarcliff A,B,M
Roberts Wesleyan College B
Rochester Business Institute A
Rochester Institute of Technology
C,A,B,M
Rockland Community College A
Russell Sage College B
Sage Junior College of Albany, A
Division of Russell Sage
College A
St. Bonaventure University B,W
St. Francis College B
St. John Fisher College C,B
St. John's University B,M
St. Joseph's College
Brooklyn B
Suffolk Campus B
St. Thomas Aquinas College B
Siena College C,B
State University of New York
Albany B,M
Binghamton B,M
Buffalo B,M,D
College of Agriculture and
Technology at Cobleskill A
College of Agriculture and
Technology at Morrisville A
College at Brockport B
College at Fredonia B
College at Geneseo B
College at New Paltz B
College at Old Westbury B
College at Plattsburgh B
College of Technology at
Alfred A
College of Technology at
Canton A
College of Technology at
Delhi A
College of Technology at
Farmingdale A
Institute of Technology at
Utica/Rome B
Oswego B
Suffolk County Community College
Eastern Campus A
Selden C,A
Western Campus C,A
Sullivan County Community
College A
Syracuse University B,M,D
Taylor Business Institute A
Tompkins-Cortland Community
College C,A
Touro College A,B
Union College W
University of the State of New
York: Regents College B
Utica College of Syracuse
University B
Utica School of Commerce A
Wagner College B
Westchester Business Institute A
Westchester Community College
C,A
Yeshiva University B

North Carolina

Alamance Community College A
Anson Community College A
Appalachian State University B,M
Asheville Buncombe Technical
Community College C,A
Barber-Scotia College B
Barton College B
Beaufort County Community
College A
Belmont Abbey College B
Bennett College B
Brevard College A
Caldwell Community College and
Technical Institute A
Campbell University B
Cape Fear Community College A
Catawba College B
Catawba Valley Community College
C,A
Cecils College C
Central Carolina Community
College A
Central Piedmont Community
College A
Chowan College A
Cleveland Community College A
Coastal Carolina Community
College A
Craven Community College A
Davidson County Community
College A
Durham Technical Community
College A
East Carolina University B,M
Edgecombe Community College A
Elizabeth City State University B
Elon College B
Fayetteville State University B
Fayetteville Technical Community
College A
Forsyth Technical Community
College A
Gardner-Webb College B
Gaston College A
Greensboro College B
Guilford College B
Guilford Technical Community
College A
High Point University B
James Sprunt Community
College A
Johnson C. Smith University B
Johnston Community College A
Lenoir-Rhyne College B
Livingstone College B
Mars Hill College B
Martin Community College A
Mayland Community College C,A
McDowell Technical Community
College A
Methodist College A,B
Mitchell Community College A
Montgomery Community College A
Mount Olive College A,B
Nash Community College A
North Carolina Agricultural and
Technical State University B
North Carolina Central
University B
North Carolina State University B
North Carolina Wesleyan College B
Pamlico Community College A
Pfeiffer College B
Piedmont Community College A
Pitt Community College A
Queens College B
Richmond Community College C,A
Roanoke-Chowan Community
College C
Robeson Community College A
Rockingham Community College A

St. Augustine's College B
Salem College B
Sampson Community College A
Sandhills Community College A
Shaw University B
Southwestern Community
College A
Stanly Community College A
Surry Community College A
Tri-County Community College A
University of North Carolina
Asheville B
Chapel Hill M,D
Charlotte B
Greensboro B,M
Wilmington B
Vance-Granville Community
College A
Wake Forest University B
Wake Technical Community
College A
Wayne Community College A
Western Carolina University B
Western Piedmont Community
College A
Wilkes Community College A
Wilson Technical Community
College A
Wingate College A,B
Winston-Salem State University B

North Dakota

Dickinson State University B
Jamestown College B
Little Hoop Community College A
Minot State University A,B
North Dakota State College of
Science A
North Dakota State University B
Turtle Mountain Community
College C
University of Mary A,B
University of North Dakota
Grand Forks B
Lake Region A
Williston A

Ohio

Ashland University B
Baldwin-Wallace College C,B
Bluffton College B
Bowling Green State University
Bowling Green B,M
Firelands College C,A
Bradford School C,A
Bryant & Stratton Business
Institute: Great Northern C,A
Capital University B
Case Western Reserve University
B,M,D
Cedarville College B
Central Ohio Technical College A
Central State University B
Cincinnati Metropolitan College A
Cincinnati Technical College A
Clark State Community College A
Cleveland State University B,M
College of Mount St. Joseph A,B
Columbus State Community
College A
Cuyahoga Community College
Metropolitan Campus A
Western Campus A
Davis Junior College of Business A
Defiance College B
DeVry Institute of Technology:
Columbus B
Dyke College A,B
Edison State Community College
C,A
Franciscan University of
Steubenville A,B

Franklin University *A,B*
Heidelberg College *B*
Hocking Technical College *A*
ITT Technical Institute:
Youngstown *A*
Jefferson Technical College *A*
John Carroll University *B*
Kent State University
Ashtabula Regional Campus *A*
East Liverpool Regional
Campus *A*
Kent *B,M,D*
Salem Regional Campus *A*
Tuscarawas Campus *A*
Lake Erie College *B*
Lakeland Community College *C,A*
Lorain County Community
College *A*
Malone College *B*
Marietta College *B*
Marion Technical College *C,A*
Miami University
Hamilton Campus *A*
Oxford Campus *B,M*
Miami-Jacobs College *A*
Mount Union College *B*
Mount Vernon Nazarene College *B*
Muskingum Area Technical College
C,A
Muskingum College *B*
North Central Technical College *A*
Northwest Technical College *A*
Northwestern College *C,A*
Notre Dame College of Ohio *B*
Ohio Dominican College *C,B*
Ohio Northern University *B*
Ohio State University: Columbus
Campus *B,M,D*
Ohio University *B,M*
Ohio Valley Business College *A*
Ohio Wesleyan University *B*
Otterbein College *B*
Owens Technical College: Toledo
C,A
Shawnee State University *A*
Sinclair Community College *A*
Southern Ohio College *A*
Southern State Community
College *A*
Stark Technical College *A*
Terra Technical College *A*
Tiffin University *A,B*
Union Institute *B,D*
University of Akron *A,B,M*
University of Cincinnati
Access Colleges *A*
Cincinnati *B,M,D*
Clermont College *A*
Raymond Walters College *C,A*
University of Dayton *B*
University of Findlay *A,B*
University of Rio Grande *A,B*
University of Toledo *A,B,M*
Urbana University *B*
Ursuline College *B*
Walsh College *A,B*
Washington State Community
College *A*
Wilberforce University *B*
Wilmington College *B*
Wittenberg University *B*
Wright State University
Dayton *B,M*
Lake Campus *A*
Xavier University *B*
Youngstown State University
A,B,M

Oklahoma

Bacone College *A*
Bartlesville Wesleyan College *A,B*
Cameron University *B*

Connors State College *A*
East Central University *B*
Eastern Oklahoma State College *A*
Langston University *B*
Northeastern State University *B*
Northern Oklahoma College *A*
Northwestern Oklahoma State
University *B*
Oklahoma Baptist University *B*
Oklahoma Christian University of
Science and Arts *B*
Oklahoma City University *B,M*
Oklahoma Junior College *A*
Oklahoma Panhandle State
University *B*
Oklahoma State University
Oklahoma City *A*
Stillwater *B,M*
Technical Branch:
Okmulgee *A*
Oral Roberts University *B*
Phillips University *B*
Redlands Community College *A*
Rogers State College *A*
Rose State College *A*
St. Gregory's College *A*
Southeastern Oklahoma State
University *B*
Southwestern Oklahoma State
University *B*
Tulsa Junior College *A*
University of Central Oklahoma *B*
University of Oklahoma *B,M*
University of Science and Arts of
Oklahoma *B*
University of Tulsa *C,B,M*

Oregon

Central Oregon Community College
C,A
Chemeketa Community College *A*
Clackamas Community College *A*
Clatsop Community College *A*
Linfield College *B*
Linn-Benton Community College
C,A
Mount Hood Community College
C,A
Oregon Institute of Technology *A*
Oregon State University *B*
Portland Community College *C,A*
Portland State University *B*
Rogue Community College *C*
Southern Oregon State College
A,B,M
Southwestern Oregon Community
College *C,A*
Umpqua Community College *A*
University of Oregon
Eugene *B,M,D*
Robert Donald Clark Honors
College *B*
University of Portland *B*
Western Baptist College *B*

Pennsylvania

Albright College *B*
Allentown College of St. Francis de
Sales *B*
Alvernia College *A,B*
Beaver College *B*
Berean Institute *A*
Bloomsburg University of
Pennsylvania *B*
Bucknell University *B,M*
Bucks County Community
College *A*
Butler County Community
College *A*
Cabrini College *B*
California University of
Pennsylvania *A,B*

Carlow College *B*
Carnegie Mellon University *M,D,W*
Cedar Crest College *B*
Central Pennsylvania Business
School *A*
Chestnut Hill College *A,B*
Churchman Business School *A*
Clarion University of Pennsylvania
A,B,M
College Misericordia *B*
Community College of Beaver
County *A*
Community College of
Philadelphia *A*
Delaware County Community
College *C,A*
Delaware Valley College *B*
Drexel University *B,M,D*
DuBois Business College *C,A*
Duquesne University *C,B,M*
Eastern College *B*
Edinboro University of
Pennsylvania *B*
Elizabethtown College *B*
Franklin and Marshall College *B*
Gannon University *A,B*
Geneva College *B*
Gettysburg College *B*
Grove City College *B*
Gwynedd-Mercy College *A,B*
Harrisburg Area Community
College *C,A*
Holy Family College *B*
ICS Center for Degree Studies *A*
Immaculata College *A,B*
Indiana University of
Pennsylvania *B*
Juniata College *B*
King's College *A,B*
Kutztown University of
Pennsylvania *B*
La Roche College *B*
La Salle University *A,B,M*
Lackawanna Junior College *C,A*
Lansdale School of Business *C,A*
Lebanon Valley College of
Pennsylvania *B*
Lehigh County Community College
C,A
Lehigh University *B*
Lincoln University *B*
Luzerne County Community
College *A*
Lycoming College *B*
Manor Junior College *A*
Marywood College *B*
Mercyhurst College *C,B*
Messiah College *B*
Montgomery County Community
College *C,A*
Moravian College *B*
Mount Aloysius College *A*
Muhlenberg College *B*
Neumann College *B*
Northampton County Area
Community College *C,A*
Northeastern Christian Junior
College *A*
Peirce Junior College *C,A*
Penn State
Erie Behrend College *B*
Harrisburg Capital College *B*
University Park Campus *B*
Pennsylvania College of
Technology *A*
Philadelphia College of Textiles and
Science *A,B,M*
Point Park College *C,A,B*
Reading Area Community College
C,A
Robert Morris College *B,M*
Rosemont College *B*

Carlow College *B*
St. Francis College *B*
St. Joseph's University *C,A,B,M*
St. Vincent College *B*
Seton Hill College *B*
Shippensburg University of
Pennsylvania *B*
Slippery Rock University of
Pennsylvania *B*
Spring Garden College *C,A,B*
Susquehanna University *B*
Temple University *B,M,D*
Thiel College *A,B*
University of Pennsylvania
A,B,M,D
University of Pittsburgh
Greensburg *B*
Johnstown *B*
Pittsburgh *B*
Titusville *A*
University of Scranton *B*
Villanova University *B*
Washington and Jefferson College *B*
Waynesburg College *B*
West Chester University of
Pennsylvania *B,M*
Westminster College *B*
Westmoreland County Community
College *A*
Widener University *B,M*
Wilkes University *B*
York College of Pennsylvania *B*

Puerto Rico

American University of Puerto Rico
A,B
Bayamon Central University *B*
Caribbean University *A,B*
ICPR Junior College *A*
Instituto Tecnico Comercial Junior
College *A*
Inter American University of Puerto
Rico
Arecibo Campus *A,B*
Metropolitan Campus *A,B,M*
San German Campus *A,B,M*
Pontifical Catholic University of
Puerto Rico *B*
Puerto Rico Junior College *A*
Turabo University *A,B,M*
Universidad Metropolitana *B*
University of Puerto Rico
Arecibo Campus *A,B*
Bayamon Technological
University College *A,B*
Cayey University College *B*
Humacao University College
A,B
La Montana Regional
College *A*
Mayaguez Campus *B,M*
Ponce Technological
University College *A,B*
Rio Piedras Campus *B,M*
University of the Sacred Heart *A,B*

Rhode Island

Bryant College *B,M*
Community College of Rhode
Island *A*
Johnson & Wales University *A,B*
Providence College *B*
Rhode Island College *B*
Roger Williams College *B*
Salve Regina University *B,M*
University of Rhode Island *B,M*

South Carolina

Aiken Technical College *C,A*
Benedict College *B*
Bob Jones University *B*
Central Wesleyan College *B*
Charleston Southern University *B*

Chesterfield-Marlboro Technical
College *C,A*
Clemson University *B,M*
Coker College *B*
College of Charleston *B*
Columbia College *B*
Columbia Junior College of
Business *A*
Converse College *B*
Erskine College *B*
Florence-Darlington Technical
College *A*
Francis Marion College *B*
Furman University *B*
Greenville Technical College *A*
Lander College *B*
Limestone College *B*
Midlands Technical College *A*
Newberry College *B*
North Greenville College *A*
Presbyterian College *B*
South Carolina State College *B*
Sumter Area Technical College *A*
Technical College of the
Lowcountry *C*
Tri-County Technical College *A*
Trident Technical College *A*
University of South Carolina
Aiken *B*
Coastal Carolina College *B*
Columbia *B,M*
Wofford College *B*

South Dakota

Augustana College *B*
Black Hills State University *B*
Dakota Wesleyan University *B*
Kilian Community College *A*
Mitchell Vocational Technical
Institute *C,A*
Mount Marty College *A,B*
National College *A,B*
Northern State University *A,B*
Presentation College *C,A*
Sinte Gleska College *A*
Sioux Falls College *B*
University of South Dakota *B,M*

Tennessee

Austin Peay State University *B*
Belmont University *B*
Bethel College *B*
Bristol University *A*
Carson-Newman College *B*
Chattanooga State Technical
Community College *A*
Christian Brothers University *C,B,M*
Cleveland State Community
College *C*
Columbia State Community
College *A*
Cumberland University *B*
David Lipscomb University *B*
East Tennessee State University
B,M
Fisk University *B*
Free Will Baptist Bible College *A*
Freed-Hardeman University *B*
Hiwassee College *A*
Knoxville Business College *A*
Knoxville College *B*
Lambuth University *B*
LeMoyne-Owen College *B*
Lincoln Memorial University *B*
Martin Methodist College *A*
McKenzie College *A*
Memphis State University *B,M*
Middle Tennessee State University
B,M
Milligan College *B*
Motlow State Community
College *A*

Nashville State Technical
Institute *A*
Northeast State Technical
Community College *C,A*
Pellissippi State Technical
Community College *A*
Roane State Community College *A*
Shelby State Community College *A*
Southern College of Seventh-day
Adventists *A,B*
State Technical Institute at
Memphis *A*
Tennessee State University *A,B*
Tennessee Technological
University *B*
Tennessee Temple University *B*
Tennessee Wesleyan College *B*
Trevecca Nazarene College *B*
Union University *B*
University of Tennessee
Chattanooga *B,M*
Knoxville *B,M*
Martin *B,M*
William Jennings Bryan College *B*

Texas

Abilene Christian University *B*
Alvin Community College *A*
Amarillo College *A*
Amber University *B*
Angelina College *A*
Angelo State University *B,M*
Austin Community College *A*
Baylor University *B*
Bee County College *A*
Brookhaven College *A*
Central Texas College *A*
Cisco Junior College *A*
College of the Mainland *A*
Collin County Community College
District *A*
Concordia Lutheran College *B*
Corpus Christi State University *B,M*
Dallas Baptist University *B*
Del Mar College *A*
DeVry Institute of Technology:
Irving *B*
East Texas Baptist University *B*
East Texas State University
Commerce *B*
Texarkana *B*
Eastfield College *A*
El Centro College *C,A*
El Paso Community College *C,A*
Galveston College *A*
Hardin-Simmons University *B*
Houston Baptist University *B,M*
Houston Community College *C,A*
Howard College *A*
Howard Payne University *B*
Huston-Tillotson College *B*
Incarnate Word College *B*
Jacksonville College *A*
Jarvis Christian College *B*
Kilgore College *A*
Lamar University—Beaumont *B*
Laredo Junior College *C,A*
Laredo State University *B*
Lee College *A*
LeTourneau University *B*
Lubbock Christian University *B*
McLennan Community College *C,A*
McMurry University *B*
Midland College *C,A*
Midwestern State University *B*
Mountain View College *C,A*
Navarro College *A*
North Harris Montgomery
Community College District *A*
North Lake College *A*
Northeast Texas Community
College *A*

Odessa College *C*
Our Lady of the Lake University of
San Antonio *B*
Panola College *A*
Paul Quinn College *B*
Prairie View A&M University *B*
Rice University *M*
Richland College *A*
St. Edward's University *B*
St. Mary's University *B,M*
St. Philip's College *A*
Sam Houston State University *B,M*
San Antonio College *A*
Schreiner College *B*
South Plains College *A*
Southern Methodist University *B*
Southwest Texas State University *B*
Southwestern Adventist College *B*
Southwestern Christian College *A*
Southwestern University *B*
Stephen F. Austin State
University *B*
Sul Ross State University *B,M*
Tarleton State University *B*
Tarrant County Junior College *A*
Texas A&I University *B,M*
Texas A&M University *B,M,D*
Texas Christian University *B*
Texas Southern University *B*
Texas Southmost College *A*
Texas State Technical College
Harlingen *A*
Sweetwater *C,A*
Texas Tech University *B,M*
Texas Wesleyan University *B*
Texas Woman's University *B*
Trinity Valley Community
College *A*
University of Central Texas *B*
University of Houston
Clear Lake *B,M*
Downtown *B*
Houston *B,M,D*
Victoria *B*
University of Mary Hardin-
Baylor *B*
University of North Texas *B,M,D*
University of St. Thomas *B*
University of Texas
Arlington *B,M*
Austin *B,M,D*
Dallas *B,M*
El Paso *B,M*
Pan American *B*
Permian Basin *B*
San Antonio *B,M*
Tyler *B*
Vernon Regional Junior College *A*
Victoria College *A*
West Texas State University *B,M*
Western Texas College *A*

Utah

Brigham Young University *B,M*
College of Eastern Utah *C*
Dixie College *A*
LDS Business College *C,A*
Phillips Junior College: Salt Lake
City Campus *C,A*
Southern Utah University *B,M*
Stevens-Henager College of
Business *A*
University of Utah *B,M,D*
Utah State University *B,M*
Utah Valley Community College
C,A
Weber State University *B,M*
Westminster College of Salt Lake
City *B*

Vermont

Castleton State College *B*
Champlain College *A,B*
College of St. Joseph in Vermont
A,B
Green Mountain College *B*
Johnson State College *A*
Lyndon State College *B*
Norwich University *B*
St. Michael's College *B*
Southern Vermont College *A,B*
Trinity College of Vermont *C,A,B*
University of Vermont *B*

Virginia

Averett College *B*
Blue Ridge Community College *A*
Bluefield College *B*
Bridgewater College *B*
Central Virginia Community College
C,A
Christopher Newport College *B*
Clinch Valley College of the
University of Virginia *B*
College of William and Mary *B*
Commonwealth *C,A*
Eastern Mennonite College *B*
Emory and Henry College *B*
Ferrum College *B*
George Mason University *B,M*
Hampton University *B*
James Madison University *B,M*
John Tyler Community College *A*
Liberty University *B*
Lord Fairfax Community College *A*
Lynchburg College *B*
Marymount University *B,M*
Mountain Empire Community
College *A*
National Business College *C,A,B*
New River Community College *C,A*
Norfolk State University *B*
Northern Virginia Community
College *A*
Old Dominion University *B,M*
Patrick Henry Community
College *A*
Piedmont Virginia Community
College *A*
Radford University *B*
St. Paul's College *B*
Southwest Virginia Community
College *A*
Strayer College *A,B,M*
Tidewater Community College *A*
University of Richmond *B*
University of Virginia *M*
Virginia Commonwealth University
B,M
Virginia Highlands Community
College *C,A*
Virginia Polytechnic Institute and
State University *B,M,D*
Virginia State University *B*
Virginia Union University *B*
Virginia Wesleyan College *B*
Washington and Lee University *B*
Wytheville Community College *A*

Washington

Bellevue Community College *C,A*
Big Bend Community College *A*
Central Washington University *B*
Centralia College *A*
City University *B*
Clark College *C,A*
Eastern Washington University *B*
Edmonds Community College *C,A*
Everett Community College *C,A*
Gonzaga University *B*
Grays Harbor College *A*
Green River Community College *A*

Griffin College C,A,B
Lower Columbia College A
North Seattle Community
College A
Olympic College C,A
Pacific Lutheran University B
Peninsula College A
Pierce College C,A
St. Martin's College B
Seattle Central Community College
C,A
Seattle Pacific University C,B
Seattle University B,M
Shoreline Community College C,A
Skagit Valley College A
South Puget Sound Community
College C,A
Spokane Community College A
Spokane Falls Community College
C,A
Tacoma Community College A
University of Puget Sound B
University of Washington B,M
Walla Walla College A,B
Walla Walla Community College A
Washington State University M
Wenatchee Valley College C,A
Western Washington University B
Whatcom Community College A
Whitworth College B
Yakima Valley Community College
C,A

West Virginia

Alderson-Broaddus College B
Bethany College B
Bluefield State College A,B
College of West Virginia B
Davis and Elkins College A,B
Fairmont State College A,B
Glenville State College B
Marshall University A,B,M
Ohio Valley College A
Potomac State College of West
Virginia University A
Salem-Teikyo University A,B
Shepherd College A,B
University of Charleston A,B
West Liberty State College B
West Virginia Institute of
Technology A,B
West Virginia Northern Community
College A
West Virginia State College A,B
West Virginia University B,M
West Virginia Wesleyan College B
Wheeling Jesuit College B

Wisconsin

Cardinal Stritch College B
Carroll College B
Carthage College B
Chippewa Valley Technical
College A
Concordia University Wisconsin B
Edgewood College B
Fox Valley Technical College C,A
Lakeland College B
Madison Area Technical College A
Madison Junior College of
Business A
Marian College of Fond du Lac B
Marquette University B
Mid-State Technical College C,A
Milwaukee College of Business C,A
Moraine Park Technical College A
Mount Mary College B
Mount Senario College B
Northeast Wisconsin Technical
College A
Northland College B
St. Norbert College B

Silver Lake College B
Stratton College C,A
University of Wisconsin
Eau Claire B
Green Bay B
La Crosse B
Madison B,M,D
Milwaukee B
Oshkosh B
Platteville B
River Falls B
Stevens Point B
Superior B
Whitewater B,M
Viterbo College B
Waukesha County Technical
College A
Western Wisconsin Technical
College A
Wisconsin Indianhead Technical
College A

Wyoming

Casper College C,A
Central Wyoming College C,A
Eastern Wyoming College A
Laramie County Community
College C
Northwest College A
Sheridan College A
University of Wyoming B
Western Wyoming Community
College A

**American Samoa, Caroline
Islands, Guam, Marianas,
Virgin Islands**

Community College of
Micronesia A
Guam Community College C,A
Northern Marianas College A
University of Guam B
University of the Virgin Islands A,B

Canada

McGill University C,B,M,D

Mexico

Sistema Instituto Tecnologico y de
Estudios Superiores de
Monterrey B

Switzerland

American College of Switzerland B

Actuarial sciences

Arizona

Northern Arizona University B

Colorado

University of Northern Colorado B

Connecticut

Central Connecticut State
University B
Quinnipiac College B
University of Connecticut B
University of Hartford B

Florida

Florida Agricultural and Mechanical
University B

Georgia

Georgia State University B,M

Idaho

University of Idaho B

Illinois

Bradley University B
College of St. Francis B
De Paul University B
Illinois Central College A
Morton College A
Roosevelt University B,M
University of Illinois at Urbana-
Champaign B

Indiana

Ball State University B
Butler University B
Indiana University
Bloomington B
Northwest B
Purdue University B

Iowa

Drake University B
University of Iowa B,M

Kansas

Tabor College B

Kentucky

Bellarmine College B

Maryland

Frostburg State University B

Massachusetts

Westfield State College B
Worcester Polytechnic Institute B

Michigan

Central Michigan University B
Eastern Michigan University B
University of Michigan B,M

Missouri

Central Missouri State University B
Maryville University B

Nebraska

University of Nebraska
Kearney B
Lincoln B,M

New Hampshire

Plymouth State College of the
University System of New
Hampshire B

New Jersey

New Jersey Institute of
Technology B
Rider College B
Stockton State College B

New York

City University of New York:
Baruch College B
College of Insurance B,M
Dominican College of Blauvelt B
New York University B
St. Thomas Aquinas College B
Utica College of Syracuse
University B

North Carolina

University of North Carolina at
Asheville B

North Dakota

Jamestown College B

Ohio

Ohio State University: Columbus
Campus B

Oklahoma

University of Central Oklahoma B

Oregon

Oregon State University B

Pennsylvania

Carnegie Mellon University B
Clarion University of
Pennsylvania B
Elizabethtown College B
Lebanon Valley College of
Pennsylvania B
Mansfield University of
Pennsylvania B
Penn State University Park
Campus B
Temple University B,M,D
Thiel College B
University of Pennsylvania B,M,D

Rhode Island

Bryant College B

Tennessee

Bethel College B
Middle Tennessee State
University B
University of Tennessee:
Chattanooga B

Utah

Brigham Young University B

Washington

Central Washington University B

Wisconsin

University of Wisconsin: Madison
B,M

Administration of special
education

Alabama

Alabama Agricultural and
Mechanical University M
University of Alabama M

Arizona

University of Phoenix M

Arkansas

University of Central Arkansas B,M

California

Azusa Pacific University M
California Lutheran University M
California State University
Bakersfield M
Fresno M
Los Angeles M
Northridge M
St. Mary's College of California
B,M
University of California: Riverside
M,D

Colorado

University of Northern Colorado D

District of Columbia

Gallaudet University M,D
Trinity College M

Florida

Nova University *M*
Stetson University *M*

Georgia

Georgia College *M*
Georgia Southern University *B,M*
Georgia State University *D*
University of Georgia *M*

Illinois

National-Louis University *M*
Northern Illinois University *M*
Southern Illinois University at Carbondale *M,D*

Indiana

Butler University *M*
Indiana State University *M*
Indiana University Bloomington *M,D*

Iowa

Drake University *M*
University of Iowa *M,D*

Massachusetts

American International College *B*
Lesley College *M*
Suffolk University *M*
Westfield State College *M*

Michigan

Eastern Michigan University *M*
Grand Valley State University *M*
Michigan State University *D*
Wayne State University *D*

Minnesota

Winona State University *B,M*

Missouri

St. Louis University *D*
University of Missouri: Columbia *M,D*

New Jersey

Monmouth College *M*
Rutgers—The State University of New Jersey *M*

New York

Bank Street College of Education *M,W*
City University of New York: City College *M*
Fordham University *M,D*
Manhattan College *B,M*
Syracuse University *D*

North Carolina

Appalachian State University *B,M*

Ohio

Ohio University *M*
Union Institute *D*
University of Cincinnati *M,D*
Wright State University *M*

Oklahoma

Northeastern State University *M*

Oregon

Western Oregon State College *M*

Pennsylvania

Bucknell University *M*
California University of Pennsylvania *M*
Slippery Rock University of Pennsylvania *B*
Temple University *D*

Rhode Island

Rhode Island College *W*

South Carolina

Furman University *M*
University of South Carolina *D*

Texas

Texas Woman's University *M,D*
University of Houston *M,D*
University of Mary Hardin-Baylor *B,M*

Vermont

Johnson State College *M*

Virginia

Virginia Polytechnic Institute and State University *D,W*

Washington

Central Washington University *M*
University of Washington *M*
Western Washington University *M*

West Virginia

Marshall University *M*

Wisconsin

University of Wisconsin: Oshkosh *M*

Adult and continuing education administration

Alabama

Alabama State University *M*
Troy State University at Montgomery *M*
University of Alabama *M,W*

Alaska

Alaska Pacific University *M*

Arizona

University of Phoenix *M*

Arkansas

University of Arkansas
Fayetteville *M*
Little Rock *M*

California

San Francisco State University *M*

Colorado

Colorado State University *M*
Lamar Community College *A*

District of Columbia

George Washington University *M,D*

Florida

Florida Agricultural and Mechanical University *M*
Florida Atlantic University *M,D*
Florida International University *M,D*
Nova University *D*
University of Florida *M*
University of South Florida *M*

Georgia

University of Georgia *M,D*

Illinois

Loyola University of Chicago *M*
National-Louis University *M*
Northwestern University *D*

Roosevelt University *M*

Indiana

Ball State University *M,D*
Indiana University—Purdue University at Indianapolis *M,D*
Purdue University *M*

Iowa

Drake University *M,D*
Iowa State University *M,D*

Kentucky

Morehead State University *M*

Louisiana

Louisiana State University and Agricultural and Mechanical College *M,D*

Maine

University of Southern Maine *M*

Maryland

Coppin State College *M*

Massachusetts

Boston University *M,W*
Suffolk University *M*

Michigan

Eastern Michigan University *M*
Michigan State University *M,D*
University of Michigan *M,D*

Minnesota

University of St. Thomas *M*

Mississippi

University of Southern Mississippi *M*

Missouri

Central Missouri State University *M*
University of Missouri: Columbia *M,D*

Nebraska

University of Nebraska—Lincoln *M*

New Jersey

Rutgers—The State University of New Jersey *M*

New York

City University of New York: City College *M*
University of Rochester *M,D*

North Carolina

Appalachian State University *M*
North Carolina Agricultural and Technical State University *M*
North Carolina State University *M,D*

Ohio

Union Institute *D*

Oklahoma

University of Oklahoma *M,D*

Oregon

Oregon State University *M*

Pennsylvania

Cheyney University of Pennsylvania *M*
Indiana University of Pennsylvania *M*

South Carolina

University of South Carolina *M*

Texas

Texas A&I University *M*
Texas A&M University *B,M,D*
Texas Woman's University *M,D*

Virginia

Virginia Polytechnic Institute and State University *M,D,W*

Washington

Washington State University *M*
Western Washington University *M*

West Virginia

Marshall University *M*

Wisconsin

University of Wisconsin: Madison *M,D*

Wyoming

University of Wyoming *M,D*

Adult and continuing education research

Alabama

Auburn University *B,M,D*

Alaska

Alaska Pacific University *M*
University of Alaska Anchorage *M*

Arizona

Prescott College *B*

California

California State University: Los Angeles *M*
Pacific Oaks College *M*
University of Southern California *M,D*

Connecticut

Southern Connecticut State University *M*

District of Columbia

Howard University *M*

Florida

Florida State University *M,D*
Nova University *M,D*

Georgia

Georgia Southern University *M*
University of Georgia *M*

Illinois

National-Louis University *M*
Northern Illinois University *M,D*
Northwestern University *D*
Roosevelt University *M*
State Community College *C*

Indiana

Ball State University *D*
Indiana University Bloomington *M,D*

Iowa

Drake University *M,D*

Kansas

Kansas State University *M,D*

Maine
University of Southern Maine *M*

Maryland
Baltimore Hebrew University *B,M*

Massachusetts
Lesley College *B,M,D*

Michigan
Grand Valley State University *M*
University of Michigan *M,D*
Wayne State University *M*

Minnesota
University of St. Thomas *M*

Missouri
Central Missouri State
University *M*

Montana
Montana State University *M,D*

Nebraska
University of Nebraska—Lincoln *M*

New Jersey
Rutgers—The State University of
New Jersey *M*

New Mexico
University of New Mexico *M*

New York
Adelphi University *M*
Cornell University *M,D*

North Carolina
Appalachian State University *M*
East Carolina University *M*
North Carolina State University
M,D

Ohio
Ohio State University: Columbus
Campus *B,M*
Union Institute *B,D*
University of Toledo *B*
Wittenberg University *B*

Oklahoma
University of Oklahoma *M,D*

Pennsylvania
California University of
Pennsylvania *M*
Gratz College *M*
Penn State
Erie Behrend College *M*
Harrisburg Capital College *D*
University Park Campus *M,D*
Temple University *M,D*

Rhode Island
University of Rhode Island *M*

Tennessee
University of Tennessee: Knoxville
M,D

Texas
Incarnate Word College *M*
Texas A&I University *M*
University of Houston *M,D*

Virginia
Norfolk State University *M*
Virginia Commonwealth
University *M*
Virginia Polytechnic Institute and
State University *M,D,W*

Washington
Heritage College *M*

West Virginia
Marshall University *M*

Wyoming
University of Wyoming *M,D*

Advertising

Alabama
Spring Hill College *B*
University of Alabama *B,M*

Alaska
University of Alaska Anchorage *B*

Arizona
Northern Arizona University *B*

Arkansas
Arkansas State University *B*
Harding University *B*
University of Arkansas at Little
Rock *B*

California
Academy of Art College *C,B,M*
Art Center College of Design *B,M*
California Lutheran University *B*
California State University
Fresno *B*
Fullerton *B,M*
Los Angeles *B*
Chapman University *B*
Cosumnes River College *A*
Long Beach City College *C,A*
Los Angeles City College *A*
Mount San Antonio College *A*
Orange Coast College *A*
Otis/Parsons School of Art and
Design *C,A,B*
Pepperdine University *B*
Saddleback College *C,A*
San Jose State University *B*
University of San Francisco *B*

Colorado
Adams State College *B*
University of Colorado at
Boulder *B*
University of Denver *M*
University of Northern Colorado *B*
University of Southern Colorado *B*

Connecticut
Quinnipiac College *B,M*
University of Bridgeport *B*

Florida
Daytona Beach Community
College *A*
Florida Southern College *B*
Florida State University *B*
Gulf Coast Community College *A*
International Fine Arts College *A*
Lynn University *B*
University of Florida *B,M,D*
University of Miami *B,M*

Georgia
Clark Atlanta University *B*
Georgia Southern University *B*
University of Georgia *B*

Idaho
University of Idaho *B*

Illinois
Bradley University *B*
College of St. Francis *B*
Columbia College *B*
International Academy of
Merchandising and Design *A,B*
Northwestern University *M*
Parkland College *A*
Roosevelt University *B*
Southern Illinois University at
Carbondale *B*
University of Illinois at Urbana-
Champaign *B,M*

Indiana
Ball State University *B*
Franklin College *B*
Indiana University at South Bend *B*
Purdue University *B*
St. Mary-of-the-Woods College *B*
University of Evansville *B*

Iowa
Clarke College *B*
Drake University *B*
St. Ambrose University *B*
Teikyo Marycrest University *B*

Kansas
Coffeyville Community College *A*
Colby Community College *A*
Highland Community College *A*
Kansas State University *B*
Pittsburg State University *B*
University of Kansas *B*

Kentucky
Eastern Kentucky University *B*
Kentucky Wesleyan College *B*
Morehead State University *B*
University of Kentucky *B*
Western Kentucky University *B*

Louisiana
Louisiana College *B*
Louisiana State University and
Agricultural and Mechanical
College *B*
Loyola University *B*

Maryland
Montgomery College: Rockville
Campus *A*
University of Baltimore *B*
University of Maryland: College
Park *B*

Massachusetts
Becker College: Leicester
Campus *A*
Boston University *B,M*
Emerson College *B,M*
Endicott College *B*
Mount Ida College *A*
Northeastern University *C*
Salem State College *B*
Simmons College *B*

Michigan
Ferris State University *B*
Grand Valley State University *B*
Kendall College of Art and
Design *B*
Lansing Community College *A*
Michigan State University *B,M*
Northwood Institute *A*
University of Detroit Mercy *B*
Western Michigan University *B*

Minnesota
College of Associated Arts *B*
Concordia College: Moorhead *B*

Moorhead State University *B*
Rainy River Community College *A*
St. Cloud State University *B*
University of St. Thomas *B*
Vermilion Community College *A*
Winona State University *B*

Mississippi
University of Mississippi *B*
University of Southern
Mississippi *B*

Missouri
Park College *B*
St. Louis Community College at
Florissant Valley *A*
Southeast Missouri State
University *B*
University of Missouri: Columbia *B*
Webster University *B*

Nebraska
Creighton University *B*
Hastings College *B*
Midland Lutheran College *B*
University of Nebraska
Kearney *B*
Lincoln *B*

New Hampshire
Franklin Pierce College *B*
New England College *B*
New Hampshire Technical College:
Manchester *A*
White Pines College *A*

New Jersey
Glassboro State College *B*
Seton Hall University *B*
Stockton State College *B*

New Mexico
New Mexico State University *B*

New York
Cazenovia College *A*
City University of New York
Baruch College *B,M*
New York City Technical
College *A*
College of New Rochelle *B*
Fashion Institute of Technology *A*
Iona College *B*
Manhattan College *B*
Medaille College *B*
Mohawk Valley Community College
C,A
New York Institute of
Technology *B*
Parsons School of Design *B*
Pratt Institute *B*
Rochester Institute of
Technology *B*
School of Visual Arts *B*
State University of New York
College of Technology at
Farmingdale *A*
Syracuse University *B,M*

North Carolina
Campbell University *B*
Central Piedmont Community
College *A*
Queens College *B*

North Dakota
University of North Dakota *B*

Ohio
Bowling Green State University *B*
Cincinnati Metropolitan College *A*
Kent State University *B*

Marietta College *B*
Ohio State University: Columbus
  Campus *B,M,D*
Ohio University *B*
University of Akron *B*
University of Findlay *B*
University of Toledo *B*
Youngstown State University *A,B*

Oklahoma
Oklahoma Christian University of
  Science and Arts *B*
Oklahoma City University *B*
Oklahoma State University *B*
University of Central Oklahoma *B*
University of Oklahoma *B*

Oregon
University of Oregon
  Eugene *B,M*
  Robert Donald Clark Honors
    College *B*

Pennsylvania
California University of
  Pennsylvania *B*
Clarion University of
  Pennsylvania *B*
Duquesne University *B*
Harcum Junior College *A*
Hussian School of Art *A*
Lycoming College *B*
Penn State University Park Campus
  B,M
University of Scranton *B*

Puerto Rico
University of Puerto Rico: Carolina
  Regional College *A*
University of the Sacred Heart *B*

Rhode Island
Johnson & Wales University *A*

South Carolina
University of South Carolina *B*

South Dakota
South Dakota State University *B*
University of South Dakota *B,M*

Tennessee
Austin Peay State University *A*
East Tennessee State University *B*
Lambuth University *B*
Memphis College of Art *B*
Middle Tennessee State
  University *B*
Union University *B*
University of Tennessee
  Chattanooga *B*
  Knoxville *B*

Texas
Abilene Christian University *B*
Lamar University—Beaumont *B*
Northwood Institute: Texas
  Campus *A*
Panola College *A*
Southern Methodist University *B*
Texas Christian University *B*
Texas Tech University *B*
Texas Wesleyan University *B*
Texas Woman's University *B*
University of Texas at Austin
  B,M,D
Western Texas College *A*

Utah
Brigham Young University *B*
Southern Utah University *B*

Vermont
Champlain College *A*

Virginia
Averett College *B*
Tidewater Community College *A*

Washington
Edmonds Community College *C*
Pacific Lutheran University *B*
Washington State University *B*

West Virginia
Bethany College *B*
Marshall University *B*
West Virginia State College *A*
West Virginia University *B*

Wisconsin
Marquette University *B,M*
University of Wisconsin
  Eau Claire *B*
  Oshkosh *B*

Aeronautical technology

Alabama
Community College of the Air
  Force *A*
Wallace State Community College
  at Hanceville *A*

Arizona
Arizona State University *B,M*
Embry-Riddle Aeronautical
  University: Prescott Campus *B*

California
Bakersfield College *A*
Chaffey Community College *C,A*
City College of San Francisco *C,A*
College of the Redwoods *C*
Glendale Community College *A*
Kings River Community College *A*
Merced College *A*
Mount San Antonio College *A*
Ohlone College *A*
Orange Coast College *C,A*
Palomar College *C,A*
San Diego Miramar College *A*
San Jose State University *B*
Santa Rosa Junior College *C,A*
Solano Community College *A*
Southwestern College *A*

Colorado
United States Air Force
  Academy *B*

Connecticut
Housatonic Community College *A*
Thames Valley State Technical
  College *A*

Delaware
Delaware Technical and
  Community College: Terry
  Campus *A*

District of Columbia
University of the District of
  Columbia *A*

Florida
Broward Community College *A*
Embry-Riddle Aeronautical
  University *A,B*
Gulf Coast Community College *A*
Manatee Community College *A*

Miami-Dade Community College *A*
Pensacola Junior College *C*

Georgia
Clayton State College *A*
Georgia Southwestern College *A*

Hawaii
University of Hawaii: Honolulu
  Community College *A*

Illinois
City Colleges of Chicago: Richard J.
  Daley College *A*
Lewis University *A,B*
Moody Bible Institute *B*
Parks College of St. Louis
  University *A,B*
Rock Valley College *A*
Southern Illinois University at
  Carbondale *A*

Indiana
Purdue University *A,B*
Vincennes University *A*

Kansas
Central College *A*
Hesston College *A*
Johnson County Community
  College *A*

Maryland
Frederick Community College *A*

Massachusetts
Roxbury Community College *A*
Wentworth Institute of
  Technology *A*

Michigan
Andrews University *A*
Baker College of Muskegon *A,B*
Jackson Community College *A*
Lansing Community College *A*
Macomb Community College *A*
Northern Michigan University *A*
Western Michigan University *B*

Minnesota
Northwestern Electronics
  Institute *A*

Mississippi
Hinds Community College *A*

Missouri
Central Missouri State University
  A,B
Maple Woods Community
  College *C*

New Hampshire
New Hampshire Technical College:
  Nashua *A*

New York
College of Aeronautics *A,B*
State University of New York
  College of Technology at
  Farmingdale *A*

North Carolina
Guilford Technical Community
  College *A*
Wayne Community College *C,A*

North Dakota
University of North Dakota: Lake
  Region *A*

Ohio
Bowling Green State University *B*
Cincinnati Technical College *A*
Kent State University *B*
Ohio University *A,B*

Oklahoma
National Education Center: Spartan
  School of Aeronautics Campus *A*

Pennsylvania
Pennsylvania Institute of
  Technology *A*
Pittsburgh Institute of
  Aeronautics *A*

Tennessee
Hiwassee College *A*
Motlow State Community
  College *A*

Texas
Houston Community College *C*
LeTourneau University *A,B*
Mountain View College *C,A*
North Harris Montgomery
  Community College District *C,A*
San Jacinto College: Central
  Campus *A*
Tarrant County Junior College *A*
Texarkana College *A*
Texas State Technical College:
  Waco *C,A*

Utah
Dixie College *A*
Utah State University *A,B*

Virginia
Northern Virginia Community
  College *A*

Washington
Everett Community College *A*
Green River Community College *A*
Spokane Community College *A*

West Virginia
Marshall University *A*

Aerospace/aeronautical/
astronautical engineering

Alabama
Alabama Aviation and Technical
  College *C,A*
Auburn University *B,M,D*
Tuskegee University *B*
University of Alabama *B,M*

Arizona
Arizona State University *B,M,D*
Embry-Riddle Aeronautical
  University: Prescott Campus *B*
University of Arizona *B,M,D*

Arkansas
Westark Community College *A*

California
California Institute of Technology
  B,M,D,W
California Polytechnic State
  University: San Luis Obispo *B,M*
California State Polytechnic
  University: Pomona *B*
California State University
  Long Beach *M*
  Northridge *B,M*

11

Merced College *A*
Naval Postgraduate School *M,D*
San Diego State University *B,M*
San Jose State University *B*
Southwestern College *A*
Stanford University *M,D*
University of California
    Davis *B*
    Los Angeles *B,M,D*
    San Diego *M,D*
University of Southern California
  B,M,D,W
West Coast University *M*

Colorado
United States Air Force
  Academy *B*
University of Colorado at Boulder
  B,M,D

Connecticut
University of Connecticut *M,D*

Delaware
Delaware State College *B*

District of Columbia
George Washington University *M,D*

Florida
Embry-Riddle Aeronautical
  University *B,M*
Florida Institute of Technology *B*
University of Central Florida *B*
University of Florida *B,M,D*
University of Miami *B*

Georgia
Georgia Institute of Technology
  B,M,D
Mercer University *B*
Middle Georgia College *A*

Illinois
Aero-Space Institute *A,B*
Illinois Benedictine College *B*
Illinois Institute of Technology
  B,M,D
Parks College of St. Louis
  University *B,M*
Richland Community College *A*
University of Illinois at Urbana-
  Champaign *B,M,D*

Indiana
Purdue University *B,M,D,W*
Tri-State University *B*
University of Notre Dame *B,M,D*

Iowa
Iowa State University *B,M,D*

Kansas
University of Kansas *B,M,D*
Wichita State University *B,M,D*

Maryland
College of Notre Dame of
  Maryland *B*
United States Naval Academy *B*
University of Maryland
  Baltimore County *M,D*
  College Park *B,M,D*
  Eastern Shore *B*

Massachusetts
Boston University *B,M,D*
Eastern Nazarene College *B*
Massachusetts Institute of
  Technology *B,M,D,W*
Northeastern University *B*
Worcester Polytechnic Institute *B*

Michigan
University of Michigan *B,M,D*
Western Michigan University *B*

Minnesota
University of Minnesota: Twin
  Cities *B,M,D*
Willmar Community College *A*

Mississippi
Mississippi College *B*
Mississippi State University *B,M*

Missouri
St. Louis University *B,M*
University of Missouri
  Columbia *M,D*
  Rolla *B,M,D*

New Hampshire
Daniel Webster College *A*

New Jersey
Princeton University *B,M,D*
Rutgers—The State University of
  New Jersey
  College of Engineering *B*
  New Brunswick *M,D*

New York
City University of New York: City
  College *B*
Clarkson University *B*
Cornell University *M,D*
Pace University
  College of White Plains *B*
  Pleasantville/Briarcliff *B*
Polytechnic University
  Brooklyn *B,M*
  Long Island Campus *B,M,D*
Rensselaer Polytechnic Institute
  B,M,D
Rochester Institute of
  Technology *B*
State University of New York at
  Buffalo *B,M,D*
Syracuse University *B,M,D*

North Carolina
North Carolina State University *B*
St. Augustine's College *B*

Ohio
Air Force Institute of Technology
  M,D
Case Western Reserve University
  B,M,D
Ohio State University: Columbus
  Campus *B,M,D*
University of Cincinnati *B,M,D*
University of Dayton *M,D*

Oklahoma
Oklahoma State University *B*
Southeastern Oklahoma State
  University *B*
University of Oklahoma *B,M,D*

Pennsylvania
Lock Haven University of
  Pennsylvania *B*
Penn State University Park Campus
  B,M,D
Pennsylvania Institute of
  Technology *A*

Tennessee
Middle Tennessee State
  University *B*
Motlow State Community
  College *A*
Tennessee State University *B*

University of Tennessee: Knoxville
  B,M,D

Texas
Rice University *M,D*
Texas A&M University *B,M,D*
University of Texas
  Arlington *B,M,D*
  Austin *B,M,D*

Virginia
University of Virginia *B,M,D*
Virginia Polytechnic Institute and
  State University *B,M,D*

Washington
University of Washington *B,M,D*

West Virginia
West Virginia University *B,M,D*
West Virginia Wesleyan College *B*

Aerospace science (Air Force)

Alabama
Marion Military Institute *A*

Colorado
United States Air Force
  Academy *B*

Michigan
Eastern Michigan University *B*

Missouri
Columbia College *B*

Ohio
Ohio State University: Columbus
  Campus *B*

Oklahoma
Oklahoma State University *B*

Oregon
University of Portland *B*

Pennsylvania
West Chester University of
  Pennsylvania *C*

South Dakota
South Dakota State University *B*

Tennessee
Tennessee State University *B*

Texas
Texas Wesleyan University *B*

Utah
Weber State University *A*

African languages

Alabama
Marion Military Institute *A*

California
University of California: Los
  Angeles *B*

District of Columbia
Howard University *B*

Massachusetts
Harvard and Radcliffe Colleges *B*

New York
City University of New York: City
  College *B*

Ohio
Ohio State University: Columbus
  Campus *B*

Pennsylvania
University of Pennsylvania *B*

Wisconsin
University of Wisconsin: Madison
  B,M,D

African studies

California
Naval Postgraduate School *M*
Palomar College *C*
San Diego City College *A*
Southwestern College *A*
Stanford University *B*
University of California: Los
  Angeles *M*

Connecticut
Trinity College *B*
Wesleyan University *B*
Yale University *B,M*

District of Columbia
Howard University *M,D*

Florida
University of South Florida *B*

Georgia
Clark Atlanta University *M*
Emory University *B*
Morris Brown College *B*
University of Georgia *B*

Illinois
University of Chicago *B,M*
University of Illinois at Urbana-
  Champaign *M*

Indiana
Earlham College *B*
Indiana University Bloomington *C*
University of Notre Dame *B*

Iowa
Luther College *B*
University of Iowa *C*

Kansas
University of Kansas *B*

Maryland
Coppin State College *B*
Morgan State University *B*

Massachusetts
Boston University *B*
Brandeis University *B*
Hampshire College *B*
Harvard and Radcliffe Colleges *B*
Tufts University *B,M*
Williams College *B*

Michigan
Eastern Michigan University *B*
Oakland University *B*
University of Michigan *B*

Western Michigan University *B*

Minnesota

University of Minnesota: Twin
Cities *B*

New Hampshire

Dartmouth College *B*

New Jersey

Rutgers—The State University of
New Jersey
Douglass College *B*
Livingston College *B*
Newark College of Arts and
Sciences *B*
Rutgers College *B*
University College New
Brunswick *B*
William Paterson College of New
Jersey *B*

New York

Bard College *B*
City University of New York
Brooklyn College *B*
City College *B*
Hostos Community College *A*
Queens College *B*
Columbia University
Columbia College *B*
New York *M,D*
Cornell University *B,M,D*
Fordham University *B*
Hofstra University *B*
Sarah Lawrence College *B*
State University of New York
Binghamton *B*
Stony Brook *B*
Vassar College *B*

North Carolina

University of North Carolina at
Chapel Hill *B*

Ohio

Antioch College *B*
College of Wooster *B*
Kent State University *B*
Ohio University *B,M*
Union Institute *B,D*

Pennsylvania

Bryn Mawr College *B*
Penn State University Park
Campus *C*

Rhode Island

Rhode Island College *B*

Tennessee

Memphis State University *C*

Vermont

Marlboro College *B*

Canada

McGill University *B*

Afro-American (black) studies

California

California State University
Dominguez Hills *B*
Fullerton *B*
Hayward *B*
Long Beach *C,B*
Los Angeles *B*
Northridge *B*
Sacramento *B*
City College of San Francisco *A*
Claremont McKenna College *B*
De Anza College *A*
Fresno City College *A*
Laney College *A*
Los Angeles City College *A*
Loyola Marymount University *B*
Pitzer College *B*
Pomona College *B*
San Diego City College *A*
San Diego State University *B*
San Francisco State University *B*
San Jose State University *B*
Santa Barbara City College *A*
Scripps College *B*
Solano Community College *A*
Sonoma State University *B*
Southwestern College *A*
Stanford University *B*
University of California
Berkeley *B*
Davis *B*
Los Angeles *B,M*
Santa Barbara *B*
University of the Pacific *B*
Ventura College *A*

Colorado

Metropolitan State College of
Denver *B*
University of Colorado at
Boulder *B*
University of Northern Colorado *B*

Connecticut

Trinity College *B*
Wesleyan University *B*
Yale University *B,M*

District of Columbia

Howard University *B*

Florida

Florida Agricultural and Mechanical
University *B*
Florida Atlantic University *C*
University of South Florida *B*

Georgia

Clark Atlanta University *M*
Emory University *B,D*
Mercer University *B*
Morris Brown College *B*
University of Georgia *B*

Illinois

City Colleges of Chicago: Olive-
Harvey College *A*
Eastern Illinois University *B*
Knox College *B*
Northwestern University *B*
Richland Community College *A*
Roosevelt University *B*
University of Chicago *B*
University of Illinois at Chicago *B*

Indiana

Earlham College *B*
Indiana State University *B*
Indiana University
Bloomington *B*
Northwest *B*
Martin University *B*
Purdue University *B*
University of Notre Dame *B*

Iowa

Luther College *B*
University of Iowa *B,M*

Kansas

University of Kansas *B*
Wichita State University *B*

Kentucky

University of Louisville *B*

Maine

Bates College *B*
Bowdoin College *B*

Maryland

Coppin State College *B*
Morgan State University *B,M*
University of Maryland
Baltimore County *B,M*
College Park *B*

Massachusetts

Amherst College *B*
Boston University *M*
Brandeis University *B*
Hampshire College *B*
Harvard and Radcliffe Colleges *B*
Mount Holyoke College *B*
Northeastern University *B*
Simmons College *B*
Smith College *B*
Tufts University *B*
University of Massachusetts
Amherst *B*
Boston *B*
Wellesley College *B*
Williams College *B*

Michigan

Lansing Community College *A*
Oakland University *B*
University of Michigan
Ann Arbor *B*
Flint *B*
Wayne State University *B*

Minnesota

Carleton College *B*
Mankato State University *B*
St. Olaf College *B*
University of Minnesota: Twin
Cities *B*

Missouri

Washington University *B*

Nebraska

University of Nebraska—Omaha *B*

New Hampshire

Dartmouth College *B*

New Jersey

Bloomfield College *B*
Monmouth College *C*
Passaic County Community
College *A*

Rutgers—The State University of
New Jersey
Camden College of Arts and
Sciences *B*
Douglass College *B*
Livingston College *B*
Newark College of Arts and
Sciences *B*
Rutgers College *B*
University College Camden *B*
University College New
Brunswick *B*
Seton Hall University *B*
Stockton State College *C*
William Paterson College of New
Jersey *B*

New York

City University of New York
Brooklyn College *B,M*
City College *B*
College of Staten Island *B*
Hostos Community College *A*
Hunter College *B*
Lehman College *B*
York College *B*
Colgate University *B*
Columbia University: Columbia
College *B*
Cornell University *B,M,D*
Fordham University *B*
Hobart College *B*
Nassau Community College *A*
New York University *B,M*
Sarah Lawrence College *B*
State University of New York
Albany *B,M*
Binghamton *B*
Buffalo *B*
College at Brockport *B*
College at Cortland *B*
College at Geneseo *B*
College at New Paltz *B*
Syracuse University *B*
Vassar College *B*
William Smith College *B*

North Carolina

Duke University *B*
St. Augustine's College *B*
University of North Carolina
Chapel Hill *B*
Charlotte *B*

Ohio

Antioch College *B*
College of Wooster *B*
Denison University *B*
Kent State University *B*
Miami University: Oxford
Campus *B*
Oberlin College *B*
Ohio State University: Columbus
Campus *B,M*
Ohio University *B*
Ohio Wesleyan University *B*
Union Institute *B,D*
University of Cincinnati *B*
Youngstown State University *B*

Pennsylvania

Edinboro University of
Pennsylvania *B*
Gettysburg College *B*
Lehigh University *B*
Penn State University Park Campus
C,B
Swarthmore College *B*
Temple University *B,M,D*
University of Pennsylvania *B,M,D*
University of Pittsburgh *B*

Rhode Island

Brown University *B*
Rhode Island College *B*

South Carolina

University of South Carolina *B*

Tennessee

Shelby State Community College *A*
University of Tennessee:
  Knoxville *B*
Vanderbilt University *B*

Texas

Southern Methodist University *B*
University of Texas at Austin *B*

Vermont

Goddard College *B*

Virginia

University of Virginia *B*

Washington

University of Washington *B*

Wisconsin

University of Wisconsin
    Madison *B,M*
    Milwaukee *B*

Agribusiness

Alabama

Alabama Agricultural and
  Mechanical University *B,M*
Auburn University *B*
Chattahoochee Valley Community
  College *A*
Gadsden State Community
  College *A*
Snead State Junior College *A*
Tuskegee University *B,M*

Arizona

Arizona State University *B*
Arizona Western College *A*
Eastern Arizona College *A*
Glendale Community College *A*

Arkansas

Arkansas State University
    Beebe Branch *A*
    Jonesboro *B*
Arkansas Tech University *B*
Mississippi County Community
  College *A*
North Arkansas Community
  College *A*
Phillips County Community
  College *A*
Southern Arkansas University *B*
University of Arkansas *B*
Westark Community College *A*

California

California Polytechnic State
  University: San Luis Obispo *B*
California State Polytechnic
  University: Pomona *B*
California State University
    Chico *B*
    Fresno *B,M*
College of the Desert *A*
Cosumnes River College *C,A*
Fresno City College *C,A*
Imperial Valley College *A*
Kings River Community College *A*
Los Angeles Pierce College *A*

Merced College *A*
Modesto Junior College *A*
Mount San Antonio College *A*
Oxnard College *A*
San Joaquin Delta College *C,A*
Santa Clara University *M*
Santa Rosa Junior College *C,A*
Ventura College *C,A*
West Hills Community College *A*
Yuba College *A*

Colorado

Colorado State University *B*
Fort Lewis College *B*
Front Range Community College *C*
Morgan Community College *A*
Northeastern Junior College *A*
Otero Junior College *C*

Delaware

Delaware State College *B*
Delaware Technical and
    Community College: Southern
    Campus *A*

Florida

Florida Agricultural and Mechanical
    University *B*
Miami-Dade Community College *A*
Pensacola Junior College *A*

Georgia

Abraham Baldwin Agricultural
    College *A*
Georgia Southern University *B*
Georgia Southwestern College *B*
South Georgia College *A*
University of Georgia *B*
Young Harris College *A*

Hawaii

University of Hawaii at Hilo *B*

Idaho

College of Southern Idaho *C,A*
University of Idaho *B*

Illinois

Black Hawk College: East
    Campus *A*
Carl Sandburg College *A*
Highland Community College *A*
Illinois Central College *A*
Illinois Eastern Community
    Colleges: Wabash Valley
    College *A*
Illinois State University *B,M*
Illinois Valley Community
    College *A*
Joliet Junior College *A*
Kishwaukee College *C,A*
Lake Land College *C,A*
Lewis and Clark Community
    College *A*
Parkland College *C*
Rend Lake College *A*
Richland Community College *A*
Southern Illinois University at
    Carbondale *B,M*
University of Illinois at Urbana-
    Champaign *B*

Indiana

Purdue University *B,M,D*
Vincennes University *A*

Iowa

Des Moines Area Community
    College *A*
Dordt College *B*
Iowa Central Community College *A*
Iowa Lakes Community College *A*

Iowa State University *B*
Kirkwood Community College *A*
Morningside College *B*
Muscatine Community College *A*
North Iowa Area Community
    College *A*
Northeast Iowa Community
    College *A*
Northwest Iowa Technical
    College *A*
Southeastern Community College:
    North Campus *A*
Waldorf College *A*

Kansas

Allen County Community
    College *A*
Butler County Community
    College *A*
Central College *A*
Cloud County Community
    College *A*
Coffeyville Community College *A*
Colby Community College *A*
Cowley County Community
    College *A*
Dodge City Community College *A*
Fort Scott Community College *A*
Highland Community College *A*
McPherson College *B*
MidAmerica Nazarene College *A,B*
Pratt Community College *C,A*
Seward County Community
    College *A*

Kentucky

Berea College *B*
Eastern Kentucky University *B*
Lindsey Wilson College *A*
Morehead State University *A*
Murray State University *B*
St. Catharine College *A*

Louisiana

Louisiana State University and
    Agricultural and Mechanical
    College *B*
Louisiana Tech University *B*
McNeese State University *B*
Nicholls State University *B*
Northeast Louisiana University *B*
Southern University and
    Agricultural and Mechanical
    College *B*
University of Southwestern
    Louisiana *B*

Maine

University of Maine
    Fort Kent *B*
    Orono *B,M*

Maryland

Frederick Community College *A*
University of Maryland: College
    Park *B,M,D*

Michigan

Delta College *A*
Glen Oaks Community College *C*
Michigan State University *B*
Southwestern Michigan College *A*

Minnesota

Southwest State University *A,B*
University of Minnesota
    Crookston *A*
    Twin Cities *B*
Vermilion Community College *A*
Willmar Community College *A*
Willmar Technical College *C,A*
Worthington Community College *A*

Mississippi

Hinds Community College *A*
Mississippi State University *B*

Missouri

Central Missouri State University *B*
College of the Ozarks *B*
Missouri Valley College *B*
Missouri Western State College *B*
Moberly Area Community
    College *A*
North Central Missouri College *A*
Northwest Missouri State
    University *B*
Southeast Missouri State
    University *B*
Southwest Missouri State
    University *B*
State Fair Community College *A*

Montana

Dawson Community College *A*
Montana State University *B*
Northern Montana College *A*

Nebraska

Central Community College *C,A*
Chadron State College *A,B*
McCook Community College *A*
Northeast Community College *A*
University of Nebraska
    Kearney *B*
    Lincoln *B*
Wayne State College *B*
Western Nebraska Community
    College: Scottsbluff Campus *A*

Nevada

University of Nevada: Reno *B*

New Hampshire

University of New Hampshire *B*

New Jersey

Rutgers—The State University of
    New Jersey: Cook College *B*

New Mexico

Eastern New Mexico University *B*
New Mexico State University *B,M*

New York

Cornell University *B,M,D*
State University of New York
        College of Agriculture and
            Technology at Cobleskill *A*
        College of Agriculture and
            Technology at Morrisville *A*
        College of Technology at
            Alfred *A*

North Carolina

James Sprunt Community
    College *A*
North Carolina Agricultural and
    Technical State University *B*
North Carolina State University *B*
Surry Community College *A*
Wayne Community College *A*

North Dakota

Bismarck State College *C,A*
Dickinson State University *A*
North Dakota State College of
    Science *A*
North Dakota State University:
    Bottineau and Institute of
    Forestry *A*
University of North Dakota
    Lake Region *C,A*
    Williston *A*

Ohio

Clark State Community College *A*
Ohio State University
    Agricultural Technical
        Institute *A*
    Columbus Campus *B,M,D*
Ohio University *B*
Owens Technical College: Toledo *A*

Oklahoma

Connors State College *A*
Northern Oklahoma College *A*
Northwestern Oklahoma State
    University *B*
Oklahoma Panhandle State
    University *B*
Redlands Community College *A*
Rogers State College *A*

Oregon

Treasure Valley Community
    College *A*

Pennsylvania

Delaware Valley College *B*

Puerto Rico

University of Puerto Rico:
    Mayaguez Campus *B*

South Carolina

Clemson University *B*
South Carolina State College *B,M*

South Dakota

Dakota Wesleyan University *B*
Mitchell Vocational Technical
    Institute *C,A*
South Dakota State University *B*
Western Dakota Vocational
    Technical Institute *C,A*

Tennessee

Freed-Hardeman University *B*
Hiwassee College *A*
Martin Methodist College *A*
Middle Tennessee State
    University *B*
Motlow State Community
    College *A*
Tennessee Technological
    University *B*
University of Tennessee
    Knoxville *B*
    Martin *B*

Texas

Abilene Christian University *B*
Angelo State University *B*
Cisco Junior College *A*
Howard College *A*
Lubbock Christian University *B*
Navarro College *A*
Panola College *A*
Sam Houston State University *B,M*
South Plains College *A*
Southwest Texas State University *B*
Stephen F. Austin State
    University *B*
Sul Ross State University *B,M*
Tarleton State University *B*
Texas A&I University *B,M*
Texas A&M University *B,M*
Texas Tech University *B*
Weatherford College *A*
West Texas State University *B,M*
Western Texas College *A*

Utah

Southern Utah University *B*
Utah State University *B*

Virginia

Virginia Polytechnic Institute and
    State University *A*

Washington

Columbia Basin College *A*
Pierce College *A*
Skagit Valley College *A*
Spokane Community College *A*
Walla Walla Community College
    C,A
Washington State University *B*
Yakima Valley Community College
    C,A

Wisconsin

Chippewa Valley Technical
    College *A*
Fox Valley Technical College *A*
University of Wisconsin
    Madison *B*
    Platteville *B*
    River Falls *B*
Western Wisconsin Technical
    College *A*
Wisconsin Indianhead Technical
    College *A*

Wyoming

Casper College *A*
Central Wyoming College *A*
Eastern Wyoming College *A*
Northwest College *A*
Sheridan College *A*
University of Wyoming *B*

American Samoa, Caroline Islands, Guam, Marianas, Virgin Islands

Northern Marianas College *A*

Agricultural business and management

Alabama

Alabama Agricultural and
    Mechanical University *B*
Enterprise State Junior College *A*
James H. Faulkner State
    Community College *A*
Jefferson State Community
    College *A*
Lurleen B. Wallace State Junior
    College *A*
Snead State Junior College *A*

California

Bakersfield College *A*
California State Polytechnic
    University: Pomona *B*
California State University:
    Fresno *B*
College of the Redwoods *C,A*
Cosumnes River College *A*
Imperial Valley College *A*
Kings River Community College *A*
MiraCosta College *C,A*
San Joaquin Delta College *A*
Santa Rosa Junior College *C,A*
University of California: Davis *B*
West Hills Community College *A*
Yuba College *A*

Colorado

Aims Community College *C,A*
Colorado Northwestern Community
    College *C*
Colorado State University *B*
Lamar Community College *A*

Otero Junior College *C*

Delaware

University of Delaware *B*

Florida

Indian River Community College *A*
University of Florida *M*

Georgia

Abraham Baldwin Agricultural
    College *A*
Fort Valley State College *B*
South Georgia College *A*

Idaho

Ricks College *A*
University of Idaho *B*

Illinois

Belleville Area College *A*
Carl Sandburg College *A*
Illinois Central College *A*
Illinois Eastern Community
    Colleges: Wabash Valley
    College *A*
Illinois Valley Community
    College *A*
Joliet Junior College *A*
Lake Land College *C,A*
Lincoln Land Community
    College *A*
Parkland College *A*
Rend Lake College *A*
Shawnee Community College *A*
Southern Illinois University at
    Carbondale *B,M*
Spoon River College *A*

Indiana

Purdue University *B,M,D*

Iowa

Hawkeye Institute of Technology *A*
Iowa Lakes Community College *A*
Iowa State University *B,M*
Iowa Western Community
    College *A*
Kirkwood Community College *A*
Muscatine Community College *A*
North Iowa Area Community
    College *A*
Northwest Iowa Technical
    College *A*
St. Ambrose University *B*

Kansas

Allen County Community
    College *A*
Butler County Community
    College *A*
Cloud County Community
    College *A*
Coffeyville Community College *A*
Colby Community College *A*
Fort Hays State University *B*
Fort Scott Community College *A*
Hutchinson Community College *A*
Kansas State University *B*
Pratt Community College *C,A*

Kentucky

Eastern Kentucky University *B*
St. Catharine College *A*

Louisiana

University of Southwestern
    Louisiana *B*

Maine

University of Maine *B*

Maryland

Garrett Community College *A*

Michigan

Delta College *A*
Southwestern Michigan College *A*

Minnesota

Northland Community College *A*
Southwest State University *A,B*
University of Minnesota
    Crookston *A*
    Twin Cities *B*
Vermilion Community College *A*
Willmar Community College *A*
Willmar Technical College *C,A*
Worthington Community College *A*

Mississippi

Mississippi Delta Community
    College *A*

Missouri

Central Missouri State University
    B,M
Moberly Area Community
    College *A*
State Fair Community College *A*
Three Rivers Community College *A*

Nebraska

Nebraska College of Technical
    Agriculture *A*
Northeast Community College *A*
Southeast Community College:
    Beatrice Campus *A*
University of Nebraska—Lincoln *B*
Western Nebraska Community
    College: Sidney Campus *A*

New Jersey

County College of Morris *A*

New Mexico

Eastern New Mexico University *B*
New Mexico State University *B,M*

New York

Cornell University *B,M,D*
State University of New York
    College of Agriculture and
        Technology at Cobleskill *A*
    College of Technology at
        Alfred *A*

North Carolina

James Sprunt Community
    College *A*
North Carolina State University *B*

North Dakota

Bismarck State College *C,A*
Dickinson State University *A,B*
North Dakota State College of
    Science *A*
North Dakota State University:
    Bottineau and Institute of
    Forestry *C,A*
Standing Rock College *A*
University of North Dakota
    Lake Region *C,A*
    Williston *A*

Ohio

Clark State Community College *A*
Northwest Technical College *A*
Ohio State University Agricultural
    Technical Institute *A*

Oklahoma

Connors State College *A*
Langston University *B*

Redlands Community College *A*

Oregon
Eastern Oregon State College *B*
Linn-Benton Community College *A*
Oregon State University *B*

Pennsylvania
Penn State University Park Campus *A,B*

Puerto Rico
University of Puerto Rico: La Montana Regional College *A*

South Carolina
Bob Jones University *C,A,B*

South Dakota
Mitchell Vocational Technical Institute *C,A*

Tennessee
Jackson State Community College *A*
Tennessee Technological University *B*

Texas
Central Texas College *A*
Southwest Texas State University *B*
Sul Ross State University *B*
Texarkana College *A*
Texas State Technical College: Harlingen *C,A*
Wharton County Junior College *A*

Utah
Brigham Young University *B*
Utah State University *B,M*

Vermont
Vermont Technical College *A*

Virginia
Lord Fairfax Community College *A*

Washington
Columbia Basin College *A*
Evergreen State College *B*
Skagit Valley College *A*
Spokane Community College *A*
Wenatchee Valley College *A*

Wisconsin
Fox Valley Technical College *A*
Moraine Park Technical College *C*
Northeast Wisconsin Technical College *A*
University of Wisconsin
    Madison *B*
    River Falls *B*
Western Wisconsin Technical College *C*

Wyoming
Central Wyoming College *A*
Laramie County Community College *A*
Northwest College *A*
Sheridan College *A*
University of Wyoming *B*
Western Wyoming Community College *A*

Agricultural economics

Alabama
Alabama Agricultural and Mechanical University *B*
Auburn University *B,M,D*
Chattahoochee Valley Community College *A*
Tuskegee University *M*

Arizona
Prescott College *B*
University of Arizona *B,M*

Arkansas
Arkansas State University *B*
University of Arkansas
    Fayetteville *B,M*
    Pine Bluff *B*
Westark Community College *A*

California
California State Polytechnic University: Pomona *B*
California State University: Fresno *B*
Kings River Community College *A*
San Joaquin Delta College *A*
Stanford University *M,D*
University of California
    Berkeley *B,M,D*
    Davis *B,M,D*

Colorado
Colorado State University *B,M,D*
Lamar Community College *A*
Northeastern Junior College *A*

Connecticut
University of Connecticut *B,M,D*

Delaware
University of Delaware *B,M*

Florida
University of Florida *B,M,D*

Georgia
Fort Valley State College *B*
University of Georgia *B,M,D*
Young Harris College *A*

Hawaii
University of Hawaii at Manoa *B,M,D*

Idaho
University of Idaho *B,M*

Illinois
Southern Illinois University at Carbondale *B,M*
University of Illinois at Urbana-Champaign *B,M,D*

Indiana
Purdue University *A,B,M,D,W*
Vincennes University *A*

Iowa
Iowa State University *M,D*
Kirkwood Community College *A*
North Iowa Area Community College *A*

Kansas
Cloud County Community College *A*
Coffeyville Community College *A*
Colby Community College *A*

Fort Scott Community College *A*
Kansas State University *B,M,D*
McPherson College *B*

Kentucky
Murray State University *B*
University of Kentucky *B,M,D*

Louisiana
Louisiana State University and Agricultural and Mechanical College *B,M,D*
Southern University and Agricultural and Mechanical College *B*

Maine
University of Maine *B,M*

Maryland
University of Maryland: College Park *B,M,D*

Massachusetts
University of Massachusetts at Amherst *B,M,D*

Michigan
Michigan State University *M,D*

Minnesota
University of Minnesota
    Crookston *A*
    Twin Cities *M,D*
Willmar Community College *A*

Mississippi
Alcorn State University *B,M*
Mississippi State University *B,M,D*

Missouri
Central Missouri State University *B*
Northeast Missouri State University *B*
Northwest Missouri State University *B*
University of Missouri: Columbia *B,M,D*

Montana
Montana State University *B,M*

Nebraska
University of Nebraska—Lincoln *B,M,D*

Nevada
University of Nevada: Reno *M*

New Jersey
Rutgers—The State University of New Jersey
    Cook College *B*
    New Brunswick *M*

New Mexico
New Mexico State University *B,M*

New York
Cornell University *B,M,D*

North Carolina
North Carolina Agricultural and Technical State University *B,M*
North Carolina State University *B,M*

North Dakota
North Dakota State University *B,M*
University of North Dakota: Williston *A*

Ohio
Ohio State University: Columbus Campus *B,M,D*

Oklahoma
Eastern Oklahoma State College *A*
Langston University *B*
Oklahoma State University *B,M,D*

Oregon
Eastern Oregon State College *B*
Oregon State University *B,M,D*

Pennsylvania
Penn State University Park Campus *B,M,D*

Puerto Rico
University of Puerto Rico: Mayaguez Campus *B,M*

South Carolina
Clemson University *B,M,D*

South Dakota
South Dakota State University *B*

Tennessee
Hiwassee College *A*
Tennessee Technological University *B*
University of Tennessee: Knoxville *B,M,D*

Texas
Howard College *A*
Prairie View A&M University *B,M*
Stephen F. Austin State University *B*
Tarleton State University *B*
Texas A&M University *B,M,D*
Texas Tech University *B,M,D*
West Texas State University *B,M*

Utah
Brigham Young University *B,M*
Southern Utah University *B*
Utah State University *B,M*

Vermont
University of Vermont *B,M*

Virginia
Virginia Polytechnic Institute and State University *B,M,D*

Washington
Washington State University *B,M,D*

West Virginia
West Virginia University *B,M*

Wisconsin
University of Wisconsin
    Madison *B,M,D*
    Platteville *B*
    River Falls *B,M*

Wyoming
Northwest College *A*
University of Wyoming *M*

Canada
McGill University *B,M*

Agricultural education

Alabama

Alabama Agricultural and
Mechanical University *B,M*
Auburn University *B,M,D*
Brewer State Junior College *A*
Snead State Junior College *A*

Arizona

University of Arizona *B,M*
University of Phoenix *M*

Arkansas

Arkansas State University *B,M*
University of Arkansas
Fayetteville *B*
Pine Bluff *B*

California

California Polytechnic State
University: San Luis Obispo *B*
California State University
Fresno *B*
Sacramento *B*
University of California: Davis *B*

Colorado

Colorado State University *B,M*

Connecticut

University of Connecticut *B*

Delaware

Delaware State College *B*
University of Delaware *B,M*

Florida

Florida Agricultural and Mechanical
University *M*
Pensacola Junior College *A*
University of Florida *B*

Georgia

University of Georgia *B,M*

Idaho

University of Idaho *M*

Illinois

Southern Illinois University at
Carbondale *B*
University of Illinois at Urbana-
Champaign *B,M*
Western Illinois University *B*

Indiana

Purdue University *B,M,D*
Vincennes University *A*

Iowa

Iowa Lakes Community College *A*
Iowa State University *B,M,D*
Kirkwood Community College *A*

Kansas

Colby Community College *A*
Kansas State University *B*

Kentucky

Eastern Kentucky University *B,M*
Morehead State University *B*
Murray State University *B*
Western Kentucky University *M*

Louisiana

Louisiana State University and
Agricultural and Mechanical
College *B*
Louisiana Tech University *B*

Southern University and
Agricultural and Mechanical
College *B,M*
University of Southwestern
Louisiana *B*

Massachusetts

Lesley College *M*

Michigan

Michigan State University *B,M,D*

Minnesota

Rainy River Community College *A*
University of Minnesota: Twin
Cities *B,M*
Willmar Community College *A*

Mississippi

Alcorn State University *B,M*
Jones County Junior College *A*
Mississippi State University *B,M*
Northeast Mississippi Community
College *A*

Missouri

Central Missouri State University *B*
College of the Ozarks *B*
Northwest Missouri State
University *B,M*
Southwest Missouri State
University *B*
University of Missouri: Columbia *B*

Montana

Montana State University *B,M*

Nebraska

University of Nebraska—Lincoln
B,M

Nevada

University of Nevada: Reno *B*

New Jersey

Rutgers—The State University of
New Jersey: Cook College *B*

New Mexico

Eastern New Mexico University *B*
New Mexico State University *B,M*

New York

Cornell University *B,M,D*

North Carolina

North Carolina Agricultural and
Technical State University *B,M*
North Carolina State University
B,M

North Dakota

Bismarck State College *A*
North Dakota State University *B,M*

Ohio

Ohio State University: Columbus
Campus *B,M,D*

Oklahoma

Cameron University *B*
Oklahoma Panhandle State
University *B*
Oklahoma State University *B,M,D*

Oregon

Oregon State University *M*

Pennsylvania

Delaware Valley College *B*
Penn State University Park Campus
B,M,D

Puerto Rico

University of Puerto Rico:
Mayaguez Campus *B*

South Carolina

Clemson University *B,M*

Tennessee

Tennessee Technological
University *B*
University of Tennessee
Knoxville *M*
Martin *B*

Texas

East Texas State University *B,M*
Prairie View A&M University *M*
Sam Houston State University *B,M*
Southwest Texas State
University *M*
Tarleton State University *B*
Texas A&I University *B*
Texas A&M University *B,M,D*
Texas Tech University *B,M*

Utah

Utah State University *B,M*

Vermont

University of Vermont *B*

Virginia

Ferrum College *B*
Virginia Polytechnic Institute and
State University *B,M*
Virginia State University *M*

Washington

Washington State University *B*

West Virginia

West Virginia University *B,M*

Wisconsin

University of Wisconsin
Madison *B,M*
Platteville *B,M*
River Falls *B,M*

Wyoming

University of Wyoming *B*

American Samoa, Caroline Islands, Guam, Marianas, Virgin Islands

University of Guam *B*

Agricultural engineering

Alabama

Auburn University *B,M,D*

Arizona

University of Arizona *B,M,D*

Arkansas

Arkansas State University *B*
University of Arkansas *B,M*
Westark Community College *A*

California

California Polytechnic State
University: San Luis Obispo *B*
California State Polytechnic
University: Pomona *B*
Santa Rosa Junior College *A*
University of California: Davis
B,M,D

Colorado

Colorado State University *B,M,D*

Connecticut

University of Connecticut *B*

Delaware

University of Delaware *B,M*

Florida

University of Florida *B,M*

Georgia

Abraham Baldwin Agricultural
College *A*
Atlanta Metropolitan College *A*
Clayton State College *A*
DeKalb College *A*
Fort Valley State College *B*
Gordon College *A*
Middle Georgia College *A*
University of Georgia *B,M,D*

Hawaii

University of Hawaii at Manoa *M*

Idaho

College of Southern Idaho *A*
North Idaho College *A*
University of Idaho *B,M,D*

Illinois

University of Illinois at Urbana-
Champaign *B,M,D*

Indiana

Purdue University *B,M,D,W*
Vincennes University *A*

Iowa

Iowa State University *B,M,D*

Kansas

Cloud County Community
College *A*
Kansas State University *B,M,D*

Kentucky

University of Kentucky *B,M,D*

Louisiana

Louisiana State University and
Agricultural and Mechanical
College *B,M*
University of Southwestern
Louisiana *B*

Maine

University of Maine *B,M*

Maryland

University of Maryland: College
Park *B,M,D*

Michigan

Michigan State University *B,M,D*

Minnesota

University of Minnesota: Twin
Cities *B,M,D*
Willmar Community College *A*

Mississippi

Mississippi State University *B,M*

Missouri

University of Missouri: Columbia
B,M,D

Montana

Montana State University *B,M*

Nebraska
University of Nebraska—Lincoln
B,M

New Jersey
Rutgers—The State University of
New Jersey
College of Engineering B
Cook College B
New Brunswick M

New Mexico
New Mexico State University
B,M,D

New York
Cornell University B,M,D
State University of New York
College of Agriculture and
Technology at Cobleskill A
College of Agriculture and
Technology at Morrisville A

North Carolina
North Carolina Agricultural and
Technical State University B
North Carolina State University
B,M,D
St. Augustine's College B

North Dakota
North Dakota State University B,M

Ohio
Ohio State University: Columbus
Campus B,M,D

Oklahoma
Oklahoma State University B,M,D

Oregon
Oregon State University M,D

Pennsylvania
Lock Haven University of
Pennsylvania B
Penn State University Park Campus
C,B,M,D

South Carolina
Clemson University B,M,D

South Dakota
South Dakota State University B,M

Tennessee
Hiwassee College A
Tennessee Technological
University B
University of Tennessee: Knoxville
B,M,D

Texas
Prairie View A&M University B
Texas A&M University B,M,D
Texas Tech University B,M

Utah
Utah State University B,M,D

Virginia
Virginia Polytechnic Institute and
State University B,M,D

Washington
Washington State University B

Wisconsin
University of Wisconsin
Madison B,M,D
Platteville B
River Falls B

Wyoming
University of Wyoming B,M

Canada
McGill University B,M,D

Agricultural mechanics

Arkansas
University of Arkansas B

California
Bakersfield College A
California Polytechnic State
University: San Luis Obispo B
California State University:
Fresno B
College of the Desert C,A
Imperial Valley College C,A
Kings River Community College C
Lassen College A
Merced College C,A
Modesto Junior College A
Mount San Antonio College C,A
Oxnard College C,A
San Joaquin Delta College C,A
West Hills Community College C,A
Yuba College C

Florida
University of Florida M

Georgia
University of Georgia B

Idaho
Lewis Clark State College A
Ricks College A
University of Idaho B

Illinois
Black Hawk College: East
Campus C
Carl Sandburg College C,A
Illinois Central College C,A
Illinois Valley Community
College A
Kishwaukee College C,A
Lake Land College C,A
Rend Lake College C,A
Southern Illinois University at
Carbondale B,M
University of Illinois at Urbana-
Champaign B

Indiana
Purdue University A,B
Vincennes University A

Iowa
Iowa Lakes Community College C
Iowa State University B
Kirkwood Community College A
Southwestern Community
College C
William Penn College B

Kansas
Dodge City Community College
C,A
Hutchinson Community College
C,A
Kansas State University B,M
Pratt Community College C,A

Kentucky
Eastern Kentucky University A,B
Murray State University B
Western Kentucky University C,A

Louisiana
Louisiana State University and
Agricultural and Mechanical
College B

Minnesota
Alexandria Technical College C
University of Minnesota:
Crookston A

Mississippi
Hinds Community College C,A

Missouri
Northwest Missouri State
University B
University of Missouri: Columbia
B,M

Montana
Dawson Community College C
Montana State University B

Nebraska
Nebraska College of Technical
Agriculture A
Southeast Community College:
Beatrice Campus A
University of Nebraska—Lincoln
B,M

New Jersey
Thomas Edison State College A,B

New York
State University of New York
College of Agriculture and
Technology at Cobleskill A
College of Agriculture and
Technology at Morrisville A

North Carolina
Beaufort County Community
College A
North Carolina State University A

North Dakota
North Dakota State University B
University of North Dakota: Lake
Region C

Ohio
Northwest Technical College A

Oklahoma
Oklahoma State University B

Oregon
Lane Community College A
Portland Community College A

Pennsylvania
Penn State University Park
Campus B

Puerto Rico
University of Puerto Rico:
Mayaguez Campus B

South Carolina
Horry-Georgetown Technical
College C

South Dakota
Mitchell Vocational Technical
Institute C,A

Texas
Sam Houston State University B,M
Southwest Texas State University B
Tarleton State University B
Texas A&M University B,M

Utah
Utah State University C,A

Virginia
Tidewater Community College C

Washington
Spokane Community College A
Walla Walla Community College
C,A
Washington State University B
Yakima Valley Community
College A

West Virginia
West Virginia University B

Wisconsin
Madison Area Technical College C
Moraine Park Technical College C
University of Wisconsin: River
Falls B
Wisconsin Indianhead Technical
College C

Wyoming
Casper College A
Eastern Wyoming College A

Agricultural production

Alabama
Wallace State Community College
at Hanceville C

California
MiraCosta College C,A
San Joaquin Delta College A
Santa Rosa Junior College C

Colorado
Northeastern Junior College C

Illinois
Black Hawk College: East
Campus A
Carl Sandburg College A
Highland Community College C,A
Joliet Junior College C,A
Kishwaukee College C
Lake Land College C,A
Rend Lake College C,A
Richland Community College A
Southern Illinois University at
Carbondale B

Iowa
Hawkeye Institute of Technology A
Iowa Lakes Community College A
Iowa State University M
Kirkwood Community College A
Muscatine Community College A
North Iowa Area Community
College C
Southeastern Community College:
North Campus A

Kansas
Barton County Community
College A
Butler County Community
College A
Cloud County Community
College A
Coffeyville Community College A
Cowley County Community
College A
Pratt Community College C,A

Kentucky

Morehead State University A
University of Kentucky B
Western Kentucky University A

Massachusetts

University of Massachusetts at
Amherst A

Michigan

Michigan State University B

Minnesota

University of Minnesota:
Crookston A
Willmar Community College A
Willmar Technical College C,A

Missouri

North Central Missouri College A
Northwest Missouri State
University C

Montana

Miles Community College C

Nebraska

Central Community College C,A
McCook Community College A
Nebraska College of Technical
Agriculture A
Southeast Community College:
Beatrice Campus A

North Carolina

North Carolina State University A

Ohio

Southern State Community
College A

Oklahoma

Northern Oklahoma College A

Oregon

Linn-Benton Community College A

South Dakota

Mitchell Vocational Technical
Institute C,A
Western Dakota Vocational
Technical Institute C,A

Texas

Texas A&M University M
Texas Southmost College A

Utah

Brigham Young University B

Virginia

Lord Fairfax Community College A

Washington

Columbia Basin College A
Spokane Community College A
Walla Walla Community College
C,A
Yakima Valley Community College
C,A

Wisconsin

Chippewa Valley Technical
College A
Wisconsin Indianhead Technical
College C

Wyoming

Central Wyoming College C
Northwest College C,A
Sheridan College A

American Samoa, Caroline Islands, Guam, Marianas, Virgin Islands

Northern Marianas College A

Mexico

Sistema Instituto Tecnologico y de
Estudios Superiores de
Monterrey B,M

Agricultural products and processing

California

California State Polytechnic
University: Pomona B

Florida

University of Florida M

Illinois

Illinois Valley Community
College A

Indiana

Vincennes University A

Iowa

Iowa State University M,D

Kansas

Coffeyville Community College A
Colby Community College A

New York

State University of New York
College of Agriculture and
Technology at Morrisville A

North Carolina

North Carolina State University A

Ohio

Ohio State University Agricultural
Technical Institute A

Texas

Sul Ross State University A

Washington

Pierce College A

Mexico

Sistema Instituto Tecnologico y de
Estudios Superiores de
Monterrey B

Agricultural sciences

Alabama

Alabama Southern Community
College A
Auburn University B
Brewer State Junior College A
Chattahoochee Valley Community
College A
James H. Faulkner State
Community College A
John C. Calhoun State Community
College A
Shoals Community College A
Snead State Junior College A

Arizona

Arizona State University M
Arizona Western College A

Cochise College A
Eastern Arizona College A
Mesa Community College A
Pima Community College A
University of Arizona B

Arkansas

Arkansas State University
Beebe Branch A
Jonesboro B,M
Arkansas Tech University B
East Arkansas Community
College A
Mississippi County Community
College A
Southern Arkansas University B
University of Arkansas
Fayetteville B,M
Monticello B

California

California Polytechnic State
University: San Luis Obispo M
California State Polytechnic
University: Pomona B,M
California State University
Chico B,M
Fresno B,M
Cerritos Community College A
College of the Desert A
College of the Sequoias A
Cosumnes River College A
Imperial Valley College A
Kings River Community College A
Lassen College A
Los Angeles Pierce College C,A
Merced College A
Modesto Junior College A
Napa Valley College A
San Joaquin Delta College A
Santa Rosa Junior College C,A
Sierra College C,A
Ventura College A
West Hills Community College A

Colorado

Colorado State University B,M
Fort Lewis College A
Lamar Community College A
Mesa State College A
Northeastern Junior College A
Trinidad State Junior College A

Connecticut

University of Connecticut B

Delaware

Delaware State College B
University of Delaware B
Wesley College A

Florida

Chipola Junior College A
Daytona Beach Community
College A
Florida Agricultural and Mechanical
University B
Indian River Community College A
Manatee Community College A
Pensacola Junior College A
South Florida Community
College A

Georgia

Abraham Baldwin Agricultural
College A
Andrew College A
Atlanta Metropolitan College A
Bainbridge College A
Clayton State College A
Darton College A
DeKalb College A

East Georgia College A
Floyd College A
Fort Valley State College B
Gainesville College A
Gordon College A
Macon College A
Middle Georgia College A
South Georgia College C,A
Young Harris College A

Hawaii

University of Hawaii
Hilo B
Manoa B

Idaho

College of Southern Idaho A
Ricks College A
University of Idaho B

Illinois

Black Hawk College: East
Campus A
City Colleges of Chicago: Wright
College A
Highland Community College A
Illinois State University B,M
Illinois Valley Community
College A
Joliet Junior College A
Kishwaukee College A
Lake Land College A
Lincoln Land Community
College A
Rend Lake College A
Shawnee Community College A
Southern Illinois University at
Carbondale B
University of Illinois at Urbana-
Champaign B
Western Illinois University B

Indiana

Purdue University C,A,B
Vincennes University A

Iowa

Dordt College A,B
Kirkwood Community College A
North Iowa Area Community
College A

Kansas

Barton County Community
College A
Butler County Community
College A
Coffeyville Community College A
Colby Community College A
Cowley County Community
College A
Dodge City Community College A
Fort Hays State University B
Fort Scott Community College A
Highland Community College A
Hutchinson Community College A
Kansas City Kansas Community
College A
McPherson College B
MidAmerica Nazarene College A,B
Pratt Community College A
Seward County Community
College A

Kentucky

Berea College B
Eastern Kentucky University A,B
Morehead State University B
Murray State University B,M
St. Catharine College A
University of Kentucky B
Western Kentucky University B,M

Louisiana

McNeese State University *B*
University of Southwestern
Louisiana *B*

Maine

University of Maine
Orono *B*
Presque Isle *B*

Maryland

Frederick Community College *A*
University of Maryland
College Park *B*
Eastern Shore *B,M*

Massachusetts

Hampshire College *B*

Michigan

Andrews University *B*
Southwestern Michigan College *A*

Minnesota

Bethany Lutheran College *A*
Northland Community College *A*
Rainy River Community College *A*
Rochester Community College *A*
University of Minnesota
Crookston *A*
Twin Cities *B*
Willmar Community College *A*
Worthington Community College *A*

Mississippi

Alcorn State University *B,M*
Jones County Junior College *A*
Mississippi Delta Community
College *A*
Mississippi State University *B*

Missouri

College of the Ozarks *B*
Lincoln University *B*
Mineral Area College *A*
Missouri Western State College *B*
Moberly Area Community
College *A*
Northeast Missouri State
University *B*
Northwest Missouri State
University *B,M*
Southeast Missouri State
University *B*
Southwest Missouri State
University *B*
Three Rivers Community College *A*
University of Missouri: Columbia *B*

Montana

Miles Community College *C,A*
Northern Montana College *A*

Nebraska

Northeast Community College *A*
Southeast Community College:
Beatrice Campus *A*
University of Nebraska—Lincoln
C,B
Western Nebraska Community
College: Scottsbluff Campus *A*

New Hampshire

University of New Hampshire *B*

New Jersey

Cumberland County College *C,A*
Rutgers—The State University of
New Jersey: Cook College *B*

New Mexico

Eastern New Mexico University *B*
New Mexico Junior College *A*
New Mexico State University *B,M*

New York

Cornell University *B*
State University of New York
College of Agriculture and
Technology at Cobleskill
A,B
College of Agriculture and
Technology at Morrisville
C,A
College of Technology at
Alfred *A*

North Carolina

Brevard College *A*
Chowan College *A*
College of the Albemarle *A*
North Carolina Agricultural and
Technical State University *B,M*
North Carolina State University
A,M
Surry Community College *A*
Western Piedmont Community
College *A*

North Dakota

North Dakota State University
Bottineau and Institute of
Forestry *A*
Fargo *B,M*
University of North Dakota
Lake Region *A*
Williston *A*

Ohio

Ohio State University: Columbus
Campus *B,M*
Wilmington College *B*

Oklahoma

Cameron University *B*
Connors State College *A*
Eastern Oklahoma State College *A*
Langston University *B*
Murray State College *A*
Northern Oklahoma College *A*
Oklahoma State University *B,M*
Redlands Community College *A*

Oregon

Central Oregon Community
College *A*
Linn-Benton Community College
C,A
Oregon State University *B,M*
Treasure Valley Community
College *A*

Pennsylvania

Penn State University Park Campus
C,B

Puerto Rico

University of Puerto Rico:
Mayaguez Campus *B*

Rhode Island

University of Rhode Island *B*

South Carolina

Clemson University *M*
Sumter Area Technical College *A*

South Dakota

South Dakota State University *A,B*

Tennessee

Austin Peay State University *B*
Columbia State Community
College *A*
Martin Methodist College *A*
Tennessee State University *B,M*
Tennessee Technological
University *B*
University of Tennessee: Martin *B*
Walters State Community
College *A*

Texas

Abilene Christian University *A,B*
Angelina College *A*
Bee County College *A*
Blinn College *A*
Central Texas College *A*
Cisco Junior College *A*
Cooke County College *A*
East Texas State University *B,M*
Hardin-Simmons University *B*
Houston Community College *A*
Howard College *A*
Kilgore College *A*
Lubbock Christian University *B*
McLennan Community College *A*
Navarro College *A*
Northeast Texas Community
College *A*
Panola College *A*
Prairie View A&M University *B*
Sam Houston State University *B,M*
South Plains College *A*
Southwest Texas State University *B*
Stephen F. Austin State University
B,M
Tarleton State University *B,M*
Texas A&M University *B,M*
Texas Southmost College *A*
Texas Tech University *M,D*
Trinity Valley Community
College *A*
Vernon Regional Junior College *A*
West Texas State University *B,M*
Western Texas College *A*
Wharton County Junior College *A*

Utah

Southern Utah University *A*

Vermont

Goddard College *B,M*
Sterling College *A*

Virginia

Ferrum College *B*
Virginia State University *B*

Washington

Centralia College *A*
Evergreen State College *B*
Skagit Valley College *A*
Spokane Community College *A*
Washington State University *B*
Wenatchee Valley College *A*
Yakima Valley Community
College *A*

West Virginia

Potomac State College of West
Virginia University *A*
West Virginia University *B,M*

Wisconsin

University of Wisconsin
Platteville *B,M*
River Falls *B*

Wyoming

Casper College *A*
Central Wyoming College *A*

Eastern Wyoming College *A*
Laramie County Community
College *A*
Northwest College *A*
Sheridan College *A*
University of Wyoming *B*

American Samoa, Caroline Islands, Guam, Marianas, Virgin Islands

Community College of
Micronesia *A*
Micronesian Occupational College
C,A
University of Guam *B*
University of the Virgin Islands *A*

Canada

McGill University *B,M,D*

Agronomy

Alabama

Auburn University *B,M,D*

Arizona

Mesa Community College *C*
University of Arizona *B,M,D*

Arkansas

University of Arkansas
Fayetteville *B,M,D*
Pine Bluff *B*
Westark Community College *A*

California

California State Polytechnic
University: Pomona *B*
California State University:
Fresno *B*
Kings River Community College *A*
Merced College *A*
Modesto Junior College *A*
San Joaquin Delta College *A*
Santa Rosa Junior College *A*
Sierra College *C,A*
University of California: Davis *M*
Ventura College *C,A*
West Hills Community College *A*

Colorado

Colorado State University *B,M,D*
Lamar Community College *A*

Connecticut

University of Connecticut *B*

Delaware

University of Delaware *B*

Florida

Florida Agricultural and Mechanical
University *B*
University of Florida *B,M,D*

Georgia

Fort Valley State College *B*
University of Georgia *B,M,D*

Hawaii

University of Hawaii at Manoa
B,M,D

Idaho

Ricks College *C,A*

Illinois

Illinois Valley Community
College *C*

Southern Illinois University at
Carbondale *B,M*
University of Illinois at Urbana-
Champaign *B,M,D*

Indiana

Purdue University *A,B,M,D,W*
Vincennes University *A*

Iowa

Iowa State University *B,M,D*
Kirkwood Community College *A*

Kansas

Cowley County Community
College *A*
Kansas State University *B,M,D*
Sterling College *B*

Kentucky

Murray State University *B*
University of Kentucky *B,M,D*

Louisiana

Louisiana State University and
Agricultural and Mechanical
College *B,M,D*
Louisiana Tech University *B*
McNeese State University *B*

Maryland

University of Maryland: College
Park *B,M,D*

Michigan

Michigan State University *B,M,D*
Southwestern Michigan College *A*

Minnesota

University of Minnesota
Crookston *A*
Twin Cities *M,D*
Willmar Community College *A*

Mississippi

Alcorn State University *B,M*
Mississippi State University *B,M,D*

Missouri

Northeast Missouri State
University *B*
Northwest Missouri State
University *B*
Southeast Missouri State
University *B*
Southwest Missouri State
University *B*
University of Missouri: Columbia
B,M,D

Montana

Montana State University *B,M*

Nebraska

McCook Community College *A*
Northeast Community College *A*
University of Nebraska—Lincoln
B,M,D

New Hampshire

University of New Hampshire *B*

New Jersey

Rutgers—The State University of
New Jersey: Cook College *B*

New Mexico

New Mexico State University
B,M,D

New York

Cornell University *B,M,D*
State University of New York
College of Agriculture and
Technology at Cobleskill *A*
College of Agriculture and
Technology at Morrisville *A*
College of Technology at
Alfred *A*

North Carolina

North Carolina State University *B*

North Dakota

North Dakota State University
B,M,D

Ohio

Ohio State University
Agricultural Technical
Institute *A*
Columbus Campus *B,M,D*

Oklahoma

Eastern Oklahoma State College *A*
Oklahoma Panhandle State
University *A*
Oklahoma State University *B,M,D*

Oregon

Oregon State University *B,M,D*

Pennsylvania

Delaware Valley College *B*
Penn State University Park Campus
C,B,M,D

Puerto Rico

University of Puerto Rico:
Mayaguez Campus *B,M*

South Carolina

Clemson University *B,M,D*

South Dakota

South Dakota State University
B,M,D

Tennessee

Tennessee Technological
University *B*

Texas

Abilene Christian University *B*
Howard College *A*
Prairie View A&M University *B*
Stephen F. Austin State
University *B*
Texas A&I University *M*
Texas A&M University *B,M,D*
Texas Tech University *D*
West Texas State University *B,M*
Western Texas College *A*

Utah

Brigham Young University *B,M*
Southern Utah University *A,B*
Utah State University *B*

Virginia

Virginia Polytechnic Institute and
State University *B,M,D*

Washington

Spokane Community College *A*
Washington State University *B,M,D*
Yakima Valley Community College
C,A

West Virginia

West Virginia University *B,M,D*

Wisconsin

University of Wisconsin
Madison *B,M,D*
Platteville *B*
River Falls *B*

Wyoming

Northwest College *A*
University of Wyoming *M,D*

Canada

McGill University *B,M,D*

Air conditioning/
heating/refrigeration
mechanics

Alabama

Bessemer State Technical College *C*
Brewer State Junior College *A*
Central Alabama Community
College: Childersburg Campus *C*
Community College of the Air
Force *A*
Douglas MacArthur State Technical
College *C*
Gadsden State Community College
C,A
George C. Wallace State
Community College at Selma *A*
John C. Calhoun State Community
College *C,A*
Shoals Community College *C*
Walker State Technical College *C,A*
Wallace State Community College
at Hanceville *C*

Arizona

Arizona Western College *A*
Mohave Community College *C*
Pima Community College *C,A*
Rio Salado Community College *A*

Arkansas

Phillips County Community
College *A*

California

Cerro Coso Community College
C,A
Citrus College *C,A*
College of the Desert *C,A*
College of the Sequoias *C,A*
El Camino College *C,A*
Fresno City College *C,A*
Laney College *C,A*
Long Beach City College *C,A*
Los Angeles Trade and Technical
College *C,A*
Los Medanos College *C,A*
Modesto Junior College *A*
Mount San Antonio College *C,A*
Orange Coast College *C,A*
San Diego City College *C,A*
San Joaquin Delta College *C,A*
San Jose City College *A*
Southwestern College *C*

Colorado

Arapahoe Community College *C*
Community College of Denver *C,A*
Denver Institute of Technology *C*
Pikes Peak Community College *C,A*
Pueblo Community College *C,A*

Delaware

Delaware Technical and
Community College: Southern
Campus *A*

District of Columbia

University of the District of
Columbia *C*

Florida

Brevard Community College *C*
Central Florida Community
College *C*
Daytona Beach Community
College *C*
Hillsborough Community College *A*
Indian River Community College *A*
Miami-Dade Community College *A*
New England Institute of
Technology *A*
Santa Fe Community College *C*
Seminole Community College *C*
South Florida Community
College *C*

Georgia

Athens Area Technical Institute *C*
Atlanta Metropolitan College *A*
Augusta Technical Institute *C*
Bainbridge College *C*
Chattahoochee Technical
Institute *C*
Darton College *A*
DeKalb Technical Institute *C*
Floyd College *A*
Gainesville College *A*
Savannah Technical Institute *C*

Hawaii

University of Hawaii: Honolulu
Community College *C,A*

Idaho

Boise State University *C*
College of Southern Idaho *C,A*
North Idaho College *C,A*

Illinois

Belleville Area College *C,A*
Black Hawk College *C*
City Colleges of Chicago: Chicago
City-Wide College *C*
College of DuPage *C,A*
College of Lake County *C,A*
Elgin Community College *C,A*
Illinois Central College *C*
Illinois Eastern Community
Colleges: Lincoln Trail College
C,A
John A. Logan College *C*
Joliet Junior College *C*
Lincoln Land Community
College *C*
Moraine Valley Community
College *C*
Morton College *C,A*
Oakton Community College *C,A*
Prairie State College *C*
Rend Lake College *C*
State Community College *C*
Triton College *C,A*
Waubonsee Community College
C,A
William Rainey Harper College *A*

Indiana

Indiana University—Purdue
University at Indianapolis *C*

Indiana Vocational Technical College
    Central Indiana *C,A*
    Columbus *C,A*
    Eastcentral *C,A*
    Kokomo *C,A*
    Lafayette *C,A*
    Northcentral *C,A*
    Northeast *C,A*
    Northwest *C,A*
    Southcentral *C,A*
    Southwest *C,A*
    Wabash Valley *C*
    Whitewater *C*
ITT Technical Institute: Indianapolis *C*
Oakland City College *C,A*

Iowa

Des Moines Area Community College *C*
Hawkeye Institute of Technology *C*
Indian Hills Community College *C*
Kirkwood Community College *A*
North Iowa Area Community College *A*
Northeast Iowa Community College *C*
Northwest Iowa Technical College *C,A*
Scott Community College *C*
Southeastern Community College
    North Campus *C*
    South Campus *C*

Kansas

Coffeyville Community College *A*
Kansas City Kansas Community College *A*
Labette Community College *A*
Neosho County Community College *C,A*
Pittsburg State University *C*

Kentucky

Eastern Kentucky University *B*
St. Catharine College *A*

Maine

Eastern Maine Technical College *A*
Southern Maine Technical College *A*

Maryland

Cecil Community College *C,A*
Chesapeake College *C*
Dundalk Community College *C,A*

Massachusetts

Springfield Technical Community College *A*

Michigan

Grand Rapids Community College *C,A*
Jackson Community College *A*
Lansing Community College *A*
Macomb Community College *C,A*
Mid Michigan Community College *C,A*
Northern Michigan University *C,A*
Oakland Community College *A*

Minnesota

St. Paul Technical College *C*

Mississippi

Copiah-Lincoln Community College *C*
East Central Community College *C*
Hinds Community College *C*
Jones County Junior College *C*

Mississippi Delta Community College *C*
Mississippi Gulf Coast Community College: Jefferson Davis Campus *C*
Southwest Mississippi Community College *C*

Missouri

East Central College *C,A*
Jefferson College *C,A*
Penn Valley Community College *C,A*
Ranken Technical College *A*

Nebraska

Central Community College *C,A*
Metropolitan Community College *C,A*
Northeast Community College *A*
Southeast Community College: Milford Campus *A*

Nevada

Community College of Southern Nevada *C,A*
Truckee Meadows Community College *C,A*

New Hampshire

New Hampshire Technical College: Manchester *C,A*

New Jersey

Mercer County Community College *C*

New Mexico

Albuquerque Technical-Vocational Institute *C*
Clovis Community College *C,A*
Dona Ana Branch Community College of New Mexico State University *C,A*
New Mexico State University *C,A*
Parks College *C*

New York

Dutchess Community College *C*
Erie Community College: North Campus *C*
Hudson Valley Community College *A*
Jamestown Community College *A*
Mohawk Valley Community College *C,A*
Niagara County Community College *C*
State University of New York College of Technology at Delhi *C,A*
Technical Career Institutes *C*

North Carolina

Alamance Community College *C,A*
Anson Community College *C*
Asheville Buncombe Technical Community College *C*
Blue Ridge Community College *C*
Brunswick Community College *C*
Caldwell Community College and Technical Institute *C*
Cape Fear Community College *C*
Carteret Community College *C*
Catawba Valley Community College *A*
Central Piedmont Community College *A*
Cleveland Community College *C*
Coastal Carolina Community College *C*
College of the Albemarle *C*

Craven Community College *C,A*
Davidson County Community College *C*
Forsyth Technical Community College *A*
Gaston College *C*
Guilford Technical Community College *C*
Johnston Community College *C*
Martin Community College *C*
Mitchell Community College *C*
Montgomery Community College *C*
Piedmont Community College *C*
Pitt Community College *C*
Roanoke-Chowan Community College *C*
Robeson Community College *C*
Rockingham Community College *C*
Southeastern Community College *C*
Vance-Granville Community College *C*
Wake Technical Community College *C*
Wilson Technical Community College *C*

North Dakota

Bismarck State College *C,A*
North Dakota State College of Science *C,A*

Ohio

Columbus State Community College *A*
ITT Technical Institute: Dayton *C*
Owens Technical College: Toledo *C,A*
Sinclair Community College *A*
Terra Technical College *C*
University of Cincinnati: Access Colleges *C*
Washington State Community College *A*

Oklahoma

Oklahoma State University
    Oklahoma City *A*
    Technical Branch: Okmulgee *A*
Tulsa Junior College *A*

Oregon

Lane Community College *A*
Linn-Benton Community College *C,A*
Portland Community College *C*

Pennsylvania

Lehigh County Community College *C,A*
Pennsylvania College of Technology *A*
Spring Garden College *C*
Triangle Tech: Greensburg School *A*
Westmoreland County Community College *A*

Rhode Island

New England Institute of Technology *A*

South Carolina

Aiken Technical College *C*
Chesterfield-Marlboro Technical College *C,A*
Denmark Technical College *C*
Florence-Darlington Technical College *A*
Greenville Technical College *C*
Horry-Georgetown Technical College *A*

Midlands Technical College *A*
Sumter Area Technical College *C*
Technical College of the Lowcountry *A*
Trident Technical College *C*
Williamsburg Technical College *C*

South Dakota

Mitchell Vocational Technical Institute *C,A*

Tennessee

Chattanooga State Technical Community College *C,A*

Texas

Alvin Community College *C,A*
Amarillo College *C,A*
Austin Community College *A*
Bee County College *C,A*
Brazosport College *C,A*
Central Texas College *A*
College of the Mainland *C,A*
Del Mar College *C,A*
Eastfield College *A*
El Paso Community College *C*
Houston Community College *C*
Howard College *C*
Lamar University—Beaumont *A*
Laredo Junior College *C*
Lee College *A*
Midland College *A*
North Harris Montgomery Community College District *C,A*
Northeast Texas Community College *C,A*
Odessa College *C,A*
St. Philip's College *A*
South Plains College *C,A*
Tarrant County Junior College *C,A*
Texarkana College *C*
Texas Southmost College *A*
Texas State Technical College
    Amarillo *A*
    Harlingen *C,A*
    Sweetwater *C*
    Waco *C,A*
Trinity Valley Community College *A*
Victoria College *C,A*
Wharton County Junior College *C*

Utah

Utah Valley Community College *C,A*

Virginia

Central Virginia Community College *C*
John Tyler Community College *C*
Mountain Empire Community College *C*
Northern Virginia Community College *C,A*
Patrick Henry Community College *C*
Piedmont Virginia Community College *C*
Southside Virginia Community College *C*
Tidewater Community College *C*
Virginia Highlands Community College *C*

Washington

Columbia Basin College *C*
North Seattle Community College *A*
Spokane Community College *A*
Walla Walla Community College *C,A*
Wenatchee Valley College *A*

Yakima Valley Community
College *C*

West Virginia

West Virginia Northern Community
College *A*

Wisconsin

Chippewa Valley Technical
College *A*
Western Wisconsin Technical
College *C*

Wyoming

Eastern Wyoming College *C,A*

**American Samoa, Caroline
Islands, Guam, Marianas,
Virgin Islands**

Guam Community College *C*
Micronesian Occupational College
C,A

Air conditioning/
heating/refrigeration
technology

Alabama

Bessemer State Technical College *C*
Brewer State Junior College *A*
Central Alabama Community
College: Childersburg Campus *C*
Community College of the Air
Force *A*
John C. Calhoun State Community
College *C,A*
John M. Patterson State Technical
College *A*
Shelton State Community College
C,A
Walker State Technical College *C,A*
Wallace State Community College
at Hanceville *C*

Arizona

Arizona Western College *A*
Mohave Community College *C*
Rio Salado Community College *A*

Arkansas

Phillips County Community
College *C*

California

Citrus College *C*
City College of San Francisco *C*
College of the Desert *C,A*
College of the Sequoias *C,A*
El Camino College *C,A*
Fresno City College *C,A*
Long Beach City College *C,A*
Los Angeles Trade and Technical
College *C,A*
Mount San Antonio College *C,A*
Orange Coast College *C,A*
Oxnard College *A*
San Diego City College *C,A*
San Joaquin Delta College *C,A*

Colorado

Community College of Denver *C,A*

Connecticut

Hartford State Technical College *A*
Waterbury State Technical
College *C*

Delaware

Delaware Technical and
Community College: Southern
Campus *A*

Florida

Brevard Community College *C,A*
Central Florida Community
College *C*
Daytona Beach Community
College *A*
Florida Community College at
Jacksonville *A*
Hillsborough Community College *A*
Indian River Community College *A*
New England Institute of
Technology *A*
Okaloosa-Walton Community
College *C,A*
Santa Fe Community College *C*
Seminole Community College *C*
South Florida Community
College *C*

Georgia

DeKalb Technical Institute *C*
Floyd College *A*
Georgia Southwestern College *A*
Savannah Technical Institute *C*

Hawaii

University of Hawaii: Honolulu
Community College *C,A*

Idaho

Boise State University *A*
College of Southern Idaho *C,A*

Illinois

Belleville Area College *C,A*
Black Hawk College *A*
City Colleges of Chicago: Chicago
City-Wide College *C*
College of DuPage *C,A*
College of Lake County *C,A*
Elgin Community College *C,A*
Illinois Eastern Community
Colleges: Lincoln Trail College
C,A
John A. Logan College *C*
Joliet Junior College *C*
Lake Land College *C*
Lincoln Land Community
College *C*
Moraine Valley Community
College *C*
Morton College *C,A*
Oakton Community College *C,A*
Prairie State College *C*
Triton College *C,A*
Waubonsee Community College
C,A
William Rainey Harper College *C,A*

Indiana

Oakland City College *C,A*

Iowa

Kirkwood Community College *A*
North Iowa Area Community
College *A*
Northeast Iowa Community
College *C*
Northwest Iowa Technical College
C,A
Scott Community College *C*
Southeastern Community College
North Campus *C*
South Campus *C*

Kansas

Johnson County Community
College *C,A*
Kansas City Kansas Community
College *A*
Neosho County Community College
C
Pittsburg State University *C*

Kentucky

Eastern Kentucky University *A*
St. Catharine College *A*

Maine

Eastern Maine Technical College *A*
Southern Maine Technical
College *A*

Maryland

Chesapeake College *C*

Massachusetts

Massasoit Community College *A*
Springfield Technical Community
College *A*

Michigan

Charles Stewart Mott Community
College *C,A*
Ferris State University *A*
Grand Rapids Community College
C,A
Henry Ford Community College
C,A
Jackson Community College *C,A*
Kalamazoo Valley Community
College *C,A*
Lansing Community College *A*
Macomb Community College *C,A*
Mid Michigan Community College
C,A
Northern Michigan University *C,A*
Oakland Community College *A*

Minnesota

St. Paul Technical College *C*

Mississippi

Copiah-Lincoln Community
College *C*
Holmes Community College *C*
Jones County Junior College *C*
Meridian Community College *A*
Mississippi Delta Community
College *C*

Missouri

Central Missouri State University *A*
East Central College *C,A*
Jefferson College *C,A*
Penn Valley Community College
C,A

Nebraska

Central Community College *C,A*
Metropolitan Community College
C,A
Southeast Community College:
Milford Campus *A*

Nevada

Community College of Southern
Nevada *C,A*
Truckee Meadows Community
College *C,A*

New Hampshire

New Hampshire Technical College:
Manchester *C,A*

New Jersey

Mercer County Community
College *A*

New Mexico

Clovis Community College *C*
Dona Ana Branch Community
College of New Mexico State
University *C,A*

New York

City University of New York: New
York City Technical College *A*
Dutchess Community College *C*
Hudson Valley Community
College *A*
Jamestown Community College *A*
Mohawk Valley Community College
C,A
Monroe Community College *C,A*
State University of New York
College of Technology at
Alfred *A*
College of Technology at
Canton *A*
College of Technology at
Delhi *A*

North Carolina

Alamance Community College *C,A*
Anson Community College *C,A*
Asheville Buncombe Technical
Community College *C*
Blue Ridge Community College *C*
Cape Fear Community College *C*
Central Piedmont Community
College *A*
Coastal Carolina Community
College *C*
Craven Community College *A*
Fayetteville Technical Community
College *A*
Forsyth Technical Community
College *C*
Martin Community College *A*
Montgomery Community College *C*
Roanoke-Chowan Community
College *C*
Wilson Technical Community
College *C*

North Dakota

North Dakota State College of
Science *A*

Ohio

Columbus State Community
College *A*
Owens Technical College: Toledo *A*
Sinclair Community College *C,A*
Terra Technical College *C,A*
University of Cincinnati: Access
Colleges *A*
University of Toledo *A*
Washington State Community
College *A*

Oklahoma

Oklahoma State University
Oklahoma City *C,A*
Technical Branch:
Okmulgee *A*
Tulsa Junior College *C,A*

Pennsylvania

CHI Institute *C*
Delaware County Community
College *A*
Lehigh County Community College
C,A
Penn State University Park
Campus *C*

Triangle Tech
    Greensburg School *A*
    Pittsburgh Campus *A*
Westmoreland County Community
    College *A*

Puerto Rico
Huertas Junior College *C*

Rhode Island
New England Institute of
    Technology *A*

South Carolina
Chesterfield-Marlboro Technical
    College *A*
Greenville Technical College *C*
Sumter Area Technical College *C*
Tri-County Technical College *A*
Trident Technical College *C*
Williamsburg Technical College *C*

South Dakota
Mitchell Vocational Technical
    Institute *C,A*

Tennessee
Chattanooga State Technical
    Community College *C*

Texas
Alvin Community College *A*
Austin Community College *C,A*
Brazosport College *C,A*
Central Texas College *A*
Eastfield College *C,A*
El Paso Community College *C,A*
Lamar University—Beaumont *A*
Laredo Junior College *C*
Midland College *A*
Northeast Texas Community
    College *C,A*
St. Philip's College *A*
South Plains College *C,A*
Texas Southmost College *A*
Texas State Technical College
    Harlingen *A*
    Waco *A*
Trinity Valley Community
    College *A*

Utah
Utah Valley Community College
    C,A

Virginia
Central Virginia Community
    College *C*
John Tyler Community College *C*
Mountain Empire Community
    College *C*
Northern Virginia Community
    College *C,A*
Patrick Henry Community
    College *C*
Tidewater Community College *C*
Virginia Highlands Community
    College *C*

Washington
North Seattle Community
    College *A*
Spokane Community College *A*
Walla Walla Community College
    C,A
Wenatchee Valley College *A*

West Virginia
West Virginia Northern Community
    College *A*

Wisconsin
Chippewa Valley Technical
    College *A*
Moraine Park Technical College *A*
Northeast Wisconsin Technical
    College *A*
Western Wisconsin Technical
    College *A*

Air pollution control technology

District of Columbia
University of the District of
    Columbia *A*

Florida
Santa Fe Community College *A*

Illinois
Waubonsee Community College
    C,A

Iowa
Iowa Lakes Community College *A*

Minnesota
Vermilion Community College *A*

New York
City University of New York: New
    York City Technical College *A*
Westchester Community College *C*

Ohio
Muskingum Area Technical
    College *A*
University of Toledo *A*

Pennsylvania
Penn State University Park Campus
    C,M

Mexico
Sistema Instituto Tecnologico y de
    Estudios Superiores de
    Monterrey *M*

Air traffic control

Alabama
Community College of the Air
    Force *A*
Judson College *B*

Alaska
University of Alaska Anchorage *A*

Arizona
Glendale Community College *A*

California
Mount San Antonio College *A*
San Diego Mesa College *A*
Southwestern College *C,A*

Delaware
Delaware State College *B*

Florida
Embry-Riddle Aeronautical
    University *B*
Florida Memorial College *B*

Illinois
Lincoln Land Community
    College *A*
Parks College of St. Louis
    University *A,B*
Southern Illinois University at
    Carbondale *B*

Indiana
Purdue University *A,B*

Kansas
Kansas State University *A*

Louisiana
Northeast Louisiana University *B*

Maryland
Catonsville Community College *A*

Massachusetts
Bridgewater State College *C*
North Shore Community College *A*

Minnesota
Anoka-Ramsey Community
    College *A*
Inver Hills Community College *A*

Mississippi
Delta State University *B*

Missouri
St. Louis Community College at
    Meramec *C*
St. Louis University *B*

New Hampshire
Daniel Webster College *B*

New Jersey
Thomas Edison State College *A,B*

New York
Dowling College *B*

North Carolina
Guilford Technical Community
    College *C*

Ohio
Kent State University *B*

Pennsylvania
Community College of Beaver
    County *A*
Westmoreland County Community
    College *A*

Texas
Mountain View College *A*

Virginia
Averett College *A*
Hampton University *B*

Washington
Green River Community College *A*

Aircraft mechanics

Alabama
Alabama Aviation and Technical
    College *C,A*
Brewer State Junior College *A*
Community College of the Air
    Force *A*

Alaska
University of Alaska
    Anchorage *C,A*
    Fairbanks *C,A*

Arizona
Cochise College *A*
Pima Community College *C*

Arkansas
Southern Arkansas University:
    Technical Branch *A*

California
Chaffey Community College *C,A*
City College of San Francisco *C,A*
Gavilan Community College *A*
Kings River Community College *A*
Long Beach City College *C,A*
Merced College *A*
Napa Valley College *A*
Orange Coast College *C,A*
Solano Community College *A*

Colorado
Colorado Northwestern Community
    College *C,A*
Community College of Denver *A*

Connecticut
Quinebaug Valley Community
    College *A*

District of Columbia
University of the District of
    Columbia *A*

Florida
Embry-Riddle Aeronautical
    University *A,B*
Pensacola Junior College *C*

Georgia
Atlanta Metropolitan College *A*
Clayton State College *A*

Hawaii
University of Hawaii: Honolulu
    Community College *A*

Idaho
Idaho State University *A*

Illinois
Belleville Area College *C,A*
Lewis University *A,B*
Parks College of St. Louis
    University *A,B*
Rock Valley College *A*
Southern Illinois University at
    Carbondale *A*

Indiana
Purdue University *A,B*
Vincennes University *A*

Iowa
Hawkeye Institute of Technology *A*
Indian Hills Community College *A*
Iowa Western Community
    College *A*

Kansas
Barton County Community
    College *A*
Cowley County Community College
    C,A
Pratt Community College *A*

Kentucky
Eastern Kentucky University *B*

Maryland

Chesapeake College *C,A*
Frederick Community College *C,A*

Michigan

Kirtland Community College *C,A*
Lansing Community College *A*
Macomb Community College *C,A*
Northern Michigan University *A*
William Tyndale College *A,B*

Minnesota

Northland Community College *A*

Missouri

Maple Woods Community
College *A*

Nebraska

Western Nebraska Community
College: Sidney Campus *C,A*

New Hampshire

New Hampshire Technical College
Nashua *A*
Stratham *C*

New Jersey

Cumberland County College *A*
Thomas Edison State College *A,B*

New Mexico

Eastern New Mexico University:
Roswell Campus *A*

New York

Clinton Community College *C*
College of Aeronautics *A,B*
State University of New York
College of Technology at
Farmingdale *C,A*

North Carolina

Guilford Technical Community
College *C,A*
Tri-County Community College *A*

Ohio

Columbus State Community College
C,A

Oklahoma

National Education Center: Spartan
School of Aeronautics Campus
C,A

Oregon

Lane Community College *A*
Portland Community College *A*

Pennsylvania

Pennsylvania College of Technology
C,A
Pittsburgh Institute of
Aeronautics *A*

South Carolina

Bob Jones University *A*
Florence-Darlington Technical
College *A*
Greenville Technical College *A*
Trident Technical College *A*

Texas

Houston Community College *C*
LeTourneau University *A*
St. Philip's College *A*
Tarrant County Junior College *A*
Texas State Technical College
Amarillo *A*
Waco *C,A*

Utah

Dixie College *C*
Utah State University *B*

Washington

Big Bend Community College *A*
Everett Community College *A*
Spokane Community College *A*

Airline piloting and navigation

Alabama

Alabama Aviation and Technical
College *A*
Wallace State Community College
at Hanceville *A*

Alaska

University of Alaska
Anchorage *A*
Fairbanks *A*

Arizona

Cochise College *A*
Embry-Riddle Aeronautical
University: Prescott Campus *A,B*

Arkansas

Henderson State University *A*

California

Foothill College *A*
Glendale Community College *C*
Long Beach City College *C,A*
Mount San Antonio College *A*
Ohlone College *C,A*
Orange Coast College *C,A*
Palomar College *C,A*

Colorado

Aims Community College *C,A*
Colorado Northwestern Community
College *A*
Metropolitan State College of
Denver *B*

Connecticut

University of New Haven *C,A*

Delaware

Delaware State College *B*
Delaware Technical and
Community College: Terry
Campus *A*

Florida

Broward Community College *A*
Embry-Riddle Aeronautical
University *A,B,M*
Florida Community College at
Jacksonville *A*
Florida Institute of Technology *B*
Gulf Coast Community College *A*
Lynn University *B*
Miami-Dade Community College *A*
Palm Beach Community College *A*
St. Petersburg Junior College *A*

Illinois

Belleville Area College *C,A*
Elgin Community College *A*
Lewis University *B*
Parks College of St. Louis
University *A,B*
Prairie State College *A*
Southern Illinois University at
Carbondale *A*

University of Illinois at Urbana-
Champaign *C*

Indiana

Indiana State University *A,B*
Purdue University *A,B*
Vincennes University *A*

Iowa

Indian Hills Community College *A*
Iowa Central Community College *A*
Iowa Lakes Community College *A*

Kansas

Central College *A*
Fort Scott Community College *C,A*
Kansas State University *A*

Kentucky

Eastern Kentucky University *C*
Western Kentucky University *C*

Louisiana

Louisiana Tech University *B*
Nicholls State University *A*
Northeast Louisiana University *B*

Maryland

Catonsville Community College *A*

Massachusetts

Bridgewater State College *B*
North Shore Community College *A*

Michigan

Lansing Community College *A*
Northwestern Michigan College *A*
Western Michigan University *B*
William Tyndale College *C,A,B*

Minnesota

Inver Hills Community College *A*
Vermilion Community College *A*
Winona State University *A*

Mississippi

Delta State University *B*

Missouri

Central Missouri State University
A,B
St. Louis Community College at
Meramec *C*
St. Louis University *B*

Montana

Rocky Mountain College *B*

Nebraska

Grace College of the Bible *B*
University of Nebraska—Omaha *C*

New Hampshire

Daniel Webster College *A,B*

New Jersey

Mercer County Community
College *A*
Thomas Edison State College *A,B*

New Mexico

Dona Ana Branch Community
College of New Mexico State
University *A*
Eastern New Mexico University:
Roswell Campus *A*
San Juan College *A*

New York

Dowling College *B*
Fulton-Montgomery Community
College *A*

St. John's University *B*
State University of New York
College of Technology at
Farmingdale *A*

North Carolina

Guilford Technical Community
College *A*

North Dakota

University of North Dakota *B*

Ohio

Cuyahoga Community College:
Metropolitan Campus *A*
Kent State University *B*
Ohio University *B*

Oklahoma

National Education Center: Spartan
School of Aeronautics Campus *C*
Rose State College *A*

Oregon

Lane Community College *A*
Mount Hood Community
College *A*
Treasure Valley Community
College *A*

Pennsylvania

Community College of Beaver
County *A*
Lehigh County Community
College *A*
Luzerne County Community
College *A*

South Carolina

Bob Jones University *B*
Technical College of the
Lowcountry *C*

Texas

Baylor University *B*
Central Texas College *A*
LeTourneau University *B*
Mountain View College *A*
Texas State Technical College:
Waco *A*
University of Central Texas *B*

Utah

Dixie College *C*

Virginia

Averett College *B*
Northern Virginia Community
College *A*

Washington

Big Bend Community College *A*
Central Washington University *B*
Green River Community College *A*
Walla Walla College *C*

West Virginia

Salem-Teikyo University *B*
West Virginia Northern Community
College *A*

Wisconsin

Concordia University Wisconsin *B*
Fox Valley Technical College *A*

Allied health

Alabama

Alabama Southern Community
    College A
Bishop State Community College A
Brewer State Junior College A
Chattahoochee Valley Community
    College A
Community College of the Air
    Force A
Faulkner University A
Lawson State Community
    College A
Lurleen B. Wallace State Junior
    College A
Shelton State Community
    College A
Snead State Junior College A
University of Alabama in
    Birmingham B
Walker College A

Arizona

Pima Community College C

Arkansas

Shorter College A

California

Barstow College A
California College for Health
    Sciences C,A
California State University: Los
    Angeles B
Chabot College A
Citrus College A
Crafton Hills College A
Cuesta College A
East Los Angeles College C,A
El Camino College A
Gavilan Community College A
Kings River Community College A
Mission College A
Orange Coast College C,A
Pasadena City College C,A
San Joaquin Delta College A
Santa Rosa Junior College A
Skyline College A
Ventura College A

Colorado

Pikes Peak Community College A

Connecticut

Sacred Heart University A
University of Connecticut M

Delaware

Delaware Technical and
    Community College: Southern
    Campus A

District of Columbia

Mount Vernon College B

Florida

Barry University B
Brevard Community College A
Daytona Beach Community
    College A
Jones College A,B
Lake City Community College A
Okaloosa-Walton Community
    College A
University of Florida B
University of North Florida B,M

Georgia

Albany State College B
Clark Atlanta University B
Dalton College A
East Georgia College A
Gainesville College A
Georgia State University M
Meadows College of Business C
Morris Brown College B
South Georgia College A

Idaho

College of Southern Idaho A
Northwest Nazarene College A

Illinois

College of DuPage A
Kendall College A
National-Louis University B
Northern Illinois University B,M
Rend Lake College A
Robert Morris College: Chicago
    C,A
Southern Illinois University at
    Carbondale A
Trinity Christian College B

Indiana

Ball State University B
Franklin College B
Manchester College B
Marian College B
St. Francis College B
Valparaiso University A

Iowa

Buena Vista College B
Cornell College B
Northeast Iowa Community
    College A

Kansas

Allen County Community
    College A
Central College A
Colby Community College A
Fort Scott Community College C,A
Highland Community College A
Kansas City Kansas Community
    College A
Washburn University of Topeka C

Kentucky

Cumberland College B
Jefferson Community College A
Lees College A
Sue Bennett College A

Louisiana

Centenary College of Louisiana B
Dillard University B
Nicholls State University B
Our Lady of Holy Cross College B

Maryland

Catonsville Community College A
Essex Community College A
Villa Julie College A

Massachusetts

Bunker Hill Community College C
Endicott College A
Massachusetts Bay Community
    College C
Massachusetts College of Pharmacy
    and Allied Health Sciences B
Merrimack College B
Mount Ida College A
Springfield Technical Community
    College A

Michigan

Eastern Michigan University B
Great Lakes Junior College of
    Business C,A
Jordan College A
Kalamazoo Valley Community
    College A
Madonna University B
Marygrove College A,B
Southwestern Michigan College A
Suomi College A

Minnesota

Bethany Lutheran College A
Northland Community College A
University of Minnesota: Twin
    Cities M,D
Willmar Community College A

Mississippi

Holmes Community College A
Jones County Junior College A
Phillips Junior College of the
    Mississippi Gulf Coast A

Missouri

East Central College A
Hannibal-LaGrange College A

Nebraska

Central Community College A
Chadron State College B
Concordia College B
Dana College B
Doane College B
McCook Community College A
Union College A
York College A

New Jersey

Montclair State College B

New Mexico

Eastern New Mexico University
    B,M

New York

City University of New York
    Brooklyn College B,M
    Hunter College M
College of Mount St. Vincent B
Daemen College B
Herkimer County Community
    College A

North Carolina

Brevard College A
Mars Hill College B
St. Andrews Presbyterian College B
St. Augustine's College B
Wingate College B

Ohio

Baldwin-Wallace College B
Bowling Green State University:
    Firelands College A
Columbus State Community College
    C,A
Heidelberg College B
Hocking Technical College A
Kettering College of Medical
    Arts A
Malone College B
Marietta College B
Mount Vernon Nazarene College A
Notre Dame College of Ohio B
Ohio State University: Columbus
    Campus M
Union Institute B,D
Youngstown State University B

Oklahoma

Connors State College A
Redlands Community College A
Southwestern Oklahoma State
    University B
Tulsa Junior College A
University of Central Oklahoma B

Oregon

Central Oregon Community
    College A
University of Portland B

Pennsylvania

Bloomsburg University of
    Pennsylvania A
Bucks County Community
    College A
California University of
    Pennsylvania B
Harcum Junior College A
Juniata College B
Keystone Junior College A
Lebanon Valley College of
    Pennsylvania B
Manor Junior College A
Pennsylvania Institute of
    Technology C,A
Point Park College A
Slippery Rock University of
    Pennsylvania B
University of Pittsburgh B,M
Ursinus College B
West Chester University of
    Pennsylvania B
Widener University B

Puerto Rico

Puerto Rico Junior College A

South Carolina

Erskine College B
Newberry College B
North Greenville College A

South Dakota

Huron University A

Tennessee

Chattanooga State Technical
    Community College A
Dyersburg State Community
    College A
Knoxville College B
McKenzie College A

Texas

College of the Mainland A
Dallas Baptist University B
East Texas Baptist University A
El Paso Community College A
Galveston College A
Incarnate Word College B
San Antonio College A
San Jacinto College: Central
    Campus A
Southwest Texas State University
    B,M
Texas Southmost College A
University of Houston: Clear
    Lake B
University of Texas
    El Paso B
    Tyler B

Utah

Weber State University B

Vermont

Community College of Vermont A
Johnson State College B

Virginia
Bluefield College *A*
Virginia Intermont College *A*

Washington
North Seattle Community
College *A*
Seattle University *B*
Tacoma Community College *A*

Wisconsin
Ripon College *B*

**American Samoa, Caroline
Islands, Guam, Marianas,
Virgin Islands**
Community College of
Micronesia *A*

American Indian studies

Alaska
University of Alaska Fairbanks *B*

Arizona
Navajo Community College *A*
Pima Community College *A*
Prescott College *B*
University of Arizona *M*

California
California State University
Hayward *B*
Long Beach *C*
Sacramento *B*
Fresno City College *A*
Humboldt State University *C*
Santa Barbara City College *A*
University of California
Berkeley *B*
Davis *B*
Los Angeles *M*

Florida
Florida Atlantic University *C*

Illinois
NAES College *B*

Iowa
Morningside College *B*

Kansas
Haskell Indian Junior College *A*

Massachusetts
Hampshire College *B*

Minnesota
Bemidji State University *B*
College of St. Scholastica *B*
Itasca Community College:
Arrowhead Region *A*
Mankato State University *B*
University of Minnesota: Twin
Cities *B*

Montana
Dull Knife Memorial College *A*
Fort Peck Community College *A*
Little Big Horn College *A*
Northern Montana College *A,B*
Salish Kootenai College *C,A*

Nebraska
Nebraska Indian Community
College *A*

New Hampshire
Dartmouth College *B*

New York
Colgate University *B*

North Dakota
Standing Rock College *A*
Turtle Mountain Community
College *A*
University of North Dakota *B*

Ohio
Union Institute *D*

Oklahoma
Bacone College *A*
Northeastern State University *B*
University of Science and Arts of
Oklahoma *B*
University of Tulsa *C*

South Dakota
Black Hills State University *B*
Dakota Wesleyan University *B*

Vermont
Goddard College *B*

Washington
Northwest Indian College *A*
University of Washington *B*

Wisconsin
Northland College *B*

American literature

Arizona
Prescott College *B*

California
California State University:
Bakersfield *B,M*
Claremont McKenna College *B*
Pomona College *B*
San Joaquin Delta College *A*
San Jose State University *M*
University of California
Berkeley *M,D*
San Diego *B,M,D*
Santa Cruz *B,D*
University of Southern California *B*

Connecticut
Wesleyan University *B*

District of Columbia
George Washington University
B,M,D

Florida
Eckerd College *B*
Indian River Community College *A*
Miami-Dade Community College *A*
New College of the University of
South Florida *B*
University of Florida *M,D*

Georgia
Emory University *B,M,D*

Hawaii
Hawaii Pacific University *B*

Illinois
Concordia University *B*
Joliet Junior College *A*
KAES College *B*

Lincoln Land Community
College *A*
Northwestern University *B*
Richland Community College *A*
Shimer College *B*
Southern Illinois University at
Edwardsville *B,M*
University of Illinois at Chicago *B*

Indiana
Ball State University *D*
Indiana University
Bloomington *B,M,D*
South Bend *B*
Purdue University *B,D*
University of Notre Dame *B,M,D*

Iowa
Drake University *B*
Grinnell College *B*

Maryland
Johns Hopkins University *B,M,D*

Massachusetts
Brandeis University *B,M,D*
Clark University *B,M*
Emerson College *M*
Emmanuel College *B*
Hampshire College *B*
Harvard and Radcliffe Colleges *B*
Harvard University *D*
Simmons College *B*
Tufts University *B,M,D*
Williams College *B*

Michigan
Eastern Michigan University *B,M*
Lansing Community College *A*
Michigan State University *M*
University of Michigan *M,D*

Minnesota
St. Olaf College *B*
Willmar Community College *A*

Montana
Rocky Mountain College *B*

Nebraska
York College *A*

New Jersey
Ramapo College of New Jersey *B*
Rutgers—The State University of
New Jersey *B*
Stevens Institute of Technology *B*

New York
Bard College *B*
City University of New York
Brooklyn College *B,M*
City College *B,M*
Hunter College *B,M*
Queens College *B*
Columbia University *M,D*
Cornell University *M,D*
D'Youville College *B*
Eugene Lang College/New School
for Social Research *B*
Fordham University *B*
Hofstra University *B*
Manhattan College *B*
Manhattanville College *B*
New York University *B,M,D*
Sarah Lawrence College *B*
Syracuse University *M,D*

North Carolina
Brevard College *A*

Ohio
Capital University *B*
Case Western Reserve University
B,M,D
College of Wooster *B*
Kenyon College *B*
Ohio State University: Columbus
Campus *B,M,D*
Union Institute *B,D*
Wittenberg University *B*

Oregon
George Fox College *B*

Pennsylvania
Bucknell University *B*
California University of
Pennsylvania *B*
Carnegie Mellon University *B,M*
Chatham College *B*
Grove City College *B*
Immaculata College *B*
La Salle University *B*
Penn State Harrisburg Capital
College *B*
West Chester University of
Pennsylvania *B*

Rhode Island
Brown University *B,M,D*

Tennessee
Union University *B*

Texas
Lon Morris College *A*
University of Houston *M,D*
University of Texas of the Permian
Basin *B,M*

Vermont
Bennington College *B*
Castleton State College *B*
Marlboro College *B*
Middlebury College *B*

Virginia
Virginia Wesleyan College *B*

Washington
Eastern Washington University *B*
Everett Community College *A*
Evergreen State College *B*
Seattle Central Community
College *A*
Tacoma Community College *A*
Western Washington University
B,M

West Virginia
Bethany College *B*
Shepherd College *B*

Wisconsin
Beloit College *B*

American studies

Alabama
Faulkner University *B*
University of Alabama *B,M*

Arizona
Prescott College *B*

Arkansas
Harding University *B*
Hendrix College *B*

California

California State Polytechnic
University: Pomona *B*
California State University
Chico *B*
Fullerton *B,M*
Long Beach *B*
San Bernardino *B*
Claremont McKenna College *B*
Cosumnes River College *A*
El Camino College *A*
Foothill College *A*
Glendale Community College *A*
Lassen College *A*
Los Angeles Mission College *A*
Los Angeles Valley College *A*
Mills College *B*
Mount St. Mary's College *B*
Occidental College *B*
Pepperdine University *M*
Pitzer College *B*
Pomona College *B*
Saddleback College *A*
San Diego State University *B,M*
San Francisco State University *B*
San Jose State University *B*
Scripps College *B*
Stanford University *B*
University of California
Davis *B*
Santa Cruz *B*
University of the Pacific *B,M*
University of Southern California *B*

Colorado

University of Colorado at
Boulder *B*
University of Denver *B*
Western State College of
Colorado *B*

Connecticut

Eastern Connecticut State
University *B*
Fairfield University *B*
Mattatuck Community College *A*
St. Joseph College *B,M*
Trinity College *B,M*
Wesleyan University *B*
Western Connecticut State
University *B*
Yale University *B,M,D*

Delaware

University of Delaware *B*

District of Columbia

American University *B*
Catholic University of America *B*
Gallaudet University *B*
George Washington University *M,D*
Georgetown University *B*
Trinity College *B*

Florida

Eckerd College *B*
Florida State University *B,M*
Miami-Dade Community College *A*
New College of the University of
South Florida *B*
Stetson University *B*
University of Florida *B*
University of South Florida *B,M*

Georgia

Emory University *M,D*
Oglethorpe University *B*
Reinhardt College *A*

Hawaii

Chaminade University of
Honolulu *B*

Hawaii Pacific University *B*
University of Hawaii
Manoa *B,M,D*
West Oahu *B*

Idaho

Idaho State University *B*
University of Idaho *B*

Illinois

De Paul University *B*
Elmhurst College *B*
KAES College *B*
Kendall College *B*
Knox College *B*
Lake Forest College *B*
Millikin University *B*
Northwestern University *B*
Richland Community College *A*
Roosevelt University *B*
Rosary College *B*

Indiana

Anderson University *B*
Butler University *B*
Franklin College *B*
Indiana University Bloomington *D*
Indiana University—Purdue
University at Fort Wayne *C*
Purdue University *B,M,D*
St. Francis College *B*
University of Notre Dame *B,M*
Valparaiso University *B*

Iowa

Grinnell College *B*
Teikyo Marycrest University *A,B*
University of Iowa *B,M,D*
University of Northern Iowa *B*

Kansas

Highland Community College *A*
Ottawa University *B*
University of Kansas *B,M,D*
Wichita State University *B*

Kentucky

Georgetown College *B*
Sue Bennett College *A*
Thomas More College *B*
University of Louisville *B*

Louisiana

Tulane University *B*

Maine

Bates College *B*
Colby College *B*
Westbrook College *B*

Maryland

Anne Arundel Community
College *A*
Goucher College *B*
Mount St. Mary's College *B*
Prince George's Community
College *A*
University of Maryland
Baltimore County *B*
College Park *B,M,D*
Washington College *B*
Western Maryland College *B*

Massachusetts

Amherst College *B*
Babson College *B*
Boston College *M*
Boston University *B,M,D*
Bradford College *B*
Brandeis University *B*
Elms College *B*
Greenfield Community College *A*

Hampshire College *B*
Harvard and Radcliffe Colleges *B*
Lesley College *B*
Massachusetts Institute of
Technology *B*
Mount Holyoke College *B*
Pine Manor College *B*
Smith College *C,B,M*
Springfield College *B*
Stonehill College *B*
Tufts University *B,M*
University of Massachusetts
Boston *B,M*
Lowell *B*
Wellesley College *B*
Wheaton College *B*
Williams College *B*

Michigan

Albion College *B*
Calvin College *B*
Central Michigan University *B*
Hillsdale College *B*
Michigan State University *B,M*
Olivet College *B*
Siena Heights College *B*
University of Michigan
Ann Arbor *B,M,D*
Dearborn *B*
Wayne State University *B*
Western Michigan University *B*

Minnesota

Bethany Lutheran College *A*
Carleton College *B*
Hamline University *B*
Mankato State University *B*
Moorhead State University *B*
St. Cloud State University *B*
St. Olaf College *B*
University of Minnesota
Duluth *B*
Twin Cities *B,M,D*
University of St. Thomas *B*

Mississippi

University of Southern
Mississippi *B*

Missouri

Maryville University *B*
St. Louis University *B,M,D*
Southeast Missouri State
University *B*
Stephens College *B*
University of Missouri: Kansas
City *B*

Nebraska

Creighton University *B*
Midland Lutheran College *B*

New Hampshire

Colby-Sawyer College *B*
Keene State College *B*
Plymouth State College of the
University System of New
Hampshire *B*

New Jersey

Caldwell College *C*
Drew University *B*
Ramapo College of New Jersey *B*
Rider College *B*

Rutgers—The State University of
New Jersey
Douglass College *B*
Livingston College *B*
Newark College of Arts and
Sciences *B*
Rutgers College *B*
University College New
Brunswick *B*
St. Peter's College *B*

New Mexico

Eastern New Mexico University *B*
University of New Mexico *B,M,D*

New York

Adelphi University *B*
Bard College *B*
Barnard College *B*
City University of New York
Brooklyn College *B*
City College *B*
College of Staten Island *B*
Hostos Community College *A*
Lehman College *B*
Queens College *B*
College of New Rochelle *B*
College of St. Rose *B*
Columbia University: School of
General Studies *M*
Cornell University *B,M,D*
Dominican College of Blauvelt *B*
Elmira College *B*
Eugene Lang College/New School
for Social Research *B*
Fordham University *B*
Fulton-Montgomery Community
College *A*
Hamilton College *B*
Hobart College *B*
Hofstra University *B*
Iona College *B*
Long Island University: C. W. Post
Campus *B*
Manhattanville College *B*
Marist College *B*
Marymount College *B*
Nazareth College of Rochester *B*
New York University *M,D*
Paul Smith's College *A*
St. John's University *B*
Sarah Lawrence College *B*
Siena College *B*
Skidmore College *B*
State University of New York
Binghamton *B*
Buffalo *B,M,D*
College at Brockport *B*
College at Geneseo *B*
College at Old Westbury *B*
Oswego *B*
Syracuse University *B*
Union College *B*
United States Military Academy *B*
Vassar College *B*
Wells College *B*
William Smith College *B*

North Carolina

Barton College *B*
Lenoir-Rhyne College *B*
Meredith College *B*
Salem College *B*
University of North Carolina
Chapel Hill *B,M,D*
Greensboro *B*
Warren Wilson College *B*
Wingate College *B*

North Dakota

University of North Dakota *B*

Ohio

Ashland University *B*
Bowling Green State University *B,M,D*
Case Western Reserve University *B,M,D*
Cedarville College *B*
Kent State University *B*
Kenyon College *B*
Miami University: Oxford Campus *B*
Mount Union College *B*
Muskingum College *B*
Oberlin College *B*
Ohio State University: Columbus Campus *B,M,D*
Union Institute *B,D*
University of Dayton *B,M*
University of Rio Grande *B*
University of Toledo *B*
Ursuline College *B*
Wittenberg University *B*
Youngstown State University *B*

Oklahoma

Oklahoma Baptist University *B*
Phillips University *B*

Oregon

Oregon State University *B*
Reed College *B*
Warner Pacific College *B*
Willamette University *B*

Pennsylvania

Albright College *B*
Bucks County Community College *A*
Cabrini College *B*
California University of Pennsylvania *B*
Dickinson College *B*
Eastern College *B*
Franklin and Marshall College *B*
Gettysburg College *B*
Kutztown University of Pennsylvania *B*
Lafayette College *B*
Lebanon Valley College of Pennsylvania *B*
Lehigh University *B*
Lycoming College *B*
Muhlenberg College *B*
Penn State
    Harrisburg Capital College *B,M*
    University Park Campus *B*
Rosemont College *B*
St. Francis College *B*
St. Joseph's University *C*
Temple University *B*
University of Pennsylvania *B,M,D*
University of Pittsburgh
    Bradford *B*
    Johnstown *B*
West Chester University of Pennsylvania *B*

Puerto Rico

University of Puerto Rico: Mayaguez Campus *B*

Rhode Island

Brown University *B,M,D*
Providence College *B*
Salve Regina University *B*

Tennessee

David Lipscomb University *B*
East Tennessee State University *B*
Freed-Hardeman University *B*
Martin Methodist College *A*

Memphis State University *B*
Rhodes College *B*
University of the South *B*
University of Tennessee
    Chattanooga *B*
    Knoxville *B*

Texas

Austin College *B*
Baylor University *B,M*
Our Lady of the Lake University of San Antonio *B*
Southwest Texas State University *B*
Southwestern University *B*
University of Texas
    Austin *B,M,D*
    Dallas *B*
    San Antonio *B*

Utah

Brigham Young University *B*
Utah State University *B,M*

Vermont

College of St. Joseph in Vermont *B*
Goddard College *B*
Marlboro College *B*
Middlebury College *B*
St. Michael's College *B*

Virginia

College of William and Mary *M,D*
George Mason University *B*
Hollins College *B*
Lord Fairfax Community College *A*
Lynchburg College *B*
Mary Washington College *B*
Shenandoah University *B*
Sweet Briar College *B*
University of Richmond *B*
Virginia Wesleyan College *B*

Washington

Evergreen State College *B*
Washington State University *B,M,D*
Western Washington University *B*
Whitworth College *B*

West Virginia

Shepherd College *B*

Wisconsin

Edgewood College *B*
University of Wisconsin: River Falls *B*

Wyoming

University of Wyoming *B,M*

Analytical chemistry

California

California State University: Fullerton *M*
San Jose State University *B*
University of California: Berkeley *B,M,D*

District of Columbia

George Washington University *M,D*

Florida

Florida State University *B,M,D*
New College of the University of South Florida *B*
University of Florida *M,D*
University of South Florida *B*

Georgia

Emory University *D*

Illinois

Governors State University *M*
Judson College *B*
Northwestern University *B*
Southern Illinois University at Carbondale *B,M,D*
University of Chicago *B,M,D*

Indiana

Indiana University Bloomington *D*
Purdue University *M,D,W*

Iowa

Iowa State University *M,D*

Kansas

Kansas State University *M,D*

Massachusetts

Massachusetts Institute of Technology *B,M,D,W*
Tufts University *M,D*
Worcester Polytechnic Institute *B*

Michigan

Eastern Michigan University *B*
Michigan State University *M,D*
Michigan Technological University *B*
University of Michigan *M,D*

Missouri

University of Missouri: Kansas City *M,D*

Nevada

University of Nevada: Las Vegas *M*

New Hampshire

University of New Hampshire *M,D*

New Jersey

Stevens Institute of Technology *B,M,D*

New Mexico

New Mexico Institute of Mining and Technology *M,D*

New York

Columbia University *M,D*
Cornell University *M,D*
Sarah Lawrence College *B*
State University of New York College of Environmental Science and Forestry *B,M,D*

North Carolina

University of North Carolina at Chapel Hill *M,D*

Ohio

Ohio State University: Columbus Campus *B,M,D*
Ohio University *M,D*

Pennsylvania

Bucknell University *B*
Carnegie Mellon University *B,M,D,W*
Drexel University *M,D*
Lehigh University *M,D*

Rhode Island

Brown University *B,M,D*

Texas

University of Houston *M,D*

Vermont

Marlboro College *B*

West Virginia

Alderson-Broaddus College *B*

Wisconsin

Marquette University *M,D*

Canada

McGill University *M,D*

Anatomy

Alabama

Auburn University *M,D*
University of Alabama in Birmingham *M,D*
University of South Alabama *D*

Arizona

University of Arizona *M,D*

Arkansas

University of Arkansas for Medical Sciences *M,D*

California

California State University: Sacramento *B*
Chabot College *A*
Citrus College *A*
San Joaquin Delta College *A*
University of California
    Berkeley *M,D*
    Los Angeles *M,D*
    San Francisco *D*
University of Southern California *M,D*

Colorado

Colorado State University *M,D*

District of Columbia

George Washington University *D*
Georgetown University *D*
Howard University *M,D*

Florida

University of Florida *D*
University of Miami *D*

Georgia

Emory University *D*
Medical College of Georgia *M,D*
Oxford College of Emory University *A*
University of Georgia *M*

Illinois

Loyola University of Chicago *M,D*
Northwestern University *M,D*
Rush University *M,D*
University of Chicago *M,D*
University of Health Sciences: The Chicago Medical School *M,D,W*
University of Illinois
    Chicago *M,D*
    Urbana-Champaign *B,M,D*

Indiana

Indiana University Bloomington *M,D*
Indiana University—Purdue University at Indianapolis *M,D,W*

Iowa

Iowa State University *M,D*
Kirkwood Community College *A*
Palmer Chiropractic University *M*
University of Iowa *M,D*

Kansas

Coffeyville Community College *A*
Colby Community College *A*
Kansas State University *M*
University of Kansas
   Lawrence *M,D*
   Medical Center *M,D*

Kentucky

University of Kentucky *M,D*
University of Louisville *M,D*

Louisiana

Louisiana State University Medical
   Center *M,D*
Tulane University *M,D*

Maryland

Uniformed Services University of
   the Health Sciences *M,D*
University of Maryland: Baltimore
   M,D

Massachusetts

Boston University *D*
Harvard University *D*
Roxbury Community College *A*
Tufts University *D*

Michigan

Michigan State University *M,D*
University of Michigan *M,D*
Wayne State University *M,D*

Minnesota

University of Minnesota: Twin
   Cities *M,D*
Vermilion Community College *A*

Mississippi

University of Mississippi Medical
   Center *M,D*

Missouri

St. Louis University *M,D*
University of Missouri: Columbia
   M,D
Washington University *D*

Nebraska

Creighton University *M,D*
University of Nebraska Medical
   Center *M,D*
York College *A*

New York

Albany Medical College *M,D*
Columbia University *M,D*
Cornell University *B,M,D*
State University of New York
   Buffalo *M,D*
   Health Science Center at
     Brooklyn *D*
   Health Science Center at
     Syracuse *M,D*
   Health Sciences Center at
     Stony Brook *D*
University of Rochester *M,D,W*
Yeshiva University *M,D*

North Carolina

Duke University *B,D*
East Carolina University *D*
University of North Carolina at
   Chapel Hill *M,D*

Vance-Granville Community
   College *A*
Wake Forest University *M,D*

North Dakota

University of North Dakota *M,D*

Ohio

Case Western Reserve University *D*
Ohio State University: Columbus
   Campus *M,D*
University of Cincinnati *D*
Wright State University *M*

Oklahoma

University of Oklahoma
   Health Sciences Center *M,D*
   Norman *M,D*

Oregon

Oregon Health Sciences University
   M,D

Pennsylvania

Hahnemann University School of
   Health Sciences and Humanities
   M,D
Medical College of Pennsylvania
   M,D
Penn State Milton S. Hershey
   Medical Center *M,D*
Temple University *M,D*
University of Pennsylvania *M,D*
University of Pittsburgh *M,D*

Puerto Rico

University of Puerto Rico: Medical
   Sciences Campus *M,D*

South Dakota

University of South Dakota *M,D*

Tennessee

East Tennessee State University
   M,D
University of Tennessee: Memphis
   M,D
Vanderbilt University *M,D*

Texas

Baylor College of Dentistry *M*
Baylor University *M*
Howard College *A*
Jacksonville College *A*
Lon Morris College *A*
Panola College *A*
Texas A&M University *M,D*
Texas Tech University *M,D*
Texas Tech University Health
   Science Center *M,D,W*
University of Texas Health Science
   Center at Houston *M,D,W*
Western Texas College *A*

Utah

University of Utah *M,D*

Vermont

Marlboro College *B*
University of Vermont *D*

Virginia

Averett College *B*
University of Virginia *M,D*
Virginia Commonwealth University
   M,D

Washington

Evergreen State College *B*
Lower Columbia College *A*

West Virginia

West Virginia University *M,D*

Wisconsin

Medical College of Wisconsin *M,D*
University of Wisconsin: Madison
   M,D

Canada

McGill University *B,M,D*

Animal sciences

Alabama

Alabama Agricultural and
   Mechanical University *B,M*
Auburn University *B,M,D*
Tuskegee University *B,M*

Arizona

Arizona Western College *A*
Mesa Community College *C*
University of Arizona *B,M*

Arkansas

Arkansas State University
   Beebe Branch *A*
   Jonesboro *B*
University of Arkansas
   Fayetteville *B,M,D*
   Pine Bluff *B*
Westark Community College *A*

California

Bakersfield College *A*
California Polytechnic State
   University: San Luis Obispo *B*
California State Polytechnic
   University: Pomona *B,M*
California State University: Fresno
   B,M
College of the Redwoods *C,A*
College of the Sequoias *C*
Cosumnes River College *C,A*
Kings River Community College *A*
Los Angeles Pierce College *C,A*
Merced College *A*
Modesto Junior College *A*
Moorpark College *C,A*
Mount San Antonio College *C,A*
Orange Coast College *C,A*
San Joaquin Delta College *C,A*
Santa Rosa Junior College *C,A*
Sierra College *C,A*
University of California: Davis *B,M*
Ventura College *C,A*
West Hills Community College *C,A*

Colorado

Colorado State University *B,M,D*
Lamar Community College *A*
Northeastern Junior College *A*

Connecticut

University of Connecticut *C,B,M,D*

Delaware

University of Delaware *B,M,D*

District of Columbia

University of the District of
   Columbia *B*

Florida

Florida Agricultural and Mechanical
   University *B*
University of Florida *B,M,D*

Georgia

Abraham Baldwin Agricultural
   College *A*
Berry College *B*
Fort Valley State College *B*
University of Georgia *B,M,D*

Hawaii

University of Hawaii
   Hilo *B*
   Manoa *B,M*

Idaho

Ricks College *C,A*
University of Idaho *B,M*

Illinois

Black Hawk College: East
   Campus *C*
Lake Land College *C*
Parkland College *A*
Southern Illinois University at
   Carbondale *B,M*
University of Illinois at Urbana-
   Champaign *B,M,D*

Indiana

Purdue University *C,A,B,M,D,W*
Vincennes University *A*

Iowa

Dordt College *B*
Hawkeye Institute of Technology *A*
Iowa State University *B,M,D*
Kirkwood Community College *A*

Kansas

Barton County Community
   College *A*
Cloud County Community
   College *A*
Coffeyville Community College *A*
Colby Community College *A*
Cowley County Community
   College *A*
Dodge City Community College *A*
Kansas State University *B,M,D*
Seward County Community
   College *C*

Kentucky

Eastern Kentucky University *B*
Murray State University *B*
University of Kentucky *B,M,D*

Louisiana

Louisiana State University and
   Agricultural and Mechanical
   College *B,M,D*
Louisiana Tech University *B*
McNeese State University *B*
Southern University and
   Agricultural and Mechanical
   College *B*

Maine

University of Maine *B,M,D*

Maryland

University of Maryland: College
   Park *B,M,D*

Massachusetts

Becker College: Leicester
   Campus *A*
Hampshire College *B*
Mount Ida College *A,B*
University of Massachusetts at
   Amherst *A,B,M,D*

Michigan

Michigan State University *B,M,D*

Minnesota

University of Minnesota
 Crookston *A*
 Twin Cities *B,M,D*
Willmar Community College *A*

Mississippi

Alcorn State University *B,M*
Mississippi State University *B,M*

Missouri

Northeast Missouri State
 University *B*
Northwest Missouri State
 University *B*
Southeast Missouri State
 University *B*
Southwest Missouri State
 University *B*
University of Missouri: Columbia
 B,M,D

Montana

Dawson Community College *C*
Montana State University *B,M*

Nebraska

McCook Community College *A*
Northeast Community College *A*
Southeast Community College:
 Beatrice Campus *A*
University of Nebraska—Lincoln
 B,M,D

Nevada

University of Nevada: Reno *B,M*

New Hampshire

University of New Hampshire
 A,B,M,D

New Jersey

Camden County College *A*
Rutgers—The State University of
 New Jersey
 Cook College *B*
 New Brunswick *M,D*

New Mexico

New Mexico State University
 B,M,D

New York

Cornell University *B,M,D*
Niagara County Community
 College *A*
State University of New York
 College of Agriculture and
  Technology at Cobleskill *A*
 College of Agriculture and
  Technology at Morrisville *A*
 College of Technology at
  Alfred *A*

North Carolina

Alamance Community College *A*
James Sprunt Community
 College *A*
North Carolina Agricultural and
 Technical State University *B*
North Carolina State University
 B,M,D
Wayne Community College *A*

North Dakota

North Dakota State University
 B,M,D

Ohio

Columbus State Community
 College *A*
Northwest Technical College *A*
Ohio State University
 Agricultural Technical
  Institute *A*
 Columbus Campus *B,M,D*

Oklahoma

Eastern Oklahoma State College *A*
Langston University *B*
Oklahoma Panhandle State
 University *B*
Oklahoma State University *B,M,D*

Oregon

Linn-Benton Community College *A*
Oregon State University *B,M,D*

Pennsylvania

Delaware Valley College *B*
Harcum Junior College *A*
Penn State University Park Campus
 C,B,M,D

Puerto Rico

University of Puerto Rico
 Arecibo Campus *A*
 La Montana Regional
  College *A*
 Mayaguez Campus *B,M*
 Medical Sciences Campus *B*

Rhode Island

University of Rhode Island *B,M*

South Carolina

Clemson University *B*

South Dakota

National College *C*
South Dakota State University
 B,M,D

Tennessee

Hiwassee College *A*
Middle Tennessee State
 University *B*
Tennessee State University *B,M*
Tennessee Technological
 University *B*
University of Tennessee
 Knoxville *B,M,D*
 Martin *B*

Texas

Abilene Christian University *B*
Angelo State University *B,M*
Central Texas College *A*
East Texas State University *B*
Prairie View A&M University *B,M*
Sam Houston State University *B*
Southwest Texas State University *B*
Southwestern University *B*
Stephen F. Austin State
 University *B*
Sul Ross State University *B,M*
Tarleton State University *B*
Texas A&I University *B,M*
Texas A&M University *B,M,D*
Texas Southmost College *A*
Texas Tech University *B,M,D*
West Texas State University *B,M*
Western Texas College *A*

Utah

Brigham Young University *B,M*
Southern Utah University *A*
Utah State University *B,M,D*

Vermont

Sterling College *A*
University of Vermont *B,M,D*

Virginia

Northern Virginia Community
 College *A*
Virginia Polytechnic Institute and
 State University *A,B,M,D*

Washington

Spokane Community College *A*
Washington State University *B,M,D*
Yakima Valley Community College
 C,A

West Virginia

West Virginia University *B,M*

Wisconsin

University of Wisconsin
 Madison *B,M,D*
 Platteville *B*
 River Falls *B*

Wyoming

Casper College *A*
Central Wyoming College *A*
Northwest College *A*
Sheridan College *A*
University of Wyoming *B,M,D*

Canada

McGill University *B,M,D*

Mexico

Sistema Instituto Tecnologico y de
 Estudios Superiores de
 Monterrey *B*

Anthropology

Alabama

Auburn University
 Auburn *B*
 Montgomery *B*
University of Alabama
 Birmingham *B*
 Tuscaloosa *B,M*
University of South Alabama *B*

Alaska

University of Alaska
 Anchorage *B*
 Fairbanks *B,M,D*

Arizona

Arizona State University *B,M,D*
Cochise College *A*
Eastern Arizona College *A*
Northern Arizona University *B,M*
Pima Community College *A*
Prescott College *B*
University of Arizona *B,M,D*
Yavapai College *A*

Arkansas

University of Arkansas *B,M*

California

Bakersfield College *A*
California Institute of Integral
 Studies *M*
California State Polytechnic
 University: Pomona *B*

California State University
 Bakersfield *B*
 Chico *C,B,M*
 Dominguez Hills *B*
 Fresno *B*
 Fullerton *B,M*
 Hayward *B,M*
 Long Beach *B,M*
 Los Angeles *B,M*
 Northridge *B,M*
 Sacramento *B,M*
 San Bernardino *B*
 Stanislaus *B*
Cerritos Community College *A*
Chaffey Community College *A*
Christ College Irvine *B*
College of the Desert *A*
Columbia College *A*
Crafton Hills College *A*
De Anza College *A*
El Camino College *A*
Foothill College *A*
Fresno City College *A*
Fuller Theological Seminary *W*
Humboldt State University *B*
Imperial Valley College *A*
Irvine Valley College *A*
La Sierra University *B*
Los Medanos College *A*
Merced College *A*
Modesto Junior College *A*
Napa Valley College *A*
Occidental College *B*
Ohlone College *A*
Orange Coast College *A*
Oxnard College *A*
Pitzer College *B*
Pomona College *B*
Saddleback College *A*
San Diego State University *B,M*
San Francisco State University *B,M*
San Jose State University *B*
Santa Barbara City College *A*
Santa Clara University *B*
Santa Rosa Junior College *A*
Scripps College *B*
Sonoma State University *B,M*
Southern California College *B*
Southwestern College *A*
Stanford University *B,M,D*
University of California
 Berkeley *B,D*
 Davis *B,M,D*
 Irvine *B*
 Los Angeles *B,M,D*
 Riverside *B,M,D*
 San Diego *B,M,D*
 San Francisco *D*
 Santa Barbara *B,M,D*
 Santa Cruz *B,M,D*
University of the Pacific *B*
University of Redlands *B*
University of San Diego *B*
University of Southern California
 B,M,D
Ventura College *A*
Whittier College *B*

Colorado

Colorado College *B*
Colorado State University *B,M*
Fort Lewis College *B*
Mesa State College *A*
Metropolitan State College of
 Denver *B*
Pikes Peak Community College *A*
Trinidad State Junior College *A*
University of Colorado
 Boulder *B,M,D*
 Colorado Springs *B*
 Denver *B,M*
University of Denver *B,M*

Connecticut

Central Connecticut State
University *B*
Connecticut College *B*
University of Connecticut *B,M,D*
Wesleyan University *B,M*
Western Connecticut State
University *B*
Yale University *B,M,D*

Delaware

University of Delaware *B*

District of Columbia

American University *B,M,D*
Catholic University of America
B,M,D
George Washington University *B,M*
Howard University *B,M,D*
University of the District of
Columbia *B*

Florida

Daytona Beach Community
College *A*
Eckerd College *B*
Florida Atlantic University *B,M*
Florida International University *B*
Florida State University *B,M,D*
Gulf Coast Community College *A*
Miami-Dade Community College *A*
New College of the University of
South Florida *B*
Palm Beach Community College *A*
Rollins College *B*
University of Central Florida *B*
University of Florida *B,M,D*
University of Miami *B*
University of South Florida *B,M,D*
University of West Florida *B*

Georgia

Atlanta Metropolitan College *A*
DeKalb College *A*
Emory University *B,M,D*
Gainesville College *A*
Georgia Southern University *B*
Georgia State University *B,M*
Gordon College *A*
Oxford College of Emory
University *A*
University of Georgia *B,M,D*
Valdosta State College *B*
West Georgia College *B*

Hawaii

Hawaii Pacific University *B*
University of Hawaii
Hilo *B*
Manoa *B,M,D*
West Oahu *B*

Idaho

Albertson College *B*
Boise State University *B*
College of Southern Idaho *A*
Idaho State University *B,M*
North Idaho College *A*
University of Idaho *B,M*

Illinois

Black Hawk College *A*
Chicago State University *B*
De Paul University *B*
Illinois State University *B*
Judson College *B*
Knox College *B*
Lake Forest College *B*
Lincoln Land Community
College *A*
Loyola University of Chicago *B*
North Central College *B*

North Park College and Theological
Seminary *B*
Northeastern Illinois University *B*
Northern Illinois University *B,M*
Northwestern University *B,M,D*
Olivet Nazarene University *B*
Rockford College *B*
Sangamon State University *B*
Southern Illinois University
Carbondale *B,M,D*
Edwardsville *B*
Triton College *A*
University of Chicago *B,M,D*
University of Illinois
Chicago *B,M*
Urbana-Champaign *B,M,D*

Indiana

Ball State University *B,M*
DePauw University *B*
Earlham College *B*
Hanover College *B*
Indiana State University *B*
Indiana University Bloomington
B,M,D
Indiana University—Purdue
University
Fort Wayne *B*
Indianapolis *B*
Manchester College *B*
Purdue University *B,M,D*
University of Notre Dame *B,M,D*
Vincennes University *A*

Iowa

Central College *B*
Cornell College *B*
Grinnell College *B*
Iowa State University *B,M*
Luther College *B*
University of Iowa *B,M,D*
University of Northern Iowa *B*

Kansas

Kansas State University *B*
University of Kansas *B,M,D*
Washburn University of Topeka *B*
Wichita State University *B,M*

Kentucky

Centre College *B*
Eastern Kentucky University *B*
Northern Kentucky University *B*
University of Kentucky *B,M,D*
University of Louisville *B*
Western Kentucky University *B*

Louisiana

Grambling State University *B*
Louisiana State University and
Agricultural and Mechanical
College *B,M*
Northwestern State University *B*
Tulane University *B,M,D*
University of New Orleans *B*
University of Southwestern
Louisiana *B*

Maine

Bates College *B*
Bowdoin College *B*
Colby College *B*
University of Maine *B*
University of Southern Maine *B*

Maryland

Johns Hopkins University *B,D*
St. Mary's College of Maryland *B*
Salisbury State University *B*
Towson State University *B*
University of Maryland: College
Park *B,M,D*

Massachusetts

Amherst College *B*
Boston University *B,M,D*
Brandeis University *B,M,D*
Bridgewater State College *B*
Hampshire College *B*
Harvard and Radcliffe Colleges *B*
Harvard University *M,D*
Massachusetts Institute of
Technology *B*
Mount Holyoke College *B*
North Adams State College *B*
Northeastern University *B,M*
Smith College *B*
Tufts University *B*
University of Massachusetts
Amherst *B,M,D*
Boston *B*
Dartmouth *B*
Wellesley College *B*
Wheaton College *B*
Williams College *B*

Michigan

Albion College *B*
Central Michigan University *B*
Eastern Michigan University *B*
Grand Valley State University *B*
Kalamazoo College *B*
Lansing Community College *A*
Michigan State University *B,M,D*
Oakland University *B*
Olivet College *B*
University of Michigan
Ann Arbor *B,M,D*
Dearborn *B*
Flint *B*
Wayne State University *B,M,D*
Western Michigan University *B,M*

Minnesota

Carleton College *B*
Crown College *A*
Gustavus Adolphus College *B*
Hamline University *B*
Macalester College *B*
Mankato State University *B*
Moorhead State University *B*
Rainy River Community College *A*
St. Cloud State University *B*
University of Minnesota
Duluth *B*
Twin Cities *B,M,D*
University of St. Thomas *B*

Mississippi

Mississippi State University *B*
University of Mississippi *B,M*
University of Southern Mississippi
B,M

Missouri

East Central College *A*
Southeast Missouri State
University *B*
University of Missouri
Columbia *B,M,D*
St. Louis *B*
Washington University *B,M,D*
Webster University *B*
Westminster College *B*

Montana

Montana State University *B*
Rocky Mountain College *B*
University of Montana *B,M*

Nebraska

Creighton University *B*
University of Nebraska—Lincoln
B,M

Nevada

University of Nevada
Las Vegas *B,M*
Reno *B,M,D*

New Hampshire

Dartmouth College *B*
Franklin Pierce College *B*
Plymouth State College of the
University System of New
Hampshire *B*
University of New Hampshire *B*

New Jersey

Drew University *B*
Monmouth College *B*
Montclair State College *B,M*
Princeton University *B,D*
Rutgers—The State University of
New Jersey
Douglass College *B*
Livingston College *B*
New Brunswick *M,D*
Newark College of Arts and
Sciences *B*
Rutgers College *B*
University College New
Brunswick *B*
Seton Hall University *B*
Stockton State College *B*
Thomas Edison State College *B*
Upsala College *B*
William Paterson College of New
Jersey *B,M*

New Mexico

Eastern New Mexico University
B,M
New Mexico State University *B,M*
University of New Mexico *B,M,D*

New York

Adelphi University *B*
Bard College *B*
Barnard College *B*
Canisius College *B*
City University of New York
Brooklyn College *B*
City College *B,M*
College of Staten Island *B*
Graduate School and
University Center *D*
Hunter College *B,M*
Lehman College *B*
Queens College *B*
York College *B*
Colgate University *B,M*
Columbia University
Columbia College *B*
New York *M,D*
School of General Studies *B*
Cornell University *B,M,D*
Dowling College *B*
Elmira College *B*
Eugene Lang College/New School
for Social Research *B*
Fordham University *B*
Hamilton College *B*
Hartwick College *B*
Hobart College *B*
Hofstra University *B*
Ithaca College *B*
Jamestown Community College *A*
Long Island University: Brooklyn
Campus *B*
Nazareth College of Rochester *B*
New York University *B,M,D*
Pace University
College of White Plains *B*
New York *B*
Pleasantville/Briarcliff *B*
St. John Fisher College *B*

St. John's University *B*
St. Lawrence University *B*
Sarah Lawrence College *B*
Skidmore College *B*
State University of New York
    Albany *B,M,D*
    Binghamton *B,M,D*
    Buffalo *B,M,D*
    Purchase *B*
    Stony Brook *B,M,D*
    College at Brockport *B*
    College at Buffalo *B*
    College at Cortland *B*
    College at Fredonia *B*
    College at Geneseo *B*
    College at New Paltz *B*
    College at Oneonta *B*
    College at Plattsburgh *B*
    College at Potsdam *B*
    Oswego *B*
Sullivan County Community
    College *A*
Syracuse University *B,M,D*
University of Rochester *B,M,D*
Vassar College *B*
Wagner College *B*
William Smith College *B*

North Carolina

Appalachian State University *B*
Barber-Scotia College *B*
Davidson College *B*
Duke University *B,D*
East Carolina University *B*
Guilford College *B*
North Carolina State University *B*
North Carolina Wesleyan College *B*
University of North Carolina
    Chapel Hill *B,M,D*
    Charlotte *B*
    Greensboro *B*
    Wilmington *B*
Wake Forest University *B,M*
Western Carolina University *B*

North Dakota

University of North Dakota *B*

Ohio

Case Western Reserve University
    B,M,D
Central State University *B*
Cleveland State University *B*
Denison University *B*
Heidelberg College *B*
Kent State University *B,M*
Kenyon College *B*
Miami University: Oxford Campus
    B,M
Oberlin College *B,M*
Ohio State University: Columbus
    Campus *B,M,D*
Ohio University *B*
Ohio Wesleyan University *B*
Union Institute *B,D*
University of Akron *B*
University of Cincinnati *B,M*
University of Dayton *B*
University of Toledo *B*
Wright State University *B*
Youngstown State University *B*

Oklahoma

University of Oklahoma *B,M,D*
University of Tulsa *B,M*

Oregon

Central Oregon Community
    College *A*
Eastern Oregon State College *B*
Lewis and Clark College *B*
Linfield College *B*

Northwest Christian College *B*
Oregon State University *B,M*
Portland Community College *A*
Portland State University *B,M*
Reed College *B*
University of Oregon
    Eugene *B,M,D*
    Robert Donald Clark Honors
        College *B*

Pennsylvania

Allegheny College *B*
Bloomsburg University of
    Pennsylvania *B*
Bryn Mawr College *B,M,D*
Bucknell University *B*
California University of
    Pennsylvania *B*
Clarion University of
    Pennsylvania *B*
Dickinson College *B*
Drexel University *B*
Edinboro University of
    Pennsylvania *B*
Franklin and Marshall College *B*
Gannon University *B*
Gettysburg College *B*
Haverford College *B*
Indiana University of
    Pennsylvania *B*
Juniata College *B*
Kutztown University of
    Pennsylvania *B*
Lafayette College *B*
Lehigh University *B*
Lock Haven University of
    Pennsylvania *B*
Lycoming College *B*
Mansfield University of
    Pennsylvania *B*
Mercyhurst College *B*
Millersville University of
    Pennsylvania *B*
Penn State University Park Campus
    B,M,D
St. Francis College *B*
Slippery Rock University of
    Pennsylvania *B*
Swarthmore College *B*
Temple University *B,M,D*
University of Pennsylvania
    A,B,M,D
University of Pittsburgh *B,M,D*
Ursinus College *B*
West Chester University of
    Pennsylvania *B*

Puerto Rico

University of Puerto Rico: Rio
    Piedras Campus *B*

Rhode Island

Brown University *B,M,D*
Rhode Island College *B*
Salve Regina University *B*
University of Rhode Island *B*

South Carolina

College of Charleston *B*
University of South Carolina *B,M*

South Dakota

University of South Dakota *B*

Tennessee

East Tennessee State University *B*
Memphis State University *B,M*
Middle Tennessee State
    University *B*
Rhodes College *B*
University of the South *B*

University of Tennessee
    Chattanooga *B*
    Knoxville *B,M,D*
Vanderbilt University *B,M,D*

Texas

Baylor University *B*
East Texas State University *B*
Rice University *B,M,D*
Southern Methodist University
    B,M,D
Southwest Texas State University *B*
Texas A&M University *B,M*
Texas Southmost College *A*
Texas Tech University *B,M*
Trinity University *B*
University of Houston
    Clear Lake *B*
    Houston *B,M*
University of North Texas *B*
University of Texas
    Arlington *B*
    Austin *B,M,D*
    El Paso *B*
    Permian Basin *B*
    San Antonio *B,M*

Utah

Brigham Young University *B,M*
University of Utah *B,M,D*
Weber State University *A*

Vermont

Bennington College *B*
Johnson State College *B*
Marlboro College *B*
Middlebury College *B*
University of Vermont *B*

Virginia

College of William and Mary *B,M*
George Mason University *B*
James Madison University *B*
Longwood College *B*
Old Dominion University *B*
Sweet Briar College *B*
University of Virginia *B,M,D*
Virginia Commonwealth
    University *B*
Virginia Wesleyan College *B*
Washington and Lee University *B*

Washington

Central Washington University *B*
Eastern Washington University *B*
Everett Community College *A*
Evergreen State College *B*
Lower Columbia College *A*
Olympic College *A*
Pacific Lutheran University *B*
Seattle Pacific University *B*
Spokane Community College *A*
Spokane Falls Community
    College *A*
Tacoma Community College *A*
University of Washington *B,M,D*
Washington State University *B,M,D*
Western Washington University
    B,M
Whitman College *B*

West Virginia

Marshall University *B*
Shepherd College *B*
West Virginia University *B,M*

Wisconsin

Beloit College *B*
Edgewood College *B*
Lawrence University *B*
Marquette University *B*
Ripon College *B*

University of Wisconsin
    Madison *B,M,D*
    Milwaukee *B,M,D*
    Oshkosh *B*
    Stevens Point *B*

Wyoming

Casper College *A*
Laramie County Community
    College *A*
University of Wyoming *B,M*
Western Wyoming Community
    College *A*

**American Samoa, Caroline
Islands, Guam, Marianas,
Virgin Islands**

University of Guam *B*

Canada

McGill University *B,M,D*

Arab Republic of Egypt

American University in Cairo *B,M*

Apparel and accessories marketing

California

Chabot College *A*
Fashion Institute of Design and
    Merchandising
        Los Angeles *A*
        San Francisco *A*
Mount San Antonio College *C,A*
Orange Coast College *C,A*
Phillips Junior College: Fresno
    Campus *C,A*
Saddleback College *C*

Colorado

Colorado Institute of Art *A*

Connecticut

Teikyo-Post University *B*

Florida

Florida Community College at
    Jacksonville *A*
International Fine Arts College *A*
Miami-Dade Community College *A*
Pensacola Junior College *A*

Georgia

Savannah Technical Institute *C,A*

Idaho

Northwest Nazarene College *B*

Illinois

Southern Illinois University at
    Carbondale *B*

Indiana

Purdue University *B*

Iowa

Des Moines Area Community
    College *A*
Iowa Lakes Community College
    C,A

Kansas

Kansas State University *B*

Louisiana

Phillips Junior College: New
    Orleans *A*

Massachusetts

Endicott College *A*
Mount Ida College *A*
University of Massachusetts at
Amherst *B*

Michigan

Northwood Institute *A*

Minnesota

Lakewood Community College *A*

Missouri

University of Missouri: Columbia
B,M

New York

Parsons School of Design *B*
Tobe-Coburn School for Fashion
Careers *A*

Ohio

Columbus State Community
College *A*

Oklahoma

Tulsa Junior College *C,A*

Pennsylvania

Lehigh County Community
College *A*
Mansfield University of
Pennsylvania *B*
Philadelphia College of Textiles and
Science *B,M*

Vermont

Champlain College *A*

Washington

Seattle Central Community
College *A*

Applied mathematics

Alabama

Auburn University *B,M*
University of Alabama
Birmingham *D*
Huntsville *D*
Tuscaloosa *B*

Arizona

Northern Arizona University *B*
University of Arizona *M,D*

Arkansas

Arkansas College *B*
University of Arkansas at Little
Rock *M*
University of Central Arkansas *B*

California

Biola University *B*
California Institute of Technology
B,D,W
California State University
Fresno *B*
Fullerton *B,M*
Hayward *M*
Long Beach *B,M*
Los Angeles *B,M*
Northridge *B,M*
Sacramento *B*
Stanislaus *B*
Chapman University *B*
Harvey Mudd College *B*
Holy Names College *B*
Humboldt State University *M*

Mount St. Mary's College *B*
Naval Postgraduate School *M,D*
Pacific Union College *B*
Pitzer College *B*
San Diego City College *A*
San Francisco State University *B*
San Jose State University *B*
Santa Clara University *M*
Stanford University *M,D*
University of California
Berkeley *B,M,D*
Davis *M,D*
Los Angeles *B*
Riverside *M*
San Diego *B,M*
Santa Barbara *M*
Santa Cruz *B,M*
University of the Pacific *B*
University of Southern California
M,D

Colorado

Colorado School of Mines
B,M,D,W
Mesa State College *B*
University of Colorado
Boulder *B,M,D*
Colorado Springs *B,M*
Denver *B,M,D*
University of Northern Colorado *B*

Connecticut

Connecticut College *B*
Southern Connecticut State
University *B,M*
University of Connecticut *B*
University of New Haven *B*
Yale University *B*

District of Columbia

American University *B,M*
Catholic University of America *B*
George Washington University *B,M*

Florida

Florida Institute of Technology
B,M,D
Florida International University
B,M
University of Central Florida *M*
University of Florida *M,D*
University of Miami *M*
University of Tampa *B*
University of West Florida *B*

Georgia

Armstrong State College *B*
Georgia Institute of Technology
B,M
University of Georgia *M*
Valdosta State College *B*

Idaho

University of Idaho *B*

Illinois

De Paul University *B*
Eastern Illinois University *B*
Illinois Institute of Technology *M*
Northern Illinois University *M*
Northwestern University *B,M,D*
University of Chicago *B,M,D*
University of Illinois at Urbana-
Champaign *M*

Indiana

Franklin College *B*
Indiana University
Bloomington *B,M,D*
South Bend *B*
Oakland City College *B*

Purdue University
Calumet *B,M*
West Lafayette *B,M,D,W*
Rose-Hulman Institute of
Technology *B*
University of Evansville *B*

Iowa

Grand View College *B*
Iowa State University *M,D*
University of Iowa *B,D*

Kansas

Kansas State University *M,D*
Tabor College *B*

Kentucky

Asbury College *B*
Brescia College *B*
Kentucky State University *B*
Murray State University *B*
University of Kentucky *M*
University of Louisville *M*

Louisiana

Grambling State University *B*
Louisiana College *B*
Nicholls State University *M*
Tulane University *M*

Maryland

Bowie State University *B*
Johns Hopkins University *B,M,D*
Salisbury State University *B*
University of Maryland
Baltimore County *M,D*
College Park *M,D*

Massachusetts

Boston University *B,M,D*
Hampshire College *B*
Harvard and Radcliffe Colleges *B*
Harvard University *M,D*
Massachusetts Institute of
Technology *B,M,D,W*
Roxbury Community College *A*
Salem State College *B*
Tufts University *B,M*
University of Massachusetts
Boston *B*
Lowell *A,B*
Williams College *B*
Worcester Polytechnic Institute
B,M

Michigan

Alma College *B*
Ferris State University *B*
GMI Engineering & Management
Institute *B*
Grand Valley State University *B*
Lansing Community College *A*
Michigan State University *M,D*
Michigan Technological
University *B*
Oakland University *M*
Olivet College *B*
University of Detroit Mercy *B*
University of Michigan
Ann Arbor *B,M*
Flint *B*
Wayne State University *M*
Western Michigan University *M*

Minnesota

University of Minnesota: Duluth *M*
University of St. Thomas *B*
Willmar Community College *A*

Mississippi

Alcorn State University *B*

Missouri

Central Missouri State
University *M*
Missouri Valley College *B*
Northeast Missouri State
University *B*
University of Missouri
Columbia *M*
Rolla *B,M*
St. Louis *B*
Washington University *B,M,D*

Montana

Carroll College *B*
Montana College of Mineral
Science and Technology *B*

Nebraska

Creighton University *B*
Hastings College *B*
University of Nebraska—Omaha *B*

Nevada

University of Nevada: Las Vegas *B*

New Hampshire

Plymouth State College of the
University System of New
Hampshire *B*
University of New Hampshire *B*

New Jersey

Centenary College *B*
Kean College of New Jersey *B*
New Jersey Institute of Technology
B,M,D
Princeton University *D*
Rutgers—The State University of
New Jersey
New Brunswick *M,D*
Newark College of Arts and
Sciences *B*
Stevens Institute of Technology
B,M,D

New Mexico

College of Santa Fe *B*
New Mexico Institute of Mining
and Technology *B,M*

New York

Alfred University *B*
City University of New York
Brooklyn College *B,M*
Hunter College *M*
Queens College *B*
Columbia University
Columbia College *B*
School of Engineering and
Applied Science *B,D*
School of General Studies *B*
Cornell University *M,D*
Dowling College *B*
Hofstra University *M*
Long Island University: C. W. Post
Campus *M*
Manhattan College *B*
New York University *B,M*
Polytechnic University *B*
Rensselaer Polytechnic Institute *M*
Rochester Institute of Technology
A,B
St. Thomas Aquinas College *B*
State University of New York
Stony Brook *B,M,D*
College at New Paltz *B*
Oswego *B*
United States Military Academy *B*
University of Rochester *B,M*

North Carolina

Elizabeth City State University *B*
North Carolina Agricultural and Technical State University *M*
North Carolina State University *B,M,D*
University of North Carolina
  Asheville *B*
  Chapel Hill *B*
Western Carolina University *M*

Ohio

Air Force Institute of Technology *M,D*
Case Western Reserve University *B,M,D*
Defiance College *B*
Kent State University *B,M,D*
Kenyon College *B*
Marietta College *B*
Ohio State University: Columbus Campus *M,D*
Ohio University *B,M,D*
Union Institute *B,D*
University of Akron *B,M*
University of Cincinnati *B*
University of Dayton *M*
University of Toledo *B*
Wright State University *B*

Oklahoma

Oklahoma State University *M*
University of Central Oklahoma *B,M*
University of Tulsa *B,M*

Oregon

Oregon State University *B*
Southern Oregon State College *B*

Pennsylvania

Bucknell University *B,M*
California University of Pennsylvania *B*
Carnegie Mellon University *B,M,D,W*
Clarion University of Pennsylvania *B*
Delaware Valley College *B*
Drexel University *M,D*
Elizabethtown College *B*
Geneva College *B*
Gettysburg College *B*
Indiana University of Pennsylvania *B,M*
Lehigh University *M,D*
Penn State Harrisburg Capital College *B*
Philadelphia College of Textiles and Science *B*
Point Park College *B*
Seton Hill College *B*
University of Pittsburgh
  Bradford *B*
  Greensburg *B*
  Pittsburgh *B,M*
Ursinus College *B*
Widener University *B*

Puerto Rico

University of Puerto Rico:
  Mayaguez Campus *B,M*

Rhode Island

Brown University *B,M,D*
Salve Regina University *B*
University of Rhode Island *D*

South Carolina

Charleston Southern University *B*
University of South Carolina:
  Coastal Carolina College *B*

South Dakota

Augustana College *B*
Sioux Falls College *B*

Tennessee

Bethel College *B*
David Lipscomb University *B*
Tennessee Technological University *M*
University of Tennessee:
  Chattanooga *B*

Texas

Abilene Christian University *B*
Jacksonville College *A*
Lamar University—Beaumont *B*
McMurry University *B*
Rice University *B,M,D*
Texas A&M University *B*
University of Houston
  Downtown *B*
  Houston *B,M*
University of Mary Hardin-Baylor *B*
University of Texas
  Dallas *B,M,D*
  El Paso *B*
West Texas State University *B*

Utah

Weber State University *B*

Virginia

Averett College *B*
Emory and Henry College *B*
Longwood College *B*
Old Dominion University *B,M,D*
Radford University *M*
University of Virginia *B,M,D*
Virginia Wesleyan College *B*

Washington

University of Washington *M,D*
Western Washington University *B*

West Virginia

Alderson-Broaddus College *B*
Bethany College *B*
Davis and Elkins College *B*
Shepherd College *B*
West Virginia State College *B*
Wheeling Jesuit College *B*

Wisconsin

Lakeland College *B*
University of Wisconsin
  Madison *B*
  Milwaukee *B*
  Stout *B*

Wyoming

University of Wyoming *B*

Canada

McGill University *M,D*

Arabic

California

University of California
  Berkeley *B,M,D*
  Los Angeles *B*

District of Columbia

Georgetown University *B,M,D*
Howard University *B*

Illinois

University of Chicago *B,M,D*

Indiana

Indiana University Bloomington *B,M,D*

Maryland

Baltimore Hebrew University *B,M*

Massachusetts

Harvard and Radcliffe Colleges *B*
Harvard University *M,D*
Simon's Rock College of Bard *B*

Michigan

University of Michigan *B,M,D*

Minnesota

University of Minnesota: Twin Cities *M*

New York

Columbia University
  Columbia College *B*
  New York *M,D*
New York University *B,M,D*
State University of New York at Binghamton *B*
United States Military Academy *B*

Ohio

Ohio State University: Columbus Campus *B,M*

Pennsylvania

University of Pennsylvania *B,M,D*

Utah

Brigham Young University *M*

Washington

University of Washington *B,M*

Arab Republic of Egypt

American University in Cairo *B,M*

Archeology

Alabama

University of Alabama *B*

Arizona

Pima Community College *C*
Prescott College *B*

California

Fresno City College *C*
Imperial Valley College *C*
Merced College *A*
Palomar College *C,A*
University of California
  Berkeley *M,D*
  Los Angeles *M,D*
  Santa Barbara *B*

Connecticut

Wesleyan University *B*
Yale University *B,M*

District of Columbia

George Washington University *B*

Florida

Florida State University *B,M*
Gulf Coast Community College *A*
University of Florida *M,D*

Illinois

Black Hawk College *A*
Southern Illinois University at Carbondale *B,M,D*
University of Chicago *M,D*
Wheaton College *B*

Indiana

Purdue University *M,D*
University of Evansville *B*
Vincennes University *A*

Kansas

University of Kansas *B*

Maine

Bowdoin College *B*

Maryland

Baltimore Hebrew University *B,M,D*

Massachusetts

Boston University *B,M,D*
Bridgewater State College *B*
Hampshire College *B*
Harvard and Radcliffe Colleges *B*
Harvard University *M,D*
Massachusetts Institute of Technology *B*
Tufts University *B*
Wellesley College *B*

Michigan

University of Michigan *B,D*

Missouri

University of Missouri: Columbia *B,M,D*
Washington University *B,M,D*

New Hampshire

Franklin Pierce College *B*

New Jersey

Princeton University *B,D*
Thomas Edison State College *B*

New York

Bard College *B*
City University of New York
  Brooklyn College *B*
  Hunter College *B*
Columbia University: Columbia College *B*
Cornell University *B,M,D*
State University of New York at Albany *B,M*

Ohio

College of Wooster *B*
Kenyon College *B*
Oberlin College *B*
Union Institute *D*
University of Cincinnati *M,D*

Oregon

Oregon State University *B*

Pennsylvania

Bryn Mawr College *B,M,D*
Haverford College *B*
Mercyhurst College *B*
University of Pennsylvania *M,D*

Rhode Island

Brown University *B,M,D*

Texas

Baylor University *B*
Rice University *B*
Texas A&M University *D*

Texas Southmost College *A*
University of Texas at Austin *B*

Utah

Southern Utah University *B*
Weber State University *A*

Canada

McGill University *M*

Architectural engineering

Arkansas

Westark Community College *A*

California

California Polytechnic State
University: San Luis Obispo *B*
Laney College *C,A*
Modesto Junior College *A*
San Joaquin Delta College *A*
Southwestern College *A*
University of Southern California
B,M

Colorado

University of Colorado at
Boulder *B*

Florida

Miami-Dade Community College *A*
University of Miami *B,M*

Illinois

University of Illinois at Urbana-
Champaign *M*

Indiana

University of Notre Dame *B,M*

Kansas

Kansas State University *B,M*
Pratt Community College *A*
University of Kansas *B,M*

Massachusetts

Franklin Institute of Boston *A*
Massachusetts Institute of
Technology *B,M,D,W*
Tufts University *B*

Missouri

East Central College *A*
Washington University *M*

Nebraska

Southeast Community College:
Milford Campus *A*

New Jersey

Union County College *A*

North Carolina

North Carolina Agricultural and
Technical State University *B,M*

Oklahoma

Oklahoma State University *B,M*

Pennsylvania

Drexel University *B*
Penn State University Park Campus
B,M,D
Pennsylvania Institute of
Technology *A*

Tennessee

Motlow State Community
College *A*
Tennessee State University *B*

Texas

Amarillo College *A*
Texas Southmost College *A*
University of Texas at Austin *B,M*

Wisconsin

Milwaukee School of Engineering *B*

Wyoming

University of Wyoming *B*

Architectural technologies

Alaska

University of Alaska Anchorage *A*

Arizona

Yavapai College *C,A*

California

Chabot College *A*
Chaffey Community College *C,A*
City College of San Francisco *A*
College of the Desert *C,A*
Golden West College *C,A*
Laney College *C,A*
Los Angeles Harbor College *C,A*
Los Angeles Pierce College *C,A*
Los Angeles Trade and Technical
College *C,A*
MiraCosta College *C,A*
Mount San Antonio College *C,A*
Orange Coast College *C,A*
San Joaquin Delta College *C,A*
Santa Monica College *C,A*
Santa Rosa Junior College *A*
Southwestern College *C,A*
Ventura College *A*

Colorado

Arapahoe Community College *C,A*
Denver Institute of Technology *A*
Denver Technical College *A*
Front Range Community College
C,A
Pikes Peak Community College *A*

Connecticut

Hartford State Technical College *A*
Norwalk State Technical College *A*
University of Hartford *B*
Waterbury State Technical
College *A*

Delaware

Delaware Technical and
Community College
Southern Campus *A*
Stanton/Wilmington
Campus *A*
Terry Campus *A*

District of Columbia

University of the District of
Columbia *A*

Florida

Broward Community College *A*
Daytona Beach Community
College *A*
Florida Agricultural and Mechanical
University *B*

Florida Community College at
Jacksonville *A*
ITT Technical Institute: Tampa *A*
Miami-Dade Community College *A*
New England Institute of
Technology *A*
St. Petersburg Junior College *A*
Seminole Community College *A*
Valencia Community College *A*

Idaho

Ricks College *A*

Illinois

City Colleges of Chicago
Chicago City-Wide College
C,A
Olive-Harvey College *C,A*
College of Lake County *C,A*
Illinois Central College *C,A*
Lake Land College *A*
Lincoln Land Community
College *A*
Morrison Institute of Technology *A*
Oakton Community College *C,A*
Southern Illinois University at
Carbondale *A*
Triton College *C,A*
William Rainey Harper College *A*

Indiana

Indiana State University *A*
Indiana University—Purdue
University
Fort Wayne *A*
Indianapolis *A,B*
ITT Technical Institute
Fort Wayne *A*
Indianapolis *A*
Purdue University: North Central
Campus *A*
Vincennes University *A*

Iowa

Iowa Western Community
College *A*

Kentucky

Lexington Community College *A*
Louisville Technical Institute *A*
Morehead State University *A*

Louisiana

Louisiana State University and
Agricultural and Mechanical
College *B*
Northeast Louisiana University *B*

Maine

Central Maine Technical College
C,A

Maryland

Anne Arundel Community
College *A*
Chesapeake College *C*
Montgomery College: Rockville
Campus *A*

Massachusetts

Franklin Institute of Boston *A*
Massasoit Community College *A*
Northeastern University *A*
Wentworth Institute of Technology
A,B

Michigan

Charles Stewart Mott Community
College *A*
Delta College *A*
Ferris State University *A*
Henry Ford Community College *A*

Kirtland Community College *C*
Macomb Community College *C,A*
Oakland Community College *A*
Schoolcraft College *C,A*

Minnesota

St. Paul Technical College *C*

Mississippi

Holmes Community College *A*
Mississippi Delta Community
College *A*
University of Southern
Mississippi *B*

Missouri

Jefferson College *A*
St. Louis Community College at
Meramec *A*
Southwest Missouri State
University *B*
Three Rivers Community College *A*

Nebraska

Southeast Community College:
Milford Campus *A*

Nevada

Community College of Southern
Nevada *C,A*
Truckee Meadows Community
College *C,A*

New Jersey

Burlington County College *A*
Essex County College *A*
Mercer County Community
College *A*
Thomas Edison State College *A,B*

New Mexico

Albuquerque Technical-Vocational
Institute *A*

New York

City University of New York: New
York City Technical College *A*
Dutchess Community College *A*
Erie Community College: South
Campus *A*
Institute of Design and
Construction *A*
New York Institute of Technology
A,B
Onondaga Community College *A*
Orange County Community
College *A*
Rochester Institute of
Technology *A*
State University of New York
College of Technology at
Alfred *A*
College of Technology at
Delhi *A*
College of Technology at
Farmingdale *A*

North Carolina

Catawba Valley Community
College *A*
Central Piedmont Community
College *A*
Coastal Carolina Community
College *A*
Durham Technical Community
College *C*
Fayetteville Technical Community
College *A*
Forsyth Technical Community
College *A*
Guilford Technical Community
College *A*

Nash Community College *A*
Pitt Community College *A*
Roanoke-Chowan Community College *A*
Sandhills Community College *C,A*
Wake Technical Community College *A*

North Dakota

North Dakota State College of Science *A*

Ohio

Bowling Green State University *B*
Cincinnati Technical College *A*
Clark State Community College *A*
Columbus State Community College *A*
Edison State Community College *A*
Lakeland Community College *C*
Owens Technical College: Toledo *C,A*
Sinclair Community College *A*
Terra Technical College *C,A*
University of Cincinnati
  Access Colleges *A*
  Cincinnati *B*
University of Toledo *A*

Oklahoma

Oklahoma State University: Oklahoma City *A*

Oregon

Chemeketa Community College *A*
Mount Hood Community College *C,A*
Portland Community College *C,A*

Pennsylvania

Butler County Community College *A*
Community College of Beaver County *A*
Community College of Philadelphia *A*
Delaware County Community College *A*
Harrisburg Area Community College *C,A*
Luzerne County Community College *C,A*
Northampton County Area Community College *A*
Penn State University Park Campus *A*
Pennsylvania College of Technology *A*
Pennsylvania Institute of Technology *A*

South Carolina

Greenville Technical College *A*
Midlands Technical College *A*

Tennessee

Cleveland State Community College *A*
Memphis State University *B*
Nashville State Technical Institute *A*
State Technical Institute at Memphis *A*

Texas

Del Mar College *A*
El Centro College *A*
ITT Technical Institute: Houston *A*
Midland College *A*
Southwest Texas State University *B*
Tarrant County Junior College *A*

Utah

Weber State University *A*

Vermont

Vermont Technical College *A*

Virginia

Central Virginia Community College *A*
John Tyler Community College *A*
Mountain Empire Community College *A*
New River Community College *A*

Washington

Spokane Community College *A*

West Virginia

Bluefield State College *A,B*
Fairmont State College *A,B*
West Virginia State College *A*

Wisconsin

Chippewa Valley Technical College *A*
Northeast Wisconsin Technical College *A*

American Samoa, Caroline Islands, Guam, Marianas, Virgin Islands

Guam Community College *A*

Architecture

Alabama

Auburn University *B*
Tuskegee University *B*

Arizona

Arizona State University *B,M*
Pima Community College *C*
University of Arizona *B,M*
Yavapai College *C,A*

Arkansas

University of Arkansas *B*
Westark Community College *A*

California

Allan Hancock College *C,A*
Bakersfield College *A*
California College of Arts and Crafts *B*
California Polytechnic State University: San Luis Obispo *B,M*
California State Polytechnic University: Pomona *B,M*
Cerritos Community College *A*
Chabot College *A*
City College of San Francisco *A*
College of the Desert *A*
College of Marin: Kentfield *A*
College of the Sequoias *A*
Cosumnes River College *A*
Diablo Valley College *A*
El Camino College *A*
Fresno City College *A*
Golden West College *A*
Laney College *C,A*
Long Beach City College *A*
Los Angeles City College *A*
Los Angeles Harbor College *C,A*
Modesto Junior College *A*
Orange Coast College *C,A*
Saddleback College *A*
San Diego Mesa College *A*
San Joaquin Delta College *C,A*
Santa Monica College *C,A*

Southern California Institute of Architecture *B,M*
Southwestern College *A*
University of California
  Berkeley *B,M,D*
  Los Angeles *M,D*
  San Diego *B,M,D*
University of Southern California *B,M*
Ventura College *A*
West Valley College *A*
Woodbury University *B*

Colorado

Denver Institute of Technology *A*
Denver Technical College *A*
Front Range Community College *C,A*
University of Colorado at Denver *M*

Connecticut

Hartford State Technical College *A*
Norwalk State Technical College *A*
Waterbury State Technical College *C*
Wesleyan University *B*
Yale University *B,M*

Delaware

Delaware Technical and Community College
  Stanton/Wilmington Campus *A*
  Terry Campus *A*

District of Columbia

Catholic University of America *B,M*
Howard University *B,M*
University of the District of Columbia *A*

Florida

Broward Community College *A*
Chipola Junior College *A*
Daytona Beach Community College *A*
Florida Agricultural and Mechanical University *B,M*
Gulf Coast Community College *A*
Hillsborough Community College *A*
Indian River Community College *A*
Manatee Community College *A*
Miami-Dade Community College *A*
New England Institute of Technology *A*
Palm Beach Community College *A*
University of Florida *B,M,D*
University of Miami *B,M*
University of South Florida *M*

Georgia

Georgia Institute of Technology *B,M,D*
Middle Georgia College *A*
Morehouse College *B*
Morris Brown College *B*
Savannah College of Art and Design *B*
Southern College of Technology *B*

Hawaii

University of Hawaii at Manoa *B,M*

Idaho

University of Idaho *B,M*

Illinois

City Colleges of Chicago
  Chicago City-Wide College *C,A*
  Olive-Harvey College *A*
  Richard J. Daley College *A*
  Wright College *C,A*
College of Lake County *C,A*
Illinois Central College *A*
Illinois Institute of Technology *B,M*
Kishwaukee College *A*
Lake Land College *A*
Lincoln Land Community College *A*
Morton College *A*
Oakton Community College *C,A*
Rend Lake College *A*
Southern Illinois University at Carbondale *A*
Triton College *C,A*
University of Illinois
  Chicago *B,M*
  Urbana-Champaign *B,M*

Indiana

Ball State University *B,M*
Indiana State University *A*
ITT Technical Institute: Fort Wayne *A*
University of Notre Dame *B,M*

Iowa

Coe College *B*
Iowa State University *B,M*

Kansas

Bethel College *B*
Central College *A*
Coffeyville Community College *A*
Fort Scott Community College *A*
Hutchinson Community College *A*
Kansas State University *B,M*
University of Kansas *B,M*

Kentucky

University of Kentucky *B*

Louisiana

Louisiana State University and Agricultural and Mechanical College *B,M*
Louisiana Tech University *B*
Southern University and Agricultural and Mechanical College *B*
Tulane University *B,M*
University of Southwestern Louisiana *B*

Maine

Maine Maritime Academy *A*
University of Maine at Augusta *A*

Maryland

Anne Arundel Community College *A*
Morgan State University *M*
University of Maryland: College Park *B,M*

Massachusetts

Boston Architectural Center *B*
Hampshire College *B*
Harvard University *M,D*
Massachusetts College of Art *B*
Massachusetts Institute of Technology *B,M,D,W*
Smith College *B*
Wellesley College *B*
Wentworth Institute of Technology *A,B*

Michigan
Andrews University *B*
Grand Rapids Community
College *A*
Lawrence Technological
University *B*
St. Clair County Community
College *A*
University of Detroit Mercy *B*
University of Michigan *B,M,D*

Minnesota
Northland Community College *A*
Northwest Technical Institute *A*
Rainy River Community College *A*
University of Minnesota: Twin
Cities *B,M*

Mississippi
Copiah-Lincoln Community
College *A*
Mississippi Delta Community
College *A*
Mississippi State University *B,M*

Missouri
Drury College *B*
East Central College *A*
St. Louis Community College at
Meramec *A*
Washington University *B,M*

Montana
Montana State University *B*

Nebraska
Central Community College *A*
McCook Community College *A*
Southeast Community College:
Milford Campus *A*
University of Nebraska—Lincoln
B,M

Nevada
Truckee Meadows Community
College *C,A*
University of Nevada: Las Vegas
B,M

New Jersey
Burlington County College *C,A*
Mercer County Community
College *A*
New Jersey Institute of Technology
B,M
Princeton University *B,M,D*

New Mexico
Dona Ana Branch Community
College of New Mexico State
University *C,A*
New Mexico Junior College *A*
University of New Mexico *B,M*

New York
Barnard College *B*
Cazenovia College *A*
City University of New York
City College *B*
College of Staten Island *A*
Columbia University
Columbia College *B*
New York *M*
School of General Studies *B*
Cooper Union *B*
Cornell University *B,M,D*
Erie Community College: South
Campus *A*
Hobart College *B*
Institute of Design and
Construction *A*

New York Institute of
Technology *B*
Onondaga Community College *A*
Orange County Community
College *A*
Parsons School of Design *B,M*
Pratt Institute *B,M*
Rensselaer Polytechnic Institute
B,M
Rochester Institute of
Technology *C*
State University of New York
Buffalo *B,M*
College of Technology at
Delhi *A*
Syracuse University *B,M*

North Carolina
Brevard College *A*
Catawba Valley Community
College *A*
Central Piedmont Community
College *A*
Forsyth Technical Community
College *A*
Guilford Technical Community
College *C,A*
Mayland Community College *C*
North Carolina State University
B,M
Pitt Community College *A*
University of North Carolina at
Charlotte *B,M*

North Dakota
North Dakota State University *B,M*

Ohio
Cincinnati Technical College *A*
Columbus State Community
College *A*
Cuyahoga Community College:
Metropolitan Campus *A*
ITT Technical Institute: Dayton *A*
Kent State University *B,M*
Miami University: Oxford
Campus *M*
Ohio State University: Columbus
Campus *B,M*
Sinclair Community College *A*
Union Institute *D*
University of Cincinnati *B,M*
University of Toledo *A*

Oklahoma
Connors State College *A*
Oklahoma State University
Oklahoma City *A*
Stillwater *B,M*
University of Oklahoma *B,M*

Oregon
University of Oregon
Eugene *B,M*
Robert Donald Clark Honors
College *B*

Pennsylvania
Butler County Community
College *A*
Carnegie Mellon University
B,M,D,W
Community College of Beaver
County *A*
Delaware County Community
College *A*
Drexel University *B*
Lehigh University *B*
Penn State University Park Campus
B,M
Pennsylvania Institute of
Technology *A*

Philadelphia College of Textiles and
Science *B*
Spring Garden College *B*
Temple University *B*
University of the Arts *B,M*
University of Pennsylvania *M,D*

Puerto Rico
University of Puerto Rico: Rio
Piedras Campus *M*

Rhode Island
Rhode Island School of Design *B*
Roger Williams College *B*

South Carolina
Aiken Technical College *C,A*
Clemson University *B,M*
Denmark Technical College *C*

Tennessee
Tennessee State University *B*
University of Tennessee:
Knoxville *B*

Texas
Amarillo College *A*
Austin Community College *A*
Central Texas College *A*
El Centro College *C,A*
El Paso Community College *A*
Midland College *A*
Mountain View College *A*
Prairie View A&M University *B*
Rice University *B,M,D,W*
San Antonio College *A*
Texas A&M University *M,D*
Texas Southmost College *A*
Texas Tech University *B,M*
University of Houston *B,M*
University of Texas
Arlington *B,M*
Austin *B,M*

Utah
University of Utah *B,M*
Weber State University *A*

Vermont
Bennington College *B*
Norwich University *B*
Vermont Technical College *A*

Virginia
Hampton University *B*
Mountain Empire Community
College *A*
Northern Virginia Community
College *C,A*
University of Virginia *B,M*
Virginia Polytechnic Institute and
State University *B,M*

Washington
University of Washington *B,M*
Washington State University *B*

Wisconsin
Chippewa Valley Technical
College *A*
Madison Area Technical College *A*
Northeast Wisconsin Technical
College *A*
University of Wisconsin: Milwaukee
B,M,D
Wisconsin Indianhead Technical
College *A*

Canada
McGill University *B,M*

Mexico
Sistema Instituto Tecnologico y de
Estudios Superiores de
Monterrey *B*

Archival science

Louisiana
University of New Orleans *M*

Michigan
University of Michigan *M*
Wayne State University *M*

Pennsylvania
Duquesne University *M*

Puerto Rico
Inter American University of Puerto
Rico: Metropolitan Campus *M*

Washington
Western Washington University *M*

Art conservation

California
John F. Kennedy University *M*

Delaware
University of Delaware *M*

District of Columbia
Mount Vernon College *B*

New Mexico
Institute of American Indian
Arts *A*

New York
New York University *M,W*
State University of New York
College at Buffalo *M*

Art education

Alabama
Alabama Agricultural and
Mechanical University *B,M*
Alabama Southern Community
College *A*
Alabama State University *B*
Auburn University at
Montgomery *B*
Birmingham-Southern College *B*
Huntingdon College *B*
John C. Calhoun State Community
College *A*
Samford University *B*
Snead State Junior College *A*
University of Alabama
Birmingham *B,M*
Tuscaloosa *B,M,W*
University of Montevallo *B,M*
University of North Alabama *B*
University of South Alabama *B*

Arizona
Arizona State University *B,D*
Cochise College *A*
Eastern Arizona College *A*
Grand Canyon University *B*
Northern Arizona University *B,M*

University of Arizona *B,M*

Arkansas

Arkansas State University *B*
Arkansas Tech University *B*
Harding University *B*
Henderson State University *B,M*
Ouachita Baptist University *B*
University of Arkansas
    Fayetteville *B*
    Monticello *B*
    Pine Bluff *B*
University of Central Arkansas *B*
University of the Ozarks *B*
Westark Community College *A*

California

Academy of Art College *B,M*
Azusa Pacific University *B*
Biola University *B*
California Baptist College *B*
California Lutheran University *B*
California State University
    Bakersfield *B*
    Fresno *B*
    Fullerton *B*
    Long Beach *B*
    Los Angeles *B,M*
    Northridge *B*
Chapman University *B*
Christ College Irvine *B*
Mount St. Mary's College *B*
Point Loma Nazarene College *B*
University of the Pacific *B*
University of Redlands *B*
University of San Francisco *B*
Westmont College *B*

Colorado

Adams State College *M*
Colorado Christian University *B*
Colorado State University *B*
University of Colorado at Boulder *B,M*
University of Denver *B*
University of Northern Colorado *B*

Connecticut

Central Connecticut State University *B,M*
St. Joseph College *B*
Southern Connecticut State University *B,M*
University of Bridgeport *B,M*

Delaware

Delaware State College *B*
University of Delaware *B*

District of Columbia

Gallaudet University *B*
University of the District of Columbia *B*

Florida

Flagler College *B*
Florida Agricultural and Mechanical University *B*
Florida Atlantic University *B,M*
Florida International University *B,M*
Florida Southern College *B*
Florida State University *B,M,D*
Jacksonville University *B,M*
Pensacola Junior College *A*
Stetson University *B*
University of Central Florida *B,M*
University of Florida *B,M*
University of Miami *M*
University of North Florida *B*
University of South Florida *B,M*
University of Tampa *B*

University of West Florida *B*

Georgia

Armstrong State College *B*
Augusta College *B*
Berry College *B*
Clayton State College *A*
Columbus College *B*
Gainesville College *A*
Georgia College *B*
Georgia Southern University *B,M*
Georgia Southwestern College *B*
Georgia State University *B,M*
Kennesaw State College *B*
Middle Georgia College *A*
North Georgia College *B,M*
Piedmont College *B*
Shorter College *B*
University of Georgia *B,M,D*
Valdosta State College *B,M*
West Georgia College *M*

Hawaii

Brigham Young University-Hawaii *B*
Chaminade University of Honolulu *B*

Idaho

Boise State University *B,M*
College of Southern Idaho *A*
Northwest Nazarene College *B*
University of Idaho *M*

Illinois

Augustana College *B*
Blackburn College *B*
Columbia College *M*
Concordia University *B*
Elmhurst College *B*
Greenville College *B*
Illinois State University *D*
Illinois Wesleyan University *B*
MacMurray College *B*
McKendree College *B*
Millikin University *B*
Monmouth College *B*
North Central College *B*
North Park College and Theological Seminary *B*
Northern Illinois University *B,M*
Northwestern University *B,M*
Olivet Nazarene University *B*
Quincy College *B*
School of the Art Institute of Chicago *B,M*
Southern Illinois University
    Carbondale *B*
    Edwardsville *M*
University of Illinois
    Chicago *M*
    Urbana-Champaign *B,M,D*
Western Illinois University *B,M*
Wheaton College *B*

Indiana

Anderson University *B*
Ball State University *B,M*
Calumet College of St. Joseph *B*
Franklin College *B*
Goshen College *B*
Huntington College *B*
Indiana State University *B,M*
Indiana University Bloomington *M*
Indiana University—Purdue University at Indianapolis *B,M*
Indiana Wesleyan University *B*
Manchester College *B*
Marian College *B*
Martin University *B*
Oakland City College *B*
Purdue University *B,M*

St. Francis College *B*
St. Mary-of-the-Woods College *B*
Taylor University *B*
University of Evansville *B*
University of Indianapolis *B*
University of Southern Indiana *B*
Vincennes University *A*

Iowa

Briar Cliff College *B*
Buena Vista College *B*
Clarke College *B*
Coe College *B*
Cornell College *B*
Drake University *B,M*
Iowa Lakes Community College *A*
Iowa State University *B*
Iowa Wesleyan College *B*
Loras College *B*
Luther College *B*
Morningside College *B*
Mount Mercy College *B*
St. Ambrose University *B*
Simpson College *B*
Teikyo Marycrest University *B*
University of Iowa *B,M,D*
Upper Iowa University *B*
Wartburg College *B*
William Penn College *B*

Kansas

Baker University *B*
Bethany College *B*
Colby Community College *A*
Emporia State University *B*
Friends University *B*
Kansas State University *B*
Kansas Wesleyan University *B*
McPherson College *B*
Pittsburg State University *B*
Southwestern College *B*
University of Kansas *B,M,D*
Wichita State University *B,M*

Kentucky

Asbury College *B*
Bellarmine College *B*
Berea College *B*
Brescia College *B*
Campbellsville College *B*
Cumberland College *B*
Eastern Kentucky University *B,M*
Georgetown College *B*
Kentucky State University *B*
Kentucky Wesleyan College *B*
Morehead State University *M*
Murray State University *B*
Northern Kentucky University *B*
Pikeville College *B*
Thomas More College *B*
Transylvania University *B*
University of Kentucky *B*
Western Kentucky University *B,M*

Louisiana

Dillard University *B*
Grambling State University *B*
Louisiana College *B*
Louisiana State University
    Agricultural and Mechanical College *B*
    Shreveport *B*
Louisiana Tech University *B,M*
McNeese State University *B*
Nicholls State University *B*
Northeast Louisiana University *B*
Northwestern State University *B*
Southeastern Louisiana University *B*
Southern University and Agricultural and Mechanical College *B*

Tulane University *M*
University of Southwestern Louisiana *B*
Xavier University of Louisiana *B*

Maine

University of Maine *B*

Maryland

Columbia Union College *B*
Maryland Institute College of Art *B,M*
Montgomery College
    Germantown Campus *A*
    Rockville Campus *A*
    Takoma Park Campus *A*
Morgan State University *B*
Towson State University *M*
Western Maryland College *B*

Massachusetts

Anna Maria College for Men and Women *B*
Boston University *B,M*
Bridgewater State College *M*
Elms College *B*
Emmanuel College *B*
Framingham State College *B*
Hampshire College *B*
Lesley College *M*
Massachusetts College of Art *B,M*
School of the Museum of Fine Arts *B,M*
Tufts University *B,M*
University of Massachusetts
    Amherst *B,M*
    Dartmouth *B,M*
Westfield State College *B*

Michigan

Adrian College *B*
Andrews University *M*
Calvin College *B,M*
Central Michigan University *B,M*
Concordia College *B*
Eastern Michigan University *B,M*
Grand Valley State University *B*
Hillsdale College *B*
Lansing Community College *A*
Madonna University *B*
Marygrove College *B*
Michigan State University *B*
Northern Michigan University *B,M*
Saginaw Valley State University *B*
University of Michigan: Flint *B*
Wayne State University *B,M*
Western Michigan University *B*

Minnesota

Bemidji State University *B*
Bethel College *B*
College of St. Catherine: St. Catherine Campus *B*
Concordia College: Moorhead *B*
Concordia College: St. Paul *B*
Gustavus Adolphus College *B*
Mankato State University *B*
Moorhead State University *B,M*
Northland Community College *A*
Northwestern College *B*
Pillsbury Baptist Bible College *B*
Rainy River Community College *A*
St. Cloud State University *B*
St. Olaf College *B*
Southwest State University *B*
University of Minnesota
    Duluth *B*
    Twin Cities *B,M*
Willmar Community College *A*
Winona State University *B*

Mississippi

Jones County Junior College *A*
Mississippi College *B,M*
Mississippi Delta Community
   College *A*
Mississippi Gulf Coast Community
   College: Jefferson Davis
   Campus *A*
Mississippi University for Women *B*
Northeast Mississippi Community
   College *A*
University of Mississippi *M*
University of Southern
   Mississippi *M*

Missouri

Central Missouri State University
   B,M
College of the Ozarks *B*
Columbia College *B*
Culver-Stockton College *B*
Evangel College *B*
Fontbonne College *B*
Maryville University *B*
Missouri Western State College *B*
Northeast Missouri State
   University *M*
Northwest Missouri State
   University *B,M*
Park College *B*
Southeast Missouri State
   University *B*
Southwest Baptist University *B*
Southwest Missouri State
   University *B*
University of Missouri: Columbia
   B,M,D
Washington University *B,M*
Webster University *B*
Westminster College *B*
William Woods College *B*

Montana

Eastern Montana College *B*
Montana State University *B*
Rocky Mountain College *B*
University of Montana *B*
Western Montana College of the
   University of Montana *B*

Nebraska

Chadron State College *B*
College of St. Mary *B*
Concordia College *B*
Creighton University *B*
Dana College *B*
Doane College *B*
Hastings College *B*
Peru State College *B*
Union College *B*
University of Nebraska
   Kearney *B,M*
   Lincoln *B*
Wayne State College *B*

Nevada

Sierra Nevada College *B*

New Hampshire

Colby-Sawyer College *B*
Franklin Pierce College *B*
New England College *B*
Notre Dame College *B*
Plymouth State College of the
   University System of New
   Hampshire *B*
Rivier College *B*
University of New Hampshire *B*

New Jersey

Caldwell College *B*
Georgian Court College *B*

Glassboro State College *B,M*
Jersey City State College *B,M*
Kean College of New Jersey *B,M*
Rutgers—The State University of
   New Jersey
     Camden College of Arts and
      Sciences *B*
     New Brunswick *M,D*
     Newark College of Arts and
      Sciences *B*
     University College Newark *B*
Seton Hall University *B*
Trenton State College *B*

New Mexico

Eastern New Mexico University *B*
New Mexico Highlands
   University *B*
New Mexico State University *B*
University of New Mexico *B,M*
Western New Mexico University *B*

New York

Adelphi University *B,M*
Alfred University *B,M*
City University of New York
   Brooklyn College *B*
   Hunter College *B,M*
   Lehman College *M*
   Queens College *B,M*
College of New Rochelle *B,M*
College of St. Rose *B,M*
Daemen College *B*
Dowling College *B*
Elmira College *B*
Hofstra University *B,M*
Houghton College *B*
Long Island University
   C. W. Post Campus *B,M*
   Southampton Campus *B*
Manhattanville College *M*
Marymount College *B*
Mohawk Valley Community
   College *A*
Nazareth College of Rochester *B,M*
New York Institute of
   Technology *B*
New York University *B,M,D*
Parsons School of Design *B*
Pratt Institute *B*
Roberts Wesleyan College *B*
Rochester Institute of
   Technology *M*
St. John's University *B*
St. Thomas Aquinas College *B*
School of Visual Arts *B*
Skidmore College *B*
State University of New York
   Buffalo *B,M*
   College at Buffalo *B,M*
   College at New Paltz *B,M*
Syracuse University *B,M,D*
Wells College *B*

North Carolina

Appalachian State University *B,M*
Barton College *B*
Brevard College *A*
East Carolina University *B,M*
Gaston College *A*
High Point University *B*
Lenoir-Rhyne College *B*
Mars Hill College *B*
Methodist College *A,B*
North Carolina Agricultural and
   Technical State University *B,M*
North Carolina Central
   University *B*
Pembroke State University *B*
St. Andrews Presbyterian College *B*
Salem College *B*

University of North Carolina
   Asheville *C*
   Greensboro *B,M*
Western Carolina University *B,M*
Wingate College *B*
Winston-Salem State University *B*

North Dakota

Bismarck State College *A*
Dickinson State University *B*
Minot State University *B*
University of North Dakota *B*
Valley City State University *B*

Ohio

Ashland University *B*
Baldwin-Wallace College *B*
Bluffton College *B*
Bowling Green State University *B*
Capital University *B*
Case Western Reserve University
   B,M
College of Mount St. Joseph *B*
Defiance College *B*
Kent State University *B,M*
Miami University: Oxford Campus
   B,M
Mount Union College *B*
Mount Vernon Nazarene College *B*
Muskingum College *B*
Ohio Dominican College *B*
Ohio State University: Columbus
   Campus *B,M,D*
Ohio University *B*
Otterbein College *B*
University of Cincinnati *B,M,D*
University of Dayton *B*
University of Findlay *B*
University of Rio Grande *B*
University of Toledo *B*
Wittenberg University *B*
Wright State University *B,M*
Xavier University *B*
Youngstown State University *B*

Oklahoma

East Central University *B*
Oklahoma Baptist University *B*
Oklahoma Christian University of
   Science and Arts *B*
Oklahoma City University *B*
Oral Roberts University *B*
Phillips University *B*
Southeastern Oklahoma State
   University *B,M*
Southwestern Oklahoma State
   University *B,M*
University of Central Oklahoma
   B,M
University of Science and Arts of
   Oklahoma *B*
University of Tulsa *B,M*

Oregon

Linfield College *B*
Willamette University *M*

Pennsylvania

Beaver College *B,M*
Carlow College *B*
Edinboro University of
   Pennsylvania *B,M*
Gannon University *B*
Harrisburg Area Community
   College *A*
Indiana University of
   Pennsylvania *B*
Kutztown University of
   Pennsylvania *B,M*
Lycoming College *B*
Mansfield University of
   Pennsylvania *B,M*

Marywood College *B,M*
Mercyhurst College *B*
Millersville University of
   Pennsylvania *B*
Moore College of Art and Design *B*
Penn State University Park Campus
   B,M,D
St. Vincent College *B*
Seton Hill College *B*
Temple University *B,M*
University of the Arts *M*
Washington and Jefferson College *B*
Westminster College *B*
Wilkes University *B*

Puerto Rico

Inter American University of Puerto
   Rico: San German Campus *B*
Pontifical Catholic University of
   Puerto Rico *B*
University of Puerto Rico: Rio
   Piedras Campus *B*

Rhode Island

Rhode Island College *B,M*
Rhode Island School of Design *M*
Salve Regina University *B*

South Carolina

Benedict College *B*
Bob Jones University *B*
Claflin College *B*
Coker College *B*
Columbia College *B*
Francis Marion College *B,M*
Lander College *B*
Limestone College *B*
Presbyterian College *B*
South Carolina State College *B*
University of South Carolina
   Coastal Carolina College *B*
   Columbia *B,M*

South Dakota

Augustana College *B*
Black Hills State University *B*
Dakota State University *B*
Dakota Wesleyan University *B*
Northern State University *B,M*
Sioux Falls College *B*
South Dakota State University *B*
University of South Dakota *B*

Tennessee

Bethel College *B*
East Tennessee State University
   B,M
Freed-Hardeman University *B*
Lincoln Memorial University *B*
Roane State Community College *A*
Tennessee Technological
   University *B*
Union University *B,M*
University of Tennessee
   Chattanooga *B,M*
   Knoxville *B,M*
   Martin *B*

Texas

Abilene Christian University *B*
Angelo State University *B*
Baylor University *B*
Del Mar College *A*
Hardin-Simmons University *B*
Houston Baptist University *B*
Incarnate Word College *B*
McMurry University *B*
Midwestern State University *B*
North Harris Montgomery
   Community College District *A*
St. Edward's University *B*
Sam Houston State University *B*

Schreiner College *B*
Sul Ross State University *B,M*
Texas A&I University *B*
Texas Christian University *B*
Texas College *B*
Texas Lutheran College *B*
Texas Southmost College *A*
Texas Tech University *B,M*
Texas Wesleyan University *B*
Texas Woman's University *M*
University of Dallas *B*
University of Houston *M*
University of Mary Hardin-
Baylor *B*
University of North Texas *B,M,D*
University of Texas
Austin *M*
El Paso *M*
West Texas State University *B,M*

Utah

Brigham Young University *B,M*
Weber State University *B*

Vermont

Castleton State College *B*
Johnson State College *B*
St. Michael's College *B*
University of Vermont *B*

Virginia

Averett College *B*
Bluefield College *B*
Emory and Henry College *B*
Northern Virginia Community
College *A*
Old Dominion University *B*
Radford University *M*
Virginia Commonwealth
University *B*
Virginia Intermont College *B*
Virginia State University *B*
Virginia Wesleyan College *B*

Washington

Central Washington University *B*
Eastern Washington University *B*
Pacific Lutheran University *B*
Seattle Pacific University *B*
University of Puget Sound *M*
Washington State University *B*
Western Washington University *B*

West Virginia

Concord College *B*
Davis and Elkins College *B*
Fairmont State College *B*
Glenville State College *B*
Shepherd College *B*
University of Charleston *B*
West Liberty State College *B*
West Virginia State College *B*
West Virginia University *B,M*
West Virginia Wesleyan College *B*

Wisconsin

Alverno College *B*
Beloit College *B*
Cardinal Stritch College *B*
Carroll College *B*
Carthage College *B*
Lawrence University *B*
Marian College of Fond du Lac *B*
Mount Mary College *B*
Mount Senario College *B*
Northland College *B*
St. Norbert College *B*
Silver Lake College *B*

University of Wisconsin
Eau Claire *B*
Green Bay *B*
La Crosse *B*
Madison *B,M*
Platteville *B,M*
River Falls *B*
Stevens Point *B*
Stout *B*
Whitewater *B*

Wyoming

University of Wyoming *B,M*

American Samoa, Caroline Islands, Guam, Marianas, Virgin Islands

University of Guam *B*

Canada

McGill University *B,M*

Art history

Alabama

Birmingham-Southern College *B*
Chattahoochee Valley Community
College *A*
Judson College *B*
Mobile College *B*
Troy State University *B*
University of Alabama
Birmingham *B,M*
Huntsville *B*
Tuscaloosa *B,M*
University of South Alabama *B*

Arizona

Northern Arizona University *B*
University of Arizona *B,M*

Arkansas

Hendrix College *B*

California

California State University
Dominguez Hills *B*
Fresno *B*
Fullerton *B,M*
Long Beach *B*
Los Angeles *B,M*
Northridge *B,M*
San Bernardino *B*
Stanislaus *B*
Chapman University *B*
Cosumnes River College *A*
De Anza College *C*
Dominican College of San Rafael *B*
El Camino College *A*
Glendale Community College *C*
Grossmont Community College *A*
Humboldt State University *B*
Long Beach City College *A*
Los Angeles Valley College *A*
Loyola Marymount University *B*
Mendocino College *C,A*
Mills College *B*
Monterey Peninsula College *C,A*
Occidental College *B*
Pacific Union College *B*
Pitzer College *B*
Pomona College *B*
St. Mary's College of California *B*
San Diego City College *A*
San Diego State University *B,M*
San Jose State University *B,M*
Santa Barbara City College *A*
Santa Clara University *B*
Scripps College *B*

Skyline College *A*
Sonoma State University *B*
University of California
Berkeley *B,M,D*
Davis *B,M*
Irvine *B*
Los Angeles *B,M,D*
Riverside *B,M*
San Diego *B*
Santa Barbara *B,M,D*
Santa Cruz *B*
University of the Pacific *B*
University of Redlands *B*
University of Southern California
B,M,D
West Hills Community College *A*
Whittier College *B*

Colorado

Colorado College *B*
University of Colorado
Boulder *B*
Denver *B*
University of Denver *M*
Western State College of
Colorado *B*

Connecticut

Albertus Magnus College *B*
Connecticut College *B*
Fairfield University *B*
St. Joseph College *B*
Southern Connecticut State
University *B*
Trinity College *B*
University of Connecticut *B*
University of Hartford *B*
Wesleyan University *B*
Yale University *B,M,D*

Delaware

University of Delaware *B,M,D*
Wesley College *A*

District of Columbia

American University *B,M*
Catholic University of America *B,M*
Gallaudet University *B*
George Washington University
B,M,D
Howard University *B,M*
Trinity College *B*

Florida

Florida Atlantic University *B*
Florida State University *B,M,D*
Jacksonville University *B*
New College of the University of
South Florida *B*
Pensacola Junior College *A*
Rollins College *B*
Stetson University *B*
University of Florida *B,M*
University of Miami *B,M*
University of North Florida *B*
University of South Florida *B,M*
University of West Florida *B*

Georgia

Emory University *B,M,D*
Georgia State University *M*
Mercer University *B*
Oxford College of Emory
University *A*
Reinhardt College *A*
Savannah College of Art and
Design *B,M*
University of Georgia *B,M*
Wesleyan College *B*
Young Harris College *A*

Hawaii

Brigham Young University-
Hawaii *B*

Illinois

Augustana College *B*
Bradley University *B*
Chicago State University *B*
Columbia College *B*
De Paul University *B*
Illinois College *B*
Illinois Wesleyan University *B*
Knox College *B*
Lake Forest College *B*
Lewis University *B*
MacMurray College *B*
Northern Illinois University *B,M*
Northwestern University *B,M,D*
Principia College *B*
Quincy College *B*
Richland Community College *A*
Rockford College *B*
Roosevelt University *B*
St. Xavier University *B*
School of the Art Institute of
Chicago *M*
Southern Illinois University
Carbondale *B*
Edwardsville *B*
University of Chicago *B,M,D*
University of Illinois
Chicago *B*
Urbana-Champaign *B,M,D*
Wheaton College *B*

Indiana

Ball State University *B*
DePauw University *B*
Earlham College *B*
Indiana State University *B,M*
Indiana University
Bloomington *B,M,D*
South Bend *B*
Indiana University—Purdue
University at Indianapolis *B*
Indiana Wesleyan University *B*
Marian College *B*
Purdue University *B*
University of Evansville *B*
University of Indianapolis *B*
University of Notre Dame *B*

Iowa

Central College *B*
Clarke College *B*
Coe College *B*
Cornell College *B*
Drake University *B*
Graceland College *B*
Grinnell College *B*
Loras College *B*
Simpson College *B*
Teikyo Marycrest University *B*
University of Iowa *B,M,D*

Kansas

Coffeyville Community College *A*
Dodge City Community College *A*
Southwestern College *B*
University of Kansas *B,M,D*
Wichita State University *B*

Kentucky

Berea College *B*
Campbellsville College *B*
University of Kentucky *B,M*
University of Louisville *B,M*

Louisiana

Grambling State University *B*
Louisiana State University and
 Agricultural and Mechanical
 College *M*
Tulane University *B,M*
University of New Orleans *B*

Maine

Bowdoin College *B*
University of Maine *B*

Maryland

Howard Community College *A*
Johns Hopkins University *B,M,D*
Montgomery College: Rockville
 Campus *A*
Morgan State University *B,M*
University of Maryland: College
 Park *B,M,D*
Washington College *B*
Western Maryland College *B*

Massachusetts

Boston College *B*
Boston University *B,M,D*
Bradford College *B*
Clark University *B*
College of the Holy Cross *B*
Emmanuel College *B*
Framingham State College *B*
Hampshire College *B*
Harvard and Radcliffe Colleges *B*
Massachusetts College of Art *B*
Massachusetts Institute of
 Technology *B*
Mount Holyoke College *B*
Pine Manor College *A,B*
School of the Museum of Fine
 Arts *B*
Simmons College *B*
Smith College *B,M*
Tufts University *B,M*
University of Massachusetts
 Amherst *B,M*
 Dartmouth *B*
Wellesley College *B*
Wheaton College *B*
Williams College *B,M*

Michigan

Alma College *B*
Aquinas College *B*
Calvin College *B*
Central Michigan University *B*
Hillsdale College *B*
Hope College *B*
Marygrove College *B*
Michigan State University *B,M*
Oakland University *B*
Olivet College *B*
University of Detroit Mercy *B*
University of Michigan
 Ann Arbor *B,M,D*
 Dearborn *B*
Wayne State University *B,M*

Minnesota

Augsburg College *B*
Bethel College *B*
Carleton College *B*
College of St. Benedict *B*
College of St. Catherine: St.
 Catherine Campus *B*
Concordia College: Moorhead *B*
Gustavus Adolphus College *B*
Hamline University *B*
Macalester College *B*
Mankato State University *B,M*
Moorhead State University *B*
Northland Community College *A*
Rainy River Community College *A*

St. Cloud State University *B,M*
St. John's University *B*
St. Olaf College *B*
University of Minnesota
 Duluth *B*
 Morris *B*
 Twin Cities *B,M,D*
University of St. Thomas *A*
Willmar Community College *A*

Mississippi

University of Mississippi *B,M*

Missouri

Central Missouri State University *B*
Drury College *B*
Jefferson College *A*
Lindenwood College *B*
University of Missouri
 Columbia *B,M,D*
 Kansas City *B,M*
 St. Louis *B*
Washington University *B,M,D*

Nebraska

Creighton University *B*
Northeast Community College *A*
University of Nebraska
 Kearney *B*
 Lincoln *B,M*
 Omaha *B*

New Hampshire

Dartmouth College *B*
Franklin Pierce College *B*
Plymouth State College of the
 University System of New
 Hampshire *B*
University of New Hampshire *B*

New Jersey

Drew University *B*
Georgian Court College *B*
Jersey City State College *B*
Kean College of New Jersey *B*
Princeton University *B,D*
Rutgers—The State University of
 New Jersey
 Camden College of Arts and
  Sciences *B*
 Douglass College *B*
 Livingston College *B*
 New Brunswick *M,D*
 Newark College of Arts and
  Sciences *B*
 Rutgers College *B*
 University College Camden *B*
 University College New
  Brunswick *B*
St. Peter's College *B*
William Paterson College of New
 Jersey *B*

New Mexico

University of New Mexico *B,M,D*

New York

Adelphi University *B*
Bard College *B*
Barnard College *B*
Canisius College *B*
City University of New York
 Brooklyn College *B,M*
 City College *B,M*
 Graduate School and
  University Center *D*
 Hunter College *B,M*
 Lehman College *B,M*
 Queens College *B,M*
College of New Rochelle *B*

Columbia University
 Columbia College *B*
 New York *M,D*
 School of General Studies *B*
Cornell University *B,M,D*
Fordham University *B*
Hamilton College *B*
Hartwick College *B*
Hobart College *B*
Hofstra University *B*
Ithaca College *B*
Long Island University: C. W. Post
 Campus *B*
Manhattanville College *B*
Marymount College *B*
Molloy College *B*
Nazareth College of Rochester *B*
New York University *A,M,D*
Parsons School of Design *M*
Sarah Lawrence College *B*
Skidmore College *B*
State University of New York
 Binghamton *B,M,D*
 Buffalo *B,M*
 Purchase *B*
 Stony Brook *B,M*
 College at Brockport *B*
 College at Buffalo *B*
 College at Fredonia *B*
 College at Geneseo *B*
 College at New Paltz *B*
 College at Oneonta *B*
 College at Plattsburgh *B*
 College at Potsdam *B*
Syracuse University *B*
University of Rochester *B*
Vassar College *B*
Wells College *B*
William Smith College *B*

North Carolina

Brevard College *A*
Davidson College *B*
Duke University *B,M*
East Carolina University *B*
Mars Hill College *B*
Queens College *B*
St. Andrews Presbyterian College *B*
Salem College *B*
University of North Carolina
 Chapel Hill *B,M,D*
 Greensboro *B*
Wake Forest University *B*

North Dakota

Dickinson State University *B*

Ohio

Baldwin-Wallace College *B*
Bowling Green State University *B*
Case Western Reserve University
 B,M,D
Cleveland State University *B*
College of Wooster *B*
Denison University *B*
Hiram College *B*
John Carroll University *B*
Kent State University *B,M*
Kenyon College *B*
Lourdes College *A,B*
Miami University: Oxford
 Campus *B*
Oberlin College *B,M*
Ohio State University: Columbus
 Campus *B,M,D*
Ohio University *B,M*
Ohio Wesleyan University *B*
Union Institute *B,D*
University of Akron *B*
University of Cincinnati *B,M*
University of Findlay *B*
University of Toledo *B*

Wittenberg University *B*
Wright State University *B*
Youngstown State University *B*

Oklahoma

Oklahoma City University *M*
Phillips University *B*
Rogers State College *A*
St. Gregory's College *A*
University of Oklahoma *B,M*
University of Tulsa *B*

Oregon

Oregon State University *B*
Reed College *B*
Southern Oregon State College *B*
University of Oregon
 Eugene *B,M,D*
 Robert Donald Clark Honors
  College *B*
Willamette University *B*

Pennsylvania

Allegheny College *B*
Beaver College *B*
Bloomsburg University of
 Pennsylvania *B,M*
Bryn Mawr College *B,M,D*
Bucknell University *B*
California University of
 Pennsylvania *B*
Chatham College *B*
Chestnut Hill College *A,B*
Eastern College *B*
Edinboro University of
 Pennsylvania *B,M*
Franklin and Marshall College *B*
Gettysburg College *B*
Haverford College *B*
Immaculata College *A*
Indiana University of
 Pennsylvania *B*
Juniata College *B*
La Salle University *B*
Lehigh University *B*
Lycoming College *B*
Mansfield University of
 Pennsylvania *B*
Messiah College *B*
Moravian College *B*
Penn State University Park Campus
 B,M,D
Rosemont College *B*
Seton Hill College *B*
Susquehanna University *B*
Swarthmore College *B*
Temple University *B,M*
University of Pennsylvania *B,M,D*
West Chester University of
 Pennsylvania *C*

Puerto Rico

University of Puerto Rico
 Mayaguez Campus *B*
 Rio Piedras Campus *B*

Rhode Island

Brown University *B,M,D*
Providence College *B*
Rhode Island College *B*
University of Rhode Island *B*

South Carolina

College of Charleston *B*
Converse College *B*
University of South Carolina *B,M*
Winthrop University *B*
Wofford College *B*

Tennessee

Belmont University *B*
East Tennessee State University *B*

Fisk University *B*
Memphis State University *B*
Rhodes College *B*
Tennessee State University *B*
University of the South *B*
University of Tennessee:
  Knoxville *B*
Vanderbilt University *M*

Texas

Abilene Christian University *B*
Baylor University *B*
Howard College *A*
Incarnate Word College *B*
Lon Morris College *A*
Rice University *B,M*
Southern Methodist University *B,M*
Southwestern University *B*
Texas Christian University *B*
Texas Tech University *B*
Texas Woman's University *B,M*
Trinity University *B*
University of Dallas *B,M*
University of Houston *B*
University of North Texas *B,M*
University of Texas
  Arlington *B*
  Austin *B,M,D*

Utah

Brigham Young University *B,M*
Dixie College *A*
University of Utah *B*

Vermont

Marlboro College *B*
University of Vermont *B*

Virginia

Averett College *B*
George Mason University *B*
Hampton University *B*
Hollins College *B*
James Madison University *B*
Longwood College *B*
Lynchburg College *B*
Mary Baldwin College *B*
Mary Washington College *B*
Old Dominion University *B*
Radford University *B,M*
Randolph-Macon Woman's
  College *B*
Sweet Briar College *B*
University of Richmond *B*
University of Virginia *M,D*
Virginia Commonwealth University
  B,M
Virginia Wesleyan College *B*
Washington and Lee University *B*

Washington

Eastern Washington University *B*
Evergreen State College *B*
Olympic College *A*
Tacoma Community College *A*
University of Puget Sound *B*
University of Washington *B,M,D*
Western Washington University *B*
Whitman College *B*
Whitworth College *B*

West Virginia

Marshall University *B*
Shepherd College *B*
West Virginia University *B,M*

Wisconsin

Beloit College *B*
Carthage College *B*
Lawrence University *B*
Ripon College *B*

University of Wisconsin
  Green Bay *B*
  Madison *B,M,D*
  Milwaukee *B,M*
  Superior *B*
  Whitewater *B*

Wyoming

Eastern Wyoming College *A*

Canada

McGill University *B,M,D*

France

American University of Paris *B*

Switzerland

Franklin College: Switzerland *A,B*

Art therapy

Alabama

Spring Hill College *B*

California

College of Notre Dame *M*
Loyola Marymount University *M*

Connecticut

Albertus Magnus College *B*

District of Columbia

George Washington University *M*

Illinois

Barat College *B*
Millikin University *B*
Northern Illinois University *M*
School of the Art Institute of
  Chicago *M*
Southern Illinois University at
  Edwardsville *M*
University of Illinois at Chicago *M*

Indiana

Marian College *B*
University of Indianapolis *B*

Kansas

Emporia State University *M*
Pittsburg State University *B*

Kentucky

University of Louisville *M*

Maryland

Western Maryland College *B*

Massachusetts

Anna Maria College for Men and
  Women *B*
Elms College *B*
Emmanuel College *B*
Lesley College *B,M*

Michigan

Marygrove College *B*

Minnesota

Willmar Community College *A*

New Jersey

Caldwell College *C*
Jersey City State College *B*
Thomas Edison State College *B*

New York

College of New Rochelle *B,M*
Hofstra University *M*

Long Island University: C. W. Post
  Campus *B,M*
New York University *M,D*
Pratt Institute *M*
Russell Sage College *B*
St. Thomas Aquinas College *B*

Ohio

Bowling Green State University *B*
Capital University *B*
Union Institute *D*
University of Findlay *B*
Ursuline College *M*
Wright State University *M*

Oregon

Marylhurst College *M*

Pennsylvania

Beaver College *B*
Hahnemann University School of
  Health Sciences and
  Humanities *M*
Marywood College *M*
Mercyhurst College *B*
St. Vincent College *B*
Seton Hill College *B*
University of the Arts *C*

Vermont

Norwich University *M*

Wisconsin

Alverno College *B*
Edgewood College *B*
Mount Mary College *B,M*

Arts management

Alabama

Spring Hill College *B*

Arizona

Northern Arizona University *B*

California

California State University:
  Dominguez Hills *M*
Humboldt State University *C*
John F. Kennedy University *M*
Scripps College *B*

Connecticut

Sacred Heart University *B*

District of Columbia

American University *M*

Florida

Barry University *B*
University of Tampa *B*

Georgia

Brenau Women's College *B*
Georgia College *B*
Wesleyan College *B*

Illinois

Columbia College *B,M*
Elmhurst College *B*
Illinois Wesleyan University *B*
Millikin University *B*
Sangamon State University *M*

Indiana

Butler University *B*
Indiana University Bloomington *M*

Iowa

Luther College *B*
Simpson College *B*

Kansas

Kansas Wesleyan University *B*

Kentucky

University of Kentucky *B*

Louisiana

University of New Orleans *M*

Massachusetts

Anna Maria College for Men and
  Women *B*
Endicott College *A*
Lesley College *M*
Simmons College *B*

Michigan

Eastern Michigan University *B*
University of Michigan *M*

Missouri

Culver-Stockton College *B*

Nebraska

McCook Community College *A*

New Hampshire

Colby-Sawyer College *B*

New York

City University of New York:
  Lehman College *B*
Long Island University
  C. W. Post Campus *B*
  Southampton Campus *B*
Medaille College *C*
New York University *M,W*
Russell Sage College *B*
State University of New York
  Binghamton *M*
  Purchase *C*
Wagner College *B*

North Carolina

Bennett College *B*
Catawba College *B*
East Carolina University *B*
Methodist College *A,B*
Pfeiffer College *B*
St. Andrews Presbyterian College *B*
Salem College *B*

North Dakota

Jamestown College *B*

Ohio

Baldwin-Wallace College *B*
Case Western Reserve
  University *M*
Marietta College *B*
Notre Dame College of Ohio *B*
Ursuline College *B*
Wright State University *B*

Oklahoma

Oklahoma City University *M*

Oregon

Linfield College *B*

Pennsylvania

Cabrini College *B*
Carnegie Mellon University *M*
Marywood College *B*
St. Vincent College *B*
Seton Hill College *B*

South Carolina
Newberry College *B*

South Dakota
Dakota State University *B*

Texas
Abilene Christian University *B*
El Paso Community College *C*
Southern Methodist University *M*

Virginia
Mary Baldwin College *B*
Randolph-Macon College *B*
Shenandoah University *B*

Washington
Evergreen State College *B*
University of Puget Sound *B*
Whitworth College *B*

West Virginia
Glenville State College *A*

Wisconsin
University of Wisconsin
    Green Bay *B*
    Stevens Point *B*
Viterbo College *B*

Asian studies

Arkansas
Hendrix College *B*

California
California State University: Long
    Beach *B,M*
Claremont McKenna College *B*
Laney College *A*
Monterey Institute of International
    Studies *M*
Naval Postgraduate School *M*
Occidental College *B*
Pitzer College *B*
Pomona College *B*
San Diego State University *B,M*
Scripps College *B*
University of California
    Berkeley *B,M,D*
    Los Angeles *M*
    Santa Barbara *B,M*
University of the Pacific *B*
University of Redlands *B*

Colorado
Colorado College *B*
University of Colorado at
    Boulder *B*

Connecticut
Connecticut College *B*
Trinity College *B*
Wesleyan University *B*

District of Columbia
Georgetown University *B*

Florida
Florida State University *B,M*
Miami-Dade Community College *A*
University of Florida *B*

Hawaii
Hawaii Loa College *B*
University of Hawaii
    Manoa *B,M*
    West Oahu *B*

Illinois
Augustana College *B*
Illinois College *B*
KAES College *B*
Lake Forest College *B*
Northwestern University *B*
Principia College *B*
University of Chicago *B*
University of Illinois at Urbana-
    Champaign *B,M*

Indiana
DePauw University *B*
Indiana University Bloomington
    C,B,M,D
University of Notre Dame *B*

Iowa
University of Iowa *B,M*
University of Northern Iowa *B*

Louisiana
Tulane University *B*

Maine
Bowdoin College *B*

Maryland
Morgan State University *B*

Massachusetts
Hampshire College *B*
Harvard and Radcliffe Colleges *B*
Mount Holyoke College *B*
Tufts University *B,M*
Wellesley College *B*
Wheaton College *B*
Williams College *B*

Michigan
Eastern Michigan University *B*
University of Michigan *B,M*
Western Michigan University *B*

Minnesota
Carleton College *B*
St. Olaf College *B*

Missouri
Washington University *B,M*
Westminster College *B*

New Hampshire
Dartmouth College *B*

New Jersey
Rutgers—The State University of
  New Jersey
    Douglass College *B*
    Livingston College *B*
    Rutgers College *B*
    University College New
      Brunswick *B*
Seton Hall University *B,M*

New Mexico
University of New Mexico *B*

New York
Bard College *B*
Barnard College *B*
City University of New York
    Brooklyn College *B*
    City College *B*
Colgate University *B*
Cornell University *B,M,D*
Hamilton College *B*
Hobart College *B*
Hofstra University *B*
Manhattanville College *B*
St. John's University *B*
St. Lawrence University *B*

Sarah Lawrence College *B*
State University of New York at
    Albany *B*
Vassar College *B*
William Smith College *B*

North Carolina
St. Andrews Presbyterian College *B*
University of North Carolina at
    Chapel Hill *B,M,D*

Ohio
Bowling Green State University *B*
Case Western Reserve University *B*
Kent State University *B*
Kenyon College *B*
Ohio State University: Columbus
    Campus *B,M,D*
Ohio University *B*
Union Institute *B,D*
University of Cincinnati *B*
University of Toledo *B*

Oklahoma
Oklahoma City University *B*
Phillips University *B*
University of Oklahoma *B*

Oregon
Northwest Christian College *B*
University of Oregon
    Eugene *B,M*
    Robert Donald Clark Honors
      College *B*
Willamette University *B*

Pennsylvania
Bucknell University *B*
Gettysburg College *B*
Penn State University Park
    Campus *C*
Swarthmore College *B*
Temple University *B*

Rhode Island
Brown University *B*

South Carolina
Furman University *B*

Tennessee
University of Tennessee:
    Knoxville *B*

Texas
Baylor University *B*
Rice University *B*
Southwest Texas State University *B*
Trinity University *B*
University of Texas at Austin *B,M*

Utah
Brigham Young University *B,M*

Vermont
Marlboro College *B*
University of Vermont *B*

Virginia
University of Virginia *M*

Washington
University of Puget Sound *B*
University of Washington *B*
Washington State University *B*

Wisconsin
University of Wisconsin: Madison *B*

**American Samoa, Caroline
Islands, Guam, Marianas,
Virgin Islands**
University of Guam *B*

Astronomy

Arizona
Northern Arizona University *B*
University of Arizona *B,M,D*

California
California Institute of Technology
    B,M,D,W
Chabot College *A*
El Camino College *A*
Modesto Junior College *A*
Napa Valley College *A*
Ohlone College *A*
Orange Coast College *A*
Palomar College *C,A*
Pomona College *B*
Saddleback College *A*
San Diego State University *B,M*
San Francisco State University *B*
Southwestern College *A*
University of California
    Berkeley *B,M,D*
    Los Angeles *B,M,D*
    Santa Cruz *D*
University of Southern California *B*

Connecticut
Wesleyan University *B,M*
Western Connecticut State
    University *B*
Yale University *B,M,D*

District of Columbia
Howard University *B*

Florida
Daytona Beach Community
    College *A*
Edison Community College *A*
Florida Institute of Technology
    B,M,D
Pensacola Junior College *A*
University of Florida *B,M,D*

Georgia
Georgia State University *D*
University of Georgia *B*
Valdosta State College *B*

Hawaii
University of Hawaii at Manoa *M,D*

Idaho
North Idaho College *A*

Illinois
Illinois Central College *A*
Morton College *A*
Northwestern University *B,M,D*
Triton College *A*
University of Chicago *B,M,D*
University of Illinois at Urbana-
    Champaign *B,M,D*

Indiana
Earlham College *B*
Indiana University Bloomington
    B,M,D

Iowa
Drake University *B*
University of Iowa *B,M*

Kansas

Benedictine College *B*
University of Kansas *B*

Louisiana

Louisiana State University and
Agricultural and Mechanical
College *B*

Maryland

Howard Community College *A*
Johns Hopkins University *B,D*
University of Maryland: College
Park *B,M,D*

Massachusetts

Amherst College *B*
Boston University *B,M,D*
Hampshire College *B*
Harvard and Radcliffe Colleges *B*
Harvard University *D*
Massachusetts Institute of
Technology *B,M,D,W*
Mount Holyoke College *B*
Smith College *B*
Tufts University *B*
University of Massachusetts at
Amherst *B,M,D*
Wellesley College *B*
Wheaton College *B*
Williams College *B*

Michigan

Michigan State University *B*
University of Michigan *B,M,D*

Minnesota

Mankato State University *B*
University of Minnesota: Twin
Cities *B,M*

Nebraska

University of Nebraska—Lincoln
M,D

New Jersey

Jersey City State College *B*

New Mexico

New Mexico State University *M,D*

New York

Colgate University *B*
Columbia University
Columbia College *B*
New York *M,D*
Cornell University *B,M,D*
State University of New York at
Stony Brook *B*
University of Rochester *D,W*
Vassar College *B*

North Carolina

University of North Carolina at
Chapel Hill *B,M,D*

Ohio

Case Western Reserve University
B,M,D
Mount Union College *B*
Ohio State University: Columbus
Campus *B,M,D*
Ohio University *M,D*
Ohio Wesleyan University *B*
University of Akron *B*
University of Toledo *D*
Youngstown State University *B*

Oklahoma

Tulsa Junior College *A*
University of Oklahoma *B*

Pennsylvania

Bryn Mawr College *B*
Eastern College *B*
Haverford College *B*
Lycoming College *B*
Penn State University Park Campus
B,M,D
Swarthmore College *B*
University of Pennsylvania *B,M,D*
University of Pittsburgh *B,M,D*
Villanova University *B*
West Chester University of
Pennsylvania *B*

Rhode Island

Brown University *B*

Tennessee

Vanderbilt University *M*

Texas

Austin Community College *A*
Lon Morris College *A*
Rice University *M,D*
University of Texas at Austin
B,M,D

Utah

Brigham Young University *D*

Vermont

Marlboro College *B*

Virginia

University of Virginia *B,M,D*

Washington

Lower Columbia College *A*
University of Washington *B,M,D*
Western Washington University *B*
Whitman College *B*

Wisconsin

University of Wisconsin: Madison
M,D

Wyoming

University of Wyoming *B*

Astrophysics

Alaska

University of Alaska Fairbanks *M,D*

California

San Francisco State University *B*
University of California
Los Angeles *B*
Santa Cruz *D*

Colorado

University of Colorado at Boulder
M,D

Connecticut

Wesleyan University *B,M,D*

Florida

University of Florida *M,D*

Georgia

Agnes Scott College *B*

Illinois

Northwestern University *B*
University of Chicago *B,M,D*

Indiana

Indiana University Bloomington *D*

Iowa

Iowa State University *M,D*

Massachusetts

Boston University *B,M,D*
Harvard University *D*
Massachusetts Institute of
Technology *B,M,D,W*
Tufts University *M,D*
Williams College *B*

Michigan

Michigan State University *B*
University of Michigan *D*

Minnesota

University of Minnesota: Twin
Cities *B,D*

New Jersey

Princeton University *B,D*

New Mexico

New Mexico Institute of Mining
and Technology *B,M,D*
University of New Mexico *B*

New York

Colgate University *B*
Columbia University
Columbia College *B*
New York *M,D*
Cornell University *M,D*

Ohio

University of Akron *B*

Oklahoma

University of Oklahoma *B*

Oregon

University of Oregon *M,D*

Pennsylvania

Penn State University Park Campus
B,M,D
Swarthmore College *B*

Rhode Island

Brown University *B*

Texas

Texas Christian University *B*

Vermont

Marlboro College *B*

Wisconsin

University of Wisconsin: Madison *B*

Atmospheric sciences and meteorology

Alaska

University of Alaska Fairbanks *M,D*

Arizona

Northern Arizona University *B*
University of Arizona *B,M,D*

California

Naval Postgraduate School *M,D*
San Francisco State University *B*
San Jose State University *B,M*

University of California
Davis *B,M,D*
Los Angeles *B,M,D*

Colorado

Colorado State University *M,D*
Metropolitan State College of
Denver *B*
University of Colorado at Boulder
M,D
University of Northern Colorado *B*

Connecticut

Western Connecticut State
University *B*

Delaware

University of Delaware *D*

Florida

Daytona Beach Community
College *A*
Florida State University *B,M,D*
Gulf Coast Community College *A*
Miami-Dade Community College *A*
University of Miami *M,D*

Georgia

Georgia Institute of Technology
M,D

Hawaii

University of Hawaii at Manoa
B,M,D

Illinois

Illinois Central College *A*
Northern Illinois University *B*
Parks College of St. Louis
University *B*
University of Chicago *B,M,D*
University of Illinois at Urbana-
Champaign *M,D*

Indiana

Purdue University *B,M,D*

Iowa

Iowa State University *B,M,D*

Kansas

University of Kansas *B,M*

Kentucky

Western Kentucky University *A*

Louisiana

Northeast Louisiana University *B*

Maryland

Howard Community College *A*

Massachusetts

Massachusetts Institute of
Technology *M,D,W*
University of Massachusetts at
Lowell *B*

Michigan

University of Michigan *B,M,D*

Minnesota

St. Cloud State University *B*

Mississippi

Jackson State University *B*

Missouri

St. Louis University *B,M,D*
University of Missouri: Columbia
B,M,D

Nebraska
Creighton University *C,B,M*
University of Nebraska—Lincoln *B*

New Hampshire
Plymouth State College of the
University System of New
Hampshire *B*

New Jersey
Kean College of New Jersey *B*
Rutgers—The State University of
New Jersey
Cook College *B*
Douglass College *B*
New Brunswick *M*

New Mexico
New Mexico Institute of Mining
and Technology *M,D*

New York
City University of New York: City
College *B,M*
Columbia University *M,D*
Cornell University *B,M,D*
State University of New York
Albany *B,M,D*
Stony Brook *B*
College at Brockport *B*
Maritime College *B*

North Carolina
North Carolina State University
B,M
University of North Carolina at
Asheville *B*

North Dakota
University of North Dakota *B*

Ohio
Ohio State University: Columbus
Campus *M,D*

Oklahoma
University of Oklahoma *B,M,D*

Oregon
Oregon Graduate Institute *M,D*
Oregon State University *B,M,D*

Pennsylvania
Butler County Community
College *A*
California University of
Pennsylvania *B*
Drexel University *B,M,D*
Millersville University of
Pennsylvania *B*
Penn State University Park Campus
B,M,D
Villanova University *B*

South Dakota
South Dakota School of Mines and
Technology *M,D*

Texas
Texas A&M University *B,M,D*
Texas Tech University *B,M*

Utah
University of Utah *B,M,D*

Vermont
Lyndon State College *B*

Washington
University of Washington *B,M,D*

Wisconsin
Northland College *B*
University of Wisconsin: Madison
B,M,D

Wyoming
University of Wyoming *M,D*

Canada
McGill University *B,M,D*

Atomic/molecular physics

Florida
New College of the University of
South Florida *B*
University of Florida *M,D*

Illinois
Northwestern University *B*
University of Chicago *B,M,D*

Kansas
Kansas State University *M,D*

Massachusetts
Brandeis University *D*
Harvard University *D*
Massachusetts Institute of
Technology *B,M,D,W*

Michigan
University of Michigan *D*

New Hampshire
University of New Hampshire *M,D*

New Jersey
Stevens Institute of Technology
B,M,D

New York
Columbia University *M,D*

Ohio
Ohio State University: Columbus
Campus *B,M,D*

Pennsylvania
Carnegie Mellon University
B,M,D,W
Lehigh University *M*

Vermont
Marlboro College *B*

Canada
McGill University *M,D*

Automotive mechanics

Alabama
Alabama Aviation and Technical
College *C*
Bessemer State Technical College *C*
Brewer State Junior College *A*
Community College of the Air
Force *A*
Douglas MacArthur State Technical
College *C*
Enterprise State Junior College *A*
Gadsden State Community
College *C*
John C. Calhoun State Community
College *C*

Lawson State Community
College *C*
Shelton State Community
College *A*
Shoals Community College *C*
Walker State Technical College *C*
Wallace State Community College
at Hanceville *C*

Alaska
University of Alaska
Anchorage *C,A*
Southeast *A*

Arizona
Eastern Arizona College *C,A*
Glendale Community College *C,A*
Mohave Community College *C,A*
Northland Pioneer College *C,A*
Pima Community College *C*
Yavapai College *C,A*

Arkansas
Phillips County Community
College *A*
Rich Mountain Community
College *A*
Westark Community College *C,A*

California
Allan Hancock College *A*
Barstow College *C,A*
Cerritos Community College *A*
Cerro Coso Community College *C*
Chabot College *A*
Chaffey Community College *C,A*
Citrus College *C,A*
College of the Desert *C,A*
College of the Sequoias *C,A*
Columbia College *A*
Cosumnes River College *C,A*
De Anza College *C,A*
El Camino College *C,A*
Fresno City College *C,A*
Gavilan Community College *A*
Glendale Community College *C*
Golden West College *C,A*
Imperial Valley College *C,A*
Lassen College *C,A*
Long Beach City College *C,A*
Los Angeles Pierce College *C,A*
Los Angeles Trade and Technical
College *C,A*
Los Medanos College *C,A*
Mendocino College *C,A*
Merced College *C,A*
MiraCosta College *C,A*
Modesto Junior College *A*
Mount San Jacinto College *C,A*
Oxnard College *A*
Palomar College *C,A*
Pasadena City College *C,A*
Porterville College *C,A*
Saddleback College *C,A*
San Diego City College *C,A*
San Joaquin Delta College *C,A*
Santa Barbara City College *C,A*
Santa Monica College *C,A*
Santa Rosa Junior College *C,A*
Sierra College *A*
Skyline College *C,A*
Solano Community College *A*
Southwestern College *C,A*
Taft College *A*
Ventura College *C,A*
West Hills Community College *C,A*
Yuba College *A*

Colorado
Aims Community College *C,A*
Arapahoe Community College *C,A*
Denver Institute of Technology *A*

Lamar Community College *C*
Mesa State College *C,A*
Morgan Community College *C*
Pikes Peak Community College *A*
Red Rocks Community College *C,A*
Trinidad State Junior College *C,A*

Connecticut
Greater New Haven State Technical
College *A*
Mattatuck Community College *A*

Delaware
Delaware Technical and
Community College: Southern
Campus *A*

Florida
Brevard Community College *C*
Central Florida Community
College *C*
Daytona Beach Community
College *C*
Indian River Community College *A*
New England Institute of
Technology *A*
Okaloosa-Walton Community
College *C,A*
Palm Beach Community College *A*
Pensacola Junior College *A*
Seminole Community College *A*
South Florida Community
College *C*

Georgia
Athens Area Technical Institute *C*
Atlanta Metropolitan College *A*
Augusta Technical Institute *C*
Bainbridge College *C,A*
Chattahoochee Technical
Institute *C*
Dalton College *C*
Darton College *A*
DeKalb Technical Institute *C,A*
Floyd College *A*
Gainesville College *A*
Savannah Technical Institute *C,A*

Hawaii
University of Hawaii
Honolulu Community College
C,A
Kauai Community College *C,A*
Leeward Community College
C,A

Idaho
Boise State University *C*
College of Southern Idaho *A*
Idaho State University *C*
Lewis Clark State College *A*
North Idaho College *C,A*
Ricks College *A*

Illinois
Black Hawk College
East Campus *A*
Moline *A*
Carl Sandburg College *C,A*
City Colleges of Chicago: Chicago
City-Wide College *C,A*
College of DuPage *C,A*
College of Lake County *C*
Elgin Community College *C,A*
Highland Community College *C,A*
Illinois Eastern Community
Colleges: Olney Central College
C,A
Illinois Valley Community College
C,A
Joliet Junior College *C,A*
Kishwaukee College *C,A*

Lake Land College *C,A*
Lewis and Clark Community College *A*
Lincoln Land Community College *C,A*
Moraine Valley Community College *C,A*
Morton College *C,A*
Parkland College *A*
Prairie State College *C,A*
Rend Lake College *C,A*
Richland Community College *C*
Rock Valley College *A*
Shawnee Community College *C,A*
Southern Illinois University at Carbondale *A*
Spoon River College *A*
State Community College *C*
Triton College *C,A*
Waubonsee Community College *C,A*

Indiana

Indiana Vocational Technical College
    Central Indiana *C,A*
    Columbus *A*
    Eastcentral *C,A*
    Kokomo *C,A*
    Lafayette *C,A*
    Northcentral *C,A*
    Northeast *C,A*
    Northwest *C,A*
    Southcentral *C,A*
    Southeast *C,A*
    Southwest *C,A*
    Wabash Valley *C,A*
    Whitewater *A*
Oakland City College *C,A*
Vincennes University *A*

Iowa

Des Moines Area Community College *A*
Hawkeye Institute of Technology *A*
Iowa Central Community College *A*
Iowa Lakes Community College *C,A*
Iowa Western Community College *C,A*
Kirkwood Community College *A*
North Iowa Area Community College *A*
Northwest Iowa Technical College *C,A*
Scott Community College *A*
Southeastern Community College: North Campus *A*
Southwestern Community College *C,A*

Kansas

Butler County Community College *C,A*
Central College *A*
Coffeyville Community College *A*
Cowley County Community College *C,A*
Dodge City Community College *C,A*
Hutchinson Community College *A*
Kansas City Kansas Community College *A*
Neosho County Community College *C,A*
Pittsburg State University *C*
Pratt Community College *C,A*

Kentucky

Eastern Kentucky University *B*
St. Catharine College *A*

Louisiana

Grambling State University *A,B*

Maine

Central Maine Technical College *C,A*
Eastern Maine Technical College *A*
Southern Maine Technical College *A*

Maryland

Catonsville Community College *A*
Montgomery College: Rockville Campus *C*

Massachusetts

Franklin Institute of Boston *A*
Massachusetts Bay Community College *A*
Mount Wachusett Community College *C,A*
Springfield Technical Community College *A*

Michigan

Alpena Community College *C*
Delta College *C,A*
Glen Oaks Community College *C*
Grand Rapids Community College *C,A*
Henry Ford Community College *A*
Kellogg Community College *C,A*
Kirtland Community College *C,A*
Lansing Community College *A*
Macomb Community College *C,A*
Mid Michigan Community College *C,A*
Montcalm Community College *C,A*
Northern Michigan University *C,A*
Northwestern Michigan College *A*
Oakland Community College *C*
Southwestern Michigan College *C,A*

Minnesota

Alexandria Technical College *C*
Inver Hills Community College *A*
Willmar Technical College *C*

Mississippi

Copiah-Lincoln Community College *C*
East Central Community College *C*
Hinds Community College *C*
Holmes Community College *C*
Jones County Junior College *C*
Mississippi Delta Community College *C*
Mississippi Gulf Coast Community College
    Jackson County Campus *A*
    Jefferson Davis Campus *C*
    Perkinston *C,A*
Northeast Mississippi Community College *C*
Southwest Mississippi Community College *C*

Missouri

East Central College *C,A*
Jefferson College *C*
North Central Missouri College *A*
Ranken Technical College *A*
State Fair Community College *C*

Montana

Dawson Community College *C*
Fort Peck Community College *C,A*
Miles Community College *C,A*
Northern Montana College *C,A,B*

Nebraska

Central Community College *C,A*
Metropolitan Community College *C,A*
Northeast Community College *A*
Southeast Community College
    Lincoln Campus *C,A*
    Milford Campus *A*
Western Nebraska Community College
    Scottsbluff Campus *C,A*
    Sidney Campus *C,A*

Nevada

Community College of Southern Nevada *C,A*
Northern Nevada Community College *A*
Truckee Meadows Community College *C,A*
Western Nevada Community College *C,A*

New Hampshire

New Hampshire Technical College
    Laconia *A*
    Manchester *C,A*
    Nashua *A*
    Stratham *C,A*

New Jersey

Brookdale Community College *A*

New Mexico

Albuquerque Technical-Vocational Institute *C*
Clovis Community College *C,A*
Dona Ana Branch Community College of New Mexico State University *C,A*
Eastern New Mexico University: Roswell Campus *A*
New Mexico Junior College *C,A*
New Mexico State University *C,A*
Northern New Mexico Community College *C,A*
San Juan College *C,A*
Western New Mexico University *C,A*

New York

Columbia-Greene Community College *A*
Corning Community College *C,A*
Fulton-Montgomery Community College *C,A*
Hudson Valley Community College *A*
State University of New York
    College of Agriculture and Technology at Morrisville *C,A*
    College of Technology at Alfred *A*
    College of Technology at Canton *C*
    College of Technology at Delhi *C,A*
    College of Technology at Farmingdale *C,A*

North Carolina

Alamance Community College *C,A*
Anson Community College *C*
Asheville Buncombe Technical Community College *C*
Beaufort County Community College *A*
Bladen Community College *C*
Blue Ridge Community College *C*
Brunswick Community College *C*

Caldwell Community College and Technical Institute *C*
Cape Fear Community College *C*
Carteret Community College *C*
Catawba Valley Community College *C,A*
Central Piedmont Community College *A*
Cleveland Community College *C*
Coastal Carolina Community College *C*
College of the Albemarle *C*
Craven Community College *C*
Davidson County Community College *C*
Durham Technical Community College *C*
Edgecombe Community College *C*
Fayetteville Technical Community College *A*
Forsyth Technical Community College *A*
Gaston College *C,A*
Guilford Technical Community College *C,A*
Haywood Community College *C*
Isothermal Community College *C*
James Sprunt Community College *C*
Johnston Community College *C*
Martin Community College *A*
Mitchell Community College *C*
Montgomery Community College *C*
Pitt Community College *C*
Richmond Community College *C*
Roanoke-Chowan Community College *C*
Robeson Community College *C*
Sandhills Community College *C*
Southwestern Community College *C*
Stanly Community College *C*
Surry Community College *C,A*
Vance-Granville Community College *C*
Wake Technical Community College *C*
Wayne Community College *A*
Western Piedmont Community College *C*
Wilkes Community College *A*
Wilson Technical Community College *C*

North Dakota

Bismarck State College *C*
North Dakota State College of Science *C,A*
University of North Dakota
    Lake Region *C,A*
    Williston *C,A*

Ohio

Cincinnati Technical College *A*
Columbus State Community College *A*
Hocking Technical College *A*
Northwestern College *C,A*
Owens Technical College: Toledo *C,A*
Sinclair Community College *C,A*
Terra Technical College *C,A*
University of Cincinnati: Raymond Walters College *A*
Washington State Community College *A*

Oklahoma

Oklahoma State University Technical Branch: Okmulgee *A*

Oregon

Central Oregon Community College
C,A
Chemeketa Community College A
Clackamas Community College C,A
Lane Community College A
Linn-Benton Community College
C,A
Portland Community College C,A
Rogue Community College C,A
Southwestern Oregon Community
College A
Treasure Valley Community College
C,A
Umpqua Community College C,A

Pennsylvania

Community College of Beaver
County C,A
Community College of
Philadelphia A
Johnson Technical Institute A
Lehigh County Community College
C,A
Luzerne County Community
College A
Montgomery County Community
College A
National Education Center: Vale
Tech Campus C
Pennsylvania College of
Technology C
Reading Area Community
College A

Puerto Rico

Huertas Junior College C

Rhode Island

New England Institute of
Technology A

South Carolina

Aiken Technical College C,A
Bob Jones University C,A
Florence-Darlington Technical
College A
Greenville Technical College A
Horry-Georgetown Technical
College A
Midlands Technical College C
Sumter Area Technical College C
Technical College of the
Lowcountry A
Trident Technical College C
Williamsburg Technical College C

South Dakota

Mitchell Vocational Technical
Institute C,A
Western Dakota Vocational
Technical Institute C,A

Tennessee

Austin Peay State University A
Chattanooga State Technical
Community College C,A
Northeast State Technical
Community College C,A
Pellissippi State Technical
Community College A

Texas

Alvin Community College C,A
Amarillo College C,A
Angelina College A
Austin Community College A
Bee County College C,A
Brazosport College C,A
Brookhaven College A
Central Texas College A
Cisco Junior College C

College of the Mainland C
Cooke County College A
Del Mar College C,A
Eastfield College C,A
Houston Community College C
Howard College C,A
Laredo Junior College C
Lee College A
Midland College A
North Harris Montgomery
Community College District C,A
Odessa College C,A
Ranger Junior College C,A
St. Philip's College A
South Plains College C,A
Tarrant County Junior College C,A
Temple Junior College A
Texarkana College C
Texas Southmost College A
Texas State Technical College
Amarillo C
Harlingen C
Sweetwater C
Waco C,A
Vernon Regional Junior College A
Wharton County Junior College C

Utah

College of Eastern Utah C
Dixie College C
Utah Valley Community College
C,A
Weber State University A

Virginia

Blue Ridge Community College C
John Tyler Community College C
Northern Virginia Community
College C,A
Patrick Henry Community
College C
Paul D. Camp Community
College C
Piedmont Virginia Community
College C
Southside Virginia Community
College C
Southwest Virginia Community
College C
Tidewater Community College C

Washington

Big Bend Community College A
Clark College A
Columbia Basin College C,A
Everett Community College A
Grays Harbor College A
Green River Community College A
Lower Columbia College A
Peninsula College A
Shoreline Community College A
Skagit Valley College C,A
South Puget Sound Community
College C,A
Spokane Community College A
Walla Walla College C,A,B
Walla Walla Community College
C,A
Yakima Valley Community College
C,A

Wisconsin

Fox Valley Technical College C
Madison Area Technical College A
Mid-State Technical College C
Moraine Park Technical College C
Northeast Wisconsin Technical
College A
Western Wisconsin Technical
College C
Wisconsin Indianhead Technical
College C

Wyoming

Casper College C,A
Central Wyoming College C,A
Laramie County Community
College C,A
Western Wyoming Community
College C,A

American Samoa, Caroline Islands, Guam, Marianas, Virgin Islands

Guam Community College C
Micronesian Occupational College
C,A

Automotive technology

Alabama

Bessemer State Technical College A
Community College of the Air
Force A
John C. Calhoun State Community
College C,A
John M. Patterson State Technical
College C
Reid State Technical College C
Shelton State Community
College C
Walker State Technical College C
Wallace State Community College
at Hanceville C

Alaska

University of Alaska Anchorage
C,A

Arizona

Arizona Western College A
Eastern Arizona College C,A
Mesa Community College A
Mohave Community College C,A
National Education Center: Arizona
Automotive Institute A
Northland Pioneer College C,A
Pima Community College C,A
Yavapai College C,A

Arkansas

East Arkansas Community
College A
Phillips County Community College
C,A
Westark Community College C,A

California

Allan Hancock College C,A
Bakersfield College A
Barstow College A
Cerritos Community College A
Cerro Coso Community College C
Chabot College A
Chaffey Community College C,A
Citrus College C,A
City College of San Francisco C
College of the Desert A
College of the Redwoods C,A
College of the Sequoias C,A
Columbia College A
Compton Community College A
Cosumnes River College A
Cuesta College A
De Anza College C,A
Don Bosco Technical Institute A
East Los Angeles College A
El Camino College A
Evergreen Valley College A
Fresno City College C,A
Golden West College C,A
Hartnell College A

Imperial Valley College C,A
Kings River Community College A
Lassen College C,A
Long Beach City College C,A
Los Angeles Harbor College C,A
Los Angeles Pierce College C,A
Los Angeles Trade and Technical
College C,A
Merced College A
MiraCosta College C,A
Modesto Junior College A
Monterey Peninsula College C,A
Mount San Jacinto College A
Napa Valley College A
Oxnard College A
Palomar College C,A
Pasadena City College C,A
Porterville College C,A
Rio Hondo College C,A
Saddleback College A
San Diego City College C,A
San Joaquin Delta College C,A
Santa Barbara City College C,A
Santa Monica College A
Santa Rosa Junior College A
Sierra College C,A
Solano Community College A
Southwestern College A
Taft College C,A
Ventura College C,A
Victor Valley College C,A
West Hills Community College A
Yuba College A

Colorado

Arapahoe Community College C,A
Denver Institute of Technology C
Front Range Community College
C,A
Lamar Community College C
Mesa State College C,A
Northeastern Junior College A
Pikes Peak Community College C,A
Pueblo Community College A
Trinidad State Junior College A
University of Southern Colorado B

Connecticut

Greater New Haven State Technical
College A
Mattatuck Community College A

Delaware

Delaware Technical and
Community College
Southern Campus C,A
Stanton/Wilmington
Campus A

Florida

Brevard Community College C
Broward Community College A
Central Florida Community
College C
Daytona Beach Community
College A
Indian River Community College A
Lake City Community College C
Miami-Dade Community College A
New England Institute of
Technology A
Okaloosa-Walton Community
College C,A
Palm Beach Community College A
Pensacola Junior College C
Santa Fe Community College C,A
Seminole Community College C,A
South Florida Community
College C

Georgia

Atlanta Metropolitan College *A*
Augusta Technical Institute *C*
DeKalb College *A*
Floyd College *A*
Gainesville College *A*

Hawaii

University of Hawaii
    Honolulu Community College
        C,A
    Kauai Community College *C,A*
    Leeward Community
        College *A*

Idaho

Boise State University *C*
College of Southern Idaho *C,A*
Idaho State University *A*
Lewis Clark State College *A*
Ricks College *A*

Illinois

Black Hawk College
    East Campus *A*
    Moline *A*
Carl Sandburg College *C,A*
City Colleges of Chicago: Chicago
    City-Wide College *C,A*
College of DuPage *C,A*
College of Lake County *C,A*
Elgin Community College *C,A*
Illinois Central College *A*
Illinois Eastern Community
    Colleges: Olney Central College
    C,A
Illinois Valley Community
    College *A*
John A. Logan College *A*
Joliet Junior College *C,A*
Kishwaukee College *A*
Lake Land College *C,A*
Lewis and Clark Community
    College *A*
Lincoln Land Community College
    C,A
Moraine Valley Community College
    C,A
Morton College *C,A*
Oakton Community College *C,A*
Parkland College *A*
Prairie State College *A*
Rock Valley College *A*
Shawnee Community College *C,A*
Southern Illinois University at
    Carbondale *A*
Spoon River College *A*
State Community College *C*
Triton College *C,A*
Waubonsee Community College
    C,A

Indiana

Indiana State University *B*
ITT Technical Institute: Fort
    Wayne *A*
Oakland City College *C,A*
Vincennes University *A*

Iowa

Des Moines Area Community
    College *A*
Hawkeye Institute of Technology *A*
Indian Hills Community College *A*
Iowa Central Community College *A*
Iowa Western Community
    College *A*
Kirkwood Community College *A*
North Iowa Area Community
    College *C,A*
Northeast Iowa Community
    College *A*

Northwest Iowa Technical
    College *A*
Scott Community College *A*
Southwestern Community
    College *A*

Kansas

Barton County Community College
    C,A
Butler County Community
    College *A*
Central College *A*
Coffeyville Community College *A*
Cowley County Community
    College *A*
Dodge City Community College
    C,A
Fort Scott Community College *A*
Hesston College *A*
Hutchinson Community College *A*
Johnson County Community
    College *A*
Kansas City Kansas Community
    College *A*
McPherson College *A*
Neosho County Community College
    C,A
Pittsburg State University *C,B*
Pratt Community College *C,A*

Kentucky

Jefferson Community College *A*
St. Catharine College *A*

Louisiana

Grambling State University *A,B*

Maine

Central Maine Technical College
    C,A
Eastern Maine Technical College *A*
Southern Maine Technical
    College *A*

Maryland

Allegany Community College *C,A*
Catonsville Community College *C,A*
Harford Community College *C,A*
Montgomery College: Rockville
    Campus *A*

Massachusetts

Franklin Institute of Boston *A*
Massachusetts Bay Community
    College *A*
Middlesex Community College *A*
Mount Wachusett Community
    College *A*
Quinsigamond Community
    College *A*
Springfield Technical Community
    College *A*

Michigan

Alpena Community College *C*
Andrews University *A,B*
Central Michigan University *B*
Charles Stewart Mott Community
    College *A*
Delta College *C,A*
Ferris State University *A*
Glen Oaks Community College *A*
Grand Rapids Community College
    C,A
Henry Ford Community College *A*
Jackson Community College *C,A*
Kalamazoo Valley Community
    College *C,A*
Kellogg Community College *C,A*
Lansing Community College *A*
Macomb Community College *C,A*

Mid Michigan Community College
    C,A
Montcalm Community College *C,A*
Muskegon Community College *A*
Northern Michigan University
    C,A,B
Northwestern Michigan College *A*
Oakland Community College *A*
Southwestern Michigan College *A*
Western Michigan University *B*

Minnesota

Mankato State University *B*
St. Paul Technical College *C*

Mississippi

Copiah-Lincoln Community
    College *A*
Hinds Community College *A*
Jones County Junior College *C*
Northeast Mississippi Community
    College *A*
Southwest Mississippi Community
    College *A*

Missouri

Central Missouri State University *A*
Jefferson College *C,A*
Longview Community College *C,A*
Moberly Area Community
    College *A*
Ranken Technical College *A*
St. Louis Community College at
    Forest Park *A*
Southwest Missouri State
    University *B*
State Fair Community College *C,A*

Montana

Miles Community College *C,A*
Northern Montana College *A,B*

Nebraska

Central Community College *C,A*
Northeast Community College *A*
Southeast Community College
    Lincoln Campus *C,A*
    Milford Campus *A*
Western Nebraska Community
    College
    Scottsbluff Campus *A*
    Sidney Campus *A*

Nevada

Community College of Southern
    Nevada *C,A*
Northern Nevada Community
    College *C,A*
Truckee Meadows Community
    College *A*
Western Nevada Community
    College *C,A*

New Hampshire

New Hampshire Technical College
    Berlin *A*
    Laconia *C,A*
    Manchester *C,A*
    Nashua *A*
    Stratham *A*

New Jersey

Brookdale Community College *A*
Camden County College *A*
County College of Morris *C*
Mercer County Community College
    C,A
Sussex County Community
    College *C*

New Mexico

Clovis Community College *C*
Dona Ana Branch Community
    College of New Mexico State
    University *C,A*
New Mexico Junior College *A*
Western New Mexico University
    C,A

New York

City University of New York: New
    York City Technical College *A*
Columbia-Greene Community
    College *A*
Corning Community College *C,A*
Erie Community College
    North Campus *A*
    South Campus *A*
Fulton-Montgomery Community
    College *A*
Monroe Community College *A*
Onondaga Community College *A*
Rockland Community College *A*
State University of New York
    College of Agriculture and
        Technology at Morrisville *A*
    College of Technology at
        Canton *A*
    College of Technology at
        Delhi *A*
    College of Technology at
        Farmingdale *A*
Suffolk County Community
    College *A*
Westchester Community College *A*

North Carolina

Alamance Community College *A*
Asheville Buncombe Technical
    Community College *C*
Caldwell Community College and
    Technical Institute *C*
Carteret Community College *A*
Catawba Valley Community
    College *A*
Central Carolina Community
    College *A*
Central Piedmont Community
    College *A*
Coastal Carolina Community
    College *A*
College of the Albemarle *C*
Durham Technical Community
    College *C*
Fayetteville Technical Community
    College *A*
Forsyth Technical Community
    College *A*
Gaston College *A*
Guilford Technical Community
    College *C,A*
Isothermal Community College *A*
Mayland Community College *C*
Montgomery Community College *C*
Pamlico Community College *A*
Southwestern Community
    College *A*
Surry Community College *A*
Vance-Granville Community
    College *A*
Wake Technical Community
    College *A*
Wayne Community College *C,A*
Wilson Technical Community
    College *C*

North Dakota

Bismarck State College *C,A*
University of North Dakota
    Lake Region *C,A*
    Williston *A*

Ohio

Cincinnati Technical College *A*
Columbus State Community
College *A*
Cuyahoga Community College:
Western Campus *A*
Hocking Technical College *A*
Muskingum Area Technical
College *A*
Northwestern College *A*
Owens Technical College: Toledo
C,A
Sinclair Community College *C,A*
Stark Technical College *A*
Terra Technical College *C,A*
Washington State Community
College *A*

Oklahoma

Southeastern Oklahoma State
University *B*

Oregon

Central Oregon Community College
C,A
Chemeketa Community College *A*
Clackamas Community College *C,A*
Linn-Benton Community College
C,A
Mount Hood Community College
C,A
Portland Community College *C,A*
Rogue Community College *C,A*
Treasure Valley Community College
C,A
Umpqua Community College *C,A*

Pennsylvania

Community College of Beaver
County *A*
Harrisburg Area Community
College *C,A*
Johnson Technical Institute *A*
Lehigh County Community College
C,A
Montgomery County Community
College *A*
Northampton County Area
Community College *C,A*
Pennsylvania College of
Technology *A*
Reading Area Community
College *A*

Puerto Rico

Electronic Data Processing College
of Puerto Rico *C,A*
Puerto Rico Junior College *A*
University of Puerto Rico: Carolina
Regional College *A*

Rhode Island

New England Institute of
Technology *A*

South Carolina

Aiken Technical College *C,A*
Chesterfield-Marlboro Technical
College *A*
Denmark Technical College *A*
Florence-Darlington Technical
College *A*
Greenville Technical College *A*
Midlands Technical College *A*
Sumter Area Technical College *A*
Trident Technical College *C*
Williamsburg Technical College *C*

South Dakota

Mitchell Vocational Technical
Institute *C,A*

Western Dakota Vocational
Technical Institute *C,A*

Tennessee

Austin Peay State University *A*
Chattanooga State Technical
Community College *C*
Nashville State Technical
Institute *A*
Northeast State Technical
Community College *A*
State Technical Institute at
Memphis *A*

Texas

Angelina College *A*
Austin Community College *C,A*
Brazosport College *C,A*
Brookhaven College *A*
Central Texas College *A*
Cisco Junior College *A*
Cooke County College *A*
Del Mar College *C,A*
Eastfield College *C,A*
El Paso Community College *C,A*
Howard College *A*
Kilgore College *A*
Laredo Junior College *C*
Lee College *A*
LeTourneau University *A*
Midland College *A*
Northeast Texas Community
College *C,A*
Odessa College *C,A*
Panola College *A*
Ranger Junior College *C,A*
St. Philip's College *A*
San Jacinto College: Central
Campus *A*
South Plains College *C,A*
Tarrant County Junior College *C,A*
Temple Junior College *A*
Texas Southmost College *A*
Texas State Technical College
Amarillo *C*
Waco *C,A*
Western Texas College *A*

Utah

College of Eastern Utah *C*
Dixie College *A*
Southern Utah University *A*
Weber State University *A,B*

Vermont

Vermont Technical College *A*

Virginia

Eastern Shore Community
College *C*
John Tyler Community College *A*
New River Community College *C*
Northern Virginia Community
College *C,A*
Paul D. Camp Community
College *C*
Southside Virginia Community
College *C*
Tidewater Community College *C,A*

Washington

Clark College *A*
Columbia Basin College *A*
Everett Community College *A*
Grays Harbor College *A*
Lower Columbia College *A*
Olympic College *C,A*
Peninsula College *A*
Pierce College *A*
Shoreline Community College *C,A*
Skagit Valley College *A*
Spokane Community College *A*

Walla Walla College *A*
Walla Walla Community College
C,A
Wenatchee Valley College *A*
Yakima Valley Community College
C,A

Wisconsin

Chippewa Valley Technical
College *A*
Fox Valley Technical College *A*
Madison Area Technical College *A*
Northeast Wisconsin Technical
College *A*
Waukesha County Technical
College *A*

Wyoming

Casper College *C,A*
Central Wyoming College *A*
Laramie County Community
College *C,A*
Western Wyoming Community
College *A*

American Samoa, Caroline Islands, Guam, Marianas, Virgin Islands

Guam Community College *C,A*

Aviation computer technology

Arizona

Embry-Riddle Aeronautical
University: Prescott Campus *B*

California

Southwestern College *A*

Florida

Embry-Riddle Aeronautical
University *B*
Florida Memorial College *B*

Illinois

Southern Illinois University at
Carbondale *B*

Iowa

Hamilton Technical College *A*

Minnesota

Northwestern Electronics
Institute *A*

Missouri

St. Louis University *B*

Nebraska

University of Nebraska
Kearney *B*
Omaha *C*

New York

College of Aeronautics *A*
Dowling College *B*

North Dakota

Bismarck State College *A*
University of North Dakota *B*

Ohio

Kent State University *B*

Oklahoma

Oklahoma State University *B*

Pennsylvania

Community College of Beaver
County *A*

Texas

Texas State Technical College:
Waco *A*
University of Central Texas *B*

Aviation management

Alabama

Auburn University *B*

Alaska

University of Alaska Anchorage *A*

Arizona

Embry-Riddle Aeronautical
University: Prescott Campus *A,B*

California

California State University: Los
Angeles *B*
Glendale Community College *C*
Golden Gate University *B*
Long Beach City College *A*
National University *B,M*
Ohlone College *C,A*
Palomar College *C,A*
San Jose State University *B*

Colorado

Metropolitan State College of
Denver *B*
Pikes Peak Community College *A*

Connecticut

University of New Haven *B*

Delaware

Delaware State College *B*
Delaware Technical and
Community College: Terry
Campus *A*
Wilmington College *B*

Florida

Broward Community College *A*
Embry-Riddle Aeronautical
University *A,B,M*
Florida Community College at
Jacksonville *A*
Florida Institute of Technology *B*
Florida Memorial College *B*
Gulf Coast Community College *C,A*
Jacksonville University *B*
Lynn University *B*
Miami-Dade Community College *A*
St. Petersburg Junior College *A*

Georgia

Mercer University Atlanta *B*

Illinois

Aero-Space Institute *A,B*
Elgin Community College *A*
Lincoln Land Community
College *A*
Midstate College *C*
Parks College of St. Louis
University *A,B*
Southern Illinois University at
Carbondale *B*

Indiana

Indiana State University *B*
Purdue University *A,B*

Iowa
Iowa Central Community College A
Iowa Lakes Community College A
University of Dubuque B

Kansas
Fort Scott Community College A
Wichita State University B

Kentucky
Northern Kentucky University A

Louisiana
Southern University in
Shreveport A

Maryland
Catonsville Community College A

Massachusetts
Bridgewater State College B
Salem State College B
Wentworth Institute of
Technology B

Michigan
Baker College
Flint B
Muskegon A,B
Eastern Michigan University B
Oakland Community College A

Minnesota
Inver Hills Community College A
Mankato State University B
Northland Community College A
St. Cloud State University B
Willmar Community College A
Winona State University A
Worthington Community College A

Mississippi
Delta State University B

Missouri
Central Missouri State
University M
St. Louis University B

Montana
Rocky Mountain College B

Nebraska
Chadron State College B
University of Nebraska
Kearney B
Omaha B

New Hampshire
Daniel Webster College A,B
New Hampshire Technical College:
Laconia A

New Jersey
Mercer County Community
College A

New Mexico
Dona Ana Branch Community
College of New Mexico State
University A

New York
Dowling College B
Mohawk Valley Community
College A
St. Francis College B

North Carolina
Guilford Technical Community
College C,A

North Dakota
University of North Dakota B

Ohio
Davis Junior College of Business A
Kent State University B
Ohio University B
Sinclair Community College A

Oklahoma
Phillips University B
Rogers State College A
Rose State College A

Pennsylvania
Central Pennsylvania Business
School A
Community College of Beaver
County A
Lehigh County Community
College A
Luzerne County Community
College A
Pittsburgh Institute of
Aeronautics A

Puerto Rico
Inter American University of Puerto
Rico: Metropolitan Campus B

South Carolina
Bob Jones University B

South Dakota
Augustana College B

Tennessee
Chattanooga State Technical
Community College A
Tennessee Wesleyan College B

Texas
Dallas Baptist University B
Mountain View College A
Texas State Technical College:
Amarillo C
University of Central Texas B

Utah
Westminster College of Salt Lake
City B

Virginia
Averett College B
Hampton University B
Northern Virginia Community
College A

Washington
St. Martin's College A
Spokane Community College C,A

West Virginia
College of West Virginia B
Salem-Teikyo University A

Bacteriology

California
Bakersfield College A
California State University:
Fresno B
University of California: Berkeley B

Georgia
Emory University M,D

Idaho
North Idaho College A
University of Idaho B,M,D

Illinois
University of Chicago B,M,D

Indiana
Purdue University D
University of Notre Dame M,D

Maryland
Howard Community College A

Massachusetts
Massachusetts Institute of
Technology B,M,D,W

Missouri
Washington University D

New York
New York University D
Rockefeller University D

North Carolina
University of North Carolina at
Chapel Hill M,D

North Dakota
North Dakota State University B

Ohio
Ohio Wesleyan University B

Pennsylvania
University of Pennsylvania M

Rhode Island
Brown University M,D

Washington
Grays Harbor College A

Wisconsin
University of Wisconsin: Madison
B,M,D

Basic clinical health sciences

Arizona
Arizona State University B

California
Barstow College C
California State University
Bakersfield B
Dominguez Hills B

Colorado
Colorado State University M,D
University of Colorado Health
Sciences Center M,D

Illinois
Illinois Benedictine College B

Iowa
Iowa State University M

Kansas
University of Kansas
Lawrence M,D
Medical Center M,D

Massachusetts
University of Massachusetts at
Lowell B,M

Minnesota
University of Minnesota: Twin
Cities M

New Jersey
Bloomfield College B

New York
City University of New York:
Brooklyn College B
Ithaca College B

Pennsylvania
Gwynedd-Mercy College B
Hahnemann University School of
Health Sciences and
Humanities M
University of Pittsburgh M,D

Rhode Island
University of Rhode Island M

Texas
Texas A&M University B
Texas Tech University Health
Science Center M,D,W
West Texas State University B

West Virginia
West Virginia University M,D

Wisconsin
University of Wisconsin:
Milwaukee B

Behavioral sciences

Alabama
Athens State College B
Mobile College B

Arizona
Prescott College B

California
California Baptist College B
California State Polytechnic
University: Pomona B
California State University
Bakersfield M
Dominguez Hills B,M
Christ College Irvine B
College of Notre Dame B
Imperial Valley College A
John F. Kennedy University B
La Sierra University B
Los Medanos College A
Marymount College A
MiraCosta College A
Mount San Jacinto College A
National University B,M
Pacific Union College B
San Diego City College A
San Jose State University B
University of California: Davis B
University of La Verne B

Colorado
Mesa State College B
Metropolitan State College of
Denver B
United States Air Force
Academy B

Connecticut
Northwestern Connecticut
Community College A
University of Connecticut M,D
Wesleyan University B

Delaware
Wilmington College *B*

Florida
Indian River Community College *A*
Lynn University *B*
New College of the University of
South Florida *B*

Georgia
Armstrong State College *B*
Georgia Southwestern College *B*

Hawaii
Chaminade University of
Honolulu *B*

Idaho
Lewis Clark State College *A*

Illinois
Barat College *B*
East-West University *B*
Illinois Central College *A*
National-Louis University *B*
University of Chicago *B,M,D*

Indiana
Vincennes University *A*

Iowa
Cornell College *B*
Grand View College *B*
Iowa Wesleyan College *B*

Kansas
Butler County Community
College *A*
Central College *A*
Ottawa University *B*
Sterling College *B*

Louisiana
Our Lady of Holy Cross College *B*

Maine
University of Maine
Fort Kent *B*
Machias *B*
Presque Isle *B*

Maryland
Garrett Community College *A*
Harford Community College *A*
Johns Hopkins University *B,M,D*

Massachusetts
Bridgewater State College *M*
Hampshire College *B*
Harvard University *M,D*
Lesley College *B*
Quincy College *A*

Michigan
Andrews University *B*
Grand Valley State University *B*
Macomb Community College *C*
University of Michigan: Dearborn *B*

Minnesota
North Central Bible College *A,B*
St. Mary's College of Minnesota *B*
Willmar Community College *A*

Missouri
Missouri Baptist College *B*

Nebraska
Midland Lutheran College *B*
Union College *B*

New Hampshire
School for Lifelong Learning *B*

New Jersey
Bergen Community College *A*
Drew University *B*
Kean College of New Jersey *M*

New York
City University of New York
Brooklyn College *B*
John Jay College of Criminal
Justice *B*
Concordia College *B*
Cornell University *B,M,D*
Eugene Lang College/New School
for Social Research *B*
Iona College *B*
Jefferson Community College *A*
Mercy College *C,B*
New York Institute of
Technology *B*
New York University *B,M,D,W*
Sarah Lawrence College *B*
State University of New York
College at Plattsburgh *B*
United States Military Academy *B*

North Carolina
Shaw University *B*

North Dakota
Dickinson State University *B*

Ohio
Antioch School for Adult and
Experiential Learning *B*
Cedarville College *B*
Marietta College *B*
Ohio State University: Columbus
Campus *B,M,D*
Ursuline College *B*
Wittenberg University *B*
Wright State University *M*

Oklahoma
Bartlesville Wesleyan College *A,B*
Cameron University *M*
Mid-America Bible College *B*
Northwestern Oklahoma State
University *M*
Oklahoma State University *M,D*

Pennsylvania
La Roche College *B*
Messiah College *B*
Point Park College *B*
Widener University *B*
Wilson College *B*
York College of Pennsylvania *B*

South Carolina
Erskine College *B*

Tennessee
Belmont University *B*
King College *B*
Southern College of Seventh-day
Adventists *B*
Trevecca Nazarene College *B*

Texas
College of the Mainland *A*
Concordia Lutheran College *B*
East Texas Baptist University *B*
Navarro College *A*
Rice University *B*
University of Houston: Clear Lake
B,M
University of Mary Hardin-
Baylor *B*

University of Texas of the Permian
Basin *M*

Utah
Southern Utah University *B*
Westminster College of Salt Lake
City *B*

Vermont
Green Mountain College *B*

Virginia
Averett College *B*

Washington
Northwest College of the
Assemblies of God *B*

Wisconsin
Lakeland College *B*
Mount Mary College *B*

Bible studies

Alabama
Faulkner University *B*
Oakwood College *A*
Samford University *A,B*
Selma University *A*
Southeastern Bible College *A,B,M*

Alaska
Alaska Bible College *C,A*

Arizona
Arizona College of the Bible *C,B*
Grand Canyon University *B*
Southwestern College *C,A,B*

Arkansas
Central Baptist College *B*
Crowley's Ridge College *A*
John Brown University *A,B*
Ouachita Baptist University *B*
Shorter College *C*
Williams Baptist College *A*

California
Azusa Pacific University *M*
Biola University *B,M*
Christian Heritage College *C,B*
Fresno Pacific College *B*
Fuller Theological Seminary *M,D,W*
Graduate Theological Union *M,D*
La Sierra University *A*
LIFE Bible College *A,B*
Master's College *C,B*
Pacific Christian College *B*
Pacific School of Religion *M*
Pacific Union College *A*
Patten College *C,A*
Point Loma Nazarene College *B*
San Jose Christian College *C,A,B*
Simpson College *C,A*
Southern California College *B,M*
University of Judaism *B*
Westminster Theological Seminary
in California *M*

Colorado
Colorado Christian University *B*
Nazarene Bible College *A,B*

District of Columbia
Catholic University of America
M,D

Florida
Florida Baptist Theological College
A,B
Florida Bible College *A,B*
Florida Christian College *B*
Hobe Sound Bible College *C,A*
Southeastern College of the
Assemblies of God *B*
Warner Southern College *A*

Georgia
Covenant College *A,B*
Emory University *M,D,W*
Toccoa Falls College *C,B*
Truett-McConnell College *A*

Idaho
Boise Bible College *C,A,B*
Northwest Nazarene College *A,B*

Illinois
Chicago Theological Seminary
M,D,W
Garrett-Evangelical Theological
Seminary *M,D,W*
Hebrew Theological College *A*
Judson College *B*
KAES College *B*
Lincoln Christian College and
Seminary *C,A,B,M*
Moody Bible Institute *B,M*
North Park College and Theological
Seminary *B*
Olivet Nazarene University *B*
Trinity College *B*
Wheaton College *B*

Indiana
Anderson University *B*
Bethel College *A,B*
Butler University *M*
Grace College *B*
Indiana Wesleyan University *A,B*
Taylor University *B*

Iowa
Emmaus Bible College *C,A,B*
Faith Baptist Bible College and
Theological Seminary *C,A,B,M*
Vennard College *A,B*
Waldorf College *A*

Kansas
Barclay College *B*
Central College *A*
Fort Scott Community College *A*
Friends University *A*
Hesston College *A*
Manhattan Christian College *A,B*
MidAmerica Nazarene College *A*
Tabor College *A*

Kentucky
Asbury College *B*
Clear Creek Baptist Bible College
C,A,B
Kentucky Christian College *B*
Louisville Presbyterian Theological
Seminary *M*
Mid-Continent Baptist Bible College
C,B

Louisiana
New Orleans Baptist Theological
Seminary: School of Christian
Education *C,A*
World Evangelism Bible College
and Seminary *C,B,M*

Maryland
Baltimore Hebrew University
B,M,D

Eastern Christian College *C,A,B*

Massachusetts
Atlantic Union College *A*
Boston College *M*
Boston University *M,D*
Eastern Nazarene College *A*
Gordon College *B*

Michigan
Grace Bible College *A*
Grand Rapids Baptist College and
    Seminary *C,A,B,M*
Great Lakes Christian College *A,B*
Michigan Christian College *B*
Reformed Bible College *C,A*
University of Michigan *B,M,D*
William Tyndale College *C,B*

Minnesota
Bethany Lutheran College *A*
Bethel Theological Seminary *M,W*
Crown College *C,A*
Minnesota Bible College *A*
Northwestern College *C,A,B*
Pillsbury Baptist Bible College *A,B*

Mississippi
Belhaven College *B*
Blue Mountain College *B*
Magnolia Bible College *B*
Northeast Mississippi Community
    College *A*
Southeastern Baptist College *C,A,B*
Wesley College *B*

Missouri
Baptist Bible College *C,M*
Berean College *A,B*
Calvary Bible College *C,A,B,M*
Central Christian College of the
    Bible *C,A*
Covenant Theological Seminary *M*
Evangel College *B*
Hannibal-LaGrange College *A*
Kenrick-Glennon Seminary *M*
Missouri Baptist College *C*
Ozark Christian College *C,A,B*
St. Louis Christian College *C,A*
Southwest Baptist University *B*

Nebraska
Grace College of the Bible *C,A*
Midland Lutheran College *A*
Nebraska Christian College *B*
York College *A*

New Jersey
Drew University *M,D*

New York
Houghton College *A,B*
Kol Yaakov Torah Center *C*
Nyack College *A,B,M*
Union Theological Seminary *M,D*
Yeshiva University *M,D*

North Carolina
Brevard College *A*
East Coast Bible College *A,B*
John Wesley College *C,B*
Livingstone College *B*
Montreat-Anderson College *B*
Piedmont Bible College *B*
Roanoke Bible College *A*
Southeastern Baptist Theological
    Seminary *M,D*

North Dakota
Trinity Bible College *B*

Ohio
Athenaeum of Ohio *M*
Cedarville College *C,B*
Cincinnati Bible College and
    Seminary *M*
Circleville Bible College *B*
Cleveland College of Jewish Studies
    B,M
Lourdes College *A,B*
Malone College *B*
Mount Vernon Nazarene College
    C,A

Oklahoma
Hillsdale Free Will Baptist College
    C,A,B
Mid-America Bible College *A*
Oklahoma Baptist University *B*
Oklahoma Christian University of
    Science and Arts *B,M*
Southwestern College of Christian
    Ministries *B*

Oregon
Eugene Bible College *C,B*
George Fox College *B*
Multnomah School of the Bible
    A,B,M
Northwest Christian College *A*
Warner Pacific College *B*
Western Baptist College *A,B*
Western Conservative Baptist
    Seminary *M*

Pennsylvania
Baptist Bible College of
    Pennsylvania *C*
Eastern College *B*
Evangelical School of Theology *M*
Geneva College *B*
Gratz College *B,M*
La Salle University *A,B*
Lancaster Bible College *C,A,B*
Northeastern Christian Junior
    College *A*
Philadelphia College of Bible *C,B*
Valley Forge Christian College *C,B*

South Carolina
Bob Jones University *A,B,M,D*
Columbia Bible College and
    Seminary *C,A,B,M*
North Greenville College *A*

South Dakota
Sioux Falls College *A*

Tennessee
American Baptist College of ABT
    Seminary *B*
Crichton College *C,B*
David Lipscomb University *B,M*
Free Will Baptist Bible College *B*
Freed-Hardeman University *B*
Hiwassee College *A*
Johnson Bible College *A,B,M*
Milligan College *B*
Tennessee Temple University *A*
Tomlinson College *A,B*
Trevecca Nazarene College *A*
University of the South *M,D*
William Jennings Bryan College *B*

Texas
Abilene Christian University
    A,B,M,D
Arlington Baptist College *B*
Criswell College *C,A,B,M*
Dallas Christian College *B*
Hardin-Simmons University *B*
Howard Payne University *B*
Institute for Christian Studies *B*

Kilgore College *A*
LeTourneau University *B*
Lon Morris College *A*
Lubbock Christian University *B,M*
San Jacinto College: Central
    Campus *A*
Southwestern Assemblies of God
    College *A,B*
Southwestern Christian College *A*

Virginia
Eastern Mennonite College *C,A,B*
Liberty University *B,M*

Washington
Lutheran Bible Institute of Seattle
    A,B
Northwest College of the
    Assemblies of God *C,B*
Puget Sound Christian College *C,B*
Seattle Pacific University *B,M*

West Virginia
Appalachian Bible College *C,A*

Wisconsin
Concordia University Wisconsin *A*
Maranatha Baptist Bible College
    C,B,M

Biblical languages

Arkansas
Harding University *B*
Ouachita Baptist University *B*

California
Christ College Irvine *B*
Fuller Theological Seminary *M,D,W*
Hebrew Union College: Jewish
    Institute of Religion *M,D*
LIFE Bible College *B*

Florida
Florida Christian College *B*

Georgia
Toccoa Falls College *B*

Idaho
Boise Bible College *B*

Illinois
Chicago Theological Seminary
    M,D,W
Concordia University *B*
Garrett-Evangelical Theological
    Seminary *M,D,W*
Hebrew Theological College *B*
Lincoln Christian College and
    Seminary *M*
Wheaton College *B*

Indiana
Grace College *B*

Iowa
Vennard College *B*

Kentucky
Louisville Presbyterian Theological
    Seminary *M*

Maryland
Baltimore Hebrew University
    B,M,D

Massachusetts
Harvard University *D*

Michigan
Andrews University *M*
Calvin Theological Seminary *M*
Concordia College *B*
Grand Rapids Baptist College and
    Seminary *B*

Minnesota
Bethany Lutheran College *A*
Bethel Theological Seminary *M,W*
Concordia College: St. Paul *B*
North Central Bible College *A,B*

Missouri
Calvary Bible College *A,B*
Covenant Theological Seminary *M*
Southwest Baptist University *B*

Nebraska
York College *A*

New York
Yeshiva University *M,D*

North Carolina
Gardner-Webb College *B*

Ohio
Ashland University *M*

Oregon
Multnomah School of the Bible *B*
Northwest Christian College *B*
Western Conservative Baptist
    Seminary *M*

Pennsylvania
Evangelical School of Theology *M*
Gratz College *B,M*
Pittsburgh Theological Seminary
    M,D,W

Tennessee
David Lipscomb University *B*
Tennessee Temple University *B*

Texas
Abilene Christian University *B,M*
Arlington Baptist College *B*
Baylor University *B*
Dallas Christian College *B*
Howard Payne University *B*
Lubbock Christian University *B*

Virginia
Bluefield College *B*

Washington
Walla Walla College *B*

Wisconsin
Concordia University Wisconsin *B*

Bilingual/bicultural education

Alaska
Alaska Pacific University *M*

Arizona
Mesa Community College *A*
Northern Arizona University *M*
Prescott College *B*
University of Arizona *M*
University of Phoenix *M*

California

California State University
    Bakersfield *M*
    Fresno *B*
    Fullerton *M*
    Los Angeles *M*
    Northridge *M*
    Sacramento *B,M*
    San Bernardino *M*
    Stanislaus *B*
Cerritos Community College *A*
De Anza College *C*
Fresno City College *A*
Fresno Pacific College *B,M*
Imperial Valley College *A*
Modesto Junior College *A*
Oxnard College *A*
Pacific Oaks College *C*
Point Loma Nazarene College *M*
San Diego City College *A*
Santa Barbara City College *C*
Southwestern College *A*
University of California
    Irvine *M*
    Santa Cruz *M*
University of the Pacific *B,M*
University of San Francisco *M,D*
University of Southern California *W*
Ventura College *A*
World College West *B*

Colorado

Fort Lewis College *B*
University of Colorado
    Boulder *M,D*
    Denver *M*
University of Northern Colorado *B*

Connecticut

Fairfield University *M*
South Central Community
    College *A*

Florida

Nova University *M*
University of Miami *M*

Illinois

Chicago State University *B*
Loyola University of Chicago *M*
National-Louis University *M*
Northeastern Illinois University *B*
Western Illinois University *B*

Indiana

Indiana University Bloomington
    B,D

Massachusetts

Boston University *B,M,W*
Mount Holyoke College *C*
University of Massachusetts at
    Boston *M*

Michigan

Central Michigan University *B*
Eastern Michigan University *B*
Saginaw Valley State University
    B,M
Wayne State University *B,M*

Minnesota

College of St. Scholastica *C*
Itasca Community College:
    Arrowhead Region *A*
Winona State University *B*

New Jersey

Fairleigh Dickinson University *M*
Kean College of New Jersey *B,M*
Rutgers—The State University of
    New Jersey *M,D*

New Mexico

College of Santa Fe *B,M*
Eastern New Mexico University *B*
New Mexico State University *B,M*
University of New Mexico *B*

New York

Adelphi University *M*
Bank Street College of Education
    M,W
City University of New York
    Brooklyn College *B,M*
    City College *B,M*
    Hunter College *M*
    La Guardia Community
        College *A*
    York College *B*
D'Youville College *B*
Hofstra University *M*
Long Island University
    Brooklyn Campus *M*
    C. W. Post Campus *B,M*
New York University *M,D*
St. John's University *M*
State University of New York
    Albany *M*
    Buffalo *M*
    College at Brockport *M*
    College at Buffalo *M*
    College at New Paltz *B*
    College at Old Westbury *B*

North Dakota

Little Hoop Community College *A*

Ohio

Ohio State University: Columbus
    Campus *B*
University of Findlay *B*

Oregon

Chemeketa Community College *A*
Western Oregon State College *B*

Pennsylvania

Gannon University *B*
Immaculata College *M*
La Salle University *M*
Marywood College *M*

Puerto Rico

Universidad Metropolitana *B*
University of the Sacred Heart *B*

Rhode Island

Rhode Island College *B,M*

Texas

Abilene Christian University *B*
Hardin-Simmons University *B*
Houston Community College *C,A*
Laredo State University *B,M*
McMurry University *B*
Richland College *A*
St. Edward's University *B*
Southwest Texas State
    University *M*
Sul Ross State University *M*
Texas A&I University *B,M,D*
Texas Tech University *M,D*
Texas Wesleyan University *B*
University of Houston *B,M*
University of North Texas *M*
University of St. Thomas *B*
West Texas State University *B*

Utah

Weber State University *B*

Washington

Central Washington University *B*
Heritage College *B,M*

Wisconsin

Marquette University *B*
Mount Mary College *B*

American Samoa, Caroline Islands, Guam, Marianas, Virgin Islands

University of Guam *B*

Biochemistry

Alabama

Auburn University *B,M,D*
Oakwood College *B*
Selma University *A*
University of Alabama
    Birmingham *M,D*
    Tuscaloosa *M,D*
University of South Alabama *D*

Arizona

University of Arizona *B,M,D*

Arkansas

University of Arkansas for Medical
    Sciences *M,D*

California

Azusa Pacific University *B*
Biola University *B*
California Lutheran University *B*
California Polytechnic State
    University: San Luis Obispo *B*
California State University
    Bakersfield *B*
    Fresno *B*
    Fullerton *B,M*
    Hayward *B,M*
    Long Beach *B,M*
    Los Angeles *B,M*
    Northridge *B*
College of Notre Dame *B*
La Sierra University *B*
Loyola Marymount University *B*
Mills College *B*
Mount St. Mary's College *B*
Occidental College *B*
Pacific Union College *B*
Pitzer College *B*
Point Loma Nazarene College *B*
Pomona College *B*
San Francisco State University *B*
San Jose State University *B*
Scripps College *B*
Stanford University *M,D*
University of California
    Berkeley *B,M,D*
    Davis *B,M,D*
    Los Angeles *B,M,D*
    Riverside *B,M,D*
    San Diego *B,D*
    San Francisco *D*
    Santa Barbara *B,M,D*
    Santa Cruz *D*
University of the Pacific *B,M*
University of Southern California *D*
Whittier College *B*

Colorado

Colorado State University *B,M,D*
University of Colorado Health
    Sciences Center *D*

Connecticut

Connecticut College *B*
Quinnipiac College *B*
Sacred Heart University *B*
St. Joseph College *B,M*

Southern Connecticut State
    University *B*
Trinity College *B*
University of Connecticut *M,D*
Wesleyan University *B,M,D*
Yale University *B,M,D*

Delaware

University of Delaware *B*

District of Columbia

Catholic University of America *B,M*
George Washington University *M,D*
Georgetown University *D*
Howard University *M,D*
Trinity College *B*

Florida

Florida Institute of Technology *B,D*
Florida State University *B*
University of Florida *M,D*
University of Miami *B,M,D*
University of Tampa *B*

Georgia

Emory University *M,D*
Medical College of Georgia *M,D*
Oxford College of Emory
    University *A*
Spelman College *B*
University of Georgia *B,M,D*

Hawaii

University of Hawaii at Manoa *M,D*

Idaho

Idaho State University *B*
University of Idaho *M,D*

Illinois

Elmhurst College *B*
Illinois Benedictine College *B*
Illinois Institute of Technology *B*
Judson College *B*
Knox College *B*
Loyola University of Chicago *M,D*
Morton College *A*
Northwestern University *B,M,D*
Rosary College *B*
Rush University *D*
Southern Illinois University at
    Carbondale *B*
University of Chicago *B,M,D*
University of Health Sciences: The
    Chicago Medical School *M,D,W*
University of Illinois
    Chicago *B,M,D*
    Urbana-Champaign *B,M,D*

Indiana

Indiana University Bloomington
    B,M,D
Indiana University—Purdue
    University at Indianapolis
    M,D,W
Purdue University *B,M,D,W*
St. Joseph's College *A,B*
University of Notre Dame *B,D*

Iowa

Iowa State University *B,M,D*
Maharishi International University
    A,B
University of Iowa *B,M,D*

Kansas

Kansas State University *B,M,D*
University of Kansas
    Lawrence *B,M,D*
    Medical Center *M,D*

Kentucky

Asbury College *B*
Centre College *B*
Murray State University *B*
University of Kentucky *M,D*
University of Louisville *D*
Western Kentucky University *B*

Louisiana

Louisiana State University
　Agricultural and Mechanical
　　College *B,M,D*
　Medical Center *M,D*
　Shreveport *B*
Southern University and
　Agricultural and Mechanical
　College *B*
Tulane University *B,M,D*
Xavier University of Louisiana *B*

Maine

Bowdoin College *B*
Colby College *B*
University of Maine *B,M*

Maryland

Columbia Union College *B*
Hood College *B*
Johns Hopkins University *B,D*
Mount St. Mary's College *B*
Uniformed Services University of
　the Health Sciences *M,D*
University of Maryland
　Baltimore *M,D*
　Baltimore County *B,D*
　College Park *B,M,D*
Western Maryland College *B*

Massachusetts

American International College *B*
Boston College *B*
Boston University *M,D*
Brandeis University *B,D*
Clark University *B,M,D*
Elms College *B*
Emmanuel College *B*
Hampshire College *B*
Harvard and Radcliffe Colleges *B*
Harvard University *D*
Massachusetts Institute of
　Technology *B,M,D,W*
Merrimack College *B*
Mount Holyoke College *B*
Northeastern University *B*
Simmons College *B*
Smith College *B*
Suffolk University *B*
Tufts University *D*
University of Massachusetts at
　Amherst *B,M,D*
Wellesley College *B*
Wheaton College *B*
Williams College *B*
Worcester Polytechnic Institute
　B,M,D

Michigan

Alma College *B*
Andrews University *B*
Calvin College *B*
Eastern Michigan University *B*
Hope College *B*
Madonna University *B*
Michigan State University *B,M,D*
Michigan Technological
　University *B*
Northern Michigan University *B*
Oakland University *B*
Olivet College *B*
Saginaw Valley State University *B*
University of Detroit Mercy *B*

University of Michigan
　Ann Arbor *M,D*
　Dearborn *B*
Wayne State University *M,D*

Minnesota

Mankato State University *B*
University of Minnesota
　Duluth *M*
　Twin Cities *B,M,D*

Mississippi

Mississippi State University *B,M*
University of Mississippi Medical
　Center *M,D*

Missouri

St. Louis University *M,D*
University of Missouri
　Columbia *B,M,D*
　Kansas City *M,D*
Washington University *D*

Montana

Montana State University *M,D*
University of Montana *M*

Nebraska

Creighton University *M,D*
University of Nebraska Medical
　Center *M,D*

Nevada

University of Nevada: Reno *B,M,D*

New Hampshire

Dartmouth College *B,M,D*
Plymouth State College of the
　University System of New
　Hampshire *B*
St. Anselm College *B*
University of New Hampshire
　B,M,D

New Jersey

Bloomfield College *B*
College of St. Elizabeth *B*
Fairleigh Dickinson University *B*
Georgian Court College *B*
Montclair State College *B*
Rider College *B*
Rutgers—The State University of
　New Jersey
　　Camden College of Arts and
　　　Sciences *B*
　　Cook College *B*
　　Douglass College *B*
　　Livingston College *B*
　　New Brunswick *M,D*
　　Newark College of Arts and
　　　Sciences *B*
　　Rutgers College *B*
　　University College Camden *B*
　　University College New
　　　Brunswick *B*
St. Peter's College *B*
Stevens Institute of Technology
　B,M,D
Upsala College *B*

New Mexico

New Mexico Institute of Mining
　and Technology *M*
New Mexico State University *B*
University of New Mexico *B*

New York

Adelphi University *B,M*
Albany Medical College *M,D*
Barnard College *B*
Canisius College *B*

City University of New York
　City College *B,M,D*
　College of Staten Island *B*
　Graduate School and
　　University Center *D*
　Hunter College *M*
　Lehman College *B*
　Queens College *B,M*
Clarkson University *D*
Colgate University *B*
College of Mount St. Vincent *B*
Columbia University
　Columbia College *B*
　New York *M,D*
Cornell University *B,M,D*
Elmira College *B*
Hamilton College *B*
Hartwick College *B*
Hofstra University *B*
Iona College *B*
Ithaca College *B*
Keuka College *B*
Manhattan College *B*
Manhattanville College *B*
Nazareth College of Rochester *B*
New York University *B,M,D*
Niagara University *B*
Pace University: Pleasantville/
　Briarcliff *B*
Rensselaer Polytechnic Institute *B*
Rochester Institute of Technology
　A,B
Rockefeller University *D*
Russell Sage College *B*
St. John Fisher College *B*
Sarah Lawrence College *B*
Skidmore College *B*
State University of New York
　Albany *M,D*
　Binghamton *B*
　Buffalo *B,M,D*
　Stony Brook *B*
　College of Environmental
　　Science and Forestry *B,M,D*
　College at Geneseo *B*
　College at New Paltz *B*
　College at Plattsburgh *B*
　Health Science Center at
　　Brooklyn *D*
　Health Science Center at
　　Syracuse *M,D*
United States Military Academy *B*
University of Rochester *B,M,D,W*
Vassar College *B*
Yeshiva University *M,D*

North Carolina

Duke University *D*
East Carolina University *B,D*
North Carolina State University
　B,M,D
Queens College *B*
St. Andrews Presbyterian College *B*
Shaw University *B*
University of North Carolina at
　Chapel Hill *M,D*
Wake Forest University *M,D*

North Dakota

North Dakota State University *M,D*
University of North Dakota *M,D*

Ohio

Ashland University *B*
Bowling Green State University *B*
Case Western Reserve University
　B,M,D
Kent State University *M,D*
Marietta College *B*
Notre Dame College of Ohio *B*
Oberlin College *B*
Ohio Northern University *B*

Ohio State University: Columbus
　Campus *B,M,D*
Ohio University *M,D*
University of Cincinnati
　Cincinnati *B,D*
　Raymond Walters College *A*
University of Dayton *B*
Wittenberg University *B*
Wright State University *M*

Oklahoma

Oklahoma Christian University of
　Science and Arts *B*
Oklahoma City University *B*
Oklahoma State University *B,M,D*
Oral Roberts University *B*
Southeastern Oklahoma State
　University *B*
University of Oklahoma
　Health Sciences Center *M,D*
　Norman *M,D*

Oregon

Lewis and Clark College *B*
Oregon Graduate Institute *M,D*
Oregon Health Sciences University
　M,D
Oregon State University *B,M,D*
Reed College *B*

Pennsylvania

Albright College *B*
Alvernia College *B*
Bryn Mawr College *B,M,D*
Bucknell University *B*
Carnegie Mellon University
　B,M,D,W
Cedar Crest College *B*
Chestnut Hill College *B*
Drexel University *B,M,D*
Duquesne University *B,M*
East Stroudsburg University of
　Pennsylvania *B*
Elizabethtown College *B*
Gettysburg College *B*
Grove City College *B*
Hahnemann University School of
　Health Sciences and Humanities
　M,D
Holy Family College *B*
Immaculata College *B*
Indiana University of
　Pennsylvania *B*
Juniata College *B*
Keystone Junior College *A*
La Salle University *B*
Lafayette College *B*
Lebanon Valley College of
　Pennsylvania *B*
Lehigh University *B,M,D*
Lock Haven University of
　Pennsylvania *B*
Medical College of Pennsylvania
　M,D
Messiah College *B*
Penn State
　Milton S. Hershey Medical
　　Center *M,D*
　University Park Campus
　　B,M,D
Philadelphia College of Pharmacy
　and Science *B*
Philadelphia College of Textiles and
　Science *B*
St. Vincent College *B*
Seton Hill College *B*
Susquehanna University *B*
Swarthmore College *B*
Temple University *B,M,D*
University of Pennsylvania *B,D*
University of Pittsburgh *B,M,D*
University of Scranton *B,M*

Ursinus College *B*
West Chester University of
Pennsylvania *B*
Wilkes University *B*

Puerto Rico

University of Puerto Rico: Medical
Sciences Campus *M,D*

Rhode Island

Brown University *B,M,D*
University of Rhode Island *M,D*

South Carolina

Clemson University *B,M,D*
College of Charleston *B*

South Dakota

Augustana College *B*
University of South Dakota *M,D*

Tennessee

David Lipscomb University *B*
East Tennessee State University
M,D
LeMoyne-Owen College *B*
Meharry Medical College *D*
Rhodes College *B*
Tennessee State University *B*
Tennessee Technological
University *B*
University of Tennessee
Knoxville *B,M,D*
Memphis *M,D*
Vanderbilt University *M,D*

Texas

Abilene Christian University *B*
Baylor College of Dentistry *M*
Baylor University *M*
Rice University *B,M,D*
St. Mary's University *B*
Texas A&M University *B,M,D*
Texas Christian University *B*
Texas Tech University *B,M,D*
Texas Tech University Health
Science Center *M,D,W*
Trinity University *B*
University of Dallas *B*
University of Houston *M,D*
University of North Texas *B*
University of Texas
Arlington *B*
Austin *B,M,D*
Health Science Center at
Houston *M,D,W*
Health Science Center at San
Antonio *M,D*
Southwestern Medical Center
at Dallas Southwestern
Allied Health Sciences
School *M,D*
Western Texas College *A*

Utah

Brigham Young University *B,M,D*
University of Utah *M,D*
Utah State University *M,D*

Vermont

Castleton State College *B*
Marlboro College *B*
Middlebury College *B*
St. Michael's College *B*
University of Vermont *B,M,D*

Virginia

Averett College *B*
Christopher Newport College *B*
Hampden-Sydney College *B*
Old Dominion University *B*
University of Virginia *D*

Virginia Commonwealth University
M,D
Virginia Polytechnic Institute and
State University *B*
Virginia Wesleyan College *B*

Washington

Eastern Washington University *B*
Evergreen State College *B*
Pacific Lutheran University *B*
Seattle University *B*
University of Washington *B,M,D*
Washington State University *B,M,D*
Western Washington University *B*

West Virginia

Bethany College *B*
West Virginia University *M,D*

Wisconsin

Beloit College *B*
Lawrence University *B*
Marian College of Fond du Lac *B*
Marquette University *B*
Medical College of Wisconsin *M,D*
University of Wisconsin
Eau Claire *B*
Madison *B,M,D*
River Falls *B*

Canada

McGill University *B,M,D*

Mexico

Sistema Instituto Tecnologico y de
Estudios Superiores de
Monterrey *B*

Bioengineering and biomedical engineering

Alabama

Community College of the Air
Force *A*
University of Alabama in
Birmingham *M,D*

Arizona

Arizona State University *B,M,D*

Arkansas

Westark Community College *A*

California

California State University
Long Beach *B*
Sacramento *M*
Napa Valley College *A*
University of California
Berkeley *B,M,D*
Davis *M,D*
San Diego *B,M,D*
San Francisco *M,D*
University of Southern California
B,M,D

Connecticut

Greater New Haven State Technical
College *A*
University of Connecticut *M,D*

Delaware

University of Delaware *M,D*

District of Columbia

Catholic University of America *B,M*
George Washington University *M,D*
Georgetown University *M*

Florida

Keiser College of Technology *A*
University of Miami *M,D*

Georgia

Georgia Institute of Technology *M*
Mercer University *B,M*
Savannah Technical Institute *C,A*

Illinois

Northwestern University *B,M,D*
University of Illinois
Chicago *B,M,D*
Urbana-Champaign *B*

Indiana

Purdue University *B,M,D,W*
Rose-Hulman Institute of
Technology *M*

Iowa

Iowa State University *M,D*
University of Iowa *B,M,D*

Kentucky

University of Kentucky *M*

Louisiana

Louisiana Tech University *B,M,D*
Tulane University *B,M,D*

Maryland

College of Notre Dame of
Maryland *B*
Johns Hopkins University *B,M,D*

Massachusetts

Berkshire Community College *A*
Boston University *B,M,D*
Eastern Nazarene College *B*
Harvard and Radcliffe Colleges *B*
Harvard University *D*
Massachusetts Institute of
Technology *B,M,D,W*
Springfield Technical Community
College *A*
Tufts University *M,D*
Western New England College *B*
Worcester Polytechnic Institute
B,M,D

Michigan

Baker College: Flint *A*
Michigan Technological
University *B*
University of Detroit Mercy *M*
University of Michigan *B,M,D*

Minnesota

University of Minnesota: Twin
Cities *M,D*

Mississippi

Mississippi State University *B,M*

Missouri

Washington University *B,M,D*

New Hampshire

Dartmouth College *D*

New Jersey

New Jersey Institute of
Technology *M*
Rutgers—The State University of
New Jersey
College of Engineering *B*
New Brunswick *M,D*
Stevens Institute of Technology *B*

New Mexico

University of New Mexico *B*

New York

Columbia University: School of
Engineering and Applied Science
B,M,D
Manhattan College *B*
Pace University
College of White Plains *B*
Pleasantville/Briarcliff *B*
Rensselaer Polytechnic Institute
B,M,D
Syracuse University *B*
University of Rochester *D*

North Carolina

Duke University *B,D*
University of North Carolina at
Chapel Hill *M,D*

Ohio

Case Western Reserve University
B,M,D
Ohio State University: Columbus
Campus *M,D*
University of Akron *B,M,D*
University of Toledo *M*
Wright State University *B*

Pennsylvania

Carnegie Mellon University
B,M,D,W
Cedar Crest College *B*
Drexel University *M,D*
Penn State University Park Campus
M,D
Temple University *B*
University of Pennsylvania *B,M,D*
University of Pittsburgh *M*

Rhode Island

Brown University *B,M,D*

South Carolina

Clemson University *M,D*

Tennessee

Memphis State University *M*
Vanderbilt University *B,M,D*

Texas

Texas A&M University *B,M,D*
University of Houston *M,D*
University of Texas
Arlington *M,D*
Austin *M,D*
Southwestern Medical Center
at Dallas Southwestern
Allied Health Sciences
School *M,D*

Utah

University of Utah *M,D*

Vermont

University of Vermont *M*

Virginia

Emory and Henry College *B*
University of Virginia *M,D*

Washington

University of Washington *M,D*
Walla Walla College *B*

Wisconsin

Marquette University *B,M,D*
Milwaukee School of Engineering *B*
University of Wisconsin:
Madison *M*

Wyoming

University of Wyoming *B,M*

Canada

McGill University *M,D*

Biological laboratory technology

Alabama

Auburn University
Auburn *B*
Montgomery *B*

California

San Francisco State University *B,M*

Colorado

United States Air Force
Academy *B*

Georgia

Athens Area Technical Institute
C,A

Maryland

Frederick Community College *A*

Massachusetts

Mount Ida College *A*

Michigan

Grand Valley State University *B*

Minnesota

University of Minnesota:
Crookston *A*

New Jersey

Bloomfield College *B*
County College of Morris *A*
Mercer County Community
College *A*
Thomas Edison State College *B*

New York

Jefferson Community College *A*
Manhattan College *B*
Rochester Institute of
Technology *A*
State University of New York
College of Agriculture and
Technology at Cobleskill *A*
College of Agriculture and
Technology at Morrisville *A*
College at Fredonia *B*
College at Plattsburgh *B*
College of Technology at
Alfred *A*
Suffolk County Community College:
Eastern Campus *A*

Ohio

Ohio State University Agricultural
Technical Institute *A*
University of Cincinnati: Raymond
Walters College *A*

Pennsylvania

Clarion University of
Pennsylvania *B*
Slippery Rock University of
Pennsylvania *B*

Rhode Island

University of Rhode Island *B*

Biological and physical sciences

Alabama

Athens State College *B*
Auburn University at
Montgomery *B*
Birmingham-Southern College *B*
Brewer State Junior College *A*
Faulkner University *B*
Oakwood College *B*
Talladega College *B*
University of Alabama in
Birmingham *B,D*
University of Montevallo *B*

Alaska

University of Alaska
Anchorage *B*
Fairbanks *B,M,D*

Arizona

Arizona State University *M*
Arizona Western College *A*
Cochise College *A*
Prescott College *B*

Arkansas

Harding University *B,M*
Henderson State University *B,M*
John Brown University *B*
Mississippi County Community
College *A*
University of the Ozarks *B*

California

Barstow College *A*
California Lutheran University *B*
California State University:
Hayward *B,M*
Cerro Coso Community College
C,A
Chapman University *B*
Christ College Irvine *B*
Claremont McKenna College *B*
College of the Sequoias *A*
Feather River College *A*
Fresno City College *A*
Fresno Pacific College *B*
Glendale Community College *A*
Golden West College *A*
Harvey Mudd College *B*
Imperial Valley College *A*
Laney College *A*
Lassen College *A*
Los Angeles Mission College *A*
Los Medanos College *A*
Master's College *B*
Modesto Junior College *A*
Mount San Jacinto College *A*
Porterville College *A*
San Jose State University *B,M*
Santa Clara University *B*
Santa Monica College *A*
Santa Rosa Junior College *A*
Scripps College *B*
Skyline College *A*
Solano Community College *A*
Southern California College *B*
University of California: Santa
Barbara *B*
University of the Pacific *B*

Washington

Eastern Washington University *B*
Shoreline Community College *A*

Wisconsin

Mount Mary College *B*

West Hills Community College *A*

Colorado

Colorado Mountain College
Alpine Campus *A*
Spring Valley Campus *A*
Timberline Campus *A*
Colorado Northwestern Community
College *A*
Fort Lewis College *B*
Lamar Community College *A*
Regis College of Regis University *B*
Trinidad State Junior College *A*
United States Air Force
Academy *B*
University of Colorado
Boulder *B*
Colorado Springs *M*
Denver *B*
University of Southern Colorado *M*

Connecticut

Albertus Magnus College *B*
Eastern Connecticut State
University *B*
Mitchell College *A*
Sacred Heart University *B*
St. Joseph College *B*
Trinity College *B*
Wesleyan University *B*
Yale University *B*

District of Columbia

American University *B*
Catholic University of America *B*
George Washington University
B,M,D

Florida

Daytona Beach Community
College *A*
Florida Atlantic University *B*
Florida Southern College *B*
Gulf Coast Community College *A*
New College of the University of
South Florida *B*
Pensacola Junior College *A*
Stetson University *B*
University of North Florida *B*
University of South Florida *B*
University of West Florida *B*

Georgia

Atlanta Metropolitan College *A*
Berry College *B*
DeKalb College *A*
Emory University *B*
Mercer University *B*
Morehouse College *B*
Shorter College *B*
Spelman College *B*
University of Georgia *B*
Young Harris College *A*

Idaho

College of Southern Idaho *A*
Lewis Clark State College *B*
Northwest Nazarene College *B*

Illinois

Augustana College *B*
Aurora University *B*
Black Hawk College: East
Campus *A*
Blackburn College *B*
Bradley University *B*
Chicago State University *B*
College of Lake County *A*
Concordia University *B*
Illinois Wesleyan University *B*
Joliet Junior College *A*
Judson College *B*

Lake Forest College *B*
Lincoln Land Community
College *A*
Millikin University *B*
Monmouth College *B*
Moraine Valley Community
College *A*
Morton College *A*
National-Louis University *B*
North Park College and Theological
Seminary *B*
Northwestern University *B*
Oakton Community College *A*
Olivet Nazarene University *B*
Richland Community College *A*
Rockford College *B*
St. Xavier University *B*
Shawnee Community College *A*
Shimer College *B*
Southern Illinois University at
Carbondale *B,M*
Triton College *A*
University of Chicago *B,M*
University of Illinois at Chicago *D*
William Rainey Harper College *A*

Indiana

Butler University *B*
Calumet College of St. Joseph *B*
DePauw University *B*
Earlham College *B*
Goshen College *B*
Indiana State University *B,M*
Indiana University
Bloomington *M*
East *A*
Kokomo *B*
Oakland City College *B*
Purdue University *B,M,D*
St. Meinrad College *B*
Tri-State University *A*
Valparaiso University *A,B*
Vincennes University *A*

Iowa

Briar Cliff College *B*
Coe College *B*
Cornell College *B*
Loras College *B*
Luther College *B*
Morningside College *B*
Northwestern College *B*
Teikyo Marycrest University *B*
University of Northern Iowa *B,M*
William Penn College *B*

Kansas

Benedictine College *B*
Bethel College *B*
Central College *A*
Cloud County Community
College *A*
Coffeyville Community College *A*
Fort Hays State University *B*
Friends University *B*
Highland Community College *A*
Hutchinson Community College *A*
Neosho County Community
College *A*
Ottawa University *B*
Pittsburg State University *B,M*
Pratt Community College *A*
Southwestern College *B*
Sterling College *B*
University of Kansas
Lawrence *B*
Medical Center *M,D*

Kentucky

Brescia College *B*
Campbellsville College *B*
Hazard Community College *A*

Louisiana

Louisiana College *B*
Louisiana State University and
 Agricultural and Mechanical
 College *M*
Tulane University *A*
University of Southwestern
 Louisiana *B*

Maine

Unity College *B*
University of Maine
 Augusta *B*
 Farmington *B*
 Machias *B*
 Orono *B,M*
University of New England *B*
University of Southern Maine *B*

Maryland

Anne Arundel Community
 College *A*
Charles County Community
 College *A*
College of Notre Dame of
 Maryland *B*
Howard Community College *A*
Johns Hopkins University *B,M*
Montgomery College
 Germantown Campus *A*
 Rockville Campus *A*
 Takoma Park Campus *A*
St. Mary's College of Maryland *B*
Salisbury State University *B*
Villa Julie College *B*

Massachusetts

Becker College: Leicester
 Campus *A*
Boston University *B,M,D*
Bradford College *B*
Brandeis University *B*
Bridgewater State College *M*
Eastern Nazarene College *B*
Elms College *B*
Endicott College *A*
Hampshire College *B*
Harvard and Radcliffe Colleges *B*
Lesley College *B*
Massachusetts Institute of
 Technology *B,M,D*
North Adams State College *B*
Northern Essex Community
 College *A*
Quincy College *A*
St. John's Seminary College *B*
Simmons College *B*
Simon's Rock College of Bard *B*
Springfield College *B*
Suffolk University *B*
Tufts University *B,M,D*
University of Massachusetts at
 Amherst *B*
Wellesley College *B*
Western New England College *B*
Westfield State College *B*
Wheaton College *B*
Worcester Polytechnic Institute *B*
Worcester State College *B*

Michigan

Andrews University *M*
Aquinas College *B*
Calvin College *B*
Charles Stewart Mott Community
 College *A*
Concordia College *B*
Eastern Michigan University *B,M*
Grand Valley State University *B*
Hope College *B*
Kalamazoo Valley Community
 College *A*

Lansing Community College *A*
Madonna University *A,B*
Michigan Christian College *A*
Michigan State University *B,M*
Mid Michigan Community
 College *A*
Northern Michigan University *B*
Oakland University *B*
Saginaw Valley State University *B*
University of Michigan
 Ann Arbor *B,M,D*
 Dearborn *B*
 Flint *B*
Wayne State University *D*
Western Michigan University *B*

Minnesota

Augsburg College *B*
Bethany Lutheran College *A*
College of St. Benedict *B*
College of St. Scholastica *B*
Concordia College: St. Paul *B*
Crown College *A*
Gustavus Adolphus College *B*
Northland Community College *A*
Rainy River Community College *A*
St. Cloud State University *B*
St. John's University *B*
St. Mary's College of Minnesota *B*
Southwest State University *B*
University of Minnesota: Twin
 Cities *B*
Winona State University *B*

Mississippi

Blue Mountain College *B*
Holmes Community College *A*
Jones County Junior College *A*
Mary Holmes College *A*
Mississippi State University *B*
Rust College *B*
William Carey College *B*

Missouri

Columbia College *B*
Maryville University *B*
Missouri Baptist College *B*
Missouri Valley College *B*
Missouri Western State College *B*
St. Louis Community College at
 Meramec *A*
St. Louis University *B*
Southeast Missouri State University
 B,M
University of Missouri: Kansas
 City *D*
Washington University *B,M*

Montana

Rocky Mountain College *B*

Nebraska

Chadron State College *B*
Doane College *B*
Hastings College *B*
Midland Lutheran College *B*
Northeast Community College *A*
Peru State College *B*
University of Nebraska—Omaha *B*
Western Nebraska Community
 College: Scottsbluff Campus *A*
York College *A*

Nevada

Community College of Southern
 Nevada *A*
University of Nevada: Las Vegas *M*
Western Nevada Community
 College *A*

New Hampshire

Franklin Pierce College *B*
Keene State College *B*
Plymouth State College of the
 University System of New
 Hampshire *B*
Rivier College *B*
St. Anselm College *B*

New Jersey

Atlantic Community College *A*
Bloomfield College *B*
Camden County College *A*
Drew University *B*
Monmouth College *B*
Ocean County College *A*
Passaic County Community
 College *A*
Rutgers—The State University of
 New Jersey
 Camden College of Arts and
  Sciences *B*
 Cook College *B*
 Douglass College *B*
 Livingston College *B*
 Newark College of Arts and
  Sciences *B*
 Rutgers College *B*
 University College Camden *B*
 University College New
  Brunswick *B*
Stevens Institute of Technology *B*
Stockton State College *B*
Thomas Edison State College *B*
Upsala College *B*
William Paterson College of New
 Jersey *B*

New Mexico

Eastern New Mexico University *B*
New Mexico Institute of Mining
 and Technology *A,B*
Northern New Mexico Community
 College *A*

New York

Adirondack Community College *A*
Alfred University *B*
Bard College *B*
City University of New York
 Baruch College *B*
 Brooklyn College *B*
 Kingsborough Community
  College *A*
 Lehman College *B*
 Queens College *B*
Colgate University *B*
Columbia University *M,D*
Columbia-Greene Community
 College *A*
Concordia College *B*
Cornell University *B*
Dowling College *B*
Dutchess Community College *A*
Elmira College *B*
Erie Community College: South
 Campus *A*
Eugene Lang College/New School
 for Social Research *B*
Fordham University *B*
Fulton-Montgomery Community
 College *A*
Genesee Community College *A*
Herkimer County Community
 College *A*
Hofstra University *B,M*
Houghton College *B*
Hudson Valley Community
 College *A*
Iona College *B*
Jamestown Community College *A*
Jefferson Community College *A*

Le Moyne College *B*
Long Island University:
 Southampton Campus *B*
Manhattan College *B*
Manhattanville College *B*
Marymount College *B*
Mohawk Valley Community
 College *A*
Monroe Community College *A*
Mount St. Mary College *B*
Nazareth College of Rochester *B*
Onondaga Community College *A*
Paul Smith's College *A*
Rensselaer Polytechnic Institute
 B,M,D
Roberts Wesleyan College *B*
Russell Sage College *B*
Sage Junior College of Albany, A
 Division of Russell Sage
 College *A*
St. Bonaventure University *B*
St. Thomas Aquinas College *B*
Sarah Lawrence College *B*
Skidmore College *B*
State University of New York
 Buffalo *M*
 Purchase *B*
 College of Environmental
  Science and Forestry *B,M,D*
 College at Fredonia *B*
 College at Potsdam *B*
 College of Technology at
  Alfred *A*
 College of Technology at
  Canton *A*
 Empire State College *A,B*
Suffolk County Community
 College *A*
Sullivan County Community
 College *A*
Syracuse University *B*
Touro College *B*
Union College *B*
University of Rochester *B,M*
Wells College *B*
Westchester Community College *A*
Yeshiva University *B*

North Carolina

Barton College *B*
Guilford Technical Community
 College *A*
Lees-McRae College *A*
Mars Hill College *B*
Methodist College *B*
St. Andrews Presbyterian College *B*
Southeastern Community College *A*
University of North Carolina at
 Chapel Hill *B*
Wayne Community College *A*

North Dakota

North Dakota State University *B,M*
University of Mary *B*
University of North Dakota
 Grand Forks *B*
 Williston *A*

Ohio

Ashland University *B*
Bluffton College *B*
Bowling Green State University
 Bowling Green *B*
 Firelands College *A*
Capital University *B*
Case Western Reserve University *B*
Cedarville College *B*
College of Mount St. Joseph *B*
Edison State Community College *A*
Heidelberg College *B*
Kent State University *B*
Kenyon College *B*

Lorain County Community College A
Lourdes College A,B
Marietta College B
Muskingum College B
Ohio State University: Columbus Campus B
Ohio University
Eastern Campus A
Zanesville Campus A
Shawnee State University B
Union Institute B,D
University of Akron B
Urbana University B
Ursuline College B
Walsh College B
Wilberforce University B
Wittenberg University B
Wright State University D
Xavier University B

Oklahoma

Eastern Oklahoma State College A
Hillsdale Free Will Baptist College A
Oklahoma City University B
Oklahoma State University B
Redlands Community College A
University of Central Oklahoma B,M

Oregon

Central Oregon Community College A
Clackamas Community College A
Lewis and Clark College B
Marylhurst College B
Oregon State University B,M,D
Portland State University B,M
Reed College B
Rogue Community College A
Southern Oregon State College B
University of Oregon
Eugene B
Robert Donald Clark Honors College B
Warner Pacific College B
Western Oregon State College B

Pennsylvania

Beaver College B
Bucknell University B
Butler County Community College A
California University of Pennsylvania B,M
Carnegie Mellon University B,M,D,W
Chatham College B
Cheyney University of Pennsylvania B
Clarion University of Pennsylvania B
Community College of Beaver County A
Delaware County Community College A
Drexel University B
East Stroudsburg University of Pennsylvania B,M
Edinboro University of Pennsylvania B
Gettysburg College B
Gwynedd-Mercy College A
Holy Family College B
Juniata College B
King's College B
Kutztown University of Pennsylvania B
La Salle University B
Lafayette College B

Lehigh County Community College A
Lehigh University B
Luzerne County Community College A
Lycoming College B
Messiah College B
Muhlenberg College B
Northeastern Christian Junior College A
Penn State University Park Campus B
Philadelphia College of Textiles and Science B
Robert Morris College A
Swarthmore College B
Temple University D
University of Pennsylvania B
University of Pittsburgh
Bradford B
Johnstown B
Pittsburgh B,M,D
Villanova University A,B

Puerto Rico

Bayamon Central University B
Inter American University of Puerto Rico: San German Campus B
Universidad Metropolitana A,B
University of Puerto Rico
Bayamon Technological University College A
Rio Piedras Campus B

Rhode Island

Brown University B
Community College of Rhode Island A

South Carolina

Charleston Southern University B
Erskine College B
Greenville Technical College A
Limestone College B
University of South Carolina
Columbia B,M
Lancaster A
Williamsburg Technical College A

South Dakota

Augustana College B
Black Hills State University B
Dakota State University B
Mount Marty College B
Northern State University B
University of South Dakota B,D

Tennessee

Bethel College B
Christian Brothers University B
Knoxville College B
LeMoyne-Owen College B
Maryville College B
Middle Tennessee State University M
Motlow State Community College A
Roane State Community College A
Shelby State Community College A
Tennessee State University B
Tennessee Wesleyan College B
Trevecca Nazarene College B
University of the South B
University of Tennessee
Chattanooga B
Knoxville D

Texas

Central Texas College A
College of the Mainland A
Collin County Community College District A

Cooke County College A
East Texas State University B,M
Houston Community College A
McMurry University B
Navarro College A
Rice University B
San Antonio College A
Southwest Texas State University B,M
Southwestern University B
Stephen F. Austin State University M
University of Texas
Dallas M
El Paso M
Health Science Center at Houston M,D
Pan American M
Vernon Regional Junior College A
West Texas State University B

Utah

Weber State University B
Westminster College of Salt Lake City B

Vermont

Bennington College B
Castleton State College B
Marlboro College B

Virginia

Christopher Newport College B
College of William and Mary B,M,D
Hampden-Sydney College B
Lord Fairfax Community College A
Lynchburg College B
Mary Baldwin College B
Marymount University B
New River Community College A
Northern Virginia Community College A
Patrick Henry Community College A
Paul D. Camp Community College A
Richard Bland College A
Southside Virginia Community College A
Southwest Virginia Community College A
Sweet Briar College B
Tidewater Community College A
Virginia Commonwealth University B
Virginia Highlands Community College A
Virginia Intermont College B
Virginia Wesleyan College B
Washington and Lee University B
Wytheville Community College A

Washington

Centralia College A
Columbia Basin College A
Eastern Washington University B
Everett Community College A
Evergreen State College B
Grays Harbor College A
Heritage College A,B
Lower Columbia College A
St. Martin's College B
Seattle University B
Skagit Valley College A
Spokane Community College A
Tacoma Community College A
University of Puget Sound B
University of Washington B,M
Walla Walla College B
Washington State University B,D
Western Washington University B

West Virginia

Bethany College B
Glenville State College B
Marshall University B,M
Salem-Teikyo University B
Shepherd College B
University of Charleston B
West Virginia University M,D

Wisconsin

Alverno College B
Carthage College B
Edgewood College B
Lakeland College B
Lawrence University B
Mount Senario College B
Northland College B
Ripon College B
St. Norbert College B
University of Wisconsin
Green Bay B
Madison M
Milwaukee M
River Falls B
Stevens Point B
Superior B
Whitewater B
Viterbo College B

Wyoming

Central Wyoming College A
Eastern Wyoming College A
Laramie County Community College A
Northwest College A
Western Wyoming Community College A

Canada

McGill University B

Biology

Alabama

Alabama Agricultural and Mechanical University B,M
Alabama Southern Community College A
Alabama State University B,M
Athens State College B
Auburn University
Auburn B
Montgomery B
Birmingham-Southern College B
Brewer State Junior College A
Chattahoochee Valley Community College A
Faulkner University B
Huntingdon College B
Jacksonville State University B,M
James H. Faulkner State Community College A
John C. Calhoun State Community College A
Judson College B
Livingston University B
Marion Military Institute A
Miles College B
Mobile College B
Oakwood College B
Samford University B
Selma University A
Shelton State Community College A
Snead State Junior College A
Spring Hill College B
Stillman College B
Talladega College B

Troy State University
   Dothan *B*
   Troy *B,M*
Tuskegee University *B,M*
University of Alabama
   Birmingham *B,M,D*
   Huntsville *B,M*
   Tuscaloosa *B,M,D*
University of Montevallo *B*
University of North Alabama *B*
University of South Alabama *B,M*

Alaska

University of Alaska
   Anchorage *B,M*
   Fairbanks *B,M,D*
   Southeast *B*

Arizona

Arizona State University *B,M*
Arizona Western College *A*
Cochise College *A*
Eastern Arizona College *A*
Glendale Community College *A*
Grand Canyon University *B*
Mohave Community College *A*
Northern Arizona University *B,M,D*
Pima Community College *A*
Prescott College *B*
University of Arizona *B,M,D*
Yavapai College *A*

Arkansas

Arkansas College *B*
Arkansas State University
   Beebe Branch *A*
   Jonesboro *B,M*
Arkansas Tech University *B*
Harding University *B*
Henderson State University *B,M*
Hendrix College *B*
John Brown University *B*
Mississippi County Community
   College *A*
Ouachita Baptist University *B*
Philander Smith College *B*
Phillips County Community
   College *A*
Southern Arkansas University *B*
University of Arkansas
   Little Rock *B*
   Monticello *B*
   Pine Bluff *B*
University of Central Arkansas *B,M*
University of the Ozarks *B*
Westark Community College *A*

California

Allan Hancock College *A*
Azusa Pacific University *B*
Bakersfield College *A*
Barstow College *A*
Biola University *B*
California Baptist College *B*
California Institute of Technology *B*
California Lutheran University *B*
California Polytechnic State
   University: San Luis Obispo *B,M*
California State Polytechnic
   University: Pomona *B,M*

California State University
   Bakersfield *B*
   Chico *B,M*
   Dominguez Hills *B,M*
   Fresno *B,M*
   Fullerton *B,M*
   Hayward *B,M*
   Long Beach *B,M*
   Los Angeles *B,M*
   Northridge *B,M*
   Sacramento *B,M*
   San Bernardino *B,M*
   San Marcos *B*
   Stanislaus *B*
Cerritos Community College *A*
Chabot College *A*
Chaffey Community College *A*
Chapman University *B*
Christ College Irvine *B*
Citrus College *A*
City College of San Francisco *A*
Claremont McKenna College *B*
College of the Desert *A*
College of Notre Dame *B*
Columbia College *A*
Crafton Hills College *A*
De Anza College *A*
Dominican College of San Rafael *B*
El Camino College *A*
Feather River College *A*
Foothill College *A*
Fresno City College *A*
Gavilan Community College *A*
Glendale Community College *A*
Grossmont Community College *A*
Harvey Mudd College *B*
Holy Names College *B*
Humboldt State University *B,M*
Irvine Valley College *A*
Kings River Community College *A*
La Sierra University *B*
Lake Tahoe Community College *A*
Long Beach City College *A*
Los Angeles City College *A*
Los Angeles Mission College *A*
Los Angeles Valley College *A*
Los Medanos College *A*
Loyola Marymount University *B*
Marymount College *A*
Master's College *B*
Mendocino College *A*
Merced College *A*
Mills College *B*
MiraCosta College *A*
Mission College *A*
Modesto Junior College *A*
Moorpark College *A*
Mount St. Mary's College *B*
Mount San Antonio College *A*
Napa Valley College *A*
Occidental College *B,M*
Ohlone College *A*
Orange Coast College *A*
Oxnard College *A*
Pacific Union College *B*
Palomar College *C,A*
Pasadena City College *C,A*
Pepperdine University *B*
Pitzer College *B*
Point Loma Nazarene College *B*
Pomona College *B*
Porterville College *A*
Saddleback College *A*
St. Mary's College of California *B*
San Diego City College *A*
San Diego Mesa College *A*
San Diego State University *B,M*
San Francisco State University *B,M*
San Joaquin Delta College *A*
San Jose City College *A*
San Jose State University *B,M*
Santa Barbara City College *A*

Santa Clara University *B*
Santa Monica College *A*
Santa Rosa Junior College *A*
Scripps College *B*
Sierra College *A*
Skyline College *A*
Solano Community College *A*
Sonoma State University *B,M*
Southern California College *B*
Southwestern College *A*
Stanford University *B,M,D*
University of California
   Berkeley *B*
   Davis *B*
   Irvine *B,M,D*
   Los Angeles *B,M,D*
   Riverside *B,M,D*
   San Diego *B,M,D*
   Santa Barbara *B,M,D*
   Santa Cruz *B,D*
University of La Verne *B*
University of the Pacific *B,M*
University of Redlands *B*
University of San Diego *B*
University of San Francisco *B,M*
University of Southern California
   B,M,D
Ventura College *A*
Victor Valley College *A*
West Hills Community College *A*
West Valley College *A*
Westmont College *B*
Whittier College *B,M*
Yuba College *A*

Colorado

Adams State College *B*
Colorado Christian University *B*
Colorado College *B*
Colorado Mountain College
   Alpine Campus *A*
   Spring Valley Campus *A*
   Timberline Campus *A*
Colorado State University *B*
Community College of Denver *A*
Fort Lewis College *B*
Lamar Community College *A*
Mesa State College *A,B*
Metropolitan State College of
   Denver *B*
Northeastern Junior College *A*
Pikes Peak Community College *A*
Regis College of Regis University *B*
Trinidad State Junior College *A*
United States Air Force
   Academy *B*
University of Colorado
   Boulder *B*
   Colorado Springs *B*
   Denver *B*
University of Denver *B,M,D*
University of Northern Colorado
   B,M
University of Southern Colorado *B*
Western State College of
   Colorado *B*

Connecticut

Albertus Magnus College *B*
Central Connecticut State
   University *B,M*
Connecticut College *B*
Eastern Connecticut State
   University *B*
Fairfield University *B*
Mitchell College *A*
Northwestern Connecticut
   Community College *A*
Quinnipiac College *B*
Sacred Heart University *A,B*
St. Joseph College *B,M*

Southern Connecticut State
   University *B,M*
Trinity College *B*
University of Bridgeport *B,M*
University of Connecticut *B*
University of Hartford *A,B,M*
University of New Haven *A,B*
Wesleyan University *B,M,D*
Western Connecticut State
   University *B*
Yale University *B,M,D*

Delaware

Delaware State College *B,M*
University of Delaware *B,M,D*
Wesley College *B*

District of Columbia

American University *B,M*
Catholic University of America
   B,M,D
Gallaudet University *B*
George Washington University
   B,M,D
Georgetown University *B,M,D*
Trinity College *B*
University of the District of
   Columbia *B*

Florida

Barry University *B,M*
Bethune-Cookman College *B*
Brevard Community College *A*
Daytona Beach Community
   College *A*
Eckerd College *B*
Edison Community College *A*
Florida Agricultural and Mechanical
   University *B*
Florida Atlantic University *B,M*
Florida Institute of Technology
   B,M,D
Florida International University
   B,M,D
Florida Memorial College *B*
Florida Southern College *B*
Florida State University *B,M,D*
Gulf Coast Community College *A*
Indian River Community College *A*
Jacksonville University *B*
Miami-Dade Community College *A*
New College of the University of
   South Florida *B*
Okaloosa-Walton Community
   College *A*
Palm Beach Atlantic College *B*
Palm Beach Community College *A*
Pensacola Junior College *A*
Rollins College *B*
St. Leo College *B*
St. Thomas University *B*
South Florida Community
   College *A*
Stetson University *B*
University of Central Florida *B,M*
University of Miami *B,M,D*
University of North Florida *B*
University of South Florida *B,D*
University of Tampa *A,B*
University of West Florida *B,M*

Georgia

Abraham Baldwin Agricultural
   College *A*
Agnes Scott College *B*
Albany State College *B*
Andrew College *A*
Armstrong State College *B*
Augusta College *B*
Bainbridge College *A*
Berry College *B*
Brenau Women's College *B*

Brewton-Parker College *A*
Brunswick College *A*
Clark Atlanta University *B,M,D*
Clayton State College *A*
Columbus College *B*
Covenant College *B*
Darton College *A*
DeKalb College *A*
East Georgia College *A*
Emory University *B,M,D*
Floyd College *A*
Fort Valley State College *B*
Gainesville College *A*
Georgia College *B,M*
Georgia Institute of Technology *B,M,D*
Georgia Southern University *B,M*
Georgia Southwestern College *B*
Georgia State University *B,M,D*
Gordon College *A*
Kennesaw State College *B*
LaGrange College *B*
Macon College *A*
Mercer University *B*
Middle Georgia College *A*
Morehouse College *B*
Morris Brown College *B*
North Georgia College *B*
Oglethorpe University *B*
Oxford College of Emory University *A*
Paine College *B*
Piedmont College *B*
Reinhardt College *A*
Savannah State College *B*
Shorter College *B*
South Georgia College *A*
Spelman College *B*
Thomas College *A*
University of Georgia *B*
Valdosta State College *B*
Waycross College *A*
Wesleyan College *B*
West Georgia College *B,M*
Young Harris College *A*

Hawaii

Brigham Young University-Hawaii *B*
Chaminade University of Honolulu *B*
University of Hawaii
    Hilo *B*
    Manoa *B*

Idaho

Albertson College *B*
Boise State University *B*
College of Southern Idaho *A*
Idaho State University *B,M,D*
Lewis Clark State College *B*
North Idaho College *A*
Northwest Nazarene College *B*
Ricks College *A*
University of Idaho *B,M*

Illinois

Augustana College *B*
Aurora University *B*
Belleville Area College *A*
Black Hawk College *A*
Blackburn College *B*
Bradley University *B*
Chicago State University *B,M*
City Colleges of Chicago
    Malcolm X College *A*
    Olive-Harvey College *A*
    Wright College *A*
College of St. Francis *B*
Concordia University *B*
De Paul University *B,M*
Elmhurst College *B*

Eureka College *B*
Governors State University *B*
Greenville College *B*
Highland Community College *A*
Illinois Benedictine College *B*
Illinois Central College *A*
Illinois College *B*
Illinois Institute of Technology *B,M,D*
Illinois State University *B,M,D*
Illinois Valley Community College *A*
Illinois Wesleyan University *B*
John A. Logan College *A*
Joliet Junior College *A*
Judson College *B*
Kishwaukee College *A*
Knox College *B*
Lake Forest College *B*
Lake Land College *A*
Lewis University *B*
Lincoln Land Community College *A*
Loyola University of Chicago *B,M*
MacMurray College *B*
McKendree College *B*
Millikin University *B*
Monmouth College *B*
Morton College *A*
National College of Chiropractic *B*
North Central College *B*
North Park College and Theological Seminary *B*
Northeastern Illinois University *B,M*
Northern Illinois University *B,M,D*
Northwestern University *B*
Olivet Nazarene University *B*
Principia College *B*
Quincy College *B*
Rend Lake College *A*
Richland Community College *A*
Rockford College *B*
Roosevelt University *B,M*
Rosary College *B*
St. Xavier University *B*
Sangamon State University *B,M*
Southern Illinois University
    Carbondale *B,M*
    Edwardsville *B,M*
State Community College *A*
Trinity Christian College *B*
Trinity College *B*
Triton College *A*
University of Chicago *B,M,D*
University of Illinois
    Chicago *B,M,D*
    Urbana-Champaign *B,M,D*
Waubonsee Community College *A*
Western Illinois University *B,M*
Wheaton College *B*
William Rainey Harper College *A*

Indiana

Ancilla College *A*
Anderson University *B*
Ball State University *B,M*
Bethel College *A,B*
Butler University *B,M*
Calumet College of St. Joseph *B*
DePauw University *B*
Earlham College *B*
Franklin College *B*
Goshen College *B*
Grace College *B*
Hanover College *B*
Huntington College *B*
Indiana State University *B,M,D*

Indiana University
    Bloomington *B,M*
    East *A*
    Kokomo *B*
    Northwest *B*
    South Bend *B*
    Southeast *B*
Indiana University—Purdue University
    Fort Wayne *B,M*
    Indianapolis *B,M*
Indiana Wesleyan University *B*
Manchester College *B*
Marian College *B*
Martin University *B*
Oakland City College *B*
Purdue University
    Calumet *B,M*
    West Lafayette *B,M,D*
St. Francis College *B*
St. Joseph's College *B*
St. Mary-of-the-Woods College *B*
St. Mary's College *B*
Taylor University *B*
Tri-State University *B*
University of Evansville *B*
University of Indianapolis *B*
University of Notre Dame *B,M,D*
University of Southern Indiana *B*
Valparaiso University *B*
Vincennes University *A*
Wabash College *B*

Iowa

Briar Cliff College *B*
Buena Vista College *B*
Central College *B*
Clarke College *B*
Clinton Community College *A*
Coe College *B*
Cornell College *B*
Dordt College *B*
Drake University *B,M*
Graceland College *B*
Grand View College *B*
Grinnell College *B*
Iowa Lakes Community College *A*
Iowa State University *B*
Iowa Wesleyan College *B*
Kirkwood Community College *A*
Loras College *B*
Luther College *B*
Maharishi International University *A,B*
Morningside College *B*
Mount Mercy College *B*
Muscatine Community College *A*
North Iowa Area Community College *A*
Northwestern College *B*
St. Ambrose University *B*
Scott Community College *A*
Simpson College *B*
Teikyo Marycrest University *B*
Teikyo Westmar University *B*
University of Dubuque *B*
University of Iowa *B,M,D*
University of Northern Iowa *B,M*
Upper Iowa University *B*
Waldorf College *A*
Wartburg College *B*
William Penn College *B*

Kansas

Allen County Community College *A*
Baker University *B*
Barton County Community College *A*
Benedictine College *B*
Bethany College *B*
Bethel College *B*

Butler County Community College *A*
Central College *A*
Cloud County Community College *A*
Coffeyville Community College *A*
Colby Community College *A*
Dodge City Community College *A*
Emporia State University *B,M*
Fort Hays State University *B,M*
Friends University *B*
Highland Community College *A*
Hutchinson Community College *A*
Kansas City Kansas Community College *A*
Kansas Newman College *B*
Kansas State University *B,M,D*
Kansas Wesleyan University *B*
Labette Community College *A*
McPherson College *B*
MidAmerica Nazarene College *B*
Neosho County Community College *A*
Ottawa University *B*
Pittsburg State University *B,M*
Pratt Community College *A*
St. Mary College *B*
Seward County Community College *A*
Southwestern College *B*
Sterling College *B*
Tabor College *B*
University of Kansas *B,M,D*
Washburn University of Topeka *B*
Wichita State University *B,M*

Kentucky

Alice Lloyd College *B*
Asbury College *B*
Bellarmine College *B*
Berea College *B*
Brescia College *B*
Campbellsville College *B*
Centre College *B*
Cumberland College *B*
Eastern Kentucky University *B,M*
Georgetown College *B*
Kentucky State University *B*
Kentucky Wesleyan College *B*
Lindsey Wilson College *A,B*
Morehead State University *B,M*
Murray State University *B,M*
Northern Kentucky University *B*
Pikeville College *B*
St. Catharine College *A*
Spalding University *B*
Sue Bennett College *A*
Thomas More College *B*
Transylvania University *B*
Union College *B*
University of Kentucky *B,M,D*
University of Louisville *B,M*
Western Kentucky University *B,M*

Louisiana

Centenary College of Louisiana *B*
Dillard University *B*
Grambling State University *B,M*
Louisiana College *B*
Louisiana State University in Shreveport *B*
Louisiana Tech University *B,M*
Loyola University *B,M*
McNeese State University *M*
Nicholls State University *B*
Northeast Louisiana University *B,M*
Northwestern State University *B*
Our Lady of Holy Cross College *B*
Southeastern Louisiana University *B,M*

Southern University
New Orleans *B*
Shreveport *A*
Southern University and Agricultural and Mechanical College *B,M*
Tulane University *B,M,D*
University of New Orleans *B,M*
University of Southwestern Louisiana *B,M*
Xavier University of Louisiana *B*

Maine

Bates College *B*
Bowdoin College *B*
Colby College *B*
St. Joseph's College *B*
University of Maine
Farmington *B*
Fort Kent *B*
Machias *B*
Orono *B,M,D*
Presque Isle *B*
University of New England *B*
University of Southern Maine *B*

Maryland

Allegany Community College *A*
Bowie State University *B*
Charles County Community College *A*
College of Notre Dame of Maryland *B*
Columbia Union College *B*
Coppin State College *B*
Frederick Community College *A*
Frostburg State University *B,M*
Goucher College *B*
Hagerstown Junior College *A*
Harford Community College *A*
Hood College *B*
Howard Community College *A*
Johns Hopkins University *B,D*
Loyola College in Maryland *B*
Morgan State University *B*
Mount St. Mary's College *B*
St. Mary's College of Maryland *B*
Salisbury State University *B*
Towson State University *B,M*
University of Maryland
Baltimore County *B,M,D*
College Park *B*
Eastern Shore *B*
Villa Julie College *A*
Washington College *B*
Western Maryland College *B*

Massachusetts

American International College *B*
Amherst College *B*
Anna Maria College for Men and Women *B,M*
Assumption College *B*
Atlantic Union College *B*
Berkshire Community College *A*
Boston College *B,M,D*
Boston University *B,M,D*
Bradford College *B*
Brandeis University *B,D*
Bridgewater State College *B,M*
Bunker Hill Community College *A*
Clark University *B,M,D*
College of the Holy Cross *B*
Curry College *B*
Dean Junior College *A*
Eastern Nazarene College *B*
Elms College *B*
Emmanuel College *B*
Fitchburg State College *B*
Framingham State College *B*
Gordon College *B*
Hampshire College *B*

Harvard and Radcliffe Colleges *B*
Harvard University *D*
Massachusetts Institute of Technology *B,M,D,W*
Merrimack College *B*
Mount Holyoke College *B,M*
Mount Ida College *A*
North Adams State College *B*
Northeastern University *B,M,D*
Northern Essex Community College *A*
Pine Manor College *A*
Regis College *B*
Roxbury Community College *A*
Salem State College *B*
Simmons College *B*
Smith College *B,M,D*
Springfield College *B*
Stonehill College *B*
Suffolk University *B*
Tufts University *B,M,D*
University of Massachusetts
Boston *B,M*
Dartmouth *B,M*
Lowell *B,M*
Wellesley College *B*
Western New England College *B*
Westfield State College *B*
Wheaton College *B*
Williams College *B*
Worcester Polytechnic Institute *B,M*
Worcester State College *B,M*

Michigan

Adrian College *A,B*
Albion College *B*
Alma College *B*
Andrews University *B,M*
Aquinas College *B*
Calvin College *B*
Central Michigan University *B,M*
Concordia College *B*
Eastern Michigan University *B,M*
Ferris State University *B*
Grand Rapids Baptist College and Seminary *B*
Grand Valley State University *B*
Hillsdale College *B*
Hope College *B*
Kalamazoo College *B*
Kellogg Community College *A*
Lake Superior State University *B*
Lansing Community College *A*
Madonna University *A,B*
Marygrove College *B*
Michigan State University *B,M*
Michigan Technological University *B,M,D*
Northern Michigan University *A,B,M*
Oakland University *B,M*
Olivet College *B*
Saginaw Valley State University *B*
St. Mary's College *B*
Siena Heights College *A,B*
Spring Arbor College *B*
University of Detroit Mercy *B,M*
University of Michigan
Ann Arbor *B,M,D.*
Dearborn *B*
Flint *B*
Wayne State University *B,M,D*
West Shore Community College *A*
Western Michigan University *B,M*

Minnesota

Augsburg College *B*
Bemidji State University *B,M*
Bethany Lutheran College *A*
Bethel College *B*
Carleton College *B*

College of St. Benedict *B*
College of St. Catherine: St. Catherine Campus *B*
College of St. Scholastica *B*
Concordia College: Moorhead *B*
Concordia College: St. Paul *B*
Crown College *A*
Gustavus Adolphus College *B*
Hamline University *B*
Macalester College *B*
Mankato State University *B,M*
Moorhead State University *B*
Northland Community College *A*
Pillsbury Baptist Bible College *B*
Rainy River Community College *A*
Rochester Community College *A*
St. Cloud State University *B,M*
St. John's University *B*
St. Mary's College of Minnesota *B*
St. Olaf College *B*
Southwest State University *B*
University of Minnesota
Duluth *B,M*
Morris *B*
Twin Cities *B*
University of St. Thomas *B*
Vermilion Community College *A*
Willmar Community College *A*
Winona State University *B*

Mississippi

Alcorn State University *B*
Belhaven College *B*
Blue Mountain College *B*
Delta State University *B*
Jackson State University *B,M*
Jones County Junior College *A*
Mary Holmes College *A*
Millsaps College *B*
Mississippi College *B*
Mississippi Delta Community College *A*
Mississippi Gulf Coast Community College: Jefferson Davis Campus *A*
Mississippi State University *B,M,D*
Mississippi University for Women *B*
Rust College *B*
Tougaloo College *B*
University of Mississippi *B,M,D*
University of Southern Mississippi *B,M,D*
William Carey College *B*

Missouri

Avila College *B*
Central Methodist College *B*
Central Missouri State University *B,M*
College of the Ozarks *B*
Columbia College *B*
Culver-Stockton College *B*
Drury College *B*
East Central College *A*
Evangel College *B*
Fontbonne College *B*
Hannibal-LaGrange College *B*
Jefferson College *A*
Lincoln University *B*
Lindenwood College *B*
Longview Community College *A*
Maple Woods Community College *A*
Maryville University *B*
Mineral Area College *A*
Missouri Baptist College *B*
Missouri Southern State College *B*
Missouri Valley College *B*
Missouri Western State College *B*
Moberly Area Community College *A*

Northeast Missouri State University *B,M*
Northwest Missouri State University *B,M*
Park College *B*
Penn Valley Community College *A*
Rockhurst College *B*
St. Louis Community College
Florissant Valley *A*
Forest Park *A*
Meramec *A*
St. Louis University *B,M,D*
Southeast Missouri State University *B,M*
Southwest Baptist University *B*
Southwest Missouri State University *B,M*
Stephens College *B*
University of Missouri
Columbia *B,M,D*
Kansas City *B,M*
Rolla *B*
St. Louis *B,M,D*
Washington University *B,M,D*
Webster University *B*
Westminster College *B*
William Jewell College *B*
William Woods College *B*

Montana

Carroll College *B*
College of Great Falls *B*
Eastern Montana College *B*
Little Big Horn College *A*
Miles Community College *A*
Montana State University *B,M,D*
Northern Montana College *A,B*
Rocky Mountain College *B*
University of Montana *B,M*

Nebraska

Central Community College *A*
Chadron State College *B*
College of St. Mary *B*
Concordia College *B*
Creighton University *B,M*
Dana College *B*
Doane College *B*
Hastings College *B*
McCook Community College *A*
Midland Lutheran College *B*
Nebraska Wesleyan University *B*
Northeast Community College *A*
Peru State College *B*
Southeast Community College: Beatrice Campus *A*
Union College *B*
University of Nebraska
Kearney *B*
Lincoln *B*
Omaha *B,M*
Wayne State College *B*
Western Nebraska Community College: Scottsbluff Campus *A*
York College *A*

Nevada

Community College of Southern Nevada *A*
University of Nevada
Las Vegas *B,M,D*
Reno *B,M*
Western Nevada Community College *A*

New Hampshire

Colby-Sawyer College *B*
Dartmouth College *B,M,D*
Franklin Pierce College *B*
Keene State College *B*
New England College *B*
Notre Dame College *B*

Plymouth State College of the
University System of New
Hampshire *B*
Rivier College *B*
St. Anselm College *B*
University of New Hampshire
Durham *B,M*
Manchester *A*

New Jersey

Atlantic Community College *A*
Bergen Community College *A*
Bloomfield College *B*
Brookdale Community College *A*
Burlington County College *A*
Caldwell College *B*
College of St. Elizabeth *B*
County College of Morris *A*
Drew University *B*
Essex County College *A*
Fairleigh Dickinson University *B,M*
Felician College *A,B*
Georgian Court College *B,M*
Glassboro State College *B*
Gloucester County College *A*
Jersey City State College *B*
Kean College of New Jersey *B*
Mercer County Community
College *A*
Monmouth College *B*
Montclair State College *B,M*
Princeton University *B,D*
Ramapo College of New Jersey *B*
Rider College *B*
Rutgers—The State University of
New Jersey
Camden College of Arts and
Sciences *B*
Cook College *B*
Douglass College *B*
Livingston College *B*
New Brunswick *M,D*
Newark College of Arts and
Sciences *B*
Rutgers College *B*
University College Camden *B*
University College New
Brunswick *B*
St. Peter's College *B*
Seton Hall University *B,M*
Stockton State College *B*
Thomas Edison State College *A,B*
Trenton State College *B*
Union County College *A*
Upsala College *B*
William Paterson College of New
Jersey *B,M*

New Mexico

College of Santa Fe *A,B*
Eastern New Mexico University *B*
New Mexico Highlands University
B,M
New Mexico Institute of Mining
and Technology *B,M,D*
New Mexico Junior College *A*
New Mexico State University
B,M,D
University of New Mexico *B,M,D*
Western New Mexico University *B*

New York

Adelphi University *B,M*
Adirondack Community College *A*
Alfred University *B*
Bard College *B*
Barnard College *B*
Canisius College *B*

City University of New York
Brooklyn College *B,M*
City College *B,M*
College of Staten Island *B*
Graduate School and
University Center *D*
Hunter College *B,M*
Kingsborough Community
College *A*
Lehman College *B,M*
Medgar Evers College *A,B*
Queens College *B,M*
Queensborough Community
College *A*
York College *B*
Clarkson University *B,M*
Colgate University *B*
College of Mount St. Vincent *B*
College of New Rochelle *B*
College of St. Rose *B,M*
Columbia University
Columbia College *B*
New York *M,D*
School of General Studies *B*
Community College of the Finger
Lakes *A*
Concordia College *B*
Cornell University *B,M,D*
Daemen College *B*
Dowling College *B*
D'Youville College *B*
Elmira College *B*
Fordham University *B,M,D*
Fulton-Montgomery Community
College *A*
Genesee Community College *A*
Hamilton College *B*
Hartwick College *B*
Herkimer County Community
College *A*
Hobart College *B*
Hofstra University *B,M*
Houghton College *B*
Hudson Valley Community
College *A*
Iona College *B*
Ithaca College *B*
Jamestown Community College *A*
Jefferson Community College *A*
Keuka College *B*
King's College *B*
Le Moyne College *B*
Long Island University
Brooklyn Campus *B,M*
C. W. Post Campus *B,M*
Southampton Campus *B*
Manhattan College *B*
Manhattanville College *B*
Marist College *B*
Marymount College *B*
Marymount Manhattan College *B*
Mercy College *B*
Mohawk Valley Community
College *A*
Molloy College *B*
Mount St. Mary College *B*
Nazareth College of Rochester *B*
New York Institute of
Technology *B*
New York University *B,M,D,W*
Niagara University *B,M*
Pace University
College of White Plains *B*
New York *B*
Pleasantville/Briarcliff *B*
Rensselaer Polytechnic Institute
B,M,D
Roberts Wesleyan College *B*
Rochester Institute of Technology
A,B
Rockefeller University *D*
Russell Sage College *B*

Sage Junior College of Albany, A
Division of Russell Sage
College *A*
St. Bonaventure University *B,M*
St. Francis College *B*
St. John Fisher College *B*
St. John's University *B,M,D*
St. Joseph's College
Brooklyn *B*
Suffolk Campus *B*
St. Lawrence University *B*
Sarah Lawrence College *B*
Siena College *B*
Skidmore College *B*
State University of New York
Albany *B,M,D*
Binghamton *B,M,D*
Buffalo *B,M,D*
Purchase *B*
Stony Brook *B,M*
College of Agriculture and
Technology at Cobleskill *A*
College of Agriculture and
Technology at Morrisville *A*
College at Brockport *B,M*
College at Buffalo *B,M*
College at Cortland *B*
College of Environmental
Science and Forestry *B,M,D*
College at Fredonia *B,M*
College at Geneseo *B,M*
College at New Paltz *B,M*
College at Old Westbury *B*
College at Oneonta *B,M*
College at Plattsburgh *B,M*
College at Potsdam *B*
College of Technology at
Canton *A*
College of Technology at
Delhi *A*
Oswego *B*
Suffolk County Community College
Eastern Campus *A*
Selden *A*
Syracuse University *B,M,D*
Touro College *B*
Ulster County Community
College *A*
Union College *B,M*
University of Rochester *B,M,D,W*
University of the State of New
York: Regents College *B*
Utica College of Syracuse
University *B*
Vassar College *B,M*
Wagner College *B*
Wells College *B*
William Smith College *B*
Yeshiva University *B*

North Carolina

Appalachian State University *B,M*
Barber-Scotia College *B*
Barton College *B*
Belmont Abbey College *B*
Bennett College *B*
Brevard College *A*
Campbell University *B*
Catawba College *B*
Chowan College *A*
Davidson College *B*
Duke University *B*
East Carolina University *B,M*
Elizabeth City State University *B*
Elon College *B*
Fayetteville State University *B*
Gardner-Webb College *B*
Gaston College *A*
Greensboro College *B*
Guilford College *B*
High Point University *B*
Johnson C. Smith University *B*

Lees-McRae College *B*
Lenoir-Rhyne College *B*
Livingstone College *B*
Mars Hill College *B*
Meredith College *B*
Methodist College *A,B*
Mount Olive College *A,B*
North Carolina Agricultural and
Technical State University *B,M*
North Carolina Central University
B,M
North Carolina State University *B*
North Carolina Wesleyan College *B*
Pembroke State University *B*
Pfeiffer College *B*
Queens College *B*
St. Andrews Presbyterian College *B*
St. Augustine's College *B*
Salem College *B*
Shaw University *B*
University of North Carolina
Asheville *B*
Chapel Hill *B,M,D*
Charlotte *B,M*
Greensboro *B,M*
Wilmington *B,M*
Vance-Granville Community
College *A*
Wake Forest University *B,M,D*
Warren Wilson College *B*
Western Carolina University *B,M*
Western Piedmont Community
College *A*
Wingate College *B*
Winston-Salem State University *B*

North Dakota

Bismarck State College *A*
Dickinson State University *B*
Jamestown College *B*
Mayville State University *B*
Minot State University *B*
North Dakota State University *B*
Turtle Mountain Community
College *A*
University of Mary *B*
University of North Dakota
Grand Forks *B,M,D*
Williston *A*
Valley City State University *B*

Ohio

Antioch College *B*
Ashland University *B*
Baldwin-Wallace College *B*
Bluffton College *B*
Bowling Green State University
Bowling Green *B,M,D*
Firelands College *A*
Capital University *B*
Case Western Reserve University
B,M,D
Cedarville College *B*
Central State University *B*
Cleveland State University *B,M,D*
College of Mount St. Joseph *B*
College of Wooster *B*
Defiance College *B*
Denison University *B*
Edison State Community College *A*
Franciscan University of
Steubenville *B*
Heidelberg College *B*
Hiram College *B*
John Carroll University *B,M*
Kent State University *B,M*
Kenyon College *B*
Lake Erie College *B*
Lakeland Community College *A*
Lorain County Community
College *A*
Lourdes College *A,B*

Malone College *B*
Marietta College *B*
Mount Union College *B*
Mount Vernon Nazarene College *B*
Muskingum College *B*
Notre Dame College of Ohio *B*
Oberlin College *B*
Ohio Dominican College *B*
Ohio Northern University *B*
Ohio State University: Columbus
   Campus *B,M,D*
Ohio Wesleyan University *B*
Otterbein College *B*
Shawnee State University *B*
Union Institute *B,D*
University of Akron *B,M*
University of Cincinnati
   Cincinnati *B,M,D*
   Raymond Walters College *A*
University of Dayton *B,M,D*
University of Findlay *B*
University of Rio Grande *C,A,B*
University of Toledo *B,M,D*
Urbana University *B*
Ursuline College *B*
Walsh College *B*
Washington State Community
   College *A*
Wilberforce University *B*
Wilmington College *B*
Wittenberg University *B*
Wright State University
   Dayton *B,M*
   Lake Campus *A*
Xavier University *B*
Youngstown State University *B,M*

Oklahoma

Bacone College *A*
Bartlesville Wesleyan College *A,B*
Cameron University *B*
Connors State College *A*
East Central University *B*
Eastern Oklahoma State College *A*
Hillsdale Free Will Baptist
   College *A*
Langston University *B*
Northeastern State University *B*
Northern Oklahoma College *A*
Northwestern Oklahoma State
   University *B*
Oklahoma Baptist University *B*
Oklahoma Christian University of
   Science and Arts *B*
Oklahoma City University *B*
Oklahoma Panhandle State
   University *B*
Oklahoma State University *B*
Oral Roberts University *B*
Phillips University *B*
Redlands Community College *A*
Rogers State College *A*
Rose State College *A*
St. Gregory's College *A*
Southeastern Oklahoma State
   University *B*
Southwestern Oklahoma State
   University *B*
Tulsa Junior College *A*
University of Central Oklahoma
   B,M
University of Science and Arts of
   Oklahoma *B*
University of Tulsa *B,M,D*

Oregon

Central Oregon Community
   College *A*
Concordia College *B*
Eastern Oregon State College *B*
George Fox College *B*
Lewis and Clark College *B*

Linfield College *B*
Linn-Benton Community College *A*
Northwest Christian College *B*
Oregon State University *B*
Pacific University *B*
Portland Community College *A*
Portland State University *B,M*
Reed College *B*
Southern Oregon State College *B*
Treasure Valley Community
   College *A*
University of Oregon
   Eugene *B,M,D*
   Robert Donald Clark Honors
     College *B*
University of Portland *B*
Warner Pacific College *B*
Western Oregon State College *B*
Willamette University *B*

Pennsylvania

Albright College *B*
Allegheny College *B*
Allentown College of St. Francis de
   Sales *B*
Alvernia College *B*
Beaver College *B*
Bloomsburg University of
   Pennsylvania *B,M*
Bryn Mawr College *B,M,D*
Bucknell University *B,M*
Bucks County Community
   College *A*
Butler County Community
   College *A*
Cabrini College *B*
California University of
   Pennsylvania *B,M*
Carlow College *B*
Carnegie Mellon University
   B,M,D,W
Cedar Crest College *B*
Chatham College *B*
Chestnut Hill College *B*
Cheyney University of
   Pennsylvania *B*
Clarion University of Pennsylvania
   B,M
College Misericordia *B*
Community College of Beaver
   County *A*
Delaware Valley College *B*
Dickinson College *B*
Drexel University *B,M,D*
Duquesne University *B,M*
East Stroudsburg University of
   Pennsylvania *B,M*
Eastern College *B*
Edinboro University of
   Pennsylvania *B,M*
Elizabethtown College *B*
Franklin and Marshall College *B*
Gannon University *B*
Geneva College *B*
Gettysburg College *B*
Grove City College *B*
Gwynedd-Mercy College *B*
Harrisburg Area Community
   College *A*
Haverford College *B*
Holy Family College *B*
Immaculata College *B*
Indiana University of Pennsylvania
   B,M
Juniata College *B*
Keystone Junior College *A*
King's College *B*
Kutztown University of
   Pennsylvania *B,M*
La Roche College *B*
La Salle University *B*
Lafayette College *B*

Lebanon Valley College of
   Pennsylvania *B*
Lehigh University *B,M,D*
Lincoln University *B*
Lock Haven University of
   Pennsylvania *B*
Lycoming College *B*
Mansfield University of
   Pennsylvania *A,B*
Marywood College *B*
Mercyhurst College *B*
Messiah College *B*
Millersville University of
   Pennsylvania *B,M*
Montgomery County Community
   College *A*
Moravian College *B*
Muhlenberg College *B*
Neumann College *B*
Northampton County Area
   Community College *A*
Northeastern Christian Junior
   College *A*
Penn State
   Erie Behrend College *B*
   University Park Campus
     B,M,D
Philadelphia College of Pharmacy
   and Science *B*
Philadelphia College of Textiles and
   Science *B*
Point Park College *B*
Reading Area Community
   College *A*
Rosemont College *B*
St. Francis College *B*
St. Joseph's University *A,B*
St. Vincent College *B*
Seton Hill College *B*
Shippensburg University of
   Pennsylvania *B,M*
Slippery Rock University of
   Pennsylvania *B*
Susquehanna University *B*
Swarthmore College *B*
Temple University *B,M,D*
Thiel College *B*
University of Pennsylvania *B,D*
University of Pittsburgh
   Bradford *B*
   Greensburg *B*
   Johnstown *B*
   Pittsburgh *B,M,D*
University of Scranton *B*
Ursinus College *B*
Villanova University *B,M*
Washington and Jefferson College *B*
Waynesburg College *B*
West Chester University of
   Pennsylvania *B,M*
Westminster College *B*
Widener University *B*
Wilkes University *B*
Wilson College *B*
York College of Pennsylvania *B*

Puerto Rico

Bayamon Central University *B*
Caribbean University *B*
Inter American University of Puerto
   Rico
   Arecibo Campus *B*
   Metropolitan Campus *B*
   San German Campus *B*
Pontifical Catholic University of
   Puerto Rico *B*
Turabo University *A,B*
Universidad Adventista de las
   Antillas *B*
Universidad Metropolitana *B*

University of Puerto Rico
   Aguadilla *A*
   Arecibo Campus *A*
   Bayamon Technological
     University College *A*
   Cayey University College *B*
   Humacao University College *B*
   Mayaguez Campus *B,M*
   Ponce Technological
     University College *A*
   Rio Piedras Campus *B,M,D*
University of the Sacred Heart *B*

Rhode Island

Brown University *B,M,D*
Providence College *B*
Rhode Island College *B,M*
Roger Williams College *B*
Salve Regina University *B*
University of Rhode Island *B*

South Carolina

Benedict College *B*
Bob Jones University *B*
Central Wesleyan College *B*
Charleston Southern University *B*
The Citadel *B*
Claflin College *B*
Clemson University *B*
Coker College *B*
College of Charleston *B*
Columbia College *B*
Converse College *B*
Erskine College *B*
Francis Marion College *B*
Furman University *B*
Lander College *B*
Limestone College *B*
Morris College *B*
Newberry College *B*
North Greenville College *A*
Presbyterian College *B*
South Carolina State College *B*
University of South Carolina
   Aiken *B*
   Coastal Carolina College *B*
   Columbia *B,M,D*
   Spartanburg *B*
Voorhees College *B*
Winthrop University *B,M*
Wofford College *B*

South Dakota

Augustana College *B*
Black Hills State University *B*
Dakota State University *B*
Dakota Wesleyan University *B*
Huron University *B*
Mount Marty College *B*
Northern State University *B*
Sioux Falls College *B*
South Dakota State University *B,M*
University of South Dakota *B,M*

Tennessee

Austin Peay State University *B,M*
Belmont University *B*
Bethel College *B*
Carson-Newman College *B*
Christian Brothers University *B*
Columbia State Community
   College *A*
Crichton College *B*
Cumberland University *A,B*
David Lipscomb University *B*
Dyersburg State Community
   College *A*
East Tennessee State University
   B,M
Fisk University *B,M*
Freed-Hardeman University *B*
Hiwassee College *A*

King College *B*
Knoxville College *B*
Lambuth University *B*
Lane College *B*
LeMoyne-Owen College *B*
Lincoln Memorial University *B*
Martin Methodist College *A*
Maryville College *B*
Memphis State University *B,M,D*
Middle Tennessee State University *B,M*
Milligan College *B*
Motlow State Community College *A*
Rhodes College *B*
Roane State Community College *A*
Southern College of Seventh-day Adventists *B*
Tennessee State University *B,M*
Tennessee Technological University *B,M*
Tennessee Temple University *B*
Tennessee Wesleyan College *B*
Tomlinson College *A*
Trevecca Nazarene College *B*
Tusculum College *B*
Union University *B*
University of the South *B*
University of Tennessee
    Chattanooga *B*
    Knoxville *B*
    Martin *B*
Vanderbilt University *B,M,D*
William Jennings Bryan College *B*

Texas

Abilene Christian University *B,M*
Alvin Community College *A*
Amarillo College *A*
Angelina College *A*
Angelo State University *B,M*
Austin College *B*
Austin Community College *A*
Baylor University *B,M*
Bee County College *A*
Blinn College *A*
Brazosport College *A*
Central Texas College *A*
Collin County Community College District *A*
Corpus Christi State University *B,M*
Dallas Baptist University *B*
Del Mar College *A*
East Texas Baptist University *B*
East Texas State University *B,M*
El Paso Community College *A*
Galveston College *A*
Hardin-Simmons University *B*
Houston Baptist University *B*
Houston Community College *A*
Howard College *A*
Howard Payne University *B*
Huston-Tillotson College *B*
Incarnate Word College *B,M*
Jarvis Christian College *B*
Kilgore College *A*
Lamar University—Beaumont *B,M*
LeTourneau University *B*
Lon Morris College *A*
Lubbock Christian University *B*
McLennan Community College *A*
McMurry University *B*
Midland College *A*
Midwestern State University *B,M*
Navarro College *A*
North Harris Montgomery Community College District *A*
Our Lady of the Lake University of San Antonio *B*
Panola College *A*
Paul Quinn College *B*
Prairie View A&M University *B,M*

Rice University *B,M,D*
St. Edward's University *B*
St. Mary's University *B*
St. Philip's College *A*
Sam Houston State University *B,M*
Schreiner College *A,B*
South Plains College *A*
Southern Methodist University *B,M,D*
Southwest Texas State University *B,M*
Southwestern Adventist College *B*
Southwestern University *B*
Stephen F. Austin State University *B,M*
Sul Ross State University *B,M*
Tarleton State University *B,M*
Texas A&I University *B,M*
Texas A&M University *B,M,D*
Texas Christian University *B,M*
Texas College *B*
Texas Lutheran College *B*
Texas Southern University *B,M*
Texas Southmost College *A*
Texas Tech University *B,M,D*
Texas Wesleyan University *B*
Texas Woman's University *B,M*
Trinity University *B*
Trinity Valley Community College *A*
University of Dallas *B*
University of Houston
    Clear Lake *B,M*
    Downtown *B*
    Houston *B,M,D*
University of Mary Hardin-Baylor *B*
University of North Texas *B,M,D*
University of St. Thomas *B*
University of Texas
    Arlington *B,M*
    Austin *B,M,D*
    Dallas *B,M,D*
    El Paso *B,M*
    Pan American *B,M*
    Permian Basin *B,M*
    San Antonio *B,M*
    Tyler *B*
Victoria College *A*
Wayland Baptist University *B*
West Texas State University *B,M*
Western Texas College *A*
Wharton County Junior College *A*
Wiley College *B*

Utah

Dixie College *A*
Southern Utah University *B*
University of Utah *B,M,D*
Utah State University *B,M,D*
Westminster College of Salt Lake City *B*

Vermont

Bennington College *B*
Castleton State College *B*
Goddard College *B,M*
Johnson State College *B*
Lyndon State College *B*
Marlboro College *B*
Middlebury College *B*
Norwich University *B*
St. Michael's College *B*
Trinity College of Vermont *B*
University of Vermont *B*

Virginia

Averett College *B*
Bluefield College *B*
Bridgewater College *B*
Christopher Newport College *B*

Clinch Valley College of the University of Virginia *B*
College of William and Mary *B,M*
Eastern Mennonite College *B*
Emory and Henry College *B*
Ferrum College *B*
George Mason University *B,M*
Hampden-Sydney College *B*
Hampton University *B,M*
Hollins College *B*
James Madison University *B,M*
Liberty University *B*
Longwood College *B*
Lynchburg College *B*
Mary Baldwin College *B*
Mary Washington College *B*
Marymount University *B*
Mountain Empire Community College *A*
Norfolk State University *B*
Old Dominion University *B,M*
Piedmont Virginia Community College *A*
Radford University *B*
Randolph-Macon College *B*
Randolph-Macon Woman's College *B*
Roanoke College *B*
St. Paul's College *B*
Shenandoah University *B*
Sweet Briar College *B*
University of Richmond *B,M*
University of Virginia *B,M,D*
Virginia Commonwealth University *B,M*
Virginia Intermont College *B*
Virginia Military Institute *B*
Virginia Polytechnic Institute and State University *B,M,D*
Virginia State University *B,M*
Virginia Union University *B*
Virginia Wesleyan College *B*
Washington and Lee University *B*

Washington

Big Bend Community College *A*
Central Washington University *B,M*
Centralia College *A*
Eastern Washington University *B,M*
Everett Community College *A*
Evergreen State College *B*
Gonzaga University *B*
Grays Harbor College *A*
Heritage College *B*
Lower Columbia College *A*
Olympic College *A*
Pacific Lutheran University *B*
St. Martin's College *B*
Seattle Central Community College *A*
Seattle Pacific University *B*
Seattle University *B*
Skagit Valley College *A*
Spokane Community College *A*
Spokane Falls Community College *A*
Tacoma Community College *A*
University of Puget Sound *B*
Walla Walla College *B,M*
Washington State University *B,M*
Wenatchee Valley College *A*
Western Washington University *B,M*
Whitman College *B*
Whitworth College *B*

West Virginia

Alderson-Broaddus College *B*
Bethany College *B*
Bluefield State College *B*
Concord College *B*
Davis and Elkins College *B*

Fairmont State College *B*
Glenville State College *B*
Marshall University *B,M*
Ohio Valley College *B*
Potomac State College of West Virginia University *A*
Salem-Teikyo University *B*
Shepherd College *B*
University of Charleston *B*
West Liberty State College *B*
West Virginia Institute of Technology *B*
West Virginia State College *B*
West Virginia University *B,M,D*
West Virginia Wesleyan College *B*
Wheeling Jesuit College *B*

Wisconsin

Alverno College *B*
Beloit College *B*
Cardinal Stritch College *B*
Carroll College *B*
Carthage College *B*
Concordia University Wisconsin *B*
Edgewood College *B*
Lakeland College *B*
Lawrence University *B*
Marian College of Fond du Lac *B*
Marquette University *B,M,D*
Mount Mary College *B*
Mount Senario College *B*
Northland College *B*
Ripon College *B*
St. Norbert College *B*
Silver Lake College *B*
University of Wisconsin
    Eau Claire *B,M*
    Green Bay *B*
    La Crosse *B,M*
    Milwaukee *B,M,D*
    Oshkosh *B,M*
    Parkside *B*
    Platteville *B*
    River Falls *B,M*
    Stevens Point *B,M*
    Superior *B*
    Whitewater *B*
Viterbo College *B*

Wyoming

Casper College *A*
Central Wyoming College *A*
Eastern Wyoming College *A*
Laramie County Community College *A*
Northwest College *A*
Sheridan College *A*
University of Wyoming *B*
Western Wyoming Community College *A*

American Samoa, Caroline Islands, Guam, Marianas, Virgin Islands

University of Guam *B,M*
University of the Virgin Islands *B*

Canada

McGill University *B,M,D*

Biomedical equipment technology

Alabama

Community College of the Air Force *A*
Gadsden State Community College *A*

Jefferson State Community
  College *A*
John C. Calhoun State Community
  College *A*
Shelton State Community
  College *A*
Shoals Community College *A*
University of Alabama in
  Birmingham *C*

Arizona
Glendale Community College *A*

Arkansas
North Arkansas Community
  College *A*

California
Cerritos Community College *A*
Los Angeles City College *C,A*
Los Angeles Valley College *C*
Napa Valley College *C*
Palomar College *C,A*
Santa Rosa Junior College *A*

Colorado
Community College of Denver *A*

Connecticut
Greater New Haven State Technical
  College *A*

Delaware
Delaware Technical and
  Community College
    Stanton/Wilmington
      Campus *A*
    Terry Campus *A*

Florida
Brevard Community College *A*
Florida Community College at
  Jacksonville *A*
Keiser College of Technology *A*
Pensacola Junior College *A*

Georgia
Augusta Technical Institute *A*
DeKalb Technical Institute *A*
Savannah Technical Institute *C,A*

Illinois
Oakton Community College *A*
Southern Illinois University at
  Carbondale *A*

Indiana
Indiana University—Purdue
  University at Indianapolis *A*
Vincennes University *A*

Iowa
Des Moines Area Community
  College *A*

Kansas
Johnson County Community
  College *A*

Kentucky
Madisonville Community College *A*

Maryland
Howard Community College *A*

Massachusetts
Franklin Institute of Boston *A*
Quinsigamond Community
  College *A*
Springfield Technical Community
  College *A*

Michigan
Baker College: Flint *A*
Lansing Community College *A*
Muskegon Community College *A*
Northern Michigan University *A*
Schoolcraft College *A*

Minnesota
Lakewood Community College *A*

Mississippi
Delta State University *B*

Missouri
St. Louis Community College at
  Forest Park *A*

Nebraska
Central Community College *A*

New Hampshire
New Hampshire Technical College:
  Manchester *C*

New Jersey
County College of Morris *A*
Thomas Edison State College *B*

New York
State University of New York
  College of Technology at
    Farmingdale *A*

North Carolina
Alamance Community College *A*
Caldwell Community College and
  Technical Institute *A*
Stanly Community College *A*

Ohio
Cincinnati Technical College *A*
Kettering College of Medical
  Arts *A*
North Central Technical College *A*
Owens Technical College: Toledo
  C,A

Oklahoma
Tulsa Junior College *A*

Pennsylvania
Community College of
  Philadelphia *A*
Delaware County Community
  College *A*
Edinboro University of
  Pennsylvania *A*
Johnson Technical Institute *A*
Lehigh County Community
  College *A*
Lehigh University *M*
Penn State University Park
  Campus *A*
Pennsylvania College of
  Technology *A*

Tennessee
State Technical Institute at
  Memphis *A*

Texas
St. Philip's College *A*
Texas State Technical College
  Harlingen *A*
  Waco *A*

Washington
North Seattle Community
  College *A*
Spokane Community College *A*
Walla Walla College *B*

Wisconsin
Western Wisconsin Technical
  College *A*

Biomedical science

Arkansas
University of Arkansas for Medical
  Sciences *A*

California
University of California
  Los Angeles *M,D*
  Riverside *B,M,D*

Connecticut
Sacred Heart University *B*
University of Connecticut *D*

Delaware
Delaware Technical and
  Community College: Stanton/
  Wilmington Campus *A*

Florida
Barry University *M*
Florida Institute of Technology *D*

Hawaii
University of Hawaii at Manoa *M,D*

Illinois
Chicago State University *M*

Maryland
Hood College *M*
Johns Hopkins University *B,M,D*

Massachusetts
Berkshire Community College *A*
Boston University *A*
Hampshire College *B*
Northeastern University *M*
Worcester Polytechnic Institute
  B,M,D

Michigan
Grand Valley State University *B*
Oakland University *D*
Western Michigan University *B,M*

Minnesota
St. Cloud State University *B*
University of Minnesota: Twin
  Cities *D*

New Jersey
Bloomfield College *B*
Rutgers—The State University of
  New Jersey
    Cook College *B*
    Douglass College *B*
    Livingston College *B*
    Rutgers College *B*
    University College New
      Brunswick *B*

New York
City University of New York
    Brooklyn College *B*
    Graduate School and
      University Center *D*
Columbia University *M,D*
State University of New York
    Albany *M,D*
    College at Fredonia *B*

North Carolina
Alamance Community College *A*

Ohio
Kent State University *M,D*
Ohio State University: Columbus
  Campus *M,D*
Ohio University *B*
Otterbein College *B*
Wright State University *D*

Oklahoma
University of Oklahoma Health
  Sciences Center *M,D*

Pennsylvania
Carnegie Mellon University
  B,M,D,W
Drexel University *M,D*

South Carolina
University of South Carolina *D*

Tennessee
Meharry Medical College *D*
University of Tennessee: Knoxville
  M,D

Texas
Baylor University *M,D*
Texas A&M University *B*

West Virginia
West Virginia University *D*

Wisconsin
University of Wisconsin:
  Parkside *M*

Biometrics and biostatistics

Alabama
University of Alabama in
  Birmingham *M,D*

California
University of California
  Berkeley *M,D*
  Los Angeles *M,D*
University of Southern California
  M,D

Colorado
University of Colorado Health
  Sciences Center *M,D*

District of Columbia
Georgetown University *M*

Florida
University of Florida *M,D*

Georgia
Emory University *M,D*

Hawaii
University of Hawaii at Manoa *D*

Illinois
Northwestern University *M*

Iowa
University of Iowa *M,D*

Louisiana
Louisiana State University Medical
  Center *M,D*
Tulane University *M,D*

Massachusetts
Boston University *M,D*
Harvard University *D*

Michigan
University of Michigan *M,D*
Western Michigan University *M*

Minnesota
University of Minnesota: Twin
Cities *B,M,D*

Nebraska
York College *A*

New Jersey
Rutgers—The State University of
New Jersey
Cook College *B*
Douglass College *B*
Livingston College *B*
Rutgers College *B*
University College New
Brunswick *B*

New York
Columbia University *M,D*
Cornell University *B,M,D*
State University of New York
Albany *M,D*
Buffalo *M*
College of Environmental
Science and Forestry *B,M,D*

North Carolina
Duke University *M*
University of North Carolina at
Chapel Hill *B,M,D*

Ohio
Case Western Reserve University
M,D
Ohio State University: Columbus
Campus *D*

Oklahoma
University of Oklahoma
Health Sciences Center *M,D*
Norman *M,D*

Pennsylvania
Temple University *M,D*
University of Pittsburgh *M,D*

South Carolina
University of South Carolina *M,D*

Tennessee
Vanderbilt University *M*

Texas
Southwestern Adventist College *B*

Utah
University of Utah *M*

Vermont
University of Vermont *M*

Virginia
Virginia Commonwealth University
M,D

Washington
University of Washington *M,D*

Wisconsin
Medical College of Wisconsin *M*

Biophysics

Alabama
Auburn University *M,D*
University of Alabama in
Birmingham *M,D*

Arizona
University of Arizona *M,D*

Arkansas
University of Arkansas for Medical
Sciences *M,D*

California
California Institute of Technology
D,W
California State University: Los
Angeles *B*
Pacific Union College *B*
Pitzer College *B*
Stanford University *M,D*
University of California
Berkeley *B,M,D*
Davis *M,D*
San Diego *B,D*
San Francisco *D*
University of San Francisco *B*
University of Southern California
M,D

Colorado
University of Colorado Health
Sciences Center *D*

Connecticut
University of Connecticut *B,M,D*
Yale University *B,M,D*

District of Columbia
Georgetown University *B*

Georgia
Emory University *M,D*

Hawaii
University of Hawaii at Manoa *M,D*

Idaho
Idaho State University *B,M*

Illinois
University of Chicago *M,D*
University of Health Sciences: The
Chicago Medical School *M,D*
University of Illinois at Urbana-
Champaign *B,M,D*

Indiana
Indiana University Bloomington
M,D
Indiana University—Purdue
University at Indianapolis
M,D,W
Purdue University *B,M,D*
University of Notre Dame *B,D*
University of Southern Indiana *B*

Iowa
Iowa State University *B,M,D*
University of Iowa *M,D*

Maryland
Johns Hopkins University *B,D*
University of Maryland: Baltimore
M,D

Massachusetts
Boston University *D*
Brandeis University *D*

Hampshire College *B*
Harvard University *D*
Massachusetts Institute of
Technology *B,M,D,W*
Mount Holyoke College *B*
Tufts University *D*

Michigan
Andrews University *B*
University of Michigan *B,D*

Minnesota
University of Minnesota: Twin
Cities *M,D*

Missouri
University of Missouri: Kansas
City *D*
Washington University *D*

Nebraska
Nebraska Wesleyan University *B*

New Jersey
Stevens Institute of Technology *B*

New York
Barnard College *B*
Columbia University
Columbia College *B*
New York *M,D*
Cornell University *M,D*
Rensselaer Polytechnic Institute *B*
Rockefeller University *D*
St. Lawrence University *B*
State University of New York
Albany *D*
Buffalo *B,M,D*
College at New Paltz *B*
College at Plattsburgh *B*
Health Science Center at
Brooklyn *D*
Syracuse University *D*
University of Rochester *M,D,W*
Yeshiva University *M,D*

North Carolina
University of North Carolina at
Chapel Hill *M,D*

Ohio
Case Western Reserve University *D*
Ohio State University: Columbus
Campus *M,D*
Wittenberg University *B*

Oklahoma
Southwestern Oklahoma State
University *B*
University of Oklahoma
Health Sciences Center *M,D*
Norman *M,D*

Oregon
Oregon State University *B,M,D*

Pennsylvania
Bucknell University *B*
Carnegie Mellon University
B,M,D,W
Drexel University *B,M,D*
East Stroudsburg University of
Pennsylvania *B*
Juniata College *B*
Lehigh University *B*
University of Pennsylvania *B,M,D*
University of Pittsburgh *B*
University of Scranton *B*
Ursinus College *B*

Rhode Island
Brown University *B,M,D*
University of Rhode Island *M,D*

South Dakota
Augustana College *B*

Tennessee
University of Tennessee: Memphis
M,D

Texas
Rice University *B,M,D*
Texas A&M University *M*
University of Houston *M,D*
University of Texas
Health Science Center at
Houston *M,D,W*
Southwestern Medical Center
at Dallas Southwestern
Allied Health Sciences
School *M,D*

Utah
University of Utah *M,D*

Vermont
University of Vermont *M,D*

Virginia
Hampden-Sydney College *B*
University of Virginia *M,D*
Virginia Commonwealth University
M,D

Washington
Eastern Washington University *B*
University of Washington *M,D*
Walla Walla College *B*

Wisconsin
Medical College of Wisconsin *M,D*
University of Wisconsin: Madison
M,D

Biotechnology

California
Menlo College *B*
MiraCosta College *C,A*
University of the Pacific *B*

Connecticut
University of Connecticut *M*

Delaware
University of Delaware *B*

Illinois
Illinois Institute of Technology *B*

Indiana
Purdue University: Calumet *B*

Iowa
University of Northern Iowa *B*

Kentucky
Western Kentucky University *B*

Maryland
Montgomery College: Takoma Park
Campus *A*
New Community College of
Baltimore *A*
Villa Julie College *A*

Massachusetts

Becker College: Leicester
Campus *A*
Boston University *M*
Massachusetts Bay Community
College *C,A*
Merrimack College *B*
Middlesex Community College *C*
Northeastern University *A,B*
Tufts University *M*
University of Massachusetts
Boston *M*
Lowell *B,M*
Worcester Polytechnic Institute
B,M

Michigan

Ferris State University *B*

Minnesota

Mankato State University *B*
St. Cloud State University *B*

Missouri

Washington University *M*

Nebraska

Central Community College *A*

New Jersey

Rutgers—The State University of
New Jersey
Cook College *B*
Douglass College *B*
William Paterson College of New
Jersey *B,M*

New York

College of Mount St. Vincent *M*
Manhattan College *B,M*
Niagara University *B*
Onondaga Community College *A*
Rochester Institute of Technology
A,B
State University of New York
College of Agriculture and
Technology at Morrisville *A*
College of Environmental
Science and Forestry *B,M,D*
College of Technology at
Alfred *A*
College of Technology at
Farmingdale *A*

North Carolina

Alamance Community College *A*
East Carolina University *M*
North Carolina State University *D*

North Dakota

North Dakota State University *B*

Oklahoma

University of Tulsa *D*

Oregon

Portland Community College *A*

Pennsylvania

Hahnemann University School of
Health Sciences and Humanities
M,D
Northampton County Area
Community College *A*
Penn State University Park
Campus *A*

Texas

North Harris Montgomery
Community College District *A*
St. Mary's University *B*

University of Texas at San
Antonio *M*

Utah

Brigham Young University *B*

Wisconsin

University of Wisconsin: River
Falls *B*

Botany

Alabama

Alabama Agricultural and
Mechanical University *B*
Auburn University *B,M,D*
Selma University *A*
University of Alabama *B*

Alaska

University of Alaska Fairbanks *M*

Arizona

Arizona State University *B,M,D*
Arizona Western College *A*
Northern Arizona University *B*
Prescott College *B*
University of Arizona *M,D*

Arkansas

Arkansas State University
Beebe Branch *A*
Jonesboro *B*
University of Arkansas *B,M,D*

California

California State Polytechnic
University: Pomona *B*
California State University
Chico *M*
Fresno *B*
Fullerton *B,M*
Long Beach *B*
Stanislaus *B*
Cerritos Community College *A*
Chabot College *A*
Citrus College *A*
El Camino College *A*
Humboldt State University *B*
Modesto Junior College *A*
Napa Valley College *A*
San Diego State University *B*
San Francisco State University *B*
San Joaquin Delta College *A*
San Jose State University *B*
Southwestern College *A*
University of California
Berkeley *B,M,D*
Davis *B,M,D*
Riverside *B,M,D*
Santa Barbara *B,M*
Ventura College *A*
West Hills Community College *A*

Colorado

Colorado State University *B,M,D*

Connecticut

Connecticut College *B,M*
Southern Connecticut State
University *B*
University of Connecticut *M,D*

District of Columbia

George Washington University *M,D*
Howard University *B,M*

Florida

Florida Atlantic University *B,M*
New College of the University of
South Florida *B*
Pensacola Junior College *A*
University of Central Florida *B*
University of Florida *B,M,D*
University of Miami *D*
University of South Florida *B,M*

Georgia

Fort Valley State College *B*
Reinhardt College *A*
University of Georgia *B,M,D*

Hawaii

University of Hawaii at Manoa
B,M,D

Idaho

College of Southern Idaho *A*
Idaho State University *B,M*
North Idaho College *A*
Ricks College *A*
University of Idaho *B,M,D*

Illinois

Eastern Illinois University *B,M*
Joliet Junior College *A*
Rend Lake College *A*
St. Xavier University *B*
Southern Illinois University at
Carbondale *B,M,D*
University of Chicago *B,M,D*

Indiana

Ball State University *B*
Indiana University Bloomington
B,M,D
Purdue University
Calumet *B*
West Lafayette *B,M,D*
Vincennes University *A*

Iowa

Iowa Lakes Community College *A*
Iowa State University *B,M,D*
Kirkwood Community College *A*
North Iowa Area Community
College *A*
University of Iowa *B,M,D*

Kansas

Central College *A*
Coffeyville Community College *A*
Colby Community College *A*
Pratt Community College *A*
University of Kansas *M,D*

Kentucky

University of Kentucky *B*
University of Louisville *B*

Louisiana

Louisiana State University and
Agricultural and Mechanical
College *B,M,D*
Louisiana Tech University *B,M*
McNeese State University *B*
Northeast Louisiana University *B*
Southern University and
Agricultural and Mechanical
College *B*

Maine

University of Maine *B,M,D*

Maryland

Howard Community College *A*
University of Maryland: College
Park *B,M,D*

Massachusetts

Hampshire College *B*
Harvard University *D*
University of Massachusetts at
Amherst *B,M,D*

Michigan

Andrews University *B*
Calvin College *B*
Kellogg Community College *A*
Michigan State University *B,M,D*
Northern Michigan University *B*
University of Michigan *B,M,D*

Minnesota

Gustavus Adolphus College *B*
Northland Community College *A*
Rainy River Community College *A*
University of Minnesota: Twin
Cities *B*
Vermilion Community College *A*
Willmar Community College *A*

Mississippi

Jones County Junior College *A*
Mary Holmes College *A*

Missouri

College of the Ozarks *B*
East Central College *A*
Moberly Area Community
College *A*
Northwest Missouri State
University *B*
Washington University *D*

Montana

University of Montana *B,M,D*

New Hampshire

University of New Hampshire
B,M,D

New Jersey

Rutgers—The State University of
New Jersey
Camden College of Arts and
Sciences *B*
Cook College *B*
Douglass College *B*
Livingston College *B*
New Brunswick *M,D*
Newark College of Arts and
Sciences *B*
Rutgers College *B*
University College New
Brunswick *B*

New Mexico

New Mexico State University *B*
Western New Mexico University *B*

New York

Cornell University *B,M,D*
State University of New York
College of Environmental Science
and Forestry *B,M,D*

North Carolina

Brevard College *A*
Duke University *D*
Mars Hill College *B*
North Carolina State University
B,M
University of North Carolina at
Chapel Hill *M,D*

North Dakota

North Dakota State University
B,M,D

Ohio

Kent State University *B,M,D*
Miami University: Oxford Campus *B,M,D*
Ohio State University: Columbus Campus *B,M,D*
Ohio University *B,M,D*
Ohio Wesleyan University *B*
University of Akron *B*
Wittenberg University *B*

Oklahoma

Connors State College *A*
Northeastern State University *B*
Oklahoma State University *B,M,D*
University of Oklahoma *B,M,D*

Oregon

Central Oregon Community College *A*
Oregon State University *B,M,D*

Pennsylvania

California University of Pennsylvania *B*
Juniata College *B*
Penn State University Park Campus *M,D*

Rhode Island

University of Rhode Island *B,M,D*

South Carolina

Clemson University *M*

South Dakota

South Dakota State University *B*

Tennessee

Martin Methodist College *A*
University of Tennessee: Knoxville *B,M,D*

Texas

Howard College *A*
Jacksonville College *A*
Lon Morris College *A*
South Plains College *A*
Southwest Texas State University *B*
Texas A&M University *B,M,D*
Texas Tech University *B,M,D*
University of Texas
  Austin *B,M,D*
  El Paso *B*
Western Texas College *A*

Utah

Brigham Young University *B,M,D*
Southern Utah University *B*
Weber State University *B*

Vermont

Goddard College *B,M*
Marlboro College *B*
University of Vermont *B,M,D*

Virginia

Averett College *B*
Virginia Polytechnic Institute and State University *M,D*

Washington

Big Bend Community College *A*
Centralia College *A*
Eastern Washington University *B*
Everett Community College *A*
Evergreen State College *B*
Lower Columbia College *A*
Olympic College *A*
Seattle Central Community College *A*
Skagit Valley College *A*

Tacoma Community College *A*
University of Washington *B,M,D*
Washington State University *M,D*

West Virginia

Marshall University *B*
Shepherd College *B*

Wisconsin

University of Wisconsin
  Eau Claire *B*
  Madison *B,M,D*
  Milwaukee *B,M,D*

Wyoming

University of Wyoming *B,M,D*

Business administration and management

Alabama

Alabama Agricultural and Mechanical University *B,M*
Alabama Southern Community College *A*
Alabama State University *B*
Athens State College *B*
Auburn University *B,M,D*
Birmingham-Southern College *B*
Chattahoochee Valley Community College *A*
Draughons Junior College *A*
Enterprise State Junior College *A*
Faulkner University *A,B*
Huntingdon College *B*
Jacksonville State University *B*
Jefferson State Community College *A*
John C. Calhoun State Community College *A*
Lawson State Community College *A*
Livingston University *B*
Miles College *B*
Mobile College *B*
Oakwood College *B*
Samford University *B*
Selma University *A*
Shelton State Community College *A*
Shoals Community College *A*
Snead State Junior College *A*
Spring Hill College *B*
Talladega College *B*
Troy State University
  Dothan *B,M*
  Montgomery *A,B*
  Troy *B*
Tuskegee University *B*
University of Alabama
  Birmingham *M*
  Huntsville *B,M*
  Tuscaloosa *M,D*
University of Montevallo *B*
University of North Alabama *M*
University of South Alabama *B,M*
Walker State Technical College *A*
Wallace State Community College at Hanceville *A*

Alaska

Alaska Pacific University *C,A,B,M*
Sheldon Jackson College *A,B*
University of Alaska
  Anchorage *A,B,M*
  Fairbanks *B,M*
  Southeast *A,B,M*

Arizona

Arizona Western College *A*
Cochise College *A*
DeVry Institute of Technology: Phoenix *B*
Embry-Riddle Aeronautical University: Prescott Campus *A,B*
Glendale Community College *C,A*
Grand Canyon University *B*
Lamson Junior College *A*
Mesa Community College *A*
Mohave Community College *A*
Navajo Community College *A*
Northern Arizona University *B,M*
Pima Community College *C,A*
University of Arizona *B,M,D*
University of Phoenix *B,M*
Western International University *B,M*
Yavapai College *A*

Arkansas

Arkansas State University *B,M*
Arkansas Tech University *B*
Capital City Junior College *A*
Harding University *B*
Henderson State University *B*
John Brown University *B*
Mississippi County Community College *A*
North Arkansas Community College *A*
Philander Smith College *B*
Phillips County Community College *A*
Shorter College *A*
Southern Arkansas Community College *A*
Southern Arkansas University
  Magnolia *B*
  Technical Branch *A*
University of Arkansas
  Fayetteville *B,M,D*
  Little Rock *B,M*
  Monticello *B*
  Pine Bluff *B*
University of Central Arkansas *B,M*
University of the Ozarks *B*
Westark Community College *A*
Williams Baptist College *A*

California

Allan Hancock College *A*
American Armenian International College *A*
Antioch Southern California
  Los Angeles *M*
  Santa Barbara *M*
Armstrong College *A,B,M*
Azusa Pacific University *B,M*
Bakersfield College *A*
Barstow College *C,A*
Biola University *B*
California Baptist College *B*
California Lutheran University *B,M*
California Maritime Academy *B*
California Polytechnic State University: San Luis Obispo *B*
California State Polytechnic University: Pomona *B,M*

California State University
  Bakersfield *B,M*
  Chico *B*
  Dominguez Hills *B,M*
  Fresno *B,M*
  Fullerton *B,M*
  Hayward *B,M*
  Long Beach *B,M*
  Los Angeles *B,M*
  Northridge *B,M*
  Sacramento *B,M*
  San Bernardino *M*
  Stanislaus *B,M*
Cerritos Community College *A*
Cerro Coso Community College *C,A*
Chaffey Community College *A*
Chapman University *B,M*
Christ College Irvine *B*
Christian Heritage College *B*
City College of San Francisco *A*
Coastline Community College *A*
Coleman College *B,M*
College of Notre Dame *B,M*
College of the Sequoias *C*
Columbia College *A*
Cuesta College *A*
De Anza College *C,A*
DeVry Institute of Technology: City of Industry *B*
Dominican College of San Rafael *B*
El Camino College *A*
Evergreen Valley College *C*
Feather River College *C,A*
Foothill College *A*
Fresno City College *A*
Fresno Pacific College *B*
Glendale Community College *C*
Golden Gate University *A,B,M,D,W*
Grossmont Community College *C,A*
Holy Names College *B,M*
Humboldt State University *B,M*
Humphreys College *B*
Imperial Valley College *A*
Irvine Valley College *A*
John F. Kennedy University *B,M*
Kelsey-Jenney College *A*
La Sierra University *B,M*
Lake Tahoe Community College *C,A*
Lassen College *A*
Lincoln University *B,M*
Long Beach City College *C,A*
Los Angeles City College *C,A*
Los Angeles Harbor College *C,A*
Los Angeles Mission College *A*
Los Angeles Pierce College *A*
Los Angeles Trade and Technical College *A*
Loyola Marymount University *B,M*
Master's College *B*
Mendocino College *C,A*
Menlo College *B*
Merced College *A*
MiraCosta College *C,A*
Mission College *A*
Modesto Junior College *A*
Moorpark College *A*
Mount St. Mary's College *B*
Mount San Antonio College *C,A*
Mount San Jacinto College *A*
National Hispanic University *M*
National University *B,M*
Naval Postgraduate School *M*
Ohlone College *C,A*
Oxnard College *C*
Pacific Christian College *B*
Pacific Union College *B*
Pepperdine University *B,M*

Phillips Junior College
 Condie Campus *A*
 Fresno Campus *C,A*
Porterville College *A*
Saddleback College *C,A*
St. Mary's College of California
 B,M
San Diego City College *A*
San Diego Mesa College *A*
San Diego State University *B*
San Francisco State University *B,M*
San Joaquin Delta College *C,A*
San Jose State University *B,M*
Santa Barbara City College *A*
Santa Clara University *B,M*
Santa Rosa Junior College *A*
Simpson College *B*
Solano Community College *A*
Sonoma State University *B,M*
Southern California College *B*
Southwestern College *A*
Stanford University *M,D*
United States International
 University *B,M,D*
University of California
 Davis *M*
 Irvine *M,D*
 Los Angeles *M,D*
 Riverside *B,M*
University of Judaism *M*
University of La Verne *A,B,M*
University of the Pacific *B*
University of Redlands *B*
University of San Diego *B,M*
University of San Francisco *B,M*
University of Southern California
 B,M,D
Ventura College *A*
West Coast University *B,M*
West Hills Community College *C,A*
West Valley College *C,A*
Whittier College *B*
Woodbury University *B,M*
World College West *B*
Yuba College *A*

Colorado

Adams State College *B*
Arapahoe Community College *C,A*
Colorado State University *B,M*
Denver Technical College *B*
Fort Lewis College *B*
Front Range Community College *A*
Mesa State College *B*
Metropolitan State College of
 Denver *B*
Morgan Community College *A*
National College *B*
Parks Junior College *A*
Regis College of Regis University
 B,M
Trinidad State Junior College *A*
United States Air Force
 Academy *B*
University of Colorado
 Boulder *M,D*
 Colorado Springs *B,M*
 Denver *B,M*
University of Denver *B,M*
University of Northern Colorado *B*
University of Southern Colorado
 B,M
Western State College of
 Colorado *B*

Connecticut

Asnuntuck Community College *A*
Central Connecticut State
 University *B,M*
Fairfield University *B*
Housatonic Community College *A*
Manchester Community College *A*

Mattatuck Community College *C,A*
Middlesex Community College *A*
Northwestern Connecticut
 Community College *A*
Norwalk Community College *A*
Quinebaug Valley Community
 College *C,A*
Quinnipiac College *B,M*
Sacred Heart University *B,M*
St. Joseph College *B*
Southern Connecticut State
 University *B*
Teikyo-Post University *A,B*
Tunxis Community College *C,A*
United States Coast Guard
 Academy *B*
University of Bridgeport *A,B,M*
University of Connecticut *M,D*
University of Hartford *B,M*
University of New Haven *C,A,B,M*
Western Connecticut State
 University *M*
Yale University *M*

Delaware

Delaware State College *B*
Goldey-Beacom College *A,B*
University of Delaware *B,M*
Wesley College *B*
Wilmington College *B,M*

District of Columbia

Catholic University of America *B*
Gallaudet University *B*
George Washington University
 B,M,D
Georgetown University *B,M*
Howard University *B,M*
Mount Vernon College *B*
Southeastern University *B,M*
Trinity College *B*
University of the District of
 Columbia *A,B,M*

Florida

Barry University *B,M*
Bethune-Cookman College *B*
Brevard Community College *A*
Broward Community College *A*
Central Florida Community
 College *A*
Daytona Beach Community
 College *A*
Eckerd College *B*
Embry-Riddle Aeronautical
 University *A,B,M*
Flagler College *B*
Florida Agricultural and Mechanical
 University *B,M*
Florida Atlantic University *B,M,D*
Florida Community College at
 Jacksonville *A*
Florida Institute of Technology
 B,M,D
Florida International University
 B,M,D
Florida Keys Community College *A*
Florida Memorial College *B*
Florida Southern College *B,M*
Florida State University *B,M,D*
Fort Lauderdale College *A,B,M*
Gulf Coast Community College *A*
Hillsborough Community College *A*
Indian River Community College *A*
Jacksonville University *B,M*
Jones College *A,B*
Lake City Community College *A*
Lynn University *B*
Manatee Community College *A*
Miami-Dade Community College *A*
Nova University *B,M,D*

Okaloosa-Walton Community
 College *A*
Orlando College *B,M*
Palm Beach Atlantic College *B,M*
Palm Beach Community College *A*
Pasco-Hernando Community
 College *A*
Pensacola Junior College *A*
Phillips Junior College:
 Melbourne *A*
Rollins College *M*
St. Johns River Community
 College *A*
St. Leo College *B*
St. Petersburg Junior College *A*
St. Thomas University *B,M*
Santa Fe Community College *A*
Schiller International University
 A,B
South College: Palm Beach Campus
 C,A
South Florida Community
 College *A*
Stetson University *B,M*
Tampa College *A,B,M*
University of Florida *B,M,D*
University of Miami *B,M,D*
University of North Florida *B*
University of South Florida *B,M*
University of Tampa *B,M*
University of West Florida *B,M*
Valencia Community College *A*
Warner Southern College *B*
Webber College *A,B*

Georgia

Albany State College *B,M*
Atlanta Metropolitan College *A*
Augusta College *B,M*
Bainbridge College *A*
Berry College *B*
Brenau Women's College *B*
Brewton-Parker College *A,B*
Brunswick College *A*
Clark Atlanta University *B*
Clayton State College *A,B*
Columbus College *B,M*
Covenant College *B*
Darton College *A*
DeKalb College *A*
DeVry Institute of Technology:
 Atlanta *B*
Emmanuel College *A*
Emory University *B,M*
Floyd College *A*
Fort Valley State College *B*
Gainesville College *A*
Georgia College *B,M*
Georgia Institute of Technology
 B,M,D
Georgia Southern University *B*
Georgia Southwestern College *B,M*
Georgia State University *B,M,D*
Gordon College *A*
Kennesaw State College *B,M*
LaGrange College *B*
Macon College *A*
Mercer University
 Atlanta *B,M*
 Macon *B,M*
Middle Georgia College *A*
Morehouse College *B*
Morris Brown College *B*
North Georgia College *B*
Oglethorpe University *B*
Reinhardt College *B*
Shorter College *B*
South Georgia College *A*
Thomas College *B*
University of Georgia *B,M,D*
Valdosta State College *B*
Wesleyan College *C,B*

West Georgia College *B,M*

Hawaii

Brigham Young University-
 Hawaii *B*
Cannon's International Business
 College of Honolulu *A*
Chaminade University of Honolulu
 A,B,M
Hawaii Pacific University *A,B,M*
University of Hawaii
 Manoa *M*
 West Oahu *B*

Idaho

Albertson College *B*
Boise State University *B*
College of Southern Idaho *A*
Idaho State University *B,M*
Lewis Clark State College *B*
North Idaho College *A*
Northwest Nazarene College *B*
Ricks College *A*

Illinois

Aero-Space Institute *B*
Augustana College *B*
Aurora University *B,M*
Barat College *B*
Belleville Area College *A*
Blackburn College *B*
Bradley University *B,M*
Chicago State University *B*
City Colleges of Chicago
 Chicago City-Wide College
 C,A
 Malcolm X College *A*
 Olive-Harvey College *A*
 Richard J. Daley College *A*
College of St. Francis *B*
Columbia College *M*
Concordia University *B*
De Paul University *B,M*
DeVry Institute of Technology
 Chicago *B*
 Lombard *B*
Eastern Illinois University *B,M*
Elgin Community College *C,A*
Elmhurst College *B*
Eureka College *B*
Gem City College *C,A*
Governors State University *B,M*
Greenville College *B*
Highland Community College *A*
Illinois Benedictine College *M*
Illinois College *B*
Illinois Institute of Technology *B,M*
Illinois State University *B,M*
Illinois Wesleyan University *B*
Joliet Junior College *A*
Judson College *B*
KAES College *B*
Kendall College *A,B*
Lake Land College *A*
Lewis University *B,M*
Lincoln Christian College and
 Seminary *B*
Lincoln Land Community
 College *A*
Loyola University of Chicago *B*
MacCormac Junior College *A*
MacMurray College *A,B*
McKendree College *B*
Midstate College *C,A*
Millikin University *B*
Monmouth College *B*
Moraine Valley Community
 College *A*
Morton College *A*
National-Louis University *B*
North Central College *B,M*

North Park College and Theological Seminary *B*
Northeastern Illinois University *B,M*
Northern Illinois University *B,M*
Northwestern University *M*
Oakton Community College *C,A*
Olivet Nazarene University *B,M*
Phillips College of Chicago *A*
Quincy College *B,M*
Rend Lake College *A*
Robert Morris College: Chicago *A*
Rock Valley College *A*
Rockford College *B,M*
Roosevelt University *B,M*
St. Augustine College *A*
St. Xavier University *B,M*
Sangamon State University *B,M*
Southern Illinois University
    Carbondale *B,M,D*
    Edwardsville *B,M*
State Community College *A*
Trinity Christian College *B*
Trinity College *B*
University of Chicago *M,D*
University of Illinois
    Chicago *B,M*
    Urbana-Champaign *B,M,D*
Waubonsee Community College *C,A*
Western Illinois University *B,M*
William Rainey Harper College *A*

Indiana

Ancilla College *A*
Anderson University *B*
Ball State University *A,B,M*
Bethel College *A,B*
Butler University *B,M*
Calumet College of St. Joseph *C,A,B*
Franklin College *B*
Goshen College *B*
Hanover College *B*
Huntington College *A,B*
Indiana Institute of Technology *A,B*
Indiana State University *B,M*
Indiana University
    Bloomington *B,M*
    East *A,B*
    Kokomo *B,M*
    Northwest *B*
    South Bend *B,M*
    Southeast *B*
Indiana University—Purdue University
    Fort Wayne *B*
    Indianapolis *B,M*
Indiana Vocational Technical College: Southeast *C,A*
Indiana Wesleyan University *B*
International Business College *A*
Manchester College *A,B*
Marian College *A,B*
Martin University *B*
Oakland City College *A,B*
Purdue University
    Calumet *B,M*
    West Lafayette *B,M,D*
St. Francis College *B,M*
St. Joseph's College *B*
St. Mary-of-the-Woods College *A,B*
St. Mary's College *B*
Taylor University *A,B*
Tri-State University *A,B*
University of Indianapolis *B,M*
University of Notre Dame *B,M*
University of Southern Indiana *B,M*
Valparaiso University *B*
Vincennes University *A*

Iowa

American Institute of Business *A*
American Institute of Commerce *A*
Buena Vista College *B*
Clarke College *B*
Clinton Community College *A*
Coe College *B*
Des Moines Area Community College *A*
Dordt College *B*
Drake University *B,M*
Graceland College *B*
Grand View College *B*
Iowa Lakes Community College *A*
Iowa State University *M*
Iowa Wesleyan College *B*
Kirkwood Community College *A*
Loras College *B*
Luther College *B*
Maharishi International University *A,B,M,D*
Morningside College *B*
Mount Mercy College *B*
Mount St. Clare College *B*
Muscatine Community College *A*
Northwestern College *B*
St. Ambrose University *B,M*
Scott Community College *A*
Simpson College *B*
Southwestern Community College *A*
Teikyo Marycrest University *B*
Teikyo Westmar University *B*
University of Dubuque *A,B,M*
University of Iowa *B,M,D*
University of Northern Iowa *B*
Upper Iowa University *B*
Wartburg College *B*
William Penn College *B*

Kansas

Allen County Community College *A*
Barclay College *B*
Benedictine College *A,B*
Bethany College *B*
Bethel College *B*
Brown Mackie College *A*
Butler County Community College *A*
Central College *A*
Cloud County Community College *A*
Coffeyville Community College *A*
Colby Community College *A*
Cowley County Community College *A*
Dodge City Community College *A*
Emporia State University *B,M*
Fort Hays State University *B,M*
Fort Scott Community College *A*
Friends University *B,M*
Haskell Indian Junior College *A*
Highland Community College *A*
Hutchinson Community College *A*
Johnson County Community College *A*
Kansas Newman College *B*
Kansas State University *B,M*
Labette Community College *A*
McPherson College *B*
MidAmerica Nazarene College *B,M*
Ottawa University *B*
Pittsburg State University *B,M*
Pratt Community College *C,A*
St. Mary College *B*
Seward County Community College *C,A*
Southwestern College *B*
Sterling College *B*
University of Kansas *M*

Washburn University of Topeka *B,M*
Wichita State University *B,M*

Kentucky

Alice Lloyd College *B*
Bellarmine College *B,M*
Berea College *B*
Campbellsville College *A,B*
Cumberland College *B*
Eastern Kentucky University *B,M*
Georgetown College *B*
Hazard Community College *A*
Kentucky Christian College *B*
Kentucky State University *B*
Kentucky Wesleyan College *A,B*
Lees College *A*
Lindsey Wilson College *A,B*
Maysville Community College *A*
Morehead State University *B*
Murray State University *B*
Northern Kentucky University *A,B,M*
Pikeville College *A,B*
Prestonburg Community College *A*
St. Catharine College *A*
Thomas More College *A,B*
Transylvania University *B*
Union College *A,B*
University of Kentucky *B,M,D*
University of Louisville *B,M*
Western Kentucky University *B*

Louisiana

Bossier Parish Community College *A*
Dillard University *B*
Grambling State University *B,M*
Louisiana College *B*
Louisiana State University
    Agricultural and Mechanical College *B,M,D*
    Shreveport *B*
Louisiana Tech University *B,M,D*
Loyola University *B,M*
McNeese State University *B*
Nicholls State University *B,M*
Northeast Louisiana University *B*
Northwestern State University *A,B,M*
Our Lady of Holy Cross College *B*
Phillips Junior College: New Orleans *A*
Southern University
    New Orleans *B*
    Shreveport *A*
University of New Orleans *B*
University of Southwestern Louisiana *B,M*
Xavier University of Louisiana *B*

Maine

Andover College *A*
Beal College *A*
Casco Bay College *A*
Eastern Maine Technical College *A*
Husson College *B*
Maine Maritime Academy *M*
St. Joseph's College *B*
Thomas College *B,M*
University of Maine
    Augusta *A,B*
    Farmington *A*
    Machias *B*
    Orono *B,M*
    Presque Isle *B*
University of New England *B*
University of Southern Maine *A,B,M*
Westbrook College *B*

Maryland

Allegany Community College *A*
Anne Arundel Community College *A*
Bowie State University *B,M*
Capitol College *B,M*
Catonsville Community College *C,A*
Cecil Community College *A*
Charles County Community College *A*
College of Notre Dame of Maryland *B*
Columbia Union College *B*
Coppin State College *B*
Dundalk Community College *A*
Frederick Community College *A*
Frostburg State University *M*
Garrett Community College *A*
Goucher College *B*
Hagerstown Business College *A*
Hagerstown Junior College *A*
Harford Community College *A*
Hood College *M*
Howard Community College *C,A*
Loyola College in Maryland *B,M*
Montgomery College
    Rockville Campus *A*
    Takoma Park Campus *A*
Morgan State University *B,M*
Mount St. Mary's College *M*
New Community College of Baltimore *A*
Prince George's Community College *A*
Salisbury State University *B,M*
Sojourner-Douglass College *B*
Towson State University *B*
University of Baltimore *B,M*
University of Maryland
    College Park *B,M,D*
    Eastern Shore *B*
Villa Julie College *A,B*
Washington College *B*
Western Maryland College *B*
Wor-Wic Tech Community College *C,A*

Massachusetts

American International College *B*
Anna Maria College for Men and Women *A,B,M*
Aquinas College at Milton *A*
Aquinas College at Newton *A*
Arthur D. Little Management Education Institute *M*
Assumption College *B,M*
Atlantic Union College *B*
Babson College *B,M*
Bay Path College *A,B*
Bay State College *A*
Becker College
    Leicester Campus *A*
    Worcester Campus *A*
Bentley College *B,M*
Berkshire Community College *A*
Boston College *B,M*
Boston University *A,B,M,D*
Bristol Community College *A*
Bunker Hill Community College *A*
Cape Cod Community College *A*
Clark University *M*
Dean Junior College *A*
Eastern Nazarene College *B*
Elms College *B*
Emmanuel College *B*
Endicott College *A*
Fisher College *A*
Fitchburg State College *B,M*
Framingham State College *B*
Gordon College *B*
Greenfield Community College *A*
Harvard University *M,D*

Holyoke Community College *A*
Lasell College *A,B*
Lesley College *B,M*
Massachusetts Institute of
    Technology *B,M,D*
Merrimack College *A,B*
Middlesex Community College *A*
Mount Ida College *A,B*
Mount Wachusett Community
    College *A*
New England Banking Institute *A*
Newbury College *A*
Nichols College *B,M*
North Adams State College *B*
North Shore Community College *A*
Northeastern University *C,A,B,M*
Pine Manor College *A,B*
Quincy College *A*
Quinsigamond Community
    College *A*
Salem State College *B,M*
Simmons College *B,M*
Springfield College *B*
Springfield Technical Community
    College *A*
Stonehill College *B*
Suffolk University *B,M*
University of Massachusetts
    Amherst *B,M,D*
    Boston *M*
    Dartmouth *B,M*
    Lowell *B,M*
Western New England College *B,M*
Westfield State College *B*
Worcester Polytechnic Institute
    B,M
Worcester State College *B*

Michigan

Adrian College *A,B*
Albion College *B*
Alma College *B*
Alpena Community College *A*
Andrews University *B,M*
Aquinas College *B*
Baker College
    Auburn Hills *A*
    Cadillac *A,B*
    Flint *A,B*
    Mount Clemens *A*
    Muskegon *B*
    Owosso *A*
    Port Huron *A,B*
Calvin College *B*
Central Michigan University *B,M*
Cleary College *C,A,B*
Davenport College of Business *A,B*
Detroit College of Business *B*
Eastern Michigan University *B,M*
Ferris State University *B*
GMI Engineering & Management
    Institute *B*
Grand Rapids Community
    College *A*
Grand Valley State University *B,M*
Great Lakes Junior College of
    Business *A*
Henry Ford Community College *A*
Hillsdale College *B*
Hope College *B*
Jackson Community College *A*
Jordan College *C,A*
Kalamazoo Valley Community
    College *A*
Kellogg Community College *A*
Kirtland Community College *A*
Lake Superior State University *B,M*
Lansing Community College *A*
Lawrence Technological
    University *B*
Macomb Community College *C,A*
Madonna University *B,M*

Marygrove College *B*
Michigan State University *M,D*
Michigan Technological
    University *B*
Mid Michigan Community
    College *A*
Montcalm Community College *A*
Northern Michigan University *B*
Northwestern Michigan College *A*
Northwood Institute *A,B*
Oakland Community College *A*
Oakland University *B,M*
Olivet College *B*
Saginaw Valley State University
    B,M
St. Mary's College *B*
Siena Heights College *A,B*
Spring Arbor College *B*
Suomi College *A*
University of Detroit Mercy *B,M*
University of Michigan
    Dearborn *B,M*
    Flint *B,M*
Walsh College of Accountancy and
    Business Administration *B*
Wayne State University *M*
Western Michigan University *B,M*
William Tyndale College *B*

Minnesota

Augsburg College *B*
Austin Community College *A*
Bemidji State University *B*
Bethel College *B*
College of St. Benedict *B*
College of St. Catherine: St.
    Catherine Campus *B*
College of St. Scholastica *B,M*
Concordia College: Moorhead *B*
Concordia College: St. Paul *B*
Crown College *A,B*
Gustavus Adolphus College *B*
Hamline University *B*
Inver Hills Community College *A*
Mankato State University *B,M*
Metropolitan State University *M*
Minneapolis Community College *A*
Moorhead State University *B,M*
National Education Center: Brown
    Institute Campus *A*
Northland Community College *A*
Northwestern College *A,B*
Pillsbury Baptist Bible College *B*
Rainy River Community College *A*
St. Cloud State University *B,M*
St. John's University *B*
St. Mary's College of Minnesota *B*
Southwest State University *A,B*
University of Minnesota
    Duluth *B,M*
    Twin Cities *M,D*
University of St. Thomas *B,M*
Willmar Community College *A*
Winona State University *B,M*
Worthington Community College *A*

Mississippi

Alcorn State University *B*
Belhaven College *B*
Copiah-Lincoln Community
    College *A*
Delta State University *B,M*
East Central Community College *A*
Holmes Community College *A*
Jackson State University *B,M*
Jones County Junior College *A*
Mary Holmes College *A*
Millsaps College *B,M*
Mississippi College *B,M*

Mississippi Gulf Coast Community
    College
    Jackson County Campus *A*
    Jefferson Davis Campus *A*
Mississippi State University *B,M,D*
Mississippi University for Women *B*
Northeast Mississippi Community
    College *A*
Phillips Junior College
    Jackson *A*
    Mississippi Gulf Coast *A*
Rust College *B*
University of Mississippi *B,M,D*
University of Southern Mississippi
    B,M
William Carey College *B,M*

Missouri

Avila College *B,M*
Central Methodist College *B*
Central Missouri State University
    B,M
College of the Ozarks *B*
Columbia College *B*
Culver-Stockton College *B*
DeVry Institute of Technology:
    Kansas City *B*
Drury College *B,M*
Evangel College *B*
Fontbonne College *B*
Hannibal-LaGrange College *B*
Lincoln University *B,M*
Lindenwood College *B,M*
Longview Community College *A*
Maryville University *B,M*
Mineral Area College *A*
Missouri Baptist College *B*
Missouri Southern State College *B*
Missouri Valley College *B*
Missouri Western State College *B*
Moberly Area Community
    College *A*
National College *A,B*
North Central Missouri College *A*
Northeast Missouri State
    University *B*
Northwest Missouri State
    University *B,M*
Park College *B*
Phillips Junior College *A*
Rockhurst College *B,M*
St. Charles Community College *A*
St. Louis Community College at
    Florissant Valley *A*
St. Louis University *B,M,D*
Southeast Missouri State
    University *B*
Southwest Baptist University *B*
Southwest Missouri State University
    B,M
Stephens College *B*
University of Missouri
    Columbia *B,M,D*
    Kansas City *M*
Webster University *B,M*
Wentworth Military Academy and
    Junior College *A*
Westminster College *B*
William Jewell College *B*
William Woods College *B*

Montana

Carroll College *A,B*
College of Great Falls *A,B*
Eastern Montana College *B*
Fort Peck Community College *A*
Little Big Horn College *A*
Miles Community College *A*
Montana College of Mineral
    Science and Technology *B*
Rocky Mountain College *B*
University of Montana *B,M*

Nebraska

Bellevue College *B*
Central Community College *C,A*
Chadron State College *B*
College of St. Mary *A,B*
Concordia College *B*
Creighton University *C,B*
Dana College *B*
Doane College *B*
Hastings College *B*
McCook Community College *A*
Midland Lutheran College *B*
Northeast Community College *A*
Peru State College *B*
Southeast Community College
    Beatrice Campus *A*
    Lincoln Campus *C,A*
Union College *A,B*
University of Nebraska
    Kearney *B,M*
    Lincoln *B,M,D*
    Omaha *B,M*
Wayne State College *B*

Nevada

Northern Nevada Community
    College *A*
Sierra Nevada College *B*
Truckee Meadows Community
    College *A*
University of Nevada
    Las Vegas *B,M*
    Reno *M*
Western Nevada Community
    College *C,A*

New Hampshire

Antioch New England Graduate
    School *M*
Castle College *A*
Colby-Sawyer College *B*
Daniel Webster College *B*
Dartmouth College *M*
Franklin Pierce College *A,B*
Hesser College *A*
Keene State College *B*
New England College *B*
New Hampshire College *A,B,M*
Plymouth State College of the
    University System of New
    Hampshire *M*
Rivier College *B,M*
School for Lifelong Learning *B*
University of New Hampshire
    Durham *B,M*
    Manchester *A,B*

New Jersey

Atlantic Community College *A*
Bergen Community College *A*
Berkeley College of Business *C,A*
Bloomfield College *C,B*
Brookdale Community College *A*
Burlington County College *A*
Caldwell College *C,B*
Camden County College *A*
Centenary College *B*
College of St. Elizabeth *C,B*
County College of Morris *A*
Cumberland County College *A*
Essex County College *A*
Fairleigh Dickinson University *B,M*
Georgian Court College *B*
Glassboro State College *B,M*
Gloucester County College *A*
Jersey City State College *B*
Mercer County Community
    College *A*
Monmouth College *B,M*
Montclair State College *B,M*
New Jersey Institute of Technology
    B,M,D

Ocean County College *A*
Passaic County Community College *A*
Ramapo College of New Jersey *B*
Rider College *B*
Rutgers—The State University of New Jersey
   Camden College of Arts and Sciences *B*
   Livingston College *B*
   New Brunswick *M,D*
   University College Camden *B*
St. Peter's College *B*
Seton Hall University *B,M*
Stevens Institute of Technology *B,D*
Stockton State College *B*
Sussex County Community College *A*
Thomas Edison State College *B*
Trenton State College *B*
Upsala College *B*
William Paterson College of New Jersey *B,M*

New Mexico

Albuquerque Technical-Vocational Institute *A*
College of Santa Fe *A,B,M*
College of the Southwest *B*
Dona Ana Branch Community College of New Mexico State University *A*
Eastern New Mexico University *B,M*
National College *A,B*
New Mexico Highlands University *B,M*
New Mexico Junior College *A*
New Mexico State University *B,M,D*
Northern New Mexico Community College *A*
Parks College *C,A*
University of New Mexico *B,M,D*
Western New Mexico University *B,M*

New York

Adelphi University *B,M*
Adirondack Community College *A*
Alfred University *B*
Berkeley College *A*
Boricua College *B*
Bramson ORT Technical Institute *A*
Broome Community College *A*
Bryant & Stratton Business Institute
   Albany *C,A*
   Buffalo *C,A*
Canisius College *B,M*
Central City Business Institute *A*
City University of New York
   Baruch College *B,M*
   Borough of Manhattan Community College *A*
   Hostos Community College *A*
   Kingsborough Community College *A*
   La Guardia Community College *A*
   Lehman College *B*
   Queensborough Community College *A*
   York College *B*
Clarkson University *B,M*
Clinton Community College *A*
College of Insurance *B,M*
College of St. Rose *B,M*
Columbia University *M,D*
Columbia-Greene Community College *A*

Community College of the Finger Lakes *A*
Cornell University *M,D*
Corning Community College *A*
Daemen College *B*
Dominican College of Blauvelt *C,B*
Dowling College *B,M*
Dutchess Community College *A*
D'Youville College *B*
Elmira College *B*
Erie Community College
   North Campus *A*
   South Campus *A*
Five Towns College *A*
Fordham University *B,M*
Fulton-Montgomery Community College *A*
Genesee Community College *A*
Hartwick College *B*
Herkimer County Community College *A*
Hilbert College *A*
Hofstra University *B,M*
Houghton College *B*
Hudson Valley Community College *A*
Iona College *A,B,M*
Ithaca College *B*
Jamestown Community College *A*
Jefferson Community College *A*
Keuka College *B*
King's College *B*
Le Moyne College *B*
Long Island University
   Brooklyn Campus *B,M*
   C. W. Post Campus *B,M*
   Southampton Campus *B*
Manhattan College *B,M*
Manhattanville College *B*
Marist College *B,M*
Marymount College *B*
Marymount Manhattan College *B*
Mater Dei College *A*
Medaille College *B*
Mercy College *B*
Mohawk Valley Community College *C,A*
Molloy College *B*
Monroe College *A*
Monroe Community College *A*
Mount St. Mary College *B*
Nassau Community College *C,A*
Nazareth College of Rochester *B*
New York Institute of Technology *A,B,M*
New York University *C,B,M*
Niagara County Community College *A*
Niagara University *B,M*
North Country Community College *A*
Nyack College *B*
Onondaga Community College *A*
Orange County Community College *A*
Pace University
   College of White Plains *B,M*
   New York *B,M,D*
   Pleasantville/Briarcliff *B,M*
Polytechnic University
   Brooklyn *M*
   Long Island Campus *M*
Rensselaer Polytechnic Institute *B,M,D*
Rochester Business Institute *C*
Rochester Institute of Technology *A,B,M*
Rockland Community College *A*
Russell Sage College *B,M*
Sage Junior College of Albany, A Division of Russell Sage College *A*

St. Bonaventure University *B,W*
St. Francis College *B*
St. John Fisher College *B,M*
St. John's University *B,M*
St. Joseph's College
   Brooklyn *B*
   Suffolk Campus *B*
St. Thomas Aquinas College *B*
State University of New York
   Albany *B,M*
   Binghamton *B,M*
   Buffalo *B,M,D*
   College of Agriculture and Technology at Cobleskill *A*
   College of Agriculture and Technology at Morrisville *A*
   College at Brockport *B*
   College at Buffalo *B*
   College at Fredonia *B*
   College at Geneseo *B*
   College at New Paltz *B*
   College at Plattsburgh *B*
   College of Technology at Alfred *A*
   College of Technology at Canton *A*
   College of Technology at Delhi *A*
   College of Technology at Farmingdale *A*
   Institute of Technology at Utica/Rome *B,M*
   Maritime College *B*
   Oswego *B*
Suffolk County Community College
   Eastern Campus *A*
   Selden *C,A*
   Western Campus *C,A*
Sullivan County Community College *A*
Syracuse University *B,M,D*
Tompkins-Cortland Community College *A*
Touro College *A,B*
Ulster County Community College *A*
Union College *M*
United States Military Academy *B*
University of Rochester *M,D*
Utica College of Syracuse University *B*
Utica School of Commerce *A*
Villa Maria College of Buffalo *A*
Wagner College *B,M*
Westchester Business Institute *A*
Westchester Community College *A*

North Carolina

Alamance Community College *A*
Anson Community College *A*
Appalachian State University *B,M*
Asheville Buncombe Technical Community College *A*
Barber-Scotia College *B*
Barton College *B*
Beaufort County Community College *A*
Belmont Abbey College *B*
Bladen Community College *A*
Blue Ridge Community College *A*
Brevard College *A*
Brunswick Community College *A*
Caldwell Community College and Technical Institute *A*
Campbell University *B,M*
Cape Fear Community College *A*
Carteret Community College *A*
Catawba College *B*
Cecils College *A*
Central Carolina Community College *A*
Chowan College *A,B*

Cleveland Community College *A*
Coastal Carolina Community College *A*
College of the Albemarle *A*
Craven Community College *A*
Davidson County Community College *C,A*
Duke University *M,D*
Durham Technical Community College *A*
East Carolina University *B,M*
Edgecombe Community College *A*
Elizabeth City State University *B*
Elon College *B,M*
Fayetteville State University *B,M*
Fayetteville Technical Community College *A*
Forsyth Technical Community College *A*
Gardner-Webb College *B*
Gaston College *A*
Guilford College *B*
Guilford Technical Community College *A*
High Point University *B*
Isothermal Community College *C,A*
Johnson C. Smith University *B*
Johnston Community College *A*
Lees-McRae College *B*
Lenoir-Rhyne College *B*
Livingstone College *B*
Mars Hill College *B*
Martin Community College *A*
Mayland Community College *A*
McDowell Technical Community College *A*
Meredith College *B,M*
Methodist College *A,B*
Mitchell Community College *A*
Montgomery Community College *A*
Mount Olive College *A,B*
Nash Community College *A*
North Carolina Agricultural and Technical State University *B*
North Carolina Central University *B,M*
North Carolina State University *B*
North Carolina Wesleyan College *B*
Pamlico Community College *A*
Pembroke State University *B*
Pfeiffer College *B,M*
Piedmont Community College *A*
Pitt Community College *A*
Queens College *B*
Roanoke-Chowan Community College *A*
Robeson Community College *A*
Rockingham Community College *A*
St. Andrews Presbyterian College *B*
St. Augustine's College *B*
Salem College *B*
Sampson Community College *A*
Sandhills Community College *A*
Shaw University *A,B*
Southeastern Community College *A*
Southwestern Community College *A*
Stanly Community College *A*
Surry Community College *A*
University of North Carolina
   Asheville *B*
   Chapel Hill *B,M,D*
   Charlotte *B,M*
   Greensboro *B,M*
   Wilmington *B,M*
Vance-Granville Community College *A*
Wake Forest University *M*
Warren Wilson College *B*
Western Carolina University *B,M*
Western Piedmont Community College *A*

Wilkes Community College *C,A*
Wilson Technical Community
College *C,A*
Wingate College *B,M*
Winston-Salem State University *B*

North Dakota

Bismarck State College *C,A*
Dickinson State University *B*
Jamestown College *B*
Mayville State University *A,B*
Minot State University *B*
North Dakota State College of
Science *A*
North Dakota State University
Bottineau and Institute of
Forestry *A*
Fargo *B,M*
Trinity Bible College *A*
Turtle Mountain Community
College *A*
University of Mary *B*
University of North Dakota
Grand Forks *M*
Lake Region *A*
Williston *A*
Valley City State University *B*

Ohio

Ashland University *B,M*
Baldwin-Wallace College *B,M*
Bluffton College *B*
Bowling Green State University
Bowling Green *B,M*
Firelands College *A*
Bryant & Stratton Business
Institute: Great Northern *C*
Capital University *B,M*
Case Western Reserve University
B,M,D
Cedarville College *B*
Central Ohio Technical College *A*
Central State University *B*
Chatfield College *A*
Cincinnati Metropolitan College *A*
Cincinnati Technical College *A*
Clark State Community College *A*
Cleveland State University *B*
Columbus State Community
College *A*
Cuyahoga Community College:
Metropolitan Campus *A*
Defiance College *A,B*
DeVry Institute of Technology:
Columbus *B*
Dyke College *A,B*
Franciscan University of
Steubenville *B,M*
Franklin University *A,B*
Heidelberg College *B*
John Carroll University *B,M*
Kent State University
East Liverpool Regional
Campus *A*
Kent *B,M,D*
Lake Erie College *B,M*
Lakeland Community College *A*
Malone College *B*
Marietta College *A,B*
Miami University: Oxford Campus
B,M
Miami-Jacobs College *A*
Mount Union College *B*
Mount Vernon Nazarene College
A,B
Muskingum Area Technical
College *A*
Muskingum College *B*
North Central Technical College
C,A
Northwestern College *A*
Notre Dame College of Ohio *B*

Ohio Dominican College *B*
Ohio Northern University *B*
Ohio State University: Columbus
Campus *B,M,D*
Ohio University
Athens *B*
Chillicothe Campus *A*
Ohio Wesleyan University *B*
Otterbein College *B*
Shawnee State University *B*
Sinclair Community College *A*
Southern Ohio College *A*
Southern State Community
College *A*
Terra Technical College *C,A*
Tiffin University *A,B*
Union Institute *B,D*
University of Akron *B,M*
University of Cincinnati
Cincinnati *B,M,D*
Clermont College *A*
University of Dayton *B*
University of Findlay *A,B*
University of Rio Grande *A,B*
University of Toledo *B,M*
Urbana University *A,B*
Ursuline College *B*
Walsh College *A,B,M*
Washington State Community
College *A*
Wilberforce University *B*
Wilmington College *B*
Wittenberg University *B*
Wright State University
Dayton *B,M*
Lake Campus *A*
Xavier University *B*
Youngstown State University
A,B,M

Oklahoma

Bacone College *A*
Cameron University *B,M*
Connors State College *A*
East Central University *B*
Langston University *B*
Northeastern State University *B,M*
Northern Oklahoma College *A*
Northwestern Oklahoma State
University *B*
Oklahoma Baptist University *B*
Oklahoma Christian University of
Science and Arts *B*
Oklahoma City University *B,M*
Oklahoma Junior College *A*
Oklahoma Panhandle State
University *B*
Oklahoma State University
Stillwater *B,M,D*
Technical Branch:
Okmulgee *A*
Oral Roberts University *B,M*
Phillips University *B,M*
Redlands Community College *C,A*
Rogers State College *A*
Rose State College *A*
Southeastern Oklahoma State
University *B,M*
Southwestern Oklahoma State
University *B,M*
University of Central Oklahoma
B,M
University of Oklahoma *B,M,D*
University of Science and Arts of
Oklahoma *B*
University of Tulsa *C,B,M*

Oregon

Central Oregon Community
College *A*
Chemeketa Community College *A*
Clackamas Community College *A*

Concordia College *A,B*
Lewis and Clark College *B*
Linfield College *B*
Linn-Benton Community College *A*
Marylhurst College *M*
Oregon Institute of Technology *B*
Oregon State University *B,M*
Pacific University *B*
Portland Community College *A*
Portland State University *B*
Rogue Community College *A*
Southern Oregon State College
A,B,M
Southwestern Oregon Community
College *A*
Umpqua Community College *A*
University of Oregon
Eugene *B,M,D*
Robert Donald Clark Honors
College *B*
University of Portland *B*
Warner Pacific College *B*
Western Baptist College *A,B*
Willamette University *M*

Pennsylvania

Albright College *B*
Allentown College of St. Francis de
Sales *B,M*
Alvernia College *A,B*
Beaver College *B*
Bloomsburg University of
Pennsylvania *B,M*
Bucknell University *B,M*
Bucks County Community
College *A*
Butler County Community
College *A*
Cabrini College *B*
California University of
Pennsylvania *A,B,M*
Carnegie Mellon University
B,M,D,W
Cedar Crest College *B*
Central Pennsylvania Business
School *A*
Churchman Business School *A*
Clarion University of Pennsylvania
B,M
College Misericordia *B*
Community College of Beaver
County *A*
Delaware County Community
College *A*
Delaware Valley College *B*
Drexel University *B,M,D*
DuBois Business College *A*
Duquesne University *B,M*
East Stroudsburg University of
Pennsylvania *B*
Eastern College *B,M*
Elizabethtown College *B*
Franklin and Marshall College *B*
Gannon University *B,M*
Geneva College *A*
Gettysburg College *B*
Grove City College *B*
Gwynedd-Mercy College *A,B*
Harrisburg Area Community
College *A*
Holy Family College *B*
Immaculata College *B*
Indiana University of Pennsylvania
A,B,M
Juniata College *B*
Keystone Junior College *A*
King's College *A,B*
Kutztown University of
Pennsylvania *B,M*
La Roche College *B*
La Salle University *A,B,M*
Lackawanna Junior College *A*

Lehigh County Community College
C,A
Lehigh University *B,M*
Lincoln University *B*
Luzerne County Community
College *A*
Lycoming College *B*
Manor Junior College *A*
Mansfield University of
Pennsylvania *B*
Marywood College *B,M*
Mercyhurst College *B*
Messiah College *B*
Millersville University of
Pennsylvania *B*
Montgomery County Community
College *A*
Moravian College *B,M*
Mount Aloysius College *A*
Muhlenberg College *B*
Neumann College *B*
Northampton County Area
Community College *A*
Northeastern Christian Junior
College *A*
Peirce Junior College *A*
Penn State
Erie Behrend College *B,M*
Great Valley Graduate
Center *M*
Harrisburg Capital College
B,M
University Park Campus
B,M,D
Pennsylvania College of
Technology *A*
Philadelphia College of Textiles and
Science *B,M*
Point Park College *A,B,M*
Reading Area Community
College *A*
Robert Morris College *B,M*
Rosemont College *B*
St. Francis College *M*
St. Joseph's University *C,A,B,M*
St. Vincent College *B*
Seton Hill College *B*
Shippensburg University of
Pennsylvania *B*
Slippery Rock University of
Pennsylvania *B*
Spring Garden College *C,A,B*
Susquehanna University *B*
Temple University *B,M,D*
Thiel College *B*
University of Pennsylvania
A,B,M,D
University of Pittsburgh
Greensburg *B*
Johnstown *B*
Pittsburgh *M,D*
University of Scranton *A,B,M*
Ursinus College *B*
Valley Forge Military College *A*
Villanova University *B,M*
Washington and Jefferson College *B*
Waynesburg College *A,B*
West Chester University of
Pennsylvania *B,M*
Westminster College *B*
Westmoreland County Community
College *C,A*
Widener University *B,M*
York College of Pennsylvania
A,B,M

Puerto Rico

Caribbean University *B*
Columbia College *B*
Electronic Data Processing College
of Puerto Rico *A,B*

Inter American University of Puerto Rico
  Arecibo Campus *B*
  San German Campus *A,B*
Pontifical Catholic University of Puerto Rico *B,M*
Turabo University *A,B,M*
Universidad Adventista de las Antillas *A,B*
Universidad Metropolitana *B*
University of Puerto Rico
  Aguadilla *A*
  Arecibo Campus *A,B*
  Bayamon Technological University College *A,B*
  Cayey University College *B*
  Humacao University College *A,B*
  Mayaguez Campus *B*
  Ponce Technological University College *A,B*
  Rio Piedras Campus *M*
University of the Sacred Heart *B*

Rhode Island

Bryant College *A,B,M*
Community College of Rhode Island *A*
Johnson & Wales University *A,B*
Providence College *B,M*
Rhode Island College *B*
Roger Williams College *B*
Salve Regina University *M*
University of Rhode Island *B,M*

South Carolina

Anderson College *A,B*
Benedict College *B*
Bob Jones University *B*
Central Wesleyan College *B,M*
Charleston Southern University *B,M*
Claflin College *B*
Clemson University *B,M*
Coker College *B*
College of Charleston *B*
Columbia College *B*
Columbia Junior College of Business *A*
Converse College *B*
Florence-Darlington Technical College *C*
Francis Marion College *B*
Furman University *B*
Lander College *B*
Limestone College *B*
Midlands Technical College *C,A*
Morris College *B*
Newberry College *B*
North Greenville College *A*
Presbyterian College *B*
South Carolina State College *B*
Trident Technical College *A*
University of South Carolina
  Aiken *B*
  Coastal Carolina College *B*
  Columbia *B,M,D*
  Spartanburg *B*
Voorhees College *B*
Winthrop University *B,M*

South Dakota

Augustana College *B*
Black Hills State University *B*
Dakota State University *A,B*
Dakota Wesleyan University *A,B*
Huron University *A,B,M*
Mount Marty College *A,B*
National College *A,B*
Northern State University *B*
Oglala Lakota College *A*
Sinte Gleska College *A*
Sioux Falls College *B*

University of South Dakota *B,M*

Tennessee

American Baptist College of ABT Seminary *B*
Austin Peay State University *B*
Belmont University *B*
Bethel College *B*
Bristol University *B*
Carson-Newman College *B*
Chattanooga State Technical Community College *A*
Christian Brothers University *B,M*
Columbia State Community College *C*
Crichton College *B*
David Lipscomb University *B*
Dyersburg State Community College *A*
East Tennessee State University *B,M*
Fisk University *B*
Freed-Hardeman University *B*
Hiwassee College *A*
King College *B*
Lambuth University *B*
LeMoyne-Owen College *B*
Lincoln Memorial University *B*
Martin Methodist College *A*
Maryville College *B*
McKenzie College *A*
Memphis State University *B,M,D*
Middle Tennessee State University *B,M*
Motlow State Community College *A*
Northeast State Technical Community College *A*
Pellissippi State Technical Community College *A*
Roane State Community College *A*
Shelby State Community College *A*
Southern College of Seventh-day Adventists *B*
Tennessee State University *B,M*
Tennessee Technological University *B,M*
Tennessee Temple University *B*
Tennessee Wesleyan College *B*
Trevecca Nazarene College *B*
Union University *B*
University of Tennessee
  Chattanooga *B,M*
  Knoxville *B,M,D*
  Martin *B,M*
Vanderbilt University *M,D*
William Jennings Bryan College *A,B*

Texas

Abilene Christian University *B,M*
Alvin Community College *A*
Amber University *B,M*
Angelina College *A*
Angelo State University *B,M*
Austin Community College *A*
Baylor University *B,M*
Bee County College *A*
Brookhaven College *A*
College of the Mainland *A*
Corpus Christi State University *B,M*
Dallas Baptist University *B,M*
Del Mar College *A*
DeVry Institute of Technology: Irving *B*
East Texas Baptist University *A,B*
East Texas State University
  Commerce *B,M*
  Texarkana *B,M*
El Centro College *A*
El Paso Community College *A*
Galveston College *A*
Hardin-Simmons University *B*

Houston Baptist University *B,M*
Houston Community College *A*
Huston-Tillotson College *B*
Incarnate Word College *B,M*
Jacksonville College *A*
Lamar University—Beaumont *B*
LeTourneau University *B*
Lubbock Christian University *B*
McLennan Community College *C,A*
McMurry University *B*
Midland College *C,A*
Midwestern State University *B*
Mountain View College *A*
North Harris Montgomery Community College District *A*
Northwood Institute: Texas Campus *B*
Our Lady of the Lake University of San Antonio *B,M*
Prairie View A&M University *M*
Rice University *B,M,D*
Richland College *C,A*
St. Edward's University *B,M*
St. Mary's University *B,M*
St. Philip's College *A*
Sam Houston State University *B,M*
San Antonio College *A*
Schreiner College *B*
Southern Methodist University *B,M*
Southwest Texas State University *B,M*
Southwestern Adventist College *B*
Southwestern Assemblies of God College *A,B*
Southwestern University *B*
Stephen F. Austin State University *B,M*
Sul Ross State University *B,M*
Tarleton State University *B,M*
Texarkana College *A*
Texas A&I University *M*
Texas A&M University *B,M,D*
Texas Christian University *B,M*
Texas College *B*
Texas Lutheran College *A,B*
Texas Southern University *B,M*
Texas Southmost College *A*
Texas Tech University *M,D*
Texas Wesleyan University *B*
Texas Woman's University *B,M*
Trinity University *B*
University of Central Texas *B*
University of Dallas *M*
University of Houston
  Clear Lake *B,M*
  Downtown *B*
  Houston *B,M,D*
  Victoria *B,M*
University of Mary Hardin-Baylor *B*
University of North Texas *B,M*
University of St. Thomas *B,M*
University of Texas
  Austin *B,M,D*
  Dallas *M*
  El Paso *M*
  Pan American *B*
  Permian Basin *B,M*
  San Antonio *B*
  Tyler *B*
Vernon Regional Junior College *A*
Wayland Baptist University *M*
West Texas State University *B*

Utah

Brigham Young University *M*
College of Eastern Utah *A*
LDS Business College *A*
Southern Utah University *B*
University of Utah *B,M,D*
Utah State University *B,M*

Utah Valley Community College *C,A*
Weber State University *B*
Westminster College of Salt Lake City *B,M*

Vermont

Castleton State College *B*
Champlain College *A,B*
Green Mountain College *B*
Johnson State College *A,B*
Lyndon State College *A,B*
Norwich University *B*
St. Michael's College *B*
Trinity College of Vermont *A,B*
University of Vermont *B,M*

Virginia

Averett College *B,M*
Bluefield College *B*
Bridgewater College *B*
Central Virginia Community College *A*
Clinch Valley College of the University of Virginia *B*
College of William and Mary *B,M*
Dabney S. Lancaster Community College *A*
Eastern Mennonite College *B*
Emory and Henry College *B*
Ferrum College *B*
George Mason University *B,M*
Hampton University *B,M*
James Madison University *B,M*
John Tyler Community College *A*
Liberty University *B*
Longwood College *B*
Lord Fairfax Community College *A*
Lynchburg College *B,M*
Mary Baldwin College *B*
Mary Washington College *B*
Marymount University *B,M*
Mountain Empire Community College *A*
National Business College *C,A,B*
New River Community College *A*
Northern Virginia Community College *A*
Old Dominion University *B,M*
Patrick Henry Community College *A*
Paul D. Camp Community College *A*
Piedmont Virginia Community College *A*
Radford University *B,M*
Roanoke College *B*
St. Paul's College *B*
Southside Virginia Community College *A*
Southwest Virginia Community College *A*
Strayer College *A,B,M*
Tidewater Community College *A*
University of Richmond *B,M*
University of Virginia *M,D*
Virginia Commonwealth University *B,M,D*
Virginia Highlands Community College *A*
Virginia Polytechnic Institute and State University *M*
Virginia State University *B*
Virginia Union University *B*
Virginia Wesleyan College *B*
Washington and Lee University *B*
Wytheville Community College *A*

Washington

Big Bend Community College *A*
Central Washington University *B*
Centralia College *A*

City University *B,M*
Clark College *C,A*
Eastern Washington University *B*
Edmonds Community College *A*
Everett Community College *A*
Evergreen State College *B*
Gonzaga University *B,M*
Heritage College *C,B*
Lower Columbia College *A*
Northwest College of the
   Assemblies of God *A,B*
Olympic College *C,A*
Pacific Lutheran University *B,M*
St. Martin's College *B,M*
Seattle Central Community
   College *A*
Seattle Pacific University *B,M*
Seattle University *B,M*
Shoreline Community College *A*
South Puget Sound Community
   College *C,A*
Spokane Community College *A*
Spokane Falls Community
   College *A*
Tacoma Community College *A*
University of Puget Sound *B*
University of Washington *B,M,D*
Walla Walla College *B*
Washington State University *B,M,D*
Western Washington University
   B,M
Whitworth College *B*
Yakima Valley Community College
   C,A

West Virginia

Alderson-Broaddus College *B*
Bethany College *B*
Bluefield State College *B*
Davis and Elkins College *A,B*
Marshall University *B,M*
Potomac State College of West
   Virginia University *A*
Salem-Teikyo University *A,B*
Shepherd College *A,B*
University of Charleston *B,M*
West Liberty State College *B*
West Virginia Graduate College *M*
West Virginia Institute of
   Technology *A,B*
West Virginia Northern Community
   College *A*
West Virginia State College *A,B*
West Virginia University
   Morgantown *B,M*
   Parkersburg *A*
West Virginia Wesleyan College
   B,M
Wheeling Jesuit College *B,M*

Wisconsin

Alverno College *B*
Beloit College *B*
Cardinal Stritch College *B,M*
Carroll College *B*
Carthage College *B*
Concordia University Wisconsin *B*
Edgewood College *B,M*
Lakeland College *B*
Marian College of Fond du Lac *B*
Marquette University *B*
Milwaukee College of Business *A*
Milwaukee School of Engineering *B*
Mount Mary College *B*
Mount Senario College *B*
Northeast Wisconsin Technical
   College *A*
Northland College *B*
Ripon College *B*
St. Norbert College *B*
Silver Lake College *B*
Stratton College *A*

University of Wisconsin
   Eau Claire *B*
   Green Bay *B*
   La Crosse *B,M*
   Madison *B,M,D*
   Milwaukee *M,D*
   Oshkosh *B,M*
   Platteville *B*
   River Falls *B*
   Stevens Point *B*
   Stout *B*
   Superior *B*
   Whitewater *B,M*
Viterbo College *B*

Wyoming

Casper College *A*
Central Wyoming College *A*
Eastern Wyoming College *A*
Laramie County Community
   College *A*
Northwest College *A*
Sheridan College *A*
University of Wyoming *B,M*
Western Wyoming Community
   College *A*

American Samoa, Caroline Islands, Guam, Marianas, Virgin Islands

University of Guam *B,M*
University of the Virgin Islands
   A,B,M

Canada

McGill University *B,M,D*

Mexico

Sistema Instituto Tecnologico y de
   Estudios Superiores de
   Monterrey *B,M*

Switzerland

American College of Switzerland *B*

Arab Republic of Egypt

American University in Cairo *B,M*

Business computer/ console/peripheral equipment operation

Alabama

Alabama Southern Community
   College *A*
Brewer State Junior College *A*
Enterprise State Junior College *A*
Walker State Technical College *C,A*

Alaska

University of Alaska Anchorage *A*

Arizona

ITT Technical Institute: Tucson *A*
Lamson Junior College *C,A*
Pima Community College *C,A*

Arkansas

Phillips County Community
   College *A*

California

Barstow College *C,A*
Cerritos Community College *A*
Chabot College *A*
Chaffey Community College *A*
College of the Desert *C,A*
Compton Community College *A*
Cuesta College *A*

De Anza College *C*
Diablo Valley College *A*
East Los Angeles College *A*
Evergreen Valley College *A*
Grossmont Community College *C,A*
Heald College: Sacramento *C,A*
Humphreys College *A*
Los Angeles City College *A*
Los Angeles Trade and Technical
   College *C,A*
Los Angeles Valley College *A*
Mission College *A*
Modesto Junior College *A*
Mount San Jacinto College *C,A*
Oxnard College *C*
Pasadena City College *A*
Phillips Junior College: Fresno
   Campus *C,A*
Saddleback College *C,A*
Southwestern College *A*
West Hills Community College *A*
Yuba College *A*

Colorado

Blair Junior College *A*
Mesa State College *A,B*
Otero Junior College *C*

Connecticut

Mattatuck Community College *A*
Norwalk Community College *A*

Delaware

Delaware Technical and
   Community College
   Stanton/Wilmington
      Campus *A*
   Terry Campus *A*

District of Columbia

Gallaudet University *A*
University of the District of
   Columbia *A*

Florida

Broward Community College *A*
Gulf Coast Community College *A*
Palm Beach Community College *A*

Georgia

Dalton College *A*
Darton College *A*
DeKalb College *A*
Georgia College *B*
Middle Georgia College *A*

Hawaii

Brigham Young University-
   Hawaii *A*
Hawaii Pacific University *A*

Idaho

Boise State University *A*
Ricks College *A*

Illinois

Black Hawk College *A*
City Colleges of Chicago: Chicago
   City-Wide College *C*
Elgin Community College *C,A*
Illinois Central College *C*
Illinois Valley Community
   College *C*
Lake Land College *A*
Midstate College *C,A*
Moraine Valley Community College
   C,A
Prairie State College *A*
Richland Community College *A*
Shawnee Community College *A*
William Rainey Harper College *C,A*

Indiana

St. Joseph's College *A,B*
University of Southern Indiana *A*
Vincennes University *A*

Iowa

American Institute of Business *A*
Iowa Lakes Community College *A*
Kirkwood Community College *A*
Southwestern Community
   College *A*

Kansas

Butler County Community
   College *A*
Central College *A*
Colby Community College *A*
Cowley County Community
   College *A*
Fort Scott Community College *C,A*
Haskell Indian Junior College *A*
Kansas City Kansas Community
   College *A*
Neosho County Community College
   C,A
Seward County Community
   College *A*

Kentucky

Eastern Kentucky University *B*
Paducah Community College *A*

Louisiana

Phillips Junior College: New
   Orleans *A*

Maine

Casco Bay College *A*
University of Maine at Machias *A*

Maryland

Allegany Community College *A*
Anne Arundel Community
   College *A*
Charles County Community
   College *C*
Frederick Community College *A*
Howard Community College *A*
Montgomery College: Rockville
   Campus *A*
Wor-Wic Tech Community
   College *A*

Massachusetts

Aquinas College at Milton *A*
Becker College
   Leicester Campus *A*
   Worcester Campus *A*
Berkshire Community College *A*
Bunker Hill Community College *A*
Endicott College *A*
Middlesex Community College *A*
Mount Ida College *A*
Northern Essex Community
   College *A*

Michigan

Baker College
   Flint *A*
   Muskegon *A*
   Port Huron *A*
Delta College *A*
Eastern Michigan University *B,M*
Grand Rapids Community College
   C,A
Great Lakes Junior College of
   Business *C,A*
Jackson Community College *A*
Kalamazoo Valley Community
   College *A*
Lansing Community College *A*
Northwestern Michigan College *A*

Minnesota

Alexandria Technical College *A*
Bethany Lutheran College *A*
Rainy River Community College *A*
St. Paul Technical College *C*
Willmar Community College *A*

Mississippi

Mississippi Gulf Coast Community College: Perkinston *C,A*
Northeast Mississippi Community College *A*

Missouri

Longview Community College *A*
Missouri Southern State College *A*
National College *C*
St. Louis Community College
    Florissant Valley *A*
    Meramec *A*

Montana

Fort Peck Community College *A*
Miles Community College *A*
Northern Montana College *A*

Nebraska

Lincoln School of Commerce *C*
McCook Community College *A*
Western Nebraska Community College: Scottsbluff Campus *C,A*

New Hampshire

New Hampshire Technical College: Nashua *A*

New Jersey

Bergen Community College *C*
Burlington County College *C*
Essex County College *A*

New Mexico

Dona Ana Branch Community College of New Mexico State University *A*
New Mexico Junior College *C,A*
New Mexico State University *A*

New York

Adirondack Community College *A*
Berkeley College *C*
Bramson ORT Technical Institute *C,A*
Briarcliffe: The College for Business *A*
Bryant & Stratton Business Institute: Rochester *A*
Central City Business Institute *A*
City University of New York
    La Guardia Community College *A*
    Lehman College *C*
Genesee Community College *A*
State University of New York College of Agriculture and Technology at Morrisville *A*
Sullivan County Community College *A*
Utica School of Commerce *C*

North Carolina

Alamance Community College *A*
Bladen Community College *A*
Brunswick Community College *C,A*
Edgecombe Community College *A*
Fayetteville Technical Community College *A*
McDowell Technical Community College *A*
Mitchell Community College *C,A*
Piedmont Community College *A*

Roanoke-Chowan Community College *C*
Robeson Community College *A*
Rockingham Community College *A*
Southwestern Community College *A*
Wake Technical Community College *A*
Western Piedmont Community College *C*

North Dakota

North Dakota State College of Science *A*
North Dakota State University: Bottineau and Institute of Forestry *A*
University of North Dakota
    Lake Region *C,A*
    Williston *A*

Ohio

Bowling Green State University: Firelands College *A*
Cincinnati Metropolitan College *A*
Cincinnati Technical College *A*
Cuyahoga Community College: Metropolitan Campus *A*
Edison State Community College *C,A*
ITT Technical Institute: Youngstown *A*
Miami-Jacobs College *A*
Mount Vernon Nazarene College *A*
Northwestern College *A*
Ohio University *B*
Ohio Valley Business College *A*
Tiffin University *A*
University of Cincinnati: Access Colleges *A*
University of Toledo *A,B*

Oklahoma

Eastern Oklahoma State College *A*
Oklahoma State University: Oklahoma City *A*
Redlands Community College *A*
Rogers State College *A*
Rose State College *A*
Southwestern Oklahoma State University *B*
Tulsa Junior College *A*
University of Central Oklahoma *B*

Oregon

Central Oregon Community College *A*
Chemeketa Community College *C,A*
Lane Community College *A*
Portland Community College *A*
Umpqua Community College *A*

Pennsylvania

CHI Institute *C*
Community College of Philadelphia *C*
Delaware County Community College *A*
Harcum Junior College *A*
La Salle University *B*
Mercyhurst College *C*
Pennsylvania College of Technology *C*

Puerto Rico

ICPR Junior College *A*
Instituto Tecnico Comercial Junior College *A*
Puerto Rico Junior College *A*

Rhode Island

Johnson & Wales University *A*

South Carolina

Aiken Technical College *C,A*
Technical College of the Lowcountry *A*

South Dakota

Mitchell Vocational Technical Institute *C,A*
National College *A*
Presentation College *A*
Western Dakota Vocational Technical Institute *C*

Tennessee

Bristol University *A*
Hiwassee College *A*
Nashville State Technical Institute *C*
State Technical Institute at Memphis *A*

Texas

Abilene Christian University *A*
Amarillo College *A*
Angelina College *A*
Bee County College *A*
Central Texas College *A*
Del Mar College *A*
Eastfield College *A*
El Centro College *C,A*
Galveston College *A*
Lamar University—Beaumont *A*
Lee College *C,A*
Lon Morris College *A*
McLennan Community College *A*
Midland College *A*
Mountain View College *A*
North Harris Montgomery Community College District *C,A*
Panola College *A*
Ranger Junior College *C,A*
Richland College *A*
San Antonio College *C,A*
San Jacinto College: Central Campus *A*
Stephen F. Austin State University *B*
Wharton County Junior College *A*

Utah

Phillips Junior College: Salt Lake City Campus *C,A*
Southern Utah University *A*
Stevens-Henager College of Business *A*
Weber State University *A*

Vermont

Champlain College *A*

Virginia

Bluefield College *B*
Dabney S. Lancaster Community College *A*

Washington

Clark College *C,A*
Edmonds Community College *A*
ITT Technical Institute: Seattle *C*
Spokane Community College *A*
Walla Walla College *A*
Wenatchee Valley College *A*

West Virginia

Glenville State College *A*
Shepherd College *A*
West Virginia Northern Community College *A*

Wisconsin

Fox Valley Technical College *A*
Madison Area Technical College *A*
Waukesha County Technical College *A*
Western Wisconsin Technical College *C*
Wisconsin Indianhead Technical College *A*

Wyoming

Casper College *A*
Western Wyoming Community College *C,A*

Business data entry equipment operation

Alabama

Alabama Southern Community College *A*
Bessemer State Technical College *C*
John C. Calhoun State Community College *C*
Northeast Alabama State Junior College *A*
Shelton State Community College *A*
Shoals Community College *C*
Walker State Technical College *C*

Arizona

Lamson Junior College *C*
Pima Community College *C*
Scottsdale Community College *A*

Arkansas

Phillips County Community College *A*

California

Barstow College *A*
Cerritos Community College *A*
Chabot College *A*
Chaffey Community College *C*
Coastline Community College *C,A*
Compton Community College *A*
Cosumnes River College *C*
Diablo Valley College *A*
D-Q University *C*
Glendale Community College *A*
Humphreys College *A*
Long Beach City College *A*
Los Angeles Valley College *A*
Modesto Junior College *A*
Orange Coast College *C,A*
Phillips Junior College
    Condie Campus *C*
    Fresno Campus *C,A*
Saddleback College *C,A*
Southwestern College *A*
Victor Valley College *A*

Colorado

Denver Technical College *C*
Mesa State College *C,A*
Otero Junior College *A*
Pueblo Community College *A*

Delaware

Delaware Technical and Community College: Stanton/Wilmington Campus *A*

District of Columbia

University of the District of Columbia *C,A*

Florida

Gulf Coast Community College *A*
Orlando College *A*
Pensacola Junior College *A*

Georgia

Abraham Baldwin Agricultural
    College *A*
Andrew College *A*
DeKalb Technical Institute *C*
Georgia College *B*
Macon College *A*
Middle Georgia College *A*
Savannah Technical Institute *C*

Illinois

Black Hawk College *A*
Carl Sandburg College *A*
City Colleges of Chicago
      Chicago City-Wide College *C*
      Malcolm X College *A*
Elgin Community College *C*
Illinois Central College *C*
Illinois Eastern Community
    Colleges: Lincoln Trail College *A*
Illinois Valley Community
    College *C*
Moraine Valley Community
    College *C*
Parkland College *A*
Prairie State College *A*
Richland Community College *A*
Southern Illinois University at
    Carbondale *A*
State Community College *C*
Triton College *C*
William Rainey Harper College *C*

Indiana

Vincennes University *A*

Iowa

American Institute of Business *C*
American Institute of Commerce *C*
Des Moines Area Community
    College *C*
Hawkeye Institute of Technology *C*
Iowa Central Community College *A*

Kansas

Brown Mackie College *C*
Butler County Community
    College *A*
Central College *A*
Coffeyville Community College *C,A*
Colby Community College *A*
Dodge City Community College *A*
Fort Scott Community College *C,A*
Kansas City Kansas Community
    College *A*
Neosho County Community College
    C,A
Seward County Community
    College *A*

Kentucky

Owensboro Junior College of
    Business *C,A*
Paducah Community College *A*

Louisiana

Phillips Junior College: New
    Orleans *C*

Maine

Casco Bay College *A*

Maryland

Charles County Community
    College *C*
Hagerstown Business College *C*

Massachusetts

Aquinas College at Milton *A*
Berkshire Community College *A*
Middlesex Community College *A*

Michigan

Baker College of Auburn Hills *C,A*
Davenport College of Business *C,A*
Detroit College of Business *C*
Jackson Community College *C,A*
Kellogg Community College *C,A*
Lansing Community College *A*
Northwestern Michigan College *C*
Southwestern Michigan College *A*

Minnesota

Rainy River Community College
    C,A
St. Paul Technical College *C*

Mississippi

Copiah-Lincoln Community
    College *A*
Northeast Mississippi Community
    College *A*
Phillips Junior College of the
    Mississippi Gulf Coast *C*
Southwest Mississippi Community
    College *C*

Missouri

Missouri Southern State College *A*
Phillips Junior College *C*

Nebraska

Northeast Community College *A*
Western Nebraska Community
    College: Scottsbluff Campus *A*

Nevada

Northern Nevada Community
    College *A*

New Jersey

Berkeley College of Business *A*
Essex County College *A*

New Mexico

New Mexico Junior College *A*
New Mexico State University *A*

New York

Bramson ORT Technical Institute
    C,A
Bryant & Stratton Business
    Institute: Rochester *A*
Central City Business Institute *A*
City University of New York: La
    Guardia Community College *A*
Columbia-Greene Community
    College *A*
Rochester Business Institute *A*
Rochester Institute of Technology
    C,A
State University of New York
    College of Agriculture and
    Technology at Morrisville *A*
Sullivan County Community
    College *A*
Utica School of Commerce *A*

North Carolina

Asheville Buncombe Technical
    Community College *A*
Central Piedmont Community
    College *C*
Chowan College *A*
Edgecombe Community College *A*
Isothermal Community College *A*
Mitchell Community College *A*
Vance-Granville Community
    College *A*

North Dakota

University of North Dakota:
    Williston *C*

Ohio

Miami-Jacobs College *A*
Southern State Community
    College *C*
Terra Technical College *A*
Tiffin University *A*
University of Toledo *A*

Oklahoma

Eastern Oklahoma State College *A*

Oregon

Central Oregon Community
    College *A*
Portland Community College *A*
Treasure Valley Community
    College *A*
Umpqua Community College *A*

Pennsylvania

CHI Institute *C*
Community College of Beaver
    County *A*
Community College of
    Philadelphia *A*
Manor Junior College *A*
Peirce Junior College *A*

Puerto Rico

Instituto Tecnico Comercial Junior
    College *A*
Puerto Rico Junior College *A*

Rhode Island

Johnson & Wales University *A*

South Carolina

Aiken Technical College *C*
Technical College of the
    Lowcountry *A*
Tri-County Technical College *C*

South Dakota

Kilian Community College *A*

Tennessee

Chattanooga State Technical
    Community College *C*
McKenzie College *A*
Motlow State Community
    College *A*
Northeast State Technical
    Community College *C*

Texas

Amarillo College *A*
Central Texas College *A*
Cisco Junior College *A*
College of the Mainland *C,A*
Cooke County College *A*
El Centro College *C,A*
Howard College *A*
Kilgore College *A*
Lamar University—Beaumont *A*
Laredo Junior College *C,A*
Lee College *A*
McLennan Community College *A*
Midland College *A*
Mountain View College *A*
Navarro College *A*
Panola College *A*
San Antonio College *C*
San Jacinto College: Central
    Campus *A*
Southwestern Christian College *A*
Texas State Technical College
    Amarillo *A*
    Harlingen *C*

Trinity Valley Community
    College *A*
Wharton County Junior College *A*

Utah

College of Eastern Utah *C*
LDS Business College *C*
Phillips Junior College: Salt Lake
    City Campus *C,A*

Virginia

Commonwealth College *C*
Dabney S. Lancaster Community
    College *C*
Mountain Empire Community
    College *C*

Washington

Clark College *A*
Grays Harbor College *A*
Griffin College *C,A*
ITT Technical Institute: Seattle *C*
Lower Columbia College *A*
North Seattle Community
    College *A*
Pierce College *C*
Yakima Valley Community
    College *C*

West Virginia

West Virginia Northern Community
    College *C*

Wisconsin

Chippewa Valley Technical
    College *A*
Fox Valley Technical College *C*
Northeast Wisconsin Technical
    College *C*
Stratton College *C,A*
Waukesha County Technical
    College *C*

Wyoming

Casper College *A*
Northwest College *A*
Western Wyoming Community
    College *C,A*

Business data processing and related programs

Alabama

Alabama Southern Community
    College *A*
Alabama State University *A*
Brewer State Junior College *A*
Chattahoochee Valley Community
    College *A*
Community College of the Air
    Force *A*
Enterprise State Junior College *A*
George C. Wallace State
    Community College at Selma *A*
Jefferson State Community
    College *A*
Lawson State Community
    College *A*
Northeast Alabama State Junior
    College *A*
Selma University *A*
Shelton State Community College
    C,A
Snead State Junior College *A*
Troy State University *A*
Walker State Technical College *C*

Alaska

University of Alaska
　Anchorage *A*
　Southeast *C*

Arizona

Cochise College *A*
Glendale Community College *C,A*
Mesa Community College *A*
Scottsdale Community College *A*
Yavapai College *C,A*

Arkansas

East Arkansas Community
　College *A*
Garland County Community
　College *C,A*
Henderson State University *B*
Mississippi County Community
　College *A*
North Arkansas Community
　College *A*
Phillips County Community
　College *A*
Rich Mountain Community
　College *A*
Southern Arkansas Community
　College *A*
Westark Community College *A*
Williams Baptist College *A*

California

Bakersfield College *A*
Barstow College *A*
Cerritos Community College *A*
Chabot College *A*
Chaffey Community College *A*
Citrus College *A*
City College of San Francisco *A*
College of the Sequoias *C,A*
Columbia College *C*
Compton Community College *A*
Cosumnes River College *C*
Diablo Valley College *A*
East Los Angeles College *C,A*
El Camino College *C,A*
Evergreen Valley College *A*
Foothill College *A*
Fresno City College *C,A*
Glendale Community College *A*
Golden West College *C,A*
Hartnell College *A*
Heald College: Sacramento *C,A*
Humphreys College *A*
Imperial Valley College *C,A*
Kelsey-Jenney College *C,A*
Kings River Community College *A*
Laney College *C,A*
Lassen College *A*
Long Beach City College *A*
Los Angeles City College *C,A*
Los Angeles Harbor College *C,A*
Los Angeles Mission College *A*
Los Angeles Pierce College *C,A*
Los Angeles Trade and Technical
　College *C,A*
Los Angeles Valley College *C,A*
Merced College *A*
MiraCosta College *C,A*
Modesto Junior College *A*
Monterey Peninsula College *C,A*
Moorpark College *A*
Mount San Jacinto College *A*
Orange Coast College *C,A*
Oxnard College *C,A*
Pacific Union College *A*
Pasadena City College *A*
Phillips Junior College
　Condie Campus *C,A*
　Fresno Campus *C,A*
　San Fernando Valley
　　Campus *A*

Porterville College *C,A*
Saddleback College *C,A*
San Diego City College *C,A*
San Diego Mesa College *A*
San Diego Miramar College *A*
San Joaquin Delta College *A*
San Jose City College *A*
Santa Barbara City College *C*
Santa Monica College *C,A*
Santa Rosa Junior College *C,A*
Southwestern College *A*
Taft College *C,A*
Ventura College *A*
Victor Valley College *A*
West Hills Community College *A*

Colorado

Adams State College *B*
Aims Community College *A*
Arapahoe Community College *C*
Colorado Mountain College:
　Timberline Campus *A*
Colorado Northwestern Community
　College *A*
Community College of Denver *C,A*
Denver Technical College *A*
Lamar Community College *A*
Mesa State College *C,A*
Northeastern Junior College *A*
Otero Junior College *A*
Pueblo Community College *A*
Trinidad State Junior College *A*

Connecticut

Greater New Haven State Technical
　College *A*
Housatonic Community College *A*
Northwestern Connecticut
　Community College *C*
Norwalk Community College *A*
Norwalk State Technical College *A*
South Central Community
　College *A*
Thames Valley State Technical
　College *A*
Waterbury State Technical
　College *A*

Delaware

Delaware Technical and
　Community College
　Southern Campus *A*
　Stanton/Wilmington
　　Campus *A*
　Terry Campus *A*

District of Columbia

University of the District of
　Columbia *A*

Florida

Broward Community College *A*
Chipola Junior College *A*
Daytona Beach Community College
　C,A
Florida Community College at
　Jacksonville *C*
Florida Institute of Technology *B*
Florida Keys Community College *C*
Gulf Coast Community College *C,A*
Indian River Community College *A*
Jones College *A,B*
Lake-Sumter Community College *C*
Miami-Dade Community College *A*
Orlando College *A*
Palm Beach Community College *A*
Pensacola Junior College *A*
Santa Fe Community College *A*
Seminole Community College *A*
South Florida Community
　College *C*
Webber College *A,B*

Georgia

Abraham Baldwin Agricultural
　College *A*
Andrew College *A*
Atlanta Metropolitan College *A*
Bainbridge College *C*
Brunswick College *C,A*
Clayton State College *C,A*
Dalton College *A*
Darton College *A*
DeKalb College *A*
Gainesville College *A*
Georgia College *B*
Gordon College *C,A*
Macon College *A*
Meadows College of Business *A*
Middle Georgia College *A*
Morris Brown College *B*
Reinhardt College *A*
Savannah Technical Institute *C,A*
South Georgia College *C*
Valdosta State College *A*

Hawaii

Brigham Young University-
　Hawaii *B*
Cannon's International Business
　College of Honolulu *C,A*
Hawaii Pacific University *A*
University of Hawaii: Kapiolani
　Community College *C,A*

Idaho

Idaho State University *C,A*
North Idaho College *A*
Ricks College *A*

Illinois

Belleville Area College *A*
Black Hawk College *C,A*
Carl Sandburg College *A*
City Colleges of Chicago
　Chicago City-Wide College
　　C,A
　Malcolm X College *A*
　Olive-Harvey College *C,A*
　Richard J. Daley College *C*
　Wright College *A*
College of DuPage *C,A*
College of Lake County *C,A*
Elgin Community College *C,A*
Highland Community College *A*
Illinois Eastern Community
　Colleges: Lincoln Trail College *A*
Illinois Valley Community College
　C,A
John A. Logan College *A*
Joliet Junior College *C,A*
Kishwaukee College *C,A*
Lake Land College *C,A*
Lewis and Clark Community
　College *A*
Lincoln Land Community
　College *A*
Midstate College *C*
Moraine Valley Community
　College *C*
Morton College *A*
National-Louis University *C*
Oakton Community College *C,A*
Parkland College *A*
Phillips College of Chicago *C*
Prairie State College *A*
Richland Community College *A*
Robert Morris College: Chicago
　C,A
Rock Valley College *A*
Shawnee Community College *C*
Southern Illinois University at
　Carbondale *A*
Spoon River College *A*
State Community College *A*

Triton College *C,A*
William Rainey Harper College *C,A*

Indiana

Ancilla College *A*
Calumet College of St. Joseph *C*
Indiana Institute of Technology *A,B*
Indiana Wesleyan University *A*
Purdue University *A,B*
St. Joseph's College *A,B*
University of Indianapolis *A*
Vincennes University *A*

Iowa

American Institute of Business *A*
Clinton Community College *A*
Des Moines Area Community
　College *A*
Dordt College *A*
Iowa Central Community College *A*
Iowa Lakes Community College *A*
Kirkwood Community College *A*
North Iowa Area Community
　College *A*
Northeast Iowa Community
　College *A*
Scott Community College *C*

Kansas

Barton County Community
　College *A*
Brown Mackie College *C*
Butler County Community
　College *A*
Central College *A*
Cloud County Community College
　C,A
Coffeyville Community College *A*
Colby Community College *A*
Cowley County Community
　College *A*
Dodge City Community College
　C,A
Emporia State University *B*
Fort Scott Community College *A*
Friends University *A*
Haskell Indian Junior College *A*
Hesston College *A*
Highland Community College *A*
Hutchinson Community College *A*
Johnson County Community
　College *C,A*
Kansas City Kansas Community
　College *A*
Neosho County Community
　College *A*
Pratt Community College *A*
Seward County Community
　College *A*
Washburn University of Topeka *A*

Kentucky

Campbellsville College *A*
Hazard Community College *A*
Jefferson Community College *A*
Lees College *A*
Madisonville Community College *A*
Maysville Community College *A*
Morehead State University *A,B*
Murray State University *A*
National Education Center:
　Kentucky College of Technology
　　Campus *A*
Owensboro Junior College of
　Business *C,A*
Paducah Community College *A*
Sullivan College *A*

Louisiana

Bossier Parish Community
　College *A*
Grambling State University *A*

Northwestern State University *A,B*

Maine

Andover College *A*
Casco Bay College *A*
Husson College *A*
Southern Maine Technical
    College *A*
University of Maine at Machias *A*

Maryland

Allegany Community College *A*
Anne Arundel Community
    College *A*
Cecil Community College *C,A*
Charles County Community
    College *A*
Frederick Community College *A*
Hagerstown Junior College *C,A*
Howard Community College *A*
Montgomery College
    Germantown Campus *A*
    Rockville Campus *A*
    Takoma Park Campus *A*
Villa Julie College *A*

Massachusetts

Aquinas College at Milton *A*
Becker College
    Leicester Campus *A*
    Worcester Campus *A*
Berkshire Community College *A*
Bunker Hill Community College *A*
Cape Cod Community College *A*
Mount Ida College *A*
Mount Wachusett Community
    College *A*
North Shore Community College *A*
Northern Essex Community
    College *A*
Quinsigamond Community
    College *A*
Roxbury Community College *A*
Springfield Technical Community
    College *A*

Michigan

Alpena Community College *A*
Baker College
    Auburn Hills *C,A*
    Flint *A*
    Muskegon *A*
    Owosso *A*
    Port Huron *A*
Charles Stewart Mott Community
    College *A*
Cleary College *A*
Davenport College of Business *C,A*
Delta College *A*
Glen Oaks Community College *A*
Grand Rapids Community College
    C,A
Great Lakes Junior College of
    Business *A*
Henry Ford Community College *A*
Jackson Community College *A*
Jordan College *C,A*
Kalamazoo Valley Community
    College *A*
Kellogg Community College *C,A*
Lake Superior State University *A*
Lansing Community College *A*
Lewis College of Business *A*
Macomb Community College *C,A*
Marygrove College *A*
Michigan Christian College *C,A*
Mid Michigan Community
    College *A*
Montcalm Community College *A*
Muskegon Community College *A*
Northern Michigan University *A,B*
Northwestern Michigan College *A*

Oakland Community College *A*
St. Clair County Community
    College *C,A*
Southwestern Michigan College *A*
Suomi College *A*
West Shore Community College
    C,A

Minnesota

Northland Community College *A*
Northwestern College *A*
Rochester Community College *A*
St. Cloud State University *B*
St. Paul Technical College *C*
Vermilion Community College *A*
Willmar Community College *A*
Worthington Community College *A*

Mississippi

Copiah-Lincoln Community
    College *A*
East Central Community College *A*
Hinds Community College *A*
Jones County Junior College *A*
Mary Holmes College *A*
Meridian Community College *A*
Mississippi College *B*
Mississippi Gulf Coast Community
    College
    Jackson County Campus *A*
    Jefferson Davis Campus *A*
Mississippi State University *B,M*
Northeast Mississippi Community
    College *A*
Phillips Junior College of the
    Mississippi Gulf Coast *A*
Southwest Mississippi Community
    College *A*

Missouri

East Central College *C,A*
Jefferson College *A*
Longview Community College *A*
Missouri Southern State College
    C,A
Missouri Western State College *A*
Moberly Area Community
    College *A*
National College *C*
North Central Missouri College *C,A*
St. Louis Community College
    Florissant Valley *C,A*
    Forest Park *A*
    Meramec *C,A*
State Fair Community College *A*

Montana

Eastern Montana College *A*
Little Big Horn College *A*
Miles Community College *A*
Western Montana College of the
    University of Montana *A*

Nebraska

Central Community College *C,A*
McCook Community College *A*
Midland Lutheran College *A*
Northeast Community College *A*
Southeast Community College:
    Milford Campus *A*
Wayne State College *B*
Western Nebraska Community
    College: Scottsbluff Campus *A*

Nevada

Community College of Southern
    Nevada *C,A*
Northern Nevada Community
    College *C,A*
Truckee Meadows Community
    College *A*

Western Nevada Community
    College *A*

New Hampshire

Hesser College *A*
Rivier College *A,B*

New Jersey

Atlantic Community College *A*
Bergen Community College *C*
Brookdale Community College *A*
Burlington County College *A*
Camden County College *A*
County College of Morris *A*
Cumberland County College *A*
Essex County College *C,A*
Felician College *C*
Gloucester County College *C,A*
Rider College *A*
St. Peter's College *A*
Thomas Edison State College *A,B*

New Mexico

Eastern New Mexico University *B*
New Mexico Junior College *A*
New Mexico State University at
    Carlsbad *C*
Northern New Mexico Community
    College *A*

New York

Adirondack Community College
    C,A
Bramson ORT Technical Institute
    C,A
Broome Community College *A*
Bryant & Stratton Business Institute
    Rochester *A*
    Syracuse *A*
Central City Business Institute *A*
City University of New York
    Hostos Community College *A*
    Kingsborough Community
        College *A*
    La Guardia Community
        College *A*
    New York City Technical
        College *A*
    Queensborough Community
        College *A*
Clarkson University *B,M*
Columbia-Greene Community
    College *C,A*
Community College of the Finger
    Lakes *A*
Corning Community College *A*
Dutchess Community College *A*
Erie Community College: North
    Campus *A*
Fulton-Montgomery Community
    College *A*
Genesee Community College *C*
Herkimer County Community
    College *C,A*
Hilbert College *A*
Hudson Valley Community College
    C,A
Jamestown Business College *A*
Jamestown Community College *A*
Jefferson Community College *A*
Mohawk Valley Community College
    C,A
Monroe College *A*
Nassau Community College *A*
New York Institute of
    Technology *A*
New York University *A*
Niagara County Community
    College *A*
Onondaga Community College *A*
Orange County Community
    College *A*

Rochester Business Institute *A*
Rochester Institute of Technology
    C,A
Rockland Community College *A*
St. Francis College *A*
St. John's University *A*
State University of New York
    College of Agriculture and
        Technology at Cobleskill *A*
    College of Agriculture and
        Technology at Morrisville *A*
    College of Technology at
        Alfred *A*
    College of Technology at
        Delhi *A*
    College of Technology at
        Farmingdale *A*
Suffolk County Community College
    Selden *A*
    Western Campus *A*
Sullivan County Community
    College *A*
Tompkins-Cortland Community
    College *A*
Ulster County Community
    College *A*
Utica School of Commerce *A*
Westchester Business Institute *A*
Westchester Community College *A*

North Carolina

Alamance Community College *A*
Anson Community College *A*
Caldwell Community College and
    Technical Institute *A*
Campbell University *A,B*
Catawba Valley Community College
    C,A
Central Carolina Community
    College *A*
Central Piedmont Community
    College *A*
Chowan College *A*
Cleveland Community College *A*
Coastal Carolina Community
    College *A*
College of the Albemarle *A*
Durham Technical Community
    College *A*
Fayetteville Technical Community
    College *A*
Gaston College *A*
Haywood Community College *A*
Isothermal Community College *A*
Louisburg College *A*
Mayland Community College *A*
McDowell Technical Community
    College *A*
Mitchell Community College *A*
Richmond Community College *C,A*
Robeson Community College *A*
Sampson Community College *A*
Sandhills Community College *C,A*
Southeastern Community College *A*
Surry Community College *A*
University of North Carolina at
    Greensboro *B*
Vance-Granville Community
    College *A*
Wake Technical Community
    College *A*
Wilkes Community College *C,A*

North Dakota

Bismarck State College *A*
Minot State University *A*
North Dakota State College of
    Science *A*
University of North Dakota
    Lake Region *C,A*
    Williston *C*

Ohio

Bowling Green State University:
  Firelands College *A*
Cincinnati Metropolitan College *A*
Cincinnati Technical College *A*
Columbus State Community
  College *A*
Cuyahoga Community College:
  Metropolitan Campus *A*
Edison State Community College
  C,A
Hocking Technical College *A*
Jefferson Technical College *A*
Kent State University: East
  Liverpool Regional Campus *A*
Lakeland Community College *C,A*
Lorain County Community
  College *A*
Miami-Jacobs College *A*
Mount Vernon Nazarene College *A*
Muskingum Area Technical
  College *C*
Northwestern College *A*
Ohio State University: Columbus
  Campus *B*
Southern State Community
  College *A*
Tiffin University *A*
University of Akron *A*
University of Cincinnati: Access
  Colleges *A*
University of Toledo *A*
Washington State Community
  College *A*
Wright State University: Lake
  Campus *A*
Youngstown State University *A*

Oklahoma

Connors State College *C,A*
Eastern Oklahoma State College *A*
Northern Oklahoma College *A*
Oklahoma Baptist University *B*
Oklahoma State University
  Oklahoma City *A*
  Technical Branch:
    Okmulgee *A*
Rose State College *A*
Southwestern Oklahoma State
  University *B*
Tulsa Junior College *A*
University of Science and Arts of
  Oklahoma *B*

Oregon

Central Oregon Community College
  C,A
Chemeketa Community College *A*
Clatsop Community College *A*
Linn-Benton Community College *A*
Oregon Institute of Technology *B*
Southwestern Oregon Community
  College *A*
Umpqua Community College *A*

Pennsylvania

Bucks County Community
  College *A*
Butler County Community
  College *A*
Clarion University of
  Pennsylvania *A*
Community College of Beaver
  County *A*
Community College of
  Philadelphia *A*
Delaware County Community
  College *A*
Harcum Junior College *A*
Harrisburg Area Community
  College *A*
La Salle University *A*

Lackawanna Junior College *C*
Lehigh County Community
  College *A*
Luzerne County Community
  College *C,A*
Manor Junior College *A*
Messiah College *B*
Montgomery County Community
  College *A*
Peirce Junior College *A*
Pennsylvania College of
  Technology *A*
Philadelphia College of Textiles and
  Science *A*
Reading Area Community
  College *A*
St. Francis College *A*
Shippensburg University of
  Pennsylvania *B*
University of Pittsburgh at
  Titusville *A*

Puerto Rico

Electronic Data Processing College
  of Puerto Rico *A*
Pontifical Catholic University of
  Puerto Rico *B*
Puerto Rico Junior College *A*

Rhode Island

Johnson & Wales University *A,B*

South Carolina

Chesterfield-Marlboro Technical
  College *A*
Columbia Junior College of
  Business *A*
Florence-Darlington Technical
  College *A*
Horry-Georgetown Technical
  College *C*
Technical College of the
  Lowcountry *A*

South Dakota

Huron University *A*
Kilian Community College *A*
National College *A,B*
Northern State University *A*
Presentation College *A*

Tennessee

Austin Peay State University *A*
Chattanooga State Technical
  Community College *C,A*
Dyersburg State Community
  College *A*
Martin Methodist College *A*
McKenzie College *A*
Motlow State Community
  College *A*
Northeast State Technical
  Community College *A*
Pellissippi State Technical
  Community College *A*
Roane State Community College *A*
Southern College of Seventh-day
  Adventists *A*
State Technical Institute at
  Memphis *A*
Trevecca Nazarene College *B*
Volunteer State Community
  College *A*
Walters State Community
  College *A*

Texas

Amarillo College *A*
Angelina College *A*
Austin Community College *A*
Bee County College *A*
Central Texas College *A*

Cisco Junior College *A*
College of the Mainland *A*
Cooke County College *A*
Del Mar College *A*
East Texas Baptist University *B*
Eastfield College *A*
El Centro College *A*
El Paso Community College *C,A*
Howard College *A*
Kilgore College *A*
Lamar University—Beaumont *A*
Lee College *A*
McLennan Community College *A*
Midland College *A*
Mountain View College *A*
Navarro College *A*
North Harris Montgomery
  Community College District *C*
North Lake College *A*
Panola College *A*
Richland College *A*
St. Philip's College *A*
San Antonio College *A*
San Jacinto College: Central
  Campus *A*
South Plains College *A*
Southwestern Christian College *A*
Temple Junior College *A*
Texarkana College *A*
Texas State Technical College:
  Sweetwater *C,A*
Trinity Valley Community
  College *A*
University of Houston:
  Downtown *B*
University of Mary Hardin-
  Baylor *B*
Vernon Regional Junior College *A*
Victoria College *A*
Weatherford College *C,A*
Western Texas College *A*
Wharton County Junior College *A*
Wiley College *A*

Utah

Dixie College *A*
LDS Business College *A*
Stevens-Henager College of
  Business *A*
Weber State University *A*

Vermont

Champlain College *A*

Virginia

Dabney S. Lancaster Community
  College *A*
Eastern Mennonite College *A*
Lord Fairfax Community College *A*
Mountain Empire Community
  College *A*
National Business College *A*
Northern Virginia Community
  College *A*
Patrick Henry Community
  College *A*
Piedmont Virginia Community
  College *C,A*
Southwest Virginia Community
  College *A*
Virginia Highlands Community
  College *A*

Washington

Big Bend Community College *A*
Centralia College *A*
Clark College *C,A*
Edmonds Community College *A*
Everett Community College *A*
Grays Harbor College *A*
ITT Technical Institute: Seattle *C*
Lower Columbia College *C,A*

North Seattle Community
  College *A*
Olympic College *C,A*
Peninsula College *A*
Pierce College *C,A*
Seattle Central Community College
  C,A
Shoreline Community College *A*
Spokane Community College *A*
Tacoma Community College *A*
Walla Walla College *A*
Whatcom Community College *C,A*
Yakima Valley Community College
  C,A

West Virginia

Davis and Elkins College *A*
Fairmont State College *A,B*
Glenville State College *A*
Marshall University *A*
Potomac State College of West
  Virginia University *A*
Shepherd College *A,B*
West Virginia Institute of
  Technology *A*
West Virginia Northern Community
  College *A*
West Virginia University at
  Parkersburg *A*

Wisconsin

Chippewa Valley Technical
  College *A*
Fox Valley Technical College *A*
Madison Area Technical College *A*
Madison Junior College of
  Business *A*
Mid-State Technical College *A*
Moraine Park Technical College *A*
Northeast Wisconsin Technical
  College *A*
Stratton College *C,A*
University of Wisconsin
  Oshkosh *B*
  Superior *B*
Waukesha County Technical
  College *A*
Western Wisconsin Technical
  College *A*

Wyoming

Casper College *A*
Central Wyoming College *C,A*
Eastern Wyoming College *C*
Northwest College *A*
Western Wyoming Community
  College *C,A*

Business data
programming

Alabama

Alabama Southern Community
  College *A*
Brewer State Junior College *A*
Douglas MacArthur State Technical
  College *A*
Enterprise State Junior College *A*
James H. Faulkner State
  Community College *A*
Jefferson State Community
  College *A*
Northeast Alabama State Junior
  College *A*
Shelton State Community
  College *A*
Troy State University *A*
Wallace State Community College
  at Hanceville *A*

Alaska

University of Alaska Anchorage *A*

Arizona

Cochise College *A*
Mesa Community College *A*
Scottsdale Community College *A*

Arkansas

Arkansas State University: Beebe
   Branch *A*
Capital City Junior College *A*
East Arkansas Community
   College *A*
Garland County Community
   College *A*
Phillips County Community
   College *A*
Southern Arkansas University
      Magnolia *A*
      Technical Branch *A*
Williams Baptist College *A*

California

Bakersfield College *A*
Barstow College *A*
California State Polytechnic
   University: Pomona *M*
Cerritos Community College *A*
Chabot College *A*
Chaffey Community College *A*
City College of San Francisco *A*
Compton Community College *A*
De Anza College *C,A*
Diablo Valley College *A*
East Los Angeles College *A*
Evergreen Valley College *A*
Gavilan Community College *A*
Glendale Community College *A*
Grossmont Community College *C,A*
Hartnell College *A*
Humphreys College *A*
Kings River Community College *A*
Lassen College *A*
Long Beach City College *A*
Los Angeles City College *A*
Los Angeles Harbor College *C,A*
Los Angeles Trade and Technical
   College *A*
Los Angeles Valley College *C,A*
Merced College *A*
Mission College *A*
Modesto Junior College *A*
Monterey Peninsula College *C,A*
Moorpark College *A*
Mount San Antonio College *C*
Mount San Jacinto College *A*
Ohlone College *A*
Orange Coast College *C,A*
Pasadena City College *A*
Phillips Junior College
      Condie Campus *A*
      Fresno Campus *C,A*
Saddleback College *C,A*
San Diego City College *C,A*
San Jose City College *A*
Santa Rosa Junior College *C,A*
Solano Community College *A*
Southwestern College *A*
Ventura College *A*
Victor Valley College *A*
West Hills Community College *A*

Colorado

Colorado Mountain College: Spring
   Valley Campus *A*
Community College of Denver *C,A*
Denver Technical College *A*
Front Range Community College
   C,A
Mesa State College *A*
Pueblo Community College *A*

Red Rocks Community College *A*
Trinidad State Junior College *A*

Connecticut

Greater New Haven State Technical
   College *A*
Middlesex Community College *C,A*
Norwalk Community College *A*
Norwalk State Technical College *A*
Thames Valley State Technical
   College *A*
Waterbury State Technical
   College *A*

Delaware

Goldey-Beacom College *A*

District of Columbia

University of the District of
   Columbia *A*

Florida

Brevard Community College *A*
Broward Community College *A*
Gulf Coast Community College *A*
Indian River Community College *A*
Jones College *A,B*
Manatee Community College *A*
Miami-Dade Community College *A*
Orlando College *A*
Palm Beach Community College *A*
Pasco-Hernando Community
   College *A*
St. Petersburg Junior College *A*
Tallahassee Community College *A*
Webber College *A*

Georgia

Abraham Baldwin Agricultural
   College *A*
Atlanta Metropolitan College *A*
Augusta Technical Institute *C*
Bainbridge College *A*
Dalton College *A*
Darton College *A*
DeKalb College *A*
DeKalb Technical Institute *A*
Georgia College *B*
Gordon College *A*
Macon College *A*
Middle Georgia College *A*
South Georgia College *A*

Hawaii

Hawaii Pacific University *A*

Idaho

Idaho State University *A*
North Idaho College *A*
Ricks College *A*

Illinois

Belleville Area College *A*
Black Hawk College *A*
Carl Sandburg College *A*
City Colleges of Chicago
      Richard J. Daley College *A*
      Wright College *A*
College of DuPage *A*
Elgin Community College *C,A*
Illinois Central College *C,A*
Illinois Eastern Community
   Colleges: Lincoln Trail College *A*
Illinois Valley Community College
   C,A
Joliet Junior College *A*
Lake Land College *A*
Lewis and Clark Community
   College *A*
Lincoln Land Community
   College *A*
Midstate College *C,A*

Moraine Valley Community
   College *C*
Oakton Community College *C,A*
Parkland College *A*
Prairie State College *A*
Richland Community College *A*
Robert Morris College: Chicago
   C,A
Rock Valley College *A*
Southern Illinois University at
   Carbondale *A*
Triton College *A*

Indiana

Ancilla College *A*
Anderson University *B*
Indiana University—Purdue
   University
      Fort Wayne *A*
      Indianapolis *A*
Indiana Wesleyan University *A*
ITT Technical Institute:
   Indianapolis *A*
Oakland City College *A*
Purdue University
      Calumet *A*
      North Central Campus *A*
      West Lafayette *A,B*
University of Southern Indiana *A*
Vincennes University *A*

Iowa

American Institute of Business *A*
Des Moines Area Community
   College *A*
Iowa Central Community College *A*
Iowa Lakes Community College *A*
Kirkwood Community College *A*
North Iowa Area Community
   College *A*
Scott Community College *A*
Waldorf College *A*

Kansas

Brown Mackie College *C*
Butler County Community
   College *A*
Central College *A*
Colby Community College *A*
Fort Scott Community College *A*
Hesston College *A*
Hutchinson Community College *A*
Kansas City Kansas Community
   College *A*
Neosho County Community
   College *A*
Seward County Community
   College *A*

Kentucky

Bellarmine College *A*
Jefferson Community College *A*
Murray State University *A*
Paducah Community College *A*
Sullivan College *A*

Louisiana

Southeastern Louisiana
   University *A*
Southern University at New
   Orleans *A*

Maine

Andover College *A*
Casco Bay College *A*
University of Maine at Machias *A*

Maryland

Allegany Community College *A*
Anne Arundel Community
   College *A*
Catonsville Community College *A*

Charles County Community
   College *A*
Chesapeake College *A*
Howard Community College *A*
Montgomery College
      Germantown Campus *A*
      Rockville Campus *A*
      Takoma Park Campus *A*

Massachusetts

Becker College: Worcester
   Campus *A*
Berkshire Community College *A*
Bunker Hill Community College *A*
Dean Junior College *A*
Endicott College *A*
Holyoke Community College *A*
Massasoit Community College *A*
Middlesex Community College *A*
Mount Ida College *A*
Mount Wachusett Community
   College *A*
North Shore Community College *A*
Northern Essex Community
   College *A*
Quinsigamond Community
   College *A*
Roxbury Community College *A*
Springfield Technical Community
   College *A*

Michigan

Andrews University *A*
Baker College
      Flint *A,B*
      Muskegon *A,B*
Davenport College of Business *A*
Delta College *A*
Grand Rapids Community
   College *A*
Great Lakes Junior College of
   Business *A*
Jackson Community College *C,A*
Kalamazoo Valley Community
   College *A*
Kellogg Community College *C,A*
Lansing Community College *A*
Marygrove College *A*
Mid Michigan Community
   College *A*
Muskegon Community College *A*
Northwestern Michigan College *A*
Northwood Institute *A*
Oakland Community College *A*
St. Clair County Community
   College *C,A*
Southwestern Michigan College *A*

Minnesota

Alexandria Technical College *A*
Normandale Community College *A*
Northland Community College *A*
Willmar Community College *A*

Mississippi

East Central Community College *A*
Hinds Community College *A*
Jones County Junior College *A*
Mississippi Delta Community
   College *A*
Northeast Mississippi Community
   College *A*
Phillips Junior College
      Jackson *A*
      Mississippi Gulf Coast *A*

Missouri

East Central College *A*
Jefferson College *A*
Longview Community College *A*
Missouri Southern State College *A*

St. Louis Community College
Florissant Valley *A*
Meramec *A*

Montana

Miles Community College *A*
Northern Montana College *A*

Nebraska

College of St. Mary *A*
McCook Community College *A*
Midland Lutheran College *A*
Northeast Community College *A*
Southeast Community College:
Milford Campus *A*
Western Nebraska Community
College: Scottsbluff Campus *A*
York College *A*

Nevada

Community College of Southern
Nevada *C,A*
Northern Nevada Community
College *A*
Truckee Meadows Community
College *A*

New Hampshire

Hesser College *A*
McIntosh College *A*

New Jersey

Bergen Community College *A*
Brookdale Community College *A*
Burlington County College *C,A*
Camden County College *A*
County College of Morris *A*
Essex County College *A*
Thomas Edison State College *A*
Union County College *A*

New Mexico

New Mexico Junior College *A*
New Mexico State University *B*
Northern New Mexico Community
College *C*

New York

Adirondack Community College *A*
Bramson ORT Technical Institute
C,A
Bryant & Stratton Business Institute
Albany *A*
Rochester *A*
Syracuse *A*
Central City Business Institute *A*
City University of New York
Kingsborough Community
College *A*
La Guardia Community
College *A*
Medgar Evers College *A*
Clarkson University *B,M*
Columbia-Greene Community
College *C,A*
Community College of the Finger
Lakes *A*
Corning Community College *C,A*
Fulton-Montgomery Community
College *A*
Herkimer County Community
College *A*
Jamestown Community College *A*
Jefferson Community College *A*
Monroe College *A*
Rochester Business Institute *A*

State University of New York
College of Agriculture and
Technology at Morrisville *A*
College of Technology at
Alfred *A*
College of Technology at
Delhi *A*
College of Technology at
Farmingdale *A*
Sullivan County Community
College *A*
Westchester Business Institute *A*

North Carolina

Alamance Community College *A*
Asheville Buncombe Technical
Community College *A*
Beaufort County Community
College *A*
Bladen Community College *A*
Brevard College *A*
Brunswick Community College *C,A*
Campbell University *A*
Cecils College *C*
Chowan College *A*
College of the Albemarle *A*
Craven Community College *C,A*
Davidson County Community
College *C,A*
Durham Technical Community
College *A*
Forsyth Technical Community
College *C,A*
Gaston College *A*
Guilford Technical Community
College *A*
Isothermal Community College *A*
Martin Community College *C,A*
McDowell Technical Community
College *A*
Methodist College *A*
Mitchell Community College *A*
Nash Community College *A*
Pitt Community College *A*
Richmond Community College *C,A*
Roanoke-Chowan Community
College *A*
Sandhills Community College *C,A*
Southwestern Community
College *A*
Stanly Community College *A*
Tri-County Community College *C,A*
Vance-Granville Community
College *A*
Wake Technical Community
College *A*
Western Piedmont Community
College *A*
Wilson Technical Community
College *C,A*

North Dakota

North Dakota State College of
Science *A*
University of North Dakota:
Williston *A*

Ohio

Bowling Green State University:
Firelands College *A*
Cincinnati Metropolitan College *A*
Cincinnati Technical College *A*
Clark State Community College *A*
Columbus State Community
College *A*
Davis Junior College of Business *A*
Edison State Community College *A*

Kent State University
Ashtabula Regional Campus *A*
East Liverpool Regional
Campus *A*
Kent *B*
Salem Regional Campus *A*
Lorain County Community
College *A*
Miami-Jacobs College *A*
Mount Vernon Nazarene College *A*
North Central Technical College *A*
Owens Technical College
Findlay Campus *A*
Toledo *A*
Terra Technical College *A*
University of Akron *A*
University of Cincinnati
Access Colleges *A*
Raymond Walters College *A*
University of Toledo *A*

Oklahoma

Bacone College *A*
Eastern Oklahoma State College *A*
Oklahoma State University:
Oklahoma City *A*
Redlands Community College *A*
Rogers State College *A*
Rose State College *A*
St. Gregory's College *A*
Tulsa Junior College *A*

Oregon

Central Oregon Community
College *A*
Chemeketa Community College *A*
Lane Community College *A*
Portland Community College *A*
Treasure Valley Community
College *A*
Umpqua Community College *A*

Pennsylvania

Berean Institute *A*
Bucks County Community
College *A*
Butler County Community
College *A*
California University of
Pennsylvania *A*
CHI Institute *C*
Clarion University of
Pennsylvania *A*
Community College of Beaver
County *A*
Community College of
Philadelphia *A*
Harrisburg Area Community
College *A*
La Salle University *A*
Lehigh County Community
College *A*
Messiah College *B*
Peirce Junior College *A*
Point Park College *C,A*
Westmoreland County Community
College *A*

Puerto Rico

Instituto Tecnico Comercial Junior
College *A*
Inter American University of Puerto
Rico: San German Campus *A,B*

Rhode Island

Johnson & Wales University *A*

South Carolina

Chesterfield-Marlboro Technical
College *A*
Midlands Technical College *C,A*
Sumter Area Technical College *C*

Technical College of the
Lowcountry *A*
Trident Technical College *C,A*

South Dakota

Augustana College *A*
Black Hills State University *A*
Kilian Community College *A*
National College *A,B*
Presentation College *A*

Tennessee

Bristol University *A*
Chattanooga State Technical
Community College *A*
Columbia State Community College
C,A
Dyersburg State Community
College *A*
Hiwassee College *A*
McKenzie College *A*
Motlow State Community
College *A*
Northeast State Technical
Community College *A*
Pellissippi State Technical
Community College *A*

Texas

Amarillo College *A*
Angelina College *A*
Austin Community College *A*
Brookhaven College *A*
Central Texas College *A*
Cisco Junior College *A*
College of the Mainland *A*
Cooke County College *A*
Del Mar College *A*
Eastfield College *A*
El Centro College *A*
Howard College *A*
Laredo Junior College *A*
Lee College *A*
McLennan Community College *A*
Midland College *A*
Mountain View College *A*
Navarro College *A*
North Harris Montgomery
Community College District *A*
Panola College *A*
Richland College *A*
St. Philip's College *A*
San Antonio College *A*
San Jácinto College: Central
Campus *A*
Southwestern Christian College *A*
Stephen F. Austin State
University *B*
Temple Junior College *A*
Texas Southmost College *A*
Texas State Technical College:
Amarillo *A*
University of Texas: Pan
American *A*
Victoria College *A*
Western Texas College *A*

Utah

LDS Business College *A*
Phillips Junior College: Salt Lake
City Campus *A*
Southern Utah University *A*
Weber State University *A*

Vermont

Champlain College *A*

Virginia

Blue Ridge Community College *A*
Bluefield College *A,B*
Mountain Empire Community
College *C*

National Business College *A*
Piedmont Virginia Community
College *C,A*

Washington

Big Bend Community College *A*
Centralia College *A*
Clark College *A*
Columbia Basin College *A*
Edmonds Community College *A*
Everett Community College *A*
Griffin College *C,A,B*
ITT Technical Institute: Seattle *C*
Lower Columbia College *A*
Olympic College *C,A*
Pierce College *C,A*
Skagit Valley College *A*
Spokane Community College *C,A*

West Virginia

Bluefield State College *A*
Davis and Elkins College *A*
Marshall University *A*
Potomac State College of West
Virginia University *A*
Shepherd College *A,B*
West Virginia Northern Community
College *A*

Wisconsin

Chippewa Valley Technical
College *A*
Fox Valley Technical College *A*
Madison Area Technical College *A*
Moraine Park Technical College *A*
Stratton College *C,A*
University of Wisconsin: Oshkosh *B*
Waukesha County Technical
College *A*

Wyoming

Casper College *A*
Laramie County Community
College *A*
Northwest College *A*
Western Wyoming Community
College *C,A*

American Samoa, Caroline Islands, Guam, Marianas, Virgin Islands

Northern Marianas College *A*

Business economics

Alabama

Alabama Agricultural and
Mechanical University *B*
Alabama State University *B*
Auburn University
Auburn *B,M,D*
Montgomery *B*
Huntingdon College *B*
Mobile College *B*
Oakwood College *B*
Samford University *B*
Selma University *A*
Spring Hill College *B*
Talladega College *B*
Troy State University *B*
University of Alabama
Birmingham *B*
Huntsville *B*
Tuscaloosa *B,M,D*
University of North Alabama *B*
University of South Alabama *B*

Arizona

Grand Canyon University *B*
Northern Arizona University *B*
University of Arizona *B*

Arkansas

Arkansas College *B*
Arkansas State University *B*
Arkansas Tech University *B*
Harding University *B*
Hendrix College *B*
Ouachita Baptist University *B*
Southern Arkansas University *B*
University of Arkansas
Fayetteville *B*
Little Rock *B*
University of Central Arkansas *B*

California

Barstow College *A*
Biola University *B*
California Lutheran University *B*
California Polytechnic State
University: San Luis Obispo *B,M*
California State University
Fresno *B*
Fullerton *B,M*
Los Angeles *B,M*
Northridge *B*
Chapman University *B*
College of the Desert *A*
College of Notre Dame *B*
Golden Gate University *B*
La Sierra University *B*
Lincoln University *B*
Mills College *B*
St. Mary's College of California *B*
San Joaquin Delta College *A*
Santa Clara University *B*
Scripps College *B*
University of California
Los Angeles *B*
Riverside *B*
Santa Barbara *B,M*
Santa Cruz *B*
University of La Verne *B*
University of the Pacific *B*
University of San Diego *B*
Ventura College *A*
Westmont College *B*

Colorado

Adams State College *B*
Colorado School of Mines *M,D*
Fort Lewis College *B*
Mesa State College *B*
Regis College of Regis University *B*
University of Denver *B,M*
University of Southern Colorado *B*

Connecticut

Albertus Magnus College *B*
Quinnipiac College *B,M*
Sacred Heart University *A,B*
St. Joseph College *B*
Southern Connecticut State
University *B,M*
University of Bridgeport *B*
University of Hartford *B,M*
University of New Haven *B*

Delaware

Delaware State College *B*
University of Delaware *M,D*
Wesley College *B*

District of Columbia

Catholic University of America
B,M,D
George Washington University *B,M*
Mount Vernon College *B*
Trinity College *B*

Florida

Barry University *B*
Daytona Beach Community
College *A*
Florida Atlantic University *B*
Florida Institute of Technology *B*
Jacksonville University *B*
University of Central Florida *B,M*
University of Miami *B,M,D*
University of North Florida *B*
University of South Florida *B,M*
University of Tampa *B*
University of West Florida *B*

Georgia

Augusta College *B*
Berry College *B*
Clark Atlanta University *B*
Columbus College *B*
Emory University *B*
Floyd College *A*
Fort Valley State College *B*
Georgia College *B*
Georgia Institute of Technology
B,M,D
Georgia Southern University *B*
Georgia State University *B,M,D*
Gordon College *A*
Kennesaw State College *B*
LaGrange College *B*
Mercer University
Atlanta *B,M*
Macon *B*
Morehouse College *B*
Morris Brown College *B*
North Georgia College *B*
Oglethorpe University *B*
Piedmont College *B*
University of Georgia *B,M,D*
Valdosta State College *B*
West Georgia College *B*

Hawaii

Hawaii Loa College *B*
Hawaii Pacific University *A,B*
University of Hawaii at Manoa *B*

Idaho

Boise State University *B*
University of Idaho *B*

Illinois

Augustana College *B*
Aurora University *B*
Barat College *B*
Bradley University *B*
De Paul University *B,M*
Elmhurst College *B*
Illinois Benedictine College *B*
Illinois College *B*
Illinois Wesleyan University *B*
Lewis University *B*
Loyola University of Chicago *B*
Millikin University *B*
Monmouth College *B*
Morton College *A*
North Central College *B*
North Park College and Theological
Seminary *B*
Northwestern University *M,D*
Olivet Nazarene University *B*
Principia College *B*
Rockford College *B*
Roosevelt University *B*
Southern Illinois University
Carbondale *B*
Edwardsville *B,M*
Trinity College *B*
University of Chicago *M,D*
University of Illinois
Chicago *D*
Urbana-Champaign *B,M,D*

Western Illinois University *B*

Indiana

Ball State University *B*
Butler University *B*
Calumet College of St. Joseph *B*
Huntington College *B*
Indiana University
Bloomington *B,M,D*
Northwest *B*
South Bend *B*
Southeast *B*
Indiana University—Purdue
University
Fort Wayne *B*
Indianapolis *B*
Indiana Wesleyan University *B*
Purdue University *B,M,D*
St. Joseph's College *B*
Taylor University *B*
University of Evansville *B*
University of Indianapolis *B*
University of Notre Dame *B*
University of Southern Indiana *B*

Iowa

Buena Vista College *B*
Central College *B*
Coe College *B*
Cornell College *B*
Graceland College *B*
Loras College *B*
Luther College *B*
Simpson College *B*
Teikyo Westmar University *B*
University of Dubuque *B*
University of Iowa *B,D*
Wartburg College *B*

Kansas

Baker University *B*
Bethany College *B*
Central College *A*
Coffeyville Community College *A*
Colby Community College *A*
Fort Scott Community College *A*
Kansas State University *B*
Pittsburg State University *B,M*
Southwestern College *B*
Tabor College *B*
Washburn University of Topeka *B*
Wichita State University *B,M*

Kentucky

Campbellsville College *B*
Eastern Kentucky University *B*
Georgetown College *B*
Morehead State University *B*
Murray State University *B,M*
Thomas More College *A,B*
University of Kentucky *B*
University of Louisville *B*
Western Kentucky University *B*

Louisiana

Dillard University *B*
Grambling State University *B*
Louisiana State University
Agricultural and Mechanical
College *B*
Shreveport *B*
Louisiana Tech University *B,M*
Loyola University *B*
McNeese State University *B*
Nicholls State University *B*
Northeast Louisiana University *B*
Southeastern Louisiana
University *B*
Southern University at New
Orleans *B*

Southern University and
Agricultural and Mechanical
College *B*
University of New Orleans *B,M,D*
University of Southwestern
Louisiana *B*
Xavier University of Louisiana *B*

Maine

Thomas College *B*
University of Maine
Farmington *B*
Orono *B*

Maryland

Morgan State University *B,M*
Sojourner-Douglass College *B*
University of Baltimore *B*
Western Maryland College *B*

Massachusetts

American International College *B*
Assumption College *B*
Babson College *B,M*
Bentley College *B,M*
Boston College *B*
Emmanuel College *B*
Harvard and Radcliffe Colleges *B*
Harvard University *M,D*
Massachusetts Institute of
Technology *B,M,D*
Merrimack College *B*
Nichols College *B*
Salem State College *B*
Westfield State College *B*

Michigan

Alma College *B*
Andrews University *B*
Calvin College *B*
Central Michigan University *B*
Eastern Michigan University *B*
Ferris State University *B*
Grand Valley State University *B*
Hope College *B*
Kalamazoo College *B*
Lake Superior State University *B*
Michigan Technological
University *B*
Northwood Institute *B*
Oakland University *B*
Olivet College *B*
Saginaw Valley State University
B,M
Spring Arbor College *B*
University of Detroit Mercy *B,M*
University of Michigan *D*
Wayne State University *B,M*
Western Michigan University *B*

Minnesota

Augsburg College *B*
Bethel College *B*
Concordia College: Moorhead *B*
Concordia College: St. Paul *B*
Mankato State University *B,M*
Northland Community College *A*
St. Mary's College of Minnesota *B*
University of Minnesota
Morris *B*
Twin Cities *B,M,D*
University of St. Thomas *B*
Willmar Community College *A*
Winona State University *B*

Mississippi

Jackson State University *B*
Mississippi College *B,M*
Mississippi State University *B*
Tougaloo College *B*
University of Mississippi *B,M,D*

University of Southern Mississippi
B,M
William Carey College *B*

Missouri

College of the Ozarks *B*
Lincoln University *B*
Missouri Southern State College *B*
Missouri Valley College *B*
Northwest Missouri State
University *B*
Park College *B*
Rockhurst College *B*
St. Louis University *B,M,D*
Southeast Missouri State
University *B*
Westminster College *B*
William Woods College *B*

Montana

Carroll College *B*
Eastern Montana College *B*
Rocky Mountain College *B*

Nebraska

Chadron State College *B*
Creighton University *B*
Dana College *B*
Hastings College *B*
Midland Lutheran College *B*
University of Nebraska
Lincoln *B,M,D*
Omaha *B*

Nevada

University of Nevada
Las Vegas *B,M*
Reno *B,M*

New Hampshire

Franklin Pierce College *B*
New England College *B*
New Hampshire College *B*
Plymouth State College of the
University System of New
Hampshire *B*
St. Anselm College *B*

New Jersey

Bloomfield College *B*
Caldwell College *C*
Fairleigh Dickinson University *B,M*
Jersey City State College *B*
Monmouth College *B*
Rider College *B*
Seton Hall University *B,M*
Stevens Institute of Technology *M*
Trenton State College *B*
William Paterson College of New
Jersey *B*

New Mexico

Eastern New Mexico University *B*
New Mexico State University *B,M*
University of New Mexico *M*
Western New Mexico University *B*

New York

Alfred University *B*
Canisius College *B*
City University of New York
Baruch College *B,M*
Brooklyn College *B*
Clarkson University *B*
College of New Rochelle *B*
Cornell University *M,D*
Daemen College *B*
Dominican College of Blauvelt *B*
Elmira College *B*
Fordham University *B*
Hilbert College *A*
Hofstra University *B*

Iona College *B,M*
Manhattan College *B*
Marist College *B*
Marymount College *B*
New York University *B,M,D*
Niagara University *B*
Pace University *B,M*
Russell Sage College *B*
St. Bonaventure University *B,W*
St. John's University *B,M*
Skidmore College *B*
State University of New York
Buffalo *D*
College at Geneseo *B*
College at New Paltz *B*
College at Oneonta *B*
College at Plattsburgh *B*
Touro College *B*
Union College *B*
Utica College of Syracuse
University *B*
Wagner College *B*

North Carolina

Appalachian State University *B,M*
Campbell University *B*
Methodist College *A*
North Carolina Agricultural and
Technical State University *B*
North Carolina Central
University *B*
North Carolina State University
B,M,D
St. Andrews Presbyterian College *B*
Salem College *B*
University of North Carolina
Greensboro *B,M*
Wilmington *B*
Warren Wilson College *B*
Western Carolina University *B*
Wingate College *B*
Winston-Salem State University *B*

North Dakota

University of North Dakota *B*

Ohio

Ashland University *B*
Bluffton College *B*
Bowling Green State University *B*
Cedarville College *B*
Central State University *B*
Cleveland State University *B*
College of Wooster *B*
Dyke College *B*
Franciscan University of
Steubenville *B*
Heidelberg College *B*
John Carroll University *B*
Kent State University *B,M*
Marietta College *B*
Miami University: Oxford
Campus *B*
Mount Union College *B*
Ohio Northern University *B*
Ohio State University: Columbus
Campus *B*
Ohio University *B*
Ohio Wesleyan University *B*
Otterbein College *B*
University of Akron *B,M*
University of Dayton *B*
University of Findlay *B*
University of Rio Grande *B*
University of Toledo *B,M*
Urbana University *B*
Wilberforce University *B*
Wilmington College *B*
Wittenberg University *B*
Wright State University
Dayton *B,M*
Lake Campus *A*

Xavier University *B*

Oklahoma

East Central University *B*
Northeastern State University *B*
Oklahoma City University *B*
Oklahoma State University *B*
Southeastern Oklahoma State
University *B*
Southwestern Oklahoma State
University *B*
Tulsa Junior College *A*
University of Central Oklahoma *B*
University of Oklahoma *B*
University of Science and Arts of
Oklahoma *B*
University of Tulsa *B*

Oregon

Eastern Oregon State College *B*
George Fox College *B*
Pacific University *B*
Willamette University *B*

Pennsylvania

Albright College *B*
Bloomsburg University of
Pennsylvania *B*
California University of
Pennsylvania *B*
Carnegie Mellon University
B,M,D,W
Chatham College *B*
Clarion University of
Pennsylvania *B*
Drexel University *B,M,D*
Duquesne University *B,M*
Edinboro University of
Pennsylvania *B*
Elizabethtown College *B*
Gannon University *B*
Geneva College *B*
Gettysburg College *B*
Indiana University of
Pennsylvania *B*
Juniata College *B*
Kutztown University of
Pennsylvania *B*
La Salle University *B*
Lafayette College *B*
Lehigh University *B,M,D*
Lincoln University *B*
Luzerne County Community
College *A*
Messiah College *B*
Moravian College *B*
Penn State
Erie Behrend College *B*
University Park Campus *B*
Robert Morris College *B,M*
Rosemont College *B*
St. Francis College *B*
Shippensburg University of
Pennsylvania *B*
Slippery Rock University of
Pennsylvania *B*
Susquehanna University *B*
Temple University *B,M,D*
University of Pennsylvania *B,M,D*
University of Pittsburgh at
Johnstown *B*
University of Scranton *B*
Ursinus College *B*
Villanova University *B*
West Chester University of
Pennsylvania *B,M*
Westminster College *B*
Widener University *B*
Wilson College *B*

Puerto Rico

Inter American University of Puerto Rico
    Arecibo Campus *B*
    Metropolitan Campus *B*
    San German Campus *B*
Pontifical Catholic University of Puerto Rico *B*
University of Puerto Rico
    Mayaguez Campus *B*
    Rio Piedras Campus *B,M*

Rhode Island

Brown University *B,M*
Bryant College *B*
Providence College *B*
Rhode Island College *B*

South Carolina

Charleston Southern University *B*
Erskine College *B*
Francis Marion College *B*
Lander College *B*
Limestone College *B*
Newberry College *B*
Presbyterian College *B*
South Carolina State College *B*
University of South Carolina
    Aiken *B*
    Columbia *B*
Wofford College *B*

South Dakota

Augustana College *B*
South Dakota State University *B,M*
University of South Dakota *B,M*

Tennessee

Austin Peay State University *B*
Belmont University *B*
Bristol University *A,B*
Carson-Newman College *B*
Christian Brothers University *B,M*
David Lipscomb University *B*
East Tennessee State University *B*
Fisk University *B*
King College *B*
Knoxville College *B*
Lincoln Memorial University *B*
Martin Methodist College *A*
Maryville College *B*
Memphis State University *B*
Middle Tennessee State University *B,M,D*
Milligan College *B*
Motlow State Community College *A*
Tennessee State University *B*
Union University *B*
University of Tennessee
    Chattanooga *B,M*
    Knoxville *B,M,D*
    Martin *B*

Texas

Angelo State University *B*
Baylor University *B,M*
Dallas Baptist University *B*
East Texas State University *B,M*
Houston Baptist University *B*
Lamar University—Beaumont *B*
Laredo State University *B*
McMurry University *B*
Midland College *A*
Midwestern State University *B*
Paul Quinn College *B*
Prairie View A&M University *B*
St. Mary's University *M*
Sam Houston State University *B*
Southwest Texas State University *B*
Stephen F. Austin State University *B*

Texas Southern University *B*
Texas Tech University *B*
Texas Wesleyan University *B*
Trinity University *B*
University of Houston *B*
University of Mary Hardin-Baylor *B*
University of North Texas *B*
University of St. Thomas *B*
University of Texas
    Arlington *B,M*
    El Paso *B,M*
    Pan American *B*
    Permian Basin *B*
    San Antonio *B*
    Tyler *B*
West Texas State University *B,M*
Western Texas College *A*

Utah

Brigham Young University *M*
University of Utah *B,M,D*
Utah State University *B,M,D*
Weber State University *B*
Westminster College of Salt Lake City *B*

Virginia

Christopher Newport College *B*
Hampden-Sydney College *B*
James Madison University *B*
Mary Baldwin College *B*
Marymount University *B,M*
Old Dominion University *B,M*
Radford University *B*
Randolph-Macon College *B*
Strayer College *B*
University of Richmond *B*
Virginia Commonwealth University *B,M*
Virginia Military Institute *B*
Virginia Polytechnic Institute and State University *B,M,D*
Virginia State University *B,M*
Virginia Wesleyan College *B*

Washington

Central Washington University *B*
Eastern Washington University *B*
Gonzaga University *B*
Olympic College *A*
St. Martin's College *B*
Seattle Pacific University *B*
Seattle University *B,M*
Spokane Community College *A*
Spokane Falls Community College *A*
Tacoma Community College *A*
Whitworth College *B*

West Virginia

Bethany College *B*
Davis and Elkins College *B*
Fairmont State College *B*
Marshall University *B*
Shepherd College *B*
West Liberty State College *B*
West Virginia Institute of Technology *A*
West Virginia University *B,M,D*

Wisconsin

Cardinal Stritch College *B*
Carroll College *B*
Lakeland College *B*
Marquette University *B,M*
Mount Senario College *B*
Northland College *B*

University of Wisconsin
    Eau Claire *B*
    La Crosse *B*
    Platteville *B*
    Stevens Point *B*
    Superior *B*
    Whitewater *B*

Wyoming

Northwest College *A*
Sheridan College *A*
University of Wyoming *B,M,D*
Western Wyoming Community College *A*

American Samoa, Caroline Islands, Guam, Marianas, Virgin Islands

University of Guam *B*

Canada

McGill University *B,M,D*

Switzerland

American College of Switzerland *B*

Business education

Alabama

Alabama Agricultural and Mechanical University *B,M*
Alabama Southern Community College *A*
Alabama State University *B*
Auburn University *B,M*
Chattahoochee Valley Community College *A*
James H. Faulkner State Community College *A*
Jefferson State Community College *A*
Lawson State Community College *A*
Livingston University *B,M*
Oakwood College *B*
University of North Alabama *B,M*
University of South Alabama *B*

Arizona

Arizona State University *B,D*
Eastern Arizona College *A*
Grand Canyon University *B*

Arkansas

Arkansas College *B*
Arkansas State University *B,M*
Arkansas Tech University *B*
Harding University *B*
Henderson State University *B,M*
John Brown University *B*
Ouachita Baptist University *B*
University of Arkansas
    Fayetteville *B*
    Monticello *B*
    Pine Bluff *B*
University of Central Arkansas *B,M*
University of the Ozarks *B*
Westark Community College *A*

California

Azusa Pacific University *B*
California Baptist College *B*
California State University
    Bakersfield *B*
    Fresno *B*
    Los Angeles *B,M*
    Northridge *B*
    Sacramento *B*
Fresno Pacific College *B*

Gavilan Community College *A*
Mount St. Mary's College *B*
Point Loma Nazarene College *B*
University of San Francisco *B*

Colorado

Colorado State University *M*

Connecticut

Central Connecticut State University *B,M*
Sacred Heart University *B,M*

Delaware

Delaware State College *B*

Florida

Bethune-Cookman College *B*
Florida Agricultural and Mechanical University *B,M*
Gulf Coast Community College *A*
Okaloosa-Walton Community College *A*
Palm Beach Community College *A*
Pensacola Junior College *A*
University of Central Florida *B,M*
University of South Florida *B,M*
University of West Florida *B*

Georgia

Andrew College *A*
Armstrong State College *B,M*
Atlanta Metropolitan College *A*
Augusta College *B*
Bainbridge College *A*
Brewton-Parker College *A,B*
Clark Atlanta University *B*
Gainesville College *A*
Georgia College *B,M*
Georgia Southern University *B,M*
Georgia Southwestern College *B,M*
Georgia State University *B,M,D*
Kennesaw State College *B*
Macon College *A*
Morris Brown College *B*
North Georgia College *B,M*
South Georgia College *A*
Thomas College *A*
University of Georgia *B,M,D*
Valdosta State College *B,M*
West Georgia College *B,M*

Hawaii

Brigham Young University-Hawaii *B*

Idaho

College of Southern Idaho *A*
North Idaho College *A*
Ricks College *A*
University of Idaho *M*

Illinois

Eastern Illinois University *B,M*
Greenville College *B*
Illinois State University *B,M*
Joliet Junior College *A*
McKendree College *B*
Northern Illinois University *B,M,D*
Roosevelt University *B*
Southern Illinois University
    Carbondale *B,M*
    Edwardsville *B,M*
Trinity Christian College *B*
University of Illinois at Urbana-Champaign *B*
Western Illinois University *B*

Indiana

Anderson University *B*
Ball State University *B,M*
Bethel College *B*

Calumet College of St. Joseph *B*
Franklin College *B*
Goshen College *B*
Huntington College *B*
Indiana State University *B,M*
Indiana University Bloomington
  B,M,D
Indiana Wesleyan University *B*
Manchester College *B*
Martin University *B*
Oakland City College *B*
St. Francis College *B*
St. Joseph's College *B*
Tri-State University *B*
University of Evansville *B*
University of Indianapolis *B*
University of Southern Indiana *B*
Vincennes University *A*

Iowa

Buena Vista College *B*
Clarke College *B*
Cornell College *B*
Dordt College *B*
Drake University *B,M*
Grand View College *B*
Iowa Lakes Community College *A*
Kirkwood Community College *A*
Morningside College *B*
Mount Mercy College *B*
Teikyo Marycrest University *B*
Teikyo Westmar University *B*
University of Northern Iowa *B,M*
Upper Iowa University *B*
William Penn College *B*

Kansas

Bethany College *B*
Butler County Community
  College *A*
Emporia State University *B,M*
Fort Hays State University *B*
Friends University *B*
Kansas State University *B*
McPherson College *B*
MidAmerica Nazarene College *B*
Southwestern College *B*
Tabor College *B*
Washburn University of Topeka *B*

Kentucky

Campbellsville College *B*
Cumberland College *B*
Eastern Kentucky University *B,M*
Georgetown College *B*
Morehead State University *B,M*
Murray State University *B*
Northern Kentucky University *B*
Pikeville College *B*
Sue Bennett College *A*
Thomas More College *B*
Union College *B*
University of Kentucky *B*
University of Louisville *M*
Western Kentucky University *B,M*

Louisiana

Grambling State University *B*
Louisiana College *B*
Louisiana State University
  Agricultural and Mechanical
    College *B*
  Shreveport *B*
Louisiana Tech University *B,M*
McNeese State University *B,M*
Nicholls State University *B*
Northeast Louisiana University *B,M*
Northwestern State University *B*
Our Lady of Holy Cross College *B*
Southeastern Louisiana
  University *B*

Southern University and
  Agricultural and Mechanical
    College *B,M*
University of New Orleans *B*
University of Southwestern
  Louisiana *B*

Maine

Casco Bay College *A*
Husson College *B*
Thomas College *B*
University of Maine at Machias *B*

Maryland

Howard Community College *A*
Montgomery College
  Germantown Campus *A*
  Rockville Campus *A*
  Takoma Park Campus *A*
Morgan State University *B*
Prince George's Community
  College *A*

Massachusetts

American International College *B*
Holyoke Community College *A*
Northern Essex Community
  College *A*
Suffolk University *B,M*
University of Massachusetts at
  Amherst *B,M*
Westfield State College *B*

Michigan

Adrian College *B*
Andrews University *M*
Central Michigan University *B,M*
Eastern Michigan University *B*
Ferris State University *B*
Grand Rapids Baptist College and
  Seminary *B*
Marygrove College *B*
Northern Michigan University *B*
Siena Heights College *B*
University of Michigan: Dearborn *B*
Wayne State University *B*
Western Michigan University *B*

Minnesota

Bethel College *B*
College of St. Catherine: St.
  Catherine Campus *B*
Concordia College: Moorhead *B*
Gustavus Adolphus College *B*
Mankato State University *B*
Moorhead State University *B,M*
Northland Community College *A*
Pillsbury Baptist Bible College *B*
Rainy River Community College *A*
St. Cloud State University *B*
St. Mary's College of Minnesota *B*
Southwest State University *B*
University of Minnesota: Twin
  Cities *B,M*
Willmar Community College *A*
Winona State University *B*

Mississippi

Alcorn State University *B,M*
Delta State University *B*
Jones County Junior College *A*
Mary Holmes College *A*
Mississippi College *B,M*
Mississippi Delta Community
  College *A*
Mississippi Gulf Coast Community
  College: Jefferson Davis
    Campus *A*
Mississippi State University *B*
Northeast Mississippi Community
  College *A*
Rust College *B*

University of Southern Mississippi
  B,M

Missouri

Central Missouri State University
  B,M
College of the Ozarks *B*
Columbia College *B*
Evangel College *B*
Missouri Western State College *B*
Northwest Missouri State
  University *B,M*
Southeast Missouri State
  University *B*
Southwest Baptist University *B*
Southwest Missouri State
  University *B*
University of Missouri: Columbia
  B,M,D

Montana

Montana State University *M*
University of Montana *B*
Western Montana College of the
  University of Montana *B*

Nebraska

Chadron State College *B*
College of St. Mary *B*
Concordia College *B*
Creighton University *B*
Dana College *B*
Doane College *B*
Hastings College *B*
Northeast Community College *A*
Peru State College *B*
Union College *B*
University of Nebraska
  Kearney *B,M*
  Lincoln *B,M*
  Omaha *B*
Wayne State College *B,M*

Nevada

Sierra Nevada College *B*

New Hampshire

New Hampshire College *B,M*
Notre Dame College *B*
Rivier College *B*

New Jersey

Essex County College *A*
Montclair State College *B,M*
Rutgers—The State University of
  New Jersey *M,D*

New Mexico

College of the Southwest *B*
Eastern New Mexico University *B*
New Mexico State University *B*
University of New Mexico *B*

New York

Alfred University *B,M*
Canisius College *B*
City University of New York
  Baruch College *B,M*
  Lehman College *B*
Concordia College *B*
Daemen College *B*
Dowling College *B*
D'Youville College *B*
Hofstra University *B,M*
Iona College *B,M*
Le Moyne College *B*
Long Island University
  Brooklyn Campus *B,M*
  C. W. Post Campus *B*
Nazareth College of Rochester *B,M*
New York Institute of
  Technology *A*

New York University *B,M,D*
Niagara University *B,M*
Pace University
  College of White Plains *B*
  New York *B*
  Pleasantville/Briarcliff *B*
St. Bonaventure University *B,M*
Siena College *B*
State University of New York
  College at Buffalo *B,M*
  College at Oneonta *B*
  Oswego *B*
Utica College of Syracuse
  University *B*

North Carolina

Appalachian State University *B*
Beaufort County Community
  College *A*
Catawba Valley Community
  College *A*
East Carolina University *B,M*
Elizabeth City State University *B*
Fayetteville State University *B*
North Carolina Agricultural and
  Technical State University *B*
North Carolina Central
  University *M*
Pembroke State University *B*
St. Augustine's College *B*
University of North Carolina at
  Greensboro *B,M*
Western Carolina University *B,M*
Winston-Salem State University *B*

North Dakota

Bismarck State College *A*
Dickinson State University *B*
Mayville State University *B*
Minot State University *B*
University of North Dakota *B,M*
Valley City State University *B*

Ohio

Ashland University *B*
Baldwin-Wallace College *B*
Bluffton College *B*
Bowling Green State University
  B,M
Cedarville College *B*
College of Mount St. Joseph *C*
Defiance College *B*
Kent State University *B,M*
Malone College *B*
Mount Vernon Nazarene College *B*
Muskingum College *B*
Ohio State University: Columbus
  Campus *B*
Ohio University *B*
University of Dayton *B*
University of Findlay *B*
University of Rio Grande *B*
University of Toledo *B*
Urbana University *B*
Walsh College *B*
Wittenberg University *B*
Wright State University *B*
Youngstown State University *B*

Oklahoma

Bartlesville Wesleyan College *B*
East Central University *B*
Langston University *B*
Northwestern Oklahoma State
  University *B*
Oklahoma Baptist University *B*
Oklahoma Panhandle State
  University *B*
Rogers State College *A*
Southeastern Oklahoma State
  University *B,M*

Southwestern Oklahoma State
University *B,M*
University of Central Oklahoma
B,M
University of Science and Arts of
Oklahoma *B*

Oregon

Portland State University *B*
Southern Oregon State College *M*
Willamette University *M*

Pennsylvania

Bloomsburg University of
Pennsylvania *B,M*
Cheyney University of
Pennsylvania *B*
Community College of
Philadelphia *A*
Delaware Valley College *B*
Gannon University *B*
Geneva College *B*
Gwynedd-Mercy College *B*
Harrisburg Area Community
College *A*
Indiana University of
Pennsylvania *B*
Mercyhurst College *B*
Reading Area Community
College *A*
Robert Morris College *B,M*
St. Joseph's University *C,B,M*
Shippensburg University of
Pennsylvania *B,M*
Temple University *M,D*
University of Pittsburgh *B*
Waynesburg College *B*
York College of Pennsylvania *B*

Puerto Rico

Caribbean University *B*
Inter American University of Puerto
Rico: Metropolitan Campus *M*
Pontifical Catholic University of
Puerto Rico *B*
University of Puerto Rico: Rio
Piedras Campus *B*

Rhode Island

Johnson & Wales University *B*
University of Rhode Island *C*

South Carolina

Bob Jones University *B*
South Carolina State College *B*
University of South Carolina *M*
Winthrop University *B,M*

South Dakota

Black Hills State University *B*
Dakota State University *B*
Dakota Wesleyan University *B*
Huron University *B*
Northern State University *B,M*

Tennessee

East Tennessee State University *B*
Lincoln Memorial University *B*
Roane State Community College *A*
Tennessee Wesleyan College *B*
Trevecca Nazarene College *B*
Union University *B,M*
University of Tennessee
Chattanooga *B,M*
Knoxville *B*
Martin *B*

Texas

Abilene Christian University *B*
Angelo State University *B*
Baylor University *B*
East Texas Baptist University *B*

East Texas State University *B,M*
Hardin-Simmons University *B*
Incarnate Word College *B*
McMurry University *B*
Midwestern State University *B*
Prairie View A&M University *B,M*
St. Edward's University *B*
St. Mary's University *B*
Sam Houston State University *B*
Sul Ross State University *B*
Tarleton State University *B*
Texas Christian University *B*
Texas College *B*
Texas Southmost College *A*
Texas Tech University *B,M,D*
Texas Woman's University *M*
University of Houston *B,M*
University of Mary Hardin-
Baylor *B*
University of North Texas *M*
West Texas State University *B*
Wiley College *B*

Utah

Brigham Young University *B,M*
Southern Utah University *B*
Utah State University *B*
Weber State University *B*

Vermont

Castleton State College *B*

Virginia

Bluefield College *B*
Norfolk State University *B*
Old Dominion University *B,M*
Radford University *M*
Virginia Commonwealth
University *B*
Virginia Intermont College *B*
Virginia Polytechnic Institute and
State University *B,M*
Virginia State University *B,M*
Virginia Union University *B*

Washington

Central Washington University *B,M*
Eastern Washington University *B*
Pacific Lutheran University *B*

West Virginia

Concord College *B*
Davis and Elkins College *B*
Fairmont State College *B*
Glenville State College *B*
Shepherd College *B*
West Liberty State College *B*
West Virginia Institute of
Technology *B*

Wisconsin

Concordia University Wisconsin *B*
Maranatha Baptist Bible College *B*
Marian College of Fond du Lac *B*
Mount Mary College *B*
Northland College *B*
University of Wisconsin
Eau Claire *B,M*
Whitewater *B*

Wyoming

Casper College *A*
Central Wyoming College *A*
University of Wyoming *B,M*

**American Samoa, Caroline
Islands, Guam, Marianas,
Virgin Islands**

University of Guam *B*

Business home economics

Arizona

Eastern Arizona College *A*

California

California State University:
Northridge *B*
Christian Heritage College *B*
Point Loma Nazarene College *B*

Georgia

Georgia Southern University *B*

Idaho

Northwest Nazarene College *B*

Illinois

KAES College *B*

Louisiana

McNeese State University *B*
Nicholls State University *B*

Michigan

Eastern Michigan University *B*

Nebraska

McCook Community College *A*
University of Nebraska—Kearney *B*

New Mexico

Eastern New Mexico University *B*
New Mexico State University *B*

New York

Cornell University *B*

North Carolina

University of North Carolina at
Greensboro *B*

Ohio

Ohio University *B*

Rhode Island

University of Rhode Island *B*

Tennessee

University of Tennessee:
Chattanooga *B*

Texas

Texas Tech University *B,M*
University of Mary Hardin-
Baylor *B*

Virginia

Virginia State University *B*

Wisconsin

University of Wisconsin: Stout *B*

Business and management

Alabama

Alabama Agricultural and
Mechanical University *B*
Alabama State University *A,B*
Athens State College *B*
Auburn University
Auburn *M*
Montgomery *B,M*
Birmingham-Southern College *B,M*
Brewer State Junior College *A*

Central Alabama Community
College: Childersburg Campus *C*
Enterprise State Junior College *A*
Faulkner University *B*
Gadsden State Community
College *A*
George C. Wallace State
Community College at Selma *A*
Huntingdon College *B*
Jacksonville State University *B,M*
James H. Faulkner State
Community College *A*
Jefferson State Community
College *A*
Judson College *B*
Livingston University *B*
Lurleen B. Wallace State Junior
College *A*
Mobile College *B,M*
Oakwood College *B*
Samford University *B,M*
Selma University *A*
Shelton State Community
College *A*
Snead State Junior College *A*
Southern Union State Junior
College *A*
Spring Hill College *M*
Stillman College *B*
Talladega College *B*
Troy State University
Montgomery *B,M*
Troy *B*
University of Alabama
Birmingham *B*
Tuscaloosa *B*
University of Montevallo *B*
University of South Alabama *B*
Walker State Technical College *A*
Wallace State Community College
at Hanceville *A*

Alaska

Alaska Pacific University *C,A,B,M*
Sheldon Jackson College *A,B*
University of Alaska
Anchorage *A,B,M*
Fairbanks *A,B,M*

Arizona

Arizona State University *B,M,D*
Arizona Western College *A*
Cochise College *A*
Eastern Arizona College *A*
Glendale Community College *A*
Grand Canyon University *B,M*
Mesa Community College *A*
Mohave Community College *C,A*
Navajo Community College *C,A*
Northland Pioneer College *C,A*
Paradise Valley Community College
C,A
Rio Salado Community College *A*
Scottsdale Community College *A*
South Mountain Community
College *A*
University of Arizona *B,M,D*

Arkansas

Arkansas Baptist College *A,B*
Arkansas College *B*
Arkansas State University
Beebe Branch *A*
Jonesboro *B*
Arkansas Tech University *B*
Central Baptist College *C,A*
East Arkansas Community
College *A*
Garland County Community
College *A*
Harding University *B*
Henderson State University *B,M*

John Brown University B
Mississippi County Community
College A
National Education Center:
Arkansas College of
Technology A
Ouachita Baptist University B
Rich Mountain Community
College A
Shorter College A
Southern Arkansas University B
University of Arkansas
Fayetteville B
Little Rock B
Monticello B
University of Central Arkansas B,M
University of the Ozarks B
Williams Baptist College A,B

California

Allan Hancock College C,A
American Armenian International
College B
American College for the Applied
Arts: Los Angeles A,B
Armstrong College A,B,M
Azusa Pacific University B
Barstow College C,A
Bethany College A
Biola University B
California Lutheran University B
California Polytechnic State
University: San Luis Obispo M
California State University
Bakersfield B
Chico M
Dominguez Hills B
Fresno B,M
Fullerton M
Hayward B,M
Long Beach B,M
Los Angeles B,M
San Bernardino B
San Marcos B
Stanislaus B
Cerritos Community College A
Chabot College A
Chaffey Community College A
Citrus College A
Coastline Community College A
College of the Desert A
College of Marin: Kentfield A
College of Notre Dame B
College of the Redwoods A
College of the Sequoias A
Columbia College A
Cosumnes River College A
Crafton Hills College A
Cuesta College A
El Camino College C,A
Feather River College A
Fresno City College A
Fresno Pacific College B
Gavilan Community College A
Golden Gate University C,A,B,M,D
Golden West College C,A
Imperial Valley College A
Irvine Valley College C,A
John F. Kennedy University B,M
Kelsey-Jenney College C
La Sierra University B,M
Lake Tahoe Community College
C,A
Lincoln University B,M
Long Beach City College C,A
Los Angeles Harbor College C,A
Los Angeles Mission College A
Los Angeles Valley College C,A
Los Medanos College C,A
Marymount College A
Mendocino College A
Merced College A

Mission College C,A
Monterey Peninsula College C,A
Mount St. Mary's College B
Mount San Antonio College A
Mount San Jacinto College A
Napa Valley College A
National University C,B,M
Ohlone College C,A
Orange Coast College C,A
Oxnard College A
Pacific Union College B
Pasadena City College A
Phillips Junior College: Fresno
Campus C,A
Point Loma Nazarene College B
Porterville College A
Rio Hondo College C
Saddleback College C,A
St. Mary's College of California B
San Diego City College C,A
San Diego Mesa College C,A
San Diego State University M
San Francisco State University B,M
San Joaquin Delta College C,A
Santa Barbara City College C,A
Santa Monica College C,A
Santa Rosa Junior College C,A
Sierra College A
Skyline College C
Solano Community College A
Southwestern College C,A
Taft College A
University of California
Berkeley B,M,D
Los Angeles M,D
Riverside B,M
University of Judaism B
University of La Verne B,M
University of the Pacific B
University of San Diego B
University of San Francisco B,M
Ventura College A
Victor Valley College C,A
West Coast University C,A,B,M
West Hills Community College C,A
West Valley College A
Whittier College B
Woodbury University B,M
World College West B
Yuba College A

Colorado

Blair Junior College A
Colorado Christian University B
Colorado Mountain College
Alpine Campus A
Spring Valley Campus A
Colorado Northwestern Community
College A
Colorado Technical College B,M
Community College of Denver C,A
Denver Technical College A,B
Fort Lewis College B
Front Range Community College
C,A
Lamar Community College A
Mesa State College A,B
National College B
Northeastern Junior College A
Otero Junior College A
Pikes Peak Community College A
Pueblo Community College A
Trinidad State Junior College A
University of Colorado
Boulder B
Colorado Springs B
Denver B,M
University of Denver B,M
University of Northern Colorado B

Connecticut

Briarwood College A
Central Connecticut State
University M
Eastern Connecticut State
University B
Middlesex Community College A
Mitchell College A
Northwestern Connecticut
Community College A
Norwalk Community College A
Quinnipiac College B,M
Sacred Heart University A,B,M
South Central Community
College A
Southern Connecticut State
University B
Teikyo-Post University A,B
University of Bridgeport B
University of Connecticut B
University of New Haven B

Delaware

Delaware State College B,M
Delaware Technical and
Community College
Southern Campus A
Stanton/Wilmington
Campus A
Terry Campus A
Goldey-Beacom College A,B
Wesley College A,B
Wilmington College B

District of Columbia

Catholic University of America B,M
Gallaudet University B
George Washington University
B,M,D
Georgetown University B
Southeastern University A,B,M

Florida

Barry University B,M
Brevard Community College A
Broward Community College A
Chipola Junior College A
Daytona Beach Community
College A
Edison Community College C,A
Florida Atlantic University B,M
Florida Institute of Technology B,M
Florida State University B,M
Fort Lauderdale College A,B
Gulf Coast Community College C,A
Hillsborough Community College A
Indian River Community College A
Jacksonville University B
Jones College A,B
Lake-Sumter Community College A
Nova University B,M,D
Okaloosa-Walton Community
College A
Orlando College A,B
Palm Beach Community College A
Pensacola Junior College A
Phillips Junior College: Melbourne
C,A
St. Thomas University B,M
Santa Fe Community College A
Schiller International University
A,B
South College: Palm Beach Campus
C,A
South Florida Community
College A
Southern College A
Stetson University B
Tallahassee Community College A
Tampa College A,B
University of Central Florida B,M,D
University of Florida M

University of Miami B
University of North Florida B,M
University of South Florida B,M,D
University of Tampa B,M
University of West Florida B,M
Webber College A,B

Georgia

Abraham Baldwin Agricultural
College A
American College for the Applied
Arts A,B
Andrew College A
Augusta College A,B
Bainbridge College A
Berry College M
Brewton-Parker College B
Clayton State College B
Columbus College B
Covenant College A,B
Darton College A
DeKalb College A
East Georgia College C,A
Emory University B,M
Floyd College A
Fort Valley State College B
Gainesville College A
Georgia College B,M
Georgia Institute of Technology
B,M,D
Georgia Southern University B,M
Georgia Southwestern College B
Georgia State University M,D
Gordon College C,A
Kennesaw State College B,M
LaGrange College B,M
Macon College C,A
Mercer University
Atlanta B,M
Macon B,M
North Georgia College B
Oglethorpe University B
Oxford College of Emory
University A
Paine College B
Piedmont College B
Savannah State College B
Savannah Technical Institute C
Shorter College B
South College A
South Georgia College A
Thomas College A
Truett-McConnell College A
University of Georgia B,M
Waycross College C,A
Young Harris College A

Hawaii

Brigham Young University-
Hawaii B
Hawaii Pacific University A,B,M
University of Hawaii
Hilo B
Leeward Community
College A
Manoa B

Idaho

Albertson College B
Boise State University B,M
Lewis Clark State College B
North Idaho College A
Northwest Nazarene College A
Ricks College A

Illinois

Augustana College B
Aurora University B
Barat College B
Belleville Area College A

Black Hawk College
   East Campus *A*
   Moline *A*
Bradley University *B,M*
City Colleges of Chicago
   Chicago City-Wide College
   C,A
   Malcolm X College *A*
   Richard J. Daley College *C*
   Wright College *A*
College of DuPage *C,A*
College of St. Francis *B*
Columbia College *B*
Concordia University *B*
De Paul University *B,M*
East-West University *B*
Elgin Community College *C,A*
Eureka College *B*
Greenville College *B*
Highland Community College *C*
Illinois Benedictine College *B*
Illinois Central College *A*
Illinois College *B*
Illinois Valley Community
   College *A*
Illinois Wesleyan University *B*
John A. Logan College *A*
Joliet Junior College *A*
Kishwaukee College *A*
Lake Forest College *B*
Lake Land College *C,A*
Lewis and Clark Community
   College *A*
Lincoln Land Community
   College *A*
Loyola University of Chicago *B,M*
MacCormac Junior College *A*
McKendree College *B*
Millikin University *B*
Monmouth College *B*
Montay College *A*
Moraine Valley Community
   College *A*
Morton College *A*
National-Louis University *M*
North Central College *B*
North Park College and Theological
   Seminary *A*
Northern Illinois University *M*
Northwestern University *M*
Oakton Community College *C,A*
Olivet Nazarene University *B*
Parkland College *A*
Prairie State College *A*
Principia College *B*
Quincy College *C*
Rend Lake College *A*
Richland Community College *C,A*
Rockford College *B*
Rosary College *B,M*
St. Augustine College *A*
Sangamon State University *B*
Shawnee Community College *A*
Shimer College *B*
Southern Illinois University at
   Carbondale *B,M,D*
Trinity Christian College *B*
Triton College *C,A*
University of Chicago *M,D*
University of Illinois at Chicago *B*
Waubonsee Community College *A*
Wheaton College *B*
William Rainey Harper College *A*

Indiana

Ancilla College *A*
Anderson University *B*
Ball State University *B,M*
Earlham College *B*
Franklin College *B*
Goshen College *B*
Grace College *B*

Indiana University
   Bloomington *C,D*
   Northwest *B,M*
   South Bend *C*
   Southeast *B*
Indiana University—Purdue
   University
   Fort Wayne *B,M*
   Indianapolis *B*
Indiana Wesleyan University *A,B,M*
ITT Technical Institute:
   Indianapolis *A*
Manchester College *A,B*
Oakland City College *A,B*
Purdue University
   Calumet *A,B*
   North Central Campus *C,A,B*
St. Francis College *A,B,M*
St. Joseph's College *B*
St. Mary-of-the-Woods College *A,B*
Tri-State University *B*
University of Indianapolis *A,B,M*
University of Notre Dame *M*
University of Southern Indiana *A,B*
Vincennes University *A*

Iowa

American Institute of Business *C,A*
American Institute of Commerce *C*
Briar Cliff College *B*
Buena Vista College *B*
Central College *B*
Clinton Community College *A*
Coe College *B*
Des Moines Area Community
   College *A*
Dordt College *B*
Drake University *B,M*
Grand View College *B*
Iowa Lakes Community College *A*
Iowa State University *B,M*
Iowa Wesleyan College *B*
Iowa Western Community
   College *A*
Kirkwood Community College *A*
Loras College *B*
Luther College *B*
Morningside College *B*
Mount Mercy College *B*
Muscatine Community College *A*
North Iowa Area Community
   College *A*
Northwest Iowa Technical
   College *A*
Northwestern College *B*
St. Ambrose University *B*
Scott Community College *A*
Simpson College *B*
Southeastern Community College
   North Campus *A*
   South Campus *A*
Southwestern Community
   College *A*
Teikyo Marycrest University *B*
Teikyo Westmar University *B*
University of Dubuque *B,M*
University of Iowa *B,M,D*
University of Northern Iowa *B,M*
Upper Iowa University *A,B*
Vennard College *B*
Waldorf College *A*
Wartburg College *B*
William Penn College *B*

Kansas

Allen County Community
   College *A*
Baker University *B,M*
Barton County Community
   College *A*
Brown Mackie College *C*

Butler County Community
   College *A*
Central College *A*
Cloud County Community
   College *A*
Coffeyville Community College *A*
Colby Community College *A*
Cowley County Community
   College *A*
Dodge City Community College *A*
Donnelly College *A*
Emporia State University *A,B*
Fort Hays State University *B*
Fort Scott Community College *A*
Friends University *B,M*
Haskell Indian Junior College *A*
Highland Community College *A*
Hutchinson Community College *A*
Kansas City Kansas Community
   College *A*
Kansas Newman College *B*
Kansas State University *B*
Kansas Wesleyan University *A,B*
Labette Community College *A*
MidAmerica Nazarene College *A,B*
Neosho County Community College
   C,A
Ottawa University *B*
Pittsburg State University *B*
Pratt Community College *C,A*
Seward County Community
   College *A*
Tabor College *B*
University of Kansas *B,M,D*
Washburn University of Topeka
   B,M
Wichita State University *B*

Kentucky

Asbury College *B*
Berea College *B*
Brescia College *A,B*
Campbellsville College *B*
Eastern Kentucky University *B*
Elizabethtown Community
   College *A*
Franklin College *B*
Georgetown College *B*
Hazard Community College *A*
Jefferson Community College *A*
Lexington Community College *A*
Lindsey Wilson College *A*
Madisonville Community College *A*
Morehead State University *B,M*
Murray State University *B,M*
Northern Kentucky University *B*
Paducah Community College *A*
St. Catharine College *A*
Southeast Community College *A*
Spalding University *A,B*
Sue Bennett College *A*
Sullivan College *A,B*
Thomas More College *A,B*
Watterson College *A*
Western Kentucky University *B*

Louisiana

Bossier Parish Community
   College *A*
Centenary College of Louisiana *B,M*
Dillard University *B*
Grambling State University *B,M*
Louisiana College *B*
Louisiana State University
   Agricultural and Mechanical
     College *B,M*
   Eunice *A*
   Shreveport *B,M*
Loyola University *B,M*
McNeese State University *B,M*
Nicholls State University *A,B*
Northeast Louisiana University *B,M*

Northwestern State University *A,B*
Phillips Junior College: New
   Orleans *A*
Southeastern Louisiana University
   B,M
Southern University at New
   Orleans *B*
Southern University and
   Agricultural and Mechanical
   College *B*
Tulane University *B,M,D*
University of New Orleans *B,M*
University of Southwestern
   Louisiana *B*

Maine

Andover College *A*
Casco Bay College *A*
Colby College *B*
Eastern Maine Technical College *A*
Husson College *A,B,M*
Kennebec Valley Technical
   College *A*
St. Joseph's College *B*
Thomas College *C,B,M*
University of Maine
   Fort Kent *A,B*
   Machias *A,B*
   Orono *A,B*
Westbrook College *B*

Maryland

Anne Arundel Community
   College *A*
Bowie State University *B*
Catonsville Community College *C,A*
Cecil Community College *A*
Charles County Community
   College *A*
College of Notre Dame of
   Maryland *B*
Columbia Union College *B*
Dundalk Community College *C,A*
Essex Community College *A*
Frederick Community College *A*
Frostburg State University *B*
Garrett Community College *A*
Harford Community College *A*
Hood College *B*
Howard Community College *A*
Montgomery College
   Germantown Campus *C,A*
   Rockville Campus *C*
   Takoma Park Campus *C*
Morgan State University *B*
New Community College of
   Baltimore *A*
Prince George's Community
   College *A*
University of Baltimore *B,M*
University of Maryland
   College Park *B*
   Eastern Shore *B*
   University College *M*
Villa Julie College *A*
Western Maryland College *B*

Massachusetts

American International College *B,M*
Anna Maria College for Men and
   Women *B,M*
Aquinas College at Milton *A*
Aquinas College at Newton *A*
Assumption College *B,M*
Babson College *B,M*
Becker College
   Leicester Campus *A*
   Worcester Campus *A*
Berkshire Community College *A*
Boston College *B,M*
Boston University *B,M,D*
Bradford College *B*

Bristol Community College *A*
Bunker Hill Community College *A*
Cape Cod Community College *A*
Clark University *B,M*
Curry College *B*
Dean Junior College *A*
Elms College *B*
Endicott College *A*
Fitchburg State College *B*
Greenfield Community College *A*
Harvard University *M*
Katharine Gibbs School *C,A*
Lasell College *A*
Lesley College *B,M*
Marian Court Junior College *A*
Massachusetts Bay Community
  College *C,A*
Massachusetts Institute of
  Technology *B,M,D,W*
Massasoit Community College *A*
Merrimack College *B*
Middlesex Community College *A*
Mount Ida College *A*
Mount Wachusett Community
  College *A*
Newbury College *A*
Nichols College *A,B,M*
North Adams State College *B*
Northeastern University *B,M*
Northern Essex Community
  College *A*
Quincy College *C,A*
Quinsigamond Community
  College *A*
Regis College *B*
Simmons College *B*
Springfield Technical Community
  College *A*
Suffolk University *M*
University of Massachusetts
  Amherst *B*
  Boston *B*
  Dartmouth *B*
  Lowell *A*
Western New England College *B,M*
Westfield State College *B*

Michigan
Adrian College *A,B*
Alma College *B*
Alpena Community College *A*
Andrews University *A*
Aquinas College *B*
Baker College
  Auburn Hills *A*
  Cadillac *A*
  Flint *A,B*
  Muskegon *C,A,B*
  Port Huron *A,B*
Calvin College *B*
Central Michigan University *B,M*
Charles Stewart Mott Community
  College *C,A*
Cleary College *B*
Concordia College *B*
Davenport College of Business *A,B*
Delta College *A*
Detroit College of Business *A,B*
Eastern Michigan University *B,M*
Ferris State University *B*
Glen Oaks Community College *C*
GMI Engineering & Management
  Institute *B*
Grace Bible College *A,B*
Grand Rapids Baptist College and
  Seminary *B*
Grand Rapids Community
  College *A*
Grand Valley State University *B,M*
Great Lakes Junior College of
  Business *A*
Henry Ford Community College *A*

Hope College *B*
Jackson Community College *A*
Kellogg Community College *C,A*
Lake Superior State University *A,B*
Lansing Community College *A*
Lawrence Technological University
  B,M
Macomb Community College *C,A*
Madonna University *A,B*
Marygrove College *A,B*
Michigan Christian College *C,A*
Michigan State University *B,M*
Mid Michigan Community
  College *A*
Muskegon Community College *A*
Northern Michigan University *A*
Northwestern Michigan College *A*
Northwood Institute *A,B*
Oakland University *B*
Olivet College *B*
Saginaw Valley State University
  B,M
St. Clair County Community
  College *C,A*
St. Mary's College *B*
Schoolcraft College *C,A*
Suomi College *A*
University of Detroit Mercy *B*
University of Michigan
  Ann Arbor *B,M*
  Dearborn *B*
  Flint *B*
Walsh College of Accountancy and
  Business Administration *B*
Wayne State University *B,M*
Western Michigan University *B,M*
William Tyndale College *B*

Minnesota
Augsburg College *B*
Austin Community College *A*
Bemidji State University *B*
Bethany Lutheran College *A*
Bethel College *B*
Brainerd Community College *A*
College of St. Catherine: St.
  Catherine Campus *B*
College of St. Scholastica *B*
Concordia College: Moorhead *B*
Concordia College: St. Paul *B*
Gustavus Adolphus College *B*
Inver Hills Community College *A*
Lakewood Community College *A*
Mankato State University *B,M*
Metropolitan State University *B*
Minneapolis Community College *A*
National Education Center: Brown
  Institute Campus *A*
North Central Bible College *A*
Northland Community College *A*
Northwestern College *A,B*
Pillsbury Baptist Bible College *B*
Rainy River Community College *A*
Rochester Community College *A*
St. Cloud State University *B*
St. Mary's College of Minnesota *B*
Southwest State University *B*
University of Minnesota
  Crookston *A*
  Twin Cities *B*
University of St. Thomas *B*
Vermilion Community College *A*
Willmar Community College *A*
Winona State University *B*
Worthington Community College *A*

Mississippi
Delta State University *B*
Jackson State University *B*
Jones County Junior College *A*
Mary Holmes College *A*
Mississippi College *B,M*

Mississippi Delta Community
  College *A*
Mississippi Gulf Coast Community
  College
    Jackson County Campus *A*
    Jefferson Davis Campus *A*
Mississippi University for Women *B*
Northeast Mississippi Community
  College *A*
Rust College *B*
University of Mississippi *B*
William Carey College *B*

Missouri
Central Methodist College *B*
College of the Ozarks *B*
Columbia College *B*
Drury College *B*
East Central College *C,A*
Evangel College *B*
Fontbonne College *B,M*
Hannibal-LaGrange College *B*
Jefferson College *C*
Longview Community College *C,A*
Maple Woods Community
  College *A*
Maryville University *B,M*
Mineral Area College *C,A*
Missouri Baptist College *C,A,B*
Missouri Southern State College
  A,B
Moberly Area Community
  College *A*
National College *A,B*
Northwest Missouri State
  University *B*
Park College *A,B*
Penn Valley Community College *A*
Phillips Junior College *A*
Rockhurst College *B,M*
St. Charles Community College *A*
St. Louis Community College
  Forest Park *A*
  Meramec *C,A*
Southwest Baptist University *B*
Southwest Missouri State
  University *B*
State Fair Community College *A*
Three Rivers Community College *A*
University of Missouri
  Columbia *B*
  Kansas City *B,M*
  St. Louis *B,M*
Washington University *B,M,D*
Webster University *B,M*
William Jewell College *B*
William Woods College *B*

Montana
Carroll College *B*
Dawson Community College *A*
Dull Knife Memorial College *A*
Eastern Montana College *B*
Flathead Valley Community
  College *A*
Little Big Horn College *A*
Miles Community College *A*
Montana College of Mineral
  Science and Technology *B*
Montana State University *B*
Northern Montana College *A,B*
Rocky Mountain College *B*
Stone Child College *A*
University of Montana *B*
Western Montana College of the
  University of Montana *A*

Nebraska
Bellevue College *M*
Central Community College *C,A*
Chadron State College *B*
Creighton University *M*

Dana College *B*
Hastings College *B*
Lincoln School of Commerce *A*
McCook Community College *A*
Metropolitan Community College *A*
Midland Lutheran College *B*
Nebraska Wesleyan University *A,B*
Northeast Community College *A*
Peru State College *B*
Southeast Community College:
  Beatrice Campus *A*
University of Nebraska
  Kearney *B*
  Lincoln *B,M,D*
  Omaha *B*
Wayne State College *B,M*
Western Nebraska Community
  College: Scottsbluff Campus *A*

Nevada
Community College of Southern
  Nevada *C,A*
Northern Nevada Community
  College *A*
Truckee Meadows Community
  College *C,A*

New Hampshire
Antioch New England Graduate
  School *M*
Castle College *A*
Daniel Webster College *A,B*
Dartmouth College *M*
Franklin Pierce College *A,B*
Hesser College *A*
New England College *B*
New Hampshire College *A*
New Hampshire Technical College
  Berlin *A*
  Laconia *A*
  Nashua *A*
  Stratham *C,A*
Notre Dame College *B*
Plymouth State College of the
  University System of New
  Hampshire *B*
Rivier College *B,M*
St. Anselm College *B*
School for Lifelong Learning *A*
University of New Hampshire *A*
White Pines College *A*

New Jersey
Atlantic Community College *A*
Bloomfield College *C,B*
Burlington County College *C,A*
Caldwell College *C*
College of St. Elizabeth *C*
County College of Morris *A*
Essex County College *A*
Felician College *C,A,B*
Jersey City State College *B*
Kean College of New Jersey *B*
Monmouth College *B,M*
Ocean County College *A*
Rider College *B,M*
Rutgers—The State University of
  New Jersey
    Camden College of Arts and
      Sciences *B*
    Douglass College *B*
    New Brunswick *M*
    University College Camden *B*
St. Peter's College *C,A,B*
Stevens Institute of Technology
  B,M,D
Stockton State College *B*
Thomas Edison State College *A,B*
Trenton State College *B*
Union County College *A*
Upsala College *B*

New Mexico

Clovis Community College A
College of Santa Fe A,B
College of the Southwest B
Dona Ana Branch Community
    College of New Mexico State
    University C,A
Eastern New Mexico University
    Portales B,M
    Roswell Campus C,A
National College C,A,B
New Mexico Institute of Mining
    and Technology B
New Mexico Junior College A
New Mexico State University
    Carlsbad A
    Las Cruces B,M
Northern New Mexico Community
    College A
San Juan College C,A
University of New Mexico B,M
Western New Mexico University B

New York

Adirondack Community College A
Berkeley College A
Berkeley School: New York City A
Bramson ORT Technical
    Institute A
Briarcliffe: The College for
    Business A
Bryant & Stratton Business
    Institute: Buffalo A
Cazenovia College A
City University of New York
    Brooklyn College B
    City College B
    College of Staten Island A,B,M
    Graduate School and
        University Center D
    La Guardia Community
        College A
    Medgar Evers College A,B
    Queensborough Community
        College A
Clarkson University B,M
Clinton Community College A
College for Human Services B,M
College of Insurance B,M
College of Mount St. Vincent A,B
College of New Rochelle B
College of St. Rose B
Columbia-Greene Community
    College C
Concordia College A,B
Cornell University B
Corning Community College A
Daemen College B
Dominican College of Blauvelt C,B
Dowling College B
D'Youville College B
Erie Community College
    City Campus A
    North Campus C
Five Towns College A
Fordham University B
Fulton-Montgomery Community
    College A
Genesee Community College A
Herkimer County Community
    College A
Hilbert College A
Hofstra University B,M
Iona College B,M
Jamestown Community College A
Jefferson Community College A
Keuka College A
Le Moyne College B
Long Island University
    Brooklyn Campus B,M
    C. W. Post Campus B,M
    Southampton Campus B

Manhattan College B,M
Maria College A
Marymount College B
Medaille College B
Mercy College C
New York University C,A,B,M
Niagara University A,B
North Country Community
    College A
Nyack College B
Onondaga Community College A
Orange County Community
    College A
Pace University
    College of White Plains A
    New York A,B,M
    Pleasantville/Briarcliff A
Paul Smith's College A
Roberts Wesleyan College B
Rochester Institute of Technology
    C,A,B,M
Russell Sage College B
Sage Junior College of Albany, A
    Division of Russell Sage
    College A
St. Bonaventure University B,M
St. John Fisher College C,B
St. Joseph's College
    Brooklyn C,B
    Suffolk Campus C
St. Thomas Aquinas College B
Skidmore College B
State University of New York
    Albany B,M
    Binghamton B
    Purchase C
    Stony Brook B
    College of Agriculture and
        Technology at Morrisville A
    College at Buffalo B
    College at Cortland B
    College at Geneseo B
    College at New Paltz B
    College at Old Westbury B
    College at Plattsburgh B
    College of Technology at
        Delhi A
    Empire State College A,B
    Institute of Technology at
        Utica/Rome A
    Maritime College B
    Oswego M
Suffolk County Community College
    Eastern Campus C,A
    Selden A
    Western Campus A
Sullivan County Community
    College A
Syracuse University B,M
Taylor Business Institute A
Touro College A,B
Ulster County Community
    College A
University of the State of New
    York: Regents College A,B
Villa Maria College of Buffalo A
Wagner College B

North Carolina

Appalachian State University B,M
Asheville Buncombe Technical
    Community College A
Barber-Scotia College B
Barton College B
Bennett College B
Brevard College A
Campbell University A,B,M
Catawba College B
Catawba Valley Community College
    C,A
Central Piedmont Community
    College A

Chowan College A,B
Coastal Carolina Community
    College A
College of the Albemarle A
Durham Technical Community
    College A
East Carolina University B
Forsyth Technical Community
    College A
Gaston College A
Greensboro College B
Guilford College B
High Point University B
Isothermal Community College A
James Sprunt Community
    College A
Johnson C. Smith University B
Livingstone College B
Louisburg College A
Mars Hill College B
Mitchell Community College A
Montreat-Anderson College B
North Carolina Central
    University B
North Carolina State University B
Peace College A
Pfeiffer College B
Piedmont Community College A
Queens College B,M
Richmond Community College C,A
St. Andrews Presbyterian College B
St. Augustine's College B
Salem College B
Southwestern Community
    College A
University of North Carolina
    Asheville B
    Chapel Hill D
Wake Forest University B
Wake Technical Community
    College A
Wayne Community College A
Wingate College A,B

North Dakota

Dickinson State University B
Little Hoop Community College
    C,A
Minot State University B
North Dakota State University:
    Bottineau and Institute of
    Forestry A
Trinity Bible College C,A,B
University of Mary A,B
University of North Dakota
    Grand Forks B
    Lake Region A
    Williston A

Ohio

Air Force Institute of
    Technology M
Antioch College B
Antioch School for Adult and
    Experiential Learning B,M
Ashland University B
Baldwin-Wallace College B
Bluffton College B
Bowling Green State University
    Bowling Green B
    Firelands College A
Bryant & Stratton Business
    Institute: Great Northern A
Capital University B
Case Western Reserve University
    B,M,D
Cedarville College B
Central Ohio Technical College A
Central State University B
Chatfield College A
Cincinnati Metropolitan College A
Clark State Community College A

Cleveland State University M,D
College of Mount St. Joseph A,B
Columbus State Community
    College A
Davis Junior College of Business A
Defiance College A,B
Dyke College A,B
Edison State Community College
    C,A
Franciscan University of
    Steubenville A,B
Heidelberg College B
Hiram College B
Hocking Technical College A
ITT Technical Institute:
    Youngstown A
Jefferson Technical College A
Kent State University
    Ashtabula Regional Campus A
    Kent B,M,D
    Salem Regional Campus A
    Tuscarawas Campus A
Lakeland Community College C,A
Lorain County Community
    College A
Lourdes College C,A,B
Malone College B
Marietta College B
Marion Technical College C,A
Miami University
    Hamilton Campus A
    Oxford Campus B,M
Miami-Jacobs College A
Muskingum Area Technical
    College C
Muskingum College B
Northwest Technical College A
Notre Dame College of Ohio A,B
Ohio Dominican College C,B
Ohio State University
    Agricultural Technical
        Institute A
    Columbus Campus B,M,D
Ohio University
    Athens B,M
    Eastern Campus B
    Southern Campus at Ironton
        A,B
Ohio Valley Business College A
Otterbein College B
Owens Technical College: Toledo A
Shawnee State University A
Sinclair Community College C
Terra Technical College C,A
Tiffin University M
Union Institute B,D
University of Akron
    Akron B
    Wayne College A
University of Cincinnati
    Access Colleges A
    Cincinnati B,M,D
    Clermont College C,A
    Raymond Walters College C,A
University of Dayton B,M
University of Rio Grande A,B
University of Toledo A,B,M
Urbana University B
Walsh College A,B
Washington State Community
    College A
Wilmington College B
Wittenberg University B
Wright State University: Lake
    Campus C,A
Xavier University A,B,M
Youngstown State University B

Oklahoma

Bacone College A
Bartlesville Wesleyan College A,B
Connors State College A

East Central University *B*
Eastern Oklahoma State College *A*
Hillsdale Free Will Baptist
College *A*
Langston University *B*
Mid-America Bible College *B*
Murray State College *A*
Northeastern State University *B*
Northern Oklahoma College *A*
Oklahoma Baptist University *B*
Oklahoma Christian University of
Science and Arts *B*
Oklahoma City University *B*
Oklahoma Junior College *A*
Oklahoma State University
Oklahoma City *C,A*
Stillwater *B*
Oral Roberts University *B*
Phillips University *A,B*
Redlands Community College *A*
Rogers State College *A*
Rose State College *C,A*
St. Gregory's College *A*
Southeastern Oklahoma State
University *B*
Southwestern Oklahoma State
University *B*
University of Central Oklahoma *B*
University of Oklahoma *B,M,D*
University of Science and Arts of
Oklahoma *B*

Oregon

Central Oregon Community College
C,A
Clackamas Community College *A*
Clatsop Community College *A*
Concordia College *A,B*
George Fox College *B*
Lane Community College *C,A*
Linfield College *B*
Linn-Benton Community College *A*
Marylhurst College *B,M*
Mount Hood Community
College *A*
Oregon State University *B*
Pacific University *B*
Portland State University *B,M*
Southern Oregon State College
A,B,M
Southwestern Oregon Community
College *A*
Treasure Valley Community
College *A*
Umpqua Community College *A*
University of Oregon
Eugene *B,M,D*
Robert Donald Clark Honors
College *B*
University of Portland *M*
Western Baptist College *A,B*
Western Oregon State College *B*
Willamette University *M*

Pennsylvania

Albright College *B*
Allentown College of St. Francis de
Sales *B*
Beaver College *A,B*
Bucknell University *B,M*
Bucks County Community
College *A*
Butler County Community
College *A*
California University of
Pennsylvania *A,B,M*
Carlow College *B*
Carnegie Mellon University
B,M,D,W
Cedar Crest College *B*
Chatham College *B*
Chestnut Hill College *A,B*

Cheyney University of
Pennsylvania *B*
Churchman Business School *A*
Clarion University of Pennsylvania
A,B
Community College of Beaver
County *A*
Community College of Philadelphia
C,A
Delaware County Community
College *A*
Drexel University *B*
DuBois Business College *A*
Duquesne University *B,M*
Edinboro University of
Pennsylvania *A,B*
Elizabethtown College *B*
Gannon University *C,A,B*
Geneva College *B*
Harcum Junior College *A*
Harrisburg Area Community
College *C,A*
Holy Family College *B*
Indiana University of Pennsylvania
B,M
Juniata College *B*
Keystone Junior College *C,A*
La Salle University *B,M*
Lackawanna Junior College *A*
Lansdale School of Business *C,A*
Lebanon Valley College of
Pennsylvania *A,B,M*
Lehigh County Community College
C,B
Lehigh University *M*
Lock Haven University of
Pennsylvania *B*
Luzerne County Community
College *A*
Lycoming College *B*
Manor Junior College *A*
Marywood College *B,M*
Mercyhurst College *A,B*
Messiah College *B*
Montgomery County Community
College *C,A*
Northeastern Christian Junior
College *A*
Peirce Junior College *C,A*
Penn State
Erie Behrend College *A*
Harrisburg Capital College
A,M
University Park Campus *C,A*
Philadelphia College of Textiles and
Science *A,B,M*
Point Park College *C,A,B*
Reading Area Community College
C,A
Robert Morris College *A,B,M*
St. Joseph's University *A,B,M*
St. Vincent College *B*
Seton Hill College *C,B*
University of Pennsylvania *M*
University of Pittsburgh
Bradford *B*
Johnstown *B*
Pittsburgh *B*
Titusville *A*
University of Scranton *B*
Valley Forge Military College *C,A*
Villanova University *B*
Washington and Jefferson College *B*
Waynesburg College *B,M*
West Chester University of
Pennsylvania *M*
Widener University *B,M*
Wilkes University *B,M*

Puerto Rico

American University of Puerto
Rico *B*

Bayamon Central University *A,B*
Caribbean University *A,B*
Columbia College *A*
ICPR Junior College *A*
Inter American University of Puerto
Rico
Arecibo Campus *A,B*
Metropolitan Campus *A,B,M*
San German Campus *A,B,M*
Pontifical Catholic University of
Puerto Rico *B,M*
Puerto Rico Junior College *A*
Turabo University *B*
Universidad Metropolitana *B*
Universidad Politecnica de Puerto
Rico *B*
University of Puerto Rico
Arecibo Campus *A,B*
Bayamon Technological
University College *A,B*
Cayey University College *B*
Humacao University College *B*
La Montana Regional
College *A*
Mayaguez Campus *M*
Rio Piedras Campus *B,M*
University of the Sacred Heart *B*

Rhode Island

Bryant College *B,M*
Community College of Rhode
Island *A*
Johnson & Wales University *A,B*
New England Technical College *B*
Providence College *A,B*
Rhode Island College *B*
Roger Williams College *B*
Salve Regina University *A,B,M*
University of Rhode Island *B*

South Carolina

Aiken Technical College *C,A*
Anderson College *A,B*
Bob Jones University *A*
Central Wesleyan College *A*
Charleston Southern University *B*
Chesterfield-Marlboro Technical
College *A*
The Citadel *B,M*
Coker College *B*
Erskine College *B*
Francis Marion College *M*
Horry-Georgetown Technical
College *A*
Lander College *B*
Limestone College *A,B*
Newberry College *B*
Spartanburg Methodist College *A*
Sumter Area Technical College *A*
Technical College of the
Lowcountry *A*
Tri-County Technical College *A*
Trident Technical College *A*
University of South Carolina
Aiken *B*
Coastal Carolina College *B*
Williamsburg Technical College *A*

South Dakota

Augustana College *B*
Black Hills State University *B*
Dakota State University *A,B*
Dakota Wesleyan University *A,B*
Kilian Community College *A*
Mount Marty College *B*
National College *A,B*
Northern State University *B*
Presentation College *C,A*
Sinte Gleska College *A*
Sioux Falls College *A,B*
Western Dakota Vocational
Technical Institute *A*

Tennessee

Austin Peay State University *B*
Belmont University *B,M*
Bethel College *B*
Bristol University *B*
Carson-Newman College *B*
Chattanooga State Technical
Community College *A*
Christian Brothers University *C,B,M*
Cleveland State Community
College *A*
Columbia State Community
College *A*
Cumberland University *A,B*
David Lipscomb University *B*
Fisk University *B*
Free Will Baptist Bible College *B*
Hiwassee College *A*
Jackson State Community College
C,A
Knoxville Business College *A*
Knoxville College *B*
Lambuth University *B*
Lane College *B*
Lincoln Memorial University *A,B*
Martin Methodist College *A*
Maryville College *B*
McKenzie College *C,A*
Middle Tennessee State
University *C*
Milligan College *B*
Motlow State Community
College *A*
Nashville State Technical
Institute *A*
Rhodes College *B*
Roane State Community College *A*
Southern College of Seventh-day
Adventists *B*
State Technical Institute at
Memphis *A*
Tennessee State University *B*
Tennessee Technological
University *B*
Tennessee Temple University *B*
Tennessee Wesleyan College *B*
Tomlinson College *A*
Trevecca Nazarene College *B,M*
Tusculum College *B*
Union University *B*
University of Tennessee
Chattanooga *B*
Knoxville *B,M,D*
Volunteer State Community
College *A*
Walters State Community
College *A*

Texas

Abilene Christian University *B*
Amarillo College *A*
Amber University *B,M*
Angelina College *A*
Angelo State University *B,M*
Austin College *B*
Austin Community College *A*
Baylor University *B*
Brazosport College *C,A*
Central Texas College *A*
College of the Mainland *A*
Collin County Community College
District *C,A*
Concordia Lutheran College *B*
Cooke County College *A*
Corpus Christi State University *B*
Dallas Baptist University *B,M*
Dallas Christian College *B*
East Texas Baptist University *B*
East Texas State University
Commerce *B,M*
Texarkana *B,M*
El Centro College *A*

El Paso Community College C,A
Hardin-Simmons University M
Houston Community College A
Howard College A
Howard Payne University B
Incarnate Word College B,M
Jacksonville College A
Kilgore College A
Lamar University—Beaumont B,M
Laredo State University B,M
LeTourneau University B
Lon Morris College A
Lubbock Christian University B
McMurry University B
Midland College C,A
Midwestern State University B,M
Mountain View College C,A
Northeast Texas Community
    College A
Northwood Institute: Texas Campus
    A,B
Odessa College A
Our Lady of the Lake University of
    San Antonio B
Panola College A
Paul Quinn College B
Rice University B
St. Edward's University B,M
St. Philip's College A
Sam Houston State University B,M
San Antonio College A
Schreiner College B
Southern Methodist University B,M
Southwest Texas State University B
Southwestern Adventist College B
Southwestern Assemblies of God
    College A,B
Southwestern University B
Stephen F. Austin State University
    B,M
Sul Ross State University B,M
Tarleton State University B
Tarrant County Junior College C,A
Temple Junior College C,A
Texas A&I University B
Texas A&M University at
    Galveston B
Texas Christian University B
Texas Southern University B
Texas Southmost College A
Texas Tech University B,M
Texas Wesleyan University B
Trinity University B
Trinity Valley Community
    College A
University of Central Texas B,M
University of Houston
    Clear Lake B
    Downtown B
University of Mary Hardin-
    Baylor B
University of North Texas B,M,D
University of Texas
    Arlington B,M,D
    Austin B
    Dallas B,M
    El Paso B
    Pan American B,M
    San Antonio M
    Tyler B,M
Victoria College A
Wayland Baptist University B
Weatherford College C,A
West Texas State University B,M
Western Texas College A
Wharton County Junior College A
Wiley College B

Utah

Brigham Young University B
LDS Business College A

Phillips Junior College: Salt Lake
    City Campus C,A
Utah State University B
Weber State University B
Westminster College of Salt Lake
    City B,M

Vermont

Champlain College C,A,B
College of St. Joseph in Vermont
    A,B
Community College of Vermont
    C,A
Goddard College B,M
Green Mountain College B
St. Michael's College B,M
Southern Vermont College A,B
University of Vermont B,M

Virginia

Averett College B
Blue Ridge Community College A
Bluefield College A,B
Bridgewater College B
Central Virginia Community
    College A
Christopher Newport College B
Commonwealth College C,A
Eastern Mennonite College B
Eastern Shore Community
    College A
Ferrum College B
Hampton University B
Hollins College B
Lord Fairfax Community College A
Mary Baldwin College B
Marymount University B,M
Mountain Empire Community
    College A
New River Community College C,A
Norfolk State University B
Northern Virginia Community
    College A
Patrick Henry Community
    College A
Paul D. Camp Community
    College A
Piedmont Virginia Community
    College C,A
Radford University B,M
Richard Bland College A
Roanoke College B
St. Paul's College B
Shenandoah University C,B,M
Southern Seminary College A
Southside Virginia Community
    College C,A
Southwest Virginia Community
    College A
Strayer College A,B
Tidewater Community College A
University of Virginia B
Virginia Commonwealth
    University M
Virginia Intermont College B
Virginia Polytechnic Institute and
    State University B,D
Virginia Wesleyan College B

Washington

Bellevue Community College A
Big Bend Community College A
Central Washington University B
Centralia College A
City University B
Clark College C,A
Eastern Washington University B,M
Everett Community College C,A
Evergreen State College B
Grays Harbor College A
Heritage College C,A,B
Lower Columbia College C,A

Northwest Indian College C,A
Olympic College C,A
Pacific Lutheran University B,M
Peninsula College A
Pierce College C,A
St. Martin's College B
Seattle Pacific University C
Seattle University B,M
Shoreline Community College C,A
Spokane Community College C,A
Spokane Falls Community
    College A
University of Puget Sound B
Walla Walla College A,B
Walla Walla Community College
    C,A
Wenatchee Valley College A
Whatcom Community College A
Yakima Valley Community College
    C,A

West Virginia

Alderson-Broaddus College B
Bethany College B
College of West Virginia A
Concord College B
Davis and Elkins College A,B
Fairmont State College B
Glenville State College B
Marshall University B,M
Ohio Valley College A
Salem-Teikyo University A,B
Shepherd College A,B
University of Charleston B
West Virginia Institute of
    Technology A,B
West Virginia State College A,B
West Virginia University at
    Parkersburg A
West Virginia Wesleyan College B

Wisconsin

Alverno College B
Beloit College B
Cardinal Stritch College A,B
Carroll College B
Chippewa Valley Technical
    College A
Concordia University Wisconsin B
Edgewood College B
Fox Valley Technical College A
Lakeland College B
Maranatha Baptist Bible College B
Marian College of Fond du Lac B
Marquette University B,M
Milwaukee College of Business A
Mount Mary College B
Mount Senario College B
Northland College B
St. Norbert College B
Stratton College A
University of Wisconsin
    Eau Claire B
    Green Bay B
    Madison B,M,D
    Milwaukee B,M
    Parkside B,M
    Platteville B
    River Falls B
    Superior B
    Whitewater B,M
Western Wisconsin Technical
    College A
Wisconsin Lutheran College B

Wyoming

Casper College A
Central Wyoming College A
Eastern Wyoming College A
Laramie County Community
    College A
Northwest College A

Sheridan College A
University of Wyoming B
Western Wyoming Community
    College C,A

**American Samoa, Caroline
Islands, Guam, Marianas,
Virgin Islands**

Community College of
    Micronesia A
University of Guam B,M

Canada

McGill University C,B,M,D

Switzerland

American College of Switzerland B
Franklin College: Switzerland C

Arab Republic of Egypt

American University in Cairo B,M

Business and office

Alabama

Alabama State University A
Athens State College B
Brewer State Junior College A
Central Alabama Community
    College: Childersburg Campus C
Chattahoochee Valley Community
    College A
Community College of the Air
    Force A
Draughons Junior College A
Faulkner University A
Gadsden State Community
    College A
James H. Faulkner State
    Community College C,A
John C. Calhoun State Community
    College C,A
Lawson State Community
    College A
Marion Military Institute A
Northeast Alabama State Junior
    College A
Reid State Technical College C
Samford University B
Selma University A
Shelton State Community College
    C,A
Snead State Junior College A
Troy State University A
Walker State Technical College C,A
Wallace State Community College
    at Hanceville C

Alaska

University of Alaska
    Anchorage C,A
    Fairbanks A
    Southeast C

Arizona

American Indian Bible College A
Arizona Western College A
Cochise College C,A
Eastern Arizona College A
Mesa Community College A
Mohave Community College A
Navajo Community College C,A
Paradise Valley Community College
    C,A
Pima Community College C
Scottsdale Community College C,A
Yavapai College A

Arkansas

Arkansas Baptist College *A*
Arkansas State University: Beebe Branch *A*
Capital City Junior College *A*
Central Baptist College *A*
East Arkansas Community College *A*
Garland County Community College *A*
Henderson State University *A*
Mississippi County Community College *A*
National Education Center: Arkansas College of Technology *C*
North Arkansas Community College *A*
Phillips County Community College *A*
Shorter College *A*
Southern Arkansas Community College *A*
Southern Arkansas University *A*
University of Central Arkansas *B*
Westark Community College *A*
Williams Baptist College *A*

California

Allan Hancock College *A*
Armstrong College *A*
Bakersfield College *A*
Barstow College *C,A*
Bethany College *A*
California State University: Los Angeles *B,M*
Cerritos Community College *A*
Cerro Coso Community College *C,A*
Chabot College *A*
Chaffey Community College *A*
Christian Heritage College *B*
Citrus College *C,A*
City College of San Francisco *A*
Coastline Community College *A*
College of the Desert *A*
College of the Sequoias *A*
Columbia College *A*
Compton Community College *A*
Cosumnes River College *A*
Crafton Hills College *A*
Cuesta College *A*
East Los Angeles College *A*
El Camino College *C,A*
Evergreen Valley College *A*
Feather River College *C*
Foothill College *A*
Fresno City College *A*
Fresno Pacific College *A*
Gavilan Community College *A*
Glendale Community College *C*
Golden West College *C,A*
Grossmont Community College *C,A*
Hartnell College *A*
Heald College: Sacramento *C,A*
Humphreys College *A*
Imperial Valley College *A*
Kings River Community College *A*
La Sierra University *A*
Lake Tahoe Community College *A*
Laney College *C,A*
Lassen College *C,A*
Long Beach City College *C,A*
Los Angeles City College *C,A*
Los Angeles Harbor College *C,A*
Los Angeles Mission College *C,A*
Los Angeles Pierce College *A*
Los Angeles Trade and Technical College *A*
Los Angeles Valley College *A*
Los Medanos College *C,A*
Merced College *A*

Mission College *A*
Modesto Junior College *A*
Monterey Peninsula College *A*
Mount St. Mary's College *A*
Mount San Antonio College *C,A*
Mount San Jacinto College *C,A*
Napa Valley College *C*
Ohlone College *A*
Orange Coast College *C,A*
Pacific Union College *A*
Palomar College *A*
Pasadena City College *C,A*
Phillips Junior College: Fresno Campus *C,A*
Porterville College *A*
Rio Hondo College *A*
Saddleback College *A*
San Diego City College *C,A*
San Diego Mesa College *C,A*
San Diego Miramar College *A*
San Joaquin Delta College *C,A*
San Jose City College *A*
Santa Barbara City College *C,A*
Santa Monica College *C,A*
Santa Rosa Junior College *C,A*
Sierra College *C,A*
Skyline College *C,A*
Solano Community College *A*
Southwestern College *A*
Taft College *A*
Ventura College *C,A*
Victor Valley College *C,A*
West Hills Community College *A*
West Valley College *A*
Yuba College *A*

Colorado

Arapahoe Community College *C,A*
Colorado Mountain College
    Alpine Campus *A*
    Spring Valley Campus *A*
    Timberline Campus *A*
Colorado Northwestern Community College *A*
Community College of Denver *C,A*
Front Range Community College *A*
Lamar Community College *A*
Mesa State College *A,B*
Morgan Community College *A*
National College *B*
Northeastern Junior College *A*
Otero Junior College *A*
Pueblo Community College *C,A*
Red Rocks Community College *C,A*
Trinidad State Junior College *A*

Connecticut

Asnuntuck Community College *C,A*
Briarwood College *A*
Housatonic Community College *A*
Middlesex Community College *A*
Mitchell College *A*
Northwestern Connecticut Community College *A*
Norwalk Community College *A*

Delaware

Delaware Technical and Community College
    Southern Campus *A*
    Stanton/Wilmington Campus *A*
    Terry Campus *A*
Goldey-Beacom College *C,A*

District of Columbia

University of the District of Columbia *A*

Florida

Brevard Community College *A*
Broward Community College *A*

Central Florida Community College *A*
Chipola Junior College *A*
Daytona Beach Community College *A*
Gulf Coast Community College *A*
Hillsborough Community College *A*
Indian River Community College *A*
Jones College *A,B*
Lake City Community College *A*
Lynn University *B*
Manatee Community College *A*
Miami-Dade Community College *A*
Okaloosa-Walton Community College *A*
Orlando College *A*
Palm Beach Community College *A*
Pensacola Junior College *A*
St. Petersburg Junior College *A*
Santa Fe Community College *A*
South Florida Community College *C,A*
Tallahassee Community College *A*
Valencia Community College *A*
Warner Southern College *A*

Georgia

Abraham Baldwin Agricultural College *A*
Andrew College *A*
Atlanta Metropolitan College *A*
Augusta Technical Institute *C*
Bainbridge College *C,A*
Chattahoochee Technical Institute *C*
Clayton State College *C,A*
Dalton College *A*
Darton College *A*
Emmanuel College *A*
Floyd College *A*
Gainesville College *A*
Georgia College *B*
Georgia Southwestern College *B*
LaGrange College *A*
Macon College *A*
Middle Georgia College *A*
Morris Brown College *B*
North Georgia College *B*
Savannah Technical Institute *C*
South Georgia College *A*
Truett-McConnell College *A*
University of Georgia *A*

Hawaii

Brigham Young University-Hawaii *A,B*
Hawaii Pacific University *A*

Idaho

Boise State University *A*
College of Southern Idaho *A*
Lewis Clark State College *A*
North Idaho College *A*
Ricks College *A*

Illinois

Black Hawk College
    East Campus *A*
    Moline *A*
Carl Sandburg College *A*
City Colleges of Chicago
    Chicago City-Wide College *C,A*
    Malcolm X College *A*
    Olive-Harvey College *C,A*
    Richard J. Daley College *A*
    Wright College *A*
College of DuPage *C,A*
Elgin Community College *C,A*

Illinois Eastern Community Colleges
    Lincoln Trail College *A*
    Olney Central College *A*
    Wabash Valley College *A*
Illinois State University *B*
Illinois Valley Community College *C,A*
John A. Logan College *A*
Joliet Junior College *A*
Kendall College *A*
Kishwaukee College *A*
Lake Land College *A*
Lewis and Clark Community College *C,A*
Lewis University *B*
Lincoln Land Community College *A*
MacCormac Junior College *A*
Moraine Valley Community College *C,A*
Oakton Community College *C,A*
Parkland College *A*
Rend Lake College *C,A*
Richland Community College *A*
Rock Valley College *A*
Spoon River College *C,A*
Triton College *C,A*
William Rainey Harper College *C,A*

Indiana

Ancilla College *A*
Anderson University *A*
Ball State University *A*
Indiana University—Purdue University
    Fort Wayne *A*
    Indianapolis *C*
Indiana Wesleyan University *A*
International Business College *A*
Purdue University: North Central Campus *A*
University of Indianapolis *A*
University of Southern Indiana *A*
Vincennes University *A*

Iowa

American Institute of Business *C,A*
Clinton Community College *A*
Des Moines Area Community College *A*
Hawkeye Institute of Technology *C*
Iowa Lakes Community College *A*
Kirkwood Community College *A*
Muscatine Community College *A*
North Iowa Area Community College *A*
Northeast Iowa Community College *A*
Scott Community College *A*
Southeastern Community College: North Campus *C*
Southwestern Community College *A*
Waldorf College *A*

Kansas

Allen County Community College *A*
Brown Mackie College *C*
Butler County Community College *A*
Central College *A*
Cloud County Community College *C,A*
Coffeyville Community College *A*
Colby Community College *A*
Cowley County Community College *A*
Dodge City Community College *A*
Fort Scott Community College *A*
Friends University *A*

Haskell Indian Junior College *A*
Hesston College *A*
Highland Community College *C,A*
Hutchinson Community College *A*
Kansas City Kansas Community
College *A*
Neosho County Community College
C,A
Pratt Community College *C,A*
Seward County Community
College *A*
Washburn University of Topeka
C,A

Kentucky

Campbellsville College *A*
Eastern Kentucky University *B*
Elizabethtown Community
College *A*
Franklin College *A*
Lees College *A*
Lindsey Wilson College *A*
Madisonville Community College *A*
Morehead State University *A*
Murray State University *A,B*
National Education Center:
Kentucky College of Technology
Campus *C*
Owensboro Junior College of
Business *C,A*
Paducah Community College *A*
St. Catharine College *A*
Southeast Community College *A*
Sue Bennett College *A*
Sullivan College *A*

Louisiana

Bossier Parish Community
College *A*
Grambling State University *A*
Louisiana College *A*
Louisiana Tech University *A*
Nicholls State University *A,B*
Northwestern State University *B*

Maine

Andover College *A*
Beal College *A*
Casco Bay College *A*
Husson College *A*
Thomas College *A,B,M*
University of Maine
Machias *A*
Orono *A*

Maryland

Allegany Community College *C,A*
Anne Arundel Community
College *A*
Catonsville Community College *C,A*
Cecil Community College *A*
Charles County Community
College *C*
Chesapeake College *C,A*
Essex Community College *A*
Frederick Community College *A*
Garrett Community College *A*
Harford Community College *C,A*
Howard Community College *A*
Montgomery College
Germantown Campus *C,A*
Rockville Campus *A*
Takoma Park Campus *A*
Morgan State University *B*
New Community College of
Baltimore *A*
Prince George's Community
College *A*
Villa Julie College *A*
Wor-Wic Tech Community
College *A*

Massachusetts

Anna Maria College for Men and
Women *B*
Aquinas College at Milton *A*
Aquinas College at Newton *C,A*
Bay Path College *A*
Bay State College *A*
Becker College
Leicester Campus *A*
Worcester Campus *A*
Berkshire Community College *A*
Bunker Hill Community College *A*
Dean Junior College *A*
Endicott College *A*
Greenfield Community College *C*
Massachusetts Bay Community
College *C,A*
Massasoit Community College *A*
Mount Ida College *A*
Mount Wachusett Community
College *A*
North Shore Community College *A*
Northern Essex Community College
C,A
Quincy College *C,A*
Quinsigamond Community College
C,A
Roxbury Community College *A*
Salem State College *B*
Springfield Technical Community
College *A*

Michigan

Alpena Community College *A*
Baker College
Auburn Hills *C,A*
Cadillac *C*
Flint *A*
Mount Clemens *A*
Muskegon *A*
Owosso *C*
Port Huron *A*
Charles Stewart Mott Community
College *A*
Davenport College of Business *C,A*
Delta College *A*
Detroit College of Business *A*
Eastern Michigan University *B*
Glen Oaks Community College *A*
Grand Rapids Community College
C,A
Great Lakes Junior College of
Business *C,A*
Henry Ford Community College *A*
Jackson Community College *A*
Kalamazoo Valley Community
College *A*
Kellogg Community College *A*
Kirtland Community College *C,A*
Lake Superior State University *A,B*
Lansing Community College *A*
Lewis College of Business *A*
Macomb Community College *C,A*
Marygrove College *A*
Michigan Christian College *C,A*
Mid Michigan Community
College *A*
Northern Michigan University *A*
Northwestern Michigan College *A*
Oakland Community College *C,A*
St. Clair County Community
College *C,A*
Southwestern Michigan College *A*
Suomi College *A*
West Shore Community College *A*

Minnesota

Bethany Lutheran College *A*
Concordia College: Moorhead *B*
Inver Hills Community College *A*
Normandale Community College *A*
Northland Community College *A*

Northwestern College *A,B*
Rainy River Community College *C*
Rochester Community College *A*
Southwest State University *A,B*
Vermilion Community College *A*
Willmar Community College *A*
Willmar Technical College *C*
Winona State University *A,B*
Worthington Community College *A*

Mississippi

Blue Mountain College *B*
East Central Community College *A*
Hinds Community College *A*
Jones County Junior College *A*
Mississippi Delta Community
College *A*
Mississippi Gulf Coast Community
College
Jefferson Davis Campus *A*
Perkinston *C*
Northeast Mississippi Community
College *A*
Phillips Junior College
Jackson *A*
Mississippi Gulf Coast *C,A*
Rust College *A*
Southeastern Baptist College *A*
Southwest Mississippi Community
College *A*

Missouri

East Central College *A*
Evangel College *A*
Longview Community College *A*
Maple Woods Community
College *A*
Mineral Area College *C,A*
Missouri Southern State College *A*
Missouri Western State College *A*
Moberly Area Community College
C,A
National College *C*
Penn Valley Community College *A*
St. Louis Christian College *A*
St. Louis Community College
Florissant Valley *A*
Meramec *A*
State Fair Community College *A*
Three Rivers Community College *A*

Montana

Dawson Community College *A*
Fort Peck Community College *A*
Little Big Horn College *A*
Miles Community College *A*
Northern Montana College *A*
University of Montana *B*
Western Montana College of the
University of Montana *A*

Nebraska

Central Community College *C,A*
Chadron State College *B*
Lincoln School of Commerce *C,A*
McCook Community College *A*
Metropolitan Community College *C*
Northeast Community College *A*
Peru State College *B*
Southeast Community College:
Beatrice Campus *C,A*
University of Nebraska—Kearney *B*
Wayne State College *B*
Western Nebraska Community
College: Scottsbluff Campus *A*

Nevada

Community College of Southern
Nevada *A*
Northern Nevada Community
College *C,A*

Truckee Meadows Community
College *C,A*
Western Nevada Community
College *C,A*

New Hampshire

Castle College *A*
Franklin Pierce College *A*
McIntosh College *A*
New Hampshire College *A,B*
New Hampshire Technical College:
Laconia *C,A*
Rivier College *B*

New Jersey

Atlantic Community College *A*
Berkeley College of Business *A*
Brookdale Community College *A*
Burlington County College *A*
Camden County College *A*
Cumberland County College *A*
Essex County College *C*
Mercer County Community
College *A*
Rider College *A*
St. Peter's College *C*
Trenton State College *B*
Union County College *A*

New Mexico

College of Santa Fe *A*
Dona Ana Branch Community
College of New Mexico State
University *C,A*
Eastern New Mexico University *A*
New Mexico Junior College *A*
New Mexico State University
Carlsbad *C,A*
Las Cruces *C,A*
Northern New Mexico Community
College *A*
Parks College *A*
University of New Mexico *A*
Western New Mexico University *A*

New York

Adirondack Community College *A*
Berkeley College *C,A*
Broome Community College *C*
Bryant & Stratton Business Institute
Buffalo *C,A*
Rochester *A*
Cazenovia College *A*
Central City Business Institute *A*
City University of New York
College of Staten Island *A*
Hostos Community College *A*
Kingsborough Community
College *A*
La Guardia Community
College *A*
Clinton Community College *A*
Columbia-Greene Community
College *A*
Community College of the Finger
Lakes *C,A*
Concordia College *A*
Corning Community College *A*
Erie Community College
City Campus *A*
North Campus *A*
South Campus *A*
Five Towns College *A*
Fulton-Montgomery Community
College *A*
Genesee Community College *A*
Herkimer County Community
College *C,A*
Hilbert College *A*
Hudson Valley Community
College *A*
Iona College *A*

Jamestown Business College *C,A*
Jefferson Community College *C,A*
Katharine Gibbs School: Melville *C*
Long Island University: Brooklyn
Campus *A,B,M*
Maria College *A*
Mohawk Valley Community
College *A*
Monroe College *A*
New York Institute of
Technology *A*
New York University *A*
Niagara County Community
College *C*
North Country Community
College *A*
Onondaga Community College *A*
Rochester Business Institute *A*
Rockland Community College *A*
St. Francis College *A*
St. John Fisher College *C*
St. John's University *A*
State University of New York
College of Agriculture and
Technology at Morrisville *A*
College at Buffalo *B*
College of Technology at
Alfred *A*
College of Technology at
Canton *A*
College of Technology at
Delhi *A*
College of Technology at
Farmingdale *A*
Suffolk County Community College
Eastern Campus *A*
Selden *A*
Western Campus *A*
Sullivan County Community
College *A*
Tompkins-Cortland Community
College *A*
Touro College *A*
Trocaire College *C,A*
Ulster County Community
College *A*
Utica School of Commerce *A*
Westchester Business Institute *A*
Westchester Community College *A*

North Carolina

Alamance Community College *A*
Anson Community College *A*
Appalachian State University *B*
Asheville Buncombe Technical
Community College *A*
Beaufort County Community
College *A*
Bladen Community College *A*
Blue Ridge Community College *A*
Brevard College *A*
Brunswick Community College *C,A*
Carteret Community College *A*
Catawba Valley Community
College *A*
Central Carolina Community
College *A*
Central Piedmont Community
College *C,A*
Coastal Carolina Community
College *A*
College of the Albemarle *A*
Durham Technical Community
College *A*
Edgecombe Community College *A*
Fayetteville State University *A,B*
Fayetteville Technical Community
College *A*
Forsyth Technical Community
College *A*
Gaston College *A*

Guilford Technical Community
College *A*
Haywood Community College *A*
Isothermal Community College *A*
James Sprunt Community
College *A*
Johnston Community College *A*
Louisburg College *C,A*
Martin Community College *C*
Mayland Community College *A*
McDowell Technical Community
College *A*
Methodist College *A*
Mitchell Community College *A*
Mount Olive College *A*
Nash Community College *A*
Pamlico Community College *A*
Piedmont Community College *A*
Richmond Community College *C,A*
Roanoke-Chowan Community
College *A*
Robeson Community College *A*
Rockingham Community College *A*
Sampson Community College *A*
Southwestern Community
College *A*
Surry Community College *A*
Tri-County Community College *A*
Vance-Granville Community
College *A*
Wake Technical Community
College *A*
Western Piedmont Community
College *A*
Wilkes Community College *C,A*
Wilson Technical Community
College *C*
Wingate College *A,B*

North Dakota

Dickinson State University *A*
North Dakota State College of
Science *C,A*
North Dakota State University:
Bottineau and Institute of
Forestry *C,A*
Standing Rock College *A*
Trinity Bible College *A,B*
University of North Dakota
Lake Region *A*
Williston *A*

Ohio

Ashland University *A*
Bowling Green State University:
Firelands College *A*
Cincinnati Metropolitan College *A*
Clark State Community College *A*
Columbus State Community
College *A*
Cuyahoga Community College
Metropolitan Campus *A*
Western Campus *A*
Davis Junior College of Business *A*
Dyke College *A,B*
Edison State Community College
C,A
Hocking Technical College *A*
ITT Technical Institute:
Youngstown *C*
Kent State University
Ashtabula Regional Campus *A*
East Liverpool Regional
Campus *A*
Salem Regional Campus *A*
Tuscarawas Campus *A*
Lorain County Community
College *A*
Miami-Jacobs College *A*
Mount Vernon Nazarene College
A,B
Northwestern College *C*

Notre Dame College of Ohio *A*
Sinclair Community College *A*
Stark Technical College *A*
Tiffin University *A*
University of Akron *A*
University of Cincinnati
Access Colleges *A*
Clermont College *A*
Raymond Walters College *A*
University of Findlay *A*
University of Rio Grande *A*
University of Toledo *C,A,B*
Wright State University: Lake
Campus *A*
Youngstown State University *A*

Oklahoma

Connors State College *A*
Eastern Oklahoma State College *A*
Hillsdale Free Will Baptist
College *A*
Northern Oklahoma College *A*
Northwestern Oklahoma State
University *C*
Oklahoma Baptist University *B*
Oklahoma Christian University of
Science and Arts *C*
Oklahoma Junior College *A*
Redlands Community College *C,A*
Rogers State College *A*
Rose State College *A*
Southeastern Oklahoma State
University *B*
Southwestern Oklahoma State
University *C*
Tulsa Junior College *C,A*
University of Central Oklahoma *B*

Oregon

Central Oregon Community College
C,A
Chemeketa Community College *A*
Clackamas Community College *C,A*
Clatsop Community College *A*
Portland Community College *A*
Rogue Community College *A*
Southern Oregon State College *A*
Southwestern Oregon Community
College *A*
Treasure Valley Community
College *A*
Umpqua Community College *A*

Pennsylvania

Berean Institute *A*
Bucks County Community
College *A*
Butler County Community
College *A*
Churchman Business School *C,A*
Community College of Beaver
County *A*
Community College of
Philadelphia *A*
Delaware County Community
College *A*
Gannon University *A*
Grove City College *B*
Harcum Junior College *A*
Harrisburg Area Community
College *A*
ICS Center for Degree Studies *A*
Immaculata College *A*
Indiana University of Pennsylvania
B,M
Keystone Junior College *A*
La Salle University *A*
Lehigh County Community College
C,A
Luzerne County Community
College *C,A*
Manor Junior College *A*

Mercyhurst College *C,A*
Montgomery County Community
College *A*
Northampton County Area
Community College *A*
Northeastern Christian Junior
College *A*
Peirce Junior College *C,A*
Pennsylvania College of
Technology *C*
Pennsylvania Institute of
Technology *C,A*
Reading Area Community College
C,A
Robert Morris College *A,B*
Waynesburg College *A*
Westmoreland County Community
College *A*

Puerto Rico

American University of Puerto
Rico *A*
Caribbean University *A*
Electronic Data Processing College
of Puerto Rico *A*
ICPR Junior College *A*
Inter American University of Puerto
Rico
Arecibo Campus *A*
Metropolitan Campus *A*
San German Campus *A,B*
Pontifical Catholic University of
Puerto Rico *A*
Puerto Rico Junior College *A*
Turabo University *A*
Universidad Metropolitana *B*

Rhode Island

Community College of Rhode
Island *C,A*
Johnson & Wales University *A,B*

South Carolina

Aiken Technical College *C*
Anderson College *A*
Bob Jones University *C*
Charleston Southern University *A,B*
Chesterfield-Marlboro Technical
College *A*
Columbia Junior College of
Business *C*
Denmark Technical College *A*
Horry-Georgetown Technical
College *C*
North Greenville College *A*
Sumter Area Technical College *A*
Technical College of the
Lowcountry *A*
University of South Carolina at
Lancaster *A*
Williamsburg Technical College *C*

South Dakota

Black Hills State University *A*
Dakota State University *A*
Dakota Wesleyan University *A,B*
Huron University *A*
Kilian Community College *A*
Mitchell Vocational Technical
Institute *C,A*
National College *A*
Northern State University *A*
Presentation College *A*
Sinte Gleska College *A*
Western Dakota Vocational
Technical Institute *C,A*

Tennessee

Austin Peay State University *A*
Bristol University *A*
Chattanooga State Technical
Community College *A*

Cleveland State Community College A
Dyersburg State Community College A
East Tennessee State University B
Hiwassee College A
Jackson State Community College A
Knoxville Business College C
Lincoln Memorial University B
Martin Methodist College A
McKenzie College A
Middle Tennessee State University B
Motlow State Community College A
Nashville State Technical Institute A
Roane State Community College A
Southern College of Seventh-day Adventists A
Tomlinson College A
Walters State Community College A

Texas
Amarillo College A
Angelina College C,A
Austin Community College A
Bee County College A
Blinn College A
Brazosport College C,A
Central Texas College A
Cisco Junior College A
College of the Mainland A
Collin County Community College District A
Cooke County College A
Del Mar College C,A
East Texas Baptist University A,B
East Texas State University B,M
Eastfield College A
El Centro College A
Galveston College C,A
Houston Community College C
Howard College C,A
Huston-Tillotson College B
Kilgore College A
Lamar University—Beaumont A
Laredo Junior College A
Lee College C,A
Lon Morris College A
McLennan Community College C,A
McMurry University A,B
Midland College C,A
Mountain View College C,A
Navarro College A
North Harris Montgomery Community College District C,A
North Lake College A
Odessa College A
Panola College A
Paul Quinn College B
St. Philip's College A
San Antonio College A
San Jacinto College: Central Campus A
Schreiner College A
South Plains College A
Stephen F. Austin State University B,M
Tarleton State University B
Tarrant County Junior College C,A
Temple Junior College A
Texarkana College A
Texas College B
Texas Southmost College A
Texas State Technical College: Harlingen C
Trinity Valley Community College A
Vernon Regional Junior College A

Victoria College A
Weatherford College C,A
Western Texas College A
Wharton County Junior College A
Wiley College B

Utah
College of Eastern Utah C
Dixie College A
LDS Business College A
Phillips Junior College: Salt Lake City Campus C,A
Stevens-Henager College of Business A
Utah State University B

Vermont
Castleton State College A
Champlain College A
Vermont Technical College A

Virginia
Blue Ridge Community College A
Bluefield College A
Central Virginia Community College A
Clinch Valley College of the University of Virginia C
Commonwealth College A
Dabney S. Lancaster Community College A
Eastern Shore Community College C,A
National Business College A
Northern Virginia Community College A
Patrick Henry Community College A
Paul D. Camp Community College A
Piedmont Virginia Community College C,A
Radford University B
Virginia Commonwealth University B
Virginia Highlands Community College A

Washington
Big Bend Community College A
Central Washington University B
Centralia College A
Clark College C,A
Columbia Basin College A
Edmonds Community College A
Everett Community College C,A
Griffin College C,A
Lower Columbia College C,A
North Seattle Community College A
Northwest College of the Assemblies of God A
Northwest Indian College C
Olympic College A
Pierce College A
Seattle Central Community College C,A
Shoreline Community College C,A
Skagit Valley College C,A
Spokane Community College A
Spokane Falls Community College A
Tacoma Community College A
Walla Walla College A
Walla Walla Community College C,A
Wenatchee Valley College A
Whatcom Community College C,A
Yakima Valley Community College C,A

West Virginia
College of West Virginia A,B
Fairmont State College A
Glenville State College A
Marshall University A
Potomac State College of West Virginia University A
Shepherd College A,B
West Virginia Institute of Technology A
West Virginia Northern Community College A
West Virginia University at Parkersburg B

Wisconsin
Chippewa Valley Technical College A
Concordia University Wisconsin B
Fox Valley Technical College C
Madison Area Technical College A
Madison Junior College of Business C,A
Mid-State Technical College A
Stratton College C,A
University of Wisconsin: Eau Claire B

Wyoming
Casper College A
Central Wyoming College A
Eastern Wyoming College A
Laramie County Community College A
Northwest College A
Sheridan College A
Western Wyoming Community College C,A

American Samoa, Caroline Islands, Guam, Marianas, Virgin Islands
Guam Community College A
Micronesian Occupational College C
Northern Marianas College A

Business statistics

Alabama
University of Alabama B,M,D

California
California State University: Long Beach B

Colorado
University of Colorado at Denver B
University of Denver B,M

District of Columbia
George Washington University M
Southeastern University B

Georgia
Georgia Institute of Technology M
Georgia State University B,M,D

Illinois
De Paul University M
Northwestern University M
University of Chicago M,D
University of Illinois at Chicago B

Indiana
Ball State University B
Indiana University Bloomington D

Kansas
Fort Scott Community College A

Maryland
University of Maryland: College Park B

Massachusetts
Harvard University M,D
Massachusetts Institute of Technology M,D,W

Michigan
University of Michigan D
Western Michigan University B

Minnesota
University of Minnesota: Twin Cities B,M,D
Willmar Community College A

New Jersey
Rider College B
Seton Hall University M

New York
City University of New York: Baruch College B,M
New York University B,M,D
Syracuse University B,M,D

Ohio
Bowling Green State University B,M
Cleveland State University B
Miami University: Oxford Campus B,M
Ohio University B
University of Toledo B

Oklahoma
Southwestern Oklahoma State University B
University of Oklahoma B

Pennsylvania
Carnegie Mellon University B,M,D,W
Drexel University B,D
La Salle University B,M
Lehigh University B
Northeastern Christian Junior College A
Robert Morris College M
Temple University B,M,D

Puerto Rico
University of Puerto Rico: Rio Piedras Campus B

Tennessee
Bristol University A,B
Motlow State Community College A
University of Tennessee: Knoxville B,M

Texas
University of Houston B,M,D

Utah
Brigham Young University B
University of Utah M

Virginia
Averett College B

Wisconsin
University of Wisconsin: Madison M,D

Canada
McGill University *B,D*

Business systems analysis

California
Barstow College *A*
California State University: Northridge *B,M*
Cerritos Community College *A*
Phillips Junior College: Fresno Campus *C,A*
Saddleback College *C,A*
Southwestern College *A*

Colorado
Community College of Denver *C,A*

Connecticut
Quinnipiac College *B,M*

Idaho
Idaho State University *A*
North Idaho College *A*

Illinois
Bradley University *B*
Elgin Community College *C,A*
Northern Illinois University *B*
State Community College *A*
William Rainey Harper College *A*

Iowa
Indian Hills Community College *A*

Kansas
Dodge City Community College *A*

Kentucky
Georgetown College *B*
Southeast Community College *A*

Louisiana
Northeast Louisiana University *B*

Maine
University of Maine at Machias *A*

Maryland
Montgomery College: Germantown Campus *A*

Michigan
Northern Michigan University *B*

Missouri
St. Louis Community College at Meramec *A*

New Jersey
St. Peter's College *C*

New York
Clarkson University *B,M*

Ohio
Ohio University *B*
University of Cincinnati: Access Colleges *A*
University of Findlay *B*

Oklahoma
Oklahoma State University: Oklahoma City *A*

Oregon
Linfield College *B*

Pennsylvania
Clarion University of Pennsylvania *A*
Delaware County Community College *C*

Puerto Rico
Puerto Rico Junior College *A*

Texas
Austin Community College *A*
Brookhaven College *A*
East Texas State University *B*
El Centro College *A*
San Antonio College *A*
Texas A&M University *B,M,D*

Utah
Phillips Junior College: Salt Lake City Campus *C,A*

Vermont
Champlain College *A*

West Virginia
Shepherd College *B*

Wisconsin
Moraine Park Technical College *A*
University of Wisconsin: Oshkosh *B*

Canadian studies

Indiana
Franklin College *B*

Massachusetts
Hampshire College *B*
Massachusetts Bay Community College *A*

New York
St. Lawrence University *B*
State University of New York College at Plattsburgh *B*

Utah
Brigham Young University *B*

Vermont
University of Vermont *B*

Washington
Western Washington University *B*

Canada
McGill University *B*

Caribbean studies

Florida
Florida State University *B*
Rollins College *B*

Georgia
Emory University *B*
University of Georgia *B*

Indiana
Indiana University Bloomington *C*

Maryland
Morgan State University *B*

Massachusetts
Hampshire College *B*

Michigan
University of Michigan *B*

New Jersey
Stockton State College *C*

New York
City University of New York
Brooklyn College *B*
City College *B*
Hostos Community College *A*
Lehman College *B*
Queens College *B*
New York University *M*
State University of New York
Albany *B*
Binghamton *B*

American Samoa, Caroline Islands, Guam, Marianas, Virgin Islands
University of the Virgin Islands *B*

Canada
McGill University *B*

Carpentry

Alabama
Bessemer State Technical College *C*
Central Alabama Community College: Childersburg Campus *C*
Douglas MacArthur State Technical College *C*
Gadsden State Community College *C*
George C. Wallace State Community College at Selma *C*
John C. Calhoun State Community College *C*
Lawson State Community College *C*
Reid State Technical College *C*
Shoals Community College *C*
Wallace State Community College at Hanceville *C*

Arizona
Mesa Community College *C,A*
Mohave Community College *C*
Northland Pioneer College *C,A*
Pima Community College *C,A*
Rio Salado Community College *A*

Arkansas
Phillips County Community College *C*
Rich Mountain Community College *A*

California
Bakersfield College *A*
Laney College *C,A*
Long Beach City College *C,A*
Los Angeles Trade and Technical College *C,A*
Modesto Junior College *A*
Palomar College *C,A*
Pasadena City College *C,A*
Porterville College *C,A*
San Joaquin Delta College *C,A*
Santa Rosa Junior College *C,A*
Sierra College *C*

Colorado
Pikes Peak Community College *C*
Red Rocks Community College *C,A*

Florida
Brevard Community College *C*
Indian River Community College *C*
South Florida Community College *C*

Georgia
Atlanta Metropolitan College *A*
Darton College *A*
Floyd College *A*
Gainesville College *A*
Savannah Technical Institute *C*

Hawaii
University of Hawaii
Honolulu Community College *C,A*
Kauai Community College *C,A*

Idaho
North Idaho College *C,A*
Ricks College *A*

Illinois
Belleville Area College *C,A*
Black Hawk College *C*
Lewis and Clark Community College *C*
State Community College *C*
Triton College *C,A*

Indiana
Vincennes University *A*

Iowa
Des Moines Area Community College *C*
Indian Hills Community College *C*
Iowa Central Community College *C*
Iowa Lakes Community College *C*
North Iowa Area Community College *C*
Northeast Iowa Community College *C*
Northwest Iowa Technical College *C*
Southwestern Community College *C*

Kansas
Allen County Community College *C*
Central College *A*
Coffeyville Community College *A*
Cowley County Community College *C,A*
Kansas City Kansas Community College *A*
Neosho County Community College *C,A*

Kentucky
Eastern Kentucky University *B*

Maine
Eastern Maine Technical College *A*
Southern Maine Technical College *A*

Maryland
Cecil Community College *C,A*
Howard Community College *C*

Michigan
Lansing Community College *C,A*
Macomb Community College *C,A*
Northern Michigan University *C*

Minnesota
Alexandria Technical College *C*
St. Paul Technical College *C*
Willmar Technical College *C*

Mississippi
East Central Community College *C*
Hinds Community College *C*
Mississippi Gulf Coast Community
College: Jefferson Davis
Campus *C*
Southwest Mississippi Community
College *C*

Missouri
East Central College *C,A*
North Central Missouri College *A*
Ranken Technical College *A*

Montana
Fort Peck Community College *C,A*
Little Big Horn College *C*
Salish Kootenai College *C*

Nebraska
Chadron State College *B*
Metropolitan Community College *C*
Nebraska Indian Community
College *A*
Northeast Community College *A*
Southeast Community College:
Milford Campus *A*

Nevada
Truckee Meadows Community
College *C,A*

New Mexico
Albuquerque Technical-Vocational
Institute *C*
San Juan College *C*
Western New Mexico University
C,A

New York
Hudson Valley Community
College *A*
Mohawk Valley Community
College *C*
State University of New York
College of Technology at
Delhi *A*

North Carolina
Alamance Community College *A*
Anson Community College *C*
Asheville Buncombe Technical
Community College *C*
Bladen Community College *C*
Blue Ridge Community College *C*
Craven Community College *C*
Durham Technical Community
College *C*
Fayetteville Technical Community
College *C*
Forsyth Technical Community
College *A*
Guilford Technical Community
College *C*
Haywood Community College *C*
Martin Community College *C*
Mayland Community College *C*
Montgomery Community College *C*
Piedmont Community College *C*
Pitt Community College *C*
Roanoke-Chowan Community
College *C*
Robeson Community College *C*
Rockingham Community College *C*
Southeastern Community College *C*
Southwestern Community
College *C*

Tri-County Community College *C*
Vance-Granville Community
College *C*
Wilson Technical Community
College *C*

North Dakota
Bismarck State College *C,A*
Little Hoop Community College *A*
Turtle Mountain Community
College *C*

Ohio
ITT Technical Institute: Dayton *A*
University of Cincinnati: Access
Colleges *C*

Oregon
Portland Community College *A*

Pennsylvania
Johnson Technical Institute *A*
Pennsylvania College of
Technology *C*
Williamson Free School of
Mechanical Trades *C*

Rhode Island
New England Institute of
Technology *A*

South Carolina
Bob Jones University *C,A*
Denmark Technical College *C*
Greenville Technical College *C*
Technical College of the
Lowcountry *C*
Williamsburg Technical College *C*

South Dakota
Mitchell Vocational Technical
Institute *C,A*
Western Dakota Vocational
Technical Institute *C*

Tennessee
Chattanooga State Technical
Community College *C*

Texas
Brazosport College *C,A*
Central Texas College *C*
North Lake College *A*
Odessa College *C,A*
Texarkana College *C*
Texas Southmost College *A*

Utah
Utah Valley Community College
C,A

Washington
Central Washington University *B*
Columbia Basin College *A*
Grays Harbor College *A*
Green River Community College *A*
Olympic College *C*
Seattle Central Community College
C,A
Spokane Community College *A*
Walla Walla Community College
C,A
Wenatchee Valley College *A*

Wisconsin
Chippewa Valley Technical
College *C*
Wisconsin Indianhead Technical
College *C*

**American Samoa, Caroline
Islands, Guam, Marianas,
Virgin Islands**
Guam Community College *C*
Micronesian Occupational College
C,A

Cell biology

Arizona
University of Arizona *B,M,D*

California
California Institute of Technology
D,W
California State University
Fresno *B*
Fullerton *B*
Northridge *B*
San Francisco State University *B,M*
Stanford University *D*
University of California
Berkeley *B*
Davis *D*
San Diego *B*
San Francisco *D*
Santa Barbara *B,M,D*
Santa Cruz *B,D*
University of Southern California
M,D

Colorado
University of Colorado
Boulder *B,M,D*
Health Sciences Center *D*
University of Northern Colorado *B*

Connecticut
University of Connecticut *B,M,D*
Wesleyan University *B*
Yale University *M,D*

Florida
Florida Agricultural and Mechanical
University *M*
Florida Institute of Technology
M,D
New College of the University of
South Florida *B*
University of Florida *M,D*
University of Miami *D*

Georgia
Emory University *M,D*

Illinois
Loyola University of Chicago *M,D*
Northwestern University *B,M,D*
University of Chicago *B,M,D*
University of Health Sciences: The
Chicago Medical School *M,D*
University of Illinois at Urbana-
Champaign *M,D*

Indiana
Ball State University *B*
Indiana University Bloomington *D*
Purdue University *B,D*
University of Notre Dame *B,M,D*

Iowa
Iowa State University *M,D*

Kansas
University of Kansas *B,M,D*

Maine
University of Maine *B*

Maryland
University of Maryland
Baltimore County *D*
College Park *D*

Massachusetts
Hampshire College *B*
Harvard University *D*
Massachusetts Institute of
Technology *B,M,D,W*
Tufts University *D*
University of Massachusetts at
Amherst *M,D*
Worcester Polytechnic Institute
B,M

Michigan
Eastern Michigan University *M*
Oakland University *D*
University of Michigan *B,M,D*

Minnesota
Mankato State University *B,M*
University of Minnesota: Twin
Cities *M,D*
Winona State University *B*

Missouri
University of Missouri: Kansas
City *D*
Washington University *D*

New Hampshire
University of New Hampshire *B*

New Jersey
Rutgers—The State University of
New Jersey
Camden College of Arts and
Sciences *B*
Cook College *B*
Douglass College *B*
Livingston College *B*
New Brunswick *M,D*
Rutgers College *B*
University College New
Brunswick *B*
Stevens Institute of Technology *B*

New York
Columbia University *M,D*
Cornell University *B,M,D*
Long Island University
Brooklyn Campus *M*
C. W. Post Campus *M*
Southampton Campus *B*
New York University *M,D*
Rockefeller University *D*
State University of New York
Albany *M,D*
Stony Brook *D*
College of Environmental
Science and Forestry *B,M,D*
College at Plattsburgh *B*
Health Science Center at
Brooklyn *D*
Health Science Center at
Syracuse *D*
University of Rochester *B*
Yeshiva University *M,D*

North Carolina
Barton College *B*
Duke University *D*
Vance-Granville Community
College *A*

Ohio
Case Western Reserve University *D*
Kent State University *M,D*
Ohio State University: Columbus
Campus *M,D*

Ohio University M,D
University of Akron B

Oklahoma

Northeastern State University B
University of Oklahoma Health Sciences Center M,D
University of Tulsa M

Oregon

Oregon Health Sciences University M,D

Pennsylvania

Bucknell University B
Carnegie Mellon University B,M,D,W
Drexel University M,D
Lehigh University B,M,D
Penn State
  Milton S. Hershey Medical Center M,D
  University Park Campus B,M,D
University of Pennsylvania M,D
University of Pittsburgh M,D
West Chester University of Pennsylvania B

Rhode Island

Brown University B,M,D

Tennessee

Vanderbilt University M,D

Texas

University of Texas
  Dallas M,D
  Health Science Center at Houston M,D,W
  Health Science Center at San Antonio M,D
  Southwestern Medical Center at Dallas Southwestern Allied Health Sciences School M,D

Utah

University of Utah D

Vermont

Marlboro College B
University of Vermont M,D

Virginia

Christopher Newport College B

Washington

Evergreen State College B
University of Washington B
Washington State University M,D

Wisconsin

Marquette University M,D

Canada

McGill University B,M,D

Ceramic engineering

Georgia

Georgia Institute of Technology B,M,D
Middle Georgia College A

Illinois

Richland Community College A
University of Illinois at Urbana-Champaign B,M,D

Iowa

Iowa State University B,M,D

Massachusetts

Massachusetts Institute of Technology B,M,D,W

Missouri

University of Missouri: Rolla B,M,D

New Jersey

Rutgers—The State University of New Jersey
  College of Engineering B
  New Brunswick M,D

New York

Alfred University B,M,D

Ohio

Case Western Reserve University M,D
Hocking Technical College A
Ohio State University: Columbus Campus B,M,D

Pennsylvania

Lock Haven University of Pennsylvania B
Penn State University Park Campus B,M,D

South Carolina

Clemson University B,M,D

Washington

University of Washington B

Ceramics

Alabama

University of Montevallo B

Arizona

Northern Arizona University B

Arkansas

Garland County Community College C

California

California College of Arts and Crafts B,M
California State University
  Fullerton B,M
  Long Beach B,M
  Los Angeles B,M
  Northridge B,M
Chabot College A
Chaffey Community College A
De Anza College C
Glendale Community College C
Grossmont Community College A
Laney College A
Monterey Peninsula College C,A
Otis/Parsons School of Art and Design B,M
Palomar College A
Pasadena City College C,A
San Jose City College A
San Jose State University B
Ventura College A

Connecticut

University of Connecticut B
University of Hartford B

District of Columbia

George Washington University M
Howard University B,M

Florida

New College of the University of South Florida B
Pensacola Junior College A
Ringling School of Art and Design B
University of Miami M
University of South Florida B,M

Georgia

LaGrange College B
University of Georgia B,M

Idaho

University of Idaho B

Illinois

Barat College B
Bradley University B
Illinois Wesleyan University B
Richland Community College A
School of the Art Institute of Chicago B,M
Southern Illinois University at Carbondale B,M

Indiana

Ball State University B
Indiana University Bloomington B,M
Indiana University—Purdue University at Indianapolis B
Purdue University B,M
Vincennes University A

Iowa

University of Iowa B,M

Kansas

Butler County Community College A
Kansas State University M
Pratt Community College A
University of Kansas B

Kentucky

Eastern Kentucky University B

Louisiana

Louisiana State University and Agricultural and Mechanical College B

Maine

Portland School of Art B

Maryland

Howard Community College A
Maryland Institute College of Art B

Massachusetts

Massachusetts College of Art B,M
School of the Museum of Fine Arts B,M
University of Massachusetts at Dartmouth B,M
Wellesley College B

Michigan

Center for Creative Studies: College of Art and Design B
Central Michigan University B,M
Eastern Michigan University B
Grand Valley State University B
Marygrove College B
Northern Michigan University B
Oakland Community College A
University of Michigan B,M

Minnesota

Moorhead State University B
St. Cloud State University B

Missouri

Kansas City Art Institute B
Washington University B,M
Webster University B

Nebraska

Hastings College B

New Jersey

Mercer County Community College A

New Mexico

Institute of American Indian Arts A

New York

Alfred University B,M
Hofstra University B
Parsons School of Design A,B
Pratt Institute B,M
Rochester Institute of Technology A,B,M
Sarah Lawrence College B
State University of New York
  College at New Paltz B,M
  College at Potsdam B
Syracuse University B,M

North Carolina

Barton College B
Brevard College A
East Carolina University B,M
Haywood Community College A
Montgomery Community College C

Ohio

Bowling Green State University B
Cleveland Institute of Art B
Lakeland Community College A
Ohio Northern University B
Ohio State University: Columbus Campus B,M
Ohio University B,M
University of Akron B
Wittenberg University B

Oklahoma

Phillips University A
University of Central Oklahoma B
University of Oklahoma B
University of Tulsa B

Oregon

Central Oregon Community College A
Pacific Northwest College of Art B
Portland State University M
University of Oregon
  Eugene B,M
  Robert Donald Clark Honors College B

Pennsylvania

Beaver College B
Carnegie Mellon University B,M
Edinboro University of Pennsylvania B,M
Immaculata College A
Marywood College B
Mercyhurst College B
Moore College of Art and Design B
Seton Hill College B
Temple University B,M
University of the Arts B

Puerto Rico

Inter American University of Puerto Rico: San German Campus *B*

Rhode Island

Rhode Island School of Design *B,M*

Tennessee

East Tennessee State University *B*
Memphis College of Art *B*

Texas

Lamar University—Beaumont *M*
McMurry University *B*
Texas Woman's University *B,M*
University of Dallas *B,M*
University of Houston *B*
University of Texas at El Paso *B*
Western Texas College *A*

Utah

Brigham Young University *B,M*

Vermont

Bennington College *B,M*
Marlboro College *B*

Washington

University of Washington *B,M*

West Virginia

Bethany College *B*
West Virginia State College *B*
West Virginia University *B,M*

Wisconsin

University of Wisconsin: Eau Claire *B*

Chemical engineering

Alabama

Auburn University *B,M,D*
Tuskegee University *B*
University of Alabama
    Huntsville *B*
    Tuscaloosa *B,M,D*
University of South Alabama *B,M*

Arizona

Arizona State University *B,M,D*
University of Arizona *B,M,D*

Arkansas

University of Arkansas *B,M*
Westark Community College *A*

California

California Institute of Technology *B,M,D,W*
California State Polytechnic University: Pomona *B*
California State University
    Long Beach *B*
    Northridge *B,M*
San Jose State University *B,M*
Santa Rosa Junior College *A*
Stanford University *B,M,D*
University of California
    Berkeley *B,M,D*
    Davis *B,M,D*
    Los Angeles *B,M,D*
    Riverside *B*
    San Diego *B,M,D*
    Santa Barbara *B,M,D*
University of Southern California *B,M,D,W*

Colorado

Colorado School of Mines *B,M,D,W*
Colorado State University *B,M,D*
University of Colorado at Boulder *B,M,D*

Connecticut

Hartford State Technical College *A*
University of Connecticut *B,M,D*
University of New Haven *B*
Yale University *B,M,D*

Delaware

Delaware State College *B*
University of Delaware *B,M,D*

District of Columbia

Howard University *B,M*

Florida

Florida Agricultural and Mechanical University *B,M,D*
Florida Institute of Technology *B,M*
Florida State University *B,M,D*
Miami-Dade Community College *A*
University of Florida *B,M,D*
University of South Florida *B,M,D*

Georgia

Clark Atlanta University *B*
Georgia Institute of Technology *B,M,D*
Middle Georgia College *A*
Morris Brown College *B*

Idaho

College of Southern Idaho *A*
North Idaho College *A*
Ricks College *A*
University of Idaho *B,M,D*

Illinois

Illinois Institute of Technology *B,M,D*
Lincoln Land Community College *A*
Northwestern University *B,M,D*
Richland Community College *A*
University of Illinois
    Chicago *B,M,D*
    Urbana-Champaign *B,M,D*

Indiana

Purdue University *B,M,D,W*
Rose-Hulman Institute of Technology *B,M*
Tri-State University *B*
University of Notre Dame *B,M,D*
Vincennes University *A*

Iowa

Iowa State University *B,M,D*
University of Iowa *B,M,D*

Kansas

Kansas State University *B,M,D*
University of Kansas *B,M,D*

Kentucky

University of Kentucky *B,M,D*
University of Louisville *B,M,D*

Louisiana

Louisiana State University and Agricultural and Mechanical College *B,M,D*
Louisiana Tech University *B,M*
McNeese State University *B*
Tulane University *B,M,D*
University of Southwestern Louisiana *B,M*

Maine

University of Maine *B,M,D*

Maryland

College of Notre Dame of Maryland *B*
Johns Hopkins University *B,M,D*
University of Maryland
    Baltimore County *B,M,D*
    College Park *B,M,D*

Massachusetts

Massachusetts Institute of Technology *B,M,D,W*
Northeastern University *B,M,D*
Tufts University *B,M,D*
University of Massachusetts
    Amherst *B,M,D*
    Lowell *B,M*
Worcester Polytechnic Institute *B,M,D*

Michigan

Kellogg Community College *A*
Michigan State University *B,M,D*
Michigan Technological University *B,M,D*
University of Detroit Mercy *B,M,D*
University of Michigan *B,M,D*
Wayne State University *B,M,D*

Minnesota

University of Minnesota
    Duluth *B*
    Twin Cities *B,M,D*
Willmar Community College *A*
Winona State University *B*

Mississippi

Mississippi College *B*
Mississippi State University *B,M*
University of Mississippi *B*

Missouri

East Central College *A*
University of Missouri
    Columbia *B,M,D*
    Rolla *B,M,D*
Washington University *B,M,D*
William Jewell College *B*

Montana

Montana State University *B,M,D*

Nebraska

University of Nebraska—Lincoln *B,M*

Nevada

University of Nevada: Reno *B*

New Hampshire

University of New Hampshire *B,M,D*

New Jersey

Burlington County College *A*
New Jersey Institute of Technology *B,M,D*
Princeton University *B,M,D*
Rutgers—The State University of New Jersey
    College of Engineering *B*
    New Brunswick *M,D*
Stevens Institute of Technology *B,M,D*

New Mexico

New Mexico Institute of Mining and Technology *B*
New Mexico State University *B,M,D*

University of New Mexico *B,M*

New York

City University of New York
    City College *B,M,D*
    Graduate School and University Center *D*
Clarkson University *B,M,D*
Columbia University: School of Engineering and Applied Science *B,M,D,W*
Cooper Union *B,M*
Cornell University *B,M,D*
Erie Community College: North Campus *A*
Manhattan College *B,M*
New York University *B*
Pace University
    College of White Plains *B*
    New York *B*
    Pleasantville/Briarcliff *B*
Polytechnic University
    Brooklyn *B,M,D*
    Long Island Campus *B*
Rensselaer Polytechnic Institute *B,M,D*
State University of New York
    Buffalo *B,M,D*
    College of Environmental Science and Forestry *B,M,D*
Syracuse University *B,M,D*
United States Military Academy *B*
University of Rochester *B,M,D,W*

North Carolina

Asheville Buncombe Technical Community College *A*
Brevard College *A*
North Carolina Agricultural and Technical State University *B*
North Carolina State University *B,M,D*
St. Augustine's College *B*

North Dakota

University of North Dakota *B,M*

Ohio

Case Western Reserve University *B,M,D*
Cleveland State University *B,M*
Ohio State University: Columbus Campus *B,M,D*
Ohio University *B,M,D*
University of Akron *B,M,D*
University of Cincinnati *B,M,D*
University of Dayton *B,M*
University of Toledo *B,M,D*
Wilberforce University *B*
Youngstown State University *B*

Oklahoma

Oklahoma State University *B,M,D*
University of Oklahoma *B,M,D*
University of Tulsa *B,M,D*

Oregon

Oregon State University *B,M,D*

Pennsylvania

Bucknell University *B,M*
California University of Pennsylvania *B*
Carnegie Mellon University *B,M,D,W*
Drexel University *B,M,D*
Gannon University *B*
Geneva College *B*
Keystone Junior College *A*
Lafayette College *B*
Lehigh University *B,M,D*

Lock Haven University of
Pennsylvania *B*
Penn State University Park Campus
B,M,D
Thiel College *B*
University of Pennsylvania *B,M,D*
University of Pittsburgh *B,M,D*
Villanova University *B,M*
Widener University *B,M*

Puerto Rico

University of Puerto Rico
Arecibo Campus *A,B*
Mayaguez Campus *B,M*

Rhode Island

Brown University *B,M,D*
University of Rhode Island *B,M,D*

South Carolina

Clemson University *B,M,D*
University of South Carolina *B,M,D*

South Dakota

South Dakota School of Mines and
Technology *B,M*

Tennessee

Christian Brothers University *B*
Tennessee Technological University
B,M
University of Tennessee
Chattanooga *B,M*
Knoxville *B,M,D*
Vanderbilt University *B,M,D*

Texas

Amarillo College *A*
Kilgore College *A*
Lamar University—Beaumont *B,D*
Prairie View A&M University *B*
Rice University *B,M,D*
Texas A&I University *B,M*
Texas A&M University *B,M,D*
Texas Southmost College *A*
Texas Tech University *B,M,D*
University of Houston *B,M,D*
University of Texas at Austin
B,M,D

Utah

Brigham Young University *B,M,D*
Southern Utah University *A*
University of Utah *B,M,D*

Virginia

Emory and Henry College *B*
Hampton University *B*
Radford University *B*
University of Virginia *B,M,D*
Virginia Polytechnic Institute and
State University *B,M,D*
Washington and Lee University *B*

Washington

Lower Columbia College *A*
University of Puget Sound *B*
University of Washington *B,M,D*
Washington State University *B,M,D*

West Virginia

West Virginia Graduate College *M*
West Virginia Institute of
Technology *B,M*
West Virginia University *B,M,D*
Wheeling Jesuit College *B*

Wisconsin

University of Wisconsin: Madison
B,M,D

Wyoming

University of Wyoming *B,M,D*

Canada

McGill University *B,M,D*

Mexico

Sistema Instituto Tecnologico y de
Estudios Superiores de
Monterrey *B*

Chemical manufacturing technology

Alabama

Lurleen B. Wallace State Junior
College *A*
Shoals Community College *C,A*

Arkansas

Southern Arkansas Community
College *A*
Westark Community College *C,A*

California

Cerritos Community College *A*
City College of San Francisco *A*
Irvine Valley College *C,A*
Los Angeles Trade and Technical
College *C,A*
San Diego Mesa College *A*

Colorado

Community College of Denver *C*

Connecticut

Thames Valley State Technical
College *A*
Waterbury State Technical
College *A*

Delaware

Delaware Technical and
Community College
Southern Campus *A*
Stanton/Wilmington
Campus *A*

Georgia

Savannah State College *B*

Idaho

Northwest Nazarene College *A*

Illinois

Belleville Area College *C*
City Colleges of Chicago: Chicago
City-Wide College *A*
College of Lake County *C,A*

Indiana

Ball State University *A*
Purdue University: Calumet *A*

Kentucky

Brescia College *A*
Jefferson Community College *A*
Northern Kentucky University *A*

Maryland

Catonsville Community College *A*
Howard Community College *A*

Massachusetts

Westfield State College *B*

Michigan

Grand Rapids Community
College *A*

Kalamazoo Valley Community
College *A*
Lawrence Technological
University *A*
Muskegon Community College *A*
Southwestern Michigan College *A*

Minnesota

St. Paul Technical College *C*

Missouri

St. Louis Community College at
Florissant Valley *A*

New Jersey

County College of Morris *A*
Essex County College *A*
Gloucester County College *A*

New York

Broome Community College *A*
Corning Community College *A*
Erie Community College: North
Campus *A*
Herkimer County Community
College *A*
Hudson Valley Community
College *A*
Mohawk Valley Community
College *A*
Monroe Community College *A*
Onondaga Community College *A*
State University of New York
College of Agriculture and
Technology at Cobleskill *A*

North Carolina

Cape Fear Community College *A*
Wake Technical Community
College *A*

North Dakota

Bismarck State College *A*

Ohio

Kent State University: Ashtabula
Regional Campus *A*
Lorain County Community
College *A*
University of Cincinnati: Access
Colleges *A*
University of Toledo *A*
Washington State Community
College *A*

Pennsylvania

Community College of
Philadelphia *A*

Puerto Rico

Inter American University of Puerto
Rico: Arecibo Campus *A,B*
University of Puerto Rico: Humacao
University College *A*

Rhode Island

Community College of Rhode
Island *C,A*

South Carolina

Trident Technical College *A*

Tennessee

Chattanooga State Technical
Community College *A*
Northeast State Technical
Community College *A*
Pellissippi State Technical
Community College *A*
State Technical Institute at
Memphis *A*

Texas

Brazosport College *A*
Galveston College *A*
Houston Community College *A*
Kilgore College *A*
Lee College *A*
San Jacinto College: Central
Campus *A*
Texas State Technical College
Amarillo *A*
Harlingen *A*

Washington

Clark College *A*
Lower Columbia College *A*
Seattle Central Community
College *A*
Shoreline Community College *A*

West Virginia

West Virginia State College *A*

Wyoming

Casper College *A*
Laramie County Community
College *A*
Western Wyoming Community
College *A*

Chemistry

Alabama

Alabama Agricultural and
Mechanical University *B*
Alabama Southern Community
College *A*
Alabama State University *B*
Athens State College *B*
Auburn University
Auburn *B,M,D*
Montgomery *B*
Birmingham-Southern College *B*
Chattahoochee Valley Community
College *A*
Huntingdon College *B*
Jacksonville State University *B*
John C. Calhoun State Community
College *A*
Judson College *B*
Livingston University *B*
Miles College *B*
Mobile College *B*
Oakwood College *B*
Samford University *B*
Snead State Junior College *A*
Spring Hill College *B*
Stillman College *B*
Talladega College *B*
Troy State University *B*
Tuskegee University *B,M*
University of Alabama
Birmingham *B,M,D*
Huntsville *B,M*
Tuscaloosa *B,M,D,W*
University of Montevallo *B*
University of North Alabama *B*
University of South Alabama *B*

Alaska

University of Alaska
Anchorage *B*
Fairbanks *B,M*

Arizona

Arizona State University *B,M,D*
Arizona Western College *A*
Cochise College *A*
Eastern Arizona College *A*
Glendale Community College *A*

Grand Canyon University *B*
Northern Arizona University *B,M*
Pima Community College *A*
University of Arizona *B,M,D*
Yavapai College *A*

Arkansas

Arkansas College *B*
Arkansas State University *B,M*
Arkansas Tech University *B*
Harding University *B*
Henderson State University *B*
Hendrix College *B*
John Brown University *B*
Ouachita Baptist University *B*
Philander Smith College *B*
Phillips County Community
    College *A*
Southern Arkansas University *B*
University of Arkansas
    Fayetteville *B,M,D*
    Little Rock *B,M*
    Monticello *B*
    Pine Bluff *B*
University of Central Arkansas *B*
University of the Ozarks *B*
Westark Community College *A*

California

Allan Hancock College *A*
Azusa Pacific University *B*
Bakersfield College *A*
Biola University *B*
California Institute of Technology
    B,D,W
California Lutheran University *B*
California Polytechnic State
    University: San Luis Obispo *B,M*
California State Polytechnic
    University: Pomona *B,M*
California State University
    Bakersfield *B*
    Chico *B*
    Dominguez Hills *B*
    Fresno *B,M*
    Fullerton *B*
    Hayward *B,M*
    Long Beach *B,M*
    Los Angeles *B,M*
    Northridge *B,M*
    Sacramento *B,M*
    San Bernardino *B*
    Stanislaus *B*
Cerritos Community College *A*
Chabot College *A*
Chaffey Community College *A*
Chapman University *B*
Citrus College *A*
City College of San Francisco *A*
Claremont McKenna College *B*
College of the Desert *A*
College of the Sequoias *A*
Columbia College *A*
Crafton Hills College *A*
Cuesta College *A*
De Anza College *A*
El Camino College *A*
Feather River College *A*
Foothill College *A*
Grossmont Community College *C,A*
Harvey Mudd College *B*
Humboldt State University *B*
Irvine Valley College *A*
La Sierra University *B*
Los Angeles City College *A*
Los Angeles Mission College *A*
Los Angeles Valley College *A*
Los Medanos College *A*
Loyola Marymount University *B*
Merced College *A*
Mills College *B*
MiraCosta College *A*

Mission College *A*
Modesto Junior College *A*
Moorpark College *A*
Mount St. Mary's College *B*
Napa Valley College *A*
Occidental College *B*
Ohlone College *A*
Orange Coast College *A*
Pacific Union College *B*
Palomar College *C,A*
Pasadena City College *A*
Pepperdine University *B*
Pitzer College *B*
Point Loma Nazarene College *B*
Pomona College *B*
Porterville College *A*
Saddleback College *A*
St. Mary's College of California *B*
San Diego City College *A*
San Diego Mesa College *A*
San Diego State University *B,M,D*
San Francisco State University *B,M*
San Joaquin Delta College *A*
San Jose City College *A*
San Jose State University *B,M*
Santa Barbara City College *A*
Santa Clara University *B*
Santa Monica College *A*
Santa Rosa Junior College *A*
Scripps College *B*
Sierra College *A*
Solano Community College *A*
Sonoma State University *B*
Southern California College *B*
Southwestern College *A*
Stanford University *B,M,D*
University of California
    Berkeley *B,M,D*
    Davis *B,M,D*
    Irvine *B,M,D*
    Los Angeles *B,M,D*
    Riverside *B,M,D*
    San Diego *B,M,D*
    Santa Barbara *B,M,D*
    Santa Cruz *B,M,D*
University of La Verne *B*
University of the Pacific *B,M,D*
University of Redlands *B*
University of San Diego *B*
University of San Francisco *B,M*
University of Southern California
    B,M,D
Ventura College *A*
West Hills Community College *A*
West Valley College *A*
Westmont College *B*
Whittier College *B*

Colorado

Adams State College *B*
Colorado Christian University *B*
Colorado College *B*
Colorado School of Mines
    B,M,D,W
Colorado State University *B,M,D*
Community College of Denver *A*
Fort Lewis College *B*
Mesa State College *A*
Metropolitan State College of
    Denver *B*
Pikes Peak Community College *A*
Regis College of Regis University *B*
Trinidad State Junior College *A*
United States Air Force
    Academy *B*
University of Colorado
    Boulder *B,M,D*
    Colorado Springs *B*
    Denver *B,M*
University of Denver *B,M,D*
University of Northern Colorado
    B,M

University of Southern Colorado *B*
Western State College of
    Colorado *B*

Connecticut

Central Connecticut State
    University *B,M*
Connecticut College *B*
Fairfield University *B*
Quinnipiac College *B*
Sacred Heart University *A,B*
St. Joseph College *B,M*
Southern Connecticut State
    University *B,M*
Trinity College *B,M*
University of Bridgeport *B*
University of Connecticut *B,M,D*
University of Hartford *B*
University of New Haven *B*
Wesleyan University *B,M,D*
Western Connecticut State
    University *B*
Yale University *B,M,D*

Delaware

Delaware State College *B,M*
University of Delaware *B,M,D*

District of Columbia

American University *B,M,D*
Catholic University of America
    B,M,D
Gallaudet University *B*
George Washington University
    B,M,D
Georgetown University *B,M,D*
Howard University *B,M,D*
Trinity College *B*
University of the District of
    Columbia *B*

Florida

Barry University *B*
Bethune-Cookman College *B*
Central Florida Community
    College *A*
Daytona Beach Community
    College *A*
Eckerd College *B*
Edison Community College *A*
Florida Agricultural and Mechanical
    University *B,M*
Florida Atlantic University *B,M*
Florida Institute of Technology
    B,M,D
Florida International University
    B,M
Florida Memorial College *B*
Florida Southern College *B*
Florida State University *B,M,D*
Gulf Coast Community College *A*
Indian River Community College *A*
Jacksonville University *B*
Miami-Dade Community College *A*
New College of the University of
    South Florida *B*
Okaloosa-Walton Community
    College *A*
Palm Beach Community College *A*
Pensacola Junior College *A*
Rollins College *B*
St. Thomas University *B*
Stetson University *B*
University of Central Florida *B*
University of Florida *B,M,D*
University of Miami *B,M,D*
University of North Florida *B*
University of South Florida *B,M,D*
University of Tampa *A,B*
University of West Florida *B*

Georgia

Abraham Baldwin Agricultural
    College *A*
Agnes Scott College *B*
Albany State College *B*
Andrew College *A*
Armstrong State College *B*
Atlanta Metropolitan College *A*
Augusta College *B*
Bainbridge College *A*
Berry College *B*
Brewton-Parker College *A*
Brunswick College *A*
Clark Atlanta University *B,M,D*
Clayton State College *A*
Columbus College *B*
Covenant College *B*
Darton College *A*
DeKalb College *A*
East Georgia College *A*
Emory University *B,M*
Floyd College *A*
Fort Valley State College *B*
Gainesville College *A*
Georgia College *B*
Georgia Institute of Technology
    B,M,D
Georgia Southern University *B*
Georgia Southwestern College *B*
Georgia State University *B,M,D*
Gordon College *A*
Kennesaw State College *B*
LaGrange College *B*
Macon College *A*
Mercer University *B*
Middle Georgia College *A*
Morehouse College *B*
Morris Brown College *B*
North Georgia College *B*
Oglethorpe University *B*
Oxford College of Emory
    University *A*
Paine College *B*
Piedmont College *B*
Reinhardt College *A*
Savannah State College *B*
Shorter College *B*
South Georgia College *A*
Spelman College *B*
University of Georgia *B,M,D*
Valdosta State College *B*
Wesleyan College *B*
West Georgia College *B*
Young Harris College *A*

Hawaii

Brigham Young University-
    Hawaii *B*
Chaminade University of
    Honolulu *B*
University of Hawaii
    Hilo *B*
    Manoa *B,M,D*

Idaho

Albertson College *B*
Boise State University *B*
College of Southern Idaho *A*
Idaho State University *B*
Lewis Clark State College *B*
North Idaho College *A*
Northwest Nazarene College *B*
Ricks College *A*
University of Idaho *B,M,D*

Illinois

Augustana College *B*
Aurora University *B*
Barat College *B*
Belleville Area College *A*
Black Hawk College *A*
Blackburn College *B*

Bradley University *B,M*
Chicago State University *B*
City Colleges of Chicago
 Olive-Harvey College *A*
 Wright College *A*
Concordia University *B*
De Paul University *B,M*
Eastern Illinois University *B,M*
Elmhurst College *B*
Eureka College *B*
Governors State University *B*
Greenville College *B*
Highland Community College *A*
Illinois Benedictine College *B*
Illinois Central College *A*
Illinois College *B*
Illinois Institute of Technology
 B,M,D
Illinois State University *B,M*
Illinois Wesleyan University *B*
John A. Logan College *A*
Joliet Junior College *A*
Judson College *B*
Kishwaukee College *A*
Knox College *B*
Lake Forest College *B*
Lewis University *B*
Lincoln Land Community
 College *A*
Loyola University of Chicago
 B,M,D
MacMurray College *B*
McKendree College *B*
Millikin University *B*
Monmouth College *B*
Morton College *A*
North Central College *B*
North Park College and Theological
 Seminary *B*
Northeastern Illinois University
 B,M
Northern Illinois University *B,M,D*
Northwestern University *B,M,D*
Olivet Nazarene University *B*
Principia College *B*
Quincy College *B*
Rend Lake College *A*
Richland Community College *A*
Rockford College *B*
Roosevelt University *B,M*
Rosary College *B*
St. Xavier University *B*
Sangamon State University *B*
Southern Illinois University
 Carbondale *B,M,D*
 Edwardsville *B,M*
State Community College *A*
Trinity Christian College *B*
Trinity College *B*
University of Chicago *B,M,D*
University of Illinois
 Chicago *B,M,D*
 Urbana-Champaign *B,M,D*
Waubonsee Community College *A*
Western Illinois University *B,M*
Wheaton College *B*
William Rainey Harper College *A*

Indiana

Anderson University *B*
Ball State University *B,M*
Bethel College *A,B*
Butler University *B,M*
Calumet College of St. Joseph *C,A*
DePauw University *B*
Earlham College *B*
Franklin College *B*
Goshen College *B*
Hanover College *B*
Huntington College *B*
Indiana State University *B,M*

Indiana University
 Bloomington *B,M,D*
 East *A*
 Kokomo *B*
 Northwest *B*
 South Bend *B*
 Southeast *B*
Indiana University—Purdue
 University
 Fort Wayne *B*
 Indianapolis *B,M*
Indiana Wesleyan University *B*
Manchester College *B*
Marian College *B*
Martin University *B*
Oakland City College *B*
Purdue University
 Calumet *B*
 West Lafayette *B*
Rose-Hulman Institute of
 Technology *B*
St. Francis College *B*
St. Joseph's College *B*
St. Mary's College *B*
Taylor University *B*
Tri-State University *B*
University of Evansville *B*
University of Indianapolis *A,B*
University of Notre Dame *B,M,D*
University of Southern Indiana *B*
Valparaiso University *B*
Vincennes University *A*
Wabash College *B*

Iowa

Briar Cliff College *B*
Buena Vista College *B*
Central College *B*
Clarke College *B*
Clinton Community College *A*
Coe College *B*
Cornell College *B*
Dordt College *B*
Drake University *B*
Graceland College *B*
Grinnell College *B*
Iowa Lakes Community College *A*
Iowa State University *B*
Iowa Wesleyan College *B*
Kirkwood Community College *A*
Loras College *B*
Luther College *B*
Maharishi International University
 A,B
Morningside College *B*
Muscatine Community College *A*
North Iowa Area Community
 College *A*
Northwestern College *B*
St. Ambrose University *B*
Scott Community College *A*
Simpson College *B*
Teikyo Marycrest University *B*
Teikyo Westmar University *B*
University of Dubuque *B*
University of Iowa *B,M,D*
University of Northern Iowa *B,M*
Wartburg College *B*
William Penn College *B*

Kansas

Allen County Community
 College *A*
Baker University *B*
Benedictine College *B*
Bethany College *B*
Bethel College *B*
Butler County Community
 College *A*
Central College *A*
Cloud County Community
 College *A*

Coffeyville Community College *A*
Colby Community College *A*
Dodge City Community College *A*
Emporia State University *B*
Fort Hays State University *B*
Fort Scott Community College *A*
Friends University *B*
Hutchinson Community College *A*
Kansas City Kansas Community
 College *A*
Kansas Newman College *B*
Kansas State University *B,M,D*
Kansas Wesleyan University *B*
Labette Community College *A*
McPherson College *B*
MidAmerica Nazarene College *B*
Neosho County Community
 College *A*
Ottawa University *B*
Pittsburg State University *B,M*
Pratt Community College *A*
St. Mary College *B*
Southwestern College *B*
Sterling College *B*
Tabor College *B*
University of Kansas *B,M,D*
Washburn University of Topeka *B*
Wichita State University *B,M,D*

Kentucky

Asbury College *B*
Bellarmine College *B*
Berea College *B*
Brescia College *B*
Campbellsville College *B*
Centre College *B*
Cumberland College *B*
Eastern Kentucky University *B,M*
Georgetown College *B*
Kentucky State University *B*
Kentucky Wesleyan College *B*
Lindsey Wilson College *A*
Morehead State University *B*
Murray State University *B,M*
Northern Kentucky University *B*
Pikeville College *B*
St. Catharine College *A*
Spalding University *B*
Sue Bennett College *A*
Thomas More College *A,B*
Transylvania University *B*
Union College *B*
University of Kentucky *B,M,D*
University of Louisville *B,M,D*
Western Kentucky University *B,M*

Louisiana

Centenary College of Louisiana *B*
Dillard University *B*
Grambling State University *B*
Louisiana College *B*
Louisiana State University
 Agricultural and Mechanical
 College *B,M,D*
 Shreveport *B*
Louisiana Tech University *B,M*
Loyola University *B*
McNeese State University *B,M*
Nicholls State University *B*
Northeast Louisiana University *B,M*
Northwestern State University *B*
Southeastern Louisiana
 University *B*
Southern University
 New Orleans *B*
 Shreveport *A*
Southern University and
 Agricultural and Mechanical
 College *B,M*
Tulane University *B,M,D*
University of New Orleans *B,M,D*

University of Southwestern
 Louisiana *B,M*
Xavier University of Louisiana *B*

Maine

Bates College *B*
Bowdoin College *B*
Colby College *B*
University of Maine *B,M,D*
University of Southern Maine *B*

Maryland

Allegany Community College *A*
Charles County Community
 College *A*
College of Notre Dame of
 Maryland *B*
Columbia Union College *B*
Coppin State College *B*
Frostburg State University *B*
Goucher College *B*
Hagerstown Junior College *A*
Harford Community College *A*
Hood College *B*
Howard Community College *A*
Johns Hopkins University *B,M,D*
Loyola College in Maryland *B*
Morgan State University *B*
Mount St. Mary's College *B*
St. Mary's College of Maryland *B*
Salisbury State University *B*
Towson State University *B*
United States Naval Academy *B*
University of Maryland
 Baltimore County *B,M,D*
 College Park *B,M,D*
 Eastern Shore *B*
Villa Julie College *A*
Washington College *B*
Western Maryland College *B*

Massachusetts

American International College *B*
Amherst College *B*
Assumption College *B*
Atlantic Union College *B*
Boston College *B,M,D*
Boston University *B,M,D*
Bradford College *B*
Brandeis University *B,M,D*
Bridgewater State College *B,M*
Clark University *B,M,D*
College of the Holy Cross *B*
Curry College *B*
Eastern Nazarene College *B*
Elms College *B*
Emmanuel College *B*
Fitchburg State College *B*
Framingham State College *B*
Gordon College *B*
Hampshire College *B*
Harvard and Radcliffe Colleges *B*
Harvard University *D*
Massachusetts College of Pharmacy
 and Allied Health Sciences *B*
Massachusetts Institute of
 Technology *B,M,D,W*
Merrimack College *B*
Mount Holyoke College *B,M*
North Adams State College *B*
Northeastern University *B,M,D*
Northern Essex Community
 College *A*
Regis College *B*
Roxbury Community College *A*
Salem State College *B*
Simmons College *B*
Smith College *B*
Springfield College *B*
Stonehill College *B*
Suffolk University *B*
Tufts University *B*

University of Massachusetts
Amherst *B,M,D*
Boston *B,M*
Dartmouth *B,M*
Lowell *A,B,M,D*
Wellesley College *B*
Western New England College *B*
Wheaton College *B*
Williams College *B*
Worcester Polytechnic Institute
B,M,D
Worcester State College *B*

Michigan

Adrian College *A,B*
Albion College *B*
Alma College *B*
Andrews University *B,M*
Aquinas College *B*
Calvin College *B*
Central Michigan University *B,M*
Charles Stewart Mott Community
College *C*
Eastern Michigan University *B,M*
Grand Valley State University *B*
Hillsdale College *B*
Hope College *B*
Kalamazoo College *B*
Kellogg Community College *A*
Lake Superior State University *A*
Lansing Community College *A*
Lawrence Technological
University *B*
Madonna University *B*
Marygrove College *B*
Michigan State University *B*
Michigan Technological University
B,M,D
Mid Michigan Community
College *A*
Northern Michigan University
A,B,M
Oakland University *B,M*
Olivet College *B*
Saginaw Valley State University *B*
St. Mary's College *B*
Siena Heights College *A,B*
Spring Arbor College *B*
University of Detroit Mercy *B,M,D*
University of Michigan
Ann Arbor *B*
Dearborn *B*
Flint *B*
Wayne State University *B,M,D*
West Shore Community College *A*
Western Michigan University *B,M*

Minnesota

Augsburg College *B*
Bemidji State University *B*
Bethel College *B*
Carleton College *B*
College of St. Benedict *B*
College of St. Catherine: St.
Catherine Campus *B*
College of St. Scholastica *B*
Concordia College: Moorhead *B*
Gustavus Adolphus College *B*
Hamline University *B*
Macalester College *B*
Mankato State University *B,M*
Moorhead State University *B,M*
Northland Community College *A*
Northwestern College *A*
Rainy River Community College *A*
St. Cloud State University *B*
St. John's University *B*
St. Mary's College of Minnesota *B*
St. Olaf College *B*
Southwest State University *B*

University of Minnesota
Duluth *B,M*
Morris *B*
Twin Cities *B,M,D*
University of St. Thomas *B*
Vermilion Community College *A*
Willmar Community College *A*
Winona State University *B*

Mississippi

Alcorn State University *B*
Belhaven College *B*
Copiah-Lincoln Community
College *A*
Delta State University *B*
Jackson State University *B,M*
Jones County Junior College *A*
Mary Holmes College *A*
Millsaps College *B*
Mississippi College *B*
Mississippi Gulf Coast Community
College: Jefferson Davis
Campus *A*
Mississippi State University *B,M,D*
Mississippi University for Women *B*
Rust College *B*
Tougaloo College *B*
University of Mississippi *B,M,D*
University of Southern Mississippi
B,M,D
William Carey College *B*

Missouri

Avila College *B*
Central Methodist College *B*
Central Missouri State University *B*
College of the Ozarks *B*
Culver-Stockton College *B*
Drury College *B*
East Central College *A*
Evangel College *B*
Lincoln University *B*
Lindenwood College *B*
Longview Community College *A*
Maple Woods Community
College *A*
Maryville University *B*
Mineral Area College *A*
Missouri Baptist College *B*
Missouri Southern State College *B*
Missouri Western State College *B*
Moberly Area Community
College *A*
Northeast Missouri State
University *B*
Northwest Missouri State
University *B*
Park College *B*
Penn Valley Community College *A*
Rockhurst College *B*
St. Louis Community College
Florissant Valley *A*
Forest Park *A*
St. Louis University *B,M*
Southeast Missouri State University
B,M
Southwest Baptist University *B*
Southwest Missouri State
University *B*
University of Missouri
Columbia *B,M,D*
Kansas City *B,M,D*
Rolla *B,M,D*
St. Louis *B,M,D*
Washington University *B,M,D*
Westminster College *B*
William Jewell College *B*
William Woods College *B*

Montana

College of Great Falls *B*
Eastern Montana College *A,B*

Montana College of Mineral
Science and Technology *B*
Montana State University *B,M,D*
Northern Montana College *A,B*
Rocky Mountain College *B*
University of Montana *B,M,D*

Nebraska

Chadron State College *B*
College of St. Mary *B*
Concordia College *B*
Creighton University *B*
Dana College *B*
Doane College *B*
Hastings College *B*
McCook Community College *A*
Midland Lutheran College *B*
Nebraska Wesleyan University *B*
Northeast Community College *A*
Peru State College *B*
Southeast Community College:
Beatrice Campus *A*
Union College *B*
University of Nebraska
Kearney *B*
Lincoln *B,M,D*
Omaha *B*
Wayne State College *B*
Western Nebraska Community
College: Scottsbluff Campus *A*
York College *A*

Nevada

University of Nevada
Las Vegas *B*
Reno *B,M,D*

New Hampshire

Dartmouth College *B,M,D*
Keene State College *A,B*
Plymouth State College of the
University System of New
Hampshire *B*
Rivier College *B*
St. Anselm College *B*
University of New Hampshire
B,M,D

New Jersey

Atlantic Community College *A*
Bergen Community College *A*
Bloomfield College *B*
Brookdale Community College *A*
Burlington County College *A*
Caldwell College *B*
College of St. Elizabeth *B*
County College of Morris *A*
Drew University *B*
Essex County College *A*
Fairleigh Dickinson University *B,M*
Georgian Court College *B*
Glassboro State College *B*
Gloucester County College *A*
Jersey City State College *B*
Kean College of New Jersey *B*
Mercer County Community
College *A*
Monmouth College *B*
Montclair State College *B,M*
Ocean County College *A*
Princeton University *B,D*
Ramapo College of New Jersey *B*
Rider College *B*

Rutgers—The State University of
New Jersey
Camden College of Arts and
Sciences *B*
Cook College *B*
Douglass College *B*
Livingston College *B*
New Brunswick *M,D*
Newark College of Arts and
Sciences *B*
Rutgers College *B*
University College Camden *B*
University College New
Brunswick *B*
St. Peter's College *B*
Seton Hall University *B,M,D*
Stevens Institute of Technology
B,M,D
Stockton State College *B*
Thomas Edison State College *A,B*
Trenton State College *B*
Upsala College *B*
William Paterson College of New
Jersey *B*

New Mexico

College of Santa Fe *A,B*
Eastern New Mexico University
B,M
New Mexico Highlands University
B,M
New Mexico Institute of Mining
and Technology *B,M,D*
New Mexico Junior College *A*
New Mexico State University
B,M,D
University of New Mexico *B,M,D*
Western New Mexico University *B*

New York

Adelphi University *B,M*
Adirondack Community College *A*
Alfred University *B*
Bard College *B*
Barnard College *B*
Canisius College *B*
City University of New York
Brooklyn College *B,M*
City College *B,M*
College of Staten Island *B*
Graduate School and
University Center *D*
Hunter College *B*
Kingsborough Community
College *A*
Lehman College *B*
Queens College *B,M*
Queensborough Community
College *A*
York College *B*
Clarkson University *B,M,D*
Colgate University *B*
College of Mount St. Vincent *B*
College of New Rochelle *B*
College of St. Rose *B*
Columbia University
Columbia College *B*
New York *M,D*
School of General Studies *B*
Community College of the Finger
Lakes *A*
Cornell University *B,M,D*
Daemen College *B*
Elmira College *B*
Fordham University *B,M*
Hamilton College *B*
Hartwick College *B*
Herkimer County Community
College *A*
Hobart College *B*
Hofstra University *B*
Houghton College *B*

Hudson Valley Community College *A*
Iona College *B*
Ithaca College *B*
Jamestown Community College *A*
Jefferson Community College *A*
Keuka College *B*
King's College *B*
Le Moyne College *B*
Long Island University
    Brooklyn Campus *B,M*
    C. W. Post Campus *B*
    Southampton Campus *B*
Manhattan College *B*
Manhattanville College *B*
Marist College *B*
Marymount College *B*
Mohawk Valley Community College *A*
Mount St. Mary College *B*
Nazareth College of Rochester *B*
New York University *B,M,D*
Niagara University *B*
Pace University
    College of White Plains *B*
    New York *B*
    Pleasantville/Briarcliff *B*
Polytechnic University
    Brooklyn *B,M,D*
    Long Island Campus *B*
Rensselaer Polytechnic Institute *B,M,D*
Roberts Wesleyan College *B*
Rochester Institute of Technology *A,B,M*
Russell Sage College *B*
Sage Junior College of Albany, A Division of Russell Sage College *A*
St. Bonaventure University *B*
St. John Fisher College *B*
St. John's University *B,M*
St. Joseph's College *B*
St. Lawrence University *B*
Sarah Lawrence College *B*
Siena College *B*
Skidmore College *B*
State University of New York
    Albany *B,M,D*
    Binghamton *B,M,D*
    Buffalo *B,M,D*
    Purchase *B*
    Stony Brook *B,M,D*
    College of Agriculture and Technology at Cobleskill *A*
    College of Agriculture and Technology at Morrisville *A*
    College at Brockport *B*
    College at Buffalo *B,M*
    College at Cortland *B*
    College of Environmental Science and Forestry *B,M,D*
    College at Fredonia *B,M*
    College at Geneseo *B*
    College at New Paltz *B,M*
    College at Old Westbury *B*
    College at Oneonta *B,M*
    College at Plattsburgh *B,M*
    College at Potsdam *B*
    College of Technology at Delhi *A*
    Oswego *B,M*
Suffolk County Community College: Eastern Campus *A*
Syracuse University *B,M,D*
Touro College *B*
Union College *B*
United States Military Academy *B*
University of Rochester *B,M,D,W*
University of the State of New York: Regents College *B*

Utica College of Syracuse University *B*
Vassar College *B,M*
Wagner College *B*
Wells College *B*
Westchester Community College *A*
William Smith College *B*
Yeshiva University *B*

North Carolina

Appalachian State University *B,M*
Barton College *B*
Belmont Abbey College *B*
Bennett College *B*
Brevard College *A*
Campbell University *B*
Cape Fear Community College *A*
Catawba College *A*
Chowan College *A*
Davidson College *B*
Duke University *B,D*
East Carolina University *B,M*
Elizabeth City State University *B*
Elon College *B*
Fayetteville State University *B*
Gardner-Webb College *B*
Greensboro College *B*
Guilford College *B*
High Point University *B*
Johnson C. Smith University *B*
Lenoir-Rhyne College *B*
Livingstone College *B*
Mars Hill College *B*
Meredith College *B*
Methodist College *A,B*
North Carolina Agricultural and Technical State University *B,M*
North Carolina Central University *B,M*
North Carolina State University *B,M,D*
North Carolina Wesleyan College *B*
Pembroke State University *B*
Pfeiffer College *B*
St. Andrews Presbyterian College *B*
St. Augustine's College *B*
Salem College *B*
Shaw University *B*
University of North Carolina
    Asheville *B*
    Chapel Hill *B,M,D*
    Charlotte *B,M*
    Greensboro *B,M*
    Wilmington *B,M*
Wake Forest University *B,M,D*
Warren Wilson College *B*
Western Carolina University *B,M*
Wingate College *B*
Winston-Salem State University *B*

North Dakota

Bismarck State College *A*
Dickinson State University *B*
Jamestown College *B*
Mayville State University *B*
Minot State University *B*
North Dakota State University *B,M,D*
University of North Dakota *B,M,D*
Valley City State University *B*

Ohio

Antioch College *B*
Ashland University *B*
Baldwin-Wallace College *B*
Bluffton College *B*
Bowling Green State University
    Bowling Green *B,M*
    Firelands College *A*
Capital University *B*
Case Western Reserve University *B,M,D*

Cedarville College *B*
Central State University *B*
Cleveland State University *B,M,D*
College of Mount St. Joseph *B*
College of Wooster *B*
Defiance College *B*
Denison University *B*
Franciscan University of Steubenville *B*
Heidelberg College *B*
Hiram College *B*
John Carroll University *B,M*
Kent State University *B,M,D*
Kenyon College *B*
Lake Erie College *B*
Lakeland Community College *A*
Lorain County Community College *A*
Lourdes College *A,B*
Malone College *B*
Marietta College *B*
Miami University: Oxford Campus *B,M,D*
Mount Union College *B*
Mount Vernon Nazarene College *B*
Muskingum College *B*
Notre Dame College of Ohio *B*
Oberlin College *B*
Ohio Dominican College *A,B*
Ohio Northern University *B*
Ohio State University: Columbus Campus *B,M,D*
Ohio University *B,M,D*
Ohio Wesleyan University *B*
Otterbein College *B*
Shawnee State University *B*
Union Institute *B,D*
University of Akron *B,M,D*
University of Cincinnati
    Cincinnati *B,M,D*
    Raymond Walters College *A*
University of Dayton *B,M*
University of Rio Grande *C,A*
University of Toledo *B,M,D*
Urbana University *B*
Walsh College *B*
Wilberforce University *B*
Wilmington College *B*
Wittenberg University *B*
Wright State University
    Dayton *B,M*
    Lake Campus *A*
Xavier University *B*
Youngstown State University *B,M*

Oklahoma

Bacone College *A*
Bartlesville Wesleyan College *A,B*
Cameron University *B*
Connors State College *A*
East Central University *B*
Eastern Oklahoma State College *A*
Langston University *B*
Northeastern State University *B*
Northern Oklahoma College *A*
Northwestern Oklahoma State University *B*
Oklahoma Baptist University *B*
Oklahoma Christian University of Science and Arts *B*
Oklahoma City University *B*
Oklahoma Panhandle State University *B*
Oklahoma State University *B,M,D*
Oral Roberts University *B*
Phillips University *B*
Redlands Community College *A*
Rogers State College *A*
Rose State College *A*
Southeastern Oklahoma State University *B*

Southwestern Oklahoma State University *B*
Tulsa Junior College *A*
University of Central Oklahoma *B*
University of Oklahoma *B,M,D*
University of Science and Arts of Oklahoma *B*
University of Tulsa *B*

Oregon

Central Oregon Community College *A*
Concordia College *B*
Eastern Oregon State College *B*
George Fox College *B*
Lewis and Clark College *B*
Linfield College *B*
Oregon Graduate Institute *M,D*
Oregon State University *B,M,D*
Pacific University *B*
Portland Community College *A*
Portland State University *B,M*
Reed College *B*
Southern Oregon State College *B*
Treasure Valley Community College *A*
University of Oregon
    Eugene *B,M,D*
    Robert Donald Clark Honors College *B*
University of Portland *B*
Western Oregon State College *B*
Willamette University *B*

Pennsylvania

Albright College *B*
Allegheny College *B*
Allentown College of St. Francis de Sales *B*
Alvernia College *B*
Beaver College *B*
Bloomsburg University of Pennsylvania *B*
Bryn Mawr College *B,M,D*
Bucknell University *B,M*
Bucks County Community College *A*
Cabrini College *B*
California University of Pennsylvania *B,M*
Carnegie Mellon University *B,M,D,W*
Cedar Crest College *B*
Chatham College *B*
Chestnut Hill College *A,B*
Cheyney University of Pennsylvania *B*
Clarion University of Pennsylvania *B*
College Misericordia *B*
Delaware Valley College *B*
Dickinson College *B*
Drexel University *B,M,D*
Duquesne University *B,M,D*
East Stroudsburg University of Pennsylvania *B*
Eastern College *B*
Edinboro University of Pennsylvania *B*
Elizabethtown College *B*
Franklin and Marshall College *B*
Gannon University *B*
Geneva College *B*
Gettysburg College *B*
Grove City College *B*
Harrisburg Area Community College *A*
Haverford College *B*
Holy Family College *B*
Immaculata College *B*
Indiana University of Pennsylvania *B,M*

Juniata College *B*
King's College *B*
Kutztown University of
Pennsylvania *B*
La Roche College *B*
La Salle University *B*
Lafayette College *B*
Lebanon Valley College of
Pennsylvania *B*
Lehigh University *B,M,D*
Lincoln University *B*
Lock Haven University of
Pennsylvania *B*
Lycoming College *B*
Mansfield University of
Pennsylvania *B*
Mercyhurst College *B*
Messiah College *B*
Millersville University of
Pennsylvania *A,B*
Moravian College *B*
Muhlenberg College *B*
Northampton County Area
Community College *A*
Northeastern Christian Junior
College *A*
Penn State
Erie Behrend College *B*
University Park Campus
B,M,D
Philadelphia College of Pharmacy
and Science *B*
Philadelphia College of Textiles and
Science *B*
Reading Area Community
College *A*
Rosemont College *B*
St. Francis College *B*
St. Joseph's University *A,B,M*
St. Vincent College *B*
Seton Hill College *B*
Shippensburg University of
Pennsylvania *B,M*
Slippery Rock University of
Pennsylvania *B*
Susquehanna University *B*
Swarthmore College *B*
Temple University *B,M,D*
Thiel College *B*
University of Pennsylvania *B,M,D*
University of Pittsburgh
Bradford *B*
Johnstown *B*
Pittsburgh *B,M,D*
University of Scranton *B,M*
Ursinus College *B*
Villanova University *B,M,D*
Washington and Jefferson College *B*
Waynesburg College *B*
West Chester University of
Pennsylvania *B,M*
Westminster College *B*
Widener University *B*
Wilkes University *B*
Wilson College *B*
York College of Pennsylvania *A*

Puerto Rico

Bayamon Central University *B*
Inter American University of Puerto
Rico
Arecibo Campus *B*
Metropolitan Campus *B*
San German Campus *B*
Pontifical Catholic University of
Puerto Rico *B,M*
Turabo University *B*
Universidad Adventista de las
Antillas *B*

University of Puerto Rico
Cayey University College *B*
Mayaguez Campus *B,M*
Ponce Technological
University College *A*
Rio Piedras Campus *B,M,D*
University of the Sacred Heart *B*

Rhode Island

Brown University *B,M,D*
Providence College *B,M,D*
Rhode Island College *B*
Roger Williams College *B*
Salve Regina University *B*
University of Rhode Island *B,M,D*

South Carolina

Benedict College *B*
Bob Jones University *B*
Central Wesleyan College *B*
Charleston Southern University *B*
The Citadel *B*
Claflin College *B*
Clemson University *B,M,D*
Coker College *B*
College of Charleston *B*
Columbia College *B*
Converse College *B*
Erskine College *B*
Francis Marion College *B*
Furman University *B,M*
Lander College *B*
Newberry College *B*
North Greenville College *A*
Presbyterian College *B*
South Carolina State College *B*
University of South Carolina
Aiken *B*
Columbia *B,M,D*
Spartanburg *B*
Winthrop University *B*
Wofford College *B*

South Dakota

Augustana College *B*
Black Hills State University *B*
Dakota State University *B*
Dakota Wesleyan University *B*
Mount Marty College *B*
Northern State University *B*
Sioux Falls College *B*
South Dakota School of Mines and
Technology *B,M*
South Dakota State University *B,M*
University of South Dakota *B,M*

Tennessee

Austin Peay State University *B*
Belmont University *B*
Carson-Newman College *B*
Christian Brothers University *B*
Columbia State Community
College *A*
Cumberland University *A,B*
David Lipscomb University *B*
Dyersburg State Community
College *A*
East Tennessee State University
B,M
Fisk University *B,M*
Freed-Hardeman University *B*
Hiwassee College *A*
King College *B*
Knoxville College *B*
Lambuth University *B*
LeMoyne-Owen College *B*
Lincoln Memorial University *B*
Maryville College *B*
Memphis State University *B,M,D*
Middle Tennessee State University
B,M
Milligan College *B*

Motlow State Community
College *A*
Rhodes College *B*
Southern College of Seventh-day
Adventists *B*
Tennessee State University *B,M*
Tennessee Technological University
B,M
Tennessee Wesleyan College *B*
Trevecca Nazarene College *B*
Union University *B*
University of the South *B*
University of Tennessee
Chattanooga *B*
Knoxville *B,M,D*
Martin *B*
Vanderbilt University *B,M,D*

Texas

Abilene Christian University *B,M*
Amarillo College *A*
Angelina College *A*
Angelo State University *B*
Austin College *B*
Austin Community College *A*
Baylor University *B,M,D*
Bee County College *A*
Blinn College *A*
Brazosport College *A*
Central Texas College *A*
Collin County Community College
District *A*
Corpus Christi State University *B*
Del Mar College *A*
East Texas Baptist University *B*
East Texas State University *B,M*
El Paso Community College *A*
Galveston College *A*
Hardin-Simmons University *B*
Houston Baptist University *B*
Houston Community College *A*
Howard College *A*
Howard Payne University *B*
Huston-Tillotson College *B*
Incarnate Word College *B*
Jacksonville College *A*
Jarvis Christian College *B*
Kilgore College *A*
Lamar University—Beaumont *B,M*
LeTourneau University *B*
Lon Morris College *A*
Lubbock Christian University *B*
McMurry University *B*
Midland College *A*
Midwestern State University *B*
North Harris Montgomery
Community College District *A*
Our Lady of the Lake University of
San Antonio *B*
Panola College *A*
Prairie View A&M University *B,M*
Rice University *B,M,D*
St. Edward's University *B*
St. Mary's University *B*
St. Philip's College *A*
Sam Houston State University *B,M*
Schreiner College *A*
South Plains College *A*
Southern Methodist University *B,M*
Southwest Texas State University
B,M
Southwestern Adventist College *B*
Southwestern University *B*
Stephen F. Austin State University
B,M
Sul Ross State University *B*
Tarleton State University *B*
Texas A&I University *B,M*
Texas A&M University *B,M,D*
Texas Christian University *B,M,D*
Texas Lutheran College *B*
Texas Southern University *B,M*

Texas Southmost College *A*
Texas State Technical College:
Waco *A*
Texas Tech University *B,M,D*
Texas Wesleyan University *B*
Texas Woman's University *B,M*
Trinity University *B*
Trinity Valley Community
College *A*
University of Dallas *B*
University of Houston
Clear Lake *B,M*
Houston *B,M,D*
University of Mary Hardin-
Baylor *B*
University of North Texas *B,M,D*
University of St. Thomas *B*
University of Texas
Arlington *B,M,D*
Austin *B,M,D*
Dallas *B,M,D*
El Paso *B,M*
Pan American *B*
Permian Basin *B*
San Antonio *B,M*
Tyler *B*
Wayland Baptist University *B*
West Texas State University *B,M*
Western Texas College *A*
Wharton County Junior College *A*
Wiley College *B*

Utah

Brigham Young University *B,M,D*
Southern Utah University *B*
University of Utah *B,M,D*
Utah State University *B,M,D*
Weber State University *B*
Westminster College of Salt Lake
City *B*

Vermont

Bennington College *B*
Castleton State College *B*
Marlboro College *B*
Middlebury College *B*
Norwich University *B*
St. Michael's College *B*
Trinity College of Vermont *B*
University of Vermont *B,M,D*

Virginia

Averett College *B*
Bluefield College *B*
Bridgewater College *B*
Clinch Valley College of the
University of Virginia *B*
College of William and Mary *B,M*
Eastern Mennonite College *B*
Emory and Henry College *B*
Ferrum College *B*
George Mason University *B,M*
Hampden-Sydney College *B*
Hampton University *B,M*
Hollins College *B*
James Madison University *B*
Liberty University *B*
Longwood College *B*
Lynchburg College *B*
Mary Baldwin College *B*
Mary Washington College *B*
Norfolk State University *B*
Old Dominion University *B,M*
Radford University *B*
Randolph-Macon College *B*
Randolph-Macon Woman's
College *B*
Roanoke College *B*
Shenandoah University *B*
Sweet Briar College *B*
University of Richmond *B,W*
University of Virginia *B,M,D*

Virginia Commonwealth University
B,M,D
Virginia Military Institute B
Virginia Polytechnic Institute and
State University B,M,D
Virginia State University B
Virginia Union University B
Virginia Wesleyan College B
Washington and Lee University B

Washington

Big Bend Community College A
Central Washington University B,M
Centralia College A
Clark College A
Eastern Washington University B
Everett Community College A
Evergreen State College B
Gonzaga University B
Heritage College B
Lower Columbia College A
Pacific Lutheran University B
St. Martin's College B
Seattle Central Community
College A
Seattle Pacific University B
Seattle University B
Skagit Valley College A
Spokane Community College A
Spokane Falls Community
College A
Tacoma Community College A
University of Puget Sound B
University of Washington B,M,D
Walla Walla College B
Washington State University B,M,D
Wenatchee Valley College A
Western Washington University
B,M
Whitman College B
Whitworth College B

West Virginia

Alderson-Broaddus College B
Bethany College B
Bluefield State College B
Concord College B
Davis and Elkins College B
Fairmont State College B
Glenville State College B
Marshall University B,M
Potomac State College of West
Virginia University A
Shepherd College B
University of Charleston B
West Liberty State College B
West Virginia Institute of
Technology B
West Virginia State College B
West Virginia University B,M,D
West Virginia Wesleyan College B
Wheeling Jesuit College B

Wisconsin

Alverno College B
Beloit College B
Cardinal Stritch College B
Carroll College B
Carthage College B
Edgewood College B
Lakeland College B
Lawrence University B
Marian College of Fond du Lac B
Marquette University B,M,D
Mount Mary College B
Northland College B
Ripon College B
St. Norbert College B

University of Wisconsin
Eau Claire B
Green Bay B
La Crosse B
Madison B,M,D
Milwaukee B,M,D
Oshkosh B
Parkside B
Platteville B
River Falls B
Stevens Point B
Superior B
Whitewater B
Viterbo College B
Wisconsin Lutheran College B

Wyoming

Casper College A
Central Wyoming College A
Eastern Wyoming College A
Laramie County Community
College A
Northwest College A
Sheridan College A
University of Wyoming B,M,D
Western Wyoming Community
College A

American Samoa, Caroline Islands, Guam, Marianas, Virgin Islands

University of Guam B
University of the Virgin Islands B

Canada

McGill University B,M,D

Mexico

Sistema Instituto Tecnologico y de
Estudios Superiores de
Monterrey B,D

Arab Republic of Egypt

American University in Cairo B

Child development/care/ guidance

Alabama

Jefferson State Community
College A
Shelton State Community
College C
Shoals Community College C

Alaska

University of Alaska
Anchorage C
Fairbanks A

Arizona

Arizona Western College A
Eastern Arizona College C,A
Glendale Community College C,A
Mesa Community College A
Mohave Community College C,A
Pima Community College A
Scottsdale Community College C,A

Arkansas

Capital City Junior College C
University of Arkansas at Pine
Bluff B
University of Central Arkansas B,M

California

Barstow College C,A
California State University
Bakersfield B
Chico B
Fresno B
Fullerton B
Los Angeles B,M
Northridge B
Cerro Coso Community College
C,A
Chabot College A
Chaffey Community College C,A
Christian Heritage College B
College of the Desert C,A
College of the Redwoods C,A
College of the Sequoias C,A
De Anza College C,A
Feather River College C,A
Fresno City College C,A
Gavilan Community College A
Grossmont Community College C,A
Humboldt State University B
Imperial Valley College A
La Sierra University A,B
Long Beach City College C,A
Los Angeles City College C,A
Los Angeles Harbor College C,A
Los Angeles Mission College C
Los Angeles Valley College C,A
Los Medanos College C,A
MiraCosta College A
Moorpark College A
Mount San Antonio College C,A
Mount San Jacinto College C,A
Ohlone College C,A
Orange Coast College C,A
Oxnard College A
Pacific Christian College B
Pacific Oaks College B,M
Pacific Union College A,B
Palomar College C
Porterville College C,A
Rio Hondo College C
Saddleback College C,A
San Diego City College C,A
San Diego Mesa College A
San Francisco State University C
San Joaquin Delta College C,A
San Jose State University B,M
Santa Barbara City College C,A
Santa Rosa Junior College C,A
Sierra College A
Southwestern College C
University of La Verne B
Ventura College C,A
Victor Valley College C,A
West Valley College C,A
Yuba College C,A

Colorado

Aims Community College C,A
Community College of Denver C,A
Morgan Community College C
Red Rocks Community College C

Connecticut

Briarwood College A
Connecticut College B
Housatonic Community College
C,A
Northwestern Connecticut
Community College A
St. Joseph College M

Delaware

Delaware State College B
Delaware Technical and
Community College
Southern Campus A
Stanton/Wilmington
Campus A

District of Columbia

Gallaudet University B
University of the District of
Columbia A

Florida

Brevard Community College C
Central Florida Community
College A
Daytona Beach Community
College A
Gulf Coast Community College C,A
Miami-Dade Community College C
Okaloosa-Walton Community
College C,A
Palm Beach Community College A
Pensacola Junior College A
Santa Fe Community College A
Seminole Community College C,A
South Florida Community
College C

Georgia

Abraham Baldwin Agricultural
College A
Athens Area Technical Institute C
Augusta Technical Institute C
Clark Atlanta University B
DeKalb Technical Institute C
Gainesville College A
Georgia Southern University B
Meadows College of Business C
Savannah Technical Institute C
Spelman College B
University of Georgia B,M
Waycross College A

Hawaii

Brigham Young University-Hawaii
C,A

Idaho

Boise State University C
College of Southern Idaho C
North Idaho College A
Northwest Nazarene College B
Ricks College A

Illinois

Belleville Area College A
Black Hawk College C,A
Carl Sandburg College A
City Colleges of Chicago
Chicago City-Wide College
C,A
Malcolm X College C,A
Olive-Harvey College C,A
College of DuPage C,A
College of Lake County A
Elgin Community College C,A
Highland Community College C,A
Illinois Central College A
Illinois Eastern Community
Colleges: Wabash Valley
College A
KAES College B
Kishwaukee College A
Lake Land College C
Lincoln Land Community
College A
Moraine Valley Community
College A
Oakton Community College C,A
Parkland College A
Prairie State College A
Rend Lake College C
Richland Community College C
Southern Illinois University at
Carbondale B
State Community College A
Triton College C,A

Waubonsee Community College
C,A
William Rainey Harper College C,A

Indiana

Indiana State University B
Indiana Vocational Technical
College
Central Indiana C
Eastcentral A
Northeast C,A
Whitewater A
Purdue University B,M
Vincennes University A

Iowa

Des Moines Area Community
College A
Hawkeye Institute of Technology A
Indian Hills Community College
C,A
Iowa Central Community College A
Iowa Lakes Community College A
Iowa State University B,M,D
Iowa Western Community
College C
Mount St. Clare College A
Muscatine Community College A
Waldorf College A

Kansas

Allen County Community
College A
Barton County Community College
C,A
Butler County Community College
C,A
Central College A
Cloud County Community
College A
Colby Community College A
Cowley County Community
College A
Dodge City Community College
C,A
Hutchinson Community College
C,A
Kansas City Kansas Community
College C
Kansas State University M
Pittsburg State University B
Pratt Community College C

Kentucky

Kentucky State University A,B
Morehead State University A
Murray State University A
Sullivan College C

Louisiana

Grambling State University A
Northeast Louisiana University A
Northwestern State University B

Maine

University of Maine B
Westbrook College B

Maryland

Charles County Community College
C,D
Chesapeake College C,A
Dundalk Community College C,A
Montgomery College
Germantown Campus C
Rockville Campus C,A
Takoma Park Campus C
Villa Julie College A

Massachusetts

Becker College: Leicester
Campus A

Bristol Community College A
Endicott College A
Fisher College A
Hampshire College B
Holyoke Community College A
Lasell College A,B
Massachusetts Bay Community
College C,A
Massasoit Community College C
Mount Ida College A
Wheelock College B,M

Michigan

Central Michigan University B
Charles Stewart Mott Community
College A
Delta College C,A
Eastern Michigan University B
Ferris State University A
Grand Rapids Community
College A
Jordan College A
Lake Superior State University A
Lansing Community College A
Macomb Community College C,A
Madonna University A,B
Marygrove College B
Michigan Christian College C,A
Montcalm Community College C
Northern Michigan University A,B
Oakland Community College A
Schoolcraft College A

Minnesota

Concordia College: Moorhead B
Inver Hills Community College A
Lakewood Community College A
Northland Community College A
University of Minnesota
Crookston A
Duluth B
Willmar Community College A

Mississippi

Hinds Community College A
Holmes Community College A
Jones County Junior College A
Mary Holmes College A
Mississippi College B
Northeast Mississippi Community
College A

Missouri

Central Missouri State University A
College of the Ozarks B
Jefferson College A
Mineral Area College C
Missouri Baptist College B
Moberly Area Community
College A
Northwest Missouri State
University C
Penn Valley Community College
C,A
St. Louis Community College
Florissant Valley A
Forest Park A
Southeast Missouri State
University A

Montana

Flathead Valley Community
College A

Nebraska

Central Community College C,A
Chadron State College A,B
McCook Community College C,A
Metropolitan Community College
C,A
Southeast Community College:
Lincoln Campus C,A

Wayne State College B

Nevada

Truckee Meadows Community
College C,A

New Hampshire

Keene State College A,B

New Jersey

Sussex County Community
College C
Thomas Edison State College A,B

New Mexico

Eastern New Mexico University
Portales A
Roswell Campus A
New Mexico State University C
San Juan College C
Western New Mexico University B

New York

Broome Community College C,A
City University of New York
College of Staten Island A
La Guardia Community
College A
Dutchess Community College A
Erie Community College: City
Campus A
Genesee Community College C
Hudson Valley Community
College A
Medaille College B
Nassau Community College A
Orange County Community
College A
Sage Junior College of Albany, A
Division of Russell Sage
College A
State University of New York
Purchase C
College of Agriculture and
Technology at Cobleskill A
Health Science Center at
Brooklyn C
Sullivan County Community
College C,A
Syracuse University B,M,D
Utica College of Syracuse
University B

North Carolina

Alamance Community College A
Appalachian State University B
Cape Fear Community College C
Central Carolina Community
College C
Central Piedmont Community
College C
Coastal Carolina Community
College C
Davidson County Community
College A
East Carolina University B,M
Guilford Technical Community
College C,A
Johnston Community College C,A
Mayland Community College A
Meredith College B
Montgomery Community College C
Nash Community College A
Southeastern Community College A
Southwestern Community
College A
University of North Carolina at
Charlotte B
Vance-Granville Community
College A
Wayne Community College A
Western Carolina University B

Wilson Technical Community
College C,A

North Dakota

Mayville State University A
North Dakota State University B,M
University of North Dakota: Lake
Region C,A

Ohio

Ashland University B
Bluffton College B
Bowling Green State University B
Central State University A
Clark State Community College A
Columbus State Community
College A
Jefferson Technical College C,A
Kent State University B
Lourdes College A,B
Muskingum Area Technical
College A
Ohio State University: Columbus
Campus B,M,D
Ohio University B
Owens Technical College: Toledo A
Sinclair Community College C,A
Terra Technical College A
University of Akron A,B,M
University of Cincinnati: Access
Colleges A
University of Rio Grande A
Washington State Community
College A
Youngstown State University A

Oklahoma

Connors State College A
Murray State College A
Oklahoma Christian University of
Science and Arts B
Rose State College A
University of Science and Arts of
Oklahoma B

Oregon

Chemeketa Community College A
Lane Community College C,A
Mount Hood Community
College A
Oregon State University B,M,D
Portland Community College A
Rogue Community College C
Umpqua Community College C,A

Pennsylvania

Albright College B
Central Pennsylvania Business
School A
Community College of
Philadelphia A
Harrisburg Area Community
College C,A
Indiana University of
Pennsylvania B
Keystone Junior College A
Northampton County Area
Community College A
Penn State University Park
Campus C
Pennsylvania College of
Technology A
Reading Area Community
College C
St. Vincent College B
University of Pittsburgh B,M
Westmoreland County Community
College C,A

Puerto Rico

University of Puerto Rico: Rio
Piedras Campus B

Rhode Island

Community College of Rhode
Island *A*

South Carolina

Aiken Technical College *C*
Bob Jones University *A*
Greenville Technical College *C*
South Carolina State College *B*
Technical College of the
Lowcountry *C*
Tri-County Technical College *C*
Trident Technical College *C*

South Dakota

Mitchell Vocational Technical
Institute *C*
Presentation College *A*
South Dakota State University *B*
Western Dakota Vocational
Technical Institute *C*

Tennessee

Carson-Newman College *B*
Chattanooga State Technical
Community College *C,A*
East Tennessee State University *B*
Tennessee Technological
University *B*
University of Tennessee: Knoxville
B,M
Walters State Community
College *A*

Texas

Abilene Christian University *A*
Alvin Community College *C,A*
Amarillo College *C,A*
Angelina College *C,A*
Austin Community College *C*
Bee County College *C,A*
Brazosport College *C,A*
Brookhaven College *A*
Central Texas College *A*
College of the Mainland *A*
Collin County Community College
District *A*
Del Mar College *C,A*
El Paso Community College *A*
Houston Community College *C,A*
Howard College *C*
Lamar University—Beaumont *A*
Laredo Junior College *C,A*
McLennan Community College *C,A*
Midland College *A*
Navarro College *A*
North Harris Montgomery
Community College District *C,A*
Odessa College *C,A*
San Antonio College *C*
Tarrant County Junior College *C,A*
Texas Southmost College *A*
Texas Tech University *B,M,D*
Texas Woman's University *B,M,D*
University of North Texas *B*
Vernon Regional Junior College *C*

Utah

College of Eastern Utah *A*
Dixie College *A*
Utah Valley Community College *A*
Weber State University *B*

Vermont

Southern Vermont College *A*

Virginia

Blue Ridge Community College *C*
Central Virginia Community
College *C*
John Tyler Community College *C,A*
New River Community College *C,A*

Northern Virginia Community
College *C,A*
Piedmont Virginia Community
College *C*
Southwest Virginia Community
College *C*
Tidewater Community College *A*

Washington

Columbia Basin College *C,A*
Edmonds Community College *C,A*
Lower Columbia College *A*
Olympic College *A*
Peninsula College *A*
Seattle Central Community
College *A*
Shoreline Community College *C,A*
Spokane Falls Community
College *A*
Walla Walla Community College
C,A
Whatcom Community College *C,A*
Yakima Valley Community College
C,A

Wisconsin

Chippewa Valley Technical
College *C*
Fox Valley Technical College *A*
Mid-State Technical College *C*
Moraine Park Technical College *A*
Northeast Wisconsin Technical
College *C*
University of Wisconsin: Stout *B*
Waukesha County Technical
College *A*
Western Wisconsin Technical
College *A*
Wisconsin Indianhead Technical
College *C*

Wyoming

Eastern Wyoming College *A*

**American Samoa, Caroline
Islands, Guam, Marianas,
Virgin Islands**

Guam Community College *C*

Chinese

Arizona

Arizona State University *B*

California

Los Angeles City College *A*
Monterey Institute of International
Studies *B,M*
Pomona College *B*
San Francisco State University *B,M*
San Jose State University *B*
Scripps College *B*
Stanford University *B,M,D*
University of California
Berkeley *B,M,D*
Davis *B*
Irvine *B*
Los Angeles *B*
San Diego *B*
Santa Barbara *B*
Whittier College *B*

Colorado

University of Colorado at Boulder
B,M

Connecticut

Connecticut College *B*
Wesleyan University *B*

Yale University *B*

District of Columbia

George Washington University *B*
Georgetown University *B*

Hawaii

Hawaii Loa College *B*
University of Hawaii at Manoa *B,M*

Illinois

KAES College *B*
University of Chicago *B,M,D*

Indiana

Ball State University *B*
Indiana University Bloomington
B,M,D

Kansas

University of Kansas *B*

Massachusetts

Harvard and Radcliffe Colleges *B*
Harvard University *M,D*
Tufts University *B*
University of Massachusetts at
Amherst *B,M*
Wellesley College *B*

Michigan

Michigan State University *B*
Oakland University *B*
University of Michigan *B,M,D*

Minnesota

University of Minnesota: Twin
Cities *B,M,D*

Missouri

Washington University *B,M,D*

New Hampshire

Dartmouth College *B*

New Jersey

Rutgers—The State University of
New Jersey
Douglass College *B*
Livingston College *B*
Rutgers College *B*
University College New
Brunswick *B*
Seton Hall University *B,M*

New York

Bard College *B*
City University of New York:
Hunter College *B*
Colgate University *B*
Columbia University
Columbia College *B*
New York *M,D*
Cornell University *B,M,D*
Hamilton College *B*
Hobart College *B*
State University of New York at
Albany *B*
United States Military Academy *B*
William Smith College *B*

North Carolina

St. Andrews Presbyterian College *B*

Ohio

Kenyon College *B*
Ohio State University: Columbus
Campus *B,M,D*
Wittenberg University *B*

Oregon

Pacific University *B*
Reed College *B*
University of Oregon
Eugene *B*
Robert Donald Clark Honors
College *B*

Pennsylvania

Penn State University Park
Campus *C*
Swarthmore College *B*
University of Pennsylvania *B,M,D*
University of Pittsburgh *B*

Rhode Island

Brown University *B,M,D*

Utah

Brigham Young University *B,M*

Vermont

Bennington College *B*
Middlebury College *B*

Washington

Grays Harbor College *A*
Spokane Falls Community
College *A*
University of Washington *B,M,D*

Wisconsin

University of Wisconsin: Madison
B,M,D

Chiropractic

Connecticut

Quinnipiac College *B*
University of Bridgeport *B,D*

Florida

Miami-Dade Community College *A*

Georgia

Gainesville College *A*

Illinois

National College of Chiropractic *B*

Iowa

Palmer Chiropractic University *M*
Wartburg College *B*

Kansas

Highland Community College *A*
Hutchinson Community College *A*
Pratt Community College *A*

Minnesota

Moorhead State University *B*
Rainy River Community College *A*
Willmar Community College *A*

Missouri

East Central College *A*

New Jersey

Bloomfield College *B*

New York

New York Institute of
Technology *B*

South Carolina

Spartanburg Methodist College *A*

Texas
Texas Southmost College *A*

Washington
Tacoma Community College *A*

Wisconsin
University of Wisconsin: Oshkosh *B*

Chiropractic (D.C.)

California
Life Chiropractic College West *F*

Connecticut
University of Bridgeport *F*

Georgia
Life College *F*

Illinois
National College of Chiropractic *F*

Iowa
Palmer Chiropractic University *F*

Minnesota
Northwestern College of
Chiropractic *F*

New York
New York Chiropractic College *F*

Oregon
Western States Chiropractic
College *F*

South Carolina
Sherman College of Straight
Chiropractic *F*

Cinematography/film

California
Art Center College of Design *B,M*
Brooks Institute of Photography *B*
California College of Arts and
Crafts *B,M*
California Institute of the Arts
C,B,M
California State University: Long
Beach *B*
Chapman University *B,M*
City College of San Francisco *A*
Columbia College: Hollywood *B*
Los Angeles City College *A*
Moorpark College *A*
Orange Coast College *A*
Pitzer College *B*
Saddleback College *A*
San Francisco Art Institute *B,M*
San Francisco State University *B,M*
University of California
Berkeley *B*
Los Angeles *B,M,D*
Santa Barbara *B*
Santa Cruz *C,B*
University of Southern California
B,M,D

Colorado
University of Colorado at
Boulder *B*

Connecticut
University of Bridgeport *B*
Wesleyan University *B*

District of Columbia
American University *B,M*

Florida
Miami-Dade Community College *A*
University of Miami *B*
University of South Florida *B,M*

Illinois
Columbia College *B,M*
Northwestern University *B*
School of the Art Institute of
Chicago *B,M*
Southern Illinois University at
Carbondale *B,M*

Indiana
University of Notre Dame *B*

Iowa
University of Iowa *B,M,D*

Maryland
Catonsville Community College *A*

Massachusetts
Clark University *B*
Emerson College *B*
Hampshire College *B*
Massachusetts College of Art *B,M*
Massachusetts Institute of
Technology *B*
School of the Museum of Fine
Arts *B*

Michigan
Central Michigan University *B,M*
Eastern Michigan University *B*
Grand Valley State University *B*
Lansing Community College *A*
Northern Michigan University *B*

Missouri
Webster University *B*

Montana
Montana State University *B*

New Hampshire
Dartmouth College *B*

New Jersey
Jersey City State College *B*

New York
Bard College *B,M*
City University of New York
Brooklyn College *B*
City College *B*
College of Staten Island *B,M*
Hunter College *B,M*
Columbia University: School of
General Studies *B*
Cornell University *B*
Eugene Lang College/New School
for Social Research *B*
Hofstra University *B*
Ithaca College *B*
Long Island University: C. W. Post
Campus *B*
New York University *B,M,D,W*
Pratt Institute *B*
Rochester Institute of Technology
A,B,M
Sarah Lawrence College *B*
School of Visual Arts *B*

State University of New York
Buffalo *B*
Purchase *B*
Syracuse University *B,M*
University of Rochester *B*

North Carolina
Wake Forest University *B*

Ohio
Denison University *B*
Kent State University *B*
Ohio State University: Columbus
Campus *B,M*
Ohio University *M*
University of Toledo *B*
Wright State University *B*

Oklahoma
University of Oklahoma *B*

Pennsylvania
Bucks County Community
College *A*
Edinboro University of
Pennsylvania *B*
Point Park College *B*
University of the Arts *B*
University of Pittsburgh *B*

Rhode Island
Rhode Island School of Design *B*

South Carolina
Bob Jones University *B,M*

Tennessee
University of Tennessee:
Knoxville *B*

Texas
Sam Houston State University *M*
Southern Methodist University *B*

Utah
Brigham Young University *B,M,D*

Washington
Evergreen State College *B*

Wisconsin
University of Wisconsin
Milwaukee *B*
Oshkosh *B*

City/community/regional planning

Alabama
Alabama Agricultural and
Mechanical University *B,M*
Auburn University *M*

Arizona
Arizona State University *B,M*
Northern Arizona University *B*
Prescott College *B*
University of Arizona *B,M*

California
California Polytechnic State
University: San Luis Obispo *B,M*
California State Polytechnic
University: Pomona *B,M*
California State University
Fresno *M*
Fullerton *B*
Chabot College *A*
Modesto Junior College *A*

San Diego State University *M*
San Jose State University *M*
Sonoma State University *B*
University of California
Berkeley *M,D*
Irvine *M*
Los Angeles *M,D*
University of Southern California
B,M,D

Colorado
Metropolitan State College of
Denver *B*
University of Colorado at
Denver *M*

District of Columbia
Catholic University of America *B*
George Washington University *M*
University of the District of
Columbia *B,M*

Florida
Florida State University *M,D*
University of Florida *M,D*
University of Miami *M*

Georgia
Georgia Institute of Technology *M*
Morris Brown College *B*

Hawaii
University of Hawaii at Manoa *M*

Illinois
City Colleges of Chicago: Chicago
City-Wide College *C,A*
Illinois Institute of Technology *M*
Lake Forest College *B*
Northwestern University *M*
Roosevelt University *B*
Southern Illinois University at
Carbondale *B,M*
University of Illinois at Urbana-
Champaign *B,M,D*

Indiana
Ball State University *B,M*
Indiana State University *B,M*
Indiana University Bloomington
B,M,D
Purdue University *B*

Iowa
Iowa State University *B,M*
University of Iowa *M*

Kansas
Fort Scott Community College *A*
Kansas State University *M*
University of Kansas *M*

Kentucky
Eastern Kentucky University *B*
Western Kentucky University *M*

Louisiana
University of New Orleans *M*
University of Southwestern
Louisiana *B,M*

Maine
Unity College *B*

Maryland
Montgomery College: Rockville
Campus *A*
Morgan State University *M*
University of Maryland: College
Park *M*

Massachusetts

Boston University *M*
Clark University *B,D*
Harvard University *M,D*
Massachusetts Institute of
Technology *B,M,D*
Tufts University *M*
University of Massachusetts at
Amherst *M,D*
Westfield State College *B*
Worcester Polytechnic Institute *B*

Michigan

Grand Valley State University *B*
Michigan State University *B,M*
Northern Michigan University *B*
University of Michigan *M,D*
Wayne State University *B,M*

Minnesota

Bemidji State University *B*
Mankato State University *B,M*
Winona State University *B*

Mississippi

Jackson State University *B*
University of Southern
Mississippi *B*

Missouri

Southwest Missouri State University
B,M
University of Missouri: Rolla *M*

Montana

University of Montana *M*

Nebraska

University of Nebraska—Lincoln *M*

Nevada

University of Nevada: Reno *M*

New Hampshire

University of New Hampshire *B*

New Jersey

Princeton University *M*
Rutgers—The State University of
New Jersey *M,D*
Stevens Institute of Technology
B,M,D

New Mexico

New Mexico State University *B*
University of New Mexico *M*

New York

City University of New York
City College *M*
Hunter College *M*
Cornell University *B,M,D*
New York University *C,M*
Pratt Institute *M*
State University of New York
Albany *B,M*
College at Buffalo *B*
College of Environmental
Science and Forestry *B,M*

North Carolina

Appalachian State University *B*
East Carolina University *B*
North Carolina State University *B*
University of North Carolina
Chapel Hill *M,D*
Greensboro *B*

Ohio

Ohio State University: Columbus
Campus *B,M,D*
Union Institute *B,D*

University of Akron *M*
University of Cincinnati *B,M*
Wittenberg University *B*
Wright State University *B*

Oklahoma

University of Oklahoma *M*

Oregon

Portland State University *M*
University of Oregon *M*

Pennsylvania

Bryn Mawr College *B,M*
California University of
Pennsylvania *B*
Carnegie Mellon University *M,D,W*
Indiana University of
Pennsylvania *B*
Mansfield University of
Pennsylvania *B*
Penn State University Park Campus
M,D
University of Pennsylvania *B,M,D*
West Chester University of
Pennsylvania *M*

Rhode Island

University of Rhode Island *B,M*

South Carolina

Clemson University *M*

South Dakota

Augustana College *B*

Tennessee

Austin Peay State University *B*
East Tennessee State University *M*
Memphis State University *M*
Middle Tennessee State
University *B*
University of Tennessee:
Knoxville *M*

Texas

Southwest Texas State University
B,M
Texas A&M University *M,D*
Texas Southern University *M*
Texas Tech University *B*
University of Texas
Arlington *M*
Austin *M*

Utah

Brigham Young University *B,M*
Utah State University *M*

Virginia

Christopher Newport College *B*
Old Dominion University *D*
University of Virginia *B,M*
Virginia Polytechnic Institute and
State University *M*

Washington

Eastern Washington University *B,M*
Evergreen State College *B*
University of Washington *M,D*
Washington State University *M*
Western Washington University *B*

Wisconsin

Carroll College *B*
Northland College *B*
University of Wisconsin
Green Bay *B*
Madison *M,D*
Milwaukee *M*

Canada

McGill University *M*

Civil engineering

Alabama

Alabama Agricultural and
Mechanical University *B*
Auburn University *B,M,D*
University of Alabama
Birmingham *B,M*
Huntsville *B*
Tuscaloosa *B,M,D*
University of South Alabama *B*

Alaska

University of Alaska
Anchorage *B,M*
Fairbanks *B,M*

Arizona

Arizona State University *B,M,D*
Northern Arizona University *B*
University of Arizona *B,M,D*

Arkansas

John Brown University *B*
University of Arkansas *B,M*
Westark Community College *A*

California

Allan Hancock College *A*
California Institute of Technology
B,M,D,W
California Polytechnic State
University: San Luis Obispo *B*
California State Polytechnic
University: Pomona *B*
California State University
Chico *B*
Fresno *B,M*
Fullerton *B,M*
Long Beach *B,M*
Los Angeles *B,M*
Northridge *B,M*
Sacramento *B,M*
City College of San Francisco *C,A*
Gavilan Community College *A*
Loyola Marymount University *B,M*
Modesto Junior College *A*
San Diego State University *B,M*
San Francisco State University *B*
San Joaquin Delta College *C*
San Jose State University *B,M*
Santa Clara University *B*
Santa Rosa Junior College *A*
Stanford University *B,M,D*
United States International
University *B*
University of California
Berkeley *B,M,D*
Davis *B,M,D*
Irvine *B*
Los Angeles *B,M,D*
University of the Pacific *B*
University of Southern California
B,M,D,W

Colorado

Colorado School of Mines *W*
Colorado State University *B,M,D*
United States Air Force
Academy *B*
University of Colorado
Boulder *B,M,D*
Denver *B,M*

Connecticut

United States Coast Guard
Academy *B*
University of Connecticut *B,M,D*
University of Hartford *B*
University of New Haven *A,B*

Delaware

Delaware State College *B*
University of Delaware *B,M,D*

District of Columbia

Catholic University of America
B,M,D
Gallaudet University *B*
George Washington University
B,M,D
Howard University *B,M*
University of the District of
Columbia *B*

Florida

Florida Agricultural and Mechanical
University *B,M*
Florida Atlantic University *M*
Florida Institute of Technology
B,M,D
Florida International University
B,M
Florida State University *B,M*
Gulf Coast Community College *C*
Manatee Community College *A*
Miami-Dade Community College *A*
Pensacola Junior College *A*
University of Central Florida *B,M,D*
University of Florida *B,M,D*
University of Miami *B,M,D*
University of South Florida *B,M,D*

Georgia

Clark Atlanta University *B*
Georgia Institute of Technology
B,M,D
Middle Georgia College *A*
Morris Brown College *B*
Savannah Technical Institute *C*

Hawaii

University of Hawaii at Manoa *B,M*

Idaho

College of Southern Idaho *A*
North Idaho College *A*
Ricks College *A*
University of Idaho *B,M,D*

Illinois

Bradley University *B,M*
Illinois Institute of Technology
B,M,D
Lake Land College *A*
Northwestern University *B,M,D*
Parkland College *A*
Richland Community College *A*
Southern Illinois University
Carbondale *B,M*
Edwardsville *B,M*
University of Illinois
Chicago *B,M,D*
Urbana-Champaign *B,M,D*

Indiana

Indiana University—Purdue
University at Indianapolis *A*
Purdue University *B,M,D,W*
Rose-Hulman Institute of
Technology *B,M*
Tri-State University *B*
University of Evansville *B*
University of Notre Dame *B,M,D*
Valparaiso University *B*
Vincennes University *A*

Iowa

Iowa State University *B,M,D*
University of Iowa *B,M,D*

Kansas

Fort Scott Community College *A*
Kansas State University *B,M,D*
University of Kansas *B,M,D*

Kentucky

University of Kentucky *B,M,D*
University of Louisville *B,M,D*

Louisiana

Louisiana State University and
  Agricultural and Mechanical
  College *B,M,D*
Louisiana Tech University *B,M*
McNeese State University *B*
Southern University and
  Agricultural and Mechanical
  College *B*
Tulane University *B,M,D*
University of New Orleans *B*
University of Southwestern
  Louisiana *B,M*

Maine

University of Maine *B,M,D*

Maryland

College of Notre Dame of
  Maryland *B*
Johns Hopkins University *B,M,D*
Morgan State University *B*
University of Maryland
  Baltimore County *M,D*
  College Park *B,M,D*

Massachusetts

Franklin Institute of Boston *A*
Massachusetts Institute of
  Technology *B,M,D,W*
Merrimack College *B*
Northeastern University *B,M,D*
Springfield Technical Community
  College *A*
Tufts University *B,M*
University of Massachusetts
  Amherst *B,M,D*
  Dartmouth *B*
  Lowell *B,M*
Worcester Polytechnic Institute
  B,M,D

Michigan

Calvin College *B*
Lawrence Technological
  University *B*
Michigan State University *B,M,D*
Michigan Technological University
  B,M,D
University of Detroit Mercy *B,M*
University of Michigan *B,M,D*
Wayne State University *B,M,D*

Minnesota

University of Minnesota: Twin
  Cities *B,M,D*
Willmar Community College *A*

Mississippi

Mississippi College *B*
Mississippi State University *B,M,D*
University of Mississippi *B*

Missouri

East Central College *A*
University of Missouri
  Columbia *B,M,D*
  Kansas City *B*
  Rolla *B,M,D*

Washington University *B,M,D*
William Jewell College *B*

Montana

Montana State University *B,M,D*

Nebraska

Southeast Community College:
  Milford Campus *A*
University of Nebraska
  Lincoln *B,M*
  Omaha *B,M*

Nevada

University of Nevada
  Las Vegas *B,M,D*
  Reno *B,M*

New Hampshire

New England College *B*
University of New Hampshire
  B,M,D

New Jersey

Brookdale Community College *C*
New Jersey Institute of Technology
  B,M,D
Ocean County College *A*
Princeton University *B,M,D*
Rutgers—The State University of
  New Jersey
  College of Engineering *B*
  New Brunswick *M,D*
Stevens Institute of Technology
  B,M,D

New Mexico

Eastern New Mexico University *A*
New Mexico State University
  B,M,D
University of New Mexico *B,M*

New York

City University of New York
  City College *B,M,D*
  Graduate School and
    University Center *D*
Clarkson University *B,M*
Columbia University: School of
  Engineering and Applied Science
  B,M,D,W
Cooper Union *B,M*
Cornell University *B,M,D*
Erie Community College: North
  Campus *A*
Manhattan College *B,M*
New York University *B*
Pace University
  College of White Plains *B*
  Pleasantville/Briarcliff *B*
Polytechnic University
  Brooklyn *B,M,D*
  Long Island Campus *B,M*
Rensselaer Polytechnic Institute
  B,M,D
State University of New York
  Buffalo *B,M,D*
  College of Environmental
    Science and Forestry *B,M,D*
Syracuse University *B,M,D*
Union College *B*
United States Military Academy *B*

North Carolina

Asheville Buncombe Technical
  Community College *A*
Duke University *B,M,D*
North Carolina Agricultural and
  Technical State University *B*
North Carolina State University
  B,M,D
St. Augustine's College *B*

University of North Carolina at
  Charlotte *B,M*
Western Piedmont Community
  College *A*

North Dakota

North Dakota State University *B,M*
University of North Dakota *B,M*

Ohio

Air Force Institute of
  Technology *M*
Case Western Reserve University
  B,M,D
Cleveland State University *B,M*
Cuyahoga Community College:
  Metropolitan Campus *A*
Ohio Northern University *B*
Ohio State University: Columbus
  Campus *B,M,D*
Ohio University *B,M*
University of Akron *B,M,D*
University of Cincinnati *B,M,D*
University of Dayton *B,M*
University of Toledo *B,M,D*
Wilberforce University *B*
Youngstown State University *B,M*

Oklahoma

Oklahoma State University *B,M,D*
University of Oklahoma *B,M,D*

Oregon

Chemeketa Community College *A*
George Fox College *B*
Oregon State University *B,M,D*
Portland State University *B,M*
Umpqua Community College *A*
University of Portland *B,M*

Pennsylvania

Bucknell University *B,M*
Carnegie Mellon University
  B,M,D,W
Drexel University *B,M,D*
Geneva College *B*
Lafayette College *B*
Lehigh University *B,M,D*
Messiah College *B*
Penn State University Park Campus
  B,M,D
Pennsylvania Institute of
  Technology *A*
Swarthmore College *B*
Temple University *B*
University of Pennsylvania *B,M,D*
University of Pittsburgh *B,M,D*
Villanova University *B,M*
Widener University *B,M*

Puerto Rico

Caribbean University *B*
Universidad Politecnica de Puerto
  Rico *B*
University of Puerto Rico:
  Mayaguez Campus *B,M*

Rhode Island

Brown University *B,M,D*
University of Rhode Island *B,M,D*

South Carolina

The Citadel *B*
Clemson University *B,M,D*
University of South Carolina *B,M,D*

South Dakota

South Dakota School of Mines and
  Technology *B,M*
South Dakota State University *B*

Tennessee

Christian Brothers University *B*
Memphis State University *B,M*
Tennessee State University *B*
Tennessee Technological University
  B,M
University of Tennessee
  Chattanooga *B,M*
  Knoxville *B,M,D*
Vanderbilt University *B,M,D*

Texas

Amarillo College *A*
Kilgore College *A*
Lamar University—Beaumont *B,D*
Prairie View A&M University *B*
Rice University *B,M,D*
Texas A&I University *B,M*
Texas A&M University *B,M,D*
Texas Southmost College *A*
Texas Tech University *B,M,D*
University of Houston *B,M,D*
University of Texas
  Arlington *B,M,D*
  Austin *B,M,D*
  El Paso *B,M*
  San Antonio *B,M*

Utah

Brigham Young University *B,M,D*
University of Utah *B,M,D*
Utah State University *M,D*

Vermont

Norwich University *B*
University of Vermont *B,M*

Virginia

Emory and Henry College *B*
Northern Virginia Community
  College *A*
Old Dominion University *B,M,D*
Tidewater Community College *A*
University of Virginia *B,M,D*
Virginia Military Institute *B*
Virginia Polytechnic Institute and
  State University *B,M,D*

Washington

Everett Community College *A*
Gonzaga University *B*
St. Martin's College *B,M*
Seattle University *B*
University of Puget Sound *B*
University of Washington *B,M,D*
Walla Walla College *B*
Washington State University *B,M,D*
Yakima Valley Community
  College *A*

West Virginia

Potomac State College of West
  Virginia Community *A*
West Virginia Institute of
  Technology *B,M*
West Virginia University *B,M,D*

Wisconsin

Concordia University Wisconsin *B*
Marquette University *B,M,D*
Northeast Wisconsin Technical
  College *A*
University of Wisconsin
  Madison *B,M,D*
  Milwaukee *B*
  Platteville *B*

Wyoming

University of Wyoming *B,M,D*

Canada

McGill University *B,M,D,W*

Mexico

Sistema Instituto Tecnologico y de
Estudios Superiores de
Monterrey *B*

Civil technology

Alabama

Alabama Agricultural and
Mechanical University *A,B*
Gadsden State Community College
C,A
Jefferson State Community
College *A*
University of Alabama *B*

Arizona

Mesa Community College *A*
Northern Arizona University *B*

California

Chabot College *A*
City College of San Francisco *C,A*
Don Bosco Technical Institute *A*
Santa Rosa Junior College *C,A*
Ventura College *A*

Colorado

Denver Institute of Technology *A*
Mesa State College *A*
Metropolitan State College of
Denver *B*
Trinidad State Junior College *A*
University of Southern Colorado *B*

Connecticut

Hartford State Technical College *A*
Norwalk State Technical College *A*
Thames Valley State Technical
College *A*

Delaware

Delaware Technical and
Community College
Southern Campus *A*
Stanton/Wilmington
Campus *A*
Terry Campus *A*

District of Columbia

University of the District of
Columbia *A*

Florida

Broward Community College *A*
Daytona Beach Community
College *A*
Florida Agricultural and Mechanical
University *B*
Florida Community College at
Jacksonville *A*
Miami-Dade Community College *A*
Pensacola Junior College *A*
Tallahassee Community College *A*
Valencia Community College *A*

Georgia

Georgia Southern University *B*
Savannah State College *A,B*
Savannah Technical Institute *C*
Southern College of Technology *B*

Idaho

Idaho State University *A*

Illinois

Black Hawk College *A*
City Colleges of Chicago: Chicago
City-Wide College *C,A*
College of Lake County *C,A*
Lake Land College *A*
Morrison Institute of Technology *A*
Southern Illinois University at
Carbondale *B*

Indiana

Indiana University—Purdue
University
Fort Wayne *A*
Indianapolis *A*
Purdue University
Calumet *A,B*
North Central Campus *A*
West Lafayette *A,B*
University of Southern Indiana *A,B*
Vincennes University *A*

Iowa

Hawkeye Institute of Technology *A*
Iowa Western Community
College *A*

Kansas

Johnson County Community
College *A*

Kentucky

Murray State University *A,B*
Western Kentucky University *B*

Louisiana

Louisiana Tech University *B*
Nicholls State University *B*

Maine

Central Maine Technical College
C,A
University of Maine *A,B*

Maryland

Catonsville Community College *A*
Howard Community College *C,A*
Montgomery College: Rockville
Campus *A*

Massachusetts

Bristol Community College *A*
Franklin Institute of Boston *A*
Massasoit Community College *A*
Northern Essex Community
College *C*
Springfield Technical Community
College *A*
University of Massachusetts at
Lowell *A,B*
Wentworth Institute of Technology
A,B

Michigan

Ferris State University *A*
Lansing Community College *A*
Lawrence Technological
University *A*
Macomb Community College *C,A*
Michigan Technological
University *A*

Minnesota

Inver Hills Community College *C*
Rochester Community College *A*
St. Paul Technical College *C*

Mississippi

Northeast Mississippi Community
College *A*

Missouri

Jefferson College *A*
Mineral Area College *C,A*
Missouri Western State College *A,B*
St. Louis Community College at
Florissant Valley *A*
Three Rivers Community College *A*
Washington University *B*

Montana

Montana State University *B*

Nebraska

Metropolitan Community College
C,A
Southeast Community College:
Milford Campus *A*

Nevada

Community College of Southern
Nevada *C,A*

New Hampshire

University of New Hampshire *A*

New Jersey

Brookdale Community College *C*
Burlington County College *A*
Essex County College *A*
Fairleigh Dickinson University *B*
Gloucester County College *A*
Mercer County Community
College *A*
New Jersey Institute of
Technology *B*
Thomas Edison State College *A,B*
Union County College *A*

New Mexico

Eastern New Mexico University *A*
New Mexico State University *A,B*

New York

Broome Community College *A*
City University of New York
College of Staten Island *A*
New York City Technical
College *A*
Hudson Valley Community
College *A*
Mohawk Valley Community
College *A*
Monroe Community College *A*
Nassau Community College *A*
Rochester Institute of Technology
A,B
State University of New York
College of Technology at
Alfred *A*
College of Technology at
Canton *A*
College of Technology at
Delhi *A*
College of Technology at
Farmingdale *A*
Westchester Community College
C,A

North Carolina

Asheville Buncombe Technical
Community College *A*
Central Piedmont Community
College *A*
Fayetteville Technical Community
College *A*
Gaston College *A*
Guilford Technical Community
College *C,A*
Sandhills Community College *A*
University of North Carolina at
Charlotte *B*

**Wake Technical Community
College *A***

North Dakota

North Dakota State College of
Science *A*

Ohio

Cincinnati Technical College *A*
Clark State Community College *A*
Columbus State Community
College *A*
Edison State Community College
C,A
Lakeland Community College *C,A*
Owens Technical College: Toledo
C,A
Sinclair Community College *A*
Stark Technical College *A*
University of Toledo *A*
Youngstown State University *A,B*

Oklahoma

Oklahoma State University:
Oklahoma City *A*

Oregon

Mount Hood Community
College *A*
Oregon Institute of Technology *B*
Portland Community College *C,A*

Pennsylvania

Butler County Community
College *A*
ICS Center for Degree Studies *A*
Penn State
Harrisburg Capital College *B*
University Park Campus *C*
Pennsylvania College of
Technology *A*
Pennsylvania Institute of
Technology *A*
Point Park College *A,B*
Spring Garden College *A,B*

Puerto Rico

University of Puerto Rico
Bayamon Technological
University College *A*
Ponce Technological
University College *A*

South Carolina

Florence-Darlington Technical
College *A*
Francis Marion College *B*
Horry-Georgetown Technical
College *A*
Midlands Technical College *A*
South Carolina State College *B*
Sumter Area Technical College *A*
Trident Technical College *A*

Tennessee

Nashville State Technical
Institute *A*
Pellissippi State Technical
Community College *A*
State Technical Institute at
Memphis *A*
University of Tennessee: Martin *B*

Texas

Houston Community College *A*
Tarrant County Junior College *A*
Texas Tech University *B*

Vermont

Vermont Technical College *A*

115

Virginia
Lord Fairfax Community College *A*
Wytheville Community College *A*

Washington
Centralia College *A*
Shoreline Community College *A*
Skagit Valley College *A*
Spokane Community College *A*
Walla Walla Community College *C,A*

West Virginia
Bluefield State College *A,B*
Fairmont State College *A,B*
West Virginia Institute of Technology *A*

Wisconsin
Chippewa Valley Technical College *A*
Mid-State Technical College *A*
Moraine Park Technical College *A*

American Samoa, Caroline Islands, Guam, Marianas, Virgin Islands
Guam Community College *A*

Classics

Alabama
University of Alabama *B*

Arizona
University of Arizona *B,M*

Arkansas
University of Arkansas *B*

California
Claremont McKenna College *B*
Foothill College *A*
Loyola Marymount University *B*
Pitzer College *B*
Pomona College *B*
San Diego State University *B*
San Francisco State University *B,M*
Santa Clara University *B*
Scripps College *B*
Stanford University *B,M,D*
University of California
    Berkeley *B,M,D*
    Davis *B,M*
    Irvine *B,M,D*
    Los Angeles *B,M,D*
    Riverside *B*
    San Diego *B*
    Santa Barbara *B,M*
    Santa Cruz *B*
University of the Pacific *B*
University of Southern California *B,M,D*

Colorado
Colorado College *B*
University of Colorado at Boulder *B,M,D*
University of Denver *B*

Connecticut
Albertus Magnus College *B*
Connecticut College *B*
Fairfield University *B*
Trinity College *B*
University of Connecticut *B*
Wesleyan University *B*
Yale University *B,M,D*

Delaware
University of Delaware *B*

District of Columbia
Catholic University of America *B,M,D*
George Washington University *B*
Georgetown University *B*
Howard University *B*

Florida
Florida State University *B,M*
New College of the University of South Florida *B*
Rollins College *B*
University of Florida *B,M*
University of South Florida *B*

Georgia
Agnes Scott College *B*
Emory University *B*
Georgia State University *B*
Oxford College of Emory University *A*
University of Georgia *B,M*

Hawaii
University of Hawaii at Manoa *B*

Idaho
University of Idaho *B*

Illinois
Augustana College *B*
Knox College *B*
Loyola University of Chicago *B,M,D*
Monmouth College *B*
North Central College *B*
Northwestern University *B,M,D*
Rockford College *B*
Shimer College *B*
Southern Illinois University at Carbondale *B*
University of Chicago *B,M,D*
University of Illinois
    Chicago *B*
    Urbana-Champaign *B,M,D*

Indiana
Earlham College *B*
Indiana University Bloomington *B,M,D*
St. Meinrad College *B*
University of Notre Dame *B,M*
Valparaiso University *B*
Wabash College *B*

Iowa
Cornell College *B*
Grinnell College *B*
Loras College *B*
Luther College *B*
University of Iowa *B,M,D*

Kansas
Benedictine College *B*
University of Kansas *B,M*

Kentucky
Asbury College *B*
University of Kentucky *B,M*

Louisiana
Louisiana College *B*
Tulane University *B*

Maine
Bowdoin College *B*
Colby College *B*
University of Southern Maine *B*

Maryland
College of Notre Dame of Maryland *B*
Johns Hopkins University *B,M,D*
Loyola College in Maryland *B*
Mount St. Mary's College *B*
University of Maryland
    Baltimore County *B*
    College Park *B,M*

Massachusetts
Amherst College *B*
Boston College *B*
Boston University *B,M,D*
Brandeis University *B*
Clark University *B*
College of the Holy Cross *B*
Harvard and Radcliffe Colleges *B*
Harvard University *D*
Hellenic College *B*
Mount Holyoke College *B*
Regis College *B*
Smith College *B*
Tufts University *B,M*
University of Massachusetts
    Amherst *B,M*
    Boston *B*
Wellesley College *B*
Wheaton College *B*
Williams College *B*

Michigan
Calvin College *B*
Concordia College *B*
Hillsdale College *B*
Hope College *B*
Michigan State University *B*
University of Michigan *B,D*
Wayne State University *B,M*

Minnesota
Carleton College *B*
College of St. Benedict *B*
Concordia College: Moorhead *B*
Gustavus Adolphus College *B*
Macalester College *B*
St. John's University *B*
St. Olaf College *B*
University of Minnesota: Twin Cities *B,M,D*

Mississippi
Millsaps College *B*
University of Mississippi *B,M*

Missouri
St. Louis University *B*
Southeast Missouri State University *B*
University of Missouri: Columbia *B,M,D*
Washington University *B,M,D*

Montana
University of Montana *B*

Nebraska
Creighton University *B*
University of Nebraska—Lincoln *B,M*

New Hampshire
Dartmouth College *B*
St. Anselm College *C,B*
University of New Hampshire *B*

New Jersey
Drew University *B*
Montclair State College *B*
Princeton University *B,D*

Rutgers—The State University of New Jersey
    Douglass College *B*
    Livingston College *B*
    New Brunswick *M,D*
    Newark College of Arts and Sciences *B*
    Rutgers College *B*
    University College New Brunswick *B*
St. Peter's College *B*
Seton Hall University *B*

New Mexico
University of New Mexico *B*

New York
Bard College *B*
Barnard College *B*
City University of New York
    Brooklyn College *B,M*
    City College *B*
    Graduate School and University Center *M,D*
    Hunter College *B*
    Lehman College *B*
    Queens College *B*
Colgate University *B*
College of New Rochelle *B*
Columbia University
    Columbia College *B*
    New York *M,D*
    School of General Studies *B*
Cornell University *B,M,D*
Elmira College *B*
Eugene Lang College/New School for Social Research *B*
Fordham University *B,M,D*
Hamilton College *B*
Hobart College *B*
Hofstra University *B*
Iona College *B*
Jewish Theological Seminary of America *D*
Manhattanville College *B*
New York University *B,M,D*
Sarah Lawrence College *B*
Skidmore College *B*
State University of New York
    Albany *B,M*
    Binghamton *B*
    Buffalo *B,M,D*
Syracuse University *B,M*
Union College *B*
University of Rochester *B,M*
Vassar College *B*
William Smith College *B*

North Carolina
Davidson College *B*
Duke University *B,D*
Guilford College *B*
Lenoir-Rhyne College *B*
University of North Carolina
    Asheville *B*
    Chapel Hill *B,M,D*
    Greensboro *B*
Wake Forest University *B*

Ohio
Bowling Green State University *B*
Case Western Reserve University *B*
Cleveland State University *B*
College of Wooster *B*
Denison University *B*
Hiram College *B*
John Carroll University *B,M*
Kent State University *B,M*
Kenyon College *B*
Miami University: Oxford Campus *B*
Oberlin College *B*

Ohio State University: Columbus
  Campus *B,M,D*
Ohio Wesleyan University *B*
Union Institute *D*
University of Akron *B*
University of Cincinnati *B,M,D*
University of Toledo *B,M*
Wright State University *B*
Xavier University *B*
Youngstown State University *B*

Oregon

Reed College *B*
University of Oregon
  Eugene *B,M*
    Robert Donald Clark Honors
    College *B*

Pennsylvania

Allegheny College *B*
Bryn Mawr College *B,M,D*
Bucknell University *B*
Chestnut Hill College *B*
Duquesne University *B*
Franklin and Marshall College *B*
Gettysburg College *B*
Haverford College *B*
La Salle University *B*
Lehigh University *B*
Moravian College *B*
Muhlenberg College *B*
Penn State University Park
  Campus *B*
Swarthmore College *B*
Temple University *B*
University of Pennsylvania *B,M,D*
University of Pittsburgh *B,M,D*
University of Scranton *B*
Villanova University *B,M*

Rhode Island

Brown University *B,M,D*
University of Rhode Island *B*

South Carolina

College of Charleston *B*
Furman University *B*
University of South Carolina *B*

South Dakota

Augustana College *B*
University of South Dakota *B*

Tennessee

Rhodes College *B*
University of the South *B*
University of Tennessee
  Chattanooga *B*
  Knoxville *B*
Vanderbilt University *B,M,D*

Texas

Austin College *B*
Rice University *B*
Southwestern University *B*
Texas Tech University *M*
Trinity University *B*
University of Houston *B*
University of Texas at Austin
  B,M,D

Utah

Brigham Young University *M*
University of Utah *B*

Vermont

Marlboro College *B*
Middlebury College *B*
St. Michael's College *B*
University of Vermont *B*

Virginia

College of William and Mary *B*
Emory and Henry College *B*
George Mason University *B*
Hampden-Sydney College *B*
Hollins College *B*
Mary Washington College *B*
Randolph-Macon College *B*
Randolph-Macon Woman's
  College *B*
Sweet Briar College *B*
University of Richmond *B,W*
University of Virginia *B,M,D*
Washington and Lee University *B*

Washington

Evergreen State College *B*
Gonzaga University *B*
Pacific Lutheran University *B*
Tacoma Community College *A*
University of Washington *B,M,D*
Western Washington University *B*

Wisconsin

Beloit College *B*
Lawrence University *B*
University of Wisconsin
  Madison *B,M,D*
  Milwaukee *B*

Canada

McGill University *B,M,D*

Clinical laboratory science

Alabama

Alabama Southern Community
  College *A*
Auburn University
  Auburn *B*
  Montgomery *B*
Community College of the Air
  Force *A*
Gadsden State Community
  College *A*
John C. Calhoun State Community
  College *A*
Judson College *B*
Livingston University *B*
Samford University *B*
Shelton State Community
  College *A*
Shoals Community College *A*
Troy State University *B*
Tuskegee University *B*

Alaska

University of Alaska Anchorage *A*

Arizona

Northern Arizona University *B*

Arkansas

Arkansas State University *B*
Arkansas Tech University *B*
Garland County Community
  College *A*
Harding University *B*
John Brown University *B*
Southern Arkansas University *B*
University of Arkansas for Medical
  Sciences *B*
University of Central Arkansas *B*

California

California State University
  Bakersfield *B*
  Dominguez Hills *B,M*
  Fresno *B*
  Sacramento *B*
City College of San Francisco *C,A*
Humboldt State University *B*
Modesto Junior College *A*
Mount St. Mary's College *B*
Pacific Union College *B*
Pasadena City College *C,A*
Saddleback College *A*
San Francisco State University *B,M*
San Jose State University *B*
Whittier College *M*

Colorado

Adams State College *B*
Colorado College *B*
Denver Technical College *C*

Connecticut

Housatonic Community College *A*
Quinnipiac College *B,M*
Sacred Heart University *B*
Western Connecticut State
  University *B*

Delaware

University of Delaware *B*

Florida

Barry University *B*
Brevard Community College *A*
Broward Community College *A*
Eckerd College *B*
Florida Atlantic University *B*
Florida State University *B*
Keiser College of Technology *A*
Miami-Dade Community College *A*
St. Leo College *B*
Stetson University *B*
University of Central Florida *B*
University of Florida *B*
University of South Florida *B*
University of West Florida *B*

Georgia

Armstrong State College *B*
Augusta Technical Institute *A*
Clayton State College *A*
Columbus College *B*
Georgia Southern University *B*
Medical College of Georgia *B,M*
Oglethorpe University *B*
Shorter College *B*
Waycross College *A*

Idaho

Idaho State University *B*
North Idaho College *A*

Illinois

Augustana College *B*
Bradley University *B*
City Colleges of Chicago: Malcolm
  X College *A*
College of St. Francis *B*
De Paul University *B*
Eastern Illinois University *B*
Eureka College *B*
Governors State University *B*
Illinois Benedictine College *B*
Illinois Wesleyan University *B*
Lake Forest College *B*
Lewis University *B*
Monmouth College *B*
National-Louis University *B*
Northern Illinois University *B*
Northwestern University *M*
Quincy College *B*

Rockford College *B*
Rush University *B*
Sangamon State University *B*
Southern Illinois University at
  Edwardsville *B*
Trinity Christian College *B*
University of Illinois at Chicago
  B,M

Indiana

Ball State University *B*
Franklin College *B*
Goshen College *B*
Huntington College *B*
Indiana State University *B,M*
Indiana University
  Northwest *A,B*
  Southeast *B*
Indiana University—Purdue
  University at Fort Wayne *B*
Indiana Wesleyan University *B*
Manchester College *B*
Marian College *B*
Purdue University
  Calumet *B*
  West Lafayette *B*
St. Francis College *B*
Taylor University *B*
Vincennes University *A*

Iowa

Des Moines Area Community
  College *A*
Dordt College *B*
Drake University *B*
Iowa Wesleyan College *B*
Luther College *B*
Northwestern College *B*
Southeastern Community College:
  North Campus *A*
Southwestern Community
  College *A*
Wartburg College *B*

Kansas

Bethel College *B*
Emporia State University *B*
Hutchinson Community College *A*
Kansas Newman College *B*
McPherson College *B*
Pittsburg State University *B*
St. Mary College *B*
Southwestern College *B*

Kentucky

Cumberland College *B*
Eastern Kentucky University *A,B*
Georgetown College *B*
Madisonville Community College *A*
Murray State University *B*
Thomas More College *B*
University of Kentucky *B*
University of Louisville *B*

Louisiana

Louisiana College *B*
Louisiana State University
  Medical Center *B*
  Shreveport *B*
Louisiana Tech University *B*
Southern University at New
  Orleans *B*
University of New Orleans *B*
University of Southwestern
  Louisiana *B*

Maine

Eastern Maine Technical College *A*
University of Maine *B*
Westbrook College *B*

Maryland

Columbia Union College *B*
Essex Community College *A*
Morgan State University *B*
Salisbury State University *B*
University of Maryland
    Baltimore *B,M*
    Eastern Shore *B*

Massachusetts

American International College *B*
Anna Maria College for Men and
    Women *A,B,M*
Assumption College *B*
Atlantic Union College *B*
Emmanuel College *B*
Fitchburg State College *B*
Merrimack College *B*
North Adams State College *B*
Northeastern University *A,B,M,D*
Salem State College *B*
Springfield College *B*
Stonehill College *B*

Michigan

Andrews University *B*
Aquinas College *B*
Eastern Michigan University *B*
Grand Valley State University *B*
Hope College *B*
Michigan State University *B,M*
Northern Michigan University
    C,A,B
Oakland Community College *A*
Oakland University *B*
Siena Heights College *B*
University of Detroit Mercy *B*

Minnesota

Bemidji State University *B*
College of St. Catherine: St.
    Catherine Campus *B*
College of St. Scholastica *B*
Concordia College: Moorhead *B*
Mankato State University *B*
Moorhead State University *B*
St. Cloud State University *B*
Southwest State University *B*
University of Minnesota: Twin
    Cities *B,M*
Willmar Technical College *C*
Winona State University *B*

Mississippi

Blue Mountain College *B*
Copiah-Lincoln Community
    College *A*
Millsaps College *B*
Mississippi College *B*
Mississippi Gulf Coast Community
    College: Jackson County
    Campus *A*
University of Mississippi *B*
William Carey College *B*

Missouri

Evangel College *B*
Maryville University *B*
Northwest Missouri State
    University *B*
St. Louis University *B*
Southwest Baptist University *B*
Three Rivers Community College *A*
University of Missouri: Kansas
    City *B*

Nebraska

Chadron State College *B*
Concordia College *B*
Dana College *B*
Midland Lutheran College *B*
Peru State College *B*

Union College *B*
University of Nebraska
    Medical Center *B*
    Kearney *B*
Wayne State College *B*

Nevada

University of Nevada
    Las Vegas *B*
    Reno *B*

New Hampshire

University of New Hampshire *B*

New Jersey

Bloomfield College *B*
Caldwell College *B*
College of St. Elizabeth *B*
Kean College of New Jersey *B*
Monmouth College *B*
Ocean County College *A*
Rutgers—The State University of
    New Jersey
        Camden College of Arts and
            Sciences *B*
        Douglass College *B*
        Livingston College *B*
        Newark College of Arts and
            Sciences *B*
        University College Camden *B*
Thomas Edison State College *B*

New Mexico

Eastern New Mexico University *B*
New Mexico Institute of Mining
    and Technology *B*
New Mexico Junior College *A*
New Mexico State University *A,B*

New York

Alfred University *B*
City University of New York
    Hostos Community College *A*
    Hunter College *B*
    New York City Technical
        College *A*
Clinton Community College *A*
Daemen College *B*
Dutchess Community College *A*
Elmira College *B*
Hartwick College *B*
Herkimer County Community
    College *A*
Iona College *B*
Keuka College *B*
Long Island University
    Brooklyn Campus *B*
    C. W. Post Campus *B,M*
Marist College *B*
Mercy College *B*
New York Institute of
    Technology *B*
Onondaga Community College *A*
Orange County Community
    College *A*
Pace University
    New York *B*
    Pleasantville/Briarcliff *B*
Rochester Institute of
    Technology *B*
Russell Sage College *B*
St. Bonaventure University *B*
St. Francis College *B*
St. John's University *B,M*
State University of New York
    College of Agriculture and
        Technology at Morrisville *A*
    College at Fredonia *B*
    College at Geneseo *B*
    College at Plattsburgh *B*
    Health Science Center at
        Syracuse *B,M*

Wagner College *B*
Westchester Community College *A*

North Carolina

Alamance Community College *A*
Appalachian State University *B*
Asheville Buncombe Technical
    Community College *A*
Beaufort County Community
    College *A*
Campbell University *B*
Coastal Carolina Community
    College *A*
Fayetteville State University *B*
Gardner-Webb College *B*
Lenoir-Rhyne College *B*
Meredith College *B*
North Carolina State University *B*
Pembroke State University *B*
Salem College *B*
Southwestern Community
    College *A*
University of North Carolina
    Chapel Hill *B,M,D*
    Charlotte *B*
    Greensboro *B*
    Wilmington *B*
Western Carolina University *B*

North Dakota

Bismarck State College *A*
Minot State University *B*

Ohio

Baldwin-Wallace College *B*
Bluffton College *B*
Bowling Green State University *B*
Case Western Reserve University *B*
Central State University *B*
Cleveland State University *B*
Columbus State Community
    College *A*
Cuyahoga Community College:
    Metropolitan Campus *A*
Franciscan University of
    Steubenville *B*
Lakeland Community College *A*
Malone College *B*
Mount Vernon Nazarene College *B*
Notre Dame College of Ohio *B*
Ohio Northern University *B*
Ohio University *B*
University of Cincinnati *B*
University of Dayton *M*
University of Rio Grande *A*
University of Toledo *B*
Walsh College *B*
Xavier University *B*
Youngstown State University *B*

Oklahoma

Cameron University *B*
Northeastern State University *B*
Oklahoma Christian University of
    Science and Arts *B*
Oklahoma Panhandle State
    University *B*
Oral Roberts University *B*
Phillips University *B*
Southeastern Oklahoma State
    University *B*
Southwestern Oklahoma State
    University *B*
Tulsa Junior College *A*
University of Central Oklahoma *B*
University of Oklahoma
    Health Sciences Center *B*
    Norman *B*

Oregon

Linfield College *B*
Portland Community College *A*

Pennsylvania

Albright College *B*
Alvernia College *B*
California University of
    Pennsylvania *B*
Clarion University of
    Pennsylvania *B*
East Stroudsburg University of
    Pennsylvania *B*
Eastern College *B*
Edinboro University of
    Pennsylvania *A,B*
Gannon University *B*
Gwynedd-Mercy College *B*
Holy Family College *B*
Indiana University of
    Pennsylvania *B*
King's College *B*
La Roche College *B*
Lebanon Valley College of
    Pennsylvania *B*
Lock Haven University of
    Pennsylvania *B*
Lycoming College *B*
Manor Junior College *A*
Mansfield University of
    Pennsylvania *B*
Mercyhurst College *B*
Messiah College *B*
Moravian College *B*
Neumann College *B*
Philadelphia College of Pharmacy
    and Science *B*
Reading Area Community
    College *A*
Seton Hill College *B*
Thiel College *B*
University of Pittsburgh *B*
University of Scranton *B*
Waynesburg College *B*
Westmoreland County Community
    College *A*
York College of Pennsylvania *B*

Rhode Island

Community College of Rhode
    Island *A*
Rhode Island College *B*
Salve Regina University *B*

South Carolina

Coker College *B*
Columbia College *B*
Converse College *B*
Lander College *B*

South Dakota

Augustana College *B*
Dakota State University *A*
Mitchell Vocational Technical
    Institute *C*
Mount Marty College *B*
Northern State University *B*
Sioux Falls College *B*
South Dakota State University *B*
University of South Dakota *B*

Tennessee

Austin Peay State University *B*
Christian Brothers University *B*
East Tennessee State University *B*
Freed-Hardeman University *B*
King College *B*
Lincoln Memorial University *B*
Memphis State University *B*
Middle Tennessee State
    University *B*
Milligan College *B*
Southern College of Seventh-day
    Adventists *B*
Tennessee State University *B*
Trevecca Nazarene College *B*

Tusculum College *B*
Union University *B*
University of Tennessee
    Chattanooga *B*
    Knoxville *B*

Texas

Abilene Christian University *B*
Angelo State University *B*
Austin Community College *A*
Central Texas College *A*
Corpus Christi State University *B*
East Texas Baptist University *B*
El Centro College *A*
Hardin-Simmons University *B*
Houston Baptist University *B*
Howard Payne University *B*
Incarnate Word College *B*
Laredo Junior College *A*
LeTourneau University *B*
McMurry University *B*
Midwestern State University *B*
Navarro College *A*
Our Lady of the Lake University of
    San Antonio *B*
Paul Quinn College *B*
Sam Houston State University *B*
Stephen F. Austin State
    University *B*
Texas Southmost College *A*
Texas Tech University *B*
Texas Wesleyan University *B*
University of Houston: Clear
    Lake *B*
University of Mary Hardin-
    Baylor *B*
University of Texas
    Arlington *B*
    Health Science Center at
        Houston *M*
    Health Science Center at San
        Antonio *B*
    Pan American *B*
    San Antonio *B*
    Southwestern Medical Center
        at Dallas Southwestern
        Allied Health Sciences
        School *B*
West Texas State University *B*

Utah

Utah State University *B*
Weber State University *A,B*

Vermont

Trinity College of Vermont *B*
University of Vermont *B,M*

Virginia

Averett College *B*
Bluefield College *A*
Bridgewater College *B*
Emory and Henry College *B*
George Mason University *B*
Longwood College *B*
Norfolk State University *B*
Northern Virginia Community
    College *A*
Old Dominion University *B,M*
Radford University *B*
Virginia Commonwealth University
    B,M
Virginia Intermont College *B*

Washington

Central Washington University *B*
Pacific Lutheran University *B*
Shoreline Community College *A*
University of Washington *B,M*
Walla Walla College *B*

West Virginia

Alderson-Broaddus College *B*
Concord College *B*
Fairmont State College *A*
Marshall University *B*
West Virginia University *B,M*

Wisconsin

Carroll College *B*
Carthage College *B*
Chippewa Valley Technical
    College *A*
Edgewood College *B*
Lakeland College *B*
Madison Area Technical College *A*
Marian College of Fond du Lac *B*
Ripon College *B*
St. Norbert College *B*
University of Wisconsin
    Eau Claire *B,M*
    Milwaukee *B,M*
    Oshkosh *B*
    Stevens Point *B*
    Superior *B*

Clinical pastoral care

California

Fuller Theological Seminary *M*
United States International
    University *M,D*

Georgia

Emory University *W*

Illinois

Garrett-Evangelical Theological
    Seminary *D,W*
Hebrew Theological College *M,D*

Iowa

University of Iowa *C*

Kansas

Benedictine College *B*

Massachusetts

Eastern Nazarene College *M*
Lesley College *B*

Michigan

Madonna University *B*
Marygrove College *M*

New York

Iona College *M*

North Carolina

Duke University *W*

Ohio

Union Institute *B,D*

Oregon

Marylhurst College *B*

Pennsylvania

La Salle University *M*

Clinical psychology

Alabama

Auburn University *M,D*
University of Alabama
    Birmingham *D*
    Tuscaloosa *M,D*

Arizona

Prescott College *B*

Arkansas

University of Central Arkansas *M*

California

Antioch Southern California at
    Santa Barbara *M*
Biola University *M,D*
California Institute of Integral
    Studies *M,D*
California School of Professional
    Psychology
    Berkeley/Alameda *D*
    Fresno *D*
    San Diego *D*
California State University
    Bakersfield *M*
    Dominguez Hills *M*
    Fullerton *M*
    Hayward *M*
    Long Beach *M*
    Los Angeles *M*
    Northridge *M*
    Stanislaus *M*
Chapman University *M*
Fuller Theological Seminary *D*
John F. Kennedy University *M*
New College of California *M*
Pepperdine University *M*
San Francisco State University *B,M*
San Jose State University *B,M*
United States International
    University *D*
University of California
    Berkeley *D*
    San Diego *D*
    Santa Cruz *B*

Colorado

Naropa Institute *M*
University of Colorado
    Boulder *D*
    Colorado Springs *M*
University of Denver *M,D*
University of Northern Colorado *M*
Western State College of
    Colorado *B*

Connecticut

University of Bridgeport *M*
University of Hartford *M,D*
University of New Haven *B*

Delaware

University of Delaware *M,D*

District of Columbia

American University *D*
Catholic University of America
    M,D
Gallaudet University *D*
George Washington University *D*
University of the District of
    Columbia *M*

Florida

Barry University *M*
Florida Institute of Technology *D*
Florida State University *B,M,D*
Nova University *D*
University of Central Florida *M*
University of Florida *D*
University of Miami *M,D*
University of South Florida *D*

Georgia

Emory University *M,D*
Oxford College of Emory
    University *A*
Toccoa Falls College *B*

Illinois

Barat College *B*
Chicago School of Professional
    Psychology *D*
De Paul University *M,D*
Illinois Institute of Technology *D*
Illinois State University *M*
Loyola University of Chicago *M,D*
Northwestern University *M,D*
Roosevelt University *M*
Rush University *D*
Sangamon State University *M*
Southern Illinois University
    Carbondale *M,D*
    Edwardsville *M*
University of Chicago *M,D*
University of Health Sciences: The
    Chicago Medical School *M,D*
University of Illinois at Urbana-
    Champaign *B,M,D*
Wheaton College *M*

Indiana

Ball State University *M*
Indiana State University *B,M,D*
Indiana University Bloomington
    M,D
Purdue University
    Calumet *M*
    West Lafayette *B,M,D*
St. Francis College *M*
University of Notre Dame *M,D*

Iowa

Loras College *B,M*
University of Iowa *D*

Kansas

Pittsburg State University *M*
University of Kansas *D*
Washburn University of Topeka *M*

Kentucky

Eastern Kentucky University *M*
Georgetown College *B,M*
Morehead State University *M*
Murray State University *M*
Spalding University *M*
University of Kentucky *M,D*
University of Louisville *M,D*

Louisiana

Northwestern State University *M*

Maine

University of Maine *D*

Maryland

Loyola College in Maryland *M*
University of Maryland Baltimore
    County *D*

Massachusetts

American International College *M*
Boston University *M,D*
Clark University *D*
Tufts University *B*
University of Massachusetts at
    Boston *D*
Westfield State College *M*

Michigan

Center for Humanistic Studies *M*
Central Michigan University *M,D*
Eastern Michigan University *M*
University of Detroit Mercy *M,D*
University of Michigan
    Ann Arbor *M,D*
    Flint *B*
Western Michigan University *M,D*

Minnesota
Mankato State University *M*
University of Minnesota: Twin
Cities *D*

Mississippi
University of Mississippi Medical
Center *W*
University of Southern Mississippi
M,D

Missouri
St. Louis University *D*
University of Missouri
Columbia *M,D*
St. Louis *D*

Montana
University of Montana *M,D*

Nebraska
University of Nebraska—Lincoln
M,D

New Hampshire
Antioch New England Graduate
School *D*
Franklin Pierce College *B*
Rivier College *M*

New Jersey
Fairleigh Dickinson University *M,D*
Rutgers—The State University of
New Jersey *D*
Seton Hall University *D*

New York
Adelphi University *D,W*
Alfred University *B*
City University of New York
Brooklyn College *B*
City College *D*
Graduate School and
University Center *D*
Queens College *M*
Fordham University *D*
Hofstra University *D*
Long Island University
Brooklyn Campus *D*
C. W. Post Campus *D*
Molloy College *B*
New York University *D,W*
St. John's University *D*
State University of New York
Albany *M,D*
Buffalo *D*
Syracuse University *M,D*
University of Rochester *D*
Yeshiva University *D*

North Carolina
Appalachian State University *M*
Duke University *D,W*
East Carolina University *M*
University of North Carolina at
Greensboro *D*
Western Carolina University *M*

North Dakota
North Dakota State University *M*
University of North Dakota *D*

Ohio
Bowling Green State University
M,D
Case Western Reserve University *D*
Cleveland State University *M*
Kent State University *M,D*
Miami University: Oxford
Campus *D*
Ohio State University: Columbus
Campus *M,D*

Ohio University *M,D*
Union Institute *D*
University of Dayton *M*
University of Toledo *B,D*
Wright State University *D*

Oklahoma
Southwestern Oklahoma State
University *M*
University of Tulsa *M,D*

Oregon
George Fox College *M,D*
Pacific University *M,D*

Pennsylvania
Bryn Mawr College *M,D*
Bucknell University *B*
Duquesne University *D*
Edinboro University of
Pennsylvania *M*
Geneva College *M*
Hahnemann University School of
Health Sciences and
Humanities *D*
Immaculata College *D*
Indiana University of Pennsylvania
M,D
La Salle University *B*
Marywood College *B,M*
Messiah College *B*
Moravian College *B*
Temple University *D*
University of Pennsylvania *M,D*
West Chester University of
Pennsylvania *M*
Widener University *D*

Puerto Rico
University of Puerto Rico: Rio
Piedras Campus *M,D*

Rhode Island
University of Rhode Island *D*

South Carolina
Francis Marion College *M*
University of South Carolina *D*

Tennessee
Austin Peay State University *M*
Fisk University *M*
Middle Tennessee State
University *M*

Texas
Abilene Christian University *M*
Baylor University *D*
Houston Baptist University *M*
Lamar University—Beaumont *M*
St. Mary's University *M*
Sam Houston State University *M*
Texas Tech University *D*
University of Houston
Clear Lake *M*
Houston *M,D*
University of North Texas *M,D*
University of Texas
El Paso *M*
Southwestern Medical Center
at Dallas Southwestern
Allied Health Sciences
School *D*
Tyler *M*

Utah
Brigham Young University *D*
University of Utah *D*

Vermont
St. Michael's College *M*
University of Vermont *D*

Virginia
Averett College *B*
College of William and Mary *D*
Marymount University *M*
Norfolk State University *M*
Old Dominion University *D*
Radford University *M*
University of Virginia *D*
Virginia Commonwealth University
M,D
Virginia Wesleyan College *B*

Washington
Eastern Washington University *M*
Washington State University *D*

West Virginia
Marshall University *M*
West Virginia University *M,D*

Wisconsin
Carroll College *B*
Marquette University *M*
University of Wisconsin
Milwaukee *D*
Oshkosh *M*

Canada
McGill University *D*

Clothing and textiles management/production/services

Alabama
Lawson State Community
College *C*

Arizona
Arizona Western College *A*
Pima Community College *C,A*

California
American College for the Applied
Arts: Los Angeles *A,B*
California State University: Los
Angeles *B*
Cerritos Community College *A*
Chabot College *A*
College of the Desert *C,A*
El Camino College *C*
Fashion Institute of Design and
Merchandising
Los Angeles *A*
San Francisco *A*
Los Angeles Mission College *A*
Los Angeles Trade and Technical
College *C,A*
Mendocino College *C*
Merced College *A*
Orange Coast College *C,A*
Saddleback College *C,A*
San Francisco State University *B*
Santa Rosa Junior College *C,A*
Sierra College *C*
Solano Community College *A*

District of Columbia
University of the District of
Columbia *B*

Florida
Florida Community College at
Jacksonville *A*
Gulf Coast Community College *A*
Santa Fe Community College *A*

Georgia
Georgia Southern University *B*
University of Georgia *B,M*

Idaho
Ricks College *A*

Illinois
KAES College *B*
Northern Illinois University *M*
Olivet Nazarene University *B*
Southern Illinois University at
Carbondale *B*
University of Illinois at Urbana-
Champaign *B*

Indiana
Indiana State University *B*
Purdue University *B,M*
Vincennes University *A*

Iowa
Hawkeye Institute of Technology *A*

Kansas
Kansas State University *M,D*

Kentucky
Kentucky State University *B*

Louisiana
Nicholls State University *A*

Massachusetts
Endicott College *A*

Michigan
Marygrove College *B*
Northern Michigan University *A,B*
Western Michigan University *B*

Minnesota
Lakewood Community College *A*
Mankato State University *B*

Mississippi
Hinds Community College *C*

Missouri
College of the Ozarks *B*
Southeast Missouri State
University *B*

North Carolina
Appalachian State University *B*
East Carolina University *B*

North Dakota
North Dakota State University *B*

Ohio
Bluffton College *B*
Bowling Green State University *M*
Kent State University *B*
Ohio State University: Columbus
Campus *B,M,D*
University of Akron *B*

Oregon
Oregon State University *B,M*

Pennsylvania
Antonelli Institute of Art and
Photography *A*
Philadelphia College of Textiles and
Science *A,B,M*
St. Vincent College *B*

South Carolina
Clemson University *B*
Williamsburg Technical College *C*

South Dakota

South Dakota State University *B*

Tennessee

Carson-Newman College *B*
East Tennessee State University *B*
Shelby State Community College *C,A*
University of Tennessee: Knoxville *B,M*

Texas

El Paso Community College *A*
Lamar University—Beaumont *B*
Texas Christian University *B*
Texas Tech University *B,M,D*
University of Mary Hardin-Baylor *B*

Utah

Southern Utah University *B*
Utah State University *M*

Vermont

University of Vermont *B*

Washington

Olympic College *C,A*
Shoreline Community College *A*

Wisconsin

University of Wisconsin: Stout *B*

Coast Guard science

Connecticut

United States Coast Guard Academy *B*

Cognitive psychology

Alabama

University of Alabama *M,D*

California

San Jose State University *B*
University of California
   Los Angeles *B*
   San Diego *B,D*

Colorado

University of Colorado at Boulder *D*

Connecticut

Wesleyan University *B*

Delaware

University of Delaware *M,D*

Florida

Florida State University *M,D*
New College of the University of South Florida *B*
University of Florida *M,D*

Georgia

Emory University *M,D*

Illinois

Loyola University of Chicago *M,D*
University of Chicago *B*
University of Illinois at Urbana-Champaign *B,M,D*

Indiana

Indiana University Bloomington *B,M*
Purdue University *B,M,D*

Kansas

Kansas State University *M,D*
University of Kansas *B*

Maryland

Johns Hopkins University *B,M,D*

Massachusetts

Hampshire College *B*
Harvard University *D*
Massachusetts Institute of Technology *B,M,D*
Tufts University *B,M,D*

Michigan

University of Michigan *M,D*

New Jersey

Rutgers—The State University of New Jersey *D*

New York

City University of New York Graduate School and University Center *D*
Columbia University *M,D*
Marymount Manhattan College *C*
Sarah Lawrence College *B*
State University of New York Albany *M,D*
   Buffalo *D*

Ohio

Ohio State University: Columbus Campus *M,D*

Pennsylvania

Carnegie Mellon University *B,M,D,W*
West Chester University of Pennsylvania *B*

Texas

University of Texas at Dallas *M*

Commercial art

Alabama

Alabama Agricultural and Mechanical University *B*
Bessemer State Technical College *C*
James H. Faulkner State Community College *A*
Samford University *B*

Arizona

Eastern Arizona College *A*
Glendale Community College *C,A*
Mesa Community College *A*
Pima Community College *C,A*

Arkansas

Arkansas Tech University *B*

California

Chabot College *A*
Chaffey Community College *C,A*
Glendale Community College *C*
Long Beach City College *A*
Los Angeles City College *A*
Los Angeles Trade and Technical College *C,A*
Merced College *A*
Mission College *C,A*

Orange Coast College *C,A*
Otis/Parsons School of Art and Design *A,B*
Palomar College *C*
Pasadena City College *C,A*
Porterville College *C,A*
San Diego City College *C,A*
Solano Community College *A*
Ventura College *C*
West Hills Community College *A*

Colorado

Arapahoe Community College *C,A*
Colorado Institute of Art *A*
Community College of Denver *A*
Mesa State College *A*
Pikes Peak Community College *C,A*
Western State College of Colorado *B*

Florida

Flagler College *B*
International Fine Arts College *A*
Jacksonville University *B*
Miami-Dade Community College *A*

Georgia

Atlanta College of Art *B*
Brenau Women's College *B*
DeKalb Technical Institute *C*
Georgia College *B*

Hawaii

Brigham Young University-Hawaii *A*

Idaho

North Idaho College *A*

Illinois

Black Hawk College *A*
City Colleges of Chicago
   Malcolm X College *C*
   Wright College *A*
College of DuPage *C,A*
Illinois Central College *A*
Southern Illinois University at Carbondale *A*

Indiana

St. Francis College *A,B*
University of Evansville *B*
Vincennes University *A*

Iowa

Des Moines Area Community College *A*
Hawkeye Institute of Technology *A*
Iowa Lakes Community College *A*
Simpson College *B*
Upper Iowa University *B*

Kansas

Highland Community College *A*
Hutchinson Community College *A*
Johnson County Community College *A*
Labette Community College *A*

Kentucky

Eastern Kentucky University *A,B*
Jefferson Community College *A*
Morehead State University *B*
Watterson College *C*
Western Kentucky University *B*

Maryland

Catonsville Community College *C,A*
Harford Community College *A*

Massachusetts

Bunker Hill Community College *A*
Endicott College *A*
Massasoit Community College *A*
Mount Ida College *A*
Northern Essex Community College *A*

Michigan

Henry Ford Community College *A*
Kellogg Community College *A*
Lansing Community College *C,A*
Macomb Community College *C,A*
Northwestern Michigan College *A*

Minnesota

Alexandria Technical College *C*
Northwestern College *B*
St. Paul Technical College *C*

Mississippi

Hinds Community College *A*
Mississippi Gulf Coast Community College: Perkinston *A*

Missouri

Central Missouri State University *B*
Columbia College *B*
Missouri Western State College *B*
Northeast Missouri State University *B*
St. Louis Community College
   Florissant Valley *A*
   Meramec *A*
William Woods College *B*

Nebraska

Central Community College *C,A*
Concordia College *B*
Dana College *B*
Metropolitan Community College *A*
Southeast Community College: Milford Campus *A*
Union College *B*
Wayne State College *B*

New Hampshire

New Hampshire Technical College: Manchester *C,A*
Notre Dame College *B*

New Jersey

Bergen Community College *C,A*

New York

Genesee Community College *A*
Long Island University: C. W. Post Campus *B,M*
Mohawk Valley Community College *C,A*
Onondaga Community College *A*
Rockland Community College *A*
St. John's University *B*
State University of New York College of Technology at Farmingdale *C,A*
Sullivan County Community College *A*
Ulster County Community College *A*

North Carolina

Alamance Community College *A*
Catawba Valley Community College *A*
Central Piedmont Community College *A*
Chowan College *B*
Fayetteville Technical Community College *A*
Gaston College *C*

Guilford Technical Community
College *A*
James Sprunt Community
College *A*
McDowell Technical Community
College *A*
Pitt Community College *A*
Southwestern Community
College *A*

North Dakota

Bismarck State College *C,A*

Ohio

Antonelli Institute of Art and
Photography *A*
Clark State Community College *A*
Davis Junior College of Business *A*
Marietta College *B*
Sinclair Community College *A*
University of Akron *A*
University of Cincinnati
Access Colleges *A*
Raymond Walters College *A*
Virginia Marti College of Fashion
and Art *A*

Oklahoma

Oklahoma Junior College *C*
Oklahoma State University
Technical Branch: Okmulgee *A*
Oral Roberts University *B*
Redlands Community College *C,A*
Southwestern Oklahoma State
University *C*
University of Central Oklahoma *B*

Oregon

Portland Community College *A*

Pennsylvania

Art Institute of Pittsburgh *C,A*
California University of
Pennsylvania *B*
Hussian School of Art *A*
Luzerne County Community
College *A*
Northampton County Area
Community College *A*
Pennsylvania College of
Technology *A*
Westmoreland County Community
College *A*

South Carolina

Greenville Technical College *C*

South Dakota

Black Hills State University *B*

Tennessee

Chattanooga State Technical
Community College *C,A*
East Tennessee State University *B*
Memphis College of Art *B*

Texas

Austin Community College *A*
Brookhaven College *A*
Central Texas College *A*
Collin County Community College
District *A*
El Paso Community College *A*
Houston Community College *C,A*
Navarro College *A*
South Plains College *A*
Southwest Texas State University *B*
Texas Southmost College *A*
Texas State Technical College
Amarillo *A*
Waco *A*

Virginia

Central Virginia Community
College *A*
Hampton University *B*
Northern Virginia Community
College *A*

Washington

Art Institute of Seattle *A*
Centralia College *A*
Seattle Central Community College
C,A

West Virginia

Marshall University *B*
Shepherd College *A,B*

Wisconsin

Madison Area Technical College *A*
Western Wisconsin Technical
College *A*

Wyoming

Northwest College *A*

Communications

Alabama

Alabama State University *B*
Auburn University at
Montgomery *B*
Chattahoochee Valley Community
College *A*
Community College of the Air
Force *A*
Enterprise State Junior College *A*
Jacksonville State University *B*
James H. Faulkner State
Community College *A*
Miles College *B*
Mobile College *B*
Oakwood College *A,B*
Samford University *B*
Selma University *A*
Spring Hill College *B*
Stillman College *B*
University of Alabama
Birmingham *B*
Huntsville *B*
Tuscaloosa *D*
University of Montevallo *B,M*
University of South Alabama *B,M*
Walker College *A*

Alaska

Alaska Pacific University *B*

Arizona

Arizona State University *B,M,D*
Arizona Western College *A*
Cochise College *A*
Grand Canyon University *B*
Northern Arizona University *B*
Pima Community College *A*
University of Arizona *B,M,D*
Yavapai College *A*

Arkansas

Arkansas College *B*
Harding University *B*
Henderson State University *B*
Hendrix College *B*
Ouachita Baptist University *B*
Southern Arkansas University *B*
University of Central Arkansas *B*
University of the Ozarks *B*

California

Azusa Pacific University *B*
Barstow College *A*
Bethany College *B*
Biola University *B*
California Baptist College *B*
California Lutheran University *B*
California State Polytechnic
University: Pomona *B*
California State University
Bakersfield *B*
Chico *B,M*
Dominguez Hills *B*
Fullerton *M*
Hayward *B*
Northridge *M*
Sacramento *B,M*
San Bernardino *B*
Stanislaus *B*
Chaffey Community College *A*
Chapman University *B*
Citrus College *A*
College of the Desert *A*
College of Marin: Kentfield *A*
College of Notre Dame *B*
College of the Sequoias *A*
Cosumnes River College *A*
Crafton Hills College *A*
Fashion Institute of Design and
Merchandising *A*
Foothill College *A*
Fresno Pacific College *B*
Golden West College *C,A*
Holy Names College *B*
Humboldt State University *B*
La Sierra University *B*
Loyola Marymount University *B,M*
Marymount College *A*
Master's College *B*
Menlo College *B*
Merced College *A*
Mills College *B*
National University *B*
Ohlone College *A*
Pacific Christian College *B*
Pacific Union College *B*
Pasadena City College *C,A*
Pepperdine University *B,M*
Point Loma Nazarene College *B*
Saddleback College *A*
St. Mary's College of California *B*
San Diego State University *M*
San Jose State University *M*
Santa Barbara City College *A*
Santa Clara University *B*
Santa Monica College *A*
Santa Rosa Junior College *C,A*
Scripps College *B*
Sierra College *A*
Sonoma State University *B*
Stanford University *B,M,D*
University of California
Berkeley *B*
Los Angeles *B*
San Diego *B,D*
Santa Barbara *B,M*
University of La Verne *B,M*
University of the Pacific *B,M*
University of San Diego *B*
University of San Francisco *B*
University of Southern California
B,M,D
Ventura College *A*
Westmont College *B*
World College West *B*
Yuba College *A*

Colorado

Colorado Christian University *B*
Fort Lewis College *B*
Lamar Community College *A*

Metropolitan State College of
Denver *B*
Northeastern Junior College *A*
Pikes Peak Community College *A*
Regis College of Regis University *B*
University of Colorado
Boulder *B,M,D*
Colorado Springs *B*
Denver *B,M*
University of Denver *B,M*
University of Northern Colorado
B,M
University of Southern Colorado *B*
Western State College of
Colorado *B*

Connecticut

Albertus Magnus College *B*
Asnuntuck Community College *A*
Central Connecticut State
University *B*
Eastern Connecticut State
University *B*
Fairfield University *B*
Housatonic Community College *A*
Manchester Community College *A*
Middlesex Community College *A*
Norwalk Community College *A*
Quinnipiac College *B*
Sacred Heart University *B*
Southern Connecticut State
University *B*
Tunxis Community College *C*
University of Bridgeport *B*
University of Hartford *A,B,M*
University of New Haven *A,B*
Western Connecticut State
University *B,M*

Delaware

Delaware State College *B*
Goldey-Beacom College *B*
University of Delaware *B,M*
Wesley College *A,B*
Wilmington College *B*

District of Columbia

American University *B*
Gallaudet University *B*
George Washington University *B*
Howard University *B,M,D*
Mount Vernon College *B*
Trinity College *B*
University of the District of
Columbia *B*

Florida

Barry University *B*
Chipola Junior College *A*
Daytona Beach Community
College *A*
Flagler College *B*
Florida Atlantic University *B,M*
Florida International University
B,M
Florida Southern College *B*
Florida State University *B*
Gulf Coast Community College *A*
Indian River Community College *A*
Jacksonville University *B*
Lynn University *B*
Manatee Community College *A*
Palm Beach Atlantic College *B*
Palm Beach Community College *A*
St. Thomas University *B*
Southeastern College of the
Assemblies of God *B*
Stetson University *B*
University of Central Florida *B,M*
University of Florida *M,D*
University of Miami *B,M*
University of North Florida *B*

University of South Florida *B,M*
University of Tampa *B*
University of West Florida *B,M*
Warner Southern College *B*

Georgia

Abraham Baldwin Agricultural
College *A*
Augusta College *B*
Berry College *B*
Brenau Women's College *B*
Clark Atlanta University *B*
Georgia Southern University *B*
Georgia State University *M*
Kennesaw State College *B*
Mercer University *B*
Morris Brown College *B*
Oglethorpe University *B*
Paine College *B*
Reinhardt College *A*
Savannah State College *B*
Shorter College *B*
South Georgia College *A*
Toccoa Falls College *B*
Valdosta State College *B*
Wesleyan College *B*
West Georgia College *B*
Young Harris College *A*

Hawaii

Brigham Young University-
Hawaii *A*
Chaminade University of
Honolulu *B*
Hawaii Loa College *B*
Hawaii Pacific University *B*
University of Hawaii at Manoa *B,M*

Idaho

Boise State University *B*
Idaho State University *B*
Lewis Clark State College *B*
North Idaho College *A*
Northwest Nazarene College *B*
Ricks College *A*
University of Idaho *B*

Illinois

Augustana College *B*
Aurora University *B*
Barat College *B*
Blackburn College *B*
Bradley University *B*
City Colleges of Chicago: Richard J.
Daley College *A*
College of DuPage *C,A*
College of St. Francis *B*
Columbia College *B*
Concordia University *B*
De Paul University *B*
Elmhurst College *B*
Eureka College *B*
Governors State University *B,M*
Greenville College *B*
Illinois Benedictine College *B*
Illinois College *B*
Illinois State University *M*
Illinois Valley Community
College *A*
Judson College *B*
Kishwaukee College *A*
Lewis and Clark Community
College *A*
Lewis University *B*
Lincoln Land Community
College *A*
Loyola University of Chicago *B*
McKendree College *B*
Millikin University *B*
Monmouth College *B*
Moody Bible Institute *B*
North Central College *B*

North Park College and Theological
Seminary *B*
Northern Illinois University *M*
Northwestern University *B,M,D*
Olivet Nazarene University *B*
Principia College *B*
Quincy College *B*
Rend Lake College *A*
Richland Community College *A*
Rosary College *B*
St. Xavier University *B*
Sangamon State University *B,M*
Southern Illinois University at
Edwardsville *B,M*
Trinity Christian College *B*
Trinity College *B*
University of Illinois
Chicago *B,M*
Urbana-Champaign *B,D*
Western Illinois University *B,M*
Wheaton College *B,M*
William Rainey Harper College *A*

Indiana

Anderson University *B*
Bethel College *B*
Butler University *B*
Calumet College of St. Joseph
C,A,B
DePauw University *B*
Goshen College *B*
Grace College *B*
Hanover College *B*
Indiana Institute of Technology *B*
Indiana State University *B,M*
Indiana University
Bloomington *B,M*
Kokomo *B*
Northwest *B*
Southeast *B*
Indiana University—Purdue
University at Fort Wayne *B*
Indiana Vocational Technical
College: Northcentral *A*
Indiana Wesleyan University *B*
Manchester College *B*
Marian College *B*
Martin University *B*
Purdue University
Calumet *B,M*
West Lafayette *B,M,D*
St. Francis College *B*
St. Joseph's College *B*
St. Mary's College *B*
Taylor University *B*
Tri-State University *B*
University of Indianapolis *B*
University of Notre Dame *B,M*
University of Southern Indiana *A,B*
Valparaiso University *B*

Iowa

Briar Cliff College *B*
Buena Vista College *B*
Central College *B*
Clarke College *A,B*
Cornell College *B*
Dordt College *B*
Drake University *B,M*
Graceland College *B*
Grand View College *B*
Iowa Lakes Community College *A*
Iowa Wesleyan College *B*
Loras College *B*
Luther College *B*
Morningside College *B*
North Iowa Area Community
College *A*
Northwestern College *B*
St. Ambrose University *B*
Scott Community College *A*
Simpson College *B*

Teikyo Marycrest University *B*
Teikyo Westmar University *B*
University of Iowa *B,M,D*
University of Northern Iowa *B*
Upper Iowa University *B*
Waldorf College *A*
Wartburg College *B*
William Penn College *B*

Kansas

Baker University *B*
Barton County Community
College *A*
Bethel College *B*
Central College *A*
Colby Community College *A*
Emporia State University *B*
Fort Hays State University *B,M*
Fort Scott Community College *A*
Friends University *B*
Haskell Indian Junior College *A*
Highland Community College *A*
Kansas Newman College *B*
Kansas Wesleyan University *B*
Labette Community College *A*
McPherson College *B*
MidAmerica Nazarene College *B*
Neosho County Community
College *A*
Ottawa University *B*
Pittsburg State University *B,M*
Pratt Community College *A*
University of Kansas *B,M,D*
Washburn University of Topeka *B*
Wichita State University *B,M*

Kentucky

Bellarmine College *A,B*
Campbellsville College *B*
Cumberland College *B*
Georgetown College *B*
Kentucky Christian College *B*
Kentucky Wesleyan College *B*
Morehead State University *B,M*
Murray State University *M*
Paducah Community College *A*
Spalding University *B*
Sue Bennett College *A*
Thomas More College *A,B*
University of Kentucky *B,M,D*
University of Louisville *B*
Western Kentucky University *B,M*

Louisiana

Dillard University *B*
Louisiana College *B*
Louisiana State University in
Shreveport *B*
Loyola University *B,M*
Nicholls State University *B*
Northeast Louisiana University *M*
Southeastern Louisiana
University *B*
Tulane University *B*
University of New Orleans *B*
University of Southwestern
Louisiana *B,M*

Maine

St. Joseph's College *B*
University of Maine
Orono *B*
Presque Isle *A,B*
University of Southern Maine *B*

Maryland

Anne Arundel Community
College *A*
Bowie State University *B,M*
College of Notre Dame of
Maryland *B*
Columbia Union College *B*

Frederick Community College *A*
Goucher College *B*
Hood College *B*
Loyola College in Maryland *B*
Morgan State University *B*
Salisbury State University *B*
Towson State University *B*
University of Baltimore *B*
University of Maryland
College Park *D*
Eastern Shore *B*
Villa Julie College *A*
Western Maryland College *B*

Massachusetts

American International College *B*
Babson College *B*
Becker College: Leicester
Campus *A*
Boston College *B*
Boston University *B,M*
Bradford College *B*
Bridgewater State College *B,M*
Bristol Community College *A*
Bunker Hill Community College *A*
Curry College *B*
Dean Junior College *A*
Eastern Nazarene College *B*
Emerson College *B,M*
Emmanuel College *B*
Endicott College *A*
Fitchburg State College *B,M*
Framingham State College *B*
Greenfield Community College *A*
Hampshire College *B*
Massachusetts Bay Community
College *A*
Massachusetts Institute of
Technology *B*
Massasoit Community College *A*
Middlesex Community College *A*
Mount Ida College *A*
North Adams State College *A*
Northeastern University *C,B*
Pine Manor College *B*
Quincy College *A*
Regis College *B*
Salem State College *B*
Simmons College *B,M*
Stonehill College *B*
Suffolk University *B,M*
University of Massachusetts
Amherst *B,M,D*
Boston *C*
Wentworth Institute of
Technology *B*
Westfield State College *B*
Worcester State College *B*

Michigan

Adrian College *A,B*
Albion College *B*
Alma College *B*
Andrews University *B,M*
Aquinas College *B*
Calvin College *B*
Central Michigan University *B,M*
Concordia College *B*
Eastern Michigan University *B,M*
Grand Valley State University *B,M*
Hillsdale College *B*
Hope College *B*
Kellogg Community College *A*
Lansing Community College *A*
Madonna University *A,B*
Marygrove College *B*
Michigan State University *B,M,D*
Northern Michigan University *B*
Oakland University *B*
Olivet College *B*
Saginaw Valley State University *B*

St. Clair County Community
    College A
St. Mary's College B
Spring Arbor College B
University of Detroit Mercy B
University of Michigan
    Ann Arbor B,M
    Flint B
Wayne State University B,M,D
Western Michigan University B,M
William Tyndale College B

Minnesota

Augsburg College B
Bethany Lutheran College A
Bethel College B
College of St. Benedict B
College of St. Catherine: St.
    Catherine Campus B
College of St. Scholastica B
Concordia College: Moorhead B
Concordia College: St. Paul B
Gustavus Adolphus College B
Hamline University B
Macalester College B
Mankato State University B
Metropolitan State University B
Moorhead State University B
North Central Bible College A,B
Northland Community College A
Northwestern College B
St. Cloud State University B,M
St. John's University B
St. Paul Technical College C
Southwest State University B
University of Minnesota
    Duluth B
    Morris B
University of St. Thomas B
Vermilion Community College A
Willmar Community College A
Winona State University B
Worthington Community College A

Mississippi

Alcorn State University B
Jackson State University B
Jones County Junior College A
Mary Holmes College A
Mississippi College B,M
Mississippi Delta Community
    College A
Mississippi State University B
Mississippi University for Women B
Rust College B
University of Southern Mississippi
    B,M,D
William Carey College B

Missouri

Avila College B
Central Methodist College B
Central Missouri State University
    B,M
College of the Ozarks B
Culver-Stockton College B
Drury College B
East Central College A
Evangel College A,B
Hannibal-LaGrange College B
Jefferson College A
Lindenwood College B,M
Maryville University B
Mineral Area College A
Missouri Baptist College B
Missouri Southern State College B
Missouri Valley College B
Missouri Western State College B
Park College B
Rockhurst College B

St. Louis Community College
    Florissant Valley A
    Forest Park A
    Meramec A
St. Louis University B,M
Southwest Baptist University B
Southwest Missouri State
    University B
Stephens College B
University of Missouri
    Columbia B,M,D
    Kansas City B,M
    St. Louis B
Webster University B,M
William Jewell College B
William Woods College B

Montana

Carroll College A,B
College of Great Falls B
Eastern Montana College B
Miles Community College A
Montana College of Mineral
    Science and Technology B
Montana State University B
Northern Montana College B

Nebraska

Bellevue College B
Central Community College A
College of St. Mary B
Concordia College B
Dana College B
Doane College B
Hastings College B
McCook Community College A
Midland Lutheran College B
Nebraska Wesleyan University B
Northeast Community College A
University of Nebraska
    Kearney B
    Lincoln B
    Omaha B
Wayne State College B

Nevada

Community College of Southern
    Nevada A
University of Nevada: Las Vegas
    B,M

New Hampshire

Colby-Sawyer College B
Franklin Pierce College B
Hesser College A
New England College B
Notre Dame College B
Rivier College B
University of New Hampshire
    Durham B
    Manchester B
White Pines College A

New Jersey

Bergen Community College A
Bloomfield College C,B
Brookdale Community College A
Burlington County College A
Caldwell College C
Camden County College A
Centenary College B
County College of Morris A
Fairleigh Dickinson University B,M
Glassboro State College B
Kean College of New Jersey B
Mercer County Community
    College A
Monmouth College B
Ramapo College of New Jersey B
Rider College B

Rutgers—The State University of
    New Jersey
    Cook College B
    Douglass College B
    Livingston College B
    New Brunswick M,D
    Newark College of Arts and
        Sciences B
    Rutgers College B
    University College New
        Brunswick B
Seton Hall University B
Thomas Edison State College B
Trenton State College B
Union County College A
Upsala College B
William Paterson College of New
    Jersey B,M

New Mexico

College of Santa Fe B
Eastern New Mexico University
    B,M
New Mexico Highlands
    University B
New Mexico Junior College A
New Mexico State University B,M
University of New Mexico M

New York

Adelphi University B
Adirondack Community College C
Alfred University B
Broome Community College A
Canisius College B
City University of New York
    Brooklyn College B
    City College B
    College of Staten Island B
    Hunter College B
    Lehman College B
    Queens College B,M
College of Mount St. Vincent B
College of New Rochelle B,M
College of St. Rose B
Community College of the Finger
    Lakes A
Cornell University B,M
Dutchess Community College A
Eugene Lang College/New School
    for Social Research B
Fashion Institute of Technology A
Fordham University B
Fulton-Montgomery Community
    College A
Genesee Community College A
Hofstra University B
Houghton College B
Iona College B,M
Ithaca College B,M
Jamestown Community College A
Long Island University
    C. W. Post Campus B
    Southampton Campus B
Manhattan College B
Marist College B
Marymount College B
Marymount Manhattan College B
Medaille College B
Molloy College B
Monroe Community College A
Mount St. Mary College B
Nassau Community College A
New York Institute of Technology
    A,B,M
New York University B,M
Niagara County Community
    College A
Niagara University B
Orange County Community
    College A

Pace University
    College of White Plains B
    Pleasantville/Briarcliff B
Rensselaer Polytechnic Institute
    B,M,D
Roberts Wesleyan College B
Rochester Institute of Technology
    C,A,B
Rockland Community College A
Sage Junior College of Albany, A
    Division of Russell Sage
    College A
St. Bonaventure University B
St. Francis College B
St. John Fisher College B
St. John's University B
St. Thomas Aquinas College B
School of Visual Arts B
State University of New York
    Albany B,M
    Buffalo B,M,D
    College at Brockport B,M
    College at Buffalo B
    College at Fredonia B
    College at Geneseo B
    College at New Paltz B
    College at Plattsburgh B
    College at Potsdam B
    Oswego B
Suffolk County Community
    College A
Sullivan County Community
    College A
Syracuse University D
Touro College B
Ulster County Community
    College A
United States Military Academy B
Westchester Community College A

North Carolina

Appalachian State University B
Barton College B
Bennett College B
Brevard College A
Campbell University B
Catawba College B
East Carolina University B,M
Gardner-Webb College B
High Point University B
Johnson C. Smith University B
Lees-McRae College B
Lenoir-Rhyne College B
Mars Hill College B
Methodist College A,B
North Carolina Agricultural and
    Technical State University B
North Carolina State University B
Queens College B
St. Andrews Presbyterian College B
St. Augustine's College B
Salem College B
University of North Carolina at
    Asheville B
Wake Forest University B,M
Wingate College B
Winston-Salem State University B

North Dakota

Dickinson State University B
North Dakota State University B,M
University of Mary B
University of North Dakota M

Ohio

Antioch College B
Ashland University B
Baldwin-Wallace College C,B
Bluffton College B
Bowling Green State University
    Bowling Green B,M,D
    Firelands College A

Capital University *B*
Case Western Reserve University *B,M,D*
Cedarville College *B*
Central State University *B*
Cleveland State University *B,M*
College of Mount St. Joseph *A,B*
College of Wooster *B*
Defiance College *B*
Denison University *B*
Franciscan University of Steubenville *B*
Franklin University *B*
Heidelberg College *B*
Hiram College *B*
John Carroll University *B*
Lake Erie College *B*
Malone College *B*
Miami University: Oxford Campus *B,M*
Mount Union College *B*
Mount Vernon Nazarene College *B*
Muskingum College *B*
Notre Dame College of Ohio *B*
Ohio Dominican College *C,B*
Ohio Northern University *B*
Ohio State University: Columbus Campus *B,M,D*
Ohio University
  Athens *B,M,D*
  Southern Campus at Ironton *A*
Otterbein College *B*
Sinclair Community College *A*
Union Institute *B,D*
University of Akron *B,M*
University of Cincinnati *B,M*
University of Dayton *B,M*
University of Findlay *B*
University of Rio Grande *A,B*
University of Toledo *B*
Urbana University *B*
Walsh College *B*
Wilmington College *B*
Wittenberg University *B*
Wright State University
  Dayton *B*
  Lake Campus *A*
Xavier University *A,B*
Youngstown State University *B*

Oklahoma

Bartlesville Wesleyan College *A,B*
Cameron University *B*
Connors State College *A*
East Central University *B*
Eastern Oklahoma State College *A*
Langston University *B*
Northern Oklahoma College *A*
Oklahoma Baptist University *B*
Oklahoma City University *B*
Oklahoma Panhandle State University *B*
Oral Roberts University *B*
Phillips University *B*
Redlands Community College *A*
Southeastern Oklahoma State University *B*
Southwestern Oklahoma State University *B*
University of Central Oklahoma *B*
University of Oklahoma *B,M,D*
University of Science and Arts of Oklahoma *B*
University of Tulsa *B*

Oregon

Central Oregon Community College *A*
George Fox College *B*
Lewis and Clark College *B*
Linfield College *B*
Marylhurst College *B*

Northwest Christian College *B*
Oregon State University *B*
Pacific University *B*
Southern Oregon State College *B*
Treasure Valley Community College *A*
University of Portland *B,M*
Western Oregon State College *B*

Pennsylvania

Albright College *B*
Allegheny College *B*
Allentown College of St. Francis de Sales *B*
Alvernia College *B*
Beaver College *B*
Bloomsburg University of Pennsylvania *B,M*
Cabrini College *B*
California University of Pennsylvania *B,M*
Carlow College *B*
Carnegie Mellon University *B,M,D*
Cedar Crest College *B*
Central Pennsylvania Business School *A*
Chatham College *B*
Cheyney University of Pennsylvania *B*
Clarion University of Pennsylvania *B,M*
Drexel University *B,M*
Duquesne University *B,M*
East Stroudsburg University of Pennsylvania *B*
Edinboro University of Pennsylvania *B,M*
Elizabethtown College *B*
Gannon University *B*
Geneva College *B*
Gettysburg College *B*
Grove City College *B*
Harcum Junior College *A*
Harrisburg Area Community College *A*
Holy Family College *B*
Juniata College *B*
Keystone Junior College *A*
King's College *B*
La Roche College *B*
Lincoln University *B*
Lock Haven University of Pennsylvania *B*
Lycoming College *B*
Mansfield University of Pennsylvania *B*
Marywood College *B*
Mercyhurst College *B*
Messiah College *B*
Millersville University of Pennsylvania *B*
Montgomery County Community College *A*
Muhlenberg College *B*
Neumann College *B*
Northeastern Christian Junior College *A*
Penn State
  Erie Behrend College *B*
  Harrisburg Capital College *B*
  University Park Campus *B,M,D*
Point Park College *A,B,M*
Robert Morris College *B*
St. Francis College *B*
St. Vincent College *B*
Seton Hill College *B*
Shippensburg University of Pennsylvania *M*
Slippery Rock University of Pennsylvania *B*
Susquehanna University *B*

Temple University *M,D*
Thiel College *B*
University of Pennsylvania *B,M,D*
University of Pittsburgh
  Bradford *B*
  Johnstown *B*
  Pittsburgh *B*
University of Scranton *B*
Ursinus College *B*
Villanova University *B*
Waynesburg College *B*
West Chester University of Pennsylvania *B*
Westminster College *B*
Widener University *B*
Wilkes University *B*
Wilson College *B*
York College of Pennsylvania *B*

Puerto Rico

Pontifical Catholic University of Puerto Rico *B*
University of Puerto Rico: Arecibo Campus *A*

Rhode Island

Bryant College *B*
Rhode Island College *B*
Roger Williams College *B*

South Carolina

Anderson College *B*
Coker College *B*
Columbia College *B*
Francis Marion College *B*
Newberry College *B*
North Greenville College *A*
University of South Carolina *B,M*
Winthrop University *B*

South Dakota

Augustana College *B*
Black Hills State University *B*
Dakota Wesleyan University *B*
Huron University *A,B*
Mount Marty College *B*
Sioux Falls College *B*
South Dakota State University *B,M*
University of South Dakota *B,M*

Tennessee

Austin Peay State University *B*
Belmont University *B*
Bethel College *B*
Carson-Newman College *B*
David Lipscomb University *B*
East Tennessee State University *B*
Freed-Hardeman University *B*
Hiwassee College *A*
Knoxville College *B*
Lambuth University *B*
Lane College *B*
Lincoln Memorial University *B*
Martin Methodist College *A*
Memphis State University *M*
Middle Tennessee State University *B*
Milligan College *B*
Motlow State Community College *A*
Tennessee State University *B*
Tennessee Temple University *B*
Tennessee Wesleyan College *B*
Trevecca Nazarene College *B*
Tusculum College *B*
Union University *B*
University of Tennessee
  Chattanooga *B*
  Knoxville *M,D*
  Martin *B*
Vanderbilt University *B*

Volunteer State Community College *A*
William Jennings Bryan College *B*

Texas

Abilene Christian University *B,M*
Austin College *B*
Austin Community College *A*
Baylor University *B,M*
Brazosport College *A*
Central Texas College *A*
Concordia Lutheran College *B*
Corpus Christi State University *B*
Dallas Baptist University *B*
East Texas Baptist University *B*
East Texas State University *B,M*
Hardin-Simmons University *B*
Houston Baptist University *B*
Howard College *A*
Howard Payne University *B*
Huston-Tillotson College *B*
Incarnate Word College *B,M*
Lamar University—Beaumont *B,M*
Lubbock Christian University *B*
McMurry University *B*
Midland College *B*
Midwestern State University *B*
Navarro College *A*
Our Lady of the Lake University of San Antonio *B*
Panola College *A*
Prairie View A&M University *B*
St. Edward's University *B*
St. Mary's University *B,M*
Sam Houston State University *B*
Southwestern Assemblies of God College *A*
Southwestern University *B*
Stephen F. Austin State University *B,M*
Sul Ross State University *B*
Tarleton State University *B*
Texas A&I University *B*
Texas Christian University *B,M*
Texas Lutheran College *B*
Texas Southern University *B,M*
Texas Southmost College *A*
Texas Tech University *M*
Texas Wesleyan University *B*
Trinity University *B*
University of Houston *M*
University of Mary Hardin-Baylor *B*
University of North Texas *B,M*
University of St. Thomas *B*
University of Texas
  El Paso *B,M*
  Pan American *B*
  Permian Basin *B*
Victoria College *A*
Wayland Baptist University *B*
West Texas State University *B,M*
Western Texas College *A*
Wharton County Junior College *A*
Wiley College *B*

Utah

Brigham Young University *B,M*
Dixie College *A*
Southern Utah University *B*
University of Utah *B,M,D*
Utah State University *M*
Weber State University *B*
Westminster College of Salt Lake City *B*

Vermont

Castleton State College *A,B*
Champlain College *A*
Goddard College *B*
Lyndon State College *A,B*
Norwich University *B*

Southern Vermont College *B*
Trinity College of Vermont *B*

Virginia
Averett College *B*
Bluefield College *B*
Clinch Valley College of the
University of Virginia *B*
Emory and Henry College *B*
George Mason University *B*
Hollins College *B*
James Madison University *B*
Lord Fairfax Community College *A*
Lynchburg College *B*
Mary Baldwin College *B*
Marymount University *B*
Norfolk State University *M*
Radford University *B*
Randolph-Macon Woman's
College *B*
Shenandoah University *B*
University of Virginia *B,M*
Virginia Commonwealth University
B,M
Virginia Polytechnic Institute and
State University *B*
Virginia Wesleyan College *B*

Washington
Central Washington University *B*
Centralia College *A*
Eastern Washington University *B*
Everett Community College *A*
Evergreen State College *B*
Grays Harbor College *A*
Green River Community College *C*
Lower Columbia College *A*
Olympic College *A*
Pacific Lutheran University *B*
Seattle Central Community
College *A*
Seattle Pacific University *B*
Seattle University *B*
Skagit Valley College *A*
University of Puget Sound *B*
University of Washington *B,M,D*
Walla Walla College *B*
Washington State University *B,M*
Wenatchee Valley College *A*
Western Washington University *B*
Whitworth College *B*

West Virginia
Alderson-Broaddus College *B*
Bethany College *B*
Concord College *B*
Davis and Elkins College *B*
Marshall University *B,M*
Ohio Valley College *A*
Salem-Teikyo University *B*
Shepherd College *B*
University of Charleston *B*
West Liberty State College *B*
West Virginia State College *A,B*
West Virginia University *B,M*

Wisconsin
Alverno College *B*
Beloit College *B*
Cardinal Stritch College *B*
Carroll College *B*
Carthage College *B*
Concordia University Wisconsin *B*
Marquette University *B,M*
Mount Mary College *B*
Ripon College *B*
St. Norbert College *B*

University of Wisconsin
Eau Claire *B*
Green Bay *B*
La Crosse *B*
Madison *B,M,D*
Milwaukee *B,M*
Oshkosh *B*
Parkside *B*
Platteville *B*
River Falls *B*
Stevens Point *B,M*
Superior *B*
Whitewater *M*
Wisconsin Lutheran College *B*

Wyoming
Casper College *A*
Eastern Wyoming College *A*
Northwest College *A*
Sheridan College *A*
University of Wyoming *B,M*
Western Wyoming Community
College *A*

**American Samoa, Caroline
Islands, Guam, Marianas,
Virgin Islands**
University of Guam *B*

Canada
McGill University *M,D*

Mexico
Sistema Instituto Tecnologico y de
Estudios Superiores de
Monterrey *B*

Arab Republic of Egypt
American University in Cairo *B,M*

Communications research

California
University of Southern California
M,D

Connecticut
Quinnipiac College *B,M*
University of Connecticut *D*

Florida
Florida State University *B,M,D*
University of Florida *M,D*

Illinois
Northwestern University *M,D*
University of Illinois at Urbana-
Champaign *M,D*

Indiana
Indiana University Bloomington
M,D
Purdue University *B,M,D*

Iowa
University of Iowa *M,D*

Kentucky
Sue Bennett College *A*

Massachusetts
Becker College: Leicester
Campus *A*
Emerson College *M*
Hampshire College *B*

Michigan
University of Michigan *D*

Missouri
St. Louis Community College at
Florissant Valley *A*

Nebraska
University of Nebraska—Omaha *M*

New York
Syracuse University *M,D*

Ohio
Kent State University *M,D*
University of Toledo *B*

Community college education administration

Arizona
Northern Arizona University *M*

California
California Lutheran University *M*
College of Notre Dame *M*
University of the Pacific *M,D*
University of San Francisco *M*

Colorado
Colorado State University *D*
University of Northern Colorado
M,D

Florida
Jacksonville University *M*

Illinois
Bradley University *M*
Chicago State University *M*
Southern Illinois University at
Carbondale *M*

Indiana
Indiana State University *M*

Iowa
University of Iowa *M,D*

Kansas
Pittsburg State University *M*

Massachusetts
Suffolk University *M*

Michigan
Eastern Michigan University *M*
Northern Michigan University *M*
University of Michigan *M,D*

Minnesota
Mankato State University *M*

Mississippi
Mississippi State University *M*

Missouri
University of Missouri: Columbia
M,D

New Jersey
Glassboro State College *M*

New York
State University of New York at
Buffalo *M,D*

North Carolina
Appalachian State University *M*
North Carolina State University
M,D

Ohio
Ohio University *M*

Oklahoma
Northeastern State University *M*
Southwestern Oklahoma State
University *M*
University of Central Oklahoma *M*

Oregon
Oregon State University *M,D*

South Carolina
Clemson University *M*

Texas
Texas Southern University *D*
University of Houston *M,D*
West Texas State University *M*

Utah
Brigham Young University *M*

Virginia
Virginia Polytechnic Institute and
State University *D,W*

Washington
Eastern Washington University *M*

Wisconsin
University of Wisconsin:
Oshkosh *M*

Community health work

Alaska
University of Alaska Fairbanks *A*

Arkansas
John Brown University *B*

California
California College for Health
Sciences *M*
California State University
Bakersfield *B*
Dominguez Hills *B*
Los Angeles *B*
Imperial Valley College *C*
San Jose State University *M*
Santa Rosa Junior College *C*

Colorado
University of Northern Colorado
B,M

Delaware
Delaware State College *B*

Georgia
Morris Brown College *B*

Illinois
National-Louis University *B*
Northern Illinois University *M*

Indiana
Ball State University *B*
Purdue University *B*

Iowa
University of Northern Iowa *B*

Kansas

Kansas State University *B*
University of Kansas *M*

Kentucky

Eastern Kentucky University *B*
Sue Bennett College *A*
University of Kentucky *B*
Western Kentucky University *B,M*

Maine

University of Maine
  Farmington *B*
  Machias *B*

Massachusetts

Northeastern University *M*
Springfield College *B,M*

Michigan

University of Michigan *M,D*
Wayne State University *M*

Minnesota

Mankato State University *B*

Nebraska

University of Nebraska—Lincoln *B*

New Hampshire

Plymouth State College of the
  University System of New
  Hampshire *B*

New Mexico

New Mexico State University *B*

New York

City University of New York
  Brooklyn College *B,M*
  City College *B*
  Hunter College *B,M*
  Kingsborough Community
    College *A*
Hofstra University *B*
Ithaca College *B*
Long Island University: Brooklyn
  Campus *M*
St. Joseph's College
  Brooklyn *B*
  Suffolk Campus *B*

North Dakota

Turtle Mountain Community
  College *A*

Ohio

Kent State University *B,M*
Ohio State University: Columbus
  Campus *B*
University of Toledo *B*

Oklahoma

Oklahoma State University *B*

Oregon

Chemeketa Community College *A*

Pennsylvania

Penn State University Park
  Campus *C*
West Chester University of
  Pennsylvania *B*

South Carolina

Morris College *B*

Texas

Texas Woman's University *B*
University of Texas at El Paso *B*

Utah

Brigham Young University *B,M,D*

Washington

Central Washington University *B*
Western Washington University *B*
Yakima Valley Community College
  C,A

West Virginia

West Virginia University *M*

Community psychology

Alaska

University of Alaska Fairbanks *M*

Arizona

Prescott College *B*

Arkansas

University of Central Arkansas *M*

California

California State University
  Fullerton *M*
  Long Beach *M*
  Northridge *M*

Connecticut

Albertus Magnus College *B*
Central Connecticut State
  University *M*
University of New Haven *M*

Florida

Florida Agricultural and Mechanical
  University *M*
Nova University *B*

Georgia

Georgia State University *M*

Illinois

Roosevelt University *M*
Southern Illinois University at
  Edwardsville *M*
University of Illinois at Urbana-
  Champaign *B,M,D*

Indiana

Martin University *B*
Purdue University *B,M*

Maryland

University of Maryland Baltimore
  County *M*

Massachusetts

University of Massachusetts at
  Lowell *M*

New Jersey

Fairleigh Dickinson University *M*
Seton Hall University *M*

New York

College of New Rochelle *M*
Hofstra University *D*
Marist College *M*
New York University *M,D*
Russell Sage College *M*
St. Bonaventure University *M*

Ohio

Cleveland State University *M*
Union Institute *D*

Pennsylvania

Hahnemann University School of
  Health Sciences and
  Humanities *M*
Mansfield University of
  Pennsylvania *M*
Penn State Harrisburg Capital
  College *M*
Temple University *M*
Widener University *B*

Puerto Rico

Puerto Rico Junior College *A*
University of Puerto Rico: Rio
  Piedras Campus *M,D*

South Carolina

University of South Carolina *D*

Texas

Lamar University—Beaumont *M*

Washington

Central Washington University *B*
St. Martin's College *M*
Seattle Pacific University *M*

West Virginia

Fairmont State College *B*

Community services

Alabama

Alabama State University *A,B*

Arizona

Prescott College *B*

California

California State University:
  Dominguez Hills *B*
Fresno City College *C,A*
Santa Rosa Junior College *A*
University of California: Davis *M*
University of San Francisco *B,M*
World College West *B*

Colorado

University of Denver *B*

Connecticut

Mitchell College *A*
Norwalk Community College *A*

Delaware

University of Delaware *B*

Hawaii

University of Hawaii: Honolulu
  Community College *C,A*

Illinois

KAES College *B*
National-Louis University *B,M*
Sangamon State University *B,M*
University of Chicago *M,D*

Iowa

Des Moines Area Community
  College *A*

Kansas

Highland Community College *A*

Kentucky

University of Louisville *M,D*

Maryland

University of Maryland: College
  Park *B*

Massachusetts

Northeastern University *B*
Springfield College *B,M*
University of Massachusetts at
  Boston *C,B*

Michigan

Ferris State University *B*
Grand Valley State University *B*
University of Detroit Mercy *B*

Minnesota

Bemidji State University *B*
Bethany Lutheran College *A*
Mankato State University *B,M*

Missouri

University of Missouri: Columbia *M*

Montana

College of Great Falls *A,M*

Nebraska

Midland Lutheran College *A*
University of Nebraska—Lincoln *D*

New Hampshire

New Hampshire Technical College:
  Manchester *C,A*

New Jersey

Cumberland County College *A*
Mercer County Community
  College *A*
Thomas Edison State College *A,B*

New Mexico

University of New Mexico *A*

New York

Alfred University *M*
City University of New York: New
  York City Technical College *A*
Clinton Community College *A*
Cornell University *B,M*
Hudson Valley Community
  College *A*
Jamestown Community College *A*
State University of New York
  Empire State College *A,B*
Ulster County Community
  College *A*

Ohio

Ohio University
  Athens *B*
  Southern Campus at Ironton *A*
University of Akron *A*
University of Cincinnati *B,M*
University of Findlay *A*
University of Toledo *B*
Urbana University *B*

Oklahoma

East Central University *B,M*

Pennsylvania

California University of
  Pennsylvania *A*
Indiana University of
  Pennsylvania *B*
Penn State University Park Campus
  M,D
Temple University *M*

Puerto Rico

Puerto Rico Junior College *A*

South Carolina

University of South Carolina at
Aiken *B*

South Dakota

Black Hills State University *B*
Northern State University *B*

Tennessee

University of Tennessee
Chattanooga *B*
Knoxville *B*

Texas

Texas Southern University *B*

Vermont

Champlain College *A*
Goddard College *B,M*
Lyndon State College *B*
School for International Training *M*

Virginia

Lynchburg College *B*
New River Community College *C,A*
Piedmont Virginia Community
College *A*
Virginia Wesleyan College *B*

Washington

Evergreen State College *B*
St. Martin's College *B*
Wenatchee Valley College *A*

West Virginia

Fairmont State College *B*
West Virginia Institute of
Technology *B*

Wisconsin

University of Wisconsin: Green
Bay *M*

Comparative literature

Alaska

Alaska Pacific University *B*

Arizona

Prescott College *B*
University of Arizona *M,D*

Arkansas

University of Arkansas *M,D*

California

California State University
Fullerton *B,M*
Long Beach *B*
Northridge *B*
Chapman University *M*
College of the Desert *A*
Humboldt State University *M*
Mills College *B*
Occidental College *B*
Pomona College *B*
San Diego State University *B*
San Francisco State University *B,M*
Scripps College *B*
Southwestern College *A*
Stanford University *B,M,D*

University of California
Berkeley *B,M,D*
Davis *B,M,D*
Irvine *B,M,D*
Los Angeles *M,D*
Riverside *B,M,D*
San Diego *M,D*
Santa Barbara *B,M,D*
Santa Cruz *B*
University of Southern California
B,M,D

Colorado

Colorado College *B*
University of Colorado at Boulder
M,D
University of Denver *B*

Connecticut

Southern Connecticut State
University *B,M*
Trinity College *B*
University of Connecticut *M,D*
Wesleyan University *B*
Yale University *B,M,D*

Delaware

University of Delaware *B*

District of Columbia

Catholic University of America
B,M,D

Florida

Eckerd College *B*
Florida Atlantic University *B,M*
New College of the University of
South Florida *B*
University of Florida *M,D*

Georgia

Emory University *B,M,D*
University of Georgia *B,M,D*

Illinois

Augustana College *B*
Black Hawk College *A*
Judson College *B*
Lake Forest College *B*
Northwestern University *B,M,D*
Richland Community College *A*
Roosevelt University *B,M*
Shimer College *B*
University of Chicago *B,M,D*
University of Illinois at Urbana-
Champaign *B,M,D*

Indiana

Indiana University
Bloomington *B,M,D*
South Bend *B*
Purdue University *B,D*
University of Notre Dame *B*

Iowa

Drake University *B*
Morningside College *B*
University of Iowa *B,M,D*

Kansas

University of Kansas *B*

Kentucky

University of Kentucky *B*

Louisiana

Louisiana State University and
Agricultural and Mechanical
College *M,D*

Maryland

Johns Hopkins University *B,M,D*
St. Mary's College of Maryland *B*
University of Maryland: College
Park *M,D*

Massachusetts

Bradford College *B*
Brandeis University *B*
Clark University *B*
Hampshire College *B*
Harvard and Radcliffe Colleges *B*
Harvard University *D*
Salem State College *B*
Simmons College *B*
Simon's Rock College of Bard *B*
Smith College *B*
Tufts University *B,M,D*
University of Massachusetts at
Amherst *B,M,D*
Wheaton College *B*
Williams College *B*

Michigan

Hillsdale College *B*
Michigan State University *M*
Olivet College *B*
University of Michigan *B,M,D*
Wayne State University *M*

Minnesota

North Central Bible College *A*
St. Olaf College *B*
University of Minnesota: Twin
Cities *M,D*

Missouri

Washington University *B,M,D*
Webster University *B*

Nebraska

Creighton University *B*

New Hampshire

Dartmouth College *B*
Plymouth State College of the
University System of New
Hampshire *B*

New Jersey

Atlantic Community College *A*
Bergen Community College *A*
Bloomfield College *B*
Montclair State College *M*
Princeton University *B,D*
Rutgers—The State University of
New Jersey
Douglass College *B*
Livingston College *B*
New Brunswick *M,D*
Rutgers College *B*
University College New
Brunswick *B*

New Mexico

University of New Mexico *B,M*

New York

Bard College *B*
City University of New York
Brooklyn College *B,M*
City College *B,M*
Graduate School and
University Center *M,D*
Hunter College *B*
Lehman College *B*
Queens College *B*
Columbia University
Columbia College *B*
New York *M,D*
School of General Studies *B*
Cornell University *B,M,D*

Eugene Lang College/New School
for Social Research *B*
Fordham University *B*
Hamilton College *B*
Hobart College *B*
Hofstra University *M*
King's College *B*
Molloy College *B*
New York University *B,M,D*
St. Lawrence University *B*
Sarah Lawrence College *B*
State University of New York
Binghamton *B,M,D*
Buffalo *M,D*
Stony Brook *B*
College at Geneseo *B*
College at New Paltz *B*
Syracuse University *B*
United States Military Academy *B*
University of Rochester *M,D*
William Smith College *B*

North Carolina

Brevard College *A*
Duke University *B,D*
St. Andrews Presbyterian College *B*
University of North Carolina at
Chapel Hill *B*

Ohio

Antioch College *B*
Case Western Reserve University
B,M
Cleveland College of Jewish Studies
B,M
College of Wooster *B*
Kent State University *M*
Kenyon College *B*
Oberlin College *B*
Ohio State University: Columbus
Campus *B,M,D*
Ohio University *M,D*
Union Institute *B,D*
University of Cincinnati *B*
Wilberforce University *B*
Wittenberg University *B*

Oklahoma

East Central University *B*

Oregon

Reed College *B*
University of Oregon
Eugene *B,M,D*
Robert Donald Clark Honors
College *B*

Pennsylvania

Bryn Mawr College *B*
Bucknell University *B*
Carnegie Mellon University *B,M*
Cedar Crest College *B*
Drexel University *B*
Haverford College *B*
Immaculata College *B*
La Salle University *B*
Lycoming College *B*
Penn State University Park Campus
C,B,M,D
Swarthmore College *B*
University of Pennsylvania *B,M,D*
West Chester University of
Pennsylvania *B*

Puerto Rico

University of Puerto Rico
Mayaguez Campus *B*
Rio Piedras Campus *B,M*

Rhode Island

Brown University *B,M,D*
University of Rhode Island *B,M*

South Carolina

Anderson College B
University of South Carolina M,D

South Dakota

Augustana College B

Tennessee

Tennessee Wesleyan College B
University of the South B
University of Tennessee:
Knoxville B
Vanderbilt University M,D

Texas

Houston Community College A
University of Houston: Clear Lake
B,M
University of Texas
Austin M,D
Dallas B,M,D

Utah

Brigham Young University B,M

Vermont

Bennington College B
Castleton State College B
Marlboro College B,M

Virginia

Averett College B
Christopher Newport College B
Clinch Valley College of the
University of Virginia B
Lynchburg College B
Randolph-Macon Woman's
College B
University of Virginia B

Washington

Eastern Washington University B
Everett Community College A
Evergreen State College B
Gonzaga University B
Pacific Lutheran University B
Seattle University B
Tacoma Community College A
University of Washington B,M,D
Washington State University D
Western Washington University
B,M

West Virginia

Bethany College B
Shepherd College B
West Virginia University B

Wisconsin

Beloit College B
Carthage College B
University of Wisconsin
Madison B,M,D
Milwaukee B

Canada

McGill University M

France

American University of Paris B

Arab Republic of Egypt

American University in Cairo B,M

Comparative psychology

Arizona

Prescott College B

Connecticut

Wesleyan University B

Florida

University of Florida M,D

Illinois

University of Illinois at Urbana-
Champaign B,M,D

New York

Sarah Lawrence College B

Computer engineering

Alabama

Auburn University B,M,D
University of Alabama
Huntsville B,M,D
Tuscaloosa B,M

Arizona

Arizona State University M
Northern Arizona University B
University of Arizona B

Arkansas

John Brown University B
University of Arkansas B,M
Westark Community College A

California

American Armenian International
College B
California Institute of Technology
B,M,D,W
California Polytechnic State
University: San Luis Obispo B
California State University
Chico B
Fresno B
Long Beach B,M
Northridge B,M
Sacramento B
San Jose State University B,M
Santa Clara University B,M,D
University of California
Davis B,M,D
San Diego B
Santa Barbara B,M,D
Santa Cruz B,M,D
University of La Verne B
University of the Pacific B
University of San Francisco B
University of Southern California
M,D

Colorado

Colorado Technical College B
University of Colorado
Boulder B,M,D
Denver B
University of Denver B

Connecticut

University of Bridgeport B,M
University of Connecticut B,M,D
University of Hartford B

District of Columbia

Gallaudet University B
George Washington University B

Florida

Florida Atlantic University M,D
Florida Institute of Technology
B,M,D
Florida International University
B,M

Florida State University B
Hillsborough Community College A
Keiser College of Technology A
Nova University B
University of Central Florida B,M,D
University of Florida M,D
University of Miami B
University of South Florida B,M,D
University of West Florida M

Georgia

Georgia Institute of Technology B
Mercer University B

Idaho

Boise State University B
College of Southern Idaho A
University of Idaho B,M

Illinois

Bradley University B
College of Lake County C,A
Illinois Benedictine College B
Illinois Institute of Technology M
Richland Community College A
University of Illinois
Chicago B
Urbana-Champaign B,M,D

Indiana

Indiana Institute of Technology B
Purdue University
Calumet B
West Lafayette B
Rose-Hulman Institute of
Technology B
University of Evansville B
University of Notre Dame B,M
Valparaiso University B

Iowa

Graceland College B
Iowa State University B,M,D
University of Iowa B,M,D

Kansas

Kansas State University B
University of Kansas B

Kentucky

Bellarmine College B
Louisville Technical Institute A
University of Louisville B,M,D

Louisiana

Grantham College of Engineering
A,B
Louisiana State University and
Agricultural and Mechanical
College B
Louisiana Tech University B
Tulane University B,M,D
University of Southwestern
Louisiana M

Maine

University of Maine B

Maryland

Johns Hopkins University B,M,D

Massachusetts

Boston University B,M,D
Eastern Nazarene College B
Franklin Institute of Boston A
Harvard and Radcliffe Colleges B
Harvard University M
Merrimack College B
Northeastern University B,M
Suffolk University B
Tufts University B,M,D

University of Massachusetts
Amherst B,M,D
Dartmouth B
Lowell M
Western New England College B
Worcester Polytechnic Institute B

Michigan

GMI Engineering & Management
Institute B
Michigan State University B
Michigan Technological
University B
Oakland University B,M
University of Detroit Mercy B
University of Michigan
Ann Arbor B,M,D
Dearborn B,M
Wayne State University M,D
Western Michigan University B

Minnesota

University of Minnesota: Duluth B
Willmar Community College A

Mississippi

Mississippi State University B,M,D
University of Mississippi B

Missouri

University of Missouri: Columbia B
Washington University B,M,D

Nebraska

University of Nebraska—Lincoln B

Nevada

University of Nevada: Las Vegas
B,M

New Hampshire

Daniel Webster College B

New Jersey

New Jersey Institute of
Technology B
Ocean County College A
Princeton University B,M,D
Rutgers—The State University of
New Jersey: College of
Engineering B
Stevens Institute of Technology
B,M,D

New Mexico

New Mexico State University
B,M,D
University of New Mexico B

New York

Clarkson University B,M
Columbia University: School of
Engineering and Applied Science
B,M,D,W
New York University B
Pace University
College of White Plains B
Pleasantville/Briarcliff B
Polytechnic University: Long Island
Campus B
Rensselaer Polytechnic Institute
B,M,D
Rochester Institute of Technology
B,M
State University of New York
College at New Paltz B
Syracuse University B,M,D

North Carolina

North Carolina State University
B,M,D
Sandhills Community College C,A

Surry Community College *A*

North Dakota

North Dakota State University *B*

Ohio

Air Force Institute of
Technology *M*
Case Western Reserve University
B,M,D
Cleveland State University *B*
Ohio State University: Columbus
Campus *B,M,D*
Ohio University *B*
Union Institute *D*
University of Akron *B,M*
University of Cincinnati *B,M,D*
University of Toledo *B*
Wright State University *B,M,D*

Oklahoma

Oklahoma Christian University of
Science and Arts *B*
Oklahoma State University *B*
University of Oklahoma *B,M,D*

Oregon

Central Oregon Community
College *A*
George Fox College *B*
Oregon Graduate Institute *M,D*
Oregon Institute of Technology *A,B*
Oregon State University *B,M,D*
Portland State University *B,M,D*

Pennsylvania

Bucknell University *B*
Carnegie Mellon University
B,M,D,W
Drexel University *B,M,D*
Elizabethtown College *B*
Lehigh University *B,M*
Penn State University Park Campus
B,M,D
Pennsylvania Institute of
Technology *A*
Thiel College *B*
University of Pennsylvania *B,M,D*
University of Scranton *B*
Widener University *M*

Puerto Rico

University of Puerto Rico:
Mayaguez Campus *B*

Rhode Island

Brown University *M,D*
Community College of Rhode
Island *A*
University of Rhode Island *B*

South Carolina

Clemson University *B,M,D*
University of South Carolina *B,M,D*

Tennessee

Christian Brothers University *B*

Texas

Amarillo College *A*
Baylor University *B*
Rice University *B,M,D*
St. Mary's University *B*
Southern Methodist University
B,M,D
Texas A&I University *B,M*
Texas A&M University *B*
University of Texas
Arlington *B,M,D*
Austin *B,M,D*
Dallas *B,M*
El Paso *B,M*

Utah

Brigham Young University *B*
University of Utah *B*

Vermont

Norwich University *B*

Virginia

Christopher Newport College *B*
George Mason University *B,M*
Old Dominion University *B*
Virginia Polytechnic Institute and
State University *B*

Washington

Cogswell College North *B*
Everett Community College *C*
Pacific Lutheran University *B*

West Virginia

West Virginia University *B,D*
Wheeling Jesuit College *B*

Wisconsin

Concordia University Wisconsin *B*
Marquette University *B,M,D*
Milwaukee School of Engineering *B*
University of Wisconsin: Madison
B,M,D

Wyoming

University of Wyoming *B*

Canada

McGill University *B*

Mexico

Sistema Instituto Tecnologico y de
Estudios Superiores de
Monterrey *B*

Computer graphics

Alabama

Central Alabama Community
College: Childersburg Campus *A*

California

Chaffey Community College *C,A*
City College of San Francisco *C*
Cosumnes River College *C*
Foothill College *C,A*
Long Beach City College *A*
Orange Coast College *C,A*
Santa Barbara City College *C,A*
Southwestern College *A*
West Coast University *C*

Connecticut

Hartford State Technical College *A*
Northwestern Connecticut
Community College *A*
Waterbury State Technical
College *A*

Florida

Ringling School of Art and
Design *B*

Georgia

Atlanta College of Art *B*

Illinois

Elgin Community College *C,A*
Elmhurst College *B*
Millikin University *B*
Parkland College *C,A*
Ray College of Design *C*
Richland Community College *A*

Robert Morris College: Chicago *A*

Indiana

Indiana State University *B*
Purdue University *A,B*
Vincennes University *A*

Iowa

Teikyo Marycrest University *B*

Kansas

Fort Scott Community College *A*

Kentucky

Asbury College *B*
Eastern Kentucky University *B*

Maryland

Catonsville Community College *C,A*

Massachusetts

Hampshire College *B*
Northern Essex Community
College *C*

Michigan

Lansing Community College *A*
Marygrove College *B*
Northern Michigan University *B*

Minnesota

Alexandria Technical College *A*

Montana

Fort Peck Community College *A*
Miles Community College *A*

Nebraska

College of St. Mary *B*
Metropolitan Community College *A*
Southeast Community College:
Milford Campus *A*

Nevada

Community College of Southern
Nevada *C,A*

New Jersey

Bergen Community College *C,A*
Mercer County Community
College *A*
Seton Hall University *B*
Stockton State College *B*

New Mexico

New Mexico Junior College *A*

New York

Columbia-Greene Community
College *C*
Corning Community College *A*
Pratt Institute *B,M*
Rochester Institute of
Technology *M*
School of Visual Arts *B,M*
State University of New York
College of Technology at
Alfred *A*
Syracuse University *B,M*
Tompkins-Cortland Community
College *C,A*

North Carolina

Forsyth Technical Community
College *C*
St. Andrews Presbyterian College *B*

Ohio

Ohio State University: Columbus
Campus *B,M,D*
Owens Technical College: Toledo *A*

Southern State Community
College *A*

Oklahoma

Oklahoma State University
Technical Branch: Okmulgee *A*

Oregon

Central Oregon Community
College *C*

Pennsylvania

California University of
Pennsylvania *A,B*
Harcum Junior College *C*
Hussian School of Art *A*
Northampton County Area
Community College *A*
Pittsburgh Technical Institute *C,A*
Robert Morris College *M*

Tennessee

Memphis College of Art *M*
Motlow State Community
College *A*
Pellissippi State Technical
Community College *A*
Southern College of Seventh-day
Adventists *A*

Texas

Lon Morris College *A*
University of Houston *B*
Vernon Regional Junior College *A*

Washington

Everett Community College *C*

West Virginia

Bethany College *B*

Computer and
information sciences

Alabama

Alabama Agricultural and
Mechanical University *B,M*
Alabama Southern Community
College *A*
Alabama State University *B*
Athens State College *B*
Auburn University *B,M,D*
Birmingham-Southern College *B*
Bishop State Community College *A*
Brewer State Junior College *A*
Central Alabama Community
College: Childersburg Campus *A*
Chattahoochee Valley Community
College *A*
Community College of the Air
Force *A*
Draughons Junior College *A*
Enterprise State Junior College *A*
Faulkner University *A*
Gadsden State Community
College *A*
George C. Wallace State
Community College at Selma *A*
Huntingdon College *B*
Jacksonville State University *B*
James H. Faulkner State
Community College *A*
Jefferson State Community
College *A*
John C. Calhoun State Community
College *A*
Judson College *B*
Livingston University *A,B*

Lurleen B. Wallace State Junior
College *A*
Marion Military Institute *A*
Mobile College *B*
Northeast Alabama State Junior
College *A*
Oakwood College *A,B*
RETS Electronic Institute *C*
Samford University *B*
Selma University *A*
Shelton State Community
College *A*
Shoals Community College *A*
Snead State Junior College *A*
Stillman College *B*
Talladega College *B*
Troy State University
Dothan *B*
Montgomery *A,B,M*
Troy *B*
Tuskegee University *B*
University of Alabama
Birmingham *B,M,D*
Huntsville *B,M,D*
Tuscaloosa *B,M*
University of North Alabama *B*
University of South Alabama *B,M*
Walker State Technical College *C,A*

Alaska

University of Alaska
Anchorage *B*
Fairbanks *B,M*

Arizona

Arizona State University *B,M,D*
Cochise College *A*
Eastern Arizona College *A*
Embry-Riddle Aeronautical
University: Prescott Campus *B*
Grand Canyon University *B*
ITT Technical Institute
Phoenix *A*
Tucson *A*
Mesa Community College *A*
Mohave Community College *A*
Navajo Community College *A*
Northern Arizona University *B*
Northland Pioneer College *C,A*
Scottsdale Community College *A*
South Mountain Community
College *A*
University of Arizona *B,M,D*
Western International University
A,B,M
Yavapai College *C,A*

Arkansas

Arkansas Baptist College *B*
Arkansas State University
Beebe Branch *A*
Jonesboro *B,M*
Arkansas Tech University *B*
Harding University *B*
Henderson State University *B*
Ouachita Baptist University *B*
Shorter College *A*
Southern Arkansas Community
College *A*
University of Arkansas
Fayetteville *B,M*
Little Rock *B,M*
Monticello *B*
Pine Bluff *B*
University of Central Arkansas *B*
Westark Community College *A*

California

Allan Hancock College *A*
Azusa Pacific University *B*
Barstow College *C,A*
Biola University *B*

California Institute of Technology
B,M,D
California Lutheran University *B*
California Polytechnic State
University: San Luis Obispo *B,M*
California State Polytechnic
University: Pomona *B,M*
California State University
Bakersfield *B*
Chico *B,M*
Dominguez Hills *B,M*
Fresno *B,M*
Fullerton *B,M*
Hayward *B,M*
Long Beach *B,M*
Los Angeles *B*
Northridge *B,M*
Sacramento *B,M*
San Bernardino *B*
San Marcos *B*
Stanislaus *B*
Cerritos Community College *A*
Cerro Coso Community College
C,A
Chabot College *A*
Chaffey Community College *C,A*
Chapman University *B*
Citrus College *C,A*
City College of San Francisco *C,A*
Claremont McKenna College *B*
Coastline Community College *C*
Cogswell Polytechnical College *A,B*
Coleman College *A,B,M*
College of the Desert *C,A*
College of Marin: Kentfield *A*
College of Notre Dame *B*
Columbia College *C,A*
Cosumnes River College *A*
Crafton Hills College *C,A*
D-Q University *C*
El Camino College *C,A*
Evergreen Valley College *A*
Foothill College *A*
Fresno City College *C,A*
Fresno Pacific College *B*
Gavilan Community College *A*
Glendale Community College *C*
Golden West College *A*
Grossmont Community College *C,A*
Harvey Mudd College *B*
Heald Business College: San Jose
C,A
Holy Names College *B*
Humboldt State University *B*
Humphreys College *A,B*
Irvine Valley College *C,A*
La Sierra University *B*
Lake Tahoe Community College
C,A
Laney College *C,A*
Lassen College *C,A*
Lincoln University *B*
Los Angeles City College *C,A*
Los Angeles Harbor College *C,A*
Los Angeles Mission College *A*
Los Angeles Pierce College *C,A*
Los Angeles Trade and Technical
College *C,A*
Los Medanos College *A*
Loyola Marymount University *B,M*
Mendocino College *C,A*
Menlo College *B*
Merced College *A*
Mills College *B,M*
Mission College *C,A*
Modesto Junior College *A*
Moorpark College *A*
Mount San Jacinto College *C,A*
Napa Valley College *C,A*
National University *B*
Naval Postgraduate School *M,D*
Orange Coast College *C,A*

Pacific Union College *B*
Palomar College *C,A*
Pepperdine University *B*
Phillips Junior College
Condie Campus *A*
Fresno Campus *C,A*
San Fernando Valley
Campus *A*
Point Loma Nazarene College *B*
Pomona College *B*
Porterville College *B*
Saddleback College *A*
San Diego City College *C,A*
San Diego State University *B,M*
San Francisco State University *B,M*
San Joaquin Delta College *C,A*
San Jose City College *A*
San Jose State University *B,M*
Santa Barbara City College *C,A*
Santa Clara University *B*
Santa Rosa Junior College *C,A*
Sierra College *A*
Skyline College *A*
Solano Community College *A*
Sonoma State University *B*
Southwestern College *C,A*
Stanford University *B,M,D*
Taft College *A*
University of California
Berkeley *B,M,D*
Davis *B,M,D*
Irvine *B,M,D*
Los Angeles *B,M,D*
Riverside *B,M*
San Diego *B,M,D*
Santa Barbara *B,M,D*
Santa Cruz *B,M,D*
University of La Verne *B*
University of the Pacific *B*
University of Redlands *B*
University of San Diego *B*
University of San Francisco *B,M*
University of Southern California
B,M,D
Ventura College *C,A*
Victor Valley College *A*
West Coast University *A,B,M*
West Hills Community College *A*
West Valley College *C,A*
Westmont College *B*
Whittier College *B*
Woodbury University *B*
Yuba College *A*

Colorado

Adams State College *B*
Colorado Christian University *A,B*
Colorado Northwestern Community
College *A*
Colorado School of Mines *B,M,D*
Colorado State University *B,M,D*
Colorado Technical College *B,M*
Community College of Denver *C,A*
Denver Technical College *A*
Fort Lewis College *B*
Front Range Community College
C,A
Lamar Community College *A*
Mesa State College *B*
Metropolitan State College of
Denver *B*
National College *B*
Parks Junior College *A*
Pikes Peak Community College *C,A*
Pueblo Community College *C*
Red Rocks Community College *C,A*
Regis College of Regis University *B*
Trinidad State Junior College *A*
United States Air Force
Academy *B*

University of Colorado
Boulder *B,M,D*
Colorado Springs *B,M*
Denver *B*
University of Denver *B,M,D*
University of Southern Colorado *B*

Connecticut

Asnuntuck Community College *C,A*
Central Connecticut State
University *B*
Eastern Connecticut State
University *B*
Fairfield University *B*
Housatonic Community College
C,A
Mitchell College *A*
Northwestern Connecticut
Community College *A*
Quinnipiac College *B,M*
Sacred Heart University *B*
Southern Connecticut State
University *B*
Thames Valley State Technical
College *A*
Trinity College *B*
Tunxis Community College *C,A*
United States Coast Guard
Academy *B*
University of Bridgeport *B,M*
University of Hartford *B*
University of New Haven *C,A,B,M*
Waterbury State Technical
College *A*
Wesleyan University *B*
Western Connecticut State
University *B*
Yale University *B,M,D*

Delaware

Delaware State College *B*
Goldey-Beacom College *C,A,B*
University of Delaware *B,M,D*
Wesley College *A,B*

District of Columbia

American University *B,M*
Catholic University of America *B*
Gallaudet University *B*
George Washington University *B,M*
Georgetown University *B*
Howard University *B,M*
Mount Vernon College *B*
Southeastern University *M*
University of the District of
Columbia *A,B*

Florida

Barry University *B,M*
Bethune-Cookman College *B*
Brevard Community College *A*
Broward Community College *A*
Chipola Junior College *A*
Daytona Beach Community
College *A*
Eckerd College *B*
Edison Community College *C,A*
Embry-Riddle Aeronautical
University *B*
Florida Agricultural and Mechanical
University *B*
Florida Atlantic University *B,M*
Florida Institute of Technology
B,M,D
Florida International University
B,M,D
Florida Keys Community College
C,A
Florida Memorial College *B*
Florida State University *B,M,D*
Gulf Coast Community College *A*
Hillsborough Community College *A*

Indian River Community College *A*
Jacksonville University *B*
Jones College *A,B*
Keiser College of Technology *A*
Lake-Sumter Community College *A*
Miami-Dade Community College *A*
New College of the University of
South Florida *B*
Nova University *B,M*
Okaloosa-Walton Community
College *A*
Orlando College *A,B*
Palm Beach Community College *A*
Pensacola Junior College *A*
Rollins College *B*
St. Thomas University *B*
Schiller International University *B*
South College: Palm Beach Campus
C,A
Stetson University *B*
Tampa College *A,B*
United Electronics Institute *C*
University of Central Florida *B,M,D*
University of Florida *B,M,D*
University of Miami *B,M*
University of North Florida *B,M*
University of South Florida *B,M,D*
University of Tampa *A,B*
University of West Florida *B,M*
Webber College *A,B*

Georgia

Albany State College *B*
Armstrong State College *B*
Atlanta Metropolitan College *A*
Augusta College *B*
Berry College *B*
Clark Atlanta University *B,M*
Clayton State College *A*
Columbus College *B*
Covenant College *B*
Dalton College *C*
Darton College *A*
DeKalb Technical Institute *A*
East Georgia College *A*
Emory University *B,M*
Floyd College *A*
Fort Valley State College *B*
Gainesville College *A*
Georgia College *B*
Georgia Institute of Technology
B,M,D
Georgia Southern University *B*
Georgia Southwestern College *B*
Georgia State University *B,M,D*
Gordon College *A*
Kennesaw State College *B*
LaGrange College *B*
Macon College *A*
Meadows College of Business *A*
Mercer University
Atlanta *B*
Macon *B*
Middle Georgia College *A*
Morehouse College *B*
Morris Brown College *B*
North Georgia College *B*
Oglethorpe University *B*
Piedmont College *A*
Reinhardt College *A*
Savannah State College *B*
Savannah Technical Institute *C,A*
Shorter College *B*
South College *C,A*
South Georgia College *A*
Spelman College *B*
University of Georgia *B,M*
Valdosta State College *B*
West Georgia College *A,B*

Hawaii

Brigham Young University-Hawaii
A,B
Chaminade University of
Honolulu *A*
Hawaii Loa College *B*
Hawaii Pacific University *B,M*
University of Hawaii
Hilo *B*
Leeward Community
College *A*
Manoa *B,M*

Idaho

Albertson College *B*
Boise State University *B*
College of Southern Idaho *A*
Idaho State University *B*
North Idaho College *A*
Northwest Nazarene College *B*
Ricks College *A*
University of Idaho *B,M*

Illinois

Augustana College *B*
Aurora University *B,M*
Barat College *B*
Black Hawk College *A*
Blackburn College *B*
Bradley University *B,M*
Chicago State University *B*
City Colleges of Chicago
Olive-Harvey College *C,A*
Richard J. Daley College *C*
College of DuPage *C,A*
College of St. Francis *B*
Concordia University *B*
De Paul University *C,B,M,D*
East-West University *A,B*
Elgin Community College *C,A*
Elmhurst College *B*
Eureka College *B*
Governors State University *B,M*
Greenville College *B*
Highland Community College *A*
Illinois Benedictine College *B*
Illinois Central College *A*
Illinois College *B*
Illinois Eastern Community
Colleges: Frontier Community
College *C*
Illinois Institute of Technology
C,B,M,D
Illinois State University *B,M*
Illinois Wesleyan University *B*
John A. Logan College *A*
Joliet Junior College *A*
Judson College *B*
Kishwaukee College *A*
Knox College *B*
Lake Forest College *B*
Lewis University *B*
Loyola University of Chicago *B,M*
MacMurray College *B*
McKendree College *B*
Midstate College *C,A*
Millikin University *B*
Monmouth College *B*
Montay College *A*
Moraine Valley Community College
C,A
Morton College *A*
National-Louis University *B*
North Central College *B,M*
Northeastern Illinois University
B,M
Northern Illinois University *B,M*
Northwestern University *B,M,D*
Olivet Nazarene University *A,B*
Parkland College *A*
Parks College of St. Louis
University *B*

Principia College *B*
Quincy College *B*
Rend Lake College *A*
Richland Community College *A*
Rock Valley College *A*
Rockford College *B*
Roosevelt University *B,M*
Rosary College *B*
St. Augustine College *C,A*
St. Xavier University *B*
Sangamon State University *B,M*
Southern Illinois University
Carbondale *B,M*
Edwardsville *B*
Trinity Christian College *B*
Trinity College *B*
Triton College *A*
University of Illinois at Urbana-
Champaign *B,M,D*
Waubonsee Community College
C,A
Western Illinois University *B,M*
William Rainey Harper College *A*

Indiana

Ancilla College *C,A*
Anderson University *B*
Ball State University *B,M*
Bethel College *A,B*
Butler University *B*
Calumet College of St. Joseph *A,B*
DePauw University *B*
Earlham College *B*
Franklin College *B*
Goshen College *B*
Huntington College *B*
Indiana Institute of Technology *A,B*
Indiana State University *B*
Indiana University
Bloomington *B,M,D*
East *A*
South Bend *A,B*
Southeast *A,B*
Indiana University—Purdue
University
Fort Wayne *A,B*
Indianapolis *B,M*
Indiana Vocational Technical
College: Southcentral *C,A*
Indiana Wesleyan University *B*
Manchester College *A,B*
Martin University *B*
Purdue University
Calumet *A,B*
North Central Campus *C,A*
West Lafayette *B,M,D*
Rose-Hulman Institute of
Technology *B*
St. Joseph's College *A,B*
St. Mary-of-the-Woods College *B*
Taylor University *B*
Tri-State University *B*
University of Indianapolis *B*
University of Notre Dame *B*
Valparaiso University *B*
Vincennes University *A*

Iowa

American Institute of Commerce *C*
Briar Cliff College *B*
Buena Vista College *B*
Central College *B*
Clarke College *B*
Clinton Community College *A*
Coe College *B*
Cornell College *B*
Divine Word College *B*
Dordt College *B*
Drake University *B*
Graceland College *B*
Grand View College *B*
Grinnell College *B*

Iowa Lakes Community College *A*
Iowa State University *B,M,D*
Iowa Wesleyan College *B*
Iowa Western Community
College *A*
Kirkwood Community College *A*
Loras College *B*
Luther College *B*
Maharishi International University
A,B,M
Morningside College *B*
Mount Mercy College *B*
Mount St. Clare College *B*
North Iowa Area Community
College *A*
Northeast Iowa Community
College *C*
Northwestern College *B*
St. Ambrose University *C,B*
Scott Community College *A*
Simpson College *B*
Southwestern Community
College *C*
Teikyo Marycrest University *B,M*
Teikyo Westmar University *B*
University of Dubuque *B*
University of Iowa *B,M,D*
University of Northern Iowa *B*
Upper Iowa University *A,B*
Waldorf College *A*
Wartburg College *B*
William Penn College *B*

Kansas

Allen County Community
College *A*
Baker University *B*
Benedictine College *B*
Bethany College *B*
Bethel College *B*
Central College *A*
Cloud County Community
College *A*
Coffeyville Community College *A*
Colby Community College *A*
Emporia State University *B*
Fort Hays State University *B*
Fort Scott Community College *C,A*
Friends University *B*
Highland Community College *A*
Hutchinson Community College *A*
Johnson County Community
College *A*
Kansas City Kansas Community
College *A*
Kansas Newman College *A*
Kansas State University *B,M,D*
Kansas Wesleyan University *A,B*
Labette Community College *A*
McPherson College *B*
MidAmerica Nazarene College *B*
Neosho County Community
College *A*
Ottawa University *B*
Pittsburg State University *B*
St. Mary College *B*
Seward County Community College
C,A
Southwestern College *B*
Sterling College *B*
Tabor College *B*
University of Kansas *B,M,D*
Washburn University of Topeka *A,B*
Wichita State University *B,M*

Kentucky

Bellarmine College *B*
Brescia College *B*
Campbellsville College *B*
Cumberland College *B*
Eastern Kentucky University *B*
Georgetown College *B*

Kentucky State University *A,B*
Kentucky Wesleyan College *B*
Lees College *A*
Lindsey Wilson College *A*
Murray State University *B*
Northern Kentucky University *B*
Owensboro Junior College of
Business *C,A*
Paducah Community College *A*
Pikeville College *B*
St. Catharine College *A*
Sue Bennett College *A*
Sullivan College *B*
Thomas More College *A,B*
Transylvania University *B*
Union College *A,B*
University of Kentucky *B,M,D*
University of Louisville *M*
Western Kentucky University
A,B,M

Louisiana

Centenary College of Louisiana *B*
Dillard University *B*
Grambling State University *A,B*
Louisiana College *B*
Louisiana State University
Agricultural and Mechanical
College *B,D*
Eunice *A*
Shreveport *B,M*
Louisiana Tech University *B,M*
Loyola University *B*
McNeese State University *B*
Nicholls State University *B*
Northeast Louisiana University *B*
Northwestern State University *B*
Southeastern Louisiana
University *B*
Southern University in
Shreveport *A*
Southern University and
Agricultural and Mechanical
College *B,M*
Tulane University *B,M,D*
University of New Orleans *B,M*
University of Southwestern
Louisiana *B,M,D*
Xavier University of Louisiana *B*

Maine

Andover College *A*
Bowdoin College *B*
Casco Bay College *A*
University of Maine
Augusta *A*
Farmington *B*
Fort Kent *A*
Machias *A*
Orono *B,M*
University of Southern Maine *B,M*

Maryland

Allegany Community College *A*
Anne Arundel Community
College *A*
Bowie State University *B,M*
Catonsville Community College *C,A*
Charles County Community
College *A*
Chesapeake College *A*
College of Notre Dame of
Maryland *B*
Columbia Union College *B*
Coppin State College *B*
Frederick Community College *A*
Frostburg State University *B*
Goucher College *B*
Hagerstown Junior College *A*
Harford Community College *A*
Hood College *B,M*
Howard Community College *A*

Loyola College in Maryland *B,M*
Montgomery College
Germantown Campus *A*
Rockville Campus *A*
Takoma Park Campus *C,A*
Morgan State University *B*
Mount St. Mary's College *B*
New Community College of
Baltimore *A*
Towson State University *B*
United States Naval Academy *B*
University of Baltimore *B*
University of Maryland
Baltimore County *B,M,D*
College Park *B,M,D*
Eastern Shore *B,M*
Villa Julie College *A,B*
Washington College *B*

Massachusetts

Amherst College *B*
Assumption College *B*
Atlantic Union College *A,B*
Becker College: Worcester
Campus *A*
Berkshire Community College *A*
Boston College *B*
Boston University *A,B,M,D*
Brandeis University *B,D*
Bridgewater State College *C,B,M*
Bristol Community College *A*
Bunker Hill Community College *A*
Cape Cod Community College *A*
Clark University *B*
Dean Junior College *A*
Eastern Nazarene College *B*
Elms College *A*
Emmanuel College *B*
Endicott College *A*
Fitchburg State College *B,M*
Framingham State College *B*
Franklin Institute of Boston *A*
Gordon College *B*
Greenfield Community College *A*
Hampshire College *B*
Harvard and Radcliffe Colleges *B*
Harvard University *M,D*
Massachusetts Bay Community
College *A*
Massachusetts Institute of
Technology *B,M,D,W*
Massasoit Community College *A*
Merrimack College *A,B*
Middlesex Community College *A*
Mount Ida College *A*
Mount Wachusett Community
College *C*
New England Banking Institute *A*
Newbury College *A*
North Adams State College *B*
North Shore Community College *A*
Northeastern University *B,M*
Northern Essex Community
College *A*
Quincy College *C,A*
Quinsigamond Community
College *A*
Roxbury Community College *A*
Salem State College *B*
Smith College *B*
Springfield College *B*
Springfield Technical Community
College *A*
Stonehill College *B*
Suffolk University *B*
Tufts University *B,M*
University of Massachusetts
Amherst *B,M,D*
Boston *C,B,M*
Dartmouth *B,M*
Lowell *B,M,D*
Wellesley College *B*

Wentworth Institute of Technology
A,B
Western New England College *B*
Westfield State College *B*
Williams College *B*
Worcester Polytechnic Institute
B,M,D
Worcester State College *B*

Michigan

Alma College *B*
Andrews University *B,M*
Aquinas College *B*
Baker College
Auburn Hills *C,A*
Owosso *B*
Port Huron *A*
Calvin College *B*
Central Michigan University *B,M*
Eastern Michigan University *B,M*
Ferris State University *B,M*
Grand Valley State University *B*
Henry Ford Community College *A*
Hope College *B*
Kalamazoo College *B*
Kirtland Community College *A*
Lake Superior State University *A*
Lansing Community College *A*
Lawrence Technological University
A,B
Macomb Community College *C,A*
Madonna University *A,B*
Marygrove College *A,B*
Michigan Christian College *C,A*
Michigan State University *B,M,D*
Michigan Technological University
B,M
Mid Michigan Community
College *A*
Muskegon Community College *A*
Northern Michigan University *A,B*
Northwood Institute *A,B*
Oakland University *B,M*
Olivet College *B*
Saginaw Valley State University *B*
St. Mary's College *B*
Schoolcraft College *C*
Siena Heights College *A,B*
Spring Arbor College *B*
Suomi College *A*
University of Detroit Mercy *B,M*
University of Michigan
Ann Arbor *B,M,D*
Dearborn *B*
Flint *B*
Walsh College of Accountancy and
Business Administration *B*
Wayne State University *B,M,D*
Western Michigan University *B,M*

Minnesota

Augsburg College *B*
Austin Community College *A*
Bemidji State University *B*
Bethel College *B*
Carleton College *B*
College of St. Benedict *B*
College of St. Catherine: St.
Catherine Campus *B*
College of St. Scholastica *B*
Concordia College: Moorhead *B*
Gustavus Adolphus College *B*
Hamline University *B*
Macalester College *B*
Mankato State University *B*
Metropolitan State University *B*
Minneapolis Community College *A*
Moorhead State University *B,M*
National Education Center: Brown
Institute Campus *A*
Northland Community College *A*
Northwestern College *B*

Northwestern Electronics
Institute *A*
Rainy River Community College *A*
Rochester Community College *A*
St. Cloud State University *B*
St. John's University *B*
St. Mary's College of Minnesota *B*
Southwest State University *B*
University of Minnesota
Duluth *B,M*
Morris *B*
Twin Cities *B,M,D*
University of St. Thomas *B*
Vermilion Community College *A*
Willmar Community College *A*
Winona State University *B*
Worthington Community College *A*

Mississippi

Alcorn State University *B*
Belhaven College *B*
Copiah-Lincoln Community
College *A*
East Central Community College *A*
Holmes Community College *C,A*
Jackson State University *B,M*
Jones County Junior College *A*
Mary Holmes College *A*
Millsaps College *B*
Mississippi College *B,M*
Mississippi Gulf Coast Community
College
Jefferson Davis Campus *A*
Perkinston *A*
Mississippi State University *B,M,D*
Rust College *B*
University of Mississippi *B*
University of Southern Mississippi
B,M

Missouri

Central Methodist College *B*
Central Missouri State University *B*
College of the Ozarks *B*
Columbia College *A,B*
East Central College *A*
Evangel College *B*
Fontbonne College *B*
Hannibal-LaGrange College *B*
Jefferson College *A*
Lincoln University *A,B*
Lindenwood College *B*
Maple Woods Community
College *A*
Mineral Area College *A*
Missouri Baptist College *B*
Missouri Southern State College *B*
Missouri Valley College *B*
National College *C,A,B*
Northeast Missouri State
University *B*
Northwest Missouri State
University *B*
Park College *B*
Rockhurst College *B*
St. Louis Community College
Florissant Valley *A*
Forest Park *A*
Meramec *C,A*
Southeast Missouri State
University *B*
Southwest Baptist University *A,B*
Southwest Missouri State
University *B*
State Fair Community College *A*
Stephens College *B*
Three Rivers Community College *A*
University of Missouri
Columbia *B,M*
Kansas City *B,M,D*
Rolla *B,M,D*
St. Louis *B*

Washington University *B,M,D*
Webster University *B*
William Jewell College *B*
William Woods College *B*

Montana

Carroll College *A,B*
Montana College of Mineral
    Science and Technology *B*
Montana State University *B,M*
Rocky Mountain College *B*
Salish Kootenai College *C,A*
Stone Child College *A*
University of Montana *B,M*
Western Montana College of the
    University of Montana *A*

Nebraska

Chadron State College *B*
College of St. Mary *B*
Concordia College *B*
Creighton University *C,A,B*
Doane College *B*
Hastings College *B*
Lincoln School of Commerce *A*
McCook Community College *A*
Midland Lutheran College *B*
Nebraska Indian Community
    College *C,A*
Nebraska Wesleyan University *B*
Peru State College *B*
Southeast Community College:
    Beatrice Campus *A*
University of Nebraska
    Kearney *B*
    Lincoln *B,M,D*
    Omaha *B,M*
Wayne State College *B*
Western Nebraska Community
    College: Scottsbluff Campus *C,A*

Nevada

Northern Nevada Community
    College *A*
Truckee Meadows Community
    College *A*
University of Nevada
    Las Vegas *B*
    Reno *B,M*
Western Nevada Community
    College *A*

New Hampshire

Daniel Webster College *B*
Dartmouth College *B,M,D*
Franklin Pierce College *A,B*
Keene State College *A,B*
New Hampshire College *B,M*
New Hampshire Technical College
    Berlin *A*
    Laconia *C*
    Stratham *C*
Plymouth State College of the
    University System of New
    Hampshire *B*
Rivier College *A,B,M*
St. Anselm College *B*
School for Lifelong Learning *C,A*
University of New Hampshire
    A,B,M,D

New Jersey

Atlantic Community College *A*
Bergen Community College *C,A*
Bloomfield College *B*
Brookdale Community College *A*
Burlington County College *C,A*
Caldwell College *C,B*
Centenary College *B*
College of St. Elizabeth *C,B*
County College of Morris *A*
Cumberland County College *A*

Drew University *B*
Essex County College *A*
Fairleigh Dickinson University *B,M*
Felician College *C,A,B*
Glassboro State College *B*
Gloucester County College *A*
Jersey City State College *B*
Kean College of New Jersey *B*
Mercer County Community College
    C,A
Monmouth College *B,M*
Montclair State College *B,M*
New Jersey Institute of Technology
    B,M,D
Ocean County College *C,A*
Passaic County Community College
    C,A
Princeton University *B,D*
Ramapo College of New Jersey *B*
Rider College *B*
Rutgers—The State University of
    New Jersey
        Camden College of Arts and
            Sciences *B*
        Cook College *B*
        Douglass College *B*
        Livingston College *B*
        New Brunswick *M,D*
        Newark College of Arts and
            Sciences *B*
        Rutgers College *B*
        University College Camden *B*
        University College New
            Brunswick *B*
        University College Newark *B*
St. Peter's College *A,B*
Seton Hall University *B*
Stevens Institute of Technology
    B,M,D
Stockton State College *B*
Thomas Edison State College *C,A,B*
Trenton State College *B*
Union County College *A*
Upsala College *B*
William Paterson College of New
    Jersey *B*

New Mexico

Clovis Community College *A*
College of Santa Fe *B*
Eastern New Mexico University
    Portales *B*
    Roswell Campus *A*
National College *C,A,B*
New Mexico Highlands University
    A,B
New Mexico Institute of Mining
    and Technology *B,M,D*
New Mexico Junior College *A*
New Mexico State University
    Carlsbad *A*
    Las Cruces *B,M,D*
Northern New Mexico Community
    College *A*
University of New Mexico *B,M,D*
Western New Mexico University *B*

New York

Adelphi University *B*
Adirondack Community College *A*
Alfred University *B*
Barnard College *B*
Bramson ORT Technical Institute
    C,A
Broome Community College *A*
Canisius College *B*

City University of New York
    Baruch College *B,M*
    Brooklyn College *B,M*
    City College *B,M,D*
    College of Staten Island
        B,M,D
    Graduate School and
        University Center *D*
    Hunter College *B,M*
    John Jay College of Criminal
        Justice *B*
    Kingsborough Community
        College *A*
    La Guardia Community
        College *A*
    Lehman College *B*
    Medgar Evers College *A*
    Queens College *B,M*
    Queensborough Community
        College *A*
Clarkson University *B,M*
Colgate University *B*
College of Mount St. Vincent *B*
College of St. Rose *B*
Columbia University
    Columbia College *B*
    School of Engineering and
        Applied Science *B,M,D,W*
    School of General Studies *B*
Columbia-Greene Community
    College *A*
Cornell University *B,M,D*
Corning Community College *A*
Dominican College of Blauvelt *B*
Dowling College *C,B*
Dutchess Community College *A*
D'Youville College *B*
Elmira College *B*
Erie Community College: North
    Campus *A*
Five Towns College *A*
Fordham University *B*
Fulton-Montgomery Community
    College *A*
Genesee Community College *A*
Hamilton College *B*
Hartwick College *B*
Herkimer County Community
    College *A*
Hobart College *B*
Hofstra University *B,M*
Iona College *B,M*
Ithaca College *B*
Jamestown Community College *A*
Jefferson Community College *A*
King's College *B*
Le Moyne College *B*
Long Island University
    Brooklyn Campus *B,M*
    C. W. Post Campus *B*
    Southampton Campus *B*
Manhattan College *B*
Manhattanville College *B*
Marist College *B*
Marymount Manhattan College *C*
Medaille College *B*
Mercy College *C,B*
Mohawk Valley Community
    College *A*
Molloy College *B*
Monroe College *A*
Monroe Community College *A*
Mount St. Mary College *B*
Nassau Community College *A*
Nazareth College of Rochester *B*
New York Institute of Technology
    B,M
New York University *C,B,M,D*
Niagara County Community
    College *A*
Niagara University *C,B*

North Country Community
    College *A*
Onondaga Community College *A*
Orange County Community
    College *A*
Pace University
    College of White Plains *B,M*
    New York *B*
    Pleasantville/Briarcliff *B*
Polytechnic University
    Brooklyn *B,M,D*
    Long Island Campus *B,M,D*
Rensselaer Polytechnic Institute
    B,M,D
Roberts Wesleyan College *B*
Rochester Institute of Technology
    A,B,M
Russell Sage College *B*
Sage Junior College of Albany, A
    Division of Russell Sage
    College *A*
St. Bonaventure University *B*
St. John Fisher College *B*
St. John's University *B*
St. Lawrence University *B*
Sarah Lawrence College *B*
Siena College *C,B*
Skidmore College *B*
State University of New York
    Albany *B,M,D*
    Binghamton *B,M,D*
    Buffalo *B,M,D*
    Purchase *C*
    Stony Brook *B,M,D*
    College of Agriculture and
        Technology at Cobleskill *A*
    College of Agriculture and
        Technology at Morrisville *A*
    College at Brockport *B*
    College at Buffalo *B*
    College at Fredonia *B*
    College at Geneseo *B*
    College at New Paltz *B,M*
    College at Old Westbury *B*
    College at Oneonta *B*
    College at Plattsburgh *B*
    College at Potsdam *B*
    College of Technology at
        Alfred *A*
    College of Technology at
        Canton *A*
    College of Technology at
        Delhi *A*
    College of Technology at
        Farmingdale *A*
    Institute of Technology at
        Utica/Rome *B,M*
    Oswego *B*
Suffolk County Community
    College *A*
Sullivan County Community
    College *A*
Syracuse University *B,M,D*
Tompkins-Cortland Community
    College *A*
Touro College *B*
Ulster County Community
    College *A*
Union College *B,M*
United States Military Academy *B*
University of Rochester *M,D*
University of the State of New
    York: Regents College *A,B*
Utica College of Syracuse
    University *B*
Vassar College *B*
Wagner College *B*
Wells College *B*
Westchester Community College *A*
William Smith College *B*
Yeshiva University *B*

134

North Carolina

Barber-Scotia College *B*
Bennett College *B*
Bladen Community College *A*
Blue Ridge Community College *C*
Brevard College *A*
Campbell University *B*
Catawba College *B*
Cecils College *C,A*
Central Piedmont Community
 College *A*
Chowan College *A*
College of the Albemarle *A*
Duke University *B,D*
East Carolina University *B*
Elizabeth City State University *B*
Elon College *B*
Fayetteville State University *B*
Fayetteville Technical Community
 College *A*
Gardner-Webb College *B*
High Point University *B*
Johnson C. Smith University *B*
Lenoir-Rhyne College *B*
Livingstone College *B*
Mars Hill College *B*
Mayland Community College *C*
Methodist College *A,B*
Montgomery Community College *A*
Mount Olive College *A,B*
North Carolina Agricultural and
 Technical State University *B*
North Carolina Central
 University *B*
North Carolina State University
 B,M
North Carolina Wesleyan College *B*
Pembroke State University *B*
Pfeiffer College *B*
Queens College *B*
St. Augustine's College *B*
Sandhills Community College *A*
Shaw University *B*
Tri-County Community College *A*
University of North Carolina
 Asheville *B*
 Chapel Hill *B,M,D*
 Charlotte *B,M*
 Wilmington *B*
Wake Forest University *B,M*
Warren Wilson College *B*
Western Carolina University *B*
Wilkes Community College *A*
Wilson Technical Community
 College *C*
Wingate College *B*
Winston-Salem State University *B*

North Dakota

Bismarck State College *A*
Dickinson State University *B*
Jamestown College *B*
Mayville State University *B*
Minot State University *B*
North Dakota State University
 Bottineau and Institute of
  Forestry *A*
 Fargo *B,M,D*
Turtle Mountain Community
 College *A*
University of Mary *B*
University of North Dakota
 Grand Forks *B,M*
 Williston *A*

Ohio

Air Force Institute of
 Technology *M*
Antioch College *B*
Ashland University *B*
Baldwin-Wallace College *C,B*
Bluffton College *B*

Bowling Green State University
 Bowling Green *B,M*
 Firelands College *A*
Capital University *B*
Case Western Reserve University
 B,M,D
Cedarville College *B*
Central State University *B*
Cincinnati Metropolitan College *A*
Cleveland State University *B,M*
College of Mount St. Joseph *A,B*
College of Wooster *B*
Columbus State Community
 College *A*
Cuyahoga Community College
 Metropolitan Campus *A*
 Western Campus *A*
Defiance College *A,B*
Denison University *B*
Franciscan University of
 Steubenville *B*
Franklin University *A,B*
Heidelberg College *B*
Hiram College *B*
Hocking Technical College *A*
John Carroll University *B*
Kent State University
 Ashtabula Regional Campus *A*
 Kent *B*
 Salem Regional Campus *A*
 Tuscarawas Campus *C*
Lorain County Community
 College *A*
Malone College *B*
Marietta College *B*
Miami University: Hamilton
 Campus *A*
Mount Union College *B*
Mount Vernon Nazarene College *B*
Muskingum Area Technical
 College *A*
Muskingum College *B*
Northwest Technical College *C*
Oberlin College *B*
Ohio Northern University *B*
Ohio State University: Columbus
 Campus *B,M,D*
Ohio University
 Athens *B,M*
 Southern Campus at Ironton *A*
Ohio Valley Business College *A*
Ohio Wesleyan University *B*
Otterbein College *B*
Sinclair Community College *A*
Southern Ohio College *A*
Stark Technical College *A*
Union Institute *B,D*
University of Akron *A*
University of Cincinnati *B,M*
University of Dayton *B,M*
University of Findlay *A,B*
University of Rio Grande *A,B*
University of Toledo *B,M*
Walsh College *B*
Wilberforce University *B*
Wilmington College *B*
Wittenberg University *B*
Wright State University
 Dayton *B,M,D*
 Lake Campus *A*
Xavier University *B*
Youngstown State University *B,M*

Oklahoma

Bacone College *A*
Bartlesville Wesleyan College *A,B*
Cameron University *B*
Connors State College *A*
East Central University *B*
Eastern Oklahoma State College *A*
Langston University *B*
Murray State College *A*

Northeastern State University *B*
Northern Oklahoma College *A*
Northwestern Oklahoma State
 University *B*
Oklahoma Baptist University *B*
Oklahoma Christian University of
 Science and Arts *B*
Oklahoma City University *B,M*
Oklahoma Panhandle State
 University *B*
Oklahoma State University *B,M,D*
Oral Roberts University *B*
Phillips University *A,B*
Redlands Community College *A*
Rose State College *A*
Southeastern Oklahoma State
 University *B*
Southwestern Oklahoma State
 University *B*
Tulsa Junior College *A*
University of Central Oklahoma *B*
University of Oklahoma *B,M,D*
University of Science and Arts of
 Oklahoma *B*
University of Tulsa *C,B,M,D*

Oregon

Central Oregon Community
 College *A*
George Fox College *B*
Lane Community College *C*
Linfield College *B*
Northwest Christian College *B*
Oregon Graduate Institute *M,D*
Oregon State University *B,M,D*
Pacific University *B*
Portland Community College *C,A*
Portland State University *B,M*
Rogue Community College *A*
Southern Oregon State College *B*
Southwestern Oregon Community
 College *A*
Treasure Valley Community
 College *A*
University of Oregon
 Eugene *B,M,D*
 Robert Donald Clark Honors
  College *B*
University of Portland *B*
Western Oregon State College *B*
Willamette University *B*

Pennsylvania

Albright College *B*
Allegheny College *B*
Allentown College of St. Francis de
 Sales *B*
Alvernia College *B*
Beaver College *A,B*
Berean Institute *A*
Bloomsburg University of
 Pennsylvania *B*
Bucknell University *B*
Bucks County Community
 College *A*
Cabrini College *B*
California University of
 Pennsylvania *B*
Carnegie Mellon University
 B,M,D,W
Cedar Crest College *B*
Chatham College *B*
Chestnut Hill College *B*
Cheyney University of
 Pennsylvania *B*
Clarion University of
 Pennsylvania *B*
College Misericordia *B*
Community College of Beaver
 County *A*
Community College of
 Philadelphia *A*

Delaware County Community
 College *A*
Dickinson College *B*
Drexel University *B,M,D*
Duquesne University *B*
East Stroudsburg University of
 Pennsylvania *B,M*
Edinboro University of
 Pennsylvania *A,B*
Elizabethtown College *B*
Gannon University *B*
Geneva College *B*
Gettysburg College *B*
Grove City College *B*
Gwynedd-Mercy College *B*
Harcum Junior College *A*
Haverford College *B*
Holy Family College *B*
ICS Center for Degree Studies *A*
Immaculata College *B*
Indiana University of
 Pennsylvania *B*
Juniata College *B*
Keystone Junior College *A*
King's College *C,A,B*
Kutztown University of
 Pennsylvania *B,M*
La Roche College *B*
La Salle University *B*
Lackawanna Junior College *A*
Lafayette College *B*
Lansdale School of Business *C,A*
Lebanon Valley College of
 Pennsylvania *B*
Lehigh County Community
 College *A*
Lehigh University *B,M,D*
Lincoln University *B*
Lock Haven University of
 Pennsylvania *B*
Luzerne County Community
 College *A*
Lycoming College *B*
Mansfield University of
 Pennsylvania *B*
Marywood College *B,M*
Mercyhurst College *B*
Messiah College *B*
Millersville University of
 Pennsylvania *A,B*
Montgomery County Community
 College *A*
Moravian College *B*
Mount Aloysius College *A*
Muhlenberg College *B*
Neumann College *B*
Northampton County Area
 Community College *A*
Northeastern Christian Junior
 College *A*
Peirce Junior College *C,A*
Penn State
 Harrisburg Capital College *B*
 University Park Campus
  A,B,M,D
Philadelphia College of Textiles and
 Science *B*
Point Park College *A,B*
Robert Morris College *B,M*
St. Joseph's University *A,B,M*
St. Vincent College *B*
Seton Hill College *C,B*
Shippensburg University of
 Pennsylvania *B,M*
Slippery Rock University of
 Pennsylvania *B*
Spring Garden College *A,B*
Susquehanna University *B*
Swarthmore College *B*
Temple University *B,M,D*
Thiel College *A,B*
University of Pennsylvania *B,M,D*

University of Pittsburgh
 Bradford *B*
 Johnstown *B*
 Pittsburgh *B,M,D*
University of Scranton *A,B*
Ursinus College *B*
Villanova University *B,M*
Washington and Jefferson College *B*
Waynesburg College *B*
West Chester University of
 Pennsylvania *B,M*
Westminster College *B*
Westmoreland County Community
 College *A*
Widener University *B*
Wilkes University *B*
York College of Pennsylvania *A,B*

Puerto Rico

Bayamon Central University *A,B*
Caribbean University *A,B*
Electronic Data Processing College
 of Puerto Rico *A,B*
ICPR Junior College *A*
Instituto Tecnico Comercial Junior
 College *A*
Inter American University of Puerto
 Rico
  Arecibo Campus *A,B*
  Metropolitan Campus *B*
  San German Campus *B*
Turabo University *B*
Universidad Adventista de las
 Antillas *A,B*
Universidad Metropolitana *B*
University of Puerto Rico
  Arecibo Campus *A*
  Bayamon Technological
   University College *A,B*
  Mayaguez Campus *B*
  Ponce Technological
   University College *A,B*
  Rio Piedras Campus *B*
University of the Sacred Heart *A,B*

Rhode Island

Brown University *B,M,D*
Bryant College *B,M*
Johnson & Wales University *A,B*
Providence College *B*
Rhode Island College *B*
Roger Williams College *B*
University of Rhode Island *B,M*

South Carolina

Benedict College *B*
Bob Jones University *B*
Charleston Southern University *B*
The Citadel *B*
Claflin College *B*
Clemson University *B,M,D*
College of Charleston *B*
Columbia Junior College of
 Business *A*
Converse College *B*
Florence-Darlington Technical
 College *A*
Francis Marion College *B*
Furman University *B*
Lander College *B*
Limestone College *A,B*
Newberry College *B*
North Greenville College *A*
South Carolina State College *B*
Technical College of the
 Lowcountry *A*
University of South Carolina
  Coastal Carolina College *B*
  Columbia *B,M,D*
  Spartanburg *B*
Voorhees College *B*
Winthrop University *B*

South Dakota

Augustana College *B*
Dakota State University *B*
National College *A,B*
Presentation College *C*
Sioux Falls College *B*
South Dakota School of Mines and
 Technology *B,M*
South Dakota State University *B*
University of South Dakota *B,M*

Tennessee

Austin Peay State University *A,B*
Belmont University *B*
Bristol University *A,B,M*
Chattanooga State Technical
 Community College *C,A*
Christian Brothers University *C,B*
Columbia State Community
 College *A*
Cumberland University *B*
David Lipscomb University *B*
East Tennessee State University
 B,M
Fisk University *B*
Freed-Hardeman University *B*
Hiwassee College *A*
Jackson State Community
 College *A*
Knoxville Business College *A*
Lambuth University *B*
Lane College *B*
LeMoyne-Owen College *B*
Lincoln Memorial University *A*
Maryville College *B*
Memphis State University *B*
Middle Tennessee State University
 B,M
Milligan College *B*
Motlow State Community
 College *A*
Pellissippi State Technical
 Community College *A*
Rhodes College *B*
Roane State Community College *A*
Southern College of Seventh-day
 Adventists *A,B*
State Technical Institute at
 Memphis *A*
Tennessee State University *B*
Tennessee Technological
 University *B*
Tennessee Temple University *B*
Tennessee Wesleyan College *B*
Trevecca Nazarene College *A,B*
Tusculum College *B*
Union University *B*
University of Tennessee
  Chattanooga *B,M*
  Knoxville *B,M,D*
  Martin *B*
Vanderbilt University *B,M,D*
Walters State Community
 College *A*

Texas

Abilene Christian University *B*
Amarillo College *A*
Angelina College *A*
Angelo State University *B,M*
Austin College *B*
Austin Community College *A*
Baylor University *B,M*
Bee County College *A*
Blinn College *A*
Brazosport College *C,A*
Central Texas College *A*
Cisco Junior College *C,A*
Collin County Community College
 District *C,A*
Corpus Christi State University *B,M*
Dallas Baptist University *B*

Del Mar College *A*
East Texas Baptist University *B*
East Texas State University *B,M*
Eastfield College *A*
El Centro College *A*
Hardin-Simmons University *B*
Howard College *C,A*
Howard Payne University *B*
Huston-Tillotson College *B*
Jacksonville College *A*
Jarvis Christian College *B*
Lamar University—Beaumont *B,M*
Laredo State University *B*
LeTourneau University *B*
Lon Morris College *A*
Lubbock Christian University *B*
McMurry University *B*
Midland College *A*
Midwestern State University *B,M*
Mountain View College *A*
Navarro College *C,A*
North Harris Montgomery
 Community College District *A*
North Lake College *A*
Northeast Texas Community
 College *C,A*
Odessa College *A*
Our Lady of the Lake University of
 San Antonio *B*
Paul Quinn College *B*
Prairie View A&M University *B*
Ranger Junior College *A*
Rice University *B,M,D*
Richland College *A*
St. Edward's University *B*
St. Mary's University *B,M*
St. Philip's College *A*
Sam Houston State University *B,M*
San Antonio College *A*
Schreiner College *A*
Southern Methodist University
 B,M,D
Southwest Texas State University
 B,M
Southwestern Adventist College *B*
Southwestern Christian College *A*
Southwestern University *B*
Stephen F. Austin State University
 B,M
Tarleton State University *B*
Texas A&M University *B,M,D*
Texas Christian University *B*
Texas College *B*
Texas Lutheran College *A,B*
Texas Southern University *B*
Texas Southmost College *A*
Texas State Technical College
  Amarillo *A*
  Waco *C,A*
Texas Tech University *B,M,D*
Texas Wesleyan University *B*
Texas Woman's University *B*
Trinity University *B*
Trinity Valley Community
 College *A*
University of Central Texas *B*
University of Houston
  Clear Lake *B,M*
  Downtown *B*
  Houston *B,M,D*
  Victoria *B*
University of Mary Hardin-
 Baylor *B*
University of North Texas *B,M,D*
University of St. Thomas *B*

University of Texas
 Arlington *B,M*
 Austin *B,M,D*
 Dallas *B,M,D*
 El Paso *B,M*
 Permian Basin *B*
 San Antonio *B,M*
 Tyler *B,M*
Victoria College *A*
Weatherford College *C,A*
West Texas State University *B,M*
Wharton County Junior College *A*
Wiley College *B*

Utah

Brigham Young University *B,M,D*
Phillips Junior College: Salt Lake
 City Campus *C,A*
Southern Utah University *B*
University of Utah *B,M,D*
Utah State University *B,M*
Utah Valley Community College
 C,A
Weber State University *A,B*
Westminster College of Salt Lake
 City *B*

Vermont

Champlain College *A*
College of St. Joseph in Vermont
 A,B
Johnson State College *A*
Marlboro College *B*
Middlebury College *B*
Norwich University *B*
St. Michael's College *B*
University of Vermont *B,M*

Virginia

Averett College *B*
Bluefield College *B*
Bridgewater College *B*
Central Virginia Community
 College *A*
Christopher Newport College *B*
College of William and Mary
 B,M,D
Commonwealth College *A*
Eastern Mennonite College *B*
Eastern Shore Community College
 C,A
Emory and Henry College *B*
Ferrum College *B*
George Mason University *B,M*
Hampton University *B*
Hollins College *B*
James Madison University *B,M*
John Tyler Community College *C,A*
Liberty University *B*
Lord Fairfax Community College *A*
Lynchburg College *B*
Mary Washington College *B*
Marymount University *B*
Mountain Empire Community
 College *A*
National Business College *A*
New River Community College *C*
Norfolk State University *B*
Northern Virginia Community
 College *A*
Old Dominion University *B,M*
Paul D. Camp Community
 College *A*
Piedmont Virginia Community
 College *C,A*
Radford University *B*
Randolph-Macon College *B*
Roanoke College *B*
Shenandoah University *B*
Southside Virginia Community
 College *C,A*

Southwest Virginia Community College *A*
University of Richmond *B*
University of Virginia *B,M,D*
Virginia Commonwealth University *B,M*
Virginia Polytechnic Institute and State University *B,M,D*
Virginia Wesleyan College *B*
Washington and Lee University *B*

Washington

Big Bend Community College *A*
Central Washington University *B*
City University *B*
Clark College *C,A*
Columbia Basin College *A*
Eastern Washington University *B*
Edmonds Community College *A*
Everett Community College *C,A*
Evergreen State College *B*
Gonzaga University *B*
Grays Harbor College *A*
Green River Community College *C,A*
Griffin College *C,A,B*
Heritage College *A,B*
ITT Technical Institute: Seattle *A*
Lower Columbia College *A*
Pacific Lutheran University *B,M*
Pierce College *A*
St. Martin's College *B*
Seattle Central Community College *C,A*
Seattle Pacific University *C,B*
Seattle University *B*
Shoreline Community College *C,A*
Skagit Valley College *C,A*
Spokane Falls Community College *A*
Tacoma Community College *A*
University of Puget Sound *B*
University of Washington *B,M,D*
Walla Walla College *A,B*
Walla Walla Community College *C,A*
Washington State University *B,M,D*
Wenatchee Valley College *A*
Western Washington University *B,M*
Whitman College *B*
Whitworth College *B*
Yakima Valley Community College *C,A*

West Virginia

Alderson-Broaddus College *B*
Bethany College *B*
Concord College *B*
Davis and Elkins College *A,B*
Fairmont State College *A,B*
Glenville State College *B*
Marshall University *B*
Potomac State College of West Virginia University *A*
Salem-Teikyo University *B*
Shepherd College *B*
West Virginia Institute of Technology *A,B*
West Virginia Northern Community College *A*
West Virginia State College *A*
West Virginia University *B,M,D*
West Virginia Wesleyan College *B*
Wheeling Jesuit College *B*

Wisconsin

Beloit College *B*
Cardinal Stritch College *A,B*
Carroll College *B*
Edgewood College *B*
Lakeland College *B*

Marquette University *B*
Mount Mary College *B*
Northeast Wisconsin Technical College *C*
Northland College *B*
Ripon College *B*
St. Norbert College *B*
Stratton College *C,A*
University of Wisconsin
    Eau Claire *B*
    Green Bay *B*
    La Crosse *B*
    Madison *B,M,D*
    Milwaukee *B,M*
    Oshkosh *B*
    Parkside *B*
    Platteville *B*
    River Falls *B*
    Superior *B*
    Whitewater *B*
Viterbo College *B*
Waukesha County Technical College *A*

Wyoming

Casper College *C,A*
Central Wyoming College *A*
Eastern Wyoming College *A*
Northwest College *A*
Sheridan College *A*
University of Wyoming *B,M,D*
Western Wyoming Community College *C,A*

American Samoa, Caroline Islands, Guam, Marianas, Virgin Islands

Guam Community College *C,A*

Canada

McGill University *B,M,D*

France

American University of Paris *B*

Mexico

Sistema Instituto Tecnologico y de Estudios Superiores de Monterrey *B,M*

Arab Republic of Egypt

American University in Cairo *B*

Computer mathematics

Alabama

Oakwood College *B*

Arkansas

Hendrix College *B*

California

California State University
    Fullerton *M*
    Long Beach *B,M*
Merced College *A*
Mission College *A*
Pepperdine University *B*
San Jose State University *M*
Santa Monica College *C*
Southwestern College *A*
University of California
    Los Angeles *B*
    San Diego *B*

Connecticut

Quinnipiac College *B,M*

Florida

Flagler College *B*
New College of the University of South Florida *B*

Georgia

Emory University *B,M*
Georgia College *B*
Piedmont College *B*

Idaho

Idaho State University *B*

Illinois

Augustana College *B*
Aurora University *B*
Barat College *B*
Concordia University *B*
Loyola University of Chicago *B*
Rosary College *B*
Southern Illinois University at Carbondale *B*
Wheaton College *B*

Indiana

Anderson University *B*
St. Joseph's College *B*
University of Notre Dame *B*

Kentucky

Bellarmine College *B*

Maryland

Anne Arundel Community College *C*

Massachusetts

Hampshire College *B*
Massachusetts Institute of Technology *B,M,D,W*
Wheaton College *B*
Worcester Polytechnic Institute *B*

Michigan

Albion College *B*
Lake Superior State University *B*
Lawrence Technological University *B*
Northern Michigan University *B*
Olivet College *B*
Saginaw Valley State University *B*

Mississippi

Holmes Community College *A*
Phillips Junior College of Jackson *A*

Missouri

Avila College *B*
St. Louis University *B*

Montana

Rocky Mountain College *B*

Nebraska

Creighton University *B,M*

New Hampshire

Franklin Pierce College *B*
Keene State College *B*

New Jersey

Rider College *B*
Stevens Institute of Technology *B,M,D*

New York

City University of New York
    Brooklyn College *B,M*
    College of Staten Island *B*
Colgate University *B*
Hofstra University *B*

Ithaca College *B*
Long Island University: C. W. Post Campus *B*
Manhattan College *B*
Marist College *B*
Marymount College *B*
Rochester Institute of Technology *B*
St. Joseph's College: Suffolk Campus *B*
St. Lawrence University *B*
State University of New York at Binghamton *B*
University of Rochester *B*
Vassar College *B*

North Carolina

Barber-Scotia College *B*
Meredith College *B*
St. Andrews Presbyterian College *B*
Sandhills Community College *A*
University of North Carolina at Greensboro *B*

Ohio

Air Force Institute of Technology *M*
Ashland University *B*
Kent State University *B,M,D*
Marietta College *B*
University of Toledo *B*
Walsh College *B*
Wittenberg University *B*

Oklahoma

University of Central Oklahoma *B*
University of Oklahoma *B*

Oregon

Lewis and Clark College *B*
Southern Oregon State College *B*

Pennsylvania

Bucknell University *B*
California University of Pennsylvania *B*
Carnegie Mellon University *B,M,D,W*
Chestnut Hill College *B,M*
Duquesne University *B*
Harrisburg Area Community College *A*
La Salle University *B*
Lock Haven University of Pennsylvania *B*
St. Francis College *B*

Puerto Rico

University of Puerto Rico
    Humacao University College *B*
    Mayaguez Campus *B,M*

Rhode Island

Providence College *B*

South Carolina

Furman University *B*
University of South Carolina at Aiken *B*
Wofford College *B*

South Dakota

Dakota State University *B*

Tennessee

Maryville College *B*
Pellissippi State Technical Community College *A*

Texas

LeTourneau University *B*
McMurry University *B*

South Plains College *A*

Virginia

Averett College *B*
Eastern Mennonite College *B*
Emory and Henry College *B*
Hampden-Sydney College *B*
Mary Baldwin College *B*
Virginia Military Institute *B*
Virginia Wesleyan College *B*

Washington

Gonzaga University *B*
University of Puget Sound *B*

West Virginia

Concord College *B*
Davis and Elkins College *B*
Shepherd College *B*
Wheeling Jesuit College *B*

Wisconsin

Cardinal Stritch College *B*
Lakeland College *B*
Lawrence University *B*
Marquette University *B*
St. Norbert College *B*

Wyoming

University of Wyoming *D*

Computer programming

Alabama

Enterprise State Junior College *C*
Huntingdon College *B*
Jefferson State Community
  College *A*
John C. Calhoun State Community
  College *A*
Selma University *A*
Shoals Community College *A*
Walker State Technical College *C,A*
Wallace State Community College
  at Hanceville *A*

Alaska

University of Alaska Anchorage *A*

Arizona

Mesa Community College *A*
Mohave Community College *C*
Navajo Community College *A*
Pima Community College *A*

Arkansas

Capital City Junior College *A*
Harding University *B*
Southern Arkansas University
    Magnolia *B*
    Technical Branch *A*
University of Arkansas at Little
  Rock *A*
University of Central Arkansas *B*

California

Barstow College *C,A*
California Lutheran University *B*
California State University:
  Fresno *B*
Cerritos Community College *A*
Chabot College *A*
City College of San Francisco *C,A*
College of Marin: Kentfield *A*
College of the Redwoods *C*
Columbia College *A*
Cosumnes River College *C,A*
De Anza College *C,A*
Evergreen Valley College *C*

Grossmont Community College *C,A*
Irvine Valley College *C,A*
Long Beach City College *C,A*
Los Angeles Pierce College *C,A*
Merced College *A*
Modesto Junior College *A*
National University *B*
Ohlone College *C,A*
Pasadena City College *C,A*
Phillips Junior College
    Condie Campus *A*
    Fresno Campus *C,A*
Saddleback College *C,A*
San Joaquin Delta College *C,A*
Santa Monica College *C,A*
Santa Rosa Junior College *C,A*
Sierra College *C,A*
Skyline College *A*
Solano Community College *A*
Sonoma State University *B*
Southwestern College *A*
Ventura College *A*
Victor Valley College *C*
West Valley College *C,A*

Colorado

Arapahoe Community College *C*
Blair Junior College *A*
Colorado Technical College *B*
Community College of Denver *C,A*
Denver Technical College *A*
Front Range Community College
  C,A
Mesa State College *B*
Northeastern Junior College *A*
University of Denver *M*

Connecticut

Greater New Haven State Technical
  College *A*
Middlesex Community College *C,A*
Northwestern Connecticut
  Community College *C,A*
Norwalk State Technical College *A*
Thames Valley State Technical
  College *A*
University of New Haven *C,B*
Waterbury State Technical
  College *A*

District of Columbia

Howard University *B*
Southeastern University *A,B,M*

Florida

Central Florida Community
  College *A*
Daytona Beach Community
  College *A*
Florida Community College at
  Jacksonville *A*
Gulf Coast Community College *C,A*
Indian River Community College *A*
Jones College *A,B*
Keiser College of Technology *A*
Lake City Community College *A*
Manatee Community College *C,A*
National School of Technology *A*
New College of the University of
  South Florida *B*
New England Institute of
  Technology *A*
Okaloosa-Walton Community
  College *A*
Palm Beach Community College *A*
St. Johns River Community
  College *A*
St. Petersburg Junior College *A*
Santa Fe Community College *A*
Seminole Community College *A*
Southern College *A*
Tampa College *A,B*

University of Tampa *B*
Valencia Community College *A*

Georgia

Athens Area Technical Institute
  C,A
Augusta Technical Institute *A*
Chattahoochee Technical Institute
  C,A
Darton College *A*
Floyd College *A*
Georgia Southwestern College *A,B*
Kennesaw State College *B*
LaGrange College *B*
Macon College *C,A*
South Georgia College *A*
Valdosta State College *B*
Waycross College *A*

Hawaii

Hawaii Pacific University *A,B*
University of Hawaii: Leeward
  Community College *A*

Idaho

College of Southern Idaho *A*
North Idaho College *A*
Northwest Nazarene College *A*
Ricks College *A*

Illinois

Aurora University *B*
Barat College *B*
Black Hawk College *A*
City Colleges of Chicago: Olive-
  Harvey College *C,A*
College of DuPage *C*
College of St. Francis *B*
Concordia University *B*
De Paul University *B,M*
Gem City College *C*
Greenville College *B*
Hebrew Theological College *C*
Joliet Junior College *A*
Judson College *B*
KAES College *B*
Midstate College *C,A*
Moraine Valley Community
  College *C*
Oakton Community College *C,A*
Parkland College *A*
Quincy College *A*
Richland Community College *A*
Southern Illinois University at
  Carbondale *A,B*
State Community College *C*

Indiana

Butler University *B*
Indiana State University *B*
Indiana University—Purdue
  University
    Fort Wayne *C*
    Indianapolis *B*
Indiana Vocational Technical
  College
    Central Indiana *A*
    Columbus *A*
    Eastcentral *C,A*
    Kokomo *C,A*
    Lafayette *A*
    Northcentral *C,A*
    Northeast *C,A*
    Northwest *C,A*
    Southcentral *C,A*
    Southeast *C,A*
    Southwest *A*
    Wabash Valley *C,A*
    Whitewater *A*
International Business College *A*
Martin University *B*
Oakland City College *A*

Purdue University
    Calumet *B*
    West Lafayette *B,M,D*
St. Joseph's College *B*
Taylor University *B*
Tri-State University *A,B*
University of Evansville *B*
Vincennes University *A*

Iowa

American Institute of Business *A*
American Institute of Commerce *C*
Clinton Community College *A*
Des Moines Area Community
  College *A*
Grand View College *B*
Iowa Lakes Community College *A*
Iowa Western Community
  College *A*
Kirkwood Community College *A*
Loras College *B*
Morningside College *B*
North Iowa Area Community
  College *A*
Northwest Iowa Technical
  College *A*
Scott Community College *A*
Southeastern Community College:
  North Campus *A*
Southwestern Community
  College *A*
Teikyo Marycrest University *B*
Teikyo Westmar University *B*
University of Dubuque *B*
Wartburg College *B*

Kansas

Brown Mackie College *C*
Coffeyville Community College *A*
Colby Community College *A*
Johnson County Community
  College *A*
Pittsburg State University *B*
Seward County Community
  College *A*
Tabor College *B*

Kentucky

Asbury College *B*
Eastern Kentucky University *B*
Franklin College *A*
Georgetown College *B*
Murray State University *B*
Sullivan College *A*
Watterson College *A*

Louisiana

Grambling State University *B*
Louisiana College *B*

Maine

Andover College *A*

Maryland

Allegany Community College *C,A*
Capitol College *A,B*
Catonsville Community College *C,A*
Charles County Community
  College *A*
Chesapeake College *C*
College of Notre Dame of
  Maryland *A*
Columbia Union College *A*
Dundalk Community College *C,A*
Frederick Community College *A*
Harford Community College *C*
Howard Community College *A*
Montgomery College
    Germantown Campus *C,A*
    Rockville Campus *C,A*
    Takoma Park Campus *C*

Prince George's Community
College *C*
University of Baltimore *B*
Wor-Wic Tech Community College
C,A

Massachusetts

Atlantic Union College *A*
Becker College: Worcester
Campus *A*
Berkshire Community College *A*
Bristol Community College *A*
Bunker Hill Community College *A*
Elms College *A*
Franklin Institute of Boston *A*
Greenfield Community College *A*
Hampshire College *B*
Massachusetts Institute of
Technology *B,M,D,W*
Massasoit Community College *A*
Middlesex Community College *A*
Mount Wachusett Community
College *A*
North Adams State College *B*
North Shore Community College *A*
Northeastern University *C*
Northern Essex Community
College *A*
Quincy College *A*
Roxbury Community College *C*
Salem State College *B*
Tufts University *B*

Michigan

Adrian College *A,B*
Alma College *B*
Baker College
Flint *A,B*
Muskegon *A,B*
Owosso *A*
Charles Stewart Mott Community
College *C,A*
Cleary College *B*
Davenport College of Business *A,B*
Delta College *A*
Detroit College of Business *B*
Grand Rapids Community
College *A*
Grand Valley State University *B*
Great Lakes Junior College of
Business *A*
Henry Ford Community College *A*
Jordan College *C,A*
Kellogg Community College *C,A*
Lansing Community College *A*
Madonna University *B*
Marygrove College *B*
Michigan Christian College *B*
Michigan Technological
University *B*
Mid Michigan Community
College *A*
Northern Michigan University *B*
Northwestern Michigan College *A*
Northwood Institute *A,B*
Oakland Community College *C,A*
Oakland University *M*
Olivet College *B*
Saginaw Valley State University *B*
St. Clair County Community
College *C,A*
Schoolcraft College *A*
Southwestern Michigan College *C,A*

Minnesota

Alexandria Technical College *A*
Inver Hills Community College *A*
Mankato State University *B*
National Education Center: Brown
Institute Campus *C*
Normandale Community College *A*
Northland Community College *A*

St. Mary's College of Minnesota *B*
St. Paul Technical College *C*
Vermilion Community College *A*
Willmar Community College *A*
Winona State University *B*

Mississippi

Copiah-Lincoln Community
College *A*
Holmes Community College *A*
Jackson State University *B*
Jones County Junior College *A*
Mary Holmes College *A*
Mississippi College *B*
Mississippi Delta Community
College *A*
Phillips Junior College of
Jackson *A*
Tougaloo College *B*

Missouri

College of the Ozarks *B*
East Central College *C,A*
Fontbonne College *B*
Longview Community College *A*
Maryville University *B*
Missouri Southern State College
A,B
Missouri Western State College *B*
Penn Valley Community College *A*
Rockhurst College *B*
St. Louis Community College
Florissant Valley *A*
Forest Park *A*
University of Missouri: St. Louis
B,M
Washington University *B*

Montana

College of Great Falls *A,B*
Miles Community College *A*
Montana College of Mineral
Science and Technology *B*
Northern Montana College *A*

Nebraska

Central Community College *C,A*
College of St. Mary *A,B*
Lincoln School of Commerce *A*
Metropolitan Community College *A*
Midland Lutheran College *A,B*
Northeast Community College *A*
Southeast Community College:
Milford Campus *A*

Nevada

Community College of Southern
Nevada *A*
Western Nevada Community
College *A*

New Hampshire

Daniel Webster College *A,B*
Franklin Pierce College *A,B*
Hesser College *A*

New Jersey

Bloomfield College *C*
Brookdale Community College *A*
Burlington County College *C,A*
Essex County College *A*
Ocean County College *A*

New Mexico

Clovis Community College *A*
Dona Ana Branch Community
College of New Mexico State
University *A*
Eastern New Mexico University *B*
New Mexico Institute of Mining
and Technology *B,M,D*
New Mexico Junior College *A*

University of New Mexico *A*

New York

Adirondack Community College *A*
Bramson ORT Technical Institute
C,A
Bryant & Stratton Business Institute
Albany *A*
Buffalo *A*
City University of New York
Borough of Manhattan
Community College *A*
Brooklyn College *B,M*
Kingsborough Community
College *A*
La Guardia Community
College *A*
Queensborough Community
College *C*
Clarkson University *B,M*
Community College of the Finger
Lakes *A*
Corning Community College *A*
Dominican College of Blauvelt *C,B*
Dutchess Community College *A*
Fulton-Montgomery Community
College *A*
Herkimer County Community
College *A*
Jamestown Community College *A*
Manhattan College *B*
Marymount College *B*
Mohawk Valley Community College
C,A
Rochester Business Institute *A*
Rochester Institute of Technology
A,B,M
St. Bonaventure University *B*
State University of New York
College at Plattsburgh *B*
Westchester Business Institute *A*

North Carolina

Alamance Community College *A*
Anson Community College *C,A*
Asheville Buncombe Technical
Community College *A*
Barber-Scotia College *B*
Beaufort County Community
College *A*
Blue Ridge Community College *A*
Brunswick Community College *A*
Central Carolina Community
College *A*
Chowan College *A*
Coastal Carolina Community
College *C,A*
Durham Technical Community
College *A*
Edgecombe Community College *A*
Forsyth Technical Community
College *C*
Guilford Technical Community
College *A*
Haywood Community College *A*
Isothermal Community College *C,A*
James Sprunt Community
College *A*
Johnston Community College *A*
Mayland Community College *A*
McDowell Technical Community
College *A*
Mitchell Community College *A*
Nash Community College *A*
Piedmont Community College *A*
Richmond Community College *A*
Roanoke-Chowan Community
College *A*
Sampson Community College *A*
Sandhills Community College *C,A*
Vance-Granville Community
College *A*

Wayne Community College *A*

North Dakota

North Dakota State College of
Science *A*

Ohio

Baldwin-Wallace College *C,B*
Bowling Green State University:
Firelands College *A*
Central Ohio Technical College *A*
Central State University *B*
Cincinnati Technical College *A*
Clark State Community College *A*
Columbus State Community
College *A*
Heidelberg College *B*
Kent State University
East Liverpool Regional
Campus *A*
Kent *B*
Tuscarawas Campus *A*
Marietta College *B*
Miami-Jacobs College *A*
North Central Technical College *A*
Northwest Technical College *A*
Ohio Dominican College *B*
Ohio State University: Columbus
Campus *B,M,D*
Owens Technical College: Toledo *A*
Southern Ohio College *A*
Southern State Community
College *A*
Stark Technical College *A*
Terra Technical College *A*
Tiffin University *A*
University of Akron *B*
University of Cincinnati
Cincinnati *B*
Clermont College *A*
Raymond Walters College *A*
University of Toledo *B*
Walsh College *B*

Oklahoma

Oklahoma Christian University of
Science and Arts *B*
Oklahoma State University
Oklahoma City *C,A*
Technical Branch:
Okmulgee *A*
Rogers State College *C,A*
St. Gregory's College *A*
Southeastern Oklahoma State
University *B*
Southwestern Oklahoma State
University *B*
Tulsa Junior College *C,A*
University of Central Oklahoma *B*

Oregon

Central Oregon Community
College *A*
Chemeketa Community College *A*
Linn-Benton Community College *A*
Oregon Institute of Technology *A,B*
Oregon Polytechnic Institute *C,A*
Portland Community College *A*
Rogue Community College *C*
Umpqua Community College *A*

Pennsylvania

Beaver College *B*
Bucknell University *B*
Bucks County Community College
C,A
Butler County Community
College *A*
California University of
Pennsylvania *A,B*
Carnegie Mellon University
B,M,D,W

Clarion University of
    Pennsylvania *B*
Delaware County Community
    College *A*
Duquesne University *B*
Gwynedd-Mercy College *A*
Harcum Junior College *C*
La Salle University *B*
Lehigh County Community
    College *A*
Lock Haven University of
    Pennsylvania *B*
Messiah College *B*
Penn State University Park
    Campus *C*
Philadelphia College of Textiles and
    Science *B*
Reading Area Community
    College *A*
Robert Morris College *B,M*
St. Francis College *B*
St. Joseph's University *C*
Seton Hill College *B*
University of Pittsburgh at
    Bradford *A*

Puerto Rico

Caribbean University *B*
Columbia College *C*
Instituto Tecnico Comercial Junior
    College *C,A*
Pontifical Catholic University of
    Puerto Rico *A*
Puerto Rico Junior College *A*
Universidad Adventista de las
    Antillas *B*
Universidad Metropolitana *B*
University of Puerto Rico:
    Aguadilla *A*

Rhode Island

Community College of Rhode
    Island *C,A*
New England Institute of
    Technology *A*
New England Technical College *B*
Rhode Island College *B*
Salve Regina University *B*

South Carolina

Charleston Southern University *A*
Denmark Technical College *A*
Greenville Technical College *A*
Tri-County Technical College *A*
Trident Technical College *C,A*

South Dakota

Dakota State University *A,B*
Huron University *A*
Kilian Community College *A*
National College *A,B*
Presentation College *A*
Sioux Falls College *B*

Tennessee

Belmont University *B*
Columbia State Community
    College *A*
Dyersburg State Community
    College *A*
East Tennessee State University *B*
Knoxville Business College *A*
Lambuth University *B*
LeMoyne-Owen College *B*
Martin Methodist College *A*
Maryville College *B*
Motlow State Community
    College *A*
Pellissippi State Technical
    Community College *A*
Tennessee State University *B*
Union University *B*

Texas

Alvin Community College *A*
Amarillo College *A*
Brookhaven College *A*
Central Texas College *A*
Eastfield College *A*
El Centro College *A*
El Paso Community College *A*
Houston Community College *C*
Lamar University—Beaumont *B*
Laredo Junior College *A*
LeTourneau University *B*
Lon Morris College *A*
Midland College *A*
Midwestern State University *A*
Panola College *A*
St. Edward's University *B*
St. Philip's College *A*
San Antonio College *A*
Temple Junior College *C,A*
Texas Christian University *M*
Texas Southmost College *A*
Texas State Technical College
    Amarillo *A*
    Harlingen *A*
    Sweetwater *C,A*
Victoria College *A*
Weatherford College *C,A*
Wiley College *A*

Utah

LDS Business College *A*
Phillips Junior College: Salt Lake
    City Campus *C,A*
Weber State University *B*

Vermont

Castleton State College *A*
Champlain College *A*
Lyndon State College *A,B*
Marlboro College *B*
St. Michael's College *B*
Trinity College of Vermont *C,A*

Virginia

Averett College *B*
Bluefield College *B*
Dabney S. Lancaster Community
    College *A*
Northern Virginia Community
    College *A*
Patrick Henry Community
    College *A*
Virginia Wesleyan College *B*

Washington

Big Bend Community College *A*
Clark College *C,A*
Everett Community College *A*
ITT Technical Institute: Seattle *C*
Lower Columbia College *A*
North Seattle Community
    College *C*
Olympic College *C,A*
Pacific Lutheran University *B,M*
Skagit Valley College *A*
Walla Walla Community College
    C,A
Western Washington University *B*

West Virginia

Bluefield State College *A,B*
College of West Virginia *A,B*
Marshall University *B*
Potomac State College of West
    Virginia University *A*
Shepherd College *B*
West Virginia State College *A*

Wisconsin

Madison Area Technical College *A*
Moraine Park Technical College *A*

Northland College *B*
Stratton College *C,A*
University of Wisconsin
    Oshkosh *A*
    Whitewater *B*

Wyoming

Central Wyoming College *A*
Northwest College *A*
Western Wyoming Community
    College *C,A*

Computer servicing technology

Alabama

Bessemer State Technical College *C*
Gadsden State Community
    College *A*
Walker State Technical College *A*

Arizona

Eastern Arizona College *C*

Arkansas

Phillips County Community
    College *C*
Southern Arkansas University:
    Technical Branch *A*
Westark Community College *A*

California

Chabot College *A*
Coastline Community College *A*
Coleman College *A,B*
Foothill College *A*
Los Angeles City College *A*
Los Angeles Trade and Technical
    College *C,A*
Mount San Antonio College *C,A*
Phillips Junior College: Fresno
    Campus *C,A*
Southwestern College *A*

Colorado

Trinidad State Junior College *A*

Florida

Brevard Community College *A*
Daytona Beach Community College
    C,A
Florida Community College at
    Jacksonville *A*
New England Institute of
    Technology *A*
Pensacola Junior College *A*
Seminole Community College *C*

Georgia

Clayton State College *A*

Idaho

Lewis Clark State College *A*
Ricks College *A*

Illinois

Belleville Area College *C*
Black Hawk College *A*
City Colleges of Chicago: Richard J.
    Daley College *A*
Illinois Central College *C*
ITT Technical Institute: Hoffman
    Estates *A*
Lewis and Clark Community
    College *A*
Southern Illinois University at
    Carbondale *A*

Indiana

Indiana Institute of Technology *C,A*
Indiana State University *B,M*
Vincennes University *A*

Iowa

Des Moines Area Community
    College *A*
Hawkeye Institute of Technology *A*
Indian Hills Community College *A*
National Education Center:
    National Institute of Technology
    Campus *A*

Kansas

Hutchinson Community College *A*
Neosho County Community College
    C,A

Kentucky

Eastern Kentucky University *A*
Louisville Technical Institute *A*
Southeast Community College *A*

Louisiana

Northwestern State University *A*

Maine

Southern Maine Technical
    College *A*

Maryland

Catonsville Community College *A*
Chesapeake College *A*
Howard Community College *A*
Montgomery College: Rockville
    Campus *A*

Massachusetts

Franklin Institute of Boston *A*
Massachusetts Bay Community
    College *A*
Northern Essex Community
    College *A*
Quinsigamond Community
    College *A*

Michigan

Baker College: Flint *A*
Grand Rapids Community
    College *A*
Lansing Community College *A*
Northern Michigan University *A*
Schoolcraft College *A*

Minnesota

National Education Center: Brown
    Institute Campus *A*
Northwestern Electronics
    Institute *A*
St. Paul Technical College *C*

Mississippi

Mississippi Gulf Coast Community
    College: Perkinston *A*

Missouri

St. Louis Community College at
    Florissant Valley *A*

Nebraska

Southeast Community College:
    Milford Campus *A*
Western Nebraska Community
    College: Sidney Campus *A*

New Hampshire

New Hampshire Technical College
    Nashua *A*
    Stratham *A*

New Jersey

Camden County College *A*

New Mexico

Dona Ana Branch Community
College of New Mexico State
University *C,A*

New York

City University of New York: New
York City Technical College *A*
Community College of the Finger
Lakes *A*
Erie Community College
North Campus *A*
South Campus *A*
Genesee Community College *A*
Jamestown Community College *A*
Mohawk Valley Community
College *A*
Onondaga Community College *A*
State University of New York
College of Agriculture and
Technology at Morrisville *A*

North Carolina

Alamance Community College *A*
Bladen Community College *C*
Cape Fear Community College *A*
College of the Albemarle *C*
Davidson County Community
College *A*
Durham Technical Community
College *C*
Forsyth Technical Community
College *A*
Southwestern Community
College *A*

North Dakota

North Dakota State College of
Science *A*

Ohio

Cincinnati Technical College *A*
Columbus State Community
College *A*
Hocking Technical College *A*
University of Rio Grande *A*

Oregon

Central Oregon Community College
C,A
Chemeketa Community College *A*
Portland Community College *A*

Pennsylvania

Delaware County Community
College *A*
Lehigh County Community
College *C*
Pennsylvania College of
Technology *A*
Pennsylvania Institute of
Technology *A*

South Carolina

Greenville Technical College *A*

South Dakota

Mitchell Vocational Technical
Institute *C,A*
Western Dakota Vocational
Technical Institute *C,A*

Tennessee

Chattanooga State Technical
Community College *A*
Memphis State University *B*
Nashville State Technical
Institute *A*

Pellissippi State Technical
Community College *A*

Texas

Central Texas College *A*
El Paso Community College *C,A*
St. Philip's College *A*
South Plains College *C,A*
Texas State Technical College
Amarillo *A*
Harlingen *A*
Sweetwater *C,A*
Waco *A*

Utah

Weber State University *A*

Vermont

Vermont Technical College *A*

Virginia

Northern Virginia Community
College *C*

Washington

Edmonds Community College *C,A*
North Seattle Community
College *A*
Skagit Valley College *A*
Spokane Community College *A*
Tacoma Community College *C*
Walla Walla College *B*
Yakima Valley Community
College *A*

Wisconsin

Chippewa Valley Technical
College *C*
Mid-State Technical College *A*
Moraine Park Technical College *A*

Wyoming

Casper College *A*

Computer technology

Alabama

Brewer State Junior College *A*

Arizona

Glendale Community College *A*

Arkansas

University of Arkansas at Little
Rock *B*

California

American Armenian International
College *B*
Barstow College *C*
Cerritos Community College *C,A*
Chabot College *A*
Cogswell Polytechnical College *B*
Coleman College *A,B*
El Camino College *C,A*
Fresno City College *C,A*
Heald Institute of Technology *C,A*
Irvine Valley College *C,A*
Los Angeles City College *C,A*
Los Angeles Pierce College *C,A*
Phillips Junior College: Condie
Campus *A*
San Jose State University *B*
Santa Barbara City College *C,A*
Southwestern College *A*
University of La Verne *B*

Colorado

Pikes Peak Community College *A*
Red Rocks Community College *C,A*
United States Air Force
Academy *B*

Connecticut

Greater New Haven State Technical
College *A*
Hartford State Technical College *A*
Norwalk State Technical College *A*
Thames Valley State Technical
College *A*
University of Hartford *A*
Waterbury State Technical
College *A*

Delaware

Delaware State College *B*
Delaware Technical and
Community College: Terry
Campus *A*

District of Columbia

Gallaudet University *B*
University of the District of
Columbia *A*

Florida

Daytona Beach Community
College *A*
Florida Community College at
Jacksonville *A*
Hillsborough Community College *A*
Keiser College of Technology *A*
Manatee Community College *A*
Seminole Community College *A*
University of Central Florida *B*
University of Florida *B,M,D*

Georgia

Savannah State College *A*
Southern College of Technology *B*

Hawaii

Hawaii Pacific University *A,B*

Idaho

Lewis Clark State College *A*
North Idaho College *A*
Ricks College *A*

Illinois

Belleville Area College *C,A*
Black Hawk College *A*
Illinois Central College *C*
Illinois Valley Community
College *A*
Moraine Valley Community
College *C*
Morrison Institute of Technology *A*
Richland Community College *A*
Triton College *C,A*
William Rainey Harper College *A*

Indiana

Indiana Institute of Technology *C*
Indiana State University *B,M*
Indiana University at Kokomo *A*
Indiana University—Purdue
University
Fort Wayne *C*
Indianapolis *A,B*
Purdue University
Calumet *A,B*
North Central Campus *A*
West Lafayette *A,B*
Tri-State University *A*
Vincennes University *A*

Iowa

Des Moines Area Community
College *A*
Indian Hills Community College *A*
National Education Center:
National Institute of Technology
Campus *A*
Northeast Iowa Community
College *A*

Kansas

Barton County Community
College *A*
Hutchinson Community College *A*
Johnson County Community
College *C,A*
Kansas City Kansas Community
College *A*
Kansas State University *B*

Kentucky

Eastern Kentucky University *A,B*
Murray State University *B*

Louisiana

Grantham College of Engineering
A,B
Northwestern State University *A*

Maryland

Capitol College *A,B*
Chesapeake College *C,A*
Essex Community College *A*
Frederick Community College *A*
Howard Community College *A*

Massachusetts

Bristol Community College *C*
Franklin Institute of Boston *C,A*
Middlesex Community College *A*
Northeastern University *A,B*
Northern Essex Community
College *A*
Wentworth Institute of Technology
A,B

Michigan

Central Michigan University *B*
Charles Stewart Mott Community
College *A*
Eastern Michigan University *B*
Grand Rapids Community
College *A*
Lake Superior State University *A*
Lansing Community College *A*
Marygrove College *A*
Northern Michigan University *A*

Minnesota

Mesabi Community College:
Arrowhead Region *A*
National Education Center: Brown
Institute Campus *A*
Normandale Community College *A*
Northwestern Electronics
Institute *A*
St. Paul Technical College *C*
Willmar Community College *A*

Mississippi

Copiah-Lincoln Community
College *A*
Jackson State University *B*
Mississippi Delta Community
College *A*
University of Southern
Mississippi *B*

Missouri

Ranken Technical College *A*
Washington University *B*

Montana

Northern Montana College *A*

Nevada

Truckee Meadows Community
College *C,A*

New Hampshire

New Hampshire Technical College:
Nashua *A*

New Jersey

New Jersey Institute of
Technology *B*
Ocean County College *C,A*
Thomas Edison State College *A,B*

New Mexico

New Mexico Highlands University
A,B
Northern New Mexico Community
College *A*

New York

Adirondack Community College
C,A
Bramson ORT Technical
Institute *A*
City University of New York
College of Staten Island *A*
La Guardia Community
College *A*
New York City Technical
College *A*
Queensborough Community
College *C,A*
Erie Community College
North Campus *A*
South Campus *A*
Fulton-Montgomery Community
College *A*
Jamestown Community College *A*
Mohawk Valley Community
College *A*
Monroe Community College *A*
Onondaga Community College *A*
Rochester Institute of Technology
A,B
State University of New York
Institute of Technology at Utica/
Rome *B*
University of the State of New
York: Regents College *A,B*

North Carolina

Brevard College *A*
Cape Fear Community College *A*
Catawba Valley Community
College *A*
Central Piedmont Community
College *A*
College of the Albemarle *A*
Davidson County Community
College *A*
Forsyth Technical Community
College *A*
Sandhills Community College *C,A*
Southwestern Community
College *A*
Stanly Community College *A*
Surry Community College *A*
Wake Technical Community
College *A*
Western Piedmont Community
College *A*

Ohio

Air Force Institute of
Technology *M*
Cincinnati Technical College *A*
Columbus State Community
College *A*

Edison State Community College *A*
Kent State University: Tuscarawas
Campus *C*
Miami University: Hamilton
Campus *A*
Owens Technical College
Findlay Campus *A*
Toledo *C,A*
Southern State Community
College *A*
Youngstown State University *A,B*

Oklahoma

Oklahoma State University *B*
Redlands Community College *A*
Rogers State College *A*

Oregon

Central Oregon Community
College *A*
Chemeketa Community College *A*
Portland Community College *C,A*

Pennsylvania

California University of
Pennsylvania *B*
CHI Institute *C,A*
Community College of
Philadelphia *A*
Electronic Institutes: Pittsburgh *A*
Penn State University Park
Campus *A*
Pennsylvania Institute of
Technology *A*
Spring Garden College *A,B*

Rhode Island

Community College of Rhode
Island *A*

South Carolina

Aiken Technical College *A*
Horry-Georgetown Technical
College *A*
Midlands Technical College *C*

South Dakota

Mitchell Vocational Technical
Institute *C,A*
National College *A*

Tennessee

Middle Tennessee State
University *B*
Nashville State Technical
Institute *A*
Northeast State Technical
Community College *A*
Pellissippi State Technical
Community College *A*
State Technical Institute at
Memphis *A*

Texas

Austin Community College *A*
Brazosport College *C,A*
Paul Quinn College *B*
Prairie View A&M University *B*
Texas Southmost College *A*
Texas State Technical College:
Harlingen *A*
University of Houston *B*

Utah

Brigham Young University *M,D*
Weber State University *A,B*

Vermont

Vermont Technical College *A*

Washington

Cogswell College North *A,B*
Eastern Washington University *B*
Edmonds Community College *A*
North Seattle Community
College *A*
Skagit Valley College *C,A*

West Virginia

Marshall University *A*
West Virginia Institute of
Technology *A*

Wisconsin

Mid-State Technical College *A*

Conservation and regulation

Arizona

Prescott College *B*

California

Moorpark College *A*
San Joaquin Delta College *A*
University of California: Berkeley *B*
University of San Francisco *B,M*

Colorado

University of Colorado at
Boulder *B*

Florida

University of Florida *M,D*

Illinois

Southern Illinois University at
Carbondale *B,M*

Indiana

Ball State University *B*

Iowa

Iowa Lakes Community College *A*

Kansas

Kansas State University *B*

Kentucky

Eastern Kentucky University *B*

Maine

Unity College *B*

Maryland

Frostburg State University *M*

Massachusetts

Berkshire Community College *A*

Michigan

Lake Superior State University *B*
Northern Michigan University *B*

Minnesota

Inver Hills Community College *A*
Itasca Community College:
Arrowhead Region *A*
University of Minnesota: Twin
Cities *M,D*
Vermilion Community College *A*
Willmar Community College *A*
Winona State University *A*

Missouri

Central Missouri State University *B*

Montana

University of Montana *B,M*

Nebraska

Nebraska College of Technical
Agriculture *A*

New Hampshire

University of New Hampshire *B*

New York

Community College of the Finger
Lakes *C,A*
Fulton-Montgomery Community
College *A*
Herkimer County Community
College *A*
State University of New York
College of Agriculture and
Technology at Morrisville *A*
College of Environmental
Science and Forestry *B,M,D*

North Carolina

North Carolina State University *B*

Ohio

Kent State University *B*
Ohio State University
Agricultural Technical
Institute *A*
Columbus Campus *B*

Oklahoma

Northwestern Oklahoma State
University *B*

Pennsylvania

California University of
Pennsylvania *B*

Tennessee

University of Tennessee: Martin *B*

Vermont

Sterling College *A*

Washington

University of Washington *B*

Wisconsin

Carthage College *B*
University of Wisconsin: River
Falls *B*

Canada

McGill University *B,M,D*

Construction

Alabama

Bessemer State Technical College *A*
Community College of the Air
Force *A*
Jefferson State Community
College *A*

Alaska

University of Alaska Southeast *A*

Arizona

Arizona State University *B*
Cochise College *C*
Northland Pioneer College *C,A*
Pima Community College *C,A*
Scottsdale Community College *A*
Yavapai College *C,A*

Arkansas

John Brown University *A,B*
Phillips County Community
College *C*
University of Arkansas at Little
Rock *A,B*

California

Allan Hancock College *C*
California Polytechnic State
University: San Luis Obispo *B*
Chabot College *A*
City College of San Francisco *A*
College of the Desert *A*
College of the Redwoods *C,A*
College of the Sequoias *C,A*
Cosumnes River College *C,A*
El Camino College *C,A*
Fresno City College *C,A*
Hartnell College *C,A*
Laney College *C,A*
Lassen College *C,A*
Los Angeles Pierce College *C,A*
Orange Coast College *C,A*
Palomar College *C,A*
Pasadena City College *C,A*
Porterville College *C*
Saddleback College *A*
San Diego Mesa College *A*
San Francisco State University *C*
San Joaquin Delta College *C,A*
San Jose City College *A*
Santa Monica College *A*
Santa Rosa Junior College *C,A*
Sierra College *A*
Southwestern College *C,A*
Victor Valley College *C*
West Valley College *C,A*

Colorado

Arapahoe Community College *C*
Colorado State University *B*
Pikes Peak Community College *A*

Connecticut

Norwalk State Technical College
C,A

Delaware

Delaware Technical and
Community College: Terry
Campus *A*

District of Columbia

University of the District of
Columbia *B*

Florida

Brevard Community College *C*
Daytona Beach Community
College *A*
Florida Community College at
Jacksonville *A*
Gulf Coast Community College *C,A*
Miami-Dade Community College *A*
Okaloosa-Walton Community
College *A*
Palm Beach Community College *A*
Pasco-Hernando Community
College *A*
Pensacola Junior College *A*
St. Petersburg Junior College *A*
Santa Fe Community College *A*
Seminole Community College *A*
South Florida Community
College *A*
University of Florida *B,M*
University of North Florida *B*

Georgia

Atlanta Metropolitan College *A*
Darton College *A*
DeKalb College *A*
Gainesville College *A*
Georgia Southern University *B*
Southern College of Technology *B*

Idaho

Boise State University *B*
Ricks College *A*

Illinois

Belleville Area College *C,A*
Bradley University *B*
City Colleges of Chicago: Chicago
City-Wide College *C,A*
College of Lake County *C,A*
Illinois Eastern Community
Colleges
Lincoln Trail College *C,A*
Olney Central College *A*
Joliet Junior College *C,A*
Lewis and Clark Community
College *A*
Rock Valley College *A*
Southern Illinois University
Carbondale *A*
Edwardsville *B*
State Community College *C*
Triton College *C,A*

Indiana

Indiana State University *B*
Indiana University—Purdue
University at Indianapolis *C*
Indiana Vocational Technical
College
Eastcentral *C,A*
Kokomo *C,A*
Northeast *C,A*
Southcentral *C,A*
Whitewater *C,A*
Purdue University: North Central
Campus *A*
Vincennes University *A*

Iowa

Kirkwood Community College *A*
Southeastern Community College:
North Campus *A*

Kansas

Allen County Community
College *A*
Central College *A*
Hutchinson Community College
C,A
Neosho County Community College
C,A
Pittsburg State University *B*

Kentucky

Eastern Kentucky University *B*
Northern Kentucky University *A*

Louisiana

Grambling State University *A,B*
Louisiana State University and
Agricultural and Mechanical
College *B*

Maine

Central Maine Technical College
C,A
Eastern Maine Technical College *A*
Southern Maine Technical
College *A*

Maryland

Catonsville Community College *C,A*
Garrett Community College *C*
Howard Community College *C*
Montgomery College: Rockville
Campus *A*
University of Maryland: Eastern
Shore *B*

Massachusetts

Cape Cod Community College *A*
Fitchburg State College *B*
Wentworth Institute of Technology
C,A,B

Michigan

Delta College *C,A*
Ferris State University *A*
Lansing Community College *C,A*
Macomb Community College *C,A*
Michigan State University *M*
Northern Michigan University *A,B*

Mississippi

Mississippi Delta Community
College *A*
Northeast Mississippi Community
College *C*

Missouri

Central Missouri State University
A,B
East Central College *C,A*
Mineral Area College *C,A*
Northwest Missouri State
University *C*

Montana

Northern Montana College *A,B*

Nebraska

Central Community College *C,A*
Chadron State College *B*
Metropolitan Community College
C,A
Nebraska Indian Community
College *C*
Peru State College *B*
Southeast Community College:
Milford Campus *A*

Nevada

Truckee Meadows Community
College *A*

New Hampshire

New Hampshire Technical College:
Manchester *C,A*

New Jersey

Fairleigh Dickinson University *B*
Kean College of New Jersey *B*
Ocean County College *C,A*
Thomas Edison State College *A,B*

New Mexico

Clovis Community College *C,A*
New Mexico State University *C,A*
Western New Mexico University
C,A

New York

City University of New York: New
York City Technical College *A*
Erie Community College: South
Campus *A*
Fulton-Montgomery Community
College *A*
Herkimer County Community
College *A*
Hudson Valley Community
College *A*
Institute of Design and
Construction *A*
Onondaga Community College *A*
Orange County Community
College *C*
State University of New York
College of Agriculture and
Technology at Morrisville *A*
College of Environmental
Science and Forestry *B,M,D*
College of Technology at
Alfred *A*
College of Technology at
Canton *C*
College of Technology at
Delhi *A*
Suffolk County Community
College *A*
Tompkins-Cortland Community
College *C*

North Carolina

Anson Community College *A*
Cape Fear Community College *C*
Piedmont Community College *C*
Robeson Community College *C*
Rockingham Community College *C*
Surry Community College *C*
Western Piedmont Community
College *C*
Wilkes Community College *C,A*

North Dakota

North Dakota State University *B*

Ohio

Columbus State Community
College *A*
Northwest Technical College *A*
Ohio State University Agricultural
Technical Institute *A*
University of Cincinnati *B*
University of Toledo *C*

Oklahoma

East Central University *B*
Northern Oklahoma College *C,A*
Oklahoma State University
Oklahoma City *A*
Technical Branch:
Okmulgee *A*

Oregon

Lane Community College *A*
Portland Community College *A*

Pennsylvania

Community College of
Philadelphia *A*
Harrisburg Area Community
College *C,A*
Johnson Technical Institute *A*
Northampton County Area
Community College *A*
Penn State University Park
Campus *C*
Pennsylvania College of
Technology *A*
Spring Garden College *C,A,B*
Williamson Free School of
Mechanical Trades *A*

Rhode Island

Roger Williams College *B*

South Carolina

Greenville Technical College *A*
Technical College of the
Lowcountry *A*

South Dakota

Mitchell Vocational Technical
Institute *C,A*

Tennessee
Austin Peay State University A
Chattanooga State Technical
    Community College A
State Technical Institute at
    Memphis A

Texas
Abilene Christian University A
Brazosport College C,A
East Texas State University B
El Paso Community College A
Houston Community College C
Howard College C
Laredo Junior College A
Odessa College C,A
St. Philip's College A
Tarrant County Junior College A
Texas Southmost College A
Texas State Technical College:
    Harlingen C,A
Texas Tech University B

Utah
Brigham Young University B
Utah Valley Community College
    C,A

Vermont
Vermont Technical College C

Virginia
John Tyler Community College C
Norfolk State University A
Northern Virginia Community
    College C
Virginia Polytechnic Institute and
    State University B

Washington
Eastern Washington University B
Edmonds Community College C,A
Northwest Indian College C
Peninsula College C
University of Washington B
Walla Walla College A

West Virginia
West Virginia State College B

Wisconsin
University of Wisconsin
    Platteville B
    Stout B

Wyoming
Casper College C,A
Laramie County Community
    College C

**American Samoa, Caroline
Islands, Guam, Marianas,
Virgin Islands**
Micronesian Occupational College
    C,A
Northern Marianas College C,A

Contract management and procurement/purchasing

Alabama
Athens State College B
Community College of the Air
    Force B
University of Alabama in
    Huntsville B

Arizona
Arizona State University B

California
Coastline Community College A
De Anza College C,A
Golden Gate University C,M
San Diego City College C,A
West Coast University M

Colorado
Colorado Technical College B

District of Columbia
American University M
George Washington University M
Southeastern University B,M

Florida
Florida Institute of Technology B,M
Florida State University B
Pensacola Junior College A

Iowa
St. Ambrose University B

Massachusetts
Northeastern University C,A
Northern Essex Community College
    C,A

Michigan
Michigan State University B,M,D
Western Michigan University B

Missouri
Avila College B
Rockhurst College C,B
Webster University M

Nebraska
Metropolitan Community College A

New Jersey
Bloomfield College B
Thomas Edison State College A,B

New York
Erie Community College: North
    Campus A

Ohio
Air Force Institute of
    Technology M
Columbus State Community
    College A
Miami University: Oxford
    Campus B
Sinclair Community College C,A

Oklahoma
Rose State College C,A

Pennsylvania
Northampton County Area
    Community College C,A
St. Joseph's University C,A,B

South Carolina
Greenville Technical College A

Texas
University of Dallas M

Virginia
Northern Virginia Community
    College C,A
Tidewater Community College A

Washington
Columbia Basin College A
Shoreline Community College C,A

Counseling psychology

Alabama
Alabama Agricultural and
    Mechanical University B,M
Auburn University D
University of North Alabama M

Alaska
Alaska Pacific University M
University of Alaska Anchorage M

Arizona
Northern Arizona University M,D
Prescott College B
University of Phoenix M

Arkansas
University of Central Arkansas B,M

California
Biola University M
California Baptist College M
California Institute of Integral
    Studies M,D
California State University
    Hayward M
    Los Angeles M
    San Bernardino M
    Stanislaus M
Chapman University M
Christian Heritage College B
College of Notre Dame M
Dominican College of San
    Rafael M
Holy Names College M
Humboldt State University M
John F. Kennedy University M
Loyola Marymount University M
Mount St. Mary's College M
National University M
New College of California M
Pacific Oaks College M
San Jose Christian College C
San Jose State University B,M
Santa Clara University M
Southern California College B
United States International
    University M
University of California: Santa
    Barbara M,D
University of La Verne M
University of the Pacific M
University of San Francisco M,D

Colorado
Adams State College M
Colorado State University M,D
Mesa State College B
Naropa Institute M
University of Denver D
University of Northern Colorado D

Connecticut
Southern Connecticut State
    University M
University of Bridgeport M

District of Columbia
Catholic University of America
    M,D
Howard University M,D

Florida
Florida State University D
New College of the University of
    South Florida B
Nova University M
St. Thomas University M
Stetson University M
University of Florida D
University of Miami M,D
University of North Florida M
University of West Florida M
Warner Southern College B

Georgia
Georgia State University D
Oxford College of Emory
    University A
Toccoa Falls College B
University of Georgia D
Valdosta State College M

Hawaii
Chaminade University of
    Honolulu M
Hawaii Pacific University B

Idaho
Albertson College M

Illinois
Bradley University M
Chicago State University M
Illinois Benedictine College M
Illinois State University M
Loyola University of Chicago M,D
Northwestern University M,D
Olivet Nazarene University B
Sangamon State University M
Southern Illinois University at
    Carbondale M,D
Trinity Christian College B
University of Illinois at Urbana-
    Champaign B,M,D

Indiana
Ball State University M,D
Grace College B
Indiana State University M,D
Martin University B
Purdue University M,D
St. Francis College M
University of Notre Dame M,D
Valparaiso University M

Iowa
Loras College M
University of Iowa D

Kansas
Kansas Wesleyan University B
Pittsburg State University M
University of Kansas D

Kentucky
Murray State University M
Spalding University M,D

Louisiana
McNeese State University M
Nicholls State University M,W
Southern University and
    Agricultural and Mechanical
    College B,M

Maine
University of Maine M,D

Maryland
Bowie State University M
Columbia Union College B
Coppin State College B
Frostburg State University M
Loyola College in Maryland M
Sojourner-Douglass College B
University of Baltimore M

Massachusetts
Anna Maria College for Men and
    Women M

Assumption College *M*
Boston College *D*
Boston University *D*
Eastern Nazarene College *M*
Emmanuel College *B*
Fitchburg State College *M*
Framingham State College *M*
Lesley College *B,M*
Northeastern University *M,D*
Springfield College *B,M*
Tufts University *M*
Westfield State College *M*

Michigan

Michigan Christian College *B*
Western Michigan University *M,D*
William Tyndale College *B*

Minnesota

Crown College *A*
St. Cloud State University *M*
St. Mary's College of Minnesota *M*
University of Minnesota
    Duluth *M*
    Twin Cities *M,D*
University of St. Thomas *M,D*
Willmar Community College *A*

Mississippi

University of Southern Mississippi *M,D*

Missouri

Avila College *M*
Central Missouri State
    University *M*
Lindenwood College *M*
Northwest Missouri State
    University *M*
Southeast Missouri State
    University *M*
Stephens College *B*
University of Missouri
    Columbia *M,D*
    Kansas City *M,D*
Webster University *M*

Montana

College of Great Falls *M*
University of Montana *M*

Nebraska

Chadron State College *B,M*
Grace College of the Bible *B*
Nebraska Indian Community
    College *A*
University of Nebraska
    Lincoln *M,D*
    Omaha *M*

New Hampshire

Antioch New England Graduate
    School *M*
Franklin Pierce College *B*
Notre Dame College *M*
Rivier College *M*

New Jersey

Kean College of New Jersey *M*
Rutgers—The State University of
    New Jersey *M,D*
Seton Hall University *M,D*
Upsala College *M*

New Mexico

College of Santa Fe *B*
Eastern New Mexico University *M*
New Mexico State University *M,D*
University of New Mexico *D*
Western New Mexico University *M*

New York

Alfred University *M*
Fordham University *M,D*
Manhattan College *M*
Marist College *M*
Molloy College *B*
New York Institute of
    Technology *M*
New York University *D*
State University of New York
    Albany *D*
    Buffalo *D*
    Oswego *M*

North Carolina

Appalachian State University *B,M*
Campbell University *B*
Gardner-Webb College *M*
John Wesley College *B*
North Carolina State University
    M,D
University of North Carolina at
    Chapel Hill *D*

North Dakota

University of North Dakota *D*

Ohio

Cleveland State University *M*
Franciscan University of
    Steubenville *M*
Heidelberg College *M*
John Carroll University *M*
Kent State University *D*
Ohio State University: Columbus
    Campus *M,D*
Ohio University *M,D*
Union Institute *D*
University of Akron *M,D*
Walsh College *B,M*
Wright State University *M*

Oklahoma

East Central University *M*
Northeastern State University *B,M*
Oklahoma City University *M*
Southeastern Oklahoma State
    University *M*
University of Central Oklahoma *M*
University of Oklahoma *D*

Oregon

Lewis and Clark College *M*
University of Portland *M*

Pennsylvania

Beaver College *M*
Bucknell University *B,M*
California University of
    Pennsylvania *M*
Chestnut Hill College *M*
Duquesne University *M*
Gannon University *M*
Geneva College *B*
Hahnemann University School of
    Health Sciences and
    Humanities *M*
Immaculata College *B,M*
Juniata College *B*
Kutztown University of
    Pennsylvania *M*
La Salle University *B,M*
Lehigh University *M,D*
Mansfield University of
    Pennsylvania *B*
Marywood College *M*
Moravian College *B*
Penn State University Park
    Campus *D*
Slippery Rock University of
    Pennsylvania *M*
Temple University *M,D*

West Chester University of
    Pennsylvania *M*
Widener University *C*

Puerto Rico

Inter American University of Puerto
    Rico: San German Campus *M*

South Carolina

Bob Jones University *B,M*
Coker College *B*
Limestone College *B*

Tennessee

Austin Peay State University *B*
East Tennessee State University *M*
Memphis State University *D*
Middle Tennessee State
    University *M*
University of Tennessee: Knoxville
    M,D

Texas

Abilene Christian University *M*
Amber University *M*
Angelo State University *M*
Dallas Baptist University *B*
East Texas State University at
    Texarkana *M*
Hardin-Simmons University *M*
Our Lady of the Lake University of
    San Antonio *M,D*
St. Mary's University *M*
Southern Methodist University *M*
Texas A&I University *M*
Texas A&M University *D*
Texas Tech University *M,D*
Texas Wesleyan University *B*
Texas Woman's University *M,D*
University of Central Texas *M*
University of North Texas *M,D*
University of Texas at Tyler *M*

Utah

University of Utah *M,D*

Virginia

Averett College *B*
Marymount University *B,M*
Radford University *M*
Virginia Commonwealth University
    M,D
Virginia Wesleyan College *B*

Washington

Central Washington University *M*
Eastern Washington University *M*
Evergreen State College *B*
Gonzaga University *M*
St. Martin's College *M*
Shoreline Community College *A*
Western Washington University *M*

West Virginia

Marshall University *M*
West Virginia University *D*

Wisconsin

Carroll College *B*
University of Wisconsin
    Madison *D*
    Milwaukee *M*
    Stout *M*
    Whitewater *M*

Court reporting

Alabama

Gadsden State Community
    College *A*
James H. Faulkner State
    Community College *A*

California

Cerritos Community College *C,A*
Chabot College *A*
City College of San Francisco *C,A*
Coastline Community College *C,A*
College of the Redwoods *C*
Humphreys College *C,A*
Kelsey-Jenney College *C,A*
Phillips Junior College: Condie
    Campus *C*
San Diego City College *C,A*
West Valley College *A*

Florida

Broward Community College *A*
Daytona Beach Community
    College *A*
Jones College *A,B*
Miami-Dade Community College *A*
Orlando College *A*
Pensacola Junior College *A*
Tallahassee Community College *A*

Illinois

Elgin Community College *C,A*
Illinois Central College *C,A*
Illinois Eastern Community
    Colleges: Wabash Valley College
    C,A
John A. Logan College *C*
Lewis and Clark Community
    College *A*
MacCormac Junior College *A*
Midstate College *C,A*
Southern Illinois University at
    Carbondale *A*
Triton College *A*

Iowa

American Institute of Business *A*
American Institute of Commerce *A*
Teikyo Westmar University *B*

Kansas

Brown Mackie College *A*
Washburn University of Topeka *A*

Maine

Husson College *A,B*

Maryland

Hagerstown Business College *A*
Villa Julie College *A*

Massachusetts

Massachusetts Bay Community
    College *A*
Massasoit Community College *A*
Springfield Technical Community
    College *A*

Michigan

Central Michigan University *B*
Ferris State University *A*
Great Lakes Junior College of
    Business *A*
Lansing Community College *A*
Macomb Community College *C*
Oakland Community College *C,A*

Minnesota

University of Minnesota:
Crookston *A*

Mississippi

Mississippi Gulf Coast Community
College
Jefferson Davis Campus *A*
Perkinston *C,A*
University of Mississippi *B*

Missouri

St. Louis Community College at
Meramec *A*
State Fair Community College *C,A*

Nebraska

Lincoln School of Commerce *A*

New Hampshire

Hesser College *A*

New Mexico

Albuquerque Technical-Vocational
Institute *A*
Parks College *A*

New York

Bryant & Stratton Business
Institute: Buffalo *A*
Central City Business Institute *A*
Herkimer County Community
College *A*
Mater Dei College *A*
State University of New York
College of Technology at
Alfred *A*
Stenotype Academy *A*

Ohio

Clark State Community College *A*
Cuyahoga Community College
Metropolitan Campus *A*
Western Campus *A*
Stark Technical College *A*
University of Cincinnati: Access
Colleges *A*
Youngstown State University *A*

Oklahoma

Rogers State College *A*
Rose State College *A*

Pennsylvania

Central Pennsylvania Business
School *A*
Manor Junior College *C,A*
Peirce Junior College *A*

Rhode Island

Johnson & Wales University *A,B*

South Carolina

Midlands Technical College *A*

Tennessee

Bristol University *A*
Chattanooga State Technical
Community College *A*
Middle Tennessee State
University *A*

Texas

Alvin Community College *C,A*
Amarillo College *A*
Del Mar College *A*
El Paso Community College *A*
Houston Community College *A*
San Antonio College *C*

Vermont

Champlain College *A*

Washington

Edmonds Community College *C,A*
Green River Community College *A*

Wisconsin

Concordia University Wisconsin
A,B
Wisconsin Indianhead Technical
College *A*

Crafts

Arizona

Arizona State University *B,M*
Prescott College *B*

California

California State University
Fullerton *B,M*
Long Beach *M*
Los Angeles *M*
El Camino College *A*
Palomar College *A*
Pasadena City College *A*
San Joaquin Delta College *A*
San Jose State University *B*

Colorado

Adams State College *B*

Connecticut

University of Bridgeport *C*

Florida

Lynn University *B*

Illinois

Chicago State University *B*
Kishwaukee College *A*
University of Illinois at Urbana-
Champaign *B*

Indiana

Indiana University—Purdue
University at Indianapolis *B*
Purdue University *B*

Iowa

Iowa State University *B*

Maryland

Howard Community College *A*

Massachusetts

Bridgewater State College *B*
Endicott College *A*
Massachusetts College of Art *B*
Quinsigamond Community College
C,A

Michigan

Center for Creative Studies: College
of Art and Design *B*
Henry Ford Community College *A*
Northern Michigan University *A*

Missouri

Kansas City Art Institute *B*

Nebraska

University of Nebraska—Kearney *B*

New Jersey

Jersey City State College *B*
Kean College of New Jersey *B*

New Mexico

Institute of American Indian
Arts *A*

New York

Fulton-Montgomery Community
College *A*
Mohawk Valley Community
College *A*
Parsons School of Design *A,B*
Rochester Institute of Technology
A,B
State University of New York
College at Buffalo *B*

North Carolina

Brevard College *A*

Ohio

Bowling Green State University *B*
Kent State University *B,M*
Ohio State University: Columbus
Campus *B,M*
University of Akron *B*

Oregon

Central Oregon Community
College *A*

Pennsylvania

Carnegie Mellon University *B,M*
Kutztown University of
Pennsylvania *B*

Tennessee

East Tennessee State University *B*
Memphis College of Art *B*
Tennessee Technological
University *B*

Texas

Lamar University—Beaumont *M*
Lon Morris College *A*
Sam Houston State University *M*
University of North Texas *B,M*
Western Texas College *A*

Vermont

Goddard College *B*

Virginia

Piedmont Virginia Community
College *C*
Southwest Virginia Community
College *C*
Virginia Commonwealth University
B,M

Washington

Northwest Indian College *C*
Olympic College *A*

West Virginia

Marshall University *B*

Creative writing

Alabama

Spring Hill College *B*
Troy State University *B*
University of Alabama *M*

Alaska

University of Alaska
Anchorage *M*
Fairbanks *M*

Arizona

Arizona State University *M*
Grand Canyon University *B*
Northern Arizona University *M*
Prescott College *B*
University of Arizona *B,M*

Arkansas

Arkansas Tech University *B*
University of Arkansas *M*

California

Barstow College *A*
California State University
Fresno *M*
Long Beach *B*
Northridge *B*
Dominican College of San Rafael *B*
Foothill College *A*
Humboldt State University *M*
Long Beach City College *A*
Mills College *B,M*
Orange Coast College *A*
San Francisco State University *B,M*
San Joaquin Delta College *A*
San Jose State University *M*
University of California
Davis *M*
Irvine *M*
Riverside *B*
San Diego *B*
Santa Cruz *B*
University of Redlands *B*
University of San Francisco *M*
University of Southern California
B,M

Colorado

Colorado State University *B,M*
Naropa Institute *B,M*
University of Colorado at Denver *B*
University of Denver *B,M,D*

Connecticut

Fairfield University *B*
University of Bridgeport *B*
Wesleyan University *B*

District of Columbia

American University *M*
Gallaudet University *B*

Florida

Eckerd College *B*
Florida International University *M*
Florida State University *B,M,D*
University of Miami *M,D*
University of Tampa *A,B*

Georgia

Agnes Scott College *B*
Emory University *B*
Georgia State University *M*
Oxford College of Emory
University *A*

Illinois

Augustana College *B*
Columbia College *B,M*
Illinois State University *M*
Judson College *B*
Knox College *B*
Lake Forest College *B*
Millikin University *B*
Northwestern University *B*
Richland Community College *A*
Rockford College *B*
Shimer College *B*
Southern Illinois University at
Carbondale *B*
University of Chicago *B*

Indiana

Indiana State University *B,M*
Indiana University Bloomington *B,M*
Indiana Wesleyan University *B*
Martin University *B*
Purdue University *B,M*
St. Mary's College *B*
Taylor University *B*
University of Evansville *B*
University of Notre Dame *M*

Iowa

Drake University *B*
Loras College *B*
Maharishi International University *M*
Morningside College *B*
University of Iowa *M,D*

Kansas

Central College *A*
Kansas City Kansas Community College *A*
Kansas State University *B*
Wichita State University *M*

Kentucky

Kentucky Wesleyan College *B*
Murray State University *B*

Louisiana

Louisiana State University and Agricultural and Mechanical College *M*
McNeese State University *M*

Maine

University of Maine
    Farmington *B*
    Presque Isle *A*

Maryland

Johns Hopkins University *B,M*
Loyola College in Maryland *B*
University of Baltimore *B,M*
University of Maryland: College Park *M*

Massachusetts

Boston University *M*
Bradford College *B*
Brandeis University *B*
Emerson College *B,M*
Hampshire College *B*
Harvard and Radcliffe Colleges *B*
Lesley College *B,M*
Massachusetts Institute of Technology *B*
North Adams State College *B*
Salem State College *M*
University of Massachusetts at Boston *C*

Michigan

Adrian College *A,B*
Alma College *B*
Eastern Michigan University *B*
Grand Valley State University *B*
Michigan State University *M*
Northern Michigan University *M*
Olivet College *B*
University of Michigan *B,M*
Western Michigan University *M*

Minnesota

Bethel College *B*
Macalester College *B*
Mankato State University *B*
St. Mary's College of Minnesota *B*
Southwest State University *B*

Missouri

Lindenwood College *B*
Park College *B*
Southwest Missouri State University *B*
Washington University *M*
Webster University *B*
Westminster College *B*

Montana

Carroll College *A,B*
University of Montana *M*

Nebraska

Creighton University *B*
Hastings College *B*
University of Nebraska—Omaha *B*

New Hampshire

Franklin Pierce College *B*
Plymouth State College of the University System of New Hampshire *B*
University of New Hampshire *M*

New Jersey

Jersey City State College *B*
Rider College *B*
Rutgers—The State University of New Jersey *M*

New Mexico

College of Santa Fe *B*
Institute of American Indian Arts *A*
University of New Mexico *B*

New York

Bard College *B,M*
Barnard College *B*
City University of New York
    Baruch College *B*
    Brooklyn College *B,M*
    City College *B,M*
    Queens College *B,M*
Columbia University: School of General Studies *B*
Cornell University *M*
D'Youville College *B*
Eugene Lang College/New School for Social Research *B*
Fordham University *B*
Hamilton College *B*
Hofstra University *B*
Houghton College *B*
King's College *B*
Long Island University
    Brooklyn Campus *M*
    Southampton Campus *B*
Nazareth College of Rochester *B*
New York University *B,M*
St. Lawrence University *B*
Sarah Lawrence College *B,M*
State University of New York
    Albany *D*
    College at Geneseo *B*
    College at New Paltz *B*
Syracuse University *M*

North Carolina

Brevard College *A*
East Carolina University *B*
High Point University *B*
Methodist College *A,B*
North Carolina State University *B*
St. Andrews Presbyterian College *B*
University of North Carolina
    Asheville *B*
    Greensboro *M*
Warren Wilson College *M*

Ohio

Antioch College *B*
Ashland University *B*
Bowling Green State University *B,M*
College of Wooster *B*
Denison University *B*
Kent State University *B*
Miami University: Oxford Campus *B,M*
Oberlin College *B*
Ohio State University: Columbus Campus *M,D*
Ohio University *B,M*
Ohio Wesleyan University *B*
Union Institute *B,D*
University of Findlay *B*
Wittenberg University *B*

Oklahoma

Oklahoma Christian University of Science and Arts *B*
University of Central Oklahoma *M*

Oregon

George Fox College *B*
Linfield College *B*
Pacific University *B*
University of Oregon *M*

Pennsylvania

Bucknell University *B*
California University of Pennsylvania *B*
Carnegie Mellon University *B,M*
Eastern College *B*
Gannon University *B*
Geneva College *B*
Immaculata College *A*
La Salle University *B*
Lycoming College *B*
University of Pittsburgh
    Greensburg *B*
    Johnstown *B*
    Pittsburgh *B*

Rhode Island

Brown University *B,M*
Roger Williams College *B*

South Carolina

Bob Jones University *B*
Columbia College *B*
University of South Carolina *M*

South Dakota

Dakota Wesleyan University *B*

Tennessee

Memphis State University *M*
University of Tennessee
    Chattanooga *M*
    Knoxville *B*

Texas

Lon Morris College *A*
St. Edward's University *B*
Southern Methodist University *B,M*
Southwest Texas State University *M*
University of Houston
    Downtown *B*
    Houston *B,M,D*
University of Texas at El Paso *B,M*
Western Texas College *A*

Utah

University of Utah *M*

Vermont

Bennington College *B*
Goddard College *M*

Johnson State College *B*
Lyndon State College *B*
Marlboro College *B*
Norwich University *M*

Virginia

Averett College *B*
Emory and Henry College *B*
George Mason University *M*
Hollins College *B,M*
Old Dominion University *M*
Randolph-Macon Woman's College *B*
Sweet Briar College *B*
University of Virginia *M*
Virginia Commonwealth University *M*
Virginia Intermont College *B*
Virginia Wesleyan College *B*

Washington

Eastern Washington University *B,M*
Everett Community College *A*
Evergreen State College *B*
Pacific Lutheran University *B*
Seattle Central Community College *A*
Tacoma Community College *A*
University of Washington *B,M*
Wenatchee Valley College *A*
Western Washington University *B,M*
Whitworth College *B*

West Virginia

Alderson-Broaddus College *B*
Davis and Elkins College *B*
Shepherd College *B*
West Virginia State College *B*
West Virginia Wesleyan College *B*

Wisconsin

Beloit College *B*
Carroll College *B*
Lakeland College *B*
Marquette University *B*
Northland College *B*
University of Wisconsin: Milwaukee *B,M*

Criminal justice studies

Alabama

Alabama State University *B*
Athens State College *B*
Auburn University
    Auburn *B*
    Montgomery *B,M*
Chattahoochee Valley Community College *A*
Community College of the Air Force *A*
Gadsden State Community College *A*
Jacksonville State University *B,M*
Jefferson State Community College *A*
John C. Calhoun State Community College *A*
Judson College *B*
Lawson State Community College *A*
Shoals Community College *A*
Snead State Junior College *A*
Troy State University at Dothan *B*
University of Alabama
    Birmingham *B,M*
    Tuscaloosa *B,M*
University of North Alabama *B*

University of South Alabama *B*

Alaska

University of Alaska
    Anchorage *B*
    Fairbanks *B*

Arizona

Arizona State University *B,M,D*
Arizona Western College *A*
Grand Canyon University *B*
Mesa Community College *A*
Northern Arizona University *B*
Scottsdale Community College *A*
University of Arizona *B*

Arkansas

Garland County Community
    College *C*
University of Arkansas
    Little Rock *B,M*
    Pine Bluff *B*
Westark Community College *A*

California

California Lutheran University *B*
California State University
    Bakersfield *B*
    Fullerton *B*
    Hayward *B*
    Long Beach *B,M*
    Los Angeles *B,M*
    Sacramento *B,M*
Chapman University *B*
Citrus College *A*
College of the Sequoias *C,A*
El Camino College *C,A*
Feather River College *C,A*
Fresno City College *C,A*
Gavilan Community College *A*
Golden West College *C,A*
Imperial Valley College *C,A*
La Sierra University *B*
Lake Tahoe Community College
    C,A
Los Angeles City College *C,A*
Mendocino College *A*
Napa Valley College *C,A*
National University *B*
San Jose State University *B,M*
Santa Barbara City College *C,A*
Santa Rosa Junior College *A*
Skyline College *C*
Southwestern College *A*
United States International
    University *M,D*
University of California: Santa
    Barbara *B*
University of La Verne *B*
West Valley College *A*
Yuba College *A*

Colorado

Colorado Northwestern Community
    College *C,A*
Fort Lewis College *B*
Mesa State College *A,B*
Metropolitan State College of
    Denver *B*
Pikes Peak Community College *C,A*
Pueblo Community College *A*
Red Rocks Community College *C,A*
University of Colorado at
    Denver *M*

Connecticut

Mattatuck Community College *C*
Northwestern Connecticut
    Community College *A*
Sacred Heart University *B*
Tunxis Community College *A*
University of Hartford *B*

University of New Haven *A,B,M*
Western Connecticut State
    University *A,B*

Delaware

Delaware State College *B*
University of Delaware *B*
Wilmington College *B*

District of Columbia

American University *B,M*
George Washington University *B,M*
University of the District of
    Columbia *B*

Florida

Barry University *B*
Bethune-Cookman College *B*
Brevard Community College *A*
Central Florida Community
    College *A*
Edison Community College *A*
Florida Agricultural and Mechanical
    University *B*
Florida Atlantic University *B*
Florida International University *B*
Florida Memorial College *B*
Florida Southern College *B*
Indian River Community College *A*
Miami-Dade Community College
    C,A
Palm Beach Community College *A*
St. Thomas University *B*
Tallahassee Community College *A*
University of Central Florida *B*
University of Florida *B*
University of North Florida *B,M*
University of South Florida *B,M*
University of West Florida *B*

Georgia

Albany State College *B,M*
Armstrong State College *B,M*
Augusta College *A*
Brenau Women's College *B*
Brewton-Parker College *A*
Brunswick College *A*
Clark Atlanta University *M*
Clayton State College *A*
Columbus College *C,A,B*
Darton College *A*
Fort Valley State College *B*
Georgia College *B*
Georgia Southern University *B*
Georgia State University *B,M*
Gordon College *A*
Macon College *C,A*
Middle Georgia College *A*
Morris Brown College *B*
North Georgia College *B*
Reinhardt College *A*
Savannah State College *B*
Savannah Technical Institute *C*
South Georgia College *A*
University of Georgia *B*
West Georgia College *A,B*

Hawaii

Chaminade University of Honolulu
    A,B,M
Hawaii Pacific University *B*
University of Hawaii: Honolulu
    Community College *A*

Idaho

Boise State University *A,B*
Idaho State University *A*
Lewis Clark State College *B*
North Idaho College *A*
Ricks College *A*
University of Idaho *B*

Illinois

Bradley University *B*
Carl Sandburg College *C,A*
Chicago State University *B,M*
City Colleges of Chicago
    Chicago City-Wide College
    C,A
    Richard J. Daley College *A*
College of St. Francis *B*
Elgin Community College *A*
Governors State University *B*
Illinois Central College *A*
Illinois State University *B,M*
Joliet Junior College *C,A*
Lewis and Clark Community
    College *A*
Lewis University *B,M*
Loyola University of Chicago *B*
McKendree College *B*
Moraine Valley Community
    College *A*
Northeastern Illinois University *B*
Olivet Nazarene University *B*
Parkland College *A*
Rend Lake College *A*
Rockford College *B*
St. Xavier University *B,M*
Sangamon State University *B*
Southern Illinois University at
    Carbondale *A,B,M*
Triton College *A*
University of Illinois at Chicago
    B,M

Indiana

Anderson University *A,B*
Ball State University *A,B*
Calumet College of St. Joseph
    C,A,B
Indiana State University *M*
Indiana University
    Bloomington *C,B,M*
    East *A*
    Kokomo *A*
    Northwest *A,B,M*
    South Bend *A,B*
Indiana University—Purdue
    University
    Fort Wayne *A,B*
    Indianapolis *A,B,M*
Indiana Wesleyan University *B*
Manchester College *A*
Purdue University *B,M,D*
Tri-State University *A,B*
University of Indianapolis *A,B*
Valparaiso University *B*
Vincennes University *A*

Iowa

Buena Vista College *B*
Des Moines Area Community
    College *A*
Grand View College *A*
Iowa Lakes Community College *A*
Iowa Wesleyan College *B*
Iowa Western Community
    College *A*
Morningside College *A,B*
Mount Mercy College *B*
St. Ambrose University *B*
Scott Community College *A*
Simpson College *B*
Southeastern Community College:
    North Campus *A*
University of Iowa *M*

Kansas

Bethany College *B*
Central College *A*
Colby Community College *A*
Fort Scott Community College *A*
Kansas Wesleyan University *A,B*

Labette Community College *A*
Neosho County Community
    College *A*
Seward County Community
    College *C*
Southwestern College *B*
Washburn University of Topeka *B*
Wichita State University *B,M*

Kentucky

Campbellsville College *A*
Eastern Kentucky University *M*
Kentucky State University *A,B*
Kentucky Wesleyan College *B*
Louisville Presbyterian Theological
    Seminary *M*
Murray State University *B*
Thomas More College *A,B*

Louisiana

Bossier Parish Community
    College *A*
Grambling State University *A,B,M*
Louisiana State University
    Agricultural and Mechanical
    College *B,M*
    Eunice *A*
Loyola University *B*
McNeese State University *A,B*
Northeast Louisiana University *B,M*
Southeastern Louisiana University
    A,B
University of Southwestern
    Louisiana *B*

Maine

Southern Maine Technical
    College *A*
University of Maine
    Augusta *A*
    Fort Kent *A*

Maryland

Bowie State University *B*
Catonsville Community College *C,A*
Coppin State College *B,M*
Frederick Community College *A*
Frostburg State University *B*
Montgomery College: Rockville
    Campus *A*
Sojourner-Douglass College *B*
University of Baltimore *B,M*
University of Maryland
    College Park *B,M,D*
    Eastern Shore *B*

Massachusetts

American International College *B,M*
Anna Maria College for Men and
    Women *B,M*
Becker College: Worcester
    Campus *A*
Berkshire Community College *A*
Boston University *A,M*
Bristol Community College *A*
Bunker Hill Community College *A*
Cape Cod Community College *A*
Dean Junior College *A*
Greenfield Community College *A*
Massachusetts Bay Community
    College *A*
Middlesex Community College *A*
Mount Ida College *A*
North Shore Community College *A*
Northeastern University *A,B,M*
Northern Essex Community
    College *A*
Quincy College *A*
Salem State College *B*
Stonehill College *B*

University of Massachusetts
  Boston *B*
  Lowell *A,B,M*
Western New England College *B,M*
Westfield State College *B*

Michigan

Adrian College *B*
Calvin College *B*
Charles Stewart Mott Community
  College *C*
Delta College *A*
Eastern Michigan University *B,M*
Grand Valley State University *B*
Kellogg Community College *A*
Lake Superior State University *A,B*
Lansing Community College *A*
Madonna University *C,A,B*
Michigan State University *B,M*
Mid Michigan Community
  College *A*
Montcalm Community College *C,A*
Northern Michigan University *A,B*
Northwestern Michigan College *A*
Oakland Community College *A*
Saginaw Valley State University *B*
Schoolcraft College *A*
Siena Heights College *A,B*
Suomi College *A*
University of Detroit Mercy *B,M*
University of Michigan: Flint *B*
Wayne State University *B,M*
West Shore Community College *A*
Western Michigan University *B*

Minnesota

Bemidji State University *B*
Concordia College: Moorhead *B*
Gustavus Adolphus College *B*
Moorhead State University *B*
Northland Community College *A*
Rainy River Community College *A*
St. Cloud State University *B*
St. Mary's College of Minnesota *B*
University of St. Thomas *B*
Willmar Community College *A*
Winona State University *A,B*

Mississippi

Alcorn State University *B*
Delta State University *B*
Jackson State University *B,M*
Jones County Junior College *A*
Mississippi College *B*
Mississippi Gulf Coast Community
  College: Jefferson Davis
  Campus *A*
University of Southern Mississippi
  B,M

Missouri

Central Missouri State University
  B,M
College of the Ozarks *B*
Columbia College *A,B*
Culver-Stockton College *B*
East Central College *A*
Hannibal-LaGrange College *B*
Lincoln University *B*
Lindenwood College *B*
Missouri Southern State College *B*
Missouri Western State College *B*
Northeast Missouri State
  University *B*
Park College *B*
St. Louis Community College
  Forest Park *C*
  Meramec *A*
St. Louis University *B*
Southeast Missouri State
  University *B*

University of Missouri: Kansas City
  B,M
Webster University *M*

Montana

College of Great Falls *A,B*
Fort Peck Community College *A*
Montana State University *B*

Nebraska

Bellevue College *B*
Chadron State College *B*
McCook Community College *A*
Northeast Community College *A*
University of Nebraska
  Kearney *B*
  Omaha *B,M*
Wayne State College *B*

Nevada

Community College of Southern
  Nevada *C,A*
Northern Nevada Community
  College *A*
Truckee Meadows Community
  College *C,A*
University of Nevada
  Las Vegas *B,M*
  Reno *B*
Western Nevada Community
  College *A*

New Hampshire

Hesser College *A*
St. Anselm College *B*

New Jersey

Atlantic Community College *A*
Bergen Community College *A*
Bloomfield College *B*
Brookdale Community College *A*
Burlington County College *A*
Caldwell College *C*
County College of Morris *A*
Essex County College *A*
Glassboro State College *B*
Jersey City State College *B,M*
Monmouth College *B*
Ocean County College *C,A*
Passaic County Community College
  C,A
Rutgers—The State University of
  New Jersey
    Livingston College *B*
    New Brunswick *M,D*
    Newark College of Arts and
      Sciences *B*
    Rutgers College *B*
    University College New
      Brunswick *B*
    University College Newark *B*
Seton Hall University *B*
Stockton State College *B*
Thomas Edison State College *A,B*
Trenton State College *B*
Union County College *A*

New Mexico

Clovis Community College *A*
Eastern New Mexico University:
  Roswell Campus *A*
New Mexico State University
  Carlsbad *A*
  Las Cruces *A,B,M*
University of New Mexico *B*
Western New Mexico University *B*

New York

Adirondack Community College *A*
Alfred University *B*
Broome Community College *C,A*

City University of New York
  Graduate School and
    University Center *D*
  John Jay College of Criminal
    Justice *B,M,D*
Columbia-Greene Community
  College *A*
Community College of the Finger
  Lakes *C,A*
Corning Community College *A*
Dutchess Community College *A*
Elmira College *B*
Erie Community College
  City Campus *A*
  North Campus *A*
Fordham University *B,M,D*
Fulton-Montgomery Community
  College *C,A*
Genesee Community College *C,A*
Herkimer County Community
  College *A*
Hilbert College *A*
Iona College *B,M*
Jamestown Community College *A*
Jefferson Community College *A*
Long Island University: C. W. Post
  Campus *B,M*
Marist College *B*
Mater Dei College *B*
Medaille College *B*
Mercy College *C,B*
Mohawk Valley Community
  College *A*
Monroe Community College *A*
New York Institute of
  Technology *B*
Niagara County Community
  College *A*
Niagara University *B*
North Country Community
  College *A*
Onondaga Community College *A*
Orange County Community
  College *A*
Pace University: Pleasantville/
  Briarcliff *B*
Roberts Wesleyan College *B*
Rochester Institute of
  Technology *B*
Russell Sage College *B*
Sage Junior College of Albany, A
  Division of Russell Sage
  College *A*
St. Francis College *A*
St. John's University *B*
St. Joseph's College: Suffolk
  Campus *C*
St. Thomas Aquinas College *B*
State University of New York
  Albany *B,M,D*
  College at Brockport *B*
  College at Buffalo *B,M*
  College at Plattsburgh *B*
  College of Technology at
    Farmingdale *C,A*
  Oswego *B*
Suffolk County Community College
  Eastern Campus *C,A*
  Selden *A*
Sullivan County Community
  College *A*
Tompkins-Cortland Community
  College *C*
Utica College of Syracuse
  University *B*
Westchester Community College *A*

North Carolina

Appalachian State University *B*
Barber-Scotia College *B*
Cleveland Community College *A*

Durham Technical Community
  College *A*
East Carolina University *B*
Elizabeth City State University *B*
Fayetteville State University *B*
Gardner-Webb College *B*
Gaston College *A*
Guilford College *B*
Lees-McRae College *B*
Mitchell Community College *A*
Montgomery Community College *A*
North Carolina State University *B*
North Carolina Wesleyan College *B*
Pfeiffer College *B*
St. Augustine's College *B*
Shaw University *A,B*
Surry Community College *A*
University of North Carolina
  Chapel Hill *B*
  Wilmington *B*

North Dakota

Bismarck State College *A*
Minot State University *A,B,M*
Standing Rock College *A*
University of North Dakota *B*

Ohio

Ashland University *A,B*
Baldwin-Wallace College *B*
Bluffton College *B*
Bowling Green State University
  Bowling Green *B*
  Firelands College *A*
Capital University *B*
Cedarville College *B*
Columbus State Community
  College *A*
Defiance College *A,B*
Franciscan University of
  Steubenville *B*
Kent State University
  Kent *B,M*
  Tuscarawas Campus *A*
Mount Vernon Nazarene College *B*
Ohio Dominican College *B*
Ohio Northern University *B*
Ohio State University: Columbus
  Campus *B*
Ohio University
  Athens *B*
  Zanesville Campus *B*
Union Institute *B,D*
University of Akron *A*
University of Cincinnati
  Cincinnati *B,M*
  Clermont College *A*
University of Dayton *B*
University of Toledo *B*
Wilmington College *B*
Wright State University *B*
Xavier University *A,B,M*

Oklahoma

Cameron University *A,B*
East Central University *B*
Northeastern State University *B,M*
Oklahoma City University *B,M*
Redlands Community College *A*
Rogers State College *A*
Rose State College *A*
Southeastern Oklahoma State
  University *B*
Southwestern Oklahoma State
  University *B*
Tulsa Junior College *A*
University of Central Oklahoma
  B,M
University of Tulsa *C*

Oregon

Central Oregon Community
College *A*
Lane Community College *A*
Linn-Benton Community College *A*
Rogue Community College *C,A*
Southern Oregon State College *B*
Southwestern Oregon Community
College *A*

Pennsylvania

Allentown College of St. Francis de
Sales *B*
Alvernia College *B*
Community College of Philadelphia
C,A
Duquesne University *B*
Edinboro University of
Pennsylvania *B*
Gannon University *B*
Harrisburg Area Community
College *A*
Holy Family College *B*
King's College *A,B*
Kutztown University of
Pennsylvania *B*
La Salle University *B*
Lehigh County Community
College *A*
Lincoln University *B*
Lycoming College *B*
Mansfield University of
Pennsylvania *B*
Marywood College *M*
Mercyhurst College *A,B,M*
Montgomery County Community
College *A*
Moravian College *B*
Northampton County Area
Community College *A*
Penn State
Harrisburg Capital College *B*
University Park Campus
B,M,D
St. Francis College *B*
St. Joseph's University *C,A,B,M*
Shippensburg University of
Pennsylvania *B,M*
Temple University *B,M*
University of Pittsburgh
Greensburg *B*
Pittsburgh *B,M*
University of Scranton *A,B*
Valley Forge Military College *C,A*
Waynesburg College *B*
West Chester University of
Pennsylvania *B,M*
Westmoreland County Community
College *A*
Widener University *C,A*

Puerto Rico

Inter American University of Puerto
Rico
Arecibo Campus *B*
Metropolitan Campus *B,M*

Rhode Island

Salve Regina University *A,B,M*

South Carolina

Benedict College *B*
Bob Jones University *B*
Charleston Southern University *B*
Coker College *B*
Morris College *B*
South Carolina State College *B*
Spartanburg Methodist College *A*

University of South Carolina
Aiken *A*
Columbia *B*
Lancaster *A*
Spartanburg *B*
Voorhees College *B*
Williamsburg Technical College *C*

South Dakota

Black Hills State University *B*
Dakota Wesleyan University *A*
Huron University *A,B*
Northern State University *A*
University of South Dakota *A,B*

Tennessee

Aquinas Junior College *A*
Belmont University *B*
Dyersburg State Community
College *A*
East Tennessee State University
B,M
Memphis State University *B,M*
Middle Tennessee State University
B,M
Shelby State Community College
C,A
Tennessee State University *B,M*
Tennessee Technological
University *A*
University of Tennessee
Chattanooga *B,M*
Martin *B*

Texas

Abilene Christian University *B*
Alvin Community College *C,A*
Angelo State University *B*
Bee County College *A*
Collin County Community College
District *A*
Cooke County College *A*
Corpus Christi State University *B*
Dallas Baptist University *B*
Del Mar College *A*
East Texas State University *B*
El Centro College *A*
Hardin-Simmons University *B*
Houston Community College *A*
Lamar University—Beaumont *B*
McMurry University *B*
Midwestern State University *B*
Navarro College *A*
North Harris Montgomery
Community College District *A*
Northeast Texas Community
College *C,A*
Paul Quinn College *B*
St. Edward's University *B*
St. Mary's University *B*
Sam Houston State University *D*
Southwest Texas State University
B,M
Stephen F. Austin State
University *B*
Sul Ross State University *B*
Tarleton State University *B*
Texas Christian University *B*
Texas Southern University *B*
Texas Southmost College *A*
Texas Wesleyan University *B*
Texas Woman's University *B*
University of Central Texas *B,M*
University of Houston:
Downtown *B*
University of North Texas *B*
University of Texas
Arlington *B*
El Paso *B*
Permian Basin *B*
San Antonio *B*
Tyler *B*

Weatherford College *A*
West Texas State University *B*
Western Texas College *A*
Wharton County Junior College *A*

Utah

Weber State University *A,B*

Vermont

Castleton State College *A,B*
Champlain College *A*
Norwich University *B*
Southern Vermont College *A,B*
Trinity College of Vermont *B*

Virginia

Averett College *B*
Bluefield College *B*
Christopher Newport College *B*
Hampton University *B*
Northern Virginia Community
College *C,A*
Old Dominion University *B*
Radford University *B,M*
Roanoke College *B*
University of Richmond *B*
Virginia Commonwealth University
B,M
Virginia Highlands Community
College *A*
Virginia Wesleyan College *B*

Washington

Central Washington University *B*
City University *M*
Clark College *A*
Eastern Washington University *B*
Everett Community College *C,A*
Olympic College *A*
Pierce College *A*
St. Martin's College *B*
Seattle University *B*
Shoreline Community College *A*
Tacoma Community College *A*
Whatcom Community College *A*
Yakima Valley Community
College *A*

West Virginia

Bluefield State College *B*
Fairmont State College *A,B*
Marshall University *B,M*
Salem-Teikyo University *A,B*
West Liberty State College *B*
West Virginia State College *A,B*
West Virginia University at
Parkersburg *C,A*
Wheeling Jesuit College *B*

Wisconsin

Carroll College *B*
Carthage College *B*
Edgewood College *B*
Marian College of Fond du Lac *B*
Marquette University *A,B*
Mount Senario College *B*
University of Wisconsin
Eau Claire *B*
Green Bay *B*
Milwaukee *B,M*
Oshkosh *B*
Platteville *B*
Superior *B*

Wyoming

Casper College *A*
Central Wyoming College *A*
Eastern Wyoming College *A*
University of Wyoming *B*

**American Samoa, Caroline
Islands, Guam, Marianas,
Virgin Islands**

University of Guam *B*

Criminal justice technology

Alabama

Gadsden State Community
College *A*
Jefferson State Community
College *A*
John C. Calhoun State Community
College *A*
Shoals Community College *A*
Wallace State Community College
at Hanceville *A*

Arizona

Pima Community College *A*

Arkansas

East Arkansas Community
College *A*
North Arkansas Community
College *A*
Southern Arkansas Community
College *A*
University of Arkansas at Pine
Bluff *A*

California

California State University: Los
Angeles *M*
Chaffey Community College *C,A*
City College of San Francisco *C,A*
Fresno City College *C,A*
Grossmont Community College *C,A*
San Joaquin Delta College *C,A*
Santa Monica College *C,A*
Taft College *A*
Ventura College *A*

Colorado

Aims Community College *A*
Arapahoe Community College *C,A*
Colorado Mountain College: Spring
Valley Campus *A*
Trinidad State Junior College *A*

Connecticut

Northwestern Connecticut
Community College *A*
Tunxis Community College *C*

Delaware

Delaware State College *B*
Delaware Technical and
Community College
Southern Campus *A*
Stanton/Wilmington
Campus *A*
Terry Campus *A*

District of Columbia

University of the District of
Columbia *A*

Florida

Broward Community College *A*
Central Florida Community
College *A*
Daytona Beach Community
College *A*
Florida Community College at
Jacksonville *A*
Florida Keys Community College *A*
Gulf Coast Community College *C,A*

Hillsborough Community College *A*
Indian River Community College *C*
Lake City Community College *A*
Lake-Sumter Community College *A*
Manatee Community College *A*
Okaloosa-Walton Community
  College *A*
Pensacola Junior College *A*
Phillips Junior College:
  Melbourne *A*
St. Johns River Community
  College *A*
St. Petersburg Junior College *A*
Santa Fe Community College *A*
Seminole Community College *A*
South Florida Community
  College *A*
Valencia Community College *A*

Illinois

College of DuPage *C,A*
College of Lake County *C,A*
Rend Lake College *C,A*
Southern Illinois University at
  Carbondale *A,B,M*
Spoon River College *C*
Triton College *C,A*
Waubonsee Community College
  C,A
William Rainey Harper College *C,A*

Iowa

Clinton Community College *A*
Indian Hills Community College *A*

Louisiana

Nicholls State University *A*
Northeast Louisiana University *A*
University of Southwestern
  Louisiana *A*

Maine

University of Maine at Presque Isle
  A,B

Maryland

Allegany Community College *C,A*
Harford Community College *A*
Wor-Wic Tech Community College
  C,A

Massachusetts

Bay Path College *A*
Becker College: Worcester
  Campus *A*
Massasoit Community College *A*

Michigan

Charles Stewart Mott Community
  College *A*
Kellogg Community College *A*
Kirtland Community College *A*
Macomb Community College *A*
Suomi College *A*
West Shore Community College *A*

Minnesota

Willmar Community College *A*

Missouri

East Central College *C,A*
Longview Community College *A*
Maple Woods Community
  College *A*
Mineral Area College *C,A*
Missouri Western State College *A*
Penn Valley Community College
  C,A
St. Charles Community College *A*
Three Rivers Community College *A*

New Mexico

Northern New Mexico Community
  College *A*
San Juan College *A*

New York

Adirondack Community College *A*
Erie Community College: North
  Campus *A*
Genesee Community College *C,A*
Hudson Valley Community
  College *A*
Rockland Community College *A*
St. Joseph's College: Suffolk
  Campus *C*
State University of New York
  College of Technology at
  Canton *A*
Ulster County Community
  College *A*

North Carolina

Alamance Community College *A*
Cape Fear Community College *A*
Carteret Community College *A*
Central Carolina Community
  College *A*
Coastal Carolina Community
  College *A*
Craven Community College *A*
Durham Technical Community
  College *C*
Edgecombe Community College *A*
Fayetteville Technical Community
  College *A*
Guilford Technical Community
  College *A*
Haywood Community College *A*
Isothermal Community College *A*
Richmond Community College *A*
Roanoke-Chowan Community
  College *A*
Robeson Community College *A*
Rockingham Community College *A*
Sampson Community College *A*
Southeastern Community College
  C,A
Southwestern Community
  College *A*
Stanly Community College *A*
Surry Community College *A*
Wilkes Community College *A*
Wilson Technical Community
  College *A*

Ohio

Central Ohio Technical College *A*
Clark State Community College *A*
Columbus State Community
  College *A*
Edison State Community College *A*
Hocking Technical College *A*
Muskingum Area Technical
  College *A*
North Central Technical College *A*
Terra Technical College *A*
University of Akron *A*
University of Cincinnati: Clermont
  College *A*

Oregon

Chemeketa Community College *A*
Clackamas Community College *A*
Clatsop Community College *A*
Portland Community College *A*

Pennsylvania

Delaware County Community
  College *A*
Edinboro University of
  Pennsylvania *A*

Luzerne County Community
  College *A*
Penn State University Park
  Campus *C*

South Carolina

Denmark Technical College *C*
Florence-Darlington Technical
  College *A*
Greenville Technical College *A*
Horry-Georgetown Technical
  College *A*
Midlands Technical College *A*
Spartanburg Methodist College *A*
Sumter Area Technical College *A*
Technical College of the
  Lowcountry *A*
Trident Technical College *A*

Texas

Amarillo College *A*
Brazosport College *C,A*
Central Texas College *A*
Galveston College *A*
Midland College *A*
San Antonio College *A*

Virginia

Dabney S. Lancaster Community
  College *A*
Patrick Henry Community
  College *C*

Washington

Bellevue Community College *C*
Everett Community College *A*
Heritage College *C*
Peninsula College *A*
Shoreline Community College *A*

West Virginia

Glenville State College *A*
West Virginia Northern Community
  College *A*

Wisconsin

Mid-State Technical College *A*

Wyoming

Eastern Wyoming College *A*

**American Samoa, Caroline
Islands, Guam, Marianas,
Virgin Islands**

Guam Community College *C,A*

Criminology

Alabama

Alabama State University *M*
Auburn University *B*
Enterprise State Junior College *C*

Arkansas

Arkansas State University *B*
University of Arkansas at Pine
  Bluff *B*

California

Bakersfield College *A*
California Lutheran University *B*
California State University
  Bakersfield *B*
  Fresno *B,M*
  San Bernardino *M*
  Stanislaus *B*
Chabot College *A*
Humboldt State University *C*
Porterville College *C,A*

Southwestern College *A*
University of La Verne *B*
University of Southern California *M*
West Hills Community College *A*

Colorado

Colorado Mountain College: Spring
  Valley Campus *A*

Connecticut

Albertus Magnus College *B*
Manchester Community College
  C,A
Sacred Heart University *B*
University of Hartford *B*

Delaware

University of Delaware *M,D*

District of Columbia

University of the District of
  Columbia *A*

Florida

Central Florida Community
  College *A*
Chipola Junior College *A*
Daytona Beach Community
  College *A*
Florida Southern College *B*
Florida State University *B,M,D*
Manatee Community College *A*
St. Leo College *B*
University of Miami *B*
University of North Florida *B,M*
University of South Florida *B,M*
University of Tampa *B*

Georgia

Armstrong State College *B,M*
Atlanta Metropolitan College *A*
Clark Atlanta University *B*
Darton College *A*
Fort Valley State College *B*
Georgia Southern University *B*
Morris Brown College *B*
Valdosta State College *B*
Waycross College *A*

Illinois

City Colleges of Chicago: Olive-
  Harvey College *C*
Northern Illinois University *M*
Southern Illinois University at
  Carbondale *B,M,D*
University of Illinois at Chicago
  B,M

Indiana

Ancilla College *A*
Grace College *B*
Indiana State University *A,B,M*
Indiana University Bloomington *B*
Indiana Wesleyan University *B*
Manchester College *A*
Purdue University *B*

Iowa

University of Northern Iowa *B*

Kansas

Colby Community College *A*
Fort Scott Community College *A*
Southwestern College *B*

Kentucky

Kentucky Wesleyan College *B*
Murray State University *B*

Louisiana

Dillard University *B*
Louisiana College *B*

Maine

University of Southern Maine *B*

Maryland

University of Baltimore *B*
University of Maryland
    College Park *B,M,D*
    Eastern Shore *B*

Massachusetts

American International College *B*
Bay Path College *A*
Becker College: Worcester
    Campus *A*
Bridgewater State College *B*
Suffolk University *B*

Michigan

Central Michigan University *M*
Eastern Michigan University *B,M*
Grand Valley State University *B*
Michigan State University *B,M*
Saginaw Valley State University *B*

Minnesota

Mankato State University *B*
Northland Community College *A*
University of Minnesota: Duluth *B*
University of St. Thomas *B*
Willmar Community College *A*
Winona State University *B*

Mississippi

Alcorn State University *B*

Missouri

College of the Ozarks *B*
Drury College *B*
Park College *B*

New Jersey

Caldwell College *C*
Glassboro State College *B*
Stockton State College *B*

New Mexico

Western New Mexico University *B*

New York

Canisius College *C*
Dutchess Community College *A*
Fordham University *M,D*
Iona College *B*
Le Moyne College *B*
Niagara University *B*
Rochester Institute of
    Technology *B*
Russell Sage College *B*
St. Joseph's College
    Brooklyn *C*
    Suffolk Campus *C*
State University of New York
    Albany *B,M,D*
    College at Plattsburgh *B*

North Carolina

Methodist College *A,B*
St. Augustine's College *B*

Ohio

Bluffton College *B*
Bowling Green State University:
    Firelands College *A*
Kent State University *B*
Ohio State University: Columbus
    Campus *B,M,D*
Ohio University *B*
Union Institute *B,D*
University of Toledo *B*
Youngstown State University *B,M*

Oklahoma

East Central University *B,M*
Northeastern State University *B,M*
Oklahoma City University *B,M*
Southeastern Oklahoma State
    University *B*

Oregon

Central Oregon Community
    College *A*
Southern Oregon State College *B*
Southwestern Oregon Community
    College *A*
Western Oregon State College *B,M*

Pennsylvania

Allentown College of St. Francis de
    Sales *B*
Duquesne University *B*
Indiana University of Pennsylvania
    B,M,D
Juniata College *B*
La Salle University *B*
Lackawanna Junior College *A*
Lycoming College *B*
Mansfield University of
    Pennsylvania *B*
Mount Aloysius College *A*
Reading Area Community
    College *A*
St. Francis College *B*
University of Pittsburgh at
    Greensburg *B*

Puerto Rico

Caribbean University *B*
Pontifical Catholic University of
    Puerto Rico *B*
Puerto Rico Junior College *A*
Turabo University *B*

South Carolina

Benedict College *B*
Coker College *B*
University of South Carolina *B,M*

South Dakota

Dakota Wesleyan University *A*
Huron University *A,B*

Tennessee

Motlow State Community
    College *A*
University of Tennessee:
    Chattanooga *B*

Texas

Cooke County College *A*
Dallas Baptist University *B*
Lamar University—Beaumont *B*
Sam Houston State University
    B,M,D
South Plains College *A*
University of Texas at Arlington *B*
Wharton County Junior College *A*

Vermont

Champlain College *A*

Virginia

Christopher Newport College *B*
Old Dominion University *B*
Radford University *B*

Washington

Gonzaga University *B*

Wisconsin

Marquette University *A,B*
Mount Senario College *B*

Curriculum and instruction

Alabama

Alabama Agricultural and
    Mechanical University *M*
Auburn University *M,D*
Troy State University
    Montgomery *M*
    Troy *M*
University of Alabama *M,D*

Arizona

Arizona State University *D*
Northern Arizona University *D*

Arkansas

Arkansas State University *M*
University of Arkansas at Pine
    Bluff *B*

California

Barstow College *C,A*
California Lutheran University *M*
California Polytechnic State
    University: San Luis Obispo *M*
California State University
    Bakersfield *M*
    Dominguez Hills *M*
    Fullerton *M*
    Hayward *M*
    Long Beach *M*
    Los Angeles *M*
    Northridge *M*
    Sacramento *M*
    Stanislaus *M*
Chapman University *M*
Christ College Irvine *M*
Dominican College of San
    Rafael *M*
La Sierra University *M,D*
Laney College *A*
National University *M*
Pacific Oaks College *M*
Point Loma Nazarene College *M*
San Jose State University *M*
Sonoma State University *M*
Stanford University *M,D*
United States International
    University *M,D*
University of California
    Davis *M*
    Riverside *M,D*
    Santa Barbara *M*
    Santa Cruz *M*
University of La Verne *M*
University of the Pacific *M,D*
University of San Diego *M*
University of San Francisco *M,D*
University of Southern California
    M,D

Colorado

University of Colorado
    Boulder *M,D*
    Denver *M*
University of Denver *M,D*

Connecticut

Fairfield University *M*
University of Connecticut *D*

Delaware

Delaware State College *M*
University of Delaware *M,D*

District of Columbia

George Washington University *M,D*
Howard University *M*

Florida

Florida Atlantic University *M,D*
Florida International University *D*
Nova University *M*
Stetson University *M*
University of Central Florida *D*
University of Florida *M,D*
University of North Florida *M*
University of Sarasota *M,D*
University of South Florida *M,D*
University of West Florida *M*

Georgia

Clark Atlanta University *M*
Emory University *M*
Georgia College *B,M*
Georgia Southern University *M*
Georgia State University *D*
Kennesaw State College *M*
University of Georgia *M*

Hawaii

University of Hawaii at Manoa *D*

Idaho

Boise State University *M*
Idaho State University *M*
Northwest Nazarene College *M*

Illinois

Chicago State University *M*
Concordia University *M*
De Paul University *M*
Illinois State University *M,D*
Loyola University of Chicago *M,D*
National-Louis University *M*
Northern Illinois University *M,D*
St. Xavier University *M*
Southern Illinois University
    Carbondale *M,D*
    Edwardsville *D*
University of Illinois
    Chicago *D*
    Urbana-Champaign *M,D*

Indiana

Ball State University *M*
Grace Theological Seminary *M*
Indiana State University *M,D*
Indiana University Bloomington
    B,D
Purdue University *M,D*

Iowa

Drake University *M,D*
Iowa State University *M,D*
University of Iowa *M,D*
University of Northern Iowa *M*

Kansas

Emporia State University *M*
Kansas State University *D*
Pittsburg State University *B*
University of Kansas *M,D*
Washburn University of Topeka *M*

Kentucky

Eastern Kentucky University *M*
Union College *M*
University of Kentucky *M*

Louisiana

Louisiana State University and
    Agricultural and Mechanical
    College *D*
Nicholls State University *M*
Our Lady of Holy Cross College *M*
Tulane University *M*
University of New Orleans *M,D*
Xavier University of Louisiana *M*

Maryland

Baltimore Hebrew University *B,M*
Bowie State University *M*
Frostburg State University *M*
Loyola College in Maryland *M*
University of Maryland
    Baltimore County *M*
    College Park *M,D*
Western Maryland College *M*

Massachusetts

American International College *M*
Atlantic Union College *M*
Boston College *M,D*
Boston University *D,W*
Harvard University *M,D,W*
Lesley College *M*
Northeastern University *M*
Tufts University *B,M*
University of Massachusetts at
    Lowell *M*
Wheelock College *M*

Michigan

Andrews University *M,D*
Aquinas College *M*
Calvin College *M*
Central Michigan University *M*
Eastern Michigan University *M*
Michigan State University *M,D*
Northern Michigan University *M*
Oakland University *M*
University of Detroit Mercy *M*
University of Michigan *M,D*
Wayne State University *D*
Western Michigan University *M*

Minnesota

Bemidji State University *M*
College of St. Scholastica *M*
Mankato State University *M*
St. Cloud State University *B,M*
University of St. Thomas *M*
Winona State University *M*

Mississippi

Delta State University *M*
University of Mississippi *B,M*
University of Southern
    Mississippi *M*

Missouri

Central Missouri State
    University *M*
St. Louis University *M,D*
Southeast Missouri State
    University *M*
Southwest Baptist University *M*
University of Missouri
    Columbia *B,M,D*
    Kansas City *M*
    St. Louis *D*
Webster University *M*

Montana

Eastern Montana College *M*
Montana State University *M,D*
University of Montana *D*

Nebraska

Peru State College *M*
University of Nebraska
    Kearney *M*
    Lincoln *M,D*

Nevada

University of Nevada
    Las Vegas *M,D*
    Reno *D*

New Hampshire

Antioch New England Graduate
    School *M*
Keene State College *M*
Notre Dame College *M*
Plymouth State College of the
    University System of New
    Hampshire *M*

New Jersey

Georgian Court College *M*
Glassboro State College *M*
Kean College of New Jersey *M*
Rider College *M*
Rutgers—The State University of
    New Jersey *M,D*
Seton Hall University *M*

New Mexico

New Mexico Highlands
    University *M*
New Mexico State University *M,D*
University of New Mexico *D*

New York

City University of New York:
    Hunter College *M*
Cornell University *M,D*
Fordham University *M,D*
Long Island University: C. W. Post
    Campus *B*
Manhattanville College *M*
Mercy College *M*
New York University *M,D*
Niagara University *M*
Pace University
    College of White Plains *M*
    New York *M*
Roberts Wesleyan College *M*
St. Bonaventure University *M*
St. John's University *D*
State University of New York
    Albany *M,D*
    Buffalo *M,D*
    College at Fredonia *M*
Syracuse University *M,D*
University of Rochester *M,D*

North Carolina

Appalachian State University *B,M*
Campbell University *M*
North Carolina State University
    M,D
University of North Carolina
    Chapel Hill *M,D*
    Charlotte *M*
    Greensboro *D*
Western Carolina University *M*

Ohio

Ashland University *M*
Cleveland State University *M*
Kent State University *M,D*
Miami University: Oxford
    Campus *M*
Ohio State University: Columbus
    Campus *M,D*
Ohio University *M,D*
Otterbein College *M*
University of Cincinnati *M,D*
University of Toledo *M,D*
Wright State University *M*
Youngstown State University *M*

Oklahoma

Oklahoma State University *M,D*

Oregon

Pacific University *M*
Southern Oregon State College *M*

Pennsylvania

Bloomsburg University of
    Pennsylvania *M*
Bucknell University *M*
California University of
    Pennsylvania *M*
Gannon University *M*
Gratz College *B,M*
Immaculata College *M*
Lehigh University *M,D*
Penn State
    Great Valley Graduate
      Center *M*
    Harrisburg Capital College *M*
    University Park Campus *M,D*
Temple University *M,D*
University of Pennsylvania *M,D*
Westminster College *M*

Puerto Rico

Pontifical Catholic University of
    Puerto Rico *M*
University of Puerto Rico: Rio
    Piedras Campus *D*

Rhode Island

Rhode Island College *M,W*

South Carolina

Bob Jones University *D*
The Citadel *M*
Columbia Bible College and
    Seminary *M*
University of South Carolina *D*
Winthrop University *M*

South Dakota

Black Hills State University *B,M*
University of South Dakota *D*

Tennessee

Austin Peay State University *M*
East Tennessee State University
    B,M
Freed-Hardeman University *M*
Lincoln Memorial University *M*
Memphis State University *M,D*
Middle Tennessee State
    University *M*
Tennessee State University *M,D*
Tennessee Technological
    University *M*
Trevecca Nazarene College *M*
Union University *M*
University of Tennessee
    Chattanooga *M*
    Knoxville *M,D*
    Martin *M*
Vanderbilt University *M,D*

Texas

Baylor University *M,D*
Corpus Christi State University *M*
East Texas State University *D*
Our Lady of the Lake University of
    San Antonio *M*
Prairie View A&M University *M*
Texas A&M University *M,D*
Texas Southern University *M,D*
Texas Tech University *B,M,D*
University of Houston
    Houston *M,D*
    Victoria *M*
University of North Texas *D*
University of Texas
    Austin *M,D*
    El Paso *M*
    San Antonio *M*
    Tyler *M*

Utah

Brigham Young University *M,D*
Utah State University *D*

Vermont

Castleton State College *M*
Johnson State College *M*
Lyndon State College *M*
St. Michael's College *M*
University of Vermont *M*

Virginia

George Mason University *M*
Longwood College *M*
Lynchburg College *M*
Radford University *M*
University of Virginia *M,D*
Virginia Commonwealth
    University *M*
Virginia Polytechnic Institute and
    State University *M,D,W*

Washington

Central Washington University *M*
Eastern Washington University *M*
Gonzaga University *M*
Pacific Lutheran University *M*
St. Martin's College *M*
Seattle Pacific University *M*
Seattle University *M*
University of Puget Sound *M*
University of Washington *M,D*
Walla Walla College *M*
Western Washington University *M*

West Virginia

Salem-Teikyo University *M*
West Virginia University *D*

Wisconsin

Concordia University Wisconsin *M*
Marquette University *M,D*
University of Wisconsin
    Madison *M,D*
    Milwaukee *M*
    Oshkosh *M*
    River Falls *M*
    Superior *M*

Wyoming

University of Wyoming *M,D*

American Samoa, Caroline Islands, Guam, Marianas, Virgin Islands

University of Guam *M*

Canada

McGill University *M*

Cytotechnology

Alabama

Community College of the Air
    Force *A*
Mobile College *B*
Samford University *B*
Shelton State Community
    College *A*
University of Alabama in
    Birmingham *B*

Arkansas

University of Arkansas for Medical
    Sciences *B*

California

California State University:
    Dominguez Hills *M*

Connecticut
University of Connecticut *B*

Florida
Barry University *B*
University of Miami *B*

Illinois
Augustana College *B*
Illinois College *B*
Roosevelt University *B*

Indiana
Indiana University—Purdue
University at Indianapolis *B*
St. Mary's College *B*

Iowa
Luther College *B*
Mount St. Clare College *B*

Kansas
Hutchinson Community College *A*
Kansas Newman College *B*
Southwestern College *B*
University of Kansas
Lawrence *B*
Medical Center *B*

Kentucky
Eastern Kentucky University *B*
University of Louisville *C,B*

Louisiana
Southern University and
Agricultural and Mechanical
College *B*

Michigan
Northern Michigan University *B*
University of Detroit Mercy *B*

Minnesota
Moorhead State University *B*
St. Mary's College of Minnesota *B*
Willmar Community College *A*
Winona State University *B*

Mississippi
Mississippi College *B*
University of Mississippi Medical
Center *B*

Missouri
Avila College *B*
Rockhurst College *B*
University of Missouri: Columbia *B*

Nebraska
Nebraska Wesleyan University *A*

New Jersey
Bloomfield College *B*
Felician College *A,B*
Jersey City State College *B*
Monmouth College *B*
St. Peter's College *B*
University of Medicine and
Dentistry of New Jersey: School
of Health Related Professions
C,B

New York
College of St. Rose *B*
Long Island University: Brooklyn
Campus *B*
State University of New York
Health Science Center at
Syracuse *B*

North Carolina
East Carolina University *B*

North Dakota
University of North Dakota *B*

Ohio
Kent State University *B*
Notre Dame College of Ohio *B*
University of Akron *B*

Oklahoma
University of Oklahoma Health
Sciences Center *B*

Pennsylvania
Elizabethtown College *B*
Juniata College *B*
Keystone Junior College *A*
Lebanon Valley College of
Pennsylvania *B*
Slippery Rock University of
Pennsylvania *B*
Thiel College *B*
Thomas Jefferson University:
College of Allied Health
Sciences *B*
Villanova University *B*

Puerto Rico
University of Puerto Rico: Medical
Sciences Campus *B*

Tennessee
Union University *B*
University of Tennessee:
Memphis *B*

Texas
University of Texas Health Science
Center at Houston *W*

Vermont
Trinity College of Vermont *B*

Washington
Seattle University *B*

West Virginia
Alderson-Broaddus College *B*
Marshall University *B*

Wisconsin
Marian College of Fond du Lac *B*

Dairy

Arizona
University of Arizona *M*

Arkansas
University of Arkansas *B*

California
California Polytechnic State
University: San Luis Obispo *B*
California State University:
Fresno *B*
Modesto Junior College *A*
West Hills Community College *C,A*

Florida
University of Florida *B,M,D*

Georgia
University of Georgia *B,M,D*

Idaho
College of Southern Idaho *C*
Ricks College *A*

Illinois
Southern Illinois University at
Carbondale *B,M*
University of Illinois at Urbana-
Champaign *B,M,D*

Iowa
Iowa State University *B*
Kirkwood Community College *A*
Northeast Iowa Community
College *C*

Kansas
Kansas State University *B*

Kentucky
Eastern Kentucky University *B*

Louisiana
Louisiana State University and
Agricultural and Mechanical
College *M,D*

Minnesota
University of Minnesota:
Crookston *A*
Willmar Community College *A*

Mississippi
Mississippi State University *B,M*

Missouri
Northwest Missouri State
University *B*
University of Missouri: Columbia
M,D

New York
Cornell University *B,M,D*
State University of New York
College of Agriculture and
Technology at Cobleskill *A*
College of Agriculture and
Technology at Morrisville *A*
College of Technology at
Alfred *A*

North Carolina
Surry Community College *A*

Ohio
Ohio State University
Agricultural Technical
Institute *A*
Columbus Campus *B,M,D*

Oklahoma
Oklahoma State University *M*

Oregon
Oregon State University *B*

Pennsylvania
Delaware Valley College *B*

South Carolina
Clemson University *B,M*

South Dakota
South Dakota State University *B,M*

Texas
Texas A&M University *B,M,D*

Utah
Utah State University *C,B,M*

Vermont
University of Vermont *B*
Vermont Technical College *A*

Virginia
Virginia Polytechnic Institute and
State University *B,M,D*

Washington
Skagit Valley College *A*

Wisconsin
Chippewa Valley Technical
College *A*
University of Wisconsin
Madison *B,M,D*
River Falls *B*

Canada
McGill University *M,D*

Dance

Alabama
Birmingham-Southern College *B*
Huntingdon College *B*
University of Alabama
Birmingham
Tuscaloosa *B*

Arizona
Arizona State University *B,M*
University of Arizona *B*

Arkansas
University of Arkansas *B*

California
Allan Hancock College *A*
California Institute of the Arts
C,B,M
California State University
Fresno *B,M*
Fullerton *B,M*
Hayward *B*
Long Beach *B,M*
Los Angeles *B*
Northridge *B*
Chabot College *A*
Chapman University *B*
Columbia College *A*
Fresno City College *A*
Glendale Community College *C*
Grossmont Community College *C,A*
Laney College *A*
Long Beach City College *A*
Loyola Marymount University *B*
Mills College *B,M*
Monterey Peninsula College *C,A*
Orange Coast College *A*
Palomar College *C,A*
Pitzer College *B*
San Francisco State University *B*
San Jose State University *B,M*
Santa Clara University *B*
Santa Monica College *A*
Santa Rosa Junior College *A*
Scripps College *B*
Southwestern College *A*
University of California
Berkeley *B*
Irvine *B,M*
Los Angeles *B,M*
Riverside *B*
Santa Barbara *B*
Santa Cruz *C,B*

Colorado

Colorado College *B*
Colorado State University *B*
Naropa Institute *B*
University of Colorado at Boulder *B,M*
University of Northern Colorado *B*

Connecticut

Connecticut College *B*
Trinity College *B*
Wesleyan University *B*

District of Columbia

American University *M*
George Washington University *B,M*
Howard University *B*

Florida

Daytona Beach Community College *A*
Florida International University *B*
Florida State University *B,M*
Jacksonville University *B*
Miami-Dade Community College *A*
Palm Beach Community College *A*
Pensacola Junior College *A*
St. Leo College *B*
University of South Florida *B*

Georgia

Brenau Women's College *B*
Georgia State University *B*
University of Georgia *B*

Hawaii

University of Hawaii at Manoa *B*

Idaho

Ricks College *A*
University of Idaho *B*

Illinois

Barat College *B*
Columbia College *B*
Illinois Central College *A*
Illinois State University *B*
Northwestern University *M*
Southern Illinois University
Carbondale *B*
Edwardsville *B*
University of Illinois at Urbana-Champaign *B,M*
William Rainey Harper College *A*

Indiana

Ball State University *B*
Butler University *B,M*
Earlham College *B*
Indiana University Bloomington *B,M,D*

Iowa

Teikyo Westmar University *B*
University of Iowa *B,M*

Kansas

Friends University *B*
Kansas State University *B*
University of Kansas *B*

Louisiana

Southeastern Louisiana University *B*
University of Southwestern Louisiana *B*

Maryland

Goucher College *B*
Montgomery College: Rockville Campus *A*
Towson State University *B*

University of Maryland
Baltimore County *B*
College Park *B*

Massachusetts

Boston Conservatory *B,M*
Bradford College *B*
Dean Junior College *A*
Elms College *C*
Emerson College *B*
Hampshire College *B*
Mount Holyoke College *B*
Northern Essex Community College *A*
Smith College *B,M*
University of Massachusetts at Amherst *B*

Michigan

Alma College *B*
Eastern Michigan University *B*
Hope College *B*
Lansing Community College *A*
Marygrove College *B*
University of Michigan *B,M*
Wayne State University *B*
Western Michigan University *B*

Minnesota

Mankato State University *A*
St. Olaf College *B*
University of Minnesota: Twin Cities *B*
Winona State University *A*

Mississippi

University of Southern Mississippi *B*

Missouri

Southwest Missouri State University *B*
Stephens College *B*
University of Missouri: Kansas City *B*
Washington University *B,M*
Webster University *B*

Montana

University of Montana *B*

Nebraska

Creighton University *B*
University of Nebraska—Lincoln *B,M*

Nevada

University of Nevada: Las Vegas *B,M*

New Jersey

Bergen Community College *A*
County College of Morris *A*
Mercer County Community College *A*
Montclair State College *B*
Rutgers—The State University of New Jersey
Douglass College *B*
Livingston College *B*
Mason Gross School of the Arts *B*
Rutgers College *B*
University College New Brunswick *B*
Stockton State College *B*
Thomas Edison State College *B*

New Mexico

University of New Mexico *B,M*

New York

Adelphi University *B*
Bard College *B*
Barnard College *B*
City University of New York
Brooklyn College *B,M*
City College *B*
Hunter College *B,M*
Lehman College *B*
Queens College *B*
Queensborough Community College *A*
Cornell University *B*
Hamilton College *B*
Hobart College *B*
Hofstra University *B*
Ithaca College *B*
Juilliard School *B*
Long Island University: Brooklyn Campus *B*
Manhattanville College *B*
Marymount Manhattan College *B*
Nassau Community College *A*
New York University *B,M,D*
Sarah Lawrence College *B,M*
Skidmore College *B*
State University of New York
Buffalo *B*
Purchase *B*
College at Brockport *B,M*
College at Potsdam *B*
William Smith College *B*

North Carolina

East Carolina University *B*
Lees-McRae College *B*
Meredith College *B*
North Carolina School of the Arts *C,B*
University of North Carolina
Charlotte *B*
Greensboro *B,M*

Ohio

Antioch College *B*
Baldwin-Wallace College *B*
Bowling Green State University *B*
Case Western Reserve University *B,M*
Central State University *B*
College of Wooster *B*
Denison University *B*
Kent State University *B*
Kenyon College *B*
Lake Erie College *B*
Oberlin College *B*
Ohio State University: Columbus Campus *B,M*
Ohio University *B*
Ohio Wesleyan University *B*
Otterbein College *B*
Sinclair Community College *A*
Union Institute *D*
University of Akron *B*
University of Cincinnati *B*
Wittenberg University *B*
Wright State University *B*

Oklahoma

Oklahoma City University *B*
University of Oklahoma *B,M*

Oregon

Portland Community College *A*
Portland State University *B*
Reed College *B*
University of Oregon
Eugene *B,M*
Robert Donald Clark Honors College *B*

Pennsylvania

Allentown College of St. Francis de Sales *B*
Bryn Mawr College *B*
Mercyhurst College *B*
Point Park College *B*
Slippery Rock University of Pennsylvania *B*
Temple University *B,M,D*
University of the Arts *C,B*

Rhode Island

Roger Williams College *B*

South Carolina

Coker College *B*
Columbia College *B*
Winthrop University *B*

South Dakota

Presentation College *A*

Tennessee

University of Tennessee: Martin *B*

Texas

Austin Community College *A*
Houston Community College *C*
Lamar University—Beaumont *B*
Lon Morris College *A*
Midland College *A*
Sam Houston State University *B*
Southern Methodist University *B*
Texas Christian University *B,M*
Texas Southmost College *A*
Texas Tech University *B*
Texas Woman's University *B,M,D*
University of Houston: Clear Lake *B*
University of North Texas *B*
University of Texas
Austin *B*
El Paso *B*
West Texas State University *B*

Utah

Brigham Young University *B,M,D*
Dixie College *A*
University of Utah *B,M*
Utah State University *B*

Vermont

Bennington College *B,M*
Marlboro College *B*
Middlebury College *B*

Virginia

George Mason University *B*
James Madison University *B*
Mary Washington College *B*
Old Dominion University *B*
Radford University *B*
Randolph-Macon Woman's College *B*
Shenandoah University *B*
Sweet Briar College *B*
Virginia Commonwealth University *B*
Virginia Intermont College *B*

Washington

Cornish College of the Arts *B*
Eastern Washington University *B*
Everett Community College *A*
University of Washington *B,M*

West Virginia

West Virginia University *B*

Wisconsin

University of Wisconsin
   Milwaukee *B*
   Stevens Point *B*

Wyoming

University of Wyoming *B*
Western Wyoming Community
   College *A*

Dance therapy

California

University of California: Los
   Angeles *M*
University of the Pacific *B*

Colorado

Naropa Institute *B,M*

Illinois

Barat College *B*
Columbia College *M*

Michigan

Hope College *B*
Marygrove College *B*

Missouri

ITT Technical Institute: St. Louis *B*

New Jersey

Stockton State College *B*

New York

City University of New York:
   Hunter College *M*
New York University *B,M*
Pratt Institute *M*
Russell Sage College *B*

Ohio

Union Institute *D*
University of Toledo *B*

Pennsylvania

Hahnemann University School of
   Health Sciences and
   Humanities *M*
Mercyhurst College *B*

Utah

Brigham Young University *D*

Washington

Evergreen State College *B*

Data processing

Alabama

Bessemer State Technical College *A*
Brewer State Junior College *A*
Chattahoochee Valley Community
   College *A*
Community College of the Air
   Force *A*
Douglas MacArthur State Technical
   College *A*
John M. Patterson State Technical
   College *A*
Lawson State Community
   College *A*
Selma University *A*
Shelton State Community College
   C,A
Shoals Community College *A*

Snead State Junior College *A*
Southern Union State Junior
   College *C,A*
Troy State University *B*
Walker State Technical College *C,A*

Alaska

University of Alaska Anchorage *A*

Arizona

Arizona Western College *A*
Pima Community College *C,A*

Arkansas

Garland County Community
   College *C,A*
Harding University *B*
Mississippi County Community
   College *A*
Phillips County Community
   College *A*
Southern Arkansas University:
   Technical Branch *C*
University of Arkansas at
   Monticello *A*
University of Central Arkansas *B*

California

Bakersfield College *A*
Barstow College *A*
California State University:
   Fresno *B*
Central California Commercial
   College *A*
Cerritos Community College *A*
Chabot College *C,A*
College of the Sequoias *C*
Cosumnes River College *A*
Glendale Community College *C*
Heald Business College: Walnut
   Creek *C,A*
Heald College
   Sacramento *C,A*
   Santa Rosa *C,A*
Imperial Valley College *A*
Kelsey-Jenney College *C,A*
Long Beach City College *C,A*
Los Angeles Valley College *C,A*
Monterey Peninsula College *C,A*
Mount San Antonio College *C,A*
Pacific Union College *B*
Pasadena City College *C,A*
Phillips Junior College
   Condie Campus *A*
   Fresno Campus *C,A*
Porterville College *C*
San Diego City College *C,A*
San Diego Mesa College *A*
San Joaquin Delta College *A*
Santa Monica College *C,A*
Santa Rosa Junior College *C,A*
Sierra College *A*
Southwestern College *A*
Taft College *C,A*
Ventura College *A*
Victor Valley College *C*

Colorado

Colorado Mountain College: Alpine
   Campus *C*
Denver Technical College *C*
Mesa State College *C,A*
Pueblo Community College *A*
Trinidad State Junior College *A*

Connecticut

Greater New Haven State Technical
   College *C*
Manchester Community College
   C,A
Norwalk Community College *A*
Norwalk State Technical College *A*

Sacred Heart University *B*
South Central Community
   College *A*
Thames Valley State Technical
   College *A*
Waterbury State Technical
   College *A*

Delaware

Delaware Technical and
   Community College
   Southern Campus *A*
   Stanton/Wilmington
    Campus *A*
   Terry Campus *A*

Florida

Brevard Community College *A*
Daytona Beach Community
   College *A*
Florida Memorial College *B*
Gulf Coast Community College *A*
Hillsborough Community College *C*
Jones College *A,B*
Miami-Dade Community College *C*
National School of Technology *A*
Palm Beach Community College *A*
Phillips Junior College:
   Melbourne *C*
Santa Fe Community College *A*
Seminole Community College *C*
South Florida Community
   College *A*
Tallahassee Community College
   C,A

Georgia

Abraham Baldwin Agricultural
   College *A*
Brewton-Parker College *A*
Brunswick College *C,A*
Clayton State College *C,A*
Columbus College *C,A*
Darton College *A*
DeKalb College *A*
DeKalb Technical Institute *A*
Floyd College *A*
Gainesville College *A*
Middle Georgia College *A*
South Georgia College *C*
Truett-McConnell College *A*

Hawaii

University of Hawaii: Kapiolani
   Community College *C,A*

Idaho

Idaho State University *C,A*
North Idaho College *A*
Ricks College *A*

Illinois

Belleville Area College *C,A*
Black Hawk College
   East Campus *C*
   Moline *A*
Carl Sandburg College *A*
Chicago State University *B*
City Colleges of Chicago
   Chicago City-Wide College
    C,A
   Malcolm X College *A*
   Olive-Harvey College *C,A*
   Richard J. Daley College *A*
   Wright College *A*
College of DuPage *C,A*
College of Lake County *A*
Elgin Community College *C,A*
Kishwaukee College *A*
Lake Land College *C,A*
Lewis and Clark Community
   College *A*

Lincoln Land Community
   College *A*
Morton College *C,A*
National-Louis University *C*
Oakton Community College *C,A*
Parkland College *A*
Prairie State College *C,A*
Richland Community College *A*
Roosevelt University *B*
Shawnee Community College *C*
Southern Illinois University at
   Carbondale *A*
Spoon River College *A*
State Community College *A*
Triton College *A*
William Rainey Harper College *C,A*

Indiana

Indiana University
   Kokomo *B*
   Northwest *B*
Indiana University—Purdue
   University at Fort Wayne *C*
Purdue University *B,M,D*
University of Indianapolis *A,B*
Vincennes University *A*

Iowa

American Institute of Business *A*
American Institute of Commerce *C*
Dordt College *A*
Iowa Central Community College *A*
Iowa Lakes Community College *A*
Kirkwood Community College *C*
Waldorf College *A*

Kansas

Brown Mackie College *C*
Butler County Community College
   C,A
Central College *A*
Cowley County Community
   College *A*
Dodge City Community College
   C,A
Donnelly College *C,A*
Haskell Indian Junior College *A*
Hutchinson Community College *A*
Johnson County Community
   College *A*
Kansas City Kansas Community
   College *C,A*
Labette Community College *A*
Seward County Community
   College *A*

Kentucky

Campbellsville College *A*
Franklin College *C*
Jefferson Community College *A*
Lexington Community College *A*
Maysville Community College *A*
Owensboro Junior College of
   Business *C,A*
Thomas More College *A,B*
University of Louisville *A*

Louisiana

Bossier Parish Community
   College *A*
Northwestern State University *A,B*

Maine

Beal College *A*
Casco Bay College *A*
Husson College *A,B*

Maryland

Allegany Community College *A*
Anne Arundel Community
   College *A*
Catonsville Community College *C,A*

Cecil Community College *C,A*
Charles County Community
    College *A*
Chesapeake College *A*
Essex Community College *C,A*
Frederick Community College *A*
Hagerstown Junior College *A*
Harford Community College *C*
Howard Community College *C,A*
Montgomery College: Germantown
    Campus *A*
University of Baltimore *B*

Massachusetts

Aquinas College at Milton *A*
Berkshire Community College *A*
Massasoit Community College *A*
Quincy College *A*
Quinsigamond Community College
    C,A
Springfield Technical Community
    College *A*

Michigan

Alpena Community College *A*
Baker College
    Auburn Hills *A*
    Flint *A,B*
    Mount Clemens *A*
    Muskegon *B*
    Owosso *A*
    Port Huron *A*
Charles Stewart Mott Community
    College *C*
Cleary College *A*
Delta College *A*
Detroit College of Business *A*
Glen Oaks Community College *C*
Grand Rapids Community College
    C,A
Grand Valley State University *B*
Great Lakes Junior College of
    Business *C*
Jackson Community College *A*
Kalamazoo Valley Community
    College *A*
Kellogg Community College *C,A*
Kirtland Community College *A*
Lansing Community College *A*
Montcalm Community College *A*
Muskegon Community College *A*
Northern Michigan University *A,B*
Northwood Institute *A,B*
Oakland Community College *A*
St. Clair County Community
    College *C,A*
Suomi College *A*
West Shore Community College *A*

Minnesota

Itasca Community College:
    Arrowhead Region *A*
Lakewood Community College *A*
Mankato State University *B*
Vermilion Community College *A*
Willmar Community College *A*

Mississippi

Copiah-Lincoln Community
    College *C*
Jackson State University *B*
Jones County Junior College *A*
Mississippi College *B*
Northeast Mississippi Community
    College *A*
Phillips Junior College
    Jackson *A*
    Mississippi Gulf Coast *C,A*
William Carey College *B*

Missouri

College of the Ozarks *B*
Hannibal-LaGrange College *B*
Jefferson College *A*
Longview Community College *A*
Maple Woods Community College
    C,A
Missouri Southern State College *C*
Moberly Area Community
    College *A*
North Central Missouri College *A*
Penn Valley Community College
    C,A
Phillips Junior College *A*
St. Louis Community College
    Florissant Valley *C,A*
    Forest Park *C,A*
    Meramec *C,A*
Southwest Baptist University *B*
Washington University *B,M*

Montana

Miles Community College *A*
Rocky Mountain College *A*

Nebraska

Central Community College *C,A*
Lincoln School of Commerce *A*
Midland Lutheran College *A,B*
Western Nebraska Community
    College: Scottsbluff Campus *C,A*

Nevada

Northern Nevada Community
    College *A*
Truckee Meadows Community
    College *A*

New Jersey

Bergen Community College *C*
Burlington County College *C,A*
Kean College of New Jersey *B*
Mercer County Community College
    C,A
Rider College *B*
St. Peter's College *C*
Thomas Edison State College *C,A,B*

New Mexico

Albuquerque Technical-Vocational
    Institute *C*
New Mexico State University at
    Carlsbad *C*
Parks College *C*
San Juan College *C,A*

New York

Adirondack Community College
    C,A
Berkeley School: New York City *C*
Bramson ORT Technical Institute
    C,A
Broome Community College *A*
Bryant & Stratton Business Institute
    Albany *A*
    Buffalo *C*
City University of New York
    Hostos Community College *A*
    Kingsborough Community
        College *A*
    La Guardia Community
        College *A*
    New York City Technical
        College *A*
    Queensborough Community
        College *C*
Columbia-Greene Community
    College *A*
Community College of the Finger
    Lakes *A*
Corning Community College *A*

Erie Community College: South
    Campus *A*
Five Towns College *C,A*
Fulton-Montgomery Community
    College *A*
Herkimer County Community
    College *A*
Hilbert College *A*
Hudson Valley Community College
    C,A
Iona College *C,A*
Jefferson Community College *A*
Mohawk Valley Community College
    C,A
Monroe Community College *A*
Nassau Community College *C,A*
New York Institute of
    Technology *A*
Niagara County Community
    College *A*
Onondaga Community College *A*
Orange County Community
    College *A*
Rochester Business Institute *C*
Rockland Community College *A*
St. Francis College *C,A*
St. Joseph's College
    Brooklyn *C*
    Suffolk Campus *C*
State University of New York
    Purchase *C*
    College of Agriculture and
        Technology at Cobleskill *A*
    College of Agriculture and
        Technology at Morrisville *A*
    College of Technology at
        Alfred *A*
    College of Technology at
        Delhi *A*
    College of Technology at
        Farmingdale *C,A*
Suffolk County Community College
    Selden *A*
    Western Campus *A*
Sullivan County Community
    College *C,A*
Tompkins-Cortland Community
    College *A*
Utica School of Commerce *A*
Westchester Business Institute *A*

North Carolina

Anson Community College *C,A*
Bladen Community College *C*
Campbell University *B*
Catawba Valley Community College
    C,A
Central Piedmont Community
    College *A*
Davidson County Community
    College *C,A*
Durham Technical Community
    College *A*
Gardner-Webb College *B*
Gaston College *A*
James Sprunt Community
    College *C*
Sandhills Community College *C,A*
University of North Carolina at
    Greensboro *B*
Vance-Granville Community
    College *A*

North Dakota

University of North Dakota:
    Williston *C*

Ohio

Air Force Institute of
    Technology *M*
Central State University *B*
Cincinnati Metropolitan College *A*

Cincinnati Technical College *A*
Cuyahoga Community College:
    Metropolitan Campus *A*
Edison State Community College
    C,A
Marion Technical College *C,A*
Mount Vernon Nazarene College *B*
Muskingum Area Technical
    College *C*
Shawnee State University *A*
Terra Technical College *C*
University of Akron *A*
University of Cincinnati *B*
University of Toledo *A*
Washington State Community
    College *A*

Oklahoma

Cameron University *A*
Connors State College *C,A*
University of Central Oklahoma *B*
University of Science and Arts of
    Oklahoma *B*

Oregon

Central Oregon Community College
    C,A
Portland Community College *C,A*

Pennsylvania

Butler County Community
    College *A*
Clarion University of
    Pennsylvania *A*
Delaware County Community
    College *A*
La Salle University *B*
Lehigh County Community
    College *A*
Montgomery County Community
    College *A*
Northampton County Area
    Community College *A*
Reading Area Community
    College *A*
Robert Morris College *B,M*
St. Francis College *A*
University of Pittsburgh at
    Titusville *A*
Westmoreland County Community
    College *A*

Puerto Rico

ICPR Junior College *A*
Puerto Rico Junior College *A*

Rhode Island

Johnson & Wales University *B*

South Carolina

Aiken Technical College *C*
Bob Jones University *B*
Chesterfield-Marlboro Technical
    College *C,A*
Horry-Georgetown Technical
    College *A*
Sumter Area Technical College *A*
Technical College of the
    Lowcountry *A*
Tri-County Technical College *A*

South Dakota

National College *A,B*
Sinte Gleska College *C,A*

Tennessee

Chattanooga State Technical
    Community College *A*
Dyersburg State Community
    College *A*
Lambuth University *B*
McKenzie College *A*

Motlow State Community
College *A*
Nashville State Technical
Institute *A*
Pellissippi State Technical
Community College *A*

Texas

Alvin Community College *C*
Angelina College *A*
Austin Community College *A*
Brazosport College *A*
Central Texas College *C*
College of the Mainland *A*
Cooke County College *A*
El Centro College *C,A*
Houston Community College *A*
Howard College *C*
Kilgore College *A*
Lee College *A*
McLennan Community College *C,A*
Midland College *A*
Mountain View College *A*
North Harris Montgomery
Community College District *C,A*
North Lake College *A*
Panola College *A*
Richland College *A*
San Antonio College *A*
South Plains College *A*
Tarrant County Junior College *A*
Temple Junior College *C,A*
Texas Southmost College *A*
Texas State Technical College
Sweetwater *A*
Waco *C,A*
University of Houston:
Downtown *B*
Victoria College *A*

Utah

Dixie College *A*
LDS Business College *A*
Southern Utah University *A*
Weber State University *B*

Vermont

Champlain College *A*

Virginia

Averett College *B*
Commonwealth College *C,A*
Dabney S. Lancaster Community
College *A*
Eastern Mennonite College *A*
Lord Fairfax Community College *C*
Mountain Empire Community
College *C*
New River Community College *A*
Northern Virginia Community
College *A*

Washington

Bellevue Community College *A*
Big Bend Community College *A*
Everett Community College *A*
Grays Harbor College *A*
Griffin College *C,A,B*
ITT Technical Institute: Seattle *C*
Lower Columbia College *A*
North Seattle Community
College *A*
Northwest Indian College *C*
Olympic College *C,A*
Pacific Lutheran University *B*
Peninsula College *A*
Seattle Central Community
College *A*
South Puget Sound Community
College *C,A*
Spokane Community College *A*

Walla Walla Community College
C,A
Yakima Valley Community
College *C*

West Virginia

Fairmont State College *A*
Potomac State College of West
Virginia University *A*
Shepherd College *A,B*
West Virginia Institute of
Technology *A*
West Virginia Northern Community
College *A*

Wisconsin

Chippewa Valley Technical
College *A*
Fox Valley Technical College *A*
Madison Area Technical College *A*
Mid-State Technical College *A*
Northeast Wisconsin Technical
College *A*
Stratton College *C,A*
University of Wisconsin
Oshkosh *B*
Superior *B*
Waukesha County Technical
College *A*
Wisconsin Indianhead Technical
College *A*

Wyoming

Casper College *A*
Central Wyoming College *C,A*
Western Wyoming Community
College *C,A*

**American Samoa, Caroline
Islands, Guam, Marianas,
Virgin Islands**

University of the Virgin Islands *A*

Demography

California

University of California: Berkeley
M,D
University of Southern California *M*

District of Columbia

Georgetown University *M*

Florida

Florida State University *M*

Illinois

Northwestern University *M*
University of Chicago *M,D*

Massachusetts

Hampshire College *B*

Michigan

University of Michigan *M,D*

New Jersey

Princeton University *D*

New York

Cornell University *D*
Iona College *B,M*
State University of New York at
Albany *B,M*

Ohio

Bowling Green State University *M*
Ohio State University: Columbus
Campus *B,M,D*

Pennsylvania

Penn State University Park Campus
M,D
University of Pennsylvania *M,D*

Puerto Rico

University of Puerto Rico: Medical
Sciences Campus *M*

Rhode Island

Brown University *M,D*

Dental assistant

Alabama

Bessemer State Technical College *C*
Community College of the Air
Force *A*
James H. Faulkner State
Community College *C,A*
John C. Calhoun State Community
College *C,A*
University of Alabama in
Birmingham *C*
Walker College *A*
Wallace State Community College
at Hanceville *A*

Alaska

University of Alaska Anchorage
C,A

Arizona

Pima Community College *C*

California

Allan Hancock College *C,A*
Bakersfield College *C,A*
California State University:
Dominguez Hills *B*
Cerritos Community College *C,A*
Chabot College *C,A*
Chaffey Community College *C,A*
Citrus College *C,A*
City College of San Francisco *C,A*
College of the Redwoods *C*
Diablo Valley College *A*
Foothill College *C,A*
Kings River Community College *A*
Merced College *C,A*
Modesto Junior College *A*
Monterey Peninsula College *C,A*
Orange Coast College *C,A*
Palomar College *C,A*
Pasadena City College *C,A*
Rio Hondo College *A*
San Diego Mesa College *C,A*
San Jose City College *A*
Santa Barbara City College *C*
Santa Rosa Junior College *C,A*

Colorado

Front Range Community College *C*
Pikes Peak Community College *C,A*

Connecticut

Briarwood College *C,A*
Tunxis Community College *C*

Delaware

Delaware Technical and
Community College: Stanton/
Wilmington Campus *A*

District of Columbia

Howard University *C*

Florida

Brevard Community College *C*
Broward Community College *A*
Daytona Beach Community
College *C*
Gulf Coast Community College *C,A*
Indian River Community College *C*
Palm Beach Community College *C*
Pasco-Hernando Community
College *C*
Pensacola Junior College *A*
Santa Fe Community College *C*
Southern College *C*

Georgia

Augusta Technical Institute *C*
Gainesville College *A*
Savannah Technical Institute *C*

Hawaii

University of Hawaii: Kapiolani
Community College *C*

Idaho

Boise State University *C*
Lewis Clark State College *C*

Illinois

Black Hawk College *C*
Elgin Community College *C*
Illinois Central College *C*
Illinois Valley Community
College *C*
John A. Logan College *A*
Lewis and Clark Community
College *C*
Lincoln Land Community
College *C*
Morton College *A*
Parkland College *C*
Shawnee Community College *A*

Indiana

Indiana State University *B*
Indiana University
Northwest *C*
South Bend *C*
Indiana University—Purdue
University
Fort Wayne *C,A*
Indianapolis *C*
Indiana Vocational Technical
College: Lafayette *C*
University of Southern Indiana *A*

Iowa

Des Moines Area Community
College *C*
Hawkeye Institute of Technology *C*
Iowa Central Community College
C,A
Iowa Western Community
College *C*
Kirkwood Community College *A*
Northeast Iowa Community
College *C*

Kansas

Fort Scott Community College *C*
Haskell Indian Junior College *A*
Hutchinson Community College *A*

Louisiana

Northwestern State University *A*

Maine

Kennebec Valley Technical
College *C*
University of Maine *C*

Maryland

Allegany Community College *C*
Essex Community College *A*
Montgomery College: Takoma Park
Campus *C,A*

Massachusetts

Boston University *C*
Bunker Hill Community College *A*
Massasoit Community College *C*
Middlesex Community College *A*
Mount Ida College *C,A*
Northern Essex Community
College *C*
Springfield Technical Community
College *C*

Michigan

Charles Stewart Mott Community
College *A*
Delta College *C,A*
Grand Rapids Community
College *A*
Lansing Community College *A*
Northwestern Michigan College *A*

Minnesota

Normandale Community College *C*

Mississippi

Hinds Community College *C,A*

Missouri

East Central College *C,A*
Mineral Area College *C*
St. Louis Community College at
Forest Park *A*

Montana

Salish Kootenai College *A*

Nebraska

Central Community College *A*
Metropolitan Community College *C*
Southeast Community College:
Lincoln Campus *C*

Nevada

Truckee Meadows Community
College *C,A*

New Jersey

Camden County College *C*
University of Medicine and
Dentistry of New Jersey: School
of Health Related Professions *C*

New Mexico

University of New Mexico *C*

New York

Mohawk Valley Community
College *C*
New York University *C*

North Carolina

Alamance Community College *A*
Asheville Buncombe Technical
Community College *C*
Coastal Carolina Community
College *C*
Fayetteville Technical Community
College *C*
Guilford Technical Community
College *C*
Wake Technical Community
College *C*
Western Piedmont Community
College *C*
Wilkes Community College *C*

North Dakota

North Dakota State College of
Science *C*

Ohio

Cuyahoga Community College:
Metropolitan Campus *A*
Jefferson Technical College *C,A*
Ohio Valley Business College *A*

Oklahoma

Oklahoma State University *B*
Rose State College *C,A*

Oregon

Chemeketa Community College *C*
Lane Community College *C*
Linn-Benton Community College *C*
Oregon State University *B*
Portland Community College *C*

Pennsylvania

Community College of
Philadelphia *C*
Harcum Junior College *A*
Harrisburg Area Community
College *C*
Luzerne County Community
College *C,A*
Manor Junior College *A*
Northampton County Area
Community College *C*
West Chester University of
Pennsylvania *B*
Westmoreland County Community
College *C*

Puerto Rico

Huertas Junior College *A*
University of Puerto Rico: Medical
Sciences Campus *A*

Rhode Island

Community College of Rhode
Island *C*

South Carolina

Aiken Technical College *C*
Florence-Darlington Technical
College *C*
Greenville Technical College *C*
Midlands Technical College *C*
Tri-County Technical College *C*
Trident Technical College *C*

Tennessee

Chattanooga State Technical
Community College *C,A*
East Tennessee State University
C,A
Volunteer State Community College
C,A

Texas

Amarillo College *C*
Del Mar College *C,A*
El Paso Community College *C,A*
Houston Community College *C*
North Harris Montgomery
Community College District *C,A*
San Antonio College *C,A*
Texas State Technical College:
Waco *C*

Virginia

Wytheville Community College *C*

Washington

Northwest Indian College *C*
South Puget Sound Community
College *C,A*
Spokane Community College *C,A*

Wisconsin

Concordia University Wisconsin *C*
Fox Valley Technical College *C*
Madison Area Technical College *A*
Northeast Wisconsin Technical
College *C*
Western Wisconsin Technical
College *C*

Wyoming

Sheridan College *C*

Dental hygiene

Alabama

Community College of the Air
Force *A*
University of Alabama in
Birmingham *B*
Walker College *A*

Alaska

University of Alaska Anchorage *A*

Arizona

Northern Arizona University *B*
Pima Community College *A*

Arkansas

University of Arkansas for Medical
Sciences *A,B*

California

Cerritos Community College *C,A*
Chabot College *C,A*
Diablo Valley College *C,A*
Foothill College *A*
Fresno City College *A*
Pasadena City College *C,A*
University of California: San
Francisco *B*
University of Southern California *B*

Colorado

Colorado Northwestern Community
College *A*
Pueblo Community College *A*
University of Colorado Health
Sciences Center *B*

Connecticut

Sacred Heart University *B*
Tunxis Community College *A*
University of Bridgeport *A,B*

Delaware

Delaware Technical and
Community College
Southern Campus *A*
Stanton/Wilmington
Campus *A*
Terry Campus *A*

District of Columbia

Howard University *B*

Florida

Brevard Community College *A*
Florida Community College at
Jacksonville *A*
Indian River Community College *A*
Miami-Dade Community College *A*
Palm Beach Community College *A*
Pasco-Hernando Community
College *A*
Pensacola Junior College *A*
St. Petersburg Junior College *A*
Santa Fe Community College *A*
Tallahassee Community College *A*

Valencia Community College *A*

Georgia

Armstrong State College *A,B*
Brewton-Parker College *A*
Clayton State College *A*
Columbus College *A*
Darton College *A*
DeKalb College *A*
Floyd College *A*
Gainesville College *A*
Gordon College *A*
Macon College *A*
Medical College of Georgia *A,B,M*

Hawaii

University of Hawaii at Manoa *B*

Idaho

Idaho State University *B*
Ricks College *A*

Illinois

Illinois Central College *A*
John A. Logan College *A*
Lake Land College *A*
Loyola University of Chicago *B*
Parkland College *A*
Prairie State College *A*
Southern Illinois University at
Carbondale *A*
William Rainey Harper College *A*

Indiana

Indiana University
Bloomington *A*
Northwest *A*
South Bend *A,B*
Indiana University—Purdue
University
Fort Wayne *A,B*
Indianapolis *A,B*
University of Southern Indiana *A*
Vincennes University *A*

Iowa

Des Moines Area Community
College *A*
Hawkeye Institute of Technology *A*
University of Iowa *B,M*

Kansas

Hutchinson Community College *A*
Johnson County Community
College *A*
Wichita State University *A*

Kentucky

Lexington Community College *A*
Maysville Community College *A*
Northern Kentucky University *A*
University of Louisville *A,B*
Western Kentucky University *A,B*

Louisiana

Louisiana State University Medical
Center *B*
Northeast Louisiana University *B*

Maine

University of Maine *A*
Westbrook College *A,B*

Maryland

Allegany Community College *A*
Charles County Community
College *A*
New Community College of
Baltimore *A*
Villa Julie College *A*

Massachusetts

Bristol Community College *A*
Cape Cod Community College *A*
Endicott College *A*
Forsyth School for Dental
Hygienists *A,B*
Middlesex Community College *A*
Quinsigamond Community
College *A*
Springfield Technical Community
College *A*

Michigan

Charles Stewart Mott Community
College *A*
Delta College *A*
Ferris State University *A*
Grand Rapids Community
College *A*
Kalamazoo Valley Community
College *A*
Kellogg Community College *A*
Lansing Community College *A*
Oakland Community College *A*
University of Detroit Mercy *B*
University of Michigan *B,M*

Minnesota

Mankato State University *A*
Normandale Community College *C*
University of Minnesota: Twin
Cities *B*

Mississippi

Meridian Community College *A*
Northeast Mississippi Community
College *A*
University of Mississippi Medical
Center *B*

Missouri

Missouri Southern State College *A*
St. Louis Community College at
Forest Park *A*
University of Missouri: Kansas City
B,M

Nebraska

Central Community College *A*
University of Nebraska Medical
Center *B*

Nevada

Community College of Southern
Nevada *A*

New Jersey

Bergen Community College *A*
Camden County College *A*
Essex County College *A*
Thomas Edison State College *B*
University of Medicine and
Dentistry of New Jersey: School
of Health Related Professions *A*

New Mexico

University of New Mexico *A,B*

New York

Broome Community College *A*
City University of New York
Hostos Community College *A*
New York City Technical
College *A*
Erie Community College: North
Campus *A*
Hudson Valley Community
College *A*
Monroe Community College *A*
New York University *A*
Onondaga Community College *A*

Orange County Community
College *A*
State University of New York
College of Technology at
Farmingdale *A*

North Carolina

Asheville Buncombe Technical
Community College *A*
Central Piedmont Community
College *A*
Coastal Carolina Community
College *A*
Fayetteville Technical Community
College *A*
Guilford Technical Community
College *A*
University of North Carolina at
Chapel Hill *B*
Wayne Community College *A*

North Dakota

North Dakota State College of
Science *A*

Ohio

Cuyahoga Community College:
Metropolitan Campus *A*
Lakeland Community College *A*
Ohio State University: Columbus
Campus *C,B*
Owens Technical College: Toledo *A*
Shawnee State University *A*
Sinclair Community College *A*
University of Cincinnati: Raymond
Walters College *A*
Youngstown State University *A*

Oklahoma

Rose State College *A*
Tulsa Junior College *A*
University of Oklahoma
Health Sciences Center *B*
Norman *B*

Oregon

Lane Community College *A*
Mount Hood Community
College *A*
Oregon Health Sciences
University *B*
Oregon Institute of Technology *A,B*
Portland Community College *A*

Pennsylvania

Bloomsburg University of
Pennsylvania *B*
California University of
Pennsylvania *B*
Community College of
Philadelphia *A*
Edinboro University of
Pennsylvania *B*
Elizabethtown College *B*
Harcum Junior College *A*
Harrisburg Area Community
College *A*
Juniata College *B*
Keystone Junior College *A*
Lebanon Valley College of
Pennsylvania *B*
Luzerne County Community
College *A*
Montgomery County Community
College *A*
Northampton County Area
Community College *A*
Pennsylvania College of
Technology *A*
Thomas Jefferson University:
College of Allied Health
Sciences *B*

Villanova University *B*
West Chester University of
Pennsylvania *B*
Westmoreland County Community
College *A*

Puerto Rico

University of Puerto Rico: Medical
Sciences Campus *A*

Rhode Island

Community College of Rhode
Island *A*
University of Rhode Island *A,B*

South Carolina

Florence-Darlington Technical
College *A*
Greenville Technical College *A*
Midlands Technical College *A*
Trident Technical College *A*

South Dakota

University of South Dakota *A,B*

Tennessee

Austin Peay State University *B*
Chattanooga State Technical
Community College *A*
East Tennessee State University *A*
Hiwassee College *A*
Roane State Community College *A*
Tennessee State University *A,B*
University of Tennessee:
Memphis *B*

Texas

Amarillo College *A*
Baylor College of Dentistry *B*
Bee County College *A*
Del Mar College *A*
El Paso Community College *A*
Howard College *A*
Lamar University—Beaumont *A*
Midwestern State University *B*
Tarrant County Junior College *A*
Texas Southmost College *A*
Texas Woman's University *B*
Wharton County Junior College *A*

Utah

Weber State University *A*

Vermont

University of Vermont *A*

Virginia

Northern Virginia Community
College *A*
Old Dominion University *B,M*
Virginia Commonwealth
University *B*
Virginia Highlands Community
College *A*
Wytheville Community College *A*

Washington

Clark College *A*
Eastern Washington University *B*
Pierce College *A*
Shoreline Community College *A*
Spokane Community College *A*
Yakima Valley Community
College *A*

West Virginia

West Liberty State College *A,B*
West Virginia Institute of
Technology *A*
West Virginia University *B,M*

Wisconsin

Madison Area Technical College *A*
Marquette University *B*
Northeast Wisconsin Technical
College *A*

Wyoming

Sheridan College *A*
University of Wyoming *B*

Dental laboratory technology

Alabama

Community College of the Air
Force *A*

Arizona

Pima Community College *A*

California

City College of San Francisco *C,A*
Diablo Valley College *A*
Los Angeles City College *C,A*
Merced College *A*
Pasadena City College *C,A*

Florida

Indian River Community College *A*
Palm Beach Community College *A*
Pensacola Junior College *A*
Southern College *A*

Georgia

Atlanta Metropolitan College *A*
Augusta Technical Institute *A*
Medical College of Georgia *A*

Illinois

John A. Logan College *A*
Southern Illinois University at
Carbondale *A*
Triton College *C,A*

Indiana

Indiana University—Purdue
University at Fort Wayne *A*

Iowa

Kirkwood Community College *A*

Kentucky

Lexington Community College *A*

Louisiana

Louisiana College *B*
Louisiana State University Medical
Center *B*

Maryland

University of Maryland: Baltimore
B,M

Massachusetts

Boston University *B*
Middlesex Community College *A*

Michigan

Ferris State University *A*

Missouri

St. Louis Community College at
Meramec *C,A*

Nebraska

Central Community College *C,A*

New York
City University of New York: New
York City Technical College *A*
Erie Community College: South
Campus *A*

North Carolina
Durham Technical Community
College *A*
Shaw University *B*

Ohio
Columbus State Community
College *A*
Cuyahoga Community College:
Metropolitan Campus *A*

Oregon
Portland Community College *C,A*

Tennessee
Chattanooga State Technical
Community College *A*
East Tennessee State University *A*

Texas
Howard College *C*
Texas Southmost College *A*
Texas State Technical College:
Harlingen *A*

West Virginia
West Virginia State College *A*

Dental specialties

Alabama
University of Alabama in
Birmingham *W*

California
University of California
Los Angeles *M,W*
San Francisco *W*
University of the Pacific *W*
University of Southern California
M,D

Colorado
University of Colorado Health
Sciences Center *W*

Connecticut
University of Connecticut *M*

Florida
Southern College *A*

Georgia
Medical College of Georgia *W*

Idaho
Idaho State University *W*

Illinois
Loyola University of Chicago *W*
Northwestern University *M,W*
University of Illinois at Chicago
M,W

Indiana
Indiana University—Purdue
University at Indianapolis
M,D,W

Iowa
University of Iowa *M*

Kentucky
University of Kentucky *M*
University of Louisville *M,W*

Louisiana
Louisiana State University Medical
Center *W*

Maryland
University of Maryland: Baltimore
M,D

Massachusetts
Boston University *M,D,W*
Harvard University *W*
Tufts University *W*

Michigan
University of Detroit Mercy *W*
University of Michigan *M,D,W*

Minnesota
University of Minnesota: Twin
Cities *M*

Mississippi
University of Mississippi
Medical Center *W*
University *D*

Missouri
University of Missouri: Kansas City
M,W

Nebraska
University of Nebraska Medical
Center *M,W*

New York
Columbia University *M,W*
New York University *W*
State University of New York at
Buffalo *M,D,W*
University of Rochester *W*

North Carolina
University of North Carolina at
Chapel Hill *W*

Ohio
Case Western Reserve
University *W*
Ohio State University: Columbus
Campus *M*

Oklahoma
University of Oklahoma Health
Sciences Center *M,D*

Oregon
Oregon Health Sciences
University *M*

Pennsylvania
Temple University *M,D*
University of Pittsburgh *M,D,W*

Puerto Rico
University of Puerto Rico: Medical
Sciences Campus *W*

Tennessee
University of Tennessee:
Memphis *M*

Texas
Baylor College of Dentistry *W*
Baylor University *M*

University of Texas
Health Science Center at
Houston *W*
Health Science Center at San
Antonio *M,W*

Virginia
Virginia Commonwealth University
M,D,W

Washington
University of Washington *M,D*

West Virginia
West Virginia University *M*

Canada
McGill University *W*

Dentistry (D.D.S. or D.M.D.)

Alabama
University of Alabama in
Birmingham *F*

California
La Sierra University *F*
University of California
Los Angeles *F*
San Francisco *F*
University of the Pacific *F*
University of Southern California *F*

Colorado
University of Colorado Health
Sciences Center *F*

Connecticut
University of Connecticut *F*

District of Columbia
Howard University *F*

Florida
University of Florida *F*

Georgia
Medical College of Georgia *F*

Illinois
Loyola University of Chicago *F*
Northwestern University *F*
Southern Illinois University at
Edwardsville *F*
University of Illinois at Chicago *F*

Indiana
Indiana University—Purdue
University at Indianapolis *F*

Iowa
University of Iowa *F*

Kentucky
University of Kentucky *F*
University of Louisville *F*

Louisiana
Louisiana State University Medical
Center *F*

Maryland
University of Maryland:
Baltimore *F*

Massachusetts
Boston University *F*
Harvard University *F*

Tufts University *F*

Michigan
University of Detroit Mercy *F*
University of Michigan *F*

Minnesota
University of Minnesota: Twin
Cities *F*

Mississippi
University of Mississippi Medical
Center *F*

Missouri
University of Missouri: Kansas
City *F*

Nebraska
Creighton University *F*
University of Nebraska Medical
Center *F*

New York
New York University *F*
State University of New York
Buffalo *F*
Health Sciences Center at
Stony Brook *F*

North Carolina
University of North Carolina at
Chapel Hill *F*

Ohio
Case Western Reserve University *F*
Ohio State University: Columbus
Campus *F*

Oklahoma
University of Oklahoma
Health Sciences Center *F*
Norman *F*

Oregon
Oregon Health Sciences
University *F*

Pennsylvania
Temple University *F*
University of Pennsylvania *F*
University of Pittsburgh *F*

Puerto Rico
University of Puerto Rico: Medical
Sciences Campus *F*

Tennessee
Meharry Medical College *F*
University of Tennessee:
Memphis *F*

Texas
Baylor College of Dentistry *F*
University of Texas
Health Science Center at
Houston *F*
Health Science Center at San
Antonio *F*

Virginia
Virginia Commonwealth
University *F*

Washington
University of Washington *F*

West Virginia
West Virginia University *F*

Wisconsin

Marquette University *F*

Canada

McGill University *F*

Developmental psychology

Alabama

Alabama Agricultural and
Mechanical University *B*
University of Alabama in
Huntsville *M*

Arizona

Prescott College *B*

California

California State University
Bakersfield *B*
Stanislaus *B*
Citrus College *C*
Pacific Oaks College *M*
San Francisco State University *B,M*
San Jose State University *B*
University of California
Riverside *B*
Santa Barbara *B*
Santa Cruz *B,D*

Connecticut

Wesleyan University *B*

District of Columbia

Catholic University of America
M,D
Gallaudet University *M*
George Washington University *D*

Florida

Florida International University *D*
New College of the University of
South Florida *B*
Nova University *D*
University of Florida *M,D*
University of Miami *B*

Georgia

Emory University *M,D*
University of Georgia *D*

Illinois

Illinois State University *M*
Loyola University of Chicago *M,D*
Trinity Christian College *B*
University of Chicago *B,M,D*
University of Illinois at Urbana-
Champaign *B,M,D*

Indiana

Indiana University Bloomington
M,D
Purdue University
Calumet *B*
West Lafayette *B,M,D*
University of Notre Dame *M,D*

Iowa

University of Iowa *D*

Kansas

Kansas State University *M,D*
University of Kansas *B,M,D*

Louisiana

University of New Orleans *D*

Maryland

St. Mary's College of Maryland *B*
University of Maryland Baltimore
County *D*

Massachusetts

Boston University *M,D*
Brandeis University *M,D*
Clark University *D,W*
Emmanuel College *B*
Hampshire College *B*
Harvard University *D*
Lesley College *B*
Massachusetts Institute of
Technology *M,D*
Pine Manor College *B*
Suffolk University *B*
Tufts University *B,M,D*

Michigan

University of Detroit Mercy *B*
University of Michigan *M,D*
Wayne State University *B*

Minnesota

St. Mary's College of Minnesota *M*

Nebraska

University of Nebraska—Lincoln *M*

New Hampshire

University of New Hampshire *D*

New Jersey

Glassboro State College *M*
Rutgers—The State University of
New Jersey *D*

New York

City University of New York
Graduate School and University
Center *D*
Cornell University *M,D*
New York University *D*
Sarah Lawrence College *B*
State University of New York at
Albany *M,D*
Syracuse University *M,D*
University of Rochester *D*
Yeshiva University *D*

North Carolina

North Carolina State University
M,D

Ohio

Bowling Green State University
M,D
Case Western Reserve University *D*
Ohio State University: Columbus
Campus *M,D*
Ohio University *D*
Union Institute *D*
University of Dayton *M*
University of Toledo *M,D*

Pennsylvania

Bryn Mawr College *M,D*
Bucknell University *B*
Carnegie Mellon University
B,M,D,W
Lehigh University *B,M,D*
Temple University *D*
University of Pennsylvania *D*

Rhode Island

Brown University *B,M,D*
Rhode Island College *M*
Salve Regina University *M*

Tennessee

Vanderbilt University *B,M,D*

Texas

Houston Baptist University *B*
Laredo State University *M*
University of Houston *M,D*
University of Texas at Dallas *D*

Vermont

Marlboro College *B*

Virginia

Averett College *B*
Marymount University *B*

Washington

Central Washington University *B*
Eastern Washington University *M*

West Virginia

West Virginia University *D*

Canada

McGill University *B,M,D*

Diesel engine mechanics

Alabama

Bessemer State Technical College *C*
Central Alabama Community
College: Childersburg Campus *C*
Douglas MacArthur State Technical
College *C*
Gadsden State Community
College *C*
John M. Patterson State Technical
College *C*
Shelton State Community
College *A*
Walker State Technical College *C*
Wallace State Community College
at Hanceville *C*

Alaska

University of Alaska
Anchorage *C,A*
Fairbanks *C*
Southeast *C,A*

Arizona

Mesa Community College *C,A*
National Education Center: Arizona
Automotive Institute *A*
Rio Salado Community College *A*

Arkansas

Rich Mountain Community
College *A*

California

Allan Hancock College *C,A*
Barstow College *A*
Cerritos Community College *C*
Citrus College *C,A*
College of the Desert *C*
College of the Redwoods *C,A*
Golden West College *A*
Long Beach City College *C,A*
Los Angeles Trade and Technical
College *A*
Merced College *C,A*
Oxnard College *C,A*
Palomar College *C,A*
San Diego Miramar College *A*
San Joaquin Delta College *C,A*
Santa Rosa Junior College *C,A*
Southwestern College *C,A*
West Hills Community College *C,A*

Yuba College *C,A*

Colorado

Mesa State College *C*
Northeastern Junior College *A*
Pikes Peak Community College *C*
Red Rocks Community College *C,A*
Trinidad State Junior College *A*

Delaware

Delaware Technical and
Community College: Southern
Campus *A*

Florida

Daytona Beach Community
College *C*
Pasco-Hernando Community
College *C*

Georgia

Abraham Baldwin Agricultural
College *A*
Atlanta Metropolitan College *A*
Darton College *A*
DeKalb Technical Institute *C*
Savannah Technical Institute *C*

Hawaii

University of Hawaii: Honolulu
Community College *C,A*

Idaho

Boise State University *C*
College of Southern Idaho *C,A*
Idaho State University *A*
Lewis Clark State College *A*
North Idaho College *C,A*

Illinois

Black Hawk College *A*
Carl Sandburg College *C,A*
Highland Community College *C*
Illinois Central College *A*
Illinois Eastern Community
Colleges: Wabash Valley
College *A*
Illinois Valley Community
College *C*
John A. Logan College *C*
Kishwaukee College *C,A*
Lake Land College *C,A*
Southern Illinois University at
Carbondale *A*
Triton College *C,A*

Indiana

Vincennes University *A*

Iowa

Des Moines Area Community
College *A*
Hawkeye Institute of Technology *A*
Indian Hills Community College *A*
Iowa Central Community College *A*
Iowa Western Community College
C,A
Kirkwood Community College *A*
Northeast Iowa Community
College *C*
Northwest Iowa Technical
College *C*
Scott Community College *A*

Kansas

Barton County Community
College *A*
Coffeyville Community College *A*
Dodge City Community College
C,A
Hutchinson Community College
C,A

Neosho County Community College
  C,A
Pratt Community College C,A

Kentucky

Eastern Kentucky University B

Maine

Central Maine Technical College
  C,A
Eastern Maine Technical College A

Massachusetts

Massasoit Community College A

Michigan

Lansing Community College A
Macomb Community College C,A
Northern Michigan University A
West Shore Community College
  C,A

Minnesota

Alexandria Technical College C
St. Paul Technical College C

Mississippi

Copiah-Lincoln Community
  College C
Hinds Community College A
Mississippi Delta Community
  College C
Mississippi Gulf Coast Community
  College: Jefferson Davis
  Campus A
Northeast Mississippi Community
  College C,A
Southwest Mississippi Community
  College C

Missouri

Longview Community College A

Montana

Dawson Community College C
Northern Montana College C,A,B

Nebraska

Central Community College C,A
Northeast Community College A
Southeast Community College:
  Milford Campus A
Western Nebraska Community
  College: Sidney Campus A

Nevada

Northern Nevada Community
  College A
Truckee Meadows Community
  College A

New Mexico

Albuquerque Technical-Vocational
  Institute C
San Juan College C,A

New York

State University of New York
    College of Agriculture and
      Technology at Cobleskill A
    College of Agriculture and
      Technology at Morrisville A
    College of Technology at
      Alfred A

North Carolina

Asheville Buncombe Technical
  Community College C
Caldwell Community College and
  Technical Institute C
Cape Fear Community College C

Central Piedmont Community
  College A
Coastal Carolina Community
  College C
Forsyth Technical Community
  College A
Gaston College C
Guilford Technical Community
  College C
Johnston Community College C
Pitt Community College C
Robeson Community College C
Wake Technical Community
  College C
Wilkes Community College A
Wilson Technical Community
  College C

North Dakota

North Dakota State College of
  Science C,A
University of North Dakota
    Lake Region C
    Williston C,A

Ohio

Northwestern College C,A
Owens Technical College: Toledo
  C,A
Washington State Community
  College A

Oklahoma

Oklahoma State University
  Technical Branch: Okmulgee A

Oregon

Lane Community College A
Linn-Benton Community College
  C,A
Portland Community College C,A
Rogue Community College C,A

Pennsylvania

Community College of Beaver
  County A
Johnson Technical Institute A
National Education Center: Vale
  Tech Campus C
Pennsylvania College of Technology
  C,A
Westmoreland County Community
  College C

South Carolina

Bob Jones University C,A
Greenville Technical College C
Midlands Technical College C,A
Trident Technical College C

South Dakota

Western Dakota Vocational
  Technical Institute C

Tennessee

Chattanooga State Technical
  Community College C,A
Northeast State Technical
  Community College C,A

Texas

Amarillo College C,A
Angelina College A
Bee County College C,A
Brazosport College C,A
Central Texas College A
College of the Mainland C
Cooke County College A
Del Mar College C,A
Houston Community College C
Kilgore College A
Lamar University—Beaumont A

Lee College A
Midland College A
North Harris Montgomery
  Community College District C,A
Northeast Texas Community
  College C,A
Odessa College C,A
St. Philip's College A
South Plains College C,A
Texarkana College C
Texas Southmost College A
Texas State Technical College
    Amarillo C
    Harlingen C
    Sweetwater C
    Waco C
Western Texas College C,A

Utah

College of Eastern Utah A
Utah Valley Community College
  C,A

Virginia

Southwest Virginia Community
  College C

Washington

Centralia College A
Clark College A
Grays Harbor College A
Lower Columbia College A
Peninsula College A
Seattle Central Community
  College A
Skagit Valley College C,A
Spokane Community College A
Walla Walla Community College
  C,A

Wisconsin

Chippewa Valley Technical
  College C
Fox Valley Technical College C,A
Madison Area Technical College A
Mid-State Technical College C
Moraine Park Technical College C
Northeast Wisconsin Technical
  College C
Waukesha County Technical
  College A
Western Wisconsin Technical
  College C

Wyoming

Casper College C,A
Laramie County Community
  College C,A
Sheridan College C,A
Western Wyoming Community
  College C,A

**American Samoa, Caroline
Islands, Guam, Marianas,
Virgin Islands**

Micronesian Occupational College
  C,A

Dietetic aide/assistant

Alabama

University of Alabama in
  Birmingham C

Arkansas

University of Central Arkansas C

California

Bakersfield College A
Chaffey Community College C,A
City College of San Francisco C,A
College of the Sequoias C
Fresno City College C,A
Grossmont Community College C
Imperial Valley College A
Long Beach City College C,A
Los Angeles City College C,A
Orange Coast College C,A
Pacific Union College A
Ventura College A

Colorado

Front Range Community College
  C,A

Connecticut

Briarwood College A
South Central Community
  College A

Florida

Florida Community College at
  Jacksonville A
Gulf Coast Community College C
Palm Beach Community College A
Pensacola Junior College C
Valencia Community College A

Illinois

Illinois Central College C
KAES College B
Lexington Institute of Hospitality
  Careers A
Olivet Nazarene University A,B
University of Illinois at Urbana-
  Champaign B
William Rainey Harper College A

Iowa

Des Moines Area Community
  College C

Kansas

Barton County Community College
  C,A
Central College A

Maine

Southern Maine Technical
  College A

Maryland

Montgomery College: Rockville
  Campus C,A
Morgan State University B
New Community College of
  Baltimore C,A

Michigan

St. Clair County Community
  College A

Minnesota

Alexandria Technical College C
Lakewood Community College A
Normandale Community College A

Mississippi

Hinds Community College C

Missouri

Central Missouri State University B
Northwest Missouri State
  University B
Penn Valley Community College C

Nebraska

McCook Community College *A*
Southeast Community College:
Lincoln Campus *C,A*

New York

Erie Community College: North
Campus *A*
Rockland Community College *A*
State University of New York
College of Agriculture and
Technology at Morrisville *A*
Suffolk County Community
College *A*

Ohio

Cincinnati Technical College *A*
Columbus State Community College
C,A
Cuyahoga Community College:
Metropolitan Campus *A*
Hocking Technical College *A*
Owens Technical College: Toledo *A*
Sinclair Community College *C,A*
Youngstown State University *A*

Oregon

Oregon State University *B*
Portland Community College *A*

Pennsylvania

Community College of Philadelphia
C,A
Penn State University Park Campus
C,A
Westmoreland County Community
College *A*

Rhode Island

University of Rhode Island *B*

South Carolina

South Carolina State College *M*

Tennessee

David Lipscomb University *B*

Texas

El Paso Community College *A*
North Harris Montgomery
Community College District *C*
St. Philip's College *A*
South Plains College *C*
Texas Southmost College *A*

Virginia

Tidewater Community College *C*

Washington

Shoreline Community College *A*
Spokane Community College *C,A*
Yakima Valley Community College
C,A

Wisconsin

Madison Area Technical College *A*
Moraine Park Technical College *C*
Wisconsin Indianhead Technical
College *C*

Drafting

Alabama

Alabama Agricultural and
Mechanical University *A,B*
Bessemer State Technical College *A*
Brewer State Junior College *A*
Douglas MacArthur State Technical
College *A*

Faulkner University *A*
Gadsden State Community
College *C*
George C. Wallace State
Community College at Selma *A*
Jefferson State Community
College *C*
John C. Calhoun State Community
College *C,A*
John M. Patterson State Technical
College *A*
Lawson State Community College
C,A
Shelton State Community
College *A*
Walker State Technical College *C,A*
Wallace State Community College
at Hanceville *C,A*

Alaska

University of Alaska
Anchorage *C,A*
Fairbanks *C*

Arizona

Arizona Western College *A*
Cochise College *A*
Eastern Arizona College *C,A*
Glendale Community College *C,A*
ITT Technical Institute
Phoenix *A*
Tucson *A*
Mohave Community College *C*
National Education Center: Arizona
Automotive Institute *A*
Pima Community College *C,A*
Yavapai College *A*

Arkansas

East Arkansas Community College
C,A
Phillips County Community College
C,A
Westark Community College *C,A*

California

Bakersfield College *A*
Barstow College *C*
Cerritos Community College *A*
Cerro Coso Community College
C,A
Chabot College *A*
Chaffey Community College *C,A*
Citrus College *C,A*
City College of San Francisco *A*
College of the Desert *A*
College of the Sequoias *A*
Compton Community College *A*
Cosumnes River College *A*
Diablo Valley College *A*
East Los Angeles College *C,A*
El Camino College *C,A*
Evergreen Valley College *A*
Fresno City College *C,A*
Gavilan Community College *A*
Glendale Community College *C,A*
Golden West College *C,A*
Hartnell College *C,A*
Irvine Valley College *C,A*
ITT Technical Institute: San
Diego *A*
Long Beach City College *A*
Los Angeles City College *A*
Los Angeles Harbor College *C,A*
Los Angeles Pierce College *C,A*
Los Angeles Trade and Technical
College *A*
Los Angeles Valley College *C*
Merced College *A*
Mission College *C,A*
Modesto Junior College *A*
Monterey Peninsula College *A*

Mount San Antonio College *A*
Napa Valley College *C,A*
Ohlone College *C,A*
Orange Coast College *C,A*
Pacific Union College *A*
Pasadena City College *C,A*
Porterville College *C,A*
Rio Hondo College *A*
Saddleback College *C,A*
San Diego City College *C,A*
San Joaquin Delta College *A*
San Jose City College *A*
Santa Barbara City College *C,A*
Santa Monica College *A*
Sierra College *A*
Solano Community College *A*
Southwestern College *A*
Taft College *A*
West Valley College *A*
Yuba College *C*

Colorado

Aims Community College *A*
Arapahoe Community College *C*
Community College of Denver *C,A*
Denver Technical College *A*
Front Range Community College *A*
ITT Technical Institute: Aurora *A*
Mesa State College *A*
Pueblo Community College *A*
Red Rocks Community College *C,A*
Trinidad State Junior College *A*

Connecticut

Thames Valley State Technical
College *A*

Delaware

Delaware Technical and
Community College
Southern Campus *A*
Stanton/Wilmington
Campus *A*
Terry Campus *A*

Florida

Brevard Community College *A*
Daytona Beach Community
College *A*
Gulf Coast Community College *A*
Hillsborough Community College *A*
Indian River Community College *A*
Manatee Community College *C,A*
North Florida Junior College *C*
Palm Beach Community College *A*
Pensacola Junior College *A*
Santa Fe Community College *A*
South Florida Community
College *A*

Georgia

Athens Area Technical Institute *C*
Atlanta Metropolitan College *A*
Augusta Technical Institute *C*
Bainbridge College *A*
Chattahoochee Technical
Institute *C*
Clayton State College *A*
Dalton College *A*
DeKalb College *A*
DeKalb Technical Institute *C*
Floyd College *A*
Gainesville College *A*
Georgia Southwestern College *A*
Meadows College of Business *C*
Savannah Technical Institute *C*
Truett-McConnell College *A*

Hawaii

University of Hawaii
Honolulu Community College
C,A
Leeward Community College
C,A

Idaho

Boise State University *A*
College of Southern Idaho *C,A*
Idaho State University *A*
Lewis Clark State College *A*
North Idaho College *C,A*
Ricks College *A*

Illinois

Belleville Area College *A*
Black Hawk College *A*
Carl Sandburg College *A*
City Colleges of Chicago
Chicago City-Wide College
C,A
Richard J. Daley College *A*
Wright College *A*
College of DuPage *C,A*
Elgin Community College *A*
Highland Community College *C*
Illinois Eastern Community
Colleges: Lincoln Trail College *A*
Illinois Valley Community
College *A*
ITT Technical Institute: Hoffman
Estates *C*
John A. Logan College *A*
Kishwaukee College *C,A*
Lake Land College *C,A*
Lewis and Clark Community
College *C,A*
Moraine Valley Community
College *C*
Morton College *C,A*
Prairie State College *A*
Rend Lake College *A*
Robert Morris College: Chicago
C,A
Shawnee Community College *C,A*
Southern Illinois University at
Carbondale *A*
Triton College *C,A*

Indiana

Indiana State University *A*
Indiana University—Purdue
University at Fort Wayne *A*
Indiana Vocational Technical
College
Central Indiana *C,A*
Columbus *C,A*
Eastcentral *A*
Kokomo *C,A*
Lafayette *C,A*
Northcentral *C,A*
Northeast *C,A*
Northwest *C,A*
Southcentral *C*
Southwest *A*
Wabash Valley *A*
ITT Technical Institute:
Indianapolis *A*
Purdue University *A,B*
Tri-State University *A*
Vincennes University *A*

Iowa

Clinton Community College *A*
Des Moines Area Community
College *C*
Hawkeye Institute of Technology *C*
Iowa Central Community College *C*
Iowa Lakes Community College *A*
North Iowa Area Community
College *A*

Northwest Iowa Technical
College *C*
Scott Community College *A*
Southeastern Community College:
North Campus *C*
Southwestern Community
College *C*
Waldorf College *A*

Kansas

Barton County Community
College *A*
Butler County Community
College *A*
Coffeyville Community College *A*
Cowley County Community College
C,A
Dodge City Community College *A*
Fort Scott Community College *A*
Hutchinson Community College *A*
Johnson County Community
College *A*
Kansas City Kansas Community
College *A*
Neosho County Community
College *A*

Kentucky

Eastern Kentucky University *A,B*
Kentucky State University *A*
Louisville Technical Institute *C,A*
Morehead State University *A*
Murray State University *A*
St. Catharine College *A*
Western Kentucky University *A*

Louisiana

Grambling State University *A,B*
Southeastern Louisiana
University *A*

Maine

Southern Maine Technical
College *A*

Maryland

Anne Arundel Community
College *C*
Catonsville Community College *C,A*
Charles County Community
College *A*
Chesapeake College *C*
Frederick Community College *C,A*
Harford Community College *C*
Montgomery College: Rockville
Campus *A*
New Community College of
Baltimore *A*
Prince George's Community College
C,A

Massachusetts

Dean Junior College *A*
Franklin Institute of Boston *C,A*
Middlesex Community College *A*
Roxbury Community College *A*
Springfield Technical Community
College *C,A*
Wentworth Institute of
Technology *C*

Michigan

Andrews University *A*
Baker College: Flint *A*
Glen Oaks Community College *C*
Grand Rapids Community College
C,A
Henry Ford Community College *A*
Jackson Community College *A*
Kirtland Community College *C,A*
Lansing Community College *A*
Macomb Community College *C,A*

Mid Michigan Community College
C,A
Montcalm Community College *C,A*
Muskegon Community College *A*
Northern Michigan University *A*
Northwestern Michigan College *A*
Oakland Community College *C,A*
St. Clair County Community
College *A*
Schoolcraft College *C*
Southwestern Michigan College *A*
Western Michigan University *B*

Minnesota

Normandale Community College *A*
Northland Community College *A*
Northwest Technical Institute *A*
St. Paul Technical College *C*
Willmar Technical College *C*

Mississippi

Copiah-Lincoln Community
College *A*
East Central Community College *A*
Hinds Community College *A*
Jones County Junior College *A*
Mississippi Delta Community
College *A*
Mississippi Gulf Coast Community
College
Jefferson Davis Campus *C*
Perkinston *A*
Northeast Mississippi Community
College *A*

Missouri

East Central College *C,A*
Jefferson College *A*
Lincoln University *A*
Longview Community College *A*
Mineral Area College *C,A*
Missouri Southern State College *A*
North Central Missouri College *A*
Northwest Missouri State
University *C*
St. Louis Community College
Florissant Valley *A*
Forest Park *A*
Three Rivers Community College *A*

Montana

Northern Montana College *A,B*

Nebraska

Central Community College *C,A*
Chadron State College *B*
Metropolitan Community College *A*
Northeast Community College *A*
Southeast Community College
Lincoln Campus *C,A*
Milford Campus *A*

Nevada

Community College of Southern
Nevada *C,A*
Truckee Meadows Community
College *C,A*
Western Nevada Community
College *C,A*

New Hampshire

New Hampshire Technical College
Berlin *A*
Laconia *A*
Manchester *C,A*
Nashua *A*
Stratham *A*

New Jersey

Bergen Community College *A*
Brookdale Community College *A*
County College of Morris *C*

New Mexico

Clovis Community College *A*
Dona Ana Branch Community
College of New Mexico State
University *C,A*
Eastern New Mexico University
Portales *A*
Roswell Campus *C,A*
New Mexico Junior College *C,A*
New Mexico State University *C,A*
Northern New Mexico Community
College *C,A*
Parks College *A*
San Juan College *A*
Western New Mexico University *A*

New York

Adirondack Community College
C,A
Community College of the Finger
Lakes *A*
Dutchess Community College *A*
Genesee Community College *A*
Herkimer County Community
College *C,A*
Hudson Valley Community
College *A*
Institute of Design and
Construction *A*
Mohawk Valley Community College
C,A
Niagara County Community
College *C*
State University of New York
College of Agriculture and
Technology at Morrisville *A*
College of Technology at
Alfred *A*
College of Technology at
Canton *C*
College of Technology at Delhi
C,A
College of Technology at
Farmingdale *A*
Suffolk County Community
College *C*
Ulster County Community College
C,A
Westchester Community College *C*

North Carolina

Alamance Community College *A*
Anson Community College *A*
Appalachian State University *B*
Asheville Buncombe Technical
Community College *A*
Beaufort County Community
College *C*
Blue Ridge Community College *A*
Caldwell Community College and
Technical Institute *C,A*
Catawba Valley Community
College *A*
Central Carolina Community
College *C,A*
Central Piedmont Community
College *A*
College of the Albemarle *A*
Craven Community College *A*
Davidson County Community
College *C*
Durham Technical Community
College *C*
Forsyth Technical Community
College *A*
Guilford Technical Community
College *C,A*
Mitchell Community College *A*
Nash Community College *A*
Piedmont Community College *C*
Roanoke-Chowan Community
College *A*

Robeson Community College *C*
Wake Technical Community
College *C*
Western Piedmont Community
College *A*
Wilkes Community College *C*
Wilson Technical Community
College *A*

Ohio

Central Ohio Technical College *A*
Cincinnati Metropolitan College *A*
Columbus State Community College
C,A
Cuyahoga Community College:
Metropolitan Campus *A*
Edison State Community College *A*
Hocking Technical College *A*
ITT Technical Institute:
Youngstown *A*
Miami University: Hamilton
Campus *A*
Terra Technical College *A*
University of Akron *A*
University of Rio Grande *A*
University of Toledo *A*
Washington State Community
College *A*
Wright State University: Lake
Campus *A*
Youngstown State University *A*

Oklahoma

Cameron University *A*
Connors State College *A*
Eastern Oklahoma State College *A*
Langston University *A*
Oklahoma Panhandle State
University *A*
Oklahoma State University
Oklahoma City *A*
Technical Branch:
Okmulgee *A*
Rose State College *A*
Tulsa Junior College *A*

Oregon

Central Oregon Community
College *C*
Chemeketa Community College *A*
Clackamas Community College *A*
Lane Community College *A*
Mount Hood Community College
C,A
Portland Community College *A*
Treasure Valley Community College
C,A

Pennsylvania

Bucks County Community
College *A*
Butler County Community
College *A*
California University of
Pennsylvania *A*
Community College of Beaver
County *A*
Johnson Technical Institute *A*
Lehigh County Community College
C,A
Luzerne County Community
College *A*
Montgomery County Community
College *A*
Penn State University Park
Campus *C*
Pennsylvania College of Technology
C,A
Triangle Tech
Erie School *C,A*
Greensburg School *A*

Westmoreland County Community
College *A*

Puerto Rico

Huertas Junior College *C*
University of Puerto Rico: Ponce
Technological University
College *A*

Rhode Island

New England Institute of
Technology *A*

South Carolina

Chesterfield-Marlboro Technical
College *A*
Greenville Technical College *C,A*
Horry-Georgetown Technical
College *C*
Sumter Area Technical College *C*
Trident Technical College *C*
Williamsburg Technical College *C*

South Dakota

Black Hills State University *A,B*
Northern State University *A*

Tennessee

Chattanooga State Technical
Community College *C,A*
East Tennessee State University
A,B
Northeast State Technical
Community College *C*
Pellissippi State Technical
Community College *A*

Texas

Abilene Christian University *A*
Alvin Community College *C,A*
Amarillo College *A*
Angelina College *A*
Brazosport College *C,A*
Central Texas College *A*
Cisco Junior College *A*
College of the Mainland *A*
Cooke County College *A*
Eastfield College *A*
El Paso Community College *A*
Houston Community College *C*
Howard College *C,A*
Kilgore College *A*
Lamar University—Beaumont *A*
Lee College *A*
LeTourneau University *A*
Midland College *A*
Mountain View College *C,A*
Navarro College *A*
Odessa College *A*
St. Philip's College *C,A*
San Antonio College *A*
San Jacinto College: Central
Campus *A*
South Plains College *A*
Temple Junior College *A*
Texas Southmost College *A*
Texas State Technical College
Amarillo *A*
Waco *A*
Trinity Valley Community
College *A*
Victoria College *A*
Weatherford College *A*
Western Texas College *A*
Wharton County Junior College *A*

Utah

College of Eastern Utah *C*
Dixie College *C,A*
Southern Utah University *A*
Utah Valley Community College
C,A

Weber State University *A*

Virginia

Blue Ridge Community College *C*
Central Virginia Community
College *A*
Dabney S. Lancaster Community
College *A*
Eastern Shore Community
College *C*
Mountain Empire Community
College *A*
New River Community College *A*
Norfolk State University *A*
Paul D. Camp Community
College *C*
Southside Virginia Community
College *C*
Southwest Virginia Community
College *A*
Wytheville Community College *C*

Washington

Big Bend Community College *C*
Clark College *A*
Columbia Basin College *A*
Everett Community College *A*
Green River Community College *A*
Lower Columbia College *A*
Seattle Central Community
College *A*
Shoreline Community College *C,A*
Skagit Valley College *A*
Spokane Community College *A*

West Virginia

Bluefield State College *A*
Fairmont State College *A*
West Virginia Institute of
Technology *A,B*
West Virginia State College *A,B*

Wisconsin

Chippewa Valley Technical
College *A*
Fox Valley Technical College *A*
Madison Area Technical College *A*
Moraine Park Technical College *A*
Northeast Wisconsin Technical
College *A*
Waukesha County Technical
College *C*
Wisconsin Indianhead Technical
College *C*

Wyoming

Casper College *A*
Sheridan College *A*

Drafting and design
technology

Alabama

Bessemer State Technical College *A*
Central Alabama Community
College: Childersburg Campus *A*
Gadsden State Community College
C,A
Jefferson State Community
College *A*
John C. Calhoun State Community
College *C,A*
John M. Patterson State Technical
College *A*
Shelton State Community College
C,A
Shoals Community College *A*
Walker State Technical College *C,A*

Wallace State Community College
at Hanceville *C,A*

Alaska

University of Alaska Fairbanks *C*

Arizona

Arizona Western College *A*
Eastern Arizona College *C,A*
ITT Technical Institute
Phoenix *A*
Tucson *A*
Mesa Community College *A*
National Education Center: Arizona
Automotive Institute *A*
Pima Community College *C,A*
Yavapai College *C,A*

Arkansas

Arkansas State University: Beebe
Branch *A*
Southern Arkansas University:
Technical Branch *A*
Westark Community College *A*

California

Chabot College *C,A*
Citrus College *C,A*
City College of San Francisco *C*
College of the Desert *C,A*
College of the Redwoods *C,A*
College of the Sequoias *C,A*
Cosumnes River College *C,A*
De Anza College *C,A*
Don Bosco Technical Institute *A*
East Los Angeles College *C*
El Camino College *C,A*
Fresno City College *C,A*
Glendale Community College *C,A*
Golden West College *C,A*
Irvine Valley College *C,A*
ITT Technical Institute
Buena Park *A*
Sacramento *A*
San Diego *C,A*
Van Nuys *A*
West Covina *B*
Long Beach City College *C,A*
Los Angeles Harbor College *C,A*
Los Angeles Trade and Technical
College *C,A*
Los Medanos College *C,A*
Merced College *A*
MiraCosta College *C,A*
Mount San Antonio College *C,A*
Ohlone College *C,A*
Orange Coast College *C,A*
Pacific Union College *B*
Palomar College *C,A*
Porterville College *C,A*
Saddleback College *C,A*
San Diego City College *C,A*
San Joaquin Delta College *C,A*
San Jose State University *B*
Santa Barbara City College *C,A*
Santa Monica College *C,A*
Sierra College *C,A*
Solano Community College *A*
Southwestern College *C*
Taft College *A*
Ventura College *C,A*
Victor Valley College *C*
West Valley College *C,A*
Yuba College *A*

Colorado

Aims Community College *C*
Arapahoe Community College *C*
Community College of Denver *C,A*
Denver Institute of Technology *A*
Denver Technical College *A*

Front Range Community College
C,A
ITT Technical Institute: Aurora *A*
Mesa State College *C,A*
Otero Junior College *C,A*
Pikes Peak Community College *C*
Pueblo Community College *C,A*
Red Rocks Community College *C,A*
Trinidad State Junior College *A*

Connecticut

Greater New Haven State Technical
College *C*
Housatonic Community College *C*
Thames Valley State Technical
College *C,A*
Waterbury State Technical College
C,A

Delaware

Delaware Technical and
Community College
Southern Campus *A*
Stanton/Wilmington
Campus *A*
Terry Campus *A*

Florida

Brevard Community College *A*
Central Florida Community
College *A*
Daytona Beach Community
College *A*
Edison Community College *C*
Florida Community College at
Jacksonville *A*
Gulf Coast Community College *C,A*
Indian River Community College *A*
Keiser College of Technology *A*
Miami-Dade Community College *A*
New England Institute of
Technology *A*
Okaloosa-Walton Community
College *C,A*
Palm Beach Community College *A*
Pensacola Junior College *A*
Santa Fe Community College *A*
Seminole Community College *A*
South Florida Community
College *A*
University of Central Florida *B*
Valencia Community College *A*

Georgia

Augusta College *A*
Augusta Technical Institute *C*
Brunswick College *C,A*
Clayton State College *A*
DeKalb Technical Institute *C*
Meadows College of Business *C*
Savannah State College *A*
Savannah Technical Institute *C,A*
Truett-McConnell College *A*

Hawaii

University of Hawaii: Honolulu
Community College *C,A*

Idaho

Boise State University *A*
College of Southern Idaho *C,A*
Idaho State University *C,A*
Lewis Clark State College *A*
North Idaho College *C,A*
Ricks College *A*

Illinois

Belleville Area College *A*
Black Hawk College *A*
City Colleges of Chicago: Chicago
City-Wide College *C,A*
College of DuPage *C,A*

College of Lake County *C,A*
Elgin Community College *C,A*
Illinois Central College *C*
Illinois Eastern Community
  Colleges: Lincoln Trail College *A*
Illinois Valley Community
  College *A*
Joliet Junior College *C,A*
Lake Land College *A*
Lewis and Clark Community
  College *A*
Moraine Valley Community College
  C,A
Morrison Institute of Technology *A*
Morton College *C,A*
Richland Community College *A*
Robert Morris College: Chicago *A*
Shawnee Community College *C,A*
Southern Illinois University at
  Carbondale *A*
Triton College *C,A*
Waubonsee Community College
  C,A

Indiana

Indiana State University *A*
Indiana University—Purdue
  University
    Fort Wayne *C,A*
    Indianapolis *C,A*
Indiana Vocational Technical
  College
    Central Indiana *A*
    Columbus *C,A*
    Kokomo *C,A*
    Lafayette *C,A*
    Northcentral *C,A*
    Northeast *C,A*
    Northwest *C,A*
    Southcentral *C*
    Southwest *A*
    Wabash Valley *A*
Purdue University *A,B*
Tri-State University *A,B*
Vincennes University *A*

Iowa

Clinton Community College *A*
Hawkeye Institute of Technology *A*
Indian Hills Community College *A*
Iowa Central Community College *C*
Iowa Lakes Community College *A*
North Iowa Area Community
  College *A*
Northwest Iowa Technical
  College *A*
Scott Community College *C*
Southeastern Community College:
  North Campus *A*
Southwestern Community
  College *A*
University of Northern Iowa *B*

Kansas

Butler County Community
  College *A*
Central College *A*
Cowley County Community
  College *A*
Hutchinson Community College *A*
Johnson County Community
  College *A*

Kentucky

Eastern Kentucky University *A,B*
Kentucky State University *A*
Louisville Technical Institute *A*
Murray State University *A*
St. Catharine College *A*

Louisiana

Grambling State University *B*
McNeese State University *A*
Northwestern State University *A*
Southeastern Louisiana
  University *A*

Maine

Southern Maine Technical
  College *C*

Maryland

Anne Arundel Community
  College *C*
Catonsville Community College *A*
Charles County Community
  College *C*
Chesapeake College *C*
Essex Community College *C,A*
Frederick Community College *C,A*
Montgomery College: Germantown
  Campus *C,A*
New Community College of
  Baltimore *C,A*

Massachusetts

Bristol Community College *C*
Franklin Institute of Boston *A*
Greenfield Community College *C*
Middlesex Community College *A*
North Shore Community College
  C,A
Springfield Technical Community
  College *C,A*

Michigan

Alpena Community College *A*
Baker College
    Flint *A,B*
    Owosso *A*
Central Michigan University *B*
Charles Stewart Mott Community
  College *C,A*
Delta College *C*
Ferris State University *A*
Glen Oaks Community College *C*
Grand Rapids Community College
  C,A
Henry Ford Community College *A*
Jackson Community College *C,A*
Kalamazoo Valley Community
  College *C,A*
Kellogg Community College *A*
Kirtland Community College *C,A*
Lake Superior State University *A*
Lansing Community College *A*
Macomb Community College *C,A*
Mid Michigan Community College
  C,A
Montcalm Community College *C,A*
Muskegon Community College *A*
Northern Michigan University *A,B*
Northwestern Michigan College *A*
Oakland Community College *A*
St. Clair County Community
  College *A*
Schoolcraft College *C,A*
Western Michigan University *B*

Minnesota

Normandale Community College *A*
St. Paul Technical College *C*
Willmar Technical College *C,A*

Mississippi

Alcorn State University *B*
Copiah-Lincoln Community
  College *A*
Hinds Community College *A*
Holmes Community College *A*
Jones County Junior College *A*
Meridian Community College *A*

Mississippi Delta Community
  College *A*
Mississippi Gulf Coast Community
  College
    Jackson County Campus *A*
    Jefferson Davis Campus *A*
    Perkinston *C,A*
Northeast Mississippi Community
  College *A*

Missouri

Central Missouri State University
  A,B
East Central College *C,A*
ITT Technical Institute: St. Louis *A*
Jefferson College *A*
Lincoln University *A*
Longview Community College *A*
Mineral Area College *C,A*
Missouri Southern State College *A*
St. Louis Community College at
  Florissant Valley *C*
Southeast Missouri State
  University *A*
Southwest Missouri State
  University *B*

Montana

Northern Montana College *A,B*

Nebraska

Metropolitan Community College
  C,A
Southeast Community College
    Lincoln Campus *C,A*
    Milford Campus *C,A*
University of Nebraska
    Lincoln *A,B*
    Omaha *A,B*

Nevada

Community College of Southern
  Nevada *C,A*
Truckee Meadows Community
  College *C,A*

New Hampshire

Keene State College *A,B*
New Hampshire Technical College
    Manchester *C,A*
    Nashua *A*
    Stratham *A*

New Jersey

Bergen Community College *A*
Brookdale Community College *A*
Burlington County College *A*
Camden County College *A*
County College of Morris *C*
Gloucester County College *A*
Kean College of New Jersey *B*
Mercer County Community College
  C,A
Thomas Edison State College *A,B*

New Mexico

Albuquerque Technical-Vocational
  Institute *C*
New Mexico Junior College *C,A*
Northern New Mexico Community
  College *C,A*
Parks College *C,A*
San Juan College *A*
Western New Mexico University
  C,A

New York

Adirondack Community College
  C,A

City University of New York
    New York City Technical
      College *A*
    Queensborough Community
      College *A*
Dutchess Community College *A*
Genesee Community College *C,A*
Herkimer County Community
  College *C*
Mohawk Valley Community
  College *A*
Niagara County Community
  College *A*
Onondaga Community College *C*
Orange County Community
  College *C*
State University of New York
    College of Agriculture and
      Technology at Morrisville *A*
    College of Technology at
      Alfred *A*
    College of Technology at
      Canton *C*
Suffolk County Community
  College *A*
Westchester Community College *C*

North Carolina

Alamance Community College *A*
Anson Community College *A*
Asheville Buncombe Technical
  Community College *A*
Beaufort County Community
  College *A*
Blue Ridge Community College *A*
Caldwell Community College and
  Technical Institute *A*
Cape Fear Community College *A*
Central Carolina Community
  College *A*
College of the Albemarle *A*
Craven Community College *A*
Durham Technical Community
  College *C*
Gaston College *C*
Guilford Technical Community
  College *C,A*
Piedmont Community College *C*
Stanly Community College *A*
Surry Community College *C,A*
Wayne Community College *A*
Western Piedmont Community
  College *A*

Ohio

Bowling Green State University *B*
Central Ohio Technical College *A*
Cincinnati Metropolitan College *A*
Clark State Community College
  C,A
Columbus State Community
  College *A*
Edison State Community College
  C,A
ETI Technical College *A*
Hocking Technical College *A*
ITT Technical Institute:
  Youngstown *A*
Jefferson Technical College *A*
Marion Technical College *C*
North Central Technical College *A*
Northwest Technical College *C,A*
Owens Technical College
    Findlay Campus *C,A*
    Toledo *C,A*
Shawnee State University *C*
Sinclair Community College *A*
Southern Ohio College *C*
Southern State Community
  College *A*
Stark Technical College *A*
Terra Technical College *C*

University of Akron *A*
University of Cincinnati: Access
  Colleges *A*
University of Rio Grande *A*
University of Toledo *A*
Washington State Community
  College *A*
Wright State University: Lake
  Campus *A*
Youngstown State University *A*

Oklahoma
Cameron University *A,B*
Eastern Oklahoma State College *A*
Northern Oklahoma College *C,A*
Northwestern Oklahoma State
  University *C*
Oklahoma State University:
  Oklahoma City *A*
Rose State College *C,A*
Southeastern Oklahoma State
  University *B*
Tulsa Junior College *C,A*

Oregon
Central Oregon Community
  College *C*
Chemeketa Community College *A*
Clackamas Community College *A*
ITT Technical Institute: Portland *A*
Linn-Benton Community College *A*
Oregon Polytechnic Institute *C,A*
Portland Community College *C,A*
Treasure Valley Community College
  C,A

Pennsylvania
Butler County Community
  College *A*
California University of
  Pennsylvania *A,B*
Community College of Beaver
  County *A*
Community College of
  Philadelphia *C*
Dean Institute of Technology *A*
Delaware County Community
  College *A*
Johnson Technical Institute *A*
Lehigh County Community College
  C,A
Luzerne County Community
  College *C,A*
Montgomery County Community
  College *A*
Northampton County Area
  Community College *A*
Penn State University Park
  Campus *C*
Pennsylvania Institute of
  Technology *C,A*
Pittsburgh Technical Institute *C,A*
Triangle Tech: Greensburg
  School *A*
Westmoreland County Community
  College *A*

Puerto Rico
University of Puerto Rico
  Bayamon Technological
    University College *A*
  Ponce Technological
    University College *A*

Rhode Island
Johnson & Wales University *A*
New England Institute of
  Technology *A*

South Carolina
Aiken Technical College *C,A*
Greenville Technical College *C,A*

Midlands Technical College *A*
Sumter Area Technical College *A*
Trident Technical College *C*

South Dakota
Mitchell Vocational Technical
  Institute *C,A*
Western Dakota Vocational
  Technical Institute *A*

Tennessee
Chattanooga State Technical
  Community College *A*
East Tennessee State University
  A,B
Northeast State Technical
  Community College *C,A*
Pellissippi State Technical
  Community College *A*

Texas
Alvin Community College *C,A*
Amarillo College *A*
Angelina College *C,A*
Austin Community College *C,A*
Bee County College *A*
Brazosport College *C,A*
Central Texas College *A*
Collin County Community College
  District *C,A*
Cooke County College *A*
Del Mar College *C,A*
Eastfield College *A*
El Paso Community College *C,A*
Houston Community College *A*
ITT Technical Institute
  Arlington *A*
  Houston *A*
Lamar University—Beaumont *A*
LeTourneau University *A*
Midland College *A*
North Harris Montgomery
  Community College District *C,A*
Paul Quinn College *B*
Prairie View A&M University *B*
St. Philip's College *A*
San Antonio College *A*
South Plains College *A*
Tarrant County Junior College *A*
Temple Junior College *C,A*
Texarkana College *C*
Texas Southmost College *A*
Texas State Technical College
  Amarillo *A*
  Harlingen *A*
  Sweetwater *C,A*
  Waco *A*
Trinity Valley Community
  College *A*
University of Houston
  Downtown *B*
  Houston *B*
Wharton County Junior College *A*

Utah
Utah State University *A*
Weber State University *A*

Virginia
Central Virginia Community
  College *A*
Dabney S. Lancaster Community
  College *A*
Eastern Shore Community
  College *C*
Lord Fairfax Community College *C*
Mountain Empire Community
  College *A*
New River Community College *A*
Norfolk State University *A*
Northern Virginia Community
  College *C*

Patrick Henry Community
  College *C*
Paul D. Camp Community
  College *A*
Piedmont Virginia Community
  College *C,A*
Southside Virginia Community
  College *A*
Southwest Virginia Community
  College *C,A*
Tidewater Community College *C,A*
Virginia Highlands Community
  College *C,A*
Wytheville Community College *A*

Washington
Big Bend Community College *C,A*
Eastern Washington University *B*
Everett Community College *C,A*
ITT Technical Institute: Spokane *A*
Lower Columbia College *A*
North Seattle Community
  College *A*
Olympic College *C*
Seattle Central Community College
  C,A
Shoreline Community College *C,A*
South Puget Sound Community
  College *C,A*
Spokane Community College *A*

West Virginia
Fairmont State College *A*
West Virginia Institute of
  Technology *A,B*
West Virginia State College *A*

Wyoming
Casper College *A*
Sheridan College *C,A*

Dramatic arts

Alabama
Alabama State University *B*
Auburn University
  Auburn *B*
  Montgomery *B*
Birmingham-Southern College *B*
Huntingdon College *B*
Jacksonville State University *B*
Samford University *B*
Troy State University *B*
University of Alabama in
  Birmingham *B*
University of Montevallo *B,M*
University of North Alabama *B*
University of South Alabama *B*

Alaska
Alaska Pacific University *B*
University of Alaska
  Anchorage *B*
  Fairbanks *B*

Arizona
Arizona State University *B,M,D*
Arizona Western College *A*
Glendale Community College *A*
Grand Canyon University *B*
Northern Arizona University *B*
Pima Community College *A*
University of Arizona *B,M*

Arkansas
Arkansas College *B*
Arkansas State University *B,M*
Hendrix College *B*
Ouachita Baptist University *B*

Southern Arkansas University *B*
University of Arkansas
  Fayetteville *B,M*
  Little Rock *B*
  Pine Bluff *B*
University of Central Arkansas *B*
University of the Ozarks *B*

California
Allan Hancock College *C*
American Academy of Dramatic
  Arts: West *C,A*
American Conservatory Theater *M*
Barstow College *A*
California Institute of the Arts
  C,B,M
California Lutheran University *B*
California State Polytechnic
  University: Pomona *B*
California State University
  Bakersfield *B*
  Chico *B*
  Dominguez Hills *B*
  Fresno *B,M*
  Fullerton *B,M*
  Hayward *B*
  Long Beach *B,M*
  Los Angeles *B,M*
  Northridge *B,M*
  Sacramento *B,M*
  San Bernardino *B*
  Stanislaus *B*
Cerritos Community College *A*
Chapman University *B,M*
Christ College Irvine *B*
Claremont McKenna College *B*
College of the Desert *A*
College of Notre Dame *B*
Cosumnes River College *A*
El Camino College *A*
Foothill College *A*
Fresno City College *A*
Gavilan Community College *A*
Glendale Community College *C*
Humboldt State University *B,M*
Kings River Community College *A*
Los Angeles City College *C,A*
Los Angeles Mission College *A*
Los Angeles Pierce College *A*
Loyola Marymount University *B*
Mendocino College *A*
Merced College *A*
Mills College *B*
MiraCosta College *A*
Monterey Peninsula College *C,A*
Moorpark College *A*
Mount San Jacinto College *A*
Napa Valley College *A*
Occidental College *B*
Ohlone College *A*
Orange Coast College *A*
Pitzer College *B*
Point Loma Nazarene College *B*
Pomona College *B*
Saddleback College *A*
St. Mary's College of California *B*
San Diego City College *A*
San Diego Mesa College *A*
San Diego State University *B,M*
San Francisco State University *B,M*
San Jose State University *B,M*
Santa Barbara City College *A*
Santa Clara University *B*
Santa Monica College *A*
Santa Rosa Junior College *A*
Scripps College *B*
Solano Community College *A*
Sonoma State University *B*
Southern California College *B*
Southwestern College *A*
Stanford University *B,M,D*

United States International
University B,M
University of California
Berkeley B,M,D
Davis B,M,D
Irvine B,M
Los Angeles B,M,D
Riverside B
San Diego B,M
Santa Barbara B,M,D
Santa Cruz C,B
University of La Verne B
University of the Pacific B
University of San Diego M
University of Southern California
B,M
Ventura College A
West Valley College A
Westmont College B
Whittier College B,M
World College West B

Colorado

Adams State College B
Colorado College B
Colorado Mountain College: Spring
Valley Campus A
Colorado State University B
Community College of Denver A
Mesa State College A,B
Naropa Institute B
Northeastern Junior College A
Regis College of Regis University B
Trinidad State Junior College A
University of Colorado
Boulder B,M,D
Denver B
University of Northern Colorado B
Western State College of
Colorado B

Connecticut

Central Connecticut State
University B
Connecticut College B
Fairfield University B
Sacred Heart University B
Southern Connecticut State
University B
Trinity College B
University of Bridgeport B
University of Connecticut B,M
University of Hartford B
Wesleyan University B
Western Connecticut State
University B
Yale University B,M,D

Delaware

Delaware State College B
University of Delaware M
Wesley College A

District of Columbia

American University B
Catholic University of America B,M
Gallaudet University B
George Washington University B,M
Howard University B
University of the District of
Columbia B

Florida

Barry University B
Daytona Beach Community
College A
Eckerd College B
Flagler College B
Florida Agricultural and Mechanical
University B
Florida Atlantic University B,M
Florida International University B

Florida Southern College B
Florida State University B,M,D
Jacksonville University B
Miami-Dade Community College A
Palm Beach Community College A
Pensacola Junior College A
Rollins College B
St. Leo College B
Stetson University B
University of Central Florida B
University of Florida B,M
University of Miami B
University of South Florida B
University of West Florida B

Georgia

Agnes Scott College B
Berry College B
Brenau Women's College B
Clark Atlanta University B
Clayton State College A
Columbus College B
Darton College A
Emory University B
Gainesville College A
Georgia Southwestern College B
Georgia State University B
Gordon College A
LaGrange College B
Mercer University B
Middle Georgia College A
Morehouse College B
Morris Brown College B
Reinhardt College A
Shorter College B
Spelman College B
University of Georgia B,M,D
Valdosta State College B
Wesleyan College B
West Georgia College B
Young Harris College A

Hawaii

Brigham Young University-
Hawaii A
University of Hawaii at Manoa B,D

Idaho

Boise State University B
College of Southern Idaho A
Idaho State University B,M
Ricks College A
University of Idaho B,M

Illinois

Augustana College B
Barat College B
Bradley University B
Columbia College B
Concordia University B
De Paul University C,B,M
Eastern Illinois University B
Elmhurst College B
Eureka College B
Greenville College B
Illinois Central College A
Illinois College B
Illinois State University B,M
Illinois Wesleyan University B
John A. Logan College A
Joliet Junior College A
Judson College B
Knox College B
Lewis University B
Lincoln College A
Lincoln Land Community
College A
Loyola University of Chicago B
Millikin University B
Monmouth College B
National-Louis University B
North Central College B

Northeastern Illinois University B
Northern Illinois University B,M
Northwestern University B,M,D
Principia College B
Rockford College B
Roosevelt University B
Southern Illinois University
Carbondale B,M
Edwardsville B
University of Illinois at Urbana-
Champaign B,M,D
Western Illinois University B,M

Indiana

Anderson University B
Ball State University B
Butler University B
Franklin College B
Hanover College B
Indiana State University B,M
Indiana University
Bloomington B,M,D
Northwest B
South Bend B
Indiana University—Purdue
University at Fort Wayne B
Manchester College B
Marian College B
Purdue University B,M
St. Mary-of-the-Woods College B
St. Mary's College B
Taylor University B
University of Evansville B
University of Indianapolis B
University of Notre Dame B
Vincennes University A
Wabash College B

Iowa

Buena Vista College B
Central College B
Clarke College B
Coe College B
Cornell College B
Dordt College B
Drake University B
Graceland College B
Grand View College B
Grinnell College B
Morningside College B
Mount Mercy College B
Muscatine Community College A
Northwestern College B
St. Ambrose University B
Simpson College B
Teikyo Marycrest University B
Teikyo Westmar University B
University of Iowa B,M
University of Northern Iowa B

Kansas

Baker University B
Benedictine College B
Bethel College B
Butler County Community
College A
Coffeyville Community College A
Dodge City Community College A
Emporia State University B
Friends University B
Hutchinson Community College A
Kansas State University B
McPherson College B
Ottawa University B
Pratt Community College A
St. Mary College B
Southwestern College B
Sterling College B
University of Kansas B,M,D
Washburn University of Topeka B

Kentucky

Centre College B
Cumberland College B
Eastern Kentucky University B
Georgetown College B
Kentucky Wesleyan College B
Morehead State University B
Murray State University B
Northern Kentucky University B
Thomas More College A,B
Transylvania University B
Union College B
University of Kentucky B,M
University of Louisville B,M
Western Kentucky University B

Louisiana

Centenary College of Louisiana B
Dillard University B
Grambling State University B
Louisiana College B
Louisiana State University and
Agricultural and Mechanical
College B,M,D
Loyola University B
McNeese State University B
Northwestern State University B
Southeastern Louisiana
University B
Southern University and
Agricultural and Mechanical
College B
Tulane University B,M
University of New Orleans B,M
University of Southwestern
Louisiana B

Maine

Bates College B
University of Maine
Farmington B
Orono B,M
Presque Isle B
University of Southern Maine B

Maryland

Bowie State University B
Catonsville Community College A
Goucher College B
Howard Community College A
Morgan State University B
St. Mary's College of Maryland B
Salisbury State University B
Towson State University B
University of Baltimore B
University of Maryland
Baltimore County B
College Park B,M
Washington College B
Western Maryland College B

Massachusetts

Berkshire Community College A
Boston College B
Boston University B,M
Bradford College B
Brandeis University B,M
Bridgewater State College B,M
Clark University B
College of the Holy Cross B
Dean Junior College A
Emerson College B,M
Hampshire College B
Massachusetts Institute of
Technology B
Mount Holyoke College B
Northeastern University B
Northern Essex Community
College A
Pine Manor College A
Salem State College B
Smith College B,M

Suffolk University *B*
Tufts University *B,M,D*
University of Massachusetts
    Amherst *B,M*
    Boston *B*
Williams College *B*

Michigan

Alma College *B*
Central Michigan University *B,M*
Eastern Michigan University *B,M*
Grand Valley State University *B*
Henry Ford Community College *A*
Hillsdale College *B*
Kalamazoo College *B*
Lansing Community College *A*
Marygrove College *B*
Michigan State University *B,M,D*
Northern Michigan University *B*
Olivet College *B*
Saginaw Valley State University *B*
Siena Heights College *B*
University of Detroit Mercy *B*
University of Michigan
    Ann Arbor *B,M,D*
    Flint *B*
Wayne State University *B,M,D*
Western Michigan University *B*

Minnesota

Augsburg College *B*
Bemidji State University *B*
Bethel College *B*
College of St. Benedict *B*
College of St. Catherine: St.
    Catherine Campus *B*
Concordia College: Moorhead *B*
Gustavus Adolphus College *B*
Hamline University *B*
Macalester College *B*
Mankato State University *B,M*
Moorhead State University *B,M*
Northland Community College *A*
Northwestern College *B*
Rainy River Community College *A*
St. Cloud State University *B*
St. John's University *B*
St. Mary's College of Minnesota *B*
St. Olaf College *B*
Southwest State University *B*
University of Minnesota
    Duluth *B*
    Morris *B*
University of St. Thomas *B*
Willmar Community College *A*
Winona State University *B*

Mississippi

Blue Mountain College *B*
Jackson State University *B*
Millsaps College *B*
Mississippi University for Women *B*
University of Mississippi *B,M*
University of Southern Mississippi
    B,M
William Carey College *B*

Missouri

Avila College *B*
Central Methodist College *B*
Central Missouri State University
    B,M
College of the Ozarks *B*
Culver-Stockton College *B*
Drury College *B*
Evangel College *A,B*
Fontbonne College *B*
Lindenwood College *B,M*
Missouri Southern State College *B*
Missouri Valley College *B*
Missouri Western State College *B*

Moberly Area Community
    College *A*
Northeast Missouri State
    University *B*
Northwest Missouri State
    University *B*
Park College *B*
St. Louis Community College at
    Florissant Valley *A*
Southeast Missouri State
    University *B*
Southwest Baptist University *B*
Southwest Missouri State University
    B,M
Stephens College *B*
University of Missouri
    Columbia *B,M,D*
    Kansas City *B,M*
Washington University *B*
Webster University *B*
William Woods College *B*

Montana

Carroll College *B*
Montana State University *B*
Northern Montana College *B*
Rocky Mountain College *B*
University of Montana *B,M*

Nebraska

Chadron State College *B*
Concordia College *B*
Creighton University *B*
Doane College *B*
Hastings College *B*
Midland Lutheran College *B*
Nebraska Wesleyan University *B*
Northeast Community College *A*
Peru State College *B*
University of Nebraska
    Kearney *B*
    Lincoln *B,M,D*
    Omaha *B,M*
Wayne State College *B*

Nevada

University of Nevada
    Las Vegas *B,M*
    Reno *B*

New Hampshire

Dartmouth College *B*
Franklin Pierce College *B*
New England College *B*
Plymouth State College of the
    University System of New
    Hampshire *B*
University of New Hampshire *B*

New Jersey

Bergen Community College *A*
Bloomfield College *B*
Brookdale Community College *A*
County College of Morris *A*
Drew University *B*
Glassboro State College *B*
Kean College of New Jersey *B*
Mercer County Community
    College *A*
Montclair State College *B,M*

Rutgers—The State University of
    New Jersey
    Camden College of Arts and
      Sciences *B*
    Douglass College *B*
    Livingston College *B*
    Mason Gross School of the
      Arts *B,M*
    New Brunswick *M*
    Newark College of Arts and
      Sciences *B*
    Rutgers College *B*
    University College Camden *B*
    University College New
      Brunswick *B*
Upsala College *B*
William Paterson College of New
    Jersey *B*

New Mexico

College of Santa Fe *B*
Eastern New Mexico University *B*
New Mexico State University *B*
University of New Mexico *B,M*

New York

Adelphi University *B,M*
Alfred University *B*
American Academy of Dramatic
    Arts *C,A*
Bard College *B*
Barnard College *B*
City University of New York
    Brooklyn College *B,M*
    City College *B,M*
    College of Staten Island *B*
    Graduate School and
      University Center *D*
    Hunter College *M*
    Kingsborough Community
      College *A*
    Lehman College *B*
    Queens College *B*
    Queensborough Community
      College *A*
Columbia University
    Columbia College *B*
    School of General Studies *B*
Community College of the Finger
    Lakes *A*
Cornell University *B,M,D*
Dowling College *B*
Elmira College *B*
Eugene Lang College/New School
    for Social Research *B*
Fordham University *B*
Hamilton College *B*
Hartwick College *B*
Hofstra University *B*
Iona College *B*
Ithaca College *B*
Juilliard School *B*
Long Island University
    Brooklyn Campus *B*
    C. W. Post Campus *B,M*
Manhattanville College *B*
Marymount College *B*
Marymount Manhattan College *B*
Mount St. Mary College *B*
Nazareth College of Rochester *B*
New York University *B,M,D*
Niagara County Community
    College *A*
Niagara University *B*
Pace University *A,B*
St. Lawrence University *B*
Sarah Lawrence College *B,M*
Siena College *C*
Skidmore College *B*

State University of New York
    Albany *B,M*
    Binghamton *B,M*
    Buffalo *B*
    Purchase *B*
    Stony Brook *B,M*
    College at Brockport *B*
    College at Buffalo *B*
    College at Cortland *B*
    College at Fredonia *B*
    College at Geneseo *B*
    College at New Paltz *B*
    College at Oneonta *B*
    College at Plattsburgh *B*
    College at Potsdam *B*
    Oswego *B*
Syracuse University *B,M*
Utica College of Syracuse
    University *B*
Vassar College *B,M*
Westchester Community College *A*

North Carolina

Appalachian State University *B*
Brevard College *A*
Campbell University *B*
Catawba College *B*
College of the Albemarle *A*
Davidson College *B*
Duke University *B*
East Carolina University *B*
Elon College *B*
Fayetteville State University *B*
Greensboro College *B*
Guilford College *B*
Guilford Technical Community
    College *A*
High Point University *B*
Lees-McRae College *B*
Lenoir-Rhyne College *B*
Louisburg College *A*
Mars Hill College *B*
Meredith College *B*
Methodist College *A,B*
North Carolina Agricultural and
    Technical State University *B*
North Carolina Central
    University *B*
North Carolina School of the Arts
    C,B
Pfeiffer College *B*
Queens College *B*
St. Andrews Presbyterian College *B*
Shaw University *B*
University of North Carolina
    Asheville *B*
    Chapel Hill *B,M,D*
    Charlotte *B*
    Greensboro *B,M*
Wake Forest University *B*
Western Carolina University *B*
Western Piedmont Community
    College *A*
Wilkes Community College *A*

North Dakota

Dickinson State University *B*
North Dakota State University *B,M*
Trinity Bible College *B*
University of North Dakota *B,M*

Ohio

Antioch College *B*
Ashland University *B*
Baldwin-Wallace College *B*
Bowling Green State University
    B,M,D
Case Western Reserve University
    B,M
Central State University *B*
Cleveland State University *B*
College of Wooster *B*

Denison University *B*
Franciscan University of
Steubenville *B*
Heidelberg College *B*
Hiram College *B*
Kent State University *B,M,D*
Kenyon College *B*
Marietta College *B*
Miami University: Oxford
Campus *B*
Mount Union College *B*
Muskingum College *B*
Oberlin College *B*
Ohio Northern University *B*
Ohio State University: Columbus
Campus *B,M,D*
Ohio University *B,M*
Ohio Wesleyan University *B*
Otterbein College *B*
Sinclair Community College *A*
University of Akron *B,M*
University of Cincinnati *B,M*
University of Dayton *B*
University of Findlay *B*
University of Toledo *B*
Wilmington College *B*
Wright State University *B*
Youngstown State University *B*

Oklahoma

East Central University *B*
Eastern Oklahoma State College *A*
Northeastern State University *B*
Oklahoma Baptist University *B*
Oklahoma Christian University of
Science and Arts *B*
Oklahoma City University *B*
Oral Roberts University *B*
Phillips University *B*
St. Gregory's College *A*
Southeastern Oklahoma State
University *B*
Southwestern Oklahoma State
University *B*
University of Central Oklahoma *B*
University of Oklahoma *B,M*
University of Science and Arts of
Oklahoma *B*
University of Tulsa *B*

Oregon

Eastern Oregon State College *B*
Lewis and Clark College *B*
Linfield College *B*
Linn-Benton Community College *A*
Pacific University *B*
Portland Community College *A*
Portland State University *B,M*
Reed College *B*
Southern Oregon State College *A,B*
Treasure Valley Community
College *A*
University of Oregon
Eugene *B,M,D*
Robert Donald Clark Honors
College *B*
University of Portland *B,M*
Western Oregon State College *B*
Willamette University *B*

Pennsylvania

Allegheny College *B*
Allentown College of St. Francis de
Sales *B*
Beaver College *B*
Bloomsburg University of
Pennsylvania *B*
Bryn Mawr College *B*
Bucknell University *B*
California University of
Pennsylvania *B*
Carnegie Mellon University *B,M,W*

Cedar Crest College *B*
Chatham College *B*
Cheyney University of
Pennsylvania *B*
Clarion University of
Pennsylvania *B*
Dickinson College *B*
East Stroudsburg University of
Pennsylvania *B*
Edinboro University of
Pennsylvania *B*
Franklin and Marshall College *B*
Gannon University *B*
Gettysburg College *B*
Indiana University of
Pennsylvania *B*
King's College *B*
Kutztown University of
Pennsylvania *B*
Lehigh University *B*
Lock Haven University of
Pennsylvania *B*
Lycoming College *B*
Marywood College *B*
Messiah College *B*
Muhlenberg College *B*
Northeastern Christian Junior
College *A*
Penn State University Park Campus
B,M
Point Park College *B*
Rosemont College *B*
St. Vincent College *B*
Seton Hill College *B*
Slippery Rock University of
Pennsylvania *B*
Susquehanna University *B*
Temple University *B,M*
University of the Arts *B*
University of Pennsylvania *B*
University of Pittsburgh
Johnstown *B*
Pittsburgh *B,M,D*
West Chester University of
Pennsylvania *B*
Westminster College *B*
Wilkes University *B*

Puerto Rico

University of Puerto Rico: Rio
Piedras Campus *B*
University of the Sacred Heart *B*

Rhode Island

Brown University *B,M*
Community College of Rhode
Island *A*
Providence College *B*
Rhode Island College *B*
Roger Williams College *B*
Salve Regina University *B*
University of Rhode Island *B*

South Carolina

Anderson College *B*
Bob Jones University *M*
Charleston Southern University *B*
Coker College *B*
College of Charleston *B*
Columbia College *B*
Converse College *B*
Francis Marion College *B*
Furman University *B*
Lander College *B*
Newberry College *B*
Presbyterian College *B*
South Carolina State College *B*
University of South Carolina
Coastal Carolina College *B*
Columbia *B,M*
Winthrop University *B*

South Dakota

Augustana College *B*
Black Hills State University *B*
Northern State University *B*
Sioux Falls College *B*
University of South Dakota *B,M*

Tennessee

Austin Peay State University *B*
Belmont University *B*
Christian Brothers University *B*
East Tennessee State University *B*
Fisk University *B*
Freed-Hardeman University *B*
Lambuth University *B*
Memphis State University *B,M*
Middle Tennessee State
University *B*
Rhodes College *B*
Tennessee State University *B*
Trevecca Nazarene College *B*
Union University *B*
University of the South *B*
University of Tennessee
Chattanooga *B*
Knoxville *B,M*
Martin *B*
Vanderbilt University *B*

Texas

Abilene Christian University *B,M*
Alvin Community College *A*
Amarillo College *A*
Angelina College *A*
Angelo State University *B*
Austin Community College *A*
Baylor University *B,M*
Del Mar College *A*
East Texas Baptist University *B*
El Paso Community College *A*
Hardin-Simmons University *B*
Houston Community College *C,A*
Howard College *A*
Howard Payne University *B*
Incarnate Word College *B*
Kilgore College *A*
Lamar University—Beaumont *B,M*
Lon Morris College *A*
McMurry University *B*
Midwestern State University *B*
North Harris Montgomery
Community College District *A*
Our Lady of the Lake University of
San Antonio *B*
Prairie View A&M University *B*
St. Edward's University *B*
St. Philip's College *A*
Sam Houston State University *B*
Schreiner College *A*
Southern Methodist University *B,M*
Southwest Texas State University
B,M
Southwestern University *B*
Stephen F. Austin State University
B,M
Sul Ross State University *B*
Texas A&M University *B*
Texas Christian University *B*
Texas Southmost College *A*
Texas Tech University *B,M,D*
Texas Wesleyan University *B*
Texas Woman's University *B,M*
Trinity University *B*
University of Dallas *B*
University of Houston
Clear Lake *B*
Houston *B*
University of North Texas *B,M*
University of St. Thomas *B*

University of Texas
Arlington *B*
Austin *B,M,D*
El Paso *B,M*
Tyler *B*
Vernon Regional Junior College *A*
West Texas State University *B,M*
Western Texas College *A*
Wharton County Junior College *A*

Utah

Brigham Young University *B,M*
Southern Utah University *B*
University of Utah *B,M,D*
Utah State University *B,M*
Weber State University *B*
Westminster College of Salt Lake
City *B*

Vermont

Bennington College *B*
Castleton State College *B*
Johnson State College *B*
Marlboro College *B*
St. Michael's College *B*
University of Vermont *B*

Virginia

Averett College *B*
Christopher Newport College *B*
Emory and Henry College *B*
Ferrum College *B*
George Mason University *B*
Hampton University *B*
Hollins College *B*
James Madison University *B*
Liberty University *B*
Longwood College *B*
Lynchburg College *B*
Mary Baldwin College *B*
Mary Washington College *B*
Old Dominion University *B*
Radford University *B*
Randolph-Macon Woman's
College *B*
Roanoke College *B*
Shenandoah University *B*
Sweet Briar College *B*
University of Richmond *B*
University of Virginia *B,M*
Virginia Commonwealth University
B,M
Virginia Highlands Community
College *A*
Virginia Polytechnic Institute and
State University *B,M*
Virginia Wesleyan College *B*
Washington and Lee University *B*

Washington

Central Washington University *B*
Cornish College of the Arts *B*
Eastern Washington University *B*
Everett Community College *A*
Evergreen State College *B*
Gonzaga University *B*
Lower Columbia College *A*
Pacific Lutheran University *B*
Seattle Pacific University *B*
Seattle University *B*
Spokane Falls Community
College *A*
Tacoma Community College *A*
University of Puget Sound *B*
University of Washington *B,M,D*
Western Washington University
B,M
Whitman College *B*
Whitworth College *B*

West Virginia

Alderson-Broaddus College *B*
Bethany College *B*
Davis and Elkins College *A,B*
Marshall University *B*
Shepherd College *B*
West Virginia University *B,M*
West Virginia Wesleyan College *B*

Wisconsin

Beloit College *B*
Cardinal Stritch College *B*
Carroll College *B*
Carthage College *B*
Lakeland College *B*
Lawrence University *B*
Marquette University *B,M*
University of Wisconsin
    Eau Claire *B*
    Green Bay *B*
    La Crosse *B*
    Madison *B,M,D*
    Milwaukee *B,M*
    Oshkosh *B*
    Parkside *B*
    River Falls *B*
    Stevens Point *B*
    Superior *B*
    Whitewater *B*
Viterbo College *B*

Wyoming

Casper College *A*
Central Wyoming College *A*
Eastern Wyoming College *A*
Laramie County Community
    College *A*
Northwest College *A*
University of Wyoming *B*
Western Wyoming Community
    College *A*

Arab Republic of Egypt

American University in Cairo *B*

Drawing

Alabama

University of Montevallo *B*

California

Academy of Art College *C,B,M,W*
Art Institute of Southern
    California *B*
California College of Arts and
    Crafts *B,M*
California Institute of the Arts
    C,B,M
California State University
    Fullerton *B,M*
    Long Beach *B,M*
    Los Angeles *B,M*
    Northridge *B,M*
Chabot College *A*
Chaffey Community College *A*
Grossmont Community College *A*
Humboldt State University *B*
Long Beach City College *A*
Otis/Parsons School of Art and
    Design *B*
Pasadena City College *A*
San Francisco Art Institute *B,M*
San Jose State University *B*
Solano Community College *A*
University of San Francisco *B*

Connecticut

University of Bridgeport *B*
University of Hartford *B*

Florida

Lynn University *A*
New College of the University of
    South Florida *B*
Pensacola Junior College *A*
University of Florida *B,M*
University of South Florida *B,M*

Georgia

Atlanta College of Art *B*
Berry College *B*
Georgia State University *B,M*
LaGrange College *B*
Piedmont College *B*
University of Georgia *B,M*

Idaho

University of Idaho *B*

Illinois

American Academy of Art *A*
City Colleges of Chicago: Olive-
    Harvey College *A*
Illinois Wesleyan University *B*
John A. Logan College *A*
Rend Lake College *A*
Richland Community College *A*
School of the Art Institute of
    Chicago *B,M*
Southern Illinois University at
    Carbondale *B,M*

Indiana

Ball State University *B*
Indiana University Bloomington
    B,M
Purdue University *B*
University of Notre Dame *B,M*
Vincennes University *A*

Iowa

Drake University *B*
University of Iowa *B,M*
Wartburg College *B*

Kansas

Butler County Community
    College *A*
Coffeyville Community College *A*
Colby Community College *A*
Kansas State University *M*
Pratt Community College *A*

Kentucky

Eastern Kentucky University *B*

Louisiana

Louisiana State University and
    Agricultural and Mechanical
    College *B*
McNeese State University *B*

Maryland

Howard Community College *A*
Maryland Institute College of Art *B*

Massachusetts

Hampshire College *B*
Montserrat College of Art *B*
School of the Museum of Fine Arts
    C,B,M

Michigan

Alma College *B*
Center for Creative Studies: College
    of Art and Design *B*
Central Michigan University *B,M*
Eastern Michigan University *B*
Grand Valley State University *B*
Henry Ford Community College *A*
Lansing Community College *A*
Marygrove College *B*

Northern Michigan University *B*
University of Michigan *B,M*

Minnesota

College of Associated Arts *B*
Willmar Community College *A*
Winona State University *B*

Mississippi

Mississippi University for Women *B*

Missouri

Columbia College *B*
Kansas City Art Institute *B*
Maryville University *B*
Webster University *B*

Nebraska

Hastings College *B*
McCook Community College *A*
York College *A*

New Hampshire

New England College *B*
Plymouth State College of the
    University System of New
    Hampshire *B*

New Jersey

Bergen Community College *A*
Glassboro State College *B*
Rutgers—The State University of
    New Jersey
        Mason Gross School of the
        Arts *B,M*
        New Brunswick *M*
Stockton State College *B*

New York

Alfred University *B*
Bard College *B*
City University of New York
    Brooklyn College *M*
    Queens College *B*
Cooper Union *B*
Daemen College *B*
Molloy College *B*
Parsons School of Design *B*
Pratt Institute *B*
Sarah Lawrence College *B*
School of Visual Arts *B*
State University of New York
    Albany *B,M*
    Purchase *B,M*

North Carolina

Brevard College *A*
East Carolina University *B,M*
North Carolina Agricultural and
    Technical State University *B*
Wingate College *B*

Ohio

Art Academy of Cincinnati *B*
Bowling Green State University *B*
Cleveland Institute of Art *B*
Kent State University *B*
Lourdes College *A*
Ohio State University: Columbus
    Campus *B,M*
Ohio University *B*
University of Akron *B*
University of Toledo *B*
Wittenberg University *B*
Wright State University *B*

Oklahoma

Connors State College *A*
University of Central Oklahoma *B*
University of Tulsa *B*

Oregon

Pacific Northwest College of Art *B*

Pennsylvania

Bucknell University *B*
Carnegie Mellon University *B,M*
Edinboro University of
    Pennsylvania *B*
Immaculata College *A*
Marywood College *B,M*
Mercyhurst College *B*
Moore College of Art and Design *B*
Northeastern Christian Junior
    College *A*
Seton Hill College *B*

Puerto Rico

Inter American University of Puerto
    Rico: San German Campus *B*

Rhode Island

Rhode Island College *B*

South Carolina

Anderson College *B*

Tennessee

East Tennessee State University *B*
Memphis College of Art *B*
University of Tennessee:
    Chattanooga *B*

Texas

Jacksonville College *A*
Lon Morris College *A*
Sam Houston State University *M*
Stephen F. Austin State
    University *M*
Texas Wesleyan University *B*
Texas Woman's University *B,M*
University of Dallas *M*
University of North Texas *B,M*
University of Texas at El Paso *B*
Western Texas College *A*

Vermont

Bennington College *B*
Castleton State College *B*
Marlboro College *B*

Virginia

Averett College *B*
Blue Ridge Community College *C*
Virginia Wesleyan College *B*

Washington

Evergreen State College *B*
Pacific Lutheran University *B*
Tacoma Community College *A*
Wenatchee Valley College *A*

West Virginia

Bethany College *B*
West Virginia State College *B*

Wisconsin

Milwaukee Institute of Art &
    Design *B*
University of Wisconsin: Eau
    Claire *B*

Wyoming

Western Wyoming Community
    College *A*

Driver and safety education

Alabama
Alabama State University *B,M*
University of Montevallo *B,M*

Arkansas
University of Central Arkansas *C*

California
California State University:
Fresno *B*

Delaware
Delaware State College *B*

Illinois
Millikin University *B*
Southern Illinois University at
Carbondale *B*

Indiana
Bethel College *B*
Indiana University Bloomington *B*
Purdue University *B*
Vincennes University *A*

Iowa
University of Northern Iowa *B*
William Penn College *B*

Kentucky
Eastern Kentucky University *C*
Western Kentucky University *M*

Michigan
Andrews University *M*

Mississippi
Delta State University *M*

Missouri
Central Missouri State University *B*

Nebraska
Peru State College *B*

New Hampshire
Keene State College *A*

North Carolina
Appalachian State University *B,M*
North Carolina Agricultural and
Technical State University *B,M*

Oklahoma
Southeastern Oklahoma State
University *B*
University of Central Oklahoma
B,M

Pennsylvania
California University of
Pennsylvania *B*
West Chester University of
Pennsylvania *C*

Tennessee
University of Tennessee: Knoxville
M,D

Texas
University of Mary Hardin-
Baylor *B*
West Texas State University *B*

West Virginia
Glenville State College *B*
Salem-Teikyo University *B*

West Virginia Institute of
Technology *B*
West Virginia University *B*

Wisconsin
University of Wisconsin:
Whitewater *B*

Early childhood education

Alabama
Alabama Agricultural and
Mechanical University *B,M*
Alabama State University *B,M*
Auburn University
Auburn *B,M,D*
Montgomery *B,M*
Birmingham-Southern College *B*
Brewer State Junior College *A*
Huntingdon College *B*
Jacksonville State University *B,M*
Jefferson State Community
College *A*
Livingston University *B,M*
Mobile College *B,M*
Oakwood College *B*
Samford University *B,M*
Shoals Community College *A*
Snead State Junior College *A*
Spring Hill College *B*
Troy State University
Dothan *B,M*
Montgomery *M*
Troy *B,M*
Tuskegee University *B,M*
University of Alabama
Birmingham *B,M,D*
Huntsville *M*
Tuscaloosa *B,M,W*
University of Montevallo *B,M*
University of North Alabama *B,M*
University of South Alabama *B,M*

Alaska
University of Alaska
Fairbanks *B*
Southeast *A*

Arizona
Arizona State University *B*
Cochise College *A*
Northern Arizona University *B,M*
Northland Pioneer College *C,A*
Pima Community College *A*
Prescott College *B*
Scottsdale Community College *A*
University of Arizona *B*

Arkansas
Arkansas State University *B,M*
Harding University *B*
Henderson State University *B,M*
Ouachita Baptist University *B*
Southern Arkansas University *B*
University of Arkansas at Pine
Bluff *B*
University of Central Arkansas *B,M*

California
Bethany College *A*
California Lutheran University *B,M*
California State University
Bakersfield *B,M*
Fresno *B*
Los Angeles *M*
Northridge *M*
Sacramento *B,M*
Stanislaus *B*

Cerritos Community College *A*
Christ College Irvine *B*
College of Notre Dame *M*
De Anza College *C,A*
El Camino College *C,A*
Humboldt State University *C*
Imperial Valley College *C,A*
Lake Tahoe Community College *A*
Marymount College *A*
Merced College *C,A*
Mills College *M*
MiraCosta College *C,A*
Mount St. Mary's College *A*
Mount San Jacinto College *C,A*
Napa Valley College *C,A*
Orange Coast College *C,A*
Pacific Christian College *A*
Pacific Oaks College *B,M*
Pasadena City College *C,A*
Point Loma Nazarene College *M*
St. Mary's College of California
B,M
San Francisco State University *M*
San Jose State University *M*
Santa Rosa Junior College *A*
Solano Community College *A*
Sonoma State University *B,M*
Southwestern College *C,A*
Taft College *C,A*
University of California: Santa
Barbara *M,D*
University of La Verne *B,M*
University of San Francisco *B,M*
West Hills Community College *A*
West Valley College *A*
Yuba College *A*

Colorado
Mesa State College *A*
Naropa Institute *B*
Pikes Peak Community College *A*
University of Colorado at
Denver *M*
University of Northern Colorado *M*

Connecticut
Central Connecticut State
University *B,M*
Eastern Connecticut State
University *B,M*
Housatonic Community College
C,A
Mattatuck Community College *C,A*
Mitchell College *A*
Northwestern Connecticut
Community College *C,A*
Sacred Heart University *B*
St. Joseph College *B,M*
South Central Community
College *A*
Southern Connecticut State
University *B,M*
Teikyo-Post University *A*
University of Bridgeport *B,M*
University of Hartford *B,M,W*

Delaware
Delaware State College *B*
University of Delaware *B*
Wilmington College *A*

District of Columbia
Catholic University of America *B*
Gallaudet University *B*
Howard University *M*
Trinity College *B,M*

Florida
Barry University *B*
Broward Community College *A*
Florida Atlantic University *B,M,D*

Florida Community College at
Jacksonville *A*
Florida International University *M*
Florida Southern College *B*
Florida State University *B,M,D*
Lynn University *A,B*
Nova University *M,D*
Okaloosa-Walton Community
College *A*
Palm Beach Atlantic College *B*
Palm Beach Community College *A*
Pensacola Junior College *A*
St. Petersburg Junior College *A*
Santa Fe Community College *C,A*
Southeastern College of the
Assemblies of God *B*
University of Florida *B,M*
University of Miami *M*
University of South Florida *B*

Georgia
Albany State College *B,M*
Armstrong State College *C*
Atlanta Metropolitan College *A*
Bainbridge College *A*
Brenau Women's College *B*
Brewton-Parker College *B*
Columbus College *B,M*
East Georgia College *A*
Fort Valley State College *B*
Gainesville College *A*
Georgia College *B,M*
Georgia Southern University *B,M*
Georgia Southwestern College *B,M*
Georgia State University *B,M,D*
Kennesaw State College *B*
LaGrange College *B,M*
Mercer University
Atlanta *M*
Macon *B*
Morehouse College *B*
Morris Brown College *B*
North Georgia College *B,M*
Thomas College *A*
Toccoa Falls College *B*
University of Georgia *B,M,D*
Valdosta State College *B,M*
Waycross College *A*
Wesleyan College *B*

Hawaii
Brigham Young University-Hawaii
C,A
Chaminade University of
Honolulu *B*
University of Hawaii
Honolulu Community
College *A*
Kauai Community College *C*
Manoa *B*

Idaho
Idaho State University *B*
North Idaho College *A*
Ricks College *A*

Illinois
Augustana College *B*
Bradley University *B*
Chicago State University *B*
City Colleges of Chicago: Richard J.
Daley College *A*
Concordia University *B,M*
De Paul University *C,B*
Elmhurst College *B*
Governors State University *B,M*
Illinois State University *B*
Illinois Valley Community
College *A*
Kendall College *A,B*
Kishwaukee College *A*

Lincoln Christian College and
  Seminary *B*
Loyola University of Chicago *M,D*
Montay College *C,A*
National-Louis University *B,M*
North Park College and Theological
  Seminary *B*
Northeastern Illinois University *B*
Northern Illinois University *B,M*
Olivet Nazarene University *B*
Rend Lake College *A*
Rockford College *B*
Roosevelt University *B,M*
St. Xavier University *B*
Southern Illinois University
    Carbondale *B*
    Edwardsville *B*
University of Illinois at Urbana-
    Champaign *B,M*
Waubonsee Community College *A*
William Rainey Harper College *C,A*

Indiana

Anderson University *A*
Ball State University *B,M,D*
Bethel College *A*
Butler University *B,M*
Goshen College *C,B*
Indiana State University *B,M*
Indiana University
    Bloomington *B,M,D*
    South Bend *A*
Indiana University—Purdue
    University at Indianapolis *A*
Manchester College *A*
Marian College *A,B*
Purdue University *B,M,D*
St. Mary-of-the-Woods College *B*
Taylor University *B*
University of Indianapolis *A*
University of Southern Indiana *A*
Vincennes University *A*

Iowa

Clarke College *B,M*
Drake University *B*
Iowa Lakes Community College *A*
Iowa State University *B*
Iowa Wesleyan College *B*
Kirkwood Community College *A*
Morningside College *B,W*
Mount St. Clare College *A*
North Iowa Area Community
    College *A*
Simpson College *B*
Teikyo Marycrest University *B*
University of Dubuque *B,M*
University of Iowa *M,D*
University of Northern Iowa *B,M*
Vennard College *B*
Waldorf College *A*
Wartburg College *B*

Kansas

Allen County Community
    College *A*
Butler County Community
    College *A*
Donnelly College *C,A*
Emporia State University *M*
Hesston College *A*
Highland Community College *A*
Kansas Wesleyan University *A*
McPherson College *B*
MidAmerica Nazarene College *A*
Pratt Community College *A*

Kentucky

Bellarmine College *B*
Berea College *B*
Brescia College *B*
Cumberland College *B,M*

Eastern Kentucky University *B,M*
Georgetown College *B*
Jefferson Community College *A*
Kentucky State University *B*
Kentucky Wesleyan College *B*
Pikeville College *B*
Spalding University *B*
Transylvania University *B*
Union College *M*
University of Kentucky *B,M*
University of Louisville *M*

Louisiana

Dillard University *B*
Grambling State University *B,M*
Louisiana College *A*
Louisiana Tech University *B*
McNeese State University *B,M*
Nicholls State University *B,M*
Northeast Louisiana University *B*
Northwestern State University *B,M*
Southeastern Louisiana
    University *B*
Southern University in
    Shreveport *A*
Tulane University *M*
Xavier University of Louisiana *B*

Maine

University of Maine
    Farmington *A,B*
    Presque Isle *B*
Westbrook College *B*

Maryland

Baltimore Hebrew University *B,M*
Columbia Union College *A,B*
Essex Community College *C,A*
Frederick Community College *C,A*
Harford Community College *A*
Hood College *B*
Montgomery College
    Germantown Campus *A*
    Rockville Campus *A*
    Takoma Park Campus *A*
New Community College of
    Baltimore *A*
Sojourner-Douglass College *B*
Towson State University *M*
University of Maryland: College
    Park *M,D*
Villa Julie College *A*

Massachusetts

American International College *B,M*
Anna Maria College for Men and
    Women *B*
Aquinas College at Newton *A*
Bay Path College *A*
Becker College
    Leicester Campus *A*
    Worcester Campus *A*
Boston College *B,M,D*
Boston University *B,M,W*
Bridgewater State College *B,M*
Bunker Hill Community College *C*
Cape Cod Community College *A*
Dean Junior College *A*
Eastern Nazarene College *A,B,M*
Elms College *B*
Endicott College *A,B*
Fisher College *A*
Fitchburg State College *B*
Framingham State College *B*
Gordon College *B*
Greenfield Community College *C,A*
Lasell College *A,B*
Lesley College *B,M*
Massasoit Community College *A*
Middlesex Community College *A*
Mount Ida College *A*

Mount Wachusett Community
    College *C*
North Adams State College *B*
North Shore Community College *A*
Northeastern University *B*
Northern Essex Community
    College *A*
Pine Manor College *B*
Quincy College *A*
Quinsigamond Community
    College *A*
Salem State College *B*
Smith College *B,M*
Springfield College *B*
Springfield Technical Community
    College *A*
Stonehill College *B*
Tufts University *M*
Westfield State College *B*
Wheelock College *B,M*
Worcester State College *B,M*

Michigan

Andrews University *M*
Central Michigan University *B*
Concordia College *B*
Eastern Michigan University *B,M*
Ferris State University *A*
Grand Valley State University *M*
Hillsdale College *B*
Madonna University *B*
Marygrove College *B,M*
Northern Michigan University *B*
Oakland University *M*
Spring Arbor College *B*
Suomi College *A*
University of Michigan
    Ann Arbor *D*
    Dearborn *B*
    Flint *B*
Wayne State University *B,M*
Western Michigan University *M*
William Tyndale College *A*

Minnesota

Augsburg College *B*
Bemidji State University *A*
Bethel College *B*
College of St. Benedict *B*
College of St. Catherine: St.
    Catherine Campus *B*
College of St. Scholastica *B*
Concordia College: Moorhead *B*
Concordia College: St. Paul *B*
Crown College *A*
Mankato State University *B,M*
Moorhead State University *B*
North Central Bible College *A*
Northland Community College *A*
Rochester Community College *A*
St. Cloud State University *B*
St. John's University *B*
St. Mary's Campus of the College of
    St. Catherine *C*
St. Mary's College of Minnesota *B*
Southwest State University *B*
University of Minnesota
    Duluth *B*
    Twin Cities *B*
Vermilion Community College *A*
Willmar Community College *A*
Winona State University *B*

Mississippi

Jackson State University *B*
Jones County Junior College *A*
Mary Holmes College *C,A*
Mississippi College *B,M*
Mississippi University for Women *B*
Rust College *A,B*
Tougaloo College *A*

Missouri

Central Missouri State University *B*
East Central College *A*
Evangel College *A,B*
Fontbonne College *B*
Hannibal-LaGrange College *B*
Harris Stowe State College *B*
Maryville University *B*
Mineral Area College *A*
Missouri Baptist College *B*
Moberly Area Community
    College *A*
Northwest Missouri State
    University *B,M*
Park College *B*
St. Louis Community College at
    Florissant Valley *A*
St. Louis University *B*
Southeast Missouri State
    University *B*
Stephens College *B*
University of Missouri
    Columbia *B,M,D*
    Kansas City *M*
    St. Louis *B*
Webster University *B*
William Woods College *B*

Montana

College of Great Falls *A*
Dull Knife Memorial College *A*
Eastern Montana College *B,M*
Fort Peck Community College *A*
Montana State University *B*
University of Montana *B*

Nebraska

Chadron State College *A,B*
College of St. Mary *B*
Concordia College *B,M*
Metropolitan Community College *A*
Peru State College *B*
University of Nebraska
    Kearney *B*
    Lincoln *B*
    Omaha *B*
Western Nebraska Community
    College: Scottsbluff Campus *A*

Nevada

Northern Nevada Community
    College *A*

New Hampshire

Antioch New England Graduate
    School *M*
Colby-Sawyer College *B*
Franklin Pierce College *B*
Hesser College *A*
Keene State College *B*
New Hampshire Technical College:
    Manchester *A*
Notre Dame College *A,B*
Plymouth State College of the
    University System of New
    Hampshire *B*
Rivier College *A,B*
School for Lifelong Learning *C,A*
University of New Hampshire *M*

New Jersey

Brookdale Community College *A*
Centenary College *A*
Cumberland County College *C,A*
Essex County College *A*
Glassboro State College *B*
Jersey City State College *B,M*
Kean College of New Jersey *B,M*
Monmouth College *B,M*
Passaic County Community
    College *A*
Rider College *B*

Rutgers—The State University of
New Jersey
  Camden College of Arts and
    Sciences *B*
  Douglass College *B*
  Livingston College *B*
  New Brunswick *M,D*
  Newark College of Arts and
    Sciences *B*
  Rutgers College *B*
  University College New
    Brunswick *B*
  University College Newark *B*
Trenton State College *B*
William Paterson College of New
  Jersey *B,M*

New Mexico

Eastern New Mexico University *A*
Northern New Mexico Community
  College *A*
Western New Mexico University *B*

New York

Bank Street College of
  Education *M*
Cazenovia College *A*
City University of New York
  Baruch College *B*
  Borough of Manhattan
    Community College *A*
  Brooklyn College *B,M*
  Hostos Community College *A*
  Kingsborough Community
    College *A*
  La Guardia Community
    College *A*
  Lehman College *B,M*
  Queens College *B,M*
College of New Rochelle *B*
College of St. Rose *M*
Concordia College *B*
Dominican College of Blauvelt *B*
Dutchess Community College *A*
Herkimer County Community
  College *A*
Iona College *A*
Keuka College *B*
King's College *B*
Long Island University: Brooklyn
  Campus *B,M*
Manhattan College *B*
Manhattanville College *M*
Maria College *A*
Marymount College *B*
Mater Dei College *A*
Medaille College *B*
Nazareth College of Rochester *M*
New York University *A,B,M,D*
Onondaga Community College *A*
Pace University *A,B*
Russell Sage College *B*
St. Joseph's College
  Brooklyn *B*
  Suffolk Campus *B*
State University of New York
  College of Agriculture and
    Technology at Cobleskill *A*
  College at Buffalo *B*
  College at Cortland *B*
  College at Fredonia *B,M*
  College at Geneseo *B,M*
  College at New Paltz *B,M*
  College at Oneonta *B*
  College at Potsdam *B,M*
Suffolk County Community College
  Eastern Campus *A*
  Selden *A*
Sullivan County Community
  College *A*
Syracuse University *B*
Trocaire College *A*

Villa Maria College of Buffalo *A*
Wagner College *B*

North Carolina

Barton College *B*
Bennett College *B*
Campbell University *B,M*
Catawba College *B,M*
Catawba Valley Community
  College *A*
Chowan College *B*
Cleveland Community College *A*
Durham Technical Community
  College *A*
East Carolina University *B*
Forsyth Technical Community
  College *A*
Gaston College *A*
High Point University *B*
Isothermal Community College *A*
Johnson C. Smith University *B*
Lenoir-Rhyne College *B,M*
Livingstone College *B*
Methodist College *B*
Montgomery Community College *A*
North Carolina Central
  University *B*
Pitt Community College *A*
Queens College *B*
Roanoke-Chowan Community
  College *A*
Rockingham Community College *C*
St. Augustine's College *B*
Southwestern Community
  College *A*
University of North Carolina
  Chapel Hill *B,M,D*
  Greensboro *B*
Wake Technical Community
  College *A*
Warren Wilson College *B*
Wingate College *B*

North Dakota

Bismarck State College *A*
Mayville State University *A*
University of Mary *B,M*
University of North Dakota *B*

Ohio

Ashland University *B*
Bluffton College *B*
Bowling Green State University *B*
Capital University *B*
Cedarville College *C*
Central State University *B*
Cleveland State University *B*
College of Mount St. Joseph *A*
Columbus State Community
  College *A*
Cuyahoga Community College
  Metropolitan Campus *A*
  Western Campus *A*
Defiance College *B*
Franciscan University of
  Steubenville *A*
John Carroll University *B*
Kent State University *B,M,D*
Lakeland Community College *A*
Lorain County Community
  College *A*
Malone College *A,M*
Mount Vernon Nazarene College *B*
Northwest Technical College *A*
Notre Dame College of Ohio *B*
Ohio Dominican College *B*
Ohio State University: Columbus
  Campus *B*
Ohio University *B*
Owens Technical College
  Findlay Campus *A*
  Toledo *A*

Terra Technical College *A*
University of Akron *B*
University of Cincinnati
  Cincinnati *B,M*
  Clermont College *A*
University of Dayton *B,M*
University of Rio Grande *A*
University of Toledo *B,M,D*
Walsh College *B*
Wright State University *B,M*
Xavier University *A,B*
Youngstown State University *B,M*

Oklahoma

East Central University *B*
Hillsdale Free Will Baptist
  College *A*
Northeastern State University *B*
Oklahoma Baptist University *B*
Oklahoma Christian University of
  Science and Arts *B*
University of Central Oklahoma
  B,M
University of Oklahoma *B*

Oregon

Central Oregon Community
  College *A*
Chemeketa Community College *A*
Linfield College *B,M*
Linn-Benton Community College *A*
Northwest Christian College *B*
Western Oregon State College *M*

Pennsylvania

Albright College *B*
Beaver College *B,M*
Bloomsburg University of
  Pennsylvania *B,M*
Bucknell University *B,M*
Cabrini College *B*
California University of
  Pennsylvania *A,B,M*
Carlow University *B,M*
Chatham College *B*
Chestnut Hill College *B,M*
Cheyney University of
  Pennsylvania *B*
Clarion University of
  Pennsylvania *B*
College Misericordia *B*
Community College of
  Philadelphia *A*
Delaware County Community
  College *A*
Duquesne University *B*
East Stroudsburg University of
  Pennsylvania *B*
Edinboro University of
  Pennsylvania *A,M*
Elizabethtown College *B*
Gannon University *B*
Gwynedd-Mercy College *B*
Harcum Junior College *A*
Holy Family College *B*
Immaculata College *B*
Indiana University of Pennsylvania
  B,M
Juniata College *B*
Keystone Junior College *A*
King's College *B*
Lehigh County Community
  College *A*
Lincoln University *B*
Lock Haven University of
  Pennsylvania *B*
Manor Junior College *A*
Marywood College *B,M*
Mercyhurst College *B*
Messiah College *B*
Montgomery County Community
  College *A*

Northampton County Area
  Community College *C*
Northeastern Christian Junior
  College *A*
Pennsylvania College of
  Technology *A*
Reading Area Community
  College *A*
St. Vincent College *C*
Seton Hill College *B*
Slippery Rock University of
  Pennsylvania *M*
Temple University *B*
University of Pennsylvania *M,D*
West Chester University of
  Pennsylvania *B*
Widener University *B,M*
Wilkes University *B*
York College of Pennsylvania *C*

Puerto Rico

Inter American University of Puerto
  Rico: Arecibo Campus *B*
University of Puerto Rico: Bayamon
  Technological University
  College *B*

Rhode Island

Rhode Island College *B,M*

South Carolina

Benedict College *B*
Bob Jones University *B*
Charleston Southern University *B*
Clemson University *B*
Coker College *B*
College of Charleston *M*
Columbia College *B,M*
Converse College *B*
Erskine College *B*
Francis Marion College *B,M*
Furman University *B,M*
Lander College *B*
Morris College *B*
Newberry College *B*
Spartanburg Methodist College *A*
University of South Carolina
  Aiken *B*
  Coastal Carolina College *B*
  Columbia *M*
  Spartanburg *B*
Winthrop University *B*

South Dakota

Augustana College *B,M*
Black Hills State University *B*
Dakota State University *B*
Sioux Falls College *A*
South Dakota State University *B*

Tennessee

Austin Peay State University *B*
Carson-Newman College *B*
Chattanooga State Technical
  Community College *A*
East Tennessee State University *B*
Free Will Baptist Bible College *B*
Freed-Hardeman University *B*
Johnson Bible College *B*
Lambuth University *B*
Lincoln Memorial University *B*
Martin Methodist College *A*
Memphis State University *B*
Middle Tennessee State
  University *B*
Roane State Community College *A*
Shelby State Community College
  C,A
Tennessee State University *B*
Tennessee Technological University
  B,M
Tennessee Temple University *B*

Tennessee Wesleyan College B
Trevecca Nazarene College B
Tusculum College B
Union University B,M
University of Tennessee
Chattanooga B
Martin B
Vanderbilt University B,M,D

Texas

Abilene Christian University B
Angelo State University B
Dallas Baptist University B,M
East Texas State University M,D
Houston Baptist University B
Incarnate Word College B
Lamar University—Beaumont B
Laredo Junior College C,A
Laredo State University B,M
Midwestern State University B
Panola College A
Southwest Texas State
University M
Texas A&I University M
Texas Christian University B
Texas College B
Texas Lutheran College B
Texas Tech University B,M,D
Texas Wesleyan University B
Texas Woman's University M,D
University of Houston
Clear Lake M
Houston B,M
University of Mary Hardin-
Baylor B
University of North Texas B,M,D
University of Texas
Permian Basin M
Tyler M

Utah

Brigham Young University B,M
College of Eastern Utah A
Utah State University B
Weber State University B,M
Westminster College of Salt Lake
City B

Vermont

Bennington College B
Castleton State College B
Champlain College A
College of St. Joseph in Vermont
B,M
Goddard College B,M
Johnson State College A,B,M
Lyndon State College B
Trinity College of Vermont B
University of Vermont B

Virginia

Averett College B,M
Bridgewater College B
Dabney S. Lancaster Community
College C
Eastern Mennonite College B
Emory and Henry College B
Hampton University B
James Madison University M
Longwood College M
Lynchburg College M
Norfolk State University M
Old Dominion University M
Patrick Henry Community
College C
Radford University B
Southern Seminary College A
Virginia Polytechnic Institute and
State University B
Virginia Wesleyan College B

Washington

Bellevue Community College C,A
Central Washington University B
Clark College C,A
Eastern Washington University B,M
Green River Community College A
Heritage College C,A
Lower Columbia College A
North Seattle Community
College A
Pacific Lutheran University B
Pierce College A
Spokane Falls Community
College A
Walla Walla College A
Wenatchee Valley College A

West Virginia

Alderson-Broaddus College B
Concord College B
Fairmont State College B
Glenville State College B
Marshall University B,M
Shepherd College B
West Liberty State College B
West Virginia State College B
West Virginia Wesleyan College B

Wisconsin

Alverno College B
Cardinal Stritch College B
Carroll College B
Concordia University Wisconsin B
Edgewood College B
Lakeland College B
Marian College of Fond du Lac B
Moraine Park Technical College C
Mount Mary College B
Mount Senario College B
Northland College B
St. Norbert College B
University of Wisconsin
Eau Claire B
Green Bay B
La Crosse B
Madison B
Milwaukee B
Oshkosh B
Platteville B
River Falls B
Stevens Point B
Stout B
Superior B
Whitewater B
Viterbo College B,M

Wyoming

Casper College A
Eastern Wyoming College A
Sheridan College C
University of Wyoming B
Western Wyoming Community
College A

**American Samoa, Caroline
Islands, Guam, Marianas,
Virgin Islands**

University of Guam B

Canada

McGill University B

Earth sciences

Alabama

Auburn University B
Troy State University B

Alaska

University of Alaska Fairbanks B

Arizona

Northern Arizona University B,M
Prescott College B
University of Arizona B

Arkansas

University of Arkansas B

California

California State Polytechnic
University: Pomona B
California State University
Dominguez Hills B
Long Beach B
Los Angeles B
Northridge B
Stanislaus B
Cerritos Community College A
Chaffey Community College A
Columbia College A
Los Angeles Valley College A
Merced College A
Modesto Junior College A
Santa Barbara City College A
Southwestern College A
Stanford University B,M,D
University of California
Berkeley B,M,D
Los Angeles B
Riverside B
San Diego B,M,D
Santa Cruz B,M,D

Colorado

Adams State College B
Colorado Mountain College: Spring
Valley Campus A
Colorado State University M,D
University of Northern Colorado
B,M

Connecticut

Central Connecticut State
University B,M
Eastern Connecticut State
University B
Southern Connecticut State
University B,M
Wesleyan University B,M
Western Connecticut State
University B,M

Florida

Pensacola Junior College A
University of West Florida B

Georgia

Georgia Institute of Technology
M,D
Georgia Southwestern College B
Mercer University B
West Georgia College B

Idaho

Boise State University B
Lewis Clark State College B
University of Idaho M

Illinois

Augustana College B
Black Hawk College A
Bradley University B
City Colleges of Chicago: Olive-
Harvey College A
Concordia University B
Illinois Central College A
Morton College A
Northeastern Illinois University
B,M

Northwestern University B
Southern Illinois University at
Edwardsville B
University of Chicago B,M,D
Waubonsee Community College A

Indiana

Ball State University M
DePauw University B
Indiana State University B,M
Indiana University
Bloomington M
East A
Indiana University—Purdue
University at Fort Wayne B
Purdue University B,M,D
University of Indianapolis B
University of Notre Dame B
Vincennes University A

Iowa

Cornell College B
Drake University B
Iowa State University B,M,D
University of Dubuque B
University of Northern Iowa B,M
Upper Iowa University B
William Penn College B

Kansas

Emporia State University B

Kentucky

Eastern Kentucky University B,M
Morehead State University B
Murray State University B
Western Kentucky University B

Louisiana

Tulane University B

Maine

University of Maine at
Farmington B

Maryland

Frostburg State University B
Johns Hopkins University B,M,D
Salisbury State University B

Massachusetts

Bridgewater State College B,M
Framingham State College B
Hampshire College B
Harvard and Radcliffe Colleges B
Harvard University D
Massachusetts Institute of
Technology B,M,D
Northern Essex Community
College A
Salem State College B
University of Massachusetts at
Lowell B,M

Michigan

Adrian College A,B
Aquinas College B
Calvin College B
Central Michigan University B
Charles Stewart Mott Community
College C
Eastern Michigan University B
Grand Valley State University B
Hope College B
Michigan State University B
Michigan Technological
University B
Northern Michigan University A,B
Western Michigan University B,M

Minnesota

Bemidji State University *B*
Gustavus Adolphus College *B*
Mankato State University *B*
St. Cloud State University *B*
Willmar Community College *A*
Winona State University *B*

Missouri

Central Missouri State University *B*
St. Louis University *B*
Southeast Missouri State
University *B*
University of Missouri: Kansas
City *B*
Washington University *B,M,D*

Montana

Montana State University *B,M*

Nebraska

Chadron State College *B*
Midland Lutheran College *B*
University of Nebraska—Kearney *B*
York College *A*

Nevada

University of Nevada: Las Vegas *B*

New Hampshire

Dartmouth College *B,M,D*
University of New Hampshire *M,D*

New Jersey

Kean College of New Jersey *B*
Rutgers—The State University of
New Jersey
Cook College *B*
Douglass College *B*

New Mexico

Eastern New Mexico University *B*
New Mexico State University *B*
Western New Mexico University *B*

New York

Adelphi University *B,M*
City University of New York:
Queens College *B*
Columbia University
Columbia College *B*
New York *M,D*
Dutchess Community College *A*
Hofstra University *B*
New York University *B*
State University of New York
Albany *B*
Stony Brook *M,D*
College at Brockport *B*
College at Cortland *B*
College at Fredonia *B*
College at Geneseo *B*
College at New Paltz *B,M*
College at Oneonta *B,M*
College at Plattsburgh *B*

North Carolina

Brevard College *A*
North Carolina State University
M,D
University of North Carolina
Charlotte *B*
Greensboro *B*

North Dakota

Dickinson State University *B*
Minot State University *B*
North Dakota State University *B*
University of North Dakota *B*

Ohio

Ashland University *B*
Bowling Green State University *B*
Central State University *B*
Kent State University *B*
Muskingum College *B*
Ohio State University: Columbus
Campus *B*
Ohio Wesleyan University *B*
University of Akron *M*
University of Cincinnati *B*
Wittenberg University *B*
Wright State University *M*
Youngstown State University *B*

Oklahoma

Redlands Community College *A*
University of Oklahoma *B*
University of Tulsa *B*

Pennsylvania

Bloomsburg University of
Pennsylvania *B*
California University of
Pennsylvania *B,M*
Clarion University of
Pennsylvania *B*
East Stroudsburg University of
Pennsylvania *B*
Edinboro University of
Pennsylvania *B*
Gannon University *B*
Indiana University of Pennsylvania
B,M
Kutztown University of
Pennsylvania *B*
La Salle University *B*
Lock Haven University of
Pennsylvania *B*
Mansfield University of
Pennsylvania *B*
Mercyhurst College *B*
Millersville University of
Pennsylvania *B,M*
Moravian College *B*
Penn State University Park Campus
B,M,D
Shippensburg University of
Pennsylvania *B*
Slippery Rock University of
Pennsylvania *B*
West Chester University of
Pennsylvania *B*
Wilkes University *B*

Puerto Rico

University of Puerto Rico: Carolina
Regional College *A*

South Carolina

University of South Carolina *M*

South Dakota

Augustana College *B*
University of South Dakota *B,M*

Tennessee

Middle Tennessee State
University *B*
University of Tennessee:
Chattanooga *B*

Texas

Baylor University *B,M*
Concordia Lutheran College *B*
East Texas State University *B,M*
Hardin-Simmons University *B*
Houston Community College *A*
Lamar University—Beaumont *B*
St. Mary's University *B*
Texas A&M University *B*
Trinity University *B*

University of Texas of the Permian
Basin *B*
Wayland Baptist University *B*

Utah

Brigham Young University *B,M*
Weber State University *B*

Vermont

Marlboro College *B*

Virginia

Longwood College *B*
Old Dominion University *B,M*
Radford University *B*
Virginia State University *M*

Washington

Central Washington University *B*
Eastern Washington University *B*
Evergreen State College *B*
Lower Columbia College *A*
Pacific Lutheran University *B*
Western Washington University
B,M

West Virginia

Shepherd College *B*

Wisconsin

Carroll College *B*
Northland College *B*
University of Wisconsin
Green Bay *B*
Madison *B*
Oshkosh *B*
Platteville *B*
River Falls *B*

Canada

McGill University *B,M,D*

East Asian studies

Arizona

University of Arizona *B,M,D*

California

Naval Postgraduate School *M*
Stanford University *B,M*
University of California
Davis *B*
Los Angeles *B,M,D*
Santa Cruz *B*
University of Southern California
B,M

Connecticut

Central Connecticut State
University *B*
Wesleyan University *B*
Yale University *B,M,D*

District of Columbia

George Washington University *B,M*
Georgetown University *D*

Hawaii

University of Hawaii at Manoa *M,D*

Illinois

KAES College *B*
Northwestern University *B*
Richland Community College *A*
University of Chicago *B,M,D*

Indiana

Earlham College *B*
Hanover College *B*

Indiana University Bloomington
C,B,M,D
Valparaiso University *B*

Kansas

University of Kansas *B,M*

Maine

Colby College *B*

Maryland

University of Maryland: College
Park *B*

Massachusetts

Boston University *B*
Hampshire College *B*
Harvard and Radcliffe Colleges *B*
Harvard University *M,D*
Tufts University *B,M*
Wellesley College *B*
Williams College *B*

Michigan

Eastern Michigan University *B*
Oakland University *B*
University of Michigan *M*
Wayne State University *B*

Minnesota

Augsburg College *B*
College of St. Catherine: St.
Catherine Campus *B*
Hamline University *B*
Macalester College *B*
St. Cloud State University *B*
University of Minnesota: Twin
Cities *B,M*
University of St. Thomas *B*

New Jersey

Princeton University *B,D*

New York

Barnard College *B*
City University of New York
Brooklyn College *B*
Queens College *B*
Columbia University
Columbia College *B*
New York *M,D*
School of General Studies *B,M*
Cornell University *M,D*
New York University *B*
St. John's University *B,M*
Union College *B*
United States Military Academy *B*

North Carolina

University of North Carolina at
Chapel Hill *D*

Ohio

College of Wooster *B*
Denison University *B*
Kenyon College *B*
Oberlin College *B*
Ohio State University: Columbus
Campus *M,D*
Union Institute *B,D*
Wittenberg University *B*

Oregon

Willamette University *B*

Pennsylvania

Bryn Mawr College *B*
Bucknell University *B*
Dickinson College *B*
Penn State University Park
Campus *B*
University of Pennsylvania *B,M,D*

University of Pittsburgh *M*
Ursinus College *B*

Rhode Island
Brown University *B*

Tennessee
Vanderbilt University *B*

Vermont
Middlebury College *B*

Virginia
Washington and Lee University *B*

Washington
University of Washington *B,M*
Western Washington University *B*

Wisconsin
Lawrence University *B*

Canada
McGill University *B*

Eastern European studies

Alabama
University of Alabama *B*

California
Monterey Institute of International
  Studies *M*
Naval Postgraduate School *M*

Connecticut
University of Connecticut *B*
Yale University *B,M*

District of Columbia
George Washington University *M*
Georgetown University *B*

Florida
Florida State University *B,M*
New College of the University of
  South Florida *B*

Georgia
Emory University *B*

Illinois
Richland Community College *A*
University of Chicago *B,M,D*

Indiana
Indiana University Bloomington *C*
University of Notre Dame *B*

Iowa
University of Iowa *B*

Kansas
University of Kansas *M*

Kentucky
University of Kentucky *B*

Louisiana
University of Southwestern
  Louisiana *B*

Massachusetts
Boston University *B*
Hampshire College *B*
Harvard and Radcliffe Colleges *B*
Tufts University *B,M*

University of Massachusetts at
  Amherst *B*
Williams College *B*

Michigan
University of Michigan *B,M*
Wayne State University *M*

Missouri
Westminster College *B*

New Jersey
Rutgers—The State University of
  New Jersey
    Douglass College *B*
    Livingston College *B*
    Rutgers College *B*
    University College New
      Brunswick *B*

New York
Bard College *B*
City University of New York:
  Brooklyn College *B*
Columbia University
  Columbia College *B*
  New York *M,D*
Long Island University: C. W. Post
  Campus *B*
State University of New York at
  Albany *B*

Ohio
Kent State University *B*
Ohio State University: Columbus
  Campus *M*
Ohio University *B*

Oregon
Willamette University *B*

Pennsylvania
California University of
  Pennsylvania *B*
University of Pennsylvania *B,M,D*

Tennessee
University of Tennessee:
  Knoxville *B*

Vermont
University of Vermont *B*

Washington
University of Washington *B,M*

Ecology

Arizona
Prescott College *B*
University of Arizona *B*

California
California Polytechnic State
  University: San Luis Obispo *B*
California State University:
  Fullerton *B*
Chabot College *A*
Orange Coast College *A*
San Diego State University *D*
San Francisco State University *B,M*
Southwestern College *A*
University of California
  Berkeley *B,M,D*
  Davis *M,D*
  San Diego *B*
  Santa Barbara *B*
  Santa Cruz *B,D*

Colorado
Regis College of Regis University *B*
Western State College of
  Colorado *B*

Connecticut
Connecticut College *B*
University of Connecticut *M,D*
Wesleyan University *B*

Delaware
University of Delaware *M,D*

District of Columbia
George Washington University *M,D*

Florida
Florida Agricultural and Mechanical
  University *M*
Florida Institute of Technology *D*
New College of the University of
  South Florida *B*
University of Central Florida *B*
University of Florida *M,D*

Georgia
Emory University *M,D*
University of Georgia *D*

Idaho
Idaho State University *B*
Ricks College *A*

Illinois
Southern Illinois University at
  Edwardsville *B*
State Community College *A*
University of Chicago *B,M,D*
University of Illinois at Urbana-
  Champaign *B*

Indiana
Indiana University Bloomington
  M,D
Purdue University *B,M*

Iowa
Iowa Lakes Community College *A*
Iowa State University *B,M,D*

Kansas
University of Kansas *B,M,D*

Kentucky
Morehead State University *B*

Louisiana
Louisiana State University and
  Agricultural and Mechanical
  College *B*

Maine
Unity College *B*
University of Maine at Machias *B*

Maryland
Frostburg State University *M*

Massachusetts
Hampshire College *B*
Mount Holyoke College *B*
Tufts University *B,M,D*
Worcester Polytechnic Institute *B*

Michigan
Eastern Michigan University *B*
Michigan Technological
  University *B*
Northern Michigan University *B*
University of Michigan *M*

Minnesota
Rainy River Community College *A*
University of Minnesota: Twin
  Cities *M,D*
Winona State University *B*

Missouri
Northwest Missouri State
  University *B*

Montana
Northern Montana College *A,B*

Nebraska
Peru State College *B*

New Hampshire
Franklin Pierce College *B*
University of New Hampshire *B*

New Jersey
Monmouth College *B*
Rutgers—The State University of
  New Jersey
    Camden College of Arts and
      Sciences *B*
    Cook College *B*
    Douglass College *B*
    Livingston College *B*
    New Brunswick *M,D*
    Rutgers College *B*
    University College New
      Brunswick *B*

New Mexico
New Mexico State University *B*

New York
Cornell University *B,M,D*
Iona College *B*
Paul Smith's College *A*
St. John's University *B*
State University of New York
  Albany *M*
  Stony Brook *D*
  College of Environmental
    Science and Forestry *B,M,D*
  College at Plattsburgh *B*

North Carolina
North Carolina State University *M*
University of North Carolina at
  Chapel Hill *M,D*

Ohio
Kent State University *M,D*
Ohio State University: Columbus
  Campus *M,D*
Ohio University *M,D*
University of Akron *B*
University of Findlay *B*

Oklahoma
Oklahoma State University *B,M,D*

Oregon
University of Oregon *M,D*

Pennsylvania
California University of
  Pennsylvania *B*
Drexel University *M,D*
Juniata College *B*
Lehigh University *M,D*
Penn State University Park Campus
  M,D
University of Pittsburgh at
  Johnstown *B*
West Chester University of
  Pennsylvania *B*

Tennessee

University of Tennessee: Knoxville
M,D

Texas

University of Texas Health Science
Center at Houston *M,D*

Utah

Utah State University *M,D*

Vermont

Johnson State College *B*
Marlboro College *B*
Sterling College *A*

Virginia

Averett College *B*

Washington

Evergreen State College *B*
Grays Harbor College *A*
Western Washington University *B*

Wisconsin

Northland College *B*

Canada

McGill University *B,M,D*

Economics

Alabama

Alabama State University *B*
Auburn University *B,M,D*
Birmingham-Southern College *B*
Jacksonville State University *B*
Judson College *B*
Samford University *B*
Talladega College *B*
Troy State University
   Dothan *B*
   Troy *B*
Tuskegee University *B*
University of Alabama
   Birmingham *B*
   Huntsville *B*
   Tuscaloosa *B,M,D,W*
University of South Alabama *B*

Alaska

University of Alaska
   Anchorage *B*
   Fairbanks *B,M*

Arizona

Arizona State University *B,M,D*
Glendale Community College *A*
Grand Canyon University *B*
Northern Arizona University *B*
University of Arizona *B,M,D*

Arkansas

Arkansas College *B*
Arkansas State University *B*
Arkansas Tech University *B*
Harding University *B*
Hendrix College *B*
Ouachita Baptist University *B*
University of Arkansas
   Fayetteville *B,M,D*
   Pine Bluff *B*
University of Central Arkansas *B*

California

Bakersfield College *A*
California Institute of Technology *B*
California Lutheran University *B*

California Polytechnic State
   University: San Luis Obispo *B*
California State Polytechnic
   University: Pomona *B,M*
California State University
   Bakersfield *B*
   Chico *B*
   Dominguez Hills *B*
   Fresno *B,M*
   Fullerton *B,M*
   Hayward *B,M*
   Long Beach *B,M*
   Los Angeles *B,M*
   Northridge *B*
   Sacramento *B,M*
   San Bernardino *B*
   San Marcos *B*
   Stanislaus *B*
Cerritos Community College *A*
Chaffey Community College *A*
Chapman University *B*
Claremont McKenna College *B*
Crafton Hills College *A*
De Anza College *A*
El Camino College *A*
Foothill College *A*
Grossmont Community College *A*
Humboldt State University *C,B*
Irvine Valley College *A*
Los Angeles Valley College *A*
Loyola Marymount University *B*
Marymount College *A*
Merced College *A*
Mills College *B*
Napa Valley College *A*
Occidental College *B*
Ohlone College *A*
Orange Coast College *A*
Pepperdine University *B*
Pitzer College *B*
Point Loma Nazarene College *B*
Pomona College *B*
Saddleback College *A*
St. Mary's College of California *B*
San Diego State University *B,M*
San Francisco State University *B,M*
San Jose State University *B,M*
Santa Barbara City College *A*
Santa Clara University *B*
Santa Rosa Junior College *A*
Scripps College *B*
Sonoma State University *B*
Southwestern College *A*
Stanford University *B,M,D*
University of California
   Berkeley *B,M,D*
   Davis *B,M,D*
   Irvine *B,M,D*
   Los Angeles *B,M,D*
   Riverside *B,M,D*
   San Diego *B,M,D*
   Santa Barbara *B,M,D*
   Santa Cruz *B,M,D*
University of La Verne *B*
University of the Pacific *B*
University of Redlands *B*
University of San Diego *B*
University of San Francisco *B,M*
University of Southern California
   B,M,D
Ventura College *A*
Westmont College *B*
Whittier College *B*

Colorado

Adams State College *B*
Colorado College *B*
Colorado State University *B,M,D*
Mesa State College *B*
Metropolitan State College of
   Denver *B*
Regis College of Regis University *B*

United States Air Force
   Academy *B*
University of Colorado
   Boulder *B,M,D*
   Colorado Springs *B*
   Denver *B,M*
University of Denver *B,M*
University of Northern Colorado *B*
Western State College of
   Colorado *B*

Connecticut

Albertus Magnus College *B*
Central Connecticut State
   University *B*
Connecticut College *B*
Eastern Connecticut State
   University *B*
Fairfield University *B*
Quinnipiac College *B*
Sacred Heart University *A,B*
St. Joseph College *B*
Southern Connecticut State
   University *B*
Trinity College *B,M*
University of Connecticut *B,M,D*
University of Hartford *B,M*
University of New Haven *B*
Wesleyan University *B*
Western Connecticut State
   University *B*
Yale University *B,M,D*

Delaware

University of Delaware *B,M*

District of Columbia

American University *B,M,D*
Catholic University of America
   B,M,D
Gallaudet University *B*
George Washington University
   B,M,D
Georgetown University *B,D*
Howard University *B,M,D*
Southeastern University *B,M*
Trinity College *B*
University of the District of
   Columbia *B*

Florida

Barry University *B*
Central Florida Community
   College *A*
Daytona Beach Community
   College *A*
Eckerd College *B*
Florida Agricultural and Mechanical
   University *B*
Florida Atlantic University *B,M*
Florida Institute of Technology *B*
Florida International University
   B,M,D
Florida Southern College *B*
Florida State University *B,M,D*
Gulf Coast Community College *A*
Jacksonville University *B*
Miami-Dade Community College *A*
New College of the University of
   South Florida *B*
Rollins College *B*
Stetson University *B*
University of Central Florida *B*
University of Florida *B,M,D*
University of Miami *B,M,D*
University of North Florida *B*
University of South Florida *B*
University of West Florida *B*

Georgia

Agnes Scott College *B*
Atlanta Metropolitan College *A*

Bainbridge College *A*
Berry College *B*
Brewton-Parker College *A*
Clark Atlanta University *B,M*
Emory University *B,M,D*
Fort Valley State College *B*
Georgia College *B*
Georgia Institute of Technology *B*
Georgia Southern University *B*
Georgia State University *B,M,D*
Gordon College *A*
Kennesaw State College *B*
LaGrange College *B*
Macon College *A*
Mercer University *B*
Morehouse College *B*
Morris Brown College *B*
North Georgia College *B*
Oglethorpe University *B*
Oxford College of Emory
   University *A*
Piedmont College *B*
Shorter College *B*
Spelman College *B*
University of Georgia *B,M,D*
West Georgia College *B*

Hawaii

Chaminade University of
   Honolulu *B*
Hawaii Pacific University *B*
University of Hawaii
   Hilo *B*
   Manoa *B,M,D*
   West Oahu *B*

Idaho

Albertson College *B*
Boise State University *B*
Idaho State University *B*
Ricks College *A*
University of Idaho *B,M*

Illinois

Augustana College *B*
Aurora University *B*
Barat College *B*
Black Hawk College *A*
Blackburn College *B*
Bradley University *B*
Chicago State University *B*
De Paul University *B,M*
Eastern Illinois University *B,M*
Elmhurst College *B*
Eureka College *B*
Illinois Benedictine College *B*
Illinois Central College *A*
Illinois College *B*
Illinois State University *B,M,D*
Illinois Wesleyan University *B*
Joliet Junior College *A*
Knox College *B*
Lake Forest College *B*
Lincoln Land Community
   College *A*
Loyola University of Chicago *B*
Millikin University *B*
Monmouth College *B*
North Central College *B*
North Park College and Theological
   Seminary *B*
Northeastern Illinois University *B*
Northern Illinois University *B,M,D*
Northwestern University *B,M,D*
Olivet Nazarene University *B*
Rockford College *B*
Roosevelt University *B,M*
Rosary College *B*
Sangamon State University *B,M*
Southern Illinois University
   Carbondale *B,M,D*
   Edwardsville *B,M*

Triton College *A*
University of Chicago *B,M,D*
University of Illinois
    Chicago *B,M*
    Urbana-Champaign *B,M,D*
Western Illinois University *B,M*
Wheaton College *B*

Indiana

Anderson University *B*
Ball State University *B,M*
DePauw University *B*
Earlham College *B*
Franklin College *B*
Goshen College *B*
Hanover College *B*
Indiana State University *B,M*
Indiana University
    Bloomington *B,M,D*
    Northwest *B*
    South Bend *B*
    Southeast *B*
Indiana University—Purdue
  University
    Fort Wayne *B*
    Indianapolis *B,M*
Indiana Wesleyan University *B*
Manchester College *B*
Purdue University *B,M,D*
Rose-Hulman Institute of
  Technology *B*
St. Joseph's College *B*
St. Mary's College *B*
Taylor University *B*
Tri-State University *B*
University of Evansville *B*
University of Indianapolis *B*
University of Notre Dame *B,M,D*
Valparaiso University *B*
Vincennes University *A*
Wabash College *B*

Iowa

Buena Vista College *B*
Central College *B*
Clarke College *B*
Coe College *B*
Cornell College *B*
Drake University *B*
Graceland College *B*
Grinnell College *B*
Iowa State University *B,M,D*
Loras College *B*
Luther College *B*
Morningside College *B*
St. Ambrose University *B*
Simpson College *B*
Teikyo Westmar University *B*
University of Dubuque *B*
University of Iowa *B,D*
University of Northern Iowa *B*
Wartburg College *B*
William Penn College *B*

Kansas

Baker University *B*
Benedictine College *B*
Bethel College *B*
Central College *A*
Coffeyville Community College *A*
Emporia State University *B*
Fort Hays State University *B*
Fort Scott Community College *A*
Kansas State University *B,M,D*
Ottawa University *B*
Pittsburg State University *B,M*
Southwestern College *B*
University of Kansas *B,M,D*
Washburn University of Topeka *B*
Wichita State University *B,M*

Kentucky

Bellarmine College *B*
Berea College *B*
Campbellsville College *B*
Centre College *B*
Eastern Kentucky University *B*
Georgetown College *B*
Murray State University *B,M*
Northern Kentucky University *B*
Pikeville College *B*
Thomas More College *A,B*
Transylvania University *B*
University of Kentucky *B*
University of Louisville *B*
Western Kentucky University *B,M*

Louisiana

Centenary College of Louisiana *B*
Dillard University *B*
Louisiana College *B*
Louisiana State University
    Agricultural and Mechanical
    College *B,M,D*
    Shreveport *B*
Loyola University *B*
McNeese State University *B*
Nicholls State University *B*
Northwestern State University *B*
Southern University at New
  Orleans *B*
Tulane University *B,M,D*
University of New Orleans *B*
University of Southwestern
  Louisiana *B*

Maine

Bates College *B*
Bowdoin College *B*
Colby College *B*
Thomas College *B*
University of Maine
    Farmington *B*
    Orono *B,M*
University of Southern Maine *B*

Maryland

College of Notre Dame of
  Maryland *B*
Frostburg State University *B*
Goucher College *B*
Hood College *B*
Howard Community College *A*
Johns Hopkins University *B,M,D*
Loyola College in Maryland *B*
Morgan State University *B,M*
Mount St. Mary's College *B*
St. Mary's College of Maryland *B*
Salisbury State University *B*
Towson State University *B*
United States Naval Academy *B*
University of Baltimore *B*
University of Maryland
    Baltimore County *B*
    College Park *B,M,D*
Washington College *B*
Western Maryland College *B*

Massachusetts

American International College *B*
Amherst College *B*
Assumption College *B*
Babson College *B*
Boston College *B,M,D*
Boston University *B,M,D*
Brandeis University *B,M*
Clark University *B,M,D*
College of the Holy Cross *B*
Emmanuel College *B*
Fitchburg State College *B*
Framingham State College *B*
Gordon College *B*
Hampshire College *B*

Harvard and Radcliffe Colleges *B*
Harvard University *D*
Massachusetts Institute of
  Technology *B,M,D,W*
Merrimack College *B*
Mount Holyoke College *B*
Nichols College *B*
North Adams State College *B*
Northeastern University *B,M,D*
Regis College *B*
Salem State College *B*
Simmons College *B*
Smith College *B*
Stonehill College *B*
Suffolk University *B*
Tufts University *B,M*
University of Massachusetts
    Amherst *B,M,D*
    Boston *B*
    Dartmouth *B*
    Lowell *B*
Wellesley College *B*
Western New England College *B*
Westfield State College *B*
Wheaton College *B*
Williams College *B*
Worcester Polytechnic Institute *B*
Worcester State College *B*

Michigan

Adrian College *A,B*
Albion College *B*
Alma College *B*
Andrews University *B*
Aquinas College *B*
Calvin College *B*
Central Michigan University *B,M*
Eastern Michigan University *B,M*
Grand Valley State University *B*
Hillsdale College *B*
Hope College *B*
Kalamazoo College *B*
Lake Superior State University *B*
Marygrove College *B*
Michigan State University *B,M,D*
Michigan Technological
  University *B*
Northern Michigan University
  A,B,M
Northwood Institute *B*
Oakland University *B*
Olivet College *B*
Saginaw Valley State University *B*
University of Detroit Mercy *B,M*
University of Michigan
    Ann Arbor *B,M,D*
    Dearborn *B*
    Flint *B*
Wayne State University *B,M,D*
Western Michigan University *B,M*

Minnesota

Augsburg College *B*
Bemidji State University *B*
Bethel College *B*
Carleton College *B*
College of St. Benedict *B*
College of St. Catherine: St.
  Catherine Campus *B*
Concordia College: Moorhead *B*
Concordia College: St. Paul *B*
Gustavus Adolphus College *B*
Hamline University *B*
Macalester College *B*
Mankato State University *B,M*
Moorhead State University *B*
Rainy River Community College *A*
St. Cloud State University *B*
St. John's University *B*
St. Mary's College of Minnesota *B*
St. Olaf College *B*

University of Minnesota
    Duluth *B*
    Morris *B*
    Twin Cities *B,M,D*
University of St. Thomas *B*
Willmar Community College *A*
Winona State University *B*

Mississippi

Alcorn State University *B*
Jackson State University *B*
Mary Holmes College *A*
Millsaps College *B*
Mississippi State University *B*
Rust College *B*
Tougaloo College *B*
University of Mississippi *B,M,D*

Missouri

Central Methodist College *B*
Central Missouri State University
  B,M
College of the Ozarks *B*
Drury College *B*
East Central College *A*
Missouri Valley College *B*
Missouri Western State College *B*
Northeast Missouri State
  University *B*
Northwest Missouri State
  University *B*
Park College *B*
Rockhurst College *B*
St. Louis University *B,M,D*
Southeast Missouri State
  University *B*
Southwest Baptist University *B*
Southwest Missouri State
  University *B*
University of Missouri
    Columbia *B,M,D*
    Kansas City *B,M*
    Rolla *B*
    St. Louis *B,M*
Washington University *B,M,D*
Westminster College *B*
William Jewell College *B*
William Woods College *B*

Montana

Carroll College *B*
Eastern Montana College *B*
Montana State University *B,M*
Rocky Mountain College *B*
University of Montana *B,M*

Nebraska

Central Community College *A*
Chadron State College *B*
Creighton University *B*
Dana College *B*
Doane College *B*
Hastings College *B*
Midland Lutheran College *B*
Nebraska Wesleyan University *B*
University of Nebraska
    Kearney *B*
    Lincoln *B,M,D*
    Omaha *B,M*
Wayne State College *B*
York College *A*

Nevada

University of Nevada: Reno *B,M*

New Hampshire

Dartmouth College *B*
Franklin Pierce College *B*
Keene State College *B*
New England College *B*
St. Anselm College *B*

University of New Hampshire
B,M,D

New Jersey

Bergen Community College *A*
Bloomfield College *B*
College of St. Elizabeth *B*
Drew University *B*
Fairleigh Dickinson University *B,M*
Glassboro State College *B*
Jersey City State College *B*
Kean College of New Jersey *B*
Monmouth College *B*
Montclair State College *B*
Princeton University *B,D*
Ramapo College of New Jersey *B*
Rider College *B*
Rutgers—The State University of
New Jersey
    Camden College of Arts and
      Sciences *B*
    Douglass College *B*
    Livingston College *B*
    New Brunswick *M,D*
    Newark College of Arts and
      Sciences *B*
    Rutgers College *B*
    University College Camden *B*
    University College New
      Brunswick *B*
    University College Newark *B*
St. Peter's College *B*
Seton Hall University *B*
Stevens Institute of Technology *B*
Stockton State College *B*
Thomas Edison State College *B*
Trenton State College *B*
Upsala College *B*
William Paterson College of New
Jersey *B,M*

New Mexico

New Mexico State University *B,M*
University of New Mexico *B,M,D*
Western New Mexico University *B*

New York

Adelphi University *B*
Alfred University *B*
Bard College *B*
Barnard College *B*
Canisius College *B*
City University of New York
    Baruch College *B,M*
    Brooklyn College *B,M*
    City College *B,M*
    College of Staten Island *B*
    Graduate School and
      University Center *D*
    Hunter College *B,M*
    Lehman College *B*
    Queens College *B,M*
    York College *B*
Clarkson University *B*
Colgate University *B*
College of Mount St. Vincent *B*
College of New Rochelle *B*
Columbia University
    Columbia College *B*
    New York *M,D*
    School of General Studies *B*
Cornell University *B,M,D*
Dominican College of Blauvelt *B*
Dowling College *B*
Elmira College *B*
Eugene Lang College/New School
for Social Research *B*
Fordham University *B,M,D*
Hamilton College *B*
Hartwick College *B*
Hobart College *B*
Hofstra University *B*

Iona College *B,M*
Ithaca College *B*
Jamestown Community College *A*
Le Moyne College *B*
Long Island University
    Brooklyn Campus *B,M*
    C. W. Post Campus *B*
Manhattan College *B*
Manhattanville College *B*
Marist College *B*
Marymount College *B*
Nazareth College of Rochester *B*
New York Institute of
Technology *B*
New York University *B,M,D*
Pace University
    College of White Plains *B*
    New York *B*
    Pleasantville/Briarcliff *B*
Rensselaer Polytechnic Institute
B,M
Rochester Institute of
Technology *B*
Russell Sage College *B*
St. Bonaventure University *B*
St. Francis College *B*
St. John Fisher College *B*
St. John's University *B,M*
St. Lawrence University *B*
Sarah Lawrence College *B*
Siena College *B*
Skidmore College *B*
State University of New York
    Albany *B,M,D*
    Binghamton *B,M,D*
    Buffalo *B,M,D*
    Purchase *C,B*
    Stony Brook *B,M,D*
    College at Brockport *B*
    College at Buffalo *B*
    College at Cortland *B*
    College at Fredonia *B*
    College at Geneseo *B*
    College at New Paltz *B*
    College at Old Westbury *B*
    College at Oneonta *B*
    College at Plattsburgh *B*
    College at Potsdam *B*
    Empire State College *A,B*
    Oswego *B*
Sullivan County Community
College *A*
Syracuse University *B,M,D*
Touro College *B*
Union College *B*
United States Military Academy *B*
University of Rochester *B,M,D*
University of the State of New
York: Regents College *B*
Utica College of Syracuse
University *B*
Vassar College *B*
Wagner College *B*
Wells College *B*
William Smith College *B*
Yeshiva University *B*

North Carolina

Appalachian State University *B,M*
Belmont Abbey College *B*
Brevard College *A*
Campbell University *B*
Davidson College *B*
Duke University *B,M,D*
East Carolina University *B*
Elon College *B*
Fayetteville State University *B*
Guilford College *B*
Johnson C. Smith University *B*
Lenoir-Rhyne College *B*
Meredith College *B*
Methodist College *A*

North Carolina State University
B,M,D
Pembroke State University *B*
Pfeiffer College *B*
St. Augustine's College *B*
Salem College *B*
University of North Carolina
    Asheville *B*
    Chapel Hill *B,M,D*
    Charlotte *B,M*
    Greensboro *B,M*
Wake Forest University *B*
Warren Wilson College *B*
Wingate College *B*

North Dakota

Minot State University *B*
North Dakota State University *B,M*
University of North Dakota *B,M*

Ohio

Antioch College *B*
Ashland University *B*
Baldwin-Wallace College *B*
Bluffton College *B*
Bowling Green State University
B,M
Capital University *B*
Case Western Reserve University *B*
Cedarville College *B*
Central State University *B*
Cleveland State University *B,M*
College of Wooster *B*
Denison University *B*
Franciscan University of
Steubenville *B*
Heidelberg College *B*
Hiram College *B*
John Carroll University *B*
Kent State University *B,M*
Kenyon College *B*
Lakeland Community College *A*
Marietta College *B*
Miami University: Oxford Campus
B,M
Muskingum College *B*
Oberlin College *B*
Ohio Dominican College *B*
Ohio State University: Columbus
Campus *B,M,D*
Ohio University *B,M*
Ohio Wesleyan University *B*
Otterbein College *B*
Union Institute *B,D*
University of Akron *B,M*
University of Cincinnati
    Cincinnati *B,M,D*
    Raymond Walters College *A*
University of Dayton *B*
University of Findlay *B*
University of Toledo *B,M*
Urbana University *B*
Wilberforce University *B*
Wilmington College *B*
Wittenberg University *B*
Wright State University *B,M*
Xavier University *B*
Youngstown State University *B,M*

Oklahoma

Langston University *B*
Northeastern State University *B*
Northwestern Oklahoma State
University *B*
Oklahoma City University *B*
Oklahoma State University *M,D*
Southeastern Oklahoma State
University *B*
Southwestern Oklahoma State
University *B*
Tulsa Junior College *A*
University of Central Oklahoma *B*

University of Oklahoma *B,M,D*
University of Science and Arts of
Oklahoma *B*
University of Tulsa *B*

Oregon

Central Oregon Community
College *A*
Lewis and Clark College *B*
Linfield College *B*
Northwest Christian College *B*
Oregon State University *B,M,D*
Pacific University *B*
Portland Community College *A*
Portland State University *B,M*
Reed College *B*
Southern Oregon State College *B*
University of Oregon
    Eugene *B,M,D*
    Robert Donald Clark Honors
      College *B*
Western Oregon State College *B*
Willamette University *B*

Pennsylvania

Albright College *B*
Allegheny College *B*
Bloomsburg University of
Pennsylvania *B*
Bryn Mawr College *B*
Bucknell University *B*
California University of
Pennsylvania *B*
Carnegie Mellon University
B,M,D,W
Chatham College *B*
Chestnut Hill College *B*
Cheyney University of
Pennsylvania *B*
Clarion University of
Pennsylvania *B*
Dickinson College *B*
Duquesne University *B,M*
East Stroudsburg University of
Pennsylvania *B*
Eastern College *B*
Edinboro University of
Pennsylvania *B*
Elizabethtown College *B*
Franklin and Marshall College *B*
Gannon University *B*
Geneva College *B*
Gettysburg College *B*
Grove City College *B*
Haverford College *B*
Holy Family College *B*
Immaculata College *B*
Indiana University of
Pennsylvania *B*
Juniata College *B*
King's College *B*
Kutztown University of
Pennsylvania *B*
La Salle University *B*
Lafayette College *B*
Lebanon Valley College of
Pennsylvania *B*
Lehigh University *B,M,D*
Lincoln University *B*
Lock Haven University of
Pennsylvania *B*
Lycoming College *B*
Mansfield University of
Pennsylvania *B*
Millersville University of
Pennsylvania *B*
Moravian College *B*
Muhlenberg College *B*
Penn State
    Erie Behrend College *B*
    University Park Campus
      B,M,D

Rosemont College *B*
St. Francis College *B*
St. Joseph's University *B*
St. Vincent College *B*
Seton Hill College *B*
Shippensburg University of
  Pennsylvania *B*
Slippery Rock University of
  Pennsylvania *B*
Susquehanna University *B*
Swarthmore College *B*
Temple University *B,M,D*
University of Pennsylvania *B,M,D*
University of Pittsburgh
  Bradford *B*
  Johnstown *B*
  Pittsburgh *B,M,D*
University of Scranton *B*
Ursinus College *B*
Villanova University *B*
Washington and Jefferson College *B*
Waynesburg College *B*
Westminster College *B*
Widener University *B*
Wilkes University *B*

Puerto Rico

Inter American University of Puerto
  Rico
    Arecibo Campus *B*
    San German Campus *B*
Turabo University *B*
University of Puerto Rico
    Cayey University College *B*
    Mayaguez Campus *B*
    Rio Piedras Campus *B,M*

Rhode Island

Brown University *B,M,D*
Bryant College *B*
Providence College *B*
Rhode Island College *B*
Salve Regina University *B,M*
University of Rhode Island *B,M*

South Carolina

Benedict College *B*
Clemson University *B,M*
College of Charleston *B*
Converse College *B*
Francis Marion College *B*
Furman University *B*
Newberry College *B*
Presbyterian College *B*
University of South Carolina
    Aiken *B*
    Columbia *B,M,D*
Wofford College *B*

South Dakota

Augustana College *B*
Northern State University *B*
South Dakota State University *B,M*
University of South Dakota *B,M*

Tennessee

Austin Peay State University *B*
Belmont University *B*
Christian Brothers University *C*
East Tennessee State University *B*
Fisk University *B*
Knoxville College *B*
LeMoyne-Owen College *B*
Lincoln Memorial University *B*
Maryville College *B*
Memphis State University *B,M*
Middle Tennessee State University
  B,M,D
Motlow State Community
  College *A*
Rhodes College *B*

Tennessee Technological
  University *B*
Union University *B*
University of the South *B*
University of Tennessee
  Chattanooga *B*
  Knoxville *B,M,D*
  Martin *B*
Vanderbilt University *B,M,D*

Texas

Angelo State University *B*
Austin College *B*
Austin Community College *A*
Baylor University *B,M*
College of the Mainland *A*
Collin County Community College
  District *A*
Dallas Baptist University *B*
East Texas State University *B,M*
Houston Baptist University *B*
Houston Community College *A*
Howard Payne University *B*
Huston-Tillotson College *B*
Kilgore College *A*
Lamar University—Beaumont *B*
Lon Morris College *A*
McMurry University *B*
Midland College *A*
Midwestern State University *B*
Odessa College *A*
Panola College *A*
Rice University *B,M,D*
St. Edward's University *B*
St. Mary's University *B,M*
St. Philip's College *A*
Sam Houston State University *B*
Southern Methodist University
  B,M,D
Southwest Texas State University *B*
Southwestern University *B*
Tarleton State University *B*
Texas A&M University *B,M,D*
Texas Christian University *B,M*
Texas Lutheran College *B*
Texas Southern University *B*
Texas Southmost College *A*
Texas Tech University *B,M,D*
Texas Woman's University *B,M*
Trinity University *B*
University of Dallas *B*
University of Houston *B,M,D*
University of Mary Hardin-
  Baylor *B*
University of North Texas *B,M*
University of St. Thomas *B*
University of Texas
  Austin *B,M,D*
  Dallas *B*
  El Paso *B,M*
  San Antonio *B*
West Texas State University *B,M*
Western Texas College *A*
Wharton County Junior College *A*

Utah

Brigham Young University *B,M*
Dixie College *A*
University of Utah *B,M,D*
Utah State University *B,M,D*
Weber State University *B*

Vermont

Bennington College *B*
Marlboro College *B*
Middlebury College *B*
St. Michael's College *B*
Trinity College of Vermont *B*
University of Vermont *B*

Virginia

Bridgewater College *B*
Christopher Newport College *B*
Clinch Valley College of the
  University of Virginia *B*
College of William and Mary *B*
Emory and Henry College *B*
George Mason University *B,M,D*
Hampden-Sydney College *B*
Hampton University *B*
Hollins College *B*
James Madison University *B*
Liberty University *B*
Lynchburg College *B*
Mary Baldwin College *B*
Mary Washington College *B*
Marymount University *B*
Norfolk State University *B*
Old Dominion University *B,M*
Radford University *B*
Randolph-Macon College *B*
Randolph-Macon Woman's
  College *B*
Roanoke College *B*
Strayer College *A,B*
Sweet Briar College *B*
University of Richmond *B*
University of Virginia *B,M,D*
Virginia Commonwealth University
  B,M
Virginia Military Institute *B*
Virginia Polytechnic Institute and
  State University *B,M*
Washington and Lee University *B*

Washington

Central Washington University *B*
Eastern Washington University *B*
Everett Community College *A*
Evergreen State College *B*
Gonzaga University *B*
Lower Columbia College *A*
Olympic College *A*
Pacific Lutheran University *B*
St. Martin's College *B*
Seattle Pacific University *B*
Seattle University *B*
Spokane Community College *A*
Spokane Falls Community
  College *A*
Tacoma Community College *A*
University of Puget Sound *B*
University of Washington *B,M,D*
Washington State University *B,M,D*
Western Washington University *B*
Whitman College *B*
Whitworth College *B*

West Virginia

Bethany College *B*
Davis and Elkins College *B*
Marshall University *B*
Potomac State College of West
  Virginia University *A*
Shepherd College *B*
West Virginia State College *B*
West Virginia University *B*
West Virginia Wesleyan College *B*

Wisconsin

Beloit College *B*
Carroll College *B*
Carthage College *B*
Edgewood College *B*
Lakeland College *B*
Lawrence University *B*
Marquette University *B,M*
Northland College *B*
Ripon College *B*
St. Norbert College *B*

University of Wisconsin
  Eau Claire *B*
  Green Bay *B*
  La Crosse *B*
  Madison *B,M,D*
  Milwaukee *B,M,D*
  Oshkosh *B*
  Parkside *B*
  Platteville *B*
  River Falls *B*
  Superior *B*
  Whitewater *B*

Wyoming

Casper College *A*
Eastern Wyoming College *A*
Laramie County Community
  College *A*
University of Wyoming *B*

**American Samoa, Caroline
Islands, Guam, Marianas,
Virgin Islands**

University of Guam *B*

Canada

McGill University *B,M,D*

France

American University of Paris *B*

Mexico

Sistema Instituto Tecnologico y de
  Estudios Superiores de
  Monterrey *B*

Switzerland

American College of Switzerland *B*

Arab Republic of Egypt

American University in Cairo *B,M*

Education

Alabama

Alabama Southern Community
  College *A*
Athens State College *B*
Auburn University at Montgomery
  B,M
Birmingham-Southern College *B*
Brewer State Junior College *A*
Faulkner University *B*
Gadsden State Community
  College *A*
John C. Calhoun State Community
  College *A*
Lawson State Community
  College *A*
Miles College *B*
Samford University *B,M*
Shelton State Community
  College *A*
Shoals Community College *A*
Snead State Junior College *A*
Southern Union State Junior
  College *A*
Spring Hill College *M*
University of Alabama in
  Huntsville *B*
University of Montevallo *B,M*
Wallace State Community College
  at Hanceville *A*

Alaska

Sheldon Jackson College *A,B*
University of Alaska
  Fairbanks *B,M*
  Southeast *M*

Arizona

Arizona Western College *A*
Eastern Arizona College *A*
Navajo Community College *A*
Pima Community College *A*
Prescott College *B,M*

Arkansas

Arkansas State University: Beebe
   Branch *A*
Central Baptist College *A*
Crowley's Ridge College *A*
Garland County Community
   College *A*
Harding University *B,M*
Mississippi County Community
   College *A*
Ouachita Baptist University *B*
Phillips County Community
   College *A*
Rich Mountain Community
   College *A*
Shorter College *A*
Southern Arkansas University:
   Technical Branch *A*
University of Arkansas
   Fayetteville *M,D*
   Pine Bluff *M*
University of Central Arkansas *B,M*
University of the Ozarks *B*
Westark Community College *A*
Williams Baptist College *B*

California

Allan Hancock College *C,A*
Azusa Pacific University *B,M*
Barstow College *C,A*
Biola University *B*
California Baptist College *B*
California Lutheran University *B,M*
California Polytechnic State
   University: San Luis Obispo *M*
California State Polytechnic
   University: Pomona *M*
California State University
   Bakersfield *B,M*
   Chico *M*
   Dominguez Hills *M*
   Fresno *M*
   Hayward *M*
   Sacramento *B,M*
   Stanislaus *M*
Chabot College *A*
Chaffey Community College *A*
Chapman University *B*
Christ College Irvine *B*
Christian Heritage College *B*
College of Notre Dame *M*
Cosumnes River College *A*
Crafton Hills College *A*
Feather River College *A*
Fresno Pacific College *B*
Gavilan Community College *A*
Holy Names College *M*
Humphreys College *A*
La Sierra University *B*
Laney College *A*
Lassen College *A*
Master's College *B*
Merced College *A*
Mills College *B,M*
Napa Valley College *A*
National University *B,M*
Pacific Oaks College *B,M*
Pacific Union College *M*
Patten College *B*
Pepperdine University *M*
Pitzer College *B*
Porterville College *A*
St. Mary's College of California
   B,M
San Diego State University *M,D*

San Francisco State University *M*
Santa Rosa Junior College *A*
Simpson College *M*
Skyline College *A*
Southern California College *B*
Southwestern College *A*
Stanford University *M,D*
United States International
   University *B,M*
University of California
   Berkeley *M,D*
   Davis *M*
   Los Angeles *M,D*
   Riverside *M,D*
   San Diego *M*
   Santa Barbara *M,D*
   Santa Cruz *M*
University of Judaism *M*
University of La Verne *B,M*
University of the Pacific *M,D*
University of San Diego *M*
University of Southern California *B*
Ventura College *A*
West Hills Community College *A*
Whittier College *M*
Yuba College *A*

Colorado

Adams State College *B,M*
Colorado Northwestern Community
   College *A*
Naropa Institute *B*
Northeastern Junior College *A*
Pikes Peak Community College *A*
Regis College of Regis University *B*
Trinidad State Junior College *A*
University of Colorado
   Colorado Springs *M*
   Denver *B,M*
University of Denver *M,D*

Connecticut

Fairfield University *M*
Mitchell College *A*
Norwalk Community College *A*
Sacred Heart University *B,M*
St. Joseph College *M*
South Central Community
   College *A*
Southern Connecticut State
   University *B*
University of Connecticut *M*
Western Connecticut State
   University *M*

Delaware

University of Delaware *B*
Wesley College *B*
Wilmington College *D*

District of Columbia

American University *M*
Catholic University of America
   B,M,D
Gallaudet University *B*
Trinity College *B,M*

Florida

Barry University *B*
Brevard Community College *A*
Central Florida Community
   College *A*
Chipola Junior College *A*
Daytona Beach Community
   College *A*
Edison Community College *A*
Gulf Coast Community College *A*
Indian River Community College *A*
Lake City Community College *A*
Lynn University *A,B*
Manatee Community College *A*
North Florida Junior College *A*

Okaloosa-Walton Community
   College *A*
Palm Beach Atlantic College *B*
Palm Beach Community College *A*
Pensacola Junior College *A*
Rollins College *B*
Seminole Community College *A*
Stetson University *B,M*
University of Miami *M;D*
University of Tampa *B*
University of West Florida *B*

Georgia

Abraham Baldwin Agricultural
   College *A*
Andrew College *A*
Atlanta Metropolitan College *A*
Brenau Women's College *B*
Brewton-Parker College *A*
Brunswick College *A*
Clark Atlanta University *B*
Clayton State College *A*
Darton College *A*
DeKalb College *A*
East Georgia College *A*
Emory University *B,M,D*
Floyd College *A*
Fort Valley State College *B*
Gainesville College *A*
Georgia College *B,M*
Georgia Southern University *A,B,M*
Georgia Southwestern College *B,M*
Gordon College *A*
Kennesaw State College *B,M*
Mercer University *B,M*
Middle Georgia College *A*
Morehouse College *B*
Reinhardt College *A*
South Georgia College *A*
Thomas College *A*
Truett-McConnell College *A*
University of Georgia *M*
Waycross College *A*
Wesleyan College *B*
Young Harris College *A*

Hawaii

Brigham Young University-
   Hawaii *B*
University of Hawaii
   Hilo *M*
   Manoa *D*

Idaho

Albertson College *M*
Boise State University *M*
College of Southern Idaho *A*
Lewis Clark State College *B*
North Idaho College *A*
Ricks College *A*
University of Idaho *M,D*

Illinois

Augustana College *B*
Aurora University *M*
Barat College *B*
Blackburn College *M*
Bradley University *B,M*
City Colleges of Chicago: Richard J.
   Daley College *A*
Concordia University *B,M*
De Paul University *B*
Elmhurst College *B*
Eureka College *B*
Governors State University *M*
Greenville College *B*
Highland Community College *A*
Illinois College *B*
Illinois Valley Community
   College *A*
Joliet Junior College *A*
Judson College *B*

Kishwaukee College *A*
Knox College *B*
Lake Forest College *B*
Lincoln Land Community
   College *A*
Loyola University of Chicago
   B,M,D
Millikin University *B*
Monmouth College *B*
Montay College *A*
Moraine Valley Community
   College *C*
Morton College *A*
National-Louis University *B,M*
North Central College *B*
Northeastern Illinois University *B*
Northwestern University *B,M*
Olivet Nazarene University *B,M*
Parkland College *A*
Rend Lake College *A*
Richland Community College *A*
Rockford College *B,M*
St. Xavier University *B*
Southern Illinois University
   Carbondale *D*
   Edwardsville *M*
State Community College *C*
Trinity Christian College *B*
Triton College *A*
University of Chicago *M,D*
University of Illinois
   Chicago *D*
   Urbana-Champaign *D*
William Rainey Harper College *A*

Indiana

Anderson University *B*
Earlham College *B*
Goshen College *B*
Indiana State University *M*
Indiana University
   Bloomington *B,M,D*
   Northwest *B,M*
Indiana University—Purdue
   University at Fort Wayne *M*
Manchester College *B*
Martin University *B*
Purdue University: Calumet *B*
St. Francis College *B*
St. Joseph's College *B*
University of Evansville *B,M*
University of Southern Indiana *B*
Valparaiso University *B,M*
Vincennes University *A*

Iowa

Buena Vista College *B*
Clinton Community College *A*
Drake University *B,M*
Graceland College *B*
Grand View College *B*
Iowa Lakes Community College *A*
Iowa State University *M,D*
Iowa Western Community
   College *A*
Kirkwood Community College *A*
Loras College *B*
Luther College *B*
Maharishi International
   University *M*
Mount Mercy College *B*
Muscatine Community College *A*
North Iowa Area Community
   College *A*
St. Ambrose University *B*
Scott Community College *A*
Simpson College *B*
Southwestern Community
   College *A*
Teikyo Marycrest University *B,M*
Teikyo Westmar University *B*
University of Dubuque *B,M*

University of Iowa *M,D*
University of Northern Iowa *D*
Upper Iowa University *B*
Vennard College *B*
Waldorf College *A*
Wartburg College *B*
William Penn College *B*

Kansas

Allen County Community
  College *A*
Baker University *B*
Barton County Community
  College *A*
Bethel College *B*
Butler County Community
  College *A*
Central College *A*
Cloud County Community
  College *A*
Coffeyville Community College *A*
Colby Community College *A*
Cowley County Community
  College *A*
Dodge City Community College *A*
Fort Scott Community College *A*
Friends University *B*
Highland Community College *A*
Hutchinson Community College *A*
Kansas City College and Bible
  School *B*
Kansas Newman College *B*
MidAmerica Nazarene College *B,M*
Neosho County Community
  College *A*
Ottawa University *B*
Pittsburg State University *B*
Pratt Community College *A*
Seward County Community
  College *A*
Southwestern College *M*
Sterling College *B*
Tabor College *B*
Washburn University of Topeka
  B,M

Kentucky

Cumberland College *B*
Eastern Kentucky University *B,M*
Kentucky Wesleyan College *B*
Lees College *A*
Louisville Presbyterian Theological
  Seminary *M*
Madisonville Community College *A*
Northern Kentucky University *M*
Pikeville College *B*
Spalding University *M*
Thomas More College *B*
Union College *M*
Western Kentucky University *M*

Louisiana

Dillard University *B*
Louisiana College *B*
Louisiana State University
    Agricultural and Mechanical
      College *M*
    Shreveport *B,M*
Loyola University *B,M*
Northwestern State University *M*
Tulane University *M*

Maine

University of Maine
    Fort Kent *B*
    Machias *B*
    Orono *B,M*
    Presque Isle *B*
University of New England *C,B*
University of Southern Maine *M*

Maryland

Allegany Community College *A*
Anne Arundel Community
  College *A*
Bowie State University *B,M*
Catonsville Community College *A*
Charles County Community
  College *A*
College of Notre Dame of
  Maryland *B*
Columbia Union College *A,B*
Essex Community College *A*
Frederick Community College *A*
Goucher College *B*
Hagerstown Junior College *A*
Howard Community College *A*
Loyola College in Maryland *B,M*
Montgomery College
    Germantown Campus *A*
    Rockville Campus *A*
    Takoma Park Campus *A*
Morgan State University *B,M*
Salisbury State University *B,M*
Towson State University *B*
University of Maryland
    College Park *B*
    Eastern Shore *B*
Western Maryland College *M*

Massachusetts

Anna Maria College for Men and
  Women *M*
Assumption College *B*
Boston College *B,M,D*
Bunker Hill Community College *A*
Clark University *M,D*
Curry College *B,M*
Dean Junior College *A*
Eastern Nazarene College *B*
Elms College *B,M*
Endicott College *A,B*
Gordon College *B*
Greenfield Community College *A*
Hampshire College *B*
Harvard University *M,D*
Lesley College *B,M,D,W*
Mount Ida College *A*
North Adams State College *B,M*
Northeastern University *B*
Northern Essex Community
  College *A*
Salem State College *B*
Simmons College *B,M*
Smith College *B,M*
Suffolk University *M*
Tufts University *M*
University of Massachusetts
    Amherst *B,M,D*
    Boston *M*
Westfield State College *B,M*

Michigan

Alma College *B*
Andrews University *M*
Aquinas College *B*
Calvin College *B,M*
Central Michigan University *B,M*
Eastern Michigan University *M*
Grand Valley State University *B,M*
Great Lakes Christian College *B*
Hope College *B*
Kalamazoo Valley Community
  College *A*
Kellogg Community College *A*
Kirtland Community College *A*
Lansing Community College *A*
Madonna University *A,B*
Northern Michigan University *B,M*
Northwestern Michigan College *A*
Olivet College *B*
Saginaw Valley State University *M*
Southwestern Michigan College *A*

Suomi College *A*
University of Detroit Mercy *B,M*
University of Michigan
    Dearborn *B,M*
    Flint *B*
Wayne State University *D*
West Shore Community College *A*
Western Michigan University *B,M*
William Tyndale College *B*

Minnesota

Bethany Lutheran College *A*
Bethel College *B*
College of St. Catherine: St.
  Catherine Campus *B*
Concordia College: Moorhead *B*
Concordia College: St. Paul *B,M*
Itasca Community College:
  Arrowhead Region *A*
Mankato State University *M*
Northland Community College *A*
Northwestern College *B*
Pillsbury Baptist Bible College *B*
Rainy River Community College *A*
Rochester Community College *A*
St. Cloud State University *B*
St. Mary's College of Minnesota *M*
Southwest State University *B*
University of Minnesota
    Duluth *M*
    Twin Cities *M,D*
University of St. Thomas *C*
Vermilion Community College *A*
Willmar Community College *A*
Winona State University *B,M*
Worthington Community College *A*

Mississippi

Copiah-Lincoln Community
  College *A*
Delta State University *D*
East Central Community College *A*
Jackson State University *B*
Jones County Junior College *A*
Mary Holmes College *A*
Mississippi Delta Community
  College *A*
Mississippi Gulf Coast Community
  College
    Jefferson Davis Campus *A*
    Perkinston *A*
Mississippi State University *D*
Northeast Mississippi Community
  College *A*
University of Mississippi *D*
University of Southern
  Mississippi *D*
William Carey College *B*

Missouri

Avila College *M*
Central Methodist College *B*
Central Missouri State University
  B,M
College of the Ozarks *B*
Columbia College *B*
Drury College *B,M*
East Central College *A*
Evangel College *A,B*
Fontbonne College *B*
Lindenwood College *B,M*
Maryville University *B,M*
Mineral Area College *A*
Missouri Baptist College *B*
Missouri Southern State College *B*
Missouri Valley College *B*
Moberly Area Community
  College *A*
Rockhurst College *B*
St. Louis Christian College *A*
St. Louis Community College at
  Meramec *A*

Southwest Baptist University *B*
Stephens College *B*
University of Missouri
    Columbia *B*
    Kansas City *D*
Washington University *B,M,D*
Webster University *B*
William Woods College *B*

Montana

College of Great Falls *A*
Dull Knife Memorial College *A*
Eastern Montana College *B*
Fort Peck Community College *A*
Montana State University *M,D*
Northern Montana College *B*
University of Montana *B,M,D*
Western Montana College of the
  University of Montana *A,B*

Nebraska

Central Community College *A*
Chadron State College *B*
College of St. Mary *B*
Creighton University *M*
Dana College *B*
Hastings College *B,M*
Midland Lutheran College *B*
Nebraska Wesleyan University *B*
Northeast Community College *A*
Southeast Community College:
  Beatrice Campus *A*
University of Nebraska
    Kearney *B,M*
    Lincoln *B,M*
Western Nebraska Community
  College: Scottsbluff Campus *A*

Nevada

Sierra Nevada College *B*

New Hampshire

Antioch New England Graduate
  School *M*
Dartmouth College *B*
Franklin Pierce College *B*
Keene State College *B*
New Hampshire Technical College:
  Berlin *A*
Notre Dame College *B*
Plymouth State College of the
  University System of New
  Hampshire *B*
Rivier College *B,M*
University of New Hampshire *M*

New Jersey

Atlantic Community College *A*
Brookdale Community College *A*
Burlington County College *A*
Caldwell College *B*
College of St. Elizabeth *B*
Essex County College *A*
Gloucester County College *A*
Montclair State College *M*
Rutgers—The State University of
  New Jersey *M*
St. Peter's College *M*
Seton Hall University *B,M*

New Mexico

College of Santa Fe *B*
Eastern New Mexico University *B*
New Mexico Junior College *A*
New Mexico State University
  B,M,D
University of New Mexico *M,D*
Western New Mexico University *B*

New York

Canisius College M
City University of New York
   Baruch College B
   Brooklyn College B,M
   College of Staten Island B
   La Guardia Community
     College A
   Medgar Evers College A
Colgate University B,M
Concordia College B
Cornell University B,M,D
Daemen College B
Dominican College of Blauvelt B
Dowling College B,M
D'Youville College B
Elmira College B
Fordham University B
Genesee Community College A
Hofstra University M,W
Iona College B
Keuka College B
Long Island University
   Brooklyn Campus B
   C. W. Post Campus B
   Southampton Campus B,M
Manhattan College B
Marymount College B
Molloy College B
Nazareth College of Rochester B,M
New York University B,M,D
Niagara University B
Russell Sage College B
St. Bonaventure University B,M
St. Joseph's College
   Brooklyn B
   Suffolk Campus B
St. Lawrence University M
St. Thomas Aquinas College B
Sarah Lawrence College M
State University of New York
   Buffalo M
   College at Cortland B
   College at Plattsburgh B,M
   Empire State College A,B
University of Rochester D
Wagner College B

North Carolina

Alamance Community College A
Anson Community College A
Appalachian State University B,M
Barton College B
Beaufort County Community
   College A
Bladen Community College A
Blue Ridge Community College A
Brevard College A
Campbell University A,B,M
Carteret Community College A
Catawba Valley Community
   College A
Central Carolina Community
   College A
Chowan College A
Cleveland Community College A
Coastal Carolina Community
   College A
Fayetteville Technical Community
   College A
Greensboro College B
Guilford College B
High Point University B
Isothermal Community College A
James Sprunt Community College
   C,A
John Wesley College A
Lenoir-Rhyne College B,M
Livingstone College B
Mars Hill College B
Methodist College A,B
Mitchell Community College A

Montgomery Community College A
Mount Olive College A
Nash Community College A
North Carolina State University B
Pamlico Community College A
Piedmont Bible College B
Queens College B
Richmond Community College A
St. Andrews Presbyterian College B
Salem College B
Sampson Community College A
Tri-County Community College C,A
Wake Forest University B
Warren Wilson College B
Western Piedmont Community
   College A
Wilkes Community College A

North Dakota

Little Hoop Community College A
North Dakota State University M
Turtle Mountain Community
   College A
University of North Dakota
   Grand Forks M
   Williston A

Ohio

Antioch College B
Ashland University B,M
Baldwin-Wallace College B,M
Bluffton College B
Bowling Green State University
   Bowling Green B
   Firelands College A
Cedarville College B
Central State University B
College of Mount St. Joseph M
Defiance College B
Denison University B
Edison State Community College A
Heidelberg College B,M
John Carroll University B,M
Kent State University B,M,D
Lake Erie College M
Lakeland Community College A
Marietta College B
Mount Vernon Nazarene College B
Muskingum College B,M
Ohio Dominican College B
Ohio State University: Columbus
   Campus B,M,D
Ohio Wesleyan University B
Otterbein College B
Southern State Community
   College A
Union Institute B,D
University of Akron B,M,D
University of Cincinnati
   Access Colleges A
   Clermont College A
   Raymond Walters College A
University of Dayton M
University of Toledo B
Urbana University B
Ursuline College B
Walsh College M
Washington State Community
   College A
Wilmington College B
Wittenberg University B
Xavier University M
Youngstown State University B,M

Oklahoma

Bacone College A
Bartlesville Wesleyan College B
Cameron University B,M
Connors State College A
Langston University B
Northeastern State University B,M
Oklahoma Baptist University B

Oklahoma City University B,M
Phillips University B
St. Gregory's College A
Southeastern Oklahoma State
   University B,M
Tulsa Junior College A
University of Central Oklahoma
   B,M
University of Oklahoma B
University of Tulsa B

Oregon

Central Oregon Community
   College A
Linfield College B,M
Oregon State University M,D
Pacific University B,M
Portland Community College A
Portland State University M
Southern Oregon State College M
Treasure Valley Community
   College A
University of Portland M
Warner Pacific College B
Western Baptist College B
Western Conservative Baptist
   Seminary A
Western Oregon State College B,M

Pennsylvania

Academy of the New Church A,B
Alvernia College B
Beaver College M
Bryn Mawr College M,D
Bucks County Community
   College A
Butler County Community
   College A
Cabrini College M
California University of
   Pennsylvania A,B,M
Clarion University of
   Pennsylvania B
College Misericordia B,M
Community College of Beaver
   County A
Community College of
   Philadelphia A
Duquesne University M
Edinboro University of
   Pennsylvania A
Gannon University B,M
Geneva College B
Gratz College B,M
Harrisburg Area Community
   College A
Holy Family College M
Indiana University of
   Pennsylvania B
Juniata College B
Keystone Junior College A
La Salle University B,M
Lancaster Bible College B
Lehigh County Community
   College A
Lehigh University M,D
Luzerne County Community
   College A
Manor Junior College A
Mansfield University of
   Pennsylvania M
Marywood College B,M
Messiah College B
Neumann College B
Northampton County Area
   Community College A
Northeastern Christian Junior
   College A
Point Park College B
Reading Area Community
   College A
St. Francis College M

St. Joseph's University M
Temple University M
University of Pennsylvania M,D
University of Pittsburgh
   Bradford B
   Pittsburgh M,D
Villanova University M
Westmoreland County Community
   College A
Wilkes University M

Puerto Rico

Caribbean University B
Inter American University of Puerto
   Rico: San German Campus A,B
Pontifical Catholic University of
   Puerto Rico A,B,M
Turabo University A,B
Universidad Metropolitana B
University of Puerto Rico
   Arecibo Campus A
   Carolina Regional College A

Rhode Island

Brown University B,M
Community College of Rhode
   Island A
Salve Regina University B,M

South Carolina

Charleston Southern University B,M
The Citadel B
Claflin College B
Coker College B
Columbia College B
Erskine College B
Limestone College A,B
Newberry College B
North Greenville College A
University of South Carolina
   Aiken B
   Coastal Carolina College B

South Dakota

Augustana College B
Black Hills State University B,M
Dakota State University B
Dakota Wesleyan University B
Huron University A,B
Mount Marty College B
Presentation College A
Sinte Gleska College A,B,M

Tennessee

Belmont University B,M
Bethel College M
Carson-Newman College B,M
Columbia State Community
   College A
Cumberland University B,M
Dyersburg State Community
   College A
Hiwassee College A
Knoxville College B
Lambuth University B
Lincoln Memorial University B,M
Martin Methodist College A
Middle Tennessee State University
   B,M
Motlow State Community
   College A
Shelby State Community College A
Tennessee State University B
Tennessee Technological
   University B
Tennessee Temple University A
Tennessee Wesleyan College B
Tomlinson College A
Trevecca Nazarene College B
Tusculum College M
Union University B,M

University of Tennessee
Chattanooga *B,M*
Knoxville *D*
Martin *B*
Vanderbilt University *B*
Walters State Community
College *A*

Texas

Angelina College *A*
Baylor University *B,M*
Bee County College *A*
Brazosport College *A*
Central Texas College *A*
Collin County Community College
District *A*
Dallas Baptist University *B,M*
Del Mar College *A*
East Texas State University at
Texarkana *M*
Houston Baptist University *B,M*
Howard College *A*
Huston-Tillotson College *B*
Incarnate Word College *B*
Lamar University—Beaumont *B*
Lon Morris College *A*
Lubbock Christian University *B*
McLennan Community College *A*
Midwestern State University *B,M*
North Harris Montgomery
Community College District *A*
Our Lady of the Lake University of
San Antonio *M*
Panola College *A*
Ranger Junior College *A*
Sam Houston State University *M*
San Antonio College *A*
Schreiner College *B*
Southwest Texas State University *B*
Southwestern Adventist College *M*
Southwestern Assemblies of God
College *A*
Southwestern Christian College *A*
Tarleton State University *B,M*
Texas Christian University *M*
Texas Southern University *M*
Texas Southmost College *A*
Texas Tech University *B,M,D*
Texas Wesleyan University *B,M*
Trinity Valley Community
College *A*
University of Dallas *B*
University of Houston *M,D*
University of Mary Hardin-Baylor
B,M
University of St. Thomas *B,M*
University of Texas
Arlington *B*
El Paso *M*
Victoria College *A*
Wayland Baptist University *B,M*
West Texas State University *M*
Western Texas College *A*
Wharton County Junior College *A*

Utah

Dixie College *A*
Southern Utah University *B,M*
Westminster College of Salt Lake
City *B,M*

Vermont

Burlington College *B*
Champlain College *A*
College of St. Joseph in Vermont *M*
Community College of Vermont
C,A
Goddard College *B,M*
Johnson State College *B*
Lyndon State College *M*
St. Michael's College *M*
Trinity College of Vermont *M*

University of Vermont *B,M*

Virginia

Averett College *B,M*
Bluefield College *B*
Central Virginia Community
College *A*
Dabney S. Lancaster Community
College *A*
Eastern Shore Community
College *A*
George Mason University *B,M,D*
Hampton University *B*
John Tyler Community College *A*
Liberty University *B*
Longwood College *B*
Lord Fairfax Community College *A*
Lynchburg College *B,M*
Mary Baldwin College *C*
Mountain Empire Community
College *A*
New River Community College *A*
Patrick Henry Community
College *A*
Paul D. Camp Community
College *A*
Piedmont Virginia Community
College *C,A*
Radford University *M*
St. Paul's College *B*
Shenandoah University *M*
Southside Virginia Community
College *A*
Southwest Virginia Community
College *A*
Tidewater Community College *A*
University of Richmond *B,M*
University of Virginia *M,D*
Virginia Highlands Community
College *A*
Virginia Union University *B*
Wytheville Community College *A*

Washington

Antioch University Seattle *M*
Central Washington University *B*
Centralia College *A*
Eastern Washington University *B,M*
Everett Community College *A*
Gonzaga University *M*
Grays Harbor College *A*
Heritage College *B,M*
Lower Columbia College *A*
Olympic College *A*
Pacific Lutheran University *B,M*
St. Martin's College *B,M*
Seattle University *M*
Skagit Valley College *A*
Spokane Community College *A*
Spokane Falls Community
College *A*
Tacoma Community College *A*
University of Puget Sound *M*
University of Washington *M,D*
Washington State University *M,D*
Wenatchee Valley College *A*
Western Washington University
B,M
Whitworth College *M*

West Virginia

Alderson-Broaddus College *B*
Bethany College *B*
Bluefield State College *A*
College of West Virginia *A*
Davis and Elkins College *B*
Glenville State College *B*
Marshall University *B,M*
Potomac State College of West
Virginia University *A*
Salem-Teikyo University *B,M*
Shepherd College *B*

West Virginia State College *B*
West Virginia Wesleyan College
B,M

Wisconsin

Beloit College *M*
Cardinal Stritch College *B,M*
Carroll College *B,M*
Carthage College *B*
Concordia University Wisconsin
B,M
Edgewood College *B,M*
Lakeland College *B,M*
Marian College of Fond du Lac
B,M
Mount Mary College *M*
Mount Senario College *B*
Northland College *B*
Ripon College *B*
St. Norbert College *B*
Silver Lake College *M*
University of Wisconsin
Green Bay *B*
La Crosse *B,M*
Madison *M,D*
Milwaukee *B,D*
Oshkosh *B,M*
River Falls *B,M*
Stevens Point *M*
Stout *M*
Whitewater *B,M*

Wyoming

Casper College *A*
Central Wyoming College *A*
Eastern Wyoming College *A*
Laramie County Community
College *A*
Northwest College *A*
Sheridan College *A*
University of Wyoming *D*
Western Wyoming Community
College *A*

**American Samoa, Caroline
Islands, Guam, Marianas,
Virgin Islands**

Northern Marianas College *A*
University of Guam *B*

Canada

McGill University *B,M*

Education administration

Alabama

Alabama Agricultural and
Mechanical University *M*
Alabama State University *M*
Auburn University
Auburn *M,D*
Montgomery *M*
Birmingham-Southern College *M*
Community College of the Air
Force *A*
Jacksonville State University *M*
Livingston University *M*
Troy State University
Dothan *M*
Montgomery *M*
Tuskegee University *M*
University of Alabama
Birmingham *M,D*
Huntsville *M*
Tuscaloosa *M,D*
University of Montevallo *M*
University of North Alabama *M*
University of South Alabama *M*

Alaska

University of Alaska
Anchorage *M*
Fairbanks *M*

Arizona

Arizona State University *M,D*
Northern Arizona University *M,D*
University of Arizona *M,D*
University of Phoenix *M*

Arkansas

Arkansas State University *M*
Henderson State University *M*
University of Arkansas
Fayetteville *M*
Little Rock *M*
University of Central Arkansas *B,M*

California

Azusa Pacific University *M,D*
Barstow College *A*
California Lutheran University *M*
California Polytechnic State
University: San Luis Obispo *M*
California State University
Bakersfield *M*
Dominguez Hills *M*
Fresno *M,D*
Fullerton *M*
Hayward *M*
Long Beach *M*
Los Angeles *M*
Northridge *M*
Sacramento *M*
San Bernardino *M*
Stanislaus *M*
Chapman University *M*
Christ College Irvine *M*
College of Notre Dame *M*
Fresno Pacific College *M*
Hebrew Union College: Jewish
Institute of Religion *M,D*
Humboldt State University *C*
La Sierra University *M,D*
Loyola Marymount University *M*
Mount St. Mary's College *M*
National University *M*
Pacific Oaks College *M*
Pepperdine University *M,D*
Point Loma Nazarene College *M*
St. Mary's College of California
B,M
San Diego State University *M*
San Francisco State University *M*
San Jose State University *M*
Santa Clara University *M*
Sonoma State University *M*
Stanford University *M,D*
United States International
University *M,D*
University of California
Davis *D*
Irvine *D*
Riverside *M,D*
Santa Barbara *M,D*
University of Judaism *M*
University of La Verne *M,D*
University of the Pacific *M,D*
University of Redlands *M*
University of San Diego *M,D*
University of San Francisco *M,D*
University of Southern California
M,D,W

Colorado

Colorado State University *M,D*
University of Colorado
Colorado Springs *M*
Denver *M,D*
University of Denver *M,D*

University of Northern Colorado
M,D

Connecticut

Central Connecticut State
University *M*
Fairfield University *M*
Southern Connecticut State
University *M*
University of Bridgeport *M,D*
University of Connecticut *D*

Delaware

University of Delaware *M,D*
Wilmington College *M*

District of Columbia

American University *M,D*
Catholic University of America *M*
Gallaudet University *M*
George Washington University *M,D*
Howard University *M*
Trinity College *M*
University of the District of
Columbia *M*

Florida

Florida Agricultural and Mechanical
University *M*
Florida Atlantic University *M,D*
Florida International University
M,D
Florida State University *M,D*
Nova University *M,D*
Stetson University *M*
University of Central Florida *M,D*
University of Florida *M,D*
University of Miami *M,D*
University of North Florida *D*
University of Sarasota *M,D*
University of South Florida *M,D*
University of West Florida *M*

Georgia

Augusta College *M*
Columbus College *M*
Georgia College *M*
Georgia Southern University *M*
Georgia State University *M,D*
University of Georgia *M,D*
Valdosta State College *M*
Waycross College *A*
West Georgia College *M*

Hawaii

University of Hawaii at Manoa *M*

Idaho

Albertson College *M*
Idaho State University *M*
University of Idaho *M,D*

Illinois

Bradley University *M*
Chicago State University *M*
Concordia University *M*
De Paul University *M*
Eastern Illinois University *M*
Governors State University *M*
Illinois State University *M,D,W*
Lewis University *M*
Loyola University of Chicago *M,D*
National-Louis University *M*
Northeastern Illinois University *M*
Northern Illinois University *M,D*
Northwestern University *M,D*
Roosevelt University *M,D*
St. Xavier University *M*
Sangamon State University *M*
Southern Illinois University
Carbondale *M,D*
Edwardsville *M,W*

University of Chicago *M,D*
University of Illinois at Urbana-
Champaign *M,D*
Western Illinois University *M,W*

Indiana

Ball State University *M,D*
Butler University *M*
Grace Theological Seminary *M*
Indiana State University *M,D*
Indiana University Bloomington
M,D
Indiana University—Purdue
University
Fort Wayne *M*
Indianapolis *M,D*
Purdue University
Calumet *M*
West Lafayette *M,D*

Iowa

Clarke College *M*
Drake University *M,D*
Iowa State University *M,D*
Loras College *M*
University of Iowa *M,D*
University of Northern Iowa *M,D*

Kansas

Benedictine College *M*
Emporia State University *M,W*
Fort Hays State University *M*
Kansas State University *M,D*
Pittsburg State University *M*
University of Kansas *M,D*
Washburn University of Topeka *M*
Wichita State University *B,M*

Kentucky

Eastern Kentucky University *M*
Murray State University *M*
Spalding University *M*
Union College *M*
University of Kentucky *M,D*
University of Louisville *M*
Western Kentucky University *M*

Louisiana

Centenary College of Louisiana *M*
Louisiana State University and
Agricultural and Mechanical
College *M,D*
Loyola University *M*
McNeese State University *M*
Nicholls State University *M*
Northeast Louisiana University *M*
Northwestern State University *M*
Our Lady of Holy Cross College *M*
Southeastern Louisiana
University *M*
Southern University and
Agricultural and Mechanical
College *M*
Tulane University *M*
University of New Orleans *M,D*
University of Southwestern
Louisiana *M*
Xavier University of Louisiana *M*

Maine

University of Maine *M,D*
University of Southern Maine *M*

Maryland

Baltimore Hebrew University *B,M*
Bowie State University *M*
Frostburg State University *M*
Morgan State University *M*
Salisbury State University *M*
University of Maryland: College
Park *M,D*
Western Maryland College *M*

Massachusetts

American International College *M*
Atlantic Union College *M*
Boston College *M,D*
Boston University *M,D,W*
Bridgewater State College *M*
Emmanuel College *M*
Fitchburg State College *M*
Framingham State College *M*
Harvard University *M,D,W*
Lesley College *M*
North Adams State College *M*
Salem State College *M*
Suffolk University *M*
University of Massachusetts
Boston *M*
Lowell *M,D*
Westfield State College *M*
Wheelock College *M*

Michigan

Andrews University *M,D*
Calvin College *M*
Central Michigan University *M*
Eastern Michigan University *M*
Grand Valley State University *M*
Madonna University *M,W*
Marygrove College *M*
Michigan State University *M,D*
Northern Michigan University *M*
Oakland University *D*
Saginaw Valley State University *M*
University of Detroit Mercy *M*
University of Michigan *M,D*
Wayne State University *D*
Western Michigan University *M,D*

Minnesota

Bemidji State University *M*
Mankato State University *M*
Moorhead State University *M*
Rainy River Community College *A*
St. Cloud State University *M*
St. Mary's College of Minnesota *M*
University of Minnesota: Twin
Cities *M,D*
University of St. Thomas *M,W*
Vermilion Community College *A*
Willmar Community College *A*
Winona State University *M*

Mississippi

Delta State University *M*
Jackson State University *M,D,W*
Jones County Junior College *A*
Mississippi College *M*
Mississippi State University *M*
University of Mississippi *M*
University of Southern
Mississippi *M*
William Carey College *M,W*

Missouri

Central Missouri State
University *M*
Lincoln University *M*
Northwest Missouri State
University *M*
St. Louis University *M,D*
Southeast Missouri State
University *M*
Southwest Missouri State
University *M*
University of Missouri
Columbia *M,D*
Kansas City *M,D*
St. Louis *M,D*
Washington University *M,D*

Montana

Montana State University *M,D*
University of Montana *D*

Nebraska

Chadron State College *M*
Concordia College *M*
Creighton University *M*
University of Nebraska
Kearney *M*
Lincoln *M,D*
Omaha *M*
Wayne State College *M*

Nevada

University of Nevada
Las Vegas *M,D*
Reno *M,D*

New Hampshire

Antioch New England Graduate
School *M*
Keene State College *M*
Notre Dame College *M*
Plymouth State College of the
University System of New
Hampshire *M*
Rivier College *M*
University of New Hampshire
Durham *M,D*
Manchester *M*

New Jersey

Glassboro State College *M*
Jersey City State College *M*
Kean College of New Jersey *M*
Monmouth College *M*
Montclair State College *M*
Rider College *M*
Rutgers—The State University of
New Jersey *M,D*
St. Peter's College *M*
Seton Hall University *M,D*
Stevens Institute of Technology
M,D
William Paterson College of New
Jersey *M*

New Mexico

Eastern New Mexico University *M*
New Mexico Highlands
University *M*
New Mexico State University *M,D*
University of New Mexico *M,D*
Western New Mexico University *M*

New York

Bank Street College of Education
M,W
Canisius College *M*
City University of New York
Baruch College *M*
Brooklyn College *C*
City College *M*
College of Staten Island *W*
Queens College *W*
College of New Rochelle *M*
College of St. Rose *M*
Cornell University *M,D*
Dowling College *C*
Fordham University *M,D*
Hofstra University *M,D,W*
Iona College *M,W*
Long Island University
Brooklyn Campus *M*
C. W. Post Campus *M*
Manhattan College *M*
New York University *M,D*
Niagara University *M*
Pace University
College of White Plains *M*
New York *M*
St. Bonaventure University *M,W*
St. John's University *M,D*
St. Lawrence University *M*

State University of New York
Albany *M,D,W*
Buffalo *M,D*
College at Brockport *M*
College at New Paltz *M*
College at Plattsburgh *M*
Oswego *B,M*
Syracuse University *M,D*
University of Rochester *M,D*

North Carolina

Appalachian State University *M,D*
Brevard College *A*
Campbell University *M*
East Carolina University *M,D*
Fayetteville State University *M*
Gardner-Webb College *M*
North Carolina Agricultural and
Technical State University *M*
North Carolina Central
University *M*
North Carolina State University
M,D
Pembroke State University *M*
University of North Carolina
Chapel Hill *M,D*
Charlotte *M*
Greensboro *M,D*
Wilmington *M*
Western Carolina University *M*

North Dakota

North Dakota State University *M*
University of Mary *M*
University of North Dakota *M,D*

Ohio

Ashland University *M*
Baldwin-Wallace College *M*
Bowling Green State University
M,D
Cleveland State University *M,D*
Franciscan University of
Steubenville *M*
John Carroll University *M*
Kent State University *M,D*
Miami University: Oxford Campus
M,D
Ohio State University: Columbus
Campus *B,M,D,W*
Ohio University
Athens *M,D*
Eastern Campus *M*
Union Institute *D*
University of Akron *M,D*
University of Cincinnati *M,D*
University of Dayton *M,D*
University of Toledo *M,D*
Ursuline College *M*
Wright State University *M*
Youngstown State University *M*

Oklahoma

East Central University *M*
Northeastern State University *M*
Oklahoma Baptist University *B*
Oklahoma State University *M,D*
Southeastern Oklahoma State
University *M*
Southwestern Oklahoma State
University *M*
University of Central Oklahoma *M*
University of Oklahoma *M,D*

Oregon

Central Oregon Community
College *A*
Lewis and Clark College *M*
Oregon State University *M,D*
Portland State University *D*
University of Oregon *M,D*

Pennsylvania

Beaver College *M*
Bucknell University *B,M*
California University of
Pennsylvania *M*
Carlow College *M*
Cheyney University of
Pennsylvania *M*
Clarion University of
Pennsylvania *M*
Duquesne University *M*
Edinboro University of
Pennsylvania *M*
Gratz College *M*
Immaculata College *M,D*
La Salle University *M*
Penn State University Park Campus
M,D
Shippensburg University of
Pennsylvania *M*
Temple University *M,D*
University of Pennsylvania *M,D*
University of Pittsburgh *M,D*
University of Scranton *M*
Westminster College *M*
Widener University *M*

Puerto Rico

Inter American University of Puerto
Rico
Metropolitan Campus *M,D*
San German Campus *B,M*
Pontifical Catholic University of
Puerto Rico *M*
Turabo University *M*
University of Puerto Rico: Rio
Piedras Campus *M,D*

Rhode Island

Providence College *M*
Rhode Island College *M,W*

South Carolina

Bob Jones University *M,D*
The Citadel *M*
Clemson University *M,W*
Converse College *W*
Furman University *M*
South Carolina State College *D*
University of South Carolina *M,D*
Winthrop University *M*

South Dakota

Northern State University *M*
South Dakota State University *M*
University of South Dakota *M,D*

Tennessee

Austin Peay State University *B,M*
East Tennessee State University
M,D
Lincoln Memorial University *M*
Memphis State University *M,D*
Middle Tennessee State
University *M*
Tennessee State University *M,D*
Tennessee Technological
University *M*
Tennessee Temple University *M*
University of Tennessee
Chattanooga *M*
Knoxville *M,D*
Martin *M*
Vanderbilt University *M,D*

Texas

Abilene Christian University *M*
Angelo State University *M*
Baylor University *M,D*
Corpus Christi State University *M*
Dallas Baptist University *M*
East Texas State University *M,D*

Houston Baptist University *M*
Lamar University—Beaumont *M*
Laredo State University *M*
Midwestern State University *M*
Our Lady of the Lake University of
San Antonio *M*
Prairie View A&M University *M*
Southwest Texas State
University *M*
Stephen F. Austin State University
M,W
Sul Ross State University *M*
Tarleton State University *M*
Texas A&I University *M*
Texas A&M University *M,D*
Texas Christian University *M*
Texas Southern University *M,D*
Texas Tech University *B,M,D*
Texas Woman's University *M*
Trinity University *M*
University of Houston
Clear Lake *M*
Houston *M,D*
Victoria *M*
University of Mary Hardin-Baylor
B,M
University of North Texas *M,D*
University of Texas
Austin *M,D*
El Paso *M*
Pan American *M*
Permian Basin *M*
San Antonio *M,D*
Tyler *M*
West Texas State University *M*

Utah

Brigham Young University *M,D*
University of Utah *M,D*

Vermont

Castleton State College *M*
Goddard College *B*
Johnson State College *M*
St. Michael's College *M*
University of Vermont *M,D*

Virginia

College of William and Mary *M,D*
George Mason University *M*
Hampton University *M*
James Madison University *M*
Liberty University *M*
Lynchburg College *M*
Old Dominion University *M*
Radford University *M*
University of Virginia *M,D*
Virginia Commonwealth
University *M*
Virginia Polytechnic Institute and
State University *M,D,W*
Virginia State University *M*

Washington

Central Washington University *M*
Eastern Washington University *M*
Gonzaga University *M*
Heritage College *M*
Pacific Lutheran University *M*
Seattle Pacific University *M*
Seattle University *M,D*
University of Puget Sound *M*
University of Washington *M,D*
Walla Walla College *M*
Washington State University *M,D*
Western Washington University *M*
Whitworth College *M*

West Virginia

Marshall University *M*
West Virginia Graduate College *M*
West Virginia University *M,D*

Wisconsin

Cardinal Stritch College *M*
Concordia University Wisconsin *M*
Maranatha Baptist Bible College *M*
Marian College of Fond du Lac *M*
Marquette University *M,D*
University of Wisconsin
Madison *M,D*
Milwaukee *M*
Oshkosh *M*
Superior *M*

Wyoming

University of Wyoming *M,D*

**American Samoa, Caroline
Islands, Guam, Marianas,
Virgin Islands**

University of Guam *M*

Canada

McGill University *M,D*

Education of the
culturally disadvantaged

Arizona

Prescott College *B*

California

California Lutheran University *M*
California State University
Los Angeles *M*
Northridge *M*

Connecticut

Southern Connecticut State
University *B,M*
Western Connecticut State
University *M*

Nebraska

University of Nebraska—
Kearney *M*

New Mexico

College of Santa Fe *B,M*

Ohio

Central State University *B*
University of Akron *M*

Oklahoma

Northeastern State University *B*

Oregon

Western Oregon State College *M*

Pennsylvania

California University of
Pennsylvania *B,M*
Lehigh University *M*

South Dakota

Augustana College *B,M*

Texas

University of Houston *M,D*

Education of the deaf
and hearing impaired

Alabama

Bishop State Community College *C*
Jacksonville State University *B*
Talladega College *B*

University of Alabama *B,M*
University of Montevallo *B*

Arkansas

University of Arkansas at Little
Rock *A,B*

California

California State University
Fresno *B,M*
Los Angeles *M*
Northridge *M*
Stanislaus *B*
Ohlone College *A*
Pasadena City College *C*
San Diego Mesa College *A*
San Francisco State University *M*
San Jose State University *M*
University of Southern California *W*

Colorado

University of Northern Colorado *M*

Connecticut

Northwestern Connecticut
Community College *A*

District of Columbia

Gallaudet University *B,M,D,W*

Florida

Flagler College *B*
Florida Atlantic University *B,M,D*
University of North Florida *B*
University of South Florida *M*

Georgia

Floyd College *A*
Georgia State University *M*

Idaho

Idaho State University *M*

Illinois

MacMurray College *B*
Northern Illinois University *B,M*

Indiana

Ball State University *B*
Indiana State University *B,M*
Indiana University Bloomington *B*
Vincennes University *A*

Kansas

Allen County Community
College *A*

Kentucky

Eastern Kentucky University *A,B,M*

Louisiana

Dillard University *B*
Louisiana State University in
Shreveport *B*
Southeastern Louisiana
University *B*
Southern University and
Agricultural and Mechanical
College *B*

Maryland

Western Maryland College *M*

Massachusetts

Boston College *M*
Boston University *B,M,W*
Elms College *B*
Northern Essex Community
College *A*
Smith College *M*

Michigan

Calvin College *B*
Eastern Michigan University *B,M*
Grand Valley State University *B,M*
Michigan State University *B,M,D*
Western Michigan University *B*

Minnesota

Itasca Community College:
Arrowhead Region *A*

Mississippi

Jackson State University *B*
Mississippi College *B*
University of Southern
Mississippi *B*

Missouri

Fontbonne College *B*
Washington University *B,M*

Nebraska

Nebraska Christian College *A*
University of Nebraska
Lincoln *B,M*
Omaha *B,M*

New Jersey

Kean College of New Jersey *B*
Seton Hall University *B*
Trenton State College *B*
Union County College *C,A*
William Paterson College of New
Jersey *M*

New York

Adelphi University *M*
Canisius College *M*
City University of New York
Brooklyn College *B,M*
Hunter College *M*
Elmira College *B*
Ithaca College *B,M*
Long Island University: C. W. Post
Campus *B,M*
Mercy College *B*
New York University *B,M,D*
Rochester Institute of Technology
A,M
State University of New York
College at Cortland *B*
College at Geneseo *M*
College at New Paltz *M*
College at Plattsburgh *B*
Syracuse University *B,M*
University of Rochester *M,D*

North Carolina

Barton College *B*
Gardner-Webb College *A,B*
Lenoir-Rhyne College *B,M*
University of North Carolina at
Greensboro *B,M*

North Dakota

Minot State University *B,M*

Ohio

Bowling Green State University *B*
Kent State University *B,M,D*
Ohio State University: Columbus
Campus *B,M,D*
Union Institute *D*
University of Cincinnati *M,D*
University of Toledo *B*

Oklahoma

University of Oklahoma Health
Sciences Center *M,D*
University of Science and Arts of
Oklahoma *B*
University of Tulsa *B*

Oregon

Chemeketa Community College *A*
Lewis and Clark College *M*
Portland Community College *C*
Western Oregon State College *M*

Pennsylvania

Bloomsburg University of
Pennsylvania *M*
California University of
Pennsylvania *B*
Clarion University of Pennsylvania
B,M
Duquesne University *B,M*
Indiana University of
Pennsylvania *B*
Temple University *M*

Puerto Rico

Turabo University *B*

South Carolina

Converse College *B*

South Dakota

Augustana College *B,M*

Tennessee

Tennessee Temple University *B*
Trevecca Nazarene College *B*

Texas

Eastfield College *A*
Incarnate Word College *M*
Lamar University—Beaumont *B,M*
Stephen F. Austin State
University *B*
Texas Christian University *B*
Texas Tech University *B*
Texas Woman's University *M*

Utah

Utah State University *M*

Virginia

Hampton University *B,M*
James Madison University *M*
Old Dominion University *B,M*

Washington

Eastern Washington University *B*
Seattle Central Community
College *A*

Wisconsin

University of Wisconsin:
Milwaukee *B*

Canada

McGill University *M*

Education of the
emotionally handicapped

Alabama

Alabama Agricultural and
Mechanical University *B,M*
Auburn University *B,M*
Jacksonville State University *B*
Troy State University *B,M*
University of Alabama *B,M*
University of South Alabama *M*

Arizona

Grand Canyon University *B*
Prescott College *B*

Arkansas

Arkansas State University *M*
University of Central Arkansas *B*

California

California Lutheran University *M*
California State University
Los Angeles *M*
Northridge *M*
Sonoma State University *M*
University of the Pacific *B,M,D*

Colorado

University of Northern Colorado *M*

Connecticut

Fairfield University *M*
Southern Connecticut State
University *B,M*

District of Columbia

American University *M*
George Washington University *M*
Trinity College *B,M*

Florida

Florida Atlantic University *B,M,D*
Florida International University
B,M
Florida Southern College *B*
Florida State University *B,M*
Jacksonville University *B*
Nova University *M*
University of Florida *M*
University of South Florida *B,M*
University of West Florida *B*

Georgia

Georgia Southern University *B,M*
Georgia State University *D*
Morris Brown College *B*
University of Georgia *M*
West Georgia College *M*

Illinois

Barat College *B*
Bradley University *B*
Chicago State University *M*
Elmhurst College *B*
Greenville College *B*
Illinois Benedictine College *B*
Loyola University of Chicago *B*
MacMurray College *B*
National-Louis University *M*
Northeastern Illinois University
B,M
Northwestern University *B,M,D*
Roosevelt University *M*
Southern Illinois University at
Edwardsville *B*
Western Illinois University *B*

Indiana

Butler University *B,M*
Indiana University Bloomington
B,M
Indiana University—Purdue
University at Indianapolis *M*
Purdue University *B*
St. Francis College *B,M*
Valparaiso University *M*
Vincennes University *A*

Iowa

Buena Vista College *B*
Drake University *M*
Morningside College *B,M*

Kansas

Bethany College *B*
Tabor College *B*

Kentucky

Eastern Kentucky University *B,M*
Murray State University *B*
University of Kentucky *B*
Western Kentucky University *B*

Louisiana

Dillard University *B*
Louisiana State University in
  Shreveport *B*
Louisiana Tech University *B*
McNeese State University *M*
Northwestern State University *M*
Southeastern Louisiana
  University *B*
University of New Orleans *M*

Maine

University of Maine at
  Farmington *B*

Maryland

Coppin State College *B,M*

Massachusetts

American International College *B,M*
Lesley College *B*
Westfield State College *B*
Wheelock College *M*

Michigan

Calvin College *B*
Central Michigan University *B,M*
Eastern Michigan University *B,M*
Grand Valley State University *B,M*
Hope College *B*
Marygrove College *B,M*
Michigan State University *B,M,D*
Oakland University *M*
Saginaw Valley State University
  B,M
University of Detroit Mercy *B,M*
Wayne State University *M,D*
Western Michigan University *B,M*

Minnesota

Mankato State University *M*
Moorhead State University *B*
University of St. Thomas *M*
Winona State University *B,M*

Mississippi

Alcorn State University *B*

Missouri

Avila College *B*
Central Missouri State
  University *M*
Fontbonne College *B*
St. Louis University *M,D*
Southeast Missouri State
  University *B*
Webster University *B*

Montana

Eastern Montana College *M*

Nebraska

Creighton University *M*
University of Nebraska
  Lincoln *M*
  Omaha *M*

New Jersey

Kean College of New Jersey *B,M*
Seton Hall University *B*
William Paterson College of New
  Jersey *M*

New York

Bank Street College of Education
  M,W

City University of New York
  Brooklyn College *B,M*
  City College *B,M*
  Lehman College *M*
College of New Rochelle *B,M*
College of St. Rose *M*
D'Youville College *B*
Fordham University *M*
Marymount College *B*
Mercy College *B*
New York University *B,M*
St. Thomas Aquinas College *B*
State University of New York
  College at Buffalo *M*
  College at Geneseo *B,M*
  College at New Paltz *M*
  College at Plattsburgh *B*

North Carolina

Greensboro College *B*
North Carolina Central
  University *M*
Salem College *B*
University of North Carolina at
  Greensboro *M*

North Dakota

University of Mary *M*

Ohio

Bowling Green State University *B*
Central State University *B*
Defiance College *B*
Franciscan University of
  Steubenville *B*
Kent State University *B,M,D*
Ohio State University: Columbus
  Campus *B*
Ohio University *B*
University of Akron *B,M*
University of Cincinnati *M,D*
University of Toledo *B*
Walsh College *B*
Wright State University *M*

Oklahoma

Northeastern State University *B*
University of Central Oklahoma
  B,M

Oregon

Chemeketa Community College *A*
Portland Community College *C*

Pennsylvania

Cabrini College *B*
California University of
  Pennsylvania *B,M*
Duquesne University *B,M*
Holy Family College *B*
Indiana University of
  Pennsylvania *M*
La Salle University *B*
Lock Haven University of
  Pennsylvania *B*
Mercyhurst College *B*
Slippery Rock University of
  Pennsylvania *B*
Temple University *M*

Puerto Rico

Turabo University *B*

Rhode Island

Rhode Island College *B,M*

South Carolina

The Citadel *M*
Converse College *B*

South Dakota

Augustana College *B,M*
Northern State University *B*

Tennessee

Vanderbilt University *B,M,D*

Texas

Incarnate Word College *B,M*
Texas Woman's University *M,D*
West Texas State University *B*

Virginia

Eastern Mennonite College *B*
Hampton University *B,M*
Lynchburg College *M*
Old Dominion University *B,M*
Radford University *M*
University of Richmond *M*
Virginia Commonwealth
  University *M*

West Virginia

Fairmont State College *B*

Wisconsin

Edgewood College *B*
Silver Lake College *B*
University of Wisconsin
  Eau Claire *M*
  La Crosse *M*
  Milwaukee *B*
  Oshkosh *M*

Education of exceptional children

Alabama

Alabama Agricultural and
  Mechanical University *B*
Auburn University at
  Montgomery *M*

Arkansas

Arkansas State University *M*
University of Arkansas *B*

California

California Lutheran University *M*
California State University: Los
  Angeles *M*
Chapman University *M*
University of San Francisco *M*

Delaware

Delaware State College *B*
University of Delaware *B,M*

District of Columbia

Gallaudet University *M*

Florida

Barry University *M*
Bethune-Cookman College *B*
Flagler College *B*
Nova University *B*

Georgia

Clark Atlanta University *M*
Georgia Southern University *B,M*
University of Georgia *M,D*
West Georgia College *B,M*

Illinois

College of Lake County *A*
National-Louis University *M*
Northeastern Illinois University *M*
Rosary College *M*

Indiana

Butler University *B,M*
University of Evansville *B*

Iowa

Morningside College *M,W*

Massachusetts

Assumption College *B,M*

Michigan

Wayne State University *B,M*

Mississippi

Jackson State University *B*

New York

College of New Rochelle *M*
Manhattanville College *M*

North Carolina

Western Carolina University *B,M*

Ohio

Kent State University *B,M*
Ohio State University: Columbus
  Campus *B,M,D*

Oklahoma

Oral Roberts University *M*

Pennsylvania

Duquesne University *B,M*
Harcum Junior College *A*
Indiana University of
  Pennsylvania *B*
Lehigh University *M,D*
Temple University *M*

Rhode Island

Rhode Island College *B,M*

South Carolina

The Citadel *M*

Tennessee

Vanderbilt University *B,M,D*

Texas

Abilene Christian University *B*

Vermont

Johnson State College *M*

Virginia

Lynchburg College *M*
Old Dominion University *B*

West Virginia

West Virginia State College *B*

Wisconsin

Edgewood College *B*
University of Wisconsin: Eau
  Claire *M*

Education of the gifted and talented

Alabama

Alabama Agricultural and
  Mechanical University *B,M*
Auburn University *M*
University of Alabama *B,M,D*
University of South Alabama *B,M*

Arizona

Grand Canyon University *M*
Northern Arizona University *M*

Arkansas

Arkansas State University *M*
Arkansas Tech University *M*
University of Arkansas at Little
    Rock *M*
University of Central Arkansas *B,M*

California

California State University
    Fresno *M*
    Hayward *M*
    Los Angeles *M*
    Northridge *M*
    Sacramento *M*
St. Mary's College of California
    B,M
San Jose State University *M*

Colorado

University of Northern Colorado *M*

Connecticut

Sacred Heart University *M*

Florida

Florida Atlantic University *M,D*
Nova University *M*
University of South Florida *M*
University of West Florida *B*

Georgia

Georgia Southern University *B,M*
Georgia State University *M,D*
University of Georgia *D*

Illinois

Aurora University *M*
Chicago State University *M*
Northeastern Illinois University *M*
Northwestern University *M,D*
Southern Illinois University at
    Edwardsville *B*

Indiana

Butler University *B,M*
Indiana State University *M*
Indiana University Bloomington *M*
Purdue University *B,M*

Iowa

Morningside College *W*
University of Northern Iowa *M*

Louisiana

Dillard University *B*
University of Southwestern
    Louisiana *M*

Michigan

Eastern Michigan University *M*
Grand Valley State University *M*
Wayne State University *M,D*

Minnesota

Mankato State University *M*
Winona State University *B*

Mississippi

Jackson State University *B*

Missouri

University of Missouri: Columbia
    M,D

Nebraska

University of Nebraska—
    Kearney *M*

New Hampshire

Notre Dame College *M*

New Jersey

Kean College of New Jersey *M*
Seton Hall University *B*

New York

College of New Rochelle *M*
Long Island University: C. W. Post
    Campus *M*
Manhattanville College *M*

North Carolina

Catawba College *B*
University of North Carolina at
    Greensboro *M*
Wake Forest University *M*
Western Carolina University *M*

Ohio

Cleveland State University *M*
Kent State University *B,M*
Ohio State University: Columbus
    Campus *B*
Union Institute *D*
University of Akron *B,M*
University of Toledo *B*
Wright State University *M*
Youngstown State University *M*

Oklahoma

Oklahoma City University *M*
University of Tulsa *M*

Oregon

University of Oregon *M*

Pennsylvania

Bloomsburg University of
    Pennsylvania *M*
California University of
    Pennsylvania *B,M*
Gannon University *C*
Indiana University of
    Pennsylvania *M*
Lehigh University *M*
Millersville University of
    Pennsylvania *M*
Temple University *M*
Widener University *M*

South Carolina

Converse College *M*

Texas

Abilene Christian University *B*
University of Houston *M*
University of Mary Hardin-Baylor
    B,M

Vermont

Johnson State College *B,M*

Virginia

Norfolk State University *M*

Washington

Whitworth College *M*

West Virginia

Alderson-Broaddus College *B*
Fairmont State College *B*
Marshall University *B,M*

Canada

McGill University *C*

Education of the
mentally handicapped

Alabama

Alabama Agricultural and
    Mechanical University *B,M*
Alabama State University *B,M*
Auburn University
    Auburn *B,M*
    Montgomery *B,M*
Jacksonville State University *B,M*
Troy State University *B,M*
Tuskegee University *B*
University of Alabama *B,M*
University of South Alabama *B,M*

Arizona

Northern Arizona University *M*
Prescott College *B*

Arkansas

Harding University *B*
University of Central Arkansas *B,M*

California

California Lutheran University *M*
California State University
    Fresno *M*
    Hayward *M*
    Los Angeles *M*
    Northridge *M*
Humboldt State University *C*
Sonoma State University *M*
University of California: Riverside
    M,D
University of the Pacific *M,D*
University of Redlands *M*
University of San Diego *M*
University of Southern California *W*

Colorado

Adams State College *M*
University of Northern Colorado *M*

Connecticut

Fairfield University *M*
Southern Connecticut State
    University *B,M*

District of Columbia

Trinity College *B,M*

Florida

Florida Agricultural and Mechanical
    University *M*
Florida Atlantic University *B,M,D*
Florida International University
    B,M
Florida State University *B,M*
Nova University *M*
St. Leo College *B*
University of Florida *B,M*
University of South Florida *B,M*
University of West Florida *B*

Georgia

Augusta College *B,M*
Brenau Women's College *B*
Columbus College *B,M*
Georgia College *B,M*
Georgia Southern University *B,M*
Georgia State University *B,D*
Mercer University *B*
Morris Brown College *B*
University of Georgia *B,M*
West Georgia College *B,M*

Illinois

Bradley University *B*
Chicago State University *B,M*

Greenville College *B*
National-Louis University *M*
Northeastern Illinois University
    B,M
Northern Illinois University *B,M*
Roosevelt University *M*
Southern Illinois University
    Carbondale *B,M,D*
    Edwardsville *B*
University of Illinois at Urbana-
    Champaign *B*
Western Illinois University *B*

Indiana

Ball State University *B*
Butler University *B,M*
Indiana State University *M*
Indiana University Bloomington
    B,M
Indiana University—Purdue
    University at Indianapolis *M*
Marian College *C*
Purdue University *B,M*
St. Francis College *B,M*
University of Evansville *B*

Iowa

Buena Vista College *B*
Drake University *M*
Loras College *B*
Luther College *B*
Morningside College *B,W*
Northwestern College *B*
University of Dubuque *B,M*
University of Iowa *B,M,D*
University of Northern Iowa *B*

Kansas

Bethany College *B*
McPherson College *B*
Pittsburg State University *M*
Tabor College *B*

Kentucky

Eastern Kentucky University *B,M*
Murray State University *B*
University of Kentucky *B*
Western Kentucky University *B*

Louisiana

Dillard University *B*
Louisiana Tech University *B*
McNeese State University *M*
Nicholls State University *B,M*
Northwestern State University *M*
Southeastern Louisiana
    University *B*
Southern University and
    Agricultural and Mechanical
    College *B*
University of New Orleans *M*

Maine

University of Maine at
    Farmington *B*

Maryland

Coppin State College *B,M*

Massachusetts

American International College *B,M*
Boston College *M*
Lesley College *B,M*
Westfield State College *B*

Michigan

Calvin College *B*
Central Michigan University *B,M*
Eastern Michigan University *B,M*
Grand Valley State University *B,M*
Marygrove College *B,M*
Michigan State University *B,M,D*

Northern Michigan University *B,M*
University of Detroit Mercy *B*
Wayne State University *B,M,D*
Western Michigan University *B,M*

Minnesota

Mankato State University *M*
Moorhead State University *B*
Winona State University *B,M*

Mississippi

Alcorn State University *B*
Jackson State University *B*

Missouri

Avila College *B*
Central Missouri State
　University *M*
Drury College *B*
Evangel College *B*
Fontbonne College *B*
Missouri Southern State College *B*
Northwest Missouri State
　University *B,M*
St. Louis University *M,D*
Southeast Missouri State University
　B,M
Southwest Missouri State University
　B,M
University of Missouri: Columbia
　B,M,D
Webster University *B*

Montana

Eastern Montana College *M*

Nebraska

Chadron State College *B*
Concordia College *B*
Hastings College *B*
University of Nebraska
　Kearney *B,M*
　Lincoln *B,M*
　Omaha *B,M*

New Jersey

Glassboro State College *B*
Kean College of New Jersey *B,M*
Seton Hall University *B*
William Paterson College of New
　Jersey *M*

New York

City University of New York
　Brooklyn College *B,M*
　City College *B,M*
　Lehman College *M*
College of New Rochelle *B,M*
College of St. Rose *B,M*
Dominican College of Blauvelt *B*
D'Youville College *B*
Fordham University *M*
Marymount College *B*
Mercy College *B*
New York University *B,M*
State University of New York
　College at Buffalo *M*
　College at Geneseo *B,M*
　College at New Paltz *M*
　College at Plattsburgh *B*
Syracuse University *M,D*

North Carolina

Catawba College *B*
East Carolina University *M*
Greensboro College *B*
North Carolina Central
　University *M*
Piedmont Bible College *B*
Shaw University *B*
University of North Carolina at
　Greensboro *M*

Western Carolina University *B,M*

North Dakota

Minot State University *B,M*
University of Mary *B*

Ohio

Ashland University *B*
Bowling Green State University *B*
Central State University *B*
Cleveland State University *B*
Defiance College *B*
Franciscan University of
　Steubenville *B*
Heidelberg College *B*
Kent State University *B,M,D*
Ohio Dominican College *B*
Ohio State University: Columbus
　Campus *B*
Ohio University *B,M*
University of Akron *B,M*
University of Cincinnati *B,M,D*
University of Dayton *B,M*
University of Rio Grande *C*
University of Toledo *B*
Urbana University *B*
Walsh College *B*
Wright State University *B,M*
Xavier University *B*
Youngstown State University *B,M*

Oklahoma

East Central University *B*
Northeastern State University *B*
Northwestern Oklahoma State
　University *B*
Oral Roberts University *M*
St. Gregory's College *A*
Southwestern Oklahoma State
　University *B,M*
University of Central Oklahoma
　B,M
University of Oklahoma *B*
University of Science and Arts of
　Oklahoma *B*

Oregon

Chemeketa Community College *A*
Portland Community College *C*
Western Oregon State College *M*

Pennsylvania

Bloomsburg University of
　Pennsylvania *B,M*
Cabrini College *B*
California University of
　Pennsylvania *B,M*
Clarion University of
　Pennsylvania *B*
Duquesne University *B,M*
Edinboro University of
　Pennsylvania *B*
Gwynedd-Mercy College *B*
Holy Family College *B*
Indiana University of Pennsylvania
　B,M
Kutztown University of
　Pennsylvania *B*
La Salle University *B*
Lehigh University *D*
Lock Haven University of
　Pennsylvania *B*
Mercyhurst College *B*
Slippery Rock University of
　Pennsylvania *B*
Temple University *M*

Puerto Rico

Turabo University *B*

Rhode Island

Rhode Island College *B,M*

South Carolina

Bob Jones University *B*
The Citadel *B*
Columbia College *B*
Converse College *B,M*
Furman University *B,M*
University of South Carolina *M*

South Dakota

Augustana College *B,M*
Northern State University *B*

Tennessee

Vanderbilt University *B,M,D*

Texas

Abilene Christian University *B*
Angelina College *A*
Incarnate Word College *B,M*
Stephen F. Austin State
　University *B*
Texas A&I University *M*
Texas Tech University *B,M,D*
Texas Woman's University *M,D*
University of Houston *B,M,D*
University of Mary Hardin-Baylor
　B,M
West Texas State University *B*

Vermont

College of St. Joseph in Vermont
　B,M

Virginia

Eastern Mennonite College *B*
Hampton University *B,M*
Lynchburg College *M*
Old Dominion University *B,M*
Radford University *B*
Virginia Commonwealth
　University *M*

Washington

Eastern Washington University *B*
Pierce College *A*

West Virginia

Alderson-Broaddus College *B*
Concord College *B*
Fairmont State College *B*
Glenville State College *B*
Marshall University *B,M*
Salem-Teikyo University *B*
West Virginia State College *B*

Wisconsin

Carthage College *B*
Silver Lake College *B*
University of Wisconsin
　Eau Claire *B,M*
　Milwaukee *B*
　Oshkosh *B,M*
　Whitewater *B*

Education of the multiple handicapped

Alabama

Jacksonville State University *M*
University of Alabama *B,M*
University of South Alabama *B*

California

California State University
　Fresno *M*
　Hayward *M*
　Los Angeles *M*
Fresno Pacific College *M*
San Francisco State University *M*
San Jose State University *M*
Sonoma State University *M*
University of California: Riverside
　M,D
University of the Pacific *M,D*

Connecticut

Southern Connecticut State
　University *B*

District of Columbia

Gallaudet University *B,M*

Georgia

Georgia State University *M*
University of Georgia *B,M,D*

Illinois

Governors State University *M*
Northern Illinois University *M*

Indiana

Ball State University *B*
Indiana University
　Bloomington *M*
　South Bend *B,M*

Iowa

Drake University *M*
Morningside College *B*
University of Dubuque *B,M*

Kansas

Cowley County Community
　College *A*

Louisiana

Northeast Louisiana University *A*
Southeastern Louisiana
　University *B*

Maine

University of Maine *M*

Maryland

Coppin State College *B,M*

Massachusetts

Boston College *B,M*
Lesley College *M*

Michigan

Eastern Michigan University *B*
Grand Valley State University *B,M*
Wayne State University *B*

Missouri

Fontbonne College *B*

Montana

Eastern Montana College *M*

Nebraska

University of Nebraska
　Kearney *B,M*
　Lincoln *B,M*

New Jersey

Seton Hall University *B*

New York

City University of New York:
　Brooklyn College *B,M*
College of New Rochelle *M*
D'Youville College *B*

New York University *B,M*
State University of New York
   College at Geneseo *B,M*
Syracuse University *B,M,D*

North Carolina
University of North Carolina at
   Greensboro *M*

North Dakota
Minot State University *M*

Ohio
Ashland University *B*
Bowling Green State University *B*
Cleveland State University *B,M*
Kent State University *B,M,D*
Ohio Dominican College *B*
Ohio State University: Columbus
   Campus *B,M,D*
Sinclair Community College *A*
University of Dayton *B,M*
University of Rio Grande *C*
University of Toledo *B*
Walsh College *B*
Wright State University *B,M*

Oklahoma
Northeastern State University *B*
University of Central Oklahoma
   B,M

Oregon
Chemeketa Community College *A*
Portland Community College *C*
University of Oregon *M,D*
Western Oregon State College *M*

Pennsylvania
Cabrini College *B*
California University of
   Pennsylvania *B,M*
Clarion University of
   Pennsylvania *B*
Duquesne University *B,M*
La Salle University *B*
Lehigh University *D*

Rhode Island
Rhode Island College *B,M*

South Dakota
Augustana College *B,M*

Tennessee
Trevecca Nazarene College *B*
Vanderbilt University *B,M,D*

Vermont
Johnson State College *M*

Virginia
Norfolk State University *M*

Washington
Yakima Valley Community
   College *C*

Education of the physically handicapped

Alabama
Auburn University *B,M*
Talladega College *B*
University of Alabama *B,M*
University of South Alabama *B*

Arizona
Prescott College *B*

Arkansas
University of Central Arkansas *B,M*

California
California State University
   Fresno *M*
   Hayward *M*
   Los Angeles *M*
   Northridge *M*
San Francisco State University *M*
San Jose State University *M*
University of San Diego *M*

Colorado
University of Northern Colorado *M*

Connecticut
Southern Connecticut State
   University *B*

Florida
Florida Atlantic University *M,D*

Georgia
Georgia College *B,M*
Georgia State University *M*
Morris Brown College *B*

Illinois
Northern Illinois University *B,M*
Southern Illinois University at
   Carbondale *B,M,D*

Indiana
Ball State University *B*
Indiana University Bloomington *M*
Purdue University *B*

Iowa
University of Iowa *B*

Kansas
McPherson College *B*

Kentucky
Eastern Kentucky University *B,M*

Louisiana
Louisiana College *B*
Louisiana State University in
   Shreveport *B*
Louisiana Tech University *B*
Northwestern State University *M*
Southeastern Louisiana
   University *B*
University of New Orleans *M*

Maryland
Coppin State College *B,M*
University of Maryland: College
   Park *B,M,D*

Massachusetts
Boston College *M*
Springfield College *B,M*

Michigan
Calvin College *B*
Eastern Michigan University *B,M*
Wayne State University *B*
Western Michigan University *B,M*

Mississippi
Jackson State University *B*

Missouri
Southeast Missouri State University
   B,M

University of Missouri: Columbia
   B,M

Montana
Eastern Montana College *M*

Nebraska
University of Nebraska
   Kearney *B,M*
   Lincoln *B,M*

New Jersey
Kean College of New Jersey *B*
Seton Hall University *B*
William Paterson College of New
   Jersey *M*

New York
City University of New York:
   Brooklyn College *B,M*
D'Youville College *B*
Manhattan College *B*
New York University *B,M*
State University of New York
   College at Buffalo *M*

North Dakota
University of Mary *B*

Ohio
Bowling Green State University *B*
Kent State University *B,D*
Ohio State University: Columbus
   Campus *B,M,D*
University of Akron *B,M*
University of Cincinnati *M,D*
University of Dayton *B,M*
University of Toledo *B*
Wright State University *M*

Oklahoma
East Central University *B*
University of Central Oklahoma *B*

Oregon
Chemeketa Community College *A*
Portland Community College *C*

Pennsylvania
Bloomsburg University of
   Pennsylvania *B,M*
Cabrini College *B*
California University of
   Pennsylvania *B,M*
Duquesne University *B,M*
Gwynedd-Mercy College *B*
Indiana University of
   Pennsylvania *M*
Kutztown University of
   Pennsylvania *B*
La Salle University *B*
Lock Haven University of
   Pennsylvania *B*
Penn State University Park
   Campus *B*
Slippery Rock University of
   Pennsylvania *B*
Temple University *M*

Puerto Rico
Universidad Metropolitana *B*
University of Puerto Rico
   Bayamon Technological
     University College *B*
   Carolina Regional College *A*

Rhode Island
Rhode Island College *B*

South Dakota
Augustana College *B,M*
Northern State University *B*

Tennessee
Vanderbilt University *B,M,D*

Texas
Texas Woman's University *M,D*
West Texas State University *B*

Washington
Eastern Washington University *B*

West Virginia
Marshall University *B,M*

Education of the visually handicapped

Alabama
Talladega College *B*

Arkansas
University of Arkansas at Little
   Rock *M*

California
California State University: Los
   Angeles *M*
San Francisco State University *M*

Colorado
University of Northern Colorado *M*

Florida
Florida Atlantic University *M,D*
Florida State University *B,M*

Georgia
Georgia State University *M*

Illinois
Northern Illinois University *B,M*

Massachusetts
Boston College *M,D*

Michigan
Eastern Michigan University *B,M*
Michigan State University *B,M,D*
Western Michigan University *B,M*

Mississippi
Jackson State University *B*

Missouri
Central Missouri State
   University *M*

New Jersey
Seton Hall University *B*

New York
Dominican College of Blauvelt *B*
D'Youville College *B*
New York University *B,M*

Ohio
Ohio State University: Columbus
   Campus *B,M,D*
University of Toledo *B*

Oregon
Chemeketa Community College *A*

Pennsylvania
Duquesne University *B,M*
Kutztown University of
   Pennsylvania *B*
Temple University *M,D*

South Carolina

University of South Carolina *M*

South Dakota

Northern State University *B*

Tennessee

Trevecca Nazarene College *B*
Vanderbilt University *B,M,D*

Texas

Stephen F. Austin State
    University *B*

Educational media technology

Alabama

Community College of the Air
    Force *A*

Arizona

University of Arizona *M*

Arkansas

Arkansas Tech University *M*
University of Arkansas at Pine
    Bluff *B*

California

Allan Hancock College *A*
California State University
        Long Beach *M*
        Los Angeles *M*
Saddleback College *A*
San Francisco State University *M*

Colorado

University of Colorado at Denver
    M,D
University of Northern Colorado
    M,D

Connecticut

Central Connecticut State
    University *M*
Southern Connecticut State
    University *M*

District of Columbia

Gallaudet University *M*

Georgia

Georgia College *M*
University of Georgia *B,M*

Idaho

Boise State University *M*

Illinois

Governors State University *M*
Illinois State University *M*
Northeastern Illinois University *M*
Northern Illinois University *M,D*
Southern Illinois University at
    Edwardsville *M*
Western Illinois University *B*

Indiana

Indiana State University *B,M*
Indiana University Bloomington
    M,D
Purdue University *B*

Iowa

Clarke College *M*

Maryland

Dundalk Community College *A*
Towson State University *M*

Massachusetts

Bridgewater State College *C,M*
Bunker Hill Community College *A*
Fitchburg State College *B*
Lesley College *M*
Newbury College *A*
University of Massachusetts at
    Boston *M*

Michigan

Andrews University *B*
Lansing Community College *A*
Wayne State University *M,D*

Minnesota

St. Cloud State University *M*

Mississippi

Hinds Community College *A*
Jackson State University *M*

Missouri

Central Missouri State
    University *M*

New York

Ithaca College *B*
Long Island University: Brooklyn
    Campus *M*
New York University *C,M,D*
Rochester Institute of
    Technology *M*
State University of New York
    College at Potsdam *M*

North Carolina

Appalachian State University *M*
East Carolina University *M*
University of North Carolina at
    Greensboro *M*

Ohio

Kent State University *M,D*
Miami University: Oxford
    Campus *M*
University of Toledo *B*

Oregon

Portland Community College *C*
Western Oregon State College *M*

Pennsylvania

Bloomsburg University of
    Pennsylvania *M*
California University of
    Pennsylvania *B*
East Stroudsburg University of
    Pennsylvania *A*
Temple University *M,D*
Westmoreland County Community
    College *A*
Widener University *B*

Puerto Rico

Bayamon Central University *A,B*
University of Puerto Rico: Humacao
    University College *A*
University of the Sacred Heart *M*

Rhode Island

Rhode Island College *M*

South Carolina

University of South Carolina *M*
Winthrop University *M*

Tennessee

Pellissippi State Technical
    Community College *A*

Texas

East Texas State University *M,D*
Tarrant County Junior College *A*

Utah

Utah State University *M*

Virginia

Radford University *M*

Washington

Eastern Washington University *B*
Western Washington University *B*

West Virginia

Marshall University *M*

Wisconsin

University of Wisconsin: La
    Crosse *M*

Wyoming

University of Wyoming *M*

Canada

McGill University *C*

Educational statistics and research

Alabama

University of Alabama
        Birmingham *M*
        Tuscaloosa *M,D*

Arkansas

University of Central Arkansas *B*

California

San Diego State University *M*
Stanford University *M,D*
University of California: Riverside
    M,D
University of the Pacific *M*
University of Southern California
    M,D

Colorado

University of Colorado at
    Boulder *D*

Connecticut

Southern Connecticut State
    University *M*

District of Columbia

Gallaudet University *M*

Florida

Florida Atlantic University *M*
Florida State University *M,D*
University of Florida *M,D*
University of Miami *M,D*
University of South Florida *D*

Georgia

Emory University *M*
Georgia State University *M,D*

Illinois

Loyola University of Chicago *M,D*
Southern Illinois University at
    Carbondale *M,D*
University of Chicago *M,D*

Indiana

Indiana State University *M*
Indiana University Bloomington
    M,D
Purdue University *M,D*

Iowa

University of Iowa *M,D*

Kansas

University of Kansas *M,D*

Kentucky

Eastern Kentucky University *M*

Louisiana

Louisiana State University and
    Agricultural and Mechanical
    College *D*

Maryland

University of Maryland: College
    Park *M,D*

Massachusetts

Boston College *M,D*
Hampshire College *B*
Northeastern University *M*

Michigan

Andrews University *M*
Eastern Michigan University *M*
Michigan State University *M,D*
University of Detroit Mercy *M*
University of Michigan *M,D*
Wayne State University *M,D*

Mississippi

University of Southern
    Mississippi *M*

Missouri

St. Louis University *M,D*
University of Missouri: Kansas
    City *M*

Nebraska

University of Nebraska—Lincoln
    M,D

New Jersey

Rutgers—The State University of
    New Jersey *M,D*

New York

City University of New York: City
    College *M*
Cornell University *M,D*
Fordham University *M,D*
Hofstra University *D*
State University of New York
        Albany *M,D*
        Buffalo *M,D*
Syracuse University *M,D*

North Dakota

University of North Dakota *M*

Ohio

Cleveland State University *M*
Miami University: Oxford
    Campus *M*
Ohio State University: Columbus
    Campus *M,D*
University of Dayton *M*
University of Toledo *M,D*

Pennsylvania

Bryn Mawr College *M,D*
Lehigh University *M,D*
West Chester University of
    Pennsylvania *M*

Puerto Rico

University of Puerto Rico: Rio
Piedras Campus *M*

Rhode Island

University of Rhode Island *M*

South Carolina

University of South Carolina *M,D*

Texas

University of Houston *M,D*
University of North Texas *D*

West Virginia

West Virginia University *M,D*

Educational supervision

Alabama

Alabama Agricultural and
Mechanical University *M*
Alabama State University *M*
Auburn University *M,D*
Jacksonville State University *M*
Livingston University *M*
Samford University *M*
Troy State University at
Montgomery *M*
Tuskegee University *M*
University of Alabama *M,D*

Arkansas

University of Central Arkansas *B,M*

California

California Lutheran University *M*
California State University
Fresno *M*
Hayward *M*
Los Angeles *M*
Northridge *M*
Stanislaus *M*
La Sierra University *M*
Point Loma Nazarene College *M*
San Jose State University *M*
University of the Pacific *M,D*

Colorado

University of Colorado at Colorado
Springs *M*

Connecticut

Central Connecticut State
University *M*
Fairfield University *M*
Southern Connecticut State
University *M*

Delaware

University of Delaware *M*

District of Columbia

Gallaudet University *W*
George Washington University *M*
Howard University *M*
Trinity College *M*
University of the District of
Columbia *M*

Florida

Florida Agricultural and Mechanical
University *M*
Florida Atlantic University *M,D*
Florida State University *M,D*
Nova University *M,D*
Stetson University *M*
University of Miami *M,D*
University of North Florida *M*

University of West Florida *M*

Georgia

Albany State College *M*
Augusta College *M*
Clark Atlanta University *M*
Georgia College *M*
Georgia Southern University *M*
University of Georgia *M,D*
Valdosta State College *B,M*
West Georgia College *M*

Idaho

Northwest Nazarene College *M*

Illinois

Bradley University *M*
Chicago State University *M*
Concordia University *M*
De Paul University *M*
Loyola University of Chicago *M,D*
National-Louis University *M*
Northern Illinois University *M,D*
Roosevelt University *M,D,W*
Southern Illinois University
Carbondale *M,D*
Edwardsville *M*
University of Illinois at Chicago *M*

Indiana

Indiana State University *M,D*
Purdue University *M,D*

Iowa

Drake University *M,D*
University of Iowa *M,D*
University of Northern Iowa *M*

Kansas

Pittsburg State University *M*

Kentucky

Eastern Kentucky University *M*
Spalding University *M*
Union College *M*
University of Kentucky *M,D*
University of Louisville *D*

Louisiana

Louisiana State University and
Agricultural and Mechanical
College *M,D*
Nicholls State University *M*
Our Lady of Holy Cross College *M*
Southeastern Louisiana
University *M*
Tulane University *M*
Xavier University of Louisiana *M*

Maine

University of Maine *M*

Maryland

Baltimore Hebrew University *B,M*
Bowie State University *M*
Loyola College in Maryland *M*
Morgan State University *M,D*
Salisbury State University *M*
University of Maryland: College
Park *M,D*

Massachusetts

American International College *M*
Boston College *M,D*
Lesley College *M*
Salem State College *M*
Suffolk University *M*
Westfield State College *M*

Michigan

Andrews University *M,D*
Saginaw Valley State University *M*

Wayne State University *M,D*
Western Michigan University *M*

Minnesota

Mankato State University *M*
Winona State University *M*

Mississippi

Jackson State University *M,W*
William Carey College *M*

Missouri

Central Missouri State
University *M*
Northwest Missouri State
University *M*
St. Louis University *M,D*
Southeast Missouri State
University *M*
University of Missouri
Columbia *M,D*
Kansas City *M*
St. Louis *D*

Nebraska

Chadron State College *M*
University of Nebraska
Kearney *M*
Lincoln *M,D*
Omaha *M*

New Hampshire

Antioch New England Graduate
School *M*
Plymouth State College of the
University System of New
Hampshire *M*

New Jersey

Georgian Court College *M*
Glassboro State College *M*
Kean College of New Jersey *M*
Monmouth College *M*
Rider College *M*
Rutgers—The State University of
New Jersey *M,D*
St. Peter's College *M*
Seton Hall University *M*
William Paterson College of New
Jersey *M*

New Mexico

Eastern New Mexico University *M*

New York

Bank Street College of Education
M,W
Canisius College *M*
City University of New York
Baruch College *M*
Brooklyn College *C*
City College *M*
College of Staten Island *W*
Queens College *W*
College of New Rochelle *M*
Fordham University *M,D*
Long Island University: C. W. Post
Campus *M*
Niagara University *M*
Parsons School of Design *M*
St. Bonaventure University *M,W*
St. John's University *M,D*
State University of New York
Albany *D*
Buffalo *M,D*
College at New Paltz *M,W*
College at Plattsburgh *M*
University of Rochester *M,D*

North Carolina

Appalachian State University *M*
East Carolina University *M*

Fayetteville State University *M*
North Carolina Agricultural and
Technical State University *M*
North Carolina Central
University *M*
North Carolina State University
M,D
University of North Carolina
Chapel Hill *M,D*
Greensboro *M*
Wilmington *M*
Western Carolina University *M*

Ohio

Ashland University *M*
Baldwin-Wallace College *M*
Bowling Green State University *M*
Cleveland State University *M*
John Carroll University *M*
Kent State University *M*
Miami University: Oxford
Campus *M*
Ohio University *M,D*
Otterbein College *M*
University of Akron *M,D*
University of Cincinnati *M,D*
University of Dayton *M,D*
University of Toledo *M,D*
Wright State University *M*
Youngstown State University *M*

Oklahoma

Northeastern State University *M*

Oregon

Southern Oregon State College *M*

Pennsylvania

Beaver College *C,M*
California University of
Pennsylvania *M*
Duquesne University *M*
Edinboro University of
Pennsylvania *M*
Indiana University of
Pennsylvania *B*
Lehigh University *M,D*
Marywood College *M*
St. Joseph's University *M*
Shippensburg University of
Pennsylvania *M*
Temple University *M*
University of Pennsylvania *M,D*
Westminster College *M*

Puerto Rico

Pontifical Catholic University of
Puerto Rico *M*

South Carolina

Bob Jones University *M*
The Citadel *M*
Clemson University *M,W*
Furman University *M*
Winthrop University *M*

Tennessee

Austin Peay State University *M*
East Tennessee State University
M,D
Memphis State University *M,D*
Middle Tennessee State
University *M*
Tennessee State University *M*
Tennessee Technological
University *M*
Trevecca Nazarene College *M*
University of Tennessee
Chattanooga *M*
Knoxville *M,D*
Martin *M*
Vanderbilt University *M,D*

Texas

Abilene Christian University *M*
Angelo State University *M*
Lamar University—Beaumont *M*
Our Lady of the Lake University of San Antonio *M*
Prairie View A&M University *M*
Sam Houston State University *M*
Sul Ross State University *M*
Texas A&I University *M*
Texas Southern University *M,D*
Texas Woman's University *M*
University of Houston
　　Houston *M,D*
　　Victoria *M*
University of North Texas *M*
University of Texas
　　El Paso *M*
　　Pan American *M*
　　Permian Basin *M*
West Texas State University *M*

Vermont

Johnson State College *M*
Trinity College of Vermont *M*

Virginia

George Mason University *M*
Hampton University *M*
Longwood College *M*
Lynchburg College *M*
Radford University *M*
University of Richmond *M*
Virginia Commonwealth University *M*
Virginia Polytechnic Institute and State University *M,D*
Virginia State University *M*

Washington

Central Washington University *M*
Eastern Washington University *M*
Seattle University *M*

West Virginia

Marshall University *M*

Wisconsin

Marquette University *M,D*
University of Wisconsin
　　Milwaukee *M*
　　River Falls *M*
　　Superior *M*

American Samoa, Caroline Islands, Guam, Marianas, Virgin Islands

University of Guam *M*
University of the Virgin Islands *M*

Educational testing, evaluation, and measurement

Alabama

Auburn University *M*
University of Alabama
　　Birmingham *M*
　　Tuscaloosa *M,D*
University of South Alabama *M*

Arizona

Arizona State University *M,D*

Arkansas

University of Central Arkansas *B*

California

California State University
　　Los Angeles *M*
　　Northridge *M*
Stanford University *M,D*
University of the Pacific *M*

Colorado

University of Colorado at Boulder *D*

Connecticut

Fairfield University *M*
Southern Connecticut State University *M*

Delaware

University of Delaware *M,D*

District of Columbia

Howard University *M*

Florida

Florida State University *M,D*

Georgia

Clark Atlanta University *M*
Georgia Southern University *M*
Georgia State University *M*
University of Georgia *M,D*

Illinois

Loyola University of Chicago *D*
Northern Illinois University *M,D*
Southern Illinois University at Carbondale *M,D*
University of Chicago *M,D*

Indiana

Butler University *M*
Indiana State University *M*
Indiana University Bloomington *M,D*
Indiana University—Purdue University at Indianapolis *M*
Purdue University *M,D*

Iowa

Iowa State University *M,D*
University of Iowa *M,D*

Kansas

University of Kansas *M,D*

Kentucky

Eastern Kentucky University *M*
University of Louisville *D*

Louisiana

University of New Orleans *M*

Maryland

University of Maryland: College Park *M,D*

Massachusetts

American International College *M*
Boston College *M,D*
Harvard University *M,D,W*
Tufts University *M*

Michigan

Andrews University *M*
Eastern Michigan University *M*
Michigan State University *M,D*
University of Michigan *D*
Wayne State University *M,D*
Western Michigan University *D*

Mississippi

University of Southern Mississippi *M*

Missouri

St. Louis University *M,D*

Nebraska

University of Nebraska—Lincoln *M,D*

New Hampshire

Rivier College *M*

New Mexico

Eastern New Mexico University *M*

New York

City University of New York: City College *M*
Cornell University *M,D*
Fordham University *M,D*
Hofstra University *M*
New York University *D*
State University of New York
　　Albany *M,D*
　　Buffalo *M,D*
Syracuse University *M,D*

North Carolina

University of North Carolina at Greensboro *M*

Ohio

Kent State University *M*
Miami University: Oxford Campus *M*
Ohio State University: Columbus Campus *M,D*

Oklahoma

Northeastern State University *M*
Northwestern Oklahoma State University *M*

Pennsylvania

Bryn Mawr College *M,D*
Bucknell University *B,M*
California University of Pennsylvania *M*
Lehigh University *M,D*
University of Pennsylvania *M,D*

Rhode Island

Rhode Island College *M*

South Carolina

University of South Carolina *M*

Texas

Angelo State University *M*
Incarnate Word College *M*
Sul Ross State University *M*
University of Houston *M,D*
University of Texas at El Paso *M*
West Texas State University *M*

Utah

Brigham Young University *M,D*

Virginia

Virginia Polytechnic Institute and State University *D*

Canada

McGill University *M*

Electrical/electronics/ communications engineering

Alabama

Auburn University *B,M,D*
Central Alabama Community College: Childersburg Campus *A*
Community College of the Air Force *A*
Tuskegee University *B,M*
University of Alabama
　　Birmingham *B,M*
　　Huntsville *B,M,D*
　　Tuscaloosa *B,M,D*
University of South Alabama *B,M*
Wallace State Community College at Hanceville *A*

Alaska

University of Alaska Fairbanks *B,M*

Arizona

Arizona State University *B,M,D*
Embry-Riddle Aeronautical University: Prescott Campus *B*
ITT Technical Institute: Tucson *A*
Northern Arizona University *B*
University of Arizona *B,M,D*

Arkansas

East Arkansas Community College *C,A*
John Brown University *B*
National Education Center: Arkansas College of Technology *A*
University of Arkansas *B,M*

California

Allan Hancock College *A*
American Armenian International College *B*
California Institute of Technology *B,M,D,W*
California Polytechnic State University: San Luis Obispo *B,M*
California State Polytechnic University: Pomona *B*
California State University
　　Chico *B*
　　Fresno *B*
　　Fullerton *B,M*
　　Long Beach *B,M*
　　Los Angeles *B,M*
　　Northridge *B,M*
　　Sacramento *B,M*
City College of San Francisco *C,A*
Cogswell Polytechnical College *B*
Fresno City College *C,A*
Los Angeles Harbor College *C,A*
Loyola Marymount University *B,M*
Merced College *A*
Mount San Jacinto College *C,A*
Napa Valley College *A*
Naval Postgraduate School *M,D*
Phillips Junior College
　　Fresno Campus *C,A*
　　San Fernando Valley Campus *A*
San Diego State University *B,M*
San Francisco State University *B*
San Jose State University *B,M*
Santa Clara University *B,M,D*
Santa Monica College *A*
Santa Rosa Junior College *A*
Southwestern College *A*
Stanford University *B,M,D*
United States International University *B*

University of California
  Berkeley *B,M,D*
  Davis *B,M,D*
  Irvine *B*
  Los Angeles *B,M,D*
  Riverside *B*
  San Diego *B,M,D*
  Santa Barbara *B,M,D*
University of La Verne *B*
University of the Pacific *B,M*
University of Redlands *B*
University of San Diego *B*
University of San Francisco *B*
University of Southern California
  B,M,D,W
West Coast University *A,B,M*

Colorado

Colorado School of Mines *W*
Colorado State University *B,M,D*
Colorado Technical College *B,M*
Denver Technical College *A*
Mesa State College *A*
United States Air Force
  Academy *B*
University of Colorado
  Boulder *B,M,D*
  Colorado Springs *B,M,D*
  Denver *B,M*
University of Denver *B,M,D*

Connecticut

Bridgeport Engineering Institute *B*
United States Coast Guard
  Academy *B*
University of Bridgeport *B,M*
University of Connecticut *B,M,D*
University of Hartford *B*
University of New Haven *A,B,M*
Yale University *B,M,D*

Delaware

Delaware State College *B*
University of Delaware *B,M,D*

District of Columbia

Catholic University of America
  B,M,D
Gallaudet University *B*
George Washington University
  B,M,D
Georgetown University *B*
Howard University *B,M,D*
University of the District of
  Columbia *B*

Florida

Florida Agricultural and Mechanical
  University *B,M*
Florida Atlantic University *B,M,D*
Florida Institute of Technology
  B,M,D
Florida International University
  B,M,D
Florida State University *B,M*
Hillsborough Community College *A*
Indian River Community College *A*
Manatee Community College *A*
Miami-Dade Community College *A*
Palm Beach Community College *A*
University of Central Florida *B,M,D*
University of Florida *B,M,D*
University of Miami *B,M,D*
University of North Florida *B*
University of South Florida *B,M,D*

Georgia

Augusta College *A*
Chattahoochee Technical
  Institute *A*
Georgia Institute of Technology
  B,M,D

Mercer University
  Atlanta *M*
  Macon *B,M*
Middle Georgia College *A*
Morris Brown College *B*
Savannah Technical Institute *C,A*

Hawaii

University of Hawaii at Manoa
  B,M,D

Idaho

Boise State University *B*
College of Southern Idaho *A*
North Idaho College *A*
Ricks College *A*
University of Idaho *B,M,D*

Illinois

Belleville Area College *C,A*
Bradley University *B,M*
City Colleges of Chicago
  Olive-Harvey College *C,A*
  Richard J. Daley College *C,A*
College of Lake County *A*
Elgin Community College *C,A*
Illinois Benedictine College *B*
Illinois Eastern Community
  Colleges: Wabash Valley College
  C,A
Illinois Institute of Technology
  B,M,D
John A. Logan College *A*
Northern Illinois University *B,M*
Northwestern University *B,M,D*
Parks College of St. Louis
  University *B*
Richland Community College *A*
Rock Valley College *A*
Southern Illinois University
  Carbondale *B,M*
  Edwardsville *B,M*
University of Illinois
  Chicago *B,M,D*
  Urbana-Champaign *B,M,D*

Indiana

Indiana Institute of Technology *B*
Indiana University—Purdue
  University at Indianapolis *B,M*
Purdue University
  Calumet *B*
  West Lafayette *B,M,D,W*
Rose-Hulman Institute of
  Technology *B,M*
Tri-State University *B*
University of Evansville *B*
University of Notre Dame *B,M,D*
Valparaiso University *B*
Vincennes University *A*

Iowa

Des Moines Area Community
  College *A*
Dordt College *B*
Iowa State University *B,M,D*
Kirkwood Community College *A*
Maharishi International
  University *B*
University of Iowa *B,M,D*

Kansas

Allen County Community
  College *A*
Kansas State University *B,M,D*
University of Kansas *B,M,D*
Wichita State University *B,M,D*

Kentucky

Louisville Technical Institute *A*
Southeast Community College *A*
University of Kentucky *B,M,D*

University of Louisville *B,M*

Louisiana

Grantham College of Engineering
  A,B
Louisiana State University and
  Agricultural and Mechanical
  College *B,M,D*
Louisiana Tech University *B,M*
McNeese State University *B*
Southern University and
  Agricultural and Mechanical
  College *B*
Tulane University *B,M,D*
University of New Orleans *B*
University of Southwestern
  Louisiana *B*

Maine

University of Maine *B,M*
University of Southern Maine *B,M*

Maryland

Capitol College *A,B*
College of Notre Dame of
  Maryland *B*
Howard Community College *C,A*
Johns Hopkins University *B,M,D*
Loyola College in Maryland *B*
Morgan State University *B*
United States Naval Academy *B*
University of Maryland
  Baltimore County *M,D*
  College Park *B,M,D*

Massachusetts

Berkshire Community College *A*
Boston University *B,M,D*
Eastern Nazarene College *B*
Franklin Institute of Boston *A*
Harvard and Radcliffe Colleges *B*
Massachusetts Institute of
  Technology *B,M,D,W*
Merrimack College *B*
Northeastern University *B,M,D*
Simmons College *B*
Springfield Technical Community
  College *A*
Suffolk University *B*
Tufts University *B,M,D*
University of Massachusetts
  Amherst *B,M,D*
  Dartmouth *B,M*
  Lowell *B,M,D*
Wentworth Institute of
  Technology *B*
Western New England College *B,M*
Worcester Polytechnic Institute
  B,M,D

Michigan

Baker College: Flint *A*
Calvin College *B*
Glen Oaks Community College *C*
GMI Engineering & Management
  Institute *B,M*
Grand Valley State University *B*
Lawrence Technological
  University *B*
Michigan State University *B,M,D*
Michigan Technological University
  B,M,D
Oakland University *B,M*
Saginaw Valley State University *B*
University of Detroit Mercy *B,M,D*
University of Michigan *B,M,D*
Wayne State University *B,M,D*
Western Michigan University *B,M*

Minnesota

Mankato State University *B*
National Education Center: Brown
  Institute Campus *A*
Northwestern Electronics
  Institute *A*
St. Cloud State University *B*
University of Minnesota: Twin
  Cities *B,M,D*
Willmar Community College *A*

Mississippi

Mississippi College *B*
Mississippi State University *B,M,D*
Phillips Junior College of the
  Mississippi Gulf Coast *A*
University of Mississippi *B*

Missouri

Longview Community College *A*
St. Louis University *B*
University of Missouri
  Columbia *B*
  Kansas City *B*
  Rolla *B,M,D*
Washington University *B,M,D*
William Jewell College *B*

Montana

Montana State University *B,M,D*

Nebraska

Southeast Community College:
  Milford Campus *A*
University of Nebraska—Lincoln
  B,M

Nevada

Community College of Southern
  Nevada *C,A*
University of Nevada
  Las Vegas *B,M,D*
  Reno *B,M*

New Hampshire

New Hampshire Technical College:
  Manchester *A*
University of New Hampshire
  B,M,D

New Jersey

Camden County College *A*
Fairleigh Dickinson University *B,M*
Mercer County Community
  College *A*
Monmouth College *B,M*
New Jersey Institute of Technology
  B,M,D
Ocean County College *A*
Princeton University *B,M,D*
Rutgers—The State University of
  New Jersey
  College of Engineering *B*
  New Brunswick *M,D*
Stevens Institute of Technology
  B,M,D

New Mexico

New Mexico Institute of Mining
  and Technology *B*
New Mexico State University
  B,M,D
University of New Mexico *B,M*

New York

Alfred University *B,M*
City University of New York
  City College *B,M,D*
  Graduate School and
    University Center *D*
Clarkson University *B,M*
College of Aeronautics *A*

Columbia University: School of
Engineering and Applied Science
B,M,D,W
Community College of the Finger
Lakes A
Cooper Union B,M
Cornell University B,M,D
Erie Community College: North
Campus A
Manhattan College B,M
New York Institute of
Technology B
New York University B
Pace University
College of White Plains B
New York B
Pleasantville/Briarcliff B
Polytechnic University
Brooklyn B,M,D
Long Island Campus B,M,D
Rensselaer Polytechnic Institute
B,M,D
Rochester Institute of Technology
B,M
State University of New York
Binghamton B,M
Buffalo B,M,D
Stony Brook B,M,D
College at New Paltz B
Maritime College B
Syracuse University B,M,D
Union College B,M
United States Military Academy B
University of Rochester B,M,D,W
Utica College of Syracuse
University B

North Carolina

Duke University B,M,D
Edgecombe Community College A
Mitchell Community College C,A
North Carolina Agricultural and
Technical State University B,M
North Carolina State University
B,M,D
Richmond Community College A
St. Augustine's College B
Sandhills Community College C,A
Southwestern Community
College A
University of North Carolina at
Charlotte B,M

North Dakota

North Dakota State University B,M
University of North Dakota B,M

Ohio

Air Force Institute of Technology
M,D
Case Western Reserve University
B,M,D
Cedarville College B
Central State University B
Cleveland State University B,M
Cuyahoga Community College:
Metropolitan Campus A
Hocking Technical College A
Ohio Northern University B
Ohio State University: Columbus
Campus B,M,D
Ohio University B,M,D
University of Akron B,M,D
University of Cincinnati B,M,D
University of Dayton B,M,D
University of Toledo B,M,D
Wilberforce University B
Wright State University B,M
Youngstown State University B,M

Oklahoma

Oklahoma Christian University of
Science and Arts B
Oklahoma State University B,M,D
Redlands Community College A
Rogers State College A
University of Oklahoma B,M,D
University of Tulsa B,M

Oregon

Central Oregon Community
College A
Chemeketa Community College A
George Fox College B
Oregon Graduate Institute M,D
Oregon State University B,M,D
Portland State University B,M,D
University of Portland B,M

Pennsylvania

Bucknell University B,M
Carnegie Mellon University
B,M,D,W
Drexel University B,M,D
Gannon University B
Geneva College B
Grove City College B
Lafayette College B
Lehigh County Community
College A
Lehigh University B,M,D
Lock Haven University of
Pennsylvania B
Messiah College B
Penn State University Park Campus
C,B,M,D
Pennsylvania Institute of
Technology A
Reading Area Community
College A
Swarthmore College B
Temple University B,D
University of Pennsylvania B,M,D
University of Pittsburgh B,M,D
University of Scranton A,B
Villanova University B,M
Westmoreland County Community
College A
Widener University B,M
Wilkes University B,M

Puerto Rico

Universidad Politecnica de Puerto
Rico B
University of Puerto Rico:
Mayaguez Campus B,M

Rhode Island

Brown University B,M,D
Community College of Rhode
Island C,A
Johnson & Wales University A,B
University of Rhode Island B,M,D

South Carolina

Bob Jones University B
The Citadel B
Clemson University B,M,D
Technical College of the
Lowcountry A
University of South Carolina B,M,D

South Dakota

South Dakota School of Mines and
Technology B,M
South Dakota State University B

Tennessee

Christian Brothers University B
Memphis State University B,M
Tennessee State University B

Tennessee Technological University
B,M
University of Tennessee
Chattanooga B,M
Knoxville B,M,D
Vanderbilt University B,M,D

Texas

Abilene Christian University B
Amarillo College A
Baylor University B
Del Mar College A
ITT Technical Institute: Houston A
Kilgore College A
Lamar University—Beaumont B,D
LeTourneau University B
Mountain View College A
Prairie View A&M University B
Rice University B,M,D
St. Mary's University B,M
Southern Methodist University
B,M,D
Texas A&I University B,M
Texas A&M University B,M,D
Texas Southmost College A
Texas Tech University B,M,D
University of Houston B,M,D
University of Texas
Arlington B,M,D
Austin B,M,D
Dallas B,M,D
El Paso B,M,D
San Antonio B,M
Victoria College A

Utah

Brigham Young University B,M,D
University of Utah B,M,D
Utah State University B,M,D

Vermont

Norwich University B
University of Vermont B,M,D

Virginia

Blue Ridge Community College C
Emory and Henry College B
George Mason University B,M
Hampton University B
Norfolk State University B
Northern Virginia Community
College C,A
Old Dominion University B,M,D
Tidewater Community College A
University of Virginia B,M,D
Virginia Military Institute B
Virginia Polytechnic Institute and
State University B,M,D

Washington

Cogswell College North B
Gonzaga University B,M
Lower Columbia College A
Pacific Lutheran University B
Pierce College A
Seattle Pacific University B
Seattle University B
University of Puget Sound B
University of Washington B,M,D
Walla Walla College B
Washington State University B,M,D

West Virginia

Potomac State College of West
Virginia University A
West Virginia Institute of
Technology B,M
West Virginia State College A
West Virginia University B,M,D

Wisconsin

Concordia University Wisconsin B
Marquette University B,M,D
Milwaukee School of Engineering B
University of Wisconsin
Madison B,M,D
Milwaukee B
Platteville B

Wyoming

University of Wyoming B,M,D

Canada

McGill University B,M,D

Mexico

Sistema Instituto Tecnologico y de
Estudios Superiores de
Monterrey B

Electrical and electronics equipment repair

Alabama

Alabama Aviation and Technical
College C,A
Bessemer State Technical College C
Brewer State Junior College A
Community College of the Air
Force A
Douglas MacArthur State Technical
College A
Gadsden State Community College
C,A
George C. Wallace State
Community College at Selma A
John C. Calhoun State Community
College C,A
John M. Patterson State Technical
College A
Lawson State Community College
C,A
Walker State Technical College C,A

Alaska

University of Alaska Anchorage
C,A

Arizona

Eastern Arizona College A
ITT Technical Institute
Phoenix A
Tucson A
Mohave Community College C,A
Rio Salado Community College A

Arkansas

Westark Community College C,A

California

Allan Hancock College C,A
Cerritos Community College A
Chabot College A
Chaffey Community College C,A
Coastline Community College C,A
Hartnell College A
Long Beach City College C,A
Los Angeles City College A
Los Angeles Harbor College C,A
Los Angeles Mission College C,A
Los Angeles Trade and Technical
College C,A
Mendocino College C,A
Modesto Junior College A
Mount San Antonio College C,A
Orange Coast College C,A
Oxnard College C
Palomar College C,A

San Jose City College *A*
Southwestern College *C,A*
Yuba College *C,A*

Colorado

Community College of Denver *C,A*
Denver Institute of Technology *A*
ITT Technical Institute: Aurora *A*
Pikes Peak Community College *C,A*
Red Rocks Community College *A*
Trinidad State Junior College *A*

Connecticut

University of Hartford *A*

Delaware

Delaware Technical and
 Community College: Terry
 Campus *A*

Florida

Central Florida Community
 College *A*
Gulf Coast Community College *A*
New England Institute of
 Technology *A*
Pensacola Junior College *A*
South Florida Community
 College *C*

Georgia

Athens Area Technical Institute *C*
Atlanta Metropolitan College *A*
Augusta College *A*
Augusta Technical Institute *C*
Clayton State College *A*
Dalton College *C,A*
Darton College *A*
Gainesville College *A*
Savannah Technical Institute *C*
Truett-McConnell College *A*

Hawaii

Brigham Young University-Hawaii
 C,A
University of Hawaii: Honolulu
 Community College *A*

Idaho

Boise State University *A*
College of Southern Idaho *C*
Lewis Clark State College *A*
Ricks College *A*

Illinois

Carl Sandburg College *A*
City Colleges of Chicago
 Chicago City-Wide College *C*
 Richard J. Daley College *A*
College of Lake County *A*
Illinois Central College *C*
John A. Logan College *C*
Lake Land College *A*
Lincoln Land Community College
 C,A
Moraine Valley Community College
 C,A
Oakton Community College *C*
Rend Lake College *A*
Richland Community College *A*
Shawnee Community College *C*
Southern Illinois University at
 Carbondale *A*
Triton College *C,A*

Indiana

Indiana Vocational Technical
 College: Lafayette *A*
ITT Technical Institute:
 Evansville *C*
Vincennes University *A*

Iowa

Des Moines Area Community
 College *A*
Hamilton Technical College *A*
Hawkeye Institute of Technology *C*
Indian Hills Community College *C*
Kirkwood Community College *A*
Northwest Iowa Technical
 College *A*

Kansas

Allen County Community
 College *A*
Butler County Community
 College *A*
Dodge City Community College
 C,A
Kansas City Kansas Community
 College *A*
Neosho County Community College
 C,A
Pittsburg State University *C*

Kentucky

Eastern Kentucky University *A,B*
Institute of Electronic
 Technology *A*
Louisville Technical Institute *A*
Murray State University *A*
St. Catharine College *A*

Maine

Eastern Maine Technical College *A*
Southern Maine Technical
 College *A*

Maryland

Cecil Community College *C,A*
Dundalk Community College *C,A*
Montgomery College: Rockville
 Campus *A*

Massachusetts

Bunker Hill Community College *A*
Massachusetts Bay Community
 College *C,A*
Mount Ida College *A*
Quinsigamond Community
 College *A*
Springfield Technical Community
 College *A*
Wentworth Institute of
 Technology *A*

Michigan

Baker College: Flint *A*
Delta College *C*
Grand Rapids Community College
 C,A
Great Lakes Junior College of
 Business *C,A*
Henry Ford Community College *A*
Lansing Community College *A*
Macomb Community College *C,A*
Northern Michigan University *A*
Northwestern Michigan College *A*
West Shore Community College
 C,A

Minnesota

Alexandria Technical College *C,A*
Lakewood Community College *A*
Northwestern Electronics Institute
 C,A
Rainy River Community College *A*

Mississippi

Copiah-Lincoln Community
 College *A*
Mississippi Delta Community
 College *C*

Phillips Junior College of the
 Mississippi Gulf Coast *A*

Missouri

East Central College *C,A*
North Central Missouri College *A*
Northwest Missouri State
 University *C*
State Fair Community College *A*

Montana

Miles Community College *C,A*
Northern Montana College *A,B*

Nebraska

Central Community College *C,A*
Chadron State College *B*
Northeast Community College *A*
Southeast Community College
 Lincoln Campus *C,A*
 Milford Campus *A*

Nevada

Truckee Meadows Community
 College *C,A*

New Hampshire

New Hampshire Technical College
 Manchester *A*
 Nashua *A*
 Stratham *A*

New Mexico

Dona Ana Branch Community
 College of New Mexico State
 University *C,A*
Eastern New Mexico University:
 Roswell Campus *C,A*
New Mexico State University *C,A*

New York

Bramson ORT Technical
 Institute *A*
City University of New York: New
 York City Technical College *A*
College of Aeronautics *A*
Community College of the Finger
 Lakes *A*
Genesee Community College *A*
Mohawk Valley Community College
 C,A
State University of New York
 College of Agriculture and
 Technology at Morrisville *A*
 College of Technology at
 Alfred *A*
 College of Technology at
 Farmingdale *C*
Technical Career Institutes *C,A*

North Carolina

Alamance Community College *A*
Bladen Community College *C*
Central Piedmont Community
 College *A*
College of the Albemarle *A*
Craven Community College *C,A*
Davidson County Community
 College *C*
Durham Technical Community
 College *C*
Edgecombe Community College *C*
Forsyth Technical Community
 College *A*
Guilford Technical Community
 College *C,A*
Johnston Community College *C*
Mitchell Community College *C,A*
Pitt Community College *C*
Richmond Community College *C*
Roanoke-Chowan Community
 College *C*

Robeson Community College *C*
Sandhills Community College *C*
Southwestern Community
 College *C*
Wake Technical Community
 College *C*
Wilson Technical Community
 College *C*

North Dakota

Bismarck State College *C,A*
University of North Dakota: Lake
 Region *A*

Ohio

Cincinnati Metropolitan College *A*
Columbus State Community
 College *A*
Sinclair Community College *C*
Stark Technical College *A*
University of Rio Grande *A*

Oklahoma

National Education Center: Spartan
 School of Aeronautics Campus *A*
Oklahoma State University
 Oklahoma City *A*
 Technical Branch:
 Okmulgee *A*
Rogers State College *A*
Tulsa Junior College *A*

Oregon

Central Oregon Community College
 C,A
Chemeketa Community College *A*
Lane Community College *A*
Mount Hood Community College
 C,A
Portland Community College *C,A*
Rogue Community College *C,A*
Umpqua Community College *C,A*

Pennsylvania

Bucks County Community
 College *A*
Community College of Beaver
 County *A*
Electronic Institutes: Pittsburgh *A*
Johnson Technical Institute *A*
Lincoln University *C*
Spring Garden College *C*
Triangle Tech: Erie School *C,A*
Westmoreland County Community
 College *A*

Puerto Rico

Columbia College *A*
Huertas Junior College *C*

South Carolina

Greenville Technical College *A*
Horry-Georgetown Technical
 College *A*
Midlands Technical College *C*
Technical College of the
 Lowcountry *A*
Tri-County Technical College *C*

South Dakota

Mitchell Vocational Technical
 Institute *C,A*
Western Dakota Vocational
 Technical Institute *C,A*

Tennessee

Austin Peay State University *A*
Chattanooga State Technical
 Community College *C,A*
Pellissippi State Technical
 Community College *A*

Texas

Alvin Community College *A*
Amarillo College *C,A*
Angelina College *A*
Brazosport College *A*
Central Texas College *A*
Del Mar College *C,A*
Houston Community College *C*
Lamar University—Beaumont *A*
Midland College *A*
Mountain View College *A*
South Plains College *A*
Tarrant County Junior College *C*
Texas Southmost College *A*
Texas State Technical College
    Harlingen *C*
    Waco *A*

Utah

College of Eastern Utah *C*
Utah State University *B*

Virginia

Blue Ridge Community College *C*
Dabney S. Lancaster Community
    College *C*
Mountain Empire Community
    College *A*
Northern Virginia Community
    College *C,A*
Paul D. Camp Community
    College *A*
Piedmont Virginia Community
    College *C*
Southwest Virginia Community
    College *C,A*
Tidewater Community College *C*

Washington

Centralia College *A*
Edmonds Community College *C,A*
ITT Technical Institute: Seattle *A*
Lower Columbia College *A*
North Seattle Community
    College *A*
Spokane Community College *A*

West Virginia

Shepherd College *A*
West Virginia Institute of
    Technology *A,B*
West Virginia Northern Community
    College *A*

Wisconsin

Chippewa Valley Technical
    College *A*
Mid-State Technical College *A*
Moraine Park Technical College *A*
Stratton College *A*
Waukesha County Technical
    College *C*
Western Wisconsin Technical
    College *C*
Wisconsin Indianhead Technical
    College *C*

Wyoming

Casper College *A*
Western Wyoming Community
    College *C,A*

American Samoa, Caroline Islands, Guam, Marianas, Virgin Islands

Micronesian Occupational College
    C,A

Electrical installation

Alabama

Bessemer State Technical College *C*
Central Alabama Community
    College: Childersburg Campus *A*
Gadsden State Community College
    C,A
George C. Wallace State
    Community College at Selma *A*
John C. Calhoun State Community
    College *C*
Lawson State Community College
    C,A
Shoals Community College *C*

Arizona

Mohave Community College *C*
Rio Salado Community College *A*

Arkansas

Phillips County Community
    College *C*

California

Allan Hancock College *C*
Bakersfield College *A*
Chabot College *A*
Coastline Community College *C,A*
Palomar College *A*
San Diego City College *C,A*
San Joaquin Delta College *C,A*
San Jose City College *A*
Santa Rosa Junior College *A*

Colorado

Red Rocks Community College *C,A*

Florida

Brevard Community College *C*
Pensacola Junior College *C*

Georgia

Atlanta Metropolitan College *A*
Augusta Technical Institute *C*
Gainesville College *A*
Savannah Technical Institute *C*

Hawaii

University of Hawaii
    Honolulu Community College
        C,A
    Kauai Community College *C,A*

Illinois

Belleville Area College *C,A*
Black Hawk College *C*
College of Lake County *C,A*
Illinois Eastern Community
    Colleges: Olney Central
    College *C*
Lake Land College *C*
Lewis and Clark Community
    College *C*
Moraine Valley Community
    College *A*
State Community College *C*

Iowa

Northeast Iowa Community
    College *A*
Northwest Iowa Technical College
    C,A

Kansas

Coffeyville Community College *A*
Pittsburg State University *C*

Kentucky

St. Catharine College *A*

Maine

Eastern Maine Technical College *C*
Southern Maine Technical
    College *A*

Maryland

Cecil Community College *C,A*

Massachusetts

Mount Ida College *A*

Michigan

Kellogg Community College *A*
Lansing Community College *A*

Minnesota

Northland Community College *A*

Mississippi

Hinds Community College *C*
Mississippi Delta Community
    College *C*
Mississippi Gulf Coast Community
    College: Jefferson Davis
    Campus *C*

Nebraska

Central Community College *C,A*
Chadron State College *B*
Nebraska Indian Community
    College *A*
Northeast Community College *A*
Southeast Community College:
    Milford Campus *A*

Nevada

Truckee Meadows Community
    College *C,A*

New Hampshire

New Hampshire Technical College
    Laconia *A*
    Stratham *C*

New Jersey

Bergen Community College *A*

New Mexico

Albuquerque Technical-Vocational
    Institute *C*
Northern New Mexico Community
    College *C,A*

New York

Hudson Valley Community
    College *A*
Mohawk Valley Community College
    C,A
State University of New York
    College of Technology at
        Alfred *A*
    College of Technology at
        Canton *C*
    College of Technology at
        Delhi *A*

North Carolina

Anson Community College *C*
Beaufort County Community
    College *C*
Bladen Community College *C*
Blue Ridge Community College *C*
Cape Fear Community College *C*
Catawba Valley Community College
    C,A
Cleveland Community College *C*
Coastal Carolina Community
    College *C*
College of the Albemarle *C*

Craven Community College *C*
Durham Technical Community
    College *C*
Fayetteville Technical Community
    College *C*
Forsyth Technical Community
    College *A*
Gaston College *C*
Guilford Technical Community
    College *C*
Haywood Community College *C*
Isothermal Community College *C*
James Sprunt Community
    College *C*
Johnston Community College *C*
Martin Community College *C*
Mayland Community College *C*
Mitchell Community College *C*
Pitt Community College *C*
Richmond Community College *C*
Robeson Community College *C*
Rockingham Community College *C*
Southeastern Community College *C*
Southwestern Community
    College *C*
Surry Community College *C*
Tri-County Community College *C*
Vance-Granville Community
    College *C*
Wake Technical Community
    College *C*
Wilson Technical Community
    College *C*

Ohio

Terra Technical College *C*

Oklahoma

Oklahoma State University
    Technical Branch: Okmulgee *A*

Pennsylvania

Luzerne County Community
    College *C,A*
Penn State University Park
    Campus *C*
Pennsylvania College of
    Technology *C*
Triangle Tech: Erie School *C,A*

South Carolina

Denmark Technical College *C*
Greenville Technical College *C*

South Dakota

Mitchell Vocational Technical
    Institute *C,A*
Western Dakota Vocational
    Technical Institute *C*

Tennessee

Chattanooga State Technical
    Community College *C,A*
Northeast State Technical
    Community College *C,A*

Texas

College of the Mainland *A*
Houston Community College *C*
Laredo Junior College *C,A*
North Lake College *A*
St. Philip's College *A*
Texarkana College *C*

Virginia

Central Virginia Community
    College *C*
Paul D. Camp Community
    College *C*
Piedmont Virginia Community
    College *C*

Southside Virginia Community
College *C*
Tidewater Community College *C*
Virginia Highlands Community
College *C*

Washington

Spokane Community College *A*

Wisconsin

Chippewa Valley Technical
College *C*

**American Samoa, Caroline
Islands, Guam, Marianas,
Virgin Islands**

Guam Community College *C*

Electrical technology

Alabama

Community College of the Air
Force *A*
Gadsden State Community
College *A*
John C. Calhoun State Community
College *C,A*
Reid State Technical College *A*
Shelton State Community College
C,A
University of Alabama *B*
Walker State Technical College *C,A*
Wallace State Community College
at Hanceville *C,A*

Arizona

Mesa Community College *C,A*
Northern Arizona University *B*
Rio Salado Community College *A*

California

Cerritos Community College *C,A*
Chabot College *A*
Chaffey Community College *C,A*
City College of San Francisco *C,A*
Fresno City College *C,A*
Heald College: Santa Rosa *A*
Heald Institute of Technology *A*
Irvine Valley College *C,A*
ITT Technical Institute: San
Diego *A*
Los Angeles Trade and Technical
College *C,A*
San Diego City College *C,A*
San Joaquin Delta College *C,A*
Southwestern College *A*

Colorado

Pikes Peak Community College *A*
United States Air Force
Academy *B*

Connecticut

Greater New Haven State Technical
College *A*
Hartford State Technical College *A*
Norwalk State Technical College *A*
Thames Valley State Technical
College *A*
Waterbury State Technical
College *A*

Delaware

Delaware Technical and
Community College
Southern Campus *A*
Stanton/Wilmington
Campus *A*
Terry Campus *A*

District of Columbia

Gallaudet University *C,B*
University of the District of
Columbia *A*

Florida

Brevard Community College *A*
Broward Community College *A*
Central Florida Community
College *C*
Edison Community College *C,A*
Manatee Community College *A*
Seminole Community College *C*
University of North Florida *B*
University of West Florida *B*

Georgia

Augusta Technical Institute *A*
Bainbridge College *C*
Clayton State College *C*
Georgia Southern University *B*
Southern College of Technology *B*

Hawaii

University of Hawaii: Honolulu
Community College *C,A*

Idaho

Idaho State University *C,A*
North Idaho College *A*

Illinois

Kishwaukee College *C*
Moraine Valley Community
College *A*
Parks College of St. Louis
University *A*

Indiana

Indiana Institute of Technology *A,B*
Indiana State University *M*
Indiana University
Kokomo *A,B*
Southeast *A*
Indiana University—Purdue
University at Fort Wayne *A,B*
Purdue University
Calumet *A,B*
North Central Campus *A*
West Lafayette *A,B*
University of Southern Indiana *A,B*
Vincennes University *A*

Iowa

Indian Hills Community College *C*
Northwest Iowa Technical
College *A*

Kansas

Butler County Community College
C,A
Hutchinson Community College *A*
Pittsburg State University *C*

Kentucky

Lexington Community College *A*
Madisonville Community College *A*
Murray State University *A,B*
University of Louisville *A*
Western Kentucky University *A,B*

Louisiana

Grambling State University *A,B*
McNeese State University *A,B*
Nicholls State University *B*

Maine

Eastern Maine Technical College *A*
Kennebec Valley Technical
College *A*
Southern Maine Technical
College *A*

University of Maine *A,B*

Maryland

Anne Arundel Community
College *A*
Howard Community College *A*
University of Maryland: Eastern
Shore *B*

Massachusetts

Franklin Institute of Boston *A*
Mount Ida College *A*
Northeastern University *A,B*
Springfield Technical Community
College *A*
University of Massachusetts at
Dartmouth *B*
Wentworth Institute of
Technology *A*

Michigan

Ferris State University *B*
Henry Ford Community College *A*
Kalamazoo Valley Community
College *C,A*
Kellogg Community College *A*
Lake Superior State University *A,B*
Lansing Community College *A*
Lawrence Technological
University *A*
Michigan Technological
University *A*
Northern Michigan University *A,B*
Oakland Community College *A*
Wayne State University *B*

Minnesota

Mankato State University *B*
Northland Community College *A*
St. Paul Technical College *C*
Southwest State University *A,B*

Mississippi

East Central Community College *C*
Northeast Mississippi Community
College *A*

Missouri

Central Missouri State University
A,B
Ranken Technical College *A*
St. Louis Community College
Florissant Valley *A*
Forest Park *A*
Washington University *B*

Montana

Montana State University *B*

Nebraska

Southeast Community College:
Milford Campus *A*

New Hampshire

New Hampshire Technical College
Laconia *A*
Manchester *A*
University of New Hampshire *B*

New Jersey

Bergen Community College *A*
Fairleigh Dickinson University *B*
Mercer County Community College
C,A
New Jersey Institute of
Technology *B*
Thomas Edison State College *A,B*

New Mexico

New Mexico Highlands University
A,B

New York

Bramson ORT Technical Institute
C,A
City University of New York
College of Staten Island *A*
New York City Technical
College *A*
Community College of the Finger
Lakes *A*
Corning Community College *A*
Dutchess Community College *A*
Erie Community College: North
Campus *A*
Fulton-Montgomery Community
College *A*
Genesee Community College *A*
Hudson Valley Community
College *A*
Jamestown Community College *A*
Mohawk Valley Community College
C,A
New York Institute of
Technology *A*
Niagara County Community
College *A*
Onondaga Community College *A*
Orange County Community
College *A*
Rochester Institute of Technology
A,B
Rockland Community College *A*
State University of New York
College of Agriculture and
Technology at Morrisville *A*
College at Buffalo *B*
College of Technology at
Alfred *A,B*
College of Technology at
Canton *A*
College of Technology at
Delhi *A*
College of Technology at
Farmingdale *A,B*
Institute of Technology at
Utica/Rome *B*
Suffolk County Community
College *A*
Tompkins-Cortland Community
College *C,A*
Westchester Community College *A*

North Carolina

Anson Community College *C*
Beaufort County Community
College *A*
Central Piedmont Community
College *A*
Craven Community College *A*
Durham Technical Community
College *C*
Isothermal Community College *A*
Pamlico Community College *A*
Rockingham Community College *C*
Southeastern Community College *A*
University of North Carolina at
Charlotte *B*

North Dakota

North Dakota State College of
Science *A*

Ohio

Bowling Green State University:
Firelands College *A*
Clark State Community College *A*
Cleveland Institute of Electronics *C*
Cuyahoga Community College:
Metropolitan Campus *A*
Jefferson Technical College *A*
Kent State University: Tuscarawas
Campus *A*
Marion Technical College *A*

Miami University: Hamilton
Campus *A*
Muskingum Area Technical
College *A*
Owens Technical College
Findlay Campus *A*
Toledo *C,A*
Southern State Community
College *A*
Stark Technical College *A*
Terra Technical College *C,A*
University of Cincinnati
Access Colleges *A*
Cincinnati *B*
Clermont College *A*
Washington State Community
College *A*
Youngstown State University *A,B*

Oklahoma

East Central University *B*
Langston University *A*
Oklahoma State University
Technical Branch: Okmulgee *A*
Rogers State College *A*
Tulsa Junior College *A*

Oregon

Central Oregon Community
College *A*

Pennsylvania

California University of
Pennsylvania *B*
Dean Institute of Technology *A*
Gannon University *A,B*
ICS Center for Degree Studies *A*
Lehigh County Community
College *A*
Luzerne County Community
College *C,A*
Penn State
Erie Behrend College *B*
Harrisburg Capital College *B*
Pennsylvania College of
Technology *A*
Point Park College *A,B*
Reading Area Community
College *A*

Rhode Island

New England Institute of
Technology *A*

South Carolina

Chesterfield-Marlboro Technical
College *C*
Midlands Technical College *A*
South Carolina State College *B*
Tri-County Technical College *A*
Williamsburg Technical College *C*

South Dakota

Mitchell Vocational Technical
Institute *C,A*
Western Dakota Vocational
Technical Institute *C,A*

Tennessee

Chattanooga State Technical
Community College *A*
Middle Tennessee State
University *B*
Nashville State Technical Institute
C,A
Northeast State Technical
Community College *A*
Pellissippi State Technical
Community College *A*
State Technical Institute at
Memphis *A*
University of Tennessee: Martin *B*

Texas

Angelina College *A*
Brookhaven College *A*
Collin County Community College
District *C,A*
Del Mar College *A*
ITT Technical Institute:
Arlington *A*
Laredo Junior College *C,A*
LeTourneau University *B*
Mountain View College *A*
Odessa College *C,A*
Prairie View A&M University *B*
St. Philip's College *A*
Texas Southmost College *A*
Texas State Technical College:
Waco *C,A*
Texas Tech University *B*
University of Houston
Downtown *B*
Houston *B*

Utah

Weber State University *A,B*

Vermont

Vermont Technical College *A*

Virginia

Dabney S. Lancaster Community
College *C*
New River Community College *A*
Patrick Henry Community
College *C*
Southwest Virginia Community
College *A*
Virginia Highlands Community
College *C*

Washington

Cogswell College North *B*
Spokane Community College *A*

West Virginia

Bluefield State College *A,B*
West Virginia Institute of
Technology *A,B*
West Virginia State College *A*

Wisconsin

Mid-State Technical College *C*
Milwaukee School of Engineering *B*
Waukesha County Technical
College *A*

Wyoming

Sheridan College *A*

Mexico

Sistema Instituto Tecnologico y de
Estudios Superiores de
Monterrey *M*

Electrodiagnostic technologies

Alabama

John C. Calhoun State Community
College *A*
Lawson State Community
College *A*
Northeast Alabama State Junior
College *A*
Walker College *A*

California

Orange Coast College *C,A*
San Joaquin Delta College *A*

Florida

Barry University *B*
Miami-Dade Community College
C,A
Santa Fe Community College *A*

Iowa

Kirkwood Community College *A*
Scott Community College *A*

Maryland

Harford Community College *A*

Massachusetts

Laboure College *A*
Middlesex Community College *A*

Minnesota

Anoka-Ramsey Community
College *A*

New Hampshire

New Hampshire Technical College:
Stratham *A*

New York

Niagara County Community College
C,A

Ohio

Cincinnati Technical College *C*
University of Toledo *C,A*

Washington

Spokane Community College *A*

Wisconsin

Western Wisconsin Technical
College *A*

Electromechanical technology

Alabama

Alabama Agricultural and
Mechanical University *A,B*
Bessemer State Technical College *C*
Community College of the Air
Force *A*
Jefferson State Community
College *A*

Arizona

Mesa Community College *C*
Pima Community College *C,A*
Rio Salado Community College *A*

Arkansas

North Arkansas Community
College *A*
Southern Arkansas University:
Technical Branch *A*

California

Chabot College *A*
City College of San Francisco *A*
Cosumnes River College *C*
Long Beach City College *C,A*
Los Angeles Harbor College *C,A*
Los Angeles Mission College *A*
Los Angeles Trade and Technical
College *C,A*
Moorpark College *A*
Ohlone College *C,A*

Connecticut

Norwalk State Technical College *A*
Thames Valley State Technical
College *A*

Delaware

Delaware Technical and
Community College: Terry
Campus *A*

Florida

Broward Community College *A*
Central Florida Community
College *A*
Daytona Beach Community
College *A*
Gulf Coast Community College *A*
Manatee Community College *A*
Miami-Dade Community College *A*

Georgia

Athens Area Technical Institute *A*
Augusta Technical Institute *A*
Clayton State College *A*
DeKalb Technical Institute *A*
Gainesville College *A*
Savannah Technical Institute *C,A*

Idaho

Idaho State University *A*

Illinois

College of DuPage *A*
College of Lake County *C,A*
Illinois Central College *C,A*
Joliet Junior College *A*
Lewis and Clark Community
College *A*
Morrison Institute of Technology *A*

Indiana

Indiana State University *B*
Purdue University *A,B*

Iowa

Des Moines Area Community
College *A*
Kirkwood Community College *A*
North Iowa Area Community
College *A*
Northwest Iowa Technical
College *A*

Kentucky

Morehead State University *A*

Maine

Central Maine Technical College
C,A

Maryland

Allegany Community College *A*
Cecil Community College *A*
Montgomery College: Germantown
Campus *A*

Massachusetts

Berkshire Community College *A*
Bristol Community College *A*
Franklin Institute of Boston *A*
Massasoit Community College *A*
North Shore Community College *A*
Springfield Technical Community
College *A*

Michigan

Charles Stewart Mott Community
College *A*
Jordan College *A*
Lansing Community College *A*
Macomb Community College *A*
Michigan Technological
University *A*
Northern Michigan University *A*
Oakland Community College *A*
Wayne State University *B*

Minnesota

Northwestern Electronics
Institute *A*
St. Paul Technical College *C*

Mississippi

Southwest Mississippi Community
College *A*

Missouri

Southwest Missouri State
University *B*

Nebraska

Central Community College *C,A*
Southeast Community College:
Milford Campus *A*

New Hampshire

New Hampshire Technical College
Berlin *A*
Manchester *A*
Nashua *A*
Stratham *A*

New Jersey

Camden County College *A*
Fairleigh Dickinson University *B*
Union County College *A*

New Mexico

New Mexico State University
Carlsbad *A*
Las Cruces *A,B*

New York

Bramson ORT Technical
Institute *A*
Broome Community College *A*
City University of New York
City College *B*
College of Staten Island *A*
New York City Technical
College *A*
Dutchess Community College *A*
Erie Community College: North
Campus *A*
New York Institute of
Technology *B*
Rockland Community College *A*
State University of New York
College of Agriculture and
Technology at Morrisville *A*
College at Buffalo *B*
College of Technology at
Alfred *A,B*
College of Technology at
Canton *A*
Westchester Community College *A*

North Carolina

Alamance Community College *A*
Bladen Community College *C*
Blue Ridge Community College *A*
Durham Technical Community
College *C*
Forsyth Technical Community
College *A*
Haywood Community College *A*
Rockingham Community College *A*
Wake Technical Community
College *A*
Wilkes Community College *C,A*

North Dakota

North Dakota State College of
Science *A*

Ohio

Central Ohio Technical College *A*
Cincinnati Technical College *A*

Columbus State Community
College *A*
Edison State Community College *A*
Lorain County Community
College *A*
Miami University: Hamilton
Campus *A*
Northwest Technical College *A*
Owens Technical College
Findlay Campus *A*
Toledo *C,A*
Shawnee State University *A*
Sinclair Community College *A*
Southern State Community
College *A*
Terra Technical College *C,A*

Oklahoma

Rose State College *A*
Tulsa Junior College *A*

Oregon

Chemeketa Community College *A*

Pennsylvania

Butler County Community
College *A*
Luzerne County Community
College *A*
Northampton County Area
Community College *A*
Pennsylvania Institute of
Technology *A*

South Carolina

Aiken Technical College *A*
Tri-County Technical College *A*

South Dakota

Western Dakota Vocational
Technical Institute *C,A*

Tennessee

Cleveland State Community
College *C*

Texas

Angelina College *A*
Brookhaven College *C,A*
Lee College *A*
Mountain View College *A*
Richland College *A*
San Jacinto College: Central
Campus *A*
Tarrant County Junior College *A*
Texas State Technical College
Amarillo *A*
Harlingen *A*
Western Texas College *A*

Utah

Utah Valley Community College *A*
Weber State University *A*

Vermont

Vermont Technical College *A*

Virginia

Tidewater Community College *C*

Washington

Clark College *A*
North Seattle Community
College *A*
Pierce College *A*

Wisconsin

Chippewa Valley Technical
College *A*
Fox Valley Technical College *A*
Moraine Park Technical College *A*

Northeast Wisconsin Technical
College *A*
Western Wisconsin Technical
College *A*

Wyoming

Sheridan College *A*

Mexico

Sistema Instituto Tecnologico y de
Estudios Superiores de
Monterrey *B*

Electron physics

Florida

University of Florida *M,D*

Illinois

Southern Illinois University at
Carbondale *B*

Massachusetts

Massachusetts Institute of
Technology *B,M,D,W*

New Jersey

Stevens Institute of Technology
B,M,D

New York

Columbia University *M,D*

Ohio

Ohio State University: Columbus
Campus *B,M,D*

Puerto Rico

University of Puerto Rico: Humacao
University College *B*

Electronic technology

Alabama

Athens State College *B*
Bessemer State Technical College *A*
Community College of the Air
Force *A*
Gadsden State Community
College *A*
Jefferson State Community
College *A*
John C. Calhoun State Community
College *C,A*
John M. Patterson State Technical
College *A*
Reid State Technical College *A*
RETS Electronic Institute *A*
Shelton State Community College
C,A
Shoals Community College *A*
Snead State Junior College *A*
Walker State Technical College *C,A*
Wallace State Community College
at Hanceville *C,A*

Alaska

University of Alaska
Anchorage *C,A*
Fairbanks *A*

Arizona

Arizona State University *B*
Cochise College *A*
DeVry Institute of Technology:
Phoenix *A,B*

Eastern Arizona College *A*
Glendale Community College *A*
ITT Technical Institute
Phoenix *A*
Tucson *A*
Mesa Community College *C,A*
Northland Pioneer College *C,A*
Pima Community College *C,A*
Rio Salado Community College *A*
Scottsdale Community College *A*
Yavapai College *C*

Arkansas

Arkansas State University: Beebe
Branch *A*
Garland County Community
College *A*
National Education Center:
Arkansas College of
Technology *A*
Southern Arkansas University:
Technical Branch *A*
University of Arkansas at Little
Rock *A,B*
Westark Community College *A*

California

Allan Hancock College *C,A*
American Armenian International
College *B*
Barstow College *C*
California State University: Long
Beach *B*
Cerro Coso Community College
C,A
Chabot College *A*
Chaffey Community College *C,A*
City College of San Francisco *C,A*
Cogswell Polytechnical College *A,B*
College of the Redwoods *C,A*
College of the Sequoias *A*
Cosumnes River College *A*
De Anza College *C,A*
DeVry Institute of Technology: City
of Industry *A,B*
Don Bosco Technical Institute *A*
Evergreen Valley College *C*
Foothill College *A*
Fresno City College *C,A*
ITT Technical Institute
Buena Park *A,B*
Sacramento *A*
West Covina *A*
Long Beach City College *C,A*
Los Angeles City College *C,A*
Los Angeles Pierce College *C,A*
Los Angeles Trade and Technical
College *C,A*
Los Angeles Valley College *C,A*
Moorpark College *A*
Mount San Antonio College *C,A*
Mount San Jacinto College *C*
Napa Valley College *C*
Ohlone College *C,A*
Orange Coast College *C,A*
Oxnard College *A*
Pacific Union College *A,B*
Palomar College *C,A*
Phillips Junior College
Condie Campus *C,A*
Fresno Campus *C,A*
Saddleback College *C,A*
San Diego City College *C,A*
San Jose State University *B*
Santa Barbara City College *C,A*
Santa Monica College *C,A*
Santa Rosa Junior College *C,A*
Sierra College *C,A*
Solano Community College *A*
Southwestern College *C,A*
Taft College *A*

United States International
University *B*
University of La Verne *B*
Ventura College *A*
Victor Valley College *C,A*
Yuba College *C,A*

Colorado

Aims Community College *A*
Arapahoe Community College *A*
Colorado Technical College *A,B*
Community College of Denver *C,A*
Denver Institute of Technology *A*
Denver Technical College *A*
Front Range Community College
C,A
ITT Technical Institute: Aurora *A,B*
Mesa State College *C,A*
Metropolitan State College of
Denver *B*
Morgan Community College *A*
Pikes Peak Community College *A*
Pueblo Community College *A*
Red Rocks Community College *C,A*
Trinidad State Junior College *A*
University of Southern Colorado *B*

Connecticut

Thames Valley State Technical
College *C*
University of Hartford *A,B*
Waterbury State Technical
College *A*

Delaware

Delaware Technical and
Community College
Southern Campus *A*
Stanton/Wilmington
Campus *A*
Terry Campus *A*

District of Columbia

University of the District of
Columbia *A*

Florida

Brevard Community College *A*
Central Florida Community
College *A*
Daytona Beach Community College
C,A
Florida Agricultural and Mechanical
University *B*
Florida Community College at
Jacksonville *A*
Florida Keys Community College *A*
Gulf Coast Community College *C,A*
Indian River Community College *A*
ITT Technical Institute: Tampa *A*
Lake City Community College *A*
Manatee Community College *A*
Miami-Dade Community College
C,A
National Education Center: Bauder
Campus *A*
New England Institute of
Technology *A*
Okaloosa-Walton Community
College *C,A*
Palm Beach Community College *A*
Pasco-Hernando Community
College *C,A*
Pensacola Junior College *A*
St. Johns River Community
College *A*
St. Petersburg Junior College *A*
Santa Fe Community College *A*
Seminole Community College *A*
South Florida Community
College *A*
Southern College *A*

United Electronics Institute *A*
University of Central Florida *B*
Valencia Community College *A*

Georgia

Athens Area Technical Institute *A*
Augusta College *A*
Augusta Technical Institute *A*
Bainbridge College *A*
Brunswick College *C,A*
Chattahoochee Technical
Institute *C*
Clayton State College *C,A*
Columbus College *A*
DeKalb Technical Institute *A*
DeVry Institute of Technology:
Atlanta *A,B*
Floyd College *A*
Georgia Southwestern College *A*
Macon College *A*
Savannah State College *A,B*
Savannah Technical Institute *C,A*
Waycross College *A*

Hawaii

Brigham Young University-Hawaii
A,B
University of Hawaii
Honolulu Community
College *A*
Kauai Community College *C,A*

Idaho

Boise State University *A*
Idaho State University *A*
ITT Technical Institute: Boise *A*
Lewis Clark State College *A*
Ricks College *A*

Illinois

Belleville Area College *C,A*
Black Hawk College *A*
City Colleges of Chicago: Richard J.
Daley College *C,A*
College of DuPage *C,A*
College of Lake County *C,A*
DeVry Institute of Technology
Chicago *A,B*
Lombard *A,B*
East-West University *A,B*
Elgin Community College *C,A*
Highland Community College *A*
Illinois Central College *A*
Illinois Eastern Community
Colleges: Wabash Valley
College *A*
Illinois Valley Community
College *A*
ITT Technical Institute: Hoffman
Estates *A*
John A. Logan College *A*
Joliet Junior College *C,A*
Kishwaukee College *A*
Lake Land College *C,A*
Lincoln Land Community College
C,A
Moraine Valley Community College
C,A
Morton College *C,A*
Oakton Community College *C,A*
Parkland College *A*
Parks College of St. Louis
University *A,B*
Prairie State College *A*
Richland Community College *A*
Rock Valley College *A*
Roosevelt University *B*
Shawnee Community College *A*
Southern Illinois University at
Carbondale *A,B*
Triton College *C,A*

Waubonsee Community College
C,A
William Rainey Harper College *A*

Indiana

Indiana Institute of Technology *A,B*
Indiana State University *B*
Indiana University—Purdue
University at Indianapolis *A,B*
Indiana Vocational Technical
College
Central Indiana *A*
Columbus *C,A*
Eastcentral *C,A*
Kokomo *C,A*
Lafayette *C,A*
Northcentral *C,A*
Northeast *C,A*
Northwest *C,A*
Southcentral *C,A*
Southeast *A*
Southwest *A*
Wabash Valley *A*
Whitewater *A*
ITT Technical Institute
Evansville *A*
Fort Wayne *A*
Indianapolis *A,B*
Vincennes University *A*

Iowa

Clinton Community College *A*
Des Moines Area Community
College *A*
Hamilton Technical College *A,B*
Hawkeye Institute of Technology *A*
Indian Hills Community College *A*
Iowa Central Community College *A*
Iowa Western Community
College *A*
Kirkwood Community College *A*
National Education Center:
National Institute of Technology
Campus *A*
North Iowa Area Community
College *A*
Northeast Iowa Community
College *A*
Northwest Iowa Technical
College *A*
Southeastern Community College:
North Campus *A*
Southwestern Community
College *A*

Kansas

Allen County Community
College *A*
Butler County Community College
C,A
Dodge City Community College
C,A
Hesston College *A*
Hutchinson Community College *A*
Johnson County Community
College *A*
Kansas City Kansas Community
College *A*
Kansas State University *B*
Neosho County Community College
C,A
Pittsburg State University *B*
Washburn University of Topeka *A*

Kentucky

Institute of Electronic
Technology *A*
Jefferson Community College *A*
Kentucky State University *A*
Lexington Community College *A*
Louisville Technical Institute *A*
Maysville Community College *A*

Morehead State University *A*
National Education Center:
Kentucky College of Technology
Campus *A*
Northern Kentucky University *A,B*
St. Catharine College *A*

Louisiana

Grambling State University *B*
Grantham College of Engineering
A,B
Louisiana Tech University *B*
McNeese State University *A,B*
Northwestern State University *A,B*
Phillips Junior College: New
Orleans *A*
Southern University in
Shreveport *A*
Southern University and
Agricultural and Mechanical
College *A,B*

Maine

Central Maine Technical College
C,A
Eastern Maine Technical College *A*
Southern Maine Technical
College *A*

Maryland

Capitol College *A,B*
Catonsville Community College *C,A*
Cecil Community College *C,A*
Charles County Community College
C,A
Chesapeake College *C,A*
Frederick Community College *A*
Hagerstown Junior College *A*
Harford Community College *C,A*
Howard Community College *C,A*
Montgomery College: Rockville
Campus *A*
New Community College of
Baltimore *A*
Prince George's Community College
C,A
University of Maryland: Eastern
Shore *B*

Massachusetts

Bristol Community College *A*
Bunker Hill Community College
C,A
Fitchburg State College *B*
Franklin Institute of Boston *C,A*
Holyoke Community College *A*
Massachusetts Bay Community
College *C,A*
Massasoit Community College *A*
Middlesex Community College *A*
Mount Wachusett Community
College *A*
Northern Essex Community
College *A*
Quinsigamond Community
College *A*
Roxbury Community College *A*
Springfield Technical Community
College *A*
University of Massachusetts at
Lowell *A,B*
Wentworth Institute of Technology
A,B

Michigan

Baker College: Flint *A,B*
Central Michigan University *B*
Charles Stewart Mott Community
College *A*
Delta College *A*
Ferris State University *B*
Glen Oaks Community College *C*

Grand Rapids Community College
C,A
Henry Ford Community College A
Jackson Community College A
Kalamazoo Valley Community
College C,A
Kellogg Community College A
Lansing Community College A
Macomb Community College C,A
Montcalm Community College A
Muskegon Community College A
Northern Michigan University A,B
Northwestern Michigan College A
Oakland Community College C,A
St. Clair County Community
College A
Schoolcraft College C,A
Southwestern Michigan College A
Wayne State University B
West Shore Community College A

Minnesota

Alexandria Technical College A
Mankato State University B
National Education Center: Brown
Institute Campus A
Northwestern Electronics
Institute A
Rochester Community College A
St. Paul Technical College C
Willmar Technical College C

Mississippi

Alcorn State University B
Copiah-Lincoln Community
College A
Hinds Community College A
Holmes Community College A
Jackson State University B
Jones County Junior College A
Meridian Community College A
Mississippi Delta Community
College A
Mississippi Gulf Coast Community
College
Jackson County Campus A
Jefferson Davis Campus A
Northeast Mississippi Community
College A
Phillips Junior College
Jackson A
Mississippi Gulf Coast A

Missouri

Central Missouri State University A
DeVry Institute of Technology:
Kansas City A,B
East Central College A
ITT Technical Institute: St. Louis A
Jefferson College A
Lincoln University A
Longview Community College C,A
Maple Woods Community College
C,A
Mineral Area College C,A
Missouri Western State College A,B
Moberly Area Community College
C,A
Penn Valley Community College
C,A
St. Charles Community College A
St. Louis Community College
Florissant Valley A
Forest Park A
Meramec A
Southeast Missouri State University
C,B
Southwest Missouri State
University B
State Fair Community College C,A
Washington University B

Montana

Miles Community College C,A
Montana State University B
Northern Montana College A,B

Nebraska

Metropolitan Community College
C,A
Peru State College B
Southeast Community College
Lincoln Campus C,A
Milford Campus A
University of Nebraska
Lincoln A,B
Omaha A,B
Western Nebraska Community
College: Sidney Campus A

Nevada

Truckee Meadows Community
College C,A
Western Nevada Community
College C,A

New Hampshire

Keene State College A,B
New Hampshire Technical College
Manchester A
Nashua A
Stratham C,A

New Jersey

Atlantic Community College C,A
Brookdale Community College A
Burlington County College A
Camden County College A
County College of Morris A
Essex County College A
Gloucester County College C,A
Kean College of New Jersey B
Mercer County Community College
C,A
Ocean County College A
Thomas Edison State College C,A,B
Trenton State College B
Union County College A

New Mexico

Albuquerque Technical-Vocational
Institute A
Eastern New Mexico University A
New Mexico Highlands University
A,B
New Mexico State University
Carlsbad A
Las Cruces A,B
Northern New Mexico Community
College C,A
San Juan College A

New York

Bramson ORT Technical Institute
C,A
Bryant & Stratton Business Institute
Albany A
Buffalo A
City University of New York:
Queensborough Community
College A
College of Aeronautics A
Corning Community College A
Mohawk Valley Community College
C,A
Monroe Community College C,A
Orange County Community
College A
State University of New York
College of Agriculture and
Technology at Morrisville A
College of Technology at
Canton A
Taylor Business Institute A

University of the State of New
York: Regents College A,B
Westchester Community College C

North Carolina

Alamance Community College A
Anson Community College C,A
Asheville Buncombe Technical
Community College A
Beaufort County Community
College A
Blue Ridge Community College A
Brunswick Community College C,A
Caldwell Community College and
Technical Institute A
Cape Fear Community College A
Catawba Valley Community
College A
Central Carolina Community
College A
Central Piedmont Community
College A
Cleveland Community College A
Coastal Carolina Community
College A
College of the Albemarle A
Craven Community College A
Davidson County Community
College A
Durham Technical Community
College C,A
Edgecombe Community College C
Fayetteville Technical Community
College A
Forsyth Technical Community
College A
Gaston College A
Guilford Technical Community
College C,A
Haywood Community College A
Isothermal Community College C
James Sprunt Community
College C
Johnston Community College A
Mayland Community College A
McDowell Technical Community
College A
Nash Community College A
Piedmont Community College C
Pitt Community College A
Sampson Community College A
Sandhills Community College C,A
Southwestern Community
College A
Stanly Community College A
Surry Community College A
Wake Technical Community
College A
Western Carolina University B
Wilkes Community College C,A

North Dakota

Bismarck State College C,A
North Dakota State College of
Science A
University of North Dakota: Lake
Region A

Ohio

Bowling Green State University
Bowling Green B
Firelands College A
Central Ohio Technical College A
Cincinnati Metropolitan College A
Cincinnati Technical College A
Clark State Community College C
Cleveland Institute of Electronics
C,A
Cleveland State University B
Columbus State Community
College A

Cuyahoga Community College:
Metropolitan Campus A
DeVry Institute of Technology:
Columbus A,B
Edison State Community College
C,A
ETI Technical College B
Franklin University A,B
Hocking Technical College A
ITT Technical Institute
Dayton A
Youngstown A
Jefferson Technical College A
Kent State University
Kent B
Tuscarawas Campus C,A
Lakeland Community College C,A
Marion Technical College A
Muskingum Area Technical
College A
North Central Technical College A
Northwest Technical College A
Owens Technical College
Findlay Campus A
Toledo C,A
Sinclair Community College A
Southern Ohio College C
Southern State Community
College A
Stark Technical College A
Terra Technical College A
University of Akron A,B
University of Dayton B
University of Rio Grande A
University of Toledo A,B
Washington State Community
College A
Wright State University: Lake
Campus A

Oklahoma

Cameron University B
Eastern Oklahoma State College A
Oklahoma Junior College A
Oklahoma State University
Oklahoma City A
Stillwater B
Technical Branch:
Okmulgee A
Redlands Community College C,A
Rose State College C,A
Southeastern Oklahoma State
University B
Tulsa Junior College C,A

Oregon

Central Oregon Community
College A
Chemeketa Community College A
Clatsop Community College C
ITT Technical Institute: Portland A
Linn-Benton Community College A
Mount Hood Community College
C,A
Oregon Institute of Technology A,B
Portland Community College C,A
Southwestern Oregon Community
College A
Umpqua Community College C,A

Pennsylvania

Berean Institute A
Butler County Community
College A
CHI Institute A
Community College of Beaver
County A
Community College of Philadelphia
C,A
Delaware County Community
College A

Harrisburg Area Community
College C,A
ICS Center for Degree Studies A
Johnson Technical Institute A
Lehigh County Community
College A
Luzerne County Community
College C,A
Montgomery County Community
College A
Northampton County Area
Community College A
Penn State
Erie Behrend College A
University Park Campus C,A
Penn Technical Institute A
Pennsylvania College of
Technology A
Pennsylvania Institute of
Technology A
Reading Area Community
College A
Spring Garden College A,B
Westmoreland County Community
College A

Puerto Rico

Columbia College A
Electronic Data Processing College
of Puerto Rico A
Inter American University of Puerto
Rico
Metropolitan Campus B
San German Campus B
University of Puerto Rico
Aguadilla A
Bayamon Technological
University College A,B
Humacao University
College A

Rhode Island

Community College of Rhode
Island A
Johnson & Wales University A
New England Institute of
Technology A
New England Technical College B

South Carolina

Aiken Technical College A
Bob Jones University B
Chesterfield-Marlboro Technical
College A
Denmark Technical College A
Florence-Darlington Technical
College A
Francis Marion College B
Greenville Technical College A
Horry-Georgetown Technical
College A
Midlands Technical College C,A
Nielsen Electronics Institute A
Sumter Area Technical College A
Technical College of the
Lowcountry C
Tri-County Technical College C,A
Trident Technical College A

South Dakota

Mitchell Vocational Technical
Institute C,A
National College A
South Dakota State University B
Western Dakota Vocational
Technical Institute C,A

Tennessee

Austin Peay State University A,B
Chattanooga State Technical
Community College A

Columbia State Community College
C,A
East Tennessee State University B
ITT Technical Institute:
Nashville A
Memphis State University B
Motlow State Community
College A
Nashville State Technical
Institute A
Northeast State Technical
Community College A
Pellissippi State Technical
Community College A
State Technical Institute at
Memphis A

Texas

Alvin Community College C,A
Amarillo College A
Angelina College A
Austin Community College C,A
Collin County Community College
District C,A
Cooke County College A
Del Mar College A
DeVry Institute of Technology:
Irving A,B
Eastfield College A
El Paso Community College C,A
Houston Community College A
ITT Technical Institute:
Arlington A
Lamar University—Beaumont A
Laredo Junior College C,A
Midland College A
Midwestern State University B
Mountain View College C,A
North Harris Montgomery
Community College District C,A
North Lake College A
Odessa College C,A
Richland College C,A
St. Philip's College A
San Antonio College A
South Plains College A
Tarrant County Junior College A
Temple Junior College A
Texas Southmost College A
Texas State Technical College
Amarillo A
Harlingen A
Sweetwater C,A
Waco A
University of Houston
Downtown B
Houston B
Vernon Regional Junior College A
Weatherford College C,A
Wharton County Junior College A

Utah

Brigham Young University B
ITT Technical Institute: Salt Lake
City A
Utah Valley Community College
C,A
Weber State University A,B

Vermont

Champlain College A
Vermont Technical College A

Virginia

Blue Ridge Community College A
Central Virginia Community
College A
Commonwealth College A
Dabney S. Lancaster Community
College A
Eastern Shore Community College
C,A

John Tyler Community College C,A
Lord Fairfax Community College A
Mountain Empire Community
College A
New River Community College A
Norfolk State University A
Northern Virginia Community
College C
Patrick Henry Community
College A
Paul D. Camp Community
College A
Piedmont Virginia Community
College C,A
Southside Virginia Community
College A
Southwest Virginia Community
College C,A
Virginia Highlands Community
College A
Wytheville Community College A

Washington

Central Washington University B
Centralia College A
Clark College A
Cogswell College North A,B
Columbia Basin College A
Eastern Washington University B
Edmonds Community College C,A
Everett Community College A
Green River Community College A
ITT Technical Institute
Seattle A
Spokane A
Lower Columbia College A
North Seattle Community
College A
Olympic College C,A
Peninsula College A
Pierce College A
Skagit Valley College C,A
South Puget Sound Community
College A
Spokane Community College A
Western Washington University B

West Virginia

College of West Virginia A
Fairmont State College A,B
Marshall University A
Potomac State College of West
Virginia University A
Shepherd College A
West Virginia Institute of
Technology B
West Virginia Northern Community
College A
West Virginia State College A
West Virginia University at
Parkersburg A

Wisconsin

Chippewa Valley Technical
College A
Fox Valley Technical College A
Madison Area Technical College A
Mid-State Technical College A
Northeast Wisconsin Technical
College A
Stratton College A
Western Wisconsin Technical
College A
Wisconsin School of Electronics A

Wyoming

Casper College A

**American Samoa, Caroline
Islands, Guam, Marianas,
Virgin Islands**

Guam Community College C,A

Elementary education

Alabama

Alabama Agricultural and
Mechanical University B,M
Alabama Southern Community
College A
Alabama State University B,M
Athens State College B
Auburn University
Auburn B,M,D
Montgomery B,M
Birmingham-Southern College B
Brewer State Junior College A
Chattahoochee Valley Community
College A
Faulkner University B
Huntingdon College B
Jacksonville State University B,M
James H. Faulkner State
Community College A
John C. Calhoun State Community
College A
Judson College B
Livingston University B,M
Miles College B
Mobile College B,M
Oakwood College B
Samford University B,M
Shelton State Community
College A
Snead State Junior College A
Southeastern Bible College B
Spring Hill College B,M
Stillman College B
Troy State University
Dothan B,M
Montgomery M
Troy B,M
Tuskegee University B,M
University of Alabama
Birmingham B,M
Huntsville B
Tuscaloosa B,M,D,W
University of Montevallo B,M
University of North Alabama B,M
University of South Alabama B,M

Alaska

Alaska Pacific University B,M
Sheldon Jackson College B
University of Alaska
Anchorage B,M
Fairbanks B
Southeast B

Arizona

American Indian Bible College B
Arizona College of the Bible B
Arizona State University B,M,D
Eastern Arizona College A
Grand Canyon University B,M
Navajo Community College A
Northern Arizona University B,M
Pima Community College A
Prescott College B
Southwestern College B
University of Arizona B,M,D
Yavapai College A

Arkansas

Arkansas Baptist College B
Arkansas College B
Arkansas State University B,M

Arkansas Tech University *B,M*
Central Baptist College *B*
Harding University *B,M*
Henderson State University *B,M*
Hendrix College *B*
John Brown University *B*
Ouachita Baptist University *B*
Philander Smith College *B*
Shorter College *A*
Southern Arkansas University *B,M*
University of Arkansas
    Fayetteville *B,M*
    Little Rock *B,M*
    Monticello *B*
    Pine Bluff *B*
University of Central Arkansas *B,M*
University of the Ozarks *B*
Westark Community College *A*

California

Azusa Pacific University *B*
Barstow College *C,A*
Bethany College *B*
Biola University *B*
California Baptist College *B*
California Lutheran University *B,M*
California Polytechnic State
    University: San Luis Obispo *B*
California State University
    Bakersfield *B,M*
    Dominguez Hills *M*
    Fresno *B*
    Fullerton *M*
    Long Beach *M*
    Los Angeles *M*
    Northridge *M*
    Sacramento *B,M*
    San Bernardino *M*
Chapman University *B*
Christ College Irvine *B*
Christian Heritage College *B*
College of Notre Dame *M*
Crafton Hills College *A*
Fresno Pacific College *B*
Humboldt State University *C*
Imperial Valley College *A*
John F. Kennedy University *M*
Kings River Community College *A*
La Sierra University *B,M*
Master's College *B*
Mills College *M*
Mount St. Mary's College *B*
National Hispanic University *B*
National University *M*
Occidental College *M*
Pacific Christian College *B*
Pacific Oaks College *B,M*
Pacific Union College *B,M*
Patten College *C*
Pepperdine University *B,M*
Point Loma Nazarene College *M*
St. Mary's College of California *B,M*
San Diego State University *M*
San Francisco State University *M*
San Jose State University *M*
Santa Clara University *M*
Simpson College *B*
Sonoma State University *B*
Southern California College *B*
United States International
    University *B,M*
University of California
    Los Angeles *M*
    Santa Barbara *M*
University of La Verne *B,M*
University of the Pacific *B,M,D*
University of Redlands *B*
University of San Diego *B*
University of San Francisco *B,M*
University of Southern California *B,M,W*

Westmont College *B*

Colorado

Adams State College *B,M*
Colorado Christian University *B*
Colorado College *M*
Fort Lewis College *B*
Regis College of Regis University *B*
University of Colorado
    Boulder *B*
    Colorado Springs *B,M*
    Denver *B,M*
University of Northern Colorado *M,D*
University of Southern Colorado *B*
Western State College of
    Colorado *B*

Connecticut

Central Connecticut State
    University *B,M*
Connecticut College *M*
Eastern Connecticut State
    University *B,M*
Sacred Heart University *B,M*
St. Joseph College *B,M*
Southern Connecticut State
    University *B,M*
University of Bridgeport *B,M*
University of Connecticut *B*
University of Hartford *B,M,W*
Western Connecticut State
    University *B,M*

Delaware

Delaware State College *B*
University of Delaware *B*
Wesley College *B*
Wilmington College *B*

District of Columbia

American University *B,M*
Catholic University of America *B*
Gallaudet University *B*
George Washington University *M*
Howard University *B,M*
Trinity College *B,M*
University of the District of
    Columbia *B*

Florida

Barry University *B*
Bethune-Cookman College *B*
Central Florida Community
    College *A*
Daytona Beach Community
    College *A*
Eckerd College *B*
Flagler College *B*
Florida Agricultural and Mechanical
    University *B,M*
Florida Atlantic University *B,M,D*
Florida Bible College *A,B*
Florida Christian College *B*
Florida International University *B,M*
Florida Memorial College *B*
Florida Southern College *B*
Florida State University *B,M,D*
Gulf Coast Community College *A*
Hobe Sound Bible College *B*
Indian River Community College *A*
Jacksonville University *B,M*
Lynn University *B*
Manatee Community College *A*
Miami-Dade Community College *A*
Nova University *B,M,D*
Okaloosa-Walton Community
    College *A*
Palm Beach Atlantic College *B*
Palm Beach Community College *A*
Pensacola Junior College *A*

Rollins College *B,M*
St. Leo College *B*
St. Thomas University *B,M*
Southeastern College of the
    Assemblies of God *B*
Stetson University *B,M*
University of Central Florida *B,M*
University of Florida *B,M*
University of Miami *B,M*
University of North Florida *B,M*
University of South Florida *B,M*
University of Tampa *B*
University of West Florida *B,M*
Warner Southern College *B*

Georgia

Andrew College *A*
Armstrong State College *B,M*
Atlanta Christian College *B*
Atlanta Metropolitan College *A*
Augusta College *B,M*
Bainbridge College *A*
Berry College *B,M*
Brenau Women's College *B*
Brewton-Parker College *A,B*
Clark Atlanta University *B*
Clayton State College *A*
Columbus College *B,M*
Covenant College *B*
Darton College *A*
East Georgia College *A*
Emory University *B,M*
Floyd College *A*
Fort Valley State College *B,M*
Gainesville College *A*
Georgia College *B,M*
Georgia Southern University *B,M*
Georgia Southwestern College *B,M*
Kennesaw State College *B*
LaGrange College *B,M*
Macon College *A*
Mercer University
    Atlanta *M*
    Macon *B,M*
Morehouse College *B*
Morris Brown College *B*
North Georgia College *B,M*
Oglethorpe University *B,M*
Paine College *B*
Piedmont College *B*
Shorter College *B*
Thomas College *A*
University of Georgia *B,M,D*
Valdosta State College *B,M*
Waycross College *A*
Wesleyan College *B*
West Georgia College *B,M*

Hawaii

Brigham Young University-
    Hawaii *B*
Chaminade University of
    Honolulu *B*
University of Hawaii
    Hilo *W*
    Manoa *B,M*

Idaho

Albertson College *B,M*
Boise State University *B,M*
College of Southern Idaho *A*
Idaho State University *B,M*
Lewis Clark State College *B*
North Idaho College *A*
Northwest Nazarene College *B,M*
Ricks College *A*
University of Idaho *B,M*

Illinois

Augustana College *B*
Aurora University *B*
Barat College *B*

Belleville Area College *A*
Black Hawk College *A*
Blackburn College *B*
Bradley University *B,M*
Chicago State University *B,M*
City Colleges of Chicago: Wright
    College *A*
College of St. Francis *B*
Columbia College *M*
Concordia University *B,M*
De Paul University *B*
Eastern Illinois University *B,M*
Elmhurst College *B*
Eureka College *B*
Governors State University *B*
Greenville College *B*
Hebrew Theological College *B*
Illinois Benedictine College *B*
Illinois Central College *A*
Illinois College *B*
Illinois State University *B*
Illinois Valley Community
    College *A*
Illinois Wesleyan University *B*
John A. Logan College *A*
Joliet Junior College *A*
Judson College *B*
Kishwaukee College *A*
Knox College *B*
Lake Forest College *B*
Lewis University *B*
Lincoln Christian College and
    Seminary *B*
Lincoln Land Community
    College *A*
Loyola University of Chicago *B,M*
MacMurray College *B*
McKendree College *B*
Millikin University *B*
Monmouth College *B*
National-Louis University *B,M*
North Central College *B*
North Park College and Theological
    Seminary *B*
Northeastern Illinois University *B*
Northern Illinois University *B,M,D*
Northwestern University *M*
Olivet Nazarene University *B,M*
Principia College *B*
Quincy College *B*
Rend Lake College *A*
Rock Valley College *A*
Rockford College *B,M*
Roosevelt University *B,M*
St. Xavier University *B*
Southern Illinois University
    Carbondale *B,M,D*
    Edwardsville *B,M*
Trinity Christian College *B*
Trinity College *B*
University of Chicago *M,D*
University of Illinois
    Chicago *B*
    Urbana-Champaign *B,M,D*
Waubonsee Community College *A*
Western Illinois University *B,M*
Wheaton College *B*

Indiana

Anderson University *B*
Ball State University *B,M,D*
Bethel College *B*
Butler University *B,M*
Calumet College of St. Joseph *B*
DePauw University *B*
Franklin College *B*
Goshen College *B*
Grace College *B*
Grace Theological Seminary *M*
Hanover College *B*
Huntington College *B*
Indiana State University *B,M,D*

Indiana University
    Bloomington *B,M,D*
    East *B*
    Kokomo *B,M*
    Northwest *B,M*
    South Bend *B,M*
    Southeast *B,M*
Indiana University—Purdue
  University
    Fort Wayne *B,M*
    Indianapolis *B,M*
Indiana Wesleyan University *B*
Manchester College *B,M*
Marian College *B*
Martin University *B*
Oakland City College *B*
Purdue University
    Calumet *B,M*
    North Central Campus *B,M*
    West Lafayette *B,M,D*
St. Francis College *B,M*
St. Joseph's College *B*
St. Mary-of-the-Woods College *B*
St. Mary's College *B*
Taylor University *B*
Tri-State University *B*
University of Evansville *B*
University of Indianapolis *B,M*
University of Southern Indiana *B*
Valparaiso University *B*
Vincennes University *A*

Iowa
Briar Cliff College *B*
Buena Vista College *B*
Central College *B*
Clarke College *B,M*
Coe College *B*
Cornell College *B*
Dordt College *B*
Drake University *B,M*
Faith Baptist Bible College and
  Theological Seminary *B*
Graceland College *B*
Grand View College *B*
Iowa Lakes Community College *A*
Iowa State University *B,M*
Iowa Wesleyan College *B*
Kirkwood Community College *A*
Loras College *B,M*
Luther College *B*
Maharishi International
  University *M*
Morningside College *B,M*
Mount Mercy College *B*
Mount St. Clare College *B*
North Iowa Area Community
  College *A*
Northwestern College *B,M*
St. Ambrose University *B*
Simpson College *B*
Teikyo Marycrest University *B,M*
Teikyo Westmar University *B*
University of Dubuque *B,M*
University of Iowa *B,M,D*
University of Northern Iowa *B,M*
Upper Iowa University *B*
Vennard College *B*
Wartburg College *B*
William Penn College *B*

Kansas
Allen County Community
  College *A*
Baker University *B*
Barclay College *B*
Benedictine College *B*
Bethany College *B*
Bethel College *B*
Central College *A*
Coffeyville Community College *A*
Colby Community College *A*

Cowley County Community
  College *A*
Emporia State University *B,M*
Fort Hays State University *B,M*
Friends University *B*
Hutchinson Community College *A*
Kansas City College and Bible
  School *B*
Kansas City Kansas Community
  College *A*
Kansas Newman College *B*
Kansas State University *B,M*
Kansas Wesleyan University *B*
Labette Community College *A*
McPherson College *B*
MidAmerica Nazarene College *B*
Neosho County Community
  College *A*
Ottawa University *B*
Pittsburg State University *B,M*
Pratt Community College *A*
St. Mary College *B*
Seward County Community
  College *A*
Southwestern College *B*
Sterling College *B*
Tabor College *B*
University of Kansas *B*
Washburn University of Topeka *B*
Wichita State University *B,M*

Kentucky
Alice Lloyd College *B*
Asbury College *B*
Bellarmine College *B,M*
Berea College *B*
Campbellsville College *B*
Centre College *B*
Cumberland College *B,M*
Eastern Kentucky University *B,M*
Georgetown College *B,M*
Kentucky Christian College *B*
Kentucky State University *B*
Kentucky Wesleyan College *B*
Lindsey Wilson College *B*
Louisville Presbyterian Theological
  Seminary *M*
Morehead State University *B,M*
Murray State University *B,M*
Northern Kentucky University *B,M*
Pikeville College *B*
St. Catharine College *A*
Southeast Community College *A*
Spalding University *B,M*
Sue Bennett College *A*
Thomas More College *B*
Transylvania University *B*
Union College *B,M*
University of Kentucky *B,M*
University of Louisville *B,M*
Western Kentucky University *B,M*

Louisiana
Centenary College of Louisiana *B,M*
Dillard University *B*
Grambling State University *B,M*
Louisiana College *B*
Louisiana State University
    Agricultural and Mechanical
      College *B,M*
    Shreveport *B,M*
Louisiana Tech University *B,M*
Loyola University *B*
McNeese State University *B,M*
Nicholls State University *B,M*
Northeast Louisiana University *B,M*
Northwestern State University *B,M*
Our Lady of Holy Cross College *B*
Southeastern Louisiana University
  B,M
Southern University at New
  Orleans *B*

Southern University and
  Agricultural and Mechanical
  College *B,M*
Tulane University *M*
University of New Orleans *B*
University of Southwestern
  Louisiana *B,M*
World Evangelism Bible College
  and Seminary *B*
Xavier University of Louisiana *B*

Maine
St. Joseph's College *B*
University of Maine
    Farmington *B*
    Fort Kent *B*
    Machias *B*
    Orono *B,M*
    Presque Isle *B*
University of New England *B*
Westbrook College *B*

Maryland
Anne Arundel Community
  College *A*
Baltimore Hebrew University *B,M*
Bowie State University *M*
Catonsville Community College *A*
Cecil Community College *A*
Charles County Community
  College *A*
Chesapeake College *A*
College of Notre Dame of
  Maryland *B*
Columbia Union College *B*
Coppin State College *B*
Dundalk Community College *A*
Frederick Community College *A*
Frostburg State University *M*
Garrett Community College *A*
Goucher College *M*
Harford Community College *A*
Howard Community College *A*
Montgomery College
    Germantown Campus *A*
    Rockville Campus *A*
    Takoma Park Campus *A*
Morgan State University *B,M*
Mount St. Mary's College *B,M*
Prince George's Community
  College *A*
Salisbury State University *M*
Sojourner-Douglass College *B*
Towson State University *M*
University of Maryland: College
  Park *M,D*
Villa Julie College *A*
Western Maryland College *M*

Massachusetts
American International College *B,M*
Anna Maria College for Men and
  Women *B,M*
Assumption College *B*
Atlantic Union College *B*
Boston College *B,M*
Boston University *B,M*
Bradford College *C*
Bridgewater State College *B,M*
Bristol Community College *A*
Curry College *B*
Dean Junior College *A*
Eastern Nazarene College *B,M*
Elms College *B*
Emmanuel College *B*
Endicott College *A,B*
Fitchburg State College *B,M*
Framingham State College *B*
Gordon College *B*
Hampshire College *B*
Hellenic College *B*
Holyoke Community College *A*

Lasell College *B*
Lesley College *B,M*
Merrimack College *B*
Middlesex Community College *A*
North Adams State College *B*
Northeastern University *B*
Pine Manor College *B*
Salem State College *B,M*
Simmons College *B,M*
Smith College *B,M*
Springfield College *B*
Stonehill College *B*
Suffolk University *B,M*
Tufts University *B,M*
Westfield State College *B,M*
Wheelock College *B,M*
Worcester State College *B*

Michigan
Adrian College *B*
Alma College *B*
Andrews University *B,M*
Aquinas College *B*
Calvin College *B*
Central Michigan University *B,M*
Concordia College *B*
Eastern Michigan University *B,M*
Grand Valley State University *B,M*
Hillsdale College *B*
Hope College *B*
Kellogg Community College *A*
Lansing Community College *A*
Madonna University *B*
Marygrove College *B*
Michigan State University *B*
Mid Michigan Community
  College *A*
Muskegon Community College *A*
Northern Michigan University *B,M*
Oakland University *B,M*
Olivet College *B*
Saginaw Valley State University
  B,M
Siena Heights College *B,M*
Spring Arbor College *B*
Suomi College *A*
University of Detroit Mercy *B,M*
University of Michigan
    Ann Arbor *B*
    Flint *B*
Wayne State University *B,M*
Western Michigan University *B,M*

Minnesota
Augsburg College *B*
Bemidji State University *B*
Bethany Lutheran College *A*
Bethel College *B*
College of St. Benedict *B*
College of St. Catherine: St.
  Catherine Campus *B*
College of St. Scholastica *B*
Concordia College: Moorhead *B*
Concordia College: St. Paul *B*
Crown College *B*
Dr. Martin Luther College *B*
Gustavus Adolphus College *B*
Macalester College *B*
Mankato State University *B,M*
Moorhead State University *B,M*
North Central Bible College *B*
Northland Community College *A*
Northwestern College *B*
Pillsbury Baptist Bible College *B*
Rainy River Community College *A*
St. Cloud State University *B,M*
St. John's University *B*
St. Mary's College of Minnesota *B*
St. Olaf College *B*
Southwest State University *B*

University of Minnesota
    Duluth *B*
    Morris *B*
    Twin Cities *B,M*
University of St. Thomas *B*
Vermilion Community College *A*
Willmar Community College *A*
Winona State University *B,M*

Mississippi

Alcorn State University *B,M*
Belhaven College *B*
Blue Mountain College *B*
Copiah-Lincoln Community
    College *A*
Delta State University *B,M*
Holmes Community College *A*
Jackson State University *M,D*
Jones County Junior College *A*
Mary Holmes College *A*
Millsaps College *B*
Mississippi College *B,M*
Mississippi Delta Community
    College *A*
Mississippi Gulf Coast Community
    College
        Jackson County Campus *A*
        Jefferson Davis Campus *A*
Mississippi State University *B,M*
Mississippi University for Women *B*
Northeast Mississippi Community
    College *A*
Rust College *B*
Tougaloo College *B*
University of Mississippi *B,M*
University of Southern
    Mississippi *B*
William Carey College *B,M,W*

Missouri

Avila College *B*
Baptist Bible College *B*
Calvary Bible College *B*
Central Methodist College *B*
Central Missouri State University
    B,M
College of the Ozarks *B*
Columbia College *B*
Culver-Stockton College *B*
Drury College *B*
East Central College *A*
Evangel College *B*
Fontbonne College *B*
Hannibal-LaGrange College *B*
Harris Stowe State College *B*
Jefferson College *A*
Lincoln University *B,M*
Lindenwood College *B,M*
Maryville University *B*
Mineral Area College *A*
Missouri Baptist College *B*
Missouri Southern State College *B*
Missouri Valley College *B*
Missouri Western State College *B*
Moberly Area Community
    College *A*
Northeast Missouri State
    University *M*
Northwest Missouri State
    University *B,M*
Park College *B*
Rockhurst College *B*
St. Louis Community College at
    Meramec *A*
St. Louis University *B*
Southeast Missouri State University
    B,M
Southwest Baptist University *B*
Southwest Missouri State University
    B,M
Stephens College *B*

University of Missouri
    Columbia *B,M,D*
    Kansas City *B,M*
    St. Louis *B,M*
Webster University *B*
Westminster College *B*
William Jewell College *B*
William Woods College *B*

Montana

Carroll College *B*
College of Great Falls *B*
Eastern Montana College *A,B,M*
Miles Community College *A*
Montana State University *B*
Northern Montana College *B,M*
Rocky Mountain College *B*
Salish Kootenai College *A*
Stone Child College *A*
University of Montana *B,M*
Western Montana College of the
    University of Montana *B*

Nebraska

Chadron State College *B,M*
College of St. Mary *B*
Concordia College *B,M*
Creighton University *B,M*
Dana College *B*
Doane College *B*
Grace College of the Bible *B*
Hastings College *B,M*
McCook Community College *A*
Midland Lutheran College *B*
Nebraska Christian College *B*
Nebraska Wesleyan University *B*
Northeast Community College *A*
Peru State College *B,M*
Southeast Community College:
    Beatrice Campus *A*
Union College *B*
University of Nebraska
    Kearney *B,M*
    Lincoln *B,M*
    Omaha *B,M*
Wayne State College *B,M*
Western Nebraska Community
    College: Scottsbluff Campus *A*

Nevada

Sierra Nevada College *B*
University of Nevada
    Las Vegas *B,M,D*
    Reno *B,M*

New Hampshire

Antioch New England Graduate
    School *M*
Colby-Sawyer College *B*
Franklin Pierce College *B*
Keene State College *B*
New England College *B*
Notre Dame College *B*
Plymouth State College of the
    University System of New
    Hampshire *B,M*
Rivier College *B,M*
University of New Hampshire *B,M*

New Jersey

Centenary College *B*
College of St. Elizabeth *B*
Essex County College *A*
Felician College *B*
Glassboro State College *B,M*
Jersey City State College *B*
Kean College of New Jersey *B,M*
Monmouth College *B,M*
Ocean County College *A*
Rider College *B*

Rutgers—The State University of
    New Jersey
        Camden College of Arts and
            Sciences *B*
        Douglass College *B*
        Livingston College *B*
        New Brunswick *M,D*
        Newark College of Arts and
            Sciences *B*
        Rutgers College *B*
        University College New
            Brunswick *B*
        University College Newark *B*
St. Peter's College *B*
Seton Hall University *B,M*
Trenton State College *B,M*
Union County College *A*

New Mexico

College of Santa Fe *B*
College of the Southwest *B*
Eastern New Mexico University
    B,M
New Mexico Highlands University
    A,B
New Mexico Junior College *A*
New Mexico State University *B,M*
University of New Mexico *A,B,M*
Western New Mexico University
    B,M

New York

Adelphi University *B,M*
Alfred University *B,M*
Bank Street College of
    Education *M*
Boricua College *B*
Canisius College *B*
City University of New York
    Baruch College *B,M*
    Brooklyn College *B,M*
    City College *B,M*
    College of Staten Island *M*
    Hunter College *B,M*
    La Guardia Community
        College *A*
    Lehman College *B,M*
    Medgar Evers College *B*
    Queens College *B,M*
    York College *B*
Colgate University *B*
College of New Rochelle *B,M*
College of St. Rose *B,M*
Concordia College *B*
Daemen College *B*
Dominican College of Blauvelt *B*
Dowling College *B,M*
D'Youville College *B*
Elmira College *B*
Fordham University *B,M,D*
Fulton-Montgomery Community
    College *A*
Genesee Community College *A*
Hofstra University *B,M*
Houghton College *B*
Iona College *B,M*
Keuka College *B*
King's College *B*
Le Moyne College *B*
Long Island University
    Brooklyn Campus *B,M*
    C. W. Post Campus *B,M*
    Southampton Campus *B,M*
Manhattan College *B*
Manhattanville College *M*
Marymount College *B*
Medaille College *B*
Molloy College *B*
Mount St. Mary College *B,M*
Nazareth College of Rochester *B,M*
New York University *A,B,M,D*
Niagara University *B,M*

Nyack College *B*
Pace University
    College of White Plains *B*
    Pleasantville/Briarcliff *B*
Roberts Wesleyan College *B*
Russell Sage College *B,M*
Sage Junior College of Albany, A
    Division of Russell Sage
    College *A*
St. Bonaventure University *B,M*
St. Francis College *B*
St. John Fisher College *C*
St. John's University *B,M*
St. Joseph's College
    Brooklyn *B*
    Suffolk Campus *B*
St. Thomas Aquinas College *B*
Sarah Lawrence College *M*
Skidmore College *B*
State University of New York
    Binghamton *M*
    Buffalo *M,D*
    College at Brockport *B,M*
    College at Buffalo *B,M*
    College at Cortland *B,M*
    College at Fredonia *B,M*
    College at Geneseo *B,M*
    College at New Paltz *B,M*
    College at Old Westbury *B*
    College at Oneonta *B,M*
    College at Plattsburgh *B,M*
    College at Potsdam *B,M*
    Oswego *B,M*
Syracuse University *B,M,D*
University of Rochester *M*
Villa Maria College of Buffalo *A*
Wagner College *B,M*
Wells College *B*
Yeshiva University *B*

North Carolina

Appalachian State University *B,M*
Barber-Scotia College *B*
Barton College *B*
Beaufort County Community
    College *A*
Belmont Abbey College *B*
Bennett College *B*
Brevard College *A*
Campbell University *B,M*
Catawba College *B,M*
Catawba Valley Community
    College *A*
Chowan College *B*
Coastal Carolina Community
    College *A*
College of the Albemarle *A*
East Carolina University *B,M*
East Coast Bible College *B*
Elizabeth City State University *B*
Elon College *B,M*
Fayetteville State University *B,M*
Gardner-Webb College *B,M*
Gaston College *A*
Greensboro College *B*
Guilford College *B*
High Point University *B*
Isothermal Community College *A*
John Wesley College *B*
Johnson C. Smith University *B*
Lees-McRae College *B*
Lenoir-Rhyne College *B,M*
Livingstone College *B*
Mars Hill College *B*
Martin Community College *A*
Meredith College *M*
Methodist College *B*
North Carolina Agricultural and
    Technical State University *B,M*
North Carolina Central University
    B,M
North Carolina Wesleyan College *B*

Pembroke State University *B,M*
Pfeiffer College *B*
Piedmont Bible College *B*
Pitt Community College *A*
Queens College *B,M*
St. Andrews Presbyterian College *B*
St. Augustine's College *B*
Salem College *M*
Shaw University *B*
University of North Carolina
   Asheville *C*
   Chapel Hill *B,M,D*
   Charlotte *B,M*
   Greensboro *B,M*
   Wilmington *B,M*
Wake Forest University *B,M*
Warren Wilson College *B*
Western Carolina University *B,M*
Western Piedmont Community
   College *A*
Wingate College *B,M*
Winston-Salem State University *B*

North Dakota

Dickinson State University *B*
Jamestown College *B*
Mayville State University *B*
Minot State University *B,M*
North Dakota State University *B*
Trinity Bible College *B*
Turtle Mountain Community
   College *A*
University of Mary *B,M*
University of North Dakota *B,M*
Valley City State University *B*

Ohio

Ashland University *B*
Baldwin-Wallace College *B*
Bluffton College *B*
Bowling Green State University
   Bowling Green *B,M*
   Firelands College *A*
Capital University *B*
Cedarville College *B*
Central State University *B*
Circleville Bible College *A,B*
Cleveland State University *B,M*
College of Mount St. Joseph *B*
College of Wooster *B*
Defiance College *B*
Franciscan University of
   Steubenville *B*
Heidelberg College *B*
Hiram College *B*
John Carroll University *B,M*
Kent State University *B,M,D*
Lake Erie College *B*
Lorain County Community
   College *A*
Malone College *B*
Marietta College *B*
Miami University: Oxford Campus
   B,M
Mount Union College *B*
Mount Vernon Nazarene College *B*
Muskingum College *B,M*
Notre Dame College of Ohio *B*
Ohio Dominican College *B*
Ohio Northern University *B*
Ohio State University
   Columbus Campus *B,M*
   Lima Campus *B*
   Mansfield Campus *B*
   Marion Campus *B*
   Newark Campus *B*
Ohio University
   Athens *B,M,D*
   Eastern Campus *B,M*
   Southern Campus at Ironton
      A,B
   Zanesville Campus *B*

Ohio Wesleyan University *B*
Otterbein College *B*
Shawnee State University *B*
University of Akron *B,M,D*
University of Cincinnati
   Cincinnati *B,M,D*
   Raymond Walters College *A*
University of Dayton *B,M*
University of Findlay *B*
University of Rio Grande *B*
University of Toledo *B,M,D*
Urbana University *B*
Ursuline College *B*
Walsh College *B*
Wilmington College *B*
Wittenberg University *B*
Wright State University *B,M*
Xavier University *B*
Youngstown State University *B,M*

Oklahoma

Bartlesville Wesleyan College *B*
Cameron University *B,M*
Connors State College *A*
East Central University *B,M*
Eastern Oklahoma State College *A*
Langston University *B,M*
Mid-America Bible College *B*
Murray State College *A*
Northeastern State University *B,M*
Northern Oklahoma College *A*
Northwestern Oklahoma State
   University *B,M*
Oklahoma Baptist University *B*
Oklahoma Christian University of
   Science and Arts *B*
Oklahoma City University *B,M*
Oklahoma Panhandle State
   University *B*
Oklahoma State University *B*
Oral Roberts University *B,M*
Phillips University *B,M*
Rogers State College *A*
Rose State College *A*
Southeastern Oklahoma State
   University *B,M*
Southwestern Oklahoma State
   University *B,M*
University of Central Oklahoma
   B,M
University of Oklahoma *B,M,D*
University of Science and Arts of
   Oklahoma *B*
University of Tulsa *B,M*

Oregon

Central Oregon Community
   College *A*
Concordia College *C,B*
Eastern Oregon State College *B,M*
George Fox College *B*
Linfield College *B*
Oregon State University *M*
Pacific University *B,M*
Southern Oregon State College *B,M*
Treasure Valley Community
   College *A*
University of Portland *B*
Warner Pacific College *B*
Western Baptist College *B*
Western Oregon State College *B,M*
Willamette University *M*

Pennsylvania

Academy of the New Church *B*
Albright College *B*
Allegheny College *B*
Alvernia College *B*
Baptist Bible College of
   Pennsylvania *B,M*
Beaver College *B,M*

Bloomsburg University of
   Pennsylvania *B,M*
Bryn Mawr College *M,D*
Bucknell University *B,M*
Butler County Community
   College *A*
Cabrini College *B*
California University of
   Pennsylvania *B,M*
Carlow College *B*
Cedar Crest College *B*
Chatham College *B*
Chestnut Hill College *B,M*
Cheyney University of Pennsylvania
   C,B,M
Clarion University of Pennsylvania
   B,M
College Misericordia *B*
Duquesne University *B,M*
East Stroudsburg University of
   Pennsylvania *B,M*
Eastern College *B*
Edinboro University of
   Pennsylvania *B,M*
Elizabethtown College *B*
Gannon University *B,M*
Geneva College *B*
Gettysburg College *B*
Gratz College *B,M*
Grove City College *B*
Gwynedd-Mercy College *B*
Harrisburg Area Community
   College *A*
Holy Family College *B,M*
Immaculata College *B*
Indiana University of Pennsylvania
   B,M,D
Juniata College *B*
King's College *B*
Kutztown University of
   Pennsylvania *B,M*
La Salle University *B*
Lancaster Bible College *B*
Lebanon Valley College of
   Pennsylvania *B*
Lehigh University *M*
Lincoln University *B*
Lock Haven University of
   Pennsylvania *B*
Lycoming College *B*
Mansfield University of
   Pennsylvania *B,M*
Marywood College *B,M*
Mercyhurst College *B*
Messiah College *B*
Millersville University of
   Pennsylvania *B,M*
Montgomery County Community
   College *A*
Moravian College *B*
Neumann College *B*
Northeastern Christian Junior
   College *A*
Penn State
   Harrisburg Capital College *B*
   University Park Campus *B*
Philadelphia College of Bible *B*
Point Park College *B*
Reading Area Community
   College *A*
St. Francis College *B*
St. Joseph's University *B,M*
St. Vincent College *C*
Seton Hill College *B*
Shippensburg University of
   Pennsylvania *B,M*
Slippery Rock University of
   Pennsylvania *B,M*
Susquehanna University *B*
Temple University *B,M,D*
Thiel College *C*
University of Pennsylvania *B,M,D*

University of Pittsburgh
   Bradford *C*
   Johnstown *B*
University of Scranton *B,M*
Waynesburg College *B*
West Chester University of
   Pennsylvania *B,M*
Westminster College *B,M*
Widener University *B,M*
Wilkes University *B,M*
Wilson College *B*
York College of Pennsylvania *B*

Puerto Rico

American University of Puerto
   Rico *B*
Bayamon Central University *B*
Caribbean University *B*
Inter American University of Puerto
   Rico
   Arecibo Campus *A,B*
   Metropolitan Campus *M*
   San German Campus *B*
Pontifical Catholic University of
   Puerto Rico *B*
Turabo University *B*
Universidad Adventista de las
   Antillas *B*
Universidad Metropolitana *B*
University of Puerto Rico
   Arecibo Campus *A,B*
   Bayamon Technological
      University College *B*
   Cayey University College *B*
   Humacao University College *B*
   Ponce Technological
      University College *A,B*
   Rio Piedras Campus *B*
University of the Sacred Heart *B*

Rhode Island

Community College of Rhode
   Island *A*
Providence College *B*
Rhode Island College *B,M*
Salve Regina University *B*
University of Rhode Island *B,M*

South Carolina

Anderson College *B*
Benedict College *B*
Bob Jones University *B,M*
Central Wesleyan College *B*
Charleston Southern University *B,M*
Claflin College *B*
Clemson University *B,M*
Coker College *B*
College of Charleston *B,M*
Columbia Bible College and
   Seminary *B*
Columbia College *B,M*
Converse College *B,M*
Erskine College *B*
Francis Marion College *B,M*
Furman University *B,M*
Lander College *B,M*
Limestone College *B*
Morris College *B*
Newberry College *B*
North Greenville College *A*
Presbyterian College *B*
South Carolina State College *B,M*
University of South Carolina
   Aiken *B*
   Coastal Carolina College *B*
   Columbia *M,D*
   Spartanburg *B*
Winthrop University *B,M*

South Dakota

Augustana College *B,M*
Black Hills State University *B,M*

Dakota State University *B*
Dakota Wesleyan University *B,M*
Huron University *B*
Mount Marty College *B*
Northern State University *B,M*
Oglala Lakota College *B*
Presentation College *A*
Sinte Gleska College *B*
Sioux Falls College *B*
South Dakota State University *B*
University of South Dakota *B,M*

Tennessee

Austin Peay State University *B,M*
Belmont University *B*
Bethel College *B*
Carson-Newman College *B,M*
Christian Brothers University *B*
Cleveland State Community
College *A*
Columbia State Community
College *A*
Crichton College *B*
Cumberland University *B*
David Lipscomb University *B*
East Tennessee State University
B,M
Fisk University *B*
Free Will Baptist Bible College *B*
Freed-Hardeman University *B*
Hiwassee College *A*
Johnson Bible College *B*
Knoxville College *B*
Lambuth University *B*
Lane College *B*
Lincoln Memorial University *B*
Memphis State University *B*
Middle Tennessee State
University *B*
Milligan College *B,M*
Motlow State Community
College *A*
Roane State Community College *A*
Southern College of Seventh-day
Adventists *B*
Tennessee State University *B,M*
Tennessee Technological University
B,M
Tennessee Temple University *B,M*
Tennessee Wesleyan College *B*
Trevecca Nazarene College *B,M*
Tusculum College *B*
Union University *B,M*
University of Tennessee
Chattanooga *B,M*
Knoxville *B*
Martin *B*
Vanderbilt University *B,M,D*
Volunteer State Community
College *A*
Walters State Community
College *A*
William Jennings Bryan College *B*

Texas

Abilene Christian University *M*
Amarillo College *A*
Angelina College *A*
Angelo State University *B,M*
Arlington Baptist College *B*
Austin College *M*
Baylor University *B*
Bee County College *A*
Brazosport College *A*
College of the Mainland *A*
Concordia Lutheran College *B*
Corpus Christi State University *B,M*
Dallas Baptist University *B,M*
East Texas Baptist University *B*
East Texas State University
Commerce *B,M*
Texarkana *M*

El Paso Community College *A*
Hardin-Simmons University *B,M*
Houston Baptist University *B*
Houston Community College *C,A*
Huston-Tillotson College *B*
Incarnate Word College *B,M*
Jarvis Christian College *B*
Kilgore College *A*
Lamar University—Beaumont *B,M*
Laredo State University *B,M*
Lon Morris College *A*
Lubbock Christian University *B*
McMurry University *B*
Midwestern State University *B,M*
Navarro College *A*
North Harris Montgomery
Community College District *A*
Our Lady of the Lake University of
San Antonio *B,M*
Panola College *A*
Paul Quinn College *B*
Prairie View A&M University *B,M*
Ranger Junior College *A*
St. Edward's University *B*
St. Mary's University *B*
Sam Houston State University *B,M*
Schreiner College *B*
Southwest Texas State
University *M*
Southwestern Adventist College *B*
Southwestern Assemblies of God
College *B*
Southwestern Christian College *A*
Sul Ross State University *B*
Tarleton State University *B,M*
Texas A&I University *B,M*
Texas Christian University *B,M*
Texas College *B*
Texas Lutheran College *B*
Texas Southern University *B,M*
Texas Southmost College *A*
Texas Tech University *B,M,D*
Texas Wesleyan University *B,M*
Texas Woman's University *M*
Trinity University *M*
Trinity Valley Community
College *A*
University of Dallas *B*
University of Houston
Clear Lake *B,M*
Houston *M*
Victoria *B*
University of Mary Hardin-Baylor
B,M
University of North Texas *B,M*
University of St. Thomas *B,M*
University of Texas
Pan American *B,M*
Permian Basin *M*
Victoria College *A*
Wayland Baptist University *B*
West Texas State University *B,M*
Wiley College *B*

Utah

Brigham Young University *B,M*
Southern Utah University *B*
University of Utah *B,M,D*
Utah State University *B,M*
Weber State University *B,M*
Westminster College of Salt Lake
City *B*

Vermont

Bennington College *B*
Castleton State College *B*
Champlain College *A*
College of St. Joseph in Vermont
B,M
Goddard College *B,M*
Green Mountain College *B*
Johnson State College *B,M*

Lyndon State College *B*
Norwich University *B*
St. Michael's College *B*
Trinity College of Vermont *B*
University of Vermont *B,M*

Virginia

Averett College *B,M*
Bluefield College *B*
Bridgewater College *B*
Clinch Valley College of the
University of Virginia *B*
College of William and Mary *M*
Eastern Mennonite College *B*
Emory and Henry College *B*
George Mason University *M*
Hampton University *B,M*
James Madison University *M*
Longwood College *M*
Lynchburg College *B,M*
Mary Baldwin College *C*
Marymount University *M*
Mountain Empire Community
College *A*
Norfolk State University *B*
Old Dominion University *B,M*
Radford University *B,M*
Roanoke College *B*
University of Richmond *B,M*
Virginia Commonwealth
University *M*
Virginia Polytechnic Institute and
State University *M,D*
Virginia State University *B,M*
Virginia Wesleyan College *B*

Washington

Central Washington University *B*
City University *M*
Eastern Washington University *B,M*
Evergreen State College *M*
Grays Harbor College *C*
Heritage College *B*
Lower Columbia College *A*
Northwest College of the
Assemblies of God *B*
Pacific Lutheran University *B,M*
St. Martin's College *B,M*
Seattle University *M*
University of Puget Sound *M*
Walla Walla College *B*
Washington State University *B*
Western Washington University
B,M
Whitworth College *B*

West Virginia

Alderson-Broaddus College *B*
Bethany College *B*
Bluefield State College *B*
Concord College *B*
Davis and Elkins College *B*
Fairmont State College *B*
Glenville State College *B*
Marshall University *B,M*
Potomac State College of West
Virginia University *A*
Salem-Teikyo University *B,M*
Shepherd College *B*
University of Charleston *B*
West Liberty State College *B*
West Virginia Graduate College *M*
West Virginia State College *B*
West Virginia University
Morgantown *B,M*
Parkersburg *B*
West Virginia Wesleyan College *B*

Wisconsin

Alverno College *B*
Beloit College *B,M*
Cardinal Stritch College *B*

Carroll College *B*
Carthage College *B*
Concordia University Wisconsin *B*
Edgewood College *B*
Lakeland College *B*
Lawrence University *B*
Maranatha Baptist Bible College *B*
Marian College of Fond du Lac *B*
Marquette University *B*
Mount Mary College *B*
Mount Senario College *B*
Northland College *B*
Ripon College *C*
St. Norbert College *B*
Silver Lake College *B*
University of Wisconsin
Eau Claire *B,M*
Green Bay *B*
La Crosse *B,M*
Madison *B*
Milwaukee *B*
Oshkosh *B,M*
Platteville *B,M*
River Falls *B,M*
Stevens Point *B,M*
Superior *B,M*
Whitewater *B*
Viterbo College *B,M*
Wisconsin Lutheran College *B*

Wyoming

Casper College *A*
Central Wyoming College *A*
Eastern Wyoming College *A*
Laramie County Community
College *A*
Northwest College *A*
Sheridan College *A*
University of Wyoming *B,M*
Western Wyoming Community
College *A*

American Samoa, Caroline Islands, Guam, Marianas, Virgin Islands

Community College of
Micronesia *A*
University of Guam *B,M*
University of the Virgin Islands
B,M

Canada

McGill University *B,M*

Elementary particle physics

Florida

University of Florida *M,D*

Illinois

University of Chicago *B,M,D*

Indiana

Purdue University *M,D*
University of Notre Dame *M,D*

Massachusetts

Massachusetts Institute of
Technology *B,M,D,W*
Tufts University *M,D*

Michigan

Michigan State University *D*
University of Michigan *D*

New Jersey

Stevens Institute of Technology
B,M,D

New York

Columbia University *M,D*

Pennsylvania

Carnegie Mellon University
B,M,D,W
Lehigh University *M*

Rhode Island

Brown University *M,D*

Canada

McGill University *M,D*

Embryology

California

University of the Pacific *B*

Georgia

Emory University *M,D*

Illinois

University of Chicago *M,D*

Massachusetts

Tufts University *M*

New York

Cornell University *M,D*

Virginia

Averett College *B*

Emergency/disaster science

Alabama

Community College of the Air
Force *A*

California

Crafton Hills College *C,A*

Florida

Central Florida Community
College *A*

Georgia

DeKalb Technical Institute *C*

Illinois

Illinois Eastern Community
Colleges: Frontier Community
College *C*

Kansas

Hutchinson Community College *A*

Louisiana

University of Southwestern
Louisiana *A*

Maryland

University of Maryland
Baltimore *B*
Baltimore County *B,M*

Massachusetts

Cape Cod Community College *C*
Quinsigamond Community
College *C*

Missouri

Jefferson College *A*
Southwest Baptist University *A*

New York

Hudson Valley Community
College *C*

Ohio

Hocking Technical College *A*

Pennsylvania

California University of
Pennsylvania *A*

Texas

University of North Texas *B*

Emergency medical technologies

Alabama

Alabama Southern Community
College *A*
Bessemer State Technical College *C*
Chattahoochee Valley Community
College *A*
Enterprise State Junior College *A*
Faulkner University *A*
Gadsden State Community
College *A*
George C. Wallace State
Community College at Selma *A*
James H. Faulkner State
Community College *A*
Jefferson State Community
College *A*
Livingston University *A*
Lurleen B. Wallace State Junior
College *A*
Northeast Alabama State Junior
College *A*
Shelton State Community
College *C*
Shoals Community College *C,A*
Southern Union State Junior
College *C,A*
University of Alabama in
Birmingham *C*
University of South Alabama *C*
Walker College *A*
Wallace State Community College
at Hanceville *C,A*

Alaska

University of Alaska Anchorage *C*

Arizona

Glendale Community College *C*
Mesa Community College *C*
Pima Community College *C*
Yavapai College *C*

Arkansas

East Arkansas Community
College *C*
Garland County Community
College *A*
North Arkansas Community
College *A*
Southern Arkansas Community
College *A*
University of Arkansas for Medical
Sciences *C,A*
Westark Community College *A*

California

Allan Hancock College *C*
Bakersfield College *A*
Barstow College *C*
Cerro Coso Community College *C*
Citrus College *C*
College of the Desert *C*

Crafton Hills College *A*
Imperial Valley College *C*
Mount San Antonio College *C,A*
Orange Coast College *C,A*
Palomar College *C,A*
Saddleback College *A*
San Joaquin Delta College *C,A*
Skyline College *C*
Southwestern College *C,A*
Ventura College *A*

Colorado

Aims Community College *C*
Arapahoe Community College *C,A*
Morgan Community College *C*
Pikes Peak Community College *C*

Connecticut

Mattatuck Community College *C*

District of Columbia

George Washington University *B*

Florida

Brevard Community College *C*
Broward Community College *A*
Central Florida Community
College *A*
Daytona Beach Community College
C,A
Edison Community College *C,A*
Florida Community College at
Jacksonville *C,A*
Gulf Coast Community College *C,A*
Hillsborough Community College *C*
Indian River Community College *A*
Lake City Community College *A*
Lake-Sumter Community College *A*
Miami-Dade Community College
C,A
Palm Beach Community College
C,A
Pasco-Hernando Community
College *C,A*
Pensacola Junior College *C,A*
St. Johns River Community
College *A*
St. Petersburg Junior College *C,A*
Santa Fe Community College *C,A*
Seminole Community College *C,A*
South Florida Community
College *C*
Tallahassee Community College
C,A
Valencia Community College *C,A*

Georgia

Augusta Technical Institute *C*
DeKalb College *A*
Floyd College *A*
Gainesville College *A*
Savannah Technical Institute *C*
Valdosta State College *A*

Hawaii

University of Hawaii: Kapiolani
Community College *C,A*

Idaho

Ricks College *C,A*

Illinois

Belleville Area College *A*
City Colleges of Chicago
Chicago City-Wide College
C,A
Malcolm X College *C*
Illinois Central College *C*
Illinois Eastern Community
Colleges: Frontier Community
College *C,A*

Moraine Valley Community
College *C*
Parkland College *C*
Rend Lake College *C*

Iowa

Des Moines Area Community
College *C*
Hawkeye Institute of Technology *C*
Southeastern Community College:
North Campus *A*

Kansas

Barton County Community
College *A*
Coffeyville Community College *A*
Dodge City Community College *C*
Hutchinson Community College
C,A
Johnson County Community
College *C,A*
Southwestern College *C*
Wichita State University *C*

Kentucky

Eastern Kentucky University *C,A*
Western Kentucky University *C*

Maine

Kennebec Valley Technical
College *A*

Maryland

Anne Arundel Community College
C,A
Essex Community College *C,A*
New Community College of
Baltimore *C,A*

Massachusetts

Bunker Hill Community College *C*
Cape Cod Community College *C*
Middlesex Community College *A*
North Shore Community College *C*
Northeastern University *C,A*
Quinsigamond Community
College *C*

Michigan

Baker College of Mount Clemens *C*
Davenport College of Business *A*
Henry Ford Community College
C,A
Kalamazoo Valley Community
College *C*
Kellogg Community College *A*
Lansing Community College *A*
Macomb Community College *C,A*
Madonna University *A*
Montcalm Community College *C*
Oakland Community College *A*

Minnesota

Lakewood Community College *A*

Mississippi

Hinds Community College *C,A*
Jones County Junior College *C*
Mississippi Gulf Coast Community
College: Jefferson Davis
Campus *A*

Missouri

East Central College *C,A*
Jefferson College *C*
Missouri Southern State College *C*
Moberly Area Community
College *A*
Penn Valley Community College *A*
St. Louis Community College
Forest Park *A*
Meramec *A*

Southwest Baptist University *A*

Nevada

Community College of Southern
Nevada *A*
Truckee Meadows Community
College *C*

New Jersey

Essex County College *A*
University of Medicine and
Dentistry of New Jersey: School
of Health Related Professions
C,A

New Mexico

Dona Ana Branch Community
College of New Mexico State
University *A*
Eastern New Mexico University:
Roswell Campus *A*
New Mexico Junior College *A*
New Mexico State University *C*
University of New Mexico *C*

New York

City University of New York
Borough of Manhattan
Community College *A*
La Guardia Community
College *A*
Erie Community College: South
Campus *C*
Hudson Valley Community
College *C*
Suffolk County Community
College *C*

North Carolina

Asheville Buncombe Technical
Community College *A*
Catawba Valley Community
College *A*
Fayetteville Technical Community
College *A*
Forsyth Technical Community
College *C*
Gaston College *A*
Guilford Technical Community
College *C,A*
Wake Technical Community
College *A*
Western Carolina University *B*
Wilson Technical Community
College *C,A*

Ohio

Clark State Community College *A*
Columbus State Community
College *A*
Cuyahoga Community College:
Metropolitan Campus *A*
Edison State Community College *C*
Hocking Technical College *A*
Lakeland Community College *C*
Lorain County Community
College *C*
Sinclair Community College *A*
University of Cincinnati: Raymond
Walters College *A*
University of Toledo *A*
Youngstown State University *A*

Oklahoma

Redlands Community College *C*

Oregon

Central Oregon Community
College *C*
Chemeketa Community College *A*
Linn-Benton Community College *C*
Portland Community College *C*

Southwestern Oregon Community
College *C*
Umpqua Community College *C*

Pennsylvania

California University of
Pennsylvania *A*
Hahnemann University School of
Health Sciences and Humanities
C,A,B,M
Harrisburg Area Community
College *C,A*
Luzerne County Community
College *A*

Puerto Rico

Electronic Data Processing College
of Puerto Rico *A*
University of Puerto Rico: Medical
Sciences Campus *A*

South Carolina

Greenville Technical College *A*

South Dakota

Mitchell Vocational Technical
Institute *C*

Tennessee

Chattanooga State Technical
Community College *C*
Dyersburg State Community
College *A*
Jackson State Community College
C,A
Northeast State Technical
Community College *C,A*
Roane State Community College *C*
Shelby State Community College
C,A
Volunteer State Community College
C,A

Texas

Amarillo College *C,A*
Angelina College *C,A*
Austin Community College *A*
Collin County Community College
District *A*
Cooke County College *A*
El Paso Community College *C*
Houston Community College *C*
Howard College *A*
Laredo Junior College *C,A*
Midland College *C*
Navarro College *A*
North Harris Montgomery
Community College District *C,A*
Odessa College *A*
Tarrant County Junior College *C,A*
Texarkana College *A*
Texas Southmost College *A*
Texas State Technical College:
Sweetwater *C,A*
Weatherford College *C,A*

Utah

Weber State University *A*

Virginia

College of Health Sciences *C,A*
Mountain Empire Community
College *C*
Northern Virginia Community
College *C,A*
Tidewater Community College *C*

Washington

Central Washington University *B*
Columbia Basin College *C*
Lower Columbia College *A*
Pierce College *C*

Tacoma Community College *A*

West Virginia

Fairmont State College *C*
Marshall University *C,A*

Wyoming

Casper College *A*
Sheridan College *C,A*

**American Samoa, Caroline
Islands, Guam, Marianas,
Virgin Islands**

Guam Community College *C*

Enameling

California

California State University: Los
Angeles *B,M*

Massachusetts

School of the Museum of Fine
Arts *B*

Ohio

Cleveland Institute of Art *B*
University of Akron *B*

Pennsylvania

Carnegie Mellon University *B,M*

Energy conservation and use technology

Alabama

Shoals Community College *C*

California

Coastline Community College *A*
Humboldt State University *M*
Orange Coast College *C,A*

Colorado

Colorado Mountain College:
Timberline Campus *A*

Illinois

Moraine Valley Community College
C,A

Iowa

University of Northern Iowa *B*

Kansas

Johnson County Community
College *A*

Michigan

Henry Ford Community College *A*
Jordan College *C,A,B*
Lansing Community College *A*

Minnesota

Moorhead State University *B*

North Carolina

Wilson Technical Community
College *C,A*

Ohio

University of Cincinnati: Access
Colleges *A*

Pennsylvania

California University of
Pennsylvania *B*
Delaware County Community
College *B*

Washington

Evergreen State College *B*

Engineering

Alabama

Alabama Southern Community
College *A*
Alabama State University *B*
Brewer State Junior College *A*
Chattahoochee Valley Community
College *A*
Jefferson State Community
College *A*
Marion Military Institute *A*
Shelton State Community
College *A*
Shoals Community College *A*
Snead State Junior College *A*
University of Alabama
Huntsville *B*
Tuscaloosa *M*
Walker College *A*
Wallace State Community College
at Hanceville *A*

Arizona

Arizona Western College *A*
Eastern Arizona College *A*
Glendale Community College *A*
Pima Community College *A*
Yavapai College *A*

Arkansas

Arkansas State University *B*
Arkansas Tech University *B*
John Brown University *B*
University of Arkansas *M,D*
Westark Community College *A*

California

Allan Hancock College *A*
California Institute of Technology *B*
California Polytechnic State
University: San Luis Obispo *M*
California State Polytechnic
University: Pomona *M*
California State University
Fresno *B,M*
Long Beach *B,M,D*
Los Angeles *B*
Northridge *B,M*
Sacramento *B,M*
Chabot College *A*
Chaffey Community College *A*
Citrus College *A*
City College of San Francisco *A*
College of the Sequoias *A*
Crafton Hills College *A*
De Anza College *A*
Diablo Valley College *A*
El Camino College *A*
Foothill College *A*
Fresno City College *A*
Gavilan Community College *A*
Harvey Mudd College *B*
Imperial Valley College *A*
Kings River Community College *A*
Long Beach City College *A*
Los Angeles City College *A*
Merced College *A*
Mission College *A*
Modesto Junior College *A*

Mount San Antonio College *A*
Mount San Jacinto College *C,A*
Napa Valley College *A*
Ohlone College *A*
Palomar College *A*
St. Mary's College of California *B*
San Diego City College *C,A*
San Diego Mesa College *A*
San Diego State University *B*
San Francisco State University *B*
San Joaquin Delta College *A*
San Jose State University *B,M*
Santa Barbara City College *A*
Santa Clara University *B,M*
Santa Rosa Junior College *A*
Solano Community College *A*
Southwestern College *A*
Stanford University *B,M*
Taft College *A*
University of California
    Irvine *B,M,D*
    Los Angeles *B,M,D*
    Riverside *B*
    San Diego *B*
University of Redlands *B*
University of Southern California *D*
Ventura College *A*
West Hills Community College *A*
West Valley College *A*
Yuba College *A*

Colorado

Colorado School of Mines *B,W*
Lamar Community College *A*
Mesa State College *A*
Northeastern Junior College *A*
Otero Junior College *A*
Trinidad State Junior College *A*
United States Air Force
    Academy *B*
University of Colorado at
    Boulder *M*

Connecticut

Bridgeport Engineering Institute *A*
Mitchell College *A*
Sacred Heart University *B*
Trinity College *B*
University of Bridgeport *B*
University of Hartford *B*
Yale University *B,M,D*

Delaware

Delaware State College *B*
Wesley College *A*

District of Columbia

Catholic University of America
    B,M,D
Gallaudet University *B*
George Washington University
    B,M,D

Florida

Brevard Community College *A*
Central Florida Community
    College *A*
Daytona Beach Community
    College *A*
Gulf Coast Community College *A*
Hillsborough Community College *A*
Indian River Community College *A*
Lake City Community College *A*
Manatee Community College *A*
Miami-Dade Community College *C*
Okaloosa-Walton Community
    College *A*
Palm Beach Community College *A*
Pensacola Junior College *A*
University of Central Florida *M*
University of Florida *B,M,D*
University of South Florida *B,M*

Georgia

Andrew College *A*
Clayton State College *A*
Covenant College *B*
Darton College *A*
DeKalb College *A*
Floyd College *A*
Gainesville College *A*
Macon College *A*
Mercer University *B*
Middle Georgia College *A*
Morehouse College *B*
Spelman College *B*
Wesleyan College *B*

Hawaii

Hawaii Loa College *B*

Idaho

College of Southern Idaho *A*
Idaho State University *B*
North Idaho College *A*
Ricks College *A*

Illinois

Black Hawk College *A*
Bradley University *B,M*
City Colleges of Chicago: Richard J.
    Daley College *A*
Eastern Illinois University *B*
Highland Community College *A*
Illinois Central College *A*
Illinois College *B*
Illinois Valley Community
    College *A*
John A. Logan College *A*
Joliet Junior College *A*
Kishwaukee College *A*
Lake Land College *A*
Lincoln Land Community
    College *A*
Morton College *A*
Oakton Community College *A*
Olivet Nazarene University *B*
Parkland College *A*
Principia College *B*
Rend Lake College *A*
Richland Community College *A*
Rock Valley College *A*
Southern Illinois University at
    Carbondale *B,M,D*
State Community College *A*
Triton College *A*
University of Illinois
    Chicago *B,M,D*
    Urbana-Champaign *B,M*
Waubonsee Community College *A*

Indiana

Hanover College *B*
Indiana Institute of Technology *B*
Indiana University—Purdue
    University
    Fort Wayne *B,M*
    Indianapolis *B,M*
Purdue University
    Calumet *B,M*
    West Lafayette *B*
University of Notre Dame *B,M,D*
Vincennes University *A*

Iowa

Cornell College *B*
Dordt College *B*
Grand View College *A*
Kirkwood Community College *A*
Loras College *B*
Luther College *B*
North Iowa Area Community
    College *A*
University of Iowa *B*

Kansas

Allen County Community
    College *A*
Barton County Community
    College *A*
Butler County Community
    College *A*
Central College *A*
Cloud County Community
    College *A*
Coffeyville Community College *A*
Colby Community College *A*
Cowley County Community
    College *A*
Fort Scott Community College *A*
Highland Community College *A*
Hutchinson Community College *A*
Kansas City Kansas Community
    College *A*
Kansas State University *D*
Labette Community College *A*
Neosho County Community
    College *A*
Pratt Community College *A*
Seward County Community
    College *A*

Kentucky

Asbury College *B*
Brescia College *A*
Georgetown College *B*
Sue Bennett College *A*

Louisiana

Centenary College of Louisiana *B*
Dillard University *B*
Louisiana State University and
    Agricultural and Mechanical
    College *M*
Louisiana Tech University *M,D*
McNeese State University *M*
Tulane University *B*
University of Southwestern
    Louisiana *M*

Maine

University of Maine *B,M*

Maryland

Allegany Community College *A*
Anne Arundel Community
    College *A*
Catonsville Community College *A*
Charles County Community
    College *A*
College of Notre Dame of
    Maryland *B*
Columbia Union College *A*
Frederick Community College *A*
Hagerstown Junior College *A*
Harford Community College *A*
Johns Hopkins University *B*
Montgomery College
    Germantown Campus *A*
    Rockville Campus *A*
    Takoma Park Campus *A*
New Community College of
    Baltimore *A*
Prince George's Community
    College *A*
United States Naval Academy *B*
University of Maryland: College
    Park *B*

Massachusetts

Anna Maria College for Men and
    Women *A*
Berkshire Community College *A*
Boston University *B,M*
Bristol Community College *A*
Cape Cod Community College *A*
Clark University *B*

Emmanuel College *B*
Harvard and Radcliffe Colleges *B*
Harvard University *M,D*
Holyoke Community College *A*
Massachusetts Bay Community
    College *A*
Massachusetts Institute of
    Technology *B*
North Shore Community College *A*
Northeastern University *B*
Quinsigamond Community
    College *A*
Springfield Technical Community
    College *A*
Tufts University *B*
University of Massachusetts at
    Dartmouth *B*
Wellesley College *B*
Western New England College *B,M*
Worcester Polytechnic Institute *B*

Michigan

Andrews University *B*
Calvin College *B*
GMI Engineering & Management
    Institute *B*
Grand Valley State University *B*
Henry Ford Community College *A*
Kellogg Community College *A*
Kirtland Community College *A*
Lansing Community College *A*
Michigan Technological University
    A,B
Oakland University *B,M*
Southwestern Michigan College *A*
University of Detroit Mercy *B,D*
University of Michigan
    Ann Arbor *B*
    Dearborn *B,M*

Minnesota

Anoka-Ramsey Community
    College *A*
Bethany Lutheran College *A*
Inver Hills Community College *A*
Itasca Community College:
    Arrowhead Region *A*
Northland Community College *A*
Rainy River Community College *A*
Rochester Community College *A*
Vermilion Community College *A*
Willmar Community College *A*
Worthington Community College *A*

Mississippi

Copiah-Lincoln Community
    College *A*
East Central Community College *A*
Holmes Community College *A*
Jones County Junior College *A*
Mary Holmes College *A*
Mississippi Delta Community
    College *A*
Mississippi Gulf Coast Community
    College
    Jackson County Campus *A*
    Jefferson Davis Campus *A*
Mississippi State University *D*
Northeast Mississippi Community
    College *A*
University of Mississippi *B*

Missouri

East Central College *A*
Hannibal-LaGrange College *A*
Jefferson College *A*
Longview Community College *A*
Maple Woods Community
    College *A*
Mineral Area College *A*
Penn Valley Community College *A*

St. Louis Community College
  Florissant Valley *A*
  Forest Park *A*
  Meramec *C,A*
Washington University *B*
Westminster College *B*

Montana

Miles Community College *A*
Montana College of Mineral
  Science and Technology *A*
Rocky Mountain College *B*

Nebraska

McCook Community College *A*
Union College *A*
University of Nebraska—Lincoln *D*
Western Nebraska Community
  College: Scottsbluff Campus *A*

Nevada

University of Nevada: Reno *D*

New Hampshire

Daniel Webster College *A*
Dartmouth College *B,M,D*

New Jersey

Bergen Community College *A*
Brookdale Community College *A*
Burlington County College *A*
Camden County College *A*
Cumberland County College *A*
Essex County College *A*
Ocean County College *A*
Stevens Institute of Technology *B*
Union County College *A*

New Mexico

New Mexico Institute of Mining
  and Technology *B*
New Mexico Junior College *A*
University of New Mexico *B,D*

New York

Adirondack Community College *A*
Clarkson University *B*
Columbia University: School of
  Engineering and Applied
  Science *B*
Community College of the Finger
  Lakes *A*
Cooper Union *B*
Corning Community College *A*
Dutchess Community College *A*
Erie Community College: North
  Campus *A*
Fulton-Montgomery Community
  College *A*
Genesee Community College *A*
Herkimer County Community
  College *A*
Hofstra University *B*
Hudson Valley Community
  College *A*
Jamestown Community College *A*
Jefferson Community College *A*
Manhattan College *B,M*
Mohawk Valley Community
  College *A*
Monroe Community College *A*
Nassau Community College *A*
Niagara University *A*
Onondaga Community College *A*
Orange County Community
  College *A*
Rensselaer Polytechnic Institute
  B,M,D
State University of New York
  Stony Brook *B*
  College of Technology at
    Farmingdale *A*

Suffolk County Community
  College *A*
Sullivan County Community
  College *A*
Ulster County Community
  College *A*
Westchester Community College *A*
Yeshiva University *B*

North Carolina

Brevard College *A*
Chowan College *A*
College of the Albemarle *A*
Livingstone College *B*
Louisburg College *A*
North Carolina Agricultural and
  Technical State University *M*
North Carolina State University *M*
Rockingham Community College *A*
Salem College *B*

North Dakota

Minot State University *A*
North Dakota State University *B,D*
Turtle Mountain Community
  College *A*

Ohio

Air Force Institute of Technology
  M,D
Bowling Green State University:
  Firelands College *A*
Case Western Reserve University
  B,M
Cleveland State University *D*
Cuyahoga Community College:
  Metropolitan Campus *A*
Lakeland Community College *A*
Lorain County Community
  College *A*
Marietta College *B*
Oberlin College *B*
Ohio State University: Columbus
  Campus *B,M,D*
Union Institute *D*
University of Akron *B,M*
University of Cincinnati *B,M,D*
University of Dayton *B,M*
University of Toledo *B*
Washington State Community
  College *A*
Wittenberg University *B*

Oklahoma

Eastern Oklahoma State College *A*
Oklahoma Baptist University *B*
Oklahoma State University
  Oklahoma City *A*
  Stillwater *B,M,D*
Oral Roberts University *B*
Redlands Community College *A*
Rogers State College *A*
Rose State College *A*
St. Gregory's College *A*
Tulsa Junior College *A*
University of Oklahoma *B,M,D*

Oregon

Central Oregon Community
  College *A*
George Fox College *B*
Linn-Benton Community College *A*
Portland Community College *A*
Treasure Valley Community
  College *A*

Pennsylvania

Albright College *B*
Beaver College *B*
Bucks County Community
  College *A*

Butler County Community
  College *A*
California University of
  Pennsylvania *B*
Carnegie Mellon University
  B,M,D,W
Community College of
  Philadelphia *A*
Delaware County Community
  College *A*
Drexel University *B,M*
Elizabethtown College *B*
Gannon University *M*
Geneva College *A,B*
Gettysburg College *B*
Keystone Junior College *A*
Lafayette College *B*
Lebanon Valley College of
  Pennsylvania *B*
Lehigh County Community
  College *A*
Lock Haven University of
  Pennsylvania *B*
Messiah College *B*
Moravian College *B*
Northampton County Area
  Community College *A*
Northeastern Christian Junior
  College *A*
Penn State
  Erie Behrend College *B*
  University Park Campus *C*
Reading Area Community
  College *A*
St. Francis College *B*
Swarthmore College *B*
Westmoreland County Community
  College *A*
Widener University *B*
York College of Pennsylvania *A*

Puerto Rico

Turabo University *B*
University of the Sacred Heart *B*

Rhode Island

Brown University *B*
Community College of Rhode
  Island *A*
Roger Williams College *B*

South Dakota

South Dakota State University *M*

Tennessee

Columbia State Community
  College *A*
Dyersburg State Community
  College *A*
Hiwassee College *A*
Lane College *B*
LeMoyne-Owen College *B*
Martin Methodist College *A*
Memphis State University *D*
Motlow State Community
  College *A*
Roane State Community College *A*
Southern College of Seventh-day
  Adventists *A*
Tennessee State University *B,M*
Tennessee Technological University
  B,M,D
University of Tennessee:
  Chattanooga *B,M*
Vanderbilt University *B,M,D*
Volunteer State Community
  College *A*
Walters State Community
  College *A*

Texas

Amarillo College *A*
Angelina College *A*
Austin Community College *A*
Baylor University *B*
Bee County College *A*
Brazosport College *A*
Central Texas College *A*
Collin County Community College
  District *A*
Howard College *A*
Huston-Tillotson College *B*
Lamar University—Beaumont *M,D*
Lee College *A*
LeTourneau University *B*
Lon Morris College *A*
Navarro College *A*
North Harris Montgomery
  Community College District *A*
Panola College *A*
Prairie View A&M University *M*
St. Mary's University *B,M*
Schreiner College *A*
South Plains College *A*
Southwestern Christian College *A*
Texas A&I University *M*
Texas A&M University *M,D*
Texas Southmost College *A*
Texas Tech University *B,M,D*
Trinity University *B*
University of Texas
  Arlington *D*
  El Paso *M*
Victoria College *A*
Western Texas College *A*
Wharton County Junior College *A*

Utah

Dixie College *A*
Southern Utah University *A*

Virginia

Bluefield College *A*
Emory and Henry College *B*
Northern Virginia Community
  College *A*
Patrick Henry Community
  College *A*
Piedmont Virginia Community
  College *A*
Southwest Virginia Community
  College *A*
Tidewater Community College *A*

Washington

Big Bend Community College *A*
Centralia College *A*
Clark College *A*
Everett Community College *A*
Grays Harbor College *A*
Lower Columbia College *A*
Olympic College *A*
Pierce College *A*
Seattle Central Community
  College *A*
Shoreline Community College *A*
Skagit Valley College *A*
Spokane Falls Community
  College *A*
Tacoma Community College *A*
University of Puget Sound *B*
University of Washington *B,M*
Walla Walla College *B*
Washington State University *M*
Wenatchee Valley College *A*

West Virginia

Davis and Elkins College *B*
Shepherd College *A*
West Virginia Graduate College *M*

Wisconsin

Beloit College *B*
Concordia University Wisconsin *B*
Lakeland College *B*
Ripon College *B*
University of Wisconsin
    Madison *M*
    Milwaukee *B,M,D*

Wyoming

Casper College *A*
Laramie County Community
    College *A*
Northwest College *A*
Sheridan College *A*
Western Wyoming Community
    College *A*

Arab Republic of Egypt

American University in Cairo *B*

Engineering and engineering-related technologies

Alabama

Alabama Agricultural and
    Mechanical University *A,B*
Brewer State Junior College *A*
Community College of the Air
    Force *A*
Enterprise State Junior College *A*
John C. Calhoun State Community
    College *A*
Lawson State Community
    College *A*
Snead State Junior College *A*

Arizona

Arizona State University *M*
Arizona Western College *A*
Glendale Community College *A*
Pima Community College *A*
Yavapai College *A*

Arkansas

East Arkansas Community
    College *A*
Garland County Community
    College *C*
John Brown University *A*
Mississippi County Community
    College *A*
Phillips County Community
    College *A*
University of Arkansas at Little
    Rock *A*

California

Allan Hancock College *C,A*
Bakersfield College *A*
Barstow College *A*
California Polytechnic State
    University: San Luis Obispo *B*
California State Polytechnic
    University: Pomona *B*
Central California Commercial
    College *A*
Cerritos Community College *A*
Cerro Coso Community College
    C,A
Chabot College *A*
Chaffey Community College *A*
Citrus College *A*
City College of San Francisco *A*
Cogswell Polytechnical College *A,B*
College of the Desert *A*
College of Marin: Kentfield *A*
College of the Sequoias *C,A*

Compton Community College *A*
Cuesta College *A*
De Anza College *A*
Diablo Valley College *A*
Don Bosco Technical Institute *A*
East Los Angeles College *A*
Evergreen Valley College *A*
Foothill College *A*
Fresno City College *A*
Gavilan Community College *A*
Golden West College *A*
Hartnell College *A*
ITT Technical Institute: Van
    Nuys *A*
Kings River Community College *A*
Los Angeles City College *C,A*
Los Angeles Harbor College *A*
Los Angeles Valley College *A*
Merced College *A*
Mission College *A*
Modesto Junior College *A*
Mount San Antonio College *A*
Mount San Jacinto College *A*
Pacific Union College *A,B*
Pasadena City College *C,A*
Saddleback College *A*
San Diego City College *C,A*
San Joaquin Delta College *C,A*
San Jose City College *A*
Santa Barbara City College *A*
Santa Rosa Junior College *A*
Southwestern College *A*
Taft College *A*
Ventura College *A*
West Coast University *A,B*
West Hills Community College *A*

Colorado

Aims Community College *A*
Colorado Technical College *A,B*
Mesa State College *A*
United States Air Force
    Academy *B*

Connecticut

Central Connecticut State
    University *B*
Greater New Haven State Technical
    College *A*
Hartford State Technical College *A*
Mitchell College *A*
Norwalk State Technical College *A*
Thames Valley State Technical
    College *A*
Waterbury State Technical
    College *A*

Delaware

Delaware State College *B*
Delaware Technical and
    Community College
    Stanton/Wilmington
        Campus *A*
    Terry Campus *A*
University of Delaware *B*

District of Columbia

University of the District of
    Columbia *A*

Florida

Brevard Community College *A*
Broward Community College *A*
Daytona Beach Community
    College *A*
Edison Community College *C,A*
Embry-Riddle Aeronautical
    University *B*
Gulf Coast Community College *C,A*
Hillsborough Community College *A*
Indian River Community College *A*
Manatee Community College *A*

University of Florida *B,M*
University of South Florida *B*
Valencia Community College *A*

Georgia

Atlanta Metropolitan College *A*
Brunswick College *A*
Clayton State College *A*
Dalton College *A*
Darton College *A*
DeKalb College *A*
Floyd College *A*
Fort Valley State College *A*
Gainesville College *A*
Georgia Southern University *B,M*
Macon College *A*
Meadows College of Business *A*
Middle Georgia College *A*
Savannah State College *A*
Southern College of Technology *M*
Valdosta State College *A*

Hawaii

University of Hawaii: Honolulu
    Community College *C,A*

Idaho

North Idaho College *A*
Northwest Nazarene College *A*
Ricks College *A*

Illinois

Belleville Area College *A*
Black Hawk College *A*
City Colleges of Chicago
    Richard J. Daley College *A*
    Wright College *A*
Elgin Community College *A*
Highland Community College *A*
Illinois Eastern Community
    Colleges: Wabash Valley
    College *A*
Illinois Valley Community
    College *A*
John A. Logan College *A*
Joliet Junior College *A*
Kishwaukee College *A*
Lake Land College *A*
Lewis and Clark Community
    College *A*
Lincoln Land Community
    College *A*
Moraine Valley Community College
    C,A
Morrison Institute of Technology *A*
Morton College *A*
Northern Illinois University *B*
Olivet Nazarene University *A*
Parkland College *A*
Rend Lake College *A*
Rock Valley College *A*
Southern Illinois University at
    Carbondale *B*
Triton College *C,A*
William Rainey Harper College *A*

Indiana

Indiana University East *A*
Indiana University—Purdue
    University at Fort Wayne *A,B*
Purdue University
    Calumet *A,B*
    West Lafayette *A*
University of Southern Indiana *A*
Vincennes University *A*

Iowa

Kirkwood Community College *A*
North Iowa Area Community
    College *A*
Scott Community College *A*

Southeastern Community College:
    North Campus *A*
University of Northern Iowa *B*

Kansas

Butler County Community
    College *A*
Central College *A*
Coffeyville Community College *A*
Colby Community College *A*
Donnelly College *C*
Fort Scott Community College *A*
Hutchinson Community College *A*
Kansas State University *B*
Neosho County Community
    College *A*
Pittsburg State University *A,B,M*
Southwestern College *B*

Kentucky

Brescia College *A*
Institute of Electronic
    Technology *A*
Jefferson Community College *A*
Lexington Community College *A*
Louisville Technical Institute *A*
Murray State University *A,B,M*
Sue Bennett College *A*

Louisiana

Nicholls State University *A*
Northwestern State University *B*
University of Southwestern
    Louisiana *A*

Maine

Maine Maritime Academy *B*

Maryland

Allegany Community College *A*
Anne Arundel Community
    College *A*
Charles County Community
    College *A*
Hagerstown Junior College *A*
Howard Community College *A*
Montgomery College
    Germantown Campus *A*
    Rockville Campus *A*
    Takoma Park Campus *A*
Prince George's Community
    College *A*
University of Maryland: Eastern
    Shore *B*

Massachusetts

Berkshire Community College *A*
Bristol Community College *A*
Franklin Institute of Boston *A*
Massasoit Community College *A*
Northern Essex Community
    College *A*
Quinsigamond Community
    College *C*
Roxbury Community College *A*
Springfield Technical Community
    College *A*
University of Massachusetts at
    Dartmouth *B*
Wentworth Institute of Technology
    A,B

Michigan

Andrews University *A,B*
Baker College of Muskegon *A*
Charles Stewart Mott Community
    College *A*
Delta College *A*
Eastern Michigan University *B*
Ferris State University *A*
Grand Rapids Community
    College *A*

Jackson Community College *A*
Kellogg Community College *A*
Lansing Community College *A*
Lawrence Technological
University *B*
Macomb Community College *C,A*
Mid Michigan Community
College *A*
Muskegon Community College *A*
Northwestern Michigan College *A*
Oakland Community College *A*
Schoolcraft College *A*
Southwestern Michigan College *A*

Minnesota

Itasca Community College:
Arrowhead Region *A*
Mankato State University *B*
Normandale Community College *A*
Rainy River Community College *A*
Rochester Community College *A*
St. Cloud State University *B*
Southwest State University *A,B*
Vermilion Community College *A*

Mississippi

Hinds Community College *A*
Holmes Community College *A*
Jones County Junior College *A*
Mississippi Delta Community
College *A*
University of Southern
Mississippi *B*

Missouri

Central Missouri State University
A,B
Culver-Stockton College *A,B*
Hannibal-LaGrange College *A*
Maple Woods Community
College *A*
Mineral Area College *C,A*
Penn Valley Community College *A*
St. Louis Community College
Florissant Valley *A*
Forest Park *A*

Montana

Montana College of Mineral
Science and Technology *A*

Nebraska

Central Community College *A*
McCook Community College *A*
Southeast Community College:
Milford Campus *A*
University of Nebraska—Lincoln
A,B

Nevada

Community College of Southern
Nevada *A*
Truckee Meadows Community
College *C,A*

New Jersey

Brookdale Community College *A*
Burlington County College *A*
Camden County College *A*
County College of Morris *A*
Essex County College *A*
Thomas Edison State College *A,B*
Union County College *A*

New Mexico

Albuquerque Technical-Vocational
Institute *A*
Eastern New Mexico University *A*
New Mexico State University *A,B*

New York

Adirondack Community College *A*
Bramson ORT Technical Institute
C,A
Broome Community College *A*
City University of New York
Borough of Manhattan
Community College *A*
College of Staten Island *A*
Kingsborough Community
College *A*
New York City Technical
College *A*
College of Aeronautics *A*
Community College of the Finger
Lakes *A*
Corning Community College *A*
Dutchess Community College *A*
Erie Community College: North
Campus *A*
Fulton-Montgomery Community
College *A*
Genesee Community College *A*
Herkimer County Community
College *A*
Hudson Valley Community
College *A*
Jamestown Community College *A*
Mohawk Valley Community
College *A*
New York Institute of
Technology *B*
Niagara County Community
College *A*
Onondaga Community College *A*
State University of New York
College of Agriculture and
Technology at Morrisville *A*
College of Technology at
Alfred *A*
College of Technology at
Canton *A*
College of Technology at
Delhi *A*
College of Technology at
Farmingdale *A*
Suffolk County Community
College *A*
Tompkins-Cortland Community
College *A*
Ulster County Community
College *A*
University of the State of New
York: Regents College *A,B*
Westchester Community College *A*

North Carolina

Alamance Community College *A*
Brevard College *A*
Catawba Valley Community
College *A*
Central Piedmont Community
College *A*
Chowan College *A*
Craven Community College *A*
Edgecombe Community College *A*
Gaston College *A*
Isothermal Community College *A*
Mitchell Community College *A*
Sandhills Community College *A*
Wake Technical Community
College *A*
Wayne Community College *A*
Western Piedmont Community
College *A*
Wilson Technical Community
College *A*

North Dakota

Bismarck State College *A*

Ohio

Bowling Green State University:
Firelands College *A*
Columbus State Community
College *A*
Cuyahoga Community College:
Metropolitan Campus *A*
Edison State Community College
C,A
ETI Technical College *A,B*
Kent State University
Ashtabula Regional Campus *A*
Tuscarawas Campus *A*
Marion Technical College *A*
Miami University: Hamilton
Campus *A*
Muskingum Area Technical
College *A*
North Central Technical College *A*
Owens Technical College
Findlay Campus *A*
Toledo *C,A*
Sinclair Community College *A*
Stark Technical College *A*
Terra Technical College *A*
University of Akron *A*
University of Cincinnati: Access
Colleges *A*
University of Dayton *B*
University of Toledo *A*
Washington State Community
College *A*
Wright State University: Lake
Campus *A*

Oklahoma

Cameron University *B*
Connors State College *A*
Murray State College *A*
Oklahoma State University
Oklahoma City *A*
Stillwater *B*
Phillips University *B*
Redlands Community College *A*
Rogers State College *A*
Rose State College *A*
Tulsa Junior College *A*

Oregon

Central Oregon Community
College *A*
Chemeketa Community College *A*
ITT Technical Institute: Portland *A*
Oregon Institute of Technology *A*
Oregon Polytechnic Institute *C,A*
Portland Community College *A*
Umpqua Community College *A*

Pennsylvania

Bucks County Community
College *A*
Butler County Community
College *A*
California University of
Pennsylvania *B*
CHI Institute *A*
Community College of Beaver
County *A*
Community College of
Philadelphia *A*
Drexel University *B*
Edinboro University of
Pennsylvania *A*
Gannon University *A,B*
Harrisburg Area Community
College *A*
Lincoln University *B*
Luzerne County Community
College *A*
Montgomery County Community
College *A*

Pennsylvania College of
Technology *A*
Pennsylvania Institute of
Technology *A*
Reading Area Community College
C,A
Westmoreland County Community
College *A*

Puerto Rico

Caribbean University *A*

Rhode Island

Community College of Rhode
Island *A*
Johnson & Wales University *A,B*
Rhode Island College *B*

South Carolina

Aiken Technical College *A*
Claflin College *B*
Florence-Darlington Technical
College *A*
Greenville Technical College *A*
Midlands Technical College *A*
Trident Technical College *A*

Tennessee

Austin Peay State University *B*
Columbia State Community
College *A*
Dyersburg State Community
College *A*
East Tennessee State University
B,M
Hiwassee College *A*
Maryville College *B*
Middle Tennessee State
University *B*
Motlow State Community
College *A*
Nashville State Technical
Institute *A*
Pellissippi State Technical
Community College *A*
Roane State Community College *A*
University of Tennessee: Martin *B*

Texas

Amarillo College *A*
Angelina College *A*
Brazosport College *C,A*
Central Texas College *A*
Cisco Junior College *A*
Cooke County College *A*
Del Mar College *A*
El Paso Community College *A*
Houston Community College *A*
Kilgore College *A*
Laredo Junior College *C*
Lee College *A*
LeTourneau University *B*
Midwestern State University *B*
Mountain View College *C*
Richland College *A*
San Antonio College *A*
Schreiner College *A*
Southwest Texas State University *B*
Tarrant County Junior College *A*
Texas A&M University *B*
Texas State Technical College:
Waco *A*
Texas Tech University *B*
West Texas State University *B,M*

Utah

Brigham Young University *M*
Dixie College *A*
Weber State University *A,B*

Vermont

Champlain College *A*
Vermont Technical College *A*

Virginia

Central Virginia Community
    College *A*
Commonwealth College *A*
Dabney S. Lancaster Community
    College *A*
Lord Fairfax Community College *A*
Northern Virginia Community
    College *A*
Old Dominion University *B*
Patrick Henry Community
    College *A*
Virginia Highlands Community
    College *A*
Virginia State University *B*

Washington

Bellevue Community College *A*
Centralia College *A*
Clark College *A*
Cogswell College North *A,B*
Columbia Basin College *A*
Everett Community College *A*
Lower Columbia College *A*
North Seattle Community
    College *A*
Olympic College *C,A*
Peninsula College *A*
Shoreline Community College *A*
Skagit Valley College *A*
Walla Walla Community College
    C,A
Yakima Valley Community
    College *A*

West Virginia

Marshall University *A*
Potomac State College of West
    Virginia University *A*
Salem-Teikyo University *A,B*
Shepherd College *A*
West Virginia Institute of
    Technology *A,B*
West Virginia University at
    Parkersburg *A*

Wisconsin

Concordia University Wisconsin *B*
Fox Valley Technical College *A*
Madison Area Technical College *A*
Moraine Park Technical College *A*
University of Wisconsin: Parkside *B*
Waukesha County Technical
    College *A*
Western Wisconsin Technical
    College *A*

Wyoming

Laramie County Community
    College *C,A*
Sheridan College *A*
Western Wyoming Community
    College *A*

Engineering management

Alaska

University of Alaska Anchorage *M*

California

Oxnard College *C*
Santa Clara University *M*
United States International
    University *B*
University of the Pacific *B*

University of Southern California *M*
West Coast University *M*

Colorado

Fort Lewis College *B*
United States Air Force
    Academy *B*

Connecticut

Thames Valley State Technical
    College *A*
University of Bridgeport *M*

District of Columbia

George Washington University *M,D*

Florida

Florida Institute of Technology *M*
Schiller International University *B*

Idaho

University of Idaho *M*

Illinois

Northern Illinois University *M*
Northwestern University *M*
University of Illinois at Chicago *B*

Indiana

Indiana Institute of Technology *B*
Purdue University *B*
Tri-State University *B*
University of Evansville *B,M*

Kansas

Fort Scott Community College *A*
University of Kansas *M*

Louisiana

University of Southwestern
    Louisiana *M*

Maryland

University of Maryland
        Baltimore County *M*
        University College *M*

Massachusetts

Boston University *B*
University of Massachusetts at
    Amherst *M*
Western New England College *B*
Worcester Polytechnic Institute *B*

Michigan

GMI Engineering & Management
    Institute *B*
Michigan Technological
    University *B*
Oakland University *M*
University of Detroit Mercy *M*
Western Michigan University *M*

Missouri

University of Missouri: Rolla *B,M,D*

New Jersey

Stevens Institute of Technology
    B,M
Union County College *A*

New York

Rensselaer Polytechnic Institute
    B,M
United States Military Academy *B*

North Carolina

University of North Carolina at
    Asheville *B*

North Dakota

University of North Dakota *B*

Ohio

Air Force Institute of
    Technology *M*
Dyke College *B*
University of Dayton *M*

Oklahoma

Oral Roberts University *B*
University of Tulsa *M*

Oregon

Portland State University *M*
University of Portland *B*

Pennsylvania

Drexel University *M*
Indiana University of
    Pennsylvania *B*
Lehigh University *M*
Widener University *B*
Wilkes University *B*
York College of Pennsylvania *B*

Puerto Rico

University of Puerto Rico:
    Mayaguez Campus *M*

South Dakota

South Dakota School of Mines and
    Technology *M*

Tennessee

Christian Brothers University *M*
University of Tennessee:
    Chattanooga *B*

Texas

Dallas Baptist University *B*
Lamar University—Beaumont *B*
Southern Methodist University *M,D*
University of Dallas *M*

Utah

Brigham Young University *M*

Vermont

University of Vermont *B*

Virginia

Old Dominion University *M*
Paul D. Camp Community
    College *C*

Washington

City University *M*
St. Martin's College *M*
Washington State University *M*

West Virginia

West Virginia Graduate College *M*

Wisconsin

Milwaukee School of
    Engineering *M*

Engineering mechanics

Alabama

University of Alabama *M,D*

Arizona

University of Arizona *M,D*

California

California State University
        Fresno *B*
        Northridge *B,M*
City College of San Francisco *C,A*
Santa Clara University *M*
University of California: San Diego
    B,M,D
University of Southern California
    B,M

Colorado

Colorado School of Mines *M*
United States Air Force
    Academy *B*

Connecticut

University of Connecticut *D*

District of Columbia

George Washington University
    B,M,D

Florida

University of Florida *M,D*
University of South Florida *B,M,D*

Georgia

Georgia Institute of Technology
    B,M,D

Illinois

Bradley University *M*
Richland Community College *A*
Southern Illinois University at
    Carbondale *B,M*
University of Illinois
        Chicago *B,M,D*
        Urbana-Champaign *B,M,D*

Iowa

Iowa State University *M,D*

Maryland

Johns Hopkins University *B,M,D*

Massachusetts

Boston University *M*
Tufts University *B*
Worcester Polytechnic Institute *B*

Michigan

Michigan State University *B,M,D*
Michigan Technological University
    M,D
University of Michigan *B,M,D*

Mississippi

Mississippi State University *M*

Missouri

East Central College *A*
University of Missouri: Rolla *M,D*
Washington University *B,M,D*

Montana

Montana State University *M*

Nebraska

University of Nebraska—Lincoln
    B,M

New Mexico

New Mexico Institute of Mining
    and Technology *B*

New York

Columbia University: School of
    Engineering and Applied Science
    B,M,D,W
Rensselaer Polytechnic Institute
    M,D

State University of New York at
Buffalo *D*

Ohio

Ohio State University: Columbus
Campus *B,M,D*
University of Cincinnati *B,M,D*

Pennsylvania

Drexel University *M,D*
Lehigh University *B,M,D*
Lock Haven University of
Pennsylvania *B*
Messiah College *B*
Penn State University Park
Campus *M*
Widener University *M*

South Carolina

Clemson University *M,D*

Texas

University of Texas
Arlington *M,D*
Austin *M,D*

Virginia

Old Dominion University *M,D*
University of Virginia *B*
Virginia Polytechnic Institute and
State University *B,M,D*

Washington

Spokane Falls Community
College *A*

Wisconsin

University of Wisconsin: Madison
B,M,D

Engineering and other disciplines

Arizona

Arizona State University *B*

California

Claremont McKenna College *B*
Harvey Mudd College *B*
Los Angeles City College *A*
Modesto Junior College *A*
Mount San Jacinto College *A*
Napa Valley College *A*
Naval Postgraduate School *M*
University of California: Los
Angeles *D*
University of Southern California
B,M
West Hills Community College *A*

Colorado

Metropolitan State College of
Denver *B*
University of Colorado at
Boulder *B*

Connecticut

Fairfield University *B*
Mitchell College *A*
University of Bridgeport *B*
University of Hartford *B*
University of New Haven *M*
Wesleyan University *B*
Yale University *B*

Delaware

University of Delaware *M,D*

District of Columbia

Catholic University of America *B*
George Washington University
B,M,D

Florida

Daytona Beach Community
College *A*
Florida Institute of Technology *M*
Gulf Coast Community College *A*
Pensacola Junior College *A*
University of Miami *M*

Georgia

Clark Atlanta University *B*
DeKalb College *A*
Georgia Institute of Technology
B,M

Idaho

College of Southern Idaho *A*
Idaho State University *B,M*
Northwest Nazarene College *B*

Illinois

Augustana College *B*
Aurora University *B*
Bradley University *B,M*
City Colleges of Chicago: Richard J.
Daley College *A*
Joliet Junior College *A*
Lincoln Land Community
College *A*
Olivet Nazarene University *B*
Richland Community College *A*

Indiana

DePauw University *B*
Indiana Institute of Technology *B*
Purdue University
Calumet *B,M*
West Lafayette *B,M,D*
University of Notre Dame *B*
Vincennes University *A*

Iowa

Coe College *B*
Cornell College *B*

Kansas

Coffeyville Community College *A*
University of Kansas *M,D*

Maine

University of Maine *B*

Maryland

Allegany Community College *A*
Johns Hopkins University *B*
Loyola College in Maryland *B*
Montgomery College
Rockville Campus *A*
Takoma Park Campus *A*

Massachusetts

Boston University *B,M*
Emmanuel College *B*
Harvard and Radcliffe Colleges *B*
Harvard University *M,D*
Massachusetts Institute of
Technology *B,M,D*
Northeastern University *M*
Simmons College *B*
Springfield Technical Community
College *A*
Tufts University *B,M,D*
University of Massachusetts
Amherst *M,D*
Lowell *B,M*
Western New England College *B*
Williams College *B*
Worcester Polytechnic Institute *B*

Michigan

Calvin College *B*
Hope College *B*
Lawrence Technological
University *B*
Michigan State University *B*
Michigan Technological
University *B*
Oakland University *B*
Saginaw Valley State University *B*
Schoolcraft College *A*
University of Michigan
Ann Arbor *B,M,D*
Dearborn *B*
Wayne State University *D*
Western Michigan University *B*

Minnesota

Bethany Lutheran College *A*
Northland Community College *A*
University of Minnesota: Twin
Cities *B,M,D*
Winona State University *B*

Mississippi

Mississippi State University *D*

Missouri

Central Missouri State University *B*
St. Louis University *B*
Washington University *B*

Montana

Montana College of Mineral
Science and Technology *A*

New Hampshire

Daniel Webster College *A*
New England College *B*
St. Anselm College *B*

New Jersey

Bergen Community College *A*
Camden County College *A*
New Jersey Institute of
Technology *B*
Passaic County Community
College *A*
Stevens Institute of Technology *B*
Stockton State College *B*

New Mexico

New Mexico Institute of Mining
and Technology *B*

New York

Clarkson University *B*
Columbia University
Columbia College *B*
School of Engineering and
Applied Science *M,D*
Cornell University *B*
Fulton-Montgomery Community
College *A*
Genesee Community College *A*
Herkimer County Community
College *A*
Hofstra University *B*
Hudson Valley Community
College *A*
Jefferson Community College *A*
Manhattan College *B*
Mohawk Valley Community
College *A*
New York University *B*
Rochester Institute of Technology
B,M
St. Thomas Aquinas College *B*

State University of New York
College at Fredonia *B*
College at Geneseo *B*
College of Technology at
Alfred *A*
Suffolk County Community
College *A*
Syracuse University *B*
United States Military Academy *B*
University of Rochester *B*
Westchester Community College *A*

North Carolina

Caldwell Community College and
Technical Institute *A*
Johnson C. Smith University *B*
North Carolina Agricultural and
Technical State University *B*

North Dakota

North Dakota State College of
Science *A*
University of North Dakota:
Williston *A*

Ohio

Case Western Reserve University
B,M
John Carroll University *B*
Marietta College *B*
Ohio Northern University *B*
Union Institute *B,D*
University of Akron *B*
University of Cincinnati *B*

Oklahoma

Eastern Oklahoma State College *A*
Rose State College *A*
University of Oklahoma *M*
University of Tulsa *M*

Oregon

Central Oregon Community
College *A*

Pennsylvania

Bucknell University *B*
California University of
Pennsylvania *B*
Carnegie Mellon University
B,M,D,W
Duquesne University *B*
Edinboro University of
Pennsylvania *B*
Lafayette College *B*
Lehigh University *B*
Penn State University Park Campus
C,M,D
St. Vincent College *B*
Swarthmore College *B*
University of Pennsylvania *B*

Puerto Rico

University of Puerto Rico:
Mayaguez Campus *B*

Rhode Island

Brown University *B*

South Dakota

Augustana College *B*

Tennessee

Maryville College *B*
Motlow State Community
College *A*
Tennessee State University *B*
University of Tennessee:
Knoxville *M*

Texas

Central Texas College *A*
College of the Mainland *A*
Texas A&M University *B*
Texas Tech University *M,D*

Virginia

Emory and Henry College *B*
Old Dominion University *B*
Virginia Commonwealth
University *M*

Washington

Columbia Basin College *A*
Everett Community College *A*
Grays Harbor College *A*
Skagit Valley College *A*
University of Washington *B*

West Virginia

Bethany College *B*

Wisconsin

Carthage College *B*

Wyoming

Laramie County Community
College *A*
Northwest College *A*
Western Wyoming Community
College *A*

Engineering physics

Alabama

Samford University *B*

Arizona

University of Arizona *B*

Arkansas

Ouachita Baptist University *B*
Southern Arkansas University *B*

California

La Sierra University *A*
Naval Postgraduate School *M,D*
Point Loma Nazarene College *B*
Santa Clara University *B*
University of California
Berkeley *B*
San Diego *B,M,D*
University of the Pacific *B*
University of San Francisco *B*
Westmont College *B*

Colorado

Colorado School of Mines
B,M,D,W
United States Air Force
Academy *B*
University of Colorado
Boulder *B*
Denver *B*

Florida

Embry-Riddle Aeronautical
University *B*

Idaho

Northwest Nazarene College *B*

Illinois

Bradley University *B*
Northwestern University *B*
Richland Community College *A*
University of Illinois
Chicago *B*
Urbana-Champaign *B,M,D*

Iowa

Loras College *B*
St. Ambrose University *B*

Kansas

University of Kansas *B*

Kentucky

Murray State University *B*

Maine

University of Maine *B,M*

Maryland

Morgan State University *B*

Massachusetts

Brandeis University *B*
Eastern Nazarene College *B*
Harvard and Radcliffe Colleges *B*
Harvard University *M,D*
Massachusetts Institute of
Technology *B,M,D,W*
Merrimack College *B*
Tufts University *B*
University of Massachusetts at
Boston *B*
Worcester Polytechnic Institute *B*

Michigan

Eastern Michigan University *B*
Hope College *B*
Michigan Technological University
B,D
Oakland University *B*
University of Michigan *B,D*

Minnesota

Bemidji State University *B*
Willmar Community College *A*

Missouri

East Central College *A*
Southeast Missouri State
University *B*
Washington University *B,M,D*

Nevada

University of Nevada: Reno *B*

New Jersey

Stevens Institute of Technology
B,M,D

New York

Columbia University: School of
Engineering and Applied Science
B,M,D
Cornell University *B,M*
New York University *B*
Rensselaer Polytechnic Institute
B,M,D
St. Bonaventure University *B*
State University of New York at
Buffalo *B*
United States Military Academy *B*

North Carolina

North Carolina Agricultural and
Technical State University *B*

North Dakota

North Dakota State University *B*
University of North Dakota *B*

Ohio

Air Force Institute of Technology
M,D
John Carroll University *B*
Miami University: Oxford
Campus *B*

Ohio State University: Columbus
Campus *B*
Ohio University *B*
University of Toledo *B*
Wright State University *B*

Oklahoma

Northeastern State University *B*
Oklahoma Christian University of
Science and Arts *B*
Southwestern Oklahoma State
University *B*
University of Oklahoma *B,M,D*
University of Tulsa *B*

Oregon

Linfield College *B*
Oregon State University *B*

Pennsylvania

Elizabethtown College *B*
Lehigh University *B,M,D*
Shippensburg University of
Pennsylvania *B*
Thiel College *B*
University of Pittsburgh *B*

South Carolina

Benedict College *B*
Bob Jones University *B*

South Dakota

Augustana College *B*
South Dakota State University *B*

Tennessee

Christian Brothers University *B*
University of Tennessee:
Knoxville *B*

Texas

Abilene Christian University *B*
Texas Tech University *B*

Vermont

University of Vermont *M*

Virginia

George Mason University *M*
University of Virginia *M,D*
Washington and Lee University *B*

Washington

Pacific Lutheran University *B*

West Virginia

West Virginia Wesleyan College *B*

Engineering science

Arizona

Arizona State University *B,M,D*
Mesa Community College *A*

Arkansas

University of Arkansas *B,M*
Westark Community College *A*

California

California Polytechnic State
University: San Luis Obispo *B*
California State University:
Fullerton *B,M*
Naval Postgraduate School *M*
Stanford University *M*
University of California
Berkeley *B*
San Diego *B,M,D*
University of Redlands *B*

University of Southern California
M,D

Colorado

Colorado School of Mines *M*
Colorado State University *B*
Mesa State College *A*
Pikes Peak Community College *A*
United States Air Force
Academy *B*

Connecticut

Yale University *B,M,D*

Florida

University of Florida *M,D*
University of Miami *B*
University of South Florida *B,M,D*

Georgia

Georgia Institute of Technology
B,M,D

Illinois

Aurora University *B*
Bradley University *B*
Illinois Benedictine College *B*
Northwestern University *B*
Southern Illinois University at
Carbondale *M,D*

Indiana

Manchester College *B*
Purdue University *B*

Iowa

Dordt College *B*
Iowa State University *B*

Kentucky

Georgetown College *B*

Louisiana

Louisiana State University and
Agricultural and Mechanical
College *M,D*
University of New Orleans *M*

Maryland

Loyola College in Maryland *B,M*

Massachusetts

Boston University *D*
Greenfield Community College *A*
Harvard and Radcliffe Colleges *B*
Merrimack College *A*
Middlesex Community College *A*
Tufts University *B*

Michigan

Calvin College *B*
University of Michigan
Ann Arbor *B*
Flint *B*

Mississippi

University of Mississippi *M,D*

Montana

Montana College of Mineral
Science and Technology *B,M*

New Jersey

Camden County College *A*
County College of Morris *A*
Gloucester County College *A*
Mercer County Community
College *A*
New Jersey Institute of Technology
B,M

New Mexico

New Mexico Institute of Mining and Technology *B*

New York

Broome Community College *A*
City University of New York
  Borough of Manhattan Community College *A*
  College of Staten Island *B*
  Kingsborough Community College *A*
Clarkson University *M,D*
Erie Community College
  City Campus *A*
  North Campus *A*
Herkimer County Community College *A*
Hofstra University *B*
Hudson Valley Community College *A*
Jefferson Community College *A*
Onondaga Community College *A*
Rensselaer Polytechnic Institute *B,M,D*
State University of New York
  Buffalo *B,M,D*
  College of Agriculture and Technology at Morrisville *A*
  College of Technology at Alfred *A*
  College of Technology at Canton *A*
  College of Technology at Delhi *A*
  College of Technology at Farmingdale *A*
Sullivan County Community College *A*
University of Rochester *B*
Westchester Community College *A*

Ohio

Franciscan University of Steubenville *B*
Lakeland Community College *A*
University of Cincinnati *B,M,D*
University of Toledo *B,M,D*

Oregon

University of Portland *B*

Pennsylvania

Carnegie Mellon University *B,M,D,W*
Drexel University *B*
Lock Haven University of Pennsylvania *B*
Penn State
  Erie Behrend College *B*
  Great Valley Graduate Center *M*
  Harrisburg Capital College *M*
  University Park Campus *B,M*
Swarthmore College *B*
Wilkes University *B*

South Carolina

Bob Jones University *B*

Tennessee

David Lipscomb University *B*
University of Tennessee: Knoxville *B,M,D*
Vanderbilt University *B*

Texas

Lamar University—Beaumont *M*
St. Mary's University *B,M*

Virginia

University of Virginia *B*
Virginia Polytechnic Institute and State University *B*

Washington

Seattle Pacific University *B*
Washington State University *D*

Wisconsin

University of Wisconsin: Milwaukee *B*

English

Alabama

Alabama Agricultural and Mechanical University *B,M*
Alabama Southern Community College *A*
Alabama State University *B*
Athens State College *B*
Auburn University
  Auburn *B,M,D*
  Montgomery *B*
Birmingham-Southern College *B*
Brewer State Junior College *A*
Faulkner University *B*
Huntingdon College *B*
Jacksonville State University *B,M*
James H. Faulkner State Community College *A*
John C. Calhoun State Community College *A*
Judson College *B*
Lawson State Community College *A*
Livingston University *B*
Miles College *B*
Mobile College *B*
Oakwood College *B*
Samford University *B,M*
Spring Hill College *B*
Stillman College *B*
Talladega College *B*
Troy State University
  Dothan *B*
  Montgomery *B*
  Troy *B*
Tuskegee University *B*
University of Alabama
  Birmingham *B,M*
  Huntsville *B,M*
  Tuscaloosa *B,M,D*
University of Montevallo *B,M*
University of North Alabama *B*
University of South Alabama *B,M*

Alaska

University of Alaska
  Anchorage *B,M*
  Fairbanks *B,M*

Arizona

Arizona State University *B,M,D*
Arizona Western College *A*
Cochise College *A*
Eastern Arizona College *A*
Glendale Community College *A*
Grand Canyon University *B*
Mohave Community College *A*
Northern Arizona University *B,M*
Prescott College *B*
University of Arizona *B,M,D*
Yavapai College *A*

Arkansas

Arkansas College *B*
Arkansas State University
  Beebe Branch *A*
  Jonesboro *B,M*
Arkansas Tech University *B*
Harding University *B,M*
Henderson State University *B,M*
Hendrix College *B*
John Brown University *B*
Mississippi County Community College *A*
Ouachita Baptist University *B*
Philander Smith College *B*
Southern Arkansas University *B*
University of Arkansas
  Fayetteville *B,M,D*
  Little Rock *B*
  Monticello *B*
  Pine Bluff *B*
University of Central Arkansas *B,M*
University of the Ozarks *B*
Westark Community College *A*

California

Azusa Pacific University *B*
Bakersfield College *A*
Barstow College *A*
Bethany College *B*
Biola University *B*
California Baptist College *B*
California Lutheran University *B*
California Polytechnic State University: San Luis Obispo *B,M*
California State Polytechnic University: Pomona *B,M*
California State University
  Bakersfield *B,M*
  Chico *B,M*
  Dominguez Hills *B,M*
  Fresno *B*
  Fullerton *B,M*
  Hayward *B,M*
  Long Beach *B,M*
  Los Angeles *B,M*
  Northridge *B,M*
  Sacramento *B,M*
  San Bernardino *B,M*
  San Marcos *B*
  Stanislaus *B,M*
Cerritos Community College *A*
Chabot College *A*
Chaffey Community College *A*
Chapman University *B,M*
Christ College Irvine *B*
Christian Heritage College *B*
Citrus College *A*
Claremont McKenna College *B*
College of the Desert *A*
College of Notre Dame *B,M*
College of the Sequoias *A*
Columbia College *A*
De Anza College *A*
El Camino College *A*
Feather River College *A*
Foothill College *A*
Fresno Pacific College *B*
Gavilan Community College *A*
Glendale Community College *A*
Holy Names College *B*
Humboldt State University *B,M*
Imperial Valley College *A*
Kings River Community College *A*
La Sierra University *B,M*
Laney College *A*
Long Beach City College *A*
Los Angeles City College *A*
Los Angeles Mission College *A*
Los Angeles Valley College *A*
Loyola Marymount University *B,M*
Marymount College *A*
Master's College *B*

Mendocino College *A*
Merced College *A*
Mills College *B*
MiraCosta College *A*
Mount St. Mary's College *B*
Napa Valley College *A*
Occidental College *B*
Ohlone College *A*
Orange Coast College *A*
Oxnard College *A*
Pacific Union College *B*
Pepperdine University *B,M*
Pitzer College *B*
Pomona College *B*
Porterville College *A*
St. John's Seminary College *B*
St. Mary's College of California *B*
San Diego City College *A*
San Diego State University *B,M*
San Francisco State University *B,M*
San Joaquin Delta College *A*
San Jose City College *A*
San Jose State University *B,M*
Santa Barbara City College *A*
Santa Clara University *B*
Santa Monica College *A*
Santa Rosa Junior College *A*
Scripps College *B*
Simpson College *B*
Skyline College *A*
Solano Community College *A*
Sonoma State University *B,M*
Southern California College *B*
Southwestern College *A*
Stanford University *B,M,D*
Taft College *A*
United States International University *B*
University of California
  Berkeley *B,M,D*
  Davis *B,M,D*
  Irvine *B,M,D*
  Los Angeles *B,M,D*
  Riverside *B,M,D*
  San Diego *B*
  Santa Barbara *B,M,D*
University of Judaism *B*
University of La Verne *B*
University of the Pacific *B,M*
University of Redlands *B*
University of San Diego *B,M*
University of San Francisco *B*
University of Southern California *B,M,D*
Ventura College *A*
West Valley College *A*
Westmont College *B*
Whittier College *B,M*

Colorado

Adams State College *B*
Colorado Christian University *B*
Colorado College *B*
Colorado State University *B,M*
Fort Lewis College *B*
Mesa State College *A,B*
Metropolitan State College of Denver *B*
Pikes Peak Community College *A*
Regis College of Regis University *B*
United States Air Force Academy *B*
University of Colorado
  Boulder *B,M,D*
  Colorado Springs *B*
  Denver *B,M*
University of Denver *B*
University of Northern Colorado *B,M*
University of Southern Colorado *B*
Western State College of Colorado *B*

Connecticut

Albertus Magnus College *B*
Central Connecticut State
University *B,M*
Connecticut College *B*
Eastern Connecticut State
University *B*
Fairfield University *B*
Mitchell College *A*
Northwestern Connecticut
Community College *A*
Quinnipiac College *B*
Sacred Heart University *A,B*
St. Joseph College *B,M*
Southern Connecticut State
University *B,M*
Teikyo-Post University *A,B*
Trinity College *B,M*
University of Bridgeport *B*
University of Connecticut *B,M,D*
University of Hartford *B*
University of New Haven *B*
Wesleyan University *B*
Western Connecticut State
University *B,M*

Delaware

Delaware State College *B*
University of Delaware *B,M,D*

District of Columbia

Catholic University of America
B,M,D
Gallaudet University *B*
George Washington University *B*
Georgetown University *B,M*
Howard University *B,M,D*
Trinity College *B*
University of the District of
Columbia *B*

Florida

Barry University *B,M*
Bethune-Cookman College *B*
Brevard Community College *A*
Central Florida Community
College *A*
Daytona Beach Community
College *A*
Edison Community College *A*
Flagler College *B*
Florida Agricultural and Mechanical
University *B*
Florida Atlantic University *B,M*
Florida International University *B*
Florida Memorial College *B*
Florida Southern College *B*
Florida State University *B,M,D*
Gulf Coast Community College *A*
Indian River Community College *A*
Jacksonville University *B*
Manatee Community College *A*
Miami-Dade Community College *A*
New College of the University of
South Florida *B*
Palm Beach Atlantic College *B*
Pensacola Junior College *A*
Rollins College *B*
St. Leo College *B*
St. Thomas University *B*
Santa Fe Community College *A*
Stetson University *B,M*
University of Central Florida *B,M*
University of Florida *B,M,D*
University of Miami *B,M,D*
University of North Florida *B,M*
University of South Florida *M*
University of Tampa *A,B*
University of West Florida *B,M*
Warner Southern College *B*

Georgia

Abraham Baldwin Agricultural
College *A*
Agnes Scott College *B*
Andrew College *A*
Armstrong State College *B*
Atlanta Metropolitan College *A*
Augusta College *B*
Bainbridge College *A*
Berry College *B*
Brenau Women's College *B*
Clark Atlanta University *B,M*
Clayton State College *A*
Columbus College *B*
Covenant College *B*
Darton College *A*
East Georgia College *A*
Emory University *B,M,D*
Fort Valley State College *B*
Gainesville College *A*
Georgia College *B*
Georgia Southern University *B,M*
Georgia Southwestern College *B*
Georgia State University *B,M,D*
Gordon College *A*
Kennesaw State College *B*
LaGrange College *B*
Macon College *A*
Mercer University *B*
Middle Georgia College *A*
Morehouse College *B*
North Georgia College *B*
Oglethorpe University *B*
Oxford College of Emory
University *A*
Paine College *B*
Piedmont College *B*
Reinhardt College *A*
Savannah State College *B*
Shorter College *B*
South Georgia College *A*
Spelman College *B*
Toccoa Falls College *B*
University of Georgia *B,M,D*
Valdosta State College *B,M*
Waycross College *A*
Wesleyan College *B*
West Georgia College *B,M*
Young Harris College *A*

Hawaii

Brigham Young University-
Hawaii *B*
Chaminade University of
Honolulu *B*
Hawaii Pacific University *B*
University of Hawaii
Hilo *B*
Manoa *B,M,D*
West Oahu *B*

Idaho

Albertson College *B*
Boise State University *B,M*
College of Southern Idaho *A*
Idaho State University *B,M,D*
Lewis Clark State College *A,B*
North Idaho College *A*
Northwest Nazarene College *B*
Ricks College *A*
University of Idaho *B,M*

Illinois

Augustana College *B*
Aurora University *B*
Barat College *B*
Black Hawk College *A*
Blackburn College *B*
Bradley University *B,M*
Chicago State University *B,M*
City Colleges of Chicago: Wright
College *A*

College of St. Francis *B*
Concordia University *B*
De Paul University *B,M*
Eastern Illinois University *B,M*
Elmhurst College *B*
Eureka College *B*
Governors State University *B,M*
Greenville College *B*
Illinois Benedictine College *B*
Illinois Central College *A*
Illinois College *B*
Illinois Institute of Technology *B*
Illinois State University *B,M,D*
Illinois Valley Community
College *A*
Illinois Wesleyan University *B*
Joliet Junior College *A*
Judson College *B*
KAES College *B*
Kishwaukee College *A*
Knox College *B*
Lake Forest College *B*
Lake Land College *A*
Lewis University *B*
Lincoln Land Community
College *A*
Loyola University of Chicago
B,M,D
MacMurray College *B*
McKendree College *B*
Millikin University *B*
Monmouth College *B*
National-Louis University *B*
North Central College *B*
North Park College and Theological
Seminary *B*
Northeastern Illinois University *B*
Northern Illinois University *B,M,D*
Northwestern University *B,M,D*
Olivet Nazarene University *B*
Principia College *B*
Quincy College *B*
Rend Lake College *A*
Richland Community College *A*
Rockford College *B*
Roosevelt University *B,M*
Rosary College *B*
St. Xavier University *B*
Sangamon State University *B,M*
Shimer College *B*
Southern Illinois University
Carbondale *B,M,D*
Edwardsville *B,M*
Trinity Christian College *B*
Trinity College *B*
Triton College *A*
University of Chicago *B,M,D*
University of Illinois
Chicago *M,D*
Urbana-Champaign *B,M,D*
Waubonsee Community College *A*
Western Illinois University *B,M*
William Rainey Harper College *A*

Indiana

Ancilla College *A*
Anderson University *B*
Ball State University *B,M,D*
Bethel College *B*
Butler University *B,M*
Calumet College of St. Joseph *A,B*
Earlham College *B*
Franklin College *B*
Goshen College *B*
Grace College *B*
Hanover College *B*
Huntington College *B*
Indiana State University *B,M*

Indiana University
Bloomington *B,M,D*
East *B*
Kokomo *B*
Northwest *B*
South Bend *B*
Southeast *B*
Indiana University—Purdue
University
Fort Wayne *B,M*
Indianapolis *B*
Indiana Wesleyan University *B*
Manchester College *B*
Marian College *B*
Martin University *B*
Oakland City College *B*
Purdue University
Calumet *B*
North Central Campus *B*
West Lafayette *B,M,D*
St. Francis College *B*
St. Joseph's College *B*
St. Mary-of-the-Woods College *B*
St. Meinrad College *B*
Taylor University *B*
Tri-State University *B*
University of Evansville *B*
University of Indianapolis *B,M*
University of Notre Dame *B,M,D*
University of Southern Indiana *B*
Valparaiso University *B,M*
Vincennes University *A*
Wabash College *B*

Iowa

Briar Cliff College *B*
Buena Vista College *B*
Central College *B*
Clarke College *B*
Clinton Community College *A*
Coe College *B*
Cornell College *B*
Divine Word College *B*
Dordt College *B*
Drake University *B,M*
Graceland College *B*
Grand View College *B*
Grinnell College *B*
Iowa Lakes Community College *A*
Iowa State University *B,M*
Iowa Wesleyan College *B*
Kirkwood Community College *A*
Loras College *B*
Luther College *B*
Mount Mercy College *B*
Muscatine Community College *A*
North Iowa Area Community
College *A*
Northwestern College *B*
St. Ambrose University *B*
Scott Community College *A*
Simpson College *B*
Teikyo Marycrest University *A,B*
Teikyo Westmar University *B*
University of Dubuque *B*
University of Iowa *B,M,D*
University of Northern Iowa *B,M*
Upper Iowa University *B*
Wartburg College *B*
William Penn College *B*

Kansas

Allen County Community
College *A*
Baker University *B*
Benedictine College *B*
Bethany College *B*
Bethel College *B*
Butler County Community
College *A*
Central College *A*

Cloud County Community
College *A*
Coffeyville Community College *A*
Colby Community College *A*
Dodge City Community College *A*
Emporia State University *B,M*
Fort Hays State University *B,M*
Haskell Indian Junior College *A*
Highland Community College *A*
Hutchinson Community College *A*
Kansas City College and Bible
School *B*
Kansas Newman College *B*
Kansas State University *B,M*
Kansas Wesleyan University *B*
McPherson College *B*
MidAmerica Nazarene College *B*
Neosho County Community
College *A*
Ottawa University *B*
Pittsburg State University *B,M*
Pratt Community College *A*
St. Mary College *B*
Seward County Community
College *A*
Southwestern College *B*
Sterling College *B*
Tabor College *B*
University of Kansas *B,M,D*
Washburn University of Topeka *B*
Wichita State University *B,M*

Kentucky

Asbury College *B*
Bellarmine College *B*
Berea College *B*
Brescia College *B*
Campbellsville College *B*
Centre College *B*
Cumberland College *B*
Eastern Kentucky University *B,M*
Georgetown College *B*
Kentucky State University *B*
Kentucky Wesleyan College *B*
Lindsey Wilson College *A,B*
Morehead State University *B,M*
Murray State University *B,M*
Northern Kentucky University *B*
Pikeville College *B*
Spalding University *B*
Sue Bennett College *A*
Thomas More College *A,B*
Transylvania University *B*
Union College *B*
University of Kentucky *B,M,D*
University of Louisville *B,M*
Western Kentucky University *B,M*

Louisiana

Centenary College of Louisiana *B*
Dillard University *B*
Grambling State University *B*
Louisiana College *B*
Louisiana State University
Agricultural and Mechanical
College *B,M,D*
Shreveport *B*
Louisiana Tech University *B,M*
Loyola University *B*
McNeese State University *B,M*
Nicholls State University *B*
Northeast Louisiana University *B,M*
Northwestern State University *B,M*
Our Lady of Holy Cross College *B*
Southeastern Louisiana University
B,M
Southern University at New
Orleans *B*
Southern University and
Agricultural and Mechanical
College *B*
Tulane University *B,M,D*

University of New Orleans *B,M*
University of Southwestern
Louisiana *B,M,D*
Xavier University of Louisiana *B*

Maine

Bates College *B*
Bowdoin College *B*
Colby College *B*
St. Joseph's College *B*
University of Maine
Augusta *B*
Fort Kent *B*
Machias *B*
Orono *B,M*
Presque Isle *B*
University of Southern Maine *B*
Westbrook College *B*

Maryland

Bowie State University *B*
College of Notre Dame of
Maryland *B*
Columbia Union College *B*
Coppin State College *B*
Frederick Community College *A*
Frostburg State University *B*
Goucher College *B*
Harford Community College *A*
Hood College *B*
Howard Community College *A*
Johns Hopkins University *B,M,D*
Loyola College in Maryland *B*
Morgan State University *B,M*
Mount St. Mary's College *B*
St. Mary's College of Maryland *B*
Salisbury State University *B,M*
Towson State University *B*
United States Naval Academy *B*
University of Baltimore *B*
University of Maryland
Baltimore County *B*
College Park *B,M,D*
Eastern Shore *B*
Western Maryland College *B*

Massachusetts

American International College *B*
Amherst College *B*
Anna Maria College for Men and
Women *B*
Assumption College *B*
Atlantic Union College *B*
Boston College *B,M,D*
Boston University *B,M,D*
Bradford College *B*
Brandeis University *B*
Bridgewater State College *B,M*
Bunker Hill Community College *A*
Clark University *B,M*
College of the Holy Cross *B*
Curry College *B*
Dean Junior College *A*
Eastern Nazarene College *B*
Elms College *B*
Emmanuel College *B*
Framingham State College *B*
Gordon College *B*
Hampshire College *B*
Harvard and Radcliffe Colleges *B*
Merrimack College *B*
Mount Holyoke College *B*
North Adams State College *B*
Northeastern University *B,M*
Pine Manor College *A,B*
Quincy College *A*
Regis College *B*
Roxbury Community College *A*
Salem State College *B,M*
Simmons College *B,M*
Simon's Rock College of Bard *B*
Smith College *B*

Springfield College *B*
Suffolk University *B*
Tufts University *B,M,D*
University of Massachusetts
Amherst *B,M,D*
Boston *B,M*
Dartmouth *B*
Lowell *B*
Wellesley College *B*
Western New England College *B*
Westfield State College *B,M*
Wheaton College *B*
Williams College *B*
Worcester State College *B*

Michigan

Adrian College *A,B*
Albion College *B*
Alma College *B*
Andrews University *B,M*
Aquinas College *B*
Calvin College *B*
Central Michigan University *B,M*
Concordia College *B*
Eastern Michigan University *B,M*
Grand Rapids Baptist College and
Seminary *B*
Grand Valley State University *B*
Hillsdale College *B*
Hope College *B*
Kalamazoo College *B*
Kalamazoo Valley Community
College *A*
Kellogg Community College *A*
Lake Superior State University *B*
Lansing Community College *A*
Madonna University *A,B*
Marygrove College *B*
Michigan State University *B,M,D*
Michigan Technological
University *B*
Northern Michigan University
A,B,M
Oakland University *B,M*
Olivet College *B*
Saginaw Valley State University *B*
St. Mary's College *B*
Siena Heights College *B*
Spring Arbor College *B*
Suomi College *A*
University of Detroit Mercy *B,M*
University of Michigan
Ann Arbor *B,M,D*
Dearborn *B*
Flint *B*
Wayne State University *B,M,D*
Western Michigan University *B,M*
William Tyndale College *B*

Minnesota

Augsburg College *B*
Bemidji State University *B,M*
Bethany Lutheran College *A*
Bethel College *B*
Carleton College *B*
College of St. Benedict *B*
College of St. Catherine: St.
Catherine Campus *B*
College of St. Scholastica *B*
Concordia College: Moorhead *B*
Concordia College: St. Paul *B*
Crown College *A,B*
Gustavus Adolphus College *B*
Hamline University *B*
Macalester College *B*
Mankato State University *B,M*
Moorhead State University *B*
Northland Community College *A*
Northwestern College *B*
Pillsbury Baptist Bible College *B*
Rainy River Community College *A*
St. Cloud State University *B,M*

St. John's University *B*
St. Mary's College of Minnesota *B*
St. Olaf College *B*
Southwest State University *B*
University of Minnesota
Duluth *B,M*
Morris *B*
Twin Cities *B,M,D*
University of St. Thomas *B*
Vermilion Community College *A*
Willmar Community College *A*
Winona State University *B,M*

Mississippi

Alcorn State University *B*
Belhaven College *B*
Blue Mountain College *B*
Delta State University *B*
Jackson State University *B,M*
Jones County Junior College *A*
Mary Holmes College *A*
Millsaps College *B*
Mississippi College *B,M*
Mississippi Gulf Coast Community
College: Jefferson Davis
Campus *A*
Mississippi State University *B,M*
Mississippi University for Women *B*
Northeast Mississippi Community
College *A*
Rust College *B*
Tougaloo College *B*
University of Mississippi *B,M,D*
University of Southern Mississippi
B,M,D
William Carey College *B*

Missouri

Avila College *B*
Central Methodist College *B*
Central Missouri State University
B,M
College of the Ozarks *B*
Columbia College *A,B*
Culver-Stockton College *B*
Drury College *B*
East Central College *A*
Evangel College *B*
Fontbonne College *B*
Hannibal-LaGrange College *B*
Jefferson College *A*
Lincoln University *B*
Lindenwood College *B*
Maryville University *B*
Mineral Area College *A*
Missouri Baptist College *B*
Missouri Southern State College *B*
Missouri Valley College *B*
Missouri Western State College *B*
Moberly Area Community
College *A*
Northeast Missouri State University
B,M
Northwest Missouri State
University *B,M*
Park College *B*
Rockhurst College *B*
St. Louis University *B,M,D*
Southeast Missouri State University
B,M
Southwest Baptist University *B*
Southwest Missouri State University
B,M
Stephens College *B*
University of Missouri
Columbia *B,M,D*
Kansas City *B,M,D*
Rolla *B*
St. Louis *B,M*
Washington University *B,M,D*
Webster University *B*
Westminster College *B*

William Jewell College *B*
William Woods College *B*

Montana

Carroll College *A,B*
College of Great Falls *B*
Eastern Montana College *B*
Miles Community College *A*
Montana State University *B*
Northern Montana College *B*
Rocky Mountain College *B*
University of Montana *B,M*

Nebraska

Bellevue College *B*
Chadron State College *B*
College of St. Mary *B*
Concordia College *B*
Creighton University *B,M*
Dana College *B*
Doane College *B*
Hastings College *B*
McCook Community College *A*
Midland Lutheran College *B*
Nebraska Wesleyan University *B*
Northeast Community College *A*
Peru State College *B*
Southeast Community College:
  Beatrice Campus *A*
Union College *B*
University of Nebraska
  Kearney *B*
  Lincoln *B,M,D*
  Omaha *B,M*
Wayne State College *B*
Western Nebraska Community
  College: Scottsbluff Campus *A*
York College *A*

Nevada

Community College of Southern
  Nevada *A*
Sierra Nevada College *B*
University of Nevada
  Las Vegas *B,M,D*
  Reno *B,M,D*

New Hampshire

Dartmouth College *B*
Franklin Pierce College *B*
Keene State College *B*
New England College *B*
New Hampshire College *B*
Notre Dame College *B*
Plymouth State College of the
  University System of New
  Hampshire *B*
Rivier College *B,M*
St. Anselm College *B*
University of New Hampshire
  Durham *B,M,D*
  Manchester *B*

New Jersey

Bloomfield College *B*
Brookdale Community College *A*
Burlington County College *A*
Caldwell College *B*
Centenary College *B*
College of St. Elizabeth *B*
Drew University *B*
Felician College *A,B*
Georgian Court College *B*
Jersey City State College *B*
Kean College of New Jersey *B*
Monmouth College *B*
Montclair State College *B*
Ocean County College *A*
Princeton University *B,D*

Rutgers—The State University of
  New Jersey
  Camden College of Arts and
    Sciences *B*
  Douglass College *B*
  Livingston College *B*
  New Brunswick *M,D*
  Newark College of Arts and
    Sciences *B*
  Rutgers College *B*
  University College Camden *B*
  University College New
    Brunswick *B*
  University College Newark *B*
St. Peter's College *B*
Seton Hall University *B,M*
Stevens Institute of Technology *B*
Stockton State College *B*
Thomas Edison State College *B*
Trenton State College *B,M*
William Paterson College of New
  Jersey *B,M*

New Mexico

College of Santa Fe *A,B*
Eastern New Mexico University
  B,M
New Mexico Highlands
  University *B*
New Mexico State University *B,M*
University of New Mexico *B,M,D*
Western New Mexico University *B*

New York

Adelphi University *B,M*
Adirondack Community College *A*
Alfred University *B*
Bard College *B*
Barnard College *B*
Canisius College *B*
City University of New York
  Baruch College *B*
  Brooklyn College *B,M*
  City College *B*
  College of Staten Island *B,M*
  Hunter College *B*
  Lehman College *B,M*
  Queens College *B*
  York College *B*
Colgate University *B,M*
College of Mount St. Vincent *B*
College of New Rochelle *B*
College of St. Rose *B,M*
Columbia University
  Columbia College *B*
  New York *M,D*
Columbia-Greene Community
  College *A*
Concordia College *B*
Cornell University *B,M,D*
Daemen College *B*
Dominican College of Blauvelt *B*
Dowling College *B*
D'Youville College *B*
Elmira College *B*
Eugene Lang College/New School
  for Social Research *B*
Fordham University *B,M,D*
Fulton-Montgomery Community
  College *A*
Hamilton College *B*
Hartwick College *B*
Hobart College *B*
Hofstra University *B,M*
Houghton College *B*
Iona College *B,M*
Ithaca College *B*
Jamestown Community College *A*
Keuka College *B*
King's College *B*
Le Moyne College *B*

Long Island University
  Brooklyn Campus *B,M*
  C. W. Post Campus *B,M*
  Southampton Campus *B*
Manhattan College *B*
Manhattanville College *B*
Marist College *B*
Marymount College *B*
Marymount Manhattan College *B*
Mercy College *B*
Mohawk Valley Community
  College *A*
Molloy College *B*
Mount St. Mary College *B*
Nazareth College of Rochester *B*
New York University *B,M,D*
Niagara University *B*
Nyack College *B*
Pace University
  College of White Plains *B*
  New York *B*
Roberts Wesleyan College *B*
Russell Sage College *B*
St. Bonaventure University *B,M*
St. Francis College *B*
St. John Fisher College *B*
St. John's University *B,M,D*
St. Joseph's College
  Brooklyn *B*
  Suffolk Campus *B*
St. Thomas Aquinas College *B*
Sarah Lawrence College *B*
Siena College *B*
Skidmore College *B*
State University of New York
  Albany *B,M,D*
  Binghamton *B,M,D*
  Buffalo *B,M,D*
  Stony Brook *B,M,D*
  College at Brockport *B,M*
  College at Buffalo *B,M*
  College at Cortland *B*
  College at Fredonia *B,M*
  College at Geneseo *B*
  College at New Paltz *B,M*
  College at Oneonta *B,M*
  College at Plattsburgh *B*
  College at Potsdam *B,M*
  Oswego *B*
Syracuse University *B,M,D*
Touro College *B*
Union College *B*
University of Rochester *B,M,D*
Utica College of Syracuse
  University *B*
Vassar College *B*
Wagner College *B*
Wells College *B*
William Smith College *B*
Yeshiva University *B*

North Carolina

Appalachian State University *B,M*
Barber-Scotia College *B*
Barton College *B*
Belmont Abbey College *B*
Bennett College *B*
Brevard College *A*
Campbell University *B*
Catawba College *B*
Chowan College *A*
Davidson College *B*
Duke University *B,D*
East Carolina University *B,M*
Elizabeth City State University *B*
Elon College *B*
Fayetteville State University *B*
Gardner-Webb College *B*
Greensboro College *B*
Guilford College *B*
High Point University *B*
Johnson C. Smith University *B*

Lees-McRae College *B*
Lenoir-Rhyne College *B*
Livingstone College *B*
Mars Hill College *B*
Meredith College *B*
Methodist College *A,B*
Montreat-Anderson College *B*
Mount Olive College *A,B*
North Carolina Agricultural and
  Technical State University *B,M*
North Carolina Central University
  B,M
North Carolina State University
  B,M
North Carolina Wesleyan College *B*
Pembroke State University *B,M*
Pfeiffer College *B*
Queens College *B*
St. Andrews Presbyterian College *B*
St. Augustine's College *B*
Salem College *B*
Shaw University *B*
University of North Carolina
  Chapel Hill *B,M,D*
  Charlotte *B,M*
  Greensboro *B,M,D*
  Wilmington *B,M*
Wake Forest University *B,M*
Warren Wilson College *B*
Western Carolina University *B,M*
Wingate College *B*
Winston-Salem State University *B*

North Dakota

Bismarck State College *A*
Dickinson State University *B*
Jamestown College *B*
Mayville State University *B*
Minot State University *B*
North Dakota State University *B,M*
University of Mary *B*
University of North Dakota *B,M,D*
Valley City State University *B*

Ohio

Ashland University *B*
Baldwin-Wallace College *B*
Bluffton College *B*
Bowling Green State University
  B,M,D
Capital University *B*
Case Western Reserve University
  B,M,D
Cedarville College *B*
Central State University *B*
Cleveland State University *B,M*
College of Mount St. Joseph *B*
College of Wooster *B*
Defiance College *B*
Denison University *B*
Edison State Community College *A*
Franciscan University of
  Steubenville *B*
Heidelberg College *B*
Hiram College *B*
John Carroll University *B,M*
Kent State University *B,M,D*
Kenyon College *B*
Lake Erie College *B*
Lourdes College *A,B*
Malone College *B*
Marietta College *B*
Mount Union College *B*
Mount Vernon Nazarene College *B*
Muskingum College *B*
Notre Dame College of Ohio *B*
Oberlin College *B*
Ohio Dominican College *B*
Ohio Northern University *B*
Ohio State University: Columbus
  Campus *B,M,D*
Ohio University *B,M,D*

Ohio Wesleyan University *B*
Otterbein College *B*
Pontifical College Josephinum *B*
Shawnee State University *B*
Union Institute *B,D*
University of Akron *B,M*
University of Cincinnati
    Cincinnati *B*
    Clermont College *A*
University of Dayton *B,M*
University of Findlay *B*
University of Rio Grande *B*
University of Toledo *B,M,D*
Urbana University *B*
Ursuline College *B*
Walsh College *B*
Wilberforce University *B*
Wilmington College *B*
Wittenberg University *B*
Wright State University
    Dayton *B,M*
    Lake Campus *A*
Xavier University *B,M*
Youngstown State University *B,M*

Oklahoma

Bartlesville Wesleyan College *B*
Cameron University *B*
Connors State College *A*
East Central University *B*
Eastern Oklahoma State College *A*
Hillsdale Free Will Baptist
    College *A*
Langston University *B*
Mid-America Bible College *B*
Northeastern State University *B*
Northern Oklahoma College *A*
Northwestern Oklahoma State
    University *B*
Oklahoma Baptist University *B*
Oklahoma Christian University of
    Science and Arts *B*
Oklahoma City University *B*
Oklahoma Panhandle State
    University *B*
Oklahoma State University *B,M,D*
Phillips University *B*
Redlands Community College *A*
Rogers State College *A*
Rose State College *A*
St. Gregory's College *A*
Southeastern Oklahoma State
    University *B*
Southwestern Oklahoma State
    University *B*
Tulsa Junior College *A*
University of Central Oklahoma
    B,M
University of Oklahoma *B,M,D*
University of Science and Arts of
    Oklahoma *B*
University of Tulsa *B,M,D*

Oregon

Central Oregon Community
    College *A*
Eastern Oregon State College *B*
Lewis and Clark College *B*
Linfield College *B*
Northwest Christian College *B*
Oregon State University *B*
Pacific University *B*
Portland Community College *A*
Portland State University *B,M*
Southern Oregon State College *B*
University of Oregon
    Eugene *B,M,D*
    Robert Donald Clark Honors
        College *B*
University of Portland *B*
Warner Pacific College *B*
Western Baptist College *B*

Western Oregon State College *B*
Willamette University *B*

Pennsylvania

Albright College *B*
Allegheny College *B*
Allentown College of St. Francis de
    Sales *B*
Alvernia College *B*
Beaver College *B,M*
Bloomsburg University of
    Pennsylvania *B*
Bryn Mawr College *B*
Bucknell University *B,M*
Butler County Community
    College *A*
Cabrini College *B*
California University of
    Pennsylvania *B,M*
Carlow College *B*
Carnegie Mellon University
    B,M,D,W
Cedar Crest College *B*
Chatham College *B*
Cheyney University of
    Pennsylvania *B*
Clarion University of Pennsylvania
    B,M
College Misericordia *B*
Delaware Valley College *B*
Dickinson College *B*
Duquesne University *B,M,D*
East Stroudsburg University of
    Pennsylvania *B*
Edinboro University of
    Pennsylvania *B*
Elizabethtown College *B*
Franklin and Marshall College *B*
Gannon University *B,M*
Geneva College *B*
Gettysburg College *B*
Gwynedd-Mercy College *B*
Haverford College *B*
Holy Family College *B*
Immaculata College *B*
Indiana University of Pennsylvania
    B,M,D
Juniata College *B*
King's College *B*
Kutztown University of
    Pennsylvania *B,M*
La Roche College *B*
La Salle University *B*
Lafayette College *B*
Lebanon Valley College of
    Pennsylvania *B*
Lehigh University *B,M,D*
Lincoln University *B*
Lock Haven University of
    Pennsylvania *B*
Lycoming College *B*
Mansfield University of
    Pennsylvania *B*
Marywood College *B*
Mercyhurst College *B*
Messiah College *B*
Millersville University of
    Pennsylvania *B,M*
Moravian College *B*
Muhlenberg College *B*
Neumann College *B*
Northeastern Christian Junior
    College *A*
Penn State
    Erie Behrend College *B*
    University Park Campus
        B,M,D
Point Park College *B*
Robert Morris College *B*
St. Francis College *B*
St. Joseph's University *B*
St. Vincent College *B*

Seton Hill College *B*
Shippensburg University of
    Pennsylvania *B,M*
Slippery Rock University of
    Pennsylvania *B,M*
Susquehanna University *B*
Temple University *B,M,D*
Thiel College *B*
University of Pennsylvania
    A,B,M,D
University of Pittsburgh
    Greensburg *B*
    Pittsburgh *B,M,D*
University of Scranton *B,M*
Ursinus College *B*
Villanova University *B,M*
Washington and Jefferson College *B*
Waynesburg College *B*
West Chester University of
    Pennsylvania *M*
Westminster College *B*
Widener University *B*
Wilkes University *B*
Wilson College *B*
York College of Pennsylvania *B*

Puerto Rico

Bayamon Central University *B*
Electronic Data Processing College
    of Puerto Rico *C*
Inter American University of Puerto
    Rico
    Arecibo Campus *B*
    Metropolitan Campus *B,M*
    San German Campus *B*
Pontifical Catholic University of
    Puerto Rico *B*
University of Puerto Rico
    Cayey University College *B*
    Mayaguez Campus *B*
    Rio Piedras Campus *B,M*
University of the Sacred Heart *B*

Rhode Island

Brown University *B,M,D*
Bryant College *B*
Providence College *B*
Rhode Island College *B,M*
Roger Williams College *B*
Salve Regina University *B*
University of Rhode Island *B,M,D*

South Carolina

Benedict College *B*
Bob Jones University *B*
Central Wesleyan College *B*
Charleston Southern University *B*
The Citadel *B*
Claflin College *B*
Clemson University *B,M*
Coker College *B*
College of Charleston *B*
Columbia College *B,M*
Converse College *B*
Erskine College *B*
Francis Marion College *B*
Furman University *B*
Lander College *B*
Limestone College *B*
Morris College *B*
Newberry College *B*
North Greenville College *A*
Presbyterian College *B*
South Carolina State College *B*
University of South Carolina
    Aiken *B*
    Coastal Carolina College *B*
    Columbia *B,M,D*
    Spartanburg *B*
Winthrop University *B,M*
Wofford College *B*

South Dakota

Augustana College *B*
Black Hills State University *B*
Dakota State University *B*
Dakota Wesleyan University *B*
Mount Marty College *B*
Northern State University *B*
Sioux Falls College *B*
South Dakota State University *B,M*
University of South Dakota *B,M*

Tennessee

Austin Peay State University *B,M*
Belmont University *B*
Bethel College *B*
Carson-Newman College *B*
Christian Brothers University *B*
Columbia State Community
    College *A*
David Lipscomb University *B*
Dyersburg State Community
    College *A*
East Tennessee State University
    B,M
Fisk University *B*
Free Will Baptist Bible College *B*
Freed-Hardeman University *B*
King College *B*
Knoxville College *B*
Lambuth University *B*
Lane College *B*
LeMoyne-Owen College *B*
Lincoln Memorial University *B*
Maryville College *B*
Memphis State University *B,M*
Middle Tennessee State University
    B,M,D
Milligan College *B*
Motlow State Community
    College *A*
Rhodes College *B*
Shelby State Community College *A*
Southern College of Seventh-day
    Adventists *B*
Tennessee State University *B,M*
Tennessee Technological University
    B,M
Tennessee Temple University *B*
Tennessee Wesleyan College *B*
Trevecca Nazarene College *B*
Union University *B*
University of the South *B*
University of Tennessee
    Chattanooga *B*
    Knoxville *B,M,D*
    Martin *B*
Vanderbilt University *B,M,D*
William Jennings Bryan College *B*

Texas

Abilene Christian University *B,M*
Amarillo College *A*
Angelina College *A*
Angelo State University *B,M*
Austin College *B*
Baylor University *B,M,D*
Bee County College *A*
Blinn College *A*
Brazosport College *A*
Central Texas College *A*
Collin County Community College
    District *A*
Concordia Lutheran College *B*
Corpus Christi State University *B*
Dallas Baptist University *B*
Del Mar College *A*
East Texas Baptist University *B*
East Texas State University
    Commerce *B,M*
    Texarkana *B*
El Paso Community College *A*
Hardin-Simmons University *B,M*

Houston Baptist University *B*
Houston Community College *A*
Howard College *A*
Howard Payne University *B*
Huston-Tillotson College *B*
Incarnate Word College *B,M*
Jacksonville College *A*
Jarvis Christian College *B*
Kilgore College *A*
Lamar University—Beaumont *B,M*
Laredo State University *B,M*
LeTourneau University *B*
Lon Morris College *A*
Lubbock Christian University *B*
McLennan Community College *A*
McMurry University *B*
Midland College *A*
Midwestern State University *B,M*
Our Lady of the Lake University of San Antonio *B,M*
Panola College *A*
Paul Quinn College *B*
Prairie View A&M University *B,M*
Rice University *B,M,D*
St. Edward's University *B*
St. Mary's University *B,M*
St. Philip's College *A*
Sam Houston State University *B,M*
South Plains College *A*
Southwest Texas State University *B,M*
Southwestern Adventist College *B*
Southwestern Assemblies of God College *A*
Southwestern University *B*
Stephen F. Austin State University *B,M*
Sul Ross State University *B,M*
Tarleton State University *B,M*
Texas A&I University *B,M*
Texas A&M University *B,M,D*
Texas Christian University *B,M,D*
Texas College *B*
Texas Lutheran College *B*
Texas Southern University *B,M*
Texas Southmost College *A*
Texas Tech University *B,M,D*
Texas Wesleyan University *B*
Texas Woman's University *B,M*
Trinity University *B*
Trinity Valley Community College *A*
University of Houston
    Houston *B,M,D*
    Victoria *B*
University of Mary Hardin-Baylor *B*
University of North Texas *B,M,D*
University of St. Thomas *B*
University of Texas
    Arlington *B,M*
    Austin *B,M,D*
    El Paso *B,M*
    Pan American *B,M*
    San Antonio *B,M*
    Tyler *B,M*
Victoria College *A*
Wayland Baptist University *B*
West Texas State University *B,M*
Western Texas College *A*
Wharton County Junior College *A*
Wiley College *B*

Utah

Brigham Young University *A,B,M*
Dixie College *A*
Southern Utah University *B*
University of Utah *B,M,D*
Utah State University *B,M*
Weber State University *B*
Westminster College of Salt Lake City *B*

Vermont

Bennington College *B*
Castleton State College *B*
College of St. Joseph in Vermont *B*
Goddard College *B,M*
Green Mountain College *B*
Johnson State College *B*
Marlboro College *B*
Middlebury College *B*
Norwich University *B*
St. Michael's College *B*
Southern Vermont College *B*
Trinity College of Vermont *B*
University of Vermont *B,M*

Virginia

Averett College *B*
Bluefield College *B*
Bridgewater College *B*
Christendom College *B*
Christopher Newport College *B*
College of William and Mary *B,M*
Eastern Mennonite College *B*
Emory and Henry College *B*
Ferrum College *B*
George Mason University *B,M*
Hampden-Sydney College *B*
Hampton University *B,M*
Hollins College *B,M*
James Madison University *B,M*
Liberty University *B*
Longwood College *B,M*
Lynchburg College *B*
Mary Baldwin College *B*
Mary Washington College *B*
Marymount University *B*
Norfolk State University *B*
Old Dominion University *B,M*
Radford University *B,M*
Randolph-Macon College *B*
Randolph-Macon Woman's College *B*
Roanoke College *B*
St. Paul's College *B*
Shenandoah University *B*
Sweet Briar College *B*
University of Richmond *B,M*
University of Virginia *B,M,D*
Virginia Commonwealth University *B,M*
Virginia Intermont College *B*
Virginia Military Institute *B*
Virginia Polytechnic Institute and State University *B,M*
Virginia State University *B,M*
Virginia Union University *B*
Virginia Wesleyan College *B*
Washington and Lee University *B*

Washington

Big Bend Community College *A*
Central Washington University *B,M*
Centralia College *A*
Eastern Washington University *B,M*
Everett Community College *A*
Evergreen State College *B*
Gonzaga University *B,M*
Grays Harbor College *A*
Heritage College *B*
Lower Columbia College *A*
Pacific Lutheran University *B*
St. Martin's College *B*
Seattle Central Community College *A*
Seattle Pacific University *B*
Seattle University *B*
Skagit Valley College *A*
Spokane Community College *A*
Spokane Falls Community College *A*
Tacoma Community College *A*
University of Puget Sound *B*

University of Washington *B,M,D*
Walla Walla College *B*
Washington State University *B,M,D*
Wenatchee Valley College *A*
Western Washington University *B,M*
Whitman College *B*
Whitworth College *B*

West Virginia

Bethany College *B*
Bluefield State College *B*
Concord College *B*
Davis and Elkins College *B*
Fairmont State College *B*
Glenville State College *B*
Marshall University *B,M*
Potomac State College of West Virginia University *A*
Shepherd College *B*
University of Charleston *B*
West Liberty State College *B*
West Virginia State College *B*
West Virginia University *B,M,D*
West Virginia Wesleyan College *B*
Wheeling Jesuit College *B*

Wisconsin

Alverno College *B*
Beloit College *B*
Cardinal Stritch College *B*
Carroll College *B*
Carthage College *B*
Concordia University Wisconsin *B*
Edgewood College *B*
Lakeland College *B*
Lawrence University *B*
Marian College of Fond du Lac *B*
Marquette University *B,M,D*
Mount Mary College *B*
Mount Senario College *B*
Northland College *B*
Ripon College *B*
St. Norbert College *B*
Silver Lake College *B*
University of Wisconsin
    Eau Claire *B,M*
    Green Bay *B*
    La Crosse *B*
    Madison *B,M,D*
    Milwaukee *B,M,D*
    Oshkosh *B*
    Parkside *B*
    Platteville *B*
    River Falls *B*
    Stevens Point *B,M*
    Superior *B*
    Whitewater *B*
Viterbo College *B*
Wisconsin Lutheran College *B*

Wyoming

Casper College *A*
Central Wyoming College *A*
Eastern Wyoming College *A*
Laramie County Community College *A*
Northwest College *A*
Sheridan College *A*
University of Wyoming *B,M*
Western Wyoming Community College *A*

American Samoa, Caroline Islands, Guam, Marianas, Virgin Islands

University of Guam *B*
University of the Virgin Islands *B*

Canada

McGill University *B,M,D*

English education

Alabama

Alabama Agricultural and Mechanical University *B,M*
Alabama State University *B,M*
Auburn University
    Auburn *B,M,D*
    Montgomery *B*
Birmingham-Southern College *B*
Faulkner University *B*
Huntingdon College *B*
Jacksonville State University *B,M*
John C. Calhoun State Community College *A*
Judson College *B*
Lawson State Community College *A*
Livingston University *B,M*
Mobile College *B,M*
Oakwood College *B*
Samford University *B,M*
Spring Hill College *B*
Troy State University
    Dothan *B,M*
    Montgomery *M*
University of Alabama *B*
University of Montevallo *B,M*
University of North Alabama *B,M*

Alaska

University of Alaska
    Anchorage *M*
    Fairbanks *M*

Arizona

Arizona State University *B*
Eastern Arizona College *A*
Grand Canyon University *B*
Northern Arizona University *B,M*
University of Arizona *B*

Arkansas

Arkansas College *B*
Arkansas State University *B,M*
Arkansas Tech University *M*
Harding University *B*
Henderson State University *B,M*
John Brown University *B*
Ouachita Baptist University *B*
University of Arkansas
    Fayetteville *B*
    Monticello *B*
    Pine Bluff *B*
University of Central Arkansas *B,M*
University of the Ozarks *B*
Westark Community College *A*

California

Azusa Pacific University *B*
Bethany College *B*
Biola University *B*
California Baptist College *B*
California Lutheran University *B*
California Polytechnic State University: San Luis Obispo *B*
California State University
    Bakersfield *B*
    Fresno *B*
    Los Angeles *B*
    Northridge *B*
    Sacramento *B*
Christ College Irvine *B*
Christian Heritage College *B*
College of Notre Dame *M*
Fresno Pacific College *B*
Loyola Marymount University *M*
Mount St. Mary's College *B*
Occidental College *M*
Pacific Christian College *B*

Point Loma Nazarene College *B*
Simpson College *B*
University of the Pacific *B*
University of Redlands *B*
University of San Francisco *B*
Westmont College *B*

Colorado

Colorado State University *B*
University of Colorado at Colorado
  Springs *B*
University of Northern Colorado *B*
Western State College of
  Colorado *B*

Connecticut

Sacred Heart University *B,M*
St. Joseph College *B*
Southern Connecticut State
  University *B,M*
University of Bridgeport *B,M*
University of Hartford *B*
Western Connecticut State
  University *B*

Delaware

Delaware State College *B*
University of Delaware *B*

Florida

Bethune-Cookman College *B*
Flagler College *B*
Florida Agricultural and Mechanical
  University *B,M*
Florida Atlantic University *B,M*
Florida International University
  B,M
Florida State University *B,M,D*
Gulf Coast Community College *A*
Hobe Sound Bible College *B*
Jacksonville University *M*
Nova University *M*
Pensacola Junior College *A*
St. Thomas University *B*
Southeastern College of the
  Assemblies of God *B*
Stetson University *B,M*
University of Central Florida *B,M*
University of Florida *B,M*
University of Miami *M*
University of South Florida *B,M*
University of Tampa *B*
University of West Florida *B*
Warner Southern College *B*

Georgia

Armstrong State College *B,M*
Augusta College *M*
Berry College *B*
Brenau Women's College *B*
Brewton-Parker College *B*
Columbus College *B,M*
Georgia College *B,M*
Georgia Southern University *B,M*
Georgia Southwestern College *B,M*
Georgia State University *M,D*
Kennesaw State College *B*
Mercer University *M*
North Georgia College *B,M*
Piedmont College *B*
Shorter College *B,M*
Toccoa Falls College *B*
University of Georgia *B,M,D*
Valdosta State College *B,M*
Wesleyan College *B*

Hawaii

Chaminade University of
  Honolulu *B*
Hawaii Pacific University *B*

Idaho

Albertson College *B*
Boise State University *B,M*
College of Southern Idaho *A*
Northwest Nazarene College *B*
University of Idaho *M*

Illinois

Augustana College *B*
Aurora University *B*
Barat College *B*
Blackburn College *B*
Columbia College *M*
Concordia University *B*
De Paul University *B*
Elmhurst College *B*
Governors State University *B*
Greenville College *B*
Illinois College *B*
Illinois Wesleyan University *B*
Judson College *B*
MacMurray College *B*
Millikin University *B*
North Central College *B*
Northwestern University *B,M*
Olivet Nazarene University *B*
Quincy College *B*
Roosevelt University *B*
Southern Illinois University
      Carbondale *B,M,D*
      Edwardsville *B*
Trinity Christian College *B*
Trinity College *B*
University of Illinois
      Chicago *B*
      Urbana-Champaign *B,M*
Western Illinois University *B*
Wheaton College *B*

Indiana

Anderson University *B*
Ball State University *B*
Bethel College *B*
Butler University *B*
Calumet College of St. Joseph *B*
Franklin College *B*
Goshen College *B*
Huntington College *B*
Indiana State University *B,M*
Indiana University
      Bloomington *B,M,D*
      South Bend *B*
      Southeast *B*
Indiana University—Purdue
  University
      Fort Wayne *B,M*
      Indianapolis *B*
Indiana Wesleyan University *B*
Manchester College *B,M*
Marian College *B*
Martin University *B*
Oakland City College *B*
Purdue University *B,M,D*
St. Francis College *B*
St. Joseph's College *B*
St. Mary-of-the-Woods College *B*
Taylor University *B*
Tri-State University *B*
University of Evansville *B,M*
University of Indianapolis *B*
University of Southern Indiana *B*
Vincennes University *A*

Iowa

Briar Cliff College *B*
Buena Vista College *B*
Clarke College *B*
Cornell College *B*
Drake University *B,M*
Grand View College *B*
Iowa Lakes Community College *A*
Iowa Wesleyan College *B*

Loras College *B*
Luther College *B*
Morningside College *B*
Mount Mercy College *B*
Simpson College *B*
Teikyo Marycrest University *B*
Teikyo Westmar University *B*
University of Dubuque *B*
University of Iowa *B,M,D*
Upper Iowa University *B*
Wartburg College *B*
William Penn College *B*

Kansas

Baker University *B*
Bethany College *B*
Colby Community College *A*
Emporia State University *B*
Friends University *B*
Kansas State University *B*
McPherson College *B*
MidAmerica Nazarene College *B*
Pittsburg State University *B,M*
St. Mary College *B*
Southwestern College *B*
Tabor College *B*
University of Kansas *B*
Washburn University of Topeka *B*

Kentucky

Asbury College *B*
Bellarmine College *B*
Berea College *B*
Campbellsville College *B*
Cumberland College *B*
Eastern Kentucky University *B,M*
Georgetown College *B*
Murray State University *B*
Pikeville College *B*
Sue Bennett College *A*
Thomas More College *B*
Transylvania University *B*
Union College *B*
University of Kentucky *B*
Western Kentucky University *M*

Louisiana

Dillard University *B*
Grambling State University *B*
Louisiana College *B*
Louisiana State University
  Agricultural and Mechanical
  College *B*
      Shreveport *B*
Louisiana Tech University *B,M*
McNeese State University *B,M*
Nicholls State University *B*
Northeast Louisiana University *B,M*
Northwestern State University *B*
Our Lady of Holy Cross College *B*
Southeastern Louisiana
  University *B*
Southern University and
  Agricultural and Mechanical
  College *B*
Tulane University *M*
University of New Orleans *B,M*
University of Southwestern
  Louisiana *B*
Xavier University of Louisiana *B*

Maine

St. Joseph's College *B*
University of Maine
      Farmington *B*
      Orono *M*
      Presque Isle *B*

Maryland

Columbia Union College *B*
Morgan State University *B*
Mount St. Mary's College *B*

Western Maryland College *B*

Massachusetts

Boston College *B*
Boston University *B,M,W*
Bridgewater State College *M*
Eastern Nazarene College *B,M*
Elms College *B*
Fitchburg State College *B*
Framingham State College *B,M*
Hampshire College *B*
Merrimack College *B*
Pine Manor College *B*
Salem State College *M*
Springfield College *B*
Tufts University *B,M*
Westfield State College *B*
Worcester State College *M*

Michigan

Adrian College *B*
Andrews University *M*
Calvin College *B,M*
Central Michigan University *M*
Concordia College *B*
Eastern Michigan University *B,M*
Grand Valley State University *B*
Lansing Community College *A*
Madonna University *B*
Marygrove College *B*
Michigan State University *B*
Northern Michigan University *B,M*
Oakland University *M*
Saginaw Valley State University
  B,M
University of Michigan *D*
Wayne State University *B,M*
Western Michigan University *B*

Minnesota

Bemidji State University *B,M*
Bethel College *B*
College of St. Catherine: St.
  Catherine Campus *B*
College of St. Scholastica *B*
Concordia College: Moorhead *B*
Concordia College: St. Paul *B*
Crown College *B*
Gustavus Adolphus College *B*
Mankato State University *B*
Moorhead State University *B*
Northland Community College *A*
Northwestern College *B*
Pillsbury Baptist Bible College *B*
Rainy River Community College *A*
St. Cloud State University *B*
St. Mary's College of Minnesota *B*
St. Olaf College *B*
Southwest State University *B*
University of Minnesota
      Duluth *B*
      Twin Cities *B*
Willmar Community College *A*
Winona State University *B*

Mississippi

Alcorn State University *B,M*
Blue Mountain College *B*
Delta State University *B,M*
Mississippi College *B,M*
Mississippi Gulf Coast Community
  College: Jefferson Davis
  Campus *A*
Mississippi University for Women *B*
Northeast Mississippi Community
  College *A*
Rust College *B*
University of Mississippi *B*

Missouri

Central Missouri State University
  B,M

College of the Ozarks *B*
Columbia College *B*
Culver-Stockton College *B*
Evangel College *B*
Fontbonne College *B*
Maryville University *B*
Missouri Baptist College *B*
Missouri Western State College *B*
Northeast Missouri State
    University *M*
Northwest Missouri State
    University *B,M*
Park College *B*
Southeast Missouri State University
    B,M
Southwest Missouri State
    University *B*
University of Missouri
        Columbia *M,D*
        Kansas City *B*
Washington University *B,M*
Webster University *B*
Westminster College *B*
William Woods College *B*

Montana

Carroll College *B*
Eastern Montana College *B*
Montana State University *B*
Northern Montana College *B*
Rocky Mountain College *B*
University of Montana *B*
Western Montana College of the
    University of Montana *B*

Nebraska

Chadron State College *B*
College of St. Mary *B*
Concordia College *M*
Creighton University *B*
Dana College *B*
Doane College *B*
Hastings College *B*
Peru State College *B*
Union College *B*
University of Nebraska
        Kearney *B,M*
        Lincoln *B*
        Omaha *B*
Wayne State College *B,M*

Nevada

Sierra Nevada College *B*
University of Nevada: Reno *M*

New Hampshire

Franklin Pierce College *B*
Keene State College *B*
New England College *B*
New Hampshire College *B*
Notre Dame College *B*
Plymouth State College of the
    University System of New
    Hampshire *B*
Rivier College *B*
University of New Hampshire *B,M*

New Jersey

Caldwell College *B*
Fairleigh Dickinson University *M*
Glassboro State College *B,M*
Jersey City State College *B*
Kean College of New Jersey *B*
Rider College *B*

Rutgers—The State University of
    New Jersey
        Camden College of Arts and
            Sciences *B*
        Douglass College *B*
        Livingston College *B*
        New Brunswick *M,D*
        Newark College of Arts and
            Sciences *B*
        Rutgers College *B*
        University College New
            Brunswick *B*
        University College Newark *B*
Seton Hall University *B*
Stockton State College *B*
Trenton State College *B*

New Mexico

College of the Southwest *B*
Eastern New Mexico University *B*
New Mexico Highlands
    University *B*
New Mexico State University *B*

New York

Adelphi University *B,M*
Canisius College *B*
City University of New York
        Brooklyn College *B,M*
        Hunter College *B,M*
        Lehman College *M*
        Queens College *B,M*
College of Mount St. Vincent *B*
Concordia College *B*
Cornell University *B,M,D*
Daemen College *B*
Dominican College of Blauvelt *B*
Dowling College *B*
D'Youville College *B*
Elmira College *B*
Hofstra University *B,M*
Houghton College *B*
Iona College *B,M*
Ithaca College *B*
Le Moyne College *B*
Long Island University
        C. W. Post Campus *B,M*
        Southampton Campus *B*
Manhattan College *B*
Manhattanville College *M*
Marymount College *B*
New York University *B,M,D*
Niagara University *B,M*
Russell Sage College *B*
St. Bonaventure University *B,M*
St. John's University *B,M*
St. Joseph's College
        Brooklyn *B*
        Suffolk Campus *B*
St. Thomas Aquinas College *B*
Siena College *B*
State University of New York
        Albany *B,M*
        Binghamton *M*
        Buffalo *B,M,D*
        College at Brockport *M*
        College at Buffalo *M*
        College at Cortland *B,M*
        College at Fredonia *M*
        College at Geneseo *B*
        College at New Paltz *B,M*
        College at Oneonta *B,M*
        College at Plattsburgh *B*
        College at Potsdam *B,M*
        Oswego *B,M*
• Syracuse University *B,M,D*
Union College *M*
University of Rochester *M,D*
Utica College of Syracuse
    University *B*
Wells College *B*

North Carolina

Appalachian State University *B,M*
Barton College *B*
Bennett College *B*
Campbell University *B*
Catawba College *B*
Chowan College *B*
East Carolina University *B,M*
Elizabeth City State University *B*
Fayetteville State University *B*
Gardner-Webb College *B,M*
Johnson C. Smith University *B*
Lees-McRae College *B*
Livingstone College *B*
Mars Hill College *B*
Montreat-Anderson College *B*
North Carolina Agricultural and
    Technical State University *B,M*
North Carolina Central University
    B,M
North Carolina State University *B*
North Carolina Wesleyan College *B*
St. Andrews Presbyterian College *B*
St. Augustine's College *B*
Salem College *B*
University of North Carolina
        Asheville *C*
        Greensboro *M*
Western Carolina University *B,M*
Wingate College *B*

North Dakota

Bismarck State College *A*
Dickinson State University *B*
Jamestown College *B*
Mayville State University *B*
Minot State University *B*
North Dakota State University *B,M*
Turtle Mountain Community
    College *A*
University of Mary *B*
University of North Dakota *B,M*
Valley City State University *B*

Ohio

Ashland University *B*
Baldwin-Wallace College *B*
Bluffton College *B*
Bowling Green State University *B*
Capital University *B*
Case Western Reserve University *B*
College of Mount St. Joseph *C*
Defiance College *B*
Heidelberg College *B*
Kent State University *B,M*
Malone College *B*
Miami University: Oxford
    Campus *B*
Mount Union College *B*
Mount Vernon Nazarene College *B*
Ohio Dominican College *B*
Ohio State University: Columbus
    Campus *B*
Ohio University *B*
Otterbein College *B*
University of Dayton *B*
University of Findlay *B*
University of Rio Grande *B*
University of Toledo *B*
Urbana University *B*
Walsh College *B*
Wittenberg University *B*
Wright State University *B*
Youngstown State University *B*

Oklahoma

Bartlesville Wesleyan College *B*
East Central University *B*
Mid-America Bible College *B*
Northwestern Oklahoma State
    University *B*
Oklahoma Baptist University *B*

Oklahoma Christian University of
    Science and Arts *B*
Oklahoma City University *B*
Oklahoma Panhandle State
    University *B*
Oral Roberts University *B*
Phillips University *B*
Southeastern Oklahoma State
    University *B,M*
Southwestern Oklahoma State
    University *B,M*
University of Central Oklahoma
    B,M
University of Science and Arts of
    Oklahoma *B*
University of Tulsa *B,M*

Oregon

George Fox College *B*
Oregon State University *M*
Southern Oregon State College *M*
Western Baptist College *B*
Western Oregon State College *B,M*
Willamette University *M*

Pennsylvania

Albright College *B*
Allentown College of St. Francis de
    Sales *B,M*
Beaver College *B,M*
Bloomsburg University of
    Pennsylvania *B*
Cabrini College *B*
California University of
    Pennsylvania *B,M*
Chatham College *B*
Cheyney University of
    Pennsylvania *B*
Clarion University of
    Pennsylvania *B*
Delaware Valley College *B*
Duquesne University *B,M*
East Stroudsburg University of
    Pennsylvania *B*
Eastern College *B*
Edinboro University of
    Pennsylvania *B*
Elizabethtown College *B*
Gannon University *B*
Geneva College *B*
Gettysburg College *B*
Grove City College *B*
Gwynedd-Mercy College *B*
Harrisburg Area Community
    College *A*
Holy Family College *B*
Immaculata College *B*
Indiana University of Pennsylvania
    B,M
Juniata College *B*
La Salle University *B*
Lincoln University *B*
Lock Haven University of
    Pennsylvania *B*
Lycoming College *B*
Mansfield University of
    Pennsylvania *B*
Marywood College *B*
Mercyhurst College *B*
Messiah College *B*
Moravian College *B*
Penn State Harrisburg Capital
    College *B*
Philadelphia College of Bible *B*
Point Park College *B*
Robert Morris College *B*
St. Francis College *C*
St. Joseph's University *C,B,M*
Seton Hill College *B*
Slippery Rock University of
    Pennsylvania *B*
Temple University *M,D*

University of Pennsylvania *B,M,D*
University of Pittsburgh
    Bradford *C,B*
    Johnstown *B*
University of Scranton *B,M*
Washington and Jefferson College *B*
Waynesburg College *B*
West Chester University of
    Pennsylvania *B*
Widener University *M*
Wilkes University *B,M*
York College of Pennsylvania *B*

Puerto Rico

Bayamon Central University *B*
Caribbean University *B*
Inter American University of Puerto
    Rico
    Arecibo Campus *B*
    San German Campus *B*
Pontifical Catholic University of
    Puerto Rico *B*
Turabo University *M*
Universidad Metropolitana *B*
University of Puerto Rico
    Mayaguez Campus *M*
    Rio Piedras Campus *B,M*

Rhode Island

Providence College *B*
Rhode Island College *B,M*
University of Rhode Island *M*

South Carolina

Benedict College *B*
Bob Jones University *B,M,D*
Charleston Southern University *M*
The Citadel *M*
Claflin College *B*
Coker College *B*
Columbia College *B*
Converse College *M*
Erskine College *B*
Francis Marion College *M*
Lander College *B*
Limestone College *B*
Morris College *B*
Presbyterian College *B*
South Carolina State College *B*
University of South Carolina
    Aiken *B*
    Coastal Carolina College *B*

South Dakota

Augustana College *B*
Black Hills State University *B*
Dakota State University *B*
Dakota Wesleyan University *B*
Mount Marty College *B*
Northern State University *B,M*
Sioux Falls College *B*
South Dakota State University *B*
University of South Dakota *B*

Tennessee

Crichton College *B*
David Lipscomb University *B*
East Tennessee State University
    B,M
Free Will Baptist Bible College *B*
Freed-Hardeman University *B*
Lincoln Memorial University *B*
Middle Tennessee State
    University *B*
Milligan College *B*
Tennessee Technological
    University *B*
Tennessee Wesleyan College *B*
Union University *B,M*

University of Tennessee
    Chattanooga *B,M*
    Knoxville *B*
    Martin *B*
Vanderbilt University *M,D*
William Jennings Bryan College *B*

Texas

Abilene Christian University *B*
Angelo State University *B*
Baylor University *B*
Dallas Baptist University *B*
Del Mar College *A*
East Texas Baptist University *B*
East Texas State University *D*
Hardin-Simmons University *B*
Incarnate Word College *B*
McMurry University *B*
Midwestern State University *B*
Our Lady of the Lake University of
    San Antonio *M*
Prairie View A&M University *M*
Ranger Junior College *A*
St. Edward's University *B*
St. Mary's University *B*
Schreiner College *B*
Southwest Texas State
    University *M*
Texas A&I University *B*
Texas Christian University *B*
Texas College *B*
Texas Wesleyan University *B*
University of Dallas *B*
University of Houston *B,M*
University of Mary Hardin-
    Baylor *B*
University of Texas at San
    Antonio *M*
West Texas State University *B,M*
Wiley College *B*

Utah

Brigham Young University *B*
Southern Utah University *B*
Weber State University *B*

Vermont

Castleton State College *B*
Goddard College *B*
Lyndon State College *B*
St. Michael's College *B*
University of Vermont *B*

Virginia

Averett College *B*
Bluefield College *B*
Eastern Mennonite College *B*
Emory and Henry College *B*
Ferrum College *B*
George Mason University *M*
Lynchburg College *M*
Old Dominion University *B,M*
Radford University *M*
Virginia Intermont College *B*
Virginia Polytechnic Institute and
    State University *B,M*
Virginia State University *B*
Virginia Union University *B*
Virginia Wesleyan College *B*

Washington

Central Washington University *B,M*
Eastern Washington University *B*
Heritage College *B*
Pacific Lutheran University *B*
Seattle Pacific University *B,M*
University of Puget Sound *M*
University of Washington *B*
Washington State University *B*
Western Washington University
    B,M

West Virginia

Bethany College *B*
Bluefield State College *B*
Concord College *B*
Davis and Elkins College *B*
Fairmont State College *B*
Glenville State College *B*
Shepherd College *B*
West Liberty State College *B*
West Virginia Institute of
    Technology *B*
West Virginia State College *B*
West Virginia University *B*
West Virginia Wesleyan College *B*

Wisconsin

Alverno College *B*
Cardinal Stritch College *B*
Carroll College *B*
Carthage College *B*
Concordia University Wisconsin *B*
Lakeland College *B*
Lawrence University *B*
Maranatha Baptist Bible College *B*
Marian College of Fond du Lac *B*
Marquette University *B*
Mount Mary College *B*
Mount Senario College *B*
Northland College *B*
St. Norbert College *B*
University of Wisconsin
    Eau Claire *B*
    Green Bay *B*
    La Crosse *B*
    Madison *M*
    Oshkosh *B*
    Platteville *B*
    River Falls *B*
    Stevens Point *B*
    Whitewater *B*
Wisconsin Lutheran College *B*

Wyoming

University of Wyoming *B*

Canada

McGill University *B,M*

English literature

Alabama

Samford University *B,M*
University of Alabama *B,M,D*

Arizona

Arizona Western College *A*
Grand Canyon University *B*
Prescott College *B*
University of Arizona *B*

Arkansas

Ouachita Baptist University *B*

California

California Institute of Technology *B*
California State University
    Bakersfield *B,M*
    Dominguez Hills *B,M*
    Fresno *B*
    Long Beach *B*
    Northridge *B*
Chabot College *A*
Christ College Irvine *B*
Claremont McKenna College *B*
Dominican College of San Rafael *B*
Fresno Pacific College *B*
Irvine Valley College *A*
Long Beach City College *A*
Loyola Marymount University *B*

Mills College *M*
Modesto Junior College *A*
Pitzer College *B*
Point Loma Nazarene College *B*
Pomona College *B*
Saddleback College *A*
San Francisco State University *B*
San Jose State University *M*
Scripps College *B*
Stanford University *B,M,D*
University of California
    Berkeley *B,M,D*
    Riverside *B,M,D*
    San Diego *B,M,D*
University of Judaism *B*
University of Redlands *B*
University of Southern California *B*
Westmont College *B*

Colorado

Lamar Community College *A*
Mesa State College *B*
University of Colorado at Denver *B*
University of Denver *B*

Connecticut

Fairfield University *B*
Southern Connecticut State
    University *B,M*
Trinity College *B*
University of Hartford *B*
University of New Haven *B*
Wesleyan University *B*
Yale University *B,M,D*

District of Columbia

American University *B,M*
Catholic University of America
    B,M,D
Gallaudet University *B*
George Washington University
    B,M,D
Trinity College *B*

Florida

Barry University *M*
Eckerd College *B*
Indian River Community College *A*
Miami-Dade Community College *A*
New College of the University of
    South Florida *B*
University of Florida *M,D*
University of North Florida *B*

Georgia

Agnes Scott College *B*
Andrew College *A*
Darton College *A*
Emory University *B,M,D*
Morris Brown College *B*
University of Georgia *B,M,D*

Idaho

Albertson College *B*

Illinois

Augustana College *B*
Aurora University *B*
Bradley University *B*
Chicago State University *B*
Concordia University *B*
Illinois College *B*
Judson College *B*
KAES College *B*
Lincoln College *A*
Northeastern Illinois University *M*
Northwestern University *B*
Olivet Nazarene University *B*
Richland Community College *A*
Rockford College *B*
Shimer College *B*

Southern Illinois University
  Carbondale *B,M,D*
  Edwardsville *B,M*
University of Chicago *B,M,D*
University of Illinois
  Chicago *B*
  Urbana-Champaign *M,D*
Wheaton College *B*

Indiana

DePauw University *B*
Indiana State University *B,M*
Indiana University Bloomington
  B,M,D
Indiana University—Purdue
  University at Fort Wayne *B*
Manchester College *A*
Purdue University
  Calumet *B*
  West Lafayette *D*
St. Mary's College *B*
Taylor University *B*
University of Evansville *B*
University of Notre Dame *B,M,D*

Iowa

Coe College *B*
Drake University *B*
Graceland College *B*
Grinnell College *B*
Luther College *B*
Maharishi International University
  A,B,M
Morningside College *B*
University of Iowa *M,D*
Wartburg College *B*

Kansas

Baker University *B*
MidAmerica Nazarene College *B*

Kentucky

Kentucky Wesleyan College *B*
Sue Bennett College *A*

Maine

University of Maine at
  Farmington *B*

Maryland

Coppin State College *B*
Johns Hopkins University *B,M,D*
Salisbury State University *B,M*
University of Baltimore *B*
University of Maryland: College
  Park *B,M,D*
Washington College *B,M*

Massachusetts

Assumption College *B*
Bentley College *B*
Bradford College *B*
Brandeis University *B,M,D*
Clark University *B,M*
Elms College *B*
Emmanuel College *B*
Fitchburg State College *B*
Hampshire College *B*
Harvard and Radcliffe Colleges *B*
Harvard University *D*
Massachusetts Institute of
  Technology *B*
Mount Holyoke College *B*
North Adams State College *B*
Roxbury Community College *A*
Salem State College *B*
Simmons College *B,M*
Simon's Rock College of Bard *B*
Smith College *B*
Stonehill College *B*
Tufts University *B,M,D*

University of Massachusetts at
  Dartmouth *B*
Wheaton College *B*
Williams College *B*

Michigan

Adrian College *A,B*
Alma College *B*
Calvin College *B*
Eastern Michigan University *B,M*
Grand Valley State University *B*
Lake Superior State University *B*
Northern Michigan University *B*
Oakland University *B,M*
Olivet College *B*
University of Michigan *M,D*
Wayne State University *B,M,D*

Minnesota

Bethel College *B*
Carleton College *B*
Gustavus Adolphus College *B*
St. Mary's College of Minnesota *B*
St. Olaf College *B*
Willmar Community College *A*

Mississippi

Jackson State University *B*

Missouri

Central Methodist College *B*
Fontbonne College *B*
Maryville University *B*
Park College *B*
Washington University *B,M,D*

Montana

Montana State University *B*
Rocky Mountain College *B*

Nebraska

Concordia College *B*
Hastings College *B*
York College *A*

Nevada

Sierra Nevada College *B*

New Hampshire

Franklin Pierce College *B*
Plymouth State College of the
  University System of New
  Hampshire *B*
St. Anselm College *B*

New Jersey

Drew University *B,M,D*
Fairleigh Dickinson University *B,M*
Glassboro State College *B*
Kean College of New Jersey *B*
Ramapo College of New Jersey *B*
Rider College *B*
Rutgers—The State University of
  New Jersey *M,D*
Seton Hall University *M*
Stevens Institute of Technology *B*
Stockton State College *B*
Thomas Edison State College *B*
Upsala College *B*
William Paterson College of New
  Jersey *B*

New Mexico

College of Santa Fe *B*

New York

Bard College *B*
City University of New York
  Brooklyn College *B,M*
  City College *B,M*
  Graduate School and
    University Center *D*
  Hunter College *B,M*
  Lehman College *M*
  Queens College *B,M*
  York College *B*
Columbia University
  New York *M,D*
  School of General Studies *B*
Cornell University *M,D*
Dominican College of Blauvelt *B*
Elmira College *B*
Eugene Lang College/New School
  for Social Research *B*
Fordham University *B,M,D*
Hamilton College *B*
Hofstra University *B,M*
Houghton College *B*
Iona College *B*
Long Island University:
  Southampton Campus *B*
Manhattan College *B*
Manhattanville College *B*
Mercy College *B*
Molloy College *B*
Nazareth College of Rochester *B*
New York University *B,M,D*
St. John's University *B*
Sarah Lawrence College *B*
State University of New York
  Purchase *B*
  College at Oneonta *B*
Syracuse University *M,D*
Touro College *B*
University of the State of New
  York: Regents College *B*
Wagner College *B*

North Carolina

Brevard College *A*
Fayetteville State University *B*
Guilford College *B*
High Point University *B*
North Carolina State University
  B,M
Queens College *B*
University of North Carolina at
  Asheville *B*

Ohio

Ashland University *B*
Baldwin-Wallace College *B*
Capital University *B*
Case Western Reserve University
  B,M,D
Central State University *B*
College of Wooster *B*
Denison University *B*
Franciscan University of
  Steubenville *B*
Heidelberg College *B*
Kenyon College *B*
Miami University: Oxford Campus
  B,M,D
Ohio State University: Columbus
  Campus *M,D*
Ohio University *B,M,D*
Ohio Wesleyan University *B*
Pontifical College Josephinum *B*
Union Institute *B,D*
University of Cincinnati *B,M,D*
University of Toledo *B*
Wittenberg University *B*

Oklahoma

Northeastern State University *B*
Oral Roberts University *B*

University of Central Oklahoma *M*
University of Tulsa *B,M,D*

Oregon

George Fox College *B*
Reed College *B*
University of Oregon
  Eugene *B,M,D*
  Robert Donald Clark Honors
    College *B*

Pennsylvania

Bryn Mawr College *B*
Bucknell University *B,M*
California University of
  Pennsylvania *B*
Carnegie Mellon University
  B,M,D,W
Chatham College *B*
Chestnut Hill College *B*
Duquesne University *B,M*
Eastern College *B*
Elizabethtown College *B*
Geneva College *B*
Grove City College *B*
Gwynedd-Mercy College *B*
Immaculata College *B*
Indiana University of Pennsylvania
  M,D
La Roche College *B*
La Salle University *B*
Mansfield University of
  Pennsylvania *B*
Messiah College *B*
Rosemont College *B*
St. Francis College *B*
Swarthmore College *B*
University of Pittsburgh
  Greensburg *B*
  Johnstown *B*
  Pittsburgh *B*
West Chester University of
  Pennsylvania *B*

Puerto Rico

Inter American University of Puerto
  Rico: Metropolitan Campus *B*

Rhode Island

Brown University *B,M,D*
Rhode Island College *B*
Salve Regina University *B*

South Carolina

Columbia College *B*

South Dakota

Black Hills State University *B*

Tennessee

Austin Peay State University *B,M*
Knoxville College *B*
Tennessee Wesleyan College *B*
Tusculum College *B*
Union University *B*
University of the South *B*
University of Tennessee
  Chattanooga *B,M*
  Knoxville *B*

Texas

Jacksonville College *A*
Lon Morris College *A*
St. Edward's University *B*
St. Mary's University *M*
Schreiner College *A,B*
Southern Methodist University *B,M*
University of Dallas *B,M,D*
University of Houston *M,D*
University of Texas
  El Paso *B,M*
  Permian Basin *B,M*

Western Texas College *A*

Utah

Southern Utah University *B*
Weber State University *B*

Vermont

Bennington College *B*
Castleton State College *B*
Lyndon State College *B*
Marlboro College *B*
St. Michael's College *B*

Virginia

Averett College *B*
Christopher Newport College *B*
Emory and Henry College *B*
George Mason University *M*
Virginia Wesleyan College *B*

Washington

Eastern Washington University *B,M*
Everett Community College *A*
Evergreen State College *B*
Olympic College *A*
Pacific Lutheran University *B*
Seattle Central Community
College *A*
Seattle University *B*
Tacoma Community College *A*
University of Puget Sound *B*
Western Washington University
B,M
Whitworth College *B*

West Virginia

Alderson-Broaddus College *B*
Bethany College *B*
Davis and Elkins College *B*
Shepherd College *B*
Wheeling Jesuit College *B*

Wisconsin

Beloit College *B*
Lakeland College *B*
Northland College *B*

Wyoming

Eastern Wyoming College *A*

Canada

McGill University *B,M,D*

Switzerland

American College of Switzerland *B*

Arab Republic of Egypt

American University in Cairo *B,M*

Entomology

Alabama

Auburn University *B,M,D*

Arizona

University of Arizona *B,M,D*

Arkansas

University of Arkansas *M,D*

California

California State University
Fresno *B*
Stanislaus *B*
San Jose State University *B*
University of California
Berkeley *B,M,D*
Davis *B,M,D*
Riverside *B,M,D*

West Hills Community College *A*

Colorado

Colorado State University *M,D*

Connecticut

University of Connecticut *M,D*

Delaware

University of Delaware *B,M*

Florida

Florida Agricultural and Mechanical
University *B*
University of Florida *B,M,D*

Georgia

University of Georgia *B,M,D*

Hawaii

University of Hawaii at Manoa
B,M,D

Idaho

University of Idaho *B,M,D*

Illinois

University of Illinois at Urbana-
Champaign *B,M,D*

Indiana

Purdue University *B,M,D,W*
University of Notre Dame *M,D*

Iowa

Iowa State University *B,M,D*

Kansas

Kansas State University *M,D*
University of Kansas *M,D*

Kentucky

University of Kentucky *B,M,D*

Louisiana

Louisiana State University and
Agricultural and Mechanical
College *M,D*

Maine

University of Maine *B,M*

Maryland

University of Maryland: College
Park *B,M,D*

Massachusetts

University of Massachusetts at
Amherst *B,M,D*

Michigan

Michigan State University *B,M,D*

Minnesota

University of Minnesota: Twin
Cities *M,D*

Mississippi

Mississippi State University *B,M,D*

Missouri

University of Missouri: Columbia
M,D

Montana

Montana State University *M*

Nebraska

University of Nebraska—Lincoln
M,D

New Hampshire

University of New Hampshire *B,M*

New Jersey

Rutgers—The State University of
New Jersey
Camden College of Arts and
Sciences *B*
Cook College *B*
Douglass College *B*
Livingston College *B*
New Brunswick *M,D*
Rutgers College *B*
University College New
Brunswick *B*

New Mexico

New Mexico State University *M*

New York

Cornell University *B,M,D*
State University of New York
College of Environmental Science
and Forestry *B,M,D*

North Carolina

North Carolina State University
B,M,D

North Dakota

North Dakota State University
B,M,D

Ohio

Ohio State University: Columbus
Campus *B,M,D*
Ohio University *M,D*

Oklahoma

Oklahoma State University *B,M,D*

Oregon

Oregon State University *B,M,D*

Pennsylvania

Penn State University Park Campus
C,B,M,D

South Carolina

Clemson University *B,M,D,W*

South Dakota

South Dakota State University *M*

Tennessee

University of Tennessee:
Knoxville *M*

Texas

Texas A&M University *B,M,D*
Texas Tech University *B,M*

Utah

Brigham Young University *B,M,D*

Vermont

Marlboro College *B*

Virginia

Virginia Polytechnic Institute and
State University *M,D*

Washington

Everett Community College *A*
Washington State University *B,M,D*

West Virginia

West Virginia University *M*

Wisconsin

University of Wisconsin: Madison
B,M,D

Wyoming

University of Wyoming *B,M,D*

Canada

McGill University *B,M,D*

Environmental design

Alabama

Auburn University *B*

Arizona

Prescott College *B*

California

Art Center College of Design *B,M*
California State University:
Fullerton *B*
City College of San Francisco *A*
Cosumnes River College *C,A*
Los Angeles Mission College *A*
Otis/Parsons School of Art and
Design *C,B*
San Diego City College *A*
Southwestern College *A*
University of California
Davis *B*
Los Angeles *M,D*
World College West *B*

Colorado

Rocky Mountain College of Art &
Design *A,B*
University of Colorado at
Boulder *B*

Connecticut

Yale University *M*

Georgia

Southern College of Technology *B*
University of Georgia *B,M*

Illinois

Augustana College *B*
Southern Illinois University at
Carbondale *B,M*

Indiana

Ball State University *B*
Indiana University Bloomington
B,M
Purdue University *B,M*

Maryland

Morgan State University *B,M*

Massachusetts

Hampshire College *B*
Harvard and Radcliffe Colleges *B*
Massachusetts Institute of
Technology *B,M,D*
University of Massachusetts at
Amherst *B*

Michigan

Aquinas College *B*
Center for Creative Studies: College
of Art and Design *B*
Grand Valley State University *B*
Northern Michigan University *B*
University of Michigan *B,M,D*

Minnesota

University of Minnesota: Twin
Cities *B*

Missouri

University of Missouri
    Columbia *B,M,D*
    Rolla *M*

New Jersey

Rutgers—The State University of
    New Jersey: Cook College *B*
Stevens Institute of Technology
    B,M,D

New Mexico

University of New Mexico *B*

New York

Cornell University *B,M*
Parsons School of Design *B*
State University of New York
    Buffalo *B*
    College of Environmental
      Science and Forestry *B,M*
Suffolk County Community
    College *A*
Syracuse University *B*
United States Military Academy *B*

North Carolina

North Carolina State University *B*

North Dakota

North Dakota State University *B*

Ohio

Bowling Green State University *B*
Miami University: Oxford
    Campus *B*
Ohio State University: Columbus
    Campus *B*

Oklahoma

University of Oklahoma *B*

Pennsylvania

Delaware Valley College *B*
University of Pennsylvania *B*

Puerto Rico

University of Puerto Rico: Rio
    Piedras Campus *B*

Texas

Texas A&M University *B*
Texas Southmost College *A*
University of Houston *B*

Vermont

Marlboro College *B*

Virginia

Virginia Polytechnic Institute and
    State University *D*

Washington

Evergreen State College *B*
Western Washington University *B*

Wisconsin

University of Wisconsin: Green
    Bay *B*

Environmental health engineering

Alabama

Community College of the Air
    Force *A*
University of Alabama *M*

Alaska

University of Alaska
    Anchorage *M*
    Fairbanks *M*

Arkansas

University of Arkansas *M*

California

California Polytechnic State
    University: San Luis Obispo *B*
Loyola Marymount University *M*
Santa Rosa Junior College *A*
University of California
    Berkeley *M*
    Los Angeles *D*
University of Southern California
    B,M,D

Connecticut

University of Connecticut *D*
University of New Haven *M*

District of Columbia

George Washington University *M,D*

Florida

Florida Institute of Technology *B,M*
Florida International University *M*
University of Central Florida *B,M,D*
University of Florida *B,M,D*
University of Miami *M*

Georgia

Georgia Institute of Technology
    M,D

Illinois

Illinois Institute of Technology
    B,M,D
Northwestern University *B*
Southern Illinois University at
    Carbondale *B,M*
University of Illinois at Urbana-
    Champaign *M,D*

Indiana

Purdue University *B,M,D,W*
University of Notre Dame *M*

Iowa

University of Iowa *M,D*

Kansas

Fort Scott Community College *A*
University of Kansas *M,D*

Massachusetts

Harvard University *M,D*
Massachusetts Institute of
    Technology *B*
Springfield Technical Community
    College *A*
Tufts University *B,M*
University of Massachusetts at
    Amherst *M*
Worcester Polytechnic Institute *B*

Michigan

Michigan State University *M,D*
University of Michigan *B,M,D*

Missouri

University of Missouri: Rolla *M*

Montana

Montana College of Mineral
    Science and Technology *B*
Montana State University *M*

New Jersey

Burlington County College *C*
New Jersey Institute of
    Technology *M*
Rutgers—The State University of
    New Jersey *M*
Stevens Institute of Technology
    B,M,D

New Mexico

New Mexico Institute of Mining
    and Technology *B*

New York

Cornell University *B,M,D*
Manhattan College *B,M*
Polytechnic University *M*
Rensselaer Polytechnic Institute
    B,M,D
State University of New York
    College of Environmental Science
      and Forestry *B,M,D*
Syracuse University *B,M*
United States Military Academy *B*

North Carolina

University of North Carolina at
    Chapel Hill *B,M,D*

North Dakota

University of North Dakota *B*

Ohio

University of Cincinnati *B,M,D*
University of Dayton *B*

Oklahoma

Oklahoma State University *M*
University of Oklahoma *B,M,D*

Pennsylvania

Carnegie Mellon University
    B,M,D,W
Drexel University *M,D*
Lock Haven University of
    Pennsylvania *B*
Penn State University Park Campus
    M,D
Swarthmore College *B*
Temple University *B*
Wilkes University *B*

Rhode Island

Brown University *B,M,D*

South Carolina

Clemson University *M,D*

Tennessee

University of Tennessee:
    Knoxville *M*
Vanderbilt University *M,D*

Texas

Lamar University—Beaumont *B,M*
Rice University *B,M,D*
Southern Methodist University *M*
Texas A&I University *M*
University of Houston *M,D*
University of Texas at Austin *M*

Utah

Utah State University *B*

Virginia

Virginia Polytechnic Institute and
    State University *M,D*

Washington

Seattle University *B*
Washington State University *M*

West Virginia

West Virginia University *M*

Environmental science

Alabama

Alabama Agricultural and
    Mechanical University *B*
Auburn University
    Auburn *B*
    Montgomery *B*
Livingston University *B*
Samford University *B*
Troy State University *B*
Tuskegee University *M*
University of North Alabama *B*

Alaska

Alaska Pacific University *B*

Arizona

Grand Canyon University *B*
Northern Arizona University *B*
Prescott College *B,M*

Arkansas

University of Arkansas
    Fayetteville *B*
    Little Rock *B*
University of the Ozarks *B*

California

California State University
    Fresno *B*
    Fullerton *M*
    Hayward *B*
    Sacramento *B*
    San Bernardino *B*
    Stanislaus *B*
Christ College Irvine *B*
College of the Desert *A*
Loyola Marymount University *B,M*
Pitzer College *B*
San Jose State University *B*
Santa Barbara City College *A*
Sonoma State University *B*
Southwestern College *A*
University of California
    Berkeley *B*
    Los Angeles *D*
    Riverside *B*
    Santa Barbara *B,M,D*
    Santa Cruz *B*
University of La Verne *B*
University of Redlands *B*
University of San Francisco *B,M*
Whittier College *B*
World College West *B*

Colorado

Adams State College *B*
Colorado Mountain College:
    Timberline Campus *A*
Fort Lewis College *B*
Regis College of Regis University *B*
University of Colorado at Boulder
    B,M,D
University of Denver *B*

Connecticut

Eastern Connecticut State
    University *B*
Mattatuck Community College *A*
Middlesex Community College *A*
Trinity College *B*
University of New Haven *A,B,M*
Wesleyan University *B,M*
Western Connecticut State
    University *B*

Delaware

University of Delaware *B*
Wesley College *B*

District of Columbia

American University *B*
Catholic University of America *B*
George Washington University *B,M*
University of the District of
Columbia *B*

Florida

Eckerd College *B*
Florida Institute of Technology
B,M,D
Florida International University *B*
Jacksonville University *B*
New College of the University of
South Florida *B*
Pensacola Junior College *A*
Rollins College *B*
University of Florida *M,D*
University of Miami *B*

Georgia

Emory University *M*
LaGrange College *B*
Macon College *A*
Savannah State College *B*
Shorter College *B*

Idaho

Boise State University *B*

Illinois

Augustana College *B*
Aurora University *B*
Bradley University *B*
College of DuPage *A*
College of St. Francis *B*
Concordia University *B*
De Paul University *B*
Eastern Illinois University *B,M*
Illinois Central College *A*
Illinois State University *B*
Lake Forest College *B*
Northeastern Illinois University *B*
Olivet Nazarene University *B*
Southern Illinois University at
Edwardsville *M*
University of Chicago *B,M,D*
University of Illinois at Urbana-
Champaign *M,D*

Indiana

Ball State University *B*
Butler University *B*
Indiana University Bloomington
B,M,D
Manchester College *B*
Purdue University *B,M,D*
St. Francis College *A,B*
Taylor University *B*
Tri-State University *B*
University of Evansville *B*

Iowa

Central College *B*
Cornell College *B*
Dordt College *B*
Drake University *B*
Iowa Lakes Community College *A*
Luther College *B*
Simpson College *B*
University of Dubuque *B*
William Penn College *B*

Kansas

Baker University *B*
Bethel College *B*
Friends University *B*
McPherson College *B*

Pittsburg State University *B*
University of Kansas *B*

Kentucky

Eastern Kentucky University *B*
Georgetown College *B*
Western Kentucky University *B*

Louisiana

Louisiana State University and
Agricultural and Mechanical
College *M*
McNeese State University *B,M*
University of Southwestern
Louisiana *D*

Maine

Bowdoin College *B*
St. Joseph's College *B*
Southern Maine Technical
College *A*
Unity College *B*
University of Maine
Farmington *B*
Machias *B*
Presque Isle *A,B*
University of New England *B*

Maryland

Frostburg State University *B*
Hood College *B*
Salisbury State University *B*
University of Maryland
Baltimore *M,D*
Eastern Shore *B,M,D*

Massachusetts

Anna Maria College for Men and
Women *B*
Berkshire Community College *A*
Boston College *B*
Boston University *B,M,D*
Bradford College *B*
Clark University *B,M*
Fitchburg State College *B*
Hampshire College *B*
Harvard and Radcliffe Colleges *B*
Harvard University *M,D*
Holyoke Community College *A*
Lesley College *B,M*
Massachusetts Institute of
Technology *B,M*
Merrimack College *B*
Simmons College *B*
Simon's Rock College of Bard *B*
Springfield College *B*
Suffolk University *B*
Tufts University *B*
University of Massachusetts
Amherst *B*
Boston *M,D*
Lowell *B*
Worcester Polytechnic Institute *B*

Michigan

Adrian College *B*
Aquinas College *B*
Grand Valley State University *B*
Hillsdale College *B*
Lake Superior State University *B*
Lansing Community College *A*
Michigan State University *B*
Northern Michigan University *B*
Oakland University *B*
University of Michigan: Dearborn *B*
Western Michigan University *B*

Minnesota

Bemidji State University *B,M*
Concordia College: St. Paul *B*
Hamline University *B*
Macalester College *B*

Mankato State University *B,M*
St. Mary's College of Minnesota *B*
University of Minnesota: Twin
Cities *M,D*
Willmar Community College *A*
Winona State University *B*

Mississippi

Delta State University *B*
Jackson State University *M,D*

Missouri

Fontbonne College *B*
Missouri Southern State College
A,B

Montana

Fort Peck Community College *A*
University of Montana *M*

Nebraska

Dana College *B*
Doane College *B*

Nevada

Sierra Nevada College *B*
University of Nevada: Las Vegas *B*

New Hampshire

Antioch New England Graduate
School *M*
Franklin Pierce College *B*
Keene State College *B*
New England College *B*
Plymouth State College of the
University System of New
Hampshire *B*
University of New Hampshire *B*

New Jersey

Bloomfield College *B*
Caldwell College *C*
County College of Morris *A*
Fairleigh Dickinson University *B*
Glassboro State College *B*
Kean College of New Jersey *B*
Monmouth College *B*
Montclair State College *M*
New Jersey Institute of Technology
M,D
Ramapo College of New Jersey *B*
Rutgers—The State University of
New Jersey
Cook College *B*
New Brunswick *M,D*
Stevens Institute of Technology *B*
Stockton State College *B*
Union County College *A*
William Paterson College of New
Jersey *B*

New Mexico

College of Santa Fe *B*
Eastern New Mexico University *B*
New Mexico Highlands
University *B*
New Mexico Institute of Mining
and Technology *B*
New Mexico State University *B*

New York

Alfred University *B*
Bard College *B,M*
Barnard College *B*
City University of New York
College of Staten Island *M*
Kingsborough Community
College *A*
Queens College *B*
Colgate University *B*
Columbia University: Columbia
College *B*

Concordia College *B*
Elmira College *B*
Genesee Community College *A*
Hobart College *B*
Hudson Valley Community
College *A*
Long Island University
C. W. Post Campus *M*
Southampton Campus *B*
Manhattan College *B,M*
Marist College *B*
Nazareth College of Rochester *B*
New York Institute of
Technology *A*
New York University *M,D*
Paul Smith's College *A*
Polytechnic University *M*
Rochester Institute of
Technology *B*
St. John's University *B*
St. Lawrence University *B*
State University of New York
Binghamton *B*
Purchase *C,B*
College of Environmental
Science and Forestry *B,M,D*
College at Geneseo *B*
College at Plattsburgh *B*
Sullivan County Community
College *A*
William Smith College *B*

North Carolina

Barton College *B*
Brevard College *A*
Duke University *B*
Lenoir-Rhyne College *B*
North Carolina Wesleyan College *B*
University of North Carolina
Asheville *B*
Chapel Hill *B,M,D*
Wilmington *B*
Warren Wilson College *B*

North Dakota

Dickinson State University *B*

Ohio

Antioch College *B*
Ashland University *B*
Bowling Green State University *B*
Defiance College *B*
Heidelberg College *B*
Miami University: Oxford
Campus *M*
Oberlin College *B*
Ohio State University: Columbus
Campus *M,D*
Ohio University *B,M*
Ohio Wesleyan University *B*
Otterbein College *B*
University of Cincinnati *M,D*
Wright State University *B*

Oklahoma

East Central University *B*
Langston University *B*
Rose State College *C*
University of Oklahoma
Health Sciences Center *M,D*
Norman *B,M,D*

Oregon

Marylhurst College *B*
Oregon Graduate Institute *M,D*
Oregon State University *B*
Portland State University *D*
Willamette University *B*

Pennsylvania

Albright College *B*
Allegheny College *B*

Beaver College *M*
Bucknell University *B*
California University of
 Pennsylvania *B,M*
Clarion University of
 Pennsylvania *C*
Dickinson College *C*
Drexel University *B,M,D*
East Stroudsburg University of
 Pennsylvania *B*
Edinboro University of
 Pennsylvania *B*
Elizabethtown College *B*
Gettysburg College *B*
Juniata College *B*
Keystone Junior College *A*
Kutztown University of
 Pennsylvania *B*
Lehigh University *B,M,D*
Lock Haven University of
 Pennsylvania *B*
Lycoming College *B*
Marywood College *B*
Mercyhurst College *B*
St. Francis College *B*
Slippery Rock University of
 Pennsylvania *B*
Thiel College *B*
University of Pennsylvania *B*
Westminster College *B*
Wilkes University *B*

Puerto Rico

University of Puerto Rico
 Medical Sciences Campus *M*
 Rio Piedras Campus *B*

Rhode Island

Brown University *B*

South Carolina

Benedict College *B*

South Dakota

Augustana College *B*
Northern State University *B*
South Dakota State University *B*

Tennessee

East Tennessee State University
 B,M
Middle Tennessee State
 University *B*
University of Tennessee:
 Chattanooga *B*

Texas

Baylor University *B,M*
Concordia Lutheran College *B*
Lamar University—Beaumont *B*
Sam Houston State University *B*
Southwest Texas State University
 B,M
Stephen F. Austin State
 University *B*
Texas A&M University *B*
Texas Christian University *B,M*
Texas Wesleyan University *B*
University of Texas Health Science
 Center at Houston *M,D*

Utah

Brigham Young University *B*

Vermont

Bennington College *B*
Johnson State College *B*
Lyndon State College *B*
Marlboro College *B*
Middlebury College *B*
St. Michael's College *B*
Southern Vermont College *A,B*

Sterling College *A*
University of Vermont *B*

Virginia

Averett College *B*
Clinch Valley College of the
 University of Virginia *B*
Ferrum College *B*
George Mason University *D*
Lynchburg College *B*
Mary Washington College *B*
Old Dominion University *B*
Randolph-Macon College *B*
Shenandoah University *B*
Southwest Virginia Community
 College *A*
Sweet Briar College *B*
University of Virginia *B,M,D*
Virginia Polytechnic Institute and
 State University *B*
Virginia Wesleyan College *B*

Washington

Eastern Washington University *B*
Everett Community College *A*
Evergreen State College *B,M*
Heritage College *B*
Seattle Pacific University *B*
Shoreline Community College *A*
University of Washington *B*
Washington State University *B,M*
Western Washington University
 B,M

West Virginia

Davis and Elkins College *B*
Salem-Teikyo University *B*
University of Charleston *B*
West Virginia Graduate College *M*

Wisconsin

Beloit College *B*
Carroll College *B*
Carthage College *B*
Edgewood College *B*
Northland College *B*
St. Norbert College *B*
University of Wisconsin
 Green Bay *B,M*
 Madison *M,D*
 Milwaukee *B*

Wyoming

Casper College *A*

Equestrian science

Arizona

Scottsdale Community College *A*

California

Cosumnes River College *C,A*
Feather River College *C,A*
Los Angeles Pierce College *C,A*
Merced College *A*
Moorpark College *A*

Colorado

Colorado State University *B*
Lamar Community College *A*
Northeastern Junior College *A*
Pikes Peak Community College *C*

Connecticut

Teikyo-Post University *C,A,B*

Georgia

Brenau Women's College *B*

Idaho

College of Southern Idaho *A*

Illinois

Black Hawk College: East
 Campus *A*
Parkland College *C,A*
Southern Illinois University at
 Carbondale *B*

Indiana

St. Mary-of-the-Woods College
 C,A,B

Iowa

Kirkwood Community College *A*

Kansas

Allen County Community
 College *A*
Colby Community College *A*
Dodge City Community College *A*
Johnson County Community
 College *A*
Kansas State University *B*

Kentucky

Murray State University *A*

Massachusetts

Mount Ida College *A*
University of Massachusetts at
 Amherst *A*

Minnesota

University of Minnesota:
 Crookston *A*

Missouri

Northeast Missouri State
 University *B*
Park College *B*
Stephens College *B*
William Woods College *B*

Montana

Rocky Mountain College *A,B*

New Jersey

Centenary College *A,B*

New York

Cazenovia College *A*
Pace University: Pleasantville/
 Briarcliff *A*
State University of New York
 College of Agriculture and
 Technology at Cobleskill *A*
 College of Agriculture and
 Technology at Morrisville *A*

North Carolina

Martin Community College *A*

Ohio

Lake Erie College *B*
Ohio State University Agricultural
 Technical Institute *A*
Otterbein College *B*
University of Findlay *A,B*

Oklahoma

Connors State College *C,A*
Oklahoma State University:
 Oklahoma City *A*
Redlands Community College *A*
Rogers State College *C,A*

Oregon

Treasure Valley Community College
 C,A

Pennsylvania

Delaware Valley College *A,B*
Harcum Junior College *A*
Wilson College *B*

Rhode Island

Johnson & Wales University *A,B*

Tennessee

Hiwassee College *A*

Texas

Central Texas College *A*
Cooke County College *A*
Sul Ross State University *B*
Tarleton State University *B*

Virginia

Averett College *B*
Bluefield College *B*
Southern Seminary College *A*
Virginia Intermont College *B*

West Virginia

Salem-Teikyo University *A,B,M*

Wisconsin

University of Wisconsin: River
 Falls *B*

Wyoming

Central Wyoming College *C,A*
Laramie County Community
 College *A*
Northwest College *C,A*

European studies

California

Claremont McKenna College *B*
Loyola Marymount University *B*
Naval Postgraduate School *M*
Pitzer College *B*
San Diego State University *B*
San Jose State University *B*
Scripps College *B*
University of California: Los
 Angeles *B,D*
University of the Pacific *B*

Connecticut

Connecticut College *B*
Wesleyan University *B*

District of Columbia

Catholic University of America *B*
George Washington University *B*

Florida

New College of the University of
 South Florida *B*
Schiller International University *B*

Georgia

Reinhardt College *A*

Hawaii

University of Hawaii: West Oahu *B*

Illinois

Richland Community College *A*
Rosary College *B*

Indiana

University of Notre Dame *B*

Iowa

University of Northern Iowa *B*

Kentucky
Georgetown College *B*

Maryland
Anne Arundel Community
College *A*
Goucher College *B*
Morgan State University *B*
St. John's College *B,M*

Massachusetts
Amherst College *B*
Bradford College *B*
Brandeis University *B*
Emerson College *B*
Hampshire College *B*
Harvard and Radcliffe Colleges *B*
Mount Holyoke College *B*
Tufts University *B,M*
Wellesley College *B*

Michigan
Calvin College *B*
Hillsdale College *B*
Western Michigan University *B*

Minnesota
University of Minnesota: Morris *B*

Missouri
Stephens College *B*
Westminster College *B*

New Hampshire
Plymouth State College of the
University System of New
Hampshire *B*

New York
Bard College *B*
Barnard College *B*
City University of New York
Brooklyn College *B*
City College *B*
Eugene Lang College/New School
for Social Research *B*
Sarah Lawrence College *B*

North Carolina
Queens College *B*
University of North Carolina
Chapel Hill *D*
Greensboro *B*

Ohio
Kenyon College *B*
Ohio State University: Columbus
Campus *M,D*
University of Toledo *B*
Wittenberg University *B*

Oklahoma
Phillips University *B*
University of Oklahoma *B*

Pennsylvania
California University of
Pennsylvania *B*
Carnegie Mellon University *B*
Gettysburg College *B*
St. Joseph's University *C*

Puerto Rico
University of Puerto Rico:
Mayaguez Campus *B*

Rhode Island
Brown University *B*

Tennessee
Vanderbilt University *B*

Texas
Southwest Texas State University *B*
Trinity University *B*

Utah
Brigham Young University *B*

Vermont
Goddard College *B*
Marlboro College *B*
University of Vermont *B*

Virginia
George Mason University *B*

Washington
Evergreen State College *B*
Gonzaga University *B*
Seattle Pacific University *B*

France
American University of Paris *B*

Switzerland
American College of Switzerland *B*
Franklin College: Switzerland *A,B*

Experimental psychology

Alabama
University of Alabama *M,D*

California
California State University
Northridge *M*
Stanislaus *B*
Southern California College *B*
University of California
San Diego *B,M,D*
Santa Barbara *B*
Santa Cruz *B,D*

Colorado
Colorado State University *M,D*

Connecticut
University of Hartford *M*
Wesleyan University *B,M*

District of Columbia
American University *M,D*
Catholic University of America
M,D
George Washington University *D*

Florida
Florida State University *B,M,D*
New College of the University of
South Florida *B*
University of Florida *M,D*
University of Miami *M,D*
University of South Florida *D*

Georgia
Emory University *M,D*

Illinois
De Paul University *M,D*
Illinois State University *M*
Loyola University of Chicago *M,D*
Millikin University *B*
Southern Illinois University at
Carbondale *M,D*
University of Chicago *B,M,D*
University of Health Sciences: The
Chicago Medical School *M,D*
University of Illinois at Urbana-
Champaign *B,M,D*

Indiana
Indiana State University *M*
Indiana University Bloomington
M,D
University of Notre Dame *M,D*

Iowa
University of Iowa *D*

Kansas
Kansas State University *M,D*
University of Kansas *D*

Kentucky
University of Kentucky *M,D*
University of Louisville *M,D*

Louisiana
Northeast Louisiana University *M*

Maine
University of Maine *M,D*

Maryland
Johns Hopkins University *B,M,D*

Massachusetts
Boston University *M,D*
Brandeis University *D*
Emmanuel College *B*
Harvard University *D*
Massachusetts Institute of
Technology *M,D*
Northeastern University *D*
Tufts University *B,M,D*

Michigan
Western Michigan University *M,D*

Mississippi
University of Southern Mississippi
M,D

Missouri
St. Louis University *D*
University of Missouri
Columbia *M,D*
St. Louis *D*

New Hampshire
Franklin Pierce College *B*
University of New Hampshire *D*

New Jersey
Fairleigh Dickinson University *M*

New Mexico
New Mexico Institute of Mining
and Technology *B*

New York
Alfred University *B*
City University of New York
Graduate School and University
Center *D*
Colgate University *B*
Columbia University *M,D*
Cornell University *M,D*
Fordham University *D*
Long Island University: C. W. Post
Campus *M*
New York University *M,D,W*
St. John's University *M*
Sarah Lawrence College *B*
State University of New York at
Buffalo *D*
Syracuse University *M,D*
Yeshiva University *D*

North Carolina
Duke University *D*

North Dakota
North Dakota State University *M*
University of North Dakota *D*

Ohio
Bowling Green State University
M,D
Case Western Reserve University *D*
Cleveland State University *M*
Kent State University *M,D*
Miami University: Oxford
Campus *D*
Ohio State University: Columbus
Campus *M,D*
Ohio University *B,M,D*
Union Institute *D*
University of Dayton *M*
University of Toledo *B,D*
Wright State University *B*
Xavier University *M*

Oklahoma
University of Oklahoma Health
Sciences Center *M,D*

Oregon
Oregon Health Sciences University
M,D

Pennsylvania
Bryn Mawr College *B*
Bucknell University *B,M*
Carnegie Mellon University
B,M,D,W
Juniata College *B*
La Salle University *B*
Lehigh University *M,D*
Mansfield University of
Pennsylvania *M*
Messiah College *B*
Moravian College *B*
Temple University *D*
University of Pennsylvania *M,D*

Rhode Island
Brown University *B,M,D*
University of Rhode Island *D*

South Carolina
University of South Carolina *B,M,D*

Tennessee
Middle Tennessee State
University *M*

Texas
Baylor University *M,D*
Southern Methodist University *M*
Southwestern University *B*
Texas Tech University *M,D*
University of Houston *D*
University of North Texas *M,D*
University of Texas at El Paso *M*

Utah
Brigham Young University *M,D*

Vermont
Goddard College *B*
Marlboro College *B*

Virginia
Averett College *B*
Virginia Wesleyan College *B*

Washington
Central Washington University *B,M*
Eastern Washington University *M*
Washington State University *D*

West Virginia

Bethany College *B*
West Virginia University *D*

Canada

McGill University *B,M,D*

Family and community services

California

California State University: Los
    Angeles *B*
University of California: Davis *M*

Connecticut

Tunxis Community College *C,A*

Delaware

University of Delaware *B*

Georgia

Georgia Southern University *B*

Hawaii

Hawaii Pacific University *B*

Illinois

KAES College *B*
National-Louis University *B,M*
Northern Illinois University *B*
Olivet Nazarene University *B*
Shawnee Community College *A*
Southern Illinois University at
    Carbondale *B*
State Community College *A*

Indiana

Purdue University *B,M*

Iowa

Iowa State University *B*
University of Northern Iowa *B*

Kansas

Kansas State University *B,D*
Pittsburg State University *B*

Michigan

Adrian College *B*
Marygrove College *B*
Michigan State University *B,M*

Minnesota

Willmar Community College *A*

New Hampshire

New Hampshire Technical College:
    Manchester *A*

New Jersey

Thomas Edison State College *A,B*

New Mexico

Eastern New Mexico University *B*

New York

Cazenovia College *A*
Cornell University *B,M,D*
Jefferson Community College *A*
State University of New York
    College at Plattsburgh *B*
Ulster County Community
    College *A*

Ohio

Bowling Green State University *B*
Kent State University *B*

Ohio State University: Columbus
    Campus *B,M,D*
Ohio University *B*
University of Akron *A*

Oklahoma

Oklahoma Christian University of
    Science and Arts *B*

Oregon

Oregon State University *B*

Pennsylvania

Indiana University of
    Pennsylvania *B*
Seton Hill College *B*

Tennessee

Shelby State Community College
    C,A

Texas

Lamar University—Beaumont *B*
Prairie View A&M University *B*
Texas Tech University *B,M,D*
University of Mary Hardin-
    Baylor *B*

Virginia

Eastern Mennonite College *B*

Family/consumer resource management

Alabama

Auburn University *B,M*
University of Alabama *B,M*

Arizona

University of Arizona *B,M,D*

California

California State University
    Fresno *B*
    Long Beach *B*
    Northridge *B*
Cosumnes River College *A*
Grossmont Community College *C,A*
Los Angeles Mission College *A*
Ohlone College *C,A*
Pacific Union College *A*

Colorado

Colorado State University *B,M*

Connecticut

St. Joseph College *B*

Delaware

University of Delaware *B,D*

Florida

Okaloosa-Walton Community
    College *A*

Georgia

Berry College *B*
Georgia Southern University *B*
University of Georgia *B,M*

Illinois

KAES College *B*
Olivet Nazarene University *B*
Southern Illinois University at
    Carbondale *B*
University of Illinois at Urbana-
    Champaign *B,M,D*

Indiana

Ball State University *B*
Indiana State University *B,M*
Indiana University Bloomington *B*
Purdue University *B,M*

Iowa

Iowa State University *B*

Kentucky

Murray State University *B*
University of Kentucky *B,M*

Louisiana

Louisiana Tech University *B*
Southeastern Louisiana
    University *B*
University of Southwestern
    Louisiana *B*

Maryland

University of Maryland: College
    Park *B,M,D*

Massachusetts

Framingham State College *B*

Michigan

Adrian College *B*
Andrews University *B*
Central Michigan University *B*
Eastern Michigan University *B,M*
Madonna University *B*
Marygrove College *B*
Michigan State University *B*

Minnesota

College of St. Scholastica *B*
Mankato State University *B,M*
St. Olaf College *B*

Missouri

College of the Ozarks *B*
Northwest Missouri State
    University *B*
Southeast Missouri State
    University *B*
University of Missouri: Columbia
    B,M,D

Nebraska

McCook Community College *A*
University of Nebraska
    Lincoln *B*
    Omaha *B*

New Hampshire

University of New Hampshire *B,M*

New Mexico

New Mexico State University *B*
University of New Mexico *B*

New York

City University of New York:
    Queens College *B*
Cornell University *B,M,D*
State University of New York
    College at Buffalo *B*
    College at Oneonta *B*
Syracuse University *B,M*

North Carolina

University of North Carolina at
    Greensboro *B,M,D*

North Dakota

North Dakota State University *B,M*

Ohio

Bluffton College *B*
Bowling Green State University *B*

Kent State University *B*
Miami University: Oxford
    Campus *B*
Ohio State University: Columbus
    Campus *B,M,D*
Ohio University *B*
University of Dayton *B*

Oklahoma

Oklahoma State University *B,M*

Oregon

Oregon State University *B,M,D*

Pennsylvania

Immaculata College *B*
Indiana University of
    Pennsylvania *B*
St. Vincent College *B*
Seton Hill College *B*

Rhode Island

University of Rhode Island *B*

South Dakota

South Dakota State University *B*

Tennessee

Carson-Newman College *B*
Tennessee Technological
    University *B*
University of Tennessee
    Chattanooga *B*
    Knoxville *M*

Texas

Southwest Texas State University *B*
Stephen F. Austin State
    University *B*
Texas Tech University *B,M,D*
Texas Woman's University *B,M,D*
University of Mary Hardin-
    Baylor *B*

Utah

Brigham Young University *B,M*
University of Utah *B*
Utah State University *B,M*
Weber State University *B*

Vermont

University of Vermont *B*

Virginia

Norfolk State University *B*
Virginia Polytechnic Institute and
    State University *B,M,D*

Washington

Central Washington University *B,M*
Seattle Pacific University *B*

West Virginia

West Virginia University *B*

Wisconsin

University of Wisconsin: Madison
    B,M

Fashion design

Alabama

Alabama Agricultural and
    Mechanical University *B*
Samford University *B*
University of Alabama *B*

Arizona

Pima Community College *A*

Arkansas

University of Arkansas
    Fayetteville *B*
    Pine Bluff *B*
University of Central Arkansas *C*

California

Academy of Art College *C,B,M,W*
Allan Hancock College *C,A*
American College for the Applied
    Arts: Los Angeles *A,B*
Brooks College *A*
California State University: Los
    Angeles *B*
Chaffey Community College *C,A*
College of the Desert *C*
College of the Sequoias *C*
Diablo Valley College *A*
El Camino College *C,A*
Fashion Institute of Design and
    Merchandising
        Los Angeles *A*
        San Francisco *A*
Glendale Community College *C*
Long Beach City College *C,A*
Los Angeles Trade and Technical
    College *A*
Louise Salinger Academy of
    Fashion *C,A,B*
Modesto Junior College *A*
Ohlone College *C,A*
Orange Coast College *C,A*
Otis/Parsons School of Art and
    Design *A,B*
Saddleback College *C,A*
San Joaquin Delta College *C,A*
University of San Francisco *B*
Ventura College *C,A*
West Valley College *C,A*
Woodbury University *B*

Colorado

Colorado Institute of Art *A*

Connecticut

University of New Haven *C*

Delaware

University of Delaware *B*

Florida

Daytona Beach Community
    College *A*
Florida Community College at
    Jacksonville *A*
Florida State University *B*
International Fine Arts College *A*
Miami-Dade Community College *A*
Okaloosa-Walton Community
    College *A*
Palm Beach Community College *A*
Pensacola Junior College *A*
Santa Fe Community College *A*

Georgia

American College for the Applied
    Arts *A,B*
Bauder College *A*
Clark Atlanta University *B*
Georgia Southern University *B*
Morris Brown College *B*
Savannah College of Art and
    Design *B,M*
Savannah Technical Institute *C*

Hawaii

University of Hawaii
    Honolulu Community College
        C,A
    Manoa *B*

Idaho

Ricks College *A*

Illinois

Chicago State University *B*
College of DuPage *C,A*
Columbia College *B*
International Academy of
    Merchandising and Design *A,B*
KAES College *B*
Olivet Nazarene University *B*
Ray College of Design *A,B*
Rosary College *B*
School of the Art Institute of
    Chicago *B*
Southern Illinois University at
    Carbondale *B*
University of Illinois at Urbana-
    Champaign *B*
William Rainey Harper College *C,A*

Indiana

Ball State University *B*
Indiana University Bloomington *B*
Purdue University *B,M*
Vincennes University *A*

Iowa

Iowa State University *B*

Kansas

Central College *A*
Cloud County Community
    College *A*
Coffeyville Community College *A*
Colby Community College *A*
Kansas State University *B*
Pittsburg State University *B*

Louisiana

Southeastern Louisiana
    University *B*
University of Southwestern
    Louisiana *B*

Maine

Casco Bay College *C*

Maryland

New Community College of
    Baltimore *C,A*
University of Maryland: Eastern
    Shore *B*

Massachusetts

Endicott College *A*
Massachusetts College of Art *B*
Mount Ida College *A,B*
Newbury College *A*

Michigan

Delta College *A*
Marygrove College *B*

Mississippi

Mississippi College *B*

Missouri

Columbia College *B*
Penn Valley Community College *A*
Stephens College *B*
Washington University *B,M*

New Jersey

Centenary College *B*
College of St. Elizabeth *B*

New Mexico

Dona Ana Branch Community
    College of New Mexico State
    University *A*

New York

Cazenovia College *A*
Fashion Institute of Technology *A,B*
Jefferson Community College *A*
Marist College *B*
Marymount College *C,B*
Parsons School of Design *A,B*
Pratt Institute *B*
Syracuse University *B*

North Carolina

Appalachian State University *B*
Campbell University *B*
Southwestern Community
    College *A*
University of North Carolina at
    Greensboro *B*

Ohio

Bowling Green State University *B*
Kent State University *B*
Ohio State University: Columbus
    Campus *B,M,D*
University of Akron *A*
University of Cincinnati *B*
Virginia Marti College of Fashion
    and Art *C,A*

Oklahoma

Oklahoma Panhandle State
    University *A*
Southeastern Oklahoma State
    University *B*
University of Central Oklahoma *B*

Oregon

Bassist College *A,B*

Pennsylvania

Drexel University *B,M*
Harcum Junior College *A*
Mansfield University of
    Pennsylvania *B*
Philadelphia College of Textiles and
    Science *B*
Tracey-Warner School *A*

Puerto Rico

Pontifical Catholic University of
    Puerto Rico *A*

Rhode Island

Rhode Island School of Design *B*
University of Rhode Island *B*

Tennessee

Carson-Newman College *B*
Freed-Hardeman University *B*
Hiwassee College *B*
O'More College of Design *A*
Shelby State Community College *C*
Tennessee Technological
    University *B*

Texas

Bauder Fashion College *A*
Baylor University *B*
El Centro College *A*
El Paso Community College *A*
Houston Community College *C,A*
Incarnate Word College *B*
Lamar University—Beaumont *B*
Miss Wade's Fashion
    Merchandising College *A*
Prairie View A&M University *B*
Sam Houston State University *B*
Texas Tech University *B*

Texas Woman's University *B,M,D*
University of Mary Hardin-
    Baylor *B*
University of North Texas *B,M*

Utah

Brigham Young University *B*
Dixie College *A*

Vermont

University of Vermont *B*

Virginia

Hampton University *B*
Marymount University *B*
Radford University *B*
Virginia Commonwealth
    University *B*
Virginia Polytechnic Institute and
    State University *B,M,D*

Washington

Art Institute of Seattle *A*
Central Washington University *B*
Seattle Central Community College
    C,A
Shoreline Community College *A*

West Virginia

Marshall University *B*

Wisconsin

Mount Mary College *B*

Fashion merchandising

Alabama

Auburn University *B*
Jacksonville State University *B*
James H. Faulkner State
    Community College *A*
University of Alabama *B*
University of North Alabama *B*
Wallace State Community College
    at Hanceville *A*

Alaska

University of Alaska Anchorage *C*

Arizona

Mesa Community College *A*
Northern Arizona University *B*
University of Arizona *B*

Arkansas

University of Arkansas
    Fayetteville *B*
    Pine Bluff *B*
University of Central Arkansas *C*
Westark Community College *A*

California

Allan Hancock College *A*
Brooks College *C,A*
Chabot College *A*
Chaffey Community College *C,A*
City College of San Francisco *C,A*
College of the Desert *C*
Cuesta College *A*
El Camino College *C,A*
Evergreen Valley College *A*
Fashion Institute of Design and
    Merchandising
        Los Angeles *A*
        San Francisco *A*
Fresno City College *C,A*
Glendale Community College *A*
Grossmont Community College *C,A*
Kings River Community College *A*

Long Beach City College *A*
Los Angeles Trade and Technical
    College *C,A*
Los Angeles Valley College *C,A*
Marymount College *A*
Modesto Junior College *A*
Mount San Antonio College *C,A*
Ohlone College *C,A*
Orange Coast College *C,A*
Pacific Union College *B*
Palomar College *C,A*
Pasadena City College *C,A*
Phillips Junior College: Fresno
    Campus *C,A*
Saddleback College *C,A*
San Diego Mesa College *C,A*
San Joaquin Delta College *C,A*
San Jose City College *A*
Santa Monica College *C,A*
Santa Rosa Junior College *A*
Skyline College *C,A*
Solano Community College *A*
Ventura College *A*
West Valley College *C,A*
Woodbury University *B*

Colorado

Arapahoe Community College *C,A*
Colorado Institute of Art *A*
Northeastern Junior College *A*
Parks Junior College *A*

Connecticut

Briarwood College *A*
Teikyo-Post University *A,B*
Tunxis Community College *C,A*
University of Bridgeport *A,B*

Delaware

University of Delaware *B*
Wesley College *A,B*

District of Columbia

University of the District of
    Columbia *A*

Florida

Brevard Community College *A*
Broward Community College *A*
Daytona Beach Community
    College *A*
Florida Community College at
    Jacksonville *A*
Florida State University *B,M*
Gulf Coast Community College *A*
Indian River Community College *A*
International Fine Arts College *A*
Lynn University *A,B*
Manatee Community College *A*
Miami-Dade Community College *A*
National Education Center: Bauder
    Campus *A*
Pensacola Junior College *A*
St. Petersburg Junior College *A*
Santa Fe Community College *A*
Webber College *A*

Georgia

Abraham Baldwin Agricultural
    College *A*
American College for the Applied
    Arts *A,B*
Bauder College *A*
Berry College *B*
DeKalb Technical Institute *C,A*
Gainesville College *A*
Georgia Southern University *B*
Middle Georgia College *C,A*
Morris Brown College *B*
University of Georgia *B,M*

Hawaii

University of Hawaii
    Honolulu Community College
        C,A
    Manoa *B*

Idaho

College of Southern Idaho *C*
Ricks College *A*

Illinois

Black Hawk College *A*
Bradley University *B*
Carl Sandburg College *C,A*
Chicago State University *B*
College of DuPage *A*
Columbia College *B*
Gem City College *C*
International Academy of
    Merchandising and Design *A,B*
John A. Logan College *A*
Joliet Junior College *A*
MacCormac Junior College *A*
Midstate College *C,A*
Moraine Valley Community
    College *C*
Northern Illinois University *B*
Olivet Nazarene University *B*
Ray College of Design *A,B*
Rosary College *B*
Southern Illinois University at
    Carbondale *B*
Triton College *C,A*
William Rainey Harper College *A*

Indiana

Ball State University *B*
Indiana University Bloomington *B*
Marian College *A,B*
Purdue University *B*
Vincennes University *A*

Iowa

American Institute of Commerce *C*
Des Moines Area Community
    College *A*
Hawkeye Institute of Technology *A*
Iowa Central Community College *A*
Iowa Lakes Community College
    C,A
Iowa State University *B*
Iowa Western Community
    College *A*
Kirkwood Community College *A*
North Iowa Area Community
    College *A*
Scott Community College *C,A*

Kansas

Baker University *B*
Central College *A*
Coffeyville Community College *A*
Dodge City Community College
    C,A
Friends University *A*
Highland Community College *A*
Hutchinson Community College *A*
Johnson County Community
    College *A*
Pittsburg State University *B*

Kentucky

Eastern Kentucky University *B*
Georgetown College *B*
Morehead State University *A*
Murray State University *A*
Owensboro Junior College of
    Business *C,A*

Louisiana

Louisiana State University and
    Agricultural and Mechanical
    College *B*
Phillips Junior College: New
    Orleans *A*
Southeastern Louisiana
    University *B*
University of Southwestern
    Louisiana *B*

Maine

Casco Bay College *C*
Thomas College *A,B*
University of Maine *A*

Maryland

Montgomery College: Rockville
    Campus *A*
New Community College of
    Baltimore *A*
University of Maryland
    College Park *B*
    Eastern Shore *B*

Massachusetts

Aquinas College at Milton *A*
Bay Path College *A*
Bay State College *A*
Becker College: Worcester
    Campus *A*
Bunker Hill Community College *A*
Dean Junior College *A*
Endicott College *A,B*
Essex Agricultural and Technical
    Institute *A*
Lasell College *A,B*
Middlesex Community College *A*
Mount Ida College *A,B*
Newbury College *A*

Michigan

Adrian College *B*
Baker College
    Flint *A*
    Muskegon *A*
    Owosso *A*
Davenport College of Business *A*
Delta College *A*
Eastern Michigan University *B*
Ferris State University *A*
Grand Rapids Community
    College *A*
Lansing Community College *A*
Macomb Community College *C,A*
Madonna University *B*
Marygrove College *B*
Mid Michigan Community
    College *A*
Northern Michigan University *B*
Northwood Institute *A*
Oakland Community College *A*
Siena Heights College *A,B*
Southwestern Michigan College *A*
Wayne State University *B,M*
Western Michigan University *B*

Minnesota

Alexandria Technical College *A*
College of St. Catherine: St.
    Catherine Campus *B*
Lakewood Community College *A*
Rochester Community College *C,A*
University of Minnesota:
    Crookston *A*

Mississippi

Delta State University *B*
Hinds Community College *A*
Holmes Community College *A*
Mississippi College *B*

Mississippi Gulf Coast Community
    College
    Jackson County Campus *A*
    Jefferson Davis Campus *A*
Mississippi University for Women *B*
Northeast Mississippi Community
    College *A*
University of Southern
    Mississippi *B*

Missouri

Central Missouri State University *A*
Columbia College *B*
Fontbonne College *B*
Lincoln University *B*
Northwest Missouri State
    University *B*
Penn Valley Community College *A*
St. Louis Community College at
    Florissant Valley *A*
Southeast Missouri State
    University *B*
Southwest Baptist University *A*
Stephens College *B*
William Woods College *B*

Nebraska

Chadron State College *B*
McCook Community College *A*
Metropolitan Community College *A*
Southeast Community College:
    Lincoln Campus *C,A*
University of Nebraska—Omaha *B*
Wayne State College *B*

New Hampshire

Hesser College *A*
New Hampshire College *A*

New Jersey

Berkeley College of Business *C,A*
Brookdale Community College *A*
Centenary College *A,B*
Jersey City State College *B*
Ocean County College *C*

New Mexico

Dona Ana Branch Community
    College of New Mexico State
    University *A*
New Mexico State University *B*

New York

Berkeley College *C,A*
Berkeley School: New York City *A*
Bryant & Stratton Business Institute
    Albany *A*
    Rochester *A*
    Syracuse *A*
Cazenovia College *A,B*
Central City Business Institute *A*
City University of New York
    Kingsborough Community
        College *A*
    New York City Technical
        College *A*
Erie Community College: City
    Campus *A*
Fashion Institute of Technology *A,B*
Genesee Community College *A*
Herkimer County Community
    College *A*
Jefferson Community College *C,A*
Laboratory Institute of
    Merchandising *A,B*
Marymount College *C,B*
Monroe Community College *C,A*
Nassau Community College *A*
Parsons School of Design *B*
Pratt Institute *B*

Sage Junior College of Albany, A
  Division of Russell Sage
  College A
Tobe-Coburn School for Fashion
  Careers A

North Carolina
Alamance Community College A
Campbell University B
Central Carolina Community
  College A
Central Piedmont Community
  College A
Chowan College A
Cleveland Community College A
Davidson County Community
  College A
Gaston College A
Mars Hill College B
Meredith College B
Peace College A
Southwestern Community
  College A
Wayne Community College A

North Dakota
University of North Dakota: Lake
  Region C,A

Ohio
Antonelli Institute of Art and
  Photography C,A
Ashland University B
Bluffton College B
Bowling Green State University B
Columbus State Community
  College A
Davis Junior College of Business A
Kent State University B
Miami-Jacobs College A
Muskingum Area Technical
  College A
Ohio Dominican College B
Ohio University B
Owens Technical College: Toledo A
Stark Technical College A
University of Akron A
University of Dayton B
Ursuline College B
Virginia Marti College of Fashion
  and Art A
Youngstown State University B

Oklahoma
East Central University B
Eastern Oklahoma State College
  C,A
Northern Oklahoma College A
Oklahoma Junior College A
Rose State College A
University of Central Oklahoma B

Pennsylvania
Albright College B
Antonelli Institute of Art and
  Photography A
Art Institute of Pittsburgh A
Community College of Philadelphia
  C,A
Drexel University B
Harcum Junior College A
Immaculata College A,B
Indiana University of
  Pennsylvania B
Keystone Junior College A
Lehigh County Community
  College A
Mansfield University of
  Pennsylvania B
Marywood College B
Mercyhurst College B

Northampton County Area
  Community College C,A
Peirce Junior College A
Philadelphia College of Textiles and
  Science B
Point Park College B
St. Vincent College B
Seton Hill College B
Tracey-Warner School A
Westmoreland County Community
  College A

Rhode Island
Community College of Rhode
  Island A
Johnson & Wales University A
University of Rhode Island B

South Carolina
Anderson College A,B
Columbia Junior College of
  Business A
Florence-Darlington Technical
  College C,A
Greenville Technical College C
Midlands Technical College C
Sumter Area Technical College A
Tri-County Technical College C

South Dakota
South Dakota State University B

Tennessee
Carson-Newman College B
David Lipscomb University B
Lambuth University B
Middle Tennessee State
  University B
O'More College of Design A,B
Shelby State Community College A
Tennessee Technological
  University B
Volunteer State Community
  College A

Texas
Abilene Christian University B
Alvin Community College C,A
Amarillo College A
Austin Community College A
Bauder Fashion College A
Baylor University B
Bee County College A
Brookhaven College A
Collin County Community College
  District A
El Centro College A
El Paso Community College A
Houston Community College A
Incarnate Word College B
Kilgore College A
Lamar University—Beaumont B
McLennan Community College A
Midland College A
Miss Wade's Fashion
  Merchandising College A
Northwood Institute: Texas
  Campus A
Odessa College A
San Jacinto College: Central
  Campus A
South Plains College A
Southwest Texas State University B
Tarleton State University B
Tarrant County Junior College C,A
Temple Junior College A
Texarkana College A
Texas Tech University B,M
Texas Woman's University B,M,D
Trinity Valley Community
  College A
University of Houston B

University of Mary Hardin-
  Baylor B

Utah
Brigham Young University B
College of Eastern Utah C
Dixie College C,A
LDS Business College A
Utah State University B
Utah Valley Community College
  C,A
Weber State University A

Vermont
Champlain College A

Virginia
Commonwealth College C,A
Hampton University B
Marymount University B
National Business College C,A
New River Community College C,A
Northern Virginia Community
  College A
Radford University B
Virginia Intermont College B

Washington
Art Institute of Seattle A
Bellevue Community College A
Central Washington University B
Clark College A
Edmonds Community College A
Everett Community College A
Olympic College C,A
Pierce College C,A
Shoreline Community College A
Spokane Falls Community College
  C,A

West Virginia
Davis and Elkins College A,B
Marshall University B
Shepherd College A,B
West Liberty State College B
West Virginia State College A
West Virginia University B
West Virginia Wesleyan College B

Wisconsin
Chippewa Valley Technical
  College A
Fox Valley Technical College A
Madison Area Technical College A
Milwaukee College of Business C,A
Mount Mary College B
Northeast Wisconsin Technical
  College A
University of Wisconsin
  Stevens Point B
  Stout B
Waukesha County Technical
  College A
Western Wisconsin Technical
  College A
Wisconsin Indianhead Technical
  College A

Fiber/textiles/weaving

Arizona
Northern Arizona University B

California
California College of Arts and
  Crafts B,M
California State University
  Long Beach B,M
  Los Angeles B,M

Otis/Parsons School of Art and
  Design C,B

Florida
University of Miami M

Georgia
Savannah College of Art and
  Design B,M

Illinois
School of the Art Institute of
  Chicago B,M
Southern Illinois University at
  Carbondale B,M

Indiana
Ball State University B
Indiana University Bloomington
  B,M
Purdue University B,M

Iowa
University of Iowa B

Kansas
University of Kansas B

Maryland
Howard Community College A
Maryland Institute College of Art B

Massachusetts
Massachusetts College of Art B,M
University of Massachusetts at
  Dartmouth B,M

Michigan
Center for Creative Studies: College
  of Art and Design B
Central Michigan University B,M
University of Michigan B,M

Missouri
Kansas City Art Institute B

New Jersey
Glassboro State College B

New Mexico
Institute of American Indian
  Arts A

New York
Cornell University B,M,D
Parsons School of Design A,B
Rochester Institute of Technology
  A,B,M
Syracuse University B,M

North Carolina
Haywood Community College A
North Carolina State University B

Ohio
Bowling Green State University B
Cleveland Institute of Art B
Lourdes College A
Ohio State University: Columbus
  Campus B,M
Ohio University B
University of Akron B

Oregon
University of Oregon B,M

Pennsylvania
Carnegie Mellon University B,M
Edinboro University of
  Pennsylvania B,M
Mercyhurst College B
Moore College of Art and Design B

Philadelphia College of Textiles and
  Science *B,M*
Seton Hill College *B*
Temple University *B,M*
University of the Arts *B*

Rhode Island
Rhode Island School of Design *B,M*

Tennessee
East Tennessee State University *B*
Memphis College of Art *B,M*

Texas
Texas Woman's University *B,M*

Utah
Brigham Young University *B*

Virginia
Radford University *M*

Washington
University of Washington *B,M*

West Virginia
West Virginia State College *B*

Wisconsin
University of Wisconsin: Eau
  Claire *B*

Film animation

California
California Institute of the Arts
  C,B,M

Illinois
Columbia College *B*
Southern Illinois University at
  Carbondale *B*

Massachusetts
Hampshire College *B*
School of the Museum of Fine
  Arts *B*

New York
New York University *B,M*
Rochester Institute of
  Technology *M*
School of Visual Arts *B*

Pennsylvania
University of the Arts *B*

Rhode Island
Rhode Island School of Design *B*

Washington
Evergreen State College *B*

Film arts

Alabama
John C. Calhoun State Community
  College *A*

California
Allan Hancock College *A*
American Film Institute Center for
  Advanced Film and Television
  Studies *M*
California State University: Chico *B*
Claremont McKenna College *B*

Columbia College: Hollywood *B*
De Anza College *A*
Long Beach City College *A*
Los Angeles City College *A*
Occidental College *B*
Orange Coast College *A*
Saddleback College *A*
San Francisco State University *B,M*
San Jose State University *B*
University of California
  Irvine *B*
  San Diego *B*
  Santa Barbara *B*
  Santa Cruz *C,B*
University of Southern California
  B,M

Colorado
University of Colorado at
  Boulder *B*
University of Denver *B,M*

Connecticut
Sacred Heart University *B*
Yale University *B*

District of Columbia
American University *B*
University of the District of
  Columbia *B*

Florida
Tallahassee Community College *A*
University of Central Florida *B*
Valencia Community College *A*

Georgia
Emory University *B*
Georgia State University *B*

Illinois
Columbia College *B,M*
Olivet Nazarene University *B*
Southern Illinois University at
  Carbondale *B*

Indiana
Indiana University Bloomington *C*
University of Notre Dame *B*

Kansas
Southwestern College *B*
University of Kansas *B*

Massachusetts
Emerson College *B*
Hampshire College *B*
Montserrat College of Art *B*
School of the Museum of Fine
  Arts *B*

Michigan
Northern Michigan University *B*
University of Michigan *B*
Wayne State University *B*

Missouri
Kansas City Art Institute *B*
Webster University *C*

Montana
Montana State University *B*

New Hampshire
Keene State College *B*

New Jersey
Jersey City State College *B*
Rutgers—The State University of
  New Jersey: Mason Gross School
  of the Arts *B*

New York
Bard College *B,M*
City University of New York
  Brooklyn College *B,M*
  Queens College *B*
Columbia University: Columbia
  College *B*
Eugene Lang College/New School
  for Social Research *B*
Fordham University *B*
Ithaca College *B*
Long Island University: C. W. Post
  Campus *B*
New York University *B,M,W*
Onondaga Community College *A*
Pratt Institute *B*
Rochester Institute of Technology
  A,B
Sarah Lawrence College *B*
School of Visual Arts *B*
State University of New York at
  Binghamton *B*
Syracuse University *B,M*

North Carolina
Duke University *B*
University of North Carolina at
  Greensboro *B*

Ohio
Bowling Green State University *B*
Ohio State University: Columbus
  Campus *B,M*
Ohio University *B,M*

Pennsylvania
Drexel University *B*
Penn State University Park Campus
  B,M
University of the Arts *B*

South Carolina
University of South Carolina *B,M*

Texas
Texas Southmost College *A*

Vermont
Marlboro College *B*
Middlebury College *B*

Washington
Evergreen State College *B*

Wisconsin
University of Wisconsin:
  Milwaukee *B*

Finance

Alabama
Alabama Agricultural and
  Mechanical University *B*
Alabama State University *B*
Auburn University
  Auburn *B*
  Montgomery *B*
Chattahoochee Valley Community
  College *A*
Enterprise State Junior College *A*
Faulkner University *B*
Gadsden State Community
  College *A*
Huntingdon College *B*
Jacksonville State University *B*
James H. Faulkner State
  Community College *A*
Jefferson State Community
  College *A*

John C. Calhoun State Community
  College *A*
Lurleen B. Wallace State Junior
  College *A*
Mobile College *B*
Northeast Alabama State Junior
  College *A*
Samford University *B*
Shelton State Community
  College *A*
Shoals Community College *C*
Snead State Junior College *A*
Southern Union State Junior
  College *A*
Spring Hill College *B*
Troy State University
  Montgomery *A,B*
  Troy *B*
Tuskegee University *B*
University of Alabama
  Birmingham *B*
  Huntsville *B*
  Tuscaloosa *B,M,D*
University of Montevallo *B*
University of North Alabama *B*
University of South Alabama *B*
Wallace State Community College
  at Hanceville *A*

Alaska
University of Alaska
  Anchorage *B*
  Fairbanks *A,B*

Arizona
Arizona State University *B*
Arizona Western College *A*
Cochise College *A*
Eastern Arizona College *A*
Glendale Community College *A*
Grand Canyon University *B*
Mesa Community College *A*
Mohave Community College *C,A*
Northern Arizona University *B*
Pima Community College *C,A*
Rio Salado Community College *A*
Scottsdale Community College *C,A*
University of Arizona *B,M*
Western International University *B*

Arkansas
Arkansas State University *B*
East Arkansas Community
  College *A*
Garland County Community
  College *A*
Southern Arkansas University *B*
University of Arkansas
  Fayetteville *B*
  Little Rock *B*
University of Central Arkansas *B*
Westark Community College *A*
Williams Baptist College *A*

California
Armstrong College *A,B,M*
Bakersfield College *A*
Barstow College *C*
California State Polytechnic
  University: Pomona *B*
California State University
  Bakersfield *B*
  Dominguez Hills *B*
  Fresno *B*
  Fullerton *B,M*
  Hayward *B,M*
  Long Beach *B*
  Los Angeles *B,M*
  Northridge *B,M*
  Sacramento *B*
  Stanislaus *B*
Cerritos Community College *A*

Chabot College *A*
Chaffey Community College *A*
City College of San Francisco *C,A*
Coastline Community College *A*
College of the Desert *C,A*
College of Notre Dame *B*
Compton Community College *A*
Diablo Valley College *A*
El Camino College *C,A*
Fresno City College *C,A*
Glendale Community College *A*
Golden Gate University *B,M*
Grossmont Community College *C,A*
Hartnell College *A*
Imperial Valley College *C,A*
Lake Tahoe Community College *C,A*
Laney College *C,A*
Long Beach City College *A*
Los Angeles City College *C,A*
Los Angeles Mission College *A*
Los Angeles Valley College *C*
Merced College *A*
Mission College *A*
Modesto Junior College *A*
Monterey Peninsula College *C,A*
Moorpark College *A*
Mount San Antonio College *C,A*
Napa Valley College *A*
National University *B,M*
Ohlone College *C,A*
Palomar College *A*
Pasadena City College *C,A*
Porterville College *C,A*
San Diego Miramar College *A*
San Diego State University *B*
San Francisco State University *B,M*
San Joaquin Delta College *C,A*
San Jose City College *A*
San Jose State University *B*
Santa Barbara City College *C,A*
Santa Clara University *B*
Santa Monica College *C,A*
Santa Rosa Junior College *C*
Sierra College *A*
Skyline College *A*
Solano Community College *A*
Southern California College *B*
Southwestern College *C,A*
United States International University *D*
University of the Pacific *B*
University of San Francisco *B,M*
Ventura College *A*
West Coast University *M*
Yuba College *C*

Colorado

Adams State College *B*
Arapahoe Community College *C,A*
Colorado State University *B,M*
Fort Lewis College *B*
Mesa State College *B*
Metropolitan State College of Denver *B*
Pikes Peak Community College *C,A*
Regis College of Regis University *B*
University of Colorado
　　Boulder *B*
　　Colorado Springs *B*
　　Denver *B,M*
University of Denver *B,M*
University of Northern Colorado *B*
Western State College of Colorado *B*

Connecticut

Central Connecticut State University *B*
Fairfield University *B,M*
Mattatuck Community College *A*
Quinnipiac College *B,M*

Sacred Heart University *B*
Southern Connecticut State University *B*
Teikyo-Post University *B*
University of Bridgeport *B*
University of Connecticut *B*
University of Hartford *B*
University of New Haven *B,M*
Western Connecticut State University *B,M*

Delaware

Delaware Technical and Community College: Terry Campus *A*
Goldey-Beacom College *B*
University of Delaware *B*
Wilmington College *B*

District of Columbia

American University *B,M*
George Washington University *B,M*
Georgetown University *B*
Howard University *B*
Southeastern University *A,B,M*
University of the District of Columbia *A,B*

Florida

Barry University *B*
Broward Community College *A*
Chipola Junior College *A*
Daytona Beach Community College *A*
Edison Community College *C,A*
Florida Agricultural and Mechanical University *A*
Florida Atlantic University *B*
Florida Community College at Jacksonville *A*
Florida Institute of Technology *B*
Florida International University *B,M*
Florida Southern College *B*
Florida State University *B,M*
Gulf Coast Community College *A*
Hillsborough Community College *A*
Indian River Community College *A*
Jacksonville University *B*
Lake-Sumter Community College *A*
Manatee Community College *A*
Miami-Dade Community College *A*
Okaloosa-Walton Community College *A*
Palm Beach Community College *A*
Phillips Junior College: Melbourne *C*
St. Petersburg Junior College *A*
St. Thomas University *B*
Santa Fe Community College *A*
Schiller International University *A,B*
Seminole Community College *A*
South Florida Community College *A*
Stetson University *B*
University of Central Florida *B*
University of Florida *B,M,D*
University of Miami *B*
University of North Florida *B*
University of Sarasota *M*
University of South Florida *B*
University of Tampa *B*
University of West Florida *B*
Valencia Community College *A*
Webber College *A,B*

Georgia

Augusta Technical Institute *C*
Berry College *B*
Clark Atlanta University *B,M*
Clayton State College *A*

Columbus College *B*
Dalton College *A*
Emory University *B,M*
Georgia Southern University *B*
Georgia Southwestern College *B*
Georgia State University *B,M,D*
Kennesaw State College *B,M*
Mercer University
　　Atlanta *B,M*
　　Macon *B,M*
Middle Georgia College *A*
Morehouse College *B*
North Georgia College *B*
Reinhardt College *A*
Savannah State College *B*
Shorter College *B*
South Georgia College *A*
University of Georgia *B,M*
Valdosta State College *B*
West Georgia College *B*

Hawaii

Hawaii Pacific University *A,B,M*
University of Hawaii at Manoa *B*

Idaho

Boise State University *B*
College of Southern Idaho *A*
Idaho State University *B*
Northwest Nazarene College *B*
Ricks College *A*
University of Idaho *B*

Illinois

Augustana College *B*
Aurora University *B*
Barat College *B*
Belleville Area College *A*
Black Hawk College
　　East Campus *C*
　　Moline *C,A*
Bradley University *B*
Carl Sandburg College *A*
Chicago State University *B*
City Colleges of Chicago: Chicago City-Wide College *C,A*
College of St. Francis *B*
De Paul University *B,M*
Eastern Illinois University *B*
Elgin Community College *C,A*
Elmhurst College *B*
Highland Community College *C*
Illinois Benedictine College *B*
Illinois Central College *C,A*
Illinois Eastern Community Colleges: Lincoln Trail College *C,A*
Illinois State University *B*
John A. Logan College *A*
Joliet Junior College *A*
Lake Land College *A*
Lewis and Clark Community College *A*
Lewis University *B*
Loyola University of Chicago *B*
Millikin University *B*
Moraine Valley Community College *A*
Morton College *A*
North Central College *B*
Northeastern Illinois University *B*
Northern Illinois University *B,M*
Northwestern University *M,D*
Oakton Community College *C,A*
Olivet Nazarene University *B*
Parkland College *A*
Quincy College *B*
Richland Community College *A*
Rock Valley College *A*
Rockford College *B*
Roosevelt University *B*
St. Xavier University *M*

Southern Illinois University
　　Carbondale *B*
　　Edwardsville *B*
Spoon River College *C,A*
Trinity Christian College *B*
Triton College *A*
University of Chicago *M,D*
University of Illinois
　　Chicago *B,D*
　　Urbana-Champaign *B,M,D*
Waubonsee Community College *C,A*
Western Illinois University *B*
William Rainey Harper College *C,A*

Indiana

Ball State University *B*
Franklin College *B*
Indiana State University *B*
Indiana University
　　Bloomington *B,M,D*
　　Kokomo *A*
　　South Bend *A*
Indiana University—Purdue University
　　Fort Wayne *B*
　　Indianapolis *B*
Indiana Wesleyan University *B*
International Business College *A*
Manchester College *B*
Marian College *A,B*
Purdue University *M,D*
St. Joseph's College *B*
University of Evansville *A,B*
University of Indianapolis *A,B*
University of Notre Dame *B*
University of Southern Indiana *B*
Vincennes University *A*

Iowa

American Institute of Business *A*
Buena Vista College *B*
Clinton Community College *A*
Des Moines Area Community College *A*
Drake University *B*
Iowa State University *B*
Kirkwood Community College *A*
Loras College *B*
Morningside College *B*
Muscatine Community College *A*
North Iowa Area Community College *A*
Northwest Iowa Technical College *A*
St. Ambrose University *B*
Scott Community College *A*
University of Iowa *B,M,D*
University of Northern Iowa *B*
Wartburg College *B*

Kansas

Allen County Community College *A*
Barton County Community College *A*
Central College *A*
Colby Community College *A*
Dodge City Community College *A*
Emporia State University *B*
Fort Hays State University *B*
Fort Scott Community College *A*
Hutchinson Community College *A*
Kansas City Kansas Community College *A*
Kansas State University *B*
Neosho County Community College *C,A*
Pittsburg State University *B*
Seward County Community College *C,A*
Washburn University of Topeka *B*

Wichita State University *B*

Kentucky

Eastern Kentucky University *B*
Elizabethtown Community
College *A*
Georgetown College *B*
Jefferson Community College *A*
Madisonville Community College *A*
Morehead State University *B*
Murray State University *B*
Northern Kentucky University *B*
Paducah Community College *A*
Southeast Community College *A*
University of Kentucky *B*
University of Louisville *B*
Western Kentucky University *A,B*

Louisiana

Louisiana College *B*
Louisiana State University
Agricultural and Mechanical
College *B,M,D*
Shreveport *B*
Louisiana Tech University *B,M*
Loyola University *B*
McNeese State University *B*
Nicholls State University *B*
Northeast Louisiana University *B*
Southern University in
Shreveport *A*
University of New Orleans *B*
University of Southwestern
Louisiana *B*

Maine

Husson College *B*
Thomas College *C,A*
University of Maine *B*

Maryland

Allegany Community College *C,A*
Anne Arundel Community
College *A*
Cecil Community College *C,A*
Frederick Community College *A*
Garrett Community College *A*
Harford Community College *C*
Loyola College in Maryland *M*
Montgomery College
Germantown Campus *A*
Takoma Park Campus *A*
Morgan State University *M*
Mount St. Mary's College *B*
New Community College of
Baltimore *A*
University of Baltimore *B,M*
University of Maryland: College
Park *B*
Wor-Wic Tech Community College
C,A

Massachusetts

American International College *B*
Anna Maria College for Men and
Women *B*
Babson College *B,M*
Bentley College *B,M*
Berkshire Community College *A*
Boston College *B,M,D*
Boston University *B*
Bridgewater State College *C,B*
Harvard University *M*
Massachusetts Bay Community
College *C,A*
Massachusetts Institute of
Technology *M,D,W*
Merrimack College *B*
Mount Ida College *A*
New England Banking Institute *C,A*
Newbury College *A*
Nichols College *B*

North Adams State College *B*
Northeastern University *C,A,B,M*
Northern Essex Community College
C,A
Quinsigamond Community
College *A*
Salem State College *B*
Simmons College *B*
Springfield Technical Community
College *A*
Stonehill College *B*
Suffolk University *B,M*
University of Massachusetts
Dartmouth *B*
Lowell *A,B*
Western New England College *B,M*

Michigan

Central Michigan University *B*
Charles Stewart Mott Community
College *A*
Davenport College of Business *A*
Delta College *A*
Detroit College of Business *A*
Eastern Michigan University *B,M*
Ferris State University *B*
Grand Valley State University *B,M*
Great Lakes Junior College of
Business *A*
Hillsdale College *B*
Jackson Community College *A*
Kirtland Community College *C,A*
Lake Superior State University *B*
Lansing Community College *A*
Lawrence Technological
University *B*
Macomb Community College *C,A*
Madonna University *B*
Michigan State University *B,M,D*
Mid Michigan Community
College *A*
Muskegon Community College *A*
Northern Michigan University *B*
Northwood Institute *A*
Oakland Community College *A*
Oakland University *B*
Saginaw Valley State University
B,M
University of Detroit Mercy *B*
University of Michigan
Ann Arbor *D*
Flint *B*
Walsh College of Accountancy and
Business Administration *B,M*
Wayne State University *B,M*
Western Michigan University *B,M*

Minnesota

Alexandria Technical College *A*
Augsburg College *B*
Bethel College *B*
College of St. Catherine: St.
Catherine Campus *B*
Concordia College: St. Paul *B*
Inver Hills Community College *A*
Mankato State University *B*
Moorhead State University *B*
Northland Community College *A*
Northwestern College *B*
Rainy River Community College *A*
St. Cloud State University *B*
University of Minnesota:
Crookston *A*
University of St. Thomas *B*
Willmar Community College *A*
Winona State University *B*

Mississippi

Delta State University *B*
Hinds Community College *A*
Jackson State University *B*
Meridian Community College *A*

Mississippi Gulf Coast Community
College: Jefferson Davis
Campus *A*
Mississippi State University *B*
Southwest Mississippi Community
College *A*
University of Mississippi *B*
University of Southern
Mississippi *B*

Missouri

Avila College *B,M*
Central Missouri State University *B*
Columbia College *B*
Fontbonne College *B*
Lindenwood College *M*
Mineral Area College *C,A*
Missouri Southern State College *B*
Missouri Western State College *A*
Northeast Missouri State
University *B*
Northwest Missouri State
University *B*
Park College *B*
Rockhurst College *B*
St. Charles Community College *A*
St. Louis Community College
Florissant Valley *A*
Forest Park *A*
Meramec *A*
St. Louis University *B,M,D*
Southeast Missouri State
University *B*
Southwest Missouri State
University *B*
State Fair Community College *A*
Three Rivers Community College *A*
University of Missouri: Columbia *B*
Webster University *M*

Montana

Eastern Montana College *B*
Montana College of Mineral
Science and Technology *B*
Montana State University *B*
University of Montana *B*

Nebraska

Chadron State College *B*
Creighton University *B*
Dana College *B*
Metropolitan Community College *A*
Midland Lutheran College *B*
Southeast Community College:
Beatrice Campus *A*
University of Nebraska
Lincoln *B*
Omaha *B*
Wayne State College *B*

Nevada

Community College of Southern
Nevada *A*
Truckee Meadows Community
College *A*
University of Nevada
Las Vegas *B*
Reno *B*
Western Nevada Community
College *C*

New Hampshire

Franklin Pierce College *A,B*
New England College *B*
New Hampshire College *B*

New Jersey

Atlantic Community College *A*
Bergen Community College *A*
Bloomfield College *C,B*
Burlington County College *A*
Caldwell College *C*

Camden County College *A*
County College of Morris *A*
Fairleigh Dickinson University *B,M*
Glassboro State College *B*
Gloucester County College *A*
Jersey City State College *B*
Mercer County Community
College *A*
Monmouth College *B*
Ocean County College *A*
Passaic County Community
College *A*
Rider College *B*
Rutgers—The State University of
New Jersey
Douglass College *B*
Livingston College *B*
Newark College of Arts and
Sciences *B*
Rutgers College *B*
University College New
Brunswick *B*
University College Newark *B*
St. Peter's College *A*
Seton Hall University *B,M*
Thomas Edison State College *C,A,B*
Trenton State College *B*
Union County College *A*

New Mexico

Clovis Community College *A*
Eastern New Mexico University
Portales *B*
Roswell Campus *C,A*
New Mexico Junior College *A*
New Mexico State University
Carlsbad *C*
Las Cruces *C,B,M*
San Juan College *A*
University of New Mexico *B,M*

New York

Adelphi University *B,M*
Adirondack Community College *A*
Alfred University *B*
Canisius College *B*
City University of New York
Baruch College *B,M,D*
La Guardia Community
College *A*
Clarkson University *B*
Columbia-Greene Community
College *A*
Cornell University *M,D*
Dominican College of Blauvelt *B*
Erie Community College: South
Campus *A*
Fordham University *B,M*
Fulton-Montgomery Community
College *A*
Herkimer County Community
College *A*
Hilbert College *A*
Hofstra University *B,M*
Hudson Valley Community
College *A*
Iona College *B,M*
Ithaca College *B*
Jefferson Community College *A*
Le Moyne College *B*
Long Island University
Brooklyn Campus *B*
C. W. Post Campus *B,M*
Manhattan College *B*
Medaille College *C,B*
Mohawk Valley Community
College *A*
Nassau Community College *A*
New York Institute of
Technology *B*
New York University *C,B,M,D*
Onondaga Community College *A*

Orange County Community
College *A*
Pace University
College of White Plains *B,M*
New York *A,B,M*
Pleasantville/Briarcliff *B,M*
Rochester Institute of Technology
A,B,M
Rockland Community College *A*
Russell Sage College *M*
St. Bonaventure University *B,W*
St. Francis College *C*
St. John's University *B,M*
St. Thomas Aquinas College *B*
Siena College *B*
State University of New York
Albany *B,M*
College at New Paltz *B*
College at Old Westbury *B*
College of Technology at
Alfred *A*
College of Technology at
Canton *A*
Institute of Technology at
Utica/Rome *B*
Suffolk County Community College
Eastern Campus *C*
Selden *C,A*
Western Campus *A*
Syracuse University *B,M,D*
Touro College *A,B*
Ulster County Community
College *A*
University of the State of New
York: Regents College *B*
Villa Maria College of Buffalo *C,A*
Westchester Community College *A*
Yeshiva University *B*

North Carolina

Alamance Community College *A*
Anson Community College *A*
Appalachian State University *B*
Asheville Buncombe Technical
Community College *A*
Catawba Valley Community College
C,A
Central Carolina Community
College *A*
Central Piedmont Community
College *A*
College of the Albemarle *A*
East Carolina University *B*
Fayetteville Technical Community
College *A*
Forsyth Technical Community
College *A*
Gaston College *A*
Isothermal Community College *A*
Johnson C. Smith University *B*
Mars Hill College *B*
Nash Community College *A*
North Carolina Central
University *B*
Pitt Community College *A*
Robeson Community College *A*
Southeastern Community College *A*
Southwestern Community
College *A*
University of North Carolina
Greensboro *B,M*
Wilmington *B*
Vance-Granville Community
College *A*
Western Carolina University *B*
Western Piedmont Community
College *A*
Wilson Technical Community
College *A*

North Dakota

Minot State University *B*
North Dakota State College of
Science *A*
University of North Dakota *B*

Ohio

Ashland University *B*
Baldwin-Wallace College *B*
Bowling Green State University *B*
Capital University *B*
Case Western Reserve University
M,D
Cedarville College *B*
Central Ohio Technical College *A*
Central State University *B*
Cincinnati Technical College *A*
Clark State Community College *A*
Cleveland State University *B*
Columbus State Community
College *A*
Cuyahoga Community College
Metropolitan Campus *A*
Western Campus *A*
Defiance College *B*
Dyke College *B*
Edison State Community College *A*
Franciscan University of
Steubenville *B*
Franklin University *B*
Jefferson Technical College *A*
John Carroll University *B*
Kent State University
East Liverpool Regional
Campus *A*
Kent *B,D*
Lorain County Community
College *A*
Marion Technical College *A*
Miami University: Oxford Campus
B,M
Miami-Jacobs College *A*
Northwest Technical College *A*
Notre Dame College of Ohio *B*
Ohio Northern University *B*
Ohio State University: Columbus
Campus *B,M,D*
Ohio University *B*
Otterbein College *B*
Owens Technical College: Toledo *A*
Shawnee State University *A*
Sinclair Community College *A*
Southern State Community
College *A*
Terra Technical College *C,A*
University of Akron *A,B*
University of Cincinnati
Access Colleges *A*
Cincinnati *B,M,D*
University of Dayton *B*
University of Findlay *B*
University of Toledo *B,M*
Urbana University *B*
Walsh College *B*
Washington State Community
College *A*
Wilberforce University *B*
Wilmington College *B*
Wittenberg University *B*
Wright State University *B,M*
Xavier University *B*
Youngstown State University *B,M*

Oklahoma

Bartlesville Wesleyan College *A*
Connors State College *A*
East Central University *B*
Northeastern State University *B*
Oklahoma Baptist University *B*
Oklahoma Christian University of
Science and Arts *B*
Oklahoma City University *B*

Oklahoma State University *B*
Redlands Community College *C,A*
Rogers State College *C*
Rose State College *C,A*
Southeastern Oklahoma State
University *B*
Southwestern Oklahoma State
University *B*
Tulsa Junior College *A*
University of Central Oklahoma *B*
University of Oklahoma *B*
University of Tulsa *B*

Oregon

Chemeketa Community College *A*
Lane Community College *A*
Linfield College *B*
Linn-Benton Community College *A*
Oregon State University *B*
Portland Community College *A*
Portland State University *B*
Southwestern Oregon Community
College *A*
University of Oregon
Eugene *B,M,D*
Robert Donald Clark Honors
College *B*
University of Portland *B*

Pennsylvania

Albright College *B*
Allentown College of St. Francis de
Sales *B*
Alvernia College *A,B*
Beaver College *B*
Bucknell University *B,M*
Bucks County Community
College *A*
California University of
Pennsylvania *B*
Carnegie Mellon University *M,D,W*
Central Pennsylvania Business
School *A*
Clarion University of
Pennsylvania *B*
Community College of Beaver
County *A*
Community College of
Philadelphia *A*
Delaware County Community
College *A*
Drexel University *B,M,D*
Duquesne University *C,B,M*
Elizabethtown College *B*
Gannon University *B*
Harrisburg Area Community
College *A*
ICS Center for Degree Studies *A*
Indiana University of
Pennsylvania *B*
Juniata College *B*
King's College *C,B,M*
La Roche College *B*
La Salle University *A,B,M*
Lackawanna Junior College *A*
Lehigh University *B*
Lincoln University *B*
Luzerne County Community
College *A*
Marywood College *B*
Northampton County Area
Community College *A*
Peirce Junior College *A*
Penn State
Harrisburg Capital College *B*
University Park Campus *B*
Philadelphia College of Textiles and
Science *B,M*
Point Park College *A*
Reading Area Community College
C,A
Robert Morris College *B,M*

St. Francis College *B*
St. Joseph's University *C,A,B,M*
St. Vincent College *B*
Seton Hill College *B*
Shippensburg University of
Pennsylvania *B*
Slippery Rock University of
Pennsylvania *B*
Temple University *B,M,D*
University of Pennsylvania *B,M,D*
University of Pittsburgh at
Johnstown *B*
University of Scranton *B*
Villanova University *B*
Waynesburg College *A,B*
Westmoreland County Community
College *A*
Widener University *B*

Puerto Rico

Caribbean University *A*
Inter American University of Puerto
Rico
Arecibo Campus *B*
Metropolitan Campus *B,M*
San German Campus *M*
Pontifical Catholic University of
Puerto Rico *B*
Universidad Metropolitana *B*
University of Puerto Rico
Arecibo Campus *A*
Bayamon Technological
University College *A,B*
Carolina Regional College *A*
Mayaguez Campus *B,M*
Rio Piedras Campus *B,M*

Rhode Island

Bryant College *B,M*
Johnson & Wales University *A*
Providence College *B*
University of Rhode Island *B*

South Carolina

Benedict College *B*
Bob Jones University *B*
Clemson University *B*
Coker College *B*
Francis Marion College *B*
Midlands Technical College *A*
Sumter Area Technical College *C*
University of South Carolina
Aiken *B*
Coastal Carolina College *B*
Columbia *B*
Wofford College *B*

South Dakota

Dakota Wesleyan University *B*
Northern State University *B*

Tennessee

Austin Peay State University *B*
Belmont University *B*
Bethel College *C*
Bristol University *A*
Chattanooga State Technical
Community College *A*
Christian Brothers University *B,M*
Cleveland State Community
College *C*
Columbia State Community
College *C*
David Lipscomb University *B*
Dyersburg State Community
College *A*
East Tennessee State University *B*
Fisk University *B*
Freed-Hardeman University *B*
Lincoln Memorial University *B*
Memphis State University *B,M*

Middle Tennessee State University
B,M
Motlow State Community
College A
Nashville State Technical
Institute A
Northeast State Technical
Community College A
Pellissippi State Technical
Community College A
Roane State Community College A
State Technical Institute at
Memphis A
Tennessee Technological
University B
Union University B
University of Tennessee
Chattanooga B,M
Knoxville B
Martin B

Texas

Abilene Christian University B
Amarillo College A
Angelo State University B
Austin Community College A
Baylor University B
Bee County College A
Brazosport College C,A
Central Texas College A
Cisco Junior College A
College of the Mainland A
Corpus Christi State University B
Dallas Baptist University B,M
Del Mar College A
East Texas State University B
Eastfield College A
El Paso Community College A
Galveston College A
Hardin-Simmons University B
Houston Baptist University B
Houston Community College C
Howard College A
Huston-Tillotson College B
Incarnate Word College B
Kilgore College A
Lamar University—Beaumont B,M
Laredo Junior College A
Laredo State University B
Lubbock Christian University B
McLennan Community College A
McMurry University B
Midwestern State University B
Navarro College A
North Harris Montgomery
Community College District A
Northeast Texas Community
College A
Panola College A
Prairie View A&M University B
St. Edward's University B
St. Mary's University B,M
Sam Houston State University B
San Jacinto College: Central
Campus A
Southern Methodist University B
Southwest Texas State University B
Stephen F. Austin State
University B
Sul Ross State University B
Tarleton State University B
Texarkana College A
Texas A&I University B
Texas A&M University B,M,D
Texas Christian University B
Texas Southern University B
Texas Southmost College A
Texas Tech University B
Texas Wesleyan University B
Trinity Valley Community
College A

University of Houston
Clear Lake B,M
Downtown B
Houston B,M,D
University of Mary Hardin-
Baylor B
University of North Texas B,M,D
University of Texas
Arlington B
Austin B,D
El Paso B
Pan American B
Permian Basin B
San Antonio B
Tyler B
Victoria College A
West Texas State University B

Utah

Brigham Young University B
University of Utah B,M,D
Utah State University B
Utah Valley Community College
C,A
Weber State University B
Westminster College of Salt Lake
City B

Vermont

Castleton State College B
University of Vermont B

Virginia

Averett College B
Blue Ridge Community College A
Central Virginia Community
College A
Christopher Newport College B
College of William and Mary B
Dabney S. Lancaster Community
College C
George Mason University B
Hampton University B
James Madison University B
Marymount University B,M
Old Dominion University B
Piedmont Virginia Community
College A
Radford University B
Southwest Virginia Community
College C
Tidewater Community College A
University of Richmond C,A,B
Virginia Polytechnic Institute and
State University B,D
Virginia Union University B
Wytheville Community College A

Washington

Central Washington University B
Eastern Washington University B
Gonzaga University B
Lower Columbia College A
Olympic College A
Pacific Lutheran University B
St. Martin's College B
Seattle University B
Spokane Falls Community
College A
Washington State University B

West Virginia

Bethany College B
Bluefield State College A
College of West Virginia A
Davis and Elkins College B
Fairmont State College A,B
Glenville State College B
Marshall University A,B,M
Shepherd College B
West Liberty State College B

West Virginia Institute of
Technology B
West Virginia Northern Community
College A
West Virginia State College A,B
West Virginia University B
West Virginia Wesleyan College B

Wisconsin

Carroll College B
Fox Valley Technical College A
Madison Area Technical College A
Marquette University B
Northeast Wisconsin Technical
College A
University of Wisconsin
Eau Claire B
Green Bay B
La Crosse B
Madison B,M,D
Milwaukee B
Oshkosh B
Platteville B
Whitewater B,M
Western Wisconsin Technical
College A
Wisconsin Indianhead Technical
College C,A

Wyoming

Laramie County Community
College C,A
Sheridan College A
University of Wyoming B,M
Western Wyoming Community
College A

**American Samoa, Caroline
Islands, Guam, Marianas,
Virgin Islands**

University of Guam B
University of the Virgin Islands A

Canada

McGill University B,M,D

Mexico

Sistema Instituto Tecnologico y de
Estudios Superiores de
Monterrey B

Switzerland

American College of Switzerland B

Fine arts

Alabama

Alabama Southern Community
College A
Alabama State University B
Auburn University
Auburn B,M
Montgomery B
George C. Wallace State
Community College at Selma A
Huntingdon College B
Jacksonville State University B
James H. Faulkner State
Community College A
Jefferson State Community
College A
Judson College B
Samford University B
Snead State Junior College A
Southern Union State Junior
College A
Spring Hill College B
University of North Alabama B
University of South Alabama B

Alaska

Alaska Pacific University B
University of Alaska
Anchorage B
Fairbanks B

Arizona

Arizona State University B,M
Arizona Western College A
Cochise College A
Glendale Community College A
Grand Canyon University B
Mesa Community College A
Mohave Community College C,A
Northern Arizona University B
Pima Community College A
University of Arizona B
Yavapai College A

Arkansas

Arkansas State University B,M
Harding University B
University of Arkansas at
Monticello B
University of Central Arkansas B
University of the Ozarks B
Westark Community College A

California

Academy of Art College C,B,M,W
Allan Hancock College A
Art Center College of Design B,M
Azusa Pacific University B
Barstow College A
Biola University B
California Baptist College B
California College of Arts and
Crafts B
California Institute of the Arts
C,B,M
California Lutheran University B
California State Polytechnic
University: Pomona B
California State University
Bakersfield B
Chico B
Hayward B
Long Beach B,M
Los Angeles B,M
Northridge B,M
Cerritos Community College A
Cerro Coso Community College A
Chabot College A
Chaffey Community College A
Chapman University B
Christ College Irvine B
Citrus College A
City College of San Francisco A
College of the Desert A
College of Marin: Kentfield A
College of Notre Dame B
College of the Sequoias A
Columbia College A
Cosumnes River College A
Crafton Hills College A
De Anza College A
Dominican College of San Rafael B
El Camino College A
Foothill College A
Fresno City College A
Gavilan Community College A
Glendale Community College C
Golden West College A
Imperial Valley College A
Irvine Valley College A
La Sierra University B
Lake Tahoe Community College A
Laney College A
Lassen College A
Long Beach City College A
Los Angeles City College A
Los Angeles Pierce College A

Los Angeles Valley College *A*
Los Medanos College *A*
Marymount College *A*
Merced College *A*
MiraCosta College *A*
Mission College *C,A*
Modesto Junior College *A*
Moorpark College *A*
Mount St. Mary's College *B*
Mount San Jacinto College *A*
Napa Valley College *A*
Ohlone College *A*
Orange Coast College *A*
Otis/Parsons School of Art and
Design *B,M*
Oxnard College *A*
Pacific Christian College *B*
Pacific Union College *B*
Pepperdine University *B*
Point Loma Nazarene College *B*
Porterville College *C,A*
Saddleback College *A*
San Diego City College *A*
San Diego Mesa College *A*
San Francisco Art Institute *B,M*
San Francisco State University *B,M*
San Joaquin Delta College *A*
San Jose City College *A*
San Jose State University *B,M*
Santa Monica College *A*
Santa Rosa Junior College *A*
Solano Community College *A*
Southwestern College *A*
Stanford University *B,M,D*
Taft College *A*
University of California
Berkeley *B*
Irvine *B*
Santa Cruz *B*
University of La Verne *B*
University of the Pacific *B*
University of Redlands *B*
University of San Diego *B*
University of San Francisco *B*
University of Southern California
B,M
Ventura College *A*
Victor Valley College *A*
West Valley College *A*
Westmont College *B*
Whittier College *B*

Colorado

Adams State College *B*
Colorado Christian University *B*
Colorado Institute of Art *C*
Colorado State University *B,M*
Community College of Denver *A*
Fort Lewis College *B*
Lamar Community College *A*
Mesa State College *A,B*
Northeastern Junior College *A*
Pikes Peak Community College *A*
Trinidad State Junior College *A*
University of Colorado
Boulder *M*
Colorado Springs *B*
Denver *B*
University of Denver *B*
University of Northern Colorado
B,M
Western State College of
Colorado *B*

Connecticut

Albertus Magnus College *B*
Asnuntuck Community College *A*
Central Connecticut State
University *B*
Eastern Connecticut State
University *B*
Housatonic Community College *A*

Manchester Community College *A*
Mattatuck Community College *A*
Middlesex Community College *A*
Northwestern Connecticut
Community College *A*
Paier College of Art *C,B*
Quinebaug Valley Community
College *A*
Sacred Heart University *A,B*
Tunxis Community College *A*
University of Bridgeport *B*
University of New Haven *B*
Wesleyan University *B*
Western Connecticut State
University *B*
Yale University *B,M*

Delaware

Delaware State College *B*
University of Delaware *B,M*

District of Columbia

American University *B*
Corcoran School of Art *C*
George Washington University *B*
Georgetown University *B*
Mount Vernon College *B*
Trinity College *B*

Florida

Barry University *B*
Brevard Community College *A*
Central Florida Community
College *A*
Daytona Beach Community
College *A*
Eckerd College *B*
Edison Community College *A*
Flagler College *B*
Florida Agricultural and Mechanical
University *B*
Florida Atlantic University *B*
Florida International University *B*
Gulf Coast Community College *A*
Indian River Community College *A*
Lynn University *A*
Manatee Community College *A*
Miami-Dade Community College *A*
New College of the University of
South Florida *B*
Okaloosa-Walton Community
College *A*
Palm Beach Community College *A*
Pensacola Junior College *A*
Ringling School of Art and
Design *B*
Stetson University *B*
University of Central Florida *B*
University of Miami *B,M*
University of North Florida *B*
University of Tampa *B*
University of West Florida *B*

Georgia

Abraham Baldwin Agricultural
College *A*
Agnes Scott College *B*
Armstrong State College *B*
Atlanta College of Art *B*
Atlanta Metropolitan College *A*
Brewton-Parker College *A*
Clark Atlanta University *B*
Columbus College *B*
DeKalb College *A*
Georgia Southern University *B*
Georgia Southwestern College *B*
Georgia State University *B,M*
Gordon College *A*
Kennesaw State College *B*
Middle Georgia College *A*
Morehouse College *B*
Morris Brown College *B*

North Georgia College *B*
Oglethorpe University *B*
Piedmont College *B*
Reinhardt College *A*
Spelman College *B*
Thomas College *A*
West Georgia College *B*
Young Harris College *A*

Hawaii

Brigham Young University-
Hawaii *B*
University of Hawaii
Hilo *B*
Manoa *B,M*

Idaho

Albertson College *B*
Boise State University *B,M*
Idaho State University *B,M*
Lewis Clark State College *B*
North Idaho College *A*
Northwest Nazarene College *A,B*
Ricks College *A*
University of Idaho *B,M*

Illinois

Augustana College *B*
Barat College *B*
Black Hawk College *A*
City Colleges of Chicago: Olive-
Harvey College *A*
College of St. Francis *B*
Columbia College *B*
Concordia University *B*
Eastern Illinois University *B,M*
Elmhurst College *B*
Eureka College *B*
Governors State University *B,M*
Greenville College *B*
Highland Community College *A*
Illinois Central College *A*
Illinois College *B*
Illinois Eastern Community
Colleges
Frontier Community
College *A*
Lincoln Trail College *A*
Olney Central College *A*
Wabash Valley College *A*
Illinois State University *B,M,D*
Joliet Junior College *A*
Judson College *B*
Kendall College *A*
Kishwaukee College *A*
Lincoln Land Community
College *A*
Loyola University of Chicago *B*
McKendree College *B*
Millikin University *B*
Montay College *A*
Morton College *A*
National-Louis University *B*
North Central College *B*
North Park College and Theological
Seminary *B*
Northern Illinois University *M*
Olivet Nazarene University *B*
Principia College *B*
Rend Lake College *A*
Richland Community College *A*
Rockford College *B*
Rosary College *B*
School of the Art Institute of
Chicago *B,M*
Southern Illinois University at
Carbondale *M*
Triton College *A*
University of Chicago *B,M*
University of Illinois at Urbana-
Champaign *M*
Waubonsee Community College *A*

Western Illinois University *B,M*
William Rainey Harper College *A*

Indiana

Anderson University *B*
Bethel College *B*
Calumet College of St. Joseph *B*
Earlham College *B*
Goshen College *B*
Hanover College *B*
Huntington College *B*
Indiana State University *B,M*
Indiana University
Bloomington *B,M,D*
Northwest *B*
South Bend *B*
Southeast *B*
Indiana University—Purdue
University
Fort Wayne *B*
Indianapolis *B*
Manchester College *A,B*
Oakland City College *B*
Purdue University *B,M*
St. Francis College *B*
St. Mary-of-the-Woods College *B*
St. Mary's College *B*
University of Indianapolis *M*
Valparaiso University *B*
Vincennes University *A*
Wabash College *B*

Iowa

Briar Cliff College *B*
Buena Vista College *B*
Clarke College *B*
Clinton Community College *A*
Coe College *B*
Cornell College *B*
Dordt College *B*
Grand View College *B*
Grinnell College *B*
Iowa Lakes Community College *A*
Iowa State University *B*
Kirkwood Community College *A*
Luther College *B*
Maharishi International University
A,B,M
Mount Mercy College *B*
Muscatine Community College *A*
North Iowa Area Community
College *A*
Scott Community College *A*
Teikyo Marycrest University *B*
Teikyo Westmar University *B*
University of Iowa *B,M*
University of Northern Iowa *B,M*
Upper Iowa University *B*

Kansas

Allen County Community
College *A*
Baker University *B*
Bethany College *B*
Bethel College *B*
Central College *A*
Cloud County Community
College *A*
Coffeyville Community College *A*
Colby Community College *A*
Cowley County Community
College *A*
Emporia State University *B*
Fort Hays State University *B,M*
Friends University *B*
Highland Community College *A*
Hutchinson Community College *A*
Kansas City Kansas Community
College *A*
Kansas Newman College *B*
Kansas State University *B,M*
McPherson College *B*

Neosho County Community
    College *A*
Ottawa University *B*
Pittsburg State University *B*
Pratt Community College *A*
Seward County Community
    College *A*
Sterling College *B*
Washburn University of Topeka *B*
Wichita State University *B,M*

Kentucky

Berea College *B*
Centre College *B*
Cumberland College *B*
Eastern Kentucky University *B*
Georgetown College *B*
Kentucky Wesleyan College *B*
Northern Kentucky University *B*
Pikeville College *B*
St. Catharine College *A*
Sue Bennett College *A*

Louisiana

Centenary College of Louisiana *B*
Dillard University *B*
Grambling State University *B*
Louisiana College *B*
Louisiana State University in
    Shreveport *B*
Nicholls State University *B*
Northeast Louisiana University *B*
Northwestern State University *B,M*
Southeastern Louisiana
    University *B*
Southern University and
    Agricultural and Mechanical
    College *B*
University of New Orleans *B,M*
University of Southwestern
    Louisiana *B*
Xavier University of Louisiana *B*

Maine

Bates College *B*
Colby College *B*
University of Maine
    Augusta *A*
    Farmington *B*
    Orono *B*
    Presque Isle *B*
University of Southern Maine *B*

Maryland

Anne Arundel Community
    College *A*
Bowie State University *B*
Chesapeake College *A*
College of Notre Dame of
    Maryland *B*
Frederick Community College *A*
Frostburg State University *B*
Garrett Community College *A*
Goucher College *B*
Harford Community College *A*
Hood College *B*
Howard Community College *A*
Loyola College in Maryland *B*
Maryland College of Art and
    Design *A*
Maryland Institute College of Art *B*
Montgomery College
    Germantown Campus *A*
    Takoma Park Campus *A*
Morgan State University *B*
Mount St. Mary's College *B*
St. Mary's College of Maryland *B*
Salisbury State University *B*
Towson State University *B*
University of Maryland: Eastern
    Shore *B*
Villa Julie College *A*

Western Maryland College *B*

Massachusetts

Amherst College *B*
Anna Maria College for Men and
    Women *B*
Atlantic Union College *B*
Berkshire Community College *A*
Bradford College *B*
Brandeis University *B*
Bridgewater State College *B*
Bristol Community College *C,A*
Clark University *B*
Curry College *B*
Dean Junior College *A*
Emmanuel College *B*
Greenfield Community College *A*
Hampshire College *B*
Harvard University *D*
Lasell College *A*
Massachusetts College of Art *B,M*
Middlesex Community College *A*
Montserrat College of Art *B*
Mount Wachusett Community
    College *A*
Northeastern University *B*
Regis College *B*
Salem State College *B*
School of the Museum of Fine
    Arts *B*
Simon's Rock College of Bard *B*
Tufts University *B,M*
University of Massachusetts
    Boston *B*
    Lowell *B*
Westfield State College *B*
Wheaton College *B*

Michigan

Adrian College *A,B*
Albion College *B*
Alma College *B*
Aquinas College *B*
Calvin College *B*
Center for Creative Studies: College
    of Art and Design *B*
Charles Stewart Mott Community
    College *A*
Concordia College *B*
Eastern Michigan University *B,M*
Glen Oaks Community College *A*
Grand Valley State University *B*
Hope College *B*
Kellogg Community College *A*
Kendall College of Art and
    Design *B*
Lansing Community College *A*
Madonna University *A,B*
Michigan State University *B,M*
Oakland Community College *A*
Saginaw Valley State University *B*
St. Clair County Community
    College *A*
Siena Heights College *A,B*
Spring Arbor College *B*
Suomi College *A*
University of Michigan
    Ann Arbor *M*
    Dearborn *B*
    Flint *B*
Wayne State University *B,M*
West Shore Community College *A*
Western Michigan University *B,M*

Minnesota

Bemidji State University *B*
Bethany Lutheran College *A*
Bethel College *B*
College of Associated Arts *B*
College of St. Benedict *B*
Concordia College: Moorhead *B*
Macalester College *B*

Minneapolis College of Art and
    Design *B*
Moorhead State University *B*
Northland Community College *A*
Northwestern College *B*
Pillsbury Baptist Bible College *B*
Rainy River Community College *A*
St. John's University *B*
St. Mary's College of Minnesota *B*
St. Olaf College *B*
Southwest State University *B*
Willmar Community College *A*
Winona State University *B*

Mississippi

Belhaven College *B*
Delta State University *B*
East Central Community College *A*
Jones County Junior College *A*
Mississippi Delta Community
    College *A*
Mississippi Gulf Coast Community
    College: Jefferson Davis
    Campus *A*
Mississippi University for Women *B*
University of Mississippi *B,M*
University of Southern
    Mississippi *B*

Missouri

Avila College *B*
Central Missouri State
    University *M*
College of the Ozarks *B*
Columbia College *C,B*
Culver-Stockton College *B*
East Central College *A*
Fontbonne College *B*
Hannibal-LaGrange College *A*
Jefferson College *A*
Kansas City Art Institute *B*
Maryville University *B*
Mineral Area College *A*
Missouri Southern State College *B*
Missouri Valley College *B*
Missouri Western State College *B*
Moberly Area Community
    College *A*
Northeast Missouri State
    University *B*
Northwest Missouri State
    University *B*
Park College *B*
St. Louis Community College
    Florissant Valley *A*
    Forest Park *A*
    Meramec *A*
St. Louis University *B*
Southwest Baptist University *B*
Southwest Missouri State
    University *B*
Stephens College *B*
University of Missouri
    Columbia *B,M*
    Kansas City *B*
Washington University *B,M*
Webster University *B*
Westminster College *B*
William Woods College *B*

Montana

Eastern Montana College *B*
Miles Community College *A*
Montana State University *B,M*
Rocky Mountain College *B*
University of Montana *B,M*

Nebraska

Bellevue College *B*
Central Community College *A*
Chadron State College *B*
College of St. Mary *B*

Concordia College *B*
Creighton University *B*
Dana College *B*
Doane College *B*
Midland Lutheran College *B*
Nebraska Wesleyan University *B*
Peru State College *B*
Southeast Community College:
    Beatrice Campus *A*
University of Nebraska
    Kearney *B*
    Lincoln *B*
Wayne State College *B*
York College *A*

Nevada

Community College of Southern
    Nevada *A*
Sierra Nevada College *B*
University of Nevada
    Las Vegas *B,M*
    Reno *B*

New Hampshire

Colby-Sawyer College *B*
Dartmouth College *B*
Franklin Pierce College *B*
Hesser College *C*
Keene State College *B*
Notre Dame College *B*
Plymouth State College of the
    University System of New
    Hampshire *B*
St. Anselm College *C*
University of New Hampshire *B*
White Pines College *A*

New Jersey

Bloomfield College *B*
Brookdale Community College *A*
Burlington County College *A*
Caldwell College *B*
Camden County College *A*
Centenary College *B*
College of St. Elizabeth *B*
County College of Morris *A*
Cumberland County College *A*
Essex County College *A*
Fairleigh Dickinson University *B*
Felician College *A,B*
Georgian Court College *B*
Jersey City State College *B*
Mercer County Community
    College *A*
Monmouth College *B*
Montclair State College *B,M*
Ocean County College *A*
Ramapo College of New Jersey *B*
Rider College *B*
Rutgers—The State University of
    New Jersey
    Camden College of Arts and
        Sciences *B*
    Douglass College *B*
    Livingston College *B*
    Newark College of Arts and
        Sciences *B*
    Rutgers College *B*
    University College Camden *B*
    University College New
        Brunswick *B*
Seton Hall University *B*
Stockton State College *B*
Thomas Edison State College *B*
Trenton State College *B*
Union County College *A*
Upsala College *B*
William Paterson College of New
    Jersey *B*

New Mexico

Clovis Community College *A*
College of Santa Fe *B*
Eastern New Mexico University *B*
Institute of American Indian
 Arts *A*
New Mexico Highlands
 University *B*
New Mexico Junior College *A*
New Mexico State University *B*
Northern New Mexico Community
 College *A*
University of New Mexico *B,M*
Western New Mexico University *B*

New York

Adelphi University *B*
Adirondack Community College *A*
Alfred University *B,M*
Bard College *B,M*
City University of New York
 Brooklyn College *B,M*
 City College *M*
 Hunter College *B,M*
 Kingsborough Community
  College *A*
 Lehman College *B*
 Queens College *B*
 Queensborough Community
  College *A*
 York College *B*
Colgate University *B*
College of New Rochelle *B*
Columbia-Greene Community
 College *A*
Community College of the Finger
 Lakes *A*
Cooper Union *B*
Cornell University *B*
Corning Community College *A*
Daemen College *B*
Fashion Institute of Technology *A*
Fordham University *B*
Fulton-Montgomery Community
 College *A*
Graduate School of Figurative Art
 of the New York Academy of
 Art *M*
Hartwick College *B*
Herkimer County Community
 College *A*
Hofstra University *B*
Houghton College *B*
Iona College *A*
Jamestown Community College *A*
Long Island University
 C. W. Post Campus *B,M*
 Southampton Campus *B*
Manhattan College *B*
Manhattanville College *B*
Marist College *B*
Marymount College *B*
Mohawk Valley Community
 College *A*
Molloy College *B*
Nassau Community College *A*
New York Institute of
 Technology *A*
New York University *B,M,D*
Niagara County Community
 College *A*
Onondaga Community College *A*
Pace University: Pleasantville/
 Briarcliff *A*
Parsons School of Design *A,B*
Pratt Institute *B,M*
Roberts Wesleyan College *B*
Rochester Institute of Technology
 A,B
Sage Junior College of Albany, A
 Division of Russell Sage
 College *A*

St. John's University *B*
St. Lawrence University *B*
Sarah Lawrence College *B*
School of Visual Arts *B,M*
State University of New York
 Buffalo *B,M*
 College at Brockport *B*
 College at Buffalo *B*
 College at Cortland *B*
 College at New Paltz *B*
 Empire State College *A,B*
 Oswego *B*
Suffolk County Community
 College *A*
Syracuse University *B,M*
Union College *B*
Utica College of Syracuse
 University *B*
Villa Maria College of Buffalo *A*
Wagner College *B*
Westchester Community College *A*

North Carolina

Appalachian State University *B,M*
Barton College *B*
Brevard College *A*
Campbell University *B*
Central Piedmont Community
 College *A*
Chowan College *A*
College of the Albemarle *A*
Davidson County Community
 College *A*
Elizabeth City State University *B*
Gaston College *A*
Greensboro College *B*
Guilford College *B*
Isothermal Community College *A*
Mars Hill College *B*
Meredith College *B*
Methodist College *A,B*
Mount Olive College *A,B*
North Carolina Central
 University *B*
Peace College *A*
Pembroke State University *B*
Queens College *B*
Rockingham Community College *A*
St. Andrews Presbyterian College *B*
Sandhills Community College *A*
Southeastern Community College *A*
University of North Carolina
 Asheville *B*
 Charlotte *B*
 Greensboro *B*
 Wilmington *B*
Western Carolina University *B,M*
Western Piedmont Community
 College *A*
Wilkes Community College *A*
Winston-Salem State University *B*

North Dakota

Jamestown College *B*
North Dakota State University *B*
Valley City State University *B*

Ohio

Art Academy of Cincinnati *B*
Ashland University *B*
Bowling Green State University
 Bowling Green *B,M*
 Firelands College *A*
Capital University *B*
Chatfield College *A*
College of Mount St. Joseph *B*
Columbus College of Art and
 Design *B*
Defiance College *A,B*
Edison State Community College *A*
Kent State University *B*
Lake Erie College *B*

Lakeland Community College *A*
Lorain County Community
 College *A*
Lourdes College *A,B*
Marietta College *B*
Miami University: Oxford
 Campus *B*
Mount Vernon Nazarene College *B*
Muskingum College *B*
Ohio Northern University *B*
Ohio State University: Columbus
 Campus *B,M*
Ohio University
 Athens *D*
 Eastern Campus *A*
Ohio Wesleyan University *B*
Sinclair Community College *A*
Union Institute *B,D*
University of Akron *B*
University of Cincinnati *B,M*
University of Dayton *B*
University of Rio Grande *A,B*
University of Toledo *B*
Ursuline College *B*
Wilberforce University *B*
Wittenberg University *B*
Wright State University *B*
Xavier University *B*

Oklahoma

East Central University *B*
Eastern Oklahoma State College *A*
Northern Oklahoma College *A*
Oklahoma Baptist University *B*
Oklahoma City University *B*
Oklahoma State University *B*
Phillips University *B*
Redlands Community College *A*
Southeastern Oklahoma State
 University *B*
University of Central Oklahoma
 B,M
University of Oklahoma *B*
University of Science and Arts of
 Oklahoma *B*
University of Tulsa *B,M*

Oregon

Central Oregon Community
 College *A*
Concordia College *B*
Eastern Oregon State College *B*
Lewis and Clark College *B*
Linfield College *B*
Linn-Benton Community College *A*
Marylhurst College *B*
Oregon State University *B*
Pacific Northwest College of Art *C*
Pacific University *B*
Portland Community College *A*
Portland State University *B,M*
Reed College *B*
Rogue Community College *C,A*
Southern Oregon State College *B*
Treasure Valley Community
 College *A*
University of Oregon
 Eugene *B,M*
 Robert Donald Clark Honors
  College *B*
Western Oregon State College *B*

Pennsylvania

Albright College *B*
Beaver College *B*
Bryn Mawr College *B*
Bucks County Community
 College *A*
Cabrini College *B*
California University of
 Pennsylvania *B*
Carlow College *B*

Cedar Crest College *B*
Chatham College *B*
Chestnut Hill College *B*
Cheyney University of
 Pennsylvania *B*
Clarion University of
 Pennsylvania *B*
Dickinson College *B*
East Stroudsburg University of
 Pennsylvania *B*
Edinboro University of
 Pennsylvania *B,M*
Elizabethtown College *B*
Gannon University *B*
Harcum Junior College *A*
Haverford College *B*
Holy Family College *B*
Indiana University of
 Pennsylvania *B*
Juniata College *B*
Keystone Junior College *A*
Kutztown University of
 Pennsylvania *B*
Lafayette College *B*
Lehigh County Community
 College *C*
Lock Haven University of
 Pennsylvania *B*
Lycoming College *B*
Marywood College *B*
Mercyhurst College *B*
Millersville University of
 Pennsylvania *B*
Montgomery County Community
 College *A*
Moore College of Art and Design *B*
Muhlenberg College *B*
Northeastern Christian Junior
 College *A*
Penn State University Park Campus
 B,M
Rosemont College *B*
St. Joseph's University *B*
St. Vincent College *B*
Seton Hill College *B*
Shippensburg University of
 Pennsylvania *B*
Slippery Rock University of
 Pennsylvania *B*
Susquehanna University *B*
University of Pennsylvania *B,M,D*
University of Pittsburgh *B,M,D*
University of Scranton *A*
West Chester University of
 Pennsylvania *B*
Wilkes University *B*
Wilson College *B*
York College of Pennsylvania *A,B*

Puerto Rico

Inter American University of Puerto
 Rico: San German Campus *B*
Pontifical Catholic University of
 Puerto Rico *B*
University of Puerto Rico
 Mayaguez Campus *B*
 Rio Piedras Campus *B*

Rhode Island

Rhode Island College *B*
University of Rhode Island *B*

South Carolina

Bob Jones University *B,M*
Claflin College *B*
Clemson University *B,M*
Coker College *B*
Columbia College *B*
Furman University *B*
Lander College *B*
Morris College *B*
North Greenville College *A*

Presbyterian College *B*
South Carolina State College *B*
University of South Carolina
    Columbia *M*
    Lancaster *A*
Winthrop University *B,M*

South Dakota

Augustana College *B*
Black Hills State University *B*
Dakota State University *B*
Dakota Wesleyan University *B*
Northern State University *B*
Sioux Falls College *B*
South Dakota State University *B*

Tennessee

Austin Peay State University *B*
Belmont University *B*
Bethel College *B*
Carson-Newman College *B*
Cleveland State Community
    College *A*
East Tennessee State University
    B,M
Freed-Hardeman University *B*
King College *B*
Lambuth University *B*
Lincoln Memorial University *B*
Martin Methodist College *A*
Maryville College *B*
Memphis College of Art *B,M*
Memphis State University *B,M*
Motlow State Community
    College *A*
Roane State Community College *A*
Shelby State Community College *A*
Tennessee Technological
    University *B*
Tusculum College *B*
Union University *B*
University of the South *B*
University of Tennessee:
    Knoxville *M*
Vanderbilt University *B*
Walters State Community
    College *A*

Texas

Abilene Christian University *B*
Alvin Community College *A*
Amarillo College *A*
Angelina College *A*
Angelo State University *B*
Austin College *B*
Austin Community College *A*
Brazosport College *A*
Central Texas College *A*
College of the Mainland *A*
Collin County Community College
    District *A*
Corpus Christi State University *B*
East Texas State University *B,M*
El Centro College *A*
El Paso Community College *A*
Galveston College *A*
Houston Baptist University *B*
Houston Community College *C,A*
Howard College *A*
Lamar University—Beaumont *B*
Lubbock Christian University *B*
McMurry University *B*
Midland College *A*
Midwestern State University *B*
North Harris Montgomery
    Community College District *A*
Panola College *A*
Rice University *B*
St. Edward's University *B*
St. Philip's College *A*
Sam Houston State University *B,M*
Schreiner College *B*

Southwest Texas State University *B*
Stephen F. Austin State University
    B,M
Sul Ross State University *B*
Texas A&I University *B,M*
Texas Lutheran College *B*
Texas Southmost College *A*
Texas Wesleyan University *B*
Trinity University *B*
Trinity Valley Community
    College *A*
University of Houston
    Clear Lake *B*
    Houston *B,M*
University of Mary Hardin-
    Baylor *B*
University of North Texas *B,M,D*
University of St. Thomas *B*
University of Texas
    Arlington *B*
    San Antonio *B,M*
    Tyler *B*
Vernon Regional Junior College *A*
West Texas State University *M*
Western Texas College *A*
Wharton County Junior College *A*

Utah

University of Utah *B,M*
Utah State University *B,M*
Weber State University *B*

Vermont

Bennington College *B,M*
Burlington College *B*
Castleton State College *B*
Goddard College *B*
Green Mountain College *B*
Marlboro College *B*
Middlebury College *B*
St. Michael's College *B*

Virginia

Averett College *B*
Bluefield College *A,B*
Bridgewater College *B*
Christopher Newport College *B*
College of William and Mary *B*
Eastern Mennonite College *B*
Ferrum College *B*
James Madison University *B,M*
Longwood College *B*
Lynchburg College *B*
Mary Baldwin College *B*
Mountain Empire Community
    College *C*
Norfolk State University *B*
Northern Virginia Community
    College *A*
Old Dominion University *B,M*
Patrick Henry Community
    College *A*
Piedmont Virginia Community
    College *A*
Radford University *B,M*
Randolph-Macon College *B*
Roanoke College *B*
Southwest Virginia Community
    College *C*
Tidewater Community College *A*
Virginia Commonwealth
    University *B*
Virginia Intermont College *B*
Virginia Polytechnic Institute and
    State University *B*
Virginia State University *B*
Virginia Wesleyan College *B*

Washington

Big Bend Community College *A*
Central Washington University *B,M*
Centralia College *A*

Cornish College of the Arts *B*
Eastern Washington University *B,M*
Everett Community College *A*
Evergreen State College *B*
Gonzaga University *B*
Lower Columbia College *A*
North Seattle Community College
    C,A
Northwest Indian College *C,A*
Seattle Central Community
    College *A*
Seattle Pacific University *B*
Seattle University *B*
Skagit Valley College *A*
Spokane Falls Community
    College *A*
Tacoma Community College *A*
Walla Walla College *B*
Washington State University *B,M*

West Virginia

Bethany College *B*
Davis and Elkins College *B*
Marshall University *B,M*
Shepherd College *B*
University of Charleston *B*
West Virginia State College *A,B*

Wisconsin

Cardinal Stritch College *B*
Carroll College *B*
Edgewood College *B*
Lakeland College *B*
Maranatha Baptist Bible College *B*
Marian College of Fond du Lac *B*
Mount Mary College *B*
Mount Senario College *B*
St. Norbert College *B*
University of Wisconsin
    Eau Claire *B*
    La Crosse *B*
    Madison *B,M*
    Milwaukee *B*
    Oshkosh *B*
    Platteville *B*
    Stevens Point *B*
    Stout *B*
    Whitewater *B*

Wyoming

Casper College *A*
Central Wyoming College *C,A*
Laramie County Community
    College *A*
Northwest College *A*
Sheridan College *A*
University of Wyoming *B,M*
Western Wyoming Community
    College *A*

Switzerland

American College of Switzerland *B*

Fire control and safety technology

Alabama

Athens State College *B*
Chattahoochee Valley Community
    College *A*
Community College of the Air
    Force *A*
Gadsden State Community
    College *A*
George C. Wallace State
    Community College at Selma *A*
James H. Faulkner State
    Community College *A*

Jefferson State Community
    College *A*
John C. Calhoun State Community
    College *A*
Shelton State Community
    College *A*
Shoals Community College *A*
Snead State Junior College *A*
Wallace State Community College
    at Hanceville *A*

Alaska

University of Alaska
    Anchorage *A*
    Fairbanks *C,A*

Arizona

Cochise College *A*
Glendale Community College *C,A*
Mesa Community College *C,A*
Mohave Community College *C,A*
Northland Pioneer College *C,A*
Pima Community College *C,A*
Rio Salado Community College *A*
Scottsdale Community College *C,A*
Yavapai College *C,A*

Arkansas

Garland County Community
    College *C,A*

California

Allan Hancock College *C,A*
Bakersfield College *A*
Barstow College *C,A*
California State University: Los
    Angeles *B*
Chabot College *A*
City College of San Francisco *C,A*
Cogswell Polytechnical College *B*
College of the Desert *A*
College of the Sequoias *C,A*
Columbia College *A*
Cosumnes River College *C,A*
East Los Angeles College *A*
El Camino College *C,A*
Fresno City College *C,A*
Glendale Community College *C,A*
Hartnell College *A*
Imperial Valley College *C,A*
Lake Tahoe Community College
    C,A
Long Beach City College *C,A*
Los Angeles Harbor College *C,A*
Los Medanos College *A*
Merced College *C,A*
Mission College *C,A*
Modesto Junior College *A*
Monterey Peninsula College *C,A*
Mount San Antonio College *C,A*
Napa Valley College *C,A*
Oxnard College *C,A*
Palomar College *C,A*
Pasadena City College *A*
Porterville College *C*
Rio Hondo College *A*
San Diego Miramar College *A*
San Joaquin Delta College *C,A*
Santa Monica College *C,A*
Santa Rosa Junior College *C,A*
Sierra College *C,A*
Solano Community College *A*
Southwestern College *C,A*
Victor Valley College *C,A*
Yuba College *A*

Colorado

Aims Community College *C,A*
Metropolitan State College of
    Denver *B*
Pikes Peak Community College *C,A*
Red Rocks Community College *A*

Connecticut

Greater New Haven State Technical College *A*
Hartford State Technical College *A*
Norwalk State Technical College *A*
Thames Valley State Technical College *A*
University of New Haven *C,A,B,M*
Waterbury State Technical College *A*

Delaware

Delaware Technical and Community College: Stanton/Wilmington Campus *A*

District of Columbia

University of the District of Columbia *A,B*

Florida

Brevard Community College *A*
Broward Community College *A*
Central Florida Community College *A*
Daytona Beach Community College *A*
Edison Community College *A*
Florida Community College at Jacksonville *A*
Florida Keys Community College *A*
Gulf Coast Community College *C,A*
Hillsborough Community College *A*
Indian River Community College *A*
Lake-Sumter Community College *A*
Manatee Community College *C,A*
Miami-Dade Community College *C,A*
Okaloosa-Walton Community College *C,A*
Palm Beach Community College *A*
Pasco-Hernando Community College *A*
Pensacola Junior College *A*
St. Johns River Community College *A*
St. Petersburg Junior College *A*
Santa Fe Community College *C,A*
Seminole Community College *C,A*
Tallahassee Community College *A*
Valencia Community College *C,A*

Georgia

DeKalb College *A*

Hawaii

University of Hawaii: Honolulu Community College *C,A*

Idaho

Boise State University *A*

Illinois

Belleville Area College *C,A*
Carl Sandburg College *A*
City Colleges of Chicago
Chicago City-Wide College *A*
Richard J. Daley College *A*
College of DuPage *C,A*
College of Lake County *C,A*
Elgin Community College *A*
Illinois Central College *C,A*
Illinois Eastern Community Colleges: Frontier Community College *C*
Illinois Valley Community College *A*
Joliet Junior College *C,A*
Kishwaukee College *C,A*
Lake Land College *A*
Lewis and Clark Community College *A*

Lincoln Land Community College *C,A*
Moraine Valley Community College *C,A*
Oakton Community College *C,A*
Parkland College *A*
Prairie State College *A*
Rock Valley College *A*
Spoon River College *C*
Triton College *C,A*
Waubonsee Community College *C*
William Rainey Harper College *C,A*

Indiana

Indiana Vocational Technical College
Central Indiana *C,A*
Northeast *C,A*
Northwest *C,A*

Iowa

Des Moines Area Community College *A*
Kirkwood Community College *A*

Kansas

Barton County Community College *A*
Butler County Community College *C,A*
Dodge City Community College *C,A*
Hutchinson Community College *A*
Johnson County Community College *C,A*
Kansas City Kansas Community College *A*
Labette Community College *A*

Kentucky

Eastern Kentucky University *A,B*
Jefferson Community College *A*
Northern Kentucky University *A*

Louisiana

Louisiana State University at Eunice *C,A*

Maine

Southern Maine Technical College *A*

Maryland

Montgomery College: Rockville Campus *C,A*

Massachusetts

Bristol Community College *A*
Bunker Hill Community College *A*
Cape Cod Community College *C,A*
Greenfield Community College *C,A*
Massasoit Community College *A*
Middlesex Community College *A*
North Shore Community College *A*
Quinsigamond Community College *A*
Springfield Technical Community College *A*

Michigan

Charles Stewart Mott Community College *A*
Delta College *A*
Grand Rapids Community College *A*
Henry Ford Community College *A*
Jackson Community College *C,A*
Kellogg Community College *A*
Kirtland Community College *A*
Lake Superior State University *A,B*
Lansing Community College *A*
Macomb Community College *C,A*

Mid Michigan Community College *A*
St. Clair County Community College *A*

Missouri

Central Missouri State University *B*
East Central College *A*
Jefferson College *A*
Penn Valley Community College *A*
St. Louis Community College
Florissant Valley *A*
Forest Park *A*

Montana

College of Great Falls *A*

Nebraska

Southeast Community College: Lincoln Campus *A*
University of Nebraska—Omaha *A*

Nevada

Community College of Southern Nevada *A*
Truckee Meadows Community College *C,A*
Western Nevada Community College *C,A*

New Hampshire

New Hampshire Technical College: Laconia *A*

New Jersey

Brookdale Community College *C*
Camden County College *A*
Essex County College *A*
Jersey City State College *B*
Mercer County Community College *C,A*
Ocean County College *C,A*
Passaic County Community College *A*
Union County College *A*

New Mexico

Albuquerque Technical-Vocational Institute *A*
Dona Ana Branch Community College of New Mexico State University *A*
Eastern New Mexico University: Roswell Campus *A*

New York

Broome Community College *C,A*
City University of New York: John Jay College of Criminal Justice *B,M*
Corning Community College *C,A*
Erie Community College: South Campus *A*
Mercy College *C*
Monroe Community College *A*
Onondaga Community College *A*
Rockland Community College *A*
Tompkins-Cortland Community College *A*

North Carolina

Alamance Community College *A*
Durham Technical Community College *A*
Gaston College *A*
Guilford Technical Community College *C,A*

Ohio

Cuyahoga Community College: Metropolitan Campus *A*
Hocking Technical College *A*

Lakeland Community College *A*
Lorain County Community College *A*
Sinclair Community College *A*
Stark Technical College *A*
University of Akron *A*
University of Cincinnati
Access Colleges *A*
Cincinnati *B*

Oklahoma

Oklahoma State University
Oklahoma City *A*
Stillwater *B*
Tulsa Junior College *A*

Oregon

Central Oregon Community College *A*
Chemeketa Community College *A*
Clatsop Community College *A*
Lane Community College *A*
Mount Hood Community College *C,A*
Portland Community College *A*
Rogue Community College *C,A*
Southwestern Oregon Community College *C,A*
Umpqua Community College *A*

Pennsylvania

Community College of Philadelphia *C,A*
Delaware County Community College *A*
Harrisburg Area Community College *C,A*
Holy Family College *B*
Luzerne County Community College *C,A*
Mercyhurst College *C*
Montgomery County Community College *A*
Northampton County Area Community College *A*
Westmoreland County Community College *A*

Rhode Island

Community College of Rhode Island *A*
Providence College *A,B*

South Dakota

Kilian Community College *A*

Tennessee

Chattanooga State Technical Community College *A*
Tennessee State University *A*

Texas

Amarillo College *A*
Austin Community College *A*
Bee County College *A*
Cisco Junior College *A*
College of the Mainland *A*
Collin County Community College District *C,A*
Del Mar College *A*
El Centro College *A*
El Paso Community College *A*
Galveston College *A*
Houston Community College *A*
Howard College *A*
Kilgore College *A*
Lamar University—Beaumont *A*
Midland College *A*
Navarro College *C,A*
Odessa College *C,A*
San Antonio College *A*

San Jacinto College: Central
Campus *A*
Tarrant County Junior College *A*
Temple Junior College *A*
Texarkana College *A*
Texas Southmost College *A*

Utah
Utah Valley Community College *A*

Virginia
Blue Ridge Community College *C*
Central Virginia Community
College *A*
Northern Virginia Community
College *C,A*
Tidewater Community College *A*

Washington
Bellevue Community College *A*
Everett Community College *A*
Olympic College *A*
Pierce College *A*
South Puget Sound Community
College *A*
Spokane Community College *A*
Wenatchee Valley College *A*
Yakima Valley Community
College *A*

West Virginia
Marshall University *C,A*
Shepherd College *A*

Wisconsin
Fox Valley Technical College *A*
Madison Area Technical College *A*
Northeast Wisconsin Technical
College *A*
Wisconsin Indianhead Technical
College *C*

Wyoming
Casper College *C,A*
Laramie County Community
College *A*

**American Samoa, Caroline
Islands, Guam, Marianas,
Virgin Islands**
Guam Community College *C,A*

Fire protection

Alabama
Bishop State Community College *A*
Lurleen B. Wallace State Junior
College *A*

Arizona
Mesa Community College *C*

California
Chabot College *A*
Cogswell Polytechnical College *B*
Santa Rosa Junior College *C*

Connecticut
University of New Haven *C,B*

Delaware
Delaware State College *B*

Florida
Central Florida Community
College *A*
Daytona Beach Community
College *C*

Georgia
Macon College *A*

Illinois
Southern Illinois University at
Carbondale *B*

Kansas
Johnson County Community
College *C,A*

Maryland
Catonsville Community College *C,A*
Montgomery College: Rockville
Campus *A*
University of Maryland: College
Park *B*

Massachusetts
Massachusetts Bay Community
College *A*
Worcester Polytechnic Institute *M*

Michigan
Madonna University *C,A,B*

Missouri
Penn Valley Community College *C*
St. Louis Community College at
Forest Park *C*

Nebraska
University of Nebraska
Lincoln *A*
Omaha *A*

New Hampshire
New Hampshire Technical College:
Laconia *A*

New Jersey
Thomas Edison State College *A,B*

New Mexico
Clovis Community College *C,A*
New Mexico Junior College *A*
New Mexico State University *A*

New York
City University of New York: John
Jay College of Criminal Justice
B,M
Onondaga Community College *A*

North Carolina
Alamance Community College *A*
Central Piedmont Community
College *A*
Coastal Carolina Community
College *A*
Durham Technical Community
College *A*
Guilford Technical Community
College *C,A*
Wilson Technical Community
College *A*

Ohio
Wright State University *B*

Oklahoma
Oklahoma State University:
Oklahoma City *C,A*

Oregon
Chemeketa Community College *A*
Eastern Oregon State College *B*
Western Oregon State College *B*

Pennsylvania
Mercyhurst College *C*
St. Joseph's University *M*

Texas
Howard College *C,A*
Laredo Junior College *A*
Midland College *A*

Washington
Edmonds Community College *C,A*
South Puget Sound Community
College *A*

Fishing and fisheries

Alabama
Auburn University *B,M,D*
Gadsden State Community
College *C*

Alaska
Prince William Sound Community
College *C,A*
Sheldon Jackson College *C,A,B*
University of Alaska Fairbanks *B,M*

Arizona
University of Arizona *B,M,D*

Arkansas
University of Arkansas at Pine
Bluff *B*

California
College of the Redwoods *C,A*
Feather River College *C,A*
Humboldt State University *C,B,M*
Santa Rosa Junior College *A*
Southwestern College *A*

Delaware
Delaware State College *B*

Florida
University of Florida *M,D*

Georgia
University of Georgia *B,M*

Hawaii
University of Hawaii at Hilo *B*

Idaho
College of Southern Idaho *C*
North Idaho College *A*
University of Idaho *B,M,D*

Illinois
Southern Illinois University at
Carbondale *B,M*

Indiana
Ball State University *B*
Purdue University *B,M,D*
Vincennes University *A*

Iowa
Iowa Lakes Community College *A*
Iowa State University *B,M,D*

Kansas
Kansas State University *B*
Seward County Community
College *A*

Kentucky
Eastern Kentucky University *B*

Louisiana
Louisiana State University and
Agricultural and Mechanical
College *M,D*

Maine
Unity College *B*

Maryland
Frostburg State University *B,M*
Garrett Community College *A*

Massachusetts
University of Massachusetts at
Amherst *B,M,D*

Michigan
Lake Superior State University *B*
Michigan State University *B,M,D*
University of Michigan *M*

Minnesota
Alexandria Technical College *A*
University of Minnesota: Twin
Cities *B,M,D*
Vermilion Community College *A*
Willmar Community College *A*
Winona State University *A*

Mississippi
Mississippi State University *B*

Missouri
East Central College *A*
University of Missouri: Columbia
B,M,D

Montana
Montana State University *B,M*

New Jersey
Rutgers—The State University of
New Jersey: Cook College *B*

New Mexico
New Mexico State University *B,M*

New York
City University of New York:
Kingsborough Community
College *A*
State University of New York
College of Agriculture and
Technology at Cobleskill *A*
College of Agriculture and
Technology at Morrisville *A*
College of Environmental
Science and Forestry *B,M,D*

North Carolina
North Carolina State University *B*

North Dakota
North Dakota State University *B*

Ohio
Ohio State University: Columbus
Campus *B*

Oklahoma
Southeastern Oklahoma State
University *B*

Oregon
Clatsop Community College *C*
Mount Hood Community
College *A*
Oregon State University *B,M,D*

Pennsylvania
Mansfield University of
Pennsylvania *B*
Penn State University Park Campus
B,M,D

Rhode Island
University of Rhode Island *B,M,D*

South Carolina
Clemson University *B,M*

South Dakota
South Dakota State University *B,M*

Tennessee
University of Tennessee:
Knoxville *B*

Texas
Corpus Christi State University *M*
Texas A&M University
College Station *M*
Galveston *B*
West Texas State University *B,M*

Utah
Utah State University *B,M,D*

Vermont
University of Vermont *B*

Virginia
Virginia Polytechnic Institute and
State University *M,D*

Washington
Grays Harbor College *A*
Northwest Indian College *A*
Peninsula College *A*
University of Washington *B,M,D*

Wisconsin
Northland College *B*

Flight attendants

California
Chabot College *A*
El Camino College *A*
Glendale Community College *C*
Mount San Antonio College *A*
Orange Coast College *C,A*
Saddleback College *C,A*
San Diego Mesa College *C,A*

Louisiana
Northeast Louisiana University *A*

Maryland
Catonsville Community College *A*

Minnesota
Willmar Community College *A*

New York
Herkimer County Community
College *A*

South Dakota
National College *A*

Utah
Dixie College *C*

Fluids and plasmas

Massachusetts
Massachusetts Institute of
Technology *B,M,D,W*

Minnesota
University of Minnesota: Twin
Cities *M,D*

New Jersey
Stevens Institute of Technology
B,M,D

New York
Columbia University *M,D*

Ohio
Ohio State University: Columbus
Campus *B,M,D*

Pennsylvania
Carnegie Mellon University
B,M,D,W
Lehigh University *M*

Canada
McGill University *M,D*

Folklore and mythology

Arizona
Prescott College *B*

California
Pitzer College *B*
University of California
Berkeley *M*
Los Angeles *M,D*

Florida
New College of the University of
South Florida *B*

Indiana
Indiana University Bloomington
B,M,D

Massachusetts
Hampshire College *B*
Harvard and Radcliffe Colleges *B*

New York
Sarah Lawrence College *B*

North Carolina
University of North Carolina at
Chapel Hill *M*

Ohio
Ohio State University: Columbus
Campus *M,D*

Pennsylvania
University of Pennsylvania *B,M,D*

Vermont
Marlboro College *B*

Washington
Evergreen State College *B*
Tacoma Community College *A*

Food management

Alabama
Community College of the Air
Force *A*
Jacksonville State University *B*

Alaska
University of Alaska Anchorage *A*

Arizona
Pima Community College *C,A*

California
Bakersfield College *A*
Chaffey Community College *A*
College of the Redwoods *C,A*
Columbia College *A*
Diablo Valley College *A*
El Camino College *C,A*
Fresno City College *C,A*
Glendale Community College *C*
John F. Kennedy University *B*
Long Beach City College *C,A*
Mission College *C,A*
Mount San Antonio College *C,A*
Orange Coast College *C,A*
Pasadena City College *C,A*
San Joaquin Delta College *C,A*
Yuba College *C,A*

Colorado
Pikes Peak Community College *C,A*
Red Rocks Community College *C*

Connecticut
Manchester Community College *A*
Mattatuck Community College *A*
South Central Community College
C,A

District of Columbia
Southeastern University *A,B*

Florida
Central Florida Community
College *C*
Gulf Coast Community College *C,A*
Palm Beach Community College *A*
Seminole Community College *A*
South Florida Community
College *A*

Georgia
Augusta Technical Institute *C*
Berry College *B*
Georgia Southern University *B*

Idaho
Idaho State University *C*

Illinois
Bradley University *B*
City Colleges of Chicago
Chicago City-Wide College
C,A
Malcolm X College *A*
College of DuPage *C,A*
College of Lake County *C,A*
Elgin Community College *C,A*
Joliet Junior College *C*
Kendall College *B*
Lewis and Clark Community
College *A*
Lexington Institute of Hospitality
Careers *A*
Moraine Valley Community College
C,A
Rend Lake College *C,A*
Rosary College *B*
Southern Illinois University at
Carbondale *B*
William Rainey Harper College *C,A*

Indiana
Ball State University *B*
Purdue University *A,B*
Vincennes University *A*

Iowa
Iowa Western Community
College *A*
Kirkwood Community College *A*

Kentucky
Eastern Kentucky University *B*
Jefferson Community College *A*
Kentucky State University *A*
Morehead State University *A*
Paducah Community College *A*
Sullivan College *A*

Maryland
Allegany Community College *A*
Baltimore International Culinary
College *C,A*
Montgomery College: Rockville
Campus *C,A*
Prince George's Community
College *C*
Wor-Wic Tech Community
College *C*

Massachusetts
Becker College
Leicester Campus *A*
Worcester Campus *A*
Berkshire Community College *A*
Newbury College *A*
Northeastern University *C*

Michigan
Charles Stewart Mott Community
College *A*
Ferris State University *A*
Henry Ford Community College *A*
Lansing Community College *A*
Michigan State University *M*
Northern Michigan University *B*
Northwestern Michigan College *A*
Northwood Institute *A*
Oakland Community College *A*
West Shore Community College *A*

Minnesota
College of St. Scholastica *B*
St. Paul Technical College *C*
Southwest State University *B*

Mississippi
Jones County Junior College *A*

Missouri
St. Louis Community College at
Meramec *C*

Nevada
Community College of Southern
Nevada *A*
Truckee Meadows Community
College *A*

New Hampshire
University of New Hampshire *A*

New Jersey
Atlantic Community College *A*
Brookdale Community College *A*
Burlington County College *A*
Ocean County College *C*

New York
Adirondack Community College
C,A
City University of New York: La
Guardia Community College *A*
Erie Community College
City Campus *A*
North Campus *A*
Fulton-Montgomery Community
College *A*

Herkimer County Community
College *A*
Monroe Community College *A*
Nassau Community College *A*
New York University *B,M,D*
Niagara County Community
College *A*
Niagara University *B*
Onondaga Community College *A*
Rochester Institute of Technology
A,B,M
Rockland Community College *A*
State University of New York
College of Agriculture and
Technology at Cobleskill *C*
College of Agriculture and
Technology at Morrisville *A*
College at Buffalo *B*
College of Technology at
Delhi *A*
Suffolk County Community College:
Eastern Campus *A*
Sullivan County Community
College *A*
Syracuse University *B*
Villa Maria College of Buffalo *C,A*
Westchester Community College *A*

North Carolina

Alamance Community College *A*
Asheville Buncombe Technical
Community College *A*
Campbell University *B*
Central Carolina Community
College *C*
Central Piedmont Community
College *A*
Davidson County Community
College *C*
Fayetteville Technical Community
College *A*
Guilford Technical Community
College *C,A*
Isothermal Community College *A*
Piedmont Community College *C*
Southwestern Community
College *A*
University of North Carolina at
Greensboro *B*
Wake Technical Community
College *A*
Wilkes Community College *C,A*

Ohio

Cuyahoga Community College:
Metropolitan Campus *A*
Jefferson Technical College *A*
Kent State University *B*
Miami University: Oxford
Campus *B*
Ohio State University
Agricultural Technical
Institute *A*
Columbus Campus *B*
Ohio University *B*
Owens Technical College: Toledo
C,A
Sinclair Community College *C*
University of Akron *A*
University of Toledo *C,A*

Oklahoma

Oklahoma State University
Technical Branch: Okmulgee *A*

Oregon

Chemeketa Community College *A*

Pennsylvania

Bucks County Community
College *A*

Butler County Community College
C,A
Delaware Valley College *B*
Harrisburg Area Community
College *A*
Immaculata College *A,B*
Indiana University of
Pennsylvania *B*
Keystone Junior College *A*
Luzerne County Community
College *A*
Seton Hill College *B*
Westmoreland County Community
College *A*

Rhode Island

Johnson & Wales University *A,B*

South Carolina

Denmark Technical College *C*
Greenville Technical College *A*

Tennessee

Chattanooga State Technical
Community College *C*
David Lipscomb University *B*

Texas

Austin Community College *A*
Central Texas College *A*
El Paso Community College *A*
Galveston College *C*
Lamar University—Beaumont *A*
North Harris Montgomery
Community College District *C*
St. Philip's College *A*
South Plains College *A*

Utah

Brigham Young University *B*

Vermont

New England Culinary Institute *A*

Virginia

Eastern Mennonite College *B*
Northern Virginia Community
College *C,A*
Patrick Henry Community
College *C*
Radford University *B*

Washington

Clark College *C,A*
Edmonds Community College *C,A*
Olympic College *C*
Shoreline Community College *A*
South Puget Sound Community
College *C,A*
Yakima Valley Community College
C,A

West Virginia

Glenville State College *A*

Wisconsin

Chippewa Valley Technical
College *A*
Fox Valley Technical College *A*
University of Wisconsin: Stevens
Point *B*
Wisconsin Indianhead Technical
College *A*

**American Samoa, Caroline
Islands, Guam, Marianas,
Virgin Islands**

Guam Community College *C,A*

Canada

McGill University *B*

Food production/
management/services

Alabama

Bessemer State Technical College *C*
Community College of the Air
Force *A*
Enterprise State Junior College *A*
Jefferson State Community
College *A*
Lawson State Community College
C,A
Wallace State Community College
at Hanceville *A*

Alaska

University of Alaska
Anchorage *A*
Fairbanks *A*

Arizona

Pima Community College *C,A*
Scottsdale Community College *C,A*

Arkansas

Henderson State University *A*

California

Bakersfield College *A*
Cerritos Community College *A*
Chaffey Community College *C,A*
College of the Redwoods *C,A*
El Camino College *C,A*
Fresno City College *A*
Glendale Community College *A*
Grossmont Community College *C,A*
Long Beach City College *C,A*
Los Angeles Trade and Technical
College *C,A*
Merced College *A*
Modesto Junior College *A*
Ohlone College *C,A*
Orange Coast College *C,A*
Oxnard College *C*
Pacific Union College *A*
Palomar College *C,A*
Saddleback College *C,A*
San Diego Mesa College *C,A*
San Joaquin Delta College *A*
Santa Rosa Junior College *C*
Southwestern College *C*
Yuba College *C,A*

Colorado

Pikes Peak Community College *A*
Pueblo Community College *C,A*
Red Rocks Community College *C*

Connecticut

Mattatuck Community College *A*

Delaware

Delaware Technical and
Community College
Southern Campus *A*
Stanton/Wilmington
Campus *A*

District of Columbia

University of the District of
Columbia *A*

Florida

Broward Community College *A*
Gulf Coast Community College *A*
Indian River Community College *A*
Manatee Community College *A*
Miami-Dade Community College *A*
New England Institute of
Technology *A*

Palm Beach Community College *A*
Pasco-Hernando Community
College *A*
Pensacola Junior College *A*
South Florida Community
College *C*

Georgia

Abraham Baldwin Agricultural
College *A*
Darton College *A*
Georgia Southern University *B*
University of Georgia *B,M*

Hawaii

University of Hawaii
Honolulu Community College
C,A
Kapiolani Community College
C,A
Kauai Community College *C,A*
Leeward Community
College *A*

Idaho

Boise State University *C,A*
Idaho State University *A*

Illinois

City Colleges of Chicago: Malcolm
X College *A*
College of DuPage *C,A*
College of Lake County *C,A*
Elgin Community College *C,A*
Illinois Eastern Community
Colleges: Lincoln Trail College *A*
Joliet Junior College *A*
Kendall College *A*
Lexington Institute of Hospitality
Careers *A*
Parkland College *A*
Southern Illinois University at
Carbondale *B*
University of Illinois at Urbana-
Champaign *B*
William Rainey Harper College *C,A*

Indiana

Indiana State University *B*
Indiana University—Purdue
University at Indianapolis *A*
Indiana Vocational Technical
College
Central Indiana *C,A*
Northeast *C,A*
Northwest *C,A*
Whitewater *C*
Purdue University
Calumet *A*
West Lafayette *A,B*
Valparaiso University *B*
Vincennes University *A*

Iowa

Des Moines Area Community
College *C,A*
Indian Hills Community College *A*
Iowa State University *B*
Iowa Western Community
College *A*
Kirkwood Community College *A*
Maharishi International
University *C*
Scott Community College *A*

Kansas

Central College *A*
Colby Community College *A*
Dodge City Community College *A*
Johnson County Community
College *A*
Kansas State University *B*

Pittsburg State University *B*

Kentucky

Jefferson Community College *A*
Morehead State University *A,B*
Murray State University *A*
Sullivan College *A*

Louisiana

Louisiana Tech University *A*
Nicholls State University *A*

Maine

Central Maine Technical College *C*
Southern Maine Technical
   College *A*

Maryland

Allegany Community College *A*
Anne Arundel Community College
   C,A
Baltimore International Culinary
   College *C,A*
Montgomery College: Rockville
   Campus *A*
Prince George's Community
   College *A*

Massachusetts

Bristol Community College *C*
Bunker Hill Community College *A*
Essex Agricultural and Technical
   Institute *A*
Holyoke Community College *A*
Laboure College *A*
Massasoit Community College *A*
Newbury College *A*

Michigan

Andrews University *A*
Charles Stewart Mott Community
   College *A*
Ferris State University *A*
Grand Rapids Community
   College *A*
Henry Ford Community College *A*
Lansing Community College *A*
Madonna University *B*
Montcalm Community College *C,A*
Northern Michigan University
   C,A,B
Northwestern Michigan College *A*
Oakland Community College *A*
Schoolcraft College *A*

Minnesota

Normandale Community College *A*
University of Minnesota:
   Crookston *A*

Mississippi

Copiah-Lincoln Community
   College *A*
Hinds Community College *C*
Jones County Junior College *A*
Northeast Mississippi Community
   College *A*

Missouri

St. Louis Community College
   Florissant Valley *A*
   Forest Park *A*
Southwest Missouri State
   University *B*
State Fair Community College *A*

Nebraska

Central Community College *A*
McCook Community College *A*
Metropolitan Community College *A*
Southeast Community College:
   Lincoln Campus *C,A*

Wayne State College *B*

Nevada

Community College of Southern
   Nevada *A*
Truckee Meadows Community
   College *C,A*

New Hampshire

New Hampshire College *A*
New Hampshire Technical College:
   Berlin *A*
University of New Hampshire *A*

New Jersey

Atlantic Community College *A*
Brookdale Community College *A*
Camden County College *A*

New Mexico

San Juan College *C*

New York

Adirondack Community College
   C,A
Broome Community College *C*
City University of New York: La
   Guardia Community College *A*
Culinary Institute of America *A*
Dutchess Community College *A*
Erie Community College: North
   Campus *A*
Fulton-Montgomery Community
   College *C,A*
Herkimer County Community
   College *A*
Jefferson Community College *A*
Marymount College *B*
Mohawk Valley Community
   College *A*
Monroe Community College *A*
New York Institute of
   Technology *A*
New York University *B,M,D*
Onondaga Community College *A*
Paul Smith's College *A*
Rochester Institute of Technology
   A,B,M
State University of New York
   College of Agriculture and
     Technology at Cobleskill *A*
   College of Agriculture and
     Technology at Morrisville *A*
   College at Plattsburgh *B*
   College of Technology at
     Alfred *A*
   College of Technology at
     Delhi *A*
Suffolk County Community
   College *A*
Sullivan County Community
   College *C,A*
Syracuse University *B*
Tompkins-Cortland Community
   College *A*
Westchester Community College *A*

North Carolina

Alamance Community College *A*
Appalachian State University *B*
Campbell University *B*
Catawba Valley Community
   College *A*
Central Piedmont Community
   College *A*
Fayetteville Technical Community
   College *C,A*
Guilford Technical Community
   College *C,A*
Johnston Community College *C*
Piedmont Community College *C*

Southwestern Community
   College *A*

North Dakota

North Dakota State College of
   Science *A*

Ohio

Ashland University *B*
Bowling Green State University *B*
Cincinnati Technical College *C*
Columbus State Community
   College *A*
Cuyahoga Community College:
   Metropolitan Campus *A*
Kent State University *B*
Miami University: Oxford
   Campus *B*
Ohio State University
   Agricultural Technical
     Institute *A*
   Columbus Campus *B,M,D*
Ohio University *B*
Sinclair Community College *C,A*
University of Toledo *A*
Youngstown State University *A*

Oklahoma

Oklahoma State University
   Technical Branch: Okmulgee *C*
Tulsa Junior College *A*
University of Central Oklahoma *B*

Oregon

Chemeketa Community College *A*
Lane Community College *C,A*
Linn-Benton Community College *A*
Oregon State University *B,M,D*
Portland Community College *A*
Umpqua Community College *C*

Pennsylvania

Bucks County Community
   College *A*
Butler County Community
   College *A*
Harrisburg Area Community
   College *C,A*
Immaculata College *B*
Indiana University of
   Pennsylvania *B*
Keystone Junior College *A*
Montgomery County Community
   College *A*
Northampton County Area
   Community College *A*
Penn State University Park
   Campus *C*
Pennsylvania College of Technology
   C,A
St. Vincent College *B*
Seton Hill College *B*
Westmoreland County Community
   College *C,A*

Rhode Island

Johnson & Wales University *A*
University of Rhode Island *B*

South Carolina

Greenville Technical College *A*
Horry-Georgetown Technical
   College *A*
South Carolina State College *B*
Trident Technical College *A*

South Dakota

Mitchell Vocational Technical
   Institute *C,A*

Tennessee

Chattanooga State Technical
   Community College *C,A*
Shelby State Community College
   C,A
Southern College of Seventh-day
   Adventists *A*
University of Tennessee:
   Chattanooga *B*

Texas

Austin Community College *A*
Brazosport College *C,A*
Central Texas College *A*
Del Mar College *A*
El Centro College *C,A*
Houston Community College *C*
Northeast Texas Community
   College *C,A*
St. Philip's College *A*
Sam Houston State University *B*
San Jacinto College: Central
   Campus *A*
South Plains College *A*
Tarrant County Junior College *A*
Texas Southmost College *A*
Texas State Technical College
   Harlingen *A*
   Waco *A*
Texas Tech University *B*
Texas Woman's University *B*
University of Mary Hardin-
   Baylor *B*

Utah

Dixie College *A*

Vermont

New England Culinary Institute *A*

Virginia

Northern Virginia Community
   College *A*
Radford University *B*

Washington

Clark College *A*
Everett Community College *A*
North Seattle Community
   College *A*
Olympic College *C,A*
Pierce College *A*
Seattle Central Community College
   C,A
Skagit Valley College *C,A*

West Virginia

Fairmont State College *A*
Shepherd College *A*

Wisconsin

Fox Valley Technical College *C,A*
Madison Area Technical College *A*
Mid-State Technical College *A*
Moraine Park Technical College *A*
Northeast Wisconsin Technical
   College *C*
University of Wisconsin: Stout *B*
Waukesha County Technical
   College *A*
Western Wisconsin Technical
   College *C,A*
Wisconsin Indianhead Technical
   College *C*

American Samoa, Caroline Islands, Guam, Marianas, Virgin Islands

Guam Community College *C,A*

Food science and nutrition

Alabama

Alabama Agricultural and
Mechanical University *B*
Auburn University *B,M*
Jacksonville State University *B*
Oakwood College *B*
Samford University *B*
Tuskegee University *B,M*
University of Alabama *B,M*

Arizona

Arizona Western College *A*
Northern Arizona University *B*
Pima Community College *C,A*
University of Arizona *B,M*

Arkansas

Harding University *B*
Ouachita Baptist University *B*
University of Arkansas
Fayetteville *B*
Pine Bluff *B*
University of Central Arkansas *C*

California

California Polytechnic State
University: San Luis Obispo *B*
California State Polytechnic
University: Pomona *B,M*
California State University
Chico *B,M*
Fresno *B*
Long Beach *B,M*
Los Angeles *B,M*
Northridge *B*
San Bernardino *B*
Chaffey Community College *A*
City College of San Francisco *A*
College of the Desert *A*
Cosumnes River College *C,A*
Glendale Community College *C*
Grossmont Community College *C,A*
Long Beach City College *A*
Modesto Junior College *A*
Ohlone College *C,A*
Orange Coast College *C,A*
Pacific Union College *B*
Saddleback College *C,A*
San Diego State University *B*
San Francisco State University *B*
San Joaquin Delta College *C,A*
San Jose State University *B,M*
Santa Rosa Junior College *A*
University of California: Davis
B,M,D

Colorado

Colorado State University *B,M,D*
University of Northern Colorado *B*

Connecticut

St. Joseph College *B,M*
University of Connecticut *B*
University of New Haven *B*

Delaware

Delaware State College *B*
University of Delaware *M*

District of Columbia

Gallaudet University *B*
Howard University *B,M,D*
University of the District of
Columbia *B*

Florida

Florida International University
B,M
Florida State University *B,M*
Miami-Dade Community College *A*
Palm Beach Community College *A*
University of Florida *B*

Georgia

Berry College *B*
Clark Atlanta University *B*
Fort Valley State College *B*
Georgia Southern University *B*
Georgia State University *B*
Macon College *A*
Morris Brown College *B*
University of Georgia *B,M,D*

Hawaii

University of Hawaii at Manoa *B*

Idaho

Idaho State University *B*
Ricks College *A*
University of Idaho *B*

Illinois

Eastern Illinois University *M*
Illinois Central College *A*
Joliet Junior College *A*
KAES College *B*
Northern Illinois University *B,M*
Olivet Nazarene University *B*
Rosary College *B*
Rush University *M*
Shawnee Community College *C,A*
Southern Illinois University at
Carbondale *B*
University of Illinois at Urbana-
Champaign *B,M,D*

Indiana

Ball State University *A,B*
Goshen College *B*
Indiana State University *B,M*
Indiana University Bloomington
B,M
Marian College *B*
Purdue University
Calumet *A*
West Lafayette *B,M,D*
Valparaiso University *B*
Vincennes University *A*

Iowa

Iowa State University *B,M,D*
Teikyo Marycrest University *B*
University of Northern Iowa *B*

Kansas

Central College *A*
Dodge City Community College *A*
Kansas State University *B,M,D*
Pittsburg State University *B*
Sterling College *B*

Kentucky

Berea College *B*
Eastern Kentucky University *B*
Morehead State University *B*
Murray State University *B*
University of Kentucky *B,M*
University of Louisville *B*
Western Kentucky University *B*

Louisiana

Louisiana State University and
Agricultural and Mechanical
College *B*
Louisiana Tech University *B,M*
Nicholls State University *B*
Northeast Louisiana University *B*

Southern University and
Agricultural and Mechanical
College *B*
University of Southwestern
Louisiana *B*

Maine

Southern Maine Technical
College *A*
University of Maine *B,M*

Maryland

Baltimore International Culinary
College *C,A*
Morgan State University *B*
University of Maryland
College Park *B,M*
Eastern Shore *B*

Massachusetts

Atlantic Union College *B*
Framingham State College *B,M*
Hampshire College *B*
Laboure College *A*
MGH Institute of Health
Professions *M*
University of Massachusetts at
Amherst *B*

Michigan

Andrews University *B,M*
Central Michigan University *B*
Eastern Michigan University *B,M*
Madonna University *B*
Marygrove College *B*
Michigan State University *B,M,D*
Northern Michigan University
C,A,B
Wayne State University *B,M*
Western Michigan University *B*

Minnesota

College of St. Benedict *B*
College of St. Catherine: St.
Catherine Campus *B*
College of St. Scholastica *B*
Concordia College: Moorhead *B*
Mankato State University *B,M*
St. John's University *B*
St. Olaf College *B*
University of Minnesota
Crookston *A*
Twin Cities *B,M,D*
University of St. Thomas *B*

Mississippi

Alcorn State University *B*
University of Southern
Mississippi *B*

Missouri

College of the Ozarks *B*
Fontbonne College *B*
Northwest Missouri State
University *B*
St. Louis University *M*
Southeast Missouri State
University *B*
Southwest Missouri State
University *B*
University of Missouri: Columbia
B,M,D

Montana

Montana State University *B*

Nebraska

University of Nebraska
Kearney *B*
Lincoln *B,M,D*
Omaha *B*

Nevada

University of Nevada: Reno *B,M*

New Hampshire

Keene State College *B*
University of New Hampshire *B*

New Jersey

Camden County College *A*
College of St. Elizabeth *B*
Rutgers—The State University of
New Jersey
Cook College *B*
Douglass College *B*
New Brunswick *M,D*
Rutgers College *B*
University College New
Brunswick *B*
Thomas Edison State College *B*

New Mexico

New Mexico State University *B*
University of New Mexico *B,M*

New York

Adirondack Community College
C,A
City University of New York
Brooklyn College *B,M*
Hunter College *B,M*
La Guardia Community
College *A*
Lehman College *B,M*
Queens College *B*
Cornell University *B,M,D*
Dutchess Community College *A*
D'Youville College *B,M*
Long Island University: C. W. Post
Campus *B*
Marymount College *B*
Mohawk Valley Community
College *A*
New York University *C,B,M,D*
Paul Smith's College *A*
Rochester Institute of Technology
A,B
State University of New York
College of Agriculture and
Technology at Cobleskill *A*
College at Buffalo *B,M*
College at Oneonta *B*
College at Plattsburgh *B*
College of Technology at
Farmingdale *A*
Suffolk County Community College:
Eastern Campus *A*
Syracuse University *B,M,D*
Westchester Community College *A*

North Carolina

Appalachian State University *B*
Bennett College *B*
Campbell University *B*
East Carolina University *B*
Meredith College *B*
North Carolina Agricultural and
Technical State University *B,M*
North Carolina Central
University *B*
University of North Carolina at
Greensboro *B,M,D*
Western Carolina University *B*

North Dakota

North Dakota State University *B,M*
University of North Dakota *B*

Ohio

Ashland University *B*
Baldwin-Wallace College *B*
Bluffton College *B*

Bowling Green State University
B,M
Case Western Reserve University
B,M,D
Cincinnati Technical College A
College of Mount St. Joseph B
Kent State University B,M
Miami University: Oxford
Campus B
Notre Dame College of Ohio B
Ohio State University: Columbus
Campus B,M,D
Ohio University B,M
Sinclair Community College A
University of Akron B
University of Cincinnati B,M
University of Dayton B
Youngstown State University B

Oklahoma

Langston University B
Northeastern State University B
Oklahoma State University B,M
University of Central Oklahoma
B,M

Oregon

Oregon State University B,M,D

Pennsylvania

Albright College B
Cheyney University of
Pennsylvania B
Drexel University B,M,D
Edinboro University of
Pennsylvania B
Immaculata College B,M
Indiana University of
Pennsylvania B
Mansfield University of
Pennsylvania B
Marywood College B,M
Mercyhurst College B
Messiah College B
Penn State University Park Campus
B,M,D
St. Vincent College B
Seton Hill College B
University of Pittsburgh B
Westmoreland County Community
College A

Puerto Rico

University of Puerto Rico: Rio
Piedras Campus B

Rhode Island

University of Rhode Island B,M,D

South Carolina

South Carolina State College B,M
Winthrop University B,M

South Dakota

Mount Marty College B
South Dakota State University B

Tennessee

Austin Peay State University A
Carson-Newman College B
David Lipscomb University B
East Tennessee State University
B,M
Hiwassee College A
Memphis State University M
Middle Tennessee State
University B
Tennessee State University B
Tennessee Technological
University B

University of Tennessee
Chattanooga B
Knoxville B,M

Texas

Abilene Christian University B
Baylor University B
Brazosport College C
Incarnate Word College B,M
Lamar University—Beaumont B
Prairie View A&M University B
Sam Houston State University B
South Plains College A
Southwest Texas State University B
Stephen F. Austin State
University B
Texas A&I University B
Texas A&M University B
Texas Christian University B
Texas Southern University B,M
Texas Southmost College A
Texas Tech University B,M,D
Texas Woman's University B,M,D
University of Houston B
University of Mary Hardin-
Baylor B
University of Texas
Austin B,M
Southwestern Medical Center
at Dallas Southwestern
Allied Health Sciences
School B

Utah

Brigham Young University B,M
University of Utah B,M
Utah State University B,M,D

Vermont

University of Vermont B,M

Virginia

Eastern Mennonite College B
Hampton University B,M
James Madison University B
Norfolk State University B
Radford University B
Southwest Virginia Community
College C
Virginia Polytechnic Institute and
State University B,M,D

Washington

Central Washington University B,M
Evergreen State College B
Seattle Pacific University B
University of Washington M
Washington State University B

West Virginia

Fairmont State College A
Marshall University B
West Virginia University B,M
West Virginia Wesleyan College B

Wisconsin

Mount Mary College B,M
University of Wisconsin
Green Bay B
Madison B,M,D
Stevens Point M
Stout B,M
Viterbo College B

Canada

McGill University B,M,D

Food sciences

Alabama

Alabama Agricultural and
Mechanical University B,M,D
Auburn University B,M,D

Arizona

University of Arizona B,M

Arkansas

University of Arkansas B,M,D
Westark Community College C,A

California

California Polytechnic State
University: San Luis Obispo B
California State University:
Fresno B
Chapman University B,M
Mission College C,A
Modesto Junior College A
San Joaquin Delta College A
Santa Rosa Junior College A
Southwestern College A
University of California: Davis
B,M,D

Colorado

Colorado State University B

Delaware

University of Delaware B,M

District of Columbia

University of the District of
Columbia B

Florida

Broward Community College A
Daytona Beach Community
College A
University of Florida B,M,D

Georgia

University of Georgia B,M,D

Hawaii

University of Hawaii at Manoa M

Illinois

City Colleges of Chicago: Malcolm
X College A
Parkland College C,A
University of Illinois at Urbana-
Champaign B,M,D

Indiana

Purdue University B,M,D,W
Vincennes University A

Iowa

Iowa State University B,M,D

Kansas

Kansas State University B,M,D

Kentucky

University of Kentucky B

Louisiana

Louisiana State University and
Agricultural and Mechanical
College B,M,D

Maine

University of Maine
Orono B,M
Presque Isle B

Maryland

University of Maryland: College
Park B,M,D

Massachusetts

Essex Agricultural and Technical
Institute A
Framingham State College B
Greenfield Community College A
Laboure College A
University of Massachusetts at
Amherst B,M,D

Michigan

Kellogg Community College A
Michigan State University B,M,D

Minnesota

University of Minnesota
Crookston A
Twin Cities B,M,D
Willmar Community College A

Mississippi

Hinds Community College C
Mississippi State University B,M,D

Missouri

University of Missouri: Columbia
B,M,D

Montana

Montana State University B

Nebraska

University of Nebraska—Lincoln
B,M,D

New Jersey

Rutgers—The State University of
New Jersey
Cook College B
New Brunswick M,D
University College New
Brunswick B

New Mexico

New Mexico State University B,M

New York

Cornell University B,M,D
Herkimer County Community
College A
State University of New York
College of Agriculture and
Technology at Morrisville A
College of Technology at
Alfred A
College of Technology at
Farmingdale A

North Carolina

North Carolina Agricultural and
Technical State University B
North Carolina State University
B,M,D

North Dakota

North Dakota State University B,M

Ohio

Northwest Technical College A
Ohio State University: Columbus
Campus M,D

Oklahoma

Oklahoma State University M,D

Oregon

Mount Hood Community
College A
Oregon State University B,M,D

Pennsylvania

Delaware Valley College *B*
Drexel University *B,M*
Indiana University of
Pennsylvania *B*
Mansfield University of
Pennsylvania *B*
Penn State University Park Campus
B,M,D

Puerto Rico

University of Puerto Rico
La Montana Regional
College *A*
Mayaguez Campus *M*

Rhode Island

University of Rhode Island *B*

South Carolina

Clemson University *B*

South Dakota

South Dakota State University *B*

Tennessee

Hiwassee College *A*
University of Tennessee: Knoxville
B,M,D

Texas

Stephen F. Austin State
University *B*
Texas A&M University *B,M,D*
Texas Tech University *B,M*

Utah

Brigham Young University *B,M*
Utah State University *B,M,D*

Vermont

University of Vermont *B*

Virginia

Virginia Polytechnic Institute and
State University *B,M,D*

Washington

University of Washington *B,M,D*
Washington State University *M,D*

Wisconsin

Chippewa Valley Technical
College *A*
Moraine Park Technical College *A*
Northeast Wisconsin Technical
College *A*
University of Wisconsin
Madison *B,M,D*
River Falls *B*

Wyoming

University of Wyoming *B,M*

Canada

McGill University *B,M,D*

Foreign languages education

Alabama

Alabama Agricultural and
Mechanical University *B,M*
Alabama State University *B*
Auburn University *B,M*
Birmingham-Southern College *B*
Mobile College *B*
Samford University *B*
Spring Hill College *B*

University of Alabama *B*
University of Montevallo *B*
University of North Alabama *B*

Arizona

Arizona State University *B*
Eastern Arizona College *A*
University of Arizona *B,M*

Arkansas

Arkansas College *B*
Arkansas State University *B*
Harding University *B*
Henderson State University *B*
Ouachita Baptist University *B*
University of Arkansas *B*
University of Central Arkansas *B,M*
Westark Community College *A*

California

Azusa Pacific University *B*
California Baptist College *B*
California Lutheran University *B*
California State University
Bakersfield *B*
Fresno *B*
Los Angeles *B*
Northridge *B*
Sacramento *B*
College of Notre Dame *M*
Monterey Institute of International
Studies *M*
Mount St. Mary's College *B*
Occidental College *M*
University of the Pacific *B*
University of Redlands *B*
University of San Francisco *B*

Colorado

Colorado State University *B*
University of Northern Colorado
B,M
Western State College of
Colorado *B*

Connecticut

Sacred Heart University *B,M*
St. Joseph College *B*
Southern Connecticut State
University *B,M*
University of Hartford *B*
Western Connecticut State
University *B*

Delaware

Delaware State College *B*
University of Delaware *B*

District of Columbia

Georgetown University *M*

Florida

Bethune-Cookman College *B*
Flagler College *B*
Florida Atlantic University *B,M*
Florida International University
B,M
Florida State University *B,M,D*
Jacksonville University *M*
Pensacola Junior College *A*
Stetson University *B*
University of Central Florida *B*
University of Florida *B,M*
University of Miami *M*
University of South Florida *B,M*
University of West Florida *B*

Georgia

Berry College *B*
Georgia Southern University *B,M*
Georgia Southwestern College *B*
Georgia State University *M*

Kennesaw State College *B*
North Georgia College *B,M*
Piedmont College *B*
University of Georgia *B,M,D*
Valdosta State College *B,M*

Idaho

University of Idaho *M*

Illinois

Augustana College *B*
Blackburn College *B*
Concordia University *B*
De Paul University *B*
Elmhurst College *B*
Greenville College *B*
Hebrew Theological College *B*
Illinois College *B*
Illinois Wesleyan University *B*
MacMurray College *B*
Millikin University *B*
North Central College *B*
Northwestern University *B,M*
Olivet Nazarene University *B*
Roosevelt University *B*
Southern Illinois University at
Carbondale *B*
Trinity Christian College *B*
University of Illinois
Chicago *B*
Urbana-Champaign *B,M*
Western Illinois University *B*
Wheaton College *B*

Indiana

Anderson University *B*
Ball State University *B*
Butler University *B*
Franklin College *B*
Goshen College *B*
Indiana State University *B,M*
Indiana University Bloomington
B,M,D
Indiana University—Purdue
University
Fort Wayne *B*
Indianapolis *B*
Manchester College *B*
Marian College *B*
Purdue University *B,M,D*
St. Mary-of-the-Woods College *B*
Taylor University *B*
University of Indianapolis *B*
University of Southern Indiana *B*
Vincennes University *A*

Iowa

Buena Vista College *B*
Clarke College *B*
Cornell College *B*
Dordt College *B*
Drake University *B,M*
Loras College *B*
Luther College *B*
Morningside College *B*
Simpson College *B*
Teikyo Marycrest University *B*
Teikyo Westmar University *B*
University of Dubuque *B*
University of Iowa *B,M*
Upper Iowa University *B*
Wartburg College *B*
William Penn College *B*

Kansas

Baker University *B*
Emporia State University *B*
Friends University *B*
Kansas State University *B*
McPherson College *B*
MidAmerica Nazarene College *B*
St. Mary College *B*

Southwestern College *B*
University of Kansas *B*
Washburn University of Topeka *B*

Kentucky

Asbury College *B*
Berea College *B*
Eastern Kentucky University *B,M*
Georgetown College *B*
Murray State University *B*
Sue Bennett College *A*
Transylvania University *B*
University of Kentucky *B*
University of Louisville *M*
Western Kentucky University *M*

Louisiana

Dillard University *B*
Grambling State University *B*
Louisiana College *B*
Louisiana State University
Agricultural and Mechanical
College *B*
Shreveport *B*
Louisiana Tech University *B*
McNeese State University *B*
Nicholls State University *B*
Northeast Louisiana University *B*
Southeastern Louisiana
University *B*
Southern University and
Agricultural and Mechanical
College *B*
Tulane University *M*
University of New Orleans *B*
University of Southwestern
Louisiana *B*

Maine

University of Maine at Presque
Isle *B*

Maryland

Baltimore Hebrew University *B,M*
Morgan State University *B*
Towson State University *M*
Western Maryland College *B*

Massachusetts

Boston College *B*
Boston University *B,M,W*
Bridgewater State College *M*
Eastern Nazarene College *B*
Elms College *B*
Framingham State College *B*
Pine Manor College *B*
Tufts University *M*
Westfield State College *B*

Michigan

Adrian College *B*
Andrews University *M*
Calvin College *B*
Eastern Michigan University *B*
Grand Valley State University *B*
Hillsdale College *B*
Lansing Community College *A*
Madonna University *B*
Marygrove College *B,M*
Michigan State University *B*
Northern Michigan University *B,M*
Saginaw Valley State University *B*
Wayne State University *B,M*
Western Michigan University *B*

Minnesota

Bemidji State University *B*
Bethel College *B*
College of St. Catherine: St.
Catherine Campus *B*
Concordia College: Moorhead *B*
Gustavus Adolphus College *B*

Mankato State University *B*
Moorhead State University *B*
Rainy River Community College *A*
St. Cloud State University *B*
St. Mary's College of Minnesota *B*
St. Olaf College *B*
University of Minnesota
　Duluth *B*
　Twin Cities *B,M*
Willmar Community College *A*
Winona State University *B*

Mississippi

Blue Mountain College *B*
Delta State University *B*
Mississippi College *B*
Northeast Mississippi Community
　College *A*
University of Mississippi *B*

Missouri

Central Missouri State University *B*
College of the Ozarks *B*
Evangel College *B*
Missouri Western State College *B*
Northeast Missouri State
　University *M*
Northwest Missouri State
　University *B*
Southeast Missouri State
　University *B*
Southwest Missouri State
　University *B*
University of Missouri: Columbia
　B,M,D
Washington University *B,M*
Webster University *B*
Westminster College *B*
William Woods College *B*

Montana

Carroll College *B*
Eastern Montana College *B*
Montana State University *B*
University of Montana *B*

Nebraska

Creighton University *B*
Dana College *B*
Hastings College *B*
University of Nebraska
　Kearney *B,M*
　Lincoln *B*
　Omaha *B*
Wayne State College *B*

New Hampshire

Franklin Pierce College *B*
Keene State College *B*
Plymouth State College of the
　University System of New
　Hampshire *B*
Rivier College *B*

New Jersey

Caldwell College *B*
Fairleigh Dickinson University *M*
Glassboro State College *B*
Kean College of New Jersey *B*
Rider College *B*

Rutgers—The State University of
　New Jersey
　Camden College of Arts and
　　Sciences *B*
　Douglass College *B*
　Livingston College *B*
　New Brunswick *M,D*
　Newark College of Arts and
　　Sciences *B*
　Rutgers College *B*
　University College New
　　Brunswick *B*
　University College Newark *B*
Seton Hall University *B*

New Mexico

New Mexico Highlands
　University *B*
New Mexico State University *B*
University of New Mexico *B*

New York

Adelphi University *B,M*
Canisius College *B*
City University of New York
　Brooklyn College *B,M*
　Hunter College *B,M*
　Lehman College *M*
　Queens College *B,M*
College of Mount St. Vincent *B*
College of New Rochelle *B*
Cornell University *B*
Daemen College *B*
Dowling College *B*
Elmira College *B*
Hofstra University *B,M*
Houghton College *B*
Iona College *B,M*
Ithaca College *B*
Le Moyne College *B*
Long Island University: C. W. Post
　Campus *B,M*
Manhattanville College *M*
Marymount College *B*
Mohawk Valley Community
　College *A*
New York University *B,M*
Niagara University *B,M*
Russell Sage College *B*
St. Bonaventure University *B,M*
St. John's University *B,M*
St. Joseph's College *B*
St. Thomas Aquinas College *B*
Siena College *B*
State University of New York
　Albany *B,M*
　Binghamton *M*
　Buffalo *B,M,D*
　College at Buffalo *B*
　College at Cortland *B,M*
　College at Geneseo *B*
　College at New Paltz *B,M*
　College at Old Westbury *B*
　College at Oneonta *B*
　College at Plattsburgh *B*
　College at Potsdam *B,M*
　Oswego *B,M*
Syracuse University *B,M*
Union College *M*
University of Rochester *M,D*
Wells College *B*

North Carolina

Appalachian State University *B,M*
Barton College *B*
Campbell University *B*
East Carolina University *B*
Gardner-Webb College *B*
Mars Hill College *B*
Methodist College *A,B*
North Carolina Agricultural and
　Technical State University *B*

North Carolina Central University
　B,M
North Carolina State University *B*
St. Andrews Presbyterian College *B*
St. Augustine's College *B*
Salem College *B*
University of North Carolina
　Asheville *C*
　Greensboro *M*
Western Carolina University *B*

North Dakota

Dickinson State University *B*
Minot State University *B*
North Dakota State University *B*
University of North Dakota *B*

Ohio

Ashland University *B*
Baldwin-Wallace College *B*
Bowling Green State University
　B,M
Capital University *B*
Case Western Reserve University *B*
Cedarville College *B*
Heidelberg College *B*
Kent State University *B,M*
Miami University: Oxford
　Campus *B*
Mount Union College *B*
Mount Vernon Nazarene College *B*
Ohio Dominican College *B*
Ohio State University: Columbus
　Campus *B*
Ohio University *B*
Otterbein College *B*
University of Findlay *B*
University of Toledo *B*
Walsh College *B*
Wittenberg University *B*
Wright State University *B*
Youngstown State University *B*

Oklahoma

Oklahoma Baptist University *B*
Oklahoma City University *B*
Oral Roberts University *B*
Southeastern Oklahoma State
　University *B*
University of Central Oklahoma
　B,M
University of Oklahoma *B*
University of Tulsa *B*

Oregon

University of Oregon *M*
Western Oregon State College *B,M*
Willamette University *M*

Pennsylvania

Albright College *B*
Allentown College of St. Francis de
　Sales *B*
Bloomsburg University of
　Pennsylvania *B*
Bucknell University *B*
Cabrini College *B*
California University of
　Pennsylvania *B,M*
Chatham College *B*
Cheyney University of
　Pennsylvania *B*
Clarion University of
　Pennsylvania *B*
Duquesne University *B,M*
East Stroudsburg University of
　Pennsylvania *B*
Edinboro University of
　Pennsylvania *B*
Gannon University *B*
Geneva College *B*
Gettysburg College *B*

Gratz College *C*
Grove City College *B*
Holy Family College *B*
Immaculata College *B*
Indiana University of
　Pennsylvania *B*
Juniata College *B*
La Salle University *B*
Lehigh University *M*
Lincoln University *B*
Lock Haven University of
　Pennsylvania *B*
Lycoming College *B*
Mansfield University of
　Pennsylvania *B*
Marywood College *B*
Moravian College *B*
Point Park College *B*
St. Francis College *C*
St. Joseph's University *C,B*
Seton Hill College *B*
Slippery Rock University of
　Pennsylvania *B*
Temple University *B,M,D*
University of Pennsylvania *M,D*
University of Scranton *B*
Ursinus College *B*
Washington and Jefferson College *B*
West Chester University of
　Pennsylvania *B,M*
Widener University *M*
Wilkes University *B*

Puerto Rico

University of Puerto Rico: Rio
　Piedras Campus *B,M*

Rhode Island

Providence College *B*
Rhode Island College *B,M*
University of Rhode Island *M*

South Carolina

Bob Jones University *B*
Erskine College *B*
Francis Marion College *M*
Presbyterian College *B*
South Carolina State College *B*

South Dakota

Augustana College *B*
Black Hills State University *B*
Northern State University *B*
South Dakota State University *B*
University of South Dakota *B*

Tennessee

David Lipscomb University *B*
East Tennessee State University
　B,M
Freed-Hardeman University *B*
Tennessee Technological
　University *B*
Union University *B,M*
University of Tennessee
　Chattanooga *B*
　Knoxville *B*

Texas

Abilene Christian University *B*
Angelo State University *B*
Baylor University *B*
East Texas Baptist University *B*
Hardin-Simmons University *B*
McMurry University *B*
St. Edward's University *B*
St. Mary's University *B*
Southwest Texas State
　University *M*
Texas Christian University *B*
Texas Wesleyan University *B*
University of Dallas *B*

University of Houston *B,M*
University of Mary Hardin-
    Baylor *B*
University of Texas
    Austin *M,D*
    San Antonio *M*
West Texas State University *B*

Utah

Brigham Young University *B*
Southern Utah University *B*
Weber State University *B*

Vermont

Castleton State College *B*
St. Michael's College *B*
School for International Training *M*
University of Vermont *B*

Virginia

Eastern Mennonite College *B*
Emory and Henry College *B*
George Mason University *M*
Norfolk State University *B*
Old Dominion University *B*
Virginia Polytechnic Institute and
    State University *B,M*
Virginia State University *B*
Virginia Union University *B*
Virginia Wesleyan College *B*

Washington

Central Washington University *B*
Eastern Washington University *B*
Heritage College *B*
Pacific Lutheran University *B*
University of Puget Sound *M*
University of Washington *B*
Washington State University *B*
Western Washington University
    B,M

West Virginia

Bethany College *B*
Davis and Elkins College *B*
Fairmont State College *B*
West Liberty State College *B*
West Virginia University *B*

Wisconsin

Cardinal Stritch College *B*
Carroll College *B*
Carthage College *B*
Lakeland College *B*
Lawrence University *B*
Marian College of Fond du Lac *B*
Marquette University *B,M*
Mount Mary College *B*
St. Norbert College *B*
University of Wisconsin
    Eau Claire *B*
    Green Bay *B*
    La Crosse *B*
    Madison *M*
    Oshkosh *B*
    Platteville *B*
    River Falls *B*
    Whitewater *B*

Wyoming

University of Wyoming *B*

Foreign languages
(multiple emphasis)

Alabama

Birmingham-Southern College *B*
Judson College *B*

Alaska

University of Alaska Fairbanks *B*

Arkansas

Philander Smith College *B*
Southern Arkansas University *B*

California

California State University: San
    Bernardino *B*
College of the Sequoias *A*
Fresno City College *A*
Glendale Community College *A*
Imperial Valley College *A*
Long Beach City College *C,A*
MiraCosta College *A*
Occidental College *B*
Pomona College *B*
Saddleback College *A*
San Diego City College *A*
San Diego Mesa College *A*
Santa Monica College *A*
Santa Rosa Junior College *A*
Scripps College *B*
Solano Community College *A*
Southwestern College *A*
University of California: Riverside
    B,M
West Valley College *A*
Westmont College *B*
Whittier College *B*

Colorado

Colorado College *B*
Metropolitan State College of
    Denver *B*
Pikes Peak Community College *A*
University of Colorado at Denver *B*
University of Denver *B,M*
University of Northern Colorado *M*
University of Southern Colorado *B*

Connecticut

St. Joseph College *B*
University of Connecticut *D*
University of Hartford *B*
Yale University *B,M,D*

Florida

Bethune-Cookman College *B*
Brevard Community College *A*
Daytona Beach Community
    College *A*
Eckerd College *B*
Edison Community College *A*
Gulf Coast Community College *A*
Miami-Dade Community College *A*
New College of the University of
    South Florida *B*
Stetson University *B*
University of Central Florida *B*
University of Miami *M,D*
University of South Florida *B*

Georgia

Atlanta Metropolitan College *A*
Bainbridge College *A*
Berry College *B*
Clark Atlanta University *B,M*
DeKalb College *A*
Emory University *B*
Gordon College *A*
Macon College *A*
Middle Georgia College *A*
South Georgia College *A*
University of Georgia *B,M*
Wesleyan College *B*

Hawaii

Hawaii Loa College *B*

Idaho

North Idaho College *A*
Northwest Nazarene College *B*

Illinois

Concordia University *B*
Illinois Central College *A*
Illinois State University *M*
Knox College *B*
Lincoln Land Community
    College *A*
Millikin University *B*
Olivet Nazarene University *B*
Principia College *B*
Rend Lake College *A*
Rosary College *B*
Shimer College *B*
Southern Illinois University
    Carbondale *B,M*
    Edwardsville *B*
University of Chicago *B*
Wheaton College *B*

Indiana

DePauw University *B*
Earlham College *B*
Indiana State University *B,M*
Indiana University Bloomington
    B,M,D
University of Notre Dame *B,M*

Iowa

Buena Vista College *B*
Cornell College *B*
Morningside College *B*
University of Northern Iowa *M*

Kansas

Barton County Community
    College *A*
Benedictine College *B*
Emporia State University *B*
Fort Hays State University *B*
Friends University *B*
Hutchinson Community College *A*
McPherson College *B*
MidAmerica Nazarene College *B*
Neosho County Community
    College *A*
Southwestern College *B*

Kentucky

Asbury College *B*
Georgetown College *B*
Kentucky Wesleyan College *B*

Louisiana

Centenary College of Louisiana *B*
Louisiana College *B*
Tulane University *B,M*
University of Southwestern
    Louisiana *B*

Maine

University of Maine *B*

Maryland

College of Notre Dame of
    Maryland *B*
Mount St. Mary's College *B*
Towson State University *M*

Massachusetts

Amherst College *B*
Assumption College *B*
Boston College *B,M,D*
Brandeis University *B,M,D*
Bridgewater State College *M*
Clark University *B*
College of the Holy Cross *B*
Eastern Nazarene College *B*
Elms College *B*

Emmanuel College *B*
Gordon College *B*
Harvard and Radcliffe Colleges *B*
Harvard University *M,D*
Simon's Rock College of Bard *B*
Stonehill College *B*
Tufts University *B,M*
University of Massachusetts
    Boston *B*
    Lowell *B*
Wellesley College *B*
Wheaton College *B*

Michigan

Concordia College *B*
Eastern Michigan University *B*
Grand Valley State University *B*
Hope College *B*
Lansing Community College *A*
Marygrove College *B*
Michigan Technological
    University *C*
St. Mary's College *B*
University of Detroit Mercy *B*
Wayne State University *B*

Minnesota

Bethany Lutheran College *A*
Carleton College *B*
Concordia College: St. Paul *B*
Moorhead State University *B*
St. Cloud State University *A*
St. Mary's College of Minnesota *B*

Mississippi

Blue Mountain College *B*
Mississippi College *B*
Mississippi State University *B,M*
University of Southern
    Mississippi *B*

Missouri

Central Methodist College *B*
College of the Ozarks *B*
Mineral Area College *A*
Stephens College *B*
University of Missouri
    Columbia *M,D*
    Kansas City *M*
Webster University *B*
William Woods College *B*

Nebraska

University of Nebraska—Lincoln
    B,M,D

Nevada

University of Nevada
    Las Vegas *B,M*
    Reno *M*

New Hampshire

Dartmouth College *B*
Rivier College *M*
St. Anselm College *B*

New Jersey

Bergen Community College *A*
Brookdale Community College *A*
Monmouth College *B*
Princeton University *B,D*
St. Peter's College *B*
Seton Hall University *B*
Stockton State College *B*
Thomas Edison State College *B*

New Mexico

University of New Mexico *B*

New York

Adelphi University *B*
Alfred University *B*

City University of New York
  City College *B*
  College of Staten Island *B*
  Hunter College *B*
Colgate University *B*
College of Mount St. Vincent *B*
Cornell University *M,D*
Dominican College of Blauvelt *B*
Dowling College *B*
Elmira College *B*
Eugene Lang College/New School
  for Social Research *B*
Fordham University *B*
Hamilton College *B*
Hobart College *B*
Hofstra University *B*
King's College *B*
Long Island University
  Brooklyn Campus *B*
  C. W. Post Campus *B*
Manhattan College *B*
Manhattanville College *B*
Mohawk Valley Community
  College *A*
Nazareth College of Rochester *B*
New York University *B,M,D*
Orange County Community
  College *A*
St. Bonaventure University *B*
St. Lawrence University *B*
St. Thomas Aquinas College *B*
Sarah Lawrence College *B*
State University of New York
  Purchase *B*
  Stony Brook *D*
Syracuse University *B,M,D*
Touro College *B*
Union College *B*
United States Military Academy *B*
Wagner College *B*
Wells College *B*
William Smith College *B*

North Carolina
Campbell University *B*
Peace College *A*
St. Andrews Presbyterian College *B*
University of North Carolina at
  Chapel Hill *B*

North Dakota
University of North Dakota *B*

Ohio
College of Wooster *B*
Kenyon College *B*
Lake Erie College *B*
Ohio State University: Columbus
  Campus *B,M,D*
Ohio University *B*
Union Institute *B,D*
University of Dayton *B*
Walsh College *B*
Wittenberg University *B*
Wright State University *B*

Oklahoma
Cameron University *B*
Oklahoma Baptist University *B*
Southeastern Oklahoma State
  University *B*
University of Central Oklahoma *B*

Oregon
Lewis and Clark College *B*
Pacific University *B*
Portland State University *B*
Southern Oregon State College *B*
University of Oregon
  Eugene *B,M,D*
  Robert Donald Clark Honors
   College *B*

University of Portland *B*
Western Oregon State College *B*

Pennsylvania
Allentown College of St. Francis de
  Sales *B*
Bryn Mawr College *B*
California University of
  Pennsylvania *B*
Cedar Crest College *B*
Chatham College *B*
Duquesne University *B*
Edinboro University of
  Pennsylvania *B*
Elizabethtown College *B*
Gannon University *B*
Immaculata College *B*
Juniata College *B*
Lebanon Valley College of
  Pennsylvania *B*
Rosemont College *B*
Susquehanna University *B*
Thiel College *B*
University of Pennsylvania *B,M,D*
University of Pittsburgh *M*
University of Scranton *B*
Wilson College *B*
York College of Pennsylvania *A*

South Carolina
The Citadel *B*
Clemson University *B*
Converse College *B*
Newberry College *B*
Presbyterian College *B*
Winthrop University *B*

Tennessee
Austin Peay State University *B*
King College *B*
Lambuth University *B*
Memphis State University *B,M*
Middle Tennessee State
  University *B*
University of Tennessee:
  Knoxville *D*

Texas
El Paso Community College *A*
Houston Community College *A*
Southern Methodist University *B*
Southwestern University *B*
Texas A&M University *B*
Texas Southmost College *A*
University of Dallas *B*
Victoria College *A*
Western Texas College *A*

Utah
Southern Utah University *B*

Vermont
Marlboro College *B*
St. Michael's College *B*
Trinity College of Vermont *B*

Virginia
Christopher Newport College *B*
Ferrum College *B*
George Mason University *B,M*
James Madison University *B*
Liberty University *B*
Longwood College *B*
Sweet Briar College *B*
Virginia Commonwealth
  University *B*
Virginia Military Institute *B*
Virginia State University *B*
Washington and Lee University *B*

Washington
Centralia College *A*
Evergreen State College *B*
Seattle Central Community
  College *A*
Washington State University *B,M*

West Virginia
West Virginia University *B,M*

Wisconsin
Beloit College *B*
Concordia University Wisconsin *B*
Ripon College *B*

Wyoming
Central Wyoming College *A*
Northwest College *A*
Western Wyoming Community
  College *A*

Canada
McGill University *B*

Forensic studies

Alabama
Jacksonville State University *B*
University of Alabama in
  Birmingham *M*

California
National University *M*

Connecticut
University of New Haven *B,M*

District of Columbia
George Washington University *M*

Florida
University of Central Florida *B*

Georgia
Albany State College *A*

Indiana
Indiana University Bloomington
  B,M

Kentucky
Eastern Kentucky University *B*

Michigan
Lake Superior State University *B*
Michigan State University *B*

New York
City University of New York: John
  Jay College of Criminal Justice
  B,M
Medaille College *C*
State University of New York
  College at Buffalo *B*

Ohio
Clark State Community College *A*
Ohio University *B*

Pennsylvania
York College of Pennsylvania *A*

Texas
University of Texas Southwestern
  Medical Center at Dallas
  Southwestern Allied Health
  Sciences School *M*

Virginia
New River Community College *C,A*

Forest products processing technology

Alabama
Alabama Agricultural and
  Mechanical University *B*

California
Santa Rosa Junior College *C,A*
University of California: Berkeley
  B,D

Florida
Pensacola Junior College *A*

Georgia
Waycross College *A*

Idaho
University of Idaho *B,M,D*

Illinois
Southern Illinois University at
  Carbondale *B,M*

Indiana
Purdue University *B*

Louisiana
Northeast Louisiana University *A*

Maine
University of Maine *A,B,M*

Minnesota
Itasca Community College:
  Arrowhead Region *A*
University of Minnesota: Twin
  Cities *B*
Vermilion Community College *A*

Mississippi
Jones County Junior College *A*
Mississippi State University *B,M*

New York
State University of New York
  College of Agriculture and
   Technology at Morrisville *A*
  College of Environmental
   Science and Forestry
   A,B,M,D

North Carolina
Montgomery Community College *C*
North Carolina Agricultural and
  Technical State University *B*
North Carolina State University
  B,M,D
Southeastern Community College *A*

Ohio
Hocking Technical College *A*
Ohio State University Agricultural
  Technical Institute *A*

Oregon
Oregon State University *B,M,D*

Pennsylvania
Keystone Junior College *A*
Penn State University Park Campus
  C,B
Pennsylvania College of
  Technology *A*

South Carolina

Clemson University *B*

Texas

Stephen F. Austin State
University *B*

Utah

Southern Utah University *B*

Virginia

Dabney S. Lancaster Community
College *A*

Washington

University of Washington *B*

Wisconsin

Northland College *B*

Wyoming

Casper College *A*

Forestry production and processing

Alabama

Alabama Southern Community
College *A*
Auburn University *B*
Lurleen B. Wallace State Junior
College *A*
Reid State Technical College *A*

California

Humboldt State University *B,M*

Illinois

Southern Illinois University at
Carbondale *B,M*

Indiana

Purdue University *B,M,D*
Vincennes University *A*

Iowa

Iowa State University *B,M,D*

Louisiana

Louisiana Tech University *B*

Maine

Unity College *A*

Minnesota

Itasca Community College:
Arrowhead Region *A*
Rainy River Community College *A*
University of Minnesota: Twin
Cities *B*
Vermilion Community College *A*
Willmar Community College *A*

Mississippi

Jones County Junior College *A*

New York

State University of New York
College of Environmental
Science and Forestry *B,M,D*
College of Technology at
Delhi *A*

North Carolina

Haywood Community College *A*

Ohio

Ohio State University: Columbus
Campus *B*

Oregon

Central Oregon Community
College *A*
Oregon State University *B,M,D*

Pennsylvania

Keystone Junior College *A*
Pennsylvania College of
Technology *A*

Texas

Stephen F. Austin State
University *B*

West Virginia

West Virginia University *B*

Forestry and related sciences

Alabama

Alabama Agricultural and
Mechanical University *B*
Auburn University *B,M,D*
Chattahoochee Valley Community
College *A*
James H. Faulkner State
Community College *A*
Shoals Community College *A*
Snead State Junior College *A*

Alaska

Sheldon Jackson College *C,A*

Arizona

Eastern Arizona College *A*
Northern Arizona University *B,M*
University of Arizona *B,M,D*
Yavapai College *A*

Arkansas

University of Arkansas at
Monticello *B*

California

Bakersfield College *A*
Citrus College *C*
College of the Redwoods *C,A*
Columbia College *A*
Feather River College *C,A*
Humboldt State University *C,B,M*
Kings River Community College *A*
Modesto Junior College *A*
Mount San Antonio College *C,A*
Santa Rosa Junior College *A*
Sierra College *A*
Southwestern College *A*
University of California: Berkeley
B,M

Colorado

Colorado State University *B,M,D*
Mesa State College *A*
Trinidad State Junior College *A*

Connecticut

Yale University *M,D*

Florida

Daytona Beach Community
College *A*
Gulf Coast Community College *A*
Lake City Community College *A*
Miami-Dade Community College *A*
Pensacola Junior College *A*
Stetson University *B*
University of Florida *B,M,D*

Georgia

Abraham Baldwin Agricultural
College *A*
Atlanta Metropolitan College *A*
Bainbridge College *A*
Brunswick College *A*
Clayton State College *A*
Darton College *A*
Gainesville College *A*
Georgia College *B*
Gordon College *A*
Mercer University *B*
Middle Georgia College *A*
Reinhardt College *A*
University of Georgia *B,M,D*
Young Harris College *A*

Idaho

North Idaho College *A*
Ricks College *A*
University of Idaho *B,M,D*

Illinois

Augustana College *B*
Joliet Junior College *A*
Shawnee Community College *A*
Southern Illinois University at
Carbondale *B,M*
University of Illinois at Urbana-
Champaign *B,M,D*

Indiana

Ball State University *B*
Purdue University *B,M,D*
Vincennes University *A*

Iowa

Iowa Lakes Community College *A*
Iowa State University *B,M,D*

Kansas

Baker University *B*
Colby Community College *A*
Hutchinson Community College *A*
Kansas State University *B*

Kentucky

University of Kentucky *B,M*

Louisiana

Centenary College of Louisiana *B*
Louisiana State University and
Agricultural and Mechanical
College *B,M,D*
Louisiana Tech University *B*

Maine

Unity College *A,B*
University of Maine
Fort Kent *A*
Orono *A,B,M,D*
Presque Isle *B*

Maryland

Allegany Community College *A*

Massachusetts

Berkshire Community College *A*
Harvard University *M*
University of Massachusetts at
Amherst *B,M,D*

Michigan

Eastern Michigan University *B*
Michigan State University *B,M,D*
Michigan Technological University
A,B,M,D
University of Michigan *M*

Minnesota

Itasca Community College:
Arrowhead Region *A*

Northland Community College *A*
Rainy River Community College *A*
Rochester Community College *A*
University of Minnesota
Crookston *A*
Twin Cities *M,D*
Vermilion Community College *A*
Willmar Community College *A*
Winona State University *A*

Mississippi

Holmes Community College *A*
Mississippi Delta Community
College *A*
Mississippi State University *B,M,D*

Missouri

East Central College *A*
University of Missouri: Columbia
B,M,D

Montana

Flathead Valley Community
College *A*
Salish Kootenai College *A*
University of Montana *B,M,D*

New Hampshire

New Hampshire Technical College:
Berlin *A*
University of New Hampshire *B,M*

New Jersey

Rutgers—The State University of
New Jersey: Cook College *B*
Thomas Edison State College *A,B*

New Mexico

Northern New Mexico Community
College *A*

New York

Adirondack Community College *A*
Fulton-Montgomery Community
College *A*
Herkimer County Community
College *A*
Hudson Valley Community
College *A*
Jefferson Community College *A*
Paul Smith's College *A*
State University of New York
College of Agriculture and
Technology at Morrisville *A*
College of Environmental
Science and Forestry
A,B,M,D
College at Geneseo *B*
College of Technology at
Canton *A*
College of Technology at
Delhi *A*
Sullivan County Community
College *A*
Westchester Community College *A*

North Carolina

Brevard College *A*
Chowan College *A*
College of the Albemarle *A*
Duke University *M*
Haywood Community College *A*
High Point University *B*
Montgomery Community College *C*
North Carolina State University
B,M,D
Wayne Community College *A*
Western Piedmont Community
College *A*

North Dakota

North Dakota State University: Bottineau and Institute of Forestry *C,A*

Ohio

Hocking Technical College *A*
Kent State University *B*
Marietta College *B*
Ohio State University: Columbus Campus *B,M*
Wittenberg University *B*

Oklahoma

Eastern Oklahoma State College *A*
Oklahoma State University *B,M*

Oregon

Central Oregon Community College *C,A*
Chemeketa Community College *A*
Mount Hood Community College *C,A*
Oregon State University *B,M,D*
Southwestern Oregon Community College *A*
Treasure Valley Community College *A*

Pennsylvania

Elizabethtown College *B*
Juniata College *B*
Keystone Junior College *C,A*
Lebanon Valley College of Pennsylvania *B*
Lycoming College *B*
Moravian College *B*
Penn State University Park Campus *B,M,D*
Thiel College *B*

South Carolina

Clemson University *B,M,D*
Francis Marion College *B*
Horry-Georgetown Technical College *A*

Tennessee

Hiwassee College *A*
Martin Methodist College *A*
University of the South *B*
University of Tennessee: Knoxville *B,M*

Texas

Baylor University *B*
Panola College *C*
Stephen F. Austin State University *B,M,D*
Texas A&M University *B,M,D*
Texas Southmost College *A*

Utah

Dixie College *A*
Southern Utah University *A*
Utah State University *B,M,D*

Vermont

Marlboro College *B*
Sterling College *A*
University of Vermont *B,M*

Virginia

Dabney S. Lancaster Community College *A*
Virginia Polytechnic Institute and State University *B,M,D*

Washington

Centralia College *A*
Eastern Washington University *B*
Green River Community College *A*
Spokane Community College *A*
University of Washington *B,M,D*
Washington State University *B,M*

West Virginia

College of West Virginia *A*
Davis and Elkins College *B*
Glenville State College *A*
Marshall University *B,M*
Potomac State College of West Virginia University *A*
West Virginia University *B,M,D*
West Virginia Wesleyan College *B*

Wisconsin

Mount Senario College *B*
Northland College *B*
Ripon College *B*
University of Wisconsin
    Madison *B,M,D*
    Stevens Point *B*

Wyoming

Northwest College *A*

French

Alabama

Alabama Agricultural and Mechanical University *B*
Alabama State University *B*
Auburn University *B,M*
Birmingham-Southern College *B*
Jacksonville State University *B*
Mobile College *B*
Samford University *B*
University of Alabama
    Birmingham *B*
    Huntsville *B*
    Tuscaloosa *B,M*
University of Montevallo *B*
University of North Alabama *B*
University of South Alabama *B*

Arizona

Arizona State University *B,M*
Eastern Arizona College *A*
Glendale Community College *A*
Northern Arizona University *B*
University of Arizona *B,M,D*
Yavapai College *A*

Arkansas

Arkansas State University *B*
Arkansas Tech University *B*
Harding University *B*
Hendrix College *B*
Ouachita Baptist University *B*
Southern Arkansas University *B*
University of Arkansas
    Fayetteville *B,M*
    Little Rock *B*
University of Central Arkansas *B*
Westark Community College *A*

California

California Lutheran University *B*
California State University
    Chico *B*
    Dominguez Hills *B*
    Fresno *B*
    Fullerton *B,M*
    Hayward *B*
    Long Beach *B,M*
    Los Angeles *B,M*
    Northridge *B*
    Sacramento *B,M*
    San Bernardino *B*
    Stanislaus *B*
Cerritos Community College *A*
Chabot College *A*
Chaffey Community College *A*
Chapman University *B*
Citrus College *A*
Claremont McKenna College *B*
College of the Desert *A*
College of Notre Dame *B*
De Anza College *A*
El Camino College *A*
Foothill College *A*
Grossmont Community College *C,A*
Humboldt State University *B*
Irvine Valley College *A*
Long Beach City College *C,A*
Los Angeles City College *A*
Los Angeles Mission College *A*
Los Angeles Valley College *A*
Loyola Marymount University *B*
Mendocino College *A*
Merced College *A*
Mills College *B*
MiraCosta College *A*
Modesto Junior College *A*
Monterey Institute of International Studies *B,M*
Mount St. Mary's College *B*
Napa Valley College *A*
Occidental College *B*
Ohlone College *A*
Orange Coast College *A*
Pacific Union College *B*
Pepperdine University *B*
Pitzer College *B*
Pomona College *B*
St. Mary's College of California *B*
San Diego City College *A*
San Diego State University *B,M*
San Francisco State University *B,M*
San Joaquin Delta College *A*
San Jose City College *A*
San Jose State University *B,M*
Santa Barbara City College *A*
Santa Clara University *B*
Santa Monica College *A*
Santa Rosa Junior College *A*
Scripps College *B*
Solano Community College *A*
Sonoma State University *B*
Southwestern College *A*
Stanford University *B,M,D*
University of California
    Berkeley *B,M,D*
    Davis *B,M,D*
    Irvine *B,M,D*
    Los Angeles *B,M,D*
    Riverside *B,M*
    San Diego *B,M,D*
    Santa Barbara *B,M,D*
    Santa Cruz *B,D*
University of La Verne *B*
University of the Pacific *B*
University of Redlands *B*
University of San Diego *B*
University of San Francisco *B*
University of Southern California *B,M,D*
Ventura College *A*
Westmont College *B*
Whittier College *B*

Colorado

Colorado College *B*
Colorado State University *B,M*
Regis College of Regis University *B*
University of Colorado
    Boulder *B,M,D*
    Denver *B*
University of Denver *B,M*
University of Northern Colorado *B*
Western State College of Colorado *B*

Connecticut

Albertus Magnus College *B*
Central Connecticut State University *B,M*
Connecticut College *B,M*
Fairfield University *B*
Sacred Heart University *A,B*
St. Joseph College *B*
Southern Connecticut State University *B,M*
Trinity College *B*
University of Connecticut *B,M,D*
University of Hartford *B*
Wesleyan University *B*
Yale University *B,M,D*

Delaware

Delaware State College *B*
University of Delaware *B,M*
Wesley College *A*

District of Columbia

American University *B,M*
Catholic University of America *B,M,D*
Gallaudet University *B*
George Washington University *B*
Georgetown University *B*
Howard University *B,M,D*
Trinity College *B*
University of the District of Columbia *A,B*

Florida

Barry University *B*
Eckerd College *B*
Florida Atlantic University *B,M*
Florida International University *B*
Florida Southern College *B*
Florida State University *B,M,D*
Jacksonville University *B*
Miami-Dade Community College *A*
New College of the University of South Florida *B*
Okaloosa-Walton Community College *A*
Pensacola Junior College *A*
Rollins College *B*
Stetson University *B*
University of Central Florida *B*
University of Florida *B,M,D*
University of Miami *B*
University of South Florida *B,M*
University of Tampa *A,B*
University of West Florida *B*

Georgia

Agnes Scott College *B*
Albany State College *B*
Andrew College *A*
Augusta College *B*
Berry College *B*
Clark Atlanta University *B*
Clayton State College *A*
Darton College *A*
Emory University *B,M,D*
Fort Valley State College *B*
Georgia College *B*
Georgia Southern University *B*
Georgia State University *B,M*
Kennesaw State College *B*
Mercer University *B*
Morehouse College *B*
Morris Brown College *B*
North Georgia College *B*
Oxford College of Emory University *A*
Shorter College *B*
Spelman College *B*
University of Georgia *B,M*
Valdosta State College *B*
West Georgia College *B*

Young Harris College *A*

Hawaii

Hawaii Loa College *B*
University of Hawaii at Manoa *B,M*

Idaho

Albertson College *B*
Boise State University *B*
Idaho State University *B*
Ricks College *A*
University of Idaho *B,M*

Illinois

Augustana College *B*
Black Hawk College *A*
Bradley University *B*
City Colleges of Chicago: Chicago
  City-Wide College *C*
De Paul University *B*
Eastern Illinois University *B*
Elmhurst College *B*
Greenville College *B*
Illinois College *B*
Illinois State University *B*
Illinois Wesleyan University *B*
Joliet Junior College *A*
Knox College *B*
Lake Forest College *B*
Loyola University of Chicago *B*
MacMurray College *B*
Millikin University *B*
Monmouth College *B*
North Central College *B*
Northeastern Illinois University *B*
Northern Illinois University *B,M*
Northwestern University *B,M,D*
Principia College *B*
Rend Lake College *A*
Richland Community College *A*
Rockford College *B*
Roosevelt University *B,M*
Rosary College *B*
St. Xavier University *B*
Southern Illinois University
  Carbondale *B,M*
  Edwardsville *B*
University of Chicago *B,M,D*
University of Illinois
  Chicago *B,M*
  Urbana-Champaign *B,M,D*
Western Illinois University *B*
Wheaton College *B*

Indiana

Anderson University *B*
Ball State University *B*
Butler University *B*
DePauw University *B*
Earlham College *B*
Franklin College *B*
Grace College *B*
Hanover College *B*
Indiana State University *B,M*
Indiana University
  Bloomington *B,M,D*
  Northwest *B*
  South Bend *B*
Indiana University—Purdue
  University
    Fort Wayne *B*
    Indianapolis *B*
Manchester College *B*
Marian College *B*
Purdue University
  Calumet *B*
  West Lafayette *B,M,D*
St. Mary-of-the-Woods College *B*
St. Mary's College *B*
Taylor University *B*
University of Evansville *B*
University of Indianapolis *B*

University of Notre Dame *B,M*
Valparaiso University *B*
Vincennes University *A*
Wabash College *B*

Iowa

Central College *B*
Clarke College *B*
Coe College *B*
Cornell College *B*
Drake University *B*
Graceland College *B*
Grinnell College *B*
Iowa State University *B*
Kirkwood Community College *A*
Loras College *B*
Luther College *B*
Morningside College *B*
Northwestern College *B*
St. Ambrose University *B*
Simpson College *B*
University of Dubuque *B*
University of Iowa *B,M,D*
University of Northern Iowa *B,M*
Wartburg College *B*

Kansas

Baker University *B*
Benedictine College *B*
Kansas City Kansas Community
  College *A*
Kansas State University *B,M*
Pittsburg State University *B*
Pratt Community College *A*
Southwestern College *B*
University of Kansas *B,M,D*
Washburn University of Topeka *B*
Wichita State University *B*

Kentucky

Asbury College *B*
Berea College *B*
Centre College *B*
Eastern Kentucky University *B*
Georgetown College *B*
Morehead State University *B*
Murray State University *B*
Transylvania University *B*
University of Kentucky *B,M,D*
University of Louisville *B,M*
Western Kentucky University *B*

Louisiana

Centenary College of Louisiana *B*
Dillard University *B*
Grambling State University *B*
Louisiana College *B*
Louisiana State University
  Agricultural and Mechanical
    College *B,M,D*
  Shreveport *B*
Louisiana Tech University *B,M*
Loyola University *B*
McNeese State University *B*
Nicholls State University *B*
Northeast Louisiana University *B*
Southeastern Louisiana
  University *B*
Southern University at New
  Orleans *B*
Southern University and
  Agricultural and Mechanical
  College *B*
Tulane University *B,M,D*
University of New Orleans *B,M*
University of Southwestern
  Louisiana *M*
Xavier University of Louisiana *B*

Maine

Bates College *B*
Bowdoin College *B*

Colby College *B*
University of Maine
  Fort Kent *B*
  Orono *B,M*
  Presque Isle *B*
University of Southern Maine *B*

Maryland

College of Notre Dame of
  Maryland *B*
Frostburg State University *B*
Goucher College *B*
Hood College *B*
Johns Hopkins University *B,M,D*
Loyola College in Maryland *B*
Morgan State University *B*
Mount St. Mary's College *B*
Salisbury State University *B*
Towson State University *B*
University of Maryland
  Baltimore County *B*
  College Park *B,M,D*
Washington College *B*
Western Maryland College *B*

Massachusetts

Amherst College *B*
Anna Maria College for Men and
  Women *B*
Assumption College *B*
Atlantic Union College *B*
Boston College *B,M,D*
Boston University *B,M,D*
Bradford College *B*
Brandeis University *B*
Bridgewater State College *B*
Clark University *B*
College of the Holy Cross *B*
Eastern Nazarene College *B*
Elms College *B*
Emmanuel College *M*
Framingham State College *B*
Gordon College *B*
Harvard and Radcliffe Colleges *B*
Harvard University *M,D*
Massachusetts Institute of
  Technology *B*
Mount Holyoke College *B*
Northeastern University *B*
Regis College *B*
Roxbury Community College *A*
Simmons College *B,M*
Simon's Rock College of Bard *B*
Smith College *B,M*
Suffolk University *B*
Tufts University *B,M*
University of Massachusetts
  Amherst *B,M,D*
  Boston *B*
  Dartmouth *B*
  Lowell *B*
Wellesley College *B*
Westfield State College *B*
Wheaton College *B*
Williams College *B*
Worcester State College *B*

Michigan

Adrian College *A,B*
Albion College *B*
Alma College *B*
Andrews University *B,M*
Aquinas College *B*
Calvin College *B*
Central Michigan University *B*
Eastern Michigan University *B*
Grand Valley State University *B*
Hillsdale College *B*
Hope College *B*
Kalamazoo College *B*
Lansing Community College *A*
Madonna University *B*

Marygrove College *B*
Michigan State University *B,M,D*
Northern Michigan University *B,M*
Oakland University *B*
Olivet College *B*
Saginaw Valley State University *B*
Spring Arbor College *B*
University of Detroit Mercy *B*
University of Michigan
  Ann Arbor *B,M,D*
  Flint *B*
Wayne State University *B,M*
Western Michigan University *B*

Minnesota

Augsburg College *B*
Bemidji State University *B*
Carleton College *B*
College of St. Benedict *B*
College of St. Catherine: St.
  Catherine Campus *B*
Concordia College: Moorhead *B*
Gustavus Adolphus College *B*
Hamline University *B*
Macalester College *B*
Mankato State University *B*
Moorhead State University *B*
St. Cloud State University *B*
St. John's University *B*
St. Mary's College of Minnesota *B*
St. Olaf College *B*
University of Minnesota
  Duluth *B*
  Morris *B*
  Twin Cities *B,M,D*
University of St. Thomas *B*
Winona State University *B*

Mississippi

Delta State University *B*
Millsaps College *B*
Mississippi College *B*
Rust College *B*
University of Mississippi *B,M*

Missouri

Central Methodist College *B*
Central Missouri State University *B*
College of the Ozarks *B*
Drury College *B*
East Central College *A*
Evangel College *B*
Jefferson College *A*
Lincoln University *B*
Lindenwood College *B*
Missouri Western State College *B*
Northeast Missouri State
  University *B*
Northwest Missouri State
  University *B*
Rockhurst College *B*
St. Louis University *B*
Southeast Missouri State
  University *B*
Southwest Missouri State
  University *B*
Stephens College *B*
University of Missouri
  Columbia *B,M*
  Kansas City *B*
  St. Louis *B*
Washington University *B,M,D*
Webster University *B*
Westminster College *B*
William Jewell College *B*
William Woods College *B*

Montana

Carroll College *B*
Montana State University *B*
Northern Montana College *B*
Rocky Mountain College *B*

University of Montana *B,M*

Nebraska

Creighton University *B*
Nebraska Wesleyan University *B*
University of Nebraska
    Kearney *B,M*
    Lincoln *B,M*
    Omaha *B*
Wayne State College *B*
Western Nebraska Community
    College: Scottsbluff Campus *A*

Nevada

University of Nevada
    Las Vegas *B,M*
    Reno *B*

New Hampshire

Dartmouth College *B*
Franklin Pierce College *B*
Keene State College *B*
Plymouth State College of the
    University System of New
    Hampshire *B*
Rivier College *B*
St. Anselm College *C,B*
University of New Hampshire *B*

New Jersey

Bloomfield College *B*
Brookdale Community College *A*
Caldwell College *B*
College of St. Elizabeth *B*
Drew University *B*
Fairleigh Dickinson University *B*
Georgian Court College *B*
Kean College of New Jersey *B*
Monmouth College *B*
Montclair State College *B,M*
Rider College *B*
Rutgers—The State University of
    New Jersey
    Camden College of Arts and
        Sciences *B*
    Douglass College *B*
    Livingston College *B*
    New Brunswick *M,D*
    Newark College of Arts and
        Sciences *B*
    Rutgers College *B*
    University College Camden *B*
    University College New
        Brunswick *B*
St. Peter's College *B*
Seton Hall University *B*
Stockton State College *B*
William Paterson College of New
    Jersey *B*

New Mexico

Eastern New Mexico University *B*
New Mexico State University *B*
University of New Mexico *B,M*

New York

Adelphi University *B*
Alfred University *B*
Bard College *B*
Barnard College *B*
Canisius College *B*
City University of New York
    Brooklyn College *B,M*
    City College *B*
    Graduate School and
        University Center *D*
    Hunter College *B,M*
    Lehman College *B*
    Queens College *B,M*
    Queensborough Community
        College *A*
    York College *B*

Colgate University *B*
College of Mount St. Vincent *B*
College of New Rochelle *B*
Columbia University
    Columbia College *B*
    New York *M,D*
    School of General Studies *B*
Cornell University *B,M,D*
Daemen College *B*
Elmira College *B*
Fordham University *B,M,D*
Hamilton College *B*
Hartwick College *B*
Hobart College *B*
Hofstra University *B*
Houghton College *B*
Iona College *B*
Ithaca College *B*
Jamestown Community College *A*
Le Moyne College *B*
Long Island University: C. W. Post
    Campus *B*
Manhattan College *B*
Manhattanville College *B*
Marist College *B*
Marymount College *B*
Mercy College *B*
Molloy College *B*
Nazareth College of Rochester *B*
New York University *B,M,D*
Niagara University *B*
Onondaga Community College *A*
Orange County Community
    College *A*
Pace University
    College of White Plains *B*
    New York *B*
    Pleasantville/Briarcliff *B*
Russell Sage College *B*
St. Bonaventure University *B*
St. John Fisher College *B*
St. John's University *B*
St. Joseph's College *B*
St. Lawrence University *B*
St. Thomas Aquinas College *B*
Sarah Lawrence College *B*
Siena College *B*
Skidmore College *B*
State University of New York
    Albany *B,M*
    Binghamton *B,M*
    Buffalo *B,M,D*
    Purchase *B*
    Stony Brook *B,M*
    College at Brockport *B*
    College at Buffalo *B*
    College at Cortland *B*
    College at Fredonia *B*
    College at Geneseo *B*
    College at New Paltz *B*
    College at Old Westbury *C*
    College at Oneonta *B*
    College at Plattsburgh *B*
    College at Potsdam *B*
    Oswego *B*
Syracuse University *B,M*
United States Military Academy *B*
University of Rochester *B,M*
University of the State of New
    York: Regents College *B*
Vassar College *B,M*
Wagner College *B*
Wells College *B*
William Smith College *B*
Yeshiva University *B*

North Carolina

Appalachian State University *B,M*
Barton College *B*
Brevard College *A*
Campbell University *B*
Catawba College *B*

Chowan College *A*
Davidson College *B*
Duke University *B,D*
East Carolina University *B*
Elon College *B*
Gardner-Webb College *B*
Greensboro College *B*
Guilford College *B*
High Point University *B*
Lenoir-Rhyne College *B*
Mars Hill College *B*
Meredith College *B*
Methodist College *A,B*
North Carolina Agricultural and
    Technical State University *B,M*
North Carolina Central University
    B,M
North Carolina State University *B*
Queens College *B*
St. Andrews Presbyterian College *B*
St. Augustine's College *B*
Salem College *B*
University of North Carolina
    Asheville *B*
    Chapel Hill *B,M,D*
    Charlotte *B*
    Greensboro *B,M*
    Wilmington *B*
Wake Forest University *B*
Western Carolina University *B*

North Dakota

Minot State University *B*
North Dakota State University *B*
University of North Dakota *B*

Ohio

Ashland University *B*
Baldwin-Wallace College *B*
Bowling Green State University
    B,M
Capital University *B*
Case Western Reserve University
    B,M,D
Central State University *B*
Cleveland State University *B*
College of Wooster *B*
Denison University *B*
Franciscan University of
    Steubenville *B*
Hiram College *B*
John Carroll University *B*
Kent State University *B,M*
Kenyon College *B*
Lourdes College *A,B*
Marietta College *B*
Miami University: Oxford Campus
    B,M
Mount Union College *B*
Muskingum College *B*
Notre Dame College of Ohio *B*
Oberlin College *B*
Ohio Northern University *B*
Ohio State University: Columbus
    Campus *B,M,D*
Ohio University *B,M*
Ohio Wesleyan University *B*
Otterbein College *B*
University of Akron *B,M*
University of Cincinnati *B*
University of Dayton *B*
University of Toledo *B,M*
Walsh College *B*
Wilmington College *B*
Wittenberg University *B*
Wright State University *B*
Xavier University *A,B*
Youngstown State University *B*

Oklahoma

Northeastern State University *B*
Oklahoma Baptist University *B*

Oklahoma City University *B*
Oklahoma State University *B*
Oral Roberts University *B*
Phillips University *B*
Rose State College *A*
Southeastern Oklahoma State
    University *B*
Tulsa Junior College *A*
University of Central Oklahoma *B*
University of Oklahoma *B,M,D*
University of Tulsa *B*

Oregon

Central Oregon Community
    College *A*
Lewis and Clark College *B*
Linfield College *B*
Northwest Christian College *B*
Oregon State University *B*
Pacific University *B*
Portland Community College *A*
Portland State University *B,M*
Reed College *B*
University of Oregon
    Eugene *B,M*
    Robert Donald Clark Honors
        College *B*
Willamette University *B*

Pennsylvania

Albright College *B*
Allegheny College *B*
Allentown College of St. Francis de
    Sales *B*
Alvernia College *B*
Bloomsburg University of
    Pennsylvania *B*
Bryn Mawr College *B,M*
Bucknell University *B*
Cabrini College *B*
California University of
    Pennsylvania *B*
Carnegie Mellon University *B*
Cedar Crest College *B*
Chatham College *B*
Chestnut Hill College *A,B*
Clarion University of
    Pennsylvania *B*
Dickinson College *B*
Duquesne University *B*
East Stroudsburg University of
    Pennsylvania *B*
Eastern College *B*
Edinboro University of
    Pennsylvania *B*
Elizabethtown College *B*
Franklin and Marshall College *B*
Gannon University *B*
Gettysburg College *B*
Grove City College *B*
Haverford College *B*
Holy Family College *B*
Immaculata College *A,B*
Indiana University of
    Pennsylvania *B*
Juniata College *B*
King's College *B*
Kutztown University of
    Pennsylvania *B,M*
La Roche College *C*
La Salle University *B*
Lafayette College *B*
Lebanon Valley College of
    Pennsylvania *B*
Lehigh University *B*
Lincoln University *B*
Lock Haven University of
    Pennsylvania *B*
Lycoming College *B*
Mansfield University of
    Pennsylvania *B*
Marywood College *B*

Messiah College B
Millersville University of
Pennsylvania B,M
Moravian College B
Muhlenberg College B
Northeastern Christian Junior
College A
Penn State University Park Campus
B,M,D
Rosemont College B
St. Francis College B
St. Joseph's University B
St. Vincent College B
Seton Hill College B
Shippensburg University of
Pennsylvania B
Slippery Rock University of
Pennsylvania B
Susquehanna University B
Swarthmore College B
Temple University B,M
Thiel College B
University of Pennsylvania B,M,D
University of Pittsburgh B,M,D
University of Scranton B
Ursinus College B
Villanova University B
Washington and Jefferson College B
West Chester University of
Pennsylvania B,M
Westminster College B
Widener University B
Wilkes University B

Puerto Rico

Pontifical Catholic University of
Puerto Rico B
University of Puerto Rico
Mayaguez Campus B
Rio Piedras Campus B
University of the Sacred Heart B

Rhode Island

Brown University B,M,D
Providence College B
Rhode Island College B,M
Salve Regina University B
University of Rhode Island B,M

South Carolina

Bob Jones University B
The Citadel B
Clemson University B
Coker College B
College of Charleston B
Columbia College B
Converse College B
Erskine College B
Francis Marion College B
Furman University B
Lander College B
Newberry College B
Presbyterian College B
South Carolina State College B
University of South Carolina B,M
Wofford College B

South Dakota

Augustana College B
Northern State University B
South Dakota State University B
University of South Dakota B

Tennessee

Belmont University B
Carson-Newman College B
David Lipscomb University B
East Tennessee State University B
Fisk University B
King College B
Lambuth University B
Martin Methodist College A

Middle Tennessee State University
B,M
Rhodes College B
Shelby State Community College A
Southern College of Seventh-day
Adventists B
Tennessee State University B
Tennessee Technological
University B
Union University B
University of the South B
University of Tennessee
Chattanooga B
Knoxville B,M
Martin B
Vanderbilt University B,M,D

Texas

Abilene Christian University B
Angelo State University B
Austin College B
Austin Community College A
Baylor University B
Bee County College A
Central Texas College A
Collin County Community College
District A
East Texas State University B,M
Hardin-Simmons University B
Houston Baptist University B
Kilgore College A
Lamar University—Beaumont B
Lon Morris College A
Midland College A
Rice University B,M,D
St. Mary's University B
Sam Houston State University B
Southern Methodist University B
Southwest Texas State University B
Southwestern University B
Stephen F. Austin State
University B
Texas Christian University B
Texas Southern University B
Texas Southmost College A
Texas Tech University B,M
Texas Wesleyan University B
Trinity University B
University of Dallas B
University of Houston B,M
University of North Texas B,M
University of St. Thomas B
University of Texas
Arlington B,M
Austin B,M,D
El Paso B
San Antonio B

Utah

Brigham Young University B,M
Southern Utah University B
University of Utah B
Utah State University B
Weber State University B

Vermont

Bennington College B
Castleton State College B
Marlboro College B
Middlebury College B
Norwich University B
St. Michael's College B
Trinity College of Vermont B
University of Vermont B,M

Virginia

Bridgewater College B
Christendom College B
Christopher Newport College B
College of William and Mary B
Eastern Mennonite College B
Emory and Henry College B

Ferrum College B
Hampden-Sydney College B
Hampton University M
Hollins College B
Liberty University B
Lynchburg College B
Mary Baldwin College B
Mary Washington College B
Old Dominion University B
Radford University B
Randolph-Macon College B
Randolph-Macon Woman's
College B
Roanoke College B
Sweet Briar College B
University of Richmond B,W
University of Virginia B,M,D
Virginia Commonwealth
University B
Virginia Polytechnic Institute and
State University B
Virginia Union University B
Virginia Wesleyan College B
Washington and Lee University B

Washington

Big Bend Community College A
Central Washington University B
Eastern Washington University B,M
Everett Community College A
Evergreen State College B
Gonzaga University B
Pacific Lutheran University B
Seattle Central Community
College A
Seattle University B
Spokane Falls Community
College A
Tacoma Community College A
University of Puget Sound B
University of Washington B,M,D
Walla Walla College B
Western Washington University
B,M
Whitman College B
Whitworth College B

West Virginia

Bethany College B
Davis and Elkins College B
Fairmont State College B
Marshall University B
Potomac State College of West
Virginia University A
Shepherd College B
West Virginia University B,M
Wheeling Jesuit College B

Wisconsin

Beloit College B
Cardinal Stritch College B
Carroll College B
Carthage College B
Edgewood College B
Lawrence University B
Marquette University B,M
Mount Mary College B
Ripon College B
St. Norbert College B
University of Wisconsin
Eau Claire B
Green Bay B
La Crosse B
Madison B,M,D
Milwaukee B
Oshkosh B
Platteville B
River Falls B
Stevens Point B
Whitewater B

Wyoming

Casper College A
Eastern Wyoming College A
University of Wyoming B,M
Western Wyoming Community
College A

Canada

McGill University C,B,M,D

France

American University of Paris B

Switzerland

American College of Switzerland B
Franklin College: Switzerland B

Funeral services/
mortuary science

Alabama

Bishop State Community College A
Jefferson State Community
College A

California

San Francisco College of Mortuary
Science C,A

District of Columbia

University of the District of
Columbia A

Florida

Lynn University A
Miami-Dade Community College A
St. Petersburg Junior College A

Georgia

Gupton Jones College of Funeral
Service C,A

Illinois

City Colleges of Chicago
Chicago City-Wide College
C,A
Malcolm X College A
Southern Illinois University at
Carbondale A

Indiana

Mid-America College of Funeral
Service A
Vincennes University A

Kansas

Dodge City Community College A
Hutchinson Community College A
Kansas City Kansas Community
College C,A

Louisiana

McNeese State University A

Maryland

Catonsville Community College A

Massachusetts

Mount Ida College C,A

Michigan

Ferris State University A
Wayne State University B

Minnesota

University of Minnesota: Twin
Cities B
Willmar Community College A

Missouri

St. Louis Community College at Forest Park *A*

Nebraska

Wayne State College *B*

New Jersey

Mercer County Community College *C,A*

New York

American Academy McAllister Institute of Funeral Service *C,A*
City University of New York: La Guardia Community College *A*
Columbia-Greene Community College *A*
Fulton-Montgomery Community College *A*
Herkimer County Community College *A*
Hudson Valley Community College *A*
St. John's University *B*
State University of New York College of Technology at Canton *A*

North Carolina

Fayetteville Technical Community College *A*

Ohio

Cincinnati College of Mortuary Science *A,B*

Oklahoma

University of Central Oklahoma *B*

Pennsylvania

Gannon University *A,B*
Northampton County Area Community College *C,A*
Pittsburgh Institute of Mortuary Science *C,A*
Point Park College *A,B*

South Carolina

Florence-Darlington Technical College *A*

Tennessee

John A. Gupton College *C,A*

Texas

San Antonio College *A*

Virginia

John Tyler Community College *A*

Genetics, human and animal

Alabama

Auburn University *M,D*
University of Alabama in Birmingham *M,D*

Arizona

University of Arizona *M,D*

California

California Institute of Technology *D,W*
California State University
Fresno *B*
Fullerton *B*
San Diego State University *D*

Stanford University *M,D*
University of California
Berkeley *B,M,D*
Davis *B,M,D*
San Francisco *D*

Connecticut

University of Connecticut *M,D*
Wesleyan University *B*
Yale University *M,D*

Delaware

University of Delaware *M,D*

District of Columbia

George Washington University *M,D*
Howard University *M,D*

Florida

Florida Institute of Technology *D*
New College of the University of South Florida *B*

Georgia

Emory University *M,D*
University of Georgia *B,M,D*

Hawaii

University of Hawaii at Manoa *M,D*

Illinois

Southern Illinois University at Edwardsville *B*
University of Chicago *B,M,D*
University of Illinois at Urbana-Champaign *B,D*

Indiana

Ball State University *B*
Indiana University Bloomington *M,D*
Indiana University—Purdue University at Indianapolis *M,D,W*
Purdue University *B,M,D,W*

Iowa

Iowa State University *B,M,D*
University of Iowa *D*

Kansas

Kansas State University *B,M,D*
University of Kansas *D*

Louisiana

Louisiana State University Medical Center *M,D*
Tulane University *M,D*

Maryland

University of Maryland: Baltimore *M,D*

Massachusetts

Brandeis University *D*
Hampshire College *B*
Harvard University *D*
Massachusetts Institute of Technology *B,M,D,W*
Tufts University *M,D*
Worcester Polytechnic Institute *B,M*

Michigan

Michigan State University *D*
University of Michigan *M,D*

Minnesota

University of Minnesota: Twin Cities *B,M,D*

Mississippi

Mississippi State University *M*

Missouri

University of Missouri: Columbia *M,D*
Washington University *D*

New Hampshire

University of New Hampshire *M,D*

New Jersey

Rutgers—The State University of New Jersey
Camden College of Arts and Sciences *B*
Douglass College *B*
Livingston College *B*
Rutgers College *B*
University College New Brunswick *B*
Stevens Institute of Technology *B*

New York

Cornell University *B,M,D*
New York University *D*
Rockefeller University *D*
State University of New York
Albany *D*
Stony Brook *D*
College of Environmental Science and Forestry *B,M,D*
University of Rochester *M,D*
Yeshiva University *M,D*

North Carolina

Duke University *B*
North Carolina State University *M,D*
University of North Carolina at Chapel Hill *D*

Ohio

Case Western Reserve University *D*
Ohio State University: Columbus Campus *B,M,D*
Ohio Wesleyan University *B*
Wittenberg University *B*

Oregon

Oregon State University *M,D*
University of Oregon *M,D*

Pennsylvania

Carnegie Mellon University *B,M,D,W*
Lehigh University *M,D*
Penn State
Milton S. Hershey Medical Center *M,D*
University Park Campus *M,D*
University of Pennsylvania *M,D*
University of Pittsburgh *M,D*

Texas

Texas A&M University *B,M,D*
University of Houston *M,D*
University of Texas Health Science Center at Houston *M,D,W*

Utah

Brigham Young University *M,D*

Vermont

Marlboro College *B*

Virginia

Averett College *B*
Virginia Commonwealth University *M,D*
Virginia Polytechnic Institute and State University *D*

Washington

University of Washington *M,D*
Washington State University *M,D*

West Virginia

West Virginia University *M,D*

Wisconsin

Marquette University *M,D*
University of Wisconsin: Madison *B,M,D*

Canada

McGill University *M*

Geochemistry

Arizona

Northern Arizona University *B*

California

California Institute of Technology *B,M,D,W*
California State University: Fullerton *M*
Occidental College *B*
University of California: Los Angeles *M,D*

Colorado

Colorado School of Mines *M,D,W*

District of Columbia

George Washington University *M,D*

Illinois

University of Chicago *B,M,D*

Indiana

Purdue University *B,M,D*
St. Joseph's College *B*

Massachusetts

Bridgewater State College *B*
Harvard University *M,D*
Massachusetts Institute of Technology *B,M,D,W*

Michigan

Hope College *B*
University of Michigan *M,D*

Montana

Montana College of Mineral Science and Technology *M*

Nebraska

York College *A*

Nevada

University of Nevada: Reno *M,D*

New Jersey

Princeton University *D*

New Mexico

New Mexico Institute of Mining and Technology *M,D*

New York

Colgate University *B*
Columbia University
Columbia College *B*
School of General Studies *B*
Cornell University *M,D*

State University of New York
  Albany *M,D*
    College at Cortland *B*
    College at Fredonia *B*
    College at Geneseo *B*
    Oswego *B*

Ohio

Bowling Green State University *B*
Ohio State University: Columbus
  Campus *B,M,D*

Oklahoma

University of Tulsa *M,D*

Oregon

University of Oregon *M,D*

Pennsylvania

West Chester University of
  Pennsylvania *B*

Rhode Island

Brown University *B,M,D*

Washington

Western Washington University *B*

Geography

Alabama

Auburn University *B*
Jacksonville State University *B*
University of Alabama *B,M*
University of North Alabama *B*
University of South Alabama *B*

Alaska

University of Alaska Fairbanks *B*

Arizona

Arizona State University *B,M,D*
Northern Arizona University *B,M*
Prescott College *B*
University of Arizona *B,M,D*
Yavapai College *A*

Arkansas

Arkansas State University *B*
University of Arkansas *B,M*
University of Central Arkansas *B*
Westark Community College *A*

California

Bakersfield College *A*
California State University
  Chico *B,M*
  Dominguez Hills *B*
  Fresno *B,M*
  Fullerton *B,M*
  Hayward *B,M*
  Long Beach *B,M*
  Los Angeles *B,M*
  Northridge *B,M*
  Sacramento *B*
  San Bernardino *B*
  Stanislaus *B*
Cerritos Community College *A*
Chabot College *A*
Chaffey Community College *A*
College of the Desert *A*
Crafton Hills College *A*
El Camino College *A*
Foothill College *A*
Grossmont Community College *A*
Humboldt State University *B*
Irvine Valley College *A*
Los Angeles Valley College *A*
Merced College *A*

Modesto Junior College *A*
Napa Valley College *A*
Ohlone College *A*
Orange Coast College *A*
Saddleback College *A*
San Diego State University *B,M*
San Francisco State University *B,M*
San Jose State University *B,M*
Santa Barbara City College *A*
Santa Rosa Junior College *A*
Sonoma State University *B*
Southwestern College *A*
University of California
  Berkeley *B,M,D*
  Davis *B,M,D*
  Irvine *B*
  Los Angeles *B,M,D*
  Riverside *B,M,D*
  Santa Barbara *B,M,D*
University of Southern California *B*
Ventura College *A*
West Hills Community College *A*

Colorado

Trinidad State Junior College *A*
United States Air Force
  Academy *B*
University of Colorado
  Boulder *B,M,D*
  Colorado Springs *B*
  Denver *B*
University of Denver *B,M,D*
University of Northern Colorado *B*

Connecticut

Central Connecticut State
  University *B,M*
Southern Connecticut State
  University *B*
University of Connecticut *B,M*

Delaware

University of Delaware *B,M*

District of Columbia

George Washington University *B,M*
University of the District of
  Columbia *B*

Florida

Daytona Beach Community
  College *A*
Florida Atlantic University *B,M*
Florida State University *B,M*
Jacksonville University *B*
Palm Beach Community College *A*
Stetson University *B*
University of Florida *B,M,D*
University of Miami *B,M*
University of South Florida *B,M*
University of Tampa *A*

Georgia

Atlanta Metropolitan College *A*
Georgia State University *B,M*
Morris Brown College *B*
University of Georgia *B,M,D*
West Georgia College *B*

Hawaii

University of Hawaii
  Hilo *B*
  Manoa *B,M,D*

Idaho

College of Southern Idaho *A*
Ricks College *A*
University of Idaho *B,M,D*

Illinois

Augustana College *B*
Bradley University *B*

Chicago State University *B,M*
Concordia University *B*
De Paul University *B*
Elmhurst College *B*
Illinois Central College *A*
Illinois State University *B*
Joliet Junior College *A*
Lincoln Land Community
  College *A*
Morton College *A*
Northeastern Illinois University *B*
Northern Illinois University *B,M*
Southern Illinois University
  Carbondale *B,M,D*
  Edwardsville *B,M*
Triton College *A*
University of Chicago *B,M,D*
University of Illinois
  Chicago *B,M*
  Urbana-Champaign *B,M,D*
Western Illinois University *B,M*

Indiana

Ball State University *B*
DePauw University *B*
Indiana State University *B,M,D*
Indiana University
  Bloomington *B,M,D*
  Southeast *B*
Indiana University—Purdue
  University at Indianapolis *B*
Valparaiso University *B*
Vincennes University *A*

Iowa

Drake University *B*
University of Iowa *B,M,D*
University of Northern Iowa *B,M*

Kansas

Emporia State University *B*
Kansas State University *B,M*
Pittsburg State University *B*
University of Kansas *B,M,D*

Kentucky

Eastern Kentucky University *B*
Morehead State University *B*
Murray State University *B,M*
Northern Kentucky University *B*
University of Kentucky *B,M,D*
University of Louisville *B*
Western Kentucky University *B,M*

Louisiana

Grambling State University *B*
Louisiana State University
  Agricultural and Mechanical
    College *B,M,D*
  Shreveport *B*
Louisiana Tech University *B*
Northeast Louisiana University *B*
University of New Orleans *B*
University of Southwestern
  Louisiana *B,M*

Maine

University of Maine at Farmington
  A,B
University of Southern Maine *B*

Maryland

Frostburg State University *B*
Johns Hopkins University *B,M,D*
Montgomery College: Rockville
  Campus *C*
Morgan State University *B*
Salisbury State University *B*
Towson State University *B*
University of Maryland
  Baltimore County *B*
  College Park *B,M,D*

Massachusetts

Boston University *B,M,D*
Bridgewater State College *B,M*
Clark University *B,D*
Fitchburg State College *B*
Framingham State College *B*
Hampshire College *B*
Mount Holyoke College *B*
Salem State College *B,M*
University of Massachusetts
  Amherst *B,M*
  Boston *B*
Worcester State College *B*

Michigan

Aquinas College *B*
Calvin College *B*
Central Michigan University *B*
Eastern Michigan University *B,M*
Lansing Community College *A*
Michigan State University *B,M,D*
Northern Michigan University
  A,B,M
University of Michigan: Flint *B*
Wayne State University *B,M*
Western Michigan University *B,M*

Minnesota

Bemidji State University *B*
Gustavus Adolphus College *B*
Macalester College *B*
Mankato State University *B,M*
Rainy River Community College *A*
St. Cloud State University *B,M*
University of Minnesota
  Duluth *B*
  Twin Cities *B,M,D*
Willmar Community College *A*

Mississippi

University of Southern Mississippi
  B,M

Missouri

Central Missouri State University *B*
East Central College *A*
Northwest Missouri State
  University *B*
Southeast Missouri State
  University *B*
Southwest Missouri State
  University *B*
University of Missouri
  Columbia *B,M*
  Kansas City *B*

Montana

Montana State University *B*
University of Montana *B,M*

Nebraska

Bellevue College *B*
Concordia College *B*
Peru State College *B*
University of Nebraska
  Kearney *B*
  Lincoln *B,M,D*
  Omaha *B,M*
Wayne State College *B*

Nevada

University of Nevada: Reno *B*

New Hampshire

Dartmouth College *B*
Keene State College *B*
Plymouth State College of the
  University System of New
  Hampshire *B*
University of New Hampshire *B*

New Jersey

Glassboro State College *B*
Jersey City State College *B*
Montclair State College *B*
Rutgers—The State University of
New Jersey
    Cook College *B*
    Douglass College *B*
    Livingston College *B*
    New Brunswick *M,D*
    Rutgers College *B*
    University College New
      Brunswick *B*
Thomas Edison State College *B*
William Paterson College of New
Jersey *B*

New Mexico

New Mexico State University *B,M*
University of New Mexico *B,M*

New York

City University of New York
    City College *B*
    Hunter College *B,M*
    Lehman College *B*
Colgate University *B*
Hofstra University *B*
Long Island University: C. W. Post
Campus *B*
State University of New York
    Albany *B,M*
    Binghamton *B,M*
    Buffalo *B,M,D*
    College at Buffalo *B*
    College at Cortland *B*
    College at Geneseo *B*
    College at New Paltz *B*
    College at Oneonta *B*
    College at Plattsburgh *B*
Syracuse University *B,M,D*
United States Military Academy *B*
University of the State of New
    York: Regents College *B*
Vassar College *B*

North Carolina

Appalachian State University *B,M*
East Carolina University *B,M*
Fayetteville State University *B*
North Carolina Central
    University *B*
University of North Carolina
    Chapel Hill *B,M,D*
    Charlotte *B,M*
    Greensboro *B*
    Wilmington *B*
Western Carolina University *B*

North Dakota

University of North Dakota *B,M*

Ohio

Bowling Green State University
    B,M
Central State University *B*
Kent State University *B,M,D*
Lakeland Community College *A*
Miami University: Oxford Campus
    B,M
Ohio State University: Columbus
    Campus *B,M,D*
Ohio University *B,M*
Ohio Wesleyan University *B*
Union Institute *B,D*
University of Akron *B,M*
University of Cincinnati *B,M,D*
University of Toledo *B,M*
Wittenberg University *B*
Wright State University
    Dayton *B*
    Lake Campus *A*

Youngstown State University *B*

Oklahoma

Langston University *B*
Northeastern State University *B*
Oklahoma State University *B,M*
Southwestern Oklahoma State
    University *B*
Tulsa Junior College *A*
University of Oklahoma *B,M,D*

Oregon

Central Oregon Community
    College *A*
Oregon State University *B,M,D*
Portland Community College *A*
Portland State University *B,M*
Southern Oregon State College *B*
University of Oregon
    Eugene *B,M,D*
    Robert Donald Clark Honors
      College *B*
Western Oregon State College *B*

Pennsylvania

Bloomsburg University of
    Pennsylvania *B*
Bucknell University *B*
California University of
    Pennsylvania *B,M*
Cheyney University of
    Pennsylvania *B*
Clarion University of
    Pennsylvania *B*
East Stroudsburg University of
    Pennsylvania *B*
Edinboro University of
    Pennsylvania *B*
Indiana University of Pennsylvania
    B,M
Kutztown University of
    Pennsylvania *B*
Lock Haven University of
    Pennsylvania *B*
Mansfield University of
    Pennsylvania *B*
Millersville University of
    Pennsylvania *B*
Penn State University Park Campus
    B,M,D
Shippensburg University of
    Pennsylvania *B*
Slippery Rock University of
    Pennsylvania *B*
Temple University *B,M*
University of Pittsburgh at
    Johnstown *B*
Villanova University *B*
West Chester University of
    Pennsylvania *B,M*

Puerto Rico

University of Puerto Rico: Rio
    Piedras Campus *B*

Rhode Island

Rhode Island College *B*

South Carolina

Francis Marion College *B*
University of South Carolina *B,M,D*

South Dakota

Augustana College *B*
South Dakota State University *B,M*

Tennessee

Carson-Newman College *B*
East Tennessee State University
    B,M
Memphis State University *B,M*

Middle Tennessee State
    University *B*
Motlow State Community
    College *A*
University of Tennessee
    Knoxville *B,M,D*
    Martin *B*

Texas

Collin County Community College
    District *A*
Del Mar College *A*
East Texas State University *B,M*
Prairie View A&M University *B*
Sam Houston State University *B*
Southwest Texas State University
    B,M
Stephen F. Austin State
    University *B*
Texas A&I University *B*
Texas A&M University *B,M,D*
Texas Tech University *B*
University of North Texas *B*
University of Texas
    Austin *B,M,D*
    San Antonio *B*
West Texas State University *B*
Western Texas College *A*

Utah

Brigham Young University *B,M*
University of Utah *B,M,D*
Utah State University *B*
Weber State University *B*

Vermont

Marlboro College *B*
Middlebury College *B*
University of Vermont *B,M*

Virginia

Emory and Henry College *B*
George Mason University *B,M*
James Madison University *B*
Mary Washington College *B*
Old Dominion University *B*
Radford University *B*
Virginia Polytechnic Institute and
    State University *B,M*

Washington

Central Washington University *B*
Eastern Washington University *B*
Everett Community College *A*
Olympic College *A*
Seattle Central Community
    College *A*
University of Washington *B,M,D*
Western Washington University
    B,M

West Virginia

Concord College *B*
Marshall University *B,M*
Shepherd College *B*
West Virginia University *B,M*

Wisconsin

Carroll College *B*
Carthage College *B*
University of Wisconsin
    Eau Claire *B*
    Green Bay *B*
    La Crosse *B*
    Madison *B,M,D*
    Milwaukee *B,M,D*
    Oshkosh *B*
    Parkside *B*
    Platteville *B*
    River Falls *B*
    Stevens Point *B*
    Whitewater *B*

Wyoming

University of Wyoming *B,M*

Canada

McGill University *B,M,D*

Geological engineering

Alabama

Auburn University *B*

Alaska

University of Alaska Fairbanks *B,M*

Arizona

University of Arizona *B,M,D*

California

University of California: Berkeley *B*

Colorado

Colorado School of Mines
    B,M,D,W

Idaho

North Idaho College *A*
University of Idaho *B,M*

Illinois

Bradley University *B*
University of Illinois at Chicago *D*

Indiana

Purdue University *B,M,D*
University of Notre Dame *B*

Massachusetts

Massachusetts Institute of
    Technology *B*

Michigan

Michigan Technological University
    B,M
University of Michigan *B*

Minnesota

University of Minnesota: Twin
    Cities *B,M,D*
Willmar Community College *A*

Mississippi

University of Mississippi *B*

Missouri

East Central College *A*
University of Missouri: Rolla *B,M,D*
Washington University *B*

Montana

Montana College of Mineral
    Science and Technology *B,M*

Nebraska

York College *A*

Nevada

University of Nevada: Reno *B,M*

New Mexico

New Mexico Institute of Mining
    and Technology *B,M,D*
New Mexico State University
    B,M,D

New York

Columbia University: School of
    Engineering and Applied Science
    B,M,D,W
Cornell University *M*

North Dakota

University of North Dakota *B*

Oklahoma

University of Oklahoma *B,M,D*
University of Tulsa *B,M,D*

Oregon

Oregon State University *B*

Pennsylvania

Drexel University *M,D*
Lehigh University *B*

South Dakota

South Dakota School of Mines and
  Technology *B,M,D*

Utah

Brigham Young University *B*
University of Utah *B,M,D*

Washington

Washington State University *B,M*

Wisconsin

University of Wisconsin: Madison *B*

Geology

Alabama

Auburn University *B,M*
University of Alabama
  Birmingham *B*
  Tuscaloosa *B,M,D,W*
University of South Alabama *B*

Alaska

University of Alaska Fairbanks
  B,M,D

Arizona

Arizona State University *B,M,D*
Arizona Western College *A*
Eastern Arizona College *A*
Glendale Community College *A*
Northern Arizona University *B,M*
Pima Community College *A*
Prescott College *B*
University of Arizona *B,M,D*

Arkansas

Arkansas Tech University *B*
University of Arkansas
  Fayetteville *B,M*
  Monticello *B*

California

Bakersfield College *A*
California Institute of Technology
  B,M,D,W
California Lutheran University *B*
California State Polytechnic
  University: Pomona *B*
California State University
  Bakersfield *B,M*
  Chico *B*
  Dominguez Hills *B*
  Fresno *B,M*
  Fullerton *B*
  Hayward *B,M*
  Long Beach *B,M*
  Los Angeles *B,M*
  Northridge *B,M*
  Sacramento *B*
  Stanislaus *B*
Cerritos Community College *A*
Chabot College *A*
Chaffey Community College *A*

College of the Desert *A*
De Anza College *A*
El Camino College *A*
Feather River College *A*
Foothill College *A*
Grossmont Community College *A*
Humboldt State University *B,M*
Irvine Valley College *A*
Los Angeles Valley College *A*
Modesto Junior College *A*
Moorpark College *A*
Napa Valley College *A*
Occidental College *B*
Ohlone College *A*
Orange Coast College *A*
Pomona College *B*
Saddleback College *A*
San Diego State University *B,M*
San Francisco State University *B,M*
San Joaquin Delta College *A*
San Jose State University *B,M*
Santa Barbara City College *A*
Santa Monica College *A*
Santa Rosa Junior College *A*
Sierra College *A*
Sonoma State University *B*
Southwestern College *A*
Stanford University *B,M,D*
University of California
  Berkeley *B,M,D*
  Davis *B,M,D*
  Los Angeles *B,M,D*
  Riverside *B,M,D*
  Santa Barbara *B,M,D*
  Santa Cruz *B,D*
University of the Pacific *B*
University of Southern California
  B,M,D
Ventura College *A*
West Hills Community College *A*
West Valley College *A*
Whittier College *B*

Colorado

Adams State College *B*
Colorado College *B*
Colorado School of Mines *M,D,W*
Colorado State University *B,M*
Fort Lewis College *B*
Mesa State College *A,B*
Pikes Peak Community College *A*
University of Colorado
  Boulder *B,M,D*
  Denver *B*
University of Northern Colorado *B*
Western State College of
  Colorado *B*

Connecticut

University of Connecticut *B,M,D*
Wesleyan University *B,M*
Yale University *B,M,D*

Delaware

University of Delaware *B,M,D*

District of Columbia

George Washington University
  B,M,D

Florida

Daytona Beach Community
  College *A*
Edison Community College *A*
Florida Atlantic University *B*
Florida International University
  B,M
Florida State University *B,M,D*
Gulf Coast Community College *A*
Miami-Dade Community College *A*
Pensacola Junior College *A*
University of Florida *B,M,D*

University of Miami *B*
University of South Florida *B,M*

Georgia

Atlanta Metropolitan College *A*
Columbus College *B*
Darton College *A*
DeKalb College *A*
East Georgia College *A*
Gainesville College *A*
Georgia Southern University *B*
Georgia Southwestern College *B*
Georgia State University *B,M*
Middle Georgia College *A*
University of Georgia *B,M,D*
West Georgia College *B*

Hawaii

University of Hawaii
  Hilo *B*
  Manoa *B*

Idaho

Boise State University *B,M*
Idaho State University *B,M*
Lewis Clark State College *B*
North Idaho College *A*
Ricks College *A*
University of Idaho *B,M,D*

Illinois

Augustana College *B*
Bradley University *B*
Eastern Illinois University *B*
Highland Community College *A*
Illinois Central College *A*
Illinois State University *B*
Joliet Junior College *A*
Monmouth College *B*
Northern Illinois University *B,M,D*
Northwestern University *B,M,D*
Olivet Nazarene University *B*
Southern Illinois University at
  Carbondale *B,M,D*
Triton College *A*
University of Chicago *B,M,D*
University of Illinois
  Chicago *B,M*
  Urbana-Champaign *B,M,D*
Western Illinois University *B*
Wheaton College *B*

Indiana

Ball State University *B,M*
DePauw University *B*
Earlham College *B*
Hanover College *B*
Indiana State University *B,M,D*
Indiana University
  Bloomington *B,M,D*
  Northwest *B*
Indiana University—Purdue
  University
    Fort Wayne *B*
    Indianapolis *B,M*
Purdue University *B,M,D*
St. Joseph's College *B*
University of Notre Dame *B*
University of Southern Indiana *B*
Valparaiso University *B*
Vincennes University *A*

Iowa

Cornell College *B*
Iowa State University *B,M,D*
University of Iowa *B,M,D*
University of Northern Iowa *B*

Kansas

Fort Hays State University *B,M*
Hutchinson Community College *A*
Kansas State University *B,M,D*

University of Kansas *B,M,D*
Wichita State University *B,M*

Kentucky

Eastern Kentucky University *B,M*
Morehead State University *B*
Murray State University *B*
Northern Kentucky University *B*
University of Kentucky *B,M,D*
University of Louisville *B*

Louisiana

Centenary College of Louisiana *B*
Louisiana State University and
  Agricultural and Mechanical
  College *B,M,D*
Louisiana Tech University *B*
McNeese State University *B*
Nicholls State University *B*
Northeast Louisiana University *B,M*
Northwestern State University *B*
Tulane University *B,M,D*
University of New Orleans *B,M*
University of Southwestern
  Louisiana *B,M*

Maine

Bates College *B*
Bowdoin College *B*
Colby College *B*
University of Maine
  Farmington *B*
  Orono *B,M,D*
University of Southern Maine *B*

Maryland

Johns Hopkins University *B,M,D*
University of Maryland: College
  Park *B,M,D*

Massachusetts

Amherst College *B*
Boston College *B,M*
Boston University *B,M,D*
Bridgewater State College *B*
Hampshire College *B*
Harvard and Radcliffe Colleges *B*
Harvard University *M,D*
Massachusetts Institute of
  Technology *B,M,D,W*
Mount Holyoke College *B*
Northeastern University *B*
Salem State College *B*
Smith College *B*
Tufts University *B*
University of Massachusetts
  Amherst *B,M,D*
  Lowell *B*
Wellesley College *B*
Williams College *B*

Michigan

Albion College *B*
Aquinas College *B*
Calvin College *B*
Central Michigan University *B*
Eastern Michigan University *B,M*
Grand Valley State University *B*
Hope College *B*
Lake Superior State University *B*
Michigan State University *B,M,D*
Michigan Technological University
  B,M,D
University of Michigan *B,M,D*
Wayne State University *B,M*
Western Michigan University
  B,M,D

Minnesota

Bemidji State University *B*
Carleton College *B*
Gustavus Adolphus College *B*

Macalester College *B*
St. Cloud State University *B*
University of Minnesota
 Duluth *B,M*
 Morris *B*
University of St. Thomas *B*
Winona State University *B*

Mississippi

Millsaps College *B*
Mississippi State University *B,M*
University of Mississippi *B,M*
University of Southern Mississippi *B,M*

Missouri

Central Missouri State University *B*
Northwest Missouri State University *B*
St. Louis University *B*
Southeast Missouri State University *B*
Southwest Missouri State University *B*
University of Missouri
 Columbia *B,M,D*
 Kansas City *B,D*
 Rolla *B,M,D*

Montana

Montana College of Mineral Science and Technology *M*
Montana State University *B*
Rocky Mountain College *B*
University of Montana *B,M,D*

Nebraska

University of Nebraska
 Lincoln *B,M,D*
 Omaha *B*
Wayne State College *B*

Nevada

University of Nevada
 Las Vegas *B,M*
 Reno *B,M,D*

New Hampshire

Dartmouth College *M*
Keene State College *B*
University of New Hampshire *B,M,D*

New Jersey

Jersey City State College *B*
Kean College of New Jersey *B*
Montclair State College *B,M*
Princeton University *B,D*
Rider College *B*
Rutgers—The State University of New Jersey
 Cook College *B*
 Douglass College *B*
 Livingston College *B*
 New Brunswick *M,D*
 Newark College of Arts and Sciences *B*
 Rutgers College *B*
 University College New Brunswick *B*
Stockton State College *B*

New Mexico

Eastern New Mexico University *B*
New Mexico Institute of Mining and Technology *B,M,D*
New Mexico State University *B,M*
University of New Mexico *B,M,D*
Western New Mexico University *B*

New York

Adirondack Community College *A*
Alfred University *B*
City University of New York
 Brooklyn College *B,M*
 City College *B,M*
 Graduate School and University Center *D*
 Hunter College *B*
 Lehman College *B*
 Queens College *B,M*
 York College *B*
Colgate University *B,M*
Columbia University
 Columbia College *B*
 New York *M,D*
 School of General Studies *B*
Cornell University *B,M,D*
Hamilton College *B*
Hartwick College *B*
Hofstra University *B*
Jefferson Community College *A*
Long Island University
 C. W. Post Campus *B*
 Southampton Campus *B*
Mohawk Valley Community College *A*
Rensselaer Polytechnic Institute *B,M,D*
St. Lawrence University *B*
Sarah Lawrence College *B*
Skidmore College *B*
State University of New York
 Albany *B,M,D*
 Binghamton *B,M,D*
 Buffalo *B,M,D*
 Stony Brook *B*
 College at Brockport *B*
 College at Buffalo *B*
 College at Cortland *B*
 College at Fredonia *B,M*
 College at Geneseo *B*
 College at New Paltz *B,M*
 College at Oneonta *B*
 College at Plattsburgh *B*
 College at Potsdam *B*
 Oswego *B*
Syracuse University *B,M,D*
Union College *B*
University of Rochester *B,M,D,W*
University of the State of New York: Regents College *B*
Vassar College *B*

North Carolina

Appalachian State University *B*
Brevard College *A*
Duke University *B,M,D*
East Carolina University *B,M*
Elizabeth City State University *B*
Guilford College *B*
North Carolina State University *B*
University of North Carolina
 Chapel Hill *B,M,D*
 Wilmington *B,M*
Western Carolina University *B*

North Dakota

University of North Dakota *B,M,D*

Ohio

Ashland University *B*
Baldwin-Wallace College *B*
Bowling Green State University *B,M*
Case Western Reserve University *B,M,D*
Central State University *B*
Cleveland State University *B*
College of Wooster *B*
Denison University *B*
Kent State University *B,M,D*

Lakeland Community College *A*
Marietta College *B*
Miami University: Oxford Campus *B,M,D*
Mount Union College *B*
Muskingum College *B*
Oberlin College *B*
Ohio State University: Columbus Campus *B,M,D*
Ohio University *B,M*
Ohio Wesleyan University *B*
Union Institute *B,D*
University of Akron *B,M*
University of Cincinnati *B,M,D*
University of Dayton *B*
University of Toledo *B,M*
Wittenberg University *B*
Wright State University
 Dayton *B,M*
 Lake Campus *A*
Youngstown State University *B*

Oklahoma

Northeastern State University *B*
Oklahoma State University *B,M*
Phillips University *B*
Tulsa Junior College *A*
University of Oklahoma *B,M,D*
University of Tulsa *B,M,D*

Oregon

Central Oregon Community College *A*
Northwest Christian College *B*
Oregon State University *B,M,D*
Portland Community College *A*
Portland State University *B,M*
Southern Oregon State College *B*
University of Oregon
 Eugene *B,M,D*
 Robert Donald Clark Honors College *B*

Pennsylvania

Allegheny College *B*
Bloomsburg University of Pennsylvania *B*
Bryn Mawr College *B,M,D*
Bucknell University *B*
California University of Pennsylvania *B,M*
Clarion University of Pennsylvania *B*
Dickinson College *B*
Edinboro University of Pennsylvania *B*
Franklin and Marshall College *B*
Haverford College *B*
Indiana University of Pennsylvania *B*
Juniata College *B*
Kutztown University of Pennsylvania *B*
La Salle University *B*
Lafayette College *B*
Lehigh University *B,M,D*
Mercyhurst College *B*
Millersville University of Pennsylvania *B*
Moravian College *B*
Slippery Rock University of Pennsylvania *B*
Temple University *B,M*
Thiel College *B*
University of Pennsylvania *B,M,D*
University of Pittsburgh
 Bradford *B*
 Johnstown *B*
 Pittsburgh *B,M,D*
West Chester University of Pennsylvania *B*

Puerto Rico

University of Puerto Rico:
 Mayaguez Campus *B*

Rhode Island

Brown University *B,M,D*
University of Rhode Island *B,M*

South Carolina

Clemson University *B,M*
College of Charleston *B*
Furman University *B*
University of South Carolina *B,M,D*

South Dakota

South Dakota School of Mines and Technology *B,M,D*

Tennessee

Austin Peay State University *B*
Carson-Newman College *B*
East Tennessee State University *B*
Fisk University *B*
Memphis State University *B,M,D*
Tennessee Technological University *B*
University of the South *B*
University of Tennessee
 Chattanooga *B*
 Knoxville *B,M,D*
 Martin *B*
Vanderbilt University *B,M*

Texas

Abilene Christian University *B*
Amarillo College *A*
Austin Community College *A*
Baylor University *B,M,D*
Bee County College *A*
Central Texas College *A*
Collin County Community College District *A*
Corpus Christi State University *B*
Del Mar College *A*
El Paso Community College *A*
Hardin-Simmons University *B*
Howard College *A*
Lamar University—Beaumont *B*
Midwestern State University *B*
North Harris Montgomery Community College District *A*
Rice University *B,M,D*
Sam Houston State University *B*
Southern Methodist University *B,M,D*
Stephen F. Austin State University *B,M*
Sul Ross State University *B,M*
Tarleton State University *B*
Texas A&I University *B,M*
Texas A&M University *B,M,D*
Texas Christian University *B,M*
Texas Southmost College *A*
Texas Tech University *B,M,D*
Trinity University *B*
University of Houston *B,M,D*
University of Texas
 Arlington *B,M*
 Austin *B,M,D*
 Dallas *B,M,D*
 El Paso *B,M,D*
 Permian Basin *B,M*
 San Antonio *B,M*
West Texas State University *B*

Utah

Brigham Young University *B,M*
Southern Utah University *B*
University of Utah *B,M,D*
Utah State University *B,M*
Weber State University *B*

Vermont

Castleton State College *B*
Middlebury College *B*
Norwich University *B*
University of Vermont *B,M*

Virginia

College of William and Mary *B*
George Mason University *B*
James Madison University *B*
Mary Washington College *B*
Old Dominion University *B,M,D*
Radford University *B*
Virginia Polytechnic Institute and
State University *B,M,D*
Virginia State University *B*
Washington and Lee University *B*

Washington

Central Washington University *B*
Eastern Washington University *B,M*
Everett Community College *A*
Evergreen State College *B*
Lower Columbia College *A*
Pacific Lutheran University *B*
Tacoma Community College *A*
University of Puget Sound *B*
University of Washington *B,M,D*
Washington State University *B,M,D*
Western Washington University
B,M
Whitman College *B*

West Virginia

Marshall University *B*
Potomac State College of West
Virginia University *A*
West Virginia University *B,M,D*

Wisconsin

Beloit College *B*
Lawrence University *B*
Northland College *B*
University of Wisconsin
Eau Claire *B*
Madison *B,M,D*
Milwaukee *B,M,D*
Oshkosh *B*
Parkside *B*
Platteville *B*
River Falls *B*

Wyoming

Casper College *A*
Northwest College *A*
University of Wyoming *B,M,D*
Western Wyoming Community
College *A*

Canada

McGill University *B,M,D*

Geophysical engineering

California

Stanford University *M,D*
University of California: Berkeley
M,D

Colorado

Colorado School of Mines
B,M,D,W

Massachusetts

Harvard and Radcliffe Colleges *B*
Massachusetts Institute of
Technology *B,M,D,W*
Tufts University *B,M*

Minnesota

University of Minnesota: Twin
Cities *B,M,D*

Missouri

East Central College *A*

Montana

Montana College of Mineral
Science and Technology *B,M*

New Mexico

New Mexico Institute of Mining
and Technology *M,D*

New York

Columbia University: School of
Engineering and Applied Science
B,M,D,W

Oklahoma

University of Tulsa *B,M,D*

Geophysics and seismology

Alaska

University of Alaska Fairbanks *M,D*

Arizona

Northern Arizona University *B*

California

California Institute of Technology
B,M,D,W
California State University:
Northridge *B*
Occidental College *B*
San Jose State University *B*
Stanford University *B,M,D*
University of California
Berkeley *B,M,D*
Los Angeles *B,M,D*
Riverside *B*
Santa Barbara *B,M*
Santa Cruz *B,D*
University of the Pacific *B*

Colorado

Colorado School of Mines *M,D,W*
University of Colorado at
Boulder *D*
Western State College of
Colorado *B*

Connecticut

University of Connecticut *M,D*
Yale University *B,M,D*

Delaware

University of Delaware *B*

Hawaii

University of Hawaii at Manoa *M,D*

Idaho

Boise State University *B,M*
University of Idaho *M*

Illinois

Northwestern University *B*
University of Chicago *B,M,D*

Indiana

Purdue University *B,M,D*
St. Joseph's College *B*

Kansas

Kansas State University *B*
University of Kansas *B*

Louisiana

Northeast Louisiana University *B*
University of New Orleans *B*

Massachusetts

Boston College *B,M*
Harvard and Radcliffe Colleges *B*
Harvard University *M,D*
Massachusetts Institute of
Technology *B,M,D,W*

Michigan

Eastern Michigan University *B*
Hope College *B*
Michigan Technological
University *M*
Western Michigan University *B*

Minnesota

University of Minnesota: Twin
Cities *B,M,D*

Missouri

St. Louis University *B,M,D*
University of Missouri: Rolla *B,M,D*

Montana

Montana State University *B*

Nevada

University of Nevada: Reno *B,M,D*

New Jersey

Princeton University *B,D*

New Mexico

New Mexico Institute of Mining
and Technology *B,M,D*
New Mexico State University *B*

New York

Columbia University
Columbia College *B*
New York *M,D*
School of Engineering and
Applied Science *B,M,D*
School of General Studies *B*
Cornell University *M,D*
St. Lawrence University *B*
State University of New York
Binghamton *B*
College at Fredonia *B*
College at Geneseo *B*

North Carolina

North Carolina State University *B*

Ohio

Bowling Green State University
B,M
Ohio State University: Columbus
Campus *B,M,D*
Ohio University *M*
University of Akron *B,M*
Wright State University *B*

Oklahoma

University of Oklahoma *B,M*
University of Tulsa *B,M,D*

Oregon

Oregon State University *M,D*

Pennsylvania

Lehigh University *B*

Rhode Island

Brown University *B,M,D*

South Carolina

University of South Carolina *B*

Tennessee

Memphis State University *D*

Texas

Baylor University *B*
Midwestern State University *B*
Rice University *B*
Southern Methodist University
B,M,D
Texas A&M University *B,M,D*
Texas Tech University *B,M*
University of Houston *B,M,D*
University of Texas
Austin *B*
El Paso *B,M*

Utah

University of Utah *B,M,D*

Virginia

Virginia Polytechnic Institute and
State University *B*
Washington and Lee University *B*

Washington

University of Washington *M,D*
Western Washington University *B*

Wisconsin

University of Wisconsin: Madison
B,M,D

Wyoming

University of Wyoming *B,M,D*

Canada

McGill University *B,M,D*

Geriatric aide

Colorado

Aims Community College *C*

Florida

Pasco-Hernando Community
College *C*

Iowa

Northwest Iowa Technical
College *C*

Kansas

Allen County Community
College *A*
Barton County Community
College *A*
Dodge City Community College *C*
Neosho County Community
College *C*

Maryland

Villa Julie College *A*

Michigan

Lansing Community College *A*
Macomb Community College *C,A*

Minnesota

Itasca Community College:
Arrowhead Region *C*
Rainy River Community College *C*

New Jersey

Bergen Community College *C*

New York

Herkimer County Community
College *A*
Nassau Community College *C*

North Carolina

Bladen Community College *C*
Isothermal Community College *C*
Southwestern Community
College *C*

Ohio

Columbus State Community
College *A*
University of Toledo *A*

Pennsylvania

Westmoreland County Community
College *C*

Virginia

Dabney S. Lancaster Community
College *C*
Mountain Empire Community
College *C*
Paul D. Camp Community
College *C*
Southside Virginia Community
College *C*

Geriatric services

California

Chabot College *C*

Illinois

College of Lake County *A*
Eastern Illinois University *M*
Elgin Community College *C,A*
KAES College *B*
Sangamon State University *M*

Maryland

Dundalk Community College *C,A*
Villa Julie College *A*

Michigan

Northern Michigan University *B*

New Jersey

Thomas Edison State College *B*

New York

City University of New York
Brooklyn College *M*
La Guardia Community
College *A*
New York City Technical
College *A*

North Carolina

Central Carolina Community
College *C*

Ohio

Bowling Green State University:
Firelands College *A*
Clark State Community College *A*
Columbus State Community
College *A*
Ohio State University: Columbus
Campus *B,M,D*
Union Institute *D*

Pennsylvania

Penn State University Park
Campus *C*
Westmoreland County Community
College *C*

South Dakota

Black Hills State University *B*

Virginia

Virginia Polytechnic Institute and
State University *M,D*

Washington

Lutheran Bible Institute of
Seattle *B*
Shoreline Community College *C*
Yakima Valley Community
College *C*

German

Alabama

Auburn University *B*
Birmingham-Southern College *B*
Jacksonville State University *B*
Mobile College *B*
Samford University *B*
University of Alabama
Birmingham *B*
Huntsville *B*
Tuscaloosa *B,M*
University of North Alabama *B*
University of South Alabama *B*

Arizona

Arizona State University *B,M*
Glendale Community College *A*
University of Arizona *B,M*

Arkansas

Arkansas Tech University *B*
Hendrix College *B*
University of Arkansas *B,M*

California

Bakersfield College *A*
California Lutheran University *B*
California State University
Chico *B*
Fresno *B*
Fullerton *B,M*
Hayward *B*
Long Beach *B,M*
Northridge *B*
Sacramento *B,M*
Cerritos Community College *A*
Chabot College *A*
Chaffey Community College *A*
Citrus College *A*
Claremont McKenna College *B*
College of the Desert *A*
De Anza College *A*
El Camino College *A*
Foothill College *A*
Grossmont Community College *C,A*
Humboldt State University *B*
Long Beach City College *C,A*
Los Angeles City College *A*
Los Angeles Valley College *A*
Loyola Marymount University *B*
Merced College *A*
Mills College *B*
MiraCosta College *A*
Monterey Institute of International
Studies *B,M*
Napa Valley College *A*
Occidental College *B*
Ohlone College *A*

Orange Coast College *A*
Pepperdine University *B*
Pitzer College *B*
Pomona College *B*
San Diego City College *A*
San Diego State University *B,M*
San Francisco State University *B,M*
San Joaquin Delta College *A*
San Jose City College *A*
San Jose State University *B*
Santa Barbara City College *A*
Santa Clara University *B*
Santa Monica College *A*
Santa Rosa Junior College *A*
Scripps College *B*
Solano Community College *A*
Sonoma State University *B*
Stanford University *B,M,D*
University of California
Berkeley *B,M,D*
Davis *B,M,D*
Irvine *B,M,D*
Los Angeles *B,M,D*
Riverside *B,M*
San Diego *B,M,D*
Santa Barbara *B,M,D*
Santa Cruz *B,D*
University of La Verne *B*
University of the Pacific *B*
University of Redlands *B*
University of Southern California
B,M,D
Ventura College *A*

Colorado

Colorado College *B*
Colorado State University *B,M*
University of Colorado
Boulder *B*
Denver *B*
University of Denver *B,M*
University of Northern Colorado *B*

Connecticut

Central Connecticut State
University *B*
Connecticut College *B*
Fairfield University *B*
Southern Connecticut State
University *B,M*
Trinity College *B*
University of Connecticut *B,M,D*
University of Hartford *B*
Wesleyan University *B*
Yale University *B,M,D*

Delaware

University of Delaware *B,M*

District of Columbia

American University *B*
Catholic University of America
B,M,D
Gallaudet University *B*
George Washington University *B*
Georgetown University *B,M,D*
Howard University *B,M*
University of the District of
Columbia *A,B*

Florida

Eckerd College *B*
Florida Atlantic University *B,M*
Florida International University *B*
Florida Southern College *B*
Florida State University *B,M*
Jacksonville University *B*
Miami-Dade Community College *A*
New College of the University of
South Florida *B*
Okaloosa-Walton Community
College *A*

Pensacola Junior College *A*
Rollins College *B*
Stetson University *B*
University of Florida *B,M,D*
University of Miami *B*
University of South Florida *B*

Georgia

Agnes Scott College *B*
Berry College *B*
Clark Atlanta University *B*
Emory University *B*
Georgia Southern University *B*
Georgia State University *B,M*
Mercer University *B*
Morehouse College *B*
Oxford College of Emory
University *A*
University of Georgia *B,M*

Hawaii

University of Hawaii at Manoa *B*

Idaho

Boise State University *B*
Idaho State University *B*
Ricks College *A*
University of Idaho *B,M*

Illinois

Augustana College *B*
Black Hawk College *A*
Bradley University *B*
City Colleges of Chicago: Chicago
City-Wide College *C*
Concordia University *B*
De Paul University *B*
Eastern Illinois University *B*
Elmhurst College *B*
Illinois College *B*
Illinois State University *B*
Illinois Wesleyan University *B*
Joliet Junior College *A*
Knox College *B*
Lake Forest College *B*
Loyola University of Chicago *B*
Millikin University *B*
North Central College *B*
North Park College and Theological
Seminary *B*
Northern Illinois University *B,M*
Northwestern University *B*
Principia College *B*
Richland Community College *A*
Rockford College *B*
Rosary College *B*
Southern Illinois University
Carbondale *B,M*
Edwardsville *B*
University of Chicago *B,M,D*
University of Illinois
Chicago *B,M*
Urbana-Champaign *B,M,D*
Western Illinois University *B*
Wheaton College *B*

Indiana

Anderson University *B*
Ball State University *B*
Butler University *B*
DePauw University *B*
Earlham College *B*
Goshen College *B*
Grace College *B*
Hanover College *B*
Indiana State University *B,M*
Indiana University
Bloomington *B,M,D*
South Bend *B*

Indiana University—Purdue
University
Fort Wayne *B*
Indianapolis *B*
Manchester College *B*
Marian College *B*
Purdue University
Calumet *B*
West Lafayette *B,M,D*
University of Evansville *B*
University of Indianapolis *B*
University of Notre Dame *B,M*
University of Southern Indiana *B*
Valparaiso University *B*
Vincennes University *A*
Wabash College *B*

Iowa

Central College *B*
Clarke College *B*
Coe College *B*
Cornell College *B*
Dordt College *B*
Drake University *B*
Graceland College *B*
Grinnell College *B*
Iowa State University *B*
Kirkwood Community College *A*
Loras College *B*
Luther College *B*
North Iowa Area Community
College *A*
St. Ambrose University *B*
Simpson College *B*
Teikyo Westmar University *B*
University of Dubuque *B*
University of Iowa *B,M,D*
University of Northern Iowa *B,M*
Wartburg College *B*

Kansas

Baker University *B*
Bethel College *B*
Kansas City Kansas Community
College *A*
Kansas State University *B,M*
McPherson College *B*
University of Kansas *B,M,D*
Washburn University of Topeka *B*
Wichita State University *B*

Kentucky

Berea College *B*
Centre College *B*
Eastern Kentucky University *B*
Georgetown College *B*
Murray State University *B*
University of Kentucky *B,M,D*
University of Louisville *B,M*
Western Kentucky University *B*

Louisiana

Dillard University *B*
Louisiana State University and
Agricultural and Mechanical
College *B*
Loyola University *B*
Tulane University *B,M,D*

Maine

Bates College *B*
Bowdoin College *B*
Colby College *B*
University of Maine *B*

Maryland

Hood College *B*
Johns Hopkins University *B,M,D*
Loyola College in Maryland *B*
Mount St. Mary's College *B*
Towson State University *B*

University of Maryland
Baltimore County *B*
College Park *B,M,D*
Washington College *B*
Western Maryland College *B*

Massachusetts

Amherst College *B*
Boston College *B*
Boston University *B*
Brandeis University *B*
Clark University *B*
College of the Holy Cross *B*
Harvard and Radcliffe Colleges *B*
Harvard University *M,D*
Massachusetts Institute of
Technology *B*
Mount Holyoke College *B*
Northeastern University *B*
Regis College *B*
Simon's Rock College of Bard *B*
Smith College *B*
Tufts University *B,M*
University of Massachusetts
Amherst *B,M,D*
Boston *B*
Dartmouth *B*
Wellesley College *B*
Wheaton College *B*
Williams College *B*

Michigan

Adrian College *A,B*
Albion College *B*
Alma College *B*
Andrews University *B*
Aquinas College *B*
Calvin College *B*
Central Michigan University *B*
Eastern Michigan University *B*
Grand Valley State University *B*
Hillsdale College *B*
Hope College *B*
Kalamazoo College *B*
Lansing Community College *A*
Marygrove College *B*
Michigan State University *B,M,D*
Northern Michigan University *B,M*
Oakland University *B*
University of Detroit Mercy *B*
University of Michigan
Ann Arbor *B,M,D*
Flint *B*
Wayne State University *B,M*
Western Michigan University *B*

Minnesota

Augsburg College *B*
Bemidji State University *B*
Bethany Lutheran College *A*
Carleton College *B*
College of St. Benedict *B*
College of St. Catherine: St.
Catherine Campus *B*
Concordia College: Moorhead *B*
Gustavus Adolphus College *B*
Hamline University *B*
Macalester College *B*
Mankato State University *B*
Moorhead State University *B*
St. Cloud State University *B*
St. John's University *B*
St. Olaf College *B*
University of Minnesota
Duluth *B*
Morris *B*
Twin Cities *B,M,D*
University of St. Thomas *B*
Willmar Community College *A*
Winona State University *B*

Mississippi

Delta State University *B*
Millsaps College *B*
Mississippi College *B*
Rust College *B*
University of Mississippi *B,M*

Missouri

Central Methodist College *B*
Central Missouri State University *B*
College of the Ozarks *B*
Drury College *B*
Northeast Missouri State
University *B*
St. Louis University *B*
Southwest Missouri State
University *B*
University of Missouri
Columbia *B,M*
Kansas City *B*
St. Louis *B*
Washington University *B,M,D*
Westminster College *B*
William Woods College *B*

Montana

Eastern Montana College *B*
Montana State University *B*
University of Montana *B,M*

Nebraska

Creighton University *B*
Dana College *B*
Doane College *B*
Hastings College *B*
Midland Lutheran College *B*
Nebraska Wesleyan University *B*
University of Nebraska
Kearney *B,M*
Lincoln *B,M*
Omaha *B*
Wayne State College *B*
Western Nebraska Community
College: Scottsbluff Campus *A*

Nevada

University of Nevada
Las Vegas *B,M*
Reno *B*

New Hampshire

Dartmouth College *B*
University of New Hampshire *B,M*

New Jersey

Brookdale Community College *A*
Drew University *B*
Georgian Court College *B*
Montclair State College *B*
Princeton University *B,D*
Rider College *B*
Rutgers—The State University of
New Jersey
Camden College of Arts and
Sciences *B*
Douglass College *B*
Livingston College *B*
New Brunswick *M,D*
Newark College of Arts and
Sciences *B*
Rutgers College *B*
University College Camden *B*
University College New
Brunswick *B*

New Mexico

New Mexico State University *B*
University of New Mexico *B,M*

New York

Bard College *B*
Barnard College *B*

Canisius College *B*
City University of New York
Brooklyn College *B*
City College *B*
Graduate School and
University Center *M,D*
Hunter College *B*
Lehman College *B*
Queens College *B*
Queensborough Community
College *A*
Colgate University *B*
Columbia University
Columbia College *B*
New York *M,D*
School of General Studies *B*
Cornell University *B,M,D*
Elmira College *B*
Fordham University *B*
Hamilton College *B*
Hartwick College *B*
Hobart College *B*
Hofstra University *B*
Ithaca College *B*
Long Island University: C. W. Post
Campus *B*
Nazareth College of Rochester *B*
New York University *B,M,D*
Onondaga Community College *A*
Orange County Community
College *A*
St. Bonaventure University *B*
St. John Fisher College *B*
St. John's University *B*
St. Lawrence University *B*
Sarah Lawrence College *B*
Skidmore College *B*
State University of New York
Albany *B,M,D*
Binghamton *B*
Buffalo *B,M,D*
Stony Brook *B,M,D*
College at Cortland *B*
College at Fredonia *B*
College at New Paltz *B*
College at Oneonta *B*
Oswego *B*
Syracuse University *B,M*
United States Military Academy *B*
University of Rochester *B,M*
University of the State of New
York: Regents College *B*
Vassar College *B,M*
Wagner College *B*
Wells College *B*
William Smith College *B*

North Carolina

Brevard College *A*
Davidson College *B*
Duke University *B,M*
East Carolina University *B*
Guilford College *B*
Lenoir-Rhyne College *B*
Methodist College *A*
St. Andrews Presbyterian College *B*
St. Augustine's College *B*
Salem College *B*
University of North Carolina
Asheville *B*
Chapel Hill *B,M,D*
Charlotte *B*
Greensboro *B*
Wake Forest University *B*
Western Carolina University *B*

North Dakota

Bismarck State College *A*
Minot State University *B*
North Dakota State University *B*
University of North Dakota *B*

Ohio

Baldwin-Wallace College *B*
Bowling Green State University *B,M*
Cleveland State University *B*
College of Wooster *B*
Denison University *B*
Heidelberg College *B*
Hiram College *B*
John Carroll University *B*
Kent State University *B,M*
Kenyon College *B*
Miami University: Oxford Campus *B,M*
Muskingum College *B*
Oberlin College *B*
Ohio State University: Columbus Campus *B,M,D*
Ohio University *B*
Ohio Wesleyan University *B*
University of Akron *B*
University of Cincinnati *B*
University of Dayton *B*
University of Toledo *B,M*
Wittenberg University *B*
Wright State University *B*
Youngstown State University *B*

Oklahoma

Northeastern State University *B*
Oklahoma Baptist University *B*
Oklahoma City University *B*
Oklahoma State University *B*
Oral Roberts University *B*
Rose State College *A*
Tulsa Junior College *A*
University of Central Oklahoma *B*
University of Oklahoma *B,M*

Oregon

Central Oregon Community College *A*
Lewis and Clark College *B*
Linfield College *B*
Northwest Christian College *B*
Oregon State University *B*
Pacific University *B*
Portland Community College *A*
Portland State University *B,M*
Reed College *B*
University of Oregon
    Eugene *B,M,D*
    Robert Donald Clark Honors College *B*
Willamette University *B*

Pennsylvania

Albright College *B*
Allegheny College *B*
Bloomsburg University of Pennsylvania *B*
Bryn Mawr College *B*
Bucknell University *B*
California University of Pennsylvania *B*
Carnegie Mellon University *B*
Cedar Crest College *B*
Chestnut Hill College *B*
Clarion University of Pennsylvania *B*
Dickinson College *B*
Duquesne University *B,M*
East Stroudsburg University of Pennsylvania *B*
Edinboro University of Pennsylvania *B*
Elizabethtown College *B*
Franklin and Marshall College *B*
Gannon University *B*
Gettysburg College *B*
Haverford College *B*
Immaculata College *A,B*

Indiana University of Pennsylvania *B*
Juniata College *B*
Kutztown University of Pennsylvania *B,M*
La Roche College *C*
La Salle University *B*
Lafayette College *B*
Lebanon Valley College of Pennsylvania *B*
Lehigh University *B*
Lock Haven University of Pennsylvania *B*
Lycoming College *B*
Mansfield University of Pennsylvania *B*
Messiah College *B*
Millersville University of Pennsylvania *B,M*
Moravian College *B*
Muhlenberg College *B*
Penn State University Park Campus *B,M,D*
Rosemont College *B*
St. Joseph's University *B*
Shippensburg University of Pennsylvania *B*
Slippery Rock University of Pennsylvania *B*
Susquehanna University *B*
Swarthmore College *B*
Temple University *B,M*
University of Pennsylvania *B,M,D*
University of Pittsburgh *B,M,D*
University of Scranton *B*
Ursinus College *B*
Villanova University *B*
Washington and Jefferson College *B*
West Chester University of Pennsylvania *B,M*
Westminster College *B*
Widener University *B*
Wilkes University *B*

Rhode Island

Brown University *B,M,D*
University of Rhode Island *B*

South Carolina

Bob Jones University *B*
The Citadel *B*
Clemson University *B*
College of Charleston *B*
Columbia College *B*
Furman University *B*
Presbyterian College *B*
University of South Carolina *B,M*
Wofford College *B*

South Dakota

Augustana College *B*
Northern State University *B*
South Dakota State University *B*
University of South Dakota *B*

Tennessee

Carson-Newman College *B*
David Lipscomb University *B*
East Tennessee State University *B*
Lambuth University *B*
Middle Tennessee State University *B,M*
Rhodes College *B*
Southern College of Seventh-day Adventists *B*
Tennessee Technological University *B*
University of the South *B*
University of Tennessee
    Knoxville *B,M*
    Martin *B*
Vanderbilt University *B,M,D*

Texas

Abilene Christian University *B*
Austin College *B*
Austin Community College *A*
Baylor University *B*
Bee County College *A*
Central Texas College *A*
East Texas State University *B*
Hardin-Simmons University *B*
Kilgore College *A*
Lamar University—Beaumont *B*
Rice University *B,M,D*
St. Mary's University *B*
Sam Houston State University *B*
Southern Methodist University *B*
Southwest Texas State University *B*
Southwestern University *B*
Texas Lutheran College *B*
Texas Tech University *B,M*
Trinity University *B*
University of Dallas *B*
University of Houston *B,M*
University of North Texas *B*
University of Texas
    Arlington *B,M*
    Austin *B,M,D*
    El Paso *B*
    San Antonio *B*

Utah

Brigham Young University *B,M*
Southern Utah University *B*
University of Utah *B*
Utah State University *B*
Weber State University *B*

Vermont

Bennington College *B*
Marlboro College *B*
Middlebury College *B*
Norwich University *B*
University of Vermont *B,M*

Virginia

Bridgewater College *B*
Christopher Newport College *B*
College of William and Mary *B*
Eastern Mennonite College *B*
Emory and Henry College *B*
Hampden-Sydney College *B*
Hollins College *B*
Lynchburg College *B*
Mary Washington College *B*
Old Dominion University *B*
Radford University *B*
Randolph-Macon College *B*
Randolph-Macon Woman's College *B*
Sweet Briar College *B*
University of Richmond *B,W*
University of Virginia *B,M,D*
Virginia Commonwealth University *B*
Virginia Polytechnic Institute and State University *B*
Virginia Wesleyan College *B*
Washington and Lee University *B*

Washington

Central Washington University *B*
Eastern Washington University *B,M*
Everett Community College *A*
Gonzaga University *B*
Pacific Lutheran University *B*
Seattle Central Community College *A*
Seattle University *B*
Spokane Falls Community College *A*
University of Puget Sound *B*
University of Washington *B,M,D*
Walla Walla College *B*

Western Washington University *B,M*
Whitman College *B*

West Virginia

Bethany College *B*
Marshall University *B*
Potomac State College of West Virginia University *A*
West Virginia University *B,M*

Wisconsin

Beloit College *B*
Carroll College *B*
Carthage College *B*
Concordia University Wisconsin *B*
Lakeland College *B*
Lawrence University *B*
Marquette University *B,M*
Mount Mary College *B*
Ripon College *B*
St. Norbert College *B*
University of Wisconsin
    Eau Claire *B*
    Green Bay *B*
    Madison *B,M,D*
    Milwaukee *B*
    Oshkosh *B*
    Platteville *B*
    River Falls *B*
    Stevens Point *B*
    Whitewater *B*

Wyoming

Casper College *A*
University of Wyoming *B,M*
Western Wyoming Community College *A*

Canada

McGill University *B,M,D*

Gerontology

Alabama

University of South Alabama *C*

Arkansas

University of Arkansas
    Little Rock *M*
    Pine Bluff *B*

California

California State University
    Chico *C*
    Dominguez Hills *B*
    Stanislaus *B*
Imperial Valley College *A*
Saddleback College *A*
San Francisco State University *M*
San Jose State University *M*
University of Southern California *B,M,D*

Colorado

Pikes Peak Community College *A*
University of Northern Colorado *B,M*

Connecticut

Mattatuck Community College *A*
Mitchell College *A*
Quinnipiac College *B*
St. Joseph College *C,M*
South Central Community College *A*

District of Columbia
George Washington University *M*

Florida
Lynn University *B,M*
New College of the University of South Florida *B*
Nova University *M*
Stetson University *C*
University of South Florida *B,M*

Georgia
Georgia State University *C*

Illinois
Concordia University *M*
Elgin Community College *C,A*
Greenville College *B*
Illinois Benedictine College *C*
Montay College *C,A*
National-Louis University *B,M*
Northeastern Illinois University *M*
Sangamon State University *M*
University of Health Sciences: The Chicago Medical School *M*
Western Illinois University *M*

Indiana
Ball State University *M*
Manchester College *A*
Purdue University: Calumet *B*
St. Mary-of-the-Woods College *C,A*

Kansas
Kansas State University *M,D*
Washburn University of Topeka *A*
Wichita State University *B,M*

Kentucky
Thomas More College *A*

Maine
University of Maine at Fort Kent *A*

Maryland
Morgan State University *B*
New Community College of Baltimore *C,A*

Massachusetts
Assumption College *C*
Bunker Hill Community College *C*
Cape Cod Community College *C*
Clark University *C*
Emmanuel College *B*
Endicott College *A*
Hampshire College *B*
North Shore Community College *C,A*
Springfield College *B,M*
University of Massachusetts at Boston *C,B,D*

Michigan
Charles Stewart Mott Community College *A*
Lansing Community College *A*
Madonna University *C,A,B*
Northern Michigan University *B*
Oakland Community College *A*

Minnesota
College of St. Scholastica *M*
Mankato State University *A*
Winona State University *A*

Mississippi
Mississippi College *C*

Missouri
Central Missouri State University *M*

Fontbonne College *B*
Lindenwood College *B,M*
St. Louis Community College at Forest Park *C*
Southwest Missouri State University *B*
University of Missouri: St. Louis *M*
Webster University *M*

New Jersey
Bergen Community College *C*
Caldwell College *C*
College of St. Elizabeth *C*
Gloucester County College *C*
Ocean County College *A*
Stockton State College *C*
Union County College *C,A*

New Mexico
New Mexico State University *C*

New York
Alfred University *B*
Canisius College *C*
City University of New York
    Brooklyn College *M*
    Hostos Community College *A*
    La Guardia Community College *A*
    New York City Technical College *A*
    York College *B*
College of New Rochelle *M*
Columbia University: School of Nursing *M*
Genesee Community College *C*
Herkimer County Community College *A*
Hofstra University *M*
Iona College *C*
Long Island University
    C. W. Post Campus *B,M*
    Southampton Campus *M*
Marymount Manhattan College *C*
Medaille College *A*
Mercy College *C*
Molloy College *B*
Roberts Wesleyan College *B*
St. John Fisher College *C*
St. Joseph's College
    Brooklyn *C*
    Suffolk Campus *C*
St. Thomas Aquinas College *B*
Utica College of Syracuse University *C,B*
Villa Maria College of Buffalo *A*
Wagner College *B*

North Carolina
Wayne Community College *A*
Western Piedmont Community College *C*

Ohio
Bowling Green State University *B*
Case Western Reserve University *B*
College of Mount St. Joseph *C,A,B*
Columbus State Community College *A*
Kent State University *B*
Lourdes College *C,A,B*
Miami University: Oxford Campus *M*
Ohio State University: Columbus Campus *B*
Union Institute *D*
University of Findlay *B*
University of Toledo *A*

Oklahoma
Connors State College *A*
Langston University *B*

Oklahoma State University *B*
Rogers State College *A*

Oregon
Chemeketa Community College *A*
Clackamas Community College *C*

Pennsylvania
California University of Pennsylvania *A,B*
Cedar Crest College *C*
Eastern College *C*
Gannon University *C*
Gwynedd-Mercy College *B*
King's College *C,A,B*
La Roche College *C*
Lincoln University *C*
Marywood College *M*
Millersville University of Pennsylvania *A*
St. Joseph's University *M*
University of Pittsburgh at Greensburg *C*
University of Scranton *A,B*
West Chester University of Pennsylvania *B,M*

Puerto Rico
Pontifical Catholic University of Puerto Rico *A,B*
Puerto Rico Junior College *A*
Universidad Metropolitana *B*
University of Puerto Rico: Medical Sciences Campus *M*

Rhode Island
Community College of Rhode Island *A*

South Carolina
Lander College *C*

South Dakota
Black Hills State University *B*

Tennessee
Memphis State University *M*

Texas
Abilene Christian University *C,M*
Baylor University *M*
Incarnate Word College *M*
McLennan Community College *C*
Stephen F. Austin State University *B*
Texas Tech University *M*
University of North Texas *B,M*
University of Texas
    Health Science Center at Houston *M*
    Southwestern Medical Center at Dallas Southwestern Allied Health Sciences School *B*

Vermont
Southern Vermont College *A*
Trinity College of Vermont *C*

Virginia
Hampton University *B*
Lynchburg College *C*
Norfolk State University *M*
Northern Virginia Community College *A*
Virginia Commonwealth University *M*

Washington
Central Washington University *B*
Edmonds Community College *A*
Heritage College *C*

Lutheran Bible Institute of Seattle *B*
Spokane Falls Community College *C,A*

Glass

California
California College of Arts and Crafts *B,M*
California State University: Northridge *B,M*
Palomar College *A*

Illinois
Southern Illinois University at Carbondale *B*

Massachusetts
Massachusetts College of Art *B,M*
School of the Museum of Fine Arts *B*

Michigan
Center for Creative Studies: College of Art and Design *B*

Nebraska
Hastings College *B*

New York
Alfred University *B,M*
Parsons School of Design *B*
Rochester Institute of Technology *A,B,M*

Ohio
Bowling Green State University *B*
Cleveland Institute of Art *B*
Ohio State University: Columbus Campus *B,M*
University of Toledo *B*

Pennsylvania
Carnegie Mellon University *B,M*

Rhode Island
Rhode Island School of Design *B,M*

Graphic arts technology

Alabama
Chattahoochee Valley Community College *A*
Community College of the Air Force *A*
John C. Calhoun State Community College *A*

Arizona
Pima Community College *C,A*

Arkansas
Garland County Community College *A*
Southern Arkansas University
    Magnolia *A*
    Technical Branch *A*

California
Bakersfield College *A*
Chabot College *A*
Chaffey Community College *A*
City College of San Francisco *A*
College of the Redwoods *C,A*
Compton Community College *A*

D-Q University *A*
East Los Angeles College *C,A*
El Camino College *A*
Evergreen Valley College *A*
Fashion Institute of Design and
 Merchandising *A*
Foothill College *A*
Fresno City College *C,A*
Glendale Community College *A*
Golden West College *C,A*
Los Angeles Trade and Technical
 College *A*
Los Medanos College *C,A*
Merced College *C,A*
Mission College *A*
Modesto Junior College *A*
Moorpark College *A*
Ohlone College *C,A*
Otis/Parsons School of Art and
 Design *A,B*
Pacific Union College *A*
Palomar College *C,A*
Pasadena City College *C,A*
Point Loma Nazarene College *B*
Rio Hondo College *A*
Saddleback College *C,A*
San Joaquin Delta College *A*
San Jose State University *B*
Santa Barbara City College *A*
Santa Monica College *A*
Santa Rosa Junior College *A*
Southwestern College *A*
Ventura College *A*
West Hills Community College *A*

Colorado

Colorado Institute of Art *A*
Colorado Mountain College: Spring
 Valley Campus *A*
Community College of Denver *C,A*
Mesa State College *A*
Pikes Peak Community College *A*
University of Northern Colorado *B*

Connecticut

Greater New Haven State Technical
 College *A*
Middlesex Community College *A*
Northwestern Connecticut
 Community College *A*

District of Columbia

Howard University *B*
University of the District of
 Columbia *A*

Florida

Broward Community College *A*
Daytona Beach Community
 College *A*
Florida Agricultural and Mechanical
 University *B*
Florida Community College at
 Jacksonville *A*
Gulf Coast Community College *A*
Miami-Dade Community College
 C,A
Okaloosa-Walton Community
 College *C,A*
Palm Beach Community College *A*
Valencia Community College *A*

Georgia

Augusta Technical Institute *C*
Chattahoochee Technical
 Institute *C*
Darton College *A*

Hawaii

Brigham Young University-
 Hawaii *A*

University of Hawaii
 Honolulu Community College
 C,A
 Leeward Community
 College *A*

Idaho

Lewis Clark State College *A*

Illinois

City Colleges of Chicago
 Richard J. Daley College *A*
 Wright College *A*
College of DuPage *C,A*
Elgin Community College *A*
John A. Logan College *A*
Judson College *B*
Lincoln College *C*
Parkland College *A*
Southern Illinois University at
 Carbondale *A*
State Community College *C*
Triton College *C,A*

Indiana

Ball State University *B*
Bethel College *A,B*
Indiana University—Purdue
 University at Fort Wayne *A*
Indiana Vocational Technical
 College
 Northcentral *A*
 Southcentral *C,A*
 Southwest *A*
St. Francis College *A*
Vincennes University *A*

Iowa

Hawkeye Institute of Technology *A*
Iowa Lakes Community College *C*
Iowa Western Community
 College *C*
Kirkwood Community College *A*

Kansas

Butler County Community
 College *A*
Colby Community College *A*
Dodge City Community College *A*
Fort Scott Community College *A*
Highland Community College *A*
Kansas City Kansas Community
 College *A*
Pittsburg State University *B*

Kentucky

Eastern Kentucky University *A*
Jefferson Community College *A*
Murray State University *A,B*

Maine

Central Maine Technical College
 C,A
University of Maine
 Augusta *A*
 Presque Isle *A*

Maryland

Catonsville Community College *C,A*
Columbia Union College *B*
Maryland College of Art and
 Design *A*
Montgomery College: Rockville
 Campus *A*

Massachusetts

Becker College: Worcester
 Campus *A*
Bunker Hill Community College *A*
Endicott College *A,B*
Fitchburg State College *B*
Hampshire College *B*

Mount Ida College *A*
Springfield Technical Community
 College *A*

Michigan

Alpena Community College *C,A*
Andrews University *A,B*
Eastern Michigan University *B*
Grand Rapids Community
 College *A*
Henry Ford Community College *A*
Lansing Community College *A*
Macomb Community College *C,A*
Madonna University *A,B*
Marygrove College *B*
Muskegon Community College *A*
Northern Michigan University *A*
Northwestern Michigan College *A*
Oakland Community College *A*
Schoolcraft College *A*
Southwestern Michigan College *A*

Minnesota

Northwestern College *A,B*
St. Paul Technical College *C*

Mississippi

Hinds Community College *A*
Mississippi Delta Community
 College *A*

Missouri

Central Missouri State University
 A,B
College of the Ozarks *B*
Evangel College *A*
Hannibal-LaGrange College *A*
St. Louis Community College
 Florissant Valley *A*
 Forest Park *A*
 Meramec *A*

Nebraska

Central Community College *A*
Chadron State College *B*
Metropolitan Community College
 C,A
Nebraska Indian Community
 College *A*
Nebraska Wesleyan University *A*
Southeast Community College:
 Milford Campus *A*

Nevada

Community College of Southern
 Nevada *C,A*

New Hampshire

Franklin Pierce College *B*
New Hampshire Technical College:
 Laconia *A*

New Jersey

Brookdale Community College *A*
Burlington County College *A*
Gloucester County College *C*
Kean College of New Jersey *B*
Ocean County College *A*
Union County College *A*

New Mexico

Institute of American Indian
 Arts *A*
New Mexico Junior College *A*

New York

City University of New York
 Kingsborough Community
 College *A*
 New York City Technical
 College *A*

Community College of the Finger
 Lakes *A*
Cornell University *M*
Dutchess Community College *A*
Fashion Institute of Technology *A,B*
Fulton-Montgomery Community
 College *A*
Monroe Community College *A*
New York University *B*
Onondaga Community College *A*
Pratt Institute *A*
Rochester Institute of Technology
 B,M
Rockland Community College *A*
School of Visual Arts *B*
State University of New York
 College of Technology at
 Farmingdale *A*
Sullivan County Community
 College *A*
Ulster County Community
 College *A*

North Carolina

Anson Community College *A*
Central Piedmont Community
 College *A*
Chowan College *A*
Forsyth Technical Community
 College *A*
Gaston College *A*
Guilford Technical Community
 College *A*
Johnston Community College *A*
McDowell Technical Community
 College *A*
Pitt Community College *A*
Southwestern Community
 College *A*

North Dakota

North Dakota State College of
 Science *C,A*

Ohio

Art Academy of Cincinnati *A*
Bowling Green State University *B*
Columbus State Community
 College *A*
Cuyahoga Community College:
 Metropolitan Campus *A*
Lakeland Community College *A*
Lourdes College *A*
Sinclair Community College *A*
Terra Technical College *A*
University of Akron *A*
Youngstown State University *A*

Oklahoma

Northeastern State University *B*
Northern Oklahoma College *A*
Oklahoma State University
 Technical Branch: Okmulgee *A*
Redlands Community College *A*
Rogers State College *C,A*

Oregon

Chemeketa Community College *A*
Linn-Benton Community College *A*
Mount Hood Community College
 C,A
Oregon Polytechnic Institute *C*
Portland Community College *A*

Pennsylvania

Antonelli Institute of Art and
 Photography *A*
Art Institute of Pittsburgh *A*
Bucks County Community
 College *A*
California University of
 Pennsylvania *A,B*

Carnegie Mellon University *B,M*
Edinboro University of
Pennsylvania *B*
Harrisburg Area Community
College *A*
Hussian School of Art *A*
La Roche College *B*
Luzerne County Community
College *A*
Montgomery County Community
College *A*
Northampton County Area
Community College *A*
Pennsylvania College of
Technology *A*
Seton Hill College *B*
University of the Arts *C,A,B*
West Chester University of
Pennsylvania *A*
Westmoreland County Community
College *C,A*

Puerto Rico

University of Puerto Rico: Carolina
Regional College *A*

South Carolina

Clemson University *B*
Midlands Technical College *A*
Trident Technical College *A*

South Dakota

Black Hills State University *A,B*

Tennessee

Chattanooga State Technical
Community College *A*
Memphis College of Art *B*
Nashville State Technical Institute
C,A

Texas

Amarillo College *A*
Austin Community College *A*
Bee County College *A*
Central Texas College *A*
Eastfield College *A*
Galveston College *A*
Houston Community College *A*
Kilgore College *A*
Lee College *A*
Midland College *A*
Navarro College *A*
San Jacinto College: Central
Campus *A*
Texas State Technical College
Amarillo *A*
Waco *A*
Western Texas College *A*

Utah

Dixie College *A*

Virginia

Virginia Intermont College *A*

Washington

Bellevue Community College *A*
Centralia College *A*
Clark College *C,A*
Columbia Basin College *A*
Eastern Washington University *B*
Seattle Central Community
College *A*
Shoreline Community College *A*
Skagit Valley College *C,A*
Walla Walla College *A*

West Virginia

Glenville State College *A*

Wisconsin

Cardinal Stritch College *A*
Madison Area Technical College *A*
Silver Lake College *A*
University of Wisconsin:
Platteville *B*

Wyoming

Casper College *A*
Laramie County Community
College *A*
Northwest College *A*

Graphic design

Alabama

Auburn University *B,M*
Oakwood College *A*
Samford University *B*
University of Montevallo *B*

Arizona

Grand Canyon University *B*
Yavapai College *C,A*

Arkansas

Arkansas State University *B*
John Brown University *B*

California

Academy of Art College *C,B,M,W*
American College for the Applied
Arts: Los Angeles *A,B*
Art Center College of Design *B,M*
Art Institute of Southern
California *B*
Biola University *B*
California College of Arts and
Crafts *B*
California Institute of the Arts
C,B,M
California Polytechnic State
University: San Luis Obispo *B*
California State University
Fullerton *B*
Long Beach *B*
Los Angeles *B,M*
Northridge *A*
Cerro Coso Community College *C*
City College of San Francisco *C,A*
College of Notre Dame *B*
De Anza College *C*
Golden West College *C,A*
Los Angeles Pierce College *A*
Los Angeles Valley College *C,A*
Monterey Peninsula College *C,A*
Moorpark College *A*
Otis/Parsons School of Art and
Design *C,A,B*
Pacific Christian College *B*
Palomar College *A*
Pasadena City College *C,A*
Saddleback College *C,A*
San Francisco State University *B,M*
San Jose State University *B*
Santa Monica College *A*
Southwestern College *A*
University of San Francisco *B*
West Hills Community College *C*
Woodbury University *B*

Colorado

Colorado Institute of Art *A*
Colorado Mountain College: Spring
Valley Campus *A*
Denver Institute of Technology *C*
Rocky Mountain College of Art &
Design *A,B*
University of Denver *B*

Connecticut

Housatonic Community College
C,A
Manchester Community College *A*
Northwestern Connecticut
Community College *C,A*
Norwalk Community College *A*
Paier College of Art *C,B*
Sacred Heart University *A,B*
Tunxis Community College *C,A*
University of Bridgeport *A,B*
University of Connecticut *B*
University of Hartford *B*
University of New Haven *C,A,B*
Western Connecticut State
University *B*

Delaware

University of Delaware *B*

District of Columbia

American University *B*
Corcoran School of Art *B*

Florida

Brevard Community College *A*
Daytona Beach Community
College *A*
Florida Agricultural and Mechanical
University *B*
International Fine Arts College *A*
Lake-Sumter Community College *A*
Lynn University *B*
Okaloosa-Walton Community
College *C,A*
Palm Beach Community College *A*
Pensacola Junior College *A*
Ringling School of Art and
Design *B*
St. Petersburg Junior College *A*
Santa Fe Community College *A*
Tampa College *A*
University of Florida *B*
University of Miami *M*
Valencia Community College *A*

Georgia

American College for the Applied
Arts *A,B*
Atlanta College of Art *B*
Brenau Women's College *B*
Savannah College of Art and
Design *B,M*
University of Georgia *B,M*

Idaho

University of Idaho *B*

Illinois

American Academy of Art *A*
Bradley University *B*
Chicago State University *B*
City Colleges of Chicago: Chicago
City-Wide College *C*
Columbia College *B*
Elgin Community College *A*
Illinois Institute of Technology
B,M,D
Illinois Wesleyan University *B*
Prairie State College *A*
Ray College of Design *A,B*
St. Xavier University *B*
School of the Art Institute of
Chicago *B,M*
Southern Illinois University at
Carbondale *A,B*
University of Illinois at Urbana-
Champaign *B,M*

Indiana

Anderson University *B*
Ball State University *B*

Grace College *B*
Huntington College *B*
Indiana State University *B*
Indiana University Bloomington
B,M
Indiana Vocational Technical
College
Columbus *A*
Northcentral *A*
International Business College *C*
St. Francis College *A*
University of Indianapolis *B*
Vincennes University *A*

Iowa

Drake University *B*
Graceland College *B*
Grand View College *B*
Iowa State University *B*
Morningside College *B*
St. Ambrose University *B*
Teikyo Marycrest University *B*
University of Northern Iowa *B*

Kansas

Colby Community College *A*
Hutchinson Community College *A*
Kansas Newman College *B*
Kansas State University *M*
Pratt Community College *A*
Wichita State University *B*

Kentucky

Brescia College *B*
Eastern Kentucky University *B*
Northern Kentucky University *B*

Louisiana

Louisiana College *B*
Louisiana State University and
Agricultural and Mechanical
College *B*
Louisiana Tech University *B,M*

Maine

Portland School of Art *B*

Maryland

Anne Arundel Community
College *C*
Frostburg State University *B*
Maryland Institute College of Art *B*
Morgan State University *B*
University of Baltimore *M*
Villa Julie College *A*

Massachusetts

Berkshire Community College *A*
Boston University *B,M*
Bridgewater State College *B*
Elms College *B*
Endicott College *A,B*
Greenfield Community College *A*
Massachusetts College of Art *B,M*
Montserrat College of Art *B*
Mount Ida College *A,B*
Salem State College *B*
School of the Museum of Fine
Arts *B*
Simmons College *B*
University of Massachusetts
Dartmouth *B,M*
Lowell *B*

Michigan

Alma College *B*
Aquinas College *B*
Center for Creative Studies: College
of Art and Design *B*
Central Michigan University *B,M*
Eastern Michigan University *B*
Grand Valley State University *B*

Kendall College of Art and
Design *B*
Lansing Community College *A*
Marygrove College *B*
Northern Michigan University *B*
Oakland Community College *C*
University of Michigan *B,M*

Minnesota

College of Associated Arts *B*
Moorhead State University *B*
National Education Center: Brown
Institute Campus *A*
St. Cloud State University *B*
St. Mary's College of Minnesota *B*
University of Minnesota: Duluth *B*

Mississippi

Mississippi College *B*

Missouri

Columbia College *B*
Kansas City Art Institute *B*
Missouri Southern State College *B*
Park College *B*
Southwest Missouri State
University *B*
Washington University *B,M*
Webster University *B*

Montana

Dull Knife Memorial College *A*
Montana State University *B*

Nebraska

Dana College *B*
University of Nebraska—Kearney *B*

New Hampshire

Colby-Sawyer College *B*
Franklin Pierce College *B*
Keene State College *B*
Plymouth State College of the
University System of New
Hampshire *B*
Rivier College *B*
White Pines College *A*

New Jersey

Centenary College *B*
County College of Morris *A*
Jersey City State College *B*
Mercer County Community
College *A*
Rutgers—The State University of
New Jersey
Mason Gross School of the
Arts *B*
Newark College of Arts and
Sciences *B*
Sussex County Community
College *C*
Trenton State College *B*
William Paterson College of New
Jersey *B*

New Mexico

Clovis Community College *A*
Eastern New Mexico University *B*
Institute of American Indian
Arts *A*
New Mexico Highlands
University *B*

New York

Adelphi University *B*
Alfred University *B*
Cazenovia College *A*
College of St. Rose *B*
Cooper Union *B*
Daemen College *B*

Long Island University
C. W. Post Campus *B,M*
Southampton Campus *B*
Mercy College *C,B*
Mohawk Valley Community College
C,A
New York Institute of
Technology *B*
Parsons School of Design *A,B*
Pratt Institute *A,B,M*
Rochester Institute of Technology
A,B,M
Rockland Community College *A*
Sage Junior College of Albany, A
Division of Russell Sage
College *A*
School of Visual Arts *B*
State University of New York
Purchase *B*
College at Buffalo *B*
College at New Paltz *B*
College of Technology at
Farmingdale *A*
Suffolk County Community College
Eastern Campus *A*
Selden *A*
Sullivan County Community
College *A*
Tompkins-Cortland Community
College *C*
Villa Maria College of Buffalo *C,A*

North Carolina

Barton College *B*
East Carolina University *B,M*
Mount Olive College *B*
North Carolina State University
B,M

Ohio

Art Academy of Cincinnati *A,B*
Ashland University *B*
Bowling Green State University *B*
Bradford School *C*
Cleveland Institute of Art *B*
College of Mount St. Joseph *A,B*
Columbus College of Art and
Design *B*
Kent State University *B,M*
Notre Dame College of Ohio *B*
Ohio Northern University *B*
Ohio University *B,M*
University of Akron *B*
University of Cincinnati *B*
University of Dayton *B*
Wittenberg University *B*
Youngstown State University *B*

Oklahoma

Northeastern State University *B*
Oklahoma Christian University of
Science and Arts *B*
Oklahoma State University
Technical Branch: Okmulgee *A*
Phillips University *A*
University of Central Oklahoma *B*
University of Tulsa *B*

Oregon

Lane Community College *A*
Linn-Benton Community College *A*
Mount Hood Community
College *A*
Pacific Northwest College of Art
C,B

Pennsylvania

Art Institute of Pittsburgh *A*
Beaver College *B*
Bucks County Community
College *B*

California University of
Pennsylvania *B*
Carnegie Mellon University *B,M*
Delaware County Community
College *A*
Drexel University *B*
Harcum Junior College *A*
Harrisburg Area Community
College *C,A*
Hussian School of Art *A*
La Roche College *B*
Marywood College *B*
Mercyhurst College *B*
Moore College of Art and Design *B*
Moravian College *B*
Northeastern Christian Junior
College *A*
Pittsburgh Technical Institute *C,A*
Point Park College *B*
St. Vincent College *B*
Seton Hill College *B*
Temple University *B,M*
University of the Arts *B*
Westmoreland County Community
College *A*

Rhode Island

Rhode Island School of Design *B,M*

South Carolina

Anderson College *B*
Bob Jones University *B*
Coker College *B*
University of South Carolina *B*

South Dakota

South Dakota State University *B*

Tennessee

Chattanooga State Technical
Community College *A*
East Tennessee State University *B*
Memphis College of Art *B*
O'More College of Design *C,A,B*
Union University *B*
University of Tennessee:
Knoxville *B*

Texas

Abilene Christian University *B*
Brazosport College *C*
Lamar University—Beaumont *B*
Lubbock Christian University *B*
Sam Houston State University *B*
San Antonio College *A*
Texas Christian University *B*
University of Houston *B*
University of North Texas *B,M*
University of Texas at El Paso *B*

Utah

Brigham Young University *B*
Weber State University *A*

Virginia

George Mason University *M*
Marymount University *B*
Radford University *B*
Virginia Intermont College *A*

Washington

Central Washington University *B*
Cornish College of the Arts *B*
Everett Community College *C*
Pacific Lutheran University *B*
Shoreline Community College *A*
Spokane Falls Community College
C,A
University of Washington *B,M*
Yakima Valley Community
College *A*

West Virginia

Bethany College *B*
Marshall University *B*
Shepherd College *A,B*
West Liberty State College *B*
West Virginia State College *B*
West Virginia University *B,M*

Wisconsin

Milwaukee Institute of Art &
Design *B*
Mount Mary College *B*
Mount Senario College *B*
St. Norbert College *B*
University of Wisconsin
Milwaukee *B*
Platteville *B*

Wyoming

Northwest College *A*

Graphic and printing production

Alabama

Alabama Agricultural and
Mechanical University *A*
Bessemer State Technical College *C*
Community College of the Air
Force *A*

Arizona

Pima Community College *C,A*

Arkansas

Arkansas State University *B*
Phillips County Community
College *A*

California

Allan Hancock College *A*
California Polytechnic State
University: San Luis Obispo *B*
Chaffey Community College *C,A*
City College of San Francisco *A*
Compton Community College *A*
Don Bosco Technical Institute *A*
Fresno City College *C,A*
Golden West College *C,A*
Laney College *C,A*
Los Angeles Trade and Technical
College *C,A*
Mission College *C,A*
Modesto Junior College *A*
Moorpark College *A*
Ohlone College *C,A*
Otis/Parsons School of Art and
Design *A,B*
Pasadena City College *C,A*
Saddleback College *C,A*
San Joaquin Delta College *A*
San Jose State University *B*
Santa Barbara City College *C,A*
Santa Monica College *A*

Colorado

Aims Community College *C,A*
Community College of Denver *C,A*
Denver Institute of Technology *C*
Mesa State College *A*
Pikes Peak Community College *C,A*

Connecticut

Greater New Haven State Technical
College *A*

District of Columbia

University of the District of
Columbia *A*

Florida

Miami-Dade Community College *A*
Palm Beach Community College *A*
Pensacola Junior College *A*

Georgia

Atlanta Metropolitan College *A*
Augusta Technical Institute *C*
Chattahoochee Technical
    Institute *C*
DeKalb Technical Institute *C*

Idaho

Idaho State University *A*
Lewis Clark State College *A*

Illinois

City Colleges of Chicago: Chicago
    City-Wide College *C*
College of DuPage *C,A*
Illinois Central College *A*
Southern Illinois University at
    Carbondale *A*
Triton College *C,A*

Indiana

Ball State University *A*
Indiana State University *B*
Indiana Vocational Technical
    College: Wabash Valley *A*
Vincennes University *A*

Iowa

Clinton Community College *C*
Des Moines Area Community
    College *C*
Iowa Lakes Community College *C*
Iowa Western Community
    College *C*
Kirkwood Community College *A*

Kansas

Allen County Community
    College *C*
Colby Community College *A*
Fort Scott Community College *A*
Pittsburg State University *C,B*

Kentucky

Eastern Kentucky University *A,B*
Morehead State University *A*
Murray State University *A*
Western Kentucky University *A*

Maine

Central Maine Technical College
    C,A

Maryland

Catonsville Community College *C,A*
Montgomery College: Rockville
    Campus *A*

Massachusetts

Fitchburg State College *B*
Northern Essex Community
    College *A*

Michigan

Alpena Community College *C,A*
Andrews University *A,B*
Eastern Michigan University *B*
Lansing Community College *A*
Macomb Community College *C,A*
Mid Michigan Community
    College *A*
Muskegon Community College *A*
Northern Michigan University *A,B*
Oakland Community College *A*
Southwestern Michigan College *A*
Western Michigan University *B*

Minnesota

St. Paul Technical College *C*

Mississippi

Hinds Community College *C,A*
Mississippi Delta Community
    College *C*

Missouri

Central Missouri State University
    A,B
College of the Ozarks *B*
Lincoln University *A*

Montana

Miles Community College *A*

Nebraska

Central Community College *C,A*
Chadron State College *B*
Metropolitan Community College
    C,A
Southeast Community College:
    Lincoln Campus *C*

Nevada

Community College of Southern
    Nevada *C,A*
Truckee Meadows Community
    College *C*

New Hampshire

New Hampshire Technical College:
    Laconia *A*

New Mexico

New Mexico Junior College *A*

New York

City University of New York: New
    York City Technical College *A,B*
Erie Community College: South
    Campus *A*
Fulton-Montgomery Community
    College *A*
Mohawk Valley Community College
    C,A
Onondaga Community College *A*
Rochester Institute of Technology
    A,B,M
State University of New York
    College of Technology at
    Farmingdale *A*

North Carolina

Appalachian State University *B*
Central Piedmont Community
    College *A*
Chowan College *B*
Isothermal Community College *A*
McDowell Technical Community
    College *A*

North Dakota

North Dakota State College of
    Science *C,A*

Ohio

Bowling Green State University *B*
Cincinnati Technical College *A*
Columbus State Community
    College *A*
Cuyahoga Community College:
    Western Campus *A*
Terra Technical College *A*
University of Akron *B*

Oklahoma

Northern Oklahoma College *C,A*
Oklahoma State University
    Technical Branch: Okmulgee *A*
Redlands Community College *A*

Oregon

Chemeketa Community College *A*
Linn-Benton Community College *A*
Mount Hood Community College
    C,A
Portland Community College *C,A*

Pennsylvania

California University of
    Pennsylvania *A,B*
Luzerne County Community
    College *A*
Pennsylvania College of
    Technology *A*
Westmoreland County Community
    College *A*

South Carolina

Greenville Technical College *C*
Midlands Technical College *C,A*

Tennessee

Chattanooga State Technical
    Community College *A*

Texas

Austin Community College *A*
Central Texas College *A*
College of the Mainland *C*
East Texas State University *B*
Eastfield College *A*
Houston Community College *C*
Kilgore College *A*
Lee College *A*
Midland College *A*
San Jacinto College: Central
    Campus *A*
Southwest Texas State University *B*
Tarrant County Junior College *A*
Texarkana College *A*
Texas State Technical College:
    Waco *A*
University of Houston *B*

Utah

Dixie College *A*
Utah Valley Community College
    C,A

Virginia

Tidewater Community College *A*
Virginia Intermont College *A*

Washington

Art Institute of Seattle *C*
Clark College *A*
Everett Community College *C*
Seattle Central Community College
    C,A
Shoreline Community College *C,A*
Spokane Community College *A*
Walla Walla College *C,A,B*

West Virginia

Fairmont State College *A*
West Virginia Institute of
    Technology *A,B*

Wisconsin

Fox Valley Technical College *C,A*
Madison Area Technical College *A*
University of Wisconsin:
    Platteville *B*
Western Wisconsin Technical
    College *C,A*

Wyoming

Northwest College *A*

Greek (classical)

Alabama

University of Alabama *B*

Arizona

University of Arizona *B*

California

Loyola Marymount University *B*
Pomona College *B*
St. Mary's College of California *B*
Scripps College *B*
University of California
    Berkeley *B,M,D*
    Davis *B*
    Los Angeles *B,M*
    Santa Barbara *B*
    Santa Cruz *B,D*
University of the Pacific *B*
University of Southern California *B*

Colorado

University of Colorado at
    Boulder *B*

Connecticut

Wesleyan University *B*
Yale University *B*

District of Columbia

Catholic University of America *B*

Florida

Florida State University *B,M*
New College of the University of
    South Florida *B*
University of Florida *B,M*

Georgia

Agnes Scott College *B*
Emory University *B*
Georgia State University *B*
Mercer University *B*
University of Georgia *B,M*

Illinois

Augustana College *B*
Loyola University of Chicago
    B,M,D
Monmouth College *B*
North Central College *B*
Rockford College *B*
University of Chicago *B,M,D*
University of Illinois at Urbana-
    Champaign *M*
Wheaton College *B*

Indiana

Butler University *B*
DePauw University *B*
Indiana University Bloomington
    B,M,D
University of Notre Dame *B*
Valparaiso University *B*
Wabash College *B*

Iowa

Grinnell College *B*
Loras College *B*
Luther College *B*
University of Iowa *B,M*
Wartburg College *B*

Kansas

University of Kansas *B*

Kentucky

Louisville Presbyterian Theological
    Seminary *M*

Louisiana

Tulane University *B,M*

Maryland

Johns Hopkins University *B,M,D*
Loyola College in Maryland *B*

Massachusetts

Amherst College *B*
Boston College *B,M*
Boston University *B,M*
Brandeis University *B*
College of the Holy Cross *B*
Harvard and Radcliffe Colleges *B*
Harvard University *D*
Mount Holyoke College *B*
Smith College *B*
Tufts University *B*
University of Massachusetts at
   Boston *B*
Wellesley College *B*
Wheaton College *B*
Williams College *B*

Michigan

Calvin College *B*
Concordia College *B*
Hope College *B*
University of Michigan *B,M,D*
Wayne State University *B*

Minnesota

Bethany Lutheran College *A*
Carleton College *B*
Gustavus Adolphus College *B*
Macalester College *B*
North Central Bible College *A,B*
St. Olaf College *B*
University of Minnesota: Twin
   Cities *B,M,D*

Mississippi

Millsaps College *B*
Mississippi College *B*
University of Mississippi *B,M*

Missouri

St. Louis University *B*
University of Missouri: Columbia *B*
Washington University *M*

Montana

Carroll College *B*

Nebraska

Creighton University *B*

New Hampshire

Dartmouth College *B*
University of New Hampshire *B*

New Jersey

Drew University *B*
Rutgers—The State University of
   New Jersey
      Douglass College *B*
      Livingston College *B*
      Rutgers College *B*
      University College New
         Brunswick *B*

New York

Bard College *B*
Barnard College *B*
City University of New York
   Brooklyn College *B*
   City College *B*
   Hunter College *B*
   Lehman College *B*
   Queens College *B*
Colgate University *B*

Columbia University
   Columbia College *B*
   New York *M,D*
   School of General Studies *B*
Elmira College *B*
Fordham University *B,M,D*
Hamilton College *B*
Hobart College *B*
New York University *B*
St. Bonaventure University *B*
Sarah Lawrence College *B*
State University of New York
   Albany *B*
   Binghamton *B*
Syracuse University *M*
Vassar College *B*
William Smith College *B*
Yeshiva University *B*

North Carolina

Davidson College *B*
Duke University *B*
University of North Carolina
   Chapel Hill *B,M,D*
   Greensboro *B*
Wake Forest University *B*

Ohio

College of Wooster *B*
John Carroll University *B,M*
Kenyon College *B*
Miami University: Oxford
   Campus *B*
Oberlin College *B*
Ohio State University: Columbus
   Campus *B,M*
University of Akron *B*
University of Dayton *B*
University of Toledo *B,M*
Wright State University *B*
Xavier University *B*

Oregon

University of Oregon
   Eugene *B*
   Robert Donald Clark Honors
      College *B*
Western Conservative Baptist
   Seminary *M*

Pennsylvania

Allegheny College *B*
Bryn Mawr College *B,M,D*
Bucknell University *B*
Dickinson College *B*
Duquesne University *B*
Franklin and Marshall College *B*
Gettysburg College *B*
Haverford College *B*
La Salle University *B*
Millersville University of
   Pennsylvania *B*
Muhlenberg College *B*
Susquehanna University *B*
Swarthmore College *B*
University of Pennsylvania *B,M,D*
University of Scranton *B*
Ursinus College *B*

Rhode Island

Brown University *B,M,D*

South Carolina

Furman University *B*
University of South Carolina *B*

South Dakota

Augustana College *B*
University of South Dakota *B*

Tennessee

Union University *B*
University of the South *B*
University of Tennessee:
   Chattanooga *B*
Vanderbilt University *B,M*

Texas

Abilene Christian University *B*
Baylor University *B*
Rice University *B*
Trinity University *B*
University of Dallas *B*
University of Texas at Austin *B*

Utah

Brigham Young University *B*

Vermont

Marlboro College *B*
University of Vermont *B,M*

Virginia

Hampden-Sydney College *B*
Mary Washington College *B*
Randolph-Macon College *B*
Sweet Briar College *B*
University of Richmond *B,W*

Washington

Evergreen State College *B*
Gonzaga University *B*
University of Washington *B,M,D*

West Virginia

West Virginia University *B,M*

Wisconsin

Beloit College *B*
Concordia University Wisconsin *B*
Lawrence University *B*
University of Wisconsin: Madison
   B,M,D

Greek (modern)

Alabama

University of Alabama *B*

Arizona

University of Arizona *B*

Illinois

Northwestern University *B*

Massachusetts

Boston University *B*
Harvard and Radcliffe Colleges *B*
Hellenic College *B*

New York

City University of New York:
   Queens College *B*
Columbia University *M,D*
Cornell University *B,M,D*

Ohio

Ohio State University: Columbus
   Campus *B,M*

Health care administration

Alabama

Auburn University *B*
Community College of the Air
   Force *A*
University of Alabama
   Birmingham *M,D*
   Tuscaloosa *B*

Arizona

Arizona State University *M*
Northern Arizona University *B*
University of Arizona *B*

Arkansas

Arkansas State University *B*
University of Arkansas at Little
   Rock *M*

California

Azusa Pacific University *M*
Barstow College *C*
California College for Health
   Sciences *M*
California State University
   Bakersfield *M*
   Dominguez Hills *B*
   Fresno *B*
   Long Beach *B,M*
   Los Angeles *M*
   Northridge *B*
   San Bernardino *M*
Chapman University *M*
Golden Gate University *B,M*
Mount St. Mary's College *B*
National University *M*
San Jose State University *B,M*
Santa Rosa Junior College *A*
University of Judaism *M*
University of La Verne *B,M*
University of Southern California *M*

Colorado

Denver Technical College *C*
Metropolitan State College of
   Denver *B*
Regis College of Regis University *B*

Connecticut

Quinnipiac College *B,M*
Sacred Heart University *M*
University of Connecticut *B*
University of New Haven *B,M*
Western Connecticut State
   University *M*

District of Columbia

George Washington University *M,D*
Howard University *M*

Florida

Florida Agricultural and Mechanical
   University *B*
Florida Atlantic University *B*
Florida Institute of Technology *M*
Florida International University
   B,M
Jacksonville University *M*
Lynn University *B*
Miami-Dade Community College *A*
Pensacola Junior College *A*
St. Leo College *B*
St. Petersburg Junior College *A*
University of Central Florida *B*
University of Florida *M*
University of Miami *B*
University of North Florida *M*
Valencia Community College *A*

Georgia

Augusta College *M*
Georgia State University *M,D*

Idaho

Idaho State University *B*

Illinois

Bradley University *M*
College of St. Francis *M*
Elmhurst College *B*
Governors State University *B,M*
Illinois Benedictine College *B*
Illinois Central College *C,A*
National-Louis University *B*
Northwestern University *M*
Roosevelt University *B,M*
Rush University *M*
St. Xavier University *M*
Sangamon State University *B,M*
Southern Illinois University at
  Carbondale *B*
University of Chicago *M*

Indiana

Indiana University—Purdue
  University at Indianapolis *B,M*
Indiana Vocational Technical
  College: Central Indiana *A*
University of Evansville *M*

Iowa

Des Moines Area Community
  College *A*
Indian Hills Community College *A*
Iowa Lakes Community College *A*
Simpson College *B*
University of Iowa *M,D*
University of Osteopathic Medicine
  and Health Sciences *B,M*

Kansas

Allen County Community
  College *A*
Benedictine College *A,B*
Ottawa University *B*
University of Kansas *M*
Wichita State University *B,M*

Kentucky

Bellarmine College *B*
Eastern Kentucky University *B*
Western Kentucky University *B,M*

Louisiana

Tulane University *M,D*

Maine

St. Joseph's College *M*
University of New England *B*

Maryland

Columbia Union College *B*
Sojourner-Douglass College *B*
University of Maryland Baltimore
  County *B*

Massachusetts

Boston University *M*
Bunker Hill Community College *C*
Clark University *M*
Emmanuel College *B,M*
Framingham State College *M*
Harvard University *M,D*
Lesley College *B,M*
Northeastern University *B*
Simmons College *M*
Springfield College *B,M*
Stonehill College *B*
University of Massachusetts at
  Lowell *M*

Michigan

Central Michigan University *M*
Concordia College *B*
Detroit College of Business *B*
Eastern Michigan University *B*
Ferris State University *B*
Madonna University *B,M*
Oakland Community College *A*
University of Detroit Mercy *M*
University of Michigan
  Ann Arbor *M,D*
  Flint *B*

Minnesota

College of St. Scholastica *B*
Concordia College: Moorhead *B*
St. Mary's College of Minnesota *M*
University of Minnesota: Twin
  Cities *M,D*
Willmar Community College *A*
Winona State University *B*

Mississippi

Mississippi College *M*
University of Mississippi *M,D*

Missouri

Lindenwood College *B,M*
Maryville University *C,B*
St. Louis University *M*
Southwest Baptist University *B,M*
University of Missouri
  Columbia *M*
  Kansas City *M*
Washington University *M*
Webster University *B,M*

Montana

College of Great Falls *B*

Nebraska

Central Community College *A*
Clarkson College *M*
Dana College *B*
Metropolitan Community College *A*

Nevada

University of Nevada: Las Vegas *B*

New Hampshire

University of New Hampshire *B,M*

New Jersey

Essex County College *A*
St. Peter's College *B*
Stockton State College *B*
Thomas Edison State College *A,B*

New York

Alfred University *B*
City University of New York
  Baruch College *M*
  Brooklyn College *M*
  Lehman College *B*
Cornell University *M,D*
Dominican College of Blauvelt *B*
D'Youville College *M*
Herkimer County Community
  College *A*
Hofstra University *M*
Iona College *B,M*
Ithaca College *B*
Long Island University
  Brooklyn Campus *B,M*
  C. W. Post Campus *B,M*
New York University *C,M*
Rochester Institute of
  Technology *A*
Russell Sage College *M*
St. Francis College *B*
St. John's University *B*

St. Joseph's College
  Brooklyn *B*
  Suffolk Campus *B*
State University of New York
  College at Fredonia *B*
  Institute of Technology at
    Utica/Rome *B*
Union College *M*

North Carolina

Appalachian State University *B,M*
Brevard College *A*
Duke University *M*
University of North Carolina
  Asheville *B*
  Chapel Hill *M,D*
Western Carolina University *B*

Ohio

Ashland University *B*
Bowling Green State University *B*
Cleveland State University *M*
Dyke College *B*
Heidelberg College *B*
Lake Erie College *B,M*
Ohio Dominican College *B*
Ohio State University: Columbus
  Campus *M*
Ohio University *B,M*
Union Institute *B,D*
University of Cincinnati *B,M*
University of Toledo *B,M*
Ursuline College *B*
Wilberforce University *B*
Xavier University *M*

Oklahoma

Langston University *B*
Northeastern State University *B*
Southwestern Oklahoma State
  University *B*
University of Oklahoma
  Health Sciences Center *M,D*
  Norman *M,D*

Oregon

Concordia College *C,B*
Oregon State University *B*
Portland State University *M*
University of Portland *B*

Pennsylvania

Delaware County Community
  College *A*
Eastern College *B,M*
Gannon University *M*
Gwynedd-Mercy College *B*
King's College *B*
La Salle University *B,M*
Lebanon Valley College of
  Pennsylvania *B*
Marywood College *B,M*
Penn State
  Harrisburg Capital College *B*
  University Park Campus
    C,B,M,D
Pennsylvania Institute of
  Technology *C,A*
Robert Morris College *B*
St. Joseph's University *B,M*
Temple University *M,D*
University of Pennsylvania *M,D*
University of Pittsburgh *M,D*
University of Scranton *A,B,M*
West Chester University of
  Pennsylvania *B,M*
Wilkes University *M*

Puerto Rico

University of Puerto Rico: Medical
  Sciences Campus *M*

Rhode Island

Bryant College *M*
Providence College *A,B*
Salve Regina University *M*

South Carolina

University of South Carolina *M,D*

South Dakota

Augustana College *B*
Mount Marty College *B*
University of South Dakota *B*

Tennessee

Chattanooga State Technical
  Community College *A*
East Tennessee State University *B*
Milligan College *B*
Southern College of Seventh-day
  Adventists *B*
Tennessee State University *B*
Union University *B*

Texas

Austin Community College *C*
Baylor University *M*
East Texas State University *B*
Our Lady of the Lake University of
  San Antonio *M*
Southwest Texas State University
  B,M
Texas Southern University *B*
Texas Woman's University *M*
Trinity University *M*
University of Dallas *M*
University of Houston: Clear Lake
  B,M
University of Texas
  El Paso *B*
  Health Science Center at
    Houston *M,D*
  Medical Branch at
    Galveston *B*
  Southwestern Medical Center
    at Dallas Southwestern
    Allied Health Sciences
    School *B*

Utah

Brigham Young University *B,M*
University of Utah *M*
Weber State University *B*

Virginia

College of Health Sciences *C*
Mary Baldwin College *B*
Marymount University *B*
Norfolk State University *B*
Virginia Commonwealth
  University *M*

Washington

City University *B,M*
Eastern Washington University *B*
Seattle University *B*
University of Washington *M*

West Virginia

College of West Virginia *B*
Davis and Elkins College *A,B*
Marshall University *B*
West Virginia Institute of
  Technology *B*

Wisconsin

Cardinal Stritch College *M*
Mid-State Technical College *C*
University of Wisconsin
  Eau Claire *B*
  Madison *M*
Viterbo College *B*

Health education

Alabama

Auburn University *B,M,D*
Jacksonville State University *B,M*
John C. Calhoun State Community
College *A*
Livingston University *B*
Samford University *B*
University of Alabama
Birmingham *B,M,D*
Tuscaloosa *B,M,D,W*
University of Montevallo *B*
University of North Alabama *B,M*

Arizona

Northern Arizona University *B*
University of Arizona *B,M*

Arkansas

Ouachita Baptist University *B*
University of Arkansas
Fayetteville *B,M*
Little Rock *B*
University of Central Arkansas *B,M*

California

California State University
Fresno *B*
Long Beach *B,M*
Los Angeles *B,M*
Northridge *B*
Sacramento *B*
San Jose State University *M*

Connecticut

Southern Connecticut State
University *B,M*
Western Connecticut State
University *B*

Delaware

Delaware State College *B*
University of Delaware *B*

District of Columbia

University of the District of
Columbia *B*

Florida

Florida Agricultural and Mechanical
University *M*
Florida International University
B,M
Florida State University *B,M*
Gulf Coast Community College *A*
Nova University *M*
Palm Beach Community College *A*
Pensacola Junior College *A*
University of Florida *B,M*
University of South Florida *B*

Georgia

Albany State College *B*
Brewton-Parker College *A,B*
Clark Atlanta University *B*
Georgia College *B,M*
Georgia Southern University *B,M*
Georgia State University *B*
Kennesaw State College *B*
Morris Brown College *B*
South Georgia College *B*
University of Georgia *B,M*

Idaho

Idaho State University *M*
Northwest Nazarene College *B*

Illinois

Eastern Illinois University *B*
Illinois State University *B*
North Central College *B*
St. Xavier University *M*
Southern Illinois University
Carbondale *B,M,D*
Edwardsville *B*
University of Illinois
Chicago *M*
Urbana-Champaign *B,M,D*
Western Illinois University *B*

Indiana

Ball State University *B*
Butler University *B*
Franklin College *B*
Indiana State University *B,M*
Indiana University Bloomington
B,M
Indiana University—Purdue
University at Indianapolis *B,M*
Manchester College *B*
Purdue University *B,M,D*
St. Francis College *B*
Taylor University *B*
Vincennes University *A*

Iowa

Briar Cliff College *B*
Cornell College *B*
Iowa Lakes Community College *A*
Iowa State University *B*
Luther College *B*
Simpson College *B*
University of Northern Iowa *B,M*
Upper Iowa University *B*
William Penn College *B*

Kansas

Bethany College *B*
Emporia State University *B*
Pittsburg State University *B*
Southwestern College *B*
University of Kansas *B*
Washburn University of Topeka *B*

Kentucky

Campbellsville College *B*
Cumberland College *B*
Eastern Kentucky University *B,M*
Morehead State University *B*
Murray State University *B*
University of Kentucky *B,D*
University of Louisville *B*
Western Kentucky University *B,M*

Louisiana

Dillard University *B*
Grambling State University *B*
Louisiana College *B*
Louisiana State University in
Shreveport *B*
Nicholls State University *B*
Southeastern Louisiana
University *B*
Southern University and
Agricultural and Mechanical
College *B*

Maine

University of Maine
Farmington *B*
Machias *B*
Presque Isle *B*

Maryland

Morgan State University *B*
Prince George's Community
College *A*
University of Maryland: College
Park *M,D*

Massachusetts

Boston University *B,M,W*
Bridgewater State College *M*
Northeastern University *B*
Springfield College *B,M*
University of Massachusetts at
Lowell *B*
Worcester State College *M*

Michigan

Central Michigan University *B,M*
Eastern Michigan University *B*
Michigan State University *B,M,D*
Northern Michigan University *B,M*
Wayne State University *M*
Western Michigan University *B*

Minnesota

Augsburg College *B*
Bemidji State University *B,M*
Bethel College *B*
Concordia College: Moorhead *B*
Concordia College: St. Paul *B*
Gustavus Adolphus College *B*
Mankato State University *B*
Moorhead State University *B*
Northland Community College *A*
Rainy River Community College *A*
St. Cloud State University *B*
St. Olaf College *B*
Southwest State University *B*
University of Minnesota: Duluth *B*
Vermilion Community College *A*
Willmar Community College *A*
Winona State University *B*

Mississippi

Alcorn State University *B*
Jackson State University *B,M,W*
Mary Holmes College *A*
Mississippi College *B,M*
Mississippi University for Women *B*
Northeast Mississippi Community
College *A*
University of Southern Mississippi
B,M

Missouri

Fontbonne College *B*
Missouri Baptist College *B*
Northeast Missouri State
University *M*
Northwest Missouri State
University *B*
University of Missouri
Columbia *B,M,D*
Kansas City *B*

Montana

Eastern Montana College *B*
Montana State University *B*
University of Montana *B*

Nebraska

Chadron State College *B*
Concordia College *B*
Peru State College *B*
University of Nebraska
Kearney *B*
Lincoln *B*
Omaha *B*
Wayne State College *B*

Nevada

University of Nevada: Reno *B*

New Hampshire

Keene State College *B*
Plymouth State College of the
University System of New
Hampshire *B,M*

New Jersey

Jersey City State College *B*
Kean College of New Jersey *B*
Montclair State College *B,M*
Seton Hall University *B*
Trenton State College *B*
William Paterson College of New
Jersey *B*

New Mexico

Eastern New Mexico University *B*
New Mexico State University *B*
University of New Mexico *B,M,D*
Western New Mexico University *B*

New York

Adelphi University *M*
City University of New York
Brooklyn College *B,M*
Hunter College *B,M*
Lehman College *B,M*
Queens College *B*
York College *B*
College of Mount St. Vincent *B*
Fulton-Montgomery Community
College *A*
Hofstra University *B,M*
Ithaca College *B*
Long Island University: C. W. Post
Campus *B*
Manhattan College *B*
New York Institute of Technology
A,B
New York University *B,M,D*
Russell Sage College *M*
State University of New York
Buffalo *M,D*
College at Cortland *B,M*
Syracuse University *B,M,D*

North Carolina

Appalachian State University *B*
Campbell University *B*
East Carolina University *B,M*
Elon College *B*
Fayetteville State University *B*
Gardner-Webb College *B*
Johnson C. Smith University *B*
North Carolina Central
University *B*
North Carolina State University *B*
St. Andrews Presbyterian College *B*
St. Augustine's College *B*
University of North Carolina
Charlotte *M*
Greensboro *B,M*
Western Carolina University *B*

North Dakota

Mayville State University *B*
Valley City State University *B*

Ohio

Ashland University *B*
Baldwin-Wallace College *B*
Bluffton College *B*
Bowling Green State University
B,M
Capital University *B*
Cedarville College *B*
College of Mount St. Joseph *B*
Defiance College *B*
Heidelberg College *B*
Kent State University *B,M*
Malone College *B*
Miami University: Oxford Campus
B,M
Mount Union College *B*
Ohio Northern University *B*
Ohio State University: Columbus
Campus *B,M,D*
Ohio University *B*

Otterbein College *B*
University of Cincinnati *B,M*
University of Dayton *B*
University of Findlay *B*
University of Rio Grande *B*
University of Toledo *B,M,D*
Urbana University *B*
Wittenberg University *B*
Xavier University *B*
Youngstown State University *B*

Oklahoma

Northwestern Oklahoma State
University *B*
Oklahoma City University *B*
Oklahoma State University *B*
Oral Roberts University *B*
Southeastern Oklahoma State
University *B,M*
University of Central Oklahoma
B,M
University of Oklahoma *B*

Oregon

Lewis and Clark College *B*
Linfield College *B*
Oregon State University *B,M,D*
Portland State University *B*
Southern Oregon State College *M*
Western Oregon State College *B*
Willamette University *M*

Pennsylvania

Beaver College *M*
East Stroudsburg University of
Pennsylvania *B*
Eastern College *B*
Edinboro University of
Pennsylvania *B*
Gannon University *B*
Gettysburg College *B*
Indiana University of
Pennsylvania *B*
Lehigh University *M*
Lincoln University *B*
Lock Haven University of
Pennsylvania *B*
Marywood College *B*
Messiah College *B*
Penn State
Harrisburg Capital College
M,D
University Park Campus
B,M,D
St. Joseph's University *C,M*
Slippery Rock University of
Pennsylvania *B*
Temple University *B,M,D*
University of Pennsylvania *M,D*
Ursinus College *B*
West Chester University of
Pennsylvania *B,M*

Puerto Rico

University of Puerto Rico: Medical
Sciences Campus *B,M*

Rhode Island

Rhode Island College *B,M*

South Carolina

Bob Jones University *B*
Columbia College *B*
South Carolina State College *B*
University of South Carolina *M*

South Dakota

Augustana College *B*
Black Hills State University *B*
Dakota State University *B*
Huron University *B*
South Dakota State University *B*

University of South Dakota *B,M*

Tennessee

Austin Peay State University *B,M*
Bethel College *B*
Carson-Newman College *B*
East Tennessee State University
B,M
Freed-Hardeman University *B*
Knoxville College *B*
Lincoln Memorial University *B*
Memphis State University *B,M*
Tennessee Technological University
B,M
Tennessee Wesleyan College *B*
Union University *B,M*
University of Tennessee
Chattanooga *B,M*
Knoxville *B,M,D*
Vanderbilt University *M*

Texas

Baylor University *B,M*
Collin County Community College
District *A*
Del Mar College *A*
East Texas State University *B*
Hardin-Simmons University *B*
Jarvis Christian College *B*
North Harris Montgomery
Community College District *A*
Prairie View A&M University *B,M*
Sam Houston State University *B,M*
Southwest Texas State
University *M*
Texas A&I University *B*
Texas A&M University *B,M,D*
Texas Christian University *B*
Texas Woman's University *M,D*
University of Houston *B,M,D*
University of Mary Hardin-
Baylor *B*
University of North Texas *B,M*
University of Texas
Austin *M,D*
El Paso *M*
Tyler *B,M*

Utah

Brigham Young University *B,M*
University of Utah *B,M,D*
Utah State University *B*
Weber State University *B*

Vermont

University of Vermont *B*

Virginia

Averett College *B*
Bluefield College *B*
George Mason University *B,M*
James Madison University *B,M*
Longwood College *B*
Norfolk State University *B*
Old Dominion University *B*
Virginia Commonwealth
University *B*
Virginia Polytechnic Institute and
State University *B,M*

Washington

Central Washington University *B*
Eastern Washington University *B*
Pacific Lutheran University *B*
Washington State University *B*
Western Washington University *B*

West Virginia

Davis and Elkins College *B*
Shepherd College *B*
University of Charleston *B*
West Liberty State College *B*

West Virginia Institute of
Technology *B*
West Virginia State College *B*
West Virginia University *B*
West Virginia Wesleyan College *B*

Wisconsin

Alverno College *B*
Carthage College *B*
University of Wisconsin
La Crosse *B,M*
Stevens Point *B*
Whitewater *B*

Wyoming

University of Wyoming *B*

**American Samoa, Caroline
Islands, Guam, Marianas,
Virgin Islands**

University of Guam *B*

Health sciences

Alabama

Athens State College *B*
Brewer State Junior College *A*
Community College of the Air
Force *A*
Marion Military Institute *A*
Selma University *A*
Shelton State Community
College *A*
University of South Alabama *B*

Alaska

University of Alaska Anchorage *B*

Arizona

Navajo Community College *A*

Arkansas

Shorter College *A*
University of Arkansas at Little
Rock *B*

California

Barstow College *A*
California College for Health
Sciences *C*
California Institute of Integral
Studies *M*
California State University
Bakersfield *B*
Chico *B*
Dominguez Hills *B*
Fresno *B,M*
Hayward *B*
Long Beach *B,M*
Los Angeles *B,M*
Northridge *B,M*
Sacramento *B*
San Bernardino *B*
Chapman University *B*
Citrus College *A*
Cosumnes River College *A*
Gavilan Community College *A*
Lake Tahoe Community College *A*
Mendocino College *C,A*
Mount St. Mary's College *A,B*
Mount San Jacinto College *A*
National Hispanic University *A*
St. Mary's College of California *B*
San Diego State University *M*
San Francisco State University *B,M*
San Joaquin Delta College *A*
San Jose State University *B,M*
Santa Rosa Junior College *A*
Ventura College *A*

West Coast University *C,A*
Yuba College *A*

Colorado

Naropa Institute *B*

Connecticut

Quinnipiac College *M*
Southern Connecticut State
University *B*
University of Hartford *B*

District of Columbia

George Washington University *M,D*
Mount Vernon College *B*

Florida

Barry University *B*
Daytona Beach Community
College *A*
Lake City Community College *A*
Lynn University *B,M*
Manatee Community College *A*
Okaloosa-Walton Community
College *A*
Palm Beach Atlantic College *B*
University of Central Florida *M*
University of Florida *B*
University of Miami *B*
University of North Florida *B,M*
University of South Florida *D*

Georgia

Andrew College *A*
Armstrong State College *B,M*
Brewton-Parker College *A*
Columbus College *A,B*
Covenant College *B*
East Georgia College *A*
Macon College *A*
Reinhardt College *A*

Hawaii

Hawaii Loa College *B*

Idaho

Boise State University *B*
North Idaho College *A*
Ricks College *A*

Illinois

Augustana College *B*
Aurora University *B*
Barat College *B*
City Colleges of Chicago: Malcolm
X College *A*
College of St. Francis *B*
Illinois Benedictine College *B*
KAES College *B*
Lake Land College *A*
Millikin University *B*
Montay College *A*
Morton College *A*
North Central College *B*
Rend Lake College *A*
University of Chicago *M,D*
Western Illinois University *B,M*

Indiana

Ball State University *B,M*
Indiana State University *B,M*
Indiana University Bloomington
B,M
Indiana University—Purdue
University at Indianapolis *M,D*
Manchester College *B*
Purdue University *B,M,D*
University of Southern Indiana *B*

Iowa

Graceland College *B*
Grand View College *B*

Simpson College *B*

Kansas

Central College *A*
Coffeyville Community College *A*
Colby Community College *A*
Highland Community College *A*
Kansas Newman College *A,B*
McPherson College *B*
Pratt Community College *A*
Wichita State University *B,M*

Kentucky

Asbury College *B*
University of Louisville *B*

Louisiana

Louisiana College *B*
Louisiana State University Medical Center *M*
Our Lady of Holy Cross College *B*
Tulane University *M,D*

Maine

University of Maine at Farmington *B*
University of New England *B*

Maryland

Columbia Union College *A,B*
Howard Community College *A*
Towson State University *B,M*

Massachusetts

Boston University *W*
Endicott College *A*
Hampshire College *B*
Harvard University *D*
Massachusetts College of Pharmacy and Allied Health Sciences *B*
Merrimack College *B*
Mount Ida College *A*
Northeastern University *M*
Pine Manor College *A*
Quinsigamond Community College *C*
Springfield College *B*
Tufts University *B*
Worcester State College *B*

Michigan

Andrews University *B*
Grand Valley State University *B,M*
Kalamazoo College *B*
Northern Michigan University *B*
Suomi College *A*
University of Michigan: Flint *B*
Western Michigan University *B*

Minnesota

Bemidji State University *B*
Bethany Lutheran College *A*
College of St. Scholastica *B*
Mankato State University *B*
Northland Community College *A*
Rainy River Community College *A*
St. Olaf College *B*
University of Minnesota: Twin Cities *B,M,D*
Vermilion Community College *A*
Willmar Community College *A*
Worthington Community College *A*

Mississippi

Alcorn State University *B*
Blue Mountain College *B*
Jackson State University *B*
Jones County Junior College *A*
Mississippi Gulf Coast Community College
    Jefferson Davis Campus *A*
    Perkinston *A*

Missouri

East Central College *A*
Fontbonne College *B*
Northeast Missouri State University *B*
Stephens College *B*

Nebraska

Chadron State College *B*
Dana College *B*
Midland Lutheran College *B*
Wayne State College *B*
Western Nebraska Community College: Scottsbluff Campus *A*
York College *A*

Nevada

University of Nevada: Reno *B*

New Hampshire

New Hampshire Technical College
    Manchester *C*
    Stratham *C*
Plymouth State College of the University System of New Hampshire *B*
University of New Hampshire *B*

New Jersey

Jersey City State College *B,M*
Stockton State College *B*
William Paterson College of New Jersey *B*

New Mexico

New Mexico State University *B*
University of New Mexico *M,D*

New York

City University of New York: Brooklyn College *B,M*
Fulton-Montgomery Community College *A*
Ithaca College *B*
Long Island University: Brooklyn Campus *B,M*
State University of New York
    College at Brockport *B*
    College at Cortland *B*
    Health Sciences Center at Stony Brook *M*
Touro College *B*

North Carolina

Bennett College *B*
Brevard College *A*
Campbell University *B*
Chowan College *A*
Mars Hill College *B*
McDowell Technical Community College *A*
Meredith College *B*
St. Andrews Presbyterian College *B*
Salem College *B*
Western Carolina University *M*

North Dakota

North Dakota State University *B*
University of North Dakota: Williston *A*

Ohio

Baldwin-Wallace College *B*
Bowling Green State University
    Bowling Green *B*
    Firelands College *A*
Case Western Reserve University *M,D*
Central State University *B*
Heidelberg College *B*
Lakeland Community College *A*
Malone College *B*

Mount Vernon Nazarene College *A*
Ohio State University: Columbus Campus *B,M,D*
Union Institute *B,D*
University of Rio Grande *A*
Washington State Community College *A*
Wittenberg University *B*
Youngstown State University *B*

Oklahoma

Eastern Oklahoma State College *A*
Redlands Community College *A*
Tulsa Junior College *A*

Oregon

Eastern Oregon State College *B*
Linfield College *B*
Warner Pacific College *A*

Pennsylvania

Bucks County Community College *A*
California University of Pennsylvania *B*
Carlow College *B*
Gwynedd-Mercy College *B*
Juniata College *B*
La Roche College *M*
La Salle University *B*
Lock Haven University of Pennsylvania *B*
Mount Aloysius College *A,B*
Northeastern Christian Junior College *A*
Pennsylvania Institute of Technology *C,A*
Point Park College *B*
Widener University *B*

Puerto Rico

Inter American University of Puerto Rico: Arecibo Campus *B*
Puerto Rico Junior College *A*

Rhode Island

University of Rhode Island *M*

South Carolina

Clemson University *B*
Morris College *B*

South Dakota

Black Hills State University *B*
Sioux Falls College *B*

Tennessee

Austin Peay State University *B*
Cumberland University *A,B*
Dyersburg State Community College *A*
East Tennessee State University *B*
Maryville College *B*
Motlow State Community College *A*
Union University *B*

Texas

Collin County Community College District *A*
Jacksonville College *A*
LeTourneau University *B*
Lon Morris College *A*
St. Philip's College *A*
Southwest Texas State University *B,M*
Texas Southmost College *A*
University of Mary Hardin-Baylor *B*
University of North Texas *M*

University of Texas
    El Paso *B*
    Pan American *B*
Victoria College *A*

Utah

Brigham Young University *B,M,D*
University of Utah *B,M,D*
Weber State University *B*

Vermont

Goddard College *B,M*
Johnson State College *B*

Virginia

Bridgewater College *B*
Lynchburg College *B*
Shenandoah University *B*
Tidewater Community College *C*

Washington

Centralia College *A*
Eastern Washington University *B*
Everett Community College *A*
Evergreen State College *B*
Grays Harbor College *A*
Seattle Central Community College *A*
Walla Walla College *B*

West Virginia

Bethany College *B*
Fairmont State College *B*

Wisconsin

University of Wisconsin: Milwaukee *B*

Wyoming

Eastern Wyoming College *A*
Northwest College *A*
Sheridan College *A*
Western Wyoming Community College *A*

Hebrew

California

Pomona College *B*
University of California
    Berkeley *B,M,D*
    Los Angeles *B*
University of Judaism *M*

Connecticut

Wesleyan University *B*

District of Columbia

Catholic University of America *M,D*

Georgia

Oxford College of Emory University *A*

Illinois

City Colleges of Chicago: Chicago City-Wide College *C*
Hebrew Theological College *A,B,M,D,W*
University of Chicago *B,M,D*

Indiana

Indiana University Bloomington *B,M*

Iowa

Luther College *B*

Kentucky
Louisville Presbyterian Theological
Seminary *M*

Maryland
Baltimore Hebrew University
B,M,D

Massachusetts
Harvard and Radcliffe Colleges *B*
Harvard University *D*

Michigan
Calvin Theological Seminary *M*
Concordia College *B*
University of Michigan *B,M,D*
Wayne State University *B*

Minnesota
Bethany Lutheran College *A*
North Central Bible College *A,B*
University of Minnesota: Twin
Cities *B*

New Jersey
Rutgers—The State University of
New Jersey: Newark College of
Arts and Sciences *B*

New York
City University of New York
Baruch College *B*
Brooklyn College *B*
City College *B*
Hunter College *B*
Lehman College *B*
Queens College *B*
Queensborough Community
College *A*
Columbia University
Columbia College *B*
New York *M,D*
Cornell University *M,D*
Hofstra University *B*
Long Island University: C. W. Post
Campus *B*
New York University *B,M,D*
State University of New York at
Binghamton *B*
Touro College *B*
Yeshiva University *B,M,D*

Ohio
Cleveland College of Jewish Studies
B,M
Ohio State University: Columbus
Campus *B,M*

Oregon
Western Conservative Baptist
Seminary *M*

Pennsylvania
Gratz College *B,M*
Temple University *B*
University of Pennsylvania *B,M,D*

Rhode Island
Brown University *B*

Texas
University of Texas at Austin *B*

Washington
University of Washington *B,M*

Wisconsin
Concordia University Wisconsin *B*
University of Wisconsin
Madison *B,M,D*
Milwaukee *B*

Higher education
administration

Alabama
Auburn University *M,D*

Arizona
Arizona State University *M,D*

Arkansas
University of Arkansas *M*

California
California State University
Fresno *M*
Stanislaus *M*
San Jose State University *M*
University of San Francisco *D*

Colorado
University of Denver *D*
University of Northern Colorado *D*

Connecticut
University of Connecticut *D*

District of Columbia
George Washington University *M,D*

Florida
Florida Atlantic University *M,D*
Florida State University *M,D*
Jacksonville University *M*
Nova University *D*
University of Florida *D*
University of Miami *M,D*

Georgia
Georgia College *M*
Georgia Southern University *M*
Georgia State University *D*
University of Georgia *M,D*

Hawaii
University of Hawaii at Manoa *M,D*

Illinois
Loyola University of Chicago *D*
Northwestern University *D*
Southern Illinois University at
Carbondale *M,D*
University of Illinois at Urbana-
Champaign *M,D*

Indiana
Indiana State University *M*
Indiana University Bloomington *D*
Indiana University—Purdue
University at Indianapolis *D*
Purdue University *M,D*

Iowa
Drake University *M,D*
Iowa State University *M,D*
Maharishi International
University *M*
University of Iowa *M,D*
University of Northern Iowa *D*

Kansas
Pittsburg State University *M*
University of Kansas *M,D*

Kentucky
Eastern Kentucky University *M*
University of Louisville *M*

Massachusetts
Boston College *M,D*
Suffolk University *M*

University of Massachusetts at
Boston *D*

Michigan
Michigan State University *M,D*
University of Michigan *M,D*
Wayne State University *D*

Minnesota
Mankato State University *M*
Moorhead State University *M*
St. Cloud State University *M*

Mississippi
University of Mississippi *M,D*

Missouri
Central Missouri State
University *M*
St. Louis University *M,D*
University of Missouri
Columbia *M,D*
Kansas City *M*

Montana
Montana State University *D*

Nebraska
University of Nebraska—Lincoln
M,D

New Hampshire
Antioch New England Graduate
School *M*

New Jersey
Seton Hall University *M,D*

New Mexico
Eastern New Mexico University *M*

New York
Alfred University *M*
City University of New York:
Brooklyn College *C*
Colgate University *M*
New York University *M,D*
State University of New York
Albany *D*
Buffalo *M,D*
Syracuse University *M,D*
University of Rochester *M,D*

North Carolina
Appalachian State University *M*
Campbell University *M,D*
North Carolina State University
M,D
University of North Carolina at
Greensboro *M*

Ohio
Bowling Green State University *D*
Kent State University *M*
Ohio University *M,D*
Union Institute *D*
University of Dayton *M*
University of Toledo *M,D*

Oklahoma
Oklahoma State University *M,D*
University of Oklahoma *M,D*

Oregon
Oregon State University *M,D*
Portland State University *D*
University of Portland *M*

Pennsylvania
Duquesne University *M*
Temple University *D*
University of Pennsylvania *M,D*

Widener University *D*

Rhode Island
University of Rhode Island *M*

Tennessee
Memphis State University *D*
University of Tennessee:
Knoxville *M*
Vanderbilt University *M,D,W*

Texas
Sam Houston State University *M*
Texas Tech University *M,D*
University of Houston *M,D*

Utah
Brigham Young University *D*
University of Utah *M,D*

Virginia
College of William and Mary *D*
George Mason University *D*
University of Virginia *D*
Virginia Polytechnic Institute and
State University *D*

Washington
Eastern Washington University *M*
University of Washington *M,D*
Western Washington University *M*

West Virginia
Marshall University *M*

Wisconsin
University of Wisconsin:
Oshkosh *M*

Higher education
research

Alabama
Auburn University *M,D*

Arizona
University of Arizona *M,D*

California
University of Southern California
M,D

District of Columbia
Howard University *M*

Illinois
Northwestern University *M,D*
Southern Illinois University at
Carbondale *M,D*
University of Illinois at Urbana-
Champaign *M,D*

Indiana
Indiana University Bloomington *D*

Iowa
University of Iowa *M,D*

Kentucky
Eastern Kentucky University *M*

Massachusetts
Hampshire College *B*
Suffolk University *M*

Michigan
Michigan State University *M,D*
University of Michigan *M,D*

New York

Hofstra University *D*
New York University *M,D*
State University of New York
    Albany *M,D*
    Buffalo *M,D*
Syracuse University *M,D*

North Carolina

Appalachian State University *M*

Ohio

Bowling Green State University *D*
Ohio State University: Columbus
    Campus *M,D*
Union Institute *D*

Oklahoma

Oklahoma State University *M,D*

Pennsylvania

Bucknell University *B,M*
Penn State University Park Campus
    M,D
Widener University *D*

Texas

University of Houston *M,D*
University of Texas at San
    Antonio *M*

Washington

Eastern Washington University *M*

Hispanic American studies

California

Cerritos Community College *A*
City College of San Francisco *A*
De Anza College *A*
Fresno City College *A*
Pomona College *B*
San Diego City College *A*
San Francisco State University *B*
Scripps College *B*
University of California: Santa
    Barbara *B*
Ventura College *A*

Colorado

Adams State College *B*

Connecticut

Connecticut College *B,M*

Florida

Florida Atlantic University *C*

Illinois

University of Illinois at Chicago *M*

Iowa

Luther College *B*

Massachusetts

Hampshire College *B*
Harvard and Radcliffe Colleges *B*

Minnesota

St. Olaf College *B*
University of Minnesota: Twin
    Cities *M,D*

New Jersey

Rutgers—The State University of
    New Jersey
        Douglass College *B*
        Livingston College *B*
        Newark College of Arts and
            Sciences *B*
        Rutgers College *B*

New Mexico

New Mexico State University *B*
Western New Mexico University *B*

New York

Boricua College *B*
City University of New York
    Brooklyn College *B*
    City College *B*
    Hostos Community College *A*
    Lehman College *B*
Columbia University: School of
    General Studies *B*
Hofstra University *B*
Mount St. Mary College *B*

Pennsylvania

Bryn Mawr College *B*

Rhode Island

Brown University *B,M,D*

Virginia

Sweet Briar College *B*

Washington

University of Washington *B*

Histology

Alabama

Auburn University *M*

Florida

Florida Community College at
    Jacksonville *A*

Georgia

Emory University *D*

Illinois

Northwestern University *B*
University of Chicago *M,D*

Maryland

Harford Community College *A*

Michigan

Charles Stewart Mott Community
    College *A*

New York

Cornell University *M,D*

Pennsylvania

University of Pittsburgh *M,D*

South Dakota

Presentation College *A*

Texas

Baylor College of Dentistry *M*

Washington

Shoreline Community College *A*

Historic preservation

Alabama

Auburn University *M*

Florida

South Florida Community
    College *A*

Georgia

Savannah College of Art and
    Design *B,M*
University of Georgia *B,M*

Indiana

Ball State University *M*

Maryland

Goucher College *B*

Michigan

Eastern Michigan University *M*

Missouri

Southeast Missouri State
    University *B*

New York

Columbia University
    New York *M*
    School of Engineering and
        Applied Science *M*
Iona College *M*

North Carolina

Fayetteville Technical Community
    College *A*

Oregon

University of Oregon *M*

Pennsylvania

University of Pennsylvania *M*

Rhode Island

Roger Williams College *B*

Tennessee

Middle Tennessee State University
    B,M,D
O'More College of Design *B*

Vermont

University of Vermont *M*

Virginia

Mary Washington College *B*

History

Alabama

Alabama Agricultural and
    Mechanical University *B*
Alabama Southern Community
    College *A*
Alabama State University *B,M*
Athens State College *B*
Auburn University
    Auburn *B,M,D*
    Montgomery *B*
Birmingham-Southern College *B*
Community College of the Air
    Force *A*
Huntingdon College *B*
Jacksonville State University *B,M*
Judson College *B*

Lawson State Community
    College *A*
Livingston University *B*
Mobile College *B*
Oakwood College *B*
Samford University *B,M*
Spring Hill College *B*
Stillman College *B*
Talladega College *B*
Troy State University
    Dothan *B*
    Montgomery *B*
    Troy *B*
Tuskegee University *B*
University of Alabama
    Birmingham *B,M*
    Huntsville *B,M*
    Tuscaloosa *B,M,D,W*
University of Montevallo *B,M*
University of North Alabama *B*
University of South Alabama *B,M*

Alaska

Alaska Pacific University *A,B*
Sheldon Jackson College *A*
University of Alaska
    Anchorage *B*
    Fairbanks *B*

Arizona

Arizona State University *B,M,D*
Cochise College *A*
Eastern Arizona College *A*
Glendale Community College *A*
Grand Canyon University *B*
Northern Arizona University *B,M,D*
Prescott College *B*
University of Arizona *B,M,D*
Yavapai College *A*

Arkansas

Arkansas College *B*
Arkansas State University
    Beebe Branch *A*
    Jonesboro *B,M*
Arkansas Tech University *B*
Harding University *B,M*
Henderson State University *B*
Hendrix College *B*
John Brown University *B*
Ouachita Baptist University *B*
Southern Arkansas University *B*
University of Arkansas
    Fayetteville *B,M,D*
    Little Rock *B,M*
    Monticello *B*
    Pine Bluff *B*
University of Central Arkansas *B,M*
University of the Ozarks *B*
Westark Community College *A*

California

Azusa Pacific University *B*
Bakersfield College *A*
Biola University *B*
California Baptist College *B*
California Institute of Technology *B*
California Lutheran University *B*
California Polytechnic State
    University: San Luis Obispo *B*
California State Polytechnic
    University: Pomona *B*

California State University
  Bakersfield *B,M*
  Chico *B,M*
  Dominguez Hills *B*
  Fresno *B,M*
  Fullerton *B,M*
  Hayward *B,M*
  Long Beach *B,M*
  Los Angeles *B,M*
  Northridge *B,M*
  Sacramento *B,M*
  San Bernardino *B*
  San Marcos *B*
  Stanislaus *B,M*
Cerritos Community College *A*
Chabot College *A*
Chaffey Community College *A*
Chapman University *B*
Christian Heritage College *B*
Claremont McKenna College *B*
College of the Desert *A*
College of Notre Dame *B*
Columbia College *A*
Crafton Hills College *A*
De Anza College *A*
Dominican College of San Rafael *B*
El Camino College *A*
Feather River College *A*
Foothill College *A*
Fresno Pacific College *B*
Grossmont Community College *A*
Holy Names College *B*
Humboldt State University *B*
Irvine Valley College *A*
La Sierra University *B*
Los Angeles Mission College *A*
Los Angeles Valley College *A*
Loyola Marymount University *B*
Marymount College *A*
Master's College *B*
Merced College *A*
Mills College *B*
MiraCosta College *A*
Modesto Junior College *A*
Mount St. Mary's College *B*
Napa Valley College *A*
Occidental College *B*
Ohlone College *A*
Orange Coast College *A*
Oxnard College *A*
Pacific Union College *B*
Pepperdine University *B,M*
Pitzer College *B*
Point Loma Nazarene College *B*
Pomona College *B*
Saddleback College *A*
St. Mary's College of California *B*
San Diego City College *A*
San Diego State University *B,M*
San Francisco State University *B,M*
San Jose State University *B,M*
Santa Barbara City College *A*
Santa Clara University *B*
Santa Monica College *A*
Santa Rosa Junior College *A*
Scripps College *B*
Simpson College *B*
Solano Community College *A*
Sonoma State University *B,M*
Southern California College *B*
Southwestern College *A*
Stanford University *B,M,D*
University of California
  Berkeley *B,D*
  Davis *B,M,D*
  Irvine *B,M,D*
  Los Angeles *B,M,D*
  Riverside *B,M,D*
  San Diego *B,M,D*
  San Francisco *M,D*
  Santa Barbara *B,M,D*
  Santa Cruz *B,M,D*

University of La Verne *B*
University of the Pacific *B,M*
University of Redlands *B*
University of San Diego *B,M*
University of San Francisco *B*
University of Southern California
  B,M,D
Ventura College *A*
West Valley College *A*
Westmont College *B*
Whittier College *B*

Colorado

Adams State College *B*
Colorado College *B*
Colorado State University *B,M*
Fort Lewis College *B*
Mesa State College *A,B*
Metropolitan State College of
  Denver *B*
Pikes Peak Community College *A*
Regis College of Regis University *B*
United States Air Force
  Academy *B*
University of Colorado
  Boulder *B,M,D*
  Colorado Springs *B,M*
  Denver *B,M*
University of Denver *B,M,D*
University of Northern Colorado
  B,M
University of Southern Colorado *B*
Western State College of
  Colorado *B*

Connecticut

Albertus Magnus College *B*
Central Connecticut State
  University *B,M*
Connecticut College *B*
Eastern Connecticut State
  University *B*
Fairfield University *B*
Quinnipiac College *B*
Sacred Heart University *A,B*
St. Joseph College *B,M*
Southern Connecticut State
  University *B,M*
Teikyo-Post University *A,B*
Trinity College *B,M*
University of Bridgeport *B*
University of Connecticut *B,M,D*
University of Hartford *B*
University of New Haven *B*
Wesleyan University *B*
Western Connecticut State
  University *B,M*
Yale University *B,M,D*

Delaware

Delaware State College *B*
University of Delaware *B,M,D*
Wesley College *B*

District of Columbia

American University *B,M,D*
Catholic University of America
  B,M,D
Gallaudet University *B*
George Washington University
  B,M,D
Georgetown University *B,D*
Howard University *B,M,D*
Trinity College *B*
University of the District of
  Columbia *A,B*

Florida

Barry University *B*
Bethune-Cookman College *B*
Daytona Beach Community
  College *A*

Eckerd College *B*
Flagler College *B*
Florida Agricultural and Mechanical
  University *B*
Florida Atlantic University *B,M*
Florida International University
  B,M
Florida Southern College *B*
Florida State University *B,M,D*
Gulf Coast Community College *A*
Indian River Community College *A*
Jacksonville University *B*
Lynn University *B*
Miami-Dade Community College *A*
New College of the University of
  South Florida *B*
Palm Beach Atlantic College *B*
Palm Beach Community College *A*
Pensacola Junior College *A*
Rollins College *B*
St. Leo College *B*
St. Thomas University *B*
Stetson University *B*
University of Central Florida *B,M*
University of Florida *B,M,D*
University of Miami *B,M,D*
University of North Florida *B,M*
University of South Florida *B,M*
University of Tampa *A,B*
University of West Florida *B,M*

Georgia

Abraham Baldwin Agricultural
  College *A*
Agnes Scott College *B*
Albany State College *B*
Armstrong State College *B,M*
Atlanta Metropolitan College *A*
Augusta College *B*
Bainbridge College *A*
Berry College *B*
Brenau Women's College *B*
Brewton-Parker College *A,B*
Clark Atlanta University *B,M*
Clayton State College *A*
Columbus College *B*
Covenant College *B*
Darton College *A*
DeKalb College *A*
Emory University *B,M,D*
Floyd College *A*
Fort Valley State College *B*
Gainesville College *A*
Georgia College *B,M*
Georgia Southern University *B,M*
Georgia Southwestern College *B*
Georgia State University *B,M,D*
Gordon College *A*
Kennesaw State College *B*
LaGrange College *B*
Macon College *A*
Mercer University *B*
Middle Georgia College *A*
Morehouse College *B*
Morris Brown College *B*
North Georgia College *B*
Oglethorpe University *B*
Paine College *B*
Piedmont College *B*
Reinhardt College *A*
Savannah State College *B*
Shorter College *B*
South Georgia College *A*
Spelman College *B*
Thomas College *A*
Truett-McConnell College *A*
University of Georgia *B,M,D*
Valdosta State College *B,M*
Waycross College *A*
Wesleyan College *B*
West Georgia College *B,M*
Young Harris College *A*

Hawaii

Brigham Young University-
  Hawaii *B*
Chaminade University of
  Honolulu *B*
Hawaii Pacific University *B*
University of Hawaii
  Hilo *B*
  Manoa *B,M,D*
  West Oahu *B*

Idaho

Albertson College *B*
Boise State University *B,M*
College of Southern Idaho *A*
Idaho State University *B*
Lewis Clark State College *B*
North Idaho College *A*
Northwest Nazarene College *B*
Ricks College *A*
University of Idaho *B,M,D*

Illinois

Augustana College *B*
Aurora University *B*
Black Hawk College *A*
Blackburn College *B*
Bradley University *B*
Chicago State University *B,M*
College of St. Francis *B*
Concordia University *B*
De Paul University *B,M*
Eastern Illinois University *B,M*
Elmhurst College *B*
Eureka College *B*
Greenville College *B*
Highland Community College *A*
Illinois Benedictine College *B*
Illinois Central College *A*
Illinois College *B*
Illinois Institute of Technology *B*
Illinois State University *B,M,D*
Illinois Wesleyan University *B*
John A. Logan College *A*
Joliet Junior College *A*
Judson College *B*
Knox College *B*
Lake Forest College *B*
Lewis University *B*
Lincoln Land Community
  College *A*
Loyola University of Chicago
  B,M,D
MacMurray College *B*
McKendree College *B*
Millikin University *B*
Monmouth College *B*
Morton College *A*
North Central College *B*
North Park College and Theological
  Seminary *B*
Northeastern Illinois University
  B,M
Northern Illinois University *B,M,D*
Northwestern University *B,M,D*
Olivet Nazarene University *B*
Principia College *B*
Quincy College *B*
Rend Lake College *A*
Richland Community College *A*
Rockford College *B*
Roosevelt University *B,M*
Rosary College *B*
St. Xavier University *B*
Sangamon State University *B,M*
Southern Illinois University
  Carbondale *B,M,D*
  Edwardsville *B,M*
State Community College *A*
Trinity Christian College *B*
Trinity College *B*
Triton College *A*

University of Chicago *B,M,D*
University of Illinois
    Chicago *B,M,D*
    Urbana-Champaign *B,M,D*
Waubonsee Community College *A*
Western Illinois University *B,M*
Wheaton College *B*

Indiana

Anderson University *B*
Ball State University *B,M*
Bethel College *B*
Butler University *B,M*
Calumet College of St. Joseph *B*
DePauw University *B*
Earlham College *B*
Franklin College *B*
Goshen College *B*
Hanover College *B*
Huntington College *B*
Indiana State University *B,M*
Indiana University
    Bloomington *B,M,D*
    Northwest *B*
    South Bend *B*
    Southeast *B*
Indiana University—Purdue
University
    Fort Wayne *B*
    Indianapolis *B,M*
Indiana Wesleyan University *B*
Manchester College *B*
Marian College *B*
Martin University *B*
Purdue University
    Calumet *B*
    West Lafayette *B,M,D*
St. Joseph's College *B*
St. Mary-of-the-Woods College *B*
St. Mary's College *B*
St. Meinrad College *B*
Taylor University *B*
Tri-State University *B*
University of Evansville *B*
University of Indianapolis *B,M*
University of Notre Dame *B,M,D*
University of Southern Indiana *B*
Valparaiso University *B,M*
Vincennes University *A*
Wabash College *B*

Iowa

Briar Cliff College *B*
Buena Vista College *B*
Central College *B*
Clarke College *B*
Clinton Community College *A*
Coe College *B*
Cornell College *B*
Dordt College *B*
Drake University *B*
Graceland College *B*
Grinnell College *B*
Iowa State University *B,M,D*
Loras College *B,M*
Luther College *B*
Morningside College *B*
Mount Mercy College *B*
Muscatine Community College *A*
Northwestern College *B*
St. Ambrose University *B*
Simpson College *B*
Teikyo Marycrest University *B*
Teikyo Westmar University *B*
University of Dubuque *B*
University of Iowa *B,M,D*
University of Northern Iowa *B,M*
Wartburg College *B*
William Penn College *B*

Kansas

Allen County Community
    College *A*
Baker University *B*
Benedictine College *B*
Bethany College *B*
Bethel College *B*
Butler County Community
    College *A*
Central College *A*
Coffeyville Community College *A*
Emporia State University *B,M*
Fort Hays State University *B,M*
Fort Scott Community College *A*
Friends University *B*
Hutchinson Community College *A*
Kansas City Kansas Community
    College *A*
Kansas Newman College *B*
Kansas State University *B,M,D*
Kansas Wesleyan University *B*
McPherson College *B*
MidAmerica Nazarene College *B*
Ottawa University *B*
Pittsburg State University *B,M*
Pratt Community College *A*
St. Mary College *B*
Southwestern College *B*
Sterling College *B*
University of Kansas *B,M,D*
Washburn University of Topeka *B*
Wichita State University *B,M*

Kentucky

Alice Lloyd College *B*
Asbury College *B*
Bellarmine College *B*
Berea College *B*
Brescia College *B*
Campbellsville College *B*
Centre College *B*
Cumberland College *B*
Eastern Kentucky University *B,M*
Georgetown College *B*
Kentucky State University *B*
Kentucky Wesleyan College *B*
Lees College *A*
Lindsey Wilson College *B*
Morehead State University *B*
Murray State University *B,M*
Northern Kentucky University *B*
Pikeville College *B*
Spalding University *B*
Sue Bennett College *A*
Thomas More College *A,B*
Transylvania University *B*
Union College *B*
University of Kentucky *B,M,D*
University of Louisville *B,M*
Western Kentucky University *B,M*

Louisiana

Centenary College of Louisiana *B*
Dillard University *B*
Grambling State University *B*
Louisiana College *B*
Louisiana State University
    Agricultural and Mechanical
      College *B,M,D*
    Shreveport *B*
Louisiana Tech University *B,M*
Loyola University *B*
McNeese State University *B*
Nicholls State University *B*
Northeast Louisiana University *B,M*
Northwestern State University *B,M*
Our Lady of Holy Cross College *B*
Southeastern Louisiana University
    B,M
Southern University at New
    Orleans *B*

Southern University and
    Agricultural and Mechanical
    College *B,M*
Tulane University *B,M,D*
University of New Orleans *B,M*
University of Southwestern
    Louisiana *B,M*
Xavier University of Louisiana *B*

Maine

Bates College *B*
Bowdoin College *B*
Colby College *B*
St. Joseph's College *B*
University of Maine
    Farmington *B*
    Fort Kent *B*
    Machias *B*
    Orono *B,M,D*
    Presque Isle *B*
University of Southern Maine *B*

Maryland

Bowie State University *B*
College of Notre Dame of
    Maryland *B*
Columbia Union College *B*
Coppin State College *B*
Frederick Community College *A*
Frostburg State University *B*
Goucher College *B*
Harford Community College *A*
Hood College *B*
Howard Community College *A*
Johns Hopkins University *B,M,D*
Loyola College in Maryland *B*
Morgan State University *B,M*
Mount St. Mary's College *B*
St. Mary's College of Maryland *B*
Salisbury State University *B,M*
Towson State University *B*
United States Naval Academy *B*
University of Baltimore *B*
University of Maryland
    Baltimore County *B,M*
    College Park *B,M,D*
    Eastern Shore *B*
Washington College *B,M*
Western Maryland College *B*

Massachusetts

American International College *B*
Amherst College *B*
Anna Maria College for Men and
    Women *B*
Assumption College *B*
Atlantic Union College *B*
Becker College: Leicester
    Campus *A*
Bentley College *B*
Boston College *B,M,D*
Boston University *B,M,D*
Bradford College *B*
Brandeis University *B,M,D*
Bridgewater State College *B,M*
Clark University *B,M,D*
College of the Holy Cross *B*
Curry College *B*
Eastern Nazarene College *B*
Elms College *B*
Emmanuel College *B*
Fitchburg State College *B*
Framingham State College *B*
Gordon College *B*
Hampshire College *B*
Harvard and Radcliffe Colleges *B*
Harvard University *D*
Massachusetts Institute of
    Technology *B*
Merrimack College *B*
Mount Holyoke College *B*
Nichols College *B*

North Adams State College *B*
Northeastern University *B,M*
Northern Essex Community
    College *A*
Pine Manor College *A*
Quincy College *A*
Regis College *B*
Salem State College *B,M*
Simmons College *B*
Smith College *B*
Springfield College *B*
Stonehill College *B*
Suffolk University *B*
Tufts University *B,M*
University of Massachusetts
    Amherst *B,M,D*
    Boston *B,M*
    Dartmouth *B*
    Lowell *B*
Wellesley College *B*
Western New England College *B*
Westfield State College *B*
Wheaton College *B*
Williams College *B*
Worcester State College *B*

Michigan

Adrian College *A,B*
Albion College *B*
Alma College *B*
Andrews University *B,M*
Aquinas College *B*
Calvin College *B*
Central Michigan University *B,M*
Eastern Michigan University *B,M*
Grand Rapids Baptist College and
    Seminary *B*
Grand Valley State University *B*
Hillsdale College *B*
Hope College *B*
Kalamazoo College *B*
Kirtland Community College *A*
Lake Superior State University *B*
Lansing Community College *A*
Madonna University *A,B*
Marygrove College *B*
Michigan State University *B,M,D*
Michigan Technological
    University *B*
Northern Michigan University
    A,B,M
Oakland University *B,M*
Olivet College *B*
Saginaw Valley State University *B*
Siena Heights College *B*
Spring Arbor College *B*
Suomi College *A*
University of Detroit Mercy *B*
University of Michigan
    Ann Arbor *B,M,D*
    Dearborn *B*
    Flint *B*
Wayne State University *B,M,D*
West Shore Community College *A*
Western Michigan University *B,M*

Minnesota

Augsburg College *B*
Bemidji State University *B*
Bethel College *B*
Carleton College *B*
College of St. Benedict *B*
College of St. Catherine: St.
    Catherine Campus *B*
College of St. Scholastica *B*
Concordia College: Moorhead *B*
Concordia College: St. Paul *B*
Crown College *A,B*
Gustavus Adolphus College *B*
Hamline University *B*
Macalester College *B*
Mankato State University *B,M*

Moorhead State University *B*
Northland Community College *A*
Pillsbury Baptist Bible College *B*
Rainy River Community College *A*
St. Cloud State University *B,M*
St. John's University *B*
St. Mary's College of Minnesota *B*
St. Olaf College *B*
Southwest State University *B*
University of Minnesota
    Duluth *B*
    Morris *B*
    Twin Cities *B,M,D*
University of St. Thomas *B*
Willmar Community College *A*
Winona State University *B,M*

Mississippi

Alcorn State University *B*
Belhaven College *B*
Blue Mountain College *B*
Delta State University *B*
Jackson State University *B,M*
Jones County Junior College *A*
Millsaps College *B*
Mississippi College *B,M*
Mississippi State University *B,M,D*
Mississippi University for Women *B*
Rust College *B*
Tougaloo College *B*
University of Mississippi *B,M,D*
University of Southern Mississippi *B,M,D*
William Carey College *B*

Missouri

Avila College *B*
Central Methodist College *B*
Central Missouri State University *B,M*
College of the Ozarks *B*
Columbia College *B*
Culver-Stockton College *B*
Drury College *B*
East Central College *A*
Evangel College *B*
Fontbonne College *B*
Jefferson College *A*
Lincoln University *B,M*
Lindenwood College *B*
Maryville University *B*
Missouri Baptist College *B*
Missouri Southern State College *B*
Missouri Valley College *B*
Missouri Western State College *B*
Northeast Missouri State University *B,M*
Northwest Missouri State University *B,M*
Park College *B*
Rockhurst College *B*
St. Louis University *B,M*
Southeast Missouri State University *B,M*
Southwest Baptist University *B*
Southwest Missouri State University *B,M*
Stephens College *B*
University of Missouri
    Columbia *B,M,D*
    Kansas City *B,M,D*
    Rolla *B*
    St. Louis *B,M*
Washington University *B,M,D*
Webster University *B*
Westminster College *B*
William Jewell College *B*
William Woods College *B*

Montana

Carroll College *B*
College of Great Falls *B*

Eastern Montana College *B*
Montana State University *B,M*
Rocky Mountain College *B*
University of Montana *B,M*

Nebraska

Bellevue College *B*
Central Community College *A*
Chadron State College *B*
College of St. Mary *B*
Concordia College *B*
Creighton University *C,B,M*
Dana College *B*
Doane College *B*
Hastings College *B*
Midland Lutheran College *B*
Nebraska Wesleyan University *B*
Peru State College *B*
Southeast Community College:
    Beatrice Campus *A*
Union College *B*
University of Nebraska
    Kearney *B,M*
    Lincoln *B,M,D*
    Omaha *B,M*
Wayne State College *B*
York College *A*

Nevada

University of Nevada
    Las Vegas *B,M,D*
    Reno *B,M,D*

New Hampshire

Dartmouth College *B*
Franklin Pierce College *B*
Keene State College *B*
New England College *B*
Notre Dame College *B*
Plymouth State College of the University System of New Hampshire *B*
Rivier College *B*
St. Anselm College *B*
University of New Hampshire
    Durham *B,M,D*
    Manchester *B*

New Jersey

Atlantic Community College *A*
Bergen Community College *A*
Bloomfield College *B*
Burlington County College *A*
Caldwell College *B*
Centenary College *B*
College of St. Elizabeth *B*
Drew University *B,M*
Fairleigh Dickinson University *B*
Felician College *A,B*
Georgian Court College *B*
Glassboro State College *B*
Jersey City State College *B*
Kean College of New Jersey *B*
Monmouth College *B,M*
Montclair State College *B*
Ocean County College *A*
Princeton University *B,D*
Ramapo College of New Jersey *B*
Rider College *B*

Rutgers—The State University of New Jersey
    Camden College of Arts and Sciences *B*
    Douglass College *B*
    Livingston College *B*
    New Brunswick *M,D*
    Newark College of Arts and Sciences *B*
    Rutgers College *B*
    University College Camden *B*
    University College New Brunswick *B*
    University College Newark *B*
St. Peter's College *B*
Seton Hall University *B*
Stevens Institute of Technology *B*
Stockton State College *B*
Thomas Edison State College *B*
Trenton State College *B*
Upsala College *B*
William Paterson College of New Jersey *B*

New Mexico

Eastern New Mexico University *B*
New Mexico Highlands University *B*
New Mexico State University *B,M*
University of New Mexico *B,M,D*
Western New Mexico University *B*

New York

Adelphi University *B,M*
Adirondack Community College *A*
Alfred University *B*
Bard College *B*
Barnard College *B*
Canisius College *B*
City University of New York
    Baruch College *B*
    Brooklyn College *B,M*
    City College *B,M*
    College of Staten Island *B*
    Graduate School and University Center *D*
    Hunter College *B,M*
    Lehman College *B,M*
    Queens College *B,M*
    Queensborough Community College *A*
    York College *B*
Clarkson University *B*
Colgate University *B,M*
College of Mount St. Vincent *B*
College of New Rochelle *B*
College of St. Rose *B*
Columbia University
    Columbia College *B*
    New York *M,D*
    School of General Studies *B*
Concordia College *B*
Cornell University *B,M,D*
Daemen College *B*
Dominican College of Blauvelt *B*
Dowling College *B*
D'Youville College *B*
Elmira College *B*
Eugene Lang College/New School for Social Research *B*
Fordham University *B,M,D*
Fulton-Montgomery Community College *A*
Hamilton College *B*
Hartwick College *B*
Hobart College *B*
Hofstra University *B*
Houghton College *B*
Iona College *B*
Ithaca College *B*
Jamestown Community College *A*

Jewish Theological Seminary of America *D*
Keuka College *B*
King's College *B*
Le Moyne College *B*
Long Island University
    Brooklyn Campus *B*
    C. W. Post Campus *B,M*
    Southampton Campus *B*
Manhattan College *B*
Manhattanville College *B*
Marist College *B*
Marymount College *B*
Marymount Manhattan College *B*
Mercy College *B*
Molloy College *B*
Mount St. Mary College *B*
Nazareth College of Rochester *B*
New York University *B,M,D*
Niagara University *B*
Nyack College *B*
Pace University
    College of White Plains *B*
    New York *B*
    Pleasantville/Briarcliff *B*
Roberts Wesleyan College *B*
Russell Sage College *B*
Sage Junior College of Albany, A Division of Russell Sage College *A*
St. Bonaventure University *B,M*
St. Francis College *B*
St. John Fisher College *B*
St. John's University *B,M,D*
St. Joseph's College
    Brooklyn *B*
    Suffolk Campus *B*
St. Lawrence University *B*
St. Thomas Aquinas College *B*
Sarah Lawrence College *B*
Siena College *B*
Skidmore College *B*
State University of New York
    Albany *B,M*
    Binghamton *B,M,D*
    Buffalo *B,M,D*
    Purchase *B*
    Stony Brook *B,M,D*
    College at Brockport *B,M*
    College at Buffalo *B,M*
    College at Cortland *B,M*
    College at Fredonia *B*
    College at Geneseo *B*
    College at New Paltz *B*
    College at Oneonta *B,M*
    College at Plattsburgh *B,M*
    College at Potsdam *B*
    College of Technology at Delhi *A*
    Empire State College *A,B*
    Oswego *B*
Sullivan County Community College *A*
Syracuse University *B,M,D*
Touro College *B*
Union College *B*
United States Military Academy *B*
University of Rochester *B,M,D*
University of the State of New York: Regents College *B*
Utica College of Syracuse University *B*
Vassar College *B*
Wagner College *B*
Wells College *B*
William Smith College *B*
Yeshiva University *B*

North Carolina

Appalachian State University *B,M*
Barton College *B*
Belmont Abbey College *B*

288

Brevard College *A*
Campbell University *B*
Catawba College *B*
Davidson College *B*
Duke University *B,D*
East Carolina University *B,M*
Elizabeth City State University *B*
Elon College *B*
Fayetteville State University *B*
Gardner-Webb College *B*
Greensboro College *B*
Guilford College *B*
High Point University *B*
Johnson C. Smith University *B*
Lees-McRae College *B*
Lenoir-Rhyne College *B*
Livingstone College *B*
Louisburg College *A*
Mars Hill College *B*
Meredith College *B*
Methodist College *B*
Montreat-Anderson College *B*
Mount Olive College *B*
North Carolina Agricultural and
 Technical State University *B,M*
North Carolina Central University
 B,M
North Carolina State University
 B,M
North Carolina Wesleyan College *B*
Pembroke State University *B*
Pfeiffer College *B*
Queens College *B*
St. Andrews Presbyterian College *B*
St. Augustine's College *B*
Salem College *B*
Shaw University *B*
University of North Carolina
 Asheville *B*
 Chapel Hill *B,M,D*
 Charlotte *B,M*
 Greensboro *B,M*
 Wilmington *B,M*
Wake Forest University *B,M*
Warren Wilson College *B*
Western Carolina University *B,M*
Wingate College *B*
Winston-Salem State University *B*

North Dakota

Dickinson State University *B*
Jamestown College *B*
Minot State University *B*
North Dakota State University
 Bottineau and Institute of
  Forestry *A*
 Fargo *B,M*
Turtle Mountain Community
 College *A*
University of North Dakota *B,M,D*
Valley City State University *B*

Ohio

Antioch College *B*
Ashland University *B*
Baldwin-Wallace College *B*
Bluffton College *B*
Bowling Green State University
 B,M,D
Capital University *B*
Case Western Reserve University
 B,M,D
Cedarville College *B*
Central State University *B*
Cleveland State University *B,M*
College of Mount St. Joseph *B*
College of Wooster *B*
Defiance College *B*
Denison University *B*
Franciscan University of
 Steubenville *B*
Heidelberg College *B*

Hiram College *B*
John Carroll University *B,M*
Kent State University *B,M,D*
Kenyon College *B*
Lakeland Community College *A*
Lourdes College *A,B*
Malone College *B*
Marietta College *B*
Miami University: Oxford Campus
 B,M,D
Mount Union College *B*
Mount Vernon Nazarene College *B*
Muskingum College *B*
Oberlin College *B*
Ohio Dominican College *B*
Ohio Northern University *B*
Ohio State University: Columbus
 Campus *B,M,D*
Ohio University *B,M,D*
Ohio Wesleyan University *B*
Otterbein College *B*
Pontifical College Josephinum *B*
Union Institute *B,D*
University of Akron *B,M,D*
University of Cincinnati *B,M,D*
University of Dayton *B,M*
University of Findlay *B*
University of Rio Grande *C,A,B*
University of Toledo *B,M,D*
Urbana University *B*
Ursuline College *B*
Walsh College *B*
Wilmington College *B*
Wittenberg University *B*
Wright State University
 Dayton *B,M*
 Lake Campus *A*
Xavier University *A,B,M*
Youngstown State University *B,M*

Oklahoma

Bartlesville Wesleyan College *B*
Cameron University *B*
East Central University *B*
Eastern Oklahoma State College *A*
Langston University *B*
Murray State College *A*
Northeastern State University *B*
Northwestern Oklahoma State
 University *B*
Oklahoma Baptist University *B*
Oklahoma Christian University of
 Science and Arts *B*
Oklahoma City University *B*
Oklahoma Panhandle State
 University *B*
Oklahoma State University *B,M,D*
Oral Roberts University *B*
Phillips University *B*
Redlands Community College *A*
Rogers State College *A*
Rose State College *A*
Southeastern Oklahoma State
 University *B*
Southwestern Oklahoma State
 University *B*
Tulsa Junior College *A*
University of Central Oklahoma
 B,M
University of Oklahoma *B,M,D*
University of Science and Arts of
 Oklahoma *B*
University of Tulsa *B,M*

Oregon

Central Oregon Community
 College *A*
Eastern Oregon State College *B*
George Fox College *B,D*
Lewis and Clark College *B*
Linfield College *B*
Northwest Christian College *B*

Oregon State University *B*
Pacific University *B*
Portland Community College *A*
Portland State University *B,M*
Reed College *B*
Southern Oregon State College *B*
University of Oregon
 Eugene *B,M,D*
 Robert Donald Clark Honors
  College *B*
University of Portland *B*
Warner Pacific College *B*
Western Oregon State College *B*
Willamette University *B*

Pennsylvania

Albright College *B*
Allegheny College *B*
Alvernia College *B*
Beaver College *B*
Bloomsburg University of
 Pennsylvania *B*
Bryn Mawr College *B*
Bucknell University *B*
Cabrini College *B*
California University of
 Pennsylvania *B*
Carnegie Mellon University *B,M,D*
Cedar Crest College *B*
Chatham College *B*
Chestnut Hill College *A,B*
Cheyney University of
 Pennsylvania *B*
Clarion University of
 Pennsylvania *B*
College Misericordia *B*
Dickinson College *B*
Drexel University *B*
Duquesne University *B,M*
East Stroudsburg University of
 Pennsylvania *B,M*
Eastern College *B*
Edinboro University of
 Pennsylvania *B*
Elizabethtown College *B*
Franklin and Marshall College *B*
Gannon University *B*
Geneva College *B*
Gettysburg College *B*
Grove City College *B*
Gwynedd-Mercy College *B*
Haverford College *B*
Holy Family College *B*
Immaculata College *B*
Indiana University of Pennsylvania
 B,M
Juniata College *B*
King's College *B*
Kutztown University of
 Pennsylvania *B,M*
La Roche College *B*
La Salle University *B*
Lafayette College *B*
Lebanon Valley College of
 Pennsylvania *B*
Lehigh University *B,M,D*
Lincoln University *B*
Lock Haven University of
 Pennsylvania *B*
Lycoming College *B*
Mansfield University of
 Pennsylvania *B*
Mercyhurst College *B*
Messiah College *B*
Millersville University of
 Pennsylvania *B,M*
Moravian College *B*
Muhlenberg College *B*
Northeastern Christian Junior
 College *A*

Penn State
 Erie Behrend College *B*
 University Park Campus
  B,M,D
Point Park College *B*
Rosemont College *B*
St. Francis College *B*
St. Joseph's University *B*
St. Vincent College *B*
Seton Hill College *B*
Shippensburg University of
 Pennsylvania *B,M*
Slippery Rock University of
 Pennsylvania *B,M*
Susquehanna University *B*
Swarthmore College *B*
Temple University *B,M,D*
Thiel College *B*
University of Pennsylvania *B,M,D*
University of Pittsburgh
 Bradford *B*
 Johnstown *B*
 Pittsburgh *B,M,D*
University of Scranton *B,M*
Ursinus College *B*
Villanova University *B,M*
Washington and Jefferson College *B*
Waynesburg College *B*
West Chester University of
 Pennsylvania *B,M*
Westminster College *B*
Widener University *B*
Wilkes University *B*
Wilson College *B*
York College of Pennsylvania *B*

Puerto Rico

Inter American University of Puerto
 Rico
 Arecibo Campus *B*
 Metropolitan Campus *B*
 San German Campus *B*
Pontifical Catholic University of
 Puerto Rico *B*
Universidad Adventista de las
 Antillas *B*
University of Puerto Rico
 Mayaguez Campus *B*
 Rio Piedras Campus *B,M,D*
University of the Sacred Heart *B*

Rhode Island

Brown University *B,M,D*
Bryant College *B*
Providence College *B,M,D*
Rhode Island College *B,M*
Roger Williams College *B*
Salve Regina University *B*
University of Rhode Island *B,M*

South Carolina

Bob Jones University *B*
Central Wesleyan College *B*
Charleston Southern University *B*
The Citadel *B,M*
Claflin College *B*
Clemson University *B,M*
Coker College *B*
College of Charleston *B,M*
Columbia College *B*
Converse College *B*
Erskine College *B*
Francis Marion College *B*
Furman University *B*
Lander College *B*
Limestone College *B*
Morris College *B*
Newberry College *B*
Presbyterian College *B*
South Carolina State College *B*

University of South Carolina
  Aiken *B*
  Coastal Carolina College *B*
  Columbia *B,M,D*
  Spartanburg *B*
Winthrop University *B,M*
Wofford College *B*

South Dakota

Augustana College *B*
Black Hills State University *B*
Dakota Wesleyan University *B*
Huron University *B*
Northern State University *B*
Oglala Lakota College *B*
Sioux Falls College *B*
South Dakota State University *B*
University of South Dakota *B,M*

Tennessee

Austin Peay State University *B,M*
Belmont University *B*
Carson-Newman College *B*
Christian Brothers University *B*
Cumberland University *A,B*
David Lipscomb University *B*
Dyersburg State Community
  College *A*
East Tennessee State University
  B,M
Fisk University *B*
Freed-Hardeman University *B*
King College *B*
Knoxville College *B*
Lambuth University *B*
Lane College *B*
LeMoyne-Owen College *B*
Lincoln Memorial University *B*
Maryville College *B*
Memphis State University *B,M,D*
Middle Tennessee State University
  B,M,D
Milligan College *B*
Motlow State Community
  College *A*
Rhodes College *B*
Southern College of Seventh-day
  Adventists *B*
Tennessee State University *B,M*
Tennessee Technological
  University *B*
Tennessee Temple University *B*
Tennessee Wesleyan College *B*
Trevecca Nazarene College *B*
Union University *B*
University of the South *B*
University of Tennessee
  Chattanooga *B*
  Knoxville *B,M,D*
  Martin *B*
Vanderbilt University *B,M,D*
William Jennings Bryan College *B*

Texas

Abilene Christian University *B,M*
Angelo State University *B,M*
Austin College *B*
Austin Community College *A*
Baylor University *B,M*
Bee County College *A*
College of the Mainland *A*
Collin County Community College
  District *A*
Corpus Christi State University *B*
Dallas Baptist University *B*
Del Mar College *A*
East Texas Baptist University *B*
East Texas State University
  Commerce *B,M*
  Texarkana *B*
El Paso Community College *A*
Hardin-Simmons University *B,M*

Houston Baptist University *B*
Houston Community College *A*
Howard Payne University *B*
Huston-Tillotson College *B*
Incarnate Word College *B*
Jacksonville College *A*
Jarvis Christian College *B*
Kilgore College *A*
Lamar University—Beaumont *B,M*
Laredo State University *B*
LeTourneau University *B*
Lon Morris College *A*
Lubbock Christian University *B*
McLennan Community College *A*
McMurry University *B*
Midland College *A*
Midwestern State University *B,M*
Panola College *A*
Paul Quinn College *B*
Prairie View A&M University *B,M*
Rice University *B,M,D*
St. Edward's University *B*
St. Mary's University *B,M*
St. Philip's College *A*
Sam Houston State University *B,M*
Schreiner College *B*
South Plains College *A*
Southern Methodist University *B,M*
Southwest Texas State University
  B,M
Southwestern Adventist College *B*
Southwestern University *B*
Stephen F. Austin State University
  B,M
Sul Ross State University *B,M*
Tarleton State University *B*
Texas A&I University *B,M*
Texas A&M University *B,M,D*
Texas Christian University *B,M,D*
Texas College *B*
Texas Lutheran College *B*
Texas Southern University *B,M*
Texas Southmost College *A*
Texas Tech University *B,M,D*
Texas Wesleyan University *B*
Texas Woman's University *B,M*
Trinity University *B*
University of Dallas *B*
University of Houston
  Clear Lake *B,M*
  Houston *B,M,D*
  Victoria *B*
University of Mary Hardin-
  Baylor *B*
University of North Texas *B,M,D*
University of St. Thomas *B*
University of Texas
  Arlington *B,M*
  Austin *B,M,D*
  Dallas *B*
  El Paso *B,M*
  Pan American *B*
  Permian Basin *B,M*
  San Antonio *B,M*
  Tyler *B,M*
Wayland Baptist University *B*
West Texas State University *B,M*
Western Texas College *A*
Wharton County Junior College *A*
Wiley College *B*

Utah

Brigham Young University *B,M,D*
Dixie College *A*
Southern Utah University *B*
University of Utah *B,M,D*
Utah State University *B,M*
Weber State University *B*
Westminster College of Salt Lake
  City *B*

Vermont

Bennington College *B*
Castleton State College *B*
College of St. Joseph in Vermont *B*
Johnson State College *B*
Marlboro College *B*
Middlebury College *B*
Norwich University *B*
St. Michael's College *B*
Trinity College of Vermont *B*
University of Vermont *B,M*

Virginia

Averett College *B*
Bluefield College *B*
Bridgewater College *B*
Christendom College *B*
Christopher Newport College *B*
Clinch Valley College of the
  University of Virginia *B*
College of William and Mary
  B,M,D
Eastern Mennonite College *B*
Emory and Henry College *B*
Ferrum College *B*
George Mason University *B,M*
Hampden-Sydney College *B*
Hampton University *B*
Hollins College *B*
James Madison University *B,M*
Liberty University *B*
Longwood College *B*
Lynchburg College *B*
Mary Baldwin College *B*
Mary Washington College *B*
Norfolk State University *B*
Old Dominion University *B,M*
Radford University *B*
Randolph-Macon College *B*
Randolph-Macon Woman's
  College *B*
Roanoke College *B*
Shenandoah University *B*
Sweet Briar College *B*
University of Richmond *B,M*
University of Virginia *B,M,D*
Virginia Commonwealth
  University *B*
Virginia Intermont College *B*
Virginia Military Institute *B*
Virginia Polytechnic Institute and
  State University *B,M*
Virginia State University *B,M*
Virginia Union University *B*
Virginia Wesleyan College *B*
Washington and Lee University *B*

Washington

Big Bend Community College *A*
Central Washington University *B,M*
Eastern Washington University *B,M*
Everett Community College *A*
Evergreen State College *B*
Gonzaga University *B*
Heritage College *B*
Lower Columbia College *A*
Olympic College *A*
Pacific Lutheran University *B*
St. Martin's College *B*
Seattle Pacific University *B*
Seattle University *B*
Spokane Community College *A*
Spokane Falls Community
  College *A*
Tacoma Community College *A*
University of Puget Sound *B*
University of Washington *B,M,D*
Walla Walla College *B*
Washington State University *B,M,D*
Wenatchee Valley College *A*
Western Washington University
  B,M

Whitman College *B*
Whitworth College *B*

West Virginia

Alderson-Broaddus College *B*
Bethany College *B*
Bluefield State College *B*
Concord College *B*
Davis and Elkins College *B*
Fairmont State College *B*
Glenville State College *B*
Marshall University *B,M*
Potomac State College of West
  Virginia University *A*
Salem-Teikyo University *B*
Shepherd College *B*
University of Charleston *B*
West Liberty State College *B*
West Virginia Institute of
  Technology *B*
West Virginia State College *B*
West Virginia University *B,M,D*
West Virginia Wesleyan College *B*
Wheeling Jesuit College *B*

Wisconsin

Alverno College *B*
Beloit College *B*
Cardinal Stritch College *B*
Carroll College *B*
Carthage College *B*
Concordia University Wisconsin *B*
Edgewood College *B*
Lakeland College *B*
Lawrence University *B*
Marian College of Fond du Lac *B*
Marquette University *B,M,D*
Mount Mary College *B*
Mount Senario College *B*
Northland College *B*
Ripon College *B*
St. Norbert College *B*
Silver Lake College *B*
University of Wisconsin
  Eau Claire *B,M*
  Green Bay *B*
  La Crosse *B*
  Madison *B,M,D*
  Milwaukee *B,M*
  Oshkosh *B*
  Parkside *B*
  Platteville *B*
  River Falls *B,M*
  Stevens Point *B,M*
  Superior *B*
  Whitewater *B*
Wisconsin Lutheran College *B*

Wyoming

Casper College *A*
Eastern Wyoming College *A*
Laramie County Community
  College *A*
Northwest College *A*
University of Wyoming *B,M,D*
Western Wyoming Community
  College *A*

American Samoa, Caroline Islands, Guam, Marianas, Virgin Islands

University of Guam *B*

Canada

McGill University *B,M,D*

Arab Republic of Egypt

American University in Cairo *B,M*

Home economics

Alabama

Alabama Agricultural and
  Mechanical University *B,M*
Alabama Southern Community
  College *A*
Jacksonville State University *B*
James H. Faulkner State
  Community College *A*
Judson College *B*
Oakwood College *B*
Samford University *B,M*
Shelton State Community
  College *A*
University of Alabama *B*
University of Montevallo *B*
University of North Alabama *B*

Alaska

University of Alaska Anchorage *A*

Arizona

Arizona State University *B,M*
Arizona Western College *A*
Eastern Arizona College *A*
Mesa Community College *A*
Pima Community College *C,A*
University of Arizona *B*
Yavapai College *A*

Arkansas

Harding University *B,M*
Henderson State University *B*
Ouachita Baptist University *B*
Philander Smith College *B*
University of Arkansas *B,M*
University of Central Arkansas *B,M*
Westark Community College *A*

California

Allan Hancock College *A*
Bakersfield College *A*
California Polytechnic State
  University: San Luis Obispo *B,M*
California State Polytechnic
  University: Pomona *B*
California State University
  Chico *B*
  Fresno *B,M*
  Long Beach *B,M*
  Los Angeles *B,M*
  Northridge *B,M*
  Sacramento *B*
Cerritos Community College *A*
Chaffey Community College *A*
Christian Heritage College *B*
City College of San Francisco *A*
College of the Sequoias *A*
El Camino College *A*
Fresno City College *A*
Kings River Community College *A*
Long Beach City College *A*
Los Angeles City College *A*
Los Angeles Mission College *A*
Los Angeles Valley College *A*
Master's College *B*
Merced College *A*
Modesto Junior College *A*
Monterey Peninsula College *C,A*
Moorpark College *A*
Mount San Antonio College *A*
Napa Valley College *A*
Orange Coast College *A*
Pacific Union College *B*
Point Loma Nazarene College *B*
Saddleback College *C,A*
San Diego State University *B,M*
San Francisco State University *B,M*
San Joaquin Delta College *A*

Santa Monica College *C,A*
Santa Rosa Junior College *A*
Sierra College *A*
Skyline College *A*
Solano Community College *A*
Southwestern College *A*
Ventura College *C,A*
Yuba College *A*

Colorado

Colorado State University *B,M*
Morgan Community College *A*
Trinidad State Junior College *A*

Connecticut

St. Joseph College *B,M*

Delaware

Delaware State College *B*
University of Delaware *B*

District of Columbia

Gallaudet University *B*
University of the District of
  Columbia *B*

Florida

Daytona Beach Community
  College *A*
Florida State University *B,D*
Gulf Coast Community College *C,A*
Indian River Community College *A*
Manatee Community College *A*
Miami-Dade Community College *C*
Okaloosa-Walton Community
  College *A*
Palm Beach Community College *A*
Pensacola Junior College *A*

Georgia

Abraham Baldwin Agricultural
  College *A*
Atlanta Metropolitan College *A*
Bainbridge College *A*
Brewton-Parker College *A*
Clayton State College *A*
Darton College *A*
DeKalb College *A*
Fort Valley State College *B*
Georgia Southern University *B,M*
Gordon College *A*
Middle Georgia College *A*
University of Georgia *B,M*
Young Harris College *A*

Hawaii

Brigham Young University-
  Hawaii *A*

Idaho

College of Southern Idaho *A*
Idaho State University *B*
Ricks College *A*
University of Idaho *B,M*

Illinois

Bradley University *B*
Eastern Illinois University *B,M*
Illinois Central College *A*
Illinois State University *B,M*
Illinois Valley Community
  College *A*
Kishwaukee College *A*
Olivet Nazarene University *B*
Rosary College *B*
Southern Illinois University at
  Carbondale *B*
University of Illinois at Urbana-
  Champaign *B,M*
Western Illinois University *B*

Indiana

Ball State University *B,M*
Indiana State University *B,M*
Purdue University *B*
Valparaiso University *B*
Vincennes University *A*

Iowa

Iowa State University *B*
Muscatine Community College *A*
North Iowa Area Community
  College *A*
University of Northern Iowa *B*
William Penn College *B*

Kansas

Allen County Community
  College *A*
Barton County Community
  College *A*
Bethel College *B*
Central College *A*
Cloud County Community
  College *A*
Coffeyville Community College *A*
Colby Community College *A*
Fort Hays State University *B*
Highland Community College *A*
Hutchinson Community College *A*
Kansas City Kansas Community
  College *A*
Kansas State University *B,D*
Neosho County Community
  College *A*
Pittsburg State University *B*
Pratt Community College *A*
Sterling College *B*

Kentucky

Berea College *B*
Eastern Kentucky University *B*
Georgetown College *B*
Morehead State University *B*
Murray State University *B,M*
Western Kentucky University *M*

Louisiana

Grambling State University *B*
Louisiana State University and
  Agricultural and Mechanical
  College *M*
Nicholls State University *B*
Northwestern State University *B*
Southeastern Louisiana
  University *B*
University of Southwestern
  Louisiana *B,M*

Maine

College of the Atlantic *B,M*
University of Maine *B,M*

Maryland

Hood College *B,M*
Morgan State University *B*
University of Maryland: Eastern
  Shore *B*

Massachusetts

Atlantic Union College *B*
Framingham State College *B,M*
University of Massachusetts at
  Amherst *B,M*

Michigan

Adrian College *A,B*
Andrews University *B,M*
Central Michigan University *B,M*
Eastern Michigan University *B,M*
Lansing Community College *A*
Madonna University *B*
Marygrove College *B*

Michigan Christian College *C,A*
Northern Michigan University *B,M*
Western Michigan University *M*

Minnesota

Bethany Lutheran College *A*
College of St. Catherine: St.
  Catherine Campus *B*
College of St. Scholastica *B*
Concordia College: Moorhead *B*
Mankato State University *B,M*
Northland Community College *A*
Rainy River Community College *A*
Rochester Community College *A*
University of Minnesota: Twin
  Cities *B*
University of St. Thomas *B*
Vermilion Community College *A*
Willmar Community College *A*

Mississippi

Alcorn State University *B*
Blue Mountain College *B*
Delta State University *B*
Jones County Junior College *A*
Mississippi College *B*
Mississippi Delta Community
  College *A*
Mississippi State University *B*
Mississippi University for Women *B*
Northeast Mississippi Community
  College *A*
University of Mississippi *B*
University of Southern Mississippi
  B,M

Missouri

Central Missouri State University *B*
College of the Ozarks *B*
East Central College *A*
Fontbonne College *B*
Mineral Area College *A*
Penn Valley Community College *A*
St. Louis Community College at
  Florissant Valley *A*
Southwest Missouri State
  University *B*
University of Missouri: Columbia *B*

Montana

Little Big Horn College *A*
Miles Community College *A*
Montana State University *B,M*

Nebraska

Central Community College *C,A*
Chadron State College *B*
McCook Community College *A*
University of Nebraska
  Kearney *B*
  Lincoln *M,D*
  Omaha *B,M*
Wayne State College *B*
York College *A*

Nevada

University of Nevada: Reno *B*

New Hampshire

Keene State College *B*

New Jersey

College of St. Elizabeth *B*
Montclair State College *B,M*
Rutgers—The State University of
  New Jersey *M*

New Mexico

Eastern New Mexico University *B*
New Mexico State University *B,M*

New York

City University of New York
   Brooklyn College *B*
   Queens College *B,M*
Marymount College *B*
New York University *M,D*
State University of New York
   College at Oneonta *B*
   College at Plattsburgh *B*
Syracuse University *B,M*

North Carolina

Appalachian State University *B*
Bennett College *B*
Campbell University *B*
East Carolina University *B,M*
Mars Hill College *B*
Meredith College *B*
North Carolina Agricultural and
   Technical State University *B*
North Carolina Central University
   B,M
Western Carolina University *B,M*

North Dakota

North Dakota State University *B*
Turtle Mountain Community
   College *A*

Ohio

Ashland University *B*
Baldwin-Wallace College *B*
Bluffton College *B*
Bowling Green State University *B*
Miami University: Oxford Campus
   B,M
Mount Vernon Nazarene College
   A,B
Ohio State University: Columbus
   Campus *B,M,D*
Ohio University *B,M*
University of Akron *B*
University of Dayton *B*
Youngstown State University *B*

Oklahoma

Bacone College *A*
Cameron University *B*
Connors State College *A*
East Central University *B*
Langston University *B*
Northeastern State University *B*
Northern Oklahoma College *A*
Northwestern Oklahoma State
   University *B*
Oklahoma Panhandle State
   University *B*
Oklahoma State University *D*
Rose State College *A*
Southeastern Oklahoma State
   University *B*
Southwestern Oklahoma State
   University *B*
University of Central Oklahoma *B*
University of Science and Arts of
   Oklahoma *B*

Oregon

Central Oregon Community
   College *A*
George Fox College *B*
Oregon State University *B,M*
Portland Community College *A*

Pennsylvania

Albright College *B*
Drexel University *M*
Immaculata College *B*
Indiana University of Pennsylvania
   B,M
Mercyhurst College *B*
Messiah College *B*

Northeastern Christian Junior
   College *A*
St. Vincent College *B*
Seton Hill College *B*

Puerto Rico

Pontifical Catholic University of
   Puerto Rico *B*
University of Puerto Rico: Rio
   Piedras Campus *B,M*

Rhode Island

University of Rhode Island *B*

South Carolina

Bob Jones University *B*
South Carolina State College *B*
Winthrop University *B*

South Dakota

South Dakota State University *M*

Tennessee

Carson-Newman College *B*
David Lipscomb University *B*
East Tennessee State University *B*
Freed-Hardeman University *B*
Hiwassee College *A*
Lambuth University *B*
Memphis State University *B,M*
Middle Tennessee State
   University *B*
Tennessee State University *B*
Tennessee Technological
   University *B*
Tennessee Temple University *A*
University of Tennessee
   Chattanooga *B*
   Knoxville *B,M,D*
   Martin *B,M*

Texas

Abilene Christian University *B*
Amarillo College *A*
Baylor University *B*
Bee County College *A*
Blinn College *A*
Houston Community College *A*
Lamar University—Beaumont *B,M*
Lon Morris College *A*
Lubbock Christian University *B*
Prairie View A&M University *M*
Sam Houston State University *B,M*
South Plains College *A*
Southwest Texas State University *B*
Stephen F. Austin State University
   B,M
Tarleton State University *B*
Texas A&I University *B*
Texas Southern University *B,M*
Texas Southmost College *A*
Texas Tech University *B,M,D*
University of Houston *B*
University of Mary Hardin-
   Baylor *B*
University of Texas at Austin *B*

Utah

Brigham Young University *B,M*
Dixie College *A*
Southern Utah University *B*
Utah State University *B*

Vermont

University of Vermont *B*

Virginia

Bridgewater College *B*
Hampton University *B,M*
James Madison University *B*
Liberty University *B*
Norfolk State University *B*

Washington

Central Washington University *B,M*
Everett Community College *A*
Skagit Valley College *A*
Spokane Falls Community
   College *A*
Washington State University *B,M*

West Virginia

Fairmont State College *B*
Marshall University *B,M*
Shepherd College *B*
West Virginia Wesleyan College *B*

Wisconsin

Mount Mary College *B*
University of Wisconsin
   Madison *B,M*
   Stout *B*

Wyoming

Casper College *A*
Northwest College *A*
University of Wyoming *B,M*

**American Samoa, Caroline
Islands, Guam, Marianas,
Virgin Islands**

Micronesian Occupational College
   C,A
University of Guam *B*

Home economics
education

Alabama

Alabama Agricultural and
   Mechanical University *B,M*
Auburn University *B,M*
Jacksonville State University *B*
Oakwood College *B*
Samford University *B*
Tuskegee University *B*
University of Alabama *B,M*
University of Montevallo *B,M*
University of North Alabama *B*

Arizona

Arizona State University *B*
Eastern Arizona College *A*
University of Arizona *B,M*

Arkansas

Harding University *B*
Henderson State University *B*
Ouachita Baptist University *B*
University of Arkansas
   Fayetteville *B*
   Pine Bluff *B*
University of Central Arkansas *B,M*
Westark Community College *A*

California

Allan Hancock College *A*
California State University
   Fresno *B*
   Long Beach *B*
   Los Angeles *B*
   Northridge *B*
   Sacramento *B*
Christian Heritage College *B*

Colorado

Colorado State University *B,M*

Connecticut

St. Joseph College *B*

Delaware

Delaware State College *B*
University of Delaware *B,M*

District of Columbia

Gallaudet University *B*
University of the District of
   Columbia *B*

Florida

Florida International University
   B,M
Florida State University *B,M*
Manatee Community College *A*
Pensacola Junior College *A*

Georgia

Berry College *B*
Georgia Southern University *B,M*
University of Georgia *B,M*

Idaho

College of Southern Idaho *A*
Idaho State University *M*
Northwest Nazarene College *B*
Ricks College *A*

Illinois

Bradley University *B*
Northern Illinois University *B,M*
Olivet Nazarene University *B*
Southern Illinois University at
   Carbondale *B*
Trinity Christian College *B*
University of Illinois at Urbana-
   Champaign *B,M*
Western Illinois University *B*

Indiana

Ball State University *B,M*
Indiana State University *B,M*
Purdue University *B,M,D*
St. Mary-of-the-Woods College *B*
Vincennes University *A*

Iowa

Iowa State University *B,M,D*
University of Northern Iowa *B*
William Penn College *B*

Kansas

Colby Community College *A*
Kansas State University *B*

Kentucky

Berea College *B*
Eastern Kentucky University *B,M*
Georgetown College *B*
Morehead State University *B*
Murray State University *B*
University of Kentucky *B*
University of Louisville *M*
Western Kentucky University *B,M*

Louisiana

Grambling State University *B*
Louisiana State University and
   Agricultural and Mechanical
   College *B*
Louisiana Tech University *B,M*
McNeese State University *B*
Nicholls State University *B*
Northeast Louisiana University *B*
Northwestern State University *B*
Southeastern Louisiana
   University *B*
Southern University and
   Agricultural and Mechanical
   College *B*
University of Southwestern
   Louisiana *B*

Maine

University of Maine *B*

Massachusetts

Framingham State College *B,M*

Michigan

Adrian College *B*
Andrews University *M*
Central Michigan University *B,M*
Eastern Michigan University *B,M*
Ferris State University *B*
Madonna University *A,B*
Marygrove College *B*
Michigan State University *B,M*
Northern Michigan University *B,M*
Western Michigan University *B*

Minnesota

College of St. Catherine: St.
    Catherine Campus *B*
College of St. Scholastica *B*
Concordia College: Moorhead *B*
Mankato State University *B*
Pillsbury Baptist Bible College *B*
Rainy River Community College *A*
St. Olaf College *B*
University of Minnesota
    Duluth *B*
    Twin Cities *B,M*
Willmar Community College *A*

Mississippi

Alcorn State University *B,M*
Delta State University *B*
Jones County Junior College *A*
Mississippi College *B*
Mississippi University for Women *B*
Northeast Mississippi Community
    College *A*
University of Mississippi *B*

Missouri

Central Missouri State University
    B,M
College of the Ozarks *B*
Fontbonne College *B*
Northwest Missouri State
    University *B,M*
Southeast Missouri State University
    B,M
Southwest Missouri State
    University *B*
University of Missouri: Columbia
    B,M,D

Montana

Montana State University *B*

Nebraska

Chadron State College *B*
University of Nebraska
    Kearney *B,M*
    Lincoln *B*
    Omaha *B*
Wayne State College *B*
York College *A*

New Hampshire

Keene State College *B*

New Jersey

College of St. Elizabeth *B*

New Mexico

Eastern New Mexico University *B*
New Mexico State University *B*
University of New Mexico *B*

New York

City University of New York
    Brooklyn College *B*
    Queens College *B,M*
Cornell University *B,M,D*
Marymount College *B*
New York University *M,D*
State University of New York
    College at Oneonta *B,M*
    College at Plattsburgh *B,M*
Syracuse University *M*

North Carolina

Appalachian State University *B*
Campbell University *B*
East Carolina University *B,M*
Mars Hill College *B*
North Carolina Agricultural and
    Technical State University *B*
North Carolina Central University
    B,M
University of North Carolina at
    Greensboro *B,M*
Western Carolina University *B,M*

North Dakota

North Dakota State University *B,M*
University of North Dakota *B*

Ohio

Ashland University *B*
Baldwin-Wallace College *B*
Bluffton College *B*
Bowling Green State University
    B,M
Kent State University *B,M*
Miami University: Oxford Campus
    B,M
Mount Vernon Nazarene College *B*
Ohio State University: Columbus
    Campus *B,M,D*
Ohio University *B*
Youngstown State University *B*

Oklahoma

East Central University *B*
Langston University *B*
Northwestern Oklahoma State
    University *B*
Oklahoma Panhandle State
    University *B*
Oklahoma State University *M,D*
Southeastern Oklahoma State
    University *B,M*
Southwestern Oklahoma State
    University *B,M*
University of Central Oklahoma
    B,M
University of Science and Arts of
    Oklahoma *B*

Oregon

George Fox College *B*
Oregon State University *M*

Pennsylvania

Albright College *B*
Cheyney University of
    Pennsylvania *B*
Immaculata College *B*
Indiana University of
    Pennsylvania *B*
Marywood College *B*
Mercyhurst College *B*
Messiah College *B*
Penn State University Park Campus
    B,M,D
St. Vincent College *B*
Seton Hill College *B*
Wilkes University *B*

Puerto Rico

Pontifical Catholic University of
    Puerto Rico *B*
University of Puerto Rico: Rio
    Piedras Campus *B,M*

Rhode Island

University of Rhode Island *M*

South Carolina

Bob Jones University *B*
South Carolina State College *B*
Winthrop University *B,M*

South Dakota

South Dakota State University *B*

Tennessee

Carson-Newman College *B*
East Tennessee State University *B*
Middle Tennessee State
    University *B*
Tennessee Technological
    University *B*
University of Tennessee
    Knoxville *B*
    Martin *B,M*

Texas

Abilene Christian University *B*
Prairie View A&M University *M*
Sam Houston State University *B,M*
Tarleton State University *B*
Texas A&I University *B*
Texas Tech University *B,M,D*
Texas Woman's University *M,D*
University of Houston *B*
University of Mary Hardin-
    Baylor *B*

Utah

Brigham Young University *B*
University of Utah *B*
Utah State University *B*

Vermont

University of Vermont *B*

Virginia

Liberty University *B*
Norfolk State University *B*
Virginia Polytechnic Institute and
    State University *B,M*

Washington

Central Washington University *B*
Seattle Pacific University *B*
Washington State University *B*

West Virginia

Fairmont State College *B*
Shepherd College *B*
West Virginia University *B,M*
West Virginia Wesleyan College *B*

Wisconsin

Mount Mary College *B*
University of Wisconsin
    Madison *B,M*
    Stevens Point *B,M*
    Stout *B,M*

Wyoming

University of Wyoming *B*

American Samoa, Caroline Islands, Guam, Marianas, Virgin Islands

University of Guam *B*

Home furnishings and equipment management/ production/services

Alabama

Jefferson State Community
    College *A*
University of Alabama *B*

Arizona

Arizona Western College *A*

California

California State University: Los
    Angeles *B*
Long Beach City College *C,A*
Saddleback College *C,A*

Connecticut

Teikyo-Post University *A,B*

Florida

Seminole Community College *A*

Georgia

Abraham Baldwin Agricultural
    College *A*
Georgia Southern University *B*
University of Georgia *B,M*

Illinois

KAES College *B*

Indiana

Indiana State University *B*
Purdue University *B*
Valparaiso University *B*

Iowa

Hawkeye Institute of Technology *A*

Kansas

Johnson County Community
    College *A*

Kentucky

Morehead State University *A*

Massachusetts

Endicott College *A*

Michigan

Grand Rapids Community
    College *A*

Minnesota

Lakewood Community College *A*

Missouri

Southeast Missouri State
    University *B*

North Carolina

Appalachian State University *B*
Western Carolina University *B*

Ohio

Ohio State University: Columbus
    Campus *B,M,D*

Oklahoma

Oklahoma State University *B,M*

Pennsylvania

St. Vincent College *B*

South Carolina

Bob Jones University *B*

Tennessee
Carson-Newman College *B*
East Tennessee State University *B*

Texas
St. Philip's College *C*
Sam Houston State University *B*
University of Mary Hardin-
Baylor *B*

Utah
Utah State University *M*

Wisconsin
Waukesha County Technical
College *A*

Horticultural science

Alabama
Auburn University *B,M*
John C. Calhoun State Community
College *C*

Arizona
Cochise College *C*
Mesa Community College *A*
University of Arizona *B,M,D*

California
California State Polytechnic
University: Pomona *B*
California State University:
Fresno *B*
Chabot College *A*
Cosumnes River College *A*
Golden West College *C,A*
Kings River Community College *A*
Long Beach City College *A*
Los Angeles Pierce College *C,A*
Modesto Junior College *A*
Mount San Antonio College *C,A*
Santa Rosa Junior College *C,A*
Solano Community College *A*
University of California: Davis *M*
West Hills Community College *C,A*

Colorado
Front Range Community College *A*

Delaware
Delaware State College *B*

Florida
Edison Community College *A*
Florida Southern College *B*
Hillsborough Community College *A*
Pensacola Junior College *A*
University of Florida *M,D*

Georgia
Fort Valley State College *B*
University of Georgia *B,M,D*

Hawaii
University of Hawaii at Hilo *B*

Idaho
Ricks College *C,A*
University of Idaho *B*

Illinois
Belleville Area College *A*
Black Hawk College *C*
College of DuPage *C*
Joliet Junior College *C,A*
Southern Illinois University at
Carbondale *B,M*

University of Illinois at Urbana-
Champaign *B,M,D*

Indiana
Purdue University *B,M,D,W*
Vincennes University *A*

Iowa
Hawkeye Institute of Technology *A*
Iowa Central Community College *A*
Iowa State University *B,M,D*
Kirkwood Community College *A*

Kansas
Coffeyville Community College *A*
Kansas State University *B,M,D*

Kentucky
Eastern Kentucky University *B*
Murray State University *A,B*
St. Catharine College *A*

Louisiana
Louisiana State University and
Agricultural and Mechanical
College *B*
Louisiana Tech University *B*
McNeese State University *B*
University of Southwestern
Louisiana *B*

Maryland
Allegany Community College *A*
University of Maryland: College
Park *B,M,D*

Massachusetts
Essex Agricultural and Technical
Institute *A*
University of Massachusetts at
Amherst *A*

Michigan
Michigan State University *B,M,D*
Southwestern Michigan College *A*

Minnesota
University of Minnesota
Crookston *A*
Twin Cities *M,D*
Willmar Community College *A*

Mississippi
Mississippi State University *B,M,D*

Missouri
Northwest Missouri State
University *B*
St. Louis Community College at
Meramec *C,A*
Southeast Missouri State
University *B*
Southwest Missouri State
University *B*

Nebraska
Central Community College *A*

New Hampshire
University of New Hampshire *A*

New Jersey
Rutgers—The State University of
New Jersey
Cook College *B*
New Brunswick *M,D*
Thomas Edison State College *A,B*

New Mexico
New Mexico State University *B,M*

New York
Cornell University *B,M,D*
Rockland Community College *C*
State University of New York
College of Agriculture and
Technology at Cobleskill *A*
College of Agriculture and
Technology at Morrisville *A*
College of Technology at
Delhi *A*
Suffolk County Community
College *A*

North Carolina
Alamance Community College *A*
Central Piedmont Community
College *A*
Fayetteville Technical Community
College *A*
North Carolina State University
B,M,D
Surry Community College *C,A*
Tri-County Community College *C*

North Dakota
North Dakota State University
Bottineau and Institute of
Forestry *A*
Fargo *B,M*

Ohio
Kent State University: Salem
Regional Campus *A*
Northwest Technical College *A*
Ohio State University: Columbus
Campus *B,M,D*

Oklahoma
Bacone College *C,A*
Connors State College *A*
Eastern Oklahoma State College *A*
Oklahoma State University
Oklahoma City *A*
Stillwater *B*
Tulsa Junior College *A*

Oregon
Mount Hood Community College
C,A

Pennsylvania
Delaware Valley College *B*
Penn State University Park Campus
C,B,M,D

Puerto Rico
University of Puerto Rico:
Mayaguez Campus *B,M*

South Dakota
South Dakota State University *B*

Tennessee
Walters State Community
College *A*

Texas
Austin Community College *C*
Central Texas College *A*
Lee College *A*
Richland College *A*
Southwest Texas State University *B*
Stephen F. Austin State
University *B*
Tarleton State University *B*
Tarrant County Junior College *C,A*
Texas A&M University *B,M,D*
Texas Tech University *B,M*

Utah
Brigham Young University *B,M*

Vermont
University of Vermont *B*

Washington
Clark College *C*
Spokane Community College *A*
Washington State University *B,M,D*

Wisconsin
University of Wisconsin
Madison *B,M,D*
Platteville *B*
River Falls *B*

Wyoming
Northwest College *A*

Horticulture

Alabama
Alabama Agricultural and
Mechanical University *B,M*
Shoals Community College *C*

Arizona
Mesa Community College *A*
University of Arizona *B,M,D*

Arkansas
Mississippi County Community
College *A*
University of Arkansas *B,M*

California
Bakersfield College *A*
California Polytechnic State
University: San Luis Obispo *B*
Chabot College *A*
Cosumnes River College *A*
Long Beach City College *C,A*
Los Angeles Pierce College *C,A*
Merced College *C,A*
MiraCosta College *C,A*
Modesto Junior College *A*
Ohlone College *C,A*
San Joaquin Delta College *A*
Santa Rosa Junior College *C*
Solano Community College *A*
Southwestern College *A*
University of California: Davis *M*
Ventura College *A*
Victor Valley College *C*
Yuba College *C*

Colorado
Colorado State University *B,M,D*
Front Range Community College
C,A

Connecticut
Mattatuck Community College *C*
University of Connecticut *C,B*

Florida
Central Florida Community
College *A*
Florida Southern College *B*
Hillsborough Community College *A*
Miami-Dade Community College *A*
Pensacola Junior College *A*
University of Florida *B*
Valencia Community College *A*

Georgia
Augusta College *A*
Floyd College *A*
Gainesville College *A*
Reinhardt College *A*
Savannah Technical Institute *C*

University of Georgia *B,M,D*

Hawaii
University of Hawaii at Manoa *M,D*

Idaho
Ricks College *C,A*

Illinois
Belleville Area College *C,A*
College of Lake County *C,A*
Illinois Central College *C,A*
Joliet Junior College *C,A*
Kishwaukee College *A*
Lake Land College *C*
Shawnee Community College *C,A*
Southern Illinois University at
Carbondale *B*
State Community College *C*
University of Illinois at Urbana-
Champaign *M,D*
William Rainey Harper College *A*

Indiana
Purdue University *A,B,M,D*
Vincennes University *A*

Iowa
Des Moines Area Community
College *A*
Hawkeye Institute of Technology *A*
Indian Hills Community College *C*
Iowa Lakes Community College *A*
Iowa State University *B,M,D*
Kirkwood Community College *A*

Kansas
Coffeyville Community College *A*
Kansas State University *B,M,D*

Kentucky
Eastern Kentucky University *A,B*
St. Catharine College *A*
University of Kentucky *B,M*

Louisiana
Louisiana State University and
Agricultural and Mechanical
College *B,M,D*

Maine
University of Maine *B*

Maryland
University of Maryland: College
Park *B,M,D*

Massachusetts
Essex Agricultural and Technical
Institute *A*
Springfield Technical Community
College *A*
University of Massachusetts at
Amherst *A*

Michigan
Michigan State University *B,M,D*
St. Clair County Community
College *A*

Minnesota
University of Minnesota
Crookston *A*
Twin Cities *M,D*
Willmar Community College *A*

Mississippi
Mississippi Delta Community
College *A*

Missouri
East Central College *C,A*
Northwest Missouri State
University *B*
St. Louis Community College at
Meramec *C,A*
University of Missouri: Columbia
B,M,D

Montana
Montana State University *B*

Nebraska
Central Community College *C,A*
Nebraska College of Technical
Agriculture *A*
University of Nebraska—Lincoln
B,M,D

New Hampshire
University of New Hampshire *B*

New Mexico
New Mexico State University *B,M*

New York
City University of New York: New
York City Technical College *A*
State University of New York
College of Agriculture and
Technology at Morrisville *A*
College of Technology at
Alfred *A*
College of Technology at
Delhi *A*
Suffolk County Community College
Eastern Campus *C,A*
Selden *C*

North Carolina
Blue Ridge Community College *A*
Catawba Valley Community
College *A*
Fayetteville Technical Community
College *A*
Haywood Community College *A*
Mayland Community College *C*
North Carolina State University
B,M,D
Sandhills Community College *A*
Stanly Community College *C*
Western Piedmont Community
College *A*

North Dakota
North Dakota State University *B,M*

Ohio
Clark State Community College *A*
Kent State University: Salem
Regional Campus *A*
Owens Technical College: Toledo *A*

Oklahoma
Eastern Oklahoma State College *A*
Oklahoma State University
Oklahoma City *C,A*
Stillwater *B,M*
Redlands Community College *A*

Oregon
Linn-Benton Community College
C,A
Oregon State University *B,M,D*

Pennsylvania
Delaware Valley College *B*
Penn State University Park
Campus *C*
Pennsylvania College of
Technology *A*
Temple University *A,B*

Puerto Rico
University of Puerto Rico
La Montana Regional
College *A*
Mayaguez Campus *B,M*

South Carolina
Clemson University *B,M*
Technical College of the
Lowcountry *A*
Trident Technical College *C,A*

South Dakota
South Dakota State University *B*

Tennessee
Chattanooga State Technical
Community College *C*
Tennessee Technological
University *B*

Texas
Collin County Community College
District *A*
Houston Community College *C,A*
Richland College *C,A*
Sam Houston State University *B*
Stephen F. Austin State
University *B*
Texarkana College *C*
Texas State Technical College:
Waco *A*
Texas Tech University *B,M*
Trinity Valley Community College
C,A

Utah
Utah State University *B*

Vermont
Vermont Technical College *A*

Virginia
Lord Fairfax Community College *A*
Northern Virginia Community
College *C,A*
Tidewater Community College *A*
Virginia Polytechnic Institute and
State University *B,M,D*

Washington
Clark College *A*
South Puget Sound Community
College *C,A*
Spokane Community College *A*
Washington State University *B,M,D*

West Virginia
Potomac State College of West
Virginia University *A*
West Virginia University *B,M*

Wisconsin
Madison Area Technical College *C*
University of Wisconsin
Madison *B,M,D*
River Falls *B*

Wyoming
Northwest College *A*

Canada
McGill University *B,M,D*

Hospitality and recreation marketing

Alabama
Community College of the Air
Force *A*
University of Alabama *B*

Arizona
Scottsdale Community College *A*

California
City College of San Francisco *A*
Glendale Community College *A*
Lake Tahoe Community College *A*
Los Angeles Trade and Technical
College *A*
Los Angeles Valley College *A*
Orange Coast College *C,A*
Pasadena City College *A*
San Diego Mesa College *C,A*
United States International
University *B*

Colorado
Colorado Mountain College: Alpine
Campus *A*
Mesa State College *A*

Delaware
Delaware Technical and
Community College: Southern
Campus *A*

Florida
Brevard Community College *A*
Broward Community College *A*
Daytona Beach Community
College *A*
Gulf Coast Community College *A*
Manatee Community College *C,A*
Miami-Dade Community College *A*
Valencia Community College *A*
Webber College *A,B*

Georgia
University of Georgia *B*

Hawaii
University of Hawaii: Kapiolani
Community College *C,A*

Idaho
Lewis Clark State College *A*

Illinois
College of St. Francis *B*
Elgin Community College *C,A*
MacCormac Junior College *A*
Midstate College *C*
Southern Illinois University at
Carbondale *B*

Indiana
Purdue University: Calumet *A*
Vincennes University *A*

Iowa
American Institute of Business *A*
Iowa Lakes Community College *A*

Kansas
Washburn University of Topeka *A*

Maine
Southern Maine Technical
College *A*

Maryland

Montgomery College: Rockville
   Campus *A*

Massachusetts

Bay Path College *A*
Bay State College *A*
Berkshire Community College *A*
Endicott College *A,B*
Massachusetts Bay Community
   College *C,A*

Michigan

Baker College of Muskegon *A*
Davenport College of Business *A*
Ferris State University *B*
Lansing Community College *A*
Madonna University *B*
Oakland Community College *A*

Minnesota

Normandale Community College *A*
University of Minnesota:
   Crookston *A*

Mississippi

Hinds Community College *A*
Northeast Mississippi Community
   College *A*

Missouri

East Central College *A*
Jefferson College *A*
Three Rivers Community College *A*

Nevada

Community College of Southern
   Nevada *A*
Sierra Nevada College *B*

New Jersey

Atlantic Community College *A*
Brookdale Community College *A*

New Mexico

Dona Ana Branch Community
   College of New Mexico State
   University *A*
New Mexico State University *B*

New York

Culinary Institute of America *A*
Erie Community College: City
   Campus *A*
Genesee Community College *A*
Herkimer County Community
   College *A*
Jefferson Community College *C,A*
Paul Smith's College *A*
Rochester Institute of Technology
   A,B,M
State University of New York
   College of Agriculture and
     Technology at Cobleskill *A*
   College of Agriculture and
     Technology at Morrisville *A*
   College of Technology at
     Delhi *A*
Sullivan County Community
   College *A*
Tompkins-Cortland Community
   College *A*

North Carolina

Asheville Buncombe Technical
   Community College *A*
Wake Technical Community
   College *A*

North Dakota

Bismarck State College *C,A*

Ohio

Cuyahoga Community College:
   Metropolitan Campus *A*
Hocking Technical College *A*
Ohio State University: Columbus
   Campus *B,M,D*
University of Cincinnati: Access
   Colleges *A*

Oklahoma

Tulsa Junior College *A*

Oregon

Mount Hood Community College
   C,A

Pennsylvania

Butler County Community College
   C,A
Harrisburg Area Community
   College *A*
Luzerne County Community
   College *C,A*
Mercyhurst College *C,A*
Montgomery County Community
   College *A*
Peirce Junior College *A*
Westmoreland County Community
   College *A*

Rhode Island

Johnson & Wales University *A,B*

South Carolina

Columbia Junior College of
   Business *A*
Technical College of the
   Lowcountry *A*

South Dakota

Black Hills State University *A,B*

Tennessee

Bristol University *A*
Volunteer State Community
   College *C*

Texas

Central Texas College *A*
El Centro College *A*
Galveston College *A*
San Jacinto College: Central
   Campus *A*

Utah

Dixie College *A*
Stevens-Henager College of
   Business *C*

Vermont

Champlain College *A*

Virginia

Commonwealth College *C,A*

Washington

Skagit Valley College *A*
Yakima Valley Community College
   C,A

West Virginia

Concord College *B*
Davis and Elkins College *A*
Shepherd College *B*

Wisconsin

Chippewa Valley Technical
   College *A*
Fox Valley Technical College *A*
Madison Area Technical College *A*
Stratton College *A*
University of Wisconsin: Stout *M*

Wisconsin Indianhead Technical
   College *A*

**American Samoa, Caroline
Islands, Guam, Marianas,
Virgin Islands**

Guam Community College *C,A*

Hotel/motel and restaurant management

Alabama

Auburn University *B*
Community College of the Air
   Force *A*
James H. Faulkner State
   Community College *A*
University of Alabama *B*

Arizona

Cochise College *A*
Lamson Junior College *A*
Mohave Community College *C*
Northern Arizona University *B*
Pima Community College *C,A*
Scottsdale Community College *A*
Western International University
   B,M
Yavapai College *A*

Arkansas

Arkansas Tech University *B*
Southern Arkansas University:
   Technical Branch *A*
Westark Community College *A*

California

American College for the Applied
   Arts: Los Angeles *B*
California State Polytechnic
   University: Pomona *B*
Chaffey Community College *A*
City College of San Francisco *C,A*
College of the Desert *C*
Columbia College *A*
Diablo Valley College *A*
El Camino College *A*
Golden Gate University *C,B,M*
Lake Tahoe Community College
   C,A
Long Beach City College *C,A*
Los Angeles Trade and Technical
   College *A*
MiraCosta College *C,A*
Mission College *A*
Monterey Peninsula College *C,A*
Orange Coast College *C,A*
Oxnard College *C,A*
Phillips Junior College: San
   Fernando Valley Campus *C,A*
San Diego Mesa College *C,A*
Santa Barbara City College *C,A*
United States International
   University *A*
University of San Francisco *B*

Colorado

Arapahoe Community College *A*
Blair Junior College *A*
Colorado Mountain College: Alpine
   Campus *A*
Colorado State University *B*
Community College of Denver *A*
Fort Lewis College *B*
Metropolitan State College of
   Denver *B*
University of Denver *B,M*

Connecticut

Briarwood College *A*
Manchester Community College *A*
Mattatuck Community College *C,A*
Norwalk Community College *A*
South Central Community
   College *A*
University of New Haven *C,A,B,M*

Delaware

Delaware State College *B*
Delaware Technical and
   Community College
     Southern Campus *A*
     Stanton/Wilmington
      Campus *A*
University of Delaware *B*

District of Columbia

Howard University *B*

Florida

Bethune-Cookman College *B*
Broward Community College *A*
Central Florida Community
   College *C*
Daytona Beach Community College
   C,A
Edison Community College *C,A*
Florida Community College at
   Jacksonville *A*
Florida International University
   B,M
Florida State University *B*
Fort Lauderdale College *A,B*
Gulf Coast Community College *A*
Hillsborough Community College *A*
Lake-Sumter Community College *A*
Lynn University *B*
Manatee Community College *A*
Miami-Dade Community College *A*
Nova University *B*
Okaloosa-Walton Community
   College *A*
Palm Beach Community College *A*
Pensacola Junior College *A*
Phillips Junior College:
   Melbourne *A*
St. Thomas University *B*
Schiller International University
   A,B
South Florida Community
   College *A*
United Electronics Institute *A*
University of Central Florida *B*
Webber College *A,B*

Georgia

Berry College *B*
DeKalb College *A*
Floyd College *A*
Gainesville College *A*
Georgia Southern University *B*
Georgia State University *B*
Morris Brown College *B*
South College *C,A*
University of Georgia *B*

Hawaii

Brigham Young University-Hawaii
   A,B
Cannon's International Business
   College of Honolulu *A*
Hawaii Pacific University *B,M*
University of Hawaii: Kapiolani
   Community College *A*

Idaho

College of Southern Idaho *A*

Illinois

Black Hawk College *C,A*
Chicago State University *B*
City Colleges of Chicago: Chicago City-Wide College *C,A*
College of DuPage *C,A*
Elgin Community College *A*
Illinois Eastern Community Colleges: Lincoln Trail College *A*
Joliet Junior College *C,A*
Kendall College *A,B*
Lewis and Clark Community College *A*
Lexington Institute of Hospitality Careers *A*
Midstate College *C*
Moraine Valley Community College *C,A*
Oakton Community College *C,A*
Parkland College *A*
Phillips College of Chicago *A*
Roosevelt University *B*
Southern Illinois University at Carbondale *B*
Triton College *C,A*
University of Illinois at Urbana-Champaign *B*

Indiana

Indiana State University *B*
Indiana University—Purdue University at Fort Wayne *A*
Indiana Vocational Technical College: Central Indiana *C,A*
Purdue University
  Calumet *B*
  North Central Campus *A*
  West Lafayette *A,B,M*
University of Indianapolis *A*
Vincennes University *A*

Iowa

American Institute of Business *A*
American Institute of Commerce *C,A*
Des Moines Area Community College *A*
Iowa Lakes Community College *A*
Iowa State University *B,M,D*

Kansas

Butler County Community College *C,A*
Central College *A*
Cloud County Community College *A*
Hesston College *A*
Hutchinson Community College *A*
Johnson County Community College *A*
Kansas State University *B,D*
Washburn University of Topeka *A*

Kentucky

Berea College *B*
Sullivan College *A*

Louisiana

Grambling State University *B*
Phillips Junior College: New Orleans *A*
Southern University in Shreveport *A*
University of New Orleans *B*
University of Southwestern Louisiana *B*

Maine

Beal College *A*
Husson College *C*
Southern Maine Technical College *A*

Maryland

Anne Arundel Community College *C,A*
Baltimore International Culinary College *C,A*
Essex Community College *C,A*
Hagerstown Junior College *A*
Harford Community College *A*
Montgomery College: Rockville Campus *A*
Prince George's Community College *C,A*
University of Baltimore *B*
University of Maryland: Eastern Shore *B*
Wor-Wic Tech Community College *C,A*

Massachusetts

Bay Path College *A*
Bay State College *A*
Becker College
  Leicester Campus *A*
  Worcester Campus *A*
Berkshire Community College *A*
Boston University *B*
Bunker Hill Community College *A*
Cape Cod Community College *A*
Endicott College *A,B*
Fisher College *A*
Holyoke Community College *A*
Katharine Gibbs School *C*
Lasell College *A*
Massachusetts Bay Community College *C,A*
Massasoit Community College *A*
Middlesex Community College *A*
Mount Ida College *A*
Newbury College *A*
Northeastern University *C,A*
Northern Essex Community College *C,A*
Quincy College *A*
Quinsigamond Community College *A*
University of Massachusetts at Amherst *B,M*

Michigan

Baker College
  Flint *A*
  Muskegon *B*
  Owosso *A*
Central Michigan University *B*
Davenport College of Business *A,B*
Ferris State University *B*
Grand Rapids Community College *A*
Grand Valley State University *B*
Henry Ford Community College *A*
Jackson Community College *A*
Lake Superior State University *B*
Lansing Community College *A*
Michigan State University *B,M*
Northwestern Michigan College *A*
Northwood Institute *A*
Oakland Community College *A*
Siena Heights College *A,B*
Suomi College *A*

Minnesota

Alexandria Technical College *C,A*
Moorhead State University *B*
Normandale Community College *A*
Southwest State University *B*
University of Minnesota: Crookston *A*
Willmar Community College *A*

Mississippi

Hinds Community College *A*
Meridian Community College *A*

Mississippi Gulf Coast Community College: Jefferson Davis Campus *A*
Northeast Mississippi Community College *A*
Phillips Junior College of the Mississippi Gulf Coast *A*
University of Southern Mississippi *B*

Missouri

Central Missouri State University *B*
Jefferson College *C,A*
Penn Valley Community College *C,A*
St. Louis Community College at Forest Park *C,A*
University of Missouri: Columbia *B*

Montana

Flathead Valley Community College *A*

Nebraska

Central Community College *C,A*
Metropolitan Community College *A*
University of Nebraska—Omaha *B*

Nevada

Community College of Southern Nevada *C,A*
Sierra Nevada College *B*
University of Nevada: Las Vegas *B,M,D*

New Hampshire

Franklin Pierce College *B*
Hesser College *A*
New Hampshire College *B*
New Hampshire Technical College: Laconia *C,A*
University of New Hampshire *A,B*

New Jersey

Atlantic Community College *A*
Bergen Community College *A*
Burlington County College *A*
County College of Morris *A*
Fairleigh Dickinson University *B,M*
Mercer County Community College *A*
Thomas Edison State College *A,B*

New Mexico

Dona Ana Branch Community College of New Mexico State University *A*
New Mexico State University *B*

New York

Broome Community College *A*
City University of New York: New York City Technical College *A,B*
Clinton Community College *A*
Community College of the Finger Lakes *A*
Cornell University *B,M,D*
Erie Community College: City Campus *A*
Genesee Community College *A*
Jefferson Community College *C,A*
Katharine Gibbs School
  Melville *C*
  New York *C*
Keuka College *B*
Monroe College *A*
Monroe Community College *A*
Nassau Community College *A*
New York Institute of Technology *B*
New York University *C,B*
Niagara University *B*

Onondaga Community College *A*
Paul Smith's College *A*
Rochester Institute of Technology *A,B,M*
State University of New York
  College of Agriculture and Technology at Cobleskill *A*
  College of Agriculture and Technology at Morrisville *A*
  College at Plattsburgh *B*
  College of Technology at Delhi *A*
Suffolk County Community College
  Eastern Campus *A*
  Selden *A*
Sullivan County Community College *A*
Tompkins-Cortland Community College *A*
Westchester Community College *A*

North Carolina

Appalachian State University *B*
Asheville Buncombe Technical Community College *A*
Barber-Scotia College *B*
Central Piedmont Community College *A*
College of the Albemarle *A*
North Carolina Wesleyan College *B*
Sandhills Community College *A*
Southwestern Community College *A*
Wake Technical Community College *A*
Wilkes Community College *A*

North Dakota

Bismarck State College *C,A*
North Dakota State University *B*

Ohio

Ashland University *B*
Bowling Green State University *B*
Cincinnati Technical College *A*
Columbus State Community College *A*
Cuyahoga Community College: Metropolitan Campus *A*
Hocking Technical College *A*
North Central Technical College *A*
Ohio State University: Columbus Campus *B*
Owens Technical College: Toledo *A*
Sinclair Community College *C,A*
Stark Technical College *A*
Tiffin University *A,B*
University of Akron *A*
University of Cincinnati: Clermont College *A*
Youngstown State University *A*

Oklahoma

Langston University *B*
Oklahoma State University *B*
University of Central Oklahoma *B*

Oregon

Central Oregon Community College *A*
Lane Community College *A*
Portland Community College *A*

Pennsylvania

Bucks County Community College *C,A*
Central Pennsylvania Business School *A*
Cheyney University of Pennsylvania *B*
Community College of Philadelphia *A*

Delaware County Community
College *A*
Drexel University *B*
Harcum Junior College *A*
Harrisburg Area Community
College *A*
Indiana University of
Pennsylvania *B*
Keystone Junior College *A*
Lebanon Valley College of
Pennsylvania *B*
Lehigh County Community
College *A*
Luzerne County Community
College *A*
Marywood College *B*
Mercyhurst College *A,B*
Montgomery County Community
College *A*
Mount Aloysius College *A*
Northampton County Area
Community College *A*
Peirce Junior College *A*
Point Park College *B*
Westmoreland County Community
College *A*
Widener University *B*

Puerto Rico

University of Puerto Rico: Carolina
Regional College *A*

Rhode Island

Johnson & Wales University *A,B*

South Carolina

Anderson College *A*
Horry-Georgetown Technical
College *A*
Technical College of the
Lowcountry *A*
Trident Technical College *A*
University of South Carolina *B,M*

South Dakota

Black Hills State University *A,B*
Huron University *B*
Mount Marty College *B*
Presentation College *A*
South Dakota State University *B*

Tennessee

Belmont University *B*
Knoxville College *B*
McKenzie College *C,A*
State Technical Institute at
Memphis *A*
University of Tennessee: Knoxville
B,M

Texas

Austin Community College *A*
Central Texas College *A*
Del Mar College *A*
El Centro College *A*
El Paso Community College *A*
Galveston College *A*
Houston Community College *C,A*
Huston-Tillotson College *B*
Incarnate Word College *B*
Laredo Junior College *A*
Northwood Institute: Texas
Campus *A*
St. Philip's College *C,A*
Texas Tech University *B,M*
University of Houston *B,M*
University of North Texas *B,M*
Wiley College *B*

Utah

Utah Valley Community College
C,A

Vermont

Champlain College *A*
Johnson State College *B*

Virginia

Commonwealth College *C,A*
James Madison University *B*
National Business College *A*
Northern Virginia Community
College *C,A*
Tidewater Community College *A*
Virginia Polytechnic Institute and
State University *B,M*
Virginia State University *B*

Washington

Spokane Community College *A*
Washington State University *B*

West Virginia

Concord College *B*
Davis and Elkins College *B*
Shepherd College *A,B*
West Virginia State College *A*

Wisconsin

Chippewa Valley Technical
College *A*
Lakeland College *B*
Madison Area Technical College *A*
Mid-State Technical College *A*
Mount Mary College *B*
Stratton College *A*
University of Wisconsin: Stout *B*
Waukesha County Technical
College *A*

**American Samoa, Caroline
Islands, Guam, Marianas,
Virgin Islands**

Guam Community College *C,A*
Northern Marianas College *C,A*

Human environment and housing

Alabama

Auburn University *B*

Arkansas

University of Arkansas *B*

California

California State University
Fresno *B*
Long Beach *B*
Los Angeles *B*
Northridge *B*
Fresno City College *A*
Saddleback College *C,A*

District of Columbia

Howard University *B*

Florida

Miami-Dade Community College *A*

Georgia

Georgia Southern University *B*
University of Georgia *B,M*

Illinois

KAES College *B*
Southern Illinois University at
Carbondale *B*

Indiana

Ball State University *B*
Indiana State University *B,M*

Indiana University Bloomington *B*
Purdue University *B,M*

Iowa

Iowa State University *B*
University of Northern Iowa *B*

Kansas

Kansas State University *B,M*

Kentucky

Morehead State University *B*
Murray State University *B*
University of Kentucky *B,M*
Western Kentucky University *B*

Louisiana

Louisiana State University and
Agricultural and Mechanical
College *B*
Northeast Louisiana University *B*

Maryland

University of Maryland: College
Park *B*

Michigan

Eastern Michigan University *M*
Michigan State University *B,M*
Western Michigan University *B*

Minnesota

University of Minnesota: Twin
Cities *B*

Mississippi

University of Southern
Mississippi *B*

Missouri

College of the Ozarks *B*
Northwest Missouri State
University *B*
Southeast Missouri State
University *B*
Southwest Missouri State
University *B*
University of Missouri: Columbia
B,M,D

Nebraska

McCook Community College *A*
University of Nebraska—Kearney *B*

New York

Cornell University *B,M,D*
State University of New York
College at Oneonta *B*
Syracuse University *B,M*

North Carolina

Appalachian State University *B*
Campbell University *B*
University of North Carolina at
Greensboro *B,M*
Western Carolina University *B*

North Dakota

North Dakota State University *B*

Ohio

Bowling Green State University *B*
Kent State University *B*
Miami University: Oxford
Campus *B*
Ohio State University: Columbus
Campus *B,M,D*
Ohio University *B*

Oklahoma

Cameron University *B*

Oregon

Oregon State University *B*

Pennsylvania

Indiana University of
Pennsylvania *B*
Mercyhurst College *B*
Messiah College *B*
Seton Hill College *B*

Tennessee

Freed-Hardeman University *B*

Texas

Houston Community College *C*
Stephen F. Austin State
University *B*
Texas A&I University *B*
Texas Southern University *B,M*
Texas Tech University *B,M*
Texas Woman's University *M,D*
University of North Texas *B*

Virginia

Radford University *B*
Virginia Polytechnic Institute and
State University *B,M,D*

Washington

Central Washington University *M*
Washington State University *B*

Human resources development

Alabama

Auburn University *B*
Birmingham-Southern College *B*
Faulkner University *B*
Samford University *B*
Tuskegee University *M*
University of Alabama *D*

Alaska

Alaska Pacific University *B*

Arizona

Grand Canyon University *B*

Arkansas

Harding University *B*
University of Central Arkansas *B*

California

Azusa Pacific University *M*
California State Polytechnic
University: Pomona *B*
California State University
Dominguez Hills *B*
Hayward *B,M*
Long Beach *B*
Los Angeles *B*
Sacramento *B*
Chapman University *M*
Cuesta College *A*
Golden Gate University *B,M*
John F. Kennedy University *M*
La Sierra University *B,M*
MiraCosta College *C*
National University *B,M*
San Jose State University *B*
Simpson College *B*
University of San Francisco *B,M*
Ventura College *A*

Colorado

Arapahoe Community College *C*
University of Colorado
  Boulder *B*
  Colorado Springs *B*
  Denver *B*
University of Denver *M*

Connecticut

Quinnipiac College *B,M*
Tunxis Community College *C*
University of Bridgeport *M*
University of New Haven *C,B,M*

Delaware

Wilmington College *B,M*

District of Columbia

American University *M*
George Washington University *B,M,D*
Southeastern University *B,M*
Trinity College *M*

Florida

Barry University *M*
Eckerd College *B*
Florida Institute of Technology *M*
Florida State University *B*
Okaloosa-Walton Community College *A*
St. Leo College *B*
St. Thomas University *B*
University of Miami *B*
University of North Florida *M*
University of Sarasota *M*

Georgia

Brenau Women's College *B*
Georgia Southern University *B*
Georgia State University *M,D*
Kennesaw State College *M*

Hawaii

Brigham Young University-Hawaii *B*
Hawaii Pacific University *B,M*

Idaho

Northwest Nazarene College *A*
University of Idaho *B*

Illinois

Barat College *B*
De Paul University *M*
Illinois Benedictine College *M*
National-Louis University *M*
Northeastern Illinois University *B,M*
Trinity College *B*
University of Illinois at Chicago *D*
Waubonsee Community College *A*

Indiana

Bethel College *B*
Indiana State University *M*
Indiana University Bloomington *M*
Oakland City College *B*
Purdue University *M,D*
Vincennes University *A*

Iowa

Loras College *B*
University of Iowa *B,M,D*
William Penn College *B*

Kansas

Friends University *B*
MidAmerica Nazarene College *B*
Pittsburg State University *M*

Kentucky

Kentucky Wesleyan College *B*

Maryland

Bowie State University *M*
College of Notre Dame of Maryland *M*
Frostburg State University *M*
Montgomery College: Germantown Campus *A*
Towson State University *M*
University of Baltimore *B*

Massachusetts

American International College *M*
Berkshire Community College *A*
Boston College *B*
Emmanuel College *M*
Framingham State College *M*
Hellenic College *B*
Lesley College *B,M*
Marian Court Junior College *A*
Nichols College *B*
Northeastern University *C,A,B*
Springfield College *B,M*
University of Massachusetts at Dartmouth *B*
Western New England College *B*
Worcester State College *M*

Michigan

Concordia College *B*
Eastern Michigan University *B,M*
Kalamazoo College *B*
Lawrence Technological University *B*
Marygrove College *M*
Oakland University *B*
Suomi College *A*
University of Michigan: Dearborn *B*
Western Michigan University *M,D*

Minnesota

College of St. Scholastica *B*
Crown College *B*
Mankato State University *B*
Northwestern College *B*
Rainy River Community College *A*
St. Cloud State University *M*
University of St. Thomas *B*
Winona State University *B*

Missouri

Avila College *B,M*
Lindenwood College *B,M*
Rockhurst College *B*
Webster University *B,M*

Montana

University of Montana *B*
Western Montana College of the University of Montana *A*

Nebraska

Bellevue College *B*
College of St. Mary *B*
Doane College *B*
University of Nebraska—Omaha *B*

New Hampshire

Antioch New England Graduate School *M*
New Hampshire Technical College: Stratham *C,A*
Rivier College *M*

New Jersey

Bloomfield College *C*
College of St. Elizabeth *C,B*
Fairleigh Dickinson University *M*
Glassboro State College *B*
Rider College *B*

Rutgers—The State University of New Jersey *M,D*
Stevens Institute of Technology *M,D*
Thomas Edison State College *C,A,B*
Upsala College *B,M*

New Mexico

University of New Mexico *B,M*

New York

Adelphi University *C*
Clarkson University *B,M*
College for Human Services *B*
Dominican College of Blauvelt *B*
D'Youville College *B*
Iona College *M*
Keuka College *B*
Le Moyne College *B*
Long Island University: C. W. Post Campus *M*
Marymount College *C*
Medaille College *C,B*
Mercy College *C,M*
New York University *B,M,D*
Niagara University *B*
Nyack College *B*
Roberts Wesleyan College *B*
Rochester Institute of Technology *M*
Russell Sage College *M*
St. Francis College *C*
State University of New York
  Buffalo *D*
  Institute of Technology at Utica/Rome *M*
United States Military Academy *B*
University of the State of New York: Regents College *B*

North Carolina

High Point University *B*
North Carolina State University *B*
Western Carolina University *M*

Ohio

Baldwin-Wallace College *C*
Bowling Green State University *B*
Capital University *B*
Cleveland State University *M*
Kent State University *B*
Lorain County Community College *A*
Lourdes College *B*
Marietta College *B*
Northwest Technical College *A*
Notre Dame College of Ohio *B*
Ohio State University: Columbus Campus *B,M,D*
Ohio University *B*
Union Institute *B,D*
University of Cincinnati *M*
University of Toledo *B*
Wright State University *B*
Xavier University *B*

Oklahoma

Oklahoma State University *B*
University of Central Oklahoma *B*

Oregon

Chemeketa Community College *A*
Concordia College *B*
George Fox College *B*
Marylhurst College *C*

Pennsylvania

Beaver College *B*
Bucks County Community College *A*
Cabrini College *B*

California University of Pennsylvania *B*
Cedar Crest College *C*
Central Pennsylvania Business School *A*
College Misericordia *M*
Community College of Beaver County *A*
Drexel University *B,M*
Duquesne University *B,M*
Geneva College *B*
Gettysburg College *B*
Juniata College *B*
King's College *C,B*
La Roche College *M*
La Salle University *B*
Messiah College *B*
Muhlenberg College *B*
Point Park College *B*
Reading Area Community College *C,A*
Robert Morris College *B,M*
St. Francis College *M*
St. Joseph's University *M*
Seton Hill College *B*
Temple University *B,M,D*
University of Pennsylvania *B,M*
West Chester University of Pennsylvania *M*
Widener University *B,M*

Puerto Rico

Inter American University of Puerto Rico
  Metropolitan Campus *M*
  San German Campus *M*
Universidad Metropolitana *B*
University of Puerto Rico
  Humacao University College *B*
  Rio Piedras Campus *B*

Rhode Island

Johnson & Wales University *M*
Rhode Island College *B*
Salve Regina University *M*

South Carolina

Clemson University *M*

Tennessee

Bristol University *A,B,M*
Cleveland State Community College *C*
Trevecca Nazarene College *C,B*
Vanderbilt University *M*

Texas

Abilene Christian University *B*
Austin Community College *A*
Baylor University *B*
East Texas State University *B*
Houston Baptist University *M*
Houston Community College *C*
St. Edward's University *M*
St. Mary's University *B,M*
Tarleton State University *B*
University of Central Texas *M*
University of Dallas *M*
University of Houston
  Clear Lake *M*
  Houston *B*
University of North Texas *B*
University of Texas at San Antonio *B*

Utah

Brigham Young University *B*
University of Utah *M*
Utah State University *B*
Weber State University *B*
Westminster College of Salt Lake City *B*

Vermont

Trinity College of Vermont *C*

Virginia

Bluefield College *B*
Marymount University *M*
Southside Virginia Community
  College *C,A*
University of Richmond *C*
Virginia Union University *B*
Virginia Wesleyan College *B*

Washington

Central Washington University *B*
Everett Community College *A*
Washington State University *B*
Western Washington University *B*

West Virginia

University of Charleston *M*
Wheeling Jesuit College *B*

Wisconsin

Carroll College *B*
Silver Lake College *B*
University of Wisconsin: Oshkosh *B*
Viterbo College *B*

Humanities

Alabama

Alabama Southern Community
  College *A*
Judson College *B*
Spring Hill College *B*
University of Alabama in
  Huntsville *B*

Alaska

Sheldon Jackson College *A,B*
University of Alaska Fairbanks *B*

Arizona

Arizona State University *B,M*
Northern Arizona University *B*
Prescott College *B*
Yavapai College *A*

Arkansas

Hendrix College *B*

California

Barstow College *A*
California State Polytechnic
  University: Pomona *B*
California State University
  Chico *B*
  Dominguez Hills *M*
  Hayward *B*
  Northridge *B*
Cerritos Community College *A*
Cerro Coso Community College *A*
Chaffey Community College *A*
College of Notre Dame *B*
Dominican College of San Rafael *B*
Foothill College *A*
Fresno City College *A*
Glendale Community College *A*
Golden West College *A*
Holy Names College *B*
Imperial Valley College *A*
Irvine Valley College *A*
Lake Tahoe Community College *A*
Los Angeles Harbor College *A*
Loyola Marymount University *B*
Mount San Jacinto College *A*
New College of California *A,B*
Pepperdine University *B*
Saddleback College *A*

San Francisco State University *B,M*
San Jose State University *B*
Scripps College *B*
Stanford University *B,M,D*
University of California
  Berkeley *B*
  Irvine *B*
University of the Pacific *B*
University of San Diego *B*
World College West *B*

Colorado

Fort Lewis College *B*
Pikes Peak Community College *A*
United States Air Force
  Academy *B*
University of Colorado at
  Denver *M*

Connecticut

Albertus Magnus College *B*
Middlesex Community College *A*
Sacred Heart University *B*
St. Joseph College *B*
Teikyo-Post University *A,B*
University of Hartford *A*
Wesleyan University *B*
Yale University *B*

Florida

Daytona Beach Community
  College *A*
Eckerd College *B*
Florida Institute of Technology *B*
Florida International University *B*
Florida State University *B,M,D*
New College of the University of
  South Florida *B*
Okaloosa-Walton Community
  College *A*
Stetson University *B*

Georgia

Andrew College *A*
Atlanta Metropolitan College *A*
Clark Atlanta University *D*
Covenant College *B*
Mercer University Atlanta *B*

Hawaii

Hawaii Loa College *B*
Hawaii Pacific University *B*

Idaho

Northwest Nazarene College *B*
Ricks College *A*

Illinois

Aurora University *B*
Barat College *B*
Bradley University *B*
KAES College *B*
Morton College *A*
North Central College *B*
Northwestern University *B*
Olivet Nazarene University *B*
Quincy College *B*
Richland Community College *A*
Trinity College *B*
University of Chicago *B,M*
University of Illinois at Urbana-
  Champaign *B*
William Rainey Harper College *A*

Indiana

Goshen College *B*
Indiana State University *B,M*
Indiana University at Kokomo *B*
Martin University *B*
Oakland City College *B*
St. Joseph's College *A*
St. Mary-of-the-Woods College *B*

St. Mary's College *B*
Vincennes University *A*

Iowa

Cornell College *B*
Drake University *B*
Grand View College *B*
Kirkwood Community College *A*
University of Iowa *B*
University of Northern Iowa *B*

Kansas

Kansas City College and Bible
  School *B*
Kansas State University *B*
Ottawa University *B*
Pratt Community College *A*
Southwestern College *B*
Tabor College *B*

Louisiana

Loyola University *B*

Maine

University of Maine
  Farmington *B*
  Machias *B*
  Presque Isle *B*
University of New England *B*

Maryland

Charles County Community
  College *A*
Frostburg State University *M*
Johns Hopkins University *B*
Loyola College in Maryland *B*
Montgomery College
  Germantown Campus *A*
  Takoma Park Campus *A*
Villa Julie College *B*
Washington College *B*

Massachusetts

Boston University *B,M,D*
Bradford College *B*
Bridgewater State College *M*
Dean Junior College *A*
Elms College *B*
Endicott College *A*
Greenfield Community College *A*
Hampshire College *B*
Lesley College *B*
Simon's Rock College of Bard *A,B*
Worcester Polytechnic Institute *B*

Michigan

Eastern Michigan University *B*
Lansing Community College *A*
Lawrence Technological
  University *B*
Siena Heights College *B*
University of Michigan
  Ann Arbor *B*
  Dearborn *B*
Wayne State University *B,M*
William Tyndale College *B*

Minnesota

Augsburg College *B*
Bemidji State University *B*
College of St. Benedict *B*
College of St. Scholastica *B*
Concordia College: Moorhead *B*
Crown College *A*
Macalester College *B*
North Central Bible College *A*
St. John's University *B*
University of Minnesota: Twin
  Cities *B*
Willmar Community College *A*

Missouri

Maryville University *B*
Missouri Baptist College *B*
Northwest Missouri State
  University *B*
St. Louis Christian College *A*
St. Louis University *B*
University of Missouri: Kansas
  City *D*

Nebraska

College of St. Mary *B*
Dana College *B*
York College *A*

Nevada

Sierra Nevada College *B*

New Hampshire

Colby-Sawyer College *B*
New Hampshire College *B*
University of New Hampshire
  Durham *B*
  Manchester *B*

New Jersey

Atlantic Community College *A*
Bergen Community College *A*
Brookdale Community College *A*
County College of Morris *A*
Drew University *B,M,D*
Essex County College *A*
Fairleigh Dickinson University *B*
Georgian Court College *B*
Passaic County Community
  College *A*
Rutgers—The State University of
  New Jersey: Douglass College *B*
St. Peter's College *B*
Stevens Institute of Technology *B*
Thomas Edison State College *B*

New Mexico

College of Santa Fe *B*
St. John's College *B,M*
Western New Mexico University *B*

New York

Adelphi University *B*
Adirondack Community College *A*
Bard College *B*
Canisius College *A*
Colgate University *B*
Columbia-Greene Community
  College *A*
Community College of the Finger
  Lakes *A*
Erie Community College: South
  Campus *A*
Eugene Lang College/New School
  for Social Research *B*
Fordham University *B*
Fulton-Montgomery Community
  College *A*
Genesee Community College *A*
Herkimer County Community
  College *A*
Hofstra University *M*
Houghton College *B*
Iona College *B*
Jamestown Community College *A*
Jefferson Community College *A*
Long Island University: Brooklyn
  Campus *B*
Manhattanville College *B*
Medaille College *B*
Mohawk Valley Community
  College *A*
New York University *B,M*
Nyack College *B*
Onondaga Community College *A*
St. Bonaventure University *B*

Sarah Lawrence College *B*
Skidmore College *B*
State University of New York
   Albany *D*
   Buffalo *M*
   College of Agriculture and
     Technology at Morrisville *A*
   College at Fredonia *B*
   Maritime College *B*
Suffolk County Community
   College *A*
Syracuse University *D*
Ulster County Community
   College *A*
Union College *B*
United States Military Academy *B*
Utica College of Syracuse
   University *B*
Wagner College *B*

North Carolina

Brevard College *A*
Duke University *M*
Guilford College *B*
Lees-McRae College *B*
North Carolina State University *B*
St. Andrews Presbyterian College *B*
Warren Wilson College *B*

North Dakota

North Dakota State University *B*
University of North Dakota *B*

Ohio

Antioch School for Adult and
   Experiential Learning *B*
Bluffton College *B*
Bowling Green State University:
   Firelands College *A*
College of Mount St. Joseph *B*
Franciscan University of
   Steubenville *B*
Heidelberg College *B*
John Carroll University *B,M*
Kent State University *B*
Lake Erie College *B*
Ohio State University: Columbus
   Campus *B,M*
Ohio University
   Eastern Campus *A*
   Zanesville Campus *A*
Shawnee State University *B*
Union Institute *B,D*
University of Akron *B*
University of Cincinnati
   Access Colleges *A*
   Cincinnati *B*
University of Rio Grande *B*
Ursuline College *B*
Wittenberg University *B*
Xavier University *B,M*

Oklahoma

Oklahoma City University *B*
Oral Roberts University *B*
Tulsa Junior College *A*
University of Oklahoma *B*

Oregon

Central Oregon Community
   College *A*
Linn-Benton Community College *A*
Marylhurst College *B*
Pacific University *B*
Rogue Community College *A*
Western Baptist College *B*
Western Oregon State College *B*
Willamette University *B*

Pennsylvania

Beaver College *M*
Bloomsburg University of
   Pennsylvania *B*
Butler County Community
   College *A*
California University of
   Pennsylvania *B*
Carnegie Mellon University
   B,M,D,W
Chatham College *B*
Clarion University of
   Pennsylvania *B*
Edinboro University of
   Pennsylvania *B*
Gettysburg College *B*
Holy Family College *B*
Juniata College *B*
La Salle University *A,B*
Lehigh County Community
   College *A*
Lehigh University *B*
Messiah College *B*
Muhlenberg College *B*
Northeastern Christian Junior
   College *A*
Penn State Harrisburg Capital
   College *M*
Reading Area Community
   College *A*
St. Charles Borromeo Seminary *B*
St. Joseph's University *B*
Temple University *A*
University of Pittsburgh
   Bradford *B*
   Greensburg *B*
   Johnstown *B*
   Pittsburgh *B*
York College of Pennsylvania *B*

Puerto Rico

University of Puerto Rico
   Arecibo Campus *A*
   Bayamon Technological
     University College *A*
   Carolina Regional College *A*
   Cayey University College *B*

Rhode Island

Providence College *B*
Salve Regina University *A,M,D*

South Carolina

Bob Jones University *B*
Charleston Southern University *B*
Wofford College *B*

Tennessee

Memphis State University *B*
University of Tennessee:
   Chattanooga *B*
Volunteer State Community
   College *A*

Texas

Central Texas College *A*
Midwestern State University *B*
Sam Houston State University *B*
Schreiner College *B*
Southern Methodist University *B*
Stephen F. Austin State
   University *B*
Texas Tech University *B*
University of Dallas *M*
University of Houston: Clear
   Lake *B*
University of Texas
   Arlington *M*
   Austin *B*
   Dallas *B,M,D*
   San Antonio *B*

Utah

Brigham Young University *B,M*

Vermont

Bennington College *B*
Burlington College *B*
Lyndon State College *B*
Marlboro College *B*
University of Vermont *B*

Virginia

Averett College *B*
Bluefield College *B*
Hampden-Sydney College *B*
Hollins College *M*
Lynchburg College *B*
Mary Baldwin College *B*
Marymount University *A,M*
University of Richmond *M*
Virginia Wesleyan College *B*

Washington

Eastern Washington University *B*
Evergreen State College *B*
Heritage College *A*
St. Martin's College *B*
Seattle Central Community
   College *A*
Seattle University *B*
Walla Walla College *B*
Washington State University *B*
Western Washington University *B*

West Virginia

Marshall University *B*
West Virginia Graduate College *M*

Wisconsin

Lawrence University *B*
Mount Senario College *B*
Northland College *B*
St. Norbert College *B*
University of Wisconsin: Green
   Bay *B*

Wyoming

Central Wyoming College *A*
Northwest College *A*
University of Wyoming *B*
Western Wyoming Community
   College *A*

American Samoa, Caroline Islands, Guam, Marianas, Virgin Islands

University of the Virgin Islands *B*

Canada

McGill University *B*

Switzerland

American College of Switzerland *B*
Franklin College: Switzerland *B*

Humanities and social sciences

Alabama

Athens State College *B*
Birmingham-Southern College *B*
Faulkner University *B*
Judson College *B*
Samford University *A,B*
Spring Hill College *B*
Talladega College *B*

Alaska

Sheldon Jackson College *A,B*
University of Alaska Fairbanks *B*

Arizona

Arizona State University *B,M*
Arizona Western College *A*
Prescott College *B*

Arkansas

Harding University *B*
Hendrix College *B*
Mississippi County Community
   College *A*
Shorter College *A*
University of Arkansas *M*

California

Barstow College *A*
Biola University *B*
California Lutheran University *B*
California State University
   Hayward *B,M*
   Northridge *B*
   Sacramento *B*
   San Bernardino *B*
Chaffey Community College *A*
Chapman University *B*
Christ College Irvine *B*
Claremont McKenna College *B*
College of the Sequoias *A*
Cosumnes River College *A*
Feather River College *A*
Fresno Pacific College *B*
Glendale Community College *A*
Humphreys College *A*
John F. Kennedy University *B*
Laney College *A*
Lassen College *A*
Los Angeles City College *A*
Los Angeles Mission College *A*
Marymount College *A*
Mendocino College *A*
Menlo College *B*
Modesto Junior College *A*
Mount San Jacinto College *A*
Napa Valley College *A*
Santa Clara University *B*
Santa Rosa Junior College *A*
Scripps College *B*
Skyline College *A*
Southern California College *B*
Stanford University *B,M*
University of California:
   Riverside *B*
University of La Verne *B*
University of the Pacific *B*
University of Southern California *B*
West Hills Community College *A*
World College West *B*

Colorado

Colorado Christian University *B*
Colorado College *B*
Colorado Mountain College
   Alpine Campus *A*
   Spring Valley Campus *A*
   Timberline Campus *A*
Colorado State University *B*
Fort Lewis College *B*
Lamar Community College *A*
Regis College of Regis University *B*
Trinidad State Junior College *A*
United States Air Force
   Academy *B*
University of Colorado
   Boulder *B*
   Denver *B*

Connecticut

Albertus Magnus College *B*
Eastern Connecticut State
   University *B*
Holy Apostles College and
   Seminary *B*
Housatonic Community College *A*

Mitchell College *A*
Sacred Heart University *B*
St. Joseph College *B*
Teikyo-Post University *A,B*
University of New Haven *M*
Wesleyan University *B*
Yale University *B,M,D*

District of Columbia

Catholic University of America *B*
George Washington University
 B,M,D

Florida

Florida Atlantic University *B*
Florida Southern College *B*
Gulf Coast Community College *A*
Jacksonville University *B*
Lynn University *B*
New College of the University of
 South Florida *B*
Pensacola Junior College *A*
Schiller International University *B*
University of Central Florida *B*
University of South Florida *B,M*
University of West Florida *B,M*

Georgia

Berry College *B*
Covenant College *B*
DeKalb College *A*
Emory University *B*
Shorter College *B*
University of Georgia *B*

Hawaii

Hawaii Loa College *B*
Hawaii Pacific University *B*

Idaho

Lewis Clark State College *B*
Northwest Nazarene College *B*

Illinois

Barat College *B*
Black Hawk College: East
 Campus *A*
Blackburn College *B*
Bradley University *B*
Chicago State University *B*
De Paul University *B*
Illinois Wesleyan University *B*
Joliet Junior College *A*
Judson College *B*
KAES College *B*
Lake Forest College *B*
Lincoln Land Community
 College *A*
Millikin University *B*
Monmouth College *B*
Morton College *A*
Olivet Nazarene University *B*
Rockford College *B*
Roosevelt University *B*
Rosary College *B*
St. Xavier University *B*
Trinity College *B*
University of Chicago *B,M*
University of Illinois at Chicago *B*

Indiana

Calumet College of St. Joseph *B*
DePauw University *B*
Goshen College *B*
Indiana State University *B,M*
Martin University *B*
Oakland City College *B*
Purdue University
 Calumet *A*
 West Lafayette *B,M,D*
Valparaiso University *B,M*
Vincennes University *A*

Iowa

Coe College *B*
Cornell College *B*
Drake University *B*
Grand View College *B*
Luther College *B*
Morningside College *B*
Muscatine Community College *A*
Northwestern College *B*
Teikyo Marycrest University *B*
Vennard College *B*
William Penn College *B*

Kansas

Bethel College *B*
Butler County Community
 College *A*
Cloud County Community
 College *A*
Coffeyville Community College *A*
Friends University *B*
Kansas State University *B*
MidAmerica Nazarene College *A,B*
Neosho County Community
 College *A*
Ottawa University *B*
Pratt Community College *A*
Southwestern College *B*
University of Kansas *B*

Kentucky

Hazard Community College *A*
Lindsey Wilson College *B*
Sue Bennett College *A*
Thomas More College *A,B*
University of Louisville *B,M*
Western Kentucky University *M*

Louisiana

Centenary College of Louisiana *B*
Louisiana College *B*
Louisiana State University and
 Agricultural and Mechanical
 College *M*
Loyola University *B*
Tulane University *B*

Maine

University of Maine
 Machias *B*
 Orono *B,M*
 Presque Isle *B*
University of New England *B*
University of Southern Maine *B*

Maryland

Charles County Community
 College *A*
Chesapeake College *A*
College of Notre Dame of
 Maryland *B*
Harford Community College *A*
Hood College *M*
Johns Hopkins University *B*
Loyola College in Maryland *B*
Montgomery College
 Germantown Campus *A*
 Rockville Campus *A*
 Takoma Park Campus *A*
Salisbury State University *B*
Towson State University *B*
University of Baltimore *B*

Massachusetts

Anna Maria College for Men and
 Women *B*
Atlantic Union College *B*
Becker College: Leicester
 Campus *A*
Boston University *B,M,D*
Bradford College *B*
Bunker Hill Community College *A*

Curry College *B*
Dean Junior College *A*
Elms College *B*
Endicott College *A*
Greenfield Community College *A*
Hampshire College *B*
Harvard and Radcliffe Colleges *B*
Lesley College *B*
Massachusetts Institute of
 Technology *B*
North Adams State College *B*
Quincy College *A*
Roxbury Community College *A*
St. John's Seminary College *B*
Simmons College *B*
Simon's Rock College of Bard *B*
Springfield College *B*
Suffolk University *B*
Tufts University *B,M,D*
University of Massachusetts
 Amherst *B*
 Boston *B*
 Dartmouth *B*
Wellesley College *B*
Western New England College *B*
Westfield State College *B*
Wheaton College *B*
Worcester Polytechnic Institute *B*

Michigan

Albion College *B*
Andrews University *M*
Calvin College *B*
Charles Stewart Mott Community
 College *A*
Concordia College *B*
Eastern Michigan University *B,M*
Hope College *B*
Kalamazoo Valley Community
 College *A*
Lawrence Technological
 University *B*
Marygrove College *B*
Michigan State University *B*
Michigan Technological
 University *B*
Mid Michigan Community
 College *A*
Northern Michigan University *B*
Oakland University *B*
Olivet College *B*
University of Detroit Mercy *B,M*
University of Michigan *B,M,D*
Wayne State University *D*
Western Michigan University *B*
William Tyndale College *B*

Minnesota

Bethany Lutheran College *A*
Concordia College: Moorhead *B*
Concordia College: St. Paul *B*
Gustavus Adolphus College *B*
Northland Community College *A*
St. Mary's College of Minnesota *B*
Southwest State University *B*
University of Minnesota
 Morris *B*
 Twin Cities *B,M,D*
Winona State University *B*

Mississippi

Belhaven College *B*
Jones County Junior College *A*
Mary Holmes College *A*
Rust College *B*

Missouri

Columbia College *B*
Maryville University *B*
Missouri Baptist College *B*
Missouri Valley College *B*
Rockhurst College *B*

St. Louis Community College at
 Meramec *A*
St. Louis University *B*
Southeast Missouri State
 University *B*
Southwest Missouri State
 University *B*
University of Missouri: Kansas
 City *D*
Washington University *B*
William Woods College *B*

Montana

Dull Knife Memorial College *A*
Northern Montana College *A,B*
Rocky Mountain College *B*

Nebraska

Chadron State College *B*
Dana College *B*
Doane College *B*
Hastings College *B*
Midland Lutheran College *B*
Northeast Community College *A*
University of Nebraska—Omaha *B*
York College *A*

Nevada

Community College of Southern
 Nevada *A*
Sierra Nevada College *B*
University of Nevada: Las Vegas *B*

New Hampshire

Franklin Pierce College *B*
Keene State College *B*
Plymouth State College of the
 University System of New
 Hampshire *B*
School for Lifelong Learning *B*

New Jersey

Atlantic Community College *A*
County College of Morris *A*
Drew University *B,M,D*
Essex County College *A*
Felician College *A,B*
Mercer County Community
 College *A*
Montclair State College *B*
Rutgers—The State University of
 New Jersey
 Douglass College *B*
 Livingston College *B*
 Newark College of Arts and
  Sciences *B*
 Rutgers College *B*
 University College New
  Brunswick *B*
Stevens Institute of Technology *B*
Stockton State College *B*
Upsala College *B*
William Paterson College of New
 Jersey *B*

New Mexico

College of Santa Fe *B*
Eastern New Mexico University *B*
Western New Mexico University *B*

New York

Adirondack Community College *A*
Alfred University *B*
Bard College *B*
City University of New York
 Baruch College *B*
 Lehman College *B*
 Queens College *B*
Clarkson University *B*
Clinton Community College *A*
Colgate University *B*
College of New Rochelle *B*

Columbia-Greene Community
College *A*
Community College of the Finger
Lakes *A*
Concordia College *B*
Corning Community College *A*
Daemen College *B*
Dominican College of Blauvelt *B*
Dowling College *B*
Dutchess Community College *A*
D'Youville College *B*
Elmira College *B*
Erie Community College
City Campus *A*
North Campus *A*
South Campus *A*
Eugene Lang College/New School
for Social Research *B*
Fordham University *B*
Fulton-Montgomery Community
College *A*
Genesee Community College *A*
Herkimer County Community
College *A*
Hilbert College *A*
Hofstra University *B,M*
Houghton College *B*
Hudson Valley Community
College *A*
Iona College *B*
Jamestown Community College *A*
Jefferson Community College *A*
Long Island University:
Southampton Campus *B*
Manhattan College *B*
Manhattanville College *B*
Marymount College *B*
Medaille College *B*
Mercy College *B*
Mohawk Valley Community
College *A*
Molloy College *B*
Monroe Community College *A*
Mount St. Mary College *B*
Nassau Community College *A*
Nazareth College of Rochester *B*
New York University *B*
Niagara County Community
College *A*
North Country Community
College *A*
Onondaga Community College *A*
Orange County Community
College *A*
Pace University
College of White Plains *B*
New York *B*
Polytechnic University *B*
Rensselaer Polytechnic Institute
B,M,D
Roberts Wesleyan College *B*
Rockland Community College *A*
Russell Sage College *B*
St. Bonaventure University *B*
Sarah Lawrence College *B,M*
Skidmore College *B*
State University of New York
Purchase *B*
Stony Brook *B*
College of Agriculture and
Technology at Morrisville *A*
College at Buffalo *B*
College at Fredonia *B*
College at Old Westbury *B*
College of Technology at
Alfred *A*
College of Technology at
Canton *A*
College of Technology at
Delhi *A*
Suffolk County Community
College *A*

Sullivan County Community
College *A*
Syracuse University *M,D*
Touro College *B*
Ulster County Community
College *A*
United States Military Academy *B*
Westchester Community College *A*

North Carolina

Barton College *B*
Gaston College *A*
Guilford Technical Community
College *A*
High Point University *B*
Mars Hill College *B*
North Carolina State University *B*
St. Andrews Presbyterian College *B*
University of North Carolina
Chapel Hill *D*
Greensboro *B*
Warren Wilson College *B*
Wingate College *B*

North Dakota

Bismarck State College *A*
North Dakota State University *B,M*
University of North Dakota:
Williston *A*

Ohio

Bluffton College *B*
Bowling Green State University
Bowling Green *B*
Firelands College *A*
Capital University *B*
Defiance College *B*
Dyke College *B*
Edison State Community College *A*
Heidelberg College *B*
John Carroll University *B*
Kent State University *B*
Kenyon College *B*
Lorain County Community
College *A*
Muskingum College *B*
Ohio State University: Columbus
Campus *B,M,D*
Ohio University: Zanesville
Campus *A*
Union Institute *B,D*
University of Akron *B*
University of Cincinnati: Access
Colleges *A*
University of Rio Grande *B*
University of Toledo *B*
Urbana University *B*
Ursuline College *B*
Walsh College *B*
Wittenberg University *B*
Wright State University *M*

Oklahoma

Eastern Oklahoma State College *A*
Oklahoma Baptist University *B*
Oklahoma City University *B*
University of Tulsa *M*

Oregon

Central Oregon Community
College *A*
Clackamas Community College *A*
Marylhurst College *B*
Pacific University *B*
Portland State University *B,M*
Reed College *B*
Southern Oregon State College *B*
University of Oregon
Eugene *B*
Robert Donald Clark Honors
College *B*
Warner Pacific College *B*

Western Baptist College *B*
Western Oregon State College *B*

Pennsylvania

Academy of the New Church *A,B*
Bucknell University *B*
Bucks County Community
College *A*
Butler County Community
College *A*
California University of
Pennsylvania *B,M*
Carnegie Mellon University
B,M,D,W
Chatham College *B*
Clarion University of
Pennsylvania *B*
Community College of Beaver
County *A*
Drexel University *B*
Edinboro University of
Pennsylvania *B,M*
Gannon University *B*
Gettysburg College *B*
Hahnemann University School of
Health Sciences and
Humanities *A*
Holy Family College *B*
Immaculata College *B*
Juniata College *B*
La Salle University *B*
Lafayette College *B*
Lehigh County Community
College *A*
Lehigh University *B*
Luzerne County Community
College *A*
Lycoming College *B*
Manor Junior College *A*
Mercyhurst College *B*
Messiah College *B*
Montgomery County Community
College *A*
Muhlenberg College *B*
Northeastern Christian Junior
College *A*
Penn State
Harrisburg Capital College
B,M
University Park Campus *C*
Robert Morris College *A*
Rosemont College *B*
St. Francis College *B*
St. Joseph's University *B*
Seton Hill College *B*
Swarthmore College *B*
Temple University *A*
University of Pennsylvania *B,M,D*
University of Pittsburgh
Johnstown *B*
Pittsburgh *B,M,D*
Widener University *B*

Puerto Rico

University of Puerto Rico: Rio
Piedras Campus *B*

Rhode Island

Brown University *B*
Providence College *B*
Roger Williams College *B*

South Carolina

Charleston Southern University *B*
Coker College *B*
Columbia College *B*
Limestone College *B*
University of South Carolina
Aiken *B*
Columbia *B*

South Dakota

Augustana College *B*
Black Hills State University *B*
Mount Marty College *B*
Northern State University *B*
Sioux Falls College *B*

Tennessee

Bethel College *B*
Christian Brothers University *B*
Dyersburg State Community
College *A*
East Tennessee State University *B*
Knoxville College *B*
LeMoyne-Owen College *B*
Lincoln Memorial University *B*
Martin Methodist College *A*
Memphis State University *B,M*
Middle Tennessee State
University *B*
Milligan College *B*
Motlow State Community
College *A*
Tennessee State University *B*
Tennessee Wesleyan College *B*
Trevecca Nazarene College *B*
University of the South *B*
University of Tennessee:
Chattanooga *B*

Texas

Central Texas College *A*
College of the Mainland *A*
Cooke County College *A*
Corpus Christi State University *M*
East Texas State University *B,M*
Lamar University—Beaumont *B*
Lon Morris College *A*
Navarro College *A*
Rice University *B*
Stephen F. Austin State
University *M*
Texas Southmost College *A*
Texas Wesleyan University *B*
University of Houston
Clear Lake *B,M*
Victoria *B,M*
University of Texas
Dallas *D*
Pan American *M*
Permian Basin *B*
Tyler *B,M*
Vernon Regional Junior College *A*
West Texas State University *B*

Utah

Dixie College *A*
Weber State University *B*
Westminster College of Salt Lake
City *B*

Vermont

Bennington College *B*
Goddard College *B,M*
Green Mountain College *B*
Lyndon State College *B*
Marlboro College *B*
Middlebury College *B*

Virginia

Averett College *B*
Bluefield College *B*
Christopher Newport College *B*
College of William and Mary *B*
Lynchburg College *B*
Mary Baldwin College *B*
Old Dominion University *M*
University of Richmond *C,A,B*
University of Virginia *B*
Virginia Intermont College *B*
Virginia Wesleyan College *B*

Washington
Centralia College A
Eastern Washington University B
Everett Community College A
Evergreen State College B
Grays Harbor College A
Heritage College A,B
Olympic College A
St. Martin's College B
Seattle Central Community College A
Seattle University B
Skagit Valley College A
Spokane Community College A
Spokane Falls Community College A
Tacoma Community College A
University of Puget Sound B
University of Washington B
Washington State University B
Wenatchee Valley College A

West Virginia
Bethany College B
Marshall University B,M
Ohio Valley College A

Wisconsin
Carthage College B
Concordia University Wisconsin B
Edgewood College B
Lakeland College B
Lawrence University B
Marian College of Fond du Lac B
Marquette University B
Northland College B
St. Norbert College B
University of Wisconsin
Green Bay B
Milwaukee M
Parkside B
River Falls B
Whitewater B
Viterbo College B

Wyoming
Central Wyoming College A
Eastern Wyoming College A
Northwest College A
Western Wyoming Community College A

Canada
McGill University B,M

Switzerland
American College of Switzerland B

Illustration design

Alabama
Oakwood College A

Arizona
Northern Arizona University B

Arkansas
Henderson State University B

California
Academy of Art College C,B,M,W
Art Center College of Design B,M
Art Institute of Southern California B
California College of Arts and Crafts B

California State University
Fullerton A
Long Beach B,M
Los Angeles B,M
City College of San Francisco A
Long Beach City College A
Los Angeles Pierce College A
Otis/Parsons School of Art and Design B
Palomar College A
Porterville College C
San Diego City College C,A
University of San Francisco B
West Hills Community College C

Colorado
Colorado Institute of Art A
Rocky Mountain College of Art & Design A,B

Connecticut
Paier College of Art C,B
Sacred Heart University A,B
University of Bridgeport B
University of Hartford B

Florida
Pensacola Junior College A
Ringling School of Art and Design B

Georgia
American College for the Applied Arts A,B
Atlanta College of Art B
Savannah College of Art and Design B,M

Illinois
American Academy of Art A
College of DuPage C,A
Columbia College B
Ray College of Design A,B

Indiana
Vincennes University A

Maryland
Maryland Institute College of Art B
Montgomery College: Rockville Campus A

Massachusetts
Massachusetts College of Art B,M
Montserrat College of Art B
Mount Ida College A,B
University of Massachusetts at Dartmouth B

Michigan
Aquinas College B
Center for Creative Studies: College of Art and Design B
Kendall College of Art and Design B
Lansing Community College A
Northern Michigan University A,B
Oakland Community College C

Minnesota
Bemidji State University B
College of Associated Arts B
Moorhead State University B
National Education Center: Brown Institute Campus A

Missouri
Kansas City Art Institute B
St. Louis Community College
Florissant Valley A
Meramec A
William Woods College B

New Hampshire
New Hampshire Technical College: Manchester C,A
Rivier College B
White Pines College A

New Jersey
Glassboro State College B
Union County College A

New York
Alfred University B
Cazenovia College A
Daemen College B
Fashion Institute of Technology A,B
Iona College A
Mohawk Valley Community College A
Parsons School of Design A,B
Pratt Institute A,B,M
Rochester Institute of Technology A,B,M
School of Visual Arts B,M
Syracuse University B,M

Ohio
Art Academy of Cincinnati B
Ashland University B
Cleveland Institute of Art B
Columbus College of Art and Design B
Sinclair Community College A

Oklahoma
Oklahoma State University Technical Branch: Okmulgee A

Oregon
Pacific Northwest College of Art C,B

Pennsylvania
Art Institute of Pittsburgh A
Beaver College B
Carnegie Mellon University B,M
Harcum Junior College A
Hussian School of Art A
Marywood College B
Moore College of Art and Design B
Pennsylvania College of Technology A
Point Park College B
Seton Hill College B
University of the Arts C,A,B

Rhode Island
Rhode Island School of Design B

Tennessee
Memphis College of Art B
University of Tennessee: Knoxville B

Texas
Houston Community College A
Texas Woman's University B,M

Utah
Brigham Young University B

Washington
Cornish College of the Arts B

Wisconsin
Carroll College B
Milwaukee Institute of Art & Design B

Indic languages

California
University of California: Berkeley B,M,D

Illinois
University of Chicago B,M,D

Massachusetts
Harvard and Radcliffe Colleges B
Harvard University M,D

New York
Columbia University
Columbia College B
New York M,D

Ohio
Ohio State University: Columbus Campus B,M

Pennsylvania
University of Pennsylvania B,M,D

Washington
University of Washington B,M,D

Wisconsin
University of Wisconsin: Madison B,M,D

Individual and family development

Alabama
Alabama Agricultural and Mechanical University B
Auburn University B,M,D
Oakwood College B
University of Alabama B

Arizona
Pima Community College C,A
Prescott College B
University of Arizona B

Arkansas
University of Arkansas
Fayetteville B
Pine Bluff B

California
California Polytechnic State University: San Luis Obispo B
California State University
Fresno B
Long Beach B
Los Angeles B,M
Northridge B
Los Angeles Mission College A
Merced College A
Moorpark College A
Pacific Oaks College B,M
Point Loma Nazarene College B
San Diego State University B
University of California: Davis B,M,D

Colorado
Colorado State University B,M

Connecticut
University of Connecticut B,M,D

Delaware

University of Delaware *D*

District of Columbia

Howard University *B*
University of the District of
Columbia *B*

Florida

Florida State University *B,M*

Georgia

Fort Valley State College *B*
Georgia Southern University *B*
University of Georgia *B,M,D*

Hawaii

Brigham Young University-
Hawaii *B*
University of Hawaii at Manoa *B*

Idaho

Ricks College *A*
University of Idaho *B*

Illinois

KAES College *B*
Northern Illinois University *B,M*
Southern Illinois University at
Carbondale *B*
University of Illinois at Urbana-
Champaign *B,M*

Indiana

Goshen College *B*
Indiana State University *B,M*
Indiana University Bloomington
B,M
Purdue University *B,M,D*

Iowa

Iowa State University *B,M,D*

Kansas

Dodge City Community College *A*
Friends University *B,M*
Kansas State University *B,M,D*
Sterling College *B*

Kentucky

Berea College *B*
Murray State University *B*
University of Kentucky *B,M*
Western Kentucky University *M*

Louisiana

Louisiana State University and
Agricultural and Mechanical
College *B*
Louisiana Tech University *B,M*
Northeast Louisiana University *B*
Southern University and
Agricultural and Mechanical
College *B*

Maine

University of Maine *M*

Maryland

University of Maryland: College
Park *B,M*

Massachusetts

Hampshire College *B*
University of Massachusetts at
Amherst *B*
Wheelock College *M*

Michigan

Adrian College *B*
Central Michigan University *B*
Eastern Michigan University *B,M*

Marygrove College *B*
Michigan State University *B,M,D*
Wayne State University *B*
Western Michigan University *B*

Minnesota

Bethel College *B*
College of St. Scholastica *B*
Concordia College: Moorhead *B*
Crown College *B*
Mankato State University *B,M*
St. Olaf College *B*

Mississippi

Mississippi University for Women *B*
University of Southern Mississippi
B,M

Missouri

College of the Ozarks *B*
Southeast Missouri State
University *B*
Southwest Missouri State
University *B*
University of Missouri: Columbia
B,M,D
William Woods College *B*

Montana

Montana State University *B*

Nebraska

University of Nebraska
Kearney *B*
Lincoln *B,M*
Omaha *B*

Nevada

University of Nevada: Reno *B,M*

New Hampshire

University of New Hampshire *B*

New Jersey

Kean College of New Jersey *M*

New Mexico

Eastern New Mexico University *B*
New Mexico State University *B*
University of New Mexico *B,M,D*

New York

Cornell University *B,M,D*
State University of New York
College at Oneonta *B*
College at Plattsburgh *B*
Syracuse University *B,M,D*

North Carolina

East Carolina University *B,M*
North Carolina Agricultural and
Technical State University *B*
University of North Carolina at
Greensboro *B,M,D*
Western Carolina University *B*

North Dakota

North Dakota State University *B,M*

Ohio

Ashland University *B*
Baldwin-Wallace College *B*
Bowling Green State University
B,M
Kent State University *B,M*
Ohio State University: Columbus
Campus *B,M,D*
Ohio University *B,M*
University of Akron *B,M*
Ursuline College *B*

Oklahoma

Connors State College *A*
Langston University *B*
Northeastern State University *B*
Oklahoma Baptist University *B*
Oklahoma Christian University of
Science and Arts *B*
Oklahoma State University *B,M*
St. Gregory's College *A*
University of Central Oklahoma
B,M

Oregon

Oregon State University *B,M,D*

Pennsylvania

Albright College *B*
Indiana University of
Pennsylvania *B*
Penn State University Park Campus
C,A,B,M,D
Seton Hill College *B*

Rhode Island

University of Rhode Island *B,M*

South Carolina

South Carolina State College *M*

South Dakota

South Dakota State University *B*

Tennessee

Freed-Hardeman University *B*
Tennessee State University *B*
Tennessee Technological
University *B*
University of Tennessee:
Chattanooga *B*

Texas

Abilene Christian University *B*
Austin Community College *A*
Baylor University *B*
Prairie View A&M University *B*
Southwest Texas State University *B*
Stephen F. Austin State
University *B*
Texas A&I University *B*
Texas Southern University *B,M*
Texas Southmost College *A*
Texas Tech University *B,M,D*
University of Houston *B*
University of Mary Hardin-
Baylor *B*
University of North Texas *M*
University of Texas at Austin
B,M,D

Utah

Brigham Young University *B,M*
Southern Utah University *B*
University of Utah *B*
Utah State University *B,M,D*
Weber State University *B*

Vermont

University of Vermont *B*

Virginia

Hampton University *B,M*
Norfolk State University *B*
Radford University *B*
Virginia Polytechnic Institute and
State University *B,M,D*

Washington

Central Washington University *B,M*
Seattle Central Community
College *A*
Shoreline Community College *A*
Washington State University *M*

West Virginia

West Virginia University *B,M*

Wisconsin

University of Wisconsin: Madison
B,M,D

Industrial arts education

Alabama

Alabama Agricultural and
Mechanical University *B,M*
Auburn University *B,M*
Livingston University *B*

Arizona

Northern Arizona University *B*

Arkansas

University of Arkansas
Fayetteville *B*
Pine Bluff *B*
University of Central Arkansas
A,B,M

California

California Polytechnic State
University: San Luis Obispo *M*
California State University
Fresno *B*
Long Beach *B,M*
Los Angeles *B,M*
Humboldt State University *B*
San Francisco State University *B,M*
San Jose State University *B*
Santa Rosa Junior College *A*

Colorado

Colorado State University *B*
Western State College of
Colorado *B*

Connecticut

Central Connecticut State
University *B,M*

Delaware

University of Delaware *M*

District of Columbia

University of the District of
Columbia *B*

Florida

Florida Agricultural and Mechanical
University *B,M*
Florida International University
B,M
Miami-Dade Community College *A*
Pensacola Junior College *A*
University of South Florida *B,M*
University of West Florida *B*

Georgia

Georgia Southern University *B,M*
University of Georgia *B,M*

Hawaii

University of Hawaii: Honolulu
Community College *A*

Idaho

University of Idaho *M*

Illinois

Eastern Illinois University *B*
Northern Illinois University *B,M*
Trinity Christian College *B*
Waubonsee Community College *A*

Western Illinois University *B*

Indiana
Ball State University *B,M*
Indiana State University *B,M*
Purdue University *B,M,D*
Vincennes University *A*

Iowa
Iowa Lakes Community College *A*
Iowa State University *B,M,D*
University of Northern Iowa *B,M*
William Penn College *B*

Kansas
Fort Hays State University *B*
Hutchinson Community College *A*
McPherson College *B*
Pittsburg State University *B,M*

Kentucky
Berea College *B*
Eastern Kentucky University *B,M*
Morehead State University *B*
Murray State University *B,M*
Northern Kentucky University *B*
University of Kentucky *B*
Western Kentucky University *B,M*

Louisiana
Grambling State University *B*
Louisiana State University and
    Agricultural and Mechanical
    College *B*
Northwestern State University *B*
Southeastern Louisiana
    University *B*
Southern University and
    Agricultural and Mechanical
    College *B,M*
University of Southwestern
    Louisiana *B*

Maine
University of Southern Maine *B,M*

Maryland
Prince George's Community
    College *A*

Massachusetts
Fitchburg State College *B*
Westfield State College *B*

Michigan
Andrews University *M*
Central Michigan University *B,M*
Eastern Michigan University *B,M*
Northern Michigan University *B,M*
Wayne State University *B*
Western Michigan University *B*

Minnesota
Bemidji State University *B,M*
Mankato State University *B*
Moorhead State University *B*
St. Cloud State University *B*
University of Minnesota
    Duluth *B*
    Twin Cities *B,M*
Willmar Community College *A*

Mississippi
Alcorn State University *B,M*
Mississippi State University *B*
University of Southern
    Mississippi *B*

Missouri
Central Missouri State University
    B,M
College of the Ozarks *B*

Northwest Missouri State
    University *B,M*
Southeast Missouri State
    University *B*
Southwest Missouri State
    University *B*
University of Missouri: Columbia
    B,M,D

Montana
Montana State University *B,M*
Northern Montana College *B*
Western Montana College of the
    University of Montana *B*

Nebraska
Chadron State College *B*
Peru State College *B*
University of Nebraska
    Kearney *B,M*
    Lincoln *B*
Wayne State College *B,M*

New Hampshire
Keene State College *B*

New Jersey
Glassboro State College *B,M*
Kean College of New Jersey *B*
Montclair State College *B,M*
Rutgers—The State University of
    New Jersey *M,D*

New Mexico
Eastern New Mexico University *B*
New Mexico Highlands
    University *B*
University of New Mexico *B*

New York
City University of New York: City
    College *B,M*
State University of New York
    College at Buffalo *B,M*
    Oswego *B,M*

North Carolina
Appalachian State University *B,M*
East Carolina University *B,M*
Elizabeth City State University *B*
North Carolina Agricultural and
    Technical State University *B,M*
North Carolina State University
    B,M,D
Western Carolina University *B,M*

North Dakota
University of North Dakota *B,M*
Valley City State University *B*

Ohio
Kent State University *B*
Ohio University *B*

Oklahoma
East Central University *B*
Northern Oklahoma College *A*
Northwestern Oklahoma State
    University *B*
Oklahoma Panhandle State
    University *B*
Oklahoma State University *B,M*
Rogers State College *A*
Southeastern Oklahoma State
    University *B*
Southwestern Oklahoma State
    University *B,M*
University of Central Oklahoma
    B,M

Oregon
Oregon State University *M*

Pennsylvania
California University of
    Pennsylvania *B,M*
Cheyney University of Pennsylvania
    B,M
Millersville University of
    Pennsylvania *B,M*
Temple University *B,M,D*

Puerto Rico
University of Puerto Rico: Rio
    Piedras Campus *B*

Rhode Island
Rhode Island College *B,M*

South Carolina
South Carolina State College *B*

South Dakota
Black Hills State University *B*
Northern State University *B,M*

Tennessee
East Tennessee State University *B*
Middle Tennessee State
    University *B*
Tennessee Technological
    University *B*
University of Tennessee:
    Knoxville *B*

Texas
Abilene Christian University *B*
East Texas State University *B,M*
Prairie View A&M University *B,M*
Sam Houston State University *B,M*
Southwest Texas State
    University *M*
Sul Ross State University *B,M*
Texas A&I University *B,M*
Texas A&M University *M,D*
University of Houston *B*
University of North Texas *M*
University of Texas at Tyler *B*
West Texas State University *B*

Utah
Brigham Young University *B*
Southern Utah University *B*
Utah State University *B*

Vermont
University of Vermont *B*

Virginia
Norfolk State University *B*
Old Dominion University *B*
Virginia Polytechnic Institute and
    State University *B,M*

Washington
Central Washington University *B*
Eastern Washington University *B*
Walla Walla College *B*
Washington State University *M*
Western Washington University
    B,M

West Virginia
Fairmont State College *B*
Salem-Teikyo University *B*
West Virginia Institute of
    Technology *B*

Wisconsin
University of Wisconsin
    Platteville *B*
    Stout *B,M*

Wyoming
University of Wyoming *B*

**American Samoa, Caroline
Islands, Guam, Marianas,
Virgin Islands**
University of Guam *B*

Industrial design

Alabama
Auburn University *B,M*

Arizona
Arizona State University *B,M*

California
Academy of Art College *C,B,M,W*
Art Center College of Design *B,M*
California College of Arts and
    Crafts *B*
California State University
    Long Beach *B*
    Los Angeles *B,M*
Chaffey Community College *A*
El Camino College *A*
San Francisco State University *B*
San Jose State University *B*

Colorado
Colorado Institute of Art *A*
Metropolitan State College of
    Denver *B*

Connecticut
University of Bridgeport *B*

Georgia
Morris Brown College *B*

Illinois
Illinois Institute of Technology
    B,M,D
Southern Illinois University at
    Carbondale *B*
University of Illinois at Urbana-
    Champaign *B*

Indiana
Purdue University *B,M*

Kansas
University of Kansas *B*

Kentucky
Eastern Kentucky University *B*

Massachusetts
Massachusetts College of Art *B,M*
Wentworth Institute of Technology
    A,B

Michigan
Center for Creative Studies: College
    of Art and Design *B*
Kendall College of Art and
    Design *B*
Northern Michigan University *B*
University of Michigan *B,M*

Missouri
Central Missouri State University *A*

Nebraska
Metropolitan Community College *A*

New York
Parsons School of Design *B*
Pratt Institute *B,M*

Rochester Institute of Technology
A,B,M
Syracuse University *B,M*

Ohio

Cleveland Institute of Art *B*
Columbus College of Art and
Design *B*
Kent State University *B*
Ohio State University: Columbus
Campus *B,M*
University of Cincinnati *B*

Oregon

Bassist College *A,B*

Pennsylvania

Art Institute of Pittsburgh *A*
California University of
Pennsylvania *B*
Carnegie Mellon University *B,M*
University of the Arts *B*

Rhode Island

Rhode Island School of Design *B,M*

Utah

Brigham Young University *B*

Washington

Art Institute of Seattle *A*
University of Washington *B,M*

Wisconsin

Milwaukee Institute of Art &
Design *B*

Industrial engineering

Alabama

Auburn University *B,M,D*
University of Alabama
Huntsville *B,M,D*
Tuscaloosa *B,M*

Alaska

University of Alaska Fairbanks *M*

Arizona

Arizona State University *B,M,D*
University of Arizona *B,M*

Arkansas

University of Arkansas *B,M*
Westark Community College *A*

California

California Polytechnic State
University: San Luis Obispo *B*
California State Polytechnic
University: Pomona *B*
California State University
Fresno *B*
Long Beach *B*
Northridge *B,M*
City College of San Francisco *C,A*
National University *M*
San Jose State University *B,M*
Southwestern College *A*
Stanford University *B,M,D*
University of California: Berkeley
B,M,D
University of Southern California
B,M,D,W
West Coast University *A,B,M*

Colorado

University of Southern Colorado *B*

Connecticut

University of New Haven *A,B,M*

District of Columbia

George Washington University *M,D*

Florida

Florida Agricultural and Mechanical
University *B*
Florida International University
B,M
Florida State University *B*
Manatee Community College *A*
Miami-Dade Community College *A*
University of Central Florida *B,M,D*
University of Florida *B,M,D*
University of Miami *B,M,D*
University of South Florida *B,M,D*

Georgia

Georgia Institute of Technology
B,M,D
Mercer University *B*
Middle Georgia College *A*
Morris Brown College *B*

Illinois

Bradley University *B,M*
Northern Illinois University *B,M*
Northwestern University *B,M,D*
Rend Lake College *A*
Richland Community College *A*
Roosevelt University *B*
Southern Illinois University at
Edwardsville *B*
University of Illinois
Chicago *B,M,D*
Urbana-Champaign *B,M,D*

Indiana

Indiana University—Purdue
University at Indianapolis *M*
Purdue University *B,M,D,W*

Iowa

Iowa State University *B,M,D*
St. Ambrose University *B*
University of Iowa *B,M,D*

Kansas

Kansas State University *B,M,D*
Wichita State University *B,M,D*

Kentucky

University of Louisville *B,M,D*

Louisiana

Louisiana State University and
Agricultural and Mechanical
College *B,M*
Louisiana Tech University *B,M*

Maryland

Morgan State University *B*

Massachusetts

Northeastern University *B,M,D*
Springfield Technical Community
College *A*
University of Massachusetts
Amherst *B,M,D*
Lowell *M*
Western New England College *B*
Worcester Polytechnic Institute *B*

Michigan

GMI Engineering & Management
Institute *B,M*
University of Detroit Mercy *M*
University of Michigan
Ann Arbor *B,M,D*
Dearborn *B,M*

Wayne State University *B,M,D*
Western Michigan University *B,M*

Minnesota

University of Minnesota
Duluth *B*
Twin Cities *B,M,D*
Willmar Community College *A*

Mississippi

Mississippi College *B*
Mississippi State University *B,M*

Missouri

Central Missouri State
University *M*
East Central College *A*
University of Missouri
Columbia *B,M,D*
Rolla *B,M,D*

Montana

Montana State University *B,M*

Nebraska

University of Nebraska—Lincoln
B,M

New Jersey

New Jersey Institute of Technology
B,M
Rutgers—The State University of
New Jersey
College of Engineering *B*
New Brunswick *M*

New Mexico

New Mexico State University
B,M,D

New York

Alfred University *B,M*
Columbia University: School of
Engineering and Applied Science
B,M,D,W
Cornell University *B,M,D*
Hofstra University *B*
Manhattan College *B*
New York Institute of
Technology *B*
Pace University
College of White Plains *B*
Pleasantville/Briarcliff *B*
Polytechnic University
Brooklyn *B,M,D*
Long Island Campus *B*
Rensselaer Polytechnic Institute
B,M
Rochester Institute of Technology
B,M
State University of New York
Binghamton *M*
Buffalo *B,M,D*
Syracuse University *M*

North Carolina

Edgecombe Community College *A*
North Carolina Agricultural and
Technical State University *B,M*
North Carolina State University
B,M,D
St. Augustine's College *B*
Vance-Granville Community
College *A*

North Dakota

North Dakota State University *B,M*

Ohio

Air Force Institute of
Technology *M*
Case Western Reserve University *B*

Cleveland State University *B,M*
Marietta College *B*
Ohio State University: Columbus
Campus *B,M,D*
Ohio University *B,M*
University of Cincinnati *B,M,D*
University of Toledo *B,M,D*
Youngstown State University *B*

Oklahoma

Oklahoma State University *B,M,D*
University of Oklahoma *B,M,D*

Oregon

Central Oregon Community
College *A*
Oregon State University *B,M,D*

Pennsylvania

California University of
Pennsylvania *B*
Drexel University *B*
Elizabethtown College *B*
Gannon University *B*
Geneva College *B*
Lehigh University *B,M,D*
Lock Haven University of
Pennsylvania *B*
Penn State
Great Valley Graduate
Center *M*
University Park Campus
B,M,D
Reading Area Community
College *A*
University of Pittsburgh *B,M,D*

Puerto Rico

Caribbean University *B*
Universidad Politecnica de Puerto
Rico *B*
University of Puerto Rico:
Mayaguez Campus *B,M*

Rhode Island

University of Rhode Island *B,M*

South Carolina

Clemson University *B,M,D*

South Dakota

South Dakota School of Mines and
Technology *B*

Tennessee

Memphis State University *M*
Motlow State Community
College *A*
Tennessee Technological University
B,M
University of Tennessee
Chattanooga *B,M*
Knoxville *B,M*

Texas

Lamar University—Beaumont *B,D*
St. Mary's University *B,M*
Southern Methodist University *M,D*
Texas A&I University *M*
Texas A&M University *B,M,D*
Texas Tech University *B,M,D*
University of Houston *B,M,D*
University of Texas
Arlington *B,M,D*
Austin *M*
Dallas *M*
El Paso *B,M*
West Texas State University *B*

Utah

University of Utah *B,M*

Virginia

Virginia Polytechnic Institute and
State University *B,M,D*

Washington

University of Washington *B*

West Virginia

West Virginia Graduate College *M*
West Virginia University *B,M,D*
Wheeling Jesuit College *B*

Wisconsin

Fox Valley Technical College *A*
Milwaukee School of Engineering *B*
University of Wisconsin
Madison *B,M,D*
Milwaukee *B*
Platteville *B*

Mexico

Sistema Instituto Tecnologico y de
Estudios Superiores de
Monterrey *B*

Arab Republic of Egypt

American University in Cairo *B*

Industrial equipment maintenance and repair

Alabama

Brewer State Junior College *A*
Community College of the Air
Force *A*
Gadsden State Community
College *A*
John M. Patterson State Technical
College *A*
Lawson State Community College
C,A
Livingston University *A*

Arkansas

Phillips County Community
College *A*
Westark Community College *C*

California

Chaffey Community College *C,A*
Glendale Community College *C*
Imperial Valley College *A*
Merced College *C,A*
Modesto Junior College *A*
Pacific Union College *B*

Florida

Central Florida Community
College *C*

Georgia

Athens Area Technical Institute *C*
Augusta Technical Institute *C*

Idaho

Boise State University *C*
Lewis Clark State College *A*
North Idaho College *A*

Illinois

Belleville Area College *C,A*
City Colleges of Chicago: Chicago
City-Wide College *C*
College of Lake County *C,A*
Illinois Central College *C,A*
Illinois Eastern Community
Colleges: Olney Central
College *A*
Lake Land College *C,A*

Moraine Valley Community College
C,A
Oakton Community College *C,A*
Richland Community College *A*
Triton College *C,A*
Waubonsee Community College *A*

Indiana

Indiana Vocational Technical
College
Central Indiana *C,A*
Eastcentral *A*
Kokomo *C,A*
Lafayette *C,A*
Northcentral *C,A*
Northeast *C,A*
Northwest *C,A*
Southcentral *C,A*
Southwest *C,A*
Wabash Valley *C,A*
Whitewater *A*
Vincennes University *A*

Iowa

Hawkeye Institute of Technology *C*
Kirkwood Community College *A*
North Iowa Area Community
College *A*

Kansas

Haskell Indian Junior College *A*
Kansas City Kansas Community
College *A*

Kentucky

Jefferson Community College *A*
Louisville Technical Institute *A*

Maryland

Dundalk Community College *C,A*

Michigan

Ferris State University *A*
Lansing Community College *A*

Minnesota

Northwestern Electronics
Institute *A*

Mississippi

Mississippi Delta Community
College *C*
Mississippi Gulf Coast Community
College: Jefferson Davis
Campus *C*

Nebraska

Metropolitan Community College *A*
Northeast Community College *A*
Southeast Community College:
Milford Campus *A*
Western Nebraska Community
College: Sidney Campus *A*

New Hampshire

New Hampshire Technical College
Berlin *A*
Nashua *A*

New Mexico

San Juan College *C*

New York

Mohawk Valley Community
College *A*

North Carolina

Alamance Community College *C,A*
Brunswick Community College *C*
Caldwell Community College and
Technical Institute *A*
Cape Fear Community College *C*

Central Carolina Community
College *C*
Craven Community College *A*
Fayetteville Technical Community
College *C*
Guilford Technical Community
College *C,A*
Mayland Community College *C*
Mitchell Community College *C*
Montgomery Community College *C*
Nash Community College *C*
Roanoke-Chowan Community
College *C*
Robeson Community College *C*
Rockingham Community College *C*
Sampson Community College *C*
Sandhills Community College *C*
Southeastern Community College *C*
Surry Community College *C*
Vance-Granville Community
College *C*
Wake Technical Community
College *C*
Western Piedmont Community
College *C*
Wilson Technical Community
College *C*

Ohio

Ohio State University Agricultural
Technical Institute *A*
Stark Technical College *A*

Oregon

Clackamas Community College *A*
Lane Community College *A*

Pennsylvania

Northampton County Area
Community College *A*
Penn State University Park
Campus *C*

Rhode Island

Community College of Rhode
Island *C,A*

South Carolina

Aiken Technical College *A*
Chesterfield-Marlboro Technical
College *A*
Greenville Technical College *C*
Sumter Area Technical College *A*
Tri-County Technical College *A*
Trident Technical College *C*
Williamsburg Technical College *C*

South Dakota

Western Dakota Vocational
Technical Institute *C,A*

Tennessee

Chattanooga State Technical
Community College *C,A*
Northeast State Technical
Community College *C,A*
State Technical Institute at
Memphis *A*

Texas

Amarillo College *C,A*
Angelina College *A*
Brazosport College *C,A*
Houston Community College *C*
Texas State Technical College:
Waco *A*

Virginia

New River Community College *C*
Patrick Henry Community
College *C*

Southside Virginia Community
College *C*
Tidewater Community College *C*

Washington

Grays Harbor College *A*
Lower Columbia College *A*

Wisconsin

Moraine Park Technical College *C*
Northeast Wisconsin Technical
College *A*
Waukesha County Technical
College *C*

Wyoming

Eastern Wyoming College *A*

Industrial and organizational psychology

Alabama

University of Alabama *M*

California

California School of Professional
Psychology
Berkeley/Alameda *D*
San Diego *D*
California State University
Hayward *B*
Long Beach *M*
San Bernardino *M*
John F. Kennedy University *M*
La Sierra University *B*
Point Loma Nazarene College *B*
San Francisco State University *B,M*
San Jose State University *B,M*
United States International
University *D*

Colorado

Colorado State University *M,D*
United States Air Force
Academy *B*

Connecticut

Albertus Magnus College *B*
University of Bridgeport *M*
University of New Haven *B,M*

District of Columbia

George Washington University *D*

Florida

New College of the University of
South Florida *B*
University of Central Florida *M*
University of South Florida *D*
University of West Florida *M*

Hawaii

Hawaii Pacific University *B*

Illinois

College of St. Francis *B*
De Paul University *B,M,D*
Illinois Institute of Technology *D*
Illinois State University *M*
Lewis University *B*
Northwestern University *B,M,D*
Roosevelt University *M*
St. Xavier University *B*
Southern Illinois University at
Edwardsville *M*
University of Illinois at Urbana-
Champaign *B,M,D*

Indiana

Indiana University—Purdue
University at Indianapolis *M*
Purdue University
Calumet *B*
West Lafayette *B,M,D*

Iowa

Loras College *M*
Morningside College *B*

Kansas

Kansas State University *M,D*

Maryland

University of Baltimore *M*

Massachusetts

Bridgewater State College *B*
Nichols College *B*
Springfield College *M*
Suffolk University *B*

Michigan

Central Michigan University *M,D*
University of Detroit Mercy *B*
University of Michigan *M,D*
Western Michigan University *M*

Mississippi

University of Southern Mississippi
M,D

Missouri

University of Missouri: St. Louis
B,M,D
Washington University *B,M,D*

Nebraska

University of Nebraska—Omaha *M*

New Jersey

Bloomfield College *C*
Fairleigh Dickinson University *M*
Kean College of New Jersey *M*
Rutgers—The State University of
New Jersey *D*
Stevens Institute of Technology
B,M,D

New York

City University of New York
Baruch College *B,M*
Brooklyn College *M*
Graduate School and
University Center *D*
Marymount Manhattan College *C*
New York University *M,D*
State University of New York at
Albany *D*

North Carolina

Appalachian State University *M*
High Point University *B*
North Carolina State University
M,D
University of North Carolina at
Charlotte *M*

Ohio

Bowling Green State University
M,D
Cleveland State University *M*
Ohio State University: Columbus
Campus *M,D*
Ohio University *D*
Union Institute *D*
University of Akron *D*
University of Toledo *M*

Oklahoma

University of Tulsa *M,D*

Pennsylvania

California University of
Pennsylvania *B*
Carnegie Mellon University
B,M,D,W
Hahnemann University School of
Health Sciences and
Humanities *M*
Holy Family College *B*
Juniata College *B*
King's College *B*
La Salle University *B,M*
Lincoln University *B*
Moravian College *B*
Temple University *D*
University of Pennsylvania *B*
West Chester University of
Pennsylvania *M*
Westminster College *B*

Puerto Rico

University of Puerto Rico: Rio
Piedras Campus *M,D*

South Carolina

Clemson University *M*

Tennessee

Austin Peay State University *M*
Middle Tennessee State
University *M*
Tusculum College *B*
University of Tennessee
Chattanooga *M*
Knoxville *M,D*

Texas

Lamar University—Beaumont *M*
St. Mary's University *M*
Texas A&M University *D*
University of Central Texas *M*
University of Houston *M,D*
University of North Texas *M*

Virginia

Averett College *B*
Christopher Newport College *B*
Marymount University *B,M*
Old Dominion University *D*
Radford University *M*
Virginia Wesleyan College *B*

Washington

Central Washington University *B,M*
Evergreen State College *B*
Western Washington University *B*

West Virginia

Fairmont State College *B*

Wisconsin

Concordia University Wisconsin *B*
University of Wisconsin:
Oshkosh *M*
Viterbo College *B*

Mexico

Sistema Instituto Tecnologico y de
Estudios Superiores de
Monterrey *B*

Industrial technology

Alabama

Alabama Agricultural and
Mechanical University *B*

Community College of the Air
Force *A*
Gadsden State Community
College *A*

Alaska

University of Alaska Anchorage *A*

Arizona

Arizona State University *B,M*
Mesa Community College *A*
Yavapai College *A*

Arkansas

East Arkansas Community
College *A*
Mississippi County Community
College *A*
North Arkansas Community
College *A*
Phillips County Community College
C,A
Southern Arkansas University
Magnolia *A,B*
Technical Branch *A*
University of Arkansas at Pine Bluff
A,B

California

Allan Hancock College *C,A*
Bakersfield College *A*
California Polytechnic State
University: San Luis Obispo *B*
California State University
Chico *B*
Los Angeles *B*
City College of San Francisco *C,A*
College of the Sequoias *A*
Cosumnes River College *C,A*
Cuesta College *A*
De Anza College *C,A*
El Camino College *A*
Feather River College *A*
Fresno City College *C,A*
Hartnell College *A*
Humboldt State University *B*
Los Angeles Pierce College *C,A*
Merced College *A*
Modesto Junior College *A*
Mount San Antonio College *A*
Oxnard College *A*
Pacific Union College *A*
Pasadena City College *C,A*
San Diego Mesa College *A*
San Francisco State University *B*
San Jose State University *B,M*
Sierra College *A*
Solano Community College *A*
Southwestern College *C,A*
Taft College *A*
Ventura College *A*
West Coast University *C,A,B*
West Hills Community College *A*
Yuba College *A*

Colorado

Adams State College *B*
Colorado State University *B*
Metropolitan State College of
Denver *B*
University of Southern Colorado *B*

Connecticut

Central Connecticut State
University *B*
Manchester Community College *A*
Norwalk State Technical College *A*
Thames Valley State Technical
College *A*
Waterbury State Technical
College *A*

Delaware

Delaware Technical and
Community College: Stanton/
Wilmington Campus *A*

Florida

Brevard Community College *A*
Manatee Community College *A*
Miami-Dade Community College *A*
Okaloosa-Walton Community
College *C,A*
Palm Beach Community College *A*
University of Central Florida *B*
University of North Florida *B*
University of West Florida *B*

Georgia

DeKalb College *A*
Gainesville College *A*
Georgia Southern University *B*
Middle Georgia College *A*
Southern College of Technology *B*

Idaho

University of Idaho *B*

Illinois

Belleville Area College *C,A*
Black Hawk College
East Campus *A*
Moline *A*
Eastern Illinois University *B*
Illinois Central College *A*
Illinois State University *B,M*
Illinois Valley Community
College *A*
John A. Logan College *A*
Joliet Junior College *C,A*
Kishwaukee College *A*
Moraine Valley Community College
C,A
Morrison Institute of Technology *A*
Morton College *A*
Rend Lake College *C,A*
Richland Community College *A*
Rock Valley College *A*
Southern Illinois University at
Carbondale *B*
Waubonsee Community College *A*
Western Illinois University *B,M*

Indiana

Ball State University *A*
Indiana State University *B*
Indiana University—Purdue
University at Fort Wayne *A,B*
Indiana Vocational Technical
College
Lafayette *C*
Wabash Valley *C*
Purdue University
Calumet *A,B*
North Central Campus *A*
West Lafayette *A,B,M*
University of Southern Indiana *M*

Iowa

Hawkeye Institute of Technology *A*
Iowa Central Community College *A*
Muscatine Community College *A*
National Education Center:
National Institute of Technology
Campus *A*
Northeast Iowa Community
College *A*
University of Northern Iowa *B,M,D*

Kansas

Allen County Community
College *A*
Bethel College *A,B*

Butler County Community
College *A*
Cowley County Community
College *A*
Haskell Indian Junior College *A*
Hutchinson Community College *A*
McPherson College *B*
Pittsburg State University *B*
Wichita State University *B*

Kentucky

Jefferson Community College *A*
Morehead State University *A,B*
Murray State University *A,B*
Northern Kentucky University *B*
Western Kentucky University *A,B*

Louisiana

Grambling State University *B*
Louisiana State University and
Agricultural and Mechanical
College *B*
Northwestern State University *B*
Southeastern Louisiana University
A,B

Maine

University of Maine at Presque
Isle *B*
University of Southern Maine *B*

Maryland

Catonsville Community College *A*
Chesapeake College *C*
Columbia Union College *A*

Massachusetts

Franklin Institute of Boston *A*
Greenfield Community College *A*
Massachusetts Maritime
Academy *B*
North Shore Community College *A*
Springfield Technical Community
College *A*
University of Massachusetts at
Lowell *B*

Michigan

Alpena Community College *A*
Andrews University *A*
Baker College: Flint *B*
Central Michigan University *B,M*
Charles Stewart Mott Community
College *A*
Delta College *A*
Eastern Michigan University *B,M*
Ferris State University *A*
Grand Rapids Community College
C,A
Grand Valley State University *B*
Henry Ford Community College *A*
Jackson Community College *A*
Kalamazoo Valley Community
College *A*
Kellogg Community College *A*
Lansing Community College *A*
Lawrence Technological
University *A*
Macomb Community College *C,A*
Marygrove College *A*
Mid Michigan Community
College *A*
Montcalm Community College *A*
Muskegon Community College *A*
Northern Michigan University *A,B*
Northwestern Michigan College *A*
Oakland Community College *C,A*
Saginaw Valley State University *B*
St. Clair County Community
College *A*
Southwestern Michigan College *A*
Wayne State University *B*

Western Michigan University *B*

Minnesota

Bemidji State University *B*
Moorhead State University *B*
Northwestern Electronics
Institute *A*
University of Minnesota: Duluth *B*

Mississippi

Alcorn State University *B*
Jackson State University *B*
Mississippi State University *B*
University of Southern
Mississippi *B*

Missouri

Central Missouri State University
B,M
Mineral Area College *C,A*
Moberly Area Community
College *A*
Northwest Missouri State
University *B*
St. Louis Community College
Florissant Valley *A*
Forest Park *A*
Southwest Missouri State
University *B*

Montana

Northern Montana College *A*

Nebraska

Central Community College *A*
Chadron State College *B*
Northeast Community College *A*
Peru State College *B*
Southeast Community College:
Milford Campus *A*
University of Nebraska
Lincoln *B*
Omaha *B*
Wayne State College *B*

New Hampshire

Keene State College *A,B*
New Hampshire Technical College:
Nashua *A*

New Jersey

Cumberland County College *C,A*
Kean College of New Jersey *B*
Thomas Edison State College *A,B*
Trenton State College *B*

New Mexico

San Juan College *A*

New York

Broome Community College *A*
City University of New York:
College of Staten Island *A*
Corning Community College *A*
Erie Community College
North Campus *C,A*
South Campus *A*
Fulton-Montgomery Community
College *A*
Herkimer County Community
College *A*
Hudson Valley Community
College *A*
Jefferson Community College *A*
Nassau Community College *A*
New York Institute of
Technology *B*

State University of New York
Binghamton *B*
College of Agriculture and
Technology at Morrisville *A*
College at Buffalo *B,M*
College of Technology at
Canton *A*
Institute of Technology at
Utica/Rome *B*

North Carolina

Appalachian State University *B,M*
Blue Ridge Community College *A*
Cape Fear Community College *C*
Catawba Valley Community
College *A*
Cleveland Community College *A*
College of the Albemarle *C*
East Carolina University *B,M*
Edgecombe Community College *A*
Elizabeth City State University *B*
Forsyth Technical Community
College *A*
Gaston College *A*
Guilford Technical Community
College *A*
McDowell Technical Community
College *A*
North Carolina Agricultural and
Technical State University *B*
Piedmont Community College *C*
Pitt Community College *A*
Robeson Community College *A*
Vance-Granville Community
College *A*
Wake Technical Community
College *A*
Wayne Community College *A*
Western Piedmont Community
College *A*
Wilkes Community College *C*

North Dakota

Bismarck State College *A*
University of North Dakota *B,M*

Ohio

Bowling Green State University
Bowling Green *B*
Firelands College *A*
Central Ohio Technical College *A*
Cuyahoga Community College:
Metropolitan Campus *A*
Edison State Community College
C,A
Kent State University
Ashtabula Regional Campus *A*
Kent *B,M*
Tuscarawas Campus *C,A*
Lakeland Community College *A*
Lorain County Community
College *A*
Marion Technical College *A*
Northwest Technical College *C,A*
Ohio Northern University *B*
Ohio University *B,M*
Owens Technical College
Findlay Campus *A*
Toledo *C,A*
Sinclair Community College *C,A*
Stark Technical College *A*
Terra Technical College *A*
University of Cincinnati
Access Colleges *A*
Clermont College *A*
Raymond Walters College *C,A*
University of Dayton *B*
University of Rio Grande *B*
University of Toledo *A*
Wilmington College *B*
Wright State University: Lake
Campus *A*

Oklahoma

Cameron University *B*
East Central University *B*
Northwestern Oklahoma State
University *C,B*
Oklahoma State University:
Oklahoma City *A*
Southeastern Oklahoma State
University *B*
Southwestern Oklahoma State
University *B*
Tulsa Junior College *A*
University of Central Oklahoma *B*

Oregon

Central Oregon Community College
C,A
Clackamas Community College *A*
Clatsop Community College *A*
Lane Community College *A*
Mount Hood Community College
C,A
Southwestern Oregon Community
College *A*

Pennsylvania

Butler County Community
College *A*
California University of
Pennsylvania *B,M*
Cheyney University of
Pennsylvania *B*
Gannon University *A,B*
Harrisburg Area Community
College *C,A*
Lehigh County Community College
C,A
Millersville University of
Pennsylvania *B*
Penn State University Park
Campus *C*
Pennsylvania College of
Technology *A*
Reading Area Community
College *A*
Spring Garden College *B*

Puerto Rico

University of Puerto Rico
Bayamon Technological
University College *A*
Ponce Technological
University College *A*

Rhode Island

Rhode Island College *B,M*

South Carolina

Aiken Technical College *C,A*
Greenville Technical College *A*
South Carolina State College *B*

South Dakota

Northern State University *A,B*

Tennessee

Cleveland State Community
College *A*
Columbia State Community College
C,A
Dyersburg State Community
College *A*
Hiwassee College *A*
Martin Methodist College *A*
Middle Tennessee State
University *B*
Nashville State Technical
Institute *A*
Pellissippi State Technical
Community College *A*
Southern College of Seventh-day
Adventists *A*

State Technical Institute at
Memphis *A*
Tennessee Technological
University *B*
Walters State Community
College *A*

Texas

Abilene Christian University *A*
Angelina College *C,A*
Brazosport College *C,A*
Brookhaven College *A*
Central Texas College *A*
East Texas State University *B,M*
Lamar University—Beaumont *B*
Lee College *A*
Navarro College *A*
Prairie View A&M University *B*
Sam Houston State University *B,M*
Southwest Texas State University *B*
Tarleton State University *B*
Texas A&I University *B*
University of Central Texas *B*
University of Houston *B*
University of North Texas *B,M*
University of Texas at Tyler *B*
Weatherford College *C,A*

Utah

Brigham Young University *B,M*
Utah State University *M*

Virginia

Blue Ridge Community College *A*
New River Community College *A*
Piedmont Virginia Community
College *C*

Washington

Central Washington University *B*
Clark College *A*
Lower Columbia College *A*
Seattle Central Community
College *A*
Shoreline Community College *A*
Western Washington University *B*

West Virginia

Fairmont State College *A,B*
Salem-Teikyo University *B*
West Virginia State College *B*
West Virginia University at
Parkersburg *A*

Wisconsin

Chippewa Valley Technical
College *A*
Moraine Park Technical College *A*
University of Wisconsin
Platteville *B*
Stout *B,M*
Waukesha County Technical
College *A*
Western Wisconsin Technical
College *A*
Wisconsin Indianhead Technical
College *A*

Wyoming

Western Wyoming Community
College *A*

Information sciences and systems

Alabama

Auburn University at
Montgomery *B*
Faulkner University *B*

Jacksonville State University *B*
John C. Calhoun State Community
College *A*
Oakwood College *B*
Spring Hill College *B*

Arizona

Arizona State University *B*
Cochise College *A*
DeVry Institute of Technology:
Phoenix *B*
Eastern Arizona College *A*
Northern Arizona University *B*
South Mountain Community
College *C,A*

Arkansas

Arkansas State University *A,B*
University of Arkansas at Little
Rock *B*
University of Central Arkansas *B*

California

Allan Hancock College *C,A*
Azusa Pacific University *B*
Biola University *B*
California Lutheran University *B*
California State Polytechnic
University: Pomona *B*
California State University
Bakersfield *B*
Fresno *B*
Fullerton *M*
Hayward *B,M*
Long Beach *B*
Los Angeles *B*
Stanislaus *B*
Chabot College *A*
Chaffey Community College *C*
Chapman University *B*
Christian Heritage College *B*
College of the Redwoods *C,A*
Cosumnes River College *A*
DeVry Institute of Technology: City
of Industry *A*
El Camino College *A*
Golden Gate University *C,B,M*
Humboldt State University *B*
Kings River Community College *A*
Laney College *A*
Menlo College *B*
Merced College *A*
Mission College *C,A*
Moorpark College *A*
National University *B,M*
Ohlone College *C*
Orange Coast College *C,A*
Oxnard College *C*
Pacific Union College *A,B*
Phillips Junior College: Fresno
Campus *C,A*
Point Loma Nazarene College *B*
Saddleback College *C,A*
San Diego City College *A*
San Diego State University *B*
Santa Barbara City College *C,A*
Santa Monica College *C,A*
Sierra College *A*
Southwestern College *A*
University of California: San
Diego *B*
University of La Verne *A*
University of the Pacific *B*
University of San Francisco *B*
Ventura College *C,A*
West Coast University *A,B,M*
West Hills Community College *C*
Woodbury University *B*

Colorado

Arapahoe Community College *C,A*
Denver Technical College *A*

Fort Lewis College *B*
Mesa State College *A,B*
Metropolitan State College of
Denver *B*
Regis College of Regis University *B*
University of Colorado
Boulder *B*
Colorado Springs *B*
University of Denver *M*

Connecticut

Bridgeport Engineering Institute *B*
Fairfield University *B*
Quinnipiac College *B,M*
Sacred Heart University *B*
University of Bridgeport *B,M*
University of Hartford *B*
University of New Haven *B,M*

Delaware

Goldey-Beacom College *B*
Wesley College *B*

District of Columbia

American University *B,M*
Gallaudet University *B*
George Washington University
B,M,D
Howard University *B*
Southeastern University *M*
University of the District of
Columbia *A,B*

Florida

Bethune-Cookman College *B*
Daytona Beach Community
College *A*
Embry-Riddle Aeronautical
University *B*
Florida Atlantic University *B*
Florida Community College at
Jacksonville *A*
Florida International University
B,M
Florida Southern College *B*
Fort Lauderdale College *A,B*
Hillsborough Community College *A*
Nova University *B,M,D*
Okaloosa-Walton Community
College *A*
Orlando College *B*
Palm Beach Atlantic College *B*
Phillips Junior College:
Melbourne *A*
St. Thomas University *B*
Seminole Community College *A*
Tampa College *A,B*
University of Central Florida *B*
University of Miami *B,M*
University of North Florida *B*
University of South Florida *B*
University of West Florida *B*

Georgia

Abraham Baldwin Agricultural
College *C*
Andrew College *A*
Atlanta Metropolitan College *A*
Berry College *B*
Brewton-Parker College *B*
Darton College *A*
DeKalb College *A*
DeVry Institute of Technology:
Atlanta *B*
Floyd College *A*
Georgia College *B,M*
Georgia Southern University *B*
Georgia State University *B,M,D*
Kennesaw State College *B*
Macon College *A*
Mercer University *M*
Reinhardt College *A*

Savannah State College *B*
Southern College of Technology *B*

Idaho

Northwest Nazarene College *B*

Illinois

Aurora University *B,M*
Belleville Area College *A*
Black Hawk College: East Campus
C,A
Bradley University *B*
Chicago State University *B*
College of DuPage *A*
College of St. Francis *B*
Concordia University *B*
De Paul University *C,B,M*
DeVry Institute of Technology
Chicago *B*
Lombard *B*
Eastern Illinois University *B*
Illinois College *B*
Illinois Eastern Community
Colleges
Frontier Community College
C,A
Lincoln Trail College *C,A*
Olney Central College *C,A*
Wabash Valley College *C,A*
Judson College *B*
Lewis University *B*
Loyola University of Chicago *B*
MacCormac Junior College *A*
McKendree College *B*
Millikin University *B*
Moraine Valley Community College
C,A
North Central College *B*
Northwestern University *B,M,D*
Olivet Nazarene University *B*
Quincy College *B*
Rockford College *B*
Roosevelt University *B,M*
Sangamon State University *M*
William Rainey Harper College *A*

Indiana

Ancilla College *C,A*
Franklin College *B*
Indiana Institute of Technology *A,B*
Indiana State University *B*
Indiana University
Bloomington *M,D*
Kokomo *B*
Northwest *B*
Indiana University—Purdue
University at Fort Wayne *C*
Indiana Vocational Technical
College
Central Indiana *C,A*
Columbus *A*
Eastcentral *C,A*
Kokomo *C,A*
Northcentral *C,A*
Northeast *C,A*
Northwest *C,A*
Southcentral *C,A*
Southeast *C,A*
Southwest *A*
Wabash Valley *C,A*
Whitewater *C,A*
Martin University *B*
Purdue University *B,M,D*
St. Joseph's College *B*
Taylor University *B*
Tri-State University *B*
University of Indianapolis *B*
University of Southern Indiana *A,B*
Vincennes University *A*

Iowa

American Institute of Business *A*
Buena Vista College *B*
Central College *B*
Clarke College *B*
Dordt College *B*
Drake University *B*
Graceland College *B*
St. Ambrose University *B*
University of Northern Iowa *B*
Wartburg College *B*

Kansas

Benedictine College *A,B*
Bethany College *B*
Coffeyville Community College *A*
Colby Community College *A*
Emporia State University *B*
Kansas Newman College *A,B*
Kansas State University *B*
Pittsburg State University *B*

Kentucky

Eastern Kentucky University *B*
Elizabethtown Community
    College *A*
Georgetown College *B*
Madisonville Community College *A*
Murray State University *B*
Northern Kentucky University *B*
Sue Bennett College *A*
Union College *A*
University of Louisville *B*

Louisiana

Grambling State University *B*
Louisiana College *B*
Louisiana State University and
    Agricultural and Mechanical
    College *M*
Loyola University *B*
Northwestern State University *B*
Phillips Junior College: New
    Orleans *A*
Xavier University of Louisiana *B*

Maine

Husson College *A,B*
Southern Maine Technical
    College *A*
Thomas College *A,B,M*
University of Maine at Machias *A*

Maryland

Anne Arundel Community
    College *A*
Bowie State University *M*
Catonsville Community College *A*
College of Notre Dame of
    Maryland *B*
Columbia Union College *B*
Frederick Community College *A*
Harford Community College *A*
Howard Community College *A*
Montgomery College
    Germantown Campus *A*
    Rockville Campus *A*
    Takoma Park Campus *A*
Morgan State University *B*
Prince George's Community
    College *A*
University of Baltimore *B,M*
University of Maryland
    Baltimore County *B,M,D*
    College Park *B*
Villa Julie College *B*

Massachusetts

American International College *B*
Aquinas College at Milton *A*
Assumption College *B*
Bentley College *B,M*

Boston College *B*
Bristol Community College *A*
Bunker Hill Community College *A*
Cape Cod Community College *A*
Eastern Nazarene College *B*
Hampshire College *B*
Massachusetts Bay Community
    College *C,A*
Massachusetts Institute of
    Technology *B,M,D,W*
Mount Ida College *A*
Mount Wachusett Community
    College *A*
Nichols College *B*
North Adams State College *B*
North Shore Community College *A*
Northeastern University *M*
Northern Essex Community College
    C,A
Springfield College *B*
Suffolk University *B*
Tufts University *B*
University of Massachusetts
    Dartmouth *B*
    Lowell *B*
Western New England College *B*
Westfield State College *B*
Worcester Polytechnic Institute
    B,M

Michigan

Andrews University *B*
Baker College
    Auburn Hills *A*
    Owosso *B*
Cleary College *B*
Delta College *A*
Detroit College of Business *B*
Eastern Michigan University *B,M*
GMI Engineering & Management
    Institute *A*
Grand Valley State University *B,M*
Jackson Community College *A*
Lake Superior State University *B*
Lawrence Technological
    University *B*
Madonna University *B*
Michigan Technological
    University *B*
Northern Michigan University *B*
Northwestern Michigan College *A*
Northwood Institute *A*
Saginaw Valley State University *B*
Suomi College *A*
Wayne State University *B*
Western Michigan University *B*

Minnesota

Alexandria Technical College *A*
Bemidji State University *B*
College of St. Catherine: St.
    Catherine Campus *B*
College of St. Scholastica *B*
Mankato State University *B*
Moorhead State University *B*
St. Cloud State University *B,M*
St. Mary's College of Minnesota *B*
Southwest State University *B*
University of Minnesota:
    Crookston *A*
Vermilion Community College *A*
Winona State University *B*

Mississippi

Jackson State University *B*

Missouri

Central Missouri State University *B*
College of the Ozarks *B*
DeVry Institute of Technology:
    Kansas City *B*
Fontbonne College *B*

Hannibal-LaGrange College *B*
Maryville University *B*
Mineral Area College *A*
Missouri Southern State College *B*
Missouri Western State College *B*
Park College *B*
Rockhurst College *B*
Southwest Baptist University *B*
University of Missouri: St. Louis
    B,M
Washington University *B,M*
William Jewell College *B*
William Woods College *B*

Montana

Eastern Montana College *B*
Little Big Horn College *A*
Miles Community College *A*
Montana College of Mineral
    Science and Technology *B*
University of Montana *B*

Nebraska

McCook Community College *A*
Nebraska Wesleyan University *B*
Peru State College *B*
Union College *A,B*
University of Nebraska
    Kearney *B*
    Omaha *B*
York College *A*

Nevada

Community College of Southern
    Nevada *C,A*
University of Nevada: Las Vegas *B*

New Hampshire

Daniel Webster College *A,B*
New Hampshire College *B*
Plymouth State College of the
    University System of New
    Hampshire *B*
University of New Hampshire at
    Manchester *A*

New Jersey

Caldwell College *C,B*
College of St. Elizabeth *C*
County College of Morris *A*
Glassboro State College *B*
Gloucester County College *C,A*
Kean College of New Jersey *M*
Mercer County Community
    College *C*
New Jersey Institute of
    Technology *B*
Ocean County College *C*
Rider College *B*
Rutgers—The State University of
    New Jersey
    Newark College of Arts and
        Sciences *B*
    University College Newark *B*
Stevens Institute of Technology
    B,M
Stockton State College *B*
Sussex County Community
    College *C*
Thomas Edison State College *B*
Upsala College *B*

New Mexico

Eastern New Mexico University *B*
New Mexico Highlands University
    A,B

New York

Berkeley College *A*
Canisius College *B*

City University of New York
    Baruch College *B,M*
    Borough of Manhattan
        Community College *A*
    Brooklyn College *B,M*
    La Guardia Community
        College *A*
Clarkson University *B,M*
Columbia University: School of
    Engineering and Applied Science
    B,M,D,W
Columbia-Greene Community
    College *C*
Cornell University *M,D*
Corning Community College *A*
Dominican College of Blauvelt *C,B*
Erie Community College
    City Campus *A*
    South Campus *A*
Fordham University *B*
Genesee Community College *C,A*
Hartwick College *B*
Hofstra University *B,M*
Iona College *B*
Ithaca College *B*
Jamestown Community College *A*
Long Island University
    Brooklyn Campus *B*
    C. W. Post Campus *B,M*
    Southampton Campus *B*
Manhattan College *B*
Maria College *C*
Marist College *B,M*
Marymount College *C,B*
Medaille College *B*
Mercy College *B*
Mohawk Valley Community
    College *C*
Nassau Community College *A*
New York Institute of
    Technology *B*
New York University *C,B,M,D*
Niagara University *B*
Pace University
    College of White Plains
        C,A,B,M
    New York *C,A,B,M*
    Pleasantville/Briarcliff
        C,A,B,M
Polytechnic University *M*
Rochester Institute of Technology
    A,B,M
Russell Sage College *B*
Sage Junior College of Albany, A
    Division of Russell Sage
    College *A*
State University of New York
    Binghamton *B,M,D*
    Stony Brook *B*
    College at Buffalo *B*
    College of Technology at
        Delhi *A*
    College of Technology at
        Farmingdale *A*
    Institute of Technology at
        Utica/Rome *B*
    Oswego *B*
Suffolk County Community
    College *C*
Syracuse University *B,M*
Villa Maria College of Buffalo *A*
Westchester Community College *A*

North Carolina

Appalachian State University *B*
Belmont Abbey College *B*
Brevard College *A*
Catawba College *B*
Elon College *B*
High Point University *B*
Mars Hill College *B*

North Carolina Central
University *M*
Queens College *C*
University of North Carolina at
Greensboro *B*

North Dakota

Jamestown College *B*
North Dakota State College of
Science *A*
North Dakota State University:
Bottineau and Institute of
Forestry *A*
Valley City State University *B*

Ohio

Air Force Institute of
Technology *M*
Ashland University *B*
Baldwin-Wallace College *C,B*
Bowling Green State University
Bowling Green *B*
Firelands College *A*
Bryant & Stratton Business
Institute: Great Northern *A*
Case Western Reserve University
M,D
Central State University *B*
Clark State Community College *A*
DeVry Institute of Technology:
Columbus *B*
Franciscan University of
Steubenville *B*
Heidelberg College *B*
Kent State University *B*
Lakeland Community College *C,A*
Marietta College *B*
Mount Union College *B*
Mount Vernon Nazarene College *B*
North Central Technical College *A*
Ohio State University: Columbus
Campus *B,M,D*
Ohio University *B,M*
Tiffin University *B*
Union Institute *B,D*
University of Cincinnati
Access Colleges *A*
Cincinnati *B*
University of Dayton *B*
University of Toledo *B*
Wilberforce University *B*
Xavier University *B*

Oklahoma

Bartlesville Wesleyan College *A,B*
Cameron University *B*
Northern Oklahoma College *A*
Northwestern Oklahoma State
University *B*
Oklahoma Baptist University *B*
Oklahoma City University *M*
Oklahoma Panhandle State
University *A*
Oklahoma State University *B*
Southeastern Oklahoma State
University *B*
University of Tulsa *B*

Oregon

Central Oregon Community
College *A*
Portland State University *D*

Pennsylvania

Allentown College of St. Francis de
Sales *M*
California University of
Pennsylvania *A,B*
Carnegie Mellon University
B,M,D,W
Central Pennsylvania Business
School *A*

Chatham College *B*
Clarion University of
Pennsylvania *B*
Community College of Beaver
County *A*
Delaware Valley College *B*
Drexel University *B,M,D*
Duquesne University *B*
Elizabethtown College *B*
Gannon University *B*
Harrisburg Area Community
College *C,A*
Holy Family College *B*
Indiana University of
Pennsylvania *B*
King's College *C,A,B*
La Roche College *B*
La Salle University *B,M*
Lebanon Valley College of
Pennsylvania *B*
Lehigh County Community
College *A*
Lehigh University *B,M*
Lock Haven University of
Pennsylvania *B*
Luzerne County Community
College *C,A*
Manor Junior College *A*
Mansfield University of
Pennsylvania *B*
Marywood College *B,M*
Messiah College *B*
Montgomery County Community
College *C,A*
Moravian College *B*
Muhlenberg College *B*
Northampton County Area
Community College *A*
Philadelphia College of Textiles and
Science *B*
Robert Morris College *B,M*
St. Joseph's University *B,M*
Shippensburg University of
Pennsylvania *M*
Susquehanna University *B*
Swarthmore College *B*
University of Pennsylvania *B,M,D*
University of Pittsburgh
Greensburg *B*
Pittsburgh *B,M,D*
University of Scranton *B*
Westminster College *B*
Westmoreland County Community
College *A*
Widener University *B*
Wilkes University *B*
Wilson College *A*

Puerto Rico

Electronic Data Processing College
of Puerto Rico *M*
Universidad Metropolitana *A,B*

Rhode Island

Brown University *B,M,D*
Rhode Island College *B*
Salve Regina University *B,M*

South Carolina

Charleston Southern University *B*
Clemson University *B*
College of Charleston *B*
Francis Marion College *B*

South Dakota

Augustana College *B*
Dakota State University *B*
National College *B*
Sioux Falls College *B*

Tennessee

Austin Peay State University *B*
Belmont University *B*
Carson-Newman College *B*
Chattanooga State Technical
Community College *A*
Christian Brothers University *B*
David Lipscomb University *B*
Dyersburg State Community
College *A*
East Tennessee State University *B*
Freed-Hardeman University *B*
Memphis State University *B*
Middle Tennessee State University
B,M
Motlow State Community
College *A*
Northeast State Technical
Community College *A*
Pellissippi State Technical
Community College *C,A*
State Technical Institute at
Memphis *A*
Tennessee Technological
University *B*
University of Tennessee:
Chattanooga *B*

Texas

Alvin Community College *A*
Austin Community College *A*
Baylor University *B,M*
Brookhaven College *A*
Corpus Christi State University *B*
Dallas Baptist University *B*
DeVry Institute of Technology:
Irving *B*
East Texas State University *B*
El Centro College *A*
Houston Baptist University *B,M*
Lamar University—Beaumont *B*
Mountain View College *C*
North Harris Montgomery
Community College District *A*
Richland College *A*
St. Mary's University *B,M*
South Plains College *A*
Southwest Texas State University *B*
Southwestern Adventist College *A,B*
Texas A&I University *B*
Texas State Technical College
Amarillo *A*
Harlingen *A*
Sweetwater *C,A*
Texas Tech University *B,M,D*
Texas Wesleyan University *B*
University of Central Texas *M*
University of Houston *B*
University of Mary Hardin-
Baylor *B*
University of North Texas *B,M,D*
University of Texas
El Paso *B*
Pan American *B*

Utah

Weber State University *B*

Vermont

Castleton State College *B*
Champlain College *A*

Virginia

Averett College *B*
Blue Ridge Community College *A*
Bluefield College *B*
Christopher Newport College *B*
Clinch Valley College of the
University of Virginia *B*
Commonwealth College *A*
George Mason University *M,D*
James Madison University *B*

Marymount University *M*
Mountain Empire Community
College *C*
Old Dominion University *B*
Patrick Henry Community
College *A*
Radford University *B*
Roanoke College *B*
Strayer College *C,A,B,M*
Tidewater Community College *A*
University of Richmond *C,A,B*
Virginia Commonwealth University
B,M
Virginia Highlands Community
College *C,A*
Virginia Polytechnic Institute and
State University *M*
Virginia State University *B*
Wytheville Community College *A*

Washington

Antioch University Seattle *M*
Central Washington University *B*
City University *M*
Clark College *C*
Eastern Washington University *B*
Edmonds Community College *A*
ITT Technical Institute: Seattle *A*
Olympic College *C,A*
Pacific Lutheran University *B,M*
St. Martin's College *B*
Seattle Pacific University *M*
Skagit Valley College *A*
South Puget Sound Community
College *C,A*
Tacoma Community College *A*
Walla Walla College *A*

West Virginia

Alderson-Broaddus College *B*
College of West Virginia *A,B*
Glenville State College *A*
Marshall University *A,B*
Shepherd College *B*
University of Charleston *A,B*
West Liberty State College *B*
West Virginia Graduate College *M*
West Virginia Wesleyan College *B*

Wisconsin

Carroll College *B*
Edgewood College *B*
Northland College *B*
Stratton College *C,A*
University of Wisconsin
Eau Claire *B*
Green Bay *B*
Madison *B,M,D*
Oshkosh *B*
Stevens Point *B*
Viterbo College *B*

Wyoming

Laramie County Community
College *A*
Northwest College *A*
Sheridan College *A*
University of Wyoming *B*

Canada

McGill University *C*

Mexico

Sistema Instituto Tecnologico y de
Estudios Superiores de
Monterrey *M*

Inorganic chemistry

California
California State University
Fresno *B*
Fullerton *M*
University of California: Berkeley
B,M,D

Connecticut
Wesleyan University *B*

District of Columbia
George Washington University *M,D*

Florida
Florida State University *B,M,D*
New College of the University of
South Florida *B*
University of Florida *M,D*

Georgia
Emory University *D*
Oxford College of Emory
University *A*

Illinois
Judson College *B*
Northwestern University *B*
Southern Illinois University at
Carbondale *B,M,D*
University of Chicago *B,M,D*

Indiana
Indiana University Bloomington *D*
Purdue University *M,D*

Iowa
Iowa State University *M,D*

Kansas
Kansas State University *M,D*
Pratt Community College *A*

Massachusetts
Hampshire College *B*
Harvard University *D*
Massachusetts Institute of
Technology *B,M,D,W*
Tufts University *M,D*
University of Massachusetts at
Dartmouth *B*
Worcester Polytechnic Institute *B*

Michigan
Michigan State University *M,D*
Michigan Technological
University *B*
University of Michigan *M,D*

Minnesota
Rainy River Community College *A*
Willmar Community College *A*

Missouri
University of Missouri: Kansas City
M,D

New Hampshire
University of New Hampshire *M,D*

New Jersey
Stevens Institute of Technology
B,M,D

New Mexico
New Mexico Institute of Mining
and Technology *M,D*

New York
Columbia University *M,D*
Cornell University *M,D*
Fordham University *M*
Sarah Lawrence College *B*
State University of New York at
Albany *D*

North Carolina
University of North Carolina at
Chapel Hill *M,D*

Ohio
Ohio State University: Columbus
Campus *B,M,D*
Ohio University *M,D*

Oregon
Oregon Graduate Institute *M,D*
University of Oregon *M,D*

Pennsylvania
Bucknell University *B*
Carnegie Mellon University
B,M,D,W
Drexel University *B,M,D*
Duquesne University *M*
University of Pennsylvania *M,D*

Rhode Island
Brown University *B,M,D*

Texas
Lon Morris College *A*
University of Houston *M,D*

Vermont
Marlboro College *B*

Washington
Tacoma Community College *A*

West Virginia
Alderson-Broaddus College *B*

Wisconsin
Marquette University *M,D*

Canada
McGill University *M,D*

Institutional/home management/supporting programs

Alabama
Jacksonville State University *B*
University of Alabama *B,M*

Arizona
Glendale Community College *A*

Arkansas
Harding University *B*

California
Bakersfield College *A*
California State University:
Fresno *B*
Chabot College *A*
Mission College *A*
Palomar College *A*

District of Columbia
Howard University *B*

Georgia
Georgia Southern University *B*
University of Georgia *B*

Illinois
Joliet Junior College *A*
KAES College *B*
University of Illinois at Urbana-
Champaign *B*

Indiana
Purdue University *B,M*

Iowa
Iowa State University *B,M,D*
Kirkwood Community College *A*

Kansas
Barton County Community
College *A*

Louisiana
Grambling State University *B*
University of Southwestern
Louisiana *B*

Maryland
University of Maryland: College
Park *B,M*
Villa Julie College *A*

Massachusetts
Becker College: Leicester
Campus *A*
Northern Essex Community
College *C*

Michigan
Andrews University *M*
Central Michigan University *B*
Eastern Michigan University *B*
Marygrove College *B*
Michigan State University *M*

Minnesota
College of St. Scholastica *B*
University of Minnesota:
Crookston *A*

Mississippi
Alcorn State University *B*
Mississippi College *B*
University of Southern
Mississippi *M*

Nebraska
University of Nebraska—Omaha *B*

New York
Herkimer County Community
College *A*
New York University *B,M,D*
State University of New York
College at Plattsburgh *B*

North Carolina
Campbell University *B*

North Dakota
North Dakota State University *B*

Ohio
Bowling Green State University *B*
Miami University: Oxford Campus
B,M
Ohio State University: Columbus
Campus *B,M,D*
Ohio University *B*

Oklahoma
Southeastern Oklahoma State
University *B*

Oregon
Oregon State University *B*

Pennsylvania
Mercyhurst College *B*
St. Vincent College *B*
Seton Hill College *B*

Tennessee
David Lipscomb University *B*

Texas
Austin Community College *A*
Houston Community College *C*
McLennan Community College *A*
San Jacinto College: Central
Campus *A*
Texas Southmost College *A*
Texas Woman's University *B,M,D*
University of Mary Hardin-
Baylor *B*

Virginia
John Tyler Community College *C*
Norfolk State University *B*

Wisconsin
Moraine Park Technical College *A*

Institutional management

Alabama
Community College of the Air
Force *A*
Jefferson State Community
College *A*

Arizona
Arizona State University *B*

Arkansas
University of the Ozarks *A*

California
Golden Gate University *C,B*
San Diego City College *A*

Georgia
Georgia Southern University *B*

Illinois
Illinois Central College *C,A*
Southern Illinois University at
Carbondale *B*

Indiana
Purdue University *B,M*

Kansas
Kansas State University *M*

Kentucky
Campbellsville College *B*
Western Kentucky University *B*

Maryland
Villa Julie College *A*

Massachusetts
Mount Ida College *A*

Michigan
Eastern Michigan University *B*
Henry Ford Community College *A*
Michigan State University *M*

Minnesota
University of Minnesota:
Crookston *A*
Willmar Community College *A*

Mississippi
Alcorn State University *B*

Missouri
Maryville University *B*

Nebraska
Dana College *B*

New Hampshire
Antioch New England Graduate School *M*

New Jersey
Burlington County College *A*

New York
Iona College *B*

Ohio
Bowling Green State University *B*
University of Toledo *B*

Pennsylvania
Bucks County Community College *A*
Carnegie Mellon University *M,D*
Indiana University of Pennsylvania *B*
Penn State University Park Campus *A,B,M*
St. Joseph's University *M*

Rhode Island
Johnson & Wales University *A,B*

Tennessee
Bristol University *A,B,M*

Virginia
Northern Virginia Community College *A*
Virginia Polytechnic Institute and State University *B*
Virginia Wesleyan College *B*

Instrumentation technology

Alabama
Community College of the Air Force *A*
Jefferson State Community College *A*
John M. Patterson State Technical College *A*

Alaska
University of Alaska Anchorage *A*

Arkansas
Phillips County Community College *C,A*

California
Chabot College *A*
Orange Coast College *C,A*
Pasadena City College *C,A*
West Valley College *A*
Yuba College *A*

Colorado
Colorado Northwestern Community College *C,A*

Delaware
Delaware Technical and Community College: Stanton/Wilmington Campus *A*

District of Columbia
University of the District of Columbia *A*

Florida
Brevard Community College *A*
Miami-Dade Community College *A*
Pensacola Junior College *A*
St. Johns River Community College *A*

Georgia
Gainesville College *A*

Idaho
Idaho State University *A*

Illinois
Black Hawk College *A*
Morrison Institute of Technology *A*

Indiana
Indiana State University *A*
Vincennes University *A*

Iowa
Northwest Iowa Technical College *A*

Louisiana
McNeese State University *A*

Maine
Central Maine Technical College *C,A*

Michigan
Henry Ford Community College *C,A*
Macomb Community College *A*
Muskegon Community College *A*

Minnesota
Northwestern Electronics Institute *A*

Missouri
Ranken Technical College *A*

New Mexico
San Juan College *A*

New York
Community College of the Finger Lakes *A*
Monroe Community College *C,A*
Nassau Community College *A*

North Carolina
Cape Fear Community College *A*
Central Carolina Community College *A*

North Dakota
North Dakota State College of Science *A*

Ohio
Cuyahoga Community College: Metropolitan Campus *A*
Lorain County Community College *A*
Shawnee State University *A*

Oklahoma
National Education Center: Spartan School of Aeronautics Campus *A*
Oklahoma State University: Oklahoma City *A*

Pennsylvania
Butler County Community College *A*
Community College of Philadelphia *A*
Pennsylvania College of Technology *A*

Puerto Rico
University of Puerto Rico: Bayamon Technological University College *A*

Rhode Island
Community College of Rhode Island *C,A*

Tennessee
Chattanooga State Technical Community College *A*
Northeast State Technical Community College *A*

Texas
Amarillo College *A*
Brazosport College *C,A*
Eastfield College *A*
Kilgore College *A*
Lamar University—Beaumont *A*
Lee College *A*
San Jacinto College: Central Campus *A*
Texas State Technical College
Amarillo *A*
Harlingen *A*
Waco *A*
Victoria College *A*
Western Texas College *A*

Virginia
John Tyler Community College *A*
New River Community College *A*

Washington
Columbia Basin College *A*
Lower Columbia College *A*

Wisconsin
Mid-State Technical College *A*
Northeast Wisconsin Technical College *A*

Insurance marketing

Alabama
Chattahoochee Valley Community College *A*
Enterprise State Junior College *A*
Gadsden State Community College *C*
Jefferson State Community College *A*

California
City College of San Francisco *A*
Coastline Community College *A*
Fresno City College *C,A*
Long Beach City College *A*
Pasadena City College *A*

Florida
Broward Community College *A*

Illinois
Lake Land College *A*

Indiana
Ball State University *B*
Vincennes University *A*

Iowa
Des Moines Area Community College *C*

Kansas
Dodge City Community College *A*

Michigan
Lansing Community College *A*
Muskegon Community College *A*

New Jersey
County College of Morris *A*

New York
Erie Community College: South Campus *A*
Herkimer County Community College *A*
Mohawk Valley Community College *C*
New York Institute of Technology *A*
St. John Fisher College *C*
Sullivan County Community College *A*
Westchester Community College *C,A*

North Carolina
Central Piedmont Community College *A*
Isothermal Community College *A*

North Dakota
North Dakota State College of Science *A*

Oklahoma
Tulsa Junior College *C,A*

Pennsylvania
La Salle University *A,B*

Puerto Rico
Caribbean University *A*
Inter American University of Puerto Rico: Arecibo Campus *A*

Tennessee
Motlow State Community College *A*

Texas
Austin Community College *A*
Houston Community College *C*
McLennan Community College *A*

West Virginia
Fairmont State College *A*
Marshall University *A*

Wisconsin
Fox Valley Technical College *A*
Madison Area Technical College *A*

Insurance and risk management

Alabama
Lurleen B. Wallace State Junior College *C*
Samford University *B*
Shoals Community College *C*
University of Alabama *B*

Arizona
Arizona Western College *A*

Arkansas
University of Arkansas *B*

California
California State University
　　Fresno *B*
　　Sacramento *B*
Coastline Community College *A*
Fresno City College *C,A*
Merced College *A*
San Diego Mesa College *A*
San Diego State University *B*

Colorado
Pikes Peak Community College *A*

Connecticut
South Central Community
　　College *A*
University of Connecticut *B*
University of Hartford *B,M*

District of Columbia
Howard University *B*

Florida
Broward Community College *A*
Daytona Beach Community
　　College *C*
Florida Community College at
　　Jacksonville *A*
Florida International University *B*
Florida State University *B,M*
Miami-Dade Community College *C*
Seminole Community College *C*
University of Florida *B,M,D*
University of North Florida *B*

Georgia
Georgia Southern University *B*
Georgia State University *B,M,D*
Morehouse College *B*
University of Georgia *B,M*

Illinois
Illinois Wesleyan University *B*
William Rainey Harper College *A*

Indiana
Ball State University *B*
Indiana State University *B*
Indiana University Bloomington
　　B,D
Indiana University—Purdue
　　University at Indianapolis *B*
Martin University *B*
Vincennes University *A*

Iowa
Des Moines Area Community
　　College *A*
Drake University *B*
Northwest Iowa Technical
　　College *A*

Kansas
Dodge City Community College *A*
Hutchinson Community College *A*

Kentucky
Eastern Kentucky University *B*
Thomas More College *B*

Louisiana
Louisiana State University and
　　Agricultural and Mechanical
　　College *B*
Northeast Louisiana University *B*

Maine
Casco Bay College *C*

Massachusetts
Northeastern University *B*

Michigan
Ferris State University *B*
Lansing Community College *A*
Lawrence Technological
　　University *B*
Olivet College *B*
Western Michigan University *B*

Minnesota
Mankato State University *B*
St. Cloud State University *B*
Willmar Community College *C*

Mississippi
Delta State University *B*
Mississippi State University *B*
University of Mississippi *B*
University of Southern
　　Mississippi *B*

Missouri
University of Missouri: Columbia *B*

Nebraska
Metropolitan Community College *A*
University of Nebraska—Omaha *B*

New Jersey
Brookdale Community College *A*
Thomas Edison State College *A,B*

New Mexico
New Mexico State University *B*

New York
College of Insurance *A,B,M,W*
Columbia-Greene Community
　　College *A*
Erie Community College
　　City Campus *A*
　　South Campus *C,A*
Herkimer County Community
　　College *A*
Hudson Valley Community
　　College *A*
Mohawk Valley Community College
　　C,A
Nassau Community College *C*
Onondaga Community College *A*
Pace University *B*
Suffolk County Community College
　　Selden *A*
　　Western Campus *A*
Sullivan County Community
　　College *A*
Westchester Community College
　　C,A

North Carolina
Alamance Community College *C*
Appalachian State University *B*
Central Piedmont Community
　　College *A*
Edgecombe Community College *C*
Fayetteville Technical Community
　　College *A*
Southeastern Community College *C*
University of North Carolina at
　　Greensboro *B,M*

North Dakota
North Dakota State College of
　　Science *A*

Ohio
Ohio State University: Columbus
　　Campus *B*
University of Toledo *B*

Oklahoma
Rose State College *A*
University of Central Oklahoma *B*

Pennsylvania
Delaware County Community
　　College *A*
Northampton County Area
　　Community College *A*
Penn State University Park
　　Campus *B*
Temple University *B,M,D*
University of Pennsylvania *B,M,D*

South Carolina
University of South Carolina *B*

Tennessee
Martin Methodist College *A*
Memphis State University *B*
Motlow State Community
　　College *A*
Roane State Community College *A*

Texas
Baylor University *B*
University of North Texas *B,M*

Virginia
Piedmont Virginia Community
　　College *A*
University of Richmond *A*

Washington
Washington State University *B*

West Virginia
Fairmont State College *A*
Marshall University *A,B,M*

Wisconsin
Chippewa Valley Technical
　　College *A*
Madison Area Technical College *A*
University of Wisconsin: Madison
　　B,M,D

Interior design

Alabama
Alabama Agricultural and
　　Mechanical University *B*
Auburn University *B*
Judson College *B*
Samford University *B*
University of Alabama *B,M*
University of North Alabama *B*
Wallace State Community College
　　at Hanceville *A*

Alaska
University of Alaska Anchorage
　　C,A

Arizona
Arizona State University *B,M*
Northern Arizona University *B*
Pima Community College *C,A*
University of Arizona *B*

Arkansas
University of Arkansas *B*
University of Central Arkansas *C*

California
Academy of Art College *C,B,M,W*
Allan Hancock College *C,A*
American College for the Applied
　　Arts: Los Angeles *A,B*
Bakersfield College *A*
Brooks College *C,A*
California College of Arts and
　　Crafts *B*
California State Polytechnic
　　University: Pomona *M*
California State University
　　Fresno *B*
　　Long Beach *B*
　　Los Angeles *B*
　　Sacramento *B*
Cerritos Community College *A*
Chaffey Community College *C,A*
Chapman University *B,M*
City College of San Francisco *A*
College of the Desert *A*
College of Notre Dame *B*
Cosumnes River College *C,A*
El Camino College *A*
Fashion Institute of Design and
　　Merchandising
　　　　Los Angeles *A*
　　　　San Francisco *A*
Laney College *C,A*
Long Beach City College *C,A*
Los Angeles Harbor College *A*
Marymount College *A*
Monterey Peninsula College *C,A*
Mount San Antonio College *C,A*
Ohlone College *C,A*
Orange Coast College *C,A*
Pacific Union College *A,B*
Palomar College *C,A*
Saddleback College *A*
San Diego Mesa College *C*
San Joaquin Delta College *C,A*
San Jose State University *B*
Santa Monica College *A*
Sierra College *C*
Skyline College *A*
Solano Community College *A*
Southwestern College *C,A*
University of San Francisco *B*
Ventura College *A*
West Valley College *C,A*
Woodbury University *B*

Colorado
Arapahoe Community College *C,A*
Colorado Institute of Art *A*
Colorado State University *B,M*
Rocky Mountain College of Art &
　　Design *A,B*
University of Colorado at
　　Denver *M*

Connecticut
Paier College of Art *C,B*
Sacred Heart University *B*
Teikyo-Post University *C,A,B*
University of Bridgeport *B*
University of New Haven *C,A,B*

District of Columbia
Howard University *B*
Mount Vernon College *B*

Florida
Broward Community College *A*
Central Florida Community
　　College *A*
Daytona Beach Community College
　　C,A
Florida Community College at
　　Jacksonville *A*
Florida International University *B*
Florida State University *B,M*
Hillsborough Community College *A*
Indian River Community College *A*
International Fine Arts College *A*
Lynn University *B*
Manatee Community College *A*

Miami-Dade Community College *A*
National Education Center: Bauder
Campus *A,B*
New England Institute of
Technology *A*
Palm Beach Community College *A*
Ringling School of Art and
Design *A*
St. Petersburg Junior College *A*
Southern College *A*
University of Florida *B*

Georgia

American College for the Applied
Arts *A,B*
Atlanta College of Art *B*
Bauder College *A*
Brenau Women's College *B*
Georgia Southern University *B*
Savannah College of Art and
Design *B,M*
University of Georgia *B,M*

Hawaii

Chaminade University of
Honolulu *B*

Idaho

Ricks College *A*
University of Idaho *B*

Illinois

Black Hawk College *A*
Bradley University *B*
College of DuPage *C,A*
Columbia College *B*
Harrington Institute of Interior
Design *C,A,B*
Illinois Central College *A*
International Academy of
Merchandising and Design *A,B*
Joliet Junior College *A*
Prairie State College *A*
Ray College of Design *A,B*
Roosevelt University *B*
School of the Art Institute of
Chicago *B,M*
Southern Illinois University at
Carbondale *B*
Triton College *C,A*
University of Illinois at Urbana-
Champaign *B*
William Rainey Harper College *A*

Indiana

Ball State University *B*
Indiana State University *B*
Indiana University Bloomington
B,M
Indiana University—Purdue
University at Fort Wayne *A*
Indiana Vocational Technical
College
Kokomo *C,A*
Northcentral *A*
Southwest *C,A*
Marian College *B*
Purdue University *B*
Vincennes University *A*

Iowa

Drake University *B*
Hawkeye Institute of Technology *A*
Iowa State University *B*
Kirkwood Community College *A*
Scott Community College *A*
William Penn College *B*

Kansas

Coffeyville Community College *A*
Kansas State University *B,M*
McPherson College *B*

Pittsburg State University *B*
University of Kansas *B*

Kentucky

Eastern Kentucky University *A,B*
Louisville Technical Institute *A*
Murray State University *B*
University of Kentucky *B,M*
University of Louisville *B*

Louisiana

Louisiana State University and
Agricultural and Mechanical
College *B*
Louisiana Tech University *B,M*
University of Southwestern
Louisiana *B*

Maryland

Harford Community College *C,A*
Maryland Institute College of Art *B*
Montgomery College: Rockville
Campus *A*
University of Maryland
College Park *B*
Eastern Shore *B*

Massachusetts

Atlantic Union College *B*
Bay Path College *A*
Becker College: Worcester
Campus *A*
Boston Architectural Center *C*
Endicott College *A,B*
Lasell College *A*
Massachusetts Bay Community
College *C*
Mount Ida College *C,A*
Newbury College *A*
Pine Manor College *B*
University of Massachusetts at
Amherst *B,M*
Wentworth Institute of Technology
A,B

Michigan

Adrian College *B*
Andrews University *A*
Aquinas College *B*
Baker College
Flint *A*
Muskegon *A*
Owosso *A*
Center for Creative Studies: College
of Art and Design *B*
Delta College *A*
Eastern Michigan University *B*
Henry Ford Community College
C,A
Kendall College of Art and
Design *B*
Lansing Community College *A*
Lawrence Technological
University *B*
Michigan State University *B*
Northern Michigan University *B*
University of Michigan *B,M*
Wayne State University *B,M*
Western Michigan University *B*

Minnesota

Alexandria Technical College *A*
Mankato State University *B*
University of Minnesota: Twin
Cities *B*

Mississippi

Mississippi College *B*
Mississippi University for Women *B*
University of Mississippi *B*
University of Southern
Mississippi *B*

Missouri

Central Missouri State University *B*
Maryville University *C,B*
St. Louis Community College at
Meramec *A*
Southeast Missouri State
University *B*
William Woods College *B*

Montana

Montana State University *B*

Nebraska

Central Community College *A*
Chadron State College *B*
Metropolitan Community College *A*
University of Nebraska—Omaha *B*
Wayne State College *B*

Nevada

University of Nevada: Reno *B*

New Hampshire

Hesser College *A*

New Jersey

Berkeley College of Business *C,A*
Brookdale Community College *A*
Centenary College *A,B*
Kean College of New Jersey *B*
Trenton State College *B*

New York

Cazenovia College *A*
City University of New York: City
College *B*
Cornell University *B,M*
Fashion Institute of Technology *A,B*
Marymount College *C,B*
New York Institute of
Technology *B*
New York School of Interior
Design *C,A,B*
Onondaga Community College *A*
Pace University
College of White Plains *C*
New York *C*
Pleasantville/Briarcliff *C,A*
Parsons School of Design *A,B*
Pratt Institute *B,M*
Rochester Institute of Technology
C,A,B,M
Sage Junior College of Albany, A
Division of Russell Sage
College *A*
School of Visual Arts *B*
Suffolk County Community College
Eastern Campus *A*
Selden *A*
Syracuse University *B,M*
Villa Maria College of Buffalo *C,A*

North Carolina

Carteret Community College *A*
East Carolina University *B*
Meredith College *B*
Salem College *B*
University of North Carolina at
Greensboro *B,M*
Western Piedmont Community
College *A*

North Dakota

North Dakota State University *B,M*

Ohio

Antonelli Institute of Art and
Photography *C,A*
Ashland University *B*
Bowling Green State University *B*
Cleveland Institute of Art *B*
College of Mount St. Joseph *C,A,B*

Columbus College of Art and
Design *B*
Cuyahoga Community College:
Metropolitan Campus *A*
Davis Junior College of Business *A*
Kent State University *B*
Miami University: Oxford
Campus *B*
Ohio University *A,B*
Otterbein College *B*
University of Cincinnati *B*
University of Dayton *B*
Ursuline College *B*
Virginia Marti College of Fashion
and Art *A*

Oklahoma

East Central University *B*
Oklahoma Christian University of
Science and Arts *B*
Oklahoma State University *B,M*
Rogers State College *A*
University of Central Oklahoma
B,M
University of Oklahoma *B*

Oregon

Bassist College *A,B*
Marylhurst College *B*
Portland Community College *A*
University of Oregon *B,M*

Pennsylvania

Antonelli Institute of Art and
Photography *A*
Art Institute of Pittsburgh *A*
Beaver College *B*
Drexel University *B,M*
Harcum Junior College *A*
Indiana University of
Pennsylvania *B*
La Roche College *B*
Marywood College *B*
Mercyhurst College *B*
Moore College of Art and Design *B*
Northampton County Area
Community College *A*
Philadelphia College of Textiles and
Science *B*
Pittsburgh Technical Institute *C,A*
St. Vincent College *B*
Seton Hill College *C,B*
Spring Garden College *B*
University of the Arts *A*

Puerto Rico

University of Puerto Rico: Carolina
Regional College *A*

Rhode Island

Rhode Island School of Design *B*

South Carolina

Converse College *B*

South Dakota

South Dakota State University *B*

Tennessee

Carson-Newman College *B*
Lambuth University *B*
Middle Tennessee State
University *B*
O'More College of Design *B*
Tennessee Technological
University *B*
University of Tennessee: Knoxville
B,M

Texas

Abilene Christian University *B*
Bauder Fashion College *A*

Baylor University *B*
El Centro College *A*
El Paso Community College *C,A*
Houston Community College *C,A*
Incarnate Word College *B*
Lamar University—Beaumont *B*
Lubbock Christian University *B*
Miss Wade's Fashion
    Merchandising College *A*
North Harris Montgomery
    Community College District *A*
Richland College *A*
St. Philip's College *C,A*
Southwest Texas State University *B*
Stephen F. Austin State
    University *B*
Texas A&I University *B*
Texas Southmost College *A*
Texas State Technical College:
    Amarillo *A*
Texas Tech University *B*
Texas Woman's University *B,M*
University of North Texas *B,M*
University of Texas
    Arlington *B*
    Austin *B*
    San Antonio *B*

Utah

Brigham Young University *B*
Dixie College *C,A*
LDS Business College *A*
Weber State University *A*

Virginia

John Tyler Community College *C*
Marymount University *B,M*
Northern Virginia Community
    College *A*
Radford University *B*
Southern Seminary College *A*
Tidewater Community College *A*
Virginia Commonwealth
    University *B*
Virginia Polytechnic Institute and
    State University *B,M,D*

Washington

Art Institute of Seattle *A*
Bellevue Community College *A*
Cornish College of the Arts *B*
Seattle Pacific University *B*
Spokane Falls Community College
    C,A
Washington State University *B,M*
Western Washington University *B*

West Virginia

University of Charleston *A,B*
West Virginia University *B*

Wisconsin

Concordia University Wisconsin *B*
Fox Valley Technical College *A*
Madison Area Technical College *A*
Milwaukee College of Business *C,A*
Milwaukee Institute of Art &
    Design *B*
Mount Mary College *B*
University of Wisconsin
    Madison *B*
    Stevens Point *B*
Western Wisconsin Technical
    College *A*

International agriculture

Arkansas

University of Arkansas *B*

California

California State Polytechnic
    University: Pomona *B*
University of California: Davis *B,M*

Indiana

Purdue University *B,M,D*

Kansas

MidAmerica Nazarene College *B*

New Jersey

Rutgers—The State University of
    New Jersey: Cook College *B*

New York

Cornell University *B,M*

Utah

Utah State University *B*

Virginia

Eastern Mennonite College *B*

Wyoming

University of Wyoming *B*

International business management

Alabama

Auburn University *B*
Birmingham-Southern College *B*
Samford University *B*
Spring Hill College *B*
University of Alabama *B*

Alaska

Alaska Pacific University *B*
University of Alaska Fairbanks *B*

Arizona

American Graduate School of
    International Management *M*
Grand Canyon University *B*
Pima Community College *C,A*
Western International University
    B,M

Arkansas

Arkansas State University *B*
University of Central Arkansas *B*

California

Armstrong College *A,B,M*
Azusa Pacific University *M*
California State Polytechnic
    University: Pomona *B*
California State University
    Dominguez Hills *B*
    Fresno *B*
    Fullerton *B,M*
    Hayward *M*
    Long Beach *B*
    Los Angeles *B,M*
    Northridge *B*
    Sacramento *B*
Chapman University *B*
Christian Heritage College *B*
Claremont McKenna College *B*
Coastline Community College *A*
College of Notre Dame *B*

Dominican College of San Rafael *B*
Foothill College *A*
Golden Gate University *C,B,M*
Grossmont Community College *C,A*
John F. Kennedy University *M*
Lincoln University *B,M*
Long Beach City College *A*
Los Angeles City College *C*
Monterey Institute of International
    Studies *M*
Mount St. Mary's College *B*
Oxnard College *C*
Pepperdine University *M*
St. Mary's College of California *M*
San Francisco State University *B,M*
San Jose State University *B*
Santa Clara University *B*
Scripps College *B*
United States International
    University *B,M,D*
University of La Verne *B*
University of the Pacific *B*
University of San Diego *M*
University of San Francisco *B,M*
West Coast University *C,M*
Woodbury University *B,M*
World College West *B*

Colorado

Arapahoe Community College *C,A*
Fort Lewis College *B*
Parks Junior College *A*
Regis College of Regis University *B*
University of Colorado
    Boulder *B*
    Denver *B*
University of Denver *B,M*

Connecticut

Quinnipiac College *B,M*
Sacred Heart University *B*
Teikyo-Post University *B*
University of Bridgeport *B*
University of New Haven *B,M*
Yale University *M*

Delaware

Goldey-Beacom College *B*

District of Columbia

American University *B,M*
George Washington University *B,M*
Georgetown University *B*
Howard University *B*
Southeastern University *B,M*

Florida

Brevard Community College *A*
Broward Community College *A*
Eckerd College *B*
Florida Atlantic University *B*
Florida International University
    B,M
Florida Southern College *B*
Florida State University *B*
Fort Lauderdale College *A,B*
Jacksonville University *B,M*
Lynn University *B*
Nova University *D*
Palm Beach Atlantic College *B*
St. Thomas University *B*
Schiller International University
    A,B
Tampa College *M*
University of Miami *B*
University of Tampa *B,M*

Georgia

Georgia State University *M,D*
South Georgia College *C*
University of Georgia *B,M*

Hawaii

Hawaii Pacific University *B,M*
University of Hawaii
    Manoa *B*
    West Oahu *B*

Idaho

Albertson College *B*

Illinois

Augustana College *B*
Barat College *B*
Bradley University *B*
College of DuPage *C*
De Paul University *M*
Elmhurst College *B*
Illinois Benedictine College *B*
Illinois Central College *A*
Illinois State University *B*
Millikin University *B*
National-Louis University *C*
North Central College *B*
North Park College and Theological
    Seminary *B*
Northwestern University *M*
Oakton Community College *C,A*
Rock Valley College *A*
Roosevelt University *M*
Rosary College *B*
St. Xavier University *B,M*
Southern Illinois University at
    Carbondale *B*
Triton College *A*
University of Chicago *M,D*
William Rainey Harper College *C*

Indiana

Ball State University *B*
Franklin College *B*
Indiana University Bloomington
    M,D
St. Joseph's College *B*
University of Evansville *B*
University of Indianapolis *B*
University of Notre Dame *B*
Vincennes University *A*

Iowa

Central College *B*
Cornell College *B*
Drake University *B*
Kirkwood Community College *A*
Loras College *B*
Luther College *B*
Morningside College *B*
Simpson College *B*
Teikyo Marycrest University *B*
Teikyo Westmar University *B*
Wartburg College *B*

Kansas

Baker University *B*
Friends University *B*
Southwestern College *B*
Wichita State University *B*

Louisiana

Grambling State University *M*
Louisiana State University and
    Agricultural and Mechanical
    College *B*
Loyola University *B*

Maine

St. Joseph's College *B*

Maryland

Howard Community College *A*
Loyola College in Maryland *M*
Montgomery College
    Rockville Campus *A*
    Takoma Park Campus *A*

Morgan State University *B*
University of Maryland University
College *M*

Massachusetts
American International College *B*
Assumption College *B*
Babson College *B,M*
Boston University *B*
Bunker Hill Community College *A*
Elms College *B*
Fisher College *A*
Harvard University *M,D*
Massachusetts Institute of
Technology *M,D*
Merrimack College *B*
Middlesex Community College *C*
Northeastern University *C,B*
Pine Manor College *B*
Simmons College *B*

Michigan
Adrian College *A,B*
Alma College *B*
Aquinas College *B*
Eastern Michigan University *B*
Ferris State University *B*
Hillsdale College *B*
Lansing Community College *A*
Madonna University *B,M*
Michigan State University *M*
Oakland Community College *A*
University of Michigan
Ann Arbor *D*
Dearborn *B*
Western Michigan University *B*

Minnesota
Augsburg College *B*
Bethel College *B*
College of St. Catherine: St.
Catherine Campus *B*
College of St. Scholastica *B*
Concordia College: Moorhead *B*
Gustavus Adolphus College *B*
Hamline University *B*
Mankato State University *B*
Moorhead State University *B*
Northland Community College *A*
Northwestern College *B*
St. Cloud State University *B*
St. Mary's College of Minnesota *B*
University of St. Thomas *B,M*
Willmar Community College *A*

Mississippi
University of Mississippi *B*

Missouri
Avila College *B,M*
Fontbonne College *B*
Lindenwood College *M*
Northwest Missouri State
University *B*
Park College *B*
St. Louis Community College at
Forest Park *C,A*
St. Louis University *B,M*
Webster University *M*
Westminster College *B*

Nebraska
University of Nebraska—Lincoln *B*
Wayne State College *B*

Nevada
Community College of Southern
Nevada *C*

New Hampshire
Franklin Pierce College *B*
New England College *B*

New Hampshire College *B,M*

New Jersey
Brookdale Community College *A*
Fairleigh Dickinson University *M*
Monmouth College *B*
Ramapo College of New Jersey *B*
Thomas Edison State College *A,B*
Upsala College *B*
William Paterson College of New
Jersey *B*

New Mexico
New Mexico State University *B*
University of New Mexico *B,M*
Western New Mexico University *B*

New York
Alfred University *B*
Canisius College *C*
City University of New York:
Baruch College *M*
College of Mount St. Vincent *B*
Cornell University *M,D*
Dominican College of Blauvelt *B*
Elmira College *B*
Erie Community College: City
Campus *A*
Fordham University *M*
Hofstra University *B,M*
Hudson Valley Community
College *A*
Ithaca College *B*
Long Island University: C. W. Post
Campus *M*
Manhattan College *B*
Marymount College *B*
New York University *B,M,D*
Niagara University *B*
Pace University
College of White Plains *B*
New York *B,M*
Pleasantville/Briarcliff *B*
Rochester Institute of Technology
C,B,M
St. John Fisher College *B*
State University of New York
Buffalo *D*
College at Brockport *B*
College at Geneseo *B*
College at Plattsburgh *B*
Syracuse University *M*
University of the State of New
York: Regents College *B*

North Carolina
Campbell University *B*
Catawba College *B*
Central Piedmont Community
College *A*
High Point University *B*
Lenoir-Rhyne College *B*
Mars Hill College *B*
North Carolina State University *B*
Queens College *B*
St. Andrews Presbyterian College *B*
Salem College *B*

Ohio
Baldwin-Wallace College *M*
Bowling Green State University *B*
Cedarville College *B*
Heidelberg College *B*
Hiram College *B*
Kent State University *M*
Lake Erie College *B*
Marietta College *B*
Mount Union College *B*
Muskingum College *B*
Notre Dame College of Ohio *B*
Ohio Dominican College *B*

Ohio State University: Columbus
Campus *B*
Ohio University *B*
Ohio Wesleyan University *B*
Tiffin University *B*
Union Institute *D*
University of Akron *B*
University of Rio Grande *B*
University of Toledo *B,M*
Wittenberg University *B*
Wright State University *M*

Oklahoma
Oklahoma City University *B,M*
Oklahoma State University:
Oklahoma City *A*
Oral Roberts University *B*
Tulsa Junior College *A*

Oregon
Concordia College *B*
Linfield College *B*
Mount Hood Community
College *A*
Oregon State University *B*
Portland State University *C,M*

Pennsylvania
Albright College *B*
Carnegie Mellon University *B,M,D*
Cedar Crest College *C*
Chatham College *B*
Community College of
Philadelphia *A*
Drexel University *M*
Duquesne University *B,M*
Gannon University *B*
Gettysburg College *B*
Grove City College *B*
Holy Family College *B*
King's College *B*
Kutztown University of
Pennsylvania *B*
La Roche College *B*
Lebanon Valley College of
Pennsylvania *B*
Marywood College *B,M*
Mercyhurst College *B*
Moravian College *B*
Penn State University Park
Campus *B*
Philadelphia College of Textiles and
Science *B,M*
St. Francis College *B*
Seton Hill College *B*
Temple University *B,M,D*
Thiel College *B*
University of Pennsylvania *B,M,D*
Villanova University *B*
Westminster College *B*
Widener University *C*

Rhode Island
Bryant College *B*
Johnson & Wales University *M*

South Carolina
Converse College *B*
Newberry College *B*
University of South Carolina *M*

South Dakota
Northern State University *B*

Tennessee
Bristol University *A,B,M*
Memphis State University *B*
Rhodes College *B*
University of Tennessee
Knoxville *B*
Martin *B*

Texas
Abilene Christian University *B*
Baylor University *B,M*
Dallas Baptist University *M*
El Paso Community College *C,A*
Houston Community College *C*
Incarnate Word College *B*
Laredo Junior College *A*
Laredo State University *M*
Richland College *C,A*
St. Mary's University *B,M*
Sam Houston State University *B*
Sul Ross State University *M*
Texas Tech University *B*
Texas Wesleyan University *B*
University of Dallas *M*
University of St. Thomas *M*
University of Texas
Dallas *M,D*
San Antonio *M*

Utah
Brigham Young University *B*

Virginia
Christopher Newport College *B*
James Madison University *B*
Lynchburg College *B*
Marymount University *B*
Old Dominion University *B*
University of Richmond *B*
Virginia Wesleyan College *B*

Washington
Edmonds Community College *A*
Everett Community College *C*
Gonzaga University *B*
Pacific Lutheran University *B*
St. Martin's College *B*
Seattle University *B*
Shoreline Community College *C,A*
Washington State University *B*
Whitworth College *B*

West Virginia
Bethany College *B*
Davis and Elkins College *B*
Glenville State College *B*

Wisconsin
Cardinal Stritch College *B*
Carthage College *B*
Lakeland College *B*
Marquette University *B*
Northland College *B*
Ripon College *B*
St. Norbert College *B*
University of Wisconsin
Madison *M*
Oshkosh *B*
Waukesha County Technical
College *A*

Canada
McGill University *B,M,D*

France
American University of Paris *B*

Switzerland
American College of Switzerland *B*
Franklin College: Switzerland *B*

Arab Republic of Egypt
American University in Cairo *M*

International and comparative education

California
California State University: San Bernardino *M*
University of Southern California *D*
World College West *B*

District of Columbia
American University *M*
George Washington University *M*
Howard University *M*

Florida
Eckerd College *B*
Florida International University *M*

Illinois
Loyola University of Chicago *M*
Northwestern University *D*

Indiana
Indiana University Bloomington *M*
Vincennes University *A*

Massachusetts
Boston University *M*
Hampshire College *B*

Nebraska
Doane College *B*

New York
New York University *M,D*
State University of New York
　Albany *M,D*
　Buffalo *M,D*

Ohio
Union Institute *D*

Pennsylvania
Lock Haven University of
　Pennsylvania *B*

Puerto Rico
University of the Sacred Heart *B*

Canada
McGill University *M*

International/comparative home economics

Illinois
KAES College *B*

Iowa
Iowa State University *B*

Ohio
Ohio State University: Columbus
　Campus *B,M,D*

International development

California
University of California: Davis *B,M*
World College West *B*

Connecticut
Sacred Heart University *B*

District of Columbia
American University *M*

Kansas
Bethel College *B*

Kentucky
University of Kentucky *M*

Massachusetts
Clark University *B,M*
Hampshire College *B*

Missouri
Washington University *B,M*

New York
Fordham University *B*

North Carolina
Duke University *M*

Rhode Island
Bryant College *B*

International public service

Arizona
Cochise College *A*

California
University of the Pacific *B*
University of Southern California *M*
World College West *B*

Connecticut
Sacred Heart University *B*

District of Columbia
Catholic University of America *B*

Florida
Miami-Dade Community College *A*

Illinois
Southern Illinois University at
　Carbondale *B*
University of Chicago *M,D*

Massachusetts
Bridgewater State College *B*

Michigan
University of Detroit Mercy *M*

Minnesota
Winona State University *B*

New Jersey
Princeton University *B,M,D*

New York
Cornell University *M*

Ohio
Ohio University *B*

Oklahoma
University of Central Oklahoma *M*

Oregon
University of Oregon: Robert
　Donald Clark Honors College *B*

Pennsylvania
Carnegie Mellon University *M,D,W*
Lincoln University *B*
Penn State University Park
　Campus *B*
University of Pittsburgh *M*

South Dakota
Augustana College *B*

Texas
Baylor University *B*
Texas Tech University *B*

Vermont
Marlboro College *B*
School for International Training *M*

Virginia
Christopher Newport College *B*
Virginia Wesleyan College *B*

International relations

Alabama
Samford University *B*
Spring Hill College *B*
University of Alabama *B*

Arizona
Glendale Community College *A*
Northern Arizona University *B*

Arkansas
Hendrix College *B*

California
Allan Hancock College *A*
California State University
　Bakersfield *B*
　Chico *B*
　Fresno *M*
　Sacramento *M*
　Stanislaus *B,M*
Claremont McKenna College *B*
Dominican College of San Rafael
　B,M
Golden Gate University *M*
Holy Names College *B*
Mills College *B*
Monterey Institute of International
　Studies *B,M*
Occidental College *B*
Pepperdine University *B*
Pitzer College *B*
Pomona College *B*
San Francisco State University *B,M*
Santa Barbara City College *A*
Santa Monica College *A*
Scripps College *B*
Stanford University *B*
United States International
　University *B,M*
University of California
　Davis *B,M*
　San Diego *D*
　Santa Barbara *B*
University of La Verne *B*
University of the Pacific *B*
University of Redlands *B*
University of San Diego *B,M*
University of Southern California
　B,M,D
Westmont College *B*
Whittier College *B*
World College West *B*

Colorado
United States Air Force
　Academy *B*
University of Colorado at
　Boulder *B*

Connecticut
Connecticut College *B*
Sacred Heart University *B*
Wesleyan University *B*
Yale University *B,M*

Delaware
University of Delaware *B,M*

District of Columbia
American University *B,M,D*
George Washington University *B,M*
Georgetown University *B,M*
Mount Vernon College *B*
Trinity College *B*

Florida
Barry University *B*
Eckerd College *B*
Florida International University
　B,M
Florida State University *B,M*
Jacksonville University *B*
Miami-Dade Community College *A*
New College of the University of
　South Florida *B*
Nova University *B*
Rollins College *B*
St. Thomas University *B*
Schiller International University *B*
University of Florida *M,D*
University of Miami *M,D*
University of South Florida *B*
University of West Florida *B*

Georgia
Agnes Scott College *B*
Emory University *B*
Georgia Institute of Technology *B*
Kennesaw State College *B*
Oglethorpe University *B*
Wesleyan College *B*

Hawaii
Hawaii Loa College *B*
Hawaii Pacific University *B*

Idaho
Idaho State University *B*
Northwest Nazarene College *B*

Illinois
Augustana College *B*
Bradley University *B*
College of St. Francis *B*
De Paul University *B*
Illinois College *B*
Knox College *B*
Lake Forest College *B*
McKendree College *B*
Millikin University *B*
North Central College *B*
North Park College and Theological
　Seminary *B*
Northwestern University *B*
Roosevelt University *B*
St. Xavier University *B*
Southern Illinois University at
　Carbondale *B*
University of Chicago *M,D*

Indiana
Butler University *B*
Earlham College *B*
St. Joseph's College *B*
University of Evansville *B*

University of Notre Dame *B,M,D*

Iowa

Central College *B*
Cornell College *B*
Drake University *B*
Grinnell College *B*
Simpson College *B*

Kansas

Tabor College *B*

Louisiana

Tulane University *M*

Maine

Colby College *B*
University of Maine
    Farmington *B*
    Orono *B*

Maryland

College of Notre Dame of
    Maryland *B*
Goucher College *B*
Johns Hopkins University *B,M*
Washington College *B*

Massachusetts

American International College *B*
Assumption College *B*
Boston University *B,M*
Bradford College *B*
Bridgewater State College *B*
Clark University *B*
Elms College *B*
Emmanuel College *B*
Hampshire College *B*
Harvard University *D*
Massachusetts Institute of
    Technology *B,M,D*
Mount Holyoke College *B*
Northern Essex Community
    College *A*
Simmons College *B*
Tufts University *B,M,D*
University of Massachusetts at
    Boston *C*
Wellesley College *B*
Wheaton College *B*

Michigan

Alma College *B*
Aquinas College *B*
Grand Valley State University *B*
University of Detroit Mercy *M*

Minnesota

Augsburg College *B*
Bethel College *B*
College of St. Catherine: St.
    Catherine Campus *B*
Concordia College: Moorhead *B*
Hamline University *B*
Mankato State University *B*
St. Cloud State University *B*
University of Minnesota: Twin
    Cities *B*
Willmar Community College *A*
Winona State University *B*

Missouri

Rockhurst College *B*
Webster University *B,M*
Westminster College *B*
William Jewell College *B*

Montana

Carroll College *B*

Nebraska

Creighton University *B,M*
University of Nebraska
    Lincoln *B*
    Omaha *B*

New Hampshire

New England College *B*

New Jersey

Caldwell College *C*
Drew University *M*
Fairleigh Dickinson University *B*
Princeton University *B,D*

New Mexico

New Mexico State University *B*

New York

Bard College *B*
Canisius College *B*
City University of New York
    City College *B,M*
    Hunter College *B*
Colgate University *B*
College of Mount St. Vincent *B*
College of New Rochelle *B*
Columbia University *M*
Cornell University *M,D*
Elmira College *B*
Eugene Lang College/New School
    for Social Research *B*
Fordham University *B*
Hamilton College *B*
Iona College *B*
Manhattan College *B*
Manhattanville College *B*
Marymount College *B*
Marymount Manhattan College *B*
Mohawk Valley Community
    College *A*
New York University *B,M,D*
Niagara University *B*
Sarah Lawrence College *B*
State University of New York
    College at New Paltz *B*
Syracuse University *B,M,D*
United States Military Academy *B*
Vassar College *B*

North Carolina

Catawba College *B*
Lenoir-Rhyne College *B*
St. Andrews Presbyterian College *B*
Salem College *B*
University of North Carolina at
    Chapel Hill *B,M,D*

Ohio

Capital University *B*
Central State University *B*
College of Wooster *B*
Heidelberg College *B*
Kent State University *B*
Miami University: Oxford
    Campus *B*
Muskingum College *B*
Ohio Northern University *B*
Ohio State University: Columbus
    Campus *B*
Ohio University *B,M*
Ohio Wesleyan University *B*
Otterbein College *B*
Union Institute *B,D*
University of Cincinnati *B*
University of Dayton *B*
University of Toledo *B*
Wittenberg University *B*
Xavier University *B*

Oklahoma

Northwestern Oklahoma State
    University *M*

Oregon

George Fox College *B*
Lewis and Clark College *B*
Pacific University *B*
Reed College *B*
Southern Oregon State College *B*
University of Oregon: Robert
    Donald Clark Honors College *B*

Pennsylvania

Albright College *B*
Bryn Mawr College *B*
Bucknell University *B*
California University of
    Pennsylvania *B*
Carnegie Mellon University *B,M*
Chatham College *B*
Gettysburg College *B*
Immaculata College *B*
Indiana University of Pennsylvania
    B,M
Juniata College *B*
Lafayette College *B*
Lehigh University *B*
Lock Haven University of
    Pennsylvania *B*
Lycoming College *B*
Muhlenberg College *B*
St. Francis College *B*
St. Joseph's University *B*
Swarthmore College *B*
University of Pennsylvania *B,M,D*
University of Scranton *B*
Ursinus College *B*
West Chester University of
    Pennsylvania *B*
Westminster College *B*
York College of Pennsylvania *B*

Rhode Island

Brown University *B*
Salve Regina University *M*

South Carolina

Morris College *B*
Newberry College *B*
University of South Carolina *B,M,D*

South Dakota

Augustana College *B*

Tennessee

Belmont University *B*
Lambuth University *B*
Memphis State University *B*
Middle Tennessee State
    University *B*

Texas

Angelo State University *M*
Austin College *B*
Baylor University *M*
El Paso Community College *A*
St. Mary's University *B,M*
Southwest Texas State University *B*
Southwestern Adventist College *B*
Sul Ross State University *M*
University of St. Thomas *B*

Utah

Brigham Young University *B,M*

Vermont

Bennington College *B*
Marlboro College *B*
Norwich University *B*

Virginia

Bridgewater College *B*
Christopher Newport College *B*
College of William and Mary *B*
Ferrum College *B*
George Mason University *B*
James Madison University *B*
Lynchburg College *B*
Mary Baldwin College *B*
Mary Washington College *B*
Old Dominion University *B,M*
Randolph-Macon College *B*
Randolph-Macon Woman's
    College *B*
Roanoke College *B*
Sweet Briar College *B*
University of Virginia *B,M,D*
Virginia Polytechnic Institute and
    State University *B*
Virginia State University *B*
Virginia Wesleyan College *B*

Washington

Eastern Washington University *B*
Pacific Lutheran University *B*
Whitworth College *B*

West Virginia

Marshall University *B*
Wheeling Jesuit College *B*

Wisconsin

Beloit College *B*
Carroll College *B*
St. Norbert College *B*
University of Wisconsin
    Madison *B*
    Milwaukee *B*
    Oshkosh *B*
    Whitewater *B*

Wyoming

University of Wyoming *B,M*

Canada

McGill University *B,M,D*

France

American University of Paris *B*

Mexico

Sistema Instituto Tecnologico y de
    Estudios Superiores de
    Monterrey *B*

Switzerland

American College of Switzerland *B*
Franklin College: Switzerland *A,B*

International studies

Alabama

Auburn University at
    Montgomery *B*
Spring Hill College *B*
Stillman College *B*
Troy State University at Dothan *M*
University of Alabama
    Birmingham *B*
    Tuscaloosa *B*
University of Montevallo *B*
University of South Alabama *B*

Arizona

Glendale Community College *A*
Prescott College *B*

Arkansas

Harding University *B*
University of Arkansas at Little
Rock *B*

California

Allan Hancock College *A*
Azusa Pacific University *B*
California Lutheran University *B*
California State University
Long Beach *B*
San Bernardino *M*
Claremont McKenna College *B*
Dominican College of San Rafael
B,M
Occidental College *B*
Pomona College *B*
Santa Barbara City College *A*
Scripps College *B*
Stanford University *M*
University of California: Davis *B*
University of La Verne *B*
University of the Pacific *B*
World College West *B*

Colorado

Fort Lewis College *B*
United States Air Force
Academy *B*
University of Colorado at Denver *B*
University of Denver *M,D*
University of Northern Colorado *B*

Connecticut

Central Connecticut State
University *M*
Connecticut College *C*
Sacred Heart University *B*
University of Connecticut *M*

District of Columbia

Gallaudet University *B*
George Washington University *B,M*
Mount Vernon College *B*
Trinity College *B*

Florida

Barry University *B*
Eckerd College *B*
Jacksonville University *B*
New College of the University of
South Florida *B*
Nova University *B*
Rollins College *B*
St. Leo College *B*
Schiller International University *B*
University of Miami *B*
University of West Florida *B*

Georgia

Emory University *B*
Floyd College *A*
Kennesaw State College *B*
Morehouse College *B*
Oglethorpe University *B*
University of Georgia *B*

Hawaii

Chaminade University of
Honolulu *B*
Hawaii Pacific University *B*

Idaho

Idaho State University *B*
Lewis Clark State College *B*
Northwest Nazarene College *B*
University of Idaho *B*

Illinois

Bradley University *B*
De Paul University *B*
KAES College *B*

Millikin University *B*
North Park College and Theological
Seminary *B*
Northwestern University *B*
Quincy College *B*
Roosevelt University *B*
St. Xavier University *B*
Southern Illinois University at
Carbondale *B*

Indiana

Butler University *B*
DePauw University *B*
Earlham College *B*
Hanover College *B*
Indiana State University *B*
Purdue University *B*
St. Joseph's College *B*
Taylor University *B*
University of Evansville *B*
University of Notre Dame *B*
Valparaiso University *B*

Iowa

Central College *B*
Coe College *B*
Graceland College *B*
Grinnell College *B*
Luther College *B*

Kansas

Bethel College *B*
Tabor College *B*

Kentucky

Georgetown College *B*
Northern Kentucky University *B*
Thomas More College *A,B*

Maine

University of Maine at
Farmington *B*

Maryland

Bowie State University *B*
Catonsville Community College *A*
Frostburg State University *B*
Goucher College *B*
Johns Hopkins University *B*
Morgan State University *B,M*
Mount St. Mary's College *B*
Towson State University *B*
Washington College *B*

Massachusetts

Bradford College *B*
Elms College *B*
Emmanuel College *B*
Hampshire College *B*
Lesley College *M*
Massachusetts Bay Community
College *A*
Northern Essex Community
College *A*
Stonehill College *B*

Michigan

Adrian College *A,B*
Kalamazoo College *B*
Kalamazoo Valley Community
College *C,A*
Northern Michigan University *B*
University of Michigan
Ann Arbor *B*
Dearborn *B*

Minnesota

College of St. Catherine: St.
Catherine Campus *B*
Concordia College: Moorhead *B*
Macalester College *B*

University of Minnesota
Duluth *B*
Twin Cities *B*
Winona State University *A*

Mississippi

University of Southern
Mississippi *B*

Missouri

Lindenwood College *B*
Rockhurst College *B*
Webster University *B*
Westminster College *B*
William Woods College *B*

Nebraska

Dana College *B*
Doane College *B*
Nebraska Wesleyan University *B*
Southeast Community College:
Beatrice Campus *A*
University of Nebraska—Kearney *B*
Wayne State College *B*

Nevada

University of Nevada: Reno *B*

New Hampshire

University of New Hampshire *B*

New Jersey

Centenary College *B*
County College of Morris *A*
Fairleigh Dickinson University *B*
Princeton University *B,M,D*
Ramapo College of New Jersey *B*
Union County College *A*

New York

Bard College *B*
City University of New York
College of Staten Island *B*
Hunter College *B*
Colgate University *B*
College of New Rochelle *B*
Concordia College *B*
Eugene Lang College/New School
for Social Research *B*
Fordham University *B*
Houghton College *B*
Iona College *B*
Long Island University: C. W. Post
Campus *B*
Manhattan College *B*
Manhattanville College *B*
Marymount College *B*
Mohawk Valley Community
College *A*
New York University *C,B,M,D*
Niagara University *B*
Nyack College *B*
Pace University: Pleasantville/
Briarcliff *B*
Russell Sage College *B*
St. John Fisher College *B*
Sarah Lawrence College *B*
Skidmore College *B*
State University of New York
College at Brockport *B*
College at Cortland *B*
College at Fredonia *B*
United States Military Academy *B*
Utica College of Syracuse
University *B*
Vassar College *B*

North Carolina

Campbell University *B*
High Point University *B*
Mars Hill College *B*
Meredith College *B*

Methodist College *A,B*
St. Andrews Presbyterian College *B*
Salem College *B*
Shaw University *B*
University of North Carolina at
Chapel Hill *B*
Warren Wilson College *B*

North Dakota

University of North Dakota *B*

Ohio

Antioch College *B*
Ashland University *B*
Baldwin-Wallace College *B*
Bowling Green State University *B*
Capital University *B*
Denison University *B*
Heidelberg College *B*
John Carroll University *C*
Kent State University *B*
Kenyon College *B*
Miami University: Oxford
Campus *B*
Muskingum College *B*
Ohio State University: Columbus
Campus *B,M,D*
Ohio University *B,M*
Otterbein College *B*
Union Institute *B,D*
University of Akron: Wayne
College *A*
University of Cincinnati *B*
University of Dayton *B*
University of Rio Grande *B*
University of Toledo *B*
Walsh College *B*
Wittenberg University *B*
Wright State University *B*

Oklahoma

Phillips University *B*
University of Tulsa *B*

Oregon

George Fox College *B*
Pacific University *B*
Portland Community College *C*
Portland State University *B*
Southern Oregon State College *B*
Western Oregon State College *B*
Willamette University *B*

Pennsylvania

Albright College *B*
Allegheny College *B*
Bucknell University *B*
California University of
Pennsylvania *B*
Dickinson College *B*
Drexel University *B*
Elizabethtown College *B*
Gannon University *B*
Gettysburg College *B*
Juniata College *B*
Lafayette College *B*
Lehigh University *B*
Lock Haven University of
Pennsylvania *B,M*
Lycoming College *B*
Millersville University of
Pennsylvania *B*
Muhlenberg College *B*
Susquehanna University *B*
University of Pennsylvania *M*
University of Pittsburgh at
Johnstown *C*
University of Scranton *B*
Wilkes University *B*
Wilson College *B*
York College of Pennsylvania *B*

Rhode Island
Brown University *B*
Salve Regina University *M*

South Carolina
University of South Carolina at
Spartanburg *B*

Tennessee
Maryville College *B*
Rhodes College *B*

Texas
Abilene Christian University *B*
St. Edward's University *B*
Southern Methodist University *B*
Southwest Texas State University *B*
Southwestern University *B*
Texas Wesleyan University *B*
University of Houston *M*
University of St. Thomas *B*

Utah
Brigham Young University *B,M*

Vermont
Marlboro College *B*
Middlebury College *B*
School for International Training *B*

Virginia
College of William and Mary *B*
George Mason University *B*
Lynchburg College *B*
Mary Baldwin College *B*
Northern Virginia Community
College *C,A*
Old Dominion University *M*
Randolph-Macon College *B*
University of Richmond *B*
Virginia Military Institute *B*
Virginia Polytechnic Institute and
State University *B*
Virginia State University *B*
Virginia Wesleyan College *B*

Washington
Eastern Washington University *B*
Edmonds Community College *A*
Evergreen State College *B*
Seattle University *B*
University of Washington *B,M*
Whitworth College *B*

West Virginia
Marshall University *B*
West Virginia University *B*
West Virginia Wesleyan College *B*
Wheeling Jesuit College *B*

Wisconsin
Beloit College *B*
Lawrence University *B*
Marquette University *B*
St. Norbert College *B*
University of Wisconsin
Milwaukee *B*
Parkside *B*
Platteville *B*
Whitewater *B*

Switzerland
American College of Switzerland *B*

Interpreter for the deaf

Arizona
Pima Community College *C,A*

Arkansas
University of Arkansas at Little
Rock *A*

California
College of the Sequoias *A*
Golden West College *C,A*
Los Angeles Pierce College *A*
Modesto Junior College *A*
Mount San Antonio College *C,A*
Ohlone College *C,A*
Palomar College *C,A*
Saddleback College *C,A*
San Diego Mesa College *C,A*

Colorado
Front Range Community College *A*

Connecticut
Northwestern Connecticut
Community College *C,A*

District of Columbia
Gallaudet University *M*

Florida
Hillsborough Community College *A*

Georgia
DeKalb College *A*
Floyd College *A*

Illinois
Lewis and Clark Community
College *A*
Waubonsee Community College
C,A
William Rainey Harper College *C*

Iowa
Iowa Western Community
College *A*

Kansas
Johnson County Community
College *A*

Kentucky
Eastern Kentucky University *A,B*

Louisiana
World Evangelism Bible College
and Seminary *C*

Maryland
Catonsville Community College *C*

Massachusetts
Northeastern University *C*
Northern Essex Community College
C,A

Michigan
Charles Stewart Mott Community
College *C,A*
Lansing Community College *A*
Madonna University *C,A,B*

Minnesota
Inver Hills Community College *A*
Itasca Community College:
Arrowhead Region *A*
St. Paul Technical College *C,A*

Missouri
St. Louis Community College at
Florissant Valley *A*
William Woods College *A*

Nebraska
Metropolitan Community College *C*

New Hampshire
University of New Hampshire at
Manchester *B*

New Jersey
Union County College *A*

New Mexico
University of New Mexico *B*

New York
Nassau Community College *A*
Onondaga Community College *A*
Rochester Institute of Technology
C,A
Suffolk County Community
College *A*

North Carolina
Central Piedmont Community
College *A*
Gardner-Webb College *A*

Ohio
Columbus State Community
College *A*
Sinclair Community College *A*
Terra Technical College *A*
University of Akron *A*

Oklahoma
Oklahoma State University:
Oklahoma City *C,A*
Tulsa Junior College *C,A*

Oregon
Portland Community College *C,A*
Western Oregon State College *C*

Pennsylvania
Bloomsburg University of
Pennsylvania *B*
Community College of Philadelphia
C,A
Mount Aloysius College *A*

South Dakota
Kilian Community College *A*

Tennessee
Chattanooga State Technical
Community College *C,A*
Maryville College *B*

Texas
Austin Community College *A*
El Paso Community College *C,A*
Houston Community College *C,A*
Lamar University—Beaumont *B*
Lee College *C*
McLennan Community College *A*
Tarrant County Junior College *A*

Virginia
New River Community College *C*

Washington
Seattle Central Community College
C,A
Spokane Falls Community
College *A*

Investments and securities

Alabama
University of Alabama *B*

California
California State University
Fresno *B*
Hayward *B,M*
Los Angeles *B*
Chabot College *A*
Golden Gate University *M*
Southwestern College *A*
University of San Francisco *B*

Colorado
Red Rocks Community College *C*

Connecticut
Quinnipiac College *B,M*
University of Bridgeport *B*

District of Columbia
George Washington University *M*

Illinois
De Paul University *M*
Northwestern University *M*
Oakton Community College *C,A*
Southern Illinois University at
Carbondale *B*
University of Chicago *M,D*

Iowa
Drake University *B*

Kansas
Dodge City Community College *A*

Kentucky
Eastern Kentucky University *B*

Massachusetts
Babson College *B,M*
Harvard University *M*
Nichols College *B*

Michigan
Eastern Michigan University *B*

Minnesota
Mankato State University *B*

Nebraska
York College *A*

New York
City University of New York:
Baruch College *B,M*
Clarkson University *B*
Pace University *M*
Westchester Business Institute *A*

Ohio
Kent State University *M*
University of Cincinnati *B*
University of Toledo *B*

Pennsylvania
Bucknell University *B*
Carnegie Mellon University *M,D,W*
Drexel University *B,M*
Duquesne University *B*
Lehigh University *M*
Robert Morris College *M*

Rhode Island
Bryant College *M*
Johnson & Wales University *A*

Virginia
Marymount University *B,M*

Wisconsin

University of Wisconsin
Madison *B,M,D*
Oshkosh *B*
Whitewater *B*

Iranian languages

Illinois

University of Chicago *B,M,D*

Massachusetts

Harvard University *D*

Michigan

University of Michigan *B,M,D*

New York

Columbia University *M,D*
New York University *B,D*

Ohio

Ohio State University: Columbus
Campus *B,M*

Islamic studies

California

Naval Postgraduate School *M*
University of California: Los
Angeles *M,D*

Massachusetts

Brandeis University *B,M,D*
Hampshire College *B*
Harvard and Radcliffe Colleges *B*

Michigan

University of Michigan *B*

New York

Columbia University
Columbia College *B*
New York *M,D*
School of General Studies *M*
New York University *B,M,D*

Ohio

Ohio State University: Columbus
Campus *B*

Pennsylvania

University of Pennsylvania *B,M,D*

Canada

McGill University *M,D*

Italian

Arizona

Arizona State University *B*
Glendale Community College *A*
University of Arizona *B*

California

Chabot College *A*
College of the Desert *A*
Los Angeles City College *A*
Los Angeles Valley College *A*
Modesto Junior College *A*
San Diego City College *A*
San Francisco State University *B,M*
Santa Clara University *B*

Scripps College *B*
Southwestern College *A*
Stanford University *B,M,D*
University of California
Berkeley *B,M,D*
Davis *B*
Los Angeles *B,M,D*
San Diego *B*
Santa Barbara *B*
Santa Cruz *B,D*
University of Southern California *B*

Colorado

University of Colorado at
Boulder *B*

Connecticut

Albertus Magnus College *B*
Central Connecticut State
University *B*
Connecticut College *B*
Sacred Heart University *A,B*
Southern Connecticut State
University *B,M*
Trinity College *B*
University of Connecticut *B,M,D*
University of Hartford *B*
Wesleyan University *B*
Yale University *B,M,D*

Delaware

University of Delaware *B,M*

District of Columbia

Catholic University of America *M*
Georgetown University *B*

Florida

Florida International University *B*
Florida State University *B*
Miami-Dade Community College *A*
University of South Florida *B*

Georgia

University of Georgia *B*

Illinois

City Colleges of Chicago: Chicago
City-Wide College *C*
De Paul University *B*
Loyola University of Chicago *B*
Northwestern University *B,M,D*
Rosary College *B*
University of Chicago *B,M,D*
University of Illinois
Chicago *B*
Urbana-Champaign *B,M,D*

Indiana

Indiana University Bloomington
B,M,D
University of Notre Dame *B*

Iowa

University of Iowa *B*

Kansas

University of Kansas *B*

Kentucky

University of Kentucky *B*

Louisiana

Tulane University *B*

Maryland

Johns Hopkins University *B,M,D*
University of Maryland: College
Park *B*

Massachusetts

Boston College *B,M*
Boston University *B*
Harvard and Radcliffe Colleges *B*
Harvard University *M,D*
Mount Holyoke College *B*
Northeastern University *B*
Smith College *B,M*
Tufts University *B*
University of Massachusetts
Amherst *B,M*
Boston *B*
Wellesley College *B*
Wheaton College *B*

Michigan

University of Michigan *B,M,D*
Wayne State University *B,M*

Minnesota

University of Minnesota: Twin
Cities *B,M*

Missouri

Washington University *B,M,D*

New Hampshire

Dartmouth College *B*

New Jersey

Montclair State College *B*
Rutgers—The State University of
New Jersey
Douglass College *B*
Livingston College *B*
New Brunswick *M,D*
Newark College of Arts and
Sciences *B*
Rutgers College *B*
University College New
Brunswick *B*
Seton Hall University *B*

New York

Barnard College *B*
City University of New York
Brooklyn College *B*
City College *B*
Hunter College *B,M*
Lehman College *B*
Queens College *B,M*
York College *B*
Columbia University
Columbia College *B*
New York *M,D*
School of General Studies *B*
Cornell University *B,M,D*
Fordham University *B*
Hofstra University *B*
Iona College *B*
Long Island University: C. W. Post
Campus *B*
Mercy College *B*
Nazareth College of Rochester *B*
New York University *B,M,D*
Onondaga Community College *A*
St. John Fisher College *B*
St. John's University *B*
Sarah Lawrence College *B*
State University of New York
Albany *B*
Binghamton *B,M*
Buffalo *B*
Stony Brook *B*
College at Buffalo *B*
Syracuse University *B*
Vassar College *B*
Wells College *B*

North Carolina

Duke University *B,D*
University of North Carolina at
Chapel Hill *B,M,D*

Ohio

College of Wooster *B*
Kenyon College *B*
Ohio State University: Columbus
Campus *B,M,D*
Youngstown State University *B*

Oklahoma

Tulsa Junior College *A*

Oregon

University of Oregon
Eugene *B,M*
Robert Donald Clark Honors
College *B*

Pennsylvania

Bryn Mawr College *B*
Haverford College *B*
Immaculata College *A*
La Salle University *B*
Penn State University Park Campus
C,B
Rosemont College *B*
Temple University *B*
University of Pennsylvania *B,M,D*
University of Pittsburgh *B,M*

Rhode Island

Brown University *B,M,D*
Providence College *B*
University of Rhode Island *B*

South Carolina

University of South Carolina *B*

Tennessee

University of Tennessee:
Knoxville *B*

Texas

University of Texas at Austin *B*

Utah

Brigham Young University *B*

Vermont

Marlboro College *B*
Middlebury College *B*

Virginia

University of Virginia *B,M*

Washington

Gonzaga University *B*
University of Washington *B,M,D*

Wisconsin

University of Wisconsin
Madison *B,M,D*
Milwaukee *B*

Wyoming

Casper College *A*

Canada

McGill University *B,M*

Switzerland

Franklin College: Switzerland *B*

Japanese

Arizona
Arizona State University *B*
Glendale Community College *A*

California
California State University
    Long Beach *C*
    Los Angeles *B*
El Camino College *A*
Foothill College *A*
Los Angeles City College *A*
Monterey Institute of International
    Studies *B,M*
Orange Coast College *A*
Pomona College *B*
San Francisco State University *B*
San Jose State University *B*
Scripps College *B*
Stanford University *B,M,D*
University of California
    Berkeley *B,M,D*
    Davis *B*
    Irvine *B*
    Los Angeles *B*
    Santa Barbara *B*
    Santa Cruz *B*
University of the Pacific *B*

Colorado
University of Colorado at
    Boulder *B*

Connecticut
Connecticut College *B*
Sacred Heart University *A*
Wesleyan University *B*
Yale University *B*

District of Columbia
Georgetown University *B*

Hawaii
Hawaii Loa College *B*
University of Hawaii at Manoa *B*

Illinois
Black Hawk College *A*
City Colleges of Chicago: Chicago
    City-Wide College *C*
North Central College *B*
University of Chicago *B,M,D*

Indiana
Indiana University Bloomington
    B,M,D
University of Notre Dame *B*

Kansas
University of Kansas *B*

Louisiana
Dillard University *B*

Massachusetts
Harvard and Radcliffe Colleges *B*
Harvard University *M,D*
Massachusetts Institute of
    Technology *B*
University of Massachusetts at
    Amherst *B,M*
Wellesley College *B*

Michigan
Eastern Michigan University *B*
University of Michigan *B,M,D*

Minnesota
Gustavus Adolphus College *B*
Macalester College *B*
University of Minnesota: Twin
    Cities *B,M,D*
Winona State University *A*

Missouri
Washington University *B,M,D*

New Jersey
Seton Hall University *B,M*

New York
Colgate University *B*
Columbia University
    Columbia College *B*
    New York *M,D*
Cornell University *B,M,D*
Hamilton College *B*
Hobart College *B*
University of Rochester *B*
William Smith College *B*

North Carolina
St. Andrews Presbyterian College *B*

Ohio
Kenyon College *B*
Ohio State University: Columbus
    Campus *B,M,D*
University of Findlay *B*
University of Rio Grande *C*
Wittenberg University *B*

Oklahoma
Tulsa Junior College *A*

Oregon
Pacific University *B*
Portland Community College *A*
Portland State University *B*
University of Oregon
    Eugene *B*
    Robert Donald Clark Honors
        College *B*

Pennsylvania
Bucknell University *B*
Penn State University Park
    Campus *C*
University of Pennsylvania *B,M,D*
University of Pittsburgh *B*
Ursinus College *B*

Utah
Brigham Young University *B,M*

Washington
Everett Community College *A*
Evergreen State College *B*
Grays Harbor College *A*
Seattle Central Community
    College *A*
Seattle University *B*
Spokane Falls Community
    College *A*
Tacoma Community College *A*
University of Washington *B,M,D*

West Virginia
Salem-Teikyo University *B*

Wisconsin
University of Wisconsin: Madison
    B,M

Jazz

Arizona
University of Arizona *B*

California
California Institute of the Arts
    C,B,M
California State University
    Long Beach *B*
    Los Angeles *B*
University of Southern California
    B,M

Connecticut
University of Hartford *B*

District of Columbia
Howard University *B,M*

Florida
Florida Atlantic University *B*
University of Miami *B*
University of North Florida *B*

Illinois
American Conservatory of Music
    A,B
Augustana College *B*
De Paul University *B*
Illinois Benedictine College *B*
Roosevelt University *B*
Southern Illinois University
    Carbondale *B*
    Edwardsville *B*

Indiana
Indiana University
    Bloomington *B*
    South Bend *A*

Iowa
Iowa Lakes Community College *A*
University of Iowa *B*

Kansas
Kansas City Kansas Community
    College *A*

Louisiana
Loyola University *B*

Maine
University of Maine at Augusta *A,B*

Massachusetts
Berklee College of Music *C,B*
Hampshire College *B*
New England Conservatory of
    Music *B,M,D*

Michigan
Aquinas College *B*
University of Michigan *B,M*
Wayne State University *B*
Western Michigan University *B*

Minnesota
University of Minnesota: Duluth *B*

Missouri
Webster University *B*

New Jersey
Jersey City State College *B*
Rutgers—The State University of
    New Jersey: Mason Gross School
    of the Arts *B*
William Paterson College of New
    Jersey *B*

New York
Eastman School of Music of the
    University of Rochester *M*
Five Towns College *A,B*
Hofstra University *B*
Long Island University: Brooklyn
    Campus *B*
Manhattan School of Music *B,M*
New York University *B*
University of Rochester *M*

North Carolina
Brevard College *A*

Ohio
Bowling Green State University *B*
Capital University *B*
Ohio State University: Columbus
    Campus *B*
University of Cincinnati *B*

Pennsylvania
Carnegie Mellon University *B,M*
Duquesne University *B*
Indiana University of
    Pennsylvania *B*
University of the Arts *B*
West Chester University of
    Pennsylvania *B*

Rhode Island
Community College of Rhode
    Island *A*

Texas
University of North Texas *B,M*

Vermont
Bennington College *B*

Virginia
Shenandoah University *B*

Washington
Cornish College of the Arts *B*
Pacific Lutheran University *B*
Western Washington University
    B,M

Jewish studies

Arizona
University of Arizona *B*

California
Hebrew Union College: Jewish
    Institute of Religion *B*
University of California
    Los Angeles *B*
    San Diego *B,M*
University of Judaism *B,M*
University of Southern California *B*

Colorado
University of Denver *B,M*

Connecticut
Trinity College *B*
University of Hartford *B*
Wesleyan University *B*
Yale University *B*

District of Columbia
American University *B*
George Washington University *B*

Florida
Florida Atlantic University *C*
University of Florida *B*

University of Miami *B*

Georgia
Emory University *B*

Illinois
De Paul University *B*
Hebrew Theological College
A,B,M,D,W
Northeastern Illinois University *B*
University of Illinois at Chicago *B*

Indiana
Indiana University Bloomington *C*

Louisiana
Tulane University *B*

Maryland
Baltimore Hebrew University
B,M,D
University of Maryland: College
Park *B*

Massachusetts
Brandeis University *B,M,D*
Hampshire College *B*
Harvard and Radcliffe Colleges *B*
Mount Holyoke College *B*
University of Massachusetts at
Amherst *B*
Wellesley College *B*

Michigan
University of Michigan *B*

Minnesota
University of Minnesota: Twin
Cities *B*

Missouri
University of Missouri: Kansas
City *B*
Washington University *B,M*

New Jersey
Rutgers—The State University of
New Jersey
Douglass College *B*
Livingston College *B*
Newark College of Arts and
Sciences *B*
Rutgers College *B*
University College New
Brunswick *B*
Stockton State College *C*

New York
Bramson ORT Technical
Institute *A*
City University of New York
Brooklyn College *B,M*
City College *B*
Hunter College *B*
Lehman College *B*
Queens College *B*
Columbia University
New York *M,D*
School of General Studies *M*
Hofstra University *B*
Jewish Theological Seminary of
America *B,M,D*
Kol Yaakov Torah Center *B,M*
New York University *B,M,D*
Sarah Lawrence College *B*
State University of New York
Albany *B*
Binghamton *B*
Touro College *B,M*
Yeshiva University *A,B,M,D*

North Carolina
Duke University *B*

Ohio
Cleveland College of Jewish Studies
B,M
Kent State University *B*
Oberlin College *B*
University of Cincinnati *B*

Pennsylvania
Dickinson College *B*
Gratz College *B,M*
Lehigh University *B*
University of Pennsylvania *B*

Rhode Island
Brown University *B,M,D*

Texas
University of Texas at Austin *M*

Vermont
Goddard College *B,M*

Washington
University of Washington *B*

Wisconsin
University of Wisconsin: Madison
M,D

Canada
McGill University *B,M*

Journalism

Alabama
Alabama State University *B*
Auburn University *B*
James H. Faulkner State
Community College *A*
Samford University *B*
Spring Hill College *B*
Talladega College *B*
Troy State University *B*
University of Alabama *B,M,D*
University of Montevallo *B,M*
University of North Alabama *B*
Walker College *A*

Alaska
University of Alaska
Anchorage *B*
Fairbanks *B*

Arizona
Arizona State University *B,M*
Arizona Western College *A*
Cochise College *A*
Glendale Community College *A*
Grand Canyon University *B*
Mesa Community College *A*
Northern Arizona University *B*
Northland Pioneer College *A*
University of Arizona *B,M*

Arkansas
Arkansas State University *B,M*
Arkansas Tech University *B*
Harding University *B*
Henderson State University *B*
Hendrix College *B*
John Brown University *A,B*
University of Arkansas
Fayetteville *B,M*
Little Rock *B,M*
Pine Bluff *B*
University of Central Arkansas *B*

University of the Ozarks *B*
Westark Community College *A*

California
Azusa Pacific University *B*
Bakersfield College *A*
California Polytechnic State
University: San Luis Obispo *B*
California State University
Chico *B*
Dominguez Hills *B*
Fresno *B,M*
Fullerton *B,M*
Long Beach *B*
Los Angeles *B*
Northridge *B,M*
Sacramento *B*
Cerritos Community College *A*
Chapman University *B,M*
City College of San Francisco *A*
College of the Desert *A*
College of the Sequoias *A*
Cosumnes River College *A*
De Anza College *A*
Diablo Valley College *A*
East Los Angeles College *C*
El Camino College *A*
Foothill College *A*
Fresno City College *C,A*
Glendale Community College *C*
Golden West College *C,A*
Humboldt State University *C,B*
Laney College *A*
Long Beach City College *A*
Los Angeles City College *A*
Los Angeles Mission College *A*
Los Angeles Pierce College *A*
Los Angeles Trade and Technical
College *C,A*
Los Angeles Valley College *C,A*
Los Medanos College *A*
Merced College *A*
MiraCosta College *A*
Modesto Junior College *A*
Mount San Antonio College *A*
Oxnard College *A*
Pacific Union College *B*
Palomar College *C,A*
Pasadena City College *C,A*
Pepperdine University *B*
Point Loma Nazarene College *B*
Saddleback College *C,A*
San Diego City College *A*
San Diego State University *B*
San Francisco State University *B*
San Joaquin Delta College *A*
San Jose State University *B*
Santa Monica College *A*
Santa Rosa Junior College *A*
Sierra College *A*
Skyline College *A*
Solano Community College *A*
Southern California College *B*
Southwestern College *A*
Taft College *A*
University of California:
Berkeley *M*
University of La Verne *B*
University of the Pacific *B*
University of San Francisco *B*
University of Southern California
B,M
Ventura College *A*
West Hills Community College *A*

Colorado
Adams State College *B*
Colorado State University *B,M*
Fort Lewis College *B*
Mesa State College *B*
Metropolitan State College of
Denver *B*

Pikes Peak Community College *A*
Trinidad State Junior College *A*
University of Colorado at Boulder
B,M,D
University of Denver *B*
University of Northern Colorado *B*
University of Southern Colorado *B*

Connecticut
Housatonic Community College *A*
Norwalk Community College *A*
Sacred Heart University *B*
Southern Connecticut State
University *B*
University of Bridgeport *B*
University of Connecticut *B*
University of New Haven *C,B*

Delaware
Delaware State College *B*
Delaware Technical and
Community College: Southern
Campus *A*
University of Delaware *B*

District of Columbia
American University *B,M*
George Washington University *B*
Howard University *B*
University of the District of
Columbia *B*

Florida
Barry University *B*
Central Florida Community
College *A*
Daytona Beach Community
College *A*
Florida Agricultural and Mechanical
University *B*
Florida Atlantic University *B*
Florida Southern College *B*
Florida State University *B,M,D*
Gulf Coast Community College *A*
Lynn University *B*
Manatee Community College *A*
Miami-Dade Community College *A*
Palm Beach Community College *A*
University of Central Florida *B*
University of Florida *B,M,D*
University of Miami *B,M*
University of West Florida *M*

Georgia
Abraham Baldwin Agricultural
College *A*
Atlanta Metropolitan College *A*
Bainbridge College *A*
Berry College *B*
Brenau Women's College *B*
Clark Atlanta University *B*
Clayton State College *A*
Darton College *A*
DeKalb College *A*
Floyd College *A*
Fort Valley State College *B*
Gainesville College *A*
Georgia College *B*
Georgia Southern University *B*
Georgia State University *B*
Gordon College *C,A*
Kennesaw State College *B*
Macon College *A*
Middle Georgia College *A*
Morris Brown College *B*
Savannah State College *B*
Shorter College *B*
South Georgia College *A*
Toccoa Falls College *B*
University of Georgia *B,M,D*
Wesleyan College *B*
Young Harris College *A*

Hawaii

University of Hawaii at Manoa *B*

Idaho

Idaho State University *B*
North Idaho College *A*
Ricks College *A*
University of Idaho *B*

Illinois

Black Hawk College *A*
Bradley University *B*
City Colleges of Chicago: Richard J.
Daley College *A*
College of St. Francis *B*
Columbia College *B,M*
Eastern Illinois University *B*
Illinois Central College *A*
Illinois State University *B*
Illinois Valley Community
College *A*
John A. Logan College *A*
Joliet Junior College *A*
Judson College *B*
Lewis University *B*
Lincoln Land Community
College *A*
MacMurray College *B*
McKendree College *B*
Northern Illinois University *B,M*
Northwestern University *B,M*
Olivet Nazarene University *B*
Parkland College *A*
Rend Lake College *A*
Richland Community College *A*
Roosevelt University *B,M*
Sangamon State University *M*
Southern Illinois University
Carbondale *B,M,D*
Edwardsville *B*
Triton College *A*
University of Illinois at Urbana-
Champaign *B,M*
Waubonsee Community College *A*
Western Illinois University *B*
Wheaton College *M*
William Rainey Harper College *A*

Indiana

Ball State University *B,M*
Bethel College *A*
Butler University *B*
Calumet College of St. Joseph
C,A,B
Franklin College *B*
Huntington College *B*
Indiana State University *B,M*
Indiana University
Bloomington *B,M,D*
Southeast *A*
Indiana University—Purdue
University at Indianapolis *B*
Manchester College *A*
Martin University *B*
Purdue University *B,M,D*
St. Joseph's College *B*
St. Mary-of-the-Woods College *B*
Taylor University *B*
University of Evansville *B*
University of Indianapolis *B*
University of Notre Dame *B*
Valparaiso University *B*
Vincennes University *A*

Iowa

Buena Vista College *B*
Clarke College *B*
Clinton Community College *A*
Dordt College *B*
Drake University *B,M*
Grand View College *B*
Iowa Lakes Community College *A*

Iowa State University *B,M*
Iowa Western Community
College *A*
Kirkwood Community College *A*
Loras College *B*
Morningside College *B*
Muscatine Community College *A*
North Iowa Area Community
College *A*
St. Ambrose University *B*
Teikyo Marycrest University *B*
Teikyo Westmar University *B*
University of Iowa *B,M,D*
Waldorf College *A*
Wartburg College *B*

Kansas

Allen County Community
College *A*
Baker University *B*
Benedictine College *B*
Butler County Community
College *A*
Central College *A*
Cloud County Community
College *A*
Coffeyville Community College *A*
Colby Community College *A*
Cowley County Community
College *A*
Dodge City Community College *A*
Haskell Indian Junior College *A*
Highland Community College *A*
Hutchinson Community College *A*
Kansas City Kansas Community
College *A*
Kansas State University *B,M*
Labette Community College *A*
Pratt Community College *A*
Seward County Community
College *A*
University of Kansas *B,M*
Washburn University of Topeka *B*

Kentucky

Asbury College *B*
Campbellsville College *B*
Eastern Kentucky University *B*
Kentucky Wesleyan College *B*
Morehead State University *A,B*
Murray State University *B*
Northern Kentucky University *B*
Union College *B*
University of Kentucky *B*
Western Kentucky University *B*

Louisiana

Centenary College of Louisiana *B*
Grambling State University *B*
Louisiana College *B*
Louisiana State University
Agricultural and Mechanical
College *B,M*
Shreveport *B*
Louisiana Tech University *B*
Loyola University *B*
Northeast Louisiana University *B*
Northwestern State University *B*
Southern University and
Agricultural and Mechanical
College *B,M*
University of Southwestern
Louisiana *B*
Xavier University of Louisiana *B*

Maine

University of Maine *B*

Maryland

Baltimore Hebrew University *M*
Bowie State University *B*

College of Notre Dame of
Maryland *B*
Columbia Union College *B*
Frostburg State University *B*
Garrett Community College *A*
Towson State University *B,M*
University of Maryland: College
Park *B,M*

Massachusetts

American International College *B*
Becker College: Leicester
Campus *A*
Boston University *B,M*
Emerson College *B,M*
Endicott College *A*
Fisher College *A*
Hampshire College *B*
Mount Ida College *A*
North Adams State College *B*
Northeastern University *C,B,M*
Northern Essex Community
College *A*
Quincy College *A*
Suffolk University *B*
University of Massachusetts at
Amherst *B*
Western New England College *B*

Michigan

Andrews University *B*
Central Michigan University *B*
Eastern Michigan University *B*
Ferris State University *A*
Grand Valley State University *B*
Henry Ford Community College *A*
Lansing Community College *A*
Madonna University *A,B*
Michigan State University *B,M*
Northern Michigan University *B*
Oakland University *B*
Olivet College *B*
St. Clair County Community
College *A*
University of Detroit Mercy *B*
University of Michigan *B,M*
Wayne State University *B*

Minnesota

Bemidji State University *B*
Concordia College: Moorhead *B*
Macalester College *B*
Mankato State University *B*
Moorhead State University *B*
North Central Bible College *A,B*
Northland Community College *A*
Northwestern College *B*
Rainy River Community College *A*
Rochester Community College *A*
St. Cloud State University *B*
St. Mary's College of Minnesota *B*
University of Minnesota: Twin
Cities *B,M,D*
University of St. Thomas *B*
Vermilion Community College *A*
Willmar Community College *A*
Winona State University *B*

Mississippi

Alcorn State University *B*
Jackson State University *B,M*
Mississippi College *B*
Mississippi University for Women *B*
Northeast Mississippi Community
College *A*
Rust College *B*
University of Mississippi *B,M*
University of Southern
Mississippi *B*

Missouri

Central Missouri State University *B*
College of the Ozarks *B*
East Central College *A*
Evangel College *A,B*
Lincoln University *B*
Lindenwood College *B,M*
Maryville University *B*
Missouri Southern State College *B*
Missouri Valley College *B*
Northeast Missouri State
University *B*
Northwest Missouri State
University *B*
Park College *B*
Penn Valley Community College *A*
St. Louis Community College at
Florissant Valley *A*
Southeast Missouri State
University *B*
Stephens College *B*
University of Missouri
Columbia *B,M,D*
Kansas City *B*
Webster University *B*

Montana

Miles Community College *A*
University of Montana *B,M*

Nebraska

Chadron State College *B*
Creighton University *A,B*
Dana College *B*
Doane College *B*
Hastings College *B*
Midland Lutheran College *B*
Northeast Community College *A*
Southeast Community College:
Beatrice Campus *A*
Union College *B*
University of Nebraska
Kearney *B*
Lincoln *B,M*
Omaha *B*
Wayne State College *B*
Western Nebraska Community
College: Scottsbluff Campus *A*

Nevada

University of Nevada: Reno *B,M*

New Hampshire

Franklin Pierce College *B*
Keene State College *B*
New England College *B*
University of New Hampshire *B*
White Pines College *A*

New Jersey

Brookdale Community College *A*
Burlington County College *A*
Caldwell College *C*
County College of Morris *A*
Essex County College *A*
Glassboro State College *B*
Ocean County College *A*
Rider College *B*
Rutgers—The State University of
New Jersey
Cook College *B*
Douglass College *B*
Livingston College *B*
Newark College of Arts and
Sciences *B*
Rutgers College *B*
University College New
Brunswick *B*
Seton Hall University *B*
Stockton State College *B*
Thomas Edison State College *B*
Trenton State College *B*

New Mexico

New Mexico Highlands
University *B*
New Mexico State University *B*
University of New Mexico *B*

New York

City University of New York
Baruch College *B*
Brooklyn College *B*
City College *B*
Kingsborough Community
College *A*
Lehman College *B*
College of New Rochelle *B*
Columbia University *M*
Fordham University *B*
Herkimer County Community
College *A*
Hofstra University *B*
Iona College *B*
Ithaca College *B*
Jefferson Community College *A*
Keuka College *B*
Long Island University
Brooklyn Campus *B*
C. W. Post Campus *B*
Southampton Campus *B*
Manhattan College *B*
Marymount College *B*
Medaille College *B*
Mercy College *B*
New York University *B,M*
Onondaga Community College *A*
Pace University
College of White Plains *B*
Pleasantville/Briarcliff *B*
Polytechnic University *B,M*
St. Bonaventure University *B*
St. John Fisher College *B*
St. John's University *B*
St. Thomas Aquinas College *B*
State University of New York
College of Agriculture and
Technology at Morrisville *A*
College at Buffalo *B*
College at New Paltz *B*
College at Plattsburgh *B*
Syracuse University *B,M*
Ulster County Community
College *A*
Utica College of Syracuse
University *B*

North Carolina

Appalachian State University *B*
Barber-Scotia College *B*
Bennett College *B*
Brevard College *A*
Campbell University *B*
East Carolina University *B*
Elon College *B*
Methodist College *B*
North Carolina State University *B*
North Carolina Wesleyan College *B*
Queens College *B*
St. Andrews Presbyterian College *B*
St. Augustine's College *B*
University of North Carolina at
Chapel Hill *B,M,D*
Western Piedmont Community
College *A*
Wingate College *B*

North Dakota

North Dakota State University *B,M*
Turtle Mountain Community
College *A*
University of North Dakota *B*

Ohio

Ashland University *B*
Bowling Green State University
B,M,D
Central State University *B*
Cuyahoga Community College:
Metropolitan Campus *A*
Defiance College *B*
Franciscan University of
Steubenville *B*
Kent State University *B,M*
Lorain County Community
College *A*
Malone College *B*
Marietta College *B*
Miami University: Oxford
Campus *B*
Ohio State University: Columbus
Campus *B,M*
Ohio University
Athens *B,M,D*
Southern Campus at Ironton *A*
Ohio Wesleyan University *B*
Otterbein College *B*
Union Institute *B,D*
University of Akron *B*
University of Dayton *B*
University of Findlay *B*
University of Rio Grande *B*
University of Toledo *B*
Wilberforce University *B*
Wittenberg University *B*
Wright State University *B*

Oklahoma

Bacone College *A*
Bartlesville Wesleyan College *A*
Connors State College *A*
East Central University *B*
Eastern Oklahoma State College *A*
Northeastern State University *B*
Northern Oklahoma College *A*
Northwestern Oklahoma State
University *B*
Oklahoma Baptist University *B*
Oklahoma Christian University of
Science and Arts *B*
Oklahoma City University *B,M*
Oklahoma State University *B,M*
Redlands Community College *A*
Rogers State College *A*
Rose State College *A*
St. Gregory's College *A*
Southwestern Oklahoma State
University *B*
University of Central Oklahoma *B*
University of Oklahoma *B,M*

Oregon

Central Oregon Community
College *A*
Linfield College *B*
Linn-Benton Community College *A*
Mount Hood Community
College *A*
Pacific University *B*
Portland Community College *A*
Umpqua Community College *C*
University of Oregon
Eugene *B,M*
Robert Donald Clark Honors
College *B*
University of Portland *B*

Pennsylvania

Allegheny College *B*
Bloomsburg University of
Pennsylvania *B*
Bucks County Community
College *A*
California University of
Pennsylvania *B*

Carnegie Mellon University *B,M,D*
Duquesne University *B*
Elizabethtown College *B*
Gannon University *B*
Indiana University of
Pennsylvania *B*
Keystone Junior College *A*
Lehigh University *B*
Lincoln University *B*
Lock Haven University of
Pennsylvania *B*
Luzerne County Community
College *A*
Lycoming College *B*
Mansfield University of
Pennsylvania *B*
Mercyhurst College *B*
Messiah College *B*
Moravian College *B*
Penn State University Park Campus
B,M
Pennsylvania College of
Technology *A*
Point Park College *A,B,M*
St. Francis College *B*
Seton Hill College *B*
Shippensburg University of
Pennsylvania *B*
Temple University *B,M*
University of Pittsburgh
Greensburg *B*
Johnstown *B*
University of Scranton *B*
Waynesburg College *B*
Widener University *B*

Puerto Rico

Bayamon Central University *B*
University of Puerto Rico: Rio
Piedras Campus *B,M*
University of the Sacred Heart *B*

Rhode Island

University of Rhode Island *B*

South Carolina

Anderson College *B*
Benedict College *B*
Bob Jones University *B*
Coker College *B*
University of South Carolina *B,M*

South Dakota

Augustana College *B*
Black Hills State University *B*
Dakota Wesleyan University *B*
South Dakota State University *B,M*
University of South Dakota *B,M*

Tennessee

Austin Peay State University *B*
Belmont University *B*
Carson-Newman College *B*
Christian Brothers University *B*
David Lipscomb University *B*
East Tennessee State University *B*
Lambuth University *B*
Martin Methodist College *A*
Memphis State University *B,M*
Middle Tennessee State
University *B*
Southern College of Seventh-day
Adventists *B*
Tennessee State University *B*
Tennessee Technological
University *B*
Union University *B*
University of Tennessee
Chattanooga *B*
Knoxville *B*
Martin *B*

Texas

Abilene Christian University *B*
Amarillo College *A*
Angelina College *A*
Angelo State University *B*
Baylor University *B,M*
Del Mar College *A*
East Texas State University *B,M*
El Paso Community College *A*
Houston Community College *A*
Kilgore College *A*
Lee College *A*
Lubbock Christian University *B*
McLennan Community College *A*
Midland College *A*
Midwestern State University *B*
North Harris Montgomery
Community College District *A*
Panola College *A*
Prairie View A&M University *B*
Sam Houston State University *B*
San Antonio College *A*
South Plains College *A*
Southern Methodist University *B*
Southwest Texas State University *B*
Southwestern Adventist College *B*
Southwestern Assemblies of God
College *A*
Stephen F. Austin State
University *B*
Texas A&M University *B*
Texas Christian University *B,M*
Texas Southern University *B,M*
Texas Southmost College *A*
Texas Tech University *B*
Texas Wesleyan University *B*
Texas Woman's University *B*
Trinity University *B*
Trinity Valley Community
College *A*
University of Houston *B*
University of North Texas *B,M*
University of Texas
Arlington *B*
Austin *B,M,D*
El Paso *B*
Tyler *B*
West Texas State University *B*
Western Texas College *A*

Utah

Brigham Young University *B*
Southern Utah University *B*
University of Utah *B,M*
Utah State University *B*
Weber State University *B*

Vermont

Castleton State College *B*
Goddard College *B*
Green Mountain College *B*
Johnson State College *B*
Lyndon State College *B*
St. Michael's College *B*

Virginia

Averett College *B*
Christopher Newport College *B*
Emory and Henry College *B*
Hampton University *B*
Liberty University *B*
Norfolk State University *B*
Old Dominion University *B*
Radford University *B*
University of Richmond *B*
Virginia Commonwealth University
B,M
Virginia Union University *B*
Virginia Wesleyan College *B*
Washington and Lee University *B*

Washington

Big Bend Community College *A*
Central Washington University *B*
Eastern Washington University *B*
Everett Community College *A*
Gonzaga University *B*
Olympic College *A*
Pacific Lutheran University *B*
Seattle University *B*
Spokane Community College *A*
Spokane Falls Community
  College *A*
Walla Walla College *B*
Washington State University *B*
Western Washington University *B*
Whitworth College *B*

West Virginia

Bethany College *B*
Concord College *B*
Davis and Elkins College *A,B*
Marshall University *B,M*
Potomac State College of West
  Virginia University *A*
University of Charleston *B*
West Virginia University *B,M*

Wisconsin

Carroll College *B*
Lakeland College *B*
Marquette University *B,M*
University of Wisconsin
  Eau Claire *B*
  Madison *B,M,D*
  Milwaukee *B*
  Oshkosh *B*
  River Falls *B*
  Whitewater *B*
Viterbo College *B*

Wyoming

Casper College *A*
Eastern Wyoming College *A*
Laramie County Community
  College *A*
Northwest College *A*
Sheridan College *A*
University of Wyoming *B,M*
Western Wyoming Community
  College *A*

Mexico

Sistema Instituto Tecnologico y de
  Estudios Superiores de
  Monterrey *B,M*

Arab Republic of Egypt

American University in Cairo *B,M*

Junior high education

Alabama

Alabama Agricultural and
  Mechanical University *B,M*
Athens State College *B*
Auburn University
  Auburn *B,M,D*
  Montgomery *B,M*
Faulkner University *B*
Huntingdon College *B*
Judson College *B*
Samford University *B,M*
Spring Hill College *B*
Troy State University
  Dothan *B,M*
  Troy *B,M*
University of Alabama in
  Huntsville *B*
University of Montevallo *B,M*

University of South Alabama *B,M*

Arizona

Prescott College *B*

Arkansas

Harding University *B*
John Brown University *B*
Ouachita Baptist University *B*
University of Central Arkansas *B,M*
University of the Ozarks *B*

California

Azusa Pacific University *B*
Biola University *B*
California Lutheran University *B,M*
California State University
  Bakersfield *B,M*
  Northridge *M*
Christ College Irvine *B*
College of Notre Dame *M*
Mills College *M*
Mount St. Mary's College *B*
Occidental College *M*
Pepperdine University *B,M*
St. Mary's College of California
  B,M
Sonoma State University *B*
University of California: Los
  Angeles *M*
University of La Verne *B,M*
University of the Pacific *B,M,D*
University of Redlands *B*
University of San Francisco *B,M*

Colorado

University of Colorado at
  Boulder *B*
University of Northern Colorado *M*

Connecticut

Eastern Connecticut State
  University *B*
Quinnipiac College *M*
Sacred Heart University *B,M*
St. Joseph College *B,M*
Southern Connecticut State
  University *B,M*
University of Bridgeport *B,M*

Delaware

Delaware State College *B*

District of Columbia

Trinity College *M*

Florida

Daytona Beach Community
  College *A*
Florida Agricultural and Mechanical
  University *M*
Florida Atlantic University *C*
Indian River Community College *A*
Jacksonville University *B,M*
Pensacola Junior College *A*
Stetson University *B,M*
University of West Florida *B*

Georgia

Albany State College *B,M*
Andrew College *A*
Armstrong State College *B,M*
Augusta College *B,M*
Bainbridge College *A*
Berry College *B,M*
Clark Atlanta University *B*
Columbus College *B*
Covenant College *B*
East Georgia College *A*
Floyd College *A*
Fort Valley State College *B*
Georgia College *B,M*

Georgia Southern University *B,M*
Georgia Southwestern College *B,M*
Georgia State University *B,M*
Kennesaw State College *B*
Mercer University
  Atlanta *M*
  Macon *B,M*
North Georgia College *B,M*
Oglethorpe University *B,M*
Paine College *B*
Piedmont College *B*
Shorter College *B*
Thomas College *A*
Toccoa Falls College *B*
University of Georgia *B,M,D*
Valdosta State College *B,M*
Waycross College *A*
West Georgia College *B,M*

Hawaii

Brigham Young University-
  Hawaii *B*
University of Hawaii at Hilo *W*

Idaho

Idaho State University *B*
Lewis Clark State College *B*
North Idaho College *A*

Illinois

Augustana College *B*
Aurora University *B*
Barat College *B*
Bradley University *B,M*
Concordia University *B,M*
Eastern Illinois University *B*
Eureka College *B*
Greenville College *B*
Hebrew Theological College *B*
Illinois State University *B*
Illinois Valley Community
  College *A*
Illinois Wesleyan University *B*
Kishwaukee College *A*
Knox College *B*
Lake Forest College *B*
Lincoln Christian College and
  Seminary *B*
Millikin University *B*
National-Louis University *M*
Northwestern University *M*
Olivet Nazarene University *B,M*
Rend Lake College *A*
Rockford College *B*
St. Xavier University *B*
Southern Illinois University at
  Edwardsville *M*
Trinity Christian College *B*
Trinity College *B*

Indiana

Anderson University *B*
Ball State University *B,M*
Bethel College *B*
Butler University *B,M*
Franklin College *B*
Goshen College *B*
Huntington College *B*
Indiana State University *B,M*
Indiana University
  Bloomington *B*
  East *B*
  Northwest *B,M*
  South Bend *B*
Indiana University—Purdue
  University at Fort Wayne *B*
Indiana Wesleyan University *B*
Manchester College *B*
Martin University *B*
Oakland City College *B*
Purdue University *B,M*
St. Joseph's College *B*

Taylor University *B*
Tri-State University *B*
University of Evansville *B*
University of Indianapolis *B*
University of Southern Indiana *B*
Vincennes University *A*

Iowa

Briar Cliff College *B*
Buena Vista College *B*
Iowa Lakes Community College *A*
Iowa Wesleyan College *B*
Kirkwood Community College *A*
Morningside College *B*
Northwestern College *B*
Simpson College *B*
Teikyo Marycrest University *B*
Teikyo Westmar University *B*
University of Dubuque *B,M*
University of Northern Iowa *B,M*
Upper Iowa University *B*
Wartburg College *B*
William Penn College *B*

Kansas

Benedictine College *B*
Bethany College *B*
Friends University *B*
McPherson College *B*
Neosho County Community
  College *A*
Ottawa University *B*
Sterling College *B*
Tabor College *B*
University of Kansas *B*

Kentucky

Asbury College *B*
Bellarmine College *B*
Berea College *B*
Brescia College *B*
Campbellsville College *B*
Cumberland College *B*
Eastern Kentucky University *B,M*
Kentucky Christian College *B*
Kentucky Wesleyan College *B*
Lindsey Wilson College *B*
Louisville Presbyterian Theological
  Seminary *M*
Morehead State University *B,M*
Murray State University *B,M*
Pikeville College *B*
Thomas More College *B*
Transylvania University *B*
Union College *B,M*
University of Kentucky *B*
University of Louisville *B,M*
Western Kentucky University *B,M*

Louisiana

Dillard University *B*
Louisiana College *B*
Southern University and
  Agricultural and Mechanical
  College *B*
World Evangelism Bible College
  and Seminary *B*

Maine

St. Joseph's College *B*
University of Maine
  Fort Kent *B*
  Machias *B*

Maryland

Bowie State University *M*
Goucher College *M*
Salisbury State University *M*

Massachusetts

American International College *B,M*
Assumption College *B*

Bradford College *C*
Bridgewater State College *M*
Elms College *B*
Gordon College *B*
Lesley College *B,M*
North Adams State College *B*
Simmons College *B,M*
Tufts University *M*
Westfield State College *B*
Worcester State College *M*

Michigan
Alma College *B*
Calvin College *B*
Central Michigan University *M*
Eastern Michigan University *M*
Grand Valley State University *B,M*
Hillsdale College *B*
Hope College *B*
Madonna University *B*
Northern Michigan University *B,M*
Olivet College *B*
Western Michigan University *B,M*

Minnesota
Bethel College *B*
College of St. Catherine: St.
    Catherine Campus *B*
Concordia College: Moorhead *B*
Concordia College: St. Paul *B*
Gustavus Adolphus College *B*
Mankato State University *B,M*
Moorhead State University *B*
Northland Community College *A*
Rainy River Community College *A*
St. Cloud State University *B*
St. Mary's College of Minnesota *B*
Southwest State University *B*
University of Minnesota
    Morris *B*
    Twin Cities *B*
Vermilion Community College *A*
Willmar Community College *A*
Winona State University *B,M*

Mississippi
Blue Mountain College *B*
Jones County Junior College *A*
Mississippi College *B,M*

Missouri
Central Missouri State University *B*
College of the Ozarks *B*
Columbia College *B*
East Central College *A*
Evangel College *B*
Fontbonne College *B*
Harris Stowe State College *B*
Maryville University *B*
Mineral Area College *A*
Missouri Southern State College *B*
Missouri Valley College *B*
Moberly Area Community
    College *A*
Northeast Missouri State
    University *M*
Northwest Missouri State
    University *B*
Park College *B*
Rockhurst College *B*
St. Louis University *B*
Webster University *B*
William Woods College *B*

Montana
Miles Community College *A*
Montana State University *B*
University of Montana *B,M*
Western Montana College of the
    University of Montana *B*

Nebraska
Chadron State College *B*
Concordia College *B,M*
Creighton University *B*
Hastings College *M*
Midland Lutheran College *B*
Nebraska Christian College *B*
Nebraska Wesleyan University *B*
Peru State College *B*
University of Nebraska
    Kearney *B,M*
    Lincoln *B*
    Omaha *B*

New Hampshire
Antioch New England Graduate
    School *M*
Franklin Pierce College *B*
Notre Dame College *B*
Plymouth State College of the
    University System of New
    Hampshire *B*

New Jersey
Centenary College *B*
Rutgers—The State University of
    New Jersey
    Camden College of Arts and
        Sciences *B*
    Douglass College *B*
    Livingston College *B*
    Newark College of Arts and
        Sciences *B*
    University College New
        Brunswick *B*
    University College Newark *B*

New Mexico
Eastern New Mexico University *B*
New Mexico State University *B*
Western New Mexico University
    B,M

New York
Alfred University *B,M*
City University of New York
    Brooklyn College *B,M*
    La Guardia Community
        College *A*
    Lehman College *B,M*
    Queens College *B*
College of New Rochelle *B*
Concordia College *B*
Daemen College *B*
Fordham University *B*
Houghton College *B*
Iona College *B,M*
Long Island University: Brooklyn
    Campus *B,M*
Manhattan College *B*
Manhattanville College *B*
Marymount College *B*
Molloy College *B*
Mount St. Mary College *B*
Nazareth College of Rochester *B*
New York University *B,M,D*
Niagara University *B,M*
Russell Sage College *B*
St. Joseph's College
    Brooklyn *B*
    Suffolk Campus *B*
St. Thomas Aquinas College *B*
State University of New York
    Albany *M*
    Buffalo *M,D*
    College at Cortland *B,M*
    College at Fredonia *B*
    College at New Paltz *B,M*
    College at Old Westbury *B*
    College at Oneonta *B,M*
    College at Plattsburgh *B,M*
    College at Potsdam *B,M*

University of Rochester *M,D*
Wagner College *B*

North Carolina
Appalachian State University *B,M*
Barton College *B*
Bennett College *B*
Campbell University *B,M*
Catawba College *B,M*
Catawba Valley Community
    College *A*
East Carolina University *B,M*
Elizabeth City State University *B*
Elon College *B,M*
Greensboro College *B*
High Point University *B*
Lees-McRae College *B*
Lenoir-Rhyne College *B,M*
Mars Hill College *B*
Methodist College *B*
North Carolina Central University
    B,M
North Carolina State University
    B,M
North Carolina Wesleyan College *B*
Pembroke State University *B,M*
Queens College *M*
St. Andrews Presbyterian College *B*
Salem College *B*
University of North Carolina
    Asheville *C*
    Chapel Hill *B,M,D*
    Charlotte *B,M*
    Greensboro *B*
    Wilmington *B*
Wake Forest University *B,M*
Warren Wilson College *B*
Western Carolina University *B,M*
Wingate College *B,M*
Winston-Salem State University *B*

North Dakota
Dickinson State University *B*
University of North Dakota *B*

Ohio
Baldwin-Wallace College *B*
Bluffton College *B*
Capital University *B*
Central State University *B*
Circleville Bible College *A,B*
College of Wooster *B*
Defiance College *B*
Franciscan University of
    Steubenville *B*
John Carroll University *B,M*
Kent State University *B,M,D*
Lake Erie College *B*
Mount Union College *B*
Mount Vernon Nazarene College *B*
Notre Dame College of Ohio *B*
Ohio State University: Columbus
    Campus *B,M*
Ohio University *B,M*
Ohio Wesleyan University *B*
Otterbein College *B*
University of Dayton *M*
University of Findlay *B*
University of Rio Grande *B*
University of Toledo *B,M,D*
Urbana University *B*
Walsh College *B*
Wittenberg University *B*
Wright State University *M*

Oklahoma
Oklahoma Baptist University *B*
Oral Roberts University *M*

Oregon
Central Oregon Community
    College *A*

Concordia College *C,B*
Linfield College *B*
Pacific University *M*
Southern Oregon State College *M*
Warner Pacific College *B*
Western Oregon State College *B,M*
Willamette University *M*

Pennsylvania
Bucknell University *B,M*
Cabrini College *B*
California University of
    Pennsylvania *B,M*
Chatham College *B*
Clarion University of
    Pennsylvania *B*
Edinboro University of
    Pennsylvania *B*
Elizabethtown College *B*
Gwynedd-Mercy College *B*
Immaculata College *B*
Indiana University of
    Pennsylvania *B*
La Salle University *B,M*
Lehigh University *M,D*
Lock Haven University of
    Pennsylvania *B*
Marywood College *B,M*
Messiah College *B*
Northeastern Christian Junior
    College *A*
Reading Area Community
    College *A*
St. Vincent College *C*

Puerto Rico
Inter American University of Puerto
    Rico: San German Campus *B*

Rhode Island
Rhode Island College *B,M*

South Carolina
Anderson College *B*
Erskine College *B*
University of South Carolina at
    Aiken *B*

South Dakota
Augustana College *B,M*
Dakota State University *B*
Mount Marty College *B*
Sioux Falls College *B*
South Dakota State University *B*

Tennessee
Carson-Newman College *B*
Crichton College *B*
Cumberland University *B*
East Tennessee State University *B*
Johnson Bible College *B*
Knoxville College *B*
Lambuth University *B*
Lincoln Memorial University *B*
Tennessee Wesleyan College *B*
Trevecca Nazarene College *B*
Union University *B*
University of Tennessee: Martin *B*

Texas
East Texas Baptist University *B*
Lamar University—Beaumont *B*
Panola College *A*
St. Mary's University *B*
Texas A&I University *B,M*
Texas Lutheran College *B*
Texas Wesleyan University *B*
University of Houston: Clear
    Lake *M*
University of Mary Hardin-Baylor
    B,M
University of St. Thomas *B*

Utah

Southern Utah University *B*
Weber State University *B,M*
Westminster College of Salt Lake
City *B*

Vermont

Bennington College *B*
Goddard College *B,M*
Johnson State College *B*
Trinity College of Vermont *M*

Virginia

Averett College *B*
Bluefield College *B*
Bridgewater College *B*
Eastern Mennonite College *B*
Emory and Henry College *B*
Hampton University *B*
Longwood College *M*
Mary Baldwin College *C*
Mountain Empire Community
College *A*
Old Dominion University *B*
Radford University *M*
University of Richmond *B,M*
Virginia Polytechnic Institute and
State University *B*
Virginia Wesleyan College *B*

Washington

Central Washington University *B*
City University *M*
Evergreen State College *M*
Heritage College *B*
Pacific Lutheran University *B,M*
St. Martin's College *B,M*
Seattle University *M*
University of Puget Sound *M*
Western Washington University
B,M
Whitworth College *B*

West Virginia

Alderson-Broaddus College *B*
Bethany College *B*
Bluefield State College *B*
Concord College *B*
Davis and Elkins College *B*
Glenville State College *B*
Marshall University *B,M*
Shepherd College *B*
University of Charleston *B*
West Virginia Institute of
Technology *B*
West Virginia State College *B*
West Virginia Wesleyan College *B*

Wisconsin

Alverno College *B*
Cardinal Stritch College *B*
Carthage College *B*
Concordia University Wisconsin *B*
Edgewood College *B*
Lakeland College *B*
Marian College of Fond du Lac *B*
Mount Mary College *B*
Mount Senario College *B*
Northland College *B*
Ripon College *C*
St. Norbert College *B*
University of Wisconsin
Green Bay *B*
La Crosse *B,M*
Milwaukee *B*
Oshkosh *B*
Platteville *B,M*
River Falls *B*
Superior *B*
Whitewater *B*
Wisconsin Lutheran College *B*

Wyoming

University of Wyoming *B*

Korean

Illinois

KAES College *B*
University of Chicago *B*

Massachusetts

Harvard University *D*

New York

Columbia University *M,D*

Ohio

Ohio State University: Columbus
Campus *B*

Utah

Brigham Young University *B,M*

Labor/industrial relations

Alabama

University of Alabama *B,M,D*

California

California State University
Dominguez Hills *B*
Fresno *B*
Hayward *B,M*
Los Angeles *B*
City College of San Francisco *C,A*
Long Beach City College *A*
Los Angeles Trade and Technical
College *C,A*
San Diego City College *C,A*
San Francisco State University *B*
University of San Francisco *B,M*

Connecticut

South Central Community
College *A*
University of Bridgeport *B*
University of New Haven *M*

District of Columbia

Southeastern University *M*

Georgia

Georgia State University *M,D*
University of Georgia *B,M*

Hawaii

Hawaii Pacific University *B,M*

Illinois

Black Hawk College *C,A*
City Colleges of Chicago: Chicago
City-Wide College *C,A*
Lewis and Clark Community
College *A*
Loyola University of Chicago *M*
Northwestern University *M*
Sangamon State University *B*
Southern Illinois University at
Edwardsville *B*
University of Chicago *M,D*
University of Illinois at Urbana-
Champaign *M,D*

Indiana

Ball State University *M*
Calumet College of St. Joseph *B*

Franklin College *B*
Indiana University
Bloomington *C,A,B*
Kokomo *C,A,B*
Northwest *A,B*
South Bend *B*
Indiana University—Purdue
University
Fort Wayne *B*
Indianapolis *C,A,B*
Purdue University
North Central Campus *A,B*
West Lafayette *B,D*

Iowa

Iowa State University *M*
University of Iowa *B,M,D*

Kentucky

Northern Kentucky University *A,B*
University of Kentucky *B*
University of Louisville *A*

Maryland

Dundalk Community College *C,A*
University of Maryland: College
Park *B*

Massachusetts

Babson College *M*
Hampshire College *B*
Harvard University *M,D*
Massachusetts Institute of
Technology *M,D,W*
University of Massachusetts at
Amherst *M*

Michigan

Baker College
Muskegon *B*
Owosso *A*
Eastern Michigan University *B*
Grand Valley State University *B,M*
Macomb Community College *C,A*
Michigan State University *M*
Michigan Technological
University *B*
Wayne State University *M*

Minnesota

Mankato State University *B*
University of Minnesota: Twin
Cities *M,D*
Winona State University *B*

Missouri

Rockhurst College *B*
St. Louis Community College at
Forest Park *C*
St. Louis University *B*
University of Missouri: Kansas
City *M*

Nebraska

University of Nebraska—Omaha *B*

New Jersey

Bergen Community College *A*
Fairleigh Dickinson University *M*
Rider College *B*
Rutgers—The State University of
New Jersey
Douglass College *B*
Livingston College *B*
New Brunswick *M*
Rutgers College *B*
University College New
Brunswick *B*
Thomas Edison State College *C,B*

New York

City University of New York:
Baruch College *M*
Clarkson University *B*
Cornell University *B,M,D*
Ithaca College *B*
Le Moyne College *B*
New York Institute of
Technology *M*
Niagara County Community
College *C*
Onondaga Community College *A*
Pace University *B*
State University of New York
College at Geneseo *B*
College at Old Westbury *B*
College at Potsdam *B*
Empire State College *A,B*
Syracuse University *B,M,D*
Tompkins-Cortland Community
College *A*

North Carolina

Gardner-Webb College *B*
McDowell Technical Community
College *A*

Ohio

Bowling Green State University *B*
Case Western Reserve University
M,D
Cleveland State University *M*
Cuyahoga Community College:
Western Campus *A*
Kent State University *B*
Ohio State University: Columbus
Campus *B*
Ohio University *B*
Sinclair Community College *C,A*
Terra Technical College *C,A*
Union Institute *B,D*
University of Akron *M*
University of Cincinnati *M*
University of Toledo *B,M*
Xavier University *B*
Youngstown State University *A,B*

Oregon

University of Oregon *M*

Pennsylvania

Bucks County Community
College *A*
Carnegie Mellon University *M,D,W*
Clarion University of
Pennsylvania *B*
Drexel University *B,M*
Indiana University of
Pennsylvania *M*
La Salle University *B,M*
Penn State University Park Campus
C,B
St. Francis College *M*
Shippensburg University of
Pennsylvania *B*
Temple University *B,M,D*
University of Pennsylvania *B,M,D*
Westminster College *B*
Westmoreland County Community
College *C*

Puerto Rico

Inter American University of Puerto
Rico
Arecibo Campus *B*
Metropolitan Campus *M*
University of Puerto Rico: Rio
Piedras Campus *B,M*

Rhode Island

Community College of Rhode
Island *A*

Providence College *A*
Rhode Island College *B*
University of Rhode Island *M*

Tennessee
Bristol University *A,B,M*
Martin Methodist College *A*
Tennessee Technological
University *B*

Texas
College of the Mainland *A*
San Antonio College *C*
University of North Texas *B,M,D*

Virginia
Averett College *B*
Norfolk State University *B*

Washington
Evergreen State College *B*
Pacific Lutheran University *B*
Whitworth College *B*

West Virginia
West Virginia Graduate College *M*
West Virginia Institute of
Technology *B*
West Virginia University *M*

Wisconsin
University of Wisconsin
Madison *M,D*
Milwaukee *B,M*
Parkside *B*

Canada
McGill University *B,M,D*

Landscape architecture

Alabama
Auburn University *B*

Arizona
Pima Community College *C,A*
University of Arizona *B,M*

Arkansas
University of Arkansas *B*

California
California Polytechnic State
University: San Luis Obispo *B*
California State Polytechnic
University: Pomona *B,M*
City College of San Francisco *A*
Cosumnes River College *A*
Modesto Junior College *A*
San Joaquin Delta College *C,A*
Santa Rosa Junior College *A*
Sierra College *C,A*
Southwestern College *C,A*
University of California
Berkeley *B,M*
Davis *B*
University of Southern California *M*
West Valley College *A*
Yuba College *C*

Colorado
Arapahoe Community College *C,A*
Colorado State University *B*
University of Colorado at
Denver *M*

Connecticut
University of Connecticut *B*

Florida
Broward Community College *A*
Florida Agricultural and Mechanical
University *B*
Florida International University *M*
Lake City Community College *A*
Miami-Dade Community College *A*
Tallahassee Community College *A*
University of Florida *B,M*

Georgia
Middle Georgia College *A*
University of Georgia *B,M*

Idaho
University of Idaho *B*

Illinois
Augustana College *B*
Kishwaukee College *C*
Southern Illinois University at
Carbondale *B,M*
University of Illinois at Urbana-
Champaign *B,M*

Indiana
Ball State University *B,M*
Purdue University *B,M,D*

Iowa
Iowa State University *B,M*
Kirkwood Community College *A*

Kansas
Kansas State University *B,M*

Kentucky
Eastern Kentucky University *A,B*
University of Kentucky *B*

Louisiana
Louisiana State University and
Agricultural and Mechanical
College *B,M*

Maine
Southern Maine Technical
College *A*
Unity College *B*

Maryland
Montgomery College: Germantown
Campus *C*
Morgan State University *M*

Massachusetts
Conway School of Landscape
Design *M*
Harvard University *M*
Springfield Technical Community
College *A*
University of Massachusetts at
Amherst *B,M*

Michigan
Andrews University *A*
Lansing Community College *A*
Michigan State University *B*
Oakland Community College *C,A*
University of Michigan *M,D*

Minnesota
University of Minnesota: Twin
Cities *B,M*
Willmar Community College *A*

Mississippi
Mississippi State University *B*

Montana
Montana State University *B*

Nebraska
Central Community College *A*

Nevada
Truckee Meadows Community
College *A*

New Jersey
Rutgers—The State University of
New Jersey: Cook College *B*
Union County College *C*

New York
City University of New York: City
College *B*
Community College of the Finger
Lakes *A*
Cornell University *B,M*
Herkimer County Community
College *A*
Rockland Community College *C*
State University of New York
College of Agriculture and
Technology at Morrisville *A*
College of Environmental
Science and Forestry *B,M*

North Carolina
North Carolina Agricultural and
Technical State University *B*
North Carolina State University
B,M
Wake Technical Community
College *A*

North Dakota
North Dakota State University *B*

Ohio
Columbus State Community
College *A*
Ohio State University: Columbus
Campus *B,M*

Oklahoma
Oklahoma State University *B*
University of Oklahoma *M*

Oregon
University of Oregon *B,M*

Pennsylvania
Keystone Junior College *A*
Penn State University Park Campus
C,B,M
Temple University *A,B*
University of Pennsylvania *M*

Rhode Island
Rhode Island School of Design *B,M*
University of Rhode Island *B*

South Carolina
Clemson University *B*

South Dakota
South Dakota State University *B*

Texas
Austin Community College *A*
Texas A&M University *B,M,D*
Texas Tech University *B*
University of Texas at Arlington
B,M

Utah
Utah State University *B,M*

Virginia
University of Virginia *M*
Virginia Polytechnic Institute and
State University *B,M*

Washington
Edmonds Community College *A*
University of Washington *B,M*
Washington State University *B*

West Virginia
West Virginia University *B*

Wisconsin
University of Wisconsin: Madison
B,M

Language interpretation and translation

Illinois
KAES College *B*

Kentucky
Louisville Presbyterian Theological
Seminary *M*

Nebraska
University of Nebraska—Kearney *B*

New York
Bard College *B*
City University of New York:
Brooklyn College *B*

Laser electro-optic technology

Alabama
Shoals Community College *A*
Wallace State Community College
at Hanceville *C,A*

California
American Armenian International
College *B*
Irvine Valley College *C,A*
Long Beach City College *A*
Moorpark College *A*
Pacific Union College *A*
San Diego City College *C,A*
San Jose State University *B*
Sierra College *C*
University of La Verne *B*

Colorado
Denver Institute of Technology *A*
Pikes Peak Community College *C*

Florida
Valencia Community College *A*

Idaho
Idaho State University *C,A*

Indiana
Vincennes University *A*

Iowa
Indian Hills Community College *A*

Kentucky
Madisonville Community College *A*

Maryland
Capitol College *A*

Massachusetts
Bunker Hill Community College *A*
Springfield Technical Community
College *A*

Michigan

Jackson Community College *A*
Schoolcraft College *A*

Missouri

Jefferson College *A*

New Jersey

Camden County College *A*
Union County College *A*

New Mexico

Albuquerque Technical-Vocational
Institute *A*
Northern New Mexico Community
College *A*

New York

City University of New York:
Queensborough Community
College *A*
Hudson Valley Community
College *A*

North Carolina

Central Carolina Community
College *A*

Ohio

Air Force Institute of
Technology *M*
Cincinnati Technical College *A*

Oregon

Oregon Institute of Technology *A,B*

Pennsylvania

Luzerne County Community
College *A*
Pennsylvania College of
Technology *A*

South Dakota

Mitchell Vocational Technical
Institute *C,A*

Tennessee

Pellissippi State Technical
Community College *A*

Texas

Paul Quinn College *B*
Texas State Technical College
Amarillo *A*
Harlingen *A*
Waco *A*
University of Houston: Clear Lake
B,M

Latin

Alabama

University of Alabama *B*

Arizona

University of Arizona *B*

California

Loyola Marymount University *B*
Pomona College *B*
St. Mary's College of California *B*
Scripps College *B*
University of California
Berkeley *B,M,D*
Davis *B*
Los Angeles *B,M*
Santa Barbara *B*
Santa Cruz *B,D*
University of the Pacific *B*

University of Southern California *B*

Colorado

University of Colorado at
Boulder *B*

Connecticut

Sacred Heart University *A*
University of Connecticut *M*
Wesleyan University *B*
Yale University *B*

Delaware

University of Delaware *B,M*

District of Columbia

Catholic University of America *B*

Florida

Florida State University *B,M*
New College of the University of
South Florida *B*
Pensacola Junior College *A*
University of Florida *B,M*
University of South Florida *B*

Georgia

Agnes Scott College *B*
Emory University *B*
Georgia State University *B*
Mercer University *B*
University of Georgia *B,M*

Idaho

University of Idaho *B*

Illinois

Augustana College *B*
Loyola University of Chicago
B,M,D
Monmouth College *B*
North Central College *B*
Northwestern University *B*
Rockford College *B*
University of Chicago *B,M,D*
University of Illinois at Urbana-
Champaign *M*

Indiana

Ball State University *B*
Butler University *B*
DePauw University *B*
Indiana State University *B*
Indiana University Bloomington
B,M,D
University of Notre Dame *B,M*
Valparaiso University *B*
Wabash College *B*

Iowa

Cornell College *B*
Grinnell College *B*
Loras College *B*
Luther College *B*
University of Iowa *B,M*

Kansas

Benedictine College *B*
University of Kansas *B*
Wichita State University *B*

Kentucky

Berea College *B*

Louisiana

Louisiana State University and
Agricultural and Mechanical
College *B*
Tulane University *B,M*

Maine

University of Maine *B*

Maryland

Johns Hopkins University *B,M,D*
Loyola College in Maryland *B*

Massachusetts

Amherst College *B*
Boston College *B,M*
Boston University *B,M*
Brandeis University *B*
College of the Holy Cross *B*
Harvard and Radcliffe Colleges *B*
Harvard University *D*
Mount Holyoke College *B*
Smith College *B*
Tufts University *B*
University of Massachusetts at
Boston *B*
Wellesley College *B*
Wheaton College *B*
Williams College *B*

Michigan

Calvin College *B*
Hope College *B*
Kalamazoo College *B*
Michigan State University *B*
University of Michigan *B,M,D*
Wayne State University *B,M*
Western Michigan University *B*

Minnesota

Carleton College *B*
College of St. Catherine: St.
Catherine Campus *B*
Concordia College: Moorhead *B*
Gustavus Adolphus College *B*
Macalester College *B*
St. Olaf College *B*
University of Minnesota: Twin
Cities *B,M,D*
University of St. Thomas *B*

Mississippi

Mississippi College *B*

Missouri

St. Louis University *B*
Southwest Missouri State
University *B*
University of Missouri: Columbia *B*
Washington University *B,M,D*

Montana

Carroll College *B*
University of Montana *B*

Nebraska

Creighton University *B*
University of Nebraska—Lincoln *B*

New Hampshire

Dartmouth College *B*
St. Anselm College *B*
University of New Hampshire *B*

New Jersey

Drew University *B*
Montclair State College *B*
Rutgers—The State University of
New Jersey
Douglass College *B*
Livingston College *B*
Rutgers College *B*
University College New
Brunswick *B*
Stockton State College *B*

New York

Bard College *B*
Barnard College *B*
City University of New York
Brooklyn College *B*
City College *B*
Hunter College *B*
Lehman College *B*
Queens College *B*
Colgate University *B*
College of New Rochelle *B*
Columbia University
Columbia College *B*
New York *M,D*
School of General Studies *B*
Cornell University *B,M,D*
Elmira College *B*
Fordham University *B,M,D*
Hamilton College *B*
Hobart College *B*
New York University *B,M*
St. Bonaventure University *B*
Sarah Lawrence College *B*
State University of New York
Albany *B,M*
Binghamton *B*
Buffalo *B*
Syracuse University *M,D*
Vassar College *B*
William Smith College *B*
Yeshiva University *B*

North Carolina

Davidson College *B*
Duke University *B*
University of North Carolina
Chapel Hill *B,M,D*
Greensboro *B*
Wake Forest University *B*

North Dakota

University of North Dakota *B*

Ohio

Bowling Green State University *B*
College of Wooster *B*
John Carroll University *B,M*
Kent State University *B,M*
Kenyon College *B*
Miami University: Oxford
Campus *B*
Oberlin College *B*
Ohio State University: Columbus
Campus *B,M,D*
Ohio University *B*
University of Akron *B*
University of Toledo *B,M*
Wright State University *B*
Xavier University *B*
Youngstown State University *B*

Oregon

University of Oregon
Eugene *B*
Robert Donald Clark Honors
College *B*

Pennsylvania

Allegheny College *B*
Bryn Mawr College *B,M,D*
Bucknell University *B*
Chestnut Hill College *B*
Dickinson College *B*
Duquesne University *B*
Franklin and Marshall College *B*
Gettysburg College *B*
Haverford College *B*
Immaculata College *A,B*
La Salle University *B*
Millersville University of
Pennsylvania *B,M*
Muhlenberg College *B*

Susquehanna University *B*
Swarthmore College *B*
University of Pennsylvania *B,M,D*
University of Scranton *B*
Ursinus College *B*
West Chester University of
Pennsylvania *B,M*
Westminster College *B*

Rhode Island

Brown University *B,M,D*

South Carolina

Furman University *B*
University of South Carolina *B*

South Dakota

University of South Dakota *B*

Tennessee

University of the South *B*
University of Tennessee:
Chattanooga *B*
Vanderbilt University *M*

Texas

Baylor University *B*
Collin County Community College
District *A*
Rice University *B*
Southwestern University *B*
Texas Tech University *B*
University of Dallas *B*
University of Texas at Austin *B*

Utah

Brigham Young University *B*

Vermont

Marlboro College *B*
University of Vermont *B,M*

Virginia

Emory and Henry College *B*
Hampden-Sydney College *B*
Mary Washington College *B*
Radford University *B*
Randolph-Macon College *B*
Sweet Briar College *B*
University of Richmond *B,W*

Washington

Gonzaga University *B*
Seattle Central Community
College *A*
University of Washington *B,M,D*

West Virginia

Marshall University *B*
West Virginia University *B,M*

Wisconsin

Beloit College *B*
Lawrence University *B*
Marquette University *B*
University of Wisconsin: Madison
B,M

Latin American studies

Alabama

University of Alabama *B,M*

Arizona

Northern Arizona University *B*
Prescott College *B*
University of Arizona *B,M*

California

California State University
Chico *B*
Fullerton *B*
Hayward *B*
Los Angeles *B,M*
Claremont McKenna College *B*
College of Notre Dame *B*
El Camino College *A*
Laney College *A*
Monterey Institute of International
Studies *M*
Naval Postgraduate School *M*
Pitzer College *B*
San Diego City College *A*
San Diego State University *B,M*
Scripps College *B*
Stanford University *B,M*
University of California
Berkeley *B,M,D*
Los Angeles *B,M*
Riverside *B*
Santa Barbara *B,M*
Santa Cruz *B*
University of the Pacific *B,M*
University of San Diego *B*
Whittier College *B*

Colorado

University of Colorado at
Boulder *B*
University of Denver *B*
University of Northern Colorado *B*

Connecticut

Fairfield University *B*
Trinity College *B*
University of Connecticut *B*
Wesleyan University *B*
Yale University *B*

District of Columbia

American University *B*
Gallaudet University *B*
George Washington University *B,M*
Georgetown University *B,M*

Florida

Flagler College *B*
Florida Atlantic University *B*
Florida State University *B*
Miami-Dade Community College *A*
Nova University *C*
Rollins College *B*
University of Florida *M*
University of Miami *B*

Georgia

Agnes Scott College *B*
Emory University *B*
University of Georgia *B*

Idaho

University of Idaho *B*

Illinois

De Paul University *B*
Northwestern University *B*
Rosary College *B*
University of Chicago *B,M*
University of Illinois
Chicago *B*
Urbana-Champaign *B*

Indiana

Ball State University *B*
Indiana State University *B*
Indiana University Bloomington
C,M
University of Notre Dame *B*

Iowa

Central College *B*
Cornell College *B*
Drake University *B*
Luther College *B*
University of Northern Iowa *B*

Kansas

Bethel College *B*
University of Kansas *B,M*

Kentucky

University of Kentucky *B*

Louisiana

Tulane University *B,M,D*

Maryland

Goucher College *B*
Hood College *B*
Morgan State University *B*

Massachusetts

Boston University *B,M*
Brandeis University *B*
Hampshire College *B*
Massachusetts Institute of
Technology *B*
Mount Holyoke College *B*
Smith College *B*
Tufts University *B,M*
Wellesley College *B*

Michigan

Eastern Michigan University *B*
Oakland University *B*
University of Michigan *B*
Western Michigan University *B*

Minnesota

Carleton College *B*
Hamline University *B*
Macalester College *B*
St. Cloud State University *B*
University of Minnesota
Morris *B*
Twin Cities *B*

Missouri

St. Louis University *B*
Southwest Missouri State
University *B*
University of Missouri: Columbia *B*
Washington University *B*

Nebraska

University of Nebraska—Lincoln *B*

New Jersey

Caldwell College *C*
Rutgers—The State University of
New Jersey
Camden College of Arts and
Sciences *B*
Douglass College *B*
Livingston College *B*
Rutgers College *B*
University College New
Brunswick *B*
Stockton State College *C*

New Mexico

New Mexico State University *B*
University of New Mexico *B,M*

New York

Adelphi University *B*
Bard College *B*
Barnard College *B*
Boricua College *B*

City University of New York
Brooklyn College *B*
City College *B*
Hostos Community College *A*
Lehman College *B*
Queens College *B*
Colgate University *B*
Columbia University
Columbia College *B*
New York *M,D*
Fordham University *B*
Long Island University: C. W. Post
Campus *B*
New York University *B,M*
Sarah Lawrence College *B*
State University of New York
Albany *B*
Binghamton *B*
College at Plattsburgh *B*
Syracuse University *B*
Union College *B*
United States Military Academy *B*
Vassar College *B*

North Carolina

University of North Carolina
Chapel Hill *B,M,D*
Greensboro *B*

Ohio

Bowling Green State University *B*
College of Wooster *B*
Denison University *B*
Kent State University *B*
Kenyon College *B*
Oberlin College *B*
Ohio State University: Columbus
Campus *B,M,D*
Ohio University *B,M*
Pontifical College Josephinum *B*
University of Cincinnati *B*
University of Toledo *B*

Oklahoma

University of Oklahoma *B*

Oregon

Willamette University *B*

Pennsylvania

Bucknell University *B*
Dickinson College *C*
Lehigh University *B*
Lock Haven University of
Pennsylvania *B*
Penn State University Park Campus
C,B
St. Joseph's University *C*
University of Pennsylvania *M*

Rhode Island

Brown University *B*
Providence College *B*
Rhode Island College *B*
University of Rhode Island *B*

South Carolina

University of South Carolina *B*

Tennessee

Memphis State University *B*
Rhodes College *B*
University of Tennessee:
Knoxville *B*
Vanderbilt University *B,M*

Texas

Austin College *B*
Baylor University *B*
Rice University *B*
St. Mary's University *B*
Southern Methodist University *B,M*

Texas Christian University *B*
Texas Tech University *B*
Trinity University *B*
University of Texas
    Austin *B,M,D*
    El Paso *B*
    Pan American *B*

Utah

Brigham Young University *B*

Vermont

Goddard College *B,M*
Marlboro College *B*
University of Vermont *B*

Virginia

George Mason University *B*
University of Richmond *B*

Wisconsin

Carthage College *B*
Ripon College *B*
University of Wisconsin
    Eau Claire *B*
    Madison *B,M*

Canada

McGill University *B*

Law

Alabama

Draughons Junior College *A*
Marion Military Institute *A*
University of Alabama *M*

Arizona

Arizona State University *M*

Arkansas

University of Arkansas *B*

California

Golden Gate University *W*
National University *B*
Stanford University *M,D*
University of California
    Berkeley *W*
    Los Angeles *M*
University of the Pacific *M*
University of San Diego *M,W*
University of Southern California *M*
Western State University College of
    Law
    Orange County *B*
    San Diego *B*

Colorado

University of Denver *M*

Connecticut

Yale University *M,D,W*

District of Columbia

George Washington University *M,D*
Georgetown University *M,W*
Howard University *M*

Florida

Nova University *D*
University of Florida *M*
University of Miami *M*

Georgia

Emory University *M,D,W*
Mercer University *B*
University of Georgia *M*

Illinois

De Paul University *M*
Illinois Institute of Technology *M*
Loyola University of Chicago *W*
Northwestern University *W*
Southern Illinois University at
    Carbondale *D*
University of Chicago *M,D*
University of Illinois at Urbana-
    Champaign *M,D*

Indiana

Indiana University Bloomington *M*
Indiana University—Purdue
    University at Indianapolis *W*

Iowa

University of Iowa *M*

Kansas

Central College *A*

Kentucky

Louisville Presbyterian Theological
    Seminary *M*

Louisiana

Louisiana State University and
    Agricultural and Mechanical
    College *M*
Tulane University *M,D,W*

Maryland

Chesapeake College *C,A*

Massachusetts

Boston University *M,W*
Harvard University *W*
Northeastern University *M*
University of Massachusetts at
    Boston *C,B*

Michigan

University of Michigan *M,D*
Wayne State University *M*

Minnesota

Vermilion Community College *A*
William Mitchell College of Law *M*

Mississippi

University of Mississippi *M*

Missouri

University of Missouri: Kansas
    City *M*
Washington University *M*

Nebraska

University of Nebraska—Lincoln
    B,M,D

New York

City University of New York: John
    Jay College of Criminal Justice *B*
Cornell University *M,D*
New York University *M,D*
United States Military Academy *B*

North Carolina

Chowan College *A*

Ohio

Cleveland State University *W*
Union Institute *B,D*

Oregon

Willamette University *D*

Pennsylvania

Dickinson School of Law *M*
Hahnemann University School of
    Health Sciences and
    Humanities *D*
Temple University *M*
University of Pennsylvania *D*
University of Pittsburgh *B*
Westmoreland County Community
    College *C,A*
Widener University *M,D*

South Carolina

University of South Carolina *M*

Texas

Baylor University *B*
Southern Methodist University *M,D*
University of Houston *M*
University of Texas at Austin *M*

Utah

University of Utah *M*

Vermont

Vermont Law School *M*

Virginia

College of William and Mary *M*
University of Virginia *M,D*

Washington

University of Washington *M,D*

West Virginia

Marshall University *B*

Canada

McGill University *W*

Mexico

Sistema Instituto Tecnologico y de
    Estudios Superiores de
    Monterrey *B*

Law enforcement and corrections

Alabama

Auburn University
    Auburn *B*
    Montgomery *B*
Jacksonville State University *B*
James H. Faulkner State
    Community College *A*
Samford University *B*
Troy State University
    Montgomery *B,M*
    Troy *B,M*

Arizona

Northern Arizona University *B*
Western International University *B*
Yavapai College *A*

Arkansas

University of Arkansas
    Fayetteville *B*
    Pine Bluff *B*

California

California Lutheran University *B*
California State University
    Fresno *B,M*
    Long Beach *B*
    Los Angeles *B*
    San Bernardino *B,M*
    Stanislaus *B*
Citrus College *C*

Cosumnes River College *A*
De Anza College *A*
Fresno City College *C,A*
Irvine Valley College *C,A*
MiraCosta College *C,A*
San Diego State University *B,M*
Santa Rosa Junior College *C,A*
West Hills Community College *C,A*

Colorado

Colorado Northwestern Community
    College *C,A*
Western State College of
    Colorado *B*

Connecticut

Northwestern Connecticut
    Community College *A*
Sacred Heart University *B*
University of Hartford *B*
University of New Haven *C,A,B,M*
Western Connecticut State
    University *A,B*

District of Columbia

American University *M*

Florida

Brevard Community College *C*
Daytona Beach Community College
    C,A
Lake City Community College *A*
Manatee Community College *A*
Miami-Dade Community College
    C,A
Palm Beach Community College *C*
Pasco-Hernando Community
    College *C*
Seminole Community College *C*
South Florida Community
    College *C*

Georgia

Armstrong State College *B,M*
Chattahoochee Technical Institute
    C,A
East Georgia College *A*
Gainesville College *A*
Georgia State University *B,M*
Macon College *A*
South Georgia College *A*
Valdosta State College *B*

Idaho

Idaho State University *C*
Lewis Clark State College *B*

Illinois

Black Hawk College *C,A*
Chicago State University *B,M*
City Colleges of Chicago: Chicago
    City-Wide College *C,A*
College of DuPage *A*
Illinois Central College *A*
Lake Land College *A*
MacMurray College *A,B*
Shawnee Community College *C,A*
Southern Illinois University at
    Carbondale *A,B,M*
State Community College *A*
Waubonsee Community College *A*
Western Illinois University *B,M*

Indiana

Indiana State University *M*
Indiana University
    Northwest *B*
    South Bend *B,M*
Indiana University—Purdue
    University at Indianapolis *B*
University of Indianapolis *A,B*
Vincennes University *A*

Iowa

Iowa Lakes Community College *A*
St. Ambrose University *B*
Simpson College *B*
Southeastern Community College:
　North Campus *A*
University of Iowa *M*
Wartburg College *B*
William Penn College *B*

Kansas

Allen County Community
　College *A*
Colby Community College *A*
Fort Scott Community College *A*
Hutchinson Community College *A*
Neosho County Community
　College *A*
Washburn University of Topeka *B*

Kentucky

Eastern Kentucky University *B,M*
Morehead State University *A*
Murray State University *B*
Thomas More College *A,B*
Union College *A,B*
University of Louisville *B,M*

Louisiana

Louisiana State University in
　Shreveport *B*
Southeastern Louisiana
　University *B*
Southern University and
　Agricultural and Mechanical
　College *A*

Maine

Unity College *B*

Maryland

Bowie State University *B*
Catonsville Community College *C,A*
Coppin State College *B,M*
Montgomery College: Rockville
　Campus *A*
University of Baltimore *B,M*

Massachusetts

Becker College
　Leicester Campus *A*
　Worcester Campus *A*
Berkshire Community College *A*
Dean Junior College *A*
Western New England College *B*
Westfield State College *B,M*

Michigan

Charles Stewart Mott Community
　College *C*
Delta College *A*
Ferris State University *B*
Grand Rapids Community
　College *A*
Grand Valley State University *B*
Henry Ford Community College *A*
Jackson Community College *C,A*
Lake Superior State University *A,B*
Lansing Community College *A*
Madonna University *C,A,B*
Mid Michigan Community
　College *A*
Montcalm Community College *C,A*
Northern Michigan University *A,B*
Northwestern Michigan College *A*
Oakland Community College *C,A*
Saginaw Valley State University *B*
Schoolcraft College *A*
Suomi College *C,A*
University of Detroit Mercy *B,M*
University of Michigan: Flint *B*
Western Michigan University *B*

Minnesota

Alexandria Technical College *A*
Lakewood Community College *A*
Mankato State University *B*
Normandale Community College *A*
Northland Community College *A*
St. Mary's College of Minnesota *B*
University of St. Thomas *B*
Willmar Community College *A*

Mississippi

Delta State University *B*
Jackson State University *B*
University of Mississippi *B,M*

Missouri

Central Missouri State University
　B,M
College of the Ozarks *B*
Moberly Area Community
　College *A*
Northeast Missouri State
　University *B*
Park College *B*
St. Louis Community College
　Forest Park *C*
　Meramec *C,A*
St. Louis University *B*
Southeast Missouri State
　University *B*
University of Missouri
　Kansas City *B,M*
　St. Louis *B*

Nebraska

Chadron State College *B*
University of Nebraska—Kearney *B*
Wayne State College *B*

New Hampshire

Hesser College *A*
St. Anselm College *A*

New Jersey

Burlington County College *C*
County College of Morris *A*
Glassboro State College *B*
Mercer County Community
　College *A*
Stockton State College *B*
Trenton State College *B*

New Mexico

Albuquerque Technical-Vocational
　Institute *A*
New Mexico State University *B*
Western New Mexico University
　C,B

New York

Adirondack Community College *A*
City University of New York: John
　Jay College of Criminal Justice
　A,B
Clinton Community College *A*
Elmira College *B*
Fordham University *M*
Iona College *B*
Long Island University: C. W. Post
　Campus *B,M*
Mercy College *B*
Mohawk Valley Community
　College *A*
New York Institute of
　Technology *B*
Onondaga Community College *A*
Rochester Institute of
　Technology *B*
Russell Sage College *B*
Sullivan County Community
　College *A*

North Carolina

Brunswick Community College *C*
Carteret Community College *C*
College of the Albemarle *C*
Craven Community College *C*
Davidson County Community
　College *C*
East Carolina University *B*
James Sprunt Community
　College *C*
North Carolina Central University
　B,M
Pfeiffer College *B*
Rockingham Community College *A*
Surry Community College *A*
University of North Carolina at
　Charlotte *B,M*
Western Carolina University *B*

North Dakota

University of North Dakota: Lake
　Region *C*

Ohio

Bowling Green State University *B*
Cleveland State University *B*
Columbus State Community
　College *A*
Kent State University *B*
Ohio University: Chillicothe
　Campus *A*
Terra Technical College *C*
Tiffin University *B*
Union Institute *B*
University of Akron *A,B*
University of Dayton *B*
Urbana University *B*
Youngstown State University *B,M*

Oklahoma

East Central University *B*
Eastern Oklahoma State College *A*
Langston University *B*
Northern Oklahoma College *A*
Northwestern Oklahoma State
　University *C,B*
Oklahoma City University *B,M*
Oklahoma State University
　Oklahoma City *A*
　Stillwater *M*
University of Oklahoma *B*

Oregon

Portland State University *B,M*
Southern Oregon State College *B*
Southwestern Oregon Community
　College *C*
University of Oregon *M*
Western Oregon State College *B,M*

Pennsylvania

Alvernia College *B*
Edinboro University of
　Pennsylvania *B*
King's College *A,B*
La Salle University *B*
Lehigh County Community College
　C,A
Lycoming College *B*
Mercyhurst College *C,A,B,M*
University of Pittsburgh at
　Greensburg *B*
University of Scranton *A,B*
York College of Pennsylvania *A,B*

Puerto Rico

Caribbean University *A*

Rhode Island

Community College of Rhode
　Island *A*
Roger Williams College *B*

South Carolina

Benedict College *B*
University of South Carolina *M*

South Dakota

Black Hills State University *B*
Western Dakota Vocational
　Technical Institute *C,A*

Tennessee

Austin Peay State University *A*
East Tennessee State University *B*
Middle Tennessee State University
　B,M
Tennessee State University *B,M*
University of Tennessee:
　Chattanooga *B,M*

Texas

Alvin Community College *C,A*
Angelina College *A*
Dallas Baptist University *B*
Hardin-Simmons University *B*
Lamar University—Beaumont *B*
Laredo Junior College *A*
Laredo State University *B*
McLennan Community College *C*
Prairie View A&M University *B*
Sam Houston State University *B,M*
South Plains College *A*
Southwest Texas State University *B*
Tarleton State University *B*
University of Texas: Pan
　American *B*
Wayland Baptist University *B*
Weatherford College *A*
West Texas State University *B*

Utah

Weber State University *A,B*

Vermont

Champlain College *A*

Virginia

Averett College *B*
Christopher Newport College *B*
George Mason University *B*
St. Paul's College *B*
Virginia Commonwealth University
　B,M
Wytheville Community College *C*

Washington

Central Washington University *B*
Eastern Washington University *B*
Shoreline Community College *A*
Spokane Community College *A*
Washington State University *B,M*

West Virginia

Bluefield State College *B*
Marshall University *B,M*
West Virginia State College *B*

Wisconsin

Marquette University *A,B*
Mount Senario College *B*
University of Wisconsin
　Oshkosh *B*
　River Falls *B*

Law enforcement and corrections technologies

Alabama

Chattahoochee Valley Community
　College *A*

Community College of the Air
  Force *A*
Enterprise State Junior College *A*
Jefferson State Community
  College *A*
John C. Calhoun State Community
  College *A*
Lawson State Community
  College *A*
Marion Military Institute *A*
Northeast Alabama State Junior
  College *A*
Snead State Junior College *A*
Troy State University
  Montgomery *A*
  Troy *A*
Wallace State Community College
  at Hanceville *A*

Alaska

University of Alaska Southeast *C*

Arizona

Cochise College *A*
Eastern Arizona College *C,A*
Glendale Community College *C,A*
Mohave Community College *C,A*
Northland Pioneer College *C,A*
Pima Community College *A*
Scottsdale Community College *A*

Arkansas

Arkansas State University *A*
East Arkansas Community
  College *A*
Garland County Community
  College *A*
Mississippi County Community
  College *A*
University of Arkansas
  Little Rock *A*
  Pine Bluff *A*

California

Allan Hancock College *A*
Bakersfield College *A*
Barstow College *C,A*
Cerritos Community College *A*
Cerro Coso Community College
  C,A
Chabot College *A*
City College of San Francisco *A*
College of the Desert *C,A*
College of the Redwoods *C,A*
College of the Sequoias *C,A*
Compton Community College *A*
Crafton Hills College *C,A*
Diablo Valley College *A*
East Los Angeles College *A*
El Camino College *A*
Evergreen Valley College *A*
Fresno City College *C,A*
Gavilan Community College *A*
Glendale Community College *A*
Golden West College *C,A*
Grossmont Community College *C,A*
Hartnell College *A*
Imperial Valley College *A*
Irvine Valley College *C,A*
Kings River Community College *A*
Lake Tahoe Community College *A*
Lassen College *C,A*
Long Beach City College *A*
Los Angeles City College *C,A*
Los Angeles Harbor College *C,A*
Los Angeles Valley College *C,A*
Merced College *A*
Modesto Junior College *A*
Monterey Peninsula College *C,A*
Moorpark College *A*
Mount San Antonio College *C,A*
Mount San Jacinto College *A*

Napa Valley College *C,A*
Ohlone College *C,A*
Palomar College *C,A*
Pasadena City College *C,A*
Porterville College *C,A*
Rio Hondo College *A*
Saddleback College *C,A*
San Diego Miramar College *A*
San Joaquin Delta College *A*
San Jose City College *A*
Santa Monica College *A*
Santa Rosa Junior College *C,A*
Sierra College *A*
Solano Community College *A*
Southwestern College *C,A*
Ventura College *A*
Victor Valley College *C,A*
West Hills Community College *C,A*
Yuba College *A*

Colorado

Aims Community College *C*
Arapahoe Community College *C,A*
Colorado Mountain College: Spring
  Valley Campus *A*
Morgan Community College *C*

Connecticut

Housatonic Community College
  C,A
Manchester Community College *A*
Mattatuck Community College *A*
Northwestern Connecticut
  Community College *A*
Norwalk Community College *A*

Delaware

Delaware Technical and
  Community College
  Southern Campus *A*
  Stanton/Wilmington
    Campus *A*
  Terry Campus *A*

District of Columbia

American University *M*
University of the District of
  Columbia *A*

Florida

Broward Community College *A*
Central Florida Community
  College *A*
Chipola Junior College *A*
Gulf Coast Community College *A*
Hillsborough Community College *A*
Indian River Community College *A*
Lake City Community College *A*
Manatee Community College *A*
North Florida Junior College *C*
Pasco-Hernando Community
  College *A*
Pensacola Junior College *A*
Santa Fe Community College *C*
Tallahassee Community College *A*

Georgia

Abraham Baldwin Agricultural
  College *A*
Armstrong State College *A*
Atlanta Metropolitan College *A*
Bainbridge College *A*
Dalton College *A*
Darton College *A*
Floyd College *A*
LaGrange College *A*
Middle Georgia College *A*

Hawaii

University of Hawaii: Honolulu
  Community College *A*

Idaho

College of Southern Idaho *C,A*
Lewis Clark State College *A*
North Idaho College *A*
Ricks College *A*

Illinois

Belleville Area College *A*
Black Hawk College *C,A*
Carl Sandburg College *A*
City Colleges of Chicago
  Chicago City-Wide College
    C,A
  Richard J. Daley College *A*
Illinois Eastern Community
  Colleges: Olney Central
  College *A*
Illinois Valley Community
  College *A*
John A. Logan College *A*
Joliet Junior College *C,A*
Kishwaukee College *C,A*
Lake Land College *A*
Lewis and Clark Community
  College *A*
Lincoln Land Community College
  C,A
Morton College *A*
Oakton Community College *C,A*
Parkland College *A*
Prairie State College *A*
Rend Lake College *C,A*
Rock Valley College *A*
Southern Illinois University at
  Carbondale *A,B,M*
Spoon River College *A*
Triton College *C,A*
William Rainey Harper College *C,A*

Indiana

Indiana University at South Bend *A*
Indiana Wesleyan University *A*
Vincennes University *A*

Iowa

Des Moines Area Community
  College *A*
Hawkeye Institute of Technology *A*
Iowa Central Community College *A*
Iowa Western Community
  College *A*
Kirkwood Community College *A*
North Iowa Area Community
  College *A*
Scott Community College *A*
Waldorf College *A*

Kansas

Barton County Community
  College *A*
Butler County Community
  College *A*
Cowley County Community College
  C,A
Fort Scott Community College *A*
Highland Community College *A*
Johnson County Community
  College *C,A*
Kansas City Kansas Community
  College *A*
Labette Community College *A*
Seward County Community
  College *A*
Washburn University of Topeka *A*

Kentucky

Campbellsville College *A*
Jefferson Community College *A*
Kentucky Wesleyan College *A*
Murray State University *A*
Northern Kentucky University *A*
University of Louisville *A*

Louisiana

Bossier Parish Community
  College *A*
Louisiana College *A*
Our Lady of Holy Cross College *A*
Southeastern Louisiana
  University *A*

Maine

Southern Maine Technical
  College *A*
University of Maine *A*

Maryland

Allegany Community College *A*
Anne Arundel Community
  College *A*
Catonsville Community College *C,A*
Cecil Community College *C,A*
Chesapeake College *C,A*
Essex Community College *C,A*
Hagerstown Junior College *C,A*
Montgomery College: Rockville
  Campus *A*
New Community College of
  Baltimore *A*
Prince George's Community
  College *A*
Wor-Wic Tech Community
  College *A*

Massachusetts

Becker College
  Leicester Campus *A*
  Worcester Campus *A*
Bunker Hill Community College *A*
Holyoke Community College *A*
Massasoit Community College *A*
Middlesex Community College *A*
Mount Wachusett Community
  College *A*
Quincy College *A*
Quinsigamond Community
  College *A*
Springfield Technical Community
  College *A*

Michigan

Alpena Community College *C,A*
Henry Ford Community College
  C,A
Jackson Community College *C,A*
Kalamazoo Valley Community
  College *A*
Kellogg Community College *A*
Kirtland Community College *C,A*
Lansing Community College *A*
Macomb Community College *C,A*
Madonna University *C,A*
Marygrove College *C,A*
Muskegon Community College *A*
Northwestern Michigan College *A*
Oakland Community College *C,A*
St. Clair County Community
  College *C,A*
West Shore Community College *A*

Minnesota

Inver Hills Community College *A*
Mankato State University *A*
Mesabi Community College:
  Arrowhead Region *A*
Minneapolis Community College *A*
Normandale Community College *A*
Northland Community College *A*
Rochester Community College *A*
Vermilion Community College *A*
Willmar Community College *A*

Mississippi

Hinds Community College *A*
Jones County Junior College *A*

Meridian Community College *A*
Northeast Mississippi Community
  College *A*
Southwest Mississippi Community
  College *A*

Missouri

Hannibal-LaGrange College *A*
Jefferson College *A*
Lincoln University *A*
Longview Community College *A*
Mineral Area College *C,A*
Missouri Southern State College *A*
Penn Valley Community College *A*
St. Louis Community College
    Florissant Valley *A*
    Forest Park *A*
State Fair Community College *A*
Three Rivers Community College *A*

Montana

Dawson Community College *A*

Nebraska

Metropolitan Community College *A*
Northeast Community College *A*

Nevada

Community College of Southern
  Nevada *C,A*
Northern Nevada Community
  College *A*
Truckee Meadows Community
  College *A*
Western Nevada Community
  College *C,A*

New Jersey

Atlantic Community College *A*
Bergen Community College *A*
Brookdale Community College *A*
Camden County College *A*
Cumberland County College *C,A*
Essex County College *A*
Gloucester County College *C,A*
Passaic County Community
  College *A*
Union County College *A*

New Mexico

New Mexico Junior College *A*
New Mexico State University
    Carlsbad *A*
    Las Cruces *A,B*
San Juan College *A*
Western New Mexico University *A*

New York

Adirondack Community College *A*
Columbia-Greene Community
  College *A*
Community College of the Finger
  Lakes *A*
Herkimer County Community
  College *A*
Hilbert College *A*
Hudson Valley Community
  College *A*
Jamestown Community College *A*
Jefferson Community College *C,A*
Monroe Community College *A*
Nassau Community College *A*
Onondaga Community College *A*
Orange County Community
  College *A*
St. Francis College *A*
St. John's University *A*
State University of New York
  College of Technology at
  Farmingdale *A*
Tompkins-Cortland Community
  College *A*

Ulster County Community
  College *A*
Westchester Community College *A*

North Carolina

Alamance Community College *A*
Asheville Buncombe Technical
  Community College *A*
Beaufort County Community
  College *A*
Bladen Community College *A*
Carteret Community College *A*
Central Carolina Community
  College *A*
Central Piedmont Community
  College *A*
Cleveland Community College *A*
Davidson County Community
  College *A*
Edgecombe Community College *A*
Forsyth Technical Community
  College *A*
Gaston College *A*
Guilford Technical Community
  College *A*
Haywood Community College *A*
Isothermal Community College *A*
James Sprunt Community
  College *A*
Johnston Community College *A*
McDowell Technical Community
  College *A*
Mitchell Community College *A*
Nash Community College *A*
Pitt Community College *A*
Richmond Community College *A*
Surry Community College *A*
Vance-Granville Community
  College *A*
Wake Technical Community
  College *A*
Wayne Community College *A*
Western Piedmont Community
  College *A*

North Dakota

Bismarck State College *A*

Ohio

Central Ohio Technical College *A*
Clark State Community College *A*
Columbus State Community
  College *A*
Cuyahoga Community College
    Metropolitan Campus *A*
    Western Campus *A*
Edison State Community College *A*
Hocking Technical College *A*
Jefferson Technical College *A*
Kent State University
    Ashtabula Regional Campus *A*
    East Liverpool Regional
      Campus *A*
Lakeland Community College *A*
Lorain County Community
  College *A*
Miami University: Hamilton
    Campus *A*
Muskingum Area Technical
    College *A*
Owens Technical College
    Findlay Campus *A*
    Toledo *A*
Sinclair Community College *A*
Terra Technical College *C,A*
Tiffin University *A*
University of Akron *A*
University of Toledo *A*
Youngstown State University *A*

Oklahoma

Cameron University *A*
Connors State College *A*
Oklahoma State University:
    Oklahoma City *A*
Redlands Community College *A*
Rogers State College *A*
Tulsa Junior College *A*

Oregon

Chemeketa Community College *A*
Clackamas Community College *A*
Linn-Benton Community College *A*
Portland Community College *C,A*
Southwestern Oregon Community
  College *A*
Treasure Valley Community College
  C,A

Pennsylvania

Bucks County Community
  College *A*
Community College of Beaver
  County *C,A*
Community College of
  Philadelphia *A*
Edinboro University of
  Pennsylvania *A*
Harrisburg Area Community
  College *C,A*
La Salle University *A*
Lackawanna Junior College *A*
Mercyhurst College *C,A*
Montgomery County Community
  College *A*
Mount Aloysius College *A*
Westmoreland County Community
  College *A*
York College of Pennsylvania *A*

Puerto Rico

Puerto Rico Junior College *A*
University of Puerto Rico: Carolina
  Regional College *A*

South Carolina

Tri-County Technical College *A*
University of South Carolina at
  Aiken *A*

South Dakota

Huron University *A*
Oglala Lakota College *A*

Tennessee

Dyersburg State Community
  College *A*
Middle Tennessee State
  University *A*
Roane State Community College *A*
Walters State Community
  College *A*

Texas

Alvin Community College *C,A*
Angelina College *A*
Austin Community College *A*
Bee County College *A*
Central Texas College *A*
Cisco Junior College *A*
College of the Mainland *A*
Cooke County College *A*
El Centro College *A*
El Paso Community College *C,A*
Galveston College *A*
Houston Community College *A*
Howard College *C,A*
Kilgore College *A*
Lamar University—Beaumont *A*
Lee College *C,A*
McLennan Community College *A*
Midland College *A*

Navarro College *A*
North Harris Montgomery
  Community College District *A*
Odessa College *C,A*
San Antonio College *A*
San Jacinto College: Central
    Campus *A*
South Plains College *A*
Tarrant County Junior College *A*
Temple Junior College *A*
Texarkana College *A*
Texas Southmost College *A*
Trinity Valley Community
  College *A*
University of Texas: Pan
    American *A*
Vernon Regional Junior College *A*
Victoria College *A*
Western Texas College *A*

Utah

Southern Utah University *A*
Weber State University *A,B*

Virginia

Blue Ridge Community College *C*
Central Virginia Community
  College *A*
Dabney S. Lancaster Community
  College *A*
John Tyler Community College *A*
Mountain Empire Community
  College *A*
New River Community College *C*
Paul D. Camp Community
    College *A*
Piedmont Virginia Community
  College *A*
Southside Virginia Community
  College *C,A*
Southwest Virginia Community
  College *A*
Wytheville Community College *A*

Washington

Bellevue Community College *A*
Clark College *C,A*
Columbia Basin College *A*
Eastern Washington University *B*
Green River Community College *A*
Lower Columbia College *A*
Olympic College *A*
Pierce College *A*
Shoreline Community College *A*
Skagit Valley College *C,A*
Spokane Community College *A*
Walla Walla Community College *A*

West Virginia

Fairmont State College *A*
West Virginia Northern Community
  College *A*

Wisconsin

Chippewa Valley Technical
  College *A*
Fox Valley Technical College *A*
Madison Area Technical College *A*
Mid-State Technical College *A*
Moraine Park Technical College *A*
Mount Senario College *A*
Northeast Wisconsin Technical
    College *A*
University of Wisconsin: Superior *A*
Waukesha County Technical
    College *A*

Wyoming

Casper College *A*
Central Wyoming College *A*
Eastern Wyoming College *A*

Laramie County Community
College *A*

American Samoa, Caroline Islands, Guam, Marianas, Virgin Islands

Guam Community College *A*
Micronesian Occupational College
C,A
University of the Virgin Islands *A*

Law (J.D.)

Alabama

Faulkner University *F*
Samford University *F*
University of Alabama
Huntsville *F*
Tuscaloosa *F*

Arizona

Arizona State University *F*
University of Arizona *F*

Arkansas

University of Arkansas
Fayetteville *F*
Little Rock *F*

California

Golden Gate University *F*
Humphreys College *F*
John F. Kennedy University *F*
Lincoln University *F*
Loyola Marymount University *F*
National University *F*
New College of California *F*
Pepperdine University *F*
Santa Clara University *F*
Stanford University *F*
University of California
Berkeley *F*
Davis *F*
Los Angeles *F*
University of La Verne *F*
University of the Pacific *F*
University of San Diego *F*
University of San Francisco *F*
University of Southern California *F*
University of West Los Angeles *F*
Western State University College of
Law
Orange County *F*
San Diego *F*
Whittier College *F*

Colorado

University of Colorado at
Boulder *F*
University of Denver *F*

Connecticut

University of Bridgeport *F*
University of Connecticut *F*
Yale University *F*

District of Columbia

American University *F*
Catholic University of America *F*
George Washington University *F*
Georgetown University *F*
Howard University *F*

Florida

Florida State University *F*
Nova University *F*
St. Thomas University *F*
Stetson University *F*
University of Florida *F*

University of Miami *F*

Georgia

Emory University *F*
Georgia State University *F*
Mercer University *F*
University of Georgia *F*

Hawaii

University of Hawaii at Manoa *F*

Idaho

University of Idaho *F*

Illinois

De Paul University *F*
Illinois Institute of Technology *F*
Loyola University of Chicago *F*
Northern Illinois University *F*
Northwestern University *F*
Southern Illinois University at
Carbondale *F*
University of Chicago *F*
University of Illinois at Urbana-
Champaign *F*

Indiana

Indiana University Bloomington *F*
Indiana University—Purdue
University at Indianapolis *F*
University of Notre Dame *F*
Valparaiso University *F*

Iowa

Drake University *F*
University of Iowa *F*

Kansas

University of Kansas *F*
Washburn University of Topeka *F*

Kentucky

Northern Kentucky University *F*
University of Kentucky *F*
University of Louisville *F*

Louisiana

Louisiana State University and
Agricultural and Mechanical
College *F*
Loyola University *F*
Southern University and
Agricultural and Mechanical
College *F*
Tulane University *F*

Maine

University of Maine *F*
University of Southern Maine *F*

Maryland

University of Baltimore *F*
University of Maryland:
Baltimore *F*

Massachusetts

Boston College *F*
Boston University *F*
Harvard University *F*
Northeastern University *F*
Suffolk University *F*
Western New England College *F*

Michigan

University of Detroit Mercy *F*
University of Michigan *F*
Wayne State University *F*

Minnesota

Hamline University *F*
University of Minnesota: Twin
Cities *F*

William Mitchell College of Law *F*

Mississippi

Mississippi College *F*
University of Mississippi *F*

Missouri

St. Louis University *F*
University of Missouri
Columbia *F*
Kansas City *F*
Washington University *F*

Montana

University of Montana *F*

Nebraska

Creighton University *F*
University of Nebraska—Lincoln *F*

New Jersey

Rutgers—The State University of
New Jersey *F*
Seton Hall University *F*

New Mexico

University of New Mexico *F*
Western New Mexico University *F*

New York

Cornell University *F*
Fordham University *F*
Hofstra University *F*
New York University *F*
Pace University: College of White
Plains *F*
St. John's University *F*
State University of New York at
Buffalo *F*
Syracuse University *F*
Touro College *F*
Yeshiva University *F*

North Carolina

Campbell University *F*
Duke University *F*
North Carolina Central
University *F*
University of North Carolina at
Chapel Hill *F*
Wake Forest University *F*

North Dakota

University of North Dakota *F*

Ohio

Capital University *F*
Case Western Reserve University *F*
Cleveland State University *F*
Ohio Northern University *F*
Ohio State University: Columbus
Campus *F*
University of Akron *F*
University of Cincinnati *F*
University of Dayton *F*
University of Toledo *F*

Oklahoma

Oklahoma City University *F*
University of Oklahoma *F*
University of Tulsa *F*

Oregon

Lewis and Clark College *F*
University of Oregon *F*
Willamette University *F*

Pennsylvania

Dickinson School of Law *F*
Duquesne University *F*
Temple University *F*
University of Pennsylvania *F*

University of Pittsburgh *F*
Villanova University *F*
Widener University *F*

Puerto Rico

Inter American University of Puerto
Rico: Metropolitan Campus *F*
Pontifical Catholic University of
Puerto Rico *F*
University of Puerto Rico: Rio
Piedras Campus *F*

South Carolina

University of South Carolina *F*

South Dakota

University of South Dakota *F*

Tennessee

Memphis State University *F*
University of Tennessee:
Knoxville *F*
Vanderbilt University *F*

Texas

Baylor University *F*
St. Mary's University *F*
Southern Methodist University *F*
Southwest Texas State University *F*
Texas Southern University *F*
Texas Tech University *F*
University of Houston *F*
University of Texas at Austin *F*

Utah

Brigham Young University *F*
University of Utah *F*

Vermont

Vermont Law School *F*

Virginia

College of William and Mary *F*
George Mason University *F*
University of Richmond *F*
University of Virginia *F*
Washington and Lee University *F*

Washington

Gonzaga University *F*
University of Puget Sound *F*
University of Washington *F*

West Virginia

West Virginia University *F*

Wisconsin

Marquette University *F*
University of Wisconsin: Madison *F*

Wyoming

University of Wyoming *F*

Canada

McGill University *F*

Legal assistant/paralegal

Alabama

Auburn University at
Montgomery *B*
Community College of the Air
Force *A*
Faulkner University *A*
Gadsden State Community
College *A*
James H. Faulkner State
Community College *A*

John C. Calhoun State Community
   College *A*
Samford University *A,B*
Wallace State Community College
   at Hanceville *A*

Alaska

University of Alaska Southeast *A*

Arizona

Lamson Junior College *A*
Pima Community College *A*

Arkansas

Westark Community College *A*

California

California State University: Chico *C*
Central California Commercial
   College *A*
Cerritos Community College *A*
City College of San Francisco *C,A*
Coastline Community College *C,A*
College of the Redwoods *A*
College of the Sequoias *C,A*
De Anza College *C,A*
El Camino College *A*
Fresno City College *C,A*
Gavilan Community College *C,A*
Glendale Community College *C*
Grossmont Community College *C,A*
Humphreys College *C,B*
Imperial Valley College *A*
Kelsey-Jenney College *C,A*
Lake Tahoe Community College *C*
Los Angeles City College *A*
Los Angeles Mission College *A*
National University *C*
Oxnard College *C,A*
Palomar College *C,A*
Pasadena City College *C,A*
Phillips Junior College
    Condie Campus *A*
    San Fernando Valley Campus
      C,A
Saddleback College *A*
St. Mary's College of California *C*
San Diego City College *A*
San Francisco State University *C*
Skyline College *C,A*
University of La Verne *A,B*
University of West Los Angeles *B*
West Valley College *A*

Colorado

Arapahoe Community College *C,A*
Blair Junior College *A*
Community College of Denver *C,A*
Parks Junior College *A*
Pikes Peak Community College *C,A*

Connecticut

Briarwood College *A*
Manchester Community College *A*
Mattatuck Community College *A*
Northwestern Connecticut
   Community College *A*
Norwalk Community College *A*
Quinnipiac College *B*
Sacred Heart University *A,B*
Teikyo-Post University *A,B*
University of Bridgeport *A*
University of New Haven *C,A*

Delaware

Delaware State College *C*
Delaware Technical and
   Community College: Southern
   Campus *A*
Wesley College *C,A,B*

District of Columbia

University of the District of
   Columbia *A*

Florida

Brevard Community College *A*
Central Florida Community
   College *A*
Daytona Beach Community
   College *A*
Edison Community College *A*
Florida Community College at
   Jacksonville *A*
Fort Lauderdale College *A*
Gulf Coast Community College *C*
Jones College *C,A*
Keiser College of Technology *A*
Manatee Community College *A*
Miami-Dade Community College *A*
Nova University *C*
Okaloosa-Walton Community
   College *C,A*
Orlando College *A,B*
Palm Beach Community College *A*
Pensacola Junior College *A*
St. Petersburg Junior College *A*
Santa Fe Community College *A*
Schiller International University
   A,B
Seminole Community College *A*
South Florida Community
   College *A*
Southern College *A*
Tallahassee Community College *A*
Tampa College *A*
University of Central Florida *B*
University of West Florida *B*
Valencia Community College *A*

Georgia

Athens Area Technical Institute *A*
Augusta College *C*
Floyd College *A*
Gainesville College *A*
Georgia College *B*
Morris Brown College *B*
South College *A*

Hawaii

University of Hawaii: Kapiolani
   Community College *A*

Idaho

Lewis Clark State College *A*

Illinois

Black Hawk College *A*
Elgin Community College *A*
Illinois Central College *C,A*
MacCormac Junior College *A*
Midstate College *C,A*
Robert Morris College: Chicago
   C,A
Roosevelt University *C*
Southern Illinois University at
   Carbondale *B*
William Rainey Harper College *A*

Indiana

Ball State University *A*
Indiana University at South Bend *A*
Indiana Vocational Technical
   College: Central Indiana *A*
International Business College *A*
St. Mary-of-the-Woods College
   C,A,B
University of Evansville *B*
University of Indianapolis *A*
Vincennes University *A*

Iowa

Des Moines Area Community
   College *A*
Iowa Lakes Community College *A*
Iowa Western Community
   College *A*
Kirkwood Community College *A*
Teikyo Marycrest University *C*

Kansas

Brown Mackie College *A*
Hutchinson Community College *A*
Johnson County Community
   College *C,A*
Washburn University of Topeka *A*
Wichita State University *A*

Kentucky

Eastern Kentucky University *A,B*
Morehead State University *B*
Owensboro Junior College of
   Business *A*
Sue Bennett College *A*
Sullivan College *A*
University of Louisville *A*
Watterson College *C,A*

Louisiana

McNeese State University *A*
Nicholls State University *A*
Phillips Junior College: New
   Orleans *A*
Southern University in
   Shreveport *A*
Tulane University *B*

Maine

Andover College *C,A*
Beal College *C,A*
Casco Bay College *C*
Husson College *A*

Maryland

Anne Arundel Community College
   C,A
Chesapeake College *C,A*
Dundalk Community College *A*
Frederick Community College *C,A*
Hagerstown Business College *A*
Hagerstown Junior College *C*
Harford Community College *A*
Montgomery College: Takoma Park
   Campus *C,A*
New Community College of
   Baltimore *C,A*
Villa Julie College *A,B*

Massachusetts

Anna Maria College for Men and
   Women *C,A,B*
Atlantic Union College *A*
Bay Path College *A,B*
Becker College: Worcester
   Campus *A*
Bentley College *A*
Boston University *C,B*
Bridgewater State College *C,B*
Bunker Hill Community College *C*
Elms College *C,A,B*
Endicott College *A*
Fisher College *A*
Massachusetts Bay Community
   College *C,A*
Middlesex Community College *A*
Mount Ida College *A*
Newbury College *A*
North Shore Community College *A*
Northern Essex Community College
   C,A
Quincy College *A*
Suffolk University *C*

Michigan

Charles Stewart Mott Community
   College *A*
Davenport College of Business *A*
Delta College *C,A*
Eastern Michigan University *B*
Ferris State University *A*
Great Lakes Junior College of
   Business *A*
Henry Ford Community College *A*
Kalamazoo Valley Community
   College *A*
Kellogg Community College *A*
Lake Superior State University *A,B*
Lansing Community College *A*
Macomb Community College *A*
Madonna University *A,B*
Michigan Christian College *C,A*
Montcalm Community College *C,A*
Oakland Community College *C,A*
University of Detroit Mercy *A,B*

Minnesota

Hamline University *B*
Inver Hills Community College *A*
Itasca Community College:
   Arrowhead Region *A*
Mankato State University *B*
Moorhead State University *B*
Northland Community College *A*
Winona State University *B*

Mississippi

Mississippi College *C,B*
Mississippi Gulf Coast Community
   College
    Jackson County Campus *A*
    Jefferson Davis Campus *A*
Mississippi University for Women *B*
Northeast Mississippi Community
   College *A*
Phillips Junior College
    Jackson *A*
    Mississippi Gulf Coast *A*
University of Southern
   Mississippi *B*

Missouri

Avila College *C,B*
Missouri Southern State College *A*
Missouri Western State College *C,A*
Penn Valley Community College
   C,A
Phillips Junior College *A*
Rockhurst College *C*
St. Louis Community College at
   Meramec *C,A*
Webster University *C,B*
William Woods College *B*

Montana

College of Great Falls *A,B*
Rocky Mountain College *C,A*

Nebraska

Central Community College *C,A*
College of St. Mary *C,A,B*
Lincoln School of Commerce *A*
Metropolitan Community College *A*
Midland Lutheran College *A,B*
Nebraska Wesleyan University *A*
Union College *A*

Nevada

Community College of Southern
   Nevada *C,A*
Truckee Meadows Community
   College *A*

New Hampshire

Hesser College *A*
New Hampshire Technical College: Nashua *A*
Notre Dame College *C,B*
Rivier College *B*
School for Lifelong Learning *C*

New Jersey

Atlantic Community College *A*
Bergen Community College *A*
Berkeley College of Business *A*
Brookdale Community College *A*
Caldwell College *C*
Cumberland County College *A*
Mercer County Community College *A*
Ocean County College *C,A*
Rider College *B*
Sussex County Community College *C*

New Mexico

Albuquerque Technical-Vocational Institute *A*
Dona Ana Branch Community College of New Mexico State University *A*
Eastern New Mexico University: Roswell Campus *A*
New Mexico State University Carlsbad *C*
Las Cruces *A*
San Juan College *A*

New York

Berkeley College *A*
Briarcliffe: The College for Business *A*
Broome Community College *C,A*
Bryant & Stratton Business Institute: Albany *A*
City University of New York
La Guardia Community College *A*
Lehman College *C*
New York City Technical College *A,B*
Corning Community College *A*
Erie Community College: City Campus *A*
Genesee Community College *A*
Herkimer County Community College *A*
Hilbert College *A*
Iona College *A*
Katharine Gibbs School: Melville *C*
Mercy College *B*
Nassau Community College *A*
New York University *C*
Sage Junior College of Albany, A Division of Russell Sage College *A*
St. John Fisher College *C*
St. John's University *A,B*
Stenotype Academy *A*
Suffolk County Community College
Selden *A*
Western Campus *A*
Sullivan County Community College *A*
Tompkins-Cortland Community College *A*

North Carolina

Caldwell Community College and Technical Institute *A*
Cape Fear Community College *A*
Carteret Community College *A*
Cecils College *A*
Central Carolina Community College *C,A*

Coastal Carolina Community College *A*
Davidson County Community College *C,A*
Durham Technical Community College *A*
Fayetteville Technical Community College *A*
Forsyth Technical Community College *A*
Guilford Technical Community College *C,A*
Johnston Community College *A*
Pitt Community College *A*
Rockingham Community College *A*
Southwestern Community College *A*
Surry Community College *A*
Western Piedmont Community College *A*
Wilson Technical Community College *A*

North Dakota

University of North Dakota: Lake Region *A*

Ohio

Bradford School *A*
Cincinnati Metropolitan College *A*
Clark State Community College *A*
College of Mount St. Joseph *A,B*
Columbus State Community College *A*
Cuyahoga Community College
Metropolitan Campus *A*
Western Campus *A*
Davis Junior College of Business *C,A*
Dyke College *C,A,B*
Edison State Community College *A*
Kent State University: East Liverpool Regional Campus *A*
Lake Erie College *B*
Lakeland Community College *C,A*
Marion Technical College *A*
Muskingum Area Technical College *A*
Northwestern College *C*
Notre Dame College of Ohio *A*
Ohio Dominican College *A*
Ohio Valley Business College *A*
Shawnee State University *A*
Sinclair Community College *A*
University of Cincinnati: Access Colleges *A*
University of Toledo *A*

Oklahoma

Bartlesville Wesleyan College *A*
East Central University *B*
Oklahoma City University *C*
Oklahoma Junior College *A*
Rogers State College *A*
Rose State College *A*
Tulsa Junior College *A*
University of Oklahoma *C*

Oregon

Portland Community College *A*
Southwestern Oregon Community College *C*

Pennsylvania

Cedar Crest College *C*
Central Pennsylvania Business School *C,A*
Clarion University of Pennsylvania *A*
Duquesne University *C*
Gannon University *A*
Harcum Junior College *A*

Harrisburg Area Community College *C,A*
King's College *C,A*
Lackawanna Junior College *A*
Manor Junior College *A*
Marywood College *A,B*
Mount Aloysius College *A*
Northampton County Area Community College *C*
Peirce Junior College *A*
Penn State University Park Campus *C*
Pennsylvania College of Technology *A*
Point Park College *A,B*
St. Vincent College *C*
Westmoreland County Community College *C,A*
Widener University *C,A*

Puerto Rico

Electronic Data Processing College of Puerto Rico *C*
Puerto Rico Junior College *A*

Rhode Island

Johnson & Wales University *A,B*
Roger Williams College *B*

South Carolina

Columbia Junior College of Business *C,A*
Florence-Darlington Technical College *A*
Greenville Technical College *A*
Horry-Georgetown Technical College *C*
Midlands Technical College *A*
Sumter Area Technical College *C*
Technical College of the Lowcountry *A*
Trident Technical College *C,A*

South Dakota

Kilian Community College *A*
National College *A,B*
Western Dakota Vocational Technical Institute *A*

Tennessee

Bristol University *A,B,M*
Chattanooga State Technical Community College *A*
Cleveland State Community College *A*
Knoxville Business College *A*
Memphis State University *C*
Milligan College *C,B*
Pellissippi State Technical Community College *A*
State Technical Institute at Memphis *A*
Volunteer State Community College *A*

Texas

Alvin Community College *A*
Austin Community College *A*
Central Texas College *A*
Collin County Community College District *C,A*
Cooke County College *A*
Del Mar College *A*
East Texas Baptist University *A*
East Texas State University *B*
El Centro College *A*
El Paso Community College *C,A*
Houston Community College *A*
Lee College *C,A*
McMurry University *B*
Midland College *A*
Navarro College *C*

North Harris Montgomery Community College District *C,A*
San Antonio College *A*
Southwest Texas State University *C*
Tarrant County Junior College *A*
Texas Woman's University *B*
University of St. Thomas *B*

Utah

Phillips Junior College: Salt Lake City Campus *A*
Utah Valley Community College *A*

Vermont

Champlain College *A*

Virginia

Blue Ridge Community College *C*
Bluefield College *A*
Central Virginia Community College *C*
Commonwealth College *C,A*
Eastern Mennonite College *A*
Marymount University *B*
Mountain Empire Community College *C*
Northern Virginia Community College *A*
Patrick Henry Community College *C*
Tidewater Community College *C*
University of Richmond *C,A*
Virginia Intermont College *B*

Washington

City University *A*
Clark College *C,A*
Edmonds Community College *A*
Pierce College *C,A*
South Puget Sound Community College *A*
Spokane Community College *A*
Whatcom Community College *A*

West Virginia

College of West Virginia *A*
Marshall University *A,B*
University of Charleston *C,A*

Wisconsin

Chippewa Valley Technical College *A*
Concordia University Wisconsin *B*
Northeast Wisconsin Technical College *A*
Western Wisconsin Technical College *A*

Wyoming

Casper College *C,A*
Laramie County Community College *A*
Western Wyoming Community College *C*

Legal secretary

Alabama

Draughons Junior College *C*
James H. Faulkner State Community College *A*
Lawson State Community College *A*
Shoals Community College *C*
Southern Union State Junior College *A*
Walker State Technical College *A*
Wallace State Community College at Hanceville *A*

Alaska

University of Alaska Anchorage *C*

Arizona

Cochise College *A*
Lamson Junior College *A*
Pima Community College *A*
Yavapai College *C*

Arkansas

University of Central Arkansas *C*

California

Allan Hancock College *C,A*
Chabot College *A*
Chaffey Community College *A*
City College of San Francisco *C,A*
Coastline Community College *C,A*
College of the Redwoods *C,A*
East Los Angeles College *C*
Fresno City College *C,A*
Glendale Community College *C*
Golden West College *C,A*
Heald College
　　Sacramento *C,A*
　　Santa Rosa *C*
Imperial Valley College *C,A*
Kelsey-Jenney College *C,A*
Lake Tahoe Community College
　　C,A
Lassen College *C*
Long Beach City College *C,A*
Los Angeles City College *C,A*
Los Angeles Harbor College *C,A*
Los Angeles Pierce College *C,A*
Merced College *C,A*
Napa Valley College *C,A*
Pacific Union College *A*
Palomar College *C*
Pasadena City College *A*
Phillips Junior College
　　Condie Campus *C*
　　Fresno Campus *C,A*
Porterville College *C*
Saddleback College *C,A*
San Diego Mesa College *C,A*
Santa Rosa Junior College *C,A*
Sierra College *C,A*
Skyline College *C,A*
Solano Community College *A*
Southwestern College *C,A*
Ventura College *C,A*
Yuba College *C*

Colorado

Arapahoe Community College *A*
Colorado Northwestern Community
　　College *A*
Community College of Denver *A*
Front Range Community College *A*
Mesa State College *C,A*
Northeastern Junior College *A*
Parks Junior College *A*
Red Rocks Community College *A*

Connecticut

Briarwood College *C,A*
Manchester Community College *A*
Mattatuck Community College *A*
Middlesex Community College *A*
Northwestern Connecticut
　　Community College *A*
Norwalk Community College *C,A*
South Central Community
　　College *A*
Tunxis Community College *A*

Delaware

Goldey-Beacom College *A*

Florida

Broward Community College *A*
Central Florida Community
　　College *A*
Daytona Beach Community
　　College *A*
Florida Community College at
　　Jacksonville *C*
Florida International University *C*
Florida Keys Community College *A*
Hillsborough Community College *A*
Indian River Community College *A*
Jones College *A*
Miami-Dade Community College *A*
Okaloosa-Walton Community
　　College *C,A*
Pensacola Junior College *A*
Phillips Junior College:
　　Melbourne *A*
St. Petersburg Junior College *A*
Santa Fe Community College *A*
South College: Palm Beach
　　Campus *C*
South Florida Community
　　College *A*
Valencia Community College *A*

Georgia

Athens Area Technical Institute *C*
Augusta Technical Institute *C*
Brewton-Parker College *A*
Clayton State College *A*
DeKalb Technical Institute *C*
Gainesville College *A*
Meadows College of Business *A*
South College *C*

Hawaii

Cannon's International Business
　　College of Honolulu *C,A*
University of Hawaii: Kapiolani
　　Community College *A*

Idaho

Idaho State University *C*
ITT Technical Institute: Boise *C*
Lewis Clark State College *A*
North Idaho College *A*

Illinois

Belleville Area College *A*
Black Hawk College
　　East Campus *A*
　　Moline *A*
City Colleges of Chicago
　　Chicago City-Wide College *C*
　　Richard J. Daley College *C*
College of DuPage *C*
Elgin Community College *C,A*
Gem City College *C*
John A. Logan College *C*
Joliet Junior College *C*
Kishwaukee College *C*
Lake Land College *A*
Lewis and Clark Community
　　College *C,A*
MacCormac Junior College *A*
Midstate College *A*
Moraine Valley Community
　　College *C*
Morton College *A*
Parkland College *A*
Prairie State College *A*
Rend Lake College *A*
Richland Community College *A*
Robert Morris College: Chicago
　　C,A
Rock Valley College *A*
Shawnee Community College *A*
Southern Illinois University at
　　Carbondale *A*
Triton College *C,A*

Waubonsee Community College *C*
William Rainey Harper College *C,A*

Indiana

International Business College *C*
ITT Technical Institute: Fort
　　Wayne *C*
Vincennes University *A*

Iowa

American Institute of Business *A*
American Institute of Commerce *C*
Des Moines Area Community
　　College *A*
Iowa Lakes Community College *C*
Iowa Western Community
　　College *A*
Kirkwood Community College *C*
North Iowa Area Community
　　College *C,A*
Waldorf College *A*

Kansas

Barton County Community
　　College *A*
Butler County Community
　　College *A*
Central College *A*
Cloud County Community
　　College *A*
Coffeyville Community College *A*
Colby Community College *A*
Dodge City Community College *A*
Fort Scott Community College *A*
Highland Community College *A*
Hutchinson Community College *A*
Johnson County Community
　　College *A*
Labette Community College *A*
Pratt Community College *C,A*
Tabor College *B*
Washburn University of Topeka *A*

Kentucky

Hazard Community College *A*
Lees College *A*
Owensboro Junior College of
　　Business *C,A*
St. Catharine College *A*
Sue Bennett College *A*
Sullivan College *A*

Louisiana

Phillips Junior College: New
　　Orleans *C*

Maine

Andover College *A*
Beal College *A*
Casco Bay College *A*
Husson College *A*
Kennebec Valley Technical
　　College *A*
Thomas College *A*

Maryland

Allegany Community College *A*
Catonsville Community College *A*
Chesapeake College *A*
Frederick Community College *A*
Hagerstown Business College *A*
Howard Community College *C,A*
Montgomery College: Rockville
　　Campus *A*
New Community College of
　　Baltimore *A*
Prince George's Community College
　　C,A
Villa Julie College *A*
Wor-Wic Tech Community
　　College *A*

Massachusetts

Aquinas College at Milton *A*
Aquinas College at Newton *C,A*
Atlantic Union College *A*
Bay Path College *A*
Bay State College *A*
Becker College: Worcester
　　Campus *A*
Bristol Community College *A*
Bunker Hill Community College *A*
Cape Cod Community College *C,A*
Dean Junior College *A*
Endicott College *A*
Fisher College *A*
Holyoke Community College *A*
Katharine Gibbs School *C*
Marian Court Junior College *A*
Massasoit Community College *A*
Middlesex Community College *A*
North Shore Community College *A*
Northern Essex Community
　　College *A*
Quincy College *A*
Quinsigamond Community
　　College *A*
Roxbury Community College *A*
Springfield Technical Community
　　College *A*

Michigan

Baker College
　　Flint *A*
　　Muskegon *A*
　　Owosso *A*
Central Michigan University *B*
Charles Stewart Mott Community
　　College *A*
Davenport College of Business *A*
Delta College *A*
Detroit College of Business *A*
Ferris State University *A*
Grand Rapids Baptist College and
　　Seminary *A*
Grand Rapids Community
　　College *A*
Great Lakes Junior College of
　　Business *A*
Henry Ford Community College *A*
Jackson Community College *A*
Jordan College *C,A*
Kalamazoo Valley Community
　　College *C,A*
Kellogg Community College *A*
Kirtland Community College *A*
Lake Superior State University *A*
Lansing Community College *A*
Macomb Community College *C,A*
Michigan Christian College *C,A*
Montcalm Community College *A*
Northern Michigan University *A*
Northwestern Michigan College *A*
Oakland Community College *C*
St. Clair County Community
　　College *C,A*

Minnesota

Alexandria Technical College *C*
Anoka-Ramsey Community
　　College *A*
Inver Hills Community College *C,A*
Itasca Community College:
　　Arrowhead Region *A*
National Education Center: Brown
　　Institute Campus *A*
Northwestern College *A*
Rainy River Community College *C*
Rochester Community College *C,A*
St. Paul Technical College *C*
University of Minnesota:
　　Crookston *A*
Vermilion Community College *A*
Willmar Community College *A*

Willmar Technical College *C,A*

Mississippi

Jones County Junior College *A*
Mississippi Gulf Coast Community
College: Perkinston *A*
Phillips Junior College of Jackson *C*

Missouri

Central Missouri State University *A*
East Central College *C,A*
Jefferson College *A*
Longview Community College *A*
Maple Woods Community
College *C*
Moberly Area Community
College *A*
Penn Valley Community College *C*
Phillips Junior College *C*
St. Louis Community College at
Meramec *A*
Southeast Missouri State
University *C*
State Fair Community College *A*

Montana

Dawson Community College *A*
Miles Community College *A*
Western Montana College of the
University of Montana *A*

Nebraska

Central Community College *C,A*
Lincoln School of Commerce *C*
McCook Community College *A*
Metropolitan Community College *A*
Midland Lutheran College *A*
Northeast Community College *A*
Southeast Community College
Beatrice Campus *A*
Lincoln Campus *A*

Nevada

Community College of Southern
Nevada *C,A*
Northern Nevada Community
College *C*
Truckee Meadows Community
College *A*

New Hampshire

Castle College *C,A*
Hesser College *A*

New Jersey

Berkeley College of Business *A*
Camden County College *A*
Cumberland County College *C,A*
Gloucester County College *A*
Katharine Gibbs School *C*
Rider College *B*

New Mexico

New Mexico State University *C*
Parks College *C*
Western New Mexico University
C,A

New York

Berkeley School: New York City *A*
Bryant & Stratton Business Institute
Albany *C,A*
Buffalo *C,A*
Central City Business Institute *C,A*
City University of New York
La Guardia Community
College *A*
New York City Technical
College *A*
Community College of the Finger
Lakes *A*
Concordia College *A*

Fulton-Montgomery Community
College *A*
Herkimer County Community
College *A*
Hilbert College *A*
Jamestown Business College *A*
Katharine Gibbs School: Melville *C*
Mater Dei College *A*
Mohawk Valley Community
College *A*
Monroe Community College *A*
Nassau Community College *A*
Onondaga Community College *A*
Rochester Business Institute *A*
Sage Junior College of Albany, A
Division of Russell Sage
College *A*
State University of New York
College of Agriculture and
Technology at Morrisville *A*
College of Technology at
Delhi *A*
College of Technology at
Farmingdale *A*
Suffolk County Community College
Selden *A*
Western Campus *A*
Trocaire College *A*
Utica School of Commerce *A*
Westchester Business Institute *A*
Westchester Community College *A*

North Carolina

Anson Community College *A*
Carteret Community College *A*
Cecils College *A*
Central Carolina Community
College *A*
Central Piedmont Community
College *A*
Coastal Carolina Community
College *A*
Craven Community College *A*
Edgecombe Community College *A*
Gaston College *A*
Guilford Technical Community
College *A*
Louisburg College *A*
Mount Olive College *A*
Nash Community College *A*
Piedmont Community College *A*
Rockingham Community College *A*
Stanly Community College *A*
Surry Community College *A*
Wake Technical Community
College *A*
Wayne Community College *A*
Western Piedmont Community
College *A*

North Dakota

Bismarck State College *C,A*
Dickinson State University *A*
Little Hoop Community College *C*
Minot State University *A*
North Dakota State College of
Science *A*
North Dakota State University:
Bottineau and Institute of
Forestry *A*
University of North Dakota
Lake Region *C,A*
Williston *A*

Ohio

Bradford School *C*
Bryant & Stratton Business
Institute: Great Northern *C*
Central Ohio Technical College *A*
Cincinnati Metropolitan College *A*
Clark State Community College *A*

Columbus State Community
College *A*
Dyke College *A*
Edison State Community College *A*
Hocking Technical College *C*
Jefferson Technical College *A*
Lakeland Community College *A*
Miami-Jacobs College *A*
Northwest Technical College *A*
Northwestern College *A*
Ohio University: Chillicothe
Campus *A*
Ohio Valley Business College *C*
Sinclair Community College *A*
Stark Technical College *A*
Terra Technical College *A*
University of Akron *A*
University of Cincinnati
Access Colleges *A*
Clermont College *A*
Raymond Walters College *A*
University of Rio Grande *A*
University of Toledo *A*
Wright State University: Lake
Campus *A*

Oklahoma

Bartlesville Wesleyan College *A*
Connors State College *C,A*
Eastern Oklahoma State College
C,A
Oklahoma State University
Technical Branch: Okmulgee *A*
Rose State College *A*
Southwestern Oklahoma State
University *C*
Tulsa Junior College *C,A*

Oregon

Central Oregon Community
College *A*
Chemeketa Community College *A*
Linn-Benton Community College *A*
Mount Hood Community
College *A*
Portland Community College *A*
Southwestern Oregon Community
College *C*
Treasure Valley Community
College *A*
Umpqua Community College *A*

Pennsylvania

Bucks County Community
College *A*
Butler County Community
College *A*
Central Pennsylvania Business
School *A*
Churchman Business School *A*
Clarion University of
Pennsylvania *A*
DuBois Business College *A*
Gannon University *A*
Harcum Junior College *A*
Harrisburg Area Community
College *A*
Lehigh County Community
College *A*
Luzerne County Community
College *A*
Manor Junior College *C,A*
Mercyhurst College *A*
Montgomery County Community
College *C,A*
Northampton County Area
Community College *C,A*
Peirce Junior College *A*
Pennsylvania College of
Technology *A*
Reading Area Community College
C,A

Robert Morris College *A*
Waynesburg College *A*
Westmoreland County Community
College *A*
York College of Pennsylvania *A*

Puerto Rico

Caribbean University *A*

Rhode Island

Community College of Rhode
Island *A*
Johnson & Wales University *A*

South Carolina

Aiken Technical College *C*
Greenville Technical College *C*
Midlands Technical College *A*
Technical College of the
Lowcountry *A*

South Dakota

Kilian Community College *A*
Mitchell Vocational Technical
Institute *C,A*
National College *A*
Western Dakota Vocational
Technical Institute *C*

Tennessee

Chattanooga State Technical
Community College *A*
Knoxville Business College *C*
Nashville State Technical
Institute *A*
Pellissippi State Technical
Community College *A*
Shelby State Community College *A*
Southern College of Seventh-day
Adventists *A*
State Technical Institute at
Memphis *A*

Texas

Alvin Community College *A*
Amarillo College *A*
Austin Community College *A*
Brazosport College *C,A*
Brookhaven College *A*
Central Texas College *C*
Cooke County College *A*
Del Mar College *A*
Eastfield College *A*
Houston Community College *C*
Laredo Junior College *A*
Lee College *C,A*
McLennan Community College *A*
Midland College *C,A*
Mountain View College *A*
North Harris Montgomery
Community College District *C*
Northeast Texas Community
College *C,A*
Richland College *A*
St. Philip's College *A*
San Antonio College *A*
South Plains College *A*
Southwestern Adventist College *A*
Texas Southmost College *A*
Texas State Technical College:
Harlingen *A*

Utah

LDS Business College *A*
Phillips Junior College: Salt Lake
City Campus *C,A*
Stevens-Henager College of
Business *A*
Utah Valley Community College
C,A

Vermont

Champlain College *A*

Virginia

Bluefield College *A*
Commonwealth College *A*
Mountain Empire Community
  College *A*
National Business College *A*
Tidewater Community College *C,A*

Washington

Big Bend Community College *A*
Centralia College *A*
Clark College *C,A*
Columbia Basin College *C*
Edmonds Community College *A*
Grays Harbor College *A*
Green River Community College *A*
Lower Columbia College *C,A*
Olympic College *C,A*
Pierce College *C,A*
Shoreline Community College *C,A*
South Puget Sound Community
  College *A*
Spokane Community College *C,A*
Walla Walla Community College *A*
Wenatchee Valley College *A*
Whatcom Community College *C*
Yakima Valley Community College
  C,A

West Virginia

Bluefield State College *A*
College of West Virginia *A*
Marshall University *A,B*
West Virginia Institute of
  Technology *A*
West Virginia State College *A*

Wisconsin

Chippewa Valley Technical
  College *A*
Concordia University Wisconsin *A*
Fox Valley Technical College *A*
Madison Junior College of
  Business *A*
Milwaukee College of Business *C,A*
Moraine Park Technical College *A*
Northeast Wisconsin Technical
  College *A*
Stratton College *A*
Western Wisconsin Technical
  College *A*

Wyoming

Eastern Wyoming College *A*
Western Wyoming Community
  College *C*

Liberal/general studies

Alabama

Alabama Southern Community
  College *A*
Alabama State University *A,B*
Athens State College *B*
Auburn University at Montgomery
  B,M
Birmingham-Southern College *B*
Brewer State Junior College *A*
Chattahoochee Valley Community
  College *A*
Concordia College *A*
Enterprise State Junior College *A*
Faulkner University *A,B*
Gadsden State Community
  College *A*

George C. Wallace State
  Community College at Selma *A*
Huntingdon College *A,B*
Jacksonville State University *B*
James H. Faulkner State
  Community College *A*
Jefferson State Community
  College *A*
John C. Calhoun State Community
  College *A*
Lawson State Community
  College *A*
Lurleen B. Wallace State Junior
  College *A*
Marion Military Institute *A*
Mobile College *A,B*
Northeast Alabama State Junior
  College *A*
Oakwood College *B*
Samford University *A,B*
Selma University *A*
Shelton State Community
  College *A*
Shoals Community College *A*
Snead State Junior College *A*
Southeastern Bible College *A*
Southern Union State Junior
  College *A*
Spring Hill College *B*
Troy State University
  Dothan *A*
  Montgomery *A*
  Troy *A*
University of North Alabama *B*
University of South Alabama *B*
Walker College *A*
Wallace State Community College
  at Hanceville *A*

Alaska

Alaska Pacific University *M*
Prince William Sound Community
  College *A*
Sheldon Jackson College *A,B*
University of Alaska
  Anchorage *A,B,M*
  Fairbanks *A*
  Southeast *A,B*

Arizona

Arizona State University *B*
Arizona Western College *A*
Cochise College *A*
Eastern Arizona College *A*
Glendale Community College *A*
Grand Canyon University *B*
Mohave Community College *A*
Navajo Community College *A*
Northern Arizona University *B*
Northland Pioneer College *A*
Pima Community College *A*
Prescott College *B*
Rio Salado Community College *A*
Scottsdale Community College *A*
South Mountain Community
  College *A*
Southwestern College *A*
University of Arizona *B*
Western International University
  A,B
Yavapai College *A*

Arkansas

Arkansas Baptist College *A*
Arkansas State University
  Beebe Branch *A*
  Jonesboro *A,B*
Arkansas Tech University *A*
Central Baptist College *A*
Crowley's Ridge College *A*
East Arkansas Community
  College *A*

Garland County Community
  College *A*
Hendrix College *B*
John Brown University *A,B*
Mississippi County Community
  College *A*
North Arkansas Community
  College *A*
Ouachita Baptist University *B*
Phillips County Community
  College *A*
Shorter College *A*
Southern Arkansas Community
  College *A*
Southern Arkansas University:
  Technical Branch *A*
University of Arkansas
  Little Rock *A,B*
  Pine Bluff *B*
University of the Ozarks *B*
Westark Community College *A*
Williams Baptist College *A*

California

Allan Hancock College *A*
Antioch Southern California
  Los Angeles *B*
  Santa Barbara *B*
Armstrong College *A*
Azusa Pacific University *B*
Bakersfield College *A*
Barstow College *A*
Bethany College *B*
Biola University *B*
California Baptist College *B*
California Lutheran University *B*
California Polytechnic State
  University: San Luis Obispo *B*
California State Polytechnic
  University: Pomona *B*
California State University
  Bakersfield *B*
  Chico *B,M*
  Dominguez Hills *B*
  Fullerton *B*
  Hayward *B*
  Long Beach *B*
  Los Angeles *B*
  Northridge *B*
  Sacramento *B*
  San Bernardino *B*
  San Marcos *B*
  Stanislaus *B*
Cerritos Community College *A*
Cerro Coso Community College *A*
Chabot College *A*
Chaffey Community College *A*
Chapman University *B*
Christ College Irvine *B*
Citrus College *A*
City College of San Francisco *A*
Coastline Community College *A*
College of the Desert *A*
College of Marin: Kentfield *A*
College of Notre Dame *B*
College of the Sequoias *A*
Columbia College *A*
Compton Community College *A*
Cosumnes River College *A*
Crafton Hills College *A*
Cuesta College *A*
De Anza College *A*
Diablo Valley College *A*
Dominican College of San Rafael *B*
D-Q University *A*
East Los Angeles College *A*
El Camino College *A*
Evergreen Valley College *A*
Feather River College *A*
Foothill College *A*
Fresno City College *A*
Fresno Pacific College *A,B*

Gavilan Community College *A*
Glendale Community College *A*
Golden West College *A*
Grossmont Community College *A*
Hartnell College *A*
Holy Names College *B*
Humphreys College *A*
Imperial Valley College *A*
Irvine Valley College *A*
John F. Kennedy University *B*
Kings River Community College *A*
La Sierra University *B*
Lake Tahoe Community College *A*
Laney College *A*
Lassen College *A*
Long Beach City College *A*
Los Angeles City College *A*
Los Angeles Harbor College *A*
Los Angeles Mission College *A*
Los Angeles Pierce College *A*
Los Angeles Trade and Technical
  College *A*
Los Angeles Valley College *A*
Los Medanos College *A*
Loyola Marymount University *B*
Marymount College *A*
Master's College *B*
Mendocino College *A*
Menlo College *A*
Merced College *A*
Mills College *B,M*
MiraCosta College *A*
Mission College *A*
Modesto Junior College *A*
Monterey Peninsula College *C,A*
Moorpark College *A*
Mount St. Mary's College *A*
Mount San Antonio College *A*
Mount San Jacinto College *A*
Napa Valley College *A*
National University *A,B*
Occidental College *B*
Ohlone College *A*
Oxnard College *A*
Pacific Christian College *A*
Pacific Union College *A,B*
Palomar College *A*
Pasadena City College *C,A*
Patten College *A,B*
Pepperdine University *B*
Pitzer College *B*
Point Loma Nazarene College *B*
Pomona College *B*
Porterville College *A*
Rio Hondo College *A*
Saddleback College *A*
St. John's Seminary College *B*
St. Mary's College of California *B*
San Diego City College *A*
San Diego Mesa College *A*
San Diego Miramar College *A*
San Francisco State University *B*
San Joaquin Delta College *A*
San Jose City College *A*
San Jose State University *B*
Santa Barbara City College *A*
Santa Clara University *B*
Santa Monica College *A*
Santa Rosa Junior College *A*
Scripps College *B*
Sierra College *A*
Simpson College *B*
Skyline College *A*
Solano Community College *A*
Sonoma State University *B*
Southwestern College *A*
Stanford University *B*
Taft College *A*
Thomas Aquinas College *B*
United States International
  University *A,B*

University of California
Riverside *B*
Santa Barbara *B*
University of Judaism *B*
University of La Verne *B*
University of the Pacific *B*
University of Redlands *B*
University of San Diego *B*
University of San Francisco *B*
Ventura College *A*
Victor Valley College *A*
West Hills Community College *A*
West Valley College *A*
Westmont College *B*
Whittier College *B*
World College West *B*
Yuba College *A*

Colorado

Adams State College *A*
Aims Community College *A*
Arapahoe Community College *A*
Blair Junior College *A*
Colorado Christian University *B*
Colorado College *B*
Colorado Mountain College
Alpine Campus *A*
Spring Valley Campus *A*
Timberline Campus *A*
Colorado Northwestern Community
College *A*
Community College of Denver *A*
Front Range Community College *A*
Lamar Community College *A*
Mesa State College *A,B*
Morgan Community College *A*
Naropa Institute *B*
Northeastern Junior College *A*
Otero Junior College *A*
Pikes Peak Community College *A*
Red Rocks Community College *A*
Regis College of Regis University *B*
Trinidad State Junior College *A*
United States Air Force
Academy *B*
University of Colorado
Boulder *B*
Colorado Springs *B*
Denver *B*

Connecticut

Albertus Magnus College *A,B,M*
Asnuntuck Community College *A*
Central Connecticut State
University *B*
Charter Oak College *A,B*
Eastern Connecticut State
University *A,B*
Holy Apostles College and
Seminary *A,B*
Housatonic Community College *A*
Manchester Community College *A*
Mattatuck Community College *A*
Middlesex Community College *A*
Mitchell College *A*
Northwestern Connecticut
Community College *A*
Norwalk Community College *A*
Quinebaug Valley Community
College *A*
Quinnipiac College *B*
Sacred Heart University *A,B*
South Central Community
College *A*
Southern Connecticut State
University *A,B*
Teikyo-Post University *A,B*
Tunxis Community College *A*
University of Bridgeport *A,B*
University of Connecticut *B*
University of Hartford *A*
University of New Haven *A*

Wesleyan University *B*
Western Connecticut State
University *A,B*

Delaware

Delaware Technical and
Community College: Southern
Campus *A*
University of Delaware *A,B,M*
Wesley College *A,B*
Wilmington College *A*

District of Columbia

American University *A,B*
Catholic University of America *B*
Gallaudet University *B*
George Washington University *B*
Georgetown University *B,M*
Mount Vernon College *A,B*

Florida

Barry University *B*
Brevard Community College *A*
Broward Community College *A*
Central Florida Community
College *A*
Chipola Junior College *A*
Daytona Beach Community
College *A*
Edison Community College *A*
Flagler College *B*
Florida Agricultural and Mechanical
University *A*
Florida Christian College *A*
Florida College *A*
Florida International University *B*
Florida Keys Community College *A*
Florida State University *A*
Gulf Coast Community College *A*
Hillsborough Community College *A*
Indian River Community College *A*
Jacksonville University *B*
Lake City Community College *A*
Lake-Sumter Community College *A*
Lynn University *A*
Miami-Dade Community College *A*
New College of the University of
South Florida *B*
North Florida Junior College *A*
Nova University *B,M*
Okaloosa-Walton Community
College *A*
Palm Beach Community College *A*
Pasco-Hernando Community
College *A*
Pensacola Junior College *A*
Rollins College *M*
St. Johns River Community
College *A*
St. Leo College *A*
St. Thomas University *B*
Santa Fe Community College *A*
Schiller International University
A,B
Seminole Community College *A*
Tallahassee Community College *A*
University of Central Florida *A,B*
University of Florida *A*
University of Miami *B*
University of North Florida *A,B*
University of South Florida *A,B,M*
University of West Florida *A*
Valencia Community College *A*
Warner Southern College *A*

Georgia

Abraham Baldwin Agricultural
College *A*
Andrew College *A*
Armstrong State College *A,B*
Atlanta Metropolitan College *A*
Augusta College *A*

Bainbridge College *A*
Berry College *B*
Brenau Women's College *B*
Brewton-Parker College *A,B*
Brunswick College *A*
Clayton State College *A*
Columbus College *A,B*
Covenant College *B*
Dalton College *A*
Darton College *A*
DeKalb College *A*
East Georgia College *A*
Emmanuel College *A*
Emory University *B,M,D*
Floyd College *A*
Gainesville College *A*
Georgia College *B*
Georgia Southern University *B*
Georgia State University *M*
Gordon College *A*
LaGrange College *A*
Macon College *A*
Middle Georgia College *A*
Oglethorpe University *B*
Reinhardt College *A*
Shorter College *B*
South Georgia College *A*
Thomas College *A*
Toccoa Falls College *A*
Truett-McConnell College *A*
University of Georgia *B*
Valdosta State College *A,B*
Waycross College *A*
Wesleyan College *B*
West Georgia College *B*
Young Harris College *A*

Hawaii

Hawaii Loa College *B*
Hawaii Pacific University *B*
University of Hawaii
Hilo *B*
Honolulu Community
College *A*
Kapiolani Community
College *A*
Kauai Community College *A*
Leeward Community
College *A*
Manoa *B*

Idaho

Boise State University *B,M*
College of Southern Idaho *A*
Idaho State University *B*
Lewis Clark State College *A,B*
North Idaho College *A*
Northwest Nazarene College *B*
Ricks College *A*
University of Idaho *B,M*

Illinois

Barat College *B*
Belleville Area College *A*
Black Hawk College
East Campus *A*
Moline *A*
Blackburn College *B*
Bradley University *M*
Carl Sandburg College *A*
City Colleges of Chicago
Chicago City-Wide College *A*
Malcolm X College *A*
Olive-Harvey College *A*
Richard J. Daley College *A*
Wright College *A*
College of DuPage *A*
College of Lake County *A*
Columbia College *B*
De Paul University *B,M*
Eastern Illinois University *B*
East-West University *B*

Elgin Community College *A*
Governors State University *B*
Greenville College *B*
Highland Community College *A*
Illinois Central College *A*
Illinois College *B*
Illinois Eastern Community
Colleges
Frontier Community
College *A*
Lincoln Trail College *A*
Olney Central College *A*
Wabash Valley College *A*
Illinois State University *B*
Illinois Valley Community
College *A*
John A. Logan College *A*
Joliet Junior College *A*
Kendall College *A,B*
Kishwaukee College *A*
Lake Forest College *B,M*
Lake Land College *A*
Lewis and Clark Community
College *A*
Lewis University *B*
Lincoln Land Community
College *A*
Millikin University *B*
Monmouth College *B*
Montay College *A*
Moraine Valley Community
College *A*
Morton College *A*
North Central College *B,M*
Northern Illinois University *B*
Northwestern University *M*
Oakton Community College *A*
Olivet Nazarene University *B*
Parkland College *A*
Prairie State College *A*
Rend Lake College *A*
Richland Community College *A*
Rock Valley College *A*
Rockford College *B*
Roosevelt University *B,M*
St. Augustine College *A*
St. Xavier University *B*
Sangamon State University *B*
Shawnee Community College *A*
Shimer College *B*
Southern Illinois University
Carbondale *B*
Edwardsville *B*
Spoon River College *A*
Springfield College in Illinois *A*
Trinity College *B*
Triton College *A*
University of Chicago *B*
Western Illinois University *B*
Wheaton College *B*
William Rainey Harper College *A*

Indiana

Ancilla College *A*
Ball State University *A*
Bethel College *B*
Calumet College of St. Joseph *A,B*
Goshen College *B*
Holy Cross College *A*
Indiana State University *A*
Indiana University
Bloomington *A,B*
East *A,B*
Kokomo *A,B*
Northwest *A,B*
South Bend *A,B,M*
Southeast *A,B*
Indiana University—Purdue
University
Fort Wayne *A,B*
Indianapolis *A,B*
Oakland City College *A*

Purdue University
   Calumet *A*
   North Central Campus *B*
St. Francis College *B*
St. Joseph's College *A*
St. Mary-of-the-Woods College *A,B*
University of Evansville *B*
University of Indianapolis *A*
University of Notre Dame *B*
University of Southern Indiana *M*
Valparaiso University *B,M*
Vincennes University *A*

Iowa

Briar Cliff College *A*
Buena Vista College *B*
Central College *B*
Clarke College *B*
Clinton Community College *A*
Coe College *B*
Cornell College *B*
Des Moines Area Community
   College *A*
Divine Word College *A*
Dordt College *A,B*
Drake University *B,M*
Graceland College *B*
Grand View College *A,B*
Hawkeye Institute of Technology *A*
Indian Hills Community College *A*
Iowa Central Community College *A*
Iowa Lakes Community College *A*
Iowa State University *B,M*
Iowa Wesleyan College *B*
Iowa Western Community
   College *A*
Kirkwood Community College *A*
Loras College *A,B*
Luther College *B*
Maharishi International
   University *A*
Morningside College *B*
Mount Mercy College *B*
Mount St. Clare College *A,B*
Muscatine Community College *A*
North Iowa Area Community
   College *A*
St. Ambrose University *B*
Scott Community College *A*
Southeastern Community College
   North Campus *A*
   South Campus *A*
Southwestern Community
   College *A*
Teikyo Marycrest University *A,B*
Teikyo Westmar University *B*
University of Dubuque *A*
University of Iowa *B*
University of Northern Iowa *B*
Upper Iowa University *A*
Vennard College *A*
Waldorf College *A*
Wartburg College *B*
William Penn College *B*

Kansas

Allen County Community
   College *A*
Baker University *M*
Barton County Community
   College *A*
Benedictine College *B*
Bethel College *B*
Butler County Community
   College *A*
Central College *A*
Coffeyville Community College *A*
Colby Community College *A*
Cowley County Community
   College *A*
Dodge City Community College *A*
Donnelly College *A*

Emporia State University *B*
Fort Scott Community College *A*
Friends University *B*
Haskell Indian Junior College *A*
Hesston College *A*
Highland Community College *A*
Hutchinson Community College *A*
Johnson County Community
   College *A*
Kansas Newman College *A*
Labette Community College *A*
Neosho County Community
   College *A*
Pittsburg State University *B*
Pratt Community College *A*
St. Mary College *A*
Seward County Community
   College *A*
Southwestern College *B,M*
Sterling College *B*
Tabor College *A,B*
University of Kansas *B*
Washburn University of Topeka *A,B*
Wichita State University *B,M*

Kentucky

Bellarmine College *B*
Brescia College *B*
Elizabethtown Community
   College *A*
Hazard Community College *A*
Jefferson Community College *A*
Kentucky Christian College *A*
Kentucky State University *A,B*
Lees College *A*
Lexington Community College *A*
Lindsey Wilson College *A,B*
Madisonville Community College *A*
Maysville Community College *A*
Morehead State University *A,B*
Paducah Community College *A*
Prestonburg Community College *A*
St. Catharine College *A*
Southeast Community College *A*
Spalding University *B*
Sue Bennett College *A*
Thomas More College *B*
Union College *A*
University of Kentucky *B*
University of Louisville *A,B,M*
Western Kentucky University *A,B*

Louisiana

Bossier Parish Community
   College *A*
Centenary College of Louisiana *B*
Grambling State University *M*
Louisiana College *B*
Louisiana State University
   Agricultural and Mechanical
     College *B*
   Eunice *A*
   Shreveport *B,M*
Louisiana Tech University *A,B*
Loyola University *B*
McNeese State University *A,B*
Nicholls State University *B*
Northeast Louisiana University *A,B*
Northwestern State University *A,B*
St. Joseph Seminary College *B*
Southeastern Louisiana
   University *B*
Tulane University *M*
University of New Orleans *B*
University of Southwestern
   Louisiana *A,B*

Maine

Thomas College *A*
Unity College *A,B*

University of Maine
   Augusta *A,B*
   Farmington *A,B*
   Fort Kent *A,B*
   Machias *A,B*
   Orono *A,B,M*
   Presque Isle *A,B*
University of New England *B*
University of Southern Maine *A,B*

Maryland

Allegany Community College *A*
Anne Arundel Community
   College *A*
Catonsville Community College *A*
Cecil Community College *A*
Charles County Community
   College *A*
Chesapeake College *A*
College of Notre Dame of
   Maryland *B,M*
Columbia Union College *A,B*
Dundalk Community College *A*
Essex Community College *A*
Frederick Community College *A*
Garrett Community College *A*
Hagerstown Junior College *A*
Harford Community College *A*
Howard Community College *A*
Maryland College of Art and
   Design *A*
Montgomery College
   Germantown Campus *A*
   Rockville Campus *A*
   Takoma Park Campus *A*
Mount St. Mary's College *B*
New Community College of
   Baltimore *A*
Prince George's Community
   College *A*
St. John's College *B,M*
St. Mary's College of Maryland *B*
Salisbury State University *B*
Towson State University *B,M*
University of Baltimore *B*
University of Maryland
   Baltimore County *B*
   College Park *B*
   Eastern Shore *B*
   University College *A,B*
Villa Julie College *A,B*
Western Maryland College *M*
Wor-Wic Tech Community
   College *A*

Massachusetts

American International College *B*
Anna Maria College for Men and
   Women *B*
Aquinas College at Milton *A*
Aquinas College at Newton *A*
Assumption College *B*
Bay Path College *A*
Becker College
   Leicester Campus *A*
   Worcester Campus *A*
Bentley College *B*
Berkshire Community College *A*
Boston University *B,M,D*
Bristol Community College *A*
Bunker Hill Community College *A*
Cape Cod Community College *A*
Dean Junior College *A*
Eastern Nazarene College *A*
Elms College *B*
Endicott College *A*
Fisher College *A*
Framingham State College *B*
Greenfield Community College *A*
Hampshire College *B*
Harvard University *M*
Holyoke Community College *A*

Lasell College *A*
Lesley College *B*
Massachusetts Bay Community
   College *C,A*
Massachusetts Institute of
   Technology *B*
Massasoit Community College *A*
Middlesex Community College *A*
Mount Ida College *A,B*
Mount Wachusett Community
   College *A*
North Adams State College *B*
North Shore Community College *A*
Northeastern University *A,B*
Northern Essex Community
   College *A*
Pine Manor College *A*
Quincy College *A*
Quinsigamond Community
   College *A*
Roxbury Community College *A*
St. John's Seminary College *B*
Salem State College *B*
Simmons College *B,M*
Simon's Rock College of Bard *A,B*
Springfield College *B*
Springfield Technical Community
   College *A*
Suffolk University *A*
Tufts University *B,M,D*
University of Massachusetts
   Amherst *B*
   Lowell *B*
Western New England College *A,B*
Westfield State College *B*
Wheaton College *B*

Michigan

Alma College *B*
Alpena Community College *A*
Andrews University *A,M*
Aquinas College *A,B*
Baker College: Flint *A*
Calvin College *B*
Central Michigan University *B*
Charles Stewart Mott Community
   College *A*
Concordia College *A,B*
Delta College *A*
Detroit College of Business *A*
Eastern Michigan University *B*
Ferris State University *A*
Glen Oaks Community College *A*
Grace Bible College *A*
Grand Rapids Community
   College *A*
Grand Valley State University *B*
Henry Ford Community College *A*
Hope College *B*
Jackson Community College *A*
Jordan College *A*
Kalamazoo Valley Community
   College *A*
Kellogg Community College *A*
Kirtland Community College *A*
Lake Superior State University *A*
Lansing Community College *A*
Macomb Community College *A*
Marygrove College *A,B*
Michigan Christian College *A*
Michigan State University *B,D*
Michigan Technological University
   A,B
Mid Michigan Community
   College *A*
Montcalm Community College *A*
Muskegon Community College *A*
Northern Michigan University *A*
Northwestern Michigan College *A*
Northwood Institute *A*
Oakland Community College *A*
Oakland University *B*

Olivet College *B*
Reformed Bible College *A*
Sacred Heart Major Seminary *B*
St. Clair County Community
    College *A*
St. Mary's College *B*
Schoolcraft College *A*
Siena Heights College *A,B*
Southwestern Michigan College *A*
Spring Arbor College *A*
Suomi College *A*
University of Detroit Mercy *M*
University of Michigan
    Ann Arbor *B*
    Dearborn *B*
    Flint *B,M*
Wayne State University *B*
West Shore Community College *A*
Western Michigan University *B*
William Tyndale College *A,B*

Minnesota

Anoka-Ramsey Community
    College *A*
Austin Community College *A*
Bemidji State University *A*
Bethany Lutheran College *A*
Bethel College *A*
Brainerd Community College *A*
College of St. Benedict *A*
College of St. Scholastica *B*
Concordia College: St. Paul *A,B*
Crown College *A*
Inver Hills Community College *A*
Itasca Community College:
    Arrowhead Region *A*
Lakewood Community College *A*
Mankato State University *A,B,M*
Mesabi Community College:
    Arrowhead Region *A*
Metropolitan State University *B*
Minneapolis Community College *A*
Moorhead State University *A,M*
Normandale Community College *A*
North Central Bible College *A*
Northland Community College *A*
Northwestern College *A*
Rainy River Community College *A*
Rochester Community College *A*
St. Cloud State University *B*
St. Mary's College of Minnesota *B*
Southwest State University *B*
University of Minnesota: Twin
    Cities *B*
University of St. Thomas *B*
Vermilion Community College *A*
Willmar Community College *A*
Winona State University *A,B*
Worthington Community College *A*

Mississippi

Copiah-Lincoln Community
    College *A*
East Central Community College *A*
Hinds Community College *A*
Holmes Community College *A*
Jones County Junior College *A*
Mary Holmes College *A*
Meridian Community College *A*
Mississippi Delta Community
    College *A*
Mississippi Gulf Coast Community
    College
        Jackson County Campus *A*
        Jefferson Davis Campus *A*
Mississippi State University *B*
Northeast Mississippi Community
    College *A*
Rust College *B*
Southwest Mississippi Community
    College *A*
University of Mississippi *B*

William Carey College *B*
Wood Junior College *A*

Missouri

Avila College *A,B*
Columbia College *A,B*
Cottey College *A*
East Central College *A*
Evangel College *A*
Fontbonne College *B*
Hannibal-LaGrange College *A*
Jefferson College *A*
Kemper Military School and
    College *A*
Longview Community College *A*
Maple Woods Community
    College *A*
Maryville University *B*
Mineral Area College *A*
Missouri Southern State College
    A,B
Missouri Valley College *B*
Moberly Area Community
    College *A*
North Central Missouri College *A*
Penn Valley Community College *A*
St. Louis Community College
        Florissant Valley *A*
        Forest Park *A*
        Meramec *A*
St. Louis University *B*
Southeast Missouri State
    University *B*
Southwest Baptist University *A,B*
Southwest Missouri State
    University *A*
State Fair Community College *A*
Stephens College *A,B*
Three Rivers Community College *A*
University of Missouri
        Columbia *B*
        Kansas City *B*
        St. Louis *B*
Washington University *B,M*
Webster University *B*
Wentworth Military Academy and
    Junior College *A*
William Jewell College *B*
William Woods College *B*

Montana

Carroll College *B*
College of Great Falls *B*
Dawson Community College *A*
Dull Knife Memorial College *A*
Eastern Montana College *A*
Flathead Valley Community
    College *A*
Fort Peck Community College *A*
Little Big Horn College *A*
Miles Community College *A*
Northern Montana College *A,B*
Rocky Mountain College *A,B*
Salish Kootenai College *A*
Stone Child College *A*
University of Montana *A,B*

Nebraska

Central Community College *A*
Chadron State College *B*
College of St. Mary *A*
Dana College *B*
Doane College *B*
Hastings College *B*
McCook Community College *A*
Metropolitan Community College *A*
Midland Lutheran College *B*
Nebraska Indian Community
    College *A*
Northeast Community College *A*
Southeast Community College:
    Beatrice Campus *A*

Union College *A*
University of Nebraska
    Lincoln *B*
    Omaha *B*
Western Nebraska Community
    College: Scottsbluff Campus *A*
York College *A*

Nevada

Community College of Southern
    Nevada *A*
Deep Springs College *A*
Northern Nevada Community
    College *A*
Sierra Nevada College *B*
Truckee Meadows Community
    College *A*
University of Nevada
    Las Vegas *B,M*
    Reno *B*
Western Nevada Community
    College *A*

New Hampshire

Colby-Sawyer College *A*
Daniel Webster College *A*
Dartmouth College *M*
Franklin Pierce College *A,B*
Hesser College *A*
Keene State College *A,B,M*
New England College *A,B*
New Hampshire Technical College:
    Stratham *A*
Notre Dame College *A*
Plymouth State College of the
    University System of New
    Hampshire *A,B*
Rivier College *B*
St. Anselm College *B*
School for Lifelong Learning *A,B*
University of New Hampshire
    Durham *A,B*
    Manchester *A*
White Pines College *A*

New Jersey

Assumption College for Sisters *A*
Atlantic Community College *A*
Bergen Community College *A*
Brookdale Community College *A*
Burlington County College *A*
Camden County College *A*
Centenary College *A,B*
County College of Morris *A*
Cumberland County College *A*
Drew University *B,M,D*
Essex County College *A*
Fairleigh Dickinson University:
    Edward Williams College *A*
Felician College *A,B*
Gloucester County College *A*
Kean College of New Jersey *M*
Mercer County Community
    College *A*
Monmouth College *A,B,M*
Ocean County College *A*
Passaic County Community
    College *A*
Rider College *A*
Rutgers—The State University of
    New Jersey
        Camden College of Arts and
            Sciences *B*
        Douglass College *B*
        Livingston College *B*
        Newark College of Arts and
            Sciences *B*
        Rutgers College *B*
        University College Camden *B*
        University College New
            Brunswick *B*
St. Peter's College *B*

Seton Hall University *B*
Stockton State College *B*
Sussex County Community
    College *A*
Thomas Edison State College *A*
Union County College *A*
Upsala College *B*

New Mexico

College of Santa Fe *A,B*
College of the Southwest *B*
Eastern New Mexico University
    Portales *A,B*
    Roswell Campus *A*
New Mexico Institute of Mining
    and Technology *A,B*
New Mexico Junior College *A*
New Mexico Military Institute *A*
New Mexico State University
    Carlsbad *A*
    Las Cruces *A,B*
Northern New Mexico Community
    College *A*
St. John's College *B,M*
San Juan College *A*
University of New Mexico *B*
Western New Mexico University *B*

New York

Adelphi University *A*
Adirondack Community College *A*
Alfred University *B*
Boricua College *A,B*
Broome Community College *A*
Cazenovia College *A,B*
City University of New York
        Baruch College *B*
        Borough of Manhattan
            Community College *A*
        Brooklyn College *M*
        College of Staten Island *A,M*
        Graduate School and
            University Center *M*
        Hostos Community College *A*
        Kingsborough Community
            College *A*
        La Guardia Community
            College *A*
        Lehman College *B,M*
        Medgar Evers College *A*
        New York City Technical
            College *A*
        Queens College *M*
        Queensborough Community
            College *A*
Clinton Community College *A*
College of Mount St. Vincent *A,B*
College of New Rochelle: School of
    New Resources *B*
College of St. Rose *M*
Columbia-Greene Community
    College *A*
Community College of the Finger
    Lakes *A*
Concordia College *A,B*
Cornell University *B*
Corning Community College *A*
Dominican College of Blauvelt *A,B*
Dowling College *B*
Dutchess Community College *C*
Elmira College *B*
Erie Community College
        North Campus *A*
        South Campus *A*
Eugene Lang College/New School
    for Social Research *B*
Five Towns College *A*
Fulton-Montgomery Community
    College *C,A*
Genesee Community College *A*
Hamilton College *B*

Herkimer County Community
College *A*
Hilbert College *A*
Hofstra University *B,M*
Houghton College *A*
Hudson Valley Community
College *A*
Iona College *A,B*
Ithaca College *B*
Jamestown Community College *C,A*
Jefferson Community College *A*
King's College *A*
Long Island University: C. W. Post
Campus *A*
Manhattan College *B*
Manhattanville College *M*
Maria College *A*
Marymount College *B*
Marymount Manhattan College *B*
Mater Dei College *A*
Medaille College *A,B*
Mercy College *C,A,B*
Mohawk Valley Community
College *A*
Molloy College *A*
Monroe Community College *A*
Mount St. Mary College *B*
Nassau Community College *A*
New York Institute of
Technology *B*
New York University *A,B,M*
Niagara County Community
College *A*
Niagara University *A*
Nyack College *A*
Onondaga Community College *A*
Pace University
College of White Plains *B*
New York *B*
Pleasantville/Briarcliff *B*
Paul Smith's College *A*
Roberts Wesleyan College *A*
Rochester Institute of
Technology *A*
Rockland Community College *A*
Russell Sage College *B*
Sage Junior College of Albany, A
Division of Russell Sage
College *A*
St. Bonaventure University *B*
St. Francis College *B*
St. John Fisher College *B*
St. John's University *A*
St. Joseph's College *B*
St. Thomas Aquinas College *B*
Sarah Lawrence College *B*
Skidmore College *M*

State University of New York
Albany *B,M*
Binghamton *B*
Buffalo *A,B*
Purchase *B*
Stony Brook *B,M*
College of Agriculture and
Technology at Cobleskill *A*
College of Agriculture and
Technology at Morrisville *A*
College at Brockport *B,M*
College at Buffalo *B*
College at Cortland *B*
College at Fredonia *B*
College at New Paltz *B*
College at Oneonta *B*
College at Plattsburgh *B*
College at Potsdam *B*
College of Technology at
Alfred *A*
College of Technology at
Canton *A*
College of Technology at
Delhi *A*
College of Technology at
Farmingdale *A*
Empire State College *A,B*
Institute of Technology at
Utica/Rome *B*
Suffolk County Community College
Eastern Campus *A*
Selden *A*
Western Campus *A*
Sullivan County Community
College *A*
Syracuse University *B*
Tompkins-Cortland Community
College *C,A*
Touro College *A,B*
Trocaire College *A*
Ulster County Community
College *A*
University of the State of New
York: Regents College *A,B*
Villa Maria College of Buffalo *A*
Westchester Community College *A*

North Carolina

Alamance Community College *A*
Anson Community College *A*
Appalachian State University *B*
Barton College *B*
Beaufort County Community
College *A*
Bennett College *B*
Bladen Community College *A*
Blue Ridge Community College *A*
Brevard College *A*
Brunswick Community College *A*
Caldwell Community College and
Technical Institute *A*
Central Piedmont Community
College *A*
Chowan College *A*
Cleveland Community College *A*
Coastal Carolina Community
College *A*
College of the Albemarle *A*
Craven Community College *A*
Davidson College *B*
Davidson County Community
College *A*
Duke University *M*
Durham Technical Community
College *A*
East Coast Bible College *A*
Edgecombe Community College *A*
Fayetteville State University *A*
Fayetteville Technical Community
College *A*
Gardner-Webb College *B*
Gaston College *A*

Greensboro College *B*
Guilford Technical Community
College *A*
Haywood Community College *A*
Isothermal Community College *A*
James Sprunt Community
College *A*
John Wesley College *A*
Johnston Community College *A*
Lees-McRae College *A*
Lenoir-Rhyne College *B*
Louisburg College *A*
Mars Hill College *B*
Martin Community College *A*
Mayland Community College *A*
McDowell Technical Community
College *A*
Methodist College *A*
Mitchell Community College *A*
Montreat-Anderson College *A*
Mount Olive College *A,B*
Nash Community College *A*
North Carolina State University
B,M
Piedmont Community College *A*
Pitt Community College *A*
Richmond Community College *A*
Roanoke-Chowan Community
College *A*
Rockingham Community College *A*
St. Mary's College *A*
Sampson Community College *A*
Sandhills Community College *A*
Shaw University *B*
Southeastern Community College *A*
Southwestern Community
College *A*
Surry Community College *A*
Tri-County Community College *A*
University of North Carolina
Asheville *M*
Chapel Hill *B*
Greensboro *B,M*
Vance-Granville Community
College *A*
Wake Forest University *M*
Warren Wilson College *B*
Wayne Community College *A*
Western Piedmont Community
College *A*
Wilkes Community College *A*
Wilson Technical Community
College *A*
Wingate College *A,B*

North Dakota

Bismarck State College *A*
Dickinson State University *A,B*
Mayville State University *B*
Minot State University *B*
North Dakota State College of
Science *A*
North Dakota State University
Bottineau and Institute of
Forestry *A*
Fargo *B*
Turtle Mountain Community
College *A*
University of Mary *B*
University of North Dakota
Grand Forks *B*
Lake Region *A*
Williston *A*
Valley City State University *A,B*

Ohio

Antioch College *B*
Antioch School for Adult and
Experiential Learning *M*
Ashland University *A*
Bluffton College *B*

Bowling Green State University
Bowling Green *B*
Firelands College *A*
Capital University *B*
Chatfield College *A*
College of Mount St. Joseph *A,B*
Columbus State Community
College *A*
Cuyahoga Community College:
Metropolitan Campus *A*
Defiance College *A,B*
Edison State Community College *A*
Franciscan University of
Steubenville *A*
Heidelberg College *B*
John Carroll University *B*
Kent State University
Ashtabula Regional Campus *A*
East Liverpool Regional
Campus *A*
Kent *B,M*
Salem Regional Campus *A*
Stark Campus *A*
Tuscarawas Campus *A*
Lake Erie College *B*
Lakeland Community College *A*
Lorain County Community
College *A*
Lourdes College *A,B*
Malone College *B*
Marietta College *A,B,M*
Miami University
Hamilton Campus *A*
Oxford Campus *A,B*
Mount Union College *B*
Mount Vernon Nazarene College *A*
Muskingum College *B*
Ohio Dominican College *A,B*
Ohio Northern University *B*
Ohio State University
Columbus Campus *B,M,D*
Lima Campus *A*
Mansfield Campus *A*
Marion Campus *A*
Newark Campus *A*
Ohio University
Athens *B*
Chillicothe Campus *A*
Eastern Campus *A*
Southern Campus at Ironton
A,B
Zanesville Campus *A,B*
Shawnee State University *A*
Sinclair Community College *A*
Southern State Community
College *A*
Union Institute *B,D*
University of Akron *A*
University of Cincinnati
Access Colleges *A*
Cincinnati *B*
Clermont College *A*
Raymond Walters College *A*
University of Dayton *B*
University of Findlay *A*
University of Toledo *A,B,M*
Urbana University *A*
Ursuline College *B*
Walsh College *A,B*
Wilberforce University *B*
Wilmington College *B*
Wittenberg University *B*
Xavier University *A,B*

Oklahoma

Bacone College *A*
Bartlesville Wesleyan College *A*
Cameron University *A,B*
Connors State College *A*
Hillsdale Free Will Baptist
College *A*
Mid-America Bible College *A*

Northern Oklahoma College *A*
Oklahoma Christian University of
 Science and Arts *B*
Oklahoma City University *B,M*
Oral Roberts University *B*
Redlands Community College *A*
Rogers State College *A*
Rose State College *A*
St. Gregory's College *A*
Southwestern Oklahoma State
 University *A*
Tulsa Junior College *A*
University of Central Oklahoma *B*
University of Oklahoma *B,M*
University of Science and Arts of
 Oklahoma *B*

Oregon

Central Oregon Community
 College *A*
Chemeketa Community College *A*
Clackamas Community College *A*
Clatsop Community College *A*
Concordia College *A,B*
Eastern Oregon State College *A,B*
George Fox College *B*
Lane Community College *A*
Linfield College *B*
Linn-Benton Community College *A*
Marylhurst College *B*
Mount Angel Seminary *B*
Mount Hood Community
 College *A*
Oregon Institute of Technology *A*
Oregon State University *B*
Portland Community College *A*
Portland State University *B*
Reed College *B,M*
Rogue Community College *A*
Southern Oregon State College *A,B*
Southwestern Oregon Community
 College *A*
Treasure Valley Community
 College *A*
Umpqua Community College *A*
University of Oregon
 Eugene *B*
 Robert Donald Clark Honors
 College *B*
Western Baptist College *A,B*
Western Oregon State College *A,B*

Pennsylvania

Academy of the New Church *A,B*
Allentown College of St. Francis de
 Sales *B*
Alvernia College *B*
Baptist Bible College of
 Pennsylvania *A*
Beaver College *A,B,M*
Bucks County Community
 College *A*
Butler County Community
 College *A*
Cabrini College *B*
California University of
 Pennsylvania *B,M*
Carlow College *B*
Chatham College *B*
Clarion University of Pennsylvania
 A,B
College Misericordia *B*
Community College of Beaver
 County *A*
Community College of
 Philadelphia *A*
Delaware County Community
 College *A*
Eastern College *A*
Edinboro University of
 Pennsylvania *A,B*
Gannon University *B*

Gettysburg College *B*
Gwynedd-Mercy College *A*
Harcum Junior College *A*
Harrisburg Area Community
 College *A*
Immaculata College *A*
Indiana University of
 Pennsylvania *A*
Juniata College *B*
Keystone Junior College *A*
Kutztown University of
 Pennsylvania *B*
La Salle University *A,B*
Lackawanna Junior College *A*
Lebanon Valley College of
 Pennsylvania *A,B*
Lehigh University *B*
Lock Haven University of
 Pennsylvania *B*
Luzerne County Community
 College *A*
Lycoming College *B*
Manor Junior College *A*
Mansfield University of
 Pennsylvania *A,B*
Messiah College *B*
Millersville University of
 Pennsylvania *A*
Montgomery County Community
 College *A*
Mount Aloysius College *A*
Neumann College *A,B*
Northampton County Area
 Community College *A*
Northeastern Christian Junior
 College *A*
Peirce Junior College *A*
Penn State
 Erie Behrend College *A,B*
 Harrisburg Capital College *A*
 University Park Campus *C,A,B*
Pennsylvania College of
 Technology *A*
Point Park College *A*
Reading Area Community
 College *A*
Robert Morris College *A*
St. Francis College *B*
St. Vincent College *B*
Slippery Rock University of
 Pennsylvania *B*
Swarthmore College *B*
Temple University *M*
Thiel College *A*
Thomas Jefferson University:
 College of Allied Health
 Sciences *A*
University of the Arts *B*
University of Pennsylvania *B,M,D*
University of Pittsburgh
 Bradford *B*
 Johnstown *B*
 Pittsburgh *B*
 Titusville *A*
Valley Forge Military College *C,A*
Villanova University *A,B,M*
Washington and Jefferson College *B*
West Chester University of
 Pennsylvania *A,B*
Westmoreland County Community
 College *A*
Wilkes University *B*
York College of Pennsylvania *A*

Puerto Rico

American University of Puerto
 Rico *A*
Pontifical Catholic University of
 Puerto Rico *A*
Puerto Rico Junior College *A*
Turabo University *A*
Universidad Metropolitana *A*

University of Puerto Rico
 Aguadilla *A*
 Arecibo Campus *A*
 Humacao University
 College *A*
 Ponce Technological
 University College *A*
 Rio Piedras Campus *B*

Rhode Island

Brown University *B*
Community College of Rhode
 Island *A*
Providence College *A,B*
Rhode Island College *B*

South Carolina

Anderson College *A,B*
Charleston Southern University *A*
Chesterfield-Marlboro Technical
 College *A*
Francis Marion College *B*
Greenville Technical College *A*
Lander College *B*
Limestone College *B*
Midlands Technical College *A*
Morris College *B*
North Greenville College *A*
Tri-County Technical College *A*
Trident Technical College *A*
University of South Carolina
 Aiken *B*
 Beaufort *A*
 Coastal Carolina College *A,B*
 Columbia *B*
 Salkehatchie Regional
 Campus *A*
 Spartanburg *B*
 Sumter *A*
 Union *A*
Williamsburg Technical College *C,A*

South Dakota

Augustana College *B*
Black Hills State University *A*
Dakota State University *A*
Dakota Wesleyan University *A*
Huron University *A,B*
Mount Marty College *B*
National College *A*
Northern State University *A*
Oglala Lakota College *A*
Sinte Gleska College *A*
Sioux Falls College *A,B*
South Dakota State University *B*
University of South Dakota *B*

Tennessee

Austin Peay State University *A*
Carson-Newman College *B*
Chattanooga State Technical
 Community College *A*
Cleveland State Community
 College *A*
Columbia State Community
 College *A*
Crichton College *B*
Dyersburg State Community
 College *A*
Free Will Baptist Bible College *A*
Freed-Hardeman University *B*
Hiwassee College *A*
Jackson State Community
 College *A*
Knoxville College *B*
Lincoln Memorial University *A,B*
Martin Methodist College *A*
Maryville College *B*
Memphis State University *B,M*
Motlow State Community
 College *A*
Roane State Community College *A*

Shelby State Community College *A*
Tennessee State University *A,B*
Tennessee Temple University *B*
Tennessee Wesleyan College *B*
Tomlinson College *A*
Trevecca Nazarene College *A*
University of Tennessee:
 Chattanooga *B*
Vanderbilt University *B*
Volunteer State Community
 College *A*
Walters State Community
 College *A*
William Jennings Bryan College *B*

Texas

Alvin Community College *A*
Amarillo College *A*
Amber University *B*
Angelina College *A*
Austin Community College *A*
Baylor University *B*
Bee County College *A*
Blinn College *A*
Brazosport College *A*
Central Texas College *A*
Cisco Junior College *A*
College of the Mainland *A*
Concordia Lutheran College *A,B*
Cooke County College *A*
Dallas Baptist University *B,M*
Dallas Christian College *A*
Del Mar College *A*
East Texas Baptist University *A*
East Texas State University
 Commerce *B,M*
 Texarkana *B,M*
Eastfield College *A*
El Centro College *A*
El Paso Community College *A*
Galveston College *A*
Houston Community College *A*
Howard College *A*
Howard Payne University *B*
Incarnate Word College *M*
Jacksonville College *A*
Kilgore College *A*
Lamar University—Beaumont *B*
Laredo Junior College *A*
Laredo State University *B,M*
Lee College *A*
Lon Morris College *A*
Lubbock Christian University *A,B*
McLennan Community College *A*
McMurry University *A*
Midland College *A*
Mountain View College *A*
Navarro College *A*
North Harris Montgomery
 Community College District *A*
North Lake College *A*
Odessa College *A*
Our Lady of the Lake University of
 San Antonio *B*
Panola College *A*
Ranger Junior College *A*
Rice University *B*
Richland College *A*
St. Edward's University *B*
St. Mary's University *B*
St. Philip's College *A*
San Antonio College *A*
San Jacinto College: Central
 Campus *A*
Schreiner College *A,B*
South Plains College *A*
Southern Methodist University *M*
Southwestern Christian College *A*
Tarrant County Junior College *A*
Temple Junior College *A*
Texarkana College *A*
Texas Christian University *B,M*

349

Texas Southmost College *A*
Texas Tech University *B,M*
Trinity Valley Community
   College *A*
University of Central Texas *B,M*
University of Houston:
   Downtown *B*
University of Mary Hardin-
   Baylor *B*
University of North Texas *B*
University of St. Thomas *B*
University of Texas
   Arlington *B*
   Dallas *B,M*
   El Paso *M*
   Pan American *M*
   Tyler *B,M*
Vernon Regional Junior College *A*
Victoria College *C,A*
Weatherford College *A*
West Texas State University *B*
Western Texas College *A*
Wharton County Junior College *A*
Wiley College *B*

Utah

College of Eastern Utah *A*
Dixie College *A*
LDS Business College *A*
University of Utah *B*
Utah State University *B*
Utah Valley Community College *A*
Weber State University *A,B*
Westminster College of Salt Lake
   City *B*

Vermont

Bennington College *B*
Burlington College *A,B*
Castleton State College *A*
Champlain College *A*
College of St. Joseph in Vermont
   A,B
Community College of Vermont *A*
Goddard College *B,M*
Johnson State College *A*
Landmark College *A*
Lyndon State College *A*
Marlboro College *B*
Middlebury College *B*
Southern Vermont College *A,B*
Trinity College of Vermont *A*
University of Vermont *B*

Virginia

Averett College *B*
Blue Ridge Community College *A*
Bluefield College *A,B*
Bridgewater College *B*
Central Virginia Community
   College *A*
Christendom College *A*
Christopher Newport College *B*
Clinch Valley College of the
   University of Virginia *A*
College of William and Mary *B*
Dabney S. Lancaster Community
   College *A*
Eastern Mennonite College *C,A,B*
Eastern Shore Community
   College *A*
Emory and Henry College *B*
Ferrum College *B*
George Mason University *B,M*
Hollins College *B,M*
James Madison University *B*
John Tyler Community College *A*
Liberty University *B*
Lord Fairfax Community College *A*
Mary Washington College *B,M*
Marymount University *B*

Mountain Empire Community
   College *A*
National Business College *A*
New River Community College *A*
Norfolk State University *B*
Northern Virginia Community
   College *A*
Old Dominion University *B*
Patrick Henry Community
   College *A*
Paul D. Camp Community
   College *A*
Piedmont Virginia Community
   College *A*
Radford University *B*
Richard Bland College *A*
St. Paul's College *B*
Southern Seminary College *A*
Southside Virginia Community
   College *A*
Southwest Virginia Community
   College *A*
Strayer College *A*
Tidewater Community College *A*
Virginia Commonwealth University
   B,M
Virginia Highlands Community
   College *A*
Virginia Intermont College *A,B*
Virginia Polytechnic Institute and
   State University *B*
Virginia Wesleyan College *B*
Wytheville Community College *A*

Washington

Antioch University Seattle *B*
Bellevue Community College *A*
Big Bend Community College *A*
Central Washington University *B,M*
Centralia College *A*
City University *A*
Clark College *A*
Columbia Basin College *A*
Eastern Washington University *B*
Edmonds Community College *A*
Everett Community College *A*
Evergreen State College *B*
Gonzaga University *B*
Grays Harbor College *A*
Green River Community College *A*
Heritage College *A,B*
Lower Columbia College *A*
North Seattle Community
   College *A*
Northwest College of the
   Assemblies of God *B*
Olympic College *A*
Peninsula College *A*
Pierce College *A*
St. Martin's College *A,B*
Seattle Central Community
   College *A*
Seattle Pacific University *B*
Shoreline Community College *A*
Skagit Valley College *A*
South Puget Sound Community
   College *A*
Spokane Community College *A*
Spokane Falls Community
   College *A*
Tacoma Community College *A*
University of Puget Sound *B*
University of Washington *B*
Walla Walla Community College *A*
Washington State University *B*
Wenatchee Valley College *A*
Western Washington University *B*
Whatcom Community College *A*
Yakima Valley Community
   College *A*

West Virginia

Alderson-Broaddus College *B*
Bethany College *B*
Bluefield State College *A*
College of West Virginia *A*
Concord College *B*
Fairmont State College *A,B*
Glenville State College *B*
Ohio Valley College *A*
Potomac State College of West
   Virginia University *A*
Salem-Teikyo University *A,B*
University of Charleston *A*
West Liberty State College *B*
West Virginia Northern Community
   College *A*
West Virginia State College *A,B*
West Virginia University *B,M*
Wheeling Jesuit College *B*

Wisconsin

Alverno College *A*
Cardinal Stritch College *A,B*
Carroll College *B*
Concordia University Wisconsin *B*
Edgewood College *A,B*
Lakeland College *B*
Lawrence University *B*
Madison Area Technical College *A*
Maranatha Baptist Bible College *B*
Marian College of Fond du Lac *B*
Mount Senario College *B*
Northland College *B*
Northwestern College *B*
Silver Lake College *A*
University of Wisconsin
   Eau Claire *A*
   Green Bay *A,B*
   La Crosse *A*
   Milwaukee *B*
   Oshkosh *A*
   Platteville *A*
   River Falls *B*
   Stevens Point *A*
   Superior *A*
   Whitewater *A,B*
University of Wisconsin Center
   Baraboo/Sauk County *A*
   Barron County *A*
   Fox Valley *A*
   Manitowoc County *A*
   Marathon County *A*
   Marinette County *C,A*
   Marshfield/Wood County *A*
   Richland *A*
   Sheboygan County *A*
   Washington County *A*
   Waukesha *A*
Viterbo College *B*

Wyoming

Casper College *A*
Central Wyoming College *A*
Eastern Wyoming College *A*
Laramie County Community
   College *A*
Northwest College *A*
Sheridan College *A*
Western Wyoming Community
   College *A*

**American Samoa, Caroline
Islands, Guam, Marianas,
Virgin Islands**

Community College of
   Micronesia *A*
Northern Marianas College *A*

Switzerland

American College of Switzerland *A*
Franklin College: Switzerland *A*

Library assistant

Alabama

Bishop State Community College *A*
Lawson State Community
   College *A*

Arizona

Northland Pioneer College *C,A*

California

Barstow College *C*
Chabot College *A*
Citrus College *C,A*
City College of San Francisco *A*
Foothill College *A*
Hartnell College *A*
Imperial Valley College *C*
Los Angeles Trade and Technical
   College *C,A*
Merced College *A*
Oxnard College *A*
Palomar College *C,A*
Pasadena City College *C,A*
Rio Hondo College *A*
Sierra College *A*

Connecticut

Norwalk Community College *C,A*

Florida

Indian River Community College *A*

Illinois

Black Hawk College *A*
City Colleges of Chicago: Wright
   College *A*
College of DuPage *C,A*
College of Lake County *C*
Illinois Central College *A*
Illinois Eastern Community
   Colleges: Wabash Valley
   College *A*
Joliet Junior College *C,A*
Lewis and Clark Community
   College *A*
Rock Valley College *A*

Indiana

Vincennes University *A*

Kansas

Central College *A*
Colby Community College *A*

Massachusetts

Atlantic Union College *A*

Michigan

Oakland Community College *A*

New Hampshire

School for Lifelong Learning *C*

New Jersey

Brookdale Community College *A*

New Mexico

Northern New Mexico Community
   College *C,A*

North Carolina

Wake Technical Community
   College *A*

Ohio

Cuyahoga Community College:
   Metropolitan Campus *A*
Ohio Dominican College *A*
University of Akron *A*

University of Cincinnati: Raymond Walters College *A*

Oklahoma
Rose State College *C,A*

Oregon
Portland Community College *A*

Pennsylvania
Community College of Philadelphia *A*
Northampton County Area Community College *C,A*

South Dakota
Augustana College *A*
Black Hills State University *B*

Tennessee
Hiwassee College *A*
Martin Methodist College *A*

Washington
Northwest Indian College *C*
Spokane Falls Community College *A*

West Virginia
Marshall University *A*

Library science

Alabama
Alabama State University *M*
Jacksonville State University *M*
X University of Alabama *B,M*

Arizona
Eastern Arizona College *C,A*
University of Arizona *M*

Arkansas
X University of Central Arkansas *M*

California
California State University: Los Angeles *M*
Citrus College *A*
City College of San Francisco *A*
Merced College *A*
San Jose State University *M*
Santa Rosa Junior College *A*
University of California
    Berkeley *M,D*
    Los Angeles *M,D*

Colorado
Western State College of Colorado *B*

Connecticut
Norwalk Community College *A*
Southern Connecticut State University *B,M*
Western Connecticut State University *B*

District of Columbia
Catholic University of America *M*
University of the District of Columbia *A,B*

Florida
Daytona Beach Community College *A*
Florida State University *M,D*
Gulf Coast Community College *A*
X University of South Florida *M*

Georgia
Georgia College *M*
Georgia Southern University *M*

Hawaii
University of Hawaii at Manoa *M*

Idaho
College of Southern Idaho *A*

Illinois
Chicago State University *B,M*
College of Lake County *A*
Illinois Eastern Community Colleges: Wabash Valley College *A*
Northern Illinois University *M*
Rosary College *M*
University of Illinois at Urbana-Champaign *M,D*

Indiana
Ball State University *B*
Indiana State University *B,M*
Indiana University
    Bloomington *M,D*
    South Bend *M*

Iowa
Northwestern College *B*
St. Ambrose University *C*
University of Iowa *M*
University of Northern Iowa *M*

Kansas
Allen County Community College *A*
Barton County Community College *A*
Central College *A*
Colby Community College *A*
Dodge City Community College *A*
Emporia State University *M*
Haskell Indian Junior College *A*
Hutchinson Community College *A*

Kentucky
Murray State University *B*
Spalding University *B,M*
University of Kentucky *M*
X Western Kentucky University *B,M*

Louisiana
Louisiana State University and Agricultural and Mechanical College *M*
Our Lady of Holy Cross College *C*
Southern University and Agricultural and Mechanical College *B*

Maryland
University of Maryland: College Park *M,D*
Western Maryland College *M*

Massachusetts
Bridgewater State College *M*
Bristol Community College *A*
Simmons College *M,D*

Michigan
Central Michigan University *M*
University of Michigan *M,D*
Wayne State University *M*

Minnesota
Bethany Lutheran College *A*
Mankato State University *M*
St. Cloud State University *M*
Willmar Community College *A*

Mississippi
Blue Mountain College *B*
Mississippi State University *B*
X University of Southern Missis... *B,M*

Missouri
Central Missouri State University *M*
East Central College *A*
Missouri Baptist College *C*
Northwest Missouri State University *B*
University of Missouri: Columbia ...

Nebraska
Chadron State College *B*
University of Nebraska—Omaha *B*

New Jersey
Brookdale Community College *A*
Glassboro State College *M*
Rutgers—The State University of New Jersey *M,D*

New York
City University of New York: Queens College *M*
Long Island University: C. W. Post Campus *M*
Pratt Institute *M,W*
St. John's University *M*
State University of New York
    Albany *M,W*
    Buffalo *M*
Syracuse University *M,D*

North Carolina
Appalachian State University *M*
East Carolina University *M*
North Carolina Central University *M*
University of North Carolina
    Chapel Hill *M,D*
    Greensboro *M*

North Dakota
University of North Dakota *B*

Ohio
Kent State University *M*
Ohio Dominican College *B*

Oklahoma
Northeastern State University *B*
Northwestern Oklahoma State University *B*
Phillips University *B,M*
Southwestern Oklahoma State University *B*
Tulsa Junior College *A*
University of Oklahoma *M*

Pennsylvania
Clarion University of Pennsylvania *B,M*
Drexel University *M,D*
Kutztown University of Pennsylvania *B,M*
Lock Haven University of Pennsylvania *B*
University of Pittsburgh *M,D*

Puerto Rico
Inter American University of Puerto Rico: San German Campus *M*
University of Puerto Rico: Rio Piedras Campus *M*

Rhode Island
University of Rhode Island *M*

Texas
East Texas State University *M*
Sam Houston State University *M*
Texas Woman's University *B,M,D*
University of North Texas *B,M,D*
University of Texas at Austin *M,D*

Utah
Brigham Young University *A,M*
Southern Utah University *B*

Vermont
Goddard College *B*

Virginia
Longwood College *M*
Norfolk State University *A*
Old Dominion University *M*

Washington
Eastern Washington University *M*
Seattle Central Community College *A*
University of Washington *M*

West Virginia
Concord College *B*
Marshall University *B,M*
Shepherd College *B*

Wisconsin
University of Wisconsin
    Madison *M,D*
    Milwaukee *M*
    Platteville *B*

Canada
McGill University *M*

Linguistics

Alaska
University of Alaska Fairbanks *B*

Arizona
University of Arizona *B,M,D*

California
California State University
    Bakersfield *B*
    Dominguez Hills *B*
    Fresno *B,M*
    Fullerton *B,M*
    Long Beach *M*
    Northridge *B,M*
Foothill College *A*
Pitzer College *B*
Pomona College *B*
San Diego State University *B,M*
San Jose State University *B,M*
Scripps College *B*
Stanford University *B,M,D*

Colorado

University of Colorado at Boulder B,M,D

Connecticut

Central Connecticut State University M
University of Connecticut B,M,D
University of Hartford B
Wesleyan University B
Yale University B,M,D

Delaware

University of Delaware M,D

District of Columbia

Gallaudet University M
Georgetown University B,M,D

Florida

Florida Atlantic University B,M
Florida International University M
University of Florida M,D
University of South Florida M

Georgia

Morehouse College B
University of Georgia B,M,D

Hawaii

University of Hawaii
Hilo B
Manoa M,D

Illinois

Chicago State University B
Lincoln Christian College and Seminary B
Loyola University of Chicago B
Northeastern Illinois University B,M
Northwestern University B,M,D
Southern Illinois University
Carbondale B,M
Edwardsville M
University of Chicago B,M,D
University of Illinois
Chicago M
Urbana-Champaign B,M,D

Indiana

Ball State University M,D
Indiana University Bloomington B,M,D
Purdue University B,D

Iowa

Central College B
Iowa State University B
University of Iowa B,M,D

Kansas

University of Kansas B,M,D

Kentucky

University of Kentucky B
University of Louisville B,M

Louisiana

Louisiana State University and Agricultural and Mechanical College M,D
Tulane University B

Maryland

Bowie State University B
Johns Hopkins University B,M,D
University of Maryland
Baltimore County B,M,D
College Park B,M,D

Massachusetts

Boston College B,M
Boston University B,D
Brandeis University B
Hampshire College B
Harvard and Radcliffe Colleges B
Harvard University D
Massachusetts Institute of Technology B,M,D
Northeastern University B
Salem State College B
University of Massachusetts at Amherst B,M,D

Michigan

Central Michigan University B,M
Eastern Michigan University B,M
Michigan State University B,M,D
Oakland University B,M
University of Michigan B,M,D
Wayne State University B,M
Western Michigan University B

Minnesota

Macalester College B
Mankato State University A
University of Minnesota: Twin Cities B,M,D
University of St. Thomas B

Mississippi

Jackson State University M
University of Mississippi B

Missouri

University of Missouri: Columbia B,M
Washington University B,M,D

Nebraska

Hastings College B

New Hampshire

Dartmouth College B
University of New Hampshire B

New Jersey

Montclair State College B
Rutgers—The State University of New Jersey
Douglass College B
Livingston College B
Rutgers College B
University College New Brunswick B

New Mexico

University of New Mexico B,M

New York

Barnard College B
City University of New York
Brooklyn College B
City College B
Graduate School and University Center M,D
Lehman College B
Queens College B,M
Cornell University B,M,D

Hamilton College B
Hofstra University M
New York University B,M,D
State University of New York
Albany B
Binghamton B
Buffalo B,M,D
Stony Brook B,M
Oswego B
Syracuse University B,M
University of Rochester B,M,D

North Carolina

University of North Carolina
Chapel Hill B,M,D
Greensboro B

North Dakota

University of North Dakota M

Ohio

Cleveland State University B
Miami University: Oxford Campus B,M
Ohio State University: Columbus Campus B,M,D
Ohio University M
Union Institute D
University of Akron C
University of Cincinnati B,M
University of Toledo B,M

Oklahoma

Bartlesville Wesleyan College A,B
University of Oklahoma B

Oregon

Portland State University B
Reed College B
University of Oregon
Eugene B,M,D
Robert Donald Clark Honors College B

Pennsylvania

Bucknell University B
Carnegie Mellon University B,M
Duquesne University B
Penn State University Park Campus B,M
Swarthmore College B
Temple University B,M
University of Pennsylvania B,M,D
University of Pittsburgh B,M,D

Puerto Rico

Inter American University of Puerto Rico: San German Campus B
University of Puerto Rico: Rio Piedras Campus M

Rhode Island

Brown University B
University of Rhode Island B

South Carolina

University of South Carolina M,D

Tennessee

University of Tennessee: Knoxville B
Vanderbilt University B

Texas

Rice University B,M,D
Texas Southmost College A
University of Houston M
University of Texas
Arlington M
Austin B,M,D
El Paso B,M

Utah

Brigham Young University B,M
University of Utah B,M

Vermont

Marlboro College B

Virginia

University of Virginia M

Washington

Seattle Pacific University B
University of Washington B,M,D
Western Washington University B

West Virginia

West Virginia University B,M

Wisconsin

University of Wisconsin
Green Bay B
Madison B,M,D
Milwaukee B

Canada

McGill University B,M,D

Machine tool operation/machine shop

Alabama

Bessemer State Technical College A
Gadsden State Community College C,A
George C. Wallace State Community College at Selma A
John C. Calhoun State Community College C,A
John M. Patterson State Technical College C
Shoals Community College C
Walker State Technical College C,A
Wallace State Community College at Hanceville C,A

Arizona

Eastern Arizona College C,A
Pima Community College C,A

Arkansas

Westark Community College C,A

California

Allan Hancock College C,A
Cerro Coso Community College C,A
Citrus College C,A
College of the Redwoods C,A
De Anza College C,A
El Camino College C,A
Laney College C,A
Long Beach City College C,A
Los Angeles Pierce College C,A
Los Angeles Trade and Technical College A
Los Angeles Valley College C
MiraCosta College C,A
Mount San Antonio College C,A
Orange Coast College C,A
San Joaquin Delta College C,A
San Jose City College A
Santa Barbara City College C
Santa Rosa Junior College C,A

Colorado

Arapahoe Community College C
Community College of Denver C
Mesa State College C
Pikes Peak Community College C,A

Florida

Daytona Beach Community
College *C*
South Florida Community
College *C*

Georgia

Athens Area Technical Institute *C*
Augusta Technical Institute *C*
Brunswick College *C*
DeKalb Technical Institute *C*
Floyd College *A*
Gainesville College *A*
Savannah Technical Institute *C*

Idaho

Idaho State University *A*
North Idaho College *C,A*

Illinois

Carl Sandburg College *A*
City Colleges of Chicago: Chicago
City-Wide College *C*
College of Lake County *C,A*
Illinois Central College *C*
Illinois Eastern Community
Colleges: Lincoln Trail College *A*
Kishwaukee College *C*
Lewis and Clark Community
College *A*
Moraine Valley Community
College *C*
Oakton Community College *C,A*
Southern Illinois University at
Carbondale *A*
Triton College *C,A*
Waubonsee Community College
C,A

Indiana

Indiana Vocational Technical
College
Central Indiana *C*
Eastcentral *C,A*
Kokomo *C,A*
Lafayette *C,A*
Northcentral *C,A*
Northeast *C,A*
Northwest *C,A*
Whitewater *A*
Vincennes University *A*

Iowa

Des Moines Area Community
College *C*
Hawkeye Institute of Technology *A*
Indian Hills Community College *A*
Iowa Central Community College *C*
Iowa Western Community College
C,A
Kirkwood Community College *A*
Northwest Iowa Technical
College *C*
Southeastern Community College:
North Campus *C,A*

Kansas

Barton County Community
College *A*
Cowley County Community College
C,A
Seward County Community
College *A*

Kentucky

Eastern Kentucky University *A,B*

Maine

Central Maine Technical College
C,A
Eastern Maine Technical College *A*

Southern Maine Technical
College *A*

Maryland

Catonsville Community College *A*

Massachusetts

Northern Essex Community College
C,A

Michigan

Alpena Community College *C,A*
Delta College *C,A*
Glen Oaks Community College *C*
Grand Rapids Community
College *C*
Henry Ford Community College *C*
Jackson Community College *A*
Kalamazoo Valley Community
College *C*
Kellogg Community College *A*
Kirtland Community College *C,A*
Lansing Community College *A*
Mid Michigan Community College
C,A
Montcalm Community College *C*
Oakland Community College *C*
St. Clair County Community
College *A*
West Shore Community College
C,A

Minnesota

Alexandria Technical College *C*
Willmar Technical College *C*

Mississippi

Copiah-Lincoln Community
College *C*
East Central Community College *C*
Hinds Community College *C*
Jones County Junior College *C*
Meridian Community College *C*
Mississippi Delta Community
College *C*
Mississippi Gulf Coast Community
College
Jackson County Campus *A*
Jefferson Davis Campus *C*
Northeast Mississippi Community
College *C*
Southwest Mississippi Community
College *C*

Missouri

Jefferson College *C,A*
Maple Woods Community
College *A*
Missouri Southern State College *A*
Ranken Technical College *A*
State Fair Community College *C,A*

Nebraska

Chadron State College *B*
Southeast Community College
Lincoln Campus *C,A*
Milford Campus *C,A*

Nevada

Western Nevada Community
College *C,A*

New Hampshire

New Hampshire Technical College
Berlin *A*
Nashua *A*
Stratham *C,A*

New Jersey

Passaic County Community
College *A*

New Mexico

Albuquerque Technical-Vocational
Institute *C*
New Mexico Junior College *A*
Northern New Mexico Community
College *C,A*
San Juan College *C,A*
Western New Mexico University
C,A

New York

City University of New York: New
York City Technical College *A*
Hudson Valley Community
College *A*
Mohawk Valley Community College
C,A
State University of New York
College of Technology at
Farmingdale *C*
Suffolk County Community
College *C*
Westchester Community College *C*

North Carolina

Alamance Community College *A*
Asheville Buncombe Technical
Community College *C*
Beaufort County Community
College *C*
Blue Ridge Community College *C*
Caldwell Community College and
Technical Institute *A*
Cape Fear Community College *C*
Central Carolina Community
College *C*
Cleveland Community College *C*
Coastal Carolina Community
College *C*
College of the Albemarle *C*
Craven Community College *C*
Davidson County Community
College *C*
Durham Technical Community
College *C*
Fayetteville Technical Community
College *A*
Forsyth Technical Community
College *A*
Guilford Technical Community
College *C,A*
Haywood Community College *C*
Isothermal Community College *C,A*
Johnston Community College *C*
Martin Community College *C*
Nash Community College *C*
Pitt Community College *C*
Rockingham Community College *C*
Stanly Community College *C*
Surry Community College *C,A*
Tri-County Community College *C*
Wake Technical Community
College *C*
Western Piedmont Community
College *C*
Wilson Technical Community
College *C*

North Dakota

North Dakota State College of
Science *C,A*

Ohio

Terra Technical College *A*
University of Cincinnati: Access
Colleges *C*
University of Toledo *C*

Oklahoma

Oklahoma State University
Technical Branch: Okmulgee *A*

Oregon

Central Oregon Community College
C,A
Chemeketa Community College *C,A*
Clatsop Community College *A*
Lane Community College *A*
Portland Community College *C,A*
Southwestern Oregon Community
College *A*

Pennsylvania

Johnson Technical Institute *A*
Pennsylvania College of
Technology *C*
Reading Area Community College
C,A
Spring Garden College *C*
Williamson Free School of
Mechanical Trades *C*

South Carolina

Aiken Technical College *C,A*
Chesterfield-Marlboro Technical
College *C*
Florence-Darlington Technical
College *C,A*
Greenville Technical College *C,A*
Tri-County Technical College *C,A*
Williamsburg Technical College *C*

Tennessee

Chattanooga State Technical
Community College *C,A*
Northeast State Technical
Community College *A*

Texas

Angelina College *A*
Cooke County College *A*
Del Mar College *C,A*
Houston Community College *C*
Laredo Junior College *C*
Mountain View College *C*
Odessa College *C,A*
St. Philip's College *C,A*
South Plains College *C,A*
Texas State Technical College
Amarillo *A*
Harlingen *A*
Sweetwater *C*
Waco *C,A*

Utah

College of Eastern Utah *C,A*
Utah Valley Community College
C,A
Weber State University *A*

Virginia

Central Virginia Community
College *C*
John Tyler Community College *C*
New River Community College *C,A*
Northern Virginia Community
College *C*
Patrick Henry Community
College *C*
Southwest Virginia Community
College *C*
Tidewater Community College *C*
Virginia Highlands Community
College *C*
Wytheville Community College *C*

Washington

Columbia Basin College *A*
Olympic College *A*
Shoreline Community College *C,A*
Spokane Community College *A*
Walla Walla Community College
C,A

Wisconsin

Chippewa Valley Technical
College *A*
Fox Valley Technical College *C*
Mid-State Technical College *C*
Moraine Park Technical College *C*
Northeast Wisconsin Technical
College *A*
Waukesha County Technical
College *C*
Western Wisconsin Technical
College *C*
Wisconsin Indianhead Technical
College *C*

Wyoming

Casper College *C,A*
Western Wyoming Community
College *C,A*

Management information systems

Alabama

Auburn University
Auburn *B,M*
Montgomery *B*
Community College of the Air
Force *A*
Oakwood College *B*
Samford University *B*
Spring Hill College *B*
University of Alabama
Huntsville *B,M*
Tuscaloosa *B*
University of North Alabama *B*

Alaska

University of Alaska
Anchorage *B*
Fairbanks *B*

Arizona

Arizona State University *M*
Arizona Western College *A*
Cochise College *A*
Mesa Community College *A*
University of Arizona *B,M*
Western International University *M*

California

Azusa Pacific University *B*
Biola University *B*
California State University
Bakersfield *B*
Dominguez Hills *B*
Fullerton *B,M*
Hayward *B,M*
Long Beach *B*
Los Angeles *B,M*
Northridge *B*
Sacramento *B,M*
San Marcos *B*
Stanislaus *B*
Golden Gate University *C,B,M*
Lincoln University *B*
Long Beach City College *C,A*
Mission College *A*
Orange Coast College *C,A*
Pacific Union College *B*
Phillips Junior College: Fresno
Campus *C,A*
San Francisco State University *B,M*
San Jose State University *B*
United States International
University *B,M*
University of San Francisco *B*
University of Southern California *M*
Ventura College *A*

West Coast University *C,A,B,M*
Woodbury University *B*

Colorado

Arapahoe Community College *C,A*
Colorado State University *B,M*
Fort Lewis College *B*
Mesa State College *B*
University of Colorado
Boulder *B*
Colorado Springs *B*
Denver *B*
University of Denver *M*
University of Northern Colorado *B*

Connecticut

Central Connecticut State
University *B*
Fairfield University *B*
Quinnipiac College *B,M*
Teikyo-Post University *C*
University of Connecticut *B*
University of Hartford *B*
University of New Haven *B,M,D*
Western Connecticut State
University *B*

Delaware

Goldey-Beacom College *B*

District of Columbia

American University *B,M*
George Washington University *M,D*
Southeastern University *A,B*

Florida

Barry University *B*
Broward Community College *A*
Daytona Beach Community
College *A*
Embry-Riddle Aeronautical
University *B*
Florida Atlantic University *B*
Florida Institute of Technology *B,M*
Florida International University
B,M
Florida Southern College *B*
Florida State University *B*
Fort Lauderdale College *A,B*
Jacksonville University *B*
Pensacola Junior College *A*
St. Thomas University *M*
University of Florida *M,D*
University of Miami *B,M*
University of South Florida *B*
University of West Florida *B*

Georgia

Brewton-Parker College *B*
Brunswick College *A*
Clayton State College *B*
Columbus College *B*
DeKalb College *A*
Georgia College *B,M*
Georgia Southern University *B*
Kennesaw State College *M*
Mercer University
Atlanta *M*
Macon *B*
Savannah State College *B*
Shorter College *B*
University of Georgia *B,M*
West Georgia College *B*

Hawaii

Hawaii Pacific University *B,M*
University of Hawaii at Manoa *B*

Idaho

Boise State University *B*
Northwest Nazarene College *B*
Ricks College *A*

University of Idaho *B*

Illinois

Aurora University *M*
Bradley University *B*
Chicago State University *B*
College of St. Francis *B*
De Paul University *M*
Elmhurst College *B*
Greenville College *B*
Illinois Benedictine College *M*
Lewis University *B*
Loyola University of Chicago *B*
MacMurray College *B*
Millikin University *B*
National-Louis University *B*
North Central College *B,M*
Northern Illinois University *M*
Northwestern University *M*
Quincy College *B*
Roosevelt University *M*
Rosary College *M*
St. Augustine College *A*
Sangamon State University *M*
Southern Illinois University at
Edwardsville *B,M*
University of Illinois at Chicago *D*
William Rainey Harper College *A*

Indiana

Ball State University *B,M*
Indiana State University *B*
Indiana University Bloomington
B,M,D
Indiana University—Purdue
University at Indianapolis *B*
Purdue University *M,D*
St. Joseph's College *B*
Taylor University *A*
Tri-State University *B*
University of Indianapolis *B*
University of Notre Dame *B*
Vincennes University *A*

Iowa

Buena Vista College *B*
Clarke College *B*
Dordt College *B*
Drake University *B*
Iowa Central Community College *A*
Loras College *B*
Luther College *B*
University of Iowa *M,D*
William Penn College *B*

Kansas

Coffeyville Community College *A*
Friends University *B*
Kansas State University *B*

Kentucky

Owensboro Junior College of
Business *A*
Western Kentucky University *B*

Louisiana

Louisiana College *B*
Louisiana Tech University *B*

Maine

Husson College *A,B*
University of Maine
Machias *A*
Orono *B*

Maryland

Bowie State University *M*
Frederick Community College *A*
Morgan State University *B*
Salisbury State University *B*
University of Baltimore *B,M*

University of Maryland: College
Park *B*
Villa Julie College *B*

Massachusetts

American International College *B*
Anna Maria College for Men and
Women *B*
Babson College *B,M*
Boston University *B,M*
Bridgewater State College *C,B*
Fitchburg State College *B*
Massachusetts Bay Community
College *A*
Massachusetts Institute of
Technology *M,D*
Mount Ida College *A*
New England Banking Institute *C,A*
Nichols College *B*
Northeastern University *A,B*
Salem State College *B*
Simmons College *B*
University of Massachusetts
Dartmouth *B*
Lowell *B*
Western New England College *M*
Westfield State College *B*

Michigan

Alma College *B*
Central Michigan University *B*
Cleary College *B*
Eastern Michigan University *B*
GMI Engineering & Management
Institute *B*
Grand Rapids Baptist College and
Seminary *B*
Lake Superior State University *B*
Lansing Community College *A*
Lawrence Technological
University *B*
Michigan Technological
University *B*
Northern Michigan University *B*
Northwood Institute *A*
Oakland University *B*
University of Detroit Mercy *B*
University of Michigan *D*
Walsh College of Accountancy and
Business Administration *B*
Wayne State University *B,M*
Western Michigan University *B*

Minnesota

Augsburg College *B*
National Education Center: Brown
Institute Campus *A*
Southwest State University *B*
University of St. Thomas *M*
Winona State University *B*

Mississippi

Delta State University *B*
Mississippi University for Women *B*
University of Mississippi *B*
William Carey College *B*

Missouri

Avila College *B,M*
Central Missouri State University *B*
Lindenwood College *M*
Maryville University *B*
Northwest Missouri State
University *B*
Park College *B*
St. Louis University *B*
Southwest Missouri State
University *B*
University of Missouri
Kansas City *M*
St. Louis *M*
Webster University *B,M*

Montana

Eastern Montana College *B*
University of Montana *B*
Western Montana College of the
University of Montana *A*

Nebraska

Bellevue College *B*
Creighton University *B,M*
Dana College *B*
Peru State College *B*
University of Nebraska—Omaha
B,M

Nevada

University of Nevada
Las Vegas *B*
Reno *B*

New Hampshire

Daniel Webster College *A,B*
Franklin Pierce College *A,B*
Hesser College *A*
New Hampshire College *B*

New Jersey

Caldwell College *C,B*
Fairleigh Dickinson University *M*
Glassboro State College *B*
Monmouth College *B*
New Jersey Institute of
Technology *M*
Ramapo College of New Jersey *B*
St. Peter's College *M*
Seton Hall University *B*
Stevens Institute of Technology
B,M,D
Stockton State College *B*
Trenton State College *B*

New Mexico

College of Santa Fe *B*
New Mexico State University *B*
Northern New Mexico Community
College *A*
University of New Mexico *B,M*
Western New Mexico University *B*

New York

Alfred University *B*
Bramson ORT Technical
Institute *A*
Canisius College *B*
City University of New York
Brooklyn College *B*
York College *B*
Clarkson University *B,M*
Daemen College *B*
Dominican College of Blauvelt *B*
Dowling College *B*
D'Youville College *B*
Fordham University *B*
Hofstra University *B,M*
Iona College *B,M*
Le Moyne College *C*
Long Island University
C. W. Post Campus *M*
Southampton Campus *B*
Manhattan College *B*
New York University *B,M,D*
Niagara University *B*
Pace University
College of White Plains *B*
New York *B*
Pleasantville/Briarcliff *B*
Polytechnic University
Brooklyn *B*
Long Island Campus *B*
Rochester Institute of Technology
A,B,M

State University of New York
Albany *B,M*
Buffalo *D*
College at Geneseo *B*
Syracuse University *B,M,D*
Touro College *A,B*
University of the State of New
York: Regents College *B*
Westchester Business Institute *A*
Yeshiva University *B*

North Carolina

Appalachian State University *B*
Barber-Scotia College *B*
Gardner-Webb College *B*
Rockingham Community College *A*
Salem College *B*
University of North Carolina at
Wilmington *B*
Western Piedmont Community
College *C*

North Dakota

Minot State University *B*
North Dakota State University *B*

Ohio

Air Force Institute of
Technology *M*
Bowling Green State University
Bowling Green *B*
Firelands College *A*
Case Western Reserve University
M,D
Cincinnati Metropolitan College *A*
Cincinnati Technical College *A*
Cleveland State University *B*
Franklin University *B*
Miami University
Hamilton Campus *A*
Oxford Campus *B*
Notre Dame College of Ohio *B*
Ohio University *B*
Union Institute *B,D*
University of Akron *M*
University of Cincinnati *B*
University of Dayton *B*
University of Toledo *A,B*
Wright State University *B*
Xavier University *B*

Oklahoma

Oklahoma Baptist University *B*
Oklahoma City University *B*
Oklahoma State University *B*
Oral Roberts University *B*
Southeastern Oklahoma State
University *B*
Southwestern Oklahoma State
University *B*
Tulsa Junior College *C,A*
University of Oklahoma *B*
University of Tulsa *C,B*

Oregon

Central Oregon Community
College *A*
Marylhurst College *C*
Oregon State University *B*
University of Oregon *B,M,D*

Pennsylvania

Beaver College *B*
California University of
Pennsylvania *A,B*
Carnegie Mellon University
B,M,D,W
College Misericordia *B*
Drexel University *B*
Duquesne University *C,B,M*
Gannon University *B*
Geneva College *B*

Grove City College *B*
Harrisburg Area Community
College *A*
Holy Family College *B*
Indiana University of
Pennsylvania *B*
Juniata College *B*
King's College *B*
La Salle University *B,M*
Lehigh University *M*
Lock Haven University of
Pennsylvania *B*
Marywood College *B*
Mercyhurst College *B*
Penn State
Erie Behrend College *B*
Harrisburg Capital College *B*
University Park Campus *C,B*
Philadelphia College of Textiles and
Science *B*
Robert Morris College *M*
St. Francis College *B*
St. Joseph's University *B,M*
Seton Hill College *B*
Shippensburg University of
Pennsylvania *B*
University of Pennsylvania *B,M,D*
University of Pittsburgh
Pittsburgh *M*
Titusville *A*
West Chester University of
Pennsylvania *M*
Widener University *B*

Puerto Rico

Bayamon Central University *A,B*
Inter American University of Puerto
Rico
Arecibo Campus *B*
Metropolitan Campus *B*
San German Campus *B*
Universidad Metropolitana *B*
University of Puerto Rico
Mayaguez Campus *B*
Rio Piedras Campus *B*
University of the Sacred Heart *M*

Rhode Island

Rhode Island College *B*
Roger Williams College *B*
Salve Regina University *B*
University of Rhode Island *B*

South Carolina

Charleston Southern University *B*

South Dakota

Sioux Falls College *B*
University of South Dakota *M*

Tennessee

Bristol University *A,B,M*
Christian Brothers University *B*
Dyersburg State Community
College *A*
Memphis State University *B*
Tennessee Technological
University *B*
Trevecca Nazarene College *B*
University of Tennessee: Martin *B*

Texas

Baylor University *B*
Dallas Baptist University *B*
East Texas State University
Commerce *B*
Texarkana *B*
Hardin-Simmons University *B*
Houston Community College *C*
Howard College *A*
Incarnate Word College *B*
Lamar University—Beaumont *B*

McMurry University *B*
Panola College *A*
St. Mary's University *B,M*
Southern Methodist University *B*
Southwest Texas State University *B*
Texas A&M University *M*
Texas Tech University *B,M,D*
Texas Wesleyan University *B*
University of Central Texas *M*
University of Dallas *M*
University of Houston
Downtown *B*
Houston *B,M,D*
University of Mary Hardin-
Baylor *B*
University of North Texas *B,M,D*
University of St. Thomas *B*
University of Texas
Arlington *B,M*
Austin *B,D*
El Paso *B*
San Antonio *B*

Utah

Brigham Young University *B,M*
Utah State University *B,M,D*

Vermont

Johnson State College *A*

Virginia

Blue Ridge Community College *C*
Christopher Newport College *B*
George Mason University *B,M*
Marymount University *M*
Mountain Empire Community
College *C*
Old Dominion University *B*
Radford University *B*
University of Virginia *M*
Virginia State University *B*
Virginia Union University *B*

Washington

Central Washington University *B*
Clark College *C,A*
Eastern Washington University *B*
Evergreen State College *B*
Pacific Lutheran University *B*
Shoreline Community College *A*
Washington State University *B*
Western Washington University *B*

West Virginia

Alderson-Broaddus College *B*
West Virginia Wesleyan College *B*

Wisconsin

Carroll College *B*
Chippewa Valley Technical
College *A*
Marquette University *B*
University of Wisconsin
Eau Claire *B*
Madison *B,M*
Milwaukee *B*
Oshkosh *B*
Superior *B*
Whitewater *B*
Wisconsin Indianhead Technical
College *A*

Wyoming

Northwest College *A*

Canada

McGill University *B,M,D*

Mexico

Sistema Instituto Tecnologico y de
Estudios Superiores de
Monterrey *B,M*

Management science

Alabama
Bishop State Community College *C*
John C. Calhoun State Community
College *A*
Tuskegee University *B*
University of Alabama *B,M,D*
University of North Alabama *B*

Alaska
Alaska Pacific University *B*

Arizona
Eastern Arizona College *A*
Glendale Community College *A*
Paradise Valley Community College
C,A

Arkansas
Arkansas State University *B*

California
Armstrong College *A,B,M*
California State University
Dominguez Hills *B*
Fullerton *B,M*
Hayward *B,M*
Northridge *B,M*
Sacramento *B*
San Marcos *B*
Chabot College *A*
Coastline Community College *A*
Cosumnes River College *A*
Grossmont Community College *C,A*
Lincoln University *B,M*
Los Angeles Pierce College *A*
Mission College *A*
San Diego City College *C,A*
San Francisco State University *B,M*
Santa Monica College *C,A*
Solano Community College *A*
Southwestern College *A*
University of Southern California *M*
Ventura College *A*
West Coast University *M*
Yuba College *A*

Colorado
Adams State College *B*
Fort Lewis College *B*
Mesa State College *B*
Red Rocks Community College *A*
University of Colorado at Denver *B*
University of Northern Colorado *B*
Western State College of
Colorado *B*

Connecticut
Sacred Heart University *B,M*
University of Connecticut *B*
Western Connecticut State
University *M*
Yale University *M,D*

District of Columbia
George Washington University *M,D*
Mount Vernon College *B*
Southeastern University *A,B*

Florida
Florida State University *B,M*
Miami-Dade Community College *A*
National Education Center: Bauder
Campus *B*
Pensacola Junior College *A*
Stetson University *B*
University of Central Florida *B,M*
University of Miami *M*

Georgia
Chattahoochee Technical Institute
C,A
Georgia Institute of Technology
B,D
Georgia Southwestern College *B*
Savannah Technical Institute *C*
University of Georgia *B,M*

Hawaii
Chaminade University of
Honolulu *B*

Idaho
Lewis Clark State College *B*

Illinois
Aurora University *B,M*
College of DuPage *C,A*
De Paul University *M*
Elgin Community College *C,A*
Elmhurst College *B*
Highland Community College *A*
Illinois Benedictine College *B*
Illinois Institute of Technology *D*
Illinois State University *B*
Northwestern University *M*
Roosevelt University *B,M*
Shawnee Community College *A*
Southern Illinois University
Carbondale *B*
Edwardsville *B*
University of Illinois at Chicago *B*

Indiana
Ball State University *B,M*
Indiana State University *B*
Indiana University Bloomington
B,M,D
Indiana Wesleyan University *M*
Purdue University *M*
University of Evansville *B*
University of Notre Dame *B*

Iowa
Buena Vista College *B*
Drake University *B*
Iowa State University *B*
Simpson College *B*
University of Iowa *B,M,D*

Kansas
Colby Community College *A*

Kentucky
Maysville Community College *A*
Morehead State University *B*

Louisiana
Louisiana Tech University *B*
Loyola University *B*

Maine
Thomas College *B,M*

Maryland
Capitol College *M*
Essex Community College *C,A*
Hagerstown Junior College *A*
Montgomery College
Rockville Campus *A*
Takoma Park Campus *A*
University of Maryland University
College *M*

Massachusetts
Bridgewater State College *B*
Cape Cod Community College *A*
Lesley College *B*
Massachusetts Institute of
Technology *M,D*
North Adams State College *B*

Wentworth Institute of
Technology *B*

Michigan
Aquinas College *M*
Baker College
Auburn Hills *A*
Mount Clemens *A*
Central Michigan University *B*
Grand Rapids Baptist College and
Seminary *B*
Henry Ford Community College *A*
Macomb Community College *C,A*
Madonna University *B*
Michigan State University *M*
Michigan Technological
University *B*
Muskegon Community College *A*
Northern Michigan University *B*
University of Michigan *D*
Walsh College of Accountancy and
Business Administration *M*
Wayne State University *B,M*

Minnesota
Crown College *B*
St. Mary's College of Minnesota *M*
University of St. Thomas *B*

Mississippi
Delta State University *B*

Missouri
Columbia College *A*
Fontbonne College *B*
Lindenwood College *M*
St. Louis Community College at
Meramec *C,A*
Webster University *B,M,D*

Nebraska
Creighton University *B*
Union College *B*
University of Nebraska
Lincoln *B*
Omaha *B*
Wayne State College *B*

Nevada
Community College of Southern
Nevada *A*
University of Nevada: Reno *B*

New Hampshire
Antioch New England Graduate
School *M*
Franklin Pierce College *A,B*

New Jersey
Caldwell College *C*
Jersey City State College *B*
Rutgers—The State University of
New Jersey
Camden College of Arts and
Sciences *B*
Douglass College *B*
Livingston College *B*
Newark College of Arts and
Sciences *B*
Rutgers College *B*
University College Camden *B*
University College New
Brunswick *B*
University College Newark *B*
Stevens Institute of Technology
B,M,D

New Mexico
New Mexico State University *B*
University of New Mexico *M*

New York
Alfred University *B*
City University of New York:
Baruch College *D*
Clarkson University *B,M*
Fordham University *B*
Hofstra University *B,M*
Iona College *B,M*
Manhattan College *B*
Niagara University *B*
Pace University
College of White Plains *M*
New York *B*
Pleasantville/Briarcliff *M*
St. Bonaventure University *B*
State University of New York
Albany *B,M*
Binghamton *M*
Buffalo *D*
College at Cortland *B*
College at Geneseo *B*
College at Plattsburgh *B*
Oswego *B*
United States Military Academy *B*

North Carolina
East Carolina University *B*
North Carolina State University *M*
Western Carolina University *B*
Wingate College *A,B*

North Dakota
University of Mary *M*

Ohio
Case Western Reserve University *B*
Dyke College *A,B*
Franklin University *B*
Heidelberg College *B*
Kent State University *B*
Ohio State University: Columbus
Campus *B,M,D*
Ohio University
Athens *B*
Southern Campus at Ironton *B*
University of Akron *M*
University of Cincinnati *B,M,D*
University of Dayton *M*

Oklahoma
Oklahoma State University
Oklahoma City *A*
Stillwater *B*
Southeastern Oklahoma State
University *B*
Southwestern Oklahoma State
University *B*
University of Central Oklahoma *B*
University of Tulsa *B*

Oregon
Central Oregon Community
College *A*
Chemeketa Community College *A*
Oregon State University *B*

Pennsylvania
Albright College *B*
Carnegie Mellon University
B,M,D,W
Cedar Crest College *C*
Chatham College *B*
Drexel University *M,D*
Duquesne University *B*
Gannon University *B*
La Salle University *B*
Lehigh University *M*
Lock Haven University of
Pennsylvania *B*
Penn State University Park
Campus *B*
Robert Morris College *M*

St. Joseph's University *C*
Shippensburg University of
    Pennsylvania *B*
Spring Garden College *A,B*
Waynesburg College *B*
Westminster College *B*
Widener University *M*

Puerto Rico

Bayamon Central University *B*
Inter American University of Puerto
    Rico: Metropolitan Campus *M*
University of Puerto Rico:
    Mayaguez Campus *B*
University of the Sacred Heart *B*

Rhode Island

Johnson & Wales University *A,B*
University of Rhode Island *B*

South Carolina

Clemson University *D*
Francis Marion College *B*
Greenville Technical College *A*
University of South Carolina *B*

Tennessee

Pellissippi State Technical
    Community College *A*
University of Tennessee
    Chattanooga *B,M*
    Knoxville *M,D*

Texas

Abilene Christian University *B*
Amarillo College *A*
Dallas Baptist University *B,M*
El Paso Community College *A*
Hardin-Simmons University *B*
Jarvis Christian College *B*
Midland College *C,A*
Midwestern State University *B*
North Lake College *A*
Prairie View A&M University *B*
Texas A&I University *B*
Texas Tech University *B*
University of Central Texas *M*
University of Houston
    Clear Lake *B*
    Houston *B,M,D*
University of North Texas *M,D*
University of Texas
    Arlington *B,M*
    Austin *B,D*
    Dallas *D*
    San Antonio *B*
    Tyler *B*

Utah

Weber State University *B*

Virginia

Averett College *B*
Ferrum College *B*
George Mason University *B,M*
Marymount University *B,M*
Old Dominion University *B*
Virginia Highlands Community
    College *A*
Virginia Polytechnic Institute and
    State University *B,D*

Washington

Central Washington University *B*
Eastern Washington University *B*
Gonzaga University *B*
Western Washington University *B*

West Virginia

Fairmont State College *B*
West Virginia University *B*

Wisconsin

Cardinal Stritch College *B,M*
University of Wisconsin
    Milwaukee *D*
    Oshkosh *B*

Wyoming

University of Wyoming *B*

Canada

McGill University *B,M,D*

Mexico

Sistema Instituto Tecnologico y de
    Estudios Superiores de
    Monterrey *M*

Manufacturing technology

Arizona

Arizona State University *B,M*
Arizona Western College *A*
Cochise College *A*
Mesa Community College *C*
Yavapai College *A*

Arkansas

Arkansas State University
    Beebe Branch *A*
    Jonesboro *B*
Southern Arkansas University:
    Technical Branch *A*
University of Arkansas at Little
    Rock *A,B*
Westark Community College *C,A*

California

California State University: Long
    Beach *B*
Cerritos Community College *C,A*
Don Bosco Technical Institute *A*
El Camino College *C,A*
Fashion Institute of Design and
    Merchandising *A*
Fresno City College *C,A*
ITT Technical Institute: West
    Covina *B*
Mount San Antonio College *C,A*
National University *B*
Orange Coast College *C,A*
Pacific Union College *A,B*
San Diego City College *C,A*
San Jose State University *B*
Southwestern College *C,A*
University of Southern California *M*
West Coast University *C,A,B*
Yuba College *A*

Connecticut

Central Connecticut State
    University *B*
Greater New Haven State Technical
    College *A*
Hartford State Technical College *A*
Thames Valley State Technical
    College *A*
Waterbury State Technical
    College *A*

Florida

Daytona Beach Community
    College *A*
Okaloosa-Walton Community
    College *C,A*
St. Petersburg Junior College *A*
Seminole Community College *A*
University of North Florida *B*

Georgia

Augusta Technical Institute *A*
Brunswick College *A*
Georgia Southern University *B*

Idaho

Boise State University *A,B*
Lewis Clark State College *A*
Ricks College *A*

Illinois

Black Hawk College *A*
Bradley University *B*
College of DuPage *C,A*
Eastern Illinois University *M*
Elgin Community College *C,A*
Illinois Central College *C,A*
Kishwaukee College *A*
Morrison Institute of Technology *A*
Prairie State College *A*
Rock Valley College *A*
Southern Illinois University at
    Carbondale *B*
Triton College *C,A*
Waubonsee Community College *A*
William Rainey Harper College *A*

Indiana

Ball State University *A*
Indiana State University *A,B,M*
Indiana University at Kokomo *A*
Indiana University—Purdue
    University at Indianapolis *A,B*
Indiana Vocational Technical
    College: Northwest *C,A*
ITT Technical Institute:
    Indianapolis *B*
Purdue University: Calumet *A,B*
Tri-State University *A*

Iowa

Hawkeye Institute of Technology *A*
Muscatine Community College *A*
North Iowa Area Community
    College *A*
Northwest Iowa Technical
    College *A*
University of Northern Iowa *B*

Kansas

Allen County Community
    College *A*
Hutchinson Community College *A*
Johnson County Community
    College *C,A*
Kansas State University *B*
Pittsburg State University *B*
Southwestern College *B*

Kentucky

Kentucky State University *A*
Morehead State University *A*
Murray State University *B*
Northern Kentucky University *A,B*
Western Kentucky University *A*

Maryland

Anne Arundel Community
    College *C*

Massachusetts

Fitchburg State College *B*
Franklin Institute of Boston *A*
North Shore Community College *A*
University of Massachusetts at
    Lowell *M*
Wentworth Institute of Technology
    A,B

Michigan

Central Michigan University *B*
Eastern Michigan University *B*
Ferris State University *B*
Grand Rapids Community
    College *A*
Henry Ford Community College *A*
Kellogg Community College *A*
Kirtland Community College *A*
Lansing Community College *C,A*
Macomb Community College *C,A*
Northern Michigan University *B*
Oakland Community College *C*
St. Clair County Community
    College *A*
Schoolcraft College *A*
Wayne State University *B*
Western Michigan University *B*

Minnesota

Alexandria Technical College *A*
Mankato State University *B*
St. Cloud State University *B*
St. Paul Technical College *A*
Southwest State University *A,B*

Mississippi

University of Southern
    Mississippi *M*

Missouri

Central Missouri State University *A*
Mineral Area College *C,A*
Southwest Missouri State
    University *B*
Three Rivers Community College *A*

Nebraska

Central Community College *C,A*
Chadron State College *B*
Southeast Community College
    Lincoln Campus *C,A*
    Milford Campus *A*
University of Nebraska
    Lincoln *A,B*
    Omaha *A,B*

New Hampshire

Keene State College *A,B*
New Hampshire Technical College:
    Nashua *A*

New Jersey

Gloucester County College *A*
Kean College of New Jersey *B*
New Jersey Institute of
    Technology *B*
Ocean County College *A*
Passaic County Community
    College *A*

New York

City University of New York:
    College of Staten Island *C*
College of Aeronautics *B*
Erie Community College
    City Campus *A*
    North Campus *A*
Mohawk Valley Community College
    C,A
Rochester Institute of Technology
    A,B
State University of New York
    College of Technology at
    Farmingdale *B*
Suffolk County Community College
    C,A

North Carolina

Blue Ridge Community College *A*
Central Piedmont Community
    College *A*
Forsyth Technical Community
    College *A*
Haywood Community College *A*

Pitt Community College *A*
Sandhills Community College *C,A*
University of North Carolina at
   Charlotte *B*
Wake Technical Community
   College *A*
Western Carolina University *B*
Wilson Technical Community
   College *A*

Ohio
Bowling Green State University
   Bowling Green *B,M*
   Firelands College *A*
Central State University *B*
Cincinnati Technical College *A*
Clark State Community College *A*
Cleveland State University *B*
Columbus State Community
   College *A*
Edison State Community College *A*
Kent State University
   Kent *B*
   Tuscarawas Campus *C*
Lakeland Community College *C,A*
Miami University: Oxford
   Campus *B*
North Central Technical College *A*
Owens Technical College: Toledo
   C,A
Sinclair Community College *A*
Terra Technical College *A*
University of Akron *A*
University of Cincinnati: Access
   Colleges *C*
University of Dayton *B*
University of Rio Grande *A*
University of Toledo *A,B*
Washington State Community
   College *A*
Wright State University: Lake
   Campus *A*

Oklahoma
Oklahoma State University
   Stillwater *B*
     Technical Branch:
      Okmulgee *A*
Southeastern Oklahoma State
   University *B*

Oregon
Central Oregon Community College
   C,A
Chemeketa Community College *A*
Clackamas Community College *C,A*
ITT Technical Institute: Portland *B*
Oregon Institute of Technology *A,B*

Pennsylvania
California University of
   Pennsylvania *B*
Delaware County Community
   College *A*
Edinboro University of
   Pennsylvania *A*
Harrisburg Area Community
   College *A*
Pennsylvania Institute of
   Technology *A*
Spring Garden College *A,B*

Puerto Rico
Turabo University *B*

Rhode Island
New England Institute of
   Technology *A*

South Carolina
Greenville Technical College *A*
Trident Technical College *A*

Tennessee
Austin Peay State University *B*
Dyersburg State Community
   College *A*
East Tennessee State University *B*
Memphis State University *B*
Middle Tennessee State
   University *B*
Northeast State Technical
   Community College *A*
Pellissippi State Technical
   Community College *A*

Texas
Austin Community College *C,A*
Brookhaven College *C,A*
East Texas State University *B*
Houston Community College *A*
Richland College *A*
Southwest Texas State University *B*
Texas State Technical College
   Sweetwater *A*
   Waco *C*
University of Houston *B*

Utah
Brigham Young University *B,M*
Weber State University *A,B*

Washington
Central Washington University *B*
Cogswell College North *B*
Eastern Washington University *B*
Shoreline Community College *A*
Western Washington University *B*

Wisconsin
Mid-State Technical College *A*
Milwaukee School of Engineering *B*
Northeast Wisconsin Technical
   College *A*

Mexico
Sistema Instituto Tecnologico y de
   Estudios Superiores de
   Monterrey *M*

Marine biology

Alabama
Alabama State University *B*
Auburn University
   Auburn *B*
   Montgomery *B*
Livingston University *B*
Samford University *B*
Spring Hill College *B*
Troy State University *B,M*
University of Alabama *B,M*
University of North Alabama *B*
University of South Alabama *D*

Alaska
University of Alaska Fairbanks *M*

Arkansas
University of Central Arkansas *C*
University of the Ozarks *B*

California
California State University
   Fresno *B,M*
   Fullerton *B*
   Hayward *M*
   Long Beach *B*
   Stanislaus *B,M*
Modesto Junior College *A*
San Francisco State University *B,M*
San Jose State University *B,M*

Southwestern College *A*
University of California
   Berkeley *B*
   San Diego *M,D*
   Santa Barbara *B,M,D*
   Santa Cruz *B,M*
University of San Diego *B,M*

Connecticut
Mitchell College *A*
United States Coast Guard
   Academy *B*

Delaware
University of Delaware *M,D*

District of Columbia
George Washington University *M,D*
University of the District of
   Columbia *A*

Florida
Barry University *B*
Eckerd College *B*
Florida Atlantic University *B,M*
Florida Institute of Technology
   B,M,D
Jacksonville University *B*
New College of the University of
   South Florida *B*
Nova University *B,M*
Pensacola Junior College *A*
University of Miami *B,M,D*
University of South Florida *M,D*
University of Tampa *B*
University of West Florida *B,M*

Georgia
Savannah State College *B*

Hawaii
Hawaii Loa College *B*

Idaho
Ricks College *A*

Indiana
Ball State University *B*

Iowa
Drake University *B*
Luther College *B*

Kansas
Southwestern College *B*

Louisiana
Nicholls State University *B*

Maine
Southern Maine Technical
   College *A*
Unity College *B*
University of Maine at Machias *B*
University of New England *B*

Maryland
University of Maryland
   Baltimore County *M,D*
   College Park *M,D*
   Eastern Shore *B,M*

Massachusetts
Boston University *B*
Bradford College *B*
Hampshire College *B*
Harvard University *D*
Salem State College *B*
Suffolk University *B*
University of Massachusetts at
   Dartmouth *B,M*

Minnesota
Bemidji State University *B*
Willmar Community College *A*

Mississippi
Jackson State University *B*
University of Southern Mississippi
   M,D

Nebraska
York College *A*

New Hampshire
University of New Hampshire *B*

New Jersey
Atlantic Community College *A*
Fairleigh Dickinson University *B*
Rider College *B*
Stockton State College *B*

New York
Colgate University *B*
Cornell University *M,D*
Dowling College *B*
Long Island University:
   Southampton Campus *B*
Sarah Lawrence College *B*
State University of New York at
   Stony Brook *M*

North Carolina
Brevard College *A*
Cape Fear Community College *A*
North Carolina State University *M*
University of North Carolina
   Chapel Hill *M,D*
   Wilmington *B,M*

Ohio
Wittenberg University *B*

Oklahoma
Northeastern State University *B*

Oregon
University of Oregon
   Eugene *B,M,D*
   Robert Donald Clark Honors
   College *B*

Pennsylvania
East Stroudsburg University of
   Pennsylvania *B*
Kutztown University of
   Pennsylvania *B*
St. Francis College *B*

Puerto Rico
University of Puerto Rico
   Humacao University College *B*
   Mayaguez Campus *M,D*

Rhode Island
Brown University *B,M,D*
Roger Williams College *B*

South Carolina
College of Charleston *B,M*
University of South Carolina
   Coastal Carolina College *B*
   Columbia *B,M,D*

Tennessee
Tennessee Technological
   University *B*

Texas
Lamar University—Beaumont *B*
Southwest Texas State University *B*
Texas A&M University at
   Galveston *B*

University of Texas at Austin
B,M,D

Vermont

Marlboro College *B*

Virginia

College of William and Mary *M,D*
Hampton University *B*
Old Dominion University *M,D*

Washington

Evergreen State College *B*
Grays Harbor College *A*
Olympic College *A*
Seattle University *B*
Shoreline Community College *A*
Western Washington University *B*

Wisconsin

Lawrence University *B*
Northland College *B*

American Samoa, Caroline Islands, Guam, Marianas, Virgin Islands

Community College of
Micronesia *A*
University of the Virgin Islands *B*

Canada

McGill University *B,M,D*

Mexico

Sistema Instituto Tecnologico y de
Estudios Superiores de
Monterrey *M*

Marine maintenance

Alaska

University of Alaska Southeast *C,A*

California

College of Oceaneering *A*

Florida

Seminole Community College *C*

Idaho

North Idaho College *C*

Iowa

Iowa Lakes Community College *C*
Kirkwood Community College *A*

Maine

Southern Maine Technical
College *A*

Minnesota

Alexandria Technical College *C*

Mississippi

Mississippi Gulf Coast Community
College: Jackson County
Campus *A*

New Hampshire

New Hampshire Technical College:
Laconia *C,A*

Oregon

Clatsop Community College *C*

Rhode Island

New England Institute of
Technology *A*

Washington

Northwest Indian College *C*
Seattle Central Community College
C,A
Skagit Valley College *C,A*

Wisconsin

Chippewa Valley Technical
College *C*
Wisconsin Indianhead Technical
College *C*

Marketing and distribution

Alabama

Alabama Agricultural and
Mechanical University *B*
Brewer State Junior College *A*
Community College of the Air
Force *A*
Enterprise State Junior College *A*
Gadsden State Community
College *A*
Jacksonville State University *B*
James H. Faulkner State
Community College *A*
Jefferson State Community
College *A*
John C. Calhoun State Community
College *A*
Samford University *B*
Wallace State Community College
at Hanceville *A*

Arizona

Arizona Western College *A*
Eastern Arizona College *A*
Grand Canyon University *B*
Mohave Community College *C,A*

Arkansas

Arkansas State University *B*
Capital City Junior College *A*
East Arkansas Community
College *A*
Mississippi County Community
College *A*
North Arkansas Community
College *A*
Phillips County Community
College *A*
Southern Arkansas University *B*
University of Arkansas
Fayetteville *B*
Little Rock *B*
University of Central Arkansas *A,B*
University of the Ozarks *B*

California

Armstrong College *A*
Azusa Pacific University *B*
Barstow College *A*
California State University
Bakersfield *B*
Los Angeles *B,M*
Northridge *B,M*
Cerritos Community College *A*
Chabot College *A*
City College of San Francisco *A*
Coastline Community College *A*
College of the Desert *A*
Compton Community College *A*
Crafton Hills College *A*
Cuesta College *A*
East Los Angeles College *A*
El Camino College *A*
Fashion Institute of Design and
Merchandising *A*

Fresno City College *C,A*
Gavilan Community College *A*
Glendale Community College *C,A*
Golden Gate University *B,M*
Grossmont Community College *C,A*
Hartnell College *A*
Humphreys College *A*
Imperial Valley College *A*
Kings River Community College *A*
Lake Tahoe Community College *A*
Long Beach City College *C,A*
Los Angeles Pierce College *C,A*
Los Angeles Trade and Technical
College *A*
Los Angeles Valley College *C,A*
Merced College *A*
Mission College *A*
Modesto Junior College *A*
Moorpark College *A*
Napa Valley College *A*
Ohlone College *C,A*
Orange Coast College *C,A*
Oxnard College *C,A*
Pacific Union College *B*
Pasadena City College *C,A*
Saddleback College *C,A*
San Diego City College *C,A*
San Diego Mesa College *C,A*
San Diego Miramar College *A*
San Francisco State University *B*
San Jose City College *A*
Santa Barbara City College *C,A*
Santa Monica College *C,A*
Santa Rosa Junior College *A*
Sierra College *C,A*
Skyline College *A*
Solano Community College *A*
Southwestern College *C,A*
Ventura College *A*
West Hills Community College *A*
West Valley College *C,A*
Woodbury University *B,M*
Yuba College *A*

Colorado

Arapahoe Community College *C,A*
Colorado Mountain College: Alpine
Campus *A*
Colorado State University *M*
Community College of Denver *C,A*
Front Range Community College *A*
Mesa State College *B*
Northeastern Junior College *A*
Red Rocks Community College *A*

Connecticut

Central Connecticut State
University *B*
Manchester Community College
C,A
Mattatuck Community College *C,A*
Middlesex Community College *A*
Mitchell College *A*
Northwestern Connecticut
Community College *A*
Norwalk Community College *A*
Quinnipiac College *B,M*
Teikyo-Post University *A,B*
Thames Valley State Technical
College *A*
Tunxis Community College *C,A*
University of Hartford *B*
University of New Haven *B,M*

Delaware

Delaware Technical and
Community College
Southern Campus *A*
Terry Campus *A*

District of Columbia

George Washington University *B*
Southeastern University *A*
University of the District of
Columbia *A*

Florida

Barry University *B*
Brevard Community College *A*
Broward Community College *A*
Daytona Beach Community
College *A*
Florida Institute of Technology *B*
Gulf Coast Community College *A*
Hillsborough Community College *A*
Indian River Community College *A*
Jones College *A,B*
Lynn University *B*
Manatee Community College *C,A*
Miami-Dade Community College *A*
Orlando College *A*
Palm Beach Community College *A*
St. Johns River Community
College *A*
Santa Fe Community College *A*
University of West Florida *B*
Webber College *A,B*

Georgia

Abraham Baldwin Agricultural
College *A*
Atlanta Metropolitan College *A*
Augusta College *A,B*
Augusta Technical Institute *C*
Bainbridge College *A*
Brunswick College *C,A*
Clayton State College *C,A*
Dalton College *A*
Darton College *A*
DeKalb College *A*
DeKalb Technical Institute *C,A*
Floyd College *A*
Gainesville College *A*
Georgia College *B*
Georgia Southern University *B*
Georgia State University *B,M,D*
Kennesaw State College *B,M*
Mercer University Atlanta *B*
Morehouse College *B*
North Georgia College *B*
Savannah State College *B*
South Georgia College *A*
University of Georgia *B,M*
Valdosta State College *B*
West Georgia College *B*

Hawaii

Hawaii Pacific University *A,B,M*
University of Hawaii
Kapiolani Community College
C,A
Kauai Community College *C,A*
Leeward Community
College *A*
Manoa *B*

Idaho

Boise State University *A,B*
College of Southern Idaho *C*
Idaho State University *C,A,B*
Lewis Clark State College *A*
Ricks College *A*
University of Idaho *B*

Illinois

Black Hawk College *A*
Carl Sandburg College *A*

City Colleges of Chicago
    Chicago City-Wide College
        C,A
    Malcolm X College *A*
    Richard J. Daley College *A*
    Wright College *A*
College of DuPage *C,A*
College of Lake County *C,A*
College of St. Francis *B*
Columbia College *B*
De Paul University *B,M*
Elgin Community College *C,A*
Eureka College *B*
Illinois Benedictine College *B*
Illinois Central College *A*
Illinois Eastern Community
    Colleges
        Olney Central College *A*
        Wabash Valley College *A*
Illinois Valley Community
    College *A*
John A. Logan College *A*
Joliet Junior College *A*
Kishwaukee College *C,A*
Lake Land College *A*
Lewis and Clark Community
    College *A*
Lincoln Land Community
    College *A*
Loyola University of Chicago *B*
MacCormac Junior College *A*
McKendree College *B*
Moraine Valley Community College
    C,A
Morton College *A*
North Central College *B*
Northeastern Illinois University *B*
Oakton Community College *C,A*
Parkland College *A*
Prairie State College *A*
Rend Lake College *A*
Rock Valley College *A*
Southern Illinois University
    Carbondale *B*
    Edwardsville *B*
Trinity Christian College *B*
Trinity College *B*
Triton College *A*
Western Illinois University *B*
William Rainey Harper College *A*

Indiana

Anderson University *B*
Ball State University *B*
Indiana University at South Bend *A*
Indiana University—Purdue
    University at Fort Wayne *A*
Indiana Vocational Technical
    College
        Central Indiana *A*
        Eastcentral *A*
        Kokomo *A*
        Lafayette *C,A*
        Northcentral *A*
        Northeast *C,A*
        Northwest *C,A*
        Southwest *A*
        Wabash Valley *C,A*
Martin University *B*
Purdue University: North Central
    Campus *A*
St. Joseph's College *B*
St. Mary-of-the-Woods College *B*
Tri-State University *B*
University of Evansville *B*
Vincennes University *A*

Iowa

American Institute of Business *A*
Clinton Community College *A*
Des Moines Area Community
    College *A*

Hawkeye Institute of Technology *A*
Iowa Central Community College *A*
Iowa Lakes Community College *A*
Kirkwood Community College *A*
Mount Mercy College *B*
Muscatine Community College *C*
North Iowa Area Community
    College *A*
Northeast Iowa Community
    College *A*
Northwest Iowa Technical
    College *A*
Teikyo Westmar University *B*
University of Iowa *B*
Upper Iowa University *B*
Waldorf College *A*

Kansas

Allen County Community
    College *A*
Benedictine College *B*
Brown Mackie College *A*
Butler County Community
    College *A*
Central College *A*
Colby Community College *A*
Cowley County Community College
    C,A
Dodge City Community College *A*
Emporia State University *B*
Fort Scott Community College *A*
Hutchinson Community College *A*
Kansas City Kansas Community
    College *A*
Kansas Newman College *B*
Neosho County Community
    College *A*
Pratt Community College *C,A*
Seward County Community
    College *A*

Kentucky

Georgetown College *B*
Maysville Community College *A*
Morehead State University *B*
Murray State University *A,B*
Owensboro Junior College of
    Business *C,A*
Sullivan College *A,B*
University of Kentucky *B*

Louisiana

Grambling State University *B*
Louisiana College *B*
Nicholls State University *B*
Northwestern State University *A*
Southeastern Louisiana
    University *A*
Southern University in
    Shreveport *A*
University of New Orleans *B*
University of Southwestern
    Louisiana *B*

Maine

Thomas College *B,M*
Westbrook College *B*

Maryland

Catonsville Community College *C,A*
Cecil Community College *C,A*
Frederick Community College *A*
Hagerstown Business College *A*
Howard Community College *A*
Montgomery College
    Germantown Campus *A*
    Rockville Campus *A*
    Takoma Park Campus *A*
New Community College of
    Baltimore *A*
Prince George's Community
    College *A*

Massachusetts

American International College *B*
Anna Maria College for Men and
    Women *B*
Becker College: Leicester
    Campus *A*
Berkshire Community College *A*
Bristol Community College *A*
Dean Junior College *A*
Elms College *B*
Greenfield Community College *A*
Massasoit Community College *A*
Middlesex Community College *A*
Mount Ida College *A*
Mount Wachusett Community
    College *A*
Newbury College *A*
Nichols College *B*
Quincy College *A*
Quinsigamond Community
    College *A*
Roxbury Community College *A*
Simmons College *B*
Suffolk University *B*
University of Massachusetts at
    Dartmouth *B*

Michigan

Alpena Community College *A*
Baker College
    Auburn Hills *A*
    Muskegon *A*
Charles Stewart Mott Community
    College *A*
Cleary College *A,B*
Davenport College of Business *A,B*
Delta College *A*
Detroit College of Business *A,B*
Eastern Michigan University *B,M*
Grand Rapids Community College
    C,A
Grand Valley State University *B,M*
Jackson Community College *C,A*
Kalamazoo Valley Community
    College *A*
Kirtland Community College *A*
Lake Superior State University *B*
Lansing Community College *A*
Macomb Community College *C,A*
Madonna University *B*
Marygrove College *B*
Michigan State University *B,M,D*
Mid Michigan Community
    College *A*
Muskegon Community College *A*
Northern Michigan University *B*
Northwood Institute *B*
Oakland Community College *A*
St. Clair County Community
    College *C,A*
Southwestern Michigan College *A*
Wayne State University *B,M*
West Shore Community College *A*
Western Michigan University *B*

Minnesota

Alexandria Technical College *A*
Anoka-Ramsey Community
    College *A*
Itasca Community College:
    Arrowhead Region *A*
Lakewood Community College *A*
Mesabi Community College:
    Arrowhead Region *A*
Moorhead State University *B*
Normandale Community College *A*
Northwestern College *A,B*
Rochester Community College *C,A*
St. Cloud State University *B*
St. Mary's College of Minnesota *B*
Southwest State University *A,B*

University of Minnesota:
    Crookston *A*
Willmar Technical College *C*
Worthington Community College *A*

Mississippi

Hinds Community College *A*
Holmes Community College *A*
Jackson State University *B*
Jones County Junior College *A*
Meridian Community College *A*
Mississippi Gulf Coast Community
    College
        Jackson County Campus *A*
        Jefferson Davis Campus *A*
Northeast Mississippi Community
    College *A*
Rust College *B*
Southwest Mississippi Community
    College *A*
University of Mississippi *B*

Missouri

Avila College *B,M*
Longview Community College *A*
Maple Woods Community
    College *A*
Mineral Area College *A*
Moberly Area Community
    College *A*
Northwest Missouri State
    University *B*
Penn Valley Community College *A*
Rockhurst College *B*
St. Louis Community College
    Florissant Valley *A*
    Meramec *A*
Southeast Missouri State
    University *B*
State Fair Community College *A*
University of Missouri: Columbia *B*

Montana

Miles Community College *A*
University of Montana *B*

Nebraska

Central Community College *A*
Chadron State College *B*
Metropolitan Community College *A*
Midland Lutheran College *A*
Northeast Community College *A*
Wayne State College *B*

Nevada

Community College of Southern
    Nevada *A*
Northern Nevada Community
    College *A*
Truckee Meadows Community
    College *A*
Western Nevada Community
    College *A*

New Hampshire

Daniel Webster College *A*
Franklin Pierce College *A,B*
Hesser College *A*
McIntosh College *A*
New England College *B*
New Hampshire College *B,M*
New Hampshire Technical College:
    Nashua *A*
Plymouth State College of the
    University System of New
    Hampshire *B*
Rivier College *B*
University of New Hampshire *A*

New Jersey

Atlantic Community College *A*
Berkeley College of Business *A*

Brookdale Community College *A*
Burlington County College *A*
Camden County College *A*
County College of Morris *A*
Cumberland County College *A*
Glassboro State College *B*
Gloucester County College *A*
Jersey City State College *B*
Ocean County College *A*
Passaic County Community
　College *A*
Rider College *B*
St. Peter's College *B*
Seton Hall University *B*
Stockton State College *B*
Thomas Edison State College *C,A,B*

New Mexico

Clovis Community College *C*
College of Santa Fe *B*
Dona Ana Branch Community
　College of New Mexico State
　University *C*
Eastern New Mexico University *B*
New Mexico Junior College *A*
New Mexico State University *A*

New York

Adirondack Community College *A*
Berkeley School: New York City *A*
Bramson ORT Technical Institute
　C,A
Bryant & Stratton Business
　Institute: Syracuse *A*
Central City Business Institute *A*
City University of New York
　Borough of Manhattan
　　Community College *A*
　Kingsborough Community
　　College *A*
　New York City Technical
　　College *A*
　York College *B*
Clarkson University *B*
Cornell University *M,D*
Elmira College *B*
Erie Community College: South
　Campus *A*
Fashion Institute of Technology *B*
Five Towns College *A*
Genesee Community College *A*
Herkimer County Community
　College *A*
Hilbert College *A*
Hudson Valley Community
　College *A*
Iona College *A,B*
Jamestown Business College *A*
Jamestown Community College *A*
Long Island University: C. W. Post
　Campus *B,M*
Manhattan College *B*
Monroe Community College *A*
Nassau Community College *A*
North Country Community
　College *A*
Parsons School of Design *B*
Rochester Business Institute *A*
Rochester Institute of Technology
　A,B
Rockland Community College *A*
Sage Junior College of Albany, A
　Division of Russell Sage
　College *A*
St. Bonaventure University *B,W*
St. Francis College *C*
St. Thomas Aquinas College *B*

State University of New York
　College at Plattsburgh *B*
　College of Technology at
　　Delhi *A*
　College of Technology at
　　Farmingdale *A*
　Oswego *B*
Suffolk County Community College
　Selden *A*
　Western Campus *A*
Sullivan County Community
　College *A*
Tompkins-Cortland Community
　College *A*
Utica School of Commerce *A*
Villa Maria College of Buffalo *A*
Westchester Business Institute *A*
Westchester Community College *A*

North Carolina

Alamance Community College *A*
Anson Community College *A*
Appalachian State University *B*
Asheville Buncombe Technical
　Community College *A*
Blue Ridge Community College *A*
Brevard College *A*
Catawba Valley Community
　College *A*
Central Piedmont Community
　College *A*
Coastal Carolina Community
　College *A*
Craven Community College *A*
Fayetteville State University *B*
Fayetteville Technical Community
　College *A*
Forsyth Technical Community
　College *A*
Gaston College *A*
Isothermal Community College *A*
Johnson C. Smith University *B*
McDowell Technical Community
　College *A*
Nash Community College *A*
North Carolina Central
　University *B*
Pitt Community College *A*
Robeson Community College *A*
Stanly Community College *A*
Surry Community College *A*
University of North Carolina at
　Greensboro *B*
Vance-Granville Community
　College *A*
Wake Technical Community
　College *A*
Wayne Community College *A*

North Dakota

Bismarck State College *C,A*
North Dakota State College of
　Science *A*
North Dakota State University:
　Bottineau and Institute of
　Forestry *C,A*
University of North Dakota
　Grand Forks *B*
　Lake Region *A*
　Williston *A*

Ohio

Ashland University *B*
Bowling Green State University *B*
Cedarville College *B*
Cincinnati Metropolitan College *A*
Cincinnati Technical College *A*
Cleveland State University *B*
Columbus State Community
　College *A*

Cuyahoga Community College
　Metropolitan Campus *A*
　Western Campus *A*
Defiance College *B*
Dyke College *A,B*
Edison State Community College
　C,A
Franklin University *B*
Hocking Technical College *A*
Kent State University
　East Liverpool Regional
　　Campus *A*
　Kent *B*
Lakeland Community College *C*
Lorain County Community
　College *A*
Marietta College *B*
Miami University: Oxford Campus
　B,M
Miami-Jacobs College *A*
Muskingum Area Technical
　College *A*
Northwestern College *A*
Notre Dame College of Ohio *B*
Ohio State University
　Agricultural Technical
　　Institute *A*
　Columbus Campus *B*
Ohio University *B*
Owens Technical College
　Findlay Campus *A*
　Toledo *A*
Sinclair Community College *A*
Stark Technical College *A*
Terra Technical College *A*
University of Akron *A,B*
University of Cincinnati
　Access Colleges *A*
　Raymond Walters College *A*
University of Dayton *B*
University of Toledo *A,B,M*
Wilberforce University *B*
Wilmington College *B*
Wright State University
　Dayton *B,M*
　Lake Campus *A*
Youngstown State University
　A,B,M

Oklahoma

Connors State College *A*
Eastern Oklahoma State College *A*
Oklahoma Baptist University *B*
Oklahoma Christian University of
　Science and Arts *B*
Oral Roberts University *B*
Redlands Community College *A*
Rose State College *A*
Southwestern Oklahoma State
　University *B*
Tulsa Junior College *A*
University of Central Oklahoma *B*
University of Tulsa *B*

Oregon

Central Oregon Community
　College *A*
Marylhurst College *C*
Mount Hood Community
　College *A*
Portland State University *B*
Southwestern Oregon Community
　College *A*
Treasure Valley Community
　College *A*
Umpqua Community College *A*

Pennsylvania

Allentown College of St. Francis de
　Sales *B*
Butler County Community
　College *A*

California University of
　Pennsylvania *A,B*
Clarion University of
　Pennsylvania *B*
College Misericordia *B*
Community College of Philadelphia
　C,A
Gannon University *B*
Grove City College *B*
Holy Family College *B*
ICS Center for Degree Studies *A*
Keystone Junior College *A*
La Salle University *A,B,M*
Lackawanna Junior College *A*
Lehigh County Community
　College *A*
Lehigh University *B*
Mercyhurst College *A*
Messiah College *B*
Montgomery County Community
　College *A*
Neumann College *B*
Peirce Junior College *A*
Philadelphia College of Textiles and
　Science *B*
Robert Morris College *B*
York College of Pennsylvania *B*

Puerto Rico

Bayamon Central University *B*
Caribbean University *A,B*
ICPR Junior College *A*
Instituto Tecnico Comercial Junior
　College *A*
Pontifical Catholic University of
　Puerto Rico *B*
Puerto Rico Junior College *A*
University of Puerto Rico
　Bayamon Technological
　　University College *A,B*
　Mayaguez Campus *B*
University of the Sacred Heart *B*

Rhode Island

Bryant College *M*
Johnson & Wales University *A,B*

South Carolina

Anderson College *A,B*
Charleston Southern University *B*
Coker College *B*
Converse College *B*
Florence-Darlington Technical
　College *A*
Greenville Technical College *A*
Midlands Technical College *A*
South Carolina State College *B*
Sumter Area Technical College *A*
Trident Technical College *A*
University of South Carolina
　Aiken *B*
　Columbia *B*

South Dakota

Black Hills State University *B*
Dakota Wesleyan University *B*
Northern State University *A*
Western Dakota Vocational
　Technical Institute *C*

Tennessee

Bristol University *A*
Chattanooga State Technical
　Community College *A*
Christian Brothers University *C,B*
Columbia State Community
　College *A*
David Lipscomb University *B*
Dyersburg State Community
　College *A*
East Tennessee State University *B*
Freed-Hardeman University *B*

Lambuth University *B*
Memphis State University *B*
Motlow State Community
  College *A*
Pellissippi State Technical
  Community College *A*
Southern College of Seventh-day
  Adventists *B*
Tennessee Technological
  University *B*
Trevecca Nazarene College *A*
University of Tennessee:
  Knoxville *B*
Volunteer State Community
  College *A*

Texas
Abilene Christian University *B*
Alvin Community College *C,A*
Amarillo College *A*
Austin Community College *A*
Baylor University *B*
Bee County College *A*
Blinn College *A*
Central Texas College *A*
Cisco Junior College *A*
College of the Mainland *A*
Collin County Community College
  District *C,A*
Cooke County College *A*
Del Mar College *A*
Galveston College *A*
Houston Community College *C*
Howard College *A*
Incarnate Word College *B*
Kilgore College *A*
Lamar University—Beaumont *A*
Laredo Junior College *A*
Lee College *A*
LeTourneau University *B*
McLennan Community College *A*
McMurry University *B*
Midland College *A*
Midwestern State University *B*
Mountain View College *A*
Navarro College *A*
Sam Houston State University *B*
South Plains College *A*
Stephen F. Austin State
  University *B*
Sul Ross State University *B*
Tarleton State University *B*
Tarrant County Junior College *A*
Temple Junior College *C,A*
Texas A&M University *B*
Texas Lutheran College *A,B*
Texas Tech University *B,M,D*
Texas Wesleyan University *B*
Trinity Valley Community
  College *A*
University of Central Texas *B*
University of Mary Hardin-
  Baylor *A*
University of North Texas *B,M,D*
Vernon Regional Junior College *A*
Victoria College *A*
West Texas State University *B*
Western Texas College *A*

Utah
Brigham Young University *B*
College of Eastern Utah *C*
Dixie College *C,A*
LDS Business College *A*
Southern Utah University *A*
Utah State University *B*
Utah Valley Community College
  C,A
Weber State University *B*
Westminster College of Salt Lake
  City *B*

Vermont
Castleton State College *B*
Champlain College *A*
Goddard College *B,M*

Virginia
Averett College *B*
Blue Ridge Community College *C,A*
Christopher Newport College *B*
Marymount University *B,M*
Mountain Empire Community
  College *A*
National Business College *A*
New River Community College *A*
Northern Virginia Community
  College *A*
Patrick Henry Community
  College *A*
Paul D. Camp Community
  College *A*
Piedmont Virginia Community
  College *A*
Radford University *B*
St. Paul's College *B*
Strayer College *A*
Tidewater Community College *A*

Washington
Bellevue Community College *A*
Big Bend Community College *A*
Central Washington University *B*
Clark College *A*
Columbia Basin College *A*
Eastern Washington University *B*
Edmonds Community College *A*
Everett Community College *A*
Grays Harbor College *A*
Green River Community College
  C,A
Olympic College *A*
Pacific Lutheran University *B*
Peninsula College *A*
St. Martin's College *B*
Seattle Central Community
  College *A*
Seattle University *B*
Shoreline Community College *A*
Skagit Valley College *A*
Spokane Community College *A*
Spokane Falls Community
  College *A*
Walla Walla Community College *A*
Wenatchee Valley College *A*

West Virginia
Bluefield State College *A*
Concord College *B*
Marshall University *A,B*
Potomac State College of West
  Virginia University *A*
Salem-Teikyo University *A,B*
Shepherd College *A*
University of Charleston *A,B*
West Liberty State College *B*
West Virginia State College *B*
West Virginia Wesleyan College *B*

Wisconsin
Chippewa Valley Technical
  College *A*
Fox Valley Technical College *A*
Lakeland College *B*
Madison Area Technical College *A*
Madison Junior College of
  Business *A*
Mid-State Technical College *A*
Moraine Park Technical College *A*
Northeast Wisconsin Technical
  College *A*
Stratton College *A*

University of Wisconsin
  Eau Claire *B*
  Oshkosh *B*
  Superior *B*
  Whitewater *B*
Viterbo College *B*
Waukesha County Technical
  College *A*
Western Wisconsin Technical
  College *A*
Wisconsin Indianhead Technical
  College *A*

Wyoming
Casper College *A*
Central Wyoming College *A*
Laramie County Community
  College *A*
Northwest College *A*
Sheridan College *A*
Western Wyoming Community
  College *C,A*

**American Samoa, Caroline
Islands, Guam, Marianas,
Virgin Islands**
Guam Community College *C,A*

Mexico
Sistema Instituto Tecnologico y de
  Estudios Superiores de
  Monterrey *B*

Switzerland
American College of Switzerland *B*

Marketing and
distributive education

Alabama
Auburn University *B,M*

Arkansas
University of Central Arkansas *B*

Connecticut
Central Connecticut State
  University *B,M*
Sacred Heart University *B,M*

Delaware
Delaware State College *B*

Florida
Gulf Coast Community College *A*
Pensacola Junior College *A*
University of North Florida *B*
University of South Florida *B,M*

Georgia
Gainesville College *A*
Georgia State University *B,M*
University of Georgia *B,M*

Indiana
Ball State University *M*
Indiana State University *B*
Indiana University Bloomington *B*
Vincennes University *A*

Iowa
Iowa Lakes Community College *A*
Kirkwood Community College *A*
Upper Iowa University *B*

Kansas
Cowley County Community
  College *A*

Kentucky
Murray State University *B*
University of Kentucky *B*

Louisiana
Grambling State University *B*
Northwestern State University *B*
University of Southwestern
  Louisiana *B*

Michigan
Eastern Michigan University *B*
Wayne State University *B*
Western Michigan University *B*

Minnesota
Mankato State University *B*
University of Minnesota: Twin
  Cities *B,M*

Mississippi
Mississippi State University *B*
Northeast Mississippi Community
  College *A*

Missouri
Central Missouri State University
  B,M
University of Missouri: Columbia
  B,M,D

Nebraska
Chadron State College *B*
University of Nebraska—Lincoln *B*

New Hampshire
New Hampshire College *B,M*

New Jersey
Rider College *B*
Rutgers—The State University of
  New Jersey *M,D*

New York
City University of New York:
  Baruch College *B,M*
Long Island University: Brooklyn
  Campus *B,M*
State University of New York
  College at Buffalo *B,M*

North Carolina
Appalachian State University *B*
East Carolina University *B,M*
North Carolina State University *B*
University of North Carolina at
  Greensboro *B,M*

North Dakota
Standing Rock College *A*
University of North Dakota *B*

Ohio
Baldwin-Wallace College *B*
Bowling Green State University *B*
Kent State University *B,M*
Ohio State University: Columbus
  Campus *B,M,D*
University of Toledo *B*

Oklahoma
University of Central Oklahoma
  B,M

Oregon
Oregon State University *M*

Pennsylvania
Indiana University of
  Pennsylvania *B*
Temple University *B,M,D*
University of Pittsburgh *B*

Rhode Island

Johnson & Wales University *B*

South Carolina

University of South Carolina *M*
Winthrop University *B*

South Dakota

Dakota State University *B*

Tennessee

Union University *B*
University of Tennessee:
　Knoxville *B*

Texas

University of Houston *B*
University of North Texas *M*

Utah

Utah State University *B*

Virginia

James Madison University *B*
Old Dominion University *B,M*
Virginia Polytechnic Institute and
　State University *B,M*

Washington

Central Washington University *B,M*
Eastern Washington University *B*

Wisconsin

Marian College of Fond du Lac *B*
University of Wisconsin
　Stout *B*
　Whitewater *B*

Wyoming

Laramie County Community
　College *A*
University of Wyoming *B*

Marketing management

Alabama

Alabama Agricultural and
　Mechanical University *B*
Alabama State University *B*
Auburn University
　Auburn *B*
　Montgomery *B*
Bishop State Community College *A*
Community College of the Air
　Force *A*
Faulkner University *B*
Huntingdon College *B*
James H. Faulkner State
　Community College *A*
Lurleen B. Wallace State Junior
　College *A*
Mobile College *B*
Samford University *B*
Selma University *A*
Spring Hill College *B*
Tuskegee University *B*
University of Alabama
　Birmingham *B*
　Huntsville *B*
　Tuscaloosa *B,M,D*
University of Montevallo *B*
University of North Alabama *B*
University of South Alabama *B*

Alaska

Alaska Pacific University *B*
University of Alaska
　Anchorage *B*
　Fairbanks *B*

Arizona

Arizona State University *B*
Mesa Community College *A*
Northern Arizona University *B*
University of Arizona *B,M*
Western International University *B*

Arkansas

Arkansas State University *B*
Harding University *B*
University of Arkansas at
　Monticello *B*
University of Central Arkansas *B*
University of the Ozarks *B*
Westark Community College *A*

California

Armstrong College *A,B,M*
Azusa Pacific University *B*
Biola University *B*
California Lutheran University *B*
California State Polytechnic
　University: Pomona *B*
California State University
　Bakersfield *B*
　Dominguez Hills *B*
　Fresno *B*
　Fullerton *B,M*
　Hayward *B,M*
　Long Beach *B*
　Los Angeles *B*
　Sacramento *B*
　Stanislaus *B*
Cerritos Community College *A*
Chabot College *A*
Chapman University *B*
City College of San Francisco *A*
Coastline Community College *A*
College of the Sequoias *C*
Cosumnes River College *A*
Crafton Hills College *C*
De Anza College *C,A*
El Camino College *C,A*
Fashion Institute of Design and
　Merchandising
　　Los Angeles *A*
　　San Francisco *A*
Glendale Community College *C*
Golden Gate University *B,M*
Golden West College *C,A*
Grossmont Community College *C,A*
Imperial Valley College *A*
Long Beach City College *C,A*
Los Angeles City College *C,A*
Los Angeles Pierce College *A*
Los Angeles Valley College *C*
Merced College *A*
Mission College *A*
Modesto Junior College *A*
Mount St. Mary's College *B*
Mount San Antonio College *C,A*
National University *B*
Ohlone College *C,A*
Orange Coast College *C,A*
Pacific Union College *B*
San Diego City College *C,A*
San Diego Mesa College *A*
San Francisco State University *B,M*
San Jose State University *B*
Santa Barbara City College *C,A*
Santa Clara University *B*
Solano Community College *A*
Southern California College *B*
University of the Pacific *B*
University of San Francisco *B,M*
Ventura College *A*
West Coast University *M*
West Valley College *C,A*
Woodbury University *B,M*
Yuba College *A*

Colorado

Adams State College *B*
Aims Community College *A*
Colorado Mountain College: Alpine
　Campus *A*
Colorado State University *B,M*
Community College of Denver *C,A*
Front Range Community College *A*
Metropolitan State College of
　Denver *B*
Pikes Peak Community College *C,A*
Red Rocks Community College *A*
Regis College of Regis University *B*
University of Colorado
　Boulder *B*
　Colorado Springs *B*
　Denver *B*
University of Denver *B,M*
University of Northern Colorado *B*
University of Southern Colorado *B*
Western State College of
　Colorado *B*

Connecticut

Central Connecticut State
　University *B*
Fairfield University *B*
Middlesex Community College *A*
Quinnipiac College *B,M*
Sacred Heart University *B,M*
Southern Connecticut State
　University *B*
Teikyo-Post University *A,B*
Tunxis Community College *C,A*
University of Bridgeport *B*
University of Connecticut *B*
University of Hartford *B*
University of New Haven *B,M*
Western Connecticut State
　University *B,M*

Delaware

Delaware State College *B*
Delaware Technical and
　Community College
　　Southern Campus *A*
　　Terry Campus *A*
Goldey-Beacom College *B*
University of Delaware *B*
Wesley College *B*

District of Columbia

American University *B,M*
George Washington University *B,M*
Georgetown University *B*
Howard University *B*
Mount Vernon College *B*
Southeastern University *A,B,M*

Florida

Brevard Community College *A*
Broward Community College *A*
Daytona Beach Community
　College *A*
Florida Atlantic University *B*
Florida Community College at
　Jacksonville *A*
Florida Institute of Technology *B*
Florida International University *B*
Florida Southern College *B*
Florida State University *B,M*
Fort Lauderdale College *A,B*
Gulf Coast Community College *C,A*
Jacksonville University *B,M*
Jones College *A,B*
Lake City Community College *A*
Okaloosa-Walton Community
　College *A*
Orlando College *A,B*
Palm Beach Atlantic College *B*
Pasco-Hernando Community
　College *A*

Pensacola Junior College *A*
St. Petersburg Junior College *A*
St. Thomas University *B*
Santa Fe Community College *A*
Seminole Community College *A*
South College: Palm Beach Campus
　C,A
South Florida Community
　College *A*
Stetson University *B*
Tampa College *A,B*
University of Central Florida *B*
University of Florida *B,M,D*
University of Miami *B*
University of North Florida *B*
University of Tampa *B*
Webber College *A,B*

Georgia

Abraham Baldwin Agricultural
　College *C*
Augusta Technical Institute *C,A*
Berry College *B*
Brewton-Parker College *B*
Brunswick College *C*
Chattahoochee Technical Institute
　C,A
Clark Atlanta University *B,M*
Clayton State College *A*
Columbus College *B*
DeKalb College *A*
DeKalb Technical Institute *C*
Emory University *B,M*
Floyd College *A*
Georgia College *B*
Georgia Southwestern College *B*
Georgia State University *B,M,D*
Mercer University
　Atlanta *B,M*
　Macon *B*
Morehouse College *B*
Morris Brown College *B*
Savannah State College *B*
Shorter College *B*
Valdosta State College *B*

Hawaii

Cannon's International Business
　College of Honolulu *A*

Idaho

College of Southern Idaho *A*
Idaho State University *B*
Ricks College *C,A*
University of Idaho *B*

Illinois

Augustana College *B*
Aurora University *B*
Barat College *B*
Belleville Area College *A*
Black Hawk College *A*
Bradley University *B*
Carl Sandburg College *A*
College of DuPage *C,A*
College of Lake County *C,A*
De Paul University *B,M*
Eastern Illinois University *B*
Elgin Community College *C,A*
Elmhurst College *B*
Greenville College *B*
Highland Community College *A*
Illinois Benedictine College *B*
Illinois Eastern Community
　Colleges: Wabash Valley
　College *A*
Illinois State University *B*
Illinois Valley Community
　College *A*
Lewis University *B*
Lincoln Land Community
　College *A*

Loyola University of Chicago *B*
MacMurray College *B*
McKendree College *B*
Millikin University *B*
Morton College *A*
North Central College *B*
North Park College and Theological
   Seminary *B*
Northeastern Illinois University *B*
Northern Illinois University *B,M*
Northwestern University *M,D*
Oakton Community College *C,A*
Olivet Nazarene University *B*
Parkland College *A*
Prairie State College *A*
Quincy College *B*
Rend Lake College *A*
Richland Community College *A*
Rock Valley College *A*
Roosevelt University *B*
Southern Illinois University at
   Carbondale *B*
University of Illinois
     Chicago *B,D*
     Urbana-Champaign *B*
Waubonsee Community College *A*
William Rainey Harper College *C,A*

Indiana

Ball State University *B*
Butler University *B*
Franklin College *B*
Indiana State University *B*
Indiana University Bloomington
   B,M,D
Indiana University—Purdue
   University
     Fort Wayne *B*
     Indianapolis *B*
Indiana Wesleyan University *B*
Manchester College *B*
Purdue University
     North Central Campus *A*
     West Lafayette *M,D*
St. Joseph's College *B*
St. Mary-of-the-Woods College *B*
Tri-State University *B*
University of Indianapolis *B*
University of Notre Dame *B*
University of Southern Indiana *B*
Vincennes University *A*

Iowa

American Institute of Business *A*
Buena Vista College *B*
Clarke College *B*
Des Moines Area Community
   College *A*
Drake University *B*
Hawkeye Institute of Technology *A*
Iowa State University *B*
Kirkwood Community College *A*
Loras College *B*
Morningside College *B*
Mount Mercy College *B*
North Iowa Area Community
   College *A*
Northeast Iowa Community
   College *A*
Northwest Iowa Technical
   College *A*
St. Ambrose University *B*
Southwestern Community
   College *A*
Teikyo Westmar University *B*
University of Dubuque *B,M*
University of Iowa *M,D*
University of Northern Iowa *B*
Upper Iowa University *B*
Wartburg College *B*

Kansas

Brown Mackie College *A*
Butler County Community
   College *A*
Central College *A*
Cloud County Community
   College *A*
Emporia State University *B*
Fort Hays State University *B*
Johnson County Community
   College *A*
Kansas Newman College *B*
Kansas State University *B*
Neosho County Community
   College *A*
Pittsburg State University *B*
Pratt Community College *C,A*
Washburn University of Topeka *B*
Wichita State University *B*

Kentucky

Eastern Kentucky University *B*
Georgetown College *B*
Maysville Community College *A*
Morehead State University *B*
Northern Kentucky University *B*
University of Louisville *B*
Western Kentucky University *B*

Louisiana

Louisiana College *B*
Louisiana State University
     Agricultural and Mechanical
     College *B,M,D*
     Shreveport *B*
Louisiana Tech University *B,M*
Loyola University *B*
McNeese State University *B*
Nicholls State University *B*
Northeast Louisiana University *B*
Phillips Junior College: New
   Orleans *A*
Southern University and
   Agricultural and Mechanical
   College *B*

Maine

St. Joseph's College *B*
Thomas College *C,B,M*
University of Maine
     Machias *A,B*
     Orono *B*
Westbrook College *B*

Maryland

Catonsville Community College *C,A*
Essex Community College *A*
Montgomery College
     Germantown Campus *C,A*
     Rockville Campus *A*
     Takoma Park Campus *A*
Morgan State University *B*
Prince George's Community College
   C,A
University of Baltimore *B*
University of Maryland: College
   Park *B*

Massachusetts

Anna Maria College for Men and
   Women *B*
Assumption College *B*
Babson College *B,M*
Becker College: Leicester
   Campus *A*
Bentley College *B*
Berkshire Community College *A*
Boston College *B*
Boston University *B*
Bradford College *B*
Bridgewater State College *C,B*
Bristol Community College *A*

Elms College *B*
Endicott College *A*
Fitchburg State College *B*
Lasell College *A*
Massachusetts Bay Community
   College *C,A*
Massachusetts Institute of
   Technology *M,D*
Merrimack College *B*
Mount Ida College *A*
Mount Wachusett Community
   College *A*
New England Banking Institute *C,A*
Nichols College *B*
North Adams State College *B*
North Shore Community College *A*
Northeastern University *C,A,B*
Pine Manor College *B*
Quincy College *A*
Quinsigamond Community
   College *A*
Salem State College *B*
Springfield Technical Community
   College *A*
Stonehill College *B*
University of Massachusetts
     Amherst *B*
     Lowell *B*
Western New England College *B,M*

Michigan

Adrian College *A,B*
Alma College *B*
Baker College
     Auburn Hills *A*
     Cadillac *A*
     Flint *A,B*
     Mount Clemens *A*
     Muskegon *A,B*
     Owosso *B*
     Port Huron *A*
Charles Stewart Mott Community
   College *A*
Cleary College *A,B*
Delta College *A*
Ferris State University *B*
Glen Oaks Community College *C*
GMI Engineering & Management
   Institute *B*
Grand Rapids Baptist College and
   Seminary *B*
Grand Rapids Community
   College *A*
Grand Valley State University *B,M*
Hillsdale College *B*
Lake Superior State University *B*
Lansing Community College *A*
Lawrence Technological
   University *B*
Michigan State University *B,M,D*
Michigan Technological
   University *B*
Muskegon Community College *A*
Northern Michigan University *B*
Northwood Institute *B*
Oakland University *B*
Olivet College *B*
Saginaw Valley State University
   B,M
Schoolcraft College *A*
University of Detroit Mercy *B*
University of Michigan
     Ann Arbor *D*
     Dearborn *B*
     Flint *B*
Walsh College of Accountancy and
   Business Administration *B*
West Shore Community College *A*

Minnesota

Alexandria Technical College *A*
Anoka-Ramsey Community
   College *A*
Augsburg College *B*
Bethel College *B*
College of St. Scholastica *B*
Inver Hills Community College *A*
Itasca Community College:
   Arrowhead Region *A*
Mankato State University *B*
Moorhead State University *B*
Normandale Community College *A*
Northland Community College *A*
Northwestern College *B*
Rochester Community College *A*
St. Cloud State University *B,M*
Southwest State University *A,B*
University of St. Thomas *B*
Willmar Community College *A*
Willmar Technical College *C*
Winona State University *B*

Mississippi

Delta State University *B*
Mississippi Gulf Coast Community
   College: Jackson County
   Campus *A*
Mississippi State University *B*
University of Mississippi *B*
University of Southern
   Mississippi *B*

Missouri

Central Missouri State University *B*
Columbia College *B*
Evangel College *B*
Fontbonne College *B*
Hannibal-LaGrange College *B*
Lindenwood College *M*
Maryville University *B*
Missouri Southern State College *B*
Missouri Valley College *B*
Missouri Western State College *B*
Moberly Area Community
   College *A*
Northeast Missouri State
   University *B*
Northwest Missouri State
   University *B*
Park College *B*
Rockhurst College *B*
Southeast Missouri State
   University *B*
Southwest Baptist University *B*
Southwest Missouri State
   University *B*
Three Rivers Community College *A*
University of Missouri: Kansas
   City *M*
Webster University *B,M*
William Woods College *B*

Montana

Eastern Montana College *B*
Montana State University *B*
University of Montana *B*

Nebraska

Bellevue College *B*
Creighton University *B*
Dana College *B*
Midland Lutheran College *B*
Northeast Community College *A*
Southeast Community College:
   Beatrice Campus *A*
Union College *B*
University of Nebraska
     Lincoln *B*
     Omaha *B*
Wayne State College *B*

Western Nebraska Community College
- Scottsbluff Campus *C,A*
- Sidney Campus *A*

Nevada

Community College of Southern Nevada *A*
Truckee Meadows Community College *A*
University of Nevada
- Las Vegas *B*
- Reno *B*

New Hampshire

Daniel Webster College *A*
Franklin Pierce College *B*
New Hampshire College *B*
New Hampshire Technical College: Nashua *A*
Plymouth State College of the University System of New Hampshire *B*

New Jersey

Atlantic Community College *A*
Bergen Community College *A*
Bloomfield College *C,B*
Burlington County College *A*
Caldwell College *C*
College of St. Elizabeth *C,B*
Fairleigh Dickinson University *B,M*
Glassboro State College *B*
Gloucester County College *A*
Monmouth College *B*
Rider College *B*
Rutgers—The State University of New Jersey
- Camden College of Arts and Sciences *A*
- Douglass College *B*
- Livingston College *B*
- Newark College of Arts and Sciences *B*
- Rutgers College *B*
- University College Camden *B*
- University College New Brunswick *B*
- University College Newark *B*
St. Peter's College *C,A,B*
Seton Hall University *B,M*
Thomas Edison State College *B*
Trenton State College *B*

New Mexico

College of the Southwest *B*
Dona Ana Branch Community College of New Mexico State University *C,A*
Eastern New Mexico University *B*
New Mexico State University *B,M*
University of New Mexico *B,M*
Western New Mexico University *B*

New York

Adelphi University *B,M*
Adirondack Community College *A*
Alfred University *B*
Berkeley College *A*
Bramson ORT Technical Institute *A*
Broome Community College *A*
Bryant & Stratton Business Institute: Buffalo *A*
Canisius College *B*
City University of New York
- Baruch College *B,M*
- Kingsborough Community College *A*
- New York City Technical College *A*
Clarkson University *B*

Daemen College *B*
Dominican College of Blauvelt *B*
Dowling College *B*
D'Youville College *B*
Elmira College *B*
Five Towns College *A*
Fordham University *B*
Genesee Community College *A*
Herkimer County Community College *A*
Hofstra University *B,M*
Hudson Valley Community College *A*
Iona College *B,M*
Jamestown Business College *A*
Jamestown Community College *A*
Keuka College *B*
Le Moyne College *B*
Long Island University
- Brooklyn Campus *B*
- C. W. Post Campus *B*
- Southampton Campus *B*
Manhattan College *B*
Mohawk Valley Community College *C,A*
New York University *B,M,D*
Niagara University *B*
Orange County Community College *A*
Pace University
- College of White Plains *B,M*
- New York *B,M*
- Pleasantville/Briarcliff *B,M*
Rochester Business Institute *A*
Rochester Institute of Technology *C,A,B,M*
Russell Sage College *B,M*
Sage Junior College of Albany, A Division of Russell Sage College *A*
St. Bonaventure University *B*
St. John Fisher College *B*
St. John's University *B,M*
Siena College *B*
State University of New York
- Albany *B,M*
- College at Geneseo *B*
- College at Plattsburgh *B*
- College of Technology at Alfred *A*
- College of Technology at Delhi *A*
- Oswego *B*
Syracuse University *B,M,D*
Touro College *B*
University of the State of New York: Regents College *B*
Westchester Community College *A*
Yeshiva University *B*

North Carolina

Appalachian State University *B*
Asheville Buncombe Technical Community College *A*
Catawba Valley Community College *A*
Duke University *B*
East Carolina University *B*
Forsyth Technical Community College *A*
Gaston College *A*
Mars Hill College *B*
Salem College *B*
University of North Carolina
- Asheville *B*
- Greensboro *B,M*
- Wilmington *B*
Western Carolina University *B*
Wilson Technical Community College *C*

North Dakota

Minot State University *B*
North Dakota State University: Bottineau and Institute of Forestry *C,A*
University of North Dakota: Williston *A*

Ohio

Ashland University *B*
Baldwin-Wallace College *B*
Bowling Green State University *B*
Capital University *B*
Case Western Reserve University *M,D*
Central State University *B*
Cincinnati Metropolitan College *A*
Cincinnati Technical College *A*
Cleveland State University *B*
Columbus State Community College *A*
Cuyahoga Community College: Metropolitan Campus *A*
Defiance College *B*
Dyke College *A,B*
Franciscan University of Steubenville *B*
John Carroll University *B*
Kent State University *B*
Marietta College *B*
Marion Technical College *C,A*
Miami-Jacobs College *A*
Northwest Technical College *A*
Notre Dame College of Ohio *B*
Ohio Northern University *B*
Ohio State University: Columbus Campus *B,M,D*
Ohio University *B*
Otterbein College *B*
Owens Technical College
- Findlay Campus *A*
- Toledo *A*
Shawnee State University *A*
Sinclair Community College *A*
Terra Technical College *A*
Union Institute *B,D*
University of Cincinnati: Raymond Walters College *A*
University of Dayton *B*
University of Findlay *B*
University of Rio Grande *B*
University of Toledo *A,B*
Urbana University *B*
Washington State Community College *A*
Wilmington College *B*
Wittenberg University *B*
Youngstown State University *B*

Oklahoma

East Central University *B*
Eastern Oklahoma State College *C*
Oklahoma Baptist University *B*
Oklahoma City University *B,M*
Oklahoma State University
- Stillwater *B*
- Technical Branch: Okmulgee *A*
Southeastern Oklahoma State University *B*
Southwestern Oklahoma State University *B*
Tulsa Junior College *C,A*
University of Central Oklahoma *B*
University of Oklahoma *B*
University of Tulsa *B*

Oregon

Central Oregon Community College *A*
Concordia College *B*
Marylhurst College *C*

Oregon State University *B*
Southern Oregon State College *B,M*
Southwestern Oregon Community College *A*
Umpqua Community College *A*
University of Oregon
- Eugene *B,M,D*
- Robert Donald Clark Honors College *B*
University of Portland *B*
Warner Pacific College *B*

Pennsylvania

Albright College *B*
Allentown College of St. Francis de Sales *B*
Alvernia College *B*
Beaver College *B*
Bucknell University *B*
Bucks County Community College *A*
Cabrini College *B*
California University of Pennsylvania *B*
Carnegie Mellon University *B,M,D,W*
Cedar Crest College *C*
Central Pennsylvania Business School *A*
Chestnut Hill College *B*
Clarion University of Pennsylvania *B*
College Misericordia *B*
Delaware Valley College *B*
Drexel University *B,M,D*
Duquesne University *B*
Elizabethtown College *B*
Gannon University *A,B*
Grove City College *B*
Harrisburg Area Community College *A*
Holy Family College *B*
Immaculata College *A*
Juniata College *B*
King's College *C,A,B*
Kutztown University of Pennsylvania *B*
La Salle University *B*
Marywood College *B*
Messiah College *B*
Montgomery County Community College *A*
Peirce Junior College *A*
Penn State
- Harrisburg Capital College *B*
- University Park Campus *C,B*
Philadelphia College of Textiles and Science *B*
Robert Morris College *B,M*
St. Francis College *B*
St. Joseph's University *C,A,B,M*
Seton Hill College *B*
Shippensburg University of Pennsylvania *B*
Slippery Rock University of Pennsylvania *B*
Temple University *B,M,D*
University of Pennsylvania *A,B,M,D*
University of Scranton *B*
Villanova University *B*
Waynesburg College *B*
West Chester University of Pennsylvania *B*

Puerto Rico

Caribbean University *B*
ICPR Junior College *A*

Inter American University of Puerto
Rico
    Arecibo Campus *B*
    Metropolitan Campus *B,M*
    San German Campus *B,M*
Turabo University *B*
Universidad Metropolitana *B*
University of Puerto Rico
    Ponce Technological
      University College *A,B*
    Rio Piedras Campus *B,M*
University of the Sacred Heart *A,B*

Rhode Island
Bryant College *B,M*
Johnson & Wales University *A,B*
Providence College *B*
Rhode Island College *B*
Roger Williams College *B*
University of Rhode Island *B*

South Carolina
Aiken Technical College *A*
Anderson College *B*
Bob Jones University *B*
Charleston Southern University *B*
Clemson University *B*
Coker College *B*
Francis Marion College *B*
Greenville Technical College *A*
Lander College *B*
Limestone College *B*
Midlands Technical College *A*
Tri-County Technical College *A*
University of South Carolina:
    Coastal Carolina College *B*

South Dakota
Black Hills State University *B*
National College *A,B*
Sioux Falls College *B*

Tennessee
Bristol University *A,B,M*
Christian Brothers University *B,M*
Cumberland University *B*
Dyersburg State Community
    College *A*
Hiwassee College *A*
Lambuth University *B*
Lincoln Memorial University *B*
Memphis State University *B*
Pellissippi State Technical
    Community College *A*
Union University *B*
University of Tennessee
    Chattanooga *B,M*
    Martin *B*

Texas
Abilene Christian University *B*
Angelina College *C,A*
Angelo State University *B*
Baylor University *B*
Brazosport College *C,A*
Brookhaven College *A*
Central Texas College *A*
Corpus Christi State University *B*
Dallas Baptist University *B,M*
Del Mar College *A*
East Texas State University
    Commerce *B*
    Texarkana *B*
Eastfield College *A*
Hardin-Simmons University *B*
Houston Baptist University *B*
Houston Community College *C*
Huston-Tillotson College *B*
Jarvis Christian College *B*
Lamar University—Beaumont *B*
Laredo Junior College *A*
Laredo State University *B*

Midland College *A*
North Harris Montgomery
    Community College District *A*
Northeast Texas Community
    College *A*
Northwood Institute: Texas
    Campus *B*
Prairie View A&M University *B*
St. Edward's University *B*
St. Mary's University *B,M*
Sam Houston State University *B*
Schreiner College *B*
Southern Methodist University *B*
Southwest Texas State University *B*
Stephen F. Austin State University
    B,M
Tarleton State University *B*
Texas A&I University *B*
Texas A&M University *B,M,D*
Texas Christian University *B*
Texas Southmost College *A*
Texas Tech University *B*
Texas Wesleyan University *B*
Texas Woman's University *B*
University of Central Texas *B*
University of Houston
    Clear Lake *B*
    Houston *B,M,D*
    Victoria *B*
University of St. Thomas *B*
University of Texas
    Arlington *B,M*
    Austin *B,D*
    El Paso *B*
    Permian Basin *B*
    San Antonio *B*
    Tyler *B*
Weatherford College *C,A*

Utah
Brigham Young University *B*
LDS Business College *A*
University of Utah *B,M*
Weber State University *B*

Vermont
Champlain College *A*
Norwich University *B*

Virginia
Averett College *B*
Clinch Valley College of the
    University of Virginia *B*
College of William and Mary *B*
Ferrum College *B*
George Mason University *B*
James Madison University *B*
Lynchburg College *B*
Mary Baldwin College *B*
Marymount University *B,M*
Old Dominion University *B*
Piedmont Virginia Community
    College *A*
St. Paul's College *B*
University of Richmond *B*
Virginia Commonwealth
    University *B*
Virginia Polytechnic Institute and
    State University *B,D*
Virginia State University *B*
Virginia Wesleyan College *B*

Washington
Bellevue Community College *A*
Central Washington University *B*
City University *M*
Eastern Washington University *B*
Edmonds Community College *C*
Gonzaga University *B*
Pacific Lutheran University *B*
Seattle University *B*
Spokane Community College *A*

Washington State University *B*

West Virginia
Bethany College *B*
Bluefield State College *A*
Davis and Elkins College *B*
Fairmont State College *B*
Glenville State College *B*
Salem-Teikyo University *A*
Shepherd College *A,B*
University of Charleston *B*
West Virginia State College *A*
West Virginia University *B*
Wheeling Jesuit College *B*

Wisconsin
Carroll College *B*
Carthage College *B*
Chippewa Valley Technical
    College *A*
Concordia University Wisconsin *B*
Lakeland College *B*
Marian College of Fond du Lac *B*
Marquette University *B*
Mid-State Technical College *A*
Stratton College *A*
University of Wisconsin
    La Crosse *B*
    Madison *B,M*
    Milwaukee *B*
    Oshkosh *B*
    Platteville *B*
    Superior *B*
    Whitewater *B,M*
Viterbo College *B*

Wyoming
University of Wyoming *B*
Western Wyoming Community
    College *A*

American Samoa, Caroline Islands, Guam, Marianas, Virgin Islands
University of Guam *B*

Canada
McGill University *C,B,M,D*

Switzerland
American College of Switzerland *B*

Marketing research

Alabama
University of Alabama *B*

Alaska
University of Alaska Anchorage *B*

California
California State University
    Bakersfield *B*
    Los Angeles *B*
    Northridge *B,M*
La Sierra University *B*
Los Angeles Trade and Technical
    College *C,A*
National Hispanic University *M*

Colorado
Fort Lewis College *B*
Mesa State College *B*

Connecticut
Quinnipiac College *B,M*

District of Columbia
Southeastern University *B,M*

Florida
Florida State University *B*
University of Florida *M,D*
University of Sarasota *M*

Georgia
University of Georgia *M*

Hawaii
Chaminade University of
    Honolulu *B*
University of Hawaii at Manoa *B*

Idaho
Idaho State University *B*

Illinois
Bradley University *B*
De Paul University *M*
Southern Illinois University at
    Edwardsville *M*

Indiana
Indiana University Bloomington
    M,D
University of Notre Dame *B*

Iowa
University of Dubuque *B*
Wartburg College *B*

Kansas
Dodge City Community College *A*
Fort Hays State University *B*

Massachusetts
Bay Path College *A*
Mount Ida College *A*

Michigan
Central Michigan University *B*

Minnesota
Normandale Community College *A*

Nebraska
University of Nebraska—Omaha *B*

New Hampshire
Franklin Pierce College *B*
Hesser College *A*

New York
City University of New York:
    Baruch College *B*
Clarkson University *B*
Herkimer County Community
    College *A*
Ithaca College *B*
New York University *M,D*
State University of New York
    Buffalo *D*
    Oswego *B*
Suffolk County Community College
    Selden *A*
    Western Campus *A*
Wagner College *B,M*

North Carolina
Western Piedmont Community
    College *A*

Ohio
University of Dayton *B*
University of Toledo *A,B*

Oregon
Concordia College *B*

Pennsylvania

Carnegie Mellon University
B,M,D,W
Duquesne University B
Robert Morris College M
St. Francis College B

Tennessee

Lambuth University B
Middle Tennessee State
University B
Motlow State Community
College A
University of Tennessee:
Knoxville B

Vermont

Castleton State College B

Virginia

Averett College B

Wisconsin

Lakeland College B
University of Wisconsin
Oshkosh B
Whitewater B

Marriage and family counseling

Alabama

Auburn University M

Arizona

Prescott College B
University of Arizona M

California

Azusa Pacific University M
California State University
Bakersfield M
Dominguez Hills M
Fullerton M
Long Beach M
Northridge M
Christian Heritage College B
La Sierra University M
Loyola Marymount University M
Pacific Christian College M
Pacific Oaks College M
San Francisco State University M
San Jose State University M
United States International
University M,D
University of San Francisco M,D
University of Southern California M

Colorado

University of Northern Colorado M

Connecticut

St. Joseph College M

Florida

Florida State University D
Nova University M,D
St. Thomas University M

Illinois

KAES College B
Northern Illinois University M
University of Illinois at Urbana-
Champaign M

Indiana

Anderson University B
Butler University M
Indiana State University M

Purdue University M,D

Kansas

Kansas State University M,D

Kentucky

Louisville Presbyterian Theological
Seminary M,D
Spalding University M
Sue Bennett College A

Louisiana

Northeast Louisiana University M

Massachusetts

Springfield College M

Minnesota

Willmar Community College A

Montana

Montana State University M

New Hampshire

New Hampshire Technical College:
Manchester A
University of New Hampshire M

New Mexico

Eastern New Mexico University M
Western New Mexico University M

New York

Hofstra University M
Long Island University: C. W. Post
Campus C
Syracuse University M

North Carolina

East Carolina University M

Ohio

Ohio State University: Columbus
Campus B,M,D
Union Institute D
University of Akron M
Wright State University M

Pennsylvania

La Salle University M

Rhode Island

University of Rhode Island M

Texas

Abilene Christian University M
St. Mary's University M,D
Texas Tech University D
Texas Woman's University M,D
University of Central Texas M

Utah

Brigham Young University M,D

Virginia

Hampton University M
Virginia Polytechnic Institute and
State University D

Washington

Seattle Pacific University M

Wisconsin

University of Wisconsin
Oshkosh M
Stout M

Masonry/tile setting

Alabama

Central Alabama Community
College: Childersburg Campus C
Gadsden State Community
College C
George C. Wallace State
Community College at Selma C
Lawson State Community
College C
Reid State Technical College C

Arizona

Cochise College C
Rio Salado Community College A

Arkansas

Phillips County Community
College C

California

Bakersfield College A
San Jose City College A
Santa Rosa Junior College C,A
Ventura College A

Colorado

Red Rocks Community College C

Florida

Lake City Community College C

Georgia

Atlanta Metropolitan College A
Gainesville College A

Illinois

Belleville Area College C,A
Illinois Eastern Community
Colleges: Olney Central
College C
State Community College C

Kansas

Coffeyville Community College A

Kentucky

Eastern Kentucky University B

Maine

Southern Maine Technical
College A

Maryland

Cecil Community College C,A

Michigan

Lansing Community College A
Macomb Community College C,A

Mississippi

Hinds Community College C

Missouri

Ranken Technical College A

Nebraska

Chadron State College B
Metropolitan Community College C
Nebraska Indian Community
College A
Southeast Community College:
Milford Campus A

Nevada

Truckee Meadows Community
College C,A

New Hampshire

New Hampshire Technical College:
Manchester C

New York

Mohawk Valley Community
College C
State University of New York
College of Technology at
Alfred A
College of Technology at Delhi
C,A

North Carolina

Anson Community College C
Blue Ridge Community College C
Central Carolina Community
College C
Fayetteville Technical Community
College C
Forsyth Technical Community
College A
James Sprunt Community
College C
Mayland Community College C
Piedmont Community College C
Pitt Community College C

Pennsylvania

Williamson Free School of
Mechanical Trades C

South Carolina

Denmark Technical College C
Technical College of the
Lowcountry C
Williamsburg Technical College C

Texas

Central Texas College A

Virginia

Piedmont Virginia Community
College C

Wisconsin

Chippewa Valley Technical
College C

American Samoa, Caroline Islands, Guam, Marianas, Virgin Islands

Guam Community College C

Materials engineering

Alabama

Auburn University B,M,D
University of Alabama
Birmingham B,M,D
Tuscaloosa D

Arizona

Arizona State University B,D
University of Arizona B,M,D

California

California Institute of Technology
B,M,D,W
California Polytechnic State
University: San Luis Obispo B
California State University
Long Beach B
Northridge B,M
San Jose State University B,M
Southwestern College A
Stanford University B,M,D

University of California
Berkeley *B,M,D*
Davis *B*
Los Angeles *B,M,D*
San Diego *B*
Santa Barbara *M,D*
University of Southern California *M,D,W*

Colorado
Colorado School of Mines *B,M,D,W*
University of Denver *M,D*

Delaware
University of Delaware *M,D*

District of Columbia
Catholic University of America *B,M*
George Washington University *M,D*

Florida
Bethune-Cookman College *B*
University of Florida *B,M,D*
University of South Florida *B,M,D*

Georgia
Georgia Institute of Technology *B,M,D*

Illinois
Bradley University *B*
Illinois Institute of Technology *M,D*
Northwestern University *B,M,D*
University of Illinois at Urbana-Champaign *M,D*

Indiana
Purdue University *B,M,D,W*
University of Notre Dame *M,D*

Iowa
Iowa State University *M*

Kentucky
University of Kentucky *B,M,D*

Maryland
College of Notre Dame of Maryland *B*
Johns Hopkins University *B,M,D*
University of Maryland: College Park *B,M,D*

Massachusetts
Harvard and Radcliffe Colleges *B*
Massachusetts Institute of Technology *B,M,D,W*
University of Massachusetts at Lowell *M*
Worcester Polytechnic Institute *B,M,D*

Michigan
Michigan State University *B,M,D*
University of Michigan *B,M,D*

Minnesota
University of Minnesota: Twin Cities *B,M,D*
Winona State University *B*

Mississippi
Mississippi College *B*

Missouri
Washington University *M,D*

Montana
Montana College of Mineral Science and Technology *B*

Nevada
University of Nevada: Reno *B*

New Jersey
New Jersey Institute of Technology *B*
Rutgers—The State University of New Jersey *M,D*
Stevens Institute of Technology *B,M,D*

New Mexico
New Mexico Institute of Mining and Technology *B,M,D*

New York
Columbia University: School of Engineering and Applied Science *B,M,D,W*
Cornell University *B,M,D*
Pace University
College of White Plains *B*
Pleasantville/Briarcliff *B*
Rensselaer Polytechnic Institute *B,M,D*
Rochester Institute of Technology *M*
State University of New York
Stony Brook *M,D*
College of Environmental Science and Forestry *B,M,D*
University of Rochester *M,D*

North Carolina
Duke University *B,M,D*
North Carolina State University *B,M,D*
St. Augustine's College *B*

Ohio
Case Western Reserve University *B,M,D*
Hocking Technical College *A*
Ohio State University: Columbus Campus *B,M,D*
University of Cincinnati *M,D*
University of Dayton *M,D*
Wright State University *B*
Youngstown State University *M*

Oregon
Oregon Graduate Institute *M,D*
Oregon State University *M*

Pennsylvania
Carnegie Mellon University *B,M,D,W*
Drexel University *B,M,D*
Lehigh University *B,M,D*
Penn State University Park Campus *B,M,D*
Thiel College *B*
University of Pennsylvania *B,M,D*
University of Pittsburgh *B,M,D*
Wilkes University *B*

Rhode Island
Brown University *B,M,D*
University of Rhode Island *B*

South Carolina
Clemson University *M,D*

South Dakota
South Dakota School of Mines and Technology *D*

Tennessee
Vanderbilt University *M,D*

Texas
Rice University *B,M,D*
Southern Methodist University *M,D*
University of Houston *M,D*
University of Texas
Arlington *M,D*
Austin *M,D*

Utah
University of Utah *B,M,D*

Vermont
University of Vermont *M,D*

Virginia
University of Virginia *M,D*
Virginia Polytechnic Institute and State University *B,M,D*

Washington
University of Washington *M,D*
Washington State University *B,M*

Wisconsin
University of Wisconsin
Madison *M,D*
Milwaukee *B*

Arab Republic of Egypt
American University in Cairo *B,M*

Mathematics

Alabama
Alabama Agricultural and Mechanical University *B*
Alabama Southern Community College *A*
Alabama State University *B,M*
Athens State College *B*
Auburn University
Auburn *B,M,D*
Montgomery *B*
Birmingham-Southern College *B*
Brewer State Junior College *A*
Chattahoochee Valley Community College *A*
Huntingdon College *B*
Jacksonville State University *B,M*
James H. Faulkner State Community College *A*
John C. Calhoun State Community College *A*
Judson College *B*
Lawson State Community College *A*
Livingston University *B*
Marion Military Institute *A*
Miles College *B*
Mobile College *B*
Oakwood College *B*
Samford University *B*
Selma University *A*
Shelton State Community College *A*
Snead State Junior College *A*
Spring Hill College *B*
Stillman College *B*
Talladega College *B*
Troy State University
Dothan *B*
Montgomery *B*
Troy *B*
Tuskegee University *B*
University of Alabama
Birmingham *B,M*
Huntsville *B,M*
Tuscaloosa *B,M,D*
University of Montevallo *B*

University of North Alabama *B*
University of South Alabama *B,M*

Alaska
University of Alaska
Anchorage *B*
Fairbanks *B,M,D*

Arizona
Arizona State University *B,M,D*
Arizona Western College *A*
Cochise College *A*
Eastern Arizona College *A*
Glendale Community College *A*
Grand Canyon University *B*
Mesa Community College *A*
Mohave Community College *A*
Navajo Community College *A*
Northern Arizona University *B,M*
Pima Community College *A*
University of Arizona *B,M,D*
Yavapai College *A*

Arkansas
Arkansas College *B*
Arkansas State University
Beebe Branch *A*
Jonesboro *B,M*
Arkansas Tech University *B*
Harding University *B,M*
Henderson State University *B,M*
Hendrix College *B*
John Brown University *B*
Mississippi County Community College *A*
Ouachita Baptist University *B*
Philander Smith College *B*
Phillips County Community College *A*
Southern Arkansas University *B*
University of Arkansas
Fayetteville *B,M,D*
Little Rock *B*
Monticello *B*
Pine Bluff *B*
University of Central Arkansas *B,M*
University of the Ozarks *B*
Westark Community College *A*

California
Azusa Pacific University *B*
Bakersfield College *A*
Barstow College *A*
Biola University *B*
California Lutheran University *B*
California Polytechnic State University: San Luis Obispo *B,M*
California State Polytechnic University: Pomona *B,M*
California State University
Bakersfield *B*
Chico *B*
Dominguez Hills *B*
Fresno *B,M*
Fullerton *B,M*
Hayward *B,M*
Long Beach *B,M*
Los Angeles *B,M*
Northridge *B,M*
Sacramento *B,M*
San Bernardino *B*
San Marcos *B*
Stanislaus *B*
Cerritos Community College *A*
Chabot College *A*
Chaffey Community College *A*
Christ College Irvine *B*
Citrus College *A*
Claremont McKenna College *B*
College of the Desert *A*
College of Marin: Kentfield *A*
College of the Sequoias *A*

Columbia College *A*
Cosumnes River College *A*
Crafton Hills College *A*
De Anza College *A*
Dominican College of San Rafael *B*
El Camino College *A*
Feather River College *A*
Foothill College *A*
Fresno City College *A*
Fresno Pacific College *B*
Gavilan Community College *A*
Glendale Community College *A*
Grossmont Community College *A*
Harvey Mudd College *B*
Holy Names College *B*
Humboldt State University *B*
Imperial Valley College *A*
Irvine Valley College *A*
Kings River Community College *A*
La Sierra University *B*
Lake Tahoe Community College *A*
Laney College *A*
Lassen College *A*
Long Beach City College *A*
Los Angeles City College *A*
Los Angeles Mission College *A*
Los Angeles Valley College *A*
Los Medanos College *A*
Loyola Marymount University *B*
Marymount College *A*
Master's College *B*
Mendocino College *A*
Merced College *A*
Mills College *B*
MiraCosta College *A*
Mission College *A*
Modesto Junior College *A*
Moorpark College *A*
Mount St. Mary's College *B*
Mount San Jacinto College *A*
Napa Valley College *A*
National University *B*
Occidental College *B*
Ohlone College *A*
Orange Coast College *A*
Oxnard College *A*
Pacific Union College *B*
Palomar College *A*
Pepperdine University *B*
Pitzer College *B*
Point Loma Nazarene College *B*
Pomona College *B*
Porterville College *A*
Saddleback College *A*
St. Mary's College of California *B*
San Diego City College *A*
San Diego Mesa College *A*
San Diego State University *B,M*
San Francisco State University *B,M*
San Joaquin Delta College *A*
San Jose City College *A*
San Jose State University *B,M*
Santa Barbara City College *A*
Santa Clara University *B*
Santa Monica College *A*
Santa Rosa Junior College *A*
Scripps College *B*
Skyline College *A*
Solano Community College *A*
Sonoma State University *B*
Southern California College *B*
Southwestern College *A*
Stanford University *B,M,D*
Taft College *A*

University of California
   Berkeley *B,M,D*
   Davis *B,M,D*
   Irvine *B,M,D*
   Los Angeles *B,M,D*
   Riverside *B,M,D*
   San Diego *B,M,D*
   Santa Barbara *B,M,D*
   Santa Cruz *B,M,D*
University of La Verne *B*
University of the Pacific *B*
University of Redlands *B*
University of San Diego *B*
University of San Francisco *B*
University of Southern California *B,M,D*
Ventura College *A*
Victor Valley College *A*
West Hills Community College *A*
West Valley College *A*
Westmont College *B*
Whittier College *B*

Colorado

Adams State College *B*
Colorado College *B*
Colorado Mountain College
   Alpine Campus *A*
   Spring Valley Campus *A*
Colorado State University *B,M,D*
Community College of Denver *A*
Fort Lewis College *B*
Lamar Community College *A*
Mesa State College *A,B*
Metropolitan State College of Denver *B*
Northeastern Junior College *A*
Pikes Peak Community College *A*
Regis College of Regis University *B*
Trinidad State Junior College *A*
United States Air Force Academy *B*
University of Colorado
   Boulder *B,M,D*
   Colorado Springs *B*
   Denver *B*
University of Denver *B,M,D*
University of Northern Colorado *B,M*
University of Southern Colorado *B*
Western State College of Colorado *B*

Connecticut

Albertus Magnus College *B*
Central Connecticut State University *B,M*
Connecticut College *B*
Eastern Connecticut State University *B*
Fairfield University *B*
Mattatuck Community College *A*
Mitchell College *A*
Northwestern Connecticut Community College *A*
Quinnipiac College *B*
Sacred Heart University *A,B*
St. Joseph College *B*
Southern Connecticut State University *B,M*
Trinity College *B,M*
United States Coast Guard Academy *B*
University of Bridgeport *B*
University of Connecticut *B,M,D*
University of Hartford *B*
University of New Haven *B*
Wesleyan University *B,M,D*
Western Connecticut State University *B,M*
Yale University *B,M,D*

Delaware

Delaware State College *B*
University of Delaware *B,M,D*
Wesley College *A*

District of Columbia

American University *B,M*
Catholic University of America *B,M,D*
Gallaudet University *B*
George Washington University *B,M,D*
Georgetown University *B*
Howard University *B,M,D*
Trinity College *B*
University of the District of Columbia *B,M*

Florida

Barry University *B*
Bethune-Cookman College *B*
Brevard Community College *A*
Central Florida Community College *A*
Daytona Beach Community College *A*
Eckerd College *B*
Flagler College *B*
Florida Agricultural and Mechanical University *B*
Florida Atlantic University *B,M,D*
Florida International University *B*
Florida Memorial College *B*
Florida Southern College *B*
Florida State University *B,M,D*
Gulf Coast Community College *A*
Indian River Community College *A*
Jacksonville University *B*
Manatee Community College *A*
Miami-Dade Community College *A*
New College of the University of South Florida *B*
Okaloosa-Walton Community College *A*
Palm Beach Atlantic College *B*
Palm Beach Community College *A*
Pensacola Junior College *A*
Rollins College *B*
St. Thomas University *B*
Stetson University *B*
University of Central Florida *B*
University of Florida *B,M,D*
University of Miami *B,M,D*
University of North Florida *B,M*
University of South Florida *B,M,D*
University of Tampa *A,B*
University of West Florida *B,M*

Georgia

Abraham Baldwin Agricultural College *A*
Agnes Scott College *B*
Albany State College *B*
Atlanta Metropolitan College *A*
Augusta College *B*
Bainbridge College *A*
Berry College *B*
Brewton-Parker College *A*
Brunswick College *A*
Clark Atlanta University *B*
Clayton State College *A*
Columbus College *B*
Darton College *A*
DeKalb College *A*
East Georgia College *A*
Emory University *B,M,D*
Floyd College *A*
Fort Valley State College *B*
Gainesville College *A*
Georgia College *B*
Georgia Institute of Technology *B,M,D*

Georgia Southern University *B,M*
Georgia Southwestern College *B*
Georgia State University *B,M*
Gordon College *A*
Kennesaw State College *B*
LaGrange College *B*
Macon College *A*
Mercer University *B*
Middle Georgia College *A*
Morehouse College *B*
Morris Brown College *B*
North Georgia College *B*
Oglethorpe University *B*
Oxford College of Emory University *A*
Paine College *B*
Piedmont College *B*
Reinhardt College *A*
Savannah State College *B*
Shorter College *B*
South Georgia College *A*
Southern College of Technology *B*
Spelman College *B*
Thomas College *A*
University of Georgia *B,M,D*
Valdosta State College *B*
Waycross College *A*
Wesleyan College *B*
West Georgia College *B*
Young Harris College *A*

Hawaii

Brigham Young University-Hawaii *B*
Chaminade University of Honolulu *B*
Hawaii Loa College *B*
Hawaii Pacific University *A,B*
University of Hawaii
   Hilo *B*
   Manoa *B,M,D*

Idaho

Albertson College *B*
Boise State University *B*
College of Southern Idaho *A*
Idaho State University *B,M,D*
Lewis Clark State College *B*
North Idaho College *A*
Northwest Nazarene College *B*
Ricks College *A*
University of Idaho *B,M,D*

Illinois

Augustana College *B*
Aurora University *B*
Barat College *B*
Belleville Area College *A*
Black Hawk College *A*
Blackburn College *B*
Bradley University *B*
Chicago State University *B,M*
City Colleges of Chicago
   Olive-Harvey College *A*
   Wright College *A*
College of St. Francis *B*
Concordia University *B*
De Paul University *B,M*
Eastern Illinois University *B,M*
East-West University *B*
Elmhurst College *B*
Eureka College *B*
Greenville College *B*
Highland Community College *A*
Illinois Benedictine College *B*
Illinois Central College *A*
Illinois College *B*
Illinois Institute of Technology *B,M,D*
Illinois State University *B,M,D*
Illinois Valley Community College *A*

Illinois Wesleyan University *B*
John A. Logan College *A*
Joliet Junior College *A*
Judson College *B*
Kishwaukee College *A*
Knox College *B*
Lake Forest College *B*
Lake Land College *A*
Lewis University *B*
Lincoln Land Community
  College *A*
Loyola University of Chicago *B,M*
MacMurray College *B*
McKendree College *B*
Millikin University *B*
Monmouth College *B*
Morton College *A*
National-Louis University *B*
North Central College *B*
North Park College and Theological
  Seminary *B*
Northeastern Illinois University
  B,M
Northern Illinois University *B,M,D*
Northwestern University *B,M,D*
Olivet Nazarene University *B*
Principia College *B*
Quincy College *B*
Rend Lake College *A*
Richland Community College *A*
Rockford College *B*
Roosevelt University *B*
Rosary College *B*
St. Xavier University *B*
Sangamon State University *B,M*
Southern Illinois University
  Carbondale *B,M,D*
  Edwardsville *B,M*
State Community College *A*
Trinity Christian College *B*
Trinity College *B*
Triton College *A*
University of Chicago *B,M,D*
University of Illinois
  Chicago *B,M,D*
  Urbana-Champaign *B,M,D*
Waubonsee Community College *A*
Western Illinois University *B,M*
Wheaton College *B*
William Rainey Harper College *A*

Indiana

Anderson University *B*
Ball State University *B,M*
Bethel College *B*
Butler University *B*
DePauw University *B*
Earlham College *B*
Franklin College *B*
Goshen College *B*
Grace College *B*
Hanover College *B*
Huntington College *B*
Indiana State University *B,M*
Indiana University
  Bloomington *B,M,D*
  East *B*
  Kokomo *B*
  Northwest *B*
  South Bend *B*
  Southeast *B*
Indiana University—Purdue
  University
    Fort Wayne *B,M*
    Indianapolis *B,M*
Indiana Wesleyan University *B*
Manchester College *B*
Marian College *B*
Martin University *B*
Purdue University
  Calumet *B,M*
  West Lafayette *B,M,D*

St. Joseph's College *B*
St. Mary-of-the-Woods College *B*
St. Mary's College *B*
Taylor University *B*
Tri-State University *B*
University of Evansville *B*
University of Indianapolis *B*
University of Notre Dame *B,M,D*
University of Southern Indiana *B*
Valparaiso University *B*
Vincennes University *A*
Wabash College *B*

Iowa

Briar Cliff College *B*
Buena Vista College *B*
Central College *B*
Clarke College *B*
Clinton Community College *A*
Coe College *B*
Cornell College *B*
Divine Word College *B*
Dordt College *B*
Drake University *B*
Graceland College *B*
Grinnell College *B*
Iowa Lakes Community College *A*
Iowa State University *B,M,D*
Iowa Wesleyan College *B*
Iowa Western Community
  College *A*
Kirkwood Community College *A*
Loras College *B*
Luther College *B*
Maharishi International University
  A,B,M
Morningside College *B*
Mount Mercy College *B*
Muscatine Community College *A*
North Iowa Area Community
  College *A*
Northwestern College *B*
St. Ambrose University *B*
Scott Community College *A*
Simpson College *B*
Teikyo Westmar University *B*
University of Dubuque *B*
University of Iowa *B,M,D*
University of Northern Iowa *B,M*
Upper Iowa University *B*
Waldorf College *A*
Wartburg College *B*
William Penn College *B*

Kansas

Allen County Community
  College *A*
Baker University *B*
Barton County Community
  College *A*
Benedictine College *B*
Bethany College *B*
Bethel College *B*
Butler County Community
  College *A*
Central College *A*
Cloud County Community
  College *A*
Coffeyville Community College *A*
Colby Community College *A*
Dodge City Community College *A*
Emporia State University *B,M*
Fort Hays State University *B*
Friends University *B*
Highland Community College *A*
Hutchinson Community College *A*
Kansas City Kansas Community
  College *A*
Kansas Newman College *B*
Kansas State University *B,M,D*
Kansas Wesleyan University *B*
Labette Community College *A*

McPherson College *B*
MidAmerica Nazarene College *B*
Neosho County Community
  College *A*
Ottawa University *B*
Pittsburg State University *B,M*
Pratt Community College *A*
St. Mary College *B*
Seward County Community
  College *A*
Southwestern College *B*
Sterling College *B*
Tabor College *B*
University of Kansas *B,M,D*
Washburn University of Topeka *B*
Wichita State University *B,M,D*

Kentucky

Asbury College *B*
Bellarmine College *B*
Berea College *B*
Campbellsville College *B*
Centre College *B*
Cumberland College *B*
Eastern Kentucky University *B,M*
Georgetown College *B*
Kentucky State University *B*
Kentucky Wesleyan College *B*
Lindsey Wilson College *A*
Morehead State University *B*
Murray State University *B,M*
Northern Kentucky University *B*
Pikeville College *B*
St. Catharine College *A*
Spalding University *B*
Sue Bennett College *A*
Thomas More College *A,B*
Transylvania University *B*
Union College *B*
University of Kentucky *B,M,D*
University of Louisville *B,M*
Western Kentucky University *B,M*

Louisiana

Centenary College of Louisiana *B*
Dillard University *B*
Grambling State University *B*
Louisiana College *B*
Louisiana State University
  Agricultural and Mechanical
    College *B,M,D*
  Shreveport *B*
Louisiana Tech University *B,M*
Loyola University *B*
McNeese State University *B,M*
Nicholls State University *B*
Northeast Louisiana University *B*
Northwestern State University *B*
Southeastern Louisiana
  University *B*
Southern University
  New Orleans *B*
  Shreveport *A*
Southern University and
  Agricultural and Mechanical
  College *B,M*
Tulane University *B,M,D*
University of New Orleans *B,M*
University of Southwestern
  Louisiana *B,M,D*
Xavier University of Louisiana *B*

Maine

Bates College *B*
Bowdoin College *B*
Colby College *B*
St. Joseph's College *B*
University of Maine
  Augusta *B*
  Orono *B,M*
  Presque Isle *B*
University of Southern Maine *B*

Maryland

Charles County Community
  College *A*
Chesapeake College *A*
College of Notre Dame of
  Maryland *B*
Columbia Union College *B*
Coppin State College *B*
Frederick Community College *A*
Frostburg State University *B*
Garrett Community College *A*
Goucher College *B*
Hagerstown Junior College *A*
Harford Community College *A*
Hood College *B*
Johns Hopkins University *B,M,D*
Loyola College in Maryland *B*
Montgomery College: Germantown
  Campus *A*
Morgan State University *B,M*
Mount St. Mary's College *B*
St. Mary's College of Maryland *B*
Salisbury State University *B*
Towson State University *B*
United States Naval Academy *B*
University of Maryland
  Baltimore County *B*
  College Park *B,M,D*
  Eastern Shore *B*
Washington College *B*
Western Maryland College *B*

Massachusetts

American International College *B*
Amherst College *B*
Assumption College *B*
Atlantic Union College *B*
Babson College *B*
Boston College *B,M*
Boston University *B,M,D*
Brandeis University *B,M,D*
Bridgewater State College *B,M*
Bristol Community College *A*
Bunker Hill Community College *A*
Clark University *B,M,D*
College of the Holy Cross *B*
Dean Junior College *A*
Eastern Nazarene College *B*
Elms College *B*
Emmanuel College *B*
Fitchburg State College *B*
Framingham State College *B*
Gordon College *B*
Hampshire College *B*
Harvard and Radcliffe Colleges *B*
Harvard University *D*
Massachusetts Institute of
  Technology *B,M,D,W*
Merrimack College *B*
Mount Holyoke College *B*
North Adams State College *B*
Northeastern University *B,M*
Quincy College *A*
Regis College *B*
Roxbury Community College *A*
Salem State College *B,M*
Simmons College *B*
Simon's Rock College of Bard *B*
Smith College *B*
Springfield College *B*
Stonehill College *B*
Suffolk University *B*
Tufts University *B,M,D*
University of Massachusetts
  Amherst *B,M,D*
  Dartmouth *B*
  Lowell *B,M*
Wellesley College *B*
Western New England College *B*
Westfield State College *B*
Wheaton College *B*
Williams College *B*

Worcester Polytechnic Institute *B*
Worcester State College *B*

Michigan

Adrian College *A,B*
Albion College *B*
Alma College *B*
Andrews University *B*
Aquinas College *B*
Calvin College *B*
Central Michigan University *B,M*
Charles Stewart Mott Community
 College *C*
Eastern Michigan University *B,M*
Grand Rapids Baptist College and
 Seminary *B*
Grand Valley State University *B*
Hillsdale College *B*
Hope College *B*
Kalamazoo College *B*
Kellogg Community College *A*
Lake Superior State University *B*
Lansing Community College *A*
Lawrence Technological
 University *B*
Madonna University *A,B*
Marygrove College *B*
Michigan State University *B,M,D*
Michigan Technological University
 B,M
Northern Michigan University *B,M*
Oakland University *B*
Olivet College *B*
Saginaw Valley State University *B*
Siena Heights College *A,B*
Spring Arbor College *B*
University of Detroit Mercy *B,M*
University of Michigan
 Ann Arbor *B,M,D*
 Dearborn *B*
 Flint *B*
Wayne State University *B,M,D*
Western Michigan University
 B,M,D

Minnesota

Augsburg College *B*
Bemidji State University *B,M*
Bethany Lutheran College *A*
Bethel College *B*
Carleton College *B*
College of St. Benedict *B*
College of St. Catherine: St.
 Catherine Campus *B*
College of St. Scholastica *B*
Concordia College: Moorhead *B*
Concordia College: St. Paul *B*
Gustavus Adolphus College *B*
Hamline University *B*
Macalester College *B*
Mankato State University *B,M*
Moorhead State University *B*
Northland Community College *A*
Northwestern College *B*
Pillsbury Baptist Bible College *B*
Rainy River Community College *A*
Rochester Community College *A*
St. Cloud State University *B,M*
St. John's University *B*
St. Mary's College of Minnesota *B*
St. Olaf College *B*
Southwest State University *B*
University of Minnesota
 Duluth *B*
 Morris *B*
 Twin Cities *B,M,D*
University of St. Thomas *B*
Vermilion Community College *A*
Willmar Community College *A*
Winona State University *B*

Mississippi

Alcorn State University *B*
Belhaven College *B*
Blue Mountain College *B*
Delta State University *B*
East Central Community College *A*
Holmes Community College *A*
Jackson State University *B,M*
Jones County Junior College *A*
Mary Holmes College *A*
Millsaps College *B*
Mississippi College *B,M*
Mississippi Delta Community
 College *A*
Mississippi Gulf Coast Community
 College
 Jackson County Campus *A*
 Jefferson Davis Campus *A*
Mississippi State University *B,M*
Mississippi University for Women *B*
Rust College *B*
Tougaloo College *B*
University of Mississippi *B,M,D*
University of Southern Mississippi
 B,M
William Carey College *B*

Missouri

Avila College *B*
Central Methodist College *B*
Central Missouri State University
 B,M
College of the Ozarks *B*
Columbia College *B*
Culver-Stockton College *B*
Drury College *B*
East Central College *A*
Evangel College *B*
Fontbonne College *B*
Jefferson College *A*
Lincoln University *B*
Lindenwood College *B*
Maryville University *B*
Mineral Area College *A*
Missouri Baptist College *B*
Missouri Southern State College *B*
Missouri Valley College *B*
Missouri Western State College *B*
Moberly Area Community
 College *A*
Northeast Missouri State University
 B,M
Northwest Missouri State
 University *B*
Park College *B*
Rockhurst College *B*
St. Louis Community College
 Florissant Valley *A*
 Forest Park *A*
 Meramec *A*
St. Louis University *B,M,D*
Southeast Missouri State University
 B,M
Southwest Baptist University *B*
Southwest Missouri State University
 B,M
Stephens College *B*
University of Missouri
 Columbia *B,M,D*
 Kansas City *B,M,D*
 Rolla *D*
 St. Louis *B,M*
Washington University *B,M,D*
Webster University *B*
Westminster College *B*
William Jewell College *B*
William Woods College *B*

Montana

Carroll College *B*
College of Great Falls *A,B*
Dull Knife Memorial College *A*

Eastern Montana College *B*
Little Big Horn College *A*
Miles Community College *A*
Montana College of Mineral
 Science and Technology *B*
Montana State University *B,M,D*
Northern Montana College *B*
Rocky Mountain College *B*
University of Montana *B,M,D*

Nebraska

Bellevue College *B*
Central Community College *A*
Chadron State College *B*
College of St. Mary *B*
Concordia College *B*
Creighton University *C,A,B,M*
Dana College *B*
Doane College *B*
Hastings College *B*
McCook Community College *A*
Midland Lutheran College *B*
Nebraska Wesleyan University *B*
Northeast Community College *A*
Peru State College *B*
Southeast Community College:
 Beatrice Campus *A*
Union College *B*
University of Nebraska
 Kearney *B*
 Lincoln *B,M,D*
 Omaha *B,M*
Wayne State College *B*
Western Nebraska Community
 College: Scottsbluff Campus *A*
York College *A*

Nevada

University of Nevada
 Las Vegas *B,M*
 Reno *B,M*
Western Nevada Community
 College *A*

New Hampshire

Dartmouth College *B,M,D*
Franklin Pierce College *B*
Keene State College *B*
New England College *B*
Plymouth State College of the
 University System of New
 Hampshire *B*
Rivier College *B*
St. Anselm College *B*
University of New Hampshire
 B,M,D

New Jersey

Atlantic Community College *A*
Bergen Community College *A*
Brookdale Community College *A*
Burlington County College *A*
Caldwell College *B*
College of St. Elizabeth *B*
County College of Morris *A*
Cumberland County College *A*
Drew University *B*
Essex County College *A*
Fairleigh Dickinson University *B,M*
Felician College *A,B*
Georgian Court College *B,M*
Glassboro State College *B,M*
Jersey City State College *B*
Kean College of New Jersey *B*
Mercer County Community
 College *A*
Monmouth College *B*
Montclair State College *B,M*
Ocean County College *A*
Passaic County Community
 College *A*
Princeton University *B,D*

Ramapo College of New Jersey *B*
Rider College *B*
Rutgers—The State University of
 New Jersey
 Camden College of Arts and
 Sciences *B*
 Douglass College *B*
 Livingston College *B*
 New Brunswick *M,D*
 Newark College of Arts and
 Sciences *B*
 Rutgers College *B*
 University College Camden *B*
 University College New
 Brunswick *B*
 University College Newark *B*
St. Peter's College *B*
Seton Hall University *B,M*
Stevens Institute of Technology
 B,M,D
Stockton State College *B*
Thomas Edison State College *A,B*
Trenton State College *B,M*
Upsala College *B*
William Paterson College of New
 Jersey *B*

New Mexico

College of Santa Fe *A,B*
Eastern New Mexico University
 B,M
New Mexico Highlands
 University *B*
New Mexico Institute of Mining
 and Technology *B,M*
New Mexico Junior College *A*
New Mexico State University
 B,M,D
University of New Mexico *B,M,D*
Western New Mexico University *B*

New York

Adelphi University *B,M,D*
Adirondack Community College *A*
Alfred University *B*
Bard College *B*
Barnard College *B*
Canisius College *B*
City University of New York
 Baruch College *B*
 Brooklyn College *B,M*
 City College *B,M*
 College of Staten Island *B*
 Graduate School and
 University Center *D*
 Hunter College *B,M*
 Kingsborough Community
 College *A*
 Lehman College *B,M*
 Queens College *B,M*
 York College *B*
Clarkson University *B,M,D*
Clinton Community College *A*
Colgate University *B*
College of Mount St. Vincent *B*
College of New Rochelle *B*
College of St. Rose *B*
Columbia University
 Columbia College *B*
 New York *M,D*
 School of General Studies *B*
Columbia-Greene Community
 College *A*
Community College of the Finger
 Lakes *A*
Concordia College *B*
Cornell University *B,M,D*
Corning Community College *A*
Daemen College *B*
Dominican College of Blauvelt *B*
Dowling College *B*
Dutchess Community College *A*

D'Youville College *B*
Elmira College *B*
Erie Community College
  North Campus *A*
  South Campus *A*
Eugene Lang College/New School
  for Social Research *B*
Fordham University *B,M,D*
Fulton-Montgomery Community
  College *A*
Genesee Community College *A*
Hamilton College *B*
Hartwick College *B*
Herkimer County Community
  College *A*
Hobart College *B*
Hofstra University *B,M*
Houghton College *B*
Hudson Valley Community
  College *A*
Iona College *B*
Ithaca College *B*
Jamestown Community College *A*
Jefferson Community College *A*
Keuka College *B*
King's College *B*
Le Moyne College *B*
Long Island University
  Brooklyn Campus *B*
  C. W. Post Campus *B,M*
Manhattan College *B*
Manhattanville College *B*
Marist College *B*
Marymount College *B*
Mercy College *B*
Mohawk Valley Community
  College *A*
Molloy College *B*
Mount St. Mary College *B*
Nassau Community College *A*
Nazareth College of Rochester *B*
New York University *B,M,D*
Niagara University *B*
North Country Community
  College *A*
Onondaga Community College *A*
Orange County Community
  College *A*
Pace University
  College of White Plains *B*
  New York *B*
  Pleasantville/Briarcliff *B*
Paul Smith's College *A*
Polytechnic University
  Brooklyn *B,M,D*
  Long Island Campus *B*
Rensselaer Polytechnic Institute
  B,M,D
Roberts Wesleyan College *B*
Rochester Institute of
  Technology *B*
Russell Sage College *B*
Sage Junior College of Albany, A
  Division of Russell Sage
  College *A*
St. Bonaventure University *B*
St. Francis College *B*
St. John Fisher College *B*
St. John's University *B,M*
St. Joseph's College
  Brooklyn *B*
  Suffolk Campus *B*
St. Lawrence University *B*
St. Thomas Aquinas College *B*
Sarah Lawrence College *B*
Siena College *B*
Skidmore College *B*

State University of New York
  Albany *B,M,D*
  Binghamton *B,M,D*
  Buffalo *B,M,D*
  Purchase *B*
  Stony Brook *B,M,D*
  College of Agriculture and
    Technology at Cobleskill *A*
  College of Agriculture and
    Technology at Morrisville *A*
  College at Brockport *B,M*
  College at Buffalo *B,M*
  College at Cortland *B*
  College at Fredonia *B,M*
  College at Geneseo *B*
  College at New Paltz *B,M*
  College at Old Westbury *B*
  College at Oneonta *B*
  College at Plattsburgh *B*
  College at Potsdam *B,M*
  College of Technology at
    Delhi *A*
  Oswego *B*
Suffolk County Community
  College *A*
Sullivan County Community
  College *A*
Syracuse University *B,M,D*
Touro College *B*
Trocaire College *A*
Ulster County Community
  College *A*
Union College *B*
United States Military Academy *B*
University of Rochester *B,M,D*
University of the State of New
  York: Regents College *B*
Utica College of Syracuse
  University *B*
Vassar College *B*
Wagner College *B*
Wells College *B*
Westchester Community College *A*
William Smith College *B*
Yeshiva University *B*

North Carolina

Appalachian State University *B,M*
Barber-Scotia College *B*
Barton College *B*
Belmont Abbey College *B*
Bennett College *B*
Brevard College *A*
Campbell University *B*
Catawba College *B*
Chowan College *A*
College of the Albemarle *A*
Davidson College *B*
Duke University *B,D*
East Carolina University *B,M*
Elizabeth City State University *B*
Elon College *B*
Fayetteville State University *B*
Gardner-Webb College *B*
Gaston College *A*
Greensboro College *B*
Guilford College *B*
High Point University *B*
Johnson C. Smith University *B*
Lees-McRae College *B*
Lenoir-Rhyne College *B*
Livingstone College *B*
Mars Hill College *B*
Meredith College *B*
Methodist College *A,B*
North Carolina Agricultural and
  Technical State University *B,M*
North Carolina Central University
  B,M
North Carolina State University
  B,M,D
North Carolina Wesleyan College *B*

Pembroke State University *B*
Pfeiffer College *B*
Queens College *B*
St. Andrews Presbyterian College *B*
St. Augustine's College *B*
Salem College *B*
Shaw University *B*
University of North Carolina
  Asheville *B*
  Chapel Hill *B,M,D*
  Charlotte *B,M*
  Greensboro *B,M*
  Wilmington *B,M*
Vance-Granville Community
  College *A*
Wake Forest University *B,M*
Warren Wilson College *B*
Western Carolina University *B,M*
Western Piedmont Community
  College *A*
Wilkes Community College *A*
Wingate College *B*
Winston-Salem State University *B*

North Dakota

Bismarck State College *A*
Dickinson State University *B*
Jamestown College *B*
Mayville State University *B*
Minot State University *B*
North Dakota State University
  Bottineau and Institute of
    Forestry *A*
  Fargo *B,M,D*
Turtle Mountain Community
  College *A*
University of Mary *B*
University of North Dakota
  Grand Forks *B,M*
  Williston *A*
Valley City State University *B*

Ohio

Antioch College *B*
Ashland University *B*
Baldwin-Wallace College *B*
Bluffton College *B*
Bowling Green State University
  Bowling Green *B,M,D*
  Firelands College *A*
Capital University *B*
Case Western Reserve University
  B,M,D
Cedarville College *B*
Central State University *B*
Cleveland State University *B,M*
College of Mount St. Joseph *B*
College of Wooster *B*
Defiance College *B*
Denison University *B*
Edison State Community College *A*
Franciscan University of
  Steubenville *B*
Heidelberg College *B*
Hiram College *B*
John Carroll University *B,M*
Kent State University *B*
Kenyon College *B*
Lake Erie College *B*
Lakeland Community College *A*
Lorain County Community
  College *A*
Malone College *B*
Marietta College *B*
Miami University: Oxford Campus
  B,M
Mount Union College *B*
Mount Vernon Nazarene College *B*
Muskingum College *B*
Notre Dame College of Ohio *B*
Oberlin College *B*
Ohio Dominican College *B*

Ohio Northern University *B*
Ohio State University: Columbus
  Campus *B*
Ohio University *B,M,D*
Ohio Wesleyan University *B*
Otterbein College *B*
Shawnee State University *B*
University of Akron *B,M*
University of Cincinnati *B,M,D*
University of Dayton *B,M*
University of Findlay *B*
University of Rio Grande *A,B*
University of Toledo *B,M,D*
Ursuline College *B*
Walsh College *B*
Washington State Community
  College *A*
Wilberforce University *B*
Wilmington College *B*
Wittenberg University *B*
Wright State University *B,M*
Xavier University *B*
Youngstown State University *B,M*

Oklahoma

Bacone College *A*
Bartlesville Wesleyan College *A,B*
Cameron University *B*
Connors State College *A*
East Central University *B*
Eastern Oklahoma State College *A*
Hillsdale Free Will Baptist
  College *A*
Langston University *B*
Murray State College *A*
Northeastern State University *B*
Northern Oklahoma College *A*
Northwestern Oklahoma State
  University *B*
Oklahoma Baptist University *B*
Oklahoma Christian University of
  Science and Arts *B*
Oklahoma City University *B*
Oklahoma Panhandle State
  University *B*
Oklahoma State University *B,M,D*
Oral Roberts University *B*
Phillips University *B*
Redlands Community College *A*
Rogers State College *A*
Rose State College *A*
St. Gregory's College *A*
Southeastern Oklahoma State
  University *B*
Southwestern Oklahoma State
  University *B*
Tulsa Junior College *A*
University of Central Oklahoma *B*
University of Oklahoma *B,M,D*
University of Science and Arts of
  Oklahoma *B*
University of Tulsa *B*

Oregon

Central Oregon Community
  College *A*
Eastern Oregon State College *B*
George Fox College *B*
Lewis and Clark College *B*
Linfield College *B*
Linn-Benton Community College *A*
Marylhurst College *B*
Northwest Christian College *B*
Oregon State University *B,M,D*
Pacific University *B*
Portland Community College *A*
Portland State University *B,M*
Reed College *B*
Rogue Community College *A*
Southern Oregon State College *B*
Treasure Valley Community
  College *A*

University of Oregon
  Eugene *B,M,D*
    Robert Donald Clark Honors
      College *B*
University of Portland *B*
Warner Pacific College *A,B*
Western Baptist College *B*
Western Oregon State College *B*
Willamette University *B*

Pennsylvania

Albright College *B*
Allegheny College *B*
Allentown College of St. Francis de
  Sales *B*
Alvernia College *B*
Beaver College *B*
Bloomsburg University of
  Pennsylvania *B*
Bryn Mawr College *B,M,D*
Bucknell University *B,M*
Bucks County Community
  College *A*
Butler County Community
  College *A*
Cabrini College *B*
California University of
  Pennsylvania *B,M*
Carlow College *B*
Carnegie Mellon University
  B,M,D,W
Cedar Crest College *B*
Chatham College *B*
Chestnut Hill College *B*
Cheyney University of
  Pennsylvania *B*
Clarion University of
  Pennsylvania *B*
College Misericordia *B*
Dickinson College *B*
Drexel University *B,M,D*
Duquesne University *B*
East Stroudsburg University of
  Pennsylvania *B*
Eastern College *B*
Edinboro University of
  Pennsylvania *B*
Elizabethtown College *B*
Franklin and Marshall College *B*
Gannon University *B*
Geneva College *B*
Gettysburg College *B*
Grove City College *B*
Gwynedd-Mercy College *B*
Harrisburg Area Community
  College *A*
Haverford College *B*
Holy Family College *B*
Immaculata College *B*
Indiana University of Pennsylvania
  B,M
Juniata College *B*
King's College *B*
Kutztown University of
  Pennsylvania *B,M*
La Salle University *B*
Lafayette College *B*
Lebanon Valley College of
  Pennsylvania *B*
Lehigh County Community
  College *A*
Lehigh University *B,M,D*
Lincoln University *B*
Lock Haven University of
  Pennsylvania *B*
Luzerne County Community
  College *A*
Lycoming College *B*
Mansfield University of
  Pennsylvania *B*
Marywood College *B*
Mercyhurst College *B*

Messiah College *B*
Millersville University of
  Pennsylvania *B,M*
Montgomery County Community
  College *A*
Moravian College *B*
Muhlenberg College *B*
Northampton County Area
  Community College *A*
Northeastern Christian Junior
  College *A*
Penn State
    Erie Behrend College *B*
    Great Valley Graduate
      Center *M*
    University Park Campus
      B,M,D
Rosemont College *B*
St. Francis College *B*
St. Joseph's University *B*
St. Vincent College *B*
Seton Hill College *B*
Shippensburg University of
  Pennsylvania *B,M*
Slippery Rock University of
  Pennsylvania *B*
Susquehanna University *B*
Swarthmore College *B*
Temple University *B,M,D*
Thiel College *B*
University of Pennsylvania *B,M,D*
University of Pittsburgh
    Johnstown *B*
    Pittsburgh *B,M,D*
University of Scranton *B*
Ursinus College *B*
Villanova University *B,M*
Washington and Jefferson College *B*
West Chester University of
  Pennsylvania *B,M*
Westminster College *B*
Widener University *B*
Wilkes University *B,M*
Wilson College *B*
York College of Pennsylvania *A*

Puerto Rico

Inter American University of Puerto
  Rico
    Arecibo Campus *B*
    Metropolitan Campus *B*
    San German Campus *B*
Pontifical Catholic University of
  Puerto Rico *B*
Universidad Metropolitana *B*
University of Puerto Rico
    Cayey University College *B*
    Mayaguez Campus *B,M*
    Ponce Technological
      University College *A*
    Rio Piedras Campus *B,M*
University of the Sacred Heart *B*

Rhode Island

Brown University *B,M,D*
Providence College *B*
Rhode Island College *B,M*
Roger Williams College *B*
Salve Regina University *B*
University of Rhode Island *B,M,D*

South Carolina

Benedict College *B*
Bob Jones University *B*
Central Wesleyan College *B*
Charleston Southern University *B*
The Citadel *B*
Claflin College *B*
Clemson University *B,M,D*
Coker College *B*
College of Charleston *B,M*
Columbia College *B*

Converse College *B*
Erskine College *B*
Francis Marion College *B*
Furman University *B*
Lander College *B*
Limestone College *B*
Morris College *B*
Newberry College *B*
North Greenville College *A*
Presbyterian College *B*
South Carolina State College *B*
University of South Carolina
    Columbia *B,M,D*
    Spartanburg *B*
Voorhees College *B*
Winthrop University *B,M*
Wofford College *B*

South Dakota

Augustana College *B*
Black Hills State University *B*
Dakota State University *B*
Dakota Wesleyan University *B*
Mount Marty College *B*
Northern State University *B*
Sioux Falls College *B*
South Dakota School of Mines and
  Technology *B*
South Dakota State University *B,M*
University of South Dakota *B,M*

Tennessee

Austin Peay State University *B,M*
Belmont University *B*
Carson-Newman College *B*
Christian Brothers University *B*
Columbia State Community
  College *A*
Cumberland University *A,B*
David Lipscomb University *B*
Dyersburg State Community
  College *A*
East Tennessee State University
  B,M
Fisk University *B*
Freed-Hardeman University *B*
King College *B*
Knoxville College *B*
Lambuth University *B*
Lane College *B*
LeMoyne-Owen College *B*
Lincoln Memorial University *B*
Martin Methodist College *A*
Maryville College *B*
Memphis State University *B,M,D*
Middle Tennessee State University
  B,M
Milligan College *B*
Motlow State Community
  College *A*
Rhodes College *B*
Roane State Community College *A*
Shelby State Community College *A*
Southern College of Seventh-day
  Adventists *B*
Tennessee State University *B*
Tennessee Technological University
  B,M
Tennessee Wesleyan College *B*
Trevecca Nazarene College *B*
Union University *B*
University of the South *B*
University of Tennessee
    Chattanooga *B*
    Knoxville *B,M,D*
    Martin *B*
Vanderbilt University *B,M,D*
William Jennings Bryan College *B*

Texas

Abilene Christian University *B*
Alvin Community College *A*

Amarillo College *A*
Angelina College *A*
Angelo State University *B,M*
Austin College *B*
Austin Community College *A*
Baylor University *B,M*
Bee County College *A*
Blinn College *A*
Brazosport College *A*
Central Texas College *A*
College of the Mainland *A*
Collin County Community College
  District *A*
Corpus Christi State University *B,M*
Dallas Baptist University *B*
Del Mar College *A*
East Texas Baptist University *B*
East Texas State University
    Commerce *B,M*
    Texarkana *B*
El Paso Community College *A*
Galveston College *A*
Hardin-Simmons University *B*
Houston Baptist University *B*
Houston Community College *A*
Howard College *A*
Howard Payne University *B*
Huston-Tillotson College *B*
Incarnate Word College *B*
Jacksonville College *A*
Jarvis Christian College *B*
Kilgore College *A*
Lamar University—Beaumont *B,M*
Laredo State University *B*
LeTourneau University *B*
Lon Morris College *A*
Lubbock Christian University *B*
McLennan Community College *A*
McMurry University *B*
Midland College *A*
Midwestern State University *B*
Navarro College *A*
North Harris Montgomery
  Community College District *A*
Our Lady of the Lake University of
  San Antonio *B*
Panola College *A*
Paul Quinn College *B*
Prairie View A&M University *B,M*
Ranger Junior College *A*
Rice University *B,M,D*
St. Edward's University *B*
St. Mary's University *B*
St. Philip's College *A*
Sam Houston State University *B,M*
Schreiner College *B*
South Plains College *A*
Southern Methodist University
  B,M,D
Southwest Texas State University
  B,M
Southwestern Adventist College *B*
Southwestern Christian College *A*
Southwestern University *B*
Stephen F. Austin State University
  B,M
Sul Ross State University *B*
Tarleton State University *B,M*
Texas A&I University *B,M*
Texas A&M University *B,M,D*
Texas Christian University *B,M*
Texas College *B*
Texas Lutheran College *B*
Texas Southern University *B,M*
Texas Tech University *B,M,D*
Texas Wesleyan University *B*
Texas Woman's University *B,M*
Trinity University *B*
Trinity Valley Community
  College *A*
University of Dallas *B*

University of Houston
 Clear Lake *B,M*
 Houston *B,M,D*
 Victoria *B*
University of Mary Hardin-
 Baylor *B*
University of North Texas *B,M,D*
University of St. Thomas *B*
University of Texas
 Arlington *B,M,D*
 Austin *B,M,D*
 Dallas *B,M,D*
 El Paso *B,M*
 Pan American *B,M*
 Permian Basin *B*
 San Antonio *B,M*
 Tyler *B*
Victoria College *A*
Wayland Baptist University *B*
West Texas State University *B,M*
Western Texas College *A*
Wharton County Junior College *A*
Wiley College *B*

Utah

Brigham Young University *B,M,D*
Dixie College *A*
Southern Utah University *B*
University of Utah *B,M,D*
Utah State University *B,M*
Weber State University *B*
Westminster College of Salt Lake
 City *B*

Vermont

Bennington College *B*
Castleton State College *B*
Goddard College *B,M*
Johnson State College *B*
Lyndon State College *B*
Marlboro College *B*
Middlebury College *B*
Norwich University *B*
St. Michael's College *B*
Trinity College of Vermont *B*
University of Vermont *B,M*

Virginia

Averett College *B*
Bluefield College *B*
Bridgewater College *B*
Christopher Newport College *B*
Clinch Valley College of the
 University of Virginia *B*
College of William and Mary *B,M*
Eastern Mennonite College *B*
Emory and Henry College *B*
Ferrum College *B*
George Mason University *B,M*
Hampden-Sydney College *B*
Hampton University *B,M*
Hollins College *B*
James Madison University *B*
Liberty University *B*
Longwood College *B*
Lynchburg College *B*
Mary Baldwin College *B*
Mary Washington College *B*
Marymount University *B*
Mountain Empire Community
 College *A*
Norfolk State University *B*
Northern Virginia Community
 College *A*
Old Dominion University *B*
Piedmont Virginia Community
 College *A*
Radford University *B*
Randolph-Macon College *B*
Randolph-Macon Woman's
 College *B*
Roanoke College *B*

St. Paul's College *B*
Shenandoah University *B*
Sweet Briar College *B*
University of Richmond *B,W*
University of Virginia *B,M,D*
Virginia Commonwealth University
 B,M
Virginia Military Institute *B*
Virginia Polytechnic Institute and
 State University *B,M,D*
Virginia State University *B,M*
Virginia Union University *B*
Virginia Wesleyan College *B*
Washington and Lee University *B*

Washington

Big Bend Community College *A*
Central Washington University *B,M*
Centralia College *A*
Eastern Washington University *B,M*
Everett Community College *A*
Evergreen State College *B*
Gonzaga University *B*
Grays Harbor College *A*
Heritage College *B*
Lower Columbia College *A*
Olympic College *A*
Pacific Lutheran University *B*
St. Martin's College *B*
Seattle Central Community
 College *A*
Seattle Pacific University *B*
Seattle University *B*
Skagit Valley College *A*
Spokane Community College *A*
Spokane Falls Community
 College *A*
Tacoma Community College *A*
University of Puget Sound *B*
University of Washington *B,M,D*
Walla Walla College *B*
Washington State University *B,M,D*
Wenatchee Valley College *A*
Western Washington University
 B,M
Whitman College *B*
Whitworth College *B*

West Virginia

Alderson-Broaddus College *B*
Bethany College *B*
Bluefield State College *B*
Concord College *B*
Davis and Elkins College *B*
Fairmont State College *B*
Marshall University *B,M*
Potomac State College of West
 Virginia University *A*
Salem-Teikyo University *B*
Shepherd College *B*
University of Charleston *B*
West Liberty State College *B*
West Virginia Institute of
 Technology *B*
West Virginia State College *B*
West Virginia University *B,M,D*
West Virginia Wesleyan College *B*
Wheeling Jesuit College *B*

Wisconsin

Alverno College *B*
Beloit College *B*
Cardinal Stritch College *B*
Carroll College *B*
Carthage College *B*
Concordia University Wisconsin *B*
Edgewood College *B*
Lakeland College *B*
Lawrence University *B*
Marian College of Fond du Lac *B*
Marquette University *B,M,D*
Mount Mary College *B*

Mount Senario College *B*
Northland College *B*
Ripon College *B*
St. Norbert College *B*
Silver Lake College *B*
University of Wisconsin
 Eau Claire *B,M*
 Green Bay *B*
 La Crosse *B*
 Madison *B,M,D*
 Milwaukee *B,M,D*
 Oshkosh *B,M*
 Parkside *B*
 Platteville *B*
 River Falls *B,M*
 Stevens Point *B*
 Superior *B*
 Whitewater *B*
Viterbo College *B*
Wisconsin Lutheran College *B*

Wyoming

Casper College *A*
Central Wyoming College *A*
Eastern Wyoming College *A*
Laramie County Community
 College *A*
Northwest College *A*
Sheridan College *A*
University of Wyoming *B,M,D*
Western Wyoming Community
 College *A*

**American Samoa, Caroline
Islands, Guam, Marianas,
Virgin Islands**

University of Guam *B*
University of the Virgin Islands *B*

Canada

McGill University *B,M,D*

Arab Republic of Egypt

American University in Cairo *B*

Mathematics education

Alabama

Alabama Agricultural and
 Mechanical University *B,M*
Alabama State University *B,M*
Auburn University
 Auburn *B,M,D*
 Montgomery *B,M*
Birmingham-Southern College *B*
Faulkner University *B*
Huntingdon College *B*
Jacksonville State University *B,M*
Judson College *B*
Lawson State Community
 College *A*
Livingston University *B,M*
Mobile College *B*
Oakwood College *B*
Samford University *B,M*
Spring Hill College *B*
Troy State University
 Dothan *B,M*
 Montgomery *B,M*
Tuskegee University *B*
University of Alabama
 Huntsville *B*
 Tuscaloosa *B*
University of Montevallo *B,M*
University of North Alabama *B,M*

Alaska

University of Alaska Fairbanks *M*

Arizona

Arizona State University *B,M,D*
Eastern Arizona College *A*
Grand Canyon University *B*
Northern Arizona University *B,M*
University of Arizona *B,M*

Arkansas

Arkansas College *B*
Arkansas State University *B,M*
Arkansas Tech University *M*
Harding University *B*
Henderson State University *B,M*
John Brown University *B*
Ouachita Baptist University *B*
University of Arkansas
 Fayetteville *B,M*
 Monticello *B*
 Pine Bluff *B*
University of Central Arkansas *B,M*
University of the Ozarks *B*
Westark Community College *A*

California

Azusa Pacific University *B*
Biola University *B*
California Baptist College *B*
California Lutheran University *B*
California State University
 Bakersfield *B*
 Fresno *B*
 Fullerton *B*
 Los Angeles *B*
 Northridge *B*
 Sacramento *B*
Christ College Irvine *B*
Christian Heritage College *B*
Fresno Pacific College *B,M*
Humboldt State University *B*
Loyola Marymount University *M*
Mount St. Mary's College *B*
National University *B*
Occidental College *M*
Santa Clara University *M*
University of California: Davis *M*
University of the Pacific *B*
University of Redlands *B*
University of San Francisco *B*
Westmont College *B*

Colorado

Colorado College *M*
Colorado State University *B*
University of Colorado at Colorado
 Springs *B*
University of Northern Colorado
 B,M,D
Western State College of
 Colorado *B*

Connecticut

Eastern Connecticut State
 University *M*
Sacred Heart University *B,M*
St. Joseph College *B,M*
Southern Connecticut State
 University *B,M*
University of Bridgeport *B*
University of Hartford *M*
Western Connecticut State
 University *B*

Delaware

Delaware State College *B*
University of Delaware *B*

District of Columbia

American University *D*
University of the District of
 Columbia *M*

Florida

Bethune-Cookman College *B*
Flagler College *B*
Florida Agricultural and Mechanical
   University *B,M*
Florida Atlantic University *B,M*
Florida Institute of Technology
   B,M,D
Florida International University
   B,M
Florida State University *B,M,D*
Hobe Sound Bible College *B*
Jacksonville University *M*
Nova University *M*
Pensacola Junior College *A*
St. Leo College *B*
Southeastern College of the
   Assemblies of God *B*
Stetson University *B,M*
University of Central Florida *B,M*
University of Florida *B,M*
University of Miami *M*
University of North Florida *B*
University of South Florida *B,M*
University of Tampa *B*
University of West Florida *B*

Georgia

Albany State College *B,M*
Armstrong State College *B,M*
Augusta College *M*
Berry College *B*
Columbus College *B,M*
Georgia College *B,M*
Georgia Southern University *B,M*
Georgia Southwestern College *B,M*
Georgia State University *M,D*
Kennesaw State College *B*
Mercer University *M*
North Georgia College *B,M*
Piedmont College *B*
Shorter College *B*
University of Georgia *B,M,D*
Valdosta State College *B,M*
Wesleyan College *B*

Hawaii

Brigham Young University-
   Hawaii *B*
Chaminade University of
   Honolulu *B*

Idaho

Albertson College *B*
Boise State University *B,M*
Idaho State University *M*
Northwest Nazarene College *B*
University of Idaho *M*

Illinois

Augustana College *B*
Aurora University *B*
Barat College *B*
Blackburn College *B*
Concordia University *B,M*
De Paul University *B*
Elmhurst College *B*
Eureka College *B*
Greenville College *B*
Illinois College *B*
Illinois State University *D*
Illinois Wesleyan University *B*
Judson College *B*
MacMurray College *B*
Millikin University *B*
National-Louis University *M*
North Central College *B*
Northern Illinois University *M*
Northwestern University *B,M,D*
Olivet Nazarene University *B*
Quincy College *B*
Roosevelt University *B*

St. Xavier University *M*
Southern Illinois University
   Carbondale *B*
   Edwardsville *B*
Trinity Christian College *B*
Trinity College *B*
University of Illinois
   Chicago *B,M*
   Urbana-Champaign *B,M*
Western Illinois University *B*
Wheaton College *B*

Indiana

Anderson University *B*
Ball State University *B*
Bethel College *B*
Butler University *B*
Franklin College *B*
Goshen College *B*
Huntington College *B*
Indiana State University *B,M*
Indiana University
   Bloomington *B,M,D*
   Southeast *B*
Indiana University—Purdue
   University at Fort Wayne *B,M*
Indiana Wesleyan University *B*
Manchester College *B*
Marian College *B*
Martin University *B*
Oakland City College *B*
Purdue University *B,M,D*
St. Joseph's College *B*
St. Mary-of-the-Woods College *B*
Taylor University *B*
Tri-State University *B*
University of Evansville *B,M*
University of Indianapolis *B*
University of Southern Indiana *B*
Vincennes University *A*

Iowa

Briar Cliff College *B*
Buena Vista College *B*
Clarke College *B*
Cornell College *B*
Drake University *B,M*
Grand View College *B*
Iowa Lakes Community College *A*
Iowa State University *M*
Iowa Wesleyan College *B*
Kirkwood Community College *A*
Loras College *B*
Luther College *B*
Morningside College *B*
Mount Mercy College *B*
St. Ambrose University *B*
Simpson College *B*
Teikyo Westmar University *B*
University of Dubuque *B,M*
University of Iowa *B,M,D*
University of Northern Iowa *M*
Upper Iowa University *B*
Wartburg College *B*
William Penn College *B*

Kansas

Baker University *B*
Bethany College *B*
Colby Community College *A*
Emporia State University *B*
Fort Hays State University *M*
Friends University *B*
Kansas State University *B*
McPherson College *B*
MidAmerica Nazarene College *B*
Pittsburg State University *B,M*
St. Mary College *B*
Southwestern College *B*
Tabor College *B*
University of Kansas *B*
Washburn University of Topeka *B*

Kentucky

Alice Lloyd College *B*
Asbury College *B*
Bellarmine College *B*
Berea College *B*
Campbellsville College *B*
Cumberland College *B*
Eastern Kentucky University *B,M*
Georgetown College *B*
Kentucky Christian College *B*
Murray State University *B*
Pikeville College *B*
Sue Bennett College *A*
Thomas More College *B*
Transylvania University *B*
Union College *B*
University of Kentucky *B,M*
Western Kentucky University *M*

Louisiana

Dillard University *B*
Grambling State University *B*
Louisiana College *B*
Louisiana State University
   Agricultural and Mechanical
      College *B*
   Shreveport *B*
Louisiana Tech University *B,M*
McNeese State University *B,M*
Nicholls State University *B*
Northeast Louisiana University *B*
Northwestern State University *B*
Our Lady of Holy Cross College *B*
Southeastern Louisiana
   University *B*
Southern University and
   Agricultural and Mechanical
      College *B*
Tulane University *M*
University of New Orleans *B*
University of Southwestern
   Louisiana *B*
Xavier University of Louisiana *B*

Maine

St. Joseph's College *B*
Thomas College *B*
University of Maine
   Farmington *B*
   Presque Isle *B*

Maryland

Columbia Union College *B*
Frederick Community College *A*
Montgomery College: Germantown
   Campus *A*
Morgan State University *B*
Western Maryland College *B*

Massachusetts

American International College *B*
Boston College *B*
Boston University *B,M,W*
Bridgewater State College *M*
Eastern Nazarene College *B,M*
Elms College *B*
Fitchburg State College *B*
Framingham State College *B,M*
Hampshire College *B*
Lesley College *B*
Merrimack College *B*
Salem State College *M*
Springfield College *B*
Suffolk University *B*
Tufts University *B,M*
University of Massachusetts at
   Lowell *D*
Westfield State College *B*
Worcester Polytechnic Institute *M*

Michigan

Adrian College *B*
Andrews University *M*
Calvin College *B*
Central Michigan University *B,M*
Concordia College *B*
Eastern Michigan University *B*
Ferris State University *B*
Grand Valley State University *B*
Hillsdale College *B*
Lansing Community College *A*
Madonna University *B*
Marygrove College *B*
Michigan State University *B,D*
Northern Michigan University *B,M*
Oakland University *B,M*
Saginaw Valley State University *B*
University of Detroit Mercy *M*
University of Michigan
   Ann Arbor *M,D*
   Dearborn *B*
Wayne State University *B,M*
Western Michigan University
   B,M,D

Minnesota

Bemidji State University *B,M*
Bethel College *B*
College of St. Catherine: St.
   Catherine Campus *B*
College of St. Scholastica *B*
Concordia College: Moorhead *B*
Concordia College: St. Paul *B*
Gustavus Adolphus College *B*
Mankato State University *B*
Moorhead State University *B*
Northland Community College *A*
Northwestern College *B*
Pillsbury Baptist Bible College *B*
Rainy River Community College *A*
St. Cloud State University *B*
St. Mary's College of Minnesota *B*
St. Olaf College *B*
Southwest State University *B*
University of Minnesota
   Duluth *B*
   Twin Cities *M*
Vermilion Community College *A*
Willmar Community College *A*
Winona State University *B*

Mississippi

Alcorn State University *B,M*
Blue Mountain College *B*
Delta State University *B,M*
Mary Holmes College *A*
Mississippi College *B,M*
Mississippi Gulf Coast Community
   College: Jefferson Davis
   Campus *A*
Mississippi University for Women *B*
Northeast Mississippi Community
   College *A*
Rust College *B*
University of Mississippi *B*

Missouri

Central Missouri State University
   B,M
College of the Ozarks *B*
Columbia College *B*
Culver-Stockton College *B*
Evangel College *B*
Maryville University *B*
Missouri Baptist College *B*
Missouri Valley College *B*
Northeast Missouri State
   University *M*
Northwest Missouri State
   University *B,M*
Park College *B*
Rockhurst College *B*

Southeast Missouri State University *B,M*
Southwest Missouri State University *B*
University of Missouri
    Columbia *B,M,D*
    Kansas City *B*
Washington University *B,M*
Webster University *B,M*
Westminster College *B*
William Woods College *B*

Montana

Carroll College *B*
Eastern Montana College *B*
Montana State University *B*
Northern Montana College *B*
Rocky Mountain College *B*
University of Montana *B*
Western Montana College of the University of Montana *B*

Nebraska

Chadron State College *B*
College of St. Mary *B*
Concordia College *B*
Creighton University *B*
Dana College *B*
Doane College *B*
Hastings College *B*
Nebraska Wesleyan University *B*
Peru State College *B*
Union College *B*
University of Nebraska
    Kearney *B,M*
    Lincoln *B,M*
    Omaha *B*
Wayne State College *B*

Nevada

University of Nevada: Reno *M*

New Hampshire

Franklin Pierce College *B*
Keene State College *B*
New England College *B*
New Hampshire College *B*
Plymouth State College of the University System of New Hampshire *B*
Rivier College *B*
University of New Hampshire *B,M*

New Jersey

Caldwell College *B*
Fairleigh Dickinson University *M*
Glassboro State College *B,M*
Jersey City State College *B,M*
Kean College of New Jersey *B,M*
Monmouth College *B*
Rider College *B*
Rutgers—The State University of New Jersey
    Camden College of Arts and Sciences *B*
    Douglass College *B*
    Livingston College *B*
    New Brunswick *M,D*
    Newark College of Arts and Sciences *B*
    Rutgers College *B*
    University College New Brunswick *B*
    University College Newark *B*
Seton Hall University *B*
Stockton State College *B*
Trenton State College *B,M*

New Mexico

College of the Southwest *B*
Eastern New Mexico University *B,M*

New Mexico Highlands University *B*
New Mexico State University *B*
University of New Mexico *B*

New York

Adelphi University *B,M*
Canisius College *B*
City University of New York
    Baruch College *B*
    Brooklyn College *B,M*
    City College *B,M*
    Hunter College *B,M*
    Lehman College *M*
    Queens College *B,M*
College of Mount St. Vincent *B*
College of New Rochelle *B*
Concordia College *B*
Cornell University *B,M,D*
Daemen College *B*
Dominican College of Blauvelt *B*
Dowling College *B*
D'Youville College *B*
Elmira College *B*
Hofstra University *B,M*
Houghton College *B*
Iona College *B,M*
Ithaca College *B*
Le Moyne College *B*
Long Island University: C. W. Post Campus *B,M*
Manhattanville College *M*
Marymount College *B*
Mohawk Valley Community College *A*
New York Institute of Technology *B*
New York University *B,M,D*
Niagara University *B,M*
Rensselaer Polytechnic Institute *B*
Russell Sage College *B*
St. Bonaventure University *B,M*
St. John's University *B,M*
St. Joseph's College
    Brooklyn *B*
    Suffolk Campus *B*
St. Thomas Aquinas College *B*
Siena College *B*
State University of New York
    Albany *B,M*
    Binghamton *M*
    Buffalo *B,M,D*
    College at Brockport *M*
    College at Buffalo *M*
    College at Cortland *B,M*
    College at Fredonia *M*
    College at Geneseo *B*
    College at New Paltz *B,M*
    College at Old Westbury *B*
    College at Oneonta *B,M*
    College at Plattsburgh *B,M*
    College at Potsdam *B,M*
    Oswego *B,M*
Syracuse University *B,M,D*
Union College *M*
University of Rochester *M,D*
Utica College of Syracuse University *B*
Wells College *B*

North Carolina

Appalachian State University *B,M*
Barber-Scotia College *B*
Barton College *B*
Bennett College *B*
Brevard College *A*
Campbell University *B*
Catawba College *B*
East Carolina University *B,M*
Elizabeth City State University *B*
Fayetteville State University *B*
Gardner-Webb College *B*

Johnson C. Smith University *B*
Lees-McRae College *B*
Livingstone College *B*
Mars Hill College *B*
Methodist College *A,B*
North Carolina Agricultural and Technical State University *B,M*
North Carolina Central University *B,M*
North Carolina State University *B,M,D*
North Carolina Wesleyan College *B*
Pembroke State University *M*
St. Andrews Presbyterian College *B*
St. Augustine's College *B*
Salem College *B*
University of North Carolina
    Asheville *C*
    Greensboro *M*
Western Carolina University *B,M*
Wingate College *B*
Winston-Salem State University *B*

North Dakota

Bismarck State College *A*
Dickinson State University *B*
Jamestown College *B*
Mayville State University *B*
Minot State University *B,M*
North Dakota State University *B,M*
University of Mary *B*
University of North Dakota *B,M*
Valley City State University *B*

Ohio

Ashland University *B*
Baldwin-Wallace College *B*
Bluffton College *B*
Bowling Green State University *B,M*
Capital University *B*
Case Western Reserve University *B*
Cedarville College *B*
College of Mount St. Joseph *C*
Defiance College *B*
Heidelberg College *B*
John Carroll University *B*
Kent State University *B,M,D*
Malone College *B*
Miami University: Oxford Campus *B*
Mount Union College *B*
Mount Vernon Nazarene College *B*
Ohio Dominican College *B*
Ohio State University: Columbus Campus *B,M,D*
Ohio University *B*
Otterbein College *B*
University of Dayton *B*
University of Findlay *B*
University of Rio Grande *B*
University of Toledo *B*
Urbana University *B*
Walsh College *B*
Wittenberg University *B*
Wright State University *B,M*
Youngstown State University *B*

Oklahoma

Bartlesville Wesleyan College *B*
East Central University *B*
Langston University *B*
Northwestern Oklahoma State University *B*
Oklahoma Baptist University *B*
Oklahoma Christian University of Science and Arts *B*
Oklahoma City University *B*
Oklahoma Panhandle State University *B*
Oral Roberts University *B*
Phillips University *B*

Rogers State College *A*
Southeastern Oklahoma State University *B,M*
Southwestern Oklahoma State University *B,M*
University of Central Oklahoma *B,M*
University of Oklahoma *B,D*
University of Science and Arts of Oklahoma *B*
University of Tulsa *B,M*

Oregon

George Fox College *B*
Oregon State University *M,D*
Southern Oregon State College *M*
University of Oregon *M*
Western Baptist College *B*
Western Oregon State College *B,M*
Willamette University *M*

Pennsylvania

Albright College *B*
Allentown College of St. Francis de Sales *B,M*
Beaver College *B,M*
Bloomsburg University of Pennsylvania *B*
Bucknell University *B*
Cabrini College *B*
California University of Pennsylvania *B,M*
Chatham College *B*
Cheyney University of Pennsylvania *B*
Clarion University of Pennsylvania *B,M*
Delaware Valley College *B*
Drexel University *B*
Duquesne University *B,M*
East Stroudsburg University of Pennsylvania *B*
Edinboro University of Pennsylvania *B,M*
Elizabethtown College *B*
Gannon University *B*
Geneva College *B*
Gettysburg College *B*
Grove City College *B*
Gwynedd-Mercy College *B*
Harrisburg Area Community College *A*
Holy Family College *B*
Immaculata College *B,M*
Indiana University of Pennsylvania *B,M*
Juniata College *B*
La Salle University *B*
Lehigh University *M*
Lincoln University *B*
Lock Haven University of Pennsylvania *B*
Lycoming College *B*
Mansfield University of Pennsylvania *B*
Marywood College *B*
Mercyhurst College *B*
Messiah College *B*
Moravian College *B*
Philadelphia College of Bible *B*
Point Park College *B*
St. Francis College *C*
St. Joseph's University *C,B,M*
Seton Hill College *B*
Slippery Rock University of Pennsylvania *B*
Temple University *B,M,D*
University of Pennsylvania *M,D*
University of Pittsburgh
    Bradford *C,B*
    Johnstown *B*
University of Scranton *B,M*

Washington and Jefferson College *B*
Waynesburg College *B*
West Chester University of
Pennsylvania *B,M*
Wilkes University *B,M*
York College of Pennsylvania *B*

Puerto Rico

Bayamon Central University *B*
Caribbean University *B*
Inter American University of Puerto
Rico: San German Campus *B*
Pontifical Catholic University of
Puerto Rico *B*
Universidad Metropolitana *B*
University of Puerto Rico
Mayaguez Campus *B*
Rio Piedras Campus *B,M*

Rhode Island

Providence College *B*
Rhode Island College *B,M*

South Carolina

Benedict College *B*
Bob Jones University *B,M*
Charleston Southern University *B*
The Citadel *M*
Claflin College *B*
Coker College *B*
Columbia College *B*
Converse College *M*
Erskine College *B*
Francis Marion College *M*
Lander College *B*
Limestone College *B*
Morris College *B*
Presbyterian College *B*
South Carolina State College *B*
University of South Carolina
Aiken *B*
Coastal Carolina College *B*

South Dakota

Augustana College *B*
Black Hills State University *B*
Dakota State University *B*
Dakota Wesleyan University *B*
Mount Marty College *B*
Northern State University *B,M*
Sioux Falls College *B*
South Dakota State University *B*
University of South Dakota *B*

Tennessee

Bethel College *B*
Carson-Newman College *B*
David Lipscomb University *B*
East Tennessee State University
B,M
Freed-Hardeman University *B*
Lincoln Memorial University *B*
Middle Tennessee State
University *B*
Milligan College *B*
Tennessee Technological
University *B*
Tennessee Wesleyan College *B*
Union University *B,M*
University of Tennessee
Chattanooga *B,M*
Knoxville *B*
Martin *B*
Vanderbilt University *M,D*
William Jennings Bryan College *B*

Texas

Abilene Christian University *B*
Angelo State University *B*
Baylor University *B*
Dallas Baptist University *B*
East Texas Baptist University *B*

Hardin-Simmons University *B*
Houston Baptist University *M*
Incarnate Word College *B*
McMurry University *B*
Prairie View A&M University *M*
Ranger Junior College *A*
St. Edward's University *B*
St. Mary's University *B*
Schreiner College *B*
Southwest Texas State
University *M*
Stephen F. Austin State
University *M*
Texas A&I University *B*
Texas Christian University *B*
Texas College *B*
Texas Wesleyan University *B*
University of Dallas *B*
University of Houston *B,M*
University of Mary Hardin-
Baylor *B*
University of Texas
Austin *M,D*
San Antonio *M*
West Texas State University *B,M*
Wiley College *B*

Utah

Brigham Young University *B,M*
Southern Utah University *B*
Utah State University *B*
Weber State University *B*

Vermont

Castleton State College *B*
Johnson State College *B*
St. Michael's College *B*
Trinity College of Vermont *B*
University of Vermont *B,M*

Virginia

Averett College *B*
Bluefield College *B*
Eastern Mennonite College *B*
Emory and Henry College *B*
Ferrum College *B*
George Mason University *M*
Liberty University *B*
Marymount University *B*
Old Dominion University *B*
Virginia Polytechnic Institute and
State University *B,M*
Virginia Union University *B*
Virginia Wesleyan College *B*

Washington

Central Washington University *B,M*
Eastern Washington University *B*
Heritage College *B*
Pacific Lutheran University *B*
Seattle Pacific University *B*
University of Puget Sound *M*
University of Washington *B*
Washington State University *B*
Western Washington University
B,M

West Virginia

Bethany College *B*
Bluefield State College *B*
Concord College *B*
Davis and Elkins College *B*
Fairmont State College *B*
Glenville State College *B*
Shepherd College *B*
University of Charleston *B*
West Liberty State College *B*
West Virginia Institute of
Technology *B*
West Virginia State College *B*
West Virginia University *B*
West Virginia Wesleyan College *B*

Wheeling Jesuit College *M*

Wisconsin

Alverno College *B*
Cardinal Stritch College *B*
Carroll College *B*
Carthage College *B*
Concordia University Wisconsin *B*
Lakeland College *B*
Lawrence University *B*
Maranatha Baptist Bible College *B*
Marian College of Fond du Lac *B*
Marquette University *B*
Mount Mary College *B*
Mount Senario College *B*
Northland College *B*
St. Norbert College *B*
University of Wisconsin
Eau Claire *B*
Green Bay *B*
La Crosse *B*
Madison *B,M*
Oshkosh *B*
Platteville *B*
River Falls *B*
Stevens Point *B*
Whitewater *B*
Wisconsin Lutheran College *B*

Wyoming

University of Wyoming *B,M*

**American Samoa, Caroline
Islands, Guam, Marianas,
Virgin Islands**

University of Guam *B*

Canada

McGill University *B,M*

Mechanical design technology

Alabama

Alabama Agricultural and
Mechanical University *A,B*
Community College of the Air
Force *A*
Jefferson State Community
College *A*
John C. Calhoun State Community
College *A*

Arizona

Arizona State University *B*
Northern Arizona University *B*
Pima Community College *C,A*

Arkansas

Garland County Community
College *C*
University of Arkansas at Little
Rock *A,B*
Westark Community College *C,A*

California

Chabot College *A*
Chaffey Community College *A*
City College of San Francisco *A*
Cogswell Polytechnical College *A,B*
College of the Sequoias *A*
Don Bosco Technical Institute *A*
Fresno City College *C,A*
Los Angeles Trade and Technical
College *C,A*
Los Angeles Valley College *C*
Modesto Junior College *A*
Mount San Antonio College *C,A*
Pasadena City College *C,A*

San Diego City College *C,A*
San Jose City College *A*
Southwestern College *A*
Ventura College *A*

Colorado

Arapahoe Community College *A*
Denver Institute of Technology *A*
Metropolitan State College of
Denver *A*
Pikes Peak Community College *A*
University of Southern Colorado *B*

Connecticut

Greater New Haven State Technical
College *A*
Hartford State Technical College *A*
Norwalk State Technical College *A*
Thames Valley State Technical
College *A*
Waterbury State Technical
College *A*

Delaware

Delaware Technical and
Community College: Stanton/
Wilmington Campus *A*

District of Columbia

University of the District of
Columbia *A*

Florida

Broward Community College *A*
Daytona Beach Community
College *A*
Gulf Coast Community College *A*
New England Institute of
Technology *A*

Georgia

Abraham Baldwin Agricultural
College *A*
Augusta Technical Institute *A*
Brunswick College *A*
Clayton State College *A*
Gainesville College *A*
Georgia Southern University *B*
Savannah State College *A,B*
Southern College of Technology *B*
Truett-McConnell College *A*

Idaho

Idaho State University *A*

Illinois

Black Hawk College *A*
Bradley University *B*
City Colleges of Chicago: Wright
College *A*
College of Lake County *C,A*
Elgin Community College *C,A*
Illinois Central College *A*
Illinois Valley Community
College *A*
Joliet Junior College *C,A*
Kishwaukee College *A*
Lake Land College *A*
Moraine Valley Community College
C,A
Morrison Institute of Technology *A*
Oakton Community College *C,A*
Parkland College *A*
Prairie State College *A*
Rock Valley College *A*
Waubonsee Community College
C,A
William Rainey Harper College *A*

Indiana

Ball State University *A*
Indiana State University *B*

Indiana University
Kokomo A
Southeast A
Indiana University—Purdue
University
Fort Wayne A
Indianapolis A,B
Purdue University
North Central Campus A,B
West Lafayette A,B
Vincennes University A

Iowa

Hawkeye Institute of Technology A
Iowa Western Community
College A
Kirkwood Community College A
North Iowa Area Community
College A
Northeast Iowa Community
College A
Northwest Iowa Technical
College A
Southeastern Community College:
North Campus A
University of Northern Iowa B

Kansas

Allen County Community
College A
Butler County Community
College A
Dodge City Community College
C,A
Hutchinson Community College A
Kansas State University B
Pittsburg State University B

Kentucky

Eastern Kentucky University A
Louisville Technical Institute A
Madisonville Community College A
Murray State University A,B
University of Louisville A
Western Kentucky University B

Louisiana

Nicholls State University B

Maine

Central Maine Technical College
C,A
University of Maine A,B

Maryland

Anne Arundel Community
College A
Hagerstown Junior College C,A
Montgomery College: Rockville
Campus A

Massachusetts

Bristol Community College A
Franklin Institute of Boston A
Northeastern University A,B
Roxbury Community College A
Springfield Technical Community
College A
University of Massachusetts at
Lowell A,B
Wentworth Institute of
Technology A

Michigan

Andrews University A
Central Michigan University B
Charles Stewart Mott Community
College A
Delta College A
Ferris State University A
Grand Rapids Community College
C,A

Jackson Community College A
Kalamazoo Valley Community
College A
Lansing Community College A
Lawrence Technological
University A
Macomb Community College A
Michigan Technological
University A
Mid Michigan Community College
C,A
Northwestern Michigan College A
Oakland Community College C,A
Southwestern Michigan College A
Wayne State University B

Minnesota

Alexandria Technical College A
Normandale Community College A
Rochester Community College A
St. Paul Technical College C
Southwest State University A,B

Mississippi

Hinds Community College A
University of Southern
Mississippi B

Missouri

Central Missouri State University B
Jefferson College A
St. Louis Community College
Florissant Valley A
Forest Park A
Three Rivers Community College A
Washington University B

Montana

Montana State University B
Northern Montana College A,B

Nebraska

Southeast Community College:
Milford Campus A

Nevada

University of Nevada: Las Vegas B

New Hampshire

New Hampshire Technical College
Manchester C,A
Nashua A
Stratham A

New Jersey

Camden County College A
County College of Morris A
Kean College of New Jersey B
New Jersey Institute of
Technology B
Trenton State College B
Union County College A

New Mexico

New Mexico Junior College A
New Mexico State University A,B

New York

Adirondack Community College A
Broome Community College A
City University of New York
College of Staten Island A
New York City Technical
College A
Queensborough Community
College A
Community College of the Finger
Lakes A
Corning Community College A
Dutchess Community College A

Erie Community College
North Campus A
South Campus A
Hudson Valley Community
College A
Jamestown Community College A
Mohawk Valley Community
College A
Monroe Community College A
New York Institute of
Technology B
Niagara County Community
College A
Onondaga Community College A
Rochester Institute of Technology
A,B
Rockland Community College A
State University of New York
College of Agriculture and
Technology at Morrisville A
College of Technology at
Alfred A,B
College of Technology at
Canton A
College of Technology at
Farmingdale A
Institute of Technology at
Utica/Rome B
Suffolk County Community
College A
Tompkins-Cortland Community
College A

North Carolina

Alamance Community College A
Catawba Valley Community
College A
Central Piedmont Community
College A
Forsyth Technical Community
College A
Guilford Technical Community
College C,A
Isothermal Community College A
Mitchell Community College A
Richmond Community College A
University of North Carolina at
Charlotte B
Wilson Technical Community
College A

North Dakota

North Dakota State College of
Science A

Ohio

Bowling Green State University B
Central Ohio Technical College A
Cincinnati Technical College A
Clark State Community College A
Columbus State Community
College A
Cuyahoga Community College:
Metropolitan Campus A
Franklin University A,B
Jefferson Technical College A
Kent State University
Ashtabula Regional Campus A
Salem Regional Campus A
Lakeland Community College A
Lorain County Community
College A
Marion Technical College A
Muskingum Area Technical
College A
North Central Technical College A
Northwest Technical College A
Sinclair Community College A
Terra Technical College C,A
University of Akron A
University of Dayton B
University of Rio Grande A

University of Toledo A
Washington State Community
College A
Wright State University: Lake
Campus A
Youngstown State University A,B

Oklahoma

Oklahoma State University B
Rose State College A
Tulsa Junior College A

Oregon

Chemeketa Community College A
Mount Hood Community College
C,A
Oregon Institute of Technology A,B
Portland Community College C,A
Rogue Community College A

Pennsylvania

Butler County Community
College A
California University of
Pennsylvania B
Delaware County Community
College A
Harrisburg Area Community
College C,A
Johnson Technical Institute A
Lehigh County Community
College A
Luzerne County Community
College C,A
Penn State
Erie Behrend College A,B
Harrisburg Capital College B
University Park Campus C,A
Pennsylvania College of
Technology A
Pennsylvania Institute of
Technology A
Point Park College A,B
Spring Garden College B
Triangle Tech: Pittsburgh
Campus A
Williamson Free School of
Mechanical Trades A

Puerto Rico

University of Puerto Rico: Bayamon
Technological University
College A

Rhode Island

Community College of Rhode
Island C,A
New England Institute of
Technology A

South Carolina

Aiken Technical College A
Chesterfield-Marlboro Technical
College A
Greenville Technical College A
Midlands Technical College A
South Carolina State College B
Tri-County Technical College A
Trident Technical College A

Tennessee

Chattanooga State Technical
Community College A
Nashville State Technical
Institute A
Northeast State Technical
Community College A
Pellissippi State Technical
Community College A
State Technical Institute at
Memphis A
University of Tennessee: Martin B

Texas

Angelina College *A*
Central Texas College *A*
Eastfield College *A*
Lee College *A*
LeTourneau University *A*
Prairie View A&M University *B*
Richland College *A*
Texas State Technical College
    Amarillo *A*
    Waco *A*
Texas Tech University *B*
Western Texas College *A*

Utah

Dixie College *A*
Southern Utah University *A*
Weber State University *A*

Vermont

Vermont Technical College *A*

Virginia

Blue Ridge Community College *A*
Central Virginia Community
    College *A*
Dabney S. Lancaster Community
    College *A*
John Tyler Community College *A*
Lord Fairfax Community College *A*
Virginia Highlands Community
    College *C*

Washington

Central Washington University *B*
Clark College *A*
Cogswell College North *A,B*
Lower Columbia College *A*
Shoreline Community College *A*
Spokane Community College *A*

West Virginia

Bluefield State College *A*
Fairmont State College *A,B*
West Virginia Institute of
    Technology *A,B*

Wisconsin

Chippewa Valley Technical
    College *A*
Fox Valley Technical College *A*
Madison Area Technical College *A*
Mid-State Technical College *A*
Moraine Park Technical College *A*
Northeast Wisconsin Technical
    College *A*
Waukesha County Technical
    College *A*
Western Wisconsin Technical
    College *A*
Wisconsin Indianhead Technical
    College *A*

Mechanical engineering

Alabama

Alabama Agricultural and
    Mechanical University *B*
Auburn University *B,M,D*
Tuskegee University *B,M*
University of Alabama
    Birmingham *B,M*
    Huntsville *B,M,D*
    Tuscaloosa *B,M,D*
University of South Alabama *B,M*

Alaska

University of Alaska Fairbanks *B,M*

Arizona

Arizona State University *B,M,D*
Northern Arizona University *B*
University of Arizona *B,M,D*

Arkansas

John Brown University *B*
University of Arkansas *B,M*
Westark Community College *A*

California

Allan Hancock College *C*
California Institute of Technology
    B,M,D,W
California Maritime Academy *B*
California Polytechnic State
    University: San Luis Obispo *B*
California State Polytechnic
    University: Pomona *B*
California State University
    Chico *B*
    Fresno *B*
    Fullerton *B,M*
    Long Beach *B,M*
    Los Angeles *B,M*
    Northridge *B,M*
    Sacramento *B,M*
City College of San Francisco *A*
Loyola Marymount University *B,M*
Merced College *A*
Naval Postgraduate School *M,D*
San Diego State University *B,M*
San Francisco State University *B*
San Joaquin Delta College *C,A*
San Jose State University *B,M*
Santa Clara University *B,M,D*
Santa Rosa Junior College *A*
Stanford University *B,M,D*
University of California
    Berkeley *B,M,D*
    Davis *B,M,D*
    Irvine *B*
    Los Angeles *B,M,D*
    San Diego *B,M,D*
    Santa Barbara *B,M,D*
University of the Pacific *B*
University of Redlands *B*
University of Southern California
    B,M,D,W
West Coast University *A,B,M*

Colorado

Colorado School of Mines *W*
Colorado State University *B,M,D*
United States Air Force
    Academy *B*
University of Colorado
    Boulder *B,M,D*
    Denver *B,M*
University of Denver *B,M*

Connecticut

Bridgeport Engineering Institute *B*
University of Bridgeport *B,M*
University of Connecticut *B,M,D*
University of Hartford *B*
University of New Haven *A,B,M*
Yale University *B,M,D*

Delaware

Delaware State College *B*
University of Delaware *B,M,D*

District of Columbia

Catholic University of America
    B,M,D
Gallaudet University *B*
George Washington University
    B,M,D
Georgetown University *B*
Howard University *B,M,D*

University of the District of
    Columbia *B*

Florida

Florida Agricultural and Mechanical
    University *B,M,D*
Florida Atlantic University *B,M*
Florida Institute of Technology
    B,M,D
Florida International University
    B,M
Florida State University *B,M,D*
Manatee Community College *A*
Miami-Dade Community College *A*
University of Central Florida *B,M,D*
University of Florida *B,M,D*
University of Miami *B,M,D*
University of South Florida *B,M,D*

Georgia

Augusta College *A*
Clark Atlanta University *B*
DeKalb Technical Institute *A*
Georgia Institute of Technology
    B,M,D
Mercer University *B,M*
Middle Georgia College *A*
Morris Brown College *B*
Savannah Technical Institute *C,A*

Hawaii

University of Hawaii at Manoa *B,M*

Idaho

College of Southern Idaho *A*
Ricks College *A*
University of Idaho *B,M,D*

Illinois

Bradley University *B,M*
Illinois Benedictine College *B*
Illinois Institute of Technology
    B,M,D
Northern Illinois University *B,M*
Northwestern University *B,M,D*
Richland Community College *A*
Southern Illinois University
    Carbondale *B,M*
    Edwardsville *B*
University of Illinois
    Chicago *B,M,D*
    Urbana-Champaign *B,M,D*

Indiana

Indiana Institute of Technology *B*
Indiana University—Purdue
    University at Indianapolis *B,M*
Purdue University
    Calumet *B*
    West Lafayette *B,M,D,W*
Rose-Hulman Institute of
    Technology *B,M*
Tri-State University *B*
University of Evansville *B*
University of Notre Dame *B,M,D*
Valparaiso University *B*
Vincennes University *A*

Iowa

Iowa State University *B,M,D*
Kirkwood Community College *A*
University of Iowa *B,M,D*

Kansas

Kansas State University *B,M,D*
University of Kansas *B,M,D*
Wichita State University *B,M,D*

Kentucky

University of Kentucky *B,M,D*
University of Louisville *B,M*

Louisiana

Louisiana State University and
    Agricultural and Mechanical
    College *B,M,D*
Louisiana Tech University *B,M*
McNeese State University *B*
Southern University and
    Agricultural and Mechanical
    College *B*
Tulane University *B,M,D*
University of New Orleans *B*
University of Southwestern
    Louisiana *B,M*

Maine

University of Maine *B,M*

Maryland

College of Notre Dame of
    Maryland *B*
Johns Hopkins University *B,M,D*
United States Naval Academy *B*
University of Maryland
    Baltimore County *B,M,D*
    College Park *B,M,D*

Massachusetts

Boston University *B,M,D*
Eastern Nazarene College *B*
Franklin Institute of Boston *A*
Harvard and Radcliffe Colleges *B*
Massachusetts Institute of
    Technology *B,M,D,W*
Northeastern University *B,M,D*
Springfield Technical Community
    College *A*
Tufts University *B,M,D*
University of Massachusetts
    Amherst *B,M,D*
    Dartmouth *B*
    Lowell *B,M,D*
Western New England College *B,M*
Worcester Polytechnic Institute
    B,M,D

Michigan

Calvin College *B*
GMI Engineering & Management
    Institute *B,M*
Grand Valley State University *B*
Lawrence Technological
    University *B*
Michigan State University *B,M,D*
Michigan Technological University
    B,M,D
Mid Michigan Community
    College *A*
Oakland University *B,M*
Saginaw Valley State University *B*
University of Detroit Mercy *B,M,D*
University of Michigan
    Ann Arbor *B,M,D*
    Dearborn *B,M*
Wayne State University *B,M,D*
Western Michigan University *B,M*

Minnesota

Mankato State University *B*
Northwest Technical Institute *A*
University of Minnesota: Twin
    Cities *B,M,D*
Willmar Community College *A*
Winona State University *B*

Mississippi

Mississippi College *B*
Mississippi State University *B,M,D*
University of Mississippi *B*

Missouri

University of Missouri
  Columbia *B,M,D*
  Kansas City *B*
  Rolla *B,M,D*
Washington University *B,M,D*

Montana

Montana State University *B,M,D*

Nebraska

Southeast Community College:
  Milford Campus *A*
University of Nebraska—Lincoln
  B,M

Nevada

University of Nevada
  Las Vegas *B,M,D*
  Reno *B,M*

New Hampshire

University of New Hampshire
  B,M,D

New Jersey

Mercer County Community
  College *A*
New Jersey Institute of Technology
  B,M,D
Princeton University *B,M,D*
Rutgers—The State University of
  New Jersey
    College of Engineering *B*
    New Brunswick *M,D*
Stevens Institute of Technology
  B,M,D

New Mexico

New Mexico State University
  B,M,D
University of New Mexico *B,M*

New York

Alfred University *B*
City University of New York
    City College *B,M,D*
    Graduate School and
      University Center *D*
Clarkson University *B,M*
Columbia University: School of
  Engineering and Applied Science
  B,M,D,W
Cooper Union *B,M*
Cornell University *B,M,D*
Erie Community College: North
  Campus *A*
Hofstra University *B*
Manhattan College *B,M*
New York Institute of
  Technology *B*
New York University *B*
Niagara County Community
  College *A*
Polytechnic University
    Brooklyn *B,M,D*
    Long Island Campus *B*
Rensselaer Polytechnic Institute
  B,M,D
Rochester Institute of Technology
  B,M
State University of New York
    Binghamton *B,M*
    Buffalo *B,M,D*
    Stony Brook *B,M,D*
    College of Agriculture and
      Technology at Morrisville *A*
    College of Environmental
      Science and Forestry *B,M,D*
    Maritime College *B*
Syracuse University *B,M,D*
Union College *B,M*

United States Military Academy *B*
University of Rochester *B*

North Carolina

Asheville Buncombe Technical
  Community College *A*
Central Piedmont Community
  College *A*
Duke University *B,M,D*
North Carolina Agricultural and
  Technical State University *B,M*
North Carolina State University
  B,M,D
St. Augustine's College *B*
Surry Community College *A*
University of North Carolina at
  Charlotte *B,M*

North Dakota

North Dakota State University *B,M*
University of North Dakota *B,M*

Ohio

Case Western Reserve University
  B,M,D
Cedarville College *B*
Central State University *B*
Cleveland State University *B,M*
Cuyahoga Community College:
  Metropolitan Campus *A*
Lorain County Community
  College *A*
Ohio Northern University *B*
Ohio State University: Columbus
  Campus *B,M,D*
Ohio University *B,M*
Owens Technical College: Toledo *A*
University of Akron *B,M,D*
University of Cincinnati *B,M,D*
University of Dayton *B,M,D*
University of Toledo *B,M,D*
Wilberforce University *B*
Wright State University *B*
Youngstown State University *B,M*

Oklahoma

Oklahoma Christian University of
  Science and Arts *B*
Oklahoma State University *B,M,D*
University of Oklahoma *B,M,D*
University of Tulsa *B,M,D*

Oregon

George Fox College *B*
Linfield College *B*
Oregon State University *B,M,D*
Portland State University *B,M*
University of Portland *B,M*

Pennsylvania

Bucknell University *B,M*
California University of
  Pennsylvania *B*
Carnegie Mellon University
  B,M,D,W
Drexel University *B,M,D*
Gannon University *B*
Geneva College *B*
Grove City College *B*
Lafayette College *B*
Lehigh University *B,M,D*
Lock Haven University of
  Pennsylvania *B*
Messiah College *B*
Penn State University Park Campus
  B,M,D
Pennsylvania Institute of
  Technology *A*
Reading Area Community
  College *A*
Swarthmore College *B*
Temple University *B*

University of Pennsylvania *B,M,D*
University of Pittsburgh *B,M,D*
Villanova University *B,M*
Widener University *B,M*
Wilkes University *B*

Puerto Rico

Turabo University *B*
Universidad Politecnica de Puerto
  Rico *B*
University of Puerto Rico
    Carolina Regional College *A*
    Mayaguez Campus *B,M*

Rhode Island

Brown University *B,M,D*
Community College of Rhode
  Island *A*
University of Rhode Island *B,M,D*

South Carolina

Clemson University *B,M,D*
University of South Carolina *B,M,D*

South Dakota

South Dakota School of Mines and
  Technology *B,M*
South Dakota State University *B*

Tennessee

Christian Brothers University *B*
Memphis State University *B,M*
Tennessee State University *B*
Tennessee Technological University
  B,M
University of Tennessee
    Chattanooga *B,M*
    Knoxville *B,M,D*
Vanderbilt University *B,M,D*

Texas

Amarillo College *A*
Baylor University *B*
Kilgore College *A*
Lamar University—Beaumont *B,D*
LeTourneau University *B*
Prairie View A&M University *B*
Rice University *B,M,D*
Southern Methodist University
  B,M,D
Texas A&I University *B,M*
Texas A&M University *B,M,D*
Texas Southmost College *A*
Texas Tech University *B,M,D*
University of Houston *B,M,D*
University of Texas
    Arlington *B,M,D*
    Austin *B,M,D*
    El Paso *B,M*
    San Antonio *B,M*

Utah

Brigham Young University *B,M,D*
Southern Utah University *A*
University of Utah *B,M,D*
Utah State University *B,M,D*

Vermont

Norwich University *B*
University of Vermont *B,M,D*

Virginia

Emory and Henry College *B*
Northern Virginia Community
  College *A*
Old Dominion University *B,M,D*
University of Virginia *B*
Virginia Military Institute *B*
Virginia Polytechnic Institute and
  State University *B,M,D*

Washington

Gonzaga University *B,M*
Lower Columbia College *A*
St. Martin's College *B*
Seattle University *B*
University of Puget Sound *B*
University of Washington *B,M,D*
Walla Walla College *B*
Washington State University *B,M,D*

West Virginia

Potomac State College of West
  Virginia University *A*
West Virginia Institute of
  Technology *B,M*
West Virginia University *B,M,D*

Wisconsin

Concordia University Wisconsin *B*
Marquette University *B,M,D*
Milwaukee School of Engineering *B*
University of Wisconsin
    Madison *B,M,D*
    Milwaukee *B*
    Platteville *B*

Wyoming

University of Wyoming *B,M,D*

**American Samoa, Caroline
Islands, Guam, Marianas,
Virgin Islands**

Micronesian Occupational College
  C,A

Canada

McGill University *B,M,D*

Mexico

Sistema Instituto Tecnologico y de
  Estudios Superiores de
  Monterrey *M*

Arab Republic of Egypt

American University in Cairo *B*

Medical assistant

Alabama

Alabama Southern Community
  College *A*
Brewer State Junior College *A*
Chattahoochee Valley Community
  College *A*
Community College of the Air
  Force *A*
Draughons Junior College *A*
Enterprise State Junior College *A*
Faulkner University *A*
Gadsden State Community
  College *A*
George C. Wallace State
  Community College at Selma *A*
James H. Faulkner State
  Community College *A*
Jefferson State Community
  College *A*
John C. Calhoun State Community
  College *A*
Lawson State Community
  College *A*
Livingston University *A*
Lurleen B. Wallace State Junior
  College *A*
Northeast Alabama State Junior
  College *A*
Shelton State Community
  College *A*
Shoals Community College *C,A*

Southern Union State Junior
College *A*
University of Alabama in
Birmingham *C*
Walker College *A*
Wallace State Community College
at Hanceville *A*

Alaska

University of Alaska Anchorage *A*

Arkansas

Arkansas Tech University *A*
Capital City Junior College *A*
Garland County Community
College *A*

California

Allan Hancock College *C,A*
Barstow College *C*
Cerritos Community College *C,A*
Chabot College *C,A*
Citrus College *C,A*
City College of San Francisco *C,A*
College of the Desert *A*
College of the Redwoods *C*
Compton Community College *A*
Cosumnes River College *C,A*
De Anza College *C,A*
East Los Angeles College *C,A*
El Camino College *C,A*
Fresno City College *C,A*
Glendale Community College *C,A*
Humphreys College *A*
Imperial Valley College *C*
Kelsey-Jenney College *C*
Long Beach City College *C,A*
Merced College *A*
Modesto Junior College *A*
Monterey Peninsula College *C,A*
Ohlone College *C,A*
Orange Coast College *C,A*
Palomar College *C,A*
Pasadena City College *C,A*
Saddleback College *A*
San Diego Mesa College *C,A*
Santa Rosa Junior College *C,A*
Southwestern College *C*
Victor Valley College *C*
West Valley College *C,A*

Colorado

Arapahoe Community College *C,A*
Blair Junior College *A*
Denver Institute of Technology *A*
Denver Technical College *C,A*
Parks Junior College *A*

Connecticut

Briarwood College *C,A*
Northwestern Connecticut
Community College *A*
Quinebaug Valley Community
College *A*

Delaware

Delaware Technical and
Community College
Southern Campus *A*
Stanton/Wilmington
Campus *A*

Florida

Broward Community College *A*
Gulf Coast Community College *A*
Jones College *A*
Keiser College of Technology *A*
Miami-Dade Community College *C*
National School of Technology *A*
New England Institute of
Technology *A*
Orlando College *A*

Pasco-Hernando Community
College *C*
Pensacola Junior College *C*
Phillips Junior College:
Melbourne *A*
Seminole Community College *C*
South College: Palm Beach Campus
C,A
Tampa College *A*
United Electronics Institute *C*

Georgia

Athens Area Technical Institute *C*
Augusta Technical Institute *C*
Brewton-Parker College *A*
Chattahoochee Technical
Institute *C*
Clayton State College *C*
Darton College *A*
DeKalb College *A*
DeKalb Technical Institute *C*
Gainesville College *A*
Meadows College of Business *C*
Savannah Technical Institute *C*
South College *C,A*

Hawaii

Cannon's International Business
College of Honolulu *C,A*
University of Hawaii: Kapiolani
Community College *C,A*

Illinois

Belleville Area College *C,A*
Black Hawk College *A*
Gem City College *C*
Illinois Central College *C*
Illinois Eastern Community
Colleges
Frontier Community
College *C*
Lincoln Trail College *C*
Olney Central College *C*
Wabash Valley College *C*
Midstate College *C,A*
Robert Morris College: Chicago
C,A

Indiana

Indiana Vocational Technical
College
Central Indiana *C,A*
Columbus *C*
Eastcentral *C,A*
Kokomo *C,A*
Lafayette *C*
Northcentral *C,A*
Northeast *C,A*
Northwest *C,A*
Southcentral *C,A*
Southeast *C*
Southwest *C,A*
Wabash Valley *C,A*
Whitewater *A*
International Business College *C*
Vincennes University *A*

Iowa

American Institute of Commerce *C*
Des Moines Area Community
College *C,A*
Iowa Central Community College *C*
Iowa Western Community
College *C*
Kirkwood Community College *A*
North Iowa Area Community
College *A*
Southeastern Community College:
North Campus *C*

Kansas

Barton County Community
College *A*
Dodge City Community College *C*
Fort Scott Community College *A*
Kansas City Kansas Community
College *A*

Kentucky

Eastern Kentucky University *A*
Franklin College *A*
Owensboro Junior College of
Business *C,A*
Watterson College *C,A*

Louisiana

Bossier Parish Community
College *A*
Phillips Junior College: New
Orleans *A*
Southern University in
Shreveport *A*

Maine

Andover College *A*
Beal College *A*
Husson College *A*
Kennebec Valley Technical
College *C*

Maryland

Anne Arundel Community College
C,A
Hagerstown Business College *A*
Montgomery College: Takoma Park
Campus *C,A*
Villa Julie College *A*

Massachusetts

Aquinas College at Milton *A*
Aquinas College at Newton *C,A*
Bay State College *A*
Fisher College *A*
Massasoit Community College *C*
Middlesex Community College *A*
Northern Essex Community
College *C*
Springfield Technical Community
College *A*

Michigan

Baker College
Auburn Hills *A*
Cadillac *A*
Flint *A*
Mount Clemens *A*
Muskegon *A*
Owosso *A*
Port Huron *A*
Cleary College *A*
Davenport College of Business *A*
Delta College *A*
Detroit College of Business *A*
Great Lakes Junior College of
Business *A*
Jackson Community College *A*
Kalamazoo Valley Community
College *A*
Lansing Community College *A*
Macomb Community College *C,A*
Marygrove College *A*
Northwestern Michigan College *A*
Oakland Community College *A*
Schoolcraft College *C*

Minnesota

Itasca Community College:
Arrowhead Region *C*
Rochester Community College *C*
Willmar Technical College *C*

Mississippi

Northeast Mississippi Community
College *A*
Phillips Junior College
Jackson *A*
Mississippi Gulf Coast *A*

Missouri

Springfield *A*

Nebraska

Central Community College *C,A*
Southeast Community College:
Lincoln Campus *C*

New Hampshire

Hesser College *A*
McIntosh College *A*

New Jersey

Bergen Community College *A*

New Mexico

Eastern New Mexico University *A*

New York

Broome Community College *A*
Bryant & Stratton Business Institute
Buffalo *A*
Rochester *A*
Syracuse *A*
Central City Business Institute *C*
City University of New York
College of Staten Island *C*
Queensborough Community
College *C*
Erie Community College: North
Campus *A*
Herkimer County Community
College *A*
Jamestown Business College *A*
Mohawk Valley Community
College *C*
New York University *A*
Niagara County Community
College *A*
State University of New York
College of Technology at
Alfred *A*
Tompkins-Cortland Community
College *A*
Trocaire College *A*

North Carolina

Alamance Community College *C*
Carteret Community College *A*
Cecils College *A*
Central Piedmont Community
College *A*
Chowan College *A*
Edgecombe Community College *A*
Gaston College *A*
Guilford Technical Community
College *A*
Haywood Community College *A*
James Sprunt Community
College *C*
Martin Community College *C*
Pamlico Community College *A*
Pitt Community College *A*
Stanly Community College *C*
Tri-County Community College *A*
Wake Technical Community
College *C*
Western Piedmont Community
College *A*
Wilkes Community College *C*
Wingate College *A*

Ohio

Bradford School *C*
Bryant & Stratton Business
  Institute: Great Northern *A*
Cincinnati Metropolitan College *A*
Cincinnati Technical College *A*
Cuyahoga Community College:
  Metropolitan Campus *A*
Davis Junior College of Business
  C,A
Hocking Technical College *A*
Jefferson Technical College *C,A*
Lorain County Community
  College *C*
Miami-Jacobs College *A*
Muskingum Area Technical
  College *A*
Northwestern College *C,A*
Ohio Valley Business College *A*
Southern Ohio College *A*
Southern State Community
  College *A*
Stark Technical College *A*
University of Akron *A*
University of Toledo *A*
Youngstown State University *A*

Oklahoma

Bacone College *A*
Connors State College *A*
Oklahoma Junior College *A*
Tulsa Junior College *A*

Oregon

Chemeketa Community College *C*
Clackamas Community College *C*
Lane Community College *C*
Mount Hood Community
  College *A*
Southwestern Oregon Community
  College *A*

Pennsylvania

Central Pennsylvania Business
  School *A*
Community College of
  Philadelphia *A*
Delaware County Community
  College *C,A*
Gannon University *A*
Harrisburg Area Community
  College *A*
Lansdale School of Business *C,A*
Lehigh County Community
  College *A*
Mount Aloysius College *A*
Tracey-Warner School *C*

Rhode Island

Community College of Rhode
  Island *A*
New England Institute of
  Technology *A*

South Carolina

Columbia Junior College of
  Business *A*
Sumter Area Technical College *C*
Trident Technical College *C*

South Dakota

National College *A*

Tennessee

East Tennessee State University *A*
Knoxville College *A*
McKenzie College *A*
Motlow State Community
  College *A*
Shelby State Community College *A*
Trevecca Nazarene College *A*

Texas

El Centro College *C*
El Paso Community College *C,A*
Houston Community College *C*
San Antonio College *A*
San Jacinto College: Central
  Campus *A*
Texas Southmost College *A*

Utah

LDS Business College *C,A*
Stevens-Henager College of
  Business *A*

Virginia

Commonwealth College *C,A*
National Business College *A*
Northern Virginia Community
  College *C*

Washington

Edmonds Community College *C*
North Seattle Community
  College *A*
Olympic College *C,A*
South Puget Sound Community
  College *C,A*
Tacoma Community College *C*
University of Washington *B*
Whatcom Community College *C,A*

West Virginia

College of West Virginia *C,A*
West Virginia State College *A*

Wisconsin

Concordia University Wisconsin *C*
Madison Area Technical College *A*
Mid-State Technical College *C*
Northeast Wisconsin Technical
  College *C*
Stratton College *C,A*
Waukesha County Technical
  College *A*
Western Wisconsin Technical
  College *C*
Wisconsin Indianhead Technical
  College *C*

Wyoming

Western Wyoming Community
  College *C,A*

Medical illustrating

California

Gavilan Community College *C*

Georgia

Atlanta Metropolitan College *A*
Clark Atlanta University *B*
Medical College of Georgia *M*
Morris Brown College *B*

Iowa

Iowa State University *B*

Massachusetts

Springfield College *B*

Michigan

Alma College *B*
University of Michigan *M*

New York

Rochester Institute of
  Technology *B*

North Carolina

Chowan College *A*

Ohio

Cleveland Institute of Art *B*
Ohio State University: Columbus
  Campus *C,B*

Pennsylvania

Beaver College *B*

Texas

Texas Woman's University *B*
University of Texas Southwestern
  Medical Center at Dallas
  Southwestern Allied Health
  Sciences School *M*

Washington

Bellevue Community College *A*

Medical laboratory technologies

Alabama

Alabama Agricultural and
  Mechanical University *A*
Alabama Southern Community
  College *A*
Alabama State University *B*
Auburn University
  Auburn *B*
  Montgomery *B*
Brewer State Junior College *A*
Chattahoochee Valley Community
  College *A*
Community College of the Air
  Force *A*
Enterprise State Junior College *A*
Faulkner University *A*
Gadsden State Community
  College *A*
James H. Faulkner State
  Community College *A*
Jefferson State Community
  College *A*
John C. Calhoun State Community
  College *A*
Lawson State Community
  College *A*
Livingston University *A*
Lurleen B. Wallace State Junior
  College *A*
Northeast Alabama State Junior
  College *A*
Shelton State Community
  College *A*
Shoals Community College *A*
University of Alabama in
  Birmingham *C*
University of South Alabama *B*
Walker College *A*
Wallace State Community College
  at Hanceville *A*

Alaska

University of Alaska Anchorage *A*

Arizona

University of Arizona *B*

Arkansas

Arkansas State University
  Beebe Branch *A*
  Jonesboro *A,B*
Capital City Junior College *A*
East Arkansas Community
  College *A*
Garland County Community
  College *A*
Phillips County Community
  College *A*
Southern Arkansas Community
  College *A*
Southern Arkansas University *A*
University of Arkansas for Medical
  Sciences *B*
University of Central Arkansas *B*
Westark Community College *A*

California

California State University
  Bakersfield *B*
  Los Angeles *B*
Chabot College *A*
Charles R. Drew University: College
  of Allied Health *C*
City College of San Francisco *C,A*
Pacific Union College *B*
Pasadena City College *C,A*
San Francisco State University *C,M*
San Jose State University *B*

Colorado

Arapahoe Community College *A*
Blair Junior College *A*
University of Colorado Health
  Sciences Center *B*
University of Northern Colorado *B*

Connecticut

Housatonic Community College
  C,A
Manchester Community College *A*
Quinnipiac College *C,B,M*
Sacred Heart University *B*
St. Joseph College *B*
University of Bridgeport *B*
University of Connecticut *B*
University of Hartford *B*
Western Connecticut State
  University *B*

Delaware

Delaware Technical and
  Community College: Southern
  Campus *A*
University of Delaware *B*
Wesley College *B*

District of Columbia

Catholic University of America *B*
George Washington University *B*
Howard University *B*
University of the District of
  Columbia *A*

Florida

Barry University *B*
Brevard Community College *A*
Broward Community College *A*
Florida Atlantic University *B*
Florida Community College at
  Jacksonville *A*
Florida International University
  B,M
Florida Memorial College *B*
Florida Southern College *B*
Florida State University *B*
Indian River Community College *A*
Jacksonville University *B*
Keiser College of Technology *A*
Lake City Community College *A*
Miami-Dade Community College *A*
St. Petersburg Junior College *A*
University of Florida *B*
University of Miami *B*
University of Tampa *B*
Valencia Community College *A*

Georgia

Armstrong State College *B*
Atlanta Metropolitan College *A*
Augusta College *A*
Brunswick College *A*
Clark Atlanta University *B*
Clayton State College *A*
Columbus College *A*
Dalton College *A*
Darton College *A*
DeKalb College *A*
Gainesville College *A*
Georgia Southern University *B*
Georgia State University *B*
Gordon College *A*
Macon College *A*
Medical College of Georgia *B,M*
Savannah State College *B*
Truett-McConnell College *A*
Waycross College *A*

Hawaii

University of Hawaii
    Kapiolani Community
      College *A*
    Manoa *B*

Idaho

Boise State University *B*
Lewis Clark State College *A*
North Idaho College *A*
Ricks College *A*
University of Idaho *B*

Illinois

Aurora University *B*
Barat College *B*
Belleville Area College *A*
Blackburn College *B*
Bradley University *B*
City Colleges of Chicago: Malcolm
   X College *A*
College of Lake County *A*
College of St. Francis *B*
De Paul University *B*
Illinois Central College *A*
Illinois College *B*
Illinois Valley Community
   College *A*
Illinois Wesleyan University *B*
Lewis and Clark Community
   College *A*
McKendree College *B*
Moraine Valley Community
   College *A*
National-Louis University *B*
North Central College *B*
North Park College and Theological
   Seminary *B*
Northern Illinois University *B*
Oakton Community College *A*
Olivet Nazarene University *B*
Roosevelt University *B*
University of Health Sciences: The
   Chicago Medical School *B,M*

Indiana

Butler University *B*
DePauw University *B*
Indiana State University *A,B,M*
Indiana University
   Kokomo *B*
   Northwest *A*
Indiana University—Purdue
   University
      Fort Wayne *B*
      Indianapolis *B*
Indiana Vocational Technical
   College
      Northcentral *A*
      Wabash Valley *A*
Indiana Wesleyan University *A*

Marian College *B*
Purdue University *B*
St. Joseph's College *B*
St. Mary-of-the-Woods College *B*
St. Mary's College *B*
Taylor University *B*
University of Evansville *B*
University of Indianapolis *B*
University of Southern Indiana *B*
Vincennes University *A*

Iowa

Briar Cliff College *B*
Buena Vista College *B*
Clarke College *B*
Clinton Community College *A*
Cornell College *B*
Des Moines Area Community
   College *A*
Dordt College *B*
Graceland College *B*
Hawkeye Institute of Technology *A*
Luther College *B*
Morningside College *B*
Mount Mercy College *B*
Scott Community College *A*
Simpson College *B*
Southwestern Community
   College *A*
University of Iowa *B*

Kansas

Barton County Community
   College *A*
Bethany College *B*
Bethel College *B*
Emporia State University *B*
Hutchinson Community College *A*
Kansas Newman College *A*
Kansas State University *B*
Pittsburg State University *B*
Seward County Community
   College *A*
Southwestern College *B*
Tabor College *B*
University of Kansas
   Lawrence *B*
   Medical Center *B*
Washburn University of Topeka *B*
Wichita State University *B*

Kentucky

Asbury College *B*
Brescia College *B*
Campbellsville College *B*
Cumberland College *B*
Eastern Kentucky University *A,B*
Hazard Community College *A*
Jefferson Community College *A*
Kentucky Wesleyan College *B*
Morehead State University *B*
Murray State University *A*
Northern Kentucky University *B*
Pikeville College *B*
Thomas More College *B*
University of Kentucky *B*
University of Louisville *C,B*
Western Kentucky University *B*

Louisiana

Louisiana State University Medical
   Center *B,M*
McNeese State University *B*
Northeast Louisiana University *B*
Northwestern State University *B*
Southern University in
   Shreveport *A*
Southern University and
   Agricultural and Mechanical
   College *B*

Maine

Eastern Maine Technical College *A*
University of Maine
   Augusta *A*
   Orono *M*
   Presque Isle *A*
University of New England *B*
Westbrook College *B*

Maryland

Allegany Community College *A*
Catonsville Community College *A*
Columbia Union College *A*
Essex Community College *A*
Harford Community College *A*
Montgomery College: Takoma Park
   Campus *A*
Towson State University *B*
University of Maryland:
   Baltimore *B*
Villa Julie College *A*

Massachusetts

American International College *B*
Anna Maria College for Men and
   Women *A,B*
Bay State College *A*
Boston University *C,B*
Bristol Community College *A*
Elms College *B*
Framingham State College *B*
Massachusetts Bay Community
   College *A*
Massasoit Community College *A*
Merrimack College *B*
Middlesex Community College *A*
Mount Wachusett Community
   College *A*
North Adams State College *B*
Northeastern University *A,B*
Springfield College *B*
Springfield Technical Community
   College *A*
Suffolk University *B*
University of Massachusetts
   Amherst *B*
   Boston *B*
   Dartmouth *B*
   Lowell *B*

Michigan

Alma College *B*
Central Michigan University *B*
Eastern Michigan University *B*
Ferris State University *A*
Kellogg Community College *A*
Lake Superior State University *B*
Lansing Community College *A*
Madonna University *B*
Michigan State University *B*
Michigan Technological
   University *B*
Northern Michigan University
   C,A,B
Oakland Community College *A*
Saginaw Valley State University *B*
University of Michigan: Flint *B*

Minnesota

Alexandria Technical College *A*
Bemidji State University *B*
College of St. Benedict *B*
Concordia College: Moorhead *B*
Hamline University *B*
Moorhead State University *B*
Normandale Community College *A*
Rochester Community College *A*
St. John's University *B*
St. Mary's College of Minnesota *B*
St. Paul Technical College *A*
University of Minnesota: Twin
   Cities *B*

Mississippi

Hinds Community College *A*
Meridian Community College *A*
Mississippi College *B*
Mississippi Delta Community
   College *A*
Mississippi Gulf Coast Community
   College: Jackson County
   Campus *A*
Mississippi State University *B*
Northeast Mississippi Community
   College *A*
University of Mississippi Medical
   Center *B*
University of Southern Mississippi
   B,M

Missouri

Avila College *B*
Central Missouri State University *B*
College of the Ozarks *B*
Culver-Stockton College *B*
Evangel College *A*
Fontbonne College *B*
Lindenwood College *B*
Missouri Southern State College *B*
Missouri Western State College *B*
Rockhurst College *B*
St. Louis Community College at
   Forest Park *C,A*
St. Louis University *B*
Southwest Missouri State
   University *B*
Three Rivers Community College *A*
University of Missouri
   Columbia *B*
   Kansas City *B*
William Jewell College *B*

Montana

Carroll College *B*
University of Montana *B*

Nebraska

Chadron State College *B*
College of St. Mary *B*
Dana College *B*
Southeast Community College:
   Lincoln Campus *A*
University of Nebraska Medical
   Center *B*
Wayne State College *B*

Nevada

Community College of Southern
   Nevada *A*

New Jersey

Atlantic Community College *A*
Bergen Community College *A*
Bloomfield College *B*
Brookdale Community College *A*
Caldwell College *B*
Camden County College *A*
County College of Morris *A*
Fairleigh Dickinson University *B,M*
Felician College *A,B*
Jersey City State College *B*
Mercer County Community
   College *A*
Monmouth College *B*
St. Peter's College *B*
Thomas Edison State College *B*
University of Medicine and
   Dentistry of New Jersey: School
   of Health Related Professions
   C,B

New Mexico

Albuquerque Technical-Vocational
   Institute *A*

New Mexico Institute of Mining
and Technology *B*
New Mexico Junior College *A*
New Mexico State University *A,B*

New York

Broome Community College *A*
Canisius College *B*
City University of New York
College of Staten Island *A*
Hostos Community College *A*
New York City Technical
College *A*
Queensborough Community
College *A*
York College *B*
Clinton Community College *A*
College of St. Rose *B*
Daemen College *B*
Dutchess Community College *A*
Elmira College *B*
Erie Community College: North
Campus *A*
Fordham University *B*
Fulton-Montgomery Community
College *A*
Genesee Community College *A*
Herkimer County Community
College *A*
Houghton College *B*
Hudson Valley Community
College *A*
Iona College *B*
Jamestown Community College *A*
King's College *B*
Long Island University: Brooklyn
Campus *B*
Marist College *B*
Monroe Community College *A*
Mount St. Mary College *B*
Nassau Community College *A*
North Country Community
College *A*
Onondaga Community College *A*
Orange County Community
College *A*
Rochester Institute of Technology
A,B
Rockland Community College *A*
Russell Sage College *B*
St. Bonaventure University *B*
St. Francis College *B*
St. Thomas Aquinas College *B*
State University of New York
Buffalo *B,M*
College of Agriculture and
Technology at Cobleskill *A*
College of Agriculture and
Technology at Morrisville *A*
College of Technology at
Alfred *A*
College of Technology at
Canton *A*
College of Technology at
Farmingdale *A*
Health Science Center at
Syracuse *B,M*
Health Sciences Center at
Stony Brook *B*
Tompkins-Cortland Community
College *A*
Trocaire College *A*
Wagner College *B*
Westchester Community College *A*

North Carolina

Alamance Community College *A*
Appalachian State University *B*
Asheville Buncombe Technical
Community College *A*
Barton College *B*

Beaufort County Community
College *A*
Belmont Abbey College *B*
Campbell University *B*
Catawba College *B*
Coastal Carolina Community
College *A*
Duke University *C*
Durham Technical Community
College *C*
East Carolina University *B*
Elon College *B*
Greensboro College *B*
High Point University *B*
Lenoir-Rhyne College *B*
Mars Hill College *B*
Meredith College *B*
North Carolina State University *B*
North Carolina Wesleyan College *B*
Peace College *A*
St. Augustine's College *B*
Salem College *B*
Sandhills Community College *A*
Southwestern Community
College *A*
Wake Forest University *B*
Wake Technical Community
College *A*
Western Piedmont Community
College *A*
Winston-Salem State University *B*

North Dakota

Bismarck State College *A*
North Dakota State University *B*
University of Mary *B*
University of North Dakota *B,M*

Ohio

Ashland University *B*
Baldwin-Wallace College *B*
Cincinnati Technical College *A*
Clark State Community College *A*
College of Mount St. Joseph *B*
Columbus State Community
College *A*
Cuyahoga Community College:
Metropolitan Campus *A*
Defiance College *B*
Heidelberg College *B*
Jefferson Technical College *A*
Kent State University *B*
Lakeland Community College *A*
Lorain County Community
College *A*
Malone College *B*
Marion Technical College *C,A*
Miami University: Oxford
Campus *B*
Mount Union College *B*
Mount Vernon Nazarene College *B*
Muskingum College *B*
Ohio Northern University *B*
Ohio State University: Columbus
Campus *C,B,M*
Shawnee State University *A*
Stark Technical College *A*
University of Akron *B*
University of Cincinnati: Raymond
Walters College *A*
University of Dayton *B*
University of Findlay *B*
University of Rio Grande *A*
Walsh College *B*
Washington State Community
College *A*
Wilmington College *B*
Wright State University *B*
Youngstown State University *A,B*

Oklahoma

Connors State College *A*
East Central University *B*
Eastern Oklahoma State College *A*
Northwestern Oklahoma State
University *B*
Oklahoma State University *B*
Phillips University *B*
Redlands Community College *A*
Rose State College *A*
Southeastern Oklahoma State
University *B*
Tulsa Junior College *A*
University of Oklahoma
Health Sciences Center *B*
Norman *B*
University of Science and Arts of
Oklahoma *B*

Oregon

Oregon Health Sciences University
B,M
Oregon State University *B*
Portland Community College *A*

Pennsylvania

Allentown College of St. Francis de
Sales *B*
Bloomsburg University of
Pennsylvania *B*
California University of
Pennsylvania *B*
Cedar Crest College *B*
Cheyney University of
Pennsylvania *B*
College Misericordia *B*
Community College of Beaver
County *A*
Community College of
Philadelphia *A*
Elizabethtown College *B*
Geneva College *B*
Gwynedd-Mercy College *B*
Hahnemann University School of
Health Sciences and Humanities
A,B
Harcum Junior College *A*
Harrisburg Area Community
College *A*
Holy Family College *B*
Indiana University of
Pennsylvania *B*
Juniata College *B*
Keystone Junior College *A*
King's College *B*
Kutztown University of
Pennsylvania *B*
La Roche College *B*
Lebanon Valley College of
Pennsylvania *B*
Lock Haven University of
Pennsylvania *B*
Manor Junior College *A*
Mercyhurst College *B*
Montgomery County Community
College *A*
Moravian College *B*
Mount Aloysius College *A*
Northampton County Area
Community College *A*
Penn State University Park
Campus *A*
Philadelphia College of Pharmacy
and Science *B*
Reading Area Community
College *A*
St. Francis College *B*
St. Vincent College *B*
Seton Hill College *B*
Shippensburg University of
Pennsylvania *B*

Slippery Rock University of
Pennsylvania *B*
Thiel College *B*
Thomas Jefferson University:
College of Allied Health
Sciences *B*
Villanova University *B*
Washington and Jefferson College *B*
Westmoreland County Community
College *A*
Wilkes University *B*

Puerto Rico

Inter American University of Puerto
Rico
Arecibo Campus *A*
Metropolitan Campus *B,M*
San German Campus *B*
Pontifical Catholic University of
Puerto Rico *B*
University of Puerto Rico: Medical
Sciences Campus *B*

Rhode Island

Community College of Rhode
Island *A*
Rhode Island College *B*
Salve Regina University *B,M*
University of Rhode Island *B*

South Carolina

Central Wesleyan College *B*
Chesterfield-Marlboro Technical
College *A*
Columbia College *B*
Erskine College *B*
Florence-Darlington Technical
College *A*
Francis Marion College *B*
Greenville Technical College *A*
Lander College *B*
Midlands Technical College *A*
Tri-County Technical College *A*
Trident Technical College *A*
University of South Carolina *B*
Winthrop University *B*

South Dakota

Dakota State University *A*
Presentation College *A*

Tennessee

Austin Peay State University *B*
Belmont University *B*
Christian Brothers University *B*
Cleveland State Community
College *A*
Columbia State Community
College *A*
David Lipscomb University *B*
East Tennessee State University *A*
Hiwassee College *A*
Jackson State Community
College *A*
Lincoln Memorial University *B*
Motlow State Community
College *A*
Roane State Community College *A*
Shelby State Community College
C,A
Union University *B*
University of Tennessee:
Memphis *B*
Walters State Community
College *A*

Texas

Alvin Community College *A*
Amarillo College *A*
Austin Community College *A*
Baylor University *B*
Central Texas College *A*

Del Mar College *A*
East Texas Baptist University *A,B*
El Centro College *A*
El Paso Community College *A*
Hardin-Simmons University *B*
Houston Community College *A*
Howard College *C,A*
Incarnate Word College *B*
Kilgore College *A*
Lamar University—Beaumont *B*
McLennan Community College *A*
Midwestern State University *B*
Navarro College *A*
Odessa College *A*
St. Mary's University *B*
St. Philip's College *A*
Sam Houston State University *B*
Southwest Texas State University *B*
Southwestern Adventist College *B*
Southwestern University *B*
Tarleton State University *B*
Tarrant County Junior College *A*
Temple Junior College *A*
Texas Christian University *B,M*
Texas Southmost College *A*
University of Houston
    Clear Lake *B*
    Houston *B*
University of Mary Hardin-
    Baylor *B*
University of North Texas *B*
University of Texas
    Austin *B*
    El Paso *B*
    Medical Branch at
      Galveston *B*
    Southwestern Medical Center
      at Dallas Southwestern
      Allied Health Sciences
      School *B*
    Tyler *B*
Victoria College *A*
Wharton County Junior College *A*

Utah

Brigham Young University *B,M*
University of Utah *B,M*
Weber State University *A*

Vermont

Norwich University *B*
Trinity College of Vermont *B*

Virginia

Averett College *B*
Clinch Valley College of the
    University of Virginia *B*
Eastern Mennonite College *B*
Ferrum College *B*
James Madison University *B*
Lynchburg College *B*
Mary Baldwin College *B*
Northern Virginia Community
    College *A*
Old Dominion University *B*
Roanoke College *B*
Wytheville Community College *A*

Washington

Central Washington University *B*
Eastern Washington University *B*
Lower Columbia College *A*
Seattle University *B*
Shoreline Community College *A*
Walla Walla College *B*
Wenatchee Valley College *A*

West Virginia

College of West Virginia *A*
Davis and Elkins College *B*
Fairmont State College *A*
Marshall University *A,B*

Potomac State College of West
    Virginia University *A*
Salem-Teikyo University *B*
West Liberty State College *B*
West Virginia Northern Community
    College *A*

Wisconsin

Beloit College *B*
Carthage College *B*
Chippewa Valley Technical
    College *A*
Madison Area Technical College *A*
Marian College of Fond du Lac *B*
Marquette University *B*
St. Norbert College *B*
University of Wisconsin
    Eau Claire *B,M*
    La Crosse *B*
    Madison *B*
    Superior *B*
Western Wisconsin Technical
    College *A*

Wyoming

University of Wyoming *B*

Medical radiation dosimetry

Arkansas

University of Arkansas for Medical
    Sciences *B*
University of Central Arkansas *B*

California

Orange Coast College *C,A*
San Diego State University *M*

Colorado

Community College of Denver *C,A*

Connecticut

South Central Community
    College *A*

District of Columbia

Howard University *B*

Florida

Hillsborough Community College *C*
Santa Fe Community College *A*
Valencia Community College *A*

Georgia

Emory University *B*

Idaho

Idaho State University *B*

Illinois

University of Chicago *M*

Indiana

Indiana University—Purdue
    University at Indianapolis *B*

Iowa

Briar Cliff College *B*

Kansas

Kansas Newman College *B*

Kentucky

University of Kentucky *M*

Louisiana

McNeese State University *B*
Northwestern State University *B*

Maine

Southern Maine Technical
    College *A*

Massachusetts

Laboure College *C*

Michigan

Andrews University *B*
Wayne State University *B,M*

Minnesota

University of Minnesota: Twin
    Cities *M*

Mississippi

Mississippi College *B*
William Carey College *B*

Nebraska

University of Nebraska—Kearney *B*

New Mexico

University of New Mexico *C*

New York

Long Island University: C. W. Post
    Campus *B*
Manhattan College *B*
Nassau Community College *A*
State University of New York
    Health Science Center at
      Brooklyn *B*
    Health Science Center at
      Syracuse *A*

North Carolina

Greensboro College *B*
University of North Carolina at
    Chapel Hill *B*

Ohio

Kettering College of Medical
    Arts *A*
Ohio State University: Columbus
    Campus *M*

Oklahoma

Northeastern State University *B*
University of Oklahoma
    Health Sciences Center *B*
    Norman *B,M,D*

Oregon

Oregon Institute of Technology *B*

Tennessee

Austin Peay State University *B*
Chattanooga State Technical
    Community College *C*

Texas

Amarillo College *A*
El Paso Community College *A*
Galveston College *C*

Virginia

Averett College *B*
Virginia Commonwealth
    University *B*

Washington

University of Washington *M*

Wisconsin

University of Wisconsin: Madison
    M,D

Canada

McGill University *M*

Medical records administration

Alabama

Alabama Southern Community
    College *A*
Faulkner University *C*
Lurleen B. Wallace State Junior
    College *A*
Samford University *B*
Shelton State Community
    College *A*
University of Alabama in
    Birmingham *B*

Alaska

University of Alaska Anchorage *A*

Arizona

Pima Community College *C,A*

Arkansas

Arkansas Tech University *B*

California

Barstow College *C*
Chabot College *C,A*
City College of San Francisco *C,A*
Fresno City College *C,A*
Grossmont Community College *C,A*
Imperial Valley College *A*
San Diego Mesa College *C,A*
Southwestern College *A*

Colorado

Denver Technical College *C*
Regis College of Regis University *B*

Florida

Daytona Beach Community
    College *A*
Florida Agricultural and Mechanical
    University *B*
Florida International University *B*
Gulf Coast Community College *A*
Indian River Community College *A*
Miami-Dade Community College *A*
University of Central Florida *B*

Georgia

Atlanta Metropolitan College *A*
Brewton-Parker College *A*
Clayton State College *A*
Darton College *A*
Emory University *B*
Floyd College *A*
Gainesville College *A*
Georgia State University *B*
Medical College of Georgia *B*
Middle Georgia College *A*

Idaho

Boise State University *A,B*

Illinois

Chicago State University *B*
Illinois Central College *A*
Illinois State University *B*
Shawnee Community College *C,A*
University of Illinois at Chicago *B*

Indiana

Indiana University—Purdue
    University at Indianapolis *B*
Vincennes University *A*

Iowa

Northeast Iowa Community
    College *A*

Kansas

Hutchinson Community College *A*
University of Kansas
    Lawrence *B*
    Medical Center *B*
Washburn University of Topeka *A*
Wichita State University *B*

Kentucky

Eastern Kentucky University *A,B*
Franklin College *C*

Louisiana

Louisiana Tech University *B*
University of Southwestern
    Louisiana *B*

Maine

University of Maine *A*

Maryland

Essex Community College *A*

Michigan

Baker College
    Auburn Hills *A*
    Mount Clemens *A*
    Port Huron *A*
Ferris State University *B*
Lansing Community College *A*

Minnesota

College of St. Scholastica *B*
Moorhead State University *A*
Willmar Technical College *C*

Mississippi

University of Mississippi
    Medical Center *B*
    University *B*

Missouri

St. Louis University *B*
Stephens College *B*

Nebraska

College of St. Mary *A,B*
Southeast Community College:
    Beatrice Campus *C*

Nevada

Northern Nevada Community
    College *C*

New Hampshire

New Hampshire Technical College:
    Manchester *C,A*

New Jersey

Kean College of New Jersey *B*

New York

Adirondack Community College *A*
City University of New York:
    Kingsborough Community
    College *A*
Ithaca College *B*
Long Island University: C. W. Post
    Campus *B*
Mohawk Valley Community
    College *A*
Onondaga Community College *A*
Pace University *B*
State University of New York
    Health Science Center at
    Brooklyn *C,B*
    Institute of Technology at
    Utica/Rome *B*
Touro College *B*

North Carolina

Central Piedmont Community
    College *A*
Chowan College *A*
Davidson County Community
    College *A*
East Carolina University *B*
Edgecombe Community College *A*
Guilford Technical Community
    College *A*
Western Carolina University *B*

Ohio

Bowling Green State University:
    Firelands College *A*
Bradford School *C*
Columbus State Community
    College *A*
Cuyahoga Community College:
    Metropolitan Campus *A*
Hocking Technical College *A*
Ohio State University: Columbus
    Campus *B,M*
University of Toledo *A*

Oklahoma

Rose State College *A*
Southwestern Oklahoma State
    University *B*

Oregon

Central Oregon Community College
    C,A
Portland Community College *A*

Pennsylvania

Community College of
    Philadelphia *A*
Duquesne University *B,M*
Gwynedd-Mercy College *A,B*
Lehigh County Community College
    C,A
Pennsylvania Institute of
    Technology *C,A*
Temple University *B*
University of Pittsburgh *B*
York College of Pennsylvania *B*

Puerto Rico

Inter American University of Puerto
    Rico: San German Campus *A*
Puerto Rico Junior College *A*
Universidad Adventista de las
    Antillas *A*
University of Puerto Rico: Medical
    Sciences Campus *M*

South Carolina

Trident Technical College *C*

South Dakota

Dakota State University *A,B*
National College *A*

Tennessee

Carson-Newman College *B*
Tennessee State University *B*
Trevecca Nazarene College *A*
Union University *B*
University of Tennessee
    Knoxville *B*
    Memphis *B*

Texas

Central Texas College *C*
El Centro College *A*
Lee College *C,A*
Southwest Texas State University *B*
Texas Southern University *B*
Texas Woman's University *B*
University of Texas Medical Branch
    at Galveston *B*

Utah

Weber State University *A*

Virginia

Mountain Empire Community
    College *C*
Norfolk State University *B*
Northern Virginia Community
    College *A*
Tidewater Community College *A*
Wytheville Community College *C*

Washington

Clark College *C,A*
Shoreline Community College *A*

West Virginia

Marshall University *A*

Wisconsin

Chippewa Valley Technical
    College *A*
Northeast Wisconsin Technical
    College *A*
University of Wisconsin:
    Milwaukee *B*

Medical records technology

Alabama

Alabama Southern Community
    College *A*
Chattahoochee Valley Community
    College *A*
Enterprise State Junior College *A*
Faulkner University *A*
Gadsden State Community
    College *A*
George C. Wallace State
    Community College at Selma *A*
James H. Faulkner State
    Community College *A*
Jefferson State Community
    College *A*
John C. Calhoun State Community
    College *A*
Lawson State Community
    College *A*
Livingston University *A*
Lurleen B. Wallace State Junior
    College *A*
Northeast Alabama State Junior
    College *A*
Shelton State Community
    College *A*
Shoals Community College *A*
Southern Union State Junior
    College *A*
University of Alabama in
    Birmingham *C*
Walker College *A*
Wallace State Community College
    at Hanceville *A*

Arizona

Pima Community College *C*

Arkansas

Garland County Community
    College *A*
Phillips County Community
    College *A*
University of Central Arkansas *B*

California

Cerritos Community College *A*
Chabot College *C,A*

Charles R. Drew University: College
    of Allied Health *C,A*
City College of San Francisco *C,A*
Cosumnes River College *C,A*
East Los Angeles College *C,A*
El Camino College *C,A*
Fresno City College *A*
Grossmont Community College *C,A*
Los Angeles City College *A*
Mount St. Mary's College *C*
Orange Coast College *C,A*
San Diego Mesa College *A*
Southwestern College *A*
Ventura College *A*

Colorado

Arapahoe Community College *A*
Denver Technical College *C,A*

Connecticut

Briarwood College *C,A*

Florida

Broward Community College *A*
Daytona Beach Community
    College *A*
Florida Agricultural and Mechanical
    University *B*
Gulf Coast Community College *A*
Indian River Community College *A*
Miami-Dade Community College
    C,A
Pensacola Junior College *A*
St. Petersburg Junior College *A*
Seminole Community College *C*

Georgia

Atlanta Metropolitan College *A*
Brewton-Parker College *A*
Clark Atlanta University *B*
Darton College *A*
DeKalb College *A*
Gainesville College *A*
Medical College of Georgia *A*
Morris Brown College *B*

Idaho

Boise State University *A*
Idaho State University *B*
Lewis Clark State College *A*

Illinois

Belleville Area College *A*
City Colleges of Chicago: Malcolm
    X College *A*
College of DuPage *C,A*
College of Lake County *C,A*
Illinois Central College *C,A*
Moraine Valley Community
    College *A*
Oakton Community College *C,A*
Robert Morris College: Chicago *A*

Indiana

Indiana University
    Bloomington *B*
    Kokomo *A*
    Northwest *A*
Indiana University—Purdue
    University at Fort Wayne *A*
Vincennes University *A*

Iowa

Indian Hills Community College
    C,A
Kirkwood Community College *A*
Northeast Iowa Community
    College *A*
Waldorf College *A*

Kansas

Dodge City Community College
C,A
Hutchinson Community College A
Johnson County Community
College A
Washburn University of Topeka A

Kentucky

Eastern Kentucky University A,B
Franklin College C
Western Kentucky University C,A

Louisiana

Louisiana Tech University A
Southern University in
Shreveport A

Maine

University of Maine A

Maryland

Hagerstown Business College C,A
Montgomery College: Takoma Park
Campus A
New Community College of
Baltimore C,A
Prince George's Community
College A

Massachusetts

Holyoke Community College C,A
Laboure College C,A
Massachusetts Bay Community
College C,A
Northeastern University A
Northern Essex Community College
C,A

Michigan

Baker College
Flint A
Mount Clemens A
Muskegon A
Port Huron A
Cleary College A
Davenport College of Business A
Ferris State University A
Henry Ford Community College A
Muskegon Community College A
Schoolcraft College A

Minnesota

Anoka-Ramsey Community
College A
Moorhead State University A
St. Mary's Campus of the College of
St. Catherine A
Vermilion Community College A

Mississippi

Hinds Community College A
Meridian Community College A
Mississippi Gulf Coast Community
College: Jackson County
Campus A
Northeast Mississippi Community
College A
Rust College B

Missouri

Penn Valley Community College A
St. Charles Community College A
St. Louis University B
State Fair Community College A

Montana

Carroll College B

Nebraska

College of St. Mary A

Nevada

Community College of Southern
Nevada A
Truckee Meadows Community
College C

New Hampshire

New Hampshire Technical College:
Manchester C

New Jersey

Burlington County College A

New Mexico

Eastern New Mexico University
Portales B
Roswell Campus C

New York

Adirondack Community College A
Broome Community College A
City University of New York
Borough of Manhattan
Community College A
Kingsborough Community
College A
Fulton-Montgomery Community
College C,A
Long Island University: C. W. Post
Campus B,M
Mohawk Valley Community
College A
Monroe Community College A
Onondaga Community College A
Rochester Institute of
Technology A
Rockland Community College A
State University of New York
College of Technology at
Alfred A
Institute of Technology at
Utica/Rome B
Touro College B
Trocaire College A
Utica School of Commerce A

North Carolina

Central Piedmont Community
College C,A
Chowan College A
Edgecombe Community College A
Forsyth Technical Community
College C
Pitt Community College A
Rockingham Community College A

North Dakota

North Dakota State College of
Science A

Ohio

Bowling Green State University:
Firelands College A
Cincinnati Metropolitan College A
Cincinnati Technical College A
Columbus State Community
College A
Cuyahoga Community College:
Metropolitan Campus A
Hocking Technical College A
Miami-Jacobs College A
Sinclair Community College C,A
Stark Technical College A
University of Toledo C,A

Oklahoma

Bacone College A
East Central University B
Rose State College A

Oregon

Central Oregon Community College
C,A
Chemeketa Community College C
Lane Community College C
Portland Community College C,A
Rogue Community College C

Pennsylvania

Community College of
Philadelphia A
Gannon University A
Gwynedd-Mercy College A,B
Lehigh County Community College
C,A
Mercyhurst College B
Pennsylvania Institute of
Technology C,A

Puerto Rico

Inter American University of Puerto
Rico: Arecibo Campus C
Universidad Metropolitana A

South Carolina

Columbia Junior College of
Business C
Florence-Darlington Technical
College A
Midlands Technical College A

South Dakota

Dakota State University A,B
Kilian Community College A
Presentation College A

Tennessee

Bristol University A
Chattanooga State Technical
Community College A
Motlow State Community
College A
Roane State Community College A
Tennessee State University A
Trevecca Nazarene College A
Volunteer State Community
College A

Texas

Amarillo College C
Central Texas College C
El Centro College A
El Paso Community College A
Galveston College A
Houston Community College A
Howard College C
Kilgore College A
Laredo Junior College A
St. Philip's College C,A
South Plains College A
Tarrant County Junior College C,A
Texas State Technical College:
Harlingen C,A
Texas Woman's University B
University of Texas Health Science
Center at Houston B
Wharton County Junior College A

Utah

Stevens-Henager College of
Business A
Weber State University A

Virginia

College of Health Sciences A
National Business College A
Northern Virginia Community
College A
Tidewater Community College A
Virginia Commonwealth University
B,M

Washington

Clark College C,A
Green River Community College A
Seattle University B
Shoreline Community College A
Spokane Community College C,A
Tacoma Community College A
Wenatchee Valley College A

West Virginia

Fairmont State College A
Marshall University A

Wisconsin

Chippewa Valley Technical
College A
Moraine Park Technical College A
Western Wisconsin Technical
College A

Medical secretary

Alabama

Draughons Junior College C
Gadsden State Community
College A
James H. Faulkner State
Community College A
Lawson State Community
College A
Shoals Community College C
Southern Union State Junior
College A
Walker State Technical College A
Wallace State Community College
at Hanceville A

Alaska

University of Alaska Anchorage C

Arizona

Cochise College A
Pima Community College A
Yavapai College C

Arkansas

Garland County Community
College C
Phillips County Community
College C
Shorter College A
University of Central Arkansas C

California

Barstow College C
Chaffey Community College A
City College of San Francisco A
Crafton Hills College A
Fresno City College C,A
Heald College: Sacramento C,A
Imperial Valley College C,A
La Sierra University A
Lake Tahoe Community College A
Lassen College C
Long Beach City College C,A
Los Angeles City College C,A
Los Angeles Harbor College C,A
Merced College C,A
Monterey Peninsula College C,A
Mount San Antonio College C,A
Napa Valley College C,A
Ohlone College C,A
Orange Coast College C
Pacific Union College A
Palomar College C
Pasadena City College C,A
Phillips Junior College
Condie Campus A
Fresno Campus C,A

387

San Diego Mesa College *C,A*
Santa Rosa Junior College *C*
Sierra College *C,A*
Skyline College *C*
Ventura College *C,A*
West Hills Community College *C,A*
Yuba College *C*

Colorado

Community College of Denver *A*
Denver Technical College *C*
Mesa State College *C,A*
Northeastern Junior College *A*
Red Rocks Community College *A*

Connecticut

Briarwood College *C,A*
Manchester Community College *A*
Mattatuck Community College *A*
Middlesex Community College *A*
Northwestern Connecticut
  Community College *A*
Quinebaug Valley Community
  College *C,A*
South Central Community
  College *A*
Tunxis Community College *C,A*

Delaware

Delaware Technical and
  Community College: Stanton/
  Wilmington Campus *A*
Goldey-Beacom College *A*

Florida

Broward Community College *A*
Central Florida Community
  College *A*
Daytona Beach Community
  College *A*
Florida Community College at
  Jacksonville *C*
Florida Keys Community College *A*
Hillsborough Community College *A*
Indian River Community College *A*
Jones College *A*
Miami-Dade Community College *A*
Pensacola Junior College *A*
Phillips Junior College:
  Melbourne *C*
Santa Fe Community College *A*
South College: Palm Beach
  Campus *C*
South Florida Community
  College *C*
Valencia Community College *A*

Georgia

Augusta Technical Institute *C*
Brewton-Parker College *A*
DeKalb College *A*
DeKalb Technical Institute *C*
Meadows College of Business *A*

Idaho

College of Southern Idaho *C,A*
Idaho State University *C*
ITT Technical Institute: Boise *C*
Lewis Clark State College *A*
North Idaho College *A*

Illinois

Belleville Area College *A*
Black Hawk College *A*
City Colleges of Chicago
    Chicago City-Wide College *C*
    Richard J. Daley College *C*
Elgin Community College *C,A*
Gem City College *C*
Illinois Eastern Community
  Colleges: Olney Central College
  C,A

John A. Logan College *C*
Joliet Junior College *C*
Kishwaukee College *C*
Lake Land College *A*
Midstate College *A*
Morton College *A*
Oakton Community College *C*
Parkland College *A*
Rend Lake College *A*
Richland Community College *A*
Rock Valley College *A*
Shawnee Community College *A*
Southern Illinois University at
  Carbondale *A*
Waubonsee Community College *C*
William Rainey Harper College *C,A*

Indiana

Vincennes University *A*

Iowa

American Institute of Business *A*
American Institute of Commerce *C*
Des Moines Area Community
  College *A*
Hawkeye Institute of Technology *C*
Iowa Lakes Community College *C*
Iowa Western Community
  College *A*
Kirkwood Community College *C*
North Iowa Area Community
  College *C,A*
Waldorf College *A*

Kansas

Butler County Community
  College *A*
Central College *A*
Cloud County Community
  College *A*
Coffeyville Community College *C,A*
Colby Community College *A*
Dodge City Community College *A*
Hesston College *A*
Highland Community College *A*
Hutchinson Community College *A*
Johnson County Community
  College *A*
Labette Community College *A*
Pratt Community College *C,A*
Tabor College *B*
Washburn University of Topeka *A*

Kentucky

Hazard Community College *A*
Lees College *A*
Owensboro Junior College of
  Business *C,A*
St. Catharine College *A*
Sue Bennett College *A*

Louisiana

Phillips Junior College: New
  Orleans *C*

Maine

Beal College *A*
Casco Bay College *A*
Husson College *A*
Kennebec Valley Technical
  College *A*
Thomas College *A*

Maryland

Allegany Community College *A*
Catonsville Community College *A*
Chesapeake College *A*
Columbia Union College *A*
Frederick Community College *A*
Hagerstown Business College *A*
Howard Community College *C,A*

Montgomery College: Takoma Park
  Campus *C,A*
New Community College of
  Baltimore *A*
Prince George's Community College
  C,A
Villa Julie College *A*
Wor-Wic Tech Community
  College *A*

Massachusetts

Aquinas College at Milton *A*
Aquinas College at Newton *C,A*
Atlantic Union College *A*
Bay State College *A*
Berkshire Community College *A*
Bristol Community College *A*
Bunker Hill Community College *A*
Cape Cod Community College *C,A*
Endicott College *A*
Holyoke Community College *A*
Marian Court Junior College *A*
Massasoit Community College *A*
Middlesex Community College *A*
North Shore Community College *A*
Northern Essex Community
  College *A*
Quincy College *C,A*
Quinsigamond Community
  College *A*
Roxbury Community College *A*
Springfield Technical Community
  College *A*

Michigan

Baker College
    Auburn Hills *C,A*
    Cadillac *C,A*
    Flint *C,A*
    Mount Clemens *A*
    Muskegon *A*
    Owosso *A*
    Port Huron *A*
Central Michigan University *B*
Charles Stewart Mott Community
  College *A*
Davenport College of Business *A*
Delta College *A*
Detroit College of Business *A*
Grand Rapids Baptist College and
  Seminary *A*
Grand Rapids Community
  College *A*
Great Lakes Junior College of
  Business *A*
Jackson Community College *C,A*
Jordan College *C,A*
Kalamazoo Valley Community
  College *C,A*
Kellogg Community College *A*
Kirtland Community College *A*
Lake Superior State University *A*
Lansing Community College *A*
Macomb Community College *C,A*
Montcalm Community College *A*
Northern Michigan University *A*
Northwestern Michigan College *A*
St. Clair County Community
  College *C,A*
Southwestern Michigan College *A*

Minnesota

Alexandria Technical College *C*
Anoka-Ramsey Community
  College *A*
Inver Hills Community College *C,A*
Itasca Community College:
  Arrowhead Region *A*
Rainy River Community College *C*
Rochester Community College *C,A*
St. Mary's Campus of the College of
  St. Catherine *C*

St. Paul Technical College *C*
Vermilion Community College *A*
Willmar Community College *A*
Willmar Technical College *C,A*

Mississippi

Phillips Junior College of Jackson *C*

Missouri

East Central College *C,A*
Jefferson College *A*
Longview Community College *A*
Maple Woods Community
  College *A*
Moberly Area Community
  College *A*
Northwest Missouri State
  University *C*
Penn Valley Community College *C*
Phillips Junior College *C*
Southeast Missouri State
  University *C*
Southwest Missouri State
  University *A*
State Fair Community College *C,A*

Montana

Dawson Community College *A*
Miles Community College *A*
Western Montana College of the
  University of Montana *A*

Nebraska

Central Community College *C,A*
Lincoln School of Commerce *C*
McCook Community College *A*
Metropolitan Community College
  C,A
Northeast Community College *A*
Southeast Community College
    Beatrice Campus *A*
    Lincoln Campus *A*

Nevada

Northern Nevada Community
  College *C*
Truckee Meadows Community
  College *A*

New Hampshire

Hesser College *C*
New Hampshire Technical College:
  Manchester *C,A*

New Jersey

Essex County College *A*
Gloucester County College *A*
Katharine Gibbs School *C*

New Mexico

Parks College *C*
Western New Mexico University
  C,A

New York

Adirondack Community College *A*
Bryant & Stratton Business
  Institute: Buffalo *C,A*
Central City Business Institute *C,A*
City University of New York
    Hostos Community College *A*
    New York City Technical
      College *A*
Community College of the Finger
  Lakes *A*
Concordia College *A*
Fulton-Montgomery Community
  College *A*
Herkimer County Community
  College *A*
Hilbert College *A*

Hudson Valley Community
College *A*
Jamestown Business College *C,A*
Jefferson Community College *C,A*
Mater Dei College *A*
Mohawk Valley Community
College *A*
Nassau Community College *A*
Rochester Business Institute *A*
State University of New York
College of Agriculture and
Technology at Morrisville *A*
College of Technology at
Farmingdale *A*
Suffolk County Community College
Selden *A*
Western Campus *A*
Trocaire College *A*
Utica School of Commerce *A*
Westchester Business Institute *A*

North Carolina

Alamance Community College *A*
Anson Community College *A*
Blue Ridge Community College *C*
Caldwell Community College and
Technical Institute *A*
Carteret Community College *A*
Cecils College *A*
Central Carolina Community
College *A*
Central Piedmont Community
College *A*
Cleveland Community College *A*
Coastal Carolina Community
College *A*
College of the Albemarle *A*
Craven Community College *A*
Durham Technical Community
College *A*
Edgecombe Community College *A*
Gaston College *A*
Guilford Technical Community
College *A*
Johnston Community College *A*
Louisburg College *A*
Mayland Community College *A*
Mount Olive College *A*
Nash Community College *A*
Pamlico Community College *A*
Piedmont Community College *A*
Pitt Community College *A*
Rockingham Community College *A*
Sandhills Community College *A*
Stanly Community College *A*
Surry Community College *A*
Wayne Community College *A*
Western Piedmont Community
College *A*

North Dakota

Bismarck State College *C,A*
Dickinson State University *A*
Minot State University *A*
North Dakota State College of
Science *A*
North Dakota State University:
Bottineau and Institute of
Forestry *A*
University of North Dakota
Lake Region *C,A*
Williston *A*

Ohio

Bowling Green State University:
Firelands College *C*
Bradford School *C*
Bryant & Stratton Business
Institute: Great Northern *C*
Central Ohio Technical College *A*
Cincinnati Metropolitan College *A*
Clark State Community College *A*

Columbus State Community
College *A*
Hocking Technical College *C*
Jefferson Technical College *A*
Lakeland Community College *A*
Marion Technical College *A*
Miami-Jacobs College *A*
Northwest Technical College *A*
Northwestern College *A*
Ohio University: Chillicothe
Campus *A*
Ohio Valley Business College *C*
Sinclair Community College *C*
Terra Technical College *A*
University of Akron *A*
University of Cincinnati
Access Colleges *A*
Clermont College *A*
Raymond Walters College *A*
University of Rio Grande *A*
University of Toledo *A*
Washington State Community
College *A*
Wright State University: Lake
Campus *A*

Oklahoma

Oklahoma State University
Technical Branch: Okmulgee *A*
Rose State College *A*
Southwestern Oklahoma State
University *C*
Tulsa Junior College *C,A*

Oregon

Central Oregon Community
College *A*
Chemeketa Community College *A*
Clackamas Community College *C*
Linn-Benton Community College
C,A
Mount Hood Community
College *A*
Rogue Community College *C*
Southwestern Oregon Community
College *A*
Treasure Valley Community
College *A*
Umpqua Community College *A*

Pennsylvania

Bucks County Community
College *A*
Butler County Community
College *A*
Central Pennsylvania Business
School *A*
Churchman Business School *A*
Community College of Beaver
County *A*
DuBois Business College *A*
Gannon University *A*
Lackawanna Junior College *A*
Lehigh County Community
College *A*
Luzerne County Community
College *A*
Manor Junior College *C,A*
Mercyhurst College *A*
Montgomery County Community
College *C,A*
Northampton County Area
Community College *C,A*
Peirce Junior College *A*
Pennsylvania College of
Technology *A*
Reading Area Community College
C,A
Robert Morris College *A*
Waynesburg College *A*
Westmoreland County Community
College *A*

York College of Pennsylvania *A*

Puerto Rico

Caribbean University *A*
Universidad Adventista de las
Antillas *A*

Rhode Island

Community College of Rhode
Island *A*
Johnson & Wales University *A*
New England Institute of
Technology *A*

South Carolina

Aiken Technical College *C*
Greenville Technical College *A*
Midlands Technical College *C,A*
Williamsburg Technical College *C*

South Dakota

Kilian Community College *A*
Mitchell Vocational Technical
Institute *C,A*
National College *A*
Presentation College *A*
Western Dakota Vocational
Technical Institute *C*

Tennessee

Chattanooga State Technical
Community College *A*
Knoxville Business College *C*
Pellissippi State Technical
Community College *A*
Roane State Community College
C,A
Shelby State Community College *A*
Southern College of Seventh-day
Adventists *A*

Texas

Alvin Community College *A*
Amarillo College *A*
Austin Community College *A*
Brazosport College *C,A*
Central Texas College *C*
Collin County Community College
District *C,A*
Houston Community College *C*
Lee College *C,A*
McLennan Community College *A*
Northeast Texas Community
College *C,A*
St. Philip's College *C,A*
South Plains College *A*
Southwestern Adventist College *A*
Temple Junior College *A*
Texas State Technical College:
Harlingen *A*

Utah

LDS Business College *A*
Phillips Junior College: Salt Lake
City Campus *A*
Stevens-Henager College of
Business *A*
Utah Valley Community College
C,A

Vermont

Champlain College *A*

Virginia

Bluefield College *A*
Commonwealth College *A*
Mountain Empire Community
College *A*
National Business College *A*

Washington

Big Bend Community College *A*
Centralia College *A*
Clark College *C,A*
Columbia Basin College *C*
Edmonds Community College *C*
Grays Harbor College *A*
Green River Community College *A*
Lower Columbia College *C,A*
Pierce College *C,A*
Shoreline Community College *C,A*
South Puget Sound Community
College *A*
Spokane Community College *C,A*
Tacoma Community College *A*
Walla Walla Community College *A*
Wenatchee Valley College *A*
Yakima Valley Community College
C,A

West Virginia

Bluefield State College *A*
College of West Virginia *A*
Marshall University *A*
Potomac State College of West
Virginia University *A*
West Virginia Institute of
Technology *C,A*
West Virginia State College *A*

Wisconsin

Chippewa Valley Technical
College *A*
Fox Valley Technical College *C*
Madison Junior College of
Business *A*
Milwaukee College of Business *C,A*
Moraine Park Technical College *A*
Northeast Wisconsin Technical
College *A*
Stratton College *A*
Western Wisconsin Technical
College *A*

Wyoming

Eastern Wyoming College *A*

Medical social work

California

California State University: Fresno
B,M
University of California: Los
Angeles *M*

Connecticut

Sacred Heart University *B*

Illinois

Loyola University of Chicago *M*

Massachusetts

Mount Ida College *A*
Smith College *M,D,W*

Missouri

St. Louis University *B,M*

New Jersey

Bloomfield College *B*
Stockton State College *B*

New Mexico

New Mexico Highlands University
B,M

North Carolina

University of North Carolina at
Chapel Hill *M*

Ohio
Ohio University *B*

Pennsylvania
University of Pittsburgh *D*

Texas
University of Texas Southwestern
Medical Center at Dallas
Southwestern Allied Health
Sciences School *B,M*

Virginia
Virginia Commonwealth University
B,M,D

Washington
University of Washington *M*

Canada
McGill University *M,D*

Medical specialties

Alabama
University of Alabama in
Birmingham *W*

California
Azusa Pacific University *W*
University of California: San
Francisco *W*

Colorado
University of Colorado Health
Sciences Center *W*

District of Columbia
Georgetown University *W*

Florida
University of Miami *D*

Georgia
Emory University *D*
Medical College of Georgia *W*

Illinois
Loyola University of Chicago *W*
Northwestern University *W*
University of Illinois at Chicago *W*

Indiana
Indiana University—Purdue
University at Indianapolis *W*

Iowa
University of Iowa *M,D*

Kansas
University of Kansas
Lawrence *W*
Medical Center *W*

Kentucky
University of Kentucky *W*
University of Louisville *W*

Louisiana
Louisiana State University Medical
Center *W*
Tulane University *W*

Maryland
University of Maryland: Baltimore
M,D

Massachusetts
Boston University *W*
Harvard University *D*
Tufts University *W*

Michigan
University of Michigan *M,D,W*

Minnesota
University of Minnesota: Twin
Cities *M,D*

Mississippi
University of Mississippi
Medical Center *W*
University *D*

Missouri
St. Louis University *W*

Nebraska
University of Nebraska Medical
Center *W*

New Hampshire
Dartmouth College *W*

New York
New York University *W*
State University of New York
Health Science Center at
Brooklyn *W*
Health Science Center at
Syracuse *W*
University of Rochester *W*

North Carolina
Duke University *W*
University of North Carolina at
Chapel Hill *W*

Ohio
Case Western Reserve
University *W*
Ohio State University: Columbus
Campus *M,D*
University of Cincinnati *M,D*
Wright State University *D*

Pennsylvania
Reading Area Community
College *C*
Temple University *M,D*
University of Pennsylvania *M,D*
University of Pittsburgh *M,D,W*

Puerto Rico
University of Puerto Rico: Medical
Sciences Campus *W*

Tennessee
Vanderbilt University *W*

Texas
Texas A&M University *M,D*
University of Texas Health Science
Center at San Antonio *W*

Utah
University of Utah *W*

Virginia
Virginia Commonwealth University
M,D,W

Washington
University of Washington *M,D*

Wisconsin
Medical College of Wisconsin *W*

Canada
McGill University *W*

Medicine (M.D.)

Alabama
University of Alabama
Birmingham *F*
Tuscaloosa *F*
University of South Alabama *F*

Arizona
University of Arizona *F*

Arkansas
University of Arkansas
Little Rock *F*
Medical Sciences *F*

California
La Sierra University *F*
Stanford University *F*
University of California
Davis *F*
Irvine *F*
Los Angeles *F*
San Diego *F*
San Francisco *F*
University of Southern California *F*

Colorado
University of Colorado Health
Sciences Center *F*

Connecticut
University of Connecticut *F*
Yale University *F*

District of Columbia
George Washington University *F*
Georgetown University *F*
Howard University *F*

Florida
University of Florida *F*
University of Miami *F*
University of South Florida *F*

Georgia
Emory University *F*
Medical College of Georgia *F*
Mercer University *F*

Hawaii
University of Hawaii at Manoa *F*

Illinois
Loyola University of Chicago *F*
Northwestern University *F*
Rush University *F*
Southern Illinois University at
Carbondale *F*
University of Chicago *F*
University of Health Sciences: The
Chicago Medical School *F*
University of Illinois at Chicago *F*

Indiana
Indiana University—Purdue
University at Indianapolis *F*

Iowa
University of Iowa *F*

Kansas
University of Kansas Medical
Center *F*

Kentucky
University of Kentucky *F*
University of Louisville *F*

Louisiana
Louisiana State University Medical
Center *F*
Tulane University *F*

Maryland
Johns Hopkins University *F*
Uniformed Services University of
the Health Sciences *F*
University of Maryland:
Baltimore *F*

Massachusetts
Boston University *F*
Harvard University *F*
Tufts University *F*

Michigan
Michigan State University *F*
University of Michigan *F*
Wayne State University *F*

Minnesota
University of Minnesota: Twin
Cities *F*

Mississippi
University of Mississippi
Medical Center *F*
University *F*

Missouri
St. Louis University *F*
University of Missouri
Columbia *F*
Kansas City *F*
Washington University *F*

Nebraska
Creighton University *F*
University of Nebraska Medical
Center *F*

Nevada
University of Nevada: Reno *F*

New Hampshire
Dartmouth College *F*

New Mexico
University of New Mexico *F*
Western New Mexico University *F*

New York
Cornell University *F*
New York University *F*
State University of New York
Buffalo *F*
Health Science Center at
Brooklyn *F*
Health Science Center at
Syracuse *F*
Health Sciences Center at
Stony Brook *F*
University of Rochester *F*
Yeshiva University *F*

North Carolina
Duke University *F*
East Carolina University *F*
University of North Carolina at
Chapel Hill *F*
Wake Forest University *F*

North Dakota
University of North Dakota *F*

Ohio

Case Western Reserve University *F*
Kent State University *F*
Ohio State University: Columbus Campus *F*
University of Cincinnati *F*
Wright State University *F*

Oklahoma

University of Oklahoma Health Sciences Center *F*
Norman *F*

Oregon

Oregon Health Sciences University *F*

Pennsylvania

Medical College of Pennsylvania *F*
Temple University *F*
University of Pennsylvania *F*
University of Pittsburgh *F*

Puerto Rico

University of Puerto Rico: Medical Sciences Campus *F*

Rhode Island

Brown University *F*

South Carolina

University of South Carolina *F*

South Dakota

University of South Dakota *F*

Tennessee

East Tennessee State University *F*
Meharry Medical College *F*
University of Tennessee: Memphis *F*
Vanderbilt University *F*

Texas

Southwest Texas State University *F*
Texas A&M University *F*
Texas Tech University *F*
Texas Tech University Health Science Center *F*
University of Texas
Health Science Center at Houston *F*
Health Science Center at San Antonio *F*
Southwestern Medical Center at Dallas Southwestern Allied Health Sciences School *F*

Utah

Brigham Young University *F*
University of Utah *F*

Vermont

University of Vermont *F*

Virginia

University of Virginia *F*
Virginia Commonwealth University *F*

Washington

University of Washington *F*

West Virginia

Marshall University *F*
West Virginia University *F*

Wisconsin

Medical College of Wisconsin *F*
University of Wisconsin: Madison *F*

Canada

McGill University *F*

Medieval studies

California

California State University: Long Beach *C*
University of California
Davis *B*
Santa Barbara *B,M,D*
Santa Cruz *B*

Connecticut

Connecticut College *B*
University of Connecticut *M,D*
Wesleyan University *B*
Yale University *M,D*

Florida

New College of the University of South Florida *B*
University of Florida *M,D*

Georgia

Emory University *B*
University of Georgia *C,A,B*

Illinois

University of Chicago *B,M,D*

Indiana

Indiana University Bloomington *C*
Martin University *B*
Purdue University *B*
University of Notre Dame *B,M,D*

Louisiana

Tulane University *B*

Maryland

Johns Hopkins University *B,M,D*

Massachusetts

Boston College *M,D*
Hampshire College *B*
Mount Holyoke College *B*
Smith College *B*
Wellesley College *B*

Michigan

University of Michigan *B*
Western Michigan University *M*

Minnesota

College of St. Benedict *B*
St. John's University *B*

Missouri

Washington University *B*

New Hampshire

Plymouth State College of the University System of New Hampshire *B*

New York

City University of New York: City College *M*
Columbia University
Columbia College *B*
New York *D*
School of General Studies *M*
Cornell University *B,M,D*
Fordham University *B*
Manhattanville College *B*
New York University *B*
Sarah Lawrence College *B*

State University of New York at Binghamton *B*
Syracuse University *B*
Vassar College *B*

North Carolina

Duke University *B*

Ohio

Ohio State University: Columbus Campus *B*
University of Toledo *B*

Oregon

Reed College *B*

Pennsylvania

Carnegie Mellon University *M*
Penn State University Park Campus *B*

Rhode Island

Rhode Island College *B*

Tennessee

University of the South *B*
University of Tennessee: Knoxville *B*

Vermont

Marlboro College *B*

Washington

Seattle Central Community College *A*

West Virginia

West Virginia University *B*

Mental health/human services

Alabama

Auburn University *M,D*
Gadsden State Community College *A*
Shoals Community College *A*
Wallace State Community College at Hanceville *A*

Alaska

University of Alaska
Anchorage *A*
Fairbanks *A*

Arizona

Glendale Community College *A*
Pima Community College *C*
Rio Salado Community College *A*

California

Allan Hancock College *C,A*
California State University: Fullerton *B*
Cuesta College *A*
East Los Angeles College *C,A*
Fresno City College *A*
Los Angeles City College *A*
Los Angeles Trade and Technical College *A*
Mission College *A*
Mount San Antonio College *C,A*
Napa Valley College *C,A*
Pacific Oaks College *M*
Rio Hondo College *A*
Saddleback College *A*
Santa Rosa Junior College *C,A*
Ventura College *A*
Yuba College *A*

Colorado

Metropolitan State College of Denver *B*
Naropa Institute *M*
Red Rocks Community College *C*

Connecticut

Mattatuck Community College *C,A*
Middlesex Community College *A*
Quinebaug Valley Community College *A*
South Central Community College *A*
University of Bridgeport *A,B,M*

Delaware

Delaware Technical and Community College
Southern Campus *A*
Stanton/Wilmington Campus *A*
Terry Campus *A*

District of Columbia

Gallaudet University *M*

Florida

Barry University *M*
Daytona Beach Community College *A*
Gulf Coast Community College *C,A*
Hillsborough Community College *A*
Indian River Community College *A*
Palm Beach Community College *A*
Pasco-Hernando Community College *A*
St. Petersburg Junior College *A*

Georgia

Atlanta Metropolitan College *A*
Floyd College *A*
Georgia State University *B*
Mercer University *B*

Illinois

College of DuPage *C,A*
College of Lake County *C*
Elgin Community College *A*
Governors State University *B*
Illinois Eastern Community Colleges: Wabash Valley College *A*
Millikin University *B*
National-Louis University *B,M*
Prairie State College *A*
Waubonsee Community College *C,A*

Indiana

Indiana University—Purdue University at Fort Wayne *A*
Indiana Vocational Technical College
Central Indiana *A*
Eastcentral *A*
Northeast *C*

Iowa

Iowa Lakes Community College *A*

Kansas

Colby Community College *A*
Washburn University of Topeka *C,A*

Kentucky

Jefferson Community College *A*
Northern Kentucky University *A,B*

Louisiana

Northeast Louisiana University *M*
Southern University in
Shreveport *A*

Maine

University of Maine *A*
University of New England *B*

Maryland

Allegany Community College *A*
Catonsville Community College *A*
Chesapeake College *A*
Essex Community College *A*
Frederick Community College *A*
Montgomery College: Takoma Park
Campus *A*
New Community College of
Baltimore *A*

Massachusetts

Bay Path College *A*
Endicott College *A*
Holyoke Community College *A*
Lasell College *A,B*
Lesley College *B,M*
Massasoit Community College *A*
Middlesex Community College *A*
Mount Ida College *A*
North Shore Community College *A*
Northern Essex Community College
C,A
Simmons College *B*
Springfield College *B*
Springfield Technical Community
College *A*

Michigan

Lake Superior State University *A,B*
Lansing Community College *A*
Macomb Community College *C,A*
Oakland Community College *A*
St. Clair County Community
College *A*
St. Mary's College *B*

Minnesota

Inver Hills Community College *A*
Lakewood Community College *A*
Mesabi Community College:
Arrowhead Region *A*
Northland Community College *A*
Rainy River Community College *A*
Willmar Community College *A*

Mississippi

Hinds Community College *A*
Mississippi Gulf Coast Community
College: Jackson County
Campus *A*

Missouri

Fontbonne College *B*
Longview Community College *A*

Montana

Dawson Community College *A*
Dull Knife Memorial College *A*
Eastern Montana College *B*
Flathead Valley Community
College *A*
Stone Child College *A*

Nebraska

Central Community College *C,A*
Southeast Community College:
Lincoln Campus *C,A*
Wayne State College *B*
Western Nebraska Community
College: Scottsbluff Campus *A*

New Hampshire

Castle College *A*
New Hampshire Technical College:
Berlin *A*

New Jersey

Brookdale Community College *A*
Camden County College *A*

New Mexico

Northern New Mexico Community
College *A*

New York

City University of New York
Borough of Manhattan
Community College *A*
Kingsborough Community
College *A*
La Guardia Community
College *A*
Herkimer County Community
College *A*
Hilbert College *A*
Mohawk Valley Community
College *A*
Niagara County Community
College *A*
North Country Community
College *A*
Orange County Community
College *A*
Suffolk County Community College
Selden *A*
Western Campus *A*
Westchester Community College
C,A

North Carolina

Pitt Community College *A*
Sandhills Community College *A*
Wayne Community College *A*

Ohio

Chatfield College *A*
Columbus State Community
College *A*
Cuyahoga Community College:
Metropolitan Campus *A*
Kent State University
Ashtabula Regional Campus *A*
Salem Regional Campus *A*
Muskingum Area Technical
College *A*
North Central Technical College *A*
Ohio University: Chillicothe
Campus *A*
Sinclair Community College *A*
University of Toledo *A*

Oregon

Chemeketa Community College *A*
Mount Hood Community
College *A*

Pennsylvania

Bucks County Community
College *A*
Community College of
Philadelphia *A*
Hahnemann University School of
Health Sciences and Humanities
A,B
Manor Junior College *A*
Montgomery County Community
College *A*
Pennsylvania College of
Technology *A*
Reading Area Community
College *A*

Puerto Rico

University of Puerto Rico: Cayey
University College *B*

Rhode Island

Community College of Rhode
Island *A*

South Carolina

Midlands Technical College *A*
Trident Technical College *C*

South Dakota

Black Hills State University *B*
Dakota Wesleyan University *B*

Tennessee

Carson-Newman College *B*
Cleveland State Community
College *A*

Texas

Alvin Community College *C,A*
Angelina College *A*
Austin Community College *C,A*
Collin County Community College
District *C*
Del Mar College *A*
El Paso Community College *A*
Houston Community College *C,A*
McLennan Community College *C,A*
North Harris Montgomery
Community College District *C,A*
Odessa College *A*
San Antonio College *A*
South Plains College *C,A*
Tarrant County Junior College *A*
University of Texas at El Paso *M*

Utah

Utah Valley Community College *A*

Vermont

College of St. Joseph in Vermont *B*
Community College of Vermont
C,A

Virginia

Blue Ridge Community College *C,A*
Central Virginia Community
College *C*
John Tyler Community College *A*
Northern Virginia Community
College *A*

Washington

Olympic College *A*
Pierce College *A*
Skagit Valley College *A*
Tacoma Community College *A*
Western Washington University *B*

West Virginia

Davis and Elkins College *A*

Wyoming

Central Wyoming College *C,A*

Merchant Marine

California

California Maritime Academy *B*

Maine

Maine Maritime Academy *B,M*

Massachusetts

Massachusetts Maritime
Academy *B*

New York

State University of New York
Maritime College *B*
United States Merchant Marine
Academy *B*

Metal/jewelry

Arizona

Mohave Community College *C,A*
Northern Arizona University *B*

California

California College of Arts and
Crafts *B,M*
California State University
Long Beach *B,M*
Los Angeles *B,M*
Northridge *B,M*
El Camino College *C*
Humboldt State University *B*
Monterey Peninsula College *C,A*
Otis/Parsons School of Art and
Design *B*
Palomar College *A*
Santa Rosa Junior College *C*

Florida

Pensacola Junior College *A*

Georgia

University of Georgia *B,M*

Idaho

University of Idaho *B*

Illinois

Gem City College *C*
Southern Illinois University at
Carbondale *B,M*
University of Illinois at Urbana-
Champaign *M*

Indiana

Ball State University *B*
Indiana University Bloomington
B,M
Purdue University *B,M*

Iowa

University of Iowa *B,M*

Kansas

Kansas State University *M*
University of Kansas *B*

Kentucky

Eastern Kentucky University *B*

Maine

Portland School of Art *B*

Massachusetts

Massachusetts College of Art *B,M*
School of the Museum of Fine Arts
B,M
University of Massachusetts at
Dartmouth *B,M*

Michigan

Center for Creative Studies: College
of Art and Design *B*
Central Michigan University *B,M*
Eastern Michigan University *B*
Grand Valley State University *B*
Northern Michigan University *B*
University of Michigan *B,M*

Missouri

Washington University *B,M*

New Jersey

Glassboro State College *B*

New Mexico

Institute of American Indian
Arts *A*

New York

Fashion Institute of Technology *A*
Hofstra University *B*
Parsons School of Design *A,B*
Pratt Institute *B*
Rochester Institute of Technology
A,B,M
State University of New York
College at New Paltz *B,M*
Syracuse University *B,M*

North Carolina

Haywood Community College *A*
Montgomery Community College *C*

Ohio

Bowling Green State University *B*
Cleveland Institute of Art *B*
University of Akron *B*

Oklahoma

Oklahoma State University
Technical Branch: Okmulgee *A*
University of Oklahoma *B*

Oregon

Central Oregon Community
College *A*
Portland Community College *A*
University of Oregon
Eugene *B,M*
Robert Donald Clark Honors
College *B*

Pennsylvania

Beaver College *B*
Carnegie Mellon University *B,M*
Edinboro University of
Pennsylvania *B,M*
Marywood College *B*
Moore College of Art and Design *B*
Seton Hill College *B*
Temple University *B,M*
University of the Arts *B*

Rhode Island

Rhode Island School of Design *B,M*

Tennessee

East Tennessee State University *B*
Memphis College of Art *B*

Texas

San Antonio College *A*
Texas Woman's University *B,M*
University of Houston *B*
University of Texas at El Paso *B*
Western Texas College *A*

Washington

University of Washington *B,M*

Wisconsin

Northeast Wisconsin Technical
College *C*
University of Wisconsin: Eau
Claire *B*

Metallurgical engineering

Alabama

University of Alabama *B,M,D*

Arizona

University of Arizona *B*

California

California Polytechnic State
University: San Luis Obispo *B*
Southwestern College *A*
University of California: Berkeley
B,M,D

Colorado

Colorado School of Mines
B,M,D,W

Connecticut

University of Connecticut *M,D*

Florida

University of Florida *B,M,D*

Georgia

Georgia Institute of Technology
M,D

Idaho

University of Idaho *B,M*

Illinois

Illinois Institute of Technology
B,M,D
Northwestern University *B*
University of Illinois
Chicago *B,M,D*
Urbana-Champaign *B,M,D*

Indiana

Purdue University *B,M,D*

Massachusetts

Massachusetts Institute of
Technology *B,M,D,W*

Michigan

Michigan State University *M,D*
Michigan Technological University
B,M,D
Schoolcraft College *C,A*
University of Michigan *B,M,D*
Wayne State University *B,M,D*

Missouri

East Central College *A*
University of Missouri: Rolla *B,M,D*

Montana

Montana College of Mineral
Science and Technology *B,M*

Nevada

University of Nevada: Reno *B,M,D*

New Jersey

Stevens Institute of Technology
B,M,D

New Mexico

New Mexico Institute of Mining
and Technology *B,M,D*

New York

Columbia University: School of
Engineering and Applied Science
B,M,D,W

Polytechnic University
Brooklyn *B,M*
Long Island Campus *B*

Ohio

Ohio State University: Columbus
Campus *B,M,D*
University of Cincinnati *B,M,D*
Youngstown State University *B*

Oklahoma

University of Oklahoma *M,D*

Oregon

Oregon State University *B*

Pennsylvania

Carnegie Mellon University
B,M,D,W
Lehigh University *B,M,D*
Lock Haven University of
Pennsylvania *B*
Penn State University Park Campus
B,M,D
University of Pennsylvania *B,M,D*
University of Pittsburgh *B,M,D*

South Dakota

South Dakota School of Mines and
Technology *B,M*

Tennessee

University of Tennessee: Knoxville
M,D

Texas

Rice University *B,M,D*
University of Texas at El Paso *B,M*

Utah

University of Utah *B,M,D*

Washington

University of Washington *B*

Wisconsin

University of Wisconsin: Madison
M,D

Canada

McGill University *B,M,D*

Metallurgy

California

California State University: Long
Beach *M*
Don Bosco Technical Institute *A*
University of California: Berkeley
B,M,D

Colorado

Colorado School of Mines *M,D,W*

Georgia

Georgia Institute of Technology
M,D

Idaho

University of Idaho *M*

Illinois

Moraine Valley Community
College *A*
Northwestern University *B*
University of Chicago *B,M,D*

Iowa

Iowa State University *B,M,D*

Massachusetts

Massachusetts Institute of
Technology *B,M,D*

Michigan

Eastern Michigan University *B*
Macomb Community College *C,A*
Michigan Technological
University *B*

New Jersey

Stevens Institute of Technology
B,M,D

New Mexico

New Mexico Institute of Mining
and Technology *M,D*

New York

Columbia University: School of
Engineering and Applied Science
B,M,D,W
Mohawk Valley Community
College *C*

Oregon

Linn-Benton Community College *A*
Oregon Graduate Institute *M,D*

Pennsylvania

Carnegie Mellon University
B,M,D,W
Lehigh University *B,M,D*
University of Pennsylvania *M,D*

Utah

University of Utah *M,D*

Canada

McGill University *B,M,D*

Mexican American studies

Arizona

Prescott College *B*
University of Arizona *B*

California

California State University
Dominguez Hills *B*
Fullerton *B*
Hayward *B*
Long Beach *C,B*
Los Angeles *B,M*
Northridge *B,M*
Sacramento *B*
Claremont McKenna College *B*
Fresno City College *A*
Los Angeles City College *A*
Loyola Marymount University *B*
Pitzer College *B*
Pomona College *B*
San Diego City College *A*
San Diego State University *B*
San Francisco State University *B*
San Jose State University *M*
Santa Barbara City College *A*
Santa Monica College *A*
Scripps College *B*
Solano Community College *A*
Sonoma State University *B*
Southwestern College *A*

University of California
Berkeley *B*
Davis *B*
Los Angeles *B*
Ventura College *A*

Colorado

Metropolitan State College of
Denver *B*
University of Northern Colorado *B*

Massachusetts

Hampshire College *B*

New Mexico

New Mexico State University *B*

Texas

Concordia Lutheran College *B*
Southern Methodist University *B*
Texas Southmost College *A*
University of Texas
Austin *B*
Pan American *B*

Vermont

Goddard College *B*

Microbiology

Alabama

Auburn University *B,M,D*
University of Alabama
Birmingham *M,D*
Tuscaloosa *B,M*
University of South Alabama *D*

Arizona

Arizona State University *B,M,D*
Northern Arizona University *B,M*
Pima Community College *A*
University of Arizona *B,M,D*

Arkansas

University of Arkansas
Fayetteville *B,M,D*
Medical Sciences *M,D*

California

Bakersfield College *A*
California Polytechnic State
University: San Luis Obispo *B*
California State Polytechnic
University: Pomona *B*
California State University
Chico *B*
Dominguez Hills *B*
Fresno *B,M*
Fullerton *B,M*
Long Beach *B,M*
Los Angeles *B,M*
Northridge *B*
Sacramento *B*
Cerritos Community College *A*
Crafton Hills College *A*
Modesto Junior College *A*
San Diego State University *B,M*
San Francisco State University *B,M*
San Jose State University *B,M*
Southwestern College *A*
Stanford University *B,M,D*
University of California
Berkeley *B,M,D*
Davis *B,M*
Los Angeles *B,M,D*
San Diego *B*
San Francisco *D*
Santa Barbara *B*
University of Southern California *D*

Colorado

Colorado State University *B,M,D*
University of Colorado Health
Sciences Center *D*

Connecticut

Quinnipiac College *B,M*
University of Connecticut *M,D*
University of New Haven *B*

Delaware

University of Delaware *M,D*

District of Columbia

George Washington University *M,D*
Georgetown University *D*
Howard University *B,M,D*

Florida

Florida Atlantic University *B,M*
University of Central Florida *B,M*
University of Florida *B,M,D*
University of Miami *B,M,D*
University of South Florida *B,M*

Georgia

Emory University *M,D*
Medical College of Georgia *M,D*
University of Georgia *B,M,D*

Hawaii

University of Hawaii at Manoa
B,M,D

Idaho

Idaho State University *B,M*
Ricks College *A*

Illinois

Joliet Junior College *A*
Loyola University of Chicago *M,D*
Northwestern University *B,M,D*
Southern Illinois University at
Carbondale *B,M,D*
University of Chicago *B,M,D*
University of Health Sciences: The
Chicago Medical School *M,D,W*
University of Illinois
Chicago *M,D*
Urbana-Champaign *B,M,D*

Indiana

Ball State University *B*
Indiana University Bloomington
B,M,D
Indiana University—Purdue
University at Indianapolis
M,D,W
Purdue University
Calumet *B*
West Lafayette *B,D,W*
University of Notre Dame *B,M,D*

Iowa

Iowa State University *B,M,D*
University of Iowa *B,M,D*

Kansas

Coffeyville Community College *A*
Kansas State University *B,M,D*
University of Kansas
Lawrence *B,M,D*
Medical Center *M,D*

Kentucky

Eastern Kentucky University *B*
University of Kentucky *B,M,D*
University of Louisville *M,D*

Louisiana

Louisiana State University
Agricultural and Mechanical
College *B,M,D*
Medical Center *M,D*
Louisiana Tech University *B*
McNeese State University *B*
Northeast Louisiana University *B*
Southern University and
Agricultural and Mechanical
College *B*
Tulane University *M,D*
University of Southwestern
Louisiana *M*
Xavier University of Louisiana *B*

Maine

University of Maine *B,M*

Maryland

Howard Community College *A*
Uniformed Services University of
the Health Sciences *M,D*
University of Maryland
Baltimore *M,D*
College Park *B,M,D*

Massachusetts

Boston University *M,D*
Hampshire College *B*
Harvard University *D*
Massachusetts Institute of
Technology *B,M,D,W*
Roxbury Community College *A*
Tufts University *M,D*
University of Massachusetts at
Amherst *B,M,D*
Worcester Polytechnic Institute
B,M

Michigan

Central Michigan University *B*
Eastern Michigan University *B*
Michigan State University *B,M,D*
Michigan Technological
University *B*
Northern Michigan University *B*
University of Michigan
Ann Arbor *B,M,D*
Dearborn *B*
Wayne State University *M,D*

Minnesota

Mankato State University *B,M*
University of Minnesota
Duluth *M*
Twin Cities *B,M,D*
Willmar Community College *A*

Mississippi

Mississippi State University *B*
Mississippi University for Women *B*
University of Mississippi Medical
Center *M,D*

Missouri

St. Louis University *M,D*
University of Missouri
Columbia *B,D*
Kansas City *M*
Washington University *D*

Montana

Montana State University *B,M,D*
University of Montana *B,M,D*

Nebraska

Creighton University *M,D*
University of Nebraska Medical
Center *M,D*
York College *A*

New Hampshire

University of New Hampshire
B,M,D

New Jersey

Rutgers—The State University of
New Jersey
Camden College of Arts and
Sciences *B*
Cook College *B*
Douglass College *B*
Livingston College *B*
New Brunswick *M,D*
Newark College of Arts and
Sciences *B*
Rutgers College *B*
University College New
Brunswick *B*
Seton Hall University *M*
Stevens Institute of Technology *B*

New Mexico

New Mexico State University *B*

New York

Albany Medical College *M,D*
Columbia University
Columbia College *B*
New York *M,D*
Cornell University *B,M,D*
Long Island University: Brooklyn
Campus *M*
New York University *M,D*
Rockefeller University *D*
State University of New York
Buffalo *M,D*
College of Environmental
Science and Forestry *B,M,D*
College at Plattsburgh *B*
Health Science Center at
Brooklyn *D*
Health Science Center at
Syracuse *M,D*
Health Sciences Center at
Stony Brook *D*
University of Rochester *B,M,D,W*
Wagner College *B,M*
Yeshiva University *M,D*

North Carolina

Duke University *D*
East Carolina University *D*
North Carolina State University
B,M,D
University of North Carolina at
Chapel Hill *M,D*
Wake Forest University *B,M,D*

North Dakota

North Dakota State University *B,M*
University of North Dakota *M,D*

Ohio

Bowling Green State University *B*
Case Western Reserve University *D*
Miami University: Oxford Campus
B,M,D
Ohio State University: Columbus
Campus *B,M,D*
Ohio University *B,M,D*
University of Akron *B*
University of Cincinnati *M,D*
Wittenberg University *B*
Wright State University *M*

Oklahoma

Oklahoma State University *B,M,D*
University of Oklahoma
Health Sciences Center *M,D*
Norman *B,M,D*

Oregon

Oregon Health Sciences University
  M,D
Oregon State University *B,M,D*

Pennsylvania

Duquesne University *B*
Hahnemann University School of
  Health Sciences and Humanities
  M,D
Juniata College *B*
Lehigh University *M,D*
Medical College of Pennsylvania
  M,D
Penn State
  Milton S. Hershey Medical
    Center *M,D*
  University Park Campus
    C,B,M,D
Philadelphia College of Pharmacy
  and Science *B*
Temple University *M,D*
University of Pennsylvania *M,D*
University of Pittsburgh *B,M,D*
West Chester University of
  Pennsylvania *B*

Puerto Rico

Inter American University of Puerto
  Rico: Arecibo Campus *B*
University of Puerto Rico
  Arecibo Campus *B*
  Humacao University College *B*
  Mayaguez Campus *B*
  Medical Sciences Campus *M,D*

Rhode Island

Brown University *M,D*
University of Rhode Island *B,M,D*

South Carolina

Clemson University *B,M,D*

South Dakota

South Dakota State University *B,M*
University of South Dakota *M,D*

Tennessee

East Tennessee State University
  B,M,D
Meharry Medical College *M,D*
University of Tennessee
    Knoxville *B,M,D*
    Memphis *M,D*
Vanderbilt University *M,D*

Texas

Abilene Christian University *M*
Baylor College of Dentistry *M*
Baylor University *M*
Howard College *A*
Lon Morris College *A*
Southwest Texas State University *B*
Texas A&M University *B,M,D*
Texas Tech University *B,M,D*
Texas Tech University Health
  Science Center *M,D,W*
University of Houston:
  Downtown *B*
University of Texas
    Arlington *B*
    Austin *B,M,D*
    El Paso *B*
    Health Science Center at
      Houston *M,D,W*
    Health Science Center at San
      Antonio *M,D*
    Southwestern Medical Center
      at Dallas Southwestern
      Allied Health Sciences
      School *M,D*
Western Texas College *A*

Utah

Brigham Young University *B,M,D*
University of Utah *D*
Weber State University *B*

Vermont

University of Vermont *M,D*

Virginia

Christopher Newport College *B*
University of Virginia *M,D*
Virginia Commonwealth University
  M,D
Virginia Polytechnic Institute and
  State University *M,D*

Washington

Eastern Washington University *B*
Evergreen State College *B*
University of Washington *B,M,D*
Washington State University *B,M,D*

West Virginia

Alderson-Broaddus College *B*
West Virginia University *M,D*

Wisconsin

Marquette University *M,D*
Medical College of Wisconsin *M,D*
University of Wisconsin
    La Crosse *B*
    Madison *B,M,D*
    Oshkosh *B,M*

Wyoming

Sheridan College *A*

Canada

McGill University *B,M,D*

Microcomputer software

Alabama

Lawson State Community
  College *A*
Selma University *A*

Arizona

Lamson Junior College *A*

California

California State University:
  Bakersfield *B*
Chabot College *A*
Glendale Community College *C*
Heald Business College: San Jose
  C,A
Irvine Valley College *C,A*
Los Angeles City College *C,A*
Los Angeles Mission College *C*
National University *M*
Ohlone College *C*
Orange Coast College *C,A*
Phillips Junior College
    Fresno Campus *C,A*
    San Fernando Valley
      Campus *A*
Saddleback College *C,A*
San Diego City College *A*
San Jose City College *A*
Southwestern College *A*

Colorado

Colorado Mountain College: Alpine
  Campus *C*

Connecticut

Norwalk State Technical College *C*

Delaware

Delaware Technical and
  Community College
    Stanton/Wilmington
      Campus *A*
    Terry Campus *A*

Florida

Jones College *A*
Seminole Community College *A*
Southern College *A*

Georgia

Abraham Baldwin Agricultural
  College *C*
Chattahoochee Technical
  Institute *C*
Floyd College *A*
Meadows College of Business *A*
Savannah Technical Institute *C*

Hawaii

Cannon's International Business
  College of Honolulu *C,A*

Illinois

Belleville Area College *A*
Carl Sandburg College *C*
College of Lake County *C,A*
Hebrew Theological College *C*
Illinois Central College *C*
Joliet Junior College *A*
Lincoln Land Community
  College *C*
Robert Morris College: Chicago
  C,A
William Rainey Harper College *C*

Iowa

American Institute of Business *C*
Clinton Community College *C*
Indian Hills Community College *C*
Kirkwood Community College *C*
Muscatine Community College *C*
Scott Community College *C*
Southeastern Community College
    North Campus *C,A*
    South Campus *C*

Kansas

Coffeyville Community College *A*

Kentucky

Franklin College *C*
Owensboro Junior College of
  Business *C,A*
Watterson College *C*

Maryland

Hagerstown Business College *A*
Hagerstown Junior College *C*
Howard Community College *C,A*
New Community College of
  Baltimore *C*
Prince George's Community
  College *A*

Massachusetts

Aquinas College at Milton *A*
Bristol Community College *A*
Bunker Hill Community College *A*
Marian Court Junior College *A*
Massachusetts Bay Community
  College *C*
North Shore Community College
  C,A

Michigan

Baker College
    Cadillac *A*
    Flint *A*
Detroit College of Business *B*

Minnesota

St. Paul Technical College *A*
Willmar Community College *A*
Willmar Technical College *C*

Mississippi

Holmes Community College *A*
Northeast Mississippi Community
  College *A*

Missouri

Phillips Junior College *C*
St. Louis Community College at
  Meramec *C*

Montana

Miles Community College *A*

Nebraska

Lincoln School of Commerce *C*
Metropolitan Community College *C*
Northeast Community College *C*
Southeast Community College
    Lincoln Campus *C*
    Milford Campus *A*

Nevada

Community College of Southern
  Nevada *C,A*
Truckee Meadows Community
  College *A*

New Hampshire

New Hampshire Technical College
    Nashua *A*
    Stratham *C,A*

New Jersey

Mercer County Community
  College *C*

New Mexico

Dona Ana Branch Community
  College of New Mexico State
  University *C,A*
New Mexico State University at
  Carlsbad *C*
San Juan College *A*

New York

Berkeley College *A*
Briarcliffe: The College for
  Business *A*
Bryant & Stratton Business
  Institute: Albany *A*
City University of New York
    La Guardia Community
      College *A*
    Lehman College *C*
Clarkson University *B,M*
Five Towns College *A*
Onondaga Community College *A*
Rochester Institute of
  Technology *M*
State University of New York
  College at Plattsburgh *B*
Westchester Business Institute *A*

Glen Oaks Community College *C*
Grand Rapids Community College
  C,A
Jordan College *C,A*
Kellogg Community College *C*
Lansing Community College *A*
St. Clair County Community
  College *A*
Southwestern Michigan College *C*
West Shore Community College
  C,A

North Carolina

Alamance Community College A
Caldwell Community College and
 Technical Institute A
Cecils College C
Cleveland Community College A
College of the Albemarle A
Craven Community College A
Durham Technical Community
 College A
Edgecombe Community College A
Forsyth Technical Community
 College C
Rockingham Community College A

North Dakota

North Dakota State College of
 Science A

Ohio

Cincinnati Technical College A
Cuyahoga Community College:
 Western Campus A
Edison State Community College
 C,A
Lakeland Community College C,A
Marion Technical College C,A
Miami-Jacobs College A
Owens Technical College
 Findlay Campus A
 Toledo A
Washington State Community
 College A

Oklahoma

Oklahoma Junior College A
Tulsa Junior College C

Oregon

Chemeketa Community College A
Linn-Benton Community College C
Oregon Polytechnic Institute C
Portland Community College A
Umpqua Community College A

Pennsylvania

Harrisburg Area Community
 College A
Peirce Junior College A
Penn State University Park
 Campus C
Pennsylvania Institute of
 Technology A
Robert Morris College M
Spring Garden College B

Tennessee

Chattanooga State Technical
 Community College A
Maryville College B
Motlow State Community
 College C
State Technical Institute at
 Memphis A

Texas

Amarillo College A
Brazosport College C
Collin County Community College
 District C,A
Cooke County College A
Del Mar College A
El Paso Community College A
Galveston College C,A
North Harris Montgomery
 Community College District C
South Plains College C,A

Virginia

Blue Ridge Community College C
Central Virginia Community College
 C,A

Dabney S. Lancaster Community
 College C
John Tyler Community College C
Mountain Empire Community
 College C
National Business College A
Northern Virginia Community
 College C,A

Washington

Big Bend Community College A
Central Washington University B
Edmonds Community College A
Everett Community College C
Pacific Lutheran University B,M
Seattle University M
Spokane Falls Community
 College A

Wisconsin

Northeast Wisconsin Technical
 College A

Middle Eastern studies

Arizona

University of Arizona M,D

California

American Armenian International
 College B
Naval Postgraduate School M
University of California
 Berkeley B
 Los Angeles B

Connecticut

University of Connecticut B
Wesleyan University B

District of Columbia

George Washington University B
Georgetown University B,M

Illinois

University of Chicago B,M,D

Indiana

Indiana University Bloomington
 B,M,D

Kentucky

University of Kentucky B

Maryland

Baltimore Hebrew University
 B,M,D
Johns Hopkins University B,M,D
Morgan State University B

Massachusetts

Brandeis University B
Hampshire College B
Harvard and Radcliffe Colleges B
Harvard University M,D
Tufts University B,M

Michigan

Eastern Michigan University B
University of Michigan B,M,D

Minnesota

University of Minnesota: Twin
 Cities B

New Jersey

Princeton University B,M,D
Rutgers—The State University of
 New Jersey
 Douglass College B
 Livingston College B
 Rutgers College B
 University College New
  Brunswick B

New York

Barnard College B
City University of New York:
 Brooklyn College B
Columbia University
 Columbia College B
 New York M,D
 School of General Studies B
Fordham University B
New York University B,M,D
United States Military Academy B

North Carolina

University of North Carolina at
 Chapel Hill D

Ohio

Cleveland College of Jewish Studies
 B,M
College of Wooster B
Kenyon College B
Oberlin College B
University of Toledo B

Pennsylvania

Gratz College B
Lycoming College B
Penn State University Park
 Campus C
University of Pennsylvania B,M,D

Texas

Southwest Texas State University B
University of Texas at Austin B,M

Utah

Brigham Young University B
University of Utah B,M,D

Vermont

Goddard College B,M

Washington

University of Washington M

Canada

McGill University B

Switzerland

American College of Switzerland B

Arab Republic of Egypt

American University in Cairo B,M

Military science (Army)

Arkansas

University of Central Arkansas B

Connecticut

Sacred Heart University B

Georgia

Floyd College A
Georgia College B

Kansas

U.S. Army Command and General
 Staff College M

Washburn University of Topeka B

Louisiana

Centenary College of Louisiana B

Maryland

Johns Hopkins University B

Michigan

Eastern Michigan University B

Minnesota

Mankato State University B
St. Cloud State University A

Missouri

Columbia College B
Missouri Southern State College B
Park College B

New York

St. Bonaventure University B
United States Military Academy B

North Carolina

Campbell University B
Durham Technical Community
 College A
Methodist College A

Ohio

Central State University B
Ohio State University: Columbus
 Campus B
University of Rio Grande C

Oklahoma

Oklahoma State University B
Southwestern Oklahoma State
 University B

Pennsylvania

Bucknell University B
California University of
 Pennsylvania B
Dickinson College C
Gannon University B
Valley Forge Military College A
West Chester University of
 Pennsylvania C
Widener University B

South Carolina

Erskine College B

South Dakota

South Dakota State University B

Tennessee

Middle Tennessee State
 University B

Texas

Texas Southmost College A
Texas Wesleyan University B
University of Texas: Pan
 American B

Utah

Weber State University A

Virginia

Marymount University B

Washington

Central Washington University B
Eastern Washington University B
Seattle University B
Whitworth College B

West Virginia

University of Charleston *A,B*
West Virginia Institute of
Technology *A,B*

Wisconsin

University of Wisconsin: Oshkosh *B*

Mining and mineral engineering

Alabama

University of Alabama *B,M*

Alaska

University of Alaska Fairbanks *B,M*

Arizona

University of Arizona *B,M,D*

California

University of California: Berkeley
B,M,D

Colorado

Colorado School of Mines
B,M,D,W

Idaho

North Idaho College *A*
University of Idaho *B,M,D*

Illinois

Southern Illinois University at
Carbondale *B,M*
University of Illinois at Urbana-
Champaign *M,D*

Kentucky

University of Kentucky *B,M*

Massachusetts

Massachusetts Institute of
Technology *B*

Michigan

Michigan Technological University
B,M,D

Minnesota

University of Minnesota: Twin
Cities *M,D*

Missouri

University of Missouri: Rolla *B,M,D*

Montana

Montana College of Mineral
Science and Technology *B,M*

Nevada

University of Nevada: Reno *B,M*

New Mexico

New Mexico Institute of Mining
and Technology *B,M*

New York

Columbia University: School of
Engineering and Applied Science
B,M,D,W

Ohio

Ohio State University: Columbus
Campus *B,M*
Ohio University *B*

Oregon

Oregon State University *B*

Pennsylvania

Lock Haven University of
Pennsylvania *B*
Penn State University Park Campus
B,M,D
University of Pittsburgh *M*

South Dakota

South Dakota School of Mines and
Technology *B,M*

Utah

University of Utah *B,M,D*

Virginia

Virginia Polytechnic Institute and
State University *B,M,D*

West Virginia

West Virginia University *B,M,D*

Wisconsin

University of Wisconsin: Madison
B,M,D

Wyoming

University of Wyoming *M*

Canada

McGill University *B,M,D,W*

Mining and petroleum technologies

Alabama

Walker State Technical College *C*

Alaska

University of Alaska
Anchorage *C,A*
Fairbanks *C*

California

Santa Barbara City College *C*
Taft College *A*
Ventura College *C*

Illinois

Belleville Area College *A*
Illinois Eastern Community
Colleges
Lincoln Trail College *C,A*
Wabash Valley College *C,A*
Lincoln Land Community
College *A*
Rend Lake College *C,A*
Roosevelt University *B*
Southern Illinois University at
Carbondale *B*

Indiana

Indiana Vocational Technical
College: Wabash Valley *A*

Kansas

Barton County Community
College *A*
Hutchinson Community College *A*

Kentucky

Madisonville Community College *A*
Murray State University *B*
Southeast Community College *A*

Louisiana

Nicholls State University *B*

Massachusetts

Cape Cod Community College *A*

Nevada

Northern Nevada Community
College *A*

New Mexico

Dona Ana Branch Community
College of New Mexico State
University *C,A*
Eastern New Mexico University:
Roswell Campus *C,A*
New Mexico Junior College *A*

New York

Bryant & Stratton Business
Institute: Buffalo *A*

Ohio

University of Akron: Wayne
College *A*

Pennsylvania

Penn State University Park Campus
B,M,D

Texas

Houston Community College *C,A*
Navarro College *A*
Odessa College *C,A*
South Plains College *A*

Utah

College of Eastern Utah *A*

Virginia

Mountain Empire Community
College *A*
Southwest Virginia Community
College *A*

West Virginia

Bluefield State College *B*
Fairmont State College *A,B*
Glenville State College *A*

Wyoming

Casper College *A*
Sheridan College *A*
Western Wyoming Community
College *A*

Missionary studies

Alabama

Southeastern Bible College *B*

Alaska

Alaska Bible College *B*

Arizona

Arizona College of the Bible *B*
Southwestern College *C,A,B*

Arkansas

Central Baptist College *B*
John Brown University *B*
Ouachita Baptist University *B*

California

Bethany College *B*
Christian Heritage College *B*
Fresno Pacific College *B*
Fuller Theological Seminary *M,D,W*
LIFE Bible College *B*

Pacific Christian College *A,B,M*
San Jose Christian College *B*
Simpson College *B,M*
Southern California College *B*

Colorado

Colorado Christian University *B*

Florida

Florida Bible College *A,B*
Florida Christian College *B*
Hobe Sound Bible College *B*
Southeastern College of the
Assemblies of God *B*

Georgia

Emory University *W*
Toccoa Falls College *B*

Illinois

Garrett-Evangelical Theological
Seminary *M,D,W*
Lincoln Christian College and
Seminary *B,M*
Moody Bible Institute *B*
Wheaton College *M*

Indiana

Grace Theological Seminary *M*
Taylor University *C*

Iowa

Faith Baptist Bible College and
Theological Seminary *B*
Vennard College *B*

Kansas

Barclay College *B*
Central College *A,B*
Manhattan Christian College *A,B*

Kentucky

Asbury College *B*

Louisiana

World Evangelism Bible College
and Seminary *C,B,M*

Michigan

Grace Bible College *B*
Grand Rapids Baptist College and
Seminary *M*
William Tyndale College *B*

Minnesota

Bethel College *B*
Bethel Theological Seminary *M,W*
Concordia College: St. Paul *B*
Crown College *B*
North Central Bible College *A,B*
Northwestern College *B*
Pillsbury Baptist Bible College *B*

Mississippi

Wesley College *B*

Missouri

Baptist Bible College *B*
Calvary Bible College *A,B*
Covenant Theological Seminary *M*
Evangel College *B*
Ozark Christian College *B*
St. Louis Christian College *B*

Nebraska

Grace College of the Bible *C*
Nebraska Christian College *A,B*

New York

New York Theological Seminary *D*
Nyack College *B,M*
St. John's University *M*

North Carolina
John Wesley College *B*
Montreat-Anderson College *B*

North Dakota
Trinity Bible College *B*

Ohio
Cincinnati Bible College and
Seminary *B*
Circleville Bible College *A,B*

Oklahoma
Bartlesville Wesleyan College *B*
Hillsdale Free Will Baptist
College *A*
Oklahoma Baptist University *B*
Oklahoma Christian University of
Science and Arts *B*
Oral Roberts University *B*
Southwestern College of Christian
Ministries *B*

Oregon
Eugene Bible College *B*
Western Baptist College *B*
Western Conservative Baptist
Seminary *M,D*

Pennsylvania
Evangelical School of Theology *M*
Geneva College *B*
Lancaster Bible College *B*
Philadelphia College of Bible *B*
Pittsburgh Theological Seminary *M*
Valley Forge Christian College *B*

South Carolina
Bob Jones University *A,B*
Columbia Bible College and
Seminary *B*

Tennessee
Free Will Baptist Bible College *B*
Freed-Hardeman University *B*
Milligan College *B*
Tennessee Temple University *B*

Texas
Abilene Christian University *B,M*
Arlington Baptist College *B*
Criswell College *A,B,M*
Dallas Christian College *B*
Lubbock Christian University *B*
Southwestern Assemblies of God
College *B*

Virginia
Liberty University *B,M*

Washington
Lutheran Bible Institute of
Seattle *B*
Northwest College of the
Assemblies of God *B*
Puget Sound Christian College *B*

Wisconsin
Maranatha Baptist Bible College *B*

Molecular biology

Alabama
Auburn University *B*

Arizona
University of Arizona *B,M,D*

Arkansas
University of Arkansas for Medical
Sciences *M,D*

California
California Institute of Technology
D,W
California Lutheran University *B*
California State University
Fresno *B*
Fullerton *B*
Northridge *B*
Sacramento *B*
Pomona College *B*
San Francisco State University *B,M*
San Jose State University *B*
Stanford University *D*
University of California
Berkeley *B,D*
Los Angeles *D*
San Diego *B*
Santa Barbara *B,M,D*
Santa Cruz *B,D*
University of Southern California
M,D

Colorado
Fort Lewis College *B*
University of Colorado at Boulder
B,M,D

Connecticut
Wesleyan University *B,M,D*
Yale University *B,M,D*

Delaware
University of Delaware *M,D*

Florida
Florida Agricultural and Mechanical
University *M*
Florida Institute of Technology
B,M
New College of the University of
South Florida *B*
University of Florida *M,D*
University of Miami *D*

Georgia
Emory University *M,D*

Illinois
Loyola University of Chicago *D*
Northwestern University *B,M,D*
Southern Illinois University at
Carbondale *D*
University of Chicago *B,M,D*
University of Health Sciences: The
Chicago Medical School *M,D*
University of Illinois at Urbana-
Champaign *M,D*

Indiana
Ball State University *B*
Indiana University Bloomington *D*
Purdue University *B,D*
University of Notre Dame *B,M,D*

Iowa
Clarke College *B*
Iowa State University *M,D*
University of Iowa *D*

Kentucky
Centre College *B*

Louisiana
Louisiana State University Medical
Center *M,D*

Maine
University of Maine *B*

Maryland
University of Maryland
Baltimore *M,D*
Baltimore County *B,M,D*
College Park *D*

Massachusetts
Brandeis University *D*
Clark University *B,M,D*
Hampshire College *B*
Harvard University *D*
Massachusetts Institute of
Technology *B,M,D,W*
Tufts University *D*
University of Massachusetts at
Amherst *M,D*
Williams College *B*
Worcester Polytechnic Institute
B,M

Michigan
Eastern Michigan University *M*
University of Michigan *B,M,D*
Wayne State University *M,D*

Minnesota
Bethel College *B*
Winona State University *B*

Missouri
Northwest Missouri State
University *B*
University of Missouri: Kansas
City *D*
Washington University *D*

New Hampshire
University of New Hampshire *B*

New Jersey
Montclair State College *B*
Princeton University *B,D*
Rutgers—The State University of
New Jersey
Camden College of Arts and
Sciences *B*
Cook College *B*
Douglass College *B*
Livingston College *B*
New Brunswick *M,D*
Rutgers College *B*
University College New
Brunswick *B*
Seton Hall University *D*
Stevens Institute of Technology *B*

New Mexico
New Mexico State University *M,D*

New York
Colgate University *B*
Columbia University *M,D*
Cornell University *M,D*
Hamilton College *B*
Long Island University: Brooklyn
Campus *B*
New York University *M,D*
Rockefeller University *D*
State University of New York
Albany *M,D*
Stony Brook *D*
College of Environmental
Science and Forestry *B,M,D*
Health Science Center at
Syracuse *D*
Yeshiva University *M,D*

North Carolina
Duke University *D*
East Carolina University *M*

Ohio
Case Western Reserve University *D*
Kent State University *M,D*
Ohio State University: Columbus
Campus *M,D*
Ohio University *D*
University of Cincinnati *M,D*

Oklahoma
Northeastern State University *B*
University of Oklahoma
Health Sciences Center *M,D*
Norman *M,D*
University of Tulsa *D*

Oregon
Oregon Graduate Institute *M,D*
Oregon Health Sciences University
M,D
Oregon State University *D*
University of Oregon *M,D*

Pennsylvania
Bryn Mawr College *B*
Carnegie Mellon University
B,M,D,W
Chestnut Hill College *B*
Clarion University of
Pennsylvania *B*
Drexel University *M,D*
Grove City College *B*
Hahnemann University School of
Health Sciences and Humanities
M,D
Lehigh University *B,M,D*
Penn State
Milton S. Hershey Medical
Center *M,D*
University Park Campus
B,M,D
University of Pennsylvania *B,M,D*
West Chester University of
Pennsylvania *B*
Westminster College *B*

Rhode Island
Brown University *B,M,D*

Tennessee
Vanderbilt University *B,M,D*

Texas
Incarnate Word College *M*
Texas Woman's University *D*
University of North Texas *D*
University of Texas
Austin *B*
Health Science Center at
Houston *M,D,W*
San Antonio *M*
Southwestern Medical Center
at Dallas Southwestern
Allied Health Sciences
School *M,D*

Utah
Brigham Young University *B*
University of Utah *D*

Vermont
Marlboro College *B*
Middlebury College *B*

Virginia
Hampton University *B*

Washington

Evergreen State College *B*
University of Washington *B*

Wisconsin

Beloit College *B*
Marquette University *B,M,D*
University of Wisconsin: Madison
B,M,D

Wyoming

University of Wyoming *B,M,D*

Canada

McGill University *B,M,D*

Motion picture technology

Alabama

University of Alabama *B,M*

Arizona

Scottsdale Community College *A*

California

Biola University *B*
Brooks Institute of Photography *B*
Columbia College: Hollywood *B*
Los Angeles Valley College *C*

Connecticut

University of Bridgeport *B*

Florida

Phillips Junior College:
Melbourne *A*
University of Central Florida *B*
University of Miami *B*
Valencia Community College *A*

Illinois

Columbia College *B*
Southern Illinois University at
Carbondale *B*

Kansas

Colby Community College *A*

Massachusetts

Emerson College *B*
Fitchburg State College *B*
Hampshire College *B*

Michigan

Lansing Community College *A*

Montana

Montana State University *B*

New Jersey

Jersey City State College *B*

New Mexico

College of Santa Fe *B*

New York

Hofstra University *B*
New York University *B,M*
Rochester Institute of Technology
A,B
School of Visual Arts *B*
Syracuse University *B,M*

Ohio

University of Toledo *B*

South Carolina

Bob Jones University *B,M*
Trident Technical College *C*

Utah

Brigham Young University *B,M,D*

Wisconsin

University of Wisconsin: Oshkosh *B*

Museum studies

California

California State University: Long
Beach *C*
John F. Kennedy University *M*
University of Southern California *M*

Delaware

University of Delaware *M*

District of Columbia

Gallaudet University *B*
George Washington University *M*

Indiana

Earlham College *B*

Kansas

University of Kansas *M*

Massachusetts

Framingham State College *M*

Nebraska

University of Nebraska—Lincoln *M*

New Mexico

Institute of American Indian
Arts *A*

New York

City University of New York: City
College *M*
New York University *B,M*
Rochester Institute of
Technology *M*
State University of New York
College at Oneonta *M*
Syracuse University *M*

Ohio

Case Western Reserve
University *M*
Union Institute *D*

Oklahoma

University of Central Oklahoma
B,M

Oregon

Oregon State University *M*

Pennsylvania

Immaculata College *A*

Texas

Baylor University *B*
Texas Tech University *M*

Virginia

Hampton University *M*

West Virginia

Salem-Teikyo University *B,M*

Wisconsin

Carroll College *B*

Music

Alabama

Alabama Southern Community
College *A*
Alabama State University *B*
Auburn University *B,M*
Birmingham-Southern College *B*
Brewer State Junior College *A*
Chattahoochee Valley Community
College *A*
Community College of the Air
Force *A*
Huntingdon College *B*
Jacksonville State University *B,M*
James H. Faulkner State
Community College *A*
Jefferson State Community
College *A*
John C. Calhoun State Community
College *A*
Judson College *B*
Livingston University *B*
Mobile College *B*
Oakwood College *B*
Samford University *B*
Shelton State Community
College *A*
Shoals Community College *A*
Snead State Junior College *A*
Stillman College *B*
Talladega College *B*
University of Alabama
Birmingham *B*
Huntsville *B*
Tuscaloosa *B,M*
University of South Alabama *B*

Alaska

Alaska Pacific University *B*
University of Alaska
Anchorage *B*
Fairbanks *B,M*

Arizona

Arizona State University *B*
Arizona Western College *A*
Eastern Arizona College *A*
Glendale Community College *A*
Grand Canyon University *B*
Mesa Community College *A*
Mohave Community College *A*
Northern Arizona University *B,M*
Pima Community College *A*
Yavapai College *A*

Arkansas

Arkansas College *B*
Arkansas State University *B,M*
Arkansas Tech University *B*
Central Baptist College *A*
Harding University *B*
Henderson State University *B*
Hendrix College *B*
John Brown University *A,B*
Mississippi County Community
College *A*
Ouachita Baptist University *B*
Philander Smith College *B*
Southern Arkansas University *B*
University of Arkansas
Fayetteville *B*
Little Rock *B*
Monticello *B*
Pine Bluff *B*
University of Central Arkansas *B,M*
University of the Ozarks *B*
Westark Community College *A*
Williams Baptist College *A*

California

Allan Hancock College *A*
Azusa Pacific University *B*
Bakersfield College *A*
Barstow College *A*
Bethany College *B*
Biola University *B*
California Baptist College *B*
California Institute of the Arts *C,B*
California Lutheran University *B*
California State Polytechnic
University: Pomona *B*
California State University
Bakersfield *B*
Chico *B,M*
Dominguez Hills *B*
Fresno *B,M*
Fullerton *B,M*
Hayward *B,M*
Long Beach *B,M*
Los Angeles *B,M*
Northridge *B,M*
Sacramento *B,M*
San Bernardino *B*
Stanislaus *B*
Cerritos Community College *A*
Chabot College *A*
Chaffey Community College *A*
Chapman University *B*
Christ College Irvine *B*
Citrus College *A*
Claremont McKenna College *B*
College of the Desert *A*
College of Marin: Kentfield *A*
College of Notre Dame *B,M*
College of the Sequoias *A*
Columbia College *A*
Crafton Hills College *A*
De Anza College *A*
Dominican College of San Rafael
B,M
El Camino College *A*
Foothill College *A*
Fresno City College *A*
Fresno Pacific College *B*
Gavilan Community College *A*
Grossmont Community College *A*
Holy Names College *B,M*
Humboldt State University *B*
Imperial Valley College *A*
Irvine Valley College *A*
La Sierra University *B*
Laney College *A*
Long Beach City College *A*
Los Angeles City College *A*
Los Angeles Mission College *A*
Los Angeles Pierce College *A*
Los Angeles Valley College *A*
Los Medanos College *A*
Loyola Marymount University *B*
Marymount College *A*
Master's College *B*
Mendocino College *A*
Merced College *A*
Mills College *B*
MiraCosta College *A*
Modesto Junior College *A*
Monterey Peninsula College *C,A*
Moorpark College *A*
Mount St. Mary's College *B*
Mount San Jacinto College *A*
Napa Valley College *A*
Occidental College *B*
Ohlone College *A*
Orange Coast College *A*
Pacific Christian College *B*
Pacific Union College *B*
Palomar College *A*
Pasadena City College *C,A*
Pepperdine University *B*
Pitzer College *B*
Point Loma Nazarene College *B*

Pomona College *B*
Porterville College *A*
Saddleback College *A*
San Diego City College *A*
San Diego Mesa College *A*
San Diego State University *B,M*
San Francisco State University *B,M*
San Joaquin Delta College *A*
San Jose City College *A*
San Jose State University *B,M*
Santa Barbara City College *A*
Santa Clara University *B*
Santa Monica College *A*
Santa Rosa Junior College *A*
Scripps College *B*
Simpson College *B*
Skyline College *A*
Solano Community College *A*
Sonoma State University *B*
Southern California College *B*
Southwestern College *A*
Stanford University *B,M,D*
University of California
    Berkeley *B,M,D*
    Davis *B,M,D*
    Irvine *B*
    Los Angeles *B,M,D*
    Riverside *B,M*
    San Diego *B,M,D*
    Santa Barbara *B,M,D*
    Santa Cruz *B,M*
University of La Verne *B*
University of the Pacific *B,M*
University of Redlands *B*
University of San Diego *B*
University of Southern California *B,M,D*
Ventura College *A*
West Hills Community College *A*
West Valley College *A*
Westmont College *B*
Whittier College *B*
Yuba College *A*

Colorado

Adams State College *B*
Colorado Christian University *B*
Colorado College *B*
Colorado State University *B,M*
Community College of Denver *A*
Fort Lewis College *B*
Mesa State College *A,B*
Naropa Institute *B*
Nazarene Bible College *C,A*
Northeastern Junior College *A*
Trinidad State Junior College *A*
University of Colorado at Boulder *B,M,D*
University of Denver *B,M*
University of Northern Colorado *B,M,D*
University of Southern Colorado *B*
Western State College of Colorado *B*

Connecticut

Central Connecticut State University *B*
Connecticut College *B,M*
Fairfield University *B*
Manchester Community College *A*
Mattatuck Community College *A*
Sacred Heart University *A*
Trinity College *B*
University of Bridgeport *B*
University of Connecticut *B,M,D*
University of Hartford *B*
Wesleyan University *B,M,D*
Western Connecticut State University *B*
Yale University *B,M*

Delaware

Delaware State College *B*
University of Delaware *B*

District of Columbia

American University *B,M*
Catholic University of America *B*
George Washington University *B,M*
Howard University *B,M*
Trinity College *B*
University of the District of Columbia *A,B*

Florida

Bethune-Cookman College *B*
Brevard Community College *A*
Daytona Beach Community College *A*
Eckerd College *B*
Edison Community College *A*
Florida Agricultural and Mechanical University *B*
Florida Atlantic University *B*
Florida International University *B*
Florida Southern College *B*
Florida State University *B,M,D*
Gulf Coast Community College *A*
Hillsborough Community College *A*
Indian River Community College *A*
Jacksonville University *B*
Manatee Community College *A*
Miami-Dade Community College *A*
New College of the University of South Florida *B*
Palm Beach Atlantic College *B*
Palm Beach Community College *A*
Pensacola Junior College *A*
Rollins College *B*
St. Leo College *B*
Stetson University *B*
University of Florida *M*
University of Miami *B*
University of Tampa *A,B*
University of West Florida *B*

Georgia

Abraham Baldwin Agricultural College *A*
Agnes Scott College *B*
Albany State College *B*
Andrew College *A*
Armstrong State College *B*
Atlanta Metropolitan College *A*
Augusta College *B*
Berry College *B*
Brenau Women's College *B*
Brewton-Parker College *A,B*
Clark Atlanta University *B*
Clayton State College *A*
Columbus College *B*
Covenant College *B*
Darton College *A*
DeKalb College *A*
Emmanuel College *A*
Emory University *B*
Georgia College *B*
Georgia Southern University *B*
Georgia State University *B,M*
Gordon College *A*
Kennesaw State College *B*
Macon College *A*
Mercer University *B*
Middle Georgia College *A*
Morehouse College *B*
Morris Brown College *B*
North Georgia College *B*
Piedmont College *B*
Reinhardt College *A*
Savannah State College *B*
Shorter College *B*
Spelman College *B*
Thomas College *A*

Toccoa Falls College *B*
Truett-McConnell College *A*
University of Georgia *B,M*
Valdosta State College *B*
Waycross College *C*
Wesleyan College *B*
Young Harris College *A*

Hawaii

Brigham Young University-Hawaii *A*
University of Hawaii
    Hilo *B*
    Manoa *B,M*

Idaho

Albertson College *B*
Boise State University *B*
College of Southern Idaho *A*
Idaho State University *B*
North Idaho College *A*
Northwest Nazarene College *B*
Ricks College *A*
University of Idaho *B,M*

Illinois

Augustana College *B*
Black Hawk College *A*
Blackburn College *B*
Bradley University *B*
Chicago State University *B*
City Colleges of Chicago
    Olive-Harvey College *A*
    Wright College *A*
Columbia College *B*
Concordia University *B*
De Paul University *B,M*
Eastern Illinois University *B,M*
Elmhurst College *B*
Eureka College *B*
Governors State University *B,M*
Greenville College *B*
Highland Community College *A*
Illinois Benedictine College *B*
Illinois Central College *A*
Illinois College *B*
Illinois State University *B,M*
Illinois Valley Community College *A*
Illinois Wesleyan University *B*
Joliet Junior College *A*
Kishwaukee College *A*
Knox College *B*
Lewis University *B*
Lincoln College *A*
Lincoln Land Community College *A*
MacMurray College *B*
Millikin University *B*
Monmouth College *B*
Montay College *A*
Morton College *A*
North Central College *B*
North Park College and Theological Seminary *B*
Northeastern Illinois University *B,M*
Northern Illinois University *B*
Northwestern University *B*
Olivet Nazarene University *B*
Parkland College *A*
Principia College *B*
Richland Community College *A*
Rockford College *B*
Roosevelt University *B*
Rosary College *B*
St. Xavier University *B*
Southern Illinois University
    Carbondale *B,M*
    Edwardsville *B*
Trinity Christian College *B*
Trinity College *B*

Triton College *A*
University of Chicago *B,M,D*
University of Illinois
    Chicago *B*
    Urbana-Champaign *B,M,D*
VanderCook College of Music *B,M*
Waubonsee Community College *A*
Western Illinois University *B,M*
Wheaton College *B*
William Rainey Harper College *A*

Indiana

Ancilla College *C*
Ball State University *B,M,D*
Bethel College *B*
DePauw University *B*
Earlham College *B*
Goshen College *B*
Grace College *B*
Hanover College *B*
Huntington College *B*
Indiana State University *B,M*
Indiana University
    Bloomington *B,M,D*
    South Bend *B,M*
    Southeast *B*
Indiana University—Purdue University at Fort Wayne *B*
Indiana Wesleyan University *B*
Manchester College *B*
Marian College *B*
Martin University *B*
Oakland City College *B*
St. Joseph's College *B*
St. Mary-of-the-Woods College *B*
St. Mary's College *B*
Taylor University *B*
University of Evansville *B*
University of Indianapolis *B*
University of Notre Dame *B,M*
Valparaiso University *B,M*
Vincennes University *A*
Wabash College *B*

Iowa

Briar Cliff College *B*
Buena Vista College *B*
Central College *B*
Clarke College *B*
Coe College *B*
Cornell College *B*
Dordt College *B*
Drake University *B,M*
Graceland College *B*
Grinnell College *B*
Iowa Lakes Community College *A*
Iowa State University *B*
Iowa Wesleyan College *B*
Kirkwood Community College *A*
Loras College *B*
Luther College *B*
Morningside College *B*
Mount Mercy College *B*
Muscatine Community College *A*
North Iowa Area Community College *A*
Northwestern College *B*
St. Ambrose University *B*
Simpson College *B*
Southwestern Community College *A*
Teikyo Westmar University *B*
University of Dubuque *B*
University of Iowa *B,M,D*
University of Northern Iowa *B,M*
Upper Iowa University *B*
Vennard College *B*
Waldorf College *A*
Wartburg College *B*
William Penn College *B*

Kansas

Allen County Community
  College *A*
Baker University *B*
Barclay College *B*
Barton County Community
  College *A*
Benedictine College *B*
Bethany College *B*
Bethel College *B*
Butler County Community
  College *A*
Central College *A*
Cloud County Community
  College *A*
Coffeyville Community College *A*
Colby Community College *A*
Cowley County Community
  College *A*
Dodge City Community College *A*
Emporia State University *B,M*
Fort Hays State University *B,M*
Friends University *B*
Highland Community College *A*
Hutchinson Community College *A*
Kansas City College and Bible
  School *B*
Kansas City Kansas Community
  College *A*
Kansas State University *B,M*
Kansas Wesleyan University *B*
Labette Community College *A*
McPherson College *B*
MidAmerica Nazarene College *B*
Neosho County Community
  College *A*
Ottawa University *B*
Pittsburg State University *B*
Pratt Community College *A*
St. Mary College *B*
Seward County Community
  College *A*
Southwestern College *B*
Sterling College *A,B*
Tabor College *B*
University of Kansas *B*
Wichita State University *B,M*

Kentucky

Asbury College *B*
Bellarmine College *B*
Berea College *B*
Campbellsville College *B*
Centre College *B*
Cumberland College *B*
Eastern Kentucky University *B,M*
Georgetown College *B*
Kentucky Christian College *B*
Kentucky Wesleyan College *B*
Morehead State University *B*
Murray State University *B,M*
Northern Kentucky University *B*
Union College *B*
University of Kentucky *B,M,D*
Western Kentucky University *B*

Louisiana

Centenary College of Louisiana *B*
Dillard University *B*
Grambling State University *B*
Louisiana College *B*
Louisiana State University and
  Agricultural and Mechanical
  College *M,D*
Louisiana Tech University *B*
Loyola University *B,M*
McNeese State University *B,M*
Northeast Louisiana University *B*
Northwestern State University *B,M*
Southeastern Louisiana University
  B,M

Southern University and
  Agricultural and Mechanical
  College *B*
Tulane University *B,M*
University of New Orleans *B,M*
Xavier University of Louisiana *B*

Maine

Bates College *B*
Bowdoin College *B*
Colby College *B*
University of Maine *B,M*
University of Southern Maine *B*

Maryland

Anne Arundel Community
  College *C*
Catonsville Community College *A*
College of Notre Dame of
  Maryland *B*
Columbia Union College *B*
Frederick Community College *A*
Frostburg State University *B*
Goucher College *B*
Harford Community College *A*
Howard Community College *A*
Johns Hopkins University *B,M,D*
Montgomery College: Rockville
  Campus *A*
Morgan State University *B,M*
Prince George's Community
  College *A*
St. Mary's College of Maryland *B*
Salisbury State University *B*
Towson State University *B,M*
University of Maryland
  Baltimore County *B,M,D*
  College Park *B,M,D*
  Eastern Shore *B*
Washington College *B*
Western Maryland College *B*

Massachusetts

Amherst College *B*
Anna Maria College for Men and
  Women *B*
Atlantic Union College *B*
Berkshire Community College *A*
Boston College *B*
Boston University *B,M*
Bradford College *B*
Brandeis University *B*
Bridgewater State College *B*
Clark University *B*
College of the Holy Cross *B*
Dean Junior College *A*
Eastern Nazarene College *B*
Emmanuel College *B*
Gordon College *B*
Hampshire College *B*
Harvard and Radcliffe Colleges *B*
Holyoke Community College *A*
Massachusetts Institute of
  Technology *B*
Mount Holyoke College *B*
New England Conservatory of
  Music *B,M*
Northeastern University *B*
Northern Essex Community
  College *A*
Roxbury Community College *A*
Simmons College *B*
Simon's Rock College of Bard *B*
Smith College *B,M*
Tufts University *B,M*
University of Massachusetts
  Amherst *B,M,D*
  Boston *B*
  Dartmouth *B*
  Lowell *B*
Wellesley College *B*
Westfield State College *B*

Wheaton College *B*
Williams College *B*

Michigan

Adrian College *A,B*
Albion College *B*
Alma College *B*
Andrews University *B,M*
Aquinas College *B*
Calvin College *B*
Central Michigan University *B,M*
Charles Stewart Mott Community
  College *A*
Concordia College *B*
Eastern Michigan University *B*
Grace Bible College *B*
Grand Rapids Baptist College and
  Seminary *B*
Grand Rapids Community
  College *A*
Grand Valley State University *B*
Henry Ford Community College *A*
Hillsdale College *B*
Hope College *B*
Kalamazoo College *B*
Kellogg Community College *A*
Lansing Community College *A*
Madonna University *B*
Marygrove College *B*
Michigan State University *B,M,D*
Northern Michigan University *B*
Oakland University *B,M*
Olivet College *B*
Saginaw Valley State University *B*
Siena Heights College *B*
Southwestern Michigan College *A*
Spring Arbor College *B*
Suomi College *A*
University of Michigan
  Ann Arbor *B,M,D*
  Flint *B*
Wayne State University *B,M*
Western Michigan University *B,M*
William Tyndale College *B*

Minnesota

Augsburg College *B*
Bemidji State University *B*
Bethel College *B*
Carleton College *B*
College of St. Benedict *B*
College of St. Catherine: St.
  Catherine Campus *B*
College of St. Scholastica *B*
Concordia College: Moorhead *B*
Concordia College: St. Paul *B*
Crown College *A,B*
Gustavus Adolphus College *B*
Hamline University *B*
Macalester College *B*
Mankato State University *B,M*
Moorhead State University *B*
Northland Community College *A*
Northwestern College *B*
Pillsbury Baptist Bible College *B*
Rainy River Community College *A*
Rochester Community College *A*
St. Cloud State University *B,M*
St. John's University *B*
St. Mary's College of Minnesota *B*
St. Olaf College *B*
Southwest State University *B*
University of Minnesota
  Duluth *B*
  Morris *B*
  Twin Cities *B,M,D*
University of St. Thomas *B*
Vermilion Community College *A*
Willmar Community College *A*
Winona State University *B*

Mississippi

Alcorn State University *B*
Belhaven College *B*
Blue Mountain College *B*
Delta State University *B*
East Central Community College *A*
Holmes Community College *A*
Jackson State University *B,M*
Jones County Junior College *A*
Mary Holmes College *A*
Millsaps College *B*
Mississippi College *B,M*
Mississippi University for Women *B*
Rust College *B*
Tougaloo College *B*
University of Mississippi *B,M,D*
University of Southern Mississippi
  B,M
William Carey College *B*

Missouri

Baptist Bible College *B*
Calvary Bible College *B*
Central Christian College of the
  Bible *B*
Central Methodist College *B*
Central Missouri State University
  B,M
College of the Ozarks *B*
Culver-Stockton College *B*
Drury College *B*
East Central College *A*
Evangel College *A,B*
Fontbonne College *B*
Jefferson College *A*
Lindenwood College *B*
Mineral Area College *A*
Missouri Baptist College *B*
Missouri Southern State College *B*
Missouri Western State College *B*
Moberly Area Community
  College *A*
Northeast Missouri State University
  B,M
Northwest Missouri State
  University *B*
Penn Valley Community College *A*
St. Louis Community College
  Florissant Valley *A*
  Forest Park *A*
  Meramec *A*
Southeast Missouri State
  University *B*
Southwest Baptist University *B*
University of Missouri
  Columbia *B,M*
  Kansas City *B,M*
  St. Louis *B*
Washington University *B,M,D*
Webster University *B*
William Jewell College *B*
William Woods College *B*

Montana

Eastern Montana College *B*
Miles Community College *A*
Montana State University *B*
Northern Montana College *B*
Rocky Mountain College *B*
University of Montana *B,M*

Nebraska

Chadron State College *B*
College of St. Mary *B*
Concordia College *B*
Creighton University *C*
Dana College *B*
Doane College *B*
Hastings College *B*
McCook Community College *A*
Midland Lutheran College *B*
Nebraska Wesleyan University *B*

Linfield College *B*
Marylhurst College *B*
Oregon State University *B*
Pacific University *B*
Portland Community College *A*
Portland State University *B*
Reed College *B*
Southern Oregon State College *B*
Treasure Valley Community
  College *A*
University of Oregon
  Eugene *B*
  Robert Donald Clark Honors
    College *B*
University of Portland *B,M*
Warner Pacific College *B*
Western Baptist College *B*
Western Conservative Baptist
  Seminary *M*
Western Oregon State College *B*
Willamette University *B*

Pennsylvania

Allegheny College *B*
Alvernia College *B*
Bloomsburg University of
  Pennsylvania *B*
Bryn Mawr College *B*
Bucknell University *B*
Bucks County Community
  College *A*
Carnegie Mellon University *B,M*
Cedar Crest College *B*
Chatham College *B*
Chestnut Hill College *A,B*
Cheyney University of
  Pennsylvania *B*
Clarion University of
  Pennsylvania *B*
Community College of
  Philadelphia *A*
Dickinson College *B*
Drexel University *B*
East Stroudsburg University of
  Pennsylvania *B*
Edinboro University of
  Pennsylvania *B*
Elizabethtown College *B*
Franklin and Marshall College *B*
Geneva College *B*
Gettysburg College *B*
Grove City College *B*
Haverford College *B*
Immaculata College *B*
Indiana University of Pennsylvania
  B,M
Kutztown University of
  Pennsylvania *B*
La Salle University *B*
Lebanon Valley College of
  Pennsylvania *B*
Lehigh University *B*
Lincoln University *B*
Lock Haven University of
  Pennsylvania *B*
Lycoming College *B*
Marywood College *B,M*
Mercyhurst College *B*
Messiah College *B*
Millersville University of
  Pennsylvania *B*
Moravian College *B*
Muhlenberg College *B*
Northeastern Christian Junior
  College *A*
Penn State University Park Campus
  B
Philadelphia College of Bible *B*
St. Vincent College *B*
Seton Hill College *B*
Slippery Rock University of
  Pennsylvania *B*

Susquehanna University *B*
Swarthmore College *B*
Temple University *B*
University of Pennsylvania *B,M,D*
University of Pittsburgh *B,M,D*
Valley Forge Military College *A*
West Chester University of
  Pennsylvania *B,M*
Westminster College *B*
York College of Pennsylvania *A,B*

Puerto Rico

Universidad Adventista de las
  Antillas *B*
University of Puerto Rico: Rio
  Piedras Campus *B*

Rhode Island

Brown University *B,M*
Community College of Rhode
  Island *A*
Providence College *B*
Rhode Island College *B*
Salve Regina University *B*
University of Rhode Island *B,M*

South Carolina

Anderson College *A,B*
Central Wesleyan College *B*
Claflin College *B*
Coker College *B*
College of Charleston *B*
Columbia College *B,M*
Converse College *B*
Erskine College *B*
Furman University *B*
Lander College *B*
Limestone College *B*
Newberry College *B*
North Greenville College *A*
Presbyterian College *B*
South Carolina State College *B*
University of South Carolina *B,M*
Winthrop University *B*

South Dakota

Augustana College *B*
Black Hills State University *B*
Dakota State University *B*
Mount Marty College *B*
Northern State University *B*
Sioux Falls College *B*
South Dakota State University *B*

Tennessee

Austin Peay State University *B,M*
Belmont University *B*
Bethel College *B*
Carson-Newman College *B*
Cleveland State Community
  College *A*
Columbia State Community
  College *A*
David Lipscomb University *B*
Dyersburg State Community
  College *A*
East Tennessee State University *B*
Fisk University *B*
Freed-Hardeman University *B*
Hiwassee College *A*
Johnson Bible College *B*
Knoxville College *B*
Lambuth University *B*
Lane College *B*
Martin Methodist College *A*
Maryville College *B*
Memphis State University *B,M,D*
Middle Tennessee State University
  B,M
Milligan College *B*
Motlow State Community
  College *A*

Rhodes College *B*
Roane State Community College *A*
Southern College of Seventh-day
  Adventists *B*
Tennessee State University *B*
Tennessee Technological
  University *B*
Tennessee Temple University *B*
Tennessee Wesleyan College *B*
Tomlinson College *A*
Trevecca Nazarene College *B*
Tusculum College *B*
Union University *B*
University of the South *B*
University of Tennessee
  Chattanooga *B,M*
  Knoxville *B,M*
  Martin *B*
Walters State Community
  College *A*
William Jennings Bryan College *B*

Texas

Abilene Christian University *B*
Alvin Community College *A*
Amarillo College *A*
Angelina College *A*
Angelo State University *B*
Arlington Baptist College *B*
Austin College *B*
Austin Community College *A*
Baylor University *B,M*
Bee County College *A*
Brazosport College *A*
College of the Mainland *A*
Collin County Community College
  District *A*
Concordia Lutheran College *B*
Corpus Christi State University *B*
Dallas Baptist University *B*
East Texas Baptist University *B*
East Texas State University *B,M*
El Paso Community College *A*
Hardin-Simmons University *B*
Houston Baptist University *B*
Houston Community College *C,A*
Howard College *A*
Howard Payne University *B*
Huston-Tillotson College *B*
Incarnate Word College *B*
Jacksonville College *A*
Jarvis Christian College *B*
Kilgore College *A*
Lamar University—Beaumont *B,M*
Lon Morris College *A*
Lubbock Christian University *B*
McLennan Community College *A*
McMurry University *B*
Midland College *A*
Midwestern State University *B*
Navarro College *A*
North Harris Montgomery
  Community College District *A*
Odessa College *C*
Our Lady of the Lake University of
  San Antonio *B*
Panola College *A*
Paul Quinn College *B*
Prairie View A&M University *B*
Rice University *B,M,D*
St. Mary's University *B*
St. Philip's College *A*
Sam Houston State University *B,M*
South Plains College *A*
Southwest Texas State University
  B,M
Southwestern Assemblies of God
  College *B*
Southwestern University *B*
Stephen F. Austin State University
  B,M
Sul Ross State University *B*

Tarleton State University *B*
Texas A&I University *B,M*
Texas Christian University *B*
Texas College *B*
Texas Lutheran College *B*
Texas Southern University *B,M*
Texas Southmost College *A*
Texas Tech University *B,D*
Texas Wesleyan University *B*
Texas Woman's University *B,M*
Trinity University *B*
Trinity Valley Community
  College *B*
University of Houston *B,M*
University of Mary Hardin-
  Baylor *B*
University of North Texas *B*
University of St. Thomas *B*
University of Texas
  Arlington *B*
  Austin *B,M,D*
  Pan American *B*
  Permian Basin *B*
  San Antonio *B,M*
  Tyler *B*
Victoria College *A*
Wayland Baptist University *B*
West Texas State University *B,M*
Western Texas College *A*
Wharton County Junior College *A*
Wiley College *B*

Utah

Brigham Young University *B,M,D*
Dixie College *A*
Southern Utah University *B*
University of Utah *B,M,D*
Utah State University *B*
Weber State University *B*

Vermont

Bennington College *B,M*
Castleton State College *B*
Goddard College *B,M*
Johnson State College *B*
Marlboro College *B*
Middlebury College *B*
St. Michael's College *B*
University of Vermont *B*

Virginia

Averett College *B*
Bluefield College *B*
Bridgewater College *B*
Christopher Newport College *B*
College of William and Mary *B*
Eastern Mennonite College *B*
Emory and Henry College *B*
George Mason University *B,M*
Hampton University *B*
Hollins College *B*
James Madison University *B,M*
Liberty University *B*
Longwood College *B*
Lynchburg College *B*
Mary Washington College *B*
Norfolk State University *B,M*
Northern Virginia Community
  College *A*
Old Dominion University *B*
Radford University *B,M*
Randolph-Macon Woman's
  College *B*
Roanoke College *B*
Southwest Virginia Community
  College *A*
Sweet Briar College *B*
University of Richmond *B*
University of Virginia *B,M*
Virginia Commonwealth University
  B,M
Virginia Intermont College *B*

Virginia Polytechnic Institute and
State University *B*
Virginia State University *B*
Virginia Union University *B*
Virginia Wesleyan College *B*
Washington and Lee University *B*

Washington

Big Bend Community College *A*
Central Washington University *B,M*
Centralia College *A*
Cornish College of the Arts *B*
Eastern Washington University *B,M*
Everett Community College *A*
Evergreen State College *B*
Lower Columbia College *A*
Olympic College *A*
Pacific Lutheran University *B,M*
Seattle Central Community
College *A*
Seattle Pacific University *B*
Skagit Valley College *A*
Spokane Falls Community
College *A*
Tacoma Community College *A*
University of Puget Sound *B*
University of Washington *B,M*
Walla Walla College *B*
Washington State University *B,M*
Wenatchee Valley College *A*
Western Washington University
B,M
Whitman College *B*
Whitworth College *B*

West Virginia

Alderson-Broaddus College *B*
Davis and Elkins College *B*
Marshall University *B,M*
Potomac State College of West
Virginia University *A*
Shepherd College *B*
University of Charleston *B*
West Virginia Wesleyan College *B*

Wisconsin

Alverno College *B*
Beloit College *B*
Carroll College *B*
Carthage College *B*
Concordia University Wisconsin *B*
Lakeland College *B*
Lawrence University *B*
Maranatha Baptist Bible College *B*
Marian College of Fond du Lac *B*
Mount Mary College *B*
Mount Senario College *B*
Northland College *B*
Ripon College *B*
St. Norbert College *B*
Silver Lake College *B*
University of Wisconsin
Eau Claire *B,M*
Green Bay *B*
La Crosse *B*
Madison *B,M,D*
Milwaukee *B,M*
Oshkosh *B*
Parkside *B*
Platteville *B*
River Falls *B*
Stevens Point *B*
Superior *B*
Whitewater *B*
Viterbo College *B*

Wyoming

Casper College *A*
Central Wyoming College *A*
Eastern Wyoming College *A*
Laramie County Community
College *A*

Northwest College *A*
Sheridan College *A*
University of Wyoming *B,M*
Western Wyoming Community
College *A*

Canada

McGill University *B*

Music business management

Arkansas

John Brown University *B*
University of the Ozarks *B*

California

Point Loma Nazarene College *B*
Scripps College *B*
University of the Pacific *B*

Colorado

Colorado Institute of Art *A*

Connecticut

University of Hartford *B*

Florida

Florida Southern College *B*
Jacksonville University *B*
University of Miami *B*

Georgia

Berry College *B*
Georgia State University *B*
Shorter College *B*

Illinois

Columbia College *B,M*
De Paul University *B*
Elmhurst College *B*
Illinois Wesleyan University *B*
Millikin University *B*
Quincy College *B*
Roosevelt University *B*
Southern Illinois University at
Carbondale *B*

Indiana

Anderson University *B*
Butler University *B*
Indiana State University *B*
Indiana Wesleyan University *B*
St. Joseph's College *B*
University of Evansville *B*

Iowa

Drake University *B*
Luther College *B*

Kentucky

Eastern Kentucky University *B*
Union College *B*

Massachusetts

University of Massachusetts at
Lowell *B*

Michigan

Madonna University *B*
Wayne State University *B*

Minnesota

College of St. Scholastica *B*

Missouri

Fontbonne College *B*
Webster University *B*

New Jersey

William Paterson College of New
Jersey *B*

New Mexico

Eastern New Mexico University
B,M

New York

City University of New York:
Baruch College *B*
Five Towns College *A,B*
Manhattanville College *B*
New York University *B*
Onondaga Community College *A*
Syracuse University *B*
Villa Maria College of Buffalo *A*

North Carolina

Methodist College *A,B*
St. Andrews Presbyterian College *B*
Salem College *B*
Wingate College *B*
Winston-Salem State University *B*

Ohio

Baldwin-Wallace College *B*
Heidelberg College *B*
Ohio University *B*
Otterbein College *B*

Oklahoma

Oklahoma City University *B*
Phillips University *B*

Pennsylvania

Carnegie Mellon University *M*
Cheyney University of
Pennsylvania *B*
Clarion University of
Pennsylvania *B*
Geneva College *B*
Grove City College *B*
Mansfield University of
Pennsylvania *B*

South Carolina

Anderson College *B*

South Dakota

Dakota State University *B*
South Dakota State University *B*

Tennessee

Bristol University *A,B,M*
Memphis State University *B*
Middle Tennessee State
University *B*
Trevecca Nazarene College *B*

Texas

University of Texas at San
Antonio *B*
West Texas State University *B*

Virginia

Radford University *B*

Washington

Art Institute of Seattle *A*
Pierce College *A*
University of Puget Sound *B*

West Virginia

Davis and Elkins College *B*
Glenville State College *A*
West Virginia Institute of
Technology *B*

Wisconsin

Carroll College *B*
Lakeland College *B*

University of Wisconsin: Oshkosh *B*

Music education

Alabama

Alabama Agricultural and
Mechanical University *B*
Alabama Southern Community
College *A*
Alabama State University *B,M*
Auburn University *B,M,D*
Birmingham-Southern College *B*
Huntingdon College *B*
Jacksonville State University *B,M*
Jefferson State Community
College *A*
John C. Calhoun State Community
College *A*
Judson College *B*
Lawson State Community
College *A*
Livingston University *B,M*
Oakwood College *B*
Samford University *B,M*
Talladega College *B*
University of Alabama
Birmingham *B*
Huntsville *B*
Tuscaloosa *B,M*
University of Montevallo *B,M*
University of North Alabama *B,M*
University of South Alabama *B*
Wallace State Community College
at Hanceville *A*

Alaska

University of Alaska
Anchorage *B*
Fairbanks *M*

Arizona

Arizona State University *B,M,D*
Eastern Arizona College *A*
Grand Canyon University *B*
Northern Arizona University *B,M*
University of Arizona *B,M,D*
Yavapai College *A*

Arkansas

Arkansas College *B*
Arkansas State University *B,M*
Arkansas Tech University *B,M*
Harding University *B*
Henderson State University *B,M*
John Brown University *B*
Ouachita Baptist University *B*
University of Arkansas
Fayetteville *B,M*
Monticello *B*
Pine Bluff *B*
University of Central Arkansas *B,M*
University of the Ozarks *B*
Westark Community College *A*

California

Azusa Pacific University *B*
Bethany College *B*
Biola University *B*
California Lutheran University *B*
California State University
Bakersfield *B*
Fresno *B*
Fullerton *B,M*
Long Beach *B*
Los Angeles *B,M*
Northridge *B*
Sacramento *B*
Chapman University *B*
Christ College Irvine *B*

Christian Heritage College *B*
College of Notre Dame *M*
Fresno Pacific College *B*
Holy Names College *M*
Humboldt State University *B*
Mount St. Mary's College *B*
Occidental College *M*
Pacific Union College *B*
Point Loma Nazarene College *B*
Simpson College *B*
Southern California College *B*
University of California: Davis *M*
University of the Pacific *B,M*
University of Redlands *B*
University of Southern California
 B,M,D
Westmont College *B*

Colorado

Colorado Christian University *B*
Colorado State University *B*
Metropolitan State College of
 Denver *B*
University of Colorado
 Boulder *B,M,D*
 Denver *B*
University of Denver *B*
University of Northern Colorado
 B,M,D
Western State College of
 Colorado *B*

Connecticut

Central Connecticut State
 University *B,M*
University of Bridgeport *B,M*
University of Connecticut *B*
University of Hartford *B,M,D,W*
Western Connecticut State
 University *B,M*

Delaware

Delaware State College *B*
University of Delaware *B*

District of Columbia

Howard University *M*
University of the District of
 Columbia *B*

Florida

Barry University *B*
Bethune-Cookman College *B*
Florida Agricultural and Mechanical
 University *B*
Florida Atlantic University *B,M*
Florida International University
 B,M
Florida Southern College *B*
Florida State University *B,M,D*
Hobe Sound Bible College *B*
Jacksonville University *B,M*
Manatee Community College *A*
Palm Beach Community College *A*
Pensacola Junior College *A*
Southeastern College of the
 Assemblies of God *B*
Stetson University *B*
University of Central Florida *B,M*
University of Florida *B,M*
University of Miami *B,M*
University of North Florida *B*
University of South Florida *B,M*
University of Tampa *B*
University of West Florida *B*
Warner Southern College *B*

Georgia

Albany State College *B,M*
Armstrong State College *B*
Augusta College *B*
Berry College *B*

Brenau Women's College *B*
Brewton-Parker College *B*
Columbus College *B*
Covenant College *B*
Gainesville College *A*
Georgia College *B*
Georgia Southern University *B,M*
Georgia Southwestern College *B*
Georgia State University *M*
Kennesaw State College *B*
Mercer University *B*
North Georgia College *B*
Paine College *B*
Piedmont College *B*
Shorter College *B,M*
Toccoa Falls College *B*
University of Georgia *B,M,D*
Valdosta State College *B,M*
Wesleyan College *B*
West Georgia College *B,M*

Hawaii

Brigham Young University-
 Hawaii *B*

Idaho

Boise State University *B,M*
College of Southern Idaho *A*
Idaho State University *B*
North Idaho College *A*
Northwest Nazarene College *B*
Ricks College *A*

Illinois

Augustana College *B*
Blackburn College *B*
Bradley University *B*
Concordia University *B,M*
De Paul University *B,M*
Elmhurst College *B*
Eureka College *B*
Governors State University *B*
Greenville College *B*
Illinois Benedictine College *B*
Illinois State University *B,M*
Illinois Wesleyan University *B*
MacMurray College *B*
Millikin University *B*
Monmouth College *B*
Northern Illinois University *B,M*
Northwestern University *B,M,D*
Olivet Nazarene University *B*
Quincy College *B*
Roosevelt University *B,M*
Southern Illinois University
 Carbondale *B,M*
 Edwardsville *B*
Trinity Christian College *B*
Trinity College *B*
University of Illinois at Urbana-
 Champaign *B,M,D*
VanderCook College of Music *B,M*
Western Illinois University *B*
Wheaton College *B*

Indiana

Anderson University *B*
Ball State University *B*
Bethel College *B*
Butler University *B,M*
Goshen College *B*
Huntington College *B*
Indiana State University *B,M*
Indiana University
 Bloomington *B,M*
 South Bend *B*
Indiana University—Purdue
 University at Fort Wayne *B*
Indiana Wesleyan University *B*
Manchester College *B*
Marian College *B*
Martin University *B*

Oakland City College *B*
St. Joseph's College *B*
St. Mary-of-the-Woods College *B*
St. Mary's College *B*
Taylor University *B*
University of Evansville *B,M*
University of Indianapolis *B*
Valparaiso University *B*
Vincennes University *A*

Iowa

Briar Cliff College *B*
Buena Vista College *B*
Central College *B*
Clarke College *B*
Coe College *B*
Cornell College *B*
Drake University *B,M*
Iowa Lakes Community College *A*
Iowa State University *B*
Iowa Wesleyan College *B*
Kirkwood Community College *A*
Loras College *B*
Luther College *B*
Morningside College *B*
Mount Mercy College *B*
St. Ambrose University *B*
Simpson College *B*
Teikyo Westmar University *B*
University of Iowa *B,M,D*
University of Northern Iowa *B,M*
Upper Iowa University *B*
Wartburg College *B*
William Penn College *B*

Kansas

Baker University *B*
Benedictine College *B*
Bethany College *B*
Emporia State University *B*
Friends University *B*
Hutchinson Community College *A*
Kansas State University *B,M*
Kansas Wesleyan University *B*
McPherson College *B*
MidAmerica Nazarene College *B*
Pittsburg State University *M*
Southwestern College *B*
Tabor College *B*
University of Kansas *B,M,D*
Washburn University of Topeka *B*
Wichita State University *B,M*

Kentucky

Asbury College *B*
Bellarmine College *B*
Berea College *B*
Campbellsville College *B*
Cumberland College *B*
Eastern Kentucky University *B*
Georgetown College *B*
Kentucky State University *B*
Kentucky Wesleyan College *B*
Morehead State University *B,M*
Murray State University *B*
Northern Kentucky University *B*
Transylvania University *B*
Union College *B*
University of Kentucky *B*
University of Louisville *B,M*
Western Kentucky University *B,M*

Louisiana

Centenary College of Louisiana *B*
Dillard University *B*
Grambling State University *B*
Louisiana College *B*
Louisiana State University and
 Agricultural and Mechanical
 College *B,M,D*
Louisiana Tech University *B*
McNeese State University *B,M*

Nicholls State University *B*
Northeast Louisiana University *B,M*
Northwestern State University *B,M*
Southeastern Louisiana
 University *B*
Southern University and
 Agricultural and Mechanical
 College *B*
University of New Orleans *B*
University of Southwestern
 Louisiana *B*
Xavier University of Louisiana *B*

Maine

University of Maine *B*
University of Southern Maine *B*

Maryland

Columbia Union College *B*
Frederick Community College *A*
Montgomery College
 Germantown Campus *A*
 Rockville Campus *A*
Morgan State University *B*
Towson State University *M*

Massachusetts

Anna Maria College for Men and
 Women *B*
Berklee College of Music *B*
Boston Conservatory *B,M*
Boston University *B,M,D*
Eastern Nazarene College *B,M*
Emmanuel College *B*
Hampshire College *B*
New England Conservatory of
 Music *M*
Salem State College *B*
Tufts University *B,M*
University of Massachusetts at
 Lowell *B,M*
Westfield State College *B*

Michigan

Adrian College *B*
Andrews University *M*
Aquinas College *B*
Calvin College *B,M*
Central Michigan University *B,M*
Concordia College *B*
Eastern Michigan University *B,M*
Grand Rapids Baptist College and
 Seminary *B*
Grand Valley State University *B*
Hillsdale College *B*
Lansing Community College *A*
Madonna University *B*
Marygrove College *B*
Michigan State University *B,M,D*
Northern Michigan University *B,M*
Oakland University *B*
Saginaw Valley State University *B*
University of Michigan
 Ann Arbor *B*
 Flint *B*
Wayne State University *B,M*
Western Michigan University *B,M*

Minnesota

Bemidji State University *B*
Bethel College *B*
College of St. Catherine: St.
 Catherine Campus *B*
College of St. Scholastica *B*
Concordia College: Moorhead *B*
Concordia College: St. Paul *B*
Crown College *B*
Gustavus Adolphus College *B*
Mankato State University *B*
Moorhead State University *B,M*
Northland Community College *A*
Northwestern College *B*

Pillsbury Baptist Bible College *B*
Rainy River Community College *A*
St. Cloud State University *B*
St. Mary's College of Minnesota *B*
St. Olaf College *B*
Southwest State University *B*
University of Minnesota
    Duluth *B,M*
    Twin Cities *B,M*
Willmar Community College *A*
Winona State University *B*

Mississippi

Alcorn State University *B*
Blue Mountain College *B*
Delta State University *B,M*
Mississippi College *B,M*
Mississippi State University *B,M*
Mississippi University for Women *B*
Northeast Mississippi Community
    College *A*
Rust College *B*
University of Mississippi *B*
University of Southern Mississippi
    B,M,D

Missouri

Avila College *B*
Calvary Bible College *B*
Central Missouri State University
    B,M
College of the Ozarks *B*
Culver-Stockton College *B*
Evangel College *B*
Hannibal-LaGrange College *B*
Lindenwood College *B*
Missouri Baptist College *B*
Missouri Western State College *B*
Northeast Missouri State
    University *M*
Northwest Missouri State
    University *B,M*
Southeast Missouri State University
    B,M
Southwest Baptist University *B*
Southwest Missouri State
    University *B*
University of Missouri
    Columbia *B,M,D*
    Kansas City *B,M,D*
Webster University *B*

Montana

Eastern Montana College *B*
Montana State University *B*
Rocky Mountain College *B*
University of Montana *B*
Western Montana College of the
    University of Montana *B*

Nebraska

Chadron State College *B*
College of St. Mary *B*
Concordia College *B*
Dana College *B*
Doane College *B*
Grace College of the Bible *B*
Hastings College *B*
Nebraska Wesleyan University *B*
Northeast Community College *A*
Peru State College *B*
Union College *B*
University of Nebraska
    Kearney *B,M*
    Lincoln *B,M*
    Omaha *B*
Wayne State College *B*

Nevada

Sierra Nevada College *B*
University of Nevada: Reno *B*

New Hampshire

Keene State College *B*
Plymouth State College of the
    University System of New
    Hampshire *B*
University of New Hampshire *B,M*

New Jersey

Essex County College *A*
Glassboro State College *B,M*
Jersey City State College *B,M*
Kean College of New Jersey *B*
Ocean County College *A*
Rutgers—The State University of
    New Jersey
        Camden College of Arts and
        Sciences *B*
        Mason Gross School of the
        Arts *B*
        New Brunswick *M,D*
        Newark College of Arts and
        Sciences *B*
        University College Newark *B*
Seton Hall University *B*
Trenton State College *B,M*
Westminster Choir College *B,M*
William Paterson College of New
    Jersey *B*

New Mexico

Eastern New Mexico University
    B,M
New Mexico Highlands
    University *B*
New Mexico State University *B*
University of New Mexico *B,M*
Western New Mexico University *B*

New York

Adelphi University *B*
City University of New York
    Brooklyn College *B,M*
    Hunter College *B,M*
    Lehman College *M*
    Queens College *B,M*
    York College *B*
College of St. Rose *B,M*
Concordia College *B*
Dowling College *B*
Eastman School of Music of the
    University of Rochester *B,M,D*
Five Towns College *B*
Hartwick College *B*
Hofstra University *B,M*
Houghton College *B*
Ithaca College *B,M*
King's College *B*
Long Island University: C. W. Post
    Campus *B,M*
Manhattan School of Music *M*
Manhattanville College *M*
Nazareth College of Rochester *B,M*
New York University *B,M,D*
Nyack College *B*
Roberts Wesleyan College *B*
State University of New York
    Buffalo *B,M,D*
    College at Fredonia *B,M*
    College at Potsdam *B,M*
Syracuse University *B,M*
University of Rochester *B,M,D*
Wagner College *B*
Wells College *B*

North Carolina

Appalachian State University *B,M*
Barton College *B*
Bennett College *B*
Brevard College *A*
Campbell University *B*
Catawba College *B*
East Carolina University *B,M*

Elizabeth City State University *B*
Elon College *B*
Fayetteville State University *B*
Gardner-Webb College *B*
Johnson C. Smith University *B*
Lenoir-Rhyne College *B*
Livingstone College *B*
Mars Hill College *B*
Meredith College *B,M*
Methodist College *A,B*
North Carolina Agricultural and
    Technical State University *B*
North Carolina Central University
    B,M
Pembroke State University *B*
Pfeiffer College *B*
Piedmont Bible College *B*
Queens College *B*
St. Augustine's College *B*
Salem College *B*
University of North Carolina
    Chapel Hill *B*
    Greensboro *B,M,D*
Western Carolina University *B,M*
Wingate College *B*
Winston-Salem State University *B*

North Dakota

Bismarck State College *A*
Dickinson State University *B*
Jamestown College *B*
Minot State University *B,M*
North Dakota State University *B*
University of Mary *B*
University of North Dakota *B,M*
Valley City State University *B*

Ohio

Ashland University *B*
Baldwin-Wallace College *B*
Bluffton College *B*
Bowling Green State University
    B,M
Capital University *B*
Case Western Reserve University
    B,M,D
Cedarville College *B*
College of Mount St. Joseph *C*
College of Wooster *B*
Defiance College *B*
Denison University *B*
Heidelberg College *B*
Kent State University *B*
Lorain County Community
    College *A*
Malone College *B*
Miami University: Oxford Campus
    B,M
Mount Union College *B*
Mount Vernon Nazarene College *B*
Muskingum College *B*
Oberlin College *B,M*
Ohio Northern University *B*
Ohio State University: Columbus
    Campus *B*
Ohio University *B*
Otterbein College *B*
University of Cincinnati *B,M,D*
University of Dayton *B*
University of Findlay *B*
University of Rio Grande *B*
University of Toledo *B*
Wittenberg University *B*
Wright State University *B,M*
Xavier University *B*
Youngstown State University *B,M*

Oklahoma

East Central University *B*
Langston University *B*
Mid-America Bible College *B*

Northwestern Oklahoma State
    University *B*
Oklahoma Baptist University *B*
Oklahoma Christian University of
    Science and Arts *B*
Oklahoma City University *B*
Oklahoma Panhandle State
    University *B*
Oral Roberts University *B*
Phillips University *B*
Southeastern Oklahoma State
    University *B,M*
Southwestern Oklahoma State
    University *B,M*
University of Central Oklahoma
    B,M
University of Oklahoma *B*
University of Science and Arts of
    Oklahoma *B*
University of Tulsa *B,M*

Oregon

George Fox College *B*
Linfield College *B*
Oregon State University *M*
Pacific University *B*
Portland State University *M*
University of Oregon *B,M,D*
University of Portland *B*
Warner Pacific College *B*
Western Baptist College *B*
Western Oregon State College *B,M*
Willamette University *B,M*

Pennsylvania

Bucknell University *B*
Carnegie Mellon University *B*
Chestnut Hill College *B*
Clarion University of
    Pennsylvania *B*
Duquesne University *B,M*
Edinboro University of
    Pennsylvania *B*
Elizabethtown College *B*
Geneva College *B*
Gettysburg College *B*
Gratz College *B,M*
Grove City College *B*
Immaculata College *B*
Indiana University of Pennsylvania
    B,M
Lebanon Valley College of
    Pennsylvania *B*
Lincoln University *B*
Lycoming College *B*
Mansfield University of
    Pennsylvania *B,M*
Marywood College *B,M*
Mercyhurst College *B*
Messiah College *B*
Millersville University of
    Pennsylvania *B*
Moravian College *B*
Penn State University Park Campus
    B,M,D
Philadelphia College of Bible *B*
St. Vincent College *B*
Seton Hill College *B*
Slippery Rock University of
    Pennsylvania *B*
Susquehanna University *B*
Temple University *B,M,D*
University of the Arts *M*
West Chester University of
    Pennsylvania *B,M*
Westminster College *B*
Wilkes University *B*

Puerto Rico

Conservatory of Music of Puerto
    Rico *B*

Inter American University of Puerto Rico: San German Campus B
University of Puerto Rico: Rio Piedras Campus B

Rhode Island
Rhode Island College B,M
Salve Regina University B
University of Rhode Island B

South Carolina
Anderson College B
Benedict College B
Bob Jones University B,M
Charleston Southern University B
Coker College B
Columbia College B
Erskine College B
Lander College B
Limestone College B
Newberry College B
Presbyterian College B
South Carolina State College B
University of South Carolina
    Coastal Carolina College B
    Columbia B,M,D
Winthrop University B,M

South Dakota
Augustana College B
Black Hills State University B
Dakota State University B
Mount Marty College B
Northern State University B,M
Sioux Falls College B
South Dakota State University B
University of South Dakota B,M

Tennessee
Belmont University B,M
Carson-Newman College B
Crichton College B
David Lipscomb University B
East Tennessee State University B,M
Freed-Hardeman University B
Lambuth University B
Maryville College B
Middle Tennessee State University B
Milligan College B
Roane State Community College A
Tennessee Technological University B
Tennessee Wesleyan College B
Trevecca Nazarene College B
Union University B,M
University of Tennessee
    Chattanooga B,M
    Knoxville B,M
    Martin B
William Jennings Bryan College B

Texas
Abilene Christian University B
Angelo State University B,M
Baylor University B,M
Dallas Baptist University B
Del Mar College A
East Texas Baptist University B
East Texas State University B,M
Hardin-Simmons University B,M
Houston Baptist University B
Incarnate Word College B
Jarvis Christian College B
Lubbock Christian University B
McMurry University B
Midwestern State University B
Prairie View A&M University M
Ranger Junior College A
St. Mary's University B
Sam Houston State University B,M

Southern Methodist University B,M
Southwest Texas State University B,M
Sul Ross State University B
Texas A&I University B,M
Texas Christian University B,M
Texas College B
Texas Lutheran College B
Texas Tech University B,M
Texas Wesleyan University B
Texas Woman's University M
University of Houston B,M
University of Mary Hardin-Baylor B
University of North Texas M,D
University of Texas
    El Paso M
    San Antonio M
Wayland Baptist University B
West Texas State University B,M
Wiley College B

Utah
Brigham Young University B,M
Southern Utah University B
Weber State University B

Vermont
Castleton State College B
Johnson State College B
St. Michael's College B
University of Vermont B

Virginia
Bluefield College B
Eastern Mennonite College B
Emory and Henry College B
George Mason University B,M
Liberty University B
Old Dominion University B
Radford University M
Shenandoah University B,M
University of Richmond B
Virginia Commonwealth University B
Virginia Intermont College B
Virginia Polytechnic Institute and State University B,M
Virginia Union University B
Virginia Wesleyan College B

Washington
Central Washington University B
Eastern Washington University B
Gonzaga University B
Pacific Lutheran University B
Seattle Pacific University B
University of Puget Sound M
University of Washington B
Walla Walla College B
Washington State University B
Western Washington University B,M

West Virginia
Alderson-Broaddus College B
Concord College B
Fairmont State College B
Glenville State College B
Shepherd College B
University of Charleston B
West Liberty State College B
West Virginia Institute of Technology B
West Virginia State College B
West Virginia University B,M,D
West Virginia Wesleyan College B

Wisconsin
Alverno College B
Beloit College B,M
Carroll College B

Carthage College B
Lakeland College B
Lawrence University B
Maranatha Baptist Bible College B
Marian College of Fond du Lac B
Marquette University B
Mount Mary College B
Mount Senario College B
Northland College B
Ripon College C
St. Norbert College B
Silver Lake College B
University of Wisconsin
    Eau Claire B
    Green Bay B
    La Crosse B
    Madison B,M
    Oshkosh B
    Platteville B
    River Falls B
    Stevens Point B,M
    Whitewater B
Wisconsin Lutheran College B

Wyoming
University of Wyoming B

American Samoa, Caroline Islands, Guam, Marianas, Virgin Islands
University of Guam B
University of the Virgin Islands B

Music history and appreciation

Alabama
Alabama State University B
Birmingham-Southern College B

Arizona
Arizona State University M
Northern Arizona University B

Arkansas
Ouachita Baptist University B

California
California State University
    Fresno B,M
    Fullerton B,M
    Long Beach B
    Los Angeles B,M
    Northridge B,M
Chapman University B
Dominican College of San Rafael B
Mills College B
San Francisco State University B,M
San Jose State University B
Santa Clara University B
Scripps College B
University of California
    San Diego B
    Santa Barbara D
University of the Pacific B
University of Redlands B
University of Southern California M,D

Colorado
University of Colorado at Boulder B
University of Denver B,M

Connecticut
Connecticut College B
University of Hartford B,M
Wesleyan University B,M,D
Yale University M,D

District of Columbia
American University B
Catholic University of America M,D
Howard University B,M
Mount Vernon College B

Florida
Florida Atlantic University B
Florida State University B
Jacksonville University B
New College of the University of South Florida B
Pensacola Junior College A
Stetson University B
University of Florida B,M
University of Miami B,M,D
University of North Florida B
University of South Florida M

Georgia
Emory University B
Reinhardt College A
University of Georgia B,M,D
Young Harris College A

Idaho
University of Idaho B

Illinois
Augustana College B
Concordia University B
Illinois College B
Illinois Wesleyan University B
Lake Forest College B
Northern Illinois University M
Northwestern University B,M,D
Roosevelt University B,M
Southern Illinois University
    Carbondale B,M
    Edwardsville B
University of Chicago B,M,D
University of Illinois at Urbana-Champaign B
Wheaton College B

Indiana
Butler University B,M
Indiana State University M
Indiana University Bloomington B
Valparaiso University B,M

Iowa
Drake University B,M
Grinnell College B
University of Iowa B,M,D
University of Northern Iowa M

Kansas
Coffeyville Community College A
Dodge City Community College A
Kansas State University M
Pittsburg State University M
University of Kansas B

Kentucky
University of Kentucky M,D
University of Louisville B,M,D

Louisiana
Louisiana State University and Agricultural and Mechanical College M,D
University of Southwestern Louisiana B

Maryland
College of Notre Dame of Maryland B
University of Maryland: College Park B,M,D

Massachusetts

Boston University *B,M*
Brandeis University *M,D*
College of the Holy Cross *B*
Gordon College *B*
Hampshire College *B*
Harvard and Radcliffe Colleges *B*
Harvard University *D*
New England Conservatory of
Music *B,M*
Simmons College *B*
Smith College *B,M*
Tufts University *B,M*
University of Massachusetts at
Lowell *B,M*
Wellesley College *B*

Michigan

Calvin College *B*
Central Michigan University *M*
Hope College *B*
Michigan State University *M,D*
Olivet College *B*
University of Michigan
Ann Arbor *B,M,D*
Dearborn *B*
Western Michigan University *B*

Minnesota

College of St. Scholastica *B*
Concordia College: Moorhead *B*
Gustavus Adolphus College *B*
Mankato State University *B,M*
Northland Community College *A*
Rainy River Community College *A*
St. Olaf College *B*
University of Minnesota: Duluth *B*
Willmar Community College *A*

Missouri

Central Methodist College *B*
Drury College *B*
Maryville University *B*
University of Missouri: Kansas
City *M*
Webster University *B*

Montana

University of Montana *M*

Nebraska

Hastings College *B*
Northeast Community College *A*
York College *A*

New Hampshire

Franklin Pierce College *B*
University of New Hampshire *B,M*

New Jersey

Jersey City State College *B*
Princeton University *M,D*
Rutgers—The State University of
New Jersey
Camden College of Arts and
Sciences *B*
Douglass College *B*
Livingston College *B*
New Brunswick *M,D*
Newark College of Arts and
Sciences *B*
Rutgers College *B*
University College New
Brunswick *B*
Seton Hall University *B*

New Mexico

New Mexico State University *M*

New York

Bard College *B*
City University of New York
City College *B,M*
Hunter College *B,M*
Queensborough Community
College *A*
Concordia College *B*
Eastman School of Music of the
University of Rochester *M,D*
Eugene Lang College/New School
for Social Research *B*
Fordham University *B*
Hofstra University *B*
Jewish Theological Seminary of
America *M,D*
Manhattanville College *B*
Molloy College *B*
New York University *B,M,D*
Sarah Lawrence College *B*
State University of New York
Buffalo *B,M,D*
Stony Brook *M,D*
College at Fredonia *B*
College at Geneseo *B*
College at New Paltz *B*
Syracuse University *M*
University of Rochester *B*

North Carolina

Brevard College *A*
Duke University *B*
St. Andrews Presbyterian College *B*
University of North Carolina
Chapel Hill *M,D*
Greensboro *B*

North Dakota

Dickinson State University *B*

Ohio

Baldwin-Wallace College *B*
Bowling Green State University
B,M
Case Western Reserve University
B,M
Cedarville College *B*
Cleveland State University *B,M*
College of Wooster *B*
Heidelberg College *B*
Kent State University *M,D*
Kenyon College *B*
Oberlin College *B,M*
Ohio State University: Columbus
Campus *B,M,D*
Ohio University *B,M*
Ohio Wesleyan University *B*
Otterbein College *B*
University of Akron *M*
University of Cincinnati *B,M*
Wright State University *B*
Youngstown State University *B,M*

Oklahoma

University of Oklahoma *B,M*

Oregon

Lewis and Clark College *B*
Oregon State University *B*
University of Oregon *M,D*
Western Conservative Baptist
Seminary *M*

Pennsylvania

Bryn Mawr College *B*
Bucknell University *B*
Indiana University of Pennsylvania
B,M
La Salle University *B*
Lafayette College *B*
Mansfield University of
Pennsylvania *B*

Marywood College *M*
Moravian College *B*
Penn State University Park
Campus *B*
Temple University *B,M*
West Chester University of
Pennsylvania *B,M*

Rhode Island

Brown University *B,M,D*
University of Rhode Island *B*

South Carolina

Columbia College *B*
Converse College *B,M*
Furman University *B*
University of South Carolina *M*

South Dakota

University of South Dakota *M*

Tennessee

Fisk University *B*
Trevecca Nazarene College *B*
Vanderbilt University *B*

Texas

Baylor University *B,M*
Central Texas College *A*
East Texas State University *M*
Jacksonville College *A*
Lon Morris College *A*
Rice University *B,M,D*
Southern Methodist University *B,M*
Southwestern University *B*
Texas Christian University *B*
Texas Tech University *B,M*
University of Houston *B*
University of North Texas *B*

Utah

Weber State University *B*

Vermont

Marlboro College *B*

Virginia

Averett College *B*
Christopher Newport College *B*
Emory and Henry College *B*
Old Dominion University *B*
University of Richmond *B*
Virginia Commonwealth University
B,M

Washington

Central Washington University *M*
Eastern Washington University *B,M*
Evergreen State College *B*
Tacoma Community College *A*
University of Washington *B,M,D*
Western Washington University
B,M

West Virginia

Marshall University *B*
Shepherd College *B*
West Virginia University *B,M*

Wisconsin

Lawrence University *B*
University of Wisconsin
Green Bay *B*
Madison *M*
Milwaukee *B*

Canada

McGill University *B,M,D*

Music performance

Alabama

Huntingdon College *B*
Jacksonville State University *B,M*
Jefferson State Community
College *A*
Miles College *B*
Oakwood College *B*
Samford University *B*
Snead State Junior College *A*
Talladega College *B*
University of Alabama *B,M*
University of Montevallo *B*
University of North Alabama *B*
University of South Alabama *B*

Alaska

University of Alaska Anchorage *B*

Arizona

Arizona State University *B,M,D*
Grand Canyon University *B*
Northern Arizona University *B*
University of Arizona *B,M,D*

Arkansas

Arkansas State University *B*
Henderson State University *B*
Ouachita Baptist University *B*
University of Arkansas *B,M*

California

Azusa Pacific University *B*
Bethany College *B*
Biola University *B*
California Institute of the Arts
C,B,M
California State University
Dominguez Hills *B*
Fullerton *B,M*
Long Beach *B,M*
Los Angeles *B*
Northridge *B,M*
Stanislaus *B*
Chabot College *A*
Chapman University *B*
College of Notre Dame *B*
Dominican College of San Rafael
B,M
El Camino College *A*
Fresno Pacific College *B*
Gavilan Community College *A*
Golden West College *C,A*
Holy Names College *B,M*
La Sierra University *B*
Los Angeles Valley College *C*
Mills College *M*
MiraCosta College *C*
Mount St. Mary's College *B*
Pacific Union College *B*
Point Loma Nazarene College *B*
Saddleback College *A*
San Francisco Conservatory of
Music *B,M*
San Francisco State University *B,M*
San Jose State University *B,M*
Santa Clara University *B*
Scripps College *B*
Simpson College *B*
United States International
University *B,M*
University of California: Irvine *B*
University of the Pacific *B,M*
University of Redlands *B,M*
University of Southern California
B,M,D

Colorado

Adams State College *B*
Colorado Christian University *B*
Colorado State University *B,M*
Metropolitan State College of
  Denver *B*
University of Colorado
    Boulder *B*
    Denver *B*
University of Denver *M*
University of Northern Colorado
  B,M

Connecticut

Connecticut College *B*
University of Bridgeport *B*
University of Hartford *B,M,D,W*
Yale University *M,D*

Delaware

University of Delaware *B,M*

District of Columbia

American University *B,M*
Catholic University of America
  B,M,D
George Washington University *M*

Florida

Daytona Beach Community
  College *A*
Florida Agricultural and Mechanical
  University *B*
Florida Atlantic University *B*
Florida Southern College *B*
Florida State University *B,M,D*
Gulf Coast Community College *A*
Jacksonville University *B*
Palm Beach Community College *A*
Pensacola Junior College *A*
Stetson University *B*
University of Central Florida *B*
University of Florida *B,M*
University of Miami *B,M,D*
University of South Florida *B,M*
University of Tampa *B*

Georgia

Augusta College *B*
Berry College *B*
Brenau Women's College *B*
Clayton State College *A,B*
Gainesville College *A*
Georgia College *B*
Georgia Southern University *B*
Kennesaw State College *B*
Mercer University *B*
Morris Brown College *B*
Piedmont College *B*
Shorter College *B,M*
Toccoa Falls College *B*
Truett-McConnell College *A*
University of Georgia *B,M,D*
Valdosta State College *B*
Wesleyan College *B*
West Georgia College *B*

Hawaii

Brigham Young University-
  Hawaii *A*

Idaho

Boise State University *B,M*
North Idaho College *A*
University of Idaho *B*

Illinois

American Conservatory of Music
  C,B,M,D
Augustana College *B*
Columbia College *B*
Concordia University *B*

De Paul University *B,M*
Eureka College *B*
Illinois State University *B,M*
Illinois Wesleyan University *B*
Judson College *B*
Lake Forest College *B*
Millikin University *B*
North Park College and Theological
  Seminary *B*
Northern Illinois University *M*
Northwestern University *B,M,D*
Olivet Nazarene University *B*
Quincy College *B*
Roosevelt University *B,M*
St. Xavier University *B*
Southern Illinois University
    Carbondale *B,M*
    Edwardsville *B,M*
Trinity Christian College *B*
University of Illinois at Urbana-
  Champaign *B*
Wheaton College *B*

Indiana

Anderson University *B*
Ball State University *B*
Butler University *B,M*
DePauw University *B*
Huntington College *B*
Indiana State University *B,M*
Indiana University
    Bloomington *B,M,D*
    South Bend *B*
Indiana Wesleyan University *B*
St. Mary-of-the-Woods College *B*
St. Mary's College *B*
Taylor University *B*
University of Evansville *B*
University of Indianapolis *B*
University of Notre Dame *B,M*

Iowa

Cornell College *B*
Drake University *B,M*
Iowa Lakes Community College *A*
Morningside College *B*
Simpson College *B*
Southwestern Community
  College *A*
University of Iowa *B,M,D*
University of Northern Iowa *B,M*
Vennard College *B*
Wartburg College *B*

Kansas

Baker University *B*
Coffeyville Community College *A*
Friends University *B*
Kansas City College and Bible
  School *B*
Kansas State University *M*
McPherson College *B*
Ottawa University *B*
Pittsburg State University *B*
St. Mary College *B*
Southwestern College *B*
University of Kansas *B,M,D*

Kentucky

Asbury College *B*
Bellarmine College *B*
Berea College *B*
Campbellsville College *B*
Cumberland College *B*
Eastern Kentucky University *B,M*
Kentucky Christian College *B*
Kentucky State University *B*
Morehead State University *M*
Murray State University *B*
Transylvania University *B*
Union College *B*
University of Kentucky *B*

University of Louisville *B,M*
Western Kentucky University *B,M*

Louisiana

Centenary College of Louisiana *B*
Louisiana College *B*
Louisiana State University and
  Agricultural and Mechanical
  College *B,D*
Louisiana Tech University *B*
Loyola University *B,M*
McNeese State University *B*
Nicholls State University *B*
Northeast Louisiana University *B,M*
Northwestern State University *B*
University of Southwestern
  Louisiana *M*
World Evangelism Bible College
  and Seminary *B*
Xavier University of Louisiana *B*

Maine

University of Maine *B,M*
University of Southern Maine *B*

Maryland

College of Notre Dame of
  Maryland *B*
Howard Community College *A*
Johns Hopkins University *B,M,D*
Morgan State University *B*
New Community College of
  Baltimore *A*
University of Maryland: College
  Park *B*

Massachusetts

Anna Maria College for Men and
  Women *B*
Berklee College of Music *C,B*
Boston Conservatory *B,M*
Boston University *B,M,D,W*
Clark University *B*
Eastern Nazarene College *B*
Gordon College *B*
Hampshire College *B*
New England Conservatory of
  Music *B,M,D*
Simmons College *B*
University of Massachusetts
    Amherst *B*
    Lowell *B,M*

Michigan

Aquinas College *B*
Central Michigan University *M*
Eastern Michigan University *B,M*
Grand Rapids Baptist College and
  Seminary *B*
Grand Valley State University *B*
Hope College *B*
Lansing Community College *A*
Macomb Community College *C*
Madonna University *B*
Marygrove College *B*
Michigan State University *B,M,D*
Oakland University *B*
Olivet College *B*
University of Michigan *B,M,D*
Wayne State University *B,M*
Western Michigan University *B,M*
William Tyndale College *B*

Minnesota

Augsburg College *B*
Bethel College *B*
College of St. Benedict *B*
College of St. Catherine: St.
  Catherine Campus *B*
College of St. Scholastica *B*
Concordia College: Moorhead *B*
Crown College *B*

Mankato State University *B*
North Central Bible College *B*
Northwestern College *B*
St. Cloud State University *B*
St. John's University *B*
St. Mary's College of Minnesota *B*
St. Olaf College *B*
University of Minnesota: Duluth *B*
Willmar Community College *A*
Winona State University *B*

Mississippi

Belhaven College *B*
Delta State University *B*
Jackson State University *B*
Millsaps College *B*
Mississippi College *M*
Mississippi University for Women *B*
University of Southern
  Mississippi *D*

Missouri

Avila College *B*
Calvary Bible College *B*
Central Methodist College *B*
Central Missouri State University
  B,M
College of the Ozarks *B*
Evangel College *B*
Fontbonne College *B*
Jefferson College *A*
Lindenwood College *B*
Maryville University *B*
Missouri Baptist College *B*
Northeast Missouri State
  University *B*
Southeast Missouri State
  University *B*
Southwest Baptist University *B*
Southwest Missouri State
  University *B*
University of Missouri: Kansas City
  B,M,D
Webster University *B,M*
William Jewell College *B*

Montana

University of Montana *B,M*

Nebraska

Hastings College *B*
Nebraska Wesleyan University *B*
Northeast Community College *A*
Union College *B*
University of Nebraska
    Kearney *B*
    Omaha *B,M*
Wayne State College *B*
York College *A*

Nevada

University of Nevada: Reno *B*

New Hampshire

Franklin Pierce College *B*
Keene State College *B*
University of New Hampshire *B,M*

New Jersey

Burlington County College *A*
Georgian Court College *B*
Glassboro State College *B*
Jersey City State College *B*
Rutgers—The State University of
  New Jersey
      Mason Gross School of the
        Arts *B,M,D*
      New Brunswick *M,D*
Stockton State College *B*
Westminster Choir College *B,M*
William Paterson College of New
  Jersey *B*

New Mexico

New Mexico State University *M*
University of New Mexico *B,M*

New York

Bard College *B,M*
City University of New York
　Brooklyn College *B,M*
　Graduate School and
　　University Center *D*
　Hunter College *B,M*
　Lehman College *B*
　Queens College *B,M*
College of St. Rose *B*
Concordia College *B*
Eastman School of Music of the
　University of Rochester *B,M,D*
Five Towns College *A,B*
Hofstra University *B*
Houghton College *B*
Ithaca College *B,M*
Juilliard School *B,M,D*
King's College *B*
Manhattan School of Music *B,M,D*
Manhattanville College *B*
Mannes College of Music *B,M,W*
Molloy College *B*
Nassau Community College *A*
Nazareth College of Rochester *B*
New York University *B,M,D,W*
Niagara County Community
　College *A*
Nyack College *B*
Onondaga Community College *A*
Sarah Lawrence College *B*
State University of New York
　Albany *B*
　Binghamton *B,M*
　Buffalo *B,M*
　Purchase *B*
　Stony Brook *M*
　College at Fredonia *B,M*
　College at Geneseo *B*
　College at New Paltz *B*
　College at Potsdam *B,M*
Suffolk County Community
　College *A*
Syracuse University *B,M*
University of Rochester *M,D*
Wagner College *B*

North Carolina

Appalachian State University *B*
Brevard College *A*
Campbell University *B*
East Carolina University *B,M*
Elon College *B*
Lenoir-Rhyne College *B*
Mars Hill College *B*
Meredith College *B*
Methodist College *A,B*
North Carolina School of the Arts
　C,B,M
Queens College *B*
St. Andrews Presbyterian College *B*
Salem College *B*
University of North Carolina
　Chapel Hill *M,D*
　Charlotte *B*
　Greensboro *B,M,D*
Wingate College *B*

North Dakota

Jamestown College *B*
University of North Dakota *B,M*

Ohio

Ashland University *B*
Baldwin-Wallace College *B*
Bluffton College *B*
Bowling Green State University
　B,M

Capital University *B*
Case Western Reserve University
　B,M,D
Cleveland Institute of Music *B,M,D*
Cleveland State University *M*
College of Wooster *B*
Denison University *B*
Heidelberg College *B*
Kent State University *B,M*
Malone College *B*
Mount Union College *B*
Oberlin College *B*
Ohio Northern University *B*
Ohio State University: Columbus
　Campus *B,M,D*
Ohio University *B,M*
Ohio Wesleyan University *B*
Otterbein College *B*
University of Akron *B,M*
University of Cincinnati *B,M,D*
University of Dayton *B*
Wittenberg University *B*
Wright State University *B*
Youngstown State University *B,M*

Oklahoma

Langston University *B*
Oklahoma Baptist University *B*
Oklahoma City University *B,M*
Oral Roberts University *B*
Southeastern Oklahoma State
　University *B*
University of Oklahoma *B*
University of Tulsa *B,M*

Oregon

George Fox College *B*
Linfield College *B*
Marylhurst College *B*
Oregon State University *B*
Portland Community College *C,A*
Portland State University *B*
University of Oregon
　Eugene *B,M,D*
　Robert Donald Clark Honors
　　College *B*
Western Conservative Baptist
　Seminary *M*
Willamette University *B*

Pennsylvania

Bucknell University *B*
Carnegie Mellon University *B,M*
Chatham College *B*
Clarion University of
　Pennsylvania *B*
Curtis Institute of Music *C,B*
Duquesne University *B,M*
Geneva College *B*
Indiana University of Pennsylvania
　B,M
Lebanon Valley College of
　Pennsylvania *B*
Lock Haven University of
　Pennsylvania *B*
Mansfield University of
　Pennsylvania *B,M*
Marywood College *B*
Mercyhurst College *B*
Moravian College *B*
Penn State University Park
　Campus *M*
Philadelphia College of Bible *B*
St. Vincent College *B*
Seton Hill College *B*
Slippery Rock University of
　Pennsylvania *B*
Susquehanna University *B*
Temple University *B,M,D*
University of the Arts *C,B,M*
West Chester University of
　Pennsylvania *B,M*

Westminster College *B*
Wilkes University *B*

Puerto Rico

Conservatory of Music of Puerto
　Rico *B*
Inter American University of Puerto
　Rico: San German Campus *B*
Universidad Adventista de las
　Antillas *B*

Rhode Island

Rhode Island College *B*
Salve Regina University *B*
University of Rhode Island *B*

South Carolina

Anderson College *B*
Bob Jones University *B,M*
Charleston Southern University *B*
Coker College *B*
Columbia College *B*
Converse College *B,M*
Erskine College *B*
Furman University *B*
Limestone College *B*
Newberry College *B*
University of South Carolina *D*
Winthrop University *B,M*

South Dakota

Black Hills State University *B*
Sioux Falls College *B*
South Dakota State University *B*
University of South Dakota *B,M*

Tennessee

Carson-Newman College *B*
Christian Brothers University *B*
David Lipscomb University *B*
Hiwassee College *A*
Lambuth University *B*
Maryville College *B*
Tennessee Temple University *B*
Tennessee Wesleyan College *B*
Union University *B*
University of Tennessee
　Chattanooga *B,M*
　Martin *B*
Vanderbilt University *B*

Texas

Abilene Christian University *B*
Alvin Community College *A*
Baylor University *B,M*
Dallas Baptist University *B*
Del Mar College *A*
East Texas State University *B,M*
Hardin-Simmons University *B,M*
Houston Community College *A*
Incarnate Word College *B*
Lamar University—Beaumont *B,M*
Lon Morris College *A*
McMurry University *B*
Midland College *A*
Prairie View A&M University *B,M*
Rice University *B,M,D*
Sam Houston State University *B,M*
Southern Methodist University *B,M*
Southwest Texas State University
　B,M
Sul Ross State University *B*
Texas Christian University *B,M*
Texas Southmost College *A*
Texas Tech University *M*
Texas Woman's University *B,M*
Trinity University *B*
University of Houston *B,M*
University of Mary Hardin-
　Baylor *B*
University of North Texas *B,M,D*

University of Texas
　El Paso *B,M*
　San Antonio *B,M*
West Texas State University *B,M*
Wiley College *B*

Utah

Brigham Young University *B,M*
Weber State University *B*

Vermont

Bennington College *B*
Johnson State College *B*
Marlboro College *B*
University of Vermont *B*

Virginia

Averett College *B*
Bluefield College *B*
Christopher Newport College *B*
Emory and Henry College *B*
George Mason University *B*
Old Dominion University *B*
Radford University *B*
Shenandoah University *B,M*
University of Richmond *B*

Washington

Central Washington University *B,M*
Cornish College of the Arts *B*
Eastern Washington University *B,M*
Gonzaga University *B*
Green River Community College
　C,A
Pacific Lutheran University *B*
Seattle Pacific University *B*
Shoreline Community College *A*
Tacoma Community College *A*
University of Puget Sound *B*
University of Washington *B,M,D*
Walla Walla College *B*
Wenatchee Valley College *A*
Western Washington University
　B,M
Whitworth College *B*

West Virginia

Alderson-Broaddus College *B*
Davis and Elkins College *B*
Marshall University *B*
Shepherd College *B*
University of Charleston *B*
West Virginia University *B,M,D*
West Virginia Wesleyan College *B*

Wisconsin

Alverno College *B*
Beloit College *B*
Carroll College *B*
Lawrence University *B*
St. Norbert College *B*
University of Wisconsin
　Green Bay *B*
　Madison *B,M,D*
　Milwaukee *B*
　Oshkosh *B*
　Whitewater *B*

Wyoming

Casper College *A*
University of Wyoming *B*

Canada

McGill University *B,M,D*

Music theory and composition

Alabama

Huntingdon College *B*
Samford University *B,M*
University of Alabama *B,M*
University of Montevallo *B*
University of South Alabama *B*

Arizona

Arizona State University *B,M*
University of Arizona *B,M,D*

Arkansas

Henderson State University *B*
Ouachita Baptist University *B*

California

Azusa Pacific University *B,M*
Bethany College *B*
Biola University *B*
California Institute of the Arts
    C,B,M
California State University
    Dominguez Hills *B*
    Fullerton *B,M*
    Long Beach *B,M*
    Los Angeles *B,M*
    Northridge *B,M*
Chapman University *B*
Dominican College of San Rafael
    B,M
Golden West College *C,A*
Humboldt State University *B*
Mills College *M*
Mount St. Mary's College *B*
Point Loma Nazarene College *B*
San Francisco Conservatory of
    Music *B,M*
San Jose State University *B*
University of California: San
    Diego *B*
University of the Pacific *B,M*
University of Redlands *B*
University of Southern California
    B,M,D

Colorado

University of Colorado
    Boulder *B*
    Denver *B*
University of Denver *M*
University of Northern Colorado
    B,M

Connecticut

Connecticut College *B*
University of Bridgeport *B*
University of Connecticut *B*
University of Hartford *B,M,D,W*
Western Connecticut State
    University *B*

Delaware

University of Delaware *B*

District of Columbia

American University *B,M*
Catholic University of America
    B,M,D
Howard University *B,M*

Florida

Florida State University *B,M,D*
Jacksonville University *B*
New College of the University of
    South Florida *B*
Pensacola Junior College *A*
Stetson University *B*

University of Florida *M*
University of Miami *B,M,D*
University of South Florida *B,M*
University of Tampa *B*

Georgia

Clayton State College *A,B*
Georgia College *B*
Georgia Southern University *B*
Toccoa Falls College *B*
University of Georgia *B,M,D*
West Georgia College *B*

Idaho

Boise State University *B,M*
North Idaho College *A*
University of Idaho *B*

Illinois

American Conservatory of Music
    B,M
Columbia College *B*
Concordia University *B,M*
De Paul University *B*
Illinois Wesleyan University *B*
Judson College *B*
Lake Forest College *B*
Northern Illinois University *M*
Northwestern University *B,M,D*
Roosevelt University *B,M*
Southern Illinois University
    Carbondale *B,M*
    Edwardsville *B*
University of Chicago *B,M,D*
University of Illinois at Urbana-
    Champaign *B*
Wheaton College *B*

Indiana

Ball State University *B*
Butler University *B,M*
DePauw University *B*
Indiana State University *B,M*
Indiana University
    Bloomington *B,M,D*
    South Bend *B*
St. Joseph's College *A,M*
St. Mary's College *B*
Taylor University *B*
University of Notre Dame *B,M*
Valparaiso University *B*
Vincennes University *A*

Iowa

Drake University *B,M*
Loras College *B*
Southwestern Community
    College *A*
University of Iowa *B,M,D*
University of Northern Iowa *M*
Vennard College *B*
Wartburg College *B*

Kansas

Coffeyville Community College *A*
Kansas City College and Bible
    School *B*
Kansas State University *M*
Pittsburg State University *M*
Southwestern College *B*
University of Kansas *B,M,D*

Kentucky

Asbury College *B*
Eastern Kentucky University *B,M*
University of Kentucky *M*
University of Louisville *B,M*

Louisiana

Grambling State University *B*
Louisiana College *B*

Louisiana State University and
    Agricultural and Mechanical
    College *B,D*
Loyola University *B*
McNeese State University *B*
Northwestern State University *B*
University of New Orleans *B,M*
University of Southwestern
    Louisiana *B*

Maine

University of Maine *M*

Maryland

College of Notre Dame of
    Maryland *B*
Johns Hopkins University *B,M,D*
University of Maryland: College
    Park *B*

Massachusetts

Berklee College of Music *C,B*
Boston Conservatory *B,M*
Boston University *B,M,D*
Brandeis University *M,D*
Clark University *B*
Hampshire College *B*
Harvard University *D*
New England Conservatory of
    Music *B,M*
Simmons College *B*
University of Massachusetts at
    Lowell *B,M*

Michigan

Central Michigan University *B,M*
Grand Rapids Baptist College and
    Seminary *B*
Hope College *B*
Lansing Community College *A*
Marygrove College *B*
Michigan State University *B,M,D*
Olivet College *B*
University of Michigan *B,M,D*
Wayne State University *B,M*
Western Michigan University *B,M*
William Tyndale College *B*

Minnesota

Concordia College: Moorhead *B*
St. Olaf College *B*
University of Minnesota: Duluth *B*
Willmar Community College *A*
Winona State University *B*

Mississippi

Mississippi College *B,M*

Missouri

Maryville University *B*
Southeast Missouri State
    University *B*
Southwest Missouri State
    University *B*
University of Missouri: Kansas City
    B,M
Webster University *B,M*
William Jewell College *B*

Montana

University of Montana *B,M*

Nebraska

Wayne State College *B*
York College *A*

New Hampshire

Franklin Pierce College *B*
University of New Hampshire *B,M*

New Jersey

Glassboro State College *B*
Jersey City State College *B*
Princeton University *M,D*
Rutgers—The State University of
    New Jersey *M,D*
Stockton State College *B*
Westminster Choir College *B,M*
William Paterson College of New
    Jersey *B*

New Mexico

New Mexico State University *M*

New York

Bard College *B,M*
City University of New York
    Brooklyn College *B,M*
    Graduate School and
        University Center *D*
    Hunter College *B,M*
    Lehman College *B*
    Queens College *B,M*
Columbia University *M*
Concordia College *B*
Cornell University *M,D*
Eastman School of Music of the
    University of Rochester *B,M,D*
Eugene Lang College/New School
    for Social Research *B*
Five Towns College *B*
Houghton College *B*
Ithaca College *B,M*
Juilliard School *B,M,D*
Long Island University: Brooklyn
    Campus *B*
Manhattan School of Music *B,M,D*
Manhattanville College *B*
Mannes College of Music *B,M,W*
Nazareth College of Rochester *B*
New York University *B,M,D*
Nyack College *B*
Sarah Lawrence College *B*
State University of New York
    Albany *B*
    Buffalo *M,D*
    College at Fredonia *B,M*
    College at Geneseo *B*
    College at New Paltz *B*
    College at Potsdam *M*
Syracuse University *B,M*
University of Rochester *B,M,D,W*
Wagner College *B*

North Carolina

Appalachian State University *B*
Brevard College *A*
East Carolina University *B,M*
University of North Carolina
    Chapel Hill *M,D*
    Greensboro *B,M*

Ohio

Ashland University *B*
Baldwin-Wallace College *B*
Bowling Green State University
    B,M
Capital University *B*
Cleveland Institute of Music *B,M,D*
Cleveland State University *B,M*
Denison University *B*
Heidelberg College *B*
Kent State University *B,M,D*
Oberlin College *B*
Ohio State University: Columbus
    Campus *B,M,D*
Ohio University *B,M*
Otterbein College *B*
University of Akron *B,M*
University of Cincinnati *B,M,D*
University of Dayton *B*
Wittenberg University *B*

Wright State University *B*
Youngstown State University *B,M*

Oklahoma

Oklahoma Baptist University *B*
Oklahoma City University *B*
Oral Roberts University *B*
Southeastern Oklahoma State
University *B*
Southwestern Oklahoma State
University *B*
University of Oklahoma *B,M,D*
University of Tulsa *B,M*

Oregon

Linfield College *B*
Marylhurst College *B*
Oregon State University *B*
University of Oregon
Eugene *B,M,D*
Robert Donald Clark Honors
College *B*
Warner Pacific College *B*
Western Conservative Baptist
Seminary *M*

Pennsylvania

Bucknell University *B*
Carnegie Mellon University *B,M*
Curtis Institute of Music *C,B*
Duquesne University *M*
Indiana University of Pennsylvania
B,M
Mansfield University of
Pennsylvania *B*
Moravian College *B*
Penn State University Park
Campus *M*
Philadelphia College of Bible *B*
Slippery Rock University of
Pennsylvania *B*
Temple University *B,M,D*
University of the Arts *B,M*
West Chester University of
Pennsylvania *B,M*

Puerto Rico

Conservatory of Music of Puerto
Rico *B*

Rhode Island

University of Rhode Island *B*

South Carolina

Columbia College *B*
Converse College *B*
Furman University *B*
Newberry College *B*
University of South Carolina *D*

South Dakota

Black Hills State University *B*
Sioux Falls College *B*

Tennessee

Tennessee Temple University *B*
University of Tennessee:
Chattanooga *B,M*
Vanderbilt University *B*

Texas

Baylor University *B,M*
Del Mar College *A*
East Texas State University *B,M*
Hardin-Simmons University *B,M*
Houston Community College *A*
Lamar University—Beaumont *B,M*
Lon Morris College *A*
Rice University *B,M,D*
Sam Houston State University *B,M*
Southern Methodist University *B,M*
Sul Ross State University *B*

Texas Christian University *B,M*
Texas Tech University *M*
Texas Woman's University *B,M*
University of Houston *B,M*
University of North Texas *B,M,D*
University of Texas
Austin *B*
El Paso *B*
San Antonio *B*

Utah

Brigham Young University *M,D*
Weber State University *B*

Vermont

Bennington College *B*
Marlboro College *B*
University of Vermont *B*

Virginia

Averett College *B*
Bluefield College *B*
Christopher Newport College *B*
Emory and Henry College *B*
Old Dominion University *B*
Shenandoah University *B,M*
University of Richmond *B*
Virginia Commonwealth
University *B*
Virginia Wesleyan College *B*

Washington

Central Washington University *B,M*
Cornish College of the Arts *B*
Eastern Washington University *B,M*
Pacific Lutheran University *B*
Seattle Pacific University *B*
Tacoma Community College *A*
University of Washington *B,M,D*
Walla Walla College *B*
Wenatchee Valley College *A*
Western Washington University
B,M

West Virginia

Marshall University *B*
Shepherd College *B*
West Virginia University *B,M*

Wisconsin

Carroll College *B*
Lawrence University *B*
University of Wisconsin
Eau Claire *B*
Madison *B,M*
Milwaukee *B*
Oshkosh *B*
Wisconsin Lutheran College *B*

Wyoming

University of Wyoming *B*

Canada

McGill University *B,M,D*

Music therapy

Alabama

University of Alabama *B*

Arizona

Arizona State University *B*

California

California State University
Long Beach *C*
Northridge *M*
University of the Pacific *B,M*

Colorado

Colorado State University *B,M*

Florida

Florida State University *B,M*
University of Miami *B,M*

Georgia

University of Georgia *B*

Indiana

St. Mary-of-the-Woods College *B*
University of Evansville *B*

Iowa

University of Iowa *B*
Wartburg College *B*

Kansas

Baker University *B*
University of Kansas *B,M*

Louisiana

Loyola University *B,M*

Massachusetts

Anna Maria College for Men and
Women *B*
Emmanuel College *B*

Michigan

Eastern Michigan University *B*
Michigan State University *B,M*
Wayne State University *B*
Western Michigan University *B,M*

Minnesota

Augsburg College *B*
University of Minnesota: Twin
Cities *B*
Willmar Community College *A*

Missouri

Maryville University *B*

Montana

Eastern Montana College *B*

New Jersey

Montclair State College *B*

New Mexico

Eastern New Mexico University *B*

New York

Hofstra University *M*
Long Island University: C. W. Post
Campus *B*
Molloy College *B*
Nazareth College of Rochester *B*
Russell Sage College *B*
State University of New York
College at Fredonia *B*
College at New Paltz *B*

North Carolina

East Carolina University *B,M*
Queens College *B*

Ohio

Baldwin-Wallace College *B*
Cleveland State University *B*
College of Wooster *B*
Ohio University *B*
Union Institute *D*
University of Dayton *B*

Oklahoma

Phillips University *B*

Oregon

Willamette University *B*

Pennsylvania

Elizabethtown College *B*
Hahnemann University School of
Health Sciences and
Humanities *M*
Immaculata College *B,M*
Mansfield University of
Pennsylvania *B*
Marywood College *B*
Mercyhurst College *B*
Temple University *B,M*

South Carolina

Charleston Southern University *B*

Tennessee

Tennessee Technological
University *B*

Texas

Sam Houston State University *B*
Southern Methodist University *B,M*
Texas Southmost College *A*
Texas Woman's University *B,M*
West Texas State University *B*

Utah

Utah State University *B*

Virginia

Radford University *B*
Shenandoah University *B*

Wisconsin

Alverno College *B*
University of Wisconsin
Eau Claire *B*
Oshkosh *B*

Musical theater

Alabama

Huntingdon College *B*
University of Montevallo *B*

Arkansas

Ouachita Baptist University *B*

California

California State University:
Fullerton *B*
Humboldt State University *C*
United States International
University *B,M*

Colorado

Mesa State College *B*
University of Northern Colorado *B*

Connecticut

Sacred Heart University *B*
University of Hartford *B*

District of Columbia

Catholic University of America *B*

Florida

Jacksonville University *B*
Stetson University *B*
University of Florida *M*
University of Miami *B*

Georgia

Shorter College *B*

Idaho

Ricks College *A*

Illinois

Columbia College *B*
Illinois Wesleyan University *B*
Millikin University *B*
Rockford College *B*
Roosevelt University *B*
Southern Illinois University at
    Edwardsville *B*

Indiana

St. Mary-of-the-Woods College *B*
Vincennes University *A*

Iowa

Cornell College *B*
Drake University *B*
University of Northern Iowa *B*

Kentucky

Eastern Kentucky University *B*

Louisiana

Centenary College of Louisiana *B*

Massachusetts

Boston Conservatory *B,M*
Emerson College *B*
Hampshire College *B*

Michigan

Lansing Community College *A*
Michigan State University *B*
University of Michigan *B*
Western Michigan University *B*

Minnesota

College of St. Catherine: St.
    Catherine Campus *B*
Willmar Community College *A*

Mississippi

University of Mississippi *M*

Missouri

Avila College *B*
Stephens College *B*
Webster University *B*

Nebraska

University of Nebraska
    Kearney *B*
    Lincoln *B*

New Mexico

College of Santa Fe *B*

New York

City University of New York:
    Brooklyn College *B,M*
Ithaca College *B*
Long Island University: C. W. Post
    Campus *B*
New York University *B,M*
Sarah Lawrence College *B*
State University of New York
    College at Fredonia *B*
    College at New Paltz *B*
Syracuse University *B*
Wagner College *B*

North Carolina

Brevard College *A*
Catawba College *B*
Elon College *B*
Lees-McRae College *B*
Mars Hill College *B*

Ohio

Baldwin-Wallace College *B*
Bowling Green State University *B*
Kent State University *B*
Ohio Northern University *B*
Otterbein College *B*
University of Cincinnati *B*
Wittenberg University *B*

Oklahoma

Oklahoma City University *B,M*
University of Central Oklahoma *B*
University of Oklahoma *B*
University of Tulsa *B*

Pennsylvania

Carnegie Mellon University *B,M,W*
Clarion University of
    Pennsylvania *B*
Marywood College *B*
University of the Arts *B*

Texas

Alvin Community College *A*
Mountain View College *C*
Southwest Texas State University *B*
Texas Wesleyan University *B*

Utah

Brigham Young University *B*
Weber State University *B*

Virginia

Shenandoah University *B*

West Virginia

Shepherd College *B*
West Virginia University *B*

Wisconsin

University of Wisconsin: Stevens
    Point *B*

Mycology

Indiana

Purdue University *D*

New York

State University of New York
    College of Environmental Science
    and Forestry *B,M,D*

Ohio

Ohio University *M,D*

Native American languages

Alaska

University of Alaska Fairbanks *B*

Arizona

Navajo Community College *A*

Minnesota

Rainy River Community College *A*

Montana

Little Big Horn College *A*

South Dakota

Black Hills State University *B*

Wyoming

Central Wyoming College *A*

Naval architecture and marine engineering

California

California Maritime Academy *B*
University of California: Berkeley
    B,M,D

Connecticut

United States Coast Guard
    Academy *B*

Louisiana

University of New Orleans *B*

Maine

Maine Maritime Academy *B*

Maryland

United States Naval Academy *B*

Massachusetts

Massachusetts Institute of
    Technology *B,M,D,W*
Massachusetts Maritime
    Academy *B*

Michigan

University of Michigan *B,M,D*

New Jersey

Stevens Institute of Technology
    M,D

New York

State University of New York
    Maritime College *B*
United States Merchant Marine
    Academy *B*
Webb Institute of Naval
    Architecture *B*

Texas

Texas A&M University at
    Galveston *B*

Naval science (Navy, Marines)

Florida

Jacksonville University *B*

Idaho

University of Idaho *B*

Iowa

Iowa State University *B*

Maine

Maine Maritime Academy *B*

Michigan

Eastern Michigan University *B*

Missouri

Columbia College *B*

New York

State University of New York
    Maritime College *B*

Pennsylvania

Villanova University *B*
West Chester University of
    Pennsylvania *C*

Wisconsin

University of Wisconsin: Madison *B*

Neurosciences

Arizona

University of Arizona *M,D*

California

California Institute of Technology
    D,W
Stanford University *M,D*
University of California
    Berkeley *B,M,D*
    Los Angeles *D*
    San Diego *M,D*
    San Francisco *D*

Connecticut

Trinity College *B*
University of Connecticut *B*
University of Hartford *M*

Delaware

University of Delaware *D*

Florida

Florida Institute of Technology *D*
University of Miami *D*

Georgia

Emory University *M,D*

Illinois

Loyola University of Chicago *M,D*
Northwestern University *B,M,D*
University of Chicago *M,D*
University of Health Sciences: The
    Chicago Medical School *M,D*
University of Illinois at Urbana-
    Champaign *M,D*

Indiana

Indiana University Bloomington *D*
Purdue University *M,D*

Iowa

Maharishi International University
    M,D
University of Iowa *D*

Louisiana

Tulane University *M,D*

Maine

Bowdoin College *B*

Maryland

Uniformed Services University of
    the Health Sciences *D*

Massachusetts

Amherst College *B*
Boston University *D*
Brandeis University *B*
Clark University *B*
Hampshire College *B*
Harvard University *D*
Massachusetts Institute of
    Technology *M,D,W*
Tufts University *M,D*
University of Massachusetts at
    Amherst *M,D*

Michigan

University of Michigan D

Minnesota

University of Minnesota: Twin
Cities D

Missouri

Washington University D

New York

City University of New York:
College of Staten Island D
Colgate University B
Cornell University B,M,D
New York University D
Rockefeller University D
State University of New York
Albany M,D
Stony Brook D
Health Science Center at
Brooklyn D
Health Science Center at
Syracuse D
Syracuse University D
University of Rochester B,M,D,W
Yeshiva University M,D

North Carolina

Duke University B,D
University of North Carolina at
Chapel Hill D

Ohio

Case Western Reserve University D
Kent State University M,D
Oberlin College B

Oklahoma

University of Oklahoma Health
Sciences Center M,D

Oregon

University of Oregon M,D

Pennsylvania

Bryn Mawr College B,M,D
Hahnemann University School of
Health Sciences and
Humanities D
Lehigh University B,M,D
Penn State Milton S. Hershey
Medical Center M,D
University of Pennsylvania M,D
University of Pittsburgh B,M,D
University of Scranton B

Rhode Island

Brown University B,M,D

Texas

Texas Christian University B
University of Texas Health Science
Center at Houston M,D,W

Virginia

University of Virginia D

Wisconsin

Lawrence University B
University of Wisconsin: Madison
M,D

Canada

McGill University M,D

Nuclear engineering

Arizona

University of Arizona B,M,D

California

University of California
Berkeley B,M,D
Los Angeles B,M,D
Santa Barbara B,M,D
University of Southern California M

District of Columbia

Catholic University of America M

Florida

University of Florida B,M,D

Georgia

Georgia Institute of Technology
B,M,D

Idaho

Idaho State University M
University of Idaho M,D

Illinois

University of Illinois at Urbana-
Champaign B,M,D

Indiana

Purdue University B,M,D,W
University of Notre Dame M

Iowa

Iowa State University M,D

Kansas

Kansas State University B,M,D

Louisiana

Louisiana State University and
Agricultural and Mechanical
College M

Maryland

College of Notre Dame of
Maryland B
University of Maryland: College
Park B,M,D

Massachusetts

Massachusetts Institute of
Technology B,M,D,W
University of Massachusetts at
Lowell B,M
Worcester Polytechnic Institute B

Michigan

University of Michigan B,M,D

Mississippi

Mississippi State University B,M

Missouri

East Central College A
University of Missouri
Columbia M,D
Rolla B,M,D

New Jersey

Stevens Institute of Technology
B,M

New Mexico

University of New Mexico B,M

New York

Columbia University: School of
Engineering and Applied Science
M,D,W
Cornell University M,D
Manhattan College B
Pace University
College of White Plains B
Pleasantville/Briarcliff B
Rensselaer Polytechnic Institute
B,M,D
United States Military Academy B

North Carolina

North Carolina State University
B,M,D

Ohio

Air Force Institute of Technology
M,D
Ohio State University: Columbus
Campus M,D
Terra Technical College A
University of Cincinnati B,M,D

Oregon

Oregon State University B,M,D

Pennsylvania

Lock Haven University of
Pennsylvania B
Penn State University Park Campus
B,M,D

Rhode Island

Brown University B,M,D

Tennessee

University of Tennessee: Knoxville
B,M,D

Texas

Texas A&M University B,M,D

Utah

University of Utah M,D

Virginia

University of Virginia B,M,D

Washington

University of Washington B,M,D

Wisconsin

University of Wisconsin: Madison
B,M,D

Nuclear medical technology

Alabama

Community College of the Air
Force A
Mobile College B
Samford University B
University of Alabama in
Birmingham B

Arkansas

University of Arkansas for Medical
Sciences B

California

California State University:
Dominguez Hills B
Charles R. Drew University: College
of Allied Health C

Colorado

Community College of Denver C,A

Connecticut

South Central Community
College A

Delaware

Delaware Technical and
Community College: Stanton/
Wilmington Campus A

District of Columbia

George Washington University A

Florida

Barry University B
Hillsborough Community College A
Santa Fe Community College A
University of Miami B
Valencia Community College A

Georgia

Emory University A
Medical College of Georgia A,B

Illinois

College of DuPage C
College of St. Francis B
Illinois Benedictine College B
Roosevelt University B
Triton College C,A

Indiana

Ball State University A
Indiana University—Purdue
University at Indianapolis B
Purdue University B
Vincennes University A

Iowa

University of Iowa B

Kansas

Kansas Newman College B
Southwestern College B

Kentucky

Lexington Community College A
University of Louisville B

Maryland

Essex Community College A
Prince George's Community
College A

Massachusetts

Bunker Hill Community College A
Massachusetts College of Pharmacy
and Allied Health Sciences A,B
Salem State College B
Springfield Technical Community
College A

Michigan

Ferris State University A,B
University of Detroit Mercy B

Minnesota

St. Cloud State University B
St. Mary's College of Minnesota B

Missouri

St. Louis University B
University of Missouri: Columbia B

Nebraska

Dana College B
University of Nebraska Medical
Center B

New Jersey

Gloucester County College *A*
Jersey City State College *B*
Thomas Edison State College *B*
University of Medicine and
   Dentistry of New Jersey: School
   of Health Related Professions *C*

New Mexico

University of New Mexico *C*

New York

Long Island University: C. W. Post
   Campus *B*
Manhattan College *A,B*
Rochester Institute of
   Technology *B*
State University of New York
   Buffalo *B*
      Health Science Center at
         Brooklyn *C*

North Carolina

Forsyth Technical Community
   College *A*

Ohio

Kettering College of Medical
   Arts *A*
Lakeland Community College *A*
Lorain County Community
   College *A*
Notre Dame College of Ohio *B*
Owens Technical College: Toledo *A*
University of Cincinnati
   Cincinnati *B*
      Raymond Walters College *A*
University of Dayton *B*
University of Findlay *A,B*

Oklahoma

University of Oklahoma Health
   Sciences Center *B*

Pennsylvania

Cedar Crest College *B*
Edinboro University of
   Pennsylvania *B*
Harrisburg Area Community
   College *A*
York College of Pennsylvania *B*

Puerto Rico

University of Puerto Rico: Medical
   Sciences Campus *B*

South Carolina

Midlands Technical College *C*

Tennessee

Austin Peay State University *B*
Chattanooga State Technical
   Community College *A*
Roane State Community College *A*

Texas

Amarillo College *A*
El Paso Community College *C*
Galveston College *A*
Houston Baptist University *B*
Houston Community College *C,A*
Incarnate Word College *B*
McLennan Community College *A*
University of Houston *B*

Utah

Weber State University *A*

Vermont

University of Vermont *A*

Virginia

Old Dominion University *B*

West Virginia

West Virginia State College *A,B*
Wheeling Jesuit College *B*

Wisconsin

Alverno College *B*
University of Wisconsin: La
   Crosse *B*

Nuclear physics

California

Naval Postgraduate School *M*
San Jose State University *M*
University of California: Berkeley
   B,M,D

District of Columbia

George Washington University *D*

Florida

University of Florida *M,D*

Georgia

Emory University *M,D*

Illinois

Northwestern University *B*
University of Chicago *M,D*

Indiana

Purdue University *M,D*
University of Notre Dame *M,D*

Iowa

Iowa State University *M,D*

Louisiana

Louisiana State University and
   Agricultural and Mechanical
   College *M*

Maryland

Johns Hopkins University *B,D*

Massachusetts

Harvard University *D*
Massachusetts Institute of
   Technology *B,M,D,W*
Worcester Polytechnic Institute *B*

Michigan

Michigan State University *D*
University of Michigan *D*

New Hampshire

University of New Hampshire *M,D*

New Jersey

Stevens Institute of Technology
   B,M,D,W

New York

Columbia University *M,D*

Ohio

Ohio State University: Columbus
   Campus *B,M,D*
Ohio University *M,D*

Pennsylvania

Bucknell University *B*
Drexel University *M,D*
University of Pennsylvania *M,D*

Rhode Island

Brown University *B,M,D*

South Carolina

Francis Marion College *B*

Vermont

Marlboro College *B*

Canada

McGill University *M,D*

Nuclear technologies

Alabama

Community College of the Air
   Force *A*

Connecticut

Thames Valley State Technical
   College *A*

Illinois

Joliet Junior College *A*

Kansas

Kansas State University *B*

Louisiana

Louisiana State University and
   Agricultural and Mechanical
   College *M*

Massachusetts

Massachusetts College of Pharmacy
   and Allied Health Sciences *B*

Minnesota

Winona State University *A*

Mississippi

Hinds Community College *A*

New Jersey

Thomas Edison State College *A,B*

New York

City University of New York:
   Queensborough Community
   College *A*
University of the State of New
   York: Regents College *A,B*

Ohio

Terra Technical College *A*
University of Cincinnati: Raymond
   Walters College *A*

Pennsylvania

Community College of Beaver
   County *A*
Penn State University Park
   Campus *A*
Westmoreland County Community
   College *A*

South Carolina

Aiken Technical College *A*

Tennessee

Chattanooga State Technical
   Community College *A*

Texas

McLennan Community College *A*
Texas A&M University *M*
Texas State Technical College:
   Waco *A*

Washington

Columbia Basin College *A*

West Virginia

West Virginia State College *A*

Nurse anesthetist

Alabama

University of Alabama in
   Birmingham *B*

California

California State University
   Long Beach *M*
   San Bernardino *B*
University of California: Los
   Angeles *M*

Illinois

Southern Illinois University at
   Edwardsville *M*

Indiana

Ball State University *A*

Kansas

University of Kansas
   Lawrence *M*
   Medical Center *M*

Louisiana

Xavier University of Louisiana *M*

Maine

University of New England *M*

Michigan

Oakland University *M*
University of Detroit Mercy *M*
University of Michigan: Flint *M*
Wayne State University *M*

Minnesota

St. Mary's College of Minnesota *M*
University of Minnesota: Twin
   Cities *M*

New York

Albany Medical College *M*
Columbia University: School of
   Nursing *M*
State University of New York at
   Buffalo *M*

North Dakota

University of Mary *M*

Ohio

Case Western Reserve
   University *M*
Malone College *B*
Ohio State University: Columbus
   Campus *C,B,M*

Pennsylvania

California University of
   Pennsylvania *B*
Gannon University *M*
La Roche College *M*
Medical College of Pennsylvania *M*
St. Joseph's University *M*
University of Pittsburgh *M*

Puerto Rico

Pontifical Catholic University of
   Puerto Rico *M*

South Dakota

Mount Marty College *M*
University of South Dakota *B*

Texas

Texas Wesleyan University *M*
University of Texas Health Science
Center at Houston *W*

Virginia

Virginia Commonwealth
University *M*

Washington

Gonzaga University *M*

Nursing

Alabama

Alabama Southern Community
College *A*
Auburn University
Auburn *B*
Montgomery *B*
Bishop State Community College *A*
Central Alabama Community
College: Childersburg Campus *C*
Chattahoochee Valley Community
College *C,A*
Gadsden State Community
College *A*
George C. Wallace State
Community College at Selma *A*
Jacksonville State University *B*
James H. Faulkner State
Community College *A*
Jefferson State Community
College *A*
John C. Calhoun State Community
College *A*
Judson College *B*
Lawson State Community
College *A*
Livingston University *A*
Mobile College *A,B,M*
Northeast Alabama State Junior
College *A*
Oakwood College *A,B*
Samford University *A,B*
Selma University *A*
Shelton State Community
College *A*
Southern Union State Junior
College *A*
Troy State University *A,B,M*
Tuskegee University *B*
University of Alabama
Birmingham *B,M,D*
Huntsville *B,M*
Tuscaloosa *B,M*
University of North Alabama *B*
University of South Alabama *B,M*
Walker College *A*
Walker State Technical College *A*
Wallace State Community College
at Hanceville *A*

Alaska

University of Alaska Anchorage
A,B,M

Arizona

Arizona State University *B,M*
Arizona Western College *A*
Cochise College *A*
Eastern Arizona College *A*
Glendale Community College *A*
Grand Canyon University *B*
Mesa Community College *A*

Mohave Community College *A*
Northern Arizona University *B*
Pima Community College *A*
Scottsdale Community College *A*
University of Arizona *B,M,D*
University of Phoenix *B,M*
Yavapai College *A*

Arkansas

Arkansas State University *A,B,M*
Arkansas Tech University *B*
East Arkansas Community
College *A*
Garland County Community
College *A*
Harding University *B*
Henderson State University *B*
Mississippi County Community
College *A*
North Arkansas Community
College *A*
Phillips County Community
College *A*
Southern Arkansas University *A*
University of Arkansas
Fayetteville *A*
Little Rock *A*
Medical Sciences *B,M*
Monticello *A,B*
Pine Bluff *B*
University of Central Arkansas *B,M*
Westark Community College *A*

California

Allan Hancock College *C,A*
Azusa Pacific University *B,M*
Bakersfield College *A*
Barstow College *A*
Biola University *B*
California State University
Bakersfield *B,M*
Chico *B,M*
Dominguez Hills *B,M*
Fresno *B,M*
Fullerton *B*
Hayward *B*
Long Beach *B,M*
Los Angeles *B,M*
Northridge *B*
Sacramento *B,M*
San Bernardino *B*
Stanislaus *B*
Cerritos Community College *A*
Chabot College *A*
Chaffey Community College *C,A*
Citrus College *C,A*
City College of San Francisco *C,A*
College of the Desert *A*
College of the Redwoods *C,A*
College of the Sequoias *A*
Compton Community College *A*
Cuesta College *A*
De Anza College *C,A*
Dominican College of San Rafael *B*
East Los Angeles College *A*
El Camino College *A*
Evergreen Valley College *A*
Fresno City College *A*
Gavilan Community College *A*
Glendale Community College *C,A*
Golden West College *C,A*
Grossmont Community College *A*
Hartnell College *A*
Holy Names College *B*
Humboldt State University *B*
Imperial Valley College *A*
Long Beach City College *C,A*
Los Angeles Harbor College *A*
Los Angeles Pierce College *A*
Los Angeles Trade and Technical
College *C,A*
Los Angeles Valley College *C,A*

Los Medanos College *C,A*
Merced College *C,A*
Mission College *A*
Modesto Junior College *A*
Monterey Peninsula College *C,A*
Moorpark College *A*
Mount St. Mary's College *A,B*
Mount San Antonio College *C,A*
Mount San Jacinto College *C,A*
Napa Valley College *A*
National Hispanic University *A*
Ohlone College *A*
Pacific Union College *A,B*
Palomar College *A*
Pasadena City College *C,A*
Point Loma Nazarene College *B*
Rio Hondo College *A*
Saddleback College *A*
St. Mary's College of California *B*
Samuel Merritt College *B,M*
San Diego City College *A*
San Diego State University *B*
San Francisco State University *B,M*
San Joaquin Delta College *C,A*
San Jose State University *B,M*
Santa Barbara City College *A*
Santa Monica College *A*
Santa Rosa Junior College *C,A*
Sierra College *A*
Solano Community College *A*
Sonoma State University *B,M*
Southwestern College *A*
University of California
Los Angeles *B,M,D*
San Francisco *M,D*
University of San Diego *B,M,D*
University of San Francisco *B,M*
University of Southern California
B,M
Ventura College *C,A*
Victor Valley College *C,A*
Yuba College *A*

Colorado

Arapahoe Community College *A*
Community College of Denver *C,A*
Front Range Community College
C,A
Mesa State College *A,B*
Metropolitan State College of
Denver *B*
Morgan Community College *A*
Northeastern Junior College *C*
Otero Junior College *C,A*
Pikes Peak Community College *A*
Pueblo Community College *C,A*
Red Rocks Community College *C*
Regis College of Regis University *B*
Trinidad State Junior College *A*
University of Colorado Health
Sciences Center *B,M,D*
University of Northern Colorado
B,M
University of Southern Colorado *B*

Connecticut

Central Connecticut State
University *B*
Fairfield University *B*
Mattatuck Community College *A*
Norwalk Community College *A*
Quinnipiac College *B*
Sacred Heart University *B,M*
St. Joseph College *B,M*
Southern Connecticut State
University *B,M*
University of Connecticut *B,M*
University of Hartford *B,M*
Western Connecticut State
University *B,M*
Yale University *M*

Delaware

Delaware State College *B*
Delaware Technical and
Community College
Southern Campus *A*
Stanton/Wilmington
Campus *A*
Terry Campus *A*
University of Delaware *B,M*
Wesley College *A*
Wilmington College *B*

District of Columbia

Catholic University of America
B,M,D
Georgetown University *B,M*
Howard University *B,M*
Mount Vernon College *B*
University of the District of
Columbia *A,B*

Florida

Barry University *B,M*
Bethune-Cookman College *B*
Brevard Community College *A*
Broward Community College *A*
Central Florida Community
College *A*
Chipola Junior College *A*
Daytona Beach Community
College *A*
Edison Community College *A*
Florida Agricultural and Mechanical
University *B*
Florida Atlantic University *B,M*
Florida Community College at
Jacksonville *A*
Florida International University
B,M
Florida Keys Community College *A*
Florida State University *B,M*
Gulf Coast Community College *A*
Hillsborough Community College *A*
Indian River Community College *A*
Jacksonville University *B*
Keiser College of Technology *C*
Lake City Community College *A*
Lake-Sumter Community College *A*
Manatee Community College *A*
Miami-Dade Community College *A*
Palm Beach Community College *A*
Pasco-Hernando Community
College *A*
Pensacola Junior College *A*
St. Petersburg Junior College *A*
Santa Fe Community College *A*
Seminole Community College *A*
South Florida Community
College *A*
Tallahassee Community College *A*
University of Central Florida *B*
University of Florida *B,M,D*
University of Miami *B,M,D*
University of North Florida *B*
University of South Florida *B,M*
University of Tampa *B*
University of West Florida *B*
Valencia Community College *A*
Webber College *B*

Georgia

Abraham Baldwin Agricultural
College *A*
Albany State College *B,M*
Armstrong State College *A,B,M*
Athens Area Technical Institute *A*
Atlanta Christian College *A*
Atlanta Metropolitan College *A*
Augusta College *A*
Brenau Women's College *B*
Brewton-Parker College *A*
Brunswick College *A*

Clayton State College *A,B*
Columbus College *A,B*
Dalton College *A*
Darton College *A*
DeKalb College *A*
Emory University *B,M*
Floyd College *A*
Georgia College *B,M*
Georgia Southern University *B,M*
Georgia Southwestern College *A,B*
Georgia State University *B,M,D*
Gordon College *A*
Kennesaw State College *A,B*
LaGrange College *A*
Macon College *A*
Medical College of Georgia *B,M,D*
Middle Georgia College *A*
Morris Brown College *B*
North Georgia College *A,B*
Reinhardt College *A*
South Georgia College *A*
Valdosta State College *B,M*
West Georgia College *A,B*

Hawaii

Hawaii Loa College *B*
University of Hawaii
    Hilo *B*
    Kauai Community College *A*
    Manoa *B,M*

Idaho

Boise State University *A,B*
College of Southern Idaho *A*
Idaho State University *B,M*
Lewis Clark State College *A,B*
North Idaho College *A*
Ricks College *A*

Illinois

Aurora University *B,M*
Barat College *B*
Belleville Area College *A*
Black Hawk College
    East Campus *A*
    Moline *A*
Blessing-Reiman College of
    Nursing *B*
Bradley University *B,M*
Carl Sandburg College *A*
Chicago State University *B*
City Colleges of Chicago
    Malcolm X College *A*
    Olive-Harvey College *A*
    Richard J. Daley College *A*
College of DuPage *A*
College of Lake County *A*
Concordia University *B*
De Paul University *B,M*
Elgin Community College *A*
Elmhurst College *B*
Eureka College *B*
Governors State University *B,M*
Highland Community College *A*
Illinois Benedictine College *B*
Illinois Central College *A*
Illinois Eastern Community
  Colleges: Olney Central
  College *A*
Illinois Valley Community College
  C,A
Illinois Wesleyan University *B*
John A. Logan College *A*
Joliet Junior College *A*
Kishwaukee College *A*
Lake Forest College *B*
Lake Land College *C,A*
Lakeview College of Nursing *B*
Lewis and Clark Community
  College *A*
Lewis University *B,M*

Lincoln Land Community
  College *A*
Loyola University of Chicago
  B,M,D
MacMurray College *B*
McKendree College *B*
Mennonite College of Nursing *B*
Millikin University *B*
Monmouth College *B*
Moraine Valley Community
  College *A*
Morton College *A*
North Central College *B*
North Park College and Theological
  Seminary *B*
Northern Illinois University *B,M*
Oakton Community College *A*
Olivet Nazarene University *B*
Parkland College *A*
Prairie State College *A*
Rend Lake College *C,A*
Rock Valley College *A*
Rockford College *B*
Rush University *B,M,D*
St. Francis Medical Center College
  of Nursing *B*
St. Joseph College of Nursing *B*
St. Xavier University *B,M*
Sangamon State University *B*
Shawnee Community College *C,A*
Southern Illinois University at
  Edwardsville *B,M*
State Community College *A*
Trinity Christian College *B*
Triton College *A*
University of Illinois at Chicago
  B,M,D
Waubonsee Community College *A*
West Suburban College of
  Nursing *B*
William Rainey Harper College *A*

Indiana

Anderson University *B*
Ball State University *A,B,M*
Bethel College *A,B*
Franklin College *B*
Goshen College *B*
Indiana State University *A,B,M*
Indiana University
    Bloomington *B*
    East *A,B*
    Kokomo *A,B*
    Northwest *A,B*
    South Bend *A,B*
    Southeast *B*
Indiana University—Purdue
  University
    Fort Wayne *A,B*
    Indianapolis *A,B,M,D*
Indiana Vocational Technical
  College
    Central Indiana *A*
    Columbus *A*
    Lafayette *A*
    Northcentral *A*
    Southcentral *A*
    Southeast *A*
    Southwest *A*
    Whitewater *A*
Indiana Wesleyan University *B,M*
Lutheran College of Health
  Professions *A,B*
Marian College *A,B*
Purdue University
    Calumet *A,B,M*
    North Central Campus *A*
    West Lafayette *B,M*
St. Francis College *B*
St. Joseph's College *B*
St. Mary's College *B*
University of Evansville *B,M*

University of Indianapolis *A,B*
University of Southern Indiana *A,B*
Valparaiso University *B,M*
Vincennes University *A*

Iowa

Briar Cliff College *B*
Clarke College *B*
Clinton Community College *A*
Coe College *B*
Des Moines Area Community
  College *C,A*
Drake University *B,M*
Graceland College *B*
Grand View College *B*
Hawkeye Institute of Technology *A*
Indian Hills Community College *A*
Iowa Central Community College *A*
Iowa Lakes Community College
  C,A
Iowa Wesleyan College *B*
Iowa Western Community
  College *A*
Kirkwood Community College *A*
Luther College *B*
Morningside College *B*
Mount Mercy College *B*
North Iowa Area Community
  College *A*
Northeast Iowa Community
  College *A*
Northwest Iowa Technical
  College *A*
Scott Community College *A*
Southeastern Community College
    North Campus *C,A*
    South Campus *A*
Southwestern Community College
  C,A
Teikyo Marycrest University *B*
University of Dubuque *B*
University of Iowa *B,M,D*
Vennard College *B*

Kansas

Baker University *B*
Barton County Community
  College *A*
Bethel College *B*
Butler County Community
  College *A*
Cloud County Community
  College *A*
Coffeyville Community College *A*
Colby Community College *A*
Cowley County Community
  College *A*
Dodge City Community College *A*
Emporia State University *B*
Fort Hays State University *B,M*
Fort Scott Community College *A*
Hesston College *A*
Highland Community College *A*
Hutchinson Community College *A*
Johnson County Community
  College *A*
Kansas City Kansas Community
  College *A*
Kansas Newman College *A,B*
Kansas Wesleyan University *A,B*
Labette Community College *A*
MidAmerica Nazarene College *B*
Neosho County Community
  College *A*
Pittsburg State University *B*
Pratt Community College *A*
Seward County Community
  College *A*
Southwestern College *B*
University of Kansas
    Lawrence *B,M,D*
    Medical Center *B,M,D*

Washburn University of Topeka *B*
Wichita State University *B,M*

Kentucky

Asbury College *B*
Bellarmine College *B,M*
Berea College *B*
Eastern Kentucky University *A,B*
Elizabethtown Community
  College *A*
Georgetown College *B*
Hazard Community College *A*
Jefferson Community College *A*
Kentucky State University *A*
Kentucky Wesleyan College *A,B*
Lees College *A*
Lexington Community College *A*
Madisonville Community College *A*
Maysville Community College *A*
Morehead State University *B*
Murray State University *B,M*
Northern Kentucky University
  A,B,M
Paducah Community College *A*
Pikeville College *A*
Prestonburg Community College *A*
Southeast Community College *A*
Spalding University *B,M*
Thomas More College *B*
University of Kentucky *B,M,D*
University of Louisville *B,M*
Western Kentucky University *A,B*

Louisiana

Dillard University *B*
Grambling State University *B*
Louisiana College *B*
Louisiana State University Medical
  Center *B,M,D*
Louisiana Tech University *A*
Loyola University *B*
McNeese State University *B*
Nicholls State University *A,B*
Northeast Louisiana University *B*
Northwestern State University
  A,B,M
Our Lady of Holy Cross College *B*
Southeastern Louisiana University
  B,M
Southern University and
  Agricultural and Mechanical
  College *B*
University of Southwestern
  Louisiana *B,M*

Maine

Central Maine Medical Center
  School of Nursing *A*
Central Maine Technical College *A*
Eastern Maine Technical College *A*
Husson College *B*
Kennebec Valley Technical
  College *A*
St. Joseph's College *B*
Southern Maine Technical
  College *A*
University of Maine
    Augusta *A*
    Fort Kent *B*
    Orono *B*
    Presque Isle *B*
University of New England *A*
University of Southern Maine *B,M*
Westbrook College *B*

Maryland

Allegany Community College *A*
Anne Arundel Community
  College *A*
Bowie State University *B,M*
Catonsville Community College *A*
Cecil Community College *A*

Charles County Community
College *A*
College of Notre Dame of
Maryland *B*
Columbia Union College *B*
Coppin State College *B*
Essex Community College *C,A*
Frederick Community College *A*
Hagerstown Junior College *A*
Harford Community College *A*
Howard Community College *A*
Johns Hopkins University *B,M*
Montgomery College: Takoma Park
Campus *A*
New Community College of
Baltimore *A*
Prince George's Community
College *A*
Salisbury State University *B,M*
Towson State University *B*
University of Maryland
Baltimore *B,M,D*
Baltimore County *B*
Villa Julie College *B*
Wor-Wic Tech Community
College *A*

Massachusetts

American International College *B*
Anna Maria College for Men and
Women *B,M*
Atlantic Union College *A,B*
Becker College: Worcester
Campus *A*
Berkshire Community College *A*
Boston College *B,M,D*
Bristol Community College *A*
Bunker Hill Community College *A*
Cape Cod Community College *A*
Curry College *B*
Elms College *B*
Emmanuel College *B*
Endicott College *A*
Fitchburg State College *B*
Framingham State College *B*
Greenfield Community College *A*
Holyoke Community College *A*
Laboure College *A*
Massachusetts Bay Community
College *A*
Massachusetts College of Pharmacy
and Allied Health Sciences *B*
Massasoit Community College *A*
MGH Institute of Health
Professions *M*
Middlesex Community College *A*
Mount Wachusett Community
College *A*
North Shore Community College *A*
Northeastern University *B,M*
Northern Essex Community
College *A*
Quincy College *A*
Quinsigamond Community
College *A*
Roxbury Community College *A*
Salem State College *B,M*
Simmons College *B,M*
Springfield Technical Community
College *A*
University of Massachusetts
Amherst *B,M*
Boston *B,M*
Dartmouth *B,M*
Lowell *B,M*
Worcester State College *B*

Michigan

Alpena Community College *A*
Andrews University *B,M*
Calvin College *B*

Charles Stewart Mott Community
College *A*
Delta College *A*
Eastern Michigan University *B,M*
Ferris State University *A,B*
Glen Oaks Community College *C,A*
Grand Rapids Community
College *A*
Grand Valley State University *B,M*
Great Lakes Junior College of
Business *A*
Henry Ford Community College *A*
Hope College *B*
Jackson Community College *A*
Kalamazoo Valley Community
College *A*
Kellogg Community College *A*
Kirtland Community College *A*
Lake Superior State University *B*
Lansing Community College *A*
Macomb Community College *A*
Madonna University *B,M*
Michigan State University *B,M*
Mid Michigan Community
College *A*
Montcalm Community College *A*
Muskegon Community College *A*
Northern Michigan University
C,A,B,M
Northwestern Michigan College *A*
Oakland Community College *A*
Oakland University *B,M*
Saginaw Valley State University
B,M
St. Clair County Community
College *A*
Schoolcraft College *A*
Southwestern Michigan College *C,A*
Suomi College *A*
University of Detroit Mercy *B*
University of Michigan
Ann Arbor *B,M,D*
Flint *B*
Wayne State University *B,M,D*
West Shore Community College
C,A

Minnesota

Alexandria Technical College *C*
Anoka-Ramsey Community
College *A*
Augsburg College *B*
Austin Community College *A*
Bemidji State University *B*
Bethel College *B*
Brainerd Community College *A*
College of St. Benedict *B*
College of St. Catherine: St.
Catherine Campus *B,M*
College of St. Scholastica *B,M*
Concordia College: Moorhead *B*
Gustavus Adolphus College *B*
Inver Hills Community College *A*
Itasca Community College:
Arrowhead Region *C*
Lakewood Community College *A*
Mankato State University *B*
Metropolitan State University *B*
Minneapolis Community College *A*
Moorhead State University *B*
Normandale Community College *A*
Northland Community College *A*
Rochester Community College *A*
St. John's University *B*
St. Mary's Campus of the College of
St. Catherine *A*
St. Olaf College *B*
University of Minnesota: Twin
Cities *B,M,D*
Willmar Community College *A*
Willmar Technical College *C,A*
Winona State University *B,M*

Mississippi

Alcorn State University *A,B*
Delta State University *B*
East Central Community College *A*
Hinds Community College *A*
Holmes Community College *A*
Jackson State University *B*
Jones County Junior College *A*
Mary Holmes College *A*
Meridian Community College *A*
Mississippi College *B*
Mississippi Delta Community
College *A*
Mississippi Gulf Coast Community
College
Jackson County Campus *A*
Jefferson Davis Campus *A*
Mississippi University for Women
A,B,M
Northeast Mississippi Community
College *A*
Southwest Mississippi Community
College *A*
University of Mississippi
Medical Center *B,M*
University *B,M*
University of Southern Mississippi
B,M
William Carey College *B*

Missouri

Avila College *B*
Central Methodist College *A,B*
Central Missouri State University *B*
College of the Ozarks *B*
Culver-Stockton College *B*
Deaconess College of Nursing *A,B*
Drury College *B*
East Central College *A*
Hannibal-LaGrange College *A,B*
Jefferson College *A*
Lincoln University *A*
Maryville University *B*
Mineral Area College *A*
Missouri Baptist College *B*
Missouri Southern State College
A,B
Missouri Western State College *B*
Moberly Area Community
College *A*
North Central Missouri College *A*
Northeast Missouri State
University *B*
Park College *A*
Penn Valley Community College *A*
Research College of Nursing *B*
Rockhurst College *B*
St. Charles Community College *A*
St. Louis Community College
Florissant Valley *A*
Forest Park *A*
Meramec *A*
St. Louis University *B,M,D*
Southeast Missouri State University
A,B
Southwest Baptist University *B*
Southwest Missouri State University
A,B
State Fair Community College *A*
Three Rivers Community College *A*
University of Missouri
Columbia *B,M*
Kansas City *B,M*
St. Louis *B*
Webster University *B*
William Jewell College *B*

Montana

Carroll College *B*
Miles Community College *A*
Montana College of Mineral
Science and Technology *A*

Montana State University *B,M*
Northern Montana College *A,B*
Salish Kootenai College *A*

Nebraska

Central Community College *A*
Clarkson College *B,M*
College of St. Mary *A,B*
Creighton University *B,M*
Grace College of the Bible *B*
Metropolitan Community College *A*
Midland Lutheran College *B*
Nebraska Methodist College of
Nursing and Allied Health *B*
Nebraska Wesleyan University *B*
Northeast Community College *C,A*
Southeast Community College
Beatrice Campus *A*
Lincoln Campus *A*
Union College *B*
University of Nebraska Medical
Center *B,M,D*

Nevada

Community College of Southern
Nevada *A*
Northern Nevada Community
College *C,A*
Truckee Meadows Community
College *A*
University of Nevada
Las Vegas *B,M*
Reno *B,M*
Western Nevada Community
College *C,A*

New Hampshire

Colby-Sawyer College *B*
New Hampshire Technical College
Berlin *A*
Manchester *A*
Stratham *A*
Rivier College *A,B*
St. Anselm College *B*
University of New Hampshire *B,M*

New Jersey

Atlantic Community College *A*
Bergen Community College *A*
Bloomfield College *B*
Brookdale Community College *A*
Camden County College *A*
College of St. Elizabeth *B*
County College of Morris *A*
Cumberland County College *A*
Essex County College *A*
Fairleigh Dickinson University *B*
Felician College *A,B*
Gloucester County College *A*
Jersey City State College *B*
Kean College of New Jersey *B*
Mercer County Community
College *A*
Monmouth College *B,M*
Ocean County College *A*
Passaic County Community
College *A*
Rutgers—The State University of
New Jersey
Camden College of Arts and
Sciences *B*
College of Nursing *B,M,D*
New Brunswick *M,D*
St. Peter's College *B*
Seton Hall University *B,M*
Stockton State College *B*
Thomas Edison State College *B*
Trenton State College *B,M*
Union County College *A*

University of Medicine and
Dentisfry of New Jersey: School
of Health Related Professions
A,M

William Paterson College of New
Jersey *B*

New Mexico

Albuquerque Technical-Vocational
Institute *A*
Clovis Community College *C,A*
Eastern New Mexico University:
Roswell Campus *C,A*
New Mexico Junior College *A*
New Mexico State University
Carlsbad *A,B*
Las Cruces *A,B*
Northern New Mexico Community
College *A*
San Juan College *A*
University of New Mexico *B,M*
Western New Mexico University *A*

New York

Adelphi University *B,M,D*
Adirondack Community College *A*
Broome Community College *A*
Catholic Medical Center of
Brooklyn and Queens School of
Nursing *A*
City University of New York
Borough of Manhattan
Community College *A*
City College *B*
College of Staten Island *A,B*
Hostos Community College *A*
Hunter College *B,M*
Kingsborough Community
College *A*
La Guardia Community
College *A*
Lehman College *B,M*
Medgar Evers College *A,B*
New York City Technical
College *A*
Queensborough Community
College *A*
York College *B*
Clinton Community College *A*
Cochran School of Nursing-St.
John's Riverside Hospital *A*
College of Mount St. Vincent *B,M*
College of New Rochelle *B,M*
Columbia University: School of
Nursing *B,M*
Columbia-Greene Community
College *A*
Community College of the Finger
Lakes *A*
Corning Community College *A*
Daemen College *B*
Dominican College of Blauvelt *B*
Dutchess Community College *A*
D'Youville College *B,M*
Elmira College *B*
Erie Community College
City Campus *A*
North Campus *A*
Fulton-Montgomery Community
College *A*
Genesee Community College *A*
Hartwick College *B*
Helene Fuld School of Nursing *A*
Hudson Valley Community
College *A*
Iona College *A*
Jamestown Community College *A*
Jefferson Community College *A*
Keuka College *B*
King's College *B*
Long Island College Hospital School
of Nursing *A*

Long Island University
Brooklyn Campus *B*
C. W. Post Campus *B*
Maria College *A*
Mercy College *B,M*
Mohawk Valley Community
College *A*
Molloy College *B,M*
Monroe Community College *A*
Mount St. Mary College *B*
Nassau Community College *A*
Nazareth College of Rochester *B*
New York University *B,M,D*
Niagara County Community
College *A*
Niagara University *B*
North Country Community
College *A*
Onondaga Community College *A*
Orange County Community
College *A*
Pace University
New York *B*
Pleasantville/Briarcliff *A,B,M*
Phillips Beth Israel School of
Nursing *A*
Roberts Wesleyan College *B*
Rockland Community College *A*
Russell Sage College *B,M*
St. John Fisher College *B,M*
St. Joseph's College
Brooklyn *B*
Suffolk Campus *B*
St. Joseph's School of Nursing *A*
State University of New York
Binghamton *B,M,W*
Buffalo *B,M,D*
College of Agriculture and
Technology at Morrisville *A*
College at Brockport *B*
College at New Paltz *B*
College at Plattsburgh *B*
College of Technology at
Alfred *A*
College of Technology at
Canton *A*
College of Technology at
Delhi *A*
College of Technology at
Farmingdale *A*
Health Science Center at
Brooklyn *B,M*
Health Science Center at
Syracuse *B,M*
Health Sciences Center at
Stony Brook *B,M*
Institute of Technology at
Utica/Rome *B,M*
Suffolk County Community
College *A*
Sullivan County Community
College *A*
Syracuse University *B,M*
Tompkins-Cortland Community
College *A*
Trocaire College *A*
Ulster County Community
College *A*
University of Rochester *B,M,D,W*
University of the State of New
York: Regents College *A,B*
Utica College of Syracuse
University *B*
Wagner College *B,M*
Westchester Community College *A*

North Carolina

Alamance Community College *A*
Asheville Buncombe Technical
Community College *A*
Barton College *B*

Beaufort County Community
College *A*
Blue Ridge Community College *A*
Brevard College *A*
Caldwell Community College and
Technical Institute *A*
Cape Fear Community College *A*
Catawba Valley Community
College *A*
Central Carolina Community
College *A*
Central Piedmont Community
College *A*
Chowan College *A*
Cleveland Community College *A*
Coastal Carolina Community
College *C,A*
College of the Albemarle *A*
Craven Community College *A*
Davidson County Community
College *A*
Duke University *M*
Durham Technical Community
College *A*
East Carolina University *B,M*
Edgecombe Community College *A*
Fayetteville Technical Community
College *A*
Forsyth Technical Community
College *A*
Gardner-Webb College *A,B*
Gaston College *A*
Guilford Technical Community
College *C,A*
Haywood Community College *A*
James Sprunt Community College
C,A
Johnston Community College *A*
Lenoir-Rhyne College *B*
Mayland Community College *C*
Mitchell Community College *A*
Nash Community College *A*
North Carolina Agricultural and
Technical State University *B*
North Carolina Central
University *B*
Peace College *A*
Pitt Community College *A*
Queens College *B*
Richmond Community College *A*
Roanoke-Chowan Community
College *A*
Robeson Community College *C,A*
Rockingham Community College *A*
Sampson Community College *A*
Sandhills Community College *C,A*
Southeastern Community College *A*
Southwestern Community
College *A*
Stanly Community College *A*
Surry Community College *A*
Tri-County Community College *A*
University of North Carolina
Chapel Hill *B,M,D*
Charlotte *B,M*
Greensboro *B,M*
Wilmington *B*
Vance-Granville Community
College *A*
Wake Technical Community
College *A*
Wayne Community College *A*
Western Carolina University *B*
Western Piedmont Community
College *A*
Wilkes Community College *A*
Wilson Technical Community
College *A*
Wingate College *B*
Winston-Salem State University *B*

North Dakota

Dickinson State University *A,B*
Jamestown College *B*
Medcenter One College of
Nursing *B*
Minot State University *B*
North Dakota State University *B*
Turtle Mountain Community
College *A*
University of Mary *B,M*
University of North Dakota *B,M*

Ohio

Ashland University *B*
Bowling Green State University *B*
Capital University *B*
Case Western Reserve University
B,M,D
Cedarville College *B*
Central Ohio Technical College *A*
Cincinnati Technical College *A*
Clark State Community College *A*
Cleveland State University *B*
College of Mount St. Joseph *B*
Columbus State Community
College *A*
Cuyahoga Community College
Metropolitan Campus *A*
Western Campus *A*
Edison State Community College *A*
Franciscan University of
Steubenville *B*
Franklin University *B*
Hocking Technical College *A*
Kent State University
Ashtabula Regional Campus *A*
East Liverpool Regional
Campus *A*
Kent *B,M*
Tuscarawas Campus *A*
Kettering College of Medical
Arts *A*
Lakeland Community College *A*
Lorain County Community
College *A*
Lourdes College *B*
Malone College *B*
Marion Technical College *A*
Miami University
Hamilton Campus *A*
Oxford Campus *B*
North Central Technical College *A*
Northwest Technical College *A*
Ohio State University: Columbus
Campus *B,M,D*
Ohio University
Athens *B*
Eastern Campus *B*
Southern Campus at Ironton *B*
Zanesville Campus *A,B*
Otterbein College *B*
Owens Technical College
Findlay Campus *A*
Toledo *A*
Shawnee State University *A*
Sinclair Community College *A*
Southern State Community
College *A*
Stark Technical College *A*
University of Akron *B,M*
University of Cincinnati
Cincinnati *B,M,D*
Raymond Walters College *A*
University of Rio Grande *A*
University of Toledo *A,B*
Ursuline College *B*
Walsh College *A,B*
Washington State Community
College *A*
Wittenberg University *B*
Wright State University *B,M*
Xavier University *A,B*

Youngstown State University *B*

Oklahoma

Bacone College *A*
Cameron University *A*
Connors State College *A*
East Central University *B*
Eastern Oklahoma State College *A*
Hillsdale Free Will Baptist
   College *A*
Langston University *B*
Murray State College *A*
Northeastern State University *B*
Northern Oklahoma College *A*
Northwestern Oklahoma State
   University *B*
Oklahoma Baptist University *B*
Oklahoma City University *B*
Oklahoma State University:
   Oklahoma City *A*
Oral Roberts University *B,M*
Redlands Community College *A*
Rogers State College *A*
Rose State College *A*
Southwestern Oklahoma State
   University *B*
Tulsa Junior College *A*
University of Central Oklahoma *B*
University of Oklahoma
   Health Sciences Center *B,M*
   Norman *B,M*
University of Tulsa *B*

Oregon

Central Oregon Community
   College *A*
Chemeketa Community College *C,A*
Clackamas Community College *A*
Clatsop Community College *A*
Eastern Oregon State College *B*
Lane Community College *A*
Linfield College *B*
Linn-Benton Community College *A*
Mount Hood Community
   College *A*
Oregon Health Sciences University
   B,M,D
Oregon Institute of Technology *B*
Portland Community College *A*
Rogue Community College *A*
Southern Oregon State College *B*
Southwestern Oregon Community
   College *A*
Treasure Valley Community College
   C,A
Umpqua Community College *A*
University of Portland *B,M*

Pennsylvania

Allentown College of St. Francis de
   Sales *B,M*
Alvernia College *A,B*
Bloomsburg University of
   Pennsylvania *B,M*
Bucks County Community
   College *A*
Butler County Community
   College *A*
California University of
   Pennsylvania *B*
Carlow College *B*
Cedar Crest College *B*
Clarion University of Pennsylvania
   A,B
College Misericordia *C,B,M*
Community College of Beaver
   County *A*
Community College of
   Philadelphia *A*
Delaware County Community
   College *A*
Duquesne University *B,M*

East Stroudsburg University of
   Pennsylvania *B*
Eastern College *B*
Edinboro University of
   Pennsylvania *B,M*
Elizabethtown College *B*
Gannon University *A,B,M*
Gwynedd-Mercy College *A,B,M*
Hahnemann University School of
   Health Sciences and Humanities
   A,B,M
Harrisburg Area Community
   College *A*
Holy Family College *B*
Immaculata College *B*
Indiana University of Pennsylvania
   B,M
Juniata College *B*
Keystone Junior College *A*
Kutztown University of
   Pennsylvania *B*
La Roche College *B,M*
La Salle University *B*
Lehigh County Community
   College *A*
Lock Haven University of
   Pennsylvania *A*
Luzerne County Community
   College *A*
Lycoming College *B*
Mansfield University of
   Pennsylvania *B*
Marywood College *B*
Mercyhurst College *B*
Messiah College *B*
Millersville University of
   Pennsylvania *B*
Montgomery County Community
   College *A*
Mount Aloysius College *A,B*
Neumann College *B*
Northampton County Area
   Community College *A*
Northeastern Christian Junior
   College *A*
Penn State
   Harrisburg Capital College *B*
   University Park Campus *B,M*
Pennsylvania College of
   Technology *A*
Reading Area Community
   College *A*
St. Francis College *B*
Seton Hill College *B*
Slippery Rock University of
   Pennsylvania *B*
Temple University *B,M*
Thiel College *B*
Thomas Jefferson University:
   College of Allied Health Sciences
   B,M
University of Pennsylvania *B,M,D*
University of Pittsburgh
   Bradford *A*
   Pittsburgh *B,M,D*
University of Scranton *B*
Villanova University *B,M*
Waynesburg College *B*
West Chester University of
   Pennsylvania *B*
Westmoreland County Community
   College *A*
Widener University *B,M,D*
Wilkes University *B,M*
York College of Pennsylvania *B*

Puerto Rico

Bayamon Central University *B*
Caribbean University *B*
Columbia College *A*

Inter American University of Puerto
Rico
   Arecibo Campus *A,B*
   Metropolitan Campus *B*
   San German Campus *B*
Pontifical Catholic University of
   Puerto Rico *B,M*
Universidad Adventista de las
   Antillas *A,B*
Universidad Metropolitana *A,B*
University of Puerto Rico
   Arecibo Campus *A,B*
   Humacao University College
   A,B
   Mayaguez Campus *A,B*
   Medical Sciences Campus *B,M*
University of the Sacred Heart *A,B*

Rhode Island

Community College of Rhode
   Island *A*
Rhode Island College *B*
Salve Regina University *B*
University of Rhode Island *B,M,D*

South Carolina

Bob Jones University *B*
Chesterfield-Marlboro Technical
   College *A*
Clemson University *B,M*
Florence-Darlington Technical
   College *A*
Francis Marion College *B*
Greenville Technical College *A*
Lander College *B*
Midlands Technical College *A*
South Carolina State College *B*
Sumter Area Technical College *A*
Technical College of the
   Lowcountry *A*
Tri-County Technical College *A*
Trident Technical College *A*
University of South Carolina
   Aiken *A,B*
   Columbia *B,M,D*
   Lancaster *A*
   Spartanburg *A,B*
Williamsburg Technical College *C*

South Dakota

Augustana College *B*
Dakota Wesleyan University *A*
Huron University *A*
Mount Marty College *B*
Oglala Lakota College *A*
Presentation College *A,B*
South Dakota State University *B,M*
University of South Dakota *A*
Western Dakota Vocational
   Technical Institute *C*

Tennessee

Aquinas Junior College *A*
Austin Peay State University *B*
Belmont University *B*
Carson-Newman College *B*
Chattanooga State Technical
   Community College *A*
Cleveland State Community
   College *A*
Columbia State Community
   College *A*
Dyersburg State Community
   College *A*
East Tennessee State University
   A,B,M
Jackson State Community
   College *A*
Lincoln Memorial University *A,B*
Memphis State University *B*
Middle Tennessee State
   University *B*

Motlow State Community
   College *A*
Roane State Community College *A*
Shelby State Community College *A*
Southern College of Seventh-day
   Adventists *A,B*
Tennessee State University *A,B*
Tennessee Technological
   University *B*
Union University *A,B*
University of Tennessee
   Chattanooga *B,M*
   Knoxville *B,M,D*
   Martin *B*
   Memphis *B,M,D*
Vanderbilt University *M*
Walters State Community
   College *A*

Texas

Abilene Christian University *A,B*
Alvin Community College *C,A*
Amarillo College *A*
Angelina College *A*
Angelo State University *A,B*
Austin Community College *A*
Baylor University *B,M*
Bee County College *A*
Blinn College *A*
Brazosport College *A*
Brookhaven College *A*
Central Texas College *A*
College of the Mainland *A*
Collin County Community College
   District *A*
Cooke County College *A*
Corpus Christi State University *B,M*
Dallas Baptist University *B*
Del Mar College *A*
El Centro College *A*
El Paso Community College *A*
Galveston College *A*
Hardin-Simmons University *A,B*
Houston Baptist University *A,B*
Houston Community College *A*
Howard College *A*
Huston-Tillotson College *B*
Incarnate Word College *B,M*
Kilgore College *A*
Lamar University—Beaumont *A,B*
Laredo Junior College *C,A*
Lee College *A*
Lubbock Christian University *B*
McLennan Community College *A*
McMurry University *A,B*
Midland College *A*
Midwestern State University *B*
Navarro College *A*
North Harris Montgomery
   Community College District *A*
Northeast Texas Community
   College *C,A*
Odessa College *A*
Prairie View A&M University *B*
Ranger Junior College *C*
San Antonio College *A*
San Jacinto College: Central
   Campus *A*
South Plains College *A*
Southwestern Adventist College *A,B*
Stephen F. Austin State
   University *B*
Tarleton State University *A*
Tarrant County Junior College *A*
Texarkana College *A*
Texas Christian University *B*
Texas Southmost College *A*
Texas State Technical College:
   Sweetwater *C*
Texas Tech University Health
   Science Center *M*
Texas Woman's University *B,M,D*

Trinity Valley Community
College *A*
University of Houston *B*
University of Mary Hardin-
Baylor *B*
University of Texas
Arlington *B,M*
Austin *B,M,D*
El Paso *B,M*
Health Science Center at
Houston *B,M*
Health Science Center at San
Antonio *B,M,D*
Medical Branch at Galveston
B,M
Pan American *A,B*
Tyler *B,M*
Victoria College *A*
Weatherford College *C*
West Texas State University *B,M*
Wharton County Junior College *A*

Utah

Brigham Young University *B,M*
College of Eastern Utah *C,A*
Dixie College *A*
Southern Utah University *A*
University of Utah *B,M,D*
Utah Valley Community College
C,A
Weber State University *A,B*
Westminster College of Salt Lake
City *B*

Vermont

Castleton State College *A*
Norwich University *B*
Southern Vermont College *A,B*
University of Vermont *A,B*

Virginia

Blue Ridge Community College *A*
Christopher Newport College *B*
College of Health Sciences *A*
Dabney S. Lancaster Community
College *A*
Eastern Mennonite College *B*
Eastern Shore Community
College *A*
George Mason University *B,M,D*
Hampton University *B,M*
James Madison University *B*
John Tyler Community College *A*
Liberty University *B*
Lynchburg College *B*
Marymount University *A,B,M*
Mountain Empire Community
College *A*
Norfolk State University *A,B*
Northern Virginia Community
College *A*
Old Dominion University *B,M*
Patrick Henry Community
College *A*
Piedmont Virginia Community
College *A*
Radford University *B,M*
Richard Bland College *A*
Shenandoah University *A,B*
Southside Virginia Community
College *A*
Southwest Virginia Community
College *A*
Tidewater Community College *A*
University of Virginia *B,M,D*
Virginia Commonwealth University
B,M,D
Virginia Highlands Community
College *A*
Wytheville Community College *A*

Washington

Bellevue Community College *A*
Big Bend Community College *A*
Centralia College *A*
City University *B*
Clark College *A*
Columbia Basin College *A*
Eastern Washington University *B,M*
Everett Community College *C,A*
Gonzaga University *B*
Grays Harbor College *A*
Heritage College *C,A*
Lower Columbia College *A*
Olympic College *C,A*
Pacific Lutheran University *B,M*
Peninsula College *A*
St. Martin's College *B*
Seattle Central Community
College *A*
Seattle Pacific University *B,M*
Seattle University *B*
Shoreline Community College *A*
Skagit Valley College *A*
South Puget Sound Community
College *C,A*
Spokane Community College *A*
Spokane Falls Community
College *A*
Tacoma Community College *A*
University of Washington *B,M,D*
Walla Walla College *B*
Walla Walla Community College
C,A
Washington State University *B,M*
Wenatchee Valley College *A*
Whitworth College *B,M*
Yakima Valley Community College
C,A

West Virginia

Alderson-Broaddus College *B*
Bluefield State College *A,B*
College of West Virginia *B*
Davis and Elkins College *A,B*
Fairmont State College *A,B*
Glenville State College *B*
Marshall University *B,M*
Shepherd College *A,B*
University of Charleston *A,B*
West Liberty State College *B*
West Virginia Institute of
Technology *A*
West Virginia Northern Community
College *A*
West Virginia University
Morgantown *B,M*
Parkersburg *A*
West Virginia Wesleyan College *B*
Wheeling Jesuit College *B*

Wisconsin

Alverno College *B*
Bellin College of Nursing *B*
Cardinal Stritch College *A,B*
Carroll College *B*
Chippewa Valley Technical
College *A*
Columbia College of Nursing *B*
Concordia University Wisconsin *B*
Edgewood College *B*
Fox Valley Technical College *A*
Madison Area Technical College *A*
Maranatha Baptist Bible College *B*
Marian College of Fond du Lac *B*
Marquette University *B*
Moraine Park Technical College *A*
Northeast Wisconsin Technical
College *A*
Ripon College *B*
Silver Lake College *B*

University of Wisconsin
Eau Claire *B,M*
Green Bay *B*
Madison *B,M,D*
Milwaukee *B,M,D*
Oshkosh *B,M*
Viterbo College *B*
Waukesha County Technical
College *A*
Western Wisconsin Technical
College *A*
Wisconsin Indianhead Technical
College *A*

Wyoming

Casper College *A*
Central Wyoming College *A*
Laramie County Community
College *A*
Northwest College *C,A*
Sheridan College *A*
University of Wyoming *B,M*
Western Wyoming Community
College *A*

**American Samoa, Caroline
Islands, Guam, Marianas,
Virgin Islands**

Community College of
Micronesia *A*
Northern Marianas College *A*
University of the Virgin Islands *A,B*

Canada

McGill University *B,M*

Nursing education

Arkansas

University of Central Arkansas *M*

California

Azusa Pacific University *B*
San Francisco State University *B,M*

Connecticut

Southern Connecticut State
University *B,M*

Georgia

Morris Brown College *B*

Illinois

Bradley University *B*
De Paul University *M*
St. Xavier University *M*

Indiana

St. Joseph's College *B*
Vincennes University *A*

Iowa

Grand View College *B*
Kirkwood Community College *A*

Kansas

Butler County Community
College *A*

Michigan

Oakland Community College *C*

Minnesota

Northland Community College *A*
Willmar Community College *A*
Winona State University *B*

Mississippi

Jones County Junior College *A*
Northeast Mississippi Community
College *A*

New Jersey

Caldwell College *C*

New York

New York University *B,M,D*

North Carolina

Gaston College *A*

North Dakota

Turtle Mountain Community
College *A*
University of Mary *M*

Ohio

Otterbein College *B*

Pennsylvania

Widener University *D*

Nutritional education

Florida

Manatee Community College *A*

Illinois

Southern Illinois University at
Carbondale *B*

Indiana

Indiana University Bloomington
B,M
Vincennes University *A*

Louisiana

Southeastern Louisiana
University *B*

Massachusetts

Framingham State College *M*

Michigan

Marygrove College *B*

Minnesota

Concordia College: Moorhead *B*
St. Olaf College *B*
Willmar Community College *A*

Mississippi

Alcorn State University *B*
Mississippi College *B,M*

New Mexico

University of New Mexico *B*

New York

City University of New York:
Brooklyn College *B*
New York University *B,M,D*

North Carolina

Campbell University *B*

Ohio

University of Cincinnati *M*

Pennsylvania

Immaculata College *M*
Indiana University of
Pennsylvania *B*
Marywood College *B*
Temple University *M,D*

Tennessee
East Tennessee State University *B*

Texas
University of Mary Hardin-
Baylor *B*

Nutritional sciences

Alabama
Auburn University *M,D*
Community College of the Air
Force *A*
University of Alabama in
Birmingham *M,D*

Arizona
University of Arizona *B,M,D*

Arkansas
Ouachita Baptist University *B*
University of Arkansas for Medical
Sciences *M*

California
Chapman University *B,M*
John F. Kennedy University *M*
Pepperdine University *B*
San Francisco State University *B*
San Jose State University *B*
University of California
Berkeley *B,M,D*
Davis *B,M,D*

Connecticut
St. Joseph College *B,M*
University of Bridgeport *M*
University of Connecticut *B,M,D*

Delaware
University of Delaware *B,M*

Florida
University of Florida *B*

Georgia
Clark Atlanta University *B*
Emory University *M*
Fort Valley State College *B*
University of Georgia *B*

Hawaii
University of Hawaii at Manoa *M*

Illinois
Illinois Benedictine College *B*
University of Chicago *M*
University of Health Sciences: The
Chicago Medical School *M*
University of Illinois at Urbana-
Champaign *M,D*

Indiana
Indiana University Bloomington
B,M
Purdue University *M,D*

Iowa
University of Iowa *D*

Kansas
Kansas State University *B*
University of Kansas
Lawrence *M*
Medical Center *M*

Louisiana
Tulane University *M*

Maine
University of Maine *D*

Maryland
University of Maryland: College
Park *M,D*

Massachusetts
Atlantic Union College *B*
Boston University *M,D*
Hampshire College *B*
Harvard University *M,D*
Simmons College *B*
Tufts University *M,D*
University of Massachusetts at
Amherst *M,D*

Michigan
Eastern Michigan University *B*
University of Michigan *M*

Minnesota
University of Minnesota: Twin
Cities *B,M,D*

Mississippi
Alcorn State University *B*
Mississippi State University *M,D*

Nebraska
University of Nebraska
Medical Center *W*
Lincoln *M,D*

New Jersey
Rutgers—The State University of
New Jersey
Douglass College *B*
Livingston College *B*
New Brunswick *M,D*
Rutgers College *B*
University College New
Brunswick *B*

New York
City University of New York:
Brooklyn College *B*
Columbia University *M,D*
Cornell University *B,M,D*
Long Island University: C. W. Post
Campus *M*
Mohawk Valley Community
College *A*
New York Institute of
Technology *M*
Russell Sage College *B*
State University of New York at
Buffalo *M*
Syracuse University *B,M,D*

North Carolina
North Carolina State University
B,M,D
University of North Carolina at
Chapel Hill *B*

Ohio
Case Western Reserve University
B,M,D
Ohio University *B*

Pennsylvania
Drexel University *B,M*
University of Pittsburgh *B*

Puerto Rico
University of Puerto Rico: Medical
Sciences Campus *M*

South Carolina
Clemson University *M,D,W*

Tennessee
University of Tennessee: Knoxville
B,M

Texas
Texas A&M University *M,D*
Texas Woman's University *B,M,D*
University of Texas
Austin *D*
Health Science Center at
Houston *M,D,W*
Southwestern Medical Center
at Dallas Southwestern
Allied Health Sciences
School *B*

Utah
Utah State University *M*

Virginia
Virginia Polytechnic Institute and
State University *B,M,D*

Washington
Bastyr College *B,M*
University of Washington *M,D*
Washington State University *M,D*

Wisconsin
University of Wisconsin
Green Bay *B*
Madison *B,M,D*

**American Samoa, Caroline
Islands, Guam, Marianas,
Virgin Islands**
Community College of
Micronesia *A*

Canada
McGill University *B,M,D*

Mexico
Sistema Instituto Tecnologico y de
Estudios Superiores de
Monterrey *M*

Occupational safety and health technology

Alabama
Community College of the Air
Force *A*
Jacksonville State University *B*
Wallace State Community College
at Hanceville *A*

Arizona
University of Arizona *B*

California
National University *B,M*
San Diego City College *C,A*
University of Southern California *M*

Connecticut
University of New Haven *C,A,B,M*
Waterbury State Technical
College *C*

Hawaii
University of Hawaii: Honolulu
Community College *C,A*

Illinois
Illinois State University *B*
Moraine Valley Community College
C,A

Indiana
Indiana State University *B,M*
Purdue University *B,M*

Kentucky
Murray State University *A,B,M*
Western Kentucky University *A*

Maine
Central Maine Technical College
C,A

Maryland
Catonsville Community College *A*

Michigan
Madonna University *A,B*

Missouri
Central Missouri State University
B,M

Montana
Montana College of Mineral
Science and Technology *B*

New Jersey
New Jersey Institute of
Technology *M*

New York
Mercy College *C*

North Carolina
North Carolina Agricultural and
Technical State University *B*

Ohio
Columbus State Community
College *A*
Ohio University *B*
Sinclair Community College *C,A*
University of Cincinnati: Access
Colleges *A*

Oklahoma
Southeastern Oklahoma State
University *B*

Oregon
Mount Hood Community
College *A*

Pennsylvania
Millersville University of
Pennsylvania *B*
Penn State University Park
Campus *C*

South Carolina
Horry-Georgetown Technical
College *A*
Williamsburg Technical College *A*

Texas
Lamar University—Beaumont *A*
Paul Quinn College *B*
Texas State Technical College:
Waco *A*

Utah
Brigham Young University *B*

Washington
Central Washington University *B*

West Virginia
Fairmont State College *B*
Salem-Teikyo University *B*

Wisconsin

University of Wisconsin:
Platteville *B*

Wyoming

Laramie County Community
College *A*

Occupational therapy

Alabama

Samford University *B*
Tuskegee University *B*
University of Alabama in
Birmingham *B,M*

Arkansas

University of Central Arkansas *B*

California

San Jose State University *B,M*
Santa Rosa Junior College *A*
University of Southern California
B,M,D

Colorado

Colorado State University *B,M*

Connecticut

Quinnipiac College *C,B*
Sacred Heart University *B*
University of Hartford *B*

District of Columbia

Howard University *B*

Florida

Barry University *B*
Broward Community College *A*
Florida Agricultural and Mechanical
University *B*
Florida International University
B,M
Miami-Dade Community College *A*
University of Florida *B,M*

Georgia

Atlanta Metropolitan College *A*
Clayton State College *A*
Gainesville College *A*
Medical College of Georgia *B,M*
Middle Georgia College *A*

Illinois

Chicago State University *B*
Illinois Central College *A*
Illinois College *B*
Rush University *M*
University of Illinois at Chicago
B,M

Indiana

Indiana University—Purdue
University at Indianapolis *B*
University of Indianapolis *M*
Vincennes University *A*

Iowa

Central College *B*
Luther College *B*
St. Ambrose University *B*
Wartburg College *B*

Kansas

Hutchinson Community College *A*
University of Kansas
Lawrence *B,M*
Medical Center *B,M*

Kentucky

Eastern Kentucky University *B,M*

Louisiana

Louisiana State University Medical
Center *B*
Northeast Louisiana University *B*
Southern University and
Agricultural and Mechanical
College *B*

Maine

University of New England *B*

Maryland

Towson State University *B,M*

Massachusetts

Boston University *B,M,W*
Springfield College *M*
Tufts University *M*
Worcester State College *B*

Michigan

Alma College *B*
Calvin College *B*
Eastern Michigan University *B*
Lansing Community College *A*
Wayne State University *B,M*
Western Michigan University *B,M*

Minnesota

College of St. Catherine: St.
Catherine Campus *B,M*
Northland Community College *A*
Rainy River Community College *A*
Rochester Community College *A*
University of Minnesota: Twin
Cities *B*
Willmar Community College *A*

Mississippi

Mississippi College *B*
University of Mississippi Medical
Center *B*

Missouri

Maryville University *B*
Rockhurst College *B,M*
St. Louis University *B*
University of Missouri: Columbia *B*
Washington University *B,M*
William Jewell College *B*

Montana

Rocky Mountain College *B*

Nebraska

Creighton University *B*

New Hampshire

University of New Hampshire *B*

New Jersey

Kean College of New Jersey *B*

New York

City University of New York: York
College *B*
Dominican College of Blauvelt *B*
D'Youville College *B,M*
Keuka College *B*
New York University *B,M,D*
Russell Sage College *B,M*
State University of New York
Buffalo *B,M*
Health Science Center at
Brooklyn *B*
Touro College *B,M*
Utica College of Syracuse
University *B*

North Carolina

East Carolina University *B*
University of North Carolina at
Chapel Hill *M*

North Dakota

University of North Dakota *B*

Ohio

Capital University *B*
Cleveland State University *B*
Ohio State University: Columbus
Campus *C,B,M*
Wittenberg University *B*

Oklahoma

Eastern Oklahoma State College *A*
University of Oklahoma
Health Sciences Center *B*
Norman *B*

Oregon

Pacific University *B*

Pennsylvania

College Misericordia *B,M*
Duquesne University *M*
Elizabethtown College *B*
Juniata College *B*
Keystone Junior College *A*
Lebanon Valley College of
Pennsylvania *B*
Messiah College *B*
Moravian College *B*
Temple University *B,M*
Thomas Jefferson University:
College of Allied Health Sciences
B,M
University of Pittsburgh *B*
Wilkes University *B*

Puerto Rico

University of Puerto Rico: Medical
Sciences Campus *B*

South Dakota

University of South Dakota *M*

Tennessee

University of Tennessee:
Memphis *B*

Texas

Southwest Texas State University *B*
Texas Southmost College *A*
Texas Tech University *B*
Texas Woman's University *B,M*
University of Texas
Health Science Center at San
Antonio *B*
Medical Branch at
Galveston *B*
San Antonio *B*

Virginia

Virginia Commonwealth University
B,M

Washington

University of Puget Sound *B,M*
University of Washington *B,M*

West Virginia

Davis and Elkins College *B*

Wisconsin

Carthage College *B*
Mount Mary College *B*
Northland College *B*
University of Wisconsin
Madison *B*
Milwaukee *B*

Wyoming

Northwest College *A*

Canada

McGill University *B,M*

Occupational therapy assistant

Alabama

Alabama Southern Community
College *A*
Chattahoochee Valley Community
College *A*
Enterprise State Junior College *A*
Faulkner University *A*
Gadsden State Community
College *A*
George C. Wallace State
Community College at Selma *A*
James H. Faulkner State
Community College *A*
Jefferson State Community
College *A*
John C. Calhoun State Community
College *A*
Lawson State Community
College *A*
Livingston University *A*
Lurleen B. Wallace State Junior
College *A*
Northeast Alabama State Junior
College *A*
Shelton State Community
College *A*
Shoals Community College *A*
Southern Union State Junior
College *A*
University of Alabama in
Birmingham *C*
Walker College *A*
Wallace State Community College
at Hanceville *A*

Arkansas

University of Central Arkansas *B*

California

Chabot College *A*
Kings River Community College *A*
Mount St. Mary's College *C,A*

Colorado

Pueblo Community College *A*

Connecticut

Manchester Community College *A*

Florida

Palm Beach Community College *A*

Georgia

Brewton-Parker College *A*
Gainesville College *A*
Medical College of Georgia *A*

Hawaii

University of Hawaii: Kapiolani
Community College *A*

Illinois

City Colleges of Chicago
Chicago City-Wide College *A*
Wright College *A*
College of DuPage *A*
Illinois Central College *A*
Parkland College *A*

Indiana

Indiana University—Purdue
University at Indianapolis *A*

Iowa

Kirkwood Community College *A*

Kansas

Johnson County Community
College *A*

Louisiana

Northeast Louisiana University *A*

Maine

Kennebec Valley Technical
College *A*

Maryland

Catonsville Community College *A*

Massachusetts

Bay State College *A*
Becker College: Worcester
Campus *A*
Massachusetts Bay Community
College *A*
Middlesex Community College *C*
Mount Ida College *A*
North Shore Community College *A*
Quinsigamond Community
College *A*
Springfield Technical Community
College *A*

Michigan

Grand Rapids Community
College *A*
Schoolcraft College *A*

Minnesota

Anoka-Ramsey Community
College *A*
Austin Community College *A*
St. Mary's Campus of the College of
St. Catherine *A*
Vermilion Community College *A*

Missouri

Penn Valley Community College *A*
St. Louis Community College at
Meramec *A*

New Jersey

Atlantic Community College *A*
Union County College *A*

New York

City University of New York: La
Guardia Community College *A*
Erie Community College: North
Campus *A*
Herkimer County Community
College *A*
Maria College *A*
Orange County Community
College *A*
Rockland Community College *A*

North Carolina

Caldwell Community College and
Technical Institute *A*
Pitt Community College *A*
Stanly Community College *A*

North Dakota

North Dakota State College of
Science *A*

Ohio

Cincinnati Technical College *A*
Cuyahoga Community College:
Metropolitan Campus *A*
Kent State University: East
Liverpool Regional Campus *A*
Lourdes College *A*
Muskingum Area Technical
College *A*
Shawnee State University *A*
Sinclair Community College *A*
Stark Technical College *A*

Oklahoma

Tulsa Junior College *A*

Oregon

Mount Hood Community
College *A*

Pennsylvania

Harcum Junior College *A*
Lehigh County Community
College *A*
Mount Aloysius College *A*
Pennsylvania College of
Technology *A*

Puerto Rico

University of Puerto Rico
Humacao University
College *A*
Ponce Technological
University College *A*

South Carolina

Trident Technical College *A*

Tennessee

Motlow State Community
College *A*
Nashville State Technical
Institute *A*
Shelby State Community College *A*

Texas

Austin Community College *A*
Cooke County College *A*
Houston Community College *C*
St. Philip's College *A*
San Jacinto College: Central
Campus *A*

Virginia

College of Health Sciences *A*

Washington

Green River Community College *A*
Yakima Valley Community
College *A*

Wisconsin

Fox Valley Technical College *A*
Madison Area Technical College *A*

Wyoming

Casper College *A*

Ocean engineering

Alaska

University of Alaska Fairbanks *M*

California

University of California: San Diego
M,D
University of Southern California *M*

Connecticut

University of Connecticut *M*

District of Columbia

Catholic University of America *M*
George Washington University *M*

Florida

Daytona Beach Community
College *A*
Florida Atlantic University *B,M,D*
Florida Institute of Technology
B,M,D
Miami-Dade Community College *A*
University of Florida *M,D*
University of Miami *M*

Hawaii

University of Hawaii at Manoa *M,D*

Maryland

United States Naval Academy *B*

Massachusetts

Massachusetts Institute of
Technology *B,M,D,W*
Worcester Polytechnic Institute *B*

Minnesota

Willmar Community College *A*

Missouri

East Central College *A*

New Hampshire

University of New Hampshire *M*

New Jersey

Stevens Institute of Technology
B,M,D

Oregon

Oregon State University *M*

Rhode Island

University of Rhode Island *B,M,D*

Texas

Texas A&M University
College Station *B,M,D*
Galveston *B*

Virginia

Virginia Polytechnic Institute and
State University *B*

Washington

University of Washington *B*

Wisconsin

University of Wisconsin:
Madison *M*

Oceanographic technologies

California

Saddleback College *C,A*
University of California: San
Diego *D*

Florida

Nova University *B*

Hawaii

Hawaii Loa College *B*

Michigan

Lansing Community College *A*

New Jersey

Stevens Institute of Technology
M,D

Pennsylvania

Penn State University Park
Campus *C*

Washington

Shoreline Community College *A*

Oceanography

Alaska

University of Alaska Fairbanks *M,D*

Arizona

Arizona Western College *A*

California

California State University:
Fresno *M*
Humboldt State University *B*
Naval Postgraduate School *M,D*
San Jose State University *B*
Santa Rosa Junior College *A*
Southwestern College *A*
University of California: San Diego
M,D
University of San Diego *B,M*

Connecticut

University of Connecticut *M,D*
Wesleyan University *B*
Western Connecticut State
University *M*

Delaware

University of Delaware *M,D*

Florida

Eckerd College *B*
Florida Institute of Technology
B,M,D
Florida State University *M,D*
Gulf Coast Community College *A*
Nova University *B,D*
Pensacola Junior College *A*
University of Miami *M,D*
University of South Florida *M,D*

Hawaii

University of Hawaii at Manoa *M,D*

Illinois

Illinois Central College *A*
University of Chicago *B,M,D*

Louisiana

Louisiana State University and
Agricultural and Mechanical
College *M,D*

Maine

Maine Maritime Academy *B*
Southern Maine Technical
College *A*
University of Maine *M,D*

Maryland

United States Naval Academy *B*

Massachusetts

Bridgewater State College *B*
Hampshire College *B*
Harvard University *M,D*

Massachusetts Institute of
Technology *M,D,W*

Michigan

University of Michigan *B,M,D*

Minnesota

St. Cloud State University *B*
Willmar Community College *A*

New Hampshire

University of New Hampshire *M,D*

New Jersey

Atlantic Community College *A*
Rutgers—The State University of
New Jersey
Cook College *B*
Douglass College *B*
Stevens Institute of Technology
M,D
Stockton State College *B*

New York

City University of New York: City
College *B,M*
Columbia University
Columbia College *B*
New York *M,D*
Cornell University *M,D*
Long Island University:
Southampton Campus *B*
State University of New York
Maritime College *B*

North Carolina

Cape Fear Community College *A*

Oregon

Oregon State University *M,D*

Pennsylvania

California University of
Pennsylvania *B*
Millersville University of
Pennsylvania *B*

Rhode Island

University of Rhode Island *M,D*

Texas

Lamar University—Beaumont *B*
Texas A&M University *M,D*
Texas Southmost College *A*

Virginia

Old Dominion University *M,D*

Washington

Evergreen State College *B*
Lower Columbia College *A*
Tacoma Community College *A*
University of Washington *B,M,D*

Wisconsin

University of Wisconsin: Madison
M,D

Canada

McGill University *M,D*

Office supervision and management

Alabama

Alabama Agricultural and
Mechanical University *B*
Alabama State University *B*
Athens State College *B*

Bishop State Community College *A*
Chattahoochee Valley Community
College *C*
Community College of the Air
Force *A*
Enterprise State Junior College *A*
Faulkner University *B*
James H. Faulkner State
Community College *A*
John C. Calhoun State Community
College *A*
Oakwood College *A*
Reid State Technical College *C*
Shoals Community College *C,A*
Snead State Junior College *A*
Southern Union State Junior
College *A*
University of North Alabama *B*
Walker State Technical College *A*
Wallace State Community College
at Hanceville *A*

Alaska

University of Alaska
Anchorage *A*
Southeast *A*

Arizona

Cochise College *A*
Eastern Arizona College *A*
Lamson Junior College *A*
Mesa Community College *A*
Mohave Community College *C*
Rio Salado Community College *A*
Yavapai College *A*

Arkansas

Arkansas State University
Beebe Branch *A*
Jonesboro *A,B*
Garland County Community
College *C*
Harding University *A,B*
Henderson State University *A*
Ouachita Baptist University *B*
University of Arkansas at Little
Rock *B*
University of Central Arkansas *B*

California

Barstow College *C,A*
California State University: Los
Angeles *B*
Cerritos Community College *A*
Cerro Coso Community College
C,A
Chabot College *A*
College of the Desert *C,A*
El Camino College *C,A*
Glendale Community College *C*
Golden West College *C,A*
Heald College: Sacramento *C,A*
Irvine Valley College *C,A*
La Sierra University *A*
Los Angeles Harbor College *C,A*
Los Angeles Pierce College *C,A*
Los Medanos College *C,A*
Merced College *A*
MiraCosta College *C,A*
Mission College *A*
Monterey Peninsula College *C,A*
Moorpark College *C,A*
Mount San Jacinto College *C,A*
Napa Valley College *C,A*
Pacific Union College *B*
Point Loma Nazarene College *B*
Porterville College *C*
Saddleback College *C*
Santa Barbara City College *A*
Santa Monica College *A*
Santa Rosa Junior College *C*
Skyline College *C*

Southwestern College *A*
West Valley College *A*

Colorado

Aims Community College *C,A*
Mesa State College *C,A*
Pikes Peak Community College *C*
Red Rocks Community College *A*
Trinidad State Junior College *A*

Connecticut

Briarwood College *A*
Central Connecticut State
University *B*
Mattatuck Community College *A*
Northwestern Connecticut
Community College *A*
Quinebaug Valley Community
College *A*
University of New Haven *C*

Delaware

Goldey-Beacom College *A,B*

Florida

Brevard Community College *A*
Daytona Beach Community
College *A*
Florida Agricultural and Mechanical
University *B*
Florida Community College at
Jacksonville *A*
Gulf Coast Community College *C*
Hillsborough Community College *A*
Indian River Community College *A*
Jones College *A,B*
Lake-Sumter Community College *A*
Miami-Dade Community College *C*
Pensacola Junior College *A*
Phillips Junior College:
Melbourne *A*
St. Petersburg Junior College *A*
South College: Palm Beach Campus
C,A
South Florida Community
College *A*

Georgia

Abraham Baldwin Agricultural
College *A*
Atlanta Metropolitan College *A*
Augusta College *B*
Brewton-Parker College *B*
Clark Atlanta University *B*
Darton College *A*
DeKalb College *A*
Georgia College *B*
Georgia State University *B*
Gordon College *A*
Macon College *C*
North Georgia College *B*
West Georgia College *B*

Hawaii

Cannon's International Business
College of Honolulu *A*

Idaho

University of Idaho *B*

Illinois

City Colleges of Chicago: Chicago
City-Wide College *C*
College of DuPage *C,A*
Eastern Illinois University *B*
Elgin Community College *C,A*
Governors State University *B*
Illinois Central College *C*

Illinois Eastern Community
Colleges
Frontier Community
College *A*
Lincoln Trail College *C,A*
Olney Central College *C,A*
Wabash Valley College *C,A*
John A. Logan College *C*
Lincoln Land Community
College *A*
Moraine Valley Community
College *C*
Northern Illinois University *B*
Oakton Community College *C,A*
Parkland College *A*
Richland Community College *A*
Southern Illinois University at
Carbondale *A*
Waubonsee Community College *A*
Western Illinois University *B*
William Rainey Harper College *C,A*

Indiana

Indiana State University *B*
Indiana University—Purdue
University
Fort Wayne *A*
Indianapolis *C*
Purdue University *A,B*
Tri-State University *B*
University of Southern Indiana *B*

Iowa

American Institute of Business *A*
American Institute of Commerce *A*
Des Moines Area Community
College *A*
Hawkeye Institute of Technology *A*
Iowa Lakes Community College *A*
Morningside College *B*
Mount St. Clare College *B*
North Iowa Area Community
College *A*
Northeast Iowa Community
College *A*
Northwestern College *A*
Vennard College *B*

Kansas

Brown Mackie College *C*
Cloud County Community
College *A*
Emporia State University *B*
Fort Hays State University *B*
Haskell Indian Junior College *A*
Hutchinson Community College
C,A
Johnson County Community
College *A*
Neosho County Community
College *A*
Pratt Community College *C,A*
Tabor College *B*
Washburn University of Topeka *A*

Kentucky

Campbellsville College *A,B*
Franklin College *A*
Jefferson Community College *A*
Kentucky State University *A*
Morehead State University *A*
Northern Kentucky University *A,B*
St. Catharine College *A*
Sullivan College *A*
Union College *A,B*
University of Louisville *A*

Louisiana

Louisiana College *B*
Northeast Louisiana University *B*

Maine

Andover College *A*
Beal College *A*
Central Maine Technical College
 C,A
Kennebec Valley Technical
 College *A*
Southern Maine Technical
 College *A*
Thomas College *A*
University of Maine at Machias *A*

Maryland

Bowie State University *B*
Catonsville Community College *A*
Columbia Union College *C,A*
Howard Community College *A*
Montgomery College: Germantown
 Campus *C*
Morgan State University *B*
New Community College of
 Baltimore *A*
Villa Julie College *A*
Wor-Wic Tech Community
 College *A*

Massachusetts

Aquinas College at Milton *A*
Aquinas College at Newton *C,A*
Atlantic Union College *A,B*
Berkshire Community College *A*
Bunker Hill Community College *A*
Cape Cod Community College *C*
Dean Junior College *A*
Endicott College *A*
Fisher College *A*
Massachusetts Bay Community
 College *C,A*
North Shore Community College *A*
Northern Essex Community College
 C,A
Quincy College *A*
Salem State College *B*
Suffolk University *B*

Michigan

Baker College
 Auburn Hills *A*
 Flint *B*
 Mount Clemens *C,A*
 Muskegon *B*
 Owosso *B*
Cleary College *A*
Delta College *A*
Detroit College of Business *B*
Eastern Michigan University *B*
Ferris State University *B*
Grand Rapids Baptist College and
 Seminary *B*
Great Lakes Junior College of
 Business *A*
Lake Superior State University *A,B*
Lansing Community College *A*
Michigan Christian College *C,A*
Northern Michigan University *B*
Schoolcraft College *A*

Minnesota

Alexandria Technical College *A*
Anoka-Ramsey Community
 College *A*
Crown College *A*
Mankato State University *B*
Moorhead State University *B*
Normandale Community College *A*
North Central Bible College *A*
Northwestern College *B*
Southwest State University *A,B*
University of Minnesota:
 Crookston *A*
Willmar Community College *A*
Winona State University *B*

Mississippi

Delta State University *B*
Jackson State University *B*
Mississippi College *B*
Mississippi Gulf Coast Community
 College: Jefferson Davis
 Campus *A*

Missouri

Central Missouri State University *B*
Longview Community College *A*
Maple Woods Community College
 C,A
Mineral Area College *C,A*
Moberly Area Community
 College *A*
Northwest Missouri State
 University *B*
Penn Valley Community College
 C,A
St. Charles Community College *C*
St. Louis Community College
 Florissant Valley *C*
 Meramec *C*
Southeast Missouri State
 University *A*
Southwest Missouri State
 University *B*

Montana

Dull Knife Memorial College *C,A*
Western Montana College of the
 University of Montana *A*

Nebraska

Chadron State College *B*
Lincoln School of Commerce *A*
McCook Community College *A*
Southeast Community College:
 Beatrice Campus *A*
Union College *A,B*
University of Nebraska
 Kearney *B*
 Lincoln *B*

Nevada

Community College of Southern
 Nevada *C,A*
Truckee Meadows Community
 College *A*

New Hampshire

Castle College *A*
Hesser College *A*
New Hampshire Technical College
 Laconia *C,A*
 Manchester *C,A*

New Jersey

Berkeley College of Business *A*
Burlington County College *A*
Mercer County Community
 College *A*
Rider College *B*
Sussex County Community
 College *C*
Thomas Edison State College *C,A,B*
Trenton State College *B*

New Mexico

Clovis Community College *C,A*
New Mexico Highlands
 University *B*
New Mexico Junior College *C,A*
Western New Mexico University *A*

New York

Berkeley College *C,A*
Central City Business Institute *A*

City University of New York
 Baruch College *B*
 Borough of Manhattan
 Community College *A*
Clinton Community College *A*
Community College of the Finger
 Lakes *A*
Herkimer County Community
 College *A*
Jamestown Business College *C*
Maria College *A*
Nassau Community College *C*
Sage Junior College of Albany, A
 Division of Russell Sage
 College *A*
St. John Fisher College *C*
State University of New York
 College of Agriculture and
 Technology at Morrisville *A*
 College at Buffalo *B*
 College of Technology at
 Delhi *A*
 College of Technology at
 Farmingdale *A*
Suffolk County Community College
 Eastern Campus *A*
 Selden *A*
 Western Campus *A*
Sullivan County Community
 College *A*
Trocaire College *A*
Westchester Business Institute *A*

North Carolina

Alamance Community College *A*
College of the Albemarle *A*
Guilford Technical Community
 College *C,A*
Rockingham Community College *A*
University of North Carolina at
 Greensboro *B*
Wingate College *A,B*
Winston-Salem State University *B*

North Dakota

Dickinson State University *A*
Minot State University *A*
North Dakota State College of
 Science *A*
North Dakota State University:
 Bottineau and Institute of
 Forestry *A*
Trinity Bible College *A,B*
University of North Dakota
 Grand Forks *B*
 Lake Region *A*
Valley City State University *B*

Ohio

Bowling Green State University *B*
Cincinnati Metropolitan College
 C,A
Cuyahoga Community College:
 Western Campus *C,A*
Dyke College *A,B*
Kent State University
 East Liverpool Regional
 Campus *A*
 Salem Regional Campus *A*
Lakeland Community College *C,A*
Miami University: Oxford
 Campus *B*
Miami-Jacobs College *A*
Northwest Technical College *A*
Ohio State University Agricultural
 Technical Institute *A*
Ohio University: Chillicothe
 Campus *A*
Terra Technical College *C*
Tiffin University *B*
University of Akron *A*

University of Cincinnati
 Access Colleges *B*
 Clermont College *C*
 Raymond Walters College *A*

Oklahoma

East Central University *B*
Northern Oklahoma College *A*
Northwestern Oklahoma State
 University *C,B*
Oklahoma State University:
 Oklahoma City *C*
Rose State College *C,A*
Southwestern Oklahoma State
 University *A*
University of Central Oklahoma *B*

Oregon

Chemeketa Community College *A*
Lane Community College *A*
Portland Community College *A*
Rogue Community College *A*
Southwestern Oregon Community
 College *A*

Pennsylvania

Bloomsburg University of
 Pennsylvania *B*
Bucks County Community
 College *A*
Central Pennsylvania Business
 School *A*
Clarion University of
 Pennsylvania *A*
Community College of Beaver
 County *A*
Delaware County Community
 College *C,A*
Gannon University *A*
Harcum Junior College *A*
Indiana University of
 Pennsylvania *B*
Luzerne County Community
 College *C,A*
Manor Junior College *A*
Mercyhurst College *A*
Northampton County Area
 Community College *A*
Peirce Junior College *A*
Reading Area Community
 College *A*
Shippensburg University of
 Pennsylvania *B*
University of Pittsburgh at
 Titusville *A*
Westmoreland County Community
 College *A*
York College of Pennsylvania *A,B*

Rhode Island

Johnson & Wales University *B*
Providence College *C,A*

South Carolina

Claflin College *B*
Midlands Technical College *A*
South Carolina State College *B*
Technical College of the
 Lowcountry *A*
University of South Carolina *B*

South Dakota

Black Hills State University *A*
Mount Marty College *C*
National College *A*
Presentation College *C,A*

Tennessee

Austin Peay State University *B*
Bristol University *A*
David Lipscomb University *B*

Dyersburg State Community College *A*
East Tennessee State University *B*
Knoxville Business College *A*
Memphis State University *B*
Middle Tennessee State University *B*
Motlow State Community College *A*
Nashville State Technical Institute *A*
Pellissippi State Technical Community College *A*
Southern College of Seventh-day Adventists *B*
Tennessee Temple University *B*
Trevecca Nazarene College *B*
University of Tennessee
    Chattanooga *B*
    Martin *B*

Texas

Amarillo College *A*
Brookhaven College *A*
Central Texas College *A*
College of the Mainland *A*
Collin County Community College District *C,A*
East Texas State University *B*
Eastfield College *C*
El Centro College *A*
El Paso Community College *C,A*
Houston Community College *C*
Mountain View College *A*
North Harris Montgomery Community College District *C,A*
Prairie View A&M University *B*
Sam Houston State University *B*
Southwest Texas State University *B*
Southwestern Adventist College *A,B*
Stephen F. Austin State University *B*
Tarleton State University *B*
Texas College *B*
Texas State Technical College: Sweetwater *C,A*
Texas Woman's University *B*
University of Houston: Downtown *B*

Utah

LDS Business College *A*
Southern Utah University *A*
Utah Valley Community College *C,A*

Vermont

Champlain College *A*

Virginia

Blue Ridge Community College *C*
Clinch Valley College of the University of Virginia *C*
Commonwealth College *A*
Dabney S. Lancaster Community College *C*
Mountain Empire Community College *A*
National Business College *A*
Radford University *B*
St. Paul's College *B*
Virginia Commonwealth University *B*

Washington

Big Bend Community College *A*
Central Washington University *B*
Centralia College *A*
Columbia Basin College *C*
Eastern Washington University *B*
Edmonds Community College *A*
Lower Columbia College *A*

Pierce College *C,A*
South Puget Sound Community College *A*
Tacoma Community College *A*
Whatcom Community College *A*

West Virginia

Bluefield State College *B*
Marshall University *A*
Shepherd College *B*
West Liberty State College *B*
West Virginia Institute of Technology *A*

Wisconsin

Moraine Park Technical College *A*
Northeast Wisconsin Technical College *A*
Stratton College *A*
University of Wisconsin
    Eau Claire *B*
    Superior *B*
    Whitewater *B*
Western Wisconsin Technical College *C*

Wyoming

Casper College *A*
Northwest College *A*
Sheridan College *A*
Western Wyoming Community College *A*

Operations research

Alabama

Auburn University at Montgomery *B*
University of Alabama
    Birmingham *B*
    Tuscaloosa *B*

Arizona

University of Arizona *B*

Arkansas

University of Central Arkansas *B*

California

California School of Professional Psychology at Fresno *M*
California State Polytechnic University: Pomona *B*
California State University
    Hayward *M*
    Long Beach *C,B*
    Los Angeles *B*
    Northridge *B,M*
    Sacramento *B*
    Stanislaus *B*
Naval Postgraduate School *M,D*
San Francisco State University *B*
Santa Clara University *B*
Stanford University *M,D*
University of California: San Diego *B*
University of San Francisco *B*

Colorado

United States Air Force Academy *B*
University of Colorado
    Boulder *B*
    Colorado Springs *B*
University of Denver *B,M*

Connecticut

Quinnipiac College *B*
University of New Haven *M*

Yale University *M,D*

Delaware

University of Delaware *M,D*

District of Columbia

George Washington University *B,M,D*

Florida

Florida Institute of Technology *M,D*
University of Tampa *B*

Georgia

Georgia Institute of Technology *M*
Georgia State University *B,M,D*

Idaho

University of Idaho *B*

Illinois

Bradley University *B*
De Paul University *M*
Lewis University *B*
Northwestern University *B,M*
Roosevelt University *B*
University of Chicago *M,D*
University of Illinois at Chicago *D*

Indiana

Ball State University *B,M*
Indiana University Bloomington *B,M,D*
Purdue University *M,D*

Louisiana

Louisiana State University and Agricultural and Mechanical College *B,M,D*
Louisiana Tech University *B,M*
Nicholls State University *B*

Massachusetts

Babson College *B,M*
Boston College *B*
Boston University *B*
Harvard University *M,D*
Massachusetts Institute of Technology *M,D*
Worcester Polytechnic Institute *B*

Michigan

Central Michigan University *B*
Eastern Michigan University *B,M*
Ferris State University *B*
Grand Valley State University *B,M*
Madonna University *M*
Michigan State University *M*
Michigan Technological University *B,M*
Wayne State University *M,D*
Western Michigan University *M*

Minnesota

St. Cloud State University *B*
University of St. Thomas *B*

Missouri

University of Missouri
    Columbia *B*
    Kansas City *M*

New Jersey

Fairleigh Dickinson University *M*
Rutgers—The State University of New Jersey *M,D*
Stevens Institute of Technology *M,D*
Thomas Edison State College *C,A,B*

New Mexico

University of New Mexico *B*

New York

City University of New York:
    Baruch College *B,M*
Clarkson University *B*
Columbia University: School of Engineering and Applied Science *B,M,D,W*
Cornell University *B,M,D*
New York University *B,M,D*
Polytechnic University *B,M*
Rensselaer Polytechnic Institute *M,D*
St. John's University *B,M*
State University of New York at Buffalo *D*
Syracuse University *B,M,D*
Union College *M*
United States Military Academy *B*
University of the State of New York: Regents College *B*

North Carolina

North Carolina State University *M,D*
University of North Carolina
    Chapel Hill *B,M,D*
    Greensboro *M*

North Dakota

North Dakota State University *M,D*

Ohio

Air Force Institute of Technology *M,D*
Bowling Green State University *B*
Case Western Reserve University *M,D*
Kent State University *M,D*
Ohio University *B*
University of Cincinnati *B,M,D*
University of Toledo *B,M*
Wittenberg University *B*
Wright State University *B,M*

Oregon

Oregon State University *M*
University of Oregon
    Eugene *B,M,D*
    Robert Donald Clark Honors College *B*

Pennsylvania

Carnegie Mellon University *B,M,D,W*
Drexel University *B,M*
La Salle University *B*
Lehigh University *M*
Penn State University Park Campus *M,D*
Philadelphia College of Textiles and Science *M*
Robert Morris College *M*
Temple University *M,D*
University of Pennsylvania *M,D*

Puerto Rico

University of Puerto Rico
    Mayaguez Campus *B*
    Rio Piedras Campus *B,M*

Rhode Island

University of Rhode Island *B*

Tennessee

Bristol University *A,B,M*
University of Tennessee:
    Chattanooga *M*

Texas
Baylor University *B*
East Texas State University *B*
Texas A&M University *B,M,D*
University of Houston
    Downtown *B*
    Houston *B,M,D*

Utah
Utah State University *B*

Virginia
George Mason University *M*

Washington
Central Washington University *B*
Eastern Washington University *B*

Wisconsin
University of Wisconsin
    Madison *B,M,D*
    Oshkosh *B*

Canada
McGill University *B,D*

Mexico
Sistema Instituto Tecnologico y de
    Estudios Superiores de
    Monterrey *M*

Ophthalmic services

Alabama
Community College of the Air
    Force *A*
Samford University *B*
Wallace State Community College
    at Hanceville *A*

Arizona
Pima Community College *A*

California
Santa Rosa Junior College *A*

Connecticut
Middlesex Community College *A*

Florida
Hillsborough Community College *C*
Miami-Dade Community College *A*
St. Petersburg Junior College *A*

Georgia
DeKalb College *A*
DeKalb Technical Institute *A*
Emory University *M*

Illinois
Triton College *A*

Indiana
Indiana University Bloomington *A*

Iowa
North Iowa Area Community
    College *A*

Maryland
Howard Community College *A*

Massachusetts
Boston University *C*
Holyoke Community College *C*
Newbury College *A*

Michigan
Ferris State University *A*

Minnesota
University of Minnesota: Twin
    Cities *M*

Nebraska
Metropolitan Community College
    C,A

Nevada
Community College of Southern
    Nevada *A*

New Jersey
Camden County College *A*
Essex County College *A*

New York
City University of New York: New
    York City Technical College *A*
Erie Community College: North
    Campus *A*
Mater Dei College *A*
Rochester Institute of Technology
    C,A

North Carolina
Duke University *C*
Durham Technical Community
    College *A*

Ohio
Cuyahoga Community College:
    Metropolitan Campus *A*
Owens Technical College: Toledo *A*
Southern Ohio College *A*

Oregon
Portland Community College *C,A*

Pennsylvania
Westmoreland County Community
    College *A*

Puerto Rico
University of Puerto Rico: Medical
    Sciences Campus *A*

Texas
El Paso Community College *C,A*

Washington
Seattle Central Community
    College *A*
Spokane Community College *A*

Wisconsin
Madison Area Technical College *A*

Optical technology

Colorado
Pikes Peak Community College *C,A*

Connecticut
Norwalk State Technical College *A*
Waterbury State Technical
    College *A*

Indiana
Indiana University Bloomington *A*

Michigan
Ferris State University *A*

New Hampshire
New Hampshire Technical College:
    Nashua *A*

New Jersey
Essex County College *A*

New York
Monroe Community College *C*
State University of New York
    Institute of Technology at Utica/
    Rome *B*

Oregon
Portland Community College *C,A*

Optics

Alabama
University of Alabama in
    Huntsville *B*

Arizona
University of Arizona *M,D*

California
San Jose State University *B*

Indiana
Rose-Hulman Institute of
    Technology *B,M*

Kansas
Kansas State University *M,D*

Massachusetts
Hampshire College *B*
Tufts University *M,D*
Worcester Polytechnic Institute *B*

Michigan
University of Michigan *D*

New Jersey
Stevens Institute of Technology
    B,M,D

New Mexico
University of New Mexico *D*

New York
University of Rochester *B,M,D,W*

Canada
McGill University *M,D*

Optometry

Alabama
Shelton State Community
    College *A*
University of Alabama in
    Birmingham *B,M,D,W*

California
University of California: Berkeley
    B,M,D

Florida
Miami-Dade Community College
    C,A

Indiana
Ancilla College *A*
Indiana University Bloomington *B*
Vincennes University *A*

Iowa
Simpson College *B*
Wartburg College *B*

Kansas
Hutchinson Community College *A*

Louisiana
University of Southwestern
    Louisiana *B*

Michigan
Ferris State University *A,B*

Minnesota
Moorhead State University *B*

Missouri
East Central College *A*

Nebraska
York College *A*

New York
State University of New York
    College of Optometry *M,D*

Ohio
Ohio State University: Columbus
    Campus *B,M*
Wittenberg University *B*

Oklahoma
Northeastern State University *B*

Pennsylvania
Beaver College *B*
La Salle University *B*
Pennsylvania College of
    Optometry *M*
Villanova University *B*

South Carolina
Greenville Technical College *C*

Tennessee
Tennessee Wesleyan College *B*
Union University *B*

Texas
Texas Southmost College *A*
University of Houston *B,M,D*

Wisconsin
University of Wisconsin: Oshkosh *B*

Optometry (O.D.)

Alabama
University of Alabama in
    Birmingham *F*

California
Southern California College of
    Optometry *F*
University of California: Berkeley *F*

Florida
Southeastern University of the
    Health Sciences: College of
    Optometry *F*

Indiana
Indiana University Bloomington *F*

Michigan
Ferris State University *F*

Missouri

University of Missouri: St. Louis *F*

New York

State University of New York College of Optometry *F*

Ohio

Ohio State University: Columbus Campus *F*

Oklahoma

Northeastern St⌐ University *F*

Oregon

Pacific University *F*

Puerto Rico

Inter American University of Puerto Rico: Metropolitan Campus *F*

Tennessee

Southern College of Optometry *F*

Texas

University of Houston *F*

Utah

Brigham Young University *F*

Organic chemistry

California

California State University
    Fresno *B*
    Fullerton *M*
University of California: Berkeley *B,M,D*

Connecticut

Wesleyan University *B*

District of Columbia

George Washington University *M,D*

Florida

Florida State University *B,M,D*
New College of the University of South Florida *B*
University of Florida *M,D*

Georgia

Emory University *D*
Oxford College of Emory University *A*

Illinois

Judson College *B*
Southern Illinois University at Carbondale *B,M,D*
University of Chicago *B,M,D*

Indiana

Indiana University Bloomington *D*
Purdue University *M,D*

Iowa

Iowa State University *M,D*

Kansas

Kansas State University *M,D*

Massachusetts

Hampshire College *B*
Harvard University *D*
Massachusetts Institute of Technology *B,M,D,W*
Tufts University *M,D*
Worcester Polytechnic Institute *B*

Michigan

Eastern Michigan University *B*
Michigan State University *M,D*
Michigan Technological University *B*
University of Michigan *M,D*

Minnesota

Rainy River Community College *A*
Willmar Community College *A*

Missouri

University of Missouri: Kansas City *M,D*

Nebraska

York College *A*

New Hampshire

University of New Hampshire *M,D*

New Jersey

Stevens Institute of Technology *B,M,D*

New York

Columbia University *M,D*
Cornell University *M,D*
Fordham University *M*
Rockefeller University *D*
Sarah Lawrence College *B*
State University of New York
    Albany *D*
    College of Environmental Science and Forestry *B,M,D*

North Carolina

University of North Carolina at Chapel Hill *M,D*

Ohio

Ohio State University: Columbus Campus *B,M,D*
Ohio University *M,D*

Oregon

Oregon Graduate Institute *M,D*
University of Oregon *M,D*

Pennsylvania

Bucknell University *B*
Carnegie Mellon University *B,M,D,W*
Drexel University *B,M,D*
Duquesne University *M*
Lehigh University *M,D*
University of Pennsylvania *M,D*

Rhode Island

Brown University *B,M,D*

Texas

Kilgore College *A*
Lon Morris College *A*
University of Houston *M,D*

Vermont

Marlboro College *B*

Washington

Tacoma Community College *A*

West Virginia

Alderson-Broaddus College *B*

Wisconsin

Marquette University *M,D*

Canada

McGill University *M,D*

Mexico

Sistema Instituto Tecnologico y de Estudios Superiores de Monterrey *M*

Organizational behavior

Alabama

University of Alabama *M,D*

California

California Institute of Integral Studies *M*
California State University: Hayward *B,M*
John F. Kennedy University *M*
National University *M*
Pepperdine University *M*
United States International University *D*
University of the Pacific *B*
University of San Francisco *B,M*
University of Southern California *M*

Colorado

United States Air Force Academy *B*
University of Colorado
    Boulder *B*
    Colorado Springs *B*

Connecticut

Quinnipiac College *B,M*
University of Hartford *M*

District of Columbia

George Washington University *M*

Florida

University of Florida *M,D*

Georgia

University of Georgia *B*

Hawaii

Hawaii Pacific University *B*

Illinois

Aurora University *M*
Elmhurst College *B*
Illinois Benedictine College *M*
Northwestern University *B,M,D*
Southern Illinois University at Edwardsville *B*

Indiana

Indiana University Bloomington *D*
Purdue University *M,D*

Maryland

Columbia Union College *B*

Massachusetts

Babson College *M*
Boston College *D*
Lesley College *B*
Massachusetts Institute of Technology *M,D*

Michigan

Eastern Michigan University *M*
Michigan State University *D*
University of Michigan
    Ann Arbor *D*
    Dearborn *B*

Minnesota

Concordia College: St. Paul *B*
Winona State University *B*

Missouri

University of Missouri: Kansas City *M*

Nebraska

Dana College *B*
University of Nebraska—Omaha *B*

New Hampshire

Antioch New England Graduate School *M*

New Jersey

Bloomfield College *C*
Rider College *B*
Stevens Institute of Technology *M,D*

New York

City University of New York: Baruch College *D*
Iona College *M*
New York University *C,M,D*
State University of New York
    Albany *D*
    Buffalo *D*
Syracuse University *M*

Ohio

Bowling Green State University *M*
Case Western Reserve University *M,D*
Lourdes College *B*
Miami University: Oxford Campus *B*
Union Institute *B,D*

Oregon

University of Oregon *D*

Pennsylvania

Bucknell University *B*
Carnegie Mellon University *B,M,D,W*
Drexel University *M*
La Salle University *B*
Robert Morris College *M*
St. Joseph's University *B*
University of Pennsylvania *M*
Westminster College *B*

Puerto Rico

University of Puerto Rico: Mayaguez Campus *B*

South Dakota

Huron University *B*
Sioux Falls College *B*

Tennessee

Bristol University *A,B,M*
Tusculum College *B*

Texas

Southern Methodist University *B*
University of Houston *B,M,D*

Utah

Brigham Young University *M*

Washington

Central Washington University *B*
Evergreen State College *B*

Wisconsin

Carroll College *B*
Marquette University *B*

Canada

McGill University *B*

Ornamental horticulture

Alabama

Auburn University *B,M*
Bessemer State Technical College *A*
Wallace State Community College
at Hanceville *C*

Arizona

Glendale Community College *A*

California

Bakersfield College *A*
California Polytechnic State
University: San Luis Obispo *B*
California State Polytechnic
University: Pomona *B*
California State University:
Fresno *B*
Cerritos Community College *A*
Chabot College *A*
City College of San Francisco *C,A*
College of the Desert *C,A*
College of the Sequoias *C,A*
El Camino College *C,A*
Foothill College *C,A*
Merced College *C,A*
Modesto Junior College *A*
Monterey Peninsula College *C,A*
Moorpark College *A*
Mount San Antonio College *C*
Napa Valley College *C,A*
Orange Coast College *C,A*
Saddleback College *C,A*
San Joaquin Delta College *A*
Santa Barbara City College *C,A*
Santa Rosa Junior College *C,A*
Sierra College *C,A*
Solano Community College *A*
Southwestern College *A*
Ventura College *A*
Victor Valley College *C,A*
Yuba College *C*

Colorado

Colorado State University *B*
Front Range Community College *A*

Delaware

University of Delaware *B,M*

District of Columbia

University of the District of
Columbia *B*

Florida

Brevard Community College *C*
Broward Community College *A*
Florida Agricultural and Mechanical
University *B*
Florida Southern College *B*
Palm Beach Community College *A*
Pasco-Hernando Community
College *C*
Pensacola Junior College *A*
Santa Fe Community College *A*
Tallahassee Community College *A*
University of Florida *B,M,D*

Georgia

Abraham Baldwin Agricultural
College *A*
Augusta Technical Institute *C*
Floyd College *A*
Gainesville College *A*
Reinhardt College *A*
University of Georgia *B,M*

Idaho

Boise State University *A*
Ricks College *A*
University of Idaho *B*

Illinois

City Colleges of Chicago: Chicago
City-Wide College *C*
College of DuPage *C,A*
College of Lake County *C,A*
Joliet Junior College *C,A*
Kishwaukee College *C,A*
Lincoln Land Community
College *A*
Southern Illinois University at
Carbondale *B,M*
Spoon River College *C*
Triton College *C,A*
University of Illinois at Urbana-
Champaign *B*

Indiana

Purdue University *B,M,D*
Vincennes University *A*

Iowa

Des Moines Area Community
College *A*
Iowa State University *B,M,D*
Kirkwood Community College *A*

Kansas

Dodge City Community College *C*
Kansas State University *B*

Kentucky

Eastern Kentucky University *A,B*
Murray State University *B*

Louisiana

Louisiana Tech University *B*
Nicholls State University *A*
University of Southwestern
Louisiana *B*

Maine

Southern Maine Technical
College *A*
University of Maine *A,B*

Maryland

Dundalk Community College *C,A*
University of Maryland: College
Park *B,M,D*

Michigan

Ferris State University *A*
Michigan State University *B*

Minnesota

University of Minnesota:
Crookston *A*

Mississippi

Jones County Junior College *A*
Meridian Community College *A*
Mississippi Gulf Coast Community
College: Perkinston *A*

Missouri

St. Louis Community College at
Meramec *C,A*

Nebraska

Metropolitan Community College *A*

Nevada

Community College of Southern
Nevada *C,A*

New Jersey

Bergen Community College *A*
Cumberland County College *C,A*
Mercer County Community College
C,A

New York

Community College of the Finger
Lakes *C,A*
Cornell University *B,M,D*
Niagara County Community
College *C*
State University of New York
College of Agriculture and
Technology at Cobleskill *A*
College of Technology at
Alfred *A*
College of Technology at
Farmingdale *A*
Suffolk County Community College:
Eastern Campus *A*

North Carolina

Catawba Valley Community
College *A*
Forsyth Technical Community
College *A*
North Carolina State University *B*
Sampson Community College *A*
Western Piedmont Community
College *C*

North Dakota

North Dakota State University
Bottineau and Institute of
Forestry *C,A*
Fargo *B,M*

Ohio

Cincinnati Technical College *A*
Clark State Community College *A*
Ohio State University Agricultural
Technical Institute *A*

Oklahoma

Oklahoma State University *B,M*

Oregon

Clackamas Community College *C,A*
Mount Hood Community
College *A*

Pennsylvania

Delaware Valley College *B*
Penn State University Park
Campus *C*
Pennsylvania College of
Technology *A*
Westmoreland County Community
College *A*

South Carolina

Horry-Georgetown Technical
College *A*
Technical College of the
Lowcountry *C*

Tennessee

Hiwassee College *A*
University of Tennessee: Knoxville
B,M
Walters State Community
College *A*

Texas

Alvin Community College *C*
Galveston College *A*
Richland College *A*
Texas A&I University *B*
Texas A&M University *B,M*
Trinity Valley Community
College *A*

Utah

Utah State University *C,A*

Virginia

Christopher Newport College *B*

Washington

Clark College *C*
Edmonds Community College *C,A*
Skagit Valley College *C*
Spokane Community College *A*

Wyoming

Northwest College *A*

Osteopathic medicine (D.O.)

Iowa

University of Osteopathic Medicine
and Health Sciences *F*

Maine

University of New England *F*

Michigan

Michigan State University *F*

New York

New York Institute of
Technology *F*

Ohio

Ohio University *F*

Oklahoma

Oklahoma State University *F*

Pacific area studies

Alaska

Alaska Pacific University *A,B,M*

California

Naval Postgraduate School *M*
University of California: San Diego
M,D

Hawaii

Hawaii Loa College *B*
University of Hawaii
Manoa *M*
West Oahu *B*

Massachusetts

Hampshire College *B*

Washington

Evergreen State College *B*

Painting

Alabama

University of Alabama *M*
University of Montevallo *B*

Arizona

Northern Arizona University *B*

California

Academy of Art College *C,B,M,W*
Art Center College of Design *B,M*

Art Institute of Southern
California *B*
California College of Arts and
Crafts *B,M*
California Institute of the Arts
C,B,M
California State University
Fullerton *B,M*
Long Beach *B,M*
Los Angeles *B,M*
Northridge *B,M*
Chabot College *A*
Chaffey Community College *A*
De Anza College *C*
Grossmont Community College *A*
Humboldt State University *B*
Long Beach City College *A*
Otis/Parsons School of Art and
Design *B,M*
Pasadena City College *A*
San Francisco Art Institute *B,M*
San Jose State University *B*
Solano Community College *A*
University of California: Santa Cruz
C,B
University of San Francisco *B*

Colorado

Rocky Mountain College of Art &
Design *A,B*

Connecticut

Paier College of Art *C,B*
Sacred Heart University *A,B*
University of Bridgeport *B*
University of Connecticut *B*
University of Hartford *B*

District of Columbia

American University *M*
George Washington University *M*
Howard University *B,M*

Florida

Lynn University *A*
New College of the University of
South Florida *B*
Pensacola Junior College *A*
Ringling School of Art and
Design *B*
University of Florida *B,M*
University of Miami *M*
University of South Florida *B,M*

Georgia

Atlanta College of Art *B*
Berry College *B*
LaGrange College *B*
Piedmont College *B*
Savannah College of Art and
Design *B,M*
University of Georgia *B,M*

Idaho

University of Idaho *B*

Illinois

American Academy of Art *A*
Bradley University *B,M*
City Colleges of Chicago: Olive-
Harvey College *A*
Illinois Wesleyan University *B*
John A. Logan College *A*
Northwestern University *B*
Rend Lake College *A*
Richland Community College *A*
School of the Art Institute of
Chicago *B,M*
Southern Illinois University at
Carbondale *B,M*
University of Illinois at Urbana-
Champaign *B,M*

Indiana

Ball State University *B*
Indiana University Bloomington
B,M
Indiana University—Purdue
University at Indianapolis *B*
Purdue University *B,M*
University of Notre Dame *B,M*
Vincennes University *A*

Iowa

Drake University *B,M*
Teikyo Marycrest University *B*
University of Iowa *B,M*

Kansas

Butler County Community
College *A*
Coffeyville Community College *A*
Colby Community College *A*
Kansas State University *M*
Pratt Community College *A*
University of Kansas *B*
Wichita State University *B,M*

Kentucky

Eastern Kentucky University *B*

Louisiana

Louisiana State University and
Agricultural and Mechanical
College *B*
McNeese State University *B*

Maine

Portland School of Art *B*

Maryland

Howard Community College *A*
Maryland Institute College of Art
B,M

Massachusetts

Boston University *B,M*
Hampshire College *B*
Massachusetts College of Art *B,M*
Montserrat College of Art *B*
School of the Museum of Fine Arts
C,B,M
University of Massachusetts at
Dartmouth *B,M*

Michigan

Alma College *B*
Center for Creative Studies: College
of Art and Design *B*
Central Michigan University *B,M*
Eastern Michigan University *B*
Grand Valley State University *B*
Henry Ford Community College *A*
Lansing Community College *A*
Marygrove College *B*
Northern Michigan University *B*
Olivet College *B*
University of Michigan *B,M*

Minnesota

College of Associated Arts *B*
Moorhead State University *B*
Southwest State University *B*
Willmar Community College *A*
Winona State University *B*

Mississippi

Mississippi University for Women *B*

Missouri

Columbia College *B*
Kansas City Art Institute *B*
Washington University *B,M*
Webster University *B*

Nebraska

Hastings College *B*
York College *A*

New Hampshire

New England College *B*
Plymouth State College of the
University System of New
Hampshire *B*

New Jersey

Caldwell College *B*
Glassboro State College *B*
Rutgers—The State University of
New Jersey
Mason Gross School of the
Arts *B,M*
New Brunswick *M*

New Mexico

Institute of American Indian
Arts *A*

New York

Adelphi University *B*
Alfred University *B*
Bard College *B,M*
City University of New York
Brooklyn College *M*
Queens College *B,M*
Columbia University: School of
General Studies *B*
Cooper Union *B*
Cornell University *M*
Daemen College *B*
Graduate School of Figurative Art
of the New York Academy of
Art *M*
Hofstra University *B*
New York University *B,M,D*
Parsons School of Design *A,B,M*
Pratt Institute *B,M*
Rochester Institute of Technology
A,B,M
Sarah Lawrence College *B*
School of Visual Arts *B*
State University of New York
Albany *B,M*
Purchase *B,M*
College at Buffalo *B*
College at New Paltz *B,M*
College at Potsdam *B*
Syracuse University *B,M*

North Carolina

Barton College *B*
Brevard College *A*
East Carolina University *B,M*
North Carolina Agricultural and
Technical State University *B*
University of North Carolina at
Greensboro *B*
Wingate College *B*

Ohio

Art Academy of Cincinnati *B*
Bowling Green State University *B*
Cleveland Institute of Art *B*
Kent State University *B*
Lourdes College *A*
Ohio Northern University *B*
Ohio State University: Columbus
Campus *B,M*
Ohio University *B,M*
University of Akron *B*
University of Toledo *B*
Wittenberg University *B*
Wright State University *B*

Oklahoma

Phillips University *B*
University of Central Oklahoma *B*

University of Oklahoma *B*
University of Tulsa *B*

Oregon

Pacific Northwest College of Art *B*
Portland State University *B,M*
University of Oregon
Eugene *B,M*
Robert Donald Clark Honors
College *B*

Pennsylvania

Beaver College *B*
Bucknell University *B*
Carnegie Mellon University *B,M*
Edinboro University of
Pennsylvania *B,M*
Immaculata College *A*
Marywood College *B,M*
Mercyhurst College *B*
Moore College of Art and Design *B*
Northeastern Christian Junior
College *A*
Seton Hill College *B*
Temple University *B,M*
University of the Arts *C,B*

Puerto Rico

Inter American University of Puerto
Rico: San German Campus *B*

Rhode Island

Rhode Island College *B*
Rhode Island School of Design *B,M*

South Carolina

Anderson College *B*

Tennessee

East Tennessee State University *B*
Memphis College of Art *B,M*
University of Tennessee:
Chattanooga *B*

Texas

Houston Community College *C*
Jacksonville College *A*
Lon Morris College *A*
McMurry University *B*
Sam Houston State University *M*
Stephen F. Austin State
University *M*
Texas Woman's University *B,M*
University of Dallas *B,M*
University of Houston *B*
University of North Texas *B,M*
University of Texas at El Paso *B*

Utah

Brigham Young University *B,M*

Vermont

Bennington College *B*
Castleton State College *B*
Marlboro College *B*

Virginia

Averett College *B*
Blue Ridge Community College *C*
Virginia Commonwealth University
B,M
Virginia Wesleyan College *B*

Washington

Evergreen State College *B*
Pacific Lutheran University *B*
Tacoma Community College *B*
University of Washington *B,M*
Wenatchee Valley College *A*

West Virginia
Bethany College *B*
Davis and Elkins College *B*
Marshall University *B*
Shepherd College *B*
West Virginia State College *B*
West Virginia University *B,M*

Wisconsin
Milwaukee Institute of Art &
Design *B*
University of Wisconsin: Eau
Claire *B*

Wyoming
Western Wyoming Community
College *A*

Paleontology

California
University of California: Berkeley
B,M,D

District of Columbia
George Washington University *M,D*

Illinois
University of Chicago *B,M,D*

Indiana
Purdue University *B,M,D*

Louisiana
Tulane University *D*

Massachusetts
Harvard University *M,D*

New York
Columbia University *M,D*
Cornell University *M,D*

Ohio
Bowling Green State University *B*
Ohio State University: Columbus
Campus *B,M,D*
Ohio University *M*

South Dakota
South Dakota School of Mines and
Technology *M*

Paper engineering

Georgia
Institute of Paper Science and
Technology *M,D*

Michigan
Western Michigan University *B,M*

New York
State University of New York
College of Environmental Science
and Forestry *B,M,D*

Ohio
Miami University: Oxford Campus
B,M

Virginia
Dabney S. Lancaster Community
College *A*

Wisconsin
University of Wisconsin: Stevens
Point *B*

Parasitology

Alabama
Auburn University *M,D*

California
University of California: Berkeley
M,D

Georgia
University of Georgia *M,D*

Iowa
Iowa State University *M*

Louisiana
Louisiana State University Medical
Center *M,D*
Tulane University *M,D*

New York
New York University *M,D*
Rockefeller University *D*
State University of New York at
Albany *D*

Pennsylvania
University of Pennsylvania *M,D*

Texas
Texas A&M University *M*

Canada
McGill University *M,D*

Parks and recreation management

Alabama
Alabama State University *A,B*
Auburn University *B*
Huntingdon College *B*
Jacksonville State University *B*
Jefferson State Community
College *A*
Stillman College *B*
University of North Alabama *B*

Alaska
Sheldon Jackson College *B*

Arizona
Arizona State University *B,M*
Northern Arizona University *B*
Prescott College *B*

Arkansas
Arkansas Tech University *B*
Henderson State University *B*
University of Arkansas at Pine
Bluff *B*

California
California Polytechnic State
University: San Luis Obispo *B*
California State Polytechnic
University: Pomona *B*

California State University
  Chico *B,M*
  Dominguez Hills *B*
  Fresno *B,M*
  Hayward *B*
  Long Beach *B*
  Sacramento *B,M*
College of the Desert *A*
Humboldt State University *B*
Mount San Antonio College *A*
Pacific Union College *B*
Palomar College *C,A*
San Francisco State University *B,M*
San Jose State University *B,M*
Santa Rosa Junior College *C,A*
West Valley College *C,A*

Colorado
Colorado Mountain College: Spring
Valley Campus *A*
Colorado State University *B,M,D*
Mesa State College *B*
Metropolitan State College of
Denver *B*
University of Colorado at
Boulder *B*
University of Northern Colorado
B,M
University of Southern Colorado *B*
Western State College of
Colorado *B*

Connecticut
Northwestern Connecticut
Community College *A*
Norwalk Community College *A*
University of Connecticut *B*

Delaware
Delaware State College *B*
University of Delaware *B*

Florida
Daytona Beach Community
College *A*
Flagler College *B*
Florida International University
B,M
Florida Southern College *B*
Lynn University *B*
Santa Fe Community College *A*
University of Florida *M*

Georgia
Columbus College *B*
Georgia Southern University *B,M*
Georgia State University *B,M*
Savannah State College *B*
Shorter College *B*
South Georgia College *A*
University of Georgia *B,M,D*
Young Harris College *A*

Idaho
University of Idaho *B*

Illinois
Aurora University *B,M*
College of DuPage *C*
College of St. Francis *B*
Eastern Illinois University *B*
Illinois Eastern Community
Colleges: Wabash Valley
College *A*
Illinois State University *B*
Moraine Valley Community
College *A*
Northeastern Illinois University *B*
Southern Illinois University at
Carbondale *B,M*
Western Illinois University *B,M*
William Rainey Harper College *C,A*

Indiana
Bethel College *B*
Huntington College *B*
Indiana Institute of Technology *A,B*
Indiana State University *B,M*
Indiana University Bloomington
B,M,D
Indiana Wesleyan University *B*
Purdue University *B,M,D*
Taylor University *B*

Iowa
Graceland College *B*
Iowa Lakes Community College *A*
Iowa State University *B*
Kirkwood Community College *A*
Morningside College *B*
University of Iowa *B,M*
University of Northern Iowa *B*
Upper Iowa University *B*

Kansas
Central College *A*
Dodge City Community College *A*
Hutchinson Community College *A*
Kansas State University *B*
Pittsburg State University *B*

Kentucky
Asbury College *B*
Eastern Kentucky University *A,B,M*
Morehead State University *B*
Murray State University *B*
University of Louisville *B*
Western Kentucky University *B,M*

Louisiana
Grambling State University *B*
Louisiana Tech University *B*
Southern University and
Agricultural and Mechanical
College *B,M*

Maine
Unity College *B*
University of Maine
  Machias *A,B*
  Orono *B,M*
University of New England *B*

Maryland
Catonsville Community College *C,A*
Frederick Community College *A*
Frostburg State University *B*
University of Maryland: College
Park *B,M,D*

Massachusetts
Becker College: Leicester
Campus *A*
Dean Junior College *A*
Northeastern University *B,M*
Springfield College *B,M*
University of Massachusetts at
Amherst *B*

Michigan
Central Michigan University *B,M*
Eastern Michigan University *B*
Ferris State University *B*
Lake Superior State University *B*
Michigan State University *B,M,D*
Northern Michigan University *B*
Wayne State University *B,M*
Western Michigan University *B*

Minnesota
Bemidji State University *B*
Mankato State University *B*
Rainy River Community College *A*

University of Minnesota
Crookston *A*
Twin Cities *B*
Vermilion Community College *A*
Willmar Community College *A*
Winona State University *B*

Mississippi

University of Mississippi *B,M*
University of Southern Mississippi *B,M*

Missouri

Culver-Stockton College *B*
Missouri Valley College *B*
Missouri Western State College *B*
Moberly Area Community College *A*
Southeast Missouri State University *B*
Southwest Missouri State University *B*
University of Missouri: Columbia *B,M*

Montana

University of Montana *B,M*

Nebraska

University of Nebraska
Kearney *B*
Omaha *A*

New Hampshire

Franklin Pierce College *B*
University of New Hampshire *B*

New Jersey

Gloucester County College *A*
Kean College of New Jersey *B*
Montclair State College *B*

New Mexico

New Mexico State University *B*

New York

City University of New York:
Lehman College *M*
Herkimer County Community College *A*
Ithaca College *B*
Long Island University: C. W. Post Campus *B*
New York University *B,M,D*
North Country Community College *A*
Onondaga Community College *A*
Paul Smith's College *A*
St. Joseph's College: Suffolk Campus *B*
State University of New York
College of Agriculture and Technology at Cobleskill *A*
College of Agriculture and Technology at Morrisville *A*
College at Brockport *B,M*
College of Technology at Delhi *A*

North Carolina

Appalachian State University *B*
Barber-Scotia College *B*
Brevard College *A*
Catawba College *B*
Catawba Valley Community College *A*
East Carolina University *B*
Elon College *B*
Mars Hill College *B*
Montreat-Anderson College *A,B*
Mount Olive College *A,B*

North Carolina Agricultural and Technical State University *B*
North Carolina Central University *B,M*
North Carolina State University *B,M*
Southeastern Community College *A*
University of North Carolina
Chapel Hill *B,M*
Greensboro *B*
Wilmington *B*
Western Carolina University *B*
Wingate College *B*

North Dakota

North Dakota State University:
Bottineau and Institute of Forestry *A*
University of North Dakota *B*

Ohio

Bluffton College *B*
Bowling Green State University *B*
Hocking Technical College *A*
Kent State University *B*
Mount Vernon Nazarene College *A*
Muskingum Area Technical College *A*
Ohio State University: Columbus Campus *B,M*
Ohio University *B*
University of Toledo *B*

Oklahoma

Eastern Oklahoma State College *A*
Oklahoma Baptist University *B*

Oregon

Oregon State University *B*

Pennsylvania

Butler County Community College *A*
California University of Pennsylvania *B*
Cheyney University of Pennsylvania *B*
East Stroudsburg University of Pennsylvania *B*
Lock Haven University of Pennsylvania *B*
Penn State University Park Campus *C*
Slippery Rock University of Pennsylvania *B,M*
Temple University *B,M,D*

South Carolina

Benedict College *B*
Clemson University *B,M,D*
Horry-Georgetown Technical College *A*
North Greenville College *A*

South Dakota

South Dakota State University *B*
University of South Dakota *B*

Tennessee

Bristol University *A,B*
Martin Methodist College *A*
Memphis State University *B*
University of Tennessee: Martin *B*

Texas

Abilene Christian University *B*
Hardin-Simmons University *B*
Southwest Texas State University *B*
Stephen F. Austin State University *B*
Texas A&M University *B,M,D*
Texas Tech University *B,M*

Texas Woman's University *B,M,D*
West Texas State University *B*
Western Texas College *A*

Utah

Brigham Young University *B,M*
University of Utah *B*
Utah State University *B,M,D*

Vermont

Green Mountain College *B*
Lyndon State College *B*
University of Vermont *B*

Virginia

Averett College *B*
Christopher Newport College *B*
Ferrum College *B*
George Mason University *B*
Norfolk State University *B*
Northern Virginia Community College *A*
Old Dominion University *B*
Radford University *B,M*
Virginia Commonwealth University *B,M*
Virginia Union University *B*
Virginia Wesleyan College *B*

Washington

Central Washington University *B*
Eastern Washington University *B*
Everett Community College *A*
Evergreen State College *B*
Pierce College *A*
Skagit Valley College *C*
Spokane Community College *A*
Washington State University *B*
Western Washington University *B*

West Virginia

Concord College *B*
Marshall University *B*
Shepherd College *B*
West Virginia State College *B*
West Virginia University *B,M*

Wisconsin

Carthage College *B*
Northland College *B*
University of Wisconsin
La Crosse *B,M*
Madison *B,M*
River Falls *B*

Wyoming

Northwest College *A*

Pathology, human and animal

Alabama

Auburn University *M*
University of Alabama in Birmingham *M,D*

Arkansas

University of Arkansas for Medical Sciences *M*

California

University of California
Berkeley *M,D*
Davis *M,D*
Los Angeles *M,D*
University of Southern California *D*

Colorado

Colorado State University *M,D*
University of Colorado Health Sciences Center *D*

Connecticut

University of Connecticut *B,M,D*
Yale University *M,D*

District of Columbia

George Washington University *D*
Georgetown University *M,D*

Florida

University of Florida *M,D*

Georgia

Emory University *M,D*
University of Georgia *M,D*

Illinois

Northwestern University *M,D*
University of Chicago *M,D*
University of Health Sciences: The Chicago Medical School *M,D,W*

Indiana

Indiana University Bloomington *M,D*
Indiana University—Purdue University at Indianapolis *M,D,W*

Iowa

Iowa State University *M,D*
University of Iowa *M*

Kansas

Kansas State University *B,M,D*
University of Kansas
Lawrence *M,D*
Medical Center *M,D*

Louisiana

Louisiana State University Medical Center *M,D*

Maryland

Uniformed Services University of the Health Sciences *D*
University of Maryland: Baltimore *M,D*

Massachusetts

Boston University *D*
Hampshire College *B*
Harvard University *D*
Tufts University *M,D*

Michigan

Michigan State University *M,D*
Wayne State University *D*

Mississippi

Jackson State University *B*
University of Mississippi Medical Center *M,D*

Missouri

St. Louis University *M,D*
University of Missouri: Columbia *M,D*
Washington University *D*

Nebraska

University of Nebraska Medical Center *M*

New York

Albany Medical College *M,D*
Columbia University *M,D*
Cornell University *M,D*

New York University *D*
State University of New York
  Buffalo *M,D*
  Health Science Center at
    Brooklyn *D*
  Health Sciences Center at
    Stony Brook *D*
University of Rochester *M,D,W*
Yeshiva University *M,D*

North Carolina
Duke University *D*
East Carolina University *D*
University of North Carolina at
  Chapel Hill *M,D*
Vance-Granville Community
  College *A*
Wake Forest University *M,D*

Ohio
Case Western Reserve University *D*
Ohio State University: Columbus
  Campus *M,D*
University of Cincinnati *M,D*

Oklahoma
University of Oklahoma
  Health Sciences Center *M,D*
  Norman *M,D*

Pennsylvania
Hahnemann University School of
  Health Sciences and Humanities
  M,D
Temple University *D*
University of Pennsylvania *M,D*
University of Pittsburgh *M,D*

Puerto Rico
University of Puerto Rico: Medical
  Sciences Campus *M,D*

Tennessee
University of Tennessee: Memphis
  M,D
Vanderbilt University *M,D*

Texas
Texas A&M University *M,D*
Texas Tech University *M,D*
University of Texas Health Science
  Center at Houston *M,D,W*

Utah
University of Utah *D*

Vermont
University of Vermont *M*

Virginia
Virginia Commonwealth University
  M,D

Washington
University of Washington *M,D*

Wisconsin
Medical College of Wisconsin *M,D*
University of Wisconsin: Madison
  M,D

Canada
McGill University *M,D*

Peace studies

Arizona
Prescott College *B*

California
Chapman University *B*
Humboldt State University *C*
University of California
  Berkeley *B*
  Santa Cruz *B*
World College West *B*

Colorado
Colorado College *B*

Florida
New College of the University of
  South Florida *B*

Illinois
Garrett-Evangelical Theological
  Seminary *M,D,W*

Indiana
Earlham College *B*
Manchester College *B*

Iowa
Clarke College *B*
St. Ambrose University *B*

Kansas
Bethel College *B*

Massachusetts
Berkshire Community College *A*
Hampshire College *B*
Wellesley College *B*

Michigan
Wayne State University *B*

Minnesota
College of St. Benedict *B*
St. John's University *B*

Missouri
Southwest Missouri State
  University *M*

New York
Colgate University *B*
Manhattan College *B*
Molloy College *B*
Niagara University *B*

North Carolina
Guilford College *B*
University of North Carolina at
  Chapel Hill *B*

North Dakota
University of North Dakota *B*

Ohio
Antioch College *B*
Kent State University *B*

Oregon
Oregon State University *C*
Portland Community College *C*
University of Portland *C*

Pennsylvania
Bryn Mawr College *B*
Elizabethtown College *B*
Gettysburg College *B*
Juniata College *B*
University of Pennsylvania *B,M,D*
West Chester University of
  Pennsylvania *C*

Texas
Incarnate Word College *M*

Vermont
Norwich University *B*

Washington
Evergreen State College *B*
University of Washington *B*
Whitworth College *B*

Wisconsin
Northland College *B*
University of Wisconsin:
  Milwaukee *B*

Personal services

Alabama
Lawson State Community
  College *A*
Shelton State Community
  College *A*

Arkansas
Phillips County Community
  College *A*

California
Chabot College *A*
Coastline Community College *A*
Compton Community College *A*
El Camino College *A*
Merced College *A*
Pasadena City College *A*
San Diego Miramar College *A*
San Jose City College *A*
Santa Rosa Junior College *C*

Colorado
Northeastern Junior College *A*

Florida
Broward Community College *A*
Manatee Community College *A*

Illinois
Carl Sandburg College *A*
Lake Land College *A*
Lewis and Clark Community
  College *A*

Indiana
Vincennes University *A*

Iowa
Iowa Lakes Community College *A*
Northeast Iowa Community
  College *A*

Kansas
Barton County Community
  College *A*
Dodge City Community College *A*

Massachusetts
Becker College: Leicester
  Campus *A*

Michigan
Lansing Community College *A*
Oakland Community College *A*

Minnesota
Willmar Community College *A*

Mississippi
Hinds Community College *A*
Jones County Junior College *A*

New York
Herkimer County Community
  College *A*

Ohio
Ohio State University: Columbus
  Campus *B*

Texas
Central Texas College *A*
Cisco Junior College *A*
McLennan Community College *A*
North Harris Montgomery
  Community College District *A*
Panola College *A*
San Jacinto College: Central
  Campus *A*
Trinity Valley Community
  College *A*
Western Texas College *A*

Utah
Dixie College *A*
Utah State University *B*

Virginia
National Business College *C*

Washington
Seattle Central Community
  College *A*

Wisconsin
Chippewa Valley Technical
  College *A*

Wyoming
Eastern Wyoming College *A*

Personality psychology

California
San Jose State University *B*
University of California
  Santa Barbara *B*
  Santa Cruz *B*

Delaware
University of Delaware *M,D*

Indiana
Purdue University *B,M,D*

Kansas
Kansas State University *M,D*

Massachusetts
Hampshire College *B*
Suffolk University *B*

Michigan
University of Michigan *M,D*

New Jersey
Bloomfield College *B*

New York
Cornell University *M,D*
Sarah Lawrence College *B*

Rhode Island
Rhode Island College *M*

Utah
Brigham Young University *D*

Personnel management

Alabama

Auburn University at
  Montgomery *B*
Community College of the Air
  Force *A*
Shoals Community College *C*
Troy State University
  Dothan *M*
  Montgomery *M*
University of Alabama *B*
Wallace State Community College
  at Hanceville *A*

Arizona

University of Arizona *B*

Arkansas

University of Arkansas *B*
University of Central Arkansas *B,M*

California

California State University
  Dominguez Hills *B*
  Fresno *B*
  Hayward *B,M*
  Los Angeles *B*
  Northridge *B,M*
  Sacramento *B*
  Stanislaus *B*
Cerritos Community College *A*
City College of San Francisco *A*
Coastline Community College *A*
College of Marin: Kentfield *A*
National University *B*
Naval Postgraduate School *M*
San Francisco State University *B*
University of San Francisco *B*
University of Southern California *M*
Ventura College *B*
Yuba College *C,A*

Colorado

Mesa State College *B*
University of Colorado
  Boulder *B*
  Colorado Springs *B*
  Denver *B*
Western State College of
  Colorado *B*

Connecticut

Quinnipiac College *B,M*

District of Columbia

American University *B,M*
George Washington University *M*

Florida

Florida International University *B*
Florida Southern College *B*
Florida State University *B*
Nova University *M*
Tampa College *B*
University of North Florida *M*

Georgia

Brenau Women's College *B*
Kennesaw State College *M*
Middle Georgia College *A*

Hawaii

Hawaii Pacific University *B,M*

Illinois

Barat College *B*
De Paul University *M*
Elmhurst College *B*
Joliet Junior College *C*

Loyola University of Chicago *B*
Millikin University *B*
Quincy College *B*
Roosevelt University *B*
Southern Illinois University at
  Edwardsville *B*
Western Illinois University *B*

Indiana

Ball State University *B*
Indiana University
  Bloomington *B,M*
  South Bend *B*
Indiana University—Purdue
  University
  Fort Wayne *B*
  Indianapolis *B*
Purdue University
  North Central Campus *A,B*
  West Lafayette *B,M*

Iowa

Morningside College *B*

Kansas

University of Kansas *B*
Wichita State University *B*

Kentucky

Eastern Kentucky University *B*
University of Kentucky *B*

Louisiana

Louisiana Tech University *B*
Nicholls State University *B*
University of Southwestern
  Louisiana *B*

Maine

University of Maine
  Augusta *C*
  Orono *B*

Maryland

Essex Community College *A*
University of Maryland: College
  Park *B*

Massachusetts

American International College *B*
Harvard University *M,D*
University of Massachusetts at
  Dartmouth *B*
Western New England College *B*

Michigan

Andrews University *B*
Central Michigan University *B*
Ferris State University *B*
Grand Valley State University *B,M*
Lansing Community College *A*
Michigan State University *B,M,D*
Oakland University *B*
Olivet College *B*
University of Detroit Mercy *B*
University of Michigan *D*

Minnesota

Mankato State University *B*
Moorhead State University *B*
St. Paul Technical College *A*
Willmar Community College *A*
Winona State University *B*

Mississippi

University of Southern
  Mississippi *B*

Missouri

Central Missouri State University *B*
Northwest Missouri State
  University *B*

Rockhurst College *B*
St. Louis University *B*
Southeast Missouri State
  University *B*
University of Missouri
  Columbia *B*
  Kansas City *M*
Webster University *B,M*

Nebraska

Hastings College *B*
University of Nebraska—Omaha *B*

New Hampshire

Antioch New England Graduate
  School *M*

New Jersey

Bloomfield College *C,B*
Brookdale Community College *A*
Burlington County College *A*
Cumberland County College *A*
Fairleigh Dickinson University *M*
Rider College *B*
Stevens Institute of Technology *M*
Thomas Edison State College *B*

New Mexico

Eastern New Mexico University *B*
New Mexico State University *B*
Western New Mexico University *B*

New York

City University of New York
  Baruch College *B*
  Kingsborough Community
    College *A*
Ithaca College *B*
Le Moyne College *C,B*
Marymount College *C*
New York University *C*
Niagara University *B*
Rochester Institute of Technology
  A,M
State University of New York
  Buffalo *D*
  College at Geneseo *B*
Syracuse University *B,M,D*

North Carolina

Davidson County Community
  College *A*
Methodist College *B*
Pitt Community College *A*
Rockingham Community College *A*
University of North Carolina
  Asheville *B*
  Greensboro *B,M*

Ohio

Bowling Green State University *B*
Cleveland State University *B*
Columbus State Community
  College *A*
Franklin University *B*
John Carroll University *B*
Kent State University *B,M,D*
Lourdes College *B*
Miami University: Oxford
  Campus *B*
Ohio University *B*
Union Institute *B,D*
University of Cincinnati *B*
University of Toledo *B,M*
Urbana University *B*

Oklahoma

Langston University *B*
Southwestern Oklahoma State
  University *B*
Tulsa Junior College *C,A*
University of Central Oklahoma *B*

Oregon

Clackamas Community College *C*
Southern Oregon State College *B,M*
University of Oregon *D*

Pennsylvania

Beaver College *B*
Bucknell University *B*
California University of
  Pennsylvania *B*
Central Pennsylvania Business
  School *A*
Drexel University *B,M*
Duquesne University *C,B*
Indiana University of
  Pennsylvania *B*
Juniata College *B*
La Roche College *M*
La Salle University *B,M*
Mansfield University of
  Pennsylvania *B*
Robert Morris College *B*
St. Francis College *M*
Seton Hill College *B*
University of Pennsylvania *B,M,D*
Widener University *C,M*

Puerto Rico

Inter American University of Puerto
  Rico: Arecibo Campus *B*

Rhode Island

Rhode Island College *B*
University of Rhode Island *B*

South Carolina

Central Wesleyan College *B*
University of South Carolina *M*

Tennessee

Bristol University *A,B,M*
Cleveland State Community
  College *C*
Tennessee Technological
  University *B*
Union University *B*
University of Tennessee
  Chattanooga *B*
  Knoxville *B*

Texas

East Texas State University *B*
Huston-Tillotson College *B*
Lamar University—Beaumont *B*
Panola College *A*
Tarleton State University *B*
University of Central Texas *M*
University of Texas at San
  Antonio *B*
Weatherford College *C,A*
Western Texas College *A*

Utah

Utah State University *B*

Virginia

Averett College *B*
Lynchburg College *M*
Marymount University *B,M*
Old Dominion University *B*
University of Richmond *A*
Virginia Wesleyan College *B*

Washington

Eastern Washington University *B*
Evergreen State College *B*
Pacific Lutheran University *B*
Washington State University *B*

Wisconsin

Carroll College *B*
Marquette University *B*

Mid-State Technical College *A*
University of Wisconsin
  Green Bay *B*
  Oshkosh *B*
  Platteville *B*
  Superior *B*
  Whitewater *B*
Viterbo College *B*

Wyoming
Western Wyoming Community
  College *A*

**American Samoa, Caroline
Islands, Guam, Marianas,
Virgin Islands**
Northern Marianas College *A*

Canada
McGill University *C,B,M,D*

Petroleum engineering

Alabama
University of Alabama *B,M*

Alaska
University of Alaska Fairbanks *B,M*

California
California State University:
  Bakersfield *B*
Coastline Community College *A*
Stanford University *B,M,D*
University of California: Berkeley
  B,M,D
University of Southern California
  B,M,D,W

Colorado
Colorado School of Mines
  B,M,D,W

Kansas
University of Kansas *B,M,D*

Louisiana
Louisiana State University and
  Agricultural and Mechanical
  College *B,M,D*
Louisiana Tech University *B,M*
University of Southwestern
  Louisiana *B,M*

Minnesota
Willmar Community College *A*

Mississippi
Mississippi State University *B,M*

Missouri
East Central College *A*
University of Missouri: Rolla *B,M,D*

Montana
Montana College of Mineral
  Science and Technology *B,M*

New Mexico
New Mexico Institute of Mining
  and Technology *B,M,D*

North Dakota
North Dakota State University *B*

Ohio
Marietta College *B*

Oklahoma
Oklahoma State University
  Oklahoma City *A*
  Stillwater *B*
University of Oklahoma *B,M,D*
University of Tulsa *B,M,D*

Pennsylvania
Lock Haven University of
  Pennsylvania *B*
Penn State University Park Campus
  B,M,D
University of Pittsburgh *M*

Texas
Amarillo College *A*
Kilgore College *A*
Texas A&I University *B,M*
Texas A&M University *B,M,D*
Texas Southmost College *A*
Texas Tech University *B,M*
University of Houston *M,D*
University of Texas at Austin
  B,M,D

Utah
University of Utah *B,M,D*

Washington
University of Puget Sound *B*

West Virginia
West Virginia University *B,M*

Wyoming
University of Wyoming *B,M,D*

Pharmaceutical chemistry

California
San Jose State University *B*
University of California: San
  Francisco *D*
University of the Pacific *M,D*

Florida
University of Florida *M,D*

Georgia
Clark Atlanta University *B*

Illinois
University of Chicago *M,D*

Indiana
Butler University *M*
Purdue University *M,D*
Vincennes University *A*

Kansas
Kansas State University *M,D*
University of Kansas *M,D*

Maryland
University of Maryland: Baltimore
  M,D

Massachusetts
Massachusetts College of Pharmacy
  and Allied Health Sciences *M,D*
Massachusetts Institute of
  Technology *B,M,D,W*
Northeastern University *D*
Worcester Polytechnic Institute *B*

Michigan
University of Michigan *M,D*

Minnesota
Willmar Community College *A*

Mississippi
University of Mississippi *M,D*

Missouri
University of Missouri: Kansas City
  M,D

Nebraska
University of Nebraska Medical
  Center *M,D*

New Jersey
Rutgers—The State University of
  New Jersey *M,D*

New York
Columbia University *M,D*
State University of New York at
  Buffalo *B,M,D*

North Dakota
North Dakota State University *M,D*

Pennsylvania
Duquesne University *M,D*
Philadelphia College of Pharmacy
  and Science *M*
Temple University *M,D*
University of Pennsylvania *D*

Rhode Island
University of Rhode Island *D*

Virginia
Virginia Commonwealth University
  M,D

Wisconsin
University of Wisconsin: Madison
  M,D

Canada
McGill University *M,D*

Pharmacology, human and animal

Alabama
Auburn University *M*
University of Alabama in
  Birmingham *M,D*
University of South Alabama *D*

Arizona
University of Arizona *M,D*

Arkansas
University of Arkansas for Medical
  Sciences *M,D*

California
Stanford University *M,D*
University of California
  Davis *M,D*
  Irvine *M,D*
  Los Angeles *M,D*
  San Diego *M,D*
  San Francisco *D*
  Santa Barbara *B*
University of Southern California *D*

Colorado
University of Colorado Health
  Sciences Center *D*

Connecticut
Yale University *M,D*

District of Columbia
George Washington University *M,D*
Georgetown University *D*
Howard University *M,D*

Florida
Florida Agricultural and Mechanical
  University *M*
University of Florida *M,D*
University of Miami *D*

Georgia
Emory University *M,D*
Medical College of Georgia *M,D*
University of Georgia *M,D*

Hawaii
University of Hawaii at Manoa *M,D*

Illinois
Loyola University of Chicago *M,D*
Northwestern University *M,D*
Rush University *M,D*
Southern Illinois University at
  Carbondale *M,D*
University of Chicago *M,D*
University of Health Sciences: The
  Chicago Medical School *M,D,W*
University of Illinois at Chicago
  M,D

Indiana
Butler University *M*
Indiana University Bloomington
  M,D
Indiana University—Purdue
  University at Indianapolis
  M,D,W
Purdue University *M,D,W*

Iowa
University of Iowa *M,D*

Kansas
University of Kansas
  Lawrence *M,D*
  Medical Center *M,D*

Kentucky
University of Kentucky *M,D*
University of Louisville *M,D*

Louisiana
Louisiana State University Medical
  Center *M,D*
Tulane University *M,D*

Maryland
Uniformed Services University of
  the Health Sciences *M,D*
University of Maryland: Baltimore
  M,D

Massachusetts
Boston University *M,D*
Harvard University *D*
Massachusetts College of Pharmacy
  and Allied Health Sciences *M,D*
Northeastern University *M,D*
Tufts University *M*

Michigan
Michigan State University *M,D*
University of Michigan *M,D*
Wayne State University *M,D*

Minnesota
University of Minnesota
Duluth *M*
Twin Cities *M,D*

Mississippi
University of Mississippi
Medical Center *M,D*
University *D*

Missouri
St. Louis University *M,D*
University of Missouri
Columbia *M,D*
Kansas City *M,D*
Washington University *D*

Nebraska
Creighton University *M,D*
University of Nebraska Medical
Center *M,D*

New Hampshire
Dartmouth College *D*

New Jersey
Rutgers—The State University of
New Jersey *M,D*

New York
Albany Medical College *M,D*
Columbia University *M,D*
Cornell University *M,D*
New York University *D*
State University of New York
Buffalo *M,D*
Health Science Center at
Brooklyn *D*
Health Science Center at
Syracuse *M,D*
Health Sciences Center at
Stony Brook *D*
University of Rochester *M,D,W*
Yeshiva University *M,D*

North Carolina
Duke University *D*
East Carolina University *D*
University of North Carolina at
Chapel Hill *M,D*
Wake Forest University *M,D*

North Dakota
North Dakota State University *M*
University of North Dakota *M*

Ohio
Case Western Reserve University *D*
Kent State University *M,D*
Ohio State University: Columbus
Campus *M,D*
Ohio University *M,D*
University of Cincinnati *D*

Oklahoma
University of Oklahoma
Health Sciences Center *M,D*
Norman *M,D*

Pennsylvania
Duquesne University *B,M*
Hahnemann University School of
Health Sciences and Humanities
M,D
Medical College of Pennsylvania
M,D
Penn State Milton S. Hershey
Medical Center *M,D*
Philadelphia College of Pharmacy
and Science *B,M,D*
Temple University *M,D*
University of Pennsylvania *M,D*

University of Pittsburgh *M,D*

Puerto Rico
University of Puerto Rico: Medical
Sciences Campus *M,D*

Rhode Island
Brown University *M,D*
University of Rhode Island *M,D*

South Dakota
University of South Dakota *M,D*

Tennessee
East Tennessee State University
M,D
Meharry Medical College *D*
University of Tennessee: Memphis
M,D
Vanderbilt University *M,D*

Texas
Baylor College of Dentistry *M*
Baylor University *M*
Texas Tech University *M,D*
Texas Tech University Health
Science Center *M,D,W*
University of Houston *M,D*
University of Texas
Health Science Center at
Houston *M,D,W*
Health Science Center at San
Antonio *M,D*
Southwestern Medical Center
at Dallas Southwestern
Allied Health Sciences
School *M,D*

Utah
University of Utah *M,D*

Vermont
University of Vermont *M,D*

Virginia
University of Virginia *M,D*
Virginia Commonwealth University
M,D

Washington
University of Washington *M,D*
Washington State University *D*

West Virginia
West Virginia University *M,D*

Wisconsin
Medical College of Wisconsin *M,D*
University of Wisconsin: Madison
M,D

Canada
McGill University *M,D*

Pharmacy

Alabama
Auburn University *B,M,D*
Community College of the Air
Force *A*
Samford University *B*
Shelton State Community
College *A*

Arizona
Pima Community College *C,A*
University of Arizona *B,M,D*

Arkansas
University of Arkansas for Medical
Sciences *M*

California
Chabot College *A*
University of California: San
Francisco *W*
University of the Pacific *M,D,W*
University of Southern California
M,D

Colorado
University of Colorado
Boulder *B,M,D*
Health Sciences Center *B,M,D*

Connecticut
University of Connecticut *B,M,D*

District of Columbia
Howard University *B,M,D*

Florida
Florida Agricultural and Mechanical
University *B,M,D*
Manatee Community College *A*
University of Florida *B,M,D*

Georgia
Andrew College *A*
Bainbridge College *A*
Brewton-Parker College *A*
Mercer University *B*
University of Georgia *B,M,D*

Idaho
Idaho State University *M,D*

Illinois
University of Illinois at Chicago
B,M,D

Indiana
Butler University *B,M*
Purdue University *B,M,D*
Vincennes University *A*

Iowa
Clinton Community College *A*
Drake University *B*
Muscatine Community College *A*
Scott Community College *A*
University of Iowa *B,M,D*
Wartburg College *B*

Kansas
Hutchinson Community College *A*
University of Kansas *B,M*

Kentucky
University of Kentucky *B,W*

Louisiana
Northeast Louisiana University
B,M,D
Xavier University of Louisiana *B*

Maryland
University of Maryland: Baltimore
B,M

Massachusetts
Massachusetts College of Pharmacy
and Allied Health Sciences
B,M,D
Northeastern University *B,M,D*
Simmons College *B*
Western New England College *B*

Michigan
Ferris State University *B*
University of Michigan *B,M,D*
Wayne State University *B,M,D*

Minnesota
Rainy River Community College *A*
University of Minnesota: Twin
Cities *B,M,D*

Mississippi
Jackson State University *B*
University of Mississippi *B,M,D*

Missouri
St. Louis College of Pharmacy *B,M*
University of Missouri: Kansas City
B,M,D

Montana
University of Montana *B,M*

Nebraska
Creighton University *B*
University of Nebraska Medical
Center *M*

New Jersey
Rutgers—The State University of
New Jersey: College of
Pharmacy *B*

New Mexico
University of New Mexico *B,M,D*

New York
Albany College of Pharmacy *B*
Long Island University: Brooklyn
Campus *B,M*
Mercy College *B*
St. John's University *B,M,D*
State University of New York at
Buffalo *B,M,D*

North Carolina
Campbell University *D*
Central Piedmont Community
College *C*
Chowan College *A*
Davidson County Community
College *C*
Duke University *W*
Durham Technical Community
College *C*
Livingstone College *B*
University of North Carolina at
Chapel Hill *B,M,D*

North Dakota
North Dakota State University
B,M,D

Ohio
Ohio Northern University *B*
Ohio State University: Columbus
Campus *B,M,D*
University of Cincinnati *B,M,D*
University of Toledo *B,M*

Oklahoma
Southwestern Oklahoma State
University *B*
University of Oklahoma
Health Sciences Center *B,M,D*
Norman *B,M*

Oregon
Oregon State University *B,M,D*
Southwestern Oregon Community
College *C*

Pennsylvania
Duquesne University *B,M,D*
Philadelphia College of Pharmacy
and Science *B,M,D*
Temple University *B,M,D*
University of Pittsburgh *B,M,D*

Puerto Rico
Huertas Junior College *A*
Puerto Rico Junior College *A*
University of Puerto Rico: Medical
Sciences Campus *B,M*

Rhode Island
University of Rhode Island *B,M,D*

South Carolina
Greenville Technical College *C*
Sumter Area Technical College *C*
Trident Technical College *C*
University of South Carolina *B,M,D*

South Dakota
South Dakota State University *B*

Tennessee
Roane State Community College *A*
Union University *B*
Vanderbilt University *M,D*

Texas
El Paso Community College *C*
Texas Southern University *B*
University of Houston *B,M,D*
University of Texas
Austin *B,M,D*
Health Science Center at
Houston *M,D*

Utah
University of Utah *B,M,D*

Virginia
Mountain Empire Community
College *C*
Virginia Commonwealth University
B,M,D

Washington
University of Washington *B,M,D*
Washington State University *B,M,D*

West Virginia
West Virginia University *B,M,D*

Wisconsin
University of Wisconsin
Madison *B,M,D*
Oshkosh *B*

Wyoming
University of Wyoming *B*

Pharmacy (Pharm. D)

Alabama
Auburn University *F*
Samford University *F*

Arizona
University of Arizona *F*

Arkansas
University of Arkansas for Medical
Sciences *F*

California
University of California: San
Francisco *F*

University of the Pacific *F*
University of Southern California *F*

Colorado
University of Colorado at
Boulder *F*

District of Columbia
Howard University *F*

Florida
Florida Agricultural and Mechanical
University *F*
University of Florida *F*

Georgia
Mercer University
Atlanta *F*
Macon *F*
University of Georgia *F*

Idaho
Idaho State University *F*

Illinois
University of Illinois at Chicago *F*

Indiana
Butler University *F*
Purdue University *F*

Iowa
Drake University *F*
University of Iowa *F*

Kansas
University of Kansas *F*

Kentucky
University of Kentucky *F*

Louisiana
Xavier University of Louisiana *F*

Maryland
University of Maryland:
Baltimore *F*

Massachusetts
Massachusetts College of Pharmacy
and Allied Health Sciences *F*
Northeastern University *F*

Michigan
Ferris State University *F*
University of Michigan *F*
Wayne State University *F*

Minnesota
University of Minnesota: Twin
Cities *F*

Mississippi
University of Mississippi *F*

Missouri
St. Louis College of Pharmacy *F*
University of Missouri: Kansas
City *F*

Nebraska
Creighton University *F*
University of Nebraska Medical
Center *F*

Nevada
University of Nevada: Reno *F*

New Jersey
Rutgers—The State University of
New Jersey
College of Pharmacy *F*
Rutgers College *F*

New Mexico
Western New Mexico University *F*

New York
Albany College of Pharmacy *F*
St. John's University *F*
State University of New York at
Buffalo *F*

North Carolina
Campbell University *F*
University of North Carolina at
Chapel Hill *F*

North Dakota
North Dakota State University *F*

Ohio
Ohio Northern University *F*
Ohio State University: Columbus
Campus *F*
University of Cincinnati *F*
University of Toledo *F*

Oklahoma
University of Oklahoma *F*

Pennsylvania
Duquesne University *F*
Philadelphia College of Pharmacy
and Science *F*
Temple University *F*

Rhode Island
University of Rhode Island *F*

South Carolina
University of South Carolina *F*

Tennessee
University of Tennessee:
Memphis *F*

Texas
Southwest Texas State University *F*
Texas Southern University *F*
University of Houston *F*
University of Texas
Austin *F*
Health Science Center at San
Antonio *F*

Utah
Brigham Young University *F*
University of Utah *F*

Virginia
Virginia Commonwealth
University *F*

Washington
University of Washington *F*
Washington State University *F*

Wisconsin
University of Wisconsin: Madison *F*

Philosophy

Alabama
Athens State College *B*
Auburn University *B*
Birmingham-Southern College *B*

Huntingdon College *B*
Spring Hill College *B*
University of Alabama
Birmingham *B*
Huntsville *B*
Tuscaloosa *B,M*
University of South Alabama *B*

Alaska
University of Alaska Fairbanks *B*

Arizona
Arizona State University *B,M*
Glendale Community College *A*
Northern Arizona University *B*
Prescott College *B*
University of Arizona *B,M,D*

Arkansas
Arkansas College *B*
Arkansas State University *B*
Hendrix College *B*
Ouachita Baptist University *B*
Philander Smith College *B*
University of Arkansas
Fayetteville *B,M,D*
Little Rock *B*
University of Central Arkansas *B*
University of the Ozarks *B*

California
Azusa Pacific University *B*
Bakersfield College *A*
California Institute of Integral
Studies *M,D*
California Lutheran University *B*
California State Polytechnic
University: Pomona *B*
California State University
Bakersfield *B*
Chico *B*
Dominguez Hills *B*
Fresno *B*
Fullerton *B*
Hayward *B*
Long Beach *B,M*
Los Angeles *B,M*
Northridge *B*
Sacramento *B*
San Bernardino *B*
Stanislaus *B*
Cerritos Community College *A*
Chaffey Community College *A*
Chapman University *B*
Claremont McKenna College *B*
College of the Desert *A*
College of Notre Dame *B*
Columbia College *A*
De Anza College *A*
Dominican School of Philosophy
and Theology *B,M*
El Camino College *A*
Foothill College *A*
Grossmont Community College *A*
Holy Names College *B*
Humboldt State University *B*
Irvine Valley College *A*
Los Angeles Valley College *A*
Loyola Marymount University *B*
Marymount College *A*
Merced College *A*
Mills College *B*
MiraCosta College *A*
Mount St. Mary's College *B*
Napa Valley College *A*
Occidental College *B*
Ohlone College *A*
Orange Coast College *A*
Oxnard College *A*
Pepperdine University *B*
Pitzer College *B*
Point Loma Nazarene College *B*

Pomona College *B*
Saddleback College *A*
St. John's Seminary College *B*
St. Mary's College of California *B*
San Diego City College *A*
San Diego State University *B,M*
San Francisco State University *B,M*
San Jose State University *B,M*
Santa Barbara City College *A*
Santa Clara University *B*
Santa Rosa Junior College *A*
Scripps College *B*
Sonoma State University *B*
Southwestern College *A*
Stanford University *B,M,D*
University of California
    Berkeley *B,M,D*
    Davis *B,M,D*
    Irvine *B,M,D*
    Los Angeles *B,M,D*
    Riverside *B,M,D*
    San Diego *B,M,D*
    Santa Barbara *B,M,D*
    Santa Cruz *B*
University of La Verne *B*
University of the Pacific *B*
University of Redlands *B*
University of San Diego *B*
University of San Francisco *B*
University of Southern California
    B,M,D
Ventura College *A*
Westmont College *B*
Whittier College *B*
World College West *B*

Colorado

Colorado College *B*
Colorado State University *B,M*
Fort Lewis College *B*
Metropolitan State College of
    Denver *B*
Regis College of Regis University *B*
University of Colorado
    Boulder *B,M,D*
    Colorado Springs *B*
    Denver *B*
University of Denver *B,M*
University of Northern Colorado *B*

Connecticut

Albertus Magnus College *B*
Central Connecticut State
    University *B*
Connecticut College *B*
Fairfield University *B*
Holy Apostles College and
    Seminary *B*
Sacred Heart University *A,B*
St. Joseph College *B*
Southern Connecticut State
    University *B*
Trinity College *B,M*
University of Connecticut *B,M,D*
University of Hartford *B*
Wesleyan University *B*
Yale University *B,M,D*

Delaware

University of Delaware *B*

District of Columbia

American University *B,M*
Catholic University of America
    B,M,D
Gallaudet University *B*
George Washington University *B,M*
Georgetown University *B,M,D*
Howard University *B,M*
Oblate College *B*
Trinity College *B*

University of the District of
    Columbia *A,B*

Florida

Barry University *B*
Daytona Beach Community
    College *A*
Eckerd College *B*
Edison Community College *A*
Flagler College *B*
Florida Agricultural and Mechanical
    University *B*
Florida Atlantic University *B*
Florida International University *B*
Florida State University *B,M,D*
Gulf Coast Community College *A*
Jacksonville University *B*
Miami-Dade Community College *A*
New College of the University of
    South Florida *B*
Pensacola Junior College *A*
Rollins College *B*
St. John Vianney College
    Seminary *B*
Stetson University *B*
University of Central Florida *B*
University of Florida *B,M,D*
University of Miami *B,M,D*
University of South Florida *B,M*
University of Tampa *A,B*
University of West Florida *B*

Georgia

Agnes Scott College *B*
Berry College *B*
Clark Atlanta University *B*
Clayton State College *A*
DeKalb College *A*
Emory University *B,M,D*
Floyd College *A*
Georgia State University *B,M*
Mercer University *B*
Morehouse College *B*
Morris Brown College *B*
Oglethorpe University *B*
Oxford College of Emory
    University *A*
Paine College *B*
Shorter College *B*
South Georgia College *A*
Spelman College *B*
Toccoa Falls College *B*
University of Georgia *B,M,D*
Valdosta State College *B*
Wesleyan College *B*
West Georgia College *B*
Young Harris College *A*

Hawaii

Chaminade University of
    Honolulu *B*
University of Hawaii
    Hilo *B*
    Manoa *B,M,D*
    West Oahu *B*

Idaho

Albertson College *B*
Boise State University *B*
Idaho State University *B*
Northwest Nazarene College *B*
University of Idaho *B*

Illinois

Augustana College *B*
Aurora University *B*
Black Hawk College *A*
Bradley University *B*
City Colleges of Chicago: Olive-
    Harvey College *A*
Concordia University *B*
De Paul University *B,M,D*

Eastern Illinois University *B*
Elmhurst College *B*
Eureka College *B*
Garrett-Evangelical Theological
    Seminary *D,W*
Greenville College *B*
Illinois Benedictine College *B*
Illinois College *B*
Illinois Institute of Technology *B*
Illinois State University *B*
Illinois Wesleyan University *B*
John A. Logan College *A*
Judson College *B*
Kishwaukee College *A*
Knox College *B*
Lake Forest College *B*
Lewis University *B*
Lincoln Christian College and
    Seminary *M*
Lincoln Land Community
    College *A*
Loyola University of Chicago
    B,M,D
MacMurray College *B*
McKendree College *B*
Millikin University *B*
Monmouth College *B*
Morton College *A*
North Central College *B*
North Park College and Theological
    Seminary *B*
Northeastern Illinois University *B*
Northern Illinois University *B,M*
Northwestern University *B,M,D*
Olivet Nazarene University *B*
Principia College *B*
Quincy College *B*
Richland Community College *A*
Rockford College *B*
Roosevelt University *B,M*
Rosary College *B*
St. Xavier University *B*
Shimer College *B*
Southern Illinois University
    Carbondale *B,M,D*
    Edwardsville *B,M*
Trinity Christian College *B*
Trinity College *B*
Triton College *A*
University of Chicago *B,M,D*
University of Illinois
    Chicago *B,M,D*
    Urbana-Champaign *B,M,D*
Western Illinois University *B*
Wheaton College *B*

Indiana

Anderson University *B*
Ball State University *B*
Butler University *B*
Calumet College of St. Joseph *B*
DePauw University *B*
Earlham College *B*
Franklin College *B*
Hanover College *B*
Huntington College *B*
Indiana State University *B,M*
Indiana University
    Bloomington *B,M,D*
    Northwest *B*
    South Bend *B*
    Southeast *B*
Indiana University—Purdue
    University
    Fort Wayne *B*
    Indianapolis *B*
Indiana Wesleyan University *A,B*
Manchester College *B*
Marian College *B*
Purdue University
    Calumet *B*
    West Lafayette *B,M,D*

St. Joseph's College *B*
St. Mary's College *B*
St. Meinrad College *B*
Taylor University *B*
University of Evansville *B*
University of Indianapolis *B*
University of Notre Dame *B,M,D*
University of Southern Indiana *B*
Valparaiso University *B*
Vincennes University *A*
Wabash College *B*

Iowa

Buena Vista College *B*
Central College *B*
Clarke College *B*
Coe College *B*
Cornell College *B*
Divine Word College *B*
Dordt College *B*
Drake University *B*
Grinnell College *B*
Iowa State University *B*
Loras College *B*
Luther College *B*
Morningside College *B*
Northwestern College *B*
St. Ambrose University *B*
Simpson College *B*
Teikyo Marycrest University *A*
Teikyo Westmar University *B*
University of Dubuque *B*
University of Iowa *B,M,D*
University of Northern Iowa *B,M*
Vennard College *B*
Wartburg College *B*
William Penn College *B*

Kansas

Baker University *B*
Barton County Community
    College *A*
Benedictine College *B*
Bethany College *B*
Bethel College *B*
Central College *A*
Fort Hays State University *B*
Kansas State University *B*
McPherson College *B*
Ottawa University *B*
Southwestern College *B*
Sterling College *B*
University of Kansas *B,M,D*
Washburn University of Topeka *B*
Wichita State University *B*

Kentucky

Asbury College *B*
Bellarmine College *B*
Berea College *B*
Centre College *B*
Eastern Kentucky University *B*
Georgetown College *B*
Kentucky Wesleyan College *B*
Lees College *A*
Morehead State University *B*
Murray State University *B*
Northern Kentucky University *B*
Spalding University *B*
Thomas More College *A,B*
Transylvania University *B*
Union College *B*
University of Kentucky *B,M,D*
University of Louisville *B,M*
Western Kentucky University *B*

Louisiana

Centenary College of Louisiana *B*
Dillard University *B*
Grambling State University *B*
Louisiana College *B*

Louisiana State University
  Agricultural and Mechanical
    College *B,M*
    Shreveport *B*
Loyola University *B*
Tulane University *B,M,D*
University of New Orleans *B*
University of Southwestern
  Louisiana *B*
Xavier University of Louisiana *B*

Maine

Bates College *B*
Bowdoin College *B*
Colby College *B*
University of Maine *B*
University of Southern Maine *B*

Maryland

Baltimore Hebrew University
  B,M,D
Coppin State College *B*
Frederick Community College *A*
Frostburg State University *B*
Goucher College *B*
Harford Community College *A*
Hood College *B*
Johns Hopkins University *B,M,D*
Loyola College in Maryland *B*
Morgan State University *B*
Mount St. Mary's College *B*
St. Mary's College of Maryland *B*
Salisbury State University *B*
Towson State University *B*
University of Maryland
    Baltimore County *B*
    College Park *B,M,D*
Washington College *B*
Western Maryland College *B*

Massachusetts

American International College *B*
Amherst College *B*
Assumption College *B*
Becker College: Leicester
  Campus *A*
Bentley College *B*
Boston College *B,M,D*
Boston University *B,M,D*
Bradford College *B*
Brandeis University *B*
Bridgewater State College *B*
Clark University *B*
College of the Holy Cross *B*
Curry College *B*
Elms College *A*
Emmanuel College *B*
Framingham State College *B*
Gordon College *B*
Hampshire College *B*
Harvard and Radcliffe Colleges *B*
Harvard University *D*
Massachusetts Institute of
  Technology *B,M,D*
Merrimack College *B*
Mount Holyoke College *B*
North Adams State College *B*
Northeastern University *B*
St. Hyacinth College and Seminary
  C,A,B
St. John's Seminary College *B*
Simmons College *B*
Smith College *B,M*
Stonehill College *B*
Suffolk University *B*
Tufts University *B,M*
University of Massachusetts
    Amherst *B,M,D*
    Boston *B*
    Dartmouth *B*
    Lowell *B*
Wellesley College *B*

Wheaton College *B*
Williams College *B*

Michigan

Adrian College *A,B*
Albion College *B*
Alma College *B*
Aquinas College *B*
Calvin College *B*
Central Michigan University *B*
Eastern Michigan University *B*
Grand Valley State University *B*
Hillsdale College *B*
Hope College *B*
Kalamazoo College *B*
Lansing Community College *A*
Marygrove College *B*
Michigan State University *B,M,D*
Northern Michigan University *A,B*
Oakland University *B*
Sacred Heart Major Seminary *B*
St. Mary's College *B*
Siena Heights College *B*
Spring Arbor College *B*
University of Detroit Mercy *B*
University of Michigan
    Ann Arbor *B,M,D*
    Dearborn *B*
    Flint *B*
Wayne State University *B,M,D*
Western Michigan University *B,M*

Minnesota

Augsburg College *B*
Bemidji State University *B*
Bethel College *B*
Carleton College *B*
College of St. Benedict *B*
College of St. Catherine: St.
  Catherine Campus *B*
Concordia College: Moorhead *B*
Gustavus Adolphus College *B*
Hamline University *B*
Macalester College *B*
Mankato State University *B*
Moorhead State University *B*
North Central Bible College *A*
Northland Community College *A*
St. Cloud State University *B*
St. John's University *B*
St. Mary's College of Minnesota *B*
St. Olaf College *B*
University of Minnesota
    Duluth *B*
    Morris *B*
    Twin Cities *B,M,D*
University of St. Thomas *B*
Winona State University *A*

Mississippi

Belhaven College *B*
Millsaps College *B*
Mississippi State University *B*
University of Mississippi *B,M*
University of Southern Mississippi
  B,M

Missouri

Central Methodist College *B*
College of the Ozarks *B*
Drury College *B*
East Central College *A*
Lincoln University *B*
Maryville University *B*
Missouri Southern State College *B*
Missouri Valley College *B*
Northeast Missouri State
  University *B*
Northwest Missouri State
  University *B*
Rockhurst College *B*
St. Louis University *B,M,D*

Southeast Missouri State
  University *B*
Southwest Missouri State
  University *B*
Stephens College *B*
University of Missouri
    Columbia *B,M,D*
    Kansas City *B,D*
    Rolla *B*
    St. Louis *B*
Washington University *B,M,D*
Webster University *B*
Westminster College *B*
William Jewell College *B*
William Woods College *B*

Montana

Carroll College *B*
Montana State University *B*
Rocky Mountain College *B*
University of Montana *B,M*

Nebraska

Bellevue College *B*
Creighton University *B*
Doane College *B*
Hastings College *B*
Nebraska Wesleyan University *B*
University of Nebraska
    Lincoln *B,M,D*
    Omaha *B*

Nevada

University of Nevada
    Las Vegas *B*
    Reno *B,M*

New Hampshire

Dartmouth College *B*
New England College *B*
Plymouth State College of the
  University System of New
  Hampshire *B*
St. Anselm College *B*
University of New Hampshire *B*

New Jersey

Bergen Community College *A*
Bloomfield College *B*
Burlington County College *A*
College of St. Elizabeth *B*
Cumberland County College *A*
Drew University *B*
Fairleigh Dickinson University *B*
Jersey City State College *B*
Kean College of New Jersey *B*
Monmouth College *B*
Montclair State College *B*
Princeton University *B,D*
Ramapo College of New Jersey *B*
Rider College *B*
Rutgers—The State University of
  New Jersey
    Camden College of Arts and
      Sciences *B*
    Douglass College *B*
    Livingston College *B*
    New Brunswick *M,D*
    Newark College of Arts and
      Sciences *B*
    Rutgers College *B*
    University College Camden *B*
    University College New
      Brunswick *B*
    University College Newark *B*
St. Peter's College *B*
Seton Hall University *B*
Stevens Institute of Technology *B*
Stockton State College *B*
Thomas Edison State College *B*
Trenton State College *B*
Upsala College *B*

William Paterson College of New
  Jersey *B*

New Mexico

New Mexico State University *B*
University of New Mexico *B,M,D*

New York

Adelphi University *B*
Alfred University *B*
Bard College *B*
Barnard College *B*
Canisius College *B*
City University of New York
    Baruch College *B*
    Brooklyn College *B*
    City College *B*
    College of Staten Island *B*
    Graduate School and
      University Center *M,D*
    Hunter College *B*
    Lehman College *B*
    Queens College *B,M*
    York College *B*
Colgate University *B,M*
College of Mount St. Vincent *B*
College of New Rochelle *B*
Columbia University
    Columbia College *B*
    New York *M,D*
    School of General Studies *B*
Cornell University *B,M,D*
D'Youville College *B*
Elmira College *B*
Eugene Lang College/New School
  for Social Research *B*
Fordham University *B,M,D*
Hamilton College *B*
Hartwick College *B*
Hobart College *B*
Hofstra University *B*
Houghton College *B*
Iona College *B*
Ithaca College *B*
Le Moyne College *B*
Long Island University
    Brooklyn Campus *B*
    C. W. Post Campus *B*
Manhattan College *B*
Manhattanville College *B*
Marymount College *B*
Molloy College *B*
Nazareth College of Rochester *B*
New York University *B,M,D*
Niagara University *B*
Nyack College *B*
Rensselaer Polytechnic Institute
  B,M
St. Bonaventure University *B*
St. John Fisher College *B*
St. John's University *B,M*
St. Lawrence University *B*
St. Thomas Aquinas College *B*
Sarah Lawrence College *B*
Siena College *B*
Skidmore College *B*
State University of New York
    Albany *B,M*
    Binghamton *B,M,D*
    Buffalo *B,M,D*
    Purchase *B*
    Stony Brook *B,M,D*
    College at Brockport *B*
    College at Buffalo *B*
    College at Cortland *B*
    College at Fredonia *B*
    College at Geneseo *B*
    College at New Paltz *B*
    College at Oneonta *B*
    College at Plattsburgh *B*
    College at Potsdam *B*
    Oswego *B*

Sullivan County Community
College *A*
Syracuse University *B,M,D*
Touro College *B*
Union College *B*
United States Military Academy *B*
University of Rochester *B,M,D*
University of the State of New
York: Regents College *B*
Utica College of Syracuse
University *B*
Vassar College *B*
Wadhams Hall Seminary-College
C,B
Wagner College *B*
Wells College *B*
William Smith College *B*
Yeshiva University *B*

North Carolina

Appalachian State University *B*
Barton College *B*
Belmont Abbey College *B*
Brevard College *A*
Campbell University *B*
Catawba College *B*
Davidson College *B*
Duke University *B,D*
East Carolina University *B*
Elon College *B*
Guilford College *B*
High Point University *B*
Lenoir-Rhyne College *B*
Methodist College *A,B*
North Carolina Central
University *B*
North Carolina State University *B*
North Carolina Wesleyan College *B*
Queens College *B*
St. Andrews Presbyterian College *B*
Salem College *B*
University of North Carolina
Asheville *B*
Chapel Hill *B,M,D*
Charlotte *B*
Greensboro *B*
Wilmington *B*
Wake Forest University *B*

North Dakota

Jamestown College *B*
University of North Dakota *B*

Ohio

Antioch College *B*
Ashland University *B*
Baldwin-Wallace College *B*
Bluffton College *B*
Bowling Green State University
B,M,D
Capital University *B*
Case Western Reserve University
B,M
Central State University *B*
Cleveland State University *B,M*
College of Wooster *B*
Defiance College *B*
Denison University *B*
Franciscan University of
Steubenville *B*
Heidelberg College *B*
Hiram College *B*
John Carroll University *B*
Kent State University *B*
Kenyon College *B*
Lakeland Community College *A*
Marietta College *B*
Miami University: Oxford Campus
B,M
Mount Union College *B*
Mount Vernon Nazarene College *B*
Muskingum College *B*

Oberlin College *B*
Ohio Dominican College *B*
Ohio Northern University *B*
Ohio State University: Columbus
Campus *B,M,D*
Ohio University *B,M*
Ohio Wesleyan University *B*
Otterbein College *B*
Pontifical College Josephinum *B*
Union Institute *B,D*
University of Akron *B*
University of Cincinnati *B,M,D*
University of Dayton *B,M*
University of Findlay *B*
University of Toledo *B,M*
Urbana University *B*
Ursuline College *B*
Walsh College *B*
Wilmington College *B*
Wittenberg University *B*
Wright State University *B*
Xavier University *B*
Youngstown State University *B*

Oklahoma

Bartlesville Wesleyan College *A*
Oklahoma Baptist University *B*
Oklahoma City University *B*
Oklahoma State University *B,M*
Phillips University *B*
Tulsa Junior College *A*
University of Central Oklahoma *B*
University of Oklahoma *B,M,D*
University of Tulsa *B*

Oregon

Lewis and Clark College *B*
Linfield College *B*
Mount Angel Seminary *B*
Oregon State University *B*
Pacific University *B*
Portland Community College *A*
Portland State University *B*
Reed College *B*
University of Oregon
Eugene *B,M,D*
Robert Donald Clark Honors
College *B*
University of Portland *B*
Willamette University *B*

Pennsylvania

Albright College *B*
Allegheny College *B*
Alvernia College *B*
Beaver College *B*
Bloomsburg University of
Pennsylvania *B*
Bryn Mawr College *B*
Bucknell University *B*
Cabrini College *B*
California University of
Pennsylvania *B*
Carnegie Mellon University *B*
Cedar Crest College *B*
Chatham College *B*
Clarion University of
Pennsylvania *B*
Dickinson College *B*
Duquesne University *B,M,D*
East Stroudsburg University of
Pennsylvania *B*
Eastern College *B*
Edinboro University of
Pennsylvania *B*
Elizabethtown College *B*
Franklin and Marshall College *B*
Gannon University *B*
Geneva College *B*
Gettysburg College *B*
Gratz College *B*
Haverford College *B*

Holy Family College *B*
Indiana University of
Pennsylvania *B*
Juniata College *B*
King's College *B*
Kutztown University of
Pennsylvania *B*
La Salle University *B*
Lafayette College *B*
Lebanon Valley College of
Pennsylvania *B*
Lehigh University *B*
Lincoln University *B*
Lock Haven University of
Pennsylvania *B*
Lycoming College *B*
Mansfield University of
Pennsylvania *B*
Mercyhurst College *B*
Millersville University of
Pennsylvania *B*
Moravian College *B*
Muhlenberg College *B*
Penn State University Park Campus
B,M,D
Rosemont College *B*
St. Charles Borromeo Seminary *B*
St. Francis College *B*
St. Joseph's University *B*
St. Vincent College *B*
Seton Hill College *B*
Slippery Rock University of
Pennsylvania *B*
Susquehanna University *B*
Swarthmore College *B*
Temple University *B,M,D*
Thiel College *B*
University of Pennsylvania *B,M,D*
University of Pittsburgh *B,M,D*
University of Scranton *B*
Ursinus College *B*
Villanova University *B,M*
Washington and Jefferson College *B*
West Chester University of
Pennsylvania *B,M*
Westminster College *B*
Wilkes University *B*
Wilson College *B*
York College of Pennsylvania *A*

Puerto Rico

Bayamon Central University *B*
Pontifical Catholic University of
Puerto Rico *B*
University of Puerto Rico
Mayaguez Campus *B*
Rio Piedras Campus *B,M*

Rhode Island

Brown University *B,M,D*
Providence College *B*
Rhode Island College *B*
Roger Williams College *B*
Salve Regina University *B*
University of Rhode Island *B,M*

South Carolina

Clemson University *B*
College of Charleston *B*
Francis Marion College *B*
Furman University *B*
Newberry College *B*
University of South Carolina *B,M*
Winthrop University *B*
Wofford College *B*

South Dakota

Augustana College *B*
Dakota Wesleyan University *B*
University of South Dakota *B*

Tennessee

Austin Peay State University *B*
Belmont University *B*
Carson-Newman College *B*
East Tennessee State University *B*
Lambuth University *B*
Martin Methodist College *A*
Memphis State University *B,M,D*
Middle Tennessee State
University *B*
Motlow State Community
College *A*
Rhodes College *B*
Union University *B*
University of the South *B*
University of Tennessee
Chattanooga *B*
Knoxville *B,M,D*
Vanderbilt University *B,M,D*

Texas

Austin College *B*
Baylor University *B,M*
Collin County Community College
District *A*
Hardin-Simmons University *B*
Houston Community College *A*
Howard Payne University *B*
Incarnate Word College *B*
Lon Morris College *A*
McLennan Community College *A*
McMurry University *B*
Our Lady of the Lake University of
San Antonio *B*
Rice University *B,M,D*
St. Edward's University *B*
St. Mary's University *B*
Schreiner College *B*
Southern Methodist University *B*
Southwest Texas State University *B*
Southwestern University *B*
Texas A&M University *B,M*
Texas Christian University *B*
Texas Lutheran College *B*
Texas Tech University *B,M*
Texas Wesleyan University *B*
Trinity University *B*
University of Dallas *B,M,D*
University of Houston *B,M*
University of North Texas *B*
University of St. Thomas *B,M,D*
University of Texas
Arlington *B*
Austin *B,M,D*
El Paso *B*
Wiley College *B*

Utah

Brigham Young University *B*
Southern Utah University *B*
University of Utah *B,M,D*
Utah State University *B*
Westminster College of Salt Lake
City *B*

Vermont

Bennington College *B*
Goddard College *B,M*
Marlboro College *B*
Middlebury College *B*
St. Michael's College *B*
Trinity College of Vermont *B*
University of Vermont *B*

Virginia

Bluefield College *B*
Bridgewater College *B*
Christendom College *B*
Christopher Newport College *B*
College of William and Mary *B*
Emory and Henry College *B*
Ferrum College *B*

George Mason University *B*
Hampden-Sydney College *B*
Hollins College *B*
James Madison University *B*
Liberty University *B,M*
Lynchburg College *B*
Mary Baldwin College *B*
Mary Washington College *B*
Marymount University *B*
Old Dominion University *B*
Radford University *B*
Randolph-Macon College *B*
Randolph-Macon Woman's
 College *B*
Sweet Briar College *B*
University of Richmond *B*
University of Virginia *B,M,D*
Virginia Commonwealth
 University *B*
Virginia Polytechnic Institute and
 State University *B*
Virginia Union University *B*
Virginia Wesleyan College *B*
Washington and Lee University *B*

Washington

Central Washington University *B*
Eastern Washington University *B*
Everett Community College *A*
Evergreen State College *B*
Gonzaga University *B,M*
Lower Columbia College *A*
Pacific Lutheran University *B*
Seattle Central Community
 College *A*
Seattle Pacific University *B*
Seattle University *B*
Spokane Community College *A*
Spokane Falls Community
 College *A*
Tacoma Community College *A*
University of Puget Sound *B*
University of Washington *B,M,D*
Washington State University *B*
Western Washington University *B*
Whitman College *B*
Whitworth College *B*

West Virginia

Bethany College *B*
Davis and Elkins College *B*
Marshall University *B*
University of Charleston *B*
West Virginia University *B*
West Virginia Wesleyan College *B*
Wheeling Jesuit College *B*

Wisconsin

Alverno College *B*
Beloit College *B*
Carroll College *B*
Carthage College *B*
Lakeland College *B*
Lawrence University *B*
Marquette University *B,M,D*
Mount Mary College *B*
Northland College *B*
Ripon College *B*
St. Norbert College *B*
University of Wisconsin
 Eau Claire *B*
 Green Bay *B*
 La Crosse *B*
 Madison *B,M,D*
 Milwaukee *B,M*
 Oshkosh *B*
 Parkside *B*
 Platteville *B*
 Stevens Point *B*

Wyoming

Laramie County Community
 College *A*
Northwest College *A*
University of Wyoming *B,M*

Canada

McGill University *B,M,D*

Photographic technology

Alabama

Bessemer State Technical College *C*
Community College of the Air
 Force *A*
John C. Calhoun State Community
 College *A*

Arizona

Northland Pioneer College *A*
Rio Salado Community College *A*

California

Academy of Art College *C,B,M*
Allan Hancock College *A*
Bakersfield College *A*
Barstow College *C*
Brooks Institute of Photography
 B,M
California State University:
 Fullerton *B*
Chabot College *A*
Chaffey Community College *C,A*
City College of San Francisco *A*
Compton Community College *A*
Cosumnes River College *A*
East Los Angeles College *C,A*
El Camino College *C,A*
Fresno City College *A*
Glendale Community College *A*
Long Beach City College *C,A*
Los Angeles City College *A*
Los Angeles Trade and Technical
 College *C,A*
Modesto Junior College *A*
Moorpark College *A*
Mount San Antonio College *C,A*
Mount San Jacinto College *C,A*
Napa Valley College *C,A*
Orange Coast College *C,A*
Otis/Parsons School of Art and
 Design *A,B,M*
Palomar College *C,A*
Pasadena City College *C,A*
Rio Hondo College *A*
Saddleback College *A*
San Diego City College *A*
San Joaquin Delta College *A*
San Jose City College *A*
Santa Monica College *A*
Solano Community College *A*
Southwestern College *A*
Ventura College *A*
Yuba College *C,A*

Colorado

Colorado Institute of Art *A*
Colorado Mountain College: Spring
 Valley Campus *A*
Community College of Denver *A*

Connecticut

Greater New Haven State Technical
 College *A*
University of Bridgeport *A,B*

Florida

Brevard Community College *A*
Daytona Beach Community
 College *A*
Manatee Community College *A*
Miami-Dade Community College *A*

Idaho

Idaho State University *B*

Illinois

Bradley University *B*
City Colleges of Chicago: Richard J.
 Daley College *A*
College of DuPage *C,A*
Columbia College *B*
Prairie State College *A*
Southern Illinois University at
 Carbondale *A*

Indiana

Calumet College of St. Joseph *C,A*
Indiana Vocational Technical
 College
 Columbus *A*
 Northcentral *A*
 Southcentral *C*
 Southwest *A*
 Wabash Valley *C*
Purdue University *B,M*

Iowa

Hawkeye Institute of Technology *A*
Kirkwood Community College *A*

Kansas

Butler County Community
 College *A*
Colby Community College *A*
Fort Scott Community College *A*

Kentucky

Brescia College *A*
Jefferson Community College *A*

Maine

University of Maine at Augusta *A*

Maryland

Catonsville Community College *C*
Cecil Community College *C,A*
Dundalk Community College *A*
Montgomery College: Rockville
 Campus *A*

Massachusetts

Endicott College *A*
Fitchburg State College *B*
Hampshire College *B*

Michigan

Lansing Community College *A*
Northern Michigan University *A*
Oakland Community College *C,A*
Southwestern Michigan College *A*

Minnesota

College of Associated Arts *B*
St. Cloud State University *A,B*

Mississippi

Northeast Mississippi Community
 College *A*

Missouri

St. Louis Community College at
 Forest Park *C*

Montana

Montana State University *B*

Nebraska

Metropolitan Community College *A*
Northeast Community College *A*

New Jersey

Brookdale Community College *A*
County College of Morris *A*
Jersey City State College *B*
Ocean County College *A*

New York

Fashion Institute of Technology *A*
Herkimer County Community
 College *A*
Onondaga Community College *A*
Rochester Institute of Technology
 A,B,M
St. John's University *A*
School of Visual Arts *B*
Sullivan County Community
 College *A*
Syracuse University *B,M*
Villa Maria College of Buffalo *C,A*

North Carolina

Anson Community College *A*
Carteret Community College *A*
Chowan College *A*

Ohio

Antonelli Institute of Art and
 Photography *A*
Ohio Institute of Photography *C,A*

Pennsylvania

Antonelli Institute of Art and
 Photography *A*
Community College of Beaver
 County *A*
Community College of Philadelphia
 C,A
Harrisburg Area Community
 College *A*
Moore College of Art and Design *B*
Westmoreland County Community
 College *A*

South Carolina

Technical College of the
 Lowcountry *C*

Texas

Amarillo College *A*
Austin Community College *A*
Cisco Junior College *A*
Cooke County College *A*
El Paso Community College *A*
Houston Community College *A*
Kilgore College *A*
Lee College *A*
Midland College *A*
North Harris Montgomery
 Community College District *C,A*
Odessa College *A*
Sam Houston State University *B*

Utah

Brigham Young University *B*

Virginia

Northern Virginia Community
 College *A*

Washington

Eastern Washington University *B*
Everett Community College *A*
Seattle Central Community
 College *A*
Spokane Falls Community College
 C,A

Wisconsin
Madison Area Technical College *A*
University of Wisconsin: Oshkosh *B*

Wyoming
Casper College *A*
Northwest College *A*
Western Wyoming Community
College *A*

Photography

Alabama
Bessemer State Technical College *C*
John C. Calhoun State Community
College *A*
University of Montevallo *B*

Arizona
Arizona Western College *A*
Northern Arizona University *B*
Prescott College *B*
University of Arizona *B*

Arkansas
Arkansas State University *B*

California
Academy of Art College *C,B,M,W*
Allan Hancock College *A*
Art Center College of Design *B,M*
Bakersfield College *A*
Brooks Institute of Photography
B,M
California College of Arts and
Crafts *B,M*
California Institute of the Arts
C,B,M
California State University
Fullerton *B,M*
Long Beach *B*
Cerritos Community College *A*
Chabot College *A*
Chaffey Community College *C,A*
City College of San Francisco *C,A*
Columbia College *A*
Cosumnes River College *A*
De Anza College *A*
El Camino College *C,A*
Foothill College *A*
Fresno City College *C,A*
Glendale Community College *C*
Grossmont Community College *A*
Irvine Valley College *A*
Laney College *C,A*
Long Beach City College *C,A*
Los Angeles City College *A*
Los Angeles Pierce College *A*
Los Angeles Trade and Technical
College *C,A*
Merced College *A*
Modesto Junior College *A*
Monterey Peninsula College *C,A*
Moorpark College *A*
Mount San Antonio College *C,A*
Mount San Jacinto College *C,A*
Napa Valley College *A*
Orange Coast College *A*
Otis/Parsons School of Art and
Design *A,B,M*
Pacific Union College *A*
Saddleback College *A*
San Francisco Art Institute *B,M*
San Jose State University *B*
Santa Monica College *A*
Santa Rosa Junior College *C,A*
Sierra College *C,A*
Solano Community College *A*
Southwestern College *A*

University of California
San Diego *B*
Santa Cruz *C,B*
University of San Francisco *B*
University of Southern California *B*
Yuba College *A*

Colorado
Colorado Institute of Art *A*
Colorado Mountain College: Spring
Valley Campus *A*
University of Colorado at Denver *B*

Connecticut
Paier College of Art *A*
University of Bridgeport *A,B*
University of Connecticut *B*
University of Hartford *B*
University of New Haven *C,A,B*
Wesleyan University *B*

District of Columbia
Corcoran School of Art *B*
Howard University *B*

Florida
Barry University *B*
Daytona Beach Community
College *A*
Palm Beach Community College *A*
University of Miami *B,M*
University of South Florida *B,M*

Georgia
Atlanta College of Art *B*
LaGrange College *B*
Savannah College of Art and
Design *B,M*
University of Georgia *B*

Idaho
College of Southern Idaho *A*
Ricks College *A*

Illinois
American Academy of Art *A*
Bradley University *B*
City Colleges of Chicago: Olive-
Harvey College *A*
College of DuPage *C,A*
Columbia College *B,M*
Illinois Institute of Technology *M,D*
Prairie State College *A*
Ray College of Design *A*
School of the Art Institute of
Chicago *B,M*
Southern Illinois University at
Carbondale *B,M*
University of Chicago *M*
University of Illinois at Urbana-
Champaign *B*

Indiana
Ball State University *B*
Indiana University Bloomington
B,M
Indiana University—Purdue
University at Indianapolis *B*
Indiana Vocational Technical
College: Northcentral *A*
Purdue University *B,M*
University of Notre Dame *B,M*

Iowa
Hawkeye Institute of Technology *A*
Morningside College *B*
University of Iowa *M*

Kentucky
Brescia College *A*
Morehead State University *B*
Western Kentucky University *B*

Louisiana
Louisiana Tech University *B,M*

Maine
Portland School of Art *B*
University of Maine at Augusta *A*

Maryland
Anne Arundel Community
College *C*
Catonsville Community College *A*
College of Notre Dame of
Maryland *B*
Harford Community College *C,A*
Howard Community College *A*
Maryland Institute College of Art
B,M
Montgomery College: Rockville
Campus *A*
Morgan State University *B*

Massachusetts
Endicott College *A*
Hampshire College *B*
Massachusetts College of Art *B,M*
Massachusetts Institute of
Technology *B,M*
Montserrat College of Art *B*
Salem State College *B*
School of the Museum of Fine
Arts *B*
University of Massachusetts at
Dartmouth *B*

Michigan
Center for Creative Studies: College
of Art and Design *B*
Central Michigan University *B,M*
Charles Stewart Mott Community
College *C*
Grand Valley State University *B*
Lansing Community College *A*
Macomb Community College *C,A*
Northern Michigan University *B*
Oakland Community College *C*
University of Michigan *B,M*
Wayne State University *B,M*

Minnesota
College of Associated Arts *B*
Moorhead State University *B*
Willmar Community College *A*

Missouri
Columbia College *B*
Kansas City Art Institute *B*
Lindenwood College *M*
St. Louis Community College
Forest Park *A*
Meramec *A*
Washington University *B,M*
Webster University *B*

Montana
Montana State University *B*

Nebraska
Metropolitan Community College *A*
Northeast Community College *A*
Southeast Community College:
Beatrice Campus *A*

New Hampshire
New England College *B*
White Pines College *A*

New Jersey
Burlington County College *A*
County College of Morris *A*
Jersey City State College *B*
Mercer County Community
College *A*

Rutgers—The State University of
New Jersey: Mason Gross School
of the Arts *B,M*
Stockton State College *B*
Thomas Edison State College *B*

New Mexico
Institute of American Indian
Arts *A*

New York
Adirondack Community College
C,A
Alfred University *B*
Bard College *B,M*
City University of New York
City College *B*
La Guardia Community
College *C,A*
Queensborough Community
College *C,A*
Cornell University *B*
Hofstra University *B*
Ithaca College *B*
Long Island University: C. W. Post
Campus *B*
Mercy College *C*
Mohawk Valley Community College
C,A
Nassau Community College *C*
New York University *B*
Onondaga Community College *A*
Parsons School of Design *A,B*
Pratt Institute *B,M*
Rochester Institute of Technology
A,B,M
Sage Junior College of Albany, A
Division of Russell Sage
College *A*
St. John's University *B*
Sarah Lawrence College *B*
School of Visual Arts *B,M*
State University of New York
Albany *B,M*
Purchase *B*
College at Buffalo *B*
College at New Paltz *B,M*
College at Potsdam *B*
Sullivan County Community
College *A*
Syracuse University *B,M*
Villa Maria College of Buffalo *C,A*

North Carolina
Barton College *B*
Brevard College *A*
Carteret Community College *C*
Chowan College *A*
Guilford Technical Community
College *C*

Ohio
Antonelli Institute of Art and
Photography *A*
Art Academy of Cincinnati *B*
Bowling Green State University *B*
Cleveland Institute of Art *B*
Columbus College of Art and
Design *B*
Kent State University *B*
Lakeland Community College *A*
Ohio Institute of Photography *C,A*
Ohio State University: Columbus
Campus *B,M*
Ohio University *B,M*
University of Akron *B*
University of Dayton *B*
Wright State University *B*

Oklahoma
Oklahoma State University
Technical Branch: Okmulgee *A*

University of Central Oklahoma *B*
University of Oklahoma *B*

Oregon
Pacific Northwest College of Art *B*

Pennsylvania
Art Institute of Pittsburgh *A*
Beaver College *B*
Community College of
    Philadelphia *A*
Edinboro University of
    Pennsylvania *B*
Harrisburg Area Community
    College *C,A*
Lycoming College *B*
Marywood College *B*
Moore College of Art and Design *B*
Northampton County Area
    Community College *C*
Point Park College *B*
St. Vincent College *B*
Seton Hill College *B*
Temple University *B,M*
University of the Arts *C,B*
Westmoreland County Community
    College *A*

Puerto Rico
Inter American University of Puerto
    Rico: San German Campus *B*

Rhode Island
Rhode Island School of Design *B,M*

South Carolina
Coker College *B*
University of South Carolina *B*

Tennessee
Carson-Newman College *B*
Middle Tennessee State
    University *B*
Nashville State Technical Institute
    C,A

Texas
Austin Community College *A*
Collin County Community College
    District *A*
East Texas State University *B*
Kilgore College *A*
Lamar University—Beaumont *M*
Sam Houston State University *B,M*
Texas Southern University *B*
Texas Woman's University *B,M*
University of Houston *B,M*
University of North Texas *B,M*
Western Texas College *A*

Utah
Brigham Young University *B*
Weber State University *A,B*

Vermont
Bennington College *B*

Virginia
Central Virginia Community
    College *C*
Northern Virginia Community
    College *A*
Virginia Intermont College *B*

Washington
Art Institute of Seattle *C,A*
Eastern Washington University *B*
Everett Community College *A*
Evergreen State College *B*
Olympic College *A*
Seattle Central Community
    College *A*

Shoreline Community College *A*
University of Washington *B,M*

West Virginia
Shepherd College *A,B*
West Virginia State College *B*

Wisconsin
Milwaukee Institute of Art &
    Design *B*
University of Wisconsin
    Eau Claire *B*
    Green Bay *B*
    Milwaukee *B*
    Superior *B*

Wyoming
Casper College *A*
Northwest College *A*
Western Wyoming Community
    College *A*

Physical chemistry

California
California State University
    Fresno *B*
    Fullerton *M*
San Diego State University *B*
University of California: Berkeley
    B,M,D
University of Southern California *D*

Connecticut
Wesleyan University *B*

District of Columbia
George Washington University *M,D*

Florida
Florida State University *B,M,D*
New College of the University of
    South Florida *B*
University of Florida *M,D*

Georgia
Emory University *D*

Illinois
Judson College *B*
Northwestern University *B*
University of Chicago *B,M,D*

Indiana
Indiana University Bloomington *D*
Purdue University *M,D,W*
University of Notre Dame *D*

Iowa
Iowa State University *M,D*

Kansas
Kansas State University *M,D*

Kentucky
University of Kentucky *D*

Maryland
University of Maryland: College
    Park *M,D*

Massachusetts
Harvard University *D*
Massachusetts Institute of
    Technology *B,M,D,W*
Tufts University *M,D*
University of Massachusetts at
    Lowell *M,D*
Worcester Polytechnic Institute *B*

Michigan
Eastern Michigan University *B*
Michigan State University *B,M,D*
University of Michigan *M,D*

Missouri
University of Missouri: Kansas City
    M,D

New Hampshire
University of New Hampshire *M,D*

New Jersey
Princeton University *D*
Stevens Institute of Technology
    B,M,D

New York
Columbia University
    Columbia College *B*
    New York *M,D*
Cornell University *M,D*
Fordham University *M*
Mohawk Valley Community
    College *A*
Rockefeller University *D*
State University of New York
    Albany *D*
    College of Environmental
        Science and Forestry *B,M,D*

North Carolina
University of North Carolina at
    Chapel Hill *M,D*

Ohio
Ohio State University: Columbus
    Campus *B,M,D*
Ohio University *M,D*

Oregon
University of Oregon *M,D*

Pennsylvania
Bucknell University *B*
Carnegie Mellon University
    B,M,D,W
Drexel University *M,D*
Duquesne University *M*
Lehigh University *M,D*
University of Pennsylvania *M,D*

Puerto Rico
University of Puerto Rico: Rio
    Piedras Campus *D*

Rhode Island
Brown University *B,M,D*

Tennessee
Motlow State Community
    College *A*

Texas
Rice University *B,M,D*
University of Houston *M,D*

Virginia
Hampden-Sydney College *B*

West Virginia
Alderson-Broaddus College *B*

Wisconsin
Marquette University *M,D*

Canada
McGill University *M,D*

Mexico
Sistema Instituto Tecnologico y de
    Estudios Superiores de
    Monterrey *M*

Physical education

Alabama
Alabama Agricultural and
    Mechanical University *B*
Alabama Southern Community
    College *A*
Alabama State University *B,M*
Auburn University
    Auburn *B,M,D*
    Montgomery *B,M*
Chattahoochee Valley Community
    College *A*
Faulkner University *B*
Huntingdon College *B*
Jacksonville State University *B,M*
James H. Faulkner State
    Community College *A*
Jefferson State Community
    College *A*
John C. Calhoun State Community
    College *A*
Lawson State Community
    College *A*
Livingston University *B,M*
Mobile College *B,M*
Oakwood College *B*
Samford University *B*
Snead State Junior College *A*
Southeastern Bible College *B*
Tuskegee University *B*
University of Alabama
    Birmingham *B,M*
    Tuscaloosa *B,M,D,W*
University of Montevallo *B,M*
University of North Alabama *B,M*
University of South Alabama *B,M*

Alaska
University of Alaska
    Anchorage *B*
    Fairbanks *B*

Arizona
Arizona State University *B,M,D*
Cochise College *A*
Eastern Arizona College *A*
Grand Canyon University *B*
Northern Arizona University *B,M*
University of Arizona *B*
Yavapai College *A*

Arkansas
Arkansas College *B*
Arkansas State University *B,M*
Arkansas Tech University *B,M*
Harding University *B*
Henderson State University *B,M*
John Brown University *B*
Ouachita Baptist University *B*
University of Arkansas
    Fayetteville *B,M*
    Monticello *B*
    Pine Bluff *B*
University of Central Arkansas *B,M*
University of the Ozarks *B*
Westark Community College *A*

California
Azusa Pacific University *B*
Biola University *B*
California Baptist College *B*
California Lutheran University *B*

California State Polytechnic
University: Pomona *B,M*
California State University
Bakersfield *B*
Chico *B*
Dominguez Hills *M*
Fresno *B*
Fullerton *B,M*
Long Beach *B,M*
Los Angeles *B,M*
Northridge *B*
Sacramento *B*
Chapman University *B*
Christ College Irvine *B*
Christian Heritage College *B*
Foothill College *A*
Fresno Pacific College *B*
Humboldt State University *B*
Master's College *B*
Pacific Christian College *B*
Pacific Union College *B*
Pepperdine University *B*
Point Loma Nazarene College *B*
San Jose State University *B,M*
Santa Rosa Junior College *A*
Sonoma State University *M*
Taft College *A*
United States International
University *B*
University of California: Davis *B,M*
University of La Verne *B*
University of the Pacific *B*
University of San Francisco *B*
West Hills Community College *A*
Westmont College *B*

Colorado

Adams State College *M*
Colorado Christian University *B*
Colorado Northwestern Community
College *A*
Colorado State University *B,M*
Metropolitan State College of
Denver *B*
University of Northern Colorado
M,D
University of Southern Colorado *B*

Connecticut

Central Connecticut State
University *B,M*
Eastern Connecticut State
University *B*
Southern Connecticut State
University *B,M*
University of Connecticut *B*

Delaware

Delaware State College *B*
University of Delaware *B,M*
Wesley College *B*

District of Columbia

Gallaudet University *B*
Howard University *B,M*
University of the District of
Columbia *B*

Florida

Bethune-Cookman College *B*
Daytona Beach Community
College *A*
Flagler College *B*
Florida Agricultural and Mechanical
University *B,M*
Florida Atlantic University *M*
Florida International University
B,M
Florida Memorial College *B*
Florida Southern College *B*
Florida State University *B,M,D*
Gulf Coast Community College *A*

Jacksonville University *B,M*
Miami-Dade Community College *A*
Nova University *M*
Pensacola Junior College *A*
St. Leo College *B*
Stetson University *B*
University of Central Florida *B,M*
University of Florida *B,M*
University of Miami *M*
University of North Florida *B*
University of South Florida *B,M*
University of Tampa *B*
University of West Florida *B*
Warner Southern College *B*

Georgia

Albany State College *B,M*
Armstrong State College *B*
Augusta College *B*
Berry College *B*
Brewton-Parker College *A,B*
Clark Atlanta University *B*
Clayton State College *A*
Columbus College *B*
Fort Valley State College *B*
Gainesville College *A*
Georgia College *B,M*
Georgia Southern University *B,M*
Georgia Southwestern College *B,M*
Georgia State University *B,M*
Kennesaw State College *B*
Macon College *A*
Morris Brown College *B*
North Georgia College *B,M*
University of Georgia *B,M,D*
Valdosta State College *B,M*
West Georgia College *B,M*

Hawaii

Brigham Young University-
Hawaii *B*
University of Hawaii at Manoa *B*

Idaho

Albertson College *B*
Boise State University *B*
College of Southern Idaho *A*
Idaho State University *B,M*
Lewis Clark State College *B*
Northwest Nazarene College *B*
Ricks College *A*
University of Idaho *M*

Illinois

Augustana College *B*
Aurora University *B*
Blackburn College *B*
Concordia University *B*
De Paul University *B*
Eastern Illinois University *B,M*
Elmhurst College *B*
Eureka College *B*
Greenville College *B*
Illinois Benedictine College *B*
Illinois Central College *A*
Illinois College *B*
Illinois State University *B*
Lewis University *B*
MacMurray College *B*
McKendree College *B*
Millikin University *B*
Monmouth College *B*
North Central College *B*
North Park College and Theological
Seminary *B*
Northeastern Illinois University *B*
Northern Illinois University *B,M*
Olivet Nazarene University *B*
Quincy College *B*
Southern Illinois University
Carbondale *B,M,D*
Edwardsville *M*

Trinity Christian College *B*
Trinity College *B*
University of Illinois
Chicago *B,M*
Urbana-Champaign *B,M,D*
Western Illinois University *B*
Wheaton College *B*

Indiana

Anderson University *B*
Ball State University *B*
Bethel College *B*
Butler University *B*
Franklin College *B*
Goshen College *B*
Grace College *B*
Huntington College *B*
Indiana State University *B,M*
Indiana University Bloomington
B,M,D
Indiana University—Purdue
University at Indianapolis *B*
Indiana Wesleyan University *B*
Manchester College *B*
Marian College *B*
Oakland City College *B*
Purdue University *B,M,D*
St. Joseph's College *B*
Taylor University *B*
Tri-State University *B*
University of Evansville *B,M*
University of Indianapolis *B*
University of Southern Indiana *B*
Valparaiso University *B*
Vincennes University *A*

Iowa

Briar Cliff College *B*
Buena Vista College *B*
Clarke College *B*
Coe College *B*
Cornell College *B*
Dordt College *B*
Iowa Lakes Community College *A*
Iowa State University *B,M*
Iowa Wesleyan College *B*
Kirkwood Community College *A*
Loras College *B,M*
Luther College *B*
Morningside College *B*
St. Ambrose University *B*
Simpson College *B*
Teikyo Westmar University *B*
University of Dubuque *B,M*
University of Iowa *B,M,D*
University of Northern Iowa *B,M*
Upper Iowa University *B*
Wartburg College *B*
William Penn College *B*

Kansas

Baker University *B*
Benedictine College *B*
Bethany College *B*
Colby Community College *A*
Emporia State University *B,M*
Fort Hays State University *B,M*
Friends University *B*
Hutchinson Community College *A*
Kansas State University *B,M*
McPherson College *B*
MidAmerica Nazarene College *B*
Pittsburg State University *B,M*
Southwestern College *B*
Tabor College *B*
University of Kansas *B,M,D*
Washburn University of Topeka *B*
Wichita State University *B,M*

Kentucky

Alice Lloyd College *B*
Asbury College *B*

Berea College *B*
Campbellsville College *B*
Eastern Kentucky University *B,M*
Georgetown College *B*
Kentucky State University *B*
Kentucky Wesleyan College *B*
Morehead State University *B,M*
Murray State University *B*
Northern Kentucky University *B*
St. Catharine College *A*
Transylvania University *B*
Union College *B*
University of Kentucky *B*
University of Louisville *B,M*
Western Kentucky University *B,M*

Louisiana

Centenary College of Louisiana *B*
Dillard University *B*
Grambling State University *B*
Louisiana College *B*
Louisiana State University and
Agricultural and Mechanical
College *B,M,D*
Louisiana Tech University *B,M*
McNeese State University *B,M*
Nicholls State University *B*
Northeast Louisiana University *B,M*
Northwestern State University *B,M*
Southeastern Louisiana
University *B*
Southern University and
Agricultural and Mechanical
College *B,M*
University of New Orleans *B,M*
University of Southwestern
Louisiana *B*
Xavier University of Louisiana *B*

Maine

St. Joseph's College *B*
University of Maine
Orono *B,M*
Presque Isle *B*

Maryland

Chesapeake College *A*
Frostburg State University *M*
Garrett Community College *A*
Hagerstown Junior College *A*
Montgomery College
Germantown Campus *A*
Rockville Campus *A*
Morgan State University *B,M*
Western Maryland College *M*

Massachusetts

Becker College: Leicester
Campus *A*
Berkshire Community College *A*
Boston University *B,M,W*
Bridgewater State College *B,M*
Dean Junior College *A*
Eastern Nazarene College *B,M*
Endicott College *A*
Mount Ida College *A*
Northeastern University *B,M*
Salem State College *B*
Springfield College *B,M,D*
University of Massachusetts
Amherst *B*
Boston *B*
Westfield State College *B*

Michigan

Adrian College *B*
Andrews University *M*
Calvin College *B*
Central Michigan University *B,M*
Concordia College *B*
Eastern Michigan University *B,M*

Grand Rapids Baptist College and
Seminary *B*
Grand Valley State University *B*
Hillsdale College *B*
Lansing Community College *A*
Michigan State University *B,M,D*
Northern Michigan University *B,M*
Olivet College *B*
Saginaw Valley State University *B*
Spring Arbor College *B*
University of Michigan *B,M*
Wayne State University *B,M*
Western Michigan University *B,M*

Minnesota

Augsburg College *B*
Bemidji State University *B,M*
Bethel College *B*
College of St. Catherine: St.
Catherine Campus *B*
Concordia College: Moorhead *B*
Concordia College: St. Paul *B*
Crown College *B*
Gustavus Adolphus College *B*
Mankato State University *B*
Moorhead State University *B*
Northland Community College *A*
Northwestern College *B*
Pillsbury Baptist Bible College *B*
Rainy River Community College *A*
St. Cloud State University *B*
St. Olaf College *B*
Southwest State University *B*
University of Minnesota
Duluth *B*
Twin Cities *B,M,D*
Willmar Community College *A*
Winona State University *B*

Mississippi

Alcorn State University *B,M*
Blue Mountain College *B*
Delta State University *B,M*
Jackson State University *B,M,W*
Mary Holmes College *A*
Mississippi College *B*
Mississippi State University *B,M*
Mississippi University for Women *B*
Northeast Mississippi Community
College *A*
Rust College *B*
University of Mississippi *B,M*
University of Southern Mississippi
B,M,D

Missouri

Calvary Bible College *B*
Central Missouri State University
B,M
College of the Ozarks *B*
Culver-Stockton College *B*
Evangel College *B*
Missouri Baptist College *B*
Missouri Valley College *B*
Northeast Missouri State
University *M*
Northwest Missouri State
University *B,M*
Southeast Missouri State University
B,M
Southwest Baptist University *B*
Southwest Missouri State
University *B*
University of Missouri
Columbia *B,M,D*
Kansas City *B*
Westminster College *B*
William Woods College *B*

Montana

Carroll College *B*
College of Great Falls *B*

Eastern Montana College *B*
Montana State University *B,M*
Northern Montana College *B*
Rocky Mountain College *B*
University of Montana *B,M*
Western Montana College of the
University of Montana *B*

Nebraska

Bellevue College *B*
Chadron State College *B*
Concordia College *B*
Creighton University *B*
Dana College *B*
Doane College *B*
Hastings College *B*
Nebraska Wesleyan University *B*
Northeast Community College *A*
Peru State College *B*
Union College *B*
University of Nebraska
Kearney *B,M*
Lincoln *B,M*
Omaha *B*
Wayne State College *B,M*

Nevada

University of Nevada: Reno *B,M*

New Hampshire

Keene State College *B*
New England College *B*
Plymouth State College of the
University System of New
Hampshire *B*
University of New Hampshire *B,M*

New Jersey

County College of Morris *C*
Essex County College *A*
Glassboro State College *B,M*
Gloucester County College *A*
Kean College of New Jersey *B*
Montclair State College *B,M*
Rutgers—The State University of
New Jersey
Cook College *B*
Douglass College *B*
Livingston College *B*
Rutgers College *B*
University College New
Brunswick *B*
Seton Hall University *B*
Trenton State College *B,M*
William Paterson College of New
Jersey *B*

New Mexico

College of the Southwest *B*
Eastern New Mexico University *B*
New Mexico Highlands University
B,M
New Mexico State University *B*
University of New Mexico *B,M,D*
Western New Mexico University *B*

New York

Adelphi University *B,M*
Canisius College *B*
City University of New York
Brooklyn College *B*
City College *B*
Hunter College *B,M*
Lehman College *M*
Queens College *B,M*
York College *B*
College of Mount St. Vincent *B*
Fulton-Montgomery Community
College *A*
Herkimer County Community
College *A*
Hofstra University *B,M*

Houghton College *B*
Hudson Valley Community
College *A*
Ithaca College *B,M*
King's College *B*
Long Island University
Brooklyn Campus *B,M*
C. W. Post Campus *B*
Manhattan College *B*
Mohawk Valley Community
College *A*
New York University *M*
Niagara County Community
College *A*
St. Bonaventure University *B*
St. Francis College *B*
St. Lawrence University *B*
State University of New York
College at Brockport *B,M*
College at Cortland *B,M*
Syracuse University *B,M,D*

North Carolina

Appalachian State University *B,M*
Barber-Scotia College *B*
Barton College *B*
Brevard College *A*
Campbell University *B,M*
Catawba College *B*
Chowan College *B*
East Carolina University *B,M*
Elizabeth City State University *B*
Elon College *B*
Fayetteville State University *B*
Gardner-Webb College *B,M*
Guilford College *B*
High Point University *B*
Johnson C. Smith University *B*
Livingstone College *B*
Mars Hill College *B*
Methodist College *A,B*
North Carolina Agricultural and
Technical State University *B,M*
North Carolina Central University
B,M
North Carolina Wesleyan College *B*
Peace College *A*
Pembroke State University *B*
Pfeiffer College *B*
Piedmont Bible College *B*
St. Andrews Presbyterian College *B*
St. Augustine's College *B*
University of North Carolina
Greensboro *B,M,D*
Wilmington *B*
Western Carolina University *B,M*
Winston-Salem State University *B*

North Dakota

Bismarck State College *A*
Dickinson State University *B*
Jamestown College *B*
Mayville State University *B*
Minot State University *B*
North Dakota State University *B,M*
University of Mary *B*
University of North Dakota *B,M*
Valley City State University *B*

Ohio

Ashland University *B*
Baldwin-Wallace College *B*
Bluffton College *B*
Bowling Green State University
B,M
Capital University *B*
Cedarville College *B*
Cleveland State University *B,M*
College of Mount St. Joseph *B*
Defiance College *B*
Denison University *B*
Heidelberg College *B*

John Carroll University *B*
Kent State University *B*
Malone College *B*
Miami University: Oxford Campus
B,M
Mount Union College *B*
Mount Vernon Nazarene College *B*
Muskingum College *B*
Ohio Dominican College *B*
Ohio Northern University *B*
Ohio State University: Columbus
Campus *B*
Ohio University *B*
Otterbein College *B*
Sinclair Community College *A*
University of Dayton *B*
University of Findlay *B*
University of Rio Grande *A,B*
University of Toledo *B,M,D*
Urbana University *B*
Walsh College *B*
Wittenberg University *B*
Wright State University *B*
Xavier University *B*
Youngstown State University *B*

Oklahoma

Bartlesville Wesleyan College *B*
East Central University *B*
Hillsdale Free Will Baptist
College *A*
Langston University *B*
Northern Oklahoma College *A*
Northwestern Oklahoma State
University *B*
Oklahoma Baptist University *B*
Oklahoma Christian University of
Science and Arts *B*
Oklahoma City University *B*
Oklahoma Panhandle State
University *B*
Oklahoma State University *B*
Oral Roberts University *B*
Phillips University *B*
Southeastern Oklahoma State
University *B,M*
Southwestern Oklahoma State
University *B,M*
Tulsa Junior College *A*
University of Central Oklahoma
B,M
University of Oklahoma *B,M*
University of Science and Arts of
Oklahoma *B*

Oregon

George Fox College *B*
Linfield College *B*
Oregon State University *B,M,D*
Pacific University *B*
Southern Oregon State College *M*
Treasure Valley Community
College *A*
University of Portland *B*
Warner Pacific College *B*
Western Baptist College *B*
Western Oregon State College *B*
Willamette University *M*

Pennsylvania

East Stroudsburg University of
Pennsylvania *B,M*
Eastern College *B*
Edinboro University of
Pennsylvania *B*
Gannon University *B*
Gettysburg College *B*
Harrisburg Area Community
College *A*
Indiana University of
Pennsylvania *B*
Lincoln University *B*

Lock Haven University of
Pennsylvania *B*
Luzerne County Community
College *A*
Marywood College *B*
Messiah College *B*
Montgomery County Community
College *A*
Northeastern Christian Junior
College *A*
Philadelphia College of Bible *B*
Slippery Rock University of
Pennsylvania *B,M*
Temple University *B,M,D*
University of Pittsburgh *B*
Ursinus College *B*
West Chester University of
Pennsylvania *B,M*

Puerto Rico

American University of Puerto
Rico *B*
Bayamon Central University *B*
Inter American University of Puerto
Rico
Metropolitan Campus *M*
San German Campus *B,M*
Pontifical Catholic University of
Puerto Rico *B*
University of Puerto Rico
Cayey University College *B*
Rio Piedras Campus *B,M*
University of the Sacred Heart *A*

Rhode Island

Rhode Island College *B*
University of Rhode Island *B,M*

South Carolina

Bob Jones University *B,M*
Central Wesleyan College *B*
Charleston Southern University *B*
The Citadel *B,M*
Claflin College *B*
Coker College *B*
College of Charleston *B*
Columbia College *B*
Erskine College *B*
Lander College *B*
Limestone College *B*
Newberry College *B*
South Carolina State College *B*
University of South Carolina
Aiken *B*
Coastal Carolina College *B*
Columbia *B,M,D*
Spartanburg *B*
Winthrop University *B,M*

South Dakota

Augustana College *B*
Black Hills State University *B*
Dakota State University *B*
Dakota Wesleyan University *B*
Huron University *B*
Mount Marty College *B*
Northern State University *B,M*
Sioux Falls College *B*
South Dakota State University *B*
University of South Dakota *B*

Tennessee

Austin Peay State University *B*
Bethel College *B*
Carson-Newman College *B*
David Lipscomb University *B*
East Tennessee State University
B,M
Free Will Baptist Bible College *B*
Freed-Hardeman University *B*
Knoxville College *B*
Lambuth University *B*

Lane College *B*
Lincoln Memorial University *B*
Memphis State University *B,M*
Middle Tennessee State University
B,D
Milligan College *B*
Roane State Community College *A*
Tennessee State University *B*
Tennessee Technological University
B,M
Tennessee Wesleyan College *B*
Tusculum College *B*
Union University *B,M*
University of Tennessee
Chattanooga *B,M*
Knoxville *B,M,D*
Martin *B*

Texas

Abilene Christian University *B*
Alvin Community College *A*
Angelo State University *B,M*
Austin College *B*
Baylor University *B,M*
Corpus Christi State University *B*
Dallas Baptist University *B*
Del Mar College *A*
East Texas Baptist University *B*
East Texas State University *B,M*
El Paso Community College *A*
Hardin-Simmons University *B,M*
Incarnate Word College *B*
Jarvis Christian College *B*
McMurry University *B*
Midwestern State University *B,M*
North Harris Montgomery
Community College District *A*
Prairie View A&M University *B,M*
Ranger Junior College *A*
Rice University *B*
St. Edward's University *B*
St. Mary's University *B*
Sam Houston State University *B,M*
Schreiner College *B*
Southwest Texas State
University *M*
Sul Ross State University *B,M*
Tarleton State University *B,M*
Texas A&I University *B,M*
Texas A&M University *B,M,D*
Texas Christian University *B,M*
Texas College *B*
Texas Lutheran College *B*
Texas Southmost College *A*
Texas Tech University *B,M*
Texas Wesleyan University *B*
Texas Woman's University *M,D*
Trinity Valley Community
College *A*
University of Houston *B,M,D*
University of Mary Hardin-
Baylor *B*
University of North Texas *B*
University of Texas
Arlington *B*
Austin *M,D*
El Paso *M*
Permian Basin *B,M*
Tyler *B,M*
Wayland Baptist University *B*
West Texas State University *B,M*
Wiley College *B*

Utah

Brigham Young University *B*
University of Utah *B*
Utah State University *B,M*
Weber State University *B*

Vermont

Castleton State College *B*
Johnson State College *B*

Lyndon State College *B*
Norwich University *B,M*
University of Vermont *B*

Virginia

Averett College *B*
Bluefield College *B*
College of William and Mary *B*
Eastern Mennonite College *B*
Emory and Henry College *B*
George Mason University *B,M*
Hampton University *B*
James Madison University *B,M*
Liberty University *B*
Longwood College *B*
Norfolk State University *B*
Old Dominion University *B,M*
Radford University *M*
Roanoke College *B*
Shenandoah University *B*
University of Richmond *B,M*
University of Virginia *B,M,D*
Virginia Commonwealth
University *B*
Virginia Polytechnic Institute and
State University *B,M*
Virginia State University *B*

Washington

Central Washington University *B*
Eastern Washington University *B*
Gonzaga University *B,M*
Pacific Lutheran University *B*
Seattle Pacific University *B,M*
Spokane Community College *A*
University of Puget Sound *M*
Walla Walla College *B*
Washington State University *B*
Western Washington University
B,M
Whitworth College *B*

West Virginia

Alderson-Broaddus College *B*
Bethany College *B*
Bluefield State College *B*
Concord College *B*
Davis and Elkins College *B*
Fairmont State College *B*
Glenville State College *B*
Salem-Teikyo University *A,B,M*
Shepherd College *B*
University of Charleston *B*
West Liberty State College *B*
West Virginia Institute of
Technology *B*
West Virginia State College *B*
West Virginia University *B,M,D*
West Virginia Wesleyan College *B*

Wisconsin

Carroll College *B*
Carthage College *B*
Concordia University Wisconsin *B*
Maranatha Baptist Bible College *B*
Ripon College *C*
University of Wisconsin
Eau Claire *B*
La Crosse *B,M*
Madison *B,M,D*
Oshkosh *B,M*
Platteville *B*
River Falls *B*
Stevens Point *B*
Whitewater *B*

Wyoming

Casper College *A*
Central Wyoming College *A*
Laramie County Community
College *A*
University of Wyoming *B,M*

Canada

McGill University *B,M*

Physical sciences

Alabama

Auburn University at
Montgomery *B*
Judson College *B*
Livingston University *B*
Troy State University
Dothan *B*
Troy *B*

Arizona

Arizona Western College *A*
Glendale Community College *A*
Northern Arizona University *B*
Prescott College *B*
Yavapai College *A*

Arkansas

Arkansas State University
Beebe Branch *A*
Jonesboro *B*
Arkansas Tech University *B*
Henderson State University *B,M*
Mississippi County Community
College *A*
Ouachita Baptist University *B*
University of Arkansas at
Monticello *B*
University of Central Arkansas *B,M*
University of the Ozarks *B*

California

Barstow College *A*
Biola University *B*
California Baptist College *B*
California Polytechnic State
University: San Luis Obispo *B*
California State University
Chico *B,M*
Fresno *B*
Hayward *B*
Los Angeles *B*
Northridge *B*
Sacramento *B*
Stanislaus *B*
Cerro Coso Community College *A*
Chabot College *A*
Chaffey Community College *A*
Chapman University *B*
Citrus College *A*
College of Notre Dame *B*
College of the Sequoias *A*
El Camino College *A*
Feather River College *A*
Fresno City College *A*
Fresno Pacific College *B*
Gavilan Community College *A*
Glendale Community College *A*
Golden West College *A*
Humboldt State University *B*
Imperial Valley College *A*
Irvine Valley College *A*
Kings River Community College *A*
Lassen College *A*
Long Beach City College *A*
Los Angeles Mission College *A*
Marymount College *A*
Master's College *B*
Mendocino College *A*
Merced College *A*
MiraCosta College *A*
Modesto Junior College *A*
Mount San Antonio College *A*
Napa Valley College *A*
Occidental College *B*

Ohlone College *A*
Orange Coast College *A*
Pacific Union College *B*
Porterville College *A*
Saddleback College *A*
San Diego City College *A*
San Diego State University *B*
San Joaquin Delta College *A*
San Jose City College *A*
San Jose State University *B*
Santa Monica College *A*
Santa Rosa Junior College *A*
Skyline College *A*
Southwestern College *A*
Taft College *A*
University of California
    Berkeley *A*
    Riverside *B*
University of La Verne *B*
University of the Pacific *B*
University of Southern California *B*
Ventura College *A*
Victor Valley College *A*
West Hills Community College *A*
Westmont College *B*

Colorado

Adams State College *B*
Arapahoe Community College *A*
Colorado Mountain College
    Alpine Campus *A*
    Spring Valley Campus *A*
Colorado Northwestern Community
    College *A*
Colorado State University *B*
Fort Lewis College *B*
Lamar Community College *A*
Northeastern Junior College *A*
Trinidad State Junior College *A*
United States Air Force
    Academy *B*
University of Colorado at Denver *B*
University of Denver *B*
University of Northern Colorado *B*

Connecticut

Albertus Magnus College *B*
Central Connecticut State
    University *B*
Mattatuck Community College *A*
Mitchell College *A*
Northwestern Connecticut
    Community College *A*
Trinity College *B*
United States Coast Guard
    Academy *B*
University of Hartford *A*

Delaware

Wesley College *A*

District of Columbia

University of the District of
    Columbia *A*

Florida

Brevard Community College *A*
Central Florida Community
    College *A*
Edison Community College *A*
Gulf Coast Community College *A*
Indian River Community College *A*
New College of the University of
    South Florida *B*
Palm Beach Community College *A*
Pensacola Junior College *A*
South Florida Community
    College *A*
University of North Florida *B*

Georgia

Abraham Baldwin Agricultural
    College *A*
Andrew College *A*
Armstrong State College *B*
Augusta College *B*
Berry College *B*
Covenant College *B*
Darton College *A*
LaGrange College *B*
Oxford College of Emory
    University *A*
Shorter College *B*
South Georgia College *A*
Waycross College *A*
Young Harris College *A*

Hawaii

Brigham Young University-
    Hawaii *B*

Idaho

Lewis Clark State College *B*
North Idaho College *A*
Ricks College *A*
University of Idaho *B,M*

Illinois

Augustana College *B*
Belleville Area College *A*
Bradley University *B*
City Colleges of Chicago: Wright
    College *A*
Concordia University *B*
Eureka College *B*
Greenville College *B*
Illinois Eastern Community
    Colleges
        Frontier Community
            College *A*
        Lincoln Trail College *A*
        Wabash Valley College *A*
Illinois Valley Community
    College *A*
John A. Logan College *A*
Judson College *B*
Kishwaukee College *A*
Lincoln Land Community
    College *A*
Monmouth College *B*
Morton College *A*
Olivet Nazarene University *B*
Parkland College *A*
Rend Lake College *A*
Richland Community College *A*
Rockford College *B*
Southern Illinois University at
    Edwardsville *B*
Triton College *A*
University of Chicago *B,M*
University of Illinois at Urbana-
    Champaign *M*
William Rainey Harper College *A*

Indiana

Ball State University *B*
Goshen College *B*
Indiana State University *B*
Indiana University—Purdue
    University at Fort Wayne *B*
St. Francis College *B*
Tri-State University *B*
University of Indianapolis *B*
University of Notre Dame *B,M,D*
Vincennes University *A*

Iowa

Buena Vista College *B*
Dordt College *B*
Drake University *M*
Graceland College *B*
Iowa Lakes Community College *A*

Iowa Western Community
    College *A*
Kirkwood Community College *A*
Loras College *B*
Luther College *B*
North Iowa Area Community
    College *A*
William Penn College *B*

Kansas

Allen County Community
    College *A*
Barton County Community
    College *A*
Butler County Community
    College *A*
Cloud County Community
    College *A*
Coffeyville Community College *A*
Colby Community College *A*
Dodge City Community College *A*
Emporia State University *B,M*
Fort Hays State University *B,M*
Fort Scott Community College *A*
Highland Community College *A*
Hutchinson Community College *A*
Kansas City Kansas Community
    College *A*
Kansas State University *B*
McPherson College *B*
Neosho County Community
    College *A*
Pittsburg State University *B*
Seward County Community
    College *A*
Southwestern College *B*
Washburn University of Topeka *A*

Kentucky

Sue Bennett College *A*
Western Kentucky University *B*

Louisiana

Northwestern State University *B*
Southern University and
    Agricultural and Mechanical
    College *B*

Maine

St. Joseph's College *B*
University of Maine at
    Farmington *B*

Maryland

Charles County Community
    College *A*
College of Notre Dame of
    Maryland *B*
Frostburg State University *B*
Howard Community College *A*
Montgomery College
    Germantown Campus *A*
    Rockville Campus *A*
    Takoma Park Campus *A*
Salisbury State University *B*
United States Naval Academy *B*
University of Maryland: College
    Park *B*

Massachusetts

Bridgewater State College *M*
Clark University *B,M,D*
Greenfield Community College *C*
Hampshire College *B*
Harvard and Radcliffe Colleges *B*
Massachusetts Institute of
    Technology *B*
Roxbury Community College *A*
Westfield State College *B*
Worcester Polytechnic Institute *B*

Michigan

Aquinas College *B*
Calvin College *B*
Central Michigan University *B*
Concordia College *B*
Eastern Michigan University *B,M*
Grand Valley State University *B*
Hope College *B*
Kalamazoo Valley Community
    College *A*
Madonna University *A,B*
Michigan State University *B,M*
Oakland University *B*
Schoolcraft College *A*
University of Michigan
    Dearborn *B*
    Flint *B*
Western Michigan University *B*

Minnesota

Bemidji State University *B*
Bethany Lutheran College *A*
Bethel College *B*
Concordia College: Moorhead *B*
Concordia College: St. Paul *B*
Mankato State University *B*
Moorhead State University *B*
Northland Community College *A*
Northwestern College *A*
Rainy River Community College *A*
St. Cloud State University *B,M*
St. Mary's College of Minnesota *B*
Southwest State University *B*
University of Minnesota: Twin
    Cities *B*
Vermilion Community College *A*
Willmar Community College *A*
Winona State University *B*

Mississippi

Belhaven College *B*
Blue Mountain College *B*
Delta State University *B*
Jones County Junior College *A*
Mississippi College *M*
Mississippi Delta Community
    College *A*
Mississippi University for Women *B*

Missouri

College of the Ozarks *B*
East Central College *A*
Jefferson College *A*
Maryville University *B*
Mineral Area College *A*
Missouri Southern State College *B*
Moberly Area Community
    College *A*
St. Louis Community College
    Forest Park *A*
    Meramec *A*
Washington University *B,M,D*

Montana

Little Big Horn College *A*
Miles Community College *A*

Nebraska

Central Community College *A*
Chadron State College *B*
Concordia College *B*
Doane College *B*
Hastings College *B*
McCook Community College *A*
Midland Lutheran College *B*
Northeast Community College *A*
Peru State College *B*
Southeast Community College:
    Beatrice Campus *A*

University of Nebraska
Kearney *B*
Lincoln *B,M,D*
Omaha *B*
Western Nebraska Community
College: Scottsbluff Campus *A*
York College *A*

Nevada

Community College of Southern
Nevada *A*
Western Nevada Community
College *A*

New Hampshire

Plymouth State College of the
University System of New
Hampshire *B*

New Jersey

Burlington County College *A*
Glassboro State College *B*
Gloucester County College *A*
Ocean County College *A*
Thomas Edison State College *A,B*
Union County College *A*

New Mexico

College of Santa Fe *A*
Eastern New Mexico University *B*
New Mexico Institute of Mining
and Technology *B,M,D*
New Mexico State University *B*
Western New Mexico University *B*

New York

Adirondack Community College *A*
Bard College *B*
City University of New York
Brooklyn College *B,M*
City College *B,M,D*
Kingsborough Community
College *A*
Medgar Evers College *A*
Colgate University *B*
Columbia University: Columbia
College *B*
Dowling College *B*
Eugene Lang College/New School
for Social Research *B*
Fordham University *B*
Fulton-Montgomery Community
College *A*
Herkimer County Community
College *A*
Hudson Valley Community
College *A*
Jamestown Community College *A*
Manhattan College *B*
Mohawk Valley Community
College *A*
Molloy College *B*
New York University *B,M*
Paul Smith's College *A*
Sage Junior College of Albany, A
Division of Russell Sage
College *A*
St. John's University *B*
Sarah Lawrence College *B*
Suffolk County Community
College *A*
Sullivan County Community
College *A*
Tompkins-Cortland Community
College *A*
United States Military Academy *B*

North Carolina

Brevard College *A*
Chowan College *A*
College of the Albemarle *A*
Johnson C. Smith University *B*

Lees-McRae College *A*
Methodist College *A,B*
Rockingham Community College *A*
St. Augustine's College *B*
University of North Carolina at
Chapel Hill *M*
Western Carolina University *M*

North Dakota

Dickinson State University *B*
Mayville State University *B*
Minot State University *B*
North Dakota State University *B,M*
University of North Dakota
Grand Forks *B*
Williston *A*

Ohio

Ashland University *B*
Bluffton College *B*
Bowling Green State University:
Firelands College *A*
Defiance College *B*
Edison State Community College *A*
Heidelberg College *B*
Lakeland Community College *A*
Muskingum College *B*
Ohio State University: Columbus
Campus *B,M,D*
Shawnee State University *B*
Union Institute *B,D*
University of Dayton *B*
Urbana University *B*
Washington State Community
College *A*
Wittenberg University *B*

Oklahoma

Bacone College *A*
Bartlesville Wesleyan College *A*
Connors State College *A*
Eastern Oklahoma State College *A*
Langston University *B*
Northeastern State University *B*
Oklahoma Baptist University *B*
Oklahoma City University *B*
Oklahoma Panhandle State
University *B*
Oklahoma State University *B*
Redlands Community College *A*
St. Gregory's College *A*
Southwestern Oklahoma State
University *B*
Tulsa Junior College *A*
University of Oklahoma *M*

Oregon

Central Oregon Community
College *A*
Linfield College *B*
Pacific University *B*
Portland Community College *A*
Rogue Community College *A*
Southern Oregon State College *B*
Treasure Valley Community
College *A*
Warner Pacific College *B*
Western Oregon State College *B*

Pennsylvania

Butler County Community
College *A*
California University of
Pennsylvania *B,M*
Carnegie Mellon University
B,M,D,W
Clarion University of
Pennsylvania *B*
East Stroudsburg University of
Pennsylvania *B*
Edinboro University of
Pennsylvania *B*

Gannon University *B*
Geneva College *B*
Harrisburg Area Community
College *A*
Juniata College *B*
Keystone Junior College *A*
La Salle University *B*
Lincoln University *B*
Lock Haven University of
Pennsylvania *B*
Luzerne County Community
College *A*
Montgomery County Community
College *A*
Northampton County Area
Community College *A*
Northeastern Christian Junior
College *A*
Penn State Erie Behrend College *B*
Point Park College *B*
Slippery Rock University of
Pennsylvania *B*
University of Pittsburgh
Bradford *B*
Johnstown *B*
Pittsburgh *B*
Valley Forge Military College *C,A*
West Chester University of
Pennsylvania *M*
Widener University *B*
York College of Pennsylvania *B*

Puerto Rico

Inter American University of Puerto
Rico: Metropolitan Campus *B*
University of Puerto Rico:
Mayaguez Campus *B,M*

Rhode Island

Rhode Island College *B,M*

South Carolina

Columbia College *B*
Limestone College *B*
Newberry College *B*
North Greenville College *A*

South Dakota

Black Hills State University *B*

Tennessee

Belmont University *B*
Cumberland University *B*
Freed-Hardeman University *B*
Knoxville College *B*
Lambuth University *B*
Martin Methodist College *A*
Memphis State University *B*
Middle Tennessee State
University *B*
Motlow State Community
College *A*
Roane State Community College *A*
Tennessee State University *B*
Tennessee Temple University *B*
Tomlinson College *A*
Union University *B*
University of Tennessee:
Chattanooga *B*
Vanderbilt University *M,D*

Texas

Abilene Christian University *B*
Alvin Community College *A*
Amarillo College *A*
Angelina College *A*
Austin Community College *A*
Bee County College *A*
Central Texas College *A*
Howard College *A*
Kilgore College *A*
Lon Morris College *A*

McLennan Community College *A*
McMurry University *B*
Midland College *A*
Panola College *A*
Schreiner College *A*
Texas Southmost College *A*
University of Houston: Clear Lake
B,M
Victoria College *A*
Western Texas College *A*

Utah

Southern Utah University *B*
Weber State University *B*
Westminster College of Salt Lake
City *B*

Vermont

Bennington College *B*
Goddard College *B,M*
Lyndon State College *B*
Marlboro College *B*

Virginia

Bluefield College *B*
Bridgewater College *B*
Dabney S. Lancaster Community
College *A*
John Tyler Community College *A*
Marymount University *B*
Piedmont Virginia Community
College *A*
Radford University *B*
St. Paul's College *A*
Tidewater Community College *A*
Virginia Wesleyan College *B*

Washington

Big Bend Community College *A*
Centralia College *A*
Eastern Washington University *B*
Everett Community College *A*
Evergreen State College *B*
Grays Harbor College *A*
Lower Columbia College *A*
Seattle Central Community
College *A*
Seattle University *B*
Skagit Valley College *A*
Spokane Falls Community
College *A*
Wenatchee Valley College *A*
Western Washington University
B,M

West Virginia

Bethany College *B*
Marshall University *B,M*
Shepherd College *B*
Wheeling Jesuit College *B*

Wisconsin

Edgewood College *B*
Lawrence University *B*
Northland College *B*
St. Norbert College *B*
University of Wisconsin
Eau Claire *B*
Green Bay *B*
Platteville *B*
River Falls *B*
Superior *B*

Wyoming

Central Wyoming College *A*
Eastern Wyoming College *A*
Laramie County Community
College *A*
Northwest College *A*
Western Wyoming Community
College *A*

American Samoa, Caroline Islands, Guam, Marianas, Virgin Islands

University of Guam *B*

Physical therapy

Alabama

University of Alabama in Birmingham *M*
University of South Alabama *B*

Arizona

Northern Arizona University *B,M*

Arkansas

University of Central Arkansas *B,M*

California

California State University
    Fresno *B*
    Long Beach *B*
    Northridge *B*
Chapman University *M*
Mount San Antonio College *C*
Samuel Merritt College *M*
University of California: San Francisco *M*
University of the Pacific *B,M*
University of Southern California *M,D*

Colorado

University of Colorado Health Sciences Center *M*

Connecticut

Quinnipiac College *B,M*
Sacred Heart University *B*
University of Connecticut *B*

Delaware

University of Delaware *M*

District of Columbia

Howard University *B*

Florida

Barry University *B,M*
Daytona Beach Community College *A*
Florida Agricultural and Mechanical University *B*
Florida International University *B,M*
Gulf Coast Community College *A*
Miami-Dade Community College *A*
University of Florida *B,M*
University of Miami *M*
University of North Florida *B*

Georgia

Atlanta Metropolitan College *A*
Brewton-Parker College *A*
Clark Atlanta University *B*
Clayton State College *A*
Emory University *M*
Gainesville College *A*
Georgia State University *B*
Macon College *A*
Medical College of Georgia *B,M*
Middle Georgia College *A*
Morris Brown College *B*
North Georgia College *M*
Reinhardt College *A*

Idaho

Idaho State University *M*

Illinois

Barat College *B*
Bradley University *B*
Illinois Central College *A*
Northern Illinois University *B*
Northwestern University *M*
University of Health Sciences: The Chicago Medical School *B,M*
University of Illinois at Chicago *B,M*

Indiana

Indiana University—Purdue University at Indianapolis *B*
University of Evansville *B*
University of Indianapolis *M*

Iowa

Iowa Wesleyan College *B*
Luther College *B*
St. Ambrose University *M*
University of Iowa *M*
University of Osteopathic Medicine and Health Sciences *M*
Wartburg College *B*

Kansas

Hutchinson Community College *A*
Pratt Community College *A*
University of Kansas
    Lawrence *B*
    Medical Center *M*
Wichita State University *M*

Kentucky

University of Kentucky *B,M*
University of Louisville *B*

Louisiana

Louisiana College *B*
Louisiana State University Medical Center *B,M*
Southern University and Agricultural and Mechanical College *B*

Maine

University of New England *B*

Maryland

University of Maryland
    Baltimore *B*
    Eastern Shore *B,M*

Massachusetts

Becker College: Worcester Campus *A*
Boston University *B,M*
MGH Institute of Health Professions *M*
Northeastern University *B,M*
Simmons College *B*
Springfield College *B,M*
University of Massachusetts at Lowell *M*

Michigan

Andrews University *B,M*
Grand Valley State University *M*
Lansing Community College *A*
Oakland University *B,M*
University of Michigan: Flint *M*
Wayne State University *B*

Minnesota

College of St. Catherine: St. Catherine Campus *M*
College of St. Scholastica *B,M*
Rainy River Community College *A*
Rochester Community College *A*
St. Mary's Campus of the College of St. Catherine *M*

St. Mary's College of Minnesota *B*
University of Minnesota: Twin Cities *B,M*
Willmar Community College *A*

Mississippi

Mississippi College *B*
University of Mississippi
    Medical Center *B*
    University *B*

Missouri

Maryville University *B*
Rockhurst College *B,M*
St. Louis University *B,M*
Southwest Baptist University *B*
University of Missouri: Columbia *B*
Washington University *M*

Montana

Rocky Mountain College *B*
University of Montana *B*

Nebraska

University of Nebraska Medical Center *M*

Nevada

University of Nevada: Las Vegas *M*

New Jersey

Kean College of New Jersey *B*
Rutgers—The State University of New Jersey *M*
Stockton State College *B*
University of Medicine and Dentistry of New Jersey: School of Health Related Professions *B,M*

New Mexico

University of New Mexico *B*

New York

City University of New York: Hunter College *B*
Daemen College *B*
D'Youville College *B,M*
Herkimer County Community College *A*
Ithaca College *B,M*
Long Island University: Brooklyn Campus *B,M*
New York University *B,M,D*
Russell Sage College *B*
State University of New York
    Buffalo *B*
    Health Science Center at Brooklyn *B*
    Health Science Center at Syracuse *B*
    Health Sciences Center at Stony Brook *B*
Touro College *B,M*

North Carolina

Chowan College *A*
Duke University *M*
East Carolina University *B*
Louisburg College *A*
Shaw University *B*
University of North Carolina at Chapel Hill *B,M*

North Dakota

University of North Dakota *B,M*

Ohio

Bowling Green State University *B*
Cleveland State University *B*
Ohio State University: Columbus Campus *C,B,M*

Ohio University *B*
University of Toledo *B*

Oklahoma

Eastern Oklahoma State College *A*
Langston University *B*
University of Oklahoma
    Health Sciences Center *B*
    Norman *B*

Oregon

Pacific University *M*

Pennsylvania

Beaver College *M*
College Misericordia *B,M*
Duquesne University *M*
Elizabethtown College *B*
Gannon University *M*
Hahnemann University School of Health Sciences and Humanities *M,D*
Juniata College *B*
Keystone Junior College *A*
Lebanon Valley College of Pennsylvania *B*
Messiah College *B*
Philadelphia College of Pharmacy and Science *M*
Slippery Rock University of Pennsylvania *M*
Temple University *M*
Thomas Jefferson University: College of Allied Health Sciences *M*
University of Pittsburgh *M*
University of Scranton *M*
Villanova University *B*
Wilkes University *B*

Puerto Rico

University of Puerto Rico: Medical Sciences Campus *B*

Rhode Island

University of Rhode Island *B,M*

South Dakota

University of South Dakota *M*

Tennessee

Austin Peay State University *B*
Hiwassee College *A*
Trevecca Nazarene College *B*
Union University *B*
University of Tennessee
    Chattanooga *B*
    Memphis *B,M*

Texas

Baylor University *M*
McLennan Community College *A*
San Antonio College *A*
Southwest Texas State University *B*
Texas Southmost College *A*
Texas Tech University *B*
Texas Woman's University *M,D*
University of Texas
    Health Science Center at San Antonio *B*
    Medical Branch at Galveston *B*
    San Antonio *B*
    Southwestern Medical Center at Dallas Southwestern Allied Health Sciences School *B*

Utah

University of Utah *B*

Vermont

University of Vermont *B*

Virginia

Old Dominion University *M*
Shenandoah University *M*
Virginia Commonwealth University
    B,M

Washington

Eastern Washington University *B*
University of Puget Sound *M*
University of Washington *B,M*

West Virginia

Potomac State College of West
    Virginia University *A*
West Virginia University *B*
Wheeling Jesuit College *B*

Wisconsin

Marquette University *M*
University of Wisconsin
    La Crosse *B*
    Madison *B,M*

Wyoming

Northwest College *A*

Canada

McGill University *B,M*

Physical therapy assistant

Alabama

Alabama Southern Community
    College *A*
Bishop State Community College *A*
Brewer State Junior College *A*
Chattahoochee Valley Community
    College *A*
Community College of the Air
    Force *A*
Enterprise State Junior College *A*
Faulkner University *A*
Gadsden State Community
    College *A*
George C. Wallace State
    Community College at Selma *A*
James H. Faulkner State
    Community College *A*
Jefferson State Community
    College *A*
John C. Calhoun State Community
    College *A*
Lawson State Community
    College *A*
Livingston University *A*
Lurleen B. Wallace State Junior
    College *A*
Northeast Alabama State Junior
    College *A*
Shelton State Community
    College *A*
Shoals Community College *A*
Southern Union State Junior
    College *A*
University of Alabama in
    Birmingham *C*
Walker College *A*
Wallace State Community College
    at Hanceville *A*

Arkansas

University of Central Arkansas *A,B*

California

Cerritos Community College *A*
De Anza College *A*
Mount St. Mary's College *A*
San Diego Mesa College *A*

Colorado

Arapahoe Community College *A*
Denver Technical College *A*
Morgan Community College *A*
Pueblo Community College *A*

Connecticut

Housatonic Community College *A*

Delaware

Delaware Technical and
    Community College: Stanton/
    Wilmington Campus *A*

Florida

Broward Community College *A*
Miami-Dade Community College *A*
Palm Beach Community College *A*
Pensacola Junior College *A*
St. Petersburg Junior College *A*
Seminole Community College *A*

Georgia

Gainesville College *A*
Medical College of Georgia *A*

Hawaii

University of Hawaii: Kapiolani
    Community College *A*

Illinois

Belleville Area College *A*
Black Hawk College *A*
Illinois Central College *A*
Illinois Eastern Community
    Colleges
        Frontier Community
            College *C*
        Lincoln Trail College *C*
        Olney Central College *C*
Morton College *A*
Oakton Community College *A*
Southern Illinois University at
    Carbondale *A*

Indiana

University of Evansville *A*
Vincennes University *A*

Iowa

Indian Hills Community College *A*

Kansas

Colby Community College *A*
Dodge City Community College *A*
Johnson County Community
    College *A*
Kansas City Kansas Community
    College *A*
Washburn University of Topeka *A*

Kentucky

Jefferson Community College *A*
Paducah Community College *A*

Maine

Kennebec Valley Technical
    College *A*

Maryland

New Community College of
    Baltimore *A*

Massachusetts

Bay State College *A*
Becker College: Worcester
    Campus *A*
Berkshire Community College *A*
Lasell College *A*
Newbury College *A*
North Shore Community College *A*
Springfield Technical Community
    College *A*

Michigan

Delta College *A*
Henry Ford Community College *A*
Kellogg Community College *A*
Macomb Community College *A*

Minnesota

Anoka-Ramsey Community
    College *A*
St. Mary's Campus of the College of
    St. Catherine *A*
Vermilion Community College *A*

Missouri

Penn Valley Community College *A*
St. Louis Community College at
    Meramec *A*

Nevada

Community College of Southern
    Nevada *A*

New Jersey

Atlantic Community College *A*
Essex County College *A*
Fairleigh Dickinson University *A*
Union County College *A*

New York

Broome Community College *A*
City University of New York
    Kingsborough Community
        College *A*
    La Guardia Community
        College *A*
Genesee Community College *A*
Herkimer County Community
    College *A*
Maria College *A*
Nassau Community College *A*
New York University *A*
Niagara County Community
    College *A*
Onondaga Community College *A*
Orange County Community
    College *A*
Suffolk County Community
    College *A*

North Carolina

Caldwell Community College and
    Technical Institute *A*
Central Piedmont Community
    College *A*
Fayetteville Technical Community
    College *A*
Martin Community College *A*
Nash Community College *A*
Southwestern Community
    College *A*
Stanly Community College *A*

Ohio

Central Ohio Technical College *A*
Cuyahoga Community College:
    Metropolitan Campus *A*
Kent State University: East
    Liverpool Regional Campus *A*
Owens Technical College: Toledo *A*
Shawnee State University *A*
Sinclair Community College *A*

Stark Technical College *A*
University of Cincinnati: Access
    Colleges *A*

Oklahoma

Rogers State College *A*
Tulsa Junior College *A*

Oregon

Mount Hood Community
    College *A*

Pennsylvania

Alvernia College *A*
Central Pennsylvania Business
    School *A*
Hahnemann University School of
    Health Sciences and
    Humanities *A*
Harcum Junior College *A*
Lehigh County Community
    College *A*
Penn State University Park
    Campus *A*

Puerto Rico

University of Puerto Rico
        Humacao University
            College *A*
        Ponce Technological
            University College *A*

Rhode Island

Community College of Rhode
    Island *A*

South Carolina

Florence-Darlington Technical
    College *A*
Greenville Technical College *A*
Trident Technical College *A*

Tennessee

Chattanooga State Technical
    Community College *A*
Jackson State Community
    College *A*
Motlow State Community
    College *A*
Roane State Community College *A*
Shelby State Community College *A*
Volunteer State Community
    College *A*
Walters State Community
    College *A*

Texas

Amarillo College *A*
Austin Community College *A*
El Paso Community College *A*
Houston Community College *C*
Laredo Junior College *A*
Odessa College *A*
St. Philip's College *A*
Tarrant County Junior College *A*
Texas Southmost College *A*
Wharton County Junior College *A*

Virginia

College of Health Sciences *A*
John Tyler Community College *A*
Northern Virginia Community
    College *A*
Tidewater Community College *A*
Virginia Highlands Community
    College *A*
Wytheville Community College *A*

Washington

Green River Community College *A*

Wisconsin

Northeast Wisconsin Technical
College *A*
Western Wisconsin Technical
College *A*

Physician's assistant

Alabama

Gadsden State Community
College *A*
John C. Calhoun State Community
College *A*
Lawson State Community
College *C*
Shoals Community College *A*
University of Alabama in
Birmingham *B*

California

California State University:
Dominguez Hills *B*
Charles R. Drew University: College
of Allied Health *C,B*
City College of San Francisco *A*
Foothill College *C,A*

Colorado

University of Colorado Health
Sciences Center *M*

Connecticut

Housatonic Community College *A*
Quinnipiac College *M*

District of Columbia

George Washington University *B*
Howard University *C,B*

Florida

Daytona Beach Community
College *A*
Gulf Coast Community College *A*
University of Florida *B*

Georgia

DeKalb Technical Institute *C*
Emory University *M*
Medical College of Georgia *B*

Illinois

City Colleges of Chicago
Chicago City-Wide College *A*
Malcolm X College *A*
University of Health Sciences: The
Chicago Medical School *B*

Iowa

University of Iowa *B*
University of Osteopathic Medicine
and Health Sciences *B*

Kansas

Wichita State University *C,B*

Kentucky

Eastern Kentucky University *A*
University of Kentucky *B*

Maryland

Essex Community College *A*

Michigan

Andrews University *B*
Lansing Community College *A*
Western Michigan University *B*

Missouri

St. Louis University *B*

Nebraska

Concordia College *B*
Metropolitan Community College *A*
Union College *B*
University of Nebraska Medical
Center *B*

New Jersey

Rutgers—The State University of
New Jersey: Livingston
College *B*
University of Medicine and
Dentistry of New Jersey: School
of Health Related Professions *B*

New York

City University of New York: City
College *B*
Hudson Valley Community
College *A*
Long Island University: Brooklyn
Campus *B*
St. John's University *B*
State University of New York
Health Science Center at
Brooklyn *B*
Health Sciences Center at
Stony Brook *B*
Touro College *B*
Wagner College *B*

North Carolina

Catawba College *B*
Duke University *M*
Gardner-Webb College *B*
Greensboro College *B*
Lenoir-Rhyne College *B*
Wake Forest University *B*

Ohio

Cuyahoga Community College
Metropolitan Campus *A*
Western Campus *A*
Kettering College of Medical
Arts *A*

Oklahoma

University of Oklahoma
Health Sciences Center *B*
Norman *B*

Pennsylvania

Gannon University *B*
Hahnemann University School of
Health Sciences and Humanities
A,B
King's College *B*
Lehigh County Community
College *A*
St. Francis College *B*

Tennessee

Trevecca Nazarene College *B*

Texas

Austin Community College *A*
San Antonio College *A*
University of Texas
Medical Branch at
Galveston *B*
Southwestern Medical Center
at Dallas Southwestern
Allied Health Sciences
School *B*

West Virginia

Alderson-Broaddus College *B,M*

Wisconsin

University of Wisconsin: Madison *B*

Physics

Alabama

Alabama Agricultural and
Mechanical University *B,M,D*
Alabama Southern Community
College *A*
Athens State College *B*
Auburn University *B,M,D*
Birmingham-Southern College *B*
Chattahoochee Valley Community
College *A*
Jacksonville State University *B*
Samford University *B*
Shelton State Community
College *A*
Snead State Junior College *A*
Stillman College *B*
Talladega College *B*
Tuskegee University *B*
University of Alabama
Birmingham *B,M,D*
Huntsville *B,M,D*
Tuscaloosa *B,M,D,W*
University of North Alabama *B*
University of South Alabama *B*

Alaska

University of Alaska Fairbanks
B,M,D

Arizona

Arizona State University *B,M,D*
Arizona Western College *A*
Eastern Arizona College *A*
Glendale Community College *A*
Northern Arizona University *B*
Pima Community College *A*
University of Arizona *B,M,D*
Yavapai College *A*

Arkansas

Arkansas State University *B*
Arkansas Tech University *B*
Harding University *B*
Henderson State University *B*
Hendrix College *B*
Ouachita Baptist University *B*
University of Arkansas
Fayetteville *B,M,D*
Little Rock *B*
Monticello *B*
Pine Bluff *B*
University of Central Arkansas *B*
Westark Community College *A*

California

Allan Hancock College *A*
Azusa Pacific University *B*
Bakersfield College *A*
California Institute of Technology
B,D,W
California Lutheran University *B*
California Polytechnic State
University: San Luis Obispo *B*
California State Polytechnic
University: Pomona *B*

California State University
Bakersfield *B*
Chico *B*
Dominguez Hills *B*
Fresno *B,M*
Fullerton *B*
Hayward *B*
Long Beach *B,M*
Los Angeles *B,M*
Northridge *B,M*
Sacramento *B*
San Bernardino *B*
Stanislaus *B*
Cerritos Community College *A*
Chabot College *A*
Chaffey Community College *A*
Citrus College *A*
Claremont McKenna College *B*
College of the Desert *A*
Crafton Hills College *A*
De Anza College *A*
El Camino College *A*
Foothill College *A*
Grossmont Community College *A*
Harvey Mudd College *B*
Humboldt State University *B*
La Sierra University *B*
Los Angeles City College *A*
Los Angeles Valley College *A*
Loyola Marymount University *B*
Merced College *A*
MiraCosta College *A*
Modesto Junior College *A*
Moorpark College *A*
Napa Valley College *A*
Naval Postgraduate School *M,D*
Occidental College *B*
Ohlone College *A*
Orange Coast College *A*
Pacific Union College *B*
Pitzer College *B*
Point Loma Nazarene College *B*
Pomona College *B*
Saddleback College *A*
St. Mary's College of California *B*
San Diego City College *A*
San Diego Mesa College *A*
San Diego State University *B,M*
San Francisco State University *B,M*
San Joaquin Delta College *A*
San Jose City College *A*
San Jose State University *B,M*
Santa Barbara City College *A*
Santa Clara University *B*
Santa Monica College *A*
Scripps College *B*
Solano Community College *A*
Sonoma State University *B*
Southwestern College *A*
Stanford University *B,M,D*
University of California
Berkeley *B,M,D*
Davis *B,M,D*
Irvine *B,M,D*
Los Angeles *B,M,D*
Riverside *B,M,D*
San Diego *B,M,D*
Santa Barbara *B,M,D*
Santa Cruz *B,M,D*
University of La Verne *B*
University of the Pacific *B,M*
University of Redlands *B*
University of San Diego *B*
University of San Francisco *B*
University of Southern California
B,M,D
Ventura College *A*
West Hills Community College *A*
West Valley College *A*
Westmont College *B*
Whittier College *B*

Colorado

Adams State College *B*
Colorado College *B*
Colorado School of Mines
  B,M,D,W
Colorado State University *B,M,D*
Community College of Denver *A*
Fort Lewis College *B*
Mesa State College *A,B*
Metropolitan State College of
  Denver *B*
Pikes Peak Community College *A*
United States Air Force
  Academy *B*
University of Colorado
  Boulder *B,M,D*
  Colorado Springs *B*
  Denver *B*
University of Denver *B,M,D*
University of Northern Colorado *B*
University of Southern Colorado *B*
Western State College of
  Colorado *B*

Connecticut

Central Connecticut State
  University *B,M*
Connecticut College *B*
Fairfield University *B*
Mitchell College *A*
St. Joseph College *B,M*
Southern Connecticut State
  University *B*
Trinity College *B*
University of Bridgeport *B*
University of Connecticut *B,M,D*
University of Hartford *B*
University of New Haven *B*
Wesleyan University *B,M,D*
Yale University *B,M,D*

Delaware

Delaware State College *B,M*
University of Delaware *B,M,D*

District of Columbia

American University *B,M,D*
Catholic University of America
  B,M,D
Gallaudet University *B*
George Washington University
  B,M,D
Georgetown University *B*
Howard University *B,M,D*
University of the District of
  Columbia *B*

Florida

Brevard Community College *A*
Central Florida Community
  College *A*
Daytona Beach Community
  College *A*
Eckerd College *B*
Edison Community College *A*
Florida Agricultural and Mechanical
  University *B*
Florida Atlantic University *B,M,D*
Florida Institute of Technology
  B,M,D
Florida International University
  B,M
Florida Southern College *B*
Florida State University *B,M,D*
Gulf Coast Community College *A*
Indian River Community College *A*
Jacksonville University *B*
Miami-Dade Community College *A*
New College of the University of
  South Florida *B*
Okaloosa-Walton Community
  College *A*

Pensacola Junior College *A*
Rollins College *B*
Stetson University *B*
University of Central Florida *B,M,D*
University of Florida *B,M,D*
University of Miami *B,M,D*
University of South Florida *B,M*
University of West Florida *B*

Georgia

Agnes Scott College *B*
Andrew College *A*
Augusta College *B*
Bainbridge College *A*
Berry College *B*
Brewton-Parker College *A*
Clark Atlanta University *B,M*
Clayton State College *A*
Darton College *A*
DeKalb College *A*
Emory University *B*
Floyd College *A*
Fort Valley State College *B*
Gainesville College *A*
Georgia Institute of Technology
  B,M,D
Georgia Southern University *B*
Georgia Southwestern College *B*
Georgia State University *B,M,D*
Gordon College *A*
Macon College *A*
Mercer University *B*
Middle Georgia College *A*
Morehouse College *B*
Morris Brown College *B*
North Georgia College *B*
Oglethorpe University *B*
South Georgia College *A*
Southern College of Technology *B*
Spelman College *B*
University of Georgia *B,M,D*
Valdosta State College *B*
West Georgia College *B*
Young Harris College *A*

Hawaii

University of Hawaii
  Hilo *B*
  Manoa *B,M,D*

Idaho

Boise State University *B*
College of Southern Idaho *A*
Idaho State University *B,M*
North Idaho College *A*
Northwest Nazarene College *B*
Ricks College *A*
University of Idaho *B,M,D*

Illinois

Augustana College *B*
Aurora University *B*
Belleville Area College *A*
Bradley University *B*
Chicago State University *B*
City Colleges of Chicago
  Olive-Harvey College *A*
  Wright College *A*
Concordia University *B*
De Paul University *B,M*
Eastern Illinois University *B*
Elmhurst College *B*
Greenville College *B*
Highland Community College *A*
Illinois Benedictine College *B*
Illinois Central College *A*
Illinois College *B*
Illinois Institute of Technology
  B,M,D
Illinois State University *B*
Illinois Wesleyan University *B*
John A. Logan College *A*

Joliet Junior College *A*
Kishwaukee College *A*
Knox College *B*
Lake Forest College *B*
Lewis University *B*
Lincoln Land Community
  College *A*
Loyola University of Chicago *B*
MacMurray College *B*
Millikin University *B*
Monmouth College *B*
Morton College *A*
North Central College *B*
North Park College and Theological
  Seminary *B*
Northeastern Illinois University
  B,M
Northern Illinois University *B,M*
Northwestern University *B,M,D*
Principia College *B*
Rend Lake College *A*
Richland Community College *A*
Roosevelt University *B*
Southern Illinois University
  Carbondale *B,M*
  Edwardsville *B,M*
State Community College *A*
Triton College *A*
University of Chicago *B,M,D*
University of Illinois
  Chicago *B,M,D*
  Urbana-Champaign *B,M,D*
Waubonsee Community College *A*
Western Illinois University *B,M*
Wheaton College *B*
William Rainey Harper College *A*

Indiana

Anderson University *B*
Ball State University *B,M*
Butler University *B*
DePauw University *B*
Earlham College *B*
Franklin College *B*
Goshen College *B*
Hanover College *B*
Indiana State University *B,M*
Indiana University
  Bloomington *B,M,D*
  South Bend *B*
Indiana University—Purdue
  University
  Fort Wayne *B*
  Indianapolis *B,M*
Manchester College *B*
Martin University *B*
Purdue University
  Calumet *B*
  West Lafayette *A,B,M,D*
Rose-Hulman Institute of
  Technology *B*
Taylor University *B*
University of Evansville *B*
University of Indianapolis *B*
University of Notre Dame *B,M,D*
Valparaiso University *B*
Vincennes University *A*
Wabash College *B*

Iowa

Buena Vista College *B*
Central College *B*
Clinton Community College *A*
Coe College *B*
Cornell College *B*
Dordt College *B*
Drake University *B,M*
Grinnell College *B*
Iowa Lakes Community College *A*
Iowa State University *B,M,D*
Kirkwood Community College *A*
Loras College *B*

Luther College *B*
Maharishi International University
  A,B,M,D
Morningside College *B*
North Iowa Area Community
  College *A*
Northwestern College *B*
St. Ambrose University *B*
Scott Community College *A*
Teikyo Westmar University *B*
University of Dubuque *B*
University of Iowa *B,M,D*
University of Northern Iowa *B,M*
Wartburg College *B*

Kansas

Allen County Community
  College *A*
Baker University *B*
Benedictine College *B*
Bethel College *B*
Butler County Community
  College *A*
Cloud County Community
  College *A*
Coffeyville Community College *A*
Colby Community College *A*
Dodge City Community College *A*
Emporia State University *B*
Fort Hays State University *B*
Fort Scott Community College *A*
Hutchinson Community College *A*
Kansas State University *B,M,D*
Kansas Wesleyan University *B*
McPherson College *B*
MidAmerica Nazarene College *B*
Neosho County Community
  College *A*
Pittsburg State University *B,M*
Pratt Community College *A*
Southwestern College *B*
University of Kansas *B,M,D*
Washburn University of Topeka *B*
Wichita State University *B,M*

Kentucky

Berea College *B*
Centre College *B*
Cumberland College *B*
Eastern Kentucky University *B,M*
Georgetown College *B*
Kentucky Wesleyan College *B*
Morehead State University *B*
Murray State University *B,M*
Northern Kentucky University *B*
Thomas More College *A,B*
Transylvania University *B*
Union College *B*
University of Kentucky *B,M,D*
University of Louisville *B,M*
Western Kentucky University *B*

Louisiana

Centenary College of Louisiana *B*
Dillard University *B*
Grambling State University *B*
Louisiana State University
  Agricultural and Mechanical
    College *B,M,D*
  Shreveport *B*
Louisiana Tech University *B,M*
Loyola University *B*
McNeese State University *B*
Northeast Louisiana University *B*
Northwestern State University *B*
Southeastern Louisiana
  University *B*
Southern University at New
  Orleans *B*
Southern University and
  Agricultural and Mechanical
  College *B*

Tulane University *B,M,D*
University of New Orleans *B,M*
University of Southwestern
    Louisiana *B,M*
Xavier University of Louisiana *B*

Maine

Bates College *B*
Bowdoin College *B*
Colby College *B*
University of Maine *B,M,D*
University of Southern Maine *B*

Maryland

Charles County Community
    College *A*
College of Notre Dame of
    Maryland *B*
Columbia Union College *B*
Frostburg State University *B*
Hagerstown Junior College *A*
Harford Community College *A*
Howard Community College *A*
Johns Hopkins University *B,D*
Loyola College in Maryland *B*
Morgan State University *B*
St. Mary's College of Maryland *B*
Salisbury State University *B*
Towson State University *B*
United States Naval Academy *B*
University of Maryland
    Baltimore County *B,M*
    College Park *B,M,D*
Washington College *B*
Western Maryland College *B*

Massachusetts

Amherst College *B*
Boston College *B,M,D*
Boston University *B,M,D*
Brandeis University *B,D*
Bridgewater State College *B,M*
Clark University *B,M,D*
College of the Holy Cross *B*
Curry College *B*
Eastern Nazarene College *B*
Emmanuel College *B*
Gordon College *B*
Hampshire College *B*
Harvard and Radcliffe Colleges *B*
Harvard University *D*
Massachusetts Institute of
    Technology *B,M,D,W*
Merrimack College *B*
Mount Holyoke College *B*
North Adams State College *B*
Northeastern University *B,M,D*
Northern Essex Community
    College *A*
Roxbury Community College *A*
Smith College *B*
Suffolk University *B*
Tufts University *B,M,D*
University of Massachusetts
    Amherst *B,M,D*
    Boston *B*
    Dartmouth *B,M*
    Lowell *B,M,D*
Wellesley College *B*
Wheaton College *B*
Williams College *B*
Worcester Polytechnic Institute
    B,M,D
Worcester State College *B*

Michigan

Adrian College *A,B*
Albion College *B*
Alma College *B*
Andrews University *B,M*
Aquinas College *B*
Calvin College *B*

Central Michigan University *B,M*
Eastern Michigan University *B,M*
Grand Valley State University *B*
Hillsdale College *B*
Hope College *B*
Kalamazoo College *B*
Kellogg Community College *A*
Kirtland Community College *A*
Lansing Community College *A*
Lawrence Technological
    University *B*
Marygrove College *B*
Michigan State University *B,M,D*
Michigan Technological University
    B,M
Northern Michigan University
    A,B,M
Oakland University *B,M*
Saginaw Valley State University *B*
University of Michigan
    Ann Arbor *B,M*
    Dearborn *B*
    Flint *B*
Wayne State University *B,M,D*
Western Michigan University
    B,M,D

Minnesota

Augsburg College *B*
Bemidji State University *B*
Bethel College *B*
Carleton College *B*
College of St. Benedict *B*
College of St. Catherine: St.
    Catherine Campus *B*
Concordia College: Moorhead *B*
Gustavus Adolphus College *B*
Hamline University *B*
Macalester College *B*
Mankato State University *B,M*
Moorhead State University *B*
Northland Community College *A*
Northwestern College *A*
Rainy River Community College *A*
St. Cloud State University *B*
St. John's University *B*
St. Mary's College of Minnesota *B*
St. Olaf College *B*
Southwest State University *B*
University of Minnesota
    Duluth *B,M*
    Morris *B*
    Twin Cities *B,M,D*
University of St. Thomas *B*
Vermilion Community College *A*
Willmar Community College *A*
Winona State University *B*

Mississippi

Jackson State University *B*
Jones County Junior College *A*
Mary Holmes College *A*
Millsaps College *B*
Mississippi College *B*
Mississippi Gulf Coast Community
    College: Jefferson Davis
    Campus *A*
Mississippi State University *B,M*
Rust College *B*
Tougaloo College *B*
University of Mississippi *B,M,D*
University of Southern Mississippi
    B,M

Missouri

Central Methodist College *B*
Central Missouri State University *B*
Drury College *B*
East Central College *A*
Lincoln University *B*
Missouri Southern State College *B*

Moberly Area Community
    College *A*
Northeast Missouri State
    University *B*
Northwest Missouri State
    University *B*
Penn Valley Community College *A*
Rockhurst College *B*
St. Louis Community College
    Florissant Valley *A*
    Forest Park *A*
St. Louis University *B*
Southeast Missouri State
    University *B*
Southwest Missouri State
    University *B*
University of Missouri
    Columbia *B,M,D*
    Kansas City *B,M,D*
    Rolla *B,M,D*
    St. Louis *B,M,D*
Washington University *B,M,D*
Westminster College *B*
William Jewell College *B*
William Woods College *B*

Montana

Montana State University *B,M,D*
University of Montana *B,M*

Nebraska

Chadron State College *B*
Creighton University *B,M*
Hastings College *B*
Nebraska Wesleyan University *B*
Northeast Community College *A*
Southeast Community College:
    Beatrice Campus *A*
Union College *B*
University of Nebraska
    Kearney *B*
    Lincoln *B,M,D*
    Omaha *B*
York College *A*

Nevada

University of Nevada
    Las Vegas *B,M,D*
    Reno *B,M,D*

New Hampshire

Dartmouth College *B,M,D*
Keene State College *B*
University of New Hampshire
    B,M,D

New Jersey

Bergen Community College *A*
Brookdale Community College *A*
Burlington County College *A*
Drew University *B*
Georgian Court College *B*
Kean College of New Jersey *B*
Mercer County Community
    College *A*
Monmouth College *B*
Montclair State College *B*
Ocean County College *A*
Princeton University *B,D*
Rider College *B*

Rutgers—The State University of
    New Jersey
    Camden College of Arts and
        Sciences *B*
    Douglass College *B*
    Livingston College *B*
    New Brunswick *M,D*
    Newark College of Arts and
        Sciences *B*
    Rutgers College *B*
    University College Camden *B*
    University College New
        Brunswick *B*
St. Peter's College *B*
Seton Hall University *B*
Stevens Institute of Technology
    B,M,D
Stockton State College *B*
Thomas Edison State College *A,B*
Trenton State College *B*

New Mexico

Eastern New Mexico University *B*
New Mexico Institute of Mining
    and Technology *B,M,D*
New Mexico Junior College *A*
New Mexico State University
    B,M,D
University of New Mexico *B,M,D*

New York

Adelphi University *B,M,D*
Adirondack Community College *A*
Alfred University *B*
Bard College *B*
Barnard College *B*
Canisius College *B*
City University of New York
    Brooklyn College *B,M*
    City College *B,M,D*
    College of Staten Island *B*
    Graduate School and
        University Center *D*
    Hunter College *B,M*
    Kingsborough Community
        College *A*
    Lehman College *B*
    Queens College *B,M*
    York College *B*
Clarkson University *B,M,D*
Colgate University *B*
College of Mount St. Vincent *B*
College of New Rochelle *B*
Columbia University
    Columbia College *B*
    New York *M,D*
    School of General Studies *B*
Community College of the Finger
    Lakes *A*
Cornell University *B,M,D*
Fordham University *B,M*
Hamilton College *B*
Hartwick College *B*
Herkimer County Community
    College *A*
Hobart College *B*
Hofstra University *B*
Houghton College *B*
Iona College *B*
Ithaca College *B*
Jamestown Community College *A*
Jefferson Community College *A*
Le Moyne College *B*
Long Island University: C. W. Post
    Campus *B*
Manhattan College *B*
Manhattanville College *B*
Mohawk Valley Community
    College *A*
New York Institute of
    Technology *B*
New York University *B,M,D*

Polytechnic University *B,M,D*
Rensselaer Polytechnic Institute
B,M,D
Roberts Wesleyan College *B*
Rochester Institute of Technology
A,B
Rockefeller University *D*
St. Bonaventure University *B,M*
St. John Fisher College *B*
St. John's University *B*
St. Lawrence University *B*
Sarah Lawrence College *B*
Siena College *B*
Skidmore College *B*
State University of New York
Albany *B,M,D*
Binghamton *B,M*
Buffalo *B,M,D*
Purchase *B*
Stony Brook *B,M,D*
College of Agriculture and
Technology at Morrisville *A*
College at Brockport *B*
College at Buffalo *B,M*
College at Cortland *B*
College at Fredonia *B*
College at Geneseo *B*
College at New Paltz *B,M*
College at Oneonta *B*
College at Plattsburgh *B*
College at Potsdam *B*
College of Technology at
Delhi *A*
Oswego *B*
Syracuse University *B,M,D*
Union College *B*
United States Military Academy *B*
University of Rochester *B,M,D,W*
University of the State of New
York: Regents College *B*
Utica College of Syracuse
University *B*
Vassar College *B*
Wagner College *B*
William Smith College *B*
Yeshiva University *B*

North Carolina

Appalachian State University *B*
Brevard College *A*
Davidson College *B*
Duke University *B,D*
East Carolina University *B,M*
Elizabeth City State University *B*
Elon College *B*
Guilford College *B*
Johnson C. Smith University *B*
Lenoir-Rhyne College *B*
North Carolina Agricultural and
Technical State University *B*
North Carolina Central
University *B*
North Carolina State University
B,M,D
St. Augustine's College *B*
University of North Carolina
Asheville *B*
Chapel Hill *B,M,D*
Charlotte *B*
Greensboro *B,M*
Wilmington *B*
Wake Forest University *B,M,D*
Western Carolina University *B*

North Dakota

Minot State University *B*
North Dakota State University
B,M,D
University of North Dakota *B,M,D*

Ohio

Air Force Institute of Technology
M,D
Antioch College *B*
Ashland University *B*
Baldwin-Wallace College *B*
Bluffton College *B*
Bowling Green State University
Bowling Green *B,M*
Firelands College *A*
Case Western Reserve University
B,M,D
Central State University *B*
Cleveland State University *B,M*
College of Wooster *B*
Defiance College *B*
Denison University *B*
Heidelberg College *B*
Hiram College *B*
John Carroll University *B,M*
Kent State University *B,M,D*
Kenyon College *B*
Lakeland Community College *A*
Lorain County Community
College *A*
Marietta College *B*
Miami University: Oxford Campus
B,M
Mount Union College *B*
Muskingum College *B*
Oberlin College *B*
Ohio Northern University *B*
Ohio State University: Columbus
Campus *B,M,D*
Ohio University *B,M,D*
Ohio Wesleyan University *B*
Otterbein College *B*
Union Institute *B,D*
University of Akron *B,M*
University of Cincinnati *B,M,D*
University of Dayton *B,M*
University of Rio Grande *C*
University of Toledo *B,M,D*
Wittenberg University *B*
Wright State University *B,M*
Xavier University *B*
Youngstown State University *B*

Oklahoma

Cameron University *B*
East Central University *B*
Eastern Oklahoma State College *A*
Northeastern State University *B*
Northern Oklahoma College *A*
Northwestern Oklahoma State
University *B*
Oklahoma Baptist University *B*
Oklahoma City University *B*
Oklahoma State University *B,M,D*
Oral Roberts University *B*
Phillips University *B*
Redlands Community College *A*
Rogers State College *A*
Rose State College *A*
Southeastern Oklahoma State
University *B*
Southwestern Oklahoma State
University *B*
Tulsa Junior College *A*
University of Central Oklahoma
B,M
University of Oklahoma *B,M,D*
University of Science and Arts of
Oklahoma *B*
University of Tulsa *B*

Oregon

Central Oregon Community
College *A*
Eastern Oregon State College *B*
Lewis and Clark College *B*
Linfield College *B*

Northwest Christian College *B*
Oregon Graduate Institute *M,D*
Oregon State University *B,M,D*
Pacific University *B*
Portland Community College *A*
Portland State University *B,M*
Reed College *B*
Southern Oregon State College *B*
University of Oregon
Eugene *B,M,D*
Robert Donald Clark Honors
College *B*
University of Portland *B*
Willamette University *B*

Pennsylvania

Albright College *B*
Allegheny College *B*
Bloomsburg University of
Pennsylvania *B*
Bryn Mawr College *B,M,D*
Bucknell University *B*
California University of
Pennsylvania *B,M*
Carnegie Mellon University
B,M,D,W
Clarion University of
Pennsylvania *B*
Dickinson College *B*
Drexel University *B,M,D*
Duquesne University *B*
East Stroudsburg University of
Pennsylvania *B*
Edinboro University of
Pennsylvania *B*
Elizabethtown College *B*
Franklin and Marshall College *B*
Gannon University *B*
Geneva College *B*
Gettysburg College *B*
Grove City College *B*
Haverford College *B*
Immaculata College *A*
Indiana University of Pennsylvania
B,M
Juniata College *B*
King's College *B*
Kutztown University of
Pennsylvania *B*
La Salle University *B*
Lafayette College *B*
Lebanon Valley College of
Pennsylvania *B*
Lehigh University *B,M,D*
Lincoln University *B*
Lock Haven University of
Pennsylvania *B*
Lycoming College *B*
Mansfield University of
Pennsylvania *B*
Mercyhurst College *B*
Messiah College *B*
Millersville University of
Pennsylvania *B*
Moravian College *B*
Muhlenberg College *B*
Northeastern Christian Junior
College *A*
Penn State University Park Campus
B,M,D
St. Joseph's University *B*
St. Vincent College *B*
Seton Hill College *B*
Shippensburg University of
Pennsylvania *B*
Slippery Rock University of
Pennsylvania *B*
Susquehanna University *B*
Swarthmore College *B*
Temple University *B,M,D*
Thiel College *B*
University of Pennsylvania *B,M,D*

University of Pittsburgh *B,M,D*
University of Scranton *B*
Ursinus College *B*
Villanova University *B*
Washington and Jefferson College *B*
West Chester University of
Pennsylvania *B*
Westminster College *B*
Widener University *B*
Wilkes University *B,M*
York College of Pennsylvania *A*

Puerto Rico

Inter American University of Puerto
Rico: San German Campus *B*
Pontifical Catholic University of
Puerto Rico *B*
University of Puerto Rico
Mayaguez Campus *B,M*
Ponce Technological
University College *A*
Rio Piedras Campus *B,M*

Rhode Island

Brown University *B,M,D*
Rhode Island College *B*
University of Rhode Island *B,M,D*

South Carolina

Benedict College *B*
Bob Jones University *B*
Charleston Southern University *B*
The Citadel *B*
Clemson University *B,M,D*
College of Charleston *B*
Erskine College *B*
Francis Marion College *B*
Furman University *B*
North Greenville College *A*
Presbyterian College *B*
South Carolina State College *B*
University of South Carolina *B,M,D*
Wofford College *B*

South Dakota

Augustana College *B*
Dakota State University *B*
South Dakota School of Mines and
Technology *B,M*
South Dakota State University *B*
University of South Dakota *B*

Tennessee

Austin Peay State University *B*
Belmont University *B*
Carson-Newman College *B*
Christian Brothers University *B*
Cumberland University *A*
David Lipscomb University *B*
East Tennessee State University
B,M
Fisk University *B,M*
King College *B*
Knoxville College *B*
Lambuth University *B*
Memphis State University *B,M*
Middle Tennessee State
University *B*
Motlow State Community
College *A*
Rhodes College *B*
Southern College of Seventh-day
Adventists *B*
Tennessee State University *B*
Tennessee Technological
University *B*
Union University *B*
University of the South *B*
University of Tennessee
Chattanooga *B*
Knoxville *B,M,D*
Vanderbilt University *B,M,D*

Texas

Abilene Christian University *B*
Amarillo College *A*
Angelina College *A*
Angelo State University *B*
Austin College *B*
Austin Community College *A*
Baylor University *B,M,D*
Bee County College *A*
Blinn College *A*
Brazosport College *A*
Central Texas College *A*
Collin County Community College
District *A*
Del Mar College *A*
East Texas State University *B,M*
El Paso Community College *A*
Galveston College *A*
Hardin-Simmons University *B*
Houston Community College *A*
Howard College *A*
Jacksonville College *A*
Lamar University—Beaumont *B*
Lon Morris College *A*
Midland College *A*
North Harris Montgomery
Community College District *A*
Panola College *A*
Prairie View A&M University *B*
Rice University *B,M,D*
St. Mary's University *B*
Sam Houston State University *B,M*
Schreiner College *A*
South Plains College *A*
Southern Methodist University
B,M,D
Southwest Texas State University
B,M
Southwestern Adventist College *B*
Southwestern University *B*
Stephen F. Austin State University
B,M
Tarleton State University *B*
Texas A&I University *B*
Texas A&M University *B,M,D*
Texas Christian University *B,M,D*
Texas Southern University *B*
Texas Southmost College *A*
Texas Tech University *B,M,D*
Trinity University *B*
Trinity Valley Community
College *A*
University of Dallas *B*
University of Houston *B,M,D*
University of North Texas *B,M,D*
University of Texas
Arlington *B,M,D*
Austin *B,M,D*
Dallas *B,M,D*
El Paso *B,M*
Pan American *B*
San Antonio *B*
West Texas State University *B*
Western Texas College *A*
Wharton County Junior College *A*
Wiley College *B*

Utah

Brigham Young University *B,M,D*
University of Utah *B,M,D*
Utah State University *B,M,D*
Weber State University *B*
Westminster College of Salt Lake
City *B*

Vermont

Bennington College *B*
Marlboro College *B*
Middlebury College *B*
Norwich University *B*
St. Michael's College *B*
University of Vermont *B,M*

Virginia

Bridgewater College *B*
Christopher Newport College *B*
College of William and Mary
B,M,D
Emory and Henry College *B*
George Mason University *B*
Hampden-Sydney College *B*
Hampton University *B,M*
Hollins College *B*
James Madison University *B*
Longwood College *B*
Lynchburg College *B*
Mary Washington College *B*
Norfolk State University *B*
Old Dominion University *B,M,D*
Randolph-Macon College *B*
Randolph-Macon Woman's
College *B*
Roanoke College *B*
Sweet Briar College *B*
University of Richmond *B,W*
University of Virginia *B,M,D*
Virginia Commonwealth University
B,M,D
Virginia Military Institute *B*
Virginia Polytechnic Institute and
State University *B,M,D*
Virginia State University *B,M*
Virginia Wesleyan College *B*
Washington and Lee University *B*

Washington

Big Bend Community College *A*
Central Washington University *B*
Centralia College *A*
Eastern Washington University *B*
Everett Community College *A*
Evergreen State College *B*
Gonzaga University *B*
Lower Columbia College *A*
Pacific Lutheran University *B*
Seattle Central Community
College *A*
Seattle Pacific University *B*
Seattle University *B*
Skagit Valley College *A*
Spokane Community College *A*
Spokane Falls Community
College *A*
Tacoma Community College *A*
University of Puget Sound *B*
University of Washington *B,M,D*
Walla Walla College *B*
Washington State University *B,M,D*
Western Washington University *B*
Whitman College *B*
Whitworth College *B*

West Virginia

Bethany College *B*
Bluefield State College *B*
Marshall University *B,M*
Potomac State College of West
Virginia University *A*
West Virginia Institute of
Technology *B*
West Virginia State College *B*
West Virginia University *B,M,D*
West Virginia Wesleyan College *B*
Wheeling Jesuit College *B*

Wisconsin

Beloit College *B*
Carroll College *B*
Carthage College *B*
Lawrence University *B*
Marquette University *B,M*
Ripon College *B*
St. Norbert College *B*

University of Wisconsin
Eau Claire *B*
Green Bay *B*
La Crosse *B*
Madison *B,M,D*
Milwaukee *B,M,D*
Oshkosh *B,M*
Parkside *B*
Platteville *B*
River Falls *B*
Stevens Point *B*
Superior *B*
Whitewater *B*

Wyoming

Casper College *A*
Eastern Wyoming College *A*
Northwest College *A*
University of Wyoming *B,M,D*
Western Wyoming Community
College *A*

American Samoa, Caroline Islands, Guam, Marianas, Virgin Islands

University of the Virgin Islands *A*

Canada

McGill University *B,M,D*

Arab Republic of Egypt

American University in Cairo *B*

Physiological psychology

California

San Francisco State University *M*

Connecticut

Wesleyan University *B*

District of Columbia

Catholic University of America
M,D

Florida

New College of the University of
South Florida *B*
University of Miami *D*

Illinois

University of Illinois at Urbana-
Champaign *B,M,D*

Indiana

Indiana University Bloomington
M,D

Iowa

University of Iowa *D*

Kansas

Kansas State University *M,D*

Massachusetts

Hampshire College *B*
Massachusetts Institute of
Technology *M,D*

New Jersey

Rutgers—The State University of
New Jersey *M,D*

New York

New York University *D*
Sarah Lawrence College *B*

Ohio

Ohio State University: Columbus
Campus *M,D*

Pennsylvania

Bucknell University *B*
Lehigh University *B,M,D*
University of Pennsylvania *B,D*

Rhode Island

Brown University *B,M,D*

Vermont

Marlboro College *B*

Washington

University of Washington *D*

Canada

McGill University *B,M,D*

Physiology, human and animal

Alabama

Auburn University *M,D*
University of Alabama in
Birmingham *M,D*
University of South Alabama *D*

Arizona

University of Arizona *M,D*

Arkansas

University of Arkansas for Medical
Sciences *M,D*

California

California State University
Fresno *B*
Long Beach *B*
Sacramento *B*
Chabot College *A*
Modesto Junior College *A*
San Francisco State University *B,M*
Stanford University *D*
University of California
Berkeley *B,M,D*
Davis *B,M,D*
Los Angeles *M,D*
San Diego *B,M,D*
San Francisco *D*
Santa Barbara *B*
University of Southern California
M,D

Colorado

Colorado State University *M,D*
University of Colorado Health
Sciences Center *D*

Connecticut

University of Connecticut *B,M,D*
Yale University *M,D*

Delaware

University of Delaware *M,D*

District of Columbia

George Washington University *M,D*
Georgetown University *M,D*
Howard University *M,D*

Florida

New College of the University of
South Florida *B*
University of Florida *M,D*
University of Miami *D*

Georgia
Emory University *M,D*
Medical College of Georgia *M,D*
University of Georgia *M,D*

Hawaii
University of Hawaii at Manoa *M,D*

Illinois
Loyola University of Chicago *M,D*
Northwestern University *B,M,D*
Rush University *D*
Southern Illinois University at
    Carbondale *B,M,D*
University of Chicago *B,M,D*
University of Health Sciences: The
    Chicago Medical School *M,D,W*
University of Illinois
    Chicago *M,D*
    Urbana-Champaign *B,M,D*

Indiana
Ball State University *M*
Indiana University Bloomington
    M,D
Indiana University—Purdue
    University at Indianapolis
    M,D,W
Purdue University *B,M,D*

Iowa
Iowa State University *M,D*
Maharishi International University
    M,D
University of Iowa *M,D*

Kansas
Kansas State University *B,M,D*
University of Kansas
    Lawrence *M,D*
    Medical Center *M,D*

Kentucky
University of Kentucky *M,D*
University of Louisville *M,D*

Louisiana
Louisiana State University
    Agricultural and Mechanical
        College *M,D*
    Medical Center *M,D*
Northeast Louisiana University *B*
Tulane University *M,D*

Maryland
Howard Community College *A*
Uniformed Services University of
    the Health Sciences *D*
University of Maryland: Baltimore
    M,D

Massachusetts
Boston University *B,D*
Hampshire College *B*
Harvard University *D*
Massachusetts Institute of
    Technology *D,W*
Tufts University *M,D*
Worcester Polytechnic Institute *B*

Michigan
Eastern Michigan University *B,M*
Michigan State University *B,M,D*
Northern Michigan University *B*
University of Michigan *M,D*
Wayne State University *M,D*

Minnesota
University of Minnesota
    Duluth *M*
    Twin Cities *B,M,D*

Mississippi
Mississippi State University *M,D*
University of Mississippi Medical
    Center *M,D*

Missouri
St. Louis University *M,D*
University of Missouri: Columbia
    M,D
Washington University *D*

Montana
Miles Community College *A*

Nebraska
Creighton University *M,D*
University of Nebraska Medical
    Center *M,D*

New Hampshire
Dartmouth College *D*

New Jersey
Rutgers—The State University of
    New Jersey
    Camden College of Arts and
        Sciences *B*
    Cook College *B*
    Douglass College *B*
    Livingston College *B*
    New Brunswick *M,D*
    Newark College of Arts and
        Sciences *B*
    Rutgers College *B*
    University College New
        Brunswick *B*

New Mexico
New Mexico State University *B*

New York
Albany Medical College *M,D*
Columbia University *M,D*
Cornell University *B,M,D*
Long Island University: Brooklyn
    Campus *M*
New York University *M,D*
Rockefeller University *D*
State University of New York
    Buffalo *M,D*
    College of Environmental
        Science and Forestry *B,M,D*
    Health Science Center at
        Brooklyn *D*
    Health Science Center at
        Syracuse *M,D*
University of Rochester *M,D,W*
Yeshiva University *M,D*

North Carolina
East Carolina University *D*
North Carolina State University
    M,D
University of North Carolina at
    Chapel Hill *M,D*
Vance-Granville Community
    College *A*
Wake Forest University *M,D*

North Dakota
University of North Dakota *M,D*

Ohio
Case Western Reserve University *D*
Kent State University *M,D*
Ohio State University: Columbus
    Campus *M,D*
Ohio University *M,D*
University of Akron *B*
University of Cincinnati *M,D*
Wright State University *M*

Oklahoma
Oklahoma State University *B,M,D*
University of Oklahoma
    Health Sciences Center *M,D*
    Norman *M,D*

Pennsylvania
Drexel University *M,D*
Hahnemann University School of
    Health Sciences and Humanities
    M,D
Lehigh University *M,D*
Medical College of Pennsylvania
    M,D
Penn State
    Milton S. Hershey Medical
        Center *M,D*
    University Park Campus *M,D*
Temple University *M,D*
University of Pennsylvania *M,D*
University of Pittsburgh *D*

Puerto Rico
University of Puerto Rico: Medical
    Sciences Campus *M,D*

Rhode Island
Brown University *M,D*

South Carolina
Clemson University *M,D,W*

South Dakota
University of South Dakota *M,D*

Tennessee
East Tennessee State University
    M,D
Meharry Medical College *D*
Motlow State Community
    College *A*
University of Tennessee: Memphis
    M,D
Vanderbilt University *D*

Texas
Baylor College of Dentistry *M*
Baylor University *M*
Southwest Texas State University *B*
Texas A&M University *M,D*
Texas Tech University *M,D*
Texas Tech University Health
    Science Center *M,D,W*
University of Texas
    Health Science Center at
        Houston *M,D,W*
    Health Science Center at San
        Antonio *M,D*
    Southwestern Medical Center
        at Dallas Southwestern
        Allied Health Sciences
        School *M,D*

Utah
University of Utah *D*

Vermont
Marlboro College *B*
University of Vermont *M,D*

Virginia
Averett College *B*
University of Virginia *M,D*
Virginia Commonwealth University
    M,D

Washington
Central Washington University *B*
University of Washington *M,D*
Washington State University *D*

West Virginia
West Virginia University *M,D*

Wisconsin
Marquette University *M,D*
Medical College of Wisconsin *M,D*
University of Wisconsin
    Green Bay *B*
    Madison *M,D*

Canada
McGill University *B,M,D*

Planetary science

Arizona
University of Arizona *M,D*

California
California Institute of Technology *B*

Colorado
University of Colorado at Boulder
    M,D

Florida
Florida Institute of Technology
    B,M,D

Maryland
Johns Hopkins University *B,M,D*

Massachusetts
Boston University *B*
Harvard University *D*
Massachusetts Institute of
    Technology *B,M,D*

New York
Columbia University *M,D*

Pennsylvania
West Chester University of
    Pennsylvania *B*

Plant genetics

Arizona
University of Arizona *M,D*

California
University of California
    Berkeley *B,M,D*
    Riverside *D*

Florida
University of Florida *M,D*

Georgia
Oxford College of Emory
    University *A*

Illinois
University of Chicago *B,M,D*

Indiana
Purdue University *B,M,D*

Massachusetts
Hampshire College *B*
Harvard University *D*

Minnesota
University of Minnesota: Twin
    Cities *B,M,D*

New Hampshire
University of New Hampshire *M,D*

New York
Cornell University *B,M,D*
Rockefeller University *D*
State University of New York
    College of Environmental Science
    and Forestry *B,M,D*

Utah
Brigham Young University *M,D*

West Virginia
West Virginia University *M,D*

Plant pathology

Alabama
Auburn University *M,D*

Arizona
University of Arizona *B,M,D*

Arkansas
University of Arkansas *M,D*

California
University of California
    Berkeley *B,M,D*
    Davis *M,D*
    Riverside *M,D*

Colorado
Colorado State University *M,D*

Delaware
University of Delaware *B*

Florida
University of Florida *B,M,D*

Georgia
University of Georgia *B,M,D*

Hawaii
University of Hawaii at Manoa *M,D*

Illinois
University of Illinois at Urbana-
    Champaign *M,D*

Indiana
Purdue University *B,M,D*

Iowa
Iowa State University *B,M,D*

Kansas
Kansas State University *M,D*

Kentucky
University of Kentucky *B,M,D*

Louisiana
Louisiana State University and
    Agricultural and Mechanical
    College *M,D*

Maine
University of Maine *B,M*

Massachusetts
University of Massachusetts at
    Amherst *B,M,D*

Michigan
Michigan State University *M,D*

Minnesota
University of Minnesota: Twin
    Cities *D*

Mississippi
Mississippi State University *M,D*

Missouri
University of Missouri: Columbia *M*
Washington University *D*

Montana
Montana State University *M,D*

New Jersey
Rutgers—The State University of
    New Jersey *M,D*

New Mexico
New Mexico State University *M*

New York
Cornell University *B,M,D*
State University of New York
    College of Environmental Science
    and Forestry *B,M,D*

North Carolina
North Carolina State University
    M,D

North Dakota
North Dakota State University
    B,M,D

Ohio
Ohio State University: Columbus
    Campus *B,M,D*
Ohio University *M,D*

Oklahoma
Oklahoma State University *M,D*
Tulsa Junior College *A*

Oregon
Oregon State University *M,D*

Pennsylvania
Penn State University Park Campus
    M,D

South Carolina
Clemson University *B,M,D*

South Dakota
South Dakota State University *M*

Tennessee
University of Tennessee:
    Knoxville *M*

Texas
Texas A&M University *M,D*

Vermont
Marlboro College *B*

Virginia
Virginia Polytechnic Institute and
    State University *M,D*

Washington
Washington State University *M,D*

West Virginia
West Virginia University *M,D*

Wisconsin
University of Wisconsin: Madison
    B,M,D

Wyoming
University of Wyoming *M*

Canada
McGill University *B,M,D*

Plant pharmacology

Indiana
Vincennes University *A*

Massachusetts
Harvard University *D*
Massachusetts College of Pharmacy
    and Allied Health Sciences *M,D*

Minnesota
University of Minnesota
    Duluth *M*
    Twin Cities *M,D*

Mississippi
University of Mississippi *D*

Missouri
Washington University *D*

Wisconsin
University of Wisconsin: Madison
    M,D

Plant physiology

California
California State University:
    Sacramento *B*
University of California
    Berkeley *M,D*
    Davis *M,D*
    Riverside *D*

Florida
Florida Agricultural and Mechanical
    University *M*
Florida Institute of Technology *D*
University of Florida *M,D*

Georgia
University of Georgia *B,M,D*

Hawaii
University of Hawaii at Manoa *M,D*

Illinois
University of Chicago *B,M,D*

Indiana
Purdue University *M,D*

Kentucky
University of Kentucky *M,D*

Louisiana
Louisiana State University and
    Agricultural and Mechanical
    College *B*

Massachusetts
Hampshire College *B*

Minnesota
University of Minnesota: Twin
    Cities *M,D*

New Hampshire
University of New Hampshire
    B,M,D

New Jersey
Rutgers—The State University of
    New Jersey *M,D*

New York
Cornell University *M,D*
State University of New York
    Albany *D*
    College of Environmental
    Science and Forestry *B,M,D*

Ohio
Ohio State University: Columbus
    Campus *M,D*
Ohio University *M,D*

Oregon
Oregon State University *M,D*

Pennsylvania
Drexel University *M,D*
Penn State University Park Campus
    M,D

South Carolina
Clemson University *D*

Texas
Texas A&M University *M,D*

Vermont
Marlboro College *B*

Virginia
Virginia Polytechnic Institute and
    State University *M,D*

Washington
Evergreen State College *B*
Washington State University *M,D*

Wisconsin
University of Wisconsin: Madison
    M,D

Plant protection

Alabama
Auburn University *B,M*

Arkansas
University of Arkansas *B*

California
California State Polytechnic
    University: Pomona *B*
San Joaquin Delta College *A*
University of California
    Davis *M*
    Riverside *M*
Ventura College *A*

Florida
Broward Community College *A*
Palm Beach Community College *A*

Georgia
University of Georgia *B,M*

Hawaii
University of Hawaii at Hilo *B*

Idaho
University of Idaho *B*

Illinois

Southern Illinois University at
Carbondale *B,M*

Indiana

Purdue University *B*

Kansas

Kansas State University *B,M*

Massachusetts

University of Massachusetts at
Amherst *B*

Mississippi

Mississippi State University *B,M*

Missouri

University of Missouri: Columbia
M,D

Montana

Montana State University *B*

Nebraska

University of Nebraska—Lincoln *B*

Nevada

University of Nevada: Reno *M*

New Jersey

County College of Morris *A*

New Mexico

New Mexico State University *B*

New York

Cornell University *B,M*
State University of New York
College of Environmental Science
and Forestry *B,M,D*

North Carolina

North Carolina State University *B*

Oregon

Oregon State University *B*

Puerto Rico

University of Puerto Rico
La Montana Regional
College *A*
Mayaguez Campus *B,M*

South Carolina

Clemson University *M*

South Dakota

South Dakota State University *M*

Texas

Texas A&M University *M*
Texas Tech University *B,M*

Washington

Spokane Community College *A*

Canada

McGill University *B,M,D*

Mexico

Sistema Instituto Tecnologico y de
Estudios Superiores de
Monterrey *M,D*

Plant sciences

Alabama

Auburn University *M,D*
Tuskegee University *B,M*

Arizona

Arizona Western College *A*
University of Arizona *B*

Arkansas

Arkansas State University *B*
University of Arkansas *D*

California

California Polytechnic State
University: San Luis Obispo *B*
California State Polytechnic
University: Pomona *B*
College of the Desert *A*
College of the Redwoods *C,A*
College of the Sequoias *C*
Cosumnes River College *C,A*
Mendocino College *C,A*
Modesto Junior College *A*
Napa Valley College *C,A*
San Joaquin Delta College *A*
University of California
Davis *B*
Riverside *M*
Santa Cruz *B,D*
Ventura College *A*
Yuba College *C*

Connecticut

University of Connecticut *M,D*

Delaware

Delaware State College *B*
University of Delaware *B,M,D*

Florida

University of Florida *B*

Georgia

Abraham Baldwin Agricultural
College *A*
University of Georgia *B,M,D*

Idaho

Idaho State University *B*
Ricks College *C,A*
University of Idaho *M,D*

Illinois

Southern Illinois University at
Carbondale *B,M*
University of Illinois at Urbana-
Champaign *M,D*

Indiana

Purdue University *C,B,M,D*

Iowa

Dordt College *B*
Iowa State University *B,M,D*

Kansas

Coffeyville Community College *A*
Kansas State University *B*

Louisiana

Southeastern Louisiana
University *B*
Southern University and
Agricultural and Mechanical
College *B*

Maine

University of Maine
Orono *B,M*
Presque Isle *B*

Maryland

Howard Community College *C*

Massachusetts

Hampshire College *B*
Springfield Technical Community
College *A*
University of Massachusetts at
Amherst *B,M,D*

Minnesota

University of Minnesota
Duluth *M*
Twin Cities *B*
Willmar Community College *A*

Mississippi

Mississippi State University *B,M,D*

Missouri

University of Missouri: Columbia *M*

Montana

Montana State University *B,D*

Nebraska

University of Nebraska—Lincoln *B*

Nevada

University of Nevada: Reno *M*

New Hampshire

University of New Hampshire
B,M,D

New Jersey

Mercer County Community
College *A*
Ocean County College *C*
Rutgers—The State University of
New Jersey
Cook College *B*
New Brunswick *M,D*

New Mexico

New Mexico State University *B,M*

New York

Cornell University *B,M,D*
State University of New York
College of Agriculture and
Technology at Cobleskill *A*
College of Agriculture and
Technology at Morrisville *A*
College of Environmental
Science and Forestry *B,M,D*
College of Technology at
Delhi *A*

North Carolina

North Carolina State University
M,D

North Dakota

North Dakota State University
B,M,D

Ohio

Cuyahoga Community College:
Metropolitan Campus *A*

Oklahoma

Oklahoma Panhandle State
University *B*

Pennsylvania

Delaware Valley College *B*
Penn State University Park
Campus *B*

Puerto Rico

University of Puerto Rico:
Mayaguez Campus *M*

Rhode Island

University of Rhode Island *B,M,D*

South Carolina

Technical College of the
Lowcountry *C*

South Dakota

South Dakota State University *B*

Tennessee

Hiwassee College *A*
Middle Tennessee State
University *B*
Tennessee Technological
University *B*
University of Tennessee
Knoxville *B,M,D*
Martin *B*

Texas

Cisco Junior College *A*
Southwest Texas State University *B*
Tarleton State University *B*
Texas A&I University *B,M*
Texas A&M University *B,M,D*
West Texas State University *B,M*

Utah

Utah State University *B,M,D*

Vermont

University of Vermont *B,M,D*

Virginia

Virginia Polytechnic Institute and
State University *A,M,D*

Washington

Spokane Community College *A*

West Virginia

West Virginia University *B*

Wisconsin

University of Wisconsin: River
Falls *B*

Wyoming

Sheridan College *A*
University of Wyoming *B*

Canada

McGill University *B,M,D*

Mexico

Sistema Instituto Tecnologico y de
Estudios Superiores de
Monterrey *M*

Plastic technology

California

Cerritos Community College *C,A*
Los Angeles Trade and Technical
College *A*
San Diego City College *C,A*

Connecticut

Waterbury State Technical
College *C*

Delaware

Delaware Technical and
Community College: Stanton/
Wilmington Campus *A*

Hawaii

University of Hawaii: Honolulu
Community College *C,A*

Illinois

College of DuPage *C,A*
Elgin Community College *C*

Indiana

Indiana Vocational Technical
College
Northcentral *C,A*
Southwest *A*
Wabash Valley *A*
Vincennes University *A*

Kansas

Pittsburg State University *B*

Massachusetts

Massachusetts Bay Community
College *C,A*

Michigan

Eastern Michigan University *B*
Ferris State University *A,B*
Grand Rapids Community
College *A*
Kalamazoo Valley Community
College *C,A*
Lansing Community College *C,A*
Macomb Community College *C,A*
St. Clair County Community
College *A*
University of Detroit Mercy *B*

Nebraska

Central Community College *A*
Southeast Community College:
Milford Campus *A*

New Jersey

Cumberland County College *C,A*

Ohio

Kent State University: Ashtabula
Regional Campus *A*
Northwest Technical College *A*
Shawnee State University *A,B*
Terra Technical College *C,A*
University of Toledo *A*

Pennsylvania

Delaware County Community
College *A*
Penn State Erie Behrend College *B*
Pennsylvania College of
Technology *A*

Washington

Clark College *A*
Western Washington University *B*

West Virginia

Marshall University *A*

Plumbing/pipefitting/steamfitting

Alabama

Bessemer State Technical College *C*
Gadsden State Community
College *C*
Lawson State Community
College *C*

Arizona

Rio Salado Community College *A*

Arkansas

Phillips County Community
College *C*

California

Allan Hancock College *C*
Bakersfield College *A*
Los Angeles Trade and Technical
College *C,A*
Modesto Junior College *A*
Orange Coast College *C,A*
San Diego City College *C,A*
San Jose City College *A*
Santa Rosa Junior College *C,A*
Ventura College *A*

Colorado

Red Rocks Community College *C*

Florida

North Florida Junior College *C*
Palm Beach Community College *C*

Georgia

Gainesville College *A*

Hawaii

University of Hawaii: Honolulu
Community College *A*

Illinois

Belleville Area College *C,A*
Black Hawk College *C*
Prairie State College *C*
Triton College *C,A*

Iowa

Northwest Iowa Technical
College *C*

Kansas

Neosho County Community College
C,A

Kentucky

Eastern Kentucky University *B*

Maine

Southern Maine Technical
College *A*

Maryland

Cecil Community College *C,A*

Michigan

Kellogg Community College *C*
Lansing Community College *A*
Macomb Community College *C,A*

Minnesota

St. Paul Technical College *C*

Mississippi

Mississippi Gulf Coast Community
College: Jefferson Davis
Campus *C*

Nebraska

Nebraska Indian Community
College *A*
Southeast Community College:
Milford Campus *A*

Nevada

Truckee Meadows Community
College *C,A*

New Mexico

Albuquerque Technical-Vocational
Institute *C*
Northern New Mexico Community
College *C,A*

New York

State University of New York
College of Technology at
Alfred *A*
College of Technology at
Canton *C*
College of Technology at Delhi
C,A

North Carolina

Blue Ridge Community College *C*
Fayetteville Technical Community
College *C*
Forsyth Technical Community
College *A*
Southwestern Community
College *C*
Tri-County Community College *C*

North Dakota

North Dakota State College of
Science *C*

Oklahoma

Oklahoma State University
Technical Branch: Okmulgee *A*

Pennsylvania

Pennsylvania College of
Technology *C*

Rhode Island

New England Institute of
Technology *A*

South Carolina

Denmark Technical College *C*

Tennessee

Chattanooga State Technical
Community College *C*

Texas

Brazosport College *C,A*
St. Philip's College *A*

Virginia

Tidewater Community College *C*

Washington

Lower Columbia College *A*

Wisconsin

Chippewa Valley Technical
College *C*

**American Samoa, Caroline
Islands, Guam, Marianas,
Virgin Islands**

Guam Community College *C*

Podiatry or podiatric medicine

Tennessee

Union University *B*

Wisconsin

University of Wisconsin: Oshkosh *B*

Podiatry or podiatric medicine (D.P.M.)

California

California College of Podiatric
Medicine *F*

Florida

Barry University *F*

Iowa

University of Osteopathic Medicine
and Health Sciences *F*

Utah

Brigham Young University *F*

Political science and government

Alabama

Alabama Agricultural and
Mechanical University *B*
Alabama State University *B*
Athens State College *B*
Auburn University
Auburn *B,M*
Montgomery *M*
Birmingham-Southern College *B*
Jacksonville State University *B,M*
Mobile College *B*
Spring Hill College *B*
Troy State University
Montgomery *B*
Troy *B*
Tuskegee University *B*
University of Alabama
Birmingham *B*
Huntsville *B*
Tuscaloosa *B,M,D,W*
University of Montevallo *B*
University of North Alabama *B*
University of South Alabama *B*

Alaska

University of Alaska
Anchorage *B*
Fairbanks *B*
Southeast *B*

Arizona

Arizona State University *B,M,D*
Cochise College *A*
Eastern Arizona College *A*
Glendale Community College *A*
Northern Arizona University *B,M,D*
Prescott College *B*
University of Arizona *B,M,D*

Arkansas

Arkansas State University *B,M*
Arkansas Tech University *B*
Harding University *B*
Henderson State University *B*
Hendrix College *B*

Ouachita Baptist University *B*
Southern Arkansas University *B*
University of Arkansas
    Fayetteville *B,M*
    Little Rock *B*
    Monticello *B*
    Pine Bluff *B*
University of Central Arkansas *B*
University of the Ozarks *B*
Westark Community College *A*

California

Azusa Pacific University *B*
Bakersfield College *B*
California Baptist College *B*
California Lutheran University *B*
California Polytechnic State
    University: San Luis Obispo *B*
California State Polytechnic
    University: Pomona *B*
California State University
    Bakersfield *B*
    Chico *B,M*
    Dominguez Hills *B*
    Fresno *B,M*
    Fullerton *B,M*
    Hayward *B*
    Long Beach *B,M*
    Los Angeles *B,M*
    Northridge *B*
    Sacramento *B,M*
    San Bernardino *B*
    San Marcos *B*
    Stanislaus *B*
Cerritos Community College *A*
Chabot College *A*
Chaffey Community College *A*
Chapman University *B*
Claremont McKenna College *B*
College of the Desert *A*
College of Notre Dame *B*
Crafton Hills College *A*
De Anza College *A*
Dominican College of San Rafael *B*
El Camino College *A*
Feather River College *A*
Foothill College *A*
Fresno City College *A*
Golden Gate University *B*
Grossmont Community College *A*
Humboldt State University *B*
Irvine Valley College *A*
La Sierra University *B*
Los Angeles Valley College *A*
Loyola Marymount University *B*
Master's College *B*
Merced College *A*
Mills College *B*
Monterey Institute of International
    Studies *B*
Mount St. Mary's College *B*
Napa Valley College *A*
Occidental College *B*
Ohlone College *A*
Orange Coast College *A*
Pacific Union College *B*
Pepperdine University *B*
Pitzer College *B*
Point Loma Nazarene College *B*
Pomona College *B*
Saddleback College *A*
St. Mary's College of California *B*
San Diego City College *A*
San Diego State University *B,M*
San Francisco State University *B,M*
San Jose State University *B,M*
Santa Barbara City College *A*
Santa Clara University *B*
Santa Monica College *A*
Santa Rosa Junior College *A*
Scripps College *B*
Sonoma State University *B*

Southern California College *B*
Southwestern College *A*
Stanford University *B,M,D*
University of California
    Berkeley *B,M,D*
    Davis *B,M,D*
    Irvine *B,D*
    Los Angeles *B,M,D*
    Riverside *B,M,D*
    San Diego *B,M,D*
    Santa Barbara *B,M,D*
    Santa Cruz *B*
University of Judaism *B*
University of La Verne *B*
University of the Pacific *B*
University of Redlands *B*
University of San Diego *B*
University of San Francisco *B*
University of Southern California
    B,M,D
Ventura College *A*
Westmont College *B*
Whittier College *B,M*

Colorado

Adams State College *B*
Colorado College *B*
Colorado State University *B,M,D*
Fort Lewis College *B*
Mesa State College *A,B*
Metropolitan State College of
    Denver *B*
Pikes Peak Community College *A*
Regis College of Regis University *B*
United States Air Force
    Academy *B*
University of Colorado
    Boulder *B,M,D*
    Colorado Springs *B*
    Denver *B,M*
University of Denver *B*
University of Northern Colorado *B*
University of Southern Colorado *B*
Western State College of
    Colorado *B*

Connecticut

Albertus Magnus College *B*
Central Connecticut State
    University *B*
Connecticut College *B*
Eastern Connecticut State
    University *B*
Fairfield University *B*
Mitchell College *A*
Sacred Heart University *A,B*
St. Joseph College *B*
Southern Connecticut State
    University *B,M*
Trinity College *B*
United States Coast Guard
    Academy *B*
University of Bridgeport *B*
University of Connecticut *B,M,D*
University of Hartford *B*
University of New Haven *B*
Wesleyan University *B*
Western Connecticut State
    University *B*
Yale University *B,M,D*

Delaware

Delaware State College *B*
University of Delaware *B,M,D*
Wesley College *B*

District of Columbia

American University *B,M,D*
Catholic University of America
    B,M,D
Gallaudet University *B*

George Washington University
    B,M,D
Georgetown University *B,D*
Howard University *B,M,D*
Mount Vernon College *B*
Trinity College *B*
University of the District of
    Columbia *B*

Florida

Barry University *B*
Bethune-Cookman College *B*
Eckerd College *B*
Florida Agricultural and Mechanical
    University *B*
Florida Atlantic University *B,M*
Florida International University *B*
Florida Southern College *B*
Florida State University *B,M,D*
Gulf Coast Community College *A*
Jacksonville University *B*
Lynn University *B*
Miami-Dade Community College *A*
New College of the University of
    South Florida *B*
Palm Beach Atlantic College *B*
Palm Beach Community College *A*
Rollins College *B*
St. Leo College *B*
St. Thomas University *B*
Stetson University *B*
University of Central Florida *B,M*
University of Florida *B,M,D*
University of Miami *B,M*
University of North Florida *B,M*
University of South Florida *B,M*
University of Tampa *A,B*
University of West Florida *B,M*

Georgia

Agnes Scott College *B*
Albany State College *B*
Armstrong State College *B*
Atlanta Metropolitan College *A*
Augusta College *B*
Bainbridge College *A*
Berry College *B*
Brenau Women's College *B*
Brewton-Parker College *A*
Clark Atlanta University *B*
Clayton State College *A*
Columbus College *B*
Darton College *A*
DeKalb College *A*
Emory University *B,M,D*
Floyd College *A*
Fort Valley State College *B*
Gainesville College *A*
Georgia College *B,M*
Georgia Southern University *B,M*
Georgia Southwestern College *B*
Georgia State University *B,M,D*
Gordon College *A*
Kennesaw State College *B*
LaGrange College *B*
Macon College *A*
Mercer University *B*
Middle Georgia College *A*
Morehouse College *B*
Morris Brown College *B*
North Georgia College *B*
Oglethorpe University *B*
Savannah State College *B*
Shorter College *B*
South Georgia College *A*
Spelman College *B*
Thomas College *A*
University of Georgia *B,M,D*
Valdosta State College *B*
Waycross College *A*
Wesleyan College *B*
West Georgia College *B*

Young Harris College *A*

Hawaii

Brigham Young University-
    Hawaii *B*
Chaminade University of
    Honolulu *B*
Hawaii Pacific University *B*
University of Hawaii
    Hilo *B*
    Manoa *B,M,D*
    West Oahu *B*

Idaho

Albertson College *B*
Boise State University *B*
College of Southern Idaho *A*
Idaho State University *B,M,D*
North Idaho College *A*
Northwest Nazarene College *B*
Ricks College *A*
University of Idaho *B,M,D*

Illinois

Augustana College *B*
Aurora University *B*
Barat College *B*
Black Hawk College *A*
Blackburn College *B*
Bradley University *B*
Chicago State University *B*
College of St. Francis *B*
Concordia University *B*
De Paul University *B*
Eastern Illinois University *B,M*
Elmhurst College *B*
Eureka College *B*
Governors State University *M*
Greenville College *B*
Highland Community College *A*
Illinois Benedictine College *B*
Illinois Central College *A*
Illinois College *B*
Illinois Institute of Technology *B*
Illinois State University *B,M*
Illinois Wesleyan University *B*
John A. Logan College *A*
Joliet Junior College *A*
Knox College *B*
Lake Forest College *B*
Lewis University *B*
Lincoln Land Community
    College *A*
Loyola University of Chicago
    B,M,D
MacMurray College *B*
McKendree College *B*
Millikin University *B*
Monmouth College *B*
Morton College *A*
North Central College *B*
North Park College and Theological
    Seminary *B*
Northeastern Illinois University
    B,M
Northern Illinois University *B,M,D*
Northwestern University *B,M,D*
Olivet Nazarene University *B*
Principia College *B*
Quincy College *B*
Rend Lake College *A*
Rockford College *B*
Roosevelt University *B,M*
Rosary College *B*
St. Xavier University *B*
Sangamon State University *B,M*
Southern Illinois University
    Carbondale *B,M,D*
    Edwardsville *B,M*
State Community College *A*
Triton College *A*
University of Chicago *B,M,D*

University of Illinois
  Chicago *B,M*
  Urbana-Champaign *B,M,D*
Waubonsee Community College *A*
Western Illinois University *B,M*
Wheaton College *B*

Indiana

Anderson University *B*
Ball State University *B,M*
Butler University *B,M*
Calumet College of St. Joseph *B*
DePauw University *B*
Earlham College *B*
Franklin College *B*
Goshen College *B*
Hanover College *B*
Indiana State University *B,M*
Indiana University
  Bloomington *B,M,D*
  Northwest *B*
  South Bend *B*
  Southeast *B*
Indiana University—Purdue
  University
    Fort Wayne *B*
    Indianapolis *B*
Indiana Wesleyan University *B*
Manchester College *B*
Martin University *B*
Purdue University
  Calumet *B*
  West Lafayette *B,M,D*
St. Joseph's College *B*
St. Mary-of-the-Woods College *B*
St. Mary's College *B*
Taylor University *B*
University of Evansville *B*
University of Indianapolis *B*
University of Notre Dame *B,M,D*
University of Southern Indiana *B*
Valparaiso University *B*
Vincennes University *A*
Wabash College *B*

Iowa

Buena Vista College *B*
Central College *B*
Clarke College *B*
Coe College *B*
Cornell College *B*
Dordt College *B*
Drake University *B*
Grinnell College *B*
Iowa State University *B,M*
Loras College *B*
Luther College *B*
Maharishi International University
  A,B
Morningside College *B*
Mount Mercy College *B*
Northwestern College *B*
St. Ambrose University *B*
Simpson College *B*
University of Dubuque *B*
University of Iowa *B,M,D*
University of Northern Iowa *B,M*
Wartburg College *B*
William Penn College *B*

Kansas

Baker University *B*
Benedictine College *B*
Bethany College *B*
Butler County Community
  College *A*
Coffeyville Community College *A*
Emporia State University *B*
Fort Hays State University *B,M*
Fort Scott Community College *A*
Friends University *B*
Hutchinson Community College *A*

Kansas State University *B,M*
Ottawa University *B*
Pittsburg State University *B,M*
Pratt Community College *A*
St. Mary College *B*
Southwestern College *B*
Sterling College *B*
University of Kansas *B,M,D*
Washburn University of Topeka *B*
Wichita State University *B,M*

Kentucky

Bellarmine College *B*
Berea College *B*
Campbellsville College *B*
Centre College *B*
Cumberland College *B*
Eastern Kentucky University *B,M*
Georgetown College *B*
Kentucky State University *B*
Kentucky Wesleyan College *B*
Morehead State University *B*
Murray State University *B*
Northern Kentucky University *B*
Pikeville College *B*
Thomas More College *A*
Transylvania University *B*
Union College *B*
University of Kentucky *B,M,D*
University of Louisville *B,M*
Western Kentucky University *B*

Louisiana

Centenary College of Louisiana *B*
Dillard University *B*
Grambling State University *B*
Louisiana College *B*
Louisiana State University
  Agricultural and Mechanical
    College *B,M,D*
  Shreveport *B*
Louisiana Tech University *B*
Loyola University *B*
McNeese State University *B*
Nicholls State University *B*
Northeast Louisiana University *B*
Northwestern State University *B*
Southeastern Louisiana
  University *B*
Southern University at New
  Orleans *B*
Southern University and
  Agricultural and Mechanical
  College *B,M*
Tulane University *B,M,D*
University of New Orleans *B,M,D*
University of Southwestern
  Louisiana *B*
Xavier University of Louisiana *B*

Maine

Bates College *B*
Bowdoin College *B*
Colby College *B*
University of Maine
  Farmington *B*
  Orono *B*
  Presque Isle *B*
University of Southern Maine *B*

Maryland

Bowie State University *B*
College of Notre Dame of
  Maryland *B*
Frederick Community College *A*
Frostburg State University *B*
Goucher College *B*
Harford Community College *A*
Hood College *B*
Howard Community College *A*
Johns Hopkins University *B,D*
Loyola College in Maryland *B*

Morgan State University *B*
Mount St. Mary's College *B*
St. Mary's College of Maryland *B*
Salisbury State University *B*
Towson State University *B*
United States Naval Academy *B*
University of Baltimore *B*
University of Maryland
  Baltimore County *B*
  College Park *B,M,D*
Washington College *B*
Western Maryland College *B*

Massachusetts

American International College *B*
Amherst College *B*
Anna Maria College for Men and
  Women *B*
Assumption College *B*
Becker College: Leicester
  Campus *A*
Boston College *B,M,D*
Boston University *B,M,D*
Bradford College *B*
Brandeis University *B,M,D*
Bridgewater State College *B*
Clark University *B*
College of the Holy Cross *B*
Curry College *B*
Emmanuel College *B*
Framingham State College *B*
Gordon College *B*
Hampshire College *B*
Harvard and Radcliffe Colleges *B*
Harvard University *D*
Massachusetts Institute of
  Technology *B,M,D*
Merrimack College *B*
Mount Holyoke College *B*
North Adams State College *B*
Northeastern University *B,M*
Northern Essex Community
  College *A*
Quincy College *A*
Regis College *B*
Salem State College *B*
Simmons College *B*
Smith College *B*
Springfield College *B*
Stonehill College *B*
Suffolk University *B*
Tufts University *B*
University of Massachusetts
  Amherst *B,M,D*
  Boston *B*
  Dartmouth *B*
  Lowell *B*
Wellesley College *B*
Western New England College *B*
Westfield State College *B*
Wheaton College *B*
Williams College *B*

Michigan

Adrian College *A,B*
Albion College *B*
Alma College *B*
Andrews University *B*
Aquinas College *B*
Calvin College *B*
Central Michigan University *B,M*
Eastern Michigan University *B*
Grand Valley State University *B*
Hillsdale College *B*
Hope College *B*
Kalamazoo College *B*
Lake Superior State University *B*
Lansing Community College *A*
Marygrove College *B*
Michigan State University *B,M,D*
Northern Michigan University
  A,B,M

Oakland University *B*
Saginaw Valley State University *B*
University of Detroit Mercy *B,M*
University of Michigan
  Ann Arbor *B,M,D*
  Dearborn *B*
  Flint *B*
Wayne State University *B,M,D*
Western Michigan University *B,M*

Minnesota

Augsburg College *B*
Bemidji State University *B*
Bethel College *B*
Carleton College *B*
College of St. Benedict *B*
College of St. Catherine: St.
  Catherine Campus *B*
Concordia College: Moorhead *B*
Concordia College: St. Paul *B*
Gustavus Adolphus College *B*
Hamline University *B*
Macalester College *B*
Mankato State University *B,M*
Moorhead State University *B*
Northland Community College *A*
Rainy River Community College *A*
St. Cloud State University *B*
St. John's University *B*
St. Mary's College of Minnesota *B*
St. Olaf College *B*
Southwest State University *B*
University of Minnesota
  Duluth *B*
  Morris *B*
  Twin Cities *B,M,D*
University of St. Thomas *B*
Willmar Community College *A*
Winona State University *B,M*

Mississippi

Alcorn State University *B*
Delta State University *B*
Jackson State University *B,M*
Millsaps College *B*
Mississippi College *B*
Mississippi State University *B,M*
Rust College *B*
Tougaloo College *B*
University of Mississippi *B,M,D*
University of Southern Mississippi
  B,M,D

Missouri

Avila College *B*
Central Methodist College *B*
Central Missouri State University
  B,M
College of the Ozarks *B*
Columbia College *B*
Drury College *B*
East Central College *A*
Evangel College *B*
Jefferson College *A*
Lincoln University *B*
Lindenwood College *B*
Maryville University *B*
Missouri Southern State College *B*
Missouri Valley College *B*
Missouri Western State College *B*
Northeast Missouri State
  University *B*
Northwest Missouri State
  University *B*
Park College *B*
Rockhurst College *B*
St. Louis University *B*
Southeast Missouri State
  University *B*
Southwest Baptist University *B*
Southwest Missouri State
  University *B*

Stephens College *B*
University of Missouri
    Columbia *B,M,D*
    Kansas City *B,M*
    St. Louis *B,M,D*
Washington University *B,M,D*
Webster University *B*
Westminster College *B*
William Jewell College *B*
William Woods College *B*

Montana
Carroll College *B*
College of Great Falls *B*
Montana State University *B*
Rocky Mountain College *B*
University of Montana *B,M*

Nebraska
Bellevue College *B*
Central Community College *A*
Chadron State College *B*
Creighton University *B*
Doane College *B*
Hastings College *B*
Nebraska Wesleyan University *B*
Southeast Community College:
    Beatrice Campus *A*
University of Nebraska
    Kearney *B*
    Lincoln *B,M,D*
    Omaha *B,M*
Wayne State College *B*
York College *A*

Nevada
University of Nevada
    Las Vegas *B,M*
    Reno *B,M,D*

New Hampshire
Dartmouth College *B*
Franklin Pierce College *B*
Keene State College *B*
New England College *B*
Plymouth State College of the
    University System of New
    Hampshire *B*
Rivier College *B*
St. Anselm College *B*
University of New Hampshire *B,M*

New Jersey
Bergen Community College *A*
Bloomfield College *B*
Brookdale Community College *A*
Burlington County College *A*
Drew University *B*
Fairleigh Dickinson University *B,M*
Glassboro State College *B*
Jersey City State College *B*
Kean College of New Jersey *B*
Monmouth College *B*
Montclair State College *B*
Ocean County College *A*
Princeton University *B,D*
Ramapo College of New Jersey *B*
Rider College *B*
Rutgers—The State University of
    New Jersey
    Camden College of Arts and
        Sciences *B*
    Douglass College *B*
    Livingston College *B*
    New Brunswick *M,D*
    Newark College of Arts and
        Sciences *B*
    Rutgers College *B*
    University College Camden *B*
    University College New
        Brunswick *B*
    University College Newark *B*

St. Peter's College *B*
Seton Hall University *B*
Stockton State College *B*
Thomas Edison State College *B*
Trenton State College *B*
Upsala College *B*
William Paterson College of New
    Jersey *B,M*

New Mexico
Eastern New Mexico University *B*
New Mexico Highlands
    University *B*
New Mexico State University *B,M*
University of New Mexico *B,M,D*

New York
Adelphi University *B*
Adirondack Community College *A*
Alfred University *B*
Bard College *B*
Barnard College *B*
Canisius College *B*
City University of New York
    Baruch College *B*
    Brooklyn College *B,M*
    City College *B*
    College of Staten Island *B*
    Graduate School and
        University Center *M,D*
    Hunter College *B*
    John Jay College of Criminal
        Justice *B*
    Lehman College *B*
    Queens College *B,M*
    Queensborough Community
        College *A*
    York College *B*
Colgate University *B*
College of New Rochelle *B*
College of St. Rose *B,M*
Columbia University
    Columbia College *B*
    New York *M,D*
    School of General Studies *B*
Cornell University *B,M,D*
Dominican College of Blauvelt *B*
Elmira College *B*
Eugene Lang College/New School
    for Social Research *B*
Fordham University *B,M,D*
Fulton-Montgomery Community
    College *A*
Hamilton College *B*
Hartwick College *B*
Hobart College *B*
Hofstra University *B*
Houghton College *B*
Iona College *B*
Ithaca College *B*
Jamestown Community College *A*
Keuka College *B*
Le Moyne College *B*
Long Island University
    Brooklyn Campus *B,M*
    C. W. Post Campus *B,M*
    Southampton Campus *B*
Manhattan College *B*
Manhattanville College *B*
Marist College *B*
Marymount College *B*
Marymount Manhattan College *B*
Medaille College *A,B*
Mercy College *B*
Molloy College *B*
Nazareth College of Rochester *B*
New York Institute of
    Technology *B*
New York University *B,M,D*
Niagara University *B*

Pace University
    College of White Plains *B*
    New York *B*
    Pleasantville/Briarcliff *B*
Russell Sage College *B*
St. Bonaventure University *B*
St. Francis College *B*
St. John Fisher College *B*
St. John's University *B,M*
St. Lawrence University *B*
Sarah Lawrence College *B*
Siena College *B*
Skidmore College *B*
State University of New York
    Albany *B,M,D*
    Binghamton *B,M,D*
    Buffalo *B,M,D*
    Purchase *B*
    Stony Brook *B,M,D*
    College at Brockport *B*
    College at Buffalo *B*
    College at Cortland *B*
    College at Fredonia *B*
    College at Geneseo *B*
    College at New Paltz *B*
    College at Old Westbury *B*
    College at Oneonta *B*
    College at Plattsburgh *B*
    College at Potsdam *B*
    Oswego *B*
Sullivan County Community
    College *A*
Syracuse University *B,M,D*
Touro College *B*
Union College *B*
United States Military Academy *B*
University of Rochester *B,M,D*
University of the State of New
    York: Regents College *B*
Utica College of Syracuse
    University *B*
Vassar College *B*
Wagner College *B*
Wells College *B*
William Smith College *B*
Yeshiva University *B*

North Carolina
Appalachian State University *B,M*
Barton College *B*
Belmont Abbey College *B*
Bennett College *B*
Brevard College *A*
Campbell University *B*
Catawba College *B*
Davidson College *B*
Duke University *B,M,D*
East Carolina University *B,M*
Elizabeth City State University *B*
Elon College *B*
Fayetteville State University *B*
Gardner-Webb College *B*
Greensboro College *B*
Guilford College *B*
High Point University *B*
Johnson C. Smith University *B*
Lenoir-Rhyne College *B*
Livingstone College *B*
Louisburg College *A*
Mars Hill College *B*
Meredith College *B*
Methodist College *A,B*
North Carolina Agricultural and
    Technical State University *B*
North Carolina Central
    University *B*
North Carolina State University
    B,M
North Carolina Wesleyan College *B*
Pembroke State University *B*
Queens College *B*
St. Andrews Presbyterian College *B*

St. Augustine's College *B*
Salem College *B*
University of North Carolina
    Asheville *B*
    Chapel Hill *B,M,D*
    Charlotte *B*
    Greensboro *B,M*
    Wilmington *B*
Wake Forest University *B*
Western Carolina University *B*
Winston-Salem State University *B*

North Dakota
Dickinson State University *B*
Jamestown College *B*
North Dakota State University *B,M*
University of North Dakota *B,M*

Ohio
Antioch College *B*
Ashland University *B*
Baldwin-Wallace College *B*
Bowling Green State University
    B,M
Capital University *B*
Case Western Reserve University
    B,M,D
Cedarville College *B*
Central State University *B*
Cleveland State University *B*
College of Wooster *B*
Denison University *B*
Franciscan University of
    Steubenville *B*
Heidelberg College *B*
Hiram College *B*
John Carroll University *B*
Kent State University *B,M,D*
Kenyon College *B*
Lakeland Community College *A*
Marietta College *B*
Miami University: Oxford Campus
    B,M,D
Mount Union College *B*
Muskingum College *B*
Oberlin College *B*
Ohio Dominican College *B*
Ohio Northern University *B*
Ohio State University: Columbus
    Campus *B,M,D*
Ohio University *B,M*
Ohio Wesleyan University *B*
Otterbein College *B*
Union Institute *B,D*
University of Akron *B,M*
University of Cincinnati *B,M,D*
University of Dayton *B,M*
University of Findlay *B*
University of Rio Grande *A*
University of Toledo *B,M*
Walsh College *B*
Wilberforce University *B*
Wittenberg University *B*
Wright State University *B*
Xavier University *A,B*
Youngstown State University *B*

Oklahoma
Bartlesville Wesleyan College *B*
Cameron University *B*
East Central University *B*
Eastern Oklahoma State College *A*
Northeastern State University *B*
Northwestern Oklahoma State
    University *B*
Oklahoma Baptist University *B*
Oklahoma City University *B*
Oklahoma State University *B,M*
Oral Roberts University *B*
Phillips University *B*
Redlands Community College *A*
Rogers State College *A*

Rose State College A
Southeastern Oklahoma State
University B
Southwestern Oklahoma State
University B
Tulsa Junior College A
University of Central Oklahoma
B,M
University of Oklahoma B,M,D
University of Science and Arts of
Oklahoma B
University of Tulsa B

Oregon

Central Oregon Community
College A
Lewis and Clark College B
Linfield College B
Northwest Christian College B
Oregon State University B
Pacific University B
Portland Community College A
Portland State University B,M
Reed College B
Southern Oregon State College B
University of Oregon
Eugene B,M,D
Robert Donald Clark Honors
College B
University of Portland B
Western Oregon State College B
Willamette University B

Pennsylvania

Albright College B
Allegheny College B
Allentown College of St. Francis de
Sales B
Alvernia College B
Beaver College B
Bloomsburg University of
Pennsylvania B
Bryn Mawr College B
Bucknell University B
Cabrini College B
California University of
Pennsylvania B,M
Carnegie Mellon University B,M,D
Cedar Crest College B
Chatham College B
Chestnut Hill College B
Cheyney University of
Pennsylvania B
Clarion University of
Pennsylvania B
Dickinson College B
Drexel University B
Duquesne University B,M
East Stroudsburg University of
Pennsylvania B,M
Eastern College B
Edinboro University of
Pennsylvania B
Elizabethtown College B
Franklin and Marshall College B
Gannon University B
Geneva College B
Gettysburg College B
Grove City College B
Haverford College B
Immaculata College B
Indiana University of Pennsylvania
B,M
Juniata College B
King's College B
Kutztown University of
Pennsylvania B,M
La Salle University B
Lafayette College B
Lebanon Valley College of
Pennsylvania B
Lehigh University B,M,D

Lincoln University B
Lock Haven University of
Pennsylvania B
Lycoming College B
Mansfield University of
Pennsylvania B
Mercyhurst College B
Messiah College B
Millersville University of
Pennsylvania B
Moravian College B
Muhlenberg College B
Neumann College B
Penn State
Erie Behrend College B
Harrisburg Capital College D
University Park Campus
B,M,D
Point Park College B
Rosemont College B
St. Francis College B
St. Joseph's University B
St. Vincent College B
Seton Hill College B
Shippensburg University of
Pennsylvania B
Slippery Rock University of
Pennsylvania B
Susquehanna University B
Swarthmore College B
Temple University B,M,D
Thiel College B
University of Pennsylvania B,M,D
University of Pittsburgh
Bradford B
Greensburg B
Johnstown B
Pittsburgh B,M,D
University of Scranton A,B
Ursinus College B
Villanova University B,M
Washington and Jefferson College B
Waynesburg College B
West Chester University of
Pennsylvania B,M
Westminster College B
Widener University B
Wilkes University B
Wilson College B
York College of Pennsylvania B

Puerto Rico

Inter American University of Puerto
Rico
Arecibo Campus B
Metropolitan Campus B
San German Campus B
Pontifical Catholic University of
Puerto Rico B
Turabo University B
University of Puerto Rico
Mayaguez Campus B
Rio Piedras Campus B

Rhode Island

Brown University B,M,D
Providence College B
Rhode Island College B
Roger Williams College B
Salve Regina University B
University of Rhode Island B,M

South Carolina

Benedict College B
Charleston Southern University B
The Citadel B
Clemson University B
Coker College B
College of Charleston B
Converse College B
Francis Marion College B
Furman University B

Lander College B
Morris College B
Newberry College B
Presbyterian College B
South Carolina State College B
University of South Carolina
Aiken B
Coastal Carolina College B
Columbia B,M,D
Spartanburg B
Voorhees College B
Winthrop University B
Wofford College B

South Dakota

Augustana College B
Black Hills State University B
Dakota Wesleyan University B
Northern State University B
Sioux Falls College B
South Dakota State University B
University of South Dakota B,M

Tennessee

Austin Peay State University B
Belmont University B
Carson-Newman College B
David Lipscomb University B
East Tennessee State University B
Fisk University B
King College B
Knoxville College B
LeMoyne-Owen College B
Maryville College B
Memphis State University B,M
Middle Tennessee State University
B,M
Motlow State Community
College A
Rhodes College B
Tennessee State University B
Tennessee Technological
University B
University of the South B
University of Tennessee
Chattanooga B,M
Knoxville B,M,D
Martin B
Vanderbilt University B,M,D

Texas

Abilene Christian University B
Angelo State University B
Austin College B
Austin Community College A
Baylor University B,M
Bee County College A
College of the Mainland A
Collin County Community College
District A
Corpus Christi State University B
Dallas Baptist University B
Del Mar College A
East Texas State University B,M
El Paso Community College A
Hardin-Simmons University B
Houston Baptist University B
Houston Community College A
Howard Payne University B
Huston-Tillotson College B
Incarnate Word College B
Jacksonville College A
Jarvis Christian College B
Lamar University—Beaumont B,M
Laredo State University B
LeTourneau University B
Lon Morris College A
McMurry University B
Midland College A
Midwestern State University B,M
Panola College A
Prairie View A&M University B

Rice University B,M,D
St. Edward's University B
St. Mary's University B,M
St. Philip's College A
Sam Houston State University B,M
South Plains College A
Southern Methodist University B
Southwest Texas State University
B,M
Southwestern University B
Stephen F. Austin State
University B
Sul Ross State University B,M
Tarleton State University B
Texas A&I University B,M
Texas A&M University B,M
Texas Christian University B
Texas College B
Texas Lutheran College B
Texas Southern University B
Texas Southmost College A
Texas Tech University B,M,D
Texas Wesleyan University B
Texas Woman's University B,M
Trinity University B
University of Dallas B,M,D
University of Houston
Clear Lake B
Houston B,M,D
University of Mary Hardin-
Baylor B
University of North Texas B,M,D
University of St. Thomas B
University of Texas
Arlington B,M
Austin B,M,D
Dallas B
El Paso B,M
Pan American B
Permian Basin B
San Antonio B
Tyler B
Wayland Baptist University B
West Texas State University B,M
Western Texas College A
Wharton County Junior College A

Utah

Brigham Young University B,M
Dixie College A
Southern Utah University B
University of Utah B,M,D
Utah State University B,M
Weber State University B
Westminster College of Salt Lake
City B

Vermont

Bennington College B
College of St. Joseph in Vermont B
Johnson State College B
Marlboro College B
Middlebury College B
Norwich University B
St. Michael's College B
University of Vermont B,M

Virginia

Bridgewater College B
Christendom College B
Christopher Newport College B
Clinch Valley College of the
University of Virginia B
College of William and Mary B,M
Emory and Henry College B
Ferrum College B
George Mason University B
Hampden-Sydney College B
Hampton University B
Hollins College B
James Madison University B
Liberty University B

Longwood College *B*
Lynchburg College *B*
Mary Baldwin College *B*
Mary Washington College *B*
Marymount University *B*
Norfolk State University *B*
Old Dominion University *B*
Radford University *B*
Randolph-Macon College *B*
Randolph-Macon Woman's
  College *B*
Roanoke College *B*
St. Paul's College *B*
Sweet Briar College *B*
University of Richmond *B,M*
University of Virginia *B,M,D*
Virginia Commonwealth
  University *B*
Virginia Intermont College *B*
Virginia Polytechnic Institute and
  . State University *B,M*
Virginia State University *B*
Virginia Union University *B*
Virginia Wesleyan College *B*
Washington and Lee University *B*

Washington
Central Washington University *B*
Eastern Washington University *B*
Everett Community College *A*
Evergreen State College *B*
Gonzaga University *B*
Heritage College *B*
Lower Columbia College *A*
Olympic College *A*
Pacific Lutheran University *B*
St. Martin's College *B*
Seattle Pacific University *B*
Seattle University *B*
Spokane Community College *A*
Spokane Falls Community
  College *A*
Tacoma Community College *A*
University of Puget Sound *B*
University of Washington *B,M,D*
Washington State University *B,M,D*
Wenatchee Valley College *A*
Western Washington University
  B,M
Whitman College *B*
Whitworth College *B*

West Virginia
Alderson-Broaddus College *B*
Bethany College *B*
Concord College *B*
Davis and Elkins College *B*
Fairmont State College *B*
Marshall University *B,M*
Potomac State College of West
  Virginia University *A*
Shepherd College *B*
University of Charleston *B*
West Liberty State College *B*
West Virginia State College *B*
West Virginia University *B,M,D*
West Virginia Wesleyan College *B*
Wheeling Jesuit College *B*

Wisconsin
Beloit College *B*
Carroll College *B*
Carthage College *B*
Edgewood College *B*
Lawrence University *B*
Marquette University *B,M*
Northland College *B*
Ripon College *B*
St. Norbert College *B*

University of Wisconsin
  Eau Claire *B*
  Green Bay *B*
  La Crosse *B*
  Madison *B,M,D*
  Milwaukee *B,M,D*
  Oshkosh *B*
  Parkside *B*
  Platteville *B*
  River Falls *B*
  Stevens Point *B*
  Superior *B*
  Whitewater *B*

Wyoming
Casper College *A*
Central Wyoming College *A*
Eastern Wyoming College *A*
Laramie County Community
  College *A*
Northwest College *A*
Sheridan College *A*
University of Wyoming *B,M*
Western Wyoming Community
  College *A*

American Samoa, Caroline Islands, Guam, Marianas, Virgin Islands
University of Guam *B,M*

Canada
McGill University *B,M,D*

Switzerland
American College of Switzerland *B*

Arab Republic of Egypt
American University in Cairo *B,M*

Population and family planning

Massachusetts
Hampshire College *B*

Michigan
University of Michigan *M,D*

Ohio
Ohio State University: Columbus
  Campus *M*

Portuguese

Arizona
University of Arizona *B*

California
Chabot College *A*
University of California
  Berkeley *B*
  Los Angeles *B,M*
  Santa Barbara *B*

Connecticut
University of Connecticut *B*
Yale University *M,D*

District of Columbia
Georgetown University *B*

Florida
Florida International University *B*
Miami-Dade Community College *A*

Illinois
University of Chicago *B*
University of Illinois at Urbana-
  Champaign *B,M,D*

Indiana
Indiana University Bloomington
  B,M

Iowa
University of Iowa *B*

Louisiana
Tulane University *B,M*

Massachusetts
Harvard and Radcliffe Colleges *B*
Harvard University *M,D*
University of Massachusetts
  Amherst *B*
  Dartmouth *B*

Michigan
University of Michigan *M,D*

Minnesota
University of Minnesota: Twin
  Cities *B*

New Jersey
Rutgers—The State University of
  New Jersey
    Douglass College *B*
    Livingston College *B*
    Rutgers College *B*
    University College New
      Brunswick *B*

New Mexico
University of New Mexico *B,M*

New York
City University of New York:
  Queens College *B*
Columbia University: Columbia
  College *B*
New York University *B,M,D*
United States Military Academy *B*

North Carolina
University of North Carolina at
  Chapel Hill *B,M,D*

Pennsylvania
University of Pennsylvania *B,M,D*

Rhode Island
Brown University *B,M*

Tennessee
Vanderbilt University *B,M*

Texas
University of Texas at Austin
  B,M,D

Utah
Brigham Young University *B,M*

Vermont
Marlboro College *B*

Wisconsin
University of Wisconsin: Madison
  B,M,D

Poultry

Alabama
Auburn University *B,M,D*
Tuskegee University *B,M*

Arizona
University of Arizona *M*

Arkansas
University of Arkansas *B*

California
California Polytechnic State
  University: San Luis Obispo *B*
California State University:
  Fresno *B*
Modesto Junior College *A*
University of California: Davis *B,M*

Delaware
Delaware Technical and
  Community College: Southern
  Campus *A*

Florida
University of Florida *B,M*

Georgia
University of Georgia *B,M,D*

Idaho
University of Idaho *B*

Illinois
Southern Illinois University at
  Carbondale *B,M*

Iowa
Iowa State University *M,D*

Kansas
Kansas State University *B*

Louisiana
Louisiana State University and
  Agricultural and Mechanical
  College *M*

Maryland
University of Maryland
    College Park *B,M,D*
    Eastern Shore *B*

Mississippi
Mississippi State University *B,M*

New York
Cornell University *B,M,D*

North Carolina
North Carolina State University
  B,M
Wayne Community College *A*

Ohio
Ohio State University: Columbus
  Campus *B,M,D*

Oklahoma
Oklahoma State University *M*

Oregon
Oregon State University *B,M,D*

Pennsylvania
Penn State University Park Campus
  C,B,M

South Carolina

Clemson University *B*

Texas

Central Texas College *A*
Texas A&M University *B,M,D*

Virginia

Virginia Polytechnic Institute and
State University *B,M*

Wisconsin

University of Wisconsin: Madison
B,M,D

Canada

McGill University *M,D*

Power plant operation and maintenance

Alabama

Community College of the Air
Force *A*

Arizona

Northland Pioneer College *C,A*
Rio Salado Community College *A*

California

Lassen College *C,A*

Florida

Miami-Dade Community College *A*

Idaho

Idaho State University *C*

Illinois

College of DuPage *C*
Lincoln Land Community
College *A*
Moraine Valley Community
College *C*
Oakton Community College *C,A*
Richland Community College *A*

Kansas

Cowley County Community
College *A*
Haskell Indian Junior College *A*

Maine

Maine Maritime Academy *B*

Maryland

Dundalk Community College *C,A*

Michigan

Henry Ford Community College *A*
Jackson Community College *C,A*
Macomb Community College *C,A*

Nevada

Truckee Meadows Community
College *C,A*

New Hampshire

New Hampshire Technical College:
Laconia *A*

New York

College of Aeronautics *A*

North Dakota

Bismarck State College *A*

Pennsylvania

Spring Garden College *C*
Williamson Free School of
Mechanical Trades *C,A*

Tennessee

Chattanooga State Technical
Community College *A*

Texas

Angelina College *A*
Houston Community College *C*
Odessa College *C,A*
St. Philip's College *A*
Texas State Technical College:
Waco *A*

Washington

Walla Walla College *A,B*

Wisconsin

Fox Valley Technical College *C*
Mid-State Technical College *A*

Practical nursing

Alabama

Bessemer State Technical College *C*
Douglas MacArthur State Technical
College *C*
Gadsden State Community
College *C*
George C. Wallace State
Community College at Selma *C*
John C. Calhoun State Community
College *A*
Reid State Technical College *C*
Shelton State Community
College *C*
Shoals Community College *C*
Walker State Technical College *C*
Wallace State Community College
at Hanceville *A*

Arizona

Mesa Community College *C,A*
Mohave Community College *C,A*
Pima Community College *C*
Scottsdale Community College *C,A*

Arkansas

Arkansas State University *A,B*
Shorter College *A*
Westark Community College *C*

California

Allan Hancock College *C,A*
Bakersfield College *A*
Barstow College *A*
California State University:
Bakersfield *B,M*
Cerritos Community College *A*
Cerro Coso Community College
C,A
Chaffey Community College *A*
Citrus College *A*
College of the Desert *C,A*
College of the Redwoods *C*
College of the Sequoias *A*
Compton Community College *A*
El Camino College *A*
Fresno City College *C,A*
Gavilan Community College *A*
Glendale Community College *A*
Hartnell College *A*
Imperial Valley College *C,A*
Lassen College *C,A*
Long Beach City College *C,A*

Los Angeles Trade and Technical
College *A*
Merced College *C,A*
MiraCosta College *C,A*
Mission College *A*
Modesto Junior College *A*
Mount San Jacinto College *A*
Napa Valley College *C,A*
Pasadena City College *C,A*
Porterville College *C,A*
Rio Hondo College *A*
Saddleback College *A*
San Diego City College *C,A*
San Joaquin Delta College *A*
Santa Barbara City College *C,A*
Santa Rosa Junior College *A*
Sierra College *C,A*
Southwestern College *A*
Ventura College *A*
Yuba College *A*

Colorado

Community College of Denver *C*
Front Range Community College
C,A
Lamar Community College *C*
Mesa State College *A*
Northeastern Junior College *A*
Otero Junior College *C*
Trinidad State Junior College *A*

Delaware

Delaware Technical and
Community College
Southern Campus *A*
Terry Campus *C*

Florida

Brevard Community College *C*
Central Florida Community
College *C*
Chipola Junior College *C*
Daytona Beach Community
College *C*
Gulf Coast Community College *A*
Hillsborough Community College *A*
Indian River Community College *C*
North Florida Junior College *A*
Pasco-Hernando Community
College *C*
Pensacola Junior College *C*
Santa Fe Community College *C*
Seminole Community College *C*
South Florida Community
College *C*
University of Tampa *B*

Georgia

Athens Area Technical Institute *C*
Augusta Technical Institute *C*
Bainbridge College *C*
Berry College *B*
Brunswick College *C*
Chattahoochee Technical
Institute *C*
DeKalb Technical Institute *A*
Georgia Southern University *B,M*
Kennesaw State College *A,B*
Savannah Technical Institute *C*

Hawaii

University of Hawaii
Hilo *C*
Kapiolani Community
College *C*
Kauai Community College *C*

Idaho

Boise State University *C*
College of Southern Idaho *C*
Idaho State University *C*
Lewis Clark State College *A*

North Idaho College *A*

Illinois

Black Hawk College
East Campus *C*
Moline *C*
Carl Sandburg College *C,A*
City Colleges of Chicago: Richard J.
Daley College *A*
Highland Community College *C*
Illinois Central College *C*
Illinois Eastern Community
Colleges: Olney Central
College *C*
Illinois Valley Community
College *C*
John A. Logan College *A*
Kishwaukee College *C*
Lake Land College *C,A*
Morton College *A*
Parkland College *A*
Rend Lake College *C,A*
Shawnee Community College *A*
Spoon River College *C*
Triton College *C*
William Rainey Harper College *A*

Indiana

Indiana Vocational Technical
College
Central Indiana *C*
Columbus *C*
Eastcentral *C*
Lafayette *C*
Northcentral *C*
Northeast *C*
Northwest *C*
Southcentral *C*
Southeast *C*
Southwest *C*
Wabash Valley *C*
Whitewater *C*
St. Joseph's College *B*
Vincennes University *C*

Iowa

Clinton Community College *C*
Des Moines Area Community
College *C*
Hawkeye Institute of Technology *C*
Indian Hills Community College *C*
Iowa Central Community College *C*
Iowa Lakes Community College *C*
Iowa Western Community
College *C*
Kirkwood Community College *A*
Muscatine Community College *C*
North Iowa Area Community
College *A*
Northeast Iowa Community
College *A*
Northwest Iowa Technical
College *C*
Scott Community College *C*
Southeastern Community College
North Campus *C*
South Campus *C*
Southwestern Community
College *C*

Kansas

Baker University *B*
Barton County Community College
C,A
Butler County Community
College *A*
Coffeyville Community College *A*
Colby Community College *A*
Dodge City Community College *A*
Fort Scott Community College *A*
Highland Community College *A*

Neosho County Community
College *C*
Pratt Community College *A*
Seward County Community College
C,A

Kentucky

Eastern Kentucky University *A,B*
Morehead State University *A*
Northern Kentucky University *M*

Louisiana

Louisiana State University at
Eunice *A*

Maine

Central Maine Technical College *C*
Eastern Maine Technical College *A*
Kennebec Valley Technical
College *C*
Southern Maine Technical
College *A*

Maryland

Allegany Community College *C*
Charles County Community
College *C*
Columbia Union College *C*
Frederick Community College *C*
Harford Community College *C*
Wor-Wic Tech Community
College *C*

Massachusetts

Berkshire Community College *C*
Essex Agricultural and Technical
Institute *C*
Massachusetts Bay Community
College *C*
Northern Essex Community
College *C*
Quincy College *C*

Michigan

Alpena Community College *C*
Charles Stewart Mott Community
College *A*
Delta College *A*
Glen Oaks Community College *C,A*
Grand Rapids Community
College *C*
Great Lakes Junior College of
Business *C*
Jackson Community College *C*
Kalamazoo Valley Community
College *A*
Kellogg Community College *A*
Kirtland Community College *C*
Lansing Community College *A*
Mid Michigan Community
College *A*
Montcalm Community College *C*
Muskegon Community College *C,A*
Northern Michigan University *C*
Northwestern Michigan College *C*
Oakland Community College *A*
St. Clair County Community
College *C*
Schoolcraft College *C*
Southwestern Michigan College *A*
West Shore Community College *A*

Minnesota

Alexandria Technical College *C*
Concordia College: Moorhead *B*
Rainy River Community College *C*
St. Paul Technical College *C*
Willmar Technical College *A*
Worthington Community College *C*

Mississippi

Copiah-Lincoln Community
College *C*
Hinds Community College *C*
Holmes Community College *C*
Jones County Junior College *A*
Meridian Community College *A*
Mississippi Delta Community
College *C*
Mississippi Gulf Coast Community
College
    Jackson County Campus *C*
    Jefferson Davis Campus *C*
    Perkinston *C*
Northeast Mississippi Community
College *C,A*
Rust College *B*
Southwest Mississippi Community
College *C*

Missouri

Jefferson College *A*
Mineral Area College *C*
Moberly Area Community
College *A*
North Central Missouri College *C*
St. Charles Community College *C*
State Fair Community College *C*

Montana

Carroll College *B*
Fort Peck Community College *C*
Northern Montana College *A,B*

Nebraska

Central Community College *A*
Metropolitan Community College *C*
Southeast Community College
    Beatrice Campus *C,A*
    Lincoln Campus *C*
Western Nebraska Community
College: Scottsbluff Campus *C,A*

Nevada

Community College of Southern
Nevada *C*

New Hampshire

New Hampshire Technical College
    Manchester *C*
    Stratham *A*
University of New Hampshire *B*

New Jersey

Burlington County College *A*
Passaic County Community
College *A*
Union County College *C*

New Mexico

Eastern New Mexico University:
Roswell Campus *C*
New Mexico Junior College *A*
New Mexico State University *A,B*
Northern New Mexico Community
College *C*

New York

City University of New York:
Hostos Community College *A*
Helene Fuld School of Nursing *A*
Iona College *A*
Niagara County Community
College *C*
North Country Community
College *C*
State University of New York
College of Technology at Delhi
C,A
Westchester Community College *C*

North Carolina

Alamance Community College *A*
Anson Community College *C*
Asheville Buncombe Technical
Community College *C*
Beaufort County Community
College *A*
Brunswick Community College *C*
Caldwell Community College and
Technical Institute *C*
Cape Fear Community College *C*
Central Carolina Community
College *C*
Cleveland Community College *C*
Coastal Carolina Community
College *C*
College of the Albemarle *C,A*
Davidson County Community
College *C*
Durham Technical Community
College *C*
Edgecombe Community College *A*
Fayetteville Technical Community
College *C*
Forsyth Technical Community
College *A*
Guilford Technical Community
College *C,A*
Isothermal Community College *A*
Montgomery Community College *C*
Nash Community College *C*
Piedmont Community College *A*
Richmond Community College *C*
Roanoke-Chowan Community
College *A*
Robeson Community College *C*
Rockingham Community College *C*
Sampson Community College *C*
Sandhills Community College *C*
Southeastern Community College *C*
Southwestern Community
College *C*
Surry Community College *A*
Tri-County Community College *C*
Vance-Granville Community
College *C*
Wilson Technical Community
College *C*

North Dakota

North Dakota State College of
Science *A*
University of North Dakota:
Williston *A*

Ohio

Clark State Community College *C*
Hocking Technical College *A*
Jefferson Technical College *C*
Lorain County Community
College *C*
North Central Technical College *C*
Northwest Technical College *C*
Southern State Community
College *C*
Washington State Community
College *A*

Oregon

Central Oregon Community College
C,A
Chemeketa Community College *C,A*
Clackamas Community College *C*
Clatsop Community College *C*
Lane Community College *C*
Portland Community College *A*
Rogue Community College *A*
Southwestern Oregon Community
College *C*
Treasure Valley Community
College *C*
Umpqua Community College *C*

Pennsylvania

Community College of Beaver
County *A*
Geneva College *B*
Harrisburg Area Community
College *C*
Lebanon Valley College of
Pennsylvania *B*
Lehigh County Community
College *C*
Northampton County Area
Community College *C*
Pennsylvania College of
Technology *C*
Reading Area Community
College *C*
Westmoreland County Community
College *A*

Puerto Rico

Columbia College *A*
Inter American University of Puerto
Rico: Arecibo Campus *C*
Universidad Adventista de las
Antillas *A*

Rhode Island

Community College of Rhode
Island *C*

South Carolina

Aiken Technical College *C*
Greenville Technical College *C*
Horry-Georgetown Technical
College *C*
Midlands Technical College *C*
Technical College of the
Lowcountry *C*
Tri-County Technical College *C*
Trident Technical College *C*

South Dakota

Oglala Lakota College *A*
Western Dakota Vocational
Technical Institute *C*

Tennessee

Chattanooga State Technical
Community College *C*
Tennessee State University *A*
University of Tennessee: Knoxville
B,M,D

Texas

Alvin Community College *C*
Amarillo College *C*
Angelina College *A*
Austin Community College *C,A*
Bee County College *C*
Brazosport College *A*
Central Texas College *A*
Cisco Junior College *A*
College of the Mainland *A*
Cooke County College *C*
Del Mar College *C,A*
Eastfield College *A*
El Centro College *C*
El Paso Community College *A*
Galveston College *C*
Houston Community College *C*
Howard College *A*
Kilgore College *A*
Lamar University—Beaumont *A*
Lee College *A*
McLennan Community College *A*
Midland College *C*
Navarro College *C,A*
North Harris Montgomery
Community College District *C*
Northeast Texas Community
College *A*
Odessa College *C*

Panola College *A*
Ranger Junior College *C*
St. Philip's College *C,A*
Schreiner College *C*
South Plains College *A*
Sul Ross State University *A*
Tarleton State University *A*
Temple Junior College *C*
Texarkana College *C*
Texas Southmost College *A*
Trinity Valley Community
  College *A*
University of Texas Health Science
  Center at Houston *B,M*
Vernon Regional Junior College *C*
Victoria College *A*
Weatherford College *A*
Western Texas College *A*
Wharton County Junior College *C*

Utah

Dixie College *A*
Southern Utah University *A*
Utah Valley Community College *C*
Weber State University *A,B*

Virginia

New River Community College *C*
Southside Virginia Community
  College *C*

Washington

Big Bend Community College *A*
Centralia College *A*
Clark College *A*
Columbia Basin College *A*
Everett Community College *C,A*
Grays Harbor College *A*
Green River Community College *C*
Lower Columbia College *A*
North Seattle Community
  College *A*
Olympic College *C*
Skagit Valley College *C,A*
South Puget Sound Community
  College *C*
Spokane Community College *C*
Walla Walla Community College *C*
Wenatchee Valley College *C*
Yakima Valley Community
  College *C*

Wisconsin

Madison Area Technical College *A*
Moraine Park Technical College *A*
Northeast Wisconsin Technical
  College *C*
Western Wisconsin Technical
  College *C*

Wyoming

Laramie County Community
  College *A*
Northwest College *C*
Sheridan College *C*
Western Wyoming Community
  College *C*

**American Samoa, Caroline
Islands, Guam, Marianas,
Virgin Islands**

Northern Marianas College *C*
University of Guam *B*

Precision metal work

Alabama

Gadsden State Community
  College *C*

George C. Wallace State
  Community College at Selma *C*
Shelton State Community
  College *A*

Alaska

University of Alaska Southeast *C*

Arizona

Arizona Western College *A*
Cochise College *A*
Rio Salado Community College *A*
Yavapai College *A*

Arkansas

Phillips County Community
  College *A*
Rich Mountain Community
  College *A*

California

Bakersfield College *A*
Cerritos Community College *A*
Chabot College *A*
College of the Redwoods *C,A*
College of the Sequoias *A*
Compton Community College *A*
Cuesta College *A*
Diablo Valley College *A*
Evergreen Valley College *A*
Fresno City College *C,A*
Hartnell College *C,A*
Imperial Valley College *A*
Kings River Community College *A*
Laney College *C,A*
Long Beach City College *C,A*
Los Angeles Trade and Technical
  College *A*
Los Angeles Valley College *C*
Mendocino College *C,A*
Merced College *C,A*
Modesto Junior College *A*
Napa Valley College *A*
Orange Coast College *C,A*
Palomar College *C,A*
Pasadena City College *C,A*
Rio Hondo College *A*
San Diego City College *C,A*
San Joaquin Delta College *A*
Santa Monica College *A*
Santa Rosa Junior College *C,A*
Sierra College *A*
Ventura College *C,A*
West Hills Community College *C,A*
Yuba College *A*

Colorado

Aims Community College *C,A*
Front Range Community College *A*
Pueblo Community College *A*
Trinidad State Junior College *A*

Florida

Brevard Community College *C*
Daytona Beach Community
  College *A*

Georgia

Bainbridge College *C,A*
Brunswick College *A*
Gainesville College *A*

Hawaii

University of Hawaii: Honolulu
  Community College *C,A*

Idaho

Lewis Clark State College *A*
North Idaho College *A*

Illinois

Black Hawk College *A*
Carl Sandburg College *A*
City Colleges of Chicago: Chicago
  City-Wide College *C*
Elgin Community College *A*
Illinois Eastern Community
  Colleges: Olney Central
  College *C*
John A. Logan College *A*
Joliet Junior College *A*
Moraine Valley Community
  College *C*
Prairie State College *A*
Rend Lake College *A*
Southern Illinois University at
  Carbondale *A*
Triton College *C,A*

Indiana

Vincennes University *A*

Iowa

Des Moines Area Community
  College *A*
Hawkeye Institute of Technology *A*
Northeast Iowa Community
  College *A*
Waldorf College *A*

Kansas

Coffeyville Community College *A*
Dodge City Community College *A*
Fort Scott Community College *A*
Johnson County Community
  College *C*
Pratt Community College *A*

Louisiana

University of Southwestern
  Louisiana *A*

Maine

Central Maine Technical College
  C,A
Eastern Maine Technical College *A*

Massachusetts

Roxbury Community College *A*

Michigan

Grand Rapids Community
  College *A*
Jackson Community College *A*
Kalamazoo Valley Community
  College *A*
Kellogg Community College *A*
Lansing Community College *A*
Muskegon Community College *A*
Oakland Community College *A*
Southwestern Michigan College *A*
West Shore Community College
  C,A
Western Michigan University *B*

Minnesota

Alexandria Technical College *C*
St. Paul Technical College *C*

Mississippi

Copiah-Lincoln Community
  College *A*
East Central Community College *A*
Hinds Community College *A*
Mississippi Delta Community
  College *C*
Northeast Mississippi Community
  College *A*

Missouri

Jefferson College *A*
North Central Missouri College *A*

Northwest Missouri State
  University *C*
State Fair Community College *A*

Montana

Northern Montana College *C,A*

Nebraska

Central Community College *C,A*
Southeast Community College:
  Milford Campus *A*
Western Nebraska Community
  College
    Scottsbluff Campus *C,A*
    Sidney Campus *C,A*

Nevada

Community College of Southern
  Nevada *C,A*
Northern Nevada Community
  College *A*
Truckee Meadows Community
  College *C,A*
Western Nevada Community
  College *C,A*

New Mexico

New Mexico Junior College *A*
Western New Mexico University
  C,A

New York

Mohawk Valley Community College
  C,A

North Carolina

Alamance Community College *A*
Anson Community College *C*
Catawba Valley Community
  College *A*
College of the Albemarle *C*
Surry Community College *C*
Vance-Granville Community
  College *A*
Wake Technical Community
  College *C*

North Dakota

Bismarck State College *C,A*

Ohio

Terra Technical College *A*

Oklahoma

Oklahoma Panhandle State
  University *A*
Tulsa Junior College *A*

Oregon

Central Oregon Community
  College *A*
Chemeketa Community College *A*
Linn-Benton Community College
  C,A
Portland Community College *A*

Pennsylvania

Johnson Technical Institute *A*
Pennsylvania College of Technology
  C,A
Westmoreland County Community
  College *A*

Puerto Rico

University of Puerto Rico: Ponce
  Technological University
  College *A*

South Carolina

Chesterfield-Marlboro Technical
  College *A*
Greenville Technical College *C*

Horry-Georgetown Technical
College *A*
Midlands Technical College *C,A*
Sumter Area Technical College *A*
Trident Technical College *C,A*

South Dakota

Black Hills State University *B*

Tennessee

Chattanooga State Technical
Community College *C,A*

Texas

Austin Community College *A*
Cooke County College *A*
Eastfield College *A*
Houston Community College *C*
Kilgore College *A*
Lamar University—Beaumont *A*
Lee College *A*
Mountain View College *A*
Navarro College *A*
Odessa College *C,A*
Panola College *A*
San Jacinto College: Central
Campus *A*
South Plains College *A*
Tarrant County Junior College *A*
Victoria College *C*
Weatherford College *A*
Western Texas College *A*

Utah

Southern Utah University *A*
Utah Valley Community College
C,A
Weber State University *A*

Virginia

Paul D. Camp Community
College *C*
Wytheville Community College *A*

Washington

Clark College *A*
Everett Community College *A*
Grays Harbor College *A*
Green River Community College *A*
Lower Columbia College *A*
Shoreline Community College *C,A*
South Puget Sound Community
College *C,A*
Spokane Community College *A*

Wisconsin

Chippewa Valley Technical
College *A*
Fox Valley Technical College *A*
Madison Area Technical College *A*
Waukesha County Technical
College *A*

Wyoming

Casper College *A*
Eastern Wyoming College *C,A*
Laramie County Community
College *A*
Northwest College *A*
Western Wyoming Community
College *C,A*

American Samoa, Caroline
Islands, Guam, Marianas,
Virgin Islands

Guam Community College *C*

Predentistry

Alabama

Alabama Southern Community
College *A*
Auburn University *B*
Huntingdon College *B*
James H. Faulkner State
Community College *A*
John C. Calhoun State Community
College *A*
Judson College *B*
Lawson State Community
College *A*
Mobile College *B*
Shelton State Community
College *A*
Shoals Community College *A*
Snead State Junior College *A*
Spring Hill College *B*
University of Alabama *B*
Wallace State Community College
at Hanceville *A*

Arizona

Eastern Arizona College *A*
Glendale Community College *A*
Grand Canyon University *B*
Northern Arizona University *B*
Pima Community College *A*

Arkansas

Hendrix College *B*
Ouachita Baptist University *B*
University of Central Arkansas *B*
University of the Ozarks *B*
Westark Community College *A*

California

Azusa Pacific University *B*
Bakersfield College *A*
California State University:
Stanislaus *B*
Cerritos Community College *A*
Chabot College *A*
Chapman University *B*
Christ College Irvine *B*
City College of San Francisco *A*
College of Notre Dame *B*
Dominican College of San Rafael *B*
El Camino College *A*
Foothill College *A*
Humboldt State University *B*
Marymount College *A*
Mount St. Mary's College *B*
Pacific Union College *B*
St. Mary's College of California *B*
Santa Clara University *B*
Santa Rosa Junior College *A*
Scripps College *B*
Southern California College *B*
University of the Pacific *B*
University of San Francisco *B*
Ventura College *A*
West Coast University *C*
West Hills Community College *A*
Westmont College *B*

Colorado

Adams State College *B*
Fort Lewis College *B*
Lamar Community College *A*
Northeastern Junior College *A*
Regis College of Regis University *B*
Trinidad State Junior College *A*
University of Denver *B*
Western State College of
Colorado *B*

Connecticut

Albertus Magnus College *B*
Eastern Connecticut State
University *B*
Quinnipiac College *B*
Sacred Heart University *B*
St. Joseph College *B*
Southern Connecticut State
University *B*
University of Bridgeport *B*
University of Hartford *B*
University of New Haven *B*

Delaware

University of Delaware *B*

District of Columbia

American University *B*

Florida

Barry University *B*
Daytona Beach Community
College *A*
Eckerd College *B*
Florida Agricultural and Mechanical
University *B*
Florida Atlantic University *B*
Florida Institute of Technology *B*
Florida International University *B*
Florida Southern College *B*
Florida State University *B*
Gulf Coast Community College *A*
Indian River Community College *A*
Jacksonville University *B*
Manatee Community College *A*
Miami-Dade Community College *A*
New College of the University of
South Florida *B*
Nova University *B*
Okaloosa-Walton Community
College *A*
Pensacola Junior College *A*
Rollins College *B*
Santa Fe Community College *A*
Stetson University *B*
University of Miami *B*
University of Tampa *B*

Georgia

Andrew College *A*
Brewton-Parker College *A*
Clayton State College *A*
Columbus College *B*
Darton College *A*
Floyd College *A*
Gainesville College *A*
Georgia College *B*
Georgia Southern University *B*
Gordon College *A*
Kennesaw State College *B*
Macon College *A*
Middle Georgia College *A*
Morehouse College *B*
Oglethorpe University *B*
Piedmont College *B*
Reinhardt College *A*
Shorter College *B*
Truett-McConnell College *A*
University of Georgia *B*
Wesleyan College *B*

Hawaii

Hawaii Loa College *B*
University of Hawaii at Hilo *B*

Idaho

Boise State University *B*
College of Southern Idaho *A*
Idaho State University *B*
North Idaho College *A*
Northwest Nazarene College *B*
Ricks College *A*

Illinois

Augustana College *B*
Aurora University *B*
Black Hawk College *A*
Blackburn College *B*
City Colleges of Chicago: Richard J.
Daley College *A*
Concordia University *B*
De Paul University *B*
Elmhurst College *B*
Eureka College *B*
Governors State University *B*
Highland Community College *A*
Illinois Central College *A*
Illinois Wesleyan University *B*
Joliet Junior College *A*
Judson College *B*
Kishwaukee College *A*
Lincoln Land Community
College *A*
MacMurray College *B*
Millikin University *B*
North Central College *B*
North Park College and Theological
Seminary *B*
Olivet Nazarene University *B*
Quincy College *B*
Rend Lake College *A*
Rockford College *B*
Roosevelt University *B*
St. Xavier University *B*
Southern Illinois University at
Carbondale *B*
Trinity College *B*
William Rainey Harper College *A*

Indiana

Ball State University *B*
Butler University *B*
Franklin College *B*
Goshen College *B*
Huntington College *B*
Indiana State University *B*
Indiana University
Bloomington *B*
Southeast *B*
Indiana Wesleyan University *B*
Manchester College *B*
Marian College *B*
Purdue University
Calumet *B*
West Lafayette *B*
St. Francis College *B*
St. Joseph's College *B*
St. Mary-of-the-Woods College *B*
Taylor University *B*
University of Evansville *B*
University of Indianapolis *B*
University of Notre Dame *B*
University of Southern Indiana *B*
Vincennes University *A*

Iowa

Briar Cliff College *B*
Buena Vista College *B*
Central College *B*
Clarke College *B*
Clinton Community College *A*
Coe College *B*
Cornell College *B*
Dordt College *B*
Drake University *B*
Grinnell College *B*
Iowa Lakes Community College *A*
Iowa State University *B*
Iowa Wesleyan College *B*
Kirkwood Community College *A*
Loras College *B*
Luther College *B*
Muscatine Community College *A*
North Iowa Area Community
College *A*

Simpson College *B*
Teikyo Marycrest University *B*
Teikyo Westmar University *B*
Upper Iowa University *B*
Wartburg College *B*
William Penn College *B*

Kansas

Allen County Community
College *A*
Baker University *B*
Barton County Community
College *A*
Bethany College *B*
Bethel College *B*
Butler County Community
College *A*
Coffeyville Community College *A*
Colby Community College *A*
Dodge City Community College *A*
Friends University *B*
Hutchinson Community College *A*
Kansas City Kansas Community
College *A*
Kansas Newman College *B*
Kansas State University *B*
Neosho County Community
College *A*
Pittsburg State University *B*
Pratt Community College *A*
Tabor College *B*
University of Kansas *B*
Washburn University of Topeka *B*

Kentucky

Bellarmine College *B*
Campbellsville College *B*
Centre College *B*
Cumberland College *B*
Georgetown College *B*
Lees College *A*
St. Catharine College *A*
Spalding University *B*
Sue Bennett College *A*
Thomas More College *B*
Union College *B*

Louisiana

Dillard University *B*
Louisiana College *B*
Louisiana State University and
Agricultural and Mechanical
College *B*
Loyola University *B*
McNeese State University *B*
Nicholls State University *B*
Northeast Louisiana University *B*
Southeastern Louisiana
University *B*
University of Southwestern
Louisiana *B*
Xavier University of Louisiana *B*

Maine

St. Joseph's College *B*

Maryland

Anne Arundel Community
College *A*
College of Notre Dame of
Maryland *B*
Columbia Union College *B*
Coppin State College *B*
Frostburg State University *B*
Goucher College *B*
Howard Community College *A*
Montgomery College
Germantown Campus *A*
Rockville Campus *A*
Takoma Park Campus *A*
Morgan State University *B*
Mount St. Mary's College *B*

Salisbury State University *B*
University of Maryland: Eastern
Shore *B*
Villa Julie College *B*
Western Maryland College *B*

Massachusetts

American International College *B*
Anna Maria College for Men and
Women *B*
Assumption College *B*
Boston University *B*
Bridgewater State College *B*
Clark University *B*
Eastern Nazarene College *B*
Elms College *B*
Emmanuel College *B*
Framingham State College *B*
Hampshire College *B*
Massachusetts Bay Community
College *A*
Massachusetts College of Pharmacy
and Allied Health Sciences *B*
Massachusetts Institute of
Technology *B*
Merrimack College *B*
Salem State College *B*
Simon's Rock College of Bard *B*
Springfield College *B*
Springfield Technical Community
College *A*
Stonehill College *B*
University of Massachusetts at
Amherst *B*
Worcester Polytechnic Institute *B*

Michigan

Alma College *B*
Eastern Michigan University *B*
Ferris State University *A*
Grand Valley State University *B*
Hope College *B*
Kellogg Community College *A*
Lake Superior State University *B*
Lansing Community College *A*
Macomb Community College *A*
Madonna University *B*
Marygrove College *B*
Michigan State University *B*
Michigan Technological
University *B*
Northern Michigan University *B*
Olivet College *B*
Saginaw Valley State University *B*
Siena Heights College *B*
University of Detroit Mercy *B*
Western Michigan University *B*

Minnesota

Bethel College *B*
College of St. Benedict *B*
College of St. Catherine: St.
Catherine Campus *B*
Concordia College: Moorhead *B*
Itasca Community College:
Arrowhead Region *A*
Moorhead State University *B*
Rochester Community College *A*
St. Cloud State University *B*
St. John's University *B*
St. Olaf College *B*
University of Minnesota: Twin
Cities *B*
Willmar Community College *A*
Winona State University *B*

Mississippi

Alcorn State University *B*
East Central Community College *A*
Holmes Community College *A*
Jackson State University *B*
Jones County Junior College *A*

Mary Holmes College *A*
Millsaps College *B*
Mississippi College *B*
Mississippi Delta Community
College *A*
Mississippi Gulf Coast Community
College: Jefferson Davis
Campus *A*
Mississippi University for Women *B*
Northeast Mississippi Community
College *A*
Rust College *B*
University of Mississippi *B*
University of Southern
Mississippi *B*

Missouri

Central Methodist College *B*
College of the Ozarks *B*
East Central College *A*
Evangel College *B*
Northeast Missouri State
University *B*
Northwest Missouri State
University *B*
Park College *B*
St. Louis Community College at
Florissant Valley *A*
Webster University *B*
Wentworth Military Academy and
Junior College *A*
Westminster College *B*

Montana

Rocky Mountain College *B*
University of Montana *B*

Nebraska

Chadron State College *B*
College of St. Mary *B*
Concordia College *B*
Hastings College *B*
McCook Community College *A*
Midland Lutheran College *B*
Peru State College *B*
University of Nebraska—Lincoln *B*

Nevada

Community College of Southern
Nevada *A*
Sierra Nevada College *B*
University of Nevada: Reno *B*

New Hampshire

Colby-Sawyer College *B*
Franklin Pierce College *B*
Rivier College *B*
St. Anselm College *B*

New Jersey

Bloomfield College *B*
Georgian Court College *B*
Glassboro State College *B*
Jersey City State College *B*
Monmouth College *B*
Rider College *B*
Stevens Institute of Technology *B*

New Mexico

Eastern New Mexico University *B*
New Mexico Institute of Mining
and Technology *B*
New Mexico Junior College *A*
New Mexico State University *B*
University of New Mexico *B*
Western New Mexico University *A*

New York

Alfred University *B*
Bard College *B*
Canisius College *B*

City University of New York
Brooklyn College *B*
City College *B*
Hunter College *B*
Queens College *B*
Colgate University *B*
College of Mount St. Vincent *B*
Daemen College *B*
D'Youville College *B*
Elmira College *B*
Fordham University *B*
Houghton College *B*
Iona College *B*
Ithaca College *B*
Long Island University
Brooklyn Campus *B*
C. W. Post Campus *B*
Manhattan College *B*
Manhattanville College *B*
New York University *B*
Niagara University *B*
Pace University *B*
Rochester Institute of
Technology *B*
Russell Sage College *B*
St. Bonaventure University *B*
St. John Fisher College *B*
Sarah Lawrence College *B*
Siena College *B*
State University of New York
College of Environmental
Science and Forestry *B*
College at Geneseo *B*
College at New Paltz *B*
Oswego *B*
Sullivan County Community
College *A*
Touro College *B*
Wagner College *B*
Yeshiva University *B*

North Carolina

Appalachian State University *B*
Barton College *B*
Brevard College *A*
Campbell University *B*
Catawba College *B*
College of the Albemarle *A*
Elon College *B*
Gaston College *A*
Lenoir-Rhyne College *B*
Livingstone College *B*
Louisburg College *A*
Mars Hill College *B*
North Carolina State University *B*
Peace College *A*
Pfeiffer College *B*
Rockingham Community College *A*
St. Andrews Presbyterian College *B*
Salem College *B*
University of North Carolina at
Greensboro *B*
Western Piedmont Community
College *A*
Wingate College *B*

North Dakota

Bismarck State College *A*
Jamestown College *B*
Turtle Mountain Community
College *A*

Ohio

Ashland University *B*
Baldwin-Wallace College *B*
Bowling Green State University *B*
Capital University *B*
Cedarville College *B*
Defiance College *B*
Franciscan University of
Steubenville *B*
Heidelberg College *B*

John Carroll University *B*
Kent State University *B*
Kenyon College *B*
Malone College *B*
Marietta College *B*
Mount Vernon Nazarene College *B*
Muskingum College *B*
Notre Dame College of Ohio *B*
Ohio University *B*
Otterbein College *B*
Shawnee State University *A*
University of Akron *B*
University of Cincinnati: Raymond
    Walters College *A*
University of Dayton *B*
University of Toledo *B*
Urbana University *B*
Walsh College *B*
Wilmington College *B*
Wittenberg University *B*
Xavier University *B*
Youngstown State University *B*

Oklahoma

Bartlesville Wesleyan College *B*
Connors State College *A*
East Central University *B*
Eastern Oklahoma State College *A*
Northwestern Oklahoma State
    University *B*
Oklahoma Baptist University *B*
Oklahoma Christian University of
    Science and Arts *B*
Oklahoma City University *B*
Oral Roberts University *B*
Phillips University *B*
Redlands Community College *A*
Rose State College *A*
University of Tulsa *B*

Oregon

Central Oregon Community
    College *A*
Eastern Oregon State College *B*
George Fox College *B*
Linfield College *B*
Northwest Christian College *B*
Oregon State University *B*
Portland Community College *A*
Southern Oregon State College *B*
University of Portland *B*

Pennsylvania

Albright College *B*
Allegheny College *B*
Allentown College of St. Francis de
    Sales *B*
Bucknell University *B*
California University of
    Pennsylvania *B*
College Misericordia *B*
Duquesne University *B*
Edinboro University of
    Pennsylvania *B*
Elizabethtown College *B*
Gannon University *B*
Gettysburg College *B*
Grove City College *B*
Gwynedd-Mercy College *B*
Holy Family College *B*
Immaculata College *B*
Indiana University of
    Pennsylvania *B*
Juniata College *B*
La Roche College *B*
La Salle University *B*
Lehigh University *B*
Lock Haven University of
    Pennsylvania *B*
Lycoming College *B*
Mercyhurst College *B*
Messiah College *B*

Moravian College *B*
Philadelphia College of Textiles and
    Science *B*
Reading Area Community
    College *A*
St. Francis College *B*
Seton Hill College *B*
Susquehanna University *B*
University of Pittsburgh
    Bradford *B*
    Greensburg *B*
    Johnstown *B*
University of Scranton *B*
Ursinus College *B*
Villanova University *B*
Washington and Jefferson College *B*
Waynesburg College *B*
Widener University *B*
Wilkes University *B*
York College of Pennsylvania *B*

Rhode Island

Rhode Island College *B*
Roger Williams College *B*
Salve Regina University *B*

South Carolina

Bob Jones University *B*
Charleston Southern University *B*
Clemson University *B*
College of Charleston *B*
Converse College *B*
Erskine College *B*
Francis Marion College *B*
Lander College *B*
Morris College *B*
University of South Carolina:
    Coastal Carolina College *B*
Wofford College *B*

South Dakota

Augustana College *B*
Dakota Wesleyan University *B*
Sioux Falls College *B*
South Dakota State University *B*

Tennessee

Carson-Newman College *B*
Cumberland University *B*
David Lipscomb University *B*
East Tennessee State University *B*
Lane College *B*
Lincoln Memorial University *B*
Martin Methodist College *A*
Middle Tennessee State
    University *B*
Roane State Community College *A*
Tusculum College *B*
Union University *B*
University of the South *B*
University of Tennessee
    Chattanooga *B*
    Knoxville *B*
    Martin *B*
Volunteer State Community
    College *A*
Walters State Community
    College *A*

Texas

Abilene Christian University *B*
Amarillo College *A*
Angelina College *A*
Angelo State University *B*
Austin Community College *A*
Baylor University *B*
Bee County College *A*
Collin County Community College
    District *A*
Del Mar College *A*
East Texas State University *B*
El Paso Community College *A*

Hardin-Simmons University *B*
Houston Community College *A*
Howard College *A*
Huston-Tillotson College *B*
Lamar University—Beaumont *B*
Lon Morris College *A*
Lubbock Christian University *B*
McMurry University *B*
Midland College *A*
Navarro College *A*
North Harris Montgomery
    Community College District *A*
Panola College *A*
St. Edward's University *B*
St. Mary's University *B*
St. Philip's College *A*
San Antonio College *A*
Schreiner College *B*
South Plains College *A*
Stephen F. Austin State
    University *B*
Tarleton State University *B*
Texas A&I University *B*
Texas Lutheran College *B*
Texas Southmost College *A*
Texas Wesleyan University *B*
University of Dallas *B*
University of Houston *B*
University of Mary Hardin-
    Baylor *B*
University of St. Thomas *B*
West Texas State University *B*

Utah

Brigham Young University *B*
Utah State University *B*
Weber State University *B*

Virginia

Averett College *B*
Christopher Newport College *B*
Eastern Mennonite College *B*
Emory and Henry College *B*
Mountain Empire Community
    College *A*
Old Dominion University *B*
Radford University *B*
Randolph-Macon College *B*
Virginia Commonwealth
    University *B*
Virginia Intermont College *B*
Virginia Polytechnic Institute and
    State University *B*
Virginia Wesleyan College *B*

Washington

Centralia College *A*
Eastern Washington University *B*
Lower Columbia College *A*
Pacific Lutheran University *B*
Spokane Falls Community
    College *A*
Tacoma Community College *A*
Wenatchee Valley College *A*

West Virginia

Alderson-Broaddus College *B*
Bethany College *B*
Concord College *B*
Davis and Elkins College *B*
Glenville State College *B*
Marshall University *B*
Potomac State College of West
    Virginia University *A*
Shepherd College *B*
University of Charleston *B*
West Virginia Wesleyan College *B*
Wheeling Jesuit College *B*

Wisconsin

Alverno College *B*
Cardinal Stritch College *B*

Carroll College *B*
Carthage College *B*
Lakeland College *B*
Lawrence University *B*
Marian College of Fond du Lac *B*
Marquette University *B*
Mount Mary College *B*
Northland College *B*
Ripon College *B*
St. Norbert College *B*
University of Wisconsin
    Green Bay *B*
    La Crosse *B*
    Milwaukee *B*
    Oshkosh *B*
Viterbo College *B*

Wyoming

Casper College *A*
Northwest College *A*
Western Wyoming Community
    College *A*

Preengineering

Alabama

James H. Faulkner State
    Community College *A*
John C. Calhoun State Community
    College *A*
Judson College *B*
Spring Hill College *B*

Arizona

Cochise College *A*

Arkansas

University of Arkansas at Pine
    Bluff *B*
University of the Ozarks *B*

California

City College of San Francisco *A*
Claremont McKenna College *B*
Los Angeles Pierce College *A*
Westmont College *B*

Colorado

Red Rocks Community College *A*

Connecticut

Bridgeport Engineering Institute *A*
Fairfield University *B*
Housatonic Community College *A*
Mattatuck Community College *A*
Northwestern Connecticut
    Community College *A*

District of Columbia

American University *B*

Florida

Indian River Community College *A*
Manatee Community College *A*
Rollins College *B*
University of Tampa *B*

Georgia

Georgia College *B*
Gordon College *A*
Oglethorpe University *B*
University of Georgia *B*
Valdosta State College *B*

Idaho

Albertson College *B*

Illinois

Augustana College *B*
Aurora University *B*
Belleville Area College *A*
Eureka College *B*
Illinois Wesleyan University *B*
Judson College *A,B*
Lincoln Land Community
College *A*
MacMurray College *B*
Millikin University *B*
North Central College *B*
Richland Community College *A*
Rockford College *B*
William Rainey Harper College *A*

Indiana

Ball State University *B*
DePauw University *B*
Taylor University *B*
University of Southern Indiana *B*

Iowa

Central College *B*
Clarke College *B*
Clinton Community College *A*
Coe College *B*
Cornell College *B*
Kirkwood Community College *A*
Morningside College *B*
Muscatine Community College *A*
Scott Community College *A*
Simpson College *B*
Wartburg College *B*

Kansas

Allen County Community
College *A*
Baker University *B*
Central College *A*
Donnelly College *C*
Neosho County Community
College *A*
Pittsburg State University *B*

Kentucky

Campbellsville College *B*
Georgetown College *B*
Thomas More College *B*
Transylvania University *B*
Union College *B*

Louisiana

Xavier University of Louisiana *B*

Maryland

Frostburg State University *B*
Howard Community College *A*

Massachusetts

Mount Ida College *A*

Michigan

Alma College *B*
Aquinas College *B*
Eastern Michigan University *B*
Hope College *B*
Kalamazoo Valley Community
College *A*
Macomb Community College *A*
Mid Michigan Community
College *A*
Northwestern Michigan College *A*
Siena Heights College *A*
Suomi College *A*
West Shore Community College *A*

Minnesota

Bethany Lutheran College *A*
Bethel College *B*
Brainerd Community College *A*
College of St. Benedict *B*

College of St. Catherine: St.
Catherine Campus *B*
Concordia College: Moorhead *B*
Mesabi Community College:
Arrowhead Region *A*
Northland Community College *A*
Northwestern College *B*
Rochester Community College *A*
St. Cloud State University *A*
St. John's University *B*
St. Olaf College *B*
Willmar Community College *A*
Winona State University *A*
Worthington Community College *A*

Mississippi

Alcorn State University *A*

Missouri

Rockhurst College *B*
Webster University *B*
William Woods College *B*

Nebraska

Hastings College *B*
Metropolitan Community College *A*
Southeast Community College:
Beatrice Campus *A*

New Hampshire

Keene State College *A*

New Jersey

County College of Morris *C*
Stockton State College *B*

New Mexico

New Mexico Junior College *A*
University of New Mexico *A*

New York

City University of New York:
Queensborough Community
College *A*
Houghton College *B*
Wagner College *B*
Wells College *B*

North Carolina

Elon College *B*
Lenoir-Rhyne College *B*
Methodist College *A*
Pfeiffer College *B*
Rockingham Community College *A*
St. Andrews Presbyterian College *B*
Wingate College *B*

North Dakota

Bismarck State College *A*

Ohio

Baldwin-Wallace College *B*
Edison State Community College *A*
Heidelberg College *B*
Kenyon College *B*
Mount Union College *B*
Muskingum College *B*
Otterbein College *B*
University of Findlay *B*
Xavier University *B*

Oklahoma

Northern Oklahoma College *A*
Northwestern Oklahoma State
University *B*
Rose State College *A*

Oregon

Central Oregon Community
College *A*
Treasure Valley Community
College *A*

Pennsylvania

Elizabethtown College *B*
Indiana University of
Pennsylvania *B*
Juniata College *B*
Lincoln University *B*
Mansfield University of
Pennsylvania *B*
Reading Area Community
College *A*
St. Vincent College *B*
Seton Hill College *B*
University of Scranton *A*
West Chester University of
Pennsylvania *B*
Westminster College *B*

Rhode Island

Providence College *B*

South Carolina

Bob Jones University *B*
Charleston Southern University *B*
Furman University *B*
North Greenville College *A*

South Dakota

Augustana College *B*
Dakota Wesleyan University *B*
Northern State University *A*

Tennessee

Carson-Newman College *B*
David Lipscomb University *B*
Freed-Hardeman University *B*
Hiwassee College *A*
Union University *B*
University of the South *B*

Texas

Amarillo College *A*
Del Mar College *A*
El Paso Community College *A*
Houston Community College *A*
McLennan Community College *A*
St. Philip's College *A*
Tarleton State University *B*
Weatherford College *A*

Utah

Weber State University *B*

Vermont

St. Michael's College *B*

Virginia

Longwood College *B*
Sweet Briar College *B*

Washington

North Seattle Community
College *A*
South Puget Sound Community
College *A*

West Virginia

Alderson-Broaddus College *A*
Bluefield State College *A*

Wisconsin

Carroll College *B*
University of Wisconsin: Green
Bay *B*

Prelaw

Alabama

Alabama Southern Community
College *A*

Auburn University
Auburn *B*
Montgomery *B*
Brewer State Junior College *A*
Chattahoochee Valley Community
College *A*
Enterprise State Junior College *A*
Faulkner University *B*
Huntingdon College *B*
James H. Faulkner State
Community College *A*
John C. Calhoun State Community
College *A*
Judson College *B*
Lawson State Community
College *A*
Mobile College *B*
Shelton State Community
College *A*
Shoals Community College *A*
Snead State Junior College *A*
Spring Hill College *B*
University of Alabama *B*
Wallace State Community College
at Hanceville *A*

Alaska

Alaska Pacific University *B*

Arizona

Cochise College *A*
Eastern Arizona College *A*
Glendale Community College *A*
Grand Canyon University *B*
Northern Arizona University *B*

Arkansas

Arkansas State University *B*
Harding University *B*
Hendrix College *B*
University of Central Arkansas *B*
University of the Ozarks *B*
Westark Community College *A*

California

Azusa Pacific University *B*
Bakersfield College *A*
California Lutheran University *B*
California State University
Bakersfield *B*
Dominguez Hills *B*
Los Angeles *B*
Stanislaus *B*
Chabot College *A*
Chapman University *B*
Christ College Irvine *B*
Claremont McKenna College *B*
College of Notre Dame *B*
De Anza College *A*
El Camino College *A*
Foothill College *A*
Golden Gate University *B*
Humboldt State University *C,B*
La Sierra University *B*
Marymount College *A*
MiraCosta College *A*
Modesto Junior College *A*
Mount St. Mary's College *B*
St. Mary's College of California *B*
San Diego City College *A*
San Joaquin Delta College *A*
Santa Clara University *B*
Santa Rosa Junior College *A*
Scripps College *B*
Southern California College *B*
Southwestern College *A*
United States International
University *B*
University of Judaism *B*
University of La Verne *B*
University of the Pacific *B*
University of Redlands *B*

Ventura College *A*
Westmont College *B*
Whittier College *B*

Colorado

Adams State College *B*
Colorado Christian University *B*
Community College of Denver *C*
Fort Lewis College *B*
Mesa State College *B*
Northeastern Junior College *A*
Regis College of Regis University *B*
Trinidad State Junior College *A*
United States Air Force
 Academy *B*
University of Denver *B*
Western State College of
 Colorado *B*

Connecticut

Albertus Magnus College *B*
Eastern Connecticut State
 University *B*
Sacred Heart University *B*
St. Joseph College *B*
Teikyo-Post University *B*
University of Bridgeport *B*
University of Hartford *B*
University of New Haven *B*
Wesleyan University *B*

Delaware

Delaware State College *C*
University of Delaware *B*
Wesley College *B*

District of Columbia

American University *B*
George Washington University *B*

Florida

Barry University *B*
Daytona Beach Community
 College *A*
Eckerd College *B*
Edison Community College *A*
Flagler College *B*
Florida Institute of Technology *B*
Florida Southern College *B*
Gulf Coast Community College *A*
Indian River Community College *A*
Jacksonville University *B*
Lynn University *B*
Manatee Community College *A*
Miami-Dade Community College *A*
New College of the University of
 South Florida *B*
Nova University *B*
Pensacola Junior College *A*
Rollins College *B*
St. Leo College *B*
Stetson University *B*
University of Miami *B*
University of Tampa *B*
University of West Florida *B*

Georgia

Berry College *B*
Brewton-Parker College *A*
Clayton State College *A*
Columbus College *B*
East Georgia College *A*
Georgia College *B*
Georgia Southern University *B*
Gordon College *A*
Kennesaw State College *B*
LaGrange College *B*
Macon College *A*
Middle Georgia College *A*
Morehouse College *B*
Oglethorpe University *B*

Oxford College of Emory
 University *A*
Reinhardt College *A*
Shorter College *B*
South Georgia College *A*
Thomas College *A*
Truett-McConnell College *A*
University of Georgia *B*
Valdosta State College *B*
Wesleyan College *B*
Young Harris College *A*

Hawaii

Hawaii Loa College *B*
Hawaii Pacific University *B*
University of Hawaii at Hilo *B*

Idaho

College of Southern Idaho *A*
Idaho State University *B*
North Idaho College *A*
Northwest Nazarene College *B*
Ricks College *A*

Illinois

Augustana College *B*
Aurora University *B*
Barat College *B*
Black Hawk College *A*
Blackburn College *B*
City Colleges of Chicago
 Richard J. Daley College *A*
 Wright College *A*
Concordia University *B*
De Paul University *B*
Elmhurst College *B*
Eureka College *B*
Governors State University *B*
Illinois Central College *A*
Illinois Eastern Community
 Colleges: Olney Central
 College *A*
Illinois Valley Community
 College *A*
Joliet Junior College *A*
Judson College *B*
Kishwaukee College *A*
Lincoln Land Community
 College *A*
MacCormac Junior College *A*
MacMurray College *B*
McKendree College *B*
Millikin University *B*
Montay College *A*
Morton College *A*
North Central College *B*
North Park College and Theological
 Seminary *B*
Olivet Nazarene University *B*
Quincy College *B*
Rend Lake College *A*
Richland Community College *A*
Rock Valley College *A*
Rockford College *B*
Roosevelt University *B*
St. Xavier University *B*
Sangamon State University *B,M*
Shimer College *B*
Southern Illinois University at
 Carbondale *B*
Trinity Christian College *B*
Trinity College *B*
William Rainey Harper College *A*

Indiana

Anderson University *B*
Butler University *B*
Franklin College *B*
Goshen College *B*
Grace College *B*
Hanover College *B*
Huntington College *B*

Indiana State University *B*
Indiana University
 Bloomington *B*
 Southeast *B*
Indiana Wesleyan University *B*
Manchester College *B*
Marian College *B*
Oakland City College *A*
Purdue University *B*
St. Francis College *B*
St. Joseph's College *B*
St. Mary-of-the-Woods College *B*
Taylor University *B*
University of Evansville *B*
University of Indianapolis *B*
University of Southern Indiana *B*
Vincennes University *A*

Iowa

Briar Cliff College *B*
Buena Vista College *B*
Central College *B*
Clarke College *B*
Clinton Community College *A*
Coe College *B*
Cornell College *B*
Dordt College *B*
Drake University *B*
Grand View College *B*
Iowa Lakes Community College *A*
Iowa State University *B*
Iowa Wesleyan College *B*
Kirkwood Community College *A*
Luther College *B*
Morningside College *B*
Mount Mercy College *B*
Mount St. Clare College *A*
North Iowa Area Community
 College *A*
Simpson College *B*
Teikyo Marycrest University *B*
Teikyo Westmar University *B*
University of Dubuque *B*
Upper Iowa University *B*
Wartburg College *B*
William Penn College *B*

Kansas

Allen County Community
 College *A*
Baker University *B*
Barton County Community
 College *A*
Benedictine College *B*
Bethany College *B*
Bethel College *B*
Butler County Community
 College *A*
Central College *A*
Cloud County Community
 College *A*
Coffeyville Community College *A*
Colby Community College *A*
Cowley County Community
 College *A*
Dodge City Community College *A*
Friends University *B*
Highland Community College *A*
Hutchinson Community College *A*
Kansas City Kansas Community
 College *A*
Kansas State University *B*
Kansas Wesleyan University *B*
McPherson College *B*
Neosho County Community
 College *A*
Ottawa University *B*
Pittsburg State University *B*
Pratt Community College *A*
Sterling College *B*
Washburn University of Topeka *B*

Kentucky

Bellarmine College *B*
Brescia College *B*
Campbellsville College *B*
Centre College *B*
Cumberland College *B*
Eastern Kentucky University *B*
Georgetown College *B*
Lees College *A*
Lindsey Wilson College *A*
St. Catharine College *A*
Spalding University *B*
Sue Bennett College *A*
Thomas More College *A,B*
Union College *B*

Louisiana

Dillard University *B*
Grambling State University *B*
Louisiana College *B*
Louisiana State University and
 Agricultural and Mechanical
 College *B*
Louisiana Tech University *B*
Loyola University *B*
Northeast Louisiana University *B*
Northwestern State University *B*
Southeastern Louisiana
 University *B*
University of Southwestern
 Louisiana *B*
Xavier University of Louisiana *B*

Maine

St. Joseph's College *B*
Unity College *B*

Maryland

Catonsville Community College *A*
College of Notre Dame of
 Maryland *B*
Frostburg State University *B*
Goucher College *B*
Howard Community College *A*
Morgan State University *B*
Mount St. Mary's College *B*
Salisbury State University *B*
University of Baltimore *B*
University of Maryland: Eastern
 Shore *B*
Villa Julie College *B*
Western Maryland College *B*

Massachusetts

American International College *B*
Anna Maria College for Men and
 Women *B*
Assumption College *B*
Boston University *B*
Bridgewater State College *B*
Clark University *B*
Curry College *B*
Eastern Nazarene College *B*
Elms College *B*
Emmanuel College *B*
Framingham State College *B*
Gordon College *B*
Hampshire College *B*
Massachusetts Institute of
 Technology *B*
North Adams State College *B*
Simmons College *B*
Simon's Rock College of Bard *B*
Springfield College *B*
Stonehill College *B*
University of Massachusetts at
 Amherst *B*
Wellesley College *B*
Western New England College *B*
Wheaton College *B*
Worcester Polytechnic Institute *B*

Michigan

Alma College *B*
Calvin College *B*
Eastern Michigan University *B*
Ferris State University *A*
Grand Rapids Baptist College and
   Seminary *B*
Grand Valley State University *B*
Hope College *B*
Kellogg Community College *A*
Kirtland Community College *A*
Lake Superior State University *B*
Lansing Community College *A*
Lawrence Technological
   University *B*
Macomb Community College *A*
Madonna University *B*
Marygrove College *B*
Michigan State University *B*
Northern Michigan University *B*
Northwestern Michigan College *A*
Olivet College *B*
Saginaw Valley State University *B*
Siena Heights College *B*
Suomi College *A*
University of Detroit Mercy *B*
Western Michigan University *B*

Minnesota

Bethel College *B*
College of St. Benedict *B*
College of St. Catherine: St.
   Catherine Campus *B*
College of St. Scholastica *B*
Concordia College: Moorhead *B*
Concordia College: St. Paul *C*
Hamline University *B*
Mankato State University *B*
Moorhead State University *B*
Northland Community College *A*
Rochester Community College *A*
St. Cloud State University *B*
St. John's University *B*
St. Olaf College *B*
Southwest State University *B*
University of Minnesota
   Morris *B*
   Twin Cities *B*
Vermilion Community College *A*
Willmar Community College *A*
Winona State University *B*

Mississippi

Alcorn State University *B*
Belhaven College *B*
Copiah-Lincoln Community
   College *A*
Jackson State University *B*
Jones County Junior College *A*
Mary Holmes College *A*
Millsaps College *B*
Mississippi College *B*
Mississippi Delta Community
   College *A*
Mississippi Gulf Coast Community
   College: Jefferson Davis
   Campus *A*
Mississippi University for Women *B*
Northeast Mississippi Community
   College *A*
Rust College *B*
University of Southern
   Mississippi *B*

Missouri

Central Methodist College *B*
College of the Ozarks *B*
Columbia College *A,B*
East Central College *A*
Evangel College *B*
Fontbonne College *B*
Jefferson College *A*

Maryville University *B*
Mineral Area College *A*
Missouri Southern State College *B*
Missouri Valley College *B*
Northeast Missouri State
   University *B*
Northwest Missouri State
   University *B*
Southwest Baptist University *B*
Webster University *B*
Westminster College *B*
William Woods College *B*

Montana

Carroll College *B*
Miles Community College *A*
Rocky Mountain College *B*
University of Montana *B*

Nebraska

Chadron State College *B*
College of St. Mary *C,A,B*
Concordia College *B*
Creighton University *B*
Dana College *B*
Hastings College *B*
McCook Community College *A*
Midland Lutheran College *B*
Peru State College *B*
Southeast Community College:
   Beatrice Campus *A*
University of Nebraska
   Lincoln *B*
   Omaha *B*
Wayne State College *B*
Western Nebraska Community
   College: Scottsbluff Campus *A*

New Hampshire

Colby-Sawyer College *B*
Franklin Pierce College *B*
New England College *B*
Rivier College *B*
St. Anselm College *B*

New Jersey

Atlantic Community College *A*
Georgian Court College *B*
Glassboro State College *B*
Jersey City State College *B*
Monmouth College *B*
Rider College *B*
Stevens Institute of Technology *B*
Stockton State College *B*
Trenton State College *B*

New Mexico

College of the Southwest *B*
New Mexico Highlands
   University *B*
New Mexico Institute of Mining
   and Technology *B*
New Mexico Junior College *A*
New Mexico State University *B*
University of New Mexico *B*
Western New Mexico University *A*

New York

Adirondack Community College *A*
Alfred University *B*
Bard College *B*
Canisius College *B*
City University of New York
   Brooklyn College *B*
   City College *B*
   Hunter College *B*
   John Jay College of Criminal
      Justice *B*
Clarkson University *B*
Colgate University *B*
College of New Rochelle *B*
Daemen College *B*

Dominican College of Blauvelt *B*
D'Youville College *B*
Elmira College *B*
Fordham University *B*
Houghton College *B*
Iona College *B*
Ithaca College *B*
Keuka College *B*
Long Island University
   Brooklyn Campus *B*
   C. W. Post Campus *B*
   Southampton Campus *B*
Manhattan College *B*
Manhattanville College *B*
Marist College *B*
Marymount College *B*
Medaille College *B*
Molloy College *B*
Mount St. Mary College *B*
New York University *B*
Niagara University *B*
Onondaga Community College *A*
Pace University
   College of White Plains *B*
   New York *B*
   Pleasantville/Briarcliff *B*
Rensselaer Polytechnic Institute *B*
Rochester Institute of
   Technology *B*
Russell Sage College *B*
St. Bonaventure University *B*
St. Francis College *B*
St. John Fisher College *B*
Sarah Lawrence College *B*
Siena College *B*
State University of New York
   Purchase *B*
   College of Environmental
      Science and Forestry *B*
   College at Geneseo *B*
   College at New Paltz *B*
   College at Oneonta *B*
Sullivan County Community
   College *A*
Wagner College *B*
Yeshiva University *B*

North Carolina

Appalachian State University *B*
Barton College *B*
Brevard College *A*
Campbell University *B*
Catawba College *B*
College of the Albemarle *A*
Elon College *B*
Gaston College *A*
Guilford College *B*
Isothermal Community College *A*
Johnson C. Smith University *B*
Lenoir-Rhyne College *B*
Mars Hill College *B*
Methodist College *A,B*
Mount Olive College *A,B*
North Carolina State University *B*
North Carolina Wesleyan College *B*
Peace College *A*
Pfeiffer College *B*
Rockingham Community College *A*
St. Andrews Presbyterian College *B*
St. Augustine's College *B*
Salem College *B*
University of North Carolina at
   Greensboro *B*
Western Piedmont Community
   College *A*
Wingate College *B*

North Dakota

Bismarck State College *A*
Minot State University *B*
Turtle Mountain Community
   College *A*

Ohio

Ashland University *B*
Baldwin-Wallace College *B*
Bluffton College *B*
Bowling Green State University *B*
Capital University *B*
Cedarville College *B*
Central State University *B*
College of Mount St. Joseph *C*
Defiance College *B*
Franciscan University of
   Steubenville *B*
Heidelberg College *B*
Kent State University *B*
Kenyon College *B*
Lake Erie College *B*
Lorain County Community
   College *A*
Malone College *B*
Marietta College *B*
Mount Union College *B*
Mount Vernon Nazarene College *B*
Muskingum College *B*
Notre Dame College of Ohio *B*
Oberlin College *B*
Ohio Dominican College *B*
Ohio State University: Columbus
   Campus *B*
Ohio University
   Athens *B*
   Southern Campus at Ironton *A*
   Zanesville Campus *B*
Ohio Wesleyan University *B*
Otterbein College *B*
Shawnee State University *B*
Union Institute *B*
University of Akron *B*
University of Cincinnati
   Cincinnati *B*
   Clermont College *A*
University of Dayton *B*
University of Findlay *B*
University of Rio Grande *B*
University of Toledo *B*
Urbana University *B*
Ursuline College *B*
Walsh College *B*
Wilmington College *B*
Wittenberg University *B*
Xavier University *B*
Youngstown State University *B*

Oklahoma

Bartlesville Wesleyan College *B*
Connors State College *A*
East Central University *B*
Northern Oklahoma College *A*
Northwestern Oklahoma State
   University *B*
Oklahoma Baptist University *B*
Oklahoma Christian University of
   Science and Arts *B*
Oklahoma City University *B*
Oral Roberts University *B*
Phillips University *B*
Rogers State College *B*
Rose State College *A*
Southwestern Oklahoma State
   University *B*
University of Tulsa *B*

Oregon

Central Oregon Community
   College *A*
George Fox College *B*
Linfield College *B*
Northwest Christian College *B*
Pacific University *B*
Southern Oregon State College *B*
Treasure Valley Community
   College *A*
University of Portland *B*

Western Baptist College *B*
Western Oregon State College *B*

Pennsylvania

Albright College *B*
Allegheny College *B*
Allentown College of St. Francis de Sales *B*
Bucknell University *B*
California University of Pennsylvania *B*
Carlow College *B*
College Misericordia *B*
Duquesne University *B*
Edinboro University of Pennsylvania *B*
Elizabethtown College *B*
Gannon University *B*
Gettysburg College *B*
Grove City College *B*
Gwynedd-Mercy College *B*
Immaculata College *B*
Indiana University of Pennsylvania *B*
Juniata College *B*
King's College *B*
La Roche College *B*
La Salle University *B*
Lock Haven University of Pennsylvania *B*
Lycoming College *B*
Mansfield University of Pennsylvania *B*
Marywood College *B*
Messiah College *B*
Moravian College *B*
Neumann College *B*
Northeastern Christian Junior College *A*
Penn State
    Erie Behrend College *B*
    University Park Campus *B*
Reading Area Community College *A*
St. Francis College *B*
Seton Hill College *B*
Susquehanna University *B*
University of Pittsburgh
    Bradford *B*
    Greensburg *B*
    Johnstown *B*
University of Scranton *B*
Ursinus College *B*
Washington and Jefferson College *B*
Waynesburg College *B*
West Chester University of Pennsylvania *B*
Westmoreland County Community College *A*
Widener University *B*
York College of Pennsylvania *B*

Puerto Rico

Caribbean University *B*

Rhode Island

Salve Regina University *B*

South Carolina

Bob Jones University *B*
Charleston Southern University *B*
Clemson University *B*
Coker College *B*
Columbia College *B*
Converse College *B*
Erskine College *B*
Francis Marion College *B*
Limestone College *B*
Morris College *B*
North Greenville College *A*
South Carolina State College *B*

University of South Carolina
    Aiken *B*
    Coastal Carolina College *B*
Wofford College *B*

South Dakota

Augustana College *B*
Black Hills State University *B*
Dakota State University *B*
Dakota Wesleyan University *B*
Huron University *B*
Sioux Falls College *B*
South Dakota State University *B*

Tennessee

Belmont University *B*
Carson-Newman College *B*
Christian Brothers University *B*
Cumberland University *B*
East Tennessee State University *B*
Hiwassee College *A*
Knoxville College *B*
Lane College *B*
Lincoln Memorial University *B*
Maryville College *B*
Middle Tennessee State University *B*
Pellissippi State Technical Community College *A*
Tennessee Technological University *B*
Union University *B*
University of the South *B*
University of Tennessee
    Chattanooga *B*
    Martin *B*
William Jennings Bryan College *B*

Texas

Angelina College *A*
Bee County College *A*
Brazosport College *A*
Central Texas College *A*
Collin County Community College District *A*
Concordia Lutheran College *B*
Dallas Baptist University *B*
Del Mar College *A*
East Texas State University *B*
Hardin-Simmons University *B*
Huston-Tillotson College *B*
Jarvis Christian College *B*
Lamar University—Beaumont *B*
LeTourneau University *B*
Lon Morris College *A*
Lubbock Christian University *B*
McMurry University *B*
Midland College *A*
Panola College *A*
St. Edward's University *B*
St. Philip's College *A*
San Antonio College *A*
Schreiner College *B*
South Plains College *A*
Tarleton State University *B*
Texas A&I University *B*
Texas Lutheran College *B*
Texas Southmost College *A*
Texas Wesleyan University *B*
University of Dallas *B*
University of Houston
    Clear Lake *B*
    Houston *B*
University of Mary Hardin-Baylor *B*
University of St. Thomas *B*
University of Texas at Arlington *B*
West Texas State University *B*

Utah

Southern Utah University *B*
Utah State University *B*

Weber State University *B*
Westminster College of Salt Lake City *B*

Vermont

College of St. Joseph in Vermont *B*
Green Mountain College *B*
St. Michael's College *B*

Virginia

Averett College *B*
Bluefield College *B*
Christopher Newport College *B*
Emory and Henry College *B*
Hampton University *B*
Longwood College *B*
Mountain Empire Community College *A*
Radford University *B*
Virginia Commonwealth University *B*
Virginia Intermont College *B*
Virginia Wesleyan College *B*

Washington

Centralia College *A*
Eastern Washington University *B*
Everett Community College *A*
Evergreen State College *B*
Heritage College *B*
Lower Columbia College *A*
Pacific Lutheran University *B*
Seattle Pacific University *B*
Spokane Falls Community College *A*
Washington State University *B*

West Virginia

Alderson-Broaddus College *B*
Bethany College *B*
Concord College *B*
Davis and Elkins College *B*
Marshall University *B*
Potomac State College of West Virginia University *A*
Salem-Teikyo University *B*
Shepherd College *B*
University of Charleston *B*
West Virginia Wesleyan College *B*
Wheeling Jesuit College *B*

Wisconsin

Alverno College *B*
Beloit College *B*
Cardinal Stritch College *B*
Carroll College *B*
Carthage College *B*
Concordia University Wisconsin *B*
Lakeland College *B*
Lawrence University *B*
Marian College of Fond du Lac *B*
Marquette University *B*
Mount Mary College *B*
Mount Senario College *B*
Northland College *B*
Ripon College *B*
St. Norbert College *B*
University of Wisconsin
    Green Bay *B*
    Oshkosh *B*
    Superior *B*
    Whitewater *B*
Viterbo College *B*

Wyoming

Casper College *A*
Central Wyoming College *A*
Northwest College *A*
Western Wyoming Community College *A*

Switzerland

American College of Switzerland *B*

Premedicine

Alabama

Alabama Southern Community College *A*
Auburn University *B*
Birmingham-Southern College *B*
Huntingdon College *B*
James H. Faulkner State Community College *A*
John C. Calhoun State Community College *A*
Judson College *B*
Lawson State Community College *A*
Selma University *A*
Shelton State Community College *A*
Shoals Community College *A*
Snead State Junior College *A*
Spring Hill College *B*
University of Alabama
    Huntsville *B*
    Tuscaloosa *B*
Wallace State Community College at Hanceville *A*

Arizona

Eastern Arizona College *A*
Glendale Community College *A*
Grand Canyon University *B*
Northern Arizona University *B*
Pima Community College *A*

Arkansas

Hendrix College *B*
Ouachita Baptist University *B*
University of Central Arkansas *B*
University of the Ozarks *B*
Westark Community College *A*

California

Azusa Pacific University *B*
Bakersfield College *A*
California Institute of Technology *B*
California Lutheran University *B*
California State University: Stanislaus *B*
Cerritos Community College *A*
Chabot College *A*
Chapman University *B*
Christ College Irvine *B*
City College of San Francisco *A*
Claremont McKenna College *B*
College of Notre Dame *B*
Dominican College of San Rafael *B*
El Camino College *A*
Foothill College *A*
Fresno Pacific College *B*
Humboldt State University *B*
Marymount College *A*
Mount St. Mary's College *B*
Pacific Union College *B*
St. Mary's College of California *B*
Santa Clara University *B*
Santa Rosa Junior College *A*
Scripps College *B*
Southern California College *B*
Southwestern College *A*
University of California: San Diego *B*
University of the Pacific *B*
University of San Francisco *B*
Ventura College *A*
West Coast University *C*
West Hills Community College *A*

Westmont College *B*

Colorado

Adams State College *B*
Colorado Christian University *B*
Fort Lewis College *B*
Mesa State College *A*
Northeastern Junior College *A*
Pikes Peak Community College *A*
Regis College of Regis University *B*
Trinidad State Junior College *A*
University of Denver *B*
Western State College of
 Colorado *B*

Connecticut

Albertus Magnus College *B*
Eastern Connecticut State
 University *B*
Quinnipiac College *B*
Sacred Heart University *B*
St. Joseph College *B*
University of Bridgeport *B*
University of Hartford *B*
University of New Haven *B*
Wesleyan University *B*

Delaware

University of Delaware *B*

District of Columbia

American University *B*
George Washington University *B*

Florida

Barry University *B*
Daytona Beach Community
 College *A*
Eckerd College *B*
Florida Agricultural and Mechanical
 University *B*
Florida Atlantic University *B*
Florida Institute of Technology *B*
Florida International University *B*
Florida Southern College *B*
Florida State University *B*
Gulf Coast Community College *A*
Indian River Community College *A*
Jacksonville University *B*
Manatee Community College *A*
Miami-Dade Community College *A*
New College of the University of
 South Florida *B*
Nova University *B*
Okaloosa-Walton Community
 College *A*
Pensacola Junior College *A*
Rollins College *B*
Santa Fe Community College *A*
Stetson University *B*
University of Miami *B*
University of Tampa *B*

Georgia

Andrew College *A*
Brewton-Parker College *A*
Clayton State College *A*
Columbus College *B*
Darton College *A*
Floyd College *A*
Gainesville College *A*
Georgia College *B*
Georgia Southern University *B*
Gordon College *A*
Kennesaw State College *B*
Macon College *A*
Middle Georgia College *A*
Morehouse College *B*
Oglethorpe University *B*
Piedmont College *B*
Reinhardt College *A*
Shorter College *B*

Truett-McConnell College *A*
University of Georgia *B*
Wesleyan College *B*

Hawaii

Hawaii Loa College *B*
University of Hawaii at Hilo *B*

Idaho

Boise State University *B*
College of Southern Idaho *A*
Idaho State University *B*
North Idaho College *A*
Northwest Nazarene College *B*
Ricks College *A*

Illinois

Augustana College *B*
Aurora University *B*
Barat College *B*
Black Hawk College *A*
Blackburn College *B*
Chicago State University *B*
City Colleges of Chicago: Richard J.
 Daley College *A*
Concordia University *B*
De Paul University *B*
Elmhurst College *B*
Eureka College *B*
Governors State University *B*
Highland Community College *A*
Illinois Central College *A*
Illinois Institute of Technology *B*
Illinois Wesleyan University *B*
Joliet Junior College *A*
Judson College *B*
Kishwaukee College *A*
Lincoln Land Community
 College *A*
MacMurray College *B*
Millikin University *B*
Morton College *A*
North Central College *B*
North Park College and Theological
 Seminary *B*
Olivet Nazarene University *B*
Quincy College *B*
Rend Lake College *A*
Rockford College *B*
Roosevelt University *B*
St. Xavier University *B*
Southern Illinois University at
 Carbondale *B*
Trinity College *B*
William Rainey Harper College *A*

Indiana

Ball State University *B*
Butler University *B*
Franklin College *B*
Goshen College *B*
Huntington College *B*
Indiana State University *B*
Indiana University
 Bloomington *B*
 Southeast *B*
Indiana Wesleyan University *B*
Manchester College *B*
Marian College *B*
Purdue University
 Calumet *B*
 West Lafayette *B*
St. Francis College *B*
St. Joseph's College *B*
St. Mary-of-the-Woods College *B*
Taylor University *B*
Tri-State University *B*
University of Evansville *B*
University of Indianapolis *B*
University of Notre Dame *B*
University of Southern Indiana *B*
Vincennes University *A*

Iowa

Briar Cliff College *B*
Buena Vista College *B*
Central College *B*
Clarke College *B*
Clinton Community College *A*
Coe College *B*
Cornell College *B*
Dordt College *B*
Drake University *B*
Grinnell College *B*
Iowa Lakes Community College *A*
Iowa State University *B*
Iowa Wesleyan College *B*
Kirkwood Community College *A*
Loras College *B*
Luther College *B*
Morningside College *B*
Muscatine Community College *A*
North Iowa Area Community
 College *A*
Scott Community College *A*
Simpson College *B*
Teikyo Marycrest University *B*
Teikyo Westmar University *B*
University of Dubuque *B*
Upper Iowa University *B*
Wartburg College *B*
William Penn College *B*

Kansas

Allen County Community
 College *A*
Baker University *B*
Barton County Community
 College *A*
Bethany College *B*
Bethel College *B*
Butler County Community
 College *A*
Coffeyville Community College *A*
Colby Community College *A*
Dodge City Community College *A*
Friends University *B*
Hutchinson Community College *A*
Kansas City Kansas Community
 College *A*
Kansas Newman College *B*
Kansas State University *B*
Neosho County Community
 College *A*
Pittsburg State University *B*
Pratt Community College *A*
St. Mary College *B*
Tabor College *B*
University of Kansas *B*
Washburn University of Topeka *B*

Kentucky

Bellarmine College *B*
Campbellsville College *B*
Centre College *B*
Cumberland College *B*
Georgetown College *B*
Lees College *A*
Lindsey Wilson College *A*
St. Catharine College *A*
Spalding University *B*
Sue Bennett College *A*
Thomas More College *B*
Union College *B*

Louisiana

Dillard University *B*
Louisiana College *B*
Louisiana State University and
 Agricultural and Mechanical
 College *B*
Loyola University *B*
McNeese State University *B*
Nicholls State University *B*
Northeast Louisiana University *B*

Southeastern Louisiana
 University *B*
Southern University and
 Agricultural and Mechanical
 College *B*
University of Southwestern
 Louisiana *B*
Xavier University of Louisiana *B*

Maine

St. Joseph's College *B*
University of New England *B*

Maryland

Anne Arundel Community
 College *A*
College of Notre Dame of
 Maryland *B*
Columbia Union College *B*
Coppin State College *B*
Frostburg State University *B*
Goucher College *B*
Howard Community College *A*
Montgomery College
 Germantown Campus *A*
 Rockville Campus *A*
 Takoma Park Campus *A*
Morgan State University *B*
Mount St. Mary's College *B*
Salisbury State University *B*
University of Maryland: Eastern
 Shore *B*
Villa Julie College *B*
Western Maryland College *B*

Massachusetts

American International College *B*
Anna Maria College for Men and
 Women *B*
Assumption College *B*
Boston University *B*
Bridgewater State College *B*
Clark University *B*
Eastern Nazarene College *B*
Elms College *B*
Emmanuel College *B*
Framingham State College *B*
Hampshire College *B*
Massachusetts Bay Community
 College *A*
Massachusetts College of Pharmacy
 and Allied Health Sciences *B*
Massachusetts Institute of
 Technology *B*
Merrimack College *B*
Salem State College *B*
Simon's Rock College of Bard *B*
Springfield College *B*
Springfield Technical Community
 College *A*
Stonehill College *B*
University of Massachusetts at
 Amherst *B*
Wellesley College *B*
Wheaton College *B*
Worcester Polytechnic Institute *B*

Michigan

Alma College *B*
Aquinas College *B*
Concordia College *B*
Eastern Michigan University *B*
Ferris State University *A*
Grand Valley State University *B*
Hope College *B*
Kellogg Community College *A*
Lake Superior State University *B*
Lansing Community College *A*
Macomb Community College *A*
Madonna University *B*
Marygrove College *B*
Michigan State University *B*

Michigan Technological
University *B*
Northern Michigan University *B*
Olivet College *B*
Saginaw Valley State University *B*
Siena Heights College *B*
University of Detroit Mercy *B*
Western Michigan University *B*

Minnesota

Bemidji State University *B*
Bethel College *B*
College of St. Benedict *B*
College of St. Catherine: St.
Catherine Campus *B*
Concordia College: Moorhead *B*
Itasca Community College:
Arrowhead Region *A*
Moorhead State University *B*
Rochester Community College *A*
St. Cloud State University *B*
St. John's University *B*
St. Olaf College *B*
University of Minnesota
Morris *B*
Twin Cities *B*
Willmar Community College *A*
Winona State University *B*

Mississippi

Alcorn State University *B*
East Central Community College *A*
Holmes Community College *A*
Jackson State University *B*
Jones County Junior College *A*
Mary Holmes College *A*
Millsaps College *B*
Mississippi College *B*
Mississippi Gulf Coast Community
College: Jefferson Davis
Campus *A*
Mississippi University for Women *B*
Northeast Mississippi Community
College *A*
Rust College *B*
University of Mississippi *B*
University of Southern
Mississippi *B*

Missouri

Avila College *B*
Central Methodist College *B*
College of the Ozarks *B*
East Central College *A*
Evangel College *B*
Fontbonne College *B*
Jefferson College *A*
Northeast Missouri State
University *B*
Northwest Missouri State
University *B*
Park College *B*
St. Louis Community College at
Florissant Valley *A*
Webster University *B*
Wentworth Military Academy and
Junior College *A*
Westminster College *B*
William Woods College *B*

Montana

Rocky Mountain College *B*
University of Montana *B*

Nebraska

Chadron State College *B*
College of St. Mary *B*
Concordia College *B*
Hastings College *B*
McCook Community College *A*
Midland Lutheran College *B*
Peru State College *B*

Southeast Community College:
Beatrice Campus *A*
University of Nebraska—Lincoln *B*

Nevada

Sierra Nevada College *B*
University of Nevada: Reno *B*

New Hampshire

Colby-Sawyer College *B*
Franklin Pierce College *B*
Rivier College *B*
St. Anselm College *B*

New Jersey

Bloomfield College *B*
Essex County College *A*
Georgian Court College *B*
Glassboro State College *B*
Jersey City State College *B*
Monmouth College *B*
Rider College *B*
Stevens Institute of Technology *B*
Stockton State College *B*
Trenton State College *B*

New Mexico

College of Santa Fe *B*
Eastern New Mexico University *B*
New Mexico Institute of Mining
and Technology *B*
New Mexico Junior College *A*
New Mexico State University *B*
University of New Mexico *B*
Western New Mexico University *A*

New York

Alfred University *B*
Bard College *B*
Canisius College *B*
City University of New York
Brooklyn College *B*
City College *B*
Hunter College *B*
Queens College *B*
Clarkson University *B*
Colgate University *B*
College of Mount St. Vincent *B*
College of New Rochelle *B*
Daemen College *B*
D'Youville College *B*
Elmira College *B*
Fordham University *B*
Houghton College *B*
Iona College *B*
Ithaca College *B*
Long Island University
Brooklyn Campus *B*
C. W. Post Campus *B*
Southampton Campus *B*
Manhattan College *B*
Manhattanville College *B*
New York University *B*
Niagara University *B*
Pace University *B*
Rochester Institute of
Technology *B*
Russell Sage College *B*
Sage Junior College of Albany, A
Division of Russell Sage
College *A*
St. Bonaventure University *B*
St. Francis College *B*
St. John Fisher College *B*
Sarah Lawrence College *B*
Siena College *B*
State University of New York
College of Environmental
Science and Forestry *B*
College at Geneseo *B*
College at New Paltz *B*
Oswego *B*

Sullivan County Community
College *A*
Touro College *B*
Wagner College *B*
Yeshiva University *B*

North Carolina

Appalachian State University *B*
Barton College *B*
Brevard College *A*
Campbell University *B*
Catawba College *B*
College of the Albemarle *A*
Elon College *B*
Gaston College *A*
Isothermal Community College *A*
Lenoir-Rhyne College *B*
Louisburg College *A*
Mars Hill College *B*
Methodist College *B*
North Carolina State University *B*
Peace College *A*
Pfeiffer College *B*
Rockingham Community College *A*
St. Andrews Presbyterian College *B*
St. Augustine's College *B*
Salem College *B*
University of North Carolina at
Greensboro *B*
Warren Wilson College *B*
Western Piedmont Community
College *A*
Wingate College *B*

North Dakota

Bismarck State College *A*
Jamestown College *B*
Minot State University *B*
Turtle Mountain Community
College *A*

Ohio

Ashland University *B*
Baldwin-Wallace College *B*
Bluffton College *B*
Bowling Green State University *B*
Capital University *B*
Cedarville College *B*
Defiance College *B*
Franciscan University of
Steubenville *B*
Heidelberg College *B*
John Carroll University *B*
Kent State University *B*
Kenyon College *B*
Lake Erie College *B*
Lorain County Community
College *A*
Malone College *B*
Marietta College *B*
Mount Vernon Nazarene College *B*
Muskingum College *B*
Notre Dame College of Ohio *B*
Ohio University *B*
Otterbein College *B*
Shawnee State University *A*
University of Akron *B*
University of Cincinnati: Raymond
Walters College *A*
University of Dayton *B*
University of Findlay *B*
University of Toledo *B*
Urbana University *B*
Walsh College *B*
Wilmington College *B*
Wittenberg University *B*
Xavier University *B*
Youngstown State University *B*

Oklahoma

Bartlesville Wesleyan College *B*
Connors State College *A*

East Central University *B*
Eastern Oklahoma State College *A*
Langston University *B*
Northern Oklahoma College *A*
Northwestern Oklahoma State
University *B*
Oklahoma Baptist University *B*
Oklahoma Christian University of
Science and Arts *B*
Oklahoma City University *B*
Oral Roberts University *B*
Phillips University *B*
Redlands Community College *A*
Rogers State College *A*
Rose State College *A*
University of Tulsa *B*

Oregon

Central Oregon Community
College *A*
Eastern Oregon State College *B*
George Fox College *B*
Linfield College *B*
Northwest Christian College *B*
Oregon State University *B*
Pacific University *B*
Portland Community College *A*
Southern Oregon State College *B*
University of Portland *B*

Pennsylvania

Albright College *B*
Allegheny College *B*
Allentown College of St. Francis de
Sales *B*
Bucknell University *B*
California University of
Pennsylvania *B*
College Misericordia *B*
Duquesne University *B*
East Stroudsburg University of
Pennsylvania *B*
Edinboro University of
Pennsylvania *B*
Elizabethtown College *B*
Gannon University *B*
Gettysburg College *B*
Grove City College *B*
Gwynedd-Mercy College *B*
Hahnemann University School of
Health Sciences and
Humanities *B*
Holy Family College *B*
Immaculata College *B*
Indiana University of
Pennsylvania *B*
Juniata College *B*
La Roche College *B*
La Salle University *B*
Lehigh University *B*
Lock Haven University of
Pennsylvania *B*
Lycoming College *B*
Mercyhurst College *B*
Messiah College *B*
Moravian College *B*
Penn State University Park
Campus *B*
Philadelphia College of Textiles and
Science *B*
Reading Area Community
College *A*
St. Francis College *B*
Seton Hill College *B*
Susquehanna University *B*
University of Pittsburgh
Bradford *B*
Greensburg *B*
Johnstown *B*
University of Scranton *B*
Ursinus College *B*
Villanova University *B*

Washington and Jefferson College *B*
Waynesburg College *B*
West Chester University of
Pennsylvania *B*
Widener University *B*
Wilkes University *B*
York College of Pennsylvania *B*

Puerto Rico
Caribbean University *B*
Inter American University of Puerto
Rico
Arecibo Campus *B*
San German Campus *B*
Universidad Metropolitana *B*
University of Puerto Rico:
Mayaguez Campus *B*

Rhode Island
Providence College *B*
Rhode Island College *B*
Roger Williams College *B*
Salve Regina University *B*

South Carolina
Bob Jones University *B*
Charleston Southern University *B*
Clemson University *B*
Coker College *B*
College of Charleston *B*
Columbia College *B*
Converse College *B*
Erskine College *B*
Francis Marion College *B*
Lander College *B*
Morris College *B*
North Greenville College *A*
University of South Carolina:
Coastal Carolina College *B*
Wofford College *B*

South Dakota
Augustana College *B*
Dakota State University *B*
Dakota Wesleyan University *B*
Sioux Falls College *B*
South Dakota State University *B*

Tennessee
Carson-Newman College *B*
Cumberland University *B*
David Lipscomb University *B*
Dyersburg State Community
College *A*
East Tennessee State University *B*
Fisk University *B*
Jackson State Community
College *A*
Lane College *B*
Lincoln Memorial University *B*
Martin Methodist College *A*
Maryville College *B*
Middle Tennessee State
University *B*
Roane State Community College *A*
Tusculum College *B*
Union University *B*
University of the South *B*
University of Tennessee
Chattanooga *B*
Knoxville *B*
Martin *B*
Volunteer State Community
College *A*
Walters State Community
College *A*

Texas
Abilene Christian University *B*
Amarillo College *A*
Angelina College *A*
Angelo State University *B*

Austin Community College *A*
Baylor University *B*
Bee County College *A*
Central Texas College *A*
Collin County Community College
District *A*
Dallas Baptist University *B*
Del Mar College *A*
East Texas State University *B*
El Paso Community College *A*
Hardin-Simmons University *B*
Houston Community College *A*
Howard College *A*
Huston-Tillotson College *B*
Lamar University—Beaumont *B*
LeTourneau University *B*
Lon Morris College *A*
Lubbock Christian University *B*
McMurry University *B*
Midland College *A*
Navarro College *A*
North Harris Montgomery
Community College District *A*
Panola College *A*
St. Edward's University *B*
St. Mary's University *B*
St. Philip's College *A*
San Antonio College *A*
Schreiner College *B*
South Plains College *A*
Stephen F. Austin State
University *B*
Tarleton State University *B*
Texas A&I University *B*
Texas Lutheran College *B*
Texas Southmost College *A*
Texas Wesleyan University *B*
University of Dallas *B*
University of Houston
Clear Lake *B*
Houston *B*
University of Mary Hardin-
Baylor *B*
University of St. Thomas *B*
West Texas State University *B*

Utah
Brigham Young University *B*
Utah State University *B*
Weber State University *B*

Vermont
Marlboro College *B*

Virginia
Averett College *B*
Bluefield College *A*
Christopher Newport College *B*
Eastern Mennonite College *B*
Emory and Henry College *B*
Hampton University *B*
Mountain Empire Community
College *A*
Old Dominion University *B*
Radford University *B*
Randolph-Macon College *B*
Virginia Commonwealth
University *B*
Virginia Intermont College *B*
Virginia Polytechnic Institute and
State University *B*
Virginia Wesleyan College *B*

Washington
Centralia College *A*
Eastern Washington University *B*
Evergreen State College *B*
Lower Columbia College *A*
Pacific Lutheran University *B*
Spokane Falls Community
College *A*
Tacoma Community College *A*

Wenatchee Valley College *A*

West Virginia
Alderson-Broaddus College *B*
Bethany College *B*
Concord College *B*
Davis and Elkins College *B*
Glenville State College *B*
Marshall University *B*
Potomac State College of West
Virginia University *A*
Shepherd College *B*
University of Charleston *B*
West Virginia Wesleyan College *B*
Wheeling Jesuit College *B*

Wisconsin
Alverno College *B*
Cardinal Stritch College *B*
Carroll College *B*
Carthage College *B*
Concordia University Wisconsin *B*
Lakeland College *B*
Lawrence University *B*
Marian College of Fond du Lac *B*
Marquette University *B*
Mount Mary College *B*
Northland College *B*
Ripon College *B*
St. Norbert College *B*
University of Wisconsin
Green Bay *B*
La Crosse *B*
Milwaukee *B*
Oshkosh *B*
Viterbo College *B*

Wyoming
Casper College *A*
Northwest College *A*
Western Wyoming Community
College *A*

Preoptometry

Alabama
Auburn University *B*
Huntingdon College *B*
Shelton State Community
College *A*
Shoals Community College *A*
Spring Hill College *B*
University of Alabama *B*

Arizona
Eastern Arizona College *A*

Arkansas
Hendrix College *B*
Ouachita Baptist University *B*
University of Central Arkansas *B*

California
Chabot College *A*
Santa Rosa Junior College *A*
University of San Francisco *B*

Colorado
Northeastern Junior College *A*

Connecticut
Albertus Magnus College *B*
Eastern Connecticut State
University *B*
Sacred Heart University *B*
University of Hartford *B*

Florida
Daytona Beach Community
College *A*
Florida Atlantic University *B*
Florida International University *B*
Florida State University *B*
Gulf Coast Community College *A*
Indian River Community College *A*
Manatee Community College *A*
Nova University *B*
Pensacola Junior College *A*
Rollins College *B*

Georgia
Brewton-Parker College *A*
Floyd College *A*
Gainesville College *A*
Georgia College *B*
Oglethorpe University *B*
Piedmont College *B*

Idaho
College of Southern Idaho *A*
Idaho State University *B*
North Idaho College *A*
Ricks College *A*

Illinois
Augustana College *B*
City Colleges of Chicago: Richard J.
Daley College *A*
Morton College *A*
Olivet Nazarene University *B*
Rockford College *B*
Southern Illinois University at
Carbondale *B*

Indiana
Indiana State University *B*
Taylor University *B*
University of Evansville *B*
University of Southern Indiana *A*
Vincennes University *A*

Iowa
Buena Vista College *B*
Central College *B*
Clarke College *B*
Dordt College *B*
Drake University *B*
Iowa Lakes Community College *A*
Iowa State University *B*
Loras College *B*
Luther College *B*
North Iowa Area Community
College *A*
Simpson College *B*
Upper Iowa University *B*

Kansas
Bethany College *B*
Dodge City Community College *A*
Kansas State University *B*
Neosho County Community
College *A*

Kentucky
Bellarmine College *B*
Campbellsville College *B*
Cumberland College *B*
Spalding University *B*

Louisiana
Dillard University *B*
Louisiana College *B*
Nicholls State University *B*
University of Southwestern
Louisiana *B*

Maryland

Montgomery College
Germantown Campus *A*
Rockville Campus *A*
Salisbury State University *B*
Western Maryland College *B*

Massachusetts

American International College *B*
Elms College *B*
Massachusetts Bay Community
College *A*
Springfield Technical Community
College *A*

Michigan

Eastern Michigan University *B*
Ferris State University *A*
Macomb Community College *A*
Michigan Technological
University *B*

Minnesota

Concordia College: Moorhead *B*
Rochester Community College *A*
St. Cloud State University *B*
St. Olaf College *B*
Willmar Community College *A*
Winona State University *B*

Mississippi

East Central Community College *A*
Jones County Junior College *A*
Mississippi Gulf Coast Community
College: Jefferson Davis
Campus *A*

Missouri

College of the Ozarks *B*
Northeast Missouri State
University *B*

Montana

Rocky Mountain College *B*
University of Montana *B*

Nebraska

Chadron State College *B*
Concordia College *B*
McCook Community College *A*
Southeast Community College:
Beatrice Campus *A*

New Hampshire

St. Anselm College *B*

New Jersey

Bloomfield College *B*
Glassboro State College *B*

New York

City University of New York
Hunter College *B*
Queens College *B*
Houghton College *B*
Niagara University *B*
Rochester Institute of
Technology *B*
St. John Fisher College *B*
Siena College *B*
State University of New York
College at Geneseo *B*

North Carolina

Elon College *B*

North Dakota

Bismarck State College *A*
Jamestown College *B*
Turtle Mountain Community
College *A*

Ohio

Baldwin-Wallace College *B*
Capital University *B*
Franciscan University of
Steubenville *B*
Otterbein College *B*
Shawnee State University *A*
Walsh College *B*
Xavier University *B*

Oklahoma

East Central University *B*
Oklahoma Baptist University *B*
Oral Roberts University *B*
Phillips University *B*

Oregon

Eastern Oregon State College *B*
Oregon State University *B*
Pacific University *B*

Pennsylvania

Albright College *B*
Allentown College of St. Francis de
Sales *B*
California University of
Pennsylvania *B*
College Misericordia *B*
Duquesne University *B*
Elizabethtown College *B*
Gannon University *B*
Gettysburg College *B*
Juniata College *B*
Lycoming College *B*
Mercyhurst College *B*
Messiah College *B*
St. Francis College *B*
Seton Hill College *B*
Susquehanna University *B*
University of Scranton *B*
Villanova University *B*
Washington and Jefferson College *B*
Widener University *B*
Wilkes University *B*
York College of Pennsylvania *B*

Rhode Island

Rhode Island College *B*

South Carolina

Converse College *B*

South Dakota

Dakota Wesleyan University *B*

Tennessee

Carson-Newman College *B*
Cumberland University *B*
Lincoln Memorial University *B*
Martin Methodist College *A*
Union University *B*
University of Tennessee
Knoxville *B*
Martin *B*
Volunteer State Community
College *A*

Texas

Abilene Christian University *B*
Amarillo College *A*
Baylor University *B*
Lamar University—Beaumont *B*
Lubbock Christian University *B*
St. Edward's University *B*
Stephen F. Austin State
University *B*
Texas Lutheran College *B*

Virginia

Virginia Commonwealth
University *B*
Virginia Intermont College *B*

Washington

Pacific Lutheran University *B*

West Virginia

Marshall University *B*
West Virginia Wesleyan College *B*

Wisconsin

Lakeland College *B*
Ripon College *B*
St. Norbert College *B*
University of Wisconsin
La Crosse *B*
Oshkosh *B*
Viterbo College *B*

Prepharmacy

Alabama

Alabama Southern Community
College *A*
Huntingdon College *B*
James H. Faulkner State
Community College *A*
John C. Calhoun State Community
College *A*
Judson College *B*
Lawson State Community
College *A*
Shelton State Community
College *A*
Shoals Community College *A*
University of Alabama *B*
Wallace State Community College
at Hanceville *A*

Arizona

Eastern Arizona College *A*
Glendale Community College *A*
Grand Canyon University *B*
Northern Arizona University *B*
Pima Community College *A*

Arkansas

Hendrix College *B*
Ouachita Baptist University *B*
University of Central Arkansas *B*
University of the Ozarks *B*
Westark Community College *A*

California

Bakersfield College *A*
California State University:
Stanislaus *B*
Cerritos Community College *A*
Chabot College *A*
Christ College Irvine *B*
City College of San Francisco *A*
College of Notre Dame *B*
El Camino College *A*
Foothill College *A*
Marymount College *A*
St. Mary's College of California *B*
Santa Rosa Junior College *A*
University of the Pacific *B*
University of San Francisco *B*
Ventura College *A*
West Coast University *C*
West Hills Community College *A*
Westmont College *B*

Colorado

Adams State College *B*
Fort Lewis College *B*
Lamar Community College *A*
Mesa State College *B*
Northeastern Junior College *A*
Trinidad State Junior College *A*

Connecticut

Quinnipiac College *B*
Sacred Heart University *B*

Florida

Barry University *B*
Daytona Beach Community
College *A*
Florida Atlantic University *B*
Florida State University *B*
Gulf Coast Community College *A*
Indian River Community College *A*
Miami-Dade Community College *A*
Nova University *B*
Okaloosa-Walton Community
College *A*
Pensacola Junior College *A*
Rollins College *B*
Santa Fe Community College *A*
Stetson University *B*

Georgia

Andrew College *A*
Brewton-Parker College *A*
Clayton State College *A*
Columbus College *B*
Darton College *A*
Emmanuel College *A*
Floyd College *A*
Gainesville College *A*
Georgia College *B*
Georgia Southern University *B*
Gordon College *A*
Kennesaw State College *B*
Macon College *A*
Middle Georgia College *A*
Oglethorpe University *B*
Piedmont College *B*
Reinhardt College *A*
Shorter College *B*
Truett-McConnell College *A*
Wesleyan College *B*

Hawaii

Hawaii Loa College *B*

Idaho

College of Southern Idaho *A*
Idaho State University *B*
North Idaho College *A*
Northwest Nazarene College *B*
Ricks College *A*

Illinois

Augustana College *B*
Aurora University *B*
Black Hawk College *A*
City Colleges of Chicago: Richard J.
Daley College *A*
Concordia University *B*
De Paul University *B*
Elmhurst College *B*
Eureka College *B*
Highland Community College *A*
Illinois Central College *A*
Illinois Wesleyan University *B*
Joliet Junior College *A*
Kishwaukee College *A*
Lincoln Land Community
College *A*
Morton College *A*
Olivet Nazarene University *B*
Rend Lake College *A*
Roosevelt University *B*
St. Xavier University *B*
Southern Illinois University at
Carbondale *B*
William Rainey Harper College *A*

Indiana

Ball State University *B*
Franklin College *B*

Goshen College *B*
Indiana State University *B*
Indiana University Bloomington *B*
Indiana Wesleyan University *B*
Purdue University: Calumet *B*
Taylor University *B*
University of Evansville *B*
University of Notre Dame *B*
University of Southern Indiana *B*
Vincennes University *A*

Iowa

Briar Cliff College *B*
Buena Vista College *B*
Central College *B*
Clarke College *B*
Clinton Community College *A*
Cornell College *B*
Dordt College *B*
Grinnell College *B*
Iowa Lakes Community College *A*
Iowa State University *B*
Iowa Wesleyan College *B*
Kirkwood Community College *A*
Loras College *B*
Luther College *B*
Muscatine Community College *A*
North Iowa Area Community
    College *A*
Scott Community College *A*
Simpson College *B*
Upper Iowa University *B*
Wartburg College *B*
William Penn College *B*

Kansas

Allen County Community
    College *A*
Baker University *B*
Barton County Community
    College *A*
Bethany College *B*
Butler County Community
    College *A*
Coffeyville Community College *A*
Colby Community College *A*
Dodge City Community College *A*
Hutchinson Community College *A*
Kansas City Kansas Community
    College *A*
Kansas Newman College *B*
Kansas State University *B*
Neosho County Community
    College *A*
Pittsburg State University *B*
Pratt Community College *A*
St. Mary College *B*
Washburn University of Topeka *B*

Kentucky

Bellarmine College *B*
Campbellsville College *B*
Cumberland College *B*
Georgetown College *B*
Lees College *A*
St. Catharine College *A*
Spalding University *B*
Sue Bennett College *A*
Thomas More College *B*
Union College *B*

Louisiana

Dillard University *B*
Louisiana College *B*
Loyola University *B*
Southeastern Louisiana
    University *B*

Maine

St. Joseph's College *B*

Maryland

Anne Arundel Community
    College *A*
College of Notre Dame of
    Maryland *B*
Columbia Union College *B*
Coppin State College *B*
Frostburg State University *B*
Howard Community College *A*
Montgomery College
    Germantown Campus *A*
    Rockville Campus *A*
    Takoma Park Campus *A*
Morgan State University *B*
Salisbury State University *B*
University of Maryland
    College Park *B*
    Eastern Shore *B*
Villa Julie College *B*

Massachusetts

Eastern Nazarene College *B*
Massachusetts Bay Community
    College *A*
Simon's Rock College of Bard *B*
Springfield Technical Community
    College *A*

Michigan

Eastern Michigan University *B*
Ferris State University *A*
Kellogg Community College *A*
Lansing Community College *A*
Macomb Community College *A*
Madonna University *B*
Michigan Technological
    University *B*
Olivet College *B*
Siena Heights College *B*

Minnesota

Bethel College *B*
College of St. Benedict *B*
College of St. Catherine: St.
    Catherine Campus *A*
Concordia College: Moorhead *B*
Itasca Community College:
    Arrowhead Region *A*
Rochester Community College *A*
St. Cloud State University *A*
St. John's University *B*
St. Olaf College *B*
University of Minnesota: Twin
    Cities *B*
Willmar Community College *A*
Winona State University *B*

Mississippi

Alcorn State University *B*
East Central Community College *A*
Holmes Community College *A*
Jackson State University *B*
Jones County Junior College *A*
Mary Holmes College *A*
Mississippi College *B*
Mississippi Delta Community
    College *A*
Mississippi Gulf Coast Community
    College: Jefferson Davis
    Campus *A*
Mississippi University for Women *B*
Northeast Mississippi Community
    College *A*
Rust College *B*
University of Southern
    Mississippi *B*

Missouri

Central Methodist College *B*
College of the Ozarks *B*
East Central College *A*

Northeast Missouri State
    University *B*
St. Louis Community College at
    Florissant Valley *A*

Montana

Rocky Mountain College *B*

Nebraska

Chadron State College *B*
College of St. Mary *B*
Concordia College *B*
Hastings College *B*
McCook Community College *A*
Midland Lutheran College *B*
Peru State College *B*
Southeast Community College:
    Beatrice Campus *A*
University of Nebraska—Lincoln *B*

New Hampshire

Notre Dame College *A*
St. Anselm College *B*

New Jersey

Bloomfield College *B*
Glassboro State College *B*
Jersey City State College *B*

New Mexico

Eastern New Mexico University *B*
New Mexico Institute of Mining
    and Technology *B*
New Mexico Junior College *A*
New Mexico State University *B*
Western New Mexico University *A*

New York

City University of New York
    Brooklyn College *B*
    Hunter College *B*
    New York City Technical
        College *A*
    Queensborough Community
        College *A*
Colgate University *B*
Herkimer County Community
    College *A*
Long Island University
    Brooklyn Campus *B*
    C. W. Post Campus *B*
Manhattan College *B*
Monroe Community College *A*
Niagara University *B*
Rochester Institute of
    Technology *B*
Sage Junior College of Albany, A
    Division of Russell Sage
    College *A*
St. Bonaventure University *B*
St. John Fisher College *B*
State University of New York
    College of Environmental
        Science and Forestry *B*
    College at Geneseo *B*
Sullivan County Community
    College *A*
Touro College *B*
Wagner College *B*

North Carolina

Appalachian State University *B*
Barton College *B*
Brevard College *A*
College of the Albemarle *A*
Gaston College *A*
Isothermal Community College *A*
Lenoir-Rhyne College *B*
Louisburg College *A*
Mars Hill College *B*
Peace College *A*
Rockingham Community College *A*

St. Andrews Presbyterian College *B*
Salem College *B*
University of North Carolina at
    Greensboro *B*
Wingate College *B*

North Dakota

Bismarck State College *A*
Jamestown College *B*
Turtle Mountain Community
    College *A*

Ohio

Ashland University *B*
Baldwin-Wallace College *B*
Capital University *B*
Cedarville College *B*
Kent State University *B*
Lorain County Community
    College *A*
Malone College *B*
Marietta College *B*
Mount Vernon Nazarene College *B*
Ohio University *B*
Otterbein College *B*
Shawnee State University *A*
University of Akron *B*
University of Cincinnati
    Clermont College *A*
    Raymond Walters College *A*
Walsh College *B*
Wittenberg University *B*
Xavier University *A*

Oklahoma

Connors State College *A*
East Central University *B*
Eastern Oklahoma State College *A*
Oklahoma Baptist University *B*
Oklahoma City University *B*
Oral Roberts University *B*
Phillips University *B*
Redlands Community College *A*
Rogers State College *A*
Rose State College *A*
University of Tulsa *B*

Oregon

Central Oregon Community
    College *A*
Eastern Oregon State College *B*
George Fox College *B*
Oregon State University *B*
Portland Community College *A*
Southern Oregon State College *B*
University of Portland *B*

Pennsylvania

Albright College *B*
California University of
    Pennsylvania *B*
East Stroudsburg University of
    Pennsylvania *B*
Edinboro University of
    Pennsylvania *B*
Elizabethtown College *B*
Gannon University *B*
Gettysburg College *B*
Holy Family College *B*
Immaculata College *B*
Indiana University of
    Pennsylvania *B*
Juniata College *B*
La Salle University *B*
Lock Haven University of
    Pennsylvania *B*
Luzerne County Community
    College *A*
Lycoming College *B*
Mercyhurst College *B*
Reading Area Community
    College *A*

University of Pittsburgh at
  Bradford *B*
University of Scranton *B*
Wilkes University *B*
York College of Pennsylvania *B*

Rhode Island

Salve Regina University *B*

South Carolina

Charleston Southern University *B*
Clemson University *B*
Coker College *B*
Converse College *B*
Erskine College *B*
Francis Marion College *B*
Lander College *B*
Morris College *B*
University of South Carolina:
  Coastal Carolina College *B*
Wofford College *B*

South Dakota

Augustana College *B*
Dakota Wesleyan University *B*
Sioux Falls College *B*

Tennessee

Carson-Newman College *B*
Cumberland University *B*
David Lipscomb University *B*
East Tennessee State University *B*
Lincoln Memorial University *B*
Martin Methodist College *A*
Middle Tennessee State
  University *B*
Roane State Community College *A*
Tusculum College *B*
Union University *B*
University of Tennessee
  Chattanooga *B*
  Knoxville *B*
  Martin *B*
Volunteer State Community
  College *A*
Walters State Community
  College *A*

Texas

Amarillo College *A*
Angelina College *A*
Austin Community College *A*
Baylor University *B*
Bee County College *A*
Dallas Baptist University *B*
Del Mar College *A*
El Paso Community College *A*
Houston Community College *A*
Howard College *A*
Huston-Tillotson College *B*
Lamar University—Beaumont *B*
Lon Morris College *A*
Lubbock Christian University *B*
McMurry University *B*
Midland College *A*
Navarro College *A*
North Harris Montgomery
  Community College District *A*
Panola College *A*
St. Edward's University *B*
St. Mary's University *B*
San Antonio College *A*
Schreiner College *B*
South Plains College *A*
Stephen F. Austin State
  University *B*
Tarleton State University *B*
Texas A&I University *B*
Texas Lutheran College *B*
Texas Southmost College *A*
Texas Wesleyan University *B*
University of Dallas *B*

University of Houston *B*
University of Mary Hardin-
  Baylor *B*
West Texas State University *B*

Utah

Weber State University *B*

Virginia

Averett College *B*
Bluefield College *A*
Christopher Newport College *B*
Eastern Mennonite College *B*
Mountain Empire Community
  College *A*
Old Dominion University *B*
Radford University *B*
Virginia Commonwealth
  University *B*
Virginia Intermont College *B*
Virginia Wesleyan College *B*

Washington

Centralia College *A*
Eastern Washington University *B*
Lower Columbia College *A*
Pacific Lutheran University *B*
Spokane Falls Community
  College *A*
Tacoma Community College *A*
Wenatchee Valley College *A*

West Virginia

Alderson-Broaddus College *B*
Concord College *B*
Davis and Elkins College *A*
Glenville State College *B*
Marshall University *B*
Potomac State College of West
  Virginia University *A*
Shepherd College *B*
West Virginia Wesleyan College *B*

Wisconsin

Carroll College *B*
Carthage College *B*
Lakeland College *B*
Lawrence University *B*
Marian College of Fond du Lac *B*
Northland College *B*
Ripon College *B*
St. Norbert College *B*
University of Wisconsin
  Green Bay *B*
  La Crosse *B*
  Milwaukee *B*
  Oshkosh *B*
Viterbo College *B*

Wyoming

Casper College *A*
Northwest College *A*
Western Wyoming Community
  College *A*

Prephysical therapy

Alabama

Auburn University *B*

Arizona

Eastern Arizona College *A*

California

Humboldt State University *B*
University of San Francisco *B*
Whittier College *B*

Colorado

Mesa State College *A*
Trinidad State Junior College *A*
Western State College of
  Colorado *B*

Connecticut

Sacred Heart University *B*

Delaware

University of Delaware *B*

Florida

Pensacola Junior College *A*
Santa Fe Community College *A*
University of Miami *B*

Georgia

Andrew College *A*
Brewton-Parker College *A*
Georgia College *B*

Idaho

College of Southern Idaho *A*
Idaho State University *B*
North Idaho College *A*
Ricks College *A*

Illinois

Augustana College *B*
Concordia University *B*
MacMurray College *B*
Millikin University *B*
North Central College *B*
Southern Illinois University at
  Carbondale *B*

Indiana

Franklin College *B*
Indiana State University *B*
Purdue University *B*
St. Joseph's College *B*
Taylor University *B*
University of Southern Indiana *A*

Iowa

Buena Vista College *B*
Clarke College *B*
Clinton Community College *A*
Coe College *B*
Iowa State University *B*
Loras College *B*
Simpson College *B*
Upper Iowa University *B*

Kansas

Baker University *B*
Colby Community College *A*
Dodge City Community College *A*
Kansas State University *B*
McPherson College *B*
Neosho County Community
  College *A*
Pittsburg State University *B*

Kentucky

Campbellsville College *B*
Union College *B*

Maryland

Anne Arundel Community
  College *B*
Coppin State College *B*
Frostburg State University *B*
Villa Julie College *A*
Western Maryland College *B*

Massachusetts

Endicott College *A*

Michigan

Alma College *B*
Hope College *B*
Michigan Technological
  University *B*

Minnesota

College of St. Benedict *B*
College of St. Catherine: St.
  Catherine Campus *B*
St. Cloud State University *B*
St. John's University *B*
St. Olaf College *B*
Willmar Community College *A*
Winona State University *B*

Mississippi

Mississippi Gulf Coast Community
  College: Jefferson Davis
  Campus *A*

Missouri

Northeast Missouri State
  University *B*

Nebraska

Concordia College *B*
Dana College *B*
Midland Lutheran College *B*
Southeast Community College:
  Beatrice Campus *A*
University of Nebraska—Lincoln *B*

Nevada

University of Nevada: Reno *B*

New York

City University of New York:
  Queensborough Community
  College *A*
Manhattan College *B*
Sage Junior College of Albany, A
  Division of Russell Sage
  College *A*

Ohio

Heidelberg College *B*
Kettering College of Medical
  Arts *A*
University of Rio Grande *B*

Oklahoma

Oklahoma Baptist University *B*
Oral Roberts University *B*
Rose State College *A*

Oregon

Linfield College *B*
Southern Oregon State College *B*

Pennsylvania

California University of
  Pennsylvania *B*
Gannon University *B*
Hahnemann University School of
  Health Sciences and
  Humanities *B*
Lock Haven University of
  Pennsylvania *B*
University of Pittsburgh at
  Johnstown *B*

Puerto Rico

Universidad Metropolitana *B*

Rhode Island

Rhode Island College *B*

South Carolina

Bob Jones University *B*
Clemson University *B*
Coker College *B*

Francis Marion College *B*
Lander College *B*

South Dakota

South Dakota State University *B*

Tennessee

Carson-Newman College *B*
Martin Methodist College *A*
University of Tennessee:
    Knoxville *B*

Texas

Angelina College *A*
Dallas Baptist University *B*
South Plains College *A*
Tarleton State University *B*
University of Houston *B*
West Texas State University *B*

West Virginia

Alderson-Broaddus College *B*
Marshall University *B*
West Virginia Wesleyan College *B*

Wisconsin

Ripon College *B*

Wyoming

Casper College *A*

Preveterinary

Alabama

Alabama Agricultural and
    Mechanical University *B*
Alabama Southern Community
    College *A*
Auburn University *B*
Huntingdon College *B*
James H. Faulkner State
    Community College *A*
John C. Calhoun State Community
    College *A*
Judson College *B*
Mobile College *B*
Shelton State Community
    College *A*
Shoals Community College *A*
Wallace State Community College
    at Hanceville *A*

Arizona

Eastern Arizona College *A*
Grand Canyon University *B*
Northern Arizona University *B*
Pima Community College *A*

Arkansas

Hendrix College *B*
Ouachita Baptist University *B*
University of Central Arkansas *B*
University of the Ozarks *B*
Westark Community College *A*

California

Bakersfield College *A*
California State University:
    Stanislaus *B*
Cerritos Community College *A*
Chabot College *A*
Chapman University *B*
Christ College Irvine *B*
College of Notre Dame *B*
Dominican College of San Rafael *B*
El Camino College *A*
Foothill College *A*
Humboldt State University *B*
Marymount College *A*

Mount St. Mary's College *B*
Pacific Union College *B*
St. Mary's College of California *B*
Santa Clara University *B*
Scripps College *B*
Southern California College *B*
Southwestern College *A*
University of the Pacific *B*
University of San Francisco *B*
Ventura College *A*
West Coast University *C*
Westmont College *B*

Colorado

Adams State College *B*
Fort Lewis College *B*
Lamar Community College *A*
Mesa State College *A*
Northeastern Junior College *A*
Trinidad State Junior College *A*
University of Denver *B*

Connecticut

Albertus Magnus College *B*
Eastern Connecticut State
    University *B*
Quinnipiac College *B*
Sacred Heart University *B*
University of Bridgeport *B*
University of New Haven *B*

Delaware

University of Delaware *B*

District of Columbia

American University *B*

Florida

Barry University *B*
Daytona Beach Community
    College *A*
Eckerd College *B*
Florida Atlantic University *B*
Florida Institute of Technology *B*
Florida International University *B*
Florida Southern College *B*
Florida State University *B*
Gulf Coast Community College *A*
Indian River Community College *A*
Jacksonville University *B*
Manatee Community College *A*
Miami-Dade Community College *A*
New College of the University of
    South Florida *B*
Nova University *B*
Okaloosa-Walton Community
    College *A*
Pensacola Junior College *A*
Rollins College *B*
Stetson University *B*
University of Tampa *B*

Georgia

Andrew College *A*
Brewton-Parker College *A*
Clayton State College *A*
Columbus College *B*
Floyd College *A*
Gainesville College *A*
Georgia College *B*
Georgia Southern University *B*
Gordon College *A*
Kennesaw State College *B*
Macon College *A*
Middle Georgia College *A*
Oglethorpe University *B*
Piedmont College *B*
Reinhardt College *A*
Truett-McConnell College *A*
University of Georgia *B*
Wesleyan College *B*

Hawaii

Hawaii Loa College *B*
University of Hawaii at Hilo *B*

Idaho

Boise State University *B*
College of Southern Idaho *A*
Idaho State University *B*
North Idaho College *A*
Northwest Nazarene College *B*
Ricks College *A*
University of Idaho *B,M*

Illinois

Augustana College *B*
Aurora University *B*
Blackburn College *B*
De Paul University *B*
Elmhurst College *B*
Eureka College *B*
Governors State University *B*
Highland Community College *A*
Illinois Central College *A*
Illinois Wesleyan University *B*
Joliet Junior College *A*
Kishwaukee College *A*
Lincoln Land Community
    College *A*
MacMurray College *B*
Millikin University *B*
Morton College *A*
North Central College *B*
North Park College and Theological
    Seminary *B*
Olivet Nazarene University *B*
Quincy College *B*
Rend Lake College *A*
Rockford College *B*
Roosevelt University *B*
St. Xavier University *B*
Southern Illinois University at
    Carbondale *B*
Trinity College *B*
William Rainey Harper College *A*

Indiana

Franklin College *B*
Goshen College *B*
Indiana State University *B*
Indiana University Bloomington *B*
Indiana Wesleyan University *B*
Manchester College *B*
Marian College *B*
Purdue University: Calumet *B*
St. Francis College *B*
St. Joseph's College *B*
St. Mary-of-the-Woods College *B*
Taylor University *B*
University of Evansville *B*
University of Indianapolis *B*
University of Notre Dame *B*
University of Southern Indiana *B*
Vincennes University *A*

Iowa

Briar Cliff College *B*
Buena Vista College *B*
Central College *B*
Clarke College *B*
Clinton Community College *A*
Cornell College *B*
Dordt College *B*
Drake University *B*
Grinnell College *B*
Iowa Lakes Community College *A*
Iowa State University *B*
Iowa Wesleyan College *B*
Kirkwood Community College *A*
Loras College *B*
Luther College *B*
Muscatine Community College *A*

North Iowa Area Community
    College *A*
Scott Community College *A*
Simpson College *B*
Teikyo Marycrest University *B*
Teikyo Westmar University *B*
Upper Iowa University *B*
Wartburg College *B*
William Penn College *B*

Kansas

Allen County Community
    College *A*
Baker University *B*
Barton County Community
    College *A*
Bethany College *B*
Bethel College *B*
Butler County Community
    College *A*
Coffeyville Community College *A*
Colby Community College *A*
Dodge City Community College *A*
Friends University *B*
Hutchinson Community College *A*
Kansas Newman College *B*
Kansas State University *B*
Neosho County Community
    College *A*
Pittsburg State University *B*
Pratt Community College *A*
St. Mary College *B*
Tabor College *B*
Washburn University of Topeka *B*

Kentucky

Bellarmine College *B*
Campbellsville College *B*
Centre College *B*
Cumberland College *B*
Georgetown College *B*
Lees College *A*
St. Catharine College *A*
Spalding University *B*
Thomas More College *B*
Union College *B*

Louisiana

Dillard University *B*
Louisiana College *B*
Loyola University *B*
University of Southwestern
    Louisiana *B*

Maine

St. Joseph's College *B*

Maryland

Anne Arundel Community
    College *A*
College of Notre Dame of
    Maryland *B*
Columbia Union College *B*
Frostburg State University *B*
Howard Community College *A*
Salisbury State University *B*
University of Maryland
    College Park *B*
    Eastern Shore *B*
Villa Julie College *B*
Western Maryland College *B*

Massachusetts

American International College *B*
Anna Maria College for Men and
    Women *B*
Clark University *B*
Eastern Nazarene College *B*
Elms College *B*
Framingham State College *B*
Hampshire College *B*

Massachusetts Bay Community
College *A*
Massachusetts Institute of
Technology *B*
Salem State College *B*
Simon's Rock College of Bard *B*
Springfield College *B*
Springfield Technical Community
College *A*
University of Massachusetts at
Amherst *B*
Worcester Polytechnic Institute *B*

Michigan

Alma College *B*
Eastern Michigan University *B*
Ferris State University *A*
Hope College *B*
Kellogg Community College *A*
Lake Superior State University *B*
Lansing Community College *A*
Macomb Community College *A*
Madonna University *B*
Michigan State University *B*
Michigan Technological
University *B*
Olivet College *B*
Siena Heights College *B*

Minnesota

Bethel College *B*
College of St. Benedict *B*
College of St. Catherine: St.
Catherine Campus *B*
Concordia College: Moorhead *B*
Itasca Community College:
Arrowhead Region *A*
Moorhead State University *B*
Rochester Community College *A*
St. Cloud State University *B*
St. John's University *B*
St. Olaf College *B*
University of Minnesota: Twin
Cities *B*
Willmar Community College *A*
Winona State University *B*

Mississippi

Alcorn State University *B*
East Central Community College *A*
Holmes Community College *A*
Jackson State University *B*
Jones County Junior College *A*
Mary Holmes College *A*
Millsaps College *B*
Mississippi College *B*
Mississippi Delta Community
College *A*
Mississippi Gulf Coast Community
College: Jefferson Davis
Campus *A*
Mississippi University for Women *B*
Northeast Mississippi Community
College *A*
University of Southern
Mississippi *B*

Missouri

Central Methodist College *B*
College of the Ozarks *B*
East Central College *A*
Evangel College *B*
Jefferson College *A*
Northeast Missouri State
University *B*
Northwest Missouri State
University *B*
Park College *B*
Westminster College *B*
William Woods College *B*

Montana

Rocky Mountain College *B*
University of Montana *B*

Nebraska

Chadron State College *B*
College of St. Mary *B*
Hastings College *B*
McCook Community College *A*
Metropolitan Community College *A*
Midland Lutheran College *B*
Peru State College *B*
Southeast Community College:
Beatrice Campus *A*

Nevada

Sierra Nevada College *B*
University of Nevada: Reno *B*

New Hampshire

Colby-Sawyer College *B*
Franklin Pierce College *B*
Rivier College *B*
University of New Hampshire *B*

New Jersey

Bloomfield College *B*
Glassboro State College *B*
Jersey City State College *B*
Monmouth College *B*

New Mexico

College of Santa Fe *B*
Eastern New Mexico University *B*
New Mexico Institute of Mining
and Technology *B*
New Mexico State University *B*
University of New Mexico *B*
Western New Mexico University *A*

New York

Alfred University *B*
Bard College *B*
Canisius College *B*
City University of New York
Brooklyn College *B*
City College *B*
Hunter College *B*
Queensborough Community
College *A*
Colgate University *B*
Daemen College *B*
D'Youville College *B*
Fordham University *B*
Houghton College *B*
Long Island University
C. W. Post Campus *B*
Southampton Campus *B*
Manhattan College *B*
Manhattanville College *B*
New York University *B*
Niagara University *B*
Rochester Institute of
Technology *B*
Russell Sage College *B*
St. Bonaventure University *B*
St. John Fisher College *B*
Siena College *B*
State University of New York
College of Agriculture and
Technology at Morrisville *A*
College of Environmental
Science and Forestry *B*
College at Geneseo *B*
College at New Paltz *B*
Oswego *B*
Sullivan County Community
College *A*
Touro College *B*
Wagner College *B*

North Carolina

Barton College *B*
Brevard College *B*
College of the Albemarle *A*
Elon College *B*
Gaston College *A*
Isothermal Community College *A*
Louisburg College *A*
Mars Hill College *B*
Methodist College *B*
North Carolina State University *B*
Pfeiffer College *B*
Rockingham Community College *A*
St. Andrews Presbyterian College *B*
Salem College *B*
University of North Carolina at
Greensboro *B*
Warren Wilson College *B*
Western Piedmont Community
College *B*
Wingate College *B*

North Dakota

Jamestown College *B*
Turtle Mountain Community
College *A*

Ohio

Ashland University *B*
Baldwin-Wallace College *B*
Bowling Green State University *B*
Capital University *B*
Cedarville College *B*
Defiance College *B*
Franciscan University of
Steubenville *B*
Heidelberg College *B*
John Carroll University *B*
Kent State University *B*
Kenyon College *B*
Lake Erie College *B*
Lorain County Community
College *A*
Malone College *B*
Marietta College *B*
Mount Vernon Nazarene College *B*
Muskingum College *B*
Notre Dame College of Ohio *B*
Ohio University *B*
Otterbein College *B*
Shawnee State University *A*
University of Akron *B*
University of Findlay *B*
Walsh College *B*
Wilmington College *B*
Wittenberg University *B*
Xavier University *B*
Youngstown State University *B*

Oklahoma

Bartlesville Wesleyan College *B*
Connors State College *A*
East Central University *B*
Eastern Oklahoma State College *A*
Langston University *B*
Murray State College *A*
Northwestern Oklahoma State
University *B*
Oklahoma Baptist University *B*
Oklahoma City University *B*
Oklahoma State University *B*
Oral Roberts University *B*
Phillips University *B*
Rose State College *A*
University of Tulsa *B*

Oregon

Central Oregon Community
College *A*
Eastern Oregon State College *B*
George Fox College *B*
Linfield College *B*

Oregon State University *B*
Portland Community College *A*
Southern Oregon State College *B*
University of Portland *B*

Pennsylvania

Albright College *B*
Allegheny College *B*
Allentown College of St. Francis de
Sales *B*
Bucknell University *B*
California University of
Pennsylvania *B*
College Misericordia *B*
Duquesne University *B*
Edinboro University of
Pennsylvania *B*
Elizabethtown College *B*
Gannon University *B*
Gettysburg College *B*
Grove City College *B*
Gwynedd-Mercy College *B*
Holy Family College *B*
Immaculata College *B*
Indiana University of
Pennsylvania *B*
Juniata College *B*
La Roche College *B*
La Salle University *B*
Lehigh University *B*
Lock Haven University of
Pennsylvania *B*
Lycoming College *B*
Manor Junior College *A*
Mercyhurst College *B*
Messiah College *B*
Moravian College *B*
Philadelphia College of Textiles and
Science *B*
St. Francis College *B*
Seton Hill College *B*
Susquehanna University *B*
University of Pittsburgh
Bradford *B*
Johnstown *B*
University of Scranton *B*
Ursinus College *B*
Washington and Jefferson College *B*
Widener University *B*
Wilkes University *B*
York College of Pennsylvania *B*

Puerto Rico

University of Puerto Rico:
Mayaguez Campus *B*

Rhode Island

Rhode Island College *B*
Roger Williams College *B*
Salve Regina University *B*

South Carolina

Bob Jones University *B*
Clemson University *B*
Coker College *B*
Converse College *B*
Erskine College *B*
Francis Marion College *B*
Lander College *B*
Morris College *B*
University of South Carolina:
Coastal Carolina College *B*
Wofford College *B*

South Dakota

Augustana College *B*
Dakota Wesleyan University *B*
Sioux Falls College *B*
South Dakota State University *B*

Tennessee

Carson-Newman College *B*
Cumberland University *B*
David Lipscomb University *B*
Dyersburg State Community
College *A*
East Tennessee State University *B*
Lincoln Memorial University *B*
Maryville College *B*
Middle Tennessee State
University *B*
Tusculum College *B*
Union University *B*
University of the South *B*
University of Tennessee
Chattanooga *B*
Knoxville *B*
Martin *B*
Volunteer State Community
College *A*

Texas

Abilene Christian University *B*
Amarillo College *A*
Angelina College *A*
Austin Community College *A*
Bee County College *A*
Collin County Community College
District *A*
Dallas Baptist University *B*
Del Mar College *A*
East Texas State University *B*
El Paso Community College *A*
Houston Community College *A*
LeTourneau University *B*
Lon Morris College *A*
Lubbock Christian University *B*
McMurry University *B*
Navarro College *A*
North Harris Montgomery
Community College District *A*
Panola College *A*
St. Edward's University *B*
San Antonio College *A*
Schreiner College *B*
South Plains College *A*
Stephen F. Austin State
University *B*
Tarleton State University *B*
Texas A&I University *B*
Texas Lutheran College *B*
Texas Southmost College *A*
University of Dallas *B*
University of Houston *B*
University of St. Thomas *B*
West Texas State University *B*

Utah

Brigham Young University *B*
Utah State University *B*
Weber State University *B*

Virginia

Averett College *B*
Bluefield College *A*
Christopher Newport College *B*
Eastern Mennonite College *B*
Emory and Henry College *B*
Old Dominion University *B*
Radford University *B*
Virginia Commonwealth
University *B*
Virginia Intermont College *B*
Virginia Polytechnic Institute and
State University *B*
Virginia Wesleyan College *B*

Washington

Centralia College *A*
Eastern Washington University *B*
Evergreen State College *B*
Lower Columbia College *A*

Pacific Lutheran University *B*
Spokane Falls Community
College *A*
Tacoma Community College *A*
Wenatchee Valley College *A*

West Virginia

Alderson-Broaddus College *B*
Bethany College *B*
Glenville State College *B*
Marshall University *B*
Potomac State College of West
Virginia University *A*
Shepherd College *B*
University of Charleston *B*
West Virginia University *B*
West Virginia Wesleyan College *B*
Wheeling Jesuit College *B*

Wisconsin

Alverno College *B*
Cardinal Stritch College *B*
Carroll College *B*
Carthage College *B*
Lakeland College *B*
Lawrence University *B*
Marian College of Fond du Lac *B*
Mount Mary College *B*
Northland College *B*
Ripon College *B*
St. Norbert College *B*
University of Wisconsin
Green Bay *B*
La Crosse *B*
Oshkosh *B*
Viterbo College *B*

Wyoming

Casper College *A*
Northwest College *A*
Western Wyoming Community
College *A*

Printmaking

Alabama

University of Montevallo *B*

Arizona

Northern Arizona University *B*

Arkansas

Phillips County Community College
C,A

California

Academy of Art College *C,B,M,W*
California College of Arts and
Crafts *B,M*
California Institute of the Arts
C,B,M
California State University
Fullerton *B,M*
Long Beach *B,M*
Northridge *B,M*
Stanislaus *B*
City College of San Francisco *C,A*
De Anza College *C*
Long Beach City College *A*
Modesto Junior College *A*
Otis/Parsons School of Art and
Design *B*
Palomar College *A*
Pasadena City College *C,A*
Saddleback College *A*
San Jose State University *B*
Santa Rosa Junior College *C*
University of California: Santa Cruz
C,B

Colorado

Mesa State College *A*

Connecticut

University of Bridgeport *B*
University of Connecticut *B*
University of Hartford *B*

District of Columbia

American University *M*
George Washington University *M*
Howard University *B,M*

Florida

Pensacola Junior College *A*
Ringling School of Art and
Design *B*
University of Miami *M*

Georgia

Atlanta College of Art *B*
University of Georgia *B,M*

Idaho

University of Idaho *B*

Illinois

Bradley University *B,M*
Illinois Wesleyan University *B*
Richland Community College *A*
School of the Art Institute of
Chicago *B,M*
Southern Illinois University at
Carbondale *B,M*

Indiana

Ball State University *B*
Indiana University Bloomington
B,M
Indiana University—Purdue
University at Indianapolis *B*
Purdue University *B,M*
Vincennes University *A*

Iowa

Drake University *B,M*
University of Iowa *B,M*

Kansas

Kansas City Kansas Community
College *A*
Kansas State University *M*
University of Kansas *B*

Kentucky

Eastern Kentucky University *B*

Louisiana

Louisiana State University and
Agricultural and Mechanical
College *B*

Maine

Portland School of Art *B*

Maryland

Maryland Institute College of Art *B*

Massachusetts

Massachusetts College of Art *B,M*
Montserrat College of Art *B*
School of the Museum of Fine Arts
B,M
University of Massachusetts at
Dartmouth *B,M*

Michigan

Center for Creative Studies: College
of Art and Design *B*
Central Michigan University *B*
Eastern Michigan University *B*
Grand Valley State University *B*

Marygrove College *B*
Northern Michigan University *B*
University of Michigan *B,M*

Minnesota

College of Associated Arts *B*
Moorhead State University *B*

Missouri

Kansas City Art Institute *B*
Washington University *B,M*
Webster University *B*

New Hampshire

Plymouth State College of the
University System of New
Hampshire *B*

New Jersey

Rutgers—The State University of
New Jersey: Mason Gross School
of the Arts *B*

New Mexico

Institute of American Indian
Arts *A*

New York

Alfred University *B*
Daemen College *B*
Parsons School of Design *B*
Pratt Institute *B,M*
Rochester Institute of Technology
A,B,M
Sarah Lawrence College *B*
School of Visual Arts *B*
State University of New York
College at Buffalo *B*
College at Potsdam *B*
Syracuse University *B,M*

North Carolina

Barton College *B*
Brevard College *A*
East Carolina University *B,M*

Ohio

Art Academy of Cincinnati *B*
Bowling Green State University *B*
Cleveland Institute of Art *B*
Lourdes College *A*
Ohio Northern University *B*
Ohio State University: Columbus
Campus *B,M*
Ohio University *B,M*
University of Akron *B*
University of Toledo *B*
Wittenberg University *B*
Wright State University *B*

Oklahoma

University of Oklahoma *B*
University of Tulsa *B*

Oregon

Pacific Northwest College of Art *B*
University of Oregon
Eugene *B*
Robert Donald Clark Honors
College *B*

Pennsylvania

Beaver College *B*
Carnegie Mellon University *B,M*
Edinboro University of
Pennsylvania *B,M*
Immaculata College *A*
Marywood College *B*
Moore College of Art and Design *B*
Seton Hill College *B*
Temple University *B,M*
University of the Arts *B,M*

Rhode Island
Rhode Island School of Design *B*

South Carolina
South Carolina State College *B*

Tennessee
Memphis College of Art *B,M*

Texas
Lamar University—Beaumont *M*
Lon Morris College *A*
Sam Houston State University *M*
Texas Woman's University *B,M*
University of Dallas *B,M*
University of Houston *B*
University of North Texas *B,M*
University of Texas at El Paso *B*

Utah
Brigham Young University *B*

Vermont
Bennington College *B,M*

Virginia
Virginia Commonwealth University *B,M*

Washington
Evergreen State College *B*
University of Washington *B,M*
Wenatchee Valley College *A*

West Virginia
Marshall University *B*
Shepherd College *B*
West Virginia State College *B*
West Virginia University *B,M*

Wisconsin
Milwaukee Institute of Art & Design *B*

Protective services

Alabama
Community College of the Air Force *A*
George C. Wallace State Community College at Selma *A*

Arkansas
Mississippi County Community College *A*

California
Bakersfield College *A*
Chabot College *A*
Citrus College *A*
Compton Community College *A*
Crafton Hills College *A*
De Anza College *C,A*
D-Q University *A*
East Los Angeles College *A*
Modesto Junior College *A*
Napa Valley College *A*
Pasadena City College *A*
San Joaquin Delta College *A*
San Jose City College *A*

Connecticut
Manchester Community College *A*
Mitchell College *A*

District of Columbia
Southeastern University *M*

Florida
Brevard Community College *A*

Georgia
Atlanta Metropolitan College *A*

Illinois
Black Hawk College *A*
Carl Sandburg College *A*
City Colleges of Chicago: Richard J. Daley College *C*
Illinois Central College *C,A*
Illinois Eastern Community Colleges: Frontier Community College *C*
Joliet Junior College *C,A*
Moraine Valley Community College *C*
Western Illinois University *B*

Iowa
Iowa Central Community College *A*
Kirkwood Community College *A*

Louisiana
Louisiana State University at Eunice *A*

Maryland
Cecil Community College *C,A*
Montgomery College: Rockville Campus *A*

Massachusetts
Dean Junior College *A*

Michigan
Lansing Community College *A*
Macomb Community College *C,A*
Madonna University *C,A,B*
Southwestern Michigan College *A*

Minnesota
Bethany Lutheran College *A*
Concordia College: St. Paul *A*
Mesabi Community College: Arrowhead Region *A*
Normandale Community College *C*
Willmar Community College *A*

Mississippi
Phillips Junior College of the Mississippi Gulf Coast *A*

Missouri
Central Missouri State University *M*

Nebraska
Metropolitan Community College *A*

Nevada
Community College of Southern Nevada *A*
Northern Nevada Community College *A*

New Jersey
Camden County College *A*

New York
Adirondack Community College *A*
City University of New York: John Jay College of Criminal Justice *A,B*
Hudson Valley Community College *A*
Mercy College *B*
St. John's University *B*
Tompkins-Cortland Community College *A*

Ulster County Community College *A*

North Carolina
Central Piedmont Community College *A*
Edgecombe Community College *A*
Guilford Technical Community College *A*
Mayland Community College *C*
Mitchell Community College *A*
Western Piedmont Community College *A*

Ohio
Columbus State Community College *A*
Lakeland Community College *A*
Mount Vernon Nazarene College *A*
Ohio University: Chillicothe Campus *A*
Sinclair Community College *A*
University of Toledo *A*

Oregon
Central Oregon Community College *A*

Texas
Central Texas College *A*
San Antonio College *A*

Virginia
John Tyler Community College *C*
Northern Virginia Community College *C,A*
Piedmont Virginia Community College *C,A*
Tidewater Community College *A*

Wisconsin
Western Wisconsin Technical College *A*
Wisconsin Indianhead Technical College *C,A*

Wyoming
Sheridan College *A*

Psychobiology

California
Claremont McKenna College *B*
La Sierra University *B*
Occidental College *B*
Pitzer College *B*
Pomona College *B*
Scripps College *B*
University of California
Los Angeles *B*
Riverside *B*
Santa Barbara *B*
Santa Cruz *B*
University of Southern California *B*

Colorado
Western State College of Colorado *B*

Connecticut
Quinnipiac College *B*
Wesleyan University *B*

Florida
New College of the University of South Florida *B*
University of Miami *B,D*

Illinois
University of Chicago *B,M,D*

Indiana
Purdue University *B,M,D*
University of Evansville *B*

Iowa
Luther College *B*

Kansas
Kansas State University *M,D*

Kentucky
Centre College *B*

Louisiana
University of New Orleans *D*

Maryland
Hood College *B*
Mount St. Mary's College *B*
Western Maryland College *B*

Massachusetts
Hampshire College *B*
Mount Holyoke College *B*
Pine Manor College *B*
Simmons College *B*
Wellesley College *B*

Michigan
University of Michigan *M,D*

Missouri
Northwest Missouri State University *B*

Nebraska
University of Nebraska
Kearney *B*
Omaha *D*

New Jersey
Drew University *B*
Rutgers—The State University of New Jersey *D*

New York
City University of New York Graduate School and University Center *D*
Columbia University: School of General Studies *B*
Hamilton College *B*
Long Island University
C. W. Post Campus *B*
Southampton Campus *B*
New York University *B*
Sarah Lawrence College *B*
State University of New York
Albany *M,D*
Binghamton *B*
Buffalo *D*
Vassar College *B*

Ohio
Hiram College *B*
Oberlin College *B*
Ohio State University: Columbus Campus *M,D*

Pennsylvania
Albright College *B*
Beaver College *B*
Holy Family College *B*
Juniata College *B*
Lafayette College *B*
Lebanon Valley College of Pennsylvania *B*
Swarthmore College *B*
Temple University *D*

Westminster College *B*

Wisconsin

Ripon College *B*

Psycholinguistics

California

University of Southern California *B*

Connecticut

Wesleyan University *B*

Florida

New College of the University of
South Florida *B*

Illinois

University of Chicago *B,M,D*

Kansas

Kansas State University *M,D*

Massachusetts

Hampshire College *B*
Massachusetts Institute of
Technology *B,M,D*

New Hampshire

University of New Hampshire *D*

New York

Sarah Lawrence College *B*

Pennsylvania

Swarthmore College *B*

Psychology

Alabama

Alabama Agricultural and
Mechanical University *B*
Alabama Southern Community
College *A*
Alabama State University *B*
Athens State College *B*
Auburn University
Auburn *B,M,D*
Montgomery *B,M*
Birmingham-Southern College *B*
Faulkner University *B*
Huntingdon College *B*
Jacksonville State University *B,M*
Judson College *B*
Lawson State Community
College *A*
Marion Military Institute *A*
Mobile College *B*
Oakwood College *B*
Samford University *B*
Selma University *A*
Spring Hill College *B*
Talladega College *B*
Troy State University
Dothan *B*
Montgomery *B*
Troy *B*
Tuskegee University *B*
University of Alabama
Birmingham *B,M*
Huntsville *B*
Tuscaloosa *B,M,D*
University of Montevallo *B*
University of North Alabama *B*
University of South Alabama *B,M*

Alaska

Alaska Pacific University *B*
University of Alaska
Anchorage *B*
Fairbanks *B*

Arizona

Arizona State University *B,M,D*
Cochise College *A*
Eastern Arizona College *A*
Glendale Community College *A*
Grand Canyon University *B*
Mesa Community College *A*
Mohave Community College *A*
Northern Arizona University *B,M*
Prescott College *B,M*
University of Arizona *B,M,D*
Yavapai College *A*

Arkansas

Arkansas College *B*
Arkansas State University *B*
Arkansas Tech University *B*
Harding University *B,M*
Henderson State University *B*
Hendrix College *B*
John Brown University *B*
Mississippi County Community
College *A*
Ouachita Baptist University *B*
Philander Smith College *B*
Southern Arkansas University *B*
University of Arkansas
Fayetteville *B,M,D*
Little Rock *B,M*
Monticello *B*
Pine Bluff *B*
University of Central Arkansas *B*
University of the Ozarks *B*
Westark Community College *A*

California

Antioch Southern California at Los
Angeles *M*
Azusa Pacific University *B*
Bakersfield College *A*
Barstow College *A*
Bethany College *B*
Biola University *B*
California Baptist College *B*
California Institute of Integral
Studies *M,D*
California Lutheran University *B*
California State Polytechnic
University: Pomona *B*
California State University
Bakersfield *B,M*
Chico *B,M*
Dominguez Hills *B,M*
Fresno *B,M*
Fullerton *B,M*
Hayward *B*
Long Beach *B,M*
Los Angeles *B,M*
Northridge *B,M*
Sacramento *B,M*
San Bernardino *B,M*
San Marcos *B*
Stanislaus *B,M*
Cerritos Community College *A*
Chabot College *A*
Chaffey Community College *A*
Chapman University *B*
Christ College Irvine *B*
Citrus College *A*
Claremont McKenna College *B*
College of the Desert *A*
College of Notre Dame *B*
Columbia College *A*
Crafton Hills College *A*
De Anza College *A*
Dominican College of San Rafael *B*

El Camino College *A*
Feather River College *A*
Foothill College *A*
Fresno City College *A*
Fresno Pacific College *B*
Holy Names College *B*
Humboldt State University *B,M*
Imperial Valley College *A*
Irvine Valley College *A*
Kings River Community College *A*
La Sierra University *B*
Los Angeles City College *A*
Los Angeles Mission College *A*
Los Angeles Valley College *A*
Los Medanos College *A*
Loyola Marymount University *B*
Marymount College *A*
Master's College *B*
Mendocino College *A*
Menlo College *B*
Merced College *A*
Mills College *B*
MiraCosta College *A*
Modesto Junior College *A*
Mount St. Mary's College *B*
Napa Valley College *A*
National University *B*
New College of California *M*
Occidental College *B,M*
Ohlone College *A*
Orange Coast College *A*
Pacific Christian College *B*
Pacific Union College *B*
Palomar College *C,A*
Pasadena City College *A*
Pepperdine University *B,M,D*
Pitzer College *B*
Point Loma Nazarene College *B*
Pomona College *B*
Saddleback College *A*
St. Mary's College of California
B,M
San Diego City College *A*
San Diego Mesa College *A*
San Diego State University *B,M*
San Francisco State University *B,M*
San Joaquin Delta College *A*
San Jose City College *A*
San Jose State University *B,M*
Santa Barbara City College *A*
Santa Clara University *B*
Santa Rosa Junior College *A*
Saybrook Institute *M,D*
Scripps College *B*
Simpson College *B*
Skyline College *A*
Solano Community College *A*
Sonoma State University *B,M*
Southern California College *B*
Southwestern College *A*
Stanford University *B,M,D*
United States International
University *B*
University of California
Berkeley *B,D*
Davis *B,M,D*
Irvine *B,D*
Los Angeles *B,M,D*
Riverside *B,M,D*
San Diego *B,M,D*
Santa Barbara *B,M,D*
Santa Cruz *B,D*
University of Judaism *B*
University of La Verne *B*
University of the Pacific *B,M*
University of Redlands *B*
University of San Diego *B*
University of San Francisco *B*
University of Southern California
B,D
Ventura College *A*
West Hills Community College *A*

West Valley College *A*
Westmont College *B*
Whittier College *B*

Colorado

Adams State College *B*
Colorado Christian University *B*
Colorado College *B*
Colorado Mountain College: Spring
Valley Campus *A*
Colorado State University *B,M,D*
Community College of Denver *A*
Fort Lewis College *B*
Lamar Community College *A*
Mesa State College *A,B*
Metropolitan State College of
Denver *B*
Naropa Institute *B*
Northeastern Junior College *A*
Pikes Peak Community College *A*
Regis College of Regis University *B*
Trinidad State Junior College *A*
United States Air Force
Academy *B*
University of Colorado
Boulder *B,M,D*
Colorado Springs *B*
Denver *B,M*
University of Denver *B,M,D*
University of Northern Colorado
B,M
University of Southern Colorado *B*
Western State College of
Colorado *B*

Connecticut

Albertus Magnus College *B*
Central Connecticut State
University *B,M*
Connecticut College *B,M*
Eastern Connecticut State
University *B*
Fairfield University *B*
Quinnipiac College *B*
Sacred Heart University *A,B*
St. Joseph College *B*
Southern Connecticut State
University *B,M*
Teikyo-Post University *A,B*
Trinity College *B*
University of Bridgeport *B,M*
University of Connecticut *B,M,D*
University of Hartford *B,M*
University of New Haven *B*
Wesleyan University *B,M*
Western Connecticut State
University *B*
Yale University *B,M,D*

Delaware

Delaware State College *B*
University of Delaware *B,M,D*
Wesley College *B*

District of Columbia

American University *B,M*
Catholic University of America
B,M,D
Gallaudet University *B*
George Washington University
B,M,D
Georgetown University *B,D*
Howard University *B*
Mount Vernon College *B*
Trinity College *B*
University of the District of
Columbia *B*

Florida

Barry University *B*
Bethune-Cookman College *B*

Central Florida Community
College *A*
Daytona Beach Community
College *A*
Eckerd College *B*
Edison Community College *A*
Flagler College *B*
Florida Agricultural and Mechanical
University *B*
Florida Atlantic University *B,M,D*
Florida Institute of Technology *B*
Florida International University
B,M
Florida Memorial College *B*
Florida Southern College *B*
Florida State University *B,M,D*
Gulf Coast Community College *A*
Indian River Community College *A*
Jacksonville University *B*
Lynn University *B*
Manatee Community College *A*
Miami-Dade Community College *A*
New College of the University of
South Florida *A*
Nova University *B*
Palm Beach Atlantic College *B*
Palm Beach Community College *A*
Pensacola Junior College *A*
Rollins College *B*
St. Leo College *B*
St. Thomas University *B*
South Florida Community
College *A*
Southeastern College of the
Assemblies of God *B*
Stetson University *B*
University of Central Florida *B,D*
University of Florida *B,M,D*
University of Miami *B,M,D*
University of North Florida *B*
University of South Florida *B,M*
University of Tampa *A,B*
University of West Florida *B,M*

Georgia
Abraham Baldwin Agricultural
College *A*
Agnes Scott College *B*
Albany State College *B*
Andrew College *A*
Armstrong State College *B*
Atlanta Metropolitan College *A*
Augusta College *B,M*
Bainbridge College *A*
Berry College *B*
Brenau Women's College *B*
Brewton-Parker College *A,B*
Clark Atlanta University *B*
Clayton State College *A*
Columbus College *B*
Covenant College *B*
Darton College *A*
DeKalb College *A*
East Georgia College *A*
Emory University *B,M,D*
Floyd College *A*
Fort Valley State College *B*
Gainesville College *A*
Georgia College *B,M*
Georgia Institute of Technology
B,M,D
Georgia Southern University *B,M*
Georgia Southwestern College *B*
Georgia State University *B,M,D*
Gordon College *A*
Kennesaw State College *B*
LaGrange College *B*
Macon College *A*
Mercer University *B*
Middle Georgia College *A*
Morehouse College *B*
Morris Brown College *B*

North Georgia College *B*
Oglethorpe University *B*
Oxford College of Emory
University *A*
Paine College *B*
Piedmont College *B*
Reinhardt College *A*
Shorter College *B*
South Georgia College *A*
Spelman College *B*
Thomas College *A*
Toccoa Falls College *B*
Truett-McConnell College *A*
University of Georgia *B,M,D*
Valdosta State College *B,M*
Waycross College *A*
Wesleyan College *B*
West Georgia College *B,M*
Young Harris College *A*

Hawaii
Chaminade University of
Honolulu *B*
Hawaii Pacific University *B*
University of Hawaii
Hilo *B*
Manoa *B,M,D*
West Oahu *B*

Idaho
Albertson College *B*
Boise State University *B*
College of Southern Idaho *A*
Idaho State University *B,M*
North Idaho College *A*
Northwest Nazarene College *A,B*
Ricks College *A*
University of Idaho *B,M*

Illinois
Augustana College *B*
Aurora University *B*
Barat College *B*
Belleville Area College *A*
Black Hawk College *A*
Blackburn College *B*
Bradley University *B,M*
Chicago State University *B*
College of St. Francis *B*
Concordia University *B,M*
De Paul University *B*
Eastern Illinois University *B,M*
Elmhurst College *B*
Eureka College *B*
Governors State University *B,M*
Greenville College *B*
Highland Community College *A*
Illinois Benedictine College *B*
Illinois Central College *A*
Illinois College *B*
Illinois Institute of Technology
B,M,D
Illinois State University *B*
Illinois Valley Community
College *A*
Illinois Wesleyan University *B*
John A. Logan College *A*
Joliet Junior College *A*
Judson College *B*
Kishwaukee College *A*
Knox College *B*
Lake Forest College *B*
Lake Land College *A*
Lewis University *B*
Lincoln Land Community
College *A*
Loyola University of Chicago
B,M,D
MacMurray College *B*
McKendree College *B*
Millikin University *B*
Monmouth College *B*

Morton College *A*
National-Louis University *B*
North Central College *B*
North Park College and Theological
Seminary *B*
Northeastern Illinois University *B*
Northern Illinois University *B,M,D*
Northwestern University *B,M,D*
Olivet Nazarene University *B*
Quincy College *B*
Rend Lake College *A*
Richland Community College *A*
Rockford College *B*
Roosevelt University *B,M*
Rosary College *B*
St. Augustine College *A*
St. Xavier University *B*
Sangamon State University *B,M*
Southern Illinois University
Carbondale *B*
Edwardsville *B,M*
State Community College *A*
Trinity Christian College *B*
Trinity College *B*
Triton College *A*
University of Chicago *B,M,D*
University of Illinois
Chicago *B,M,D*
Urbana-Champaign *B,M,D*
Waubonsee Community College *A*
Western Illinois University *B,M*
Wheaton College *B*
William Rainey Harper College *A*

Indiana
Anderson University *B*
Ball State University *B,M*
Bethel College *B*
Butler University *B*
Calumet College of St. Joseph *B*
DePauw University *B*
Earlham College *B*
Franklin College *B*
Goshen College *B*
Grace College *B*
Hanover College *B*
Huntington College *B*
Indiana State University *B,M,D*
Indiana University
Bloomington *B,M,D*
East *B*
Kokomo *B*
Northwest *B*
South Bend *B*
Southeast *B*
Indiana University—Purdue
University
Fort Wayne *B*
Indianapolis *B,M*
Indiana Wesleyan University *B*
Manchester College *B*
Marian College *B*
Martin University *B*
Purdue University
Calumet *B*
West Lafayette *B*
St. Francis College *B,M*
St. Joseph's College *B*
St. Mary-of-the-Woods College *B*
St. Mary's College *B*
St. Meinrad College *B*
Taylor University *B*
University of Evansville *B*
University of Indianapolis *B*
University of Notre Dame *B,M,D*
University of Southern Indiana *B*
Valparaiso University *B,M*
Vincennes University *A*
Wabash College *B*

Iowa
Briar Cliff College *B*
Buena Vista College *B*
Central College *B*
Clarke College *B*
Clinton Community College *A*
Coe College *B*
Cornell College *B*
Dordt College *B*
Drake University *B,M*
Graceland College *B*
Grinnell College *B*
Iowa Lakes Community College *A*
Iowa State University *B,M,D*
Iowa Wesleyan College *B*
Iowa Western Community
College *A*
Kirkwood Community College *A*
Loras College *B,M*
Luther College *B*
Maharishi International University
B,M,D
Morningside College *B*
Mount Mercy College *B*
Muscatine Community College *A*
North Iowa Area Community
College *A*
Northwestern College *B*
St. Ambrose University *B*
Scott Community College *A*
Simpson College *B*
Teikyo Marycrest University *B*
Teikyo Westmar University *B*
University of Dubuque *B*
University of Iowa *B,M,D*
University of Northern Iowa *B,M*
Upper Iowa University *B*
Vennard College *B*
Wartburg College *B*
William Penn College *B*

Kansas
Allen County Community
College *A*
Baker University *B*
Barton County Community
College *A*
Benedictine College *B*
Bethany College *B*
Bethel College *B*
Butler County Community
College *A*
Central College *A*
Cloud County Community
College *A*
Coffeyville Community College *A*
Colby Community College *A*
Cowley County Community
College *A*
Dodge City Community College *A*
Emporia State University *B,M*
Fort Hays State University *B,M*
Fort Scott Community College *A*
Friends University *B*
Highland Community College *A*
Hutchinson Community College *A*
Kansas City Kansas Community
College *A*
Kansas Newman College *B*
Kansas State University *B,M,D*
Kansas Wesleyan University *B*
Labette Community College *A*
McPherson College *B*
MidAmerica Nazarene College *B*
Neosho County Community
College *A*
Ottawa University *B*
Pittsburg State University *B,M*
Pratt Community College *A*
St. Mary College *B*
Seward County Community
College *A*

Southwestern College *B*
Sterling College *B*
University of Kansas *B,M,D*
Washburn University of Topeka *B*
Wichita State University *B,M,D*

Kentucky

Asbury College *B*
Bellarmine College *B*
Berea College *B*
Brescia College *B*
Campbellsville College *B*
Centre College *B*
Cumberland College *B*
Eastern Kentucky University *B*
Georgetown College *B*
Kentucky Christian College *B*
Kentucky State University *B*
Kentucky Wesleyan College *B*
Lees College *A*
Morehead State University *B,M*
Murray State University *B,M*
Northern Kentucky University *B*
Pikeville College *B*
Spalding University *B*
Sue Bennett College *A*
Thomas More College *A,B*
Transylvania University *B*
Union College *B*
University of Kentucky *B*
University of Louisville *B,M*
Western Kentucky University *B,M*

Louisiana

Centenary College of Louisiana *B*
Dillard University *B*
Grambling State University *B*
Louisiana College *B*
Louisiana State University
    Agricultural and Mechanical
       College *B,M,D*
    Shreveport *B*
Louisiana Tech University *B*
Loyola University *B*
McNeese State University *B*
Nicholls State University *B*
Northeast Louisiana University *B,M*
Northwestern State University *B,M*
Southeastern Louisiana University
    B,M
Southern University at New
    Orleans *B*
Southern University and
    Agricultural and Mechanical
    College *B*
Tulane University *B,M,D*
University of New Orleans *B,M*
University of Southwestern
    Louisiana *B,M*
Xavier University of Louisiana *B*

Maine

Bates College *B*
Bowdoin College *B*
Colby College *B*
St. Joseph's College *B*
University of Maine
    Farmington *B*
    Orono *B,M,D*
    Presque Isle *B*
University of New England *B*
University of Southern Maine *B*
Westbrook College *B*

Maryland

Allegany Community College *A*
Bowie State University *B*
College of Notre Dame of
    Maryland *B*
Columbia Union College *B*
Coppin State College *B*
Frederick Community College *A*

Frostburg State University *B*
Garrett Community College *A*
Goucher College *B*
Harford Community College *A*
Hood College *B*
Howard Community College *A*
Johns Hopkins University *B,M,D*
Loyola College in Maryland *B,M*
Morgan State University *B*
Mount St. Mary's College *B*
St. Mary's College of Maryland *B*
Salisbury State University *B,M*
Towson State University *B,M*
University of Baltimore *B*
University of Maryland
    Baltimore County *B*
    College Park *B,M,D*
Washington College *B,M*
Western Maryland College *B*

Massachusetts

American International College *B*
Amherst College *B*
Anna Maria College for Men and
    Women *B*
Assumption College *B,M*
Atlantic Union College *B*
Bay Path College *B*
Boston College *B,D*
Boston University *B,M,D*
Bradford College *B*
Brandeis University *B,M,D*
Bridgewater State College *B,M*
Bunker Hill Community College *A*
Clark University *B,M,D*
College of the Holy Cross *B*
Curry College *B*
Eastern Nazarene College *B*
Elms College *B*
Emmanuel College *B*
Endicott College *A,B*
Fitchburg State College *B*
Framingham State College *B*
Gordon College *B*
Hampshire College *B*
Harvard and Radcliffe Colleges *B*
Harvard University *D*
Lesley College *B*
Massachusetts Institute of
    Technology *B*
Merrimack College *B*
Mount Holyoke College *B*
Nichols College *B*
North Adams State College *B*
Northeastern University *B,M,D*
Pine Manor College *A,B*
Quincy College *A*
Regis College *B*
Salem State College *B*
Simmons College *B*
Smith College *B*
Springfield College *B*
Stonehill College *B*
Suffolk University *B*
Tufts University *B,M,D*
University of Massachusetts
    Amherst *B,M,D*
    Boston *B*
    Dartmouth *B,M*
    Lowell *B*
Wellesley College *B*
Western New England College *B*
Westfield State College *B*
Wheaton College *B*
Williams College *B*
Worcester State College *B*

Michigan

Adrian College *A,B*
Albion College *B*
Alma College *B*
Andrews University *B*

Aquinas College *B*
Calvin College *B*
Central Michigan University *B,M*
Concordia College *B*
Eastern Michigan University *B,M*
Grand Rapids Baptist College and
    Seminary *B*
Grand Valley State University *B*
Hillsdale College *B*
Hope College *B*
Kalamazoo College *B*
Lake Superior State University *B*
Lansing Community College *A*
Madonna University *B*
Marygrove College *A,B*
Michigan State University *B,M,D*
Northern Michigan University *A,B*
Oakland University *B*
Olivet College *B*
Saginaw Valley State University *B*
St. Mary's College *B*
Siena Heights College *A,B*
Spring Arbor College *B*
University of Detroit Mercy *B,M*
University of Michigan
    Ann Arbor *B*
    Dearborn *B*
    Flint *B*
Wayne State University *B,M,D*
West Shore Community College *A*
Western Michigan University
    B,M,D

Minnesota

Augsburg College *B*
Bemidji State University *B*
Bethany Lutheran College *A*
Bethel College *B*
Carleton College *B*
College of St. Benedict *B*
College of St. Catherine: St.
    Catherine Campus *B*
College of St. Scholastica *B*
Concordia College: Moorhead *B*
Concordia College: St. Paul *B*
Crown College *A,B*
Gustavus Adolphus College *B*
Hamline University *B*
Macalester College *B*
Mankato State University *B,M*
Moorhead State University *B*
Northland Community College *A*
Northwestern College *B*
Rainy River Community College *A*
St. Cloud State University *B,M*
St. John's University *B*
St. Mary's College of Minnesota *B*
St. Olaf College *B*
Southwest State University *B*
University of Minnesota
    Duluth *B*
    Morris *B*
    Twin Cities *B,M,D*
University of St. Thomas *B*
Vermilion Community College *A*
Willmar Community College *A*
Winona State University *B,M*

Mississippi

Alcorn State University *B*
Belhaven College *B*
Blue Mountain College *B*
Delta State University *B*
Jackson State University *B*
Jones County Junior College *A*
Mary Holmes College *A*
Millsaps College *B*
Mississippi College *B*
Mississippi Delta Community
    College *A*

Mississippi Gulf Coast Community
    College: Jefferson Davis
    Campus *A*
Mississippi State University *B,M*
Northeast Mississippi Community
    College *A*
Tougaloo College *B*
University of Mississippi *B,M,D*
University of Southern Mississippi
    B,M,D
William Carey College *B*

Missouri

Avila College *B*
Central Methodist College *B*
Central Missouri State University
    B,M
College of the Ozarks *B*
Columbia College *B*
Culver-Stockton College *B*
Drury College *B*
East Central College *A*
Evangel College *B*
Jefferson College *A*
Lincoln University *B*
Lindenwood College *B*
Maryville University *B*
Mineral Area College *A*
Missouri Baptist College *B*
Missouri Southern State College *B*
Missouri Valley College *B*
Missouri Western State College *B*
Moberly Area Community
    College *A*
Northeast Missouri State
    University *B*
Northwest Missouri State
    University *B*
Park College *B*
Rockhurst College *B*
St. Louis Community College
    Florissant Valley *A*
    Forest Park *A*
St. Louis University *B,M*
Southeast Missouri State
    University *B*
Southwest Baptist University *B*
Southwest Missouri State
    University *B*
Stephens College *B*
University of Missouri
    Columbia *B*
    Kansas City *B,M,D*
    Rolla *B*
    St. Louis *B,M*
Washington University *B,M,D*
Webster University *B*
Westminster College *B*
William Jewell College *B*
William Woods College *B*

Montana

Carroll College *B*
Eastern Montana College *A,B*
Little Big Horn College *A*
Miles Community College *A*
Montana State University *B*
Rocky Mountain College *B*
University of Montana *B,M,D*

Nebraska

Bellevue College *B*
Central Community College *A*
Chadron State College *B*
Concordia College *B*
Creighton University *C,B*
Dana College *B*
Doane College *B*
Hastings College *B*
McCook Community College *A*
Midland Lutheran College *B*
Nebraska Wesleyan University *B*

Northeast Community College *A*
Peru State College *B*
Southeast Community College:
Beatrice Campus *A*
Union College *B*
University of Nebraska
Kearney *B*
Lincoln *B,M,D*
Omaha *B,M,D*
Wayne State College *B*
Western Nebraska Community
College: Scottsbluff Campus *A*
York College *A*

Nevada

University of Nevada
Las Vegas *B,M*
Reno *B,M,D*

New Hampshire

Antioch New England Graduate
School *M*
Colby-Sawyer College *B*
Dartmouth College *B,M,D*
Franklin Pierce College *B*
Keene State College *B*
New England College *B*
Notre Dame College *B*
Plymouth State College of the
University System of New
Hampshire *B*
Rivier College *B*
St. Anselm College *B*
University of New Hampshire
Durham *B,D*
Manchester *B*

New Jersey

Atlantic Community College *A*
Bergen Community College *A*
Bloomfield College *B*
Brookdale Community College *A*
Burlington County College *A*
Caldwell College *B*
Centenary College *B*
College of St. Elizabeth *B*
Drew University *B*
Fairleigh Dickinson University *B,M*
Felician College *A,B*
Georgian Court College *B*
Glassboro State College *B*
Jersey City State College *B*
Kean College of New Jersey *B,M*
Monmouth College *B*
Montclair State College *B,M*
Ocean County College *A*
Princeton University *B,D*
Ramapo College of New Jersey *B*
Rider College *B*
Rutgers—The State University of
New Jersey
Camden College of Arts and
Sciences *B*
Douglass College *B*
Livingston College *B*
New Brunswick *M,D*
Newark College of Arts and
Sciences *B*
Rutgers College *B*
University College Camden *B*
University College New
Brunswick *B*
University College Newark *B*
St. Peter's College *B*
Seton Hall University *B,M*
Stevens Institute of Technology *B*
Stockton State College *B*
Thomas Edison State College *B*
Trenton State College *B*
Upsala College *B*
William Paterson College of New
Jersey *B*

New Mexico

Clovis Community College *A*
College of Santa Fe *B*
College of the Southwest *B*
Eastern New Mexico University
A,B,M
New Mexico Highlands University
B,M
New Mexico Institute of Mining
and Technology *B*
New Mexico Junior College *A*
New Mexico State University
B,M,D
University of New Mexico *B,M,D*
Western New Mexico University *B*

New York

Adelphi University *B,M,D*
Adirondack Community College *A*
Alfred University *B*
Bard College *B*
Barnard College *B*
Canisius College *B*
City University of New York
Baruch College *B*
Brooklyn College *B,M*
City College *B,M*
College of Staten Island *B*
Hunter College *B,M*
John Jay College of Criminal
Justice *B,M*
Lehman College *B*
Medgar Evers College *B*
Queens College *B,M*
Queensborough Community
College *A*
York College *B*
Clarkson University *B*
Colgate University *B,M*
College of Mount St. Vincent *A,B*
College of New Rochelle *B*
College of St. Rose *B*
Columbia University
Columbia College *B*
School of General Studies *B*
Cornell University *B,M,D*
Daemen College *B*
Dominican College of Blauvelt *B*
Dowling College *B*
Elmira College *B*
Eugene Lang College/New School
for Social Research *B*
Fordham University *B,M,D*
Fulton-Montgomery Community
College *A*
Genesee Community College *A*
Hamilton College *B*
Hartwick College *B*
Herkimer County Community
College *A*
Hobart College *B*
Hofstra University *B*
Houghton College *B*
Iona College *B*
Ithaca College *B*
Jamestown Community College *A*
Keuka College *B*
King's College *B*
Le Moyne College *B*
Long Island University
Brooklyn Campus *B,M*
C. W. Post Campus *B,M*
Southampton Campus *B*
Manhattan College *B*
Manhattanville College *B*
Marist College *B*
Marymount College *B*
Marymount Manhattan College *B*
Mercy College *B*
Mohawk Valley Community
College *A*
Molloy College *B*

Mount St. Mary College *B*
Nazareth College of Rochester *B*
New York University *B,M*
Niagara University *B*
Nyack College *B*
Pace University
College of White Plains *B*
New York *B*
Pleasantville/Briarcliff *B*
Rensselaer Polytechnic Institute
B,M
Roberts Wesleyan College *B*
Russell Sage College *B*
Sage Junior College of Albany, A
Division of Russell Sage
College *A*
St. Bonaventure University *B,M*
St. Francis College *B*
St. John Fisher College *B*
St. John's University *B*
St. Joseph's College
Brooklyn *B*
Suffolk Campus *B*
St. Lawrence University *B*
St. Thomas Aquinas College *B*
Sarah Lawrence College *B*
Siena College *B*
Skidmore College *B*
State University of New York
Albany *B,M,D*
Binghamton *B,M,D*
Buffalo *B,M*
Purchase *B*
Stony Brook *B,M,D*
College at Brockport *B,M*
College at Buffalo *B*
College at Cortland *B,M*
College at Fredonia *B*
College at Geneseo *B*
College at New Paltz *B,M*
College at Old Westbury *B*
College at Oneonta *B*
College at Plattsburgh *B*
College at Potsdam *B*
College of Technology at
Delhi *A*
Empire State College *A,B*
Institute of Technology at
Utica/Rome *B*
Oswego *B*
Sullivan County Community
College *A*
Syracuse University *B,M,D*
Touro College *B*
Union College *B*
United States Military Academy *B*
University of Rochester *B,M,D*
University of the State of New
York: Regents College *B*
Utica College of Syracuse
University *B*
Vassar College *B*
Wagner College *B*
Wells College *B*
William Smith College *B*
Yeshiva University *B,M*

North Carolina

Appalachian State University *B,M*
Barton College *B*
Belmont Abbey College *B*
Bennett College *B*
Brevard College *A*
Campbell University *B*
Catawba College *B*
Chowan College *A*
Davidson College *B*
Duke University *B,D*
East Carolina University *B,M*
Elizabeth City State University *B*
Elon College *B*
Fayetteville State University *B*

Gardner-Webb College *B*
Gaston College *A*
Greensboro College *B*
Guilford College *B*
High Point University *B*
Johnson C. Smith University *B*
Lenoir-Rhyne College *B*
Livingstone College *B*
Mars Hill College *B*
Meredith College *B*
Methodist College *A,B*
Mount Olive College *B*
North Carolina Agricultural and
Technical State University *B*
North Carolina Central University
B,M
North Carolina State University
B,M,D
North Carolina Wesleyan College *B*
Pembroke State University *B*
Pfeiffer College *B*
Queens College *B*
St. Andrews Presbyterian College *B*
St. Augustine's College *B*
Salem College *B*
University of North Carolina
Asheville *B*
Chapel Hill *B,M,D*
Charlotte *B,M*
Greensboro *B,M,D*
Wilmington *B*
Wake Forest University *B,M*
Warren Wilson College *B*
Western Carolina University *B,M*
Wingate College *B*
Winston-Salem State University *B*

North Dakota

Bismarck State College *A*
Jamestown College *B*
Minot State University *B*
North Dakota State University *B,M*
Trinity Bible College *B*
University of North Dakota
Grand Forks *B,M,D*
Williston *A*

Ohio

Antioch College *B*
Ashland University *B*
Baldwin-Wallace College *B*
Bluffton College *B*
Bowling Green State University
Bowling Green *B,M,D*
Firelands College *A*
Capital University *B*
Case Western Reserve University
B,M,D
Central State University *B*
Cleveland State University *B*
College of Wooster *B*
Defiance College *B*
Denison University *B*
Edison State Community College *A*
Franciscan University of
Steubenville *B*
Heidelberg College *B,M*
Hiram College *B*
John Carroll University *B*
Kent State University *B*
Kenyon College *B*
Lake Erie College *B*
Lakeland Community College *A*
Lorain County Community
College *A*
Lourdes College *A,B*
Malone College *B*
Marietta College *B*
Miami University: Oxford Campus
B,M
Mount Union College *B*
Mount Vernon Nazarene College *B*

Muskingum College *B*
Notre Dame College of Ohio *B*
Oberlin College *B*
Ohio Dominican College *B*
Ohio Northern University *B*
Ohio State University: Columbus
   Campus *B,M,D*
Ohio University *B*
Ohio Wesleyan University *B*
Otterbein College *B*
Pontifical College Josephinum *B*
Union Institute *B,D*
University of Akron *B,M,D*
University of Cincinnati *B,M,D*
University of Dayton *B,M*
University of Findlay *B*
University of Rio Grande *A,B*
University of Toledo *B,M,D*
Urbana University *B*
Ursuline College *B*
Walsh College *B*
Wilberforce University *B*
Wilmington College *B*
Wittenberg University *B*
Wright State University
   Dayton *B*
   Lake Campus *A*
Xavier University *A,B,M*
Youngstown State University *B*

Oklahoma

Bacone College *A*
Bartlesville Wesleyan College *A,B*
Cameron University *B*
Connors State College *A*
East Central University *B*
Eastern Oklahoma State College *A*
Hillsdale Free Will Baptist
   College *A*
Langston University *B*
Mid-America Bible College *B*
Northeastern State University *B*
Northwestern Oklahoma State
   University *B*
Oklahoma Baptist University *B*
Oklahoma Christian University of
   Science and Arts *B*
Oklahoma City University *B*
Oklahoma Panhandle State
   University *B*
Oklahoma State University *B,M,D*
Oral Roberts University *B*
Phillips University *B*
Redlands Community College *A*
Rose State College *A*
St. Gregory's College *A*
Southeastern Oklahoma State
   University *B*
Southwestern Oklahoma State
   University *B,M*
Tulsa Junior College *A*
University of Central Oklahoma *B*
University of Oklahoma *B,M,D*
University of Science and Arts of
   Oklahoma *B*
University of Tulsa *B*

Oregon

Central Oregon Community
   College *A*
Concordia College *B*
Eastern Oregon State College *B*
George Fox College *B*
Lewis and Clark College *B*
Linfield College *B*
Northwest Christian College *B*
Oregon State University *B*
Pacific University *B*
Portland Community College *A*
Portland State University *B,M*
Reed College *B*
Southern Oregon State College *B*

Treasure Valley Community
   College *A*
University of Oregon
   Eugene *B,M,D*
   Robert Donald Clark Honors
    College *B*
University of Portland *B*
Warner Pacific College *B*
Western Baptist College *B*
Western Oregon State College *B*
Willamette University *B*

Pennsylvania

Albright College *B*
Allegheny College *B*
Allentown College of St. Francis de
   Sales *B*
Alvernia College *B*
Beaver College *B*
Bloomsburg University of
   Pennsylvania *B*
Bryn Mawr College *B,M,D*
Bucknell University *B,M*
Bucks County Community
   College *A*
Cabrini College *B*
California University of
   Pennsylvania *B,M*
Carlow College *B*
Carnegie Mellon University
   B,M,D,W
Cedar Crest College *B*
Chatham College *B*
Chestnut Hill College *A,B*
Cheyney University of
   Pennsylvania *B*
Clarion University of
   Pennsylvania *B*
College Misericordia *B*
Dickinson College *B*
Drexel University *B*
Duquesne University *B,M,D*
East Stroudsburg University of
   Pennsylvania *B*
Eastern College *B*
Edinboro University of
   Pennsylvania *B*
Elizabethtown College *B*
Franklin and Marshall College *B*
Gannon University *B*
Geneva College *B*
Gettysburg College *B*
Grove City College *B*
Gwynedd-Mercy College *B*
Harrisburg Area Community
   College *A*
Haverford College *B*
Holy Family College *B*
Immaculata College *B*
Indiana University of Pennsylvania
   B,M
Juniata College *B*
King's College *B*
Kutztown University of
   Pennsylvania *B*
La Roche College *B*
La Salle University *B*
Lafayette College *B*
Lebanon Valley College of
   Pennsylvania *B*
Lehigh University *B,M,D*
Lincoln University *B*
Lock Haven University of
   Pennsylvania *B*
Lycoming College *B*
Manor Junior College *A*
Mansfield University of
   Pennsylvania *B*
Marywood College *B,M*
Mercyhurst College *B*
Messiah College *B*

Millersville University of
   Pennsylvania *B,M*
Moravian College *B*
Muhlenberg College *B*
Neumann College *B*
Northeastern Christian Junior
   College *A*
Penn State
   Erie Behrend College *B*
   University Park Campus
    B,M,D
Philadelphia College of Textiles and
   Science *B*
Point Park College *B*
Reading Area Community
   College *A*
Rosemont College *B*
St. Francis College *B*
St. Joseph's University *B*
St. Vincent College *B*
Seton Hill College *B*
Shippensburg University of
   Pennsylvania *B,M*
Slippery Rock University of
   Pennsylvania *B*
Susquehanna University *B*
Swarthmore College *B*
Temple University *B,M,D*
Thiel College *B*
University of Pennsylvania *B,M,D*
University of Pittsburgh
   Bradford *B*
   Greensburg *B*
   Johnstown *B*
   Pittsburgh *B,M,D*
University of Scranton *B*
Ursinus College *B*
Villanova University *B,M*
Washington and Jefferson College *B*
Waynesburg College *B*
West Chester University of
   Pennsylvania *B,M*
Westminster College *B*
Widener University *B*
Wilkes University *B*
York College of Pennsylvania *B*

Puerto Rico

Bayamon Central University *B*
Inter American University of Puerto
   Rico
   Arecibo Campus *B*
   Metropolitan Campus *B,M*
   San German Campus *B,M*
Pontifical Catholic University of
   Puerto Rico *B*
Turabo University *B*
Universidad Metropolitana *B*
University of Puerto Rico
   Cayey University College *B*
   Mayaguez Campus *B*
   Rio Piedras Campus *B,M,D*
University of the Sacred Heart *B*

Rhode Island

Brown University *B,M,D*
Providence College *B*
Rhode Island College *B*
Roger Williams College *B*
Salve Regina University *B*
University of Rhode Island *B,M*

South Carolina

Central Wesleyan College *B*
Charleston Southern University *B*
The Citadel *B*
Clemson University *B*
Coker College *B*
College of Charleston *B*
Columbia College *B*
Converse College *B*
Erskine College *B*

Francis Marion College *B*
Furman University *B*
Lander College *B*
Limestone College *B*
North Greenville College *A*
Presbyterian College *B*
South Carolina State College *B*
University of South Carolina
   Aiken *B*
   Coastal Carolina College *B*
   Spartanburg *B*
Winthrop University *B*
Wofford College *B*

South Dakota

Augustana College *B*
Black Hills State University *B*
Dakota Wesleyan University *B,M*
Northern State University *B*
Sioux Falls College *B*
South Dakota State University *B*
University of South Dakota *B,M,D*

Tennessee

Austin Peay State University *B,M*
Belmont University *B*
Bethel College *B*
Carson-Newman College *B*
Christian Brothers University *B*
Columbia State Community
   College *A*
Crichton College *B*
Cumberland University *B*
David Lipscomb University *B*
Dyersburg State Community
   College *A*
East Tennessee State University
   B,M
Fisk University *B,M*
Freed-Hardeman University *B*
Hiwassee College *A*
King College *B*
Knoxville College *B*
Lambuth University *B*
Lincoln Memorial University *B*
Martin Methodist College *A*
Maryville College *B*
Memphis State University *B,M,D*
Middle Tennessee State University
   B,M
Milligan College *B*
Motlow State Community
   College *A*
Rhodes College *B*
Southern College of Seventh-day
   Adventists *B*
Tennessee State University *B,M*
Tennessee Technological
   University *B*
Tennessee Temple University *B*
Tennessee Wesleyan College *B*
Trevecca Nazarene College *B*
Tusculum College *B*
Union University *B*
University of the South *B*
University of Tennessee
   Chattanooga *B,M*
   Knoxville *B,M,D*
   Martin *B*
Vanderbilt University *B,M,D*
William Jennings Bryan College *B*

Texas

Abilene Christian University *B*
Amarillo College *A*
Angelina College *A*
Angelo State University *B,M*
Austin College *B*
Austin Community College *A*
Baylor University *B,M,D*
Bee County College *A*
Brazosport College *A*

Central Texas College *A*
College of the Mainland *A*
Collin County Community College District *A*
Corpus Christi State University *B,M*
Dallas Baptist University *B*
Del Mar College *A*
East Texas Baptist University *B*
East Texas State University
  Commerce *B,M,D*
  Texarkana *B*
El Paso Community College *A*
Galveston College *A*
Hardin-Simmons University *B*
Houston Baptist University *B*
Houston Community College *A*
Howard College *A*
Howard Payne University *B*
Incarnate Word College *B*
Jacksonville College *A*
Kilgore College *A*
Lamar University—Beaumont *B,M*
Laredo State University *B*
Lon Morris College *A*
Lubbock Christian University *B*
McLennan Community College *A*
McMurry University *B*
Midland College *A*
Midwestern State University *B,M*
Navarro College *A*
North Harris Montgomery Community College District *A*
Our Lady of the Lake University of San Antonio *B*
Panola College *A*
Prairie View A&M University *B*
Rice University *B,M,D*
St. Edward's University *B*
St. Mary's University *B,M*
St. Philip's College *A*
Sam Houston State University *B,M*
Schreiner College *B*
South Plains College *A*
Southern Methodist University *B,M,D*
Southwest Texas State University *B*
Southwestern Adventist College *B*
Southwestern Assemblies of God College *A*
Southwestern University *B*
Stephen F. Austin State University *B,M*
Sul Ross State University *B*
Texas A&I University *B,M*
Texas A&M University *B,M,D*
Texas Christian University *B,M,D*
Texas Lutheran College *B*
Texas Southern University *B,M*
Texas Southmost College *A*
Texas Tech University *B,M,D*
Texas Wesleyan University *B*
Texas Woman's University *B,M,D*
Trinity University *B*
Trinity Valley Community College *A*
University of Central Texas *B*
University of Dallas *B*
University of Houston
  Clear Lake *B,M*
  Houston *B,M,D*
  Victoria *B,M*
University of Mary Hardin-Baylor *B,M*
University of North Texas *B,M,D*
University of St. Thomas *B*

University of Texas
  Arlington *B,M,D*
  Austin *B,M,D*
  Dallas *B*
  El Paso *B,M*
  Pan American *B*
  Permian Basin *B*
  San Antonio *B*
  Tyler *B,M*
Victoria College *A*
Wayland Baptist University *B*
West Texas State University *B,M*
Western Texas College *A*
Wharton County Junior College *A*

Utah

Brigham Young University *B,M*
Southern Utah University *B*
University of Utah *B,M,D*
Utah State University *B,M,D*
Weber State University *B*
Westminster College of Salt Lake City *B*

Vermont

Bennington College *B*
Burlington College *B*
Castleton State College *B*
College of St. Joseph in Vermont *B*
Goddard College *B,M*
Johnson State College *B*
Lyndon State College *B*
Marlboro College *B*
Middlebury College *B*
Norwich University *B*
St. Michael's College *B*
Trinity College of Vermont *B*
University of Vermont *B,M,D*

Virginia

Averett College *B*
Bluefield College *B*
Bridgewater College *B*
Christopher Newport College *B*
Clinch Valley College of the University of Virginia *B*
College of William and Mary *B,M*
Eastern Mennonite College *B*
Emory and Henry College *B*
Ferrum College *B*
George Mason University *B,M,D*
Hampden-Sydney College *B*
Hampton University *B*
Hollins College *B,M*
James Madison University *B,M*
Liberty University *B*
Longwood College *B*
Lynchburg College *B*
Mary Baldwin College *B*
Mary Washington College *B*
Marymount University *B,M*
Mountain Empire Community College *A*
Norfolk State University *B*
Old Dominion University *B,M,D*
Radford University *B,M*
Randolph-Macon College *B*
Randolph-Macon Woman's College *B*
Roanoke College *B*
Shenandoah University *B*
Sweet Briar College *B*
University of Richmond *B,M*
University of Virginia *B,M,D*
Virginia Commonwealth University *B,M,D*
Virginia Intermont College *B*
Virginia Polytechnic Institute and State University *B,M,D*
Virginia State University *B,M*
Virginia Union University *B*
Virginia Wesleyan College *B*

Washington and Lee University *B*

Washington

Antioch University Seattle *M*
Big Bend Community College *A*
Central Washington University *B,M*
Centralia College *A*
Eastern Washington University *B,M*
Everett Community College *A*
Evergreen State College *B*
Gonzaga University *B*
Grays Harbor College *A*
Heritage College *A,B*
Lower Columbia College *A*
Olympic College *A*
Pacific Lutheran University *B*
St. Martin's College *B*
Seattle Central Community College *A*
Seattle Pacific University *B*
Seattle University *B*
Skagit Valley College *A*
Spokane Community College *A*
Spokane Falls Community College *A*
Tacoma Community College *A*
University of Puget Sound *B*
University of Washington *B,M,D*
Walla Walla College *B*
Washington State University *B,M,D*
Wenatchee Valley College *A*
Western Washington University *B,M*
Whitman College *B*
Whitworth College *B*

West Virginia

Alderson-Broaddus College *B*
Bethany College *B*
Concord College *B*
Davis and Elkins College *A,B*
Fairmont State College *B*
Marshall University *B,M*
Potomac State College of West Virginia University *A*
Shepherd College *B*
University of Charleston *B*
West Liberty State College *B*
West Virginia Graduate College *M*
West Virginia State College *B*
West Virginia University *B*
West Virginia Wesleyan College *B*
Wheeling Jesuit College *B*

Wisconsin

Alverno College *B*
Beloit College *B*
Cardinal Stritch College *B*
Carroll College *B*
Carthage College *B*
Concordia University Wisconsin *B*
Edgewood College *B*
Lakeland College *B*
Lawrence University *B*
Marian College of Fond du Lac *B*
Marquette University *B,M*
Mount Senario College *B*
Northland College *B*
Ripon College *B*
St. Norbert College *B*

University of Wisconsin
  Eau Claire *B*
  Green Bay *B*
  La Crosse *B*
  Madison *B,M,D*
  Milwaukee *B,M,D*
  Oshkosh *B,M*
  Parkside *B*
  Platteville *B*
  River Falls *B,M*
  Stevens Point *B*
  Stout *B*
  Superior *B*
  Whitewater *B*
Viterbo College *B*
Wisconsin Lutheran College *B*

Wyoming

Casper College *A*
Central Wyoming College *A*
Eastern Wyoming College *A*
Laramie County Community College *A*
Northwest College *A*
Sheridan College *A*
University of Wyoming *B,M,D*
Western Wyoming Community College *A*

American Samoa, Caroline Islands, Guam, Marianas, Virgin Islands

University of Guam *B*
University of the Virgin Islands *B*

Canada

McGill University *B,M,D*

Arab Republic of Egypt

American University in Cairo *B*

Psychometrics

Alabama

University of Alabama in Huntsville *M*

Georgia

University of Georgia *M*

Illinois

University of Chicago *M,D*

Indiana

Indiana State University *M*
St. Francis College *M*

Louisiana

Northeast Louisiana University *M*

New York

City University of New York: Baruch College *B*
Fordham University *D*
Syracuse University *M,D*

Oklahoma

Southwestern Oklahoma State University *M*

Rhode Island

Brown University *B,M,D*

Public administration

Alabama

Auburn University
    Auburn *B,M,D*
    Montgomery *M,D*
Jacksonville State University *M*
Samford University *B*
Talladega College *B*
University of Alabama
    Birmingham *M*
    Huntsville *M*
    Tuscaloosa *M*
University of South Alabama *M*

Alaska

University of Alaska
    Anchorage *M*
    Southeast *M*

Arizona

Arizona State University *M,D*
Cochise College *A*
Northern Arizona University *B,M*
Pima Community College *A*
Scottsdale Community College *A*
University of Arizona *B,M*

Arkansas

Arkansas State University *M*
Henderson State University *B*
University of Arkansas
    Fayetteville *B,M*
    Little Rock *M*
University of Central Arkansas *B*
University of the Ozarks *B*

California

California Baptist College *B*
California Lutheran University *M*
California State University
    Bakersfield *B,M*
    Chico *C,B,M*
    Dominguez Hills *B,M*
    Fresno *B,M*
    Fullerton *B,M*
    Hayward *M*
    Long Beach *M*
    Los Angeles *B,M*
    Northridge *M*
    Sacramento *B,M*
    San Bernardino *B,M*
    Stanislaus *B,M*
College of Notre Dame *M*
Fresno City College *C,A*
Golden Gate University *M,D*
National University *M*
Palomar College *C,A*
San Diego State University *B,M*
San Francisco State University *M*
San Jose State University *B,M*
Santa Rosa Junior College *A*
Skyline College *C,A*
Sonoma State University *M*
Southwestern College *A*
University of California
    Irvine *M*
    Los Angeles *M*
University of La Verne *B,M,D*
University of San Francisco *B,M*
University of Southern California *B,M,D*
World College West *B*

Colorado

Red Rocks Community College *A*
University of Colorado
    Colorado Springs *M*
    Denver *M,D*

Connecticut

Eastern Connecticut State
    University *B*
Housatonic Community College *A*
University of Hartford *B,M*
University of New Haven *B,M*

Delaware

University of Delaware *M*

District of Columbia

American University *M,D*
George Washington University *M,D*
Howard University *M*
Southeastern University *B*
University of the District of
    Columbia *B,M*

Florida

Daytona Beach Community
    College *A*
Florida Agricultural and Mechanical
    University *M*
Florida Atlantic University *B,M,D*
Florida International University *B,M,D*
Florida State University *M,D*
Jacksonville University *B*
Nova University *M,D*
St. Leo College *B*
St. Thomas University *B*
Tampa College *M*
University of Central Florida *B,M*
University of Miami *M*
University of North Florida *M*
University of South Florida *M*
University of West Florida *B,M*

Georgia

Brenau Women's College *B*
Clark Atlanta University *M*
Columbus College *B*
Darton College *A*
Georgia College *B,M*
Georgia Southern University *M*
Georgia Southwestern College *B*
Georgia State University *M*
Macon College *A*
Middle Georgia College *A*
University of Georgia *M,D*
Valdosta State College *M*
West Georgia College *M*

Hawaii

Hawaii Pacific University *B*
University of Hawaii: West Oahu *B*

Idaho

Boise State University *M*
Idaho State University *M*
University of Idaho *M*

Illinois

Augustana College *B*
Blackburn College *B*
De Paul University *M*
Governors State University *B,M*
Illinois Institute of Technology *M*
Lewis University *B*
Morton College *A*
Northern Illinois University *M*
Rockford College *B*
Roosevelt University *B,M*
Sangamon State University *M*
Southern Illinois University
    Carbondale *M*
    Edwardsville *M*
University of Chicago *M*
University of Illinois at Chicago *M*

Indiana

Ball State University *A*
Indiana State University *M*
Indiana University
    Bloomington *B,M,D*
    Northwest *B,M*
    South Bend *B,M*
Indiana University—Purdue
    University at Indianapolis *B,M*

Iowa

Drake University *B,M*
Iowa State University *B,M*
St. Ambrose University *B*
University of Iowa *M*
University of Northern Iowa *B*

Kansas

Colby Community College *A*
Fort Scott Community College *A*
Hutchinson Community College *A*
Kansas State University *M*
University of Kansas *M*
Washburn University of Topeka *B*
Wichita State University *M*

Kentucky

Eastern Kentucky University *M*
Kentucky State University *B*
Murray State University *M*
Northern Kentucky University *B,M*
University of Kentucky *M,D*
Western Kentucky University *M*

Louisiana

Grambling State University *B,M*
Louisiana College *B*
Louisiana State University
    Agricultural and Mechanical
        College *B,M*
    Shreveport *B*
University of New Orleans *M*

Maine

University of Maine
    Augusta *B*
    Orono *B,M*
    Presque Isle *C,M*
University of Southern Maine *M*

Maryland

Bowie State University *B,M*
Sojourner-Douglass College *B*
University of Baltimore *M*
University of Maryland: College
    Park *M*

Massachusetts

American International College *B,M*
Boston University *M*
Clark University *M*
Framingham State College *M*
Harvard University *M,D*
Nichols College *B*
Northeastern University *M*
Stonehill College *B*
Suffolk University *M*

Michigan

Alma College *B*
Central Michigan University *B,M*
Eastern Michigan University *B,M*
Grand Valley State University *B,M*
Madonna University *A,B*
Michigan State University *B,M*
Northern Michigan University *B,M*
Oakland University *B,M*
Saginaw Valley State University *B*
Siena Heights College *A,B*
University of Detroit Mercy *M*

University of Michigan
    Ann Arbor *M*
    Dearborn *B,M*
    Flint *B,M*
Wayne State University *M*
Western Michigan University
    B,M,D

Minnesota

Hamline University *M*
Mankato State University *B,M*
Moorhead State University *M*
St. Cloud State University *B*
St. Mary's College of Minnesota *B*
University of St. Thomas *B*
Winona State University *B*

Mississippi

Jackson State University *M,D*
Mississippi College *B*
Rust College *B*
University of Mississippi *B,M*

Missouri

Avila College *B*
Central Missouri State
    University *M*
East Central College *A*
Evangel College *B*
Lincoln University *B*
Missouri Valley College *B*
Northwest Missouri State
    University *B*
Park College *B*
St. Louis University *M*
Southwest Missouri State University
    B,M
University of Missouri
    Columbia *M*
    Kansas City *M,D*
    St. Louis *M*
Webster University *M*

Montana

Carroll College *B*
Montana State University *M*
University of Montana *M*

Nebraska

Doane College *B*
University of Nebraska—Omaha *M*
Wayne State College *B*

Nevada

University of Nevada
    Las Vegas *M*
    Reno *M*

New Hampshire

Plymouth State College of the
    University System of New
    Hampshire *B*
University of New Hampshire *M*

New Jersey

Caldwell College *C*
County College of Morris *A*
Fairleigh Dickinson University *M*
Kean College of New Jersey *B,M*
Princeton University *B,M,D*
Rider College *B,M*
Rutgers—The State University of
    New Jersey *M*
Seton Hall University *M*
Thomas Edison State College *A,B*
Trenton State College *B*
Upsala College *B*
William Paterson College of New
    Jersey *B,M*

New Mexico

College of Santa Fe *A,B*
New Mexico State University *M*
University of New Mexico *M*
Western New Mexico University *B*

New York

Alfred University *B*
Canisius College *M*
City University of New York
　Baruch College *B,M*
　Brooklyn College *M*
　Hostos Community College *A*
　John Jay College of Criminal
　　Justice *A,B,M*
　Medgar Evers College *A,B*
Columbia University *M*
Cornell University *M,D*
Dominican College of Blauvelt *B*
Eugene Lang College/New School
　for Social Research *B*
Fordham University *M*
Herkimer County Community
　College *A*
Iona College *M*
Keuka College *B*
Long Island University
　Brooklyn Campus *B,M*
　C. W. Post Campus *B,M*
Marist College *M*
Medaille College *B*
New York University *C,B,M,D*
Onondaga Community College *A*
Pace University: College of White
　Plains *M*
Russell Sage College *M*
St. John's University *B*
State University of New York
　Albany *M,D*
　College at Brockport *M*
Syracuse University *M,D*
Wagner College *B*

North Carolina

Campbell University *B*
East Carolina University *M*
Elon College *B*
Fayetteville State University *B*
Fayetteville Technical Community
　College *A*
North Carolina Central
　University *M*
North Carolina State University *M*
Shaw University *B*
University of North Carolina
　Chapel Hill *M*
　Charlotte *M*
　Greensboro *B,M*
Western Carolina University *M*
Winston-Salem State University *B*

North Dakota

Turtle Mountain Community
　College *A*
University of North Dakota *B,M*

Ohio

Ashland University *B*
Bowling Green State University
　B,M
Capital University *B*
Cedarville College *B*
Central State University *B*
Cleveland State University *M*
Dyke College *A,B*
Franklin University *A,B*
Heidelberg College *B*
Kent State University *M,D*
Lakeland Community College *A*
Miami University: Oxford
　Campus *B*

Ohio State University: Columbus
　Campus *M,D*
Ohio University *B,M*
Union Institute *B,D*
University of Akron *M*
University of Cincinnati *M*
University of Dayton *M*
University of Toledo *M*
Youngstown State University *B*

Oklahoma

Rose State College *A*
University of Central Oklahoma *B*
University of Oklahoma *B,M*

Oregon

Lewis and Clark College *M*
Portland Community College *A*
Portland State University *M,D*
University of Oregon: Robert
　Donald Clark Honors College *B*
Western Oregon State College *B*
Willamette University *M*

Pennsylvania

Albright College *B*
California University of
　Pennsylvania *B*
Carnegie Mellon University
　B,M,D,W
Cedar Crest College *B*
Drexel University *M*
Elizabethtown College *B*
Gannon University *M*
Juniata College *B*
Kutztown University of
　Pennsylvania *B,M*
La Salle University *B*
Lehigh County Community
　College *A*
Marywood College *M*
Mercyhurst College *B*
Mount Aloysius College *B*
Penn State
　Harrisburg Capital College
　　M,D
　University Park Campus *M*
Point Park College *B*
Reading Area Community
　College *A*
St. Francis College *B*
St. Joseph's University *B*
Shippensburg University of
　Pennsylvania *B,M*
Slippery Rock University of
　Pennsylvania *B,M*
Temple University *M*
University of Pennsylvania *B,M*
University of Pittsburgh *B,M,D*
University of Scranton *A,B*
Waynesburg College *B*
West Chester University of
　Pennsylvania *M*
York College of Pennsylvania *B*

Puerto Rico

Inter American University of Puerto
　Rico
　Arecibo Campus *B*
　Metropolitan Campus *B*
　San German Campus *B*
University of Puerto Rico: Rio
　Piedras Campus *M*

Rhode Island

Bryant College *M*
Rhode Island College *B*
Roger Williams College *B*
University of Rhode Island *M*

South Carolina

Benedict College *B*
College of Charleston *M*
University of South Carolina *M*

South Dakota

University of South Dakota *M*

Tennessee

Austin Peay State University *B*
David Lipscomb University *B*
Fisk University *B*
Maryville College *B*
Memphis State University *M*
Tennessee State University *M*
University of Tennessee
　Chattanooga *M*
　Knoxville *B,M*
　Martin *B*

Texas

Angelo State University *M*
Baylor University *B*
Corpus Christi State University *M*
Dallas Baptist University *M*
Del Mar College *A*
Lamar University—Beaumont *M*
LeTourneau University *B*
Midwestern State University *M*
Our Lady of the Lake University of
　San Antonio *B*
St. Mary's University *M*
San Antonio College *A*
Southwest Texas State University
　B,M
Stephen F. Austin State
　University *B*
Sul Ross State University *M*
Texas A&I University *B*
Texas A&M University *M*
Texas Southern University *B,M*
Texas Tech University *M*
University of Central Texas *M*
University of Houston
　Clear Lake *B,M*
　Houston *M*
University of North Texas *M*
University of Texas
　Dallas *B*
　El Paso *M*
　San Antonio *M*
　Tyler *M*
West Texas State University *B*

Utah

Brigham Young University *M*
University of Utah *M*
Utah State University *M*

Vermont

Goddard College *B*
St. Michael's College *M*
University of Vermont *M*

Virginia

Christopher Newport College *B*
Ferrum College *B*
George Mason University *B,M,D*
James Madison University *B,M*
Old Dominion University *M*
University of Richmond *A*
University of Virginia *M*
Virginia Commonwealth University
　M,D
Virginia Polytechnic Institute and
　State University *B*
Virginia State University *B*
Virginia Wesleyan College *B*

Washington

City University *M*
Eastern Washington University *M*

Evergreen State College *B,M*
Heritage College *C*
Seattle University *B,M*
University of Puget Sound *B*
University of Washington *M*

West Virginia

Bethany College *B*
West Virginia University *M*
West Virginia Wesleyan College *B*

Wisconsin

Carthage College *B*
Edgewood College *B*
University of Wisconsin
　Green Bay *B,M*
　La Crosse *B*
　Madison *M,D*
　Milwaukee *M*
　Oshkosh *B,M*
　Stevens Point *B*
　Whitewater *B*

Wyoming

Laramie County Community
　College *C*
Northwest College *A*
University of Wyoming *M*

**American Samoa, Caroline
Islands, Guam, Marianas,
Virgin Islands**

University of Guam *B,M*
University of the Virgin Islands *M*

Arab Republic of Egypt

American University in Cairo *M*

Public affairs

Alabama

Community College of the Air
　Force *A*

California

Chabot College *A*
Citrus College *A*
Claremont McKenna College *B*
College of the Sequoias *A*
Compton Community College *A*
East Los Angeles College *A*
El Camino College *A*
Imperial Valley College *A*
Modesto Junior College *A*
Moorpark College *A*
Oxnard College *A*
Pasadena City College *A*
Saddleback College *A*
San Jose City College *A*
Santa Rosa Junior College *A*
Solano Community College *A*
Southwestern College *A*
Ventura College *A*
World College West *B*

Colorado

University of Denver *B*

Connecticut

Manchester Community College *A*
Mitchell College *A*
Thames Valley State Technical
　College *A*
University of Connecticut *M*

District of Columbia

George Washington University *M*
Southeastern University *A*

University of the District of
Columbia A

Florida
Broward Community College A
Florida Atlantic University B
Gulf Coast Community College A
Miami-Dade Community College A

Georgia
Atlanta Metropolitan College A
Darton College A
Georgia State University M
Kennesaw State College B

Idaho
Boise State University M

Illinois
Black Hawk College A
Lincoln Land Community
College A
Southern Illinois University at
Carbondale M

Indiana
Indiana University
Bloomington A,B,M
Northwest A,B
South Bend A,B
Indiana University—Purdue
University
Fort Wayne C,A,B,M
Indianapolis A,B,M
Vincennes University A

Iowa
Iowa Central Community College A
Kirkwood Community College A
University of Iowa M

Kansas
Butler County Community
College A
Hutchinson Community College A
St. Mary College B

Kentucky
Kentucky State University M

Maryland
Villa Julie College A

Massachusetts
University of Massachusetts at
Boston M

Michigan
Alma College B
Lansing Community College A
Michigan State University B
Muskegon Community College A
Wayne State University B

Minnesota
University of Minnesota: Twin
Cities M
Willmar Community College A

Missouri
Central Missouri State
University M
East Central College A
Park College M

Montana
Carroll College B

Nebraska
Northeast Community College A
University of Nebraska—Lincoln M

New Hampshire
Plymouth State College of the
University System of New
Hampshire A

New Jersey
Camden County College A
County College of Morris A
St. Peter's College A

New Mexico
New Mexico Highlands
University M
Western New Mexico University A

New York
Cornell University B,M
Eugene Lang College/New School
for Social Research B
Hudson Valley Community
College A
Jefferson Community College A
State University of New York at
Albany B

North Carolina
Brevard College A
Mayland Community College A
Mitchell Community College A
University of North Carolina at
Greensboro M

North Dakota
Bismarck State College A

Ohio
Ashland University B
Miami University: Hamilton
Campus A
Muskingum College B
Ohio State University: Columbus
Campus B,M,D
Sinclair Community College A
Union Institute B,D
University of Toledo A,B
Youngstown State University A

Oklahoma
University of Central Oklahoma M

Oregon
Central Oregon Community
College A
Willamette University M

Pennsylvania
California University of
Pennsylvania A
Carnegie Mellon University B,M
Community College of Beaver
County A
Harrisburg Area Community
College A
Indiana University of
Pennsylvania B
La Salle University A
Lincoln University B
Penn State University Park Campus
C,B
University of Pittsburgh M,D
Westmoreland County Community
College A

Puerto Rico
Puerto Rico Junior College A
Turabo University M

Rhode Island
University of Rhode Island M

South Carolina
Clemson University M
Columbia College B
Winthrop University B

South Dakota
Northern State University A

Tennessee
Tennessee State University A

Texas
College of the Mainland A
Del Mar College A
Galveston College A
San Antonio College A
University of Texas
Austin M
Dallas M
Western Texas College A

Virginia
University of Richmond A

Washington
Eastern Washington University M

Wisconsin
University of Wisconsin: Oshkosh B

Public health laboratory science

Alabama
University of Alabama in
Birmingham M,D

California
California State University
Long Beach M
Northridge M
San Diego State University M
San Jose State University B,M
Santa Rosa Junior College A
University of California
Berkeley M,D
Los Angeles B,M,D
University of Southern California D

Connecticut
Southern Connecticut State
University B,M
Yale University M,D

District of Columbia
George Washington University M

Florida
University of Miami M
University of South Florida M

Georgia
Columbus College B
Emory University M

Hawaii
University of Hawaii at Manoa M,D

Illinois
Northwestern University M
University of Illinois at Chicago
M,D

Indiana
Ball State University B
Indiana State University B
Indiana University Bloomington B
Indiana University—Purdue
University at Indianapolis B

Iowa
University of Iowa M

Kansas
University of Kansas
Lawrence M
Medical Center M

Kentucky
Eastern Kentucky University B
University of Kentucky B

Maryland
Johns Hopkins University B,M
Uniformed Services University of
the Health Sciences M
University of Maryland: Baltimore
M,D

Massachusetts
Boston University C,M,D
Harvard University M,D
Springfield College B
Tufts University B
University of Massachusetts
Amherst B,M,D
Lowell M,D

Michigan
Grand Valley State University B
University of Michigan M,D

Minnesota
Mankato State University B
St. Cloud State University B
University of Minnesota: Twin
Cities M,D

Missouri
East Central College A

Nebraska
Chadron State College B

New Jersey
Rutgers—The State University of
New Jersey
Cook College B
Douglass College B
Livingston College B
New Brunswick M,D
Rutgers College B
University College New
Brunswick B
Stockton State College B

New Mexico
New Mexico State University B

New York
Columbia University M,D
State University of New York
Albany M,D
Buffalo M
Wagner College B

North Carolina
University of North Carolina at
Chapel Hill B,M,D

Ohio
Case Western Reserve University
M,D
Kent State University B
Ohio State University: Columbus
Campus M
University of Cincinnati B
University of Toledo B,M

Oklahoma

Eastern Oklahoma State College *A*
University of Oklahoma
    Health Sciences Center *M,D*
    Norman *M,D*

Pennsylvania

Temple University *M*
University of Pittsburgh *M,D*
West Chester University of
    Pennsylvania *B,M*

Puerto Rico

University of Puerto Rico: Medical
    Sciences Campus *M*

South Carolina

University of South Carolina *M,D*

Tennessee

Austin Peay State University *M*
East Tennessee State University *M*
Meharry Medical College *M*

Texas

Austin Community College *C*
Texas A&M University *M,D*
University of Texas Health Science
    Center at Houston *M*

Utah

Utah State University *B*

Virginia

James Madison University *B*
Old Dominion University *B*
University of Virginia *M*
Virginia Commonwealth
    University *M*

Washington

Central Washington University *B*
Evergreen State College *B*
University of Washington *M,D*

Wisconsin

University of Wisconsin: Eau Claire
    B,M

Canada

McGill University *M,D*

Public policy studies

California

Occidental College *B*
San Jose State University *B*
Stanford University *B*
University of California: Berkeley
    M,D
University of Southern California
    M,D

Connecticut

Trinity College *B*
University of New Haven *C*
Wesleyan University *B*

District of Columbia

American University *M*
George Washington University *M,D*

Florida

New College of the University of
    South Florida *B*

Illinois

Barat College *B*
College of St. Francis *B*

Lake Forest College *B,M*
Northwestern University *M,D*
Southern Illinois University at
    Edwardsville *M*
University of Chicago *B,M*
University of Illinois at Chicago *D*

Indiana

Indiana University
    Bloomington *B*
    Northwest *B*

Iowa

University of Northern Iowa *M*

Maryland

St. Mary's College of Maryland *B*
University of Maryland
    Baltimore County *M,D*
    College Park *M*

Massachusetts

Bridgewater State College *C*
Emmanuel College *M*
Hampshire College *B*
University of Massachusetts at
    Boston *B,D*

Michigan

Oakland University *B*
University of Michigan *M,D*

Mississippi

Mississippi State University *M,D*

Missouri

St. Louis University *M,D*
University of Missouri: Columbia *M*

New Jersey

Bloomfield College *B*
Rutgers—The State University of
    New Jersey *M*

New York

City University of New York:
    Brooklyn College *M*
Cornell University *M,D*
Eugene Lang College/New School
    for Social Research *B*
Hamilton College *B*
Sarah Lawrence College *B*
State University of New York
    Albany *M*
    Stony Brook *M*
University of Rochester *M*

North Carolina

Duke University *B,M*

Ohio

Ohio State University: Columbus
    Campus *M,D*
Union Institute *B,D*

Oregon

Willamette University *M*

Pennsylvania

Carnegie Mellon University
    B,M,D,W
Duquesne University *M*
Indiana University of
    Pennsylvania *B*
Penn State Harrisburg Capital
    College *B*
University of Pennsylvania *B,M,D*
University of Pittsburgh *M*

Tennessee

Vanderbilt University *B,M,D*

Texas

Abilene Christian University *B*
Baylor University *M*
University of Texas
    Austin *D*
    Dallas *D*

Utah

Brigham Young University *B,M*

Virginia

Christopher Newport College *B*
Virginia Wesleyan College *B*
Washington and Lee University *B*

Washington

Evergreen State College *B*
Whitworth College *B*

West Virginia

Bethany College *B*

Wisconsin

Lakeland College *B*
Northland College *B*

Public relations

Alabama

Alabama State University *B*
Auburn University *B*
Spring Hill College *B*
University of Alabama *B,M*
University of North Alabama *B*

Alaska

University of Alaska Anchorage *B*

Arizona

Glendale Community College *A*
Grand Canyon University *B*
Mesa Community College *A*
Northern Arizona University *B*
Scottsdale Community College *C,A*

Arkansas

Arkansas State University *B*
Garland County Community
    College *C*
John Brown University *A,B*
Ouachita Baptist University *B*

California

California State University
    Dominguez Hills *B*
    Fullerton *B,M*
    Los Angeles *B*
Chapman University *B*
College of Marin: Kentfield *A*
Cosumnes River College *A*
Golden Gate University *M*
Golden West College *C,A*
Long Beach City College *A*
Los Angeles City College *A*
Pacific Union College *B*
Pepperdine University *B*
San Jose State University *B*
University of the Pacific *B*
University of Southern California
    B,M

Colorado

Colorado Christian University *B*
University of Northern Colorado *B*
University of Southern Colorado *B*

Connecticut

Quinnipiac College *B,M*
University of New Haven *B*

District of Columbia

American University *B,M*
Howard University *B*

Florida

Barry University *B*
Central Florida Community
    College *A*
Florida Southern College *B*
Florida State University *B*
Gulf Coast Community College *A*
Lynn University *B*
University of Florida *B,M,D*
University of Miami *B,M*

Georgia

Berry College *B*
Brenau Women's College *B*
Clark Atlanta University *B*
Georgia Southern University *B*
Morris Brown College *B*
Shorter College *B*
Toccoa Falls College *B*
University of Georgia *B*
Wesleyan College *B*

Idaho

University of Idaho *B*

Illinois

Black Hawk College *A*
Bradley University *B*
Columbia College *B*
Illinois State University *B*
Parkland College *A*
Ray College of Design *A,B*
Roosevelt University *B*
Southern Illinois University at
    Carbondale *B*

Indiana

Ball State University *B,M*
Butler University *B*
Franklin College *B*
Indiana State University *B*
Purdue University *B,M,D*
St. Mary-of-the-Woods College *B*
University of Evansville *B*
Valparaiso University *B*
Vincennes University *A*

Iowa

Buena Vista College *B*
Clarke College *B*
Cornell College *B*
Drake University *B*
Kirkwood Community College *A*
Loras College *B*
Mount Mercy College *B*
St. Ambrose University *B*
Teikyo Marycrest University *B*
University of Northern Iowa *B*
Wartburg College *B*

Kansas

Cloud County Community
    College *A*
Colby Community College *A*
Fort Scott Community College *A*
Highland Community College *A*
Kansas State University *B*
MidAmerica Nazarene College *B*
Pittsburg State University *B*
Washburn University of Topeka *B*

Kentucky

Eastern Kentucky University *B*
Kentucky Wesleyan College *B*
Western Kentucky University *B*

Louisiana

Louisiana State University in
  Shreveport *B*
Loyola University *B*
Northeast Louisiana University *B*
University of Southwestern
  Louisiana *B*

Maryland

Harford Community College *A*
University of Maryland: College
  Park *B*

Massachusetts

Aquinas College at Milton *A*
Becker College: Leicester
  Campus *A*
Boston University *B,M*
Emerson College *B,M*
Endicott College *A,B*
North Adams State College *B*
Northeastern University *B*
Salem State College *B*
Simmons College *B*
Suffolk University *B,M*

Michigan

Adrian College *B*
Eastern Michigan University *B*
Ferris State University *B*
Grand Valley State University *B*
Michigan State University *M*
Northern Michigan University *B*
University of Detroit Mercy *B*
Wayne State University *B*
Western Michigan University *B*

Minnesota

Concordia College: Moorhead *B*
Mankato State University *B*
Moorhead State University *B*
St. Cloud State University *B*
St. Mary's College of Minnesota *B*
Southwest State University *B*
Vermilion Community College *A*
Willmar Community College *A*
Winona State University *B*

Mississippi

Jackson State University *B*
Mississippi College *B*
University of Southern
  Mississippi *M*

Missouri

Central Missouri State University *B*
East Central College *A*
Fontbonne College *B*
Northwest Missouri State
  University *B*
Park College *B*
St. Louis Community College at
  Florissant Valley *A*
Southeast Missouri State
  University *B*
Southwest Missouri State
  University *B*
Stephens College *B*
Webster University *B*
William Jewell College *B*

Montana

Carroll College *B*

Nebraska

Creighton University *C,A*
Hastings College *B*
Union College *B*
University of Nebraska—Omaha *B*

New Hampshire

New England College *B*

New Jersey

Brookdale Community College *A*
Glassboro State College *B,M*
Rider College *B*
Seton Hall University *M*
Stockton State College *B*

New Mexico

New Mexico State University *B*

New York

Daemen College *B*
Herkimer County Community
  College *A*
Iona College *B*
Long Island University
  C. W. Post Campus *B*
  Southampton Campus *B*
Manhattan College *B*
Medaille College *B*
Mount St. Mary College *B*
Rochester Institute of
  Technology *C*
State University of New York
  College at Buffalo *B*
Syracuse University *B,M*
Utica College of Syracuse
  University *B*

North Carolina

Appalachian State University *B*
Campbell University *B*
Mars Hill College *B*
Mount Olive College *A,B*
North Carolina State University *B*
Queens College *B*
Wingate College *B*

North Dakota

University of North Dakota *B*

Ohio

Ashland University *B*
Bowling Green State University *B*
Capital University *B*
Defiance College *B*
Heidelberg College *B*
Kent State University *B,M*
Marietta College *B*
Miami University: Oxford
  Campus *B*
Ohio Dominican College *B*
Ohio Northern University *B*
Ohio State University: Columbus
  Campus *B,M,D*
Ohio University *B*
Otterbein College *B*
University of Akron *B*
University of Dayton *B*
University of Findlay *B*
University of Rio Grande *B*
University of Toledo *B*
Ursuline College *B*
Xavier University *A,B*
Youngstown State University *B*

Oklahoma

Eastern Oklahoma State College *A*
Northwestern Oklahoma State
  University *B*
Oklahoma Baptist University *B*
Oklahoma Christian University of
  Science and Arts *B*
Oklahoma City University *B*
Oklahoma State University *B*
University of Central Oklahoma *B*
University of Oklahoma *B*

Oregon

Marylhurst College *C*
University of Oregon
  Eugene *B,M*
  Robert Donald Clark Honors
    College *B*

Pennsylvania

California University of
  Pennsylvania *B*
Community College of Beaver
  County *A*
Duquesne University *B*
Elizabethtown College *B*
Lock Haven University of
  Pennsylvania *B*
Lycoming College *B*
Mansfield University of
  Pennsylvania *B*
Marywood College *B*
Mercyhurst College *B*
Pennsylvania College of
  Technology *A*
St. Francis College *B*
University of Pittsburgh at
  Bradford *B*
University of Scranton *B*
Westminster College *B*
Widener University *B*

Puerto Rico

University of the Sacred Heart *M*

Rhode Island

Johnson & Wales University *A*
Rhode Island College *B*

South Carolina

Bob Jones University *B*
University of South Carolina *B*

South Dakota

Black Hills State University *A,B*
Huron University *A,B*
Sioux Falls College *B*
University of South Dakota *B,M*

Tennessee

Bristol University *A*
David Lipscomb University *B*
East Tennessee State University *B*
Freed-Hardeman University *B*
Lambuth University *B*
Middle Tennessee State
  University *B*
Southern College of Seventh-day
  Adventists *B*
Union University *B*
University of Tennessee
  Chattanooga *B*
  Martin *B*

Texas

Abilene Christian University *B*
El Paso Community College *A*
Hardin-Simmons University *B*
Lubbock Christian University *B*
Southern Methodist University *B*
Texas Tech University *B*
West Texas State University *B*

Utah

Brigham Young University *B*
Southern Utah University *B*
Weber State University *B*

Vermont

Champlain College *A*
Green Mountain College *B*

Virginia

Averett College *B*
Hampton University *B*
Radford University *B,M*
University of Richmond *A*
Virginia Wesleyan College *B*

Washington

Central Washington University *B*
Eastern Washington University *B*
Gonzaga University *B*
Pacific Lutheran University *B*
Washington State University *B*

West Virginia

Bethany College *B*
Concord College *B*
Marshall University *B,M*
West Virginia University *B*
West Virginia Wesleyan College *B*

Wisconsin

Marquette University *B*
Mount Mary College *B*
University of Wisconsin
  Oshkosh *B*
  Platteville *B*

Arab Republic of Egypt

American University in Cairo *B*

Public utilities

Indiana

Indiana University Bloomington
  B,M,D

Wisconsin

Northeast Wisconsin Technical
  College *C*

Pure mathematics

California

California Institute of Technology
  B,D,W
California State University
  Los Angeles *B,M*
  Northridge *B*
University of California: Santa Cruz
  B,M,D

Connecticut

Wesleyan University *B*

Florida

University of Florida *M,D*
University of Miami *D*

Georgia

Armstrong State College *B*

Illinois

Concordia University *B*
De Paul University *B*
Northern Illinois University *M*
Trinity College *B*
University of Chicago *B,M,D*

Indiana

Franklin College *B*
Oakland City College *B*
Purdue University *M,D*
University of Notre Dame *B,M,D*

Iowa

University of Iowa *B*

Kansas

Kansas State University *M,D*

Maine

University of Maine at
Farmington *B*

Maryland

Bowie State University *B*

Massachusetts

Boston University *B,M,D*
Brandeis University *M,D*
Hampshire College *B*
Harvard and Radcliffe Colleges *B*
Massachusetts Institute of
Technology *B,M,D,W*
Salem State College *B*
University of Massachusetts at
Boston *B*
Williams College *B*
Worcester Polytechnic Institute *B*

Minnesota

Willmar Community College *A*

Montana

Montana College of Mineral
Science and Technology *B*

Nebraska

Hastings College *B*

New Jersey

Centenary College *B*
Rutgers—The State University of
New Jersey *M,D*
Seton Hall University *M*
Stevens Institute of Technology
B,M,D

New York

City University of New York
Brooklyn College *B,M*
Queens College *B*
Colgate University *B*
Columbia University *M,D*
St. Thomas Aquinas College *B*

Ohio

Case Western Reserve University
B,M,D
Defiance College *B*
Kent State University *B,M,D*
Kenyon College *B*
Ohio State University: Columbus
Campus *B,M,D*
Ohio University *B,M,D*
Union Institute *D*
University of Toledo *B*
Wright State University *B*

Oregon

Oregon State University *B*

Pennsylvania

Bucknell University *B,M*
Carnegie Mellon University
B,M,D,W
Elizabethtown College *B*

Puerto Rico

Inter American University of Puerto
Rico: San German Campus *B*
University of Puerto Rico:
Mayaguez Campus *B,M*

Virginia

Averett College *B*
Emory and Henry College *B*
Virginia Wesleyan College *B*

Washington

University of Washington *M,D*

West Virginia

Shepherd College *B*

Quality control technology

Alabama

John C. Calhoun State Community
College *C*
Shelton State Community College
C,A

Arizona

Glendale Community College *A*
Mesa Community College *C*
Pima Community College *C,A*
Rio Salado Community College *A*

Arkansas

Arkansas State University: Beebe
Branch *A*
Westark Community College *A*

California

Allan Hancock College *C,A*
California State University: Long
Beach *B*
Cerro Coso Community College *A*
Chaffey Community College *A*
Citrus College *C*
Coastline Community College *A*
De Anza College *C,A*
El Camino College *C,A*
Los Angeles Pierce College *C,A*
Mount San Antonio College *C,A*
Palomar College *C,A*
Rio Hondo College *C*
San Diego City College *C,A*
San Diego Mesa College *C,A*
San Jose State University *B,M*
Ventura College *A*

Connecticut

Waterbury State Technical College
C,A

Florida

Brevard Community College *A*
Manatee Community College *C*

Illinois

Illinois Eastern Community
Colleges: Frontier Community
College *C*
Illinois Valley Community
College *A*
Kishwaukee College *C*
Moraine Valley Community College
C,A
Rock Valley College *A*
Waubonsee Community College
C,A

Indiana

Indiana Vocational Technical
College
Columbus *C,A*
Kokomo *C,A*
Northeast *C,A*
Wabash Valley *A*

Kansas

Cowley County Community
College *A*

Kentucky

Eastern Kentucky University *A,B*

Michigan

Baker College of Mount Clemens *C*
Grand Rapids Community College
C,A
Henry Ford Community College *A*
Jackson Community College *C,A*
Lansing Community College *A*
Oakland Community College *C,A*
Schoolcraft College *C,A*
Wayne State University *B*

Missouri

Central Missouri State
University *M*
Longview Community College *A*
St. Louis Community College at
Florissant Valley *A*

Nebraska

Southeast Community College:
Milford Campus *A*

New Hampshire

New Hampshire Technical College:
Nashua *A*

New Jersey

Gloucester County College *C*

New York

Monroe Community College *A*
Onondaga Community College *A*

Ohio

Clark State Community College
C,A
Columbus State Community
College *A*
Edison State Community College *A*
Lakeland Community College *A*
Lorain County Community
College *A*
Marion Technical College *C*
Northwest Technical College *C,A*
Ohio State University: Columbus
Campus *B,M,D*
Owens Technical College: Toledo
C,A
Sinclair Community College *C,A*
Terra Technical College *C,A*
University of Cincinnati: Access
Colleges *A*
University of Toledo *A*
Wright State University: Lake
Campus *C*

Oklahoma

National Education Center: Spartan
School of Aeronautics Campus *A*
Rose State College *C,A*

Pennsylvania

Penn State University Park
Campus *C*

Puerto Rico

University of Puerto Rico:
Aguadilla *A*

South Carolina

Tri-County Technical College *C,A*

Tennessee

Cleveland State Community
College *C*

Pellissippi State Technical
Community College *A*

Texas

Austin Community College *C,A*
Brazosport College *A*
Brookhaven College *A*
El Paso Community College *C*
Mountain View College *A*
Richland College *C,A*
Tarrant County Junior College *A*
Texas State Technical College
Amarillo *A*
Waco *A*

Virginia

Central Virginia Community
College *C*

Washington

Everett Community College *A*

Wisconsin

Mid-State Technical College *A*
Northeast Wisconsin Technical
College *A*
Western Wisconsin Technical
College *A*

Mexico

Sistema Instituto Tecnologico y de
Estudios Superiores de
Monterrey *M*

Quantitative psychology

California

California State University
Long Beach *B*
Northridge *M*

Florida

New College of the University of
South Florida *B*

Illinois

Illinois State University *M*
University of Chicago *M,D*
University of Illinois at Urbana-
Champaign *B,M,D*

Indiana

Purdue University *B,M,D*

New Jersey

Stevens Institute of Technology
M,D

New York

Syracuse University *M,D*

Ohio

Ohio State University: Columbus
Campus *M,D*

Pennsylvania

Carnegie Mellon University
B,M,D,W
Temple University *D*

Rhode Island

Brown University *B,M,D*

Wisconsin

Carroll College *B*

Radio/television broadcasting

Alabama

Alabama State University *B*
Auburn University *B,M*
Gadsden State Community
   College *A*
Jefferson State Community
   College *A*
Lurleen B. Wallace State Junior
   College *A*
Spring Hill College *B*
Troy State University *B*
University of Alabama *B,M*
University of North Alabama *B*
Walker College *A*

Alaska

Prince William Sound Community
   College *C,A*

Arizona

Arizona State University *B*
Arizona Western College *A*
Grand Canyon University *B*
Northern Arizona University *B*
University of Arizona *B*

Arkansas

Arkansas State University *B,M*
Capital City Junior College *A*
Harding University *B*
John Brown University *A,B*
Ouachita Baptist University *B*
Philander Smith College *B*
Southern Arkansas University *B*
University of Arkansas at Little
   Rock *B*
University of Central Arkansas *B*

California

Bakersfield College *A*
California State University
   Bakersfield *B*
   Fullerton *B,M*
   Long Beach *B*
   Los Angeles *B*
   Northridge *B,M*
Chabot College *A*
Chaffey Community College *C,A*
Chapman University *B*
City College of San Francisco *C,A*
College of Marin: Kentfield *A*
Columbia College: Hollywood *A,B*
Cosumnes River College *A*
Foothill College *A*
Laney College *C,A*
Long Beach City College *C,A*
Los Angeles City College *C,A*
Los Angeles Valley College *C,A*
Modesto Junior College *A*
Moorpark College *A*
Mount San Antonio College *C,A*
Ohlone College *C,A*
Orange Coast College *C,A*
Palomar College *C,A*
Pasadena City College *C,A*
Saddleback College *A*
San Diego City College *A*
San Diego State University *B,M*
San Francisco State University *B,M*
San Joaquin Delta College *A*
San Jose State University *B*
Santa Monica College *A*
Santa Rosa Junior College *C,A*
Southern California College *B*
Southwestern College *A*
University of La Verne *B*
University of the Pacific *B*

University of San Francisco *B*
University of Southern California
   B,M

Colorado

Colorado Christian University *B*
Mesa State College *B*
Pikes Peak Community College *C,A*
University of Colorado at
   Boulder *B*
University of Southern Colorado *B*
Western State College of
   Colorado *B*

Connecticut

Briarwood College *A*
Middlesex Community College *C,A*
Sacred Heart University *B*

District of Columbia

American University *B,M*
George Washington University *B*
Howard University *B*
University of the District of
   Columbia *B*

Florida

Bethune-Cookman College *B*
Daytona Beach Community
   College *A*
Edison Community College *A*
Florida Southern College *B*
Florida State University *B*
Gulf Coast Community College *A*
Lake City Community College *A*
Miami-Dade Community College
   C,A
National Education Center: Bauder
   Campus *C*
University of Florida *B,M,D*
University of Miami *B,M*
University of West Florida *M*

Georgia

Brenau Women's College *B*
Clark Atlanta University *B*
Georgia Southern University *B*
Morris Brown College *B*
Savannah State College *B*
Shorter College *B*
Toccoa Falls College *B*
University of Georgia *B*
Valdosta State College *B*

Idaho

Idaho State University *B*
Ricks College *A*

Illinois

Black Hawk College *A*
Bradley University *B*
Chicago State University *B*
College of St. Francis *B*
Columbia College *B*
Illinois Central College *A*
Illinois College *B*
Illinois Eastern Community
   Colleges: Wabash Valley
   College *A*
Lake Land College *A*
Lewis and Clark Community
   College *A*
North Central College *B*
Northwestern University *B,M,D*
Olivet Nazarene University *B*
Parkland College *A*
Roosevelt University *B*
Southern Illinois University
   Carbondale *B*
   Edwardsville *B*
University of Illinois at Urbana-
   Champaign *B*

Western Illinois University *M*
Wheaton College *M*

Indiana

Ball State University *B*
Butler University *B,M*
Franklin College *B*
Huntington College *B*
Indiana State University *B,M*
Indiana University Bloomington
   B,M,D
Indiana University—Purdue
   University at Fort Wayne *B*
Manchester College *A,B*
Purdue University
   Calumet *B*
   West Lafayette *B*
St. Joseph's College *B*
Taylor University *B*
University of Indianapolis *B*
Vincennes University *A*

Iowa

American Institute of Commerce *C*
Buena Vista College *B*
Dordt College *B*
Drake University *B*
Grand View College *B*
Iowa Central Community College *A*
Iowa Lakes Community College *A*
Iowa Western Community
   College *A*
Kirkwood Community College *A*
Loras College *B*
Morningside College *B*
St. Ambrose University *B*
Scott Community College *A*
Teikyo Marycrest University *B*
Teikyo Westmar University *B*
University of Iowa *B,M,D*
University of Northern Iowa *B*
Waldorf College *A*
Wartburg College *B*

Kansas

Cloud County Community
   College *A*
Coffeyville Community College *A*
Colby Community College *A*
Dodge City Community College *A*
Hutchinson Community College *A*
Kansas State University *B*
Pittsburg State University *B*
University of Kansas *B*
Washburn University of Topeka *B*

Kentucky

Asbury College *B*
Campbellsville College *B*
Eastern Kentucky University *B*
Kentucky Wesleyan College *B*
Morehead State University *A,B*
Murray State University *B*
Northern Kentucky University *B*
Western Kentucky University *B*

Louisiana

Louisiana College *B*
Louisiana State University and
   Agricultural and Mechanical
   College *B*
Loyola University *B*
McNeese State University *B*
Northeast Louisiana University *B*
Southern University and
   Agricultural and Mechanical
   College *B*
University of Southwestern
   Louisiana *B*
World Evangelism Bible College
   and Seminary *C,A*
Xavier University of Louisiana *B*

Maine

Beal College *A*
Husson College *A*
St. Joseph's College *B*
University of Maine *B*

Maryland

Columbia Union College *B*
Hagerstown Junior College *A*
Harford Community College *C,A*
Montgomery College: Rockville
   Campus *A*
Morgan State University *B*
Salisbury State University *B*
University of Maryland: College
   Park *B,M*

Massachusetts

Becker College: Leicester
   Campus *A*
Boston University *B,M*
Curry College *B*
Dean Junior College *A*
Emerson College *B,M*
Endicott College *A*
Hampshire College *B*
Mount Ida College *A*
Mount Wachusett Community
   College *A*
Newbury College *A*
North Adams State College *B*
Suffolk University *B*

Michigan

Adrian College *A,B*
Andrews University *B*
Central Michigan University *B,M*
Delta College *A*
Eastern Michigan University *B*
Grand Rapids Baptist College and
   Seminary *A*
Grand Valley State University *B*
Henry Ford Community College *A*
Kellogg Community College *A*
Lansing Community College *A*
Michigan State University *B,M*
Northern Michigan University *B*
Oakland Community College *A*
Olivet College *B*
St. Clair County Community
   College *A*
Schoolcraft College *A*
University of Detroit Mercy *B*
Wayne State University *B*

Minnesota

Austin Community College *A*
Bemidji State University *B*
Bethel College *B*
Concordia College: Moorhead *B*
Moorhead State University *B*
National Education Center: Brown
   Institute Campus *C,A*
North Central Bible College *A,B*
Northwestern College *A,B*
Rainy River Community College *A*
St. Cloud State University *B*
Southwest State University *B*
Willmar Community College *A*
Winona State University *B*

Mississippi

Jackson State University *B*
Mississippi University for Women *B*
Rust College *B*
University of Mississippi *B,M*
University of Southern
   Mississippi *B*

Missouri

Calvary Bible College *A,B*
Central Missouri State University *B*

College of the Ozarks *B*
East Central College *A*
Evangel College *A,B*
Fontbonne College *B*
Lincoln University *B*
Missouri Valley College *B*
Northwest Missouri State
   University *B*
Park College *B*
St. Louis Community College at
   Florissant Valley *A*
Southeast Missouri State
   University *B*
Southwest Missouri State
   University *B*
Stephens College *B*
University of Missouri: Columbia *B*
Webster University *B*
William Woods College *B*

Montana

College of Great Falls *A,B*
University of Montana *B*

Nebraska

Central Community College *C,A*
Creighton University *B*
Dana College *B*
Grace College of the Bible *B*
Hastings College *B*
Northeast Community College *A*
Southeast Community College:
   Beatrice Campus *A*
University of Nebraska
   Kearney *B*
   Lincoln *B*
   Omaha *B*
Wayne State College *B*

New Hampshire

Franklin Pierce College *B*
New England College *B*
White Pines College *A*

New Jersey

Bergen Community College *A*
Brookdale Community College *A*
Caldwell College *C*
County College of Morris *A*
Glassboro State College *B*
Jersey City State College *B*
Rider College *B*
Seton Hall University *B*
Stockton State College *B*

New Mexico

College of Santa Fe *B*
Eastern New Mexico University
   B,M
New Mexico State University *B*
San Juan College *A*

New York

Adirondack Community College
   C,A
City University of New York
   Brooklyn College *B,M*
   Kingsborough Community
      College *A*
   Queens College *B*
College of New Rochelle *B*
Fordham University *B*
Herkimer County Community
   College *C,A*
Hofstra University *B*
Iona College *A,B*
Ithaca College *B*
Jefferson Community College *A*
Long Island University
   C. W. Post Campus *B*
   Southampton Campus *B*
Manhattan College *B*

Medaille College *B*
Mercy College *B*
Mount St. Mary College *B*
Nassau Community College *A*
New York University *B,M*
Onondaga Community College *A*
St. Thomas Aquinas College *B*
School of Visual Arts *B*
State University of New York
   College at Buffalo *B*
   College at Cortland *B*
   College at Geneseo *B*
   College at New Paltz *B*
   College at Plattsburgh *B*
   Oswego *B*
Sullivan County Community
   College *A*
Syracuse University *B,M*
Ulster County Community
   College *A*

North Carolina

Appalachian State University *B*
Campbell University *B*
Central Carolina Community
   College *A*
Davidson County Community
   College *A*
East Carolina University *B*
Elon College *B*
Isothermal Community College *A*
North Carolina State University *B*
St. Augustine's College *B*
Shaw University *B*
Southwestern Community
   College *A*
University of North Carolina
   Chapel Hill *B,M*
   Greensboro *B*
Wilkes Community College *C,A*
Wingate College *B*

North Dakota

Minot State University *B*
University of North Dakota *B*

Ohio

Ashland University *A,B*
Baldwin-Wallace College *B*
Bowling Green State University *B*
Capital University *B*
Cedarville College *B*
Central State University *B*
Cuyahoga Community College:
   Metropolitan Campus *A*
Defiance College *B*
Franciscan University of
   Steubenville *B*
Heidelberg College *B*
Kent State University *B,M*
Malone College *B*
Marietta College *B*
Miami University: Oxford Campus
   B,M
Mount Vernon Nazarene College *B*
Muskingum College *B*
Ohio Northern University *B*
Ohio State University: Columbus
   Campus *B,M,D*
Ohio University
   Athens *B,M,D*
   Zanesville Campus *A*
Ohio Wesleyan University *B*
Otterbein College *B*
University of Akron *B*
University of Cincinnati *B,M*
University of Dayton *B*
University of Findlay *B*
University of Toledo *B*
Washington State Community
   College *A*
Xavier University *A,B*

Oklahoma

East Central University *B*
Langston University *B*
Northern Oklahoma College *A*
Northwestern Oklahoma State
   University *B*
Oklahoma Baptist University *B*
Oklahoma Christian University of
   Science and Arts *B*
Oklahoma City University *B*
Oklahoma State University *B*
Oral Roberts University *B*
Rogers State College *A*
Rose State College *A*
University of Central Oklahoma *B*
University of Oklahoma *B*

Oregon

Lane Community College *A*
Linfield College *B*
Mount Hood Community
   College *A*
University of Oregon
   Eugene *B,M*
   Robert Donald Clark Honors
      College *B*

Pennsylvania

California University of
   Pennsylvania *B*
Duquesne University *B*
Elizabethtown College *B*
Gannon University *B*
Geneva College *B*
Keystone Junior College *A*
Kutztown University of
   Pennsylvania *B,M*
Lock Haven University of
   Pennsylvania *B*
Lycoming College *B*
Mansfield University of
   Pennsylvania *B*
Marywood College *B*
Mercyhurst College *B*
Messiah College *B*
Northampton County Area
   Community College *A*
Penn State University Park Campus
   C,B
Temple University *B,M*
University of Scranton *B*
Waynesburg College *B*
Westminster College *B*
York College of Pennsylvania *A,B*

Puerto Rico

University of the Sacred Heart *B*

Rhode Island

Rhode Island College *B*

South Carolina

Anderson College *B*
Benedict College *B*
Bob Jones University *B,M*
Trident Technical College *C*
University of South Carolina *B*

South Dakota

Black Hills State University *A,B*
Sioux Falls College *B*
South Dakota State University *B*
University of South Dakota *B,M*

Tennessee

Austin Peay State University *A*
Belmont University *B*
Carson-Newman College *B*
Chattanooga State Technical
   Community College *A*
East Tennessee State University *B*
Freed-Hardeman University *B*

Lambuth University *B*
Lincoln Memorial University *B*
Middle Tennessee State
   University *B*
Southern College of Seventh-day
   Adventists *B*
Trevecca Nazarene College *B*
Union University *B*
University of Tennessee
   Chattanooga *B*
   Knoxville *B*
   Martin *B*

Texas

Abilene Christian University *B*
Alvin Community College *C,A*
Amarillo College *A*
Central Texas College *A*
Del Mar College *A*
East Texas State University *B*
El Paso Community College *A*
Huston-Tillotson College *B*
Kilgore College *A*
Lamar University—Beaumont *B*
Midland College *A*
Navarro College *A*
Odessa College *A*
Prairie View A&M University *B*
Sam Houston State University *B*
Southern Methodist University *B,M*
Southwestern Adventist College *B*
Stephen F. Austin State
   University *B*
Texarkana College *A*
Texas Christian University *B,M*
Texas Southern University *B,M*
Texas Southmost College *A*
Texas Tech University *B*
Texas Wesleyan University *B*
Texas Woman's University *B*
University of Houston *B*
University of North Texas *B,M*
University of Texas
   Arlington *B*
   Austin *B,M,D*
   El Paso *B*
West Texas State University *B*

Utah

Brigham Young University *B*
Weber State University *B*

Vermont

Castleton State College *B*
Goddard College *B*
Lyndon State College *B*

Virginia

Emory and Henry College *B*
Hampton University *B*
Norfolk State University *B,M*
Radford University *B*
Virginia Wesleyan College *B*

Washington

Central Washington University *B*
Centralia College *A*
Clark College *A*
Eastern Washington University *B*
Gonzaga University *B*
Green River Community College
   C,A
Pacific Lutheran University *B*
Spokane Falls Community
   College *A*
Washington State University *B*
Western Washington University *B*
Yakima Valley Community
   College *A*

West Virginia

Alderson-Broaddus College *B*
Bethany College *B*
College of West Virginia *A*
Concord College *B*
Davis and Elkins College *B*
Marshall University *B,M*
Ohio Valley College *A*
Salem-Teikyo University *A,B*
Shepherd College *B*
West Virginia University *B*

Wisconsin

Marquette University *B,M*
University of Wisconsin
    Eau Claire *B*
    Madison *B,M,D*
    Milwaukee *B*
    Oshkosh *B*
    Platteville *B*
    River Falls *B*
    Superior *B,M*

Wyoming

Central Wyoming College *A*
University of Wyoming *B*

Arab Republic of Egypt

American University in Cairo *M*

Radio/television technology

Alabama

Chattahoochee Valley Community
    College *A*
Community College of the Air
    Force *A*
Douglas MacArthur State Technical
    College *A*
Jefferson State Community
    College *A*

Alaska

University of Alaska Anchorage *B*

Arizona

Glendale Community College *A*
Northern Arizona University *B*
Rio Salado Community College *A*

Arkansas

Arkansas State University *B*
Harding University *B*
Henderson State University *B*
John Brown University *A,B*
Southern Arkansas University *B*

California

Biola University *B*
California State University: Los
    Angeles *B*
Chabot College *C,A*
Columbia College: Hollywood *A,B*
Cosumnes River College *A*
De Anza College *C,A*
Golden West College *C,A*
Grossmont Community College *C,A*
La Sierra University *B*
Laney College *C,A*
Los Angeles City College *C,A*
Los Angeles Trade and Technical
    College *C,A*
Moorpark College *A*
Pasadena City College *C,A*
San Diego City College *A*
San Francisco State University *B*
San Jose City College *A*
San Jose State University *B*

Southwestern College *A*
University of La Verne *B*

Colorado

Colorado Institute of Art *A*
University of Colorado at
    Boulder *B*

Connecticut

Southern Connecticut State
    University *B*

District of Columbia

Howard University *B*

Florida

Florida Community College at
    Jacksonville *A*
Florida State University *B*
Gulf Coast Community College *C,A*
Jones College *A*
Lake City Community College *A*

Georgia

Clark Atlanta University *B*
Georgia Southern University *B*
University of Georgia *B,M,D*

Hawaii

University of Hawaii: Leeward
    Community College *C*

Idaho

Idaho State University *B*

Illinois

Bradley University *B*
Columbia College *B*
Illinois College *B*
Northwestern University *B,M*
Parkland College *A*
St. Xavier University *B*
Southern Illinois University
    Carbondale *B*
    Edwardsville *B*

Indiana

Ball State University *B*
Indiana State University *B,M*
Indiana University Bloomington
    B,M,D
Indiana Vocational Technical
    College: Northcentral *A*
Vincennes University *A*

Iowa

Kirkwood Community College *A*
Teikyo Marycrest University *B*

Kansas

Coffeyville Community College *A*
Colby Community College *A*
Dodge City Community College *A*
Kansas State University *B*

Kentucky

Eastern Kentucky University *A,B*
Kentucky Wesleyan College *B*
Morehead State University *A*

Louisiana

Northeast Louisiana University *A*

Maryland

Allegany Community College *A*
Catonsville Community College *C,A*
College of Notre Dame of
    Maryland *B*
Montgomery College: Rockville
    Campus *A*
University of Maryland: College
    Park *B*

Villa Julie College *B*

Massachusetts

Dean Junior College *A*
Emerson College *B,M*
Endicott College *A*
Fitchburg State College *B*
Hampshire College *B*
Massachusetts Institute of
    Technology *B*
Mount Wachusett Community
    College *A*
Newbury College *A*
Suffolk University *B*

Michigan

Central Michigan University *B,M*
Eastern Michigan University *B*
Ferris State University *B*
Lansing Community College *A*
Northern Michigan University *B*
Oakland Community College *A*

Minnesota

Bemidji State University *B*
College of St. Scholastica *B*
National Education Center: Brown
    Institute Campus *A*
Northland Community College *A*
Northwestern College *A,B*
Northwestern Electronics
    Institute *A*
Rainy River Community College *A*

Mississippi

Jackson State University *B*

Missouri

East Central College *A*
Evangel College *B*
Missouri Southern State College *B*
Webster University *B*
William Woods College *B*

Montana

University of Montana *B*

Nebraska

Central Community College *C,A*

New Jersey

Caldwell College *C*
Essex County College *A*
Jersey City State College *B*
Mercer County Community
    College *A*

New Mexico

Eastern New Mexico University *B*

New York

Adirondack Community College *A*
City University of New York:
    Queens College *B*
Fordham University *B*
Herkimer County Community
    College *A*
Hofstra University *B*
Iona College *B*
Long Island University
    Brooklyn Campus *B*
    C. W. Post Campus *B*
Manhattan College *B*
New York University *B,M*
Onondaga Community College *A*
School of Visual Arts *B*
State University of New York
    College at Plattsburgh *B*
Sullivan County Community
    College *A*
Syracuse University *B,M*

Tompkins-Cortland Community
    College *A*

North Carolina

Campbell University *B*
Cleveland Community College *A*
Isothermal Community College *A*
Southwestern Community
    College *A*
Wilkes Community College *C,A*

Ohio

Ashland University *B*
Bowling Green State University *B*
Cedarville College *B*
Central State University *B*
Cuyahoga Community College:
    Metropolitan Campus *A*
Kent State University *B*
Miami University: Oxford Campus
    B,M
Ohio University: Zanesville
    Campus *A*
Southern Ohio College *A*
University of Akron *B*
University of Toledo *B*

Oklahoma

Langston University *B*
Rogers State College *A*
Rose State College *A*

Oregon

George Fox College *B*
Lane Community College *A*

Pennsylvania

California University of
    Pennsylvania *B*
Cheyney University of
    Pennsylvania *B*
Community College of Beaver
    County *A*
Duquesne University *B*
Gannon University *B*
King's College *B*
Lehigh County Community
    College *A*
Mansfield University of
    Pennsylvania *B*
Marywood College *B*
Pennsylvania College of
    Technology *A*
Pennsylvania Institute of
    Technology *A*
Temple University *B,M*

South Carolina

Bob Jones University *B*
Tri-County Technical College *A*
University of South Carolina *B*

South Dakota

Black Hills State University *A*
Mitchell Vocational Technical
    Institute *C,A*
Sioux Falls College *B*

Tennessee

Austin Peay State University *B*
Belmont University *B*
Pellissippi State Technical
    Community College *A*
Southern College of Seventh-day
    Adventists *B*

Texas

Abilene Christian University *B,M*
Amarillo College *A*
Bee County College *C,A*
Central Texas College *A*
Lamar University—Beaumont *B*

Our Lady of the Lake University of
San Antonio *B*
San Antonio College *A*
Southern Methodist University *B,M*
Stephen F. Austin State
University *B*
Texas Southern University *B,M*
Texas State Technical College:
Waco *C*
Texas Tech University *B*

Utah

Brigham Young University *B,M,D*

Vermont

Goddard College *B,M*
Lyndon State College *B*

Virginia

Patrick Henry Community
College *C*
Radford University *B*

Washington

Pacific Lutheran University *B*

West Virginia

Bethany College *B*
Marshall University *B,M*
Salem-Teikyo University *B*

Wisconsin

University of Wisconsin
Oshkosh *B*
Platteville *B*
Stout *M*
Superior *B,M*
Western Wisconsin Technical
College *A*

Radiobiology

Colorado

Colorado State University *M,D*

Illinois

University of Chicago *M,D*

Iowa

University of Iowa *M,D*

Massachusetts

Harvard University *D*

Minnesota

University of Minnesota: Twin
Cities *M*

New Jersey

Rutgers—The State University of
New Jersey
Cook College *B*
New Brunswick *M*

Ohio

University of Cincinnati *M*

Oklahoma

University of Oklahoma Health
Sciences Center *M,D*

Pennsylvania

Hahnemann University School of
Health Sciences and Humanities
M,D

Texas

Texas Woman's University *D*
University of Texas
Health Science Center at
Houston *B,M,D,W*
Health Science Center at San
Antonio *D*
Southwestern Medical Center
at Dallas Southwestern
Allied Health Sciences
School *M,D*

Radiograph medical technology

Alabama

Alabama Southern Community
College *A*
Chattahoochee Valley Community
College *A*
Community College of the Air
Force *A*
Faulkner University *A*
Gadsden State Community
College *A*
George C. Wallace State
Community College at Selma *A*
James H. Faulkner State
Community College *A*
Jefferson State Community
College *A*
John C. Calhoun State Community
College *A*
Lawson State Community
College *A*
Livingston University *A*
Lurleen B. Wallace State Junior
College *A*
Northeast Alabama State Junior
College *A*
Samford University *B*
Shelton State Community
College *A*
Shoals Community College *A*
University of Alabama in
Birmingham *C,B*
University of South Alabama *C*
Walker College *A*
Wallace State Community College
at Hanceville *A*

Arizona

Pima Community College *A*

Arkansas

Arkansas State University *A*
Garland County Community
College *A*
Phillips County Community
College *A*
Southern Arkansas Community
College *A*
University of Central Arkansas *B*
University of the Ozarks *B*
Westark Community College *A*

California

Bakersfield College *A*
Chaffey Community College *C,A*
Charles R. Drew University: College
of Allied Health *C,A*
City College of San Francisco *C,A*
Compton Community College *A*
Crafton Hills College *C,A*
El Camino College *C,A*
Foothill College *A*
Fresno City College *A*
Long Beach City College *A*
Los Angeles City College *A*

Merced College *C,A*
Mount San Antonio College *C,A*
Orange Coast College *C,A*
Pasadena City College *C,A*
San Diego Mesa College *A*
Santa Barbara City College *A*
Santa Rosa Junior College *C,A*
Yuba College *A*

Colorado

Aims Community College *A*
Community College of Denver *A*
Mesa State College *A*
Pueblo Community College *A*

Connecticut

Mattatuck Community College *A*
Middlesex Community College *A*
Quinnipiac College *B*
South Central Community
College *A*
University of Hartford *B*

Delaware

Delaware Technical and
Community College
Southern Campus *A*
Stanton/Wilmington
Campus *A*

District of Columbia

University of the District of
Columbia *A*

Florida

Brevard Community College *A*
Broward Community College *A*
Gulf Coast Community College *A*
Hillsborough Community College *C*
Indian River Community College *A*
Manatee Community College *A*
Miami-Dade Community College *A*
Palm Beach Community College *A*
Pensacola Junior College *C,A*
St. Petersburg Junior College *A*
Santa Fe Community College *A*
Tallahassee Community College *A*
University of Central Florida *B*
Valencia Community College *A*

Georgia

Armstrong State College *A*
Athens Area Technical Institute *A*
Atlanta Metropolitan College *A*
Brunswick College *A*
Gainesville College *A*
Gordon College *A*
LaGrange College *A*
Medical College of Georgia *A*

Hawaii

University of Hawaii: Kapiolani
Community College *A*

Idaho

Boise State University *A,B*
Idaho State University *A,B*
North Idaho College *A*

Illinois

Belleville Area College *A*
Black Hawk College *A*
Carl Sandburg College *A*
City Colleges of Chicago
Malcolm X College *A*
Wright College *A*
College of DuPage *A*
College of Lake County *A*
Illinois Central College *A*
Illinois Valley Community
College *A*
Kishwaukee College *A*

Lincoln Land Community
College *A*
Moraine Valley Community
College *A*
National-Louis University *B*
Parkland College *A*
Southern Illinois University at
Carbondale *A*
Triton College *A*

Indiana

Ball State University *A*
Indiana University
Kokomo *A*
Northwest *A*
South Bend *A*
Indiana University—Purdue
University
Fort Wayne *A*
Indianapolis *B*
Indiana Vocational Technical
College
Central Indiana *A*
Wabash Valley *A*
Marian College *A,B*
St. Francis College *A*
University of Southern Indiana *A*

Iowa

Indian Hills Community College *A*
Northeast Iowa Community
College *A*
Scott Community College *A*

Kansas

Fort Hays State University *A*
Hutchinson Community College *A*
Johnson County Community
College *A*
Kansas Newman College *A*
Labette Community College *A*
Southwestern College *B*
University of Kansas
Lawrence *B*
Medical Center *B*
Washburn University of Topeka *A*

Kentucky

Lexington Community College *A*
Madisonville Community College *A*
Morehead State University *A*
Northern Kentucky University *A,B*
University of Louisville *A*

Louisiana

Northeast Louisiana University *B*
Southern University in
Shreveport *A*

Maine

Eastern Maine Technical College *A*
St. Joseph's College *A,B*
Southern Maine Technical
College *A*

Maryland

Allegany Community College *A*
Anne Arundel Community College
C,A
Chesapeake College *A*
Essex Community College *C,A*
Hagerstown Junior College *A*
Hood College *B*
Prince George's Community
College *A*
Wor-Wic Tech Community
College *A*

Massachusetts

Bunker Hill Community College *A*
Holyoke Community College *A*
Laboure College *A*

Massachusetts Bay Community
College *A*
Massachusetts College of Pharmacy
and Allied Health Sciences *A,B*
Massasoit Community College *A*
Middlesex Community College *A*
North Shore Community College *A*
Northeastern University *A*
Northern Essex Community
College *A*
Quinsigamond Community
College *A*
Springfield Technical Community
College *A*

Michigan

Andrews University *A,B*
Delta College *A*
Grand Rapids Community
College *A*
Jackson Community College *A*
Kellogg Community College *A*
Lansing Community College *A*
Madonna University *B*
Marygrove College *A*
Mid Michigan Community
College *A*
Montcalm Community College *A*
St. Mary's College *B*

Minnesota

Lakewood Community College *A*
Rochester Community College *A*
University of Minnesota: Twin
Cities *M,D*
Willmar Community College *A*

Mississippi

Copiah-Lincoln Community
College *A*
Jones County Junior College *A*
Meridian Community College *A*
Mississippi Delta Community
College *A*
Mississippi Gulf Coast Community
College: Jackson County
Campus *A*

Missouri

Avila College *B*
Missouri Southern State College *A*
Penn Valley Community College *A*
St. Louis Community College at
Forest Park *A*
Southwest Missouri State
University *B*
University of Missouri: Columbia *B*

Nebraska

Clarkson College *A,B*
Dana College *B*
Nebraska Methodist College of
Nursing and Allied Health *B*
Southeast Community College:
Lincoln Campus *A*
University of Nebraska
Medical Center *B*
Kearney *B*
Western Nebraska Community
College
Scottsbluff Campus *A*
Sidney Campus *A*

Nevada

Truckee Meadows Community
College *A*
University of Nevada: Las Vegas *B*

New Jersey

Bergen Community College *A*
Burlington County College *A*
Cumberland County College *A*

Essex County College *A*
Fairleigh Dickinson University *A,B*
Mercer County Community
College *A*
Passaic County Community
College *A*
Thomas Edison State College *A,B*
Union County College *A*
University of Medicine and
Dentistry of New Jersey: School
of Health Related Professions *C*

New Mexico

Dona Ana Branch Community
College of New Mexico State
University *A*
New Mexico Junior College *A*
New Mexico State University
Carlsbad *A*
Las Cruces *A*
Northern New Mexico Community
College *A*
University of New Mexico *A*

New York

Broome Community College *A*
City University of New York
Hostos Community College *A*
New York City Technical
College *A*
Erie Community College: City
Campus *A*
Hudson Valley Community
College *A*
Monroe Community College *A*
Nassau Community College *A*
Niagara County Community
College *A*
North Country Community
College *A*
State University of New York
Health Science Center at
Brooklyn *C*
Health Science Center at
Syracuse *A*
Trocaire College *A*
Westchester Community College *A*

North Carolina

Asheville Buncombe Technical
Community College *A*
Caldwell Community College and
Technical Institute *A*
Carteret Community College *A*
Cleveland Community College *A*
Edgecombe Community College *A*
Fayetteville Technical Community
College *A*
Forsyth Technical Community
College *A*
Johnston Community College *A*
Pitt Community College *A*
Roanoke-Chowan Community
College *A*
Sandhills Community College *A*
Southwestern Community
College *A*
Vance-Granville Community
College *A*
Wake Technical Community
College *A*

North Dakota

Minot State University *B*
University of Mary *A,B*

Ohio

Central Ohio Technical College *A*
Cuyahoga Community College
Metropolitan Campus *A*
Western Campus *A*
Jefferson Technical College *A*

Kent State University: Salem
Regional Campus *A*
Kettering College of Medical
Arts *A*
Lorain County Community
College *A*
Muskingum Area Technical
College *A*
North Central Technical College *A*
Ohio State University: Columbus
Campus *C,B,M*
Owens Technical College: Toledo *A*
Shawnee State University *A*
Sinclair Community College *A*
University of Akron *A*
University of Cincinnati: Raymond
Walters College *A*
Xavier University *A*

Oklahoma

Bacone College *A*
Rose State College *A*
Tulsa Junior College *A*
University of Oklahoma *B*

Oregon

Oregon Institute of Technology *A*
Portland Community College *A*

Pennsylvania

Bloomsburg University of
Pennsylvania *B*
California University of
Pennsylvania *B*
College Misericordia *A,B*
Community College of
Philadelphia *A*
Gannon University *A*
Hahnemann University School of
Health Sciences and Humanities
C,A
Harrisburg Area Community
College *A*
Holy Family College *A*
Juniata College *B*
Keystone Junior College *A*
La Roche College *B*
Lebanon Valley College of
Pennsylvania *B*
Mansfield University of
Pennsylvania *A*
Northampton County Area
Community College *A*
Penn State University Park
Campus *A*
Pennsylvania College of
Technology *A*
Reading Area Community
College *A*
Robert Morris College *A*
Thomas Jefferson University:
College of Allied Health
Sciences *B*
Widener University *B*

Puerto Rico

Inter American University of Puerto
Rico: San German Campus *A*
Puerto Rico Junior College *A*
University of Puerto Rico: Medical
Sciences Campus *A*

Rhode Island

Rhode Island College *B*

South Carolina

Florence-Darlington Technical
College *A*
Greenville Technical College *A*
Midlands Technical College *A*
Trident Technical College *A*

South Dakota

Presentation College *A*
Sioux Falls College *B*

Tennessee

Austin Peay State University *B*
Chattanooga State Technical
Community College *A*
Columbia State Community
College *A*
East Tennessee State University *A*
Jackson State Community
College *A*
Motlow State Community
College *A*
Roane State Community College *A*
Shelby State Community College *A*
Volunteer State Community
College *A*
Walters State Community
College *A*

Texas

Amarillo College *A*
Angelina College *A*
Austin Community College *A*
Del Mar College *A*
El Centro College *A*
El Paso Community College *A*
Galveston College *A*
Houston Community College *A*
Howard College *A*
Lamar University—Beaumont *A*
Laredo Junior College *A*
McLennan Community College *A*
Midland College *A*
Midwestern State University *A,B*
Navarro College *A*
Odessa College *A*
St. Philip's College *A*
San Jacinto College: Central
Campus *A*
South Plains College *A*
Tarrant County Junior College *A*
Texas Southmost College *A*
Wharton County Junior College *A*

Utah

Utah Valley Community College *A*
Weber State University *A,B*

Vermont

Champlain College *A*
University of Vermont *A*

Virginia

Central Virginia Community
College *A*
Northern Virginia Community
College *A*
Southwest Virginia Community
College *A*
Tidewater Community College *A*
Virginia Commonwealth
University *A*
Virginia Highlands Community
College *A*
Wytheville Community College *A*

Washington

Bellevue Community College *A*
Tacoma Community College *A*
Wenatchee Valley College *A*
Yakima Valley Community
College *A*

West Virginia

Alderson-Broaddus College *B*
Bluefield State College *A*
Marshall University *A*
Salem-Teikyo University *B*
University of Charleston *A,B*

West Virginia State College *A*

Wisconsin

Chippewa Valley Technical College *A*
Marian College of Fond du Lac *B*
Western Wisconsin Technical College *A*

Wyoming

Casper College *A*
Laramie County Community College *A*
Western Wyoming Community College *A*

Range management

Arizona

University of Arizona *B,M,D*

California

California State University:
Fresno *B*
Humboldt State University *B*
Southwestern College *A*
University of California
Berkeley *M*
Davis *B*

Colorado

Colorado State University *B,M,D*
Lamar Community College *A*
Trinidad State Junior College *C*

Idaho

University of Idaho *B,M*

Indiana

Purdue University *B*

Iowa

Iowa State University *B,M*

Kansas

Colby Community College *A*
Kansas State University *B*
Pratt Community College *A*

Maine

Unity College *B*

Montana

Montana State University *B,M*

Nebraska

Northeast Community College *A*
University of Nebraska—Lincoln *B*

New Mexico

New Mexico State University *B,M,D*

North Dakota

North Dakota State University *B,M,D*

Ohio

Ohio State University Agricultural Technical Institute *A*

Oklahoma

Connors State College *C*
Eastern Oklahoma State College *C,A*
Oklahoma State University *B*
Rogers State College *A*
Southeastern Oklahoma State University *B*

Oregon

Eastern Oregon State College *B*
Oregon State University *B,M,D*
Treasure Valley Community College *A*

South Dakota

South Dakota State University *B*

Texas

Abilene Christian University *B*
Angelo State University *B*
Central Texas College *A*
Cisco Junior College *A*
Navarro College *A*
Southwest Texas State University *B*
Stephen F. Austin State University *B*
Sul Ross State University *B,M*
Tarleton State University *B*
Texas A&I University *B,M*
Texas A&M University *B,M,D*
Texas Tech University *B,M,D*
Trinity Valley Community College *A*

Utah

Brigham Young University *B,M*
Utah State University *B,M,D*

Wyoming

Northwest College *A*
Sheridan College *A*
University of Wyoming *B,M,D*

Reading education

Alabama

Alabama Agricultural and Mechanical University *M*
Alabama State University *M*
Auburn University
Auburn *B,M,D*
Montgomery *M*
Spring Hill College *M*
University of Alabama
Birmingham *M*
Tuscaloosa *M*

Alaska

University of Alaska Anchorage *M*

Arizona

Arizona State University *M*
Grand Canyon University *M*
University of Arizona *M,D*

Arkansas

Arkansas State University *M*
Harding University *B*
Henderson State University *M*
University of Central Arkansas *M*

California

Azusa Pacific University *M*
California Lutheran University *B*
California Polytechnic State University: San Luis Obispo *M*
California State University
Bakersfield *M*
Dominguez Hills *M*
Fullerton *M*
Los Angeles *M*
San Bernardino *M*
Chapman University *M*
Loyola Marymount University *M*
Sonoma State University *M*
University of La Verne *M*
University of the Pacific *B*

Colorado

University of Colorado at Colorado Springs *M*
University of Northern Colorado *M,D*

Connecticut

Central Connecticut State University *M*
Eastern Connecticut State University *M*
Southern Connecticut State University *M*
University of Hartford *M,W*
Western Connecticut State University *M*

Delaware

University of Delaware *M,D*

District of Columbia

Howard University *M*
University of the District of Columbia *B,M*

Florida

Barry University *M*
Florida Atlantic University *M*
Florida International University *M*
Florida State University *M,D*
Jacksonville University *M*
Nova University *M*
Pensacola Junior College *A*
University of Central Florida *M*
University of Florida *M*
University of Miami *M,D*
University of South Florida *M*

Georgia

Clark Atlanta University *M*
Columbus College *M*
Georgia Southern University *M*
Georgia State University *M,D*
Mercer University *M*
University of Georgia *B,M,D*
West Georgia College *M*

Idaho

Boise State University *M*
Idaho State University *M*

Illinois

Aurora University *M*
Concordia University *M*
Illinois State University *M*
Lewis University *M*
Loyola University of Chicago *M*
National-Louis University *M,D*
North Central College *B*
Northeastern Illinois University *M*
Northern Illinois University *M,D*
Northwestern University *D*
Olivet Nazarene University *M*
Roosevelt University *M*
St. Xavier University *M*
Southern Illinois University at Carbondale *B*
Western Illinois University *M*

Indiana

Butler University *B,M*
Indiana State University *M*
Indiana University Bloomington *M,D*
Purdue University *B,D*
St. Francis College *M*
Vincennes University *A*

Iowa

Briar Cliff College *B*
Buena Vista College *B*
Clarke College *M*
Drake University *B,M*
Luther College *B*
Morningside College *B,M,W*
St. Ambrose University *C*
Teikyo Marycrest University *B*
University of Northern Iowa *B,M*
Upper Iowa University *B*
Wartburg College *B*

Kentucky

Eastern Kentucky University *M*
Murray State University *M*
Spalding University *M*
Union College *M*
University of Louisville *M*
Western Kentucky University *M*

Louisiana

Dillard University *B*
Louisiana State University and Agricultural and Mechanical College *M*
Louisiana Tech University *M*
McNeese State University *M*
Northeast Louisiana University *M*
Northwestern State University *M*
Our Lady of Holy Cross College *B*

Maine

University of Maine *M*

Maryland

Bowie State University *M*
Frostburg State University *M*
Morgan State University *B,M*
Towson State University *M*
Western Maryland College *M*

Massachusetts

Boston College *M*
Boston University *M,W*
Bridgewater State College *M*
Eastern Nazarene College *M*
Framingham State College *M*
Hampshire College *B*
Lesley College *M*
Northeastern University *M*
Salem State College *M*
Tufts University *B,M*
University of Massachusetts at Lowell *M,D*
Westfield State College *M*

Michigan

Andrews University *M*
Aquinas College *B*
Calvin College *M*
Central Michigan University *M*
Eastern Michigan University *M*
Grand Valley State University *B*
Marygrove College *B,M*
Michigan State University *M*
Oakland University *M,D*
University of Michigan *M,D*
Wayne State University *M*
Western Michigan University *M*

Minnesota

Moorhead State University *M*
Rainy River Community College *A*
St. Cloud State University *B*
Southwest State University *C*
Willmar Community College *A*
Winona State University *B*

Mississippi

University of Southern Mississippi *M*

Missouri

Central Missouri State University *M*

Northwest Missouri State
University *M*
Southeast Missouri State
University *M*
Southwest Missouri State
University *M*
University of Missouri
Columbia *M,D*
Kansas City *M*

Montana

Eastern Montana College *M*

Nebraska

Concordia College *B,M*
University of Nebraska
Kearney *M*
Lincoln *B*

New Hampshire

Rivier College *M*
University of New Hampshire *M*

New Jersey

Glassboro State College *B,M*
Jersey City State College *M*
Kean College of New Jersey *M*
Monmouth College *M*
Montclair State College *M*
Rider College *M*
Rutgers—The State University of
New Jersey *M,D*
St. Peter's College *M*
Trenton State College *M*

New Mexico

Eastern New Mexico University
B,M
Western New Mexico University
B,M

New York

Adelphi University *M*
Alfred University *M*
Bank Street College of
Education *M*
Canisius College *M*
City University of New York
Brooklyn College *B,M*
City College *M*
Lehman College *M*
Queens College *M*
College of New Rochelle *M*
Dowling College *M*
Hofstra University *M,D,W*
Long Island University
Brooklyn Campus *M*
C. W. Post Campus *M*
Manhattanville College *M*
Medaille College *B*
Nazareth College of Rochester *M*
New York University *M,D*
Russell Sage College *M*
St. Bonaventure University *M*
St. John's University *B,M*
State University of New York
Albany *M,D,W*
Binghamton *M*
Buffalo *M,D*
College at Brockport *M*
College at Buffalo *M*
College at Cortland *M*
College at Fredonia *M*
College at Geneseo *B*
College at New Paltz *M*
College at Plattsburgh *M*
College at Potsdam *M*
Oswego *B,M*
Syracuse University *M,D*
University of Rochester *M,D*

North Carolina

Appalachian State University *B*
Campbell University *B*
Catawba College *B*
East Carolina University *M*
North Carolina Agricultural and
Technical State University *M*
Salem College *B,M*
University of North Carolina
Asheville *C*
Chapel Hill *M*
Charlotte *M*
Greensboro *M*
Wilmington *M*
Western Carolina University *M*
Wingate College *B*

North Dakota

University of Mary *M*
University of North Dakota *M*

Ohio

Baldwin-Wallace College *M*
Bowling Green State University *M*
Defiance College *B*
Kent State University *M,D*
Miami University: Oxford
Campus *M*
Mount Vernon Nazarene College *C*
Ohio University *M*
Otterbein College *M*
University of Cincinnati *M*
University of Dayton *M*
University of Rio Grande *B,M*
University of Toledo *B,M*
Walsh College *B*
Wittenberg University *B*
Wright State University *B*
Youngstown State University *B*

Oklahoma

Northwestern Oklahoma State
University *M*
Southeastern Oklahoma State
University *M*
Southwestern Oklahoma State
University *M*
University of Central Oklahoma
B,M
University of Oklahoma *M,D*
University of Science and Arts of
Oklahoma *B*
University of Tulsa *M*

Oregon

Southern Oregon State College *M*
Western Oregon State College *M*
Willamette University *M*

Pennsylvania

Beaver College *M*
Bloomsburg University of
Pennsylvania *M*
California University of
Pennsylvania *B,M*
Clarion University of
Pennsylvania *M*
East Stroudsburg University of
Pennsylvania *M*
Edinboro University of
Pennsylvania *M*
Gannon University *M*
Gwynedd-Mercy College *M*
Holy Family College *M*
Kutztown University of
Pennsylvania *M*
Lehigh University *M,D*
Lincoln University *C*
Marywood College *M*
Millersville University of
Pennsylvania *M*

Penn State University Park
Campus *M*
St. Joseph's University *C,M*
Shippensburg University of
Pennsylvania *M*
Slippery Rock University of
Pennsylvania *M*
Temple University *M,D*
University of Pennsylvania *M,D*
University of Scranton *M*
West Chester University of
Pennsylvania *M*
Widener University *M*

Rhode Island

Rhode Island College *M*
University of Rhode Island *M*

South Carolina

The Citadel *M*
Clemson University *M*
University of South Carolina *M,D*
Winthrop University *M*

South Dakota

Sioux Falls College *M*

Tennessee

East Tennessee State University
B,M
Tennessee Technological
University *M*
Vanderbilt University *M,D*

Texas

Abilene Christian University *M*
Angelo State University *M*
Dallas Baptist University *B,M*
East Texas Baptist University *B*
East Texas State University *M,D*
Hardin-Simmons University *B,M*
Houston Baptist University *M*
Incarnate Word College *B*
Laredo State University *B,M*
McMurry University *B*
Midwestern State University *M*
Prairie View A&M University *M*
St. Edward's University *B*
St. Mary's University *B*
Sam Houston State University *M*
Southwest Texas State
University *M*
Sul Ross State University *M*
Texas A&I University *M*
Texas Christian University *B*
Texas Tech University *M,D*
Texas Wesleyan University *B*
Texas Woman's University *M,D*
University of Houston *B,M*
University of Mary Hardin-
Baylor *B*
University of North Texas *M,D*
University of Texas
El Paso *M*
Permian Basin *M*
San Antonio *M*
Tyler *M*

Utah

Brigham Young University *M,D*

Vermont

Castleton State College *B*
College of St. Joseph in Vermont *M*
St. Michael's College *M*
University of Vermont *B,M*

Virginia

Averett College *B,M*
George Mason University *M*
James Madison University *M*
Longwood College *M*

Norfolk State University *B*
Old Dominion University *M*
Radford University *M*
University of Richmond *M*
Virginia Polytechnic Institute and
State University *M*

Washington

Central Washington University *M*
Eastern Washington University *M*
Pacific Lutheran University *B*
Seattle Pacific University *M*
Washington State University *B*
Western Washington University *M*
Whitworth College *M*

West Virginia

Concord College *B*
West Virginia Graduate College *M*
West Virginia University *M,D*

Wisconsin

Cardinal Stritch College *M*
Carthage College *M*
University of Wisconsin
Eau Claire *M*
La Crosse *M*
Oshkosh *M*
Platteville *B,M*
River Falls *M*

Wyoming

University of Wyoming *B*

Canada

McGill University *M*

Real estate

Alabama

Chattahoochee Valley Community
College *A*
Enterprise State Junior College *A*
Jefferson State Community
College *A*
John C. Calhoun State Community
College *A*
Lurleen B. Wallace State Junior
College *C*
Northeast Alabama State Junior
College *A*
Samford University *B*
Shoals Community College *C*
Snead State Junior College *A*
University of Alabama *B*
Wallace State Community College
at Hanceville *A*

Arizona

Arizona State University *B*
Arizona Western College *A*
Glendale Community College *A*
Mesa Community College *C*
Mohave Community College *C*
Pima Community College *C,A*
Rio Salado Community College *A*
Scottsdale Community College *C,A*
University of Arizona *B*

Arkansas

Arkansas State University *B*
East Arkansas Community
College *A*
Garland County Community
College *A*
University of Arkansas *B*
Williams Baptist College *A*

California

Allan Hancock College *C,A*
Bakersfield College *A*
Barstow College *C,A*
California State University
    Dominguez Hills *B*
    Fresno *B*
    Hayward *B*
    Los Angeles *B*
    Northridge *B*
    Sacramento *B*
Cerritos Community College *C,A*
Chabot College *A*
Chaffey Community College *C,A*
Citrus College *C*
City College of San Francisco *C,A*
Coastline Community College *C,A*
College of the Desert *C,A*
College of Marin: Kentfield *C,A*
College of the Redwoods *C,A*
College of the Sequoias *C*
Compton Community College *A*
Cuesta College *A*
De Anza College *C,A*
Diablo Valley College *A*
East Los Angeles College *C,A*
El Camino College *C,A*
Foothill College *C,A*
Fresno City College *C,A*
Glendale Community College *C,A*
Golden West College *C,A*
Hartnell College *A*
Humphreys College *A*
Imperial Valley College *C,A*
Irvine Valley College *C,A*
Lake Tahoe Community College
  C,A
Lassen College *A*
Long Beach City College *C,A*
Los Angeles City College *C,A*
Los Angeles Harbor College *A*
Los Angeles Mission College *C,A*
Los Angeles Pierce College *A*
Los Angeles Trade and Technical
  College *C,A*
Los Angeles Valley College *C*
Los Medanos College *C,A*
Mendocino College *C,A*
Merced College *A*
MiraCosta College *C,A*
Mission College *A*
Modesto Junior College *A*
Monterey Peninsula College *C,A*
Moorpark College *C,A*
Mount San Antonio College *C,A*
Mount San Jacinto College *C,A*
Napa Valley College *C,A*
Ohlone College *C,A*
Oxnard College *A*
Palomar College *C,A*
Pasadena City College *C,A*
Porterville College *C,A*
Rio Hondo College *A*
Saddleback College *C,A*
San Diego City College *C,A*
San Diego Mesa College *C,A*
San Diego Miramar College *A*
San Diego State University *B*
San Francisco State University *B*
San Joaquin Delta College *C,A*
San Jose City College *A*
Santa Barbara City College *C,A*
Santa Monica College *C,A*
Santa Rosa Junior College *C*
Sierra College *A*
Solano Community College *A*
Southwestern College *C,A*
University of Southern California *M*
Ventura College *C,A*
Victor Valley College *C,A*
West Hills Community College *A*
West Valley College *C,A*

Yuba College *C,A*

Colorado

Aims Community College *C*
Arapahoe Community College *C*
Colorado State University *B*
Red Rocks Community College *C,A*
University of Colorado
    Boulder *B*
    Colorado Springs *B*
    Denver *B*
University of Denver *B,M*

Connecticut

Manchester Community College
  C,A
University of Connecticut *B*

District of Columbia

American University *B,M*

Florida

Broward Community College *A*
Edison Community College *C,A*
Florida Atlantic University *B*
Florida Community College at
  Jacksonville *A*
Florida International University *B*
Florida State University *B*
Gulf Coast Community College *C,A*
Manatee Community College *C,A*
Miami-Dade Community College
  C,A
Okaloosa-Walton Community
  College *C,A*
St. Petersburg Junior College *A*
South Florida Community
  College *C*
University of Florida *B,M*
University of Miami *B*
Valencia Community College *A*

Georgia

DeKalb Technical Institute *C*
Georgia Southern University *B*
Georgia State University *B,M,D*
Morehouse College *B*
University of Georgia *B,M*
West Georgia College *B*

Hawaii

University of Hawaii at Manoa *B*

Idaho

College of Southern Idaho *A*
Lewis Clark State College *C*

Illinois

Belleville Area College *A*
Black Hawk College *C,A*
Carl Sandburg College *C,A*
City Colleges of Chicago
    Chicago City-Wide College *C*
    Malcolm X College *C,A*
    Olive-Harvey College *C*
College of DuPage *C,A*
College of Lake County *C*
De Paul University *M*
Elgin Community College *C,A*
Highland Community College *C*
Illinois Central College *C,A*
Joliet Junior College *C,A*
Kishwaukee College *C*
Lake Land College *A*
Lewis and Clark Community
  College *A*
Lincoln Land Community
  College *A*
Moraine Valley Community
  College *A*
Morton College *A*
Northwestern University *M*

Oakton Community College *C,A*
Parkland College *A*
Prairie State College *A*
Richland Community College *A*
Triton College *C,A*
Waubonsee Community College
  C,A
William Rainey Harper College *C,A*

Indiana

Ball State University *B*
Indiana University Bloomington
  B,D
Indiana University—Purdue
  University at Indianapolis *B*

Iowa

University of Northern Iowa *B*

Kansas

Butler County Community
  College *A*
Dodge City Community College *A*
Neosho County Community
  College *C*
Wichita State University *B*

Kentucky

Eastern Kentucky University *B*
Elizabethtown Community
  College *A*
Jefferson Community College *A*
Lexington Community College *A*
Madisonville Community College *A*
Morehead State University *A,B*
Murray State University *A,B*
Northern Kentucky University *A*
Paducah Community College *A*
Prestonburg Community College *A*
Western Kentucky University *C,A*

Louisiana

Louisiana State University and
  Agricultural and Mechanical
  College *B*
Northeast Louisiana University *B*
Southern University at New
  Orleans *A*
University of New Orleans *B*

Maine

Andover College *A*
Thomas College *C*
University of Maine at Augusta *C*

Maryland

Catonsville Community College *C,A*
Charles County Community
  College *C*
Dundalk Community College *C,A*
Harford Community College *C*
Villa Julie College *A*

Massachusetts

Bristol Community College *A*
Greenfield Community College *C*
Harvard University *M*
Massachusetts Bay Community
  College *A*
Massachusetts Institute of
  Technology *M,D*
Nichols College *B*
North Shore Community College *A*
Northeastern University *C,A*
Northern Essex Community
  College *A*

Michigan

Central Michigan University *B*
Eastern Michigan University *B*
Ferris State University *C,A,B*
Lansing Community College *A*

Muskegon Community College *C*
Western Michigan University *B*

Minnesota

Inver Hills Community College *C*
Itasca Community College:
  Arrowhead Region *C*
Mankato State University *B*
St. Cloud State University *B*
University of Minnesota:
  Crookston *A*
Willmar Community College *C,A*

Mississippi

Delta State University *B*
Hinds Community College *A*
Mississippi State University *B*
University of Mississippi *B*
University of Southern
  Mississippi *B*

Missouri

East Central College *A*
St. Louis Community College at
  Meramec *C,A*
University of Missouri: Columbia *B*
Webster University *B,M*

Nebraska

Chadron State College *B*
McCook Community College *C,A*
Metropolitan Community College
  C,A
Northeast Community College *A*
University of Nebraska—Omaha *B*
Western Nebraska Community
  College: Scottsbluff Campus *A*

Nevada

Community College of Southern
  Nevada *C,A*
Northern Nevada Community
  College *A*
Truckee Meadows Community
  College *A*
University of Nevada: Las Vegas *B*
Western Nevada Community
  College *A*

New Hampshire

New Hampshire Technical College:
  Stratham *C*

New Jersey

Bergen Community College *C,A*
Burlington County College *A*
Camden County College *C*
Gloucester County College *C*
Ocean County College *C,A*
Thomas Edison State College *A,B*

New Mexico

Clovis Community College *A*
New Mexico Junior College *A*
New Mexico State University *B*
San Juan College *C,A*

New York

City University of New York
  Borough of Manhattan
    Community College *A*
  Lehman College *C*
  Queensborough Community
    College *A*
Columbia-Greene Community
  College *C,A*
Erie Community College: City
  Campus *A*
Five Towns College *A*
Herkimer County Community
  College *A*

Hudson Valley Community
College *A*
Mohawk Valley Community
College *C*
Nassau Community College *C*
New York University *C,M*
Orange County Community
College *A*
Pace University *B*
Rochester Institute of Technology
C,A
State University of New York
College of Technology at
Alfred *A*
Suffolk County Community College
Eastern Campus *C*
Selden *C,A*
Western Campus *C,A*
Sullivan County Community
College *C,A*
Utica School of Commerce *C*
Westchester Community College
C,A

North Carolina

Alamance Community College *A*
Appalachian State University *B*
Blue Ridge Community College *C*
Brunswick Community College *C,A*
Catawba Valley Community
College *A*
Central Carolina Community
College *A*
Central Piedmont Community
College *A*
Cleveland Community College *C*
Durham Technical Community
College *C*
East Carolina University *B*
Edgecombe Community College *C*
Fayetteville Technical Community
College *A*
Forsyth Technical Community
College *A*
Guilford Technical Community
College *C*
Isothermal Community College *A*
Montgomery Community College *C*
Southeastern Community College *C*
Southwestern Community
College *A*
Wayne Community College *C*
Western Piedmont Community
College *A*
Wilson Technical Community
College *C*

North Dakota

Bismarck State College *A*
North Dakota State College of
Science *A*

Ohio

Bryant & Stratton Business
Institute: Great Northern *C*
Cincinnati Technical College *A*
Columbus State Community
College *A*
Cuyahoga Community College
Metropolitan Campus *A*
Western Campus *A*
Dyke College *A,B*
Edison State Community College *A*
Franklin University *A,B*
Jefferson Technical College *A*
Kent State University
Ashtabula Regional Campus *A*
East Liverpool Regional
Campus *A*
Kent *B,M*
Lakeland Community College *C*

Lorain County Community
College *A*
Malone College *C*
Northwest Technical College *A*
Ohio State University: Columbus
Campus *B*
Ohio University: Chillicothe
Campus *C*
Shawnee State University *A*
Sinclair Community College *A*
Southern Ohio College *A*
Southern State Community
College *A*
Terra Technical College *A*
University of Akron *A*
University of Cincinnati
Access Colleges *C,A*
Cincinnati *B*
Clermont College *C,A*
Raymond Walters College *C,A*
University of Rio Grande *C*
University of Toledo *C*
Xavier University *C*
Youngstown State University *A*

Oklahoma

Redlands Community College *C,A*
Rogers State College *A*
Rose State College *A*
Tulsa Junior College *A*
University of Central Oklahoma *B*
University of Oklahoma *B*
University of Tulsa *B*

Oregon

Chemeketa Community College *A*
Clackamas Community College *C*
Lane Community College *C,A*
Portland Community College *A*
Southwestern Oregon Community
College *C*
Treasure Valley Community
College *C*

Pennsylvania

Bucks County Community College
C,A
Clarion University of
Pennsylvania *B*
Community College of
Philadelphia *A*
Duquesne University *C,B,M*
Harrisburg Area Community
College *A*
Immaculata College *A*
Lehigh County Community College
C,A
Luzerne County Community
College *A*
Montgomery County Community
College *C,A*
Northampton County Area
Community College *C*
Penn State University Park Campus
C,B
Robert Morris College *C*
St. Francis College *A*
Shippensburg University of
Pennsylvania *B*
Temple University *B,M*
University of Pennsylvania *B,M*
Westmoreland County Community
College *C*
York College of Pennsylvania *A*

Puerto Rico

Caribbean University *A*

Rhode Island

Community College of Rhode
Island *A*

South Carolina

University of South Carolina
Coastal Carolina College *B*
Columbia *B*

South Dakota

Kilian Community College *A*
National College *C*

Tennessee

Bristol University *A,B,M*
East Tennessee State University *B*
Jackson State Community
College *A*
Martin Methodist College *A*
Memphis State University *B*
Motlow State Community
College *A*

Texas

Amarillo College *A*
Angelina College *A*
Angelo State University *B*
Austin Community College *A*
Baylor University *B*
Bee County College *A*
Brazosport College *C,A*
Central Texas College *A*
Cisco Junior College *A*
College of the Mainland *A*
Collin County Community College
District *C,A*
Cooke County College *A*
Dallas Baptist University *B*
Del Mar College *A*
Eastfield College *A*
El Paso Community College *A*
Galveston College *A*
Houston Community College *C,A*
Howard College *A*
Kilgore College *A*
Lamar University—Beaumont *A*
Laredo Junior College *A*
Lee College *A*
McLennan Community College *C,A*
Midland College *C,A*
Navarro College *A*
North Harris Montgomery
Community College District *C,A*
North Lake College *A*
Northeast Texas Community
College *A*
Odessa College *C,A*
Panola College *A*
Richland College *A*
San Antonio College *A*
San Jacinto College: Central
Campus *A*
Schreiner College *B*
South Plains College *A*
Southern Methodist University *B*
Tarrant County Junior College *C,A*
Temple Junior College *A*
Texarkana College *A*
Texas A&I University *B*
Texas A&M University *M*
Texas Christian University *C*
Texas Southmost College *A*
Trinity Valley Community
College *A*
University of Houston:
Downtown *B*
University of North Texas *B,M*
University of Texas
Arlington *B,M*
El Paso *B*
Victoria College *A*
Wayland Baptist University *A*

Utah

Dixie College *C,A*
Southern Utah University *C,A*

Virginia

Blue Ridge Community College *C*
Christopher Newport College *B*
John Tyler Community College *C*
Mountain Empire Community
College *C*
Northern Virginia Community
College *C,A*
Paul D. Camp Community
College *C*
Piedmont Virginia Community
College *A*
Southwest Virginia Community
College *C*
Tidewater Community College *A*
University of Richmond *C,A*

Washington

Bellevue Community College *C,A*
Clark College *A*
Columbia Basin College *A*
Everett Community College *C,A*
Green River Community College *A*
North Seattle Community College
C,A
Olympic College *C,A*
Pierce College *C,A*
Spokane Falls Community College
C,A
Washington State University *B*

West Virginia

Bluefield State College *C*
Davis and Elkins College *A*
Fairmont State College *A*
Marshall University *A,B,M*

Wisconsin

Chippewa Valley Technical
College *A*
Madison Area Technical College *A*
University of Wisconsin
Madison *B,M,D*
Milwaukee *B*
Waukesha County Technical
College *A*

Canada

McGill University *C,B,M*

Recreation and community services technologies

Alabama

Alabama Agricultural and
Mechanical University *A*
Community College of the Air
Force *A*
Enterprise State Junior College *A*
John C. Calhoun State Community
College *A*
Lawson State Community
College *A*

Arizona

Northland Pioneer College *C,A*
Prescott College *B*
University of Arizona *B*

Arkansas

John Brown University *B*
Southern Arkansas University *A*
University of Arkansas *B,M*
Williams Baptist College *A*

California

Allan Hancock College *C,A*
Bakersfield College *A*

California State Polytechnic
    University: Pomona *B*
California State University
    Long Beach *B,M*
    Northridge *B,M*
Cerritos Community College *A*
Chabot College *A*
College of the Desert *A*
Compton Community College *A*
Cuesta College *A*
East Los Angeles College *A*
El Camino College *A*
Feather River College *A*
Fresno City College *A*
Glendale Community College *A*
Grossmont Community College *A*
Hartnell College *A*
Los Angeles Valley College *A*
Merced College *A*
Modesto Junior College *A*
Mount San Antonio College *A*
Pacific Union College *B*
Palomar College *C,A*
Pasadena City College *A*
San Diego Mesa College *A*
San Jose City College *A*
San Jose State University *B*
Santa Barbara City College *C,A*
Santa Monica College *C,A*
Santa Rosa Junior College *C*
Skyline College *C,A*
Southwestern College *A*
Taft College *A*
Ventura College *A*

Colorado

Colorado Mountain College: Spring
    Valley Campus *A*

Connecticut

Mitchell College *A*
Northwestern Connecticut
    Community College *A*
Norwalk Community College *A*
Southern Connecticut State
    University *B*

Delaware

Delaware State College *B*
Delaware Technical and
    Community College: Southern
    Campus *A*
University of Delaware *B*

District of Columbia

Gallaudet University *B*

Florida

Broward Community College *A*
Lynn University *B*
Miami-Dade Community College *A*
Okaloosa-Walton Community
    College *A*
Palm Beach Community College *A*
University of Florida *B,M*

Georgia

Abraham Baldwin Agricultural
    College *A*
Atlanta Metropolitan College *A*
Brewton-Parker College *A*
Brunswick College *A*
Columbus College *A*
Georgia Southern University *B,M*
North Georgia College *B*
South Georgia College *A*
West Georgia College *B*

Hawaii

University of Hawaii: Leeward
    Community College *A*

Idaho

Northwest Nazarene College *A,B*
Ricks College *A*

Illinois

City Colleges of Chicago: Chicago
    City-Wide College *C,A*
College of St. Francis *B*
Judson College *B*
KAES College *B*
Rend Lake College *A*
Southern Illinois University at
    Edwardsville *B*

Indiana

Indiana Institute of Technology *A,B*
Indiana University Southeast *A*
Vincennes University *A*

Iowa

Central College *B*
Des Moines Area Community
    College *A*
Iowa Lakes Community College *A*
Kirkwood Community College *A*
Northwestern College *B*
Teikyo Westmar University *B*
University of Iowa *M*
Waldorf College *A*

Kansas

Bethany College *B*
Bethel College *B*
Butler County Community
    College *A*
Central College *A*
Colby Community College *A*
Cowley County Community
    College *A*
Dodge City Community College *A*
Emporia State University *B*
Fort Scott Community College *A*
Friends University *A*
Highland Community College *A*
Hutchinson Community College *A*
Kansas City Kansas Community
    College *A*
Tabor College *B*

Louisiana

University of Southwestern
    Louisiana *A*

Maine

University of Maine
    Machias *A,B*
    Presque Isle *A,B*

Maryland

Allegany Community College *A*
Anne Arundel Community
    College *A*
Catonsville Community College *A*
Morgan State University *B,M*
Salisbury State University *B*

Massachusetts

Becker College: Leicester
    Campus *A*
Bridgewater State College *B*
Greenfield Community College *C,A*
Mount Ida College *A*

Michigan

Calvin College *B*
Charles Stewart Mott Community
    College *A*
Jordan College *A*
Lansing Community College *A*
Michigan State University *B,M,D*
Muskegon Community College *A*
Northern Michigan University *A*

Minnesota

Northland Community College *A*
St. Cloud State University *B*
University of Minnesota: Twin
    Cities *B,M*
Vermilion Community College *A*

Mississippi

Alcorn State University *B*
Northeast Mississippi Community
    College *A*

Missouri

Central Missouri State University *B*
Evangel College *B*
Hannibal-LaGrange College *A*
Northwest Missouri State
    University *A*
Southwest Baptist University *B*

Montana

College of Great Falls *A*

Nebraska

Midland Lutheran College *A*
University of Nebraska
    Lincoln *B*
    Omaha *B*
Wayne State College *B*
York College *A*

New Jersey

Bergen Community College *A*
Camden County College *A*

New Mexico

University of New Mexico *B,M*

New York

City University of New York
    Brooklyn College *M*
    Kingsborough Community
        College *A*
    Lehman College *M*
Dutchess Community College *A*
Erie Community College: South
    Campus *A*
Herkimer County Community
    College *A*
Mohawk Valley Community
    College *A*
Monroe Community College *A*
North Country Community
    College *A*
Onondaga Community College *A*
Orange County Community
    College *A*
St. Joseph's College: Suffolk
    Campus *A*
State University of New York
    College at Cortland *B,M*
Suffolk County Community
    College *A*
Tompkins-Cortland Community
    College *A*
Ulster County Community
    College *A*

North Carolina

Belmont Abbey College *B*
Brevard College *A*
Carteret Community College *A*
Central Piedmont Community
    College *A*
Fayetteville Technical Community
    College *A*
Isothermal Community College *A*
Montreat-Anderson College *B*
University of North Carolina at
    Greensboro *B*
Vance-Granville Community
    College *A*

North Dakota

North Dakota State University *B*

Ohio

Ashland University *B*
Kent State University *B*
Lourdes College *A*
Ohio State University: Columbus
    Campus *B,M*
Ohio University *M*
University of Akron *A*
University of Toledo *A*
Urbana University *B*

Oklahoma

Oklahoma Panhandle State
    University *B*
Southeastern Oklahoma State
    University *B*
Southwestern Oklahoma State
    University *B*

Oregon

Warner Pacific College *A*

Pennsylvania

Cabrini College *B*
California University of
    Pennsylvania *B*
Gannon University *B*
Lincoln University *B*
West Chester University of
    Pennsylvania *M*
York College of Pennsylvania *B*

Puerto Rico

Inter American University of Puerto
    Rico: Arecibo Campus *A*
Puerto Rico Junior College *A*
University of Puerto Rico: Rio
    Piedras Campus *B*

Rhode Island

Johnson & Wales University *A*

South Carolina

Horry-Georgetown Technical
    College *A*
Morris College *B*
North Greenville College *A*

South Dakota

Augustana College *A*
Northern State University *B*
Oglala Lakota College *A*

Tennessee

Hiwassee College *A*
Knoxville College *B*
Martin Methodist College *A*

Texas

Central Texas College *A*
Cisco Junior College *A*
Eastfield College *A*
Hardin-Simmons University *B*
McLennan Community College *A*
University of Mary Hardin-
    Baylor *B*
University of Texas: Pan
    American *A*
West Texas State University *B*

Utah

Dixie College *A*

Vermont

Green Mountain College *B*

Virginia

Averett College *B*
Bluefield College *B*

Eastern Mennonite College *B*
Marymount University *B*
Tidewater Community College *A*

Washington
Bellevue Community College *A*
Central Washington University *B*
Eastern Washington University *B*
Everett Community College *A*
Pierce College *A*
Seattle Central Community
    College *A*
Walla Walla Community College *A*

West Virginia
Alderson-Broaddus College *B*
Davis and Elkins College *B*
Glenville State College *A*

Wisconsin
Fox Valley Technical College *A*
Madison Area Technical College *A*

Recreation therapy

Arkansas
John Brown University *B*

California
California State University:
    Fresno *B*
Grossmont Community College *C,A*
San Jose State University *B*
Skyline College *C,A*

Colorado
University of Northern Colorado
    B,M

Connecticut
Mitchell College *A*
Northwestern Connecticut
    Community College *A*
South Central Community
    College *C*
Teikyo-Post University *A*

District of Columbia
Gallaudet University *B*

Georgia
Morris Brown College *B*
University of Georgia *B*

Illinois
Aurora University *B*
College of St. Francis *B*
Moraine Valley Community
    College *A*
Southern Illinois University at
    Carbondale *B*

Indiana
Indiana Institute of Technology *A,B*
Indiana State University *B*
Vincennes University *A*

Iowa
St. Ambrose University *B*
University of Iowa *B,M*
University of Northern Iowa *B*

Kansas
Kansas City Kansas Community
    College *A*
Pittsburg State University *B*

Maine
University of Southern Maine *A,B*

Massachusetts
Aquinas College at Milton *A*
Boston University *B,M*
Northeastern University *C,A*
Springfield College *B,M*

Michigan
Eastern Michigan University *B*
Grand Valley State University *B*
Lake Superior State University *B*

Minnesota
Mankato State University *B*
Northland Community College *A*
Willmar Community College *A*
Winona State University *B*

New Hampshire
University of New Hampshire *B*

New York
City University of New York:
    Lehman College *M*
Houghton College *B*
Medaille College *C*
Mercy College *B*
Mohawk Valley Community
    College *B*
Monroe Community College *A*
New York University *M,D*
Onondaga Community College *A*
St. Joseph's College: Suffolk
    Campus *A*
Suffolk County Community
    College *A*
Utica College of Syracuse
    University *B*

North Carolina
Carteret Community College *A*
Vance-Granville Community
    College *A*
Western Piedmont Community
    College *A*
Winston-Salem State University *B*

Ohio
Defiance College *B*
Kent State University *B*
North Central Technical College *A*
Ohio University *B*
University of Toledo *B*

Pennsylvania
Gannon University *A,B*
Lincoln University *B*
York College of Pennsylvania *B*

Texas
Abilene Christian University *B*
Texas Woman's University *B,M,D*

Utah
Brigham Young University *B,M*

Vermont
Green Mountain College *B*

Virginia
Hampton University *B*
Radford University *B*
Virginia Wesleyan College *B*

Washington
Eastern Washington University *B*

West Virginia
Shepherd College *B*
West Virginia State College *B*

Wisconsin
University of Wisconsin: La Crosse
    B,M

Rehabilitation counseling/services

Alabama
Auburn University *B,M,D*
University of Alabama in
    Birmingham *M*

Arkansas
Arkansas State University *M*
University of Arkansas *M*
University of Central Arkansas *M*

California
California State University
    Los Angeles *B,M*
    San Bernardino *M*
Imperial Valley College *C,A*
San Francisco State University *M*
University of San Francisco *M*

Colorado
University of Northern Colorado
    B,M,D

Connecticut
Asnuntuck Community College *A*
Manchester Community College *A*
Quinebaug Valley Community
    College *A*
South Central Community
    College *A*
Tunxis Community College *A*
University of Connecticut *B*

District of Columbia
Gallaudet University *M*
Howard University *M*

Florida
Barry University *M*
Florida State University *B,M,D*
University of Florida *M*

Georgia
Georgia State University *M*
University of Georgia *M,D*

Illinois
De Paul University *M*
Illinois Institute of Technology
    B,M,D
Moraine Valley Community
    College *C*
National-Louis University *C,B,M*
St. Xavier University *M*
Southern Illinois University at
    Carbondale *M,D*
University of Illinois at Urbana-
    Champaign *M*

Iowa
University of Iowa *M,D*

Kansas
Dodge City Community College *A*
Emporia State University *B,M*

Kentucky
Murray State University *B*
University of Kentucky *M*

Louisiana
Louisiana State University Medical
    Center *B*

Phillips Junior College: New
    Orleans *A*
Southern University and
    Agricultural and Mechanical
    College *B*

Maine
University of Maine at
    Farmington *B*

Maryland
Dundalk Community College *C,A*
Montgomery College: Rockville
    Campus *A*
University of Maryland: Eastern
    Shore *B*

Massachusetts
Boston University *B,M,D,W*
Emmanuel College *B*
Northeastern University *M*
Springfield College *B,M*

Michigan
Eastern Michigan University *M*
Northern Michigan University *A*

Minnesota
St. Cloud State University *M*
Willmar Community College *A*

Mississippi
Jackson State University *M*
Phillips Junior College of the
    Mississippi Gulf Coast *A*
University of Southern
    Mississippi *B*

Montana
College of Great Falls *A*
Dull Knife Memorial College *A*
Eastern Montana College *A,B,M*

Nebraska
Grace College of the Bible *B*
Metropolitan Community College *A*
Nebraska Methodist College of
    Nursing and Allied Health *A*
Southeast Community College:
    Lincoln Campus *A*

New Jersey
Thomas Edison State College *A,B*

New York
City University of New York:
    Hunter College *M*
Hofstra University *M,W*
Medaille College *C*
New York University *B,M,D*
Niagara County Community
    College *C*
State University of New York at
    Buffalo *M*
Syracuse University *M,D*

North Carolina
East Carolina University *M*
Roanoke-Chowan Community
    College *A*

Ohio
Bowling Green State University *M*
Columbus State Community
    College *A*
Kent State University *M*
Wright State University *B*

Oregon
Western Oregon State College *M*

Pennsylvania

Clarion University of Pennsylvania
A,B
Edinboro University of
Pennsylvania M
Northampton County Area
Community College A
University of Scranton M

Puerto Rico

University of Puerto Rico: Rio
Piedras Campus M

Rhode Island

Rhode Island College M

South Carolina

South Carolina State College M

Tennessee

Memphis State University B
University of Tennessee:
Knoxville M

Texas

Howard College A
Incarnate Word College M
Lee College A
Stephen F. Austin State
University M
University of North Texas M
University of Texas Southwestern
Medical Center at Dallas
Southwestern Allied Health
Sciences School B,M

Washington

Northwest Indian College C
Pierce College A
Seattle Central Community
College A

West Virginia

Marshall University B,M
West Virginia University M
West Virginia Wesleyan College B

Wisconsin

Chippewa Valley Technical
College A
University of Wisconsin:
Oshkosh M

Wyoming

Central Wyoming College C,A

Religion

Alabama

Athens State College B
Auburn University B
Birmingham-Southern College B
Faulkner University B
Gadsden State Community College
C,A
Huntingdon College B
Judson College B
Mobile College B,M
Oakwood College B
Samford University B
Southern Christian University B,M
Stillman College B
University of Alabama B
Wallace State Community College
at Hanceville A

Arizona

Arizona State University B,M
Grand Canyon University B

Northern Arizona University B
Prescott College B
University of Arizona B

Arkansas

Arkansas Baptist College B
Arkansas College B
Harding University B,M
Hendrix College B
John Brown University B
Ouachita Baptist University B
Philander Smith College B
University of the Ozarks B

California

American Armenian International
College B
Azusa Pacific University B
Biola University B
California Baptist College B
California Institute of Integral
Studies M,D
California Lutheran University B
California State University
Bakersfield B
Chico B
Fresno B
Fullerton B
Long Beach B
Northridge B
Chaffey Community College A
Chapman University B
Christ College Irvine B
Claremont McKenna College B
College of Notre Dame B
Dominican College of San Rafael B
Fresno Pacific College B
Graduate Theological Union M,D
Hebrew Union College: Jewish
Institute of Religion B,M,D
Holy Names College B,M
Humboldt State University B
John F. Kennedy University B,M
La Sierra University B,M
Los Angeles Pierce College A
Marymount College A
Master's College B
Mount St. Mary's College B,M
Occidental College B
Orange Coast College A
Pacific Christian College B
Pacific Union College B
Patten College A,B
Pepperdine University B,M
Point Loma Nazarene College B
Pomona College B
Queen of the Holy Rosary
College A
St. Mary's College of California B
San Diego State University B
San Francisco State University B
San Jose State University B
Santa Clara University B,M
Scripps College B
Southern California College B,M
Stanford University B,M,D
University of California
Berkeley B
Davis B
Los Angeles B
Riverside B
Santa Barbara B,M,D
Santa Cruz B
University of La Verne B
University of the Pacific B,M
University of Redlands B
University of San Diego B
University of San Francisco B,M
University of Southern California
B,M,D
Westmont College B
Whittier College B

World College West B

Colorado

Colorado College B
Naropa Institute B,M
Nazarene Bible College C
Regis College of Regis University B
University of Colorado at Boulder
B,M
University of Denver B,M,D

Connecticut

Albertus Magnus College B
Connecticut College B
Fairfield University B
Holy Apostles College and
Seminary B
Sacred Heart University A,B,M
St. Joseph College B,M
Trinity College B
Wesleyan University B
Yale University B,M,D

Delaware

Wesley College C

District of Columbia

American University B
Catholic University of America
B,M,D
Gallaudet University B
George Washington University B
Georgetown University B
Howard University M,D
Trinity College B

Florida

Daytona Beach Community
College A
Eckerd College B
Flagler College B
Florida Agricultural and Mechanical
University B
Florida Christian College B
Florida International University B
Florida Memorial College B
Florida Southern College B
Florida State University B,M
Gulf Coast Community College A
Hobe Sound Bible College B
Miami-Dade Community College A
New College of the University of
South Florida B
Palm Beach Atlantic College B
Pensacola Junior College A
Rollins College B
St. Leo College B
St. Thomas University B
Stetson University B
University of Florida B,M
University of Miami B
University of South Florida B,M
University of West Florida B
Warner Southern College B

Georgia

Agnes Scott College B
Andrew College A
Atlanta Christian College B
Berry College B
Brewton-Parker College B
Clark Atlanta University B
Emmanuel College A,B
Emory University B,M,D,W
LaGrange College B
Mercer University B
Morehouse College B
Morris Brown College B
Oxford College of Emory
University A
Paine College B
Reinhardt College A

Shorter College B
Spelman College B
Toccoa Falls College B
Truett-McConnell College A
University of Georgia B,M
Wesleyan College B
Young Harris College A

Hawaii

Chaminade University of
Honolulu B
University of Hawaii at Manoa B,M

Idaho

Albertson College B
Northwest Nazarene College A,B

Illinois

Augustana College B
Aurora University B
Bradley University B
Chicago Theological Seminary
M,D,W
Concordia University B
De Paul University B
Elmhurst College B
Eureka College B
Garrett-Evangelical Theological
Seminary M,D,W
Greenville College B
Hebrew Theological College
B,M,D,W
Illinois Benedictine College B
Illinois College B
Illinois Wesleyan University B
Judson College B
KAES College B
Knox College B
Lewis University B
MacMurray College B
McKendree College B
Millikin University B
Monmouth College B
North Central College B
North Park College and Theological
Seminary B
Northwestern University B,M,D
Olivet Nazarene University C,B
Principia College B
Rockford College B
Rosary College B
St. Xavier University B
Southern Illinois University at
Carbondale B
State Community College A
Trinity Christian College B
University of Chicago B,M,D
University of Illinois at Urbana-
Champaign B
Wheaton College B

Indiana

Anderson University B,M
Ball State University B
Butler University B,M
Calumet College of St. Joseph C,A
DePauw University B
Earlham College B
Franklin College B
Goshen College B
Indiana State University B
Indiana University Bloomington
B,M,D
Indiana University—Purdue
University at Indianapolis B
Indiana Wesleyan University A,B
Manchester College A,B
Martin University B
Oakland City College B
Purdue University B
St. Francis College B
St. Mary-of-the-Woods College B

St. Mary's College *B*
Taylor University *B*
University of Evansville *B*
University of Indianapolis *B*
University of Notre Dame *B,M,D*
Valparaiso University *B*
Wabash College *B*

Iowa

Buena Vista College *B*
Central College *B*
Clarke College *B*
Coe College *B*
Cornell College *B*
Drake University *B,M*
Graceland College *B*
Grinnell College *B*
Iowa State University *B*
Loras College *B*
Luther College *B*
Morningside College *B*
Mount Mercy College *B*
Northwestern College *B*
Simpson College *B*
Teikyo Marycrest University *A*
Teikyo Westmar University *B*
University of Dubuque *B,M*
University of Iowa *B,M,D*
University of Northern Iowa *B*
Wartburg College *B*
William Penn College *B*

Kansas

Baker University *B*
Barton County Community
    College *A*
Benedictine College *B*
Bethany College *B*
Bethel College *B*
Central College *A,B*
Friends University *B*
Kansas City College and Bible
    School *B*
Kansas Wesleyan University *B*
Manhattan Christian College *B*
McPherson College *B*
MidAmerica Nazarene College *B*
Ottawa University *B*
St. Mary College *B*
Southwestern College *B*
Sterling College *B*
Tabor College *B*
University of Kansas *B,M*
Washburn University of Topeka *B*

Kentucky

Berea College *B*
Brescia College *B*
Campbellsville College *B*
Centre College *B*
Clear Creek Baptist Bible College
    C,A,B
Cumberland College *B*
Eastern Kentucky University *B*
Georgetown College *B*
Kentucky Christian College *B*
Kentucky Wesleyan College *B*
Lees College *A*
Mid-Continent Baptist Bible
    College *B*
Pikeville College *B*
Spalding University *B,M*
Thomas More College *A,B*
Transylvania University *B*
Union College *B*
Western Kentucky University *B*

Louisiana

Centenary College of Louisiana *B*
Louisiana College *B*

Louisiana State University and
    Agricultural and Mechanical
    College *B*
Loyola University *B,M*
Tulane University *B*

Maine

Bates College *B*
Bowdoin College *B*
Colby College *B*
St. Joseph's College *B*

Maryland

Baltimore Hebrew University
    B,M,D
College of Notre Dame of
    Maryland *B*
Columbia Union College *B*
Goucher College *B*
Hood College *B*
Morgan State University *B*
Western Maryland College *B*

Massachusetts

Amherst College *B*
Assumption College *B,M*
Atlantic Union College *B*
Boston University *B,M,D*
College of the Holy Cross *B*
Eastern Nazarene College *A,B,M*
Elms College *B,M*
Emmanuel College *B*
Hampshire College *B*
Harvard and Radcliffe Colleges *B*
Harvard University *M,D*
Hellenic College *B*
Merrimack College *B*
Mount Holyoke College *B*
St. Hyacinth College and
    Seminary *A*
Smith College *B,M*
Stonehill College *B*
Tufts University *B*
Wellesley College *B*
Wheaton College *B*
Williams College *B*

Michigan

Adrian College *A,B*
Albion College *B*
Alma College *B*
Andrews University *B,M*
Aquinas College *B*
Calvin College *B*
Central Michigan University *B*
Grand Rapids Baptist College and
    Seminary *B*
Hillsdale College *B*
Hope College *B*
Kalamazoo College *B*
Lansing Community College *A*
Madonna University *A,B*
Marygrove College *B*
Michigan State University *B*
Siena Heights College *B*
Spring Arbor College *B*
University of Detroit Mercy *B,M*
University of Michigan *B*
Western Michigan University *B,M*

Minnesota

Augsburg College *B*
Bethel College *B*
Bethel Theological Seminary *M*
Carleton College *B*
College of St. Scholastica *B*
Concordia College: Moorhead *B*
Concordia College: St. Paul *A,B*
Gustavus Adolphus College *B*
Hamline University *B*
Luther Northwestern Theological
    Seminary *M*

Macalester College *B*
Mankato State University *B*
Northwestern College *B*
St. Olaf College *B*
United Theological Seminary of the
    Twin Cities *M*
University of Minnesota: Twin
    Cities *B,M*

Mississippi

Mary Holmes College *A*
Millsaps College *B*
Mississippi College *B*
Southeastern Baptist College *B*
Wesley College *B*

Missouri

Avila College *B*
Baptist Bible College *B*
Central Christian College of the
    Bible *B*
Central Methodist College *B*
College of the Ozarks *B*
Culver-Stockton College *B*
Drury College *B*
East Central College *B*
Hannibal-LaGrange College *B*
Maryville University *B*
Missouri Baptist College *A,B*
Missouri Valley College *B*
Northeast Missouri State
    University *B*
Park College *M*
St. Louis Christian College *A,B*
Southwest Baptist University *B*
Southwest Missouri State
    University *B*
Stephens College *B*
University of Missouri: Columbia *B*
Washington University *B*
Webster University *B*
Westminster College *B*
William Jewell College *B*

Montana

Carroll College *B*
College of Great Falls *A*
Rocky Mountain College *B*

Nebraska

Dana College *B*
Doane College *B*
Hastings College *B*
Midland Lutheran College *B*
Nebraska Christian College *B*
Nebraska Wesleyan University *B*
Union College *B*
University of Nebraska—Omaha *B*

New Hampshire

Dartmouth College *B*
Notre Dame College *B*

New Jersey

Bergen Community College *A*
Bloomfield College *B*
Caldwell College *B*
Cumberland County College *A*
Drew University *B*
Felician College *A,B*
Georgian Court College *B*
Montclair State College *B*
Princeton University *B,D*
Rutgers—The State University of
    New Jersey
    Douglass College *B*
    Livingston College *B*
    Rutgers College *B*
    University College New
        Brunswick *B*
Seton Hall University *B*
Stockton State College *B*

Thomas Edison State College *B*
Upsala College *B*

New Mexico

College of Santa Fe *B*
Eastern New Mexico University *B*
University of New Mexico *B*

New York

Bard College *B*
Barnard College *B*
Canisius College *B*
City University of New York
    Baruch College *B*
    Brooklyn College *B*
    Hunter College *B*
    Queens College *B*
Colgate University *B,M*
College of Mount St. Vincent *B*
College of New Rochelle *B*
College of St. Rose *B*
Columbia University
    Columbia College *B*
    New York *M,D*
    School of General Studies *B*
Concordia College *B*
Cornell University *B*
Daemen College *B*
Fordham University *B,M,D*
Hamilton College *B*
Hartwick College *B*
Hobart College *B*
Houghton College *B*
Iona College *B*
Ithaca College *B*
King's College *B*
Le Moyne College *C,B*
Manhattan College *B*
Manhattanville College *B*
Marymount College *B*
Molloy College *B*
Nazareth College of Rochester *B*
New York University *B,M*
Niagara University *B*
Nyack College *B*
St. John Fisher College *B*
St. John's University *B,M*
St. Lawrence University *B*
St. Thomas Aquinas College *B*
Sarah Lawrence College *B*
Siena College *B*
State University of New York at
    Stony Brook *B*
Syracuse University *B,M,D*
Touro College *B*
University of Rochester *B*
Vassar College *B*
Wadhams Hall Seminary-College
    C,B
Wagner College *B*
Wells College *B*
William Smith College *B*

North Carolina

Appalachian State University *B*
Barton College *B*
Brevard College *A*
Campbell University *B*
Catawba College *B*
Chowan College *B*
Davidson College *B*
Duke University *B,D*
Elon College *B*
Gardner-Webb College *B*
Greensboro College *B*
Guilford College *B*
High Point University *B*
John Wesley College *B*
Lees-McRae College *A*
Lenoir-Rhyne College *B*
Mars Hill College *B*
Meredith College *B*

Methodist College *A,B*
Montreat-Anderson College *B*
Mount Olive College *A,B*
North Carolina Wesleyan College *B*
Pfeiffer College *B*
Queens College *B*
St. Andrews Presbyterian College *B*
Salem College *B*
Shaw University *B*
University of North Carolina
    Chapel Hill *B,M,D*
    Charlotte *B*
    Greensboro *B*
    Wilmington *B*
Wake Forest University *B,M*
Wingate College *B*

North Dakota
Jamestown College *B*
University of North Dakota *B*

Ohio
Ashland University *B*
Athenaeum of Ohio *M*
Baldwin-Wallace College *B*
Bluffton College *B*
Capital University *B*
Case Western Reserve University *B*
Cedarville College *B*
Cleveland State University *B*
College of Mount St. Joseph *B*
College of Wooster *B*
Defiance College *B*
Denison University *B*
Heidelberg College *B*
Hiram College *B*
John Carroll University *B,M*
Kenyon College *B*
Lourdes College *A,B*
Malone College *B*
Marietta College *B*
Miami University: Oxford Campus
    B,M
Mount Union College *B*
Mount Vernon Nazarene College *B*
Muskingum College *B*
Oberlin College *B*
Ohio Northern University *B*
Ohio State University: Columbus
    Campus *B*
Ohio Wesleyan University *B*
Otterbein College *B*
Pontifical College Josephinum *B*
Union Institute *B,D*
University of Dayton *B,M*
University of Findlay *A,B*
Urbana University *B*
Ursuline College *B*
Walsh College *B*
Wilmington College *B*
Wittenberg University *B*
Wright State University *B*
Youngstown State University *B*

Oklahoma
Bacone College *A*
Bartlesville Wesleyan College *A,B*
Mid-America Bible College *B*
Oklahoma Baptist University *B*
Oklahoma Christian University of
    Science and Arts *B,M*
Oklahoma City University *B,M*
Phillips University *B*
Southwestern College of Christian
    Ministries *A,B*
University of Oklahoma *B*

Oregon
Concordia College *B*
George Fox College *B*
Lewis and Clark College *B*
Linfield College *B*

Northwest Christian College *M*
Pacific University *B*
Reed College *B*
University of Oregon
    Eugene *B*
    Robert Donald Clark Honors
      College *B*
Warner Pacific College *B,M*
Willamette University *B*

Pennsylvania
Academy of the New Church *B*
Albright College *B*
Allegheny College *B*
Bryn Mawr College *B*
Bucknell University *B*
Cabrini College *B*
Chatham College *B*
Dickinson College *B*
Duquesne University *B,M,D*
Elizabethtown College *B*
Evangelical School of Theology *M*
Franklin and Marshall College *B*
Gettysburg College *B*
Gratz College *B*
Grove City College *B*
Haverford College *B*
Holy Family College *B*
Juniata College *B*
King's College *B*
La Roche College *B*
La Salle University *B,M*
Lafayette College *B*
Lancaster Bible College *B*
Lebanon Valley College of
    Pennsylvania *B*
Lehigh University *B*
Lycoming College *B*
Marywood College *B*
Mercyhurst College *B*
Messiah College *B*
Moravian College *B*
Muhlenberg College *B*
Neumann College *B*
Northeastern Christian Junior
    College *A*
Penn State University Park
    Campus *B*
Pittsburgh Theological Seminary
    M,D,W
Rosemont College *B*
St. Francis College *B*
St. Joseph's University *B*
Seton Hill College *B*
Susquehanna University *B*
Swarthmore College *B*
Temple University *B,M,D*
Thiel College *B*
University of Pennsylvania *B,M,D*
University of Pittsburgh *B,M,D*
Ursinus College *B*
Villanova University *B,M*
West Chester University of
    Pennsylvania *B*
Westminster College *B*
Wilson College *B*

Puerto Rico
Bayamon Central University *B*
Universidad Adventista de las
    Antillas *A,B*

Rhode Island
Brown University *B,M,D*
Providence College *B,M*
Salve Regina University *B*

South Carolina
Anderson College *B*
Benedict College *B*
Central Wesleyan College *B*
Charleston Southern University *B*

Coker College *B*
Columbia College *B*
Converse College *B*
Erskine College *B*
Francis Marion College *B*
Furman University *B*
North Greenville College *A*
Presbyterian College *B*
University of South Carolina *B,M*
Winthrop University *B*
Wofford College *B*

South Dakota
Augustana College *B*
Dakota Wesleyan University *B*
Mount Marty College *B*
Sioux Falls College *B*

Tennessee
Belmont University *B*
Bethel College *B*
Carson-Newman College *B*
David Lipscomb University *M*
King College *B*
Lambuth University *B*
Lane College *B*
Martin Methodist College *A*
Maryville College *B*
Memphis Theological Seminary *M*
Rhodes College *B*
Southern College of Seventh-day
    Adventists *B*
Tennessee Wesleyan College *B*
Tomlinson College *A,B*
Trevecca Nazarene College *B,M*
Union University *B*
University of the South *B*
University of Tennessee
    Chattanooga *B*
    Knoxville *B*
Vanderbilt University *B,M,D*

Texas
Amarillo College *A*
Austin College *B*
Baptist Missionary Association
    Theological Seminary *B,M*
Baylor University *B,M,D*
Dallas Baptist University *B,M*
East Texas Baptist University *B*
Hardin-Simmons University *M*
Houston Baptist University *B*
Incarnate Word College *B,M*
Institute for Christian Studies *B*
Jacksonville College *A*
Jarvis Christian College *B*
Lon Morris College *A*
Lubbock Christian University *B*
McLennan Community College *A*
McMurry University *B*
Our Lady of the Lake University of
    San Antonio *B*
Paul Quinn College *B*
Rice University *B,M,D*
St. Edward's University *B*
Schreiner College *B*
Southern Methodist University
    B,M,D
Southwestern Adventist College *B*
Southwestern University *B*
Texas Christian University *B*
Texas Wesleyan University *B*
Trinity University *B*
University of Mary Hardin-
    Baylor *B*
Wayland Baptist University *B*
Wiley College *B*

Utah
Westminster College of Salt Lake
    City *B*

Vermont
Goddard College *B*
Marlboro College *B*
Middlebury College *B*
St. Michael's College *B,M*
University of Vermont *B*

Virginia
Averett College *B*
Bluefield College *B*
Bridgewater College *B*
Christopher Newport College *B*
College of William and Mary *B*
Eastern Mennonite College *B*
Emory and Henry College *B*
Ferrum College *B*
Hampden-Sydney College *B*
Hollins College *B*
James Madison University *B*
Liberty University *A*
Lynchburg College *B*
Mary Baldwin College *B*
Mary Washington College *B*
Marymount University *B*
Old Dominion University *B*
Radford University *B*
Randolph-Macon College *B*
Randolph-Macon Woman's
    College *B*
Shenandoah University *B*
Sweet Briar College *B*
University of Richmond *B*
University of Virginia *B,M,D*
Virginia Commonwealth
    University *B*
Virginia Intermont College *B*
Virginia Union University *B*
Virginia Wesleyan College *B*
Washington and Lee University *B*

Washington
Central Washington University *B*
Gonzaga University *B,M*
Lutheran Bible Institute of Seattle
    A,B
Northwest College of the
    Assemblies of God *B*
Pacific Lutheran University *B*
St. Martin's College *B,M*
Seattle Pacific University *B*
Seattle University *B,M*
University of Puget Sound *B*
University of Washington *B,M*
Walla Walla College *B*
Whitworth College *B*

West Virginia
Alderson-Broaddus College *B*
Bethany College *B*
Davis and Elkins College *B*
Marshall University *B*
University of Charleston *B*
West Virginia University *B*
West Virginia Wesleyan College *B*
Wheeling Jesuit College *B*

Wisconsin
Alverno College *B*
Beloit College *B*
Cardinal Stritch College *A,B,M*
Carroll College *B*
Carthage College *B*
Concordia University Wisconsin *B*
Edgewood College *B,M*
Lakeland College *B*
Lawrence University *B*
Mount Mary College *B*
Northland College *B*
Ripon College *B*
St. Norbert College *B*
Silver Lake College *B*

University of Wisconsin
Eau Claire *B*
Milwaukee *B*
Oshkosh *B*
Viterbo College *B*

Canada
McGill University *B,M,D*

Religious education

Alabama
Faulkner University *B*
Huntingdon College *B*
Mobile College *B*
Oakwood College *B*
Samford University *B*
Selma University *B*
Southeastern Bible College *B*

Alaska
Alaska Bible College *B*

Arizona
American Indian Bible College *B*
Arizona College of the Bible *A,B*
Southwestern College *C,A,B*

Arkansas
Central Baptist College *B*
Harding University *B*
John Brown University *B*
Ouachita Baptist University *B*
University of the Ozarks *B*
Williams Baptist College *A,B*

California
Azusa Pacific University *B*
Bethany College *B*
Biola University *B,M,D*
California Lutheran University *B*
Christ College Irvine *B,M*
College of Notre Dame *B,M*
Fresno Pacific College *B*
Fuller Theological Seminary *M,W*
Hebrew Union College: Jewish Institute of Religion *M,D*
La Sierra University *B,M*
LIFE Bible College *B*
Loyola Marymount University *M*
Mount St. Mary's College *M*
Pacific Christian College *B*
Pacific School of Religion *M*
Pacific Union College *B*
Patten College *B*
Point Loma Nazarene College *B,M*
San Jose Christian College *B*
Simpson College *B,M*
Southern California College *B*
University of Judaism *M*
University of San Diego *M*
University of San Francisco *M*
Westmont College *B*

Colorado
Nazarene Bible College *A,B*
Regis College of Regis University *B,M*

Connecticut
Fairfield University *M*

District of Columbia
Catholic University of America *B,M*

Florida
Bethune-Cookman College *B*
Eckerd College *B*

Florida Baptist Theological College *A,B*
Florida Bible College *A,B*
Florida Christian College *B*
Florida Southern College *B*
Southeastern College of the Assemblies of God *B*

Georgia
Andrew College *A*
Atlanta Christian College *B*
Brewton-Parker College *A*
Emory University *M,D,W*
LaGrange College *B*
Toccoa Falls College *B*
Wesleyan College *B*

Idaho
Boise Bible College *A,B*
Northwest Nazarene College *A,B*

Illinois
Chicago Theological Seminary *M,D,W*
Concordia University *B,M*
Garrett-Evangelical Theological Seminary *M,D,W*
Hebrew Theological College *B,M,D,W*
Lincoln Christian College and Seminary *B,M*
Loyola University of Chicago *M*
McKendree College *B*
Moody Bible Institute *B*
Olivet Nazarene University *B*
Quincy College *B*
St. Xavier University *B*
Trinity Christian College *B*
Trinity College *B*
Wheaton College *B,M*

Indiana
Anderson University *B*
Christian Theological Seminary *M*
Grace Theological Seminary *M,W*
Huntington College *B,M*
Indiana Wesleyan University *A,B*
Marian College *B*
St. Mary-of-the-Woods College *B*
Taylor University *B*

Iowa
Faith Baptist Bible College and Theological Seminary *B,M*
Loras College *B*
Vennard College *B*
Wartburg College *B*

Kansas
Barclay College *B*
Kansas Wesleyan University *B*
Manhattan Christian College *A,B*
MidAmerica Nazarene College *A,B*
Sterling College *B*

Kentucky
Asbury College *B*
Brescia College *A*
Campbellsville College *B*
Clear Creek Baptist Bible College *C,A,B*
Cumberland College *B*
Kentucky Christian College *B*
Louisville Presbyterian Theological Seminary *M*
Mid-Continent Baptist Bible College *B*
Union College *B*

Louisiana
Centenary College of Louisiana *B*
Louisiana College *B*

Loyola University *M*
New Orleans Baptist Theological Seminary: School of Christian Education *A*
World Evangelism Bible College and Seminary *C,B,M*

Maryland
Baltimore Hebrew University *B,M,D*

Massachusetts
Assumption College *B,M*
Atlantic Union College *B*
Boston College *M,D*
Eastern Nazarene College *B*

Michigan
Andrews University *B,M,D*
Calvin College *B*
Calvin Theological Seminary *M*
Grace Bible College *A,B*
Grand Rapids Baptist College and Seminary *M*
Great Lakes Christian College *B*
Olivet College *B*
Reformed Bible College *B*
Sacred Heart Major Seminary *C*
St. Mary's College *B*

Minnesota
Bethany Lutheran College *A*
Bethel Theological Seminary *M,D,W*
College of St. Benedict *B*
College of St. Scholastica *B*
Concordia College: Moorhead *B*
Concordia College: St. Paul *B*
Crown College *B*
Luther Northwestern Theological Seminary *M*
Minnesota Bible College *B*
North Central Bible College *B*
Northwestern College *B*
Pillsbury Baptist Bible College *B*
St. John's University *B,M*
St. Mary's College of Minnesota *B*

Mississippi
Blue Mountain College *B*
Mississippi College *B*
Southeastern Baptist College *B*
Wesley College *B*
William Carey College *B*

Missouri
Baptist Bible College *B*
Berean College *B*
Calvary Bible College *A,B*
Central Christian College of the Bible *B*
Hannibal-LaGrange College *B*
Missouri Baptist College *B*
Missouri Valley College *B*
Ozark Christian College *B*
St. Louis Christian College *B*
St. Louis University *M*
Southwest Baptist University *B*

Montana
Carroll College *B*

Nebraska
Concordia College *B*
Grace College of the Bible *B*
Nebraska Christian College *A,B*
Union College *B*

New Jersey
College of St. Elizabeth *C*
Seton Hall University *B*

New York
Fordham University *M*
Houghton College *B*
Jewish Theological Seminary of America *M*
Le Moyne College *B*
Manhattan College *B*
Mater Dei College *A*
Molloy College *B*
New York Theological Seminary *D*
New York University *M,D*
Nyack College *B*
Ohr Somayach Tanenbaum Education Center *B,M*
Siena College *B*
Union Theological Seminary *M*
Villa Maria College of Buffalo *A*

North Carolina
Brevard College *A*
Campbell University *B*
Duke University *M*
East Coast Bible College *A,B*
Gardner-Webb College *B*
Greensboro College *B*
John Wesley College *B*
Lenoir-Rhyne College *B*
Livingstone College *B*
Mars Hill College *B*
Methodist College *A*
Mount Olive College *A,B*
Pfeiffer College *B,M*
Piedmont Bible College *C,B*
Roanoke Bible College *B*
Southeastern Baptist Theological Seminary *M*

North Dakota
Trinity Bible College *B*

Ohio
Ashland University *B*
Capital University *B*
Cedarville College *B*
Cincinnati Bible College and Seminary *M*
Circleville Bible College *A,B*
College of Mount St. Joseph *B*
Defiance College *A,B*
Malone College *B*
Mount Vernon Nazarene College *B*
Muskingum College *B*
Notre Dame College of Ohio *A,B*
University of Dayton *B,M*
Walsh College *B*

Oklahoma
Hillsdale Free Will Baptist College *A*
Mid-America Bible College *B*
Oklahoma Baptist University *B*
Oklahoma Christian University of Science and Arts *B*
Oklahoma City University *M*
Oral Roberts University *B*
St. Gregory's College *A*
Southwestern College of Christian Ministries *B*

Oregon
Eugene Bible College *B*
Multnomah School of the Bible *B,M*
Northwest Christian College *B*
University of Portland *C*
Warner Pacific College *A,B*
Western Baptist College *B*
Western Conservative Baptist Seminary *M,D*

Pennsylvania

Albright College *B*
Baptist Bible College of
  Pennsylvania *B*
Evangelical School of Theology *M*
Gannon University *B,M*
Gratz College *B,M*
Holy Family College *B*
Juniata College *B*
La Roche College *B*
La Salle University *B,M*
Lancaster Bible College *B*
Lincoln University *B*
Lutheran Theological Seminary at
  Gettysburg *M*
Mercyhurst College *C,A,B*
Messiah College *B*
Philadelphia College of Bible *B*
Pittsburgh Theological Seminary
  M,D,W
St. Vincent College *B*
Seton Hill College *B*
Thiel College *B*
Valley Forge Christian College *B*
Westminster College *B*

Puerto Rico

Pontifical Catholic University of
  Puerto Rico *M*

Rhode Island

Providence College *M*

South Carolina

Bob Jones University *B*
Columbia Bible College and
  Seminary *B*
Columbia College *B*
Erskine College *B*
Morris College *B*
North Greenville College *A*

South Dakota

Augustana College *B*
Mount Marty College *B*
Presentation College *A*

Tennessee

Belmont University *B*
Bethel College *B*
Free Will Baptist Bible College *B*
Milligan College *B*
Southern College of Seventh-day
  Adventists *B*
Tennessee Temple University
  B,M,D
Tomlinson College *A,B*
Trevecca Nazarene College *B*
Union University *B*
William Jennings Bryan College *B*

Texas

Abilene Christian University *B,M*
Arlington Baptist College *B*
Baptist Missionary Association
  Theological Seminary *M*
Dallas Baptist University *B*
Dallas Christian College *B*
East Texas Baptist University *B*
Hardin-Simmons University *B*
Howard Payne University *B*
Jacksonville College *A*
Lubbock Christian University *B*
McMurry University *B*
St. Mary's University *M*
Southern Methodist University *M*
Southwestern Assemblies of God
  College *B*
Southwestern Christian College *B*
Southwestern University *B*
Texas Christian University *M*
University of Dallas *M*

University of St. Thomas *B,M*

Vermont

St. Michael's College *M*

Virginia

Averett College *B*
Bluefield College *B*
Liberty University *B,M*

Washington

Lutheran Bible Institute of
  Seattle *B*
Northwest College of the
  Assemblies of God *B*
Puget Sound Christian College *B*
Seattle Pacific University *B*
Seattle University *M*

West Virginia

Davis and Elkins College *B*
West Virginia Wesleyan College *B*
Wheeling Jesuit College *M*

Wisconsin

Cardinal Stritch College *B,M*
Concordia University Wisconsin *B*
Edgewood College *B*
Mount Mary College *B*
St. Norbert College *B*
Viterbo College *B*

Religious music

Alabama

Huntingdon College *B*
Samford University *B,M*
Southeastern Bible College *B*

Arizona

Arizona College of the Bible *B*
Grand Canyon University *B*
Southwestern College *C,A,B*

Arkansas

Arkansas State University *B*
Central Baptist College *B*
Harding University *B*
John Brown University *B*
Ouachita Baptist University *B*
Williams Baptist College *B*

California

Azusa Pacific University *B*
Biola University *M*
Christ College Irvine *B*
Christian Heritage College *B*
Fresno Pacific College *B*
La Sierra University *B*
Mount St. Mary's College *B*
Pacific Christian College *B*
Patten College *B*
Point Loma Nazarene College *B*
Santa Clara University *M*
Simpson College *B*
University of Southern California
  M,D

Colorado

Colorado Christian University *B*
Nazarene Bible College *A,B*

Connecticut

University of Hartford *M*

District of Columbia

Catholic University of America *M*

Florida

Florida Baptist Theological College
  A,B
Florida Christian College *B*
Florida Southern College *B*
Hobe Sound Bible College *B*
Southeastern College of the
  Assemblies of God *B*
Stetson University *B*
Warner Southern College *B*

Georgia

Atlanta Christian College *B*
Brewton-Parker College *A*
Emory University *M*
Middle Georgia College *A*
Shorter College *B,M*
Toccoa Falls College *B*
University of Georgia *B*
Wesleyan College *B*

Idaho

Boise Bible College *A,B*
Northwest Nazarene College *B*

Illinois

Augustana College *B*
Concordia University *B,M*
Elmhurst College *B*
Garrett-Evangelical Theological
  Seminary *M,D,W*
Illinois Benedictine College *B*
Illinois Wesleyan University *B*
Judson College *B*
Lincoln Christian College and
  Seminary *B*
Millikin University *B*
Moody Bible Institute *B*
Olivet Nazarene University *B*
St. Xavier University *B*

Indiana

Anderson University *B*
Bethel College *A,B*
Christian Theological Seminary *M*
Goshen College *C*
Grace College *B*
Indiana Wesleyan University *B*
Manchester College *B*
St. Mary-of-the-Woods College *B*
Taylor University *B*

Iowa

Drake University *B*
Faith Baptist Bible College and
  Theological Seminary *B*
Vennard College *B*

Kansas

Barclay College *B*
Central College *A,B*
Friends University *B*
Manhattan Christian College *B*
MidAmerica Nazarene College *A,B*
Ottawa University *B*

Kentucky

Asbury College *B*
Campbellsville College *B*
Clear Creek Baptist Bible College
  C,A,B
Cumberland College *B*
Kentucky Wesleyan College *B*
Union College *B*

Louisiana

Centenary College of Louisiana *B*
Louisiana College *B*
New Orleans Baptist Theological
  Seminary: School of Christian
  Education *A*

World Evangelism Bible College
  and Seminary *C,B*

Massachusetts

Boston University *M*

Michigan

Aquinas College *A,B*
Grace Bible College *B*
Great Lakes Christian College *B*
Hope College *B*
Madonna University *B*
Olivet College *B*
Wayne State University *B*
William Tyndale College *C,B*

Minnesota

Bethany Lutheran College *A*
Bethel College *B*
College of St. Benedict *B*
Concordia College: St. Paul *B*
Crown College *B*
Gustavus Adolphus College *B*
Luther Northwestern Theological
  Seminary *M*
North Central Bible College *B*
Pillsbury Baptist Bible College *B*
St. John's University *B*
St. Olaf College *B*

Mississippi

Millsaps College *B*
Mississippi College *B*
Southeastern Baptist College *A,B*
William Carey College *B*

Missouri

Baptist Bible College *B*
Calvary Bible College *A,B*
Central Christian College of the
  Bible *B*
Evangel College *B*
Hannibal-LaGrange College *B*
Missouri Baptist College *B*
Ozark Christian College *C,B*
St. Louis Christian College *B*
Southwest Baptist University *B*

Nebraska

Concordia College *B*
Grace College of the Bible *B*
Nebraska Christian College *A,B*
Union College *B*

New Jersey

Westminster Choir College *B,M*

New York

Concordia College *B*
Manhattan School of Music *M,D*
Nyack College *B*

North Carolina

Brevard College *A*
Campbell University *B*
Catawba College *B*
East Carolina University *B,M*
East Coast Bible College *A,B*
Gardner-Webb College *B*
Greensboro College *B*
Mars Hill College *B*
Pfeiffer College *B*
Piedmont Bible College *B*
Southeastern Baptist Theological
  Seminary *M*

North Dakota

Trinity Bible College *B*

Ohio

Ashland University *M*
Bowling Green State University *B*

Cedarville College B
Cincinnati Bible College and
    Seminary B
Circleville Bible College A,B
Malone College B
Mount Vernon Nazarene College
    A,B
Wittenberg University B

Oklahoma
Hillsdale Free Will Baptist
    College A
Mid-America Bible College B
Oklahoma Baptist University B
Oral Roberts University B
Southwestern College of Christian
    Ministries B
Southwestern Oklahoma State
    University B

Oregon
Eugene Bible College B
Northwest Christian College B
Warner Pacific College B
Western Baptist College B
Western Conservative Baptist
    Seminary M

Pennsylvania
Baptist Bible College of
    Pennsylvania B
Duquesne University B,M
Gratz College B,M
Immaculata College A
Lancaster Bible College B
Lebanon Valley College of
    Pennsylvania B
Lutheran Theological Seminary at
    Gettysburg M
Marywood College B,M
Messiah College B
Philadelphia College of Bible B
Pittsburgh Theological Seminary
    M,D
St. Vincent College B
Seton Hill College C,B
Susquehanna University B
Valley Forge Christian College B
Westminster College B

South Carolina
Bob Jones University B,M
Charleston Southern University B
Columbia Bible College and
    Seminary B
Columbia College B
Newberry College B

Tennessee
Belmont University B
Carson-Newman College B
Crichton College B
Free Will Baptist Bible College B
Johnson Bible College B
Milligan College B
Trevecca Nazarene College B
Union University B

Texas
Arlington Baptist College B
Baylor University B,M
Concordia Lutheran College B
Dallas Baptist University B
Dallas Christian College B
East Texas Baptist University B
Hardin-Simmons University B
Houston Baptist University B
Howard Payne University B
Jacksonville College A
McMurry University B
Southern Methodist University M

Southwestern Assemblies of God
    College B
Southwestern University B
University of Mary Hardin-
    Baylor B

Virginia
Averett College B
Bluefield College B
Emory and Henry College B
Shenandoah University B,M
Virginia Commonwealth University
    B,M

Washington
Northwest College of the
    Assemblies of God B
Pacific Lutheran University B
Puget Sound Christian College B
Seattle Pacific University B,M
Whitworth College B

West Virginia
West Virginia State College A

Wisconsin
Alverno College A,B
Carthage College B
Concordia University Wisconsin B
Maranatha Baptist Bible College B
Viterbo College B

Remedial education

California
California Lutheran University M
University of the Pacific B,M,D

Georgia
Georgia College B

Indiana
Vincennes University A

Iowa
University of Iowa M

Louisiana
Grambling State University M,D

Maryland
Morgan State University B

Massachusetts
Lesley College M

Michigan
Madonna University B

Minnesota
Mankato State University M
University of St. Thomas M
Winona State University B,M

Mississippi
Jackson State University B

Missouri
Northwest Missouri State
    University B,M

New Jersey
Kean College of New Jersey M

New York
City University of New York:
    Brooklyn College B,M

State University of New York
    Buffalo M,D
    College at New Paltz M

Ohio
Central State University B
University of Toledo M

Texas
Southwest Texas State
    University M
University of Mary Hardin-Baylor
    B,M

Washington
Eastern Washington University B

Renewable natural resources

Alaska
Alaska Pacific University B
Sheldon Jackson College A,B
University of Alaska Fairbanks B,M

Arizona
Arizona State University B,M
Northern Arizona University B
Prescott College B
University of Arizona M,D

California
California Polytechnic State
    University: San Luis Obispo B
College of the Desert A
Columbia College A
Feather River College C,A
Humboldt State University C,B,M
Kings River Community College A
Los Angeles Pierce College A
Mendocino College C,A
Sierra College C
Southwestern College A
University of California
    Berkeley M,D
    Davis B
University of San Francisco B,M
Ventura College A

Colorado
Colorado State University B
Trinidad State Junior College A

Connecticut
University of Connecticut B,M

Delaware
Delaware State College B

Florida
University of Florida M,D
University of West Florida B

Georgia
University of Georgia B,M,D

Idaho
Idaho State University B
North Idaho College A
University of Idaho B

Illinois
Southern Illinois University at
    Carbondale B,M

Indiana
Ball State University B,M
Martin University B
Purdue University A,B,M,D

Vincennes University A

Iowa
Kirkwood Community College A
Muscatine Community College A

Kansas
Fort Scott Community College A
Haskell Indian Junior College A
Kansas State University B

Kentucky
Eastern Kentucky University B

Maine
Unity College B
University of Maine B,M

Maryland
Garrett Community College A
University of Maryland: College
    Park B

Massachusetts
Greenfield Community College A
Springfield College B
University of Massachusetts at
    Amherst B

Michigan
Grand Valley State University B
Jordan College A,B
Lake Superior State University A
Michigan State University B,M,D
University of Michigan B,M,D

Minnesota
Itasca Community College:
    Arrowhead Region A
Mankato State University B
Rainy River Community College A
University of Minnesota
    Crookston A
    Twin Cities B
Vermilion Community College A
Willmar Community College A

Montana
Montana State University B,M
Salish Kootenai College A
University of Montana M

Nebraska
Nebraska College of Technical
    Agriculture A
University of Nebraska—Lincoln
    B,M

New Hampshire
New Hampshire Technical College:
    Berlin A
University of New Hampshire
    B,M,D

New Jersey
Rutgers—The State University of
    New Jersey: Cook College B
Stockton State College B

New Mexico
New Mexico State University B,M
Northern New Mexico Community
    College A

New York
Community College of the Finger
    Lakes A
Cornell University B,M,D
Dutchess Community College A
State University of New York
    College of Environmental Science
    and Forestry B,M,D

North Carolina

Western Carolina University *B*

North Dakota

North Dakota State University
  Bottineau and Institute of
    Forestry *A*
  Fargo *M*

Ohio

Kent State University *B*
Marietta College *B*
Mount Vernon Nazarene College *A*
Ohio State University: Columbus
  Campus *B,M*

Oklahoma

Murray State College *A*
Phillips University *B*
Southeastern Oklahoma State
  University *B*

Pennsylvania

California University of
  Pennsylvania *M*
Penn State University Park
  Campus *B*

Rhode Island

University of Rhode Island *B,M,D*

South Dakota

Sinte Gleska College *C,A*
South Dakota State University *B*

Tennessee

Tennessee Technological
  University *B*
University of the South *B*
University of Tennessee: Martin *B*

Texas

Texas A&M University *M*
University of Texas at San
  Antonio *M*
Western Texas College *A*

Utah

Utah State University *B,M,D*

Vermont

Goddard College *B,M*
Sterling College *C,A*
University of Vermont *B,M*

Virginia

Christopher Newport College *B*
St. Paul's College *B*

Washington

Evergreen State College *B*
Heritage College *A*
Spokane Community College *A*
Washington State University *B,M*

Wisconsin

Fox Valley Technical College *A*
Northland College *B*
University of Wisconsin
  Green Bay *B,M*
  River Falls *B*
  Stevens Point *B,M*

Wyoming

Central Wyoming College *A*

Canada

McGill University *B,M,D*

Respiratory therapy

Alabama

Enterprise State Junior College *A*
Faulkner University *A*
Gadsden State Community
  College *A*
George C. Wallace State
  Community College at Selma *A*
John C. Calhoun State Community
  College *A*
Shelton State Community
  College *A*
Shoals Community College *A*
Wallace State Community College
  at Hanceville *A*

Arkansas

University of Central Arkansas *B*
Westark Community College *A*

California

College of the Desert *A*
El Camino College *C,A*
Los Angeles Valley College *C,A*
Napa Valley College *A*
Ohlone College *A*
Santa Monica College *A*
Santa Rosa Junior College *C*
Skyline College *C*

Colorado

Front Range Community College *A*

Connecticut

Manchester Community College *A*
Quinnipiac College *B*
Sacred Heart University *A*
University of Bridgeport *B*
University of Hartford *B*

Delaware

Delaware Technical and
  Community College: Stanton/
  Wilmington Campus *A*

Florida

Daytona Beach Community
  College *C*
Flagler Career Institute *A*
Florida Agricultural and Mechanical
  University *B*
Florida Community College at
  Jacksonville *A*
Gulf Coast Community College *C*
Indian River Community College *A*
Manatee Community College *A*
Miami-Dade Community College *A*
Palm Beach Community College *C*
Pensacola Junior College *C,A*
St. Petersburg Junior College *A*
University of Central Florida *B*

Georgia

Brewton-Parker College *A*
Floyd College *A*
Georgia State University *B*
Medical College of Georgia *A,B*
Middle Georgia College *A*

Hawaii

University of Hawaii: Kapiolani
  Community College *C,A*

Idaho

Boise State University *A,B*

Illinois

Belleville Area College *C*
Black Hawk College *C,A*

College of DuPage *C,A*
Moraine Valley Community
  College *A*
National-Louis University *B*
Southern Illinois University at
  Carbondale *A*
Triton College *C,A*

Indiana

Indiana University—Purdue
  University at Indianapolis *B*
Marian College *A*
Vincennes University *A*

Iowa

Des Moines Area Community
  College *A*
Hawkeye Institute of Technology *C*
Kirkwood Community College *A*
Scott Community College *A*

Kansas

Johnson County Community
  College *A*
Kansas City Kansas Community
  College *A*
Labette Community College *A*
University of Kansas
  Lawrence *B*
  Medical Center *B*

Kentucky

Morehead State University *A*
Northern Kentucky University *A*

Louisiana

Bossier Parish Community College
  C,A
Louisiana State University Medical
  Center *M*
Nicholls State University *A*
Southeastern Louisiana
  University *A*

Maryland

Columbia Union College *B*
New Community College of
  Baltimore *A*
Salisbury State University *B*

Massachusetts

Berkshire Community College *A*
Newbury College *A*
North Shore Community College *A*
Springfield Technical Community
  College *A*

Michigan

Charles Stewart Mott Community
  College *A*
Delta College *A*
Ferris State University *A*
Henry Ford Community College *A*
Kalamazoo Valley Community
  College *A*
Lansing Community College *A*
Macomb Community College *A*
Marygrove College *A*

Minnesota

Rochester Community College *A*
St. Mary's Campus of the College of
  St. Catherine *A*
St. Paul Technical College *A*

Missouri

Penn Valley Community College
  C,A
St. Louis Community College at
  Forest Park *A*
University of Missouri: Columbia *B*

Montana

College of Great Falls *A*

Nebraska

Metropolitan Community College
  C,A
Midland Lutheran College *B*
Southeast Community College:
  Lincoln Campus *A*

Nevada

Community College of Southern
  Nevada *A*

New Jersey

Atlantic Community College *A*
Camden County College *A*
Fairleigh Dickinson University *A*
Thomas Edison State College *B*
Union County College *A*
University of Medicine and
  Dentistry of New Jersey: School
  of Health Related Professions
  C,A

New York

Erie Community College: North
  Campus *A*
Hudson Valley Community
  College *A*
Long Island University: Brooklyn
  Campus *B*
Mohawk Valley Community
  College *A*
Monroe Community College *A*
Onondaga Community College *A*
Rockland Community College *A*
State University of New York
  Health Science Center at
    Syracuse *A,B*
  Health Sciences Center at
    Stony Brook *B*
Westchester Community College *A*

North Carolina

Carteret Community College *A*
Durham Technical Community
  College *A*
Edgecombe Community College *A*
Forsyth Technical Community
  College *A*
Robeson Community College *A*
Southwestern Community
  College *A*

North Dakota

North Dakota State University *B*

Ohio

Bowling Green State University:
  Firelands College *A*
College of Mount St. Joseph *A*
Columbus State Community College
  C,A
Cuyahoga Community College:
  Metropolitan Campus *A*
Ohio State University: Columbus
  Campus *C,B,M*
Sinclair Community College *A*
University of Toledo *A*
Youngstown State University *A*

Oklahoma

Tulsa Junior College *C,A*

Oregon

Mount Hood Community
  College *A*
Rogue Community College *A*

Pennsylvania

Gannon University B
Gwynedd-Mercy College C,A
Harrisburg Area Community
College A
Indiana University of
Pennsylvania B
Lehigh County Community
College A
Mansfield University of
Pennsylvania A
University of Pittsburgh at
Johnstown A
West Chester University of
Pennsylvania A
York College of Pennsylvania C,A,B

Rhode Island

Community College of Rhode
Island A

South Carolina

Greenville Technical College A

South Dakota

Dakota State University A,B

Tennessee

Roane State Community College A
Volunteer State Community College
C,A

Texas

Amarillo College A
Angelina College A
El Centro College C,A
Houston Community College C
Lamar University—Beaumont A
Midland College A
North Harris Montgomery
Community College District C,A
Odessa College C,A
St. Philip's College C
South Plains College C
Texas Southmost College A
University of Texas Health Science
Center at Houston B

Utah

Weber State University A

Vermont

Champlain College A

Virginia

Mountain Empire Community
College A
Northern Virginia Community
College C,A
Shenandoah University A,B
Tidewater Community College C,A

Washington

Seattle Central Community
College A
Spokane Community College A
Walla Walla Community College A

West Virginia

University of Charleston A,B
Wheeling Jesuit College B

Wisconsin

Madison Area Technical College A
Mid-State Technical College A
Northeast Wisconsin Technical
College A

Respiratory therapy technology

Alabama

Alabama Southern Community
College A
Chattahoochee Valley Community
College A
Enterprise State Junior College A
Faulkner University A
Gadsden State Community
College A
James H. Faulkner State
Community College A
Jefferson State Community
College A
John C. Calhoun State Community
College A
Lawson State Community
College A
Livingston University A
Lurleen B. Wallace State Junior
College A
Northeast Alabama State Junior
College A
Shelton State Community
College A
Shoals Community College A
Southern Union State Junior
College A
University of Alabama in
Birmingham C
University of South Alabama B
Walker College A
Wallace State Community College
at Hanceville A

Arizona

Pima Community College C,A

Arkansas

University of Arkansas for Medical
Sciences C,A
University of Central Arkansas B
University of the Ozarks B

California

California College for Health
Sciences A
College of the Desert A
Compton Community College A
Crafton Hills College C,A
East Los Angeles College C,A
El Camino College C,A
Foothill College A
Fresno City College A
Grossmont Community College C,A
Imperial Valley College C
Long Beach City College A
Los Angeles Valley College C,A
Modesto Junior College A
Mount San Antonio College C,A
Napa Valley College A
Ohlone College A
Orange Coast College C,A
Rio Hondo College A
Santa Monica College A
Santa Rosa Junior College C,A
Skyline College C
Victor Valley College C,A

Colorado

Community College of Denver A
Front Range Community College A
Pueblo Community College A

Connecticut

Manchester Community College A
Mattatuck Community College C
Norwalk Community College A

Quinnipiac College C,B
Sacred Heart University A
University of Bridgeport B

Delaware

Delaware Technical and
Community College: Stanton/
Wilmington Campus A

District of Columbia

University of the District of
Columbia A

Florida

Brevard Community College A
Broward Community College A
Daytona Beach Community
College A
Edison Community College A
Florida Agricultural and Mechanical
University B
Florida Community College at
Jacksonville A
Gulf Coast Community College A
Indian River Community College A
Manatee Community College A
Miami-Dade Community College
C,A
Palm Beach Community College A
Pensacola Junior College C,A
St. Petersburg Junior College A
Santa Fe Community College A
Seminole Community College A
Tallahassee Community College A
Valencia Community College A

Georgia

Armstrong State College A
Athens Area Technical Institute
C,A
Augusta Technical Institute C
Brewton-Parker College A
Columbus College A
DeKalb College A
Gainesville College A
Georgia State University B

Hawaii

University of Hawaii: Kapiolani
Community College C

Idaho

Boise State University C,A,B
North Idaho College A

Illinois

Belleville Area College C
Black Hawk College C,A
City Colleges of Chicago
Malcolm X College A
Olive-Harvey College C
College of DuPage C,A
Illinois Central College C,A
Lincoln Land Community
College A
Moraine Valley Community
College A
National-Louis University B
Parkland College A
Rock Valley College A
Shawnee Community College A
Southern Illinois University at
Carbondale A
Triton College C,A

Indiana

Ball State University A
Indiana University Northwest A
Indiana University—Purdue
University at Indianapolis A

Indiana Vocational Technical
College
Central Indiana A
Lafayette C
Northeast C,A
Northwest C,A
Marian College A
University of Southern Indiana A
Vincennes University A

Iowa

Des Moines Area Community
College A
Hawkeye Institute of Technology C
Kirkwood Community College A
Northeast Iowa Community
College C
Scott Community College A

Kansas

Colby Community College A
Johnson County Community
College C,A
Kansas City Kansas Community
College A
Seward County Community College
C,A
Southwestern College B
Washburn University of Topeka A
Wichita State University A

Kentucky

Jefferson Community College A
Lexington Community College A
Madisonville Community College A
Morehead State University A
University of Louisville A,B

Louisiana

Bossier Parish Community
College A
Louisiana State University
Eunice A
Medical Center B
Nicholls State University A
Our Lady of Holy Cross College B
Southeastern Louisiana
University A
Southern University in
Shreveport A

Maine

Kennebec Valley Technical
College C
Southern Maine Technical
College A

Maryland

Allegany Community College A
Columbia Union College A
Essex Community College A
New Community College of
Baltimore C,A
Prince George's Community
College A

Massachusetts

Berkshire Community College A
Massasoit Community College A
Northern Essex Community College
C,A
Quinsigamond Community
College A
Springfield Technical Community
College A

Michigan

Charles Stewart Mott Community
College A
Delta College A
Henry Ford Community College A

Kalamazoo Valley Community
College *A*
Lansing Community College *A*
Macomb Community College *A*
Marygrove College *A*
Muskegon Community College *A*
Oakland Community College *A*

Minnesota

Rochester Community College *A*
St. Mary's Campus of the College of
St. Catherine *A*

Mississippi

Hinds Community College *A*
Mississippi College *B*
Mississippi Gulf Coast Community
College: Jackson County
Campus *C*
Northeast Mississippi Community
College *C,A*

Missouri

Avila College *B*
Penn Valley Community College *A*
St. Louis Community College at
Forest Park *A*
Southwest Missouri State
University *B*
State Fair Community College *C*
University of Missouri: Columbia *B*

Nebraska

Metropolitan Community College
C,A
Midland Lutheran College *A,B*
Nebraska Methodist College of
Nursing and Allied Health *A*
Southeast Community College:
Lincoln Campus *A*
University of Nebraska—Kearney *B*

Nevada

Community College of Southern
Nevada *A*

New Jersey

Bergen Community College *A*
Brookdale Community College *A*
Camden County College *A*
Gloucester County College *C,A*
Passaic County Community
College *C*
Thomas Edison State College *B*
Union County College *A*
University of Medicine and
Dentistry of New Jersey: School
of Health Related Professions *C*

New Mexico

Albuquerque Technical-Vocational
Institute *C,A*
University of New Mexico *C,A*

New York

City University of New York:
Borough of Manhattan
Community College *A*
Genesee Community College *A*
Hudson Valley Community
College *A*
Mohawk Valley Community
College *A*
Molloy College *B*
Nassau Community College *A*
Onondaga Community College *C,A*
Pace University *B*
Rockland Community College *A*
Westchester Community College *A*

North Carolina

Carteret Community College *A*
Catawba Valley Community
College *A*
Central Piedmont Community
College *A*
Durham Technical Community
College *C,A*
Edgecombe Community College
C,A
Fayetteville Technical Community
College *A*
Forsyth Technical Community
College *A*
Pitt Community College *A*
Robeson Community College *A*
Sandhills Community College *A*
Southwestern Community
College *A*
Stanly Community College *A*

North Dakota

University of Mary *A,B*

Ohio

Bowling Green State University:
Firelands College *A*
Cincinnati Technical College *A*
Columbus State Community College
C,A
Cuyahoga Community College
Metropolitan Campus *A*
Western Campus *A*
Jefferson Technical College *A*
Kettering College of Medical
Arts *A*
Lakeland Community College *A*
North Central Technical College *A*
Ohio State University: Columbus
Campus *B*
Shawnee State University *A*
Stark Technical College *C,A*
University of Akron *A*
University of Toledo *A*
Youngstown State University *A*

Oklahoma

Rose State College *A*
Tulsa Junior College *A*

Oregon

Lane Community College *A*
Mount Hood Community
College *A*
Rogue Community College *C*

Pennsylvania

Community College of
Philadelphia *A*
Delaware County Community
College *A*
Gwynedd-Mercy College *C,A*
Harrisburg Area Community
College *A*
La Roche College *B*
Lehigh County Community College
C,A
Luzerne County Community
College *C,A*
Mansfield University of
Pennsylvania *A*
Point Park College *A*
Reading Area Community
College *A*
Thiel College *C,B*
West Chester University of
Pennsylvania *A*

Puerto Rico

Universidad Adventista de las
Antillas *A*
Universidad Metropolitana *A,B*

South Carolina

Florence-Darlington Technical
College *C,A*
Greenville Technical College *A*
Midlands Technical College *C,A*
Trident Technical College *A*

South Dakota

Dakota State University *A,B*

Tennessee

Chattanooga State Technical
Community College *C,A*
Columbia State Community
College *A*
Dyersburg State Community
College *A*
East Tennessee State University
C,A
Jackson State Community
College *A*
Motlow State Community
College *A*
Roane State Community College *A*

Texas

Alvin Community College *C,A*
Amarillo College *A*
Angelina College *A*
Collin County Community College
District *C,A*
Del Mar College *A*
El Centro College *C,A*
El Paso Community College *C,A*
Houston Community College *C*
Howard College *C*
Lamar University—Beaumont *A*
McLennan Community College *C,A*
Midland College *A*
North Harris Montgomery
Community College District *C,A*
Odessa College *C,A*
St. Philip's College *C*
San Jacinto College: Central
Campus *A*
South Plains College *C,A*
Southwest Texas State University *A*
Tarrant County Junior College *A*
Temple Junior College *A*
Texas Southmost College *A*
University of Texas Health Science
Center at Houston *B*
Victoria College *A*

Utah

Weber State University *A,B*

Vermont

Champlain College *A*

Virginia

Central Virginia Community
College *C*
College of Health Sciences *A*
Northern Virginia Community
College *C,A*
Southwest Virginia Community
College *C*

Washington

Seattle Central Community
College *A*
Spokane Community College *A*
Tacoma Community College *A*
Walla Walla Community College *A*

West Virginia

College of West Virginia *A*
University of Charleston *A,B*
West Virginia Northern Community
College *A*
Wheeling Jesuit College *B*

Wisconsin

Madison Area Technical College *A*
Mid-State Technical College *A*
Western Wisconsin Technical
College *A*

Wyoming

Western Wyoming Community
College *A*

Retailing

Alabama

Bessemer State Technical College *A*
Gadsden State Community
College *A*
Jefferson State Community
College *A*
John C. Calhoun State Community
College *A*
University of Alabama *B*

California

California State University: Los
Angeles *B*
Chabot College *A*
College of the Desert *A*
Fashion Institute of Design and
Merchandising *A*
Golden West College *C,A*
Grossmont Community College *C,A*
MiraCosta College *C,A*
Pasadena City College *A*
Phillips Junior College: Fresno
Campus *C,A*
Saddleback College *C,A*
Santa Clara University *B*
Santa Rosa Junior College *C,A*
Southwestern College *A*

Colorado

Arapahoe Community College *C,A*

Connecticut

Briarwood College *A*
Quinnipiac College *B,M*
University of Bridgeport *A,B*

Florida

Florida Community College at
Jacksonville *A*
Indian River Community College *A*
International Fine Arts College *A*
Palm Beach Community College *A*
Webber College *B*

Georgia

Athens Area Technical Institute
C,A
Georgia Southern University *B*
Macon College *A*

Hawaii

University of Hawaii: Kapiolani
Community College *C,A*

Idaho

College of Southern Idaho *C*

Illinois

Black Hawk College: East
Campus *C*
City Colleges of Chicago: Chicago
City-Wide College *C,A*
College of DuPage *C,A*
College of Lake County *C,A*
Elgin Community College *C,A*
John A. Logan College *C*
Joliet Junior College *C*

Lincoln Land Community
College *A*
MacCormac Junior College *A*
Oakton Community College *A*
Richland Community College *A*
Robert Morris College: Chicago
C,A
Rock Valley College *A*
Southern Illinois University at
Carbondale *B*
Triton College *C,A*
Waubonsee Community College
C,A

Indiana

Ball State University *B*
International Business College *C,A*
Purdue University *B,M,D*
Vincennes University *A*

Iowa

Clinton Community College *A*
Des Moines Area Community
College *C,A*
Iowa Central Community College *A*
Iowa Western Community College
C,A
Kirkwood Community College *A*
North Iowa Area Community
College *A*

Kansas

Barton County Community
College *A*
Coffeyville Community College *A*
Hutchinson Community College *A*
Pittsburg State University *B*

Kentucky

Madisonville Community College *A*
Western Kentucky University *A*

Maine

Thomas College *A,B*
Westbrook College *B*

Maryland

Allegany Community College *C,A*
Charles County Community
College *C*
Harford Community College *C,A*
Howard Community College *A*
Montgomery College: Germantown
Campus *C,A*

Massachusetts

Aquinas College at Milton *A*
Bay Path College *A*
Bay State College *A*
Becker College: Worcester
Campus *A*
Bristol Community College *A*
Cape Cod Community College *A*
Dean Junior College *A*
Endicott College *A,B*
Holyoke Community College *A*
Lasell College *A,B*
Massachusetts Bay Community
College *A*
Middlesex Community College *A*
Mount Ida College *A,B*
Northern Essex Community
College *A*
Quincy College *C,A*
Quinsigamond Community
College *A*

Michigan

Cleary College *A*
Davenport College of Business *A*
Ferris State University *B*
Henry Ford Community College *A*

Lansing Community College *A*
Michigan State University *B*
Western Michigan University *B*

Minnesota

Alexandria Technical College *C*
Itasca Community College:
Arrowhead Region *A*
Willmar Technical College *C*

Missouri

East Central College *C,A*
Fontbonne College *B*
Jefferson College *A*
Missouri Western State College *A*

Nebraska

Metropolitan Community College *C*
Peru State College *B*

New Hampshire

Hesser College *A*
New Hampshire College *B*

New Jersey

Atlantic Community College *A*
Bergen Community College *A*
Bloomfield College *C,B*
Camden County College *A*
County College of Morris *A*
Gloucester County College *A*
Passaic County Community College
C,A
Thomas Edison State College *A,B*

New Mexico

Clovis Community College *A*
Dona Ana Branch Community
College of New Mexico State
University *C*
New Mexico State University *C,B*

New York

Adirondack Community College *A*
Central City Business Institute *A*
City University of New York:
Baruch College *B*
Community College of the Finger
Lakes *C*
Dutchess Community College *A*
Erie Community College: City
Campus *A*
Five Towns College *A*
Genesee Community College *A*
Hilbert College *A*
Iona College *A*
Jamestown Community College *A*
Jefferson Community College *C,A*
Laboratory Institute of
Merchandising *A,B*
Mohawk Valley Community College
C,A
Nassau Community College *A*
Niagara County Community
College *A*
Orange County Community
College *A*
Pace University
College of White Plains *B*
New York *B*
Pleasantville/Briarcliff *B*
Sage Junior College of Albany, A
Division of Russell Sage
College *A*
State University of New York
College of Technology at
Alfred *A*
College of Technology at
Canton *A*
Suffolk County Community College
Selden *A*
Western Campus *A*

Sullivan County Community
College *A*
Syracuse University *B*
Tompkins-Cortland Community
College *A*
Ulster County Community
College *A*
Utica School of Commerce *A*
Villa Maria College of Buffalo *A*
Westchester Community College *A*

North Carolina

Western Piedmont Community
College *C*

North Dakota

University of North Dakota
Grand Forks *B*
Lake Region *C,A*

Ohio

Bradford School *C,A*
Clark State Community College *C*
Columbus State Community
College *A*
Jefferson Technical College *A*
Miami University: Oxford
Campus *B*
Miami-Jacobs College *A*
Northwest Technical College *A*
Northwestern College *C*
Ohio Valley Business College *C*
Sinclair Community College *A*
University of Akron *A*
University of Cincinnati: Access
Colleges *A*
University of Toledo *A*
Youngstown State University *B*

Oklahoma

Southwestern Oklahoma State
University *B*
University of Central Oklahoma *B*
University of Science and Arts of
Oklahoma *B*

Oregon

Bassist College *A,B*
Lane Community College *C*
Mount Hood Community
College *A*
Portland Community College *C*

Pennsylvania

Bucks County Community
College *A*
Butler County Community College
C,A
Cedar Crest College *C*
Central Pennsylvania Business
School *A*
Community College of Philadelphia
C,A
Delaware County Community
College *A*
Drexel University *B*
Harcum Junior College *A*
Harrisburg Area Community
College *A*
Lackawanna Junior College *A*
Lehigh County Community
College *C*
Peirce Junior College *A*
Pennsylvania College of
Technology *A*
Philadelphia College of Textiles and
Science *B*
Seton Hill College *B*
Tracey-Warner School *A*
Westmoreland County Community
College *A*
York College of Pennsylvania *A*

Rhode Island

Community College of Rhode
Island *A*
Johnson & Wales University *A,B*

South Carolina

Aiken Technical College *C*
Technical College of the
Lowcountry *C*
University of South Carolina *B*

Texas

Amarillo College *A*
Austin Community College *A*
Lamar University—Beaumont *B*
Laredo Junior College *A*
Texas Southmost College *A*

Utah

Brigham Young University *B*
Weber State University *A,B*

Vermont

Champlain College *A*
Green Mountain College *B*

Virginia

Averett College *B*
Marymount University *B*

Washington

Edmonds Community College *A*
Pierce College *C*
Shoreline Community College *A*
Spokane Falls Community
College *A*
Walla Walla Community College *A*

West Virginia

Fairmont State College *A*
Marshall University *A,B*

Wisconsin

Marian College of Fond du Lac *B*
Mid-State Technical College *A*
Western Wisconsin Technical
College *A*

Wyoming

Casper College *C,A*

Rhetoric

Arizona

Northern Arizona University *M*

California

California State University: Long
Beach *B*
Chapman University *M*
University of California
Berkeley *B,M,D*
Davis *B,M*

Florida

Barry University *M*

Illinois

University of Illinois at Urbana-
Champaign *B*

Indiana

Purdue University *D*

Maine

Bates College *B*

Maryland
Mount St. Mary's College *B*

New Jersey
Rutgers—The State University of
New Jersey *M,D*

New York
State University of New York
Albany *B,M*
Binghamton *B*

North Carolina
Brevard College *A*

Ohio
Kent State University *B,M,D*
Ohio State University: Columbus
Campus *M,D*

Pennsylvania
Allegheny College *B*
Carnegie Mellon University *M*

Texas
East Texas State University *D*
Texas Woman's University *D*
University of Texas at El Paso *M*

Vermont
Marlboro College *B*

Robotics

California
Cerritos Community College *A*
Coastline Community College *A*
Modesto Junior College *A*
Orange Coast College *C*
Pacific Union College *B*
San Diego City College *A*
University of California: Santa
Barbara *B,M*
West Coast University *B*

Colorado
Denver Institute of Technology *A*
Denver Technical College *A*
Red Rocks Community College *C*

Connecticut
Waterbury State Technical
College *A*

Delaware
Delaware Technical and
Community College: Stanton/
Wilmington Campus *A*

Florida
Gulf Coast Community College *A*
Pensacola Junior College *A*
Valencia Community College *A*

Illinois
Illinois Central College *C,A*
Triton College *A*
Waubonsee Community College
C,A

Indiana
Indiana Vocational Technical
College
Central Indiana *A*
Columbus *A*
Eastcentral *C,A*
Kokomo *A*
Lafayette *A*
Northcentral *A*
Northeast *A*
Northwest *C,A*
Southcentral *C,A*
Southeast *A*
Southwest *A*
Wabash Valley *A*
Whitewater *A*
Purdue University
North Central Campus *A*
West Lafayette *B,M,D*
Taylor University *B*
Vincennes University *A*

Iowa
Des Moines Area Community
College *A*
Hawkeye Institute of Technology *A*
Indian Hills Community College *A*
North Iowa Area Community
College *A*
Southeastern Community College:
North Campus *A*

Kansas
Kansas City Kansas Community
College *A*

Kentucky
Eastern Kentucky University *A,B*
Louisville Technical Institute *A*

Massachusetts
Massachusetts Institute of
Technology *M,D,W*
Northern Essex Community
College *C*

Michigan
Charles Stewart Mott Community
College *A*
Eastern Michigan University *B*
Henry Ford Community College *A*
Jackson Community College *A*
Kellogg Community College *A*
Lake Superior State University *B*
Lansing Community College *A*
Macomb Community College *A*
Oakland Community College *C,A*
St. Clair County Community
College *A*

Minnesota
Alexandria Technical College *C*

Mississippi
Holmes Community College *A*
Southwest Mississippi Community
College *A*

Missouri
Jefferson College *A*

Nebraska
Peru State College *B*
Southeast Community College:
Milford Campus *A*

New Hampshire
New Hampshire Technical College:
Nashua *A*

New Jersey
Atlantic Community College *A*
Brookdale Community College *A*
Stevens Institute of Technology
B,M,D

New York
Bramson ORT Technical Institute
C,A
Erie Community College: City
Campus *A*
Herkimer County Community
College *A*
State University of New York
College at Plattsburgh *B*

North Carolina
Catawba Valley Community
College *A*
Wake Technical Community
College *A*

Ohio
Lorain County Community
College *A*
Sinclair Community College *A*
Southern State Community
College *A*
Terra Technical College *A*
University of Cincinnati: Access
Colleges *A*

Oklahoma
Oklahoma State University
Technical Branch: Okmulgee *A*
Tulsa Junior College *A*

Oregon
Central Oregon Community
College *A*
Mount Hood Community
College *A*

Pennsylvania
California University of
Pennsylvania *A*
Carnegie Mellon University
B,M,D,W
CHI Institute *A*
Community College of Beaver
County *A*
Delaware County Community
College *A*
Gannon University *A*
Lehigh County Community
College *C*
Lehigh University *M*
Luzerne County Community
College *A*
Pennsylvania Institute of
Technology *A*
University of Pennsylvania *B*
Westmoreland County Community
College *A*

South Dakota
Mitchell Vocational Technical
Institute *C,A*

Tennessee
Chattanooga State Technical
Community College *A*
Motlow State Community
College *C*

Texas
Brookhaven College *A*
Central Texas College *A*
Lamar University—Beaumont *A*
Richland College *C,A*

Texas State Technical College
Harlingen *A*
Sweetwater *A*
University of Texas at Arlington *M*

Washington
Skagit Valley College *A*
Spokane Community College *A*

Wisconsin
Chippewa Valley Technical
College *A*
University of Wisconsin: Oshkosh *B*

Rural sociology

Alabama
Auburn University *B,M*

Arkansas
University of Arkansas *M*

Florida
New College of the University of
South Florida *B*

Kansas
Kansas State University *M*

Louisiana
Louisiana State University and
Agricultural and Mechanical
College *B*

Minnesota
Northland Community College *A*

Missouri
University of Missouri: Columbia
B,M,D

New York
Cornell University *B,M*
Sarah Lawrence College *B*

North Carolina
North Carolina State University *B*

Ohio
Ohio State University: Columbus
Campus *B,M,D*

Pennsylvania
Penn State University Park Campus
M,D

South Dakota
South Dakota State University *B,M*

Texas
Texas A&M University *M*

Washington
Eastern Washington University *B*

Wisconsin
University of Wisconsin: Madison
B,M

Russian

Alabama
University of Alabama *B*
University of South Alabama *B*

Arizona

Arizona State University *B*
Glendale Community College *A*
University of Arizona *B,M*

California

California State University:
    Fresno *B*
Chabot College *A*
El Camino College *A*
Monterey Institute of International
    Studies *B,M*
Pomona College *B*
San Diego City College *A*
San Diego State University *B,M*
San Francisco State University *B,M*
Stanford University *M*
University of California
    Berkeley *B,M,D*
    Davis *B,M*
    Irvine *B*
    Los Angeles *B*
    Riverside *B*
    San Diego *B*
    Santa Barbara *B*
    Santa Cruz *B*
University of Southern California *B*

Colorado

University of Colorado at
    Boulder *B*
University of Denver *B*

Connecticut

Connecticut College *B*
Trinity College *B*
University of Connecticut *B*
Wesleyan University *B*
Yale University *B*

Delaware

University of Delaware *B*

District of Columbia

American University *B,M*
Gallaudet University *B*
George Washington University *B*
Georgetown University *B*
Howard University *B,M*

Florida

Eckerd College *B*
Florida State University *B*
Miami-Dade Community College *A*
New College of the University of
    South Florida *B*
University of Florida *B*
University of South Florida *B*

Georgia

Emory University *B*

Hawaii

University of Hawaii at Manoa *B*

Idaho

Ricks College *A*

Illinois

Black Hawk College *A*
City Colleges of Chicago: Chicago
    City-Wide College *C*
Knox College *B*
Northern Illinois University *B,M*
Northwestern University *B*
Principia College *B*
Southern Illinois University at
    Carbondale *B*
University of Chicago *B,M,D*
University of Illinois
    Chicago *B*
    Urbana-Champaign *B,M,D*

Indiana

Grace College *B*
Indiana State University *B*
Indiana University Bloomington
    B,M,D
Purdue University *B,M*
University of Notre Dame *B,M*

Iowa

Cornell College *B*
Grinnell College *B*
Iowa State University *B*
St. Ambrose University *B*
University of Iowa *B,M*

Kansas

Kansas State University *B*
University of Kansas *B,M,D*

Kentucky

University of Kentucky *B*
University of Louisville *B*

Louisiana

Loyola University *B*
Tulane University *B*

Maine

Bates College *B*
Bowdoin College *B*

Maryland

Goucher College *B*
University of Maryland
    Baltimore County *B*
    College Park *B*

Massachusetts

Amherst College *B*
Boston College *B,M*
Boston University *B*
Brandeis University *B*
College of the Holy Cross *B*
Harvard and Radcliffe Colleges *B*
Harvard University *D*
Massachusetts Institute of
    Technology *B*
Mount Holyoke College *B*
Northeastern University *B*
Simon's Rock College of Bard *B*
Smith College *B*
Tufts University *B*
University of Massachusetts
    Amherst *B*
    Boston *B*
Wellesley College *B*
Wheaton College *B*
Williams College *B*

Michigan

Michigan State University *B,M,D*
University of Michigan *B,M,D*
Wayne State University *B,M*

Minnesota

Carleton College *B*
College of St. Catherine: St.
    Catherine Campus *B*
Gustavus Adolphus College *B*
Macalester College *B*
St. Olaf College *B*
University of Minnesota: Twin
    Cities *B*
University of St. Thomas *B*

Missouri

St. Louis University *B*
University of Missouri: Columbia *B*
Washington University *B*

Montana

University of Montana *B*

Nebraska

University of Nebraska—Lincoln *B*

New Hampshire

Dartmouth College *B*
St. Anselm College *C*
University of New Hampshire *B*

New Jersey

Drew University *B*
Princeton University *B,M*
Rider College *B*
Rutgers—The State University of
    New Jersey
    Douglass College *B*
    Livingston College *B*
    Newark College of Arts and
        Sciences *B*
    Rutgers College *B*
    University College New
        Brunswick *B*

New Mexico

New Mexico State University *B*

New York

Bard College *B*
Barnard College *B*
City University of New York
    Brooklyn College *B*
    City College *B*
    Hunter College *B*
    Lehman College *B*
    Queens College *B*
Colgate University *B*
Columbia University
    Columbia College *B*
    New York *M,D*
    School of General Studies *B*
Cornell University *B,M,D*
Fordham University *B,M*
Hamilton College *B*
Hobart College *B*
Hofstra University *B*
Marist College *B*
New York University *B,M*
Sarah Lawrence College *B*
State University of New York
    Albany *B,M*
    Buffalo *B*
    Stony Brook *B*
    Oswego *B*
Syracuse University *B,M*
United States Military Academy *B*
University of Rochester *B*
Vassar College *B*
Wells College *B*
William Smith College *B*

North Carolina

Duke University *B,M*
University of North Carolina at
    Chapel Hill *B,M,D*
Wake Forest University *B*

North Dakota

University of North Dakota *B*

Ohio

Bowling Green State University *B*
Kent State University *B*
Kenyon College *B*
Miami University: Oxford
    Campus *B*
Oberlin College *B*
Ohio State University: Columbus
    Campus *B,M,D*
Ohio University *B*
Wittenberg University *B*

Montana — *(see column above)*

Youngstown State University *B*

Oklahoma

Oklahoma State University *B*
Tulsa Junior College *A*
University of Oklahoma *B*

Oregon

Northwest Christian College *B*
Portland Community College *A*
Portland State University *B*
Reed College *B*
University of Oregon
    Eugene *B,M*
    Robert Donald Clark Honors
        College *B*

Pennsylvania

Allegheny College *B*
Bryn Mawr College *B,M,D*
Bucknell University *B*
California University of
    Pennsylvania *B*
Dickinson College *B*
Edinboro University of
    Pennsylvania *B*
Haverford College *B*
Immaculata College *A*
Juniata College *B*
Kutztown University of
    Pennsylvania *B,M*
La Salle University *B*
Lafayette College *B*
Millersville University of
    Pennsylvania *B*
Penn State University Park
    Campus *B*
Swarthmore College *B*
Temple University *B*
University of Pennsylvania *B,M,D*
University of Pittsburgh *B*
West Chester University of
    Pennsylvania *B*

Rhode Island

Brown University *B,M,D*
University of Rhode Island *B*

Tennessee

University of the South *B*
University of Tennessee:
    Knoxville *B*
Vanderbilt University *B*

Texas

Baylor University *B*
Rice University *B*
Southern Methodist University *B*
Trinity University *B*
University of Texas
    Arlington *B*
    Austin *B*

Utah

Brigham Young University *B,M*
University of Utah *B*

Vermont

Marlboro College *B*
Middlebury College *B*
Norwich University *B,M*
University of Vermont *B*

Virginia

Ferrum College *B*
Old Dominion University *B*
University of Richmond *W*

Washington

Evergreen State College *B*
Seattle Pacific University *B*

Spokane Falls Community
College *A*
University of Washington *B,M,D*
Western Washington University *B*

West Virginia

West Virginia University *B,M*

Wisconsin

Beloit College *B*
Lawrence University *B*
University of Wisconsin
Madison *B,M,D*
Milwaukee *B*

Wyoming

University of Wyoming *B*

Canada

McGill University *B,M,D*

Russian and Slavic studies

Alabama

Auburn University *B*
University of Alabama
Huntsville *B*
Tuscaloosa *B*

Alaska

University of Alaska Fairbanks *B*

Arizona

University of Arizona *B*

California

California State University
Fullerton *B*
Long Beach *C*
Naval Postgraduate School *M*
San Diego State University *B*
University of California
Berkeley *B,M,D*
Los Angeles *B,M,D*
Riverside *B*
Santa Cruz *B*
University of Southern California
B,M,D

Colorado

Colorado College *B*
University of Denver *B*

Connecticut

Connecticut College *B*
Trinity College *B*
University of Connecticut *B*
Wesleyan University *B*
Yale University *B,M*

District of Columbia

American University *B*
George Washington University *B,M*
Georgetown University *B,M*

Florida

Eckerd College *B*
Florida State University *B,M*
New College of the University of
South Florida *B*
Rollins College *B*
Stetson University *B*

Georgia

Emory University *B*

Illinois

Illinois State University *B*
Knox College *B*
Northwestern University *B,M,D*
Principia College *B*
University of Chicago *B,M,D*
University of Illinois
Chicago *M*
Urbana-Champaign *B*

Indiana

DePauw University *B*
Indiana University Bloomington
C,B,M,D
University of Notre Dame *B*

Iowa

Cornell College *B*
University of Northern Iowa *B*

Kansas

University of Kansas *B,M*

Kentucky

University of Kentucky *B*
University of Louisville *B*

Louisiana

Louisiana State University and
Agricultural and Mechanical
College *B*
Tulane University *B*

Maine

Colby College *B*
University of Maine at Presque
Isle *C*

Maryland

Goucher College *B*
University of Maryland: College
Park *B*

Massachusetts

Boston College *B,M*
Boston University *B*
Brandeis University *B*
Hampshire College *B*
Harvard and Radcliffe Colleges *B*
Harvard University *M*
Massachusetts Institute of
Technology *B*
Mount Holyoke College *B*
Tufts University *B,M*
Wellesley College *B*
Wheaton College *B*
Williams College *B*

Michigan

Eastern Michigan University *B*
Grand Valley State University *B*
University of Michigan *B,M*

Minnesota

Augsburg College *B*
Carleton College *B*
College of St. Catherine: St.
Catherine Campus *B*
Gustavus Adolphus College *B*
Hamline University *B*
Macalester College *B*
St. Olaf College *B*
University of Minnesota: Twin
Cities *B,M*

Missouri

University of Missouri: Columbia *B*

New Hampshire

Dartmouth College *B*
St. Anselm College *C*

New Jersey

Drew University *B*
Princeton University *B,M*
Rutgers—The State University of
New Jersey
Douglass College *B*
Livingston College *B*
Newark College of Arts and
Sciences *B*
Rutgers College *B*
University College New
Brunswick *B*

New Mexico

New Mexico State University *B*
University of New Mexico *B*

New York

Bard College *B*
Barnard College *B*
City University of New York
Brooklyn College *B*
City College *B*
Hunter College *M*
Lehman College *B*
Colgate University *B*
Columbia University
Columbia College *B*
New York *M,D*
School of General Studies *B*
Cornell University *B,M,D*
Fordham University *B*
Hamilton College *B*
Hobart College *B*
Long Island University: C. W. Post
Campus *B*
Manhattanville College *B*
New York University *B*
Sarah Lawrence College *B*
State University of New York at
Albany *B,M*
Syracuse University *B*
United States Military Academy *B*
Wells College *B*
William Smith College *B*

North Carolina

University of North Carolina
Chapel Hill *B,M,D*
Greensboro *B*

North Dakota

University of North Dakota *B*

Ohio

Bowling Green State University *B*
College of Wooster *B*
Kent State University *B*
Kenyon College *B*
Oberlin College *B*
Ohio State University: Columbus
Campus *B,M,D*
Wittenberg University *B*

Oklahoma

Oklahoma State University *B*
University of Oklahoma *B*

Oregon

Willamette University *B*

Pennsylvania

Bryn Mawr College *B,M,D*
California University of
Pennsylvania *B*
Dickinson College *B*
Kutztown University of
Pennsylvania *B*
Lehigh University *B*
Muhlenberg College *B*
Penn State University Park
Campus *C*

University of Pennsylvania *B,M,D*

Rhode Island

Brown University *B,M,D*

Tennessee

Rhodes College *B*
University of the South *B*
University of Tennessee:
Knoxville *B*
Vanderbilt University *B*

Texas

Baylor University *B*
Rice University *B*
Southern Methodist University *B*

Vermont

Marlboro College *B*
Middlebury College *B*
University of Vermont *B*

Virginia

George Mason University *B*
Randolph-Macon Woman's
College *B*
University of Richmond *B*
Washington and Lee University *B*

Washington

Evergreen State College *B*
University of Washington *B,M*

West Virginia

West Virginia University *B*

Wisconsin

Lawrence University *B*

Canada

McGill University *B,M,D*

Sanitation technology

California

Humboldt State University *M*
University of Southern California *M*

Minnesota

Vermilion Community College *A*

Scandinavian languages

California

University of California
Berkeley *B,M,D*
Los Angeles *B,M*

Illinois

Augustana College *B*
North Park College and Theological
Seminary *B*
University of Chicago *B,M,D*

Iowa

Luther College *B*

Massachusetts

Harvard and Radcliffe Colleges *B*

Michigan

Suomi College *A*
University of Michigan *B*

Minnesota

Augsburg College *B*
Concordia College: Moorhead *B*
Gustavus Adolphus College *B*
Mankato State University *B*
St. Olaf College *B*
University of Minnesota: Twin
Cities *B*

Missouri

Washington University *B,M*

New York

Columbia University: Columbia
College *B*

North Dakota

University of North Dakota *B*

Pennsylvania

University of Pennsylvania *B*

Texas

University of Texas at Austin *B*

Utah

Brigham Young University *M*

Washington

Pacific Lutheran University *B*
University of Washington *B,M,D*

Wisconsin

University of Wisconsin: Madison
B,M,D

Scandinavian studies

Illinois

Augustana College *B*

Iowa

Luther College *B*

Massachusetts

Hampshire College *B*
Harvard and Radcliffe Colleges *B*

Michigan

University of Michigan *B*

Minnesota

Augsburg College *B*
Concordia College: Moorhead *B*
Gustavus Adolphus College *B*
Mankato State University *B*
University of Minnesota: Twin
Cities *M,D*

Washington

Pacific Lutheran University *B*

Wisconsin

University of Wisconsin: Madison
B,M,D

School psychology

Alabama

Alabama Agricultural and
Mechanical University *B,M*
Auburn University *M*
Troy State University *B*
University of Alabama
Birmingham *M*
Tuscaloosa *M,D*

University of South Alabama *M*

Arizona

Arizona State University *M,D*
Northern Arizona University *M,D*
Prescott College *B*
University of Arizona *M,D*

Arkansas

University of Central Arkansas *B,M*

California

California Lutheran University *M*
California State University
Fresno *M*
Hayward *M*
Long Beach *M*
Los Angeles *M*
Northridge *M*
Chapman University *M*
Fresno Pacific College *M*
Loyola Marymount University *M*
San Jose State University *M*
Stanford University *D*
University of California
Davis *M*
Riverside *M,D*
Santa Barbara *M,D*
University of the Pacific *M,D*
University of San Diego *M*
University of San Francisco *M,D*

Colorado

University of Colorado
Boulder *M,D*
Denver *M*
University of Northern Colorado *D*

Connecticut

Fairfield University *M*
Southern Connecticut State
University *M*
University of Bridgeport *M*
University of Connecticut *D*
University of Hartford *M*

Delaware

University of Delaware *M*

District of Columbia

Gallaudet University *B,W*
Howard University *M,D*

Florida

Florida Agricultural and Mechanical
University *M*
Florida International University *M*
Nova University *M*
University of Central Florida *M*
University of Florida *M,D*
University of Miami *M*
University of North Florida *M*
University of South Florida *M*

Georgia

Fort Valley State College *B*
Georgia Southern University *M*
Georgia State University *D*
University of Georgia *M,D*
Valdosta State College *B,M*

Hawaii

University of Hawaii at Manoa *D*

Idaho

Idaho State University *M*

Illinois

Governors State University *M*
Illinois State University *M,D*
Loyola University of Chicago *M,D*
National-Louis University *M,D*

Northern Illinois University *M,D*
Southern Illinois University at
Carbondale *M,D*
University of Chicago *M,D*

Indiana

Ball State University *M,D*
Butler University *M*
Indiana State University *M*
Indiana University Bloomington
M,D
Indiana University—Purdue
University at Indianapolis *M*
Purdue University *M,D*
St. Francis College *M*
Valparaiso University *M*

Iowa

Iowa State University *M*
University of Iowa *M,D*
University of Northern Iowa *M*

Kansas

Emporia State University *M,W*
Fort Hays State University *M*
Kansas State University *D*
Pittsburg State University *B*
University of Kansas *D*

Kentucky

Eastern Kentucky University *M*
University of Kentucky *M,D*

Louisiana

Louisiana State University in
Shreveport *B,M*
McNeese State University *B*
Nicholls State University *M*
Northeast Louisiana University *M*

Maine

University of New England *M*
University of Southern Maine *M*

Massachusetts

American International College *M*
Boston University *D*
Harvard University *M,D,W*
Northeastern University *D*
Tufts University *M*
University of Massachusetts at
Boston *M*
Westfield State College *M*

Michigan

Andrews University *M,D*
Central Michigan University *M,D*
Eastern Michigan University *M*
Michigan State University *D*
University of Detroit Mercy *M*
University of Michigan *M,D*
Wayne State University *M,D*
Western Michigan University *M*

Minnesota

Bethel College *B*
Moorhead State University *M*
St. Cloud State University *M*
University of Minnesota: Twin
Cities *B,M,D*
Willmar Community College *A*

Mississippi

Delta State University *M*
Jackson State University *B*
Mississippi State University *B,M,D*
University of Mississippi *D*
University of Southern Mississippi
M,D

Missouri

St. Louis University *M,D*
University of Missouri: Columbia
M,D

Nebraska

Chadron State College *M*
University of Nebraska
Kearney *M*
Lincoln *M,D*
Omaha *M*

Nevada

University of Nevada: Las Vegas *M*

New Jersey

Glassboro State College *M*
Kean College of New Jersey *M*
Montclair State College *M*
Rutgers—The State University of
New Jersey *M,D*
Seton Hall University *M*

New Mexico

New Mexico State University *M,D*
University of New Mexico *D*

New York

Alfred University *M*
City University of New York
Brooklyn College *M*
City College *M*
Graduate School and
University Center *D*
Queens College *M*
College of New Rochelle *M*
College of St. Rose *M*
Cornell University *M,D*
Fordham University *M,D*
Hofstra University *M,D*
Long Island University: Brooklyn
Campus *M*
Manhattanville College *M*
New York University *M,D*
Pace University *M,D*
Rochester Institute of
Technology *M*
St. John's University *M*
St. Lawrence University *M*
State University of New York
Albany *D*
Buffalo *M*
College at Plattsburgh *M*
Oswego *M*
Syracuse University *M,D*
Yeshiva University *D*

North Carolina

Campbell University *B*
East Carolina University *M*
Gardner-Webb College *M*
North Carolina State University *M*
University of North Carolina
Chapel Hill *M,D*
Greensboro *M*
Western Carolina University *M*

Ohio

Bowling Green State University *M*
Kent State University *D*
Miami University: Oxford
Campus *M*
Ohio State University: Columbus
Campus *M,D*
Ohio University *M*
Union Institute *D*
University of Cincinnati *M,D*
University of Dayton *M*
University of Toledo *M,D*
Wright State University *M*

Oklahoma

Northeastern State University *B*
Southeastern Oklahoma State
University *M*
University of Central Oklahoma
B,M
University of Oklahoma *M,D*

Oregon

University of Oregon *M,D*

Pennsylvania

Bryn Mawr College *M,D*
Bucknell University *M*
California University of
Pennsylvania *M*
Duquesne University *M*
Edinboro University of
Pennsylvania *M*
Gannon University *M*
Immaculata College *M*
Indiana University of Pennsylvania
M,D
Juniata College *B*
La Salle University *B*
Lehigh University *D*
Marywood College *M*
Penn State University Park Campus
M,D
Temple University *M,D*
University of Pennsylvania *M,D*
University of Pittsburgh *M,D*

Puerto Rico

Pontifical Catholic University of
Puerto Rico *M*

Rhode Island

Rhode Island College *M*
University of Rhode Island *M,D*

South Carolina

The Citadel *M*
University of South Carolina *M,D*
Winthrop University *M*

Tennessee

Austin Peay State University *M*
East Tennessee State University *M*
Memphis State University *M*
Motlow State Community
College *A*
Tennessee State University *D*
Tennessee Technological
University *M*
University of Tennessee
Chattanooga *M*
Knoxville *M,D*
Vanderbilt University *M,D*

Texas

Abilene Christian University *B*
Baylor University *M,D*
East Texas State University *D*
Houston Baptist University *M*
Our Lady of the Lake University of
San Antonio *M*
Sam Houston State University *M*
Southwest Texas State
University *M*
Texas A&M University *M,D*
Texas Tech University *B,M,D*
Texas Woman's University *M,D*
Trinity University *M*
University of Houston: Clear
Lake *M*
University of North Texas *M,D*
University of Texas
El Paso *M*
San Antonio *M*
Tyler *M*
West Texas State University *M*

Utah

Brigham Young University *M,D*
University of Utah *M,D*

Virginia

College of William and Mary *M*
James Madison University *M*
Radford University *M*
University of Virginia *M,D*
Virginia Union University *B*

Washington

Central Washington University *M*
Eastern Washington University *M*
Pacific Lutheran University *B,M*
Seattle University *W*
University of Washington *M,D*
Western Washington University *M*

Wisconsin

Marquette University *M,D*
University of Wisconsin
Eau Claire *M*
La Crosse *M*
Madison *M,D*
Milwaukee *M*
River Falls *M*
Stout *M*
Superior *M*
Whitewater *M*

Wyoming

Eastern Wyoming College *A*

Canada

McGill University *M,D*

Science education

Alabama

Alabama Agricultural and
Mechanical University *B,M*
Alabama State University *B,M*
Auburn University
Auburn *B,M,D*
Montgomery *B,M*
Birmingham-Southern College *B*
Huntingdon College *B*
Jacksonville State University *B,M*
Judson College *B*
Lawson State Community
College *A*
Livingston University *B,M*
Mobile College *B*
Oakwood College *B*
Samford University *B,M*
Spring Hill College *B*
Troy State University at Dothan
B,M
Tuskegee University *B,M*
University of Alabama *B*
University of Montevallo *B,M*
University of North Alabama *B,M*
University of South Alabama *B*

Alaska

University of Alaska
Anchorage *M*
Fairbanks *M*

Arizona

Arizona State University *B,M,D*
Eastern Arizona College *A*
Grand Canyon University *B*

Arkansas

Arkansas College *B*
Arkansas State University *B*
Arkansas Tech University *M*

Harding University *B*
Henderson State University *B,M*
John Brown University *B*
Ouachita Baptist University *B*
University of Arkansas
Fayetteville *B*
Monticello *B*
Pine Bluff *B*
University of Central Arkansas *B,M*
University of the Ozarks *B*
Westark Community College *A*

California

California Baptist College *B*
California Lutheran University *B*
California State University
Bakersfield *B*
Fresno *B*
Fullerton *M*
Christ College Irvine *B*
College of Notre Dame *M*
Fresno Pacific College *B,M*
Loyola Marymount University *M*
Occidental College *M*
University of the Pacific *B*
University of Redlands *B*
University of San Francisco *B*
Westmont College *B*

Colorado

Colorado College *M*
Colorado State University *B*
University of Colorado
Boulder *M*
Colorado Springs *B*
University of Northern Colorado
B,M,D
Western State College of
Colorado *B*

Connecticut

Eastern Connecticut State
University *M*
Sacred Heart University *B,M*
St. Joseph College *B,M*
Southern Connecticut State
University *B,M*
University of Hartford *B*

Delaware

Delaware State College *B,M*
University of Delaware *B*
Wesley College *B*

Florida

Bethune-Cookman College *B*
Florida Agricultural and Mechanical
University *B,M*
Florida Atlantic University *B,M*
Florida Institute of Technology
B,M,D
Florida International University
B,M
Florida State University *B,M,D*
Gulf Coast Community College *A*
Nova University *M*
Palm Beach Community College *A*
Pensacola Junior College *A*
Southeastern College of the
Assemblies of God *B*
Stetson University *B*
University of Central Florida *B,M*
University of Florida *B,M*
University of Miami *M*
University of North Florida *B*
University of South Florida *B,M*
University of Tampa *B*
University of West Florida *B*
Warner Southern College *B*

Georgia

Albany State College *B,M*
Armstrong State College *B,M*
Berry College *B*
Columbus College *B,M*
Georgia College *B,M*
Georgia Southern University *B,M*
Georgia Southwestern College *B,M*
Georgia State University *M,D*
Kennesaw State College *B*
Mercer University *M*
North Georgia College *M*
Piedmont College *B*
Shorter College *B*
Thomas College *A*
University of Georgia *B,M,D*
Valdosta State College *B,M*
Wesleyan College *B*
West Georgia College *B*

Hawaii

Brigham Young University-
Hawaii *B*
Chaminade University of
Honolulu *B*

Idaho

Albertson College *B*
Boise State University *B*
Idaho State University *M*
Northwest Nazarene College *B*

Illinois

Aurora University *B*
Blackburn College *B*
Columbia College *M*
Concordia University *B*
De Paul University *B*
Eastern Illinois University *M*
Elmhurst College *B*
Eureka College *B*
Governors State University *B*
Greenville College *B*
Illinois College *B*
Illinois Wesleyan University *B*
Judson College *B*
MacMurray College *B*
Millikin University *B*
National-Louis University *M*
North Central College *B*
North Park College and Theological
Seminary *B*
Northern Illinois University *M*
Northwestern University *B,M*
Olivet Nazarene University *B,M*
Quincy College *B*
Southern Illinois University
Carbondale *B*
Edwardsville *B*
Trinity Christian College *B*
Trinity College *B*
University of Illinois
Chicago *B*
Urbana-Champaign *B,M*
Wheaton College *B*

Indiana

Anderson University *B*
Ball State University *B,M,D*
Bethel College *B*
Butler University *B*
Calumet College of St. Joseph *B*
Franklin College *B*
Goshen College *B*
Huntington College *B*
Indiana State University *B,M*
Indiana University
Bloomington *B,M,D*
South Bend *B*
Southeast *B*
Indiana University—Purdue
University at Fort Wayne *B*

Indiana Wesleyan University *B*
Manchester College *B,M*
Marian College *B*
Martin University *B*
Oakland City College *B*
Purdue University *B,M,D*
St. Francis College *B*
St. Joseph's College *B*
St. Mary-of-the-Woods College *B*
Taylor University *B*
Tri-State University *B*
University of Evansville *B,M*
University of Indianapolis *B*
University of Southern Indiana *B*
Vincennes University *A*

Iowa

Briar Cliff College *B*
Buena Vista College *B*
Clarke College *B*
Cornell College *B*
Drake University *B,M*
Grand View College *B*
Iowa Lakes Community College *A*
Iowa Wesleyan College *B*
Loras College *B*
Morningside College *B*
Mount Mercy College *B*
Simpson College *B*
Teikyo Marycrest University *B*
Teikyo Westmar University *B*
University of Dubuque *B,M*
University of Iowa *B,M,D*
University of Northern Iowa *B,M*
Upper Iowa University *B*
Wartburg College *B*
William Penn College *B*

Kansas

Baker University *B*
Bethany College *B*
Colby Community College *A*
Emporia State University *B,M*
Friends University *B*
Kansas State University *B,D*
McPherson College *B*
MidAmerica Nazarene College *B*
Pittsburg State University *B*
St. Mary College *B*
Tabor College *B*
University of Kansas *B*
Washburn University of Topeka *B*
Wichita State University *M*

Kentucky

Alice Lloyd College *B*
Asbury College *B*
Berea College *B*
Campbellsville College *B*
Eastern Kentucky University *B*
Georgetown College *B*
Kentucky Christian College *B*
Morehead State University *B*
Murray State University *B*
Pikeville College *B*
Sue Bennett College *A*
Thomas More College *B*
Transylvania University *B*
Union College *B*
University of Kentucky *B*
Western Kentucky University *B,M*

Louisiana

Centenary College of Louisiana *B*
Dillard University *B*
Grambling State University *B*
Louisiana College *B*
Louisiana State University
    Agricultural and Mechanical
      College *B*
    Shreveport *B*
Louisiana Tech University *B,M*

McNeese State University *B,M*
Nicholls State University *B*
Northeast Louisiana University *B*
Northwestern State University *B*
Our Lady of Holy Cross College *B*
Southeastern Louisiana
    University *B*
Southern University and
    Agricultural and Mechanical
    College *B*
Tulane University *M*
University of New Orleans *B,M*
University of Southwestern
    Louisiana *B*
Xavier University of Louisiana *B*

Maine

St. Joseph's College *B*
University of Maine
    Farmington *B*
    Orono *M*
    Presque Isle *B*
University of New England *B*

Maryland

Columbia Union College *B*
Frostburg State University *M*
Montgomery College
    Germantown Campus *A*
    Rockville Campus *A*
    Takoma Park Campus *A*
Morgan State University *B*
Western Maryland College *B*

Massachusetts

American International College *B*
Boston College *B*
Boston University *B,M,W*
Bridgewater State College *M*
Eastern Nazarene College *B,M*
Elms College *B*
Fitchburg State College *B*
Framingham State College *B*
Hampshire College *B*
Lesley College *B*
Merrimack College *B*
Salem State College *M*
Springfield College *B*
Suffolk University *B*
Tufts University *B,M*
University of Massachusetts at
    Lowell *D*
Westfield State College *B*
Worcester Polytechnic Institute *M*

Michigan

Adrian College *B*
Calvin College *B,M*
Central Michigan University *B,M*
Concordia College *B*
Eastern Michigan University *B,M*
Ferris State University *B*
Grand Rapids Baptist College and
    Seminary *B*
Grand Valley State University *B*
Hillsdale College *B*
Lansing Community College *A*
Madonna University *B*
Marygrove College *B*
Michigan State University *B*
Michigan Technological
    University *B*
Northern Michigan University *B,M*
Saginaw Valley State University
    B,M
University of Michigan
    Ann Arbor *M*
    Dearborn *B*
Wayne State University *B,M*
Western Michigan University
    B,M,D

Minnesota

Bemidji State University *B,M*
Bethel College *B*
College of St. Scholastica *B*
Concordia College: Moorhead *B*
Concordia College: St. Paul *B*
Gustavus Adolphus College *B*
Macalester College *B*
Mankato State University *B*
Moorhead State University *B*
Northland Community College *A*
Pillsbury Baptist Bible College *B*
Rainy River Community College *A*
St. Cloud State University *B*
St. Mary's College of Minnesota *B*
St. Olaf College *B*
Southwest State University *B*
University of Minnesota
    Duluth *B*
    Twin Cities *B*
Vermilion Community College *A*
Willmar Community College *A*
Winona State University *B*

Mississippi

Alcorn State University *B,M*
Blue Mountain College *B*
Delta State University *B,M*
Mississippi College *B,M*
Mississippi Gulf Coast Community
    College: Jefferson Davis
    Campus *A*
Mississippi University for Women *B*
Northeast Mississippi Community
    College *A*
Rust College *B*
University of Mississippi *B*
University of Southern Mississippi
    B,M,D

Missouri

Central Missouri State University *B*
College of the Ozarks *B*
Columbia College *B*
Culver-Stockton College *B*
Evangel College *B*
Fontbonne College *B*
Maryville University *B*
Missouri Baptist College *B*
Missouri Valley College *B*
Northeast Missouri State
    University *M*
Northwest Missouri State
    University *B,M*
Park College *B*
Rockhurst College *B*
Southeast Missouri State University
    B,M
Southwest Missouri State
    University *B*
University of Missouri
    Columbia *B,M,D*
    Kansas City *B*
Washington University *B,M*
Webster University *B,M*
Westminster College *B*
William Woods College *B*

Montana

Carroll College *B*
College of Great Falls *B*
Eastern Montana College *B*
Montana State University *B*
Northern Montana College *B*
University of Montana *B*
Western Montana College of the
    University of Montana *B*

Nebraska

Chadron State College *B*
College of St. Mary *B*
Concordia College *B*

Creighton University *B*
Dana College *B*
Doane College *B*
Hastings College *B*
Nebraska Wesleyan University *B*
Peru State College *B*
Union College *B*
University of Nebraska
    Kearney *B,M*
    Lincoln *B*
    Omaha *B*
Wayne State College *B,M*

New Hampshire

Antioch New England Graduate
    School *M*
Colby-Sawyer College *B*
Franklin Pierce College *B*
Keene State College *B*
Plymouth State College of the
    University System of New
    Hampshire *B*
Rivier College *B*

New Jersey

Caldwell College *B*
Fairleigh Dickinson University *M*
Glassboro State College *B,M*
Jersey City State College *B*
Kean College of New Jersey *B,M*
Rider College *B*
Rutgers—The State University of
    New Jersey
    Camden College of Arts and
      Sciences *B*
    Cook College *B*
    Douglass College *B*
    Livingston College *B*
    New Brunswick *M,D*
    Newark College of Arts and
      Sciences *B*
    Rutgers College *B*
    University College New
      Brunswick *B*
    University College Newark *B*
St. Peter's College *M*
Seton Hall University *B*
Stockton State College *B*
Trenton State College *B*

New Mexico

College of the Southwest *B*
New Mexico Highlands
    University *B*
New Mexico Institute of Mining
    and Technology *M*
New Mexico State University *B*
University of New Mexico *B*

New York

Adelphi University *B,M*
Canisius College *B*
City University of New York
    Brooklyn College *B,M*
    City College *B,M*
    Hunter College *B,M*
    Lehman College *M*
    Queens College *B,M*
College of Mount St. Vincent *B*
College of New Rochelle *B*
Concordia College *B*
Cornell University *M,D*
Daemen College *B*
Dominican College of Blauvelt *B*
Dowling College *B*
D'Youville College *B*
Elmira College *B*
Hofstra University *B*
Houghton College *B*
Iona College *B,M*
Ithaca College *B*
Le Moyne College *B*

Long Island University
  Brooklyn Campus *M*
  C. W. Post Campus *B,M*
  Southampton Campus *B*
Manhattan College *B*
Manhattanville College *M*
Marymount College *B*
Mohawk Valley Community
  College *A*
New York Institute of
  Technology *B*
New York University *B,M,D*
Niagara University *B,M*
Rensselaer Polytechnic Institute *B*
Russell Sage College *B*
St. Bonaventure University *B,M*
St. John's University *B,M*
St. Joseph's College *B*
Siena College *B*
State University of New York
  Albany *B,M*
  Binghamton *M*
  Buffalo *B,M,D*
  College at Brockport *M*
  College at Buffalo *M*
  College at Cortland *B,M*
  College of Environmental
    Science and Forestry *B*
  College at Fredonia *M*
  College at Geneseo *B*
  College at New Paltz *B,M*
  College at Old Westbury *B*
  College at Oneonta *B,M*
  College at Plattsburgh *B*
  College at Potsdam *B,M*
  Oswego *B,M*
Syracuse University *B,M,D*
Union College *M*
University of Rochester *M,D*
Utica College of Syracuse
  University *B*
Wells College *B*

North Carolina

Appalachian State University *B*
Barton College *B*
Bennett College *B*
Brevard College *A*
Campbell University *B*
Catawba College *B*
East Carolina University *B,M*
Elizabeth City State University *B*
Elon College *B*
Fayetteville State University *B*
Gardner-Webb College *B*
Lees-McRae College *B*
Livingstone College *B*
Mars Hill College *B*
North Carolina Central University
  B,M
North Carolina State University
  B,M,D
North Carolina Wesleyan College *B*
Pembroke State University *B*
St. Augustine's College *B*
Salem College *B*
University of North Carolina
  Asheville *C*
  Chapel Hill *B*
  Greensboro *M*
Western Carolina University *B*
Wingate College *B*

North Dakota

Bismarck State College *A*
Dickinson State University *B*
Jamestown College *B*
Mayville State University *B*
Minot State University *B*
North Dakota State University *B,M*
University of Mary *B*
University of North Dakota *B*

Valley City State University *B*

Ohio

Baldwin-Wallace College *B*
Bluffton College *B*
Bowling Green State University *B*
Capital University *B*
Case Western Reserve University *B*
Cedarville College *B*
College of Mount St. Joseph *C*
Defiance College *B*
Heidelberg College *B*
Kent State University *B,M*
Malone College *B*
Miami University: Oxford
  Campus *B*
Mount Union College *B*
Mount Vernon Nazarene College *B*
Ohio Dominican College *B*
Ohio State University: Columbus
  Campus *B*
Ohio University *B*
Otterbein College *B*
University of Dayton *B*
University of Rio Grande *B*
University of Toledo *B*
Urbana University *B*
Walsh College *B*
Wittenberg University *B*
Wright State University *B,M*
Youngstown State University *B*

Oklahoma

Bartlesville Wesleyan College *B*
East Central University *B*
Northwestern Oklahoma State
  University *B*
Oklahoma Baptist University *B*
Oklahoma Christian University of
  Science and Arts *B*
Oklahoma City University *B*
Oklahoma Panhandle State
  University *B*
Oral Roberts University *B*
Phillips University *B*
Southeastern Oklahoma State
  University *B,M*
Southwestern Oklahoma State
  University *B,M*
University of Central Oklahoma
  B,M
University of Oklahoma *B,M,D*
University of Science and Arts of
  Oklahoma *B*
University of Tulsa *B,M*

Oregon

George Fox College *B*
Oregon State University *M,D*
Southern Oregon State College *M*
Warner Pacific College *B*
Western Oregon State College *B,M*
Willamette University *M*

Pennsylvania

Albright College *B*
Allentown College of St. Francis de
  Sales *B,M*
Beaver College *B,M*
Bloomsburg University of
  Pennsylvania *B*
Bucknell University *B*
Cabrini College *B*
California University of
  Pennsylvania *B,M*
Cedar Crest College *B*
Chatham College *B*
Cheyney University of Pennsylvania
  B,M
Clarion University of Pennsylvania
  B,M
Delaware Valley College *B*

Drexel University *B*
East Stroudsburg University of
  Pennsylvania *B,M*
Edinboro University of
  Pennsylvania *B,M*
Elizabethtown College *B*
Gannon University *B*
Gettysburg College *B*
Grove City College *B*
Gwynedd-Mercy College *B*
Harrisburg Area Community
  College *A*
Holy Family College *B*
Immaculata College *B*
Indiana University of
  Pennsylvania *B*
Juniata College *B*
La Salle University *B*
Lehigh University *M*
Lincoln University *B*
Lock Haven University of
  Pennsylvania *B*
Lycoming College *B*
Mansfield University of
  Pennsylvania *B*
Marywood College *B*
Mercyhurst College *B*
Messiah College *B*
Moravian College *B*
Point Park College *B*
St. Francis College *C*
St. Joseph's University *C,B,M*
Seton Hill College *B*
Shippensburg University of
  Pennsylvania *B*
Slippery Rock University of
  Pennsylvania *B*
Temple University *B,M,D*
University of Pennsylvania *M,D*
University of Pittsburgh
  Bradford *C,B*
  Johnstown *B*
University of Scranton *B,M*
Washington and Jefferson College *B*
Waynesburg College *B*
West Chester University of
  Pennsylvania *B,M*
Wilkes University *B,M*
York College of Pennsylvania *B*

Puerto Rico

Bayamon Central University *B*
Caribbean University *B*
Inter American University of Puerto
  Rico
    Metropolitan Campus *M*
    San German Campus *B,M*
Pontifical Catholic University of
  Puerto Rico *B*
Universidad Metropolitana *B*
University of Puerto Rico: Rio
  Piedras Campus *B,M*

Rhode Island

Providence College *B*
Rhode Island College *B,M*
University of Rhode Island *M*

South Carolina

Benedict College *B*
Bob Jones University *B,M*
Charleston Southern University *B,M*
The Citadel *M*
Coker College *B*
Columbia College *B*
Converse College *M*
Erskine College *B*
Francis Marion College *M*
Lander College *B*
Presbyterian College *B*

University of South Carolina
  Aiken *B*
  Coastal Carolina College *B*

South Dakota

Augustana College *B*
Black Hills State University *B*
Dakota State University *B*
Dakota Wesleyan University *B*
Huron University *B*
Mount Marty College *B*
Northern State University *B,M*
Sioux Falls College *B*
South Dakota State University *B*
University of South Dakota *B*

Tennessee

Belmont University *B*
Bethel College *B*
Carson-Newman College *B*
Crichton College *B*
David Lipscomb University *B*
East Tennessee State University *B*
Freed-Hardeman University *B*
Lincoln Memorial University *B*
Milligan College *B*
Tennessee Technological
  University *B*
Tennessee Wesleyan College *B*
Trevecca Nazarene College *B*
Union University *B,M*
University of Tennessee
  Chattanooga *B,M*
  Knoxville *B*
  Martin *M*
Vanderbilt University *M,D*
William Jennings Bryan College *B*

Texas

Abilene Christian University *B*
Angelo State University *B*
Baylor University *B*
Dallas Baptist University *B*
East Texas Baptist University *B*
Hardin-Simmons University *B*
Incarnate Word College *B*
McMurry University *B*
Prairie View A&M University *M*
St. Edward's University *B*
St. Mary's University *B*
Southwest Texas State University
  B,M
Sul Ross State University *B*
Texas Christian University *B*
Texas Southmost College *A*
Texas Wesleyan University *B*
University of Dallas *B*
University of Houston *B,M*
University of Mary Hardin-
  Baylor *B*
University of Texas
  Austin *M,D*
  San Antonio *M*
West Texas State University *B*

Utah

Brigham Young University *M*
University of Utah *M*
Weber State University *B*

Vermont

Castleton State College *B*
Johnson State College *B*
Lyndon State College *B,M*
St. Michael's College *B*
Trinity College of Vermont *B*
University of Vermont *B,M*

Virginia

Averett College *B*
Bluefield College *B*
Eastern Mennonite College *B*

Emory and Henry College *B*
Ferrum College *B*
George Mason University *M*
Old Dominion University *B*
Radford University *M*
Virginia Intermont College *B*
Virginia Polytechnic Institute and
State University *B,M*
Virginia Union University *B*
Virginia Wesleyan College *B*

Washington

Central Washington University *B,M*
Eastern Washington University *B*
Heritage College *B*
Pacific Lutheran University *B*
Seattle Pacific University *B*
University of Puget Sound *M*
University of Washington *B*
Washington State University *B*
Western Washington University
B,M

West Virginia

Bethany College *B*
Bluefield State College *B*
Concord College *B*
Davis and Elkins College *B*
Fairmont State College *B*
Glenville State College *B*
Shepherd College *B*
University of Charleston *B*
West Liberty State College *B*
West Virginia Institute of
Technology *B*
West Virginia State College *B*
West Virginia University *B*
West Virginia Wesleyan College *B*
Wheeling Jesuit College *M*

Wisconsin

Alverno College *B*
Beloit College *B*
Cardinal Stritch College *B*
Carroll College *B*
Concordia University Wisconsin *B*
Lakeland College *B*
Lawrence University *B*
Marquette University *B*
Mount Mary College *B*
Mount Senario College *B*
Northland College *B*
St. Norbert College *B*
University of Wisconsin
Eau Claire *B*
Green Bay *B*
La Crosse *B*
Madison *B,M*
Oshkosh *B*
Platteville *B*
River Falls *B*
Stevens Point *B*
Whitewater *B*
Wisconsin Lutheran College *B*

Wyoming

University of Wyoming *B,M*

Canada

McGill University *B,M*

Science technologies

Alabama

Alabama Southern Community
College *A*
Chattahoochee Valley Community
College *A*

Lawson State Community
College *A*
Mobile College *B*

Alaska

Sheldon Jackson College *A*

Arizona

Navajo Community College *A*

Arkansas

John Brown University *A*
Westark Community College *A*
Williams Baptist College *A*

California

Bakersfield College *A*
Barstow College *A*
Chabot College *A*
Chaffey Community College *A*
College of Oceaneering *A*
College of the Sequoias *A*
Compton Community College *A*
Crafton Hills College *A*
Fresno City College *A*
Fresno Pacific College *A*
Kings River Community College *A*
Lake Tahoe Community College *A*
Los Angeles Harbor College *A*
Merced College *A*
Modesto Junior College *A*
Mount San Antonio College *A*
Mount San Jacinto College *A*
Napa Valley College *A*
Ohlone College *A*
Pasadena City College *A*
Saddleback College *A*
San Diego Miramar College *A*
San Joaquin Delta College *A*
San Jose City College *A*
Santa Rosa Junior College *A*
Skyline College *A*
Southwestern College *A*
Victor Valley College *A*
West Hills Community College *A*
Yuba College *A*

Colorado

Front Range Community College *A*
Mesa State College *A*
United States Air Force
Academy *B*

Delaware

Delaware Technical and
Community College: Southern
Campus *A*
Wesley College *A*

Florida

Brevard Community College *A*
Central Florida Community
College *A*
Indian River Community College *A*

Georgia

Abraham Baldwin Agricultural
College *A*
Atlanta Metropolitan College *A*
Brewton-Parker College *A*
Dalton College *A*
DeKalb College *A*
Floyd College *A*
Gordon College *A*

Idaho

Lewis Clark State College *A*

Illinois

Black Hawk College
East Campus *A*
Moline *A*

Carl Sandburg College *A*
City Colleges of Chicago: Wright
College *A*
Joliet Junior College *A*
Lincoln Land Community
College *A*
Olivet Nazarene University *A*
Southern Illinois University at
Edwardsville *B*

Indiana

Vincennes University *A*

Iowa

Iowa Lakes Community College *A*
Kirkwood Community College *A*
Scott Community College *A*

Kansas

Butler County Community
College *A*
Central College *A*
Colby Community College *A*
Dodge City Community College *A*
Fort Scott Community College *A*
Friends University *A*
Highland Community College *A*
Hutchinson Community College *A*
Johnson County Community
College *A*
Kansas City Kansas Community
College *A*
Neosho County Community
College *A*
Seward County Community
College *A*

Louisiana

Southern University in
Shreveport *A*

Maryland

Cecil Community College *A*
Charles County Community
College *A*
Harford Community College *A*
New Community College of
Baltimore *A*
Villa Julie College *B*

Massachusetts

Becker College: Leicester
Campus *A*
Hampshire College *B*
Mount Ida College *A*
Mount Wachusett Community
College *A*

Michigan

Andrews University *A*
Charles Stewart Mott Community
College *A*
Lansing Community College *A*
Madonna University *A,B*
Michigan State University *B*
Muskegon Community College *A*
Oakland Community College *A*
Schoolcraft College *A*
West Shore Community College *A*

Minnesota

Concordia College: St. Paul *A*
St. Cloud State University *B*
University of Minnesota:
Crookston *A*
Vermilion Community College *A*
Willmar Community College *A*
Winona State University *A*

Mississippi

Copiah-Lincoln Community
College *A*

Mississippi Gulf Coast Community
College: Jefferson Davis
Campus *A*

Missouri

Hannibal-LaGrange College *A*
St. Louis Community College at
Forest Park *A*
Webster University *B*

Montana

Flathead Valley Community
College *A*

Nebraska

McCook Community College *A*
Northeast Community College *A*
Southeast Community College:
Lincoln Campus *A*

New Jersey

Atlantic Community College *A*
Burlington County College *A*
Camden County College *A*

New Mexico

Northern New Mexico Community
College *A*

New York

Adirondack Community College *A*
City University of New York
La Guardia Community
College *A*
Medgar Evers College *A*
Columbia-Greene Community
College *A*
Community College of the Finger
Lakes *A*
Erie Community College: City
Campus *A*
Fulton-Montgomery Community
College *A*
Herkimer County Community
College *A*
Jefferson Community College *A*
Mohawk Valley Community
College *A*
Monroe Community College *A*
Niagara County Community
College *A*
Onondaga Community College *A*
Roberts Wesleyan College *A*
State University of New York
College of Agriculture and
Technology at Cobleskill *A*
College of Agriculture and
Technology at Morrisville *A*
College of Technology at
Alfred *A*
College of Technology at
Canton *A*
Suffolk County Community
College *A*
Trocaire College *A*
Ulster County Community
College *A*

North Carolina

Brevard College *A*
Isothermal Community College *A*
Mount Olive College *A*
Southwestern Community
College *A*
Western Piedmont Community
College *A*
Wilkes Community College *A*

North Dakota

Turtle Mountain Community
College *A*

University of North Dakota:
  Williston *A*

Ohio

Lakeland Community College *A*
Lorain County Community
  College *A*
Mount Vernon Nazarene College *A*
Ohio State University Agricultural
  Technical Institute *A*
University of Cincinnati: Access
  Colleges *A*
University of Toledo *A*
Wittenberg University *B*

Oklahoma

Eastern Oklahoma State College *A*
Redlands Community College *A*
Tulsa Junior College *A*

Oregon

Central Oregon Community
  College *A*

Pennsylvania

Butler County Community
  College *A*
California University of
  Pennsylvania *B*
Community College of
  Philadelphia *A*
Penn State University Park
  Campus *A*
Reading Area Community College
  C,A
Robert Morris College *A*

Puerto Rico

Turabo University *A*

Tennessee

Cumberland University *A*
Hiwassee College *A*
Knoxville College *A*
Motlow State Community
  College *A*

Texas

Angelina College *A*
Austin Community College *A*
College of the Mainland *A*
Cooke County College *A*
Galveston College *A*
Lee College *A*
Navarro College *A*
Southwestern Christian College *A*
Texarkana College *A*
Western Texas College *A*

Utah

Dixie College *A*

Vermont

Sterling College *A*

Virginia

Central Virginia Community
  College *A*
Eastern Shore Community
  College *A*
Patrick Henry Community
  College *A*
Virginia Polytechnic Institute and
  State University *M,D*

Washington

Evergreen State College *B*
Lower Columbia College *A*
Skagit Valley College *A*

West Virginia

Marshall University *A*
Ohio Valley College *A*
West Virginia State College *A*

Wyoming

Central Wyoming College *A*
Western Wyoming Community
  College *A*

Sculpture

Alabama

University of Alabama *M*
University of Montevallo *B*

Arizona

Northern Arizona University *B*

California

Academy of Art College *C,B,M,W*
California College of Arts and
  Crafts *B,M*
California Institute of the Arts
  C,B,M
California State University
  Fullerton *B,M*
  Long Beach *B,M*
  Los Angeles *B,M*
  Northridge *B,M*
Chabot College *A*
De Anza College *C*
Grossmont Community College *A*
Humboldt State University *B*
Long Beach City College *A*
Otis/Parsons School of Art and
  Design *B,M*
Palomar College *A*
Pasadena City College *A*
San Francisco Art Institute *B,M*
San Jose State University *B*
Santa Rosa Junior College *C*
Solano Community College *A*
University of California: Santa Cruz
  C,B
University of San Francisco *B*

Colorado

Rocky Mountain College of Art &
  Design *A,B*

Connecticut

University of Bridgeport *B*
University of Connecticut *B*
University of Hartford *B*

District of Columbia

American University *M*
George Washington University *M*
Howard University *B,M*

Florida

New College of the University of
  South Florida *B*
Pensacola Junior College *A*
Ringling School of Art and
  Design *B*
University of Florida *B,M*
University of Miami *M*
University of South Florida *B,M*

Georgia

Atlanta College of Art *B*
LaGrange College *B*
University of Georgia *B,M*

Idaho

University of Idaho *B*

Illinois

Bradley University *B,M*
Illinois Wesleyan University *B*
John A. Logan College *A*
School of the Art Institute of
  Chicago *B,M*
Southern Illinois University at
  Carbondale *B,M*
University of Illinois at Urbana-
  Champaign *B,M*

Indiana

Ball State University *B*
Indiana University Bloomington
  B,M
Indiana University—Purdue
  University at Indianapolis *B*
Purdue University *B,M*
University of Notre Dame *B,M*
Vincennes University *A*

Iowa

Drake University *B*
Teikyo Marycrest University *B*
University of Iowa *B,M*

Kansas

Coffeyville Community College *A*
Kansas State University *M*
University of Kansas *B*

Kentucky

Eastern Kentucky University *B*

Louisiana

Louisiana State University and
  Agricultural and Mechanical
  College *B*
McNeese State University *B*

Maine

Portland School of Art *B*

Maryland

Howard Community College *A*
Maryland Institute College of Art
  B,M

Massachusetts

Boston University *B,M*
Hampshire College *B*
Massachusetts College of Art *B,M*
Montserrat College of Art *B*
School of the Museum of Fine Arts
  C,B,M
University of Massachusetts at
  Dartmouth *B,M*

Michigan

Alma College *B*
Center for Creative Studies: College
  of Art and Design *B*
Central Michigan University *B,M*
Eastern Michigan University *B*
Grand Valley State University *B*
Northern Michigan University *B*
Olivet College *B*
University of Michigan *B,M*

Minnesota

College of Associated Arts *B*
Moorhead State University *B*
Southwest State University *B*
Winona State University *B*

Missouri

Kansas City Art Institute *B*
Washington University *B,M*
Webster University *B*

Nebraska

Hastings College *B*

New Hampshire

Plymouth State College of the
  University System of New
  Hampshire *B*

New Jersey

Caldwell College *B*
Glassboro State College *B*
Mercer County Community
  College *A*
Rutgers—The State University of
  New Jersey
    Mason Gross School of the
    Arts *B,M*
    New Brunswick *M*

New Mexico

Institute of American Indian
  Arts *A*

New York

Alfred University *B,M*
Bard College *B,M*
City University of New York
    Brooklyn College *M*
    Queens College *B,M*
Columbia University: School of
  General Studies *B*
Cooper Union *B*
Cornell University *M*
Daemen College *B*
Graduate School of Figurative Art
  of the New York Academy of
  Art *M*
Hofstra University *B*
New York University *B,M,D*
Parsons School of Design *A,B,M*
Pratt Institute *B,M*
Rochester Institute of Technology
  A,B,M
Sarah Lawrence College *B*
School of Visual Arts *B*
State University of New York
    Albany *B,M*
    Purchase *B,M*
    College at Buffalo *B*
    College at New Paltz *B,M*
    College at Potsdam *B*
Syracuse University *B,M*

North Carolina

Barton College *B*
Brevard College *A*
East Carolina University *B,M*
University of North Carolina at
  Greensboro *B*

Ohio

Art Academy of Cincinnati *B*
Bowling Green State University *B*
Cleveland Institute of Art *B*
Kent State University *B*
Lourdes College *B*
Ohio Northern University *B*
Ohio State University: Columbus
  Campus *B,M*
Ohio University *B,M*
University of Akron *B*
University of Toledo *B*
Wittenberg University *B*
Wright State University *B*

Oklahoma

University of Central Oklahoma *B*
University of Oklahoma *B*
University of Tulsa *B*

Oregon

Pacific Northwest College of Art *B*
Portland State University *B,M*
University of Oregon
  Eugene *B,M*
  Robert Donald Clark Honors
    College *B*

Pennsylvania

Bucknell University *B*
Carnegie Mellon University *B,M*
Edinboro University of
  Pennsylvania *B,M*
Immaculata College *A*
Lycoming College *B*
Marywood College *B*
Mercyhurst College *B*
Moore College of Art and Design *B*
Seton Hill College *B*
Temple University *B,M*
University of the Arts *B*

Rhode Island

Rhode Island College *B*
Rhode Island School of Design *B,M*

Tennessee

East Tennessee State University *B*
Memphis College of Art *B,M*
University of Tennessee:
  Chattanooga *B*

Texas

Houston Community College *C*
Sam Houston State University *M*
Stephen F. Austin State
  University *M*
Texas Woman's University *B,M*
University of Dallas *B,M*
University of Houston *B*
University of North Texas *B,M*
University of Texas at El Paso *B*

Utah

Brigham Young University *B,M*

Vermont

Bennington College *B*
Marlboro College *B*

Virginia

Averett College *B*
Virginia Commonwealth University
  B,M

Washington

Evergreen State College *B*
Pacific Lutheran University *B*
Tacoma Community College *A*
University of Washington *B,M*

West Virginia

Bethany College *B*
Marshall University *B*
West Virginia State College *B*
West Virginia University *B,M*

Wisconsin

Milwaukee Institute of Art &
  Design *B*
University of Wisconsin: Eau
  Claire *B*

Secondary education

Alabama

Alabama Agricultural and
  Mechanical University *B,M*

Alabama Southern Community
  College *A*
Alabama State University *B,M*
Athens State College *B*
Auburn University
  Auburn *B,M,D*
  Montgomery *B,M*
Birmingham-Southern College *B*
Brewer State Junior College *A*
Chattahoochee Valley Community
  College *A*
Faulkner University *B*
Huntingdon College *B*
Jacksonville State University *B,M*
James H. Faulkner State
  Community College *A*
John C. Calhoun State Community
  College *A*
Judson College *B*
Livingston University *B,M*
Lurleen B. Wallace State Junior
  College *A*
Miles College *B*
Oakwood College *B*
Samford University *B,M*
Snead State Junior College *A*
Southeastern Bible College *B*
Spring Hill College *B*
Troy State University
  Dothan *B,M*
  Montgomery *M*
  Troy *B,M*
University of Alabama
  Birmingham *B,M*
  Huntsville *B*
  Tuscaloosa *B,M,D,W*
University of Montevallo *B,M*
University of North Alabama *B,M*
University of South Alabama *B,M*

Alaska

Sheldon Jackson College *B*
University of Alaska
  Anchorage *B,M*
  Fairbanks *B*
  Southeast *B*

Arizona

Arizona State University *B,M,D*
Eastern Arizona College *A*
Grand Canyon University *B,M*
Northern Arizona University *B,M*
Pima Community College *A*
Prescott College *B*
University of Arizona *B,M,D*
Yavapai College *A*

Arkansas

Arkansas Baptist College *B*
Arkansas Tech University *B,M*
Harding University *B,M*
Henderson State University *B,M*
Hendrix College *B*
John Brown University *B*
Ouachita Baptist University *B*
Southern Arkansas University *B,M*
University of Arkansas
  Fayetteville *B,M*
  Little Rock *M*
  Monticello *B*
  Pine Bluff *B*
University of Central Arkansas *B,M*
University of the Ozarks *B*
Westark Community College *A*

California

Academy of Art College *M*
Azusa Pacific University *B*
Biola University *B*
California Baptist College *B*
California Lutheran University *B,M*

California State University
  Bakersfield *B,M*
  Dominguez Hills *M*
  Fresno *B*
  Long Beach *M*
  Los Angeles *M*
  Northridge *M*
  Sacramento *B,M*
  San Bernardino *M*
Christ College Irvine *B*
Christian Heritage College *B*
College of Notre Dame *M*
Crafton Hills College *A*
Fresno Pacific College *B*
Kings River Community College *A*
La Sierra University *M*
Master's College *B*
Mills College *M*
Mount St. Mary's College *B*
National Hispanic University *B*
National University *M*
Occidental College *M*
Pacific Christian College *B*
Pepperdine University *B,M*
Point Loma Nazarene College *M*
St. Mary's College of California
  B,M
San Diego State University *M*
San Francisco State University *M*
San Jose State University *M*
Santa Clara University *M*
Simpson College *B*
Sonoma State University *B*
Southern California College *B*
Stanford University *M*
United States International
  University *B,M*
University of California
  Los Angeles *M*
  Santa Barbara *M*
University of La Verne *B,M*
University of the Pacific *B,M,D*
University of Redlands *B*
University of San Diego *B*
University of San Francisco *B,M*
University of Southern California
  M,W
Westmont College *B*

Colorado

Adams State College *B,M*
Colorado Christian University *B*
Colorado College *M*
Fort Lewis College *B*
Regis College of Regis University *B*
University of Colorado
  Colorado Springs *B,M*
  Denver *B,M*
University of Southern Colorado *B*
Western State College of
  Colorado *B*

Connecticut

Connecticut College *M*
Eastern Connecticut State
  University *B,M*
Fairfield University *B,M*
Quinnipiac College *M*
Sacred Heart University *B,M*
St. Joseph College *B,M*
Southern Connecticut State
  University *B,M*
University of Bridgeport *B,M*
University of Connecticut *B*
University of Hartford *B,M,W*
Western Connecticut State
  University *B,M*

Delaware

University of Delaware *B,M*
Wesley College *B*

District of Columbia

American University *M*
Catholic University of America *B*
Gallaudet University *B*
George Washington University *M*
Howard University *B*
Trinity College *M*
University of the District of
  Columbia *B*

Florida

Central Florida Community
  College *A*
Daytona Beach Community
  College *A*
Eckerd College *B*
Flagler College *B*
Florida Agricultural and Mechanical
  University *M*
Florida Atlantic University *C*
Florida Bible College *B*
Florida Institute of Technology
  B,M,D
Florida International University *M*
Florida Southern College *B*
Gulf Coast Community College *A*
Indian River Community College *A*
Jacksonville University *B,M*
Manatee Community College *A*
Miami-Dade Community College *A*
Nova University *B*
Okaloosa-Walton Community
  College *A*
Pensacola Junior College *A*
St. Thomas University *B*
Southeastern College of the
  Assemblies of God *B*
Stetson University *B,M*
University of Florida *M*
University of Miami *B,M*
University of North Florida *B,M*
University of West Florida *B,M*
Warner Southern College *B*

Georgia

Albany State College *B,M*
Andrew College *A*
Armstrong State College *B,M*
Augusta College *M*
Bainbridge College *A*
Berry College *B*
Brenau Women's College *B*
Brewton-Parker College *B*
Clark Atlanta University *B*
Clayton State College *A*
Columbus College *B,M*
Covenant College *B*
Darton College *A*
East Georgia College *A*
Emory University *B,M*
Floyd College *A*
Fort Valley State College *B*
Gainesville College *A*
Georgia College *B,M*
Georgia Southern University *B,M*
Kennesaw State College *B*
LaGrange College *B*
Macon College *A*
Mercer University *B*
Morehouse College *B*
Oglethorpe University *B*
Piedmont College *B*
Shorter College *B*
Thomas College *A*
Toccoa Falls College *B*
University of Georgia *B,M,D*
Valdosta State College *B,M*
Waycross College *A*
Wesleyan College *B*
West Georgia College *B,M*

Hawaii

Brigham Young University-
  Hawaii *B*
Chaminade University of
  Honolulu *B*
University of Hawaii
  Hilo *W*
  Manoa *B,M*

Idaho

College of Southern Idaho *A*
Idaho State University *B,M*
Lewis Clark State College *B*
North Idaho College *A*
Northwest Nazarene College *B*
University of Idaho *B,M*

Illinois

Augustana College *B*
Aurora University *B*
Barat College *B*
Belleville Area College *A*
Black Hawk College *A*
Bradley University *B,M*
Chicago State University *B*
City Colleges of Chicago: Wright
  College *A*
College of St. Francis *B*
Concordia University *B,M*
De Paul University *B*
Eureka College *B*
Greenville College *B*
Hebrew Theological College *B*
Illinois Central College *A*
Illinois College *B*
Illinois Valley Community
  College *A*
Illinois Wesleyan University *B*
Joliet Junior College *A*
Judson College *B*
Kishwaukee College *A*
Knox College *B*
Lake Forest College *B*
Lewis University *B*
Lincoln Christian College and
  Seminary *B*
Loyola University of Chicago *B*
MacMurray College *B*
McKendree College *B*
Millikin University *B*
Monmouth College *B*
North Central College *B*
North Park College and Theological
  Seminary *B*
Northeastern Illinois University *B*
Northern Illinois University *M,D*
Northwestern University *B*
Olivet Nazarene University *B,M*
Principia College *B*
Rend Lake College *A*
Rock Valley College *A*
Rockford College *B,M*
Roosevelt University *B*
St. Xavier University *B*
Southern Illinois University
  Carbondale *B,M,D*
  Edwardsville *B,M*
Trinity Christian College *B*
Trinity College *B*
University of Chicago *M,D*
University of Illinois
  Chicago *B*
  Urbana-Champaign *B,M,D*
Waubonsee Community College *A*
Wheaton College *B*

Indiana

Anderson University *B*
Ball State University *B,M*
Bethel College *B*
Butler University *B,M*
Calumet College of St. Joseph *B*

Earlham College *B*
Franklin College *B*
Goshen College *B*
Grace College *B*
Hanover College *B*
Huntington College *B*
Indiana State University *B,M,D*
Indiana University
  Bloomington *B*
  East *B*
  Northwest *B,M*
  South Bend *B,M*
  Southeast *B,M*
Indiana University—Purdue
  University
  Fort Wayne *B,M*
  Indianapolis *B,M*
Indiana Wesleyan University *B*
Manchester College *B,M*
Marian College *B*
Martin University *B*
Oakland City College *B*
Purdue University
  Calumet *B,M*
  West Lafayette *B*
St. Francis College *B,M*
St. Joseph's College *B*
St. Mary-of-the-Woods College *B*
Taylor University *B*
Tri-State University *B*
University of Evansville *B*
University of Indianapolis *B*
University of Notre Dame *B*
University of Southern Indiana *B,M*
Vincennes University *A*
Wabash College *C*

Iowa

Briar Cliff College *B*
Buena Vista College *B*
Clarke College *B*
Coe College *B*
Cornell College *B*
Dordt College *B*
Drake University *B,M*
Graceland College *B*
Grand View College *B*
Iowa Lakes Community College *A*
Iowa Wesleyan College *B*
Kirkwood Community College *A*
Loras College *B,M*
Luther College *B*
Maharishi International
  University *M*
Morningside College *B*
Mount Mercy College *B*
North Iowa Area Community
  College *A*
Northwestern College *B*
St. Ambrose University *B*
Simpson College *B*
Teikyo Marycrest University *B*
Teikyo Westmar University *B*
University of Dubuque *B,M*
University of Iowa *B,M,D*
Upper Iowa University *B*
Wartburg College *B*
William Penn College *B*

Kansas

Allen County Community
  College *A*
Baker University *B*
Bethany College *B*
Central College *A*
Coffeyville Community College *A*
Colby Community College *A*
Cowley County Community
  College *A*
Emporia State University *B,M*
Fort Hays State University *M*
Friends University *B*

Hutchinson Community College *A*
Kansas City Kansas Community
  College *A*
Kansas Newman College *B*
Kansas State University *B,M*
Labette Community College *A*
McPherson College *B*
Neosho County Community
  College *A*
Ottawa University *B*
Pittsburg State University *B,M*
Pratt Community College *A*
Seward County Community
  College *A*
Sterling College *B*
Tabor College *B*
University of Kansas *B*
Washburn University of Topeka *B*
Wichita State University *M*

Kentucky

Alice Lloyd College *B*
Asbury College *B*
Bellarmine College *B*
Berea College *B*
Brescia College *B*
Campbellsville College *B*
Cumberland College *B,M*
Eastern Kentucky University *B,M*
Georgetown College *B,M*
Kentucky Christian College *B*
Kentucky Wesleyan College *B*
Louisville Presbyterian Theological
  Seminary *M*
Morehead State University *M*
Murray State University *M*
Northern Kentucky University *B,M*
Pikeville College *B*
St. Catharine College *A*
Spalding University *B,M*
Sue Bennett College *A*
Thomas More College *B*
Transylvania University *B*
Union College *B,M*
University of Kentucky *M*
University of Louisville *M*
Western Kentucky University *M*

Louisiana

Centenary College of Louisiana *B,M*
Dillard University *B*
Louisiana College *B*
Louisiana State University
  Agricultural and Mechanical
    College *M*
  Shreveport *B,M*
McNeese State University *B,M*
Nicholls State University *B*
Northeast Louisiana University *M*
Northwestern State University *M*
Our Lady of Holy Cross College *B*
Southeastern Louisiana University
  B,M
Southern University at New
  Orleans *B*
Southern University and
  Agricultural and Mechanical
  College *B,M*
Tulane University *M*
University of New Orleans *B*
University of Southwestern
  Louisiana *M*
World Evangelism Bible College
  and Seminary *B*

Maine

St. Joseph's College *B*
University of Maine
  Farmington *B*
  Machias *B*
  Orono *B,M*
  Presque Isle *B*

University of New England *C*

Maryland

Anne Arundel Community
  College *A*
Bowie State University *M*
Catonsville Community College *A*
Cecil Community College *A*
Charles County Community
  College *A*
Chesapeake College *A*
College of Notre Dame of
  Maryland *B*
Columbia Union College *B*
Coppin State College *B*
Dundalk Community College *A*
Frostburg State University *M*
Garrett Community College *A*
Goucher College *M*
Harford Community College *A*
Howard Community College *A*
Johns Hopkins University *M*
Loyola College in Maryland *M*
Montgomery College
  Germantown Campus *A*
  Rockville Campus *A*
  Takoma Park Campus *A*
Morgan State University *B*
Mount St. Mary's College *B*
Prince George's Community
  College *A*
Salisbury State University *M*
Towson State University *M*
University of Maryland: College
  Park *M,D*
Western Maryland College *M*

Massachusetts

American International College *B,M*
Assumption College *B*
Atlantic Union College *B*
Boston College *B,M*
Bridgewater State College *M*
Eastern Nazarene College *B,M*
Elms College *B*
Emmanuel College *B*
Fitchburg State College *B*
Framingham State College *B*
Hampshire College *B*
Merrimack College *B*
North Adams State College *B*
Simmons College *B,M*
Smith College *B,M*
Springfield College *B*
Stonehill College *B*
Suffolk University *B,M*
Tufts University *M*
Wellesley College *B*
Western New England College *B*
Westfield State College *B,M*
Worcester State College *M*

Michigan

Alma College *B*
Andrews University *M*
Aquinas College *B*
Calvin College *B*
Central Michigan University *B,M*
Concordia College *B*
Eastern Michigan University *B,M*
Ferris State University *A*
Grand Valley State University *B,M*
Hillsdale College *B*
Hope College *B*
Kellogg Community College *A*
Lansing Community College *A*
Madonna University *B*
Marygrove College *B*
Michigan State University *B*
Michigan Technological
  University *B*

Mid Michigan Community
College *A*
Northern Michigan University *B,M*
Oakland University *B,M*
Olivet College *B*
Saginaw Valley State University *B*
Siena Heights College *M*
Spring Arbor College *B*
Suomi College *A*
University of Detroit Mercy *B*
University of Michigan
Ann Arbor *B*
Flint *B*
Wayne State University *B,M*
Western Michigan University *B,M*

Minnesota
Augsburg College *B*
Bemidji State University *B*
Bethel College *B*
College of St. Benedict *B*
College of St. Catherine: St.
Catherine Campus *B*
College of St. Scholastica *B*
Concordia College: Moorhead *B*
Concordia College: St. Paul *B*
Crown College *B*
Dr. Martin Luther College *B*
Gustavus Adolphus College *B*
Macalester College *B*
Mankato State University *B,M*
Moorhead State University *B*
Northland Community College *A*
Pillsbury Baptist Bible College *B*
Rainy River Community College *A*
St. Cloud State University *B*
St. John's University *B*
St. Mary's College of Minnesota *B*
St. Olaf College *B*
Southwest State University *B*
University of Minnesota
Morris *C*
Twin Cities *M*
University of St. Thomas *B,M*
Vermilion Community College *A*
Willmar Community College *A*
Winona State University *B,M*

Mississippi
Alcorn State University *B,M*
Blue Mountain College *B*
Copiah-Lincoln Community
College *A*
Delta State University *B,M*
Holmes Community College *A*
Jackson State University *B,M,W*
Jones County Junior College *A*
Mary Holmes College *A*
Millsaps College *B*
Mississippi College *B,M*
Mississippi Delta Community
College *A*
Mississippi Gulf Coast Community
College
Jackson County Campus *A*
Jefferson Davis Campus *A*
Mississippi State University *B,M*
Mississippi University for Women *B*
Northeast Mississippi Community
College *A*
Rust College *B*
Tougaloo College *B*
University of Mississippi *B,M*
University of Southern
Mississippi *B*

Missouri
Calvary Bible College *B*
Central Methodist College *B*
Central Missouri State University
B,M
College of the Ozarks *B*

Columbia College *B*
Culver-Stockton College *B*
Drury College *B*
East Central College *A*
Evangel College *B*
Fontbonne College *B*
Hannibal-LaGrange College *B*
Jefferson College *A*
Lincoln University *M*
Lindenwood College *M*
Maryville University *B*
Mineral Area College *A*
Missouri Baptist College *B*
Missouri Southern State College *B*
Missouri Valley College *B*
Missouri Western State College *B*
Moberly Area Community
College *A*
Northeast Missouri State
University *M*
Northwest Missouri State
University *B*
Park College *B*
Rockhurst College *B*
St. Louis Community College at
Meramec *A*
St. Louis University *B*
Southeast Missouri State University
B,M
Southwest Missouri State
University *M*
University of Missouri
Columbia *B,M,D*
Kansas City *B,M*
St. Louis *M*
Washington University *B,M*
Webster University *B*
Westminster College *B*
William Jewell College *B*
William Woods College *B*

Montana
College of Great Falls *B*
Eastern Montana College *B,M*
Miles Community College *A*
Montana State University *B,M*
Northern Montana College *B*
Rocky Mountain College *B*
University of Montana *B,M*
Western Montana College of the
University of Montana *B*

Nebraska
Chadron State College *B*
College of St. Mary *B*
Concordia College *B,M*
Creighton University *B,M*
Dana College *B*
Hastings College *B,M*
Midland Lutheran College *B*
Nebraska Christian College *B*
Nebraska Wesleyan University *B*
Northeast Community College *A*
Peru State College *B*
Southeast Community College:
Beatrice Campus *A*
Union College *B*
University of Nebraska
Kearney *B,M*
Lincoln *B,M*
Omaha *B,M*
Western Nebraska Community
College: Scottsbluff Campus *A*

Nevada
Sierra Nevada College *B*
University of Nevada
Las Vegas *B,M,D*
Reno *B,M*

New Hampshire
Colby-Sawyer College *B*
Franklin Pierce College *B*
Keene State College *B*
New England College *B*
Notre Dame College *B*
Plymouth State College of the
University System of New
Hampshire *B,M*
Rivier College *B,M*
St. Anselm College *B*
University of New Hampshire *M*

New Jersey
Burlington County College *A*
Centenary College *B*
Essex County College *A*
Glassboro State College *M*
Jersey City State College *B*
Kean College of New Jersey *B*
Monmouth College *B,M*
Montclair State College *M*
Rider College *B*
Rutgers—The State University of
New Jersey
Camden College of Arts and
Sciences *B*
Douglass College *B*
Livingston College *B*
New Brunswick *M,D*
Newark College of Arts and
Sciences *B*
Rutgers College *B*
University College New
Brunswick *B*
University College Newark *B*
St. Peter's College *B*
Seton Hall University *B,M*
Stockton State College *B*
Trenton State College *M*
William Paterson College of New
Jersey *B,W*

New Mexico
College of Santa Fe *B*
College of the Southwest *B*
Eastern New Mexico University
B,M
New Mexico Highlands
University *B*
New Mexico Institute of Mining
and Technology *B*
New Mexico Junior College *A*
New Mexico State University *B,M*
University of New Mexico *M,D*
Western New Mexico University
B,M

New York
Adelphi University *B,M*
Alfred University *B,M*
Canisius College *B,M*
City University of New York
Brooklyn College *B,M*
City College *B,M*
College of Staten Island *M*
Hunter College *B,M*
La Guardia Community
College *A*
Lehman College *B,M*
Queens College *B,M*
Colgate University *B,M*
College of New Rochelle *B*
College of St. Rose *B,M*
Concordia College *B*
Daemen College *B*
Dominican College of Blauvelt *B*
Dowling College *B,M*
D'Youville College *B*
Elmira College *B*
Fordham University *B,M*

Fulton-Montgomery Community
College *A*
Hofstra University *B,M*
Houghton College *B*
Iona College *B,M*
Keuka College *B*
Le Moyne College *B*
Long Island University
Brooklyn Campus *B,M*
C. W. Post Campus *B,M*
Southampton Campus *B*
Manhattan College *B,M*
Manhattanville College *M*
Marymount College *B*
Molloy College *B*
Mount St. Mary College *B*
Nazareth College of Rochester *B,M*
New York University *B,M,D*
Niagara University *B,M*
Nyack College *B*
Pace University
College of White Plains *B*
Pleasantville/Briarcliff *B*
Russell Sage College *B*
St. Bonaventure University *B,M*
St. Francis College *B*
St. John Fisher College *C*
St. John's University *B,M*
St. Joseph's College
Brooklyn *B*
Suffolk Campus *B*
St. Thomas Aquinas College *B*
Siena College *B*
State University of New York
Albany *M*
Binghamton *M*
Buffalo *M,D*
College at Brockport *M*
College at Fredonia *B,M*
College at Geneseo *B,M*
College at New Paltz *B,M*
College at Oneonta *B,M*
College at Plattsburgh *B,M*
College at Potsdam *B,M*
Oswego *B,M*
Syracuse University *B,M*
Union College *M*
University of Rochester *M,D*
Wagner College *B*
Wells College *B*

North Carolina
Appalachian State University *B,M*
Barber-Scotia College *B*
Barton College *B*
Beaufort County Community
College *A*
Belmont Abbey College *B*
Bennett College *B*
Campbell University *B,M*
Catawba Valley Community
College *A*
Chowan College *B*
Coastal Carolina Community
College *A*
Duke University *M*
East Carolina University *B,M*
Elon College *B*
Fayetteville State University *B*
Gardner-Webb College *B,M*
Gaston College *A*
Greensboro College *B*
Guilford College *B*
High Point University *B*
Isothermal Community College *A*
Johnson C. Smith University *B*
Lees-McRae College *B*
Lenoir-Rhyne College *B*
Mars Hill College *B*
Martin Community College *A*
Methodist College *B*

North Carolina Central University
B,M
North Carolina State University
B,M
North Carolina Wesleyan College B
Pfeiffer College B
Pitt Community College A
Queens College B
St. Andrews Presbyterian College B
St. Augustine's College B
Salem College B
Shaw University B
University of North Carolina
Asheville C
Chapel Hill B,M,D
Charlotte M
Wake Forest University B,M
Warren Wilson College B
Western Carolina University B,M
Western Piedmont Community
College A
Wingate College B

North Dakota

Dickinson State University B
Jamestown College B
Mayville State University B
Minot State University B
Turtle Mountain Community
College A
University of Mary B
University of North Dakota M,D

Ohio

Ashland University B
Baldwin-Wallace College B
Bluffton College B
Bowling Green State University
Bowling Green M
Firelands College A
Capital University B
Case Western Reserve University B
Cedarville College B
Central State University B
Cleveland State University B,M
College of Mount St. Joseph C,B
College of Wooster B
Defiance College B
Franciscan University of
Steubenville B
Heidelberg College B
John Carroll University B,M
Kent State University B,M,D
Lake Erie College B
Lorain County Community
College A
Malone College B
Marietta College B
Miami University: Oxford Campus
B,M
Mount Union College B
Mount Vernon Nazarene College B
Muskingum College B,M
Notre Dame College of Ohio B
Ohio Dominican College B
Ohio State University: Columbus
Campus B,M
Ohio University M,D
Ohio Wesleyan University B
Otterbein College B
University of Akron B,M,D
University of Cincinnati
Cincinnati B,M,D
Clermont College A
Raymond Walters College A
University of Dayton B,M
University of Findlay B
University of Rio Grande B
University of Toledo B,M,D
Urbana University B
Walsh College B
Wilmington College B

Wittenberg University B
Wright State University B,M
Xavier University B
Youngstown State University B,M

Oklahoma

Bartlesville Wesleyan College B
Connors State College A
East Central University M
Eastern Oklahoma State College A
Langston University B
Mid-America Bible College B
Northeastern State University B,M
Northern Oklahoma College A
Northwestern Oklahoma State
University B,M
Oklahoma Baptist University B
Oklahoma City University B,M
Oklahoma Panhandle State
University B
Oklahoma State University B
Oral Roberts University B,M
Phillips University B,M
Rogers State College A
Rose State College A
Southeastern Oklahoma State
University B,M
Southwestern Oklahoma State
University B,M
University of Central Oklahoma M
University of Oklahoma M,D
University of Science and Arts of
Oklahoma B
University of Tulsa B,M

Oregon

Central Oregon Community
College A
Concordia College B
Eastern Oregon State College B,M
George Fox College B
Linfield College B,M
Linn-Benton Community College A
Oregon State University M
Pacific University M
Portland State University B,M
Southern Oregon State College M
Treasure Valley Community
College A
University of Portland B
Warner Pacific College B
Western Baptist College B
Western Oregon State College B,M
Willamette University M

Pennsylvania

Albright College B
Allegheny College B
Allentown College of St. Francis de
Sales M
Alvernia College B
Baptist Bible College of
Pennsylvania B
Beaver College B,M
Bloomsburg University of
Pennsylvania B,M
Bryn Mawr College M,D
Bucknell University B,M
Butler County Community
College A
Cabrini College B
California University of
Pennsylvania B,M
Cedar Crest College B
Chatham College B
Cheyney University of Pennsylvania
C,B
Clarion University of
Pennsylvania B
College Misericordia B
Dickinson College C
Duquesne University B,M

East Stroudsburg University of
Pennsylvania B,M
Eastern College B
Edinboro University of
Pennsylvania B
Elizabethtown College B
Gannon University B,M
Geneva College B
Gettysburg College B
Gratz College B,M
Grove City College B
Gwynedd-Mercy College B
Harrisburg Area Community
College A
Holy Family College B
Immaculata College B
Indiana University of Pennsylvania
B,M
Juniata College B
King's College B
Kutztown University of
Pennsylvania B
La Salle University B,M
Lebanon Valley College of
Pennsylvania B
Lehigh University M,D
Lincoln University B
Lock Haven University of
Pennsylvania B
Lycoming College B
Mansfield University of
Pennsylvania B,M
Marywood College B,M
Mercyhurst College B
Messiah College B
Montgomery County Community
College A
Moravian College B
Neumann College B
Northeastern Christian Junior
College A
Penn State University Park
Campus B
Philadelphia College of Bible B
Reading Area Community
College A
St. Francis College C
St. Joseph's University B,M
St. Vincent College C
Seton Hill College B
Slippery Rock University of
Pennsylvania B,M
Temple University B,M,D
Thiel College C
University of Pennsylvania M,D
University of Pittsburgh
Bradford C
Johnstown B
University of Scranton B,M
Ursinus College B
Villanova University B,M
Washington and Jefferson College B
Waynesburg College B
West Chester University of
Pennsylvania M
Westminster College B
Widener University B,M
Wilkes University B
York College of Pennsylvania B

Puerto Rico

American University of Puerto
Rico B
Bayamon Central University B
Caribbean University B
Inter American University of Puerto
Rico
Arecibo Campus B
San German Campus B
Pontifical Catholic University of
Puerto Rico B
Turabo University B

Universidad Adventista de las
Antillas B
Universidad Metropolitana B
University of Puerto Rico
Cayey University College B
Rio Piedras Campus B,M

Rhode Island

Brown University M
Providence College B
Rhode Island College B,M
Salve Regina University B
University of Rhode Island B,M

South Carolina

Charleston Southern University B,M
The Citadel M
Claflin College B
Clemson University B,M
Columbia College B,M
Converse College M
Erskine College B
Francis Marion College M
Limestone College B
Morris College B
North Greenville College A
South Carolina State College M
University of South Carolina
Aiken B
Coastal Carolina College B
Columbia M,D
Spartanburg B
Winthrop University M

South Dakota

Augustana College B,M
Black Hills State University B,M
Dakota State University B
Dakota Wesleyan University B
Huron University B
Mount Marty College B
Presentation College A
Sioux Falls College B
South Dakota State University B
University of South Dakota B,M

Tennessee

Austin Peay State University B,M
Belmont University B
Bethel College B
Carson-Newman College B
Christian Brothers University B
Cleveland State Community
College A
Columbia State Community
College A
Crichton College B
Cumberland University B
East Tennessee State University
B,M
Free Will Baptist Bible College B
Freed-Hardeman University B
Hiwassee College A
Knoxville College B
Lambuth University B
LeMoyne-Owen College B
Lincoln Memorial University B
Milligan College B,M
Motlow State Community
College A
Roane State Community College A
Tennessee State University B,M
Tennessee Technological University
B,M
Tennessee Temple University B,M
Tennessee Wesleyan College B
Trevecca Nazarene College B
Tusculum College B
Union University B,M

University of Tennessee
Chattanooga *B,M*
Knoxville *B*
Martin *B*
Vanderbilt University *B,M,D*
Volunteer State Community
College *A*
Walters State Community
College *A*

Texas

Abilene Christian University *M*
Amarillo College *A*
Angelina College *A*
Austin College *M*
Baylor University *B*
Bee County College *A*
Brazosport College *A*
College of the Mainland *A*
Concordia Lutheran College *B*
Corpus Christi State University *B,M*
Dallas Baptist University *B*
East Texas Baptist University *B*
East Texas State University
Commerce *B,M*
Texarkana *M*
El Paso Community College *A*
Hardin-Simmons University *M*
Houston Baptist University *B*
Houston Community College *A*
Huston-Tillotson College *B*
Incarnate Word College *B*
Jarvis Christian College *B*
Kilgore College *A*
Lamar University—Beaumont *B,M*
Laredo State University *B,M*
LeTourneau University *B*
Lon Morris College *A*
Lubbock Christian University *B*
McMurry University *B*
Midwestern State University *B,M*
Navarro College *A*
North Harris Montgomery
Community College District *A*
Our Lady of the Lake University of
San Antonio *B,M*
Panola College *A*
Paul Quinn College *B*
Prairie View A&M University *B*
Ranger Junior College *A*
Rice University *M*
St. Edward's University *B*
St. Mary's University *B*
Sam Houston State University *B,M*
Schreiner College *B*
Southwest Texas State
University *M*
Southwestern Christian College *A*
Sul Ross State University *M*
Tarleton State University *M*
Texas A&I University *B,M*
Texas Christian University *B,M*
Texas Lutheran College *B*
Texas Southern University *B,M*
Texas Southmost College *A*
Texas Tech University *B,M,D*
Texas Wesleyan University *B,M*
Trinity University *M*
Trinity Valley Community
College *A*
University of Dallas *B*
University of Houston
Houston *M*
Victoria *M*
University of Mary Hardin-Baylor
B,M
University of North Texas *M*
University of St. Thomas *B,M*
University of Texas
Pan American *B,M*
Permian Basin *M*
Victoria College *A*

Wayland Baptist University *B*
West Texas State University *B,M*
Wiley College *B*

Utah

Brigham Young University *B,M,D*
University of Utah *B,M*
Utah State University *B,M*
Weber State University *B,M*
Westminster College of Salt Lake
City *B*

Vermont

Castleton State College *B*
College of St. Joseph in Vermont *B*
Goddard College *B,M*
Johnson State College *B*
Lyndon State College *B*
St. Michael's College *B*
Trinity College of Vermont *B*
University of Vermont *B,M*

Virginia

Averett College *B*
Bluefield College *B*
Bridgewater College *B*
Christopher Newport College *M*
College of William and Mary *M*
Eastern Mennonite College *B*
Emory and Henry College *B*
Ferrum College *B*
George Mason University *M*
Hampton University *B,M*
James Madison University *M*
Longwood College *M*
Lynchburg College *M*
Mary Baldwin College *C*
Marymount University *M*
Mountain Empire Community
College *A*
Norfolk State University *M*
Old Dominion University *B,M*
Radford University *B,M*
University of Richmond *B,M*
Virginia Polytechnic Institute and
State University *B,M,D*
Virginia Wesleyan College *B*

Washington

Central Washington University *B*
Eastern Washington University *B,M*
Evergreen State College *M*
Heritage College *B*
Lower Columbia College *A*
Pacific Lutheran University *B,M*
St. Martin's College *B,M*
Seattle University *M*
University of Puget Sound *M*
University of Washington *C*
Walla Walla College *B,M*
Washington State University *B*
Western Washington University
B,M
Whitworth College *B*

West Virginia

Alderson-Broaddus College *B*
Bethany College *B*
Bluefield State College *B*
Concord College *B*
Davis and Elkins College *B*
Fairmont State College *B*
Glenville State College *B*
Marshall University *B,M*
Potomac State College of West
Virginia University *A*
Salem-Teikyo University *B,M*
Shepherd College *B*
University of Charleston *B*
West Liberty State College *B*
West Virginia Graduate College *M*

West Virginia Institute of
Technology *B*
West Virginia State College *B*
West Virginia University *B,M*
West Virginia Wesleyan College *B*

Wisconsin

Alverno College *B*
Beloit College *B,M*
Cardinal Stritch College *B*
Carroll College *B*
Carthage College *B*
Concordia University Wisconsin *B*
Edgewood College *B*
Lakeland College *B*
Lawrence University *B*
Marian College of Fond du Lac *B*
Marquette University *B*
Mount Mary College *B*
Mount Senario College *B*
Northland College *B*
Ripon College *C*
St. Norbert College *B*
University of Wisconsin
Eau Claire *M*
Green Bay *B*
La Crosse *B,M*
Milwaukee *B*
Oshkosh *B*
Platteville *B,M*
River Falls *B,M*
Stevens Point *B*
Superior *B*
Whitewater *B*
Wisconsin Lutheran College *B*

Wyoming

Central Wyoming College *A*
Eastern Wyoming College *A*
Laramie County Community
College *A*
Northwest College *A*
Sheridan College *A*
University of Wyoming *B*
Western Wyoming Community
College *A*

American Samoa, Caroline Islands, Guam, Marianas, Virgin Islands

University of Guam *B,M*

Canada

McGill University *B,M*

Secretarial and related programs

Alabama

Alabama Southern Community
College *A*
Alabama State University *A,B*
Bessemer State Technical College *A*
Bishop State Community College *A*
Brewer State Junior College *A*
Central Alabama Community
College: Childersburg Campus *C*
Chattahoochee Valley Community
College *A*
Community College of the Air
Force *A*
Draughons Junior College *C*
Enterprise State Junior College *C,A*
Faulkner University *A*
Gadsden State Community
College *A*
George C. Wallace State
Community College at Selma *A*

James H. Faulkner State
Community College *C,A*
Jefferson State Community College
C,A
John C. Calhoun State Community
College *C,A*
John M. Patterson State Technical
College *C*
Lawson State Community College
C,A
Livingston University *A*
Lurleen B. Wallace State Junior
College *C,A*
Northeast Alabama State Junior
College *A*
Reid State Technical College *C*
Selma University *A*
Shelton State Community
College *A*
Shoals Community College *C,A*
Snead State Junior College *A*
Southern Union State Junior
College *A*
Troy State University *A,B*
Walker College *C*
Walker State Technical College *A*
Wallace State Community College
at Hanceville *A*

Alaska

Prince William Sound Community
College *C,A*
University of Alaska
Anchorage *C,A*
Fairbanks *A*
Southeast *C,A*

Arizona

Arizona Western College *A*
Cochise College *C,A*
Eastern Arizona College *C*
Glendale Community College *C,A*
Lamson Junior College *C*
Mesa Community College *A*
Mohave Community College *C,A*
Navajo Community College *C,A*
Northland Pioneer College *C,A*
Pima Community College *A*
Rio Salado Community College *A*
Scottsdale Community College *A*
Yavapai College *C*

Arkansas

Arkansas Baptist College *A*
Arkansas State University
Beebe Branch *A*
Jonesboro *C,A,B*
Arkansas Tech University *A*
Capital City Junior College *A*
Central Baptist College *A*
East Arkansas Community College
C,A
Garland County Community
College *C,A*
Harding University *A,B*
Henderson State University *A,B,M*
John Brown University *A,B*
Mississippi County Community
College *A*
North Arkansas Community
College *A*
Ouachita Baptist University *A*
Philander Smith College *B*
Phillips County Community College
C,A
Rich Mountain Community
College *A*
Shorter College *A*
Southern Arkansas Community
College *C,A*

Southern Arkansas University
Magnolia *A,B*
Technical Branch *A*
University of Arkansas
Fayetteville *A,B*
Monticello *A,B*
University of Central Arkansas *A,B*
University of the Ozarks *A*
Westark Community College *C,A*
Williams Baptist College *A*

California

Allan Hancock College *C,A*
Bakersfield College *A*
Barstow College *C,A*
Central California Commercial College *A*
Cerritos Community College *A*
Cerro Coso Community College *C,A*
Chabot College *C,A*
Chaffey Community College *A*
City College of San Francisco *C,A*
Coastline Community College *C,A*
College of the Desert *C,A*
College of the Redwoods *C,A*
College of the Sequoias *C,A*
Columbia College *C,A*
Compton Community College *A*
Cosumnes River College *A*
Crafton Hills College *C,A*
Cuesta College *A*
De Anza College *C,A*
Diablo Valley College *A*
East Los Angeles College *C,A*
El Camino College *C,A*
Evergreen Valley College *A*
Feather River College *C,A*
Foothill College *A*
Fresno City College *C,A*
Gavilan Community College *A*
Glendale Community College *C,A*
Golden West College *C,A*
Grossmont Community College *C,A*
Hartnell College *A*
Heald Business College
San Jose *C,A*
Walnut Creek *C,A*
Heald College
Sacramento *C,A*
Santa Rosa *C,A*
Humphreys College *C,A*
Imperial Valley College *C,A*
Kelsey-Jenney College *C,A*
Kings River Community College *A*
La Sierra University *A,B*
Lake Tahoe Community College *C,A*
Laney College *C,A*
Lassen College *A*
Long Beach City College *C,A*
Los Angeles City College *C,A*
Los Angeles Harbor College *C,A*
Los Angeles Mission College *C,A*
Los Angeles Pierce College *C,A*
Los Angeles Trade and Technical College *C,A*
Los Angeles Valley College *C,A*
Los Medanos College *C,A*
Mendocino College *C,A*
Merced College *C,A*
MiraCosta College *C,A*
Mission College *A*
Modesto Junior College *A*
Monterey Peninsula College *C,A*
Moorpark College *C,A*
Mount San Antonio College *C,A*
Mount San Jacinto College *C,A*
Napa Valley College *C,A*
Ohlone College *C,A*
Orange Coast College *C,A*
Oxnard College *A*

Pacific Union College *A,B*
Palomar College *C,A*
Pasadena City College *C,A*
Phillips Junior College
Condie Campus *C,A*
San Fernando Valley Campus *C*
Point Loma Nazarene College *C*
Porterville College *A*
Rio Hondo College *A*
Saddleback College *C,A*
San Diego City College *C,A*
San Diego Mesa College *C,A*
San Diego Miramar College *A*
San Joaquin Delta College *A*
San Jose City College *A*
Santa Monica College *C,A*
Santa Rosa Junior College *C,A*
Sierra College *C,A*
Skyline College *C,A*
Solano Community College *A*
Southwestern College *C,A*
Taft College *A*
Ventura College *C,A*
Victor Valley College *C,A*
West Hills Community College *A*
West Valley College *C,A*
Yuba College *C,A*

Colorado

Adams State College *B*
Arapahoe Community College *C,A*
Blair Junior College *A*
Colorado Mountain College:
Timberline Campus *A*
Colorado Northwestern Community College *C,A*
Community College of Denver *C,A*
Denver Technical College *C*
Front Range Community College *C,A*
Lamar Community College *C*
Mesa State College *C,A*
Morgan Community College *A*
Northeastern Junior College *A*
Otero Junior College *C,A*
Parks Junior College *C,A*
Pikes Peak Community College *A*
Pueblo Community College *C,A*
Red Rocks Community College *C,A*
Trinidad State Junior College *A*

Connecticut

Asnuntuck Community College *C,A*
Briarwood College *C,A*
Housatonic Community College *C,A*
Manchester Community College *A*
Mattatuck Community College *C,A*
Middlesex Community College *C,A*
Mitchell College *A*
Northwestern Connecticut Community College *C,A*
Norwalk Community College *A*
Quinebaug Valley Community College *A*
South Central Community College *A*
Tunxis Community College *A*
University of New Haven *C*

Delaware

Delaware State College *B*
Delaware Technical and Community College
Southern Campus *A*
Stanton/Wilmington Campus *A*
Terry Campus *A*
Goldey-Beacom College *C,A*

District of Columbia

University of the District of Columbia *C,A,B*

Florida

Brevard Community College *C,A*
Broward Community College *A*
Central Florida Community College *A*
Chipola Junior College *A*
Daytona Beach Community College *A*
Edison Community College *C,A*
Florida Community College at Jacksonville *C,A*
Florida Keys Community College *A*
Gulf Coast Community College *C,A*
Hillsborough Community College *C*
Hobe Sound Bible College *A*
Indian River Community College *A*
Jones College *A,B*
Lake-Sumter Community College *C*
Manatee Community College *A*
Miami-Dade Community College *C,A*
New England Institute of Technology *A*
Okaloosa-Walton Community College *A*
Palm Beach Community College *A*
Pasco-Hernando Community College *C,A*
Pensacola Junior College *A*
Phillips Junior College:
Melbourne *A*
St. Johns River Community College *A*
Santa Fe Community College *A*
Seminole Community College *C*
South College: Palm Beach Campus *C*
South Florida Community College *C,A*
Southern College *A*
Tallahassee Community College *C,A*
Valencia Community College *C,A*
Webber College *A*

Georgia

Abraham Baldwin Agricultural College *A*
Albany State College *B*
Athens Area Technical Institute *C,A*
Atlanta Christian College *A,B*
Atlanta Metropolitan College *A*
Augusta College *A*
Augusta Technical Institute *C,A*
Brewton-Parker College *A*
Brunswick College *C,A*
Chattahoochee Technical Institute *C,A*
Clark Atlanta University *B*
Clayton State College *A*
Dalton College *C,A*
Darton College *A*
DeKalb College *A*
DeKalb Technical Institute *C*
East Georgia College *A*
Emmanuel College *A*
Floyd College *A*
Fort Valley State College *A,B*
Gainesville College *A*
Georgia Southern University *B*
Gordon College *A*
Macon College *A*
Meadows College of Business *A*
Middle Georgia College *C,A*
Morris Brown College *B*
North Georgia College *A,B*
Reinhardt College *A*

Savannah Technical Institute *C,A*
South College *C,A*
South Georgia College *C,A*
Truett-McConnell College *A*
Valdosta State College *B*
Waycross College *A*
West Georgia College *A*

Hawaii

Brigham Young University-Hawaii *C,A,B*
Cannon's International Business College of Honolulu *C,A*
University of Hawaii
Honolulu Community College *C,A*
Kapiolani Community College *C,A*
Kauai Community College *C,A*
Leeward Community College *C,A*

Idaho

Boise State University *C,A*
College of Southern Idaho *C*
Idaho State University *C*
ITT Technical Institute: Boise *C*
Lewis Clark State College *A*
North Idaho College *A*
Ricks College *C*
University of Idaho *B*

Illinois

Belleville Area College *C,A*
Black Hawk College
East Campus *A*
Moline *C,A*
Carl Sandburg College *C,A*
City Colleges of Chicago
Chicago City-Wide College *C,A*
Malcolm X College *C,A*
Olive-Harvey College *C,A*
Richard J. Daley College *A*
Wright College *C,A*
College of DuPage *C,A*
College of Lake County *C,A*
Elgin Community College *C,A*
Gem City College *C*
Highland Community College *C,A*
Illinois Central College *C,A*
Illinois Eastern Community Colleges
Frontier Community College *C,A*
Lincoln Trail College *C,A*
Olney Central College *C,A*
Wabash Valley College *C,A*
Illinois Valley Community College *A*
John A. Logan College *A*
Joliet Junior College *A*
Kishwaukee College *C,A*
Lake Land College *C,A*
Lewis and Clark Community College *A*
Lincoln Christian College and Seminary *B*
Lincoln Land Community College *C,A*
MacCormac Junior College *A*
Midstate College *C,A*
Moraine Valley Community College *C,A*
Morton College *C,A*
Oakton Community College *C,A*
Parkland College *A*
Prairie State College *A*
Rend Lake College *C,A*
Richland Community College *C,A*
Robert Morris College: Chicago *C,A*

Rock Valley College *A*
St. Augustine College *C,A*
Shawnee Community College *C,A*
Southern Illinois University at
    Carbondale *A*
Spoon River College *C,A*
State Community College *A*
Triton College *C,A*
Waubonsee Community College
    C,A
Western Illinois University *B*
William Rainey Harper College *C,A*

Indiana

Ancilla College *C,A*
Anderson University *A*
Ball State University *A,B*
Bethel College *A*
Calumet College of St. Joseph *C,A*
Huntington College *A*
Indiana State University *A*
Indiana University at Kokomo *C*
Indiana Vocational Technical
    College
        Central Indiana *C,A*
        Columbus *C,A*
        Eastcentral *C,A*
        Kokomo *C,A*
        Lafayette *C,A*
        Northcentral *C,A*
        Northeast *C,A*
        Northwest *C,A*
        Southcentral *C,A*
        Southeast *C,A*
        Southwest *C,A*
        Wabash Valley *C,A*
        Whitewater *C,A*
International Business College *A*
ITT Technical Institute
        Evansville *C*
        Fort Wayne *C*
Oakland City College *C,A*
Tri-State University *A*
University of Southern Indiana *A*
Vincennes University *A*

Iowa

American Institute of Business *C,A*
American Institute of Commerce *C*
Clinton Community College *C,A*
Des Moines Area Community
    College *C,A*
Dordt College *A*
Faith Baptist Bible College and
    Theological Seminary *A*
Hawkeye Institute of Technology
    C,A
Indian Hills Community College *C*
Iowa Central Community College *A*
Iowa Lakes Community College *C*
Iowa Western Community College
    C,A
Kirkwood Community College *C,A*
Morningside College *B*
Muscatine Community College *A*
North Iowa Area Community
    College *A*
Northeast Iowa Community
    College *C*
Northwest Iowa Technical
    College *C*
Northwestern College *A*
Scott Community College *C,A*
Southeastern Community College
        North Campus *C*
        South Campus *C*
Southwestern Community College
    C,A
Vennard College *A,B*
Waldorf College *A*

Kansas

Allen County Community
    College *A*
Barton County Community College
    C,A
Brown Mackie College *C*
Butler County Community College
    C,A
Central College *A*
Cloud County Community
    College *A*
Coffeyville Community College *C,A*
Colby Community College *C,A*
Cowley County Community
    College *A*
Dodge City Community College *A*
Emporia State University *A*
Fort Hays State University *A*
Fort Scott Community College *C,A*
Friends University *A,B*
Haskell Indian Junior College *A*
Hesston College *A*
Highland Community College *C,A*
Hutchinson Community College
    C,A
Johnson County Community
    College *C,A*
Kansas City Kansas Community
    College *C,A*
Labette Community College *A*
Neosho County Community College
    C,A
Pratt Community College *C,A*
Seward County Community College
    C,A
Southwestern College *B*
Tabor College *A,B*
Washburn University of Topeka
    C,A

Kentucky

Clear Creek Baptist Bible College *A*
Cumberland College *B*
Eastern Kentucky University *A,B*
Elizabethtown Community
    College *A*
Franklin College *A*
Hazard Community College *A*
Jefferson Community College *A*
Lees College *A*
Lexington Community College *A*
Lindsey Wilson College *A*
Madisonville Community College *A*
Maysville Community College *A*
Morehead State University *A*
Murray State University *A,B*
Owensboro Junior College of
    Business *C,A*
Paducah Community College *A*
St. Catharine College *C,A*
Southeast Community College *A*
Sue Bennett College *A*
Sullivan College *A*
Union College *A,B*
University of Louisville *B*
Western Kentucky University *A*

Louisiana

Bossier Parish Community
    College *A*
Grambling State University *A,B*
Louisiana College *A,B*
Louisiana State University at Eunice
    C,A
Louisiana Tech University *A*
McNeese State University *A,B*
Nicholls State University *A,B*
Northeast Louisiana University *C,A*
Northwestern State University *A,B*
Phillips Junior College: New
    Orleans *C,A*

Southeastern Louisiana University
    A,B
Southern University
        New Orleans *A,B*
        Shreveport *A*
University of New Orleans *A*
University of Southwestern
    Louisiana *A,B*
World Evangelism Bible College
    and Seminary *A*

Maine

Andover College *A*
Beal College *A*
Casco Bay College *A*
Husson College *C,A,B*
Southern Maine Technical
    College *A*
Thomas College *A*
University of Maine at Machias *A*

Maryland

Allegany Community College *C,A*
Anne Arundel Community
    College *A*
Catonsville Community College *C,A*
Cecil Community College *C,A*
Charles County Community
    College *C*
Chesapeake College *C,A*
Columbia Union College *A*
Dundalk Community College *C,A*
Essex Community College *C,A*
Frederick Community College *A*
Garrett Community College *C*
Hagerstown Business College *A*
Hagerstown Junior College *C,A*
Harford Community College *C,A*
Howard Community College *C,A*
Montgomery College
        Germantown Campus *C,A*
        Rockville Campus *C,A*
        Takoma Park Campus *C,A*
Morgan State University *B*
New Community College of
    Baltimore *A*
Prince George's Community College
    C,A
Villa Julie College *A*
Wor-Wic Tech Community College
    C,A

Massachusetts

Aquinas College at Milton *A*
Aquinas College at Newton *A*
Atlantic Union College *A,B*
Bay Path College *A*
Bay State College *A*
Becker College: Worcester
    Campus *A*
Berkshire Community College *C,A*
Bristol Community College *C,A*
Bunker Hill Community College *A*
Cape Cod Community College *C,A*
Dean Junior College *A*
Endicott College *A*
Fisher College *A*
Greenfield Community College *C,A*
Holyoke Community College *A*
Katharine Gibbs School *A*
Marian Court Junior College *A*
Massachusetts Bay Community
    College *C,A*
Massasoit Community College *A*
Middlesex Community College *A*
Mount Ida College *A*
Mount Wachusett Community
    College *A*
North Shore Community College *A*
Northern Essex Community
    College *A*
Quincy College *A*

Quinsigamond Community College
    C,A
Roxbury Community College *A*
Salem State College *B*
Springfield Technical Community
    College *C,A*

Michigan

Alpena Community College *A*
Andrews University *A,B*
Baker College
        Auburn Hills *A*
        Cadillac *C,A*
        Flint *C,A*
        Mount Clemens *C*
        Muskegon *C,A*
        Owosso *A*
        Port Huron *A*
Central Michigan University *B*
Charles Stewart Mott Community
    College *C,A*
Cleary College *A,B*
Davenport College of Business *C,A*
Delta College *C,A*
Detroit College of Business *A,B*
Eastern Michigan University *B*
Ferris State University *A*
Glen Oaks Community College *C*
Grand Rapids Baptist College and
    Seminary *A*
Grand Rapids Community College
    C,A
Great Lakes Junior College of
    Business *C,A*
Henry Ford Community College *A*
Jackson Community College *C,A*
Jordan College *C,A*
Kalamazoo Valley Community
    College *A*
Kellogg Community College *C,A*
Kirtland Community College *C,A*
Lake Superior State University *A*
Lansing Community College *A*
Lewis College of Business *A*
Macomb Community College *C,A*
Marygrove College *A,B*
Michigan Christian College *C,A*
Mid Michigan Community College
    C,A
Montcalm Community College *A*
Muskegon Community College *A*
Northern Michigan University
    C,A,B,M
Northwestern Michigan College *A*
Oakland Community College *A*
St. Clair County Community
    College *C,A*
Schoolcraft College *C,A*
Southwestern Michigan College *A*
Suomi College *A*
West Shore Community College
    C,A

Minnesota

Alexandria Technical College *C*
Anoka-Ramsey Community
    College *A*
Bethany Lutheran College *A*
Concordia College: Moorhead *B*
Gustavus Adolphus College *B*
Inver Hills Community College *A*
Itasca Community College:
    Arrowhead Region *A*
Lakewood Community College *A*
Mankato State University *A,B*
Mesabi Community College:
    Arrowhead Region *A*
Moorhead State University *A*
Normandale Community College *A*
North Central Bible College *A*
Northland Community College *A*
Northwestern College *A*

Pillsbury Baptist Bible College *A,B*
Rainy River Community College *A*
Rochester Community College *C,A*
St. Cloud State University *A,B*
St. Paul Technical College *C*
Southwest State University *A,B*
University of Minnesota:
    Crookston *A*
Vermilion Community College *C,A*
Willmar Community College *A*
Willmar Technical College *C,A*
Winona State University *A,B*

Mississippi

Alcorn State University *B*
Blue Mountain College *B*
Copiah-Lincoln Community
    College *A*
Delta State University *B*
East Central Community College
    C,A
Hinds Community College *C,A*
Holmes Community College *C,A*
Jackson State University *B,M*
Jones County Junior College *A*
Mary Holmes College *A*
Meridian Community College *A*
Mississippi College *B*
Mississippi Delta Community
    College *C,A*
Mississippi Gulf Coast Community
    College
        Jackson County Campus *C,A*
        Jefferson Davis Campus *A*
        Perkinston *C,A*
Northeast Mississippi Community
    College *A*
Phillips Junior College
        Jackson *C,A*
        Mississippi Gulf Coast *C,A*
Rust College *A,B*
Southeastern Baptist College *C,A*
Southwest Mississippi Community
    College *A*
William Carey College *B*

Missouri

Baptist Bible College *A,B*
Central Missouri State University *A*
East Central College *C,A*
Evangel College *A,B*
Hannibal-LaGrange College *A*
Jefferson College *A*
Lincoln University *A,B*
Longview Community College *A*
Maple Woods Community College
    C,A
Mineral Area College *C,A*
Missouri Southern State College
    C,A
Missouri Western State College *C,A*
Moberly Area Community
    College *A*
North Central Missouri College *C,A*
Northwest Missouri State
    University *C*
Penn Valley Community College
    C,A
Phillips Junior College *A*
St. Charles Community College *C*
St. Louis Christian College *A*
St. Louis Community College
        Florissant Valley *C,A*
        Forest Park *C,A*
        Meramec *C,A*
Southeast Missouri State
    University *B*
Southwest Baptist University *A*
Southwest Missouri State
    University *C*
State Fair Community College *C,A*
Three Rivers Community College *A*

Montana

Dawson Community College *C,A*
Flathead Valley Community
    College *A*
Fort Peck Community College *C*
Little Big Horn College *C,A*
Miles Community College *A*
Northern Montana College *A*
Salish Kootenai College *C,A*
Western Montana College of the
    University of Montana *A*

Nebraska

Central Community College *C,A*
Lincoln School of Commerce *C,A*
McCook Community College *C,A*
Metropolitan Community College
    C,A
Midland Lutheran College *A,B*
Nebraska Christian College *A*
Nebraska Indian Community
    College *A*
Northeast Community College *A*
Southeast Community College
        Beatrice Campus *A*
        Lincoln Campus *C,A*
Wayne State College *B*
Western Nebraska Community
    College
        Scottsbluff Campus *C,A*
        Sidney Campus *A*
York College *A*

Nevada

Community College of Southern
    Nevada *C,A*
Northern Nevada Community
    College *C,A*
Truckee Meadows Community
    College *A*

New Hampshire

Castle College *C,A*
Hesser College *A*
McIntosh College *A*
New Hampshire Technical College
        Berlin *A*
        Laconia *C,A*
        Manchester *A*
        Stratham *C,A*
Plymouth State College of the
    University System of New
    Hampshire *B*

New Jersey

Atlantic Community College *A*
Bergen Community College *C,A*
Berkeley College of Business *C,A*
Brookdale Community College *A*
Burlington County College *A*
Camden County College *A*
County College of Morris *A*
Cumberland County College *C,A*
Essex County College *A*
Gloucester County College *C,A*
Katharine Gibbs School *C,A*
Ocean County College *A*
Passaic County Community
    College *C*
Rider College *A,B*
Sussex County Community College
    C,A
Union County College *A*

New Mexico

Albuquerque Technical-Vocational
    Institute *A*
Clovis Community College *C,A*
College of Santa Fe *A*
Dona Ana Branch Community
    College of New Mexico State
    University *C,A*

Eastern New Mexico University
    Portales *A*
    Roswell Campus *C,A*
New Mexico Junior College *C,A*
New Mexico State University
    Carlsbad *C,A*
    Las Cruces *C,A*
Northern New Mexico Community
    College *C,A*
Parks College *C*
San Juan College *C,A*
Western New Mexico University *A*

New York

Adirondack Community College
    C,A
Berkeley College *C,A*
Berkeley School: New York City
    C,A
Bramson ORT Technical Institute
    C,A
Briarcliffe: The College for Business
    C,A
Broome Community College *A*
Bryant & Stratton Business Institute
        Albany *A*
        Buffalo *C,A*
        Rochester *A*
        Syracuse *A*
Cazenovia College *A*
Central City Business Institute *C,A*
City University of New York
        Baruch College *B*
        Hostos Community College *A*
        Kingsborough Community
            College *A*
        La Guardia Community
            College *A*
        Lehman College *B*
        Medgar Evers College *A*
        New York City Technical
            College *A*
        Queensborough Community
            College *A*
Clinton Community College *C,A*
Columbia-Greene Community
    College *C,A*
Community College of the Finger
    Lakes *A*
Concordia College *A*
Corning Community College *C,A*
Dutchess Community College *A*
Erie Community College
        City Campus *A*
        North Campus *C,A*
        South Campus *C,A*
Five Towns College *A*
Fulton-Montgomery Community
    College *C,A*
Genesee Community College *C,A*
Herkimer County Community
    College *C,A*
Hilbert College *A*
Hofstra University *B*
Hudson Valley Community
    College *A*
Iona College *C*
Jamestown Business College *C,A*
Jefferson Community College *C,A*
Katharine Gibbs School
        Melville *C,A*
        New York *C,A*
Maria College *A*
Mater Dei College *C,A*
Mohawk Valley Community College
    C,A
Monroe College *A*
Monroe Community College *A*
Nassau Community College *A*
New York Institute of
    Technology *A*

Niagara County Community College
    C,A
Onondaga Community College *A*
Orange County Community
    College *A*
Pace University
        College of White Plains *C,A,B*
        New York *C,A,B*
        Pleasantville/Briarcliff *C*
Rochester Business Institute *A*
Rockland Community College *A*
Sage Junior College of Albany, A
    Division of Russell Sage
    College *A*
State University of New York
        College of Agriculture and
            Technology at Cobleskill
            C,A
        College of Agriculture and
            Technology at Morrisville *A*
        College of Technology at
            Alfred *A*
        College of Technology at
            Canton *A*
        College of Technology at
            Delhi *A*
        College of Technology at
            Farmingdale *A*
Suffolk County Community College
        Eastern Campus *C,A*
        Selden *C,A*
        Western Campus *A*
Taylor Business Institute *C,A*
Technical Career Institutes *A*
Tompkins-Cortland Community
    College *C,A*
Trocaire College *C,A*
Ulster County Community
    College *A*
Utica School of Commerce *A*
Villa Maria College of Buffalo *C*
Westchester Business Institute *C,A*
Westchester Community College
    C,A
Wood School *C,A*

North Carolina

Alamance Community College *A*
Anson Community College *A*
Asheville Buncombe Technical
    Community College *A*
Beaufort County Community
    College *A*
Bennett College *A*
Bladen Community College *A*
Blue Ridge Community College *A*
Brunswick Community College *A*
Caldwell Community College and
    Technical Institute *A*
Carteret Community College *A*
Catawba Valley Community
    College *A*
Cecils College *C,A*
Central Carolina Community
    College *A*
Central Piedmont Community
    College *A*
Cleveland Community College *A*
Coastal Carolina Community
    College *A*
College of the Albemarle *A*
Craven Community College *A*
Davidson County Community
    College *C,A*
Durham Technical Community
    College *A*
East Carolina University *B*
Edgecombe Community College *A*
Fayetteville State University *A*
Fayetteville Technical Community
    College *A*

Forsyth Technical Community
College *A*
Gaston College *A*
Guilford Technical Community
College *C,A*
Haywood Community College *A*
Isothermal Community College *A*
James Sprunt Community
College *A*
Johnston Community College *A*
Louisburg College *C*
Martin Community College *A*
Mayland Community College *C,A*
McDowell Technical Community
College *A*
Mitchell Community College *A*
Montgomery Community College
C,A
Mount Olive College *A*
Nash Community College *A*
North Carolina Agricultural and
Technical State University *B*
Pamlico Community College *A*
Peace College *A*
Piedmont Community College *A*
Pitt Community College *A*
Richmond Community College *C,A*
Roanoke-Chowan Community
College *A*
Robeson Community College *A*
Rockingham Community College *A*
Sampson Community College *A*
Sandhills Community College *C,A*
Southeastern Community College
C,A
Southwestern Community
College *A*
Stanly Community College *A*
Surry Community College *A*
Tri-County Community College *A*
University of North Carolina at
Greensboro *B*
Vance-Granville Community
College *A*
Wake Technical Community
College *A*
Wayne Community College *A*
Western Carolina University *B*
Western Piedmont Community
College *A*
Wilkes Community College *A*
Wilson Technical Community
College *C,A*

North Dakota

Bismarck State College *C,A*
Dickinson State University *A*
Little Hoop Community College
C,A
Mayville State University *A,B*
Minot State University *A*
North Dakota State College of
Science *C,A*
North Dakota State University:
Bottineau and Institute of
Forestry *A*
Standing Rock College *A*
Turtle Mountain Community
College *C*
University of North Dakota
Lake Region *C,A*
Williston *A*
Valley City State University *A*

Ohio

Bowling Green State University
Bowling Green *A*
Firelands College *A*
Bradford School *C,A*
Bryant & Stratton Business
Institute: Great Northern *A*
Cedarville College *A,B*

Central Ohio Technical College *A*
Central State University *B*
Cincinnati Metropolitan College *A*
Cincinnati Technical College *A*
Clark State Community College
C,A
Columbus State Community
College *A*
Cuyahoga Community College
Metropolitan Campus *A*
Western Campus *C,A*
Davis Junior College of Business
C,A
Dyke College *A,B*
Edison State Community College
C,A
Hocking Technical College *A*
ITT Technical Institute:
Youngstown *C*
Jefferson Technical College *C,A*
Kent State University
Ashtabula Regional Campus *A*
East Liverpool Regional
Campus *A*
Salem Regional Campus *A*
Tuscarawas Campus *C,A*
Lorain County Community
College *A*
Marion Technical College *C*
Miami University: Hamilton
Campus *A*
Miami-Jacobs College *C,A*
Mount Vernon Nazarene College
A,B
Muskingum Area Technical
College *A*
North Central Technical College *A*
Northwest Technical College *C,A*
Northwestern College *C,A*
Ohio University: Chillicothe
Campus *A*
Ohio Valley Business College *A*
Owens Technical College
Findlay Campus *C,A*
Toledo *C,A*
Shawnee State University *A*
Sinclair Community College *C,A*
Southern Ohio College *A*
Southern State Community College
C,A
Stark Technical College *A*
Terra Technical College *C,A*
University of Akron
Akron *A*
Wayne College *C*
University of Cincinnati
Access Colleges *A*
Clermont College *C,A*
Raymond Walters College *A*
University of Findlay *A*
University of Rio Grande *C,A*
University of Toledo *A*
Washington State Community
College *A*
Wright State University: Lake
Campus *C,A*
Youngstown State University *A*

Oklahoma

Bacone College *C,A*
Bartlesville Wesleyan College *A*
Connors State College *C,A*
East Central University *B*
Eastern Oklahoma State College
C,A
Langston University *B*
Murray State College *A*
Northeastern State University *C,B*
Northern Oklahoma College *C,A*
Oklahoma Junior College *A*
Oklahoma Panhandle State
University *B*

Oklahoma State University
Technical Branch: Okmulgee *A*
Redlands Community College *C,A*
Rogers State College *C,A*
Rose State College *C,A*
Southeastern Oklahoma State
University *C,B*
Southwestern Oklahoma State
University *C,B*
Tulsa Junior College *C,A*
University of Central Oklahoma *B*

Oregon

Central Oregon Community College
C,A
Chemeketa Community College *C,A*
Clackamas Community College *C*
Clatsop Community College *C,A*
Eastern Oregon State College *A*
Lane Community College *C,A*
Linn-Benton Community College
C,A
Mount Hood Community College
C,A
Oregon Institute of Technology *A*
Portland Community College *C,A*
Rogue Community College *C,A*
Southern Oregon State College *A*
Southwestern Oregon Community
College *C,A*
Treasure Valley Community College
C,A
Umpqua Community College *C,A*

Pennsylvania

Baptist Bible College of
Pennsylvania *A,B*
Berean Institute *A*
Bucks County Community
College *A*
Butler County Community College
C,A
Central Pennsylvania Business
School *A*
Churchman Business School *C,A*
Clarion University of
Pennsylvania *A*
Community College of Beaver
County *A*
Community College of Philadelphia
C,A
Delaware County Community
College *C*
DuBois Business College *C,A*
Edinboro University of
Pennsylvania *A*
Gannon University *A*
Harcum Junior College *A*
Harrisburg Area Community
College *A*
Lackawanna Junior College *C,A*
Lansdale School of Business *A*
Lehigh County Community
College *A*
Luzerne County Community
College *A*
Manor Junior College *A*
Mercyhurst College *C,A*
Montgomery County Community
College *C,A*
Northampton County Area
Community College *A*
Northeastern Christian Junior
College *A*
Peirce Junior College *C,A*
Penn State University Park
Campus *C*
Pennsylvania College of
Technology *A*
Pennsylvania Institute of
Technology *C,A*

Reading Area Community College
C,A
Robert Morris College *A,B*
Waynesburg College *A*
Westmoreland County Community
College *A*
York College of Pennsylvania *A*

Puerto Rico

American University of Puerto Rico
A,B
Bayamon Central University *A,B*
Caribbean University *A,B*
Columbia College *A*
Electronic Data Processing College
of Puerto Rico *A*
Huertas Junior College *C*
ICPR Junior College *A*
Instituto Tecnico Comercial Junior
College *A*
Inter American University of Puerto
Rico
Arecibo Campus *A,B*
Metropolitan Campus *A,B*
San German Campus *A,B*
Pontifical Catholic University of
Puerto Rico *A,B*
Puerto Rico Junior College *A*
Turabo University *A,B*
Universidad Adventista de las
Antillas *C,A,B*
University of Puerto Rico
Aguadilla *A*
Arecibo Campus *A,B*
Bayamon Technological
University College *A,B*
Carolina Regional College *A*
Cayey University College *A*
Humacao University College
A,B
La Montana Regional
College *A*
Mayaguez Campus *A,B*
Ponce Technological
University College *A,B*
Rio Piedras Campus *A,B*
University of the Sacred Heart *A,B*

Rhode Island

Community College of Rhode
Island *C*
Johnson & Wales University *C,A*
New England Institute of
Technology *A*

South Carolina

Aiken Technical College *C*
Anderson College *A*
Benedict College *B*
Bob Jones University *A,B*
Chesterfield-Marlboro Technical
College *A*
Columbia Junior College of
Business *A*
Denmark Technical College *A*
Florence-Darlington Technical
College *C,A*
Greenville Technical College *A*
Horry-Georgetown Technical
College *A*
Midlands Technical College *A*
Sumter Area Technical College *A*
Technical College of the
Lowcountry *A*
Tri-County Technical College *C,A*
Trident Technical College *C,A*
University of South Carolina at
Lancaster *A*
Williamsburg Technical College *A*

South Dakota

Black Hills State University *A,B*
Dakota State University *A*
Kilian Community College *A*
Mitchell Vocational Technical
    Institute *C,A*
Mount Marty College *C,A*
National College *A*
Northern State University *A,B*
Sioux Falls College *A,B*

Tennessee

Austin Peay State University *A,B*
Belmont University *B*
Bristol University *A*
Chattanooga State Technical
    Community College *A*
Cleveland State Community
    College *A*
Columbia State Community College
    C,A
Dyersburg State Community
    College *A*
East Tennessee State University *B*
Free Will Baptist Bible College *A*
Hiwassee College *A*
Jackson State Community College
    C,A
Knoxville Business College *C,A*
Knoxville College *A,B*
Lincoln Memorial University *A,B*
Martin Methodist College *A*
McKenzie College *A*
Middle Tennessee State
    University *A*
Milligan College *A,B*
Motlow State Community
    College *A*
Nashville State Technical
    Institute *C*
Northeast State Technical
    Community College *C,A*
Pellissippi State Technical
    Community College *A*
Roane State Community College
    C,A
Shelby State Community College
    C,A
Southern College of Seventh-day
    Adventists *A,B*
Tennessee State University *A,B*
Tennessee Temple University *A,B*
Tomlinson College *A*
Trevecca Nazarene College *A,B*
Volunteer State Community
    College *A*
Walters State Community College
    C,A

Texas

Alvin Community College *A*
Amarillo College *C,A*
Angelina College *C,A*
Austin Community College *A*
Bee County College *C,A*
Blinn College *C*
Brazosport College *C,A*
Central Texas College *A*
Cisco Junior College *C,A*
College of the Mainland *C,A*
Collin County Community College
    District *A*
Cooke County College *A*
Dallas Christian College *A*
Del Mar College *C,A*
Eastfield College *A*
El Centro College *A*
Galveston College *A*
Houston Community College *A*
Howard College *C,A*
Howard Payne University *B*

ITT Technical Institute:
    Arlington *C*
Jacksonville College *C*
Kilgore College *A*
Lamar University—Beaumont *A,B*
Laredo Junior College *C,A*
Lee College *A*
Lubbock Christian University *A,B*
McLennan Community College *C,A*
McMurry University *A,B*
Midland College *C,A*
Mountain View College *A*
Navarro College *C,A*
North Lake College *A*
Northeast Texas Community
    College *C,A*
Odessa College *C,A*
Panola College *A*
Ranger Junior College *C,A*
Richland College *C,A*
St. Philip's College *C,A*
San Antonio College *A*
San Jacinto College: Central
    Campus *A*
Schreiner College *A*
South Plains College *C,A*
Southwestern Adventist College *A,B*
Southwestern Christian College *A*
Stephen F. Austin State
    University *B*
Sul Ross State University *B*
Temple Junior College *C,A*
Texarkana College *C,A*
Texas Southern University *B*
Texas Southmost College *A*
Texas State Technical College
    Amarillo *C,A*
    Harlingen *A*
    Sweetwater *A*
Texas Tech University *B*
Texas Woman's University *B*
Trinity Valley Community
    College *A*
University of Houston:
    Downtown *B*
University of Texas: Pan
    American *B*
Vernon Regional Junior College *A*
Victoria College *A*
Wayland Baptist University *C*
Weatherford College *C,A*
Western Texas College *A*
Wharton County Junior College *C*
Wiley College *A*

Utah

College of Eastern Utah *C,A*
Dixie College *C,A*
LDS Business College *C,A*
Phillips Junior College: Salt Lake
    City Campus *C,A*
Southern Utah University *C,A*
Stevens-Henager College of
    Business *A*
Utah State University *A*
Utah Valley Community College
    C,A
Weber State University *A,B*

Vermont

Champlain College *C,A*

Virginia

Blue Ridge Community College *A*
Bluefield College *A*
Central Virginia Community
    College *A*
Commonwealth College *C,A*
Dabney S. Lancaster Community
    College *A*
Eastern Shore Community
    College *A*

Hampton University *B*
James Madison University *B*
John Tyler Community College *C,A*
Lord Fairfax Community College
    C,A
Mountain Empire Community
    College *A*
National Business College *C,A*
New River Community College *A*
Norfolk State University *A,B*
Northern Virginia Community
    College *C,A*
Patrick Henry Community
    College *A*
Paul D. Camp Community
    College *A*
Piedmont Virginia Community
    College *A*
Southside Virginia Community
    College *C,A*
Southwest Virginia Community
    College *C,A*
Tidewater Community College *A*
Virginia Highlands Community
    College *C,A*
Virginia Intermont College *A,B*
Wytheville Community College *C,A*

Washington

Bellevue Community College *C,A*
Big Bend Community College *C,A*
Centralia College *A*
Clark College *A*
Columbia Basin College *C*
Edmonds Community College *C,A*
Everett Community College *A*
Grays Harbor College *A*
Green River Community College
    C,A
Griffin College *C,A*
Lower Columbia College *C,A*
North Seattle Community
    College *A*
Northwest College of the
    Assemblies of God *A*
Northwest Indian College *C,A*
Olympic College *C,A*
Peninsula College *A*
Pierce College *C,A*
Seattle Central Community
    College *A*
Shoreline Community College *A*
Skagit Valley College *A*
South Puget Sound Community
    College *C,A*
Spokane Community College *C,A*
Spokane Falls Community College
    C,A
Tacoma Community College *A*
Walla Walla College *A,B*
Walla Walla Community College
    C,A
Wenatchee Valley College *A*
Whatcom Community College *C,A*
Yakima Valley Community College
    C,A

West Virginia

Bluefield State College *A*
College of West Virginia *C,A*
Concord College *B*
Davis and Elkins College *A,B*
Fairmont State College *C,A,B*
Glenville State College *A*
Marshall University *A*
Ohio Valley College *A*
Potomac State College of West
    Virginia University *A*
Salem-Teikyo University *C,A*
Shepherd College *A,B*
West Virginia Institute of
    Technology *C,A*

West Virginia Northern Community
    College *A*
West Virginia State College *A*
West Virginia University at
    Parkersburg *C,A*

Wisconsin

Chippewa Valley Technical
    College *A*
Concordia University Wisconsin *A*
Fox Valley Technical College *A*
Madison Area Technical College *A*
Madison Junior College of Business
    C,A
Maranatha Baptist Bible College
    A,B
Mid-State Technical College *C,A*
Milwaukee College of Business *C,A*
Moraine Park Technical College *A*
Northeast Wisconsin Technical
    College *A*
Stratton College *A*
University of Wisconsin
    Eau Claire *B*
    Superior *B*
    Whitewater *B*
Waukesha County Technical
    College *A*
Western Wisconsin Technical
    College *A*
Wisconsin Indianhead Technical
    College *C,A*

Wyoming

Casper College *C,A*
Central Wyoming College *C,A*
Eastern Wyoming College *A*
Laramie County Community
    College *C,A*
Northwest College *C,A*
Sheridan College *C,A*
Western Wyoming Community
    College *C,A*

American Samoa, Caroline Islands, Guam, Marianas, Virgin Islands

Guam Community College *A*
Micronesian Occupational
    College *A*
Northern Marianas College *A*
University of the Virgin Islands *A*

Slavic languages

California

Stanford University *B,D*
University of California
    Berkeley *B,M,D*
    Los Angeles *B,M,D*
    Santa Barbara *B*
University of Southern California
    M,D

Connecticut

Yale University *M,D*

Florida

Florida State University *M*
University of Florida *M,D*

Georgia

University of Georgia *B*

Illinois

Northwestern University *M,D*
University of Chicago *B,M,D*

University of Illinois
  Chicago *B,D*
  Urbana-Champaign *M,D*

Indiana

Indiana University Bloomington
B,M,D

Kansas

University of Kansas *B,M,D*

Maryland

University of Maryland: College
Park *B*

Massachusetts

Boston College *B,M*
Harvard and Radcliffe Colleges *B*
Harvard University *D*

Michigan

University of Michigan *M,D*
Wayne State University *B*

New Jersey

Rutgers—The State University of
New Jersey: Newark College of
Arts and Sciences *B*

New York

Columbia University
  Columbia College *B*
  New York *M,D*
  School of General Studies *B*
Cornell University *M,D*
New York University *M,D*
State University of New York at
Stony Brook *M*
Syracuse University *M*

North Carolina

Duke University *B*
University of North Carolina at
Chapel Hill *B,M,D*

Ohio

Ohio State University: Columbus
Campus *B,M,D*

Pennsylvania

California University of
Pennsylvania *B*
University of Pennsylvania *B,M,D*
University of Pittsburgh *M,D*

Rhode Island

Brown University *B,M,D*

Tennessee

University of Tennessee:
Knoxville *B*

Texas

University of Texas at Austin *M*

Virginia

University of Virginia *B,M,D*

Washington

University of Washington *B,M,D*
Western Washington University *B*

Wisconsin

University of Wisconsin: Madison
B,M,D

Small business management and ownership

Alabama

Chattahoochee Valley Community
College *A*
University of Alabama *B*
Wallace State Community College
at Hanceville *A*

Alaska

University of Alaska Anchorage *C*

Arizona

Eastern Arizona College *A*
Mesa Community College *C*
Prescott College *B*

Arkansas

University of Central Arkansas *B*

California

California State University
  Dominguez Hills *B*
  Hayward *B,M*
  Los Angeles *B*
Chaffey Community College *C,A*
Coastline Community College *A*
College of Marin: Kentfield *C,A*
College of the Redwoods *A*
De Anza College *C*
Golden West College *C,A*
Lake Tahoe Community College
C,A
Los Angeles City College *C,A*
Los Angeles Trade and Technical
College *A*
Los Medanos College *C,A*
Mendocino College *A*
Merced College *A*
Mount San Antonio College *C,A*
Mount San Jacinto College *C*
Napa Valley College *A*
Ohlone College *C,A*
Pasadena City College *A*
Phillips Junior College: Fresno
Campus *C,A*
Saddleback College *A*
San Francisco State University *B*
Santa Monica College *C,A*
Santa Rosa Junior College *C*
Solano Community College *A*
Southwestern College *C,A*
Yuba College *A*

Colorado

Arapahoe Community College *C*
Colorado Northwestern Community
College *A*
Denver Technical College *B*
Front Range Community College *C*
Lamar Community College *C*
Mesa State College *B*
Northeastern Junior College *A*
Pueblo Community College *A*
Red Rocks Community College *C*
University of Colorado
  Boulder *B*
  Colorado Springs *B*
Western State College of
Colorado *B*

Connecticut

Middlesex Community College *C*
Quinnipiac College *B,M*

District of Columbia

Gallaudet University *B*
Southeastern University *A,B*

Florida

Broward Community College *C*
Florida Atlantic University *B*
Florida Keys Community College *C*
Florida State University *B*
Lake City Community College *C*
Lynn University *B*
Pasco-Hernando Community
College *C*
Pensacola Junior College *A*
Santa Fe Community College *C*
University of Miami *B*

Georgia

Darton College *A*

Hawaii

Hawaii Pacific University *B*

Idaho

North Idaho College *A*
Ricks College *C,A*

Illinois

Belleville Area College *A*
De Paul University *M*
Kishwaukee College *C*
National-Louis University *C*
Prairie State College *A*
Rock Valley College *A*
Southern Illinois University at
Carbondale *B*
State Community College *C*
Triton College *C*
Waubonsee Community College
C,A
William Rainey Harper College *A*

Indiana

Ball State University *B*
Indiana University Bloomington *B*
Indiana Vocational Technical
College
  Central Indiana *A*
  Columbus *A*
  Eastcentral *C,A*
  Lafayette *C,A*
  Northcentral *C,A*
  Northeast *C,A*
  Northwest *C,A*
  Southcentral *C,A*
  Southeast *C,A*
  Southwest *C,A*
  Wabash Valley *C,A*
  Whitewater *A*
Vincennes University *A*

Iowa

Buena Vista College *B*
Des Moines Area Community
College *C*
Iowa Lakes Community College *A*
Iowa Western Community
College *A*
Kirkwood Community College *A*

Kansas

Butler County Community
College *A*
Central College *A*
Coffeyville Community College *A*
Dodge City Community College *A*
Hutchinson Community College *A*
Pratt Community College *C,A*

Kentucky

Morehead State University *A*
Western Kentucky University *A*

Louisiana

Southern University in
Shreveport *A*

Maine

University of Maine
  Augusta *A,B*
  Machias *A*

Maryland

Essex Community College *C*
Garrett Community College *A*
Prince George's Community
College *C*

Massachusetts

Babson College *B,M*
Berkshire Community College *A*
Dean Junior College *A*
Endicott College *A,B*
Lasell College *A*
Massachusetts Bay Community
College *C*
Mount Wachusett Community
College *A*
Northeastern University *B*
Quinsigamond Community
College *A*

Michigan

Alpena Community College *C*
Baker College: Flint *A*
Delta College *A*
Eastern Michigan University *B*
Ferris State University *B*
Lansing Community College *C*
Lawrence Technological
University *B*
Michigan Technological
University *B*
Mid Michigan Community
College *A*
Montcalm Community College *C,A*
Schoolcraft College *A*
Suomi College *A*

Minnesota

Anoka-Ramsey Community
College *A*
Normandale Community College *A*
University of St. Thomas *B*
Willmar Community College *A*

Mississippi

Mary Holmes College *C*

Missouri

Missouri Valley College *A*
Moberly Area Community
College *A*
Northwest Missouri State
University *B*

Montana

University of Montana *B*

Nebraska

Central Community College *C*

Nevada

Sierra Nevada College *B*
Truckee Meadows Community
College *A*

New Hampshire

Antioch New England Graduate
School *M*
Franklin Pierce College *B*
Hesser College *A*
University of New Hampshire *A*
White Pines College *A*

New Jersey

Bergen Community College *C*
Brookdale Community College *A*
Burlington County College *C*

Camden County College *A*
Gloucester County College *A*

New Mexico

Albuquerque Technical-Vocational
Institute *C*
New Mexico Junior College *A*
Northern New Mexico Community
College *A*

New York

Bryant & Stratton Business Institute
Albany *C*
Rochester *A*
Columbia-Greene Community
College *C*
Erie Community College
City Campus *C*
North Campus *C*
Fashion Institute of Technology *C*
Fulton-Montgomery Community
College *A*
Herkimer County Community
College *C,A*
Medaille College *C,B*
Mohawk Valley Community
College *C*
Monroe Community College *C*
Nassau Community College *C*
Rochester Institute of Technology
C,A,B,M
Westchester Business Institute *A*

North Carolina

Edgecombe Community College *C*
Wingate College *B*

North Dakota

Standing Rock College *A*

Ohio

Columbus State Community
College *A*
Cuyahoga Community College
Metropolitan Campus *A*
Western Campus *A*
Kent State University: East
Liverpool Regional Campus *A*
Lakeland Community College *C*
Lourdes College *B*
Ohio State University Agricultural
Technical Institute *A*
Ohio University *B*
Shawnee State University *A*
Union Institute *B,D*
University of Akron *A*
Xavier University *B*

Oklahoma

Connors State College *C,A*
Rose State College *A*
Tulsa Junior College *C,A*

Oregon

Clatsop Community College *C*
Concordia College *B*
Mount Hood Community
College *A*
Portland Community College *C*
Rogue Community College *C*
Southwestern Oregon Community
College *C*
Umpqua Community College *C*

Pennsylvania

Bucks County Community
College *A*
Central Pennsylvania Business
School *A*
Gettysburg College *B*
La Salle University *B*

Northampton County Area
Community College *C*
Peirce Junior College *A*
Philadelphia College of Textiles and
Science *A*
Reading Area Community College
C,A
Waynesburg College *B*
West Chester University of
Pennsylvania *M*

Rhode Island

Johnson & Wales University *A*

South Carolina

Florence-Darlington Technical
College *A*

South Dakota

Kilian Community College *A*
Mount Marty College *C*

Tennessee

Bristol University *A,B,M*
Chattanooga State Technical
Community College *A*
Nashville State Technical
Institute *A*
Roane State Community College *A*

Texas

Baylor University *B*
Brookhaven College *A*
Collin County Community College
District *C,A*
Midland College *C,A*
Richland College *C,A*
St. Mary's University *B*
Tarrant County Junior College *A*
Texas Southmost College *A*

Utah

Southern Utah University *B*

Vermont

Champlain College *A*
Lyndon State College *A,B*
Trinity College of Vermont *C*

Virginia

Averett College *B*
Dabney S. Lancaster Community
College *C*
Ferrum College *B*
John Tyler Community College *C*
Northern Virginia Community
College *C*
Radford University *B*

Washington

Big Bend Community College *A*
Clark College *A*
Edmonds Community College *C,A*
Skagit Valley College *A*
Spokane Falls Community College
C,A
Walla Walla Community College *C*

West Virginia

Potomac State College of West
Virginia University *A*

Wisconsin

Fox Valley Technical College *C*
University of Wisconsin
Green Bay *B*
Oshkosh *B*
Wisconsin Indianhead Technical
College *C*

Wyoming

Northwest College *A*
University of Wyoming *B*

**American Samoa, Caroline
Islands, Guam, Marianas,
Virgin Islands**

Northern Marianas College *A*

Canada

McGill University *M*

Social foundations

Alabama

Troy State University
Dothan *M*
Montgomery *M*
University of Alabama *M*

Arizona

Arizona State University *M*
University of Arizona *M,D*

California

California State University
Long Beach *M*
Los Angeles *M*
Northridge *M*
La Sierra University *M*
Stanford University *M,D*
University of the Pacific *M,D*
University of Southern California
M,D

Colorado

University of Colorado
Boulder *M,D*
Denver *M*

Connecticut

Central Connecticut State
University *M*

Delaware

University of Delaware *M,D*

District of Columbia

Howard University *M*
University of the District of
Columbia *B*

Florida

Florida Atlantic University *M*
University of Florida *M,D*

Georgia

Georgia State University *M,D*
University of Georgia *M,D*

Illinois

Loyola University of Chicago *M*
Northern Illinois University *M*
Northwestern University *M,D*
Richland Community College *A*
Southern Illinois University at
Carbondale *M,D*
University of Illinois at Urbana-
Champaign *M,D*

Indiana

Indiana University Bloomington
M,D

Iowa

Iowa State University *M,D*
Maharishi International
University *M*
University of Iowa *M,D*

University of Northern Iowa *M*

Kansas

University of Kansas *M,D*

Kentucky

University of Kentucky *M,D*

Maryland

Loyola College in Maryland *M*
University of Maryland: College
Park *M,D*

Massachusetts

Hampshire College *B*
Harvard University *M,D,W*
Suffolk University *M*
Tufts University *M*

Michigan

Andrews University *M*
Eastern Michigan University *M*
University of Michigan *M,D*
Wayne State University *M,D*

Minnesota

University of Minnesota: Twin
Cities *M*

Missouri

St. Louis University *M,D*
University of Missouri: Columbia
M,D

Nebraska

University of Nebraska—Lincoln
M,D

New Hampshire

Antioch New England Graduate
School *M*

New Jersey

Rutgers—The State University of
New Jersey *M,D*

New Mexico

University of New Mexico *D*

New York

Fordham University *M*
Hofstra University *M,W*
New York University *M,D*
State University of New York at
Buffalo *M,D*

North Carolina

University of North Carolina at
Chapel Hill *D*

Ohio

Miami University: Oxford
Campus *M*
University of Akron *M*
University of Dayton *M*
University of Toledo *M,D*

Oklahoma

University of Oklahoma *M,D*

Pennsylvania

Lehigh University *D*
Penn State University Park Campus
M,D
Temple University *M,D*
University of Pennsylvania *M,D*

Rhode Island

Rhode Island College *M*

South Carolina
University of South Carolina D

Tennessee
Memphis State University M,D

Texas
Stephen F. Austin State University B,W
Texas Tech University B,M,D
University of Houston M,D

Utah
University of Utah M,D

Vermont
University of Vermont M

Wisconsin
Marquette University M,D
University of Wisconsin:
Milwaukee M

Canada
McGill University M,D

Social psychology

Arizona
Prescott College B

Arkansas
University of Central Arkansas B

California
California State University
Northridge M
Sacramento M
New College of California M
San Francisco State University M
San Jose State University B
United States International
University B
University of California: Santa Cruz B,D
University of San Francisco B

Colorado
University of Colorado at
Boulder D

Connecticut
Wesleyan University B

Delaware
University of Delaware M,D

District of Columbia
American University M
Catholic University of America M,D
George Washington University D

Florida
Florida Atlantic University B
New College of the University of
South Florida B

Illinois
Loyola University of Chicago M,D
University of Chicago M,D
University of Illinois at Urbana-
Champaign B,M,D

Indiana
Indiana University Bloomington M,D
Indiana University—Purdue
University at Indianapolis M

Purdue University B,M,D
University of Notre Dame M,D

Iowa
University of Iowa D

Kansas
Kansas State University M,D
University of Kansas D

Massachusetts
Clark University D
Elms College B
Hampshire College B
Harvard University D
Tufts University B,M,D
University of Massachusetts at
Lowell M

Michigan
University of Michigan M,D

Minnesota
Northland Community College A
Willmar Community College A

Missouri
University of Missouri
Columbia M,D
Kansas City M
St. Louis B,M,D

Nebraska
Chadron State College B

Nevada
University of Nevada: Reno B,D

New Hampshire
University of New Hampshire D

New Jersey
Rutgers—The State University of
New Jersey M,D

New York
City University of New York
Graduate School and University
Center D
Columbia University M,D
Cornell University M,D
New York University M,D
Pace University
College of White Plains B
New York B
Pleasantville/Briarcliff B
Sarah Lawrence College B
State University of New York at
Buffalo D
Syracuse University M,D
University of Rochester D

Ohio
Bowling Green State University M,D
College of Mount St. Joseph B
Miami University: Oxford
Campus D
Ohio State University: Columbus
Campus M,D
Union Institute B,D
University of Dayton M
University of Toledo B,D
Urbana University B

Oregon
Northwest Christian College M

Pennsylvania
Bucknell University B
Carnegie Mellon University B,M,D,W

La Salle University B
Lehigh University B
Temple University D
University of Pennsylvania D

Rhode Island
Rhode Island College M

Texas
University of Houston M,D

Utah
Brigham Young University D

Virginia
Averett College B
Virginia Wesleyan College B

West Virginia
Bethany College B

Canada
McGill University B,M,D

Social science education

Alabama
Alabama Agricultural and
Mechanical University B,M
Alabama State University B,M
Auburn University
Auburn B,M,D
Montgomery B,M
Birmingham-Southern College B
Huntingdon College B
Jacksonville State University B,M
Judson College B
Livingston University B,M
Miles College B
Oakwood College B
Samford University B,M
Spring Hill College B
Troy State University
Dothan B,M
Montgomery M
University of Alabama B
University of Montevallo B,M
University of North Alabama B,M

Alaska
Sheldon Jackson College B
University of Alaska
Anchorage M
Fairbanks M

Arizona
Eastern Arizona College A
Northern Arizona University B

Arkansas
Arkansas State University B,M
Harding University B
Henderson State University B,M
Ouachita Baptist University B
University of Arkansas at Pine
Bluff B
University of Central Arkansas B

California
Azusa Pacific University B
Bethany College B
California Baptist College B
California Lutheran University B
California Polytechnic State
University: San Luis Obispo B

California State University
Bakersfield B
Los Angeles B
Northridge B
Sacramento B
Christ College Irvine B
Christian Heritage College B
College of Notre Dame M
Fresno Pacific College B
Humboldt State University B
Mount St. Mary's College B
Pacific Christian College B
Simpson College B
University of the Pacific B
University of Redlands B
University of San Francisco B
Westmont College B

Colorado
University of Colorado at Colorado
Springs B
University of Northern Colorado B

Connecticut
Eastern Connecticut State
University M
St. Joseph College B
Southern Connecticut State
University B,M
University of Bridgeport B,M
Western Connecticut State
University B

Delaware
University of Delaware B
Wesley College B

Florida
Flagler College B
Florida Agricultural and Mechanical
University M
Florida Atlantic University B,M
Palm Beach Community College A
Pensacola Junior College A
Southeastern College of the
Assemblies of God B
Stetson University B
University of Central Florida B,M
University of North Florida B
University of South Florida B,M
University of Tampa B
University of West Florida B

Georgia
Albany State College B,M
Armstrong State College B,M
Augusta College M
Berry College B
Brenau Women's College B
Columbus College B,M
Georgia College B,M
Georgia Southern University B,M
Georgia Southwestern College B,M
Georgia State University M,D
Mercer University M
North Georgia College B,M
Piedmont College B
Shorter College B,M
University of Georgia B,M,D
Wesleyan College B
West Georgia College B

Hawaii
Brigham Young University-
Hawaii B

Idaho
Boise State University B
Northwest Nazarene College B

Illinois

Barat College *B*
Blackburn College *B*
Concordia University *B*
De Paul University *B*
Eastern Illinois University *B*
Elmhurst College *B*
Greenville College *B*
Illinois Wesleyan University *B*
Millikin University *B*
North Central College *B*
North Park College and Theological
Seminary *B*
Northern Illinois University *B*
Northwestern University *B,M*
Olivet Nazarene University *B*
Southern Illinois University at
Carbondale *B*
Trinity Christian College *B*
University of Illinois at Chicago
B,M
Wheaton College *B*

Indiana

Ball State University *B,M*
Butler University *B*
Calumet College of St. Joseph *B*
Indiana State University *B,M*
Indiana University Bloomington *B*
Manchester College *B*
Martin University *B*
St. Joseph's College *B*
Taylor University *B*
Tri-State University *B*
University of Southern Indiana *B*
Vincennes University *A*

Iowa

Briar Cliff College *B*
Buena Vista College *B*
Clarke College *B*
Cornell College *B*
Drake University *B*
Grand View College *B*
Iowa Lakes Community College *A*
Morningside College *B*
Mount Mercy College *B*
Simpson College *B*
Teikyo Westmar University *B*
University of Iowa *B*
University of Northern Iowa *B,M*
Upper Iowa University *B*
Wartburg College *B*
William Penn College *B*

Kansas

Bethany College *B*
Colby Community College *A*
Emporia State University *B,M*
Friends University *B*
McPherson College *B*
MidAmerica Nazarene College *B*
Pittsburg State University *B*
St. Mary College *B*
Tabor College *B*
Washburn University of Topeka *B*

Kentucky

Berea College *B*
Eastern Kentucky University *B,M*
Georgetown College *B*
Murray State University *B*
Pikeville College *B*
Sue Bennett College *A*
Thomas More College *B*
Transylvania University *B*

Louisiana

Dillard University *B*
Grambling State University *B*
McNeese State University *M*
Northwestern State University *B*

Our Lady of Holy Cross College *B*
Xavier University of Louisiana *B*

Maine

University of Maine
Farmington *B*
Presque Isle *B*

Maryland

Baltimore Hebrew University *B,M*
Montgomery College: Germantown
Campus *A*

Massachusetts

American International College *B*
Bridgewater State College *M*
Elms College *B*
Fitchburg State College *B*
Hampshire College *B*
Merrimack College *B*
Springfield College *B*
Tufts University *M*
Westfield State College *B*

Michigan

Adrian College *B*
Aquinas College *B*
Concordia College *B*
Eastern Michigan University *B,M*
Grand Rapids Baptist College and
Seminary *B*
Grand Valley State University *B*
Lansing Community College *A*
Madonna University *B*
Marygrove College *B*
Michigan State University *B*
Northern Michigan University *B*
University of Michigan *M,D*
Western Michigan University *B*

Minnesota

Bemidji State University *B*
Bethel College *B*
College of St. Scholastica *B*
Concordia College: Moorhead *B*
Concordia College: St. Paul *B*
Crown College *B*
Macalester College *B*
Mankato State University *B*
Northland Community College *A*
Rainy River Community College *A*
St. Cloud State University *B*
Southwest State University *B*
Vermilion Community College *A*
Willmar Community College *A*
Winona State University *B*

Mississippi

Alcorn State University *B,M*
Blue Mountain College *B*
Delta State University *B,M*
Jackson State University *B*
Jones County Junior College *A*
Mary Holmes College *A*
Mississippi College *B,M*
Mississippi Gulf Coast Community
College: Jefferson Davis
Campus *A*
Mississippi University for Women *B*
Northeast Mississippi Community
College *A*
Rust College *B*

Missouri

College of the Ozarks *B*
Columbia College *B*
Fontbonne College *B*
Maryville University *B*
Missouri Baptist College *B*
Northwest Missouri State
University *B,M*

Southeast Missouri State University
B,M
Southwest Missouri State
University *B*
University of Missouri: Kansas
City *B*
Washington University *B,M*
Webster University *M*
William Woods College *B*

Montana

Carroll College *B*
Eastern Montana College *B*
Northern Montana College *B*
Rocky Mountain College *B*
University of Montana *B*
Western Montana College of the
University of Montana *B*

Nebraska

Chadron State College *B*
College of St. Mary *B*
Concordia College *B*
Creighton University *B*
Dana College *B*
Doane College *B*
Hastings College *B*
Nebraska Wesleyan University *B*
Peru State College *B*
Union College *B*
University of Nebraska
Kearney *B,M*
Lincoln *B*
Omaha *B*
Wayne State College *B,M*

New Hampshire

Franklin Pierce College *B*
Keene State College *B*
Plymouth State College of the
University System of New
Hampshire *B*
Rivier College *B*

New Jersey

County College of Morris *A*
Glassboro State College *B,M*
Seton Hall University *B*
Stockton State College *B*

New Mexico

College of the Southwest *B*
New Mexico State University *B*

New York

City University of New York
Brooklyn College *B*
Hunter College *B*
Daemen College *B*
Dominican College of Blauvelt *B*
Long Island University
Brooklyn Campus *M*
Southampton Campus *B*
Manhattan College *B*
Manhattanville College *M*
Mohawk Valley Community
College *A*
Russell Sage College *B*
St. Bonaventure University *B*
Siena College *B*
State University of New York
Binghamton *M*
College at Brockport *M*
College at Geneseo *B*
College at Oneonta *B,M*
College at Plattsburgh *B*
College at Potsdam *B,M*
Syracuse University *B,M*
Wells College *B*

North Carolina

Anson Community College *A*
Appalachian State University *B*
Campbell University *B*
Catawba College *B*
Fayetteville State University *B*
Gardner-Webb College *B*
Johnson C. Smith University *B*
Livingstone College *B*
Mars Hill College *B*
Methodist College *A,B*
Montreat-Anderson College *B*
North Carolina Agricultural and
Technical State University *B,M*
St. Andrews Presbyterian College *B*
St. Augustine's College *B*
Salem College *B*
Western Carolina University *B,M*
Wingate College *B*

North Dakota

Bismarck State College *A*
Dickinson State University *B*
Mayville State University *B*
Minot State University *B*
North Dakota State University *B,M*
Turtle Mountain Community
College *A*
University of Mary *B*
University of North Dakota *B*
Valley City State University *B*

Ohio

Capital University *B*
Cedarville College *B*
Defiance College *B*
Heidelberg College *B*
Malone College *B*
Miami University: Oxford
Campus *B*
Mount Union College *B*
Ohio Dominican College *B*
Ohio State University: Columbus
Campus *B*
Ohio University *B*
University of Findlay *B*
University of Rio Grande *B*
University of Toledo *B*
Walsh College *B*
Wittenberg University *B*
Wright State University *B,M*
Youngstown State University *B*

Oklahoma

Bartlesville Wesleyan College *B*
Mid-America Bible College *B*
Northwestern Oklahoma State
University *B*
Oklahoma Baptist University *B*
Oklahoma Panhandle State
University *B*
Southeastern Oklahoma State
University *B,M*
Southwestern Oklahoma State
University *B,M*
University of Science and Arts of
Oklahoma *B*
University of Tulsa *B*

Oregon

Southern Oregon State College *M*
Warner Pacific College *B*
Western Oregon State College *B,M*
Willamette University *M*

Pennsylvania

California University of
Pennsylvania *B,M*
Carlow College *B*
Cheyney University of
Pennsylvania *B*
Gannon University *B*

Gettysburg College *B*
Grove City College *B*
Harrisburg Area Community
  College *A*
Immaculata College *B*
Indiana University of
  Pennsylvania *B*
La Salle University *B*
Lock Haven University of
  Pennsylvania *B*
Mansfield University of
  Pennsylvania *B*
Marywood College *B*
Mercyhurst College *B*
Messiah College *B*
Point Park College *B*
Seton Hill College *B*
Slippery Rock University of
  Pennsylvania *B*
University of Pittsburgh at Bradford
  C,B
University of Scranton *B*
West Chester University of
  Pennsylvania *B,M*
Wilkes University *B,M*

Puerto Rico

University of Puerto Rico: Rio
  Piedras Campus *B*

Rhode Island

University of Rhode Island *M*

South Carolina

The Citadel *M*
Columbia College *B*
Converse College *M*
University of South Carolina at
  Aiken *B*

South Dakota

Black Hills State University *B*
Dakota Wesleyan University *B*
Huron University *B*
Mount Marty College *B*
Northern State University *B,M*
Sioux Falls College *B*
South Dakota State University *B*
University of South Dakota *B*

Tennessee

Carson-Newman College *B*
Crichton College *B*
East Tennessee State University
  B,M
Lincoln Memorial University *B*
Tennessee Technological
  University *B*
Tennessee Wesleyan College *B*
Trevecca Nazarene College *B*
Union University *B,M*
University of Tennessee
  Chattanooga *B,M*
  Knoxville *B*
William Jennings Bryan College *B*

Texas

Baylor University *B*
Dallas Baptist University *B*
East Texas Baptist University *B*
Hardin-Simmons University *B*
McMurry University *B*
Prairie View A&M University *M*
St. Mary's University *B*
Schreiner College *B*
Southwest Texas State
  University *M*
Texas Christian University *B*
Texas College *B*
University of Houston *B,M*
University of Mary Hardin-
  Baylor *B*

University of Texas at San
  Antonio *M*
Wiley College *B*

Utah

Brigham Young University *B*
Weber State University *B*

Vermont

Castleton State College *B*
Lyndon State College *B*
St. Michael's College *B*
University of Vermont *B*

Virginia

Averett College *B*
Eastern Mennonite College *B*
George Mason University *M*
Liberty University *B*
Old Dominion University *B*
Virginia Wesleyan College *B*

Washington

Central Washington University *B,M*
Eastern Washington University *B,M*
Pacific Lutheran University *B*
Seattle Pacific University *B*
University of Puget Sound *M*
University of Washington *B*

West Virginia

Bethany College *B*
Concord College *B*
Glenville State College *B*
Shepherd College *B*
West Liberty State College *B*
West Virginia Institute of
  Technology *B*

Wisconsin

Alverno College *B*
Cardinal Stritch College *B*
Carroll College *B*
Carthage College *B*
Concordia University Wisconsin *B*
Lakeland College *B*
Lawrence University *B*
Marquette University *B*
Mount Senario College *B*
Northland College *B*
St. Norbert College *B*
University of Wisconsin
  Eau Claire *B*
  Green Bay *B*
  La Crosse *B*
  Madison *B,M*
  Oshkosh *B*
  Platteville *B*
  River Falls *B*
  Stevens Point *B*
  Whitewater *B*

Wyoming

University of Wyoming *B,M*

Social sciences

Alabama

Athens State College *B*
Brewer State Junior College *A*
James H. Faulkner State
  Community College *A*
Judson College *B*
Lawson State Community
  College *A*
Livingston University *B*
Marion Military Institute *A*
Miles College *B*
Oakwood College *B*

Samford University *A,B*
Selma University *A*
Shelton State Community
  College *A*
Troy State University
  Dothan *B*
  Montgomery *B*
  Troy *B*
University of Montevallo *B*

Alaska

Alaska Pacific University *A,B*
Sheldon Jackson College *B*

Arizona

Arizona Western College *A*
Eastern Arizona College *A*
Glendale Community College *A*
Grand Canyon University *B*
Navajo Community College *A*
Northern Arizona University *B*
Prescott College *B*

Arkansas

Arkansas Baptist College *B*
Arkansas State University
  Beebe Branch *A*
  Jonesboro *B*
Harding University *B,M*
Henderson State University *B*
John Brown University *B*
Ouachita Baptist University *B*
Phillips County Community
  College *A*
Shorter College *A*
University of Arkansas
  Monticello *B*
  Pine Bluff *B*
University of Central Arkansas *B,M*
University of the Ozarks *B*

California

Allan Hancock College *A*
Azusa Pacific University *B,M*
Barstow College *A*
Bethany College *B*
Biola University *B*
California Baptist College *B*
California Institute of Technology
  B,D
California Polytechnic State
  University: San Luis Obispo *B*
California State Polytechnic
  University: Pomona *B*
California State University
  Chico *B,M*
  Fresno *B*
  Fullerton *M*
  Los Angeles *B*
  Sacramento *B,M*
  San Bernardino *B,M*
  San Marcos *B*
  Stanislaus *B*
Cerro Coso Community College *A*
Chabot College *A*
Chaffey Community College *A*
Chapman University *B*
Christ College Irvine *B*
Christian Heritage College *B*
Citrus College *A*
College of the Desert *A*
College of Notre Dame *B*
College of the Sequoias *A*
Columbia College *A*
Cosumnes River College *A*
Crafton Hills College *A*
Feather River College *A*
Foothill College *A*
Fresno City College *A*
Fresno Pacific College *B*
Gavilan Community College *A*
Glendale Community College *A*

Golden West College *A*
Holy Names College *B*
Humboldt State University *B*
Imperial Valley College *A*
Kings River Community College *A*
Lake Tahoe Community College *A*
Laney College *A*
Lassen College *A*
Long Beach City College *A*
Los Angeles Mission College *A*
Los Medanos College *A*
Marymount College *A*
Mendocino College *A*
Merced College *A*
MiraCosta College *A*
Mission College *A*
Modesto Junior College *A*
Moorpark College *A*
Mount St. Mary's College *B*
Mount San Jacinto College *A*
Napa Valley College *A*
Ohlone College *A*
Pacific Christian College *B*
Pacific Union College *B*
Pasadena City College *A*
Porterville College *A*
Saddleback College *A*
San Diego City College *A*
San Diego Mesa College *A*
San Diego State University *B,M*
San Francisco State University *B,M*
San Joaquin Delta College *A*
San Jose City College *A*
San Jose State University *B,M*
Santa Monica College *A*
Santa Rosa Junior College *A*
Scripps College *B*
Simpson College *B*
Skyline College *A*
Solano Community College *A*
Southern California College *B*
Southwestern College *A*
Taft College *A*
United States International
  University *B*
University of California
  Berkeley *B*
  Irvine *B,M,D*
  Santa Barbara *B*
University of La Verne *B*
University of the Pacific *B*
University of San Diego *B*
University of San Francisco *B*
Ventura College *A*
West Hills Community College *A*
West Valley College *A*
Westmont College *B*
Whittier College *B*
Yuba College *A*

Colorado

Arapahoe Community College *A*
Colorado Christian University *B*
Colorado Mountain College
  Alpine Campus *A*
  Spring Valley Campus *A*
Colorado State University *B*
Community College of Denver *A*
Lamar Community College *A*
Mesa State College *B*
Northeastern Junior College *A*
Trinidad State Junior College *A*
United States Air Force
  Academy *B*
University of Colorado at Denver
  B,M
University of Denver *B*
University of Northern Colorado *B*
University of Southern Colorado *B*

Connecticut

Albertus Magnus College *B*
Central Connecticut State
  University *B,M*
Eastern Connecticut State
  University *B*
Holy Apostles College and
  Seminary *B*
Mitchell College *A*
Northwestern Connecticut
  Community College *A*
Sacred Heart University *B*
Southern Connecticut State
  University *B,M*
University of Hartford *A*
Wesleyan University *B*
Western Connecticut State
  University *A,B,M*

Delaware

Wesley College *A*

Florida

Brevard Community College *A*
Central Florida Community
  College *A*
Daytona Beach Community
  College *A*
Flagler College *B*
Florida Agricultural and Mechanical
  University *M*
Florida Atlantic University *B*
Florida Southern College *B*
Florida State University *B,M*
Gulf Coast Community College *A*
Indian River Community College *A*
Lynn University *B*
New College of the University of
  South Florida *B*
Okaloosa-Walton Community
  College *A*
Palm Beach Community College *A*
Pensacola Junior College *A*
South Florida Community
  College *A*
Stetson University *B*
University of Central Florida *B*
University of South Florida *B*
University of Tampa *B*
University of West Florida *B*
Warner Southern College *B*

Georgia

Abraham Baldwin Agricultural
  College *A*
Andrew College *A*
Berry College *B*
Brewton-Parker College *A*
Clark Atlanta University *B*
Darton College *A*
East Georgia College *A*
Georgia College *B*
Georgia Southern University *B*
Georgia Southwestern College *B*
Mercer University *B*
Middle Georgia College *A*
North Georgia College *B*
Reinhardt College *A*
Shorter College *B*
South Georgia College *A*
University of Georgia *B*
Waycross College *A*
Young Harris College *A*

Hawaii

Chaminade University of
  Honolulu *B*
Hawaii Loa College *B*
Hawaii Pacific University *B*
University of Hawaii: West Oahu *B*

Idaho

Boise State University *B*
Lewis Clark State College *B*
North Idaho College *A*
Northwest Nazarene College *A,B*
University of Idaho *M*

Illinois

Aurora University *B*
Barat College *B*
Bradley University *B*
City Colleges of Chicago
    Olive-Harvey College *A*
    Wright College *A*
De Paul University *B*
Eureka College *B*
Governors State University *B*
Greenville College *B*
Illinois Benedictine College *B*
Illinois State University *B*
Illinois Valley Community
  College *A*
Judson College *B*
Kendall College *B*
Kishwaukee College *A*
Lake Forest College *B*
McKendree College *B*
Monmouth College *B*
Montay College *A*
Morton College *A*
National-Louis University *B*
North Park College and Theological
  Seminary *B*
Northeastern Illinois University
  B,M
Northern Illinois University *B*
Olivet Nazarene University *B*
Rend Lake College *A*
Richland Community College *A*
Rockford College *B*
Roosevelt University *B*
Rosary College *B*
St. Augustine College *A*
St. Xavier University *B*
Shimer College *B*
Southern Illinois University at
  Carbondale *B*
Trinity College *B*
Triton College *A*
University of Chicago *B,M*
Waubonsee Community College *A*
Wheaton College *B*
William Rainey Harper College *A*

Indiana

Anderson University *B*
Ball State University *B,M*
Bethel College *A,B*
Calumet College of St. Joseph *B*
Goshen College *B*
Indiana State University *B,M*
Indiana University at Kokomo *B*
Indiana Wesleyan University *B*
St. Francis College *B*
Tri-State University *B*
University of Southern Indiana *A,B*
Vincennes University *A*

Iowa

Buena Vista College *B*
Clinton Community College *A*
Dordt College *B*
Drake University *B*
Graceland College *B*
Grand View College *B*
Iowa Lakes Community College *A*
Iowa Western Community
  College *A*
Kirkwood Community College *A*
Loras College *B*
Luther College *B*
Muscatine Community College *A*

North Iowa Area Community
  College *A*
Northwestern College *B*
Scott Community College *A*
Teikyo Westmar University *B*
University of Iowa *B,M*
University of Northern Iowa *B,M*
Upper Iowa University *B*
Vennard College *B*
Waldorf College *A*
Wartburg College *B*
William Penn College *B*

Kansas

Allen County Community
  College *A*
Baker University *B*
Barton County Community
  College *A*
Benedictine College *B*
Bethel College *B*
Butler County Community
  College *A*
Central College *A*
Cloud County Community
  College *A*
Coffeyville Community College *A*
Colby Community College *A*
Cowley County Community
  College *A*
Dodge City Community College *A*
Emporia State University *B*
Fort Scott Community College *A*
Friends University *B*
Highland Community College *A*
Hutchinson Community College *A*
Kansas City College and Bible
  School *B*
Kansas City Kansas Community
  College *A*
Kansas State University *B*
Labette Community College *A*
McPherson College *B*
Neosho County Community
  College *A*
Ottawa University *B*
Pittsburg State University *B*
Pratt Community College *A*
Seward County Community
  College *A*
Southwestern College *B*
Tabor College *B*

Kentucky

Brescia College *B*
Campbellsville College *A,B*
Kentucky Christian College *B*
Lindsey Wilson College *A,B*
Morehead State University *B*
St. Catharine College *A*
Sue Bennett College *A*
Western Kentucky University *B*

Louisiana

Grambling State University *B,M*
Louisiana College *B*
Loyola University *B*
Northwestern State University *B*
Our Lady of Holy Cross College *B*
Southern University
    New Orleans *B*
    Shreveport *A*

Maine

University of Maine
    Augusta *A,B*
    Fort Kent *B*
    Presque Isle *B*

Maryland

Baltimore Hebrew University *B,M*
Charles County Community
  College *A*
Chesapeake College *A*
College of Notre Dame of
  Maryland *B*
Coppin State College *B*
Frostburg State University *B*
Howard Community College *A*
Johns Hopkins University *B,M,D*
Montgomery College
    Germantown Campus *A*
    Rockville Campus *A*
    Takoma Park Campus *A*
Salisbury State University *B*
Towson State University *B*
University of Baltimore *B*
University of Maryland: Eastern
  Shore *B*

Massachusetts

Becker College: Leicester
  Campus *A*
Berkshire Community College *A*
Bradford College *B*
Bridgewater State College *M*
Dean Junior College *A*
Eastern Nazarene College *B*
Elms College *B*
Endicott College *A*
Greenfield Community College *A*
Hampshire College *B*
Harvard and Radcliffe Colleges *B*
Lesley College *B*
Northern Essex Community College
  C,A
Quincy College *A*
Roxbury Community College *A*
Simon's Rock College of Bard *B*
Westfield State College *B*

Michigan

Adrian College *B*
Andrews University *B*
Aquinas College *B*
Central Michigan University *B*
Concordia College *B*
Eastern Michigan University *B,M*
Glen Oaks Community College *A*
Grand Valley State University *B*
Hope College *B*
Kellogg Community College *A*
Lake Superior State University *B*
Lansing Community College *A*
Madonna University *A,B*
Marygrove College *B*
Michigan State University *B,M,D*
Michigan Technological
  University *B*
Northern Michigan University *B*
St. Mary's College *B*
Siena Heights College *B*
Spring Arbor College *B*
University of Michigan
    Ann Arbor *B*
    Flint *B*
West Shore Community College *A*
Western Michigan University *B*
William Tyndale College *B*

Minnesota

Augsburg College *B*
Bemidji State University *B,M*
Bethany Lutheran College *A*
Bethel College *B*
College of St. Benedict *B*
College of St. Catherine: St.
  Catherine Campus *B*
College of St. Scholastica *B*
Concordia College: St. Paul *B*
Gustavus Adolphus College *B*

Macalester College *B*
Mankato State University *B*
Northland Community College *A*
Northwestern College *A,B*
Rainy River Community College *A*
St. Cloud State University *B,M*
St. John's University *B*
St. Mary's College of Minnesota *B*
Southwest State University *B*
University of Minnesota
    Morris *B*
    Twin Cities *M,D*
University of St. Thomas *B*
Vermilion Community College *A*
Willmar Community College *A*
Winona State University *B*

Mississippi

Alcorn State University *B*
Blue Mountain College *B*
Delta State University *B*
Jackson State University *B*
Jones County Junior College *A*
Mary Holmes College *A*
Mississippi College *B,M*
Mississippi Delta Community
    College *A*
Mississippi Gulf Coast Community
    College: Jefferson Davis
    Campus *A*
Mississippi University for Women *B*
Rust College *B*
University of Southern
    Mississippi *B*
William Carey College *B*

Missouri

College of the Ozarks *B*
Drury College *B*
East Central College *A*
Evangel College *A,B*
Fontbonne College *B*
Jefferson College *A*
Lincoln University *B,M*
Maryville University *B*
Mineral Area College *A*
Missouri Baptist College *B*
Missouri Valley College *B*
Moberly Area Community
    College *A*
Northwest Missouri State
    University *B*
Rockhurst College *B*
St. Louis Community College
    Florissant Valley *A*
    Forest Park *A*
    Meramec *A*
Southwest Baptist University *B*
Stephens College *B*
University of Missouri: Columbia *B*
Washington University *B*
Webster University *B*

Montana

Carroll College *B*
College of Great Falls *B*
Fort Peck Community College *A*
Miles Community College *A*
Rocky Mountain College *B*

Nebraska

Bellevue College *B*
Central Community College *A*
Chadron State College *B*
College of St. Mary *B*
Concordia College *B*
Dana College *B*
Doane College *B*
McCook Community College *A*
Midland Lutheran College *B*
Northeast Community College *A*
Peru State College *B*

Southeast Community College:
    Beatrice Campus *A*
Union College *B*
University of Nebraska—Kearney
    B,M
Western Nebraska Community
    College: Scottsbluff Campus *A*
York College *A*

Nevada

Community College of Southern
    Nevada *A*
University of Nevada: Las Vegas *B*

New Hampshire

Franklin Pierce College *B*
Keene State College *B*
New Hampshire College *B*
Plymouth State College of the
    University System of New
    Hampshire *B*

New Jersey

Atlantic Community College *A*
Bergen Community College *A*
Brookdale Community College *A*
Burlington County College *A*
Caldwell College *B*
County College of Morris *A*
Cumberland County College *A*
Essex County College *A*
Glassboro State College *M*
Montclair State College *M*
St. Peter's College *A,B*
Stevens Institute of Technology *B*
Thomas Edison State College *A,B*
William Paterson College of New
    Jersey *B,M*

New Mexico

College of Santa Fe *A,B*
Eastern New Mexico University *B*
New Mexico Junior College *A*
New Mexico State University *B*
University of New Mexico *B*
Western New Mexico University *B*

New York

Adelphi University *B*
Adirondack Community College *A*
Bard College *B*
Canisius College *A*
City University of New York:
    Medgar Evers College *A*
Clarkson University *B*
Colgate University *B*
College of Mount St. Vincent *A*
Columbia-Greene Community
    College *A*
Community College of the Finger
    Lakes *A*
Cornell University *B,M,D*
Corning Community College *A*
Dominican College of Blauvelt *B*
Dowling College *B*
D'Youville College *B*
Elmira College *B*
Erie Community College
    City Campus *A*
    North Campus *A*
    South Campus *A*
Eugene Lang College/New School
    for Social Research *B*
Fordham University *B*
Fulton-Montgomery Community
    College *A*
Genesee Community College *A*
Herkimer County Community
    College *A*
Hilbert College *A*
Hofstra University *B*
Houghton College *B*

Hudson Valley Community
    College *A*
Iona College *B*
Ithaca College *B*
Jamestown Community College *A*
Jefferson Community College *A*
Long Island University
    Brooklyn Campus *B,M*
    C. W. Post Campus *B*
    Southampton Campus *B*
Manhattan College *B*
Medaille College *B*
Mohawk Valley Community
    College *A*
Molloy College *B*
Mount St. Mary College *B*
Nazareth College of Rochester *B*
New York University *B,M,D*
Niagara University *B*
Nyack College *B*
Pace University
    New York *B*
    Pleasantville/Briarcliff *B*
Polytechnic University *B,M*
Roberts Wesleyan College *B*
St. Bonaventure University *B*
St. Francis College *B*
St. John's University *B*
St. Joseph's College
    Brooklyn *B*
    Suffolk Campus *B*
St. Thomas Aquinas College *B*
Sarah Lawrence College *B*
State University of New York
    Binghamton *B,M*
    Buffalo *B,M*
    Stony Brook *B*
    College of Agriculture and
        Technology at Cobleskill *A*
    College of Agriculture and
        Technology at Morrisville *A*
    College at Potsdam *B*
    College of Technology at
        Alfred *A*
    College of Technology at
        Delhi *A*
    Empire State College *A,B*
Suffolk County Community College
    Selden *A*
    Western Campus *A*
Sullivan County Community
    College *A*
Syracuse University *M,D*
Tompkins-Cortland Community
    College *A*
Touro College *B*
Ulster County Community
    College *A*
Utica College of Syracuse
    University *B*
Westchester Community College *A*

North Carolina

Appalachian State University *B,M*
Barton College *B*
Brevard College *A*
Campbell University *B*
Chowan College *A*
Elizabeth City State University *B*
Elon College *B*
Fayetteville State University *B*
Gardner-Webb College *B*
High Point University *B*
Isothermal Community College *A*
Johnson C. Smith University *B*
Lees-McRae College *B*
Lenoir-Rhyne College *B*
Livingstone College *B*
Mars Hill College *B*
North Carolina Agricultural and
    Technical State University *B,M*

North Carolina Central
    University *B*
North Carolina State University *B*
St. Augustine's College *B*
University of North Carolina
    Chapel Hill *B*
    Wilmington *B*
Western Carolina University *B,M*
Western Piedmont Community
    College *A*
Wingate College *B*

North Dakota

Bismarck State College *A*
Dickinson State University *B*
Mayville State University *B*
Minot State University *B*
North Dakota State University *B,M*
Turtle Mountain Community
    College *A*
University of Mary *B*
University of North Dakota
    Grand Forks *B*
    Williston *A*
Valley City State University *B*

Ohio

Ashland University *B*
Baldwin-Wallace College *B*
Bluffton College *B*
Bowling Green State University
    Bowling Green *B*
    Firelands College *A*
Case Western Reserve University *B*
Cedarville College *B*
Central State University *B*
Cleveland State University *B*
Dyke College *B*
Edison State Community College *A*
Heidelberg College *B*
Hiram College *B*
Kent State University *B*
Lake Erie College *B*
Lakeland Community College *A*
Lorain County Community
    College *A*
Lourdes College *A,B*
Malone College *B*
Marietta College *B*
Mount Vernon Nazarene College *B*
Northwest Technical College *A*
Notre Dame College of Ohio *B*
Ohio Dominican College *B*
Ohio State University: Columbus
    Campus *B,M,D*
Shawnee State University *B*
Union Institute *B,D*
University of Dayton *B*
University of Findlay *A,B*
University of Rio Grande *B*
Urbana University *A,B*
Wittenberg University *B*
Wright State University: Lake
    Campus *A*
Youngstown State University *B*

Oklahoma

Bacone College *A*
Bartlesville Wesleyan College *A*
Connors State College *A*
Eastern Oklahoma State College *A*
Hillsdale Free Will Baptist
    College *A*
Langston University *B*
Northeastern State University *B*
Northern Oklahoma College *A*
Oklahoma Baptist University *B*
Oklahoma Panhandle State
    University *B*
Redlands Community College *A*
Southeastern Oklahoma State
    University *B*

Southwestern Oklahoma State
University *B*
Tulsa Junior College *A*
University of Central Oklahoma *B*
University of Oklahoma *M*

Oregon

Central Oregon Community
College *A*
Clackamas Community College *A*
George Fox College *B*
Lane Community College *A*
Linn-Benton Community College *A*
Marylhurst College *B*
Portland Community College *A*
Portland State University *B,M*
Rogue Community College *A*
Southern Oregon State College *B*
Treasure Valley Community
College *A*
Warner Pacific College *A,B*
Western Baptist College *B*
Western Oregon State College *B*

Pennsylvania

Alvernia College *B*
Bloomsburg University of
Pennsylvania *B*
Bucks County Community
College *A*
California University of
Pennsylvania *B,M*
Carnegie Mellon University
B,M,D,W
Cheyney University of
Pennsylvania *B*
Clarion University of
Pennsylvania *B*
Community College of Beaver
County *A*
Edinboro University of
Pennsylvania *B,M*
Gannon University *B,M*
Harrisburg Area Community
College *A*
Holy Family College *B*
Indiana University of
Pennsylvania *B*
Juniata College *B*
La Roche College *B*
La Salle University *B*
Lehigh County Community
College *A*
Lehigh University *B*
Lock Haven University of
Pennsylvania *B*
Luzerne County Community
College *A*
Marywood College *B*
Mercyhurst College *B*
Montgomery County Community
College *A*
Moravian College *B*
Northeastern Christian Junior
College *A*
Penn State
Harrisburg Capital College *B*
University Park Campus *A*
Reading Area Community
College *A*
Rosemont College *B*
Seton Hill College *B*
Slippery Rock University of
Pennsylvania *B,M*
Spring Garden College *B*
University of Pennsylvania
A,B,M,D
University of Pittsburgh
Bradford *B*
Greensburg *B*
Johnstown *B*
Pittsburgh *B*

Waynesburg College *B*
Widener University *B*

Puerto Rico

Caribbean University *B*
Inter American University of Puerto
Rico
Metropolitan Campus *B*
San German Campus *B*
Pontifical Catholic University of
Puerto Rico *B*
Puerto Rico Junior College *A*
Turabo University *B*
Universidad Metropolitana *B*
University of Puerto Rico
Arecibo Campus *A*
Bayamon Technological
University College *A*
Carolina Regional College *A*
Cayey University College *B*
Mayaguez Campus *B*
Ponce Technological
University College *A*
Rio Piedras Campus *B*

Rhode Island

Providence College *B*
Rhode Island College *B*

South Carolina

Benedict College *B*
Central Wesleyan College *B*
Claflin College *B*
Coker College *B*
Limestone College *B*
Morris College *B*
North Greenville College *A*
Presbyterian College *B*
South Carolina State College *B*
University of South Carolina *M*

South Dakota

Black Hills State University *B*
Dakota Wesleyan University *B*
Huron University *B*
Mount Marty College *B*
Sinte Gleska College *A,B*
Sioux Falls College *A,B*

Tennessee

Bethel College *B*
Columbia State Community
College *A*
Cumberland University *A,B*
David Lipscomb University *B*
Dyersburg State Community
College *A*
East Tennessee State University *B*
Lambuth University *B*
LeMoyne-Owen College *B*
Lincoln Memorial University *B*
Martin Methodist College *A*
Middle Tennessee State
University *B*
Motlow State Community
College *A*
Roane State Community College *A*
Southern College of Seventh-day
Adventists *B*
Tennessee State University *B*
Tennessee Wesleyan College *B*
Trevecca Nazarene College *B*
Tusculum College *B*
Union University *B*
University of Tennessee:
Chattanooga *B*

Texas

Amarillo College *A*
Angelina College *A*
Brazosport College *A*
Central Texas College *A*

Concordia Lutheran College *B*
Eastfield College *A*
El Paso Community College *A*
Howard College *A*
Howard Payne University *B*
Jarvis Christian College *B*
Kilgore College *A*
Lon Morris College *A*
McLennan Community College *A*
McMurry University *B*
Midland College *A*
Navarro College *A*
Our Lady of the Lake University of
San Antonio *B*
Panola College *A*
Ranger Junior College *A*
Southern Methodist University *B*
Southwest Texas State University *B*
Southwestern Adventist College *B*
Southwestern Assemblies of God
College *A*
Southwestern University *B*
Sul Ross State University *B,M*
Texas College *B*
Texas Wesleyan University *B*
Trinity Valley Community
College *A*
University of North Texas *B*
University of St. Thomas *B*
Vernon Regional Junior College *A*
Victoria College *A*
Wayland Baptist University *B*
West Texas State University *B,M*
Western Texas College *A*
Wiley College *B*

Utah

Southern Utah University *B*
University of Utah *B*
Utah State University *M*
Weber State University *B*
Westminster College of Salt Lake
City *B*

Vermont

Bennington College *B*
Castleton State College *B*
Goddard College *B,M*
Lyndon State College *B*
Marlboro College *B*

Virginia

Averett College *B*
Bluefield College *B*
Clinch Valley College of the
University of Virginia *B*
Eastern Mennonite College *B*
Hollins College *M*
James Madison University *B*
Lynchburg College *B*
Mountain Empire Community
College *A*
Radford University *B*
St. Paul's College *B*
Southwest Virginia Community
College *A*
Strayer College *A*
Virginia Wesleyan College *B*

Washington

Big Bend Community College *A*
Central Washington University *B*
Centralia College *A*
Eastern Washington University *B*
Everett Community College *A*
Evergreen State College *B*
Grays Harbor College *A*
Heritage College *A,B*
Lower Columbia College *A*
Olympic College *A*
Pacific Lutheran University *M*

Seattle Central Community
College *A*
Seattle University *B*
Skagit Valley College *A*
Spokane Community College *A*
Spokane Falls Community
College *A*
Washington State University *B*
Wenatchee Valley College *A*

West Virginia

Bethany College *B*
Bluefield State College *B*
Marshall University *B,M*
Shepherd College *B*
University of Charleston *B*
West Virginia Wesleyan College *B*

Wisconsin

Alverno College *B*
Cardinal Stritch College *B*
Carroll College *B*
Carthage College *B*
Concordia University Wisconsin *B*
Edgewood College *B*
Lakeland College *B*
Marquette University *B*
Mount Senario College *B*
Northland College *B*
St. Norbert College *B*
Silver Lake College *B*
University of Wisconsin
Eau Claire *B*
Green Bay *B*
Oshkosh *B*
Platteville *B*
River Falls *B*
Stevens Point *B*
Superior *B*
Whitewater *B*

Wyoming

Casper College *A*
Central Wyoming College *A*
Eastern Wyoming College *A*
Laramie County Community
College *A*
Northwest College *A*
Sheridan College *A*
University of Wyoming *B*
Western Wyoming Community
College *A*

**American Samoa, Caroline
Islands, Guam, Marianas,
Virgin Islands**

University of Guam *B*
University of the Virgin Islands *B*

Switzerland

American College of Switzerland *B*

Social studies education

Alabama

Alabama Agricultural and
Mechanical University *B,M*
Auburn University at Montgomery
B,M
Faulkner University *B*
Huntingdon College *B*
Jacksonville State University *B*
Livingston University *B,M*
Mobile College *B*
Samford University *B*
University of North Alabama *B*

Arizona

Arizona State University *B,M*
Eastern Arizona College *A*
University of Arizona *B*

Arkansas

Arkansas College *B*
Arkansas Tech University *M*
Harding University *B*
John Brown University *B*
Ouachita Baptist University *B*
University of Arkansas
    Fayetteville *B*
    Monticello *B*
University of Central Arkansas *B*
University of the Ozarks *B*

California

Azusa Pacific University *B*
California Baptist College *B*
California Lutheran University *B*
California State University
    Fresno *B*
    Northridge *B*
Fresno Pacific College *M*
Humboldt State University *B*
Loyola Marymount University *M*
Mount St. Mary's College *B*
University of the Pacific *B*

Colorado

Colorado State University *B*

Connecticut

Sacred Heart University *B,M*
St. Joseph College *B*
Southern Connecticut State
    University *B,M*
University of Bridgeport *B,M*
University of Hartford *B*
Western Connecticut State
    University *B*

Delaware

Delaware State College *B*
University of Delaware *B*

Florida

Bethune-Cookman College *B*
Flagler College *B*
Florida Agricultural and Mechanical
    University *B,M*
Florida Atlantic University *B,M*
Florida International University
    B,M
Florida State University *B,M,D*
Gulf Coast Community College *A*
Nova University *M*
Pensacola Junior College *A*
St. Thomas University *B*
Southeastern College of the
    Assemblies of God *B*
University of Florida *B,M*
University of Miami *M*

Georgia

Georgia College *B*
Georgia State University *M,D*
Kennesaw State College *B*
Piedmont College *B*
Shorter College *B*
Valdosta State College *B,M*

Hawaii

Chaminade University of
    Honolulu *B*

Idaho

Albertson College *B*

Illinois

Aurora University *B*
Blackburn College *B*
Greenville College *B*
Illinois College *B*
MacMurray College *B*
North Central College *B*
Northwestern University *B,M*
Olivet Nazarene University *B,M*
Quincy College *B*
Southern Illinois University at
    Carbondale *B*
Trinity Christian College *B*
University of Illinois at Urbana-
    Champaign *B,M*

Indiana

Anderson University *B*
Ball State University *B*
Bethel College *B*
Butler University *B*
Franklin College *B*
Goshen College *B*
Huntington College *B*
Indiana State University *B,M*
Indiana University
    Bloomington *B,M,D*
    South Bend *B*
    Southeast *B*
Indiana University—Purdue
    University
    Fort Wayne *B*
    Indianapolis *B*
Indiana Wesleyan University *B*
Manchester College *B*
Marian College *B*
Martin University *B*
Oakland City College *B*
Purdue University *B,M,D*
St. Francis College *B*
St. Joseph's College *B*
St. Mary-of-the-Woods College *B*
Taylor University *B*
University of Evansville *B,M*
University of Indianapolis *B*
University of Southern Indiana *B*
Vincennes University *A*

Iowa

Buena Vista College *B*
Clarke College *B*
Cornell College *B*
Drake University *B*
Grand View College *B*
Iowa Lakes Community College *A*
Luther College *B*
Morningside College *B*
Simpson College *B*
Teikyo Marycrest University *B*
University of Iowa *B,M,D*
Upper Iowa University *B*
Wartburg College *B*
William Penn College *B*

Kansas

Baker University *B*
Bethany College *B*
Colby Community College *A*
Friends University *B*
Kansas State University *B*
McPherson College *B*
MidAmerica Nazarene College *B*
University of Kansas *B*
Washburn University of Topeka *B*

Kentucky

Alice Lloyd College *B*
Asbury College *B*
Bellarmine College *B*
Brescia College *B*
Campbellsville College *B*
Eastern Kentucky University *B,M*

Kentucky State University *B*
Pikeville College *B*
Union College *B*
University of Kentucky *B*
Western Kentucky University *M*

Louisiana

Centenary College of Louisiana *B*
Dillard University *B*
Grambling State University *B*
Louisiana College *B*
Louisiana State University
    Agricultural and Mechanical
      College *B*
    Shreveport *B*
Louisiana Tech University *B,M*
McNeese State University *B*
Nicholls State University *B*
Northeast Louisiana University *B*
Southeastern Louisiana
    University *B*
Southern University and
    Agricultural and Mechanical
    College *B*
Tulane University *M*
University of New Orleans *B*
University of Southwestern
    Louisiana *B*

Maine

St. Joseph's College *B*
University of Maine *M*

Maryland

Montgomery College
    Rockville Campus *A*
    Takoma Park Campus *A*
Morgan State University *B*
Mount St. Mary's College *B*
Western Maryland College *B*

Massachusetts

American International College *B*
Boston University *B,M,W*
Bridgewater State College *M*
Eastern Nazarene College *B,M*
Elms College *B*
Framingham State College *B,M*
Springfield College *B*
Tufts University *B,M*

Michigan

Adrian College *B*
Calvin College *B,M*
Concordia College *B*
Eastern Michigan University *B,M*
Grand Valley State University *B*
Hillsdale College *B*
Lansing Community College *A*
Marygrove College *B*
Michigan State University *B*
Northern Michigan University *B,M*
Saginaw Valley State University *B*
University of Michigan
    Ann Arbor *M*
    Dearborn *B*
Wayne State University *B,M*

Minnesota

Bethel College *B*
College of St. Scholastica *B*
Concordia College: Moorhead *B*
Gustavus Adolphus College *B*
Mankato State University *B*
Moorhead State University *B,M*
Rainy River Community College *A*
St. Cloud State University *B*
St. Mary's College of Minnesota *B*
St. Olaf College *B*
Southwest State University *B*

University of Minnesota
    Duluth *B*
    Twin Cities *B*
Vermilion Community College *A*
Willmar Community College *A*
Winona State University *B*

Mississippi

Alcorn State University *B,M*
Mary Holmes College *A*
Mississippi College *B,M*
Northeast Mississippi Community
    College *A*

Missouri

Calvary Bible College *B*
Central Missouri State University
    B,M
Columbia College *B*
Culver-Stockton College *B*
Evangel College *B*
Missouri Valley College *B*
Northeast Missouri State
    University *M*
Park College *B*
Southwest Missouri State
    University *B*
University of Missouri
    Columbia *B,M,D*
    Kansas City *B*
Webster University *B*
Westminster College *B*

Montana

Montana State University *B*
University of Montana *B*

Nebraska

Chadron State College *B*
Concordia College *B*
Creighton University *B*
Dana College *B*
Peru State College *B*
University of Nebraska—Lincoln *B*

New Hampshire

Colby-Sawyer College *B*
Franklin Pierce College *B*
New England College *B*
Notre Dame College *B*
Plymouth State College of the
    University System of New
    Hampshire *B*

New Jersey

Caldwell College *B*
Fairleigh Dickinson University *M*
Jersey City State College *B*
Kean College of New Jersey *B*
Ocean County College *A*
Rider College *B*
Rutgers—The State University of
    New Jersey
    Camden College of Arts and
      Sciences *B*
    Douglass College *B*
    Livingston College *B*
    New Brunswick *M,D*
    Newark College of Arts and
      Sciences *B*
    Rutgers College *B*
    University College New
      Brunswick *B*
    University College Newark *B*
Seton Hall University *B*
Stockton State College *B*
Trenton State College *B*

New Mexico

Eastern New Mexico University *B*
New Mexico Highlands
    University *B*

New Mexico State University *B*
University of New Mexico *B*

New York

Adelphi University *B,M*
Canisius College *B*
City University of New York
    Brooklyn College *B,M*
    City College *B,M*
    Hunter College *B,M*
    Lehman College *M*
    Queens College *B,M*
College of Mount St. Vincent *B*
College of New Rochelle *B*
Concordia College *B*
Daemen College *B*
Dominican College of Blauvelt *B*
Dowling College *B*
D'Youville College *B*
Elmira College *B*
Hofstra University *B,M*
Houghton College *B*
Iona College *B,M*
Ithaca College *B*
Le Moyne College *B*
Long Island University
    Brooklyn Campus *M*
    C. W. Post Campus *B,M*
    Southampton Campus *B*
Manhattan College *B*
Manhattanville College *M*
Marymount College *B*
New York University *B,M*
Niagara University *B,M*
Russell Sage College *B*
St. Bonaventure University *M*
St. John's University *B*
St. Joseph's College
    Brooklyn *B*
    Suffolk Campus *B*
St. Thomas Aquinas College *B*
Siena College *B*
State University of New York
    Albany *B,M*
    Binghamton *M*
    Buffalo *B,M,D*
    College at Brockport *M*
    College at Buffalo *B*
    College at Cortland *B,M*
    College at Fredonia *B*
    College at Geneseo *B*
    College at New Paltz *B,M*
    College at Potsdam *B,M*
    Oswego *B,M*
Syracuse University *B,M*
Union College *M*
University of Rochester *M,D*
Utica College of Syracuse
    University *B*
Wells College *B*

North Carolina

Barton College *B*
Campbell University *B*
East Carolina University *M*
Elizabeth City State University *B*
Gardner-Webb College *B,M*
Lees-McRae College *B*
Livingstone College *B*
Mars Hill College *B*
Methodist College *A,B*
North Carolina Central
    University *B*
North Carolina State University *B*
North Carolina Wesleyan College *B*
Pfeiffer College *B*
St. Andrews Presbyterian College *B*
St. Augustine's College *B*
Salem College *B*
University of North Carolina
    Asheville *C*
    Greensboro *M*

Wingate College *B*
Winston-Salem State University *B*

North Dakota

Jamestown College *B*
Minot State University *B*
North Dakota State University *B,M*

Ohio

Baldwin-Wallace College *B*
Bluffton College *B*
Bowling Green State University *B*
Capital University *B*
Case Western Reserve University *B*
Cedarville College *B*
Defiance College *B*
Heidelberg College *B*
Kent State University *B,M*
Lorain County Community
    College *A*
Malone College *B*
Miami University: Oxford Campus
    B,M
Mount Union College *B*
Mount Vernon Nazarene College *B*
Ohio Dominican College *B*
Ohio State University: Columbus
    Campus *B*
Ohio University *B*
Otterbein College *B*
University of Dayton *B*
University of Findlay *B*
University of Rio Grande *B*
University of Toledo *B*
Urbana University *B*
Ursuline College *B*
Walsh College *B*
Wittenberg University *B*
Wright State University *B*
Youngstown State University *B*

Oklahoma

Bartlesville Wesleyan College *B*
East Central University *B*
Langston University *B*
Oklahoma Baptist University *B*
Oklahoma Christian University of
    Science and Arts *B*
Oklahoma City University *B*
Oral Roberts University *B*
Phillips University *B*
Southwestern Oklahoma State
    University *B,M*
University of Central Oklahoma
    B,M
University of Oklahoma *B*
University of Science and Arts of
    Oklahoma *B*
University of Tulsa *B*

Oregon

George Fox College *B*
Southern Oregon State College *M*
Western Baptist College *B*
Western Oregon State College *B,M*
Willamette University *M*

Pennsylvania

Albright College *B*
Allentown College of St. Francis de
    Sales *B*
Beaver College *B,M*
Bloomsburg University of
    Pennsylvania *B*
Bucknell University *B*
Cabrini College *B*
California University of
    Pennsylvania *B,M*
Chatham College *B*
Clarion University of
    Pennsylvania *B*

East Stroudsburg University of
    Pennsylvania *B,M*
Edinboro University of
    Pennsylvania *B,M*
Elizabethtown College *B*
Geneva College *B*
Gettysburg College *B*
Grove City College *B*
Gwynedd-Mercy College *B*
Holy Family College *B*
Immaculata College *B*
Indiana University of
    Pennsylvania *B*
Juniata College *B*
La Salle University *B*
Lehigh University *M*
Lincoln University *B*
Lock Haven University of
    Pennsylvania *B*
Lycoming College *B*
Mansfield University of
    Pennsylvania *B*
Marywood College *B*
Messiah College *B*
Millersville University of
    Pennsylvania *B*
Moravian College *B*
Philadelphia College of Bible *B*
St. Francis College *C*
St. Joseph's University *C,B,M*
Seton Hill College *B*
Slippery Rock University of
    Pennsylvania *B,M*
Temple University *B,M,D*
University of Pennsylvania *M,D*
University of Pittsburgh at Bradford
    C,B
University of Scranton *B*
Washington and Jefferson College *B*
Waynesburg College *B*
West Chester University of
    Pennsylvania *B*
Widener University *M*
Wilkes University *B,M*
York College of Pennsylvania *B*

Puerto Rico

Inter American University of Puerto
    Rico: San German Campus *B*
Pontifical Catholic University of
    Puerto Rico *B*
University of Puerto Rico: Rio
    Piedras Campus *B*

Rhode Island

Providence College *B*
Rhode Island College *B,M*

South Carolina

Benedict College *B*
Bob Jones University *B,M*
Charleston Southern University *M*
The Citadel *M*
Columbia College *B*
Erskine College *B*
Francis Marion College *M*
Lander College *B*
Limestone College *B*
Morris College *B*
Presbyterian College *B*
South Carolina State College *B*
University of South Carolina
    Aiken *B*
    Coastal Carolina College *B*

South Dakota

Augustana College *B*
Black Hills State University *B*
Dakota Wesleyan University *B*
South Dakota State University *B*
University of South Dakota *B*

Tennessee

Crichton College *B*
David Lipscomb University *B*
East Tennessee State University
    B,M
Freed-Hardeman University *B*
Lincoln Memorial University *B*
Milligan College *B*
Tennessee Wesleyan College *B*
Union University *B,M*
University of Tennessee
    Knoxville *B*
    Martin *B*
Vanderbilt University *M,D*

Texas

Abilene Christian University *B*
Angelo State University *B*
Baylor University *B*
Dallas Baptist University *B*
East Texas Baptist University *B*
Hardin-Simmons University *B*
Incarnate Word College *B*
McMurry University *B*
Prairie View A&M University *M*
St. Edward's University *B*
St. Mary's University *B*
Texas Christian University *B*
Texas College *B*
Texas Wesleyan University *B*
University of Dallas *B*
University of Houston *B,M*
University of Mary Hardin-
    Baylor *B*
West Texas State University *B,M*

Utah

Weber State University *B*

Vermont

Castleton State College *B*
Goddard College *B,M*
Johnson State College *B*

Virginia

Averett College *B*
Bluefield College *B*
Eastern Mennonite College *B*
Emory and Henry College *B*
Ferrum College *B*
Old Dominion University *B*
Virginia Polytechnic Institute and
    State University *B,M*
Virginia Wesleyan College *B*

Washington

Heritage College *B*
Pacific Lutheran University *B*
University of Puget Sound *M*
Washington State University *B*
Western Washington University
    B,M

West Virginia

Bethany College *B*
Bluefield State College *B*
Concord College *B*
Davis and Elkins College *B*
Fairmont State College *B*
Glenville State College *B*
Shepherd College *B*
University of Charleston *B*
West Virginia Institute of
    Technology *B*
West Virginia State College *B*
West Virginia University *B*
West Virginia Wesleyan College *B*

Wisconsin

Cardinal Stritch College *B*
Carroll College *B*
Carthage College *B*

Concordia University Wisconsin *B*
Lakeland College *B*
Maranatha Baptist Bible College *B*
Marian College of Fond du Lac *B*
Marquette University *B*
Mount Mary College *B*
Mount Senario College *B*
Northland College *B*
St. Norbert College *B*
University of Wisconsin
    Eau Claire *B*
    Green Bay *B*
    La Crosse *B*
    Oshkosh *B*
    Platteville *B*
    Whitewater *B*

Wyoming

University of Wyoming *B*

Canada

McGill University *B,M*

Social work

Alabama

Alabama Agricultural and
    Mechanical University *B*
Alabama State University *B*
Auburn University *B*
Community College of the Air
    Force *A*
Gadsden State Community
    College *A*
Huntingdon College *B*
Jacksonville State University *B*
Judson College *B*
Oakwood College *B*
Talladega College *B*
Troy State University *B*
Tuskegee University *B*
University of Alabama
    Birmingham *B*
    Tuscaloosa *B,M,D*
University of Montevallo *B*
University of North Alabama *B*

Alaska

University of Alaska
    Anchorage *B*
    Fairbanks *B*

Arizona

Arizona State University *B,M,D*
Cochise College *A*
Glendale Community College *A*
Northern Arizona University *B*
Northland Pioneer College *C,A*
Pima Community College *C,A*
Prescott College *B*
Yavapai College *A*

Arkansas

Arkansas College *B*
Arkansas State University *B*
Harding University *B*
Henderson State University *B,M*
Philander Smith College *B*
University of Arkansas
    Fayetteville *B*
    Little Rock *M*
    Pine Bluff *B*
Westark Community College *A*

California

Azusa Pacific University *B*
Biola University *B*
California State Polytechnic
    University: Pomona *B*

California State University
    Chico *B*
    Fresno *B,M*
    Hayward *B*
    Long Beach *B,M*
    Los Angeles *B*
    Sacramento *B,M*
    San Bernardino *B,M*
Fresno Pacific College *B*
Humboldt State University *B*
Merced College *A*
Monterey Peninsula College *C,A*
Pacific Christian College *B*
Pacific Union College *B*
San Diego State University *B,M*
San Francisco State University *B,M*
San Jose State University *B,M*
Santa Rosa Junior College *A*
Southwestern College *A*
University of California
    Berkeley *M,D*
    Los Angeles *M,D*
University of Southern California
    M,D
Whittier College *B*
Yuba College *A*

Colorado

Colorado State University *B,M*
Community College of Denver *A*
Lamar Community College *A*
Mesa State College *B*
Metropolitan State College of
    Denver *B*
Pikes Peak Community College *C,A*
University of Denver *M,D*
University of Southern Colorado *B*

Connecticut

Central Connecticut State
    University *B*
Manchester Community College *A*
Mattatuck Community College *C,A*
Norwalk Community College *A*
Quinebaug Valley Community
    College *A*
Sacred Heart University *B*
St. Joseph College *B*
Southern Connecticut State
    University *B,M*
University of Connecticut *M*
University of New Haven *B*
Western Connecticut State
    University *B*

Delaware

Delaware State College *B,M*

District of Columbia

Catholic University of America *B,M*
Gallaudet University *B*
Howard University *M,D*
University of the District of
    Columbia *B*

Florida

Barry University *M,D*
Daytona Beach Community
    College *A*
Florida Agricultural and Mechanical
    University *B*
Florida Atlantic University *B*
Florida International University
    B,M
Florida Southern College *B*
Florida State University *B,M,D*
Gulf Coast Community College *A*
Manatee Community College *A*
Miami-Dade Community College *A*
Okaloosa-Walton Community
    College *A*
St. Leo College *B*

University of Central Florida *B*
University of South Florida *B,M*
University of Tampa *B*
University of West Florida *B*
Warner Southern College *B*

Georgia

Albany State College *B*
Armstrong State College *B*
Atlanta Metropolitan College *A*
Clark Atlanta University *B*
Darton College *A*
Fort Valley State College *B*
Gainesville College *A*
Georgia State University *B*
LaGrange College *B*
Macon College *A*
Mercer University *B*
Oglethorpe University *B*
Savannah State College *B*
University of Georgia *B,M,D*

Hawaii

Brigham Young University-
    Hawaii *B*
University of Hawaii
    Leeward Community
        College *A*
    Manoa *B,M,D*

Idaho

Boise State University *B,M*
Idaho State University *B*
Lewis Clark State College *B*
Northwest Nazarene College *A,B*
Ricks College *A*

Illinois

Augustana College *B*
Aurora University *B,M*
Bradley University *B*
College of St. Francis *B*
Concordia University *B,M*
Eureka College *B*
Governors State University *B*
Greenville College *B*
Illinois College *B*
Illinois State University *B*
Illinois Wesleyan University *B*
KAES College *B*
Kendall College *A,B*
Lewis University *B*
Lincoln Land Community
    College *A*
Loyola University of Chicago
    B,M,D
MacMurray College *B*
Morton College *A*
Northeastern Illinois University *B*
Olivet Nazarene University *B*
Quincy College *B*
Rend Lake College *A*
Richland Community College *A*
Rock Valley College *A*
Rockford College *B*
Shawnee Community College *A*
Southern Illinois University
    Carbondale *B,M*
    Edwardsville *B*
University of Chicago *B,M,D*
University of Illinois
    Chicago *B,M,D*
    Urbana-Champaign *B,M,D*

Indiana

Anderson University *B*
Ball State University *B*
Calumet College of St. Joseph *A,B*
Goshen College *B*
Indiana State University *B,M*

Indiana University
    Bloomington *B*
    East *A,B*
Indiana University—Purdue
    University at Indianapolis *B,M*
Indiana Wesleyan University *B*
Manchester College *B*
Purdue University *B*
St. Francis College *B*
St. Mary's College *B*
Taylor University *B*
University of Indianapolis *B*
University of Southern Indiana *B*
Valparaiso University *B*
Vincennes University *A*

Iowa

Briar Cliff College *B*
Buena Vista College *B*
Clarke College *B*
Clinton Community College *A*
Des Moines Area Community
    College *A*
Dordt College *B*
Grand View College *B*
Iowa State University *B*
Iowa Western Community
    College *A*
Kirkwood Community College *A*
Loras College *B*
Luther College *B*
Mount Mercy College *B*
Northwestern College *B*
Scott Community College *A*
Teikyo Marycrest University *A,B*
University of Dubuque *B*
University of Iowa *B,M*
University of Northern Iowa *B*
Wartburg College *B*

Kansas

Benedictine College *B*
Bethany College *B*
Bethel College *B*
Coffeyville Community College *A*
Colby Community College *A*
Dodge City Community College *A*
Friends University *B*
Haskell Indian Junior College *A*
Kansas City Kansas Community
    College *A*
Kansas State University *B*
Neosho County Community
    College *A*
Ottawa University *B*
Pittsburg State University *B*
Southwestern College *B*
University of Kansas *B,M,D*
Washburn University of Topeka *B*
Wichita State University *B*

Kentucky

Asbury College *B*
Eastern Kentucky University *B*
Kentucky State University *B*
Morehead State University *A,B*
Murray State University *B*
Northern Kentucky University *B*
Spalding University *B*
Sue Bennett College *A*
University of Kentucky *B,M*
University of Louisville *M*
Western Kentucky University *B*

Louisiana

Dillard University *B*
Grambling State University *B,M*
Louisiana College *B*
Louisiana State University and
    Agricultural and Mechanical
    College *M*
Louisiana Tech University *B*

Northeast Louisiana University *B*
Northwestern State University *B*
Our Lady of Holy Cross College *B*
Southeastern Louisiana
   University *B*
Southern University at New Orleans
   B,M
Southern University and
   Agricultural and Mechanical
   College *B*
Tulane University *M,D*

Maine

University of Maine
   Orono *B,M*
   Presque Isle *B*
University of New England *B,M*
University of Southern Maine *B*

Maryland

Allegany Community College *A*
Baltimore Hebrew University *B*
Bowie State University *B*
Columbia Union College *B*
Coppin State College *B*
Frostburg State University *B*
Hood College *B*
Morgan State University *B*
New Community College of
   Baltimore *A*
Salisbury State University *B*
Sojourner-Douglass College *B*
University of Maryland
   Baltimore *M,D*
   Baltimore County *B*
   Eastern Shore *B*
Western Maryland College *C,B*

Massachusetts

Anna Maria College for Men and
   Women *B*
Assumption College *B*
Atlantic Union College *B*
Berkshire Community College *A*
Boston College *M,D*
Boston University *B,M*
Bridgewater State College *B*
Bristol Community College *A*
Bunker Hill Community College *A*
Dean Junior College *A*
Eastern Nazarene College *B*
Elms College *B,M*
Endicott College *A*
Fitchburg State College *B*
Gordon College *B*
Hampshire College *B*
Lesley College *B*
Massachusetts Bay Community
   College *C,A*
Massasoit Community College *A*
Mount Ida College *A*
Nichols College *B*
Regis College *B*
Salem State College *B,M*
Simmons College *M,D*
Springfield College *M*
Suffolk University *B*
Western New England College *B*
Westfield State College *B*
Wheelock College *B*

Michigan

Andrews University *B*
Calvin College *B*
Charles Stewart Mott Community
   College *A*
Eastern Michigan University *B,M*
Ferris State University *B*
Grand Rapids Baptist College and
   Seminary *B*
Grand Valley State University *B,M*
Hillsdale College *B*

Jordan College *A*
Kellogg Community College *A*
Lake Superior State University *B*
Lansing Community College *A*
Madonna University *B*
Marygrove College *B*
Michigan State University *B,M*
Northern Michigan University *B*
Saginaw Valley State University *B*
Siena Heights College *A,B*
Southwestern Michigan College *A*
Spring Arbor College *B*
Suomi College *A*
University of Detroit Mercy *B*
University of Michigan
   Ann Arbor *M,D*
   Flint *B*
Wayne State University *B,M*
West Shore Community College *A*
Western Michigan University *B,M*

Minnesota

Augsburg College *B,M*
Bemidji State University *B*
Bethel College *B*
College of St. Benedict *B*
College of St. Catherine: St.
   Catherine Campus *B,M*
College of St. Scholastica *B*
Concordia College: Moorhead *B*
Concordia College: St. Paul *B*
Itasca Community College:
   Arrowhead Region *A*
Lakewood Community College *A*
Mankato State University *B*
Moorhead State University *B,M*
Northland Community College *A*
Rainy River Community College *A*
St. Cloud State University *B*
St. John's University *B*
St. Mary's College of Minnesota *B*
St. Olaf College *B*
Southwest State University *B*
University of Minnesota
   Duluth *B*
   Twin Cities *M,D*
University of St. Thomas *B*
Willmar Community College *A*
Winona State University *B*

Mississippi

Alcorn State University *B*
Blue Mountain College *B*
Delta State University *B*
Jackson State University *B,M*
Mississippi College *B*
Mississippi State University *B*
Rust College *B*
University of Mississippi *B*
University of Southern
   Mississippi *M*

Missouri

Avila College *B*
Central Missouri State University *B*
Columbia College *B*
East Central College *A*
Evangel College *A,B*
Fontbonne College *B*
Missouri Western State College *B*
Park College *B*
St. Louis Community College at
   Meramec *A*
St. Louis University *B,M*
Southeast Missouri State
   University *B*
Southwest Baptist University *B*
Southwest Missouri State
   University *B*
University of Missouri
   Columbia *B,M*
   St. Louis *B*

Washington University *M,D*
William Woods College *B*

Montana

Carroll College *B*
Miles Community College *A*
Salish Kootenai College *A*
University of Montana *B*

Nebraska

Chadron State College *B*
College of St. Mary *B*
Creighton University *B*
Dana College *B*
Doane College *B*
Midland Lutheran College *B*
Nebraska Wesleyan University *B*
Peru State College *B*
Union College *B*
University of Nebraska
   Kearney *B*
   Omaha *B,M*

Nevada

University of Nevada
   Las Vegas *B,M*
   Reno *B,M*

New Hampshire

Franklin Pierce College *B*
Plymouth State College of the
   University System of New
   Hampshire *B*
University of New Hampshire *B*
White Pines College *A*

New Jersey

Camden County College *A*
County College of Morris *A*
Essex County College *A*
Georgian Court College *B*
Kean College of New Jersey *B*
Monmouth College *B*
Ocean County College *A*
Ramapo College of New Jersey *B*
Rutgers—The State University of
   New Jersey
   Camden College of Arts and
     Sciences *B*
   Livingston College *B*
   New Brunswick *M,D*
   Newark College of Arts and
     Sciences *B*
   University College Camden *B*
   University College Newark *B*
Seton Hall University *B*
Stockton State College *B*
Thomas Edison State College *A,B*
Upsala College *B*

New Mexico

Eastern New Mexico University:
   Roswell Campus *A*
New Mexico State University *B,M*
Western New Mexico University *B*

New York

Adelphi University *B,M,D*
Adirondack Community College *A*
Boricua College *B*
Cazenovia College *A*
City University of New York
   Graduate School and
     University Center *D*
   Hunter College *M*
   Lehman College *B*
   York College *B*
College of New Rochelle *B*
College of St. Rose *B*
Columbia University *M,D*
Concordia College *B*
Cornell University *B*

Daemen College *B*
Dominican College of Blauvelt *B*
D'Youville College *B*
Elmira College *B*
Fordham University *M,D*
Fulton-Montgomery Community
   College *A*
Herkimer County Community
   College *A*
Hilbert College *A*
Hudson Valley Community
   College *A*
Iona College *B*
Jamestown Community College *A*
Keuka College *B*
Manhattan College *B*
Marist College *B*
Marymount College *B*
Mater Dei College *A*
Medaille College *B*
Mercy College *B*
Mohawk Valley Community
   College *A*
Molloy College *B*
Nazareth College of Rochester *B*
New York University *A,B,M,D*
Niagara University *B*
Onondaga Community College *A*
Roberts Wesleyan College *B*
Rochester Institute of
   Technology *B*
Sage Junior College of Albany, A
   Division of Russell Sage
   College *A*
Siena College *B*
Skidmore College *B*
State University of New York
   Albany *B,M,D*
   Buffalo *M,D*
   College at Brockport *B*
   College at Buffalo *B*
   College at Plattsburgh *B*
   Health Sciences Center at
     Stony Brook *B,M*
Syracuse University *B,M*
Wagner College *B*
Yeshiva University *M,D*

North Carolina

Anson Community College *A*
Appalachian State University *B*
Barton College *B*
Bennett College *B*
Campbell University *B*
Coastal Carolina Community
   College *A*
East Carolina University *B,M*
Edgecombe Community College *A*
Elizabeth City State University *B*
Elon College *B*
Johnson C. Smith University *B*
Livingstone College *B*
Mars Hill College *B*
Martin Community College *A*
Meredith College *B*
Methodist College *B*
North Carolina Agricultural and
   Technical State University *B*
North Carolina State University *B*
Pembroke State University *B*
Piedmont Community College *A*
Richmond Community College *A*
St. Augustine's College *B*
University of North Carolina
   Chapel Hill *M*
   Charlotte *B*
   Greensboro *B*
   Wilmington *B*
Warren Wilson College *B*
Western Carolina University *B*
Wilkes Community College *A*

University of Wisconsin
Eau Claire *B*
Green Bay *B*
La Crosse *B*
Madison *B,M,D*
Milwaukee *B,M*
Oshkosh *B*
River Falls *B*
Superior *B*
Whitewater *B*

Wyoming

Casper College *A*
Northwest College *A*
Sheridan College *A*
University of Wyoming *B*

American Samoa, Caroline Islands, Guam, Marianas, Virgin Islands

University of Guam *B*
University of the Virgin Islands *B*

Canada

McGill University *B,M,W*

Sociology

Alabama

Alabama Agricultural and Mechanical University *B*
Alabama State University *A,B*
Athens State College *B*
Auburn University
Auburn *B,M*
Montgomery *B*
Birmingham-Southern College *B*
Jacksonville State University *B*
Judson College *B*
Lawson State Community College *A*
Livingston University *B*
Miles College *B*
Mobile College *B*
Samford University *B*
Spring Hill College *B*
Stillman College *B*
Talladega College *B*
Troy State University
Dothan *B*
Montgomery *B*
Troy *B*
Tuskegee University *B*
University of Alabama
Birmingham *B,M*
Huntsville *B*
Tuscaloosa *B,M,D,W*
University of Montevallo *B*
University of North Alabama *B*
University of South Alabama *B,M*

Alaska

University of Alaska
Anchorage *B*
Fairbanks *B*

Arizona

Arizona State University *B,M,D*
Glendale Community College *A*
Grand Canyon University *B*
Mohave Community College *A*
Northern Arizona University *B,M*
Prescott College *B*
University of Arizona *B,M,D*
Yavapai College *A*

Arkansas

Arkansas State University
Beebe Branch *A*
Jonesboro *B,M*
Arkansas Tech University *B*
Harding University *B,M*
Henderson State University *B,M*
Hendrix College *B*
Ouachita Baptist University *B*
Philander Smith College *B*
Southern Arkansas University *B*
University of Arkansas
Fayetteville *B,M*
Little Rock *B*
Pine Bluff *B*
University of Central Arkansas *B,M*
University of the Ozarks *B*
Westark Community College *A*

California

Azusa Pacific University *B*
Bakersfield College *A*
Biola University *B*
California Baptist College *B*
California Lutheran University *B*
California State Polytechnic University: Pomona *B*
California State University
Bakersfield *B*
Chico *B*
Dominguez Hills *B,M*
Fresno *B,M*
Fullerton *B,M*
Hayward *B,M*
Long Beach *B*
Los Angeles *B,M*
Northridge *B,M*
Sacramento *B,M*
San Bernardino *B*
San Marcos *B*
Stanislaus *B*
Cerritos Community College *A*
Chabot College *A*
Chaffey Community College *A*
Chapman University *B*
Christ College Irvine *B*
College of the Desert *A*
College of Notre Dame *B*
College of the Sequoias *A*
Crafton Hills College *A*
De Anza College *A*
El Camino College *A*
Foothill College *A*
Holy Names College *B*
Humboldt State University *B,M*
Irvine Valley College *A*
La Sierra University *B*
Los Angeles Valley College *A*
Los Medanos College *A*
Loyola Marymount University *B*
Marymount College *A*
Merced College *A*
Mills College *B*
MiraCosta College *A*
Modesto Junior College *A*
Mount St. Mary's College *B*
Napa Valley College *A*
Occidental College *B*
Ohlone College *A*
Orange Coast College *A*
Oxnard College *A*
Pepperdine University *B*
Pitzer College *B*
Point Loma Nazarene College *B*
Pomona College *B*
Saddleback College *A*
San Diego Mesa College *A*
San Diego State University *B,M*
San Francisco State University *B*
San Jose State University *B,M*
Santa Barbara City College *A*
Santa Clara University *B*

Santa Rosa Junior College *A*
Scripps College *B*
Sonoma State University *B*
Southern California College *B*
Southwestern College *A*
Stanford University *B,M,D*
University of California
Berkeley *B,M,D*
Davis *B,M,D*
Irvine *B*
Los Angeles *B,M,D*
Riverside *B,M,D*
San Diego *B,M,D*
San Francisco *D*
Santa Barbara *B,M,D*
Santa Cruz *B,D*
University of La Verne *B*
University of the Pacific *B,M*
University of Redlands *B*
University of San Diego *B*
University of San Francisco *B*
University of Southern California *B,M,D*
Ventura College *A*
West Valley College *A*
Westmont College *B*
Whittier College *B*

Colorado

Adams State College *B*
Colorado College *B*
Colorado State University *B,M,D*
Fort Lewis College *B*
Mesa State College *B*
Metropolitan State College of Denver *B*
Pikes Peak Community College *A*
Regis College of Regis University *B*
University of Colorado
Boulder *B,M,D*
Colorado Springs *B,M*
Denver *B*
University of Denver *B,M,D*
University of Northern Colorado *B*
University of Southern Colorado *B*
Western State College of Colorado *B*

Connecticut

Albertus Magnus College *B*
Central Connecticut State University *B*
Connecticut College *B*
Eastern Connecticut State University *B*
Fairfield University *B*
Quinnipiac College *B*
Sacred Heart University *A,B*
St. Joseph College *B*
Southern Connecticut State University *B,M*
Teikyo-Post University *A,B*
Trinity College *B*
University of Bridgeport *B*
University of Connecticut *B,M,D*
University of Hartford *B*
University of New Haven *B*
Wesleyan University *B*
Western Connecticut State University *B*
Yale University *B,M,D*

Delaware

Delaware State College *B*
University of Delaware *B,M,D*

District of Columbia

American University *B,M,D*
Catholic University of America *B,M,D*
Gallaudet University *B*

George Washington University *B,M,D*
Georgetown University *B*
Howard University *B,M,D*
Trinity College *B*
University of the District of Columbia *B*

Florida

Barry University *B*
Bethune-Cookman College *B*
Daytona Beach Community College *A*
Eckerd College *B*
Edison Community College *A*
Florida Agricultural and Mechanical University *B*
Florida Atlantic University *B,M*
Florida International University *B,M*
Florida Memorial College *B*
Florida Southern College *B*
Florida State University *B,M,D*
Indian River Community College *A*
Jacksonville University *B*
Lynn University *B*
Miami-Dade Community College *A*
New College of the University of South Florida *B*
Palm Beach Community College *A*
Rollins College *B*
St. Leo College *B*
St. Thomas University *B*
Stetson University *B*
University of Central Florida *B,M*
University of Florida *B,M,D*
University of Miami *B,M,D*
University of North Florida *B*
University of South Florida *B,M*
University of Tampa *A,B*
University of West Florida *B*
Warner Southern College *B*

Georgia

Abraham Baldwin Agricultural College *A*
Agnes Scott College *B*
Albany State College *B*
Andrew College *A*
Atlanta Metropolitan College *A*
Augusta College *B*
Bainbridge College *A*
Berry College *B*
Brewton-Parker College *A,B*
Clark Atlanta University *B,M*
Clayton State College *A*
Columbus College *B*
Covenant College *B*
Darton College *A*
DeKalb College *A*
Emory University *B,M,D*
Floyd College *A*
Fort Valley State College *B*
Gainesville College *A*
Georgia College *B*
Georgia Southern University *B,M*
Georgia Southwestern College *B*
Georgia State University *B,M,D*
Gordon College *A*
Macon College *A*
Mercer University *B*
Middle Georgia College *A*
Morehouse College *B*
Morris Brown College *B*
North Georgia College *B*
Oglethorpe University *B*
Paine College *B*
Piedmont College *B*
Savannah State College *B*
Shorter College *B*
South Georgia College *A*
Spelman College *B*

Thomas College *A*
Truett-McConnell College *A*
University of Georgia *B,M,D*
Valdosta State College *B,M*
Waycross College *A*
West Georgia College *B,M*
Young Harris College *A*

Hawaii

Hawaii Pacific University *B*
University of Hawaii
    Hilo *B*
    Manoa *B,M,D*
    West Oahu *B*

Idaho

Albertson College *B*
Boise State University *B*
College of Southern Idaho *A*
Idaho State University *B,M*
North Idaho College *A*
Northwest Nazarene College *B*
Ricks College *A*
University of Idaho *B,M*

Illinois

Augustana College *B*
Aurora University *B*
Barat College *B*
Black Hawk College *A*
Bradley University *B*
Chicago State University *B*
Concordia University *B*
De Paul University *B,M*
Eastern Illinois University *B*
Elmhurst College *B*
Eureka College *B*
Governors State University *M*
Greenville College *B*
Highland Community College *A*
Illinois Benedictine College *B*
Illinois Central College *A*
Illinois College *B*
Illinois Institute of Technology *B*
Illinois State University *B,M*
Illinois Wesleyan University *B*
John A. Logan College *A*
Joliet Junior College *A*
Judson College *B*
Knox College *B*
Lake Forest College *B*
Lewis University *B*
Lincoln Land Community
    College *A*
Loyola University of Chicago
    B,M,D
MacMurray College *B*
McKendree College *B*
Millikin University *B*
Monmouth College *B*
Morton College *A*
North Central College *B*
North Park College and Theological
    Seminary *B*
Northeastern Illinois University *B*
Northern Illinois University *B,M*
Northwestern University *B,M,D*
Olivet Nazarene University *B*
Principia College *B*
Quincy College *B*
Rend Lake College *A*
Rockford College *B*
Roosevelt University *B,M*
Rosary College *B*
St. Xavier University *B*
Sangamon State University *B*
Southern Illinois University
    Carbondale *B,M,D*
    Edwardsville *B,M*
State Community College *A*
Trinity Christian College *B*
Trinity College *B*

University of Chicago *B,M,D*
University of Illinois
    Chicago *B,M,D*
    Urbana-Champaign *B,M,D*
Waubonsee Community College *A*
Western Illinois University *B,M*
Wheaton College *B*

Indiana

Ancilla College *A*
Anderson University *B*
Ball State University *B,M*
Bethel College *B*
Butler University *B*
Calumet College of St. Joseph *B*
DePauw University *B*
Earlham College *B*
Franklin College *B*
Goshen College *B*
Grace College *B*
Hanover College *B*
Huntington College *B*
Indiana State University *B,M*
Indiana University
    Bloomington *B,M,D*
    East *B*
    Kokomo *B*
    Northwest *B*
    South Bend *B*
    Southeast *B*
Indiana University—Purdue
  University
    Fort Wayne *B*
    Indianapolis *B*
Indiana Wesleyan University *B*
Manchester College *B*
Marian College *B*
Martin University *B*
Purdue University
    Calumet *B*
    West Lafayette *B,M,D*
St. Joseph's College *B*
St. Mary's College *B*
Taylor University *B*
University of Evansville *B*
University of Indianapolis *B*
University of Notre Dame *B,M,D*
University of Southern Indiana *B*
Valparaiso University *B*
Vincennes University *A*

Iowa

Briar Cliff College *B*
Buena Vista College *B*
Central College *B*
Clarke College *B*
Clinton Community College *A*
Coe College *B*
Cornell College *B*
Divine Word College *B*
Dordt College *B*
Drake University *B*
Graceland College *B*
Grinnell College *B*
Iowa State University *B,M,D*
Iowa Wesleyan College *B*
Loras College *B*
Luther College *B*
Morningside College *B*
Mount Mercy College *B*
Muscatine Community College *A*
Northwestern College *B*
St. Ambrose University *B*
Scott Community College *A*
Simpson College *B*
Teikyo Westmar University *B*
University of Dubuque *B*
University of Iowa *B,M,D*
University of Northern Iowa *B,M*
Upper Iowa University *B*
Wartburg College *B*
William Penn College *B*

Kansas

Allen County Community
    College *A*
Baker University *B*
Benedictine College *B*
Bethany College *B*
Butler County Community
    College *A*
Central College *A*
Coffeyville Community College *A*
Emporia State University *B*
Fort Hays State University *B*
Fort Scott Community College *A*
Friends University *B*
Hutchinson Community College *A*
Kansas City Kansas Community
    College *A*
Kansas Newman College *B*
Kansas State University *B,M,D*
Kansas Wesleyan University *B*
McPherson College *B*
Pittsburg State University *B*
Pratt Community College *A*
St. Mary College *B*
Southwestern College *B*
University of Kansas *B,M,D*
Washburn University of Topeka *B*
Wichita State University *B,M*

Kentucky

Asbury College *B*
Bellarmine College *B,M*
Berea College *B*
Brescia College *B*
Campbellsville College *B*
Centre College *B*
Cumberland College *B*
Eastern Kentucky University *B*
Georgetown College *B*
Kentucky State University *B*
Kentucky Wesleyan College *B*
Lees College *A*
Morehead State University *B,M*
Murray State University *B*
Northern Kentucky University *B*
Spalding University *B*
Thomas More College *A,B*
Transylvania University *B*
Union College *B*
University of Kentucky *B,M,D*
University of Louisville *B,M*
Western Kentucky University *B,M*

Louisiana

Centenary College of Louisiana *B*
Dillard University *B*
Grambling State University *B,M*
Louisiana College *B*
Louisiana State University
    Agricultural and Mechanical
      College *B,M,D*
    Shreveport *B*
Louisiana Tech University *B*
Loyola University *B*
McNeese State University *B*
Nicholls State University *B*
Northeast Louisiana University *B*
Northwestern State University *B*
Southeastern Louisiana
    University *B*
Southern University at New
    Orleans *B*
Southern University and
    Agricultural and Mechanical
    College *B,M*
Tulane University *B,M,D*
University of New Orleans *B,M*
University of Southwestern
    Louisiana *B*
Xavier University of Louisiana *B*

Maine

Bates College *B*
Bowdoin College *B*
Colby College *B*
St. Joseph's College *B*
University of Maine
    Farmington *B*
    Orono *B*
    Presque Isle *B*
University of Southern Maine *B*

Maryland

Allegany Community College *A*
Bowie State University *B*
Frostburg State University *B*
Goucher College *B*
Harford Community College *A*
Hood College *B*
Howard Community College *A*
Johns Hopkins University *B,M,D*
Loyola College in Maryland *B*
Morgan State University *B,M*
Mount St. Mary's College *B*
St. Mary's College of Maryland *B*
Salisbury State University *B*
Towson State University *B*
University of Baltimore *B,M*
University of Maryland
    Baltimore County *B,M*
    College Park *B,M,D*
    Eastern Shore *B*
Washington College *B*
Western Maryland College *B*

Massachusetts

American International College *B*
Amherst College *B*
Assumption College *B*
Becker College: Leicester
    Campus *A*
Boston College *B,M,D*
Boston University *B,M,D*
Bradford College *B*
Brandeis University *B,M,D*
Bridgewater State College *B*
Clark University *B*
College of the Holy Cross *B*
Curry College *B*
Eastern Nazarene College *B*
Elms College *B*
Emmanuel College *B*
Endicott College *A*
Fitchburg State College *B*
Framingham State College *B*
Gordon College *B*
Hampshire College *B*
Harvard and Radcliffe Colleges *B*
Harvard University *D*
Merrimack College *B*
Mount Holyoke College *B*
Nichols College *B*
North Adams State College *B*
Northeastern University *B,M,D*
Quincy College *A*
Regis College *B*
Salem State College *B*
Simmons College *B*
Smith College *B*
Springfield College *B*
Stonehill College *B*
Suffolk University *B*
Tufts University *B*
University of Massachusetts
    Amherst *B,M,D*
    Boston *B,M*
    Dartmouth *B*
    Lowell *B*
Wellesley College *B*
Western New England College *B*
Wheaton College *B*
Williams College *B*
Worcester State College *B*

Michigan

Adrian College *A,B*
Albion College *B*
Alma College *B*
Andrews University *B*
Aquinas College *B*
Calvin College *B*
Central Michigan University *B,M*
Concordia College *B*
Eastern Michigan University *B,M*
Grand Rapids Baptist College and
  Seminary *B*
Grand Valley State University *B*
Hillsdale College *B*
Hope College *B*
Kalamazoo College *B*
Kirtland Community College *A*
Lake Superior State University *B*
Lansing Community College *A*
Madonna University *A,B*
Marygrove College *B*
Michigan State University *B,M,D*
Northern Michigan University
  A,B,M
Oakland University *B,M*
Olivet College *B*
Saginaw Valley State University *B*
Spring Arbor College *B*
University of Detroit Mercy *B*
University of Michigan
  Ann Arbor *B,M,D*
  Dearborn *B*
  Flint *B*
Wayne State University *B,M,D*
West Shore Community College *A*
Western Michigan University
  B,M,D

Minnesota

Augsburg College *B*
Bemidji State University *B*
Bethel College *B*
Carleton College *B*
College of St. Benedict *B*
College of St. Catherine: St.
  Catherine Campus *B*
College of St. Scholastica *B*
Concordia College: Moorhead *B*
Crown College *A*
Gustavus Adolphus College *B*
Hamline University *B*
Macalester College *B*
Mankato State University *B,M*
Moorhead State University *B*
Rainy River Community College *A*
St. Cloud State University *B*
St. John's University *B*
St. Mary's College of Minnesota *B*
St. Olaf College *B*
Southwest State University *B*
University of Minnesota
  Duluth *B*
  Morris *B*
  Twin Cities *B,M,D*
University of St. Thomas *B*
Willmar Community College *A*
Winona State University *B,M*

Mississippi

Delta State University *B*
Jackson State University *B,M*
Millsaps College *B*
Mississippi College *B,M*
Mississippi State University *B,M,D*
Rust College *B*
Tougaloo College *B*
University of Mississippi *B,M*
University of Southern
  Mississippi *B*

Missouri

Avila College *B*
Central Missouri State University
  B,M
College of the Ozarks *B*
Culver-Stockton College *B*
Drury College *B*
East Central College *A*
Evangel College *B*
Jefferson College *A*
Lincoln University *B,M*
Lindenwood College *B*
Maryville University *B*
Missouri Baptist College *B*
Missouri Southern State College *B*
Missouri Valley College *B*
Northeast Missouri State
  University *B*
Northwest Missouri State
  University *B*
Park College *B*
Rockhurst College *B*
St. Louis University *B*
Southeast Missouri State
  University *B*
Southwest Baptist University *B*
Southwest Missouri State
  University *B*
University of Missouri
  Columbia *B,M,D*
  Kansas City *B,M*
  St. Louis *B,M*
Washington University *B,M,D*
Webster University *B*
Westminster College *B*
William Jewell College *B*
William Woods College *B*

Montana

Carroll College *B*
College of Great Falls *B*
Eastern Montana College *A,B*
Montana State University *B*
Rocky Mountain College *B*
University of Montana *B,M,D*

Nebraska

Bellevue College *B*
Central Community College *A*
Chadron State College *B*
Concordia College *B*
Creighton University *B*
Dana College *B*
Doane College *B*
Hastings College *B*
Midland Lutheran College *B*
Nebraska Wesleyan University *B*
Peru State College *B*
Southeast Community College:
  Beatrice Campus *A*
University of Nebraska
  Kearney *B*
  Lincoln *B,M,D*
  Omaha *B,M*
Wayne State College *B*
York College *A*

Nevada

University of Nevada
  Las Vegas *B,M,D*
  Reno *B,M*

New Hampshire

Dartmouth College *B*
Franklin Pierce College *B*
Keene State College *B*
New England College *B*
Plymouth State College of the
  University System of New
  Hampshire *B*
Rivier College *B*
St. Anselm College *B*

University of New Hampshire
  B,M,D

New Jersey

Atlantic Community College *A*
Bergen Community College *A*
Bloomfield College *B*
Brookdale Community College *A*
Burlington County College *A*
Caldwell College *B*
College of St. Elizabeth *B*
Drew University *B*
Fairleigh Dickinson University *B*
Georgian Court College *B*
Glassboro State College *B*
Jersey City State College *B*
Kean College of New Jersey *B*
Monmouth College *B*
Montclair State College *B,M*
Ocean County College *A*
Princeton University *B,D*
Ramapo College of New Jersey *B*
Rider College *B*
Rutgers—The State University of
  New Jersey
  Camden College of Arts and
    Sciences *B*
  Douglass College *B*
  Livingston College *B*
  New Brunswick *M,D*
  Newark College of Arts and
    Sciences *B*
  Rutgers College *B*
  University College Camden *B*
  University College New
    Brunswick *B*
  University College Newark *B*
St. Peter's College *B*
Seton Hall University *B*
Stevens Institute of Technology *B*
Stockton State College *B*
Thomas Edison State College *B*
Trenton State College *B*
Upsala College *B*
William Paterson College of New
  Jersey *B,M*

New Mexico

Eastern New Mexico University *B*
New Mexico State University *B,M*
University of New Mexico *B,M,D*
Western New Mexico University *B*

New York

Adelphi University *B,M*
Adirondack Community College *A*
Alfred University *B*
Bard College *B*
Barnard College *B*
Canisius College *B*
City University of New York
  Baruch College *B*
  Brooklyn College *B,M*
  City College *B,M*
  Graduate School and
    University Center *D*
  Hunter College *B*
  Lehman College *B*
  Queens College *B,M*
  Queensborough Community
    College *A*
  York College *B*
Colgate University *B,M*
College of Mount St. Vincent *B*
College of New Rochelle *B*
College of St. Rose *B*
Columbia University
  Columbia College *B*
  New York *M,D*
  School of General Studies *B*
Cornell University *B,M,D*
Dominican College of Blauvelt *B*

Dowling College *B*
D'Youville College *B*
Elmira College *B*
Eugene Lang College/New School
  for Social Research *B*
Fordham University *B,M,D*
Fulton-Montgomery Community
  College *A*
Hamilton College *B*
Hartwick College *B*
Herkimer County Community
  College *A*
Hobart College *B*
Hofstra University *B*
Houghton College *B*
Iona College *B*
Ithaca College *B*
Jamestown Community College *A*
Keuka College *B*
King's College *B*
Le Moyne College *B*
Long Island University
  Brooklyn Campus *B,M*
  C. W. Post Campus *B*
  Southampton Campus *B*
Manhattan College *B*
Manhattanville College *B*
Marymount College *B*
Marymount Manhattan College *B*
Mercy College *B*
Molloy College *B*
Mount St. Mary College *B*
Nazareth College of Rochester *B*
New York University *B,M,D*
Niagara University *B*
Pace University
  College of White Plains *B*
  New York *B*
  Pleasantville/Briarcliff *B*
Roberts Wesleyan College *B*
Russell Sage College *B*
Sage Junior College of Albany, A
  Division of Russell Sage
  College *A*
St. Bonaventure University *B*
St. Francis College *B*
St. John Fisher College *B*
St. John's University *B,M*
St. Joseph's College: Suffolk
  Campus *C,B*
St. Lawrence University *B*
Sarah Lawrence College *B*
Siena College *B*
Skidmore College *B*
State University of New York
  Albany *B,M,D*
  Binghamton *B,M,D*
  Buffalo *B,M,D*
  Purchase *B*
  Stony Brook *B,M,D*
  College at Brockport *B*
  College at Buffalo *B*
  College at Cortland *B*
  College at Fredonia *B*
  College at Geneseo *B*
  College at New Paltz *B,M*
  College at Old Westbury *B*
  College at Oneonta *B*
  College at Plattsburgh *B*
  College at Potsdam *B*
  College of Technology at
    Delhi *A*
  Institute of Technology at
    Utica/Rome *B*
  Oswego *B*
Sullivan County Community
  College *A*
Syracuse University *B,M,D*
Touro College *B*
Union College *B*
United States Military Academy *B*

University of the State of New York: Regents College *B*
Utica College of Syracuse University *B*
Vassar College *B*
Wagner College *B*
Wells College *B*
William Smith College *B*
Yeshiva University *B*

North Carolina

Appalachian State University *B,M*
Barber-Scotia College *B*
Barton College *B*
Belmont Abbey College *B*
Bennett College *B*
Brevard College *A*
Catawba College *B*
Chowan College *A*
Davidson College *B*
Duke University *B,M,D*
East Carolina University *B,M*
Elizabeth City State University *B*
Elon College *B*
Fayetteville State University *B*
Gardner-Webb College *B*
Greensboro College *B*
Guilford College *B*
High Point University *B*
Johnson C. Smith University *B*
Lenoir-Rhyne College *B*
Livingstone College *B*
Louisburg College *A*
Mars Hill College *B*
Meredith College *B*
Methodist College *A,B*
North Carolina Agricultural and Technical State University *B*
North Carolina Central University *B,M*
North Carolina State University *B,M,D*
North Carolina Wesleyan College *B*
Pembroke State University *B*
Pfeiffer College *B*
Queens College *B*
St. Augustine's College *B*
Salem College *B*
Shaw University *B*
University of North Carolina
   Asheville *B*
   Chapel Hill *B,M,D*
   Charlotte *B,M*
   Greensboro *B,M*
   Wilmington *B*
Wake Forest University *B*
Warren Wilson College *B*
Western Carolina University *B*
Wingate College *B*
Winston-Salem State University *B*

North Dakota

Minot State University *B*
North Dakota State University
   Bottineau and Institute of Forestry *A*
   Fargo *B,M*
University of North Dakota *B,M*

Ohio

Antioch College *B*
Ashland University *B*
Baldwin-Wallace College *B*
Bluffton College *B*
Bowling Green State University *B,M,D*
Capital University *B*
Case Western Reserve University *B,M,D*
Cedarville College *B*
Central State University *B*
Cleveland State University *B,M*

College of Wooster *B*
Denison University *B*
Franciscan University of Steubenville *B*
Hiram College *B*
John Carroll University *B*
Kent State University *B,M,D*
Kenyon College *B*
Lakeland Community College *A*
Lourdes College *A,B*
Miami University: Oxford Campus *B,M*
Mount Union College *B*
Mount Vernon Nazarene College *A,B*
Muskingum College *B*
Oberlin College *B,M*
Ohio Dominican College *B*
Ohio Northern University *B*
Ohio State University: Columbus Campus *B,M,D*
Ohio University
   Athens *B,M*
   Southern Campus at Ironton *A*
Ohio Wesleyan University *B*
Otterbein College *B*
Union Institute *B,D*
University of Akron *B,M,D*
University of Cincinnati *B,M,D*
University of Dayton *B*
University of Findlay *B*
University of Rio Grande *A*
University of Toledo *B,M*
Urbana University *B*
Ursuline College *B*
Walsh College *B*
Wilberforce University *B*
Wilmington College *B*
Wittenberg University *B*
Wright State University
   Dayton *B*
   Lake Campus *A*
Xavier University *A,B*
Youngstown State University *B*

Oklahoma

Bartlesville Wesleyan College *A*
Cameron University *B*
Connors State College *A*
East Central University *B*
Eastern Oklahoma State College *A*
Langston University *B*
Northeastern State University *B*
Northwestern Oklahoma State University *B*
Oklahoma Baptist University *B*
Oklahoma Christian University of Science and Arts *B*
Oklahoma City University *B*
Oklahoma State University *B,M,D*
Phillips University *B*
Redlands Community College *A*
Rose State College *A*
Southeastern Oklahoma State University *B*
Southwestern Oklahoma State University *B*
Tulsa Junior College *A*
University of Central Oklahoma *B,M*
University of Oklahoma *B,M,D*
University of Science and Arts of Oklahoma *B*
University of Tulsa *B*

Oregon

Central Oregon Community College *A*
Eastern Oregon State College *B*
George Fox College *B*
Lewis and Clark College *B*
Linfield College *B*

Northwest Christian College *B*
Oregon State University *B*
Pacific University *B*
Portland Community College *A*
Portland State University *B,M*
Reed College *B*
Southern Oregon State College *B*
University of Oregon
   Eugene *B,M,D*
   Robert Donald Clark Honors College *B*
University of Portland *B*
Warner Pacific College *B*
Western Oregon State College *B*
Willamette University *B*

Pennsylvania

Albright College *B*
Allegheny College *B*
Beaver College *B*
Bloomsburg University of Pennsylvania *B*
Bryn Mawr College *B*
Bucknell University *B*
Cabrini College *B*
California University of Pennsylvania *B,M*
Carnegie Mellon University *B,M,D*
Cedar Crest College *B*
Chestnut Hill College *A,B*
Clarion University of Pennsylvania *B*
Dickinson College *B*
Drexel University *B*
Duquesne University *B,M*
East Stroudsburg University of Pennsylvania *B*
Eastern College *B*
Edinboro University of Pennsylvania *B*
Elizabethtown College *B*
Franklin and Marshall College *B*
Gannon University *B*
Geneva College *B*
Gettysburg College *B*
Gratz College *C*
Gwynedd-Mercy College *B*
Haverford College *B*
Holy Family College *B*
Immaculata College *B*
Indiana University of Pennsylvania *B,M*
Juniata College *B*
King's College *B*
Kutztown University of Pennsylvania *B*
La Roche College *B*
La Salle University *B*
Lafayette College *B*
Lebanon Valley College of Pennsylvania *B*
Lehigh University *B*
Lincoln University *B*
Lock Haven University of Pennsylvania *B*
Lycoming College *B*
Mansfield University of Pennsylvania *B*
Marywood College *B*
Mercyhurst College *B*
Messiah College *B*
Millersville University of Pennsylvania *B*
Moravian College *B*
Muhlenberg College *B*
Penn State University Park Campus *A,B,M,D*
Rosemont College *B*
St. Francis College *B*
St. Joseph's University *B*
St. Vincent College *B*
Seton Hill College *B*

Shippensburg University of Pennsylvania *B*
Slippery Rock University of Pennsylvania *B*
Susquehanna University *B*
Swarthmore College *B*
Temple University *B,M,D*
Thiel College *B*
University of Pennsylvania *B,M,D*
University of Pittsburgh
   Johnstown *B*
   Pittsburgh *B,M,D*
University of Scranton *B*
Ursinus College *B*
Villanova University *B*
Washington and Jefferson College *B*
Waynesburg College *B*
West Chester University of Pennsylvania *B*
Westminster College *B*
Widener University *B*
Wilkes University *B*
York College of Pennsylvania *B*

Puerto Rico

Inter American University of Puerto Rico
   Arecibo Campus *B*
   Metropolitan Campus *B*
   San German Campus *B*
Pontifical Catholic University of Puerto Rico *B*
Turabo University *B*
University of Puerto Rico
   Cayey University College *B*
   Mayaguez Campus *B*
   Rio Piedras Campus *B,M*

Rhode Island

Brown University *B,M,D*
Providence College *B*
Rhode Island College *B*
Salve Regina University *B*
University of Rhode Island *B*

South Carolina

Charleston Southern University *B*
Claflin College *B*
Clemson University *B,M*
Coker College *B*
College of Charleston *B*
Columbia College *B*
Converse College *B*
Francis Marion College *B*
Furman University *B*
Lander College *B*
Morris College *B*
Newberry College *B*
Presbyterian College *B*
South Carolina State College *B*
University of South Carolina
   Aiken *B*
   Coastal Carolina College *B*
   Columbia *B,M,D*
   Spartanburg *B*
Voorhees College *B*
Winthrop University *B*
Wofford College *B*

South Dakota

Augustana College *B*
Black Hills State University *B*
Dakota Wesleyan University *B*
Northern State University *B*
Sioux Falls College *B*
South Dakota State University *B,M,D*
University of South Dakota *B,M*

Tennessee

Austin Peay State University *B*
Belmont University *B*

Carson-Newman College *B*
David Lipscomb University *B*
Dyersburg State Community
   College *A*
East Tennessee State University
   B,M
Fisk University *B,M*
Hiwassee College *A*
Knoxville College *B*
Lambuth University *B*
Lane College *B*
LeMoyne-Owen College *B*
Memphis State University *B,M*
Middle Tennessee State University
   B,M
Milligan College *B*
Motlow State Community
   College *A*
Rhodes College *B*
Tennessee State University *B*
Tennessee Technological
   University *B*
Trevecca Nazarene College *B*
Union University *B*
University of Tennessee
   Chattanooga *B*
   Knoxville *B,M,D*
   Martin *B*
Vanderbilt University *B,M,D*

Texas

Abilene Christian University *B*
Angelo State University *B*
Austin College *B*
Austin Community College *A*
Baylor University *B,M*
Bee County College *A*
College of the Mainland *A*
Collin County Community College
   District *A*
Corpus Christi State University *B*
Dallas Baptist University *B*
Del Mar College *A*
East Texas Baptist University *B*
East Texas State University *B,M*
El Paso Community College *A*
Galveston College *A*
Hardin-Simmons University *B*
Houston Baptist University *B*
Houston Community College *A*
Howard Payne University *B*
Huston-Tillotson College *B*
Incarnate Word College *B*
Jacksonville College *A*
Kilgore College *A*
Lamar University—Beaumont *B*
Laredo State University *B*
Lon Morris College *A*
Lubbock Christian University *B*
McMurry University *B*
Midland College *A*
Midwestern State University *B*
Our Lady of the Lake University of
   San Antonio *B*
Paul Quinn College *B*
Prairie View A&M University *B,M*
Rice University *B*
St. Edward's University *B*
St. Mary's University *B*
St. Philip's College *A*
Sam Houston State University *B,M*
Southern Methodist University *B*
Southwest Texas State University *B*
Southwestern University *B*
Stephen F. Austin State
   University *B*
Tarleton State University *B*
Texas A&I University *B,M*
Texas A&M University *B,M,D*
Texas Christian University *B*
Texas College *B*
Texas Lutheran College *B*

Texas Southern University *B,M*
Texas Southmost College *A*
Texas Tech University *B,M*
Texas Wesleyan University *B*
Texas Woman's University *B,M,D*
Trinity University *B*
University of Houston
   Clear Lake *B,M*
   Houston *B,M*
University of Mary Hardin-
   Baylor *B*
University of North Texas *B,M,D*
University of St. Thomas *B*
University of Texas
   Arlington *B,M*
   Austin *B,M,D*
   Dallas *B*
   El Paso *B,M*
   Pan American *B*
   Permian Basin *B*
   San Antonio *B*
   Tyler *B*
West Texas State University *B,M*
Western Texas College *A*
Wharton County Junior College *A*
Wiley College *B*

Utah

Brigham Young University *B,M,D*
Dixie College *A*
Southern Utah University *B*
University of Utah *B,M,D*
Utah State University *B,M,D*
Weber State University *B*
Westminster College of Salt Lake
   City *A*

Vermont

Castleton State College *B*
Johnson State College *B*
Marlboro College *B*
Middlebury College *B*
St. Michael's College *B*
Trinity College of Vermont *B*
University of Vermont *B*

Virginia

Averett College *B*
Bridgewater College *B*
Christopher Newport College *B*
Clinch Valley College of the
   University of Virginia *B*
College of William and Mary *B,M*
Eastern Mennonite College *B*
Emory and Henry College *B*
George Mason University *B,M*
Hampton University *B*
Hollins College *B*
James Madison University *B*
Longwood College *B*
Lynchburg College *B*
Mary Baldwin College *B*
Mary Washington College *B*
Norfolk State University *B,M*
Old Dominion University *B,M*
Radford University *B*
Randolph-Macon College *B*
Randolph-Macon Woman's
   College *B*
Roanoke College *B*
St. Paul's College *B*
Sweet Briar College *B*
University of Richmond *B,W*
University of Virginia *B,M,D*
Virginia Commonwealth University
   B,M
Virginia Polytechnic Institute and
   State University *B,M,D*
Virginia State University *B*
Virginia Union University *B*
Virginia Wesleyan College *B*
Washington and Lee University *B*

Washington

Big Bend Community College *A*
Central Washington University *B*
Eastern Washington University *B*
Everett Community College *A*
Evergreen State College *B*
Gonzaga University *B*
Lower Columbia College *A*
Olympic College *A*
Pacific Lutheran University *B*
Seattle Central Community
   College *A*
Seattle Pacific University *B*
Seattle University *B*
Spokane Community College *A*
Spokane Falls Community
   College *A*
Tacoma Community College *A*
University of Puget Sound *B*
University of Washington *B,M,D*
Walla Walla College *B*
Washington State University *B,M,D*
Wenatchee Valley College *A*
Western Washington University
   B,M
Whitman College *B*
Whitworth College *B*

West Virginia

Alderson-Broaddus College *B*
Concord College *B*
Davis and Elkins College *B*
Fairmont State College *B*
Marshall University *B,M*
Potomac State College of West
   Virginia University *A*
Shepherd College *B*
West Liberty State College *B*
West Virginia State College *B*
West Virginia University *B,M*
West Virginia Wesleyan College *B*

Wisconsin

Beloit College *B*
Cardinal Stritch College *B*
Carroll College *B*
Carthage College *B*
Edgewood College *B*
Lakeland College *B*
Marquette University *B,M*
Northland College *B*
Ripon College *B*
St. Norbert College *B*
University of Wisconsin
   Eau Claire *B*
   Green Bay *B*
   La Crosse *B*
   Madison *B,M,D*
   Milwaukee *B,M*
   Oshkosh *B*
   Parkside *B*
   River Falls *B*
   Stevens Point *B*
   Superior *B*
   Whitewater *B*
Viterbo College *B*

Wyoming

Casper College *A*
Central Wyoming College *A*
Eastern Wyoming College *A*
Laramie County Community
   College *A*
Sheridan College *A*
University of Wyoming *B,M*
Western Wyoming Community
   College *A*

**American Samoa, Caroline
Islands, Guam, Marianas,
Virgin Islands**

University of Guam *B*

Canada

McGill University *B,M,D*

Arab Republic of Egypt

American University in Cairo *B,M*

Soil sciences

Alabama

Alabama Agricultural and
   Mechanical University *B,M*
Auburn University *B,M,D*
Tuskegee University *B,M*

Arizona

University of Arizona *B,M,D*

Arkansas

University of Arkansas *B*

California

California Polytechnic State
   University: San Luis Obispo *B*
California State Polytechnic
   University: Pomona *B*
California State University:
   Fresno *B*
Humboldt State University *C*
Kings River Community College *A*
Merced College *A*
Modesto Junior College *A*
San Joaquin Delta College *A*
University of California
   Berkeley *B,M,D*
   Davis *B,M,D*
   Riverside *B,M,D*
Ventura College *A*
West Hills Community College *A*

Delaware

Delaware State College *B*

Florida

University of Florida *B,M,D*

Georgia

University of Georgia *B*

Hawaii

University of Hawaii at Manoa
   B,M,D

Idaho

Ricks College *C,A*
University of Idaho *B,M,D*

Illinois

Southern Illinois University at
   Carbondale *B,M*
University of Illinois at Urbana-
   Champaign *B*

Indiana

Purdue University *C,B,M,D,W*
Vincennes University *A*

Iowa

Iowa State University *M,D*
Kirkwood Community College *A*

Kansas

Colby Community College *A*
Cowley County Community
   College *A*

Kansas State University *B*

Kentucky
Eastern Kentucky University *B*
Murray State University *B*
University of Kentucky *M,D*

Louisiana
Southern University and
Agricultural and Mechanical
College *B*

Maine
University of Maine *B,M*

Maryland
University of Maryland: College
Park *B,M,D*

Massachusetts
University of Massachusetts at
Amherst *B,M,D*

Michigan
Grand Valley State University *B*
Michigan State University *B,M,D*

Minnesota
University of Minnesota
Crookston *A*
Twin Cities *M,D*
Willmar Community College *A*

Mississippi
Alcorn State University *B*

Montana
Montana State University *B,M,D*

Nebraska
Northeast Community College *A*
University of Nebraska—Lincoln *B*

New Hampshire
University of New Hampshire *B,M*

New Jersey
Rutgers—The State University of
New Jersey
Cook College *B*
New Brunswick *M,D*

New Mexico
New Mexico State University
B,M,D

New York
Cornell University *B,M,D*
State University of New York
College of Agriculture and
Technology at Cobleskill *A*
College of Environmental
Science and Forestry *B,M,D*

North Carolina
North Carolina State University
B,M,D
Wayne Community College *A*

North Dakota
North Dakota State University
B,M,D

Ohio
Ohio State University Agricultural
Technical Institute *A*

Oklahoma
Connors State College *A*
Oklahoma Panhandle State
University *B*
Oklahoma State University *D*

Southeastern Oklahoma State
University *B*

Oregon
Eastern Oregon State College *B*
Oregon State University *M,D*

Pennsylvania
California University of
Pennsylvania *B*
Penn State University Park Campus
B,M,D

Puerto Rico
University of Puerto Rico:
Mayaguez Campus *M*

Rhode Island
University of Rhode Island *B*

South Dakota
South Dakota State University *B*

Tennessee
Hiwassee College *A*
Middle Tennessee State
University *B*
Tennessee State University *B*
Tennessee Technological
University *B*
University of Tennessee
Knoxville *B,M,D*
Martin *B*

Texas
Central Texas College *A*
Howard College *A*
Tarleton State University *B*
Texas A&I University *B,M*
Texas A&M University *B,M,D*
Texas Tech University *B*
Western Texas College *A*

Utah
Brigham Young University *B*
Southern Utah University *B*
Utah State University *B,M,D*

Vermont
University of Vermont *B,M,D*

Virginia
Mountain Empire Community
College *A*

Washington
Spokane Community College *A*
Washington State University *B,M,D*

West Virginia
West Virginia University *B*

Wisconsin
Northland College *B*
University of Wisconsin
Madison *B,M,D*
Platteville *B*
River Falls *B*
Stevens Point *B*

Wyoming
Northwest College *A*
University of Wyoming *B*

Canada
McGill University *B,M,D*

Mexico
Sistema Instituto Tecnologico y de
Estudios Superiores de
Monterrey *M*

Solar heating and cooling technology

Arizona
Pima Community College *A*
Yavapai College *C*

California
Humboldt State University *M*
San Diego City College *C,A*
Southwestern College *A*

Colorado
Colorado Mountain College: Spring
Valley Campus *C*
Red Rocks Community College *C,A*

Florida
Okaloosa-Walton Community
College *A*

Illinois
Carl Sandburg College *A*
Lewis University *C*
Southern Illinois University at
Carbondale *A*

Indiana
Vincennes University *A*

Michigan
Eastern Michigan University *B*
Henry Ford Community College *C*
Jackson Community College *A*
Jordan College *C,A*
Lansing Community College *A*
Oakland Community College *A*

Mississippi
Mississippi Gulf Coast Community
College: Perkinston *C*

Nebraska
Southeast Community College:
Milford Campus *A*
York College *A*

Nevada
Truckee Meadows Community
College *C,A*

New Mexico
New Mexico State University *A*

New York
Erie Community College: South
Campus *A*

Pennsylvania
Penn State University Park
Campus *A*
Pittsburgh Institute of
Aeronautics *A*

Utah
Dixie College *C,A*

Solid state physics

District of Columbia
George Washington University *D*

Florida
New College of the University of
South Florida *B*

Indiana
University of Notre Dame *M,D*

Iowa
Iowa State University *M,D*

Kansas
Central College *A*
Kansas State University *M,D*

Massachusetts
Brandeis University *D*
Massachusetts Institute of
Technology *B,M,D,W*
Tufts University *M,D*
Worcester Polytechnic Institute *B*

Michigan
Michigan State University *D*

New Jersey
Stevens Institute of Technology
B,M,D

New York
Columbia University *M,D*
State University of New York at
Albany *M,D*
Syracuse University *M,D*

Ohio
Ohio State University: Columbus
Campus *B,M,D*

Oregon
Oregon Graduate Institute *M,D*

Pennsylvania
Lehigh University *B,M*

Canada
McGill University *M,D*

South Asian studies

California
Naval Postgraduate School *M*
Sonoma State University *B*
University of California
Berkeley *B,M,D*
Santa Cruz *B*

Illinois
University of Chicago *B,M,D*

Massachusetts
Hampshire College *B*
Harvard and Radcliffe Colleges *B*

Michigan
Oakland University *B*
University of Michigan *M*

Minnesota
University of Minnesota: Twin
Cities *B*

Missouri
University of Missouri: Columbia *B*

New York
Columbia University
Columbia College *B*
New York *M,D*

Ohio
College of Wooster *B*

Pennsylvania

University of Pennsylvania *B,M,D*

Rhode Island

Brown University *B*

Washington

University of Washington *B,M*

Wisconsin

University of Wisconsin: Madison *B,M*

Southeast Asian studies

California

Naval Postgraduate School *M*
University of California
    Berkeley *B,M,D*
    Santa Cruz *B*

Massachusetts

Hampshire College *B*

Michigan

University of Michigan *M*

New York

Cornell University *M,D*

North Carolina

St. Andrews Presbyterian College *B*

Ohio

Ohio University *M*

Spanish

Alabama

Alabama State University *B*
Auburn University *B,M*
Birmingham-Southern College *B*
Jacksonville State University *B*
Judson College *B*
Mobile College *B*
Samford University *B*
Stillman College *B*
University of Alabama
    Birmingham *B*
    Huntsville *B*
    Tuscaloosa *B,M,D*
University of Montevallo *B*
University of North Alabama *B*
University of South Alabama *B*

Arizona

Arizona State University *B,M,D*
Arizona Western College *A*
Cochise College *A*
Eastern Arizona College *A*
Glendale Community College *A*
Grand Canyon University *B*
Northern Arizona University *B*
Prescott College *B*
University of Arizona *B,M,D*
Yavapai College *A*

Arkansas

Arkansas State University *B*
Arkansas Tech University *B*
Harding University *B,M*
Henderson State University *B*
Hendrix College *B*
Ouachita Baptist University *B*
Southern Arkansas University *B*

University of Arkansas
    Fayetteville *B,M*
    Little Rock *B*
University of Central Arkansas *B,M*
Westark Community College *A*

California

Bakersfield College *A*
California Baptist College *B*
California Lutheran University *B*
California State University
    Bakersfield *B*
    Chico *B*
    Dominguez Hills *B*
    Fresno *B,M*
    Fullerton *B,M*
    Hayward *B*
    Long Beach *B,M*
    Los Angeles *B,M*
    Northridge *B,M*
    Sacramento *B,M*
    San Bernardino *B*
    Stanislaus *B*
Cerritos Community College *A*
Chabot College *A*
Chaffey Community College *A*
Chapman University *B*
Citrus College *A*
Claremont McKenna College *B*
College of the Desert *A*
College of the Sequoias *A*
De Anza College *A*
El Camino College *A*
Feather River College *A*
Foothill College *A*
Fresno City College *A*
Gavilan Community College *A*
Glendale Community College *A*
Grossmont Community College *C,A*
Holy Names College *B*
Humboldt State University *B*
Irvine Valley College *A*
La Sierra University *B*
Long Beach City College *C,A*
Los Angeles City College *A*
Los Angeles Mission College *A*
Los Angeles Valley College *A*
Loyola Marymount University *B*
Mendocino College *A*
Merced College *A*
Mills College *B*
MiraCosta College *A*
Modesto Junior College *A*
Monterey Institute of International
    Studies *B,M*
Mount St. Mary's College *B*
Occidental College *B*
Ohlone College *A*
Orange Coast College *A*
Oxnard College *A*
Pacific Union College *B*
Pepperdine University *B*
Pitzer College *B*
Point Loma Nazarene College *B*
Pomona College *B*
St. Mary's College of California *B*
San Diego City College *A*
San Diego State University *B,M*
San Francisco State University *B,M*
San Joaquin Delta College *A*
San Jose City College *A*
San Jose State University *B,M*
Santa Barbara City College *A*
Santa Clara University *B*
Santa Monica College *A*
Santa Rosa Junior College *A*
Scripps College *B*
Solano Community College *A*
Sonoma State University *B*
Southwestern College *A*
Stanford University *B,M,D*

University of California
    Berkeley *B,M,D*
    Davis *B,M,D*
    Irvine *B,M,D*
    Los Angeles *B,M,D*
    Riverside *B,M,D*
    San Diego *B,M,D*
    Santa Barbara *B,M,D*
    Santa Cruz *B,D*
University of La Verne *B*
University of the Pacific *B*
University of Redlands *B*
University of San Diego *B*
University of San Francisco *B*
University of Southern California
    B,M,D
Ventura College *A*
Westmont College *B*
Whittier College *B*

Colorado

Adams State College *B*
Colorado College *B*
Colorado State University *B,M*
Fort Lewis College *B*
Metropolitan State College of
    Denver *B*
Northeastern Junior College *A*
Regis College of Regis University *B*
University of Colorado
    Boulder *B,M,D*
    Colorado Springs *B*
    Denver *B*
University of Denver *B,M*
University of Northern Colorado *B*
Western State College of
    Colorado *B*

Connecticut

Albertus Magnus College *B*
Central Connecticut State
    University *B,M*
Connecticut College *B,M*
Eastern Connecticut State
    University *B*
Fairfield University *B*
Sacred Heart University *A,B*
St. Joseph College *B*
Southern Connecticut State
    University *B,M*
Trinity College *B*
University of Connecticut *B,M,D*
University of Hartford *B*
Wesleyan University *B*
Western Connecticut State
    University *B*
Yale University *B,M,D*

Delaware

Delaware State College *B*
University of Delaware *B,M*
Wesley College *A*

District of Columbia

American University *B,M*
Catholic University of America
    B,M,D
Gallaudet University *B*
George Washington University *B*
Georgetown University *B,M,D*
Howard University *B,M,D*
Trinity College *B*
University of the District of
    Columbia *B*

Florida

Barry University *B*
Eckerd College *B*
Flagler College *B*
Florida Atlantic University *B,M*
Florida International University
    B,M

Florida Southern College *B*
Florida State University *B,M,D*
Indian River Community College *A*
Jacksonville University *B*
Miami-Dade Community College *A*
New College of the University of
    South Florida *B*
Okaloosa-Walton Community
    College *A*
Rollins College *B*
St. Thomas University *B*
Stetson University *B*
University of Central Florida *B*
University of Florida *B,M,D*
University of Miami *B,M*
University of North Florida *B*
University of South Florida *B,M*
University of Tampa *A,B*
University of West Florida *B*

Georgia

Agnes Scott College *B*
Albany State College *B*
Andrew College *A*
Augusta College *B*
Bainbridge College *A*
Berry College *B*
Clark Atlanta University *B*
Clayton State College *A*
Darton College *A*
Emory University *B,M,D*
Georgia College *B*
Georgia Southern University *B*
Georgia State University *B,M*
Kennesaw State College *B*
LaGrange College *B*
Mercer University *B*
Morehouse College *B*
Morris Brown College *B*
Piedmont College *B*
Shorter College *B*
South Georgia College *A*
Spelman College *B*
University of Georgia *B,M*
Valdosta State College *B*
Wesleyan College *B*
West Georgia College *B*
Young Harris College *A*

Hawaii

University of Hawaii at Manoa *B*

Idaho

Albertson College *B*
Boise State University *B*
Idaho State University *B*
Ricks College *A*
University of Idaho *B,M*

Illinois

Augustana College *B*
Black Hawk College *A*
Blackburn College *B*
Bradley University *B*
Chicago State University *B*
City Colleges of Chicago: Chicago
    City-Wide College *C*
De Paul University *B*
Eastern Illinois University *B*
Elmhurst College *B*
Eureka College *B*
Greenville College *B*
Illinois Benedictine College *B*
Illinois College *B*
Illinois State University *B*
Illinois Wesleyan University *B*
Joliet Junior College *A*
Knox College *B*
Lake Forest College *B*
Loyola University of Chicago *B,M*
MacMurray College *B*
Millikin University *B*

Monmouth College *B*
North Central College *B*
North Park College and Theological
Seminary *B*
Northeastern Illinois University *B*
Northern Illinois University *B,M*
Northwestern University *B,M,D*
Principia College *B*
Rend Lake College *A*
Richland Community College *A*
Rockford College *B*
Roosevelt University *B,M*
Rosary College *B*
St. Xavier University *B*
Southern Illinois University
Carbondale *B,M*
Edwardsville *B*
Trinity Christian College *B*
University of Chicago *B,M,D*
University of Illinois
Chicago *B*
Urbana-Champaign *B,M,D*
Western Illinois University *B*
Wheaton College *B*

Indiana

Anderson University *B*
Ball State University *B,M*
Butler University *B*
DePauw University *B*
Earlham College *B*
Franklin College *B*
Goshen College *B*
Grace College *B*
Hanover College *B*
Indiana State University *B,M*
Indiana University
Bloomington *B,M,D*
Northwest *B*
South Bend *B*
Indiana University—Purdue
University
Fort Wayne *B*
Indianapolis *B*
Indiana Wesleyan University *B*
Manchester College *B*
Marian College *B*
Purdue University
Calumet *B*
West Lafayette *B,M,D*
St. Mary-of-the-Woods College *B*
St. Mary's College *B*
St. Meinrad College *B*
Taylor University *B*
University of Evansville *B*
University of Indianapolis *B*
University of Notre Dame *B,M*
University of Southern Indiana *B*
Valparaiso University *B*
Vincennes University *A*
Wabash College *B*

Iowa

Briar Cliff College *B*
Buena Vista College *B*
Central College *B*
Clarke College *B*
Coe College *B*
Cornell College *B*
Dordt College *B*
Drake University *B,M*
Graceland College *B*
Grinnell College *B*
Iowa State University *B*
Kirkwood Community College *A*
Loras College *B*
Luther College *B*
Morningside College *B*
North Iowa Area Community
College *A*
Northwestern College *B*
St. Ambrose University *B*

Simpson College *B*
University of Dubuque *B*
University of Iowa *B,M,D*
University of Northern Iowa *B,M*
Wartburg College *B*

Kansas

Baker University *B*
Benedictine College *B*
Fort Scott Community College *C*
Friends University *B*
Kansas City College and Bible
School *B*
Kansas City Kansas Community
College *A*
Kansas State University *B,M*
Kansas Wesleyan University *B*
McPherson College *B*
MidAmerica Nazarene College *B*
Pittsburg State University *B*
Pratt Community College *A*
St. Mary College *B*
Southwestern College *B*
University of Kansas *B,M,D*
Washburn University of Topeka *B*
Wichita State University *B,M*

Kentucky

Asbury College *B*
Berea College *B*
Centre College *B*
Eastern Kentucky University *B*
Georgetown College *B*
Morehead State University *B*
Murray State University *B*
Transylvania University *B*
University of Kentucky *B,M,D*
University of Louisville *B,M*
Western Kentucky University *B*

Louisiana

Centenary College of Louisiana *B*
Dillard University *B*
Grambling State University *B*
Louisiana State University
Agricultural and Mechanical
College *B,M*
Shreveport *B*
Louisiana Tech University *B,M*
Loyola University *B*
McNeese State University *B*
Northeast Louisiana University *B*
Southeastern Louisiana
University *B*
Southern University at New
Orleans *B*
Southern University and
Agricultural and Mechanical
College *B*
Tulane University *B,M,D*
University of New Orleans *B,M*
University of Southwestern
Louisiana *M*
Xavier University of Louisiana *B*

Maine

Bates College *B*
Bowdoin College *B*
Colby College *B*
University of Maine *B*

Maryland

College of Notre Dame of
Maryland *B*
Frostburg State University *B*
Goucher College *B*
Hood College *B*
Johns Hopkins University *B,M,D*
Loyola College in Maryland *B*
Morgan State University *B*
Mount St. Mary's College *B*
Salisbury State University *B*

Towson State University *B*
University of Maryland
Baltimore County *B*
College Park *B,M,D*
Washington College *B*
Western Maryland College *B*

Massachusetts

American International College *B*
Amherst College *B*
Anna Maria College for Men and
Women *B*
Assumption College *B*
Atlantic Union College *B*
Boston College *B,M,D*
Boston University *B,M,D*
Bradford College *B*
Brandeis University *B*
Bridgewater State College *B*
Clark University *B*
College of the Holy Cross *B*
Eastern Nazarene College *B*
Elms College *B*
Emmanuel College *B*
Framingham State College *B*
Gordon College *B*
Harvard and Radcliffe Colleges *B*
Harvard University *M,D*
Massachusetts Institute of
Technology *B*
Mount Holyoke College *B*
Northeastern University *B*
Regis College *B*
Simmons College *B,M*
Suffolk University *B*
Tufts University *B*
University of Massachusetts
Amherst *B,M,D*
Boston *B*
Dartmouth *B*
Lowell *B*
Wellesley College *B*
Westfield State College *B*
Wheaton College *B*
Williams College *B*
Worcester State College *B*

Michigan

Adrian College *A,B*
Albion College *B*
Alma College *B*
Andrews University *B*
Aquinas College *B*
Calvin College *B*
Central Michigan University *B*
Eastern Michigan University *B*
Grand Valley State University *B*
Hillsdale College *B*
Hope College *B*
Kalamazoo College *B*
Lansing Community College *A*
Madonna University *B*
Marygrove College *B*
Michigan State University *B,M,D*
Northern Michigan University *B,M*
Oakland University *B*
Olivet College *B*
Saginaw Valley State University *B*
Siena Heights College *B*
Spring Arbor College *B*
University of Detroit Mercy *B*
University of Michigan
Ann Arbor *B,M,D*
Flint *B*
Wayne State University *B,M*
Western Michigan University *B,M*

Minnesota

Augsburg College *B*
Bemidji State University *B*
Bethel College *B*
Carleton College *B*

College of St. Benedict *B*
College of St. Catherine: St.
Catherine Campus *B*
Concordia College: Moorhead *B*
Gustavus Adolphus College *B*
Hamline University *B*
Macalester College *B*
Mankato State University *B*
Moorhead State University *B*
Northland Community College *A*
St. Cloud State University *B*
St. John's University *B*
St. Mary's College of Minnesota *B*
St. Olaf College *B*
University of Minnesota
Duluth *B*
Morris *B*
Twin Cities *B*
University of St. Thomas *B*
Willmar Community College *A*
Winona State University *B*

Mississippi

Delta State University *B*
Jackson State University *B*
Millsaps College *B*
Mississippi College *B*
Mississippi University for Women *B*
Rust College *B*
University of Mississippi *B,M*
William Carey College *B*

Missouri

Central Methodist College *B*
Central Missouri State University *B*
College of the Ozarks *B*
Columbia College *A*
Drury College *B*
East Central College *A*
Evangel College *B*
Jefferson College *A*
Lindenwood College *B*
Missouri Southern State College *B*
Missouri Western State College *B*
Northeast Missouri State
University *B*
Northwest Missouri State
University *B*
Rockhurst College *B*
St. Louis University *B,M*
Southeast Missouri State
University *B*
Southwest Baptist University *B*
Southwest Missouri State
University *B*
Stephens College *B*
University of Missouri
Columbia *B,M*
Kansas City *B*
St. Louis *B*
Washington University *B,M,D*
Webster University *B*
Westminster College *B*
William Jewell College *B*
William Woods College *B*

Montana

Carroll College *B*
Eastern Montana College *B*
Miles Community College *A*
Montana State University *B*
Rocky Mountain College *B*
University of Montana *B,M*

Nebraska

Bellevue College *B*
Concordia College *B*
Creighton University *B*
Dana College *B*
Doane College *B*
Hastings College *B*
Midland Lutheran College *B*

Nebraska Wesleyan University B
Union College B
University of Nebraska
 Kearney B,M
 Lincoln B,M,D
 Omaha B
Wayne State College B
Western Nebraska Community
 College: Scottsbluff Campus A
York College A

Nevada

University of Nevada
 Las Vegas B,M
 Reno B

New Hampshire

Dartmouth College B
Franklin Pierce College B
Keene State College B
Plymouth State College of the
 University System of New
 Hampshire B
Rivier College B
St. Anselm College C,B
University of New Hampshire B,M

New Jersey

Bloomfield College B
Brookdale Community College A
Caldwell College B
College of St. Elizabeth B
Drew University B
Fairleigh Dickinson University B
Georgian Court College B
Glassboro State College B
Jersey City State College B
Kean College of New Jersey B
Monmouth College B
Montclair State College B,M
Rider College B
Rutgers—The State University of
 New Jersey
  Camden College of Arts and
   Sciences B
  Douglass College B
  Livingston College B
  New Brunswick M,D
  Newark College of Arts and
   Sciences B
  Rutgers College B
  University College Camden B
  University College New
   Brunswick B
  University College Newark B
St. Peter's College B
Seton Hall University B
Stockton State College B
Upsala College B
William Paterson College of New
 Jersey B

New Mexico

Eastern New Mexico University B
New Mexico Highlands
 University B
New Mexico Junior College A
New Mexico State University B,M
University of New Mexico B,M
Western New Mexico University B

New York

Adelphi University B
Alfred University B
Bard College B
Barnard College B
Canisius College B

City University of New York
 Baruch College B
 Brooklyn College B,M
 City College B,M
 College of Staten Island B
 Graduate School and
  University Center D
 Hunter College B,M
 Lehman College B
 Queens College B,M
 Queensborough Community
  College A
 York College B
Colgate University B
College of Mount St. Vincent B
College of New Rochelle B
College of St. Rose B
Columbia University
 Columbia College B
 New York M,D
 School of General Studies B
Cornell University B,M,D
Daemen College B
Dominican College of Blauvelt B
Elmira College B
Fordham University B,M
Hamilton College B
Hartwick College B
Hobart College B
Hofstra University B
Houghton College B
Iona College B,M
Ithaca College B
Jamestown Community College A
Le Moyne College B
Long Island University: C. W. Post
 Campus B,M
Manhattan College B
Manhattanville College B
Marist College B
Marymount College B
Mercy College B
Molloy College B
Nazareth College of Rochester B
New York University B,M,D
Niagara University B
Onondaga Community College A
Orange County Community
 College A
Pace University
 College of White Plains B
 New York B
 Pleasantville/Briarcliff B
Russell Sage College B
St. Bonaventure University B
St. John Fisher College B
St. John's University B,M
St. Joseph's College B
St. Lawrence University B
St. Thomas Aquinas College B
Sarah Lawrence College B
Siena College B
Skidmore College B
State University of New York
 Albany B,M,D
 Binghamton B,M
 Buffalo B,M,D
 Purchase B
 Stony Brook B,M,D
 College at Brockport B
 College at Buffalo B
 College at Cortland B
 College at Fredonia B
 College at Geneseo B
 College at New Paltz B
 College at Old Westbury C,B
 College at Oneonta B
 College at Plattsburgh B
 College at Potsdam B
 Oswego B
Syracuse University B,M,D
United States Military Academy B

University of Rochester B,M
University of the State of New
 York: Regents College B
Vassar College B,M
Wagner College B
Wells College B
William Smith College B

North Carolina

Appalachian State University B,M
Barton College B
Brevard College A
Campbell University B
Catawba College B
Chowan College A
Davidson College B
Duke University B,D
East Carolina University B
Elon College B
Gardner-Webb College B
Greensboro College B
Guilford College B
High Point University B
Lenoir-Rhyne College B
Mars Hill College B
Meredith College B
Methodist College A,B
North Carolina Central
 University B
North Carolina State University B
Queens College B
St. Augustine's College B
Salem College B
University of North Carolina
 Asheville B
 Chapel Hill B,M,D
 Charlotte B
 Greensboro B,M
 Wilmington B
Wake Forest University B
Western Carolina University B
Winston-Salem State University B

North Dakota

Bismarck State College A
Dickinson State University B
Minot State University B
North Dakota State University B
University of North Dakota B
Valley City State University B

Ohio

Ashland University B
Baldwin-Wallace College B
Bluffton College B
Bowling Green State University
 B,M
Capital University B
Cedarville College B
Central State University B
Cleveland State University B
College of Wooster B
Denison University B
Franciscan University of
 Steubenville B
Heidelberg College B
Hiram College B
John Carroll University B
Kent State University B,M
Kenyon College B
Lourdes College A
Marietta College B
Miami University: Oxford Campus
 B,M
Mount Union College B
Mount Vernon Nazarene College B
Muskingum College B
Notre Dame College of Ohio B
Oberlin College B
Ohio Northern University B
Ohio State University: Columbus
 Campus B,M,D

Ohio University B,M
Ohio Wesleyan University B
Otterbein College B
University of Akron B,M
University of Cincinnati B
University of Dayton B
University of Findlay B
University of Toledo B,M
Walsh College B
Wilmington College B
Wittenberg University B
Wright State University B
Xavier University A,B
Youngstown State University B

Oklahoma

Northeastern State University B
Oklahoma Baptist University B
Oklahoma Christian University of
 Science and Arts B
Oklahoma City University B
Oklahoma State University B
Oral Roberts University B
Phillips University B
Rose State College A
Southeastern Oklahoma State
 University B
Tulsa Junior College A
University of Central Oklahoma B
University of Oklahoma B,M,D
University of Science and Arts of
 Oklahoma B
University of Tulsa B

Oregon

Central Oregon Community
 College A
Lewis and Clark College B
Linfield College B
Northwest Christian College B
Oregon State University B
Pacific University B
Portland Community College A
Portland State University B,M
Reed College B
Southern Oregon State College B
University of Oregon
 Eugene B,M
 Robert Donald Clark Honors
  College B
Western Oregon State College B
Willamette University B

Pennsylvania

Albright College B
Allegheny College B
Allentown College of St. Francis de
 Sales B
Alvernia College B
Bloomsburg University of
 Pennsylvania B
Bryn Mawr College B
Bucknell University B
Cabrini College B
California University of
 Pennsylvania B
Carnegie Mellon University B
Cedar Crest College B
Chatham College B
Chestnut Hill College A,B
Clarion University of
 Pennsylvania B
Dickinson College B
Duquesne University B,M
East Stroudsburg University of
 Pennsylvania B
Eastern College B
Edinboro University of
 Pennsylvania B
Elizabethtown College B
Franklin and Marshall College B
Gannon University B

Geneva College *B*
Gettysburg College *B*
Grove City College *B*
Haverford College *B*
Holy Family College *B*
Immaculata College *A,B*
Indiana University of
  Pennsylvania *B*
Juniata College *B*
King's College *B*
Kutztown University of
  Pennsylvania *B,M*
La Roche College *C*
La Salle University *B,M*
Lafayette College *B*
Lebanon Valley College of
  Pennsylvania *B*
Lehigh University *B*
Lincoln University *B*
Lock Haven University of
  Pennsylvania *B*
Lycoming College *B*
Mansfield University of
  Pennsylvania *B*
Marywood College *B*
Messiah College *B*
Millersville University of
  Pennsylvania *B,M*
Moravian College *B*
Muhlenberg College *B*
Northeastern Christian Junior
  College *A*
Penn State University Park Campus
  C,B,M,D
Rosemont College *B*
St. Francis College *B*
St. Joseph's University *B*
St. Vincent College *B*
Seton Hill College *B*
Shippensburg University of
  Pennsylvania *B*
Slippery Rock University of
  Pennsylvania *B*
Susquehanna University *B*
Swarthmore College *B*
Temple University *B,M,D*
Thiel College *B*
University of Pennsylvania *B,M,D*
University of Pittsburgh *B,M,D*
University of Scranton *B*
Ursinus College *B*
Villanova University *B*
Washington and Jefferson College *B*
West Chester University of
  Pennsylvania *B,M*
Westminster College *B*
Widener University *B*
Wilkes University *B*

Puerto Rico

Bayamon Central University *B*
Caribbean University *B*
Inter American University of Puerto
  Rico
    Arecibo Campus *B*
    Metropolitan Campus *B,M*
    San German Campus *B*
Pontifical Catholic University of
  Puerto Rico *B*
Universidad Adventista de las
  Antillas *B*
University of Puerto Rico
    Cayey University College *B*
    Mayaguez Campus *B,M*
    Rio Piedras Campus *B,M,D*
University of the Sacred Heart *B*

Rhode Island

Brown University *B,M,D*
Providence College *B*
Rhode Island College *B,M*
Salve Regina University *B*

University of Rhode Island *B,M*

South Carolina

Bob Jones University *B*
Charleston Southern University *B*
The Citadel *B*
Clemson University *B*
Coker College *B*
College of Charleston *B*
Columbia College *B*
Converse College *B*
Erskine College *B*
Francis Marion College *B*
Furman University *B*
Newberry College *B*
Presbyterian College *B*
South Carolina State College *B*
University of South Carolina *B,M*
Winthrop University *M*
Wofford College *B*

South Dakota

Augustana College *B*
Black Hills State University *B*
Northern State University *B*
South Dakota State University *B*
University of South Dakota *B*

Tennessee

Carson-Newman College *B*
David Lipscomb University *B*
East Tennessee State University *B*
Fisk University *B*
Lambuth University *B*
Martin Methodist College *A*
Middle Tennessee State University
  B,M
Rhodes College *B*
Shelby State Community College *A*
Southern College of Seventh-day
  Adventists *B*
Tennessee State University *B*
Tennessee Technological
  University *B*
Union University *B*
University of the South *B*
University of Tennessee
    Chattanooga *B*
    Knoxville *B,M*
    Martin *B*
Vanderbilt University *B,M,D*

Texas

Abilene Christian University *B*
Angelo State University *B*
Austin College *B*
Austin Community College *A*
Baylor University *B*
Bee County College *A*
Blinn College *A*
Brazosport College *A*
Central Texas College *A*
Collin County Community College
  District *A*
Concordia Lutheran College *B*
Corpus Christi State University *B*
East Texas Baptist University *B*
East Texas State University *B,M*
Hardin-Simmons University *B*
Houston Baptist University *B*
Howard Payne University *B*
Incarnate Word College *B*
Jacksonville College *A*
Kilgore College *A*
Lamar University—Beaumont *B*
Laredo State University *B*
Lon Morris College *A*
Lubbock Christian University *B*
McLennan Community College *A*
McMurry University *B*
Midland College *A*
Midwestern State University *B*

Our Lady of the Lake University of
  San Antonio *B*
Prairie View A&M University *B*
Rice University *B,M*
St. Mary's University *B*
St. Philip's College *A*
Sam Houston State University *B*
Southern Methodist University *B*
Southwest Texas State University
  B,M
Southwestern Assemblies of God
  College *A*
Southwestern University *B*
Stephen F. Austin State
  University *B*
Sul Ross State University *B*
Tarleton State University *B*
Texas A&I University *B,M*
Texas A&M University *M*
Texas Christian University *B*
Texas Lutheran College *B*
Texas Southern University *B*
Texas Southmost College *A*
Texas Tech University *B,M,D*
Texas Wesleyan University *B*
Texas Woman's University *B,M*
Trinity University *B*
Trinity Valley Community
  College *A*
University of Dallas *B*
University of Houston *B,M*
University of Mary Hardin-
  Baylor *B*
University of North Texas *B,M*
University of St. Thomas *B*
University of Texas
    Arlington *B,M*
    Austin *B,M,D*
    El Paso *B,M*
    Pan American *B*
    Permian Basin *B*
    San Antonio *B,M*
    Tyler *B*
West Texas State University *B*
Western Texas College *A*

Utah

Brigham Young University *B,M*
Southern Utah University *B*
University of Utah *B*
Utah State University *B*
Weber State University *B*

Vermont

Bennington College *B*
Castleton State College *B*
Marlboro College *B*
Middlebury College *B*
Norwich University *B*
St. Michael's College *B*
Trinity College of Vermont *B*
University of Vermont *B*

Virginia

Bridgewater College *B*
Christopher Newport College *B*
College of William and Mary *B*
Eastern Mennonite College *B*
Emory and Henry College *B*
Ferrum College *B*
Hampden-Sydney College *B*
Hollins College *B*
Liberty University *B*
Lynchburg College *B*
Mary Baldwin College *B*
Mary Washington College *B*
Old Dominion University *B*
Radford University *B*
Randolph-Macon College *B*
Randolph-Macon Woman's
  College *B*
Roanoke College *B*

Sweet Briar College *B*
University of Richmond *B,W*
University of Virginia *B,M,D*
Virginia Commonwealth
  University *B*
Virginia Polytechnic Institute and
  State University *B*
Virginia Wesleyan College *B*
Washington and Lee University *B*

Washington

Big Bend Community College *A*
Central Washington University *B*
Eastern Washington University *B,M*
Evergreen State College *B*
Gonzaga University *B*
Heritage College *B*
Pacific Lutheran University *B*
Seattle Central Community
  College *A*
Seattle Pacific University *B*
Seattle University *B*
Spokane Falls Community
  College *A*
Tacoma Community College *A*
University of Puget Sound *B*
University of Washington *B,M,D*
Walla Walla College *B*
Wenatchee Valley College *A*
Western Washington University
  B,M
Whitman College *B*
Whitworth College *B*

West Virginia

Bethany College *B*
Davis and Elkins College *B*
Marshall University *B*
Potomac State College of West
  Virginia University *A*
West Virginia University *B,M*
Wheeling Jesuit College *B*

Wisconsin

Beloit College *B*
Cardinal Stritch College *B*
Carroll College *B*
Carthage College *B*
Edgewood College *B*
Lawrence University *B*
Marquette University *B,M*
Mount Mary College *B*
Northland College *B*
Ripon College *B*
St. Norbert College *B*
University of Wisconsin
    Eau Claire *B*
    Green Bay *B*
    La Crosse *B*
    Madison *B,M,D*
    Milwaukee *B*
    Oshkosh *B*
    Parkside *B*
    Platteville *B*
    Stevens Point *B*
    Whitewater *B*

Wyoming

Casper College *A*
Eastern Wyoming College *A*
Sheridan College *A*
University of Wyoming *B,M*
Western Wyoming Community
  College *A*

American Samoa, Caroline Islands, Guam, Marianas, Virgin Islands

University of the Virgin Islands *B*

Canada
McGill University *B,M*

Mexico
Sistema Instituto Tecnologico y de
Estudios Superiores de
Monterrey *B*

Special education

Alabama
Alabama Agricultural and
Mechanical University *B,M*
Alabama State University *B,M*
Athens State College *B*
Auburn University
Auburn *M,D*
Montgomery *B,M*
Jacksonville State University *B,M*
Livingston University *B,M*
Snead State Junior College *A*
Troy State University *B,M*
University of Alabama
Birmingham *B,M*
Huntsville *M*
Tuscaloosa *B,M,D*
University of North Alabama *B,M*
University of South Alabama *B,M*

Alaska
Prince William Sound Community
College *C,A*
University of Alaska Anchorage *M*

Arizona
Arizona State University *B,M,D*
Grand Canyon University *B*
Northern Arizona University *B,M*
Pima Community College *C,A*
Prescott College *B*
University of Arizona *M,D*

Arkansas
Arkansas State University *B,M*
Harding University *B*
Henderson State University *M*
John Brown University *B*
Philander Smith College *B*
Southern Arkansas University *B*
University of Arkansas
Fayetteville *B,M*
Little Rock *M*
Pine Bluff *B,M*
University of Central Arkansas *B,M*
University of the Ozarks *B,M*

California
Azusa Pacific University *M*
California Lutheran University *B,M*
California Polytechnic State
University: San Luis Obispo *M*
California State University
Bakersfield *M*
Dominguez Hills *M*
Fresno *M*
Fullerton *M*
Hayward *M*
Long Beach *M*
Los Angeles *M,D*
Northridge *M*
Sacramento *M*
San Bernardino *M*
Cerritos Community College *A*
Chapman University *M*
College of Notre Dame *M*
Fresno City College *C*
Fresno Pacific College *M*
Long Beach City College *A*
Master's College *B*

Mount St. Mary's College *M*
National University *M*
Pacific Oaks College *M*
Pepperdine University *M*
Point Loma Nazarene College *M*
St. Mary's College of California
B,M
San Diego State University *M*
San Francisco State University *M,D*
San Jose State University *M*
Santa Clara University *M*
Santa Rosa Junior College *A*
University of California
Berkeley *D*
Los Angeles *D*
Riverside *M,D*
Santa Barbara *M,D*
University of La Verne *M*
University of the Pacific *B,M,D*
University of San Diego *M*
University of San Francisco *M*
University of Southern California
M,D

Colorado
Adams State College *M*
University of Colorado
Colorado Springs *M*
Denver *M*
University of Northern Colorado
M,D

Connecticut
Central Connecticut State
University *B,M*
Fairfield University *M*
Mitchell College *A*
St. Joseph College *B,M*
Southern Connecticut State
University *B,M*
University of Connecticut *B,D*
University of Hartford *B,M,W*

Delaware
Delaware State College *B,M*
University of Delaware *B,M*

District of Columbia
George Washington University *M,D*
Howard University *M*
Trinity College *B,M*
University of the District of
Columbia *B,M*

Florida
Daytona Beach Community
College *A*
Florida Atlantic University *B,M,D*
Florida International University *D*
Florida Southern College *B*
Florida State University *D*
Gulf Coast Community College *A*
Jacksonville University *B*
Nova University *B*
Pensacola Junior College *A*
Stetson University *M*
University of Central Florida *B,M,D*
University of Florida *M,D*
University of Miami *B,M*
University of North Florida *B,M*
University of West Florida *B,M*

Georgia
Albany State College *B,M*
Andrew College *A*
Armstrong State College *B,M*
Augusta College *B,M*
Brenau Women's College *B*
Columbus College *B,M*
Georgia College *B,M*
Georgia Southern University *B,M*
Georgia Southwestern College *B,M*

Georgia State University *D*
Mercer University *B*
North Georgia College *B,M*
Thomas College *A*
University of Georgia *M,D*
Valdosta State College *B,M*
West Georgia College *B,M*

Hawaii
University of Hawaii at Manoa *M*

Idaho
Boise State University *M*
Idaho State University *B,M*
Lewis Clark State College *B*
Northwest Nazarene College *B*
Ricks College *A*
University of Idaho *B,M*

Illinois
Barat College *B*
Bradley University *B,M*
Chicago State University *B,M*
Eastern Illinois University *B,M*
Greenville College *B*
Illinois Central College *A*
Illinois Eastern Community
Colleges: Lincoln Trail College *A*
Illinois State University *B,M,D*
John A. Logan College *A*
Joliet Junior College *C,A*
Kishwaukee College *A*
Lake Land College *A*
Loyola University of Chicago *B,M*
National-Louis University *M*
Northeastern Illinois University *B*
Northern Illinois University *B,M,D*
Parkland College *A*
Rend Lake College *A*
Southern Illinois University
Carbondale *B,M,D*
Edwardsville *B,M*
University of Illinois
Chicago *M,D*
Urbana-Champaign *M,D*
Western Illinois University *M*

Indiana
Ancilla College *A*
Ball State University *B,M,D*
Indiana State University *B,M*
Indiana University
Bloomington *B,M,D*
South Bend *B,M*
Southeast *B,M*
Indiana University—Purdue
University at Indianapolis *M*
Purdue University
Calumet *B*
West Lafayette *B,M,D*
St. Francis College *B,M*
St. Mary-of-the-Woods College *B*
University of Evansville *B,M*
Valparaiso University *M*
Vincennes University *A*

Iowa
Buena Vista College *B*
Clarke College *B,M*
Drake University *M*
Iowa State University *M*
Loras College *B*
Luther College *B*
St. Ambrose University *M*
University of Dubuque *B,M*
University of Iowa *M,D*
University of Northern Iowa *B,M*
Waldorf College *A*

Kansas
Benedictine College *B*
Bethany College *B*

Bethel College *B*
Central College *A*
Emporia State University *M*
Fort Hays State University *M*
Kansas State University *M,D*
McPherson College *B*
Pittsburg State University *M*
Sterling College *B*
Tabor College *B*
University of Kansas *M,D*
Wichita State University *M*

Kentucky
Bellarmine College *B,M*
Brescia College *A,B*
Cumberland College *B,M*
Eastern Kentucky University *B*
Kentucky Wesleyan College *B*
Morehead State University *B,M*
Murray State University *B,M*
Northern Kentucky University *B,M*
Pikeville College *B*
University of Kentucky *M,D*
University of Louisville *M,D*
Western Kentucky University *B,M*

Louisiana
Dillard University *B*
Grambling State University *B*
Louisiana College *B*
Louisiana State University
Agricultural and Mechanical
College *B,M*
Shreveport *B*
Louisiana Tech University *M*
McNeese State University *B*
Northeast Louisiana University *M*
Northwestern State University *B,M*
Southeastern Louisiana
University *M*
Southern University and
Agricultural and Mechanical
College *B,M,D*
Tulane University *B,M*
University of New Orleans *M,D*
Xavier University of Louisiana *B*

Maine
University of Maine *M*
University of New England *B*
University of Southern Maine *M*

Maryland
Baltimore Hebrew University *B,M*
Bowie State University *M*
Coppin State College *B,M*
Dundalk Community College *C,A*
Garrett Community College *C*
Goucher College *B,M*
Hood College *B*
Loyola College in Maryland *M*
Morgan State University *B*
New Community College of
Baltimore *C*
University of Maryland
College Park *B,M,D*
Eastern Shore *B,M*
Western Maryland College *M*

Massachusetts
American International College *B,M*
Assumption College *M*
Atlantic Union College *M*
Boston College *B,M,D*
Boston University *B,M,D,W*
Bridgewater State College *B,M*
Eastern Nazarene College *M*
Emmanuel College *M*
Fitchburg State College *B,M*
Framingham State College *M*
Gordon College *B*
Lesley College *B,M*

Northeastern University *M*
Simmons College *B,M*
University of Massachusetts at
    Boston *M*
Westfield State College *B,M*
Wheelock College *M*

Michigan

Calvin College *B*
Central Michigan University *B,M*
Eastern Michigan University *B,M*
Grand Valley State University *B,M*
Lansing Community College *A*
Madonna University *B*
Michigan State University *B,M,D*
Mid Michigan Community
    College *A*
Saginaw Valley State University
    B,M
University of Detroit Mercy *B,M*
Wayne State University *B,M,D*
Western Michigan University *M,D*

Minnesota

Bemidji State University *M*
Mankato State University *M*
Moorhead State University *B,M*
Northland Community College *A*
Pillsbury Baptist Bible College *B*
Rainy River Community College *A*
St. Cloud State University *B,M*
St. Mary's College of Minnesota *M*
University of Minnesota
    Duluth *C*
    Twin Cities *M*
University of St. Thomas *M*
Willmar Community College *A*
Winona State University *B,M*

Mississippi

Alcorn State University *B*
Blue Mountain College *B*
Delta State University *B,M*
Jackson State University *B,M,W*
Jones County Junior College *A*
Mary Holmes College *A*
Mississippi College *B*
Mississippi Delta Community
    College *A*
Mississippi State University *B,M*
Mississippi University for Women *B*
Northeast Mississippi Community
    College *A*
University of Mississippi *B*
University of Southern Mississippi
    B,M

Missouri

Central Missouri State University
    B,M
Drury College *B*
East Central College *A*
Evangel College *B*
Lincoln University *B*
Lindenwood College *B,M*
Missouri Southern State College *B*
Missouri Valley College *B*
Missouri Western State College *B*
Northeast Missouri State
    University *M*
Northwest Missouri State
    University *B,M*
St. Louis University *M,D*
Southeast Missouri State University
    B,M
University of Missouri
    Kansas City *M*
    St. Louis *B,M*
Webster University *B*
Westminster College *B*
William Woods College *B*

Montana

Eastern Montana College *A,B,M*

Nebraska

Chadron State College *B*
College of St. Mary *B*
Concordia College *B,M*
Creighton University *B*
Dana College *B*
Doane College *B*
Hastings College *B*
McCook Community College *A*
Nebraska Wesleyan University *B*
Peru State College *B*
University of Nebraska
    Kearney *B,M*
    Lincoln *B,M*
Wayne State College *B,M*
York College *A*

Nevada

University of Nevada
    Las Vegas *B,M,D*
    Reno *B,M*

New Hampshire

Keene State College *B,M*
Notre Dame College *B*
Plymouth State College of the
    University System of New
    Hampshire *B*
Rivier College *B,M*
University of New Hampshire *M*

New Jersey

College of St. Elizabeth *B*
Felician College *B*
Georgian Court College *B,M*
Glassboro State College *B,M*
Gloucester County College *A*
Jersey City State College *B,M*
Kean College of New Jersey *B,M*
Mercer County Community
    College *A*
Monmouth College *B,M*
Rutgers—The State University of
    New Jersey
    Douglass College *B*
    Livingston College *B*
    New Brunswick *M,D*
    Rutgers College *B*
    University College New
        Brunswick *B*
St. Peter's College *B*
Seton Hall University *B,M*
Trenton State College *B,M*
William Paterson College of New
    Jersey *B,M*

New Mexico

Eastern New Mexico University
    B,M
New Mexico Highlands University
    B,M
New Mexico State University *B,M*
University of New Mexico *B,M,D*
Western New Mexico University
    B,M

New York

Adelphi University *M*
Alfred University *B,M*
Bank Street College of Education
    M,W
Cazenovia College *A*

City University of New York
    Baruch College *B*
    Brooklyn College *B,M*
    City College *B,M*
    College of Staten Island *M*
    Hunter College *M*
    Lehman College *M*
    Medgar Evers College *B*
    Queens College *M*
    York College *B*
College of Mount St. Vincent *B*
College of New Rochelle *B,M*
College of St. Rose *B,M*
Daemen College *B*
Dominican College of Blauvelt *B*
Dowling College *B,M*
D'Youville College *B,M*
Fordham University *M*
Herkimer County Community
    College *A*
Hofstra University *M,W*
Iona College *B*
Keuka College *B*
Le Moyne College *B*
Long Island University
    Brooklyn Campus *M*
    C. W. Post Campus *B,M*
Manhattan College *B,M*
Manhattanville College *M*
Marymount College *B*
Mercy College *B*
Molloy College *B*
Mount St. Mary College *B,M*
Nazareth College of Rochester *B,M*
New York University *B,M,D*
Russell Sage College *B,M*
St. Francis College *B*
St. John's University *B,M*
St. Joseph's College
    Brooklyn *B*
    Suffolk Campus *B*
St. Thomas Aquinas College *B,M*
State University of New York
    Albany *M*
    Binghamton *M*
    Buffalo *D*
    College at Buffalo *B*
    College at Fredonia *B*
    College at Geneseo *B,M*
    College at New Paltz *M*
    College at Old Westbury *B*
    College at Plattsburgh *B,M*
    College at Potsdam *B*
Syracuse University *B,M,D*
University of Rochester *M*
Wagner College *B,M*

North Carolina

Appalachian State University *B,M*
Belmont Abbey College *B*
Bennett College *B*
Brevard College *A*
Catawba College *B*
East Carolina University *B,M*
Elizabeth City State University *B*
Fayetteville State University *M*
Greensboro College *B*
High Point University *B*
Methodist College *A,B*
North Carolina Agricultural and
    Technical State University *B*
North Carolina Central
    University *M*
North Carolina State University *M*
Pembroke State University *B*
Pfeiffer College *B*
Roanoke-Chowan Community
    College *A*
St. Augustine's College *B*
Salem College *B*

University of North Carolina
    Chapel Hill *M,D*
    Charlotte *B,M*
    Greensboro *M*
    Wilmington *B,M*
Western Carolina University *B,M*
Winston-Salem State University *B*

North Dakota

Turtle Mountain Community
    College *A*
University of Mary *B,M*
University of North Dakota
    Grand Forks *B,M*
    Williston *A*

Ohio

Ashland University *B*
Bluffton College *B*
Bowling Green State University
    Bowling Green *B,M*
    Firelands College *A*
Cedarville College *C*
Central State University *B*
College of Mount St. Joseph *B*
Defiance College *B*
Franciscan University of
    Steubenville *B*
Kent State University *M,D*
Marietta College *B*
Miami University: Oxford Campus
    B,M
Mount Vernon Nazarene College *B*
Muskingum College *B*
Ohio Dominican College *B*
Ohio State University: Columbus
    Campus *B,M,D*
Ohio University *B,M*
Sinclair Community College *A*
Union Institute *B,D*
University of Akron *B,M*
University of Cincinnati *B,M,D*
University of Dayton *B,M*
University of Findlay *B*
University of Rio Grande *B*
University of Toledo *B,M,D*
Urbana University *B*
Walsh College *B*
Wittenberg University *B*
Wright State University *B,M*
Xavier University *B*
Youngstown State University *B,M*

Oklahoma

East Central University *B,M*
Langston University *B*
Northeastern State University *B,M*
Northwestern Oklahoma State
    University *B*
Oklahoma Baptist University *B*
Oklahoma Christian University of
    Science and Arts *B*
Oklahoma State University *B*
Oral Roberts University *B,M*
Southeastern Oklahoma State
    University *M*
University of Central Oklahoma
    B,M
University of Oklahoma *B,M,D*

Oregon

Central Oregon Community
    College *A*
Southern Oregon State College *M*
University of Oregon
    Eugene *B,M,D*
    Robert Donald Clark Honors
        College *B*
University of Portland *B*
Western Oregon State College *C,M*

Pennsylvania

Beaver College *B,M*
Cabrini College *B*
California University of Pennsylvania *B,M*
Carlow College *B*
Cheyney University of Pennsylvania *C,B,M*
Clarion University of Pennsylvania *B,M*
College Misericordia *B*
Duquesne University *B,M*
East Stroudsburg University of Pennsylvania *B,M*
Edinboro University of Pennsylvania *B,M*
Gannon University *B*
Gwynedd-Mercy College *B*
Holy Family College *B*
Indiana University of Pennsylvania *B,M*
King's College *B*
Kutztown University of Pennsylvania *B*
La Salle University *B*
Lock Haven University of Pennsylvania *B*
Mansfield University of Pennsylvania *B,M*
Marywood College *B,M*
Mercyhurst College *B*
Millersville University of Pennsylvania *B,M*
Penn State
    Great Valley Graduate Center *M*
    University Park Campus *B,M,D*
Shippensburg University of Pennsylvania *M*
Slippery Rock University of Pennsylvania *B,M*
Temple University *B,M,D*
University of Pennsylvania *M,D*
West Chester University of Pennsylvania *B,M*

Puerto Rico

American University of Puerto Rico *B*
Bayamon Central University *B*
Caribbean University *B*
Inter American University of Puerto Rico
    Arecibo Campus *B*
    Metropolitan Campus *B*
    San German Campus *B,M*
Pontifical Catholic University of Puerto Rico *B*
Turabo University *B*
Universidad Metropolitana *B*
University of Puerto Rico: Rio Piedras Campus *B,M*

Rhode Island

Community College of Rhode Island *A*
Providence College *B,M*
Salve Regina University *B*

South Carolina

Benedict College *B*
Bob Jones University *M*
Central Wesleyan College *B*
The Citadel *M*
Clemson University *B,M*
Coker College *B*
College of Charleston *B,M*
Columbia College *B*
Converse College *B,M*
Erskine College *B*
Furman University *B,M*

Lander College *B*
Presbyterian College *B*
South Carolina State College *B,M*
University of South Carolina *M*
Winthrop University *B,M*

South Dakota

Augustana College *B,M*
Black Hills State University *B*
Northern State University *B*
Presentation College *A*
University of South Dakota *B,M*

Tennessee

Austin Peay State University *B,M*
Bethel College *B*
Carson-Newman College *B,M*
Chattanooga State Technical Community College *A*
East Tennessee State University *B,M*
Hiwassee College *A*
Lambuth University *B*
Memphis State University *B,M,D*
Middle Tennessee State University *B,M*
Milligan College *B*
Roane State Community College *A*
Tennessee State University *B,M*
Tennessee Technological University *B,M*
Trevecca Nazarene College *B*
Tusculum College *B*
Union University *B,M*
University of Tennessee
    Chattanooga *B,M*
    Knoxville *B,M*
    Martin *M*
Vanderbilt University *B,M,D*

Texas

Angelo State University *B,M*
Brookhaven College *C*
Corpus Christi State University *B*
East Texas State University
    Commerce *B,M,D*
    Texarkana *M*
Houston Baptist University *B*
Incarnate Word College *B,M*
Lamar University—Beaumont *B,M*
Midwestern State University *B,M*
Our Lady of the Lake University of San Antonio *B,M*
Prairie View A&M University *M*
Sam Houston State University *M*
Southwest Texas State University *C,M*
Stephen F. Austin State University *B,M*
Texas A&I University *M*
Texas Christian University *B*
Texas Southern University *B*
Texas Southmost College *A*
Texas Tech University *B,M,D*
Texas Woman's University *B,M,D*
University of Houston
    Houston *B,M,D*
    Victoria *M*
University of Mary Hardin-Baylor *B,M*
University of North Texas *M,D*
University of St. Thomas *B*
University of Texas
    Austin *M,D*
    El Paso *M*
    Pan American *B,M*
    Permian Basin *M*
    San Antonio *M*
    Tyler *B,M*
West Texas State University *M*
Wiley College *B*

Utah

Brigham Young University *B,M*
University of Utah *B,M*
Utah State University *B,M,D*

Vermont

Castleton State College *B,M*
College of St. Joseph in Vermont *A,B,M*
Green Mountain College *B*
Johnson State College *B,M*
Lyndon State College *B,M*
St. Michael's College *M*
Trinity College of Vermont *B*
University of Vermont *B,M*

Virginia

College of William and Mary *M*
George Mason University *M*
Hampton University *B*
James Madison University *M*
Longwood College *M*
Lynchburg College *B*
Norfolk State University *B*
Old Dominion University *B,M*
Radford University *B*
University of Richmond *M*
University of Virginia *M,D*
Virginia Commonwealth University *M*
Virginia State University *B,M*

Washington

Central Washington University *B,M*
Eastern Washington University *B,M*
Gonzaga University *B,M*
Pacific Lutheran University *B,M*
St. Martin's College *B,M*
Seattle Pacific University *B*
Shoreline Community College *A*
Spokane Falls Community College *A*
University of Washington *M,D*
Walla Walla College *M*
Western Washington University *B,M*
Whitworth College *M*

West Virginia

Alderson-Broaddus College *B*
Bethany College *B*
Concord College *B*
Glenville State College *B*
Marshall University *B,M*
Salem-Teikyo University *B,M*
West Virginia Graduate College *M*
West Virginia State College *B*
West Virginia University *M,D*

Wisconsin

Cardinal Stritch College *B,M*
Carthage College *B*
Edgewood College *B*
University of Wisconsin
    Eau Claire *B,M*
    La Crosse *M*
    Milwaukee *B,M*
    Oshkosh *B,M*
    Whitewater *B*

Wyoming

Eastern Wyoming College *A*
Northwest College *A*
University of Wyoming *B,M,D*

American Samoa, Caroline Islands, Guam, Marianas, Virgin Islands

Community College of Micronesia *A*
University of Guam *B,M*

Canada

McGill University *C,M*

Specific learning disabilities

Alabama

Alabama Agricultural and Mechanical University *B*
Alabama State University *B,M*
Athens State College *B*
Auburn University
    Auburn *M*
    Montgomery *M*
Jacksonville State University *M*
University of Alabama *M*
University of South Alabama *M*

Arizona

Grand Canyon University *B*
Northern Arizona University *M*
Prescott College *B*

Arkansas

Harding University *B*
University of Central Arkansas *B,M*

California

California Lutheran University *M*
California State University
    Dominguez Hills *M*
    Fresno *B,M*
    Los Angeles *M*
    Northridge *M*
    San Bernardino *M*
College of Notre Dame *M*
Fresno Pacific College *M,W*
Humboldt State University *C*
Mount St. Mary's College *M*
Pacific Oaks College *M*
St. Mary's College of California *B,M*
San Jose State University *M*
Sonoma State University *M*
University of California
    Riverside *M,D*
    Santa Barbara *M,D*
University of the Pacific *B,M,D*
University of San Diego *M*

Colorado

University of Northern Colorado *M*

Connecticut

Fairfield University *M*
Southern Connecticut State University *B,M*

District of Columbia

American University *M*

Florida

Flagler College *B*
Florida Atlantic University *B,M*
Florida International University *B,M*
Florida Southern College *B*
Florida State University *B,M*
Jacksonville University *B*
Nova University *B*
University of Florida *M*
University of Miami *M*
University of South Florida *B,M*
University of West Florida *B*

Georgia

Armstrong State College *B,M*
Columbus College *M*
Georgia Southern University *B,M*

Georgia State University *D*
Mercer University *B*
Morris Brown College *B*
University of Georgia *M*
West Georgia College *M*

Idaho

Northwest Nazarene College *B*

Illinois

Barat College *B*
Bradley University *B,M*
Chicago State University *M*
De Paul University *M*
Elmhurst College *B*
Greenville College *B*
Illinois Benedictine College *B*
MacMurray College *B*
Monmouth College *B*
National-Louis University *M*
Northeastern Illinois University *B,M*
Northern Illinois University *M*
Northwestern University *B,M,D*
Quincy College *B*
Rockford College *M*
Roosevelt University *M*
Rosary College *M*
St. Xavier University *M*
Southern Illinois University
    Carbondale *B,M,D*
    Edwardsville *B,M*

Indiana

Ball State University *M*
Butler University *B,M*
Indiana State University *M*
Indiana University—Purdue
    University at Indianapolis *M*
St. Francis College *B,M*
University of Indianapolis *B*
Vincennes University *A*

Iowa

Clarke College *M*
Drake University *M*
Iowa State University *M*
Morningside College *B,M*
Teikyo Marycrest University *M*
University of Iowa *M,D*

Kansas

Bethany College *B*
McPherson College *B*
Tabor College *B*
Washburn University of Topeka *M*

Kentucky

Bellarmine College *B*
Eastern Kentucky University *B,M*
Murray State University *B*
University of Kentucky *B*
Western Kentucky University *B*

Louisiana

Dillard University *B*
Louisiana Tech University *B*
McNeese State University *M*
University of New Orleans *M*

Maine

University of Maine at
    Farmington *B*

Maryland

Coppin State College *B,M*

Massachusetts

American International College *M,D*
Assumption College *M*
Harvard University *M,D*

Westfield State College *M*
Wheelock College *M*

Michigan

Andrews University *M*
Calvin College *B,M*
Central Michigan University *M*
Eastern Michigan University *M*
Grand Valley State University *B,M*
Hope College *B*
Madonna University *B,M*
Marygrove College *M*
Northern Michigan University *M*
Oakland University *M*
Saginaw Valley State University *B,M*
University of Detroit Mercy *B,M*
University of Michigan *M,D*
Wayne State University *M,D*

Minnesota

Mankato State University *M*
Moorhead State University *M*
University of Minnesota: Twin
    Cities *M*
Winona State University *B,M*

Missouri

Avila College *B*
Central Missouri State
    University *M*
Fontbonne College *B*
Missouri Southern State College *B*
Northwest Missouri State
    University *B,M*
St. Louis University *B,M*
Southeast Missouri State University *B,M*
Southwest Missouri State University *B,M*
University of Missouri
    Columbia *B,M,D*
    Kansas City *M*
Webster University *B*

Montana

Eastern Montana College *M*

Nebraska

Chadron State College *B*
Creighton University *M*
University of Nebraska
    Kearney *B,M*
    Omaha *M*

New Hampshire

Notre Dame College *M*
Rivier College *M*

New Jersey

Fairleigh Dickinson University *M*
Glassboro State College *M*
Kean College of New Jersey *M*
William Paterson College of New
    Jersey *M*

New York

Bank Street College of Education *M,W*
City University of New York
    Brooklyn College *B,M*
    Lehman College *M*
College of New Rochelle *B,M*
College of St. Rose *M*
D'Youville College *B*
Fordham University *M*
Manhattanville College *M*
Marymount College *B*
Mercy College *B*
Nazareth College of Rochester *B,M*
New York University *M*
St. Thomas Aquinas College *B*

State University of New York
    College at Buffalo *M*
    College at Geneseo *B,M*
    College at New Paltz *M*
    College at Plattsburgh *B*
Syracuse University *M*

North Carolina

East Carolina University *M*
Greensboro College *B*
Lenoir-Rhyne College *M*
Salem College *M*
University of North Carolina at
    Greensboro *M*
Western Carolina University *B*

North Dakota

Minot State University *M*
University of Mary *M*

Ohio

Ashland University *B*
Baldwin-Wallace College *B,M*
Bowling Green State University *B*
Central State University *B*
Cleveland State University *M*
Defiance College *B*
Heidelberg College *B*
Kent State University *M,D*
Malone College *B*
Mount Union College *B*
Mount Vernon Nazarene College *B*
Muskingum College *B*
Notre Dame College of Ohio *M*
Ohio State University: Columbus
    Campus *B*
Ohio University *B,M*
University of Akron *B,M*
University of Cincinnati *M,D*
University of Dayton *B,M*
University of Rio Grande *C,M*
University of Toledo *B,M*
Urbana University *B*
Wittenberg University *B*
Wright State University *B,M*
Xavier University *B*
Youngstown State University *B,M*

Oklahoma

Northeastern State University *B*
Northwestern Oklahoma State
    University *B*
Oral Roberts University *M*
Southwestern Oklahoma State
    University *B,M*
University of Central Oklahoma *B*
University of Oklahoma *B*
University of Science and Arts of
    Oklahoma *B*

Oregon

University of Oregon *M,D*
Western Oregon State College *M*

Pennsylvania

Cabrini College *B*
California University of
    Pennsylvania *B,M*
Indiana University of
    Pennsylvania *M*
Lehigh University *M,D*
Lock Haven University of
    Pennsylvania *B*
Mercyhurst College *B*
Slippery Rock University of
    Pennsylvania *B*
Temple University *M*

Puerto Rico

Turabo University *B*

Rhode Island

Rhode Island College *M*

South Carolina

The Citadel *M*
Converse College *B,M*
Furman University *B,M*

South Dakota

Augustana College *B,M*
Northern State University *B*

Tennessee

East Tennessee State University *M*
Vanderbilt University *B,M,D*

Texas

Houston Baptist University *B*
Lamar University—Beaumont *B*
Our Lady of the Lake University of
    San Antonio *M*
Stephen F. Austin State
    University *B*
Texas Woman's University *M,D*
West Texas State University *B*

Utah

Southern Utah University *B*

Virginia

Eastern Mennonite College *B*
Old Dominion University *B,M*
Radford University *M*
Tidewater Community College *A*
University of Richmond *M*
Virginia Commonwealth
    University *M*
Virginia Polytechnic Institute and
    State University *M*

Washington

Pacific Lutheran University *B*
Seattle University *M*

West Virginia

Alderson-Broaddus College *B*
Bethany College *B*
Fairmont State College *B*
Glenville State College *B*
Marshall University *B,M*

Wisconsin

Carthage College *B*
Edgewood College *B*
Silver Lake College *B*
University of Wisconsin
    Eau Claire *B,M*
    La Crosse *M*
    Madison *B,M,D*
    Milwaukee *B*
    Oshkosh *B,M*
    River Falls *M*
    Superior *M*
    Whitewater *B*

Speech

Alabama

Alabama State University *B*
Auburn University
    Auburn *B,M*
    Montgomery *B*
Huntingdon College *B*
Samford University *B*
Troy State University *B*
University of Alabama *B,M*
University of Montevallo *B,M*
University of North Alabama *B*

Alaska

University of Alaska Fairbanks *B*

Arizona

Arizona Western College *A*
Glendale Community College *A*
Grand Canyon University *B*
Northern Arizona University *B*
Pima Community College *A*
University of Arizona *B,M,D*

Arkansas

Arkansas State University
    Beebe Branch *A*
    Jonesboro *B,M*
Arkansas Tech University *B*
Harding University *B,M*
Henderson State University *B,M*
Ouachita Baptist University *B*
Southern Arkansas University *B*
University of Arkansas
    Fayetteville *B,M*
    Little Rock *B*
    Monticello *B*
University of Central Arkansas *B*
Westark Community College *A*

California

California Lutheran University *B*
California Polytechnic State
    University: San Luis Obispo *B*
California State University
    Fresno *B*
    Fullerton *B,M*
    Hayward *B,M*
    Long Beach *B,M*
    Los Angeles *B,M*
    Northridge *B,M*
Cerritos Community College *A*
Chabot College *A*
Chaffey Community College *A*
College of the Desert *A*
El Camino College *A*
Foothill College *A*
Glendale Community College *A*
Grossmont Community College *A*
Humboldt State University *B*
Irvine Valley College *A*
Long Beach City College *A*
Los Angeles Mission College *A*
Loyola Marymount University *B*
Mendocino College *A*
Merced College *A*
MiraCosta College *A*
Orange Coast College *A*
Palomar College *A*
Pasadena City College *C,A*
Pepperdine University *B*
Point Loma Nazarene College *B*
Saddleback College *A*
San Diego City College *A*
San Diego State University *B,M*
San Francisco State University *B,M*
San Joaquin Delta College *A*
San Jose State University *B,M*
Santa Rosa Junior College *A*
Southern California College *B*
Southwestern College *A*
University of California: Santa
    Barbara *B*
University of the Pacific *B*
Ventura College *A*
West Valley College *A*

Colorado

Adams State College *B*
Colorado State University *B,M*
Metropolitan State College of
    Denver *B*
University of Colorado at Denver *B*
University of Southern Colorado *B*

Connecticut

Southern Connecticut State
    University *B,M*
University of Connecticut *B,M*

District of Columbia

George Washington University *B*

Florida

Florida State University *B,M,D*
Gulf Coast Community College *A*
Manatee Community College *A*
Miami-Dade Community College *A*
Stetson University *B*
University of Central Florida *B*
University of Florida *B,M,D*
University of Miami *B*
University of South Florida *B,M*
University of West Florida *B*

Georgia

Andrew College *A*
Armstrong State College *B*
Atlanta Metropolitan College *A*
Bainbridge College *A*
Berry College *B*
Clark Atlanta University *B*
Columbus College *B*
Darton College *A*
Georgia Southern University *B*
Georgia Southwestern College *B*
Georgia State University *B*
Macon College *A*
Middle Georgia College *A*
Morris Brown College *B*
Shorter College *B*
University of Georgia *B,M,D*
Waycross College *A*
Wesleyan College *B*
West Georgia College *B*
Young Harris College *A*

Hawaii

Brigham Young University-
    Hawaii *A*
University of Hawaii
    Hilo *B*
    Manoa *B,M*

Idaho

Idaho State University *B,M*
Northwest Nazarene College *B*
Ricks College *A*
University of Idaho *B*

Illinois

Augustana College *B*
Blackburn College *B*
Bradley University *B*
Eastern Illinois University *B,M*
Elmhurst College *B*
Eureka College *B*
Governors State University *B*
Illinois Central College *A*
Illinois College *B*
Illinois State University *B*
Lewis University *B*
McKendree College *B*
North Central College *B*
North Park College and Theological
    Seminary *B*
Northeastern Illinois University
    B,M
Northern Illinois University *B,M*
Northwestern University *B*
Olivet Nazarene University *B*
Rend Lake College *A*
Richland Community College *A*
Roosevelt University *B*
Southern Illinois University
    Carbondale *B,M,D*
    Edwardsville *B,M*

University of Illinois at Urbana-
    Champaign *B,M,D*
Waubonsee Community College *A*
Wheaton College *B*

Indiana

Anderson University *B*
Ball State University *B,M*
Butler University *B*
Grace College *B*
Indiana State University *B,M*
Indiana University
    Bloomington *B,M,D*
    Kokomo *B*
    South Bend *B*
Indiana University—Purdue
    University at Indianapolis *B*
Manchester College *B*
Marian College *B*
Purdue University: Calumet *B*
St. Joseph's College *B*
St. Mary-of-the-Woods College *A,B*
Vincennes University *A*
Wabash College *B*

Iowa

Buena Vista College *B*
Cornell College *B*
Dordt College *B*
Graceland College *B*
Iowa Lakes Community College *A*
Iowa State University *B*
Loras College *B*
Luther College *B*
Mount Mercy College *B*
Northwestern College *B*
St. Ambrose University *B*
Teikyo Westmar University *B*
University of Dubuque *B*
University of Iowa *M,D*
University of Northern Iowa *B,M*

Kansas

Baker University *B*
Barton County Community
    College *A*
Bethel College *B*
Coffeyville Community College *A*
Highland Community College *A*
Hutchinson Community College *A*
Kansas State University *B,M*
McPherson College *B*
Neosho County Community
    College *A*
Pittsburg State University *B*
Pratt Community College *A*
Southwestern College *B*
Sterling College *B*
Washburn University of Topeka *B*

Kentucky

Asbury College *B*
Eastern Kentucky University *B*
Georgetown College *B*
Kentucky Wesleyan College *B*
Morehead State University *B*
Murray State University *B,M*
Northern Kentucky University *B*
Union College *B*
University of Kentucky *B*
University of Louisville *B*
Western Kentucky University *B,M*

Louisiana

Centenary College of Louisiana *B*
Louisiana State University
    Agricultural and Mechanical
        College *B,M,D*
    Shreveport *B*
Louisiana Tech University *B,M*
Loyola University *B*
McNeese State University *B*

Northeast Louisiana University *B*
Northwestern State University *B*
Southeastern Louisiana
    University *B*
Southern University and
    Agricultural and Mechanical
    College *B*
University of Southwestern
    Louisiana *B,M*

Maine

University of Maine
    Orono *B,M*
    Presque Isle *B*

Maryland

Bowie State University *B*
Frostburg State University *B*
Morgan State University *B*
Salisbury State University *B*
University of Maryland: College
    Park *B,M*

Massachusetts

Bridgewater State College *B,M*
Emerson College *B,M*
Suffolk University *B*

Michigan

Adrian College *A,B*
Alma College *B*
Calvin College *B*
Central Michigan University *B,M*
Eastern Michigan University *B,M*
Grand Rapids Baptist College and
    Seminary *B*
Henry Ford Community College *A*
Northern Michigan University *B,M*
Olivet College *B*
Saginaw Valley State University *B*
University of Detroit Mercy *B*
Wayne State University *B,M,D*

Minnesota

Augsburg College *B*
Bemidji State University *B*
Bethel College *B*
Concordia College: Moorhead *B*
Gustavus Adolphus College *B*
Macalester College *B*
Mankato State University *B,M*
Moorhead State University *B*
Northland Community College *A*
St. Cloud State University *B*
St. Olaf College *B*
Southwest State University *B*
University of Minnesota: Twin
    Cities *B,M,D*
Willmar Community College *A*
Winona State University *B*

Mississippi

Blue Mountain College *B*
Jackson State University *B*
University of Southern
    Mississippi *B*

Missouri

Central Missouri State University
    B,M
College of the Ozarks *B*
Culver-Stockton College *B*
East Central College *A*
Evangel College *B*
Missouri Southern State College *B*
Missouri Western State College *B*
Northeast Missouri State
    University *B*
Northwest Missouri State
    University *B*
St. Louis Community College at
    Florissant Valley *A*

Southwest Baptist University *B*
Southwest Missouri State
University *M*
University of Missouri: St. Louis *B*
William Jewell College *B*

Montana

Carroll College *B*
Montana College of Mineral
Science and Technology *A,B*

Nebraska

Chadron State College *B,M*
Concordia College *B*
Creighton University *B*
Dana College *B*
Hastings College *B*
McCook Community College *A*
Midland Lutheran College *B*
Nebraska Wesleyan University *B*
Northeast Community College *A*
Peru State College *B*
University of Nebraska
Kearney *B,M*
Lincoln *B,M,D*
Omaha *B,M*
Wayne State College *B*

Nevada

University of Nevada: Reno *B,M*

New Jersey

Bergen Community College *A*
Brookdale Community College *A*
Glassboro State College *B*
Kean College of New Jersey *B*
Ocean County College *A*
Rider College *B*
Trenton State College *B*

New Mexico

Eastern New Mexico University
B,M
New Mexico State University *B*
University of New Mexico *B*

New York

City University of New York
Brooklyn College *B,M*
City College *B*
Lehman College *B*
Queens College *B*
York College *B*
Dowling College *B*
Hofstra University *B*
Iona College *B*
Ithaca College *B*
King's College *B*
Long Island University
Brooklyn Campus *B*
C. W. Post Campus *B,M*
Mercy College *B*
Molloy College *B*
New York University *B,M*
Pace University *B*
St. John's University *B*
St. Joseph's College *B*
State University of New York
Albany *B,M*
College at Cortland *B*
College at New Paltz *B*
College at Oneonta *B*
College at Plattsburgh *B*
Syracuse University *B,M*
Touro College *B*
Utica College of Syracuse
University *B*
Yeshiva University *B*

North Carolina

Appalachian State University *B*
Fayetteville State University *B*

Meredith College *B*
North Carolina Agricultural and
Technical State University *B*
North Carolina State University *B*
University of North Carolina
Chapel Hill *B,M*
Greensboro *B,M*
Wilmington *B*
Wake Forest University *B,M*
Wingate College *B*

North Dakota

Dickinson State University *B*
North Dakota State University *B,M*
University of North Dakota *B*

Ohio

Ashland University *B*
Baldwin-Wallace College *B*
Bluffton College *B*
Bowling Green State University
B,M,D
Capital University *B*
Cedarville College *B*
Central State University *B*
Defiance College *B*
Denison University *B*
Heidelberg College *B*
Marietta College *B*
Miami University: Oxford
Campus *B*
Mount Union College *B*
Mount Vernon Nazarene College *B*
Muskingum College *B*
Ohio State University: Columbus
Campus *B,M,D*
Ohio University *B,M,D*
Union Institute *B*
University of Akron *B,M*
University of Dayton *B,M*
University of Findlay *B*
University of Rio Grande *B*
University of Toledo *B*
Wittenberg University *B*
Youngstown State University *B*

Oklahoma

Cameron University *B*
East Central University *B*
Eastern Oklahoma State College *A*
Oklahoma Baptist University *B*
Oklahoma Christian University of
Science and Arts *B*
Oklahoma City University *B*
Oklahoma Panhandle State
University *B*
Oklahoma State University *B,M*
Phillips University *B*
Redlands Community College *A*
Rose State College *A*
Southeastern Oklahoma State
University *B*
Southwestern Oklahoma State
University *B*
Tulsa Junior College *A*
University of Central Oklahoma *B*

Oregon

Oregon State University *B*
Portland Community College *A*
Portland State University *B,M*
Southern Oregon State College *B*
University of Oregon: Robert
Donald Clark Honors College *B*
Western Oregon State College *B*
Willamette University *B*

Pennsylvania

Bloomsburg University of
Pennsylvania *B*
California University of
Pennsylvania *B*

Clarion University of
Pennsylvania *B*
Duquesne University *B*
East Stroudsburg University of
Pennsylvania *B*
Edinboro University of
Pennsylvania *B*
Geneva College *B*
Kutztown University of
Pennsylvania *B*
Lock Haven University of
Pennsylvania *B*
Mansfield University of
Pennsylvania *B*
Marywood College *B*
Messiah College *B*
Penn State University Park Campus
B,M,D
Shippensburg University of
Pennsylvania *B*
Temple University *B,M,D*
University of Pittsburgh *B,M,D*
West Chester University of
Pennsylvania *B*
York College of Pennsylvania *B*

Puerto Rico

University of Puerto Rico: Rio
Piedras Campus *B*

Rhode Island

University of Rhode Island *B*

South Carolina

Anderson College *B*
Bob Jones University *B,M*
Charleston Southern University *B*
Newberry College *B*
University of South Carolina *B,M*
Winthrop University *B*

South Dakota

Augustana College *B*
Black Hills State University *B*
Dakota Wesleyan University *B*
Northern State University *B*
Sioux Falls College *B*
South Dakota State University *B*
University of South Dakota *B,M*

Tennessee

Austin Peay State University *B*
Belmont University *B*
Carson-Newman College *B*
David Lipscomb University *B*
East Tennessee State University *B*
Fisk University *B*
Lambuth University *B*
Southern College of Seventh-day
Adventists *B*
Trevecca Nazarene College *B*
Union University *B*
University of Tennessee
Chattanooga *B*
Knoxville *B*

Texas

Abilene Christian University *B,M*
Angelina College *A*
Angelo State University *B*
Baylor University *B,M*
Bee County College *A*
Central Texas College *A*
Collin County Community College
District *A*
Del Mar College *A*
East Texas Baptist University *B*
El Paso Community College *A*
Hardin-Simmons University *B*
Houston Baptist University *B*
Houston Community College *C,A*
Howard College *A*

Howard Payne University *B*
Incarnate Word College *B*
Jacksonville College *A*
Lamar University—Beaumont *B,M*
Lon Morris College *A*
Lubbock Christian University *B*
Midland College *A*
Midwestern State University *B*
North Harris Montgomery
Community College District *A*
Our Lady of the Lake University of
San Antonio *B*
Prairie View A&M University *B*
St. Mary's University *B,M*
St. Philip's College *A*
Sam Houston State University *B*
Southwest Texas State University
B,M
Tarleton State University *B*
Texas A&M University *B*
Texas Southern University *B,M*
Texas Southmost College *A*
Texas Tech University *B,M*
Texas Wesleyan University *B*
Trinity University *B*
Trinity Valley Community
College *A*
University of Houston
Houston *B,M*
Victoria *B*
University of Mary Hardin-
Baylor *B*
University of Texas
Arlington *B*
Austin *B,M,D*
El Paso *B*
Permian Basin *B*
Tyler *B*
Wayland Baptist University *B*
West Texas State University *B,M*
Western Texas College *A*

Utah

Southern Utah University *B*
Utah State University *B*
Weber State University *B*

Virginia

Liberty University *B*
Old Dominion University *B*
Radford University *B*
University of Richmond *B*
University of Virginia *B,M*

Washington

Central Washington University *B*
Eastern Washington University *B*
Gonzaga University *B*
Pacific Lutheran University *B*
Seattle Central Community
College *A*
Spokane Community College *A*
Spokane Falls Community
College *A*
University of Washington *B,M,D*
Walla Walla College *B*
Washington State University *B,M,D*
Wenatchee Valley College *A*
Western Washington University
B,M
Whitworth College *B*

West Virginia

Alderson-Broaddus College *B*
Concord College *B*
Marshall University *B,M*
Shepherd College *B*
West Virginia Wesleyan College *B*

Wisconsin

Carthage College *B*
Marquette University *B,M*

Ripon College *B*
University of Wisconsin
    Eau Claire *B*
    La Crosse *B*
    Madison *B,M,D*
    Oshkosh *B*
    Platteville *B*
    River Falls *B*
    Superior *B,M*
    Whitewater *B*

Wyoming

Casper College *A*
Laramie County Community
    College *A*
Western Wyoming Community
    College *A*

Speech/communication/ theater education

Alabama

Auburn University at
    Montgomery *B*
Jacksonville State University *B*
University of Alabama *B*
University of Montevallo *B,M*
University of North Alabama *B*

Arizona

Arizona State University *B*
Northern Arizona University *B*
University of Arizona *B*

Arkansas

Arkansas State University *B,M*
Harding University *B*
Henderson State University *B,M*
Ouachita Baptist University *B*
University of Arkansas
    Fayetteville *B*
    Monticello *B*
University of Central Arkansas *B*
Westark Community College *A*

California

California Lutheran University *B*
California State University
    Bakersfield *B*
    Fullerton *B*
    Northridge *B*
Christ College Irvine *B*
Loyola Marymount University *M*
Occidental College *M*
San Francisco State University *B,M*
University of the Pacific *B*

Colorado

Colorado State University *B*
University of Northern Colorado
    B,M
Western State College of
    Colorado *B*

Delaware

Delaware State College *B*

Florida

Manatee Community College *A*
Pensacola Junior College *A*
Stetson University *B*
University of Central Florida *M*

Georgia

Albany State College *B*
Berry College *B*
Georgia Southern University *B*
Shorter College *B*
University of Georgia *B,M*

Wesleyan College *B*

Idaho

Boise State University *B*
Idaho State University *M*
Northwest Nazarene College *B*

Illinois

Augustana College *B*
Concordia University *B*
Elmhurst College *B*
Greenville College *B*
Illinois College *B*
Millikin University *B*
North Central College *B*
Northwestern University *B,M*
Southern Illinois University at
    Carbondale *B*
Trinity Christian College *B*
University of Illinois
    Chicago *B*
    Urbana-Champaign *B,M*
Wheaton College *B*

Indiana

Anderson University *B*
Ball State University *B*
Goshen College *B*
Indiana State University *B,M*
Indiana University—Purdue
    University at Indianapolis *B*
Manchester College *B*
Martin University *B*
Purdue University *B,M*
St. Joseph's College *B*
St. Mary-of-the-Woods College *B*
Taylor University *B*
University of Indianapolis *B*
University of Southern Indiana *B*

Iowa

Clarke College *B*
Cornell College *B*
Drake University *B,M*
Loras College *B*
Morningside College *B*
Mount Mercy College *B*
Simpson College *B*
Teikyo Marycrest University *B*
University of Iowa *B,M*
Upper Iowa University *B*
Wartburg College *B*

Kansas

Baker University *B*
Colby Community College *A*
Emporia State University *B,M*
Kansas State University *B*
McPherson College *B*
MidAmerica Nazarene College *B*
St. Mary College *B*
Southwestern College *B*
Washburn University of Topeka *B*

Kentucky

Eastern Kentucky University *B*
Georgetown College *B*
Murray State University *B*
Sue Bennett College *A*
Western Kentucky University *B*

Louisiana

Grambling State University *B*
Louisiana State University and
    Agricultural and Mechanical
    College *B*
Louisiana Tech University *B*
McNeese State University *B*
Northeast Louisiana University *B*
Southeastern Louisiana
    University *B*

Southern University and
    Agricultural and Mechanical
    College *B*
University of New Orleans *B*

Maine

University of Maine at Presque
    Isle *B*

Massachusetts

Boston University *B,M*
Bridgewater State College *M*
Emerson College *B,M*
Westfield State College *B*

Michigan

Adrian College *B*
Calvin College *B*
Concordia College *B*
Eastern Michigan University *B,M*
Grand Rapids Baptist College and
    Seminary *B*
Lansing Community College *A*
Michigan State University *B*
Northern Michigan University *B,M*
Wayne State University *B*
Western Michigan University *B*

Minnesota

Bethel College *B*
Concordia College: St. Paul *B*
Gustavus Adolphus College *B*
Mankato State University *B*
Northland Community College *A*
Pillsbury Baptist Bible College *B*
Rainy River Community College *A*
St. Cloud State University *B*
St. Mary's College of Minnesota *B*
St. Olaf College *B*
Southwest State University *B*
Willmar Community College *A*
Winona State University *B*

Mississippi

Mississippi Delta Community
    College *A*
Mississippi University for Women *B*
University of Mississippi *B*

Missouri

Central Missouri State University *B*
College of the Ozarks *B*
Culver-Stockton College *B*
Fontbonne College *B*
Missouri Valley College *B*
Missouri Western State College *B*
Northeast Missouri State
    University *M*
Northwest Missouri State
    University *B,M*
Southeast Missouri State
    University *B*
University of Missouri: Columbia *B*
Washington University *B,M*

Montana

Carroll College *B*
University of Montana *B*

Nebraska

Chadron State College *B*
Creighton University *B*
Dana College *B*
Doane College *B*
Hastings College *B*
University of Nebraska
    Kearney *B,M*
    Lincoln *B*
    Omaha *B*
Wayne State College *B*

New Jersey

Glassboro State College *B*
Rutgers—The State University of
    New Jersey: Camden College of
    Arts and Sciences *B*

New Mexico

Eastern New Mexico University
    B,M
New Mexico State University *B*
University of New Mexico *B*

New York

Adelphi University *B*
City University of New York:
    Brooklyn College *B*
Hofstra University *B,M*
Iona College *B,M*
Ithaca College *B*
New York University *B,M,D*
Russell Sage College *B*
St. Joseph's College *B*
Syracuse University *B,M*

North Carolina

Brevard College *A*
Lees-McRae College *B*
Methodist College *A,B*
North Carolina Central
    University *B*
St. Andrews Presbyterian College *B*
University of North Carolina
    Asheville *C*
    Greensboro *B,M*
Western Carolina University *B*

North Dakota

Bismarck State College *A*
Dickinson State University *B*
Minot State University *B*
North Dakota State University *B,M*
University of North Dakota *B*

Ohio

Baldwin-Wallace College *B*
Bluffton College *B*
Bowling Green State University
    B,M
Cedarville College *B*
Defiance College *B*
Heidelberg College *B*
Kent State University *B*
Malone College *B*
Mount Union College *B*
Mount Vernon Nazarene College *B*
Ohio Dominican College *B*
Ohio State University: Columbus
    Campus *B,D*
Otterbein College *B*
University of Findlay *B*
University of Rio Grande *B*
University of Toledo *B*
Wright State University *B*
Youngstown State University *B*

Oklahoma

Northwestern Oklahoma State
    University *B*
Oklahoma Baptist University *B*
Oklahoma Christian University of
    Science and Arts *B*
Oklahoma City University *B*
Oklahoma Panhandle State
    University *B*
Southwestern Oklahoma State
    University *B,M*
University of Science and Arts of
    Oklahoma *B*

Oregon

Western Oregon State College *B*
Willamette University *M*

Pennsylvania

Allentown College of St. Francis de
Sales *B*
Clarion University of
Pennsylvania *B*
East Stroudsburg University of
Pennsylvania *B*
Lock Haven University of
Pennsylvania *B*
Marywood College *B*
Point Park College *B*
Slippery Rock University of
Pennsylvania *B*
University of Pittsburgh at
Johnstown *B*

Puerto Rico

University of Puerto Rico: Rio
Piedras Campus *B*

Rhode Island

Rhode Island College *B*
Salve Regina University *B*

South Carolina

Bob Jones University *B*
Columbia College *B*
Lander College *B*
North Greenville College *A*
South Carolina State College *B*

South Dakota

Augustana College *B*
Black Hills State University *B*
Dakota State University *B*
Northern State University *B*
Sioux Falls College *B*
South Dakota State University *B*
University of South Dakota *B*

Tennessee

Carson-Newman College *B*
David Lipscomb University *B*
Tennessee Technological
University *B*

Texas

Abilene Christian University *B*
Angelo State University *B*
Baylor University *B*
East Texas Baptist University *B*
Hardin-Simmons University *B*
Incarnate Word College *B*
McMurry University *B*
Midwestern State University *B*
St. Edward's University *B*
St. Mary's University *B*
Texas A&I University *B*
Texas Christian University *B*
Texas Tech University *B,M*
University of Houston *B*
University of Mary Hardin-
Baylor *B*
University of Texas at Tyler *B*
West Texas State University *B,M*

Utah

Brigham Young University *B*
Weber State University *B*

Vermont

Johnson State College *B*

Virginia

Bluefield College *B*
George Mason University *M*
Virginia Commonwealth
University *B*
Virginia Highlands Community
College *A*
Virginia Polytechnic Institute and
State University *B*

Washington

Central Washington University *B*
Eastern Washington University *B*
Pacific Lutheran University *B*
University of Puget Sound *M*
University of Washington *B*
Washington State University *B*
Western Washington University *B*

West Virginia

Bethany College *B*
Fairmont State College *B*
Glenville State College *B*
West Liberty State College *B*
West Virginia University *B*

Wisconsin

Alverno College *B*
Cardinal Stritch College *B*
Carroll College *B*
Lakeland College *B*
Lawrence University *B*
Maranatha Baptist Bible College *B*
Marquette University *B*
St. Norbert College *B*
University of Wisconsin
La Crosse *B*
Madison *B,M*
Oshkosh *B*
Platteville *B*
River Falls *B*
Whitewater *B*
Wisconsin Lutheran College *B*

Wyoming

University of Wyoming *B*

Speech correction

Alabama

Alabama Agricultural and
Mechanical University *B,M*
Auburn University *B*
University of Alabama *B*
University of Montevallo *B,M*

Arizona

University of Arizona *B,M,D*

Arkansas

Arkansas State University *B,M*
Harding University *B*
Henderson State University *B*
University of Arkansas *B,M*
University of Central Arkansas *B,M*

California

California State University
Fresno *B,M*
Long Beach *B,M*
Northridge *B,M*
University of Redlands *B,M*
Whittier College *B,M*

Connecticut

Southern Connecticut State
University *B,M*
Western Connecticut State
University *B*

District of Columbia

University of the District of
Columbia *B*

Florida

Nova University *M*
University of Florida *B,M*
University of North Florida *B*
University of South Florida *M*

Georgia

Armstrong State College *B*
Georgia State University *M*
University of Georgia *B,M,D*
Valdosta State College *B,M*

Idaho

Idaho State University *B,M*
Northwest Nazarene College *B*

Illinois

Augustana College *B*
Bradley University *B,M*
Northern Illinois University *M*
Northwestern University *B,M,D*
St. Xavier University *B*
Southern Illinois University at
Carbondale *B,M,D*

Indiana

Ball State University *B,M*
Indiana State University *B,M*
Purdue University *B,M,D*
Vincennes University *A*

Kentucky

Brescia College *B*
Eastern Kentucky University *B*
Murray State University *B,M*
University of Kentucky *B*
Western Kentucky University *B*

Louisiana

Grambling State University *B*
Louisiana State University
Agricultural and Mechanical
College *B*
Shreveport *B*
Louisiana Tech University *B*
Northeast Louisiana University *B*
Northwestern State University *M*
Southeastern Louisiana
University *B*
Southern University and
Agricultural and Mechanical
College *B*
University of Southwestern
Louisiana *B*
Xavier University of Louisiana *B*

Maine

University of Maine at
Farmington *B*

Maryland

University of Maryland: College
Park *B,M,D*

Massachusetts

Bridgewater State College *B*
Elms College *B*

Michigan

Andrews University *B*
Central Michigan University *B,M*
Eastern Michigan University *M*
Northern Michigan University *B,M*
Western Michigan University *B,M*

Minnesota

Mankato State University *M*
Moorhead State University *B,M*
St. Cloud State University *B*
University of Minnesota: Twin
Cities *B,M,D*

Mississippi

Jackson State University *B*
Mississippi College *B*

Missouri

Fontbonne College *B,M*
Northeast Missouri State University
B,M
St. Louis University *B,M*
Southeast Missouri State
University *M*
University of Missouri: Columbia
B,M,D

Nebraska

University of Nebraska
Kearney *B,M*
Lincoln *B,M*
Omaha *B,M*

New Jersey

Kean College of New Jersey *B,M*
Trenton State College *B,M*
William Paterson College of New
Jersey *B,M*

New Mexico

Eastern New Mexico University *B*
New Mexico State University *B,M*

New York

City University of New York
Brooklyn College *B,M*
City College *B,M*
Lehman College *B,M*
College of St. Rose *B,M*
Elmira College *B*
Hofstra University *B,M*
Ithaca College *B,M*
Long Island University: C. W. Post
Campus *B,M*
Mercy College *B*
Nazareth College of Rochester *B,M*
New York University *B,M,D*
State University of New York
College at Buffalo *B,M*
College at Cortland *B*
College at Fredonia *B,M*
College at Geneseo *B,M*
College at New Paltz *B,M*
College at Plattsburgh *B*
Syracuse University *B,M,D*

North Carolina

Appalachian State University *B*
North Carolina Central
University *M*
University of North Carolina at
Greensboro *B,M*
Western Carolina University *B,M*

North Dakota

Minot State University *B,M*

Ohio

Baldwin-Wallace College *B*
Bowling Green State University
B,M,D
Miami University: Oxford Campus
B,M
Ohio State University: Columbus
Campus *B*
Ohio University *B,M,D*
University of Akron *B,M*
University of Toledo *B*

Oklahoma

Northeastern State University *B*
University of Central Oklahoma
B,M
University of Oklahoma Health
Sciences Center *M,D*
University of Science and Arts of
Oklahoma *B*
University of Tulsa *B,M*

Oregon

University of Oregon: Robert
Donald Clark Honors College *B*

Pennsylvania

Bloomsburg University of
Pennsylvania *B,M*
California University of
Pennsylvania *B,M*
East Stroudsburg University of
Pennsylvania *B*
Edinboro University of
Pennsylvania *B*
Geneva College *B*
Indiana University of Pennsylvania
B,M
Kutztown University of
Pennsylvania *B*
Marywood College *B*
West Chester University of
Pennsylvania *B,M*

South Carolina

Columbia College *B*

South Dakota

Augustana College *B,M*
Northern State University *B*
South Dakota State University *B*
University of South Dakota *B,M*

Tennessee

East Tennessee State University
B,M
Lambuth University *B*
Middle Tennessee State
University *B*
Trevecca Nazarene College *B*

Texas

Abilene Christian University *B*
Baylor University *B,M*
Hardin-Simmons University *B*
Lamar University—Beaumont *M*
Our Lady of the Lake University of
San Antonio *M*
Prairie View A&M University *B*
Stephen F. Austin State
University *B*
Texas Southern University *B*
University of Texas: Pan
American *B*
West Texas State University *B*

Utah

Brigham Young University *B,M*
Utah State University *M*

Vermont

University of Vermont *B*

Virginia

Hampton University *B,M*
Old Dominion University *B,M*
Radford University *B,M*

Washington

Eastern Washington University *B,M*

West Virginia

Marshall University *B,M*

Wisconsin

University of Wisconsin
Eau Claire *B,M*
Madison *B,M,D*
River Falls *B,M*
Whitewater *B,M*

Canada

McGill University *M*

Speech pathology/audiology

Alabama

Alabama Agricultural and
Mechanical University *B*
Auburn University
Auburn *B,M*
Montgomery *B*
University of Alabama *B,M*
University of Montevallo *B,M*
University of South Alabama *B,M*

Arizona

Arizona State University *B,M,D*
Northern Arizona University *B,M*
University of Arizona *B,M,D*

Arkansas

Arkansas State University *B,M*
Harding University *B,M*
Henderson State University *B*
Ouachita Baptist University *B*
University of Arkansas
Fayetteville *B,M*
Little Rock *B,M*
Medical Sciences *M*
University of Central Arkansas *B*

California

California State University
Chico *B,M*
Fresno *B,M*
Fullerton *M*
Hayward *B,M*
Long Beach *B,M*
Los Angeles *B,M*
Northridge *B,M*
Sacramento *B,M*
Stanislaus *B*
Chabot College *A*
Point Loma Nazarene College *B*
San Diego State University *B,M*
San Francisco State University *B,M*
San Jose State University *B,M*
Southwestern College *A*
Stanford University *D*
University of California: Santa
Barbara *B,M,D*
University of the Pacific *B,M*
University of Redlands *B,M*
Whittier College *B,M*

Colorado

Colorado State University *B,M*
University of Colorado at Boulder
B,M,D
University of Denver *B,M,D*
University of Northern Colorado
B,M

Connecticut

Southern Connecticut State
University *B,M*
University of Connecticut *M,D*

District of Columbia

Gallaudet University *M*
George Washington University *B,M*
University of the District of
Columbia *B,M*

Florida

Daytona Beach Community
College *A*
Florida Atlantic University *M*
Florida State University *B,M,D*
Nova University *B*
University of Central Florida *B,M*
University of Florida *M*

University of South Florida *M*

Georgia

Armstrong State College *M*
Columbus College *B,M*
Emory University *M*
Georgia State University *M*
University of Georgia *B,M,D*

Hawaii

University of Hawaii at Manoa *B,M*

Idaho

Idaho State University *B,M*
North Idaho College *A*
Northwest Nazarene College *B*
Ricks College *A*

Illinois

Augustana College *B*
Eastern Illinois University *B,M*
Elmhurst College *B*
Governors State University *B,M*
Illinois State University *B,M*
Northern Illinois University *B,M*
Northwestern University *B,M,D*
Rush University *M*
St. Xavier University *B*
Southern Illinois University
Carbondale *B,M,D*
Edwardsville *B,M*
University of Illinois at Urbana-
Champaign *B,M,D*
Western Illinois University *B*

Indiana

Ball State University *B,M*
Butler University *B,M*
Indiana State University *B,M*
Indiana University Bloomington
B,M,D
Purdue University *B,M,D*
Valparaiso University *B*

Iowa

University of Iowa *B,M,D*
University of Northern Iowa *B,M*

Kansas

Fort Hays State University *M*
Kansas State University *B,M*
University of Kansas
Lawrence *B,M,D*
Medical Center *M,D*
Wichita State University *B,M,D*

Kentucky

Murray State University *B,M*
University of Kentucky *B,M*
University of Louisville *M*
Western Kentucky University *B,M*

Louisiana

Grambling State University *B*
Louisiana State University
Agricultural and Mechanical
College *B,M,D*
Medical Center *M*
Shreveport *B*
Louisiana Tech University *B,M*
Nicholls State University *B*
Northeast Louisiana University *M*
Southern University and
Agricultural and Mechanical
College *B*
University of Southwestern
Louisiana *B,M*
Xavier University of Louisiana *B*

Maine

University of Maine
Farmington *B*
Orono *B,M*

Maryland

Loyola College in Maryland *B,M*
Towson State University *B,M*
University of Maryland: College
Park *B,M,D*

Massachusetts

Boston University *B,M,D,W*
Bridgewater State College *B*
Elms College *B*
Emerson College *B,M,D*
Massachusetts Bay Community
College *A*
MGH Institute of Health
Professions *M*
Northeastern University *M*
University of Massachusetts at
Amherst *B,M,D*
Worcester State College *B,M*

Michigan

Andrews University *B*
Central Michigan University *B,M*
Eastern Michigan University *M*
Lansing Community College *A*
Michigan State University *B,M,D*
Northern Michigan University *B,M*
Wayne State University *M,D*
Western Michigan University *B,M*

Minnesota

Mankato State University *B,M*
Moorhead State University *B,M*
St. Cloud State University *B,M*
University of Minnesota
Duluth *B,M*
Twin Cities *M,D*
Willmar Community College *A*

Mississippi

Delta State University *B*
Mississippi College *B*
Mississippi Delta Community
College *A*
Mississippi University for Women *B*
University of Mississippi *B,M*
University of Southern Mississippi
B,M,D

Missouri

Central Missouri State University
B,M
East Central College *A*
Fontbonne College *B,M*
Northeast Missouri State University
B,M
St. Louis University *B,M*
Southeast Missouri State University
B,M
Southwest Missouri State University
B,M
University of Missouri
Columbia *B,M,D*
Kansas City *B*

Montana

University of Montana *B,M*

Nebraska

University of Nebraska
Kearney *B,M*
Lincoln *B,M*
Omaha *M*

Nevada

University of Nevada: Reno *B,M*

New Hampshire

University of New Hampshire *B,M*

New Jersey

Kean College of New Jersey *M*
Montclair State College *B,M*
Rutgers—The State University of
New Jersey
Douglass College *B*
Livingston College *B*
Rutgers College *B*
Stockton State College *B*
Trenton State College *B,M*
William Paterson College of New
Jersey *B,M*

New Mexico

Eastern New Mexico University
B,M
New Mexico State University *B,M*
University of New Mexico *B,M*

New York

Adelphi University *B,M*
City University of New York
Brooklyn College *B,M*
City College *B,M*
Graduate School and
University Center *D*
Hunter College *M*
Lehman College *B,M*
Queens College *B,M*
Elmira College *B*
Hofstra University *B,M*
Iona College *B*
Ithaca College *B,M*
Long Island University
Brooklyn Campus *B*
C. W. Post Campus *M*
Marymount Manhattan College *B*
Mercy College *B*
Molloy College *B*
Nazareth College of Rochester *B,M*
New York University *B,M,D*
Pace University *B*
St. John's University *B,M*
State University of New York
Buffalo *B,M,D*
College at Cortland *B*
College at Fredonia *B,M*
College at Geneseo *B,M*
College at New Paltz *B,M*
College at Plattsburgh *B*
Syracuse University *B,M,D*

North Carolina

Appalachian State University *B,M*
East Carolina University *B,M*
Shaw University *B*
University of North Carolina
Chapel Hill *M,D*
Greensboro *B,M*

North Dakota

Minot State University *B,M*
University of North Dakota *B,M*

Ohio

Baldwin-Wallace College *B*
Bowling Green State University *B*
Case Western Reserve University
B,M,D
Cleveland State University *B,M*
College of Wooster *B*
Kent State University *B,M,D*
Miami University: Oxford Campus
B,M
Ohio State University: Columbus
Campus *B,M,D*
Ohio University *B,M,D*
Union Institute *D*
University of Akron *B,M*

University of Cincinnati *B,M,D*
University of Toledo *B*

Oklahoma

Oklahoma State University *B*
University of Central Oklahoma
B,M
University of Oklahoma
Health Sciences Center *M,D*
Norman *M,D*
University of Tulsa *B,M*

Oregon

Portland State University *M*
University of Oregon
Eugene *B,M,D*
Robert Donald Clark Honors
College *B*

Pennsylvania

Bloomsburg University of
Pennsylvania *M*
California University of
Pennsylvania *B,M*
Clarion University of Pennsylvania
B,M
East Stroudsburg University of
Pennsylvania *B*
Edinboro University of
Pennsylvania *M*
Geneva College *B*
Indiana University of Pennsylvania
B,M
Marywood College *B*
Penn State University Park Campus
B,M,D
Temple University *B,M,D*
Thiel College *B*
University of Pittsburgh *M,D*
West Chester University of
Pennsylvania *B,M*

Puerto Rico

University of Puerto Rico: Medical
Sciences Campus *B,M*

Rhode Island

University of Rhode Island *M*

South Carolina

South Carolina State College *B,M*
University of South Carolina *M,D*

South Dakota

Augustana College *B*
Northern State University *B*
University of South Dakota *B,M*

Tennessee

East Tennessee State University
B,M
Lambuth University *B*
Memphis State University *M,D*
Tennessee State University *B*
University of Tennessee: Knoxville
B,M,D
Vanderbilt University *M,D*

Texas

Abilene Christian University *B*
Baylor University *B,M*
Hardin-Simmons University *B*
Lamar University—Beaumont *B,M*
McMurry University *B*
Our Lady of the Lake University of
San Antonio *B,M*
Southwest Texas State University
B,M
Stephen F. Austin State University
B,M
Texas Christian University *B,M*
Texas Southmost College *A*

Texas Tech University *B,M*
Texas Woman's University *B,M*
University of Houston *B,M*
University of North Texas *B,M*
University of Texas
Dallas *B,M,D*
El Paso *B,M*
Pan American *B*
West Texas State University *B,M*

Utah

Brigham Young University *M*
University of Utah *B,M,D*
Utah State University *B,M*

Vermont

University of Vermont *B,M*

Virginia

Hampton University *B,M*
James Madison University *B,M*
Longwood College *B*
Norfolk State University *B*
Old Dominion University *B,M*
Radford University *B,M*
University of Virginia *B,M*

Washington

Eastern Washington University *B,M*
University of Washington *B,M,D*
Washington State University *B,M*
Western Washington University
B,M

West Virginia

Marshall University *B,M*
West Virginia University *B,M*

Wisconsin

Marquette University *B,M*
University of Wisconsin
Eau Claire *B,M*
Madison *B,M,D*
Milwaukee *B,M*
Oshkosh *M*
River Falls *B,M*
Stevens Point *B,M*
Whitewater *B,M*

Wyoming

University of Wyoming *B,M*

Canada

McGill University *M,D*

Sports management

Alabama

Faulkner University *B*
Jefferson State Community
College *A*
University of Alabama *B*

Arkansas

Arkansas State University *B*

California

University of the Pacific *B*

Colorado

Denver Technical College *A*

Connecticut

University of New Haven *B*

Florida

Barry University *B*
Florida Southern College *B*
Lynn University *B*

St. Thomas University *B,M*
University of Miami *M*

Georgia

Georgia Southern University *M*
Georgia State University *M,D*
University of Georgia *B*

Illinois

Concordia University *B*
MacMurray College *B*
National-Louis University *B*
Principia College *B*

Indiana

Indiana Institute of Technology *A,B*
Indiana State University *B,M*
Indiana University Bloomington *B*

Iowa

Loras College *B*
Luther College *B*
William Penn College *B*

Kentucky

Eastern Kentucky University *A,B,M*

Louisiana

Grambling State University *M*

Maine

Husson College *B*

Massachusetts

Becker College: Leicester
Campus *A*
Dean Junior College *A*
Endicott College *A*
Springfield College *B,M*
University of Massachusetts at
Amherst *B,M,D*

Michigan

Concordia College *B*
University of Michigan *B*
Wayne State University *M*

Minnesota

Bemidji State University *B*
College of St. Scholastica *B*
Northwestern College *B*
University of St. Thomas *M*

Missouri

Southwest Baptist University *B*

Nebraska

Union College *B*
University of Nebraska—Kearney *B*

New Hampshire

Colby-Sawyer College *B*
Keene State College *B*
New England College *B*
New Hampshire College *B*

New Jersey

Jersey City State College *B*

New York

City University of New York:
Brooklyn College *M*
Herkimer County Community
College *A*
Sullivan County Community
College *A*

North Carolina

Barton College *B*
Belmont Abbey College *B*
Campbell University *B*
Elon College *B*

Guilford College *B*
Livingstone College *B*
Pfeiffer College *B*
Winston-Salem State University *B*

Ohio
Baldwin-Wallace College *B*
Bowling Green State University *B*
Defiance College *B*
Miami University: Oxford
    Campus *B*
Mount Union College *B*
Mount Vernon Nazarene College *B*
Ohio Northern University *B*
University of Dayton *B*
University of Rio Grande *B*
Xavier University *B*

Oklahoma
Phillips University *B*

Pennsylvania
Allentown College of St. Francis de
    Sales *B*
Indiana University of
    Pennsylvania *M*
Robert Morris College *B,M*
West Chester University of
    Pennsylvania *M*

South Carolina
Anderson College *B*
University of South Carolina
    Aiken *B*
       Columbia *B*

South Dakota
Sioux Falls College *B*

Texas
Texas Wesleyan University *B*

Vermont
Lyndon State College *B*

Virginia
Averett College *B*
Radford University *B*
University of Richmond *M*
Virginia Intermont College *B*

West Virginia
Bethany College *B*
Davis and Elkins College *B*
Glenville State College *B*
Marshall University *B*
Salem-Teikyo University *B*

Wisconsin
University of Wisconsin: Oshkosh *B*

Sports medicine

Alabama
Livingston University *B*
University of Alabama *B*

Arizona
Northern Arizona University *B*

Arkansas
John Brown University *B*

California
California Lutheran University *B*
California State University:
    Northridge *M*
Fresno Pacific College *B*
Occidental College *B*

Orange Coast College *C,A*
Pepperdine University *B*
University of the Pacific *B*
University of San Francisco *B*
Whittier College *B*

Colorado
Colorado Mountain College: Alpine
    Campus *A*
Denver Technical College *A*

Connecticut
Southern Connecticut State
    University *B*

Florida
Barry University *B*
University of Miami *M*

Georgia
Georgia State University *M*
Life College *M*
Valdosta State College *B*

Idaho
Albertson College *B*
Boise State University *M*
Idaho State University *B*
Northwest Nazarene College *B*
Ricks College *A*

Illinois
Elmhurst College *B*
Lake Land College *A*
North Central College *B*
Southern Illinois University at
    Carbondale *B*

Indiana
Anderson University *B*
Indiana State University *B*
Indiana University Bloomington
    B,M
Manchester College *A,B*
Purdue University *B*
Vincennes University *A*

Iowa
Loras College *B*
Upper Iowa University *B*

Kansas
Bethany College *B*
Cloud County Community
    College *A*
Coffeyville Community College *A*
Dodge City Community College *A*
Highland Community College *A*
Hutchinson Community College *A*
Neosho County Community
    College *A*
Pratt Community College *A*

Kentucky
Eastern Kentucky University *B*

Maine
University of New England *C*

Maryland
Salisbury State University *B*
Western Maryland College *B*

Massachusetts
Boston University *B*
Bridgewater State College *B*
North Adams State College *B*
Springfield College *M*

Michigan
Adrian College *A*
Alma College *B*

Central Michigan University *B*
Eastern Michigan University *B*
Grand Valley State University *B*
Hope College *B*
Lansing Community College *A*
Northern Michigan University *B*
Saginaw Valley State University *B*
University of Detroit Mercy *B*

Minnesota
Mankato State University *B*
Willmar Community College *A*
Winona State University *B*

Missouri
Park College *B*
Southwest Baptist University *B*

Montana
University of Montana *B*

Nebraska
Concordia College *B*

New Hampshire
Colby-Sawyer College *B*
Keene State College *B*
New Hampshire Technical College:
    Manchester *A*
Plymouth State College of the
    University System of New
    Hampshire *B*

New Mexico
New Mexico Junior College *A*
New Mexico State University *B*

New York
Canisius College *C*
College of Mount St. Vincent *B*
Herkimer County Community
    College *A*
Long Island University: Brooklyn
    Campus *B,M*
Manhattan College *B*

North Carolina
Appalachian State University *B*
Barton College *B*
Brevard College *A*
Catawba College *B*
Chowan College *A*
Elon College *B*
Guilford College *B*
Lenoir-Rhyne College *B*
Pfeiffer College *B*
Wingate College *B*

North Dakota
North Dakota State University *B*
University of North Dakota *B*

Ohio
Ashland University *B*
Baldwin-Wallace College *B*
Capital University *B*
Defiance College *B*
Heidelberg College *B*
Lorain County Community
    College *A*
Malone College *B*
Marietta College *B*
Mount Union College *B*
Mount Vernon Nazarene College *B*
Ohio Northern University *B*
Ohio University *B,M*
Otterbein College *B*
University of Akron *B,M*
University of Toledo *B*
Urbana University *B*
Walsh College *B*
Wilmington College *B*

Oklahoma
Oklahoma Baptist University *B*
Phillips University *B*
University of Oklahoma Health
    Sciences Center *M*

Oregon
George Fox College *B*
Linfield College *B*

Pennsylvania
California University of
    Pennsylvania *B,M*
Gettysburg College *B*
Lock Haven University of
    Pennsylvania *B*
Mercyhurst College *B*
Messiah College *B*
Penn State University Park
    Campus *C*
Waynesburg College *B*

South Carolina
Coker College *B*

South Dakota
Dakota Wesleyan University *B*
South Dakota State University *B*

Tennessee
Lincoln Memorial University *B*
Union University *B*

Texas
Lubbock Christian University *B*
South Plains College *A*
Southwest Texas State University *B*
Texas Tech University *M*

Vermont
Castleton State College *B*
Johnson State College *B*

Virginia
Averett College *B*
Bluefield College *A*
Hampton University *B*
Old Dominion University *B*
Radford University *B*

Washington
Pacific Lutheran University *B*
Whitworth College *B*

West Virginia
Alderson-Broaddus College *B*
Glenville State College *B*
Marshall University *B,M*
Salem-Teikyo University *B*
Shepherd College *B*
University of Charleston *B*
West Virginia Wesleyan College *B*

Wisconsin
Ripon College *B*

Statistics

Alabama
Auburn University *M*
University of Alabama *B,M,D*
University of South Alabama *B*

Alaska
University of Alaska Fairbanks *B*

Arizona
Arizona State University *M*
Northern Arizona University *B*

University of Arizona *M*

Arkansas
University of Arkansas *M*

California
California Polytechnic State
    University: San Luis Obispo *B*
California State University
    Fullerton *B,M*
    Hayward *B,M*
    Long Beach *B*
    Northridge *B*
    Stanislaus *B*
Chabot College *A*
San Diego State University *M*
San Francisco State University *B*
San Jose State University *B*
Stanford University *B,M,D*
University of California
    Berkeley *B,M,D*
    Davis *B,M,D*
    Los Angeles *B*
    Riverside *B,M,D*
    San Diego *M*
    Santa Barbara *B,M,D*
University of Southern California *M*

Colorado
Colorado State University *B,M,D*
Fort Lewis College *B*
University of Denver *B,M*
University of Northern Colorado
    B,M,D

Connecticut
University of Connecticut *B,M,D*
Wesleyan University *B*
Yale University *M,D*

Delaware
University of Delaware *B,M,D*

District of Columbia
American University *B,M,D*
George Washington University
    B,M,D

Florida
Florida International University *B*
Florida State University *B,M,D*
University of Central Florida *B,M*
University of Florida *B,M,D*
University of North Florida *B,M*
University of West Florida *B*

Georgia
Brewton-Parker College *A*
Darton College *A*
Georgia Institute of Technology *M*
University of Georgia *B,M,D*

Idaho
University of Idaho *M*

Illinois
De Paul University *B*
Illinois Institute of Technology *M*
Northern Illinois University *M*
Northwestern University *B,M*
Southern Illinois University
    Carbondale *M*
    Edwardsville *B*
University of Chicago *B,M,D*
University of Illinois
    Chicago *B*
    Urbana-Champaign *B,M,D*

Indiana
Ball State University *M*
Purdue University
    Calumet *B*
    West Lafayette *B,M,D,W*

Iowa
Iowa State University *B,M,D*
University of Iowa *B,M,D*

Kansas
Kansas Newman College *B*
Kansas State University *B,M,D*

Kentucky
Eastern Kentucky University *B,M*
University of Kentucky *M,D*

Louisiana
Grambling State University *B*
Louisiana State University and
    Agricultural and Mechanical
    College *M*
McNeese State University *B*
Tulane University *M*
University of Southwestern
    Louisiana *B,M,D*
Xavier University of Louisiana *B*

Maine
University of Southern Maine *M*

Maryland
University of Maryland
    Baltimore County *M,D*
    College Park *M,D*

Massachusetts
Boston University *B,M,D*
Hampshire College *B*
Harvard and Radcliffe Colleges *B*
Harvard University *M,D*
Massachusetts Institute of
    Technology *B,M,D,W*
Mount Holyoke College *B*
University of Massachusetts
    Amherst *M,D*
    Lowell *B,M*
Worcester Polytechnic Institute
    B,M

Michigan
Central Michigan University *B*
Eastern Michigan University *B*
GMI Engineering & Management
    Institute *B*
Grand Valley State University *B*
Michigan State University *B,M,D*
Michigan Technological University
    B,M
Oakland University *M*
University of Detroit Mercy *B*
University of Michigan *B,M,D*
Wayne State University *M*
Western Michigan University
    B,M,D

Minnesota
Mankato State University *B*
St. Cloud State University *B*
St. Mary's College of Minnesota *B*
University of Minnesota: Twin
    Cities *B,M,D*
Winona State University *B*

Mississippi
Mississippi State University *M*

Missouri
University of Missouri: Columbia
    B,M,D

Montana
Montana State University *B,M,D*

Nebraska
Creighton University *C,A,B*
University of Nebraska—Kearney *B*

New Hampshire
University of New Hampshire *B*

New Jersey
Montclair State College *M*
New Jersey Institute of
    Technology *B*
Princeton University *B,D*
Rutgers—The State University of
    New Jersey
    Douglass College *B*
    Livingston College *B*
    New Brunswick *M,D*
    Rutgers College *B*
    University College New
        Brunswick *B*
Stevens Institute of Technology
    B,M,D
Stockton State College *B*
Trenton State College *B*

New Mexico
Eastern New Mexico University *B*
New Mexico Institute of Mining
    and Technology *M*

New York
Barnard College *B*
City University of New York
    Baruch College *B,M*
    Hunter College *B*
    Queens College *M*
Columbia University
    Columbia College *B*
    New York *M,D*
    School of General Studies *B*
Cornell University *B,M,D*
Manhattan College *B*
New York University *B,M*
Polytechnic University *M,D*
Rensselaer Polytechnic Institute *M*
Rochester Institute of Technology
    B,M
St. John's University *B*
State University of New York
    Buffalo *B,M,D*
    College at Oneonta *B*
University of Rochester *B,M,D*

North Carolina
Appalachian State University *B*
Duke University *D*
North Carolina State University
    B,M,D
University of North Carolina
    Asheville *B*
    Chapel Hill *B,M,D*
    Greensboro *B*

North Dakota
North Dakota State University
    B,M,D

Ohio
Air Force Institute of Technology
    M,D
Bowling Green State University *B*
Case Western Reserve University
    B,M,D
Lake Erie College *B*
Miami University: Oxford Campus
    B,M
Ohio State University: Columbus
    Campus *B,M,D*
Union Institute *D*

University of Akron *B,M*
University of Toledo *B*
Wright State University *B*

Oklahoma
Oklahoma State University *B,M,D*

Oregon
Oregon State University *M,D*
Southern Oregon State College *B*

Pennsylvania
Bucknell University *B*
Carnegie Mellon University
    B,M,D,W
Drexel University *M,D*
Elizabethtown College *B*
Gettysburg College *B*
La Salle University *B*
Lehigh University *B,M,D*
Mansfield University of
    Pennsylvania *B*
Penn State University Park Campus
    M,D
Temple University *B*
University of Pennsylvania *B,M,D*
University of Pittsburgh *B,M*

Puerto Rico
University of Puerto Rico:
    Mayaguez Campus *M*

Rhode Island
Brown University *B,M,D*
University of Rhode Island *B,M*

South Carolina
University of South Carolina *B,M,D*

South Dakota
University of South Dakota *B*

Tennessee
Maryville College *B*
Tennessee Technological
    University *M*
University of Tennessee: Knoxville
    B,M

Texas
Baylor University *D*
Rice University *B,M,D*
Southern Methodist University
    B,M,D
Stephen F. Austin State
    University *M*
Texas A&M University *M,D*
Texas Tech University *M*
University of Houston *B*
University of Texas
    Austin *M*
    Dallas *B,M,D*
    El Paso *B,M*
    San Antonio *B,M*

Utah
Brigham Young University *B,M*
University of Utah *M*
Utah State University *B,M*

Vermont
Marlboro College *B*
University of Vermont *B,M*

Virginia
George Mason University *M*
Old Dominion University *B,M,D*
Radford University *B*
Virginia Polytechnic Institute and
    State University *B,M,D*

Washington

Olympic College *A*
Tacoma Community College *A*
University of Washington *B,M,D*

West Virginia

West Virginia University *B,M*

Wisconsin

Marquette University *B,M,D*
University of Wisconsin
    Madison *B,M,D*
    Milwaukee *B,M*

Wyoming

University of Wyoming *B,M,D*

Canada

McGill University *B,M,D*

Student counseling and personnel services

Alabama

Alabama Agricultural and
    Mechanical University *B,M*
Alabama State University *M*
Auburn University
    Auburn *M,D*
    Montgomery *M*
Jacksonville State University *M*
Livingston University *M*
Troy State University at
    Montgomery *M*
Tuskegee University *M*
University of Alabama
    Birmingham *M*
    Tuscaloosa *M,D*
University of Montevallo *B,M*
University of North Alabama *M*
University of South Alabama *M*

Alaska

University of Alaska
    Anchorage *M*
    Fairbanks *M*

Arizona

Arizona State University *M,D*
Northern Arizona University *M*
Prescott College *B*
University of Arizona *M,D*
University of Phoenix *M*

Arkansas

Arkansas State University *M*
Henderson State University *M*
Southern Arkansas University *M*
University of Arkansas
    Fayetteville *M*
    Little Rock *M*
University of Central Arkansas *B,M*

California

Azusa Pacific University *M*
Barstow College *A*
California Lutheran University *M*
California Polytechnic State
    University: San Luis Obispo *M*

California State University
    Bakersfield *M*
    Dominguez Hills *M*
    Fresno *M*
    Hayward *M*
    Long Beach *M*
    Los Angeles *M*
    Northridge *M*
    Sacramento *M*
    San Bernardino *M*
    Stanislaus *M*
Chapman University *M*
Fresno Pacific College *M*
Humboldt State University *M*
La Sierra University *M*
Loyola Marymount University *M*
Mount St. Mary's College *M*
National University *M*
Pacific Oaks College *M*
Point Loma Nazarene College *M*
St. Mary's College of California
    B,M
San Diego State University *M*
San Francisco State University *M*
San Jose State University *M*
Santa Clara University *M*
Sonoma State University *M*
University of California: Santa
    Barbara *M,D*
University of La Verne *M*
University of the Pacific *M,D*
University of Redlands *M*
University of San Diego *M*
University of San Francisco *M,D*
University of Southern California
    M,D,W
Whittier College *M*

Colorado

Adams State College *M*
Colorado State University *M*
University of Colorado
    Colorado Springs *M*
    Denver *M*
University of Denver *M,D*
University of Northern Colorado
    M,D

Connecticut

Central Connecticut State
    University *M*
Fairfield University *M*
University of Bridgeport *M*
University of Hartford *M,W*
Western Connecticut State
    University *M*

Delaware

University of Delaware *M*
Wilmington College *M*

District of Columbia

American University *D*
Gallaudet University *M*
George Washington University *M,D*
Howard University *M*
Trinity College *M*
University of the District of
    Columbia *M*

Florida

Barry University *M*
Florida Agricultural and Mechanical
    University *M*
Florida Atlantic University *M*
Florida International University *M*
Jacksonville University *M*
Nova University *M*
Rollins College *M*
St. Thomas University *M*
Stetson University *M*
University of Central Florida *M,D*

University of Florida *M,D*
University of North Florida *M*
University of South Florida *M*

Georgia

Columbus College *M*
Fort Valley State College *M*
Georgia Southern University *M*
Georgia State University *M,D*
University of Georgia *M,D*
West Georgia College *M*

Idaho

Albertson College *M*
Idaho State University *M,D*
University of Idaho *M*

Illinois

Bradley University *M*
Chicago State University *M*
Concordia University *M*
De Paul University *M*
Eastern Illinois University *M*
Illinois State University *M*
Loyola University of Chicago *M*
Northeastern Illinois University *M*
Northern Illinois University *M,D*
Northwestern University *M,D*
Roosevelt University *M*
Southern Illinois University at
    Carbondale *M,D*
University of Illinois at Urbana-
    Champaign *M,D*
Western Illinois University *M*

Indiana

Ball State University *M,D*
Butler University *M*
Indiana State University *M,D*
Indiana University
    Bloomington *M,D*
    South Bend *M*
    Southeast *M*
Indiana University—Purdue
    University
    Fort Wayne *M*
    Indianapolis *M*
Purdue University
    Calumet *M*
    West Lafayette *M,D*
St. Francis College *M*
University of Evansville *M*

Iowa

Drake University *M,D*
Iowa State University *M,D*
Loras College *M*
Morningside College *M*
University of Iowa *M,D*
University of Northern Iowa *M*

Kansas

Emporia State University *M*
Fort Hays State University *M*
Kansas State University *M,D*
University of Kansas *M,D*
Wichita State University *M*

Kentucky

Eastern Kentucky University *M*
Morehead State University *M*
Murray State University *M*
University of Kentucky *D*
University of Louisville *B,M,D*
Western Kentucky University *M*

Louisiana

Louisiana State University and
    Agricultural and Mechanical
    College *M*
Louisiana Tech University *M*
Loyola University *M*

McNeese State University *M*
Nicholls State University *M*
Northeast Louisiana University *M*
Northwestern State University *M*
Our Lady of Holy Cross College *M*
Southeastern Louisiana
    University *M*
Southern University and
    Agricultural and Mechanical
    College *M*
University of New Orleans *M,D*
University of Southwestern
    Louisiana *M*
Xavier University of Louisiana *M*

Maine

University of Maine *M,D*
University of Southern Maine *M*

Maryland

Baltimore Hebrew University *B,M*
Bowie State University *M*
Frostburg State University *M*
Loyola College in Maryland *M*
University of Maryland
    College Park *M,D*
    Eastern Shore *M*
Western Maryland College *M*

Massachusetts

Boston College *M,D*
Boston University *M,D,W*
Bridgewater State College *M*
Fitchburg State College *M*
Lesley College *M*
Salem State College *M*
Springfield College *M*
Suffolk University *M*
University of Massachusetts at
    Boston *M*
Westfield State College *M*

Michigan

Andrews University *M,D*
Central Michigan University *M*
Eastern Michigan University *M*
Michigan State University *M,D*
Oakland University *M*
Siena Heights College *M*
University of Detroit Mercy *M*
Wayne State University *B,M,D*
Western Michigan University *M,D*

Minnesota

Mankato State University *M*
Moorhead State University *M*
University of St. Thomas *M*
Willmar Community College *A*
Winona State University *M*

Mississippi

Delta State University *M*
Jackson State University *M*
Mississippi College *M*
Mississippi State University *M*
University of Mississippi *M*
University of Southern
    Mississippi *M*

Missouri

Central Missouri State
    University *M*
Lincoln University *M*
Northeast Missouri State
    University *M*
Northwest Missouri State
    University *M*
St. Louis University *M,D*
Southeast Missouri State
    University *M*
Southwest Missouri State
    University *M*

University of Missouri
  Columbia *M,D*
  Kansas City *M,D*
  St. Louis *M*

Montana

Eastern Montana College *M*
Northern Montana College *M*
University of Montana *M*

Nebraska

Chadron State College *M*
Creighton University *M*
University of Nebraska
  Kearney *M*
  Lincoln *M,D*
  Omaha *M*
Wayne State College *M*

Nevada

University of Nevada
  Las Vegas *M,D*
  Reno *M,D*

New Hampshire

Franklin Pierce College *B*
Keene State College *M*
Notre Dame College *M*
Plymouth State College of the
  University System of New
  Hampshire *M*
Rivier College *M*
University of New Hampshire *M*

New Jersey

Glassboro State College *M*
Jersey City State College *M*
Kean College of New Jersey *M*
Monmouth College *M*
Montclair State College *M*
Rider College *M*
Seton Hall University *M*
Trenton State College *M*
William Paterson College of New
  Jersey *M*

New Mexico

Eastern New Mexico University *M*
New Mexico Highlands
  University *M*
New Mexico State University *M,D*
University of New Mexico *M,D*
Western New Mexico University *M*

New York

Alfred University *M*
Canisius College *M*
City University of New York
  Brooklyn College *M*
  College of Staten Island *M*
  Hunter College *M*
  Lehman College *M*
  Queens College *M*
College of New Rochelle *M*
College of St. Rose *M*
Fordham University *M,D*
Hofstra University *M,W*
Long Island University
  Brooklyn Campus *M*
  C. W. Post Campus *M*
Manhattan College *M*
New York University *M,D*
Niagara University *M*
Russell Sage College *M*
St. Bonaventure University *M*
St. John's University *M,D*
St. Lawrence University *M*

State University of New York
  Albany *M*
  Buffalo *M,D*
  College at Brockport *M*
  College at Buffalo *M*
  College at Oneonta *M*
  College at Plattsburgh *M*
  Oswego *M*
Syracuse University *M,D*
University of Rochester *M,D*

North Carolina

Appalachian State University *M*
Campbell University *M*
East Carolina University *M*
Lenoir-Rhyne College *M,W*
North Carolina Agricultural and
  Technical State University *M*
North Carolina Central
  University *M*
North Carolina State University
  M,D
University of North Carolina
  Chapel Hill *M*
  Charlotte *M*
  Greensboro *M,D*
Wake Forest University *M*
Western Carolina University *M*

North Dakota

North Dakota State University *M*
University of North Dakota *M,D*

Ohio

Bowling Green State University *M*
Cleveland State University *M,D*
Heidelberg College *M*
John Carroll University *M*
Kent State University *M*
Miami University: Oxford
  Campus *M*
Ohio State University: Columbus
  Campus *B,M,D*
Ohio University
  Athens *M,D*
  Eastern Campus *M*
  Southern Campus at
    Ironton *M*
University of Akron *M,D*
University of Cincinnati *M,D*
University of Dayton *M*
University of Toledo *M,D*
Wright State University *M*
Youngstown State University *M*

Oklahoma

East Central University *M*
Northeastern State University *M*
Northwestern Oklahoma State
  University *M*
Oklahoma City University *M*
Oklahoma State University *M,D*
Phillips University *M*
Southeastern Oklahoma State
  University *M*
Southwestern Oklahoma State
  University *M*
University of Central Oklahoma *M*
University of Oklahoma *M,D*
University of Tulsa *M*

Oregon

Lewis and Clark College *M*
Oregon State University *M,D*
University of Oregon *M,D*
University of Portland *M*

Pennsylvania

Bryn Mawr College *M,D*
Bucknell University *M*
California University of
  Pennsylvania *M*

Duquesne University *M*
Edinboro University of
  Pennsylvania *M*
Gannon University *M*
Gwynedd-Mercy College *M*
Indiana University of
  Pennsylvania *M*
Kutztown University of
  Pennsylvania *M*
Lehigh University *M,D*
Marywood College *M*
Millersville University of
  Pennsylvania *M*
Penn State University Park Campus
  M,D
Shippensburg University of
  Pennsylvania *M*
Slippery Rock University of
  Pennsylvania *M*
Temple University *M,D*
University of Pennsylvania *M,D*
University of Scranton *M*
West Chester University of
  Pennsylvania *M*
Westminster College *M*

Puerto Rico

Inter American University of Puerto
  Rico
    Metropolitan Campus *M*
    San German Campus *M*
Pontifical Catholic University of
  Puerto Rico *M*
University of Puerto Rico: Rio
  Piedras Campus *M,D*

Rhode Island

Providence College *M*
Rhode Island College *M,W*
University of Rhode Island *M*

South Carolina

Bob Jones University *B,M*
The Citadel *M*
Clemson University *M*
Limestone College *B*
South Carolina State College *M*
University of South Carolina *M,D*
Winthrop University *M*

South Dakota

Northern State University *M*
South Dakota State University *M*

Tennessee

Austin Peay State University *M*
East Tennessee State University *M*
Lincoln Memorial University *M*
Memphis State University *M,D*
Middle Tennessee State
  University *M*
Tennessee State University *M*
Tennessee Technological
  University *M*
University of Tennessee
  Chattanooga *M*
  Knoxville *M*
  Martin *M*

Texas

Abilene Christian University *M*
Angelo State University *M*
Corpus Christi State University *M*
East Texas State University *B,M,D*
Hardin-Simmons University *M*
Houston Baptist University *B,M*
Lamar University—Beaumont *B,M*
Laredo State University *M*
Midwestern State University *M*
Prairie View A&M University *M*
Sam Houston State University *M*

Southwest Texas State
  University *M*
Stephen F. Austin State
  University *M*
Sul Ross State University *M*
Tarleton State University *M*
Texas A&I University *M*
Texas A&M University *M,D*
Texas Southern University *M,D*
Texas Woman's University *M*
University of North Texas *M,D*
University of Texas
  El Paso *M*
  Pan American *M*
  Permian Basin *M*
  San Antonio *M*
West Texas State University *M*

Utah

Brigham Young University *M,D*

Vermont

Johnson State College *M*
Lyndon State College *M*
School for International Training *M*
University of Vermont *M*

Virginia

College of William and Mary *M,D*
George Mason University *M*
James Madison University *M*
Longwood College *M*
Lynchburg College *M*
Old Dominion University *M*
Radford University *M*
University of Virginia *M,D*
Virginia Commonwealth
  University *M*
Virginia Polytechnic Institute and
  State University *M,D,W*
Virginia State University *M*

Washington

Central Washington University *M*
Eastern Washington University *M*
Heritage College *M*
Pacific Lutheran University *M*
St. Martin's College *M*
Seattle Pacific University *M*
Seattle University *M*
University of Puget Sound *M*
University of Washington *M,D*
Walla Walla College *M*
Washington State University *M*
Western Washington University *M*
Whitworth College *M*

West Virginia

Marshall University *M*
West Virginia Graduate College *M*
West Virginia University *M*

Wisconsin

Carthage College *M*
Concordia University Wisconsin *M*
Marquette University *M,D*
University of Wisconsin
  La Crosse *M*
  Madison *M,D*
  Milwaukee *M*
  Oshkosh *M*
  Platteville *M*
  River Falls *M*
  Stout *M*
  Whitewater *M*

Wyoming

University of Wyoming *M,D*

American Samoa, Caroline Islands, Guam, Marianas, Virgin Islands
University of Guam *M*
University of the Virgin Islands *M*

Canada
McGill University *M,D*

Studio art

Alabama
Spring Hill College *B*
University of Alabama
    Birmingham *B*
    Huntsville *B*
    Tuscaloosa *B,M*
University of Montevallo *B*

Alaska
University of Alaska Anchorage *B*

Arizona
Grand Canyon University *B*
Northern Arizona University *M*
University of Arizona *B,M*

Arkansas
Arkansas College *B*
Henderson State University *B*
Ouachita Baptist University *B*
University of Arkansas
    Fayetteville *B,M*
    Little Rock *B,M*

California
Biola University *B*
California College of Arts and
    Crafts *B*
California Institute of the Arts
    C,B,M
California State University
    Long Beach *B,M*
    Los Angeles *B,M*
    Stanislaus *B*
Chabot College *A*
Chapman University *B*
College of Notre Dame *B*
El Camino College *A*
Humboldt State University *B*
Los Angeles Valley College *C*
Loyola Marymount University *B*
Mills College *B,M*
Monterey Peninsula College *C,A*
Occidental College *B*
Orange Coast College *A*
Otis/Parsons School of Art and
    Design *B,M*
Oxnard College *A*
Pasadena City College *A*
Point Loma Nazarene College *B*
Pomona College *B*
Porterville College *C,A*
San Diego City College *A*
San Francisco Art Institute *B,M*
San Jose State University *B*
Santa Clara University *B*
Scripps College *B*
University of California
    Davis *B,M*
    Irvine *B,M*
    Riverside *B*
    San Diego *B*
    Santa Barbara *B,M*
    Santa Cruz *C,B*
University of the Pacific *B*
University of Southern California *B*
West Hills Community College *A*

Colorado
Colorado College *B*
University of Colorado
    Boulder *B*
    Denver *B*
University of Denver *M*
Western State College of
    Colorado *B*

Connecticut
Albertus Magnus College *B*
Connecticut College *B*
Southern Connecticut State
    University *B*
Trinity College *B*
University of Bridgeport *B*
University of Connecticut *M*
University of Hartford *B*
Wesleyan University *B*

District of Columbia
American University *B*
Catholic University of America *B,M*
Gallaudet University *B*
University of the District of
    Columbia *B*

Florida
Florida Southern College *B*
Florida State University *B,M*
Jacksonville University *B*
New College of the University of
    South Florida *B*
Pensacola Junior College *A*
Rollins College *B*
University of Miami *M*
University of West Florida *B*

Georgia
Atlanta College of Art *B*
Augusta College *B*
Brenau Women's College *B*
Clayton State College *A*
Gainesville College *A*
Georgia State University *B,M*
Macon College *A*
Mercer University *B*
Piedmont College *B*
Shorter College *B*
Wesleyan College *B*

Hawaii
Chaminade University of
    Honolulu *B*

Illinois
Barat College *B*
Blackburn College *B*
Chicago State University *B*
De Paul University *B*
Illinois Wesleyan University *B*
John A. Logan College *A*
Knox College *B*
Lake Forest College *B*
North Central College *B*
Northeastern Illinois University *B*
Northern Illinois University *B,M*
Olivet Nazarene University *B*
Principia College *B*
Quincy College *B*
School of the Art Institute of
    Chicago *B,M*
Southern Illinois University
    Carbondale *B*
    Edwardsville *B,M*
Trinity Christian College *B*
University of Chicago *M*
University of Illinois at Chicago *B*
Wheaton College *B*

Indiana
Ball State University *M*
DePauw University *B*
Franklin College *A,B*
Huntington College *B*
Indiana Wesleyan University *B*
Marian College *B*
St. Mary-of-the-Woods College *B*
St. Mary's College *B*
Taylor University *B*
University of Evansville *B*
University of Indianapolis *B*
University of Notre Dame *B,M*
Vincennes University *A*

Iowa
Clarke College *A,B*
Drake University *B*
Iowa Lakes Community College *A*
Loras College *B*
Morningside College *B*
St. Ambrose University *B*
Simpson College *B*
University of Iowa *B,M*

Kansas
Central College *A*
Kansas Wesleyan University *B*
St. Mary College *B*
Wichita State University *B,M*

Kentucky
Asbury College *B*
Bellarmine College *A,B*
Berea College *B*
Brescia College *B*
Kentucky State University *B*
Lindsey Wilson College *A*
Morehead State University *B,M*
Murray State University *B,M*
Northern Kentucky University *B*
Spalding University *B*
Thomas More College *A,B*
Transylvania University *B*
University of Kentucky *B,M*
University of Louisville *B,M*
Western Kentucky University *B*

Louisiana
Louisiana State University and
    Agricultural and Mechanical
    College *M*
Louisiana Tech University *B,M*
Tulane University *B,M*
University of New Orleans *B*

Maine
Bowdoin College *B*
Colby College *B*
University of Maine *B*

Maryland
Howard Community College *A*
Montgomery College: Rockville
    Campus *A*
Towson State University *B,M*
University of Maryland: College
    Park *B*
Western Maryland College *B*

Massachusetts
Anna Maria College for Men and
    Women *B*
Boston College *B*
Bradford College *B*
Bridgewater State College *B*
Clark University *B*
College of the Holy Cross *B*
Emmanuel College *B*
Framingham State College *B*
Hampshire College *B*
Holyoke Community College *A*
Massachusetts College of Art *B,M*
Montserrat College of Art *B*
Mount Holyoke College *B*
School of the Museum of Fine Arts
    C,B,M
Smith College *B*
University of Massachusetts at
    Amherst *B,M*
Wellesley College *B*

Michigan
Eastern Michigan University *M*
Kalamazoo College *B*
Kellogg Community College *A*
Lansing Community College *A*
Michigan State University *B,M*
Siena Heights College *B*
West Shore Community College *A*

Minnesota
Augsburg College *B*
Bethel College *B*
Carleton College *B*
College of Associated Arts *B*
College of St. Catherine: St.
    Catherine Campus *B*
Concordia College: Moorhead *B*
Hamline University *B*
Rochester Community College *A*
St. Cloud State University *B*
St. Mary's College of Minnesota *B*
St. Olaf College *B*
University of Minnesota
    Duluth *B*
    Morris *B*
    Twin Cities *B,M*
Willmar Community College *A*
Winona State University *B*

Mississippi
Mississippi University for Women *B*

Missouri
Avila College *B*
Central Missouri State University *B*
Culver-Stockton College *B*
Kansas City Art Institute *B*
Lindenwood College *B,M*
Maryville University *B*
Northeast Missouri State
    University *B*
Northwest Missouri State
    University *B*
Stephens College *B*
University of Missouri: Kansas City
    B,M
Webster University *B*
Westminster College *B*
William Jewell College *B*
William Woods College *B*

Montana
University of Montana *B,M*

Nebraska
Concordia College *B*
Creighton University *B*
Dana College *B*
Union College *A,B*
University of Nebraska—Omaha *B*

New Hampshire
Dartmouth College *B*
Franklin Pierce College *B*
Plymouth State College of the
    University System of New
    Hampshire *B*
Rivier College *A,B*
University of New Hampshire
    Durham *B*
    Manchester *A*

New Jersey
Atlantic Community College *A*
Caldwell College *B*
Drew University *B*
Georgian Court College *B*
Jersey City State College *B*
Kean College of New Jersey *B*
Montclair State College *B*
Rutgers—The State University of
New Jersey
Mason Gross School of the
Arts *B,M*
New Brunswick *M*
Trenton State College *B*

New Mexico
Institute of American Indian
Arts *A*
University of New Mexico *B,M*

New York
Adelphi University *M*
Cazenovia College *A*
City University of New York
Brooklyn College *M*
City College *B*
College of Staten Island *B*
Hunter College *B,M*
Lehman College *B*
Queens College *B*
College of New Rochelle *M*
College of St. Rose *B*
Community College of the Finger
Lakes *A*
Cooper Union *B*
Elmira College *B*
Fordham University *B*
Hamilton College *B*
Hobart College *B*
Ithaca College *B*
Long Island University
C. W. Post Campus *B*
Southampton Campus *B*
Manhattanville College *B*
Marymount College *B*
Marymount Manhattan College *B*
Nazareth College of Rochester *B*
New York University *B,M,D*
Pace University: Pleasantville/
Briarcliff *B*
Parsons School of Design *A,B,M*
Pratt Institute *B,M*
Rochester Institute of Technology
A,B,M
St. Thomas Aquinas College *B*
Sarah Lawrence College *B*
School of Visual Arts *B*
Skidmore College *B*
State University of New York
Albany *B,M*
Binghamton *B*
Buffalo *B*
Stony Brook *B,M*
College at Brockport *B*
College at Buffalo *B*
College at Cortland *B*
College at Fredonia *B*
College at Geneseo *B*
College at Oneonta *B*
College at Plattsburgh *B*
College at Potsdam *B*
Oswego *M*
University of Rochester *B*
Vassar College *B*
Wells College *B*
William Smith College *B*

North Carolina
Barton College *B*
Brevard College *A*
Chowan College *B*
Davidson College *B*

Greensboro College *B*
Guilford College *B*
Mars Hill College *B*
Queens College *B*
Salem College *B*
Sandhills Community College *A*
University of North Carolina
Chapel Hill *B,M,D*
Greensboro *B,M*
Wake Forest University *B*
Wingate College *B*

North Dakota
Valley City State University *B*

Ohio
Art Academy of Cincinnati *B*
Baldwin-Wallace College *B*
Bluffton College *B*
Cleveland State University *B*
College of Wooster *B*
Denison University *B*
Hiram College *B*
Kent State University *B,M*
Kenyon College *B*
Lourdes College *A*
Marietta College *B*
Mount Union College *B*
Notre Dame College of Ohio *B*
Oberlin College *B*
Ohio University *B,M*
University of Akron *B*
Youngstown State University *B*

Oklahoma
Cameron University *B*
Oklahoma Baptist University *B*
Oklahoma Christian University of
Science and Arts *B*
Oklahoma City University *M*
Oklahoma State University *B*
Oral Roberts University *B*
Phillips University *B*

Oregon
Oregon State University *B*
Willamette University *B*

Pennsylvania
Allegheny College *B*
Bloomsburg University of
Pennsylvania *B,M*
Bucknell University *B*
Carnegie Mellon University *B,M*
Chestnut Hill College *A,B*
Clarion University of
Pennsylvania *B*
Community College of
Philadelphia *A*
Eastern College *B*
Edinboro University of
Pennsylvania *B*
Franklin and Marshall College *B*
Gettysburg College *B*
Immaculata College *A*
Indiana University of
Pennsylvania *B*
Keystone Junior College *A*
Kutztown University of
Pennsylvania *B*
Lehigh University *B*
Mansfield University of
Pennsylvania *B*
Marywood College *M*
Mercyhurst College *B*
Moore College of Art and Design *B*
Moravian College *B*
Northeastern Christian Junior
College *A*
St. Vincent College *B*
Seton Hill College *B*
Thiel College *B*

University of Pittsburgh *B*
West Chester University of
Pennsylvania *B*
Westminster College *B*

Rhode Island
Brown University *B,M,D*
Providence College *B*
Rhode Island College *B,M*
Roger Williams College *B*
Salve Regina University *B*
University of Rhode Island *B*

South Carolina
Anderson College *B*
College of Charleston *B*
Columbia College *B*
Converse College *B*
Francis Marion College *B*
Limestone College *B*
Newberry College *B*
University of South Carolina
Coastal Carolina College *B*
Columbia *B,M*

South Dakota
University of South Dakota *B,M*

Tennessee
David Lipscomb University *B*
East Tennessee State University *B*
Lambuth University *B*
Martin Methodist College *A*
Memphis College of Art *B,M*
Memphis State University *M*
Middle Tennessee State
University *B*
Rhodes College *B*
University of the South *B*
University of Tennessee
Knoxville *B*
Martin *B*

Texas
Baylor University *B*
Bee County College *A*
Del Mar College *A*
El Paso Community College *C*
Howard Payne University *B*
Lamar University—Beaumont *B*
Lon Morris College *A*
Rice University *B,M*
Sam Houston State University *B*
San Antonio Art Institute *B*
Southern Methodist University *B,M*
Southwest Texas State University *B*
Sul Ross State University *B*
Texas Christian University *B,M*
Texas College *B*
Texas Tech University *B*
Texas Woman's University *B,M*
University of Texas
Austin *B,M*
El Paso *B,M*
Permian Basin *B*

Utah
Brigham Young University *B*

Vermont
Bennington College *B*
Castleton State College *B*
Johnson State College *B*
Marlboro College *B*
St. Michael's College *B*
University of Vermont *B*

Virginia
Averett College *B*
Emory and Henry College *B*
George Mason University *B*
Hollins College *B*

Lynchburg College *B*
Mary Baldwin College *B*
Mary Washington College *B*
Radford University *B,M*
Randolph-Macon Woman's
College *B*
Sweet Briar College *B*
University of Richmond *B*
University of Virginia *B*
Virginia Wesleyan College *B*
Washington and Lee University *B*

Washington
Eastern Washington University *B*
Evergreen State College *B*
Pacific Lutheran University *B*
Tacoma Community College *A*
University of Puget Sound *B*
Wenatchee Valley College *A*
Western Washington University
B,M
Whitman College *B*
Whitworth College *B*

West Virginia
Bethany College *B*
Concord College *B*
Shepherd College *B*
West Virginia University *B,M*
West Virginia Wesleyan College *B*

Wisconsin
Alverno College *B*
Beloit College *B*
Cardinal Stritch College *B*
Lawrence University *B*
Mount Senario College *B*
Ripon College *B*
Silver Lake College *B*
University of Wisconsin
Green Bay *B*
River Falls *B*

Surgical technology

Alabama
Community College of the Air
Force *A*

Arkansas
University of Arkansas for Medical
Sciences *C,A*
Westark Community College *C,A*

Colorado
Community College of Denver *A*

Connecticut
Manchester Community College *A*

Florida
Central Florida Community
College *C*
Daytona Beach Community
College *C*

Georgia
Athens Area Technical Institute *C*
Augusta Technical Institute *C*
Brunswick College *C*
DeKalb College *A*
Gainesville College *A*
Savannah Technical Institute *C*

Idaho
Boise State University *C*

Illinois

Elgin Community College *C*
Illinois Central College *C*
Parkland College *C*
Triton College *C*
William Rainey Harper College *C*

Indiana

Indiana Vocational Technical
   College
      Central Indiana *C*
      Lafayette *C*
      Northwest *C*
      Southwest *C*
Lutheran College of Health
   Professions *C*
Vincennes University *C*

Louisiana

Bossier Parish Community
   College *C*
Southern University in
   Shreveport *A*

Maine

Southern Maine Technical
   College *A*

Massachusetts

Essex Agricultural and Technical
   Institute *C*
Middlesex Community College *C,A*
Quincy College *C*
Springfield Technical Community
   College *A*

Michigan

Baker College
      Flint *A*
      Muskegon *A*
Delta College *C,A*
Kalamazoo Valley Community
   College *C*
Lansing Community College *A*

Minnesota

University of Minnesota: Twin
   Cities *M,D*

Mississippi

Hinds Community College *C,A*

Missouri

St. Louis Community College at
   Forest Park *A*

Nebraska

Southeast Community College:
   Lincoln Campus *C*

New Hampshire

New Hampshire Technical College:
   Stratham *C*

New Jersey

Bergen Community College *C*
University of Medicine and
   Dentistry of New Jersey: School
   of Health Related Professions *C*

New York

Nassau Community College *A*
Niagara County Community
   College *C*
Onondaga Community College *C,A*
Trocaire College *C,A*

North Carolina

Blue Ridge Community College *C*
Catawba Valley Community
   College *C*

Coastal Carolina Community
   College *C*
Edgecombe Community College *C*
Fayetteville Technical Community
   College *C*
Guilford Technical Community
   College *C*
Sandhills Community College *C*
Wilson Technical Community
   College *C*

Ohio

Cincinnati Technical College *A*
Columbus State Community
   College *A*
Cuyahoga Community College:
   Western Campus *A*
Owens Technical College
      Findlay Campus *A*
      Toledo *A*
Sinclair Community College *A*
University of Akron *A*

Oregon

Mount Hood Community
   College *A*

Pennsylvania

Delaware County Community
   College *A*
Luzerne County Community
   College *C,A*
Mount Aloysius College *C*
Pennsylvania College of
   Technology *C*

South Carolina

Florence-Darlington Technical
   College *C*
Greenville Technical College *C*
Midlands Technical College *C*
Tri-County Technical College *C*

South Dakota

Presentation College *C*

Tennessee

Chattanooga State Technical
   Community College *C*
East Tennessee State University *A*
Nashville State Technical
   Institute *C*

Texas

Amarillo College *C*
Austin Community College *C,A*
Del Mar College *A*
El Centro College *C*
El Paso Community College *A*
Houston Community College *C*
Kilgore College *A*
Odessa College *C,A*
St. Philip's College *C*
South Plains College *C*
Tarrant County Junior College *C*
Temple Junior College *C*
Texas State Technical College:
   Harlingen *C*
Trinity Valley Community
   College *C*

Washington

Seattle Central Community
   College *A*
Spokane Community College *C,A*

West Virginia

West Virginia Northern Community
   College *A*

Wisconsin

Mid-State Technical College *C*
Northeast Wisconsin Technical
   College *C*
Waukesha County Technical
   College *A*
Western Wisconsin Technical
   College *C*

Survey and mapping technology

Alabama

Community College of the Air
   Force *A*

Alaska

University of Alaska Anchorage
   A,B

California

Chabot College *A*
City College of San Francisco *C*
Palomar College *C,A*
Saddleback College *C,A*
Sierra College *A*

Colorado

Denver Institute of Technology *A*
Denver Technical College *A*
Metropolitan State College of
   Denver *B*
Red Rocks Community College *A*
Trinidad State Junior College *A*

Florida

Edison Community College *C*
Palm Beach Community College *A*
Valencia Community College *A*

Illinois

Black Hawk College *C*
Morrison Institute of Technology *A*

Indiana

Vincennes University *A*

Iowa

Hawkeye Institute of Technology *A*

Kentucky

Western Kentucky University *A*

Maryland

Catonsville Community College *A*
Montgomery College: Rockville
   Campus *A*

Massachusetts

Northeastern University *A*
Wentworth Institute of
   Technology *B*

Michigan

Ferris State University *A,B*
Lansing Community College *A*

Missouri

Southwest Missouri State
   University *B*

Nebraska

Southeast Community College:
   Milford Campus *A*

New Jersey

County College of Morris *C*
Gloucester County College *A*

Mercer County Community
   College *C*
Ocean County College *A*
Thomas Edison State College *A,B*

New Mexico

Albuquerque Technical-Vocational
   Institute *C*

New York

Mohawk Valley Community College
   C,A
Monroe Community College *C*
Orange County Community
   College *C*
Paul Smith's College *A*
State University of New York
   College of Environmental
      Science and Forestry *A*
   College of Technology at
      Alfred *A,B*
Sullivan County Community
   College *A*

North Carolina

Asheville Buncombe Technical
   Community College *A*
Coastal Carolina Community
   College *A*
Gaston College *C*
Guilford Technical Community
   College *C,A*
Sandhills Community College *A*
Wake Technical Community
   College *A*

Ohio

Cincinnati Technical College *A*
Columbus State Community
   College *C*
Sinclair Community College *C*
University of Akron *A*

Oklahoma

Oklahoma State University:
   Oklahoma City *A*

Oregon

Oregon Institute of Technology *B*
Treasure Valley Community
   College *A*

Pennsylvania

Penn State University Park
   Campus *A*

Puerto Rico

University of Puerto Rico: Bayamon
   Technological University
   College *A*

South Carolina

Midlands Technical College *C*
Trident Technical College *C*

South Dakota

National College *C,A*

Tennessee

Chattanooga State Technical
   Community College *A*
East Tennessee State University
   A,B

Texas

Austin Community College *A*
University of Houston *B*

Virginia

John Tyler Community College *C*

Washington

Spokane Community College *A*

West Virginia

Glenville State College *A*
Potomac State College of West
Virginia University *C*
West Virginia Institute of
Technology *A*

Wyoming

Sheridan College *C*

Surveying and mapping sciences

Alabama

Community College of the Air
Force *A*

Alaska

University of Alaska Anchorage *B*

California

California State University:
Fresno *B*
Mount San Antonio College *C,A*
Sierra College *A*

Florida

Miami-Dade Community College *A*
University of Florida *B*

Georgia

Savannah Technical Institute *C*

Illinois

Lincoln Land Community
College *C*

Indiana

Purdue University *B,M,D*
Vincennes University *A*

Maine

University of Maine *B,M,D*

Michigan

Michigan Technological
University *B*

Missouri

East Central College *A*

Montana

Flathead Valley Community
College *A*

Nebraska

Southeast Community College:
Milford Campus *A*

New York

Paul Smith's College *A*
State University of New York
College of Environmental Science
and Forestry *B,M,D*

North Carolina

Asheville Buncombe Technical
Community College *A*

Ohio

Ohio State University: Columbus
Campus *B,M,D*
University of Toledo *C*

Pennsylvania

Spring Garden College *B*

Puerto Rico

Universidad Politecnica de Puerto
Rico *B*

Tennessee

Pellissippi State Technical
Community College *C*

Texas

Southwest Texas State University
B,M

West Virginia

Glenville State College *A*

Systems analysis

Arkansas

Harding University *B*

California

California State University:
Fresno *B*
Cerritos Community College *A*
College of Marin: Kentfield *A*
Glendale Community College *C*
Irvine Valley College *C,A*
Phillips Junior College: Fresno
Campus *C,A*
San Diego City College *A*
Southwestern College *A*
University of California: San Diego
B,M,D
West Coast University *M*

Colorado

University of Denver *B*

Connecticut

Quinnipiac College *B,M*

District of Columbia

George Washington University *M,D*

Florida

Gulf Coast Community College *C,A*
Manatee Community College *A*
Nova University *B*
Palm Beach Community College *A*
St. Petersburg Junior College *A*
Tampa College *B*
University of Miami *B*

Georgia

Georgia Southwestern College *B*

Hawaii

Hawaii Pacific University *A,B*

Illinois

Bradley University *B*
Concordia University *B*
De Paul University *M*
Northwestern University *B,M*
Southern Illinois University at
Carbondale *A*

Indiana

Indiana State University *B*
Purdue University *B*
Taylor University *C*

Iowa

American Institute of Commerce *A*
Central College *B*

Kentucky

University of Louisville *B*

Maryland

Catonsville Community College *C,A*
Prince George's Community
College *A*

Massachusetts

Hampshire College *B*
Massachusetts Institute of
Technology *B,M,D,W*
Northeastern University *C,M*
Tufts University *B*
Worcester Polytechnic Institute
B,M

Michigan

Alma College *B*
Detroit College of Business *B*
Eastern Michigan University *B,M*
Kellogg Community College *C,A*
Lansing Community College *A*
Marygrove College *B*
Oakland Community College *A*
University of Detroit Mercy *B*

Minnesota

Mankato State University *B*
Winona State University *B*

Missouri

College of the Ozarks *B*
Missouri Southern State College *A*
Rockhurst College *B*
St. Louis Community College at
Forest Park *A*
Washington University *B,M,D*

Nebraska

Southeast Community College:
Milford Campus *A*
University of Nebraska—Omaha *B*

New Hampshire

Daniel Webster College *A,B*
New Hampshire College *B*

New Jersey

Bloomfield College *C*
Caldwell College *C*
Stevens Institute of Technology
B,M,D
Stockton State College *B*

New Mexico

Clovis Community College *A*
New Mexico Institute of Mining
and Technology *B,M,D*

New York

Bramson ORT Technical
Institute *C*
City University of New York:
Baruch College *B,M*
Clarkson University *B,M*
Elmira College *B*
Rochester Institute of Technology
B,M
State University of New York
Binghamton *B,M,D*
College at Plattsburgh *B*
University of Rochester *M,D*
Westchester Business Institute *A*

North Carolina

Western Piedmont Community
College *A*

Ohio

Air Force Institute of
Technology *M*

Central State University *B*
Cincinnati Metropolitan College *A*
Miami University: Oxford
Campus *B*
Ohio State University: Columbus
Campus *B,M,D*
Ohio University *B,M*
Union Institute *D*
University of Akron *B*
University of Cincinnati *B,M*
University of Findlay *B*
University of Toledo *B,M*

Oklahoma

Oklahoma State University:
Oklahoma City *A*

Oregon

Linfield College *B*

Pennsylvania

Albright College *B*
Carnegie Mellon University
B,M,D,W
Clarion University of
Pennsylvania *B*
Drexel University *B*
Duquesne University *B*
Indiana University of
Pennsylvania *B*
King's College *A,B*
Mansfield University of
Pennsylvania *B*
Robert Morris College *B,M*

Puerto Rico

Caribbean University *B*
Universidad Adventista de las
Antillas *B*

Rhode Island

Brown University *B,M,D*

South Dakota

Mitchell Vocational Technical
Institute *C,A*

Tennessee

Belmont University *B*
Motlow State Community
College *A*
Tennessee Technological
University *B*
University of Tennessee:
Chattanooga *B*

Texas

Central Texas College *A*
University of Houston *B*
West Texas State University *B*

Virginia

Averett College *B*

Washington

Central Washington University *B*
Evergreen State College *B*
Olympic College *C,A*
Pacific Lutheran University *B,M*

West Virginia

Marshall University *B*
Shepherd College *B*

Wisconsin

University of Wisconsin
Oshkosh *B*
Superior *B*

Wyoming

Western Wyoming Community
College *A*

Systems engineering

Alabama
University of Alabama in Huntsville
B,M,D

Arizona
University of Arizona B,M,D

California
California State University
Fullerton M
Northridge M
University of California: San Diego
B,M,D
West Coast University M

Colorado
Pikes Peak Community College A
University of Southern Colorado M

District of Columbia
Howard University M

Florida
Florida Atlantic University M
Florida State University B,M
University of Florida B

Georgia
Georgia Institute of Technology
B,M,D

Louisiana
University of Southwestern
Louisiana M

Maryland
United States Naval Academy B
University of Maryland: College
Park M

Massachusetts
Boston University B,M,D
Eastern Nazarene College B
Harvard and Radcliffe Colleges B
University of Massachusetts at
Lowell M
Worcester Polytechnic Institute B

Michigan
GMI Engineering & Management
Institute B
Oakland University B,M,D
University of Michigan M,D

Missouri
Washington University B,M,D

New York
Polytechnic University
Brooklyn M,D
Long Island Campus M,D
Rensselaer Polytechnic Institute
B,M,D
State University of New York
College of Environmental Science
and Forestry M,D
United States Military Academy B

Ohio
Air Force Institute of
Technology M
Case Western Reserve University
B,M,D
Ohio State University: Columbus
Campus B,M,D
Ohio University B,M

Oklahoma
Oklahoma State University M

Pennsylvania
Carnegie Mellon University
B,M,D,W
Lehigh University M
University of Pennsylvania B,M,D

Rhode Island
Providence College B

Tennessee
Memphis State University M

Texas
University of Houston M,D

Virginia
George Mason University B,M
University of Virginia B,M,D
Virginia Polytechnic Institute and
State University M

Mexico
Sistema Instituto Tecnologico y de
Estudios Superiores de
Monterrey M

Taxation

Alabama
University of Alabama M

Arizona
Arizona State University M

California
California State University
Fullerton M
Hayward B,M
Northridge M
De Anza College C
Golden Gate University B,M
Grossmont Community College C,A
National University M
San Jose State University M
University of Southern California M

Colorado
University of Denver M

Connecticut
Manchester Community College C
Quinnipiac College B,M
University of Hartford M
University of New Haven M

District of Columbia
American University M
George Washington University M
Georgetown University M
Southeastern University M

Florida
Broward Community College C
Florida International University M
University of Central Florida M
University of Florida M
University of Miami M

Georgia
Georgia State University M
Mercer University Atlanta M

Illinois
De Paul University M
Northern Illinois University M

Indiana
Indiana State University B

Louisiana
University of New Orleans M

Maryland
Prince George's Community
College C
University of Baltimore M

Massachusetts
Bentley College M

Michigan
Grand Valley State University M
Walsh College of Accountancy and
Business Administration M

Minnesota
University of Minnesota: Twin
Cities M

Missouri
Fontbonne College M

New Jersey
Fairleigh Dickinson University M
Seton Hall University M

New Mexico
University of New Mexico M

New York
City University of New York:
Baruch College M
Hofstra University M
Iona College M
Long Island University
Brooklyn Campus M
C. W. Post Campus M
New York University C,M,D
Pace University
College of White Plains M
New York M
St. John's University M

Ohio
Cincinnati Metropolitan College A
Union Institute B,D
University of Akron M
University of Cincinnati M
University of Toledo M

Oklahoma
University of Tulsa M

Oregon
Portland State University M

Pennsylvania
Drexel University M
Penn State University Park
Campus C
Philadelphia College of Textiles and
Science M
Robert Morris College M
Temple University M
Villanova University M
Widener University M

Rhode Island
Bryant College M

South Carolina
Midlands Technical College C
University of South Carolina M

Texas
Baylor University M
Navarro College A
Texas Southmost College A

University of Texas at Arlington M

Utah
Brigham Young University M

Virginia
College of William and Mary M
George Mason University M
Virginia Commonwealth
University M

Washington
Seattle University M
Spokane Falls Community
College A

Wisconsin
Waukesha County Technical
College A

Teacher aide

Alabama
Alabama State University A
Lawson State Community
College A

Arizona
Cochise College C
Mesa Community College C
Northland Pioneer College C,A
Pima Community College C
Scottsdale Community College A

Arkansas
John Brown University A
University of Central Arkansas C
Westark Community College A

California
Barstow College C,A
Cerritos Community College A
Chabot College A
Chaffey Community College A
City College of San Francisco C,A
Columbia College C
Compton Community College A
Cuesta College A
East Los Angeles College C,A
El Camino College A
Fresno City College A
Hartnell College A
Los Angeles Mission College A
Mount St. Mary's College A
Mount San Jacinto College C,A
Ohlone College A
Palomar College A
Saddleback College A
San Jose City College A
Santa Rosa Junior College C,A
Sierra College C,A
Solano Community College A
Southwestern College C,A
Victor Valley College A

Colorado
Otero Junior College A
Trinidad State Junior College A

Connecticut
Manchester Community College A
Norwalk Community College A
South Central Community
College A

Florida
Daytona Beach Community
College A
Edison Community College A

Florida Community College at
Jacksonville *A*
Indian River Community College *A*
South Florida Community
College *A*

Georgia

Abraham Baldwin Agricultural
College *A*
Atlanta Metropolitan College *A*
Floyd College *A*
Georgia Southern University *A*
Middle Georgia College *C*
South College *C*

Illinois

Black Hawk College *C*
City Colleges of Chicago
Chicago City-Wide College *A*
Richard J. Daley College *A*
Illinois Eastern Community
Colleges
Frontier Community
College *C*
Lincoln Trail College *A*
Illinois Valley Community
College *A*
John A. Logan College *A*
Joliet Junior College *C,A*
Lake Land College *A*
Lewis and Clark Community
College *C*
Lincoln Land Community
College *C*
Olivet Nazarene University *A*
Prairie State College *A*
Rend Lake College *A*
Richland Community College *A*
Shawnee Community College *C*
Spoon River College *A*

Indiana

Ball State University *A*
Indiana State University *A*
Indiana University—Purdue
University at Fort Wayne *A*
Vincennes University *A*

Iowa

Des Moines Area Community
College *A*
Dordt College *A*
Iowa Central Community College *A*
Kirkwood Community College *A*
North Iowa Area Community
College *A*
Vennard College *A*

Kansas

Colby Community College *A*
Dodge City Community College *A*
Friends University *A*
Neosho County Community
College *A*

Kentucky

Union College *A*

Louisiana

Louisiana College *A*
Southern University in
Shreveport *A*

Maine

University of Maine
Fort Kent *A*
Presque Isle *C*

Maryland

Allegany Community College *A*
Chesapeake College *A*
Hagerstown Junior College *A*

Montgomery College: Rockville
Campus *A*

Massachusetts

Aquinas College at Newton *A*
Atlantic Union College *A*
Becker College: Leicester
Campus *A*
Bridgewater State College *C*
Dean Junior College *A*
Endicott College *A*
Massachusetts Bay Community
College *C,A*
Mount Ida College *A*
North Shore Community College *C*

Michigan

Andrews University *A*
Kellogg Community College *C*
Kirtland Community College *C*
Muskegon Community College *A*
Southwestern Michigan College *A*
Suomi College *A*
West Shore Community College *A*

Minnesota

Concordia College: St. Paul *A*
Rainy River Community College *A*
Willmar Community College *A*

Mississippi

Jones County Junior College *A*
Mississippi Gulf Coast Community
College: Jefferson Davis
Campus *A*
Tougaloo College *A*

Missouri

East Central College *C,A*
Hannibal-LaGrange College *A*
St. Louis Community College
Florissant Valley *A*
Forest Park *A*

Nebraska

Central Community College *A*
Metropolitan Community College *C*
Midland Lutheran College *A*
Nebraska Wesleyan University *A*
Northeast Community College *A*
Peru State College *A*

Nevada

Community College of Southern
Nevada *C,A*
Northern Nevada Community
College *A*

New Hampshire

Notre Dame College *C,A*
Plymouth State College of the
University System of New
Hampshire *A*

New Jersey

Bergen Community College *A*
Brookdale Community College *A*
Burlington County College *A*
Mercer County Community
College *A*
Union County College *A*

New Mexico

Eastern New Mexico University
Portales *A*
Roswell Campus *A*
New Mexico Highlands
University *A*
New Mexico State University *C*
University of New Mexico *A*

New York

City University of New York
Kingsborough Community
College *A*
La Guardia Community
College *A*
Maria College *A*
Mater Dei College *A*
Nassau Community College *A*
New York Institute of
Technology *A*
St. John's University *A*
State University of New York
College of Technology at
Farmingdale *A*

North Carolina

Alamance Community College *A*
Anson Community College *A*
Catawba Valley Community
College *A*
Craven Community College *A*
Davidson County Community
College *A*
Edgecombe Community College *A*
Forsyth Technical Community
College *A*
Isothermal Community College *A*
McDowell Technical Community
College *A*
Nash Community College *A*
Pitt Community College *C*
Roanoke-Chowan Community
College *A*
Rockingham Community College *C*
Sandhills Community College *C,A*
Stanly Community College *C,A*
Vance-Granville Community
College *A*

North Dakota

Standing Rock College *A*

Ohio

Lourdes College *A*
University of Akron *A*
Washington State Community
College *C*

Oregon

Central Oregon Community
College *A*
Chemeketa Community College *C,A*
Portland Community College *C*

Pennsylvania

Bucks County Community
College *A*
California University of
Pennsylvania *A*
Edinboro University of
Pennsylvania *A*
Gannon University *A*
Harcum Junior College *A*
Harrisburg Area Community
College *A*
Montgomery County Community
College *A*
Mount Aloysius College *A*
Northampton County Area
Community College *A*
Reading Area Community
College *C*

Puerto Rico

Pontifical Catholic University of
Puerto Rico *A*
Turabo University *A*

South Carolina

Spartanburg Methodist College *A*

South Dakota

Oglala Lakota College *A*
Presentation College *A*
Sinte Gleska College *A*

Tennessee

Hiwassee College *A*

Texas

Angelina College *A*
Cisco Junior College *A*
Galveston College *A*
McLennan Community College *C,A*
Midland College *A*
Panola College *A*
Richland College *A*
St. Philip's College *C,A*

Utah

Dixie College *A*
Southern Utah University *A*

Vermont

Champlain College *A*
Johnson State College *A*

Virginia

Central Virginia Community
College *C*
Eastern Mennonite College *A*
John Tyler Community College *C*

Washington

Big Bend Community College *C,A*
Grays Harbor College *C*
North Seattle Community
College *A*
Shoreline Community College *C,A*
Tacoma Community College *A*
Wenatchee Valley College *A*

Wisconsin

Alverno College *A*

Wyoming

Eastern Wyoming College *A*

**American Samoa, Caroline
Islands, Guam, Marianas,
Virgin Islands**

Community College of
Micronesia *A*

Teaching English as a second language/foreign language

Alabama

University of Alabama *M*

Arizona

Arizona State University *M*
Grand Canyon University *M*
Northern Arizona University *M*
Prescott College *B*
University of Arizona *M*

California

Azusa Pacific University *M*
California State University
Dominguez Hills *M*
Fullerton *M*
Long Beach *C*
Los Angeles *M*
Chapman University *M*
Humboldt State University *C*
La Sierra University *B*
Monterey Institute of International
Studies *M*

San Francisco State University *M*
San Jose State University *M*
United States International
University *M*
University of California
Los Angeles *M*
San Diego *M*
University of the Pacific *B,M*
University of San Francisco *M*
University of Southern California *M*

Colorado
Fort Lewis College *B*
University of Colorado
Boulder *M,D*
Denver *M*

Connecticut
Central Connecticut State
University *M*

District of Columbia
Georgetown University *M*

Florida
Florida International University *M*
Nova University *M*
University of Miami *M*
University of South Florida *M*

Georgia
Georgia State University *M*

Hawaii
Brigham Young University-
Hawaii *B*
Hawaii Pacific University *B*
University of Hawaii at Manoa *B,M*

Idaho
University of Idaho *M*

Illinois
National-Louis University *M*
Northeastern Illinois University *M*
Northwestern University *M*
Southern Illinois University
Carbondale *B,M*
Edwardsville *M*
University of Illinois at Urbana-
Champaign *M*

Indiana
Ball State University *M*
Goshen College *C,B*
Indiana University Bloomington *M*
Vincennes University *A*

Iowa
Morningside College *B*
University of Northern Iowa *B,M*

Louisiana
Tulane University *M*

Maryland
University of Maryland Baltimore
County *M*

Massachusetts
Boston University *B,M,W*
Elms College *B*
University of Massachusetts at
Boston *M*

Michigan
Andrews University *B,M*
Eastern Michigan University *M*
Madonna University *W*
Wayne State University *M,D*
Western Michigan University *M*

Minnesota
Macalester College *B*
University of Minnesota
Duluth *C*
Twin Cities *B,M*

Missouri
Central Missouri State
University *M*

Nebraska
University of Nebraska—Kearney *B*

Nevada
University of Nevada: Reno *M*

New Hampshire
Notre Dame College *M*

New Jersey
Fairleigh Dickinson University *M*
Kean College of New Jersey *B,M*
Rutgers—The State University of
New Jersey *M,D*
Seton Hall University *M*

New Mexico
New Mexico State University *B*
University of New Mexico *B*

New York
Adelphi University *M*
City University of New York
Brooklyn College *B,M*
Hunter College *M*
Queens College *B,M*
College of New Rochelle *M*
Cornell University *M,D*
Hofstra University *M*
Le Moyne College *B*
Long Island University
Brooklyn Campus *M*
C. W. Post Campus *B,M*
Manhattanville College *M*
Mercy College *B*
Molloy College *B*
Nazareth College of Rochester *M*
New York University *M,D*
State University of New York
Albany *M*
Buffalo *M*
Stony Brook *B,M*
Syracuse University *M*
University of Rochester *M*

North Carolina
University of North Carolina at
Charlotte *M*

Ohio
Ohio Dominican College *B*
Ohio State University: Columbus
Campus *M*
Ohio University *M*
Union Institute *D*
University of Findlay *M*
University of Toledo *M*

Oklahoma
Bartlesville Wesleyan College *A,B*
Langston University *M*
Oklahoma Baptist University *B*
Oklahoma Christian University of
Science and Arts *B*
Oklahoma City University *M*
Oral Roberts University *M*

Oregon
Portland State University *M*
Western Oregon State College *B*

Pennsylvania
Gannon University *B*
Indiana University of
Pennsylvania *M*
Penn State University Park
Campus *M*
Temple University *M*
University of Pennsylvania *M,D*
West Chester University of
Pennsylvania *M*

Puerto Rico
American University of Puerto
Rico *B*
Inter American University of Puerto
Rico
Arecibo Campus *B*
Metropolitan Campus *B,M*
San German Campus *B,M*
Pontifical Catholic University of
Puerto Rico *B,M*
University of Puerto Rico
Humacao University College *B*
Mayaguez Campus *M*
Rio Piedras Campus *B,M*

Rhode Island
Rhode Island College *M*

Texas
Jacksonville College *A*
Texas Southmost College *A*
University of Houston *M*
University of Texas at San
Antonio *M*
West Texas State University *B*

Utah
Brigham Young University *M*

Vermont
St. Michael's College *M*
School for International Training *M*

Virginia
College of William and Mary *M*
Old Dominion University *M*
Radford University *M*
Virginia Polytechnic Institute and
State University *B,M*

Washington
Central Washington University *M*
Eastern Washington University *M*
University of Washington *B,M*
Whitworth College *M*

West Virginia
West Virginia University *B,M*

Wisconsin
University of Wisconsin:
Milwaukee *B*

Canada
McGill University *C,B,M*

Arab Republic of Egypt
American University in Cairo *M*

Technical and business writing

Alabama
Judson College *B*

Arkansas
University of Arkansas at Little
Rock *B,M*

California
California State University: Chico *C*
Chabot College *A*
De Anza College *C,A*
Humboldt State University *C*
Irvine Valley College *A*
Long Beach City College *C*
Orange Coast College *A*
Point Loma Nazarene College *B*
University of Redlands *B*

Colorado
Front Range Community College *A*

Delaware
University of Delaware *B*

Florida
Florida Institute of Technology *B,M*

Illinois
Black Hawk College *A*
Chicago State University *B*
College of Lake County *C,A*
Rosary College *B*

Indiana
Indiana Institute of Technology *B*
Manchester College *A*

Iowa
Teikyo Marycrest University *B*
University of Iowa *M*

Louisiana
Louisiana Tech University *B*

Maryland
Towson State University *M*
University of Baltimore *M*

Massachusetts
Clark University *C*
Fitchburg State College *B*
North Shore Community College *C*
Northeastern University *C,M*
University of Massachusetts
Boston *C*
Dartmouth *B,M*
Wentworth Institute of
Technology *B*
Worcester Polytechnic Institute *B*

Michigan
Eastern Michigan University *B*
Madonna University *B*
Northern Michigan University *M*

Minnesota
Concordia College: Moorhead *B*
Mankato State University *B*

Missouri
St. Louis Community College
Florissant Valley *A*
Meramec *C*
Webster University *B*

Montana
Carroll College *B*
Montana College of Mineral
Science and Technology *A,B*

New Jersey
Essex County College *A*

New Mexico
College of Santa Fe *B*
New Mexico Institute of Mining
and Technology *B*
University of New Mexico *B*

New York
Bramson ORT Technical
    Institute *A*
Clarkson University *B*
New York Institute of
    Technology *B*
Paul Smith's College *A*
Rensselaer Polytechnic Institute
    M,D
Rochester Institute of
    Technology *C*
State University of New York
    Institute of Technology at Utica/
    Rome *B*

North Carolina
East Carolina University *B*

Ohio
Bowling Green State University
    B,M
Cedarville College *B*
Cincinnati Technical College *C,A*
Miami University: Oxford Campus
    B,M
Terra Technical College *A*
University of Findlay *B*
Youngstown State University *B*

Oklahoma
East Central University *B*
Oklahoma State University:
    Oklahoma City *A·*

Oregon
Portland Community College *C*

Pennsylvania
California University of
    Pennsylvania *B*
Carnegie Mellon University *B,M*
Drexel University *M*
Edinboro University of
    Pennsylvania *B*
Elizabethtown College *B*
Immaculata College *B*
La Roche College *B*
Penn State University Park
    Campus *C*
Slippery Rock University of
    Pennsylvania *B*
Spring Garden College *B*

Rhode Island
Bryant College *B*

South Carolina
Bob Jones University *B*

South Dakota
Dakota State University *B*

Tennessee
Tennessee Technological
    University *B*

Texas
Austin Community College *A*
El Paso Community College *A*
Houston Community College *C,A*
University of Houston:
    Downtown *B*

Virginia
Northern Virginia Community
    College *C*

Washington
Clark College *A*
Eastern Washington University *B*
Tacoma Community College *A*
Wenatchee Valley College *A*

West Virginia
Alderson-Broaddus College *B*
West Virginia State College *B*

Wisconsin
Marquette University *B*

Technical education

Alabama
Livingston University *B*
Tuskegee University *B,M*

Arkansas
Ouachita Baptist University *B*
University of Arkansas *B*

California
National University *B*

Colorado
Colorado State University *B,M,D*

Connecticut
Central Connecticut State
    University *B,M*
University of Connecticut *D*

Florida
Florida International University
    B,M
Pensacola Junior College *A*
University of North Florida *B*
University of West Florida *B*

Idaho
Boise State University *M*
Idaho State University *B*
Ricks College *A*

Illinois
Southern Illinois University at
    Carbondale *B,M,D*
University of Illinois at Urbana-
    Champaign *B*

Indiana
Indiana State University *B,M*

Kansas
Pittsburg State University *M*

Kentucky
Morehead State University *A*
Western Kentucky University *A,B*

Louisiana
McNeese State University *M*

Michigan
Ferris State University *B*
Western Michigan University *B*

Minnesota
Mankato State University *B*
University of Minnesota: Duluth *B*

Mississippi
Alcorn State University *B*
Mississippi State University *M*
University of Southern
    Mississippi *B*

Montana
Eastern Montana College *M*
Northern Montana College *B*

Nebraska
University of Nebraska—Lincoln *B*

New Jersey
Rutgers—The State University of
    New Jersey
    Cook College *B*
    New Brunswick *M,D*
    University College New
        Brunswick *B*

New Mexico
New Mexico Highlands
    University *B*
University of New Mexico *B,M,D*

New York
New York Institute of Technology
    A,B
Russell Sage College *B*
State University of New York
    College at Buffalo *B,M*

North Carolina
East Carolina University *B,M*
North Carolina State University *B*

North Dakota
University of North Dakota *M*
Valley City State University *B*

Ohio
Bowling Green State University
    B,M
Heidelberg College *B*
Ohio State University: Columbus
    Campus *M,D*
University of Toledo *B*

Oklahoma
Oklahoma State University *B,M*
Southeastern Oklahoma State
    University *B*

Pennsylvania
California University of
    Pennsylvania *B,M*
Cheyney University of Pennsylvania
    B,M
West Chester University of
    Pennsylvania *M*

Rhode Island
Community College of Rhode
    Island *A*
Rhode Island College *B*

South Dakota
Dakota State University *B*
South Dakota State University *B*

Tennessee
Memphis State University *M*
University of Tennessee: Knoxville
    B,M,D

Texas
East Texas State University *M*
Texas A&M University *B*
University of Houston *B*
University of North Texas *M,D*
University of Texas at Tyler *B*

Virginia
Virginia Polytechnic Institute and
    State University *B,M,D*

Washington
Eastern Washington University *B*

West Virginia
Fairmont State College *B*

Wisconsin
University of Wisconsin: Green
    Bay *B*

Telecommunications

Alabama
Alabama Agricultural and
    Mechanical University *B*
Community College of the Air
    Force *A*
Gadsden State Community College
    C,A
Judson College *B*
University of Alabama *B,M*

Arizona
Northern Arizona University *B*
Pima Community College *C,A*

California
California State University
    Fresno *B*
    Los Angeles *B*
Chabot College *A*
Chapman University *B*
Coastline Community College *C,A*
Columbia College: Hollywood *A,B*
Cuesta College *A*
DeVry Institute of Technology: City
    of Industry *B*
Golden Gate University *C,B,M*
Golden West College *A*
Grossmont Community College *C,A*
Laney College *C,A*
Long Beach City College *C,A*
Moorpark College *A*
Napa Valley College *C,A*
Oxnard College *A*
Pasadena City College *C,A*
Pepperdine University *B*
San Diego City College *A*
Skyline College *C*
Solano Community College *A*
Southwestern College *A*
University of San Francisco *M*

Colorado
University of Colorado at
    Boulder *M*
University of Denver *B,M*
University of Northern Colorado *B*
University of Southern Colorado *B*

Connecticut
Eastern Connecticut State
    University *B*
University of New Haven *M*

District of Columbia
George Washington University *M*

Florida
Barry University *M*
Seminole Community College *C*
University of Florida *B,M,D*
University of Miami *B*

Georgia
Clayton State College *A*
Floyd College *A*
University of Georgia *B*
Valdosta State College *B*

Idaho

Idaho State University *C*
University of Idaho *B*

Illinois

City Colleges of Chicago: Richard J.
Daley College *A*
De Paul University *B,M*
DeVry Institute of Technology:
Lombard *B*
Illinois Eastern Community
Colleges: Wabash Valley College
C,A
Roosevelt University *B*
Southern Illinois University at
Carbondale *M*

Indiana

Ball State University *B*
Indiana University Bloomington
B,M,D
Purdue University *B*
University of Evansville *B*

Iowa

Des Moines Area Community
College *A*
Iowa Central Community College *A*
Kirkwood Community College *A*
Teikyo Marycrest University *B*
Waldorf College *A*

Kansas

Colby Community College *A*

Kentucky

Kentucky Wesleyan College *B*
University of Kentucky *B*

Louisiana

University of Southwestern
Louisiana *M*

Maryland

Capitol College *A,B*
Montgomery College: Germantown
Campus *C,A*
Morgan State University *B*
New Community College of
Baltimore *A*
University of Maryland University
College *M*

Massachusetts

Northeastern University *A*
Springfield Technical Community
College *A*

Michigan

Calvin College *B*
Eastern Michigan University *B*
Lansing Community College *A*
Madonna University *B*
Michigan State University *B,M*
University of Michigan *M*

Minnesota

National Education Center: Brown
Institute Campus *A*
St. Mary's College of Minnesota
B,M

Missouri

DeVry Institute of Technology:
Kansas City *B*
Jefferson College *A*
St. Louis Community College
Florissant Valley *A*
Meramec *C*
Southwest Baptist University *B*

Montana

Miles Community College *A*

Nebraska

College of St. Mary *C*
University of Nebraska—Kearney *B*
York College *A*

New Hampshire

New Hampshire Technical College:
Nashua *A*

New Jersey

Brookdale Community College *A*
Burlington County College *A*
Caldwell College *C*
County College of Morris *A*
Stevens Institute of Technology *M*

New Mexico

Eastern New Mexico University *B*

New York

City University of New York
Borough of Manhattan
Community College *A*
La Guardia Community
College *A*
New York City Technical
College *A,B*
Queens College *B*
Herkimer County Community
College *A*
Hudson Valley Community
College *A*
Iona College *M*
Ithaca College *B*
New York Institute of
Technology *B*
New York University *M*
Onondaga Community College *A*
Polytechnic University *M*
Rochester Institute of Technology
A,B,M
State University of New York
College of Agriculture and
Technology at Cobleskill *A*
Institute of Technology at
Utica/Rome *B*
Suffolk County Community
College *A*
Syracuse University *B,M*
Tompkins-Cortland Community
College *A*

North Carolina

Central Carolina Community
College *C*

Ohio

Hocking Technical College *A*
Kent State University *B,M*
Ohio University *B,M,D*
University of Toledo *B*

Oklahoma

National Education Center: Spartan
School of Aeronautics Campus *A*
Oklahoma Baptist University *B*
Oral Roberts University *B*
Tulsa Junior College *A*

Oregon

George Fox College *B*
Marylhurst College *C*
Pacific University *B*
Portland Community College *C*
University of Oregon
Eugene *B,M,D*
Robert Donald Clark Honors
College *B*

Pennsylvania

Bucks County Community
College *A*
Community College of Beaver
County *A*
Delaware County Community
College *A*
Luzerne County Community
College *A*
Penn State University Park
Campus *A*
Pennsylvania Institute of
Technology *A*
Reading Area Community
College *A*
University of Pittsburgh *M*
Westminster College *B*

Puerto Rico

University of the Sacred Heart *B*

Rhode Island

New England Institute of
Technology *A*

South Carolina

Greenville Technical College *A*
Midlands Technical College *A*

South Dakota

Mitchell Vocational Technical
Institute *C,A*

Tennessee

Christian Brothers University *C,B*
Nashville State Technical
Institute *C*
State Technical Institute at
Memphis *A*

Texas

Baylor University *B*
Central Texas College *A*
Eastfield College *A*
South Plains College *A*
Southern Methodist University *M,D*
Texas State Technical College
Amarillo *A*
Sweetwater *C,A*
Texas Tech University *B*
University of Dallas *M*

Utah

Southern Utah University *B*
Weber State University *B*

Virginia

Liberty University *B*
Tidewater Community College *A*

Washington

Eastern Washington University *B*
Seattle Central Community
College *A*

West Virginia

Salem-Teikyo University *A,B*

Wisconsin

University of Wisconsin
Eau Claire *B*
Platteville *B*
Waukesha County Technical
College *A*
Wisconsin Indianhead Technical
College *A*

Textile engineering

Alabama

Auburn University *B*

Georgia

Georgia Institute of Technology
B,M,D

Massachusetts

Massachusetts Institute of
Technology *M*

Mississippi

Mississippi College *B*

North Carolina

North Carolina State University
B,M

Pennsylvania

Philadelphia College of Textiles and
Science *B*

Textile technology

Alabama

Auburn University *B*

California

Fashion Institute of Design and
Merchandising *A*

Georgia

Gordon College *A*
LaGrange College *A*
Southern College of Technology *B*

Massachusetts

University of Massachusetts at
Dartmouth *B,M*

Michigan

Western Michigan University *B*

New York

Fashion Institute of Technology *A,B*
Fulton-Montgomery Community
College *A*

North Carolina

Isothermal Community College *A*
Vance-Granville Community
College *A*

Pennsylvania

Philadelphia College of Textiles and
Science *B*

South Carolina

Clemson University *B,M,D*
Tri-County Technical College *A*

Tennessee

Hiwassee College *A*

Virginia

Institute of Textile Technology *M*

Textiles and clothing

Alabama

Alabama Agricultural and
Mechanical University *B*

Auburn University *B,M*
Jacksonville State University *B*
Judson College *B*
Samford University *B*
Tuskegee University *B*
University of Alabama *B,M*

Arizona

University of Arizona *B*

Arkansas

Harding University *B*
Ouachita Baptist University *B*
University of Arkansas
  Fayetteville *B*
  Pine Bluff *B*
University of Central Arkansas *C*

California

California State University
  Fresno *B*
  Long Beach *B*
  Los Angeles *B*
  Northridge *B*
Chaffey Community College *C,A*
College of the Sequoias *C*
Long Beach City College *C,A*
Modesto Junior College *A*
Ohlone College *C,A*
Pacific Union College *A*
Saddleback College *C,A*
University of California: Davis *B,M*

Colorado

Colorado State University *B,M*

Connecticut

University of Connecticut *B,M*

Delaware

Delaware State College *B*
University of Delaware *B*

District of Columbia

Howard University *B*
University of the District of
  Columbia *B*

Florida

Florida State University *B,M*
International Fine Arts College *A*

Georgia

Fort Valley State College *B*
Georgia Southern University *B*
Morris Brown College *B*
University of Georgia *B,M,D*

Idaho

Idaho State University *B*
University of Idaho *B*

Illinois

Bradley University *B*
KAES College *B*
Northern Illinois University *B*
Southern Illinois University at
  Carbondale *B*
University of Illinois at Urbana-
  Champaign *B,M*

Indiana

Ball State University *B*
Indiana State University *B,M*
Indiana University Bloomington
  A,B,M
Purdue University *B,M,D*
Vincennes University *A*

Iowa

Iowa State University *B,M,D*
University of Northern Iowa *B*

Kansas

Coffeyville Community College *A*
Kansas State University *B,M,D*
Pittsburg State University *B*

Kentucky

Eastern Kentucky University *B*
Kentucky State University *B*
Morehead State University *B*
Murray State University *B*
University of Kentucky *B,M*
Western Kentucky University *B*

Louisiana

Louisiana State University and
  Agricultural and Mechanical
  College *B*
Louisiana Tech University *B*
Northeast Louisiana University *B*
Southern University and
  Agricultural and Mechanical
  College *B*

Maryland

University of Maryland: College
  Park *B,M,D*

Massachusetts

Becker College: Worcester
  Campus *A*
Endicott College *A*
Framingham State College *B*
Mount Ida College *A*

Michigan

Central Michigan University *B*
Eastern Michigan University *M*
Marygrove College *B*
Michigan State University *B,M*
Northern Michigan University *B*
Western Michigan University *B*

Minnesota

College of St. Catherine: St.
  Catherine Campus *B*
College of St. Scholastica *B*
Concordia College: Moorhead *B*
Mankato State University *B,M*
St. Paul Technical College *C*
University of Minnesota: Twin
  Cities *B*
University of St. Thomas *B*

Mississippi

Alcorn State University *B*
Mississippi University for Women *B*
University of Southern
  Mississippi *B*

Missouri

Central Missouri State University *B*
College of the Ozarks *B*
Columbia College *A,B*
Northwest Missouri State
  University *B*
Southeast Missouri State
  University *B*
Southwest Missouri State
  University *B*
University of Missouri: Columbia
  B,M,D

Montana

Montana State University *B*

Nebraska

University of Nebraska
  Lincoln *B,M*
  Omaha *B*

Nevada

University of Nevada: Reno *B*

New Jersey

Centenary College *A,B*

New Mexico

New Mexico State University *B*

New York

City University of New York:
  Queens College *B*
Cornell University *B,M,D*
Marymount College *B*
Onondaga Community College *A*
State University of New York
  College at Oneonta *B*
Syracuse University *B*

North Carolina

Appalachian State University *B*
Bennett College *B*
Campbell University *B*
North Carolina Agricultural and
  Technical State University *B*
North Carolina Central
  University *B*
University of North Carolina at
  Greensboro *B,M,D*
Western Carolina University *B*

North Dakota

North Dakota State University *B,M*
University of North Dakota *B*

Ohio

Baldwin-Wallace College *B*
Bluffton College *B*
Bowling Green State University *M*
Miami University: Oxford
  Campus *M*
Ohio State University: Columbus
  Campus *B,M,D*
Ohio University *B,M*
University of Akron *B*
Virginia Marti College of Fashion
  and Art *C*

Oklahoma

Langston University *B*
Northeastern State University *B*
Oklahoma State University *B,M*
University of Central Oklahoma
  B,M

Oregon

Oregon State University *B,M*

Pennsylvania

Albright College *B*
Cheyney University of
  Pennsylvania *B*
Immaculata College *B*
Indiana University of
  Pennsylvania *B*
Mercyhurst College *B*
Messiah College *B*
Moore College of Art and Design *B*
Philadelphia College of Textiles and
  Science *B,M*
Seton Hill College *B*

Rhode Island

University of Rhode Island *B,M*

South Dakota

South Dakota State University *B*

Tennessee

Carson-Newman College *B*
Hiwassee College *A*
Tennessee State University *B*

Tennessee Technological
  University *B*
University of Tennessee: Knoxville
  B,M

Texas

Houston Community College *C*
St. Philip's College *C,A*
Stephen F. Austin State
  University *B*
Texas A&I University *B*
Texas Southern University *B,M*
Texas Tech University *B,M*
Texas Woman's University *B,M,D*
University of Mary Hardin-
  Baylor *B*
University of North Texas *B*
University of Texas at Austin *B*

Utah

Brigham Young University *B*
Dixie College *A*
Utah State University *B*

Vermont

University of Vermont *B*

Virginia

Hampton University *B,M*
Norfolk State University *A*
Radford University *B*
Virginia Polytechnic Institute and
  State University *B,M,D*

Washington

Central Washington University *B,M*
Seattle Central Community
  College *A*
Seattle Pacific University *B*
Spokane Falls Community
  College *A*
Washington State University *B,M*

West Virginia

West Virginia University *B*

Wisconsin

Madison Area Technical College *A*
University of Wisconsin
  Madison *B,M*
  Stevens Point *B*
  Stout *B,M*

Theater design

Alabama

University of Montevallo *B*

Arizona

Mesa Community College *A*

California

California Institute of the Arts *B,M*
California State University
  Fullerton *B,M*
  Long Beach *B,M*
Chabot College *A*
Humboldt State University *B*
Santa Barbara City College *A*
University of California: Santa Cruz
  C,B
University of Southern California
  B,M

Colorado

University of Northern Colorado *B*

Connecticut

University of Connecticut *B*

District of Columbia

George Washington University *M*

Florida

Florida Atlantic University *B*
University of South Florida *B*

Illinois

De Paul University *B,M*
Illinois Wesleyan University *B*
Northern Illinois University *M*
Southern Illinois University at
Carbondale *B,M*

Indiana

Ball State University *B*
Indiana University Bloomington *A*
Purdue University *B,M*
University of Evansville *B*

Iowa

Drake University *B*
Teikyo Westmar University *B*
University of Iowa *M*
University of Northern Iowa *B*

Kansas

University of Kansas *B*

Maryland

Howard Community College *A*

Massachusetts

Brandeis University *M*
Emerson College *B,M*
Hampshire College *B*

Michigan

Eastern Michigan University *B*

Minnesota

Mankato State University *B*
University of Minnesota: Duluth *B*

Missouri

Fontbonne College *B*
University of Missouri: Kansas
City *M*
Webster University *B*

New Hampshire

Franklin Pierce College *B*

New Jersey

Bergen Community College *A*
Rutgers—The State University of
New Jersey: Mason Gross School
of the Arts *B*

New Mexico

College of Santa Fe *A*

New York

Adelphi University *B*
City University of New York:
Brooklyn College *B*
Ithaca College *B*
New York University *B,M*
Pace University *B*
Sarah Lawrence College *B*
State University of New York
Purchase *B,M*
College at New Paltz *B*

North Carolina

Brevard College *A*
North Carolina School of the Arts
C,B,M

Ohio

Case Western Reserve University
B,M
Ohio University *B,M*
Otterbein College *B*
Sinclair Community College *A*
University of Cincinnati *B,M*
Wright State University *B*

Oklahoma

Northeastern State University *B*
Oklahoma State University *B*

Pennsylvania

Allentown College of St. Francis de
Sales *B*
California University of
Pennsylvania *B*
Carnegie Mellon University *B,M*

Texas

Collin County Community College
District *A*
Lon Morris College *A*
Texas Tech University *M*

Utah

Brigham Young University *M*

Vermont

Bennington College *B*

Virginia

Averett College *B*
Lynchburg College *B*
Virginia Commonwealth University
B,M

Washington

Cornish College of the Arts *B*
Eastern Washington University *B*
Pacific Lutheran University *B*

West Virginia

Davis and Elkins College *B*
Marshall University *B*
West Virginia University *B,M*

Wisconsin

University of Wisconsin: Green
Bay *B*

Theological professions (B.Div., M.Div., Rabbinical, or Talmudical)

Alabama

Samford University *F*
Southern Christian University *F*

California

American Baptist Seminary of the
West *F*
Azusa Pacific University *F*
Biola University *F*
Dominican School of Philosophy
and Theology *F*
Franciscan School of Theology *F*
Fuller Theological Seminary *F*
Hebrew Union College: Jewish
Institute of Religion *F*
La Sierra University *F*
Pacific School of Religion *F*
Pepperdine University *F*
St. Patrick's Seminary *F*
Westminster Theological Seminary
in California *F*

Connecticut

Holy Apostles College and
Seminary *F*
Yale University *F*

District of Columbia

Catholic University of America *F*
Dominican House of Studies *F*
Howard University *F*
Oblate College *F*

Georgia

Emory University *F*

Idaho

Northwest Nazarene College *F*

Illinois

Chicago Theological Seminary *F*
Garrett-Evangelical Theological
Seminary *F*
Hebrew Theological College *F*
Lincoln Christian College and
Seminary *F*
Loyola University of Chicago *F*
North Park College and Theological
Seminary *F*
University of Chicago *F*

Indiana

Anderson University *F*
Christian Theological Seminary *F*
Grace Theological Seminary *F*
University of Notre Dame *F*

Iowa

Faith Baptist Bible College and
Theological Seminary *F*
University of Dubuque *F*

Kentucky

Lexington Theological Seminary *F*
Louisville Presbyterian Theological
Seminary *F*

Louisiana

Notre Dame Seminary School of
Theology *F*
World Evangelism Bible College
and Seminary *F*

Maryland

Mount St. Mary's College *F*
Ner Israel Rabbinical College *F*

Massachusetts

Boston University *F*
Harvard University *F*
Hellenic College *F*
Weston School of Theology *F*

Michigan

Andrews University *F*
Calvin Theological Seminary *F*
Grand Rapids Baptist College and
Seminary *F*
Sacred Heart Major Seminary *F*

Minnesota

Bethel Theological Seminary *F*
Luther Northwestern Theological
Seminary *F*
St. John's University *F*
United Theological Seminary of the
Twin Cities *F*
University of St. Thomas *F*

Missouri

Baptist Bible College *F*
Calvary Bible College *F*
Concordia Seminary *F*
Covenant Theological Seminary *F*

Kenrick-Glennon Seminary *F*

New Jersey

Drew University *F*

New York

Beth Hamedrash Shaarei Yosher
Institute *F*
Darkei No'Am Rabbinical
College *F*
Jewish Theological Seminary of
America *F*
Kol Yaakov Torah Center *F*
Machzikei Hadath Rabbinical
College *F*
Maryknoll School Of Theology *F*
Mesivta Torah Vodaath Seminary *F*
Mirrer Yeshiva Central Institute *F*
New York Theological Seminary *F*
Nyack College *F*
Ohr Somayach Tanenbaum
Education Center *F*
St. John's University *F*
Union Theological Seminary *F*
Yeshiva Karlin Stolin Beth Aron
Y'Israel Rabbinical Institute *F*

North Carolina

Duke University *F*
Livingstone College *F*

Ohio

Ashland University *F*
Pontifical College Josephinum *F*

Oklahoma

Oral Roberts University *F*
Phillips University *F*

Oregon

Mount Angel Seminary *F*
Multnomah School of the Bible *F*
Western Conservative Baptist
Seminary *F*

Pennsylvania

Academy of the New Church *F*
Baptist Bible College of
Pennsylvania *F*
Evangelical School of Theology *F*
Lutheran Theological Seminary at
Gettysburg *F*
Moravian College *F*
Pittsburgh Theological Seminary *F*
St. Charles Borromeo Seminary *F*
St. Vincent College *F*

South Carolina

Bob Jones University *F*
Columbia Bible College and
Seminary *F*

Tennessee

Memphis Theological Seminary *F*
Tennessee Temple University *F*
University of the South *F*
Vanderbilt University *F*

Texas

Abilene Christian University *F*
Criswell College *F*
Southern Methodist University *F*
Texas Christian University *F*
University of St. Thomas *F*

Virginia

Liberty University *F*
Union Theological Seminary in
Virginia *F*
Virginia Union University *F*

Washington

Gonzaga University *F*
Seattle University *F*

Canada

McGill University *F*

Theological studies

Alabama

Faulkner University *B*
Oakwood College *B*
Samford University *B*
Selma University *B*
Southeastern Bible College *B,M*
Spring Hill College *B,M*

Alaska

Alaska Bible College *B*

Arizona

Arizona College of the Bible *B*
Grand Canyon University *B*
Southwestern College *C,A,B*

Arkansas

Central Baptist College *B*
Harding University *B,M*
John Brown University *B*
Ouachita Baptist University *B*
Williams Baptist College *B*

California

American Baptist Seminary of the
  West *M*
Azusa Pacific University *B,M*
Bethany College *B*
Biola University *B,M,D*
California Lutheran University *B*
Christ College Irvine *B*
Christian Heritage College *B*
Dominican School of Philosophy
  and Theology *M,W*
Franciscan School of Theology *M*
Fuller Theological Seminary *M,D,W*
Graduate Theological Union *M,D*
Hebrew Union College: Jewish
  Institute of Religion *M,D*
La Sierra University *B*
LIFE Bible College *B*
Loyola Marymount University *B*
Mount St. Mary's College *M*
Pacific Christian College *B,M*
Pacific School of Religion *M,D,W*
Pacific Union College *B*
Patten College *B*
Pepperdine University *B*
Point Loma Nazarene College *B,M*
Queen of the Holy Rosary
  College *A*
St. Patrick's Seminary *M*
San Jose Christian College *B*
Simpson College *B*
Southern California College *B,M*
University of California: San
  Diego *B*
University of San Francisco *B,M*
Westminster Theological Seminary
  in California *M,D*

Colorado

Colorado Christian University *B*
University of Denver *D*

Connecticut

Holy Apostles College and
  Seminary *M*
Yale University *M*

District of Columbia

Catholic University of America
  M,D
Dominican House of Studies *M*
Oblate College *M*
Trinity College *B*

Florida

Barry University *B,M*
Florida Baptist Theological College
  A,B
Florida Bible College *A,B*
Florida Christian College *B*
Hobe Sound Bible College *B*
Southeastern College of the
  Assemblies of God *B*
Warner Southern College *B*

Georgia

Atlanta Christian College *B*
Emory University *M,D,W*
LaGrange College *B*
Toccoa Falls College *B*

Idaho

Boise Bible College *A,B*
Northwest Nazarene College *B*

Illinois

Chicago Theological Seminary
  M,D,W
College of St. Francis *B*
Concordia University *B*
Elmhurst College *B*
Garrett-Evangelical Theological
  Seminary *M,D,W*
Hebrew Theological College
  B,M,D,W
Lincoln Christian College and
  Seminary *C,B,M*
Loyola University of Chicago
  B,M,D
Moody Bible Institute *B*
North Park College and Theological
  Seminary *B*
Olivet Nazarene University *B,M*
Quincy College *B*
Trinity Christian College *B*
University of Chicago *M,D*
Wheaton College *M*

Indiana

Anderson University *M*
Bethel College *M*
Butler University *M*
Calumet College of St. Joseph *B*
Christian Theological Seminary
  M,D
Goshen College *B*
Grace Theological Seminary
  M,D,W
Hanover College *B*
Huntington College *B,M*
Indiana Wesleyan University *B,M*
Marian College *B*
Martin University *B*
Oakland City College *M*
St. Mary-of-the-Woods College
  C,A,B,M
University of Evansville *B*
University of Notre Dame *B,M,D*

Iowa

Briar Cliff College *B*
Divine Word College *B*
Dordt College *B*
Faith Baptist Bible College and
  Theological Seminary *B,M*
Grand View College *B*
Luther College *B*
Northwestern College *B*
St. Ambrose University *B*

Simpson College *B*
University of Dubuque *B,M*
Vennard College *B*
Wartburg College *B*

Kansas

Barclay College *B*
Bethel College *B*
Central College *A,B*
Friends University *B*
Kansas City College and Bible
  School *A*
Kansas Newman College *B*
Manhattan Christian College *B*
St. Mary College *B*
Sterling College *B*
Washburn University of Topeka *B*

Kentucky

Bellarmine College *B*
Brescia College *B*
Campbellsville College *B*
Clear Creek Baptist Bible College
  C,A,B
Kentucky Christian College *B*
Kentucky Wesleyan College *B*
Lexington Theological Seminary
  M,D
Louisville Presbyterian Theological
  Seminary *M,D*
Thomas More College *A,B*

Louisiana

Centenary College of Louisiana *B*
Notre Dame Seminary School of
  Theology *M*
World Evangelism Bible College
  and Seminary *M*
Xavier University of Louisiana *B,M*

Maryland

Baltimore Hebrew University
  B,M,D
Columbia Union College *B*
Loyola College in Maryland *B*
Mount St. Mary's College *B,M*
Ner Israel Rabbinical College
  B,M,D

Massachusetts

Assumption College *B,M*
Atlantic Union College *B*
Boston College *B,M,D*
Boston University *M,D*
Eastern Nazarene College *B*
Elms College *M*
Emmanuel College *B,M*
Gordon College *B*
Hampshire College *B*
Harvard University *M,D*
Hellenic College *M*
Merrimack College *B*
St. Hyacinth College and
  Seminary *C*
Weston School of Theology *M,W*

Michigan

Andrews University *B,M,D*
Calvin College *B*
Calvin Theological Seminary *M*
Concordia College *B*
Grace Bible College *B*
Grand Rapids Baptist College and
  Seminary *M*
Hillsdale College *B*
Sacred Heart Major Seminary *M*
St. Mary's College *B*
William Tyndale College *B*

Minnesota

Bethel College *B*
Bethel Theological Seminary
  M,D,W
College of St. Benedict *B*
College of St. Catherine: St.
  Catherine Campus *B,M*
Concordia College: St. Paul *B*
Crown College *B*
Luther Northwestern Theological
  Seminary *M,D*
Minnesota Bible College *B*
North Central Bible College *B*
Northwestern College *B*
St. John's University *B,M*
St. Mary's College of Minnesota
  B,M
United Theological Seminary of the
  Twin Cities *D*
University of St. Thomas *B*
Willmar Community College *A*

Mississippi

Southeastern Baptist College *B*
William Carey College *B*

Missouri

Baptist Bible College *B*
Calvary Bible College *A,B,M*
Central Christian College of the
  Bible *B*
Concordia Seminary *M,D,W*
Covenant Theological Seminary
  M,D
Hannibal-LaGrange College *B*
Kenrick-Glennon Seminary *M*
Missouri Baptist College *B*
Ozark Christian College *C,A,B*
Rockhurst College *B*
St. Louis Christian College *B*
St. Louis University *B,M,D*
Southwest Baptist University *B*

Montana

Carroll College *B*

Nebraska

Concordia College *B*
Creighton University *C,A,B,M*
Grace College of the Bible *B*
Nebraska Christian College *A,B*
Union College *B*
York College *A*

New Hampshire

St. Anselm College *B*

New Jersey

Assumption College for Sisters *C,A*
Drew University *M,D,W*
St. Peter's College *B*
Seton Hall University *M,D*

New Mexico

College of Santa Fe *B*
Eastern New Mexico University *B*

New York

Concordia College *B*
Fordham University *B,M,D*
Jewish Theological Seminary of
  America *B,M,D*
Manhattan College *B*
Maryknoll School Of Theology
  M,W
Molloy College *B*
New York Theological Seminary *D*
Nyack College *B*
Ohr Somayach Tanenbaum
  Education Center *B,M*
St. Bonaventure University *B,M,W*
St. John's University *B,M*

Talmudical Institute of Upstate New York *B*
Union Theological Seminary *M,D*
Yeshiva Karlin Stolin Beth Aron Y'Israel Rabbinical Institute *B*

North Carolina
Barton College *B*
Belmont Abbey College *B*
Campbell University *B*
Chowan College *B*
Duke University *M*
Gardner-Webb College *B*
John Wesley College *B*
Piedmont Bible College *B*
Roanoke Bible College *B*
St. Andrews Presbyterian College *B*
Southeastern Baptist Theological Seminary *A,M,D*

North Dakota
Trinity Bible College *B*

Ohio
Ashland University *M,D*
Athenaeum of Ohio *M*
Cincinnati Bible College and Seminary *B,M*
Circleville Bible College *B*
Franciscan University of Steubenville *A,B,M*
Lourdes College *A,B*
Malone College *B*
Mount Vernon Nazarene College *B*
Notre Dame College of Ohio *B*
Ohio Dominican College *A,B*
Pontifical College Josephinum *M*
Union Institute *B,D*
University of Dayton *B,M*
Ursuline College *M*
Walsh College *B*
Xavier University *B,M*

Oklahoma
Bartlesville Wesleyan College *A*
Mid-America Bible College *B*
Oklahoma Baptist University *B*
Oklahoma Christian University of Science and Arts *B*
Oral Roberts University *B,M*
Southwestern College of Christian Ministries *B*

Oregon
Eugene Bible College *B*
George Fox College *B*
Mount Angel Seminary *M*
Multnomah School of the Bible *B,M*
University of Portland *B,M*
Warner Pacific College *B,M*
Western Baptist College *B*
Western Conservative Baptist Seminary *M,D*

Pennsylvania
Academy of the New Church *M*
Albright College *B*
Allentown College of St. Francis de Sales *B*
Alvernia College *B*
Baptist Bible College of Pennsylvania *B,M*
Carlow College *B*
Duquesne University *B,M,D*
Evangelical School of Theology *M*
Gannon University *B*
Immaculata College *A*
King's College *B*
La Salle University *B,M*
Lancaster Bible College *B*
Marywood College *M*
Messiah College *B*

Moravian College *M*
Pittsburgh Theological Seminary *M,D,W*
St. Charles Borromeo Seminary *C,M*
St. Joseph's University *B*
Seton Hill College *C,B*
Trinity Episcopal School for Ministry *B*
University of Scranton *B*
Valley Forge Christian College *B*

Puerto Rico
Bayamon Central University *M*
Pontifical Catholic University of Puerto Rico *B*
Universidad Adventista de las Antillas *B*

South Carolina
Bob Jones University *B,M,D*
Claflin College *B*
Columbia Bible College and Seminary *B*

Tennessee
American Baptist College of ABT Seminary *B*
Crichton College *B*
Free Will Baptist Bible College *B*
Johnson Bible College *B*
Southern College of Seventh-day Adventists *B*
Tennessee Temple University *B*
Trevecca Nazarene College *B*
Union University *B*
University of the South *M,D,W*
Vanderbilt University *M,D*

Texas
Abilene Christian University *B*
Arlington Baptist College *B*
Baptist Missionary Association Theological Seminary *A,M*
Criswell College *M*
East Texas Baptist University *B*
Hardin-Simmons University *B*
Howard Payne University *B*
Lon Morris College *A*
Lubbock Christian University *B*
McMurry University *B*
St. Mary's University *B,M*
Southern Methodist University *M,D,W*
Southwestern Christian College *B*
Southwestern University *B*
Texas Christian University *M,D*
Texas Lutheran College *B*
Texas Southmost College *A*
Texas Wesleyan University *B*
University of Dallas *B,M*
University of Mary Hardin-Baylor *B*
University of St. Thomas *B,M,D*

Utah
Westminster College of Salt Lake City *B*

Vermont
St. Michael's College *M*

Virginia
Averett College *B*
Christendom College *B*
Eastern Mennonite College *B*
Liberty University *B,M*
Union Theological Seminary in Virginia *M,D*
Virginia Union University *M*

Washington
Northwest College of the Assemblies of God *B*
Pacific Lutheran University *B*
Puget Sound Christian College *B*
Seattle Pacific University *B*
Seattle University *M*
Walla Walla College *B*
Whitworth College *B*

West Virginia
Appalachian Bible College *B*
Bethany College *B*
Davis and Elkins College *B*
Ohio Valley College *B*
Wheeling Jesuit College *B*

Wisconsin
Carthage College *B*
Concordia University Wisconsin *B*
Edgewood College *B*
Lakeland College *B*
Maranatha Baptist Bible College *B,M*
Marquette University *B,M,D*
Mount Mary College *B*
Nashotah House *M*
St. Norbert College *M*
Wisconsin Lutheran College *B*

Canada
McGill University *B,M,D*

Tourism

Alaska
Alaska Pacific University *C,A,B*
University of Alaska Southeast *C,A*

Arizona
Lamson Junior College *A*
Pima Community College *C*

California
Coastline Community College *C,A*
Foothill College *A*
Long Beach City College *A*
Los Angeles City College *C,A*
Mount St. Mary's College *A*
Palomar College *C,A*
Phillips Junior College: Fresno Campus *C,A*
San Diego City College *C,A*
San Diego Mesa College *C,A*
Southwestern College *C,A*
United States International University *B*

Colorado
Arapahoe Community College *C*
Blair Junior College *A*
Colorado Mountain College: Timberline Campus *A*
Parks Junior College *A*
Red Rocks Community College *C*

Connecticut
Briarwood College *A*
University of New Haven *A,B,M*

District of Columbia
George Washington University *M*

Florida
Broward Community College *A*
Daytona Beach Community College *A*
Lynn University *B*
Miami-Dade Community College *A*

National Education Center: Bauder Campus *A*
Phillips Junior College: Melbourne *C,A*
St. Thomas University *B*
Schiller International University *A,B*
Webber College *A,B*

Hawaii
Cannon's International Business College of Honolulu *C,A*
University of Hawaii at Manoa *B*

Illinois
City Colleges of Chicago: Chicago City-Wide College *C,A*
College of DuPage *C,A*
Elgin Community College *C*
John A. Logan College *A*
Lincoln College *C*
MacCormac Junior College *A*
Midstate College *C*
Moraine Valley Community College *C,A*
Parkland College *C*
Parks College of St. Louis University *B*
Robert Morris College: Chicago *C,A*
Southern Illinois University at Carbondale *B*
Waubonsee Community College *C,A*

Indiana
Ball State University *B*
International Business College *C*
Purdue University *B,M*
University of Indianapolis *A*

Iowa
American Institute of Commerce *C*
Iowa Lakes Community College *A*

Kansas
Brown Mackie College *C*
Cloud County Community College *C,A*
Hutchinson Community College *A*

Kentucky
Sullivan College *A*

Louisiana
Phillips Junior College: New Orleans *A*

Maine
Beal College *A*
Casco Bay College *C*

Maryland
Essex Community College *C*
Villa Julie College *A*

Massachusetts
Bay Path College *A*
Bay State College *A*
Becker College: Leicester Campus *A*
Dean Junior College *A*
Endicott College *A,B*
Fisher College *A*
Lasell College *A,B*
Marian Court Junior College *C,A*
Massachusetts Bay Community College *C,A*
Massasoit Community College *C,A*
Middlesex Community College *A*
Mount Ida College *A*
Newbury College *A*

Northern Essex Community
College *C*
Quincy College *A*
Quinsigamond Community College
C,A

Michigan

Baker College
Flint *A*
Muskegon *A*
Davenport College of Business *A*
Detroit College of Business *A*
Eastern Michigan University *B*
Lansing Community College *A*
Michigan State University *B*
Northwestern Michigan College *C*
Suomi College *A*
Western Michigan University *B*

Minnesota

Willmar Community College *A*

Mississippi

Phillips Junior College
Jackson *A*
Mississippi Gulf Coast *A*

Missouri

National College *A*
St. Louis Community College at
Forest Park *A*
St. Louis University *B*

Montana

Western Montana College of the
University of Montana *A*

Nebraska

Lincoln School of Commerce *C*
University of Nebraska—Kearney *B*

New Hampshire

Hesser College *A*
New Hampshire College *B*
Plymouth State College of the
University System of New
Hampshire *B*

New Jersey

Atlantic Community College *A*
Bergen Community College *C*

New Mexico

National College *A*

New York

Adirondack Community College *A*
Berkeley College *A*
Broome Community College *A*
Bryant & Stratton Business Institute
Albany *C,A*
Buffalo *C,A*
City University of New York
Borough of Manhattan
Community College *A*
Kingsborough Community
College *A*
La Guardia Community
College *A*
Community College of the Finger
Lakes *A*
Daemen College *B*
Genesee Community College *A*
Herkimer County Community
College *A*
Jefferson Community College *C,A*
Maria College *A*
Niagara University *B*
Paul Smith's College *A*
Rochester Institute of Technology
A,B,M
Rockland Community College *A*

State University of New York
College of Agriculture and
Technology at Cobleskill *A*
College of Agriculture and
Technology at Morrisville *A*
College of Technology at
Delhi *A*
Suffolk County Community College:
Eastern Campus *A*
Sullivan County Community
College *A*
Tompkins-Cortland Community
College *A*
Westchester Business Institute *A*
Westchester Community College
C,A

North Carolina

Blue Ridge Community College *A*
Central Piedmont Community
College *A*
Rockingham Community College *A*

Ohio

Cincinnati Metropolitan College *C*
Columbus State Community
College *A*
Davis Junior College of Business *A*
Hocking Technical College *A*
Kent State University *B*
Lorain County Community
College *A*
Miami-Jacobs College *A*
Muskingum Area Technical
College *A*
Northwestern College *C*
Sinclair Community College *A*
Southern Ohio College *A*

Oklahoma

Oklahoma Junior College *A*
Tulsa Junior College *C,A*

Oregon

Mount Hood Community College
C,A
Portland Community College *A*

Pennsylvania

California University of
Pennsylvania *B*
Central Pennsylvania Business
School *A*
Gannon University *B*
Harcum Junior College *A*
Harrisburg Area Community
College *A*
Keystone Junior College *A*
Lehigh County Community
College *A*
Luzerne County Community
College *A*
Mansfield University of
Pennsylvania *B*
Mercyhurst College *C*
Mount Aloysius College *A*
Northampton County Area
Community College *C,A*
Reading Area Community
College *A*

Puerto Rico

Electronic Data Processing College
of Puerto Rico *C*
Huertas Junior College *C*
University of the Sacred Heart *A,B*

Rhode Island

Johnson & Wales University *A,B*

South Carolina

Columbia Junior College of
Business *A*
University of South Carolina *B,M*

South Dakota

Black Hills State University *B,M*
Huron University *A*
National College *B*

Tennessee

Volunteer State Community
College *C*

Texas

Amarillo College *A*
El Paso Community College *A*
Houston Community College *C,A*
North Harris Montgomery
Community College District *C,A*

Utah

Brigham Young University *B*
Dixie College *C,A*
Phillips Junior College: Salt Lake
City Campus *C,A*
Stevens-Henager College of
Business *C*

Vermont

Champlain College *A*

Virginia

National Business College *A*
Northern Virginia Community
College *C,A*

Washington

Art Institute of Seattle *A*
Edmonds Community College *C,A*
Yakima Valley Community College
C,A

West Virginia

College of West Virginia *C,A*
Concord College *B*
Davis and Elkins College *B*
West Liberty State College *B*

Wisconsin

Madison Area Technical College *A*
Milwaukee College of Business *C,A*
Stratton College *C,A*

Wyoming

Eastern Wyoming College *A*
Northwest College *A*

**American Samoa, Caroline
Islands, Guam, Marianas,
Virgin Islands**

Guam Community College *A*
Northern Marianas College *A*

Toxicology

Alabama

Auburn University *M*

Arizona

University of Arizona *M*

Arkansas

University of Arkansas for Medical
Sciences *M,D*

California

San Jose State University *M*
University of California
Davis *M,D*
Irvine *M,D*
University of San Francisco *M*
University of Southern California
M,D

District of Columbia

American University *M*
George Washington University *M,D*

Florida

University of Florida *M,D*

Illinois

University of Chicago *M,D*

Indiana

Indiana University—Purdue
University at Indianapolis
M,D,W
Purdue University *M,D*

Iowa

Iowa State University *M,D*

Kansas

University of Kansas
Lawrence *B,M,D*
Medical Center *M,D*

Kentucky

University of Kentucky *M,D*

Louisiana

Northeast Louisiana University *B*

Maryland

University of Maryland
Baltimore *M,D*
Baltimore County *M,D*
College Park *M*

Massachusetts

Harvard University *D*
Massachusetts Institute of
Technology *M,D*
Northeastern University *B,M,D*

Michigan

Eastern Michigan University *B*
Michigan State University *M,D*
University of Michigan *M,D*

Minnesota

Mankato State University *B*
University of Minnesota
Duluth *M*
Twin Cities *M,D*

Mississippi

University of Mississippi Medical
Center *D*

Missouri

University of Missouri: Kansas City
M,D

New Jersey

Bloomfield College *B*
College of St. Elizabeth *B*
Felician College *B*
Montclair State College *B*
Rutgers—The State University of
New Jersey *M,D*
St. Peter's College *B*
University of Medicine and
Dentistry of New Jersey: School
of Health Related Professions
C,B

New Mexico

New Mexico State University *M*
University of New Mexico *M,D*

New York

Albany Medical College *M,D*
Clarkson University *B*
Cornell University *M,D*
St. John's University *B,M*
State University of New York
    Albany *M,D*
    College of Environmental
      Science and Forestry *B,M,D*
University of Rochester *M,D,W*

North Carolina

Duke University *D*
North Carolina State University
  M,D
University of North Carolina at
  Chapel Hill *M,D*

Ohio

Ashland University *B*
Case Western Reserve
  University *M*

Oklahoma

University of Oklahoma Health
  Sciences Center *M,D*

Oregon

Oregon State University *M,D*

Pennsylvania

Carnegie Mellon University
  B,M,D,W
Lehigh University *M,D*
Philadelphia College of Pharmacy
  and Science *B,M*
University of Pittsburgh *M,D*

Rhode Island

University of Rhode Island *M,D*

Texas

Prairie View A&M University *M*
Texas A&M University *M,D*
University of Texas at San
  Antonio *M*

Utah

Utah State University *M,D*

Virginia

Virginia Commonwealth University
  M,D

Washington

Washington State University *D*

Wisconsin

University of Wisconsin: Madison
  M,D

Trade and industrial education

Alabama

Alabama Agricultural and
  Mechanical University *B,M*
Athens State College *B*
Auburn University *B,M*
Community College of the Air
  Force *A*

Alaska

University of Alaska Fairbanks *M*

Arizona

Northern Arizona University *B,M*

Arkansas

Arkansas State University *A*
University of Arkansas
    Fayetteville *M*
    Pine Bluff *B*
University of Central Arkansas *B,M*

California

California State University
    Chico *B*
    Fresno *B*
    Long Beach *B,M*
    Los Angeles *B,M*
San Francisco State University *B*

Colorado

Colorado State University *B,M,D*

Connecticut

Central Connecticut State
  University *B,M*

Delaware

Delaware State College *B*

Florida

Florida Agricultural and Mechanical
  University *B,M*
Florida International University
  B,M
Pensacola Junior College *A*
University of Central Florida *B,M*
University of Florida *M*

Georgia

Armstrong State College *B*
Gainesville College *A*
Georgia Southern University *B,M*
Georgia State University *B,M,D*
Middle Georgia College *A*
University of Georgia *B,M*

Hawaii

University of Hawaii: Honolulu
  Community College *A*

Idaho

Idaho State University *B*

Illinois

Southern Illinois University at
  Carbondale *B*

Indiana

Ball State University *B,M*
Indiana State University *B,M*
Indiana University—Purdue
  University at Indianapolis *M,D*
Purdue University *A,B,M,D*
Vincennes University *A*

Iowa

Iowa Lakes Community College *A*
Iowa State University *M*
University of Northern Iowa *B*
William Penn College *B*

Kansas

Butler County Community
  College *A*
Pittsburg State University *B*

Kentucky

Eastern Kentucky University *B,M*
Morehead State University *B*
Murray State University *A,B*
University of Louisville *B,M*
Western Kentucky University *B*

Louisiana

Grambling State University *B*
Louisiana State University and
  Agricultural and Mechanical
  College *M*
Southeastern Louisiana
  University *B*
University of Southwestern
  Louisiana *B*

Maine

University of Southern Maine *B*

Massachusetts

Fitchburg State College *B*

Michigan

Central Michigan University *M*
Eastern Michigan University *B,M*
Lansing Community College *A*
Madonna University *A,B*
Northern Michigan University *B,M*
Western Michigan University *B,M*

Minnesota

Bemidji State University *B,M*
Mankato State University *B*
Moorhead State University *B*
St. Cloud State University *B*
University of Minnesota: Twin
  Cities *B,M*

Mississippi

Alcorn State University *B*
Mississippi State University *B,M*
University of Southern Mississippi
  B,M

Missouri

Central Missouri State University
  B,M
College of the Ozarks *B*
Northwest Missouri State
  University *B*
University of Missouri: Columbia *B*

Montana

Northern Montana College *B*

Nebraska

University of Nebraska
    Lincoln *B*
    Omaha *B*
Wayne State College *B*

New Hampshire

University of New Hampshire *B*

New Jersey

Kean College of New Jersey *B*
Rutgers—The State University of
  New Jersey *M,D*

New Mexico

Eastern New Mexico University *A*

New York

New York Institute of Technology
  A,B
State University of New York
    College at Buffalo *B,M*
    Oswego *B,M*

North Carolina

Guilford Technical Community
  College *A*
North Carolina State University
  B,M
Southwestern Community
  College *A*

North Dakota

Little Hoop Community College *A*

Ohio

Bowling Green State University
  B,M
Kent State University *B,M*
Ohio State University: Columbus
  Campus *B*
Ohio University *B*
University of Toledo *B*

Oklahoma

East Central University *B*
Northwestern Oklahoma State
  University *B*
Oklahoma State University *B,M*
University of Central Oklahoma
  B,M

Oregon

Oregon State University *B,M*
Portland Community College *A*
Rogue Community College *C*

Pennsylvania

California University of
  Pennsylvania *B,M*
Penn State University Park Campus
  B,M,D
Temple University *B,M*
University of Pittsburgh *B*

Rhode Island

Johnson & Wales University *B*
Rhode Island College *B*

South Carolina

Clemson University *B,M*

South Dakota

Black Hills State University *B*
Dakota State University *B*
Northern State University *M*

Tennessee

East Tennessee State University
  B,M
Tennessee Technological
  University *B*
University of Tennessee:
  Knoxville *B*

Texas

Corpus Christi State University *B*
Prairie View A&M University *B*
Sam Houston State University *B,M*
Southwest Texas State
  University *M*
Texas A&M University *M,D*
Texas Southmost College *A*
University of Central Texas *B*
University of Houston *B*

Utah

Brigham Young University *B,M*

Vermont

University of Vermont *B*

Virginia

James Madison University *B*
Virginia Polytechnic Institute and
  State University *B,M*
Virginia State University *B,M*

Washington

Central Washington University *B*

West Virginia

West Virginia Institute of
  Technology *B*

Wisconsin
University of Wisconsin
Platteville *B*
Stout *B,M*

Wyoming
University of Wyoming *B*

American Samoa, Caroline Islands, Guam, Marianas, Virgin Islands
University of the Virgin Islands *B*

Canada
McGill University *B,M*

Trade and industrial supervision and management

Alabama
Central Alabama Community
College: Childersburg Campus *C*
Jefferson State Community
College *A*

Arizona
Northern Arizona University *B*

Arkansas
University of Arkansas at Little
Rock *B*

California
Citrus College *C*
Coastline Community College *A*
De Anza College *C,A*
Fashion Institute of Design and
Merchandising *A*
Foothill College *C,A*
Laney College *C,A*
Los Medanos College *C*
San Diego City College *C,A*
Solano Community College *A*

Colorado
Arapahoe Community College *C,A*
Metropolitan State College of
Denver *B*

Connecticut
Central Connecticut State
University *M*
Quinebaug Valley Community
College *A*
Quinnipiac College *B*

Delaware
Delaware Technical and
Community College: Stanton/
Wilmington Campus *A*

Florida
Daytona Beach Community
College *A*
Pensacola Junior College *A*
South Florida Community
College *A*
Tallahassee Community College *A*

Georgia
Berry College *B*
Clayton State College *A*
DeKalb College *A*
DeKalb Technical Institute *C*
Georgia Southern University *B*

Hawaii
Hawaii Pacific University *A*

Illinois
Carl Sandburg College *A*
De Paul University *M*
Kishwaukee College *C*
Lincoln Land Community College
C,A
Millikin University *B*
Moraine Valley Community
College *A*
Oakton Community College *C,A*
Southern Illinois University at
Carbondale *A,B*
Triton College *C,A*
Waubonsee Community College *A*
William Rainey Harper College *A*

Indiana
Indiana State University *A,B*
Indiana University
East *A,B*
Kokomo *A,B*
Indiana University—Purdue
University at Indianapolis *A,B*
Indiana Vocational Technical
College
Central Indiana *C,A*
Eastcentral *A*
Lafayette *C,A*
Northcentral *C,A*
Northeast *A*
Northwest *C,A*
Southwest *A*
International Business College *A*
Purdue University
North Central Campus *C,A,B*
West Lafayette *A,B*

Kansas
Allen County Community
College *A*
Barton County Community
College *A*
Cowley County Community
College *A*
Pratt Community College *C,A*

Kentucky
Morehead State University *A*
University of Louisville *A*

Louisiana
Louisiana Tech University *B*

Massachusetts
Massachusetts Institute of
Technology *M,D*
University of Massachusetts at
Lowell *B*

Michigan
Charles Stewart Mott Community
College *C,A*
Delta College *A*
GMI Engineering & Management
Institute *B*
Macomb Community College *C,A*
Michigan State University *D*
Northwestern Michigan College *A*
Western Michigan University *B,M*

Minnesota
Bemidji State University *B*
Willmar Technical College *A*

Mississippi
University of Southern
Mississippi *B*

Missouri
Northwest Missouri State
University *B*
Penn Valley Community College *C*
State Fair Community College *C,A*

Nebraska
Doane College *B*
Peru State College *B*
Wayne State College *B*

Nevada
Truckee Meadows Community
College *C*

New Hampshire
New Hampshire Technical College
Nashua *A*
Stratham *A*

New Jersey
Cumberland County College *A*

New Mexico
Dona Ana Branch Community
College of New Mexico State
University *A*
University of New Mexico *M*

New York
City University of New York:
College of Staten Island *C*
Clarkson University *B,M*
Iona College *B*
New York Institute of
Technology *B*
Niagara County Community
College *C*
Rochester Institute of Technology
A,B,M

North Carolina
Alamance Community College *A*
Central Carolina Community
College *A*
Cleveland Community College *A*
Durham Technical Community
College *C*
Edgecombe Community College *A*
Fayetteville Technical Community
College *A*
Haywood Community College *C,A*
Pitt Community College *A*
Wilson Technical Community
College *A*

Ohio
Bowling Green State University
Bowling Green *B*
Firelands College *A*
Cuyahoga Community College:
Metropolitan Campus *A*
Lakeland Community College *C*
Sinclair Community College *A*
University of Akron *B*
University of Cincinnati: Raymond
Walters College *A*
Wright State University *M*

Oklahoma
East Central University *B*

Oregon
Linn-Benton Community College
C,A
Portland Community College *C*
Southwestern Oregon Community
College *A*

Pennsylvania
California University of
Pennsylvania *B,M*

Cheyney University of
Pennsylvania *B*
Reading Area Community
College *A*

Puerto Rico
Inter American University of Puerto
Rico: San German Campus *M*

South Carolina
Bob Jones University *B*
Clemson University *B,M,D*

Tennessee
Cleveland State Community
College *A*
State Technical Institute at
Memphis *A*

Texas
Del Mar College *A*
Kilgore College *A*
LeTourneau University *B*
Texas A&M University *M*
University of Houston *B*

Virginia
John Tyler Community College *C*
Lord Fairfax Community College *A*
Lynchburg College *M*
Tidewater Community College *C,A*

Washington
Central Washington University *B*
Clark College *C,A*
Edmonds Community College *C,A*

West Virginia
Marshall University *C,A*

Wisconsin
Chippewa Valley Technical
College *A*
Mid-State Technical College *A*
Milwaukee School of Engineering *B*
Moraine Park Technical College *A*
Western Wisconsin Technical
College *A*

American Samoa, Caroline Islands, Guam, Marianas, Virgin Islands
Guam Community College *C,A*

Transportation management

Alabama
Auburn University *B*
Community College of the Air
Force *A*
Jefferson State Community
College *A*
John C. Calhoun State Community
College *A*
University of Alabama *B,M,D*

Arizona
Pima Community College *C,A*

Arkansas
Arkansas State University *B*
University of Arkansas *B*

California
California State University
Fresno *B*
Long Beach *C*
Los Angeles *B*

Chabot College A
Chaffey Community College C,A
City College of San Francisco A
De Anza College C,A
Golden Gate University C,B,M
San Francisco State University B,M
San Joaquin Delta College C

Colorado
Community College of Denver A
University of Colorado at
Boulder B

Delaware
Delaware Technical and
Community College: Stanton/
Wilmington Campus A

Florida
Embry-Riddle Aeronautical
University A,B,M
Florida International University B
Florida Memorial College B
University of North Florida B

Georgia
Georgia Southern University B

Idaho
Boise State University B

Illinois
Carl Sandburg College A
City Colleges of Chicago: Chicago
City-Wide College C,A
College of DuPage C,A
Elmhurst College B
Illinois Central College C
Moraine Valley Community College
C,A
Oakton Community College C,A
Parkland College C
Parks College of St. Louis
University B
Richland Community College A
Triton College C,A
Western Illinois University B

Indiana
Indiana University Bloomington
B,M,D

Iowa
Iowa State University B,M

Kentucky
Eastern Kentucky University B

Maine
Maine Maritime Academy B,M

Maryland
Morgan State University M
University of Maryland: College
Park B

Massachusetts
Babson College M
Bridgewater State College B
Massachusetts Institute of
Technology M,D
Massachusetts Maritime
Academy B
Northeastern University C,A,B

Michigan
Henry Ford Community College A
Lansing Community College A
Michigan State University B,M,D
Muskegon Community College C

Minnesota
St. Paul Technical College C

Mississippi
Mississippi State University B

Missouri
St. Louis University B

New Hampshire
Daniel Webster College A

New Jersey
Burlington County College A
Thomas Edison State College A,B

New York
City University of New York: New
York City Technical College A
Nassau Community College A
Niagara University B
Polytechnic University M,D
St. John's University B
State University of New York
Maritime College B,M
Syracuse University B,M

North Carolina
Catawba Valley Community
College A
Central Piedmont Community
College A
Davidson County Community
College C
Gaston College A
North Carolina Agricultural and
Technical State University B

North Dakota
North Dakota State University B
University of North Dakota B,M

Ohio
Air Force Institute of
Technology M
Cuyahoga Community College:
Metropolitan Campus A
John Carroll University B
Ohio State University: Columbus
Campus B
Sinclair Community College C,A
University of Akron A
University of Toledo A,B
Youngstown State University A,B

Oklahoma
Oklahoma State University:
Oklahoma City A

Pennsylvania
Harrisburg Area Community
College C,A
Penn State University Park Campus
C,B
Robert Morris College B
Shippensburg University of
Pennsylvania B
Temple University M,D
University of Pennsylvania B,M
Westmoreland County Community
College C

Tennessee
Martin Methodist College A
University of Tennessee:
Knoxville B

Texas
Brookhaven College A
Houston Community College C
Texas A&M University at
Galveston B

Utah
Weber State University A

Virginia
Central Virginia Community
College C
University of Richmond C,A

Washington
Green River Community College
C,A

West Virginia
Marshall University B

Wisconsin
Northeast Wisconsin Technical
College A
University of Wisconsin: Madison
B,M

Canada
McGill University C

Transportation and travel marketing

Arizona
Lamson Junior College C

Arkansas
Henderson State University B

California
Chabot College A
City College of San Francisco C,A
Coastline Community College C,A
Los Angeles City College C,A
Los Medanos College C,A
Palomar College C
Pasadena City College C,A
Phillips Junior College
Condie Campus C,A
San Fernando Valley Campus
C,A
San Francisco State University B
Southwestern College C,A
United States International
University B

Colorado
Arapahoe Community College C
Colorado Mountain College:
Timberline Campus A
Mesa State College A
National College A
Pikes Peak Community College C

Connecticut
University of New Haven C

Florida
Broward Community College A
Daytona Beach Community
College A
Lynn University B
Miami-Dade Community College A
Webber College A,B

Georgia
Georgia Southern University B

Hawaii
Brigham Young University-Hawaii
C,A,B
University of Hawaii at Manoa B

Illinois
City Colleges of Chicago: Chicago
City-Wide College C,A
College of DuPage C,A
De Paul University B
Elgin Community College C
MacCormac Junior College A
Moraine Valley Community College
C,A
Parks College of St. Louis
University B
Southern Illinois University at
Carbondale B

Iowa
American Institute of Business A
Clinton Community College C
Des Moines Area Community
College C
Iowa Lakes Community College A

Kansas
Brown Mackie College C
Hutchinson Community College A
Kansas State University B

Kentucky
Eastern Kentucky University B

Louisiana
Phillips Junior College: New
Orleans A

Maine
Beal College A
Casco Bay College C

Maryland
Villa Julie College A

Massachusetts
Bay Path College A
Bay State College A
Becker College: Leicester
Campus A
Endicott College A,B
Fisher College A
Lasell College A,B
Massasoit Community College C,A
Mount Ida College A

Michigan
Baker College
Flint A
Owosso A
Lansing Community College A

Mississippi
Phillips Junior College of Jackson C

Missouri
Columbia College A,B
East Central College A
National College A

Nebraska
Lincoln School of Commerce C

New Hampshire
Daniel Webster College A

New Mexico
New Mexico State University B

New York
Adirondack Community College A
Berkeley School: New York City A
Bryant & Stratton Business
Institute: Albany C,A

City University of New York
   Kingsborough Community
     College *A*
   La Guardia Community
     College *A*
   New York City Technical
     College *A*
Daemen College *B*
Jefferson Community College *C,A*
Nassau Community College *A*
St. John Fisher College *C*
Sullivan County Community
   College *A*
Taylor Business Institute *A*
Westchester Community College
   C,A

North Carolina
Blue Ridge Community College *A*
Cecils College *C*

North Dakota
North Dakota State University:
   Bottineau and Institute of
   Forestry *C*

Ohio
Lakeland Community College *A*
Sinclair Community College *A*
University of Akron *A*
University of Cincinnati: Access
   Colleges *A*
University of Toledo *A*

Oklahoma
Oklahoma Junior College *A*

Pennsylvania
California University of
   Pennsylvania *B*
Keystone Junior College *A*
Lehigh County Community
   College *A*
Mansfield University of
   Pennsylvania *B*
Mercyhurst College *C*
Pittsburgh Technical Institute *C*

South Dakota
Huron University *A*
National College *A*

Tennessee
Memphis State University *B*

Texas
El Paso Community College *C*
Texas Southmost College *A*

Utah
Brigham Young University *B*
Dixie College *C,A*
Stevens-Henager College of
   Business *C*

Vermont
Champlain College *A*

Virginia
National Business College *A*
Northern Virginia Community
   College *C,A*

Washington
Art Institute of Seattle *A*
Griffin College *C,A*

West Virginia
Davis and Elkins College *B*

Wisconsin
Mid-State Technical College *C*
Stratton College *A*

Ultrasound technology

Alabama
Shelton State Community
   College *A*
Shoals Community College *A*
Wallace State Community College
   at Hanceville *A*

California
Charles R. Drew University: College
   of Allied Health *C*
Foothill College *C*
Orange Coast College *C,A*

Florida
Barry University *B*
Broward Community College *A*
Hillsborough Community College *C*
Palm Beach Community College *A*
University of Miami *B*
Valencia Community College *A*

Georgia
Medical College of Georgia *B*

Illinois
City Colleges of Chicago: Wright
   College *A*
Triton College *C,A*

Kansas
Kansas Newman College *A*

Maryland
Anne Arundel Community
   College *C*

Massachusetts
Middlesex Community College *A*

Michigan
Jackson Community College *A*
Lansing Community College *A*
Marygrove College *A*
Oakland Community College *A*

Missouri
St. Louis Community College at
   Forest Park *C,A*

Nebraska
Nebraska Methodist College of
   Nursing and Allied Health *A,B*
University of Nebraska Medical
   Center *B*

New Jersey
Bergen Community College *A*
Gloucester County College *A*
University of Medicine and
   Dentistry of New Jersey: School
   of Health Related Professions *C*

New Mexico
University of New Mexico *B*

New York
Hudson Valley Community
   College *A*
Pace University *B*
Rochester Institute of
   Technology *B*

North Carolina
Caldwell Community College and
   Technical Institute *C,A*
Forsyth Technical Community
   College *A*
Pitt Community College *A*

Ohio
Central Ohio Technical College *A*
Cuyahoga Community College:
   Western Campus *A*
Kettering College of Medical Arts
   C,A
Owens Technical College: Toledo *A*

Oklahoma
University of Oklahoma Health
   Sciences Center *B*

Oregon
Portland Community College *A*

Pennsylvania
Elizabethtown College *B*
Juniata College *B*
Keystone Junior College *A*
Lebanon Valley College of
   Pennsylvania *B*
Thomas Jefferson University:
   College of Allied Health
   Sciences *B*

Puerto Rico
Puerto Rico Junior College *A*

South Carolina
Greenville Technical College *C*
Trident Technical College *C*

Texas
Austin Community College *C*
Del Mar College *A*
El Centro College *C,A*
El Paso Community College *C*
Houston Community College *C*
St. Philip's College *C*

Utah
Weber State University *A*

Virginia
Tidewater Community College *C*

Washington
Bellevue Community College *A*
Seattle University *B*
Tacoma Community College *C*

Wisconsin
Chippewa Valley Technical
   College *A*

Urban design

Alabama
Alabama Agricultural and
   Mechanical University *B*

California
Modesto Junior College *A*
University of California: Los
   Angeles *M,D*

Colorado
University of Colorado at
   Denver *M*

District of Columbia
Catholic University of America *M*

Indiana
Ball State University *B,M*
Purdue University *B,M,D*

Maryland
University of Maryland: College
   Park *B*

Massachusetts
Harvard University *M*
Massachusetts Institute of
   Technology *B,M,D*

Michigan
University of Michigan *M*

Minnesota
University of Minnesota: Twin
   Cities *B*

Missouri
Washington University *M*

New Jersey
Stevens Institute of Technology
   B,M,D

New York
City University of New York: City
   College *M*
Columbia University: School of
   Engineering and Applied
   Science *M*
Cornell University *B,M,D*
New York University *B*
Parsons School of Design *B*
Pratt Institute *M*
State University of New York
   College of Environmental Science
   and Forestry *B,M,D*

Ohio
Union Institute *B,D*
University of Cincinnati *B*

Pennsylvania
California University of
   Pennsylvania *B*
Carnegie Mellon University *M,D,W*
University of Pennsylvania *M*.

Texas
Rice University *M*
Texas Tech University *B*

Washington
Eastern Washington University *B,M*
University of Washington *M,D*

Urban planning technology

Maryland
Montgomery College: Rockville
   Campus *A*

Massachusetts
Harvard University *D*

Pennsylvania
California University of
   Pennsylvania *B*

Urban studies

Alabama
Alabama Agricultural and Mechanical University *B*
Auburn University at Montgomery *B*

Arkansas
Arkansas State University *B*

California
California State University
    Fresno *M*
    Northridge *B*
    Stanislaus *B*
Loyola Marymount University *B*
Occidental College *B*
San Francisco State University *B*
San Jose State University *M*
Stanford University *B*
University of California
    Davis *M*
    San Diego *B*
University of the Pacific *B*
University of Southern California *B,M*
Whittier College *B*

Colorado
Metropolitan State College of Denver *B*

Connecticut
Albertus Magnus College *B*
Connecticut College *B*
Southern Connecticut State University *M*
Trinity College *B*
University of Connecticut *B*
Wesleyan University *B*

Delaware
University of Delaware *M,D*

District of Columbia
Catholic University of America *B*
Mount Vernon College *B*
University of the District of Columbia *A,B*

Florida
Florida Atlantic University *B,M*
Florida International University *B*
Florida State University *M,D*
Stetson University *B*
University of Tampa *B*

Georgia
Atlanta Metropolitan College *A*
Clayton State College *A*
DeKalb College *A*
Georgia State University *B,M*
Gordon College *A*
Morehouse College *B*
Morris Brown College *B*

Hawaii
University of Hawaii at Manoa *M*

Illinois
Chicago State University *B*
De Paul University *B*
Elmhurst College *B*
North Park College and Theological Seminary *B*
Northeastern Illinois University *B,M*
Northwestern University *B*
Rockford College *B*

Roosevelt University *B*
University of Chicago *B,M,D*
University of Illinois at Chicago *M*

Indiana
Indiana State University *B,M*
Indiana University Bloomington *B,M,D*
University of Notre Dame *B*

Iowa
Central College *B*
University of Iowa *M*

Kentucky
Murray State University *B*
University of Louisville *B*

Louisiana
Dillard University *B*
University of New Orleans *M,D*

Maryland
Morgan State University *B,M*
University of Maryland: College Park *B*

Massachusetts
Boston University *B,M*
Hampshire College *B*
Massachusetts Institute of Technology *B,M,D*
Tufts University *M*
University of Massachusetts at Boston *C*
Westfield State College *B*
Worcester Polytechnic Institute *B*
Worcester State College *B*

Michigan
Aquinas College *B*
Grand Valley State University *B*
Michigan State University *B,M,D*
University of Michigan
    Ann Arbor *M*
    Flint *B*
Wayne State University *B*
William Tyndale College *C,A,B*

Minnesota
Augsburg College *B*
Bethel College *B*
Hamline University *B*
Macalester College *B*
Mankato State University *B,M*
St. Cloud State University *B*
St. Olaf College *B*
University of Minnesota
    Duluth *B*
    Twin Cities *B*
Willmar Community College *A*
Winona State University *B*

Mississippi
Jackson State University *B*

Missouri
St. Louis University *B,M*
University of Missouri: Kansas City *B*
Washington University *B,M*

Nebraska
Bellevue College *B*
University of Nebraska—Omaha *B,M*

New Jersey
Rutgers—The State University of New Jersey
    Camden College of Arts and Sciences *B*
    Douglass College *B*
    Livingston College *B*
    New Brunswick *M,D*
    Rutgers College *B*
    University College Camden *B*
    University College New Brunswick *B*
St. Peter's College *B*
Union County College *A*

New York
Barnard College *B*
Canisius College *B*
City University of New York
    Brooklyn College *B*
    Hunter College *B,M*
    Queens College *B,M*
College of Mount St. Vincent *B*
Columbia University
    Columbia College *B*
    School of General Studies *B*
Cornell University *B,M,D*
Eugene Lang College/New School for Social Research *B*
Fordham University *B*
Hobart College *B*
Iona College *B*
Long Island University: Brooklyn Campus *M*
Manhattan College *B*
New York University *B,M*
Pace University: Pleasantville/ Briarcliff *B*
Rensselaer Polytechnic Institute *M,D*
Sarah Lawrence College *B*
State University of New York at Buffalo *M*
Vassar College *B*
William Smith College *B*

North Carolina
Johnson C. Smith University *B*
St. Augustine's College *B*
University of North Carolina at Greensboro *B*
Winston-Salem State University *B*

Ohio
Cleveland State University *B,M,D*
College of Wooster *B*
Miami University: Oxford Campus *B*
Oberlin College *B*
Ohio Wesleyan University *B*
Union Institute *B,D*
University of Akron *M*
University of Cincinnati
    Cincinnati *B*
    Clermont College *A*
    Raymond Walters College *A*
University of Toledo *B*
Wittenberg University *B*
Wright State University *B*

Oklahoma
Langston University *B*

Oregon
Portland State University *M,D*

Pennsylvania
Bryn Mawr College *B*
California University of Pennsylvania *B*
Carnegie Mellon University *B,M,D,W*

Haverford College *B*
Juniata College *B*
La Salle University *B*
Lehigh University *B*
Shippensburg University of Pennsylvania *B*
Temple University *B,M,D*
University of Pennsylvania *B,M,D*
University of Pittsburgh *B*

Puerto Rico
University of the Sacred Heart *B*

Rhode Island
Brown University *B*
Community College of Rhode Island *A*
Rhode Island College *B*
University of Rhode Island *B*

South Carolina
College of Charleston *B*
Furman University *B*

Tennessee
Austin Peay State University *B*
David Lipscomb University *B*
Memphis State University *B*
Middle Tennessee State University *B*
Rhodes College *B*
University of Tennessee
    Chattanooga *B*
    Knoxville *B*
Vanderbilt University *B*

Texas
Baylor University *B*
St. Philip's College *A*
Texas Christian University *B*
Trinity University *B,M*
University of Texas at Arlington *M*

Utah
University of Utah *B*

Virginia
Christopher Newport College *B*
Norfolk State University *B,M*
Old Dominion University *M,D*
University of Richmond *B*
Virginia Commonwealth University *B*
Virginia Polytechnic Institute and State University *B*

Washington
Eastern Washington University *B,M*
Evergreen State College *B*
Seattle Pacific University *B*
Western Washington University *B*

Wisconsin
Carthage College *B*
University of Wisconsin
    Green Bay *B*
    Madison *M,D*
    Milwaukee *M,D*
    Oshkosh *B*

Vehicle and equipment operation

Alabama
Community College of the Air Force *A*

Arizona
Rio Salado Community College *A*

California
Merced College *C*

Illinois
Elgin Community College *C*
University of Illinois at Urbana-
Champaign *C*

Iowa
Hawkeye Institute of Technology *C*

Michigan
Oakland Community College *C*

Minnesota
Alexandria Technical College *C*

Mississippi
Copiah-Lincoln Community
College *C*
Mississippi Gulf Coast Community
College: Perkinston *C*
Northeast Mississippi Community
College *C*

Nebraska
Southeast Community College:
Lincoln Campus *C*

New Mexico
Albuquerque Technical-Vocational
Institute *C*

North Carolina
Wilson Technical Community
College *C*

South Carolina
Nielsen Electronics Institute *C*

Texas
Brazosport College *C,A*
Houston Community College *C*
Texas State Technical College:
Amarillo *C*

Washington
Skagit Valley College *C,A*

Wisconsin
Fox Valley Technical College *C*

Veterinarian's assistant

Alabama
Community College of the Air
Force *A*
Gadsden State Community
College *A*
Snead State Junior College *A*

California
Cosumnes River College *A*
Foothill College *A*
Hartnell College *A*
Los Angeles Pierce College *A*
San Diego Mesa College *A*
Yuba College *A*

Colorado
Bel-Rea Institute of Animal
Technology *A*
Colorado Mountain College: Spring
Valley Campus *A*

Connecticut
Quinnipiac College *B*

Delaware
Delaware Technical and
Community College: Southern
Campus *A*

Florida
St. Petersburg Junior College *A*

Illinois
Parkland College *A*

Indiana
Purdue University *A*

Iowa
Kirkwood Community College *A*

Kansas
Colby Community College *A*
Johnson County Community
College *A*

Kentucky
Morehead State University *A,B*

Louisiana
Northwestern State University *A*

Maryland
Anne Arundel Community
College *A*
Essex Community College *A*

Massachusetts
Becker College: Leicester
Campus *A*
Holyoke Community College *A*
Mount Ida College *A,B*

Michigan
Macomb Community College *C,A*

Mississippi
Hinds Community College *A*

Missouri
Jefferson College *A*
Maple Woods Community
College *A*

Nebraska
Nebraska College of Technical
Agriculture *A*

Nevada
Community College of Southern
Nevada *A*

New Hampshire
New Hampshire Technical College:
Stratham *C*
University of New Hampshire *A*

New Jersey
Camden County College *A*

New York
City University of New York: La
Guardia Community College *A*
Medaille College *A*
Mercy College *B*
State University of New York
College of Technology at
Canton *A*
College of Technology at
Delhi *A*
College of Technology at
Farmingdale *A*

North Carolina
Central Carolina Community
College *A*

Ohio
Columbus State Community
College *A*
Cuyahoga Community College:
Western Campus *A*
University of Cincinnati: Raymond
Walters College *A*

Oregon
Portland Community College *A*

Pennsylvania
Harcum Junior College *A*
Manor Junior College *A*
Wilson College *B*

Puerto Rico
University of Puerto Rico: Medical
Sciences Campus *B*

South Carolina
Tri-County Technical College *A*

South Dakota
National College *A*

Tennessee
Columbia State Community
College *A*
Lincoln Memorial University *A*

Texas
Amarillo College *A*
Houston Community College *C*
Midland College *A*
North Harris Montgomery
Community College District *A*

Vermont
Vermont Technical College *A*

Virginia
Blue Ridge Community College *A*
Northern Virginia Community
College *A*

Washington
Pierce College *A*

West Virginia
Fairmont State College *A*

Wisconsin
Madison Area Technical College *A*

Wyoming
Eastern Wyoming College *A*

Veterinary medicine (D.V.M.)

Alabama
Auburn University *F*
Tuskegee University *F*

California
University of California: Davis *F*

Colorado
Colorado State University *F*

Florida
University of Florida *F*

Georgia
University of Georgia *F*

Illinois
University of Illinois at Urbana-
Champaign *F*

Indiana
Purdue University *F*

Iowa
Iowa State University *F*

Kansas
Kansas State University *F*

Louisiana
Louisiana State University and
Agricultural and Mechanical
College *F*

Massachusetts
Tufts University *F*

Michigan
Michigan State University *F*

Minnesota
University of Minnesota: Twin
Cities *F*

Mississippi
Mississippi State University *F*

Missouri
University of Missouri: Columbia *F*

New York
Cornell University *F*

North Carolina
North Carolina State University *F*

Ohio
Ohio State University: Columbus
Campus *F*

Oklahoma
Oklahoma State University *F*

Oregon
Oregon State University *F*

Pennsylvania
University of Pennsylvania *F*

Tennessee
University of Tennessee:
Knoxville *F*

Texas
Southwest Texas State University *F*
Texas A&M University *F*

Utah
Brigham Young University *F*

Virginia
Virginia Polytechnic Institute and
State University *F*

Washington
Washington State University *F*

Wisconsin
University of Wisconsin: Madison *F*

Video

California
California College of Arts and
Crafts B,M
California Institute of the Arts
C,B,M
California State University: Long
Beach B
Columbia College: Hollywood A,B
Cosumnes River College C
Los Angeles City College C
Saddleback College A
San Francisco Art Institute B,M
Southern California College B
University of California: Santa Cruz
C,B

Colorado
Colorado Institute of Art A

Connecticut
Northwestern Connecticut
Community College A
University of Hartford B

District of Columbia
American University B,M

Florida
Fort Lauderdale College A
Phillips Junior College:
Melbourne A
University of Miami B

Georgia
Atlanta College of Art B
Georgia State University B
Savannah College of Art and
Design B,M
University of Georgia B,M,D

Illinois
Columbia College B,M
School of the Art Institute of
Chicago B,M
Southern Illinois University at
Carbondale B

Indiana
Indiana Vocational Technical
College: Northcentral A
University of Notre Dame B

Iowa
Maharishi International
University C

Maryland
Villa Julie College A,B

Massachusetts
Emerson College B
Hampshire College B
Massachusetts College of Art B,M
Massachusetts Institute of
Technology B
Montserrat College of Art B
School of the Museum of Fine
Arts B

Michigan
Eastern Michigan University B
Kendall College of Art and
Design B
Madonna University A,B

Minnesota
Worthington Community College A

Missouri
Kansas City Art Institute B
Webster University B

Montana
Montana State University B

Nebraska
Western Nebraska Community
College: Scottsbluff Campus A

New Hampshire
Franklin Pierce College B

New Jersey
Rutgers—The State University of
New Jersey: Mason Gross School
of the Arts B,M
Stockton State College B

New York
Alfred University B
City University of New York
Brooklyn College B,M
City College B
Five Towns College A,B
New York University B
Pratt Institute B
Rochester Institute of Technology
A,B
Sarah Lawrence College B
School of Visual Arts B
State University of New York at
Purchase B
Sullivan County Community
College A
Syracuse University B,M

Ohio
Ohio Institute of Photography C,A

Oklahoma
University of Oklahoma B

Pennsylvania
Art Institute of Pittsburgh A
Point Park College B

Rhode Island
New England Institute of
Technology A
Rhode Island School of Design B

South Carolina
Bob Jones University B,M

Texas
Houston Community College C,A
North Lake College A
South Plains College A

Vermont
Marlboro College B

Washington
Eastern Washington University B
Evergreen State College B
Seattle Central Community
College A
Shoreline Community College A

Visual and performing arts

Alabama
Alabama State University B
Auburn University B
Brewer State Junior College A
Chattahoochee Valley Community
College A
Faulkner University B
Huntingdon College B
Shelton State Community
College A
University of Alabama in
Birmingham B
University of Montevallo B,M

Alaska
Alaska Pacific University B

Arizona
Arizona Western College A
Eastern Arizona College A
Mesa Community College A
Prescott College B
University of Arizona B

Arkansas
Henderson State University B,M
Mississippi County Community
College A
Ouachita Baptist University B

California
California Institute of the Arts
C,B,M
California State University
Bakersfield B
Chico B,M
Fullerton B,M
Hayward B
Chapman University B
College of the Sequoias A
Cosumnes River College A
Crafton Hills College A
Grossmont Community College C,A
Irvine Valley College A
Los Angeles City College C
Marymount College A
Merced College A
Monterey Peninsula College C,A
Moorpark College A
Occidental College B
Otis/Parsons School of Art and
Design B
Pacific Union College B
Pepperdine University B
Porterville College A
Saddleback College A
San Joaquin Delta College A
San Jose City College A
San Jose State University B,M
Santa Rosa Junior College A
Scripps College B
Skyline College A
United States International
University B,M
University of California
Riverside B
Santa Barbara B,M,D
University of La Verne B
Westmont College B
World College West B

Colorado
Colorado Christian University B
Colorado Mountain College: Spring
Valley Campus A
Fort Lewis College B
Mesa State College A,B
Metropolitan State College of
Denver B
Northeastern Junior College A
Pikes Peak Community College A
University of Colorado at Denver B
University of Northern Colorado
B,M
University of Southern Colorado B

Connecticut
Fairfield University B
Manchester Community College A
Sacred Heart University B
University of Bridgeport B
University of New Haven B
Wesleyan University B

Delaware
University of Delaware M

District of Columbia
Catholic University of America B,M
Gallaudet University B
George Washington University B,M
Howard University B
Mount Vernon College B
Trinity College B

Florida
Barry University B
Brevard Community College A
Daytona Beach Community
College A
Edison Community College A
Flagler College B
Florida Agricultural and Mechanical
University B
Florida Southern College B
Indian River Community College A
Pensacola Junior College A
St. Johns River Community
College A
University of Central Florida B
University of West Florida B
Valencia Community College A

Georgia
Abraham Baldwin Agricultural
College A
Darton College A
Georgia Southwestern College B
Mercer University B
Reinhardt College A
Shorter College B
Wesleyan College B
Young Harris College A

Hawaii
Brigham Young University-
Hawaii B

Illinois
Barat College B
Black Hawk College
East Campus A
Moline A
Bradley University B,M
Columbia College B
Eureka College B
Highland Community College A
Illinois College B
Illinois Valley Community
College A
Joliet Junior College A
Judson College B
Millikin University B
Monmouth College B
Morton College A
National-Louis University B
Northern Illinois University B
Northwestern University B
Rend Lake College A
Richland Community College A
Rockford College B
Roosevelt University B,M
Rosary College B
Sangamon State University B
School of the Art Institute of
Chicago B,M
Southern Illinois University at
Carbondale M

University of Chicago *B*
William Rainey Harper College *A*

Indiana

Ball State University *B*
Earlham College *B*
Indiana State University *B,M*
Indiana University
    Bloomington *B,M*
    Northwest *B*
    South Bend *B*
Indiana University—Purdue
    University at Fort Wayne *B*
Marian College *B*
Purdue University *B,M*
St. Mary-of-the-Woods College *B*
University of Notre Dame *B,M*
University of Southern Indiana *B*
Valparaiso University *B*
Vincennes University *A*

Iowa

Briar Cliff College *B*
Kirkwood Community College *A*
Maharishi International University
    A,B,M
Muscatine Community College *A*
North Iowa Area Community
    College *A*
Teikyo Marycrest University *B*
Waldorf College *A*
William Penn College *B*

Kansas

Barton County Community
    College *A*
Bethel College *B*
Colby Community College *A*
Dodge City Community College *A*
Highland Community College *A*
Kansas State University *M*
Neosho County Community
    College *A*
Ottawa University *B*
Pratt Community College *A*
Seward County Community
    College *A*
Southwestern College *B*
University of Kansas *B,M,D*
Washburn University of Topeka *B*
Wichita State University *B*

Kentucky

Berea College *B*
Western Kentucky University *B*

Louisiana

Loyola University *B*
Southern University at New
    Orleans *B*
Southern University and
    Agricultural and Mechanical
    College *B*

Maine

Colby College *B*
University of Maine at
    Farmington *B*

Maryland

Charles County Community
    College *A*
Frostburg State University *B*
Garrett Community College *A*
Montgomery College: Rockville
    Campus *A*
Mount St. Mary's College *B*
University of Maryland Baltimore
    County *B*
Villa Julie College *A*
Western Maryland College *B*

Massachusetts

Berkshire Community College *A*
Boston University *B*
Bradford College *B*
Brandeis University *B*
College of the Holy Cross *B*
Curry College *B*
Dean Junior College *A*
Emerson College *B,M*
Hampshire College *B*
Harvard and Radcliffe Colleges *B*
Massachusetts Bay Community
    College *A*
Massachusetts College of Art *B,M*
Northern Essex Community
    College *A*
Pine Manor College *A,B*
Quinsigamond Community College
    C,A
School of the Museum of Fine Arts
    B,M
Simmons College *B*
Tufts University *B,M*
Williams College *B*

Michigan

Andrews University *B*
Calvin College *B*
Central Michigan University *B,M*
Eastern Michigan University *B,M*
Grand Valley State University *B*
Hillsdale College *B*
Kellogg Community College *A*
Kendall College of Art and
    Design *B*
Lansing Community College *A*
Olivet College *B*
Saginaw Valley State University *B*
Southwestern Michigan College *A*

Minnesota

Bethany Lutheran College *A*
College of St. Benedict *B*
College of St. Catherine: St.
    Catherine Campus *B*
Concordia College: St. Paul *B*
Gustavus Adolphus College *B*
Moorhead State University *M*
Northland Community College *A*
Rainy River Community College *A*
Rochester Community College *A*
St. John's University *B*
St. Mary's College of Minnesota *B*
University of Minnesota: Twin
    Cities *B*
Willmar Community College *A*
Winona State University *B*

Mississippi

Delta State University *B*
Jones County Junior College *A*
Mississippi State University *B*
Mississippi University for Women *B*
Tougaloo College *B*
William Carey College *B*

Missouri

Avila College *B*
Central Methodist College *B*
College of the Ozarks *B*
Culver-Stockton College *B*
Lindenwood College *B*
Moberly Area Community
    College *A*
St. Louis Community College at
    Florissant Valley *A*
St. Louis University *B*
Washington University *B,M*
Webster University *B*
Westminster College *B*
William Woods College *B*

Montana

Carroll College *A*
Miles Community College *A*
Montana State University *B*
Rocky Mountain College *B*

Nebraska

Creighton University *B*
Northeast Community College *A*
University of Nebraska
    Kearney *B*
    Lincoln *B,M*
Western Nebraska Community
    College: Scottsbluff Campus *A*

Nevada

University of Nevada: Reno *B*

New Hampshire

Dartmouth College *B*
Franklin Pierce College *B*
Keene State College *B*
Notre Dame College *B*
Plymouth State College of the
    University System of New
    Hampshire *B*

New Jersey

Atlantic Community College *A*
Bloomfield College *B*
Brookdale Community College *A*
Burlington County College *A*
Camden County College *A*
County College of Morris *A*
Jersey City State College *B*
Kean College of New Jersey *B*
Rutgers—The State University of
    New Jersey
        Douglass College *B*
        Livingston College *B*
        Mason Gross School of the
            Arts *B,M*
        New Brunswick *M*
        Rutgers College *B*
        University College New
            Brunswick *B*
Seton Hall University *B*
Stockton State College *B*
Union County College *A*
Upsala College *B*
William Paterson College of New
    Jersey *B,M*

New Mexico

College of Santa Fe *B*
New Mexico Highlands
    University *B*
New Mexico State University *B*

New York

Adirondack Community College *A*
Bard College *B,M*
Barnard College *B*
City University of New York
    Brooklyn College *B,M*
    City College *B,M*
    Queens College *B*
    York College *B*
College of New Rochelle *B*
Columbia University
    Columbia College *B*
    School of General Studies *B*
Columbia-Greene Community
    College *A*
Cornell University *M,D*
Dowling College *B*
Eugene Lang College/New School
    for Social Research *B*
Fordham University *B*
Fulton-Montgomery Community
    College *A*
Genesee Community College *A*

Hofstra University *B*
Jamestown Community College *A*
Juilliard School *B,M,W*
Long Island University
    Brooklyn Campus *B*
    C. W. Post Campus *B,M*
    Southampton Campus *B*
Molloy College *B*
Nassau Community College *A*
Nazareth College of Rochester *B*
New York University *B,M,D*
Pace University: Pleasantville/
    Briarcliff *A*
Roberts Wesleyan College *B*
Rockland Community College *A*
Sarah Lawrence College *B*
School of Visual Arts *B,M*
State University of New York
    Buffalo *B*
    College at Brockport *M*
    College at Buffalo *B*
    College at New Paltz *B,M*
    College at Old Westbury *B*
Suffolk County Community
    College *A*
Syracuse University *B,M*
Westchester Community College *A*

North Carolina

Bennett College *B*
Brevard College *A*
Central Piedmont Community
    College *A*
Coastal Carolina Community
    College *A*
Fayetteville State University *B*
Gaston College *A*
High Point University *B*
Louisburg College *A*
Mars Hill College *B*
North Carolina Wesleyan College *B*

North Dakota

Dickinson State University *B*
Minot State University *B*

Ohio

Antioch College *B*
Art Academy of Cincinnati *B*
Bluffton College *B*
Bowling Green State University
    Bowling Green *B,M*
    Firelands College *A*
Capital University *B*
Kent State University *B*
Lorain County Community
    College *A*
Ohio State University: Columbus
    Campus *B,M*
Ohio University *B,D*
Ohio Wesleyan University *B*
Sinclair Community College *A*
Union Institute *B,D*
University of Dayton *B*
University of Findlay *B*
University of Rio Grande *A,B*
University of Toledo *B*
Wittenberg University *B*
Wright State University *B*
Youngstown State University *B*

Oklahoma

Cameron University *B*
Oklahoma Baptist University *B*
Oral Roberts University *B*
Redlands Community College *A*
St. Gregory's College *A*
Southeastern Oklahoma State
    University *B*
University of Oklahoma *B*
University of Tulsa *B*

Oregon

Central Oregon Community
College *A*
Marylhurst College *B*
Oregon State University *B*
Pacific University *B*
Rogue Community College *C,A*
Western Oregon State College *B*

Pennsylvania

Allentown College of St. Francis de
Sales *B*
Beaver College *B*
Bryn Mawr College *B*
Bucks County Community
College *A*
California University of
Pennsylvania *B*
Carnegie Mellon University *B,M*
East Stroudsburg University of
Pennsylvania *B*
Elizabethtown College *B*
Indiana University of
Pennsylvania *B*
Juniata College *B*
Kutztown University of
Pennsylvania *B*
Lycoming College *B*
Marywood College *B,M*
Messiah College *B*
Moore College of Art and Design *B*
St. Vincent College *B*
Slippery Rock University of
Pennsylvania *B*
Swarthmore College *B*
Temple University *B*
Villanova University *M*
Waynesburg College *A,B*

Puerto Rico

University of the Sacred Heart *B*

Rhode Island

Community College of Rhode
Island *A*

South Carolina

Bob Jones University *B,M*
North Greenville College *A*

South Dakota

Black Hills State University *B*

Tennessee

Austin Peay State University *B*
Belmont University *B*
Christian Brothers University *B*
Lambuth University *B*
LeMoyne-Owen College *B*
Lincoln Memorial University *B*
Maryville College *B*
Memphis College of Art *B*
Memphis State University *B*
Motlow State Community
College *A*
Vanderbilt University *B*

Texas

Abilene Christian University *B*
Baylor University *B,M*
Bee County College *A*
Central Texas College *A*
Dallas Baptist University *B*
East Texas State University *B,M*
Galveston College *A*
Howard College *A*
Kilgore College *A*
Lamar University—Beaumont *M*
Lon Morris College *A*
McMurry University *B*
Rice University *B,M*
Southwestern University *B*

Texarkana College *A*
Texas Lutheran College *B*
Texas Tech University *B,M,D*
University of Mary Hardin-
Baylor *B*
University of Texas at Dallas
B,M,D
Victoria College *A*
Western Texas College *A*

Utah

Brigham Young University *B*
Weber State University *B*
Westminster College of Salt Lake
City *B*

Vermont

Bennington College *B,M*
Goddard College *B,M*
Johnson State College *B*
Marlboro College *B*
Norwich University *M*
University of Vermont *B*

Virginia

Averett College *B*
Bluefield College *B*
Christopher Newport College *B*
College of William and Mary *B*
Longwood College *B*
Lynchburg College *B*
Norfolk State University *M*
Old Dominion University *B*
Roanoke College *B*
Shenandoah University *B*
Virginia Intermont College *B*
Virginia Wesleyan College *B*

Washington

Centralia College *A*
Columbia Basin College *A*
Eastern Washington University *B*
Everett Community College *A*
Evergreen State College *B*
Olympic College *A*
Pierce College *A*
Seattle Central Community
College *A*
Seattle Pacific University *B*
Seattle University *B*
Skagit Valley College *A*
Wenatchee Valley College *A*
Western Washington University *B*

West Virginia

Bethany College *B*
Marshall University *B*
Shepherd College *B*

Wisconsin

Cardinal Stritch College *B*
Carroll College *B*
Carthage College *B*
Edgewood College *B*
Lakeland College *B*
Marquette University *B,M*
Mount Senario College *B*
Ripon College *B*
University of Wisconsin
Eau Claire *B*
Green Bay *B*
Milwaukee *B,M*
Oshkosh *B*
Parkside *B*
River Falls *B*
Stevens Point *B*
Superior *B*
Whitewater *B*

Wyoming

Casper College *A*
Central Wyoming College *A*

Eastern Wyoming College *A*
Northwest College *A*
Western Wyoming Community
College *A*

American Samoa, Caroline Islands, Guam, Marianas, Virgin Islands

University of Guam *B,M*

Water resources

Arizona

University of Arizona *M,D*

California

Mount San Antonio College *C*

District of Columbia

University of the District of
Columbia *A*

Illinois

City Colleges of Chicago: Chicago
City-Wide College *C,A*
Shawnee Community College *C*

Kansas

Fort Scott Community College *C,A*
University of Kansas *M*

Michigan

Northern Michigan University *B*
University of Michigan *M*

Minnesota

University of Minnesota: Twin
Cities *B,M*

Nevada

University of Nevada: Las Vegas *M*

New Hampshire

University of New Hampshire *B*

New Mexico

University of New Mexico *M*

New York

State University of New York
College of Technology at
Delhi *A*

Ohio

Ohio State University: Columbus
Campus *B,M*

Pennsylvania

California University of
Pennsylvania *B*

Vermont

University of Vermont *M*

Washington

Spokane Community College *A*

Wisconsin

University of Wisconsin: Stevens
Point *B*

Wyoming

University of Wyoming *M*

Water and wastewater technology

Alabama

Bishop State Community College *A*
Gadsden State Community
College *A*
James H. Faulkner State
Community College *A*
John C. Calhoun State Community
College *A*
Lurleen B. Wallace State Junior
College *A*
Shelton State Community
College *A*
Shoals Community College *A*

Arizona

Pima Community College *C,A*
Rio Salado Community College *A*

California

Fresno City College *C,A*
Humboldt State University *M*
Imperial Valley College *C,A*
Los Angeles Trade and Technical
College *C,A*
Mount San Antonio College *C,A*
San Diego City College *C,A*
San Diego Mesa College *C*
San Joaquin Delta College *C*
Ventura College *C,A*

Colorado

Colorado Mountain College:
Timberline Campus *A*
Front Range Community College *C*
Red Rocks Community College *A*

Florida

Daytona Beach Community
College *C*
Palm Beach Community College
C,A
Pensacola Junior College *A*
St. Petersburg Junior College *A*
Seminole Community College *C*
University of Central Florida *B*
Valencia Community College *A*

Georgia

Augusta Technical Institute *A*

Idaho

Boise State University *C*
Lewis Clark State College *C*

Illinois

City Colleges of Chicago: Chicago
City-Wide College *C,A*
College of Lake County *C*
Illinois Central College *C*
Illinois Eastern Community
Colleges: Lincoln Trail College *C*
Joliet Junior College *C,A*
Kishwaukee College *C,A*
Lewis and Clark Community
College *C*
Waubonsee Community College
C,A

Indiana

Indiana Vocational Technical
College: Northwest *C,A*

Iowa

Iowa Lakes Community College *A*
Kirkwood Community College *A*

Kansas

Dodge City Community College *C,A*

Fort Scott Community College *C,A*

Kansas State University *B*

Maine

Southern Maine Technical College *C*

Michigan

Grand Rapids Community College *A*

Kellogg Community College *A*

Lake Superior State University *A*

Northern Michigan University *C,A*

Minnesota

Vermilion Community College *A*

Montana

Northern Montana College *A*

Nebraska

Southeast Community College: Lincoln Campus *C*

New Jersey

Gloucester County College *A*

Thomas Edison State College *A,B*

New Mexico

Dona Ana Branch Community College of New Mexico State University *C,A*

New Mexico State University *C,A*

San Juan College *C*

New York

Paul Smith's College *A*

State University of New York College of Technology at Delhi *A*

Ulster County Community College *A*

North Carolina

Fayetteville Technical Community College *A*

Ohio

Central State University *B*

Muskingum Area Technical College *A*

Owens Technical College: Findlay Campus *C,A*

University of Toledo *A*

Oklahoma

Rose State College *A*

Oregon

Clackamas Community College *C,A*

Linn-Benton Community College *C,A*

Pennsylvania

California University of Pennsylvania *B*

Penn State Harrisburg Capital College *B*

South Carolina

Sumter Area Technical College *C*

Texas

Houston Community College *C*

Tarleton State University *B*

Utah

Utah Valley Community College *C,A*

Virginia

Mountain Empire Community College *A*

Tidewater Community College *C*

Washington

Green River Community College *A*

Spokane Community College *A*

Wisconsin

Moraine Park Technical College *A*

University of Wisconsin: Stevens Point *B*

Wyoming

Casper College *A*

American Samoa, Caroline Islands, Guam, Marianas, Virgin Islands

Guam Community College *C,A*

Mexico

Sistema Instituto Tecnologico y de Estudios Superiores de Monterrey *D*

Welding technology

Alabama

Bessemer State Technical College *C*

Brewer State Junior College *A*

Central Alabama Community College: Childersburg Campus *C*

Gadsden State Community College *C*

John C. Calhoun State Community College *A*

John M. Patterson State Technical College *A*

Reid State Technical College *C*

Shelton State Community College *C*

Alaska

University of Alaska Anchorage *A*

Arizona

Arizona Western College *A*

Cochise College *A*

Eastern Arizona College *A*

Navajo Community College *C*

Northland Pioneer College *C,A*

Pima Community College *C,A*

Yavapai College *C*

Arkansas

Phillips County Community College *C,A*

Westark Community College *C,A*

California

Allan Hancock College *C,A*

Barstow College *C,A*

Cerritos Community College *C*

Chabot College *A*

College of the Redwoods *C,A*

College of the Sequoias *A*

Cosumnes River College *C*

El Camino College *C,A*

Glendale Community College *C*

Imperial Valley College *C,A*

Lassen College *C,A*

Long Beach City College *C,A*

Los Angeles Pierce College *C,A*

Los Angeles Trade and Technical College *A*

Merced College *A*

Mount San Antonio College *C,A*

Napa Valley College *C,A*

Orange Coast College *C,A*

Porterville College *C,A*

San Joaquin Delta College *C,A*

Sierra College *C,A*

Solano Community College *A*

Ventura College *C,A*

West Hills Community College *A*

Colorado

Front Range Community College *C,A*

Lamar Community College *C*

Mesa State College *C,A*

Morgan Community College *C*

Otero Junior College *C*

Pikes Peak Community College *C,A*

Pueblo Community College *C,A*

Red Rocks Community College *C,A*

Delaware

Delaware Technical and Community College: Southern Campus *A*

Florida

Brevard Community College *C*

Central Florida Community College *C*

Okaloosa-Walton Community College *C*

Pasco-Hernando Community College *C*

Pensacola Junior College *C*

Georgia

Augusta Technical Institute *C*

Brunswick College *C*

Dalton College *C*

Floyd College *A*

Savannah Technical Institute *C*

Hawaii

University of Hawaii
Honolulu Community College *C,A*
Kauai Community College *C,A*

Idaho

Boise State University *C*

College of Southern Idaho *C,A*

Lewis Clark State College *A*

North Idaho College *C,A*

Ricks College *A*

Illinois

Belleville Area College *C,A*

Black Hawk College: East Campus *C,A*

Carl Sandburg College *C*

College of DuPage *C*

College of Lake County *C*

Elgin Community College *C,A*

Highland Community College *A*

Illinois Central College *C,A*

Illinois Eastern Community Colleges: Olney Central College *C,A*

Kishwaukee College *C*

Lake Land College *C*

Lewis and Clark Community College *C*

Lincoln Land Community College *C*

Moraine Valley Community College *C*

Morton College *C*

Rend Lake College *C*

Shawnee Community College *C*

Southern Illinois University at Carbondale *A*

Spoon River College *C*

Triton College *C,A*

Indiana

Indiana Vocational Technical College
Central Indiana *C*
Eastcentral *C*
Kokomo *C*
Lafayette *C*
Northcentral *C*
Northeast *C*
Northwest *C*
Southcentral *C,A*
Southeast *C*
Southwest *C*
Wabash Valley *C*

Oakland City College *C,A*

Vincennes University *C,A*

Iowa

Hawkeye Institute of Technology *C*

Iowa Central Community College *C*

Iowa Lakes Community College *C*

Northwest Iowa Technical College *C*

Southeastern Community College: South Campus *C*

Kansas

Butler County Community College *C,A*

Central College *A*

Pittsburg State University *C*

Kentucky

Morehead State University *A*

St. Catharine College *A*

Maine

Eastern Maine Technical College *A*

Michigan

Alpena Community College *C*

Delta College *C,A*

Ferris State University *A,B*

Glen Oaks Community College *C*

Grand Rapids Community College *C,A*

Jackson Community College *C,A*

Kalamazoo Valley Community College *C,A*

Lansing Community College *A*

Macomb Community College *C,A*

Mid Michigan Community College *C,A*

Oakland Community College *C,A*

St. Clair County Community College *C,A*

Schoolcraft College *C*

West Shore Community College *C,A*

Minnesota

St. Paul Technical College *C*

Willmar Technical College *C*

Mississippi

East Central Community College *C*

Jones County Junior College *C*

Mississippi Delta Community College *C*

Mississippi Gulf Coast Community College
Jefferson Davis Campus *C*
Perkinston *C,A*

Missouri

East Central College *C,A*

Jefferson College *C*

Moberly Area Community College *C*

State Fair Community College *C*

Montana

Northern Montana College *C*

Nebraska

Central Community College *C,A*
Metropolitan Community College *C*
Southeast Community College
    Lincoln Campus *C,A*
    Milford Campus *C,A*
Western Nebraska Community
    College
    Scottsbluff Campus *C,A*
    Sidney Campus *A*

Nevada

Community College of Southern
    Nevada *C,A*
Northern Nevada Community
    College *C*

New Hampshire

New Hampshire Technical College
    Manchester *C,A*
    Stratham *C*

New Mexico

Dona Ana Branch Community
    College of New Mexico State
    University *C,A*
Eastern New Mexico University:
    Roswell Campus *C*
New Mexico State University
    Carlsbad *C,A*
    Las Cruces *C,A*
Parks College *C*
San Juan College *A*
Western New Mexico University
    C,A

New York

Columbia-Greene Community
    College *C*
Dutchess Community College *C*
Mohawk Valley Community College
    C,A
State University of New York
    College of Technology at
    Delhi *A*

North Carolina

Alamance Community College *C,A*
Anson Community College *C*
Asheville Buncombe Technical
    Community College *C*
Bladen Community College *C*
Blue Ridge Community College *C*
Brunswick Community College *C*
Caldwell Community College and
    Technical Institute *C*
Cape Fear Community College *C*
Forsyth Technical Community
    College *C,A*
Haywood Community College *C*
Isothermal Community College *C*
James Sprunt Community
    College *C*
Mayland Community College *C*
Piedmont Community College *C*
Richmond Community College *C*
Robeson Community College *C*
Southeastern Community College *C*
Tri-County Community College *C*
Vance-Granville Community
    College *C*
Wilson Technical Community
    College *C*

North Dakota

Bismarck State College *C,A*
North Dakota State College of
    Science *C,A*

Turtle Mountain Community
    College *C*
University of North Dakota: Lake
    Region *C*

Ohio

Jefferson Technical College *A*
Lakeland Community College *C,A*
Owens Technical College: Findlay
    Campus *C*
Terra Technical College *C,A*
University of Cincinnati: Access
    Colleges *C*

Oregon

Central Oregon Community College
    C,A
Chemeketa Community College *C,A*
Lane Community College *C,A*
Linn-Benton Community College *C*
Mount Hood Community College *C*
Portland Community College *C,A*
Southwestern Oregon Community
    College *A*
Treasure Valley Community College
    C,A
Umpqua Community College *C*

Pennsylvania

Community College of Beaver
    County *C,A*
Dean Institute of Technology *C*
Delaware County Community
    College *C*
Johnson Technical Institute *A*
Northampton County Area
    Community College *C,A*
Pennsylvania College of
    Technology *A*
Westmoreland County Community
    College *C,A*

South Carolina

Aiken Technical College *C,A*
Chesterfield-Marlboro Technical
    College *C*
Greenville Technical College *C*
Williamsburg Technical College *C*

South Dakota

Mitchell Vocational Technical
    Institute *C*
Western Dakota Vocational
    Technical Institute *C*

Tennessee

Austin Peay State University *C,A*
Northeast State Technical
    Community College *C,A*

Texas

Alvin Community College *C,A*
Angelina College *C,A*
Austin Community College *C,A*
Bee County College *C,A*
Brazosport College *C,A*
Central Texas College *A*
Cisco Junior College *C*
Cooke County College *A*
Del Mar College *C,A*
El Paso Community College *C*
Lamar University—Beaumont *A*
Laredo Junior College *C*
LeTourneau University *B*
Midland College *A*
Mountain View College *C,A*
Navarro College *C*
Northeast Texas Community
    College *C*
Ranger Junior College *C,A*
St. Philip's College *C,A*
South Plains College *C,A*

Tarrant County Junior College *C,A*
Texas Southmost College *A*
Texas State Technical College
    Amarillo *C*
    Harlingen *A*
    Waco *C,A*
Weatherford College *C,A*

Utah

College of Eastern Utah *C,A*

Virginia

Dabney S. Lancaster Community
    College *C*
Eastern Shore Community
    College *C*
John Tyler Community College *C*
New River Community College *C*
Northern Virginia Community
    College *C*
Southwest Virginia Community
    College *C*
Tidewater Community College *C*

Washington

Centralia College *A*
Clark College *A*
Green River Community College *A*
Lower Columbia College *A*
Olympic College *C,A*
Skagit Valley College *C*
South Puget Sound Community
    College *A*
Spokane Community College *C*
Wenatchee Valley College *A*

West Virginia

West Virginia University at
    Parkersburg *C,A*

Wisconsin

Mid-State Technical College *C*
Northeast Wisconsin Technical
    College *C*
Western Wisconsin Technical
    College *C*

Wyoming

Casper College *C,A*
Central Wyoming College *C,A*
Laramie County Community
    College *C,A*
Northwest College *C*
Sheridan College *C,A*

Western European studies

California

Monterey Institute of International
    Studies *M*
Naval Postgraduate School *M*
University of California: Los
    Angeles *B,D*

District of Columbia

American University *B*
Gallaudet University *B*
Georgetown University *B*

Florida

New College of the University of
    South Florida *B*

Georgia

University of Georgia *B*

Indiana

Indiana University Bloomington *M*
University of Notre Dame *B*

Iowa

Central College *B*

Massachusetts

Hampshire College *B*
Tufts University *B,M*
Wellesley College *B*

Missouri

Washington University *B,M*

Nebraska

University of Nebraska—Lincoln *B*

New York

Bard College *B*
Barnard College *B*
City University of New York:
    Brooklyn College *B*
Columbia University *M,D*
Eugene Lang College/New School
    for Social Research *B*
United States Military Academy *B*
Wells College *B*

North Carolina

University of North Carolina at
    Greensboro *B*

Ohio

College of Wooster *B*
Denison University *B*
Ohio University *B*

Oregon

Willamette University *B*

Pennsylvania

Penn State University Park
    Campus *C*

Texas

Southern Methodist University *B*

Vermont

Marlboro College *B*

Virginia

Sweet Briar College *B*

West Virginia

Shepherd College *B*

Wildlife management

Alabama

Auburn University *B,M,D*

Alaska

University of Alaska Fairbanks
    B,M,D

Arizona

Northern Arizona University *B*
Prescott College *B*
University of Arizona *B,M,D*

Arkansas

Arkansas State University *B*
Arkansas Tech University *B*
University of Arkansas at
    Monticello *B*

California
Cerritos Community College *A*
Feather River College *C,A*
Humboldt State University *C,B,M*
San Joaquin Delta College *A*
Southwestern College *A*
University of California: Davis *B*

Colorado
Colorado State University *B,M,D*

Delaware
Delaware State College *B*

Florida
University of Florida *M,D*

Georgia
Abraham Baldwin Agricultural
College *A*
Reinhardt College *A*
University of Georgia *B,M*

Idaho
North Idaho College *A*
Ricks College *A*
University of Idaho *B*

Illinois
Shawnee Community College *A*
Southern Illinois University at
Carbondale *B,M,D*

Indiana
Purdue University *B,M*
Vincennes University *A*

Iowa
Iowa Lakes Community College *A*
Iowa State University *B,M,D*

Kansas
Pratt Community College *A*
Seward County Community
College *A*

Kentucky
Eastern Kentucky University *B*

Louisiana
Louisiana State University and
Agricultural and Mechanical
College *B,M,D*
Louisiana Tech University *B*
McNeese State University *B*
University of Southwestern
Louisiana *B*

Maine
Unity College *B*
University of Maine
Orono *B,M,D*
Presque Isle *B*

Maryland
Frederick Community College *A*
Frostburg State University *B,M*
University of Maryland: College
Park *B*

Massachusetts
Berkshire Community College *A*

Michigan
Lake Superior State University *B*
Michigan State University *B,M,D*
Mid Michigan Community
College *A*
Northern Michigan University *B*
University of Michigan *M*

Minnesota
Mankato State University *B*
Northland Community College *A*
Rainy River Community College *A*
University of Minnesota: Twin
Cities *M,D*
Vermilion Community College *A*
Willmar Community College *A*
Winona State University *A*

Mississippi
Mississippi State University *M*

Missouri
East Central College *A*
Northwest Missouri State
University *B*
Southwest Missouri State
University *B*
University of Missouri: Columbia
B,M,D

Montana
Montana State University *B,M*
University of Montana *B,M*

Nebraska
Peru State College *B*
Western Nebraska Community
College: Scottsbluff Campus *A*

New Hampshire
University of New Hampshire *B,M*

New Jersey
Rutgers—The State University of
New Jersey: Cook College *B*

New Mexico
Eastern New Mexico University *B*
New Mexico State University *B,M*

New York
Community College of the Finger
Lakes *A*
State University of New York
College of Agriculture and
Technology at Cobleskill *A*
College of Agriculture and
Technology at Morrisville *A*
College of Environmental
Science and Forestry *B,M,D*

North Carolina
Haywood Community College *A*
North Carolina State University *B*
Wayne Community College *A*

North Dakota
Little Hoop Community College
C,A
North Dakota State University
Bottineau and Institute of
Forestry *A*
Fargo *B*
University of North Dakota *B*

Ohio
Hocking Technical College *A*
Ohio State University: Columbus
Campus *B*

Oklahoma
Eastern Oklahoma State College *A*
Southeastern Oklahoma State
University *B*

Oregon
Central Oregon Community
College *A*
Oregon State University *B,M,D*

Pennsylvania
Penn State University Park Campus
C,A

Puerto Rico
University of Puerto Rico: Humacao
University College *B*

Rhode Island
University of Rhode Island *B*

South Dakota
South Dakota State University *B,M*

Tennessee
Lincoln Memorial University *B*
Martin Methodist College *A*
Tennessee Technological
University *B*
University of Tennessee
Knoxville *B,M*
Martin *B*

Texas
Angelo State University *B*
Stephen F. Austin State
University *B*
Sul Ross State University *B,M*
Texas A&I University *B,M*
Texas A&M University *B,M,D*
Texas Tech University *B,M,D*
West Texas State University *B,M*

Utah
Brigham Young University *B,M,D*
Dixie College *A*
Southern Utah University *A,B*
Utah State University *M,D*

Vermont
Sterling College *A*
University of Vermont *B,M*

Virginia
Christopher Newport College *B*
Virginia Polytechnic Institute and
State University *B*

Washington
Centralia College *A*
Grays Harbor College *A*
Spokane Community College *A*
University of Washington *B*
Washington State University *B*
Yakima Valley Community College
C,A

West Virginia
Shepherd College *B*
West Virginia University *B,M*

Wisconsin
Northland College *B*
University of Wisconsin
Madison *B,M,D*
Stevens Point *B*

Wyoming
Casper College *A*
Northwest College *A*
University of Wyoming *B*

Canada
McGill University *B,M,D*

Women's studies

Alabama
University of Alabama *M*

Arizona
Arizona State University *B*
Prescott College *B*
University of Arizona *B*

California
California State University
Long Beach *C*
Stanislaus *B*
Claremont McKenna College *B*
Cosumnes River College *A*
Fresno City College *A*
Humboldt State University *C*
Irvine Valley College *A*
Mills College *B*
Occidental College *B*
Pitzer College *B*
Pomona College *B*
Saddleback College *A*
San Francisco State University *B*
Scripps College *B*
Stanford University *B*
University of California
Berkeley *B*
Davis *B*
Irvine *B*
Riverside *B*
Santa Barbara *B*
Santa Cruz *B*
University of the Pacific *B*
University of Southern California *B*
West Valley College *A*

Colorado
Colorado College *B*
University of Colorado at
Boulder *B*
University of Denver *B*

Connecticut
Trinity College *B*
University of Connecticut *B*
Wesleyan University *B*
Yale University *B*

District of Columbia
George Washington University *M*

Florida
Eckerd College *B*
Florida Atlantic University *C*
New College of the University of
South Florida *B*
Nova University *C*
University of South Florida *B*

Georgia
Darton College *C,B*
Emory University *C,B*
University of Georgia *C,A*

Hawaii
University of Hawaii at Manoa *B*

Illinois
De Paul University *B*
Garrett-Evangelical Theological
Seminary *M,D,W*
KAES College *B*
Knox College *B*
Roosevelt University *B*
Southern Illinois University at
Edwardsville *M*

Indiana
DePauw University *B*
Earlham College *B*
Indiana University Bloomington
  C,A
Purdue University: Calumet *A*

Iowa
Cornell College *B*

Kansas
University of Kansas *B*
Wichita State University *B*

Louisiana
Tulane University *B*

Maine
Bates College *B*
University of Southern Maine *B*

Maryland
Goucher College *B*

Massachusetts
Amherst College *B*
Clark University *D*
Emmanuel College *B*
Hampshire College *B*
Harvard and Radcliffe Colleges *B*
Lesley College *B*
Massachusetts Institute of
  Technology *B*
Mount Holyoke College *B*
Northern Essex Community
  College *A*
Simmons College *B*
Simon's Rock College of Bard *B*
Smith College *B*
University of Massachusetts
  Amherst *B*
  Boston *C,B*
Wellesley College *B*

Michigan
University of Michigan *B*
Wayne State University *B*

Minnesota
College of St. Catherine: St.
  Catherine Campus *B*
Hamline University *B*
Macalester College *B*
Mankato State University *B,M*
St. Olaf College *B*
University of Minnesota
  Duluth *B*
  Twin Cities *B*
Willmar Community College *A*

Missouri
Washington University *B*

Nebraska
University of Nebraska—Lincoln *B*

New Jersey
Bergen Community College *A*
Monmouth College *C*
Rutgers—The State University of
  New Jersey
    Camden College of Arts and
      Sciences *B*
    Douglass College *B*
    Livingston College *B*
    Rutgers College *B*
    University College New
      Brunswick *B*
Stockton State College *C*

New York
Barnard College *B*
City University of New York
  Brooklyn College *B*
  College of Staten Island *B*
  Hunter College *B*
  Queens College *B*
Colgate University *B*
College of New Rochelle *B*
Columbia University
  Columbia College *B*
  School of General Studies *B*
Eugene Lang College/New School
  for Social Research *B*
Fordham University *B*
Hamilton College *B*
Hobart College *B*
New York University *B*
Onondaga Community College *A*
Sarah Lawrence College *B*
State University of New York
  Albany *B*
  Buffalo *B*
  College at New Paltz *B*
Suffolk County Community
  College *A*
Tompkins-Cortland Community
  College *A*
Union College *B*
University of Rochester *B*
Vassar College *B*
William Smith College *B*

North Carolina
Duke University *B*

Ohio
Antioch College *B*
Bowling Green State University *B*
College of Mount St. Joseph *B*
College of Wooster *B*
Denison University *B*
Kent State University *B*
Kenyon College *B*
Oberlin College *B*
Ohio State University: Columbus
  Campus *B*
Ohio Wesleyan University *B*
Union Institute *B,D*
University of Cincinnati: Raymond
  Walters College *C*
University of Toledo *B*
Wittenberg University *B*

Oklahoma
University of Tulsa *C*

Oregon
University of Oregon *C*

Pennsylvania
Bryn Mawr College *B*
Bucknell University *B*
Gettysburg College *B*
Penn State University Park
  Campus *C*
Temple University *B*
University of Pennsylvania *B,M,D*
West Chester University of
  Pennsylvania *C,M*

Rhode Island
Brown University *B*
Rhode Island College *B*
University of Rhode Island *B*

Tennessee
University of Tennessee:
  Knoxville *B*

Texas
El Paso Community College *A*
Rice University *B*
Southwestern University *B*

Vermont
Burlington College *B*
Goddard College *B,M*
Marlboro College *B*
Middlebury College *B*

Virginia
Mary Baldwin College *B*
University of Richmond *B*

Washington
Eastern Washington University *B*
Evergreen State College *B*
University of Washington *B*

Wisconsin
Lawrence University *B*
University of Wisconsin
  Green Bay *A*
  Madison *B*
  Milwaukee *B*

Wyoming
Casper College *A*

Canada
McGill University *B*

Woodworking

Alabama
Gadsden State Community
  College *C*
Wallace State Community College
  at Hanceville *C*

Arizona
Mohave Community College *C*

California
Bakersfield College *A*
Laney College *C,A*
Long Beach City College *C,A*
Merced College *C,A*
Saddleback College *C,A*
San Joaquin Delta College *C,A*

Colorado
Red Rocks Community College *C*

Georgia
Augusta Technical Institute *C*

Idaho
College of Southern Idaho *C,A*
Ricks College *A*

Illinois
Illinois Eastern Community
  Colleges: Olney Central
  College *A*

Kansas
Allen County Community
  College *C*
Fort Scott Community College *A*
Neosho County Community College
  C,A
Pittsburg State University *B*

Kentucky
Eastern Kentucky University *B*

Michigan
Northern Michigan University *A*
Western Michigan University *B*

Minnesota
St. Paul Technical College *C*

Mississippi
East Central Community College *C*

Nebraska
Chadron State College *B*
Southeast Community College:
  Milford Campus *A*

New Mexico
Northern New Mexico Community
  College *C,A*

New York
Rochester Institute of Technology
  A,B,M
State University of New York
  College of Environmental Science
  and Forestry *B,M,D*

North Carolina
Roanoke-Chowan Community
  College *C*
Rockingham Community College *A*
Wilson Technical Community
  College *C*

Ohio
University of Akron *B*
University of Rio Grande *A*

Oklahoma
Oklahoma Panhandle State
  University *A*

Pennsylvania
Johnson Technical Institute *A*

South Dakota
Black Hills State University *B*

Utah
Utah Valley Community College
  C,A

Virginia
Tidewater Community College *C*

Washington
Spokane Community College *A*

Wisconsin
Chippewa Valley Technical
  College *C*
Fox Valley Technical College *C*
Northeast Wisconsin Technical
  College *C*
Western Wisconsin Technical
  College *C*

Word processing

Alabama
Central Alabama Community
  College: Childersburg Campus *C*
Chattahoochee Valley Community
  College *C*
James H. Faulkner State
  Community College *A*
Jefferson State Community
  College *C*
John C. Calhoun State Community
  College *C*

Selma University *A*
Shoals Community College *C*
Southern Union State Junior
   College *C,A*

Alaska

University of Alaska Anchorage *C*

Arizona

Eastern Arizona College *C*
Lamson Junior College *C*
Mesa Community College *C*
Paradise Valley Community
   College *C*
Scottsdale Community College *C,A*
South Mountain Community
   College *C,A*
Yavapai College *C*

Arkansas

Garland County Community
   College *C,A*
Phillips County Community
   College *C*
Southern Arkansas University:
   Technical Branch *C*
Westark Community College *C,A*

California

Allan Hancock College *C,A*
Bakersfield College *A*
Barstow College *C,A*
Central California Commercial
   College *A*
Cerritos Community College *C,A*
Cerro Coso Community College *A*
Chabot College *C,A*
Chaffey Community College *C*
City College of San Francisco *C,A*
Coastline Community College *A*
College of the Desert *C,A*
College of the Redwoods *C,A*
College of the Sequoias *C,A*
Crafton Hills College *C*
De Anza College *C,A*
East Los Angeles College *C*
Foothill College *A*
Fresno City College *C,A*
Gavilan Community College *A*
Grossmont Community College *C,A*
Heald College: Sacramento *C,A*
Imperial Valley College *C,A*
Kelsey-Jenney College *C,A*
La Sierra University *A*
Laney College *C,A*
Lassen College *C,A*
Long Beach City College *C,A*
Los Angeles City College *C,A*
Los Angeles Harbor College *C,A*
Los Angeles Pierce College *C,A*
Los Angeles Valley College *C,A*
Los Medanos College *C,A*
MiraCosta College *C,A*
Modesto Junior College *A*
Monterey Peninsula College *C,A*
Napa Valley College *C,A*
Ohlone College *C,A*
Orange Coast College *C,A*
Oxnard College *A*
Pacific Union College *A*
Palomar College *C*
Phillips Junior College: Fresno
   Campus *C*
Porterville College *C*
Saddleback College *C,A*
San Diego City College *C,A*
San Diego Mesa College *C*
San Joaquin Delta College *A*
Santa Barbara City College *C*
Santa Rosa Junior College *C*
Sierra College *C,A*
Skyline College *C,A*

Solano Community College *A*
Southwestern College *C,A*
West Hills Community College *A*
West Valley College *C,A*
Yuba College *C,A*

Colorado

Arapahoe Community College *A*
Colorado Northwestern Community
   College *A*
Community College of Denver *C,A*
Denver Technical College *A*
Front Range Community College *A*
Mesa State College *C*
Morgan Community College *C*
Parks Junior College *C*
Pikes Peak Community College *C*
Red Rocks Community College *C,A*

Connecticut

Briarwood College *C,A*
Housatonic Community College *A*
Manchester Community College *C*
Mattatuck Community College *C*
Middlesex Community College *C*
Northwestern Connecticut
   Community College *C*
Norwalk Community College *C*
Quinebaug Valley Community
   College *C*
South Central Community
   College *A*
Tunxis Community College *C*

Delaware

Delaware Technical and
   Community College
      Southern Campus *C*
      Terry Campus *A*
Goldey-Beacom College *C,A*

Florida

Central Florida Community
   College *A*
Daytona Beach Community
   College *A*
Florida Community College at
   Jacksonville *C*
Indian River Community College *A*
Jones College *A*
Okaloosa-Walton Community
   College *C,A*
Pensacola Junior College *A*
St. Johns River Community
   College *A*
Seminole Community College *A*
Tallahassee Community College *C*
Valencia Community College *A*

Georgia

Abraham Baldwin Agricultural
   College *A*
Augusta Technical Institute *C*
Brewton-Parker College *A*
Clayton State College *C*
Gordon College *C*
Meadows College of Business *A*
Middle Georgia College *C*
Savannah Technical Institute *C*

Hawaii

Cannon's International Business
   College of Honolulu *C,A*
University of Hawaii: Kapiolani
   Community College *C*

Idaho

College of Southern Idaho *C*
Lewis Clark State College *A*
Ricks College *A*

Illinois

Belleville Area College *C,A*
Black Hawk College
      East Campus *C*
      Moline *A*
Carl Sandburg College *C*
City Colleges of Chicago
      Chicago City-Wide College *C*
      Malcolm X College *C,A*
College of DuPage *C*
College of Lake County *C,A*
Elgin Community College *C,A*
Gem City College *C*
Highland Community College *C,A*
Illinois Central College *C*
Illinois Valley Community
   College *C*
John A. Logan College *C*
Joliet Junior College *C,A*
Kishwaukee College *C*
Lake Land College *C*
Lewis and Clark Community
   College *C*
Lincoln Land Community College
   C,A
MacCormac Junior College *A*
Midstate College *C*
Moraine Valley Community
   College *C*
Oakton Community College *C,A*
Parkland College *A*
Rend Lake College *A*
Richland Community College *A*
Rock Valley College *A*
Shawnee Community College *C*
Southern Illinois University at
   Carbondale *A*
State Community College *A*
Triton College *C,A*
Waubonsee Community College *C*
William Rainey Harper College *C*

Indiana

Ball State University *A*
Huntington College *A*
Vincennes University *A*

Iowa

American Institute of Business *C,A*
American Institute of Commerce *C*
Des Moines Area Community
   College *C*
Iowa Lakes Community College *C*
Iowa Western Community
   College *C*
North Iowa Area Community
   College *A*
Waldorf College *A*

Kansas

Barton County Community College
   C,A
Brown Mackie College *C*
Cloud County Community
   College *C*
Coffeyville Community College *A*
Colby Community College *C,A*
Highland Community College *C*
Hutchinson Community College
   C,A
Johnson County Community
   College *A*
Kansas City Kansas Community
   College *A*
Kansas State University *B*
Neosho County Community College
   C,A
Pratt Community College *C,A*

Kentucky

Campbellsville College *C*
Owensboro Junior College of
   Business *C,A*
Watterson College *C,A*

Louisiana

Grambling State University *A*
McNeese State University *A*
Phillips Junior College: New
   Orleans *A*
Southern University in
   Shreveport *A*

Maine

Beal College *C*
Casco Bay College *C*
Husson College *A*

Maryland

Catonsville Community College *C*
Cecil Community College *C,A*
Charles County Community
   College *C*
Chesapeake College *C,A*
Howard Community College *C,A*
Montgomery College
      Germantown Campus *C,A*
      Rockville Campus *C*
      Takoma Park Campus *C*
New Community College of
   Baltimore *C,A*
Prince George's Community College
   C,A
Villa Julie College *A*
Wor-Wic Tech Community
   College *C*

Massachusetts

Aquinas College at Milton *A*
Becker College: Worcester
   Campus *A*
Berkshire Community College *A*
Bristol Community College *C,A*
Bunker Hill Community College *A*
Cape Cod Community College *C*
Dean Junior College *A*
Fisher College *C*
Greenfield Community College *C*
Holyoke Community College *C*
Marian Court Junior College *C,A*
Massachusetts Bay Community
   College *C,A*
Middlesex Community College *A*
Mount Ida College *A*
Mount Wachusett Community
   College *A*
North Shore Community College
   C,A
Northern Essex Community
   College *A*
Quinsigamond Community
   College *C*
Roxbury Community College *A*
Springfield Technical Community
   College *A*

Michigan

Baker College
      Auburn Hills *C,A*
      Flint *C,A,B*
      Mount Clemens *C,A*
      Muskegon *A*
      Owosso *C,A*
      Port Huron *A*
Charles Stewart Mott Community
   College *C,A*
Cleary College *C*
Davenport College of Business *A*
Delta College *C,A*
Detroit College of Business *A*
Eastern Michigan University *B*

Glen Oaks Community College *C*
Grand Rapids Baptist College and
Seminary *A*
Grand Rapids Community College
C,A
Great Lakes Junior College of
Business *C,A*
Henry Ford Community College *C*
Jackson Community College *C,A*
Jordan College *C,A*
Kalamazoo Valley Community
College *C*
Kellogg Community College *C,A*
Kirtland Community College *C,A*
Lake Superior State University *C*
Lansing Community College *A*
Macomb Community College *C,A*
Marygrove College *C*
Michigan Christian College *C,A*
Mid Michigan Community
College *A*
Montcalm Community College *A*
Muskegon Community College *C*
Northern Michigan University *A,B*
Northwestern Michigan College *C*
Oakland Community College *C*
St. Clair County Community
College *C,A*
Schoolcraft College *C*
Southwestern Michigan College *A*
Suomi College *C*
West Shore Community College
C,A

Minnesota

Alexandria Technical College *C*
Anoka-Ramsey Community
College *A*
Rainy River Community College *C*
St. Mary's Campus of the College of
St. Catherine *C*
St. Paul Technical College *C,A*
University of Minnesota:
Crookston *A*
Willmar Community College *A*

Mississippi

East Central Community College
C,A
Mississippi Gulf Coast Community
College
Jackson County Campus *A*
Jefferson Davis Campus *A*
Perkinston *C,A*
Phillips Junior College of Jackson *C*

Missouri

Baptist Bible College *A*
East Central College *C,A*
Jefferson College *A*
Longview Community College *C,A*
Maple Woods Community College
C,A
Missouri Western State College *A*
Moberly Area Community
College *A*
Penn Valley Community College
C,A
Phillips Junior College *C*
St. Charles Community College *C,A*
St. Louis Community College
Florissant Valley *C,A*
Meramec *C,A*
State Fair Community College *C,A*

Montana

Eastern Montana College *A*
Flathead Valley Community
College *A*
Fort Peck Community College *C*
Miles Community College *C*

Western Montana College of the
University of Montana *A*

Nebraska

Central Community College *C*
Lincoln School of Commerce *C,A*
Metropolitan Community College *C*
Northeast Community College *C*
Southeast Community College:
Lincoln Campus *A*

Nevada

Community College of Southern
Nevada *C,A*
Northern Nevada Community
College *C*
Truckee Meadows Community
College *A*
Western Nevada Community
College *C,A*

New Hampshire

Castle College *C,A*
Hesser College *C*
New Hampshire Technical College:
Manchester *C*

New Jersey

Bergen Community College *C,A*
Berkeley College of Business *C,A*
Burlington County College *C,A*
Camden County College *C,A*
County College of Morris *C*
Cumberland County College *C,A*
Essex County College *C*
Gloucester County College *C,A*
Ocean County College *C*
Passaic County Community
College *C*
Rider College *A,B*

New Mexico

Clovis Community College *A*
New Mexico Junior College *C,A*
New Mexico State University
Carlsbad *C*
Las Cruces *C,A*
Northern New Mexico Community
College *C,A*
Parks College *C*

New York

Adirondack Community College
C,A
Berkeley College *C*
Berkeley School: New York City *A*
Bramson ORT Technical Institute
C,A
Briarcliffe: The College for
Business *C*
Broome Community College *A*
Bryant & Stratton Business Institute
Albany *C,A*
Buffalo *C,A*
City University of New York
Hostos Community College *C*
La Guardia Community
College *C*
Lehman College *C*
Medgar Evers College *C*
New York City Technical
College *A*
Queensborough Community
College *C*
Clinton Community College *C*
Columbia-Greene Community
College *C,A*
Community College of the Finger
Lakes *A*
Corning Community College *C,A*
Dutchess Community College *C*

Erie Community College
City Campus *A*
North Campus *A*
South Campus *A*
Five Towns College *C*
Fulton-Montgomery Community
College *C,A*
Genesee Community College *C*
Herkimer County Community
College *C,A*
Hilbert College *C,A*
Jamestown Business College *A*
Jefferson Community College *C,A*
Katharine Gibbs School: New
York *A*
Mohawk Valley Community
College *A*
Monroe College *A*
Nassau Community College *C,A*
Onondaga Community College *C*
Orange County Community College
C,A
Rochester Business Institute *A*
State University of New York
College of Agriculture and
Technology at Cobleskill *A*
College of Agriculture and
Technology at Morrisville *C*
College of Technology at
Alfred *A*
College of Technology at
Delhi *A*
Suffolk County Community College:
Eastern Campus *C*
Sullivan County Community
College *A*
Tompkins-Cortland Community
College *C,A*
Utica School of Commerce *A*
Villa Maria College of Buffalo *A*
Westchester Business Institute *C*
Westchester Community College
C,A

North Carolina

Asheville Buncombe Technical
Community College *C,A*
Durham Technical Community
College *C*
Forsyth Technical Community
College *C*
Piedmont Community College *C*
Rockingham Community College *C*

North Dakota

Bismarck State College *C,A*
North Dakota State College of
Science *A*
Turtle Mountain Community
College *C*
University of North Dakota:
Williston *A*

Ohio

Bowling Green State University:
Firelands College *C*
Bradford School *C,A*
Central Ohio Technical College *C*
Cincinnati Metropolitan College *A*
Cincinnati Technical College *A*
Clark State Community College
C,A
Columbus State Community
College *C*
Cuyahoga Community College:
Western Campus *C,A*
Dyke College *A,B*
Edison State Community College
C,A
Hocking Technical College *C*
Lakeland Community College *A*
Marion Technical College *C*

Miami-Jacobs College *C,A*
North Central Technical College *A*
Northwest Technical College *C*
Northwestern College *C,A*
Ohio University: Chillicothe
Campus *A*
Owens Technical College
Findlay Campus *C,A*
Toledo *C,A*
Sinclair Community College *C*
Stark Technical College *A*
Terra Technical College *C*
University of Akron
Akron *A*
Wayne College *C*
University of Cincinnati
Access Colleges *A*
Clermont College *A*
Raymond Walters College *C*
University of Toledo *A*
Wright State University: Lake
Campus *C,A*

Oklahoma

Northern Oklahoma College *C*
Redlands Community College *C,A*
Rose State College *C,A*
Tulsa Junior College *C*

Oregon

Mount Hood Community College
C,A
Portland Community College *C,A*

Pennsylvania

Bucks County Community
College *C*
Butler County Community
College *A*
Churchman Business School *C*
Community College of Beaver
County *C,A*
Community College of
Philadelphia *A*
Harcum Junior College *C*
Harrisburg Area Community
College *C*
Lansdale School of Business *C*
Lehigh County Community College
C,A
Luzerne County Community
College *C*
Manor Junior College *A*
Mercyhurst College *C*
Montgomery County Community
College *A*
Northampton County Area
Community College *C*
Pennsylvania College of
Technology *A*
Pennsylvania Institute of
Technology *C,A*
Reading Area Community College
C,A
Robert Morris College *C*
Westmoreland County Community
College *A*

Puerto Rico

American University of Puerto
Rico *B*
Columbia College *A*
Electronic Data Processing College
of Puerto Rico *C*
Huertas Junior College *C*
Inter American University of Puerto
Rico: San German Campus *A,B*
Puerto Rico Junior College *A*
Universidad Adventista de las
Antillas *A*

Rhode Island

Community College of Rhode Island *C*
Johnson & Wales University *C,A*

South Carolina

Aiken Technical College *C*
Chesterfield-Marlboro Technical College *C*
Columbia Junior College of Business *A*
Denmark Technical College *C*
Greenville Technical College *C*
Horry-Georgetown Technical College *C*
Midlands Technical College *A*
Technical College of the Lowcountry *C*
Tri-County Technical College *C*
Trident Technical College *C*
Williamsburg Technical College *C*

South Dakota

Mitchell Vocational Technical Institute *C,A*
National College *A*

Tennessee

Chattanooga State Technical Community College *C*
McKenzie College *C*
Pellissippi State Technical Community College *A*
Roane State Community College *A*

Texas

Abilene Christian University *A*
Alvin Community College *C*
Amarillo College *C,A*
Austin Community College *C,A*
Bee County College *A*
Brazosport College *C,A*
Brookhaven College *A*
Central Texas College *A*
College of the Mainland *C*
Collin County Community College District *C*
Houston Community College *C*
Howard College *C*
Laredo Junior College *C,A*
Lon Morris College *A*
McLennan Community College *A*
North Harris Montgomery Community College District *C*
St. Philip's College *A*
San Antonio College *A*
South Plains College *C*
Southwestern Adventist College *C*
Texas State Technical College: Amarillo *C*
University of Houston: Downtown *B*

Utah

Dixie College *C,A*
LDS Business College *C*
Phillips Junior College: Salt Lake City Campus *C*
Stevens-Henager College of Business *A*
Utah Valley Community College *C,A*

Vermont

Champlain College *A*

Virginia

Commonwealth College *C*
John Tyler Community College *C,A*
Mountain Empire Community College *C*
National Business College *C,A*

New River Community College *A*
Northern Virginia Community College *C,A*
Tidewater Community College *C*

Washington

Big Bend Community College *A*
Centralia College *A*
Clark College *C,A*
Columbia Basin College *C*
Edmonds Community College *C,A*
Everett Community College *C*
Grays Harbor College *A*
Griffin College *C,A*
North Seattle Community College *A*
Northwest Indian College *C*
Pierce College *C,A*
Seattle Central Community College *C*
Shoreline Community College *C,A*
Spokane Community College *C,A*
Spokane Falls Community College *C,A*
Tacoma Community College *C*
Yakima Valley Community College *C*

West Virginia

College of West Virginia *C*
Davis and Elkins College *A,B*
Glenville State College *A*
Marshall University *A*
Shepherd College *A*

Wisconsin

Chippewa Valley Technical College *A*
Madison Area Technical College *A*
Mid-State Technical College *C*
Milwaukee College of Business *C,A*
Moraine Park Technical College *A*
Northeast Wisconsin Technical College *C*
Stratton College *C,A*
Wisconsin Indianhead Technical College *C*

Wyoming

Casper College *A*
Central Wyoming College *A*
Eastern Wyoming College *C,A*
Northwest College *A*
Western Wyoming Community College *C,A*

American Samoa, Caroline Islands, Guam, Marianas, Virgin Islands

Guam Community College *C*

Yiddish

Illinois

Hebrew Theological College *B*

Maryland

Baltimore Hebrew University *B,M,D*

New York

City University of New York: Queens College *B*
Columbia University *M,D*

Zoology

Alabama

Alabama Agricultural and Mechanical University *B*
Auburn University *B,M,D*
University of Alabama *B*

Alaska

University of Alaska Fairbanks *M,D*

Arizona

Arizona State University *B,M,D*
Arizona Western College *A*
Northern Arizona University *B*
University of Arizona *B*
Yavapai College *A*

Arkansas

Arkansas State University
Beebe Branch *A*
Jonesboro *B*
University of Arkansas *B,M,D*

California

California State Polytechnic University: Pomona *B*
California State University
Fresno *B*
Fullerton *B*
Long Beach *B*
Stanislaus *B*
Cerritos Community College *A*
Chabot College *A*
Citrus College *A*
El Camino College *A*
Humboldt State University *B*
Modesto Junior College *A*
San Diego State University *B*
San Francisco State University *B*
San Joaquin Delta College *A*
San Jose State University *B*
Southwestern College *A*
University of California
Berkeley *B,M,D*
Davis *B,M,D*
Santa Barbara *B,M*
Ventura College *A*

Colorado

Colorado State University *B,M,D*

Connecticut

Connecticut College *B,M*
Southern Connecticut State University *B*
University of Connecticut *M,D*

District of Columbia

George Washington University *M,D*
Howard University *B,M,D*

Florida

Florida Atlantic University *B,M*
Palm Beach Community College *A*
Pensacola Junior College *A*
University of Central Florida *B*
University of Florida *B,M,D*
University of Miami *D*
University of South Florida *B,M*

Georgia

Fort Valley State College *B*
Middle Georgia College *A*
University of Georgia *B,M,D*

Hawaii

University of Hawaii at Manoa *B,M,D*

Idaho

Albertson College *B*
Idaho State University *B*
North Idaho College *A*
Ricks College *A*
University of Idaho *B,M,D*

Illinois

Eastern Illinois University *B,M*
Joliet Junior College *A*
Rend Lake College *A*
Southern Illinois University at Carbondale *B,M,D*
University of Chicago *B,M,D*

Indiana

Ball State University *B*
Indiana University Bloomington *B,M,D*
Purdue University
Calumet *B*
West Lafayette *D*
Vincennes University *A*

Iowa

Iowa Lakes Community College *A*
Iowa State University *B,M,D*
Kirkwood Community College *A*
North Iowa Area Community College *A*

Kansas

Butler County Community College *A*
Central College *A*
Coffeyville Community College *A*
Pratt Community College *A*

Kentucky

University of Kentucky *B*
University of Louisville *B*

Louisiana

Louisiana State University and Agricultural and Mechanical College *B,M,D*
Louisiana Tech University *B,M*
McNeese State University *B*
Northeast Louisiana University *B*
Southern University and Agricultural and Mechanical College *B*

Maine

University of Maine *B,M,D*

Maryland

Howard Community College *A*
Uniformed Services University of the Health Sciences *D*
University of Maryland: College Park *B,M,D*

Massachusetts

Harvard University *D*
University of Massachusetts at Amherst *B,M,D*

Michigan

Andrews University *B*
Calvin College *B*
Michigan State University *B,M,D*
Northern Michigan University *B*

Minnesota

Gustavus Adolphus College *B*
Northland Community College *A*
Rainy River Community College *A*
St. Cloud State University *B*
University of Minnesota: Twin Cities *M,D*
Vermilion Community College *A*

Willmar Community College *A*

Mississippi

Jones County Junior College *A*
Mary Holmes College *A*

Missouri

College of the Ozarks *B*
East Central College *A*
Moberly Area Community
    College *A*
Northwest Missouri State
    University *B*
Washington University *D*

Montana

University of Montana *B,M,D*

New Hampshire

University of New Hampshire
    B,M,D

New Jersey

Rutgers—The State University of
    New Jersey
        Camden College of Arts and
            Sciences *B*
        New Brunswick *M,D*
        Newark College of Arts and
            Sciences *B*

New Mexico

New Mexico State University *B*
Western New Mexico University *B*

New York

Cornell University *M,D*
State University of New York
        College of Environmental
            Science and Forestry *B,M,D*
        Oswego *B*

North Carolina

Duke University *D*
Mars Hill College *B*
North Carolina State University
    B,M,D
University of North Carolina at
    Chapel Hill *M,D*
Vance-Granville Community
    College *A*

North Dakota

North Dakota State University
        Bottineau and Institute of
            Forestry *A*
        Fargo *B,M,D*

Ohio

Kent State University *B*
Miami University: Oxford Campus
    B,M,D
Ohio State University: Columbus
    Campus *B,M,D*
Ohio University *B,M,D*
Ohio Wesleyan University *B*
University of Akron *B*
Wittenberg University *B*

Oklahoma

Connors State College *A*
Langston University *B*
Northeastern State University *B*
Northwestern Oklahoma State
    University *B*
Oklahoma State University *B,M,D*
Redlands Community College *A*
University of Oklahoma *B,M,D*

Oregon

Central Oregon Community
    College *A*

Oregon State University *B,M,D*

Pennsylvania

Juniata College *B*
Lehigh University *M,D*

Puerto Rico

University of Puerto Rico: Medical
    Sciences Campus *M,D*

Rhode Island

University of Rhode Island *B,M,D*

South Carolina

Clemson University *M,D,W*

South Dakota

South Dakota State University *B,M*

Tennessee

Knoxville College *B*
University of Tennessee: Knoxville
    B,M,D

Texas

Howard College *A*
Jacksonville College *A*
Lon Morris College *A*
South Plains College *A*
Southwest Texas State University *B*
Texas A&M University *B,M,D*
Texas Tech University *B,M,D*
Texas Woman's University *B*
University of Texas
        Austin *B,M,D*
        El Paso *B*
Western Texas College *A*

Utah

Brigham Young University *B,M,D*
Southern Utah University *B*
Weber State University *B*

Vermont

Goddard College *B*
Marlboro College *B*
University of Vermont *B,M,D*

Virginia

Averett College *B*
Virginia Polytechnic Institute and
    State University *M,D*

Washington

Big Bend Community College *A*
Centralia College *A*
Eastern Washington University *B*
Everett Community College *A*
Grays Harbor College *A*
Lower Columbia College *A*
Olympic College *A*
Skagit Valley College *A*
Tacoma Community College *A*
University of Washington *B,M,D*
Washington State University *B,M,D*

West Virginia

Alderson-Broaddus College *B*
Marshall University *B,M*
Shepherd College *B*

Wisconsin

University of Wisconsin
        Eau Claire *B*
        Madison *B,M,D*
        Milwaukee *B,M,D*

Wyoming

Sheridan College *A*
University of Wyoming *B,M,D*

Canada

McGill University *B,M,D*

Special academic programs

Accelerated program

Alabama

Alabama Agricultural and
    Mechanical University
Alabama Southern Community
    College
Auburn University
    Auburn
    Montgomery
Birmingham-Southern College
Bishop State Community College
Central Alabama Community
    College: Childersburg Campus
Chattahoochee Valley Community
    College
George C. Wallace State
    Community College at Selma
Jacksonville State University
James H. Faulkner State
    Community College
John C. Calhoun State Community
    College
Livingston University
Lurleen B. Wallace State Junior
    College
Mobile College
Northeast Alabama State Junior
    College
Samford University
Shelton State Community College
Snead State Junior College
Spring Hill College
Troy State University
University of Alabama
University of Montevallo
University of South Alabama
Wallace State Community College
    at Hanceville

Alaska

Alaska Pacific University

Arizona

Arizona State University
DeVry Institute of Technology:
    Phoenix
Embry-Riddle Aeronautical
    University: Prescott Campus
Grand Canyon University
ITT Technical Institute: Phoenix
Pima Community College
Prescott College
Rio Salado Community College
University of Arizona
University of Phoenix
Western International University
Yavapai College

Arkansas

Arkansas State University
    Beebe Branch
    Jonesboro
Ouachita Baptist University
Southern Arkansas University
University of Arkansas
    Fayetteville
    Little Rock
University of Central Arkansas

California

Allan Hancock College
Armstrong College
Azusa Pacific University
Barstow College
Brooks Institute of Photography
California Institute of the Arts
California Lutheran University
California State University
    Bakersfield
    Dominguez Hills
    Fresno
    Fullerton
    Los Angeles
    Stanislaus
Chaffey Community College
Chapman University
Christian Heritage College
City College of San Francisco
Claremont McKenna College
Coastline Community College
Coleman College
College of Notre Dame
Columbia College: Hollywood
Compton Community College
DeVry Institute of Technology: City
    of Industry
Evergreen Valley College
Feather River College
Fresno City College
Golden Gate University
Heald College: Santa Rosa
Irvine Valley College
John F. Kennedy University
Long Beach City College
Los Angeles Harbor College
Los Angeles Mission College
Mendocino College
Menlo College
Mission College
National University
New College of California
Occidental College
Pacific Christian College
Pacific Oaks College
Pasadena City College
Pepperdine University
Phillips Junior College: Fresno
    Campus
Samuel Merritt College
San Diego City College
San Diego Miramar College
San Jose City College
San Jose State University
Santa Monica College
Scripps College
Stanford University
United States International
    University
University of California
    Davis
    Irvine
    Riverside
    San Diego
    Santa Barbara
University of La Verne
University of the Pacific
University of Redlands
University of San Francisco
University of Southern California
University of West Los Angeles
West Coast University
Western State University College of
    Law
    Orange County
    San Diego
Westmont College
Whittier College

Colorado

Adams State College
Colorado Christian University
Colorado School of Mines
Colorado Technical College
Denver Institute of Technology
Fort Lewis College
Metropolitan State College of
    Denver
National College
Pikes Peak Community College
Pueblo Community College
Red Rocks Community College
University of Colorado at Colorado
    Springs
University of Denver
Western State College of Colorado

Connecticut

Charter Oak College
Connecticut College
Eastern Connecticut State
    University
Greater New Haven State Technical
    College
Mitchell College
Quinebaug Valley Community
    College
Quinnipiac College
Sacred Heart University
Southern Connecticut State
    University
Teikyo-Post University
Trinity College
University of Bridgeport
University of New Haven
Wesleyan University
Western Connecticut State
    University
Yale University

Delaware

Delaware State College
University of Delaware
Wilmington College

District of Columbia

Catholic University of America
Gallaudet University
George Washington University
Howard University
Southeastern University
Trinity College

Florida

Barry University
Bethune-Cookman College
Brevard Community College
Broward Community College
Chipola Junior College
Eckerd College
Edison Community College
Embry-Riddle Aeronautical
    University
Florida Agricultural and Mechanical
    University
Florida Atlantic University
Florida Baptist Theological College
Florida Community College at
    Jacksonville
Florida International University
Florida State University
Fort Lauderdale College
Gulf Coast Community College
Jacksonville University

Jones College
Keiser College of Technology
Lynn University
Miami-Dade Community College
New College of the University of
    South Florida
Nova University
Orlando College
Palm Beach Community College
Pasco-Hernando Community
    College
Pensacola Junior College
Rollins College
St. Leo College
St. Petersburg Junior College
Seminole Community College
South Florida Community College
Stetson University
Tampa College
University of Miami
University of South Florida
University of West Florida

Georgia

Agnes Scott College
Armstrong State College
Augusta College
Berry College
Brenau Women's College
Clark Atlanta University
Columbus College
DeKalb College
DeVry Institute of Technology:
    Atlanta
Emory University
Georgia College
Georgia Southwestern College
Georgia State University
Meadows College of Business
Mercer University
    Atlanta
    Macon
Morris Brown College
North Georgia College
Oglethorpe University
Thomas College
University of Georgia
West Georgia College

Hawaii

Chaminade University of Honolulu
Hawaii Loa College
Hawaii Pacific University
University of Hawaii
    Manoa
    West Oahu

Idaho

Lewis Clark State College
Northwest Nazarene College
University of Idaho

Illinois

American Conservatory of Music
Augustana College
Belleville Area College
Blackburn College
Bradley University
Chicago State University
City Colleges of Chicago
    Chicago City-Wide College
    Malcolm X College
College of DuPage
College of Lake County
College of St. Francis

De Paul University
DeVry Institute of Technology
Chicago
Lombard
Greenville College
Illinois Institute of Technology
Illinois Wesleyan University
Judson College
Kishwaukee College
Knox College
Loyola University of Chicago
McKendree College
Monmouth College
National College of Chiropractic
National-Louis University
North Central College
North Park College and Theological
Seminary
Northeastern Illinois University
Northern Illinois University
Northwestern University
Olivet Nazarene University
Parkland College
Parks College of St. Louis
University
Principia College
Ray College of Design
Robert Morris College: Chicago
Rockford College
Roosevelt University
Rosary College
St. Xavier University
Shimer College
Southern Illinois University at
Carbondale
Trinity Christian College
University of Chicago
University of Illinois
Chicago
Urbana-Champaign
VanderCook College of Music
Wheaton College

Indiana

Anderson University
Ball State University
Bethel College
Butler University
Calumet College of St. Joseph
Earlham College
Franklin College
Goshen College
Indiana Institute of Technology
Indiana State University
Indiana University
Bloomington
Northwest
Southeast
Indiana University—Purdue
University at Fort Wayne
Indiana Vocational Technical
College: Southcentral
International Business College
ITT Technical Institute: Evansville
Martin University
Oakland City College
Purdue University
Rose-Hulman Institute of
Technology
St. Joseph's College
St. Mary-of-the-Woods College
Taylor University
University of Indianapolis
University of Notre Dame
Valparaiso University

Iowa

Buena Vista College
Clarke College
Clinton Community College
Coe College
Cornell College
Drake University
Iowa Central Community College

Iowa State University
Kirkwood Community College
Loras College
Luther College
Morningside College
Mount Mercy College
Northwestern College
Scott Community College
Simpson College
Teikyo Marycrest University
Teikyo Westmar University
University of Dubuque
University of Iowa
University of Osteopathic Medicine
and Health Sciences
Upper Iowa University
Wartburg College
William Penn College

Kansas

Baker University
Benedictine College
Emporia State University
Fort Hays State University
Highland Community College
Kansas Newman College
Kansas State University
MidAmerica Nazarene College
Ottawa University
Southwestern College
Sterling College

Kentucky

Bellarmine College
Campbellsville College
Cumberland College
Georgetown College
Morehead State University
Owensboro Junior College of
Business
Sullivan College
Thomas More College
University of Kentucky
University of Louisville

Louisiana

Centenary College of Louisiana
Louisiana College
Louisiana State University
Agricultural and Mechanical
College
Shreveport
Loyola University
McNeese State University
Northeast Louisiana University
Northwestern State University
Tulane University
University of Southwestern
Louisiana

Maine

Andover College
Bates College
Beal College
Bowdoin College
Colby College
Thomas College
Unity College
University of Maine
Farmington
Orono
Presque Isle
University of New England

Maryland

Baltimore Hebrew University
Baltimore International Culinary
College
Bowie State University
Capitol College
College of Notre Dame of
Maryland
Goucher College
Hagerstown Junior College

Hood College
Johns Hopkins University
Loyola College in Maryland
Maryland Institute College of Art
Montgomery College
Germantown Campus
Rockville Campus
Takoma Park Campus
Salisbury State University
Sojourner-Douglass College
Towson State University
University of Baltimore
University of Maryland
Baltimore County
Eastern Shore
Villa Julie College
Western Maryland College

Massachusetts

American International College
Anna Maria College for Men and
Women
Atlantic Union College
Babson College
Bentley College
Berklee College of Music
Boston College
Boston University
Brandeis University
Clark University
College of the Holy Cross
Elms College
Emerson College
Emmanuel College
Fitchburg State College
Gordon College
Hampshire College
Harvard and Radcliffe Colleges
Lesley College
Massachusetts Bay Community
College
Massachusetts Institute of
Technology
Montserrat College of Art
Mount Holyoke College
North Adams State College
Northeastern University
Northern Essex Community College
Pine Manor College
Simmons College
Simon's Rock College of Bard
Smith College
Tufts University
University of Massachusetts at
Dartmouth
Wellesley College
Western New England College
Williams College
Worcester Polytechnic Institute

Michigan

Albion College
Alma College
Andrews University
Aquinas College
Cleary College
Concordia College
Eastern Michigan University
Glen Oaks Community College
GMI Engineering & Management
Institute
Great Lakes Junior College of
Business
Hillsdale College
Jackson Community College
Kirtland Community College
Lansing Community College
Madonna University
Michigan State University
Northwood Institute
Oakland University
Olivet College
Reformed Bible College
Saginaw Valley State University

St. Mary's College
Siena Heights College
University of Detroit Mercy
University of Michigan
Ann Arbor
Dearborn
Wayne State University
Western Michigan University

Minnesota

Bemidji State University
College of St. Scholastica
Concordia College: Moorhead
Concordia College: St. Paul
Inver Hills Community College
Lakewood Community College
Mankato State University
St. Mary's College of Minnesota
St. Olaf College
Southwest State University
University of Minnesota: Morris
Winona State University

Mississippi

Alcorn State University
Blue Mountain College
Mississippi State University
Tougaloo College
University of Mississippi
University of Southern Mississippi
William Carey College

Missouri

Central Methodist College
Central Missouri State University
Columbia College
Culver-Stockton College
Deaconess College of Nursing
DeVry Institute of Technology:
Kansas City
Drury College
Fontbonne College
Hannibal-LaGrange College
Lincoln University
Lindenwood College
Maryville University
Missouri Southern State College
Missouri Valley College
Northeast Missouri State University
Phillips Junior College
Research College of Nursing
Rockhurst College
St. Louis Community College at
Meramec
St. Louis University
Southeast Missouri State University
Southwest Baptist University
Stephens College
University of Missouri
Columbia
Kansas City
Washington University
Webster University
Wentworth Military Academy and
Junior College
William Woods College

Montana

Eastern Montana College
Northern Montana College
Rocky Mountain College
University of Montana

Nebraska

Bellevue College
Central Community College
Chadron State College
Creighton University
Dana College
Doane College
Hastings College
Midland Lutheran College

University of Nebraska
    Kearney
    Lincoln
    Omaha
Wayne State College

New Hampshire
Colby-Sawyer College
Daniel Webster College
Dartmouth College
Franklin Pierce College
Hesser College
Keene State College
New Hampshire Technical College:
    Stratham
Notre Dame College
School for Lifelong Learning
University of New Hampshire

New Jersey
Caldwell College
College of St. Elizabeth
Cumberland County College
Fairleigh Dickinson University
Felician College
Glassboro State College
Jersey City State College
Montclair State College
New Jersey Institute of Technology
Princeton University
Ramapo College of New Jersey
Rider College
Rutgers—The State University of
    New Jersey
    Camden College of Arts and
        Sciences
    Douglass College
    Newark College of Arts and
        Sciences
St. Peter's College
Seton Hall University
Stevens Institute of Technology
Upsala College
William Paterson College of New
    Jersey

New Mexico
Eastern New Mexico University
New Mexico State University

New York
Alfred University
Bard College
Barnard College
Berkeley College
Boricua College
Bramson ORT Technical Institute
Bryant & Stratton Business Institute
    Albany
    Syracuse
City University of New York
    Brooklyn College
    City College
    Hunter College
    Kingsborough Community
        College
    Lehman College
    Queens College
Colgate University
College of Aeronautics
College for Human Services
College of Insurance
College of Mount St. Vincent
College of New Rochelle
    New Rochelle
    School of New Resources
College of St. Rose
Columbia University
    School of Engineering and
        Applied Science
    School of General Studies
    School of Nursing
Concordia College
Cornell University

Dominican College of Blauvelt
Dowling College
D'Youville College
Elmira College
Eugene Lang College/New School
    for Social Research
Hartwick College
Hobart College
Hofstra University
Houghton College
Hudson Valley Community College
Iona College
Juilliard School
Katharine Gibbs School: New York
Keuka College
Kol Yaakov Torah Center
Le Moyne College
Long Island University
    C. W. Post Campus
    Southampton Campus
Manhattan College
Manhattanville College
Marist College
Marymount Manhattan College
Medaille College
Mercy College
Molloy College
Mount St. Mary College
New York Institute of Technology
New York School of Interior
    Design
New York University
Niagara University
Ohr Somayach Tanenbaum
    Education Center
Polytechnic University: Long Island
    Campus
Pratt Institute
Rensselaer Polytechnic Institute
Rochester Business Institute
Rochester Institute of Technology
Russell Sage College
St. Bonaventure University
St. Francis College
St. John Fisher College
St. John's University
St. Joseph's College
St. Lawrence University
St. Thomas Aquinas College
Skidmore College
State University of New York
    Albany
    Buffalo
    College at Brockport
    College at Fredonia
    Empire State College
    Health Science Center at
        Syracuse
    Institute of Technology at
        Utica/Rome
Syracuse University
Tobe-Coburn School for Fashion
    Careers
Touro College
Union College
Utica College of Syracuse
    University
Utica School of Commerce
Vassar College
Wells College
William Smith College

North Carolina
Appalachian State University
Barton College
Belmont Abbey College
Bennett College
Brunswick Community College
Campbell University
Cecils College
Duke University
Elon College
Fayetteville State University
Guilford College

John Wesley College
Johnson C. Smith University
Mars Hill College
Methodist College
Montreat-Anderson College
Mount Olive College
North Carolina Agricultural and
    Technical State University
North Carolina State University
Pfeiffer College
Piedmont Bible College
Queens College
St. Augustine's College
St. Mary's College
Salem College
University of North Carolina
    Asheville
    Chapel Hill
    Charlotte
    Greensboro
Wake Forest University

North Dakota
North Dakota State University
Trinity Bible College
University of North Dakota

Ohio
Ashland University
Bowling Green State University
Capital University
Case Western Reserve University
Cedarville College
Cincinnati Metropolitan College
Cleveland Institute of Art
Cleveland State University
Cuyahoga Community College:
    Metropolitan Campus
Defiance College
DeVry Institute of Technology:
    Columbus
Dyke College
Franciscan University of
    Steubenville
Franklin University
Heidelberg College
Hiram College
Hocking Technical College
John Carroll University
Kent State University
Kenyon College
Kettering College of Medical Arts
Marietta College
Miami-Jacobs College
Mount Union College
Muskingum College
Northwestern College
Ohio University
    Athens
    Eastern Campus
Ohio Wesleyan University
Otterbein College
Pontifical College Josephinum
University of Akron
University of Cincinnati
University of Dayton
University of Findlay
University of Rio Grande
Urbana University
Ursuline College
Walsh College
Wittenberg University
Wright State University
Xavier University
Youngstown State University

Oklahoma
Oklahoma Baptist University
Oklahoma Christian University of
    Science and Arts
Oklahoma City University
Oral Roberts University
Southeastern Oklahoma State
    University

Southwestern Oklahoma State
    University
University of Oklahoma
University of Science and Arts of
    Oklahoma

Oregon
Bassist College
Concordia College
Eastern Oregon State College
Lewis and Clark College
Linfield College
Mount Hood Community College
Portland State University
Reed College
University of Portland
Warner Pacific College
Willamette University

Pennsylvania
Albright College
Allegheny College
Allentown College of St. Francis de
    Sales
Beaver College
Bryn Mawr College
Cabrini College
California University of
    Pennsylvania
Carlow College
Carnegie Mellon University
Chatham College
Chestnut Hill College
Churchman Business School
Clarion University of Pennsylvania
College Misericordia
Delaware County Community
    College
Dickinson College
Drexel University
Duquesne University
Edinboro University of
    Pennsylvania
Franklin and Marshall College
Gannon University
Geneva College
Gettysburg College
Gratz College
Grove City College
Haverford College
Holy Family College
Immaculata College
Indiana University of Pennsylvania
Juniata College
Kutztown University of
    Pennsylvania
La Roche College
La Salle University
Lehigh University
Lincoln University
Lock Haven University of
    Pennsylvania
Lycoming College
Mansfield University of
    Pennsylvania
Marywood College
Mercyhurst College
Messiah College
Millersville University of
    Pennsylvania
Moore College of Art and Design
Muhlenberg College
Northampton County Area
    Community College
Point Park College
Rosemont College
St. Charles Borromeo Seminary
St. Francis College
St. Joseph's University
Seton Hill College
Slippery Rock University of
    Pennsylvania
Spring Garden College
Susquehanna University

Swarthmore College
Temple University
University of the Arts
University of Pennsylvania
University of Pittsburgh
   Bradford
   Greensburg
   Johnstown
   Pittsburgh
University of Scranton
Ursinus College
Valley Forge Christian College
Villanova University
Washington and Jefferson College
Waynesburg College
West Chester University of
   Pennsylvania
Westminster College
Widener University
Wilkes University

Puerto Rico

Electronic Data Processing College
   of Puerto Rico
Inter American University of Puerto
   Rico
      Metropolitan Campus
      San German Campus
Pontifical Catholic University of
   Puerto Rico

Rhode Island

Brown University
Bryant College
Johnson & Wales University
Roger Williams College
Salve Regina University

South Carolina

Benedict College
Bob Jones University
Charleston Southern University
College of Charleston
Columbia College
Converse College
Francis Marion College
Lander College
Limestone College
Presbyterian College
Trident Technical College
University of South Carolina
      Aiken
      Coastal Carolina College
      Columbia
      Lancaster
Wofford College

South Dakota

Augustana College
Mount Marty College
National College
South Dakota State University
University of South Dakota

Tennessee

Austin Peay State University
Belmont University
Bethel College
Bristol University
Carson-Newman College
Christian Brothers University
David Lipscomb University
East Tennessee State University
Freed-Hardeman University
Knoxville Business College
Lincoln Memorial University
Memphis College of Art
Milligan College
Rhodes College
Southern College of Seventh-day
   Adventists
Tennessee Technological University
Tusculum College
Union University

University of the South
University of Tennessee: Memphis
Vanderbilt University

Texas

Abilene Christian University
Angelina College
Austin College
Baylor University
Criswell College
DeVry Institute of Technology:
   Irving
East Texas Baptist University
Incarnate Word College
Lamar University—Beaumont
LeTourneau University
McMurry University
Midwestern State University
Mountain View College
North Lake College
Northwood Institute: Texas Campus
Our Lady of the Lake University of
   San Antonio
St. Mary's University
Southwestern Adventist College
Southwestern University
Stephen F. Austin State University
Tarleton State University
Texas A&I University
Texas Christian University
Texas Wesleyan University
University of Mary Hardin-Baylor
University of Texas
      Dallas
      El Paso
      Health Science Center at
         Houston
      San Antonio
Wayland Baptist University

Utah

Brigham Young University
LDS Business College
Phillips Junior College: Salt Lake
   City Campus
Stevens-Henager College of
   Business
University of Utah
Utah State University
Weber State University
Westminster College of Salt Lake
   City

Vermont

Burlington College
Champlain College
New England Culinary Institute
Norwich University
Southern Vermont College

Virginia

Averett College
Blue Ridge Community College
Bluefield College
Bridgewater College
Christopher Newport College
George Mason University
Hampton University
Hollins College
James Madison University
Longwood College
Lynchburg College
Mary Baldwin College
Mary Washington College
Marymount University
Mountain Empire Community
   College
National Business College
Norfolk State University
Old Dominion University
Randolph-Macon College
Randolph-Macon Woman's College
Richard Bland College
Roanoke College

St. Paul's College
Shenandoah University
Southwest Virginia Community
   College
Strayer College
Sweet Briar College
University of Richmond
University of Virginia
Virginia Commonwealth University
Virginia Polytechnic Institute and
   State University
Virginia Wesleyan College

Washington

Art Institute of Seattle
Central Washington University
City University
Griffin College
Lutheran Bible Institute of Seattle
Pacific Lutheran University
St. Martin's College
Seattle University
Wenatchee Valley College

West Virginia

Alderson-Broaddus College
Bethany College
Davis and Elkins College
Glenville State College
Marshall University
Potomac State College of West
   Virginia University
Salem-Teikyo University
University of Charleston
West Liberty State College
West Virginia Northern Community
   College
West Virginia University
West Virginia Wesleyan College

Wisconsin

Bellin College of Nursing
Cardinal Stritch College
Carthage College
Madison Junior College of Business
Marian College of Fond du Lac
Marquette University
Mount Mary College
Northland College
Ripon College
Stratton College
University of Wisconsin
      Madison
      Parkside
      River Falls
Viterbo College
Waukesha County Technical
   College

Wyoming

Northwest College

Switzerland

American College of Switzerland

Combined bachelor's/ graduate programs in business administration

Alabama

Spring Hill College
University of Alabama
University of South Alabama

Arizona

Arizona State University
Grand Canyon University
University of Arizona

California

California Lutheran University
California State Polytechnic
   University: Pomona
California State University: Chico
Chapman University
Claremont McKenna College
John F. Kennedy University
Monterey Institute of International
   Studies
Pitzer College
Scripps College
Sonoma State University
University of California: Irvine
University of San Diego
University of San Francisco
West Coast University

Colorado

Colorado College
Fort Lewis College
University of Denver

Connecticut

Quinnipiac College
Sacred Heart University
University of Bridgeport
University of Connecticut

Delaware

University of Delaware

District of Columbia

Georgetown University
Southeastern University

Florida

Florida Agricultural and Mechanical
   University
Rollins College
University of Miami

Georgia

Clark Atlanta University
Georgia College
LaGrange College
University of Georgia

Hawaii

Chaminade University of Honolulu
Hawaii Pacific University

Idaho

Idaho State University

Illinois

Bradley University
De Paul University
Eastern Illinois University
Illinois Benedictine College
Illinois Institute of Technology
Illinois State University
Knox College
Lewis University
North Central College
Northeastern Illinois University
Northern Illinois University
Northwestern University
Quincy College
Rockford College
Rosary College
Southern Illinois University
      Carbondale
      Edwardsville
University of Chicago
University of Illinois at Urbana-
   Champaign
Western Illinois University

Indiana

Ball State University
Indiana State University
Indiana University—Purdue
   University at Fort Wayne

Indiana Wesleyan University
Purdue University
University of Notre Dame
University of Southern Indiana

Iowa

Cornell College
Drake University
Grinnell College
Iowa State University
Luther College
Maharishi International University
University of Dubuque
University of Iowa

Kansas

Fort Hays State University
Kansas State University
Pittsburg State University
Wichita State University

Kentucky

Bellarmine College
University of Kentucky

Louisiana

Loyola University
Tulane University
Xavier University of Louisiana

Maine

Thomas College

Maryland

Loyola College in Maryland
Morgan State University
University of Maryland: College
Park

Massachusetts

American International College
Bentley College
Boston University
Clark University
Massachusetts Institute of
Technology
Salem State College
Suffolk University
Wheaton College
Worcester Polytechnic Institute

Michigan

Lake Superior State University
Oakland University

Minnesota

Moorhead State University
University of Minnesota: Twin
Cities

Mississippi

Jackson State University
Millsaps College
William Carey College

Missouri

Culver-Stockton College
Lindenwood College
Rockhurst College
University of Missouri: Kansas City
Washington University
Westminster College

Nevada

University of Nevada: Reno

New Hampshire

Dartmouth College
University of New Hampshire

New Jersey

Fairleigh Dickinson University
Monmouth College
Rider College

Rutgers—The State University of
New Jersey
College of Engineering
Douglass College
Livingston College
Newark College of Arts and
Sciences
Rutgers College
University College New
Brunswick
University College Newark
Seton Hall University
Stevens Institute of Technology

New Mexico

Eastern New Mexico University
New Mexico Highlands University
St. John's College
University of New Mexico
Western New Mexico University

New York

Adelphi University
Alfred University
Bard College
Canisius College
Clarkson University
College of Insurance
Columbia University: School of
General Studies
Cornell University
Dowling College
Hobart College
Houghton College
Iona College
King's College
Long Island University
Brooklyn Campus
C. W. Post Campus
Manhattanville College
Marymount College
Mercy College
New York Institute of Technology
New York University
Pace University
College of White Plains
New York
Pleasantville/Briarcliff
Rensselaer Polytechnic Institute
Rochester Institute of Technology
Russell Sage College
St. Bonaventure University
St. John Fisher College
St. Lawrence University
Siena College
Skidmore College
State University of New York
Albany
Binghamton
Buffalo
College at Fredonia
College at Geneseo
College at Oneonta
College at Potsdam
Syracuse University
Union College
University of Rochester
Wells College
William Smith College

North Carolina

Appalachian State University
Campbell University
Duke University
Pfeiffer College
Queens College
University of North Carolina at
Greensboro

Ohio

Ashland University
Case Western Reserve University
Franciscan University of
Steubenville

Hiram College
Kenyon College
Lake Erie College
Ohio State University: Columbus
Campus
University of Akron
University of Toledo

Oklahoma

Oklahoma City University
Oral Roberts University
Southwestern Oklahoma State
University
University of Oklahoma
University of Tulsa

Oregon

Oregon State University
University of Oregon
Eugene
Robert Donald Clark Honors
College
Willamette University

Pennsylvania

Bryn Mawr College
Clarion University of Pennsylvania
Duquesne University
Gannon University
Indiana University of Pennsylvania
La Salle University
Lebanon Valley College of
Pennsylvania
Lehigh University
Moravian College
Philadelphia College of Pharmacy
and Science
Philadelphia College of Textiles and
Science
Temple University
University of Pennsylvania
University of Scranton
Waynesburg College
Widener University
Wilkes University

Puerto Rico

Inter American University of Puerto
Rico: San German Campus
Pontifical Catholic University of
Puerto Rico

Rhode Island

Bryant College
Providence College

South Carolina

Lander College
University of South Carolina at
Aiken

South Dakota

Huron University

Tennessee

Bristol University
Maryville College
Tennessee State University
University of Tennessee: Knoxville
Vanderbilt University

Texas

Incarnate Word College
Prairie View A&M University
Rice University
St. Edward's University
Southern Methodist University
Texas A&M University
Texas Christian University
Texas Southern University
University of Dallas
University of Houston
University of North Texas

Utah

Brigham Young University

Vermont

Castleton State College
St. Michael's College

Virginia

Averett College
Old Dominion University
Sweet Briar College
Virginia Commonwealth University

Washington

City University
Eastern Washington University
Gonzaga University
Pacific Lutheran University
Seattle University
Whitman College

West Virginia

Wheeling Jesuit College

Wisconsin

Beloit College
University of Wisconsin: Oshkosh

Canada

McGill University

Combined bachelor's/ graduate programs in law

Alabama

Faulkner University
Judson College

Arizona

Arizona State University

Arkansas

University of Arkansas

California

American Armenian International
College
Claremont McKenna College
John F. Kennedy University
National University
Occidental College
University of La Verne
University of San Diego
University of San Francisco
Western State University College of
Law: San Diego

Colorado

Colorado College

District of Columbia

Catholic University of America
Georgetown University
Trinity College

Florida

University of Florida
University of Miami

Georgia

Mercer University

Illinois

De Paul University
Illinois Institute of Technology
Knox College
Northern Illinois University
Southern Illinois University at
Carbondale
University of Chicago

University of Illinois at Urbana-
Champaign

Indiana
Wabash College

Iowa
Drake University
Grinnell College

Louisiana
Loyola University
Tulane University

Maine
Bowdoin College

Maryland
Frostburg State University
Salisbury State University
University of Baltimore
University of Maryland
Baltimore
Baltimore County

Massachusetts
Boston University
Northeastern University
Suffolk University

Michigan
University of Detroit Mercy
Wayne State University

Minnesota
Carleton College
Hamline University
St. Olaf College
University of Minnesota: Twin
Cities

Missouri
Southeast Missouri State University
University of Missouri: Kansas City
William Woods College

Nebraska
Creighton University
University of Nebraska—Lincoln

New Jersey
Stevens Institute of Technology

New Mexico
University of New Mexico

New York
Bard College
Barnard College
City University of New York
Brooklyn College
City College
College of St. Rose
Columbia University
Columbia College
School of General Studies
Cornell University
Fordham University
Hamilton College
Hartwick College
Hofstra University
Pace University: College of White
Plains
Rensselaer Polytechnic Institute
Russell Sage College
St. John's University
Skidmore College
State University of New York
Albany
Buffalo
Syracuse University
Union College

North Carolina
Campbell University
Duke University
North Carolina Central University
Wake Forest University

Ohio
Ohio State University: Columbus
Campus
University of Akron
University of Cincinnati
University of Toledo

Oklahoma
Oklahoma City University
University of Oklahoma

Oregon
Lewis and Clark College

Pennsylvania
Duquesne University

Puerto Rico
Pontifical Catholic University of
Puerto Rico

Tennessee
University of Tennessee: Knoxville
Vanderbilt University

Texas
Baylor University
Jarvis Christian College
Texas Southern University
University of Houston

Virginia
University of Richmond
Washington and Lee University

Washington
Gonzaga University
Whitman College

Wisconsin
University of Wisconsin: Madison

Combined bachelor's/ graduate programs in medicine

Alabama
University of South Alabama

California
Charles R. Drew University: College
of Allied Health
University of California: Riverside

District of Columbia
Georgetown University
Howard University

Florida
University of Miami

Illinois
Knox College
Northwestern University
Rush University
Southern Illinois University at
Carbondale
University of Health Sciences: The
Chicago Medical School

Iowa
Grinnell College
University of Iowa

Kansas
University of Kansas Medical
Center

Louisiana
Louisiana State University
Agricultural and Mechanical
College
Shreveport
Tulane University

Maryland
University of Maryland: Baltimore

Massachusetts
Boston University

Michigan
Michigan State University
University of Michigan

Minnesota
University of Minnesota: Twin
Cities

Missouri
University of Missouri: Kansas City

Nevada
University of Nevada: Reno

New Jersey
Rutgers—The State University of
New Jersey
Camden College of Arts and
Sciences
College of Engineering
Cook College
Douglass College
Livingston College
Rutgers College
Stevens Institute of Technology
Stockton State College
Trenton State College

New York
City University of New York
Brooklyn College
City College
Columbia University: School of
General Studies
Cornell University
New York University
Rensselaer Polytechnic Institute
Siena College
State University of New York
Health Science Center at
Brooklyn
Union College
University of Rochester

North Carolina
University of North Carolina at
Chapel Hill
Wake Forest University

Ohio
Kent State University
Ohio State University: Columbus
Campus
University of Toledo
Youngstown State University

Oklahoma
University of Oklahoma Health
Sciences Center

Pennsylvania
Duquesne University
Lehigh University
Penn State University Park Campus
University of Pittsburgh
Villanova University

Rhode Island
Brown University

Tennessee
East Tennessee State University
University of Tennessee: Knoxville
Vanderbilt University

Texas
Abilene Christian University
Baylor University
Texas A&M University
University of Texas Health Science
Center at Houston

Virginia
Old Dominion University
Virginia Commonwealth University

Wisconsin
Beloit College
University of Wisconsin: Madison

Cooperative education

Alabama
Alabama Agricultural and
Mechanical University
Alabama State University
Athens State College
Auburn University
Auburn
Montgomery
Bessemer State Technical College
Bishop State Community College
Brewer State Junior College
Central Alabama Community
College: Childersburg Campus
Chattahoochee Valley Community
College
Douglas MacArthur State Technical
College
Faulkner University
Gadsden State Community College
Huntingdon College
Jacksonville State University
James H. Faulkner State
Community College
John C. Calhoun State Community
College
Judson College
Miles College
Oakwood College
Samford University
Shoals Community College
Stillman College
Talladega College
Tuskegee University
University of Alabama
Birmingham
Huntsville
Tuscaloosa
University of Montevallo
University of North Alabama
University of South Alabama
Walker State Technical College
Wallace State Community College
at Hanceville

Alaska
Sheldon Jackson College
University of Alaska
Anchorage
Southeast

Arizona
Arizona State University
Arizona Western College
Cochise College
Eastern Arizona College

Embry-Riddle Aeronautical
· University: Prescott Campus
Glendale Community College
Navajo Community College
Northern Arizona University
Northland Pioneer College
Paradise Valley Community College
Pima Community College
Rio Salado Community College
Scottsdale Community College
South Mountain Community
College
University of Arizona

Arkansas

Arkansas College
East Arkansas Community College
Harding University
Mississippi County Community
College
Ouachita Baptist University
Philander Smith College
University of Arkansas
Fayetteville
Pine Bluff
University of Central Arkansas
University of the Ozarks
Westark Community College

California

Allan Hancock College
Azusa Pacific University
Barstow College
California Lutheran University
California Polytechnic State
University: San Luis Obispo
California State Polytechnic
University: Pomona
California State University
Bakersfield
Chico
Dominguez Hills
Fresno
Fullerton
Hayward
Long Beach
Los Angeles
Sacramento
Stanislaus
Cerritos Community College
Cerro Coso Community College
Chabot College
Chapman University
Christ College Irvine
Citrus College
Coastline Community College
College of the Redwoods
Columbia College
Compton Community College
Cosumnes River College
Crafton Hills College
De Anza College
Diablo Valley College
Don Bosco Technical Institute
East Los Angeles College
El Camino College
Feather River College
Foothill College
Golden Gate University
Golden West College
Hartnell College
Humboldt State University
Irvine Valley College
Kings River Community College
Lassen College
Long Beach City College
Los Angeles Harbor College
Los Angeles Mission College
Los Angeles Pierce College
Los Angeles Trade and Technical
College
Los Angeles Valley College
Los Medanos College
Master's College

Mendocino College
MiraCosta College
Mission College
Modesto Junior College
Mount San Jacinto College
Ohlone College
Orange Coast College
Palomar College
San Diego State University
San Joaquin Delta College
San Jose City College
San Jose State University
Santa Barbara City College
Santa Clara University
Santa Monica College
Santa Rosa Junior College
Sierra College
Skyline College
Solano Community College
Southwestern College
University of California
Berkeley
Los Angeles
Riverside
University of the Pacific
Victor Valley College
West Hills Community College
Westmont College

Colorado

Aims Community College
Arapahoe Community College
Colorado Christian University
Colorado School of Mines
Colorado State University
Colorado Technical College
Community College of Denver
Fort Lewis College
Front Range Community College
Lamar Community College
Metropolitan State College of
Denver
National College
Northeastern Junior College
Trinidad State Junior College
University of Colorado at Denver
University of Denver
University of Northern Colorado
University of Southern Colorado

Connecticut

Central Connecticut State
University
Eastern Connecticut State
University
Greater New Haven State Technical
College
Holy Apostles College and
Seminary
Housatonic Community College
Manchester Community College
Mattatuck Community College
Quinnipiac College
Sacred Heart University
Southern Connecticut State
University
Teikyo-Post University
University of Bridgeport
University of Connecticut
University of Hartford
University of New Haven
Waterbury State Technical College
Western Connecticut State
University

Delaware

Delaware State College
Delaware Technical and
Community College
Stanton/Wilmington Campus
Terry Campus
Goldey-Beacom College

District of Columbia

American University
Gallaudet University
George Washington University
Howard University
University of the District of
Columbia

Florida

Bethune-Cookman College
Brevard Community College
Broward Community College
Central Florida Community College
Chipola Junior College
Daytona Beach Community College
Edison Community College
Embry-Riddle Aeronautical
University
Florida Agricultural and Mechanical
University
Florida Atlantic University
Florida Institute of Technology
Florida International University
Florida Keys Community College
Florida Memorial College
Florida State University
Fort Lauderdale College
Gulf Coast Community College
Hillsborough Community College
Jacksonville University
Lake City Community College
Lake-Sumter Community College
Manatee Community College
Miami-Dade Community College
Nova University
Orlando College
Palm Beach Community College
Pensacola Junior College
Santa Fe Community College
Seminole Community College
South Florida Community College
University of Central Florida
University of Florida
University of North Florida
University of South Florida
University of West Florida
Valencia Community College

Georgia

Albany State College
Armstrong State College
Atlanta Metropolitan College
Augusta College
Augusta Technical Institute
Berry College
Clark Atlanta University
Clayton State College
Columbus College
Darton College
Fort Valley State College
Georgia College
Georgia Institute of Technology
Georgia Southern University
Georgia Southwestern College
Georgia State University
Kennesaw State College
Mercer University
Atlanta
Macon
Middle Georgia College
Morehouse College
Morris Brown College
North Georgia College
Oglethorpe University
Paine College
Savannah State College
Southern College of Technology
University of Georgia
Valdosta State College
West Georgia College

Hawaii

Brigham Young University-Hawaii
Hawaii Pacific University

University of Hawaii
Honolulu Community College
Kapiolani Community College
Manoa

Idaho

College of Southern Idaho
Lewis Clark State College
University of Idaho

Illinois

Augustana College
Black Hawk College: East Campus
Blackburn College
Bradley University
City Colleges of Chicago
Chicago City-Wide College
Malcolm X College
Olive-Harvey College
Richard J. Daley College
College of DuPage
College of Lake County
Elgin Community College
Greenville College
Illinois Institute of Technology
Illinois State University
ITT Technical Institute: Hoffman
Estates
John A. Logan College
Joliet Junior College
Judson College
KAES College
Lake Land College
Lexington Institute of Hospitality
Careers
Lincoln Land Community College
North Central College
Northern Illinois University
Northwestern University
Parkland College
Ray College of Design
Rend Lake College
Robert Morris College: Chicago
Rock Valley College
School of the Art Institute of
Chicago
Southern Illinois University
Carbondale
Edwardsville
Triton College
University of Illinois
Chicago
Urbana-Champaign
Western Illinois University

Indiana

Anderson University
Ball State University
Calumet College of St. Joseph
Indiana State University
Indiana University
Bloomington
Northwest
Southeast
Indiana University—Purdue
University
Fort Wayne
Indianapolis
Indiana Vocational Technical
College
Central Indiana
Southcentral
Southwest
International Business College
Oakland City College
Purdue University
Calumet
West Lafayette
Tri-State University
University of Evansville
University of Indianapolis
University of Southern Indiana
Valparaiso University

Iowa

Clarke College
Des Moines Area Community
 College
Indian Hills Community College
Iowa Central Community College
Iowa Lakes Community College
Iowa State University
Iowa Western Community College
Kirkwood Community College
Loras College
Muscatine Community College
Northwest Iowa Technical College
St. Ambrose University
Southwestern Community College
Teikyo Marycrest University
Teikyo Westmar University
University of Dubuque
University of Iowa
University of Northern Iowa
Waldorf College

Kansas

Barton County Community College
Butler County Community College
Central College
Cloud County Community College
Cowley County Community College
Dodge City Community College
Emporia State University
Haskell Indian Junior College
Hesston College
Highland Community College
Johnson County Community
 College
Kansas Newman College
Kansas State University
McPherson College
Pittsburg State University
University of Kansas
Wichita State University

Kentucky

Bellarmine College
Brescia College
Eastern Kentucky University
Jefferson Community College
Kentucky State University
Lees College
Lexington Community College
Louisville Technical Institute
Madisonville Community College
Maysville Community College
Morehead State University
Murray State University
Northern Kentucky University
Prestonburg Community College
Southeast Community College
Sue Bennett College
Thomas More College
University of Kentucky
University of Louisville
Western Kentucky University

Louisiana

Grambling State University
Louisiana State University
 Agricultural and Mechanical
  College
 Shreveport
Louisiana Tech University
McNeese State University
Southeastern Louisiana University
Southern University at New Orleans
Southern University and
 Agricultural and Mechanical
  College
University of New Orleans
Xavier University of Louisiana

Maine

Husson College
Unity College

University of Maine
 Machias
 Orono
Westbrook College

Maryland

Anne Arundel Community College
Baltimore Hebrew University
Baltimore International Culinary
 College
Bowie State University
Capitol College
Catonsville Community College
Charles County Community College
Columbia Union College
Coppin State College
Dundalk Community College
Essex Community College
Frederick Community College
Hagerstown Junior College
Harford Community College
Howard Community College
Johns Hopkins University
Morgan State University
Mount St. Mary's College
Prince George's Community College
Salisbury State University
Sojourner-Douglass College
Towson State University
University of Baltimore
University of Maryland
 Baltimore County
 College Park
 Eastern Shore
 University College
Villa Julie College

Massachusetts

Atlantic Union College
Becker College
 Leicester Campus
 Worcester Campus
Boston University
Bristol Community College
Bunker Hill Community College
Cape Cod Community College
Gordon College
Holyoke Community College
Massachusetts Bay Community
 College
Massachusetts Institute of
 Technology
Merrimack College
Middlesex Community College
Mount Wachusett Community
 College
Northeastern University
Northern Essex Community College
Quinsigamond Community College
Springfield College
Springfield Technical Community
 College
Suffolk University
University of Massachusetts
 Amherst
 Boston
 Lowell
Wentworth Institute of Technology
Westfield State College
Worcester Polytechnic Institute

Michigan

Andrews University
Aquinas College
Baker College
 Flint
 Muskegon
 Port Huron
Cleary College
Davenport College of Business
Delta College
Detroit College of Business
Eastern Michigan University

GMI Engineering & Management
 Institute
Grand Rapids Community College
Grand Valley State University
Henry Ford Community College
Kalamazoo Valley Community
 College
Kellogg Community College
Kirtland Community College
Lake Superior State University
Lansing Community College
Lawrence Technological University
Macomb Community College
Madonna University
Marygrove College
Michigan State University
Michigan Technological University
Montcalm Community College
Muskegon Community College
Northwestern Michigan College
Oakland University
Olivet College
Saginaw Valley State University
St. Mary's College
Schoolcraft College
Siena Heights College
Southwestern Michigan College
Suomi College
University of Detroit Mercy
University of Michigan
 Ann Arbor
 Dearborn
 Flint
Wayne State University
Western Michigan University

Minnesota

Anoka-Ramsey Community College
Augsburg College
Bemidji State University
Concordia College: Moorhead
Gustavus Adolphus College
Inver Hills Community College
Itasca Community College:
 Arrowhead Region
Moorhead State University
Normandale Community College
St. Mary's College of Minnesota
Southwest State University
University of Minnesota: Twin
 Cities
Vermilion Community College
Worthington Community College

Mississippi

Alcorn State University
Hinds Community College
Holmes Community College
Jackson State University
Jones County Junior College
Mary Holmes College
Mississippi College
Mississippi Gulf Coast Community
 College
 Jackson County Campus
 Jefferson Davis Campus
 Perkinston
Mississippi State University
Mississippi University for Women
Rust College
Tougaloo College
University of Mississippi
University of Southern Mississippi

Missouri

Central Missouri State University
College of the Ozarks
Fontbonne College
Lincoln University
Lindenwood College
Longview Community College
Maryville University
Missouri Valley College
Moberly Area Community College

Rockhurst College
St. Louis Community College at
 Florissant Valley
Southeast Missouri State University
Southwest Baptist University
Southwest Missouri State University
University of Missouri
 Columbia
 Kansas City
 Rolla
 St. Louis
Washington University

Montana

Carroll College
College of Great Falls
Dull Knife Memorial College
Miles Community College
Montana College of Mineral
 Science and Technology
Northern Montana College
Rocky Mountain College
Salish Kootenai College
University of Montana
Western Montana College of the
 University of Montana

Nebraska

Central Community College
Chadron State College
McCook Community College
Metropolitan Community College
Nebraska Indian Community
 College
Peru State College
Southeast Community College
 Beatrice Campus
 Lincoln Campus
 Milford Campus
University of Nebraska
 Lincoln
 Omaha
Wayne State College
Western Nebraska Community
 College
 Scottsbluff Campus
 Sidney Campus

Nevada

Northern Nevada Community
 College
Truckee Meadows Community
 College
Western Nevada Community
 College

New Hampshire

Castle College
Daniel Webster College
Hesser College
Keene State College
New Hampshire Technical College:
 Laconia

New Jersey

Atlantic Community College
Bergen Community College
Berkeley College of Business
Brookdale Community College
Burlington County College
Caldwell College
Camden County College
County College of Morris
Essex County College
Fairleigh Dickinson University
 Edward Williams College
 Madison
Glassboro State College
Gloucester County College
Jersey City State College
Kean College of New Jersey
Mercer County Community College
Monmouth College
Montclair State College

New Jersey Institute of Technology
Passaic County Community College
Ramapo College of New Jersey
Rutgers—The State University of
New Jersey: Cook College
St. Peter's College
Seton Hall University
Stevens Institute of Technology
Stockton State College

New Mexico

College of Santa Fe
Dona Ana Branch Community
College of New Mexico State
University
Eastern New Mexico University
New Mexico Highlands University
New Mexico Institute of Mining
and Technology
New Mexico State University
San Juan College
University of New Mexico
Western New Mexico University

New York

Alfred University
Berkeley College
Berkeley School: New York City
Broome Community College
City University of New York
Borough of Manhattan
Community College
City College
John Jay College of Criminal
Justice
La Guardia Community
College
Lehman College
Medgar Evers College
Queens College
Queensborough Community
College
York College
Clarkson University
College of Aeronautics
College for Human Services
College of Insurance
College of New Rochelle
Columbia-Greene Community
College
Cornell University
Daemen College
Dominican College of Blauvelt
Dowling College
Dutchess Community College
Erie Community College: North
Campus
Fashion Institute of Technology
Fulton-Montgomery Community
College
Genesee Community College
Hilbert College
Hudson Valley Community College
Iona College
Katharine Gibbs School: New York
Laboratory Institute of
Merchandising
Long Island College Hospital School
of Nursing
Long Island University
Brooklyn Campus
C. W. Post Campus
Southampton Campus
Manhattan College
Marist College
Mercy College
Molloy College
Monroe College
Monroe Community College
Mount St. Mary College
Nassau Community College
New York Institute of Technology
Niagara County Community College
Niagara University

Onondaga Community College
Orange County Community College
Pace University
College of White Plains
New York
Pleasantville/Briarcliff
Paul Smith's College
Polytechnic University
Brooklyn
Long Island Campus
Pratt Institute
Rensselaer Polytechnic Institute
Rochester Institute of Technology
State University of New York
College at Brockport
College at Buffalo
College at Cortland
College at New Paltz
College at Potsdam
Suffolk County Community College
Eastern Campus
Selden
Western Campus
Syracuse University
Tompkins-Cortland Community
College
Ulster County Community College
Utica College of Syracuse
University
Westchester Business Institute
Wood School

North Carolina

Alamance Community College
Anson Community College
Barton College
Beaufort County Community
College
Belmont Abbey College
Blue Ridge Community College
Caldwell Community College and
Technical Institute
Campbell University
Catawba Valley Community College
Central Piedmont Community
College
Coastal Carolina Community
College
College of the Albemarle
Craven Community College
East Carolina University
Edgecombe Community College
Elizabeth City State University
Elon College
Fayetteville State University
Fayetteville Technical Community
College
Forsyth Technical Community
College
Guilford Technical Community
College
Isothermal Community College
Johnson C. Smith University
Martin Community College
Mayland Community College
McDowell Technical Community
College
Meredith College
Mount Olive College
North Carolina Agricultural and
Technical State University
North Carolina Central University
North Carolina State University
North Carolina Wesleyan College
Pfeiffer College
Piedmont Community College
Pitt Community College
Richmond Community College
Roanoke-Chowan Community
College
Rockingham Community College
Sampson Community College
Sandhills Community College
Southwestern Community College

University of North Carolina
Charlotte
Wilmington
Wake Technical Community
College
Wayne Community College
Western Carolina University
Western Piedmont Community
College
Wilkes Community College
Wilson Technical Community
College
Winston-Salem State University

North Dakota

Jamestown College
Little Hoop Community College
Mayville State University
North Dakota State University
Bottineau and Institute of
Forestry
Fargo
Standing Rock College
University of Mary
University of North Dakota
Grand Forks
Lake Region
Williston

Ohio

Antioch College
Bowling Green State University
Bradford School
Case Western Reserve University
Central Ohio Technical College
Central State University
Cincinnati Technical College
Clark State Community College
Cleveland State University
College of Mount St. Joseph
Cuyahoga Community College
Metropolitan Campus
Western Campus
Defiance College
Dyke College
Hocking Technical College
John Carroll University
Kent State University
Lake Erie College
Lakeland Community College
Lorain County Community College
Malone College
Miami University: Hamilton
Campus
Mount Union College
Northwestern College
Ohio Northern University
Ohio State University
Agricultural Technical Institute
Columbus Campus
Mansfield Campus
Marion Campus
Newark Campus
Ohio University
Owens Technical College: Toledo
Sinclair Community College
Stark Technical College
University of Akron
University of Cincinnati
Access Colleges
Cincinnati
Raymond Walters College
University of Dayton
University of Toledo
Wilberforce University
Wright State University

Oklahoma

Eastern Oklahoma State College
Langston University
Northeastern State University
Oklahoma Baptist University
Oklahoma State University
Oral Roberts University

Redlands Community College
Rogers State College
University of Oklahoma

Oregon

Central Oregon Community College
Chemeketa Community College
Clackamas Community College
Clatsop Community College
Eastern Oregon State College
Linfield College
Linn-Benton Community College
Mount Hood Community College
Oregon Institute of Technology
Oregon State University
Portland State University
Rogue Community College
Umpqua Community College
University of Oregon
Eugene
Robert Donald Clark Honors
College

Pennsylvania

Academy of the New Church
Beaver College
Bloomsburg University of
Pennsylvania
Bucks County Community College
Cabrini College
California University of
Pennsylvania
Carnegie Mellon University
Chestnut Hill College
Cheyney University of Pennsylvania
College Misericordia
Delaware County Community
College
Delaware Valley College
Drexel University
DuBois Business College
Duquesne University
Gannon University
Hahnemann University School of
Health Sciences and Humanities
Holy Family College
Indiana University of Pennsylvania
Keystone Junior College
La Salle University
Lackawanna Junior College
Lincoln University
Mercyhurst College
Millersville University of
Pennsylvania
Moore College of Art and Design
Neumann College
Peirce Junior College
Penn State University Park Campus
Pennsylvania College of Technology
Pennsylvania Institute of
Technology
Philadelphia College of Textiles and
Science
Reading Area Community College
Robert Morris College
St. Joseph's University
St. Vincent College
Temple University
Thiel College
Tracey-Warner School
University of Pittsburgh
Westmoreland County Community
College
Widener University
Wilkes University

Puerto Rico

American University of Puerto Rico
Inter American University of Puerto
Rico
Arecibo Campus
San German Campus
Universidad Politecnica de Puerto
Rico

University of Puerto Rico
  Bayamon Technological
    University College
  Mayaguez Campus
University of the Sacred Heart

Rhode Island

Community College of Rhode
  Island
Johnson & Wales University
New England Institute of
  Technology
Rhode Island College
Roger Williams College

South Carolina

Aiken Technical College
Clemson University
Coker College
College of Charleston
Denmark Technical College
Erskine College
Francis Marion College
Furman University
Greenville Technical College
Lander College
Midlands Technical College
Morris College
Newberry College
North Greenville College
South Carolina State College
Sumter Area Technical College
Tri-County Technical College
Trident Technical College
University of South Carolina
  Aiken
  Columbia
Voorhees College
Winthrop University
Wofford College

South Dakota

Augustana College
Black Hills State University
National College
South Dakota School of Mines and
  Technology
South Dakota State University

Tennessee

Belmont University
Chattanooga State Technical
  Community College
Cleveland State Community College
Cumberland University
Dyersburg State Community
  College
East Tennessee State University
Fisk University
Freed-Hardeman University
Knoxville College
LeMoyne-Owen College
McKenzie College
Middle Tennessee State University
Motlow State Community College
Nashville State Technical Institute
Northeast State Technical
  Community College
Pellissippi State Technical
  Community College
Roane State Community College
Shelby State Community College
Southern College of Seventh-day
  Adventists
State Technical Institute at
  Memphis
Tennessee State University
Tennessee Technological University
University of Tennessee
  Chattanooga
  Knoxville
  Martin

Texas

Abilene Christian University
Brazosport College
Brookhaven College
College of the Mainland
Collin County Community College
  District
DeVry Institute of Technology:
  Irving
Eastfield College
El Centro College
El Paso Community College
Galveston College
Houston Community College
Huston-Tillotson College
Jarvis Christian College
Lamar University—Beaumont
Lee College
LeTourneau University
Midland College
Midwestern State University
Mountain View College
Northwood Institute: Texas Campus
Paul Quinn College
Prairie View A&M University
Richland College
St. Edward's University
St. Mary's University
San Antonio College
Southern Methodist University
Southwestern Adventist College
Texarkana College
Texas A&I University
Texas A&M University
Texas Southern University
Texas Southmost College
Texas State Technical College
  Amarillo
  Harlingen
  Sweetwater
  Waco
Texas Woman's University
University of Houston
  Clear Lake
  Downtown
  Houston
University of North Texas
University of St. Thomas
University of Texas
  Arlington
  Austin
  El Paso
  Pan American
West Texas State University

Utah

Brigham Young University
College of Eastern Utah
Dixie College
LDS Business College
Utah State University
Utah Valley Community College
Weber State University
Westminster College of Salt Lake
  City

Vermont

Johnson State College
Lyndon State College
Norwich University
Sterling College
University of Vermont

Virginia

Central Virginia Community College
Clinch Valley College of the
  University of Virginia
Dabney S. Lancaster Community
  College
George Mason University
Hampton University
Liberty University
Lord Fairfax Community College
New River Community College

Norfolk State University
Northern Virginia Community
  College
Old Dominion University
Patrick Henry Community College
Piedmont Virginia Community
  College
Randolph-Macon College
St. Paul's College
Southwest Virginia Community
  College
Strayer College
Tidewater Community College
Virginia Commonwealth University
Virginia Highlands Community
  College
Virginia Polytechnic Institute and
  State University
Virginia State University
Virginia Union University

Washington

Central Washington University
Centralia College
Clark College
Eastern Washington University
Edmonds Community College
Grays Harbor College
Green River Community College
Griffin College
Lower Columbia College
Northwest College of the
  Assemblies of God
Olympic College
Pacific Lutheran University
Pierce College
Seattle Central Community College
Seattle Pacific University
Shoreline Community College
Skagit Valley College
South Puget Sound Community
  College
Spokane Community College
University of Puget Sound
University of Washington
Walla Walla College
Walla Walla Community College
Washington State University
Wenatchee Valley College
Whatcom Community College
Whitworth College
Yakima Valley Community College

West Virginia

Marshall University
Shepherd College
West Virginia Institute of
  Technology
West Virginia State College
West Virginia University at
  Parkersburg

Wisconsin

Marian College of Fond du Lac
Marquette University
Milwaukee Institute of Art &
  Design
Mount Senario College
Northland College
St. Norbert College
University of Wisconsin
  Eau Claire
  La Crosse
  Milwaukee
  Platteville
  River Falls
  Stevens Point
  Stout
  Superior
Viterbo College
Waukesha County Technical
  College
Western Wisconsin Technical
  College

Wyoming

Central Wyoming College
Laramie County Community
  College
Northwest College
University of Wyoming
Western Wyoming Community
  College

American Samoa, Caroline Islands, Guam, Marianas, Virgin Islands

Guam Community College
Micronesian Occupational College
Northern Marianas College

Canada

McGill University

Double major

Alabama

Alabama Agricultural and
  Mechanical University
Alabama State University
Athens State College
Auburn University
  Auburn
  Montgomery
Birmingham-Southern College
Draughons Junior College
Faulkner University
George C. Wallace State
  Community College at Selma
Huntingdon College
Jacksonville State University
James H. Faulkner State
  Community College
John C. Calhoun State Community
  College
Judson College
Lawson State Community College
Miles College
Mobile College
Northeast Alabama State Junior
  College
Oakwood College
Samford University
Shelton State Community College
Southeastern Bible College
Spring Hill College
Stillman College
Troy State University
  Dothan
  Montgomery
  Troy
Tuskegee University
University of Alabama
  Birmingham
  Huntsville
  Tuscaloosa
University of Montevallo
University of North Alabama
University of South Alabama
Wallace State Community College
  at Hanceville

Alaska

Alaska Pacific University
Sheldon Jackson College
University of Alaska
  Anchorage
  Fairbanks
  Southeast

Arizona

American Indian Bible College
Arizona College of the Bible
Arizona State University
Cochise College
Grand Canyon University

Lamson Junior College
Navajo Community College
Northern Arizona University
Northland Pioneer College
Pima Community College
Prescott College
University of Arizona
University of Phoenix
Western International University

Arkansas

Arkansas Baptist College
Arkansas College
Arkansas State University
  Beebe Branch
  Jonesboro
Arkansas Tech University
Capital City Junior College
Harding University
Henderson State University
Hendrix College
John Brown University
Ouachita Baptist University
Shorter College
Southern Arkansas University
University of Arkansas
  Fayetteville
  Little Rock
  Monticello
  Pine Bluff
University of Central Arkansas
University of the Ozarks

California

Academy of Art College
Allan Hancock College
American Armenian International
  College
American College for the Applied
  Arts: Los Angeles
Antioch Southern California at Los
  Angeles
Armstrong College
Azusa Pacific University
Bakersfield College
Bethany College
Biola University
California Baptist College
California College of Arts and
  Crafts
California Institute of the Arts
California Institute of Technology
California Lutheran University
California Maritime Academy
California Polytechnic State
  University: San Luis Obispo
California State Polytechnic
  University: Pomona
California State University
  Bakersfield
  Chico
  Dominguez Hills
  Fresno
  Fullerton
  Hayward
  Long Beach
  Los Angeles
  Northridge
  Sacramento
  San Bernardino
  San Marcos
  Stanislaus
Cerro Coso Community College
Chabot College
Chapman University
Christ College Irvine
Christian Heritage College
Claremont McKenna College
Cogswell Polytechnical College
Coleman College
College of Notre Dame
College of the Redwoods
College of the Sequoias
Dominican College of San Rafael

East Los Angeles College
Evergreen Valley College
Feather River College
Fresno City College
Fresno Pacific College
Golden West College
Grossmont Community College
Harvey Mudd College
Holy Names College
Humboldt State University
Imperial Valley College
Irvine Valley College
John F. Kennedy University
Kings River Community College
La Sierra University
Lake Tahoe Community College
Louise Salinger Academy of
  Fashion
Loyola Marymount University
Master's College
Mendocino College
Menlo College
Mills College
MiraCosta College
Modesto Junior College
Monterey Institute of International
  Studies
Mount St. Mary's College
New College of California
Occidental College
Ohlone College
Pacific Christian College
Pacific Oaks College
Pacific Union College
Palomar College
Patten College
Pepperdine University
Phillips Junior College: Fresno
  Campus
Pitzer College
Pomona College
Porterville College
Saddleback College
St. Mary's College of California
Samuel Merritt College
San Diego City College
San Diego State University
San Francisco Art Institute
San Francisco State University
San Jose Christian College
San Jose State University
Santa Clara University
Scripps College
Sierra College
Simpson College
Solano Community College
Sonoma State University
Southern California College
Southwestern College
Stanford University
University of California
  Berkeley
  Davis
  Irvine
  Los Angeles
  Riverside
  San Diego
  Santa Barbara
  Santa Cruz
University of Judaism
University of La Verne
University of the Pacific
University of Redlands
University of San Diego
University of San Francisco
University of Southern California
Victor Valley College
West Valley College
Western State University College of
  Law: Orange County
Westmont College
Whittier College
Woodbury University
World College West

Colorado

Adams State College
Aims Community College
Blair Junior College
Colorado Christian University
Colorado School of Mines
Colorado State University
Colorado Technical College
Community College of Denver
Denver Technical College
Fort Lewis College
Front Range Community College
Metropolitan State College of
  Denver
Morgan Community College
Naropa Institute
National College
Pueblo Community College
Red Rocks Community College
Regis College of Regis University
Rocky Mountain College of Art &
  Design
United States Air Force Academy
University of Colorado
  Boulder
  Colorado Springs
  Denver
University of Denver
University of Northern Colorado
University of Southern Colorado
Western State College of Colorado

Connecticut

Albertus Magnus College
Briarwood College
Bridgeport Engineering Institute
Central Connecticut State
  University
Connecticut College
Eastern Connecticut State
  University
Fairfield University
Holy Apostles College and
  Seminary
Housatonic Community College
Manchester Community College
Mattatuck Community College
Norwalk State Technical College
Quinebaug Valley Community
  College
Quinnipiac College
Sacred Heart University
St. Joseph College
Teikyo-Post University
Thames Valley State Technical
  College
Trinity College
Tunxis Community College
University of Bridgeport
University of Connecticut
University of Hartford
University of New Haven
Wesleyan University
Western Connecticut State
  University
Yale University

Delaware

Delaware State College
Delaware Technical and
  Community College
    Stanton/Wilmington Campus
    Terry Campus
Goldey-Beacom College
University of Delaware
Wilmington College

District of Columbia

American University
Catholic University of America
Gallaudet University
George Washington University
Georgetown University
Howard University

Mount Vernon College
Trinity College

Florida

Barry University
Bethune-Cookman College
Brevard Community College
Eckerd College
Edison Community College
Flagler College
Florida Agricultural and Mechanical
  University
Florida Baptist Theological College
Florida Bible College
Florida Christian College
Florida Community College at
  Jacksonville
Florida International University
Florida Keys Community College
Florida Memorial College
Florida Southern College
Florida State University
Fort Lauderdale College
Hillsborough Community College
Hobe Sound Bible College
Jacksonville University
Jones College
Lynn University
New College of the University of
  South Florida
Nova University
Orlando College
Palm Beach Atlantic College
Phillips Junior College: Melbourne
Rollins College
St. Leo College
St. Thomas University
Schiller International University
South College: Palm Beach Campus
Stetson University
Tampa College
University of Central Florida
University of Miami
University of North Florida
University of South Florida
University of West Florida
Webber College

Georgia

Agnes Scott College
Albany State College
American College for the Applied
  Arts
Armstrong State College
Atlanta Christian College
Atlanta College of Art
Augusta College
Bauder College
Berry College
Brenau Women's College
Brunswick College
Clark Atlanta University
Columbus College
Covenant College
DeKalb College
Emory University
Floyd College
Georgia College
Georgia Southern University
Georgia State University
LaGrange College
Meadows College of Business
Mercer University
  Atlanta
  Macon
Middle Georgia College
Morehouse College
Morris Brown College
North Georgia College
Oglethorpe University
Oxford College of Emory University
Piedmont College
Savannah College of Art and
  Design

Savannah State College
Savannah Technical Institute
Shorter College
South College
Southern College of Technology
Spelman College
Thomas College
Toccoa Falls College
University of Georgia
Valdosta State College
Wesleyan College
West Georgia College

Hawaii

Brigham Young University-Hawaii
Cannon's International Business
  College of Honolulu
Chaminade University of Honolulu
Hawaii Loa College
Hawaii Pacific University
University of Hawaii
  Hilo
  Kapiolani Community College
  Manoa
  West Oahu

Idaho

Albertson College
Boise Bible College
Boise State University
Idaho State University
Lewis Clark State College
Northwest Nazarene College
University of Idaho

Illinois

American Academy of Art
American Conservatory of Music
Augustana College
Aurora University
Barat College
Belleville Area College
Black Hawk College: East Campus
Blackburn College
Bradley University
Chicago State University
City Colleges of Chicago: Malcolm
  X College
College of DuPage
College of St. Francis
Columbia College
Concordia University
De Paul University
Eastern Illinois University
Elmhurst College
Eureka College
Greenville College
Hebrew Theological College
Illinois Benedictine College
Illinois College
Illinois Eastern Community
  Colleges
    Frontier Community College
    Lincoln Trail College
    Olney Central College
    Wabash Valley College
Illinois Institute of Technology
Illinois State University
Illinois Wesleyan University
Judson College
KAES College
Kishwaukee College
Knox College
Lake Forest College
Lewis and Clark Community
  College
Lewis University
Lincoln Christian College and
  Seminary
Loyola University of Chicago
MacMurray College
McKendree College
Midstate College
Millikin University

Monmouth College
Moody Bible Institute
Morrison Institute of Technology
National-Louis University
North Central College
North Park College and Theological
  Seminary
Northeastern Illinois University
Northern Illinois University
Northwestern University
Olivet Nazarene University
Parks College of St. Louis
  University
Principia College
Quincy College
Rockford College
Roosevelt University
Rosary College
St. Augustine College
St. Xavier University
Sangamon State University
Shimer College
Southern Illinois University
  Carbondale
  Edwardsville
Springfield College in Illinois
Trinity Christian College
Trinity College
University of Chicago
University of Illinois
  Chicago
  Urbana-Champaign
Western Illinois University
Wheaton College

Indiana

Anderson University
Ball State University
Butler University
Calumet College of St. Joseph
DePauw University
Earlham College
Franklin College
Goshen College
Grace College
Hanover College
Huntington College
Indiana Institute of Technology
Indiana State University
Indiana University
  Bloomington
  Northwest
  South Bend
  Southeast
Indiana University—Purdue
  University
    Fort Wayne
    Indianapolis
Indiana Vocational Technical
  College
    Lafayette
    Northwest
    Southcentral
    Southwest
    Wabash Valley
Indiana Wesleyan University
International Business College
Manchester College
Marian College
Martin University
Oakland City College
Purdue University
Rose-Hulman Institute of
  Technology
St. Francis College
St. Joseph's College
St. Mary-of-the-Woods College
St. Mary's College
Taylor University
Tri-State University
University of Evansville
University of Indianapolis
University of Notre Dame
University of Southern Indiana

Valparaiso University
Vincennes University
Wabash College

Iowa

American Institute of Business
American Institute of Commerce
Briar Cliff College
Buena Vista College
Central College
Clarke College
Clinton Community College
Coe College
Cornell College
Divine Word College
Dordt College
Drake University
Faith Baptist Bible College and
  Theological Seminary
Graceland College
Grand View College
Grinnell College
Iowa State University
Iowa Wesleyan College
Loras College
Luther College
Maharishi International University
Morningside College
Mount Mercy College
Mount St. Clare College
Northwestern College
St. Ambrose University
Scott Community College
Simpson College
Teikyo Marycrest University
Teikyo Westmar University
University of Dubuque
University of Iowa
University of Northern Iowa
Upper Iowa University
Vennard College
Wartburg College
William Penn College

Kansas

Baker University
Barclay College
Benedictine College
Bethany College
Bethel College
Brown Mackie College
Central College
Cowley County Community College
Dodge City Community College
Emporia State University
Fort Hays State University
Friends University
Johnson County Community
  College
Kansas City College and Bible
  School
Kansas City Kansas Community
  College
Kansas Newman College
Kansas State University
Kansas Wesleyan University
Manhattan Christian College
McPherson College
MidAmerica Nazarene College
Ottawa University
Pittsburg State University
St. Mary College
Southwestern College
Sterling College
Tabor College
University of Kansas
  Lawrence
  Medical Center
Washburn University of Topeka
Wichita State University

Kentucky

Asbury College
Bellarmine College

Berea College
Brescia College
Campbellsville College
Centre College
Cumberland College
Eastern Kentucky University
Franklin College
Georgetown College
Kentucky Christian College
Kentucky State University
Kentucky Wesleyan College
Morehead State University
Murray State University
Northern Kentucky University
Owensboro Junior College of
  Business
Pikeville College
Spalding University
Sullivan College
Thomas More College
Transylvania University
Union College
University of Kentucky
University of Louisville
Western Kentucky University

Louisiana

Centenary College of Louisiana
Dillard University
Grambling State University
Louisiana College
Louisiana State University
  Agricultural and Mechanical
    College
  Shreveport
Louisiana Tech University
Loyola University
McNeese State University
Northeast Louisiana University
Northwestern State University
Our Lady of Holy Cross College
Southeastern Louisiana University
Southern University and
  Agricultural and Mechanical
    College
Tulane University
University of New Orleans
University of Southwestern
  Louisiana
Xavier University of Louisiana

Maine

Andover College
Bates College
Beal College
Bowdoin College
Casco Bay College
Colby College
Husson College
St. Joseph's College
Southern Maine Technical College
Unity College
University of Maine
  Farmington
  Fort Kent
  Orono
  Presque Isle
University of New England
University of Southern Maine

Maryland

Anne Arundel Community College
Baltimore Hebrew University
Baltimore International Culinary
  College
Capitol College
Chesapeake College
College of Notre Dame of
  Maryland
Columbia Union College
Coppin State College
Frostburg State University
Garrett Community College
Goucher College

Hagerstown Business College
Harford Community College
Hood College
Howard Community College
Johns Hopkins University
Loyola College in Maryland
Maryland Institute College of Art
Montgomery College
    Germantown Campus
    Rockville Campus
    Takoma Park Campus
Morgan State University
Mount St. Mary's College
New Community College of
    Baltimore
St. Mary's College of Maryland
Salisbury State University
Towson State University
United States Naval Academy
University of Baltimore
University of Maryland
    Baltimore County
    College Park
    Eastern Shore
Villa Julie College
Washington College
Western Maryland College
Wor-Wic Tech Community College

Massachusetts

American International College
Amherst College
Anna Maria College for Men and
    Women
Aquinas College at Newton
Assumption College
Atlantic Union College
Babson College
Bay State College
Berklee College of Music
Boston College
Boston Conservatory
Boston University
Brandeis University
Bridgewater State College
Bunker Hill Community College
Clark University
College of the Holy Cross
Curry College
Eastern Nazarene College
Elms College
Emerson College
Emmanuel College
Endicott College
Fitchburg State College
Framingham State College
Gordon College
Harvard and Radcliffe Colleges
Hellenic College
Lesley College
Marian Court Junior College
Massachusetts Bay Community
    College
Massachusetts College of Art
Massachusetts College of Pharmacy
    and Allied Health Sciences
Massachusetts Institute of
    Technology
Massachusetts Maritime Academy
Merrimack College
Montserrat College of Art
Mount Holyoke College
New England Conservatory of
    Music
Newbury College
Nichols College
North Adams State College
Northeastern University
Northern Essex Community College
Pine Manor College
Quinsigamond Community College
Regis College
St. John's Seminary College
Salem State College

School of the Museum of Fine Arts
Simmons College
Smith College
Springfield College
Suffolk University
Tufts University
University of Massachusetts
    Amherst
    Boston
    Dartmouth
    Lowell
Wellesley College
Wentworth Institute of Technology
Western New England College
Westfield State College
Wheaton College
Wheelock College
Williams College
Worcester Polytechnic Institute
Worcester State College

Michigan

Adrian College
Albion College
Alma College
Alpena Community College
Andrews University
Aquinas College
Baker College
    Flint
    Muskegon
    Port Huron
Calvin College
Center for Creative Studies: College
    of Art and Design
Central Michigan University
Charles Stewart Mott Community
    College
Cleary College
Concordia College
Davenport College of Business
Detroit College of Business
Eastern Michigan University
Ferris State University
GMI Engineering & Management
    Institute
Grace Bible College
Grand Rapids Baptist College and
    Seminary
Grand Valley State University
Great Lakes Junior College of
    Business
Hillsdale College
Hope College
Jordan College
Kalamazoo College
Lake Superior State University
Lansing Community College
Madonna University
Marygrove College
Michigan State University
Michigan Technological University
Muskegon Community College
Northern Michigan University
Northwood Institute
Oakland University
Olivet College
Reformed Bible College
Saginaw Valley State University
St. Clair County Community
    College
St. Mary's College
Siena Heights College
Southwestern Michigan College
Spring Arbor College
Suomi College
University of Detroit Mercy
University of Michigan
    Ann Arbor
    Dearborn
    Flint
Walsh College of Accountancy and
    Business Administration
Wayne State University

Western Michigan University
William Tyndale College

Minnesota

Augsburg College
Bemidji State University
Bethel College
Carleton College
College of Associated Arts
College of St. Benedict
College of St. Catherine: St.
    Catherine Campus
College of St. Scholastica
Concordia College: Moorhead
Concordia College: St. Paul
Crown College
Dr. Martin Luther College
Gustavus Adolphus College
Hamline University
Macalester College
Mankato State University
Minnesota Bible College
Moorhead State University
North Central Bible College
Northwestern College
Northwestern Electronics Institute
Pillsbury Baptist Bible College
St. Cloud State University
St. John's University
St. Mary's College of Minnesota
St. Olaf College
Southwest State University
University of Minnesota
    Crookston
    Duluth
    Morris
    Twin Cities
Winona State University

Mississippi

Alcorn State University
Belhaven College
Blue Mountain College
Delta State University
Jackson State University
Millsaps College
Mississippi College
Mississippi State University
Mississippi University for Women
Phillips Junior College
    Jackson
    Mississippi Gulf Coast
Rust College
Southeastern Baptist College
Tougaloo College
University of Mississippi
University of Southern Mississippi
Wesley College
William Carey College

Missouri

Avila College
Calvary Bible College
Central Christian College of the
    Bible
Central Methodist College
Central Missouri State University
College of the Ozarks
Columbia College
Culver-Stockton College
Drury College
Evangel College
Fontbonne College
Hannibal-LaGrange College
Harris Stowe State College
ITT Technical Institute: St. Louis
Jefferson College
Lincoln University
Lindenwood College
Maryville University
Missouri Baptist College
Missouri Southern State College
Missouri Valley College
Missouri Western State College

National College
North Central Missouri College
Northwest Missouri State
    University
Ozark Christian College
Park College
Phillips Junior College
Research College of Nursing
Rockhurst College
St. Louis Christian College
St. Louis Community College at
    Forest Park
St. Louis University
Southeast Missouri State University
Southwest Baptist University
Southwest Missouri State University
Stephens College
University of Missouri
    Columbia
    Kansas City
    Rolla
    St. Louis
Washington University
Webster University
Westminster College
William Jewell College
William Woods College

Montana

Carroll College
College of Great Falls
Dull Knife Memorial College
Eastern Montana College
Fort Peck Community College
Montana College of Mineral
    Science and Technology
Montana State University
Northern Montana College
Rocky Mountain College
Salish Kootenai College
University of Montana
Western Montana College of the
    University of Montana

Nebraska

Bellevue College
Central Community College
College of St. Mary
Concordia College
Creighton University
Dana College
Doane College
Hastings College
Metropolitan Community College
Midland Lutheran College
Nebraska Christian College
Nebraska Indian Community
    College
Nebraska Wesleyan University
Peru State College
Southeast Community College:
    Beatrice Campus
Union College
University of Nebraska
    Kearney
    Lincoln
    Omaha
Wayne State College
Western Nebraska Community
    College
    Scottsbluff Campus
    Sidney Campus

Nevada

Sierra Nevada College
University of Nevada
    Las Vegas
    Reno

New Hampshire

Castle College
Daniel Webster College
Dartmouth College
Franklin Pierce College

Hesser College
Keene State College
McIntosh College
New England College
New Hampshire College
New Hampshire Technical College
    Berlin
    Laconia
    Stratham
Notre Dame College
Plymouth State College of the
    University System of New
    Hampshire
Rivier College
University of New Hampshire
White Pines College

New Jersey

Berkeley College of Business
Bloomfield College
Burlington County College
Caldwell College
College of St. Elizabeth
County College of Morris
Cumberland County College
Drew University
Essex County College
Fairleigh Dickinson University
Felician College
Georgian Court College
Glassboro State College
Jersey City State College
Kean College of New Jersey
Mercer County Community College
Monmouth College
Montclair State College
New Jersey Institute of Technology
Ramapo College of New Jersey
Rider College
Rutgers—The State University of
    New Jersey
    Camden College of Arts and
        Sciences
    College of Engineering
    Cook College
    Douglass College
    Livingston College
    Newark College of Arts and
        Sciences
    Rutgers College
    University College Camden
    University College New
        Brunswick
    University College Newark
St. Peter's College
Seton Hall University
Stevens Institute of Technology
Sussex County Community College
Trenton State College
Upsala College
Westminster Choir College
William Paterson College of New
    Jersey

New Mexico

College of Santa Fe
Eastern New Mexico University
Institute of American Indian Arts
National College
New Mexico Highlands University
New Mexico Institute of Mining
    and Technology
New Mexico State University
    Carlsbad
    Las Cruces
University of New Mexico
Western New Mexico University

New York

Adelphi University
Alfred University
Bard College
Barnard College
Bramson ORT Technical Institute

Briarcliffe: The College for Business
Broome Community College
Bryant & Stratton Business
    Institute: Albany
Canisius College
Cazenovia College
City University of New York
    Brooklyn College
    College of Staten Island
    Hunter College
    Lehman College
    Queens College
Clarkson University
Colgate University
College of Mount St. Vincent
College of New Rochelle
College of St. Rose
Columbia University
    Columbia College
    School of General Studies
    School of Nursing
Community College of the Finger
    Lakes
Concordia College
Cornell University
Corning Community College
Daemen College
Dowling College
D'Youville College
Eastman School of Music of the
    University of Rochester
Elmira College
Erie Community College
    City Campus
    North Campus
    South Campus
Eugene Lang College/New School
    for Social Research
Five Towns College
Fordham University
Genesee Community College
Hamilton College
Hartwick College
Hilbert College
Hobart College
Hofstra University
Houghton College
Institute of Design and
    Construction
Iona College
Ithaca College
Jewish Theological Seminary of
    America
Keuka College
Le Moyne College
Long Island University
    Brooklyn Campus
    C. W. Post Campus
    Southampton Campus
Manhattan College
Manhattanville College
Mannes College of Music
Marist College
Marymount College
Mater Dei College
Medaille College
Mercy College
Molloy College
Mount St. Mary College
Nazareth College of Rochester
New York University
Niagara University
North Country Community College
Onondaga Community College
Paul Smith's College
Polytechnic University
    Brooklyn
    Long Island Campus
Pratt Institute
Rensselaer Polytechnic Institute
Roberts Wesleyan College
Rochester Business Institute
Rockland Community College
Russell Sage College

St. Bonaventure University
St. Francis College
St. John Fisher College
St. John's University
St. Lawrence University
St. Thomas Aquinas College
Sarah Lawrence College
School of Visual Arts
Skidmore College
State University of New York
    Albany
    Binghamton
    Buffalo
    Purchase
    Stony Brook
    College of Agriculture and
        Technology at Morrisville
    College at Brockport
    College at Buffalo
    College at Cortland
    College at Fredonia
    College at Geneseo
    College at New Paltz
    College at Old Westbury
    College at Oneonta
    College at Plattsburgh
    College at Potsdam
    College of Technology at Delhi
    Empire State College
    Health Sciences Center at
        Stony Brook
    Institute of Technology at
        Utica/Rome
    Oswego
Syracuse University
Touro College
Ulster County Community College
Union College
United States Merchant Marine
    Academy
United States Military Academy
University of Rochester
Utica College of Syracuse
    University
Vassar College
Wadhams Hall Seminary-College
Wagner College
Webb Institute of Naval
    Architecture
Wells College
Westchester Business Institute
Westchester Community College
William Smith College
Yeshiva University

North Carolina

Alamance Community College
Anson Community College
Appalachian State University
Barber-Scotia College
Barton College
Beaufort County Community
    College
Belmont Abbey College
Bennett College
Bladen Community College
Blue Ridge Community College
Brevard College
Brunswick Community College
Campbell University
Carteret Community College
Catawba College
Catawba Valley Community College
Cecils College
Central Piedmont Community
    College
Cleveland Community College
College of the Albemarle
Duke University
East Carolina University
East Coast Bible College
Edgecombe Community College
Elizabeth City State University
Elon College

Fayetteville State University
Forsyth Technical Community
    College
Gardner-Webb College
Greensboro College
Guilford College
High Point University
James Sprunt Community College
John Wesley College
Johnson C. Smith University
Johnston Community College
Lenoir-Rhyne College
Livingstone College
Mars Hill College
Mayland Community College
McDowell Technical Community
    College
Meredith College
Methodist College
Montgomery Community College
Mount Olive College
Nash Community College
North Carolina Agricultural and
    Technical State University
North Carolina Central University
North Carolina State University
North Carolina Wesleyan College
Peace College
Pembroke State University
Pfeiffer College
Piedmont Bible College
Piedmont Community College
Queens College
Richmond Community College
Roanoke Bible College
Robeson Community College
St. Andrews Presbyterian College
St. Augustine's College
Salem College
Shaw University
Southwestern Community College
Tri-County Community College
University of North Carolina
    Asheville
    Chapel Hill
    Charlotte
    Greensboro
    Wilmington
Wake Forest University
Wake Technical Community
    College
Warren Wilson College
Wayne Community College
Western Carolina University
Wilkes Community College
Wilson Technical Community
    College
Wingate College
Winston-Salem State University

North Dakota

Dickinson State University
Jamestown College
Mayville State University
Minot State University
North Dakota State University
    Bottineau and Institute of
        Forestry
    Fargo
Trinity Bible College
University of Mary
University of North Dakota
Valley City State University

Ohio

Antioch College
Antioch School for Adult and
    Experiential Learning
Art Academy of Cincinnati
Ashland University
Baldwin-Wallace College
Bluffton College

Bowling Green State University
  Bowling Green
  Firelands College
Capital University
Case Western Reserve University
Cedarville College
Central Ohio Technical College
Central State University
Cincinnati Metropolitan College
Cincinnati Technical College
Circleville Bible College
Clark State Community College
Cleveland Institute of Art
Cleveland Institute of Music
Cleveland State University
College of Mount St. Joseph
College of Wooster
Columbus College of Art and
  Design
Columbus State Community College
Defiance College
Denison University
Dyke College
Edison State Community College
ETI Technical College
Franciscan University of
  Steubenville
Franklin University
Heidelberg College
Hiram College
Hocking Technical College
Jefferson Technical College
John Carroll University
Kent State University
  East Liverpool Regional
    Campus
  Kent
  Stark Campus
  Tuscarawas Campus
Kenyon College
Kettering College of Medical Arts
Lake Erie College
Lourdes College
Malone College
Marietta College
Marion Technical College
Miami University
  Hamilton Campus
  Oxford Campus
Mount Union College
Mount Vernon Nazarene College
Muskingum College
North Central Technical College
Northwestern College
Notre Dame College of Ohio
Oberlin College
Ohio Dominican College
Ohio Institute of Photography
Ohio Northern University
Ohio State University
  Agricultural Technical Institute
  Columbus Campus
Ohio University
  Athens
  Chillicothe Campus
  Zanesville Campus
Ohio Valley Business College
Ohio Wesleyan University
Otterbein College
Owens Technical College
  Findlay Campus
  Toledo
Pontifical College Josephinum
Shawnee State University
Sinclair Community College
Stark Technical College
Terra Technical College
Tiffin University
Union Institute
University of Cincinnati
  Access Colleges
  Cincinnati
  Clermont College
University of Dayton

University of Findlay
University of Rio Grande
University of Toledo
Urbana University
Ursuline College
Walsh College
Washington State Community
  College
Wilmington College
Wittenberg University
Wright State University
  Dayton
  Lake Campus
Xavier University
Youngstown State University

Oklahoma

Bartlesville Wesleyan College
Cameron University
East Central University
Mid-America Bible College
Northeastern State University
Northwestern Oklahoma State
  University
Oklahoma Baptist University
Oklahoma City University
Oklahoma Junior College
Oklahoma Panhandle State
  University
Oklahoma State University
  Oklahoma City
  Stillwater
Oral Roberts University
Rose State College
Southeastern Oklahoma State
  University
Southwestern College of Christian
  Ministries
Southwestern Oklahoma State
  University
University of Central Oklahoma
University of Oklahoma
University of Science and Arts of
  Oklahoma
University of Tulsa

Oregon

Central Oregon Community College
Chemeketa Community College
Clatsop Community College
Concordia College
Eastern Oregon State College
George Fox College
Lewis and Clark College
Linfield College
Marylhurst College
Mount Hood Community College
Multnomah School of the Bible
Northwest Christian College
Oregon Institute of Technology
Oregon State University
Pacific University
Portland State University
Reed College
Rogue Community College
Southern Oregon State College
Southwestern Oregon Community
  College
Treasure Valley Community College
Umpqua Community College
University of Oregon
  Eugene
  Robert Donald Clark Honors
    College
University of Portland
Warner Pacific College
Western Baptist College
Western Oregon State College
Willamette University

Pennsylvania

Albright College
Allegheny College

Allentown College of St. Francis de
  Sales
Alvernia College
Baptist Bible College of
  Pennsylvania
Beaver College
Bloomsburg University of
  Pennsylvania
Bryn Mawr College
Bucknell University
Butler County Community College
Cabrini College
California University of
  Pennsylvania
Carlow College
Carnegie Mellon University
Cedar Crest College
Central Pennsylvania Business
  School
Chestnut Hill College
Cheyney University of Pennsylvania
Clarion University of Pennsylvania
College Misericordia
Community College of Beaver
  County
Delaware County Community
  College
Dickinson College
Duquesne University
East Stroudsburg University of
  Pennsylvania
Eastern College
Edinboro University of
  Pennsylvania
Elizabethtown College
Franklin and Marshall College
Gannon University
Geneva College
Gettysburg College
Gratz College
Grove City College
Gwynedd-Mercy College
Harrisburg Area Community
  College
Haverford College
Holy Family College
Immaculata College
Indiana University of Pennsylvania
Juniata College
Keystone Junior College
King's College
Kutztown University of
  Pennsylvania
La Salle University
Lackawanna Junior College
Lafayette College
Lansdale School of Business
Lebanon Valley College of
  Pennsylvania
Lehigh University
Lincoln University
Lock Haven University of
  Pennsylvania
Luzerne County Community
  College
Lycoming College
Manor Junior College
Mansfield University of
  Pennsylvania
Marywood College
Mercyhurst College
Messiah College
Millersville University of
  Pennsylvania
Moore College of Art and Design
Moravian College
Muhlenberg College
Neumann College
Penn State
  Erie Behrend College
  University Park Campus
Pennsylvania College of Technology
Pennsylvania Institute of
  Technology

Philadelphia College of Bible
Philadelphia College of Textiles and
  Science
Point Park College
Robert Morris College
Rosemont College
St. Francis College
St. Joseph's University
St. Vincent College
Seton Hill College
Shippensburg University of
  Pennsylvania
Slippery Rock University of
  Pennsylvania
Spring Garden College
Susquehanna University
Swarthmore College
Temple University
Thiel College
University of the Arts
University of Pennsylvania
University of Pittsburgh
  Bradford
  Greensburg
  Johnstown
  Pittsburgh
University of Scranton
Ursinus College
Valley Forge Christian College
Valley Forge Military College
Villanova University
Washington and Jefferson College
Waynesburg College
West Chester University of
  Pennsylvania
Westminster College
Westmoreland County Community
  College
Widener University
Wilkes University
York College of Pennsylvania

Puerto Rico

Bayamon Central University
Inter American University of Puerto
  Rico
    Metropolitan Campus
    San German Campus
Pontifical Catholic University of
  Puerto Rico
Universidad Adventista de las
  Antillas
University of Puerto Rico
  Bayamon Technological
    University College
  Mayaguez Campus
  Rio Piedras Campus
University of the Sacred Heart

Rhode Island

Brown University
Bryant College
Community College of Rhode
  Island
Johnson & Wales University
New England Institute of
  Technology
Providence College
Rhode Island College
Roger Williams College
Salve Regina University
University of Rhode Island

South Carolina

Aiken Technical College
Benedict College
Bob Jones University
Central Wesleyan College
Charleston Southern University
The Citadel
Claflin College
Clemson University
Coker College
College of Charleston

Columbia Bible College and
  Seminary
Columbia College
Columbia Junior College of Business
Converse College
Erskine College
Francis Marion College
Furman University
Lander College
Limestone College
Newberry College
North Greenville College
Presbyterian College
Technical College of the
  Lowcountry
Tri-County Technical College
Trident Technical College
University of South Carolina
  Aiken
  Coastal Carolina College
  Columbia
Winthrop University
Wofford College

South Dakota
Augustana College
Black Hills State University
Dakota State University
Dakota Wesleyan University
Huron University
Mount Marty College
National College
Northern State University
Sioux Falls College
South Dakota School of Mines and
  Technology
South Dakota State University
University of South Dakota

Tennessee
American Baptist College of ABT
  Seminary
Austin Peay State University
Belmont University
Bethel College
Carson-Newman College
Chattanooga State Technical
  Community College
Christian Brothers University
Crichton College
David Lipscomb University
East Tennessee State University
Fisk University
Free Will Baptist Bible College
Freed-Hardeman University
Johnson Bible College
King College
Knoxville Business College
Knoxville College
Lambuth University
LeMoyne-Owen College
Lincoln Memorial University
Maryville College
Memphis College of Art
Memphis State University
Middle Tennessee State University
Milligan College
Motlow State Community College
Northeast State Technical
  Community College
O'More College of Design
Pellissippi State Technical
  Community College
Rhodes College
Southern College of Seventh-day
  Adventists
State Technical Institute at
  Memphis
Tennessee State University
Tennessee Technological University
Tennessee Temple University
Tennessee Wesleyan College
Tomlinson College
Trevecca Nazarene College

Union University
University of the South
University of Tennessee
  Chattanooga
  Knoxville
  Martin
Vanderbilt University
Volunteer State Community College
William Jennings Bryan College

Texas
Abilene Christian University
Angelo State University
Arlington Baptist College
Austin College
Baylor University
Concordia Lutheran College
Corpus Christi State University
Criswell College
Dallas Baptist University
East Texas Baptist University
East Texas State University
  Commerce
  Texarkana
El Centro College
El Paso Community College
Hardin-Simmons University
Houston Baptist University
Howard Payne University
Huston-Tillotson College
Incarnate Word College
Jarvis Christian College
Lamar University—Beaumont
Laredo State University
LeTourneau University
Lubbock Christian University
McMurry University
Midwestern State University
Miss Wade's Fashion
  Merchandising College
Northwood Institute: Texas Campus
Our Lady of the Lake University of
  San Antonio
Paul Quinn College
Prairie View A&M University
Rice University
St. Edward's University
St. Mary's University
Sam Houston State University
San Antonio Art Institute
San Antonio College
Schreiner College
Southern Methodist University
Southwest Texas State University
Southwestern Adventist College
Southwestern Assemblies of God
  College
Southwestern University
Stephen F. Austin State University
Tarleton State University
Texas A&I University
Texas A&M University
  College Station
  Galveston
Texas Christian University
Texas College
Texas Lutheran College
Texas Southern University
Texas State Technical College:
  Sweetwater
Texas Tech University
Texas Wesleyan University
Texas Woman's University
Trinity University
University of Dallas
University of Houston
University of Mary Hardin-Baylor
University of North Texas
University of St. Thomas

University of Texas
  Dallas
  El Paso
  Health Science Center at
    Houston
  Pan American
  Permian Basin
  San Antonio
  Southwestern Medical Center
    at Dallas Southwestern
    Allied Health Sciences
    School
  Tyler
Wayland Baptist University
West Texas State University

Utah
Brigham Young University
College of Eastern Utah
LDS Business College
Southern Utah University
University of Utah
Utah State University
Utah Valley Community College
Weber State University
Westminster College of Salt Lake
  City

Vermont
Bennington College
Burlington College
Castleton State College
Champlain College
College of St. Joseph in Vermont
Community College of Vermont
Green Mountain College
Johnson State College
Lyndon State College
Marlboro College
Middlebury College
Norwich University
School for International Training
Southern Vermont College
Trinity College of Vermont
University of Vermont
Vermont Technical College

Virginia
Averett College
Bluefield College
Bridgewater College
Christopher Newport College
Clinch Valley College of the
  University of Virginia
College of William and Mary
Commonwealth College
Dabney S. Lancaster Community
  College
Eastern Mennonite College
Emory and Henry College
Ferrum College
George Mason University
Hampden-Sydney College
Hollins College
James Madison University
Liberty University
Longwood College
Lord Fairfax Community College
Lynchburg College
Mary Baldwin College
Mary Washington College
Marymount University
Mountain Empire Community
  College
National Business College
Norfolk State University
Northern Virginia Community
  College
Old Dominion University
Patrick Henry Community College
Radford University
Randolph-Macon College
Randolph-Macon Woman's College
Roanoke College

Shenandoah University
Southern Seminary College
Southside Virginia Community
  College
Southwest Virginia Community
  College
Strayer College
Sweet Briar College
Tidewater Community College
University of Richmond
University of Virginia
Virginia Commonwealth University
Virginia Highlands Community
  College
Virginia Intermont College
Virginia Military Institute
Virginia Polytechnic Institute and
  State University
Virginia State University
Virginia Wesleyan College
Washington and Lee University

Washington
Bastyr College
Central Washington University
Centralia College
City University
Cogswell College North
Eastern Washington University
Gonzaga University
Griffin College
Heritage College
Northwest College of the
  Assemblies of God
Pacific Lutheran University
Pierce College
Puget Sound Christian College
St. Martin's College
Seattle Pacific University
Seattle University
University of Puget Sound
University of Washington
Walla Walla College
Washington State University
Wenatchee Valley College
Western Washington University
Whitman College
Whitworth College

West Virginia
Alderson-Broaddus College
Bethany College
Concord College
Davis and Elkins College
Marshall University
Salem-Teikyo University
Shepherd College
University of Charleston
West Liberty State College
West Virginia Institute of
  Technology
West Virginia Northern Community
  College
West Virginia State College
West Virginia University
West Virginia Wesleyan College

Wisconsin
Alverno College
Beloit College
Cardinal Stritch College
Carroll College
Carthage College
Chippewa Valley Technical College
Concordia University Wisconsin
Edgewood College
Fox Valley Technical College
Lakeland College
Lawrence University
Maranatha Baptist Bible College
Marian College of Fond du Lac
Marquette University
Mid-State Technical College

Milwaukee Institute of Art &
Design
Moraine Park Technical College
Mount Mary College
Mount Senario College
Northeast Wisconsin Technical
College
Northland College
Ripon College
St. Norbert College
Silver Lake College
Stratton College
University of Wisconsin
Eau Claire
Green Bay
La Crosse
Madison
Milwaukee
Oshkosh
Parkside
Platteville
River Falls
Stevens Point
Stout
Superior
Whitewater
Viterbo College
Waukesha County Technical
College
Western Wisconsin Technical
College
Wisconsin Indianhead Technical
College
Wisconsin Lutheran College

Wyoming
Northwest College
Sheridan College
University of Wyoming

**American Samoa, Caroline
Islands, Guam, Marianas,
Virgin Islands**
University of Guam

Canada
McGill University

Mexico
Sistema Instituto Tecnologico y de
Estudios Superiores de
Monterrey

Switzerland
American College of Switzerland
Franklin College: Switzerland

Arab Republic of Egypt
American University in Cairo

External degree

Alabama
Judson College
Southeastern Bible College
Troy State University at
Montgomery
University of Alabama

Arizona
Prescott College
University of Phoenix

Arkansas
Shorter College

California
California Polytechnic State
University: San Luis Obispo
California State Polytechnic
University: Pomona

California State University
Bakersfield
Chico
Dominguez Hills
Hayward
Christian Heritage College
La Sierra University
Oxnard College
Queen of the Holy Rosary College
St. Mary's College of California
San Diego State University
Sonoma State University
University of San Francisco

Colorado
National College
University of Northern Colorado
University of Southern Colorado

Connecticut
Charter Oak College
Quinnipiac College
University of Bridgeport

District of Columbia
Southeastern University

Florida
Eckerd College
Nova University
Pensacola Junior College
Southeastern College of the
Assemblies of God
University of South Florida

Georgia
Abraham Baldwin Agricultural
College
Covenant College
Fort Valley State College
Georgia College
West Georgia College

Hawaii
University of Hawaii: Kapiolani
Community College

Illinois
Governors State University
KAES College
Northern Illinois University
Roosevelt University
Southern Illinois University at
Carbondale
Trinity Christian College
Western Illinois University

Indiana
Indiana Institute of Technology
Indiana University
Bloomington
East
Kokomo
Northwest
South Bend
Southeast
Indiana University—Purdue
University
Fort Wayne
Indianapolis
Oakland City College
St. Mary-of-the-Woods College

Iowa
Graceland College
Iowa State University
Teikyo Marycrest University
University of Iowa
University of Northern Iowa
Upper Iowa University

Kansas
Allen County Community College
Bethel College

Donnelly College
Friends University
Kansas City Kansas Community
College
Kansas State University
Pittsburg State University

Kentucky
Murray State University

Maine
St. Joseph's College

Maryland
Columbia Union College
University of Maryland University
College

Massachusetts
Atlantic Union College
Framingham State College
Lesley College
University of Massachusetts at
Amherst

Michigan
Baker College of Port Huron
Central Michigan University
Ferris State University
Northwood Institute
Siena Heights College
Spring Arbor College

Minnesota
Bemidji State University
Bethel College
Moorhead State University
St. Mary's College of Minnesota
University of Minnesota: Morris
Winona State University

Missouri
Berean College
Culver-Stockton College
Hannibal-LaGrange College
Lindenwood College
Stephens College

Nebraska
Bellevue College
Chadron State College
Clarkson College
Wayne State College

New Hampshire
Hesser College

New Jersey
Caldwell College
Mercer County Community College
Thomas Edison State College

New Mexico
College of Santa Fe

New York
New York Institute of Technology
Nyack College
Skidmore College
State University of New York
College at Brockport
Empire State College
Syracuse University
University of the State of New
York: Regents College
Utica College of Syracuse
University

North Carolina
University of North Carolina at
Charlotte

Ohio
Antioch School for Adult and
Experiential Learning
Dyke College
Kent State University: Ashtabula
Regional Campus
Ohio University
Athens
Chillicothe Campus
Eastern Campus
Union Institute

Oklahoma
Oklahoma City University
Oklahoma State University
Oral Roberts University
University of Oklahoma

Oregon
Eastern Oregon State College
Linfield College
Warner Pacific College

Pennsylvania
Elizabethtown College
ICS Center for Degree Studies
Luzerne County Community
College
Marywood College
University of Pittsburgh

Rhode Island
Roger Williams College

South Carolina
Benedict College
Central Wesleyan College

South Dakota
Presentation College
Sioux Falls College
University of South Dakota

Tennessee
Tennessee Temple University
Tomlinson College
Vanderbilt University

Texas
Northwood Institute: Texas Campus
St. Edward's University
Southwestern Adventist College
Southwestern Assemblies of God
College

Utah
Brigham Young University
Utah State University

Vermont
Burlington College
Community College of Vermont
Goddard College
Johnson State College
Norwich University

Virginia
Liberty University
Mary Baldwin College
Patrick Henry Community College
Radford University

Washington
City University
Clark College
Eastern Washington University
Skagit Valley College

West Virginia
Shepherd College
West Liberty State College
West Virginia State College

Wisconsin

Mount Senario College
Silver Lake College
University of Wisconsin
    Green Bay
    Platteville
    River Falls
    Superior
    Whitewater

Honors program

Alabama

Alabama Agricultural and
    Mechanical University
Alabama Southern Community
    College
Alabama State University
Auburn University
    Auburn
    Montgomery
Birmingham-Southern College
Bishop State Community College
Brewer State Junior College
Chattahoochee Valley Community
    College
Enterprise State Junior College
Huntingdon College
Jacksonville State University
James H. Faulkner State
    Community College
Jefferson State Community College
John C. Calhoun State Community
    College
Judson College
Livingston University
Lurleen B. Wallace State Junior
    College
Miles College
Mobile College
Northeast Alabama State Junior
    College
Oakwood College
Samford University
Shelton State Community College
Spring Hill College
Stillman College
Troy State University
    Montgomery
    Troy
Tuskegee University
University of Alabama
    Birmingham
    Huntsville
    Tuscaloosa
University of Montevallo
Walker College
Walker State Technical College

Alaska

University of Alaska Fairbanks

Arizona

Arizona State University
Arizona Western College
Glendale Community College
Grand Canyon University
ITT Technical Institute: Tucson
Mesa Community College
Northern Arizona University
Paradise Valley Community College
Pima Community College
Rio Salado Community College
Scottsdale Community College
South Mountain Community
    College
Southwestern College
University of Arizona
Yavapai College

Arkansas

Arkansas College
Arkansas State University
    Beebe Branch
    Jonesboro
Arkansas Tech University
Crowley's Ridge College
East Arkansas Community College
Harding University
Henderson State University
Hendrix College
John Brown University
North Arkansas Community College
Ouachita Baptist University
Phillips County Community College
University of Arkansas
    Fayetteville
    Little Rock
    Pine Bluff
University of Central Arkansas
Westark Community College

California

Academy of Art College
Allan Hancock College
American Armenian International
    College
Azusa Pacific University
Barstow College
Biola University
California Lutheran University
California State Polytechnic
    University: Pomona
California State University
    Bakersfield
    Chico
    Dominguez Hills
    Fullerton
    Hayward
    Long Beach
    Los Angeles
    Northridge
    Stanislaus
Cerro Coso Community College
Chaffey Community College
Chapman University
Claremont McKenna College
College of the Redwoods
Compton Community College
Cosumnes River College
Cuesta College
De Anza College
Diablo Valley College
Dominican College of San Rafael
El Camino College
Evergreen Valley College
Feather River College
Foothill College
Fresno City College
Glendale Community College
Golden West College
Holy Names College
Humphreys College
Imperial Valley College
Irvine Valley College
ITT Technical Institute: Van Nuys
Kings River Community College
La Sierra University
Lassen College
Long Beach City College
Los Angeles City College
Los Angeles Harbor College
Los Angeles Pierce College
Los Angeles Valley College
Loyola Marymount University
Marymount College
Merced College
Mills College
MiraCosta College
Mission College
Monterey Institute of International
    Studies
Mount St. Mary's College
Mount San Antonio College

Occidental College
Oxnard College
Pacific Union College
Pasadena City College
Pepperdine University
Phillips Junior College: Condie
    Campus
Pitzer College
Point Loma Nazarene College
Rio Hondo College
Saddleback College
San Diego City College
San Diego Mesa College
San Diego Miramar College
San Diego State University
San Francisco Art Institute
San Francisco State University
San Joaquin Delta College
San Jose Christian College
San Jose City College
San Jose State University
Santa Barbara City College
Santa Clara University
Santa Monica College
Scripps College
Solano Community College
Southwestern College
Stanford University
University of California
    Berkeley
    Davis
    Irvine
    Los Angeles
    Riverside
    San Diego
    San Francisco
    Santa Barbara
University of La Verne
University of the Pacific
University of Redlands
University of San Diego
University of San Francisco
University of Southern California
Ventura College
Victor Valley College
West Hills Community College
West Valley College
Westmont College
Yuba College

Colorado

Adams State College
Arapahoe Community College
Colorado Christian University
Colorado School of Mines
Colorado State University
Fort Lewis College
Front Range Community College
ITT Technical Institute: Aurora
Metropolitan State College of
    Denver
Regis College of Regis University
United States Air Force Academy
University of Colorado
    Boulder
    Colorado Springs
    Denver
University of Denver
University of Northern Colorado
University of Southern Colorado
Western State College of Colorado

Connecticut

Albertus Magnus College
Central Connecticut State
    University
Charter Oak College
Connecticut College
Eastern Connecticut State
    University
Fairfield University
Hartford State Technical College
Housatonic Community College
Manchester Community College

Norwalk Community College
Quinebaug Valley Community
    College
Quinnipiac College
Sacred Heart University
St. Joseph College
Southern Connecticut State
    University
Teikyo-Post University
United States Coast Guard
    Academy
University of Bridgeport
University of Connecticut
University of Hartford
University of New Haven
Wesleyan University
Western Connecticut State
    University
Yale University

Delaware

Delaware State College
Goldey-Beacom College
University of Delaware

District of Columbia

American University
Catholic University of America
Gallaudet University
George Washington University
Georgetown University
Howard University
Mount Vernon College
Southeastern University
University of the District of
    Columbia

Florida

Barry University
Bethune-Cookman College
Brevard Community College
Broward Community College
Central Florida Community College
Daytona Beach Community College
Eckerd College
Edison Community College
Florida Agricultural and Mechanical
    University
Florida Atlantic University
Florida Community College at
    Jacksonville
Florida International University
Florida Memorial College
Florida State University
Gulf Coast Community College
Indian River Community College
Jacksonville University
Manatee Community College
Miami-Dade Community College
New College of the University of
    South Florida
North Florida Junior College
Palm Beach Atlantic College
Palm Beach Community College
Pasco-Hernando Community
    College
Pensacola Junior College
Rollins College
St. Leo College
St. Petersburg Junior College
St. Thomas University
Santa Fe Community College
Seminole Community College
Stetson University
Tallahassee Community College
University of Central Florida
University of Florida
University of Miami
University of North Florida
University of South Florida
University of Tampa
University of West Florida
Valencia Community College

Georgia

Albany State College
Andrew College
Armstrong State College
Atlanta College of Art
Augusta College
Berry College
Brenau Women's College
Brewton-Parker College
Clark Atlanta University
Clayton State College
Covenant College
Darton College
DeKalb College
Emory University
Floyd College
Fort Valley State College
Gainesville College
Georgia College
Georgia Institute of Technology
Georgia Southern University
Georgia Southwestern College
Georgia State University
Kennesaw State College
LaGrange College
Macon College
Meadows College of Business
Morehouse College
Morris Brown College
Oglethorpe University
Paine College
Savannah State College
Shorter College
Southern College of Technology
Spelman College
Toccoa Falls College
Truett-McConnell College
University of Georgia
Valdosta State College
Wesleyan College
West Georgia College

Hawaii

Brigham Young University-Hawaii
Chaminade University of Honolulu
Hawaii Loa College
Hawaii Pacific University
University of Hawaii
    Hilo
    Kapiolani Community College
    Leeward Community College
    Manoa

Idaho

Albertson College
Boise State University
College of Southern Idaho
Idaho State University
Lewis-Clark State College
Ricks College
University of Idaho

Illinois

Augustana College
Aurora University
Blackburn College
Bradley University
Carl Sandburg College
Chicago State University
City Colleges of Chicago
    Malcolm X College
    Olive-Harvey College
    Richard J. Daley College
    Wright College
College of DuPage
College of Lake County
De Paul University
Eastern Illinois University
Elgin Community College
Elmhurst College
Eureka College
Governors State University
Greenville College
Illinois Benedictine College

Illinois Central College
Illinois Eastern Community
    Colleges
        Frontier Community College
        Lincoln Trail College
        Olney Central College
        Wabash Valley College
Illinois State University
Illinois Wesleyan University
Joliet Junior College
Judson College
Knox College
Lake Forest College
Lake Land College
Lewis and Clark Community
    College
Lewis University
Lincoln College
Lincoln Land Community College
Loyola University of Chicago
MacMurray College
McKendree College
Midstate College
Millikin University
Monmouth College
Moraine Valley Community College
Morton College
National-Louis University
North Central College
North Park College and Theological
    Seminary
Northeastern Illinois University
Northern Illinois University
Northwestern University
Oakton Community College
Olivet Nazarene University
Principia College
Quincy College
Richland Community College
Robert Morris College: Chicago
Rockford College
Roosevelt University
Rosary College
Southern Illinois University
    Carbondale
    Edwardsville
Spoon River College
Trinity College
Triton College
University of Chicago
University of Illinois
    Chicago
    Urbana-Champaign
Waubonsee Community College
Western Illinois University
Wheaton College
William Rainey Harper College

Indiana

Anderson University
Ball State University
Butler University
Calumet College of St. Joseph
DePauw University
Franklin College
Hanover College
Indiana State University
Indiana University
    Bloomington
    Northwest
    South Bend
Indiana University—Purdue
    University
        Fort Wayne
        Indianapolis
Indiana Wesleyan University
International Business College
Manchester College
Marian College
Purdue University
    Calumet
    West Lafayette
St. Francis College
St. Joseph's College

St. Mary-of-the-Woods College
St. Meinrad College
Taylor University
University of Evansville
University of Indianapolis
University of Notre Dame
Valparaiso University
Vincennes University

Iowa

Briar Cliff College
Buena Vista College
Central College
Clarke College
Clinton Community College
Coe College
Des Moines Area Community
    College
Drake University
Graceland College
Grand View College
Indian Hills Community College
Iowa Central Community College
Iowa Lakes Community College
Iowa State University
Kirkwood Community College
Loras College
Luther College
Maharishi International University
Morningside College
Mount Mercy College
Mount St. Clare College
Muscatine Community College
North Iowa Area Community
    College
Northwestern College
St. Ambrose University
Simpson College
Teikyo Westmar University
University of Dubuque
University of Iowa
University of Northern Iowa
Vennard College
Waldorf College

Kansas

Allen County Community College
Baker University
Benedictine College
Bethel College
Butler County Community College
Dodge City Community College
Donnelly College
Emporia State University
Friends University
Johnson County Community
    College
Kansas City Kansas Community
    College
Kansas Newman College
Kansas State University
McPherson College
Pittsburg State University
St. Mary College
Southwestern College
Sterling College
University of Kansas
    Lawrence
    Medical Center
Washburn University of Topeka
Wichita State University

Kentucky

Bellarmine College
Brescia College
Centre College
Cumberland College
Eastern Kentucky University
Elizabethtown Community College
Georgetown College
Hazard Community College
Lees College
Madisonville Community College
Morehead State University

Murray State University
National Education Center:
    Kentucky College of Technology
    Campus
Northern Kentucky University
Owensboro Junior College of
    Business
Paducah Community College
Sue Bennett College
Thomas More College
University of Kentucky
University of Louisville
Western Kentucky University

Louisiana

Centenary College of Louisiana
Dillard University
Grambling State University
Louisiana College
Louisiana State University
    Agricultural and Mechanical
        College
    Eunice
    Medical Center
    Shreveport
Louisiana Tech University
Loyola University
McNeese State University
Nicholls State University
Northeast Louisiana University
Northwestern State University
Southeastern Louisiana University
Southern University and
    Agricultural and Mechanical
    College
Tulane University
University of New Orleans
University of Southwestern
    Louisiana
Xavier University of Louisiana

Maine

Bates College
Colby College
University of Maine
    Augusta
    Farmington
    Fort Kent
    Orono
    Presque Isle
University of Southern Maine
Westbrook College

Maryland

Allegany Community College
Anne Arundel Community College
Baltimore Hebrew University
Bowie State University
Catonsville Community College
Chesapeake College
College of Notre Dame of
    Maryland
Coppin State College
Dundalk Community College
Essex Community College
Frederick Community College
Frostburg State University
Goucher College
Harford Community College
Hood College
Howard Community College
Johns Hopkins University
Loyola College in Maryland
Maryland Institute College of Art
Montgomery College
    Germantown Campus
    Rockville Campus
    Takoma Park Campus
Morgan State University
Mount St. Mary's College
Prince George's Community College
St. Mary's College of Maryland
Salisbury State University
Sojourner-Douglass College

Towson State University
United States Naval Academy
University of Baltimore
University of Maryland
    Baltimore County
    College Park
    Eastern Shore
Villa Julie College
Washington College
Western Maryland College

Massachusetts

American International College
Amherst College
Atlantic Union College
Babson College
Bentley College
Berkshire Community College
Boston College
Bradford College
Brandeis University
Bridgewater State College
Bunker Hill Community College
Clark University
College of the Holy Cross
Curry College
Elms College
Emerson College
Endicott College
Fitchburg State College
Framingham State College
Gordon College
Greenfield Community College
Harvard and Radcliffe Colleges
Holyoke Community College
Lasell College
Marian Court Junior College
Massachusetts Bay Community
    College
Mount Holyoke College
Mount Wachusett Community
    College
New England Conservatory of
    Music
Nichols College
North Shore Community College
Northeastern University
Pine Manor College
Regis College
Salem State College
School of the Museum of Fine Arts
Simmons College
Smith College
Springfield College
Springfield Technical Community
    College
Suffolk University
Tufts University
University of Massachusetts
    Amherst
    Boston
    Dartmouth
    Lowell
Wellesley College
Wheaton College
Wheelock College
Williams College

Michigan

Adrian College
Albion College
Alma College
Andrews University
Aquinas College
Calvin College
Central Michigan University
Charles Stewart Mott Community
    College
Delta College
Eastern Michigan University
Glen Oaks Community College
GMI Engineering & Management
    Institute
Grand Valley State University

Henry Ford Community College
Hillsdale College
Kalamazoo Valley Community
    College
Kellogg Community College
Lansing Community College
Michigan Christian College
Michigan State University
Mid Michigan Community College
Muskegon Community College
Northwestern Michigan College
Oakland University
Olivet College
Saginaw Valley State University
Schoolcraft College
Siena Heights College
Spring Arbor College
Suomi College
University of Detroit Mercy
University of Michigan
    Ann Arbor
    Dearborn
    Flint
Walsh College of Accountancy and
    Business Administration
Wayne State University
West Shore Community College
Western Michigan University

Minnesota

Anoka-Ramsey Community College
Augsburg College
Bemidji State University
Bethany Lutheran College
College of St. Benedict
College of St. Catherine: St.
    Catherine Campus
Concordia College: Moorhead
Crown College
Gustavus Adolphus College
Hamline University
Itasca Community College:
    Arrowhead Region
Lakewood Community College
Macalester College
Mankato State University
Minneapolis College of Art and
    Design
Minneapolis Community College
Moorhead State University
Northwestern Electronics Institute
Rainy River Community College
St. Cloud State University
St. John's University
St. Mary's College of Minnesota
Southwest State University
University of Minnesota
    Duluth
    Morris
    Twin Cities
University of St. Thomas
Winona State University

Mississippi

Alcorn State University
Belhaven College
Blue Mountain College
Copiah-Lincoln Community College
Delta State University
East Central Community College
Hinds Community College
Jackson State University
Jones County Junior College
Mary Holmes College
Millsaps College
Mississippi College
Mississippi Gulf Coast Community
    College
    Jackson County Campus
    Jefferson Davis Campus
    Perkinston
Mississippi State University
Mississippi University for Women
Rust College

Tougaloo College
University of Mississippi
University of Southern Mississippi
William Carey College

Missouri

Central Methodist College
Central Missouri State University
College of the Ozarks
Columbia College
Culver-Stockton College
Drury College
East Central College
Hannibal-LaGrange College
ITT Technical Institute: St. Louis
Jefferson College
Lincoln University
Longview Community College
Maple Woods Community College
Maryville University
Mineral Area College
Missouri Baptist College
Missouri Southern State College
Missouri Valley College
Missouri Western State College
Northeast Missouri State University
Park College
Penn Valley Community College
Research College of Nursing
Rockhurst College
St. Louis College of Pharmacy
St. Louis Community College
    Florissant Valley
    Forest Park
    Meramec
St. Louis University
Southeast Missouri State University
Southwest Baptist University
Southwest Missouri State University
University of Missouri
    Columbia
    Kansas City
    Rolla
    St. Louis
Washington University
Webster University
Wentworth Military Academy and
    Junior College
Westminster College
William Jewell College

Montana

Carroll College
Montana State University
Rocky Mountain College
University of Montana

Nebraska

Central Community College
Chadron State College
Concordia College
Creighton University
Doane College
Lincoln School of Commerce
Peru State College
University of Nebraska
    Medical Center
    Kearney
    Lincoln
    Omaha
Wayne State College
York College

Nevada

University of Nevada
    Las Vegas
    Reno

New Hampshire

Dartmouth College
Franklin Pierce College
Hesser College
Keene State College
New England College

New Hampshire College
Plymouth State College of the
    University System of New
    Hampshire
University of New Hampshire

New Jersey

Atlantic Community College
Bergen Community College
Bloomfield College
Brookdale Community College
Burlington County College
Caldwell College
Camden County College
College of St. Elizabeth
County College of Morris
Cumberland County College
Drew University
Essex County College
Fairleigh Dickinson University
    Edward Williams College
    Madison
Felician College
Glassboro State College
Jersey City State College
Kean College of New Jersey
Monmouth College
Montclair State College
New Jersey Institute of Technology
Ocean County College
Ramapo College of New Jersey
Rider College
Rutgers—The State University of
    New Jersey
    Camden College of Arts and
        Sciences
    College of Engineering
    College of Nursing
    College of Pharmacy
    Cook College
    Douglass College
    Livingston College
    Newark College of Arts and
        Sciences
    Rutgers College
    University College Camden
    University College New
        Brunswick
    University College Newark
St. Peter's College
Seton Hall University
Stevens Institute of Technology
Stockton State College
Sussex County Community College
Trenton State College
Union County College
Upsala College
William Paterson College of New
    Jersey

New Mexico

Clovis Community College
College of Santa Fe
Eastern New Mexico University
New Mexico Highlands University
New Mexico Institute of Mining
    and Technology
New Mexico Junior College
New Mexico State University
University of New Mexico
Western New Mexico University

New York

Adelphi University
Adirondack Community College
Alfred University
Barnard College
Berkeley College
Broome Community College
Canisius College
Cazenovia College

625

City University of New York
Baruch College
Brooklyn College
City College
College of Staten Island
Hunter College
John Jay College of Criminal Justice
Kingsborough Community College
Lehman College
Medgar Evers College
Queens College
York College
Clinton Community College
College of Mount St. Vincent
College of New Rochelle
Columbia University
School of Engineering and Applied Science
School of General Studies
Community College of the Finger Lakes
Concordia College
Cooper Union
Cornell University
Corning Community College
Dominican College of Blauvelt
Dutchess Community College
D'Youville College
Elmira College
Erie Community College
City Campus
North Campus
South Campus
Fordham University
Fulton-Montgomery Community College
Genesee Community College
Hamilton College
Hartwick College
Herkimer County Community College
Hobart College
Hofstra University
Houghton College
Iona College
Ithaca College
Jamestown Community College
Jefferson Community College
Jewish Theological Seminary of America
Juilliard School
Keuka College
Kol Yaakov Torah Center
Laboratory Institute of Merchandising
Le Moyne College
Long Island University
Brooklyn Campus
C. W. Post Campus
Southampton Campus
Manhattan College
Manhattanville College
Marymount College
Marymount Manhattan College
Medaille College
Mercy College
Mohawk Valley Community College
Monroe Community College
Mount St. Mary College
Nassau Community College
Nazareth College of Rochester
New York Institute of Technology
New York University
Niagara County Community College
Niagara University
Pace University
College of White Plains
New York
Pleasantville/Briarcliff
Polytechnic University
Brooklyn
Long Island Campus

Rensselaer Polytechnic Institute
Roberts Wesleyan College
Rockland Community College
St. Bonaventure University
St. Francis College
St. John Fisher College
St. John's University
St. Joseph's College
St. Thomas Aquinas College
Siena College
State University of New York
Albany
Binghamton
Buffalo
Stony Brook
College of Agriculture and Technology at Cobleskill
College at Brockport
College at Buffalo
College at Cortland
College at Fredonia
College at Geneseo
College at New Paltz
College at Oneonta
College at Plattsburgh
College at Potsdam
College of Technology at Alfred
Oswego
Suffolk County Community College
Eastern Campus
Selden
Western Campus
Syracuse University
Tobe-Coburn School for Fashion Careers
Touro College
Ulster County Community College
Utica College of Syracuse University
Wagner College
Westchester Community College
William Smith College
Yeshiva University

North Carolina

Appalachian State University
Barber-Scotia College
Barton College
Belmont Abbey College
Bennett College
Brevard College
Caldwell Community College and Technical Institute
Campbell University
Catawba College
Central Carolina Community College
Central Piedmont Community College
Chowan College
Davidson College
Duke University
East Carolina University
Elizabeth City State University
Elon College
Fayetteville State University
Gardner-Webb College
Gaston College
Greensboro College
Guilford College
High Point University
Isothermal Community College
Johnson C. Smith University
Lees-McRae College
Lenoir-Rhyne College
Louisburg College
Mars Hill College
Meredith College
Methodist College
Montreat-Anderson College
Mount Olive College
North Carolina Agricultural and Technical State University

North Carolina Central University
North Carolina State University
North Carolina Wesleyan College
Peace College
Pembroke State University
Pfeiffer College
Queens College
St. Andrews Presbyterian College
St. Augustine's College
Salem College
Sandhills Community College
Southeastern Baptist Theological Seminary
University of North Carolina
Asheville
Chapel Hill
Charlotte
Greensboro
Wilmington
Wake Forest University
Warren Wilson College
Western Carolina University
Wilkes Community College
Wingate College
Winston-Salem State University

North Dakota

Jamestown College
Minot State University
North Dakota State University
University of North Dakota
Grand Forks
Williston

Ohio

Antonelli Institute of Art and Photography
Ashland University
Baldwin-Wallace College
Bluffton College
Bowling Green State University
Case Western Reserve University
Cedarville College
Central Ohio Technical College
Central State University
Cleveland Institute of Art
Cuyahoga Community College
Metropolitan Campus
Western Campus
Denison University
Franciscan University of Steubenville
Heidelberg College
Jefferson Technical College
John Carroll University
Kent State University
Kent
Stark Campus
Tuscarawas Campus
Kenyon College
Marietta College
Miami University
Hamilton Campus
Oxford Campus
Miami-Jacobs College
Mount Union College
Oberlin College
Ohio Dominican College
Ohio State University
Columbus Campus
Lima Campus
Mansfield Campus
Marion Campus
Newark Campus
Ohio University
Ohio Wesleyan University
Otterbein College
Shawnee State University
Sinclair Community College
University of Akron
Akron
Wayne College
University of Cincinnati
University of Dayton

University of Findlay
University of Rio Grande
University of Toledo
Walsh College
Wilberforce University
Wittenberg University
Wright State University
Dayton
Lake Campus
Xavier University
Youngstown State University

Oklahoma

Cameron University
East Central University
Eastern Oklahoma State College
Langston University
Murray State College
Oklahoma Baptist University
Oklahoma City University
Oklahoma State University
Redlands Community College
Rose State College
St. Gregory's College
Southeastern Oklahoma State University
Southwestern Oklahoma State University
Tulsa Junior College
University of Central Oklahoma
University of Oklahoma
Health Sciences Center
Norman
University of Science and Arts of Oklahoma
University of Tulsa

Oregon

Clackamas Community College
George Fox College
ITT Technical Institute: Portland
Lewis and Clark College
Linfield College
Oregon Institute of Technology
Pacific University
Portland State University
Southern Oregon State College
Southwestern Oregon Community College
University of Oregon
Eugene
Robert Donald Clark Honors College
University of Portland
Western Oregon State College

Pennsylvania

Albright College
Allentown College of St. Francis de Sales
Beaver College
Bloomsburg University of Pennsylvania
Bryn Mawr College
Bucknell University
Bucks County Community College
Cabrini College
California University of Pennsylvania
Carlow College
Carnegie Mellon University
Cedar Crest College
Chestnut Hill College
Clarion University of Pennsylvania
College Misericordia
Community College of Philadelphia
Delaware Valley College
Dickinson College
Drexel University
Duquesne University
East Stroudsburg University of Pennsylvania
Eastern College

Edinboro University of
Pennsylvania
Elizabethtown College
Franklin and Marshall College
Gannon University
Geneva College
Gettysburg College
Grove City College
Harrisburg Area Community
College
Immaculata College
Indiana University of Pennsylvania
King's College
Kutztown University of
Pennsylvania
La Roche College
La Salle University
Lafayette College
Lebanon Valley College of
Pennsylvania
Lehigh University
Lincoln University
Lock Haven University of
Pennsylvania
Luzerne County Community
College
Lycoming College
Manor Junior College
Mansfield University of
Pennsylvania
Marywood College
Mercyhurst College
Millersville University of
Pennsylvania
Montgomery County Community
College
Moravian College
Muhlenberg College
Neumann College
Northampton County Area
Community College
Northeastern Christian Junior
College
Peirce Junior College
Penn State
Erie Behrend College
Harrisburg Capital College
University Park Campus
Philadelphia College of Textiles and
Science
Rosemont College
St. Francis College
St. Joseph's University
St. Vincent College
Seton Hill College
Shippensburg University of
Pennsylvania
Slippery Rock University of
Pennsylvania
Spring Garden College
Susquehanna University
Swarthmore College
Temple University
Thiel College
Thomas Jefferson University:
College of Allied Health Sciences
University of the Arts
University of Pennsylvania
University of Pittsburgh
University of Scranton
Ursinus College
Valley Forge Christian College
Valley Forge Military College
Villanova University
Washington and Jefferson College
Waynesburg College
West Chester University of
Pennsylvania
Westminster College
Westmoreland County Community
College
Widener University
Wilkes University
York College of Pennsylvania

Puerto Rico

American University of Puerto Rico
Caribbean University
Inter American University of Puerto
Rico
Arecibo Campus
Metropolitan Campus
San German Campus
Pontifical Catholic University of
Puerto Rico
Turabo University
Universidad Adventista de las
Antillas
Universidad Metropolitana
University of Puerto Rico
Aguadilla
Bayamon Technological
University College
Cayey University College
Humacao University College
Ponce Technological
University College
Rio Piedras Campus
University of the Sacred Heart

Rhode Island

Brown University
Bryant College
Community College of Rhode
Island
Johnson & Wales University
Providence College
Rhode Island College
University of Rhode Island

South Carolina

Anderson College
Benedict College
Central Wesleyan College
Charleston Southern University
The Citadel
Claflin College
Clemson University
College of Charleston
Columbia College
Converse College
Francis Marion College
Lander College
Limestone College
Morris College
North Greenville College
Presbyterian College
South Carolina State College
University of South Carolina
Aiken
Beaufort
Coastal Carolina College
Columbia
Lancaster
Voorhees College
Williamsburg Technical College
Winthrop University
Wofford College

South Dakota

Augustana College
Dakota State University
Dakota Wesleyan University
Northern State University
Sioux Falls College
South Dakota State University
University of South Dakota

Tennessee

Austin Peay State University
Belmont University
Bethel College
Bristol University
Carson-Newman College
Chattanooga State Technical
Community College
Christian Brothers University
Cumberland University
David Lipscomb University

East Tennessee State University
Fisk University
Freed-Hardeman University
Hiwassee College
Lambuth University
LeMoyne-Owen College
Lincoln Memorial University
Martin Methodist College
Maryville College
Memphis College of Art
Memphis State University
Middle Tennessee State University
Motlow State Community College
Rhodes College
Roane State Community College
Southern College of Seventh-day
Adventists
State Technical Institute at
Memphis
Tennessee State University
Tennessee Technological University
Tennessee Temple University
Union University
University of the South
University of Tennessee
Chattanooga
Knoxville
Martin
Vanderbilt University
Volunteer State Community College
Walters State Community College

Texas

Abilene Christian University
Amarillo College
Angelina College
Austin College
Baylor University
Brookhaven College
Collin County Community College
District
Dallas Baptist University
Del Mar College
East Texas Baptist University
East Texas State University
Eastfield College
El Centro College
El Paso Community College
Galveston College
Hardin-Simmons University
Howard Payne University
Huston-Tillotson College
Jarvis Christian College
Lamar University—Beaumont
Laredo Junior College
Lee College
LeTourneau University
McMurry University
Midwestern State University
Mountain View College
Navarro College
North Lake College
Northwood Institute: Texas Campus
Odessa College
Paul Quinn College
Prairie View A&M University
Rice University
Richland College
St. Edward's University
St. Mary's University
Sam Houston State University
San Antonio College
Schreiner College
Southern Methodist University
Southwest Texas State University
Southwestern Adventist College
Southwestern University
Tarleton State University
Tarrant County Junior College
Texas A&M University
Texas Christian University
Texas Lutheran College
Texas Southern University
Texas Southmost College

Texas Tech University
Texas Woman's University
University of Houston
University of Mary Hardin-Baylor
University of North Texas
University of St. Thomas
University of Texas
Arlington
Austin
El Paso
Pan American
San Antonio
Tyler
Wayland Baptist University
Weatherford College
West Texas State University
Western Texas College
Wiley College

Utah

Brigham Young University
Dixie College
Southern Utah University
University of Utah
Utah State University
Utah Valley Community College
Weber State University
Westminster College of Salt Lake
City

Vermont

Castleton State College
Johnson State College
Middlebury College
Norwich University
St. Michael's College
Southern Vermont College
University of Vermont

Virginia

Blue Ridge Community College
Bluefield College
Bridgewater College
Central Virginia Community College
Christendom College
Christopher Newport College
Clinch Valley College of the
University of Virginia
College of William and Mary
Dabney S. Lancaster Community
College
Eastern Mennonite College
Emory and Henry College
Ferrum College
Hampden-Sydney College
Hampton University
Hollins College
James Madison University
Liberty University
Longwood College
Lord Fairfax Community College
Lynchburg College
Mary Baldwin College
Marymount University
Mountain Empire Community
College
New River Community College
Norfolk State University
Northern Virginia Community
College
Old Dominion University
Paul D. Camp Community College
Piedmont Virginia Community
College
Radford University
Randolph-Macon College
Randolph-Macon Woman's College
Roanoke College
St. Paul's College
Shenandoah University
Southside Virginia Community
College
Southwest Virginia Community
College

Sweet Briar College
Tidewater Community College
University of Richmond
University of Virginia
Virginia Commonwealth University
Virginia Intermont College
Virginia Military Institute
Virginia Polytechnic Institute and
  State University
Virginia State University
Virginia Union University
Virginia Wesleyan College
Washington and Lee University
Wytheville Community College

Washington

Central Washington University
Centralia College
Clark College
Eastern Washington University
Edmonds Community College
Gonzaga University
Olympic College
Pacific Lutheran University
Peninsula College
Pierce College
St. Martin's College
Seattle Pacific University
Seattle University
Skagit Valley College
University of Puget Sound
University of Washington
Walla Walla College
Walla Walla Community College
Washington State University
Wenatchee Valley College
Western Washington University
Whatcom Community College
Whitman College

West Virginia

Alderson-Broaddus College
Bethany College
College of West Virginia
Concord College
Davis and Elkins College
Marshall University
Ohio Valley College
Potomac State College of West
  Virginia University
Shepherd College
University of Charleston
West Liberty State College
West Virginia Institute of
  Technology
West Virginia State College
West Virginia University
West Virginia Wesleyan College
Wheeling Jesuit College

Wisconsin

Carroll College
Carthage College
Edgewood College
Lakeland College
Lawrence University
Marquette University
Mount Mary College
Mount Senario College
Northland College
St. Norbert College
University of Wisconsin
  Eau Claire
  La Crosse
  Madison
  Milwaukee
  Oshkosh
  Parkside
  Platteville
  River Falls
  Stevens Point
  Superior
  Whitewater

University of Wisconsin Center
  Fox Valley
  Marathon County
  Waukesha
Viterbo College

Wyoming

Central Wyoming College
Northwest College
University of Wyoming

Canada

McGill University

Switzerland

Franklin College: Switzerland

Arab Republic of Egypt

American University in Cairo

Independent study

Alabama

Alabama Agricultural and
  Mechanical University
Alabama Southern Community
  College
Auburn University
  Auburn
  Montgomery
Birmingham-Southern College
Chattahoochee Valley Community
  College
Concordia College
Faulkner University
Huntingdon College
Jacksonville State University
James H. Faulkner State
  Community College
John M. Patterson State Technical
  College
Judson College
Miles College
Mobile College
Northeast Alabama State Junior
  College
Samford University
Southeastern Bible College
Southern Christian University
Spring Hill College
Stillman College
Talladega College
Troy State University
  Dothan
  Montgomery
  Troy
Tuskegee University
University of Alabama
  Birmingham
  Huntsville
  Tuscaloosa
University of Montevallo
University of North Alabama
University of South Alabama

Alaska

Alaska Pacific University
Prince William Sound Community
  College
Sheldon Jackson College
University of Alaska
  Anchorage
  Fairbanks
  Southeast

Arizona

American Indian Bible College
Arizona College of the Bible
Arizona State University
Arizona Western College
Cochise College

Embry-Riddle Aeronautical
  University: Prescott Campus
Glendale Community College
Grand Canyon University
Lamson Junior College
Mesa Community College
Mohave Community College
Navajo Community College
Northern Arizona University
Northland Pioneer College
Pima Community College
Prescott College
Rio Salado Community College
South Mountain Community
  College
University of Arizona
University of Phoenix
Western International University
Yavapai College

Arkansas

Arkansas Baptist College
Arkansas College
Arkansas State University
  Beebe Branch
  Jonesboro
Crowley's Ridge College
Garland County Community
  College
Harding University
Henderson State University
Hendrix College
John Brown University
Mississippi County Community
  College
North Arkansas Community College
Ouachita Baptist University
Phillips County Community College
Shorter College
University of Arkansas
  Fayetteville
  Little Rock
  Medical Sciences
University of Central Arkansas
University of the Ozarks
Williams Baptist College

California

Academy of Art College
Allan Hancock College
American Armenian International
  College
Antioch Southern California
  Los Angeles
  Santa Barbara
Armstrong College
Art Institute of Southern California ·
Azusa Pacific University
Barstow College
Brooks Institute of Photography
California Baptist College
California College of Arts and
  Crafts
California College for Health
  Sciences
California Institute of the Arts
California Institute of Technology
California Lutheran University
California State University
  Bakersfield
  Chico
  Dominguez Hills
  Fresno
  Fullerton
  Hayward
  Long Beach
  Los Angeles
  Northridge
  Sacramento
  San Bernardino
  Stanislaus
Cerro Coso Community College
Chabot College
Chaffey Community College

Chapman University
Charles R. Drew University: College
  of Allied Health
Christ College Irvine
Christian Heritage College
Claremont McKenna College
Coastline Community College
Cogswell Polytechnical College
Coleman College
College of the Desert
College of Notre Dame
College of the Redwoods
College of the Sequoias
Columbia College
Cosumnes River College
Crafton Hills College
Cuesta College
De Anza College
Diablo Valley College
Dominican College of San Rafael
Don Bosco Technical Institute
D-Q University
East Los Angeles College
El Camino College
Evergreen Valley College
Fashion Institute of Design and
  Merchandising
Feather River College
Foothill College
Fresno City College
Fresno Pacific College
Glendale Community College
Golden West College
Grossmont Community College
Harvey Mudd College
Holy Names College
Humboldt State University
Humphreys College
Imperial Valley College
Irvine Valley College
John F. Kennedy University
Kings River Community College
Lassen College
Long Beach City College
Los Angeles City College
Los Angeles Mission College
Los Angeles Trade and Technical
  College
Los Angeles Valley College
Los Medanos College
Loyola Marymount University
Marymount College
Master's College
Mendocino College
Menlo College
Mills College
MiraCosta College
Mission College
Modesto Junior College
Monterey Institute of International
  Studies
Monterey Peninsula College
Moorpark College
Mount St. Mary's College
Mount San Jacinto College
Napa Valley College
National University
New College of California
Occidental College
Ohlone College
Orange Coast College
Otis/Parsons School of Art and
  Design
Oxnard College
Pacific Christian College
Pacific Oaks College
Pacific Union College
Pasadena City College
Patten College
Phillips Junior College
  Fresno Campus
  San Fernando Valley Campus
Pitzer College
Pomona College

Queen of the Holy Rosary College
Rio Hondo College
Saddleback College
St. Mary's College of California
Samuel Merritt College
San Diego City College
San Diego Miramar College
San Diego State University
San Francisco Art Institute
San Francisco Conservatory of
  Music
San Francisco State University
San Joaquin Delta College
San Jose Christian College
San Jose City College
San Jose State University
Santa Barbara City College
Santa Clara University
Santa Monica College
Santa Rosa Junior College
Scripps College
Sierra College
Simpson College
Solano Community College
Sonoma State University
Southern California College
Southern California Institute of
  Architecture
Southwestern College
Stanford University
Taft College
United States International
  University
University of California
  Berkeley
  Davis
  Irvine
  Los Angeles
  Riverside
  San Diego
  Santa Barbara
  Santa Cruz
University of Judaism
University of La Verne
University of the Pacific
University of Redlands
University of San Diego
University of San Francisco
University of Southern California
Ventura College
Victor Valley College
West Hills Community College
West Valley College
Westmont College
Whittier College
Woodbury University
World College West

Colorado

Adams State College
Aims Community College
Arapahoe Community College
Blair Junior College
Colorado Christian University
Colorado College
Colorado Mountain College
  Alpine Campus
  Spring Valley Campus
  Timberline Campus
Colorado Northwestern Community
  College
Colorado School of Mines
Colorado State University
Colorado Technical College
Community College of Denver
Denver Institute of Technology
Fort Lewis College
Front Range Community College
Mesa State College
Metropolitan State College of
  Denver
Morgan Community College
Naropa Institute
National College

Northeastern Junior College
Pikes Peak Community College
Red Rocks Community College
Regis College of Regis University
Trinidad State Junior College
United States Air Force Academy
University of Colorado
  Boulder
  Colorado Springs
  Denver
  Health Sciences Center
University of Denver
University of Northern Colorado
University of Southern Colorado
Western State College of Colorado

Connecticut

Albertus Magnus College
Briarwood College
Central Connecticut State
  University
Charter Oak College
Connecticut College
Eastern Connecticut State
  University
Fairfield University
Housatonic Community College
Manchester Community College
Mattatuck Community College
Middlesex Community College
Mitchell College
Northwestern Connecticut
  Community College
Norwalk Community College
Paier College of Art
Quinebaug Valley Community
  College
Quinnipiac College
Sacred Heart University
St. Joseph College
South Central Community College
Southern Connecticut State
  University
Teikyo-Post University
Trinity College
United States Coast Guard
  Academy
University of Bridgeport
University of Connecticut
University of Hartford
University of New Haven
Wesleyan University
Western Connecticut State
  University
Yale University

Delaware

Delaware State College
Delaware Technical and
  Community College: Stanton/
  Wilmington Campus
University of Delaware
Wesley College
Wilmington College

District of Columbia

American University
Catholic University of America
Gallaudet University
George Washington University
Georgetown University
Howard University
Mount Vernon College
Oblate College
Southeastern University
University of the District of
  Columbia

Florida

Barry University
Brevard Community College
Broward Community College
Central Florida Community College
Chipola Junior College

Daytona Beach Community College
Eckerd College
Edison Community College
Embry-Riddle Aeronautical
  University
Flagler College
Florida Agricultural and Mechanical
  University
Florida Atlantic University
Florida Institute of Technology
Florida International University
Florida Keys Community College
Florida Southern College
Florida State University
Fort Lauderdale College
Gulf Coast Community College
Hillsborough Community College
Indian River Community College
Jacksonville University
Jones College
Lake City Community College
Lake-Sumter Community College
Lynn University
Manatee Community College
Miami-Dade Community College
New College of the University of
  South Florida
North Florida Junior College
Nova University
Okaloosa-Walton Community
  College
Orlando College
Palm Beach Atlantic College
Pasco-Hernando Community
  College
Pensacola Junior College
Rollins College
St. John Vianney College Seminary
St. Leo College
St. Petersburg Junior College
St. Thomas University
Santa Fe Community College
Schiller International University
Seminole Community College
South Florida Community College
Southeastern College of the
  Assemblies of God
Stetson University
Tallahassee Community College
Tampa College
University of Central Florida
University of Florida
University of Miami
University of North Florida
University of South Florida
University of Tampa
Valencia Community College

Georgia

Abraham Baldwin Agricultural
  College
Agnes Scott College
Armstrong State College
Atlanta Christian College
Atlanta College of Art
Augusta College
Berry College
Brenau Women's College
Brewton-Parker College
Brunswick College
Clark Atlanta University
Columbus College
Covenant College
Dalton College
Darton College
DeKalb Technical Institute
East Georgia College
Emmanuel College
Emory University
Floyd College
Georgia College
Georgia Institute of Technology
Georgia Southern University
Georgia State University

LaGrange College
Meadows College of Business
Mercer University
  Atlanta
  Macon
Morehouse College
Morris Brown College
Oglethorpe University
Oxford College of Emory University
Paine College
Reinhardt College
Savannah College of Art and
  Design
Savannah State College
Shorter College
South Georgia College
Spelman College
Toccoa Falls College
University of Georgia
Valdosta State College
Waycross College
Wesleyan College
West Georgia College
Young Harris College

Hawaii

Brigham Young University-Hawaii
Chaminade University of Honolulu
Hawaii Loa College
Hawaii Pacific University
University of Hawaii
  Hilo
  Honolulu Community College
  Kapiolani Community College
  Leeward Community College
  Manoa
  West Oahu

Idaho

Albertson College
Boise State University
Idaho State University
Lewis Clark State College
North Idaho College
Northwest Nazarene College
University of Idaho

Illinois

Aero-Space Institute
Augustana College
Aurora University
Barat College
Belleville Area College
Black Hawk College
  East Campus
  Moline
Blackburn College
Bradley University
Carl Sandburg College
Chicago State University
City Colleges of Chicago
  Chicago City-Wide College
  Malcolm X College
  Olive-Harvey College
  Richard J. Daley College
  Wright College
College of DuPage
College of Lake County
College of St. Francis
Columbia College
Concordia University
De Paul University
Eastern Illinois University
East-West University
Elgin Community College
Elmhurst College
Eureka College
Governors State University
Greenville College
Highland Community College
Illinois Benedictine College
Illinois College

Illinois Eastern Community
  Colleges
    Frontier Community College
    Lincoln Trail College
    Olney Central College
    Wabash Valley College
Illinois Institute of Technology
Illinois State University
Illinois Wesleyan University
John A. Logan College
Joliet Junior College
Judson College
KAES College
Kendall College
Kishwaukee College
Knox College
Lake Forest College
Lake Land College
Lakeview College of Nursing
Lewis University
Lincoln Christian College and
  Seminary
Lincoln College
Lincoln Land Community College
Loyola University of Chicago
MacMurray College
McKendree College
Mennonite College of Nursing
Midstate College
Millikin University
Monmouth College
Montay College
Moody Bible Institute
Moraine Valley Community College
NAES College
National-Louis University
North Central College
North Park College and Theological
  Seminary
Northeastern Illinois University
Northern Illinois University
Northwestern University
Oakton Community College
Olivet Nazarene University
Parkland College
Parks College of St. Louis
  University
Prairie State College
Principia College
Quincy College
Rend Lake College
Richland Community College
Rock Valley College
Rockford College
Roosevelt University
Rosary College
St. Augustine College
St. Xavier University
Sangamon State University
School of the Art Institute of
  Chicago
Shimer College
Southern Illinois University
  Carbondale
  Edwardsville
Springfield College in Illinois
Trinity Christian College
Trinity College
Triton College
University of Chicago
University of Illinois
  Chicago
  Urbana-Champaign
VanderCook College of Music
Waubonsee Community College
West Suburban College of Nursing
Western Illinois University
Wheaton College
William Rainey Harper College

Indiana

Ancilla College
Anderson University
Ball State University

Bethel College
Butler University
Calumet College of St. Joseph
DePauw University
Earlham College
Franklin College
Goshen College
Hanover College
Huntington College
Indiana Institute of Technology
Indiana State University
Indiana University
  Bloomington
  East
  Kokomo
  Northwest
  South Bend
  Southeast
Indiana University—Purdue
  University
  Fort Wayne
  Indianapolis
Indiana Vocational Technical
  College
  Kokomo
  Southwest
  Whitewater
Indiana Wesleyan University
Manchester College
Marian College
Oakland City College
Purdue University
Rose-Hulman Institute of
  Technology
St. Francis College
St. Joseph's College
St. Mary-of-the-Woods College
St. Mary's College
St. Meinrad College
Taylor University
University of Evansville
University of Indianapolis
University of Notre Dame
University of Southern Indiana
Valparaiso University
Wabash College

Iowa

Briar Cliff College
Buena Vista College
Central College
Clarke College
Clinton Community College
Coe College
Cornell College
Des Moines Area Community
  College
Divine Word College
Dordt College
Drake University
Graceland College
Grand View College
Grinnell College
Indian Hills Community College
Iowa Central Community College
Iowa State University
Iowa Wesleyan College
Iowa Western Community College
Kirkwood Community College
Loras College
Luther College
Morningside College
Mount Mercy College
Mount St. Clare College
Muscatine Community College
North Iowa Area Community
  College
Northeast Iowa Community College
Northwest Iowa Technical College
Northwestern College
St. Ambrose University
Simpson College

Southeastern Community College
  North Campus
  South Campus
Teikyo Marycrest University
Teikyo Westmar University
University of Dubuque
University of Iowa
University of Northern Iowa
Upper Iowa University
Vennard College
Waldorf College
Wartburg College
William Penn College

Kansas

Allen County Community College
Baker University
Barclay College
Barton County Community College
Benedictine College
Bethany College
Bethel College
Butler County Community College
Central College
Coffeyville Community College
Colby Community College
Cowley County Community College
Dodge City Community College
Donnelly College
Emporia State University
Fort Hays State University
Friends University
Haskell Indian Junior College
Hesston College
Highland Community College
Johnson County Community
  College
Kansas City Kansas Community
  College
Kansas Newman College
Kansas State University
Kansas Wesleyan University
McPherson College
MidAmerica Nazarene College
Ottawa University
Pittsburg State University
Pratt Community College
St. Mary College
Southwestern College
Sterling College
Tabor College
University of Kansas
Washburn University of Topeka
Wichita State University

Kentucky

Alice Lloyd College
Asbury College
Bellarmine College
Berea College
Brescia College
Campbellsville College
Centre College
Cumberland College
Eastern Kentucky University
Georgetown College
Jefferson Community College
Kentucky Wesleyan College
Lees College
Lexington Community College
Lindsey Wilson College
Madisonville Community College
Maysville Community College
Morehead State University
Murray State University
Northern Kentucky University
Owensboro Junior College of
  Business
Prestonburg Community College
St. Catharine College
Spalding University
Sue Bennett College
Transylvania University
Union College

University of Kentucky
University of Louisville
Western Kentucky University

Louisiana

Centenary College of Louisiana
Dillard University
Grambling State University
Grantham College of Engineering
Louisiana College
Louisiana State University
  Agricultural and Mechanical
    College
  Eunice
  Medical Center
  Shreveport
Louisiana Tech University
Loyola University
Our Lady of Holy Cross College
Southern University and
  Agricultural and Mechanical
    College
Tulane University
University of New Orleans
University of Southwestern
  Louisiana
Xavier University of Louisiana

Maine

Andover College
Bates College
Beal College
Bowdoin College
Central Maine Technical College
Colby College
College of the Atlantic
Husson College
Portland School of Art
Thomas College
Unity College
University of Maine
  Augusta
  Farmington
  Fort Kent
  Machias
  Orono
  Presque Isle
University of New England
University of Southern Maine
Westbrook College

Maryland

Allegany Community College
Anne Arundel Community College
Baltimore Hebrew University
Bowie State University
Capitol College
Catonsville Community College
Chesapeake College
College of Notre Dame of
  Maryland
Columbia Union College
Coppin State College
Dundalk Community College
Essex Community College
Frederick Community College
Frostburg State University
Garrett Community College
Goucher College
Hagerstown Junior College
Harford Community College
Hood College
Howard Community College
Johns Hopkins University
Loyola College in Maryland
Maryland College of Art and
  Design
Maryland Institute College of Art
Montgomery College
  Germantown Campus
  Rockville Campus
  Takoma Park Campus
Morgan State University
Mount St. Mary's College

New Community College of
  Baltimore
St. Mary's College of Maryland
Salisbury State University
Sojourner-Douglass College
Towson State University
United States Naval Academy
University of Baltimore
University of Maryland
  Baltimore County
  College Park
  Eastern Shore
  University College
Villa Julie College
Washington College
Western Maryland College

Massachusetts

American International College
Amherst College
Anna Maria College for Men and
  Women
Aquinas College at Newton
Assumption College
Atlantic Union College
Babson College
Bay Path College
Bay State College
Bentley College
Berkshire Community College
Boston Architectural Center
Boston College
Boston Conservatory
Boston University
Bradford College
Brandeis University
Bridgewater State College
Bristol Community College
Bunker Hill Community College
Cape Cod Community College
Clark University
College of the Holy Cross
Curry College
Dean Junior College
Eastern Nazarene College
Elms College
Emerson College
Emmanuel College
Fitchburg State College
Framingham State College
Gordon College
Greenfield Community College
Hampshire College
Harvard and Radcliffe Colleges
Hellenic College
Holyoke Community College
Laboure College
Lasell College
Lesley College
Marian Court Junior College
Massachusetts Bay Community
  College
Massachusetts College of Art
Massachusetts College of Pharmacy
  and Allied Health Sciences
Massachusetts Institute of
  Technology
Merrimack College
Middlesex Community College
Montserrat College of Art
Mount Holyoke College
Mount Ida College
New England Conservatory of
  Music
Nichols College
North Adams State College
North Shore Community College
Northeastern University
Pine Manor College
Quincy College
Quinsigamond Community College
Regis College
Roxbury Community College
St. Hyacinth College and Seminary

St. John's Seminary College
Salem State College
School of the Museum of Fine Arts
Simmons College
Simon's Rock College of Bard
Smith College
Springfield College
Springfield Technical Community
  College
Stonehill College
Suffolk University
Tufts University
University of Massachusetts
  Amherst
  Boston
  Dartmouth
Wellesley College
Western New England College
Westfield State College
Wheaton College
Wheelock College
Williams College
Worcester Polytechnic Institute
Worcester State College

Michigan

Adrian College
Albion College
Alma College
Andrews University
Aquinas College
Baker College
  Flint
  Port Huron
Calvin College
Center for Creative Studies: College
  of Art and Design
Central Michigan University
Cleary College
Concordia College
Davenport College of Business
Delta College
Detroit College of Business
Eastern Michigan University
Glen Oaks Community College
GMI Engineering & Management
  Institute
Grace Bible College
Grand Rapids Baptist College and
  Seminary
Grand Rapids Community College
Grand Valley State University
Great Lakes Christian College
Great Lakes Junior College of
  Business
Henry Ford Community College
Hillsdale College
Hope College
Jackson Community College
Jordan College
Kalamazoo College
Kalamazoo Valley Community
  College
Kellogg Community College
Kendall College of Art and Design
Lake Superior State University
Lansing Community College
Lawrence Technological University
Macomb Community College
Madonna University
Marygrove College
Michigan Christian College
Michigan State University
Michigan Technological University
Mid Michigan Community College
Montcalm Community College
Muskegon Community College
Northwestern Michigan College
Northwood Institute
Oakland University
Olivet College
Reformed Bible College
Saginaw Valley State University
St. Mary's College

Schoolcraft College
Siena Heights College
Southwestern Michigan College
Spring Arbor College
Suomi College
University of Detroit Mercy
University of Michigan
  Ann Arbor
  Dearborn
  Flint
Wayne State University
West Shore Community College
Western Michigan University
William Tyndale College

Minnesota

Anoka-Ramsey Community College
Augsburg College
Bemidji State University
Bethany Lutheran College
Bethel College
Carleton College
College of Associated Arts
College of St. Benedict
College of St. Catherine: St.
  Catherine Campus
College of St. Scholastica
Concordia College: Moorhead
Concordia College: St. Paul
Crown College
Dr. Martin Luther College
Gustavus Adolphus College
Hamline University
Inver Hills Community College
Itasca Community College:
  Arrowhead Region
Lakewood Community College
Macalester College
Mankato State University
Mesabi Community College:
  Arrowhead Region
Metropolitan State University
Minneapolis College of Art and
  Design
Minneapolis Community College
Moorhead State University
Normandale Community College
North Central Bible College
Pillsbury Baptist Bible College
Rochester Community College
St. Cloud State University
St. John's University
St. Mary's College of Minnesota
St. Olaf College
Southwest State University
University of Minnesota
  Duluth
  Morris
  Twin Cities
University of St. Thomas
Vermilion Community College
Willmar Community College
Willmar Technical College
Winona State University
Worthington Community College

Mississippi

Alcorn State University
Belhaven College
Delta State University
Hinds Community College
Jackson State University
Mary Holmes College
Meridian Community College
Millsaps College
Mississippi College
Mississippi Gulf Coast Community
  College: Perkinston
Mississippi State University
Mississippi University for Women
Rust College
Southeastern Baptist College
Tougaloo College
University of Mississippi

University of Southern Mississippi
Wesley College
William Carey College

Missouri

Avila College
Berean College
Calvary Bible College
Central Methodist College
Central Missouri State University
College of the Ozarks
Columbia College
Cottey College
Culver-Stockton College
Drury College
East Central College
Fontbonne College
Hannibal-LaGrange College
Jefferson College
Kansas City Art Institute
Lincoln University
Lindenwood College
Longview Community College
Maryville University
Mineral Area College
Missouri Baptist College
Missouri Southern State College
Missouri Valley College
National College
North Central Missouri College
Northeast Missouri State University
Northwest Missouri State
  University
Park College
Research College of Nursing
Rockhurst College
St. Charles Community College
St. Louis Community College
  Florissant Valley
  Forest Park
  Meramec
St. Louis University
Southeast Missouri State University
Southwest Baptist University
Stephens College
Three Rivers Community College
University of Missouri
  Columbia
  Kansas City
  Rolla
  St. Louis
Washington University
Webster University
Westminster College
William Jewell College
William Woods College

Montana

Carroll College
College of Great Falls
Dawson Community College
Eastern Montana College
Flathead Valley Community College
Fort Peck Community College
Miles Community College
Montana College of Mineral
  Science and Technology
Montana State University
Northern Montana College
Rocky Mountain College
University of Montana

Nebraska

Bellevue College
Central Community College
Chadron State College
Clarkson College
College of St. Mary
Concordia College
Creighton University
Dana College
Doane College
Grace College of the Bible
Hastings College

McCook Community College
Metropolitan Community College
Midland Lutheran College
Nebraska Christian College
Nebraska Indian Community
　College
Nebraska Methodist College of
　Nursing and Allied Health
Nebraska Wesleyan University
Peru State College
Southeast Community College
　　Beatrice Campus
　　Lincoln Campus
Union College
University of Nebraska
　　Kearney
　　Lincoln
　　Omaha
Wayne State College
Western Nebraska Community
　College
　　Scottsbluff Campus
　　Sidney Campus
York College

Nevada

Community College of Southern
　Nevada
Deep Springs College
Northern Nevada Community
　College
Sierra Nevada College
Truckee Meadows Community
　College
University of Nevada
　　Las Vegas
　　Reno

New Hampshire

Castle College
Colby-Sawyer College
Daniel Webster College
Dartmouth College
Franklin Pierce College
Hesser College
Keene State College
New England College
New Hampshire College
New Hampshire Technical College
　　Berlin
　　Manchester
　　Stratham
Notre Dame College
Plymouth State College of the
　University System of New
　Hampshire
Rivier College
St. Anselm College
School for Lifelong Learning
University of New Hampshire
　　Durham
　　Manchester
White Pines College

New Jersey

Assumption College for Sisters
Atlantic Community College
Berkeley College of Business
Bloomfield College
Brookdale Community College
Burlington County College
Caldwell College
Centenary College
College of St. Elizabeth
Cumberland County College
Drew University
Essex County College
Fairleigh Dickinson University
　　Edward Williams College
　　Madison
Felician College
Georgian Court College
Glassboro State College
Jersey City State College

Kean College of New Jersey
Mercer County Community College
Monmouth College
Montclair State College
New Jersey Institute of Technology
Princeton University
Ramapo College of New Jersey
Rider College
Rutgers—The State University of
　New Jersey
　　Camden College of Arts and
　　　Sciences
　　College of Engineering
　　College of Pharmacy
　　Cook College
　　Douglass College
　　Livingston College
　　Mason Gross School of the
　　　Arts
　　Newark College of Arts and
　　　Sciences
　　Rutgers College
　　University College Camden
　　University College New
　　　Brunswick
　　University College Newark
St. Peter's College
Seton Hall University
Stevens Institute of Technology
Stockton State College
Sussex County Community College
Thomas Edison State College
Trenton State College
University of Medicine and
　Dentistry of New Jersey: School
　of Health Related Professions
Upsala College
Westminster Choir College
William Paterson College of New
　Jersey

New Mexico

College of Santa Fe
Eastern New Mexico University
　　Portales
　　Roswell Campus
Institute of American Indian Arts
National College
New Mexico Highlands University
New Mexico Institute of Mining
　and Technology
New Mexico State University
San Juan College
University of New Mexico
Western New Mexico University

New York

Adelphi University
Adirondack Community College
Albany College of Pharmacy
Alfred University
Bard College
Barnard College
Boricua College
Broome Community College
Bryant & Stratton Business
　Institute: Albany
Canisius College
Cazenovia College

City University of New York
　Baruch College
　Borough of Manhattan
　　Community College
　Brooklyn College
　City College
　College of Staten Island
　Hunter College
　John Jay College of Criminal
　　Justice
　Kingsborough Community
　　College
　La Guardia Community
　　College
　Lehman College
　Medgar Evers College
　New York City Technical
　　College
　Queens College
　Queensborough Community
　　College
　York College
Clarkson University
Clinton Community College
Colgate University
College of Mount St. Vincent
College of New Rochelle
　　New Rochelle
　　School of New Resources
College of St. Rose
Columbia University
　　Columbia College
　　School of General Studies
　　School of Nursing
Columbia-Greene Community
　College
Concordia College
Cooper Union
Cornell University
Corning Community College
Daemen College
Dominican College of Blauvelt
Dowling College
Dutchess Community College
D'Youville College
Elmira College
Erie Community College
　　City Campus
　　North Campus
　　South Campus
Eugene Lang College/New School
　for Social Research
Five Towns College
Fordham University
Fulton-Montgomery Community
　College
Genesee Community College
Hamilton College
Hartwick College
Hilbert College
Hobart College
Hofstra University
Houghton College
Iona College
Ithaca College
Jamestown Community College
Jefferson Community College
Jewish Theological Seminary of
　America
Keuka College
King's College
Kol Yaakov Torah Center
Laboratory Institute of
　Merchandising
Le Moyne College
Long Island University
　　Brooklyn Campus
　　C. W. Post Campus
　　Southampton Campus
Machzikei Hadath Rabbinical
　College
Manhattan College
Manhattanville College
Maria College

Marist College
Marymount College
Marymount Manhattan College
Mater Dei College
Medaille College
Mercy College
Mesivta Torah Vodaath Seminary
Molloy College
Monroe Community College
Mount St. Mary College
Nazareth College of Rochester
New York Institute of Technology
New York University
Niagara County Community College
Niagara University
North Country Community College
Nyack College
Ohr Somayach Tanenbaum
　Education Center
Orange County Community College
Pace University
　　College of White Plains
　　New York
　　Pleasantville/Briarcliff
Paul Smith's College
Pratt Institute
Rensselaer Polytechnic Institute
Roberts Wesleyan College
Rochester Business Institute
Rochester Institute of Technology
Rockland Community College
Russell Sage College
Sage Junior College of Albany, A
　Division of Russell Sage College
St. Bonaventure University
St. Francis College
St. John Fisher College
St. Joseph's College
　　Brooklyn
　　Suffolk Campus
St. Lawrence University
St. Thomas Aquinas College
Sarah Lawrence College
School of Visual Arts
Skidmore College
State University of New York
　　Albany
　　Binghamton
　　Buffalo
　　Purchase
　　Stony Brook
　　College of Agriculture and
　　　Technology at Cobleskill
　　College at Brockport
　　College at Buffalo
　　College at Cortland
　　College of Environmental
　　　Science and Forestry
　　College at Fredonia
　　College at Geneseo
　　College at New Paltz
　　College at Old Westbury
　　College at Oneonta
　　College at Plattsburgh
　　College at Potsdam
　　College of Technology at
　　　Alfred
　　College of Technology at
　　　Canton
　　College of Technology at Delhi
　　Empire State College
　　Health Science Center at
　　　Syracuse
　　Health Sciences Center at
　　　Stony Brook
　　Institute of Technology at
　　　Utica/Rome
　　Oswego
Suffolk County Community College
　　Eastern Campus
　　Selden
　　Western Campus
Sullivan County Community
　College

Syracuse University
Tobe-Coburn School for Fashion
Careers
Touro College
Trocaire College
Ulster County Community College
Union College
United States Merchant Marine
Academy
United States Military Academy
University of Rochester
University of the State of New
York: Regents College
Utica College of Syracuse
University
Vassar College
Wagner College
Wells College
William Smith College
Yeshiva University

North Carolina

Alamance Community College
Anson Community College
Appalachian State University
Barber-Scotia College
Barton College
Beaufort County Community
College
Belmont Abbey College
Bennett College
Bladen Community College
Brevard College
Caldwell Community College and
Technical Institute
Campbell University
Catawba College
Catawba Valley Community College
Central Carolina Community
College
Central Piedmont Community
College
Chowan College
Cleveland Community College
Coastal Carolina Community
College
College of the Albemarle
Davidson College
Davidson County Community
College
Duke University
East Carolina University
Edgecombe Community College
Elizabeth City State University
Elon College
Fayetteville State University
Forsyth Technical Community
College
Gardner-Webb University
Gaston College
Greensboro College
Guilford College
Guilford Technical Community
College
Haywood Community College
High Point University
Isothermal Community College
John Wesley College
Johnson C. Smith University
Lenoir-Rhyne College
Livingstone College
Louisburg College
Mars Hill College
Mayland Community College
McDowell Technical Community
College
Meredith College
Methodist College
Mitchell Community College
Montgomery Community College
Montreat-Anderson College
Mount Olive College
North Carolina Agricultural and
Technical State University

North Carolina Central University
North Carolina School of the Arts
North Carolina State University
North Carolina Wesleyan College
Pamlico Community College
Peace College
Pfeiffer College
Piedmont Community College
Queens College
Richmond Community College
Roanoke-Chowan Community
College
Rockingham Community College
St. Andrews Presbyterian College
St. Augustine's College
Salem College
Sandhills Community College
Shaw University
Southeastern Community College
Southwestern Community College
Surry Community College
Tri-County Community College
University of North Carolina
Asheville
Chapel Hill
Charlotte
Greensboro
Wilmington
Vance-Granville Community
College
Wake Forest University
Warren Wilson College
Western Carolina University
Wilkes Community College
Wingate College
Winston-Salem State University

North Dakota

Dickinson State University
Jamestown College
Little Hoop Community College
Minot State University
North Dakota State University
Standing Rock College
Trinity Bible College
University of Mary
University of North Dakota

Ohio

Antioch College
Antioch School for Adult and
Experiential Learning
Art Academy of Cincinnati
Ashland University
Baldwin-Wallace College
Bluffton College
Bowling Green State University
Bowling Green
Firelands College
Capital University
Case Western Reserve University
Cedarville College
Central State University
Chatfield College
Cincinnati Bible College and
Seminary
Cincinnati Metropolitan College
Circleville Bible College
Cleveland Institute of Art
Cleveland Institute of Electronics
Cleveland Institute of Music
Cleveland State University
College of Mount St. Joseph
College of Wooster
Columbus State Community College
Cuyahoga Community College
Metropolitan Campus
Western Campus
Defiance College
Denison University
Dyke College
Edison State Community College
Franklin University
Heidelberg College

Hiram College
Hocking Technical College
Jefferson Technical College
John Carroll University
Kent State University
Ashtabula Regional Campus
East Liverpool Regional
Campus
Kent
Stark Campus
Tuscarawas Campus
Kenyon College
Lake Erie College
Lakeland Community College
Lorain County Community College
Lourdes College
Malone College
Marietta College
Marion Technical College
Miami University
Hamilton Campus
Oxford Campus
Miami-Jacobs College
Mount Union College
Mount Vernon Nazarene College
Muskingum College
Northwest Technical College
Notre Dame College of Ohio
Oberlin College
Ohio Dominican College
Ohio Northern University
Ohio State University
Agricultural Technical Institute
Columbus Campus
Lima Campus
Mansfield Campus
Marion Campus
Newark Campus
Ohio University
Athens
Chillicothe Campus
Eastern Campus
Zanesville Campus
Ohio Wesleyan University
Otterbein College
Pontifical College Josephinum
Shawnee State University
Sinclair Community College
Southern Ohio College
Stark Technical College
Tiffin University
Union Institute
University of Akron
Akron
Wayne College
University of Cincinnati
Access Colleges
Cincinnati
Clermont College
Raymond Walters College
University of Dayton
University of Findlay
University of Rio Grande
University of Toledo
Urbana University
Ursuline College
Virginia Marti College of Fashion
and Art
Walsh College
Washington State Community
College
Wilmington College
Wittenberg University
Wright State University
Dayton
Lake Campus
Xavier University

Oklahoma

Bartlesville Wesleyan College
Cameron University
East Central University
Hillsdale Free Will Baptist College
Mid-America Bible College

Northwestern Oklahoma State
University
Oklahoma Baptist University
Oklahoma Christian University of
Science and Arts
Oklahoma City University
Oklahoma Junior College
Oklahoma State University
Oklahoma City
Stillwater
Oral Roberts University
Phillips University
Redlands Community College
Rogers State College
Southeastern Oklahoma State
University
Southwestern College of Christian
Ministries
Southwestern Oklahoma State
University
University of Central Oklahoma
University of Oklahoma
Health Sciences Center
Norman
University of Science and Arts of
Oklahoma
University of Tulsa

Oregon

Chemeketa Community College
Concordia College
Eastern Oregon State College
Eugene Bible College
George Fox College
Lane Community College
Lewis and Clark College
Linfield College
Marylhurst College
Mount Hood Community College
Oregon State University
Pacific Northwest College of Art
Pacific University
Portland State University
Reed College
Rogue Community College
Southern Oregon State College
Southwestern Oregon Community
College
University of Oregon
Eugene
Robert Donald Clark Honors
College
University of Portland
Warner Pacific College
Western Baptist College
Western Oregon State College
Willamette University

Pennsylvania

Academy of the New Church
Albright College
Allegheny College
Allentown College of St. Francis de
Sales
Alvernia College
Baptist Bible College of
Pennsylvania
Beaver College
Berean Institute
Bloomsburg University of
Pennsylvania
Bryn Mawr College
Bucknell University
Bucks County Community College
Butler County Community College
Cabrini College
California University of
Pennsylvania
Carlow College
Carnegie Mellon University
Cedar Crest College
Chatham College
Chestnut Hill College
Cheyney University of Pennsylvania

Churchman Business School
Clarion University of Pennsylvania
College Misericordia
Delaware County Community
College
Dickinson College
Drexel University
Duquesne University
East Stroudsburg University of
Pennsylvania
Eastern College
Edinboro University of
Pennsylvania
Elizabethtown College
Franklin and Marshall College
Gannon University
Geneva College
Gettysburg College
Gratz College
Grove City College
Hahnemann University School of
Health Sciences and Humanities
Harcum Junior College
Harrisburg Area Community
College
Haverford College
Holy Family College
ICS Center for Degree Studies
Immaculata College
Indiana University of Pennsylvania
Juniata College
Keystone Junior College
King's College
Kutztown University of
Pennsylvania
La Roche College
La Salle University
Lackawanna Junior College
Lafayette College
Lancaster Bible College
Lebanon Valley College of
Pennsylvania
Lehigh University
Lincoln University
Lock Haven University of
Pennsylvania
Luzerne County Community
College
Lycoming College
Manor Junior College
Mansfield University of
Pennsylvania
Marywood College
Mercyhurst College
Messiah College
Millersville University of
Pennsylvania
Montgomery County Community
College
Moore College of Art and Design
Moravian College
Mount Aloysius College
Muhlenberg College
Neumann College
Northampton County Area
Community College
Northeastern Christian Junior
College
Peirce Junior College
Penn State
Erie Behrend College
Harrisburg Capital College
University Park Campus
Pennsylvania Institute of
Technology
Philadelphia College of Bible
Philadelphia College of Textiles and
Science
Pittsburgh Technical Institute
Point Park College
Reading Area Community College
Rosemont College
St. Charles Borromeo Seminary
St. Francis College

St. Joseph's University
St. Vincent College
Seton Hill College
Shippensburg University of
Pennsylvania
Slippery Rock University of
Pennsylvania
Spring Garden College
Susquehanna University
Swarthmore College
Temple University
Thiel College
Thomas Jefferson University:
College of Allied Health Sciences
University of the Arts
University of Pennsylvania
University of Pittsburgh
Bradford
Greensburg
Johnstown
Pittsburgh
University of Scranton
Ursinus College
Valley Forge Christian College
Villanova University
Washington and Jefferson College
Waynesburg College
West Chester University of
Pennsylvania
Westminster College
Widener University
Wilkes University
Wilson College
York College of Pennsylvania

Puerto Rico

Bayamon Central University
Inter American University of Puerto
Rico
Arecibo Campus
Metropolitan Campus
San German Campus
Pontifical Catholic University of
Puerto Rico
Puerto Rico Junior College
University of Puerto Rico: Cayey
University College
University of the Sacred Heart

Rhode Island

Brown University
Johnson & Wales University
Providence College
Rhode Island College
Rhode Island School of Design
Roger Williams College
Salve Regina University
University of Rhode Island

South Carolina

Anderson College
Central Wesleyan College
Chesterfield-Marlboro Technical
College
Coker College
College of Charleston
Columbia Bible College and
Seminary
Columbia College
Converse College
Denmark Technical College
Erskine College
Florence-Darlington Technical
College
Francis Marion College
Furman University
Horry-Georgetown Technical
College
Lander College
Limestone College
Newberry College
North Greenville College
Presbyterian College
Spartanburg Methodist College

Sumter Area Technical College
Technical College of the
Lowcountry
Trident Technical College
University of South Carolina
Aiken
Beaufort
Coastal Carolina College
Columbia
Lancaster
Salkehatchie Regional Campus
Spartanburg
Union
Voorhees College
Winthrop University
Wofford College

South Dakota

Augustana College
Black Hills State University
Dakota State University
Dakota Wesleyan University
Kilian Community College
Mitchell Vocational Technical
Institute
Mount Marty College
National College
Northern State University
Sinte Gleska College
Sioux Falls College
South Dakota School of Mines and
Technology
South Dakota State University
University of South Dakota

Tennessee

Belmont University
Bethel College
Bristol University
Carson-Newman College
Chattanooga State Technical
Community College
Christian Brothers University
Crichton College
Dyersburg State Community
College
East Tennessee State University
Fisk University
Free Will Baptist Bible College
Freed-Hardeman University
Hiwassee College
King College
Knoxville College
Lambuth University
Lincoln Memorial University
Martin Methodist College
Maryville College
Memphis College of Art
Memphis State University
Middle Tennessee State University
Milligan College
Rhodes College
Roane State Community College
Shelby State Community College
State Technical Institute at
Memphis
Tennessee State University
Tennessee Technological University
Tennessee Temple University
Tennessee Wesleyan College
Tomlinson College
Trevecca Nazarene College
Tusculum College
Union University
University of the South
University of Tennessee
Chattanooga
Knoxville
Martin
Vanderbilt University
Volunteer State Community College
William Jennings Bryan College

Texas

Abilene Christian University
Amber University
Austin College
Austin Community College
Baylor University
Central Texas College
Concordia Lutheran College
Corpus Christi State University
Dallas Baptist University
Del Mar College
East Texas Baptist University
East Texas State University
Commerce
Texarkana
Eastfield College
El Paso Community College
Hardin-Simmons University
Houston Baptist University
Incarnate Word College
Lamar University—Beaumont
Lee College
LeTourneau University
Lon Morris College
McMurry University
Midwestern State University
Mountain View College
Navarro College
North Harris Montgomery
Community College District
Northwood Institute: Texas Campus
Our Lady of the Lake University of
San Antonio
Prairie View A&M University
Rice University
St. Edward's University
St. Mary's University
San Antonio Art Institute
Southern Methodist University
Southwest Texas State University
Southwestern Adventist College
Southwestern Assemblies of God
College
Southwestern Christian College
Southwestern University
Sul Ross State University
Texas A&I University
Texas A&M University
Texas Christian University
Texas Lutheran College
Texas State Technical College
Harlingen
Sweetwater
Texas Tech University
Trinity University
University of Houston
Clear Lake
Downtown
Houston
University of Mary Hardin-Baylor
University of St. Thomas
University of Texas
Austin
Dallas
El Paso
Health Science Center at
Houston
Permian Basin
San Antonio
Southwestern Medical Center
at Dallas Southwestern
Allied Health Sciences
School
Tyler
West Texas State University
Western Texas College

Utah

Brigham Young University
University of Utah
Utah State University
Weber State University
Westminster College of Salt Lake
City

Vermont

Bennington College
Burlington College
Castleton State College
Champlain College
College of St. Joseph in Vermont
Community College of Vermont
Goddard College
Green Mountain College
Johnson State College
Lyndon State College
Marlboro College
Middlebury College
Norwich University
St. Michael's College
School for International Training
Southern Vermont College
Sterling College
Trinity College of Vermont
University of Vermont
Vermont Technical College

Virginia

Averett College
Bluefield College
Bridgewater College
Central Virginia Community College
Christopher Newport College
Clinch Valley College of the
    University of Virginia
College of Health Sciences
College of William and Mary
Commonwealth College
Dabney S. Lancaster Community
    College
Eastern Mennonite College
Emory and Henry College
Ferrum College
George Mason University
Hampden-Sydney College
Hampton University
Hollins College
James Madison University
John Tyler Community College
Liberty University
Longwood College
Lord Fairfax Community College
Lynchburg College
Mary Baldwin College
Mary Washington College
Marymount University
Mountain Empire Community
    College
Norfolk State University
Northern Virginia Community
    College
Old Dominion University
Patrick Henry Community College
Paul D. Camp Community College
Piedmont Virginia Community
    College
Radford University
Randolph-Macon College
Randolph-Macon Woman's College
Roanoke College
Shenandoah University
Southern Seminary College
Southwest Virginia Community
    College
Strayer College
Sweet Briar College
Tidewater Community College
University of Richmond
University of Virginia
Virginia Commonwealth University
Virginia Highlands Community
    College
Virginia Intermont College
Virginia Military Institute
Virginia Polytechnic Institute and
    State University
Virginia Union University
Virginia Wesleyan College
Washington and Lee University

Wytheville Community College

Washington

Antioch University Seattle
Central Washington University
Centralia College
City University
Clark College
Cornish College of the Arts
Eastern Washington University
Edmonds Community College
Everett Community College
Evergreen State College
Gonzaga University
Grays Harbor College
Green River Community College
Griffin College
Heritage College
Lutheran Bible Institute of Seattle
Northwest College of the
    Assemblies of God
Northwest Indian College
Olympic College
Pacific Lutheran University
Pierce College
St. Martin's College
Seattle Central Community College
Seattle Pacific University
Seattle University
Shoreline Community College
Skagit Valley College
South Puget Sound Community
    College
Spokane Community College
Spokane Falls Community College
University of Puget Sound
University of Washington
Walla Walla Community College
Washington State University
Wenatchee Valley College
Western Washington University
Whatcom Community College
Whitman College
Whitworth College
Yakima Valley Community College

West Virginia

Alderson-Broaddus College
Bethany College
Bluefield State College
Concord College
Davis and Elkins College
Marshall University
Ohio Valley College
Salem-Teikyo University
Shepherd College
University of Charleston
West Liberty State College
West Virginia Northern Community
    College
West Virginia University
    Morgantown
    Parkersburg
West Virginia Wesleyan College
Wheeling Jesuit College

Wisconsin

Bellin College of Nursing
Beloit College
Cardinal Stritch College
Carroll College
Carthage College
Chippewa Valley Technical College
Columbia College of Nursing
Concordia University Wisconsin
Edgewood College
Lakeland College
Lawrence University
Maranatha Baptist Bible College
Marian College of Fond du Lac
Marquette University
Mid-State Technical College
Milwaukee Institute of Art &
    Design

Moraine Park Technical College
Mount Mary College
Mount Senario College
Northland College
Ripon College
St. Norbert College
Silver Lake College
University of Wisconsin
    Eau Claire
    Green Bay
    La Crosse
    Madison
    Milwaukee
    Oshkosh
    Parkside
    Platteville
    River Falls
    Stevens Point
    Stout
    Superior
    Whitewater
University of Wisconsin Center
    Baraboo/Sauk County
    Fox Valley
    Manitowoc County
    Marathon County
    Marinette County
    Marshfield/Wood County
    Richland
    Sheboygan County
    Washington County
    Waukesha
Viterbo College
Waukesha County Technical
    College
Western Wisconsin Technical
    College
Wisconsin Lutheran College

Wyoming

Central Wyoming College
Eastern Wyoming College
Northwest College
Sheridan College
University of Wyoming
Western Wyoming Community
    College

American Samoa, Caroline Islands, Guam, Marianas, Virgin Islands

Guam Community College
Northern Marianas College
University of the Virgin Islands

France

American University of Paris

Switzerland

American College of Switzerland
Franklin College: Switzerland

Arab Republic of Egypt

American University in Cairo

Internships

Alabama

Alabama Agricultural and
    Mechanical University
Alabama Aviation and Technical
    College
Alabama State University
Athens State College
Auburn University
    Auburn
    Montgomery
Bessemer State Technical College
Birmingham-Southern College
Bishop State Community College

Community College of the Air
    Force
Draughons Junior College
Enterprise State Junior College
Faulkner University
Huntingdon College
Jacksonville State University
James H. Faulkner State
    Community College
Jefferson State Community College
John C. Calhoun State Community
    College
Judson College
Miles College
Mobile College
RETS Electronic Institute
Samford University
Shoals Community College
Snead State Junior College
Southern Christian University
Spring Hill College
Stillman College
Talladega College
Troy State University at Dothan
Tuskegee University
University of Alabama
    Birmingham
    Huntsville
    Tuscaloosa
University of Montevallo
University of South Alabama
Walker State Technical College
Wallace State Community College
    at Hanceville

Alaska

Alaska Bible College
Alaska Pacific University
Prince William Sound Community
    College
Sheldon Jackson College
University of Alaska
    Anchorage
    Fairbanks
    Southeast

Arizona

American Indian Bible College
Arizona College of the Bible
Arizona State University
Cochise College
Embry-Riddle Aeronautical
    University: Prescott Campus
Glendale Community College
Grand Canyon University
ITT Technical Institute: Tucson
Lamson Junior College
Mesa Community College
Navajo Community College
Northern Arizona University
Paradise Valley Community College
Prescott College
Rio Salado Community College
Southwestern College
University of Arizona
Western International University

Arkansas

Arkansas College
Arkansas State University
Capital City Junior College
Central Baptist College
Garland County Community
    College
Harding University
Hendrix College
John Brown University
Ouachita Baptist University
Shorter College
Southern Arkansas University

University of Arkansas
  Fayetteville
  Little Rock
  Monticello
  Pine Bluff
University of Central Arkansas
University of the Ozarks
Westark Community College
Williams Baptist College

California

Allan Hancock College
American Armenian International
  College
American College for the Applied
  Arts: Los Angeles
Antioch Southern California at
  Santa Barbara
Armstrong College
Art Institute of Southern California
Azusa Pacific University
Barstow College
Bethany College
Biola University
Brooks College
Brooks Institute of Photography
California Baptist College
California College of Arts and
  Crafts
California Institute of Technology
California Lutheran University
California Maritime Academy
California Polytechnic State
  University: San Luis Obispo
California State Polytechnic
  University: Pomona
California State University
  Bakersfield
  Chico
  Dominguez Hills
  Fresno
  Fullerton
  Hayward
  Long Beach
  Los Angeles
  Northridge
  Sacramento
  San Bernardino
  San Marcos
  Stanislaus
Cerro Coso Community College
Chabot College
Chapman University
Charles R. Drew University: College
  of Allied Health
Christ College Irvine
Christian Heritage College
City College of San Francisco
Claremont McKenna College
College of Notre Dame
College of the Sequoias
Columbia College: Hollywood
De Anza College
Diablo Valley College
Dominican College of San Rafael
D-Q University
Evergreen Valley College
Fashion Institute of Design and
  Merchandising
  Los Angeles
  San Francisco
Fresno City College
Fresno Pacific College
Glendale Community College
Golden Gate University
Grossmont Community College
Hebrew Union College: Jewish
  Institute of Religion
Holy Names College
Humboldt State University
Imperial Valley College
ITT Technical Institute: Van Nuys
John F. Kennedy University
Kelsey-Jenney College

La Sierra University
Lassen College
LIFE Bible College
Louise Salinger Academy of
  Fashion
Loyola Marymount University
Marymount College
Master's College
Menlo College
Merced College
Mills College
Modesto Junior College
Monterey Institute of International
  Studies
Moorpark College
Mount St. Mary's College
Mount San Jacinto College
Napa Valley College
New College of California
Occidental College
Ohlone College
Pacific Christian College
Pacific Oaks College
Pacific Union College
Pasadena City College
Pepperdine University
Phillips Junior College
  Condie Campus
  Fresno Campus
  San Fernando Valley Campus
Pitzer College
Point Loma Nazarene College
Pomona College
Queen of the Holy Rosary College
Saddleback College
St. Mary's College of California
Samuel Merritt College
San Diego City College
San Diego State University
San Francisco Art Institute
San Jose Christian College
San Jose City College
San Jose State University
Santa Barbara City College
Santa Clara University
Santa Monica College
Santa Rosa Junior College
Scripps College
Sierra College
Simpson College
Solano Community College
Sonoma State University
Southern California College
Southern California Institute of
  Architecture
Southwestern College
Stanford University
United States International
  University
University of California
  Berkeley
  Davis
  Irvine
  Los Angeles
  Riverside
  San Diego
  Santa Barbara
  Santa Cruz
University of Judaism
University of La Verne
University of the Pacific
University of Redlands
University of San Diego
University of San Francisco
University of Southern California
University of West Los Angeles
West Coast University
West Valley College
Western State University College of
  Law
  Orange County
  San Diego
Westmont College
Whittier College

Woodbury University
World College West

Colorado

Adams State College
Aims Community College
Arapahoe Community College
Bel-Rea Institute of Animal
  Technology
Blair Junior College
Colorado Christian University
Colorado College
Colorado Mountain College
  Alpine Campus
  Spring Valley Campus
  Timberline Campus
Colorado Northwestern Community
  College
Colorado State University
Colorado Technical College
Community College of Denver
Denver Technical College
Fort Lewis College
Front Range Community College
Lamar Community College
Mesa State College
Metropolitan State College of
  Denver
Naropa Institute
National College
Parks Junior College
Pikes Peak Community College
Red Rocks Community College
Regis College of Regis University
Rocky Mountain College of Art &
  Design
University of Colorado
  Boulder
  Denver
  Health Sciences Center
University of Denver
University of Northern Colorado
University of Southern Colorado
Western State College of Colorado

Connecticut

Albertus Magnus College
Asnuntuck Community College
Briarwood College
Central Connecticut State
  University
Connecticut College
Eastern Connecticut State
  University
Fairfield University
Greater New Haven State Technical
  College
Housatonic Community College
Manchester Community College
Mattatuck Community College
Middlesex Community College
Mitchell College
Northwestern Connecticut
  Community College
Norwalk Community College
Quinebaug Valley Community
  College
Quinnipiac College
Sacred Heart University
St. Joseph College
South Central Community College
Southern Connecticut State
  University
Teikyo-Post University
Trinity College
Tunxis Community College
University of Bridgeport
University of Connecticut
University of Hartford
University of New Haven
Wesleyan University
Western Connecticut State
  University

Delaware

Delaware State College
Delaware Technical and
  Community College
  Southern Campus
  Stanton/Wilmington Campus
  Terry Campus
Goldey-Beacom College
University of Delaware
Wesley College
Wilmington College

District of Columbia

American University
Catholic University of America
Corcoran School of Art
Gallaudet University
George Washington University
Georgetown University
Howard University
Mount Vernon College
Trinity College
University of the District of
  Columbia

Florida

Barry University
Bethune-Cookman College
Brevard Community College
Broward Community College
Central Florida Community College
Daytona Beach Community College
Eckerd College
Embry-Riddle Aeronautical
  University
Flagler College
Florida Agricultural and Mechanical
  University
Florida Atlantic University
Florida Baptist Theological College
Florida Christian College
Florida Community College at
  Jacksonville
Florida Institute of Technology
Florida International University
Florida Memorial College
Florida Southern College
Florida State University
Fort Lauderdale College
Gulf Coast Community College
Hobe Sound Bible College
International Fine Arts College
Jacksonville University
Jones College
Lake City Community College
Lake-Sumter Community College
Lynn University
Miami-Dade Community College
New College of the University of
  South Florida
New England Institute of
  Technology
Nova University
Okaloosa-Walton Community
  College
Orlando College
Palm Beach Atlantic College
Palm Beach Community College
Pasco-Hernando Community
  College
Pensacola Junior College
Phillips Junior College: Melbourne
Ringling School of Art and Design
Rollins College
St. Leo College
St. Petersburg Junior College
St. Thomas University
Schiller International University
South College: Palm Beach Campus
South Florida Community College
Southern College
Stetson University
Tampa College
University of Central Florida

University of Florida
University of Miami
University of North Florida
University of South Florida
University of Tampa
University of West Florida
Valencia Community College
Warner Southern College
Webber College

Georgia

Abraham Baldwin Agricultural
  College
Agnes Scott College
Albany State College
American College for the Applied
  Arts
Armstrong State College
Athens Area Technical Institute
Atlanta Christian College
Atlanta College of Art
Atlanta Metropolitan College
Augusta College
Bauder College
Berry College
Brenau Women's College
Brewton-Parker College
Chattahoochee Technical Institute
Clark Atlanta University
Clayton State College
Columbus College
Covenant College
Dalton College
DeKalb Technical Institute
Emmanuel College
Emory University
Fort Valley State College
Georgia College
Georgia Southern University
Georgia Southwestern College
Georgia State University
Kennesaw State College
LaGrange College
Macon College
Meadows College of Business
Medical College of Georgia
Mercer University
    Atlanta
    Macon
Morehouse College
Morris Brown College
North Georgia College
Oglethorpe University
Paine College
Piedmont College
Reinhardt College
Savannah College of Art and
  Design
Savannah State College
Savannah Technical Institute
Shorter College
South College
Spelman College
Toccoa Falls College
University of Georgia
Valdosta State College
Wesleyan College
West Georgia College
Young Harris College

Hawaii

Brigham Young University-Hawaii
Cannon's International Business
  College of Honolulu
Chaminade University of Honolulu
Hawaii Loa College
Hawaii Pacific University

University of Hawaii
  Hilo
  Honolulu Community College
  Kapiolani Community College
  Kauai Community College
  Leeward Community College
  Manoa
  West Oahu

Idaho

Albertson College
Boise Bible College
Boise State University
College of Southern Idaho
Idaho State University
Lewis Clark State College
North Idaho College
Northwest Nazarene College
Ricks College
University of Idaho

Illinois

Augustana College
Aurora University
Barat College
Belleville Area College
Black Hawk College
    East Campus
    Moline
Blackburn College
Bradley University
Carl Sandburg College
Chicago State University
City Colleges of Chicago
    Chicago City-Wide College
    Malcolm X College
    Olive-Harvey College
    Richard J. Daley College
    Wright College
College of DuPage
College of Lake County
College of St. Francis
Columbia College
Concordia University
De Paul University
Eastern Illinois University
Elgin Community College
Elmhurst College
Eureka College
Governors State University
Greenville College
Highland Community College
Illinois Benedictine College
Illinois Central College
Illinois College
Illinois Eastern Community
  Colleges
    Lincoln Trail College
    Olney Central College
    Wabash Valley College
Illinois Institute of Technology
Illinois State University
Illinois Valley Community College
Illinois Wesleyan University
International Academy of
  Merchandising and Design
John A. Logan College
Joliet Junior College
Judson College
Kendall College
Kishwaukee College
Knox College
Lake Forest College
Lake Land College
Lewis and Clark Community
  College
Lewis University
Lexington Institute of Hospitality
  Careers
Lincoln Christian College and
  Seminary
Lincoln Land Community College
Loyola University of Chicago
MacCormac Junior College

MacMurray College
McKendree College
Midstate College
Millikin University
Monmouth College
Montay College
Moody Bible Institute
Moraine Valley Community College
Morton College
National-Louis University
North Central College
North Park College and Theological
  Seminary
Northeastern Illinois University
Northern Illinois University
Northwestern University
Oakton Community College
Olivet Nazarene University
Parkland College
Parks College of St. Louis
  University
Phillips College of Chicago
Prairie State College
Principia College
Quincy College
Ray College of Design
Rend Lake College
Robert Morris College: Chicago
Rock Valley College
Rockford College
Roosevelt University
Rosary College
St. Augustine College
St. Xavier University
Sangamon State University
School of the Art Institute of
  Chicago
Shawnee Community College
Shimer College
Southern Illinois University
    Carbondale
    Edwardsville
Spoon River College
State Community College
Trinity Christian College
Trinity College
Triton College
University of Chicago
University of Health Sciences: The
  Chicago Medical School
University of Illinois
    Chicago
    Urbana-Champaign
VanderCook College of Music
Western Illinois University
Wheaton College
William Rainey Harper College

Indiana

Ancilla College
Anderson University
Ball State University
Bethel College
Butler University
Calumet College of St. Joseph
DePauw University
Earlham College
Franklin College
Goshen College
Grace College
Hanover College
Huntington College
Indiana Institute of Technology
Indiana State University
Indiana University
    Bloomington
    Northwest
    South Bend
    Southeast
Indiana University—Purdue
  University
    Fort Wayne
    Indianapolis

Indiana Vocational Technical
  College
    Central Indiana
    Columbus
    Eastcentral
    Kokomo
    Lafayette
    Northcentral
    Northeast
    Northwest
    Southcentral
    Southeast
    Southwest
    Wabash Valley
    Whitewater
Indiana Wesleyan University
International Business College
Manchester College
Marian College
Martin University
Purdue University
    Calumet
    West Lafayette
St. Francis College
St. Joseph's College
St. Mary-of-the-Woods College
St. Mary's College
Taylor University
Tri-State University
University of Evansville
University of Indianapolis
University of Notre Dame
University of Southern Indiana
Valparaiso University
Vincennes University
Wabash College

Iowa

American Institute of Business
American Institute of Commerce
Briar Cliff College
Buena Vista College
Central College
Clarke College
Clinton Community College
Coe College
Cornell College
Des Moines Area Community
  College
Dordt College
Drake University
Faith Baptist Bible College and
  Theological Seminary
Graceland College
Grand View College
Grinnell College
Hawkeye Institute of Technology
Indian Hills Community College
Iowa Central Community College
Iowa Lakes Community College
Iowa State University
Iowa Wesleyan College
Kirkwood Community College
Loras College
Luther College
Maharishi International University
Morningside College
Mount Mercy College
Mount St. Clare College
Muscatine Community College
Northeast Iowa Community College
Northwestern College
St. Ambrose University
Scott Community College
Simpson College
Southeastern Community College
    North Campus
    South Campus
Southwestern Community College
Teikyo Marycrest University
Teikyo Westmar University
University of Dubuque
University of Iowa
University of Northern Iowa

Upper Iowa University
Vennard College
Waldorf College
Wartburg College
William Penn College

Kansas

Allen County Community College
Baker University
Barclay College
Barton County Community College
Benedictine College
Bethany College
Bethel College
Brown Mackie College
Cloud County Community College
Coffeyville Community College
Colby Community College
Cowley County Community College
Dodge City Community College
Emporia State University
Fort Hays State University
Fort Scott Community College
Friends University
Haskell Indian Junior College
Hutchinson Community College
Johnson County Community
    College
Kansas City College and Bible
    School
Kansas City Kansas Community
    College
Kansas Newman College
Kansas State University
Kansas Wesleyan University
Manhattan Christian College
McPherson College
MidAmerica Nazarene College
Ottawa University
Pittsburg State University
Pratt Community College
St. Mary College
Seward County Community College
Southwestern College
Tabor College
University of Kansas
    Lawrence
    Medical Center
Washburn University of Topeka
Wichita State University

Kentucky

Asbury College
Bellarmine College
Berea College
Brescia College
Campbellsville College
Centre College
Clear Creek Baptist Bible College
Eastern Kentucky University
Elizabethtown Community College
Franklin College
Georgetown College
Jefferson Community College
Kentucky Christian College
Kentucky State University
Kentucky Wesleyan College
Lexington Community College
Lindsey Wilson College
Louisville Technical Institute
Madisonville Community College
Maysville Community College
Morehead State University
Murray State University
Northern Kentucky University
Owensboro Junior College of
    Business
Pikeville College
St. Catharine College
Southeast Community College
Spalding University
Sue Bennett College
Sullivan College
Thomas More College

Transylvania University
Union College
University of Kentucky
University of Louisville
Watterson College
Western Kentucky University

Louisiana

Bossier Parish Community College
Centenary College of Louisiana
Dillard University
Grambling State University
Louisiana College
Louisiana State University
    Agricultural and Mechanical
        College
    Medical Center
    Shreveport
Louisiana Tech University
Loyola University
McNeese State University
Nicholls State University
Northeast Louisiana University
Northwestern State University
Our Lady of Holy Cross College
Southeastern Louisiana University
Southern University
    New Orleans
    Shreveport
Southern University and
    Agricultural and Mechanical
        College
Tulane University
University of New Orleans
University of Southwestern
    Louisiana
World Evangelism Bible College
    and Seminary
Xavier University of Louisiana

Maine

Andover College
Bates College
Beal College
Casco Bay College
Central Maine Technical College
Colby College
College of the Atlantic
Eastern Maine Technical College
Husson College
Maine Maritime Academy
St. Joseph's College
Southern Maine Technical College
Thomas College
Unity College
University of Maine
    Augusta
    Farmington
    Fort Kent
    Machias
    Orono
    Presque Isle
University of New England
University of Southern Maine
Westbrook College

Maryland

Allegany Community College
Anne Arundel Community College
Baltimore Hebrew University
Bowie State University
Capitol College
Cecil Community College
Chesapeake College
College of Notre Dame of
    Maryland
Columbia Union College
Coppin State College
Dundalk Community College
Eastern Christian College
Essex Community College
Frostburg State University
Garrett Community College
Goucher College

Hagerstown Business College
Hagerstown Junior College
Harford Community College
Hood College
Howard Community College
Johns Hopkins University
Loyola College in Maryland
Maryland Institute College of Art
Montgomery College
    Germantown Campus
    Rockville Campus
    Takoma Park Campus
Morgan State University
Mount St. Mary's College
New Community College of
    Baltimore
St. Mary's College of Maryland
Salisbury State University
Sojourner-Douglass College
Towson State University
University of Baltimore
University of Maryland
    Baltimore County
    College Park
    Eastern Shore
Villa Julie College
Washington College
Western Maryland College
Wor-Wic Tech Community College

Massachusetts

American International College
Anna Maria College for Men and
    Women
Aquinas College at Milton
Aquinas College at Newton
Assumption College
Atlantic Union College
Babson College
Bay Path College
Bay State College
Becker College
    Leicester Campus
    Worcester Campus
Bentley College
Berkshire Community College
Boston Architectural Center
Boston College
Boston University
Bradford College
Brandeis University
Bridgewater State College
Bristol Community College
Bunker Hill Community College
Cape Cod Community College
Clark University
College of the Holy Cross
Curry College
Dean Junior College
Eastern Nazarene College
Elms College
Emerson College
Emmanuel College
Endicott College
Fisher College
Fitchburg State College
Forsyth School for Dental
    Hygienists
Framingham State College
Gordon College
Greenfield Community College
Hampshire College
Harvard and Radcliffe Colleges
Hellenic College
Holyoke Community College
Katharine Gibbs School
Lasell College
Lesley College
Marian Court Junior College
Massachusetts Bay Community
    College
Massachusetts College of Art
Massachusetts College of Pharmacy
    and Allied Health Sciences

Massachusetts Institute of
    Technology
Massachusetts Maritime Academy
Merrimack College
Middlesex Community College
Montserrat College of Art
Mount Holyoke College
Mount Ida College
Mount Wachusett Community
    College
New England Conservatory of
    Music
Newbury College
Nichols College
North Adams State College
North Shore Community College
Northeastern University
Northern Essex Community College
Pine Manor College
Quincy College
Quinsigamond Community College
Regis College
Roxbury Community College
Salem State College
Simmons College
Simon's Rock College of Bard
Smith College
Springfield College
Stonehill College
Suffolk University
Tufts University
University of Massachusetts
    Amherst
    Boston
    Dartmouth
    Lowell
Wellesley College
Western New England College
Westfield State College
Wheaton College
Wheelock College
Williams College
Worcester Polytechnic Institute
Worcester State College

Michigan

Adrian College
Albion College
Alma College
Alpena Community College
Andrews University
Aquinas College
Baker College
    Auburn Hills
    Cadillac
    Flint
    Muskegon
    Owosso
    Port Huron
Calvin College
Center for Creative Studies: College
    of Art and Design
Central Michigan University
Charles Stewart Mott Community
    College
Cleary College
Concordia College
Davenport College of Business
Delta College
Eastern Michigan University
Ferris State University
Glen Oaks Community College
Grace Bible College
Grand Rapids Baptist College and
    Seminary
Grand Rapids Community College
Grand Valley State University
Great Lakes Christian College
Great Lakes Junior College of
    Business
Hillsdale College
Hope College
Jackson Community College
Jordan College

Kalamazoo College
Kalamazoo Valley Community
College
Kendall College of Art and Design
Kirtland Community College
Lake Superior State University
Lansing Community College
Lawrence Technological University
Macomb Community College
Madonna University
Marygrove College
Michigan Christian College
Michigan State University
Michigan Technological University
Mid Michigan Community College
Montcalm Community College
Muskegon Community College
Northern Michigan University
Northwestern Michigan College
Northwood Institute
Oakland Community College
Oakland University
Olivet College
Reformed Bible College
St. Clair County Community
College
St. Mary's College
Schoolcraft College
Siena Heights College
Spring Arbor College
Suomi College
University of Detroit Mercy
University of Michigan
Ann Arbor
Dearborn
Flint
Walsh College of Accountancy and
Business Administration
Wayne State University
West Shore Community College
Western Michigan University
William Tyndale College

Minnesota

Alexandria Technical College
Anoka-Ramsey Community College
Augsburg College
Austin Community College
Bemidji State University
Bethel College
Carleton College
College of Associated Arts
College of St. Benedict
College of St. Catherine: St.
Catherine Campus
College of St. Scholastica
Concordia College: Moorhead
Concordia College: St. Paul
Crown College
Gustavus Adolphus College
Hamline University
Inver Hills Community College
Itasca Community College:
Arrowhead Region
Lakewood Community College
Macalester College
Mankato State University
Mesabi Community College:
Arrowhead Region
Metropolitan State University
Minneapolis College of Art and
Design
Minneapolis Community College
Moorhead State University
National Education Center: Brown
Institute Campus
Normandale Community College
North Central Bible College
Northland Community College
Northwestern College
Pillsbury Baptist Bible College
Rochester Community College
St. Cloud State University
St. John's University

St. Mary's Campus of the College of
St. Catherine
St. Mary's College of Minnesota
St. Olaf College
St. Paul Technical College
Southwest State University
University of Minnesota
Crookston
Duluth
Morris
Twin Cities
University of St. Thomas
Vermilion Community College
Willmar Community College
Willmar Technical College
Winona State University
Worthington Community College

Mississippi

Alcorn State University
Belhaven College
Blue Mountain College
Delta State University
Holmes Community College
Jackson State University
Mary Holmes College
Millsaps College
Mississippi College
Mississippi Gulf Coast Community
College: Jefferson Davis Campus
Mississippi State University
Mississippi University for Women
Phillips Junior College
Jackson
Mississippi Gulf Coast
Rust College
Tougaloo College
University of Mississippi
University of Southern Mississippi
Wesley College
William Carey College

Missouri

Avila College
Calvary Bible College
Central Christian College of the
Bible
Central Methodist College
Central Missouri State University
College of the Ozarks
Columbia College
Culver-Stockton College
Drury College
East Central College
Evangel College
Fontbonne College
Hannibal-LaGrange College
Harris Stowe State College
Jefferson College
Kansas City Art Institute
Lincoln University
Lindenwood College
Longview Community College
Maple Woods Community College
Maryville University
Mineral Area College
Missouri Baptist College
Missouri Southern State College
Missouri Valley College
Missouri Western State College
Moberly Area Community College
North Central Missouri College
Northeast Missouri State University
Northwest Missouri State
University
Ozark Christian College
Park College
Penn Valley Community College
Phillips Junior College
Rockhurst College
St. Charles Community College
St. Louis Christian College
St. Louis College of Pharmacy

St. Louis Community College
Florissant Valley
Meramec
St. Louis University
Southeast Missouri State University
Southwest Baptist University
Southwest Missouri State University
State Fair Community College
Stephens College
Three Rivers Community College
University of Missouri
Columbia
Kansas City
Rolla
St. Louis
Washington University
Webster University
Westminster College
William Jewell College
William Woods College

Montana

Carroll College
College of Great Falls
Dawson Community College
Dull Knife Memorial College
Eastern Montana College
Flathead Valley Community College
Little Big Horn College
Miles Community College
Montana College of Mineral
Science and Technology
Montana State University
Northern Montana College
Rocky Mountain College
University of Montana
Western Montana College of the
University of Montana

Nebraska

Bellevue College
Central Community College
Chadron State College
College of St. Mary
Concordia College
Creighton University
Dana College
Doane College
Grace College of the Bible
Hastings College
Lincoln School of Commerce
McCook Community College
Metropolitan Community College
Midland Lutheran College
Nebraska Christian College
Nebraska College of Technical
Agriculture
Nebraska Methodist College of
Nursing and Allied Health
Nebraska Wesleyan University
Southeast Community College
Beatrice Campus
Lincoln Campus
Milford Campus
Union College
University of Nebraska
Kearney
Lincoln
Omaha
Wayne State College
Western Nebraska Community
College
Scottsbluff Campus
Sidney Campus
York College

Nevada

Community College of Southern
Nevada
Sierra Nevada College
Truckee Meadows Community
College

University of Nevada
Las Vegas
Reno
Western Nevada Community
College

New Hampshire

Castle College
Colby-Sawyer College
Daniel Webster College
Dartmouth College
Franklin Pierce College
Hesser College
Keene State College
McIntosh College
New England College
New Hampshire College
New Hampshire Technical College
Berlin
Laconia
Manchester
Nashua
Stratham
Notre Dame College
Plymouth State College of the
University System of New
Hampshire
Rivier College
St. Anselm College
School for Lifelong Learning
University of New Hampshire
Durham
Manchester
White Pines College

New Jersey

Atlantic Community College
Bergen Community College
Berkeley College of Business
Bloomfield College
Brookdale Community College
Burlington County College
Caldwell College
Camden County College
Centenary College
College of St. Elizabeth
County College of Morris
Drew University
Essex County College
Fairleigh Dickinson University
Felician College
Georgian Court College
Glassboro State College
Jersey City State College
Kean College of New Jersey
Mercer County Community College
Monmouth College
Montclair State College
New Jersey Institute of Technology
Passaic County Community College
Princeton University
Ramapo College of New Jersey
Rider College
Rutgers—The State University of
New Jersey
Camden College of Arts and
Sciences
College of Engineering
College of Nursing
College of Pharmacy
Cook College
Douglass College
Livingston College
Mason Gross School of the
Arts
Newark College of Arts and
Sciences
Rutgers College
University College New
Brunswick
St. Peter's College
Seton Hall University
Stevens Institute of Technology
Stockton State College

Sussex County Community College
Trenton State College
Union County College
University of Medicine and
  Dentistry of New Jersey: School
  of Health Related Professions
Upsala College
Westminster Choir College
William Paterson College of New
  Jersey

New Mexico

Albuquerque Technical-Vocational
  Institute
Clovis Community College
College of Santa Fe
College of the Southwest
Dona Ana Branch Community
  College of New Mexico State
  University
Eastern New Mexico University
  Portales
  Roswell Campus
Institute of American Indian Arts
New Mexico Highlands University
New Mexico Institute of Mining
  and Technology
New Mexico Junior College
New Mexico State University
  Carlsbad
  Las Cruces
Northern New Mexico Community
  College
Parks College
San Juan College
University of New Mexico
Western New Mexico University

New York

Adelphi University
Adirondack Community College
Alfred University
Bard College
Barnard College
Berkeley College
Berkeley School: New York City
Boricua College
Bramson ORT Technical Institute
Broome Community College
Bryant & Stratton Business Institute
  Albany
  Buffalo
  Rochester
Canisius College
Cazenovia College
Central City Business Institute
City University of New York
  Borough of Manhattan
    Community College
  Brooklyn College
  City College
  College of Staten Island
  Hostos Community College
  Hunter College
  John Jay College of Criminal
    Justice
  La Guardia Community
    College
  Lehman College
  Medgar Evers College
  New York City Technical
    College
  Queens College
  Queensborough Community
    College
  York College
Clinton Community College
Colgate University
College for Human Services
College of Insurance
College of Mount St. Vincent
College of New Rochelle
  New Rochelle
  School of New Resources

College of St. Rose
Columbia University
  Columbia College
  School of Engineering and
    Applied Science
  School of General Studies
Columbia-Greene Community
  College
Community College of the Finger
  Lakes
Concordia College
Cooper Union
Cornell University
Corning Community College
Culinary Institute of America
Daemen College
Dominican College of Blauvelt
Dowling College
Dutchess Community College
D'Youville College
Elmira College
Erie Community College
  City Campus
  North Campus
  South Campus
Eugene Lang College/New School
  for Social Research
Fashion Institute of Technology
Five Towns College
Fordham University
Fulton-Montgomery Community
  College
Genesee Community College
Hartwick College
Herkimer County Community
  College
Hilbert College
Hobart College
Hofstra University
Houghton College
Hudson Valley Community College
Iona College
Ithaca College
Jamestown Community College
Jefferson Community College
Katharine Gibbs School: New York
Keuka College
King's College
Kol Yaakov Torah Center
Laboratory Institute of
  Merchandising
Le Moyne College
Long Island University
  Brooklyn Campus
  C. W. Post Campus
  Southampton Campus
Manhattan College
Manhattanville College
Maria College
Marist College
Marymount College
Marymount Manhattan College
Mater Dei College
Medaille College
Mercy College
Mohawk Valley Community College
Molloy College
Monroe College
Monroe Community College
Mount St. Mary College
Nassau Community College
Nazareth College of Rochester
New York Institute of Technology
New York University
Niagara County Community College
Niagara University
North Country Community College
Nyack College
Onondaga Community College
Orange County Community College
Pace University
  College of White Plains
  New York
Paul Smith's College

Pratt Institute
Rensselaer Polytechnic Institute
Roberts Wesleyan College
Rochester Institute of Technology
Rockland Community College
Russell Sage College
Sage Junior College of Albany, A
  Division of Russell Sage College
St. Bonaventure University
St. Francis College
St. John Fisher College
St. John's University
St. Joseph's College
  Brooklyn
  Suffolk Campus
St. Lawrence University
St. Thomas Aquinas College
Sarah Lawrence College
School of Visual Arts
Siena College
Skidmore College
State University of New York
  Albany
  Binghamton
  Buffalo
  Purchase
  Stony Brook
  College of Agriculture and
    Technology at Cobleskill
  College of Agriculture and
    Technology at Morrisville
  College at Brockport
  College at Buffalo
  College at Cortland
  College of Environmental
    Science and Forestry
  College at Fredonia
  College at Geneseo
  College at New Paltz
  College at Old Westbury
  College at Oneonta
  College at Plattsburgh
  College at Potsdam
  College of Technology at
    Alfred
  College of Technology at
    Canton
  College of Technology at Delhi
  Empire State College
  Health Sciences Center at
    Stony Brook
  Institute of Technology at
    Utica/Rome
  Maritime College
  Oswego
Suffolk County Community College
  Eastern Campus
  Selden
Sullivan County Community
  College
Syracuse University
Tobe-Coburn School for Fashion
  Careers
Touro College
Trocaire College
Ulster County Community College
Union College
United States Merchant Marine
  Academy
University of Rochester
Utica College of Syracuse
  University
Vassar College
Villa Maria College of Buffalo
Wagner College
Webb Institute of Naval
  Architecture
Wells College
Westchester Business Institute
Westchester Community College
William Smith College
Yeshiva University

North Carolina

Alamance Community College
Anson Community College
Appalachian State University
Asheville Buncombe Technical
  Community College
Barber-Scotia College
Barton College
Beaufort County Community
  College
Belmont Abbey College
Bennett College
Blue Ridge Community College
Brunswick Community College
Caldwell Community College and
  Technical Institute
Campbell University
Carteret Community College
Catawba College
Catawba Valley Community College
Cecils College
Central Carolina Community
  College
Central Piedmont Community
  College
Chowan College
Cleveland Community College
Coastal Carolina Community
  College
Craven Community College
Davidson County Community
  College
Duke University
Durham Technical Community
  College
East Carolina University
East Coast Bible College
Elizabeth City State University
Elon College
Fayetteville State University
Forsyth Technical Community
  College
Gardner-Webb College
Greensboro College
Guilford College
Guilford Technical Community
  College
Haywood Community College
High Point University
James Sprunt Community College
John Wesley College
Johnson C. Smith University
Johnston Community College
Lees-McRae College
Lenoir-Rhyne College
Livingstone College
Mars Hill College
Martin Community College
Mayland Community College
McDowell Technical Community
  College
Meredith College
Methodist College
Montreat-Anderson College
Mount Olive College
North Carolina Agricultural and
  Technical State University
North Carolina Central University
North Carolina School of the Arts
North Carolina State University
North Carolina Wesleyan College
Pamlico Community College
Peace College
Pembroke State University
Pfeiffer College
Piedmont Bible College
Piedmont Community College
Pitt Community College
Queens College
Roanoke Bible College
St. Andrews Presbyterian College
St. Augustine's College
St. Mary's College
Salem College

Sampson Community College
Sandhills Community College
Southeastern Community College
Southwestern Community College
Tri-County Community College
University of North Carolina
 Asheville
 Chapel Hill
 Charlotte
 Greensboro
 Wilmington
Vance-Granville Community
 College
Wake Forest University
Warren Wilson College
Wayne Community College
Western Carolina University
Western Piedmont Community
 College
Wilson Technical Community
 College
Wingate College
Winston-Salem State University

North Dakota

Bismarck State College
Dickinson State University
Jamestown College
Mayville State University
Minot State University
North Dakota State University
 Bottineau and Institute of
  Forestry
 Fargo
Trinity Bible College
Turtle Mountain Community
 College
University of Mary
University of North Dakota
 Grand Forks
 Lake Region
 Williston
Valley City State University

Ohio

Antioch College
Art Academy of Cincinnati
Ashland University
Baldwin-Wallace College
Bluffton College
Bowling Green State University
 Bowling Green
 Firelands College
Capital University
Case Western Reserve University
Cedarville College
Central State University
Chatfield College
Cincinnati Bible College and
 Seminary
Cincinnati College of Mortuary
 Science
Cincinnati Metropolitan College
Circleville Bible College
Clark State Community College
Cleveland College of Jewish Studies
Cleveland Institute of Art
Cleveland State University
College of Mount St. Joseph
College of Wooster
Columbus College of Art and
 Design
Columbus State Community College
Cuyahoga Community College:
 Metropolitan Campus
Davis Junior College of Business
Defiance College
Denison University
Dyke College
Edison State Community College
ETI Technical College
Franciscan University of
 Steubenville
Franklin University

Heidelberg College
Hiram College
Hocking Technical College
Jefferson Technical College
John Carroll University
Kent State University
 Ashtabula Regional Campus
 East Liverpool Regional
  Campus
 Kent
 Salem Regional Campus
 Tuscarawas Campus
Lake Erie College
Lourdes College
Malone College
Marietta College
Miami University: Oxford Campus
Miami-Jacobs College
Mount Union College
Mount Vernon Nazarene College
Muskingum Area Technical College
Muskingum College
Northwest Technical College
Notre Dame College of Ohio
Oberlin College
Ohio Dominican College
Ohio Institute of Photography
Ohio Northern University
Ohio State University
 Agricultural Technical Institute
 Columbus Campus
Ohio University
 Athens
 Chillicothe Campus
Ohio Valley Business College
Ohio Wesleyan University
Otterbein College
Owens Technical College
 Findlay Campus
 Toledo
Shawnee State University
Sinclair Community College
Southern Ohio College
Southern State Community College
Stark Technical College
Terra Technical College
Tiffin University
Union Institute
University of Akron
University of Cincinnati
 Access Colleges
 Cincinnati
 Clermont College
 Raymond Walters College
University of Dayton
University of Findlay
University of Rio Grande
University of Toledo
Urbana University
Ursuline College
Virginia Marti College of Fashion
 and Art
Walsh College
Washington State Community
 College
Wilberforce University
Wilmington College
Wittenberg University
Wright State University
 Dayton
 Lake Campus
Xavier University
Youngstown State University

Oklahoma

Bartlesville Wesleyan College
Connors State College
East Central University
Eastern Oklahoma State College
Hillsdale Free Will Baptist College
Langston University
Mid-America Bible College
Northeastern State University
Oklahoma Baptist University

Oklahoma Christian University of
 Science and Arts
Oklahoma City University
Oklahoma Junior College
Oklahoma State University
 Stillwater
 Technical Branch: Okmulgee
Oral Roberts University
Phillips University
Redlands Community College
Rose State College
Southeastern Oklahoma State
 University
Southwestern College of Christian
 Ministries
Southwestern Oklahoma State
 University
Tulsa Junior College
University of Central Oklahoma
University of Oklahoma
 Health Sciences Center
 Norman
University of Tulsa

Oregon

Bassist College
Central Oregon Community College
Clackamas Community College
Concordia College
Eastern Oregon State College
Eugene Bible College
George Fox College
Lane Community College
Lewis and Clark College
Linfield College
Marylhurst College
Mount Hood Community College
Northwest Christian College
Oregon Institute of Technology
Oregon State University
Pacific Northwest College of Art
Pacific University
Portland Community College
Portland State University
Reed College
Southwestern Oregon Community
 College
Umpqua Community College
University of Oregon
 Eugene
 Robert Donald Clark Honors
  College
University of Portland
Warner Pacific College
Western Baptist College
Western Oregon State College
Willamette University

Pennsylvania

Academy of the New Church
Albright College
Allegheny College
Allentown College of St. Francis de
 Sales
Alvernia College
Art Institute of Pittsburgh
Baptist Bible College of
 Pennsylvania
Beaver College
Berean Institute
Bloomsburg University of
 Pennsylvania
Bryn Mawr College
Bucknell University
Bucks County Community College
Butler County Community College
Cabrini College
California University of
 Pennsylvania
Carlow College
Carnegie Mellon University
Cedar Crest College
Central Pennsylvania Business
 School

Chatham College
Chestnut Hill College
Cheyney University of Pennsylvania
Clarion University of Pennsylvania
College Misericordia
Community College of Beaver
 County
Community College of Philadelphia
Delaware County Community
 College
Delaware Valley College
Dickinson College
DuBois Business College
Duquesne University
East Stroudsburg University of
 Pennsylvania
Eastern College
Edinboro University of
 Pennsylvania
Elizabethtown College
Franklin and Marshall College
Gannon University
Geneva College
Gettysburg College
Gratz College
Grove City College
Gwynedd-Mercy College
Harcum Junior College
Harrisburg Area Community
 College
Haverford College
Holy Family College
Hussian School of Art
Immaculata College
Indiana University of Pennsylvania
Johnson Technical Institute
Juniata College
Keystone Junior College
King's College
Kutztown University of
 Pennsylvania
La Roche College
La Salle University
Lafayette College
Lancaster Bible College
Lebanon Valley College of
 Pennsylvania
Lehigh University
Lincoln University
Lock Haven University of
 Pennsylvania
Luzerne County Community
 College
Lycoming College
Manor Junior College
Mansfield University of
 Pennsylvania
Marywood College
Mercyhurst College
Messiah College
Millersville University of
 Pennsylvania
Montgomery County Community
 College
Moore College of Art and Design
Moravian College
Mount Aloysius College
Muhlenberg College
Northampton County Area
 Community College
Peirce Junior College
Penn State University Park Campus
Pennsylvania College of Technology
Pennsylvania Institute of
 Technology
Philadelphia College of Bible
Philadelphia College of Pharmacy
 and Science
Philadelphia College of Textiles and
 Science
Point Park College
Reading Area Community College
Rosemont College
St. Charles Borromeo Seminary

St. Francis College
St. Joseph's University
St. Vincent College
Seton Hill College
Shippensburg University of
 Pennsylvania
Slippery Rock University of
 Pennsylvania
Spring Garden College
Susquehanna University
Swarthmore College
Temple University
Thiel College
Thomas Jefferson University:
 College of Allied Health Sciences
Tracey-Warner School
University of the Arts
University of Pennsylvania
University of Pittsburgh
 Bradford
 Greensburg
 Johnstown
 Pittsburgh
University of Scranton
Ursinus College
Valley Forge Christian College
Villanova University
Washington and Jefferson College
Waynesburg College
West Chester University of
 Pennsylvania
Westminster College
Westmoreland County Community
 College
Widener University
Wilkes University
Wilson College
York College of Pennsylvania

Puerto Rico

American University of Puerto Rico
Inter American University of Puerto
 Rico
 Arecibo Campus
 Metropolitan Campus
 San German Campus
Pontifical Catholic University of
 Puerto Rico
Puerto Rico Junior College
Universidad Adventista de las
 Antillas
University of Puerto Rico
 Humacao University College
 La Montana Regional College
 Mayaguez Campus
 Medical Sciences Campus
 Ponce Technological
 University College
 Rio Piedras Campus
University of the Sacred Heart

Rhode Island

Brown University
Bryant College
Community College of Rhode
 Island
Johnson & Wales University
New England Institute of
 Technology
Providence College
Rhode Island College
Rhode Island School of Design
Roger Williams College
Salve Regina University
University of Rhode Island

South Carolina

Aiken Technical College
Anderson College
Benedict College
Central Wesleyan College
Charleston Southern University
Claflin College
Coker College

College of Charleston
Columbia Bible College and
 Seminary
Columbia College
Columbia Junior College of Business
Converse College
Denmark Technical College
Erskine College
Florence-Darlington Technical
 College
Francis Marion College
Furman University
Horry-Georgetown Technical
 College
Lander College
Limestone College
Morris College
Newberry College
Presbyterian College
South Carolina State College
Sumter Area Technical College
Technical College of the
 Lowcountry
Trident Technical College
University of South Carolina
 Aiken
 Coastal Carolina College
 Columbia
 Lancaster
 Union
Voorhees College
Winthrop University
Wofford College

South Dakota

Augustana College
Black Hills State University
Dakota State University
Dakota Wesleyan University
Huron University
Kilian Community College
Mitchell Vocational Technical
 Institute
Mount Marty College
National College
Northern State University
Presentation College
Sinte Gleska College
Sioux Falls College
South Dakota State University
University of South Dakota
Western Dakota Vocational
 Technical Institute

Tennessee

Austin Peay State University
Belmont University
Bethel College
Bristol University
Carson-Newman College
Chattanooga State Technical
 Community College
Christian Brothers University
Cleveland State Community College
Crichton College
David Lipscomb University
Dyersburg State Community
 College
East Tennessee State University
Fisk University
Free Will Baptist Bible College
Freed-Hardeman University
Hiwassee College
Jackson State Community College
Johnson Bible College
King College
Knoxville Business College
Knoxville College
Lambuth University
LeMoyne-Owen College
Lincoln Memorial University
Maryville College
McKenzie College
Memphis College of Art

Memphis State University
Middle Tennessee State University
Milligan College
O'More College of Design
Pellissippi State Technical
 Community College
Rhodes College
Roane State Community College
Shelby State Community College
Southern College of Seventh-day
 Adventists
Tennessee Technological University
Tennessee Temple University
Tennessee Wesleyan College
Tomlinson College
Trevecca Nazarene College
Tusculum College
Union University
University of the South
University of Tennessee
 Chattanooga
 Knoxville
 Martin
Vanderbilt University
William Jennings Bryan College

Texas

Alvin Community College
Angelina College
Angelo State University
Austin College
Austin Community College
Baptist Missionary Association
 Theological Seminary
Bauder Fashion College
Baylor College of Dentistry
Baylor University
Bee County College
Brazosport College
Central Texas College
Collin County Community College
 District
Concordia Lutheran College
Corpus Christi State University
Dallas Baptist University
Dallas Christian College
Del Mar College
East Texas Baptist University
East Texas State University
El Centro College
El Paso Community College
Hardin-Simmons University
Houston Baptist University
Houston Community College
Howard Payne University
Huston-Tillotson College
Incarnate Word College
Institute for Christian Studies
Kilgore College
Lamar University—Beaumont
Lee College
LeTourneau University
Lubbock Christian University
McLennan Community College
McMurry University
Midland College
Midwestern State University
Miss Wade's Fashion
 Merchandising College
Navarro College
North Lake College
Northwood Institute: Texas Campus
Our Lady of the Lake University of
 San Antonio
Paul Quinn College
Prairie View A&M University
Rice University
Richland College
St. Edward's University
St. Mary's University
St. Philip's College
Sam Houston State University
San Antonio Art Institute
San Antonio College

San Jacinto College: Central
 Campus
Schreiner College
Southern Methodist University
Southwest Texas State University
Southwestern Adventist College
Southwestern Assemblies of God
 College
Southwestern Christian College
Southwestern University
Stephen F. Austin State University
Sul Ross State University
Texarkana College
Texas A&I University
Texas A&M University
Texas Christian University
Texas Lutheran College
Texas Southern University
Texas State Technical College
 Harlingen
 Sweetwater
Texas Tech University
Texas Wesleyan University
Texas Woman's University
Trinity University
Trinity Valley Community College
University of Central Texas
University of Dallas
University of Houston
 Clear Lake
 Downtown
 Houston
University of Mary Hardin-Baylor
University of North Texas
University of St. Thomas
University of Texas
 Austin
 Dallas
 El Paso
 Health Science Center at
 Houston
 Health Science Center at San
 Antonio
 Medical Branch at Galveston
 Pan American
 Permian Basin
 San Antonio
 Southwestern Medical Center
 at Dallas Southwestern
 Allied Health Sciences
 School
 Tyler
Vernon Regional Junior College
Wayland Baptist University
West Texas State University
Western Texas College
Wiley College

Utah

Brigham Young University
Dixie College
LDS Business College
Phillips Junior College: Salt Lake
 City Campus
Southern Utah University
University of Utah
Utah State University
Utah Valley Community College
Weber State University
Westminster College of Salt Lake
 City

Vermont

Bennington College
Burlington College
Castleton State College
Champlain College
College of St. Joseph in Vermont
Community College of Vermont
Goddard College
Green Mountain College
Johnson State College
Lyndon State College
Marlboro College

Middlebury College
New England Culinary Institute
Norwich University
St. Michael's College
School for International Training
Southern Vermont College
Sterling College
Trinity College of Vermont
University of Vermont
Vermont Technical College

Virginia

Averett College
Blue Ridge Community College
Bluefield College
Bridgewater College
Central Virginia Community College
Christendom College
Christopher Newport College
Clinch Valley College of the
    University of Virginia
College of Health Sciences
College of William and Mary
Commonwealth College
Dabney S. Lancaster Community
    College
Eastern Mennonite College
Emory and Henry College
Ferrum College
George Mason University
Hampden-Sydney College
Hampton University
Hollins College
James Madison University
John Tyler Community College
Liberty University
Longwood College
Lynchburg College
Mary Baldwin College
Mary Washington College
Marymount University
Mountain Empire Community
    College
National Business College
Norfolk State University
Northern Virginia Community
    College
Old Dominion University
Patrick Henry Community College
Paul D. Camp Community College
Radford University
Randolph-Macon College
Randolph-Macon Woman's College
Roanoke College
St. Paul's College
Shenandoah University
Southside Virginia Community
    College
Southwest Virginia Community
    College
Strayer College
Sweet Briar College
Tidewater Community College
University of Richmond
University of Virginia
Virginia Commonwealth University
Virginia Highlands Community
    College
Virginia Intermont College
Virginia Polytechnic Institute and
    State University
Virginia State University
Virginia Union University
Virginia Wesleyan College
Washington and Lee University
Wytheville Community College

Washington

Art Institute of Seattle
Central Washington University
Centralia College
City University
Clark College

Columbia Basin College
Cornish College of the Arts
Eastern Washington University
Edmonds Community College
Everett Community College
Evergreen State College
Gonzaga University
Griffin College
Heritage College
Lutheran Bible Institute of Seattle
Northwest College of the
    Assemblies of God
Northwest Indian College
Pacific Lutheran University
Peninsula College
Pierce College
Puget Sound Christian College
St. Martin's College
Seattle Central Community College
Seattle Pacific University
Seattle University
Shoreline Community College
Skagit Valley College
South Puget Sound Community
    College
Spokane Community College
Tacoma Community College
University of Puget Sound
University of Washington
Walla Walla College
Walla Walla Community College
Washington State University
Wenatchee Valley College
Western Washington University
Whatcom Community College
Whitman College
Whitworth College

West Virginia

Alderson-Broaddus College
Appalachian Bible College
Bethany College
Bluefield State College
Concord College
Davis and Elkins College
Glenville State College
Marshall University
Salem-Teikyo University
Shepherd College
University of Charleston
West Liberty State College
West Virginia Institute of
    Technology
West Virginia Northern Community
    College
West Virginia State College
West Virginia University
    Morgantown
    Parkersburg
West Virginia Wesleyan College
Wheeling Jesuit College

Wisconsin

Alverno College
Beloit College
Cardinal Stritch College
Carroll College
Carthage College
Chippewa Valley Technical College
Concordia University Wisconsin
Edgewood College
Fox Valley Technical College
Lakeland College
Lawrence University
Madison Area Technical College
Maranatha Baptist Bible College
Marian College of Fond du Lac
Marquette University
Mid-State Technical College
Milwaukee College of Business
Milwaukee Institute of Art &
    Design
Milwaukee School of Engineering
Moraine Park Technical College

Mount Mary College
Mount Senario College
Northeast Wisconsin Technical
    College
Northland College
Ripon College
St. Norbert College
Silver Lake College
Stratton College
University of Wisconsin
    Eau Claire
    Green Bay
    La Crosse
    Madison
    Milwaukee
    Oshkosh
    Parkside
    Platteville
    River Falls
    Stevens Point
    Stout
    Superior
    Whitewater
University of Wisconsin Center
    Fox Valley
    Marathon County
    Marshfield/Wood County
    Washington County
Viterbo College
Western Wisconsin Technical
    College
Wisconsin Indianhead Technical
    College
Wisconsin Lutheran College

Wyoming

Casper College
Eastern Wyoming College
Laramie County Community
    College
Northwest College
Sheridan College
University of Wyoming
Western Wyoming Community
    College

American Samoa, Caroline Islands, Guam, Marianas, Virgin Islands

Guam Community College
Micronesian Occupational College
Northern Marianas College
University of Guam
University of the Virgin Islands

Canada

McGill University

France

American University of Paris

Switzerland

American College of Switzerland
Franklin College: Switzerland

Liberal arts/engineering programs

Alabama

Alabama Agricultural and
    Mechanical University
Alabama State University
Auburn University
Birmingham-Southern College
Huntingdon College
Livingston University
Mobile College
Samford University
Spring Hill College
Stillman College
Talladega College

Tuskegee University

Arizona

Arizona State University
Grand Canyon University
Northern Arizona University

Arkansas

Hendrix College
John Brown University
Ouachita Baptist University
University of Arkansas
University of the Ozarks

California

American Armenian International
    College
Azusa Pacific University
Biola University
California Institute of Technology
California Lutheran University
California State University: Long
    Beach
Claremont McKenna College
Holy Names College
Mills College
Occidental College
Pacific Union College
Pitzer College
Pomona College
St. Mary's College of California
Scripps College
Stanford University
University of California: Santa Cruz
University of La Verne
University of Redlands
University of San Diego
University of Southern California
Westmont College
Whittier College

Colorado

Colorado College
Colorado State University
Fort Lewis College
Regis College of Regis University
University of Denver

Connecticut

Connecticut College
Fairfield University
University of Bridgeport
University of Hartford
Wesleyan University
Western Connecticut State
    University

Delaware

Delaware State College
University of Delaware

District of Columbia

Catholic University of America
Gallaudet University
George Washington University
Georgetown University

Florida

Barry University
Bethune-Cookman College
Eckerd College
Florida Agricultural and Mechanical
    University
Florida Atlantic University
Florida Institute of Technology
Florida Southern College
Jacksonville University
Rollins College
Stetson University

Georgia

Agnes Scott College
Albany State College
Armstrong State College

Berry College
Clark Atlanta University
Columbus College
Covenant College
Emory University
Georgia College
LaGrange College
Morehouse College
Morris Brown College
North Georgia College
Oglethorpe University
Savannah State College
Spelman College
University of Georgia
Valdosta State College
Wesleyan College
West Georgia College

Hawaii

Hawaii Loa College

Idaho

Albertson College
Northwest Nazarene College

Illinois

Aero-Space Institute
Augustana College
De Paul University
Eastern Illinois University
Eureka College
Greenville College
Illinois Benedictine College
Illinois College
Illinois Wesleyan University
Knox College
Lake Forest College
Loyola University of Chicago
MacMurray College
Monmouth College
North Central College
North Park College and Theological
   Seminary
Northern Illinois University
Principia College
Quincy College
Rockford College
Roosevelt University
University of Illinois at Urbana-
   Champaign
Wheaton College

Indiana

Bethel College
Butler University
DePauw University
Earlham College
Franklin College
Goshen College
Grace College
Hanover College
Manchester College
Purdue University
St. Joseph's College
St. Mary's College
Taylor University
University of Evansville
University of Notre Dame
Valparaiso University
Wabash College

Iowa

Briar Cliff College
Buena Vista College
Central College
Clarke College
Coe College
Cornell College
Drake University
Grinnell College
Iowa Wesleyan College
Luther College
Morningside College
St. Ambrose University

Simpson College
Teikyo Westmar University
University of Iowa
Wartburg College

Kansas

Baker University
Benedictine College
Bethany College
Bethel College
Fort Hays State University
Kansas Newman College
Kansas Wesleyan University
Ottawa University
Pittsburg State University
University of Kansas
Washburn University of Topeka

Kentucky

Asbury College
Berea College
Campbellsville College
Centre College
Cumberland College
Eastern Kentucky University
Georgetown College
Kentucky State University
Kentucky Wesleyan College
Morehead State University
Thomas More College
Transylvania University
Union College

Louisiana

Centenary College of Louisiana
Dillard University
Grantham College of Engineering
McNeese State University
Southern University and
   Agricultural and Mechanical
   College
Tulane University
University of New Orleans
Xavier University of Louisiana

Maine

Bates College
Bowdoin College
Colby College
University of Maine
   Farmington
   Orono
   Presque Isle

Maryland

College of Notre Dame of
   Maryland
Coppin State College
Frostburg State University
Hood College
Johns Hopkins University
Loyola College in Maryland
Mount St. Mary's College
St. Mary's College of Maryland
Salisbury State University
Towson State University
University of Maryland: Eastern
   Shore
Washington College
Western Maryland College

Massachusetts

Anna Maria College for Men and
   Women
Atlantic Union College
Boston University
Clark University
College of the Holy Cross
Eastern Nazarene College
Emmanuel College
Gordon College
Harvard and Radcliffe Colleges
Mount Holyoke College
Regis College

Simmons College
Simon's Rock College of Bard
Suffolk University
Tufts University
University of Massachusetts at
   Lowell
Williams College
Worcester Polytechnic Institute
Worcester State College

Michigan

Adrian College
Albion College
Alma College
GMI Engineering & Management
   Institute
Hillsdale College
Hope College
Kalamazoo College
Madonna University
Michigan State University
Michigan Technological University
Oakland University
University of Detroit Mercy
University of Michigan

Minnesota

Augsburg College
Bethel College
Carleton College
College of St. Benedict
College of St. Scholastica
Gustavus Adolphus College
Hamline University
Macalester College
Mankato State University
St. John's University
St. Mary's College of Minnesota
St. Olaf College
University of Minnesota: Twin
   Cities
University of St. Thomas

Mississippi

Millsaps College
Mississippi College
Mississippi University for Women
Rust College
Tougaloo College

Missouri

Central Methodist College
Central Missouri State University
College of the Ozarks
Culver-Stockton College
Drury College
Evangel College
Lindenwood College
Maryville University
Missouri Baptist College
Missouri Southern State College
Rockhurst College
St. Louis University
Southwest Baptist University
Stephens College
Washington University
Webster University
Westminster College
William Jewell College
William Woods College

Montana

Carroll College
Montana College of Mineral
   Science and Technology
Rocky Mountain College

Nebraska

Doane College
Hastings College

New Hampshire

Dartmouth College
New England College

St. Anselm College

New Jersey

Drew University
Georgian Court College
Glassboro State College
New Jersey Institute of Technology
Rutgers—The State University of
   New Jersey
      Camden College of Arts and
         Sciences
      College of Engineering
      Cook College
      Douglass College
      Livingston College
      Newark College of Arts and
         Sciences
      Rutgers College
      University College Camden
Seton Hall University
Stevens Institute of Technology
Stockton State College
Upsala College

New Mexico

New Mexico Institute of Mining
   and Technology

New York

Adelphi University
Alfred University
Bard College
Barnard College
Canisius College
City University of New York
   Brooklyn College
   Queens College
Clarkson University
Colgate University
College of Mount St. Vincent
College of St. Rose
Columbia University
   Columbia College
   School of Engineering and
      Applied Science
   School of General Studies
Cornell University
Dominican College of Blauvelt
Fordham University
Hamilton College
Hartwick College
Hobart College
Hofstra University
Houghton College
Iona College
Ithaca College
Keuka College
Le Moyne College
Manhattanville College
New York University
Pace University
   College of White Plains
   New York
   Pleasantville/Briarcliff
Roberts Wesleyan College
Russell Sage College
St. John Fisher College
St. John's University
St. Lawrence University
St. Thomas Aquinas College
Siena College
Skidmore College
State University of New York
   Binghamton
   College at Brockport
   College at Buffalo
   College at Cortland
   College at Fredonia
   College at Geneseo
   College at New Paltz
   College at Oneonta
   College at Plattsburgh
   College at Potsdam
   Oswego

Syracuse University
Union College
University of Rochester
Utica College of Syracuse
  University
Vassar College
Wells College
William Smith College
Yeshiva University

North Carolina
Appalachian State University
Belmont Abbey College
Bennett College
Campbell University
Davidson College
Duke University
Elon College
Guilford College
Johnson C. Smith University
Lenoir-Rhyne College
Livingstone College
Meredith College
North Carolina State University
Pfeiffer College
St. Andrews Presbyterian College
St. Augustine's College
Salem College
University of North Carolina at
  Asheville
Wake Forest University
Warren Wilson College
Wingate College

North Dakota
Jamestown College

Ohio
Antioch College
Ashland University
Baldwin-Wallace College
Capital University
Case Western Reserve University
Cedarville College
Central State University
College of Wooster
Denison University
Heidelberg College
Hiram College
John Carroll University
Kenyon College
Marietta College
Miami University: Oxford Campus
Mount Union College
Muskingum College
Notre Dame College of Ohio
Oberlin College
Ohio Northern University
Ohio Wesleyan University
University of Findlay
Wilberforce University
Wittenberg University
Xavier University

Oklahoma
Oklahoma Baptist University
Oklahoma Christian University of
  Science and Arts
Phillips University

Oregon
Eastern Oregon State College
Lewis and Clark College
Linfield College
Pacific University
Reed College
University of Oregon
Willamette University

Pennsylvania
Albright College
Allegheny College
Beaver College

Bloomsburg University of
  Pennsylvania
Bryn Mawr College
Bucknell University
California University of
  Pennsylvania
Cedar Crest College
Clarion University of Pennsylvania
Dickinson College
Duquesne University
East Stroudsburg University of
  Pennsylvania
Eastern College
Elizabethtown College
Franklin and Marshall College
Gannon University
Gettysburg College
Haverford College
Indiana University of Pennsylvania
Juniata College
Kutztown University of
  Pennsylvania
Lafayette College
Lebanon Valley College of
  Pennsylvania
Lehigh University
Lincoln University
Lock Haven University of
  Pennsylvania
Lycoming College
Mansfield University of
  Pennsylvania
Millersville University of
  Pennsylvania
Moravian College
Muhlenberg College
Penn State University Park Campus
St. Francis College
St. Vincent College
Seton Hill College
Shippensburg University of
  Pennsylvania
Slippery Rock University of
  Pennsylvania
Susquehanna University
Swarthmore College
Thiel College
University of Pennsylvania
University of Pittsburgh
University of Scranton
Ursinus College
Washington and Jefferson College
Waynesburg College
West Chester University of
  Pennsylvania
Westminster College
York College of Pennsylvania

Puerto Rico
Caribbean University

Rhode Island
Johnson & Wales University
Providence College

South Carolina
Benedict College
Charleston Southern University
College of Charleston
Erskine College
Francis Marion College
Furman University
Lander College
Newberry College
Presbyterian College
Wofford College

South Dakota
Augustana College
Mount Marty College
Sioux Falls College

Tennessee
Belmont University
Bethel College
Carson-Newman College
David Lipscomb University
Fisk University
Freed-Hardeman University
King College
Knoxville College
Lambuth University
LeMoyne-Owen College
Maryville College
Middle Tennessee State University
Union University
University of the South
Vanderbilt University

Texas
Angelo State University
Austin College
Huston-Tillotson College
Jarvis Christian College
Lubbock Christian University
Our Lady of the Lake University of
  San Antonio
Rice University
St. Mary's University
Schreiner College
Southwest Texas State University
Southwestern University
Texas Wesleyan University
University of Houston: Clear Lake
University of St. Thomas
University of Texas at Austin
Wayland Baptist University

Vermont
Castleton State College
Middlebury College
St. Michael's College

Virginia
Bridgewater College
College of William and Mary
Emory and Henry College
Hampden-Sydney College
Hampton University
Hollins College
Longwood College
Lynchburg College
Old Dominion University
Randolph-Macon College
Randolph-Macon Woman's College
Roanoke College
Sweet Briar College
Virginia Commonwealth University
Virginia Union University
Washington and Lee University

Washington
Pacific Lutheran University
University of Puget Sound
Western Washington University
Whitman College

West Virginia
Bethany College
West Virginia Institute of
  Technology
Wheeling Jesuit College

Wisconsin
Alverno College
Beloit College
Carroll College
Carthage College
Concordia University Wisconsin
Lakeland College
Lawrence University
Milwaukee School of Engineering
Northland College
Ripon College
University of Wisconsin: Superior

Arab Republic of Egypt
American University in Cairo

Liberal arts/forestry programs

Alabama
Samford University

Alaska
Sheldon Jackson College

Arizona
Northern Arizona University

Arkansas
University of Arkansas
  Fayetteville
  Monticello

Colorado
Colorado College

Florida
Florida Southern College
Rollins College
Stetson University

Georgia
Columbus College
Mercer University

Illinois
Illinois Wesleyan University
Knox College
Lake Forest College

Indiana
Butler University
Earlham College
Franklin College

Iowa
Cornell College
Iowa Wesleyan College
Luther College

Kansas
Baker University
Kansas State University
Ottawa University

Louisiana
Centenary College of Louisiana

Maine
Unity College
University of Maine
  Farmington
  Presque Isle

Maryland
University of Maryland: Eastern
  Shore
Western Maryland College

Michigan
Albion College
Alma College
Eastern Michigan University
Michigan Technological University
University of Michigan

Minnesota
University of Minnesota: Twin
  Cities

Missouri
William Jewell College

Nebraska
Doane College

New Jersey
Drew University
Upsala College

New York
Alfred University
Bard College
Canisius College
Le Moyne College
St. John Fisher College
Siena College
State University of New York
  College at Cortland
  College at Geneseo
  College at New Paltz
  College at Oneonta
  Oswego

North Carolina
Appalachian State University
Guilford College
High Point University
Lenoir-Rhyne College
North Carolina State University
University of North Carolina at
  Asheville
Wake Forest University
Warren Wilson College

Ohio
Baldwin-Wallace College
College of Wooster
Denison University
Heidelberg College
Hiram College
Kent State University
Marietta College
Miami University: Oxford Campus
Mount Vernon Nazarene College
Otterbein College
Walsh College
Wittenberg University
Youngstown State University

Oregon
Linfield College
Reed College

Pennsylvania
Albright College
Elizabethtown College
Franklin and Marshall College
Gettysburg College
Indiana University of Pennsylvania
Juniata College
Lebanon Valley College of
  Pennsylvania
Lycoming College
Moravian College
Muhlenberg College
St. Francis College
Susquehanna University
Thiel College

Rhode Island
Roger Williams College

South Carolina
Furman University
Presbyterian College

Tennessee
Middle Tennessee State University
University of the South

Texas
Stephen F. Austin State University

Vermont
Middlebury College

Virginia
Bridgewater College
College of William and Mary
Emory and Henry College
University of Richmond
Washington and Lee University

Washington
Western Washington University
Whitman College

West Virginia
Glenville State College

Wisconsin
Beloit College
Lawrence University
Mount Senario College
Northland College
Ripon College
University of Wisconsin: Superior

Liberal arts/health sciences programs

Alabama
Alabama Agricultural and
  Mechanical University
Faulkner University
Livingston University
Miles College
Mobile College
Samford University
Stillman College
Talladega College
University of Alabama in
  Birmingham

Alaska
University of Alaska Anchorage

Arizona
Northern Arizona University

Arkansas
Ouachita Baptist University
University of Central Arkansas

California
California State University
  Bakersfield
  Dominguez Hills
Chapman University
Pacific Union College
University of La Verne
Westmont College

Colorado
Colorado College
Denver Technical College

Connecticut
Quinnipiac College
University of Bridgeport
Wesleyan University

Florida
Florida Agricultural and Mechanical
  University
Rollins College
St. Leo College
Stetson University

Georgia
Albany State College
Berry College
Oglethorpe University
Shorter College
University of Georgia

Hawaii
University of Hawaii at Hilo

Illinois
Augustana College
Greenville College
Illinois College
Illinois Wesleyan University
Judson College
Knox College
Monmouth College
National-Louis University
North Central College
North Park College and Theological
  Seminary
Northeastern Illinois University
Olivet Nazarene University
Roosevelt University
Rosary College
Trinity Christian College
Wheaton College

Indiana
Ball State University
DePauw University
Earlham College
Franklin College
Goshen College
Indiana State University
Indiana University
  Bloomington
  South Bend
Manchester College
St. Joseph's College
Valparaiso University

Iowa
Briar Cliff College
Central College
Clarke College
Coe College
Cornell College
Grand View College
Grinnell College
Iowa Wesleyan College
Luther College
Morningside College
St. Ambrose University
Simpson College
Teikyo Westmar University
University of Iowa
Wartburg College
William Penn College

Kansas
Benedictine College
Emporia State University
Kansas Newman College
Kansas State University
Kansas Wesleyan University
Ottawa University
Southwestern College
University of Kansas Medical
  Center

Kentucky
Asbury College
Campbellsville College
Kentucky State University
Spalding University
Thomas More College
Union College
University of Louisville
Western Kentucky University

Louisiana
Centenary College of Louisiana
McNeese State University
Our Lady of Holy Cross College

Maine
University of Maine
  Farmington
  Presque Isle

University of New England
Westbrook College

Maryland
College of Notre Dame of
  Maryland
Frostburg State University
Goucher College
Johns Hopkins University
Salisbury State University
Washington College
Western Maryland College

Massachusetts
Atlantic Union College
Boston University
Forsyth School for Dental
  Hygienists
Gordon College
Massachusetts College of Pharmacy
  and Allied Health Sciences
Simmons College
Springfield College

Michigan
Albion College
Alma College
Calvin College
Hope College
Kalamazoo College
Marygrove College
Oakland University
St. Mary's College
Siena Heights College
University of Detroit Mercy
University of Michigan

Minnesota
Carleton College
College of St. Benedict
College of St. Catherine: St.
  Catherine Campus
Macalester College
Mankato State University
St. John's University
St. Mary's College of Minnesota
University of Minnesota: Twin
  Cities

Mississippi
Belhaven College
Blue Mountain College
Mississippi College
Rust College

Missouri
Avila College
Central Methodist College
College of the Ozarks
Culver-Stockton College
Deaconess College of Nursing
Drury College
Lindenwood College
Maryville University
Rockhurst College
Southwest Baptist University
Southwest Missouri State University
Stephens College
William Jewell College
William Woods College

Montana
Carroll College
Montana College of Mineral
  Science and Technology
Rocky Mountain College

Nebraska
Doane College
Nebraska Methodist College of
  Nursing and Allied Health
Peru State College

New Jersey

Caldwell College
College of St. Elizabeth
Rutgers—The State University of
New Jersey: Newark College of
Arts and Sciences
St. Peter's College
Stockton State College
University of Medicine and
Dentistry of New Jersey: School
of Health Related Professions
Upsala College

New Mexico

Western New Mexico University

New York

Canisius College
City University of New York
Brooklyn College
Hunter College
Clarkson University
Elmira College
Fordham University
Keuka College
Le Moyne College
Long Island University
Brooklyn Campus
C. W. Post Campus
Manhattanville College
Roberts Wesleyan College
St. Lawrence University
Siena College
State University of New York
Albany
Binghamton
College at Geneseo
College at New Paltz
College at Oneonta
Health Sciences Center at
Stony Brook
Oswego
Utica College of Syracuse
University
Yeshiva University

North Carolina

Appalachian State University
Barton College
Belmont Abbey College
Catawba College
Gardner-Webb College
Greensboro College
Guilford College
Lenoir-Rhyne College
Livingstone College
Mars Hill College
Meredith College
Salem College
University of North Carolina at
Asheville
Wake Forest University
Warren Wilson College

North Dakota

Jamestown College

Ohio

Bowling Green State University
Case Western Reserve University
Cedarville College
Denison University
Hiram College
Kent State University
Marietta College
Muskingum College
Ohio Wesleyan University
Otterbein College
University of Findlay
Walsh College
Wilberforce University
Wittenberg University

Oklahoma

Langston University
Southwestern Oklahoma State
University
University of Oklahoma Health
Sciences Center

Oregon

Concordia College
Eastern Oregon State College
Linfield College
Pacific University
Warner Pacific College

Pennsylvania

Bloomsburg University of
Pennsylvania
California University of
Pennsylvania
Cedar Crest College
Chestnut Hill College
East Stroudsburg University of
Pennsylvania
Elizabethtown College
Gannon University
Geneva College
Holy Family College
Indiana University of Pennsylvania
Juniata College
Lebanon Valley College of
Pennsylvania
Lock Haven University of
Pennsylvania
Lycoming College
Mansfield University of
Pennsylvania
Millersville University of
Pennsylvania
Moravian College
Muhlenberg College
Penn State University Park Campus
Point Park College
St. Francis College
St. Vincent College
Seton Hill College
Shippensburg University of
Pennsylvania
Susquehanna University
Thiel College
Thomas Jefferson University:
College of Allied Health Sciences
Villanova University
Washington and Jefferson College
Wilkes University

Puerto Rico

Pontifical Catholic University of
Puerto Rico

South Carolina

Charleston Southern University
College of Charleston
Erskine College
Furman University
Lander College
Newberry College
Presbyterian College
South Carolina State College
Wofford College

South Dakota

Augustana College
Black Hills State University
Northern State University

Tennessee

Austin Peay State University
Belmont University
Carson-Newman College
David Lipscomb University
East Tennessee State University
Freed-Hardeman University
Lambuth University
LeMoyne-Owen College

Maryville College
Middle Tennessee State University
Union University
University of Tennessee: Knoxville

Texas

Huston-Tillotson College
Lubbock Christian University
Midwestern State University
Texas Christian University
University of Mary Hardin-Baylor
University of St. Thomas
Wayland Baptist University

Vermont

Johnson State College
Middlebury College

Virginia

Averett College
Bluefield College
Christopher Newport College
Emory and Henry College
Hollins College
Longwood College
Lynchburg College
Randolph-Macon Woman's College
St. Paul's College

Washington

Eastern Washington University

West Virginia

Alderson-Broaddus College
Bluefield State College
Salem-Teikyo University
University of Charleston
Wheeling Jesuit College

Wisconsin

Beloit College
Carroll College
Carthage College
Columbia College of Nursing
Edgewood College
Lawrence University
Marian College of Fond du Lac
Ripon College
University of Wisconsin
Eau Claire
Green Bay

Semester at sea

Arizona

University of Arizona

California

Brooks Institute of Photography
California Lutheran University
Pitzer College
University of California: San Diego
University of San Diego

Colorado

University of Colorado
Boulder
Denver
University of Denver

Connecticut

Connecticut College
Fairfield University
Wesleyan University

Florida

Eckerd College
New College of the University of
South Florida

Indiana

DePauw University
Indiana University Bloomington
Wabash College

Iowa

Buena Vista College
Drake University

Kentucky

Murray State University

Maine

Bates College
Bowdoin College
Colby College
Maine Maritime Academy

Massachusetts

Aquinas College at Newton
Assumption College
Babson College
Boston University
Bradford College
Massachusetts Maritime Academy
Pine Manor College
Simmons College
Smith College
Tufts University
Wellesley College
Williams College

Michigan

Adrian College

Minnesota

Augsburg College
Hamline University

Missouri

Westminster College
William Woods College

New Hampshire

Colby-Sawyer College
Dartmouth College
University of New Hampshire

New Jersey

Drew University

New York

Bard College
Colgate University
Cornell University
Hobart College
Long Island University:
Southampton Campus
St. Lawrence University
Sarah Lawrence College
State University of New York
Maritime College
William Smith College

Ohio

Case Western Reserve University
Denison University
Marietta College
Mount Union College
Muskingum College
Ohio State University: Columbus
Campus
Otterbein College

Oklahoma

Oklahoma State University
University of Oklahoma
University of Tulsa

Oregon

Linfield College
University of Oregon
 Eugene
 Robert Donald Clark Honors
 College

Pennsylvania

Allegheny College
Franklin and Marshall College
Gettysburg College
Lafayette College
St. Francis College
University of Pennsylvania
University of Pittsburgh
 Bradford
 Greensburg
 Johnstown
 Pittsburgh
University of Scranton
Westminster College

Rhode Island

Bryant College

South Carolina

College of Charleston

Tennessee

University of the South

Texas

Texas A&M University
 College Station
 Galveston
Texas Christian University

Utah

University of Utah
Westminster College of Salt Lake
 City

Vermont

Castleton State College
Middlebury College

Virginia

Hampden-Sydney College
Lynchburg College
Mary Baldwin College
University of Richmond

Washington

Seattle University

West Virginia

Bethany College
West Virginia University

Student-designed major

Alabama

Auburn University at Montgomery
Birmingham-Southern College
Huntingdon College
John M. Patterson State Technical
 College
Lawson State Community College
Spring Hill College
Troy State University
University of Alabama
 Birmingham
 Tuscaloosa
University of South Alabama

Alaska

University of Alaska
 Anchorage
 Fairbanks
 Southeast

Arizona

American Indian Bible College
Arizona State University
Cochise College
Pima Community College
Prescott College
University of Arizona
Western International University

Arkansas

Arkansas College
Garland County Community
 College
Harding University
Hendrix College
John Brown University
University of Arkansas at Little
 Rock
University of the Ozarks

California

Academy of Art College
Antioch Southern California
 Los Angeles
 Santa Barbara
Armstrong College
Azusa Pacific University
California College of Arts and
 Crafts
California Institute of the Arts
California Institute of Technology
California Lutheran University
California State University
 Bakersfield
 Chico
 Dominguez Hills
 Fresno
 Fullerton
 Hayward
 Long Beach
 Los Angeles
 Northridge
 Sacramento
 San Bernardino
 Stanislaus
Chabot College
Christ College Irvine
Claremont McKenna College
College of Notre Dame
College of the Sequoias
Cuesta College
Dominican College of San Rafael
East Los Angeles College
Fresno Pacific College
Grossmont Community College
Harvey Mudd College
Holy Names College
Humboldt State University
Imperial Valley College
John F. Kennedy University
Los Angeles Pierce College
Loyola Marymount University
Mendocino College
Mills College
Mount St. Mary's College
New College of California
Occidental College
Pacific Christian College
Pacific Union College
Pepperdine University
Pitzer College
Pomona College
Saddleback College
San Diego City College
San Diego State University
San Francisco State University
San Jose State University
Santa Clara University
Scripps College
Simpson College
Sonoma State University
Stanford University

University of California
 Berkeley
 Davis
 Los Angeles
 Riverside
 San Diego
 Santa Barbara
 Santa Cruz
University of Judaism
University of La Verne
University of the Pacific
University of Redlands
University of San Francisco
University of Southern California
Westmont College
Whittier College
World College West
Yuba College

Colorado

Adams State College
Colorado Christian University
Colorado College
Fort Lewis College
Mesa State College
Metropolitan State College of
 Denver
Morgan Community College
Naropa Institute
Regis College of Regis University
University of Colorado
 Boulder
 Denver
University of Northern Colorado

Connecticut

Central Connecticut State
 University
Connecticut College
Eastern Connecticut State
 University
Middlesex Community College
Quinnipiac College
Sacred Heart University
St. Joseph College
Teikyo-Post University
Thames Valley State Technical
 College
Trinity College
University of Bridgeport
University of Connecticut
University of Hartford
University of New Haven
Wesleyan University
Western Connecticut State
 University
Yale University

Delaware

Delaware State College
University of Delaware

District of Columbia

American University
Catholic University of America
George Washington University
Georgetown University
Howard University
Mount Vernon College
Trinity College

Florida

Brevard Community College
Eckerd College
Flagler College
Florida Atlantic University
Florida Christian College
Florida Keys Community College
Fort Lauderdale College
Jacksonville University
Jones College
Lynn University
Miami-Dade Community College

New College of the University of
 South Florida
Okaloosa-Walton Community
 College
Orlando College
Rollins College
Stetson University
University of Central Florida
University of Florida
University of Miami
University of South Florida
Warner Southern College

Georgia

Agnes Scott College
Atlanta College of Art
Berry College
Brenau Women's College
Darton College
Emory University
Fort Valley State College
Georgia College
Georgia Institute of Technology
Georgia State University
Mercer University
 Atlanta
 Macon
Oglethorpe University
Shorter College
Spelman College
University of Georgia
Wesleyan College

Hawaii

Chaminade University of Honolulu
Hawaii Loa College
Hawaii Pacific University
University of Hawaii
 Hilo
 Manoa
 West Oahu

Idaho

Albertson College
Boise State University
Idaho State University
Lewis Clark State College
Northwest Nazarene College
University of Idaho

Illinois

Augustana College
Aurora University
Barat College
Blackburn College
Bradley University
Carl Sandburg College
Chicago State University
City Colleges of Chicago
 Chicago City-Wide College
 Olive-Harvey College
College of DuPage
College of Lake County
College of St. Francis
Columbia College
De Paul University
Eureka College
Governors State University
Greenville College
Highland Community College
Illinois Eastern Community
 Colleges
 Frontier Community College
 Lincoln Trail College
 Olney Central College
 Wabash Valley College
Illinois State University
Illinois Wesleyan University
Knox College
Lake Forest College
Lewis and Clark Community
 College
Lewis University
MacMurray College

McKendree College
Millikin University
Monmouth College
Morrison Institute of Technology
Morton College
North Central College
North Park College and Theological
 Seminary
Northeastern Illinois University
Northern Illinois University
Northwestern University
Olivet Nazarene University
Principia College
Quincy College
Rock Valley College
Rockford College
Roosevelt University
Rosary College
Sangamon State University
School of the Art Institute of
 Chicago
Southern Illinois University
 Carbondale
 Edwardsville
Springfield College in Illinois
Triton College
University of Chicago
University of Illinois
 Chicago
 Urbana-Champaign
Western Illinois University
Wheaton College

Indiana

Anderson University
Ball State University
Calumet College of St. Joseph
DePauw University
Earlham College
Goshen College
Hanover College
Indiana University
 Bloomington
 Northwest
 South Bend
Indiana University—Purdue
 University at Fort Wayne
Indiana Vocational Technical
 College: Northeast
Indiana Wesleyan University
Manchester College
Martin University
Purdue University
St. Joseph's College
St. Mary-of-the-Woods College
Taylor University
University of Notre Dame
University of Southern Indiana
Valparaiso University
Vincennes University

Iowa

Briar Cliff College
Buena Vista College
Central College
Clarke College
Coe College
Cornell College
Divine Word College
Drake University
Graceland College
Grand View College
Grinnell College
Iowa Wesleyan College
Kirkwood Community College
Loras College
Luther College
Morningside College
Mount Mercy College
Mount St. Clare College
North Iowa Area Community
 College
Northwestern College
St. Ambrose University

Simpson College
Teikyo Marycrest University
Teikyo Westmar University
University of Dubuque
University of Iowa
University of Northern Iowa
Wartburg College
William Penn College

Kansas

Allen County Community College
Benedictine College
Bethany College
Bethel College
Central College
Cowley County Community College
Dodge City Community College
Emporia State University
Friends University
Highland Community College
Kansas Wesleyan University
McPherson College
Ottawa University
Pittsburg State University
St. Mary College
Southwestern College
Sterling College
Tabor College
University of Kansas
Washburn University of Topeka
Wichita State University

Kentucky

Berea College
Brescia College
Centre College
Eastern Kentucky University
Georgetown College
Kentucky State University
Kentucky Wesleyan College
Morehead State University
Northern Kentucky University
Transylvania University
Union College
University of Kentucky
University of Louisville
Western Kentucky University

Louisiana

Centenary College of Louisiana
Louisiana College
Loyola University
Northwestern State University
Southeastern Louisiana University
Tulane University
University of New Orleans
University of Southwestern
 Louisiana

Maine

Bates College
Bowdoin College
Colby College
College of the Atlantic
Thomas College
Unity College
University of Maine
 Farmington
 Fort Kent
 Machias
 Orono
University of New England
University of Southern Maine

Maryland

Anne Arundel Community College
Chesapeake College
College of Notre Dame of
 Maryland
Columbia Union College
Goucher College
Hood College
Johns Hopkins University
Maryland Institute College of Art

Montgomery College
 Germantown Campus
 Rockville Campus
 Takoma Park Campus
Mount St. Mary's College
St. Mary's College of Maryland
Salisbury State University
Towson State University
University of Baltimore
University of Maryland
 Baltimore County
 College Park
Villa Julie College
Washington College
Western Maryland College

Massachusetts

American International College
Amherst College
Anna Maria College for Men and
 Women
Assumption College
Babson College
Bentley College
Berklee College of Music
Berkshire Community College
Boston College
Boston University
Bradford College
Brandeis University
Bridgewater State College
Clark University
College of the Holy Cross
Curry College
Dean Junior College
Elms College
Emerson College
Endicott College
Fitchburg State College
Framingham State College
Hampshire College
Harvard and Radcliffe Colleges
Lasell College
Lesley College
Massachusetts College of Art
Massachusetts Institute of
 Technology
Merrimack College
Montserrat College of Art
Mount Holyoke College
Mount Ida College
North Adams State College
Northeastern University
Pine Manor College
Regis College
Salem State College
School of the Museum of Fine Arts
Simmons College
Smith College
Stonehill College
Tufts University
University of Massachusetts
 Amherst
 Boston
 Dartmouth
Wellesley College
Wentworth Institute of Technology
Western New England College
Wheaton College
Williams College
Worcester Polytechnic Institute

Michigan

Adrian College
Albion College
Alma College
Aquinas College
Calvin College
Central Michigan University
Eastern Michigan University
Grand Valley State University
Hope College
Marygrove College
Michigan State University

Michigan Technological University
Northern Michigan University
Oakland University
Olivet College
Saginaw Valley State University
St. Mary's College
Siena Heights College
Spring Arbor College
University of Detroit Mercy
University of Michigan
 Ann Arbor
 Dearborn
 Flint
Western Michigan University

Minnesota

Augsburg College
Bethel College
Carleton College
College of Associated Arts
College of St. Benedict
College of St. Catherine: St.
 Catherine Campus
College of St. Scholastica
Concordia College: St. Paul
Gustavus Adolphus College
Hamline University
Inver Hills Community College
Lakewood Community College
Macalester College
Mankato State University
Metropolitan State University
Minneapolis College of Art and
 Design
Moorhead State University
Rochester Community College
St. Cloud State University
St. John's University
St. Mary's College of Minnesota
St. Olaf College
Southwest State University
University of Minnesota
 Duluth
 Morris
 Twin Cities
Winona State University
Worthington Community College

Mississippi

Tougaloo College

Missouri

Central Methodist College
Central Missouri State University
College of the Ozarks
Columbia College
Culver-Stockton College
Fontbonne College
Hannibal-LaGrange College
Lindenwood College
Missouri Baptist College
Park College
Rockhurst College
St. Louis University
Southwest Missouri State University
Stephens College
University of Missouri
 Columbia
 Kansas City
 St. Louis
Washington University
Webster University
Westminster College
William Jewell College
William Woods College

Montana

Carroll College
Flathead Valley Community College
Montana State University
Rocky Mountain College

Nebraska

Clarkson College
Concordia College
Doane College
Hastings College
McCook Community College
Midland Lutheran College
Union College
University of Nebraska
    Lincoln
    Omaha
Wayne State College
Western Nebraska Community
    College
        Scottsbluff Campus
        Sidney Campus

Nevada

Sierra Nevada College
University of Nevada: Las Vegas

New Hampshire

Castle College
Colby-Sawyer College
Dartmouth College
Franklin Pierce College
Hesser College
Keene State College
New England College
New Hampshire Technical College:
    Manchester
Plymouth State College of the
    University System of New
    Hampshire
Rivier College
School for Lifelong Learning
University of New Hampshire
    Durham
    Manchester
White Pines College

New Jersey

Bloomfield College
Burlington County College
Centenary College
Drew University
Felician College
Monmouth College
New Jersey Institute of Technology
Princeton University
Ramapo College of New Jersey
Rutgers—The State University of
    New Jersey
        Camden College of Arts and
            Sciences
        College of Engineering
        Cook College
        Douglass College
        Livingston College
        Newark College of Arts and
            Sciences
        Rutgers College
        University College Camden
        University College New
            Brunswick
        University College Newark
St. Peter's College
Stockton State College
Upsala College

New Mexico

College of Santa Fe
College of the Southwest
Eastern New Mexico University
New Mexico State University
    Carlsbad
    Las Cruces
University of New Mexico
Western New Mexico University

New York

Alfred University
Bard College
Barnard College

Broome Community College
Canisius College
Cazenovia College
City University of New York
    Baruch College
    College of Staten Island
    Hunter College
    La Guardia Community
        College
    Lehman College
    Queens College
Clarkson University
Clinton Community College
Colgate University
College of Mount St. Vincent
College of New Rochelle
    New Rochelle
    School of New Resources
College of St. Rose
Columbia University
    Columbia College
    School of General Studies
Columbia-Greene Community
    College
Concordia College
Cooper Union
Cornell University
Elmira College
Erie Community College: North
    Campus
Eugene Lang College/New School
    for Social Research
Fordham University
Fulton-Montgomery Community
    College
Hamilton College
Hartwick College
Hobart College
Hofstra University
Hudson Valley Community College
Ithaca College
Jewish Theological Seminary of
    America
Keuka College
Kol Yaakov Torah Center
Long Island University
    Brooklyn Campus
    C. W. Post Campus
Manhattanville College
Marymount College
Medaille College
Mercy College
Molloy College
Mount St. Mary College
New York Institute of Technology
New York University
Niagara County Community College
North Country Community College
Pratt Institute
Rochester Institute of Technology
Rockland Community College
Russell Sage College
St. John Fisher College
St. Lawrence University
Sarah Lawrence College
Skidmore College

State University of New York
    Albany
    Binghamton
    Buffalo
    Purchase
    Stony Brook
    College of Agriculture and
        Technology at Morrisville
    College at Brockport
    College at Cortland
    College at Fredonia
    College at New Paltz
    College at Plattsburgh
    College at Potsdam
    College of Technology at
        Alfred
    College of Technology at
        Canton
    College of Technology at Delhi
    Empire State College
    Oswego
Syracuse University
Touro College
Ulster County Community College
Union College
University of Rochester
Vassar College
Wells College
William Smith College
Yeshiva University

North Carolina

Appalachian State University
Bennett College
Catawba College
Central Piedmont Community
    College
Davidson College
Duke University
Greensboro College
Guilford College
High Point University
Lees-McRae College
Lenoir-Rhyne College
Mars Hill College
Meredith College
North Carolina State University
Richmond Community College
Rockingham Community College
St. Andrews Presbyterian College
Salem College
University of North Carolina
    Asheville
    Chapel Hill
    Greensboro
Warren Wilson College
Western Carolina University

North Dakota

Dickinson State University
Mayville State University
Minot State University
North Dakota State University
University of North Dakota

Ohio

Antioch College
Antioch School for Adult and
    Experiential Learning
Art Academy of Cincinnati
Baldwin-Wallace College
Bluffton College
Bowling Green State University
    Bowling Green
    Firelands College
Capital University
Case Western Reserve University
Cincinnati Technical College
Clark State Community College
Cleveland Institute of Art
Cleveland State University
College of Mount St. Joseph
College of Wooster
Columbus State Community College

Cuyahoga Community College:
    Metropolitan Campus
Defiance College
Denison University
Edison State Community College
Heidelberg College
Hiram College
John Carroll University
Kent State University
    Ashtabula Regional Campus
    East Liverpool Regional
        Campus
    Kent
    Stark Campus
    Tuscarawas Campus
Kenyon College
Lake Erie College
Lourdes College
Malone College
Marietta College
Marion Technical College
Miami University: Oxford Campus
Mount Union College
Muskingum Area Technical College
Muskingum College
Northwest Technical College
Oberlin College
Ohio Dominican College
Ohio State University
    Agricultural Technical Institute
    Columbus Campus
    Newark Campus
Ohio University
    Athens
    Chillicothe Campus
    Eastern Campus
    Zanesville Campus
Ohio Wesleyan University
Otterbein College
Owens Technical College
    Findlay Campus
    Toledo
Shawnee State University
Sinclair Community College
Stark Technical College
Terra Technical College
Union Institute
University of Akron
University of Cincinnati
    Access Colleges
    Cincinnati
    Raymond Walters College
University of Dayton
University of Findlay
University of Rio Grande
University of Toledo
Urbana University
Ursuline College
Walsh College
Washington State Community
    College
Wittenberg University
Wright State University
Youngstown State University

Oklahoma

Oklahoma Baptist University
Oklahoma State University
Oral Roberts University
Phillips University
University of Oklahoma
University of Tulsa

Oregon

Clatsop Community College
Eastern Oregon State College
George Fox College
Lewis and Clark College
Linfield College
Linn-Benton Community College
Marylhurst College
Oregon State University
Portland State University
Reed College

University of Portland
Warner Pacific College
Western Oregon State College

Pennsylvania

Albright College
Allegheny College
Alvernia College
Baptist Bible College of
    Pennsylvania
Beaver College
Bryn Mawr College
Bucknell University
Bucks County Community College
Cabrini College
California University of
    Pennsylvania
Carlow College
Carnegie Mellon University
Cedar Crest College
Chatham College
Chestnut Hill College
College Misericordia
Delaware County Community
    College
Dickinson College
Duquesne University
East Stroudsburg University of
    Pennsylvania
Eastern College
Edinboro University of
    Pennsylvania
Franklin and Marshall College
Geneva College
Gettysburg College
Grove City College
Harrisburg Area Community
    College
Haverford College
Hussian School of Art
Immaculata College
Indiana University of Pennsylvania
Juniata College
Keystone Junior College
King's College
Kutztown University of
    Pennsylvania
La Salle University
Lafayette College
Lebanon Valley College of
    Pennsylvania
Lehigh University
Lock Haven University of
    Pennsylvania
Lycoming College
Mansfield University of
    Pennsylvania
Marywood College
Mercyhurst College
Messiah College
Moore College of Art and Design
Moravian College
Muhlenberg College
Neumann College
Peirce Junior College
Penn State University Park Campus
Pennsylvania College of Technology
Point Park College
Reading Area Community College
Rosemont College
St. Francis College
St. Joseph's University
St. Vincent College
Seton Hill College
Susquehanna University
Swarthmore College
Temple University
University of Pennsylvania
University of Pittsburgh
    Bradford
    Greensburg
    Johnstown
    Pittsburgh
University of Scranton

Ursinus College
Washington and Jefferson College
West Chester University of
    Pennsylvania
Westminster College
Westmoreland County Community
    College
Widener University
Wilkes University
Wilson College

Rhode Island

Brown University
Providence College
Rhode Island College
Roger Williams College
University of Rhode Island

South Carolina

Coker College
Columbia College
Furman University
Lander College
Limestone College
Tri-County Technical College
University of South Carolina
    Aiken
    Beaufort
    Coastal Carolina College
    Columbia
    Salkehatchie Regional Campus
    Spartanburg
    Union
Wofford College

South Dakota

Augustana College
Dakota Wesleyan University
Huron University
Mount Marty College
Sioux Falls College
University of South Dakota

Tennessee

Bethel College
Carson-Newman College
Chattanooga State Technical
    Community College
Fisk University
Free Will Baptist Bible College
Freed-Hardeman University
Lambuth University
LeMoyne-Owen College
Maryville College
Memphis College of Art
Memphis State University
Middle Tennessee State University
Rhodes College
State Technical Institute at
    Memphis
Tennessee Wesleyan College
Tusculum College
University of the South
University of Tennessee
    Knoxville
    Martin
Vanderbilt University
William Jennings Bryan College

Texas

Abilene Christian University
Austin College
Baylor University
East Texas State University at
    Texarkana
Lubbock Christian University
Midland College
Rice University
Schreiner College
Southern Methodist University
Southwestern Adventist College
Southwestern University
Texas Christian University
Texas Lutheran College

Texas Tech University
University of Dallas
University of Houston
    Clear Lake
    Downtown
University of North Texas
University of Texas
    Austin
    Dallas
    Tyler
West Texas State University

Utah

Brigham Young University
University of Utah
Utah State University
Weber State University
Westminster College of Salt Lake
    City

Vermont

Bennington College
Burlington College
Castleton State College
Community College of Vermont
Goddard College
Marlboro College
Middlebury College
Norwich University
St. Michael's College
Southern Vermont College
Trinity College of Vermont
University of Vermont

Virginia

Averett College
Christopher Newport College
Clinch Valley College of the
    University of Virginia
College of William and Mary
Emory and Henry College
George Mason University
Hollins College
Liberty University
Mary Baldwin College
Mary Washington College
Mountain Empire Community
    College
Old Dominion University
Radford University
Randolph-Macon Woman's College
Southern Seminary College
Sweet Briar College
University of Richmond
University of Virginia
Virginia Commonwealth University
Virginia Intermont College
Virginia Polytechnic Institute and
    State University
Virginia Wesleyan College
Washington and Lee University

Washington

Antioch University Seattle
Central Washington University
Eastern Washington University
Evergreen State College
Gonzaga University
Griffin College
Heritage College
Northwest College of the
    Assemblies of God
Northwest Indian College
Pacific Lutheran University
Pierce College
Seattle Pacific University
Seattle University
University of Washington
Wenatchee Valley College
Western Washington University
Whatcom Community College
Whitman College
Whitworth College

West Virginia

Bethany College
Concord College
Davis and Elkins College
Glenville State College
University of Charleston
West Liberty State College
West Virginia University
West Virginia Wesleyan College
Wheeling Jesuit College

Wisconsin

Beloit College
Carroll College
Carthage College
Concordia University Wisconsin
Edgewood College
Lawrence University
Marian College of Fond du Lac
Marquette University
Mount Mary College
Mount Senario College
Northland College
Ripon College
St. Norbert College
Silver Lake College
University of Wisconsin
    Green Bay
    Madison
    Milwaukee
    Oshkosh
    Platteville
    River Falls
    Stevens Point
    Superior
    Whitewater
Viterbo College

Wyoming

Central Wyoming College

Canada

McGill University

Study abroad

Alabama

Alabama Agricultural and
    Mechanical University
Auburn University
    Auburn
    Montgomery
Birmingham-Southern College
Huntingdon College
Jefferson State Community College
Judson College
Mobile College
Northeast Alabama State Junior
    College
Oakwood College
Samford University
Spring Hill College
Talladega College
University of Alabama
    Birmingham
    Tuscaloosa
University of Montevallo
University of South Alabama

Alaska

Alaska Pacific University
University of Alaska
    Anchorage
    Fairbanks

Arizona

Arizona State University
Glendale Community College
Grand Canyon University
Northern Arizona University
Prescott College

University of Arizona
Western International University

Arkansas

Arkansas College
Arkansas State University
Harding University
Hendrix College
John Brown University
Ouachita Baptist University
University of Arkansas
    Fayetteville
    Little Rock

California

Allan Hancock College
American Armenian International
    College
Antioch Southern California
    Los Angeles
    Santa Barbara
Art Center College of Design
Azusa Pacific University
Biola University
California Institute of the Arts
California Lutheran University
California Polytechnic State
    University: San Luis Obispo
California State Polytechnic
    University: Pomona
California State University
    Bakersfield
    Chico
    Dominguez Hills
    Fresno
    Fullerton
    Hayward
    Long Beach
    Los Angeles
    Northridge
    Sacramento
    San Bernardino
    San Marcos
    Stanislaus
Cerro Coso Community College
Chabot College
Chaffey Community College
Chapman University
Christ College Irvine
Citrus College
City College of San Francisco
Claremont McKenna College
College of Notre Dame
College of the Sequoias
Cosumnes River College
Cuesta College
De Anza College
Diablo Valley College
Dominican College of San Rafael
East Los Angeles College
El Camino College
Fashion Institute of Design and
    Merchandising
    Los Angeles
    San Francisco
Foothill College
Fresno City College
Fresno Pacific College
Gavilan Community College
Glendale Community College
Grossmont Community College
Harvey Mudd College
Holy Names College
Humboldt State University
Irvine Valley College
Kings River Community College
La Sierra University
Long Beach City College
Los Angeles City College
Los Angeles Harbor College
Los Angeles Pierce College
Los Angeles Trade and Technical
    College
Los Medanos College

Loyola Marymount University
Marymount College
Master's College
Menlo College
Merced College
Mills College
MiraCosta College
Modesto Junior College
Monterey Institute of International
    Studies
Moorpark College
Mount St. Mary's College
Napa Valley College
New College of California
Occidental College
Ohlone College
Orange Coast College
Otis/Parsons School of Art and
    Design
Oxnard College
Pacific Union College
Palomar College
Pasadena City College
Pepperdine University
Pitzer College
Point Loma Nazarene College
Pomona College
Rio Hondo College
Saddleback College
St. Mary's College of California
Samuel Merritt College
San Diego Mesa College
San Diego State University
San Francisco Art Institute
San Francisco State University
San Joaquin Delta College
San Jose State University
Santa Barbara City College
Santa Clara University
Santa Monica College
Santa Rosa Junior College
Scripps College
Sierra College
Simpson College
Skyline College
Sonoma State University
Southern California College
Southern California Institute of
    Architecture
Southwestern College
Stanford University
United States International
    University
University of California
    Berkeley
    Davis
    Irvine
    Los Angeles
    Riverside
    San Diego
    Santa Barbara
    Santa Cruz
University of Judaism
University of La Verne
University of the Pacific
University of Redlands
University of San Diego
University of San Francisco
University of Southern California
Ventura College
Victor Valley College
Western State University College of
    Law
      Orange County
      San Diego
Westmont College
Whittier College
World College West
Yuba College

Colorado

Arapahoe Community College
Colorado College
Colorado State University

Community College of Denver
Fort Lewis College
Front Range Community College
Mesa State College
Metropolitan State College of
    Denver
Naropa Institute
Red Rocks Community College
Regis College of Regis University
United States Air Force Academy
University of Colorado
    Boulder
    Colorado Springs
    Denver
University of Denver
University of Northern Colorado
University of Southern Colorado
Western State College of Colorado

Connecticut

Albertus Magnus College
Central Connecticut State
    University
Connecticut College
Eastern Connecticut State
    University
Fairfield University
Mattatuck Community College
Norwalk Community College
Quinebaug Valley Community
    College
Quinnipiac College
Sacred Heart University
St. Joseph College
Southern Connecticut State
    University
Teikyo-Post University
Trinity College
University of Bridgeport
University of Connecticut
University of Hartford
Wesleyan University
Western Connecticut State
    University
Yale University

Delaware

University of Delaware
Wesley College

District of Columbia

American University
Catholic University of America
Corcoran School of Art
Gallaudet University
George Washington University
Georgetown University
Howard University
Mount Vernon College
Southeastern University
Trinity College

Florida

Barry University
Bethune-Cookman College
Brevard Community College
Broward Community College
Central Florida Community College
Daytona Beach Community College
Eckerd College
Edison Community College
Embry-Riddle Aeronautical
    University
Flagler College
Florida Atlantic University
Florida Community College at
    Jacksonville
Florida International University
Florida Southern College
Florida State University
Hillsborough Community College
Jacksonville University
Lake City Community College
Lake-Sumter Community College

Lynn University
Miami-Dade Community College
New College of the University of
    South Florida
Nova University
Palm Beach Atlantic College
Palm Beach Community College
Pasco-Hernando Community
    College
Pensacola Junior College
Ringling School of Art and Design
Rollins College
St. Thomas University
Schiller International University
Seminole Community College
Stetson University
University of Central Florida
University of Florida
University of Miami
University of South Florida
University of Tampa
University of West Florida
Valencia Community College
Webber College

Georgia

Abraham Baldwin Agricultural
    College
Agnes Scott College
American College for the Applied
    Arts
Atlanta Christian College
Atlanta College of Art
Augusta College
Bauder College
Berry College
Brenau Women's College
Clark Atlanta University
Clayton State College
Columbus College
Covenant College
Darton College
East Georgia College
Emory University
Floyd College
Fort Valley State College
Gainesville College
Georgia College
Georgia Institute of Technology
Georgia Southern University
Georgia Southwestern College
Georgia State University
Gordon College
Kennesaw State College
Macon College
Mercer University
    Atlanta
    Macon
Middle Georgia College
Morehouse College
Morris Brown College
Oglethorpe University
Oxford College of Emory University
Paine College
Reinhardt College
Savannah College of Art and
    Design
Shorter College
Southern College of Technology
Spelman College
Toccoa Falls College
University of Georgia
Valdosta State College
Waycross College
Wesleyan College
West Georgia College
Young Harris College

Hawaii

Hawaii Loa College
University of Hawaii
    Hilo
    Kapiolani Community College
    Manoa

Idaho

Albertson College
Boise State University
Lewis Clark State College
University of Idaho

Illinois

Augustana College
Aurora University
Barat College
Belleville Area College
Black Hawk College
    East Campus
    Moline
Blackburn College
Bradley University
Carl Sandburg College
Chicago State University
City Colleges of Chicago
    Chicago City-Wide College
    Olive-Harvey College
College of DuPage
College of Lake County
College of St. Francis
De Paul University
Eastern Illinois University
Elgin Community College
Elmhurst College
Eureka College
Greenville College
Harrington Institute of Interior
    Design
Hebrew Theological College
Highland Community College
Illinois Benedictine College
Illinois College
Illinois Institute of Technology
Illinois State University
Illinois Valley Community College
Illinois Wesleyan University
International Academy of
    Merchandising and Design
John A. Logan College
Joliet Junior College
KAES College
Kishwaukee College
Knox College
Lake Forest College
Lincoln College
Lincoln Land Community College
Loyola University of Chicago
MacMurray College
Mennonite College of Nursing
Millikin University
Monmouth College
Moody Bible Institute
Moraine Valley Community College
National-Louis University
North Central College
North Park College and Theological
    Seminary
Northeastern Illinois University
Northern Illinois University
Northwestern University
Oakton Community College
Parkland College
Parks College of St. Louis
    University
Prairie State College
Principia College
Quincy College
Rend Lake College
Rock Valley College
Rockford College
Roosevelt University
Rosary College
St. Xavier University
School of the Art Institute of
    Chicago
Shimer College
Southern Illinois University
    Carbondale
    Edwardsville
Springfield College in Illinois

Trinity Christian College
Trinity College
Triton College
University of Chicago
University of Illinois
    Chicago
    Urbana-Champaign
Waubonsee Community College
Western Illinois University
Wheaton College
William Rainey Harper College

Indiana

Anderson University
Ball State University
Bethel College
Butler University
Calumet College of St. Joseph
DePauw University
Earlham College
Franklin College
Goshen College
Grace College
Hanover College
Huntington College
Indiana State University
Indiana University
    Bloomington
    East
    Kokomo
    Northwest
    South Bend
    Southeast
Indiana University—Purdue
    University
    Fort Wayne
    Indianapolis
Indiana Wesleyan University
Manchester College
Marian College
Purdue University
Rose-Hulman Institute of
    Technology
St. Francis College
St. Joseph's College
St. Mary-of-the-Woods College
St. Mary's College
Taylor University
University of Evansville
University of Indianapolis
University of Notre Dame
Valparaiso University
Wabash College

Iowa

Briar Cliff College
Buena Vista College
Central College
Clarke College
Coe College
Cornell College
Divine Word College
Dordt College
Drake University
Graceland College
Grand View College
Grinnell College
Iowa State University
Iowa Wesleyan College
Loras College
Luther College
Maharishi International University
Morningside College
Mount Mercy College
Northwestern College
St. Ambrose University
Simpson College
Teikyo Marycrest University
Teikyo Westmar University
University of Dubuque
University of Iowa
University of Northern Iowa
Wartburg College
William Penn College

Kansas

Baker University
Barclay College
Benedictine College
Bethany College
Bethel College
Emporia State University
Johnson County Community
    College
Kansas State University
McPherson College
MidAmerica Nazarene College
Pittsburg State University
St. Mary College
Southwestern College
Sterling College
Tabor College
University of Kansas
Washburn University of Topeka
Wichita State University

Kentucky

Asbury College
Bellarmine College
Berea College
Campbellsville College
Centre College
Eastern Kentucky University
Georgetown College
Kentucky State University
Kentucky Wesleyan College
Morehead State University
Murray State University
Northern Kentucky University
Spalding University
Transylvania University
Union College
University of Kentucky
University of Louisville
Western Kentucky University

Louisiana

Centenary College of Louisiana
Dillard University
Grambling State University
Louisiana College
Louisiana State University
    Agricultural and Mechanical
      College
    Shreveport
Louisiana Tech University
Loyola University
Nicholls State University
Northeast Louisiana University
Northwestern State University
Our Lady of Holy Cross College
Southeastern Louisiana University
Tulane University
University of New Orleans
University of Southwestern
    Louisiana
World Evangelism Bible College
    and Seminary

Maine

Bates College
Bowdoin College
Casco Bay College
Colby College
Maine Maritime Academy
Portland School of Art
St. Joseph's College
University of Maine
    Farmington
    Fort Kent
    Orono
    Presque Isle
University of New England
University of Southern Maine

Maryland

Baltimore Hebrew University
Baltimore International Culinary
    College

Catonsville Community College
Charles County Community College
College of Notre Dame of
    Maryland
Columbia Union College
Frostburg State University
Goucher College
Hood College
Johns Hopkins University
Loyola College in Maryland
Maryland Institute College of Art
Montgomery College: Rockville
    Campus
Mount St. Mary's College
Ner Israel Rabbinical College
St. Mary's College of Maryland
Salisbury State University
Towson State University
University of Baltimore
University of Maryland
    Baltimore County
    College Park
Villa Julie College
Washington College
Western Maryland College

Massachusetts

American International College
Amherst College
Anna Maria College for Men and
    Women
Assumption College
Atlantic Union College
Babson College
Becker College
    Leicester Campus
    Worcester Campus
Bentley College
Boston College
Boston University
Bradford College
Brandeis University
Bridgewater State College
Bunker Hill Community College
Cape Cod Community College
Clark University
College of the Holy Cross
Curry College
Dean Junior College
Elms College
Emerson College
Emmanuel College
Endicott College
Framingham State College
Gordon College
Hampshire College
Harvard and Radcliffe Colleges
Hellenic College
Holyoke Community College
Lasell College
Lesley College
Massachusetts Bay Community
    College
Massachusetts College of Art
Massachusetts Institute of
    Technology
Merrimack College
Montserrat College of Art
Mount Holyoke College
Mount Ida College
Nichols College
North Adams State College
North Shore Community College
Northeastern University
Northern Essex Community College
Pine Manor College
Regis College
St. John's Seminary College
Salem State College
Simmons College
Simon's Rock College of Bard
Smith College
Springfield College
Stonehill College

Suffolk University
Tufts University
University of Massachusetts
    Amherst
    Boston
    Dartmouth
    Lowell
Wellesley College
Wentworth Institute of Technology
Western New England College
Westfield State College
Wheaton College
Wheelock College
Williams College
Worcester Polytechnic Institute

Michigan

Adrian College
Albion College
Alma College
Andrews University
Aquinas College
Calvin College
Center for Creative Studies: College
    of Art and Design
Central Michigan University
Charles Stewart Mott Community
    College
Concordia College
Davenport College of Business
Delta College
Eastern Michigan University
Grand Rapids Community College
Grand Valley State University
Hillsdale College
Hope College
Kalamazoo College
Lansing Community College
Lawrence Technological University
Macomb Community College
Madonna University
Marygrove College
Michigan State University
Michigan Technological University
Northern Michigan University
Northwood Institute
Oakland University
Olivet College
Reformed Bible College
Saginaw Valley State University
St. Mary's College
Siena Heights College
Spring Arbor College
Suomi College
University of Detroit Mercy
University of Michigan
    Ann Arbor
    Dearborn
    Flint
Wayne State University
Western Michigan University

Minnesota

Augsburg College
Bemidji State University
Bethel College
Carleton College
College of Associated Arts
College of St. Benedict
College of St. Catherine: St.
    Catherine Campus
College of St. Scholastica
Concordia College: Moorhead
Concordia College: St. Paul
Gustavus Adolphus College
Hamline University
Itasca Community College:
    Arrowhead Region
Macalester College
Mankato State University
Mesabi Community College:
    Arrowhead Region
Minneapolis College of Art and
    Design

Moorhead State University
Normandale Community College
North Central Bible College
St. Cloud State University
St. John's University
St. Mary's College of Minnesota
St. Olaf College
Southwest State University
University of Minnesota
    Crookston
    Duluth
    Morris
    Twin Cities
University of St. Thomas
Winona State University
Worthington Community College

Mississippi

Belhaven College
Meridian Community College
Millsaps College
Mississippi College
Mississippi State University
Mississippi University for Women
Northeast Mississippi Community
    College
Tougaloo College
University of Mississippi
University of Southern Mississippi
William Carey College

Missouri

Central Methodist College
Central Missouri State University
Columbia College
Culver-Stockton College
Drury College
East Central College
Evangel College
Fontbonne College
Hannibal-LaGrange College
Kansas City Art Institute
Lindenwood College
Maryville University
Missouri Baptist College
Missouri Southern State College
Northeast Missouri State University
Northwest Missouri State
    University
Research College of Nursing
Rockhurst College
St. Louis Community College
    Florissant Valley
    Meramec
St. Louis University
Southeast Missouri State University
Southwest Baptist University
Southwest Missouri State University
Stephens College
University of Missouri
    Columbia
    Kansas City
    Rolla
    St. Louis
Washington University
Webster University
Westminster College
William Jewell College
William Woods College

Montana

Carroll College
Montana State University
Rocky Mountain College
University of Montana

Nebraska

Chadron State College
College of St. Mary
Concordia College
Creighton University
Dana College
Doane College
Hastings College

Midland Lutheran College
Nebraska Wesleyan University
Union College
University of Nebraska
    Kearney
    Lincoln
    Omaha
Wayne State College
York College

Nevada

University of Nevada
    Las Vegas
    Reno

New Hampshire

Colby-Sawyer College
Daniel Webster College
Dartmouth College
Franklin Pierce College
Keene State College
New England College
New Hampshire College
Notre Dame College
Plymouth State College of the
    University System of New
    Hampshire
St. Anselm College
University of New Hampshire

New Jersey

Bergen Community College
Berkeley College of Business
Bloomfield College
Brookdale Community College
Caldwell College
Centenary College
College of St. Elizabeth
Drew University
Essex County College
Fairleigh Dickinson University
    Edward Williams College
    Madison
Georgian Court College
Glassboro State College
Jersey City State College
Katharine Gibbs School
Kean College of New Jersey
Mercer County Community College
Monmouth College
Montclair State College
Ocean County College
Princeton University
Ramapo College of New Jersey
Rider College
Rutgers—The State University of
    New Jersey
    Camden College of Arts and
        Sciences
    College of Engineering
    College of Nursing
    College of Pharmacy
    Cook College
    Douglass College
    Livingston College
    Mason Gross School of the
        Arts
    Newark College of Arts and
        Sciences
    Rutgers College
    University College Camden
    University College New
        Brunswick
    University College Newark
St. Peter's College
Seton Hall University
Stevens Institute of Technology
Stockton State College
Trenton State College
Upsala College
Westminster Choir College
William Paterson College of New
    Jersey

New Mexico

College of Santa Fe
Eastern New Mexico University
New Mexico Institute of Mining
    and Technology
New Mexico State University
University of New Mexico

New York

Adelphi University
Alfred University
Bard College
Barnard College
Berkeley College
Berkeley School: New York City
Broome Community College
Canisius College
Cazenovia College
City University of New York
    Baruch College
    Borough of Manhattan
        Community College
    Brooklyn College
    City College
    College of Staten Island
    Hunter College
    John Jay College of Criminal
        Justice
    Lehman College
    Medgar Evers College
    New York City Technical
        College
    Queens College
    Queensborough Community
        College
    York College
Clarkson University
Colgate University
College for Human Services
College of Insurance
College of Mount St. Vincent
College of New Rochelle
College of St. Rose
Columbia University
    Columbia College
    School of General Studies
Concordia College
Cooper Union
Cornell University
Daemen College
Dutchess Community College
D'Youville College
Elmira College
Erie Community College
    City Campus
    North Campus
    South Campus
Eugene Lang College/New School
    for Social Research
Fashion Institute of Technology
Fordham University
Fulton-Montgomery Community
    College
Hamilton College
Hartwick College
Hobart College
Hofstra University
Houghton College
Iona College
Ithaca College
Jamestown Community College
Jewish Theological Seminary of
    America
Juilliard School
Katharine Gibbs School: Melville
Keuka College
King's College
Kol Yaakov Torah Center
Laboratory Institute of
    Merchandising
Le Moyne College
Long Island University
    C. W. Post Campus
    Southampton Campus

Machzikei Hadath Rabbinical
College
Manhattan College
Manhattanville College
Marist College
Marymount College
Marymount Manhattan College
Medaille College
Mercy College
Mohawk Valley Community College
Molloy College
Monroe Community College
Mount St. Mary College
Nazareth College of Rochester
New York Institute of Technology
New York University
Niagara County Community College
Niagara University
Nyack College
Ohr Somayach Tanenbaum
Education Center
Pace University
College of White Plains
New York
Pleasantville/Briarcliff
Parsons School of Design
Paul Smith's College
Pratt Institute
Rensselaer Polytechnic Institute
Roberts Wesleyan College
Rochester Institute of Technology
Rockland Community College
Russell Sage College
Sage Junior College of Albany, A
Division of Russell Sage College
St. Bonaventure University
St. Francis College
St. John Fisher College
St. John's University
St. Lawrence University
St. Thomas Aquinas College
Sarah Lawrence College
School of Visual Arts
Siena College
Skidmore College
State University of New York
Albany
Binghamton
Buffalo
Purchase
Stony Brook
College of Agriculture and
Technology at Cobleskill
College at Brockport
College at Buffalo
College at Cortland
College of Environmental
Science and Forestry
College at Fredonia
College at Geneseo
College at New Paltz
College at Old Westbury
College at Oneonta
College at Plattsburgh
College at Potsdam
Empire State College
Institute of Technology at
Utica/Rome
Oswego
Sullivan County Community
College
Syracuse University
Tompkins-Cortland Community
College
Touro College
Ulster County Community College
Union College
University of Rochester
Utica College of Syracuse
University
Vassar College
Wagner College
Wells College
Westchester Community College

William Smith College
Yeshiva University

North Carolina

Appalachian State University
Barton College
Belmont Abbey College
Brevard College
Campbell University
Catawba College
College of the Albemarle
Davidson College
Duke University
East Carolina University
Elon College
Gardner-Webb College
Greensboro College
Guilford College
High Point University
John Wesley College
Johnson C. Smith University
Lenoir-Rhyne College
Mars Hill College
Meredith College
Methodist College
Montreat-Anderson College
Mount Olive College
North Carolina State University
North Carolina Wesleyan College
Peace College
Pfeiffer College
Queens College
St. Andrews Presbyterian College
St. Augustine's College
St. Mary's College
Salem College
University of North Carolina
Asheville
Chapel Hill
Charlotte
Greensboro
Wilmington
Wake Forest University
Warren Wilson College
Western Carolina University
Wingate College

North Dakota

North Dakota State University
University of Mary
University of North Dakota

Ohio

Antioch College
Art Academy of Cincinnati
Ashland University
Baldwin-Wallace College
Bluffton College
Bowling Green State University
Capital University
Case Western Reserve University
Cedarville College
Cleveland College of Jewish Studies
Cleveland Institute of Art
Cleveland State University
College of Mount St. Joseph
College of Wooster
Defiance College
Denison University
Franciscan University of
Steubenville
Franklin University
Heidelberg College
Hiram College
John Carroll University
Kent State University
Kenyon College
Lake Erie College
Lorain County Community College
Malone College
Marietta College
Miami University
Hamilton Campus
Oxford Campus

Mount Union College
Muskingum College
Notre Dame College of Ohio
Oberlin College
Ohio Dominican College
Ohio Northern University
Ohio State University: Columbus
Campus
Ohio University
Athens
Chillicothe Campus
Ohio Wesleyan University
Otterbein College
Sinclair Community College
Tiffin University
University of Akron
University of Cincinnati
Cincinnati
Raymond Walters College
University of Dayton
University of Findlay
University of Toledo
Virginia Marti College of Fashion
and Art
Wilberforce University
Wilmington College
Wittenberg University
Wright State University
Dayton
Lake Campus
Xavier University
Youngstown State University

Oklahoma

Oklahoma Baptist University
Oklahoma Christian University of
Science and Arts
Oklahoma City University
Oklahoma State University
Oral Roberts University
Phillips University
University of Oklahoma
University of Tulsa

Oregon

Chemeketa Community College
Clackamas Community College
Concordia College
Eastern Oregon State College
George Fox College
Lane Community College
Lewis and Clark College
Linfield College
Mount Hood Community College
Oregon State University
Pacific University
Portland Community College
Portland State University
Reed College
Rogue Community College
Southern Oregon State College
Southwestern Oregon Community
College
University of Oregon
Eugene
Robert Donald Clark Honors
College
University of Portland
Warner Pacific College
Western Oregon State College
Willamette University

Pennsylvania

Albright College
Allegheny College
Allentown College of St. Francis de
Sales
Alvernia College
Baptist Bible College of
Pennsylvania
Beaver College
Bloomsburg University of
Pennsylvania
Bryn Mawr College

Bucknell University
Bucks County Community College
Cabrini College
California University of
Pennsylvania
Carlow College
Carnegie Mellon University
Cedar Crest College
Chatham College
Chestnut Hill College
Cheyney University of Pennsylvania
Clarion University of Pennsylvania
College Misericordia
Delaware County Community
College
Delaware Valley College
Dickinson College
Drexel University
Duquesne University
East Stroudsburg University of
Pennsylvania
Eastern College
Edinboro University of
Pennsylvania
Elizabethtown College
Franklin and Marshall College
Gannon University
Geneva College
Gettysburg College
Gratz College
Grove City College
Harcum Junior College
Harrisburg Area Community
College
Haverford College
Holy Family College
Immaculata College
Indiana University of Pennsylvania
Juniata College
King's College
Kutztown University of
Pennsylvania
La Salle University
Lafayette College
Lancaster Bible College
Lebanon Valley College of
Pennsylvania
Lehigh University
Lincoln University
Lock Haven University of
Pennsylvania
Lycoming College
Mansfield University of
Pennsylvania
Marywood College
Mercyhurst College
Messiah College
Millersville University of
Pennsylvania
Moore College of Art and Design
Moravian College
Muhlenberg College
Penn State University Park Campus
Philadelphia College of Bible
Philadelphia College of Textiles and
Science
Robert Morris College
Rosemont College
St. Francis College
St. Joseph's University
St. Vincent College
Seton Hill College
Shippensburg University of
Pennsylvania
Slippery Rock University of
Pennsylvania
Spring Garden College
Susquehanna University
Swarthmore College
Temple University
Thiel College
University of Pennsylvania

University of Pittsburgh
  Bradford
  Johnstown
  Pittsburgh
University of Scranton
Ursinus College
Valley Forge Christian College
Villanova University
Washington and Jefferson College
Waynesburg College
West Chester University of
  Pennsylvania
Westminster College
Widener University
Wilkes University
Wilson College

Puerto Rico

Inter American University of Puerto
  Rico
    Metropolitan Campus
    San German Campus
Pontifical Catholic University of
  Puerto Rico
University of Puerto Rico
    Cayey University College
    Mayaguez Campus
    Rio Piedras Campus

Rhode Island

Brown University
Bryant College
Community College of Rhode
  Island
Johnson & Wales University
Providence College
Rhode Island College
Rhode Island School of Design
Roger Williams College
Salve Regina University
University of Rhode Island

South Carolina

Anderson College
Clemson University
Coker College
College of Charleston
Columbia Bible College and
  Seminary
Columbia College
Converse College
Erskine College
Furman University
Lander College
Newberry College
Presbyterian College
Tri-County Technical College
University of South Carolina
    Coastal Carolina College
    Columbia
    Salkehatchie Regional Campus
    Spartanburg
Winthrop University
Wofford College

South Dakota

Augustana College
Dakota State University
Huron University
National College
Northern State University
Sioux Falls College
University of South Dakota

Tennessee

Austin Peay State University
Belmont University
Carson-Newman College
David Lipscomb University
East Tennessee State University
Fisk University
Freed-Hardeman University
King College
LeMoyne-Owen College

Martin Methodist College
Maryville College
Memphis College of Art
Memphis State University
Middle Tennessee State University
Milligan College
O'More College of Design
Rhodes College
Southern College of Seventh-day
  Adventists
Tennessee Wesleyan College
Union University
University of the South
University of Tennessee
    Chattanooga
    Knoxville
    Martin
Vanderbilt University
William Jennings Bryan College

Texas

Abilene Christian University
Angelo State University
Austin College
Austin Community College
Baylor University
Brookhaven College
Collin County Community College
  District
Dallas Baptist University
East Texas State University
El Centro College
Hardin-Simmons University
Houston Baptist University
Incarnate Word College
Lamar University—Beaumont
Lubbock Christian University
McMurry University
Midwestern State University
Miss Wade's Fashion
  Merchandising College
North Lake College
Northwood Institute: Texas Campus
Our Lady of the Lake University of
  San Antonio
Rice University
Richland College
St. Edward's University
St. Mary's University
San Antonio College
Schreiner College
Southern Methodist University
Southwest Texas State University
Southwestern Adventist College
Southwestern University
Texarkana College
Texas A&I University
Texas A&M University
Texas Christian University
Texas Lutheran College
Texas Tech University
Texas Wesleyan University
Texas Woman's University
Trinity University
University of Dallas
University of Houston
    Clear Lake
    Houston
University of Mary Hardin-Baylor
University of North Texas
University of St. Thomas
University of Texas
    Arlington
    Austin
    El Paso
    Health Science Center at
      Houston
    San Antonio
    Tyler

Utah

Brigham Young University
University of Utah
Utah State University

Weber State University
Westminster College of Salt Lake
  City

Vermont

Bennington College
Castleton State College
Goddard College
Green Mountain College
Johnson State College
Lyndon State College
Marlboro College
Middlebury College
New England Culinary Institute
Norwich University
St. Michael's College
School for International Training
Southern Vermont College
Trinity College of Vermont
University of Vermont

Virginia

Averett College
Bluefield College
Bridgewater College
Christendom College
Christopher Newport College
College of William and Mary
Commonwealth College
Eastern Mennonite College
Emory and Henry College
Ferrum College
George Mason University
Hampden-Sydney College
Hampton University
Hollins College
James Madison University
Liberty University
Longwood College
Lynchburg College
Mary Baldwin College
Mary Washington College
Marymount University
Old Dominion University
Radford University
Randolph-Macon College
Randolph-Macon Woman's College
Richard Bland College
Roanoke College
Southern Seminary College
Sweet Briar College
University of Richmond
University of Virginia
Virginia Commonwealth University
Virginia Intermont College
Virginia Military Institute
Virginia Polytechnic Institute and
  State University
Virginia State University
Virginia Wesleyan College
Washington and Lee University

Washington

Antioch University Seattle
Central Washington University
Clark College
Columbia Basin College
Eastern Washington University
Edmonds Community College
Evergreen State College
Gonzaga University
Grays Harbor College
Green River Community College
Lower Columbia College
Olympic College
Pacific Lutheran University
Peninsula College
Seattle Central Community College
Seattle Pacific University
Seattle University
Shoreline Community College
Skagit Valley College
South Puget Sound Community
  College

University of Puget Sound
University of Washington
Walla Walla College
Washington State University
Western Washington University
Whatcom Community College
Whitman College
Whitworth College

West Virginia

Alderson-Broaddus College
Bethany College
Concord College
Davis and Elkins College
Marshall University
Salem-Teikyo University
University of Charleston
West Virginia University
West Virginia Wesleyan College
Wheeling Jesuit College

Wisconsin

Alverno College
Beloit College
Cardinal Stritch College
Carroll College
Carthage College
Columbia College of Nursing
Concordia University Wisconsin
Edgewood College
Lakeland College
Lawrence University
Marian College of Fond du Lac
Marquette University
Milwaukee Institute of Art &
  Design
Mount Mary College
Mount Senario College
Northland College
Ripon College
St. Norbert College
Silver Lake College
University of Wisconsin
    Eau Claire
    Green Bay
    La Crosse
    Madison
    Milwaukee
    Oshkosh
    Parkside
    Platteville
    River Falls
    Stevens Point
    Stout
    Superior
    Whitewater
University of Wisconsin Center
    Marathon County
    Washington County
    Waukesha
Viterbo College
Wisconsin Lutheran College

Wyoming

Northwest College
University of Wyoming

Canada

McGill University

France

American University of Paris

Mexico

Sistema Instituto Tecnologico y de
  Estudios Superiores de
  Monterrey

Switzerland

American College of Switzerland
Franklin College: Switzerland

Arab Republic of Egypt
American University in Cairo

Teacher preparation

Alabama
Alabama Agricultural and
  Mechanical University
Alabama State University
Auburn University
    Auburn
    Montgomery
Birmingham-Southern College
Community College of the Air
  Force
Faulkner University
Gadsden State Community College
Huntingdon College
Jacksonville State University
John M. Patterson State Technical
  College
Judson College
Livingston University
Mobile College
Samford University
Southeastern Bible College
Spring Hill College
Stillman College
Troy State University
    Dothan
    Montgomery
Tuskegee University
University of Alabama
    Birmingham
    Huntsville
University of Montevallo
University of North Alabama
University of South Alabama

Alaska
Alaska Pacific University
Prince William Sound Community
  College
Sheldon Jackson College
University of Alaska
    Anchorage
    Fairbanks
    Southeast

Arizona
Arizona College of the Bible
Arizona State University
Grand Canyon University
Northern Arizona University
Prescott College
Southwestern College
University of Arizona
Yavapai College

Arkansas
Arkansas College
Arkansas State University
Arkansas Tech University
Central Baptist College
Harding University
Henderson State University
Hendrix College
Ouachita Baptist University
University of Arkansas
    Fayetteville
    Little Rock
    Monticello
    Pine Bluff
University of Central Arkansas
University of the Ozarks

California
Academy of Art College
American Armenian International
  College
Azusa Pacific University

Bethany College
Biola University
California Baptist College
California Lutheran University
California Polytechnic State
  University: San Luis Obispo
California State Polytechnic
  University: Pomona
California State University
    Bakersfield
    Chico
    Dominguez Hills
    Fresno
    Fullerton
    Hayward
    Long Beach
    Los Angeles
    Northridge
    Sacramento
    San Marcos
    Stanislaus
Chapman University
Christ College Irvine
Christian Heritage College
College of Notre Dame
Crafton Hills College
Cuesta College
Dominican College of San Rafael
Fresno Pacific College
Holy Names College
Humboldt State University
Imperial Valley College
John F. Kennedy University
La Sierra University
LIFE Bible College
Loyola Marymount University
Master's College
Mills College
Mount St. Mary's College
National University
Occidental College
Pacific Christian College
Pacific Oaks College
Pacific Union College
Patten College
Pepperdine University
Point Loma Nazarene College
Queen of the Holy Rosary College
St. Mary's College of California
San Diego City College
San Diego State University
San Francisco State University
San Jose State University
Santa Clara University
Simpson College
Sonoma State University
Southern California College
United States International
  University
University of California
    Davis
    Irvine
    Riverside
    San Diego
    Santa Barbara
    Santa Cruz
University of La Verne
University of the Pacific
University of Redlands
University of San Diego
University of San Francisco
University of Southern California
West Valley College
Westmont College
Whittier College

Colorado
Adams State College
Colorado Christian University
Colorado College
Colorado State University
Fort Lewis College
Mesa State College

Metropolitan State College of
  Denver
Morgan Community College
Regis College of Regis University
University of Colorado
    Boulder
    Colorado Springs
University of Denver
University of Northern Colorado
University of Southern Colorado
Western State College of Colorado

Connecticut
Central Connecticut State
  University
Connecticut College
Eastern Connecticut State
  University
Fairfield University
Quinnipiac College
Sacred Heart University
St. Joseph College
Southern Connecticut State
  University
University of Bridgeport
University of Connecticut
University of Hartford
Wesleyan University
Western Connecticut State
  University
Yale University

Delaware
Delaware State College
University of Delaware
Wesley College
Wilmington College

District of Columbia
American University
Catholic University of America
Gallaudet University
George Washington University
Howard University
Trinity College

Florida
Barry University
Bethune-Cookman College
Eckerd College
Flagler College
Florida Agricultural and Mechanical
  University
Florida Atlantic University
Florida Bible College
Florida Christian College
Florida Institute of Technology
Florida International University
Florida Memorial College
Florida Southern College
Florida State University
Gulf Coast Community College
Hobe Sound Bible College
Jacksonville University
Lynn University
Nova University
Rollins College
St. Leo College
St. Thomas University
Southeastern College of the
  Assemblies of God
Stetson University
University of Central Florida
University of Florida
University of Miami
University of North Florida
University of South Florida
University of Tampa
University of West Florida
Warner Southern College

Georgia
Agnes Scott College
Albany State College

Armstrong State College
Augusta College
Berry College
Brenau Women's College
Brewton-Parker College
Brunswick College
Clark Atlanta University
Columbus College
Covenant College
Emory University
Fort Valley State College
Georgia College
Georgia Southern University
Georgia Southwestern College
Kennesaw State College
Mercer University
    Atlanta
    Macon
North Georgia College
Oglethorpe University
Paine College
Piedmont College
Shorter College
South College
Spelman College
Toccoa Falls College
University of Georgia
Valdosta State College
Wesleyan College
West Georgia College

Hawaii
Brigham Young University-Hawaii
Chaminade University of Honolulu
Hawaii Pacific University
University of Hawaii
    Hilo
    Kapiolani Community College
    Manoa

Idaho
Albertson College
Idaho State University
Lewis Clark State College
Northwest Nazarene College
University of Idaho

Illinois
Augustana College
Aurora University
Barat College
Blackburn College
Bradley University
Chicago State University
College of St. Francis
Concordia University
De Paul University
Eastern Illinois University
Elmhurst College
Eureka College
Governors State University
Hebrew Theological College
Illinois Benedictine College
Illinois College
Illinois State University
Kishwaukee College
Knox College
Lake Forest College
Lewis University
Lincoln Christian College and
  Seminary
Loyola University of Chicago
MacMurray College
McKendree College
Millikin University
National-Louis University
North Central College
North Park College and Theological
  Seminary
Northeastern Illinois University
Northern Illinois University
Northwestern University
Olivet Nazarene University
Quincy College

Rockford College
Roosevelt University
Rosary College
St. Xavier University
Sangamon State University
School of the Art Institute of
    Chicago
Southern Illinois University
    Carbondale
    Edwardsville
Springfield College in Illinois
State Community College
Trinity Christian College
University of Illinois
    Chicago
    Urbana-Champaign
VanderCook College of Music
Western Illinois University
Wheaton College

Indiana

Ancilla College
Ball State University
Bethel College
Butler University
DePauw University
Franklin College
Goshen College
Grace College
Hanover College
Huntington College
Indiana State University
Indiana University
    Bloomington
    East
    Kokomo
    Northwest
    Southeast
Indiana University—Purdue
    University
    Fort Wayne
    Indianapolis
Indiana Wesleyan University
Manchester College
Marian College
Oakland City College
Purdue University
    Calumet
    North Central Campus
    West Lafayette
St. Francis College
St. Joseph's College
St. Mary-of-the-Woods College
St. Mary's College
Taylor University
Tri-State University
University of Evansville
University of Indianapolis
University of Notre Dame
University of Southern Indiana
Valparaiso University
Wabash College

Iowa

Briar Cliff College
Central College
Clarke College
Coe College
Cornell College
Dordt College
Drake University
Graceland College
Grand View College
Grinnell College
Iowa State University
Iowa Wesleyan College
Loras College
Luther College
Maharishi International University
Morningside College
Mount Mercy College
Mount St. Clare College
Northwestern College
St. Ambrose University

Simpson College
Teikyo Marycrest University
Teikyo Westmar University
University of Dubuque
University of Iowa
University of Northern Iowa
Upper Iowa University
Vennard College
Wartburg College
William Penn College

Kansas

Baker University
Barclay College
Benedictine College
Bethany College
Bethel College
Cloud County Community College
Cowley County Community College
Emporia State University
Fort Hays State University
Fort Scott Community College
Friends University
Kansas City College and Bible
    School
Kansas State University
Kansas Wesleyan University
McPherson College
Ottawa University
Pittsburg State University
St. Mary College
Southwestern College
University of Kansas
Washburn University of Topeka
Wichita State University

Kentucky

Alice Lloyd College
Asbury College
Bellarmine College
Berea College
Brescia College
Campbellsville College
Centre College
Cumberland College
Eastern Kentucky University
Georgetown College
Kentucky Christian College
Kentucky State University
Kentucky Wesleyan College
Lees College
Lindsey Wilson College
Morehead State University
Murray State University
Northern Kentucky University
Pikeville College
Spalding University
Sue Bennett College
Thomas More College
Transylvania University
Union College
University of Kentucky
University of Louisville
Western Kentucky University

Louisiana

Centenary College of Louisiana
Dillard University
Grambling State University
Louisiana College
Louisiana State University
    Agricultural and Mechanical
        College
    Shreveport
Louisiana Tech University
Loyola University
McNeese State University
Nicholls State University
Northeast Louisiana University
Northwestern State University
Our Lady of Holy Cross College
Southeastern Louisiana University

Southern University and
    Agricultural and Mechanical
    College
Tulane University
University of New Orleans
University of Southwestern
    Louisiana
Xavier University of Louisiana

Maine

Bates College
Bowdoin College
Casco Bay College
Colby College
College of the Atlantic
Husson College
St. Joseph's College
Thomas College
University of Maine
    Farmington
    Fort Kent
    Machias
    Orono
    Presque Isle
University of New England
University of Southern Maine
Westbrook College

Maryland

Anne Arundel Community College
Baltimore Hebrew University
Bowie State University
Catonsville Community College
Cecil Community College
Charles County Community College
Chesapeake College
College of Notre Dame of
    Maryland
Columbia Union College
Coppin State College
Dundalk Community College
Frostburg State University
Goucher College
Hood College
Howard Community College
Johns Hopkins University
Loyola College in Maryland
Maryland Institute College of Art
Montgomery College
    Germantown Campus
    Rockville Campus
    Takoma Park Campus
Morgan State University
Mount St. Mary's College
Prince George's Community College
St. Mary's College of Maryland
Salisbury State University
Towson State University
University of Maryland
    Baltimore County
    College Park
    Eastern Shore
Villa Julie College
Washington College
Western Maryland College

Massachusetts

American International College
Anna Maria College for Men and
    Women
Aquinas College at Newton
Assumption College
Atlantic Union College
Berklee College of Music
Boston College
Boston Conservatory
Boston University
Bradford College
Brandeis University
Bridgewater State College
Clark University
Curry College
Eastern Nazarene College
Elms College

Emerson College
Emmanuel College
Fitchburg State College
Framingham State College
Gordon College
Harvard and Radcliffe Colleges
Lasell College
Lesley College
Massachusetts College of Art
Merrimack College
Mount Holyoke College
New England Conservatory of
    Music
North Adams State College
Northeastern University
Pine Manor College
Regis College
Salem State College
School of the Museum of Fine Arts
Simmons College
Smith College
Springfield College
Stonehill College
Suffolk University
Tufts University
University of Massachusetts
    Amherst
    Boston
    Dartmouth
    Lowell
Wellesley College
Western New England College
Westfield State College
Wheaton College
Wheelock College
Worcester State College

Michigan

Adrian College
Albion College
Alma College
Andrews University
Aquinas College
Calvin College
Central Michigan University
Concordia College
Eastern Michigan University
Ferris State University
Grand Rapids Baptist College and
    Seminary
Grand Valley State University
Hillsdale College
Hope College
Kalamazoo College
Lansing Community College
Madonna University
Marygrove College
Michigan State University
Michigan Technological University
Muskegon Community College
Northern Michigan University
Oakland University
Olivet College
Saginaw Valley State University
St. Mary's College
Siena Heights College
Spring Arbor College
Suomi College
University of Detroit Mercy
University of Michigan
    Ann Arbor
    Dearborn
    Flint
Western Michigan University

Minnesota

Augsburg College
Bemidji State University
Bethel College
Carleton College
College of St. Benedict
College of St. Catherine: St.
    Catherine Campus
College of St. Scholastica

Concordia College: Moorhead
Concordia College: St. Paul
Crown College
Dr. Martin Luther College
Gustavus Adolphus College
Hamline University
Macalester College
Mankato State University
Moorhead State University
Pillsbury Baptist Bible College
St. Cloud State University
St. John's University
St. Mary's College of Minnesota
St. Olaf College
Southwest State University
University of Minnesota
    Duluth
    Morris
University of St. Thomas
Winona State University

Mississippi

Alcorn State University
Belhaven College
Blue Mountain College
Delta State University
Jackson State University
Millsaps College
Mississippi College
Mississippi State University
Mississippi University for Women
Rust College
Tougaloo College
University of Mississippi
University of Southern Mississippi
William Carey College

Missouri

Avila College
Calvary Bible College
Central Methodist College
Central Missouri State University
College of the Ozarks
Columbia College
Culver-Stockton College
Drury College
Evangel College
Fontbonne College
Hannibal-LaGrange College
Harris Stowe State College
Jefferson College
Lincoln University
Lindenwood College
Maryville University
Missouri Baptist College
Missouri Southern State College
Missouri Valley College
Missouri Western State College
Northeast Missouri State University
Northwest Missouri State
    University
Park College
Rockhurst College
St. Louis Community College at
    Florissant Valley
St. Louis University
Southeast Missouri State University
Southwest Baptist University
Southwest Missouri State University
Stephens College
University of Missouri
    Columbia
    Kansas City
    Rolla
    St. Louis
Washington University
Webster University
William Jewell College
William Woods College

Montana

College of Great Falls
Eastern Montana College
Montana State University

Northern Montana College
Rocky Mountain College
University of Montana
Western Montana College of the
    University of Montana

Nebraska

Chadron State College
College of St. Mary
Concordia College
Creighton University
Dana College
Doane College
Hastings College
McCook Community College
Midland Lutheran College
Nebraska Christian College
Nebraska Wesleyan University
Peru State College
Union College
University of Nebraska
    Kearney
    Lincoln
    Omaha
Wayne State College

Nevada

Sierra Nevada College
University of Nevada
    Las Vegas
    Reno

New Hampshire

Colby-Sawyer College
Dartmouth College
Franklin Pierce College
Keene State College
New England College
New Hampshire College
Notre Dame College
Plymouth State College of the
    University System of New
    Hampshire
Rivier College
St. Anselm College
University of New Hampshire

New Jersey

Caldwell College
Centenary College
College of St. Elizabeth
Drew University
Essex County College
Fairleigh Dickinson University
Felician College
Georgian Court College
Glassboro State College
Jersey City State College
Kean College of New Jersey
Monmouth College
Montclair State College
Princeton University
Ramapo College of New Jersey
Rider College
Rutgers—The State University of
    New Jersey
    Camden College of Arts and
        Sciences
    Cook College
    Douglass College
    Livingston College
    Mason Gross School of the
        Arts
    Newark College of Arts and
        Sciences
    Rutgers College
    University College New
        Brunswick
    University College Newark
St. Peter's College
Seton Hall University
Stockton State College
Trenton State College
Upsala College

Westminster Choir College
William Paterson College of New
    Jersey

New Mexico

College of Santa Fe
College of the Southwest
Eastern New Mexico University
New Mexico Highlands University
New Mexico Institute of Mining
    and Technology
New Mexico State University
University of New Mexico
Western New Mexico University

New York

Adelphi University
Alfred University
Barnard College
Canisius College
City University of New York
    Baruch College
    Brooklyn College
    City College
    College of Staten Island
    Hunter College
    La Guardia Community
        College
    Lehman College
    Medgar Evers College
    Queens College
    York College
Colgate University
College of Mount St. Vincent
College of New Rochelle
College of St. Rose
Columbia University
    Columbia College
    School of General Studies
Concordia College
Cornell University
Daemen College
Dominican College of Blauvelt
Dowling College
D'Youville College
Elmira College
Erie Community College
    City Campus
    North Campus
    South Campus
Five Towns College
Fordham University
Genesee Community College
Hartwick College
Hobart College
Hofstra University
Houghton College
Iona College
Ithaca College
King's College
Le Moyne College
Long Island University
    Brooklyn Campus
    C. W. Post Campus
    Southampton Campus
Manhattan College
Manhattanville College
Maria College
Marist College
Marymount College
Marymount Manhattan College
Medaille College
Mercy College
Molloy College
Mount St. Mary College
Nazareth College of Rochester
New York Institute of Technology
New York University
Niagara University
Ohr Somayach Tanenbaum
    Education Center
Pace University
    College of White Plains
    New York

Parsons School of Design
Pratt Institute
Rensselaer Polytechnic Institute
Roberts Wesleyan College
Russell Sage College
St. Bonaventure University
St. Francis College
St. John Fisher College
St. John's University
St. Joseph's College
    Brooklyn
    Suffolk Campus
St. Lawrence University
St. Thomas Aquinas College
Sarah Lawrence College
School of Visual Arts
Siena College
Skidmore College
State University of New York
    Albany
    Buffalo
    Stony Brook
    College at Brockport
    College at Buffalo
    College at Cortland
    College of Environmental
        Science and Forestry
    College at Fredonia
    College at Geneseo
    College at New Paltz
    College at Old Westbury
    College at Oneonta
    College at Plattsburgh
    College at Potsdam
Syracuse University
Ulster County Community College
Union College
University of Rochester
Utica College of Syracuse
    University
Vassar College
Wells College
William Smith College
Yeshiva University

North Carolina

Appalachian State University
Barber-Scotia College
Barton College
Belmont Abbey College
Bennett College
Campbell University
Catawba College
Chowan College
Davidson College
Duke University
East Carolina University
East Coast Bible College
Elizabeth City State University
Elon College
Fayetteville State University
Greensboro College
Guilford College
High Point University
John Wesley College
Johnson C. Smith University
Lees-McRae College
Lenoir-Rhyne College
Livingstone College
Mars Hill College
Meredith College
Montreat-Anderson College
North Carolina Agricultural and
    Technical State University
North Carolina Central University
North Carolina State University
North Carolina Wesleyan College
Pembroke State University
Pfeiffer College
Piedmont Bible College
Queens College
St. Andrews Presbyterian College
St. Augustine's College
Salem College

Shaw University
University of North Carolina
    Asheville
    Chapel Hill
    Charlotte
    Greensboro
    Wilmington
Wake Forest University
Warren Wilson College
Western Carolina University
Wingate College
Winston-Salem State University

North Dakota

Dickinson State University
Jamestown College
Mayville State University
Minot State University
North Dakota State University
Trinity Bible College
University of Mary
University of North Dakota
Valley City State University

Ohio

Antioch College
Ashland University
Baldwin-Wallace College
Bluffton College
Bowling Green State University
    Bowling Green
    Firelands College
Capital University
Case Western Reserve University
Cedarville College
Circleville Bible College
Cleveland Institute of Art
Cleveland State University
College of Wooster
Defiance College
Denison University
Franciscan University of
    Steubenville
Heidelberg College
Hiram College
John Carroll University
Kent State University
Lake Erie College
Lourdes College
Malone College
Marietta College
Miami University
    Hamilton Campus
    Oxford Campus
Mount Union College
Mount Vernon Nazarene College
Muskingum College
Notre Dame College of Ohio
Ohio Dominican College
Ohio Northern University
Ohio State University
    Columbus Campus
    Lima Campus
    Mansfield Campus
    Marion Campus
    Newark Campus
Ohio University
    Athens
    Chillicothe Campus
    Eastern Campus
    Southern Campus at Ironton
    Zanesville Campus
Ohio Wesleyan University
Otterbein College
Shawnee State University
University of Akron
University of Cincinnati
    Cincinnati
    Raymond Walters College
University of Dayton
University of Findlay
University of Rio Grande
University of Toledo
Urbana University

Ursuline College
Walsh College
Wilmington College
Wittenberg University
Wright State University
Xavier University
Youngstown State University

Oklahoma

Bartlesville Wesleyan College
Cameron University
East Central University
Northeastern State University
Northwestern Oklahoma State
    University
Oklahoma Baptist University
Oklahoma Christian University of
    Science and Arts
Oklahoma Panhandle State
    University
Oklahoma State University
Oral Roberts University
Southeastern Oklahoma State
    University
Southwestern Oklahoma State
    University
University of Oklahoma
University of Tulsa

Oregon

Concordia College
Eastern Oregon State College
George Fox College
Lewis and Clark College
Linfield College
Oregon State University
Pacific University
Portland State University
University of Oregon
University of Portland
Warner Pacific College
Western Baptist College
Western Oregon State College
Willamette University

Pennsylvania

Academy of the New Church
Albright College
Allegheny College
Allentown College of St. Francis de
    Sales
Alvernia College
Beaver College
Bloomsburg University of
    Pennsylvania
Bryn Mawr College
Bucknell University
Cabrini College
California University of
    Pennsylvania
Carlow College
Carnegie Mellon University
Cedar Crest College
Chatham College
Chestnut Hill College
Cheyney University of Pennsylvania
Clarion University of Pennsylvania
College Misericordia
Delaware Valley College
Dickinson College
Drexel University
Duquesne University
East Stroudsburg University of
    Pennsylvania
Eastern College
Edinboro University of
    Pennsylvania
Elizabethtown College
Gannon University
Gettysburg College
Gratz College
Grove City College
Gwynedd-Mercy College
Haverford College

Holy Family College
Immaculata College
Indiana University of Pennsylvania
Juniata College
King's College
Kutztown University of
    Pennsylvania
La Salle University
Lancaster Bible College
Lebanon Valley College of
    Pennsylvania
Lincoln University
Lock Haven University of
    Pennsylvania
Lycoming College
Mansfield University of
    Pennsylvania
Marywood College
Mercyhurst College
Messiah College
Millersville University of
    Pennsylvania
Montgomery County Community
    College
Moore College of Art and Design
Moravian College
Muhlenberg College
Neumann College
Penn State
    Harrisburg Capital College
    University Park Campus
Philadelphia College of Bible
Point Park College
Robert Morris College
Rosemont College
St. Francis College
St. Joseph's University
St. Vincent College
Seton Hill College
Shippensburg University of
    Pennsylvania
Slippery Rock University of
    Pennsylvania
Susquehanna University
Swarthmore College
Temple University
Thiel College
University of the Arts
University of Pennsylvania
University of Pittsburgh
    Bradford
    Johnstown
    Pittsburgh
University of Scranton
Ursinus College
Villanova University
Washington and Jefferson College
Waynesburg College
West Chester University of
    Pennsylvania
Westminster College
Widener University
Wilkes University
Wilson College
York College of Pennsylvania

Puerto Rico

Caribbean University
Conservatory of Music of Puerto
    Rico
Inter American University of Puerto
    Rico
    Arecibo Campus
    San German Campus
University of Puerto Rico
    Arecibo Campus
    Bayamon Technological
        University College
    Humacao University College
    La Montana Regional College
    Mayaguez Campus
    Rio Piedras Campus
University of the Sacred Heart

Rhode Island

Brown University
Johnson & Wales University
Providence College
Rhode Island College
Rhode Island School of Design
Roger Williams College
Salve Regina University
University of Rhode Island

South Carolina

Benedict College
Bob Jones University
Central Wesleyan College
Charleston Southern University
The Citadel
Clemson University
Coker College
College of Charleston
Columbia College
Converse College
Erskine College
Francis Marion College
Furman University
Lander College
Limestone College
Morris College
Newberry College
Presbyterian College
University of South Carolina
    Aiken
    Coastal Carolina College
    Columbia
    Salkehatchie Regional Campus
    Spartanburg
Winthrop University
Wofford College

South Dakota

Augustana College
Black Hills State University
Dakota State University
Huron University
Northern State University
Sioux Falls College
South Dakota State University
University of South Dakota

Tennessee

Austin Peay State University
Belmont University
Bethel College
Carson-Newman College
Christian Brothers University
Crichton College
Cumberland University
David Lipscomb University
East Tennessee State University
Fisk University
Free Will Baptist Bible College
Freed-Hardeman University
Johnson Bible College
King College
Lambuth University
Lincoln Memorial University
Maryville College
Memphis State University
Middle Tennessee State University
Milligan College
Rhodes College
Roane State Community College
Southern College of Seventh-day
    Adventists
Tennessee State University
Tennessee Technological University
Tennessee Temple University
Tennessee Wesleyan College
Trevecca Nazarene College
Tusculum College
Union University
University of the South

University of Tennessee
  Chattanooga
  Knoxville
  Martin
Vanderbilt University
William Jennings Bryan College

Texas

Abilene Christian University
Austin College
Baylor University
Concordia Lutheran College
Dallas Baptist University
Dallas Christian College
East Texas Baptist University
East Texas State University
  Commerce
  Texarkana
El Centro College
Hardin-Simmons University
Howard Payne University
Huston-Tillotson College
Incarnate Word College
Jarvis Christian College
Lamar University—Beaumont
LeTourneau University
Lubbock Christian University
McMurry University
Our Lady of the Lake University of
  San Antonio
Prairie View A&M University
Rice University
St. Edward's University
St. Mary's University
St. Philip's College
Schreiner College
Southwest Texas State University
Southwestern Assemblies of God
  College
Southwestern University
Stephen F. Austin State University
Sul Ross State University
Texas A&I University
Texas A&M University
Texas Christian University
Texas Lutheran College
Texas Southern University
Texas Tech University
Texas Wesleyan University
Texas Woman's University
Trinity University
University of Dallas
University of Houston
  Clear Lake
  Houston
  Victoria
University of Mary Hardin-Baylor
University of North Texas
University of St. Thomas
University of Texas
  Arlington
  Austin
  Dallas
  El Paso
  Permian Basin
  San Antonio
  Tyler
Wayland Baptist University
West Texas State University

Utah

Dixie College
Southern Utah University
University of Utah
Utah State University
Westminster College of Salt Lake
  City

Vermont

Burlington College
Castleton State College
College of St. Joseph in Vermont
Goddard College
Green Mountain College

Johnson State College
Lyndon State College
Middlebury College
Norwich University
St. Michael's College
School for International Training
Trinity College of Vermont
University of Vermont

Virginia

Bluefield College
Bridgewater College
Christopher Newport College
Clinch Valley College of the
  University of Virginia
College of William and Mary
Eastern Mennonite College
Emory and Henry College
Ferrum College
George Mason University
Hampton University
Hollins College
James Madison University
John Tyler Community College
Liberty University
Longwood College
Lynchburg College
Mary Baldwin College
Mary Washington College
Marymount University
Mountain Empire Community
  College
Norfolk State University
Old Dominion University
Patrick Henry Community College
Radford University
Randolph-Macon College
Randolph-Macon Woman's College
Roanoke College
St. Paul's College
Shenandoah University
Sweet Briar College
University of Richmond
University of Virginia
Virginia Commonwealth University
Virginia Intermont College
Virginia Polytechnic Institute and
  State University
Virginia State University
Virginia Union University
Virginia Wesleyan College
Washington and Lee University

Washington

Central Washington University
City University
Eastern Washington University
Evergreen State College
Gonzaga University
Heritage College
Northwest College of the
  Assemblies of God
Pacific Lutheran University
St. Martin's College
Seattle Pacific University
Seattle University
University of Puget Sound
University of Washington
Walla Walla College
Washington State University
Western Washington University
Whitman College
Whitworth College

West Virginia

Alderson-Broaddus College
Bethany College
Bluefield State College
Concord College
Davis and Elkins College
Fairmont State College
Glenville State College
Marshall University
Salem-Teikyo University

Shepherd College
University of Charleston
West Liberty State College
West Virginia Institute of
  Technology
West Virginia State College
West Virginia University
  Morgantown
  Parkersburg
West Virginia Wesleyan College
Wheeling Jesuit College

Wisconsin

Alverno College
Beloit College
Cardinal Stritch College
Carroll College
Carthage College
Concordia University Wisconsin
Edgewood College
Lakeland College
Lawrence University
Marian College of Fond du Lac
Marquette University
Mount Mary College
Northland College
Ripon College
St. Norbert College
Silver Lake College
University of Wisconsin
  Eau Claire
  Green Bay
  La Crosse
  Madison
  Milwaukee
  Oshkosh
  Parkside
  River Falls
  Stevens Point
  Superior
  Whitewater
University of Wisconsin Center:
  Richland
Viterbo College
Wisconsin Lutheran College

Wyoming

Northwest College
University of Wyoming

American Samoa, Caroline Islands, Guam, Marianas, Virgin Islands

Community College of Micronesia
Northern Marianas College

Canada

McGill University

Telecourses

Alabama

Gadsden State Community College
Jefferson State Community College
Troy State University
  Dothan
  Montgomery

Alaska

University of Alaska Southeast

Arizona

Arizona State University
Arizona Western College
Cochise College
Glendale Community College
Mohave Community College
Rio Salado Community College
University of Arizona
Yavapai College

Arkansas

Garland County Community
  College
North Arkansas Community College
Rich Mountain Community College
University of Arkansas at Little
  Rock
Westark Community College

California

Allan Hancock College
Barstow College
California State Polytechnic
  University: Pomona
California State University
  Chico
  Fresno
  Hayward
  Los Angeles
  Northridge
Cerritos Community College
Chabot College
Citrus College
Coastline Community College
Cosumnes River College
Crafton Hills College
De Anza College
El Camino College
Glendale Community College
Lassen College
Long Beach City College
Los Angeles Harbor College
Los Angeles Pierce College
Mendocino College
MiraCosta College
Mount San Antonio College
Ohlone College
Oxnard College
Pasadena City College
San Joaquin Delta College
San Jose State University
Sierra College
Solano Community College
Southwestern College
University of California: Santa
  Barbara
Yuba College

Colorado

Arapahoe Community College
Colorado Mountain College
  Alpine Campus
  Spring Valley Campus
  Timberline Campus
Colorado Northwestern Community
  College
Colorado State University
Front Range Community College
Metropolitan State College of
  Denver
National College
Northeastern Junior College
Pikes Peak Community College
Pueblo Community College
Red Rocks Community College
University of Colorado at Colorado
  Springs
University of Southern Colorado

Connecticut

Housatonic Community College
Mattatuck Community College
Quinnipiac College
South Central Community College

Delaware

University of Delaware

Florida

Broward Community College
Daytona Beach Community College
Florida Community College at
  Jacksonville
Florida Keys Community College

Gulf Coast Community College
Hillsborough Community College
Lake City Community College
Lake-Sumter Community College
Pasco-Hernando Community
    College
Pensacola Junior College
St. Petersburg Junior College
Seminole Community College
South Florida Community College
Tallahassee Community College
University of Central Florida
Valencia Community College

Georgia

DeKalb College
Macon College

Hawaii

University of Hawaii
    Hilo
    Kauai Community College
    Leeward Community College

Idaho

College of Southern Idaho
Lewis Clark State College
University of Idaho

Illinois

Belleville Area College
City Colleges of Chicago
    Chicago City-Wide College
    Olive-Harvey College
    Richard J. Daley College
    Wright College
College of DuPage
Elgin Community College
Governors State University
Highland Community College
Illinois Institute of Technology
John A. Logan College
KAES College
Lewis and Clark Community
    College
Oakton Community College
Parkland College
Rend Lake College
Shawnee Community College
State Community College
Triton College
Waubonsee Community College
Western Illinois University
William Rainey Harper College

Indiana

Calumet College of St. Joseph
Indiana State University
Indiana Vocational Technical
    College
    Northcentral
    Northeast
Purdue University
Taylor University

Iowa

Clinton Community College
Des Moines Area Community
    College
Iowa Central Community College
Iowa Lakes Community College
Iowa State University
Iowa Wesleyan College
Kirkwood Community College
Muscatine Community College
North Iowa Area Community
    College
Scott Community College
Southwestern Community College

Kansas

Barton County Community College
Butler County Community College
Emporia State University

Fort Scott Community College
Johnson County Community
    College
Kansas City Kansas Community
    College
Labette Community College
Pratt Community College
Wichita State University

Kentucky

Lees College
Lexington Community College
Maysville Community College
Murray State University
Paducah Community College
St. Catharine College
Southeast Community College
Western Kentucky University

Louisiana

Louisiana Tech University
McNeese State University
Northeast Louisiana University
Southeastern Louisiana University
University of New Orleans
Xavier University of Louisiana

Maine

Maine Maritime Academy
University of Maine
    Augusta
    Fort Kent
    Orono
    Presque Isle
University of Southern Maine

Maryland

Anne Arundel Community College
Cecil Community College
Charles County Community College
Chesapeake College
Dundalk Community College
Garrett Community College
Hagerstown Junior College
New Community College of
    Baltimore
Prince George's Community College
Towson State University
University of Maryland
    Baltimore County
    College Park
    University College
Wor-Wic Tech Community College

Massachusetts

Boston University
Bridgewater State College
Bristol Community College
Bunker Hill Community College
Fitchburg State College
Massachusetts Bay Community
    College
North Shore Community College

Michigan

Alpena Community College
Charles Stewart Mott Community
    College
Delta College
Grand Rapids Community College
Grand Valley State University
Henry Ford Community College
Jackson Community College
Kalamazoo Valley Community
    College
Kellogg Community College
Lansing Community College
Michigan State University
Muskegon Community College
Northern Michigan University
Northwestern Michigan College
Sacred Heart Major Seminary
Wayne State University

Minnesota

Brainerd Community College
Inver Hills Community College
Itasca Community College:
    Arrowhead Region
Normandale Community College
Rochester Community College
University of Minnesota: Twin
    Cities
Willmar Technical College
Worthington Community College

Mississippi

Mississippi University for Women

Missouri

Central Missouri State University
East Central College
Park College
St. Louis Community College
    Florissant Valley
    Meramec
Southwest Missouri State University
University of Missouri: Columbia

Montana

Miles Community College
University of Montana

Nebraska

Metropolitan Community College
University of Nebraska
    Kearney
    Lincoln
Western Nebraska Community
    College: Scottsbluff Campus

Nevada

Truckee Meadows Community
    College

New Hampshire

School for Lifelong Learning

New Jersey

Atlantic Community College
Bergen Community College
Brookdale Community College
Burlington County College
County College of Morris
Cumberland County College
Gloucester County College
Mercer County Community College
New Jersey Institute of Technology
Ocean County College
Sussex County Community College
Thomas Edison State College
Union County College

New Mexico

Clovis Community College
Eastern New Mexico University
New Mexico Institute of Mining
    and Technology
University of New Mexico

New York

Canisius College
College of New Rochelle
College of St. Rose
Columbia University: School of
    Engineering and Applied Science
Erie Community College
    City Campus
    North Campus
    South Campus
Genesee Community College
Jamestown Community College
Onondaga Community College
Rensselaer Polytechnic Institute
Rochester Institute of Technology
State University of New York
    College of Technology at Canton

Suffolk County Community College
    Eastern Campus
    Selden
    Western Campus
Ulster County Community College
Westchester Community College

North Carolina

Anson Community College
Blue Ridge Community College
Brunswick Community College
Cape Fear Community College
Carteret Community College
Central Piedmont Community
    College
Cleveland Community College
Craven Community College
Davidson County Community
    College
Duke University
Durham Technical Community
    College
Edgecombe Community College
Guilford Technical Community
    College
Haywood Community College
James Sprunt Community College
Mayland Community College
McDowell Technical Community
    College
Montgomery Community College
Nash Community College
North Carolina State University
Piedmont Community College
Pitt Community College
Roanoke-Chowan Community
    College
Sandhills Community College
Stanly Community College
Wayne Community College
Winston-Salem State University

North Dakota

Mayville State University
Minot State University
North Dakota State University
    Bottineau and Institute of
        Forestry
    Fargo
University of North Dakota
    Lake Region
    Williston

Ohio

Capital University
Cedarville College
Cuyahoga Community College
    Metropolitan Campus
    Western Campus
Kent State University: Stark
    Campus
Lakeland Community College
Lorain County Community College
Ohio University: Chillicothe
    Campus

Oklahoma

Cameron University
Connors State College
East Central University
Eastern Oklahoma State College
Northwestern Oklahoma State
    University
Oklahoma State University
Redlands Community College
Rogers State College
Rose State College
University of Oklahoma
    Health Sciences Center
    Norman

Oregon

Central Oregon Community College
Clatsop Community College

Eastern Oregon State College
Lane Community College
Linn-Benton Community College
Mount Hood Community College
Oregon State University
Rogue Community College
Southwestern Oregon Community
College
Umpqua Community College
Western Oregon State College

Pennsylvania

Bloomsburg University of
Pennsylvania
Luzerne County Community
College
Montgomery County Community
College
Reading Area Community College
Robert Morris College
Westmoreland County Community
College

Puerto Rico

Universidad Metropolitana

Rhode Island

Community College of Rhode
Island

South Carolina

University of South Carolina
Beaufort
Columbia
Union
Williamsburg Technical College

Tennessee

Chattanooga State Technical
Community College
Dyersburg State Community
College
Memphis State University
Nashville State Technical Institute
Pellissippi State Technical
Community College
Shelby State Community College
Walters State Community College

Texas

Amarillo College
Angelina College
Austin College
Central Texas College
Collin County Community College
District
Corpus Christi State University
Del Mar College
El Centro College
El Paso Community College
Houston Baptist University
Houston Community College
Howard Payne University
Lee College
Mountain View College
Navarro College
North Harris Montgomery
Community College District
Odessa College
Richland College
St. Philip's College
San Antonio College
Tarrant County Junior College
University of Texas at Austin

Utah

Dixie College
University of Utah

Vermont

Community College of Vermont
Vermont Technical College

Virginia

Bridgewater College
Clinch Valley College of the
University of Virginia
Dabney S. Lancaster Community
College
John Tyler Community College
New River Community College
Northern Virginia Community
College
Old Dominion University
Shenandoah University
Southwest Virginia Community
College
University of Virginia
Virginia Highlands Community
College
Virginia Polytechnic Institute and
State University

Washington

Eastern Washington University
Edmonds Community College
Green River Community College
Pierce College
Seattle Central Community College
Seattle Pacific University
Shoreline Community College
South Puget Sound Community
College
Spokane Community College
Tacoma Community College
University of Washington
Washington State University
Whatcom Community College

West Virginia

Bluefield State College
Marshall University
West Liberty State College
West Virginia Institute of
Technology
West Virginia State College
West Virginia University
Morgantown
Parkersburg

Wisconsin

Fox Valley Technical College
University of Wisconsin: Madison
University of Wisconsin Center
Baraboo/Sauk County
Marinette County

Wyoming

Central Wyoming College
Eastern Wyoming College
Laramie County Community
College
University of Wyoming

United Nations semester

Alabama

Spring Hill College

California

Mount St. Mary's College
Occidental College
Santa Clara University
Scripps College
University of the Pacific

Florida

Florida Southern College
New College of the University of
South Florida
Stetson University

Illinois

Illinois Wesleyan University
Lincoln Land Community College
Millikin University
North Central College
Rockford College
Southern Illinois University at
Carbondale

Indiana

DePauw University
Franklin College
Hanover College
Indiana University Bloomington
Valparaiso University

Iowa

Drake University
Morningside College
Simpson College

Kansas

Fort Hays State University

Kentucky

Northern Kentucky University

Maryland

Western Maryland College

Minnesota

Hamline University

Mississippi

Millsaps College

Missouri

Park College
Westminster College
William Jewell College
William Woods College

Nebraska

Nebraska Wesleyan University

New Jersey

College of St. Elizabeth
Drew University

New Mexico

Eastern New Mexico University

New York

Alfred University
College of New Rochelle
Elmira College
Fordham University
Hobart College
Long Island University: Brooklyn
Campus
William Smith College

North Carolina

East Carolina University
Guilford College
Lenoir-Rhyne College
Meredith College
Salem College

Ohio

Ashland University
Baldwin-Wallace College
College of Wooster
Kent State University
Muskingum College

Oregon

Willamette University

Pennsylvania

Bucknell University
Gettysburg College
Seton Hill College
Susquehanna University

Thiel College
University of Scranton
Ursinus College
Wilson College

South Carolina

Winthrop University

Utah

Weber State University

Virginia

Hollins College

West Virginia

Bethany College

Wisconsin

Carroll College
University of Wisconsin: Milwaukee

Wyoming

University of Wyoming

Switzerland

American College of Switzerland

Visiting/exchange student program

Alabama

Alabama State University
Auburn University at Montgomery
Birmingham-Southern College
Miles College
Mobile College
University of Alabama
Birmingham
Tuscaloosa
University of Montevallo

Alaska

Alaska Pacific University
University of Alaska
Anchorage
Fairbanks

Arizona

Arizona State University
Glendale Community College
Grand Canyon University
Northern Arizona University
University of Arizona
Western International University

Arkansas

Arkansas State University
Hendrix College
Ouachita Baptist University
University of Arkansas
Fayetteville
Little Rock

California

Azusa Pacific University
California Polytechnic State
University: San Luis Obispo
California State Polytechnic
University: Pomona
California State University
Bakersfield
Chico
Dominguez Hills
Fresno
Hayward
Long Beach
Los Angeles
Northridge
Sacramento
Stanislaus
Chapman University

Charles R. Drew University: College
of Allied Health
Claremont McKenna College
College of Notre Dame
Dominican College of San Rafael
Fashion Institute of Design and
Merchandising
Los Angeles
San Francisco
Foothill College
Harvey Mudd College
Holy Names College
Humboldt State University
Mills College
Mount St. Mary's College
Occidental College
Otis/Parsons School of Art and
Design
Pitzer College
Pomona College
San Diego State University
San Francisco Art Institute
San Jose State University
Scripps College
Sonoma State University
Southern California College
Southern California Institute of
Architecture
Stanford University
United States International
University
University of California
Los Angeles
Riverside
San Diego
Santa Barbara
Santa Cruz
University of the Pacific
University of San Diego
University of San Francisco
Westmont College
Whittier College
World College West

Colorado

Colorado College
Colorado State University
Fort Lewis College
Metropolitan State College of
Denver
United States Air Force Academy
University of Colorado at Boulder
University of Northern Colorado
University of Southern Colorado
Western State College of Colorado

Connecticut

Central Connecticut State
University
Connecticut College
Eastern Connecticut State
University
Fairfield University
Quinnipiac College
Sacred Heart University
Trinity College
United States Coast Guard
Academy
University of Bridgeport
University of Hartford
Wesleyan University

Delaware

Delaware State College
University of Delaware
Wesley College

District of Columbia

Corcoran School of Art
Gallaudet University
George Washington University
Georgetown University
Howard University
Trinity College

Florida

Broward Community College
Eckerd College
Flagler College
Florida Atlantic University
Florida International University
Florida Southern College
Lake City Community College
Lake-Sumter Community College
New College of the University of
South Florida
Ringling School of Art and Design
Rollins College
St. Petersburg Junior College
Schiller International University
Stetson University
University of Miami
University of South Florida
Webber College

Georgia

Agnes Scott College
Emory University
Georgia College
Morehouse College
Oglethorpe University
Shorter College
Spelman College
University of Georgia

Hawaii

Hawaii Loa College
University of Hawaii
Hilo
Kapiolani Community College
Manoa

Idaho

Albertson College
Boise State University
University of Idaho

Illinois

Augustana College
Aurora University
Chicago State University
Harrington Institute of Interior
Design
Illinois Benedictine College
Illinois Institute of Technology
Illinois State University
Illinois Wesleyan University
Knox College
Lake Forest College
North Central College
North Park College and Theological
Seminary
Northeastern Illinois University
Northwestern University
Oakton Community College
St. Xavier University
School of the Art Institute of
Chicago
Southern Illinois University at
Carbondale
Trinity College
University of Illinois at Urbana-
Champaign
Western Illinois University
Wheaton College

Indiana

Ball State University
DePauw University
Franklin College
Hanover College
Indiana University at South Bend
Indiana University—Purdue
University at Fort Wayne
St. Mary-of-the-Woods College
Taylor University
University of Evansville
University of Indianapolis
University of Notre Dame

Valparaiso University
Wabash College

Iowa

Buena Vista College
Drake University
Graceland College
Iowa Wesleyan College
Kirkwood Community College
Luther College
Maharishi International University
Morningside College
Mount Mercy College
Teikyo Westmar University
University of Iowa
University of Northern Iowa
Wartburg College

Kansas

Benedictine College
Bethel College
Emporia State University
Fort Hays State University
Johnson County Community
College
Kansas State University
McPherson College
Pittsburg State University
St. Mary College
Southwestern College
University of Kansas
Lawrence
Medical Center

Kentucky

Asbury College
Berea College
Campbellsville College
Georgetown College
Kentucky State University
Morehead State University
Murray State University
Northern Kentucky University
St. Catharine College
Transylvania University
University of Kentucky
University of Louisville

Louisiana

Centenary College of Louisiana
Grambling State University
Nicholls State University
Northwestern State University
Our Lady of Holy Cross College
Tulane University
University of Southwestern
Louisiana
Xavier University of Louisiana

Maine

Bates College
Bowdoin College
Colby College
College of the Atlantic
Portland School of Art
Thomas College
University of Maine
Farmington
Orono
Presque Isle
University of New England
University of Southern Maine

Maryland

Frostburg State University
Goucher College
Maryland College of Art and
Design
Maryland Institute College of Art
St. Mary's College of Maryland
Towson State University

University of Maryland
Baltimore County
College Park
Eastern Shore
Washington College
Western Maryland College

Massachusetts

Amherst College
Anna Maria College for Men and
Women
Aquinas College at Milton
Becker College
Leicester Campus
Worcester Campus
Boston College
Boston University
Brandeis University
Bridgewater State College
Clark University
College of the Holy Cross
Elms College
Emmanuel College
Framingham State College
Gordon College
Hampshire College
Harvard and Radcliffe Colleges
Hellenic College
Lasell College
Lesley College
Massachusetts College of Art
Middlesex Community College
Montserrat College of Art
Mount Holyoke College
Northeastern University
Pine Manor College
Regis College
Salem State College
School of the Museum of Fine Arts
Simmons College
Simon's Rock College of Bard
Smith College
Stonehill College
Suffolk University
University of Massachusetts
Amherst
Boston
Dartmouth
Wellesley College
Westfield State College
Williams College
Worcester Polytechnic Institute

Michigan

Aquinas College
Center for Creative Studies: College
of Art and Design
Cleary College
Concordia College
Delta College
Eastern Michigan University
Grand Valley State University
Hillsdale College
Hope College
Kalamazoo College
Kendall College of Art and Design
Lansing Community College
Michigan State University
Michigan Technological University
Oakland University
Olivet College
University of Detroit Mercy
University of Michigan
Wayne State University

Minnesota

Augsburg College
Bethel College
College of St. Catherine: St.
Catherine Campus
Concordia College: Moorhead
Gustavus Adolphus College
Hamline University

Minneapolis College of Art and
    Design
Moorhead State University
St. Cloud State University
Southwest State University
University of Minnesota: Morris
Winona State University

Mississippi

Delta State University
Jackson State University
Mississippi College
Tougaloo College
University of Southern Mississippi

Missouri

Avila College
Central Missouri State University
Fontbonne College
Kansas City Art Institute
Lindenwood College
Maple Woods Community College
Northeast Missouri State University
Research College of Nursing
Rockhurst College
St. Louis Community College at
    Florissant Valley
Southeast Missouri State University
Southwest Missouri State University
University of Missouri
    Columbia
    Kansas City
Webster University
William Jewell College
William Woods College

Montana

Carroll College
Little Big Horn College
Montana State University
University of Montana
Western Montana College of the
    University of Montana

Nebraska

Doane College
Hastings College
Nebraska Wesleyan University
University of Nebraska
    Kearney
    Lincoln
    Omaha

Nevada

University of Nevada
    Las Vegas
    Reno

New Hampshire

Colby-Sawyer College
Dartmouth College
Franklin Pierce College
Keene State College
New England College
Notre Dame College
St. Anselm College
University of New Hampshire

New Jersey

Bloomfield College
Drew University
Fairleigh Dickinson University
Glassboro State College
Jersey City State College
Montclair State College
Ramapo College of New Jersey
Rutgers—The State University of
    New Jersey
        Camden College of Arts and
            Sciences
        College of Engineering
        Douglass College
        Rutgers College
St. Peter's College

Seton Hall University
Stevens Institute of Technology
Trenton State College
William Paterson College of New
    Jersey

New Mexico

Eastern New Mexico University
New Mexico Institute of Mining
    and Technology
New Mexico State University
University of New Mexico

New York

Alfred University
Bard College
Barnard College
City University of New York
    Baruch College
    Borough of Manhattan
        Community College
    Brooklyn College
    City College
    Hunter College
    John Jay College of Criminal
        Justice
    Lehman College
Colgate University
College of Mount St. Vincent
College of New Rochelle
College of St. Rose
Columbia University
    Columbia College
    School of General Studies
Cooper Union
Cornell University
D'Youville College
Elmira College
Eugene Lang College/New School
    for Social Research
Fordham University
Hamilton College
Hartwick College
Hobart College
Houghton College
Juilliard School
Keuka College
Kol Yaakov Torah Center
Le Moyne College
Long Island University
    Brooklyn Campus
    C. W. Post Campus
Manhattanville College
Marymount College
Marymount Manhattan College
Mount St. Mary College
Nazareth College of Rochester
New York University
Niagara University
Nyack College
Parsons School of Design
Pratt Institute
Rensselaer Polytechnic Institute
Rochester Institute of Technology
Russell Sage College
St. Bonaventure University
St. John Fisher College
Sarah Lawrence College
Siena College
Skidmore College

State University of New York
    Albany
    Binghamton
    Buffalo
    Stony Brook
    College at Brockport
    College at Buffalo
    College at Cortland
    College at Fredonia
    College at Geneseo
    College at New Paltz
    College at Old Westbury
    College at Plattsburgh
    College at Potsdam
    Institute of Technology at
        Utica/Rome
    Oswego
Sullivan County Community
    College
Syracuse University
Union College
United States Military Academy
Utica College of Syracuse
    University
Vassar College
Wagner College
Wells College
William Smith College
Yeshiva University

North Carolina

Appalachian State University
Belmont Abbey College
Bennett College
Campbell University
Duke University
East Carolina University
Forsyth Technical Community
    College
Greensboro College
Guilford College
Johnson C. Smith University
Mars Hill College
Methodist College
North Carolina State University
Queens College
St. Andrews Presbyterian College
Salem College
University of North Carolina
    Chapel Hill
    Charlotte
    Wilmington
Wake Forest University
Warren Wilson College

North Dakota

University of North Dakota

Ohio

Art Academy of Cincinnati
Baldwin-Wallace College
Bluffton College
Bowling Green State University
Cleveland State University
College of Wooster
Cuyahoga Community College:
    Metropolitan Campus
Denison University
John Carroll University
Kent State University
Kenyon College
Marietta College
Miami University: Oxford Campus
Muskingum College
Notre Dame College of Ohio
Oberlin College
Ohio Northern University
Ohio State University: Columbus
    Campus
Ohio University
Ohio Wesleyan University
University of Rio Grande
University of Toledo
Wittenberg University

Wright State University
Xavier University

Oklahoma

East Central University
Oklahoma Baptist University
Oklahoma City University
Oklahoma State University
Phillips University
Southwestern Oklahoma State
    University
University of Oklahoma

Oregon

Clackamas Community College
Eastern Oregon State College
George Fox College
Lewis and Clark College
Linfield College
Mount Hood Community College
Oregon Health Sciences University
Oregon State University
Pacific Northwest College of Art
Pacific University
Portland State University
Reed College
University of Oregon
    Eugene
        Robert Donald Clark Honors
            College
Warner Pacific College
Willamette University

Pennsylvania

Albright College
Allegheny College
Bloomsburg University of
    Pennsylvania
Bryn Mawr College
Bucknell University
California University of
    Pennsylvania
Carnegie Mellon University
Cedar Crest College
Chatham College
Chestnut Hill College
Clarion University of Pennsylvania
College Misericordia
Dickinson College
Eastern College
Edinboro University of
    Pennsylvania
Franklin and Marshall College
Haverford College
Indiana University of Pennsylvania
Juniata College
King's College
Kutztown University of
    Pennsylvania
La Salle University
Lafayette College
Lebanon Valley College of
    Pennsylvania
Lincoln University
Lock Haven University of
    Pennsylvania
Messiah College
Millersville University of
    Pennsylvania
Muhlenberg College
Philadelphia College of Textiles and
    Science
St. Vincent College
Slippery Rock University of
    Pennsylvania
Susquehanna University
Swarthmore College
Temple University
Thiel College
University of the Arts
University of Pennsylvania
West Chester University of
    Pennsylvania
Westminster College

Widener University
Wilson College

Puerto Rico

Pontifical Catholic University of
　Puerto Rico
University of Puerto Rico
　Cayey University College
　Humacao University College
　Mayaguez Campus
　Medical Sciences Campus
　Rio Piedras Campus

Rhode Island

Brown University
Bryant College
Johnson & Wales University
Providence College
Rhode Island College
Rhode Island School of Design
Salve Regina University
University of Rhode Island

South Carolina

Clemson University
Coker College
College of Charleston
Columbia College
Horry-Georgetown Technical
　College
Lander College
Tri-County Technical College
University of South Carolina
　Columbia
　Spartanburg
Winthrop University

South Dakota

Huron University
Northern State University
Sioux Falls College
South Dakota State University
University of South Dakota

Tennessee

Hiwassee College
King College
LeMoyne-Owen College
Maryville College
Memphis College of Art
Memphis State University
Rhodes College
Tennessee State University
Union University
University of Tennessee
　Knoxville
　Martin
　Memphis
Vanderbilt University

Texas

Baylor University
Houston Community College
Incarnate Word College
Laredo Junior College
Northwood Institute: Texas Campus
Rice University
Schreiner College
Southwestern University
Texas A&M University
Texas Lutheran College
Texas Wesleyan University
Texas Woman's University
University of Houston: Downtown
University of St. Thomas
University of Texas
　Austin
　Health Science Center at
　　Houston

Utah

University of Utah
Utah State University

Vermont

Middlebury College
St. Michael's College
University of Vermont

Virginia

College of William and Mary
John Tyler Community College
Lynchburg College
Mary Baldwin College
Old Dominion University
Radford University
Randolph-Macon College
Randolph-Macon Woman's College
Southside Virginia Community
　College
Sweet Briar College
University of Richmond
Virginia Commonwealth University
Virginia Wesleyan College
Washington and Lee University

Washington

Eastern Washington University
Edmonds Community College
Everett Community College
Gonzaga University
Pacific Lutheran University
Seattle Pacific University
Seattle University
University of Washington
Washington State University
Western Washington University
Whitman College
Whitworth College

West Virginia

Alderson-Broaddus College
Bluefield State College
University of Charleston
West Virginia University
West Virginia Wesleyan College
Wheeling Jesuit College

Wisconsin

Alverno College
Beloit College
Carroll College
Carthage College
Milwaukee Institute of Art &
　Design
Ripon College
St. Norbert College
University of Wisconsin
　Eau Claire
　Green Bay
　La Crosse
　Platteville
　River Falls
　Superior

Wyoming

University of Wyoming

**American Samoa, Caroline
Islands, Guam, Marianas,
Virgin Islands**

University of the Virgin Islands

Canada

McGill University

France

American University of Paris

Mexico

Sistema Instituto Tecnologico y de
　Estudios Superiores de
　Monterrey

Switzerland

American College of Switzerland
Franklin College: Switzerland

Arab Republic of Egypt

American University in Cairo

Washington semester

Alabama

Mobile College
Spring Hill College
University of Alabama

Arizona

Arizona State University
Grand Canyon University

Arkansas

Hendrix College
John Brown University

California

Azusa Pacific University
Biola University
California Baptist College
California State University: Long
　Beach
Chapman University
Claremont McKenna College
Fresno Pacific College
Loyola Marymount University
Mills College
Mount St. Mary's College
Occidental College
Orange Coast College
Pitzer College
Point Loma Nazarene College
Pomona College
Santa Clara University
Scripps College
Southern California College
Stanford University
University of California
　Davis
　Irvine
　Riverside
　San Diego
University of the Pacific
University of Redlands
University of Southern California
Westmont College

Colorado

Colorado College
University of Colorado at Boulder
University of Denver

Connecticut

Albertus Magnus College
Connecticut College
Eastern Connecticut State
　University
Fairfield University
Sacred Heart University
Trinity College
University of Bridgeport
University of Hartford
Wesleyan University

District of Columbia

American University
Trinity College

Florida

Barry University
Florida Southern College
New College of the University of
　South Florida
Palm Beach Atlantic College
Rollins College
Stetson University
University of Tampa

Georgia

Agnes Scott College
Covenant College
Emory University
Oglethorpe University
Spelman College
University of Georgia
Wesleyan College
West Georgia College

Idaho

Albertson College
Northwest Nazarene College

Illinois

Blackburn College
College of St. Francis
Elmhurst College
Greenville College
Illinois State University
Illinois Wesleyan University
Knox College
MacMurray College
Millikin University
Monmouth College
North Central College
Northwestern University
Olivet Nazarene University
Principia College
Rockford College
Rosary College
Southern Illinois University at
　Carbondale
Trinity Christian College
Trinity College
Wheaton College

Indiana

Ball State University
DePauw University
Earlham College
Franklin College
Hanover College
Huntington College
Indiana University Bloomington
St. Joseph's College
St. Mary's College
Taylor University
University of Notre Dame
Valparaiso University
Wabash College

Iowa

Briar Cliff College
Central College
Coe College
Cornell College
Dordt College
Drake University
Grand View College
Grinnell College
Iowa State University
Luther College
Morningside College
Northwestern College
Simpson College
Teikyo Westmar University
University of Iowa
University of Northern Iowa
William Penn College

Kansas

Bethany College
MidAmerica Nazarene College
Tabor College
University of Kansas
Wichita State University

Kentucky

Asbury College
Campbellsville College
Lees College
Morehead State University
Transylvania University

Louisiana

Centenary College of Louisiana
Louisiana State University in
   Shreveport
Tulane University
University of New Orleans
University of Southwestern
   Louisiana

Maine

Bates College
Bowdoin College
Colby College
Unity College
University of Southern Maine

Maryland

Hood College
Johns Hopkins University
Montgomery College: Takoma Park
   Campus
Mount St. Mary's College
Washington College
Western Maryland College

Massachusetts

American International College
Anna Maria College for Men and
   Women
Assumption College
Boston College
Boston University
Bradford College
Brandeis University
Clark University
College of the Holy Cross
Curry College
Eastern Nazarene College
Emerson College
Emmanuel College
Framingham State College
Gordon College
Lesley College
Merrimack College
Mount Holyoke College
Nichols College
Pine Manor College
Regis College
Simmons College
Smith College
Stonehill College
Suffolk University
Tufts University
University of Massachusetts
   Amherst
   Dartmouth
Wellesley College
Western New England College
Westfield State College
Wheaton College
Worcester Polytechnic Institute

Michigan

Adrian College
Albion College
Alma College
Calvin College
Eastern Michigan University
Grand Rapids Baptist College and
   Seminary
Grand Valley State University
Hillsdale College
Hope College
Marygrove College
Spring Arbor College
University of Michigan
   Ann Arbor
   Dearborn

Minnesota

Augsburg College
Bethel College
Carleton College
College of St. Benedict

Concordia College: Moorhead
Gustavus Adolphus College
Hamline University
Moorhead State University
St. John's University
St. Olaf College

Mississippi

Millsaps College
Tougaloo College

Missouri

Avila College
Drury College
Evangel College
Lindenwood College
Maryville University
Northwest Missouri State
   University
Park College
Research College of Nursing
Rockhurst College
Stephens College
Washington University
Westminster College
William Jewell College
William Woods College

Nebraska

Creighton University
Doane College
Hastings College
Nebraska Wesleyan University

Nevada

University of Nevada: Las Vegas

New Hampshire

Colby-Sawyer College
Dartmouth College
St. Anselm College
University of New Hampshire

New Jersey

College of St. Elizabeth
Drew University
Jersey City State College
Kean College of New Jersey
Monmouth College
Montclair State College
Rutgers—The State University of
   New Jersey
   Douglass College
   Livingston College
   Newark College of Arts and
      Sciences
   Rutgers College
St. Peter's College
Seton Hall University
Stockton State College
Upsala College

New Mexico

University of New Mexico

New York

Alfred University
Bard College
Canisius College
City University of New York
   Brooklyn College
   Lehman College
Colgate University
College of New Rochelle
Cornell University
Elmira College
Hamilton College
Hartwick College
Hobart College
Hofstra University
Houghton College
Jamestown Community College
Keuka College
King's College

Le Moyne College
Manhattanville College
Marist College
Marymount College
Marymount Manhattan College
Molloy College
Mount St. Mary College
Nazareth College of Rochester
New York University
Niagara University
Roberts Wesleyan College
Russell Sage College
St. Bonaventure University
St. John Fisher College
St. Lawrence University
Siena College
Skidmore College
State University of New York
   Buffalo
   Stony Brook
   College at Brockport
   College at Buffalo
   College at Cortland
   College at Fredonia
   College at Geneseo
   College at Oneonta
   Oswego
Syracuse University
Union College
University of Rochester
Utica College of Syracuse
   University
Wells College
William Smith College

North Carolina

Bennett College
Campbell University
Davidson College
Duke University
Elon College
Guilford College
Johnson C. Smith University
Lenoir-Rhyne College
Meredith College
Methodist College
Montreat-Anderson College
Queens College
St. Andrews Presbyterian College
Salem College
University of North Carolina at
   Greensboro

Ohio

Ashland University
Baldwin-Wallace College
Bowling Green State University
Capital University
Case Western Reserve University
College of Wooster
Denison University
Heidelberg College
Hiram College
Kent State University
Malone College
Marietta College
Mount Union College
Muskingum College
Oberlin College
Ohio Dominican College
Ohio Northern University
Ohio State University: Marion
   Campus
Ohio Wesleyan University
Otterbein College
University of Cincinnati
University of Findlay
Wilmington College
Wittenberg University
Xavier University

Oklahoma

Oklahoma City University
Oral Roberts University

Phillips University
University of Tulsa

Oregon

George Fox College
Lewis and Clark College
Linfield College
Pacific University
Portland State University
Willamette University

Pennsylvania

Albright College
Allegheny College
Allentown College of St. Francis de
   Sales
Alvernia College
Beaver College
Bucknell University
Carnegie Mellon University
Cedar Crest College
Chatham College
Clarion University of Pennsylvania
Dickinson College
Duquesne University
Eastern College
Edinboro University of
   Pennsylvania
Franklin and Marshall College
Gannon University
Geneva College
Gettysburg College
Indiana University of Pennsylvania
Juniata College
King's College
Lafayette College
Lebanon Valley College of
   Pennsylvania
Lehigh University
Lycoming College
Mercyhurst College
Messiah College
Moravian College
Muhlenberg College
Point Park College
Rosemont College
St. Francis College
St. Joseph's University
St. Vincent College
Seton Hill College
Shippensburg University of
   Pennsylvania
Susquehanna University
Thiel College
University of Pittsburgh
   Greensburg
   Johnstown
   Pittsburgh
University of Scranton
Ursinus College
Villanova University
Washington and Jefferson College
Westminster College
Widener University
Wilson College
York College of Pennsylvania

Puerto Rico

University of Puerto Rico: Cayey
   University College

South Carolina

Central Wesleyan College
College of Charleston
Furman University
Presbyterian College

South Dakota

Northern State University
Sioux Falls College

Tennessee

Carson-Newman College
King College

Lambuth University
Maryville College
Milligan College
Rhodes College
University of the South
Vanderbilt University
William Jennings Bryan College

Texas
Austin College
Dallas Baptist University
Hardin-Simmons University
LeTourneau University
St. Mary's University
Southwestern University
Texas Christian University
Texas Lutheran College
Trinity University
University of Dallas

Utah
Brigham Young University
University of Utah
Weber State University

Vermont
Middlebury College
St. Michael's College
University of Vermont

Virginia
Eastern Mennonite College
Hampden-Sydney College
Hollins College
Liberty University
Lynchburg College
Randolph-Macon College
Randolph-Macon Woman's College
Roanoke College
Sweet Briar College
University of Richmond
Virginia Polytechnic Institute and
    State University
Washington and Lee University

Washington
St. Martin's College
Seattle Pacific University
University of Washington
Whitman College
Whitworth College

West Virginia
Bethany College
Davis and Elkins College
Shepherd College
University of Charleston
West Virginia University
West Virginia Wesleyan College
Wheeling Jesuit College

Wisconsin
Beloit College
Carroll College
Carthage College
Lakeland College
Lawrence University
Marquette University
Mount Mary College
Ripon College
St. Norbert College
University of Wisconsin: Milwaukee

Wyoming
University of Wyoming

Weekend college

Alabama
Alabama State University
Athens State College

Auburn University at Montgomery
Bessemer State Technical College
Birmingham-Southern College
Bishop State Community College
Gadsden State Community College
Jefferson State Community College
John C. Calhoun State Community
    College
Shelton State Community College
Shoals Community College
Troy State University at Dothan
University of Alabama
    Birmingham
    Tuscaloosa
University of Montevallo
University of South Alabama
Walker State Technical College

Alaska
Alaska Pacific University

Arizona
Cochise College
Glendale Community College
Mesa Community College
Rio Salado Community College
Yavapai College

Arkansas
East Arkansas Community College
Mississippi County Community
    College
North Arkansas Community College
Shorter College

California
Allan Hancock College
Barstow College
California State University:
    Dominguez Hills
Chabot College
City College of San Francisco
Coastline Community College
Crafton Hills College
De Anza College
Diablo Valley College
East Los Angeles College
Foothill College
Fresno City College
Golden Gate University
Holy Names College
John F. Kennedy University
Long Beach City College
Los Angeles City College
Los Angeles Harbor College
Marymount College
MiraCosta College
Mission College
New College of California
Orange Coast College
Pacific Oaks College
Rio Hondo College
St. Mary's College of California
San Diego City College
San Jose City College
United States International
    University
University of La Verne
Woodbury University
World College West

Colorado
Aims Community College
Arapahoe Community College
Colorado Christian University
Community College of Denver
Denver Technical College
Metropolitan State College of
    Denver
National College
Red Rocks Community College
University of Denver

Connecticut
Eastern Connecticut State
    University
Norwalk Community College
Sacred Heart University
St. Joseph College
South Central Community College
Teikyo-Post University
University of Bridgeport

Delaware
Delaware State College
Wilmington College

District of Columbia
Mount Vernon College
Southeastern University
Trinity College
University of the District of
    Columbia

Florida
Bethune-Cookman College
Broward Community College
Daytona Beach Community College
Florida Agricultural and Mechanical
    University
Florida Atlantic University
Florida Community College at
    Jacksonville
Florida International University
Gulf Coast Community College
Hillsborough Community College
Indian River Community College
Jacksonville University
Jones College
Lake-Sumter Community College
Miami-Dade Community College
North Florida Junior College
Nova University
Palm Beach Community College
Pasco-Hernando Community
    College
St. Leo College
St. Petersburg Junior College
University of South Florida
Valencia Community College
Webber College

Georgia
Albany State College
Atlanta Christian College
Atlanta Metropolitan College
Brenau Women's College
DeKalb College
Kennesaw State College
Mercer University Atlanta
Southern College of Technology

Hawaii
Hawaii Pacific University
University of Hawaii
    Leeward Community College
    West Oahu

Idaho
Boise State University
Lewis Clark State College

Illinois
Aurora University
Belleville Area College
City Colleges of Chicago
    Chicago City-Wide College
    Malcolm X College
    Richard J. Daley College
    Wright College
College of DuPage
College of St. Francis
Concordia University
De Paul University
Elgin Community College
Elmhurst College
Governors State University

Illinois Central College
Illinois Institute of Technology
International Academy of
    Merchandising and Design
John A. Logan College
KAES College
Lewis and Clark Community
    College
Loyola University of Chicago
Midstate College
Moraine Valley Community College
North Central College
Oakton Community College
Parkland College
Prairie State College
Roosevelt University
St. Xavier University
Sangamon State University
Shimer College
Southern Illinois University
    Carbondale
    Edwardsville
Triton College
Waubonsee Community College
William Rainey Harper College

Indiana
Bethel College
Indiana University
    Northwest
    South Bend
    Southeast
Indiana University—Purdue
    University
    Fort Wayne
    Indianapolis
Indiana Vocational Technical
    College
    Central Indiana
    Kokomo
    Northwest
    Southeast
    Whitewater
Purdue University
    Calumet
    North Central Campus
St. Mary-of-the-Woods College

Iowa
Briar Cliff College
Des Moines Area Community
    College
Drake University
Iowa Lakes Community College
Iowa Western Community College
Kirkwood Community College
Mount Mercy College
St. Ambrose University
Simpson College
Teikyo Marycrest University
University of Dubuque

Kansas
Johnson County Community
    College
Kansas City Kansas Community
    College
Kansas Newman College
Kansas State University
St. Mary College

Kentucky
Brescia College
Elizabethtown Community College
Hazard Community College
Jefferson Community College
Kentucky State University
Madisonville Community College
Maysville Community College
Morehead State University
Northern Kentucky University
Paducah Community College
Spalding University
Thomas More College

University of Kentucky
University of Louisville

Louisiana

Grambling State University
Loyola University
University of New Orleans

Maine

Husson College

Maryland

Anne Arundel Community College
Capitol College
Charles County Community College
College of Notre Dame of
  Maryland
Coppin State College
Dundalk Community College
Howard Community College
Maryland College of Art and
  Design
Montgomery College
  Germantown Campus
  Rockville Campus
  Takoma Park Campus
Morgan State University
Prince George's Community College
Towson State University
University of Baltimore
University of Maryland
  Eastern Shore
  University College
Villa Julie College

Massachusetts

American International College
Anna Maria College for Men and
  Women
Aquinas College at Newton
Elms College
Emmanuel College
Lesley College
Newbury College
Northern Essex Community College
Quinsigamond Community College
Wentworth Institute of Technology

Michigan

Aquinas College
Baker College of Port Huron
Eastern Michigan University
Grand Rapids Community College
Jackson Community College
Kalamazoo Valley Community
  College
Kellogg Community College
Lansing Community College
Macomb Community College
Northern Michigan University
Northwestern Michigan College
Spring Arbor College
University of Michigan
Wayne State University
Western Michigan University
William Tyndale College

Minnesota

Anoka-Ramsey Community College
Augsburg College
Austin Community College
Brainerd Community College
College of St. Catherine: St.
  Catherine Campus
Concordia College: St. Paul
Inver Hills Community College
Mankato State University
Metropolitan State University
Minneapolis Community College
Normandale Community College
North Central Bible College
Rochester Community College
University of St. Thomas
Willmar Community College

Mississippi

Blue Mountain College
Jackson State University
Mississippi Gulf Coast Community
  College: Jefferson Davis Campus
Mississippi University for Women

Missouri

Avila College
Central Missouri State University
Culver-Stockton College
Drury College
East Central College
Fontbonne College
Jefferson College
Maryville University
Mineral Area College
North Central Missouri College
Park College
Penn Valley Community College
St. Louis Community College at
  Florissant Valley
University of Missouri: Kansas City

Montana

Rocky Mountain College
Western Montana College of the
  University of Montana

Nebraska

Clarkson College
College of St. Mary
Dana College
Metropolitan Community College

New Hampshire

Keene State College
New Hampshire College

New Jersey

Atlantic Community College
Bergen Community College
Bloomfield College
Brookdale Community College
Burlington County College
Camden County College
College of St. Elizabeth
Fairleigh Dickinson University
  Edward Williams College
  Madison
Jersey City State College
Katharine Gibbs School
Monmouth College
Montclair State College
Passaic County Community College
Ramapo College of New Jersey
Stockton State College
Union County College
Upsala College

New Mexico

College of Santa Fe
New Mexico Junior College
New Mexico State University
  Carlsbad
  Las Cruces
University of New Mexico

New York

Broome Community College
City University of New York
  Borough of Manhattan
    Community College
  Brooklyn College
  College of Staten Island
  Lehman College
  Medgar Evers College
  New York City Technical
    College
  York College
College for Human Services
College of Mount St. Vincent
Community College of the Finger
  Lakes

Dominican College of Blauvelt
Dowling College
D'Youville College
Erie Community College
  City Campus
  North Campus
  South Campus
Fashion Institute of Technology
Fulton-Montgomery Community
  College
Iona College
Jefferson Community College
Kol Yaakov Torah Center
Long Island University: C. W. Post
  Campus
Maria College
Marymount College
Marymount Manhattan College
Mercy College
Molloy College
Mount St. Mary College
New York Institute of Technology
New York University
Orange County Community College
Pace University
Rochester Institute of Technology
Rockland Community College
St. John's University
St. Joseph's College
Suffolk County Community College
  Eastern Campus
  Western Campus
Trocaire College
Westchester Business Institute

North Carolina

Alamance Community College
Barton College
Bladen Community College
Caldwell Community College and
  Technical Institute
Central Piedmont Community
  College
Craven Community College
Duke University
Durham Technical Community
  College
Fayetteville State University
Fayetteville Technical Community
  College
Greensboro College
John Wesley College
Louisburg College
North Carolina Agricultural and
  Technical State University
Sampson Community College

North Dakota

Minot State University
University of North Dakota

Ohio

Antioch School for Adult and
  Experiential Learning
Baldwin-Wallace College
Capital University
Central Ohio Technical College
Central State University
Circleville Bible College
Clark State Community College
College of Mount St. Joseph
Columbus College of Art and
  Design
Cuyahoga Community College:
  Western Campus
Defiance College
Dyke College
Franklin University
Heidelberg College
Hiram College
Hocking Technical College
Kent State University
Lake Erie College
Lakeland Community College

Lorain County Community College
Lourdes College
Marion Technical College
North Central Technical College
Northwestern College
Notre Dame College of Ohio
Ohio Dominican College
Ohio State University
  Agricultural Technical Institute
  Columbus Campus
  Marion Campus
Ohio University: Eastern Campus
Otterbein College
Terra Technical College
Tiffin University
University of Cincinnati
  Cincinnati
  Clermont College
University of Findlay
University of Toledo
Walsh College
Wittenberg University
Xavier University

Oklahoma

Bacone College
Phillips University

Oregon

Eastern Oregon State College
Lane Community College
Marylhurst College
Oregon State University
Portland Community College

Pennsylvania

Alvernia College
Carlow College
Cedar Crest College
College Misericordia
Community College of Beaver
  County
Community College of Philadelphia
Edinboro University of
  Pennsylvania
Gannon University
Keystone Junior College
Lackawanna Junior College
Lebanon Valley College of
  Pennsylvania
Luzerne County Community
  College
Mercyhurst College
Mount Aloysius College
Peirce Junior College
Pennsylvania College of Technology
Point Park College
Reading Area Community College
Robert Morris College
University of Pittsburgh
  Greensburg
  Pittsburgh
Widener University
Wilkes University

Puerto Rico

Puerto Rico Junior College

Rhode Island

Community College of Rhode
  Island
Johnson & Wales University

South Carolina

Benedict College
Greenville Technical College
Limestone College
Midlands Technical College

South Dakota

Sioux Falls College

Tennessee

Carson-Newman College
Chattanooga State Technical
    Community College
Maryville College
Shelby State Community College
State Technical Institute at
    Memphis
Tennessee State University
Vanderbilt University

Texas

Alvin Community College
Amarillo College
Amber University
Brookhaven College
Dallas Baptist University
El Centro College
El Paso Community College
Houston Community College
Huston-Tillotson College
Lamar University—Beaumont
Lee College
Northwood Institute: Texas Campus
Our Lady of the Lake University of
    San Antonio
Richland College
St. Philip's College
San Antonio College
University of Houston: Clear Lake
University of Texas
        Austin
        Dallas

Utah

Utah State University
Weber State University

Vermont

Burlington College
Community College of Vermont
Johnson State College
Norwich University
Southern Vermont College
Trinity College of Vermont

Virginia

Commonwealth College
Northern Virginia Community
    College
Patrick Henry Community College
Shenandoah University
Strayer College
Tidewater Community College
Virginia Wesleyan College

Washington

City University
Olympic College
Pierce College
Seattle Pacific University

West Virginia

Shepherd College
West Virginia University

Wisconsin

Alverno College
Carthage College
Concordia University Wisconsin
Edgewood College
Marian College of Fond du Lac
Mount Senario College
University of Wisconsin
        Oshkosh
        River Falls
        Stevens Point
Viterbo College

Colleges included in this book

Alabama

Two-year

Alabama Aviation and Technical College, Ozark 36361
Alabama Southern Community College, Monroeville 36461-2000
Bessemer State Technical College, Bessemer 35021
Bishop State Community College, Mobile 36603-5898
Brewer State Junior College, Fayette 35555
Central Alabama Community College: Childersburg Campus, Childersburg 35044
Chattahoochee Valley Community College, Phenix City 36869
Community College of the Air Force, Maxwell AFB 36112-6655
Concordia College, Selma 36701
Douglas MacArthur State Technical College, Opp 36467
Draughons Junior College, Montgomery 36104
Enterprise State Junior College, Enterprise 36331
Gadsden State Community College, Gadsden 35902-0227
George C. Wallace State Community College at Selma, Selma 36701-1049
James H. Faulkner State Community College, Bay Minette 36507
Jefferson State Community College, Birmingham 35215-3098
John C. Calhoun State Community College, Decatur 35609-2216
John M. Patterson State Technical College, Montgomery 36116
Lawson State Community College, Birmingham 35221-1717
Lurleen B. Wallace State Junior College, Andalusia 36420-1418
Marion Military Institute, Marion 36756-0420
Northeast Alabama State Junior College, Rainsville 35986
Reid State Technical College, Evergreen 36401
RETS Electronic Institute, Birmingham 35234
Shelton State Community College, Tuscaloosa 35405
Shoals Community College, Muscle Shoals 35662
Snead State Junior College, Boaz 35957
Southern Union State Junior College, Wadley 36276
Walker College, Jasper 35501
Walker State Technical College, Sumiton 35148
Wallace State Community College at Hanceville, Hanceville 35077-9080

Two-year upper-division

Athens State College, Athens 35611

Four-year

Alabama Agricultural and Mechanical University, Normal 35762
Alabama State University, Montgomery 36101-0271
Auburn University
    Auburn, Auburn 36849-5145
    Montgomery, Montgomery 36117-3596
Birmingham-Southern College, Birmingham 35254
Faulkner University, Montgomery 36109-3398
Huntingdon College, Montgomery 36106-2148
Jacksonville State University, Jacksonville 36265-9982
Judson College, Marion 36756
Livingston University, Livingston 35470
Miles College, Fairfield 35064

Mobile College, Mobile 36663-0220
Oakwood College, Huntsville 35896
Samford University, Birmingham 35229-0000
Selma University, Selma 36701
Southeastern Bible College, Birmingham 35243-4181
Southern Christian University, Montgomery 36117-3553
Spring Hill College, Mobile 36608
Stillman College, Tuscaloosa 35403
Talladega College, Talladega 35160
Troy State University
    Dothan, Dothan 36304-0368
    Montgomery, Montgomery 36103-4419
    Troy, Troy 36082
Tuskegee University, Tuskegee 36088
University of Alabama
    Birmingham, Birmingham 35294
    Huntsville, Huntsville 35899
    Tuscaloosa, Tuscaloosa 35487-0132
University of Montevallo, Montevallo 35115-6030
University of North Alabama, Florence 35632-0001
University of South Alabama, Mobile 36688

Alaska

Two-year

Prince William Sound Community College, Valdez 99686

Four-year

Alaska Bible College, Glennallen 99588
Alaska Pacific University, Anchorage 99508-4672
Sheldon Jackson College, Sitka 99835
University of Alaska
    Anchorage, Anchorage 99508-4675
    Fairbanks, Fairbanks 99775-0060
    Southeast, Juneau 99801

Arizona

Two-year

Arizona Western College, Yuma 85366-0929
Cochise College, Douglas 85607
Eastern Arizona College, Thatcher 85552-0769
Glendale Community College, Glendale 85302-3090
ITT Technical Institute
    Phoenix, Phoenix 85008
    Tucson, Tucson 85714
Lamson Junior College, Phoenix 85017
Mesa Community College, Mesa 85202
Mohave Community College, Kingman 86401
National Education Center: Arizona Automotive Institute, Glendale 85301
Navajo Community College, Tsaile 86556
Northland Pioneer College, Holbrook 86025
Paradise Valley Community College, Phoenix 85032
Pima Community College, Tucson 85709-3010
Rio Salado Community College, Phoenix 85003
Scottsdale Community College, Scottsdale 85250-2699
South Mountain Community College, Phoenix 85040
Yavapai College, Prescott 86301

Two-year upper-division

University of Phoenix, Phoenix 85040

Four-year

American Indian Bible College, Phoenix 85021-2199
Arizona College of the Bible, Phoenix 85021-5197
Arizona State University, Tempe 85287-0112
DeVry Institute of Technology: Phoenix, Phoenix 85021-2995
Embry-Riddle Aeronautical University: Prescott Campus, Prescott 32114
Grand Canyon University, Phoenix 85061-1097
Northern Arizona University, Flagstaff 86011-4082
Prescott College, Prescott 86301
Southwestern College, Phoenix 85032-7042
University of Arizona, Tucson 85721
Western International University, Phoenix 85021

Graduate study only

American Graduate School of International Management, Glendale 85306-6003

Arkansas

Two-year

Arkansas State University: Beebe Branch, Beebe 72012-1008
Capital City Junior College, Little Rock 72204
Crowley's Ridge College, Paragould 72450
East Arkansas Community College, Forrest City 72335-9598
Garland County Community College, Hot Springs 71913-9120
Mississippi County Community College, Blytheville 72316-1109
National Education Center: Arkansas College of Technology, Little Rock 72207-9979
North Arkansas Community College, Harrison 72601
Phillips County Community College, Helena 72342
Rich Mountain Community College, Mena 71953
Shorter College, North Little Rock 72114
Southern Arkansas Community College, El Dorado 71730
Southern Arkansas University: Technical Branch, Camden 71701
Westark Community College, Fort Smith 72913-3649

Four-year

Arkansas Baptist College, Little Rock 72202
Arkansas College, Batesville 72503-2317
Arkansas State University, Jonesboro 72467-1630
Arkansas Tech University, Russellville 72801-2222
Central Baptist College, Conway 72032
Harding University, Searcy 72143
Henderson State University, Arkadelphia 71923
Hendrix College, Conway 72032-3080
John Brown University, Siloam Springs 72761
Ouachita Baptist University, Arkadelphia 71998-0001
Philander Smith College, Little Rock 72202
Southern Arkansas University, Magnolia 71753
University of Arkansas
    University of Arkansas, Fayetteville 72701
    Little Rock, Little Rock 72204
    Medical Sciences, Little Rock 72205-7199
    Monticello, Monticello 71655
    Pine Bluff, Pine Bluff 71601
University of Central Arkansas, Conway 72032
University of the Ozarks, Clarksville 72830

671

Williams Baptist College, Walnut Ridge 72476

California

Two-year

Allan Hancock College, Santa Maria 93454
American Academy of Dramatic Arts: West, Pasadena 91107
Bakersfield College, Bakersfield 93305
Barstow College, Barstow 92311-9984
Brooks College, Long Beach 90804
Central California Commercial College, Fresno 93704-1706
Cerritos Community College, Norwalk 90650
Cerro Coso Community College, Ridgecrest 93555-7777
Chabot College, Hayward 94545
Chaffey Community College, Rancho Cucamonga 91701-3002
Citrus College, Glendora 91740-1899
City College of San Francisco, San Francisco 94112
Coastline Community College, Fountain Valley 92708
College of the Desert, Palm Desert 92260
College of Marin: Kentfield, Kentfield 94904
College of Oceaneering, Wilmington 90744
College of the Redwoods, Eureka 95501-9302
College of the Sequoias, Visalia 93277
Columbia College, Columbia 95310
Compton Community College, Compton 90221
Cosumnes River College, Sacramento 95823-5799
Crafton Hills College, Yucaipa 92399-1799
Cuesta College, San Luis Obispo 93403-8106
De Anza College, Cupertino 95014
Diablo Valley College, Pleasant Hill 94523
Don Bosco Technical Institute, Rosemead 91770-4299
D-Q University, Davis 95617
East Los Angeles College, Monterey Park 91754
El Camino College, Torrance 90506
Evergreen Valley College, San Jose 95135
Fashion Institute of Design and Merchandising
    Los Angeles, Los Angeles 90015
    San Francisco, San Francisco 94108-5805
Feather River College, Quincy 95971
Foothill College, Los Altos Hills 94022-4599
Fresno City College, Fresno 93741
Gavilan Community College, Gilroy 95020
Glendale Community College, Glendale 91208
Golden West College, Huntington Beach 92647-0592
Grossmont Community College, El Cajon 92020
Hartnell College, Salinas 93901
Heald Business College
    San Jose, San Jose 95130
    Walnut Creek, Walnut Creek 94596
Heald College
    Sacramento, Rancho Cordova 95670
    Santa Rosa, Santa Rosa 95403
Heald Institute of Technology, Martinez 94553
Imperial Valley College, Imperial 92251-0158
Irvine Valley College, Irvine 92720
ITT Technical Institute
    Buena Park, Buena Park 90620-1374
    Sacramento, Sacramento 95827
    San Diego, San Diego 92123
    Van Nuys, Van Nuys 91405
Kelsey-Jenney College, San Diego 92101
Kings River Community College, Reedley 93654
Lake Tahoe Community College, South Lake Tahoe 96151
Laney College, Oakland 94607
Lassen College, Susanville 96130
Long Beach City College, Long Beach 90808
Los Angeles City College, Los Angeles 90029-3589
Los Angeles Harbor College, Wilmington 90744
Los Angeles Mission College, Sylmar 91342
Los Angeles Pierce College, Woodland Hills 91371

Los Angeles Trade and Technical College, Los Angeles 90015-4181
Los Angeles Valley College, Van Nuys 91401-4096
Los Medanos College, Pittsburg 94565
Marymount College, Rancho Palos Verdes 90274
Mendocino College, Ukiah 95482
Merced College, Merced 95348-2898
MiraCosta College, Oceanside 92056-3899
Mission College, Santa Clara 95054-1897
Modesto Junior College, Modesto 95350
Monterey Peninsula College, Monterey 93940
Moorpark College, Moorpark 93021
Mount San Antonio College, Walnut 91789
Mount San Jacinto College, San Jacinto 92583-2399
Napa Valley College, Napa 94558
Ohlone College, Fremont 94539-0390
Orange Coast College, Costa Mesa 92626
Oxnard College, Oxnard 93033
Palomar College, San Marcos 92069
Pasadena City College, Pasadena 91106
Phillips Junior College
    Condie Campus, Campbell 95008
    Fresno Campus, Clovis 93612
    San Fernando Valley Campus, Northridge 91325
Porterville College, Porterville 93257
Queen of the Holy Rosary College, Fremont 94539
Rio Hondo College, Whittier 90608
Saddleback College, Mission Viejo 92692
San Diego City College, San Diego 92101
San Diego Mesa College, San Diego 92111
San Diego Miramar College, San Diego 92126-2999
San Francisco College of Mortuary Science, San Francisco 94115-3912
San Joaquin Delta College, Stockton 95207
San Jose City College, San Jose 95128-2798
Santa Barbara City College, Santa Barbara 93109-2394
Santa Monica College, Santa Monica 90405-1628
Santa Rosa Junior College, Santa Rosa 95401
Sierra College, Rocklin 95677
Skyline College, San Bruno 94066-1698
Solano Community College, Suisun City 94585
Southwestern College, Chula Vista 92010
Taft College, Taft 93268
Ventura College, Ventura 93003
Victor Valley College, Victorville 92392-9699
West Hills Community College, Coalinga 93210
West Valley College, Saratoga 95070-5698
Yuba College, Marysville 95901

Two-year upper-division

Antioch Southern California
    Los Angeles, Marina Del Rey 90292-7090
    Santa Barbara, Santa Barbara 93101
California College for Health Sciences, National City 91950
California State University: San Marcos, San Marcos 92096-0001
Dominican School of Philosophy and Theology, Berkeley 94709
Hebrew Union College: Jewish Institute of Religion, Los Angeles 90007
John F. Kennedy University, Orinda 94563
Monterey Institute of International Studies, Monterey 93940
Pacific Oaks College, Pasadena 91103
University of California: San Francisco, San Francisco 94143-0244
University of West Los Angeles, Los Angeles 90066
Western State University College of Law
    Orange County, Fullerton 92631
    San Diego, San Diego 92110

Four-year

Academy of Art College, San Francisco 94108

American Armenian International College, LaVerne 91750
American College for the Applied Arts: Los Angeles, Los Angeles 90024-5603
Armstrong College, Berkeley 94704
Art Center College of Design, Pasadena 91103
Art Institute of Southern California, Laguna Beach 92651
Azusa Pacific University, Azusa 91702-7000
Bethany College, Scotts Valley 95066-2898
Biola University, La Mirada 90639-0001
Brooks Institute of Photography, Santa Barbara 93108
California Baptist College, Riverside 92504-3297
California College of Arts and Crafts, Oakland 94618-1487
California Institute of the Arts, Valencia 91355
California Institute of Technology, Pasadena 91125
California Lutheran University, Thousand Oaks 91360-2787
California Maritime Academy, Vallejo 94590-0644
California Polytechnic State University: San Luis Obispo, San Luis Obispo 93407
California State Polytechnic University: Pomona, Pomona 91768-4019
California State University
    Bakersfield, Bakersfield 93311-1099
    Chico, Chico 95929-0720
    Dominguez Hills, Carson 90747-9960
    Fresno, Fresno 93740-0057
    Fullerton, Fullerton 92634
    Hayward, Hayward 94542-3035
    Long Beach, Long Beach 90840-0108
    Los Angeles, Los Angeles 90032
    Northridge, Northridge 91328-1286
    Sacramento, Sacramento 95819
    San Bernardino, San Bernardino 92407
    Stanislaus, Turlock 95380-0283
Chapman University, Orange 92666
Charles R. Drew University: College of Allied Health, Los Angeles 90059
Christ College Irvine, Irvine 92715-3299
Christian Heritage College, El Cajon 92019
Claremont McKenna College, Claremont 91711-6420
Cogswell Polytechnical College, Cupertino 95014
Coleman College, La Mesa 92042-1532
College of Notre Dame, Belmont 94002-9974
Columbia College: Hollywood, Los Angeles 90038
DeVry Institute of Technology: City of Industry, City of Industry 91746-3495
Dominican College of San Rafael, San Rafael 94901-8008
Fresno Pacific College, Fresno 93702
Golden Gate University, San Francisco 94105-2968
Harvey Mudd College, Claremont 91711-5990
Holy Names College, Oakland 94619-1699
Humboldt State University, Arcata 95521
Humphreys College, Stockton 95207-3896
ITT Technical Institute: West Covina, West Covina 91790
La Sierra University, Riverside 92515-8247
LIFE Bible College, San Dimas 91773-3298
Lincoln University, San Francisco 94118
Louise Salinger Academy of Fashion, San Francisco 94105
Loyola Marymount University, Los Angeles 90045
Master's College, Santa Clarita 91322-0878
Menlo College, Atherton 94027-4301
Mills College, Oakland 94613
Mount St. Mary's College, Los Angeles 90049-1597
National Hispanic University, San Jose 95122
National University, San Diego 92108-4107
New College of California, San Francisco 94110
Occidental College, Los Angeles 90041-3393

Otis/Parsons School of Art and Design, Los Angeles 90057
Pacific Christian College, Fullerton 92631
Pacific Union College, Angwin 94508
Patten College, Oakland 94601-2699
Pepperdine University, Malibu 90263
Pitzer College, Claremont 91711-6114
Point Loma Nazarene College, San Diego 92106-2899
Pomona College, Claremont 91711-6312
St. John's Seminary College, Camarillo 93012-2599
St. Mary's College of California, Moraga 94575-9988
Samuel Merritt College, Oakland 94609-9954
San Diego State University, San Diego 92182-0771
San Francisco Art Institute, San Francisco 94133-2299
San Francisco Conservatory of Music, San Francisco 94122
San Francisco State University, San Francisco 94132
San Jose Christian College, San Jose 95108-1090
San Jose State University, San Jose 95192-0009
Santa Clara University, Santa Clara 95053
Scripps College, Claremont 91711-3948
Simpson College, Redding 96003-8606
Sonoma State University, Rohnert Park 94928
Southern California College, Costa Mesa 92626-9601
Stanford University, Stanford 94305
Thomas Aquinas College, Santa Paula 93060
United States International University, San Diego 92131-1799
University of California
    Berkeley, Berkeley 94720
    Davis, Davis 95616
    Irvine, Irvine 92717
    Los Angeles, Los Angeles 90024
    Riverside, Riverside 92521
    San Diego, La Jolla 92093-0337
    Santa Barbara, Santa Barbara 93106
    Santa Cruz, Santa Cruz 95064
University of Judaism, Los Angeles 90077
University of La Verne, La Verne 91750-4443
University of the Pacific, Stockton 95211
University of Redlands, Redlands 92373-0999
University of San Diego, San Diego 92110
University of San Francisco, San Francisco 94117-1080
University of Southern California, Los Angeles 90089-0911
West Coast University, Los Angeles 90020-1765
Westmont College, Santa Barbara 93108-1099
Whittier College, Whittier 90608
Woodbury University, Burbank 91510-7846
World College West, Petaluma 94952-9510

Five-year

Southern California Institute of Architecture, Los Angeles 90066

Graduate study only

American Baptist Seminary of the West, Berkeley 94704
American Conservatory Theater, San Francisco 94102
American Film Institute Center for Advanced Film and Television Studies, Los Angeles 90027
California College of Podiatric Medicine, San Francisco 94115
California Institute of Integral Studies, San Francisco 94117
California School of Professional Psychology
    Berkeley/Alameda, Alameda 94501
    Fresno, Fresno 94109-9967
    San Diego, San Diego 92121-3205
Franciscan School of Theology, Berkeley 94709
Fuller Theological Seminary, Pasadena 91182
Graduate Theological Union, Berkeley 94709

Life Chiropractic College West, San Lorenzo 94580
Naval Postgraduate School, Monterey 93943-5000
Pacific School of Religion, Berkeley 94709
St. Patrick's Seminary, Menlo Park 94025-3509
Saybrook Institute, San Francisco 94109
Southern California College of Optometry, Fullerton 92631
Westminster Theological Seminary in California, Escondido 92027

Colorado

Two-year

Aims Community College, Greeley 80632
Arapahoe Community College, Littleton 80160-9002
Bel-Rea Institute of Animal Technology, Denver 80231
Blair Junior College, Colorado Springs 80915
Colorado Institute of Art, Denver 80203
Colorado Mountain College
    Alpine Campus, Steamboat Springs 80477
    Spring Valley Campus, Glenwood Springs 81601
    Timberline Campus, Leadville 80461
Colorado Northwestern Community College, Rangely 81648-9988
Community College of Denver, Denver 80217-3363
Denver Institute of Technology, Denver 80221
Front Range Community College, Westminster 80030
ITT Technical Institute: Aurora, Aurora 80014-1476
Lamar Community College, Lamar 81052
Morgan Community College, Fort Morgan 80701
Northeastern Junior College, Sterling 80751
Otero Junior College, La Junta 81050
Parks Junior College, Thornton 80229
Pikes Peak Community College, Colorado Springs 80906-5498
Pueblo Community College, Pueblo 81004
Red Rocks Community College, Lakewood 80401
Trinidad State Junior College, Trinidad 81082

Two-year upper-division

University of Colorado Health Sciences Center, Denver 80262

Three-year

Naropa Institute, Boulder 80302

Four-year

Adams State College, Alamosa 81102
Colorado Christian University, Denver 80226
Colorado College, Colorado Springs 80903
Colorado School of Mines, Golden 80401-9951
Colorado State University, Fort Collins 80523-0015
Colorado Technical College, Colorado Springs 80907-3896
Denver Technical College, Denver 80222-1658
Fort Lewis College, Durango 81301
Mesa State College, Grand Junction 81502
Metropolitan State College of Denver, Denver 80217-3362
National College, Denver 80222
Nazarene Bible College, Colorado Springs 80935
Regis College of Regis University, Denver 80221-1099
Rocky Mountain College of Art & Design, Denver 80224-2359
United States Air Force Academy, Colorado Springs 80840-5651
University of Colorado
    Boulder, Boulder 80309-0030
    Colorado Springs, Colorado Springs 80933-7150
    Denver, Denver 80217-3364

University of Denver, Denver 80208-0132
University of Northern Colorado, Greeley 80639
University of Southern Colorado, Pueblo 81001-4901
Western State College of Colorado, Gunnison 81231

Connecticut

Two-year

Asnuntuck Community College, Enfield 06082
Briarwood College, Southington 06489
Greater New Haven State Technical College, North Haven 06473
Hartford State Technical College, Hartford 06106
Housatonic Community College, Bridgeport 06608
Manchester Community College, Manchester 06040
Mattatuck Community College, Waterbury 06708
Middlesex Community College, Middletown 06457
Mitchell College, New London 06320
Northwestern Connecticut Community College, Winsted 06098
Norwalk Community College, Norwalk 06854
Norwalk State Technical College, Norwalk 06854
Quinebaug Valley Community College, Danielson 06239-1699
South Central Community College, New Haven 06511-5970
Thames Valley State Technical College, Norwich 06360
Tunxis Community College, Farmington 06032
Waterbury State Technical College, Waterbury 06708-3089

Four-year

Albertus Magnus College, New Haven 06511-1189
Bridgeport Engineering Institute, Fairfield 06430
Central Connecticut State University, New Britain 06050
Charter Oak College, Farmington 06032-1934
Connecticut College, New London 06320
Eastern Connecticut State University, Willimantic 06226-2295
Fairfield University, Fairfield 06430-7524
Holy Apostles College and Seminary, Cromwell 06416
Paier College of Art, Hamden 06517
Quinnipiac College, Hamden 06518-0569
Sacred Heart University, Fairfield 06432-1000
St. Joseph College, West Hartford 06117
Southern Connecticut State University, New Haven 06515
Teikyo-Post University, Waterbury 06723-2540
Trinity College, Hartford 06106
United States Coast Guard Academy, New London 06320-4195
University of Bridgeport, Bridgeport 06601
University of Connecticut, Storrs 06269-3088
University of Hartford, West Hartford 06117-0395
University of New Haven, West Haven 06516
Wesleyan University, Middletown 06457
Western Connecticut State University, Danbury 06810
Yale University, New Haven 06520

Delaware

Two-year

Delaware Technical and Community College
    Southern Campus, Georgetown 19947
    Stanton/Wilmington Campus, Wilmington 19850
    Terry Campus, Dover 19903

Four-year

Delaware State College, Dover 19901
Goldey-Beacom College, Wilmington 19808
University of Delaware, Newark 19716
Wesley College, Dover 19901-3875
Wilmington College, New Castle 19720

District of Columbia

Two-year upper-division

Oblate College, Washington 20017-1587

Four-year

American University, Washington 20016-8001
Catholic University of America, Washington 20064
Corcoran School of Art, Washington 20006
Gallaudet University, Washington 20002
George Washington University, Washington 20052
Georgetown University, Washington 20057
Howard University, Washington 20059
Mount Vernon College, Washington 20007
Southeastern University, Washington 20024
Trinity College, Washington 20017-1094
University of the District of Columbia, Washington 20008

Graduate study only

Dominican House of Studies, Washington 20017

Florida

Two-year

Brevard Community College, Cocoa 32922-9987
Broward Community College, Fort Lauderdale 33301
Central Florida Community College, Ocala 32678
Chipola Junior College, Marianna 32446
Daytona Beach Community College, Daytona Beach 32120-2811
Edison Community College, Fort Myers 33906-6210
Flagler Career Institute, Jacksonville 32216
Florida College, Temple Terrace 33617
Florida Community College at Jacksonville, Jacksonville 32202-4030
Florida Keys Community College, Key West 33040
Gulf Coast Community College, Panama City 32401-1041
Hillsborough Community College, Tampa 33631-3127
Indian River Community College, Fort Pierce 34981-5599
International Fine Arts College, Miami 33132
ITT Technical Institute: Tampa, Tampa 33634
Keiser College of Technology, Fort Lauderdale 33309
Lake City Community College, Lake City 32055
Lake-Sumter Community College, Leesburg 34788
Manatee Community College, Bradenton 34206-1849
Miami-Dade Community College, Miami 33132-2297
National School of Technology, North Miami Beach 33162
New England Institute of Technology, West Palm Beach 33407
North Florida Junior College, Madison 32340
Okaloosa-Walton Community College, Niceville 32578
Palm Beach Community College, Lake Worth 33461
Pasco-Hernando Community College, New Port Richey 34654-5199
Pensacola Junior College, Pensacola 32504
Phillips Junior College: Melbourne, Melbourne 32935

St. Johns River Community College, Palatka 32177-3897
St. Petersburg Junior College, St. Petersburg 33733
Santa Fe Community College, Gainesville 32602
Seminole Community College, Sanford 32773-6199
South College: Palm Beach Campus, West Palm Beach 33409
South Florida Community College, Avon Park 33825
Southern College, Orlando 32807
Tallahassee Community College, Tallahassee 32304-2895
United Electronics Institute, Tampa 33619
Valencia Community College, Orlando 32802-3028

Three-year

National Education Center: Bauder Campus, Fort Lauderdale 33334-3971
Ringling School of Art and Design, Sarasota 34234

Four-year

Barry University, Miami Shores 33161
Bethune-Cookman College, Daytona Beach 32115
Eckerd College, St. Petersburg 33733-9979
Embry-Riddle Aeronautical University, Daytona Beach 32114-9970
Flagler College, St. Augustine 32084
Florida Agricultural and Mechanical University, Tallahassee 32307
Florida Atlantic University, Boca Raton 33431
Florida Baptist Theological College, Graceville 32440-1830
Florida Bible College, Kissimmee 34758
Florida Christian College, Kissimmee 34744-4402
Florida Institute of Technology, Melbourne 32901-6988
Florida International University, Miami 33199
Florida Memorial College, Miami 33054
Florida Southern College, Lakeland 33801-5698
Florida State University, Tallahassee 32306-1009
Fort Lauderdale College, Fort Lauderdale 33304
Hobe Sound Bible College, Hobe Sound 33475-1065
Jacksonville University, Jacksonville 32211
Jones College, Jacksonville 32211
Lynn University, Boca Raton 33431-5598
New College of the University of South Florida, Sarasota 34243-2197
Nova University, Fort Lauderdale 33314
Orlando College, Orlando 32810
Palm Beach Atlantic College, West Palm Beach 33416-4708
Rollins College, Winter Park 32789-4499
St. John Vianney College Seminary, Miami 33165
St. Leo College, St. Leo 33574
St. Thomas University, Miami 33054
Schiller International University, Dunedin 34698-4964
Southeastern College of the Assemblies of God, Lakeland 33801
Stetson University, DeLand 32720
Tampa College, Tampa 33614
University of Central Florida, Orlando 32816
University of Florida, Gainesville 32611
University of Miami, Coral Gables 33124
University of North Florida, Jacksonville 32216
University of South Florida, Tampa 33620-6900
University of Tampa, Tampa 33606
University of West Florida, Pensacola 32514-5750
Warner Southern College, Lake Wales 33853
Webber College, Babson Park 33827

Graduate study only

Southeastern University of the Health Sciences: College of Optometry, North Miami Beach 33162
University of Sarasota, Sarasota 34236

Georgia

Two-year

Abraham Baldwin Agricultural College, Tifton 31794-2693
Andrew College, Cuthbert 31740-1395
Athens Area Technical Institute, Athens 30610-0399
Atlanta Metropolitan College, Atlanta 30310
Augusta Technical Institute, Augusta 30906
Bainbridge College, Bainbridge 31717-0953
Bauder College, Atlanta 30326-9975
Brunswick College, Brunswick 31523
Chattahoochee Technical Institute, Marietta 30060
Dalton College, Dalton 30720
Darton College, Albany 31707-3098
DeKalb College, Decatur 30021
DeKalb Technical Institute, Clarkston 30021
East Georgia College, Swainsboro 30401-2699
Floyd College, Rome 30163-1801
Gainesville College, Gainesville 30503
Gordon College, Barnesville 30204
Gupton Jones College of Funeral Service, Atlanta 30354
Macon College, Macon 31297
Meadows College of Business, Columbus 31906
Middle Georgia College, Cochran 31014
Oxford College of Emory University, Oxford 30267-1328
Reinhardt College, Waleska 30183
Savannah Technical Institute, Savannah 31499
South College, Savannah 31406
South Georgia College, Douglas 31533
Truett-McConnell College, Cleveland 30528
Waycross College, Waycross 31501
Young Harris College, Young Harris 30582-0116

Two-year upper-division

Medical College of Georgia, Augusta 30912
Mercer University Atlanta, Atlanta 30341-4115

Four-year

Agnes Scott College, Decatur 30030
Albany State College, Albany 31705-2796
American College for the Applied Arts, Atlanta 30326
Armstrong State College, Savannah 31419-1997
Atlanta Christian College, East Point 30344
Atlanta College of Art, Atlanta 30309
Augusta College, Augusta 30910
Berry College, Rome 30149
Brenau Women's College, Gainesville 30501-3697
Brewton-Parker College, Mount Vernon 30445
Clark Atlanta University, Atlanta 30314
Clayton State College, Morrow 30260-1221
Columbus College, Columbus 31993-2399
Covenant College, Lookout Mountain 30750
DeVry Institute of Technology: Atlanta, Decatur 30030-2198
Emmanuel College, Franklin Springs 30639-0129
Emory University, Atlanta 30322
Fort Valley State College, Fort Valley 31030
Georgia College, Milledgeville 31061
Georgia Institute of Technology, Atlanta 30332-0320
Georgia Southern University, Statesboro 30460-8024
Georgia Southwestern College, Americus 31709-4693
Georgia State University, Atlanta 30303-3083
Kennesaw State College, Marietta 30061
LaGrange College, LaGrange 30240
Mercer University, Macon 31207-0001
Morehouse College, Atlanta 30314
Morris Brown College, Atlanta 30314
North Georgia College, Dahlonega 30597
Oglethorpe University, Atlanta 30319-2797
Paine College, Augusta 30901
Piedmont College, Demorest 30535
Savannah College of Art and Design, Savannah 31401-3146

Savannah State College, Savannah 31404
Shorter College, Rome 30165-4298
Southern College of Technology, Marietta 30060-2896
Spelman College, Atlanta 30314-4399
Thomas College, Thomasville 31792-7499
Toccoa Falls College, Toccoa Falls 30598-0368
University of Georgia, Athens 30602
Valdosta State College, Valdosta 31698
Wesleyan College, Macon 31297-4299
West Georgia College, Carrollton 30118-0001

Graduate study only

Institute of Paper Science and Technology, Atlanta 30318
Life College, Marietta 30060

Hawaii

Two-year

Cannon's International Business College of Honolulu, Honolulu 96814-3715
University of Hawaii
Honolulu Community College, Honolulu 96817
Kapiolani Community College, Honolulu 96816
Kauai Community College, Lihue 96766
Leeward Community College, Pearl City 96782

Two-year upper-division

University of Hawaii: West Oahu, Pearl City 96782

Four-year

Brigham Young University-Hawaii, Laie 96762-1294
Chaminade University of Honolulu, Honolulu 96816-1578
Hawaii Loa College, Kaneohe 96744
Hawaii Pacific University, Honolulu 96813
University of Hawaii
Hilo, Hilo 96720-4091
Manoa, Honolulu 96822

Idaho

Two-year

College of Southern Idaho, Twin Falls 83303-1238
ITT Technical Institute: Boise, Boise 83706
North Idaho College, Coeur d'Alene 83814
Ricks College, Rexburg 83460-4104

Four-year

Albertson College, Caldwell 83605
Boise Bible College, Boise 83714-1220
Boise State University, Boise 83725
Idaho State University, Pocatello 83209
Lewis Clark State College, Lewiston 83501-2698
Northwest Nazarene College, Nampa 83686
University of Idaho, Moscow 83843

Illinois

Two-year

American Academy of Art, Chicago 60603-6191
Belleville Area College, Belleville 62221-9989
Black Hawk College
East Campus, Kewanee 61443-0489
Moline, Moline 61265
Carl Sandburg College, Galesburg 61401

City Colleges of Chicago
Chicago City-Wide College, Chicago 60606-6997
Malcolm X College, Chicago 60612
Olive-Harvey College, Chicago 60628
Richard J. Daley College, Chicago 60652
Wright College, Chicago 60634-4276
College of DuPage, Glen Ellyn 60137-6599
College of Lake County, Grayslake 60030-1198
Elgin Community College, Elgin 60123
Gem City College, Quincy 62306
Highland Community College, Freeport 61032-9341
Illinois Central College, East Peoria 61635
Illinois Eastern Community Colleges
Frontier Community College, Fairfield 62837-9801
Lincoln Trail College, Robinson 62454-9803
Olney Central College, Olney 62450
Wabash Valley College, Mount Carmel 62863-2657
Illinois Valley Community College, Oglesby 61348-1099
ITT Technical Institute: Hoffman Estates, Hoffman Estates 60195
John A. Logan College, Carterville 62918
Joliet Junior College, Joliet 60436-9985
Kishwaukee College, Malta 60150-9699
Lake Land College, Mattoon 61938
Lewis and Clark Community College, Godfrey 62035-2466
Lexington Institute of Hospitality Careers, Chicago 60643-3294
Lincoln College, Lincoln 62656
Lincoln Land Community College, Springfield 62794-9256
MacCormac Junior College, Chicago 60604-3395
Midstate College, Peoria 61602-9990
Montay College, Chicago 60659-3115
Moraine Valley Community College, Palos Hills 60465
Morrison Institute of Technology, Morrison 61270-0410
Morton College, Cicero 60650
Oakton Community College, Des Plaines 60016
Parkland College, Champaign 61821-1899
Phillips College of Chicago, Chicago 60606
Prairie State College, Chicago Heights 60411
Rend Lake College, Ina 62846
Richland Community College, Decatur 62521
Robert Morris College: Chicago, Chicago 60601
Rock Valley College, Rockford 61111
St. Augustine College, Chicago 60640
Shawnee Community College, Ullin 62992
Spoon River College, Canton 61520
Springfield College in Illinois, Springfield 62702-2694
State Community College, East St. Louis 62201
Triton College, River Grove 60171
Waubonsee Community College, Sugar Grove 60554
William Rainey Harper College, Palatine 60067-7398

Two-year upper-division

Governors State University, University Park 60466
Mennonite College of Nursing, Bloomington 61701
National College of Chiropractic, Lombard 60148
Rush University, Chicago 60612
St. Francis Medical Center College of Nursing, Peoria 61603
St. Joseph College of Nursing, Joliet 60435
Sangamon State University, Springfield 62794-9243
University of Health Sciences: The Chicago Medical School, North Chicago 60064

Four-year

Aero-Space Institute, Chicago 60605-1116

American Conservatory of Music, Chicago 60602-4792
Augustana College, Rock Island 61201-2296
Aurora University, Aurora 60506
Barat College, Lake Forest 60045
Blackburn College, Carlinville 62626
Blessing-Reiman College of Nursing, Quincy 62301
Bradley University, Peoria 61625
Chicago State University, Chicago 60628
College of St. Francis, Joliet 60435-6188
Columbia College, Chicago 60605-1996
Concordia University, River Forest 60305-1499
De Paul University, Chicago 60604
DeVry Institute of Technology
Chicago, Chicago 60618-5994
Lombard, Lombard 60148-4892
Eastern Illinois University, Charleston 61920-3099
East-West University, Chicago 60605
Elmhurst College, Elmhurst 60126-3296
Eureka College, Eureka 61530
Greenville College, Greenville 62246
Harrington Institute of Interior Design, Chicago 60605
Hebrew Theological College, Skokie 60077
Illinois Benedictine College, Lisle 60532-0900
Illinois College, Jacksonville 62650-9990
Illinois Institute of Technology, Chicago 60616
Illinois State University, Normal 61761-6901
Illinois Wesleyan University, Bloomington 61702-9965
International Academy of Merchandising and Design, Chicago 60654-1596
Judson College, Elgin 60123
KAES College, Chicago 60646
Kendall College, Evanston 60201
Knox College, Galesburg 61401-4999
Lake Forest College, Lake Forest 60045
Lakeview College of Nursing, Danville 61832
Lewis University, Romeoville 60441-2298
Lincoln Christian College and Seminary, Lincoln 62656-2111
Loyola University of Chicago, Chicago 60611
MacMurray College, Jacksonville 62650-2590
McKendree College, Lebanon 62254
Millikin University, Decatur 62522-9982
Monmouth College, Monmouth 61462
Moody Bible Institute, Chicago 60610
NAES College, Chicago 60659
National-Louis University, Evanston 60201-1796
North Central College, Naperville 60566-7063
North Park College and Theological Seminary, Chicago 60625-4987
Northeastern Illinois University, Chicago 60625
Northern Illinois University, DeKalb 60115-2854
Northwestern University, Evanston 60204-3060
Olivet Nazarene University, Kankakee 60901-0592
Parks College of St. Louis University, Cahokia 62206
Principia College, Elsah 62028-9799
Quincy College, Quincy 62301-2699
Ray College of Design, Chicago 60611
Rockford College, Rockford 61108-2393
Roosevelt University, Chicago 60605-1394
Rosary College, River Forest 60305-1099
St. Xavier University, Chicago 60655
School of the Art Institute of Chicago, Chicago 60603
Shimer College, Waukegan 60079-0500
Southern Illinois University
Carbondale, Carbondale 62901-4710
Edwardsville, Edwardsville 62026-1600
Trinity Christian College, Palos Heights 60463
Trinity College, Deerfield 60015
University of Chicago, Chicago 60637
University of Illinois
Chicago, Chicago 60680
Urbana-Champaign, Urbana 61801
VanderCook College of Music, Chicago 60616

West Suburban College of Nursing, Oak Park 60302
Western Illinois University, Macomb 61455
Wheaton College, Wheaton 60187-5593

Graduate study only

Chicago School of Professional Psychology, Chicago 60605
Chicago Theological Seminary, Chicago 60637-9990
Garrett-Evangelical Theological Seminary, Evanston 60201

Indiana

Two-year

Ancilla College, Donaldson 46513
Holy Cross College, Notre Dame 46556-0308
Indiana Vocational Technical College
    Central Indiana, Indianapolis 46206-1763
    Columbus, Columbus 47203
    Eastcentral, Muncie 47307
    Kokomo, Kokomo 46903-1373
    Lafayette, Lafayette 47903
    Northcentral, South Bend 46619
    Northeast, Fort Wayne 46805
    Northwest, Gary 46409-1499
    Southcentral, Sellersburg 47172
    Southeast, Madison 47250
    Southwest, Evansville 47710
    Wabash Valley, Terre Haute 47802
    Whitewater, Richmond 47374
International Business College, Fort Wayne 46804
ITT Technical Institute: Evansville, Evansville 47715
Mid-America College of Funeral Service, Jeffersonville 47130
Vincennes University, Vincennes 47591

Three-year

ITT Technical Institute
    Fort Wayne, Fort Wayne 46825-5532
    Indianapolis, Indianapolis 46268

Four-year

Anderson University, Anderson 46012-3462
Ball State University, Muncie 47306-0855
Bethel College, Mishawaka 46545
Butler University, Indianapolis 46208
Calumet College of St. Joseph, Hammond 46394-2195
DePauw University, Greencastle 46135-0037
Earlham College, Richmond 47374
Franklin College, Franklin 46131-2598
Goshen College, Goshen 46526-9988
Grace College, Winona Lake 46590
Hanover College, Hanover 47243-0108
Huntington College, Huntington 46750
Indiana Institute of Technology, Fort Wayne 46803
Indiana State University, Terre Haute 47809
Indiana University
    Bloomington, Bloomington 47405
    East, Richmond 47374-1289
    Kokomo, Kokomo 46904-9003
    Northwest, Gary 46408
    South Bend, South Bend 46634-7111
    Southeast, New Albany 47150
Indiana University—Purdue University
    Fort Wayne, Fort Wayne 46805
    Indianapolis, Indianapolis 46202-5143
Indiana Wesleyan University, Marion 46953-9980
Lutheran College of Health Professions, Fort Wayne 46807
Manchester College, North Manchester 46962-0365
Marian College, Indianapolis 46222
Martin University, Indianapolis 46218
Oakland City College, Oakland City 47660

Purdue University
    Calumet, Hammond 46323-2094
    North Central Campus, Westville 46391
    West Lafayette, West Lafayette 47907
Rose-Hulman Institute of Technology, Terre Haute 47803-9989
St. Francis College, Fort Wayne 46808
St. Joseph's College, Rensselaer 47978
St. Mary-of-the-Woods College, St. Mary-of-the-Woods 47876-0068
St. Mary's College, Notre Dame 46556
St. Meinrad College, St. Meinrad 47577-1030
Taylor University, Upland 46989-1001
Tri-State University, Angola 46703-0307
University of Evansville, Evansville 47722
University of Indianapolis, Indianapolis 46227-3697
University of Notre Dame, Notre Dame 46556
University of Southern Indiana, Evansville 47712
Valparaiso University, Valparaiso 46383-6493
Wabash College, Crawfordsville 47933-0352

Graduate study only

Christian Theological Seminary, Indianapolis 46208
Grace Theological Seminary, Winona Lake 46590

Iowa

Two-year

American Institute of Business, Des Moines 50321
American Institute of Commerce, Davenport 52807-2095
Clinton Community College, Clinton 52732-6299
Des Moines Area Community College, Ankeny 50021
Hawkeye Institute of Technology, Waterloo 50704
Indian Hills Community College, Ottumwa 52501
Iowa Central Community College, Fort Dodge 50501
Iowa Lakes Community College, Estherville 51334
Iowa Western Community College, Council Bluffs 51502
Kirkwood Community College, Cedar Rapids 52406
Muscatine Community College, Muscatine 52761-5396
National Education Center: National Institute of Technology Campus, West Des Moines 50265
North Iowa Area Community College, Mason City 50401
Northeast Iowa Community College, Calmar 52132
Northwest Iowa Technical College, Sheldon 51201
Scott Community College, Bettendorf 52722-6804
Southeastern Community College
    North Campus, West Burlington 52655-0605
    South Campus, Keokuk 52632-1088
Southwestern Community College, Creston 50801
Waldorf College, Forest City 50436

Two-year upper-division

University of Osteopathic Medicine and Health Sciences, Des Moines 50312

Three-year

Hamilton Technical College, Davenport 52807

Four-year

Briar Cliff College, Sioux City 51104-2100
Buena Vista College, Storm Lake 50588-1798
Central College, Pella 50219-9989
Clarke College, Dubuque 52001-3198
Coe College, Cedar Rapids 52402-9983
Cornell College, Mount Vernon 52314-1098
Divine Word College, Epworth 52045
Dordt College, Sioux Center 51250

Drake University, Des Moines 50311-4505
Emmaus Bible College, Dubuque 52001
Faith Baptist Bible College and Theological Seminary, Ankeny 50021
Graceland College, Lamoni 50140
Grand View College, Des Moines 50316
Grinnell College, Grinnell 50112-0807
Iowa State University, Ames 50011-2010
Iowa Wesleyan College, Mount Pleasant 52641
Loras College, Dubuque 52001
Luther College, Decorah 52101-1042
Maharishi International University, Fairfield 52557-1155
Morningside College, Sioux City 51106-1751
Mount Mercy College, Cedar Rapids 52402
Mount St. Clare College, Clinton 52732
Northwestern College, Orange City 51041
St. Ambrose University, Davenport 52803
Simpson College, Indianola 50125-1299
Teikyo Marycrest University, Davenport 52804-4096
Teikyo Westmar University, Le Mars 51031
University of Dubuque, Dubuque 52001
University of Iowa, Iowa City 52242-1396
University of Northern Iowa, Cedar Falls 50614-0018
Upper Iowa University, Fayette 52142-1859
Vennard College, University Park 52595
Wartburg College, Waverly 50677
William Penn College, Oskaloosa 52577

Graduate study only

Palmer Chiropractic University, Davenport 52803

Kansas

Two-year

Allen County Community College, Iola 66749
Barton County Community College, Great Bend 67530-9283
Brown Mackie College, Salina 67402-1787
Butler County Community College, Eldorado 67042-3280
Central College, McPherson 67460-5740
Cloud County Community College, Concordia 66901-1002
Coffeyville Community College, Coffeyville 67337
Colby Community College, Colby 67701
Cowley County Community College, Arkansas City 67005
Dodge City Community College, Dodge City 67801-2399
Donnelly College, Kansas City 66102
Fort Scott Community College, Fort Scott 66701
Haskell Indian Junior College, Lawrence 66046-4800
Hesston College, Hesston 67062-3000
Highland Community College, Highland 66035-0068
Hutchinson Community College, Hutchinson 67501
Johnson County Community College, Overland Park 66210-1299
Kansas City Kansas Community College, Kansas City 66112
Labette Community College, Parsons 67357
Neosho County Community College, Chanute 66720
Pratt Community College, Pratt 67124
Seward County Community College, Liberal 67905-1137

Two-year upper-division

University of Kansas Medical Center, Kansas City 66160

Four-year

Baker University, Baldwin City 66006
Barclay College, Haviland 67059
Benedictine College, Atchison 66002-1499
Bethany College, Lindsborg 67456-1897

Bethel College, North Newton 67117-9899
Emporia State University, Emporia 66801-5087
Fort Hays State University, Hays 67601-4099
Friends University, Wichita 67213
Kansas City College and Bible School, Overland Park 66204
Kansas Newman College, Wichita 67213-2097
Kansas State University, Manhattan 66506
Kansas Wesleyan University, Salina 67401-6196
Manhattan Christian College, Manhattan 66502
McPherson College, McPherson 67460
MidAmerica Nazarene College, Olathe 66061-1776
Ottawa University, Ottawa 66067-3399
Pittsburg State University, Pittsburg 66762
St. Mary College, Leavenworth 66048-5082
Southwestern College, Winfield 67156
Sterling College, Sterling 67579-9989
Tabor College, Hillsboro 67063
University of Kansas, Lawrence 66045-0215
Washburn University of Topeka, Topeka 66621
Wichita State University, Wichita 67208-1595

Graduate study only

U.S. Army Command and General Staff College, Fort Leavenworth 66027-6900

Kentucky

Two-year

Elizabethtown Community College, Elizabethtown 42701
Franklin College, Paducah 42001
Hazard Community College, Hazard 41701
Institute of Electronic Technology, Paducah 42001
Jefferson Community College, Louisville 40202
Lees College, Jackson 41339
Lexington Community College, Lexington 40506-0235
Louisville Technical Institute, Louisville 40218-4524
Madisonville Community College, Madisonville 42431
Maysville Community College, Maysville 41056
National Education Center: Kentucky College of Technology Campus, Louisville 40213
Owensboro Junior College of Business, Owensboro 42303
Paducah Community College, Paducah 42002-7380
Prestonburg Community College, Prestonburg 41653
St. Catharine College, St. Catharine 40061
Southeast Community College, Cumberland 40823
Sue Bennett College, London 40741
Watterson College, Louisville 40218

Four-year

Alice Lloyd College, Pippa Passes 41844
Asbury College, Wilmore 40390
Bellarmine College, Louisville 40205-0671
Berea College, Berea 40404
Brescia College, Owensboro 42301-3023
Campbellsville College, Campbellsville 42718-2799
Centre College, Danville 40422
Clear Creek Baptist Bible College, Pineville 40977
Cumberland College, Williamsburg 40769-6178
Eastern Kentucky University, Richmond 40475-3101
Georgetown College, Georgetown 40324-1696
Kentucky Christian College, Grayson 41143-1199
Kentucky State University, Frankfort 40601
Kentucky Wesleyan College, Owensboro 42302-1039
Lindsey Wilson College, Columbia 42728
Mid-Continent Baptist Bible College, Mayfield 42066-0357
Morehead State University, Morehead 40351

Murray State University, Murray 42071
Northern Kentucky University, Highland Heights 41099-7010
Pikeville College, Pikeville 41501-1194
Spalding University, Louisville 40203
Sullivan College, Louisville 40232
Thomas More College, Crestview Hills 41017
Transylvania University, Lexington 40508
Union College, Barbourville 40906
University of Kentucky, Lexington 40506-0054
University of Louisville, Louisville 40292
——Western Kentucky University, Bowling Green 42101

Graduate study only

Lexington Theological Seminary, Lexington 40508
Louisville Presbyterian Theological Seminary, Louisville 40205-1798

Louisiana

Two-year

Bossier Parish Community College, Bossier City 71111
Louisiana State University at Eunice, Eunice 70535
New Orleans Baptist Theological Seminary: School of Christian Education, New Orleans 70126-4858
Phillips Junior College: New Orleans, New Orleans 70121
Southern University in Shreveport, Shreveport 71107

Two-year upper-division

Louisiana State University Medical Center, New Orleans 70112-2223

Four-year

Centenary College of Louisiana, Shreveport 71134-1188
Dillard University, New Orleans 70122-3097
Grambling State University, Grambling 71245
Grantham College of Engineering, Slidell 70469-5700
Louisiana College, Pineville 71359-0560
Louisiana State University
    Agricultural and Mechanical College, Baton Rouge 70803-2750
    Shreveport, Shreveport 71115
Louisiana Tech University, Ruston 71272
Loyola University, New Orleans 70118
McNeese State University, Lake Charles 70609-2495
Nicholls State University, Thibodaux 70310
Northeast Louisiana University, Monroe 71209-0730
Northwestern State University, Natchitoches 71497
Our Lady of Holy Cross College, New Orleans 70131-7399
St. Joseph Seminary College, St. Benedict 70457-9990
Southeastern Louisiana University, Hammond 70402-0752
Southern University at New Orleans, New Orleans 70126
Southern University and Agricultural and Mechanical College, Baton Rouge 70813
Tulane University, New Orleans 70118-5680
University of New Orleans, New Orleans 70148
University of Southwestern Louisiana, Lafayette 70504
World Evangelism Bible College and Seminary, Baton Rouge 70828-8000
Xavier University of Louisiana, New Orleans 70125

Graduate study only

Notre Dame Seminary School of Theology, New Orleans 70118

Maine

Two-year

Andover College, Portland 04103
Beal College, Bangor 04401
Casco Bay College, Portland 04101-3483
Central Maine Medical Center School of Nursing, Lewiston 04240-9986
Central Maine Technical College, Auburn 04210-6498
Eastern Maine Technical College, Bangor 04401
Kennebec Valley Technical College, Fairfield 04937
Southern Maine Technical College, South Portland 04106

Four-year

Bates College, Lewiston 04240-9917
Bowdoin College, Brunswick 04011
Colby College, Waterville 04901-4799
College of the Atlantic, Bar Harbor 04609
Husson College, Bangor 04401
Maine Maritime Academy, Castine 04420-5000
Portland School of Art, Portland 04101-3987
St. Joseph's College, Windham 04062-1198
Thomas College, Waterville 04901-9986
Unity College, Unity 04988
University of Maine
    Augusta, Augusta 04330
    Farmington, Farmington 04938
    Fort Kent, Fort Kent 04743-1292
    Machias, Machias 04654
    Orono, Orono 04469-0113
    Presque Isle, Presque Isle 04769-2888
University of New England, Biddeford 04005
University of Southern Maine, Portland 04103
Westbrook College, Portland 04103

Maryland

Two-year

Allegany Community College, Cumberland 21502
Anne Arundel Community College, Arnold 21012
Baltimore International Culinary College, Baltimore 21202-1503
Catonsville Community College, Catonsville 21228
Cecil Community College, North East 21901-1999
Charles County Community College, La Plata 20646
Chesapeake College, Wye Mills 21679
Dundalk Community College, Baltimore 21222-4692
Essex Community College, Baltimore 21237-3899
Frederick Community College, Frederick 21702
Garrett Community College, McHenry 21541
Hagerstown Business College, Hagerstown 21740
Hagerstown Junior College, Hagerstown 21742-6590
Harford Community College, Bel Air 21015
Howard Community College, Columbia 21044
Maryland College of Art and Design, Silver Spring 20902
Montgomery College
    Germantown Campus, Germantown 20876
    Rockville Campus, Rockville 20850
    Takoma Park Campus, Takoma Park 20912
New Community College of Baltimore, Baltimore 21215
Prince George's Community College, Largo 20772-2199
Wor-Wic Tech Community College, Salisbury 21801

Colriges included in this book

Two-year upper-division
University of Baltimore, Baltimore 21201-5779
University of Maryland: Baltimore, Baltimore
21201

Four-year
Baltimore Hebrew University, Baltimore 21215-
3996
Bowie State University, Bowie 20715
Capitol College, Laurel 20708
College of Notre Dame of Maryland, Baltimore
21210-2476
Columbia Union College, Takoma Park 20912
Coppin State College, Baltimore 21216
Eastern Christian College, Bel Air 21014-0629
Frostburg State University, Frostburg 21532-1099
Goucher College, Baltimore 21204
Hood College, Frederick 21701-8575
Johns Hopkins University, Baltimore 21218
Loyola College in Maryland, Baltimore 21210-
2699
Maryland Institute College of Art, Baltimore
21217
Morgan State University, Baltimore 21239
Mount St. Mary's College, Emmitsburg 21727-
7796
Ner Israel Rabbinical College, Baltimore 21208-
9964
St. John's College, Annapolis 21404-2800
St. Mary's College of Maryland, St. Mary's City
20686-9999
Salisbury State University, Salisbury 21801-6862
Sojourner-Douglass College, Baltimore 21205
Towson State University, Towson 21204-7097
United States Naval Academy, Annapolis 21402-
5018
University of Maryland
Baltimore County, Baltimore 21228-5398
College Park, College Park 20742-5235
Eastern Shore, Princess Anne 21853-1299
University College, College Park 20742-1672
Villa Julie College, Stevenson 21153
Washington College, Chestertown 21620
Western Maryland College, Westminster 21157-
4390

Graduate study only
Uniformed Services University of the Health
Sciences, Bethesda 20814-4799

Massachusetts

Two-year
Aquinas College at Milton, Milton 02186
Aquinas College at Newton, Newton 02158
Bay State College, Boston 02116
Becker College
Leicester Campus, Leicester 01524
Worcester Campus, Worcester 01609
Berkshire Community College, Pittsfield 01201-
5786
Bristol Community College, Fall River 02720
Bunker Hill Community College, Boston 02129
Cape Cod Community College, West Barnstable
02668
Dean Junior College, Franklin 02038-1994
Essex Agricultural and Technical Institute,
Hathorne 01937
Fisher College, Boston 02116
Franklin Institute of Boston, Boston 02116
Greenfield Community College, Greenfield 01301
Holyoke Community College, Holyoke 01040
Katharine Gibbs School, Boston 02116
Laboure College, Boston 02124
Marian Court Junior College, Swampscott 01907-
2896
Massachusetts Bay Community College, Wellesley
Hills 02181
Massasoit Community College, Brockton 02402
Middlesex Community College, Bedford 01730

Mount Wachusett Community College, Gardner
01440
New England Banking Institute, Boston 02111
Newbury College, Brookline 02146
North Shore Community College, Danvers 01923
Northern Essex Community College, Haverhill
01830-2399
Quincy College, Quincy 02169
Quinsigamond Community College, Worcester
01606
Roxbury Community College, Boston 02120-3400
Springfield Technical Community College,
Springfield 01105

Four-year
American International College, Springfield
01109-3184
Amherst College, Amherst 01002
Anna Maria College for Men and Women,
Paxton 01612
Assumption College, Worcester 01615-0005
Atlantic Union College, South Lancaster 01561
Babson College, Babson Park 02157-0901
Bay Path College, Longmeadow 01106
Bentley College, Waltham 02154-4705
Berklee College of Music, Boston 02215
Boston College, Chestnut Hill 02167-3804
Boston Conservatory, Boston 02215
Boston University, Boston 02215
Bradford College, Bradford 01835-7393
Brandeis University, Waltham 02254-9110
Bridgewater State College, Bridgewater 02325
Clark University, Worcester 01610-1477
College of the Holy Cross, Worcester 01610-2395
Curry College, Milton 02186-9984
Eastern Nazarene College, Quincy 02170
Elms College, Chicopee 01013-2839
Emerson College, Boston 02116
Emmanuel College, Boston 02115
Endicott College, Beverly 01915-9985
Fitchburg State College, Fitchburg 01420
Forsyth School for Dental Hygienists, Boston
02115
Framingham State College, Framingham 01701
Gordon College, Wenham 01984-1899
Hampshire College, Amherst 01002
Harvard and Radcliffe Colleges, Cambridge 02138
Hellenic College, Brookline 02146
Lasell College, Newton 02166
Lesley College, Cambridge 02138-2790
Massachusetts College of Art, Boston 02115-5882
Massachusetts Institute of Technology, Cambridge
02139
Massachusetts Maritime Academy, Buzzards Bay
02532-1803
Merrimack College, North Andover 01845
Montserrat College of Art, Beverly 01915
Mount Holyoke College, South Hadley 01075-
1488
Mount Ida College, Newton Centre 02159
New England Conservatory of Music, Boston
02115
Nichols College, Dudley 01570-5000
North Adams State College, North Adams 01247
Pine Manor College, Chestnut Hill 02167
Regis College, Weston 02193
St. Hyacinth College and Seminary, Granby
01033
St. John's Seminary College, Brighton 02135
Salem State College, Salem 01970
School of the Museum of Fine Arts, Boston
02115
Simmons College, Boston 02115-5898
Simon's Rock College of Bard, Great Barrington
01230
Smith College, Northampton 01063
Springfield College, Springfield 01109
Stonehill College, North Easton 02357
Suffolk University, Boston 02108-2772
Tufts University, Medford 02155

University of Massachusetts
Amherst, Amherst 01003
Boston, Boston 02125-3393
Dartmouth, North Dartmouth 02747
Lowell, Lowell 01854
Wellesley College, Wellesley 02181-8292
Wentworth Institute of Technology, Boston 02115
Western New England College, Springfield
01119-2688
Westfield State College, Westfield 01086
Wheaton College, Norton 02766
Wheelock College, Boston 02215-4176
Williams College, Williamstown 01267
Worcester Polytechnic Institute, Worcester
01609-2280
Worcester State College, Worcester 01602-2597

Five-year
Boston Architectural Center, Boston 02115-2795
Massachusetts College of Pharmacy and Allied
Health Sciences, Boston 02115
Northeastern University, Boston 02115-9959

Graduate study only
Arthur D. Little Management Education Institute,
Cambridge 02140-2390
Conway School of Landscape Design, Conway
01341
Harvard University, Cambridge 02138
MGH Institute of Health Professions, Boston
02108
Weston School of Theology, Cambridge 02138

Michigan

Two-year
Alpena Community College, Alpena 49707
Baker College
Auburn Hills, Auburn Hills 48326
Mount Clemens, Mount Clemens 48043
Charles Stewart Mott Community College, Flint
48503
Delta College, University Center 48710
Glen Oaks Community College, Centreville
49032
Grand Rapids Community College, Grand Rapids
49503
Great Lakes Junior College of Business, Saginaw
48607
Henry Ford Community College, Dearborn 48128
Jackson Community College, Jackson 49201
Kalamazoo Valley Community College,
Kalamazoo 49009
Kellogg Community College, Battle Creek 49016-
3397
Kirtland Community College, Roscommon 48653
Lansing Community College, Lansing 48901
Lewis College of Business, Detroit 48235
Macomb Community College, Warren 48093-
3896
Mid Michigan Community College, Harrison
48625
Montcalm Community College, Sidney 48885-
9746
Muskegon Community College, Muskegon 49442
Northwestern Michigan College, Traverse City
49684
Oakland Community College, Bloomfield Hills
48304-2266
St. Clair County Community College, Port Huron
48061-5015
Schoolcraft College, Livonia 48152-2696
Southwestern Michigan College, Dowagiac 49047
Suomi College, Hancock 49930
West Shore Community College, Scottville 49454-
0277

Two-year upper-division
Walsh College of Accountancy and Business
Administration, Troy 48007-7006

Four-year

Adrian College, Adrian 49221-2575
Albion College, Albion 49224
Alma College, Alma 48801-1599
Andrews University, Berrien Springs 49104
Aquinas College, Grand Rapids 49506-1799
Baker College
    Cadillac, Cadillac 49601
    Flint, Flint 48507
    Muskegon, Muskegon 49442
    Owosso, Owosso 48867
    Port Huron, Port Huron 48060
Calvin College, Grand Rapids 49546
Center for Creative Studies: College of Art and Design, Detroit 48202
Central Michigan University, Mount Pleasant 48859
Cleary College, Ypsilanti 48197
Concordia College, Ann Arbor 48105
Davenport College of Business, Grand Rapids 49503
Detroit College of Business, Dearborn 48126-3799
Eastern Michigan University, Ypsilanti 48197-2260
Ferris State University, Big Rapids 49307-2295
Grace Bible College, Grand Rapids 49509-0910
Grand Rapids Baptist College and Seminary, Grand Rapids 49505
Grand Valley State University, Allendale 49401-9403
Great Lakes Christian College, Lansing 48917
Hillsdale College, Hillsdale 49242
Hope College, Holland 49423-3698
Jordan College, Cedar Springs 49319
Kalamazoo College, Kalamazoo 49006-3295
Kendall College of Art and Design, Grand Rapids 49503-3194
Lake Superior State University, Sault Ste. Marie 49783
Lawrence Technological University, Southfield 48075-1058
Madonna University, Livonia 48150-1173
Marygrove College, Detroit 48221
Michigan Christian College, Rochester Hills 48307-2764
Michigan State University, East Lansing 48824-1046
Michigan Technological University, Houghton 49931-1295
Northern Michigan University, Marquette 49855
Northwood Institute, Midland 48640
Oakland University, Rochester 48309-4401
Olivet College, Olivet 49076
Reformed Bible College, Grand Rapids 49505-9749
Sacred Heart Major Seminary, Detroit 48206
Saginaw Valley State University, University Center 48710-0001
St. Mary's College, Orchard Lake 48324
Siena Heights College, Adrian 49221-9937
Spring Arbor College, Spring Arbor 49283
University of Detroit Mercy, Detroit 48221
University of Michigan
    Ann Arbor, Ann Arbor 48109-1316
    Dearborn, Dearborn 48128-1491
    Flint, Flint 48502-2186
Wayne State University, Detroit 48202
Western Michigan University, Kalamazoo 49008
William Tyndale College, Farmington Hills 48331-9985

Five-year

GMI Engineering & Management Institute, Flint 48504-4898

Graduate study only

Calvin Theological Seminary, Grand Rapids 49546
Center for Humanistic Studies, Detroit 48202

Minnesota

Two-year

Alexandria Technical College, Alexandria 56308
Anoka-Ramsey Community College, Coon Rapids 55433
Austin Community College, Austin 55912
Bethany Lutheran College, Mankato 56001-4490
Brainerd Community College, Brainerd 56401
Inver Hills Community College, Inver Grove Heights 55076-3209
Itasca Community College: Arrowhead Region, Grand Rapids 55744
Lakewood Community College, White Bear Lake 55110
Mesabi Community College: Arrowhead Region, Virginia 55792
Minneapolis Community College, Minneapolis 55403
National Education Center: Brown Institute Campus, Minneapolis 55407
Normandale Community College, Bloomington 55431
Northland Community College, Thief River Falls 56701
Northwest Technical Institute, Eden Prairie 55344-5351
Northwestern Electronics Institute, Minneapolis 55421-9990
Rainy River Community College, International Falls 56649
Rochester Community College, Rochester 55904-4999
St. Mary's Campus of the College of St. Catherine, Minneapolis 55454
St. Paul Technical College, St. Paul 55102-9913
University of Minnesota: Crookston, Crookston 56716
Vermilion Community College, Ely 55731-9989
Willmar Community College, Willmar 56201
Willmar Technical College, Willmar 56201
Worthington Community College, Worthington 56187

Two-year upper-division

Metropolitan State University, St. Paul 55101-2189

Four-year

Augsburg College, Minneapolis 55454
Bemidji State University, Bemidji 56601
Bethel College, St. Paul 55112
Carleton College, Northfield 55057
College of Associated Arts, St. Paul 55102-2199
College of St. Benedict, St. Joseph 56374-2099
College of St. Catherine: St. Catherine Campus, St. Paul 55105
College of St. Scholastica, Duluth 55811-4199
Concordia College: Moorhead, Moorhead 56562-9981
Concordia College: St. Paul, St. Paul 55104-5494
Crown College, St. Bonifacius 55375-9001
Dr. Martin Luther College, New Ulm 56073-3300
Gustavus Adolphus College, St. Peter 56082
Hamline University, St. Paul 55104-1284
Macalester College, St. Paul 55105-1899
Mankato State University, Mankato 56002
Minneapolis College of Art and Design, Minneapolis 55404
Minnesota Bible College, Rochester 55902
Moorhead State University, Moorhead 56563
North Central Bible College, Minneapolis 55404
Northwestern College, Roseville 55113
Pillsbury Baptist Bible College, Owatonna 55060
St. Cloud State University, St. Cloud 56301-4498
St. John's University, Collegeville 56321
St. Mary's College of Minnesota, Winona 55987-1399
St. Olaf College, Northfield 55057
Southwest State University, Marshall 56258-1598

University of Minnesota
    Duluth, Duluth 55812-2496
    Morris, Morris 56267-2199
    Twin Cities, Minneapolis-St. Paul 55455-0213
University of St. Thomas, St. Paul 55105-1096
Winona State University, Winona 55987

Graduate study only

Bethel Theological Seminary, St. Paul 55112-6998
Luther Northwestern Theological Seminary, St. Paul 55108
Northwestern College of Chiropractic, Bloomington 55431
United Theological Seminary of the Twin Cities, New Brighton 55112
William Mitchell College of Law, St. Paul 55105

Mississippi

Two-year

Copiah-Lincoln Community College, Wesson 39191
East Central Community College, Decatur 39327
Hinds Community College, Raymond 39154-9799
Holmes Community College, Goodman 39079
Jones County Junior College, Ellisville 39437
Mary Holmes College, West Point 39773-1257
Meridian Community College, Meridian 39307
Mississippi Delta Community College, Moorhead 38761
Mississippi Gulf Coast Community College
    Jackson County Campus, Gautier 39553
    Jefferson Davis Campus, Gulfport 39507-3894
    Perkinston, Perkinston 39573
Northeast Mississippi Community College, Booneville 38829
Phillips Junior College
    Jackson, Jackson 39216
    Mississippi Gulf Coast, Gulfport 39507
Southwest Mississippi Community College, Summit 39666
Wood Junior College, Mathiston 39752

Two-year upper-division

University of Mississippi Medical Center, Jackson 39216

Four-year

Alcorn State University, Lorman 39096
Belhaven College, Jackson 39202-1789
Blue Mountain College, Blue Mountain 38610
Delta State University, Cleveland 38733
Jackson State University, Jackson 39217
Magnolia Bible College, Kosciusko 39090
Millsaps College, Jackson 39210
Mississippi College, Clinton 39058
Mississippi State University, Mississippi State 39762
Mississippi University for Women, Columbus 39701
Rust College, Holly Springs 38635-2328
Southeastern Baptist College, Laurel 39440
Tougaloo College, Tougaloo 39174
University of Mississippi, University 38677
University of Southern Mississippi, Hattiesburg 39406
Wesley College, Florence 39073-0070
William Carey College, Hattiesburg 39401

Missouri

Two-year

Cottey College, Nevada 64772
East Central College, Union 63084
ITT Technical Institute: St. Louis, St. Louis 63045
Jefferson College, Hillsboro 63050-1000

Kemper Military School and College, Boonville 65233
Longview Community College, Lee's Summit 64081
Maple Woods Community College, Kansas City 64156-1299
Mineral Area College, Flat River 63601
Moberly Area Community College, Moberly 65270
North Central Missouri College, Trenton 64683
Penn Valley Community College, Kansas City 64111
Phillips Junior College, Springfield 65804
Ranken Technical College, St. Louis 63113
St. Charles Community College, St. Peters 63376
St. Louis Community College
    Florissant Valley, St. Louis 63135
    Forest Park, St. Louis 63110
    Meramec, St. Louis 63122-5799
State Fair Community College, Sedalia 65301-2199
Three Rivers Community College, Poplar Bluff 63901-1308
Wentworth Military Academy and Junior College, Lexington 64067

Four-year

Avila College, Kansas City 64145-9990
Baptist Bible College, Springfield 65803
Berean College, Springfield 65802
Calvary Bible College, Kansas City 64147-1341
Central Christian College of the Bible, Moberly 65270-1997
Central Methodist College, Fayette 65248-1198
Central Missouri State University, Warrensburg 64093
College of the Ozarks, Point Lookout 65726-0017
Columbia College, Columbia 65216
Culver-Stockton College, Canton 63435
Deaconess College of Nursing, St. Louis 63139
DeVry Institute of Technology: Kansas City, Kansas City 64131-3626
Drury College, Springfield 65802-9977
Evangel College, Springfield 65802
Fontbonne College, St. Louis 63105
Hannibal-LaGrange College, Hannibal 63401
Harris Stowe State College, St. Louis 63103
Kansas City Art Institute, Kansas City 64111
Lincoln University, Jefferson City 65101
Lindenwood College, St. Charles 63301-1695
Maryville University, St. Louis 63141
Missouri Baptist College, St. Louis 63141
Missouri Southern State College, Joplin 64801-1595
Missouri Valley College, Marshall 65340
Missouri Western State College, St. Joseph 64507-2294
National College, Kansas City 64111
Northeast Missouri State University, Kirksville 63501-9980
Northwest Missouri State University, Maryville 64468-6001
Ozark Christian College, Joplin 64801
Park College, Parkville 64152-9970
Research College of Nursing, Kansas City 64110-2508
Rockhurst College, Kansas City 64110-2508
St. Louis Christian College, Florissant 63033
St. Louis University, St. Louis 63103-2097
Southeast Missouri State University, Cape Girardeau 63701
Southwest Baptist University, Bolivar 65613-2496
Southwest Missouri State University, Springfield 65804-0094
Stephens College, Columbia 65215-9986
University of Missouri
    Columbia, Columbia 65211
    Kansas City, Kansas City 64110-2944
    Rolla, Rolla 65401
    St. Louis, St. Louis 63121
Washington University, St. Louis 63130
Webster University, Webster Groves 63119-3194

Westminster College, Fulton 65251-1299
William Jewell College, Liberty 64068
William Woods College, Fulton 65251-1098

Five-year

St. Louis College of Pharmacy, St. Louis 63110

Graduate study only

Concordia Seminary, Clayton 63105
Covenant Theological Seminary, Saint Louis 63141
Kenrick-Glennon Seminary, St. Louis 63119

Montana

Two-year

Dawson Community College, Glendive 59330
Dull Knife Memorial College, Lame Deer 59043
Flathead Valley Community College, Kalispell 59901
Fort Peck Community College, Poplar 59255
Little Big Horn College, Crow Agency 59022
Miles Community College, Miles City 59301
Salish Kootenai College, Pablo 59855
Stone Child College, Box Elder 59521-9728

Four-year

Carroll College, Helena 59625
College of Great Falls, Great Falls 59405
Eastern Montana College, Billings 59101-0298
Montana College of Mineral Science and Technology, Butte 59701
Montana State University, Bozeman 59717-0016
Northern Montana College, Havre 59501
Rocky Mountain College, Billings 59102-1796
University of Montana, Missoula 59812
Western Montana College of the University of Montana, Dillon 59725

Nebraska

Two-year

Central Community College, Grand Island 68802-4903
Lincoln School of Commerce, Lincoln 68501-2826
McCook Community College, McCook 69001
Metropolitan Community College, Omaha 68103-3777
Nebraska College of Technical Agriculture, Curtis 69025-0069
Nebraska Indian Community College, Winnebago 68071
Northeast Community College, Norfolk 68702-0469
Southeast Community College
    Beatrice Campus, Beatrice 68310
    Lincoln Campus, Lincoln 68520
    Milford Campus, Milford 68405
Western Nebraska Community College
    Scottsbluff Campus, Scottsbluff 69361
    Sidney Campus, Sidney 69162
York College, York 68467-2699

Three-year

University of Nebraska Medical Center, Omaha 68198-4230

Four-year

Bellevue College, Bellevue 68005
Chadron State College, Chadron 69337
Clarkson College, Omaha 68132
College of St. Mary, Omaha 68124
Concordia College, Seward 68434-9989
Creighton University, Omaha 68178
Dana College, Blair 68008-1099
Doane College, Crete 68333
Grace College of the Bible, Omaha 68108
Hastings College, Hastings 68901
Midland Lutheran College, Fremont 68025

Nebraska Christian College, Norfolk 68701
Nebraska Methodist College of Nursing and Allied Health, Omaha 68114
Nebraska Wesleyan University, Lincoln 68504
Peru State College, Peru 68421
Union College, Lincoln 68506-4300
University of Nebraska
    Kearney, Kearney 68849
    Lincoln, Lincoln 68588-0417
    Omaha, Omaha 68182-0005
Wayne State College, Wayne 68787

Nevada

Two-year

Community College of Southern Nevada, North Las Vegas 89030
Deep Springs College, Dyer 89010-9803
Northern Nevada Community College, Elko 89801
Truckee Meadows Community College, Reno 89512
Western Nevada Community College, Carson City 89703

Four-year

Sierra Nevada College, Incline Village 89450-4269
University of Nevada
    Las Vegas, Las Vegas 89154-1021
    Reno, Reno 89557-0002

New Hampshire

Two-year

Castle College, Windham 03087-1297
Hesser College, Manchester 03103-9969
McIntosh College, Dover 03820
New Hampshire Technical College
    Berlin, Berlin 03570
    Laconia, Laconia 03246
    Manchester, Manchester 03102-8518
    Nashua, Nashua 03061-2052
    Stratham, Stratham 03885-0365
White Pines College, Chester 03036

Four-year

Colby-Sawyer College, New London 03257
Daniel Webster College, Nashua 03063-1699
Dartmouth College, Hanover 03755
Franklin Pierce College, Rindge 03461-0060
Keene State College, Keene 03431
New England College, Henniker 03242-0792
New Hampshire College, Manchester 03104-1394
Notre Dame College, Manchester 03104-2299
Plymouth State College of the University System of New Hampshire, Plymouth 03264
Rivier College, Nashua 03060-5086
St. Anselm College, Manchester 03102-1310
School for Lifelong Learning, Durham 03824-3545
University of New Hampshire
    Durham, Durham 03824
    Manchester, Manchester 03102

Graduate study only

Antioch New England Graduate School, Keene 03431

New Jersey

Two-year

Assumption College for Sisters, Mendham 07945-9998
Atlantic Community College, Mays Landing 08330-9888
Bergen Community College, Paramus 07652-1595
Berkeley College of Business, West Paterson 07424-0440

Brookdale Community College, Lincroft 07738
Burlington County College, Pemberton 08068-1599
Camden County College, Blackwood 08012
County College of Morris, Randolph 07869
Cumberland County College, Vineland 08360
Essex County College, Newark 07102
Fairleigh Dickinson University: Edward Williams College, Hackensack 07601
Gloucester County College, Sewell Post Office 08080
Katharine Gibbs School, Montclair 07042
Mercer County Community College, Trenton 08690-1099
Ocean County College, Toms River 08753-2001
Passaic County Community College, Paterson 07509
Sussex County Community College, Newton 07860
Union County College, Cranford 07016-1599

Four-year

Bloomfield College, Bloomfield 07003
Caldwell College, Caldwell 07006-6195
Centenary College, Hackettstown 07840-9989
College of St. Elizabeth, Morristown 07960-6989
Drew University, Madison 07940
Fairleigh Dickinson University, Madison 07070
Felician College, Lodi 07644-2198
Georgian Court College, Lakewood 08701-2697
Glassboro State College, Glassboro 08028
Jersey City State College, Jersey City 07305-1597
Kean College of New Jersey, Union 07083
Monmouth College, West Long Branch 07764-1898
Montclair State College, Upper Montclair 07043-1624
New Jersey Institute of Technology, Newark 07102-9938
Princeton University, Princeton 08544-0430
Ramapo College of New Jersey, Mahwah 07430-1680
Rider College, Lawrenceville 08648-3099
Rutgers—The State University of New Jersey
    Camden College of Arts and Sciences, Camden 08101-3740
    College of Engineering, New Brunswick 08903-2101
    College of Nursing, Newark 07102-1896
    Cook College, New Brunswick 08903-2101
    Douglass College, New Brunswick 08903-2101
    Livingston College, New Brunswick 08903-2101
    Mason Gross School of the Arts, New Brunswick 08903-2101
    Newark College of Arts and Sciences, Newark 07102-1896
    Rutgers College, New Brunswick 08903-2101
    University College Camden, Camden 08102-1499
    University College New Brunswick, New Brunswick 08903
    University College Newark, Newark 07102-1896
St. Peter's College, Jersey City 07306-5944
Seton Hall University, South Orange 07079-2689
Stevens Institute of Technology, Hoboken 07030
Stockton State College, Pomona 08240-9988
Thomas Edison State College, Trenton 08608-1176
Trenton State College, Trenton 08650-4700
University of Medicine and Dentistry of New Jersey: School of Health Related Professions, Newark 07107-3006
Upsala College, East Orange 07019
Westminster Choir College, Princeton 08540
William Paterson College of New Jersey, Wayne 07470

Five-year

Rutgers—The State University of New Jersey: College of Pharmacy, New Brunswick 08903-2101

Graduate study only

Rutgers—The State University of New Jersey, New Brunswick 08903

New Mexico

Two-year

Albuquerque Technical-Vocational Institute, Albuquerque 87106
Clovis Community College, Clovis 88101-8345
Dona Ana Branch Community College of New Mexico State University, Las Cruces 88003
Eastern New Mexico University: Roswell Campus, Roswell 88202-6000
Institute of American Indian Arts, Santa Fe 87504
New Mexico Junior College, Hobbs 88240
New Mexico Military Institute, Roswell 88201-5173
New Mexico State University at Carlsbad, Carlsbad 88220
Northern New Mexico Community College, Espanola 87532
Parks College, Albuquerque 87102
San Juan College, Farmington 87402

Four-year

College of Santa Fe, Santa Fe 87501-5634
College of the Southwest, Hobbs 88240-9987
Eastern New Mexico University, Portales 88130
National College, Albuquerque 87110
New Mexico Highlands University, Las Vegas 87701
New Mexico Institute of Mining and Technology, Socorro 87801
New Mexico State University, Las Cruces 88003-0001
St. John's College, Santa Fe 87501-4599
University of New Mexico, Albuquerque 87131
Western New Mexico University, Silver City 88062

New York

Two-year

Adirondack Community College, Queensbury 12804-1498
American Academy of Dramatic Arts, New York 10016
American Academy McAllister Institute of Funeral Service, New York 10019
Berkeley College, White Plains 10604-9990
Berkeley School: New York City, New York 10017
Bramson ORT Technical Institute, Forest Hills 11375
Briarcliffe: The College for Business, Hicksville 11801
Broome Community College, Binghamton 13902
Bryant & Stratton Business Institute
    Albany, Albany 12205
    Buffalo, Buffalo 14202
    Rochester, Rochester 14604-1381
    Syracuse, Syracuse 13202
Catholic Medical Center of Brooklyn and Queens School of Nursing, Woodhaven 11421
Central City Business Institute, Syracuse 13203

City University of New York
    Borough of Manhattan Community College, New York 10007-1097
    Hostos Community College, Bronx 10451
    Kingsborough Community College, Brooklyn 11235
    La Guardia Community College, Long Island City 11101
    Queensborough Community College, Bayside 11364
Clinton Community College, Plattsburgh 12901-4297
Cochran School of Nursing-St. John's Riverside Hospital, Yonkers 10701
Columbia-Greene Community College, Hudson 12534
Community College of the Finger Lakes, Canandaigua 14424-8399
Corning Community College, Corning 14830
Culinary Institute of America, Hyde Park 12538-1499
Dutchess Community College, Poughkeepsie 12601-1595
Erie Community College
    City Campus, Buffalo 14203-2601
    North Campus, Williamsville 14221
    South Campus, Orchard Park 14127-2199
Five Towns College, Seaford 11783-9800
Fulton-Montgomery Community College, Johnstown 12095-9609
Genesee Community College, Batavia 14020
Helene Fuld School of Nursing, New York 10035
Herkimer County Community College, Herkimer 13350-1598
Hilbert College, Hamburg 14075
Hudson Valley Community College, Troy 12180
Institute of Design and Construction, Brooklyn 11201-5380
Jamestown Business College, Jamestown 14701
Jamestown Community College, Jamestown 14701
Jefferson Community College, Watertown 13601
Katharine Gibbs School
    Melville, Melville 11747
    New York, New York 10166
Long Island College Hospital School of Nursing, Brooklyn 11201
Maria College, Albany 12208
Mater Dei College, Ogdensburg 13669
Mohawk Valley Community College, Utica 13501-9979
Monroe College, Bronx 10468
Monroe Community College, Rochester 14623
Nassau Community College, Garden City 11530-6793
Niagara County Community College, Sanborn 14132
North Country Community College, Saranac Lake 12983
Onondaga Community College, Syracuse 13215
Orange County Community College, Middletown 10940
Paul Smith's College, Paul Smiths 12970-0265
Phillips Beth Israel School of Nursing, New York 10010
Rochester Business Institute, Rochester 14622
Rockland Community College, Suffern 10901
Sage Junior College of Albany, A Division of Russell Sage College, Albany 12208
St. Joseph's School of Nursing, Syracuse 13203

State University of New York
    College of Agriculture and Technology at
        Cobleskill, Cobleskill 12043
    College of Agriculture and Technology at
        Morrisville, Morrisville 13408
    College of Technology at Alfred, Alfred
        14802-1196
    College of Technology at Canton, Canton
        13617
    College of Technology at Delhi, Delhi
        13753-1190
    College of Technology at Farmingdale,
        Farmingdale 11735
Stenotype Academy, New York 10007
Suffolk County Community College
    Eastern Campus, Riverhead 11901
    Selden, Selden 11784
    Western Campus, Brentwood 11717
Sullivan County Community College, Loch
    Sheldrake 12759
Taylor Business Institute, New York 10036
Technical Career Institutes, New York 10001
Tobe-Coburn School for Fashion Careers, New
    York 10016
Tompkins-Cortland Community College, Dryden
    13053-0139
Trocaire College, Buffalo 14220
Ulster County Community College, Stone Ridge
    12484
Utica School of Commerce, Utica 13501
Villa Maria College of Buffalo, Buffalo 14225-
    3999
Westchester Business Institute, White Plains
    10602
Westchester Community College, Valhalla 10595
Wood School, New York 10016-0190

Two-year upper-division

Columbia University: School of Nursing, New
    York 10032
State University of New York
    Health Science Center at Brooklyn,
        Brooklyn 11203-2098
    Health Sciences Center at Stony Brook,
        Stony Brook 11794-8276
    Institute of Technology at Utica/Rome,
        Utica 13504-3050

Four-year

Adelphi University, Garden City 11530
Alfred University, Alfred 14802
Bard College, Annandale-on-Hudson 12504
Barnard College, New York 10027-6598
Boricua College, New York 10032
Canisius College, Buffalo 14208-9989
Cazenovia College, Cazenovia 13035-9989
City University of New York
    Baruch College, New York 10010
    Brooklyn College, Brooklyn 11210
    City College, New York 10031
    College of Staten Island, Staten Island
        10301-4547
    Hunter College, New York 10021
    John Jay College of Criminal Justice, New
        York 10019
    Lehman College, Bronx 10468
    Medgar Evers College, Brooklyn 11225-2201
    New York City Technical College, Brooklyn
        11201-2983
    Queens College, Flushing 11367
    York College, Jamaica 11451-9989
Clarkson University, Potsdam 13676
Colgate University, Hamilton 13346-1383
College of Aeronautics, Flushing 11371
College for Human Services, New York 10014
College of Mount St. Vincent, Riverdale 10471
College of New Rochelle
    New Rochelle, New Rochelle 10805-2308
    School of New Resources, New Rochelle
        10805-2308
College of St. Rose, Albany 12203

Columbia University
    Columbia College, New York 10027
    School of Engineering and Applied Science,
        New York 10027
    School of General Studies, New York 10027
Concordia College, Bronxville 10708
Cooper Union, New York 10003-7183
Cornell University, Ithaca 14850
Daemen College, Amherst 14226
Dominican College of Blauvelt, Orangeburg
    10962
Dowling College, Oakdale 11769-1999
D'Youville College, Buffalo 14201-1084
Eastman School of Music of the University of
    Rochester, Rochester 14604-2599
Elmira College, Elmira 14901-2345
Eugene Lang College/New School for Social
    Research, New York 10114-0059
Fashion Institute of Technology, New York
    10001-5992
Fordham University, Bronx 10458
Hamilton College, Clinton 13323-1293
Hartwick College, Oneonta 13820-9989
Hobart College, Geneva 14456
Hofstra University, Hempstead 11550
Houghton College, Houghton 14744-9989
Iona College, New Rochelle 10801
Ithaca College, Ithaca 14850
Jewish Theological Seminary of America, New
    York 10027
Juilliard School, New York 10023-6590
Keuka College, Keuka Park 14478-0098
King's College, Briarcliff Manor 10510-9985
Kol Yaakov Torah Center, Monsey 10952
Laboratory Institute of Merchandising, New York
    10022-5268
Le Moyne College, Syracuse 13214-1399
Long Island University
    Brooklyn Campus, Brooklyn 11201
    C. W. Post Campus, Brookville 11548
    Southampton Campus, Southampton 11968
Manhattan College, Riverdale 10471
Manhattan School of Music, New York 10027-
    4698
Manhattanville College, Purchase 10577
Mannes College of Music, New York 10024
Marist College, Poughkeepsie 12601
Marymount College, Tarrytown 10591-3796
Marymount Manhattan College, New York 10021
Medaille College, Buffalo 14214
Mercy College, Dobbs Ferry 10522
Mirrer Yeshiva Central Institute, Brooklyn 11223
Molloy College, Rockville Centre 11570
Mount St. Mary College, Newburgh 12550
Nazareth College of Rochester, Rochester 14618-
    3790
New York Institute of Technology, Old Westbury
    11568-0170
New York School of Interior Design, New York
    10022
New York University, New York 10011-9108
Niagara University, Niagara Falls 14109
Nyack College, Nyack 10960
Pace University
    College of White Plains, White Plains
        10603-3796
    New York, New York 10038
    Pleasantville/Briarcliff, Pleasantville 10570
Parsons School of Design, New York 10011
Polytechnic University
    Brooklyn, Brooklyn 11201-2999
    Long Island Campus, Farmingdale 11735-
        3995
Pratt Institute, Brooklyn 11205
Rensselaer Polytechnic Institute, Troy 12181-
    3590
Roberts Wesleyan College, Rochester 14624-1997
Rochester Institute of Technology, Rochester
    14623-0887
Russell Sage College, Troy 12180
St. Bonaventure University, St. Bonaventure
    14778-2284

St. Francis College, Brooklyn Heights 11201
St. John Fisher College, Rochester 14618-3597
St. John's University, Jamaica 11439
St. Joseph's College
    Brooklyn, Brooklyn 11205-3688
    Suffolk Campus, Patchogue 11772-2603
St. Lawrence University, Canton 13617-1447
St. Thomas Aquinas College, Sparkill 10976
Sarah Lawrence College, Bronxville 10708
School of Visual Arts, New York 10010-3994
Siena College, Loudonville 11211-1462
Skidmore College, Saratoga Springs 12866
State University of New York
    Albany, Albany 12222
    Binghamton, Binghamton 13902-6001
    Buffalo, Buffalo 14214
    Purchase, Purchase 10577-1400
    Stony Brook, Stony Brook 11794-1901
    College at Brockport, Brockport 14420-2915
    College at Buffalo, Buffalo 14222-1095
    College at Cortland, Cortland 13045
    College of Environmental Science and
        Forestry, Syracuse 13210-2779
    College at Fredonia, Fredonia 14063
    College at Geneseo, Geneseo 14454-1471
    College at New Paltz, New Paltz 12561-
        2499
    College at Old Westbury, Old Westbury
        11568-0307
    College at Oneonta, Oneonta 13820-4016
    College at Plattsburgh, Plattsburgh 12901
    College at Potsdam, Potsdam 13676-2294
    Empire State College, Saratoga Springs
        12866-4390
    Health Science Center at Syracuse, Syracuse
        13210.
    Maritime College, Throggs Neck 10465-
        4198
    Oswego, Oswego 13126-3599
Syracuse University, Syracuse 13244-1120
Talmudical Institute of Upstate New York,
    Rochester 14607
Touro College, New York 10036
Union College, Schenectady 12308-2311
United States Merchant Marine Academy, Kings
    Point 11024
United States Military Academy, West Point
    10996-1797
University of Rochester, Rochester 14627-0251
University of the State of New York: Regents
    College, Albany 12203
Utica College of Syracuse University, Utica
    13502-4892
Vassar College, Poughkeepsie 12601
Wadhams Hall Seminary-College, Ogdensburg
    13669-9308
Wagner College, Staten Island 10301-4495
Webb Institute of Naval Architecture, Glen Cove
    11542
Wells College, Aurora 13026
William Smith College, Geneva 14456-3381
Yeshiva University, New York 10033-3299

Five-year

Albany College of Pharmacy, Albany 12208
Beth Hamedrash Shaarei Yosher Institute,
    Brooklyn 11204
College of Insurance, New York 10007-2132
Darkei No'Am Rabbinical College, Brooklyn
    11210
Machzikei Hadath Rabbinical College, Brooklyn
    11204
Mesivta Torah Vodaath Seminary, Brooklyn
    11218
Ohr Somayach Tanenbaum Education Center,
    Monsey 10952
Yeshiva Karlin Stolin Beth Aron Y'Israel
    Rabbinical Institute, Brooklyn 11204-9961

Graduate study only

Albany Medical College, Albany 12208

Bank Street College of Education, New York 10025
City University of New York Graduate School and University Center, New York 10036-8099
Columbia University, New York 10027
Graduate School of Figurative Art of the New York Academy of Art, New York 10003
Maryknoll School Of Theology, Maryknoll 10545-0304
New York Chiropractic College, Seneca Falls 13148
New York Theological Seminary, New York 10001
Rockefeller University, New York 10021
State University of New York College of Optometry, New York 10010
Union Theological Seminary, New York 10027

North Carolina

Two-year

Alamance Community College, Goraham 27253
Anson Community College, Polkton 28135
Asheville Buncombe Technical Community College, Asheville 28801
Beaufort County Community College, Washington 27889
Bladen Community College, Dublin 28332
Blue Ridge Community College, Flat Rock 28731-9624
Brevard College, Brevard 28712
Brunswick Community College, Supply 28462
Caldwell Community College and Technical Institute, Hudson 28638
Cape Fear Community College, Wilmington 28401
Carteret Community College, Morehead City 28557-2989
Catawba Valley Community College, Hickory 28602
Cecils College, Asheville 28816
Central Carolina Community College, Sanford 27330
Central Piedmont Community College, Charlotte 28235
Cleveland Community College, Shelby 28150
Coastal Carolina Community College, Jacksonville 28540-6877
College of the Albemarle, Elizabeth City 27906-2327
Craven Community College, New Bern 28560
Davidson County Community College, Lexington 27293-1287
Durham Technical Community College, Durham 27703
Edgecombe Community College, Tarboro 27886
Fayetteville Technical Community College, Fayetteville 28303-0236
Forsyth Technical Community College, Winston-Salem 27103
Gaston College, Dallas 28034-1499
Guilford Technical Community College, Jamestown 27282
Haywood Community College, Clyde 28721
Isothermal Community College, Spindale 28160
James Sprunt Community College, Kenansville 28349-0398
Johnston Community College, Smithfield 27577-2350
Louisburg College, Louisburg 27549
Martin Community College, Williamston 27892-9988
Mayland Community College, Spruce Pine 28777
McDowell Technical Community College, Marion 28752
Mitchell Community College, Statesville 28677
Montgomery Community College, Troy 27371-0787
Nash Community College, Rocky Mount 27804
Pamlico Community College, Grantsboro 28529
Peace College, Raleigh 27604-1194

Piedmont Community College, Roxboro 27573
Pitt Community College, Greenville 27835-7007
Richmond Community College, Hamlet 28345
Roanoke-Chowan Community College, Ahoskie 27910
Robeson Community College, Lumberton 28359
Rockingham Community College, Wentworth 27375-0038
St. Mary's College, Raleigh 27603-1689
Sampson Community College, Clinton 28328
Sandhills Community College, Pinehurst 28374
Southeastern Baptist Theological Seminary, Wake Forest 27587
Southeastern Community College, Whiteville 28472
Southwestern Community College, Sylva 28779
Stanly Community College, Albemarle 28001
Surry Community College, Dobson 27017
Tri-County Community College, Murphy 28906
Vance-Granville Community College, Henderson 27536
Wake Technical Community College, Raleigh 27603
Wayne Community College, Goldsboro 27533-8002
Western Piedmont Community College, Morganton 28655
Wilkes Community College, Wilkesboro 28697-0120
Wilson Technical Community College, Wilson 27893

Four-year

Appalachian State University, Boone 28608
Barber-Scotia College, Concord 28025
Barton College, Wilson 27893
Belmont Abbey College, Belmont 28012-2795
Bennett College, Greensboro 27401-3239
Campbell University, Buies Creek 27506
Catawba College, Salisbury 28144-2488
Chowan College, Murfreesboro 27855-9901
Davidson College, Davidson 28036
Duke University, Durham 27706
East Carolina University, Greenville 27858-4353
East Coast Bible College, Charlotte 28214
Elizabeth City State University, Elizabeth City 27909
Elon College, Elon College 27244-2010
Fayetteville State University, Fayetteville 28301-4298
Gardner-Webb College, Boiling Springs 28017-9980
Greensboro College, Greensboro 27401-1875
Guilford College, Greensboro 27410
High Point University, High Point 27262-3598
John Wesley College, High Point 27265-3197
Johnson C. Smith University, Charlotte 28216-5398
Lees-McRae College, Banner Elk 28604
Lenoir-Rhyne College, Hickory 28603
Livingstone College, Salisbury 28144-5213
Mars Hill College, Mars Hill 28754
Meredith College, Raleigh 27607-5298
Methodist College, Fayetteville 28311-1420
Montreat-Anderson College, Montreat 28757
Mount Olive College, Mount Olive 28365
North Carolina Agricultural and Technical State University, Greensboro 27411
North Carolina Central University, Durham 27707
North Carolina School of the Arts, Winston-Salem 27117-2189
North Carolina State University, Raleigh 27695-7103
North Carolina Wesleyan College, Rocky Mount 27804
Pembroke State University, Pembroke 28372
Pfeiffer College, Misenheimer 28109
Queens College, Charlotte 28274
Roanoke Bible College, Elizabeth City 27909
St. Andrews Presbyterian College, Laurinburg 28352-9151

St. Augustine's College, Raleigh 27610-2298
Salem College, Winston-Salem 27108
Shaw University, Raleigh 27611
University of North Carolina
    Asheville, Asheville 28804-3299
    Chapel Hill, Chapel Hill 27599-2200
    Charlotte, Charlotte 28223
    Greensboro, Greensboro 27412-5001
    Wilmington, Wilmington 28403-3297
Wake Forest University, Winston-Salem 27109
Warren Wilson College, Swannanoa 28778-2099
Western Carolina University, Cullowhee 28723
Wingate College, Wingate 28174-0157
Winston-Salem State University, Winston-Salem 27110

Five-year

Piedmont Bible College, Winston-Salem 27101-5197

North Dakota

Two-year

Bismarck State College, Bismarck 58501
Little Hoop Community College, Fort Totten 58335
North Dakota State College of Science, Wahpeton 58076
North Dakota State University: Bottineau and Institute of Forestry, Bottineau 58318-1198
Standing Rock College, Fort Yates 58538
Turtle Mountain Community College, Belcourt 58316-0340
University of North Dakota
    Lake Region, Devils Lake 58301
    Williston, Williston 58801-1326

Two-year upper-division

Medcenter One College of Nursing, Bismarck 58501

Four-year

Dickinson State University, Dickinson 58601
Jamestown College, Jamestown 58401
Mayville State University, Mayville 58257
Minot State University, Minot 58702-5002
North Dakota State University, Fargo 58105
Trinity Bible College, Ellendale 58436-1001
University of Mary, Bismarck 58504-9652
University of North Dakota, Grand Forks 58202-8070
Valley City State University, Valley City 58072

Ohio

Two-year

Antonelli Institute of Art and Photography, Cincinnati 45202
Bowling Green State University: Firelands College, Huron 44839
Bradford School, Columbus 43229
Bryant & Stratton Business Institute: Great Northern, North Olmsted 44070
Central Ohio Technical College, Newark 43055
Chatfield College, St. Martin 45118-9705
Cincinnati Metropolitan College, St. Bernard 45217
Cincinnati Technical College, Cincinnati 45223
Clark State Community College, Springfield 45501
Cleveland Institute of Electronics, Cleveland 44114-3679
Columbus State Community College, Columbus 43216-1609
Cuyahoga Community College
    Metropolitan Campus, Cleveland 44115-2878
    Western Campus, Parma 44130
Davis Junior College of Business, Toledo 43623
Edison State Community College, Piqua 45356

Colleges included in this book

Hocking Technical College, Nelsonville 45764
ITT Technical Institute
    Dayton, Dayton 45414
    Youngstown, Youngstown 44501-0779
Jefferson Technical College, Steubenville 43952
Kent State University
    Ashtabula Regional Campus, Ashtabula
        44004
    East Liverpool Regional Campus, East
        Liverpool 43920
    Salem Regional Campus, Salem 44460
    Stark Campus, Canton 44720
    Tuscarawas Campus, New Philadelphia
        44663
Kettering College of Medical Arts, Kettering
    45429
Lakeland Community College, Mentor 44060-
    7594
Lorain County Community College, Elyria 44035-
    1697
Marion Technical College, Marion 43302-5694
Miami University: Hamilton Campus, Hamilton
    45011
Miami-Jacobs College, Dayton 45401
Muskingum Area Technical College, Zanesville
    43701
North Central Technical College, Mansfield
    44901
Northwest Technical College, Archbold 43502
Northwestern College, Lima 45805
Ohio Institute of Photography, Dayton 45439
Ohio State University
    Agricultural Technical Institute, Wooster
        44691-4099
    Lima Campus, Lima 45804-3596
    Mansfield Campus, Mansfield 44906
    Marion Campus, Marion 43302
    Newark Campus, Newark 43055
Ohio University
    Chillicothe Campus, Chillicothe 45601
    Eastern Campus, St. Clairsville 43950
Ohio Valley Business College, East Liverpool
    43920
Owens Technical College
    Findlay Campus, Findlay 45840
    Toledo, Toledo 43699-1947
Sinclair Community College, Dayton 45402
Southern Ohio College, Cincinnati 45237
Southern State Community College, Hillsboro
    45133
Stark Technical College, Canton 44720
Terra Technical College, Fremont 43420
University of Akron: Wayne College, Orrville
    44667
University of Cincinnati
    Access Colleges, Cincinnati 45221
    Clermont College, Batavia 45103
    Raymond Walters College, Cincinnati 45236
Virginia Marti College of Fashion and Art,
    Lakewood 44107
Washington State Community College, Marietta
    45750
Wright State University: Lake Campus, Celina
    45822

Three-year

Antioch School for Adult and Experiential
    Learning, Yellow Springs 45387

Four-year

Antioch College, Yellow Springs 45387
Art Academy of Cincinnati, Cincinnati 45202-
    1597
Ashland University, Ashland 44805-9981
Baldwin-Wallace College, Berea 44017-2088
Bluffton College, Bluffton 45817-1196
Bowling Green State University, Bowling Green
    43403-0080
Capital University, Columbus 43209-2394
Case Western Reserve University, Cleveland
    44106-7055
Cedarville College, Cedarville 45314-0601

Central State University, Wilberforce 45384
Cincinnati Bible College and Seminary, Cincinnati
    45204-3200
Cincinnati College of Mortuary Science,
    Cincinnati 45207-1033
Circleville Bible College, Circleville 43113
Cleveland College of Jewish Studies, Beachwood
    44122
Cleveland Institute of Music, Cleveland 44106
Cleveland State University, Cleveland 44115-2403
College of Mount St. Joseph, Cincinnati 45233-
    1672
College of Wooster, Wooster 44691-2363
Columbus College of Art and Design, Columbus
    43215-3875
Defiance College, Defiance 43512-1695
Denison University, Granville 43023
DeVry Institute of Technology: Columbus,
    Columbus 43209-2764
Dyke College, Cleveland 44115
ETI Technical College, Cleveland 44103
Franciscan University of Steubenville,
    Steubenville 43952-6701
Franklin University, Columbus 43215-5399
Heidelberg College, Tiffin 44883
Hiram College, Hiram 44234
John Carroll University, University Heights
    44118-4581
Kent State University, Kent 44242-0001
Kenyon College, Gambier 43022-9623
Lake Erie College, Painesville 44077
Lourdes College, Sylvania 43560-2898
Malone College, Canton 44709
Marietta College, Marietta 45750-4005
Miami University: Oxford Campus, Oxford 45056
Mount Union College, Alliance 44601-3993
Mount Vernon Nazarene College, Mount Vernon
    43050
Muskingum College, New Concord 43762
Notre Dame College of Ohio, Cleveland 44121
Oberlin College, Oberlin 44074
Ohio Dominican College, Columbus 43219-2099
Ohio Northern University, Ada 45810-1599
Ohio State University: Columbus Campus,
    Columbus 43210-1200
Ohio University
    Ohio University, Athens 45701-2979
    Southern Campus at Ironton, Ironton 45638
    Zanesville Campus, Zanesville 43701
Ohio Wesleyan University, Delaware 43015
Otterbein College, Westerville 43081
Pontifical College Josephinum, Columbus 43085
Shawnee State University, Portsmouth 45662
Tiffin University, Tiffin 44883
Union Institute, Cincinnati 45206-1947
University of Akron, Akron 44325-2001
University of Cincinnati, Cincinnati 45221-0091
University of Dayton, Dayton 45469-1611
University of Findlay, Findlay 45840-3695
University of Rio Grande, Rio Grande 45674
University of Toledo, Toledo 43606-3398
Urbana University, Urbana 43078-2091
Ursuline College, Pepper Pike 44124-4398
Walsh College, North Canton 44720
Wilberforce University, Wilberforce 45384-1091
Wilmington College, Wilmington 45177
Wittenberg University, Springfield 45501
Wright State University, Dayton 45435
Xavier University, Cincinnati 45207-5311
Youngstown State University, Youngstown
    44555-0001

Five-year

Cleveland Institute of Art, Cleveland 44106

Graduate study only

Air Force Institute of Technology, Dayton 45433-
    6583
Athenaeum of Ohio, Cincinnati 45230

Oklahoma

Two-year

Bacone College, Muskogee 74403-1597
Connors State College, Warner 74469-0389
Eastern Oklahoma State College, Wilburton
    74578-4999
Murray State College, Tishomingo 73460
National Education Center: Spartan School of
    Aeronautics Campus, Tulsa 74158-2833
Northern Oklahoma College, Tonkawa 74653-
    0310
Oklahoma Junior College, Tulsa 74133
Oklahoma State University
    Oklahoma City, Oklahoma City 73107
    Technical Branch: Okmulgee, Okmulgee
        74447-3901
Redlands Community College, El Reno 73036
Rogers State College, Claremore 74017
Rose State College, Midwest City 73110-2799
St. Gregory's College, Shawnee 74801
Tulsa Junior College, Tulsa 74135-6101

Two-year upper-division

University of Oklahoma Health Sciences Center,
    Oklahoma City 73190

Four-year

Bartlesville Wesleyan College, Bartlesville 74006
Cameron University, Lawton 73505
East Central University, Ada 74820-6899
Hillsdale Free Will Baptist College, Moore 73153-
    1208
Langston University, Langston 73050
Mid-America Bible College, Oklahoma City
    73170
Northeastern State University, Tahlequah 74464
Northwestern Oklahoma State University, Alva
    73717
Oklahoma Baptist University, Shawnee 74801
Oklahoma Christian University of Science and
    Arts, Oklahoma City 73136-1100
Oklahoma City University, Oklahoma City 73106
Oklahoma Panhandle State University, Goodwell
    73939-0430
Oklahoma State University, Stillwater 74078
Oral Roberts University, Tulsa 74171
Phillips University, Enid 73701-6439
Southeastern Oklahoma State University, Durant
    74701
Southwestern College of Christian Ministries,
    Bethany 73008
Southwestern Oklahoma State University,
    Weatherford 73096
University of Central Oklahoma, Edmond 73034-
    0151
University of Oklahoma, Norman 73069-0520
University of Science and Arts of Oklahoma,
    Chickasha 73018
University of Tulsa, Tulsa 74104

Oregon

Two-year

Central Oregon Community College, Bend 97701-
    5998
Chemeketa Community College, Salem 97309-
    7070
Clackamas Community College, Oregon City
    97045
Clatsop Community College, Astoria 97103
Lane Community College, Eugene 97405
Linn-Benton Community College, Albany 97321-
    3779
Mount Hood Community College, Gresham
    97030
Oregon Polytechnic Institute, Portland 97214
Portland Community College, Portland 97219-
    0990
Rogue Community College, Grants Pass 97527

Southwestern Oregon Community College, Coos Bay 97420
Treasure Valley Community College, Ontario 97914
Umpqua Community College, Roseburg 97470

Three-year

ITT Technical Institute: Portland, Portland 97218-2854

Four-year

Bassist College, Portland 97201
Concordia College, Portland 97211-6099
Eastern Oregon State College, LaGrande 97850-2899
Eugene Bible College, Eugene 97405
George Fox College, Newberg 97132-9987
Lewis and Clark College, Portland 97219
Linfield College, McMinnville 97128-6894
Marylhurst College, Marylhurst 97036
Mount Angel Seminary, St. Benedict 97373
Multnomah School of the Bible, Portland 97220-5898
Northwest Christian College, Eugene 97401-9983
Oregon Health Sciences University, Portland 97201
Oregon Institute of Technology, Klamath Falls 97601-8801
Oregon State University, Corvallis 97331-2130
Pacific Northwest College of Art, Portland 97205
Pacific University, Forest Grove 97116-1797
Portland State University, Portland 97207-0751
Reed College, Portland 97202-8199
Southern Oregon State College, Ashland 97520-5032
University of Oregon
    Eugene, Eugene 97403-1217
        Robert Donald Clark Honors College, Eugene 97403-1293
University of Portland, Portland 97203-5798
Warner Pacific College, Portland 97215
Western Baptist College, Salem 97301
Western Oregon State College, Monmouth 97361-1394
Willamette University, Salem 97301-3922

Graduate study only

Oregon Graduate Institute, Beaverton 97006-1999
Western Conservative Baptist Seminary, Portland 97215
Western States Chiropractic College, Portland 97230-3099

Pennsylvania

Two-year

Antonelli Institute of Art and Photography, Plymouth Meeting 19462
Art Institute of Pittsburgh, Pittsburgh 15222
Berean Institute, Philadelphia 19130
Bucks County Community College, Newtown 18940
Butler County Community College, Butler 16003-1203
Central Pennsylvania Business School, Summerdale 17093-0309
CHI Institute, Southampton 18966
Churchman Business School, Easton 18042
Community College of Beaver County, Monaca 15061
Community College of Philadelphia, Philadelphia 19130-3991
Dean Institute of Technology, Pittsburgh 15226
Delaware County Community College, Media 19063
DuBois Business College, DuBois 15801
Electronic Institutes: Pittsburgh, Pittsburgh 15217
Harcum Junior College, Bryn Mawr 19010-3476
Harrisburg Area Community College, Harrisburg 17110-2999
ICS Center for Degree Studies, Scranton 18515

Johnson Technical Institute, Scranton 18508
Keystone Junior College, La Plume 18440-0200
Lackawanna Junior College, Scranton 18505
Lansdale School of Business, North Wales 19454
Lehigh County Community College, Schnecksville 18078
Luzerne County Community College, Nanticoke 18634-9804
Manor Junior College, Jenkintown 19046-3399
Montgomery County Community College, Blue Bell 19422-0758
National Education Center: Vale Tech Campus, Blairsville 15717
Northampton County Area Community College, Bethlehem 18017
Northeastern Christian Junior College, Villanova 19085
Peirce Junior College, Philadelphia 19102
Penn Technical Institute, Pittsburgh 15222
Pennsylvania College of Technology, Williamsport 17701-5799
Pennsylvania Institute of Technology, Media 19063-4098
Pittsburgh Institute of Aeronautics, Pittsburgh 15236
Pittsburgh Institute of Mortuary Science, Pittsburgh 15206-3706
Pittsburgh Technical Institute, Pittsburgh 15222
Reading Area Community College, Reading 19603
Tracey-Warner School, Philadelphia 19108-1084
Triangle Tech
    Erie School, Erie 16502
    Greensburg School, Greensburg 15601
    Pittsburgh Campus, Pittsburgh 15214
University of Pittsburgh at Titusville, Titusville 16354
Valley Forge Military College, Wayne 19087-3695
Westmoreland County Community College, Youngwood 15697

Two-year upper-division

Penn State Harrisburg Capital College, Middletown 17057-4898
Thomas Jefferson University: College of Allied Health Sciences, Philadelphia 19107

Three-year

Williamson Free School of Mechanical Trades, Media 19063-5299

Four-year

Academy of the New Church, Bryn Athyn 19009
Albright College, Reading 19612-5234
Allegheny College, Meadville 16335
Allentown College of St. Francis de Sales, Center Valley 18034-9568
Alvernia College, Reading 19607-1799
Baptist Bible College of Pennsylvania, Clarks Summit 18411
Beaver College, Glenside 19038-3295
Bloomsburg University of Pennsylvania, Bloomsburg 17815
Bryn Mawr College, Bryn Mawr 19010
Bucknell University, Lewisburg 17837-9988
Cabrini College, Radnor 19087-3699
California University of Pennsylvania, California 15419-1394
Carlow College, Pittsburgh 15213-3165
Carnegie Mellon University, Pittsburgh 15213-3890
Cedar Crest College, Allentown 18104-6196
Chatham College, Pittsburgh 15232
Chestnut Hill College, Philadelphia 19118-2695
Cheyney University of Pennsylvania, Cheyney 19319-0019
Clarion University of Pennsylvania, Clarion 16214
College Misericordia, Dallas 18612-9984
Curtis Institute of Music, Philadelphia 19103
Delaware Valley College, Doylestown 18901-2697
Dickinson College, Carlisle 17013-2896

Duquesne University, Pittsburgh 15282-0201
East Stroudsburg University of Pennsylvania, East Stroudsburg 18301
Eastern College, St. Davids 19087-3696
Edinboro University of Pennsylvania, Edinboro 16444
Elizabethtown College, Elizabethtown 17022-2298
Franklin and Marshall College, Lancaster 17604-3003
Gannon University, Erie 16541-0001
Geneva College, Beaver Falls 15010-3599
Gettysburg College, Gettysburg 17325-1484
Gratz College, Melrose Park 19126
Grove City College, Grove City 16127-2104
Gwynedd-Mercy College, Gwynedd Valley 19437
Hahnemann University School of Health Sciences and Humanities, Philadelphia 19102-1192
Haverford College, Haverford 19041-1392
Holy Family College, Philadelphia 19114-2094
Hussian School of Art, Philadelphia 19107
Immaculata College, Immaculata 19345
Indiana University of Pennsylvania, Indiana 15705-1088
Juniata College, Huntingdon 16652-2119
King's College, Wilkes-Barre 18711-0801
Kutztown University of Pennsylvania, Kutztown 19530
La Roche College, Pittsburgh 15237
La Salle University, Philadelphia 19141
Lafayette College, Easton 18042-1770
Lancaster Bible College, Lancaster 17601
Lebanon Valley College of Pennsylvania, Annville 17003-0501
Lehigh University, Bethlehem 18015-3094
Lincoln University, Lincoln University 19352-0999
Lock Haven University of Pennsylvania, Lock Haven 17745
Lycoming College, Williamsport 17701
Mansfield University of Pennsylvania, Mansfield 16933
Marywood College, Scranton 18509-9989
Mercyhurst College, Erie 16546
Messiah College, Grantham 17027-0800
Millersville University of Pennsylvania, Millersville 17551-0302
Moore College of Art and Design, Philadelphia 19103-1179
Moravian College, Bethlehem 18018
Mount Aloysius College, Cresson 16630
Muhlenberg College, Allentown 18104
Neumann College, Aston 19014
Penn State
    Erie Behrend College, Erie 16563
    University Park Campus, University Park 16802
Philadelphia College of Bible, Langhorne 19047-2992
Philadelphia College of Pharmacy and Science, Philadelphia 19104-4495
Philadelphia College of Textiles and Science, Philadelphia 19144
Point Park College, Pittsburgh 15222
Robert Morris College, Coraopolis 15108-1189
Rosemont College, Rosemont 19010
St. Charles Borromeo Seminary, Overbrook 19096-3099
St. Francis College, Loretto 15940
St. Joseph's University, Philadelphia 19131
St. Vincent College, Latrobe 15650-2690
Seton Hill College, Greensburg 15601-1599
Shippensburg University of Pennsylvania, Shippensburg 17257
Slippery Rock University of Pennsylvania, Slippery Rock 16057
Spring Garden College, Philadelphia 19119-1651
Susquehanna University, Selinsgrove 17870-1001
Swarthmore College, Swarthmore 19081-1397
Temple University, Philadelphia 19122-1803
Thiel College, Greenville 16125
University of the Arts, Philadelphia 19102

ITT Technical Institute: Nashville, Nashville 37214-8029
Jackson State Community College, Jackson 38301-3797
John A. Gupton College, Nashville 37203
Knoxville Business College, Knoxville 37917
Martin Methodist College, Pulaski 38478
McKenzie College, Chattanooga 37402
Motlow State Community College, Tullahoma 37388-8100
Nashville State Technical Institute, Nashville 37209
Northeast State Technical Community College, Blountville 37617
Pellissippi State Technical Community College, Knoxville 37933-0990
Roane State Community College, Harriman 37748
Shelby State Community College, Memphis 38174-0568
State Technical Institute at Memphis, Memphis 38134
Volunteer State Community College, Gallatin 37066
Walters State Community College, Morristown 37813-6899

Two-year upper-division

University of Tennessee: Memphis, Memphis 38163

Four-year

American Baptist College of ABT Seminary, Nashville 37207
Austin Peay State University, Clarksville 37044
Belmont University, Nashville 37212-3757
Bethel College, McKenzie 38201
Bristol University, Bristol 37625
Carson-Newman College, Jefferson City 37760
Christian Brothers University, Memphis 38104-5581
Crichton College, Memphis 38175-7830
Cumberland University, Lebanon 37087
David Lipscomb University, Nashville 37204-3951
East Tennessee State University, Johnson City 37614-0002
Fisk University, Nashville 37208
Free Will Baptist Bible College, Nashville 37205-0117
Freed-Hardeman University, Henderson 38340
Johnson Bible College, Knoxville 37998
King College, Bristol 37620-2699
Knoxville College, Knoxville 37921
Lambuth University, Jackson 38301
Lane College, Jackson 38301
LeMoyne-Owen College, Memphis 38126
Lincoln Memorial University, Harrogate 37752
Maryville College, Maryville 37801
Memphis College of Art, Memphis 38112
Memphis State University, Memphis 38152
Middle Tennessee State University, Murfreesboro 37132
Milligan College, Milligan College 37682
O'More College of Design, Franklin 37065
Rhodes College, Memphis 38112-1690
Southern College of Seventh-day Adventists, Collegedale 37315
Tennessee State University, Nashville 37203
Tennessee Technological University, Cookeville 38505
Tennessee Temple University, Chattanooga 37404
Tennessee Wesleyan College, Athens 37371-0040
Tomlinson College, Cleveland 37320-3030
Trevecca Nazarene College, Nashville 37203
Tusculum College, Greeneville 37743
Union University, Jackson 38305
University of the South, Sewanee 37375-1000
University of Tennessee
    Chattanooga, Chattanooga 37403
    Knoxville, Knoxville 37996-0230
    Martin, Martin 38238

Vanderbilt University, Nashville 37212-9976
William Jennings Bryan College, Dayton 37321-7000

Graduate study only

Meharry Medical College, Nashville 37208
Memphis Theological Seminary, Memphis 38104-4395
Southern College of Optometry, Memphis 38104

Texas

Two-year

Alvin Community College, Alvin 77511
Amarillo College, Amarillo 79178
Angelina College, Lufkin 75902-1768
Austin Community College, Austin 78714
Bauder Fashion College, Arlington 76010
Bee County College, Beeville 78102
Blinn College, Brenham 77833
Brazosport College, Lake Jackson 77566
Brookhaven College, Farmers Branch 75244
Central Texas College, Killeen 76541
Cisco Junior College, Cisco 76437
College of the Mainland, Texas City 77591
Collin County Community College District, McKinney 75070-2906
Cooke County College, Gainesville 76240
Del Mar College, Corpus Christi 78404-3897
Eastfield College, Mesquite 75150
El Centro College, Dallas 75202
El Paso Community College, El Paso 79998
Galveston College, Galveston 77550
Houston Community College, Houston 77270
Howard College, Big Spring 79720
ITT Technical Institute
    Arlington, Arlington 76011
    Houston, Houston 77099
Jacksonville College, Jacksonville 75766
Kilgore College, Kilgore 75662-3299
Laredo Junior College, Laredo 78040
Lee College, Baytown 77520-4703
Lon Morris College, Jacksonville 75766
McLennan Community College, Waco 76708
Midland College, Midland 79705
Miss Wade's Fashion Merchandising College, Dallas 75258
Mountain View College, Dallas 75211-6599
Navarro College, Corsicana 75110
North Harris Montgomery Community College District, Houston 77060
North Lake College, Irving 75038-3899
Northeast Texas Community College, Mount Pleasant 75455-1307
Odessa College, Odessa 79764-7127
Panola College, Carthage 75633
Ranger Junior College, Ranger 76470
Richland College, Dallas 75243-2199
St. Philip's College, San Antonio 78203-2098
San Antonio College, San Antonio 78212-4299
San Jacinto College: Central Campus, Pasadena 77505-2007
South Plains College, Levelland 79336
Tarrant County Junior College, Fort Worth 76102-6599
Temple Junior College, Temple 76504-7435
Texarkana College, Texarkana 75501
Texas Southmost College, Brownsville 78520
Texas State Technical College
    Amarillo, Amarillo 79111
    Harlingen, Harlingen 78550-3697
    Sweetwater, Sweetwater 79556
    Waco, Waco 76705
Trinity Valley Community College, Athens 75751
Vernon Regional Junior College, Vernon 76384-4092
Victoria College, Victoria 77901
Weatherford College, Weatherford 76086
Western Texas College, Snyder 79549
Wharton County Junior College, Wharton 77488-0080

Two-year upper-division

Amber University, Garland 75041-5595
Baylor College of Dentistry, Dallas 75246-2098
Corpus Christi State University, Corpus Christi 78412
East Texas State University at Texarkana, Texarkana 75505-0518
Institute for Christian Studies, Austin 78705
Laredo State University, Laredo 78040-9960
University of Central Texas, Killeen 76540-1416
University of Houston
    Clear Lake, Houston 77058-1080
    Victoria, Victoria 77901
University of Texas
    Health Science Center at Houston, Houston 77225
    Health Science Center at San Antonio, San Antonio 78284-7702
    Medical Branch at Galveston, Galveston 77555-1305
    Permian Basin, Odessa 79762
    Southwestern Medical Center at Dallas Southwestern Allied Health Sciences School, Dallas 75235-9024
    Tyler, Tyler 75701-6699

Four-year

Abilene Christian University, Abilene 79699
Angelo State University, San Angelo 76909
Arlington Baptist College, Arlington 76012-3425
Austin College, Sherman 75091-1177
Baptist Missionary Association Theological Seminary, Jacksonville 75766
Baylor University, Waco 76798-7056
Concordia Lutheran College, Austin 78705-2799
Criswell College, Dallas 75246
Dallas Baptist University, Dallas 75211-9800
Dallas Christian College, Dallas 75234
DeVry Institute of Technology: Irving, Irving 75038-4299
East Texas Baptist University, Marshall 75670-1498
East Texas State University, Commerce 75429-3011
Hardin-Simmons University, Abilene 79698
Houston Baptist University, Houston 77074
Howard Payne University, Brownwood 76801-2794
Huston-Tillotson College, Austin 78702
Incarnate Word College, San Antonio 78209-6397
Jarvis Christian College, Hawkins 75765
Lamar University—Beaumont, Beaumont 77710
LeTourneau University, Longview 75607-7001
Lubbock Christian University, Lubbock 79407
McMurry University, Abilene 79697-0001
Midwestern State University, Wichita Falls 76308
Northwood Institute: Texas Campus, Cedar Hill 75104
Our Lady of the Lake University of San Antonio, San Antonio 78207-4666
Paul Quinn College, Dallas 75241
Prairie View A&M University, Prairie View 77446
Rice University, Houston 77251
St. Edward's University, Austin 78704-6489
St. Mary's University, San Antonio 78228-8503
Sam Houston State University, Huntsville 77341-2418
San Antonio Art Institute, San Antonio 78209-0092
Schreiner College, Kerrville 78028
Southern Methodist University, Dallas 75275-0296
Southwest Texas State University, San Marcos 78666
Southwestern Adventist College, Keene 76059
Southwestern Assemblies of God College, Waxahachie 75165
Southwestern Christian College, Terrell 75160
Southwestern University, Georgetown 78626
Stephen F. Austin State University, Nacogdoches 75962

City University, Bellevue 98008

Four-year

Central Washington University, Ellensburg 98926
Cogswell College North, Kirkland 98033
Cornish College of the Arts, Seattle 98102
Eastern Washington University, Cheney 99004-2496
Evergreen State College, Olympia 98505
Gonzaga University, Spokane 99258-0001
Griffin College, Seattle 98121
Heritage College, Toppenish 98948
Lutheran Bible Institute of Seattle, Issaquah 98027
Northwest College of the Assemblies of God, Kirkland 98083-0579
Pacific Lutheran University, Tacoma 98447-0003
Puget Sound Christian College, Edmonds 98020-3171
St. Martin's College, Lacey 98503-1297
Seattle Pacific University, Seattle 98119-1997
Seattle University, Seattle 98122
University of Puget Sound, Tacoma 98416
University of Washington, Seattle 98195
Walla Walla College, College Place 99324-1198
Washington State University, Pullman 99164-1036
Western Washington University, Bellingham 98225
Whitman College, Walla Walla 99362-2085
Whitworth College, Spokane 99251-0002

West Virginia

Two-year

College of West Virginia, Beckley 25802-2830
Potomac State College of West Virginia University, Keyser 26726
West Virginia Northern Community College, Wheeling 26003
West Virginia University at Parkersburg, Parkersburg 26101-9577

Four-year

Alderson-Broaddus College, Philippi 26416
Appalachian Bible College, Bradley 25818-1353
Bethany College, Bethany 26032
Bluefield State College, Bluefield 24701
Concord College, Athens 24712
Davis and Elkins College, Elkins 26241
Fairmont State College, Fairmont 26554
Glenville State College, Glenville 26351-1292
Marshall University, Huntington 25755
Ohio Valley College, Parkersburg 26101-9975
Salem-Teikyo University, Salem 26426
Shepherd College, Shepherdstown 25443-1569
University of Charleston, Charleston 25304-1099
West Liberty State College, West Liberty 26074
West Virginia Institute of Technology, Montgomery 25136-2436
West Virginia State College, Institute 25112-0335
West Virginia University, Morgantown 26506-6009
West Virginia Wesleyan College, Buckhannon 26201-2998
Wheeling Jesuit College, Wheeling 26003

Graduate study only

West Virginia Graduate College, Institute 25112

Wisconsin

Two-year

Chippewa Valley Technical College, Eau Claire 54701
Fox Valley Technical College, Appleton 54913-2277
Madison Area Technical College, Madison 53704-2599

Madison Junior College of Business, Madison 53705-1399
Mid-State Technical College, Wisconsin Rapids 54494
Milwaukee College of Business, Milwaukee 53203
Moraine Park Technical College, Fond du Lac 54935
Northeast Wisconsin Technical College, Green Bay 54307-9042
Stratton College, Milwaukee 53202-2608
University of Wisconsin Center
  Baraboo/Sauk County, Baraboo 53913-1098
  Barron County, Rice Lake 54868
  Fox Valley, Menasha 54952-8002
  Manitowoc County, Manitowoc 54220-6699
  Marathon County, Wausau 54401-5396
  Marinette County, Marinette 54143
  Marshfield/Wood County, Marshfield 54449
  Richland, Richland Center 53581
  Sheboygan County, Sheboygan 53081-4789
  Washington County, West Bend 53095
  Waukesha, Waukesha 53188-2799
Waukesha County Technical College, Pewaukee 53072
Western Wisconsin Technical College, La Crosse 54602-0908
Wisconsin Indianhead Technical College, Shell Lake 54871
Wisconsin School of Electronics, Madison 53704

Four-year

Alverno College, Milwaukee 53215-3922
Bellin College of Nursing, Green Bay 54305-3400
Beloit College, Beloit 53511-5595
Cardinal Stritch College, Milwaukee 53217
Carroll College, Waukesha 53186
Carthage College, Kenosha 53140
Columbia College of Nursing, Milwaukee 53186
Concordia University Wisconsin, Mequon 53092-9650
Edgewood College, Madison 53711
Lakeland College, Sheboygan 53082-0359
Lawrence University, Appleton 54912-9986
Maranatha Baptist Bible College, Watertown 53094
Marian College of Fond du Lac, Fond du Lac 54935-4699
Marquette University, Milwaukee 53233-9988
Milwaukee Institute of Art & Design, Milwaukee 53202
Milwaukee School of Engineering, Milwaukee 53201-0644
Mount Mary College, Milwaukee 53222-4597
Mount Senario College, Ladysmith 54848
Northland College, Ashland 54806
Northwestern College, Watertown 53094-4899
Ripon College, Ripon 54971
St. Norbert College, De Pere 54115-2099
Silver Lake College, Manitowoc 54220-9391
University of Wisconsin
  Eau Claire, Eau Claire 54701
  Green Bay, Green Bay 54311-7001
  La Crosse, La Crosse 54601
  Madison, Madison 53706-1490
  Milwaukee, Milwaukee 53201
  Oshkosh, Oshkosh 54901
  Parkside, Kenosha 53141-2000
  Platteville, Platteville 53818
  River Falls, River Falls 54022
  Stevens Point, Stevens Point 54481
  Stout, Menomonie 54751
  Superior, Superior 54880
  Whitewater, Whitewater 53190-1791
Viterbo College, La Crosse 54601
Wisconsin Lutheran College, Milwaukee 53226

Graduate study only

Medical College of Wisconsin, Milwaukee 53226
Nashotah House, Nashotah 53058-9990

Wyoming

Two-year

Casper College, Casper 82601
Central Wyoming College, Riverton 82501
Eastern Wyoming College, Torrington 82240
Laramie County Community College, Cheyenne 82007
Northwest College, Powell 82435
Sheridan College, Sheridan 82801-1500
Western Wyoming Community College, Rock Springs 82901

Four-year

University of Wyoming, Laramie 82071-3435

American Samoa, Caroline Islands, Guam, Marianas, Virgin Islands

Two-year

Community College of Micronesia, Ponape 96941
Guam Community College, Guam 96921
Micronesian Occupational College, Koror 96940-9999
Northern Marianas College, Saipan 96950

Four-year

University of Guam, Mangilao, Guam 96923
University of the Virgin Islands, Charlotte Amalie 00802

Canada

McGill University, Montreal, Quebec H3A 2T5

France

American University of Paris, Paris 75007

Mexico

Sistema Instituto Tecnologico y de Estudios Superiores de Monterrey, Monterrey, Neuvo Leon 64849

Switzerland

American College of Switzerland, Leysin 02110
Franklin College: Switzerland, Lugano

Arab Republic of Egypt

American University in Cairo, Cairo

Alphabetic index of fields of study